RESTAURANTS

2008 · 2009

PUDLO
FRANCE

by Gilles Pudlowski

HOTELS

About the Author

GILLES PUDLOWSKI is the restaurant critic and journalist for the French weekly magazine, *Le Point*; a contributor to *Saveurs* and *Bon Voyage* magazines; cultural commentator and critic; a historian of French culinary traditions; and the author of two cookbooks, *The France the Beautiful Cookbook* and *Great Women Chefs of Europe*, as well as many other books and guides. He is the author of *Pudlo Paris*, which is also published by The Little Bookroom.

About the Translators

SIMON BEAVER (chief text translator) grew up in the South of England, but moved to Paris nearly 30 years ago. For two and a half decades now, he has been adapting books, TV and movie scripts, songs and biographies into English, writing subtitles and recording voice overs. Whenever he can, he spends time at his second home on the Normandy coast, in England or in Andalusia.

ALICE BRINTON is a former news journalist who now specializes in French wine and gastronomy.

LIAM GAVIN is an independent translator who works on both technical and literary projects.

CATHERINE SPENCER is a freelance editor, translator, and writer who has lived in France and now lives in Morocco. She specializes in non-fiction and literary translation.

LUCY VANEL (chief food translator) is a food journalist, photographer, and writer who has lived and worked in Lyon, France since 2000. She serves as a Manager of the eGullet Society for Culinary Arts and Letters, and is co-host of the France forum there. She records her experiences though the seasons in a blog about living, writing and cooking in Lyon, France, Lucy's Kitchen Notebook. http://kitchen-notebook.blogspot.com

PHYLLIS FLICK is an American living in Paris who has written about Paris and French life for various publications including the *TimeOut Eating and Drinking Guide to Paris*. She is also co-host of the eGullet Society for Culinary Arts and Letters France forum.

RESTAURANTS

2008 · 2009

PUDLO
FRANCE

by Gilles Pudlowski

HOTELS

TRANSLATED BY SIMON BEAVER
with Alice Brinton, Liam Gavin and Catherine Spencer

Food Translation by Lucy Vanel with Phyllis Flick

The Little Bookroom • New York

Originally published in French by Michel Lafon as
Guide Le Pudlo France 2007 by Gilles Pudlowski

With the assistance of Alain Angenost, Marc Baise, Olivier Binst, Francis Brayer,
Dominique Bruiere, Didier Chambeau, Jean-Pierre Espiard, Phyllis Flick, Maryse
Grimont, Sylvain Knecht, Denys Michel, Jean-Francois Neyroud, Marc Horwitz,
Jérome Berger, Sophie Elusse, Véronique Gauthier, Michele Maublanc, Francois Morel,
Elisabeth Morin, Albert Nahmias, Didier Nicolas, Sylvie Nouaille, Sylvie Pistono, Muriel
Pragier-Pudlowski, Michael Pudlowski, Sylvie Rouge-Pullon, Elisabeth Rocher, Maurice
Rougemont, Jean-Daniel Sudres.

English edition © 2008 The Little Bookroom
English translation: Simon Beaver
with Alice Brinton, Liam Gavin and Catherine Spencer
Food translation: Lucy Vanel with Phyllis Flick

www.pudloguide.com

Book design: Louise Fili Ltd

Library of Congress Cataloging-in-Publication Data

Pudlowski, Gilles, 1950–
Pudlo France, 2008-2009 / by Gilles Pudlowski ;
translated by Simon Beaver with Alice Brinton ... [et al.].
p. cm.
Includes index.
ISBN-13: 978-1-892145-51-2 (alk. paper)
ISBN-10: 1-892145-51-0 (alk. paper)
1. Hotels--France--Paris--Directories.
2. Restaurants--France--Directories. I. Title.
TX907.5.F7P94 2008
647.94025'4--dc22
2007038133

Published by The Little Bookroom
435 Hudson Street, 3rd floor
New York NY 10014
editorial@littlebookroom.com
www.littlebookroom.com

Distributed by Random House, Random House International,
and in the UK and Ireland by Signature Book Services

PUDLO FRANCE 2008·2009
TABLE OF CONTENTS

INTRODUCTION: A TIME OF TURMOIL

Megève is mourning Marc Veyrat and his Ferme de mon Père. Strasbourg is already missing Antoine Westermann, gone from his Buerehiesel. Vézalay is anxiously awaiting news of Marc Meneau and his Espérance. Aside from these stars, there are other hosts who closed shop discreetly, suffer and seethe, or simply keep quiet (although they have plenty on their minds). Then there are those who pack their bags and move on in search of greener pastures, or those who once set out with stars in their eyes, but who would now happily settle for a quiet little bistro in the country. Finally, there are the optimists, those who have struck the right balance between quality and value from the outset and are vibrantly celebrated in this guide.

Clearly, this 2008–2009 edition, our first in English (following seven French editions of *Pudlo France* and seventeen of *Pudlo Paris*), comes at a time of great upheaval. Broadly speaking, a third of the hotels and restaurants reviewed in these pages have changed hands, name or identity, and many more will follow. Chefs have always played musical chairs on the Côte d'Azur (one delightful eatery, the Bastide Saint-Tropez, went through three in one season!) and the Parisians are nomadic by nature, so no change there.

Yet the disease (?) now seems to have spread to the whole of France. Is it the 35-hour work week, fear of recession, economic conditions, a difficult new era, a different generation, or wave of retirements? Or could it just be difficulties in finding "good," sound, motivated staff (as the delightful Chantal Chagny of the Cep in Fleurie-en-Beaujolais wrote on her poetic menu), coupled with a clientele ready to spend more time at the table, over lunch or in the countryside? Running a well-known regional establishment outside the cities is no longer automatically a sinecure in France.

Having said this, we still have been able to come up with many new award winners, ambitious young chefs, intriguing inns and pleasant regions for your consideration. Take Brittany, for instance, which has astounded us with some compelling revelations over the last few years, including Luc Mobihan at the Saint-Placide in Saint-Malo and Olivier Bellin at the Glaziks in Plomodiern; or Lorraine, now on track with—at last!—the opening of the Eastern high-speed rail line, where Lutz Janisch officiates at the Strasbourg in Bitche and Patrick Tanésy in the eponymous Nancy eatery. And how could we forget Lyon, where Martin and Magali Schmied have scored a generous hit with their generously priced fare at the marvelous Magali & Martin, a good, simple bistro. Then there are our enduringly prolific and talented culinary artisans: a skillful pastry maker (Frédéric Cassel in Fontainebleau), an expert baker (Patrick Dinel in Strasbourg) and a triumphant cheesemonger (Olivier Nivesse in Clermont-Ferrand).

In its every corner, France tells a wonderfully culinary tale, from the Landes with their gourmand *mères* (Maïté in Rion and Hélene Darroze in Paris) to the Drôme (where Denis Bertrand is our Sommelier of the Year at Pic in Valence). The country is moving and changing, but remains ever loyal to its protean *gourmandise.* We who refuse to place our trust in *espumas* or fashion for fashion's sake, and argue for common sense, roots, soil and tradition—"outdated" concepts that still have the power to move us—continue to voice our justified optimism. The France we are describing here, the France we continue to believe in with passion and pride, is a gourmet, timeless place. In Savoy (do you know the Meilleurs in Saint-Martin de Belleville?), Normandy (the crazy Tartarin in Le Havre's Villa du Havre), Beaujolais (the admirable Château de Bagnols) and Alsace of course; in the Basque country, Picardy and Vendée, we have never eaten so well, despite all these changes in people and places. We should remember that.

GILLES PUDLOWSKI

HOW TO USE THIS GUIDE

Listings—The hotels and restaurants in the guide are listed by town/city. These towns and cities are in alphabetical order ignoring articles or prepositions—le, la, les, etc. (so Le Havre is listed under the letter H). Under the heading of each town or city you will find hotels and restaurants listed in our order of preference—hotels according to their appeal and facilities, followed by restaurants according to the quality of their food. A hotel with a restaurant that we particularly like (that is not listed separately) is classified as a restaurant. At the back of the guide there is an alphabetical index of all venues.

Ratings and symbols—The names of hotels and restaurants are followed by symbols showing our ratings.

●	Restaurant
■	Hotel
○	Very good table
◎	Excellent table
◎◎	Grand table
♠	Good value for money
❀	Very peaceful hotel
⊓	Historical significance
⬆	Promotion *(higher rating than previously)*
⚘	New to the guide

Restaurant/Hotel :

SIM/⌂	Simple
COM/⌂	Comfortable
V.COM/⌂	Very comfortable
LUX/⌂	Luxurious
V.LUX/⌂	Very luxurious

Blue indicates a particularly charming establishment.

In the Paris listings only:

€	Meals for under 30€
⟲	Disappointing table

AWARD WINNERS

Chef of the Year—Hélène Darroze, *Hélène Darroze*, Paris, page 680

Discovery of the Year—Isabelle and Luc Mobihan, *Le Saint-Placide*, Saint-Malo, page 921

Young Chef of the Year—Olivier Bellin, *Auberge des Glaziks*, Plomodiern, page 793

Young Chef of the Year—Lutz Janisch, *Le Strasbourg*, Bitche, page 131

Bistro of the Year—Patrick Tanésy, *Chez Tanésy*, Nancy, page 584

Best Value for Money of the Year—Martin and Magali Schmied, *Magali & Martin*, Lyon, page 472

Innkeeper of the Year—Maité, *Chez Maité*, Rion des Landes, page 849

Sommelier of the Year—Denis Bertrand, *Pic*, Valence, page 1086

Baker of the Year—Patrick Dinel, *Au Pain de mon Grand-Père*, Strasbourg, page 1011

Cheesemonger of the Year—Olivier Nivesse, *Olivier Nivesse*, Clermont-Ferrand, page 243

Pastry Chef of the Year—Frédéric Cassel, *Frédéric Cassel*, Fontainebleau, page 336

THE BEST
TABLES OF FRANCE

THE BEST TABLES

HOW TO USE THE REGIONAL MAPS OF FRANCE

The regional maps of France show towns and cities where there are very good, excellent and grand tables (○, ○○, ○○○), our good value for money selections (○), grand hotels (🏨, 🏨) and particularly charming hotels, whatever their level of category (○) and outstandingly peaceful hotels (❀). Towns or cities with a hotel or restaurant of another kind featured in the guide are in bold type with a red location dot, but no symbol.

The small map of France located on each map gives the map number for the corresponding map of the region.

Bon voyage!

2. ALSACE

GERMANY

Woustviller
Hambach

Puttelange-
aux-Lacs

Sarralbe

Rohrbach-
les-Bitche

Bitche

Parc

des Vosges

du Nord

Oberbronn

Reichshoffen

Niedersteinbach

Obersteinbach

Lembach   Climbach

Niederbronn-
les-Bains

Soultz-sous-

Wissembourg

Merkwiller-
Pechelbronn

Sarre-
Union

Hinsingen

Domnissel

Reipertswiller

Ingwiller

Morsbronn-
les-Bains

Gundershoffen

Leutenhe

La Petite-
Pierre

Obermodern

Uberach

Schweighouse-
sur-Moder

Haguenau

Soufflenhe

Fénétrange

Réding

Pfaffenhoffen

Bouxwiller   Ringendorf

Dossenheim-
sur-Zinsel

A4

Sessenhe

Bischwiller

Drüsenhe

BAS-
RHIN

Hochfelden

A35

Phalsbourg

Sarrebourg

Saverne

Heming

Marmoutier

MOSELLE

Landersheim

Mittelhausen

Brumath

Hoerdt

Weyersheim

Kilstett

Willgottheim

Birkenwald

Wasselonne

Dabo

Obersteigen

Wangenbourg

Traenheim

Oberhaslach

Urmatt

Molsheim

Wiwersheim

Marlenheim

Stutzheim-
Offenheim

Handschuheim

Scharrachbergheim

Dachstein

Lingolsheim

La Wantzena

STRASBOURG

Vendenheim

Truchtersheim

MEURTHE

ET

-MOSELLE

Niederhaslach

Mollkirch

Mutzig

A35

Grendelbruch

Rosheim

Blaesheim

Geispolsheim

Eschau

Plobsheim

Krautergersheim

Bron-
l'Étape

Senones

Moyenmoutier

Schirmeck

Fouday

Étival-
Clairefontaine

Saulxures

VOSGES

Saint-Dié-
des-Vosges

Sainte-
Marguerite

Boersch

Le Hohwald

Colroy-
la-Roche

Villé

La Vancelle

Kintzheim

Ste-Marie-
aux-Mines

Ottrott

Andlau

Blienschwiller

Châtenois

Obernai

Heiligenstein

Barr

Mittelbergheim

Itterswiller

Dambach-
la-Ville

Sélestat

Erstein

Osthouse

Benfeld

Gerstheim

Ebersmunster

Rhinau

Baldenheim

Marckolsheim

Parc des

Ballons

des Vosges

Riquewihr

HAUT-RHIN

Kaysersberg

Orbey

Ingersheim

Colmar

Elsenheim

Marckolsheim

Biesheim

Gérardmer

Munster

A35

Winzenheim

Neuf-
Brisach

Volgelsheim

0   20 km

Anould

Fraize

Saint-Dié

MAP:2

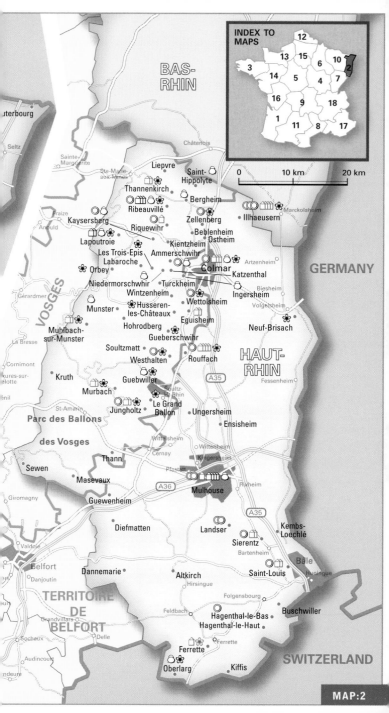

3: BRITTANY (BRETAGNE)

ENGLISH CHANNE

Perros-
Trégastel Guirec Penvén
Ploumanac'h Tré
Trébeurden Lannion
Pontriε
Locquirec B
Laumeur Bégard
Roscoff Louargat Guinguar
Brignogan- Plouignεau Belle-Isle- Plouma
Plages Saint-Pol- Carantec en-Terre
Aber-Wrac'h de-Léon Morlaix Bourbriac
Kerlouan Taulé Callac
Plouguerneau Goulven Plouzévédé
Île Ploudalmézeau Lesneven Landivisiau Saint- Huelgoat
d'Ouessant Thégonnec Carhaix-Plouguer
Lampaul- Plabennec Landerneau Sizun
Plouarzel Gouesnou Rostrene
Saint- Guipavas Le Relecq-Kerhuon FINISTÈRE
Renan Brest Châteauneuf-
Picugastel Daoulas du-Faou Plouray Clé
Le Conquet Daoulas Parc d'Armorique Gourin Guér
Camaret-sur-Mer Pont-de-Buis-lès-Quimerch sur-S
Crozon Châteaulin Le Faouët MORBIHA
Pleyben Coray Scaër Bubry
Plomodiern Rosporden
Sainte-Anne- Châteauneuf- Plouay
la-Palud Briec du-Faou La Forêt- Quimperlé
Cleden- Douarnenez Fouesnant Concarneau Pont-
Cap-Sizun Quimper Pont-Aven Scorff Henneb
Plogoff Audierne Guidel Plu
Plozévet Sainte- Lorient Port-Louis
Ploneour-Lanvern Marine Larmor-Plage
Bénodet Balz
Pont- Trégunc Moëlan-
l'Abbé Riec-sur- sur-Mer
Saint- Belon
Guénolé Île des Carnac
Glénan La Trinit
sur-M
Île de Groix
Quiberon

Belle-Ile-en-Mer Le Pal

INDEX TO MAPS

```
        12
   13  15     10
          6        2
14     5   4   7
   16     9     18
   1   11   8   17
```

3

ATLANTIC OCEAN

MAP:3

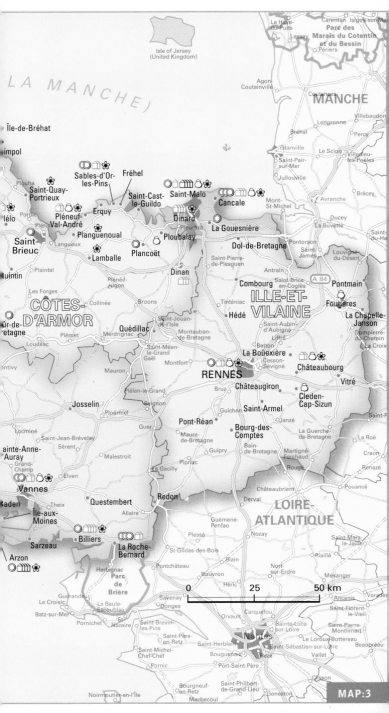

MAP:3

4: BURGUNDY (BOURGOGNE)

MAP:4

INDEX TO MAPS

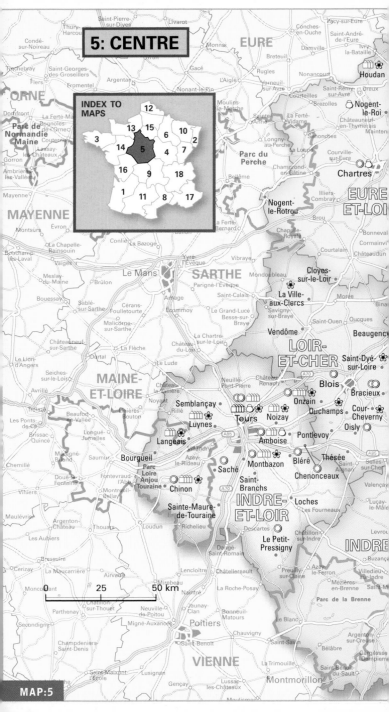

5: CENTRE

INDEX TO MAPS

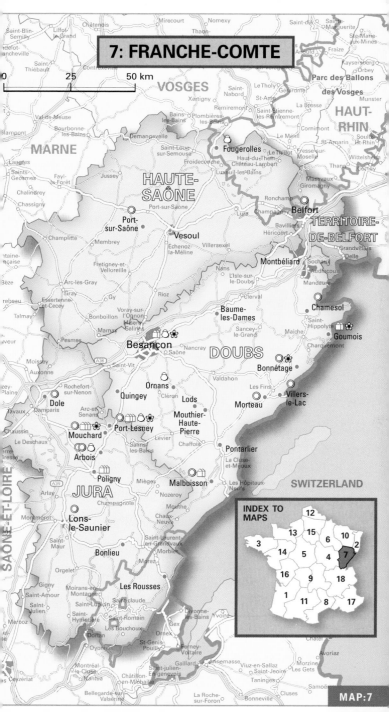

8: LANGUEDOC/ROUSSILLON

CANTAL

0   25   50 km

LOT

Mortignac
la-Villedieu
Argentat
Les Eyzies-de-Tayac-Sireuil
Buisson-Cadouin
Belvès
Rocamadour
Gramat
Saint-Céré
Cayrols
Chaudes-Aigues
Saint-Chély-d'Apcher
La Chaldette
Aumont-Aubrac
Maurs
Montsalvy
Laguiole
Entraygues-sur-Truyère
Aubrac
Marvejol
Puy-l'Évêque
Prayssac
Cahors
Figeac
Decazeville
Capdenac-Gare
Firmi
Aubin
Espalion
Bozouls
Saint-Laurent-d'Olt
Montayral
Villeséque
Montcuq
Saint-Cirq-Lapopie
Limogne-en-Quercy
Villefranche-de-Rouergue
Sébazac-Concourès
Onet-le-Château
Rodez
Luc Olemps
Sévérac-le-Château
Lauzerte
Lafrançaise
Caussade
Septfonds
Saint-Antonin-Noble-Val
Najac
Rieupeyroux
La Salvetat-Peyralès
Baraqueville
Salmiech
Boulocc
Le Rozier
Moissac
Albias
Negrepelisse
Cordes-sur-Ciel
AVEYRON
Villefranche-de-Panat
A75
Aguessa

TARN-ET-GARONNE
Montech
Bressols
Labastide-Saint-Pierre
Saint-Étienne-de-Tulmont
Puycelci
Castelnau-de-Montmiral
Marssac-sur-Tarn
Gaillac
Carmaux
Saint-Juéry
Puygouzon
Saint-Sernin-sur-Rance
Saint-Pierre
Millau
Villefranche-de-Panat
Saint-Rome-de-Cernon
Saint-Affrique
Avène-les-Bains
Beaumont-de-Lomagne
Grisolles
Grenade
Villemur-sur-Tarn
Castelnau-d'Estrétefonds
Buzet-sur-Tarn
Rabastens
Saint-Sulpice
ALBI
Réalmont
Vielmur
Montredon-Labessonnié
Grands Causses Haut-Languedoc
Montaigut-sur-Save
Blagnac
L'Union
Castelginest
Montrabé
Montastruc-la-Conseillère
Verfeil
Lavaur
Graulhet
TARN
Lautrec
Saint-Paul-Cap-de-Joux
Roquecourbe
Brassac
Viane
Lacaune
Lamalou-les-Bains
Bédarieux
L'Isle-Jourdain
Colomiers
Tournefeuille
Pibrac
Cugnaux
Saint-Lys
Balma
Saint-Orens-de-Gameville
Ramonville-Saint-Agne
Venerque
Puylaurens
Soual
Labruguière
Mazamet
Aussillon
Labastide-Rouairoux
La Salvetat-sur-Agout
Saint-Pons-de-Thomières
Parc du Haut-Languedoc
HÉRAULT
Cessenon-sur-Orb
St-Chinian
Béziers
Rieumes
HAUTE-GARONNE
Toulouse
Saint-Félix-Lauragais
Revel
Villefranche-de-Lauragais
La Pomarède
Saissac
Saint-Papoul
Caunes-Minervois
Minerve
Siran
Bize-Minervois
Ouveillan
Montady
Valras-Plage
Coursan
Auterive
Cintegabelle
Carbonne
Lézat-sur-Lèze
Saverdun
Mazères
Castelnaudary
Bram
Castres
Lastours
Aragon
Conques-sur-Orbiel
Trèbes
A61
Lézignan-Corbières
Narbonne
Narbonne-Plage
Martres-Tolosane
Montesquieu-Volvestre
Salat
Pailhès
Pamier
La Tour-du-Crieu
Saint-Jean-du-Falga
Varilhes
Caudeval
Mirepoix
Carcassonne
AUDE
Gruissan
La Bastide
ARIÈGE
Félix
Laroque-d'Olmes
Lavelanet
Espéraza
Saint-Polycarpe
Arques
Villerouge-Termenès
Fontjoncouse
Sigean
Port-la-Nouvelle
aint-Sernin
Massat
Tarascon-sur-Ariège
Montségur
Quillan
Tautavel
Estagel
Salses-le-Château
Le Barcarès
Leucate
SPAIN
ANDORRA
Ax-les-Thermes
L'Hospitalet-près-l'Andorre
Quérigut
PYRÉNÉES ORIENTALES
St-Paul-de-Fenouillet
Montner
Millas
St-Estève
Le Soler
Thuir
Molitg-les-Bains
Villefranche-de-Conflent
Perpignan
Canet-Pla
Saint-Cyprien
Bages
Argelès-sur-Mer
Port-Ven
Font-Romeu
Mont-Louis
Ur
Olivia
Céret
Arles-s-Tech
Amélie-les-Bain-Palalda
Prats-de-Mollo
Collioure
Banyuls

MAP: 8

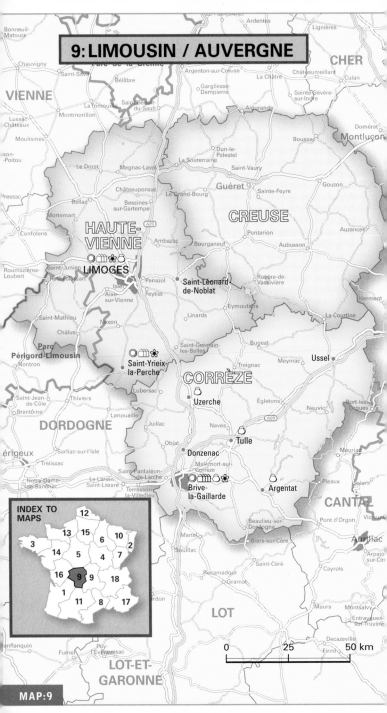

MAP:11

12: NORD/PAS-DE-CALAIS

ENGLISH CHANNEL (LA MANCHE)

Bray-Dunes

Dunkerque

Grande-Synthe

Hondschoote

Calais

Oye-Plage

Gravelines

Sangatte

Marck

Bergues

Bourbourg

Wissant

Coulogne

Audruicq

Wormhout

Guînes

Watten

Marquise

Cassel

Steenvoorde

Wimereux

Le Wast

Saint-omer

Longuenesse

Arques

Baill

Boulogne-sur-Mer

Desvres

Lumbres

Hazebrouck

Saint-Etienne-au-Mont

Parc des Caps
Marais d'Opale

Samer

Thérouanne

Aire-sur-la-Lys

Aire-sur-la-Lys

Merville

Lestrem

Hardelot-Plage

Neufchâtel-Hardelot

Isbergues

Lavent

Maninghem

Fruges

Lillers

Béthune

Le Touquet-
Paris-Plage

Étaples

Auchel

Bruay-la-Buissier

Montreuil

Beaurainville

PAS-DE-
CALAIS

Anvin

Berck

A16

Hesdin

Saint-Pol-sur-
Ternoise

Saint-La
Bi

Rue

Arras

Achicourt

Le Crotoy

Frévent

Auxi-
le-Château

Saint-Valery-
sur-Somme

Saint-Riquier

Doullens

SEINE-
MARITIME

Abbeville

Mers-
les-Bains

Friville-
Escarbotin

SOMME

Mailly-
Maillet

Le Tréport

Gamaches

Flixecourt

Flesselles

Albert

Blangy-
sur-Bresle

Airaines

Ailly-sur-Somme

Villers-
Bretonneux

Amiens

Longueau

Saloual

Boves

Aumale

Poix-
de-Picardie

Ailly-
sur-Noye

Moreuil

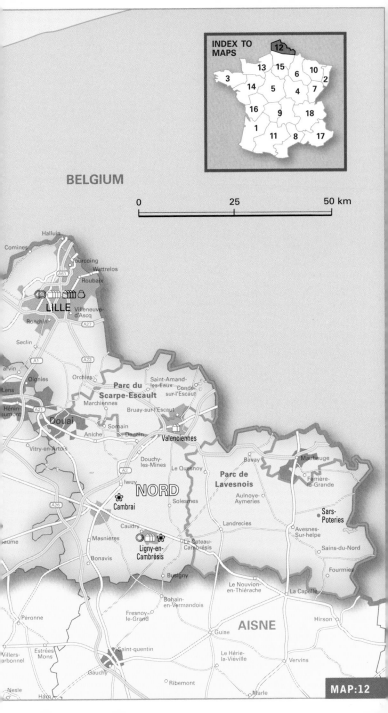

13: NORMANDY (NORMANDIE)

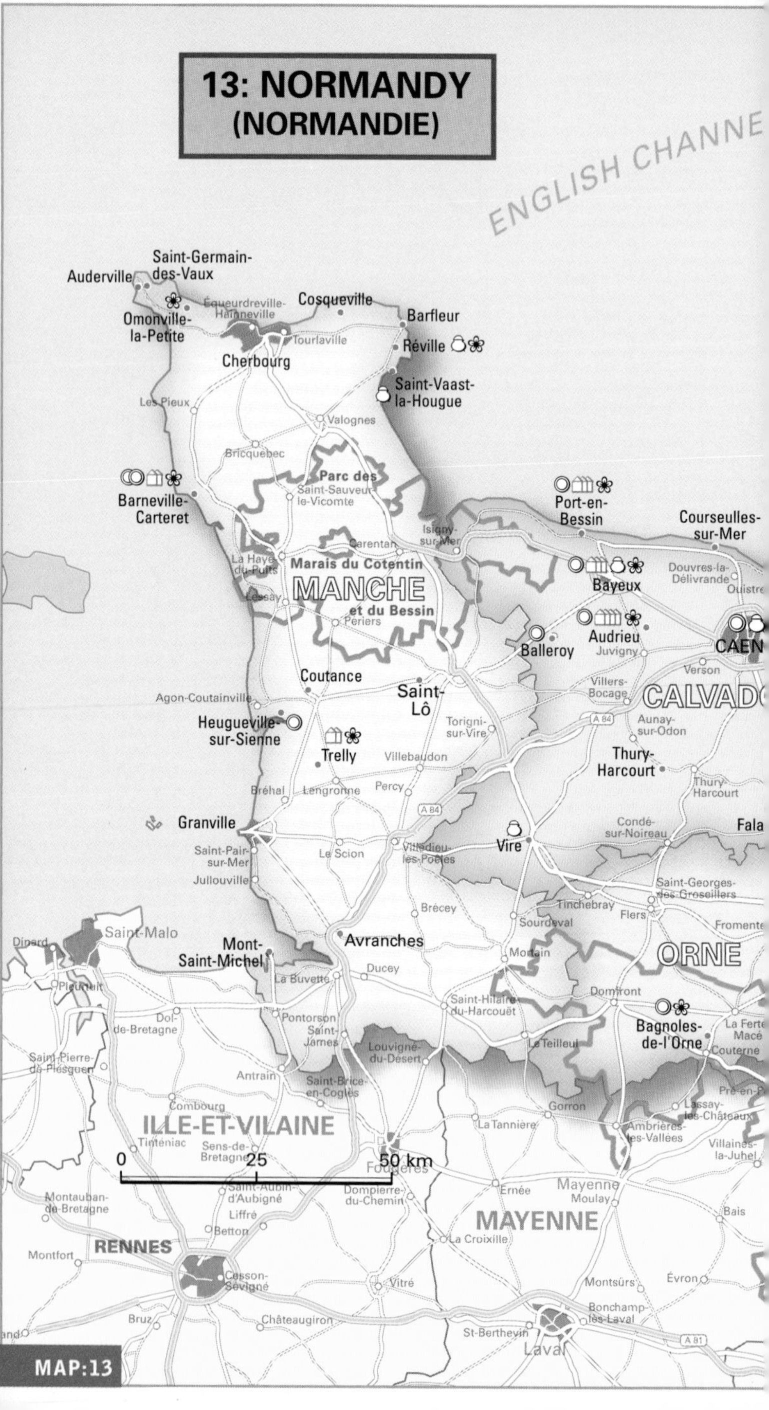

ENGLISH CHANNEL

Auderville
Saint-Germain-des-Vaux
Cosqueville
Barfleur
Omonville-la-Petite
Réville
Équeurdreville-Hainneville
Tourlaville
Cherbourg
Saint-Vaast-la-Hougue
Les Pieux
Valognes
Bricquebec
Parc des
Saint-Sauveur-le-Vicomte
Port-en-Bessin
Courseulles-sur-Mer
Barneville-Carteret
Isigny-sur-Mer
Douvres-la-Délivrande
Ouistre
Carentan
Bayeux
La Haye-du-Puits
Marais du Cotentin
MANCHE
et du Bessin
Lessay
Périers
Balleroy
Audrieu
Juvigny
CAEN
Coutances
Saint-Lô
Villers-Bocage
CALVAD
Agon-Coutainville
Verson
Aunay-sur-Odon
Heugueville-sur-Sienne
Torigni-sur-Vire
A 84
Trelly
Villebaudon
Thury-Harcourt
Percy
Thury Harcourt
Bréhal
Lengronne
A 84
Condé-sur-Noireau
Fala
Granville
Le Scion
Villedieu-les-Poêles
Vire
Saint-Pair-sur-Mer
Saint-Georges-des-Groseillers
Julliouville
Bréceyt
Tinchebray
Flers
Fromente
Dinard
Saint-Malo
Avranches
Sourdeval
ORNE
Mont-Saint-Michel
Ducey
Mortain
Piguelt
La Buvette
Domfront
Dol-de-Bretagne
Pontorson
Saint-James
Saint-Hilaire-du-Harcouët
Bagnoles-de-l'Orne
La Ferté-Macé
Saint-Pierre-du-Plesguen
Louvigné-du-Désert
Le Teilleul
Couterne
Antrain
Saint-Brice-en-Coglès
Pré-en-Pail
Combourg
Gorron
Lassay-les-Châteaux
Ambrières-les-Vallées
Villaines-la-Juhel
ILLE-ET-VILAINE
Timéniac
Sens-de-Bretagne
La Tanniere
Montauban-de-Bretagne
Fougères
Ernée
Mayenne
Moulay
Bais
RENNES
Saint-Aubin-d'Aubigné
Dompierre-du-Chemin
La Croixille
MAYENNE
Montfort
Liffré
Cesson-Sévigné
Bettom
Montsûrs
Évron
Bruz
Châteaugiron
Vitré
St-Berthevin
Bonchamp-lès-Laval
Laval
A 81

0   25   50 km

MAP:13

LA MANCHE)

Le Crotoy
Saint-Valery-
sur-Somme
Le Tréport
Mers-les-
Bains
Friville-
Escarbotin
Eu
Criel-
sur-Mer
Gamaches
Varengeville-
sur-Mer
Dieppe
Blangy-
sur-Bresle
Saint-Valery-
en-Caux
Arques-la-Bataille
Aumale
Veules-
les-Roses
Le Bourg-
Dun
Fécamp
Cany-Barville
Neufchâtel-
en-Bray
Etretat
Doudeville
SEINE-
MARITIME
Yerville
Tôtes
La Boissière
Forges-
les-Eaux
Octeville-
sur-Mer
Goderville
Yvetot
Former
Montivilliers
Bolbec
Barentin
Notre-Dame-
de-Bondeville
Gournay-en-Bray
La Feuillie
Le Havre
Gonfreville-
l'Orcher
Lillebonne
Notre-Dame-
de-Gravenchon
Le Trait
Canteleu
Darnétal
ROUEN
Neuf-
Marché
Parc de
Brotonne
Honfleur
Deauville
Trouville-s-Mer
Pont-
Audemer
Grand-
Couronne
Tourville-
la-Rivière
Pont-de-l'Arche
Lyons-
la-Forêt
Fleur-
sur-Andelle
Étrépagny
Beaumont-
en-Auge
Beuzeville
Bourgtheroulde
Infreville
Elbeuf
Val-de-
Reuil
Connelles
Les Thilliers-
en-Vexin
Gisors
Pont-l'Évêque
Pierrefitte-en-Auge
Lieurey
Le Bec-
Hellouin
La Saussaye
Louviers
Gaillon
Les Andelys
Maghy-
en-Vexin
Le Breuil-
en-Auge
Brionne
Le Neubourg
Parc de
Vexin
français
Cambremer
Crèvecœur-
en-Auge
Lisieux
La Rivière-
Thibouville
Beaumont-
le-Roger
Gravigny
Fourges
Vernon
Bernay
St-Sébastien-
de-Morsent
Pacy-sur-Eure
Livarot
Orbec
EURE
Evreux
A 13
Vimoutiers
Conches-
en-Ouche
Saint-André-
de-l'Eure
Monnai
Damville
Ivry-la-
Bataille
Anet
Thoiry
Gacé
Breteuil
Houdan
Argentan
Rugles
Nonancourt
Dreux
Nonant-le-Pin
L'Aigle
Verneuil-
sur-Avre
Saint-Rémy-
sur-Avre
Vernouillet
Moulins-
la-Marche
Courteilles
Brezolles
EURE-ET-
LOIR
Nogent-
le-Roi
Sées
Sainte-Anne
La Ferté-
Vidame
Châteauneuf-
Épernon
Parc de
Normandie
Maine
Longny-
au-Perche
Senonches
Alençon
Bellême
Mortagne-
au-Perche
La Loupe
Parc du
Perche
Nogent-
le-Rotrou
Fresnay-
sur-Sarthe
La Route
La Hutte
Mamers
Beaumont-
sur-Sarthe
Guillaume
Bonnétable
Ballon
Savigny-
l'Évêque
La Ferté-
Bernard
SARTHE
A 11
Chapelle-
Royale
La Bazoge
Yvré-
l'Évêque
Vibraye
Cormainville

INDEX TO
MAPS

12
13 | 13 | 15
3 | 14 | 5 | 6 | 10 | 2
16 | 9 | 4 | 7 | 18
1 | 11 | 8 | 17

MAP:13

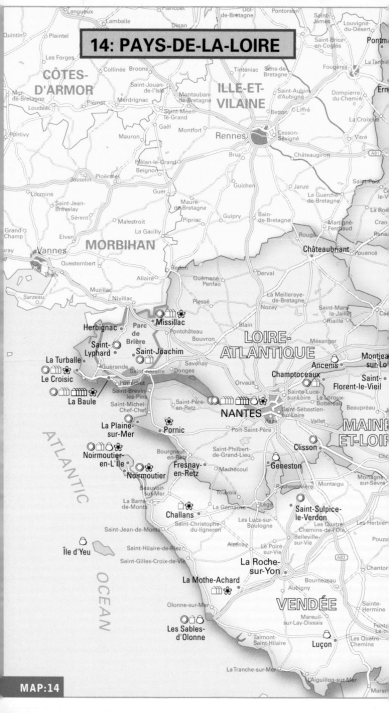

MAP:14

16: POITOU/CHARENTES

MAP:16

17: PROVENCE/ALPES/COTE D'AZUR

Montfaucon-en-Velay
Saint-Vallier
Saint-Marcellin
Grenoble
Seyssinet-Pariset
Le Pont-de-Claix
St-Martin-d'Hères
Echirolles

Saint-Agrève
Saint-Marcel-les-Valence
Bourg-de-Péage
ISÈRE

Lamastre
Saint-Péray
Bourg-lès-Valence
Montelier
La Chapelle-en-Vercors
La Mure

Guilherand-Granges
Chabeuil
Saint-Michel-les-Portes
Corps

Le Cheylard
Vernoux-en-Vivarais
Valence
Léoncel
Parc du Vercors

ARDÈCHE
Portes-lès-Valence
Étoile-sur-Rhône
Saint-Michel-les-Portes
Mens

Mézilhac
La Voulte-sur-R
Livron-sur-Drôme
Pontaix
Die

Privas
Le Pouzin
Loriol-sur-Drôme
Crest
Saint-Étienne-en-Dévoluy

a Chavade
Chirols
Chomérac
DRÔME
Luc-en-Diois

Vals-les-Bains
Cruas
Veyne

Aubenas
St-Étienne-de-Fontbellon
Montélimar
La Bégude-de-Mazenc
Bourdeaux
Serres

Villeneuve-de-Berg
LeTeil
Châteauneuf-du-Rhône
Dieulefit
La Charce
Eyguians
Laragne-Montéglin

Joyeuse
Viviers
Le Pègue
Rémuzat
Rosans
Sisteron

Vallon-Pont-d'Arc
Donzère
Cornillon-sur-l'Oule
Montguers

Les Vans
Bourg-St-Andéol
Grignan
Valréas
Nyons
Buis-les-Baronnies
Saint-Vince-sur-Jabron

Pierrelatte
Saint-Paul-Trois-Châteaux
Peyruis

St-Ambroix
Lapalud
Suze-la-Rousse
Vaison-la-Romaine
Savoillans

Rousson
Pont-Saint-Esprit
Bollène
Malaucène
Sault

Saint-Privat-des-Vieux
Bagnols-sur-Cèze
Mornas
Gigondas
Crillon-le-Brave

Vallérargues
Piolenc
Carpentras

St-Christol-lès-Alès
Laudun
Orange
Caromb
Mazan
VAUCLUSE
Forcalquier

GARD
Uzès
Châteauneuf-du-Pape
Sarrians
Monteux
Gordes
Joucas
Roussillon
Manosque

gnan
Marguerittes
Roquemaure
Pernes-les-Fontaines
Apt
Volx

uissac
Redessan
L'Isle-sur-la-Sorgue
Cabrières-d'Avignon

Nîmes
Avignon
Noves
Cavaillon
Ménerbes
Bonnieux
Cucuron
Vinon-sur-Verdo

Caveirac
Milhaud
Caissargues
Saint-Rémy-de-Provence
Eygalières
Lourmarin
Parc du Lubéron

Calvisson
Uchaud
Garons
Fontvieille
Saint-Martin-de-la-Brasque

Vergèze
Vauvert
Les Baux-de-Provence
Eyguières
Rognes
Jouques
Rians

Lunel
Aimargues
Saint-Gilles
Arles
Lambesc
Peyrolles-en-Provence

Baillargues
Lansargues
Albaron
Maussane-les-Alpilles
Salon-de-Provence
Saint-Cannat
Venelles
Aix-en-Provence
Pourriè

Mauguio
Aigues-Mortes
Istres
Saint-Chamas
Lançon-Provence
Beaurecueil

Grande-Motte
La Grau-du-Roi
Parc de Camargue
BOUCHES-DU-RHÔNE
Berre-l'Étang
Vitrolles
Gardanne
Saint-Maximin-la-Sainte-Baume

Saintes-Maries-de-la-Mer
Fos-sur-Mer
Cabriès
Marignane
Nans-les-Pins

Port-Saint-Louis-du-Rhône
Martigues
Gémenos
Gémenos

Carry-Le-Rouet
Pont-de-Bouc
Aubagne
Cuges-les-Pins
Le Beaus

Marseille
Cassis
La Cadière-d'Azur
La Se

MEDITERRANEAN SEA

MAP:17

ITALY

Valloire Val-Fréjus

La Grave

es Deux
pes

Serre-Chevalier

Briançon

Montgenèvre

Pelvoux

Parc des
Écrins

Vallouise

Puy-
Saint-Vincent

Les Vigneaux

L'Argentière-
la-Bessée

Arvieux

aint-
Firmin

HAUTES-
ALPES

aint-Bonnet-
n-Champsaur

Mont-Dauphin
Guillestre

Saint-Véran-
en-Queyras

Parc du
Queyras

Gap

Chorges

Embrun

Vars

Les Orres

lard

Jausiers

Pra-Loup
Les Agneliers

Seyne

La Foux
d'Allos

ALPES-DE-
HAUTE-
PROVENCE

Saint-Étienne-
de-Tinée

Allos

Le Brusquet

Colmars

Isola 2000

Saint-Martin-
d'Entraunes

Parc du
Mercantour

Saint-Martin-
Vésubie

Tende

teau-
oux

Digne-
les-Bains

Valberg

Châteauredon

Saint-André-
les-Alpes

Annot

Puget-
Théniers

Tourtoret

Utelle

Breil-
sur-Roya

Moustiers-
Sainte-Marie

oisson

Barrême

ALPES-MARITIMES

Sospel

Roquebrune-
Cap-Martin

Parc du
Verdon

Aiguines

Castellane

Bargème

Vence

Saint-
Martin-
du-Var

Coaraze

La Turbie

z

Trigance

Saint-Paul-
de-Vence

Peillon

Menton

Châteaudouble

Tourrettes-sur-Loup

Carros

Monaco

iso

Tourrettes

La Colle-sur-Loup

Èze-Village

Villefranche-s-Mer

Ampus

Mor

Grasse

Nice

Beaulieu-s-Mer

ols

Tourtour

Callas

Fayence

Auribeau-
sur-Siagne

Biot

Cagnes-s-Mer

Saint-Jean-
Cap-Ferrat

VAR

Draguignan

Trans-en-
Provence

Montauroux

Mougins

Valbonne

Correns

Lorgues

Le Muy

Mandelieu-
la-Napoule

Cannes

Antibes

Le Val

Vidauban

Théoule-sur-Mer

Celle

Luc

Le Cannet-
des-Maures

Fréjus

Saint-Raphaël

Juan-les-Pins

oult

Cuers

Pignans

Les Issambres

Golfe-Juan

s-
as

Carneules

Sainte-Maxime

Pierrefeu-
du-Var

Grimaud

au

Bormes-
les-Mimosas

Cogolin

Gassin

Saint-Tropez

Hyères

Cavalière

Ramatuelle

ulon

Giens

Le Lavandou

Le Rayol-
Canadel-
sur-Mer

Île de Port-Cros

Parc de
Port-Cros

Île de
Porquerolles

0   25   50 km

MAP:17

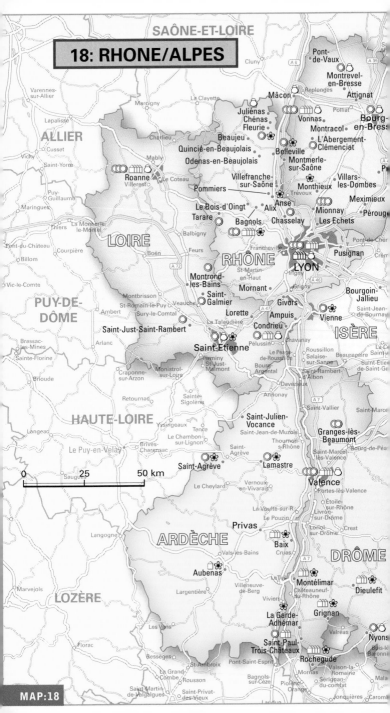

JURA
Les Rousses
oirans-en-
Montagne
Saint-Lupicin
St-Claude
La Faucille
(col de)
Divonne-
les-Bains
Lac Léman
Evian-les-Bains
Thonon-
les-Bains
La Chapelle-
d'Abondance
Gex
Yvoire
Oyonnax
Thoiry
Ferney-
Voltaire
HAUTE-
SAVOIE
Châtel
SWITZERLAND
Chézery-Forens
Annemasse
Morzine
Avoriaz
Montréal
-la-Cluse
A 40
Saint-Julien-
en-Genevois
Bonneville
Taninges
Nantua
Bellegarde-
sur-Valserine
La Roche-
sur-Foron
Cluses
Samoëns
AIN
Cruseilles
A 40
Saint-Gervais-
les-Bains
Hauteville-
Lompnes
Annecy
Le Grand-
Bornand
Sallanches
Chamonix-
Mont-Blanc
osges
Bluffy
(col de)
La Clusaz
Cordon
Combloux
Culoz
Seynod
Rumilly
Albens
A 41
Sévrier
Talloires
Manigod
N.-D.-de-Bellecombe
Megève
Belley
Doussard
Les Saisies
Hauteluce
Aix-les-
Bains
Yenne
Gilly-
sur-Isère
Albertville
Bourg-
Saint-Maurice
Le Bourget-
du-Lac
ur-du-Pin
Saint-Pierre-
d'Albigny
A 430
Aime
es Abrets
Le Pont-de-
Beauvoisin
Chambéry
SAVOIE
Moûtiers
Tignes
Montmélian
La Rochette
Valmorel
Saint-Laurent-
du-Pont
Pontcharra
Allevard
A 43
Courchevel
Val-d'Isère
Voiron
Le Touvet
Saint-Pierre-
d'Allevard
Méribel
aps
Voreppe
Saint-Martin-
de-Belleville
Les Ménuires
Villard-Bonnot
assenage
Saint-Michel-
de-Maurienne
Val-Thorens
Grenoble
St-Martin-d'Hères
Modane
inet-Parise
Saint-Hilaire-
du-Rosier
Uriage-
les-Bains
Vizille
L'Alpe-d'Huez
ITALY
Villard-
de-Lans
Le Bourg-
d'Oisans
Les Deux-
Alpes
La Mure
Briançon
HAUTES-
ALPES
Gap
Veynes
ALPES-DE-
HAUTE-
PROVENCE
Laragne-
Montéglin
Sisteron
Château-Arnoux-
Saint-Auban

INDEX TO
MAPS
12
13   15   6   10
3   2
14   5   4   7
16   9   18
1   11   8   17

MAP:18

ABBEVILLE

80100 Somme. Paris 186 – Amiens 51 –
Boulogne-sur-Mer 80 – Rouen 106.
office.tourisme.abbeville@wanadoo.fr.
This town in Picardy was devastated by bombardment in 1940. Beside the Somme river, it has a splendid collegiate church and period residences.

 | HOTELS-RESTAURANTS

■ Relais Vauban

4, bd Vauban.
Tel. 03 22 25 38 00. Fax 03 22 31 75 97.
relaisvauban@wanadoo.fr / www.relaisvauban.com
Closed Christmas–New Year's.
22 rooms: 47–62€.

Practically located in the town center, this hotel offers functional rooms in light beige, green and blue shades. Supervised parking, a warm welcome and well-behaved prices.

● L'Escale en Picardie ■COM

15, rue des Teinturiers.
Tel.-Fax 03 22 24 21 51.
Closed Sun. dinner, Mon., Thu. dinner,
Feb. vac., mid-Aug.–beg. Sept.
Prix fixe: 20€, 30€, 49,50€.

This Picardy stopover provides a combination of low prices and good food. We enjoy the lively seafood cuisine by the fireplace and under the broad beams of its friendly, rustic dining room. The set menus are shrewd and the service attentive. Salmon tartare, pike-perch filet and frozen nougat live up to their promise.

● La Corne SIM

32, chaussée du Bois.
Tel. 03 22 24 06 34. Fax 03 22 24 03 65.
Closed Sat., Sun., Christmas–New Year's.
Prix fixe: 17€. A la carte: 50€.

Yves and Maryse Lematelot look after their guests well, in the dining room and kitchen respectively. They serve up a polished cuisine reflecting current tastes. Langoustines simmered in sweet wine and presented in puff pastry, pain d'épice–

encrusted Atlantic sea bass with pantossed chanterelles and the roasted figs to conclude are astute choices.

● L'Etoile du Jour SIM

2, chaussée Marcadé.
Tel. 03 22 24 06 90. Fax 03 22 20 55 06.
www.letoiledujour.com
Closed Sun. dinner, Mon. dinner.
Prix fixe: 20€, 30€, 40€.
A la carte: 45–50€.

Annick Paris offers a warm welcome and Jean-Louis Laffitte cooks with soul. House foie gras, sole meunière, sirloin steak with morels and the two-chocolate dessert are prepared in a straightforward classical vein. The wood and white Norman-style inn setting is convivial.

L'ABERGEMENT-CLEMENCIAT

01400 Ain. Paris 413 – Mâcon 23 –
Bourg-en-Bresse 24 – Lyon 58.
officetourisme.chatillon@wanadoo.fr.
A corner of the Dombes region with its lakes and forest, and the pretty town of Châtillon-sur-Chalaronne nearby.

● | RESTAURANTS

● Le Saint-Lazare ◎COM

Le Bourg.
Tel. 04 74 24 00 23. Fax 04 74 24 00 62.
lesaintlazare@aol.com
Closed Sun. dinner, Wed., Thu., Nov. 1,
Christmas, Feb. vac., 2 weeks end July.
Prix fixe: 31€ (weekday lunch), 36€, 82€.
A la carte: 75€.

This unobtrusive village inn deserves a visit. Formerly at the Crillon and Martinez, Christian Bidard offers a new take on tradition without getting lost along the way. In his hands, produce from the surrounding area or further afield expresses its full flavor in a series of lively preparations. The marinated monkfish served with a parmesan biscuit, the roasted young Bresse chicken breast and the grilled Victoria pineapple are delights, as are Christine's welcome and the precise service.

ABER-WRAC'H

29870 Finistère. Paris 605 – Brest 28 –
Landerneau 36 – Morlaix 69 – Quimper 94.
www.abers-tourisme.com.
This seaside patch of Brittany located on one of
the region's prettiest fiords is a first-rate *finis
terrae* whose heart beats to the ebb and flow of
the majestic ocean.

 HOTELS-RESTAURANTS

■ La Baie des Anges
350, rte des Anges, port of l'Aber-Wrac'h.
Tel. 02 98 04 90 04. Fax 02 98 04 92 27.
www.baie-des-anges.com
Closed Jan.
18 rooms: 75–165€. 2 suites: 165–210€.

Whether you choose the hotel or its charming but simpler adjunct, the Villa des Anges (45, route des Anges. Tel. +33 (0)2 98 04 90 04), France Barré and the jovial Jacques Briant will immediately make you feel at home. Aber-Wrac'h is a magnificent natural setting and the décor of the very Côte Ouest rooms is extremely refined. Breakfast is a genuine treat for connoisseurs.

● Le Brennig `SIM`
Le Port-L'Aber-Wrac'h Am Ode Bri Landéda.
Tel.-Fax 02 98 04 81 12.
Closed Tue., end Sept.–beg. Apr.
Prix fixe: 25€, 28€, 9€ (child). A la carte: 55€.

The marina is just opposite and we can see the boats in the estuary from upstairs. Geneviève Falc'hun has handed over the kitchen to David Autret, whose cuisine is exclusively dedicated to the sea. A scallop carpaccio with vanilla-infused olive oil, and an oven-browned sea bass plus a caramel vacherin for dessert make a delightful impression.

● Captain' `SIM`
16, rte des Anges.
Tel.-Fax 02 98 04 82 03.
Closed Sat., Sun., (exc. July–Aug.), Mon.
(exc. July–Aug.), mid-Nov.–mid-Feb.
A la carte: 30€.

Annie Ronvel delights her customers with more than fine buckwheat crêpes in her *crêperie* and bistro opposite the estuary. Her cuisine has character. Skate terrine with sweet peppers, scallop and potato parmentier, boneless rib steak and the rice pudding with salted-butter caramel are all first rate. Frédéric Gorrias provides a very lively welcome.

ABLIS

78660 Yvelines. Paris 63 – Chartres 32 –
Versailles 49 – Mantes 65 – Rambouillet 15.
www.ablis.fr.
Here, the Yvelines look out on the Eure-et-Loir district and rivers lap against exquisite chateaux in a verdant setting.

 HOTELS-RESTAURANTS

In Saint-Symphorien-le-Château (28700).
6 km w via D168.
■ Château d'Esclimont
Tel. 02 37 31 15 15. Fax 02 37 31 57 91.
esclimont@grandesetapes.fr / www.esclimont.fr
48 rooms: 140–380€. 5 suites: 590–890€.
Prix fixe: 52€, 89€.

Ever sumptuous, this 19th-century château that belonged to the La Rochefoucauld family is just the place for a perfect weekend break. Luxury rooms, vast grounds, a swimming pool and fine lounges are equal to the task. Eric Lurthy's cuisine meets the same high standards, offering a new take on classic dishes. A foie gras mille-feuille with horseradish cream, sautéed Scottish salmon with carrot coulis, a rabbit haunch glazed with licorice root–infused sauce and the house chocolate dessert are accompanied by selected wines, with a clear preference for the Loire region.

ABRESCHVILLER

57560 Moselle. Paris 456 – Strasbourg 80 –
Phalsbourg 23 – Saverne 17.
abreschtourisme@wanadoo.fr.
This is Alexandre Chatrian's native district, where the poetry of the Moselle Vosges reigns: a land of hills, crystal factories and forests.

Pierre Moinot set his *Guetteur d'Ombre* here in this woodcutters' village.

HOTELS-RESTAURANTS

■ Les Cigognes   🏠
74, rue Jordy.
Tel. 03 87 03 70 09. Fax 03 87 03 79 06.
lescigognes57@wanadoo.fr
Closed Mon. (off season).
18 rooms: 60–120€.
Prix fixe: 13€, 22€, 32€, 10€ (child).
A la carte: 35–40€.

Bernard Mayeux now manages this village hotel set on the edge of the forest and recently renovated. Inseparable from his stove, Michaël Schmitt prepares regional classics with no faults or frills. Ham and wild boar sausage, Sarre trout or wild boar with mushrooms slip down smoothly. A heated swimming pool.

In Lettenbach (57560). 0,5 km via road to St-Quirin.

● Auberge de la Forêt   🍴COM
276, rue des Verriers.
Tel. 03 87 03 71 78. Fax 03 87 03 79 96.
www.aubergedelaforet57.com
Closed Mon., Tue. lunch, New Year's.
Prix fixe: 11€ (lunch), 22€, 28€, 33€,
37€. A la carte: 40€.

On the edge of the forest, this huge inn refurbished in contemporary style is the best bargain to be found in the Abreschviller district. With a little help from her daughter, Alexandra Schmitt, Nicole Risch provides a charming welcome, while in the kitchen, her brother Hubert concocts dishes with a modern flavor. His cuisine has an easy charm, with its marinated eggplant with olive oil and goat cheese, foie gras terrine with mirabelle plum chutney, pike-perch with chorizo and fork-mashed potatoes, veal chop with chanterelles and finally variations on the cherry (meringue, sorbet, fruit with alcohol).

AGDE

34300 Hérault. Paris 762 – Montpellier 55 – Béziers 24 – Sète 25.

ot-agde@wanadoo.fr.
The Mediterranean, modern buildings constructed a little too hastily on every side and the Cap-d'Agde campsite's legendary appeal for nature lovers are all obvious local features, but there is also a good restaurant here.

HOTELS-RESTAURANTS

● La Table de Stéphane   COM
2, rue des Moulins-à-Huile.
Tel.-Fax 04 67 26 45 22.
www.latabledestephane.com
Closed Sat. lunch, Sun. dinner, Mon.,
Jan. 2–Jan. 15.
Prix fixe: 15€ (lunch), 26€, 42€, 59€, 12€
(child). A la carte: 55–75€.

Almost as soon as he could walk, Stéphane Lavaux began to totter around his parents' restaurant. Since then, he has been put through some serious training by the Pourcel brothers in Montpellier and Jacques Maximin. His rabbit with foie gras, graced with a summer truffle cappuccino, the red mullet wrapped in caul lace and served with a thin bacon tart and his thyme-seasoned roasted pigeon filet, accompanied by the thighs (served stuffed) are gratifying dishes. For dessert, we succumb to the temptation of the light vanilla ice cream with chocolate croustillant and silky chocolate cream. Considerate hostess Caroline Lavaux knows just which regional wine will best go with her husband's preparations. A relaxed atmosphere and bargain prices for such quality.

In Le Cap-d'Agde (34300). 5 km. se via D32.

■ Capaô   🏨
Av des Corsaires.
Tel. 04 67 26 99 44. Fax 04 67 26 55 41.
contact@capao.com / www.capao.com
Closed mid-Oct.–beg. Apr.
55 rooms: 68–130€.
A la carte: 50–60€.

This seaside hotel set in exotic gardens offers colorful Mediterranean rooms, a swimming pool and a fitness center. The beach restaurant serves grilled fish, meats grilled at the table and salads. In the evening, we meet at the Manhattan for a meat-filled parrillada served royal style or a bouillabaisse. The service is pleasant and the prices far from negligible.

In Le Cap-d'Agde.

■ Hôtel du Golfe

Ile des Loisirs.
Tel. 04 67 26 87 03. Fax 04 67 26 26 89.
hotel.golf@tahoe.fr / www.hotel-du-golf.com
Hotel closed Jan., Feb. Rest. closed lunch,
Sun., Mon., Jan., Feb., Mar.
50 rooms: 95–155€. 3 suites: 265–315€.
Prix fixe: 30€, 45€.

The contemporary rooms are spacious. The swimming pool, private beach, steam bath, sailing and golf course nearby complete the range of leisure activities. Corinne Marie-Rêne gives a free hand to chef Nicolas Gros, who prepares quality produce at the Caladoc. Foie gras terrine, cod filet, slow-cooked lamb shanks and a pear croustillant "bonbon" are washed down with vinic finds from the Langue-doc-Roussillon region, recommended by the competent Laurent Saint-Dizier.

In Le Cap-d'Agde.

● Le Brasero   SIM

Port Richelieu.
Tel.-Fax 04 67 26 24 75.
Closed Thu. (Nov.–May), Jan.
Prix fixe: 11€, 14€, 18€, 30€,
6€ (child). A la carte: 36€.

Georges Millares has turned this good-natured bistro into a good-natured restaurant, with a teak terrace and salmon-colored interior. The fresh lemon-seasoned anchovies, small squid in their ink, a cod-stuffed squid and the tarte Tatin are faultless.

AGEN

47000 Lot-et-Garonne. Paris 669 – Auch 74 – Bordeaux 141 – Pau 163 – Toulouse 116.
osti.agen@wanadoo.fr.
The world's prune capital suns itself on the banks of the Garonne river. We come to visit the art gallery and Jacobins' church and to lose ourselves in the old town.

    HOTELS-RESTAURANTS

■ Château des Jacobins

1 ter, pl des Jacobins.
Tel. 05 53 47 03 31. Fax 05 53 47 02 80.
www.chateau-des-jacobins.com
15 rooms: 72–140€.

This 19th-century town house in the heart of the old quarter near the church is surrounded by generous wooded grounds. Its rooms of character boast carefully chosen period furniture.

● Mariottat   ◎V.COM

25, rue Louis-Vivent.
Tel. 05 53 77 99 77. Fax 05 53 77 99 79.
contact@restaurant-mariottat.com
www.restaurant-mariottat.com
Closed Sat. lunch, Sun. dinner, Mon.,
1 week Dec., Feb. vac., 1 week at Easter.
Prix fixe: 25€ (lunch), 38€, 49€, 62€.
A la carte: 90€.

Eric Mariottat, who trained with Daguin then Lajarrige in Paris, has returned home, but remained loyal to tradition. In his charming establishment opening on to a garden, he constantly reinterprets grandmotherly recipes, taking care to gently modernize them. The soft poached egg over truffled potatoes, the sea bass cooked skin-side down in peanut oil, lamb cooked two ways and the Agen prunes served with an Armagnac flan are fine things indeed. The welcome is enchanting, the service attentive and the wine list well devised. But then comes the check…

● Philippe Vannier   ■V.COM

66, rue Camille-Desmoulins.
Tel. 05 53 66 63 70. Fax 05 53 95 64 72.
restaurant-philippe-vannier@tiscali.fr
Closed Sat. lunch, Sun. dinner.
Prix fixe: 14,50€, 20€, 28€, 40€.

Philippe Vannier, a Breton from Fougères who worked with Marcon and Bardet, surfs on a wave of tradition, adding a touch of modernity here and there. Minced rabbit with apples, trout encrusted with couscous and capers, pan-seared sirloin steak with shallots and the candied ginger rice pudding are impressive. A fine selection of regional wines and an affordable check.

● Margoton   COM
52, rue Richard-Coeur-de-Lion.
Tel.-Fax 05 53 48 11 55.
contact@lemargoton.com / www.lemargoton.com
Closed Sat. lunch, Sun., Mon., 2 weeks Dec.,
1 week Feb.
Prix fixe: 16€, 23€, 28€, 34€.
A la carte: 43€.

Frédéric Fabre is the modest local chef. Véronique welcomes us warmly and we sit down to foie gras terrine, grilled lobster, escalope of veal sweetbreads and a Grand Marnier soufflé: dishes that have the ring of truth. A refined, modern décor, prompt service and well-devised menus.

● Washington   COM
7, cours Washington.
Tel. 05 53 48 25 50. Fax 05 53 48 25 55.
patrick.pinard4@wanadoo.fr
www.le-washington.com
Closed Sat., Sun., 3 weeks Dec.–beg. Jan.,
1 week May, 2 weeks Aug.
Prix fixe: 13€ (lunch, wine inc.),
19€ (lunch), 35€. A la carte: 50–65€.

The Pinards offer a warm welcome in their contemporary décor in shades of gray, plum, ochre and red. Marie Costa recommends wines from greater southwest France that go well with the tuna carpaccio, sea lamprey cooked in wine with vegetables and herbs, rack of lamb presented in its cooking juices and a creamy mousse with berry sauce, all skillfully prepared by Patrick.

● Le Saint Jacques   SIM
Av Jean-Monnet.
Tel. 05 53 87 90 09. Fax 05 53 87 90 10.
le.saint-jacques@wanadoo.fr
www.le-saint-jacques.fr
Closed Sat. lunch, Sun., 1 week at end July,
3 weeks Aug.
Prix fixe: 18€, 29€, 35€. A la carte: 40–45€.

Philippe Lopez-Burgos tends fondly to the dining room and Sébastien Gilbert's cuisine reflects the offerings of the market. Foie gras poached in wine, cod-and potato-stuffed piquillo peppers, scallop and chorizo lasagne and the honey-glazed duck breast are not bad. The dining room in white, burgundy and yellow is trim indeed and the rum-seasoned pineapple beignets a success.

In Laplume (47310). 12 km via N21, rte d'Auch and D268.

■ Château de Lassalle
Brimont.
Tel. 05 53 95 10 58. Fax 05 53 95 13 01.
info@chateaudelassalle.com
www.chateaudelassalle.com
Closed Christmas–New Year's.
Rest. closed Sun. dinner.
15 rooms: 119–149€. 2 suites: 189€.
Prix fixe: 30€, 32€, 42€, 56€.
A la carte: 50€.

In the heart of vast grounds with a duck pond, this château offers peaceful, bucolic rooms, a swimming pool and a restaurant serving voguish regional dishes.

64210 Pyrénées-Atlantiques. Paris 786 – Bayonne 19 – Biarritz 10 – Saint-Jean-de-Luz 12. This patch of Labourdin land between the hills and sea offers views of the Rhune, the holy mountain of the Basques. This is already the heart of the country.

 HOTELS-RESTAURANTS

■ La Ferme Ostalapia
Chemin d'Ostalapia.
Tel. 05 59 54 87 42. Fax 05 59 54 98 85.
ostalapia@wanadoo.fr / www.ostalapia.com
Closed Dec.–mid-Jan.
Rest. closed Wed., Thu.
5 rooms: 65–155€.
Prix fixe: 14,50€.
A la carte: 40€.

Affable host, dealer in delights, occasional humorist, retired rugby player and sporadic angler, Christian Duplaissy looks every inch the urbane gentleman farmer.

He has a polite word for ladies and a kiss for children, and recommends a solid rib eye steak, axoa (Basque veal stew with hot peppers), oven-crisped lamb sweetbreads with pasta, succulent grilled boudin with goose fat fries, followed by the Amatchi tart (sautéed apples on a shortbread crust with caramelized cream). His farm is a picture postcard inn, where we taste sparkling Txakoli, ruby red Ribera del Duero Pinna and an affable Irouléguy produced by his friend and neighbor Jean Brana. Exquisite, rustic rooms.

L'AIGLE

61300 Orne. Paris 139 – Alençon 61 – Chartres 81 – Dreux 61 – Evreux 56 – Lisieux 59.
otlaigle@wanadoo.fr.
This provincial Norman town is a traditional staging post on the old road from Paris to Brittany.

 HOTELS-RESTAURANTS

■ Le Dauphin
Pl de la Halle.
Tel. 02 33 84 18 00. Fax 02 33 34 09 28.
regis.ligot@free.fr / www.hoteldudauphin.free.fr
Rest. closed Sun. dinner.
30 rooms: 62–85€.
Prix fixe: 33€, 38€.

Régis Ligot has brought a modern touch to this old post house halfway between the French capital and Brittany. The rooms are comfortable and luxurious, the welcome graceful and the restaurant first-rate. The pan-tossed jumbo shrimp and shredded ginger, scallops with curry-seasoned cream sauce, veal cutlet with reduced truffle-seasoned gravy and the chocolate pyramid dessert all look good.

AIGUEBELLE see LE LAVANDOU

AIGUES-MORTES

30220 Gard. Paris 749 – Montpellier 39 – Nîmes 39 – Arles 48 – Sète 56.
ot.aiguesmortes@wanadoo.fr.
The town walls, Constance tower, Notre-Dame-des-Sablons church and Pénitents and Salines chapels are the sights to see in this town, once the departure point for knights setting off on their crusade to the Holy Land.

HOTELS-RESTAURANTS

■ Les Templiers ❀ 🏨
21-23, rue de la République.
Tel. 04 66 53 66 56. Fax 04 66 53 69 61.
Rest. closed lunch, Sun. dinner, Thu. dinner.
11 rooms: 100–250€. 3 suites: 150–250€.
A la carte: 56€.

Anne and Igor Allary have turned this 17th-century convent into a snug nest equipped with painted furniture and Provençal fabrics. The patio is fragrant with the scent of the *maquis* and the swimming pool is handy when you need to cool off. The restaurant serves up light reinterpretations of classics: Provençal-style eggplant, pan-simmered artichokes, grilled pike-perch, Aubrac beef rib eye and the classic fruit tart all have an easy charm. The wine list offers a tour of the Languedoc and Roussillon regions, with the Côtes-du-Rhône district an added bonus.

■ Les Arcades
23, bd Gambetta.
Tel. 04 66 53 81 13. Fax 04 66 53 75 46.
info@les-arcades.fr / www.les-arcades.fr
Rest. closed Mon., Tue. lunch, Thu. lunch.
9 rooms: 95–138€.
Prix fixe: 34€, 42€. A la carte: 45–50€.

Marie-Pierre Mercier provides a solicitous welcome in her 17th-century residence. The rooms breathe a blend of old-fashioned charm and modern comfort. Jean-Marie Mercier serves up Thau oysters served hot, zucchini flower with seafood, simply prepared local catch of the day and a pigeon breast braised with spices. For dessert, the three-chocolate dessert never fails to please. Delightful service and shrewd set menus.

● La Camargue
19, rue de la République.
Tel. 04 66 53 86 88. Fax 04 66 53 72 69.

Closed Mon. (off season), end Oct.–mid-Nov.
Prix fixe: 32€. A la carte: 45€.

This 16th-century establishment in Camargue-Provençal style offers set menus to match the surroundings. Anchoïade, oven-grilled oysters with slow-cooked leeks, parrillada, toro rib eye grilled over a wood fire and the strawberry gazpacho are washed down with cheerful regional vintages. Simple, good and reasonably priced.

AILLANT-SUR-THOLON

89110 Yonne. Paris 145 – Auxerre 20 – Briare 71 – Clamecy 61 – Gien 81 – Montargis 61.
ot.aillant@wanadoo.fr.
A stretch of green, hilly Yonne countryside and a golf course just next door.

 HOTELS-RESTAURANTS

● **Domaine du Roncemay**
In Chassy (89110), 7 km via D955, D57.
Tel. 03 86 73 50 50. Fax 03 86 73 69 46.
roncemay@aol.com / www.roncemay.com
Rest. closed Mon., Tue. lunch, Jan.
15 rooms: 100–250€. 3 suites: 280–360€.
Prix fixe: 42€, 52€.

Located next to one of the region's finest golf courses, this fully equipped hotel (fitness center, swimming pools, steam bath and Jacuzzi) also has delights in store for food lovers. Marc Meneau from the Espérance in Vézelay has taken over the establishment from Hubert Couilloux, who was Bernard Loiseau's dining room lieutenant in Saulieu. In the gourmet restaurant, Steeve Delamaire serves a meticulous, subtly domestic cuisine. Roasted langoustines with eggplant cream and preserved lemons, turbot with sesame poached in an aromatic herb milk and the smoked rack of lamb with thyme and Paimpol coco beans are exactly right. Strawberry tartare provides a fresh note in conclusion before a nap in one of the hotel's pleasant rooms. The Club House provides a less expensive option.

AINCILLE see **SAINT-JEAN-PIED-DE-PORT**

 AINHOA

64250 Pyrénées-Atlantiques. Paris 795 – Biarritz 28 – Saint-Jean-de-Luz 26 – Pau 128.
A superlatively Basque village at the foot of the Pyrénées, with its row of half-timbered houses on a splendid main street. Spain is just a stone's throw away.

HOTELS-RESTAURANTS

● **Ithurria**
Pl du Fronton.
Tel. 05 59 29 92 11. Fax 05 59 29 81 28.
hotel@ithurria.com / www.ithurria.com
Closed beg. Nov.–beg. Apr.
Rest. closed Wed., Thu. lunch.
27 rooms: 100–150€. 2 suites: 230–290€.
Prix fixe: 35€, 52€. A la carte: 65€.

The inseparable Isabal family are a reliable choice in the Basque hinterland. Their set menus are treasures and their dishes part of a leisurely local tradition. Maurice the father and Xavier the younger son serve up pinxos (Basque tapas) with ham and foie gras, soft-cooked Aldudes bacon chunks with chickpeas, whiting with piquillo peppers and a potato purée with black olives, crispy slow-cooked Pyrénées lamb with zucchini, while Stéphane, the elder son, recommends the best Irouléguy wines to accompany this cordial cuisine. Charming rooms, a swimming pool, a fitness center and a terrace on the village square.

■ **Argi Eder**
Rte de la Chapelle.
Tel. 05 59 93 72 00. Fax 05 59 93 72 13.
argi.eder@wanadoo.fr / www.argi-eder.com
Closed beg. Nov.–end Mar.
Rest. closed Sun. dinner (exc. July–Aug.), Mon. lunch, Wed. lunch.
19 rooms: 90–110€. 7 suites: 110–150€.
Prix fixe: 25€, 36€.

The Dottax family welcomes its guests like old friends. Philippe has taken over from his father Jean-Pierre in the kitchen and rewritten the family recipe book. Foie gras and pear Tatin, roasted monkfish and creamy chorizo-seasoned jus and the squab breast on toast, served with its thigh and wing in seasoned gravy, have plenty of character. The cellar is well stocked and the service, which owes a great deal to the personal touch of Philippe's wife Eliane, soon develops a personal synergy. The rooms have been recently renovated. Swimming pool and tennis court.

■ Oppoca
Pl du Fronton.
Tel. 05 59 29 90 72. Fax 05 59 29 81 03.
oppoca@wanadoo.fr / www.oppoca.com
Hotel closed Jan. Rest. closed Sun. dinner, Mon., 12 Nov.–19 Dec.
12 rooms: 45–65€. 1 suite: 65–75€.
Prix fixe: 20€, 45€, 12€ (child).
A la carte: 45–50€.

This typical building with its wood facade and bright colors is a former post house on the road to Spain. The rooms (with a terrace or a balcony on the mountain side) are cozy, and Dominique Massonde's local cuisine avoids any hint of the commonplace. Sautéed squid and fava beans, pan-seared tuna with pepper-seasoned cannelloni, whiting filet with pepper-seasoned jus and the pineapple carpaccio with frozen lime parfait refresh the repertoire.

AIRE-SUR-L'ADOUR

40800 Landes. Paris 727 – Mont-de-Marsan 32 – Auch 84 – Pau 53 – Condom 68.
otsi.aire@wanadoo.fr.
At the crossroads of Armagnac and the Béarn, this Chalosse stronghold with its bullfights, Landes races, Saint-Jean-Baptiste cathedral, opulent Sainte-Quitterie-du-Mas-d'Aire church and grain market is splendid indeed.

 HOTELS-RESTAURANTS

■ Chez l'Ahumat
2, rue Mendès-France.
Tel. 05 58 71 82 61.
Closed 2 weeks beg. Sept., 2 weeks Mar.
Rest. closed Tue. dinner, Wed.
12 rooms: 26–37€.

Prix fixe: 10,50€, 17,50€, 20,50€, 26,50€, 7,50€ (child). A la carte: 30–35€.

Colette Labrouche offers a warm welcome in this fine village hostelry, while Françoise and Roland Dubois prepare its regional cuisine. Fresh duck liver with apples and a steamed trout with farm-raised dove in seasoned sauce grace the pleasant set menus, followed by the Armagnac-flambéed covered fruit pie.

■ Le Relais des Landes
28, rue du Quatre-Septembre.
Tel. 05 58 71 66 17. Fax 05 58 71 87 66.
31 rooms: 39–46€.

This affable little hotel standing on the bank of the Adour boasts a swimming pool and air-conditioned rooms. Breakfast is served on the terrace and ensures a bright start to the day. WiFi and heated pool.

In Segos (32400). 9 km sw via N134 and D260.
■ Domaine de Bassibé
Bassibé.
Tel. 05 62 09 46 71. Fax 05 62 08 40 15.
bassibe@wanadoo.fr / www.bassibe.fr
Closed Easter. Rest. closed lunch, Tue., Wed.
10 rooms: 130€. 7 suites: 190€.
Prix fixe: 46€.

Located in the middle of a former farm estate whose main house dates from the 13th century, this Relais & Châteaux establishment promises cozy rooms, delicious breakfasts and relaxation by the swimming pool. Converted from a former *pressoir*, the restaurant with its huge fireplace opens onto a terrace shaded by plane trees. Sébastien Gozzer, who prepares regional produce with an expert touch, delights his guests with a pork trotter and cep spring roll, sardine filets, tomato Tatin with herb vinaigrette, grilled minced goose, a royal cut of black-tailed pork and the apple and pear pastilla flavored with Armagnac. The wine list covers Madiran, Tursan and Jurançon. The prices hold no nasty shocks for us and Sylvie and Olivier Lacroix's welcome makes us feel very much at home.

AIRE-SUR-LA-LYS

62120 Pas-de-Calais. Paris 237
– Calais 61 – Arras 57 – Lille 58.
tourisme.airelys@wanadoo.fr.
This small town is still laid out on medieval
lines. Its hilly side is to be explored at a stroll,
as in a Fielding or Sterne tale. Make sure you
see the bailiff's court and collegiate church of
Saint-Pierre.

 HOTELS-RESTAURANTS

■ Hostellerie des Trois Mousquetaires

Château du fort de la Redoute, RN43.
Tel. 03 21 39 01 11. Fax 03 21 39 50 10.
www.hostelleriedes3mousquetaires.com
Closed Christmas–20 Jan.
31 rooms: 52,50–138€. 2 suites: 170€.
Prix fixe: 32€, 43€, 63€.

Set in its own grounds, this impressive
19th-century abode is built on the ruins
of Vauban's town walls. The Venets offer
a warm welcome. The rooms are cozy and
the restaurant improvises imaginatively
on Northern French flavors. Philippe skillfully prepares duck foie gras presented
with a cider vinegar–seasoned apple chutney, grilled pike-perch with fennel-seasoned béarnaise sauce, Liques poultry
with pan-tossed Saint-Omer vegetables or
pear gratin with an almond pastry cream.
A fine wine list.

AIX-EN-PROVENCE

13100 Bouches-du-Rhône. Paris 759 –
Marseille 31 – Avignon 84 – Nice 177.
loisirs@aixenprovencetourism.com.
Summer always ends under the lime trees of
Aix. Under the plane trees, too, from the Cours
Mirabeau to the terrace of the Deux Garçons.
Old houses with courtyards, ornate bell towers
and shady little squares: charm abounds in this
aristocratic city with its Provençal village flavor. Food is a tradition here. This is the country of the calisson, still made by hand, melons
and almonds. Mont Sainte-Victoire is close by,
a treat for walkers.

■ HOTELS

■ Villa Gallici

18 bis, av Violette.
Tel. 04 42 23 29 23. Fax 04 42 96 30 45.
reservation@villagallici.com
www.villagallici.com
Rest. closed Tue. (off season).
18 rooms: 220–590€. 4 suites: 400–700€.
Prix fixe: 80€ (wine inc.). A la carte: 82–105€.

This was the great secret: a Relais & Châteaux villa just outside the town center,
with charming rooms, cozy lounges and
a riot of colored fabrics. Under the supervision of Roberto Polito, it has become a
convivial hostelry, with its restaurant now
open to non-residents. Chef Christophe
Gavot, formerly at the Roquebrune Vista
Palace, offers a very "Côte d'Azur" repertoire. Squid ink tagliatelli, John Dory
with shellfish sauce and the rack of lamb
with chickpeas make a visit worthwhile.
In the shade near the swimming pool, he
offers simple lunchtime delights, including a salade niçoise, tuna and goat cheese
tart, linguini with pesto and cheesecake
with berry sauce. Away from the clamor
of the center, surrounded by lavender-
blue shutters and neo-antique statues,
we imagine ourselves to be somewhere
between Lucca and Sienna.

■ Le Pigonnet

5, av du Pigonnet.
Tel. 04 42 59 02 90. Fax 04 42 59 47 77.
reservation@hotelpigonnet.com
www.hotelpigonnet.com
Rest. closed Sat. lunch.
51 rooms: 140–570€.
Prix fixe: 46€. A la carte: 74€.

The renovation has not detracted from this
hotel's timeless charm. Walking the paths
trod by Cézanne, we succumb to the lure
of the shady grounds. The rooms provide a
view of Mont Sainte-Victoire. At the stove,
Thierry Granero has revived a series of
trusted classics. Pan-tossed langoustines
with slow-cooked beets and the slice of
stuffed and rolled veal and sesame pastilla
are splendid. A fine Sunday brunch.

■ Aquabella

2, rue des Etuves.
Tel. 04 42 99 15 00. Fax 04 42 99 15 01.
info@aquabella.fr / www.aquabella.fr
110 rooms: 135–185€.
Prix fixe: 13€, 21€, 25€, 12€ (child).
A la carte: 35–40€.

A modern, functional extension to the Sextius thermal baths, this huge Partouche group property is worth a visit for its range of facilities and Fabrice Lemesle's cuisine. Red mullet over mixed greens with tapenade, Atlantic sea bass with artichokes and the honey-roasted lamb set the tone. The "Fitness and Relaxation" area offers a sauna, steam bath, whirlpool bath, cardio training machines and outdoor swimming pool.

■ Grand Hôtel Roi René

24, bd Roi-René.
Tel. 04 42 37 61 00. Fax 04 42 37 61 11.
h1169@accor.com / www.mercure.com
131 rooms: 165–250€. 3 suites: 320€.
Prix fixe: 28€, 38€.

Opposite the old town, this contemporary hotel with swimming pool is a practical place to stay. Its neat rooms are peaceful and relaxing. Christine Latour prepares the classical, well-crafted cuisine. Duck foie gras seasoned with Muscat, Mediterranean sea bass with tapenade and lamb medallions with slow-cooked garlic are unpretentious.

■ Hôtel Cézanne

40, av Victor-Hugo.
Tel. 04 42 91 11 11. Fax 04 42 91 11 10.
hotelcezanne@hotelaix.com
www.hotelaix.com
53 rooms: 120–170€. 2 suites: 195€.

Near the station, this hotel, devoted to the painter of Sainte-Victoire, boasts charming rooms with all modern conveniences, a free minibar and broadband. Attractive Provençal furniture.

■ Grand Hôtel Nègre Coste

33, cours Mirabeau.
Tel. 04 42 27 74 22. Fax 04 42 26 80 93.
contact@hotelnegrecoste.com
www.hotelnegrecoste.com
40 rooms: 85–145€.

Right in the heart of the Cours Mirabeau, this 18th-century town house is still a prime address for lovers of this city. The rooms have been refurbished with all modern facilities but still have a charming, old-fashioned feel to them.

■ Hôtel en Ville

2, pl Bellegarde.
Tel. 04 42 63 34 16. Fax 04 42 23 34 76.
contact@hotelenville.fr / www.hotelenville.fr
10 rooms: 75€.

This delightful little corner hotel opposite the old town makes for a choice break. A friendly bar and relaxing, contemporary, refined rooms.

■ Les Quatre Dauphins

54, rue Roux-Alpheran.
Tel. 04 42 38 16 39. Fax 04 42 38 60 19.
lesquatredauphins@wanadoo.fr
13 rooms: 55–120€.

This city center hostelry offers some of the best local value for money. The air-conditioned rooms with double glazing are not very large but attractively decorated.

● RESTAURANTS

● Le Clos de la Violette

10, av de la Violette.
Tel. 04 42 23 30 71. Fax 04 42 21 93 03.
restaurant@closdelaviolette.fr
www.closdelaviolette.fr
Closed Sun., Mon. lunch, Wed. lunch,
2 weeks Aug.
Prix fixe: 54€ (lunch), 90€, 130€.
A la carte: 140€.

Artist Banzo is in excellent form. Our "Two Plate" chef from the avenue de la Violette has been running his fine house and garden on the edge of the old town for exactly twenty years now, and has recently opened a new establishment, the Villa Madie, in Cassis. Like Cadet

Rousselle with his three homes, Jean-Marc Banzo has the power of ubiquity. Seconded by Enrico Bernardo, his former sommelier who became world champion in his category at the Paris George V, he will be keeping more than a foot in Aix. The setting at his Clos, refurbished contemporary-style in shades of brown, is chic and handsome. The cuisine displays a flawless refinement and stunning honesty. The herb-stuffed squid with squid ink ravioli, the vegetable anthology with pain d'épice crumbs and foie gras, grilled red mullet filet with bouillabaisse mousseline and, finally, the juicy lamb served with a bulgur pesto involve no fuss or frills, just the truth of pure, flavorful produce. On top of this, there are some exceptional desserts (spéculos cookies with raspberry, nougat Tropézienne). Washed down by a splendid, direct-pressing *rosé* from Sainte-Roseline, all of this forms a dazzlingly fresh spread.

● **Yamato** ⊙COM

21, av des Belges.
Tel. 04 42 38 00 20. Fax 04 42 38 52 65.
yamato.kojiyuriko@wanadoo.fr
www.restaurant-yamato.com
Closed Mon. lunch, Tue. lunch, July.
Prix fixe: 48€, 63€. A la carte: 62€.

The best Japanese restaurant outside Paris? Koji Someya's. This town house with its Zen garden, teak terrace and neat tables exudes an easy charm. Yuriko welcomes guests in traditional costume, while Koji, who worked at the Fenière for six years, prepares squid brochettes, cold soba noodles, a variety of very fresh sushi, mushroom chawanmushi (egg flan), beef okonomiyaki (cake), shrimp, fish and vegetable tempura and a highly subtle caramelized chicken yakitori. The Franco-Japanese desserts (mascarpone and shaved ice with green tea syrup, mango and fromage blanc) are enchanting and the wine list a treasure trove of delicious surprises.

● **Le Formal** ■COM

32, rue Espariat.
Tel.-Fax 04 42 27 08 31.

Closed Sat. lunch, Sun., Mon. lunch, 1 week Jan., mid-June–mid-July.
Prix fixe: 18€ (lunch), 22€ (lunch), 29,50€, 46€.

Yvonne and Jean-Luc Formal take great pride in both their welcome and their cuisine. Along a busy street, their unobtrusive facade conceals a vaulted 15th-century cellar, a haven of coolness where guests savor pan-seared scallops, symphony of foie gras, grilled Atlantic sea bass, mushroom-stuffed lamb in basil crust and the "Cezanne's palette" dessert. The contemporary pictures on the walls, smiling service and low prices inspire enthusiasm and provide a delightfully simple moment of relaxation.

● **Les Deux Frères** ⓃCOM

4, av Reine-Astrid.
Tel. 04 42 27 90 32.
Closed Sun. dinner (off season), 3 Nov.
Prix fixe: 26€.

This antique restaurant in the heart of a residential quarter in the old town, five minutes on foot from the Cours Mirabeau, has been fully refurbished. The new décor is contemporary and refined and the cuisine still has a Mediterranean feel to it. In the center, a giant, translucent screen shows the dishes being prepared in the kitchen. A contemporary art exhibition is held every two months and cooking lessons are given.

● **Le Sud** ⓃCOM

Petite rue Saint-Jean.
Tel. 04 42 26 14 60.
Closed Sun., Mon.
Prix fixe: 29€, 38€.

Near the law courts, this contemporary bistro with its stools, vaults and shades of gray is the latest attraction in town. Culinary enthusiast Pascal Monty sold his gyms to open this relaxed restaurant, which has rapidly gained a following. It serves subtle, healthy, fresh and very topical dishes. Duck breast carpaccio heightened with a mustard vinaigrette, sesame-seasoned sea bream, lamb kidneys stuffed with tapenade and the ginger-seasoned apple dessert with shaved manzana verde ice and honey jelly provide a succession of sweet surprises. The wine list pays tribute to the greater South of France without too much harm to our pockets.

● **L'Aixquis** COM

22, rue Leydet.
Tel. 04 42 27 76 16. Fax 04 42 93 10 61.
www.aixquis.fr
Closed Sun., Mon. lunch, mid-Aug.–10 Sept.
A la carte: 60€.

Benoît Strohm focuses on carefully chosen produce and unfussy dishes. His simple, tasty preparations include gazpacho with lobster mousseline, grilled Mediterranean sea bass with mushroom- and ham-stuffed artichokes simmered in wine and the lamb wrapped in caul lace with thyme-seasoned gravy. The chocolate crêpes Suzette dessert almost eats itself. A very considerate welcome from Eliane Strohm.

● **L'Amphitryon** COM

2-4, rue Paul-Doumer.
Tel. 04 42 26 54 10. Fax 04 42 38 36 15.
amphitryon22@wanadoo.fr
Closed Sun., Mon., mid-Aug.–end Aug.
Prix fixe: 21€, 26€, 35€, 15€ (child).
A la carte: 45–50€.

No unpleasant surprises from Bruno Ungaro, who offers sensible set menus and market-based cuisine. Tomato and cucumber salad, two of today's catch served in one dish, oven-roasted pork tenderloin medallion with slow-cooked apricots and the frozen coconut soufflé with mango slip down effortlessly. Patrice Lesne chooses the right bottle for us from his stock of fine wines from Provence.

● **La Rotonde** COM

Pl du Général-de-Gaulle.
Tel. 04 42 91 61 70. Fax 04 42 27 71 97.
fontaine.mirabeau@wanadoo.fr
www.larotonde-aix.com
Prix fixe: 24,50€, 10€ (child). A la carte: 60€.

Chefs change, but the brasserie spirit remains in this modern, timeless eatery. The Thai chicken salad, eggplant dish,

whole grilled Mediterranean sea bass, stir-fried chicken with citrus preceeding the dark chocolate cake with cookie ice cream are all smoothly prepared under the eye of Philippe Sublet. The prices are pitiless, though.

● **La Chimère Café** SIM

15, rue Brueys.
Tel. 04 42 38 30 00. Fax 04 42 27 29 57.
Closed lunch, Sun., Christmas–New Year's.
Prix fixe: 26,50€.

This former nightclub converted into a restaurant is still a fashionable haunt assiduously frequented by the people of Aix, so it is best to reserve if you want a chance to taste Stéphane Marie's low-priced classics. If the Pont-l'évêque with yellow apples and peppered cider caramel, the grilled red tuna with slow-cooked fennel, the duck breast with roasted figs and spicy red wine sauce and the frozen walnut and coconut soufflé are anything to judge by, his success is in no danger of decline.

● **Le Passage** SIM

10, rue Villars.
Tel. 04 42 37 09 00.
contact@le-passage.fr
Prix fixe: 22€ (tasting menu), 35€.
A la carte: 50€.

This former chocolate shop, turned into a contemporary restaurant by the Sammuts from the Fenière, still has its cast-iron framework. The conversion has been a success. On the first or second floor, guests savor well-thought-out dishes by Franck Dumont. As well as a gourmet theater, the house serves as a tearoom, wine library, cooking school and exhibition center. Its success shows no sign of faltering and this has not a little to do with the "discovery" option at 22 . Tomato and goat cheese crumble, poultry liver terrine with onion compote, fish escabeche served with heirloom tomatoes and the grilled veal tenderloin with walnut-seasoned mashed potatoes are well crafted. The sweet things, Paris-Brest (a choux pastry ring with almonds and butter cream) and the frozen blackberry parfait, are a regression to our childhood. Noisy atmosphere and brisk service.

● Chez Grand-Mère

11, rue Isolette / Pl Raphin-Gilly.
Tel. 04 42 53 33 47.
Closed Sun., Mon. lunch.
Prix fixe: 24,50€, 34,50€.

This colorful bistro with its frescos, appealing facade and terrace opposite a fountain conjures up the Provence of yesteryear. Offering a rabbit terrine, red mullet in aspic or a toro rump roast with a caramel Tropézienne for dessert, it is modest, fresh, eloquent and not too expensive. In short, a delightful place.

● Icone   SIM

3, rue Frédéric-Mistral.
Tel. 04 42 27 59 82. Fax 04 42 93 03 84.
Closed Mon., Wed., 10 days Aug.
Prix fixe: 18€, 21€. A la carte: 50€.

The contemporary décor is attractive and Yvan Croisier's cuisine deft enough. The Provençal fried squid, risotto-stuffed fish or the baba au rhum do no harm to our stomach or pocket.

● Le Saïgon   SIM

2 bis, rue Aumône-Vieille.
Tel. 04 42 26 05 48.
Prix fixe: 12€ (lunch), 14€ (lunch), 15€ (dinner), 24€ (dinner), 9€ (child). A la carte: 25–30€.

The Amiants run this fine Vietnamese eatery in old Aix. A spicy shrimp soup, the bo buns, "*trois bonheurs de la mer*" and the caramelized pork ribs are reliably served in a very polished setting.

● Yôji   SIM

7, av Victor-Hugo.
Tel. 04 42 38 48 76. Fax 04 42 38 47 01.
Closed Sun., Mon. lunch.
Prix fixe: 22€, 27€, 29€. A la carte: 35–40€.

The refined décor with its aquariums and paneling, and the terrace with its Japanese garden, are a temple to "shunju", the new Japanese cuisine based on seasonal produce. Shrimp tempura, mushroom salad,

sushi, sashimi, sukiyaki, fujikama and Korean barbecue, as well as the crunchy chocolate tempura dessert, are not bad.

● Le Zinc d'Hugo   SIM

22-24, rue Lieutaud.
Tel.-Fax 04 42 27 69 69.
Closed Sun., Mon., Christmas, 1 week Feb., 3 weeks July.
Prix fixe: 14€ (lunch), 19,50€ (dinner) 10€ (child). A la carte: 45€.

Christophe Formeau has energetically taken on this affable eatery in the heart of the city center. Refined dishes (sometimes fusion style) and wines to match are served in the modern bistro dining room. Lamb pastilla, slow-cooked monkfish with ginger, duck filet with almonds and truffled mushroom ravioli and the quince chutney tiramisu make a fine impression.

73100 Savoie. Paris 543 – Annecy 34 – Bourg-en-Bresse 111 – Chambéry 18 – Lyon 107.
otta@aixlesbains.com.
On the shore of the Lac du Bourget immortalized by Lamartine, this spa town is reputed for the curative effect on respiratory tract and rheumatological disorders. Standing over it, Mont Revard is a joy for hikers in summer and skiers in winter.

▣ HOTELS-RESTAURANTS

■ Radisson SAS Hôtel Aix   🏨

Avenue Charles-de-Gaulle.
Tel. 04 79 34 19 19. Fax 04 79 88 11 49.
info.aixlesbains@radissonsas.com
www.radissonsas.com
92 rooms: 95–135€. 10 suites: 135–185€.
Prix fixe: 19€, 22€, 24€, 29€, 9,15€ (child).

This luxury hotel in the great spa tradition boasts spacious, refined rooms on the casino grounds. To keep yourself in shape, try the indoor swimming pool and steam bath and take advantage of theraputic treatments provided by specialists. Julien serves up dishes with a contemporary flavor: tomato gazpacho, the Périgord-style duo with peach sweet-and-sour reduction,

breaded and fried veal sweetbread escalope and roasted pineapple with coconut
ice cream are enchanting.

■ Mercure Ariana

Avenue Marlioz, in Marlioz (1,5 km).
Tel. 04 79 61 79 79. Fax 04 79 61 79 00.
h2945@accor-hotels.com / www.mercure.com
Closed Sept.
60 rooms: 86–140€.
Prix fixe: 24€, 32€.

Near the rail station, this thirties residence,
now part of the Marlioz spa complex, boasts
spacious rooms, some with a balcony looking out on the mountains. We enjoy the
wealth of equipment available (balneotherapy, fitness center, steam bath, swimming
pool and Jacuzzi), before recovering at the
Grand Café Adélaïde, where Christophe
Coutaz serves lobster salad, grilled shrimp
brochette, beef filet pan tossed in olive oil
and a frozen chocolate parfait.

● Brasserie de la Poste `COM`

32, av Victoria.
Tel. 04 79 35 00 65.
Closed Mon.
Prix fixe: 11€, 20€, 29€, 7€ (child).
A la carte: 35€.

The sixties setting is lively, the atmosphere—presided over by Olivier Ouvrier-
Neyret—is pleasant and Bruno Boulanger's
cuisine is sufficiently adept. Quail terrine,
pike-perch seared skin-side down, veal
kidneys with whole grain mustard and
the tart of the day are simple and flavorsome. Reasonable prices.

ALBARET-SAINTE-MARIE see
SAINT-CHELY-D'APCHER

ALBERTVILLE

73200 Savoie. Paris 584 – Annecy 45 –
Chambéry 51 – Grenoble 81.
tourisme@albertville.com.
On the road to the ski runs, this town conjures up
memories of the Winter Olympics with its wonderful sports facilities. Old Conflans reminds us
of the Savoy villages of yesteryear.

■ HOTELS-RESTAURANTS

■ Million

8, pl de la Liberté.
Tel. 04 79 32 25 15. Fax 04 79 32 25 36.
hotel.million@wanadoo.fr / www.hotelmillion.com
Rest. closed Sat. lunch, Sun. dinner, Mon.,
2 weeks beg. Nov., 2 weeks beg. May.
26 rooms: 70–87€.
Prix fixe: 26€, 52€, 70€. A la carte: 80€.

This hotel had its golden age under
Philippe Million. The rooms here are neat
and perfectly equipped. José de Anacleto
concocts a market-based, seasonal cuisine
including a crab cake with baby vegetables
and poultry stock emulsion, pan-tossed
fennel-seasoned John Dory with sundried
tomatoes and roasted rack of lamb with a
parmesan risotto. The lemon dessert with
assorted sorbets provides a light, sweet
conclusion. The cellar is capital, the service lively and the check honest, especially
if we choose from the set menus.

ALBI

81000 Tarn. Paris 680 – Toulouse 75 –
Béziers 149.
accueil@albitourisme.com.
The red brick cathedral of Sainte-Cécile, Toulouse-Lautrec's home, the old quarter with its
alleys and the Tarn flowing below all contribute
to Albi's charm and price. The town also has a
natural love of food and boasts a *pâtisserie* that
is well worth a visit.

■ HOTELS-RESTAURANTS

■ La Réserve

Rte de Cordes.
Tel. 05 63 60 80 80. Fax 05 63 47 63 60.
lareserve@relaischateaux.com
www.relaischateaux.com/reservealbi
Closed end Oct.–beg. May. Rest. closed Mon.
lunch, Wed. lunch, Thu. lunch.
21 rooms: 150–295€. 2 suites: 395€.
Prix fixe: 38€, 58€. A la carte: 75–85€.

In her vast, shady abode on the bank of
the Tarn, Hélène Hijosa-Rieux is a skilled

hostess. She has even received the Queen of England, which really says all we need to know about the quality of her welcome. We enjoy the soothing tranquility of the grounds, the comfort of the rooms overlooking the swimming pool and a spot of relaxation after a session in the fitness center or Jacuzzi, before we sit down to eat in the dining room or on the terrace, savoring the delicate dishes carefully prepared by Jean-Pierre Emonet, among them crayfish mille-feuille, creamy langoustine risotto, tasty squab and a Grand Marnier soufflé.

■ Hostellerie Saint-Antoine

17, rue Saint-Antoine.
Tel. 05 63 54 04 04. Fax 05 63 47 10 47.
hotel@saint-antoine-albi.com
www.saint-antoine-albi.com
44 rooms: 76–185€. 3 suites: 185–225€.

This hostelry's fortunes are inseparably linked to those of the Rieux family, since it has been in their hands for five generations. Today, in place of the monastery founded in 1734, there is a hotel with huge, fully equipped rooms. The flower garden, gourmet breakfasts, swimming pool and tennis court are additional arguments in its favor.

■ Grand Hôtel d'Orléans

Pl Stalingrad.
Tel. 05 63 54 16 56. Fax 05 63 54 43 41.
hoteldorleans@wanadoo.fr
Rest. closed Sat. (exc. dinner Apr.–Oct.),
Sun., 1 week Dec., 1 week Jan.,
1 week Feb., 2 weeks Aug.
48 rooms: 60–132€.

Since 1902, this traditional establishment opposite the rail station has been greeting guests with great warmth. Functional rooms, regional cuisine and service by the pool when the sun shines.

■ Mercure-Albi-Bastides

41 bis, rue Porta.
Tel. 05 63 47 66 66. Fax 05 63 46 18 40.
h1211@accor-hotels.com / www.mercure.com
Rest. closed Sat. lunch (off season), Sun.
lunch (off season), end Dec.–end Jan.
56 rooms: 76–95€.

Prix fixe: 18€, 23€, 28€.
A la carte: 35–40€.

This former mill whose windows open onto the Tarn and cathedral provides a personal welcome, pleasantly furnished rooms and a decorous restaurant. Pascal Poirier's marbled foie gras terrine presented in strips and the pike-perch with ceps are in very good taste. Excellent local vintages recommended with gusto by Jérome Cathala.

■ Le Vieil Alby

23-25, rue Toulouse-Lautrec.
Tel. 05 63 54 14 69 / 05 63 38 28 23.
Fax 05 63 54 96 75.
levieilalby@orange.fr
perso.orange.fr/le-vieil-alby
Closed Sat. lunch (hotel open), Sun. dinner,
Mon., 3 weeks Jan., 2 weeks July.
9 rooms: 47€.
Prix fixe: 14€ (weekday lunch), 20€, 27€,
30€, 35€, 45 €, 10€ (child). A la carte: 35€.

The Sicards always provide a warm welcome. The rooms and dining room here display character. Claude greets the guests, while Christophe works in the kitchen, preparing monkfish with ham, pike-perch ballotine with crayfish and lamb medallions with pink garlic cream. Johanne provides lively, prompt service.

● L'Esprit du Vin

11, quai Choiseul.
Tel. 05 63 54 60 44. Fax 05 63 54 54 79.
lespritduvin@free.fr
Closed Sun., Mon., 2 weeks Jan., 1 week July.
Prix fixe: 30€ (weekday lunch),
15€ (child). A la carte: 75€.

The new star of Albi is David Enjalran. This native of Carmaux worked with Dutournier in Paris for three years, then at the Waterside in Bray-on-Thames, before returning home. A modest exponent of clear-cut tastes, he concocts talented preparations that show great respect for their produce. In the two vaulted dining rooms in pink brick, we taste creamy asparagus soup served with a poached egg and heightened with smoked herring caviar, filet of turbot and pork trotter presented carpaccio style with arugula, a Mont Royal pigeon with licorice root–seasoned jumbo shrimp and delicately crafted desserts ("club café" with light cream, meringue, coconut sorbet, nougatine cone with chocolate mousse), highly successful in a light, fresh manner. The finest wines from Gaillac or Rotier accompany his dishes. In short, this is an eatery where we would happily dine on a regular basis.

● **Jardin des Quatre Saisons**   `COM`
19, bd de Strasbourg.
Tel.-Fax 05 63 60 77 76.
lejardindes4saisons@tiscali.fr
http://lejardindes4saisons.chez-alice.fr
Closed Sun. dinner, Mon.
Prix fixe: 20€, 26€, 33€.

No à la carte dishes, but set menus at moderate prices put together by Georges Bermont with an eye to local produce and flattered by shrewdly chosen wines, especially vintages from the Southwest, a successful concept that segues from the marbled duck terrine with foie gras and seafood pot-au-feu to the roasted lamb shank seasoned with thyme and the chocolate dessert with pain d'épice ice cream.

● **Le Lautrec**   `N` `COM`
13, rue Henri Toulouse-Lautrec.
Tel. 05 63 54 86 55
www.restaurant-le-lautrec.com
Closed Sun. dinner, Mon., 15 Feb.–Mar. 1, last week Aug.
Prix fixe: 16€ (lunch, weekday.), 28€, 30€.

Sandrine and Antoine Caramelli have energetically taken over this corner eatery opposite Toulouse-Lautrec's house. The tables are neat and the flavors of the Tarn are showcased in set menus devoted to local produce. The local garlic and gizzard salad with melsat (a Tarn white sausage), the saffron-seasoned escargots with pink garlic and the famous cod cassoulet deserve praise, as does the "tartouillat" with fresh fruit in season and assorted house ice creams.

● **L'Epicurien**   `N` `SIM`
42, pl Jean-Jaurès.
Tel. 05 63 53 10 70.

www.restaurantlepicurien.com
Closed Sun., Mon., 3 days end Dec., beg. Aug.–end Aug.
Prix fixe: 18€ (lunch), 34€, 39€.

Rikard Hult, a Swede who has succumbed to the lures of the land of plenty, has made a lasting success of this serviceable eatery decorated in beige and gray. The place is chic and the service energetic. Behind the panoramic windows, Rikard cooks to order. Lox with radishes and asparagus, cod filet with artichoke terrine and lamb saddle with cannelloni are the epitome of freshness. The sweet treats (tart with slow-cooked rhubarb and fresh fromage blanc mousse) would not disgrace the neighboring *pâtisserie* Belin.

● **Stéphane Laurens**   `N` `SIM`
10, pl Monseigneur Mignot.
Tel. 05 63 43 62 41.
Closed Tue., 1 week Feb. vac.
Prix fixe: 24€. A la carte: 40€.

After training with Noël in Réalmont, the Oustal del Barry in Najac and Veyrat in Annecy, then moving on to cater for Formula 1 Grand Prix motor racing, Stéphane Laurens has set up business by the cathedral in this refined setting of stone and wood with parquet flooring and timber work, where he prepares a sensible, tasty cuisine. Tartiflette, softly poached salmon with cilantro, grilled squid served with pan-seared foie gras, veal sweetbreads meunière with vegetable purée and the airy hot citrus soufflé with Grand Marnier are all gratifying.

● **La Table du Sommelier**   `SIM`
20, rue Porta.
Tel.-Fax 05 63 46 20 10.
Closed Sun., Mon., Bank holidays.
Prix fixe: 16€ (lunch), 20€ (dinner), 25€, 30€ (wine inc.).

Daniel Pestre is at home in Castres, Gaillac and Albi. This magician of fine wines and dishes has a secret: teamwork. His Albi restaurant is founded on reliability, not only his own, but also that of his chef Ludovic Chuzeaud and sommeliers Baptiste Bleuzé and Benjamin Massuyes. We savor a Prieuré Saint-Roch Minervois, a Brousse Gaillac and a Ramos Pinto white at reasonable prices. Country meat pâté, goat cheese and pepper cake, osso bucco and a fruit minestrone with Grand Marnier slip down smooth as velvet.

ALBIAS see MONTAUBAN

LES ALDUDES see
SAINT-ETIENNE-DE-BAÏGORRY

ALENÇON

61000 Orne. Paris 194 – Chartres 118 –
Le Mans 50 – Laval 90 – Rouen 148.
alencon.tourisme@wanadoo.fr.
The capital of the Orne is worth a detour for the antique charm of its alleyways, its fine lace museum, art gallery and Notre-Dame church with sculpted porches and stained glass windows.

 HOTELS-RESTAURANTS

■ Mercure
187, av Général-Leclerc.
Tel. 02 33 28 64 64.
Closed Christmas–New Year's.
53 rooms: 56–60€.

Quite a way out of town, right on the Le Mans road, this modern establishment offers genuine standardized comfort with neat rooms for a good night's rest.

■ Le Grand Cerf
21, rue Saint-Blaise.
Tel. 02 33 26 00 51. Fax 02 33 26 63 07.
www.hotelgrandcerf.61.com
Closed end Dec.–beg. Jan. Rest. closed Sun.
22 rooms: 47–63€.
Prix fixe: 14€ (lunch), 18€, 26€,
8€ (child). A la carte: 30–35€.

Although Michel Bouvet pays tribute to Norman produce, for some time now he has been adding a deliberate touch of the South. This is an amusing, harmless trick, as evinced by duck breast stuffed with foie gras served with a melon sauce, niçoise-style red mullet filet and the pork tenderloin medallion seasoned with green peppercorns. The chocolate croustillant served with custard cream is delightful. The welcome and service are pleasant, the rooms comfortable (rather than luxurious) and the prices hold no surprises.

● Au Petit Vatel
72, pl Cdt-Desmeulles.
Tel. 02 33 26 23 78. Fax 02 33 82 64 57.
Closed Sun. dinner, Wed., July–beg. Aug.
Prix fixe: 16€ (lunch), 19€, 25,50€,
29,50€, 37,50€, 69€. A la carte: 38–45€.

The Fuleps run this good-natured institution in the town center. Jean-Pierre, who worked at the Dauphin in L'Aigle, juggles with the region's finest produce to perform genuinely worthwhile classical tricks. Fried Camembert salad, sea trout tart seasoned with cider, the mixed lobster dish with garden vegetables and the duck breast with a locally inspired sauce are dishes with a delightful regional connotation. Make sure you leave room for an apple croustillant with Calvados and especially the seventeen ice creams served in their silver pots (both the rum raisin and the coffee are superb).

● Le Chapeau Rouge
117, rue de Bretagne.
Tel. 02 33 26 57 33.
Closed 2 weeks Sept., Sat., Sun.
Prix fixe: 12,50€ (lunch), 15,80€, 21,50€,
24€. A la carte: 32€.

In their modest, roadside setting with tables covered in yellow and red cloths, Sophie and James Henry present practical set menus whose options allow us to wander extensively through the dishes. A native of Sologne from La Ferté Saint-Aubin, James formerly worked with Michel Peignaud at the Belle Epoque de Châteaufort, in Alsace at the Trois Epis Grand Hôtel and at the Lisbon Intercontinental, all of which suggests a penchant for travel, a conclusion borne out by his cuisine, which is not short on imagination and even displays some fine creative impulses. Pain d'épice flan with goat cheese and pears, whiting filets with olives and quince with a side of saffron-seasoned celery root salad, before the orange carpaccio with saffron syrup and olive confiture, which packs a pretty punch.

● Le Bistro
21, rue de la Sarthe.
Tel. 02 33 26 51 69.
Closed Sun., Mon., Bank holidays,
1 week Christmas–New Year's, 1 week May,
3 weeks Aug.
Prix fixe: 12,80€ (lunch), 19€.

Annie and Philippe Charbonnier run this cheerful town center bistro where they serve timeless dishes with an informal touch. Red checked tablecloths, affable set menus, carefree wines and charming service are all ingredients of their long-term success. Choosing from the blackboard, we enjoy fish soup, escargots with walnut-infused vinegar, monkfish filet with creamed leeks and grilled boneless rib steak with sel de Guérande. The madeleines prepared like pain perdu and the Norman-style dessert are sweet treats.

ALIX

69380 Rhône. Paris 444 – Lyon 30 – Villefranche-sur-Saône 12.
Beaujolais starts with the land of golden stones.

●	RESTAURANTS

● Le Vieux Moulin   COM
Chemin du Vieux-Moulin.
Tel. 04 78 43 91 66. Fax 04 78 47 98 46.
lemoulindalix@wanadoo.fr
Closed Mon., Tue., mid-Aug.–mid-Sept.
Prix fixe: 27€, 38€, 50€. A la carte: 45–50€.

The Umhauers have turned this mill into a good, reliable eatery. Annie offers a smiling welcome, while Jean-Pierre's cooking comes straight from the heart. House foie gras, monkfish in cream sauce, sirloin steak with morels and the house ice cream are washed down with very honest Beaujolais wines.

ALLEYRAS

43580 Haute-Loire. Paris 556 – Le Puy 32 – Brioude 71 – Langogne 43 – Saint-Chély-d'Apcher 59.
The heart of the Velay region, mountain air at a height of over 700 meters, the land of the Noisettes Sauvages and healthy appetites that are promptly sated.

■/●	HOTELS-RESTAURANTS

● Haut-Allier   ◎ ❀ 🏠
Pont d'Alleyras, 2 km n via D40.
Tel. 04 71 57 57 63. Fax 04 71 57 57 99.
hot.rest.hautallier@wanadoo.fr
www.hotel-lehautallier.com
Closed mid-Nov.–mid-Mar.
Rest. closed Mon. and Tue. (exc. July–Aug.).
8 rooms: 85–95€. 5 suites: 110–120€.
Prix fixe: 28€, 88€. A la carte: 63€.

The pleasure we feel at returning to the Bruns' establishment as loyal converts is not blunted by our slow climb up the road that winds along the gorges of the Allier. Our reward is commensurate with the effort involved. Michelle is terribly attentive and her welcome more than compensates for any hardship. With its view plunging down into the valley, the restaurant presents the finest dishes prepared by Philippe Brun, who studied with Jamin and at the Marée and Taillevent. This expert technician demonstrates his skills with crayfish simmered in white wine, shallots and oyster mushrooms, seasonal vegetables in truffle-seasoned broth and a gently cooked salmon trout with herb sauce. We also love the more rustic rabbit saddle terrine stuffed with olives or the roasted Velay lamb served with thin tomato cakes. The "geometric" dessert with green tea sauce and Thuao chocolate provides a choice conclusion. The wine list features 550 vintages and Michelle supplies sound advice to help us choose among them. The service has energy to spare. The large, bright rooms exude a simple elegance. Finally, we should not forget the steam bath, heated swimming pool and fitness center that add the final touch to a dream stay in this little corner of paradise.

ALOXE-CORTON see BEAUNE

L'ALPE-D'HUEZ

38750 Isère. Paris 630 – Grenoble 62 –
Le Bourg-d'Oisans 13 – Briançon 72.
info@alpedhuez.com.

This star resort in the Oisans massif has clung to its former charm, but still manages to flirt with modern tastes. After we have done a little skiing on the pistes and admired the panoramic view from the peak of Lac-Blanc, we soon warm up in a relaxed hostelry. A healthy appetite is the best counsel here.

 HOTELS-RESTAURANTS

■ Au Chamois d'Or

Rond-point des Pistes.
Tel. 04 76 80 31 32. Fax 04 76 80 34 90.
resa@chamoisdor-alpedhuez.com
www.chamoisdor-alpedhuez.com
Closed end Apr.–mid-Dec.
40 rooms: 230–300€. 4 suites: 650–930€.
Prix fixe: 31,50€ (lunch), 36,50€ (lunch),
49€, 53,50€, 59€.

The star of L'Alpe-d'Huez, Jean-Pierre and Philippe Seigle's chalet hotel has true mountain chic. Its heated pool, Jacuzzi and steam bath are prized by skiers. The rooms are handsome exercises in woodwork. In the restaurant, we listen intently as the affable majordomo presents the meticulous classical menu. Truffle omelet, strips of sole with white wine and chive sauce, veal medallion with mushroom cream sauce and the raspberry gratin with frozen parfait are an unqualified pleasure.

■ Royal Ours Blanc

Av des Jeux.
Tel. 04 79 65 07 65 (by reserv.).
resa@eurogroup-vacances.com
Closed end Apr.–mid-Dec.
47 rooms: 119–229€ per person half board.

Eighties luxury in this large, rather impersonal vessel. Thermal baths and swimming pool on site.

■ Les Grandes Rousses

Rte du Signal.
Tel. 04 76 80 33 11. Fax 04 76 80 69 57.
hmcdesgrandesrousses@hmc-hotels.com
www.hmc-hotels.com
Closed beg. Sept.–beg. Dec.,
mid-Apr.–beg. July.
60 rooms: 101–200€. 10 suites: 181–418€.

This large renovated chalet in the middle of the resort offers smart mountain rooms.

■ Le Printemps de Juliette

Av des Jeux.
Tel. 04 76 11 44 38. Fax 04 76 11 44 37.
www.leprintempsdejuliette.com
4 rooms: 80–120€. 4 suites: 190–240€.
Half board: 110–215€.

Juliette Collomb's chalet and tearoom in the heart of the resort is a charming place to stay. This has more than a little to do with our hostess' smile, not to mention the elegantly refurbished rooms in light wood and toile de Jouy. The house pastries make a delightful afternoon snack.

■ L'Ancolie

Av de l'Eglise, Huez.
Tel. 04 76 11 13 13. Fax 04 76 11 13 11.
www.hebergement-florineige.com
16 rooms: 52–94€.

Ski instructors the Forestiers have appealingly renovated this antique abode in the heart of the old village. The rooms are charming and light, and there is a delightful little restaurant just next door, dynamically managed by a young Touraine chef who has rallied round the Dauphiné flag.

● Au P'tit Creux

Chemin des Bergers.
Tel. 04 76 80 62 80. Fax 04 76 80 39 37.
Closed Sept.–beg. Dec., May–end June.
Prix fixe: 40€. A la carte: 50–55€.

Bernadette and Jean-Marie Géhin still work their wonders in an elegantly refurbished dining room on the mountainside, and on their terrace, which overlooks the peaks. Cooking comes as naturally to Bernadette as song to a thrush. Arugula cream with Réblochon cheese and ratte potatoes, pumpkin cappuccino with crispy bacon, guinea hen with Vin Jaune and the frozen soufflé with chestnuts are remarkably delicate dishes. Fine Savoy wines in the bargain.

● Le Passe-Montagne 🔒SIM

Rte de la Poste.
Tel. 04 76 11 31 53.
le.passe.montagne@wanadoo.fr
Closed Wed. lunch (off season).
Prix fixe: 18€ (lunch), 25€ (dinner),
10€ (child). A la carte: 40€.

The rustic dining room here has a mountain chic, the set menus are a steal and the Lanots pull out all the stops to make sure their guests enjoy their visit. As Valérie welcomes us, Philippe concocts his shrewd, sensible dishes. Saint-Marcellin cheese in a salad sprinkled with nuts, pike-perch meunière, layered potato and oxtail casserole with foie gras and the apple croustillant are fleeting moments of joy.

● L'Altiport SIM

Altiport Henry-Giraud.
Tel.-Fax 04 76 80 41 15.
du-chamond@wanadoo.fr
Closed mid-Sept.–end Nov., May–mid-June.
Prix fixe: 12€, 25€, 8€ (child).
A la carte: 40€.

The view of the mountains from the terrace is superb and Philippe Piloz's cuisine is enchanting. His variations on theme of foie gras (terrine, soft-cooked with potatoes and with creamy morel sauce) and the frog legs with crayfish and the Saint-Jean ravioli add to our stock of pleasant memories.

● L'Authentique SIM

Av des Jeux.
Tel. 04 76 80 43 31.
contact@lauthentique.eu / www.lauthentique.eu
Closed beg. Sept.–end Nov., May–mid-June.
Prix fixe: 19,90€, 25,90€, 9€ (child).
A la carte: 40€.

This "pasta hut" with its timber setting presents an antipasti plate, asparagus fritata, salmon trout with chanterelles and a selection of enjoyable desserts (tiramisu, a big macaron with mocha cream).

René Peltier energetically presides over his small world.

● La Cabane du Poutat SIM

Secteur des Bergers.
Tel.-Fax 04 76 80 42 88.
Closed dinner (weekdays, exc. by reserv.),
mid-Apr.–mid-Dec.
A la carte: 40€.

Thierry Cheviron has turned this mountain cabin into a very special establishment. In the evening, guests arrive on their snowmobiles to enjoy the timber décor and friendly atmosphere. The foie gras, nice cuts of beef and the tiramisu justify the trip.

● Les Caves de l'Alpe SIM

Rte du Coulet.
Tel. 04 76 80 92 44. Fax 04 50 02 40 03.
Closed May–mid-Dec.
A la carte: 40–48€.

We are fond of this charming cabin with its fine fir woodwork and black and white photos. The cuisine, which includes herb- and cream-stuffed ravioli, house crayfish gratin, blanquette de veau with rice and a Genepi sorbet for dessert have an easy charm.

ALTKIRCH

68130 Haut-Rhin. Paris 458 –
Colmar 61 – Bâle 35 – Thann 27.
ot-altkirch.com.
The Museum of Popular Tradition here reminds us that this sleepy little sub-prefecture perched on high ground was the capital of the Sundgau region. It watches over the surrounding lakes, orchards and "Route de la Carpe Frite" (Fried Carp Route) and cherishes the memory of Jean-Jacques Henner, son of Bernwiller and glorious painter of this peaceful countryside.

 HOTELS-RESTAURANTS

In Bettendorf (68560). 9 km via D432 and D9b.

■ Au Cheval Blanc 🏠

4, rue de Hirsingue.
Tel.-Fax 03 89 40 50 58.
Closed Wed. din., Thu., 2 weeks Dec., 2 weeks Apr.

7 rooms: 26–42€.
Prix fixe: 9€, 13€, 18€, 24€.
A la carte: 30€.

Philippe Petit-Richard watches over this rustic inn, delighting his following with classical but tasty concoctions. The chef's terrine, hot Munster cheese with cumin cream sauce, salmon served on a bed of sauerkraut, veal kidneys and the sliced block of cinnamon ice cream are precisely prepared and sensibly priced. A charming welcome and neat rooms.

In Carspach (68130).
■ Auberge Sundgovienne 🏠
Baerenhute, rte de Belfort 3 km w via D419.
Tel. 03 89 40 97 18. Fax 03 89 40 67 73.
www.auberge-sundgovienne.fr
Hotel closed Christmas–end Jan.
Rest. closed Sun. dinner, Mon., Tue. lunch,
Christmas–end Jan., 1 week beg. July.
28 rooms: 42–80€. 1 suite: 87–105€.
Prix fixe: 12€, 21€, 27€, 38€, 48€,
11€ (child). A la carte: 45–55€.

This contemporary motel is looking healthy indeed. Véronique Hermann provides a cordial welcome, the rooms are neat as a pin and Jean-Bernard concocts dishes with a contemporary flavor. An absolutely delicious escargot cake, seared pike-perch filet, oven-crisped pork trotter with foie gras and the pear crêpe are splendid. Well-chosen wines by the glass.

In Hirtzbach (68118). 4 km s, then D432 and D7.
● Hostellerie de l'Illberg V.COM
17, rue de Lattre-de-Tassigny.
Tel. 03 89 40 93 22. Fax 03 89 08 85 19.
hostelillberg@tiscali.fr
www.hostelillberg.fr
Closed Sun. dinner, Mon.
Prix fixe: 23€ (weekday lunch), 33€, 43€,
59,50€, 90€. A la carte: 60€.

Jean-Luc Wahl has enlarged his establishment, adding a pleasant little bistro (Le Bistro d'Arthur), and continues to offer his own individual reinterpretation of Alsace tradition. Duck foie gras, escargots in tempura mille-feuille and the grilled sirloin steak with a bone mar-

row tartine favorably impress. The tarte Tatin is excellent and Delphine Midou's service elegant and friendly.

ALTWILLER see SARRE-UNION

AMBOISE

37400 Indre-et-Loire. Paris 224 – Tours 26 – Blois 37 – Loches 36 – Vierzon 91.
tourisme.amboise@wanadoo.fr.
Naturally, the route of the royal châteaux passes through this town, which stretches nonchalantly down the Loire valley. Do not miss the Chanteloup pagoda and Clos-Lucé manor just a few minutes away by car.

 HOTELS-RESTAURANTS

● Le Choiseul 🔵🏨
36, quai Charles-Guinot.
Tel. 02 47 30 45 45. Fax 02 47 30 46 10.
choiseul@grandesetapes.fr
www.le-choiseul.com
30 rooms: 125–335€. 2 suites: 335€.
Prix fixe: 59€, 90€. A la carte: 90€.

On the banks of the Loire, this Traversac hostelry conveys an immediate charm. Josette and Gérard Guerlais welcome guests to their 18th-century abode with its prehistoric caves and show them to their traditional, snug rooms. In the restaurant, Pascal Bouvier serves a polished, produce-based cuisine. Pressed foie gras terrine, Loire pike-perch with red mustard and salsify with country bacon, squab with three types of cabbage and the bruschetta topped with ground meat are a paean to a land overflowing with treasures. To conclude, the chocolate feuille à feuille with vanilla-seasoned mango sauce makes a fine impression. As for the cellar, Jean-Christophe Ardibus' selection includes some surprising finds.

■ Manoir des Minimes 🏠
34, quai Charles-Guinot.
Tel. 02 47 30 40 40. Fax 02 47 30 40 77.
www.manoirlesminimes.com
Closed mid-Nov.–mid-Mar.
13 rooms: 110–170€. 2 suites: 240€.

Eric Deforges and Patrice Longet's manor is a sumptuous 18th-century residence overlooking the Loire. The peaceful rooms are magnificently elegant and superbly furnished. The breakfast does justice to the setting.

■ Le Pavillon des Lys

9, rue d'Orange.
Tel. 02 47 30 01 01. Fax 02 47 30 01 90.
pavillondeslys@wanadoo.fr
www.pavillondeslys.com
Closed end Nov.–mid-Dec., beg. Jan.–mid-Jan.
Rest. closed Tue.
7 rooms: 90–180€.
Prix fixe: 22€, 33€.

Sébastien Bégouin, a native of Poitou who trained in Lyon, has put down roots in the Loire Valley in this 18th-century residence with its meticulous welcome and handful of delicious rooms. The atmosphere is friendly and the set menus quite delightful. At 33 , the *grande dégustation* option includes creamed coco beans with truffle oil, poached foie gras with dried fruit compote, oysters and scallops with soy milk, cod with mandarin orange–seasoned potato purée, a tender sirloin steak with glazed turnips, tiramisu and an apple tart served with pain d'épice ice cream. Do not worry: all this is as light as down, and the Mabileau Saint Nicolas de Bourgueil glides over the whole like a breeze.

● Le 36   🍷COM

36, quai Charles-Guinot.
Tel. 02 47 30 45 45. Fax 02 47 30 46 10.
choiseul@grandesetapes.fr
www.le-choiseul.com
Closed Sun.
Prix fixe: 15€, 23€, 29€.

For a lunch that will leave your pocketbook relatively unscathed, the Choiseul's winter-garden-style adjunct offers bargain price set menus meticulously concocted by Guillaume Dallay and served only at noon. We enjoy fried whitefish, glazed whiting, Breton-style shellfish stew, veal belly with sour cherries and the quick-cooked lamb seasoned with lemon. The

strawberry, pistachio and lemon dessert is a delicacy and the wines selected by Edouard Mineau are just the thing. When the weather is fine, we enjoy the garden.

● L'Epicerie   🅝COM

46, pl Michel-Debré.
Tel. 02 47 57 08 94. Fax 02 47 57 08 89.
Closed Mon. and Tue. (exc. July, Aug., Sept.).
Prix fixe: 19,50€, 23,50€, 29,50€, 37,50€.

Opposite the château car park, this fine half-timbered abode (which used to be a grocer's more than twenty years ago, but looks nothing like one now) holds an appealing dining room graced with beams and mirrors. Alexandre Habert, a native of Chartres who trained at the Henri IV and then in Paris, executes a comfortably reinterpreted classical cuisine. Creamy carrot soup seasoned with orange, cod filet in garlic oil and a chocolate banana crumble with pecans work wonders in the set menu at 19,50 .

66110 Pyrénées-Orientales. Paris 887 –
Perpignan 37 – Montpellier 194 –
Toulouse 241.
omtt.amelie@little-france.com.
Known since ancient times for its Roman baths, Amélie has enjoyed 100 years of pleasant prosperity as a small spa town with new and old thermal baths, casino and hotels.

●	RESTAURANTS

● Le Carré d'As   COM

In the Casino, 4, av du Docteur-Bouix.
Tel. 04 68 39 20 00. Fax 04 68 39 01 02.
casino.amelie@moliflore.com
Prix fixe: 26€, 14,70€, 9€ (child).
A la carte: 40€.

Jean-Louis Ricart has taken the helm in the kitchen of this casino restaurant, which also extends to a brasserie. He adds a seasonal touch to the house cuisine. Anchoïade, cod filet, duck with sweet-and-sour sauce and the berry mille-feuille are well crafted. Appealing regional wines at sensible prices.

AMIENS

80000 Somme. Paris 137 – Lille 123 –
Rouen 121 – Saint-Quentin 77 – Reims 174.
ot@amiens-metropole.com
The capital of good-natured Picardy has a
number of treasures: a Gothic cathedral with
remarkable stalls, a museum of great interest to
visitors keen on improving their knowledge of
the region and the marshlands by the Somme
river, which offer a bucolic welcome to the city.

    HOTELS-RESTAURANTS

■ Le Carlton

42, rue Noyon.
Tel. 03 22 97 72 22. Fax 03 22 97 72 00.
reservation@lecarlton.fr / www.lecarlton.fr
24 rooms: 71–100€. 1 suite: 130€.
Prix fixe: 12€ (lunch), 16€, 19€, 25€,
5,80€ (child). A la carte: 20–25€.

Near the rail station, this fine late-19th-
century establishment provides comfortable rooms and brasserie cuisine in a
very Parisian setting. The regional dishes
(smoked eel tartare with leeks) and buffet
option are pleasant. Friendly service and
sensible prices.

■ Mercure Cathédrale

17, pl au Feurre.
Tel. 03 22 22 00 20. Fax 03 22 91 86 57.
mercure.amiens@escalotel.com
www.mercure.com
47 rooms: 71–102€.

The 18th-century facade, professional welcome and modern rooms decorated with
light wood all impress us favorably. At the
end of the afternoon, we meet up in the Tour
du Monde bar, which has a large terrace.

● Les Marissons   V.COM

Pont de la Dodane, quartier Saint-Leu.
Tel. 03 22 92 96 66. Fax 03 22 91 50 50.
les-marissons@les-marissons.fr
www.les-marissons.fr
Closed Sat. lunch, Sun., Wed. lunch.
Prix fixe: 18,50€, 34€, 49€.
A la carte: 60–65€.

This former 15th-century boat yard has
been converted into a gourmet haunt by
Antoine Benoît. This apt pupil of the Château de Locguénolé in Hennebont and the
Vivarois in Paris has not forgotten the lessons he learned there. His raw material is
drawn from local sources and he prepares
it with skill. Smoked eel *verrine*, monkfish
roasted with apricots, rosemary-seasoned
lamb and the soft-centered chocolate cake
are just the thing. Well-chosen set menus.

● Au Relais des Orfèvres   N.COM

14, rue des Orfèvres.
Tel. 03 22 92 36 01.
Closed Sat. lunch, Sun., Mon., Feb. vac., Aug.
Prix fixe: 26€, 39€, 48€.

Jean-Michel Descloux, formerly at the
Bistro du Sommelier in Paris, is a paragon of modesty. The dishes he serves up
are attractive, sometimes outsized and
often enchanting. His set menus gratify. On the day of our visit, for instance,
the "tradition" option at 26 included little goat cheese ravioli with caramelized
shallot cream, roasted halibut filet served
on a bed of red cabbage, a local cheese
plate and pleasant desserts (soft chocolate marquise with Montelimar nougat
cream). Sylvie Descloux provides an elegant welcome.

● Brasserie Jules   COM

18, bd Alsace-Lorraine.
Tel. 03 22 71 18 40. Fax 03 22 71 18 45.
l.letellier@brasserie-jules.fr
www.brasserie-jules.fr
Prix fixe: 17€, 19€, 25€. A la carte: 35€.

A step away from the rail station, this
Parisian-style brasserie remains modest
despite its star status. Patrick Letellier has
turned the unremarkable first floor of a
modern building into a charming haunt
indeed. The large dining room with its
velvet banquettes and patinated parquet
offers a cozy comfort and the large selection of oysters, grilled fish, a grilled boneless rib steak and tête de veau have soul.
We wash them down with a delightfully
fruity Brouilly and end our meal with a
polished dessert (orange-seasoned lin-

got beans, the chocolate mousse in the local style and crème brûlée).

● Le Vivier   COM

593, rte de Rouen.
Tel. 03 22 89 12 21. Fax 03 22 45 27 36.
vivier.le@wanadoo.fr / www.levivier-amiens.com
Closed Sun., Mon., Christmas–New Year's,
beg. Aug.–end Aug.
Prix fixe: 26€, 35€, 40€, 78€,
20€ (child). A la carte: 70€.

Marc-Etienne Mont pays fitting tribute to seafood here, sometimes marrying it to farm produce. Foie gras salad with langoustines and veal jus, the crab turnover and the Atlantic sea bass cooked skinside down are splendid. Christine Mont is an exquisite hostess and her wine recommendations are invaluable.

● Le Bistro des Chefs   N ● SIM

12, rue Flatters.
Tel. 03 22 92 75 46.
www.bistro deschefs.com
Closed Sun., Mon., 1 week Christmas–New Year's, 1 week Easter vac., 2 weeks end Aug.
Prix fixe: 22€, 25€.

This shrewd corner bistro is Eric Boutté's excellent idea. He has put together an efficient team under Stéphane Pecquet. The blackboard presents flavorsome tricks that reflect the vagaries of the market: Belles de Fontenay potatoes with escargots, cauliflower cream with Avruga (Spanish herring) caviar, fish duo with shellfish and tripe in the style of Caen. The produce is fresh, the desserts charming (pain perdu with vanilla ice cream, coconut macaron dessert) and the prices measured. As we wash all this down with a cheerful wine or two, we decide that life is sweet in Amiens.

● 7e Art   N SIM

7, bd de Belfort.
Tel. 03 22 67 17 17.
A la carte: 20–25€.

Next to the Gaumont multiplex, this designer setting welcomes young customers intent on eating well without paying through the nose for it. Ficelle

picarde (ham and mushroom crêpes in mornay sauce), avocado tartare, duck-and potato-layered casserole and the stir-fried chicken combine different genres in a rewarding way. The desserts (liégoise-style waffle, mandarin tiramisu) are true delicacies. Behind this success stands Laurence Letellier, whose dad runs Brasserie Jules just round the corner. Blood is thicker than water.

● Le Bouchon   SIM

10, rue Alexandre-Fatton.
Tel. 03 22 92 14 32. Fax 03 22 91 12 58.
www.lebouchon.fr
Closed Sun. (exc. lunch July–Aug.).
Prix fixe: 12,50€, 22€, 34€ (wine inc.),
42€.

Laurent Lefèvre has opted for good-natured simplicity, local produce and imagination at the stove. We savor the terrine duo, crab tartare, chitterling sausage and veal belly Marengo, all prepared without fuss.

In Dury (80480). 6 km s via N1.

● L'Aubergade   ⓥ V.COM

78, rte Nationale.
Tel. 03 22 89 51 41. Fax 03 22 95 44 05.
aubergade.dury@wanadoo.fr
www.aubergade.dury.com
Closed Sun., Mon., 2 weeks end Sept.–beg. Oct., Christmas–beg. Jan., 1 week Aug.
Prix fixe: 39€, 55€, 70€. A la carte: 81€.

Eric Boutté knows his classics and has an impressive résumé, which includes Delaveyne, Robuchon, Lorain, Le Divellec and Ghislaine Arabian. Local epicures quietly reserve a table and trust in the skillfully balanced set menus. Who could resist the pressed foie gras terrine with caramelized new turnips, roasted thin strips of John Dory with gray shrimp sauce, stuffed squab thighs with a slice of celery and the stuffed cabbage, a studied tribute to Jean Delaveyne? The desserts, including the famous marinated raspberry mille-feuille with mint salad, are equally delightful. Turning to the cellar, we are easily won over by the charms of Jérôme Parcheval's astute choices. He has a gift for unearthing just the right bottle to flatter the different dishes. Appealingly set tables and an elegant setting.

AMMERSCHWIHR

68770 Haut-Rhin. Paris 438 –
Colmar 8 – Sélestat 26 – Saint-Dié 48.
ma.ammer@calixo.net.
The Tour des Sorcières (Witches' Tower), the fortified gate opening onto the vineyards and the sundial are the landmarks in this village at the gates of Colmar, whose pride and joy is its Kaefferkopf wine.

 HOTELS-RESTAURANTS

■ A l'Arbre Vert

7, rue des Cigognes.
Tel. 03 89 47 12 23. Fax 03 89 78 27 21.
arbre.vert@wanadoo.fr / info@arbre-vert.net
www.arbre-vert.net
Closed mid-Nov.–mid-Feb.
Rest. closed lunch, Tue.
16 rooms: 39–62€. 3 suites: 48–72€.
Prix fixe: 21€, 35€, 47€.

It would be hard to come up with anything more Alsatian than this large house, once the property of a village luminary and now a welcoming hostelry in the hands of Joël Tournier offering comfortable rooms, a range of facilities and a restaurant that remains staunchly loyal to local tradition. Foie gras served hot and cold, pike-perch with beer-seasoned cream sauce, pan-seared veal steak and the warm soufflé with seasonal fruits go well together, at reasonable prices, with a string of Alsace wines.

■ Aux Trois Merles

5, rue de la 5e-DB.
Tel. 03 89 78 24 35. Fax 03 89 78 13 06.
auxtroismerles@wanadoo.fr
www.auxtroismerles.com
Closed Sun. dinner, Mon., mid-Jan.–mid-Feb.
12 rooms: 28–54€.
Prix fixe: 14,50€, 42€. A la carte: 50€.

Didier Louveau has adopted Alsace, but his Norman roots have left him with an abiding taste for seafood. The scallop and jumbo shrimp salad, cod tagine with lemon and sundried tomatoes and the roasted monkfish with a fine ratatouille display true skill. A fine pressed chestnut terrine for dessert and tremendously friendly service. Simple rooms for overnight stays.

● Les Armes de France   ◎ LUX

1, Grand-Rue.
Tel. 03 89 47 10 12. Fax 03 89 47 38 12.
aux-armes-de-france@wanadoo.fr
www.aux.armes.de.france.com
Closed Wed., Thu.
Prix fixe: 25€ (weekday lunch), 30€, 32€ (Sat., Sun. lunch), 42€. A la carte: 55€.

It is always delightful to visit Philippe Gaertner, a convert to the cause of simplicity. Having inherited his precision and sureness of hand from his father Pierre, a student of Point, he uses these talents to leisurely reinterpret fine regional produce. On the plate, this results in escargot and parmesan mille-feuille, sturgeon filet served on a bed of julienned fennel and the duck foie gras medallion with dried fruit chutney. Desserts, which include rice pudding served with vanilla-seasoned rhubarb compote, are a return to childhood. Supervised by the friendly Simone, the service is absolutely flawless. The wine list is rich in regional vintages and the check is very reasonable given the joys to be found here.

AMNEVILLE

57360 Moselle. Paris 318 – Metz 21 –
Thionville 17 – Verdun 65.
otamn@ville-amneville.fr.
No nostalgia for the spa towns of yesteryear, but a casino and modern therapeutic facilities in and around the forest.

 RESTAURANTS

● La Forêt   🍴 COM

Tourism and spa center.
Tel. 03 87 70 34 34. Fax 03 87 70 34 25.
resto.laforet@wanadoo.fr
www.restaurant-laforet.com
Closed Sun. dinner, Mon., 2 weeks
Christmas–New Year's, 1 week at end July,

1 week at beg. Aug.
Prix fixe: 18,50€, 23€ (weekend lunch), 38€.

The Stalters' eatery continues to delight lovers of classical dishes revised in a modern manner. In Denis' hands, pan-seared foie gras escalope seasoned with lime, scallops and endive, thick-cut Iberian pork tenderloin served with mushroom jus and the bergamot-infused crème brûlée show true skill. In the dining room, Jean-Jacques tends to our every need, even helping to choose the right wine to accompany our culinary choices.

AMPUIS

69420 Rhône. Paris 495 – Lyon 37 – Condrieu 5 – Givors 18 – Vienne 8.
The Rhône flows by in the valley and the Côte-Rôtie district lives up to its vinic reputation.

●	RESTAURANTS

● Le Bistro à Vins de Serine
16, bd des Allées (pl de l'Eglise).
Tel. 04 74 56 15 19. Fax 04 74 56 03 06.
bistroavindeserine@wanadoo.fr
Closed dinner (exc. weekends),
Sun., Mon., Christmas–New Year's, 1 week Feb. vac., 2 weeks end Aug., 10 days beg. Sept.
Prix fixe: 18€.

Daniel Viron has turned this bistro into a convivial haunt. His daughter Alexandra greets guests with a smile, while chef Christophe Chêne whips up a poached egg with mushrooms, a fish filet with beurre blanc and a prune-stuffed rabbit haunch, all washed down with fine vintages from the Rhône Valley. The single set menu rules out any unpleasant surprises.

AMPUS

83111 Var. Paris 839 – Castellane 57 – Draguignan 15 – Toulon 96.
Built on a hill overlooking the Nartuby river, this splendid Haut Var village at a respectable altitude (600 meters) has an unaffected charm.

●	RESTAURANTS

● La Fontaine d'Ampus
Pl de la Mairie.
Tel. 04 94 70 98 08.
Closed Mon., Tue., Oct., Feb.
Prix fixe: 38€. A la carte: 55€.

Early in the morning, Marc Haye visits the region's markets to buy his produce from local farmers, then passes by the fishmonger to inspect the day's catch. When he gets back, he sets to work in the kitchen, preparing a farinette (little crêpe) with chestnuts, eggs and tomato-seasoned béarnaise sauce, almond milk–flavored mullet with ceps, sliced duck and a soft-roasted pork trotter served with slow-cooked carrots. The light quince caramel macaron with Victoria pineapple ice cream is not bad and excellent Var vintages provide a natural accompaniment.

ANCENIS

44150 Loire-Atlantique. Paris 347 – Nantes 38 – Angers 53 – Cholet 48.
office.tourisme.ancenis@wanadoo.fr.
Cheerful slopes bedecked with vines, the Loire promenade and its anglers: in short, another heart of France and the delightful Loire Valley.

■/●	HOTELS-RESTAURANTS

■ Akwaba
Bd Dr-Moutel.
Tel. 02 40 83 30 30. Fax 02 40 83 25 10.
hotelakwaba@yahoo.fr / www.hotel-akwaba.com
Rest. closed Fri. dinner, Sun., 1 week Christmas–New Year's, 3 weeks Aug.
56 rooms: 52–67€.
Prix fixe: 18€, 22€, 6,50€ (child).
A la carte: 25–30€.

This modern, easy-to-reach hotel (three kilometers from the Océane turnpike) bids us welcome in the tongue of the Ivory Coast. Functional rooms and carefree cuisine at the Calao.

● **Les Terrasses de Bel Air**

RD 723, locale known as Bel-Air.
Tel. 02 40 83 02 87. Fax 02 40 83 33 46.
Closed Sun. dinner, Mon.
Prix fixe: 25€ (lunch, wine inc.), 38€ (wine
inc.), 45€ (wine inc.), 49€,
8€ (child), 12€ (child).

On the banks of the Loire, this establishment is something of a treat. It boasts Geneviève Gasnier's warm welcome, a dining room equipped with Louis-Philippe furniture and a terrace and garden, as well as noble dishes prepared by Jean-Paul, who deftly employs quality produce. Duck foie gras with figs and hazelnuts, lobster and vegetable "casse croute", farm-raised squab with a potato and bacon gratin and fresh goat cheese followed by pears and caramel in puff pastry with chocolate sauce inspire us with an urge to take up residence here.

● **La Toile à Beurre** ⬛SIM

82, rue Saint-Pierre.
Tel. 02 40 98 89 64. Fax 02 40 96 01 49.
Closed Sun. dinner, Mon., Wed. dinner.
Prix fixe: 25€, 33€, 45€.

This 1753 abode found minor culinary glory under the Baron/Lefèvre partnership, before they left for Nantes. Today, the modest, reliable Florence Quintin and Pierre-Yves Ladoire are at the helm. The setting remains authentic, with its beams, red hexagonal floor tiles, fine stone and fireplace. We also enjoy the shady terrace and Florence's attentive welcome, as well as the carefully chosen, unobjectionably priced Loire wines. Stuffed smoked quail legs, roasted pike-perch, duck medallions with herbs and the soft-centered chocolate cake with cherry marmalade and white chocolate mille-feuille are all in very good taste.

LES ANDELYS

27700 Eure. Paris 104 – Rouen 39 –
Evreux 38 – Mantes-la-Jolie 52.
The ruins of Richard the Lionheart's Château Gaillard watch over a bend in the Seine and this old Norman town with its engaging skyline.

 HOTELS-RESTAURANTS

■ **La Chaîne d'Or** ✿ 🏠

27, rue Grande.
Tel. 02 32 54 00 31. Fax 02 32 54 05 68.
chaineor@wanadoo.fr
wwwhotel-lachainedor.com
Closed 1 week Christmas–New Year's, 3 weeks
Jan. Rest. closed Mon. lunch, Tue. lunch.
10 rooms: 75–115€. 2 suites: 129€.
Prix fixe: 28€, 44€, 57€, 72€.
A la carte: 70–90€.

This 18th-century post house was once a toll station (with a chain across the Seine to halt the river traffic). Gérard and Sylvia Millet have now restored its culinary credentials. We enjoy the good neo-Norman dishes prepared by Christophe Bouche. Pan-tossed escargots, Atlantic sea bass, pan-fried veal sweetbreads and a warm apple tart are served in the elegant dining room overlooking the river and accompanied by wines adeptly selected by Krystelle Sénéchal. The tastefully equipped rooms make fine weekend hideaways.

ANDLAU

67140 Bas-Rhin. Paris 500 – Sélestat 17 –
Molsheim 25 – Strasbourg 39.
otandlau@netcourrier.com
This is one of the melting pots of the Alsace wine-growing region, with its theatrical scenery, abbey dedicated to St. Richard, Bear fountain, amphitheater of vines and great Kastelberg, Moenchberg and Clos du Val d'Eléon vintages.

🔲 HOTELS-RESTAURANTS

■ **Zinckhôtel** 🏠

13, rue de la Marne.
Tel. 03 88 08 27 30. Fax 03 88 08 42 50.
zinck.hotel@wanadoo.fr / www.zinckhotel.com
18 rooms: 59–95€.

Each room in this former mill is different. Guests can choose between Thousand and One Nights, Zen or fifties décor. Daniel Zinck has also fitted out large reception rooms.

● **Au Boeuf Rouge**   COM

6, rue du Dr-Stoltz.
Tel. 03 88 08 96 26. Fax 03 88 08 99 29.
auboeufrouge@wanadoo.fr
Closed Wed. dinner (off season), Thu. (off
season), 10 days Feb., 3 weeks June–July.
Prix fixe: 15€, 24€, 30€. A la carte: 48–53€.

This 17th-century post house is coming
back to life in the hands of Pierre Kieffer. Formerly with Jung in Strasbourg, he
excels at preparing his region's produce
with subtlety and lightness of touch. A
foie gras medallion, Anna Kieffer pike fish
quenelles, pike-perch served on baked
vegetables and potatoes and the apple
and cherry dessert pay serene tribute to
timeless Alsace. On the *winstub* side, the
spread includes tartes flambées (regional
flat savory tarts), a local head cheese and
aspic terrine and choucroute. A professional welcome and prompt service.

● **L'Auberge de**   NSIM
   l'Ancienne Scierie

73, rue du Maréchal-Joffre.
Tel. 03 88 08 23 65. Fax 03 88 08 84 51.
Closed Tue. dinner (exc. Bank holidays), Wed.
(exc. Bank holidays).
Prix fixe: 9,50€ (lunch), 27€. A la carte: 35€.

Monique Kientz, a woman of character,
runs this great paneled tavern on the edge
of the forest towards the Hohwald region.
There, we savor traditional specialties and
pleasant dishes of the day, not to mention
food roasted in the huge fireplace. Tourte
vigneronne (a covered pie with minced
veal and pork in cream), beer-braised ham
shank, mixed brochette, the veal escalope
with Munster cheese, rum savarin and the
tartes flambées served in the evenings are
a delight for all.

● **Le Relais de la Poste**   SIM

1, rue des Forgerons.
Tel. 03 88 08 95 91. Fax 03 88 08 57 16.
Closed Mon. (off season), Tue. (off season),
Jan., Feb.
Prix fixe: 16€, 7€ (child). A la carte: 35–40€.

A strict Alsatian décor with contemporary artwork in this establishment run

by Pierre Zinck, which combines quality, simplicity and generosity. A creamy
cep soup, crayfish and goat cheese salad,
stuffed pork trotters and a fig Tatin are
meticulously served and gently priced.
Andlau and Mittelbergheim wines are on
the agenda.

● **Au Val d'Eléon**   SIM

19, rue du Dr-Stoltz.
Tel. 03 88 08 93 23. Fax 03 88 08 53 74.
contact@valdeleon.com
www.valdeleon.com
Closed Sun. dinner, Mon.
Prix fixe: 11€, 12,50€. A la carte: 30€.

Dominique Philippe has turned this corner *winstub* into a pleasant spot. Goose
foie gras with potatoes, pike-perch with
noodles and the frozen Marc de Gewurz
kouglhopf are splendid.

ANDUZE

30140 Gard. Paris 720 – Alès 14 –
Montpellier 60 – Nîmes 46.
anduze@ot-anduze.fr.
Surrounded by the Cévennes, the Mas Soubey-
ran, desert museum, Trabuc caves and Prafrance
bamboo garden draw the crowds in summer.
Off season, this small town is an oasis of calm
and tranquility.

   HOTELS-RESTAURANTS

■ **Les Demeures du Ranquet**   ❀ 🏠

Rte de Saint-Hippolyte-du-Fort, Tornac.
Tel. 04 66 77 51 63. Fax 04 66 77 55 62.
ranquet@tiscali.fr / www.ranquet.com
Hotel closed mid-Nov.–mid-Dec., 1 week Mar.
Rest. closed Mon. lunch, Tue., Wed.,
beg. June–mid-Sept.
10 rooms: 130–215€.
Prix fixe: 20€, 80€. A la carte: 85€.

At the Majourel family's hostelry, Jean-Luc
welcomes guests, while his wife Anne tends
to the stove, creatively preparing fine local
produce. Home-style ratatouille, sage-seasoned monkfish tail with butter and smoked
bacon, Aveyron lamb chop sprinkled with
black olives and the sugared eggplant beig-

nets play on tradition and fashion without spreading themselves too thin. On the wine side, Mickael Rieusset offers sound advice. Ten appealing rooms and a swimming pool complete the picture.

● Moulin de Corbès `COM`

4 km nw via rte de Saint-Jean-du-Gard.
Tel. 04 66 61 61 83. Fax 04 66 61 68 06.
4 rooms: 70–80€.
Prix fixe: 35€, 50€. A la carte: 55–60€.

Formerly in Nyons, Christian Cormont prepares his market produce with a singular lack of fuss. The foie gras, pike-perch with grapes, Mediterranean sea bass with melon and the herb-seasoned lamb are a success. Muriel welcomes guests and serves the wine with great charm. Three delightful guest rooms.

In Générargues (30140). 5,5 km nw via D129 and D50.

■ Auberge des Trois Barbus

Rte de Mialet.
Tel. 04 66 61 72 12. Fax 04 66 61 72 74.
les3barbus@free.fr
www.aubergeles3barbus.com
Closed Jan.–beg. Feb.
Rest. closed Mon., Tue. lunch.
34 rooms: 61–118€.
Prix fixe: 27€, 49€. A la carte: 60€.

When setting off on a tour of the Cévennes, head for this chic inn offering elegant rooms, some of them with a balcony or even a terrace looking out on the valley of the Camisards. We have a pleasant time in the swimming pool or at the bar before sitting down to savor Christian Achour's sun-kissed cuisine. His wife Véronique eloquently suggests salt-cured salmon, pan-tossed trout on a Provençal-style tart, duck served three ways and a soft-centered chocolate cake served with orange sorbet.

ANGERS

49100 Maine-et-Loire. Paris 295 – Laval 79 – Le Mans 96 – Nantes 91 – Saumur 50.
accueil@angers-tourisme.com.
This sweet, good-tempered city on the Loire, with its drinkable wines, pleasant restaurants, lively inns and unobtrusive artisans, marks its territory firmly without overdoing its accent. We might think it should be a little more lively and stimulating, but in the end, it offers the modest pleasures of a peaceful region. Surrounded by the vineyards of Savennières and the Layon (which have their annual fair, along with all the other wines of the Loire Valley) and rich truck farming lands, it is also home to the Cointreau plant, located in its outskirts. All are characteristic of its riches and source of its pleasures. To complete its culinary prestige, it only needs a local star.

■	HOTELS

■ Hôtel d'Anjou

1, bd du Maréchal-Foch.
Tel. 02 41 21 12 11. Fax 02 41 87 22 21.
info@hoteldanjou.fr / www.hoteldanjou.fr
53 rooms: 104–168€.

In the heart of the city, this 19th-century establishment is a very pleasant hostelry, offering a warm welcome, lounges adorned with art deco mosaics and charming rooms. (See Restaurants: La Salamandre.)

■ Mercure-Centre

1, pl Mendès-France.
Tel. 02 41 60 34 81. Fax 02 41 60 57 84.
h0540@accor-hotels.com / www.mercure.com
Closed Christmas, New Year's.
84 rooms: 69–142€.
Prix fixe: 14,50€, 19,50€.

Ultramodern, adjacent to the convention center and opposite the botanical gardens, this fine establishment offers good-sized, functional rooms, a wine bar (L'Andegave) and a restaurant (Le Grand Jardin). Near the Lac de Maine and three kilometers from the city center is a second Mercure (Tel. +33 (0)2 41 48 02 12).

■ Hôtel du Mail

8-10, rue des Ursules.
Tel. 02 41 25 05 25. Fax 02 41 86 91 20.
hoteldumailangers@yahoo.fr
www.hotel-du-mail.com
Closed Sun., Bank holidays.
26 rooms: 39–75€.

Pass through the great wrought-iron gates and enter this 17th-century convent, now converted into a charming establishment. It offers enchanting, quiet rooms, a delightful breakfast and a welcome that reflects its high standards.

■ Hôtel Saint-Julien

9, pl du Ralliement.
Tel. 02 41 88 41 62. Fax 02 41 20 95 19.
s-julien@wanadoo.fr
www.destination-anjou.com
34 rooms: 47–59€.

The Besnards greet guests with a smile and have furnished the rooms delightfully. The TGV rail station is very close by.

In Avrillé (49240). 8 km via rte de Laval.

■ Le Cavier

La Croix-Cadeau.
Tel. 02 41 42 30 45. Fax 02 41 42 40 32.
lecavier@wanadoo.fr / www.lacroixcadeau.fr
Rest. closed Sun., Christmas–New Year's.
38 rooms: 53–67,50€.
Prix fixe: 18,60€, 28€, 35,50€,
10,60€ (child). A la carte: 45–50€.

This 1730 mill with its simple, neat rooms, swimming pool and play area makes a fine impression. Franck Houdebine's cuisine is deft enough and includes pike-perch with beurre blanc and a duck breast with crushed sugared almonds. Jean-Luc Huez provides a congenial welcome.

●   RESTAURANTS

● La Salamandre   V.COM

1, bd du Maréchal-Foch.
Tel. 02 41 88 99 55. Fax 02 41 88 98 32.
la.salamandre.angers@wanadoo.fr
Closed Sun.
Prix fixe: 26€, 36€, 46€, 75€.
A la carte: 65–70€.

Daniel Louboutin is the city's great classicist. His frescoed neo-Renaissance setting on the first floor of the Hôtel d'Anjou has its fair share of elegance. The cuisine focuses on fresh produce prepared with no undue affectation. Grilled herb-seasoned breaded oysters, roasted turbot with mushroom- and ham-stuffed artichokes simmered in wine, boneless squab with truffle oil and berry macaron with fruit jelly are very tasteful. Under the supervision of Loïc Moreau, the serried ranks of fine Loire vintages stand ready for inspection.

● Le Lucullus   COM

5, rue Hoche.
Tel.-Fax 02 41 87 00 44.
lelucullus@orange.fr
Closed Sun. (exc. Mother's Day), Mon.,
Feb. vac., end July–end Aug.
Prix fixe: 16€ (lunch), 22,30€, 40€, 58€
(wine inc.), 10€ (child). A la carte: 40–45€.

Pascal Houssay pays tribute to his region's fine produce. Egg and morel emulsion, monkfish fricasee with saffron cream sauce, shredded oxtail with Anjou wine sauce and the pear poached in Coteaux du Layon wine zealously sing the praises of the Loire in a contemporary setting where Véronique Houssay offers an enthusiastic welcome.

● Provence Caffé   COM

9, pl du Ralliement.
Tel.-Fax 02 41 87 44 15.
www.provence-caffe.com
Closed Sun., Mon., 2 weeks Dec.,
3 weeks Aug.
Prix fixe: 15€ (lunch), 20€, 26€, 30€.
A la carte: 35–45€.

We duly appreciate François Derouet's Mediterranean dishes. Herb risotto with "chips" of ham, roasted red mullet with pistou in salad, cod filet with brandade and a shellfish stew, not to mention the sage-seasoned pork tenderloin medallion, form a truly sun-kissed feast here.

● Le Relais   COM

9, rue de la Gare.
Tel. 02 41 88 42 51. Fax 02 41 24 75 20.
c.noel10@wanadoo.fr
Closed Sun., Mon., 10 days Christmas–New Year's, 3 weeks Aug.
Prix fixe: 20€, 37€. A la carte: 55–60€.

Christophe Noël, erstwhile stalwart at the Gavroche in London and Girardet in Switzerland before he took over in the kitchen at this inn close to the rail station, is an old hand at his trade. He wins us over with the tian of vegetables, served with crab and onion chutney, red mullet seared skin-side down and finished under the broiler with an Antibes-style vinaigrette or the thyme-seasoned rack of lamb, which, along with the strawberry tart with rhubarb compote, all impress favorably. Gérard Pelletier presides over the dining room and offers competent advice on the choice of wine.

● La Treille   COM
12, rue Montault.
Tel. 02 41 88 45 51.
gael.truffreau@wanadoo.fr
Closed Sun. lunch, Mon. dinner.
Prix fixe: 10,30€ (lunch), 14,40€, 18,50€, 22,90€. A la carte: 25–30€.

A likable bistro with two options. On the second floor, Gaël Truffreau serves the crayfish cassolette, pike-perch filet, duck breast and wonderful tarte Tatin. On the first floor, he has set up a wine bar with his colleague Emmanuel Micheneau. Nibbling on a little sausage, we taste vintages from the Loire Valley and further afield.

● Le Petit Comptoir   N🏠SIM
40, rue David d'Angers.
Tel. 02 41 88 81 57.
Closed Sun., Mon., 10 days in Jan.,
3 weeks Aug.
Prix fixe: 17€, 19€ (lunch), 26€.

We met Laetitia Cosnier at the Papilles in Paris. Now she is here with her husband Stéphane, who also learned his trade at great gourmet establishments (Bristol, Taillevent, Ledoyen). They work in a closet-sized kitchen for the greater pleasure of twenty or so guests. The blackboard displays the ideas of the day. The "starter + main course" and "main course + dessert" options offer honest pleasures at friendly prices. On the blackboard menu of the day, scallops with Avruga on a bed of cauliflower, jumbo shrimp wrapped in angel-hair pasta served with a coriander orange sauce, creamy risotto with clams and flat parsley, farm-raised guinea hen, frog legs with piquillo peppers in a cocotte with garlic and parsley butter find plenty of takers. For dessert, home-style apple caramel cake and a soft macaron with passion fruit are splendid.

● La Ferme   SIM
2, pl Freppel.
Tel. 02 41 87 09 90. Fax 02 41 20 92 82.
www.la.ferme.fr
Closed Sun. dinner, Wed.,
end Dec.–beg. Jan., end July–mid-Aug.
Prix fixe: 12€ (weekday lunch), 17,40€, 19,50€, 26€, 33€. A la carte: 30–35€.

The Muriers have turned this old-fashioned restaurant into a tasteful establishment. The cuisine is a candid tribute to local tradition. Foie gras, pike-perch with beurre rouge sauce, tête de veau with sauce ravigote, coq au vin and the local pear poached in red Anjou wine are hardly voguish, but very tasty.

● Aux Six Régals   SIM
14, rue Cordelle.
Tel.-Fax 02 41 86 06 31.
Closed Sun., Mon. lunch.
Prix fixe: 9,90€ (weekday lunch), 12,90€, 17,90€, 24,90€. A la carte: 34€.

Arnaud Faucher greets guests and tends to both the dining room and kitchen, all with a personal touch. Salad in the style of Périgord, perch filet, duck breast with foie gras, and frozen Cointreau soufflé make no waves.

In Saint-Sylvain-d'Anjou (49480).
6 km via N23.

● Auberge d'Eventard   V.COM
Rond-point du Bon-Puits.
Tel. 02 41 43 74 25. Fax 02 41 34 89 20.
contact@auberge-eventard.com
www.auberge-eventard.com
Closed Sat. lunch, Sun. dinner, Mon.,
1 week beg. Jan., 1 week beg. May.
Prix fixe: 23€, 55€, 68€, 78€.
A la carte: 65–75€.

For four decades, Jean-Pierre Maussion has presided over this cottage in the suburbs of Angers. During this time, his cuisine has grown more polished. Produce is still his prime criterion. Blue lobster poached in local wine, smoked salmon with horseradish cream, grilled John Dory with a cream sauce and preserved limes, pike-perch grilled skin-side down with sel de Guérande and traditional braised veal sweetbreads make a fine impression. A broad choice of Loire wines recommended by Thierry Bienvenu.

ANGLET see BIARRITZ

ANGOULEME

16000 Charente. Paris 449 – Bordeaux 120 – Limoges 103 – Niort 115 – Périgueux 85.
angoulemetourisme@wanadoo.fr.
Where sea and countryside meet, this first gateway to the South, capital of the Charente region, has a nonchalant charm. Its paved streets lined with elegant 17th-century houses, its festivals devoted to comic books and gastronomy and the mildness of its special climate are all good reasons to linger here. Digging deep into the baskets of Gascony and the nets of its fishing boats, the local restaurants serve up oysters, stuffed cabbage, ceps, foie gras and fresh goat cheese after a glass of Pineau. Peace, light and pleasures of the senses are now just two hours from Paris by high-speed train.

 HOTELS-RESTAURANTS

■ Hôtel Européen

1, pl G.-Perrot.
Tel. 05 45 92 06 42. Fax 05 45 94 88 29.
europeenhotel@wanadoo.fr
www.europeenhotel.com
Closed Christmas–New Year's.
31 rooms: 49–66€.

The breakfast buffet provides a perfect wake-up call in this welcoming hotel offering pleasant rooms and competitive prices near the high-speed rail station.

■ Mercure Hôtel de France

1, pl des Halles-Centrales.
Tel. 05 45 95 47 95. Fax 05 45 92 02 70.
h1213@accor-hotels.com / www.mercure.com
Rest. closed Sat. lunch, Sun. lunch,
lunch Bank holidays.
84 rooms: 101–111€. 5 suites: 126–136€.
A la carte: 35€.

This chain hotel is an address to remember in the city. The rooms are conventional, the service perfect and Bruno Ribe's regional cuisine deftly crafted. Foie gras terrine, Barbezieux chicken stuffed with crayfish and the chocolate quenelle stand up well to scrutiny.

■ Le Saint-Antoine

31, rue Saint-Antoine.
Tel. 05 45 68 38 21. Fax 05 45 69 10 31.
www.hotel-saint-antoine.com
Closed Christmas–New Year's.
Rest. closed Sat., Sun.
32 rooms: 37–61€.
Prix fixe: 13€. A la carte: 30€.

A classical hotel with large, comfortable rooms and a strategic location in the city center. The cuisine is by Monique Guinot, who prepares for resident guests and visitors marinated salmon, monkfish medallions with shellfish sauce, duck breast with berry sauce, not forgetting the molten chocolate cake.

● La Ruelle   ◎ V.COM

6, rue des Trois-Notre-Dame.
Tel. 05 45 95 15 19. Fax 05 45 92 94 64.
laruelle16@wanadoo.fr / www.laruelle16.fr
Closed Sun., Mon., 2 weeks Aug.
Prix fixe: 31€, 38€, 43€.

Two old houses separated by an alley provide this charming eatery's unique appeal. Virginie Combeau welcomes guests with a smile, while her husband Christophe, a disciple of Marc Meneau and Jean Ramet, prepares subtle dishes in the colors of the South of France. Shrewd combinations and precise cooking make the duck foie gras terrine with slow-cooked sweet peppers, the roasted sea bream with julienned fennel, the veal scallop served with macaroni with morel cream sauce and vegetables roasted in the local style appetizing indeed. In conclusion, the Amaretto-seasoned strawberry blanc-manger is equal to its task. A fine wine list covering all regions.

● Côté Gourmet
23, pl de la Gare.
Tel.-Fax 05 45 95 00 27.
Closed Sat. lunch, Sun., Tue. dinner,
1 week at end Feb., 3 weeks Aug.
Prix fixe: 14,50€ (lunch, wine inc.), 21,50€,
32€. A la carte: 38€.

Spirit and setting are both contemporary here. Fabrice Salzat deftly reels off celery root mousse with minced fresh tomatoes, scallops with orange-seasoned cream sauce, honey-roasted suckling pig and panna cotta with sour cherry. Very reasonable prices and a delightfully convivial atmosphere.

● Le Palma   COM
4, rampe d'Aguesseau.
Tel. 05 45 95 22 89. Fax 05 45 94 26 66.
lepalma@tiscali.fr
Closed Sun. (exc. hotel by reserv.),
2 weeks Christmas–New Year's.
9 rooms: 55–60€.
Prix fixe: 14,30€, 19,50€, 30€,
10€ (child). A la carte: 40€.

The Alemany family offers a charming welcome and reliable cuisine. Jean and Colette at the desk and in the dining room and Sébastien in the kitchen make every effort to please. The foamy scallop cream, Atlantic sea bass roasted skin-side down in a basil crust, duck "bonbon" with pears and the brioche perdu with caramel sauce are gratifying. We also enjoy the bodega with its Barcelona-style tapas. The rooms are not all huge, but each one has its charm.

● Le Terminus   COM
3, pl de la Gare.
Tel. 05 45 95 27 13. Fax 05 45 94 04 09.
le-terminus16@neuf.fr / www.le-terminus.com
Closed Sun.
Prix fixe: 16€, 24€, 30€. A la carte: 45€.

In these contemporary black and white surroundings opposite the high-speed train station, the oysters and fish come direct from La Cotinière and Anthony Pinoteau comes to order. The foie gras glazed in aspic, lightly sautéed minced drum fish, slice of Atlantic sea bass grilled with sesame oil or Thai-style "crying tiger" with fried potato wedges favorably impress. The macaron is a true delicacy.

● La Chouc'   SIM
16, pl du Palet.
Tel.-Fax 05 45 95 18 13.
Closed Sat. lunch, Sun., Mon., Aug.
Prix fixe: 18,50€, 28€, 33€, 40€.

Pascal Diouf promotes his creative cuisine in this former *winstub*. Orange-marinated salmon, Breton lobster sashimi, traditionally prepared tête de veau and lemon meringue tart display a comprehensive eclecticism. An appealing wine list.

● Le Passe-Muraille   SIM
5, rue Saint-André.
Tel. 05 45 92 05 02.
Closed Sun., Mon., Christmas–New Year's,
2 weeks Aug.
A la carte: 35–40€.

The Nicolases briskly run this Parisian-style bistro decorated with photographs of writers and magazine covers from the thirties. Jean-François greets his guests warmly and Fatima cooks with soul. Eggplant and Gorgonzola canapés, Portuguese-style squid fricassée, duck confit with cinnamon and almonds and the fig and raspberry crumble show plenty of energy.

● La Tour des Valois   SIM
7, rue Massillon.
Tel. 05 45 95 23 64. Fax 05 45 38 14 55.
la-tour-des-vallois@wanadoo.fr
Closed Sun. dinner, Mon., 14 Feb.–6 Mar.
Prix fixe: 12€, 17€, 24€, 8€ (child).
A la carte: 40–45€.

The period setting with its stone and beams has plenty of character, as do Christian Leclercq's welcome and Christophe Baron's cuisine. Pan-seared foie gras with a caramelized fruit tartare, roasted pike-perch with Pineau sauce, duck breast with pain d'épice and the frozen Cognac parfait slip down smooth as velvet.

In Asnières-sur-Nouère (16290).
10 km via N141 and D120, rte de Cognac.

■ Hostellerie du Maine Brun ❀ 🏠
Le Maine-Brun.
Tel. 05 45 90 83 00. Fax 05 45 96 91 14.
www.hotel-mainebrun.com
Hotel closed mid-Oct.–20 Jan.
Rest. closed Mon. lunch, Tue. lunch.
16 rooms: 90–110€. 2 suites: 165€.
Prix fixe: 29€, 38€.

On the banks of the Nouère, in the heart of a huge winegrowing estate, this former mill turned convivial guesthouse has been tastefully styled by Sophie Ménager. The rooms with their rural view are spacious and equipped with period furniture. The ambient calm lends itself to relaxation. A few lengths of the swimming pool leave us with an appetite we will have no trouble dealing with, thanks to Cédric Garot, who offers his own take on the classics of local cuisine: duck foie gras terrine with dried fruit compote, Charentes-style fish stew with shellfish and Pineau sauce, veal sweetbreads sautéed with white wine, not forgetting the house frozen coffee and Cognac parfait.

ANNECY

74000 Haute-Savoie. Paris 540 –
Aix-les-Bains 34 – Lyon 140 – Genève 45.
ancytour-@cybercable.tm.fr.

An island of green by the lake. Queen of Savoy, town of art and water, Annecy shines with a thousand fires, a natural crucible of light. The dazzling location and the tricks of the avenue d'Albigny, which seems to lead away to the mountains, cloak it in a very special aura. Annecy is also a frontier town (give or take fifty kilometers), breathing deeply in the fresh open air. Geneva's high society comes to feast in one or another of its great restaurants on the outskirts. At the Eridan, Marc Veyrat has purloined the halo of gourmet fame that once graced the Père Bise. A whole world now lies between Veyrier and Talloires. The culinary spirit of today comes to us

from the mountains, which impart their majesty to the dishes of the moment. Herbs, vegetables and fruit from the high pastures, fish from the lakes and fine smoked produce: here, the cuisine is rooted in the land and the town's artisans are worthy of its tremendous natural talent.

■	HOTELS

■ La Maison de Marc Veyrat ❀ 🏠
In Veyrier-du-Lac, 5.5 km via rte du Lac D909. 13, vieille route des Pensières.
Tel. 04 50 60 24 00. Fax 04 50 60 23 63.
contact@marcveyrat.fr / www.marcveyrat.fr
Closed Sun. dinner, Mon., Tue.,
beg. Nov–mid-Feb.
11 rooms: 300–685€. 2 suites: 695–800€.

In its superb natural setting, this chic chalet by the lake is a very special place to stay. We catch ourselves daydreaming when we first view the timelessly elegant rooms here. In the morning, we enjoy a breakfast exceptional in every way, preferably on the balcony, surrounded by nature's grandiose display. The stay comes at a high price, but it is an unforgettable experience. (See Restaurants.)

■ Impérial Palace ❀ 🏠
Allée de l'Impériale.
Tel. 04 50 09 30 00. Fax 04 50 09 33 33.
reservation@hotel-imperial-palace.com
www.imperial-annecy.com
99 rooms: 300–950€.
Prix fixe: 35€, 42€.

The handsome 1900 facade, grounds, view out over the lake, fitness center and contemporary rooms all wield an effortless charm. Add to this the flawless classical cuisine served at the Voile and you will start to think that this is an outstanding place to spend a weekend. Slice of duck foie gras, scallop gratin served with risotto, calf's liver with parsley and apple mousseline are enchanting. Italian-style supper is served until 2 a.m. at the Rotonde, the casino restaurant.

Les Trésoms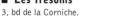

3, bd de la Corniche.
Tel. 04 50 51 43 84. Fax 04 50 45 56 49.
info@lestresoms.com / www.lestresoms.com
50 rooms: 95–250€.
Prix fixe: 49€, 63€, 97€. A la carte: 89€.

This thirties residence enjoys a plunging view down on the lake from the heart of its ten acres of grounds. The tranquil, comfortable rooms are a haven of peace and the relaxation continues in a vast complex including outdoor and indoor swimming pools, steam bath, Jacuzzi and fitness center. The fine restaurant is run by chef Nicolas Muller. Landes duck foie gras, Atlantic shellfish, Alpine lake fish, langoustines in olive oil, Simmental beef and the Valrhona chocolate dessert are all based on quality produce. Turning to the cellar, the bottles chosen by Rodrig Beucquillon provide a perfect counterpoint.

Carlton

5, rue des Glières.
Tel. 04 50 10 09 09. Fax 04 50 10 09 60.
www.bestwestern-carlton.com
55 rooms: 76–150€.

The rooms here offer impeccable comfort. Over 100 years old, this hotel is ideally situated between the rail station and the city center.

Novotel-Atria

1, av Berthollet.
Tel. 04 50 33 54 54. Fax 04 50 45 50 68.
h1357@accor-hotels.com / www.accorhotels.com
95 rooms: 84–140€. 2 suites: 140€.
Prix fixe: 18€, 25€, 8€ (child).
A la carte: 30–35€.

Just a minute from the high-speed train station, this hotel and convention center complex offers functional rooms. The restaurant is the Côté Jardin.

Splendid

4, quai E.-Chappuis.
Tel. 04 50 45 20 00. Fax 04 50 45 52 23.
splenditel@aol.com / www.splendidhotel.fr
Closed Christmas–New Year's.
50 rooms: 96–140€.

This hotel by the peaceful Vassé canal has a distinctive thirties facade. The rooms are well designed and the welcome and service first rate.

Les Allobroges

11, rue Sommeiller.
Tel. 04 50 45 03 11. Fax 04 50 51 88 32.
info@allobroges.com / www.allobroges.com
47 rooms: 78–128€.

All the rooms in this central hotel have every modern convenience, with satellite TV and Internet connection. The welcome is warm and the prices extremely honest.

Palais de l'Isle

13, rue Perrière.
Tel. 04 50 45 86 87. Fax 04 50 51 87 15.
palisle@wanadoo.fr / www.hotels-annecy.net
33 rooms: 65–140€. 2 suites: 200–240€.

Right in the heart of the old town, this 18th-century establishment has been carefully renovated and its stylish interior architecture has real character. The rooms are convivial and the restorative breakfast buffet sets us up splendidly for our tour of the town.

In Annecy-le-Vieux (74940).

Le Flamboyant

52, rue des Mouettes.
Tel. 04 50 23 61 69. Fax 04 50 23 05 03.
www.hotel-le-flamboyant.com
31 rooms: 50–140€.

This great modern chalet near the town and mountains offers neat rooms, copious breakfasts and an English pub-style bar, Les Boucaniers.

In Chavoires (74290). 4,5 km via rte du Lac D909.

Demeure de Chavoire

71, rte d'Annecy.
Tel. 04 50 60 04 38. Fax 04 50 60 05 36.
www.demeuredechavoire.com
9 rooms: 126–140€. 3 suites: 225–275€.

Just a few kilometers from the Aravis range, a hotel of character whose cozy rooms bear the names of some of the region's most remarkable locations. An appealing terrace with a view over the lake.

● | RESTAURANTS

● **La Maison de**   COLUX
  Marc Veyrat

In Veyrier-du-Lac, 5,5 km via rte du Lac D909.
13, vieille route des Pensières.
Tel. 04 50 60 24 00. Fax 04 50 60 23 63.
contact@marcveyrat.fr / www.marcveyrat.fr
Closed Mon., Tue., Wed. lunch,
beg. Nov.–end Apr.
Prix fixe: 295€, 385€. A la carte: 290€.

Marc Veyrat, who continues to spring surprises on us, has closed his Megève farm, but is continuing his alchemical culinary opus in this blue-and-white haven on the shore of the Lac d'Annecy. He is still very much a wizard of the stove, this man who has reconstructed the cuisine of his day, wielding pipette and syringe. So is he a madman of the high pastures? If so, his madness certainly inspires belief, to such an extent that he can fill his dining room with the promise of a presentation menu at 385 (not including wine). Indeed, he is so crazy that following a Homeric skiing accident, he has returned in a wheelchair, his mind brimming over with fresh tricks. The "soda vera", the herb-seasoned scampi, cubes of foie gras in yogurt, the sugar snap peas served in their shell and as a mousse, the squash with smoked pork served two ways in two tubes, cardamine-seasoned egg, parmesan noodles with hogweed sorbet, the crunchy rice sausage, the turbot in a spice-seasoned cube of lemongrass ice, and the verbena-seasoned lobster "bonbon" are just some of his current creations. Sometimes, his ideas veer dangerously close to gimmickry (scallops served cold and warm with lentils, sage, pineapple), but ultimately land on their feet with the shellfish gnocchi, the hen with pistachio-seasoned aspic or the duckling bouillon with corn-and-caraway-seed bonbon, or achieve the sublime with the decomposed paella with thick-cut bacon, rice and shellfish in cubes.

In passing, let us not forget the pigeon baked in clay, the lamb and moussaka. We admire the Savoie cheese platter and immerse ourselves in his daughter Carine's desserts: sorbets à la farine, the chicory and wildflower crèmes brûlées, the wild licorice mousse with sesame crisp, the lemon roll, the soufflé "ruined" with ginger ice cream. Guests do not just "eat" at Veyrat's, they enjoy a unique experience at the hands of an army of young, enthusiastic waitstaff. Maestro Audibert comments, explains and leads the dance in his role as master of ceremonies. At the curtain call, Marco the First in his black hat notes the audience's delight with the performance. Our culinary Jérôme Savary is exercising his art in Savoy and the show is utterly unique.

● **L'Atelier Gourmand**   V.COM

2, rue Saint-Maurice.
Tel. 04 50 51 19 71. Fax 04 50 51 36 48.
www.atelier-gourmand.net
Prix fixe: 12€ (lunch), 19€.
A la carte: 60€.

A revolution among the Leloups: Ligismond-Thierry is now devoting himself to sculpture and painting, while his two sons, Hugues and Aurélien, are currently aiming at greater simplicity. The experimental dishes have disappeared from the menu, the prices have been trimmed, the restaurant is open every day and simplicity has become their watchword. In the contemporary setting, we savor beef carpaccio, pan-seared lake whiting filet served with endive and a Beaufort sauce, a veal cutlet with oyster mushrooms and asparagus and a preserved fruit Brillat-Savarin, all delicately crafted dishes that easily find a match in the cellar, which is rich in surprises.

● **La Ciboulette**   V.COM

Cour du Pré-Carré/10, rue Vaugelas.
Tel. 04 50 45 74 57. Fax 04 50 45 76 75.
georges.paccard@wanadoo.fr
Closed Sun., Mon., Nov. 1 vac.,
Feb. vac., July.
Prix fixe: 27€, 40€, 50€. A la carte: 65€.

With its flowery terrace, light woodwork and baroque mirror, the Ciboulette deserves a protracted visit. Enthusiastically presented by Franck Petit, Georges Paccard's dishes make our mouths water. The thick grilled slice of foie gras served with purple figs in verbena jus, the Annecy lake salmon trout cooked in seasoned butter, whole veal sweetbread and soft Gentiane liqueur croustille or the rack of lamb, seasoned with parsley and served with thin-sliced eggplant, are splendid. The hot soufflé prepared in honor of the monks of the Grande Chartreuse monastery is a pure joy. We have a wonderful time, especially since the welcome is delightful and the service flawless.

● **Le Clos des Sens**   ◉ V.COM

13, rue Jean-Mermoz.
Tel. 04 50 23 07 90. Fax 04 50 66 56 54.
artisanculinaire@closdessens.com
www.closdessens.com
Closed 2 weeks Sept., 2 weeks Jan.,
2 weeks Apr. Rest. closed Sun. dinner, Mon.,
Tue. lunch.
4 suites: 150–200€.
Prix fixe: 29€ (lunch), 45€ (lunch), 70€,
90€. A la carte: 90€.

Laurent Petit creates endlessly. This culinary artisan composes original dishes that encompass successful new combinations. Seasonal produce is opportunely wed in short, magically mischievous preparations. Duck foie gras cooked in salt, smoked lake whiting, line-caught Atlantic sea bass cooked to exactly forty-four degrees Celsius, served with cryogenized Aglandau olive oil and the mountain-raised milk-fed lamb, crispy and melting, served with thin-sliced root vegetables, astonish and enchant. The desserts, such as the rosemary nougatine, are in the same vein. Turning to the wine, we find a suitable bottle with the help of Frédéric Gille's advice. There is no credit card meltdown when the check arrives and we set off back to our appealing rooms with a light heart.

● **Le Belvédère**   V.COM

7, chemin du Belvédère, rte du Semnoz.
Tel. 04 50 45 04 90. Fax 04 50 45 67 25.
reception@belvedere-annecy.com
www.belvedere-annecy.com
Closed Sun. dinner, Tue. dinner, Wed.,
Christmas–New Year's, Jan.
Prix fixe: 32€, 50€, 65€, 13€ (child).

Vincent Lugrin's cuisine is a relatively unconventional gourmet tribute to gastronomy's adventurers. He owes much of his audacity to neighbor Marc Veyrat, who introduced him to the art. Pan-tossed chanterelles seasoned with wild thyme and served with a jus emulsion in the style of a carpaccio sets the tone and the sirloin steak seared simply on one side and finished under the broiler with a cloud of Echiré butter, the beef shaped to receive a creamy cinnamon seasoned-mustard sauce with Tonka beans, forms an appealing sequel. The strawberry and lime mousse with yogurt accompanied by a strawberry jelly is a sparkling dessert to conclude a remarkable feast. The charming, restful view over the lake completes this anthology of the unexpected.

● **Le Bistro de l'Amandier**   V.COM

91, rte d'Annecy.
Tel. 04 50 60 01 22. Fax 04 50 60 03 25.
www.bistro-amandier.com
Closed Sun. dinner, Mon., end Oct.–beg. May.
A la carte: 45€.

Alain Cortési plays the chic bistro card here by the lake. Goat cheese nougat with dried fruit, a slab of grilled lake whiting with hazelnut oil, slow-cooked thyme-seasoned lamb shanks and the banana and coconut crumble are not short on ideas. The broad terrace provides a view of the far shore. Affordable prices and smiling service.

● **Le Bilboquet**   COM

14, faubourg Sainte-Claire.
Tel.-Fax 04 50 45 21 68.
eric.besson@.neuf.fr
Closed Sun. (exc. July–Aug.), Mon.
Prix fixe: 19€ (lunch), 25€ (lunch, wine
inc.), 34€, 12€ (child). A la carte: 50€.

Zealous technician Eric Besson gratifies his guests without eating too far into their budgets. The foie gras tasting plate with four presentations, pressed lake whiting terrine with pistou, duck breast with peaches and the duo of raspberry and vanilla crèmes brûlées are very well crafted. The service is brimming with energy and the check remains polite.

● **Le Vertumne**
13, rue Sommeiller.
Tel. 04 50 45 92 96.
Closed Sun., Mon., 3 weeks Aug.
Prix fixe: 26,50€, 34,50€.

The décor in this small establishment is Provençal, but the cuisine is devoted to local produce selected for its freshness and quality. Efficiently seconded by Christian Levet in the dining room, Stéphane Jacquerez consolidates his deserved success with eggplant mille-feuille, lake whiting filet (from the nearby lake), poultry breast in an almond crust and a chocolate moelleux with a peach sorbet. A delicious, attractive restaurant with highly affordable set menus.

● **Nature & Saveur** SIM
Pl des Cordeliers.
Tel. 04 50 45 82 29.
www.nature-saveur.com
Closed dinner (exc. weekends), Sun., Mon.
Prix fixe: 18€, 20€, 22€, 42€.

Laurence Salomon has set up a culinary workshop here. Each Wednesday at noon, she runs a lunchtime session where she explains how to make good, healthy, digestible meals. Her students eat the dishes they have prepared. On other days, there is a choice between vegetable variations, agricultural arrangements and marine medleys. Dessert is not off-limits and the orange-chocolate fondant with wheat milk and flakes is not bad at all.

● **Rôtisserie du Thiou** SIM
1, passage de l'Evêché.
Tel. 04 50 45 03 10.
rotisserie-du-thiou@wanadoo.fr
www.populus.ch

Closed Sun. dinner, Mon., 1 week at beg. Jan., 1 week at end June.
Prix fixe: 20€, 30€. A la carte: 35€.

This simple, pleasant rotisserie with its exposed stone is an attractive idea. So are the Alpine croustade (a tart made with many layers of thin pastry), foie gras, frog legs, perch filet and the nice rib eye steak.

ANNECY-LE-VIEUX see ANNECY

69480 Rhône. Paris 437 – Lyon 28 – Villefranche-sur-Saône 7 – Mâcon 49.
ot.pierresdorees.anse@wanadoo.fr.
This is the heart of the Beaujolais district, with its plump hills, pleasant vines and gentlemanly winegrowers fond of the good things in life.

 HOTELS-RESTAURANTS

■ **Saint-Romain**
Rte de Graves.
Tel. 04 74 60 24 46. Fax 04 74 67 12 85.
hotel-saint-romain@wanadoo.fr
www.hotel-saint-romain.fr
Hotel and rest. closed Sun. dinner (Sept.–end Apr.). Rest. closed Mon. lunch (Sept.–Apr.).
24 rooms: 45–86€.
Prix fixe: 20€ (exc. Sun. and Bank holidays), 24,50€, 32€, 46€, 17€ (child).
A la carte: 40–45€.

In this Beaujolais farmhouse, Guy Levet carries on a tradition of hospitality. Based on regional produce, Philippe Dufour and Jean-Pierre Lachize's cuisine obligingly strives to showcase local vintages. With a hearty appetite we devour the warm sausage, poultry liver terrine, pollock medallions with a creamy white vegetable sauce and the pork sausage cakes wrapped in caul and served with Port jus. Comfortable rooms, affable service and moderate prices.

ANTHY-SUR-LEMAN see THONON-LES-BAINS

ANTIBES

06600 Alpes-Maritimes. Paris 913 –
Cannes 10 – Nice 23 – Aix-en-Provence 160.
accueil@antibes-juanlespins.com.
Old walls and ancient alleyways, snatches of
jazz in the night, fifties music on the Mediterranean shore.

 HOTELS-RESTAURANTS

■ Le Mas Djoliba　　　　❀🏠
29, av de Provence.
Tel. 04 93 34 02 48. Fax 04 93 34 05 81.
hotel.djoliba@wanadoo.fr
www.hotel-djoliba.com
Closed Nov., Jan.
14 rooms: 69–110€. 1 suite: 163€.
Half board: 88–148€.

An oasis of tranquility a step away from
the town center, this twenties Provençal
house surrounded by greenery is a very
special place to stay. The cooler rooms
looking out on the garden compete for
our favors with those upstairs overlooking the sea.

● Les Vieux Murs　　　　V.COM
25, promenade Amiral-de-Grasse.
Tel. 04 93 34 06 73. Fax 04 93 34 81 08.
lesvieuxmurs@wanadoo.fr
www.lesvieuxmurs.com
Closed Mon., Tue. lunch, mid-Nov.–beg. Dec.
Prix fixe: 39€, 42€. A la carte: 70–80€.

A panoramic view over the bay of Nice
and the Cap d'Antibes, freestone and red
ochre make up the extraordinary décor of
this fine restaurant nestling in the walls
of the old town. Philippe Bensimon greets
guests warmly, while Thierry Grattarola
works at the stove, improvising with fresh
seasonal produce. Langoustine tartare
with shellfish aspic, aromatic herb-seasoned John Dory with eggplant marmalade and the squab roasted with figs and
fresh almonds are not bad. The soft peach
mille-feuille brooks no resistance.

● Oscar's　　　　📷COM
8, rue du Dr-Rostan.
Tel.-Fax 04 93 34 90 14.
www.oscars-antibes.com
Closed Sun., Mon., 2 weeks Dec.–beg. Jan.,
3 weeks May–June.
Prix fixe: 26€, 49€.

Oscar Iannaccone's Italian roots perfectly
complement Provençal inspiration to
produce shrewd set menus, especially a
more affordable option at 26€, featuring
small lasagnes made with fricasséed basil,
monkfish medallion in a grapefruit seafood
broth, suckling pig tenderloin with fresh
local ewe's cheese rolled in Parma ham and
the white chocolate and mascarpone millefeuille. Cuisine as precise and charming as
Martine Iannaccone's service.

● La Jarre　　　　COM
14, rue St-Esprit-les-Remparts.
Tel. 04 93 34 50 12. Fax 04 93 34 94 25.
info@lajarre.com / www.lajarre.com
Closed Wed. (exc. off season).
Prix fixe: 32€ (lunch, wine inc.), 40€ (Sat.,
Sun., lunch), 45€ (Sat., Sun., lunch).
A la carte: 42–68€.

A staunch native of the Auvergne gone
over to the Côte d'Azur, Frédéric Ramos
has turned his patio into one of the town's
gourmet strongholds. Fried basil-seasoned zucchini flowers, John Dory with
artichokes and the roasted duck breast
with figs do us a world of good. Matias
Mary presents Provençal wines that are
full of character.

● Le Sucrier　　　　COM
6, rue des Bains, Vieil-Antibes.
Tel.-Fax 04 93 34 85 40.
info@lesucrier.com / www.lesucrier.com
Closed lunch (July–Aug.), Mon. (exc. July–
Aug.), 1 week Nov., 3 weeks Jan.
Prix fixe: 14,50€ (lunch), 19,50€, 33€,
38,50€, 110€ (for 2). A la carte: 55€.

Roberto Pirani has taken over this eatery
in the heart of the old town, where he promotes sweet and savory dishes and timeless Provençal recipes. In the convivial
dining room and garden, we savor foie

gras pan-seared with honey and cinnamon, stuffed vegetables in the local style, a monkfish daube and lamb chops with wild blueberries.

● **Taverne du Safranier** SIM

1, pl du Safranier.
Tel. 04 93 34 80 50.
Closed Sun. dinner (exc. July–Aug.),
Mon. (exc. July–Aug.), Nov., Dec.
Prix fixe: 15€ (lunch). A la carte: 45–55€.

This casual bistro has an untrammeled Provençal approach. Fish soup, a mini-bouillabaisse, fennel-seasoned grilled Mediterranean sea bass, Provençal daube and a lemon meringue tart whet the most jaded appetites. An excellent, casually friendly atmosphere.

In Cap d'Antibes (06160).

■ **Impérial Garoupe**

770, chemin de la Garoupe.
Tel. 04 92 93 31 61. Fax 04 92 93 31 62.
cap@hotelimperialgaroupe.com
www.imperial-garoupe.com
Hotel closed Nov.–mid-Apr.
Rest. closed Wed., Nov.
30 rooms: 260–600€. 4 suites: 400–800€.
Prix fixe: 60€. A la carte: 100€.

Gilbert Irontelle, who has just joined the Relais & Châteaux chain, has turned this fine, sunny property into a dream setting. Rooms in pastel shades, swimming pool, terrace and private mini-garden set the tone. The kitchen, which made its great leap forward under Dominique Bucaille (who has sadly left for Haute Provence), is looking for a new chef. We have fond memories of the creamed potatoes with truffle oil and the grilled Mediterranean sea bass.

In Cap d'Antibes.

● **Le Bacon**

Bd de Bacon.
Tel. 04 93 61 50 02. Fax 04 93 61 65 19.
Closed Mon., Tue. lunch, Nov.–end Feb.
Prix fixe: 49€, 79€. A la carte: 141€.

The Sordello brothers have made seafood their standard. Offering a panoramic view of the cape, their dining room and terrace

have a refined elegance and there can be no quarrel about the cuisine. We feast on warm tarragon-seasoned red mullet fricassée, bouillabaisse (the best in the world!), the home-style capon and a light-as-gauze mille-feuille. A superb cellar, Biot glass fish adorning the tables and a healthy check.

In Cap d'Antibes.

● **Keller Plage**

La Garoupe.
Tel. 04 93 61 33 74.
Closed beg. Oct.–end Mar.
A la carte: 50–70€.

Dany (whose sister Nicole runs the Petite Maison in Nice) and Victor Bensimon watch over this charming, chic eatery on La Garoupe. The house shows a certain simplicity at lunchtime and greater sophistication in the evening, under the supervision of the faithful Olivier Condat. Mild peppers in olive oil, seafood tartare, fresh red mullet fried in virgin olive oil, artichoke raviolini and Provençal-style thyme-seasoned rack of lamb favorably impress. John Dory, capon, sea bream and Mediterranean sea bass are served by weight and depend on the catch of the day. The prices keep a cool head and the little Les Domaniers *rosé* chosen by Ott is a bargain.

APREMONT see CHANTILLY

APREMONT-SUR-AIRE see
VIENNE LE CHATEAU

APT

84400 Vaucluse. Paris 730 – Aix-en-Provence 51 – Avignon 54 – Cavaillon 32.
tourism@commune-apt-provence.org.
Candied fruit, antique earthenware and ochres bright as in neighboring Roussillon define the character of this happy sentinel of the Grand Luberon mountains, which comes to life on market days.

 HOTELS-RESTAURANTS

■ **Auberge du Luberon**

8, pl du Faubourg-du-Ballet.
Tel. 04 90 74 12 50. Fax 04 90 04 79 49.

serge.peuzin@free.fr
www.auberge-luberon-peuzin.com
Closed mid-Nov.–mid-Dec., Christmas.
Rest. closed Sun. (off season), Mon. (exc.
dinner, in season), Tue. lunch (in season).
13 rooms: 58–98€.
Prix fixe: 29€, 49€, 54€, 59€, 68€.

Serge Peuzin continues in the chic classical vein of his region and town. Pan-seared foie gras with dried fruit, the local onion, anchovy and olive bread, Mediterranean sea bass with morels, rabbit with figs and the trolley offering thirteen Provençal desserts are impressive as ever. The service is efficient, there is a proliferation of set menus and the Luberon wines stand ready for inspection. Spruced up rooms in the Provençal style.

● **Le Carré des Sens**

57, cours Lauze-de-Perret.
Tel. 04 90 74 74 00.
carre-des-sens@wanadoo.fr
Closed Mon., Tue. lunch, beg. Jan.–end Feb.
A la carte: 38€.

Heads: a wine bistro (with its set menus for under 25) and an area set aside for the sale of local produce, as well as a bar and tearoom. Tails: a restaurant dining room opening onto a patio. When the weather is fine, we lunch or dine on the broad terraces. The kitchens are deftly run by Julien Pilati, who started out with Lallemand in Epernay and Dutournier and Darroze in Paris. On the set menu are three sea urchins with their mousse on a bed of slow-cooked celery root, tomato mille-feuille with eggplant spread, rack of lamb served with potato cakes and cod with fennel slow-cooked in olive oil. The desserts are a heady experience, especially the molten dark chocolate dessert with vanilla ice cream and fresh berries. The wines are shrewdly picked by one of the region's greatest oenologists, Jacques Combes. We are greeted with a smile by Anne and Pierre Sauvanet, the two Parisian aficionados who saved this 18th-century town house located in the historic center of Apt.

In Le Chêne (84400). 4 km via N100.

● **Bernard Mathys**

Tel. 04 90 04 84 64. Fax 04 90 74 69 78.
Closed lunch, Tue., Wed., mid-Jan.–mid-Feb.
Prix fixe: 48€, 60€, 85€.
A la carte: 100€.

We only visit Bernard Mathys in the evening, when we have a chance to talk to the inventive cook turned master of the house, while in the kitchen, his faithful lieutenant Luc Raquin sets to work. Baby vegetable pot-au-feu in a langoustine broth, Mediterranean sea bass filet (pan-seared on one side and finished under the broiler, served with black truffle–seasoned wild rice) and the roasted saddle of rabbit pay tribute to local produce in a series of impeccably presented dishes. On the dessert side, our friend René Solnon prepares his ambitious classics, including vanilla mille-feuille. The wine list has the region's interests at heart; the check the bank's.

In Saint-Saturnin-lès-Apt (84490).
9 km n via D943.

● **Les Andéols**

Les Andéols.
Tel. 04 90 75 50 63. Fax 04 90 75 43 22.
info@domainedesandeols.com
www.domainedesandeols.com
Closed end Oct.–Easter.
Rest. closed Tue. dinner.
9 suites: 210–250€.
Prix fixe: 39€, 47€, 58€.

Imagine an estate with its streams, swimming pool, teak terrace, mountain scenery, vines and copses. Then imagine nine rooms, enclosed areas punctuated by black, white and red furniture. In short, a world apart. Art fanatics Patricia and Olivier Massart have left the keys to their property with Alain Ducasse and every evening, guests come to taste the intelligently evolving set menu of the day. The prices are reasonable and the service efficient under gentle giant Emmanuel Argillos, who made such a success of the Basque Auberge Iparla. Meat risotto with asparagus and pan juices, the Mediterranean whiting with herb sauce, Préalpes lamb rubbed with summer savory and served with sweet peas form a natural progression created by apt Apt pupil Albert Boronat, who trained at the Louis XV. There remain the cheeses with mixed greens, calisson (the local sugared-almond sweet) with melon sorbet, the vacherin, the chef's strawberries and crème vanillée and his chocolate-covered meringue cookie. Ah! If we could only spend all summer at Les Andéols…

ARAGON

11600 Aude. Paris 773 – Toulouse 97 – Carcassonne 14 – Castres 54.
The road travels on through mountains and valleys, immersed in a sea of green slopes, until it becomes a rustic lane leading to a village of dolls and shepherds in Cabardès country. Here, the people are fiercely set on preserving both tradition and building, restoring dry stone walls and *capitelles* (shepherds' huts).

●   RESTAURANTS

● La Bergerie
Allée Pech-Marie.
Tel. 04 68 26 10 65. Fax 04 68 77 02 23.
www.labergerie-aragon.com
Closed Mon., Tue., 3 weeks Jan., 2 weeks Oct.
Prix fixe: 20€, 55€. A la carte: 60€.

The location alone is worth a trip to the Cabardès district. The view from this *bergerie* (sheepfold) will take your breath away. In the kitchen, Fabien Galibert, formerly at the Pyramide in Vienne, Barbacane in Carcassonne and Petite Provence in Oslo, serves up his region on a platter. Foie gras in aspic with figs and praline mini-waffles, Atlantic sea bass with escargots, lamb saddle and chops and praline crème brûlée with an almond hazelnut biscuit pay tribute to surrounding nature. To wash down these dishes of character, nothing but the local wines will do.

ARBOIS

39600 Jura. Paris 394 – Besançon 47 – Dôle 35 – Lons-le-Saulnier 39.
otsi@arbois.com.

The old houses, the yellow roofs, the winding Cuisance, the place de la Liberté with its arcades and merry winegrowers: Pasteur's town is also the capital of Jura wine, which comes in red, white and yellow varieties with its walnut bouquet.

    HOTELS-RESTAURANTS

● Jean-Paul Jeunet
9, rue de l'Hôtel-de-Ville.
Tel. 03 84 66 05 67. Fax 03 84 66 24 20.
jpjeunet@wanadoo.fr
www.jeanpauljeunet.com
Closed Tue., Wed., Dec., Jan.
19 rooms: 85–115€. 2 suites: 105–130€.
Prix fixe: 48€, 68€, 95€, 128€.
A la carte: 95€.

In the center of the village, this hostelry has been allowed to be itself. Its plain interior is a fusion of stone, wood and glass, joined in utter simplicity. Jean-Paul Jeunet, who inherited his love of cooking from his father André, has returned to his roots, after studying under the masters (Troisgros, Cousseau and Chapel). He makes good use of the Jura's crops in preparations faithful to tradition, but anchored in their time. Foie gras, soy-seasoned sweet potatoes or the herb-seasoned red mullet are divine surprises. The langoustines work beautifully with the fresh tang of tarragon. Then the large Saint-Gilles sole is subtly enhanced by morels and fresh almonds. More morels accompany the famous Bresse poultry cooked in the Vin Jaune. Left to the capable Stéphane Planche, the wines take us on a tour of Savagnin, Chardonnay, Poulsard and Trousseau. When dessert time comes around, we again succumb to the charms the cherry "transparence" dessert or the strawberries with pistachios and milk. This great chef has plenty of followers, but despite his growing success, he has kept his feet firmly on the ground.

■ Les Messageries
2, rue de Courcelles.
Tel. 03 84 66 15 45. Fax 03 84 37 41 09.
www.hoteldesmessageries.com
Closed Dec., Jan.
26 rooms: 30€.

Three minutes from Jeunet's, a very simple establishment with a warm welcome, comfortable rooms and appealing prices.

● Balance Mets et Vins   `COM`

47, rue de Courcelles.
Tel. 03 84 37 45 00. Fax 03 84 66 14 55.
Closed Mon. (summer), Tue. dinner (exc. summer), Wed. (exc. summer),
20 Nov.–beg. Feb., 1 week at end June.
Prix fixe: 26€. A la carte: 55€.

Jura wines star in the meals prepared by Thierry Moyne. Fish also plays a central role and when he adapts traditional local recipes, he plays on their highly distinctive aromas. Tempura-style breaded and fried trout with nuoc-mâm sauce with Vin Jaune and the aromatic herb-stuffed pigeon are the hallmarks of a highly modern, gourmet Franche-Comté. The Vin Jaune ice cream profiteroles are delectable.

● Le Caveau d'Arbois   `SIM`

3, rte de Besançon.
Tel. 03 84 66 10 70. Fax 03 84 37 49 62.
www.caveau-arbois.com
Prix fixe: 18,50€, 28€, 42€. A la carte: 40€.

José Ortola champions the region's cuisine with conviction. We like the oven-crisped tête de veau, the morel and trout sausage and a Macvin-seasoned crème brûlée, all in very good taste.

● La Finette   `SIM`

22, av Louis-Pasteur.
Tel. 03 84 66 06 78. Fax 03 84 66 08 82.
info@finette.com / www.finette.com
Prix fixe: 15,50€ (lunch), 48€.
A la carte: 30€.

The wines from Henri Maire, the owner here, express themselves harmoniously with the vineyard-keeper's salad, smoked sausage with Cancoillote, chicken cooked in Vin Jaune with morels and grape ice cream. Pleasant service and the same goes for the set menus.

In Pupillin (39600). 3 km via rte de Champagnole.

● Auberge du Grapiot

Rue Bagier.
Tel. 03 84 37 49 44. Fax 03 84 37 46 78.
Closed Sun. dinner, Mon.,
Thu. dinner (off season), Christmas, Jan.,
10 days at end June.
Prix fixe: 16€ (weekday lunch), 38€.
A la carte: 35€.

Samuel Richardet, former *chef de partie* at the Château de Germigney, has turned this small village eatery into a select inn. We come to enjoy Julie's affable welcome, the sound local wines, low prices and sensible dishes. Oven-crisped smoked bacon poached in Macvin, Chardonnay-flavored ham-and-parsley terrine, poultry breast served in ballottine with Comté cheese sauce and the dark chocolate spring rolls with lychee sorbet are very pleasant.

ARCACHON

33120 Gironde. Paris 651 – Bordeaux 74 – Bayonne 184 – Royan 191 – Agen 196.
www.arcachon.com.
A summer vacation vibe floats over the Basin. The oyster route, the Pylat dune, the Arguin bank and small boats nodding gently in the wind send our thoughts scudding out over the open waves. This winter watering place boasts many fine Second Empire residences.

■ HOTELS-RESTAURANTS

■ Novotel-Thalazur

Avenue du Parc, quartier des Abatilles.
Tel. 05 57 72 06 72. Fax 05 57 72 06 72.
h3382@accor-hotels.com
www.novotel.com
94 rooms: 130–162€.

A hundred meters from the beach, this modern establishment built in the heart of a pine grove offers all the comfort of a large chain hotel combined with the luxurious facilities of a thalassotherapy complex: two swimming pools (one indoor, one outdoor) and a fitness center with Jacuzzi, steam bath and sauna. The rooms are spacious and the Côte d'Arguin restaurant is worth taking time to enjoy.

■ Mercure "Park Inn"

4, rue Pr.-Jolyet.
Tel. 05 56 83 99 91. Fax 05 56 83 87 92.
reservations.arcachon@rezidorparkinn.com
www.parkinn.fr
57 rooms: 87–159€. 3 suites: 144–209€.

The staff are attentive in this yacht club–style establishment. Near the casino and convention center, it provides attractive rooms, some of them overlooking the Basin.

■ Aquamarina

82, bd de la Plage.
Tel. 05 56 83 67 70. Fax 05 57 52 08 26.
www.hotel-aquamarina.com
Closed Christmas–New Year's vac.
33 rooms: 40–113€.

This chic hotel is advantageously situated halfway between the marina and the beach. The rooms are spacious and equipped for a comfortable stay.

■ Le Dauphin

7, av Gounod.
Tel. 05 56 83 02 89. Fax 05 56 54 84 90.
www.dauphin-arcachon.com
50 rooms: 50–100€. Half board: 80–140€.

The strong points of this hostelry are its friendly welcome and bright, well-equipped rooms. Ideal for a vacation with the sea just a stone's throw away. Flower garden and swimming pool.

■ Grand Hôtel Richelieu

185, bd de la Plage.
Tel. 05 56 83 16 50. Fax 05 56 83 47 78.
www.grand-hotel-richelieu.com
Closed beg. Nov.–mid-Mar.
43 rooms: 65–170€.

This seaside hotel provides large, comfortable rooms furnished in period style. The grounds are a delightful oasis of greenery.

■ Hôtel Point France

1, rue Grenier.
Tel. 05 56 83 46 74. Fax 05 56 22 53 24.
www.hotel-point-france.com
Closed Nov.–beg. Mar.
34 rooms: 78–181€.

Each room in this hotel in the town center has been decorated in its own style. The finest among them have a terrace looking out on the Basin. A professional welcome and friendly service.

■ Les Vagues

9, bd de l'Océan.
Tel. 05 56 83 03 75. Fax 05 56 83 77 16.
Info@hotel-les-vagues.com / www.lesvagues.fr
27 rooms: 68–123€.

A "sea and sand" hotel, a friendly team led by Jean-Michel Latappy and quiet rooms, the most pleasant of them overlooking the beach.

● Diego-l'Ecailler-Plage `COM`

Waterfront, 2, bd Veyrier-Montagnières.
Tel. 05 56 83 84 46. Fax 05 56 54 28 20.
www.diegoplage.com
Closed 24 Dec.–25 Dec.
Prix fixe: 25€, 36€. A la carte: 50€.

Formerly at the Mérignac bowling alley, Carole and Robert Huvelle have taken over this place without changing its founding principles: fresh produce and cuisine with an Iberian flavor. The "ostrich farmer's" plate, the sea bream cooked in a salt crust and the rib eye steak with piquillo peppers are quality dishes. Spanish wines still rule the list. Dominique Mazet is a pleasant dining room manager and the prices have not changed.

● Le Patio `COM`

10, bd de la Plage.
Tel. 05 56 83 02 72. Fax 05 56 54 89 98.
Closed Mon., Tue. (exc. lunch July–Aug.),
Wed. lunch (exc. July–Aug.), 2 weeks Nov.,
2 weeks Feb.
Prix fixe: 30€ (lunch, wine inc.).
A la carte: 50€.

Two strong points: Michelle Falgueirettes' charming, friendly welcome and the shrewd lunchtime set menu. Based on select produce, Bruno's cuisine is consistency itself. The cep and spicy slow-cooked eggplant tart, the langoustine and veal sweetbread salad and the veal cutlet seasoned with licorice and lime are of excellent quality. The little imperial-style mandarin orange crêpe provides a fitting conclusion.

● **Chez Pierre**   SIM

1, bd Veyrier-Montagnères.
Tel. 05 56 22 52 94. Fax 05 56 22 53 11.
lecafedelaplage@wanadoo.fr
www.cafedelaplage.com
Prix fixe: 25€, 19€. A la carte: 45€.

William Techoueyres and Bernard Laporte have taken over Arcachon's fashionable society address. Aficionados of marine fare continue to come here for the beautifully garnished seafood platters. The assorted seafood (cod, monkfish, salmon, scallops, prawns and shrimp) served with vegetables sautéed in olive oil and an exquisite house aïoli and the rib eye steak with sea salt are appealing propositions.

● **Chez Yvette**   SIM

59, bd Général-Leclerc.
Tel. 05 56 83 05 11. Fax 05 56 22 51 62.
Prix fixe: 19€, 10,50€ (child).
A la carte: 45–55€.

We arrange to meet at Laurette Dominguez's eatery in her old neo-Basque villa for the seafood, grilled Atlantic sea bass with beurre blanc and pan-seared veal kidney with chanterelles. A warm welcome and friendly atmosphere.

In 33120 Le Moulleau. 5 km sw
■ **Les Buissonnets**   ❀⌂

12, rue L.-Garros, au Moulleau.
Tel. 05 56 54 00 83. Fax 05 56 22 55 13.
hotelbuissonnets.monsite.wanadoo.fr
Closed Oct.
13 rooms: 75–90€.

This late-19th-century villa clad in Virginia creeper provides rooms with a personal touch that almost all overlook the garden. Copious breakfasts.

In Le Moulleau
■ **Hôtel Yatt**   ⌂

253, bd de la Côte-d'Argent.
Tel. 05 57 72 03 72. Fax 05 56 22 51 34.
information@yatt-hotel.com
www.yatt-hotel.com
Closed beg. Nov.–beg. Apr.
27 rooms: 45–70€. 2 suites: 85–125€.

Modern furniture, blue-and-yellow tones and a Miami-style art deco facade: this new look hotel provides a refreshing change of scenery.

ARÇAIS

79210 Deux-Sèvres. Paris 432 –
Poitiers 100 – Niort 23.
The heart of the Poitou marshland and an old village that has lost none of its character.

●	RESTAURANTS

● **La Gourmandise d'Arçais**

24, rue du Marais.
Tel. 05 49 33 22 93.
Closed weekdays. (winter), Sun. dinner, Mon., beg. Jan.–beg. Feb.
Prix fixe: 13,50€ (lunch), 18€, 29,50€.

Lydie and Pierre-Alain Mahuteau are the Tom Thumbs of the Poitou marshes. Their village establishment is delectable, the décor very simple and their hospitality genuine. They wholeheartedly champion their region's produce and traditions. Local house pâté, cabbage stuffed with vegetables, herbs and pork, served in broth, the escargots rolled in Swiss chard leaves, frog legs tossed in white wine and shallots, with local beurre de baratte and the pan-fried eels flambéed in Cognac bear vibrant witness to their cause. An impeccable welcome and friendly prices.

ARCANGUES see BIARRITZ
ARCINS see MARGAUX

ARGELES-GAZOST

65400 Hautes-Pyrénées. Paris 874 – Pau 58
– Lourdes 13 – Tarbes 31.

A highland spa (elevation 462 meters), this balcony looking out on the Pyrénées is the perfect place for a break in the mountain air.

 HOTELS-RESTAURANTS

■ Les Cimes
Pl Ourout.
Tel. 05 62 97 00 10. Fax 05 62 97 10 19.
www.hotel-lescimes.com
Closed beg. Nov.–mid-Dec.
26 rooms: 45–74€.

This changeless establishment has a discreet fifties charm. The rooms are comfortable and the studio apartments can be rented at a reasonable price for the week. We enjoy the garden and the indoor swimming pool.

■ Miramont
44, av Pyrénées.
Tel. 05 62 97 01 26. Fax 05 62 97 56 67.
hotel-miramont@sudfr.com
www.hotelmiramont.com
19 rooms: 42–122€. Half board: 72–182€.

The rooms and art deco furniture are bright and pleasantly arranged. Breakfast will set you up for a determined assault on the backpacking trails.

■ Le Soleil Levant
17, av Pyrénées.
Tel. 05 62 97 08 68. Fax 05 62 97 04 60.
hsoleillevant@aol.com
www.lesoleillevant.com
Closed end Nov.–23 Dec., 2 Jan.–31 Jan.,
1 week May.
35 rooms: 38,50–47€.

The friendly Sandrine Jaussant runs this classical hotel with its attractively turned-out rooms. The cuisine is simple and tasty. A good place to return to after a day spent walking.

In Saint-Savin (65400). 4 km s via D101.

■ Viscos
1, rue Lamarque.
Tel. 05 62 97 02 28. Fax 05 62 97 04 95.
www.hotel-leviscos.com

Closed Sun. dinner, Mon., 2 weeks Jan.
6 rooms: 65–105€. 2 suites: 105€.
Prix fixe: 26€, 36€, 52€, 75€.
A la carte: 56€.

The Saint-Martins have turned their hotel into a convivial port of call. The rooms have character and the furniture has long been in the family. In the winter, we make new acquaintances by the fireside, and in summer, we laze on the terrace when we return from our trek. Jean-Pierre takes orders before setting to work at the stove, preparing a foie gras mosaic, trout trilogy, stuffed lamb and a peach cake. Françoise unearths regional wines from both sides of the France-Spain border.

ARGELES-SUR-MER

66700 Pyrénées-Orientales. Paris 877 –
Perpignan 22 – Céret 28 – Port-Vendres 9 –
Prades 66.
infos@argeles-sur-mer.com.
Beach and mountains on the shoreline of the Côte Vermeille. Schistose rocks color the shore.

 HOTELS-RESTAURANTS

■ Le Cottage
Rue A.-Rimbaud.
Tel. 04 68 81 07 33. Fax 04 68 81 59 69.
info@hotel-lecottage.com
www.hotel-lecottage.com
Closed mid-Oct.–beg. Apr.
30 rooms: 60–173€. 4 suites: 130–284€.

In the heart of the residential district, this pleasant Mediterranean "cottage" promises a relaxing stay in its attractive, meticulously fitted-out rooms. Swimming pool, steam bath, Jacuzzi and garden complete the setting.

● L'Auberge du Roua
1,5 km w via rte de Sorède, chemin du Roua.
Tel. 04 68 95 85 85. Fax 04 68 95 83 50.
Closed mid-Nov.–beg. Mar.
14 rooms: 60–129€.

Magali Tonjum, who worked with her Norwegian husband to renovate this fine abode surrounded by vineyards, came up with the minimalist but hi-tech design for the rooms. She has entrusted the kitchen to the experienced Philippe Polin, who prepares an honest cuisine based on quality produce. We enjoy the lively, subtle, fresh, reliably flavored dishes formerly concocted at the Neptune in Collioure by this nomadic native of Valenciennes: peppers with a squid stuffing, pan-seared foie gras with apples and sweet potato chutney, scallops with artichokes, red mullet with fennel and lemon and a pine nut-and bulgur-stuffed lamb saddle. A clear, tasty feast accompanied by the best local wines and some highly appropriate desserts (cherry crumble with vanilla ice cream, frozen vacherin seasoned with Marc de Banyuls).

◾ Les Charmettes

30 av du Tech.
Tel. 04 68 81 09 84. Fax 04 68 81 33 62.
www.lescharmettes.com
10 rooms: 39–90€.

The Barbieuxs, who met at Bérard's in La Cadière d'Azur, have preserved the family spirit of this neo-Catalan establishment. Laurence greets guests with a smile, and Marc shuns complexity when preparing his anchovy plate, the little bouilabaisse with jumbo shrimp and salmon half-moon ravioli, not to forget the lamb shanks seasoned with a lavender emulsion. A great deal of thoughtfulness goes into all this and even the pricing of the set menus.

● L'Amadeus   ⓃCOM

Av des Platanes.
Tel.-Fax 04 68 81 12 38.
Closed Wed. (off season), 20 Nov.–mid-Dec.,
beg. Jan.–beg. Feb.
Prix fixe: 24€, 33€, 39€.

Emmanuel Robin has enthusiastically adopted this restaurant that backs onto the beach. The faux-rustic cottage with its fireplace and shades of white is very pleasant and the dishes served at reasonable prices are very competently prepared. Atlantic sea bass served warm, the slow-cooked vegetables, the cod mille-feuille

and the rack of lamb glazed in thyme confiture are well chosen. The variations on theme of foie gras and the duck breast are a reminder that Emmanuel learned his trade in Toulouse.

In Port-Argelès 66700. 3 km e.

● Le Manureva   SIM

Place Magellan. Résidence Atalaya.
Tel. 04 68 81 69 67.
www.le-manureva.com
Closed Tue. dinner, Wed., 4 Dec.–11 Jan.
Prix fixe: 18€, 27€, 49€.
A la carte: 40–45€.

Geneviève Pascual keenly commends the dishes prepared by her husband Jean-Claude. The foie gras degustation platter, parrillada, rib eye steak with ceps and the dessert of cold fresh fruit in jelly slip down effortlessly.

ARGENT-SUR-SAULDRE

18410 Cher. Paris 171 – Orléans 61 –
Bourges 58 – Gien 21.
info@coeur-de-france.com.
The gates of the Sologne region and the land of the Grand Meaulnes. This is peaceful, wooded Berry.

   HOTELS-RESTAURANTS

■ Le Relais de la Poste

3, rue Nationale.
Tel. 02 48 81 53 90. Fax 02 48 81 30 62.
relaisdelaposte@aol.com
Closed Sun. dinner, Mon.
10 rooms: 49–60€.
Prix fixe: 23€, 28€, 37€, 15€ (child).
A la carte: 45–50€.

Laurent and Peggy Guénot have breathed new life into this old coaching inn. In the kitchen and dining room respectively, they leave no stone unturned in their efforts to please. Crayfish gratin, fish stew with potatoes, onions and vermouth, veal sweetbreads with Sancerre sauce and the puff pastry and fig tart are well crafted. Tidy rooms and sensible prices.

ARGENTAT

19400 Corrèze. Paris 503 – Aurillac 54 – Brive 45 – Tulle 29.

The banks of the Dordogne lend a nonchalant charm to this large Corrèze village with its fine old houses.

 HOTELS-RESTAURANTS

■ Hôtel Fouillade

11, pl Gambetta.
Tel. 05 55 28 10 17.
www.fouillade.com
Closed end Nov.–Christmas.
Rest. closed Sun. dinner, Mon. (off season).
15 rooms: 44–62€.
Prix fixe: 13€, 32€.

This antique central hotel has been renovated in contemporary style with modern rooms. Regional cuisine served under the exposed beams of the dining room.

● Auberge des Gabariers

15, quai Lestourgie.
Tel. 05 55 28 05 87.Fax 05 55 28 69 63.
www.aubergedesgabarriers.com
Closed mid-Nov.–mid-Mar. Rest. closed Tue. dinner, Wed. (exc. summer).
2 rooms: 76–90€.
Prix fixe: 15€, 26€, 34€.

Pascal Jacquinot still has the moustache he wore when we met him at the Crémaillère in Brive, but he has dropped grand cuisine in favor of the simple dishes that the dreams of travelers arriving in Corrèze are made on. Cep omelet, slice of duck foie gras, veal sweetbread fricassée with ceps, garlic and shallots and finally the generous frozen chestnut crème with its liqueur all feature in the bargain set menus here, and if you should want to stay overnight, there are two charming rooms overlooking the river and the old houses of Argentat. Delightful service provided by a young team under his wife Marie-Claude.

ARLES

13200 Bouches-du-Rhône. Paris 721 – Avignon 36 – Nîmes 32 – Marseille 95 – Aix-en-Provence 78.

ot-arles@visitprovence.com.

The brand new pedestrian center enables undisturbed exploration of this genuinely Provençal town, with its authentic folklore, international photography fair, arenas, ancient theater and Alyscamps garden, where poet Paul-Jean Toulet bade us "beware the sweetness of things".

 HOTELS-RESTAURANTS

■ Jules César

9, bd des Lices.
Tel. 04 90 52 52 52. Fax 04 90 52 52 53.
julescesar2@wanadoo.fr
www.hotel-julescesar.fr
Rest. closed Sat.
56 rooms: 160–180€. 3 suites: 385€.
Prix fixe: 32€, 47€, 52€.

Michel Albagnac's establishment has become a monument in much the same way as the antique theater and arenas here. In the kitchen, the Pascal Renaud-Joseph Kriz partnership steers a course between regional and creative cuisine. Wild rabbit and foie gras terrine with chestnut cream, roasted pike-perch with sautéed zucchini and veal cutlet served on kidney risotto, not to overlook the roasted pineapple flambéed with aged rum, are not bad. This former convent provides distinctive rooms and relaxation by its pool or in its Jacuzzi.

■ Mas de Peint

2,5 km via rte de Salins. Le Sambuc.
Tel. 04 90 97 20 62. Fax 04 90 97 22 20.
hotel@masdepeint.net / www.masdepeint.com
Closed mid-Nov.–mid-Dec., beg. Jan.–20 Mar.
Rest. closed Wed., Tue., Thu. lunch.
8 rooms: 205–265€. 3 suites: 335–381€.
Prix fixe: 50€ (dinner).

A haven of peace in the heart of the country, Jacques Bon's place has charm to spare with its colorful rooms and swimming pool. In the kitchen, mushroom- and ham-stuffed artichokes simmered in wine in a cocotte with smoked-bacon broth, thyme-seasoned John Dory served with a bean risotto or the toro tenderloin with seasonal vegetables are meticulously prepared by Antoine Thibault. All Camargue is served on a platter here.

■ L'Hôtel Particulier

4, rue de la Monnaie.
Tel. 04 90 52 51 40. Fax 04 90 96 16 70.
contact@hotel-particulier.com
www.hotel-particulier.com
4 rooms: 189–239€. 10 suites: 209–289€.

Brigitte Pagès de Oliveira has turned this 1826 residence into an island of charm. It offers rooms and suites looking out onto the shady garden, a swimming pool, a spa bath in the vaulted basement and a guesthouse atmosphere. The decoration is exquisite and the comfort and service flawless. Here, in the center of town, the shade of centennial trees and, in winter, the fire blazing in the immense hearth invite us to enjoy the passage of time.

■ Hôtel d'Arlatan

26, rue du Sauvage.
Tel. 04 90 93 56 66. Fax 04 90 49 68 45.
hotel-arlatan@wanadoo.fr
www.hotel-arlatan.fr
Closed beg. Jan.–beg. Feb.
30 rooms: 77–153€. 10 suites: 127–243€.

This town center hotel has parking, a significant advantage. The delicious breakfasts, garden and rooms with a Provençal flavor are its other assets.

■ Nord-Pinus

Pl du Forum.
Tel. 04 90 93 44 44. Fax 04 90 93 34 00.
info@nord-pinus.com / www.nord-pinus.com
19 rooms: 140–190€. 7 suites: 285–320€.

Anne Igou has preserved the old-fashioned charm of this hostelry where the small world of bullfighting gathers. The spirits of Picasso and Cocteau fill the rooms. The bar is the kitschiest spot in town and the Brasserie du Nord-Pindus the haunt of a happy few.

■ Hôtel de l'Amphithéâtre

5-7, rue Diderot.
Tel. 04 90 96 10 30. Fax 04 90 93 98 69.
contact@hotelamphitheatre.fr
www.hotelamphitheatre.fr
26 rooms: 45–99€. 2 suites: 99–145€.

A step or two away from the arenas and the Roman theater, this marvelously restored 17th-century abode provides highly charming, flawlessly furnished and equipped rooms. The terrace suite offers a spectacular view over the town. A pleasant welcome and superb value for money.

● La Chassagnette

Chassagnette, rte du Sambuc.
17 km via D570 and D36.
Tel. 04 90 97 26 96. Fax 04 90 97 26 95.
restaurantchassa@aol.com
www.chassagnette.fr
Closed Wed., end Dec.–beg. Mar.
Prix fixe: 34€ (lunch), 64€, 80€.
A la carte: 45€.

Michel Mialhe, a new chef from the Ducasse stable, tends to his clientele in this bright establishment decorated with a colorful fresco. The simplified cuisine continues to pay tribute to the region with quality organic fare. Tomato gazpacho, whiting with salted butter and coco beans, olive-seasoned toro steak with simmered Swiss chard and the Camargue rice pudding served with fruit now form set menus at more sensible prices.

● L'Atelier de Jean-Luc Rabanel

7, rue des Carmes.
Tel. 04 90 91 07 69.
jlr@cuisinetc.com / www.rabanel.com
Closed Mon., Tue. lunch, 1 week beg. Oct., 3 weeks end Jan.–mid-Feb.
Prix fixe: 17€ (lunch), 20€ (lunch), 37€ (lunch), 50€ (dinner).

Jean-Luc Rabanel has left the Chassagnette to set up on his own in an appealing side street. We succumb to the charm of the modern-chic bistro décor, all in black and white. There are thirty places inside and a few more tables on the terrace.

Turning to the cuisine, Rabanel sticks to his principles: organic produce, savory then sweet tapas and between the two a meat or fish course. The other day was an emotional experience, with—among other dishes—Swiss chard ravioli, beet spring rolls with jelly, calico artichokes in a grain and ginger bouillon. There followed a grilled tuna accompanied by vegetables harvested that very morning and seared in the wok, all of virginal purity. Desserts included a giddying strawberry beignet with fresh passion fruit vinaigrette sauce. All in all, a light, lively cuisine that sparkles like spring water in the sun. The service displays a laser-like precision and a southern French conviviality under the guidance of the faithful Sébastien.

● **Le Cilantro**

31, rue Porte-de-Laure.
Tel. 04 90 18 25 05. Fax 04 90 18 25 10.
infocilantro@aol.com
Closed Sat. lunch, Sun., Mon. lunch,
2 weeks beg. Jan., 2 weeks end Mar.
Prix fixe: 20€ (lunch), 25€ (lunch),
43€ (dinner).

Westermann, Loiseau and Ducasse (the Louis XV) were the exalted masters of Jérôme Laurent, the local who set up here two years ago under the sign of the Cilantro (coriander in Occitan), a step away from the ancient theater and arenas. The comfortable designer setting in bright colors has room for forty or so guests and there are a few tables on the terrace, which is so pleasant when the weather is fine. Creativity, lightness of touch and Mediterranean authenticity are Laurent's watchwords. The marbled goose foie gras and artichokes, sautéed squid with preserved lemon and vegetables in chilled egg custard sauce, cut into cubes, red tuna and foie gras Rossini, oven-browned lamb with dried fruit and nuts served with black raisins and slow-cooked sweet-pepper polenta compose a symphony that ends on a sweet note: pistachio parfait with a topping of raspberries simmered in Banyuls. This is a chef whose career we will follow carefully. In the dining room, William brings to the

service a cheerful, discreet efficiency we value so much.

● **Le Jardin de Manon**

14, av des Alyscamps.
Tel. 04 90 93 38 68. Fax 04 90 49 62 03.
sabrine.ginoux@wanadoo.fr
Closed Tue. dinner, Wed., Nov. 1 vac.,
Feb. vac.
Prix fixe: 17€ (lunch), 21€, 28€, 46€.
A la carte: 40€.

It is worth a detour to visit Alain Ginoux's restaurant just outside the town center. The patio behind the house provides a small haven of greenery and tranquility, pleasant indeed in the summer heat. We thoroughly enjoy the cold cake of sundried tomatoes and fresh local goat cheese, stuffed sea bream served with crunchy grilled vegetables, boneless spit-roasted rabbit, rosemary-seasoned goat cheese and the fig gratin. The Languedoc and Roussillon wines are choice accompaniments.

ARLEUF see CHATEAU-CHINON
ARNAGE see LE MANS

ARNAY-LE-DUC

21230 Côte-d'Or. Paris 285 – Beaune 36 –
Dijon 59 – Saulieu 29.
ot@arnay-le-duc.com.
The museum of table arts in the heart of this small Burgundy town on the edge of the Morvan nature reserve leaves us with a healthy appetite.

■ ⧄ HOTELS-RESTAURANTS

■ **Chez Camille**   ⌂

1, pl E.-Herriot.
Tel. 03 80 90 01 38. Fax 03 80 90 04 64.
chez-camille@wanadoo.fr / www.chez-camille.fr
Open daily. Rest. closed 24 Dec. dinner.
11 rooms: 79€.
Prix fixe: 20€, 37€, 80€.

Camille is a good daughter and Armand Poinsot a conscientious cook. Her name is in capitals over the door and he meticulously prepares domestic dishes in the kitchen. The duck terrine with breast and foie gras makes a copious *amuse-bouche*, followed by the "high tide" plate, with shellfish, monkfish and other seafood or, in a more regional vein, the veal sweetbreads with a reduced spinach jus and orange zest. The hot orange soufflé is a quite an event. The Burgundy vintages—not the most famous, but all of excellent quality—are not excessively priced. The rooms are neat and tidy and the family welcome dependably warm.

ARPAILLARGUES-ET-AUREILLAC see UZES
ARRADON see VANNES

ARRAS

62000 Pas-de-Calais. Paris 179 – Lille 53 – Amiens 63 – Calais 111.
arras.tourisme@wanadoo.fr.
Capital of the Artois region with its two main squares bordered by houses with gables and fine arcades, its thirty or so kilometers of tunnels where the British army took cover during the Great War, and its art gallery in the abbey of Saint-Vaast, Arras is now just fifty minutes from Paris by high-speed train. An opportunity to enjoy authentic beauty and a natural love of food.

 HOTELS-RESTAURANTS

■ Hôtel de l'Univers
Restaurant Le Clusius
3, pl de la Croix-Rouge.
Tel. 03 21 71 34 01. Fax 03 21 71 41 42.
univers.hotel@najeti.com
www.hotel-univers-arras.com
38 rooms: 79–139€.
Prix fixe: 19€ (weekday lunch), 35€ (weekday lunch), 37€ (dinner), 53€ (dinner), 20€ (child).

In the 18th century, the Jesuits turned this immense building into a refuge for the destitute and sick. Today, it is a hotel with a more conventional clientele. Its restaurant, Le Clusius, presents an eclectic menu, with duck foie gras with local beer eau-de-vie, turbot filet served on a potato cake with slow-cooked leeks and waffles with chickory mousseline and crème gla-

cée. In short, wholesome, tempting dishes and conscientious service.

■ Holiday Inn
3, rue du Dr-Brassart.
Tel. 03 21 60 88 88. Fax 03 21 60 89 00.
www.holidayinn-arras.com
86 rooms: 78€. 12 suites: 89€.

In this hotel by the train station, priority has been given to practical considerations: functional rooms, WiFi, meeting facilities and parking are valid assets. A suitable welcome.

■ Hôtel d'Angleterre
7, pl Foch.
Tel. 03 21 51 51 16. Fax 03 21 71 38 20.
www.pilortec.fr/hotelangleterre
Rest. closed Sat. lunch, Sun. dinner, Mon.
20 rooms: 80–97€. 2 suites: 145€.
Prix fixe: 13,90€, 16,90€, 25,90€.

Opposite the station, this well-equipped establishment provides a friendly welcome and decent food (cold shrimp mousse in aspic, pot-au-feu nougat in aspic), all at reasonable prices.

■ Mercure-Atria
58, bd Carnot.
Tel. 03 21 23 88 88. Fax 03 21 23 88 89.
H1560@accor-hotels.com / www.accor.com
Rest. closed Sat. lunch, Sun. lunch.
80 rooms: 74–115€.
Prix fixe: 14,60€.

We are familiar with the "Atria" concept: a hotel plus convention center in the heart of town. This establishment five minutes from the train station follows the pattern. The rooms are functional and the restaurant offers a regionalized cuisine (sole with crabmeat, chickory ice cream) as well as a good selection of wines.

■ Le Moderne
1, bd Faidherbe.
Tel. 03 21 23 39 57. Fax 03 21 71 55 42.
www.hotel-moderne-arras.com
Closed Christmas, New Year's.
54 rooms: 75–80€.

This twenties hotel (that has been widely renovated since) provides fully equipped modern rooms. A friendly welcome, quality regional cuisine and a "local option" at an affordable price.

■ Les 3 Luppars

49, Grand-Place.
Tel. 03 21 60 02 03. Fax 03 21 24 24 80.
www.hostel-les-3luppars.com
42 rooms: 44–60€.

A Gothic facade, pure white rooms and contemporary furniture. We are on the main square and the revelry often goes on until late at night.

● Le Between   N COM

12, rue de la Taillerie.
Tel. 03 21 73 57 79.
Closed Sat. lunch, Sun. dinner, Mon.,
2 weeks beg. Aug.
Prix fixe: 22,50€, 23,50€, 31€.

Between the two fine squares, this vaulted cellar serves a topical cuisine. Spicy red tuna, pan-seared foie gras with red beets, Atlantic sea bass filet with leek cannelloni, veal scallop with salsify and asparagus and a lemon mille-feuille are the house's persuasive credentials, all washed down with a fine Mas Neuf Costière de Nîmes.

● La Coupole d'Arras   COM

26, bd de Strasbourg.
Tel. 03 21 71 88 44. Fax 03 21 71 52 46.
Closed Sun. dinner (off season).
Prix fixe: 25€, 30€, 15€ (child).
A la carte: 50–55€.

This neo-1900 Parisian-style brasserie is a fine-looking place with its patinated décor, attentive service, oyster bar and elegant dishes. Foie gras, fish choucroute and the house veal kidney with onion, mustard and white wine sauce make an excellent impression.

● Le Carnot   SIM

10-12, pl Foch.
Tel. 03 21 71 08 14 / 03 21 71 29 78.
Fax 03 21 71 60 95.
Closed Christmas, New Year's.

29 rooms: 50–64€.
Prix fixe: 17€, 32€, 45€, 8€ (child).
A la carte: 45–60€.

On one side, a traditional brasserie where we lunch on steak tartare, pork cuts and charcuterie served hot over sauerkraut, potjevlesch (a local veal, chicken and rabbit pâté); on the other, a gourmet restaurant. White truffle and scallop ravioli, sirloin steak with ceps and the nougat cornucopia are not bad.

In Saint-Laurent-Blangy (62223).

● Les Jardins de Saint-Laurent   COM

1, rue Laurent Gers.
Tel. 03 21 50 81 00. Fax 03 21 48 51 20.
www.les-jardins-de-st-laurent.fr
Closed 1 week July, 2 weeks beg. Aug.
Prix fixe: 18€, 24,50€, 35€,
13€ (child). A la carte: 40€.

Dorothée and William Basdevant have turned this residence surrounded by flower gardens into an attractive spot, providing a first-rate welcome and domestic cuisine. We enjoy the fried smoked herring cakes, veal in raisin brioche and the chitterling sausage cassolette with morels, all just right. The set menus are well chosen and the check shows leniency.

ARS-EN-RE see ILE DE RE

56640 Morbihan. Paris 489 – Vannes 33 –
Lorient 91 – Auray 51 – Quiberon 79.
crouesty@crouesty.com.
The Rhuys peninsula, a mild, almost Mediterranean Brittany, new and old harbors, healthy cuisine and fresh air.

 HOTELS-RESTAURANTS

■ Miramar-Crouesty

In Port-du-Crouesty. 2 km sw. BP32.
Tel. 02 97 53 49 00. Fax 02 97 53 49 99.
www.miramarcrouesty.com
Closed 3 weeks Dec.
108 rooms 220–370€. 12 suites: 270–500€.
Prix fixe: 49€.

The architecture of this building suggests an ocean liner setting out on a cruise. Calm, luxury and sensual pleasure are all within reach. First, there is the Louison Bobet thalassotherapy institute and its many facilities (swimming pools, steam bath, Jacuzzi, fitness center). Then, when our thoughts turn to food, we can choose between the Ruban Bleu—preferred by those receiving therapy, since it serves quality health food—and the more gastronomic Salle à Manger, where Yves Toublanc freely expresses his skills. There, we feast on crab ravioli, cilantro-seasoned catfish, Atlantic sea bass pan tossed with herbs, roasted squab with artichoke and fennel or the pralined ricotta and chocolate dome for dessert. The rooms are luxurious. The blue-and-white interior mirrors the colors of the ocean. Friendly service and an elegant welcome.

■ Le Crouesty 🏠

In Port-du-Crouesty. 2 km sw.
Tel. 02 97 53 87 91. Fax 02 97 53 66 76.
Closed Dec., Jan.
26 rooms: 64–90€.

For those who wish to enjoy the benefits of Port Crouesty but avoid its preppier side, this is an excellent address, providing neat rooms at reasonable prices.

● Le Grand Largue ⊙V.COM

In Port-du-Crouesty. 2 km sw.
Tel. 02 97 53 71 58. Fax 02 97 53 92 20.
largueadam@wanadoo.fr
http://grand-largue.ifrance.com
Closed Mon., Tue. (exc. July–Aug.),
mid-Nov.–mid-Dec., Jan.
Prix fixe: 35€, 58€.

This restaurant with its view of the rumbling sea, the boats entering and leaving the harbor and the setting sun draws inspiration from its charming surroundings. Proof comes in the set menus chosen by Serge Adam. Langoustines with artichokes flavored with summer truffles, Atlantic sea bass with shellfish jus and basil oil and the red mullet with tomato, cucumber and marjoram play to a perfectly local score. For dessert, the strawberry soup with tarragon and olive oil accompanied by a lychee sorbet provides a refreshing sweet conclusion. Anxious not to spoil our pleasure, the prices keep a low profile.

● Le Cap Horn SIM

In Port-du-Crouesty. 2 km sw.
39, quai des Voiliers.
Tel.-Fax 02 97 53 60 04.
Closed Tue. (Oct.–Dec. exc. vac.), Jan.
Prix fixe: 13€ (lunch, wine inc.), 22€, 26€,
28€, 6€ (child). A la carte: 35€.

Right on the harbor, this brasserie—also a pub—serves an honest market-based cuisine in the form of bargain set menus. Fish soup, grilled Atlantic sea bass with beurre blanc, beef tartare are all very pleasant.

■ Glann ar Mor 🏠

In Port-Navalo. 27, rue des Fontaines.
Tel. 02 97 53 88 30. Fax 02 97 53 68 47.
glannarmor@aol.com / www.glannarmor.fr
Closed beg. Jan.–beg. Mar.
9 rooms: 59–75€.

Jean-François Rousseau and Philippe Rigoulot share the same passion: the love of a job well done. This makes them interchangeable, something their customers, who enjoy the relaxed atmosphere the two have brought to the place, would not hold against them. The rooms are simple and comfortable, and the cuisine looks to the ocean, with its oven-browned seafood trio, presented in shells, haddock served with minced scallops and the grilled turbot filet with langoustines. The soft-centered chocolate and sour cherry cake is not bad at all!

ASCAIN see SAINT-JEAN-DE-LUZ

ASNIERES-SUR-NOUERE see ANGOULEME

ASTAFFORT

47220 Lot-et-Garonne. Paris 731 – Agen 19 – Lectoure 20 – Auvillar 29 – Condom 34.
ot-astaffort@wanadoo.fr.
At the crossroads of the Agen and Gers regions, the village of singer-songwriter Francis Cabrel unobtrusively illustrates the pleasures of France.

HOTELS-RESTAURANTS

● **Michel Latrille Le Square**

5-7, pl de la Craste.
Tel. 05 53 47 20 40. Fax 05 53 47 10 38.
latrille.michel@wanadoo.fr / www.latrille.com
Closed Jan. Rest. closed Sun. dinner.
14 rooms: 50–140€.
Prix fixe: 25€, 37€, 56€. A la carte: 90€.

Singer Francis Cabrel very discreetly acquired this charming hotel with its refined rooms. Sylvie Latrille at the desk and in the dining room and her husband Michel in the kitchen are attentive to their guests' enjoyment. In the modern dining room, they serve up their region a touch at a time, with a degustation of duck foie gras, langoustine ravioli with truffles, veal cutlet with morels and the raspberry pain perdu. These almost changeless, sincere dishes are washed down with wines from the four corners of France and beyond.

ATTIGNAT

01340 Ain. Paris 422 – Mâcon 35 –
Bourg-en-Bresse 13 – Tournus 42.
Simply a staging post village in the heart of portly, food-loving Bresse.

 HOTELS-RESTAURANTS

■ **Dominique Marcepoil**

481, Grande-Rue, D975.
Tel. 04 74 30 92 24. Fax 04 74 25 93 48.
www.dominiquemarcepoil.com
Closed 1 week beg. Oct., 2 weeks mid-Feb.–
beg. Mar., Sun. Rest. closed Sun., Mon. lunch
(exc. Bank holidays).
11 rooms: 50–66€.
Prix fixe: 20€, 30€ (wine inc.), 35€, 38€,
46€, 62€ (wine inc.), 13€ (child).
A la carte: 60–70€.

Dominique Marcepoil and his wife Brigitte have fitted out nine trim rooms and added an indoor swimming pool. The restaurant is reputable indeed. The foie gras duo, pan-seared and in terrine, frog legs sautéed Dombes style and the rolled Bresse chicken Rossini display true skill.

AUBAGNE

13400 Bouches-du-Rhône. Paris 795 –
Marseille 18 – Toulon 47 –
Aix-en-Provence 38 – Brignoles 49.
aubagnetour@aubagne.com.
With a population of over 40,000, Marcel Pagnol's home town has changed a great deal since the days of *My Mother's Castle*.

 HOTELS-RESTAURANTS

■ **Hostellerie de la Source**

Locale known as Saint-Pierre.
Tel. 04 42 04 09 19. Fax 04 42 04 58 72.
hoteldelasource@aol.com
www.hdelasource.com
26 rooms: 96–170€.
Prix fixe: 49€.

Isabelle and Yves Barral's hostelry has the discreet charm of an earlier age, but its rooms are decorated in contemporary style. The grounds are large, the terrace the ideal place to read or daydream, the tennis court open to enthusiasts and the benefits of the swimming pool and Jacuzzi available to all. The center of Marseille is just twenty minutes away.

● **L'Auberge de la Ferme** SIM

Sentier Marcel-Pagnol.
Tel.-Fax 04 42 03 29 67.
www.aubergelaferme.com
Closed Sat., Sun. lunch, Mon., Aug.
Prix fixe: 50€.

Jean-Louis and Patricia Zenezini offer a warm welcome here at their "farm". The inn is charming, as is its cuisine. Fig beignets rolled in Parma ham, eggplant and brandade mille-feuille, beef cheek and oxtail braised with purple artichokes favorably impress, just like the crème Provençale served with honey caramel.

AUBENAS

07200 Ardèche. Paris 632 – Alès 76 –
Montélimar 41 – Privas 31.
ot.aubenas.ardeche@en-france.com.
With its feel of a sprawling Provençal village, this
Ardèche town with its colorful Saturday market
on the château square (straight from a song by
Bécaud) wears the colors of the Great South. Do
not miss the Dôme Saint-Benoît, the 17th-cen-
tury mausoleum of the Maréchal d'Ornano.

 HOTELS-RESTAURANTS

● Le Fournil   COM
34, rue du Quatre-Septembre.
Tel.-Fax 04 75 93 58 68.
www.restaurant-le-fournil.com
Closed Sun., Mon., Nov. 1 vac., Christmas–
New Year's vac., Feb. vac.
Prix fixe: 19€, 26€, 33€, 10€ (child).
A la carte: 40–45€.

Aubenas' most authoritative establishment.
With an expert touch, Michel Leynaud concocts sun-drenched dishes. Creamy morel
mushroom flan, skate with parsley and garlic, rack of lamb served Provençal style and
aniseed mousse with berry sauce make a
delightful impression. Valérie's welcome is
delectable and so are the prices.

In Vinezac (07110). 13 km s via D104 and D423.

■ La Bastide du Soleil   ❀ ⌂
Le Bourg.
Tel. 04 75 36 91 66. Fax 04 75 36 91 59.
bastidesoleil@wanadoo.fr
Closed Jan.
4 rooms: 85–115€. 1 suite: 90€.
Prix fixe: 15€, 23€, 35€. A la carte: 40€.

Xavier Gillé has taken over this 17th-cen-
tury Sepulcri château and deliberately left
its comfortable, modern rooms very much
alone. In the kitchen, Thierry Moreau prepares conventional, time-honored dishes.
Pan-seared foie gras, trout with almonds,
traditionally prepared pork tenderloiin
and the berry sabayon slip down easily.

AUCH

32000 Gers. Paris 733 – Toulouse 77 –
Agen 74 – Bordeaux 206.
ot-auch@wanadoo.fr.
Capital of the Gers district and great exponent
of the art of living, a town of bucolic delights,
musketeers and foie gras.

 HOTELS-RESTAURANTS

● Hôtel de France   ○⌂🏨
Pl de la Libération, BP 124.
Tel. 05 62 61 71 71. Fax 05 62 61 71 81.
roland.garreau@wanadoo.fr
www.hoteldefrance-auch.com
Closed 2 weeks Christmas–New Year's.
Rest. closed Sun. dinner.
27 rooms: 69–138€. 2 suites: 210–320€.
Prix fixe: 27€, 52€. A la carte: 72€.

This former post house boasts spacious
rooms—one of which is featured in the
movie *Le bonheur est dans le pré*—and
a quality restaurant that owes a lot to
Roland Garreau, 1991 winner of the Meilleur Ouvrier de France award and former cookery teacher at Lenôtre. Moldings,
woodwork and stained glass are part of
the scenery. In the dining room, we enjoy
the best local produce meticulously prepared: foie gras served with various flavors, lobster and turbot in papillote with
slow-cooked leeks, turbot with poultry
jus, roasted duck breast and a fresh pear
Tatin with caramelized nuts. The cellar
offers great wines from Bordeaux and elsewhere, and also boasts a fine collection of
vintage Armagnacs.

● La Table d'Oste   SIM
7, rue Lamartine.
Tel.-Fax 05 62 05 55 62.
www.table-oste-restaurant.com
Closed Sat. dinner (mid-June–end Oct.), Sun.,
Mon. lunch (mid-June–end Oct.).
Prix fixe: 16€ (weekday lunch),
24€ (dinner), 35€ (dinner), 10 € (child).

In the heart of town, Camille and Patrick Bonnans have brought a new energy
to this charming inn near the cathedral.

The cozy setting and cuisine of Gers go well together. We come for the goat cheese in puff pastry, the "hamber-Gers" (pan-seared duck breast and foie gras), the duck carpaccio and the catch of the day. The apple croustade, a local tart made with many layers of thin pastry, could almost eat itself and the Gers wines form the foundation.

● **Le Darolles**   SIM

4, pl de la Libération.
Tel.-Fax 05 62 05 00 51.
Prix fixe: 16,50€, 28€. A la carte: 35–40€.

This piano bar and brasserie has changed hands. The welcome leaves a little to be desired, but Bernard Caumont's dishes are flavorsome. Mille-feuille of foie gras terrine, the all-duck plate (confit, wing, foie gras and breast) and the rib eye are splendid classics.

AUDERVILLE

50440 Manche. Paris 385 –
Barneville-Carteret 50 – Cherbourg 28 –
Nez de Jobourg 5.

Didier Decoin wrote of his home here at World's End. This granite village on the cape of La Hague is the most pleasant of promontories.

    RESTAURANTS

● **La Malle aux Epices**

Le Bourg.
Tel. 02 33 52 77 44.
Closed Sat. lunch, Mon. dinner, Tue.
Prix fixe: 15€ (lunch), 16€, 22€.
A la carte: 30€.

An Auvergnat from Clermont who trained with Loiseau in Saulieu, Christophe Barjettas worked at the Mandala in Saint-Barth and at Jean Georges' in New York, and this has left him with a taste for majestically prepared fusion cuisine. The dishes in kit form presented on the blackboard include the tuna tataki, John Dory carpaccio, Chinese cabbage salad, fish spring roll, pollock tempura as well as salmon marinated in creole spices, shrimp curry

and a pan-tossed turbot with oyster sauce, ginger and sake. In his old granite inn perched on the cape of La Hague (at the very end of World's End), this remarkable chef with his pirate's bandana sets sail for flavors new. The results are wildly unpredictable, but have a habit of coming out right in the end.

● **Auberge de Goury**

Pt de Goury.
Tel. 02 33 52 77 01.
www.aubergedegoury.com
Closed Jan.
Prix fixe: 15,50€, 25€, 30€, 50€.

Oysters from the English Channel, carpaccio of the day, whole Atlantic sea bass, sea bream, sole, Hague-style grilled leg of lamb: free of frills, this is what awaits us in the tavern at World's End, just opposite the Goury lighthouse, frequented by neighbor and literary luminary Didier Decoin.

AUDIERNE

29770 Finistère. Paris 601 – Quimper 37 –
Douarnenez 21 – Pont-l'Abbé 33.

ot.cap.sizun.pointe.du.raz@wanadoo.fr.

This famous port in South Finistère watches over its ocean shore. With its landing stage leading on to the Ile de Sein, long beach, crayfish crawls, houses clustered around the estuary and cape, the village is a staging post on the way to the pointe du Raz (fifteen kilometers away), the pointe du Van and the baie des Trépassés.

    HOTELS-RESTAURANTS

■ **Le Goyen**

At the port, pl Jean-Simon.
Tel. 02 98 70 08 88. Fax 02 98 70 18 77.
hotel.le.goyen@wanadoo.fr
www.chateauxhotels.com//goyen
Closed 11 Nov.–29 Dec., Jan. 1–end Mar.
Rest. closed Mon., Tue. lunch.
20 rooms: 77–108€. 8 suites: 105–158€.
Prix fixe: 25€ (weekday lunch), 35€, 52€,
10–12€ (child).

Serge Vervoitte conscientiously tends to the old Bosser place by the harbor, which has undergone some necessary renovation. Chef Nicolas Fornaro performs tunefully to a refined score that is based on the best of local produce. Cap Breton snail cassoulet with Fourme d'Ambert cheese, grilled Atlantic sea bass with ceps and reduced meat jus, a lobster and champagne stew from the local crawls are all fine tricks. The Breton honey-roasted duckling with applesauce and cider-cooked celery root is an appealing sweet and savory composition. The desserts (citrus croustillant with orange marmalade and mandarin orange sorbet or the almond pistachio dacquoise with white chocolate cream and mixed fruit) are well crafted.

■ La Plage

Waterfront, 21, bd Manu-Brusq.
Tel. 02 98 70 01 07. Fax 02 98 75 04 69.
hotel.laplage@wanadoo.fr
www.hotel-finistere.com
Closed mid-Nov.–Christmas,
beg. Jan.–end Mar.
26 rooms: 49–70€.
Prix fixe: 25€ (dinner), 38€ (dinner),
9€ (child). A la carte: 35–45€.

Adolphe Bosser has an eye on the kitchens in this hotel by the ocean and beaches, so it comes as no surprise that the house stuffed crab, fisherman's style, the assorted catch of the day plate with ginger butter, the breast of guinea hen pan tossed with ceps and the tarte Tatin are excellent dishes. We also enjoy the "deep sea" aspect of the décor, the simple, attractive rooms, the friendly service and shrewd set menus.

■ Le Roi Gradlon

Waterfront.
Tel. 02 98 70 04 51. Fax 02 98 70 14 73.
accueil@auroigradlon.com
www.auroigradlon.com
Closed beg. Dec.–beg. Feb. Rest. closed Wed.
19 rooms: 46–75€.
Prix fixe: 17€ (lunch, wine inc.),
20€ (weekday dinner), 25€, 34€,
9,50€ (child). A la carte: 45–50€.

This beach hotel provides handome rooms in blue and gold, as well as a restaurant

devoted to the sea and local produce. We delight in the young spinach salad with three fish from Plogloff's smokehouse, a simply poached artichoke with three accompaniments, the red mullet filet in herb crust with fennel risotto or poached John Dory with a pepper and fried basil sauce, served with grated potato cake.

● L'Iroise   COM

8, quai Camille-Pelletan.
Tel. 02 98 70 15 80. Fax 02 98 70 20 82.
www.restaurant-liroise.com
Closed Tue. (off season), end Jan.–10 Feb.
Prix fixe: 18,90€ (weekday lunch), 23,90€,
15€ (child). A la carte: 60–65€.

Eric Lavallée, who worked with Boyer in Reims, plays variations on theme of land and sea. Stuffed squid with chitterling sausage, scallops cut in thin strips served with chorizo, monkfish with Serrano ham and Paimpol white beans and also the steamed langoustines and the buttered peppers and leeks with cilantro sauce are not bad. Christelle has a ready smile and the Champagnes are served with feeling.

09800 Ariège. Paris 788 – Toulouse 108 –
Saint-Gaudens 58.
Couserans Ariège: a rough, fresh, genuine region.

■ / ● HOTELS-RESTAURANTS

● L'Auberge

Le Village.
Tel. 05 61 96 11 80. Fax 05 61 96 82 96.
www.auberge-audressein.com
Closed Sun. dinner (off season exc. vac.),
Mon. (off season exc. vac.),
10 days end Sept.–beg. Oct., Jan.
7 rooms: 45–65€.
Prix fixe: 16€ (exc. Bank holidays), 33€,
66€, 85€, 12€ (child). A la carte: 55€.

In the heart of the land of eighteen valleys, this former 19th-century forge boasts well-kept, old-fashioned rooms and especially a first-rate restaurant. Yves Atelin concocts regional dishes full of imagination, with proof in the form of young garden shoots and vegetables, scallops with truffle sauce, veal sweetbreads with lemon verbena and a chocolate and sour cherry gratin.

AUDRIEU

14250 Calvados. Paris 240 – Caen 25 – Balleroy 22 – Bayeux 13.
Bessin Normandy with its gray, windswept houses flirts with the Cotentin region nearby.

 HOTELS-RESTAURANTS

● **Château d'Audrieu**
Tel. 02 31 80 21 52. Fax 02 31 80 24 73.
www.chateaudaudrieu.com
Closed 10 Dec.–beg. Feb.
Rest. closed weekday lunch, Mon.
25 rooms: 130–420€. 4 suites: 335–455€.
Prix fixe: 38€ (Sat., Sun., lunch),
52€ (dinner), 95€ (dinner), 15€ (child).
A la carte: 100€.

Gérard and Violaine Livry-Level have turned this sumptuous 18th-century abode with its woodwork, fireplaces and period furniture, surrounded by vast English-style grounds, into a modern hotel. It boasts a swimming pool, rooms equipped like private museums and Cyril Haberland's enchanting cuisine. Precise cooking, studied seasoning and quality produce go to make the delightful foamy white bean soup with vinegar caviar and Carrouges cheese, the crab with raspberry and truffle vinegar, the grilled Atlantic sea bass with seasonal mushrooms, the lamb slow-cooked with Espelette peppers. We end with the hot coffee with Nikka White whiskey and Michel Cluizel's chestnut confit. This dream Relais & Châteaux establishment makes for a delicious weekend break.

AUENHEIM see SOUFFLENHEIM
AULNOY-LEZ-VALENCIENNES see VALENCIENNES

AULON

65240 Hautes-Pyrénées. Paris 829 – Lannemezan 39 – Saint-Lary-Soulan 12.
At a height of 1,200 meters in the heart of the Pyrénées, a delightful village with its slate roofs.

●   RESTAURANTS

● **Auberge des Aryelets**
Place de la Mairie.
Tel.-Fax 05 62 39 95 59.
www.aubergedesaryelets.fr
Closed Sun. dinner (exc. vac.), Mon. (exc. vac.), Tue. (exc. vac.), 2 weeks beg. Oct., mid-Nov.–mid-Dec., 10 days beg. June.
Prix fixe: 20,50€, 24€, 26,50€, 34,50€, 12€ (child). A la carte: 55€.

In Bénédicte and Philippe Raffié's old Pyrenean barn, ham and ricotta croustillant, turbot roasted with morel tapenade, roasted black pig tenderloin with a mango sauce and a blueberry crème brûlée are astonishing.

AUMONT-AUBRAC

48130 Lozère. Paris 556 – Aurillac 118 – Mende 40 – Espalion 57 – Marvejols 24.
The heart of the Lozère, the haughty solitude of its plateaus in winter, the beauty of the Causse and the Aveyron gorges.

 HOTELS-RESTAURANTS

● **Grand Hôtel Prouhèze**
2, rte du Languedoc.
Tel. 04 66 42 80 07. Fax 04 66 42 87 78.
prouheze@prouheze.com / www.prouheze.com
Closed beg. Nov.–end Nov. Rest. closed Tue. (exc. July–Aug.), Wed. lunch (exc. July–Aug.). Compostelle bistro open daily.
25 rooms: 50–110€.
Prix fixe: 36€, 62€ (At the Compostelle bistro: 19,50€, 27€). A la carte: 60€.

Our friend Prouhèze must be relieved: Pierre Roudgé has succeeded him brilliantly at the helm and stove of this fine

Lozère establishment. The large, quiet rooms are still a success and, most importantly, the chef and owner's cuisine delights his guests. Monkfish salad with cold tomato sauce, Fario trout with cured ham and steamed potatoes, pork cheek daube served with an aligot (a local fresh cheese and potato specialty) and the almond praline and hazelnut mille-feuille provide an eloquent tour of the locality. In the Compostelle bistro, the same produce provides the basis for more traditional preparations at a lower price.

AURAY

56400 Morbihan. Paris 478 – Vannes 19 – Lorient 41 – Quimper 100.
officetourismemeauray@wanadoo.fr.
The Loch promenade, the Saint-Goustan quarter and the glorious Pardon in season: this is the true heart of Brittany.

 HOTELS-RESTAURANTS

■ **Hôtel du Loch**
La Sterne
La Forêt.
Tel. 02 97 56 48 33. Fax 02 97 56 63 55.
www.hotel-du-loch.com
Closed mid-Dec.–beg. Jan. Rest. closed Sat. lunch, Sun. dinner (off season).
30 rooms: 55–73€.
Prix fixe: 15–44€, 11€ (child).

This modern establishment with its trim rooms plays its cards close to its chest. The welcome is warm, the garden pleasant and the cuisine showcases local produce. The scallop salad with apples and Guillevic cider, the John Dory with artichokes and the veal scallop with onion slices are well crafted. The chocolate "sausage" is amusing and the service pleasant.

● **La Closerie de Kerdrain** ◎V.COM
20, rue L.-Billet.
Tel. 02 97 56 61 27. Fax 02 97 24 15 79.
Closed Mon., 2 weeks at beg. Dec.,
2 weeks at beg. Mar.
Prix fixe: 25€, 35€, 48€, 75€.

Right in the town center, Fernand Corfmat's manor is a delicious embassy for its region. The finest produce its growers, farmers and fishermen have to offer provides inspiration for its cuisine. On the table, this means oysters and green apples served in a fish broth, oven-crisped lobster with summer vegetables and a rack of lamb seasoned with oregano, served with eggplant and zucchini rolls. The enchanting desserts include a poached peach served on shaved ice flavored with Anjou wine and our glasses lead us on a tour of France's vineyards. In short, a first-rate restaurant where we get off lightly when the check arrives.

AURIBEAU-SUR-SIAGNE

06810 Alpes-Maritimes. Paris 905 –
Cannes 14 – Grasse 9 – Nice 43 –
Draguignan 63.
Here in the Grasse hinterland, we are already entering the fragrant highlands of Provence, far from the clamor of the coast.

 HOTELS-RESTAURANTS

■ **Auberge de la Vignette Haute**
370, rte du Village.
Tel. 04 93 42 20 01. Fax 04 93 42 31 16.
info@vignettehaute.com
www.vignettehaute.com
Rest. closed Mon., Tue. lunch, Wed. lunch.
18 rooms: 180–330€. 1 suite: 330€.
Prix fixe: 45€, 85€, 115€, 30€ (child).
A la carte: 90€.

Less than a quarter of an hour from the Croisette in Cannes, this inn-museum, whose rooms are decorated with rare medieval objects and furniture, offers a refreshing change with its perfectly manicured gardens and Roman swimming pool. On the food side, Sébastien Giannini prepares cauliflower risotto with creamy olive oil mousse, lobster in its shell with slow-cooked potatoes and grilled rib eye steak that raise the tone.

AURIGNAC

31420 Haute-Garonne. Paris 750 –
Bagnères-de-Luchon 69 – Saint-Gaudens 23
– Saint-Girons 41 – Toulouse 80.
A Pyrenean aerie overlooking the Comminges
region, with its castle and Bishops' palace.

 HOTELS-RESTAURANTS

■ Le Cerf Blanc

Rue Saint-Michel.
Tel. 05 61 98 95 76. Fax 05 61 98 76 80.
Closed Sun. dinner (exc. July–Aug.),
Mon. (exc. July–Aug.).
8 rooms: 36–50€.
Prix fixe: 14€ (weekday lunch), 24€, 34€,
49€, 10€ (child). A la carte: 60€.

In this ancient stronghold of the Counts of Comminges, Dominique Picard fights like a lion. In his neo-rustic restaurant in salmon tones, the chef serves a keenly paced cuisine of regional inspiration. In the dining room, this means cep mousse with scallops and wine sauce, a turbot filet with slow-cooked rhubarb, a wild rabbit saddle with dark chocolate sauce and the delectable dessert cart where fifteen or so sweets jostle for position. All this is sufficient to fuel some delicious dreams when we return to our rooms, which are in different styles, some of them accommodations under the gables.

AURILLAC

15000 Cantal. Paris 560 – Brive 98 –
Clermont-Ferrand 161 – Laguiole 78.
aurillac.tourisme@wanadoo.fr.
The capital of the Cantal district is genial and food loving. Remarkable artisans, pleasant restaurants and a natural thoughtfulness are its fortes. Do not miss the volcano museum in the Château Saint-Etienne.

 HOTELS-RESTAURANTS

■ Grand Hôtel de Bordeaux

4, av de la République.
Tel. 04 71 48 01 84. Fax 04 71 48 49 93.
www.hotel-de-bordeaux.fr
Closed 1 week Christmas–New Year's.
33 rooms: 60–92€. 4 suites: 98–135€.

Everything in this town center hotel is designed with functionality in mind. It is competently run and the rooms are fully equipped.

■ Grand Hôtel Saint-Pierre

16, cours Monthyon.
Tel. 04 71 48 00 24 / 04 71 48 37 60 (rest.).
Fax 04 71 64 81 83.
stpierre@ac-hotel.com / www.ac-hotel.com
33 rooms: 50–95€. 2 suites: 110€.
Prix fixe: 16,50€, 23€, 35€.

This hotel combines modern comfort and tradition. The lobby is worth inspection for its registered woodwork. The spacious rooms are fitted out in period style. The "regionalistic" cuisine is not bad (Salers beef carpaccio with shavings of Cantal cheese, frozen parfait with pain d'épice).

● Les Quatre Saisons

10, rue Champeil.
Tel. 04 71 64 85 38.
www.lesquatressaisons.fr
Closed Sun. dinner, Mon., 1 week Aug.
Prix fixe: 20€, 27,50€, 36,50€.

Pierre Bordel's seasonal cuisine, which he reinterprets to match his mood, still wields its charm. Based on market produce, the lamb sweetbreads in a pastry crust, the pike-perch served on a bed of vegetables, the veal medallion with porcini cream sauce and the raspberry gratin are washed down with cheerful Côtes d'Auvergne. The service is delightful and the check honest.

● La Reine Margot

19, rue Guy-de-Veyre.
Tel. 04 71 48 26 46. Fax 04 71 48 92 39.
Closed Sat. lunch, Sun., Mon. dinner,
2 weeks Nov., 1 week at end Jan.,
2 weeks July.
Prix fixe: 20€, 22,60€, 36,80€.
A la carte: 35€.

Alexandre Cayron runs one of the busiest restaurants in town. Rudolf Delaby prepares its solid regional dishes. Foie gras terrine, the Mediterranean sea bass soup, tripous (a local veal variety meat specialty) and ceps in a crêpe pouch, as well as a warm apple tart, enchant without effort and are priced with probity.

● **Les Relais d'Alsace** `COM`
2, pl Sénard.
Tel. 04 71 43 06 00. Fax 04 71 43 06 03.
Prix fixe: 16,50€, 17,50€, 25€.
A la carte: 30–45€.

In this cozy tavern, new host Philippe Morillon presents a fairly muted version of Alsace. Soft-boiled egg with crumbled foie gras, monkfish with chanterelles, pork tenderloin prepared in the style of Alsace and the pineapple in puff pastry with passion fruit sauce provide a circumspect change of air. Riesling and Pinot Noir are very much the thing here.

● **Le Bouchon Fromager** `SIM`
et le Terroir du Cantal
3, rue du Buis.
Tel. 04 71 48 07 80 / 04 71 64 31 26.
Closed Sun. lunch, Mon., 1 week at end Aug.
Prix fixe: 20€. A la carte: 25€.

Jean-Pierre Morin, cheese expert, has brought in the Vaur brothers—Daniel in the dining room, Michel at the stove—to run this dual establishment. Stuffed cabbage, tripous, salmon filet prepared Auvergne style, breaded slice of Cantal cheese and the beef steak with blue cheese sauce and truffade (a local specialty of potato and young Tomme cheese) favorably impress. The crème brûlée with Velay verbena provides a sweet conclusion to a solid spread.

In Vézac (15130). 10 km s via rte de Rodez (D920, D990).

■ **Hostellerie du** ✿ 🏠
Château de Salles
Tel. 04 71 62 41 41. Fax 04 71 62 44 14.
chateaudesalles@wanadoo.fr / www.salles.com
Closed end Oct.–Easter.
20 rooms: 92–102€. 10 suites: 185–201€.
Prix fixe: 23€, 42€.

Now run by Jean-Marc Banquet, this château opposite the Cantal mountains holds an immediate charm. Heated swimming pool, steam bath, Jacuzzi, fitness center and well-equipped rooms offer comfort and relaxation. In the restaurant, the new chef and boss promotes a polished domestic cuisine, including marbled foie gras terrine, the house trout dish, lamb shanks served in the style of Provence and the soft-centered chocolate cake for dessert.

AUXERRE

89000 Yonne. Paris 165 – Sens 60 – Troyes 81 – Dijon 152 – Bourges 144.
tourisme@auxerre.com.
The location on the Yonne river, the old houses lining the lanes in the town center, the cathedral of Saint-Etienne and the old Saint-Germain abbey: there is more than just the Abbé-Deschamps soccer stadium to see here.

 | HOTELS-RESTAURANTS

■ **Le Parc des Maréchaux** 🏠
6, av Foch.
Tel. 03 86 51 43 77. Fax 03 86 51 31 72.
www.hotel-parcmarechaux.com
25 rooms: 75–95€. 6 suites: 95–115€.

In this Second Empire residence, the rooms are still equipped with period furniture and named after Marshals of France. Elegance and comfort are very much the thing and Pascal and Marie-Jeanne Leclerc provide a warm welcome. The swimming pool, fitness center and grounds with their century-old trees are conducive to relaxation.

■ **Le Maxime** 🏠
2, quai de la Marine.
Tel. 03 86 52 14 19. Fax 03 86 52 21 70.
contact@lemaxime.com / www.lemaxime.com
26 rooms: 65–125€. 1 suite: 120–125€.

On the bank of the Yonne in the heart of town, the Leclercs' second establishment provides cozy rooms with all modern conveniences, Internet included.

● **Jean-Luc Barnabet** ⊙LUX
14, quai de la République.
Tel. 03 86 51 68 88. Fax 03 86 52 96 85.
www.jlbarnabet.com
Closed Sun. dinner, Mon., Tue. lunch,
20 Dec.–beg. Feb.
Prix fixe: 32€, 35€, 46€, 50€ (wine inc.),
57€, 73€ (wine inc.), 17,50€ (child).
A la carte: 85€.

In their restaurant by the Yonne river, Marie and Jean-Luc Barnabet welcome their guests warmly before showing them through to the flowered courtyard or dining room in contemporary style. In the kitchen, the master of the house prepares topical dishes that change with the season. Pan-tossed langoustines and asparagus, Atlantic sea bass and saffron-seasoned mussels served in a seafood broth and the lamb medallion with almonds and sundried tomatoes take no liberties with the fine produce. The yogurt and lime ice creams provide a refreshing break. There are set menus on a Burgundy truffle theme in winter.

● **Le Jardin Gourmand** V.COM
56, bd Vauban.
Tel. 03 86 51 53 52. Fax 03 86 52 33 82.
www.lejardingourmand.com
Closed Tue., Wed., 2 weeks Mar.,
2 weeks June.
Prix fixe: 40€ (lunch), 50€, 60€, 85€, 18€
(child). A la carte: 95–105€.

Pierre Boussereau likes to acquire his produce at source, i.e. from the garden he lovingly tends. Its fresh, colorful notes structure the menu, forming a rich palette of petits farcis (stuffed vegetables in the local style), such as the zucchini with tapenade, tomatoes with anchovies and fennel, peppers with mussels, a fried zucchini flower with veal and eggplant. Among the 250 vintages on the list, Olivier Laplaine knows just which one will complement the roasted turbot with seafood risotto and the herb-seasoned grilled Morvan leg of lamb seasoned with Chartreuse and white garlic. The apricot and berry dessert and the minted apricot tart with Tahiti vanilla ice cream will make you melt. The cozy

side of this place, once a well-to-do family house, makes it the perfect setting for a romantic dinner.

● **Le Bistro du Palais** SIM
65, rue de Paris.
Tel. 03 86 51 47 02.
Closed Sun., Mon., 2 weeks Christmas–New Year's, mid-July–beg. Sept.
A la carte: 30€.

Joseph Carino, who treats everyone like an old friend, has made the "bistro spirit" his philosophy. Stéphane Drochon cunningly concocts pan-simmered pork ears, head cheese, minced meat and potato casserole or a blanquette before a solid chocolate cake. Excellent Burgundy vintages at modest prices.

● **La Salamandre** SIM
84, rue de Paris.
Tel. 03 86 52 87 87. Fax 03 86 52 05 85.
la-salamandre@wanadoo.fr
Closed Sat. lunch, Sun., Wed. dinner.
Prix fixe: 35€, 49€, 59€, 13€ (child).
A la carte: 55€.

Seafood is Serge Colas' guiding principle. Jumbo shrimp salad, fresh scallops in season, wild tubot in a potato crust and a roasted Williams pear with almond cream make a light spread. With the marine flavors, Chablis wines find themselves in the front line.

In 89290 Vincelottes. N6 and D38: 16 km.
● **Auberge les Tilleuls** COM
12, quai de l'Yonne.
Tel. 03 86 42 22 13. Fax 03 86 42 23 51.
www.auberge-les-tilleuls.com
Closed Tue., Wed., mid-Dec.–end Feb.
5 rooms: 53–75€.
Prix fixe: 25€, 36€, 45€.
A la carte: 50–65€.

Alain Renaudin has turned his inn on the Yonne river into a convivial hostelry. We enjoy feasting on the terrace in summer and, when the weather grows cold, in his dining room with its exposed stone and antique beams. Wild boar terrine with trumpet mushrooms, pan-seared tuna and a thick-cut veal cutlet seasoned with Aberlour Scotch whiskey make an excellent impression. The baba au rhum is a fine dessert and the wine list an incitement to tour the vineyards of Northern Burgundy. Five charming rooms for overnight guests.

AVALLON

89200 Yonne. Paris 213 – Auxerre 53 – Beaune 107 – Vézelay 16 – Chaumont 134. avallon.otsi@wanadoo.fr.
This traditional milestone on the turnpike was once a classic staging post on the Paris-Côte d'Azur road. There remain the walls, the old town and the Morvan region close by.

 HOTELS-RESTAURANTS

■ Le Relais Fleuri
6 km ne, N6, rte de Saulieu. La Cerce.
Tel. 03 86 34 02 85. Fax 03 86 34 09 98.
relais-fleuri@wanadoo.fr
www.relais-fleuri.com
48 rooms: 76–101€.
Prix fixe: 19,50€, 60€. A la carte: 50€.

Easy to reach from the A6 turnpike, this hotel complex covering 10 hectares boasts tennis courts, a swimming pool and ground-level rooms. Apart from the pleasures of a peaceful stay, we enjoy the gourmet lunches overseen by Richard Doit. Aparagus and foie gras terrine, roasted pike-perch, veal kidneys with whole-grain mustard, mushroom fricassée and the chocolate tartlette with pistacho ice cream topped with strawberry sauce are fine examples of the fare here, washed down by local wines.

■ Hostellerie de la Poste
13, pl Vauban.
Tel. 03 86 34 16 16. Fax 03 86 34 19 19.
www.hostelleriedelaposte.com
Closed Jan.–end Feb. Rest. closed Sun., Mon.
13 rooms: 86–124€. 17 suites: 146–197€.
Prix fixe: 40€. A la carte: 50–60€.

Sandrine Macchia is running this old coaching inn loaded with history. The rooms still have their vintage style. François-Xavier Gross' cuisine is not yet quite sure what it wants to be. The foie gras and mushroom ficassee, pan-tossed escargots with peppers, sirloin steak with Epoisses cheese sauce and the veal kidney with whole grain mustard are not bad. In conclusion, the nougatine crème brûlée with toasted brioche is a divine surprise.

In Pontaubert (89200). 6 km via D427.

■ Moulin des Ruats
Vallée du Cousin.
Tel. 03 86 34 97 00. Fax 03 86 31 65 47.
contact@moulin-des-ruats.com
www.moulin-des-ruats.com
Closed 11 Nov.–mid-Feb. Rest. closed Mon.
24 rooms: 73–150€. 1 suite: 150€.
Prix fixe: 25€, 33€, 46€, 12€ (child).
A la carte: 57€.

In the heart of the Cousin valley, this 18th-century flour mill has been skillfully transformed into a guesthouse. Its rooms have an old-fashioned charm and the library bar and hushed lounge show character. On the food side, we enjoy Jean-Pierre Rossi's fine offerings: Burgundy-style escargots in parsley, shallot and garlic butter, trout meunière with almonds, veal cutlet with morel and white mushroom cream sauce and a seasonal fruit financier.

In Pontaubert.

■ Moulin des Templiers
Vallée du Cousin.
Tel. 03 86 34 10 80. Fax 03 86 34 03 05.
www.hotel-moulin-des-templiers.com
Closed Jan.
15 rooms: 42–60€. 1 suite: 60–65€.

This attractive mill is a haven of tranquility. Guests laze on the riverside terrace or settle down to read by the fire in the lounge. The rooms are tastefully decorated and the breakfasts delightful.

In Valloux (89200): 6 km nw via N6.

● Auberge des Chenêts
10, rte Nationale 6
Tel. 03 86 34 23 34.
Closed Sun. dinner, Mon., Tue. dinner (Oct.–Mar.), 1 week at end Sept., mid-Nov.–beg. Dec., 1 week June.
Prix fixe: 23€ (lunch, weekdays), 25€, 45€.

This fine rustic inn with its fireplace cultivates a traditional family welcome, Burgundian produce (escargots, parsleyed local ham terrine, coq au vin and pears with blackcurrants) and a love of fine Yonne wines.

AVIGNON

84000 Vaucluse. Paris 685 –
Aix-en-Provence 84 – Arles 36 –
Nîmes 47 – Marseille 100.
information@ot-avignon.fr.
Visit Avignon off season, when the place du Palais des Papes is left to enjoy its solitude, space and theatrical beauty, and the Bénézet bridge yawns alone and unemployed over the Rhône. In early spring and fall, the days are delicious and the lanes havens of coolness. We can stroll around the museums, such as the little-known Angladon-Dubrujeaud foundation or the Hôtel Calvet, at our leisure. The rue Joseph-Vernet's elegant store windows stand unobstructed. Provençal gastronomy reigns congenially here and there and charm rules from one hotel to the next. From Luberon to Alpilles, Avignon is ripe for discovery.

■   HOTELS

■ La Mirande
Pl de l'Amirande.
Tel. 04 90 85 93 93. Fax 04 90 86 26 85.
mirande@la-mirande.fr / www.la-mirande.fr
19 rooms: 295–475€. 1 suite: 720€.

This former cardinal's palace converted into a charming luxury hotel provides a choice setting for visitors in search of peace and quiet. We enjoy the delights of the patio, then make our way to the 19th-century kitchen with its *table d'hôte* each Tuesday and Wednesday, a great opportunity to taste the region's produce before retiring to our room, furnished in perfect taste. Fine decorative items, elegant fabrics and delicious bathrooms. (Also see Restaurants).

■ Hôtel d'Europe
12, pl Crillon.
Tel. 04 90 14 76 76. Fax 04 90 14 76 71.

reservations@heurope.com / www.heurope.com
41 rooms: 163–467€. 3 suites: 697–792€.

This 16th-century town house still has all the charm of a bygone age. Fine rooms and elegant suites furnished in period style. Delightful views of the city from the upper floors. (See Restaurants: La Vieille Fontaine.)

■ Hôtel Cloître Saint-Louis
20, rue du Portail-Boquier.
Tel. 04 90 27 55 55. Fax 04 90 82 24 01.
www.cloitre-saint-louis.com
Rest. closed Sat. (off season), Sun. dinner (off season).
76 rooms: 100–250€. 4 suites: 200€.
Prix fixe: 28€.

This 17th-century cloister turned into a contemporary hotel by Jean Nouvel provides lively rooms, a wooded garden and a welcome swimming pool. The cuisine plays to an unconstrained Provençal score: the brandade and artichoke gratin, quick-seared tuna with spelt wheat risotto, sautéed toro with red wine sauce.

■ Mercure Cité des Papes
1, rue Jean-Vilar.
Tel. 04 90 80 93 00. Fax 04 90 80 93 01.
h1952@accor-hotels.com / www.mercure.com
Closed end Sept.–beg. Apr.
89 rooms: 93–130€. 1 suite: 150€.
Prix fixe: 9€, 15€, 7€ (child).

An architectural blot, but an excellent location in the heart of the city. The welcome and service are professional and the rooms functional.

■ Mercure Pont d'Avignon
Rue Ferruce, quartier de la Balance.
Tel. 04 90 80 93 93. Fax 04 90 80 93 94.
h549@accor-hotels.com / www.mercure.com
87 rooms: 93–130€. 1 suite: 200€.

The papal palace and the famous Pont d'Avignon are just a step away, but visitors take their cars anyway. The rooms are primarily functional.

■ Hôtel de Blauvac

11, rue Bancasse.
Tel. 04 90 86 34 11. Fax 04 90 86 27 41.
blauvac@aol.com / www.hotel-blauvac.com
16 rooms: 55–80€.

In the shelter of the city walls, this 17th-century abode in the heart of Avignon provides contemporary comfort. Polished breakfasts.

■ L'Anastasy

Ile de la Barthelasse, chemin des Poiriers.
Tel. 04 90 85 55 94.
lanastasy@wanadoo.fr
www.olga-manguin.com
Closed Christmas–New Year's.
5 rooms: 69–89€.

When Olga Manguin's establishment on the Ile de la Barthelasse was severely damaged by flooding, there was a silver lining: everything was refurbished as new. The ultramodern rooms are fully equipped and the swimming pool, terrace and garden are perfectly suited to relaxation. Reasonably priced and the welcome is so friendly that guests soon feel at home.

■ Hôtel de Garlande

20, rue Galante.
Tel. 04 90 80 08 85. Fax 04 90 27 16 58.
www.hoteldegarlande.com
Closed Sun. (off season), mid-Jan.–mid-Feb.
10 rooms: 70–118€.

Rather than go to a hotel, we decide to go and stay at a bed and breakfast. We feel totally at home in Michèle's town house in the pedestrian area. An address only to be shared with friends.

In Montfavet (84140). 7 km e.

■ Hôtellerie Les Frênes

645, av des Vertes-Rives.
Tel. 04 90 31 17 93. Fax 04 90 23 95 03.
frenes@wanadoo.fr / www.lesfrenes.com
Closed beg. Nov.–end Mar.
12 rooms: 160–550€. 6 suites: 385–750€.
Prix fixe: 30€, 50€, 70€.
A la carte: 75€.

The Biancones run this 1800 residence refurbished with a family Relais & Châteaux chic. Some of the elegant rooms are furnished in period style, others have been revamped in contemporary fashion. We enjoy the lush grounds, the coolness of the pool and the benefits of the Jacuzzi. Antoine, who has worked with Hiély, Troisgros, Le Cirque in New York and Pinchiorri in Florence, meticulously prepares the tomato, basil and garlic aspic with asparagus, swordfish medallions, the sirloin steak with roasted coco bean sauce and fresh soft goat cheese with berries for dessert. The wines recommended by Eliane always beautifully complement the food.

In Le Pontet (84130). 4 km via rte de Carpentras.

● Auberge de Cassagne

450, allée de Cassagne.
Tel. 04 90 31 04 18. Fax 04 90 32 25 09.
resa@aubergedecassagne.com
www.aubergedecassagne.com
Closed Jan.
36 rooms: 110–350€. 4 suites: 386–550€.
Prix fixe: 34€, 55€, 71€, 92€.

This 19th-century residence with its grounds and swimming pool boasts Provençal rooms, as well as a steam bath, fitness center and Jacuzzi. In the kitchen, Philippe Boucher (who trained with Bocuse and Blanc) puts together finely sculpted dishes. Marinated duck foie gras with spicy poached figs, soft-cooked monkfish with crunchy vegetables and the braised pork cheeks and summer savory served with sweet peas and new onions are pretty tricks indeed. The wine is recommended by the knowledgeable André Trestour, the service is dynamic and the menus are well chosen.

In Le Pontet.

■ Les Agassins

52, av Charles-de-Gaulle.
Tel. 04 90 32 42 91. Fax 04 90 32 08 29.
avignon@agassins.com / www.agassins.com
Closed Jan.–end Feb. Rest. closed Sat. lunch.
26 rooms: 90–400€.
Prix fixe: 32€, 58€. A la carte: 70€.

Jean-François Mariani's Provençal cottage boasts a flower garden, swimming pool, peaceful rooms and, in the kitchen, the imaginative Jean-Rémy Joli. Fresh goat cheese with eggplant spread and pesto, monkfish with sundried tomatoes and stuffed zucchini flowers and the sautéed veal medallion with a lemon- and vanilla-infused sauce have plenty of character. An appealing local wine list.

● | RESTAURANTS

● La Mirande ○LUX

4, pl de l'Amirande.
Tel. 04 90 85 93 93. Fax 04 90 86 26 85.
mirande@la-mirande.fr / www.la-mirande.fr
Closed Tue., Wed.
Prix fixe: 33€ (lunch), 105€.
A la carte: 120€.

This former cardinal's palace is undoubtedly the most beautiful of France's urban hotels, with its refined fabrics, patio, garden and wonderfully attentive staff. In the noble dining room, Ludovic Duprat, who was Darroze's maître d' in Langon, breathes new life into the establishment. At the stove, the young Sébastien Aminot, formerly with Ducasse at the Plaza in Paris, plays to a tasteful, modern Provençal score. Eggs served with shellfish and asparagus, quick-seared rouget with fennel and preserved lemons and the oven-crisped veal sweetbreads with sweet peas are high fashion indeed. The cherries flambéed at the table and served with lemon and fromage blanc sorbet offer a fine demonstration of the waiter's art and the wines chosen by the shrewd David Ripetti include a wealth of excellent finds.

● La Vieille Fontaine ○LUX

At Hôtel de l'Europe, 12, pl Crillon.
Tel. 04 90 14 76 76. Fax 04 90 14 76 71.
reservations@heurope.com / www.heurope.com
Closed Sun., Mon., 1 week at end Nov.–beg.
Dec., 2 weeks Jan., 20 Aug.–beg. Sept.
Prix fixe: 34€ (lunch), 48€, 65€, 82€.

The restaurant in this luxury city hotel is the best in Avignon and the most discreet of its kind. Bruno d'Angelis, who previously served with Chabran in the Drôme before coming here to work for himself, plays to an agile, fresh, astute score, employing local produce without overpowering it. We enjoy his individual terrine of blonde poultry livers served with Guémené chitterling sausage and oyster mushrooms in a hazelnut oil vinaigrette and his cod filet cooked in olive oil with young vegetables and a bouillabaisse-style sauce. The roasted duck breast and spelt wheat risotto with a sweet-and-sour cherry sauce accompanied by a chanterelle cappuccino with Argan oil is a masterpiece. The desserts (soft-cooked pineapple, fruit sorbet, pineapple brunoise with star anise and the frozen green apple parfait with lemon jelly and Manzana apple liqueur over shaved ice with a slice of caramelized apple) are full of spirit. The mansion décor is luxurious, but a little short on warmth. The wine list is resourceful and the service well trained.

● Christian Etienne ○V.COM

10, rue de Mons.
Tel. 04 90 86 16 50. Fax 04 90 86 67 09.
contact@christian-etienne.fr
www.christian-etienne.fr
Closed Sun., Mon.
Prix fixe: 55€, 60€, 75€, 105€.
A la carte: 90€.

This restaurant ensconced in an old bailiff's house is a runaway success and deservedly so. Christian Etienne is forever introducing new ideas while preserving the traditions and flavors of his Mediterranean produce. In season, tomatoes and truffles form the basis of some very festive set menus, and pulled slow-roasted pork, pan-tossed rouget served on a bed of brandade and the lamb baked in a garlic crust are pure, potted Provence. With their chocolate and apricot themes, the desserts are delightful. Add the great Southern French wines selected by Kelly McAuliffe and any remaining doubts will melt away.

● Les 5 Sens

Pl plaisance, au 28, rue Joseph-Vernet.
Tel. 04 90 85 26 51.

Closed Sun. (exc. festival), Mon. (exc. festival), 1 week Nov. 1 vac., 1 week Christmas vac., Feb. vac.
Prix fixe: 35€.

Holder of the Meilleur Ouvrier de France award, caterer and delicatessen expert Thierry Baucher has taken over the former Café Ventilo in this small yard near the place de l'Horloge. The contemporary setting, with its parquet flooring, tables and chairs in precious woods and small terrace, is a haven of cool. The melon frappe with cucumber gazpacho, the grilled cod with green lentil stew and the oven-crisped rouget with Vitelotte potatoes are delightful. The wine list focuses on local libations and the desserts (rum-flambéed biscuit, Gascon apple pastis) are splendid.

● **Brunel** 🔒COM
46, rue de la Balance.
Tel. 04 90 85 24 83. Fax 04 90 86 26 67.
restaurantbrunel@wanadoo.fr
Closed Sun., Mon., 2 weeks Aug.
Prix fixe: 30€. A la carte: 35–40€.

In this handsome, elegant setting a stone's throw from the Papal palace, Robert Brunel is never short of ideas. The proof is in the slow-cooked eggplant with tomatoes and parmesan, grilled salmon with pan-tossed spinach, beef with sautéed potatoes and the apricot tart, all precise, intelligent dishes that attract a clientele of connoisseurs (although without inflating the check). François Marcoux provides courteous service and the well-constructed wine list is based around a selection of vintages from the greater South of France.

● **Hiély-Lucullus** 🍴COM
5, rue de la République.
Tel. 04 90 86 17 07. Fax 04 90 86 32 38.
contact@hiely.net / www.hiely.net
Prix fixe: 28€, 35€, 45€, 15€ (child).

The chefs may change, but this fine establishment (which reminds us more of a 1900 brasserie than the venerable dwelling it once was) modestly continues on its way. Hervé Mina now presides at the stove, diligently producing flavorsome, light, creative dishes. We have no complaints about the truffle and white mushroom in chilled egg custard sauce, cut into cubes, the salmon trout poached in sweet wine, nor the oven-crisped veal sweetbreads seasoned with licorice root and served with a creamy polenta. The caramelized apples with creamy chestnut in a shell of flambéed chocolate are not bad at all.

● **La Compagnie des Comptoirs** COM
83, rue Joseph-Vernet.
Tel. 04 90 85 99 04. Fax 04 90 85 89 24.
www.lacompagniedescomptoirs.com
Closed Sun., Mon.
Prix fixe: 26€ (lunch). A la carte: 55€.

Replacing the Cloître des Arts, the Pourcels' Avignon branch is an attractive proposition indeed, with its contemporary café look, terrace/patio, colorful dining room and suggestions of the day. The cold zucchini soup with mozzarella, the tuna steak with sesame vinaigrette and the pork tenderloin with mustard sauce, before the pastry with pears and maple caramel, make an excellent impression.

● **La Fourchette** COM
17, rue Racine.
Tel. 04 90 85 20 93. Fax 04 90 85 57 60.
restaurant.la.fourchette@wanadoo.fr
Closed Sat., Sun., 3 weeks Aug.
Prix fixe: 24,50€, 26,50€, 30€.
A la carte: 40–45€.

Philippe Hiély, nephew of the great Pierre, serves up domestic dishes of obvious sincerity. We welcome the poultry liver parfait, the sardine marinated with coriander seed, the beef daube and the baba au rhum. Unassuming regional wines and amiable checks.

● **Le Jardin de la Tour** COM
9, rue de la Tour.
Tel. 04 90 85 66 50. Fax 04 90 27 90 72.
jeanmarc.larrue@free.fr / www.jardindelatour.fr
Closed Sun., Mon., 2 weeks Aug.
Prix fixe: 18€, 25€, 29€, 35€,
16€ (child). A la carte: 65–80€.

It is best to visit Jean-Marc Larrue's eatery at lunchtime and stick to the set menus. That is the only way to keep the check down to a manageable level. The zucchini flan with rouget and saffron-seasoned vegetables, the lobster ragout seasoned with nectarines, the simmered veal medallions and the soft-centered chocolate dessert are not bad at all, but excessively priced à la carte. Amusing set menus are entirely devoted to the apple in the winter and the peach in summer.

● **L'Isle Sonnante**   SIM

7, rue Racine.
Tel.-Fax 04 90 82 56 01.
Closed Sun. (exc. July–Aug.), Mon. (exc. July–Aug.), Nov. 1 vac., Feb. vac.
Prix fixe: 24€, 27€, 36€.

Boris Chevtchenko has brought a gourmet oomph to this charming bistro. The pretty wall lamps and elegant tables are easy on the eye, and the well-crafted dishes totally fail to disappoint. A cep ravioli gratin with pan-seared foie gras, marinated squid with saffron-seasoned potatoes, roasted dorade with coriander, rabbit medallions with Nyons olives, served under the fiat of a shrewd set menu, are very well done. Then there is the praline chocolate macaron and a selection of unpretentious wines.

● **Le Crillon**   SIM

15, pl Crillon.
Tel.-Fax 04 90 27 17 01.
Closed Sun., Tue. dinner (exc. July–Aug.), 2 weeks Nov., 2 weeks Feb.
Prix fixe: 28€. A la carte: 40–45€.

Jean-Pierre Ladreyet has turned this former blue collar café into a select eatery. We savor with renewed pleasure the pork trotter and chicken medallions served with chanterelles. Chef Michel Peyaud puts the finishing touches on a crayfish ravioli cassolette, a rouget and jumbo shrimp parrillada, quail pie, veal sweetbreads in Port sauce with capers, a frozen spéculos cookie and sour cherry mille-feuille, all new, subtle takes on classic dishes. The renovated dining room is very spruce with its garnet

shades and contemporary style and there is a terrace on the Grand'Place.

● **Entrée des Artistes**   SIM

1, pl des Carmes.
Tel. 04 90 82 46 90. Fax 04 90 14 03 40.
Closed Sat. lunch, Sun., 1 week Christmas–New Year's, 2 weeks end Aug.–beg. Sept.
Prix fixe: 25€.

Ladies and gentlemen, step right up, the show is about to begin! Dominique Parment is a true artist in the kitchen. His most successful tricks include a sausage Tatin, a pan-tossed rouget with grape juice, oxtail and cheek stew and a black cherry tartelette. Tickets are moderately priced and the crowd calls out for more.

● **Le Grand Café**   SIM

Cour Maria-Casarès.
Tel.-Fax 04 90 86 86 77.
Closed Sun., Mon., 1 week beg. Sept., 3 weeks Jan.
Prix fixe: 20€ (lunch), 30€ (dinner).
A la carte: 40€.

Behind the Papal palace, this café is impressive indeed with its imposing dimensions and many mirrors. The people of Avignon like to meet here for supper after a movie or to enjoy simple but flavorsome dishes. A Nyons olive tart, oven-roasted Mediterranean sea bass, sirloin steak with a house vegetable purée and baba au rhum all slip down effortlessly.

● **Le Moutardier**   SIM

15, pl du Palais-des-Papes.
Tel. 04 90 85 34 76. Fax 04 90 86 42 18.
moutardier@numericable.fr
www.moutardier.com
Closed 2 weeks Jan.
Prix fixe: 27€, 30€, 39€. A la carte: 55–60€.

Opposite the Papal palace, Emmanuel Perrin works his charm, preparing dishes with a very Mediterranean accent. The terrace and fresco décor are popular, and the crispy swordfish bits in a sweet pepper marinade, pan-seared tuna with asparagus, roasted duck breast with celery root and the crème brûlée in five flavors (licorice, vanilla, lavender, Carambar candy and pistachio) make an excellent impression. The wine list is cleverly compiled, with a distinct preference for Côtes du Rhône.

● Numéro 75 `SIM`

75, rue Guillaume-Puy.
Tel. 04 90 27 16 00. Fax 04 90 27 10 69.
numero75.brunel@wanadoo.fr
Closed Sun. (exc. July–Aug.),
Christmas–New Year's.
Prix fixe: 10€ (lunch), 16€ (lunch), 26€ (lunch), 30€ (dinner). A la carte: 35–40€.

Robert Brunel, who already owns a local establishment that trades in his name, has turned this former stately home into a stylish restaurant. Guests dine on mushroom and cod ravioli served with a Provençal gratin. Lunch is a lighter business, with composed salads, meats grilled at the table, daily specials. Duck foie gras terrine with mango, nettle pasta with calamari, the young guinea hen simmered in a cocotte with mushrooms and a berry crumble served with raspberry sorbet are all gratifying.

● Le Petit Bedon `SIM`

70, rue Joseph Vernet.
Tel. 04 90 82 33 98. Fax 04 90 85 58 64.
Closed Sun., Mon. lunch, 2 weeks Feb.,
2 weeks beg. June, 2 weeks Aug.
Prix fixe: 27€, 34€. A la carte: 45–50€.

Francine Bouley provides a warm welcome in this delightful "little tummy". Chef Laurent Wellcam, a newcomer to the kitchen here, prepares, with an eye firmly on Provence, an individual pressed-vegetable terrine, roasted Mediterranean sea bass with fennel seed, rack of lamb with crunchy vegetables and a tian of caramelized oranges served with apricot marmalade, while sommelier Christophe Siret matches food and wine. Sensible set menus.

● Le Vernet `SIM`

58, rue Joseph-Vernet.
Tel. 04 90 86 64 53. Fax 04 90 85 98 14.
clareton@levernet.fr
Closed beg. Nov.–end Feb.
Prix fixe: 19€, 25€.

This 18th-century residence opposite the Vernet museum has its charm. Olivier Dupuis' market-inspired cuisine is deft enough. Foie gras, grilled tuna steak, house lamb dish and the profiteroles are not bad. The welcome is convivial and the summer service in the garden a bonus.

AVORIAZ

74110 Haute-Savoie. Paris 620 – Thonon-les-Bains 41 – Morzine 15 – Genève 84.
info@avoriazski.com.

A mountain resort or a UFO? Avoriaz is first and foremost a car-free village, whose futuristic dwellings form an Alpine mini-Manhattan at night. It was founded in 1962 by the people of Morzine, who wanted to develop this "worthless" mountain top (its name in Savoyard). Since the fantasy movie festival ended, life has gone on in Avoriaz, which is still a skiers' paradise and now (and this is new) a fine gourmet haunt.

■ ◇ HOTELS-RESTAURANTS

■ Les Dromonts

Quartier des Dromonts.
Tel. 04 50 74 08 11. Fax 04 50 74 02 79.
www.christophe-leroy.com
Closed beg. May–mid-Dec.
29 rooms: 230–530€. 6 suites: 478–700€.

Avoriaz's emblematic fir cone lies behind the design of this late-sixties hotel. Its solid timber architecture underscores the warm, informal impression sought by Christophe Leroy. The lounges, therapy center, fireside areas, restaurants in purple and orange tones, cozy rooms in slate shades with an antique patina and ski slopes just by the hotel all help to make the Dromonts a quintessential Alpine hostelry.

■ Hôtel de la Falaise

Tel. 04 50 74 26 00. Fax 04 50 74 26 20.
www.pierreetvacances.fr
Closed end Apr.–mid-Dec.
30 suites: 107–157€.

This luxury establishment in the heart of the Falaise quarter provides well-designed suites for three or four people and direct access to the slopes, as well as good times at the Chapka restaurant, bar and fireside lounge in the Résidence les Balcons du Soleil.

● A la Table du Marché Christophe Leroy ○COM

At Les Dromonts.
Tel. 04 50 74 08 11. Fax 04 50 74 02 79.
info@christophe-leroy.com
www.christophe-leroy.com
Closed end Apr.–mid-Dec.
Prix fixe: 18€ (lunch)–64€. A la carte: 95€.

Like Alain Ducasse, his master and model, Christophe Leroy is running more and more restaurants. Also established in Saint-Tropez, Ramatuelle and Marrakech, this conquering, forty-something Norman serves subtle, deft mountain produce in Avoriaz. A born classicist, he adds a mischievously light touch to tradition, playing bistro or gourmet cards with the same energy. We enjoy his ingenious variations on the Beaufort soufflé, trout meunière with almonds with a side of broccoli purée, the (splendid) oven-crisped sage-seasoned bacon, undoubtedly his masterwork, not to mention the squab roasted woodcock style, the crayfish risotto and the salmon trout meunière, all of which offer proof of his genuine skills. The classical desserts (ah, his pain perdu!) win general acclaim. Leroy is a charmer, make no mistake about it.

● La Réserve COM

Résidence de l'Epicéa.
Tel.-Fax 04 50 74 02 01.
www.la reserve.com
Closed end Apr.–beg. Dec.
Prix fixe: 22€ (lunch), 27€ (dinner), 32€ (dinner). A la carte: 58–68€.

This is indubitably one of the resort's great addresses. Set among the pistes, skier Annie Famose's establishment warms our hearts. Aimé Stoesser welcomes guests with a ready smile, confident in the talent of David Didelot, who reliably concocts precise, lightened versions of regional dishes. Creamed lentils with pan-fried

country bacon and pan-seared foie gras, the lake whitefish with wild mushrooms and butter sauce, a real potée savoyarde (a local root vegetable and pork stew) and the dessert buffet raise our spirits, especially with the help of fine vintages from Alsace and the Savoie. The setting is friendly, the atmosphere relaxed and the service assiduous.

● Le Bistro SIM

Pl Centrale.
Tel. 04 50 74 14 08. Fax 04 50 74 06 57.
Closed Sept.–mid-Dec., May, June.
Prix fixe: 25€, 34€, 11€ (child).
A la carte: 45€.

Part of the Famose empire, this very central brasserie offers more than just Savoy specialties, although its morel mushroom fondue is as delectable as it is original. We delight in the pan-seared foie gras with blueberries, the thyme-seasoned rack of lamb, the lake whiting filet and the chocolate moelleux with mint cream. An informal ambiance and reasonable prices.

● Au Briska SIM

Pl Centrale,
Immeuble les Fontaines blanches.
Tel. 04 50 74 09 40. Fax 04 50 74 39 94.
info@aubriska-avoriaz.com
Closed Sept.–end Oct., May–end June.
Prix fixe: 25€. A la carte: 30–40€.

A pleasant terrace when the sun shines and a satisfyingly warm "wood" interior on days when the mercury drops. The salads are meals in themselves and the grillade (meats grilled at the table) first-rate. As we ponder the merits of raclette, tartiflette (a local potato and Réblochon cheese specialty) or Réblochonnade (Réblochon grilled at the table with potatoes), let us not forget that the truite Morvinoise is also a well-devised local trout dish. The Genepi liqueur–flavored crème brûlée is not bad either. Alert service and moderate prices.

● La Cabane SIM

Immeuble Ruches.
Tel. 04 50 74 20 60.

Closed lunch, Sept.–beg. Dec. Apr.–beg. July.
Prix fixe: 26€, 39€, 11€ (child).
A la carte: 45–50€.

This restaurant celebrates more than just the region. In a wood cabin entirely renovated in shades of red, we eagerly savor the smart, half-Savoyard half-Southern cuisine. The roasted ham and mozzarella, the lake whiting with vanilla-seasoned beurre blanc and a pan-roasted spice-glazed duck breast prepared by Emmanuelle Neu slip down smoothly. The ginger-flavored frozen nougat brings us to attention.

● **Le Crépy**   SIM
Promenade des Ardoisières.
Tel. 04 50 74 12 80.
Closed Sept.–mid-Dec., end Apr.–end June.
A la carte: 25–35€.

At mealtimes, visitors flock here to savor cooked meats from the mountains, pierrades (meats cooked on a hot stone at the table) and fondues. Yet it is the house soup, the salmon trout and the pork tenderloin with mustard sauce that attract our attention, along with a crème brûlée trio. A warm welcome, lively service and a restrained check.

● **Les Fontaines Blanches**   SIM
Pl Centrale.
Tel. 04 50 74 12 73. Fax 04 50 74 14 97.
Closed Sept.–mid-Dec., May, June.
Prix fixe: 23€, 11,50€ (child).
A la carte: 45–55€.

This restaurant serves true French cuisine at reasonable prices. A snail cassolette with oyster mushrooms, salmon filet with langoustine sauce and John Limosino's signature langoustine mille-feuille are not bad at all.

● **Les Intrets**   SIM
Immeuble Les Intrets.
Tel. 04 50 74 15 45. Fax 04 50 74 06 57.
Closed Sept.–Nov., May–June.
Prix fixe: 24€, 34€, 9,90€ (child).
A la carte: 40€.

In this mountain brasserie, the cuisine reflects the colors of the sun: the onion gratin, tuna Rossini, rack of lamb with hazelnuts and the three crème brûlées are very honest.

● **Chez Lenvers**   SIM
"Le Chalet d'Avoriaz"
Tel. 04 50 74 01 30.
Closed Sept.–Nov., May–June.
A la carte: 40–45€.

The Lenverses' welcome is cordial and the mountain décor pleasant. The restaurant is Savoyard and offers all those things we love on vacation here: country-style charcuterie, a copious pierrade and the house melted cheese dish. The blueberry and apple tarts are splendid.

In Montriond-les-Bains (74110). 6 km w.
● **La Chalande**   COM
Ardent.
Tel. 04 50 79 19 69. Fax 04 50 79 23 37.
lachalande@aol.com
Closed Mon., lunch (exc. weekends),
lunch in winter, Nov.–mid-Dec., May.
Prix fixe: 28€, 39€. A la carte: 45–50€.

Head over to Montriond lake and visit Karine and Gilles Lanvers' chalet. The woods are charming and the dishes change to reflect the market's offerings. Gifted with great imagination, Gilles brings out the best in his produce. Potted salmon on a bed of lentils, pikeperch with a Mondeuse wine reduction, venison noisettes with pepper sauce and the pain d'épice breaded lamb with its flavorful pan drippings. The chocolate fondant is a delicacy. A fine Savoy wine list.

In Montriond-les-Bains.
● **La Crémaillère**   SIM
Les Lindarets.
Tel. 04 50 74 11 68. Fax 04 50 75 91 19.
Closed dinner (exc. summer),
mid-Oct.–mid-Dec., end Apr.–beg. June.
Prix fixe: 17€, 35€. A la carte: 45–55€.

At lunchtime between two sessions on the slopes or in the evening after a few hours' hiking, we are not disappointed when we sit down in the restaurant of the Braizes' Chalet des Lindarets to enjoy shepherd's salad, locally-fished trout, sirloin steak with morels and a nice blueberry tart. Washed down with a Savoy wine or Swiss vintage, the pleasant spreads here are reasonably priced.

AVRANCHES

50300 Manche. Paris 335 – Caen 103 – Rennes 83 – Saint-Malo 60.
avranchestourisme@wanadoo.fr.
From Avranches, we can see the abbey of Mont-Saint-Michel, whose manuscripts—priceless parchments illuminated between the 13th and 15th centuries—are displayed each year in the excellent Fonds Ancien library in the town hall. Visitors should also take a look at the houses that show the influence of the large British community in the 19th century. In the cemetery is the step where Henry II, King of England and Duke of Normandy, knelt to do penitence for the murder of Thomas Becket in Canterbury Cathedral.

 HOTELS-RESTAURANTS

■ La Croix d'Or

83, rue de la Constitution.
Tel. 02 33 58 04 88. Fax 02 33 58 06 95.
www.hoteldelacroixdor.fr
Closed Jan., Sun. dinner (exc. rest. in season).
27 rooms: 55–95€.
Prix fixe: 17€, 25€. A la carte: 55–60€.

This Norman-style former post house with its bright rooms promotes a modish cuisine. A salmon and catfish tartare with artichoke hearts, turbot in a potato crust with creamy mushroom sauce and an oven-baked Atlantic sea bass filet with Indian spices are subtle pastimes. A pleasant welcome and service.

■ La Ramade

2, rte de la Côte.
Tel. 02 33 58 27 40. Fax 02 33 58 29 30.
hotel@laramade.fr / www.laramade.fr
Closed 10 days end Nov., Jan.
27 rooms: 68–115€.

Véronique Morvan greets her guests warmly. She has named her rooms for different flowers and the décor reflects this rustic spirit.

In Champeaux (50530). 10 km w via D911.

● Le Marquis de Tombelaine SIM

25, Rte des Falaises.
Tel. 02 33 61 85 94. Fax 02 33 61 21 52.
claude.giard@wanadoo.fr
Closed Tue. dinner (exc. July–Aug.), Wed. (exc. July–Aug.), 1 week Nov., Jan.
Prix fixe: 21,90€, 32,90€, 54,60€.
A la carte: 67–92€.

In his eatery on the mainland cliff opposite the Mont Saint-Michel, Claude Giard serves a langoustine omelet, Atlantic sea bass in puff pastry, catfish filet and rack of salt marsh lamb. The house frozen nougat served on a plate napped with blueberry sauce brings back childhood memories.

AVRILLE see ANGERS

AX-LES-THERMES

09110 Ariège. Paris 801 – Carcassonne 105 – Foix 45 – Prades 96.
A spa and ski resort at an altitude of 720 meters (with skiing up to 2,400 meters) in the pure mountain air. For winter sports fans, the Saquet resort is eight kilometers away.

 HOTELS-RESTAURANTS

■ Auberge l'Orry Le Saquet

RN 20, route d'Espagne.
Tel. 05 61 64 31 30. Fax 05 61 64 00 31.
www.auberge-lorry.com
Closed Tue. (off season), Wed. (off season), Nov. 1 vac., Easter vac.
11 rooms: 60€. 4 suites: 100–110€.
Prix fixe: 23€, 28€, 35€, 45€, 14€ (child). A la carte: 45€.

Almost fifteen years ago, Sylvie and Marc Heinrich moved into this snug chalet. Each room has been carefully decorated to reflect the flower it is named for. The same care is apparent in the kitchen, where the Alsatian owner and chef prepares polished, sunny dishes: a crayfish cappuccino with a parmesan lace biscuit, a plaice filet with Banyuls wine sauce with esclivade (a Catalan dish of roasted summer vegetables), a spicy breaded rabbit saddle and a chestnut and rum soufflé.

■ L'Auzeraie

1, av Delcassé.
Tel. 05 61 64 20 70. Fax 05 61 64 38 50.
auzeraie@auzeraie.com / www.auzeraie.com
Closed 3 weeks Nov., 3 weeks Dec.
Rest. closed Tue. (exc. dinner in season).
30 rooms: 40–74€.
Prix fixe: 12€ (weekday lunch), 19€,
24€, 38€, 8€ (child). A la carte: 35–44€.

With its woodwork and antique pink tones, Michelle Marty's modern hotel boasts well-appointed rooms, some with balconies (pleasant when the sun shines) and an entire floor just for families. In the bistro-style restaurant with its old posters and rust colors, Didier Ocipsky concocts traditional dishes on a duck theme: we savor duck foie gras medallions with Hypocras aspic and a fish soup, then enjoy jumbo shrimp prepared in the style of Provence, followed by a duck confit cassoulet or a whole duck breast with ceps, before visiting the casino just across from the terrace.

■ Le Chalet

4, av Turrel.
Tel. 05 61 64 24 31. Fax 05 61 03 55 50.
lechalet@club-internet.fr / www.le-chalet.fr
Closed mid-Nov.–mid-Dec.
Rest. closed Sun. dinner (exc. vac.),
Mon. (exc. vac.).
19 rooms: 46–52€.
Prix fixe: 21€, 34€, 44€, 9€ (child).
A la carte: 40€.

By thermal baths and just a stone's throw from the Donézan plateau ski slopes, this Ariège chalet is enjoying a second youth. Entirely renovated in 2006, it offers appealing, well-equipped rooms in contemporary tones. Frédéric Debèves serves a lively *pension* cuisine. Jumbo shrimp ravioli with parsley, scallops with spinach shoots and citrus seasonings, lamb shoulder with glazed prunes soaked in Banyuls wine and a chocolate macaron accompanied by a chestnut liqueur sorbet have effortless charm.

AYTRE see LA ROCHELLE

BADEFOLS-SUR-DORDOGNE

24150 Dordogne. Bergerac 25 – Lalinde 5.
The banks of the Dordogne and a village in the heart of gentle Périgord.

 HOTELS-RESTAURANTS

■ Côté Rivage
Tel. 05 53 23 65 00.
Closed mid-Oct.–Easter.
7 rooms: 55–90€.
Prix fixe: 25€, 32€.

This inn wages a charm offensive on the banks of the "River of Hope", with its low prices and pleasant set menus of subtle, chic dishes. In the dining room with its bay window, the foie gras terrine, the chicken and salsify pie and the tarte Tatin with vanilla ice cream never stale.

BADEN

56870 Morbihan. Paris 475 – Vannes 15 – Lorient 53 – Quiberon 40 – Auray 10.
A haven by "Ar Bro", Morbihan's little sea, and a gateway to the islands. Here, oyster farmers ply their trade under the soft, clement sky.

 HOTELS-RESTAURANTS

In Toulbroch (56870). 2 km via rte de Vannes.
● Le Gavrinis
1, rue de l'Ile-Gavrinis.
Tel. 02 97 57 00 82. Fax 02 97 57 09 47.
gavrinis@wanadoo.fr
www.gavrinis.com
Closed 1 week at end Nov.–beg. Dec.,
mid-Jan.–mid-Feb.
Rest. closed Sat. lunch, Sun. dinner (exc. summer), Mon. (exc. summer).
18 rooms: 55–115€.
Prix fixe: 18,50€ (weekday lunch),
21,50€, 28€.

Serge Ligniers serves his personal interpretation of local cuisine in his restaurant refurbished in contemporary style. The Guémené chitterling sausage pâté served warm, an Atlantic sea bass with ginger-seasoned spinach and celery root roasted in a clay pot, the pan-tossed veal sweetbreads and mushroom fricassée and the warm chocolate fondant with raspberry sauce are well mannered. We enjoy a peaceful stay in the rooms redecorated in beige and gray.

BAERENTHAL

57230 Moselle. Paris 448 – Strasbourg 64 – Bitche 16 – Niederbronn 11.
This is Bitcherland, with its forests and streams, and the North Vosges park where Moselle and Alsace meet. It owes a great deal of its glory to one famous inn.

 HOTELS-RESTAURANTS

■ Hôtel K
Locale known as Untermulthal.
Tel. 03 87 06 50 85. Fax 03 87 06 57 67.
www.arnsbourg.com
Closed Tue., Wed., 4–19 Sept., Jan.
12 rooms: 195–400€.

This brand new, minimalist timber hostelry is the height of luxury. Chic, refined and unfailingly tasteful, it has rooms like jewel boxes, with views of the surrounding nature (perfect for romantic evenings), huge bathrooms and a spacious lobby furnished with high stools for breakfast and boasting a fine ham slicer and red couch, adding a raw touch to the silken setting. Astonishing!

■ Le Kirchberg
8, impasse de la Forêt.
Tel. 03 87 98 97 70. Fax 03 87 98 97 91.
www.le-kirchberg.com
Closed Jan.
20 rooms: 40–76€.

In the heart of the Moselle regional park, this hotel with its modern architecture is just the place for those in search of a little peace in a hushed environment, with spacious, comfortable rooms and charming studios to rent by the week or just for a weekend.

L'Arnsbourg CO LUX

Locale known as Untermulthal.
Tel. 03 87 06 50 85. Fax 03 87 06 57 67.
l.arnsbourg@wanadoo.fr / www.arnsbourg.com
Closed Tue., Wed., Jan., mid-Sept.–end Sept.
Prix fixe: 52€ (lunch), 95€, 120€.
A la carte: 130€.

There are different ways of looking at the Arnsbourg. You can see it as a UFO in the Pays de Bitche on the edge of Alsace (the Untermuhtlal clearing is just two kilometers from Zinswiller). Or you can look on it as a remarkable restaurant serving both experimental cuisine and local dishes. Or, finally (a third option available since the inauguration of its brand new hotel adjunct), you could view it as a delightful, contemporary lodging house deep in the woods. The Kleins, never satisfied, are constantly trying to improve their upmarket reputation, but without becoming too pretentious. "We are the artisans of French cuisine," the late lamented Alain Chapel of Mionnay remarked with splendid modesty when asked to sum up his philosophy. Jean-Georges Klein could adopt this claim as his own. He and his wife Nicole have just opened the Hôtel K, which is opposite the restaurant but higher up: a minimalist version of the house in the woods. Like the owners, the kitchen sets its sights ever higher, but without neglecting the local cuisine. Its "petits savoureux aperitifs" (flavorsome little appetizers and before-dinner cocktails), the most delicate of hors d'oeuvres, are the ne plus ultra of today's creations. They include the truffles with bacon, a local bread of onion, anchovy and olive served with a Mauresque cocktail (a textured Orgeat syrup bite), a diminutive turnip cake, the "Nipps" (funny little tubes with tomato and lovage, a delicious mixture), the escargots in slow-cooked garlic mousse, a foie gras nougat followed by a sea-flavored fantasy of an oyster: always absolutely extraordinary! In the attractive paneled dining room shrewdly supervised by Cathy Klein, mistress of the house, we look out onto the clearing and forest as we savor the taste of the foie gras grillade with slow-cooked apricot, the grilled sea bream with orange marmalade, the roasted John Dory with tomato and warm basil-seasoned watermelon or the more regional (and magnificent!) frog legs seasoned with cilantro and other herbs and the honey-glazed suckling pork chop. We feel free to pick out these works of art from the menu, since the set menus are devoted to more topical notions. In fact, the hotel is not the only innovation at the Arnsbourg: there are also the "real desserts" brought by a pastry chef from Argentina, come to train here for a few months. Cherry brochettes on a bed of lavender and an apricot and almond tart called the Mirliton, an exemplary baba au rhum and a raspberry shortbread cookie with rose-seasoned mascarpone and pineapple sorbet add a new touch. The wine list is grandiose and the fine oriental-style lounge is perfectly suited to relaxation and the enjoyment of the finest cigars. Finally, let us end with a rare compliment: the prices in this Three Plate establishment in the North Vosges are barely higher than in a single Plate restaurant on the Côte d'Azur.

BAGNOLES-DE-L'ORNE

61140 Orne. Paris 240 – Alençon 49 – Argentan 39 – Domfront 19 – Falaise 49.
bagnolesdelorne.tourisme@wanadoo.fr.
A spa town with its period thermal baths, lake, charming park, delicious air and footpaths near the Andaine forest. The allure of an old-fashioned vacation, like a remake of Modiano's *The Scent of Yvonne*, fuels our dreams of spa society life in days gone by.

 HOTELS-RESTAURANTS

Manoir du Lys ○❀🏠

2 km nw, rte de Juvigny-sous-Andaine.
Tel. 02 33 37 80 69. Fax 02 33 30 05 80.
manoir-du-lys@wanadoo.fr
www.manoir-du-lys.fr
Closed Sun. dinner and Mon. (Nov.–end Mar.), beg. Jan.–mid-Feb.
30 rooms: 65–250€.
Prix fixe: 29€, 46€, 80€. A la carte: 80€.

In the heart of nature, this pleasant establishment with its swimming pool is Quinton territory. As Paul and Virginie watch over their children, Franck in the kitchen and his wife and sister Stéphanie in the dining room have taken over with flying colors. Refurbished in contemporary style, the rooms are sweetly inviting. On the food side, the restaurant refuses to be outdone. A cep and aromatic herb sauté, the olive oil–fried abalone served with cold thin-sliced mutton trotter in salad, little pork trotter mouthfuls and finally a salted butter quince shortbread biscuit are washed down with wines produced by Yvon, Franck's brother-in-law.

■ Bois Joli
Av Philippe-du-Rozier.
Tel. 02 33 37 92 77. Fax 02 33 37 07 56.
boisjoli@wanadoo.fr / www.hotelboisjoli.com
20 rooms: 66–142€.
Prix fixe: 19€, 30€, 41€, 62€.
A la carte: 60€.

With its Anglo-Norman architecture, this manor bearing the "Châteaux et Hôtels de France" seal of approval provides a warm welcome, refined Regency-style rooms and the domestic cuisine of Loïc Malfilâtre, formerly in Les Andelys at the Chaîne d'Or.

■ Les Camélias
Av du Château-de-Couterne.
Tel. 02 33 37 93 11. Fax 02 33 37 48 32.
cameliashotel@wanadoo.fr
www.cameliashotel.com
Closed Sun. dinner, Mon. (off season),
mid-Dec.–beg. Feb.
26 rooms: 50–64€.
Prix fixe: 22€, 28€, 11€ (child).

This early-20th-century Norman establishment has been taken over by Denis Leroutier, whose cuisine has a moderately "regionalistic" flavor. Duck foie gras, rouget filet in puff pastry, veal cutlet in a crust of crushed pistachios and a rose-flavored crème brûlée make a good impression.

69620 Rhône. Paris 488 – Lyon 36 – Villefranche-sur-Saône 15 – Tarare 19.
In this fine country of golden stone, an extremely rich Englishwoman, Helen Hamlyn, has poured a fortune into the keen, historically accurate renovation of the most sumptuous of medieval castles. We rediscover the village.

 HOTELS-RESTAURANTS

● Château de Bagnols
Le Bourg.
Tel. 04 74 71 40 00. Fax 04 74 71 40 49.
info@bagnols.com / www.bagnols.com
Closed beg. Jan.–mid-Mar.
8 rooms: 427,50–580€.
13 suites: 603–2395€.
Prix fixe: 45€ (weekday lunch), 78€, 120€, 30€ (child). A la carte: 90–125€.

A fairytale castle with its moat, high walls, honey-colored stone and magical guest rooms with views of the surrounding vineyards. The large open kitchen and spacious dining room with its huge Gothic fireplace (the largest of any private French property) are unforgettable. Helen Hamlyn, a wealthy Englishwoman with a love of France, has renovated—or should we resurrected?—the place. Inspecting the courtyard paved in traditional style, great wooded garden and period-style furniture, fabrics and comforts, we could imagine ourselves in a museum. The Rocco Forte group now runs the property. An Italian veteran of the Paris Ritz, Franco Mora, is the manager. Under his supervision, the youthful staff hurry about their work, offering a smiling, enthusiastic welcome. But most importantly, the restaurant run by the discreet Matthieu Fontaine is worth the visit on its own. This Norman in his forties—a native of the Eure district who worked at the Amphyclès with Philippe Groult, then with Lacombe at the Léon in Lyon, before taking over at the Château de Divonne—prepares a precise, intelligent cuisine employing modern techniques to the greater glory of fresh, high-quality produce. He draws his inspiration from the Rhône-Alpes region, though not slavishly. We delight in his fabulous oven-crisped potato and pork trotter Tatin with seasonal mushrooms (so crunchy), his soft and mild truffle emulsion, his pan-seared Lake Léman whiting with vegetables, capers and basil oil, not to mention the masterly Bresse hen, carved in the dining room and served for two, the breast, spit-roasted and seasoned with sage, the thighs having been slowly roasted. His potatoes seasoned with truffles: great art, lively and full of flavor. Along with this come the vegetable pistou, a basil- and garlic-seasoned minestrone soup, sole served on the bone accompanied by a Carnaroli risotto. As a bonus, the desserts are refined works of art (the fine chocolate and caramel mille-feuille, lemon soufflé with sauce Suzette and basil lemon sorbet) and we admire the wines from Beaujolais and neighboring Burgundy. The enthusiastic waitstaff carve expertly at side tables in this picture postcard setting. There is even a little lunchtime menu that might almost lead us to imagine that this royal château is an ordinary domestic eatery, were the castle not such a dazzling sight.

BAGNOLS-SUR-CEZE

30200 Gard. Paris 657 –
Nîmes 58 – Avignon 34 – Alès 53 –
Orange 30 – Pont-Saint-Esprit 11.
Just a step away from the fashionable cities of the South and their busy festivals, the peaceful Gard has kept its rural character. Its châteaux and vineyards cohabit harmoniously.

 HOTELS-RESTAURANTS

● **Château de Montcaud**
Rte d'Alès, 5 km w via D6 and D143.
Tel. 04 66 89 60 60. Fax 04 66 89 45 04.
montcaud@relaischateaux.com
www.chateau-de-montcaud.com
Closed Nov. 1–beg. Apr.
21 rooms: 210–320€. 7 suites: 310–460€.
Prix fixe: 25€ (lunch), 45€. A la carte: 90€.

With its attractive flowery grounds, swimming pool, garden, fitness center, sauna and steam bath, this fine Relais & Châteaux establishment in a 19th-century mansion has plenty of arguments in its favor. The Second Empire–style rooms are peaceful indeed and guests are only in a hurry to leave them at mealtimes. In the brightly colored dining room, Marc Buffet prepares a spirited Southern French cuisine. The fresh tomato and caper terrine, Mediterranean sea bass filet with fennel, rosemary-seasoned rack of lamb and the Breton shortbread with roasted apricots pay tribute to the region. In a second eatery, the Bistro de Montcaud, the Southern dishes are more competitively priced.

 ## BAINS-LES-BAINS

88240 Vosges. Paris 366 –
Epinal 27 – Luxeuil 28 – Vittel 42.
A 19th-century spa awakened from its slumbers like Sleeping Beauty.

■ / HOTELS-RESTAURANTS

■ **Hôtel de la Promenade**
8, av Colonel-Chavane.
Tel. 03 29 36 30 06. Fax 03 29 30 44 28.
hotelpromenade.ifrance.com
Closed mid-Nov.–end Nov.
19 rooms: 32–44€.
Prix fixe: 14€, 38€. A la carte: 35€.

Alain Béguin prepares a pleasant cuisine served in the rustic dining room in yellow and rust tones: duck foie gras, trout meunière, veal kidneys and a blueberry or mirabelle plum tart will sharpen the weakest of appetites. The contemporary rooms are pleasant, the welcome is warm and everything is sensibly priced.

BAIX

07210 Ardèche. Paris 592 – Montélimar 23 – Privas 17 – Valence 32.
At the foot of the Ardèche mountains, an admirable, timeless staging post by the Rhône.

■	HOTELS

■ La Cardinale et sa Résidence

Quai du Rhône, quartier Serre-Petoux, in Pouzin (07250).
Tel. 04 75 85 80 40. Fax 04 75 85 82 07.
bonjour@lacardinale.com
Closed Jan.–beg. Mar.
Rest. Mon., Tue. (Sept.–Apr.).
9 suites: 179–339€.

The Cardinale owes its name to Richelieu, who stayed here in 1642. Today, we settle comfortably into its rooms in various styles: classical (in the colors of Provence) or more contemporary. The hotel also boasts a swimming pool and shady grounds.

BALDENHEIM

67600 Bas-Rhin. Paris 440 – Colmar 28 – Strasbourg 52 – Sélestat 9.
Close by the border, this Ried district village built on alluvial Rhineland soil is in Alsace hunting country. The game here—waterfowl, mallard, woodcock and teal—takes flight with a flurry of wings.

●	RESTAURANTS

● La Couronne

45, rue de Sélestat.
Tel. 03 88 85 32 22. Fax 03 88 85 36 27.
la-couronne-baldenheim@wanadoo.fr
Closed Sun. dinner, Mon., Thu. dinner,
2 weeks beg. Jan., 1 week at end July,
1 week beg. Aug.
Prix fixe: 32€, 47€, 59€, 68€.
A la carte: 70€.

In the heart of the village, Angèle Trébis' inn is a magnet for gourmets of every kind who all appreciate her son-in-law Daniel Rubiné's traditional tricks. In the hushed dining room with its fine woodwork and meticulously laid tables, they make short work of the frog legs, monkfish medallions Rossini, the venison medallions with fresh chanterelles and the seasonal fruit vacherin. All these regional dishes of good stamp are washed down with Alsatian wines. The service is very enthusiastic and the check still honest.

BALLEROY

14490 Calvados. Paris 277 – Saint-Lô 23 – Bayeux 15 – Caen 44.
The fine Louis XIII château here was turned into a balloon museum by American magnate Malcolm Forbes, an aficionado of lighter-than-air flight. Nearby, the forest of Cerisy and its abbey are worth a visit.

●	RESTAURANTS

● Manoir de la Drôme ◎ V.COM

129, rue des Forges.
Tel. 02 31 21 60 94. Fax 02 31 21 88 67.
leclerc@wanadoo.fr
www.manoir-de-la-drome.com
Closed Sun. dinner, Mon., Wed.,
Nov. 1 vac., Feb. vac.
Prix fixe: 48€, 68€. A la carte: 80€.

In the heart of an estate crossed by the Drôme river, Christine and Denis Leclerc's 17th-century manor is home to an up-to-date restaurant. Both the smiling welcome and the menu, which presents fine dishes from the region and further afield, have an easy charm. In the contemporary dining room, Fernard Contes' signature langoustines, sole and foie gras fricassée, a soy- and honey-seasoned duckling filet and the cold seasonal fruit cream dessert provide delicious alternatives to traditional Norman cuisine.

BAN SAINT-MARTIN see METZ

BANNEGON

18210 Cher. Paris 288 – Bourges 42 – Sancoins 19 – Moulins 71.
This little corner of the Berry region is delicious, with its lush countryside and fine mill providing the perfect destination for a weekend break.

HOTELS-RESTAURANTS

■ Le Moulin de Chameron ✿ 🏠

3 km via D76 and secondary road.
Tel. 02 48 61 83 80 / 02 48 61 84 48 (rest.).
Fax 02 48 61 84 92.
moulindechameron@wanadoo.fr
Closed end Nov.–mid-Mar.
Rest. closed Mon. dinner, Tue. lunch.
13 rooms: 67–111€.
Prix fixe: 30€, 52€. A la carte: 55–60€.

By the Auron river, this 18th-century mill seems to have leapt straight from a postcard. Jean and Corinne Mérilleau have turned it into a charming hostelry indeed, with appealing, old-fashioned rooms and a spirited regional cuisine. The restaurant, A l'Annexe, serves oxtail presented in a crêpe pouch, a pain d'épice–breaded halibut filet, squab served with potato cakes and a thin caramelized apple tart, all enchanting dishes.

BANYULS-SUR-MER

66650 Pyrénées-Orientales. Paris 898 – Cerbère 10 – Port-Vendres 7 – Perpignan 38.
banyuls@banyuls-sur-mer.com.
This famous wine-producing village with its ancient cellars and great fortified vintages ageing in casks in the open air also has a very seaside charm.

HOTELS-RESTAURANTS

■ Les Elmes et la Littorine 🏠

Plage des Elmes.
Tel. 04 68 88 03 12. Fax 04 68 88 53 03.
www.hotel-des-elmes.com
Closed mid-Nov.–end Dec.
Rest. closed Sun. dinner, Mon. lunch and Tue. lunch (off season).
31 rooms: 46–147€.
Prix fixe: 24€, 28€, 30€, 40€, 56€.

A hotel by the beach, a very lively welcome from Jean Sannac, sensible set menus and Jean-Marie Patrouix's light version of Catalan cuisine, currently focusing closely on sweet and sour, all encourage us to lin-

ger awhile here. We feast on the Catalan-style pork belly, an anchovy and monkfish dish, eggplant crème caramel served with a mackerel filet and aioli-seasoned potatoes plus an oven-roasted white boudin sausage served with peach chutney. The local menu at 24 is a bargain.

● Al Fanal & Hôtel El Llagut Ⓝ 🍴 COM

Av du Fontaulé
Tel. 04 68 88 00 81.
al.fanal@wanadoo.fr
Closed 3 weeks Dec., 3 weeks Feb.
Rest. closed Wed., Thu. (Oct.–Mar.).
13 rooms: 50–65€
Prix fixe: 24€, 29€, 37€.

Down by Banyuls harbor, Laurent Sagols is a staunch guardian of Catalan tradition. Guests are attracted by the warm welcome, modern marine setting and traditional dishes reinterpreted to reflect contemporary tastes. The variations on the anchovy theme, a red sea bream with lentils, the strip loin steak with coarse ground pepper and a slow-cooked beef cheek served in enriched stewing juices have spirit and soul. The tender bras de gitan, a rolled genoise and pastry cream dessert, is a delightful delicacy.

BARBAZAN

31510 Haute-Garonne. Paris 779 – Bagnères-de-Luchon 32 – Lannemezan 27 – Saint-Gaudens 14 – Tarbes 67.
A spa town in the heart of the Comminges region, with its park and natural lake for anglers.

HOTELS-RESTAURANTS

● Hostellerie de l'Aristou Ⓝ COM

Rue de Sauveterre.
Tel. 05 61 88 30 67. Fax 05 61 95 55 66.
Closed Sun. dinner, Mon., end Nov.–end Feb.
6 rooms: 55–60€. 1 suite: 95€.
Prix fixe: 20€, 25€, 31€, 45€, 9€ (child).
A la carte: 50€.

Philippe Géraud good naturedly welcomes visitors to this old farm with its manorial guest rooms. In the antique dining room, he serves reliable domestic dishes, including foie gras poached in Maury wine, a pike-perch with endive and orange infusion, a sirloin steak with pepper and Armagnac sauce and a frozen nougat served with a raspberry coulis.

BARBERAZ see **CHAMBERY**

BARBEZIEUX

16300 Charente. Paris 483 – Bordeaux 85 – Cognac 37 – Angoulême 36.
Made famous by Jacques Boutelleau (pen name Jacques Chardonne), who wrote of his happy life here in the Thirties, this Charente town is still a peaceful stop with its white houses and château visible from the N10 highway.

 HOTELS-RESTAURANTS

■ **La Boule d'Or**
9, bd Gambetta.
Tel. 05 45 78 64 13. Fax 05 45 78 63 83.
laboule.dor@wanadoo.com
Closed end Dec.–beg. Jan. Rest. closed Fri. dinner (Oct.–Apr.), Sun. dinner (Oct.–Apr.).
20 rooms: 47–60€.
Prix fixe: 12€, 24€. A la carte: 45€.

Jean Charrier's hotel provides spacious, practical rooms in varied shades and traditional cuisine served in the handsome, contemporary dining room or on the shady terrace. We savor the truffle oil-seasoned scallop and cep salad, salmon steak served with roasted garlic and bacon chunks, veal medallions also with roasted garlic and a warm chocolate fondant napped with pear coulis. We cast an eye over the cellar, rich in fine bottles at sensible prices.

BARBIZON

77630 Seine-et-Marne. Paris 56 – Fontainebleau 11 – Etampes 40 – Melun 13.
The Auberge du Père Ganne, the memory of great painters, the face of Théodore Rousseau frozen in stone, Fontainebleau forest with its sands and paths, and finally the inn, where a hearty fire blazes.

 HOTELS-RESTAURANTS

● **Hôtellerie du Bas-Bréau**
22, rue Grande.
Tel. 01 60 66 40 05. Fax 01 60 69 22 89.
basbreau@wanadoo.fr / www.bas-breau.com
16 rooms: 150–390€. 4 suites: 420–520€.
Prix fixe: 54€ (weekday lunch),
76€ (dinner). A la carte: 130€.

The great and good regularly stay at Jean-Pierre and Dominique Fava's Relais & Châteaux establishment. The flower-filled grounds, swimming pool, meeting facilities, old-fashioned rooms, suites and private villa suit them wonderfully. The cuisine arouses the same enthusiasm as Sébastien Tasset deftly prepares his ambitious classics. Lobster salad, pan-tossed sole, rack and saddle of lamb and hot Grand Marnier soufflé are accompanied by great vintages from Burgundy. In season, the game, particularly the Scottish grouse, is celebrated to dazzling effect. Elegant summer service on the shady terrace.

BARCUS

64130 Pyrénées-Atlantiques. Paris 815 – Pau 53 – Mauléon-Licharre 15 – Saint-Jean-Pied-de-Port 55.
Visit Soule, the Basque country's wildest, most secret province, with the Osquich pass, Saint-Antoine de Musculdy chapel and Madeleine hill with its superb panoramic view. Marvelous treks start and end in the village.

 HOTELS-RESTAURANTS

● **Chilo**
Tel. 05 59 28 90 79. Fax 05 59 28 93 10.
martine.chilo@wanadoo.fr
www.hotel-chilo.com
Closed 2 weeks Jan., 2 weeks Mar.
Rest. closed Sun. dinner,
Mon. and Tue. lunch (off season).
11 rooms: 45–95€.
Prix fixe: 18€ (weekday lunch), 28€, 38€, 65€. A la carte: 45€.

In his charming establishment with its swimming pool and colorful rooms looking out on Soule country, Pierre Chilo, king of local cuisine, pays tribute to his region. The warm spring vegetable cake, the slice of wild turbot with new onions and meat jus, the thyme-seasoned rack of lamb with ewe's cheese ravioli and variations on the chocolate theme deftly and artistically reinterpret family recipes from the surrounding district.

BARFLEUR

50760 Manche. Paris 352 – Carentan 49 – Valognes 26 – Cherbourg 29.
This small port with its lighthouse and granite houses is a perfect Cotentin postcard.

 HOTELS-RESTAURANTS

■ Le Conquérant

18, rue Saint-Thomas.
Tel. 02 33 54 00 82. Fax 02 33 54 65 25.
Closed mid-Nov.–mid-Mar.
10 rooms: 63–105€.

This pretty 17th-century abode boasts a delightful formal garden and charming rooms refurbished in a regional style.

● Le Moderne   COM

1, pl du Général-de-Gaulle.
Tel. 02 33 23 12 44. Fax 02 33 23 91 58.
www.hotel-restaurant-moderne-barfleur.com
Closed Tue. dinner (exc. mid-July–mid-Sept.), Wed. (exc. mid-July–mid-Sept.),
10 days beg. Jan.
Prix fixe: 19€, 26€, 38€, 10,50€ (child). A la carte: 55€.

Founded in 1898, this "Moderne" is now not very, although Roselyne and Frédéric Cauchemez have plans for its renovation. For the moment, the double dining room has a retro style with plywood ceiling and high wooden chairs. Formerly at the Aubergade in Pontchartrain, Frédéric effortlessly reels off classics and is not averse to lightening them a little. The milky leek and potato soup, the bacon-wrapped cod and the simmered suckling pig chops in cocotte favorably impress. The caramelized apple dessert with Calvados sauce is a sin of omission.

● Le Café de France   Ⓝ SIM

12, quai H.-Chardon.
Tel. 02 33 54 00 38.
Closed dinner (off season), Wed., Jan.
Prix fixe: 14,90€, 19,90€.

Right on the harbor, this authentic fishermen's café run by Olivier Chardon welcomes customers at any time for breakfast or drinks, and at lunchtime, there are set menus at giveaway prices. Marinated mackerel, stuffed mussels, Saint-Vaast oysters, skate with cream sauce, Caen-style simmered tripe and the boneless rib steak with fries are attractive propositions. For dessert, the Norman-style apple and almond tart is a ritual.

BAR-LE-DUC

55000 Meuse. Paris 253 – Châlons-en-Champagne 71 – Nancy 85 – Verdun 57.
The upper town is worth a visit for its fine hotels, Ligier Richier's superb "transi" in the church of Saint-Etienne, skilled artisans and views of the hills. The red currant jam that Hitchcock adored is also a local specialty.

 HOTELS-RESTAURANTS

● La Meuse Gourmande   COM

1, rue François-de-Guise.
Tel. 03 29 79 28 40. Fax 03 29 45 40 71.
Closed Sun. dinner, Wed., Feb. vac.,
10 days end Aug.
Prix fixe: 14,50€ (lunch), 24,50€, 47€.
A la carte: 40€.

This old priory on the town heights has an easy charm. In the modern dining room in warm colors, Franck Damien, who learned his trade in the luxury hotels of Switzerland, delights his guests with quail pastilla with almonds, crab and slow-cooked vegetable-stuffed shell pasta with parmesan, a banana leaf-wrapped turbot filet with vanilla sauce, pan-tossed calf's liver with slow-cooked shallots and a blackcurrant and cream sauce and an almond biscuit with ice cream, which dances to a pleasantly exotic little tune.

● **Le Bistro Saint-Jean**

132, bd de La Rochelle.
Tel. 03 29 45 40 40. Fax 03 29 45 40 45.
Closed Sat. lunch, Sun., Mon. dinner, 1 week at end Jan.–beg. Feb., mid-July–mid-Aug.
A la carte: 50€.

Jean-Christophe Cordel trained with Loiseau and Savoy. He has chosen to practice his art in modest style in this bistro on a busy boulevard next to the his father's *pâtisserie*. The pork and foie gras house special, a shellfish and seafood in minestrone, the roasted cod with creamy shrimp risotto, a poultry and potato parmentier with meat jus and an almond and dark chocolate financier with Arabica sauce have great energy.

In Trémont-sur-Saulx (55000). 9,5 km via D3.

■ **La Source** 🌸🏠

2, rte de Beurey.
Tel. 03 29 75 45 22. Fax 03 29 75 48 55.
hotel-restaurant-lasource@wanadoo.fr
Closed 2 weeks beg. Jan., 3 weeks Aug.
Rest. closed Sun. dinner, Mon. lunch.
26 rooms: 65–105€.
Prix fixe: 28,50€, 38,50€, 12,50€ (child).
A la carte: 60€.

Deep in the country, this eighties hotel is in the upmarket motel vein. Its functional rooms and modern facilities (sauna, balneotherapy) are well conceived, as is Jacky Rondeaux's cuisine. In the dining room refurbished in modern style, the truffle-seasoned foie gras and layered potato casserole, the turbot with chanterelles, a rosemary-seasoned rack of lamb and the hot mirabelle plum soufflé are genuinely good.

50270 Manche. Paris 349 – Cherbourg 39 – Saint-Lô 63 – Carentan 43 – Coutances 48.
tourisme.barneville-carteret@wanadoo.fr.
A Cotentin port at World's End with a beach and tasteful inn: an obscure but hospitable corner of Normandy.

 HOTELS-RESTAURANTS

● **La Marine**

11, rue de Paris-Carteret.
Tel. 02 33 53 83 31. Fax 02 33 53 39 60.
infos@hotelmarine.com
www.hotelmarine.com
Closed mid-Nov.–1 Mar.
Rest. closed Sun. dinner, Mon., Thu. lunch.
21 rooms: 80–160€. 6 suites: 150–160€.
Prix fixe: 31€, 46€, 83€. A la carte: 85€.

Like his neighbor Roellinger in Cancale, Laurent Cesne took up the culinary arts by chance and discovered a passion. Several decades ago, this medical student took charge of the family hostelry by the beach and Carteret marina. He trained in Burgundy, with Lorain in Joigny and Loiseau in Saulieu, before settling in at this hotel, run by the Cesne family since 1876. Mother is still at the desk, elegant and dependable. Waitstaff in black jackets tend to the double dining room with its picture windows looking directly out over the sea. The hotel has been handsomely refurbished and spruced up. In the kitchen, Laurent—who shuns pretension—prepares the finest produce of land and sea with great skill and true dexterity, infusing it with a personal music and motion. Before the banquet, there are the Denneville oysters in a chilled seafood and cornichon-seasoned broth, the cumin-dusted tuna in sesame oil, and a mini-abalone, breaded and fried with garlic and parsley, served with mashed potatoes, all pure delights. Next? The "seafood bites", mixing gray shrimp and whelk aspic, concentrating all that is seafood of the region, a distilled essence of Cotentin sea flavor. Then comes the langoustine bouillon (with the crustaceans cooked to perfection, down to the exact second, keeping them delightfully firm) with sweet peas and crispy bacon: a miracle of flavor and precision. Then the oven-roasted line-fished Atlantic sea bass, with its tender flesh and crispy skin, served with mushroom- and ham-stuffed artichokes simmered in wine, followed by a sliced lobster with new potatoes, roasted garlic, its claw on a bed of fines herbes: luscious child's play! We yield to the temptation of the region's sublime cheese, represented by the butter churn of Camembert, with cider jelly, raisins and pine nuts, rice pudding with Gariguette strawberries, rhubarb and raspberry sorbet glazed in sweet gelatine and finally a fine passion fruit soufflé with an exotic fruit minestrone and coconut sorbet. The well-stocked cellar provides shrewd wines and a collection of Groult Calvados … for in these days of triumphant standardization and stifled local culture, Laurent has not forgotten that he is first and foremost a Norman.

■ Hôtel des Ormes

Promenade Barbey d'Aurevilly.
Tel. 02 33 52 23 50.
www.hoteldesormes.fr
12 rooms: 75–175€.
Prix fixe: 35€, 45€.

Flavia and José de Mello have turned an old family guesthouse into a charming hotel with a very Côté Ouest décor, furniture by Blanc d'Ivoire and Flamand, and snug rooms with a sea or garden view. The cozy dining room offers equally voguish dishes, including sucrine lettuce salad with with shredded cod, a pan-seared rouget on potato cakes and a lamb saddle with pesto. An urbane welcome and service.

BARNEVILLE-LA-BERTRAN see HONFLEUR

BARR

67140 Bas-Rhin. Paris 434 – Colmar 39 – Strasbourg 35.
mairie.barr.ot@wanadoo.fr.
This winegrowing town with its period houses, vineyards, theatrical main square and exhumed canals has many charms.

 HOTELS-RESTAURANTS

■ Château Landsberg ❀🏠

133, vallée de Saint-Ulrich.
Tel. 03 88 08 52 22. Fax 03 88 08 40 50.
www.chateau-landsberg.com
Closed beg. Jan.–end Mar.
Rest. closed Mon.–Thu.
3 rooms: 65–125€. 7 suites: 99–140€.
Prix fixe: 30€. A la carte: 35€.

Fatima Wehrling and Corinne Sekula's old fortified farm offers many pleasures. Along with its light, peaceful rooms, it boasts a Jacuzzi and heated swimming pool. In the restaurant, the duck foie gras terrine, saffron-seasoned salmon, pork cheeks in Pinot Noir sauce and a raspberry shortbread cookie are accompanied by lively local wines.

■ Au Château d'Andlau ❀🏠

113, vallée de Saint-Ulrich.
Tel. 03 88 08 96 78. Fax 03 88 08 00 93.
www.hotelduchateau-andlau.fr
Rest. closed Sun. dinner, Mon., 2 weeks Nov., 2 weeks Jan.
22 rooms: 44–65€.
Prix fixe: 25€, 35€. A la carte: 35–40€.

This hotel standing between river and forest provides a range of rustic rooms and a pleasant restaurant. Honed by Christian Boulard, the Alsatian-style crayfish bavarois, lemon-mint-seasoned skate wing, Indian-style monkfish filet, Middle Eastern-style lamb in a crêpe bundle and the spiced chicory candy are up to scratch. A superb wine list.

■ Le Brochet 🏠

9, pl de l'Hôtel-de-Ville.
Tel. 03 88 08 92 42. Fax 03 88 08 48 15.
hotel@brochet.com / www.brochet.com
Closed New Year's.
23 rooms: 50–69€.
Prix fixe: 15€, 18€, 21€, 7,50€ (child).
A la carte: 30€.

This half-timbered 16th-century residence is now a traditional hotel with friendly rooms in yellow shades with a tasteful regional restaurant. The onion tart, the three-fish choucroute, the honey-glazed duck breast and a frozen kouglof are pleasant.

■ **Le Manoir** ⌂
11, rue Saint-Marc.
Tel. 03 88 08 03 40. Fax 03 88 08 53 71.
info@hotel-manoir.com
www.hotel-manoir.com
Closed Jan.–end Feb.
18 rooms: 59–89€. Half board: 80–131€.

Right in the heart of town, this hotel is a strategic staging post for families exploring Alsace. The traditional rooms are pleasant and the discount prices from the fourth night on are welcome.

● **Le Potin** SIM
11, rue du Général-Vandenberg.
Tel. 03 88 08 88 84.
Closed Mon., Tue.
A la carte: 28–35€.

This "Parisian" bistro in the heart of a winegrowing town—Hervé Duhamel's rural replica of the Café Flore—is very pleasant. At any hour, customers can read the day's papers, enjoy a coffee or beer on tap and snack on a country platter or an onion tart. The pike-perch filet simmered in wine, the pork cuts and charcuterie on a bed of sauerkraut prepared with goose fat and the lemon or chocolate tart frankly deserve an ovation. An interesting choice of wines and a terrace in summer.

● **Winstub du Manoir** ⓃSIM
6, rue Saint-Marc.
Tel. 03 88 08 07 36.
Closed Sat. lunch, Mon., Jan.
Prix fixe: 25€. A la carte: 30€.

Laurent Finck, who worked at the Zimmer-Sengel in Strasbourg, has just taken over this tavern in the town center with its rough plaster and beams, where he presents a varied menu that willingly

wanders away from the beaten path. Local head cheese and aspic terrine, the grilled pike-perch with coriander-seasoned cream, the oven-crisped Munster and marinated herring served with fried potatoes and a warm cherry tart make an excellent impression.

● **S'Barrer Stubel** SIM
4, pl de l'Hôtel de Ville.
Tel. 03 88 08 57 44.
Closed Mon., Jan.
Prix fixe: 18€. A la carte: 25–35€.

In the first floor dining room with its low ceiling and woodwork, or on the less convivial second floor, Jacky Schmitter (who owns the Brochet just opposite) serves foie gras seasoned with Gewurztraminer, pike-perch served in the local-style on a bed of sauerkraut, ham braised in Pinot Noir and house spätzle, followed by a frozen kouglof seasoned with Marc de Gewurtz.

In Gertwiller (67140). 1 km e via N422.

● **Auberge du Maennelstein** SIM
154 A, rte de Strasbourg.
Tel. 03 88 08 09 80. Fax 03 88 08 10 37.
Closed Mon. dinner, Tue. dinner, Wed. dinner,
27 Dec.–8 Jan.
Prix fixe: 13€, 19€, 8€ (child).
A la carte: 35€.

This large, modern, crossroads hostelry is also a *winstub*. Eric and Marie-Claude Schoen's shrewd preparations champion the local cuisine. A quail and Port sauce *verrine*, Munster cheese in puff pastry, a four-fish choucroute, stuffed quail with flavorful meat sauce and variations on the chocolate theme for dessert are up to scratch.

10200 Aube. Paris 228 – Chaumont 41 –
Troyes 53 – Vitry-le-François 66.
ot-bar@barsuraube.net.
The Côte des Bars, southern Champagne vineyards, houses of character and the fine church of Saint-Pierre.

HOTELS-RESTAURANTS

● **La Toque Baralbine**

18, rue Nationale.
Tel.-Fax 03 25 27 20 34.
toquebaralbine@wanadoo.fr
www.latoquebaralbine.fr.st
Closed Sun. dinner (exc. holidays and summer), Mon.
Prix fixe: 20€,25€,36€,55€,10€ (child).
A la carte: 60€.

This rustic, inn in the town center is an ambitious enterprise. Sylvie Phelizot provides a very friendly welcome, while in the kitchen, her husband Daniel, who trained with Jacques Chibois and Christian Constant, prepares noble produce in a topical manner. The fruits of his labor include langoustine and lobster ravioli in a fines herbes–seasoned seafood broth, turbot filet with simmered basil-seasoned mushroom- and ham-stuffed artichokes simmered in wine and a boneless squab napped with wild thyme-seasoned jus. For dessert, the hot prune and Ratafia liqueur soufflé warms our hearts.

In Dolancourt (10200).
9 km nw via rte de Troyes.

■ **Le Moulin du Landion**

Dolancourt.
Tel. 03 25 27 92 17. Fax 03 25 27 94 44.
www.moulindulandion.com
Closed 1 week at end Dec.
16 rooms: 74–84€.
Prix fixe: 22€, 49€. A la carte: 55€.

On a bank of the Landion, this mill offering old-style guest rooms has an easy charm. The Aubertin-Heckmann family welcome visitors with a broad smile, while in the kitchen, Loic Rapart concocts authentic regional dishes, such as hot pan-seared foie gras with citrus sauce, a turbot with champagne sauce, caramelized veal sweetbreads with walnuts and a pineapple charlotte.

LES BAS-RUPTS see **GERARDMER**
BASSE-GOULAINE see **NANTES**

LA BAULE

44500 Loire-Atlantique. Paris 450 – Rennes 124 – Vannes 70 – Nantes 80.
tourisme.la.baule@wanadoo.fr.

La Baule was born in the late 19th-century and launched at the start of the 20th after the other watering places on this coast (Pornichet and Le Pouliguen). A few short decades on, it was vying with Biarritz and Deauville. So has it overtaken them now? It offers the longest beach in Europe—a 12-kilometer stretch of light sand—windsurfing, horse riding, water sports, sailing schools, tennis, golf, concerts and many other leisure activities for visitors. Together, Le Croisic, with its exotic Breton traditionalism, the salt marshes and collegiate church of Guérande, the ornithological park of Ker Anas and the waterways of the Grande Brière form its rich surroundings. Surely all this should be enough to bury La Baule's former "Concrete-on-Sea" image.

■ HOTELS

■ **Hermitage-Barrière**

5, esplanade Lucien-Barrière.
Tel. 02 40 11 46 46. Fax 02 40 11 46 45.
hermitage@lucienbarriere.com
www.hermitage-barriere.com
Closed mid-Nov.–21 Dec., beg. Jan.–end Mar.
201 rooms: 183–534€. 10 suites: 360–1600€.

This twenties luxury hotel by the ocean is an imposing sight. We admire its Anglo-Norman architecture, spacious rooms looking out to sea and luxurious décor by Jacques Garcia, not to mention the many facilities for rest and recreation: the fitness center, steam bath, sauna, seawater swimming pools, children's club, piano bar and garden. There is something for every taste and the best-stocked wallets. Culinary pleasures also abound, with the Ambassadeurs and Eden Beach (see Restaurants).

■ **Royal Thalasso Barrière**

6, av Pierre-Loti.
Tel. 02 40 11 48 48. Fax 02 40 11 48 45.
royalthalasso@lucienbarriere.com

www.lucienbarriere.com
Closed Dec.
85 rooms: 162–382€. 6 suites: 425–650€.

This 1900 residence has a belle époque charm. All in marble and wood, the thalassotherapy center boasts the latest equipment. The rooms are equipped with period furniture and shimmering fabrics, and the surrounding grounds border the sea. When mealtimes come, guests have a choice between traditional and health food at the Rotonde, or beach cuisine at the Ponton (see Restaurants).

■ Castel Marie-Louise
1, av Andrieu.
Tel. 02 40 11 48 38. Fax 02 40 11 48 35.
marielouise@relaischateaux.com
www.relaischateaux.com
Closed Jan., Feb.
29 rooms: 159–487€. 2 suites: 349–548€.

This beachside Relais & Châteaux establishment has adopted an English cottage chic. With its neatly kept garden, cozy ambiance, rooms equipped with Louis XIII furniture, attentive service, dining room (see Restaurants) and pine-shaded terrace, it has everything its guests could wish for.

■ Mercure Majestic
14, esplanade Lucien-Barrière.
Tel. 02 40 60 24 86. Fax 02 40 42 03 13.
h5692-sb@accor-hotels.com
www.mercure.com
Rest. closed 2 weeks Jan.
83 rooms: 85–345€. 7 suites: 190–355€.
Prix fixe: 27€, 50€.

Purchased by the Accor group, this 1930 luxury hotel is perfectly situated between the casino and the beach. Refurbished in art deco style, its rooms are charming indeed. At the Ruban Bleu, Didier Cadiet's cuisine is very honest. The tuna tartare with lime, a thin Saint-Pierre and red onion tart, caramelized veal sweetbreads served with mashed potatoes and the creamy berry Nantais for dessert are bright creations indeed.

■ Bellevue Plage
27, bd de l'Océan.
Tel. 02 40 60 28 55. Fax 02 40 60 10 18.
www.hotel-bellevue-plage.fr
Closed end Dec.–beg. Feb.
35 rooms: 95–170€. 2 suites: 145–175€.

The lounge and terrace look out over the roofs of the town, while pine groves and the Atlantic stretch out on the other side of this hotel boasting modern rooms. The restaurant is also worth a visit (see Restaurants: La Véranda).

■ Le Saint-Christophe
Pl Notre-Dame.
Tel. 02 40 62 40 00. Fax 02 40 62 40 40.
info@st-christophe.com
www.st-christophe.com
40 rooms: 65–165€. 5 suites: 110–180€.
Half board: 82–312€.

These three early-20th-century seaside villas surrounded by garden promise a peaceful stay with their trim, tastefully furnished rooms decorated here and there with antique ornaments. The restaurant has plenty of character with its shady terrace and traditional cuisine.

■ Alcyon
Pl du Marché / 19, av des Pétrels.
Tel. 02 40 60 19 37. Fax 02 40 42 71 33.
info@alcyon-hotel.com
www.alcyon-hotel.com
Closed Nov.–beg. Mar.
32 rooms: 64–122€.

This modern building by the market with its contemporary décor offers comfortable, soundproof rooms. All have a balcony except for those on the top floor.

■ Le Christina
26, bd Hennecart.
Tel. 02 40 60 22 44. Fax 02 40 11 04 31.
www.hotel-le-christina.com
38 rooms: 70–120€. 2 suites: 135–155€.

This centrally located hotel is a practical place to stay, with its moderately priced, comfortable, conventional rooms.

■ La Concorde ⌂

1 bis, av de la Concorde.
Tel. 02 40 60 23 09. Fax 02 40 42 72 14.
www.hotel-la-concorde.com
Closed 1 Oct.–beg. Apr.
47 rooms: 77–125€.

Located just a step away from the beach, this sixties hotel with its bright, comfortable rooms and warm welcome is practical indeed. It has been completely renovated this year.

■ Lutétia ⌂

13, av Olivier-Guichard.
Tel. 02 40 60 25 81. Fax 02 40 42 73 52.
www.lutetia-rossini.com
26 rooms: 45–149€.

Made up of two houses, this hotel is on a busy street. No need to worry, though: the classically styled rooms are perfectly soundproofed. An attractive art deco setting and a pleasant restaurant (see Restaurants: Le Rossini).

■ Hostellerie du Bois ⌂

65, av Lajarrige.
Tel. 02 40 60 24 78. Fax 02 40 42 05 88.
www.hostellerie-du-bois.com
Closed mid-Nov.–mid-Mar.
15 rooms: 60–73€.

Surrounded by a pretty little garden, this twenties establishment offers old-fashioned rooms for vacationers. Comfort and refinement are on the agenda.

■ Hôtel Marini ⌂

22, av G.-Clemenceau.
Tel. 02 40 60 23 29. Fax 02 40 11 16 98.
www.hotel-marini.com
33 rooms: 50–125€.

Located between the train station and sea, this very practical hotel offers neat, soundproofed rooms, a fitness center and a swimming pool. Reasonable prices.

In Pornichet (44380). 6 km e via D92.

■ Le Sud Bretagne ⌂

42, bd de la République.
Tel. 02 40 11 65 00. Fax 02 40 61 73 70.
sud-bretagne@wanadoo.fr
www.hotelsudbretagne.com
26 rooms: 100–180€. 4 suites: 200–280€.

The Bardouil family has been running this hotel for nearly 100 years. Along with the individualized rooms, each decorated (and colored) according to a different theme, it offers a swimming pool, spa, massage facility and seafood cuisine (see Restaurants).

In Saint-André des-Eaux (44117). 10 km ne.

■ Hôtel du Golf International ❀⌂

Rte de Brangoure.
Tel. 02 40 17 57 57. Fax 02 40 17 57 58.
hoteldugolflabaule@lucienbarrière.com
www.lucienbarriere.com
Closed Nov.–end Mar.
148 rooms: 89–663€.
Half board: 106–696€.

A genuine hotel complex built in the heart of the golf course designed by Jack Nicklaus, this succession of suites and villas (all equipped with kitchenettes) offers a memorable stay, with lunch at the pool house and dinner at the Green, where guests enjoy salads, grilled meats and various pastries. We end the evening with a drink at the Fairway.

● RESTAURANTS

● Le Castel Marie-Louise ◎ V.COM

At the Castel Marie-Louise. 1, av Andrieu.
Tel. 02 40 11 48 38. Fax 02 40 11 48 35.
marielouise@relaischateaux.com
www.castel-marie-louise.com
Closed lunch, beg. Jan.–beg. Feb.
Prix fixe: 24€ (lunch), 52€, 60€.

For more than twenty-five years now, Eric Mignard has been officiating at the stove of this 1900 pocket castle, part of the Relais & Châteaux association. In the dining room, this native of Lyon who trained at Mère Brazier's establishment serves an honest, gourmand cuisine. Local produce plays a starring role in the "coucou de Rennes" (a locally bred chicken) in pork bouillon aspic, lobster and langoustines served with ratte potatoes and dates and a pork shoulder with spicy jus and roasted fruit. For dessert, the vanilla-seasoned apple mille-feuille are a return to childhood. (See Hotels).

● La Terrasse   N V.COM

At the Hermitage, 5, esplanade Lucien-Barrière.
Tel. 02 40 11 46 46. Fax 02 40 11 46 45.
hermitage@lucienbarriere.com
www.hermitage-barriere.com
Closed outside vac.
Prix fixe: 25€, 13€ (child). A la carte: 56€.

The Hermitage's refined restaurant has changed in name, but not style. New chef Robert Becerril concocts traditional dishes based on quality produce. In the elegant dining room in blue and beige or on the terrace, crispy buckwheat crêpes with crabmeat and mild spices, monkfish and white beans with Catalan spices, a veal escalope à la Milanaise, pine nut tagliatelle and the pralines in puff pastry with chocolate sauce make an excellent impression. A buffet only at lunchtime and à la carte dishes in the evening.

● La Rotonde   V.COM

At the Royal Thalasso, 6, av Pierre-Loti.
Tel. 02 40 11 48 48. Fax 02 40 11 48 45.
www.lucienbarriere.com
Closed 1 Dec.–15 Dec.
Prix fixe: 41€, 18,50€ (child).
A la carte: 55€.

Gilles Demaure, a specialist in light cuisine, works wonders in the thirties lounges of this luxury hotel dedicated to thalassotherapy. The chicken oyster salad with shrimp and crunchy vegetables, red tuna tartare with lime juice and the haddock with herring caviar and sweet pea and onion mousseline favorably impress, as do the veal kidneys simmered in Bugundy wine and served with herb-seasoned tagliatelli. The Reine-Claude plum tourte with heavy cream and mirabelle plum-flavored eau-de-vie is a treat.

● La Véranda   V.COM

At the Bellevue Plage, 27, bd de l'Océan.
Tel. 02 40 60 57 77. Fax 02 40 24 00 22.
www.restaurant-laveranda.com
Closed Mon. lunch, Wed., Dec.–end Jan.
Prix fixe: 20€ (lunch), 49€, 65€, 80€, 15€ (child). A la carte: 70€.

The dining room is as contemporary as it is bright and Olivier Androuin's cuisine is lively and spirited. Proof takes the form of a pan-seared foie gras with chocolate flavors served with dried fruit chutney and a vanilla oil-marinated line-fished Atlantic sea bass served with langoustines. Roasted John Dory served under a layer of Bellota chorizo and beans and the thick-cut free-range pork chop served with chanterelles are excellent, bucolic and refined distractions. We would sell our souls for the warm pistachio madeleine with lavender honey ice cream. Isabelle Androuin's welcome is delightful.

● La Maison Blanche   N COM

20 bis, av Pavie.
Tel. 02 40 23 00 00. Fax 02 40 23 03 60.
lamaisonblanche@wanadoo.fr
Closed Sun. dinner, Mon., 1 Jan.–beg. Feb.
Prix fixe: 18€, 24€, 38€. A la carte: 55€.

Exit the Steak and Lobster. This New England-style cabin has changed course, keeping its piano bar, terrace and black and white dining room, but serving a more down-to-earth cuisine. Smoked duck breast with shavings of parmesan and minced cabbage, a skate wing with seaweed cream sauce, rack of lamb braised in a rosemary crust and the desserts (strawberries in soup and in pain perdu) are quite well done.

● Eden Beach   COM

At the Hermitage, 5, esplanade Lucien-Barrière.
Tel. 02 40 11 46 16 / 02 40 11 46 46.
Fax 02 40 11 46 45.
www.lucienbarriere.com
Prix fixe: 32€. A la carte: 65€.

The hotel Hermitage's brasserie has a new chef, but the style remains the same. Robert Becerril concocts limpid dishes with their fair share of energy. We admire the sea view as we savor lobster salad, the house foie gras plate, Atlantic sea bass baked in a sel de Guérande crust, rack of lamb with baby vegetables and a raspberry croustillant.

● Nossy-Be `COM`

Bd Darlu.
Tel. 02 40 60 42 25. Fax 02 40 60 68 91.
contact@nossybe.com / www.nossybe.com
Closed Mon. (off season),
Tue. (off season), Jan.
Prix fixe: 26€. A la carte: 50–55€.

A voguish old address? Try this contemporary beach restaurant in mauve, where we enjoy refined, subtle dishes to the sound of the waves. Sylvain Hevochon concocts a promising tuna sashimi, roasted John Dory, pan-tossed veal sweetbreads served with a Cajun sauce, rack of lamb roasted in pecan crust and a salted-butter caramel macaron.

● Le Ponton `COM`

At the Royal Thalasso, 6, av Pierre-Loti.
Tel. 02 40 60 52 05. Fax 02 40 11 48 45.
Closed dinner (Nov.–Mar. exc. Sat.),
2 weeks beg. Dec.
Prix fixe: 23€ (wine inc.) 10€ (child).
A la carte: 46€.

On the Royal's beach, Sylvain Verron's cuisine sates the appetites of passersby with its Southern leanings. Crab rillettes with niçoise-style vegetables, fish couscous seasoned with cumin, grilled rib eye steak and a seasonal fruit crumble have the excellent tang of simple skills and do very little damage to our pockets.

● Le Rossini `COM`

At the Lutétia, 13, av des Evens.
Tel. 02 40 60 25 81. Fax 02 40 42 73 52.
contact@lutetia-rossini.com
www.lutetia-rossini
Closed Sun. dinner, Mon. (off season), Tue. lunch, Jan.
Prix fixe: 23€, 46€. A la carte: 45–50€.

Still at the stove, Grégoire Quincay prepares spirited, tasty dishes in this pleasant hotel restaurant. We enjoy the avocado and crab with tomato dressed with a wal-

nut oil vinaigrette, the roasted Atlantic sea bass with julienned fennel and a lime butter sauce, the legendary beef filet Rossini and the soft-centered chocolate moelleux with apricot and tarragon sorbets.

● Le Portofino `SIM`

14, av de Pavie.
Tel. 02 40 60 09 21. Fax 02 40 60 28 99.
jjchgennari@wanadoo.fr
Closed Sun. (off season),
Mon. (off season), Jan.
Prix fixe: 9,50€, 13,50€. A la carte: 40€.

Christine Gennari celebrates Italy *a mezza voce* in this red and yellow trattoria. The vegetable and charcuterie antipasti, scampi fritti, veal escalope Milanaise and tiramisu slip down smooth as velvet.

● La Villa `SIM`

18, av du Général-de-Gaulle.
Tel. 02 40 23 06 00. Fax 02 40 00 89 78.
lavillabrasserie@wanadoo.fr
Closed Christmas.
Prix fixe: 13,60€ (lunch), 21,90€.
A la carte: 40€.

We come here for the bright, contemporary setting, appealingly set tables, amiable prices, pleasant welcome, cheerful service and topical cuisine. Tuna tartare with dill, garlic-seasoned shrimp cassolette, a thyme-seasoned rack of lamb and the baba au rhum are extremely well done.

In Pornichet (44380). 6 km e via D92.

● Le Sud Bretagne `COM`

At Le Sud Bretagne, 42, bd de la République.
Tel. 02 40 11 65 00. Fax 02 40 61 73 70.
www.hotelsudbretagne.com
Closed Fri. dinner, Sun., 2 weeks Oct.,
2 weeks Mar.
Prix fixe: 40€, 50€, 15€ (child).

Marc-Antoine Bardouil tends to his guests' every need, while Gilles Laurent carries on the tradition of good food. In the baroque dining room in shades of orange or on the cool patio, we feast on green bean salad with strips of duck breast with honey, minced monkfish with ginger and arugula, rib eye steak with pepper and a caramel croquant.

In Pornichet.

● Le Sunset SIM

138, bd Océanides, plage de Pornichet.
Tel. 02 40 61 29 29. Fax 02 40 61 23 21.
isabellejonneau@libertysurf.fr
www.lesunset.com
Closed Sun. lunch, Mon., Tue. dinner.
Prix fixe: 25€, 17€ (child). A la carte: 70€.

This beach restaurant serves an honest fusion cuisine by the waves. Flambéed jumbo shrimp with fine champagne sauce, lobster pastilla with ginger sauce, braised squab on a bed of slow-cooked vegetables with warmed sesame oil and the Mara des Bois strawberry crème brûlée with ice cream offer an amiable change of air.

25110 Doubs. Paris 440 – Belfort 62 –
Besançon 30 – Montbéliard 45.
A village in a lush setting and the picturesque site of an ancient abbey.

 HOTELS-RESTAURANTS

■ Hostellerie le Château d'As ○□

24, rue du Château Gaillard.
Tel. 03 81 84 00 66. Fax 03 81 84 39 67.
Closed 3 weeks end Oct.–mid-Nov., end Jan.–beg. Feb., Sun. dinner, Mon. dinner. Rest. closed Sun. dinner, Mon., Tue. lunch.
6 rooms: 57–74€.
Prix fixe: 19€ (weekdays, lunch), 29€, 69€.

This thirties villa perched on the heights is reliably run by the Cachot brothers. It boasts a large, circular dining room in a rather dated style, colorful renovated rooms and dishes that offer a successful new take on local produce. Duck foie gras terrine, poultry breast cooked in Vin Jaune with morels and the chocolate fondant with Fougerolles sour cherries are classics that never stale.

In Pont-les-Moulins (25110). 6 km s via D50.

■ L'Auberge des Moulins ○□

Rte de Pontarlier.
Tel. 03 81 84 09 99.
auberge.desmoulins@wanadoo.fr
Closed 22 Dec.–22 Jan., Fri. dinner (exc. July–Aug.), Sun. dinner (exc. July–Aug.). Rest. closed Fri. lunch, Sat. lunch.
14 rooms: 42–51€.
Prix fixe: 20€, 26€.

This inn in the heart of the Cusancin valley has a rustic charm. The rooms are snug and friendly. In the well-kept dining room, the cuisine performs an appealing regional repertoire (with local trout much in evidence).

13520 Bouches-du-Rhône. Paris 714 –
Avignon 29 – Arles 18 – Marseille 87 –
Nîmes 52.
tourisme@lesbauxdeprovence.com.
The sun that never sets on the Baumanière empire lingers over the fine village of Baux.

 HOTELS-RESTAURANTS

● Oustau de Baumanière ○○※□

Le Val d'Enfer.
Tel. 04 90 54 33 07. Fax 04 90 54 40 46.
contact@oustaudebaumaniere.com
www.oustaudebaumaniere.com
Closed Jan. Rest. closed Wed. lunch.
27 rooms: 225–390€. 3 suites: 415–490€.
Prix fixe: 175€ (for 2), 150€.
A la carte: 180€.

Jean-André Charial, who grandly modernized this fine establishment founded by his grandfather Raymond Thuillier, with its ancillary villas, charming contemporary rooms, secret manor (La Guigou) and dining room with handsomely refurbished vaulted ceiling, has renovated the house's culinary style this year without departing from tradition. Bringing in the young Wahid brothers (Sylvestre at the stove and Jonathan as pastry chef), he has encouraged them to reinterpret the repertoire here in a lighter vein. With the spider crab with lightly spiced minced young vegetables, a duck foie gras with wine and peppery Saville orange preserves, blue lobster with basil pesto and the Mediterranean sea bass with flatleaf parsley sauce and preserved lemon, this Provençal monument remains at the peak of its form. The leek and truffle ravioli, basil-seasoned rouget and the Alpilles lamb in a pastry crust are still in evidence, with their produce emphasized by Sylvestre, a pupil of Ducasse who still remembers the master's lesson: "Better a turbot with no genius than a genius with no turbot". However, at Baumanière, genius seems to be a naturally occurring commodity. The fine sweet score falls just short of excess with the whipped strawberry, champagne and rose-seasoned dessert and the "grand cru" chocolate dessert with a strawberry and raspberry accompaniment. To accompany this magical feast, the finest Provence, Baux and Rhône Valley wines stand ready for inspection, shrewdly presented by the expert Gilles Ozello.

● **La Cabro d'Or**

Rte d'Arles.
Tel. 04 90 54 33 21. Fax 04 90 54 45 98.
contact@lacabrodor.com / www.lacabrodor.com
Closed mid-Nov.–20 Dec.
Rest. closed Mon. (off season), Tue. lunch.
22 rooms: 180–245€. 9 suites: 370–435€.
Prix fixe: 45€ (wine inc. weekdays),
65€ (wine inc. weekdays), 80€ (Sat., Sun.),
98€. A la carte: 100€.

In the heart of the Domaine de Baumanière, the Cabro d'Or issues an invitation to explore the beauty and culinary joys of Provence. Its elegant rooms (Relais & Châteaux approved), swimming pool and olive-scented garden serenaded by crickets are hidden at the foot of the old village of Les Baux. Michel Hulin, who trained with Guérard and at the Crayères, deftly transforms local produce into a regional cuisine exquisite from every point of view. We are moved by the thin langoustine, zucchini and leek ravioli which has been finished in the pan with tarragon, the grilled Mediterranean sea bass with fleur de sel de Camargue,

the caramelized veal sweetbreads with golden brown croutons and the crunchy fresh raspberry mille-feuille with honey of Provence.

■ **Auberge de la Benvengudo**

Rte d'Arles, vallon d'Arcoule.
Tel. 04 90 54 32 54. Fax 04 90 54 42 58.
contact@benvengudo.com
www.benvengudo.com
Closed beg. Nov.–beg. Apr.
Rest. closed lunch, Sun., Mon.
24 rooms: 135–190€. 4 suites: 190–280€.
Prix fixe: 45€. A la carte: 65€.

Among the pines and centennial olive trees, this country house promises peace and quiet by the pool and in its old-style rooms in pastel tones. In the kitchen, Daniel Beaupied, the brand new chef and boss, has a wonderful time concocting Southern French dishes with a topical flavor. The asparagus mikado with gratinéed speck, the pan-seared red sea bream in a thin vegetable tart, grilled cockerel with celery root purée and the chocolate raspberry moelleux bring cheer to our souls.

■ **Mas de l'Oulivié**

Chemin départemental 78.
Tel. 04 90 54 35 78. Fax 04 90 54 41 31.
contact@masdeloulivie.com
www.masdeloulivie.com
Closed Nov.–mid-Mar.
25 rooms: 100–245€. 2 suites: 290–490€.

Nestling in the heart of an olive grove, this gloriously situated, authentic Provençal country house, boasting rooms with patinated furniture and a fabulous landscaped swimming pool, is a paragon of charm.

BAVENT-RANVILLE see CABOURG
BAYE see QUIMPERLE

BAYEUX

14400 Calvados. Paris 261 – Caen 29 – Cherbourg 95 – Saint-Lô 36.
bayeux-tourisme@mail.cpod.fr.
This is the place for a date with history, from Queen Mathilda's tapestries to General de

Gaulle's speech. Then there are the Notre-Dame cathedral and the Normandy Landing beaches just a step away.

 HOTELS-RESTAURANTS

● Château de Sully

Rte de Port-en-Bessin, 3 km nw via D6.
Tel. 02 31 22 29 48. Fax 02 31 22 64 77.
chsully@club-internet.fr
www.chateau-de-sully.com
Closed mid-Dec.–mid-Mar. Rest. closed lunch
13 rooms: 100–190€. 9 suites: 190–360€.
A la carte: 70€.

Hidden in its wooded grounds with a swimming pool, tennis court, gym and billiard room, this 18th-century château mainly attracts gourmets who come to enjoy Philippe Peudenier's lively, spirited seafood dishes. In the hands of this former pupil of Alain Senderens and Jacques Cagna, langoustines with watercress ravioli, Atlantic sea bass steamed over seaweed, breaded and fried squid with its ink and a pineapple mille-feuille steer a delightful course between tradition and modernity.

■ Grand Hôtel du Luxembourg

25, rue des Bouchers.
Tel. 02 31 92 00 04. Fax 02 31 92 54 26.
hotel.luxembourg@wanadoo.fr
www.hotels-bayeux-14.com
24 rooms: 70–135€. 3 suites: 90–185€.
Prix fixe: 15€, 45€. A la carte: 45€.

Admittedly, the welcome here is not always what it should be. However, this fine 18th-century town house still boasts pretty guest rooms decorated with toile de Jouy fabrics and a pleasant regional cuisine (Camembert tart, roasted monkfish, tripe prepared in the style of Caen and long-simmered pork trotters in cider).

■ Le Lion d'Or

71, rue Saint-Jean.
Tel. 02 31 92 06 90. Fax 02 31 22 15 64.
lion.d-or.bayeux@wanadoo.fr
www.liondor-bayeux.fr
Closed 20 Dec.–20 Jan.

Rest. closed Sat. lunch, Mon. lunch.
27 rooms: 75–95€. 1 suite: 155–235€.
Prix fixe: 20€ (lunch), 36€, 50€,
13€ (child). A la carte: 60€.

Visiting celebrities regularly stay at this former post house. The well-equipped rooms (three of them new), spruce tearoom and spirited cuisine served in the classical dining room are all enchanting. The duck foie gras terrine served with a spoon of lightly spiced apple chutney, the roasted turbot with its variation on the citrus theme, the olive-stuffed rabbit saddle and the Tatin-style roasted apples cannot be faulted.

■ Hôtel de Brunville

9, rue Genas-Duhomme.
Tel. 02 31 21 18 00. Fax 02 31 92 54 26.
hotel.brunville@wanadoo.fr
www.bestwestern.fr
31 rooms: 70–200€.
Prix fixe: 15€, 45€. A la carte: 50€.

This hotel on the edge of the old town is Alain Dolbeau's other establishment. Behind its attractive facade lie compact but modern rooms. In the restaurant with its photos of actors, we are faithful to the haddock filet with spinach, the basil-seasoned tuna steak, Caen-style tripe and the tarte Tatin prepared to order.

● Le Bistro de Paris   ■SIM

3, rue du Dr-Guillet.
Tel.-Fax 02 31 92 00 82.
Closed Sat. lunch, Sun., Mon. dinner,
2 weeks Feb., 2 weeks Aug.
Prix fixe: 11€ (lunch), 16,50€, 29€.
A la carte: 35€.

This resourceful bistro attracts a boisterous clientele and aficionados of roguish dishes, such as the paprika-seasoned potted salmon, crispy skate wing, pork tenderloin medallions and a thin apple tart, all accompanied by mischievous little wines, cheerful service and an affable check.

BAYONNE

64100 Pyrénées-Atlantiques.
Paris 771 – Biarritz 9 – Bordeaux 192 –
Saint-Sébastien 57.
bayonne.tourisme@wanadoo.fr.
The true capital of the Basque country? Bayonne, with its market, bullfights, ancient side
streets, cathedral of Sainte-Marie, precious
Bonnat museum, quays on the Nive river, fine
atmosphere, choice artisans and delicious restaurants. In short, the spirit of the Basque country, even out of season.

 | HOTELS-RESTAURANTS

■ Le Grand Hôtel   ⌂
21, rue Thiers.
Tel. 05 59 59 62 00. Fax 05 59 59 62 01.
www.bw-legrandhotel.com
54 rooms: 60–178€.

Charmed by the central location, smiling
service and promise of peace and quiet
offered by the charming rooms overlooking the interior courtyard, we feel an urge
to move in here.

■ Loustau   ⌂
1, pl de la République.
Tel. 05 59 55 08 08. Fax 05 59 55 69 36.
info@hotel-loustau.co
www.hotel-loustau.com
45 rooms: 77–119€.

A step away from the rail station and the
Adour, behind the 18th-century facade,
this hotel offers functional rooms and an
honest regional restaurant.

■ Adour Hotel   ⌂
13, pl Sainte-Ursule.
Tel. 05 59 55 11 31. Fax 05 59 55 86 40.
adourhotel@numericable.fr
www.adourhotel.net
12 rooms: 60–85€.

The fortes of this hotel near the rail station are its amiable prices and rooms
with amusing Basque cultural themes.

● Auberge du Cheval Blanc   ◎ V.COM
68, rue Bourg-Neuf.
Tel. 05 59 59 01 33. Fax 05 59 59 52 26.
Closed Sat. lunch, Sun. dinner, Mon., Feb.
vac., 1 week beg. July, 1 week beg. Aug.
Prix fixe: 28€, 38€, 80€. A la carte: 65€.

Reliability is still very much Jean-Claude
Tellechea's trademark. For years, this local
son has been serving dishes of unvaryingly
high quality inspired by the Adour valley. In the modern dining room, individual smoked trout terrine, roasted whiting
with slightly caramelized golden minced
onions and the oven-braised caul-wrapped
packets of pigeon with foie gras continue
to seduce us. At the end of the meal, the
hot Grand Marnier soufflé remains a paradigm. Given the pleasures on offer here,
the prices are well mannered.

● François Muira   ◎ COM
24, rue Marengo.
Tel. 05 59 59 49 89.
Closed Sun. dinner, Wed., 2 weeks Mar.
Prix fixe: 20€, 31€. A la carte: 55€.

François Muira's restaurant is still a must
and we are always delighted to take our
seats to enjoy the lively, precise regional
cuisine in the contemporary setting surrounded by stone walls. The slow-cooked
tomato and tuna belly and the stuffed
squid and grilled pigeon sprinkled with
chickory jus brook no criticism. For dessert, the pear eau-de-vie soufflé with praline-flavored custard cream sauce lends
us wings.

● El Asador   ⬤ SIM
Pl Montaut.
Tel.-Fax 05 59 59 08 57.
Closed Sun. dinner, Mon., 2 weeks Dec.,
1 week beg. Jan., 3 weeks June.
Prix fixe: 19,10€. A la carte: 40€.

At Maria Jesus Freitas' tavern, Spain is
celebrated on the walls, in the dishes and
in our glasses. Under posters illustrating
the festivities in Pamplona, grilled anchovies, line-fished whiting koskera (a spicy
Basque dish with asparagus), blood sausage served with mashed potatoes and the

almond ice cream are washed down with Spanish wines in a relaxed atmosphere.

● Le Bayonnais

38, quai des Corsaires.
Tel. 05 59 25 61 19. Fax 05 59 59 00 64.
Closed Sun., Mon., 3 weeks Christmas–New Year's, 2 weeks June.
Prix fixe: 15€. A la carte: 40€.

Trained by Alain Dutournier and Bernard Pacaud, the dependable Christophe Pascal serves up his region. In the rustic, colorful dining room, we savor the squid in parsley and garlic, marbled beef cheek dish, oven-crisped whiting, pan-simmered lamb sweetbreads and the fig pastilla. The menu barely changes, but the pleasure remains.

● La Feuillantine

Quai Amiral-Dubourdieu.
Tel.-Fax 05 59 46 14 94.
nvae@wanadoo.fr
Closed Sun., Wed. dinner,
3 days at Christmas, Feb. vac.
Prix fixe: 15€. A la carte: 38€.

Here by the Nive, Nicolas Borteyru provides the best value for money in the Basque country. There is no terrace, but the bargain prices make up for that and more. A thin tomato tart with shavings of ewe's cheese, the cod-stuffed piquillos, the layered casserole of duck and potato served with a seafood pasta salad, plus the brioche perdu served with fresh fruit salad, concocted by this veteran of Gagnaire, Loiseau, the Marée, Vié and the Bristol in Del Burgo's time, are a divine surprise.

● La Garburada Rose

34, rue d'Espagne.
Tel. 05 59 59 39 50.
Closed Sun., Mon., 23 June–10 July, 26 Aug.–11 Sept.
A la carte: 40€.

"Hélène's cousin" Alain has left the Béarn to open this Darroze temple devoted to garbure, a Southwestern stew made with cabbage, ham, bacon and preserved goose

or duck. The décor in this simple haunt is misleading, more suited to a tasting room than a cheerful inn. Here, Alain describes his own, personal Gascony, with the grilled foie gras medallion, garbure served cold in aspic, honey-glazed xamango (ham on the bone) with hints of citrus flavors, the lamb served three ways (rack with parsley and garlic, sweetbreads with ceps in ravioli, and variety cuts) and half of a tender pigeon, first roasted and then finished in wine sauce. The apple, prune and Armagnac dessert is in quite the same vein.

● La Grange

26, quai Galuperie.
Tel. 05 59 46 17 84.
Closed Sun.
Prix fixe: 18,50€. A la carte: 40€.

Jacques Diharce, who ran the Clair de la Nive just next door, has moved two numbers down the street to expand his territory. This expert technician who trained at the Crillon with Bonin, and with Coussau and Rostang, has not forgotten the valuable lessons they taught him. On the blackboard, he lists his impeccable, very eighties dishes, including tomatoes stuffed with shellfish, ricotta ravioli served with a lobster medallion, whiting with garlic petals and the gratined fresh fruit with a Grand Marnier sabayon, all an incitement to eat here on a regular basis.

● Le Chistera

42, rue du Port-Neuf.
Tel.-Fax 05 59 59 25 93.
marmouyet@lechistera.com
www.lechistera.com
Closed Mon. (off season), Tue. dinner (off season), Wed. dinner (off season).
Prix fixe: 14,70€, 7,50€ (child).
A la carte: 30€.

Jean-Pierre Marmouyet's love of the Basque country shows in his whiting salad, Bayonne ham plate, koskera whiting, veal kidney brochette and rice pudding.

● La Rôtisserie du Roy Léon SIM

8, rue de Coursic.
Tel. 05 59 59 55 84. Fax 05 59 59 55 46.
Closed Sat. lunch, Sun. 15–30 Sept.,
23 Dec.–3 Jan.
Prix fixe: 22€, 29€.

Meat lovers gather around a splendid set menu in this rustic dining room, setting to work on the grilled squid, duckling, a rack of lamb and other spit-roasted meats. For dessert, the berry gratin provides a light final act. The check is sweet, but the reception slightly sour.

BAZAS

33430 Gironde. Paris 641 – Bordeaux 62 – Agen 83 – Mont-de-Marsan 70.
bazas@fnotsi.net.
The capital of Bazas beef has a medieval elegance. Its fine markets are well worth a visit, as is its Saint-Jean cathedral. The Graves wine region is just next door.

 HOTELS-RESTAURANTS

■ Domaine de Fompeyre

Rte de Mont-de-Marsan.
Tel. 05 56 25 98 00. Fax 05 56 25 16 25.
www.monalisahotels.com
Rest. closed Sun. dinner.
40 rooms: 95–153€.
Prix fixe: 25€, 62€, 63€.

Spacious rooms, a wooded park, indoor and outdoor swimming pools, tennis, steam bath, Jacuzzi, fitness center and meeting facilities are among the assets of this hotel complex, not to mention a restaurant and winter garden–style veranda. We sit down to a veal sweetbread salad and ceps with truffle-infused oil, the pike-perch or rouget filet, the duck breast and a frozen chocolate parfait.

BAZEILLES see SEDAN

BEAUCAIRE

30300 Gard. Paris 706 – Avignon 26 – Arles 18 – Nîmes 25.

beaucaire@mnet.fr.
The château, the Rhône, the bridge and a maze of streets in the old town opposite Tarascon…

 RESTAURANTS

● L'Ail Heure COM

43, rue du Château.
Tel. 04 66 59 67 75.
lailheure@wanadoo.fr
Closed Sat. lunch, Sun., Jan.
Prix fixe: 16€ (lunch), 34€ (dinner).
A la carte: 45€.

Five minutes from the Château de Beaucaire, Luc Andreu's restaurant meets with unanimous approval. It offers a traditional setting with stone and beams, a bright, smiling welcome and especially fine tricks performed by a chef who trained with Guérard, Daguin and Baumanière. The foie gras escalope served with figs, a Mediterranean sea bass in bouillabaisse with chantrelles, the toro steak served with slow-cooked beef cheeks and the strawberry mille-feuille with vanilla-infused cream sauce cannot be faulted.

LE BEAUCET see CARPENTRAS

BEAUGENCY

45190 Loiret. Paris 154 – Orléans 31 – Blois 36 – Châteaudun 42.
tourisme.beaugency@wanadoo.fr.
A string of towers, gray stone houses, a keep that now only has to defend against a flight of birds, a Renaissance château turned quiet museum, an old bridge arching its back over the impetuous Loire and a majestic old abbey: this is a delightfully iconic, impeccably French town. At the gates of the Sologne region, this peaceful sentinel of the Loire Valley is a history book in itself.

 HOTELS-RESTAURANTS

■ L'Ecu de Bretagne

Pl du Martroi.
Tel. 02 38 44 67 60. Fax 02 38 44 68 07.
ecu-de-bretagne@wanadoo.fr

www.ecudebretagne.fr
Rest. closed Sun. dinner (exc. summer),
Mon. (Nov.–Mar.).
34 rooms: 43–80€.
Prix fixe: 21€, 28€, 35€, 10€ (child).
A la carte: 45–50€.

This 17th-century post house delights us with its welcome and calm, comfortable rooms refurbished in a modern rustic style. The dining room pays tribute to the region with a foie gras terrine, pike fish quenelles with beurre blanc sauce and steamed potatoes, house specials, wild boar stew with blood sauce served with celery root purée and a thin apple tart with cinnamon ice cream and caramel sauce, all washed down with engaging Loire wines.

● **Le P'tit Bateau**   `COM`

54, rue du Pont.
Tel. 02 38 44 56 38. Fax 02 38 46 44 37.
leptitbateau@orange.fr
Closed Mon., 2 weeks Jan.
Prix fixe: 21€, 36€, 45€. A la carte: 55–60€.

The seafood plate, scallops with garlic butter and ceps and the wild duck cooked woodcock-style play on simplicity and good taste in the two old-fashioned dining rooms of this antique establishment. Soaring checks.

BEAUJEU

69430 Rhône. Paris 432 – Mâcon 35 – Lyon 63 – Roanne 62 – Bourg-en-Bresse 57.
beaujeu.beaujolais@wanadoo.fr.
The amiable capital of Beaujolais, with its old markets and wine fair.

 HOTELS-RESTAURANTS

■ **Anne de Beaujeu**   ⌂

28, rue de la République.
Tel. 04 74 04 87 58. Fax 04 74 69 22 13.
rongeatdav@aol.com / www.beaujeu.com
Closed Sun. dinner, Mon., Tue. lunch.
7 rooms: 52,50–65€.
Prix fixe: 20€, 28€, 38€, 48€.
A la carte: 42€.

Dominique and Jany-Joël Cancella are still on track in their 19th-century residence, with its restful, relaxing grounds and seven charming rooms all in pink. At the stove, David Rongeat prepares meticulous regional dishes like a house rabbit terrine, Burgundy-style escargots, pike-perch served with shellfish and chitterling sausage with mustard sauce.

BEAULIEU-SUR-MER

06310 Alpes-Maritimes. Paris 941 – Nice 10 – Menton 25.
tourisme@ot.beaulieu-sur-mer.fr.
With its Belle Epoque casino, Kérylos Greek villa, views over the open sea, marina and luxury hotels, this port standing guard on the French Riviera north of Cap Ferrat has resisted the predations of fashion and time.

 HOTELS-RESTAURANTS

● **La Réserve de Beaulieu**

5, bd du Maréchal-Leclerc.
Tel. 04 93 01 00 01. Fax 04 93 01 28 99.
reservation@reservebeaulieu.com
www.reservebeaulieu.com
Rest. closed Sun., Mon., 11 Nov.–19 Dec.
30 rooms: 499–882€. 7 suites: 1449–2683€.
Prix fixe: 150€, 190€. A la carte: 190–202€.

A while back, this turn-of-the-century luxury hotel built like a Florentine villa with its swimming pool defying the sea had begun to show its age. Now, the Delions (who own the Pinède in Saint-Tropez) have smartened it up, rejuvenating the place without sapping its character. Concierges, chambermaids and dining room staff (including the dynamic Roger Heyd and sommelier and actor Jean-Louis Valla) form the most efficient team on the coast. And how could we forget chef Olivier Brulard, a Norman from the Orne district who trained with Chapel and Guérard, who concocts a very "French Riviera" cuisine? The flavorful sweet pea soup with julienned snowpeas, the crusty baguettes, multicolored mouthfuls (lobster brunoise, langoustines, squid) are all stunningly authentic. The olive-seasoned rouget with tender herb-seasoned fresh ewe's cheese and ricotta ravioli is the finest "sea and garden" preparation to be found on the coast today. We use our fingers to tackle the rack and saddle of Aveyron lamb with navarin garnish like some sweetmeat and later, we can always discuss the Carros strawberry gratin with Menton lemons and the frozen vanilla rhubarb dessert graced with the divine inspiration of crushed candied almonds and the prodigious wine list we pored over to finally settle on a Saint-Baillon Roudaï red. Finally, we conclude that if there is such a thing as paradise, it cannot be far from this Réserve, with its delightful ceilings decorated with freizes.

■ **Comté de Nice**

25, bd Marinoni.
Tel. 04 93 01 19 70. Fax 04 93 01 23 09.
www.hotel-comtedenice.com
32 rooms: 65–120€.

This town center hotel a step away from the harbor is very practical, offering contemporary rooms, some with a mini-terrace.

■ **Frisia**

2, bd Eugène-Gauthier.
Tel. 04 93 01 01 04. Fax 04 93 01 31 92.
www.frisia-beaulieu.com
Closed mid-Nov.–mid-Dec.
32 rooms: 50–126€. 2 suites: 110–195€.

On the marina, Daniel Hoeffly shows delighted guests to their bright, comfortable rooms.

■ **Le Havre Bleu**

29, bd du Maréchal-Joffre.
Tel. 04 93 01 01 40. Fax 04 93 01 29 92.
www.hotel-lehavrebleu.fr
Closed Nov.
20 rooms: 48–70,50€.

This hotel between the rail station and beach is a very pleasant port-of-call with its warm welcome and peaceful rooms in Provençal colors. Breakfast on the terrace and affable prices.

● **African Queen**　　　　　Ⓝ SIM

Port de Plaisance.
Tel. 04 93 01 10 85.
Closed Jan.–beg. Feb., 24 Dec., 31 Dec.
A la carte: 30–90€.

The cheerful Gilbert Vissian's fine, friendly, distinctive terrace is the sort we wish we could find in every French port. Here, the superior produce is simply prepared. Straightforward, tasty concoctions—ravioli in pesto, tagliatelli Napolitaine, pizzas (choice of "the truffle" is divine), fresh fish (Mediterranean sea bass, sea bream and sole meunière) and the choice meats (calf's liver with shallots, Simmenthal de Baviere beef) are the recipes of a restaurant that has made simplicity its watchword and sincerity its virtue.

● **Le Petit Darkoum**　　　　SIM

18, bd du Général-Leclerc.
Tel. 04 93 01 48 59.
Closed Mon., Tue., mid-Jan.–mid-July.
Prix fixe: 20€ (lunch). A la carte: 40–45€.

Michel and Saadia Guguen lead us on an exploration of Morocco. The dishes in this Maghribi setting exude authenticity. The assorted briouates (pastries stuffed with meat), grilled sardines, lamb tagine and house pastries all live up to their promise.

BEAUMES-DE-VENISE see CARPENTRAS

BEAUMONT-EN-AUGE

14950 Calvados. Paris 197 – Caen 41 –
Le Havre 45 – Deauville 11.
Perched on its hill, this Norman village (the birthplace of physicist Laplace) boasts a panoramic view of the Pays d'Auge's hedgerows and promises a peaceful overnight stay.

●	RESTAURANTS

● **Auberge de l'Abbaye**　　　🍴COM

2, rue de la Libération.
Tel. 02 31 64 82 31.
www.aubergel'abbaye.com
Closed Tue., Wed., 1 week Oct., 3 weeks Jan.
Prix fixe: 30€, 40€, 54€. A la carte: 80€.

The duck foie gras, the line-fished Atlantic sea bass, the strips of duck breast with honey-roasted figs and fresh foie gras and the thin apple tart with vanilla ice cream or the Grand Marnier soufflé make an excellent impression in this Norman-style inn with its three rustic dining rooms run by Christian Girault, who was such a success at Deauville casino. Watch out for the à la carte prices.

BEAUNE

21200 Côte-d'Or. Paris 312 – Auxerre 152 – Châlon-sur-Saône 30 – Dijon 45.
ot.beaune@wanadoo.fr.
The Hôtel-Dieu with its colored roof is famous throughout the world. The town itself, with its old hotels, ramparts, winding cobbled backstreets and great merchants' homes has more than one (vinic) string to its bow.

 HOTELS-RESTAURANTS

■ Hôtel de la Poste
5, bd G.-Clemenceau.
Tel. 03 80 22 08 11. Fax 03 80 24 19 71.
www.hoteldelapostebeaune.com
Closed beg. Jan.–beg. Feb.
26 rooms: 130–220€. 10 suites: 300–550€.
Prix fixe: 35€, 56€, 15€ (child).
A la carte: 60€.

A stone's throw from the beltway, this 19th-century post house carries on at its own pace. The regularly renovated rooms are comfortable and the restaurant holds a range of delights. Under the eye of Marc Le Ouedec, skate terrine with condiments and aromatic herbs, cod filet with cured ham, pork loin with braised vegetables and the coffee and chocolate dessert make up delicious set menus.

■ L'Hôtel de Beaune
5, rue Samuel-Legay.
Tel. 03 80 25 94 14. Fax 03 80 25 94 14.
www.lhoteldebeaune.com
Closed 3 weeks Dec.–beg. Jan.
8 rooms: 250–335€.

A step away from the Hospices and the delightful place Carnot, this fine 19th-century residence has been turned into a luxury guesthouse. The style is neo-art deco and there is a wine tasting area serving vintages from the region and further afield (Tuscany) in the cellar and at the bar.

■ La Closerie ❀ 🏠
61, rte de pommard, via N74.
Tel. 03 80 22 15 07. Fax 03 80 24 16 22.
www.hotel-lacloserie-beaune.com
Closed 23 Dec.–mid–Jan.
46 rooms: 80–110€. 1 suite: 130€.

This hotel close to the town center has a few rooms that have been spruced up in quite a pleasant modern style, as well as an apartment. It also offers a shady flower garden and heated outdoor swimming pool.

● Le Jardin des Remparts ○
10, rue de l'Hôtel-Dieu.
Tel. 03 80 24 79 41. Fax 03 80 24 92 79.
lejardin@club-internet.fr
www.le-jardin-des-remparts.com
Closed Sun., Mon., Feb.
Prix fixe: 30€ (lunch), 52€, 62€, 78€.
A la carte: 75€.

With its terrace garden running along the old town walls, this elegant thirties residence has oodles of appeal. Refurbished in a very contemporary style, the décor leaves nothing to chance. The furniture is in good taste and each item is in its proper place, thanks to Emmanuelle Chanliaud's efforts. In the kitchen, Roland applies the skills he learned with Marc Meneau as he prepares his special favorites: langoustines, presented fried and also in sorbet, line-fished Atlantic sea bass with sardine-seasoned butter, Charolais beef, wine caramel and the brown beer soufflé with powdered sugar. Laetitia Nicod expertly selects the right bottle from among the 450 wines stored in the cellar.

● Bernard Morillon   V.COM
31, rue Maufoux.
Tel. 03 80 24 12 06. Fax 03 80 22 66 22.
www.restaurant-morillon.com
Closed Sat. lunch, Mon., Tue. lunch,

Feb. vac., 1 week Aug.
Prix fixe: 20€ (lunch), 53€, 77€,
15€ (child). A la carte: 85–100€.

In an 18th-century setting a stone's throw from the Hospices de Beaune, Bernard Morillon plays to rather a successful chic rustic score. Escargots in puff pastry, langoustine tails, milk-fed veal tenderloin medallions and a strawberry and chocolate mille-feuille are opportune alliances of tradition and quality.

● Le Benaton ○COM

25, rue du faubourg-Bretonnière.
Tel. 03 80 22 00 26. Fax 03 80 22 51 95.
lebenaton@clubinternet.fr
Closed Wed., Thu., end Nov.–beg. Dec.
Prix fixe: 38€, 63€, 68€. A la carte: 85€.

On the edge of the center, Bruno Monnoir runs an ambitious restaurant with terrace and garden. In modern, refined surroundings, the polished cuisine boldly reinterprets local tradition, in the form of a roasted tête de veau served with big langoustines, a lightly salted cod with vegetables and a Bresse pigeon breast in a pastry crust, its thigh stuffed with a legume and olive oil stuffing. The same modern spirit defines the desserts, which include a chocolate cake served hot with blackcurrant sauce and ice cream made with the same local berries. Delectable service, but the check is increasingly unruly.

● Le Conty 🎥COM

1, rue Ziem.
Tel. 03 80 22 63 94. Fax 03 80 24 20 42.
Closed Sun., Mon., mid-Feb.–mid-Mar.
Prix fixe: 12,50€, 18€, 26€, 29€.
A la carte: 39–49€.

The Parras pay tribute to Burgundian tradition here. Isabelle's welcome and Laurent's cuisine make this establishment an oasis of conviviality. Quality produce and skillful preparation go into a rabbit terrine with pistachio coulis, scallop risotto, veal filet medallion with chanterelles and pan-tossed truffles and vanilla rice pudding over apricot compote. The vineyards of Burgundy are everywhere on the wine list, which has a wealth of fine regional vintages at reasonable prices.

● La Ciboulette 🎥SIM

69, rue de Lorraine.
Tel. 03 80 24 70 72. Fax 03 80 22 79 71.
Closed Mon., Tue., 3 weeks Feb.,
2 weeks Aug.
Prix fixe: 19,50€, 20,50€. A la carte: 36€.

With its traditional, Burgundy-inspired dishes, amiable prices and good-natured atmosphere, this little Beaune restaurant is a valued find. We are drawn by Alban Demougeot's ham and parsley terrine, pan-tossed langoustine tails, a slow-cooked pork cheek medallion and Laurent Male's signature frozen nougat. While we are here, we raise our glass to some excellent local libations.

● Le P'tit Paradis 🎥SIM

25, rue Paradis.
Tel. 03 80 24 91 00.
Closed Sat., Sun., 2 weeks Feb., 2 weeks Aug.
Prix fixe: 20€ (lunch), 25€, 32€.
A la carte: 45€.

A cobbled, semi-pedestrian street near the Hospices holds a small corner of paradise. This is a special place indeed with its trim dining room in pastel colors and Jean-Marie Daloz's local cuisine and bargain set menus. Regulars flock here to enjoy the langoustine salad, herb-seasoned pollock filet, veal sweetbread lasagne with morels followed by a chocolate pot de crème or white chocolate ice cream. On the cellar side, Auxey-Duresses and Comte Armand Volnay vie for our favors without bathing us in a cold sweat when the check arrives.

● Dame Tartine SIM

3, rue Nicolas-Rolin.
Tel. 03 80 22 64 20. Fax 03 80 22 32 87.
Prix fixe: 10€, 9€ (child). A la carte: 30€.

Despite the passing years, Dame Tartine is as fresh as ever. With undiminished pleasure, we take our seats in this contemporary setting to enjoy salmon tartare, pike-perch filet braised with leeks, minced duck breast with sour cherries and a frozen soufflé with prunes and almonds.

● **Ma Cuisine** `SIM`

Passage Sainte-Hélène (pl Carnot).
Tel. 03 80 22 30 22. Fax 03 80 24 99 79.
macuisine@wanadoo.fr
Closed Sat., Sun., Wed., Dec., Aug.
Prix fixe: 20€. A la carte: 40€.

In his bistro clad all in yellow, Fabienne Escoffier concocts a half-Burgundian, half-Southern French, 100% seasonal cuisine. The tuna tartare, ham and parsley terrine, skate wing with capers, spicy grilled cockerel and the dessert cart are of genuine worth. A fine collection of wines by the glass.

In Aloxe-Corton (21420). 6 km n via N74.

■ **Villa Louise** ❀ 🏠

9, rue Franche.
Tel. 03 80 26 46 70. Fax 03 80 26 47 16.
www.hotel-villa-louise.fr
Closed mid-Jan.–mid-Feb.
11 rooms: 95–150€. 1 suite: 190€.

This 18th-century winegrower's residence with its garden giving onto a few plots of Corton-Charlemagne is the domain of knowledgeable hostess Véronique Perrin. The renovated rooms (one of them with a terrace), cozy lounges, swimming pool, steam bath, Jacuzzi and gourmand breakfasts make our stay a happy one.

In Chorey-lès-Beaune (21200). 4 km n via rte de Dijon. N74.

● **Ermitage de Corton** `LUX`

Tel. 03 80 22 05 28. Fax 03 80 24 64 51.
ermitagecorton@wanadoo.fr
www.ermitagecorton.com
Closed 21 Feb.–mid-Mar. Rest. closed lunch (exc. Sun. lunch and by reserv.), Wed. dinner.
1 room: 150€. 9 suites: 200–250€.
Prix fixe: 23€ (lunch), 30€ (lunch), 70€ (dinner). A la carte: 75€.

Now the Parras have gone and Pascal Garnier is here, this large inn seems to have lost a little of its soul. Yes, the apartments are as richly decorated as ever, but the introduction of a bar with a lounge *cum* smoking room and the renovation of the classically styled dining room mark the end of an era. This is confirmed in the kitchen, where André Parra's eternal lieutenant Patrick Casetti has finally stood down. New chef Nicolas Peutin strives to champion the region's produce in traditional recipes. Individual vegetable terrine with duck foie gras, line-fished Atlantic sea bass with chanterelles, pepper-seasoned duck breast and the house chocolate dessert are pleasant, but sometimes rather two dimensional. Fortunately, the great Côtes wines have lost none of their splendor.

In Levernois (21200). 5 km via rte de Verdun-sur-le-Doubs (D970 and D111).

● **Hostellerie de Levernois**

Rue du golf.
Tel. 03 80 24 73 58. Fax 03 80 22 78 00.
levernois@relaischateaux.com
www.levernois.com
Closed end Jan.–mid-Mar.
Rest. closed Wed., Thu. lunch.
15 rooms: 130–305€. 1 suite: 245–350€.
Prix fixe: 65€, 80€, 98€. A la carte: 110€.

Just outside Beaune, Levernois is something of a model village with its spruced-up houses and ochre walls. This exemplary Relais & Châteaux establishment has found a new vitality in the enthusiastic hands of Jean-Louis Bottigliero, formerly the chain's vice president. Red hexagonal floor tiles and wood set the tone in its guest rooms, with their modern, grayish-beige bathrooms. Turning to the dining room, the refined cuisine is prepared by Vincent Maillard, a nomadic Burgundian formerly with Ducasse in Monaco and at the Belle Otéro in Cannes. Marinated tuna and monkfish served with romaine hearts, escargots baked in a sealed cocotte, turbot with white beans and pesto, the veal cutlet and the kidney brochette with spicy breading are delightful, although a little more regionalism would better suit visiting gourmets. The desserts (a variation on pain d'épice, suprising blackcurrant ice cream), the magnificent cheese trolley and the great wine list (paying tribute to the three Côtes: Beaune, Nuits and Chalonnaise) are irresistibly tempting.

In Levernois.

● Le Bistro du Bord de l'Eau

Rue du Golf.
Tel. 03 80 24 73 58.
Closed dinner, Sun., end Jan.–beg. Mar.
Prix fixe: 28€, 32€.

If you want excellent value for money in the Beaune area today, the waterside bistro opened by Jean-Louis Bottigliero is the very place. This easygoing, rustic adjunct presents chef Vincent Maillard's finest ideas of the moment at lenient prices. The friendly staff serve with a smile dishes of unsurpassed freshness. Mild garlic soup with escargots and parsley jus, cuttlefish tempura served with tartare sauce, aromatic herb-seasoned braised lamb shank, ricotta gnocchi served with gremolata (an Italian minced parsley and garlic sauce), a prune mille-feuille and a chocolate raspberry tart are pleasantly accompanied by a Merlin Moulin à Vent. The covered garden is delightful and the stone dining room chic.

In Levernois.

● La Garaudière SIM

10, Grand-Rue.
Tel. 03 80 22 47 70. Fax 03 80 22 64 01.
Closed Mon., Dec.–mid-Jan.
Prix fixe: 16€, 27€.

This Beaune country inn is worth a stop. Set menus at gentle prices, amiable service and fine table-top grilled meats await us in its pleasant setting. We like poached eggs in vineyard-keeper's sauce, lamb saddle or a grilled duck breast served with an excellent gratin Dauphinois. The finest growers of the Côtes de Beaune and Nuits districts are represented on the wine list.

In Puligny-Montrachet (21190). 12 km via N74.

● Le Montrachet

10, pl des Marronniers.
Tel. 03 80 21 30 06. Fax 03 80 21 39 06.

info@le-montrachet.com
www.le-montrachet.com
Closed end Nov.–10 Jan.
26 rooms: 110–140€. 4 suites: 180€.
Prix fixe: 30€ (lunch), 55€, 65€, 13€ (child). A la carte: 75€.

This village hostelry dating from 1824 wages its elegant, rustic charm offensive with a fair degree of success. Thierry Gazagnes' friendly welcome and the meticulous service, refined rooms and excellent cellar are convincing arguments. In the kitchen, Thierry Berger, a talented youngster formerly at the Plaza and Vernet, and our 2006 Chef of the Year, serves up sunny, specialist dishes including a langoustine and chanterelle fricassée served with celery seed consommé, tuna belly in a chorizo crust, roasted pigeon in a salt crust, its thighs the stuffing for accompanying zucchini flowers) and the hot melon soufflé with a frozen spice-seasoned center. Do not miss his take on the escargots in croustade, a local tart made with many layers of thin pastry and the grilled Charolais beef. A fine selection of wines from the three great Côtes (Beaune, Nuits and Chalonnaise).

In Puligny-Montrachet.

● La Table d'Olivier SIM

1, pl du Monument.
Tel. 03 80 21 37 65. Fax 03 80 21 33 94.
www.olivier-leflaive.com
Closed dinner, Sun., end Dec.–mid-Feb.
Prix fixe: 39€ (wine inc.), 49€ (wine inc.).

Wine merchant Olivier Leflaive runs the restaurant that bears his name on the first floor of his pale stone residence. A set menu, whose price depends on the number of wines tasted with the dishes, matches Rully, Meursault, Chassagne, Chablis, Volnay and Pommard with charcuterie, slow-simmered Bresse poultry with a honey cream sauce, aged cheeses and coffee with Valrhona chocolate squares. Chef Florence Boyeaux and sommelier Pascal Wagner answer our questions, while the master of the house tells of wines past and offers insights into the future. A hotel has been added this year.

BEAURECUEIL

13100 Bouches-du-Rhône.
Paris 783 – Avignon 90 – Marseille 37 –
Aix-en-Provence 10.
At the foot of Mont Sainte-Victoire, an island of
calm, unspoiled scenery, like a Cézanne canvas.

 HOTELS-RESTAURANTS

● **Relais de la Sainte-Victoire**
Av Sylvain-Gautier.
Tel. 04 42 66 94 98. Fax 04 42 66 85 96.
www.relais-sainte-victoire.com
Closed 1 week Jan., Nov. 1 vac.
Rest. closed Sun. dinner, Mon., Fri. lunch.
15 rooms: 61–122€.
Prix fixe: 25€, 75€.

The Jugy-Bergèses' country house offers
a delightful view of Mont Sainte-Victoire. Its porch and guest rooms in Provençal colors inspire equal enthusiasm.
In the kitchen, René, a devotee of the Aix
region, serves up shrewd, rich dishes
with an eye to both past and present.
The poached eggs with truffled cream
sauce, lobster fricassée with mild spices,
the oven-roasted milk-fed lamb and
variations on theme of the calisson (a
regional almond paste sweet) are
washed down with appealing regional
wines. Garden and swimming pool.

LE BEAUSSET

83330 Var. Paris 823 – Toulon 18 –
Aix-en-Provence 66 – Marseille 46.
A medieval village in the Var, with vineyards
and the racetrack nearby.

 HOTELS-RESTAURANTS

● **Le Castellet**
3001, RN8, Les Hauts-du-Camp.
Tel. 04 94 98 37 77. Fax 04 94 98 37 78.
www.hotelducastellet.com
Rest. closed Mon. lunch.
47 rooms: 300–600€.
2 suites: 600€.
Prix fixe: 40€ (lunch), 90€.

This luxurious residence—half hacienda,
half Italian villa—opposite the Paul-Ricard
racetrack, works its charm with cheerful colors and a vast, lush estate. Its assets include
a fitness center, steam bath, spa and swimming pool. In the kitchen, Nicolas Sale from
the Hyatt Madeleine in Paris sets the tone
with a lightened, classical, Provence-fla-
vored cuisine. Asparagus in vinaigrette with
a soft boiled egg, sole served with oyster
mushrooms and a fennel bouillon, rack of
oven-roasted Sisteron with Pata Negra jus
impress us favorably. The desserts (strawberries in sweet Muscat gelatin served with
a Breton-style shortbread cookie) are well
crafted, the service is up to the same standard and the wine list boasts fine vintages
from all over France.

BEAUVAIS

60000 Oise. Paris 88 – Compiègne 61 –
Amiens 61 – Rouen 83.
ot.beauvaisis@wanadoo.fr.
The capital of the Oise is well worth a visit with
its cathedral of Saint-Pierre and stained glass
(including the Arbre de Jessé), as well as the
district museum in the former bishop's palace.

 HOTELS-RESTAURANTS

■ **Hotel du Cygne**
24, rue Carnot.
Tel. 03 44 48 68 40. Fax 03 44 45 16 76.
www.hotelducygne-beauvais.com
21 rooms: 37–72€.

In the town's old quarter, this good, traditional hotel offers comfortable rooms
at very affable prices.

● **Le Bellevue** COM
3, av Rhin-Danube. 5 km s via N1.
Tel. 03 44 02 17 11. Fax 03 44 02 54 44.
www.restaurantlebellevue.com
Closed Sat., Sun., 2 weeks Aug.
A la carte: 45€.

A step away from a shopping precinct,
Jacques Delong plays the traditional innkeeper, serving up dishes in contrasting

flavors and colors. The snail and morel cassolette, cod filet served with leeks, beef filet with Roquefort and the tête de veau with sauce ravigote (a spicy mustard, pickle and caper vinaigrette), followed by rhubarb and strawberry "parchment" with ice cream, are worth a trip to sample.

BEAUZAC

43590 Haute-Loire. Paris 561 – Le Puy 47 – Saint-Etienne 44 – Craponne 31.
The two ruined towers and fine church with its bell wall and crypt arouse our curiosity, leading us to explore this sizable village and the Basset valley nearby.

 HOTELS-RESTAURANTS

In Bransac (43590). 3 km s via D42.
■ **La Table du Barret**
Tel. 04 71 61 47 74. Fax 04 71 61 52 73.
sandy.caire@wanadoo.fr
Closed 2 weeks beg. Nov., Jan.
Rest. closed Sun. dinner, Tue., Wed.
9 rooms: 53–58€.
Prix fixe: 19€ (lunch), 27€, 43€.
A la carte: 65€.

The hotel exudes calm and simplicity, as does the highly imaginative, subtle cuisine prepared by Sandy Caire, who studied with the great Marcon nearby. Proof comes in the shape of a crayfish "transparence" with its creamy cumin-seasoned cauliflower, skate wing poached in citrusand star anise–seasoned broth served with Puy lentil ratatouille and an oven-roasted young rabbit with pain d'épice and slowcooked sweet-and-sour carrots. The softcentered chocolate biscuit with vanilla ice cream provides a choice conclusion. Fine Rhône Valley wines.

In Confolent (43590). At 4 km e via D461.
■ **L'Air du Temps**
Hameau Confolent-Beauzac (hamlet of Confolent-Beauzac).
Tel. 04 71 61 49 05. Fax 04 71 61 50 91.
air.du.temps.hotel@wanadoo.fr
www.airdutemps.frst
Closed Jan. Rest. closed Sun. dinner, Mon.

8 rooms: 45–65€.
Prix fixe: 16€ (lunch), 21€, 51€.
A la carte: 45–55€.

This twenties establishment with its bright dining room has lost none of its charm. The guest rooms are neat and the dishes prepared by Gisèle Grangeon (seconded in the dining room by her husband Christophe) include a pan-seared escalope of foie gras, rouget filet with creamy eggplant, rabbit medallion glazed in sage jus and thyme-seasoned pan-simmered peaches with apricot sauce and thyme ice cream, all well crafted.

BEBLENHEIM

68980 Haut-Rhin. Paris 438 – Colmar 11 – Ribeauvillé 5 – Sélestat 19.
This small village on the Alsace wine route boasts listed vintages, such as Mandelberg and Sonnenglanz, redolent of sun and almond trees.

 RESTAURANTS

● **L'Auberge du Bouc Bleu**   SIM
2, rue du 5-Décembre.
Tel. 03 89 47 88 21. Fax 03 89 86 01 04.
Closed Wed., Thu., 2 weeks Feb. vac.
Prix fixe: 25€, 32€, 10€ (child).
A la carte: 70€.

Daniel Friess plays to an unusual score in this charming inn on the wine route. A native of the Bas-Rhin village of Blaesheim converted to the joys of Gascony, he combines produce from the two regions rather successfully. Duck foie gras terrine or seared escalope, duck breast and cep salad, monkfish blanquette with seasonal vegetables, beef shoulder roast served with slow-simmered shallot and the fine vanilla bean, Armagnac and brown sugar crème brûlée are frankly gratifying. Keep an eye on the à la carte prices, which tend to add up rapidly!

LE BEC-HELLOUIN

27800 Eure. Paris 151 – Rouen 41 – Evreux 48 – Pont-Audemer 24.

The abbey is a majestic monument indeed and the pretty village by the Risle river is worth a halt too.

 HOTELS-RESTAURANTS

■ Auberge de l'Abbaye

12, pl Guillaume-le-Conquérant.
Tel. 02 32 44 86 02. Fax 02 32 46 32 23.
www.auberge-abbaye-bec-hellouin.com
Closed Tue., Wed., mid-Nov.–mid-Dec.,
2 weeks Jan.
8 rooms: 65–75€. 1 suite: 110€.
Prix fixe: 19€ (weekdays), 20€ (Sat., Sun.
and Bank holidays), 28€, 30€, 10€ (child).

Catherine and Fabrice Conroux have taken over the gentle Madame Sergent's celebrated inn and preserved its admirable traditional spirit. They offer a warm welcome in the 18th-century Norman residence with its English-style guest rooms, smart function room and pleasant interior garden. In the kitchen, Christophe Lhermeroult concocts reliable dishes, including sole and rouget in puff pastry, seafood choucroute with shellfish, duck breast with apples and a crème brûlée.

BEHUARD

49170 Maine-et-Loire. Paris 310 –
Angers 18 – Laval 88 – Nantes 88 –
La Roche-sur-Yon 118.
On a Loire island, a charming hamlet with all the sweetness of Anjou.

 RESTAURANTS

● Les Tonnelles

Bossé, 12, rue du Chevalier-Buhard.
Tel. 02 41 72 21 50. Fax 02 41 72 81 10.
lestonnelles49@free.fr
Closed Sun. dinner, Mon., Wed. dinner (off season), 1 week Oct., 3 weeks Jan.,
1 week at end Mar.–beg. Apr.
Prix fixe: 24€ (lunch), 40€, 63€,
83€ (dinner), 16€ (child). A la carte: 65€.

This cozy restaurant with its chic contemporary décor and pleasant rustic terrace is run by the discreet Gérard Bossé. This deft technician, who, in the words of his compatriot Curnonsky, believes that "good cuisine is when things taste of what they are", takes a mischievous delight in reinterpreting local tradition in a series of honest, well-constructed dishes, such as grilled foie gras with seasonal mushrooms, Loire fish with beurre blanc sauce, a stew of braised sea lamprey with onions, veal cutlet braised in Quart de Chaume wine and the pretty seasonal fruit tarts.

BELCASTEL

12390 Aveyron. Paris 617 –
Villefranche-de-Rouergue 37 –
Rodez 27 – Decazeville 31.
A beautiful village perched above the river with an old, arched, stone-lined bridge, an inn at one end and a hotel at the other.

 HOTELS-RESTAURANTS

● Le Vieux Pont

Le Bourg.
Tel. 05 65 64 52 29. Fax 05 65 64 44 32.
www.hotelbelcastel.com
Closed Jan.–mid-Mar. Rest. closed Sun.
dinner (exc. July–Aug.), Mon.
7 rooms: 75–198€.
Prix fixe: 26€, 48€, 78€. A la carte: 65€.

Just cross the bridge to Belcastel, a jewel in the dazzling setting of romantic France. In this hotel at the end of the world, the Fagegaltier sisters welcome guests with disarming warmth. On each side of the old bridge, the trim, comfortable rooms whisper an invitation to stay a while longer. The kitchen is the spiritual home of Nicole and her husband Bruno Rouquier. Their meticulously prepared dishes surprise us with their entertaining accompaniments: veal trotter and oyster ravioli, pan-fried whiting filet with lemon-seasoned minced sea whelks, pigeon in a dried cep crust with garlic- and apple-seasoned pan drippings and the sausage with hazelnuts are the pearls of a cuisine that focuses on regional produce. Enthusiastically recommended by Michèle, the selection of wines from the greater South is worth the visit.

BELFORT

90000 Territoire-de-Belfort. Paris 421 – Besançon 94 – Mulhouse 40 – Bâle 77.
otbtb@essor-info.fr.
A citadel defending the border, with its bronze lion, entrenched camp, town walls and old quarter: a history lesson is laid out before us.

 HOTELS-RESTAURANTS

■ Novotel Atria
Av de l'Espérance.
Tel. 03 84 58 85 00. Fax 03 84 58 85 01.
h1742@accor.com / www.novotel.fr
78 rooms: 102–185€.
Prix fixe: 16€, 21€. A la carte: 37€.

Next to the convention center, this practical hotel offers pleasant rooms refurbished contemporary style. Tomato tartare served in a glass, minced seasonal vegetables, roasted pike-perch with whelks, scallops seasoned with pain d'épice and the floating island with pralines will sate your appetite.

● Hostellerie du Château Servin V.COM
9, rue du Général-Négrier.
Tel. 03 84 21 41 85. Fax 03 84 57 05 57.
Closed Fri., Sun. dinner, Aug.
8 rooms: 62–67€. 1 suite: 77€.
Prix fixe: 20€ (lunch), 31€, 39€, 57€.
A la carte: 55–60€.

Madame Servin continues to preside over this local institution, still with its Louis XVI dining room and love of fine traditions. Chef Dominique Mathy busies himself at the stove, delighting us with such classics as a snail cassolette with herb-seasoned butter, sole filet and crayfish, stuffed rabbit saddle and a hot sour cherry soufflé. When it is time for a nap, the old-fashioned rooms are inviting indeed.

● Le Pot-au-Feu COM
27 bis, Grand-Rue.
Tel. 03 84 28 57 84. Fax 03 84 58 17 65.

mf.lunois@wanadoo.fr
Closed Sat. lunch, Sun., Mon. lunch, 10 days beg. Jan., 2 weeks beg. Aug.
Prix fixe: 11€, 14€, 19,50€, 29€, 10€ (child). A la carte: 60€.

Marie-France Guyot-Jeannin provides a smiling welcome in her contemporary bistro where Annette Denis concocts pleasantly priced set menus. The morels with Vin Jaune cream sauce served in puff pastry, Jésus de Morteau sausage gratin with aged Comté cheese, pike-perch simmered in Vin Jaune, pot-au-feu and Saint-Jean grilottes are pleasant fare indeed. A fine cellar.

In Danjoutin (90400). 3 km s.

● Le Pot d'Etain ◎ V.COM
4, rue de la République.
Tel. 03 84 28 31 95. Fax 03 84 21 70 15.
le.pot.detain.danjoutin@wanadoo.fr
www.lepotdetain.free.fr
Closed Sat. lunch, Sun. dinner, Mon., 1 week Feb. vac., 2 weeks end Aug.
Prix fixe: 29€ (weekday lunch), 48€, 58€, 72€. A la carte: 85€.

Frédéric Roy's market-based cuisine is very flavorsome. Its fresh, polished dishes take us to the four corners of France and beyond. At the contemporary *table d'hôte* or in the more traditional section of the dining room, the fare includes tuna carpaccio served cold in aspic with a basil sorbet, spiced cod filet with fresh chanterelles, farm-raised pigeon in pastilla with apricots and sage and fresh fruit accompanied by cherry mousse and currant sorbet.

In Sevenans (90400). 6 km s via N19.

● Auberge de la Tour Penchée COM
2, rue de Delle.
Tel. 03 84 56 06 52. Fax 03 84 56 16 04.
www.la tourpenchee.com
Closed Sat. lunch, Sun. dinner, Mon.
Prix fixe: 25€, 47€, 55€, 75€.
A la carte: 85€.

In a secluded little village between Montbéliard and Belfort, the five tables of François Duthey's inn are a blessing. This former pupil of Haeberlin, Loiseau and Veyrat concocts alluring dishes. In the baroque-style orange-toned dining room, warm lobster on salad, pike-perch mille-feuille, tagine-style leg of lamb and the chocolate dessert plate are impressive indeed. A reservation is vital and the prices soar sky high.

60540 Oise. Paris 52 – Compiègne 66 – Beauvais 32 – Pontoise 29.
This little village on the lush Thelle plateau illustrates the rural nature of French Vexin. Do not miss the fine churches of Neuilly-en-Thelle and Amblainville.

 RESTAURANTS

● **La Grange de Belle-Eglise**
28, bd René-Aimé-Lagabrielle.
Tel. 03 44 08 49 00. Fax 03 44 08 45 97.
Closed Sun. dinner, Mon., Feb. vac., 2 weeks Aug.
Prix fixe: 23€ (lunch), 58€, 85€.
A la carte: 100€.

In this former coal barn with its fine exposed beams, Marc Duval takes great pleasure in creating short, lively preparations that deftly combine the best of land and sea. The frog legs, monkfish with chanterelles and foie gras, milk-fed veal medallions with asparagus and the frozen Grand Marnier soufflé, served with cookies and chocolate ice cream, are accompanied by a small selection of shrewd wines.

BELLE-ILE-EN-MER

56360 Morbihan.
Three quarters of an hour from Quiberon by boat, a little Breton paradise at World's End.

 HOTELS-RESTAURANTS

● **Castel Clara**
Port-Goulphar, in Bangor.
Tel. 02 97 31 84 21. Fax 02 97 31 51 69.
contact@castel-clara.com
www.castel-clara.com
Closed mid-Nov.–mid-Feb.

36 rooms: 140–310€. 3 suites: 327–569€.
Prix fixe: 85€, 130€.

We come to the Castel to enjoy the beauty of the setting by the rocks of Port Goulphar and the needles (spiky geological formations rising out of the sea) of Port Coton close by, as well as the peace and comfort of a Relais & Châteaux hostelry that still offers coziness and non-stop thalassotherapy. The highly dynamic Christophe Goumy has brought a new youth to the place and Christophe Hardouin prepares a very charming, modern Breton cuisine. Lobster risotto with a smoked garlic sabayon, polenta and vegetable tartlette, grilled Atlantic sea bass filet, steamed cod with a potato mille-feuille and variations on the Jouan farm leg of lamb are finely crafted work. In conclusion, the traou mad, a local shortbread cookie, with Belle-Ile beer sorbet takes your breath away.

■ **La Désirade**
Rte de Port-Goulphar, in Bangor.
Hameau du Petit Cosquet.
Tel. 02 97 31 70 70. Fax 02 97 31 89 63.
hotel-la-desirade@wanadoo.fr
www.hotel-la-desirade.com
Closed mid-Nov.–end Dec., beg. Jan.–end Mar.
28 rooms: 99–160€. 4 suites: 220–340€.
Prix fixe: 20€ (lunch), 28€, 33€,
12€ (child). A la carte: 60€.

This charming hotel is made up of five "longhouses" that open onto the swimming pool. Each holds spacious, cozy rooms, redecorated this year. Another novelty is the new wellness center with its spa pool, Jacuzzi, steam bath and therapy. At the stove, Pacôme Epron serves up sunny, topical dishes, such as the croustillant of shellfish "mikado," grilled Atlantic sea bass filet served with vegetable and parmesan crumble, slow-cooked lamb shank served with Paimpol white beans and flambéed bananas with licorice syrup.

■ **Le Cardinal**
Port-Bellec, Sauzon.
Tel. 02 97 31 61 60. Fax 02 97 31 66 87.
www.hotel-cardinal.fr
Closed beg. Oct.–mid-Mar.
63 rooms: 151–228€.

Prix fixe: 25€, 32€, 40€, 12€ (child).
A la carte: 55€.

From its terrace and bar, this seventies establishment offers a view of the ocean stretching out to the horizon. The very seventies rooms are in blue and white. In the dining room, the domestic preparations are equal to their task.

■ Le Saint-Amant ⌂

14, av Carnot, Le Palais.
Tel.-Fax 02 97 31 36 71 / 02 97 31 49 79.
hotel.lesaintamant@wanadoo.fr
Closed Jan.
13 rooms: 44–52€.

Immediately by the harbor, behind the handsome red facade is a convivial hotel offering a back garden and small rooms with modern furniture.

● Roz Avel COM

Rue du Lieutenant-Riou, Sauzon.
Tel.-Fax 02 97 31 61 48.
Closed Wed., 31 Dec.–mid-Mar.
Prix fixe: 26€ (lunch), 40€ (dinner).
A la carte: 100€.

Formerly at the Castel Clara, Christophe Didoune enjoys combining local produce with less indigenous flavors. In the dining room, with its Breton furniture and cream tones, we set off on our culinary journey in the company of oysters, roasted monkfish that has been marinated in thirty-five spices, pan-seared beef filet medallions with shallots slow cooked with honey and a hazelnut and caramelized apple financier with green apple sorbet. This year, the entire terrace is available for lunch in the high season.

● Le Contre-Quai ☎COM

Rue Saint-Nicolas, Sauzon.
Tel. 02 97 31 60 60. Fax 02 97 31 01 87.
Closed Sun. (exc. July–Aug.), Mon. (exc. July–Aug.), end Sept.–Easter.
Prix fixe: 25€. A la carte: 50€.

All Sauzon's charm is summed up in this bistro, which would not change its style or décor for all the tea in China. Naturalized islander Lucien Coquant favors Belle Ile produce, especially the local catch, which he prepares with an appealing, honest simplicity. We savor stuffed crab, Atlantic sea bass served with warm oysters, Belle-Ile rack of lamb and a hot apple and ginger tart. The wine list includes some of the best elixirs of the Loire Valley and Jean-Michel's service is pleasant.

● L'Annexe SIM

3, quai de l'Yser, Le Palais.
Tel.-Fax 02 97 31 81 53.
Closed lunch, Mon. (Nov.–Apr.),
Tue. (Nov.–Apr.), Mar.
Prix fixe: 25€ (dinner). A la carte: 35€.

Below the Vauban citadel, the Graviers' gray and burgundy bistro decorated with old black and white photos serves invigorating home cooking. Pierre energetically concocts a house special with spider crab, a tuna steak, a slice of local leg of lamb and an apple prune crumble with Armagnac and pain d'épice ice cream. A small terrace.

● Le Bistro du Port SIM

Quai Joseph-Naudin, Sauzon.
Tel. 02 97 31 60 55. Fax 02 97 31 66 21.
lebistro chezcarole@hotmail.fr
Closed Sun. dinner, mid-Nov.–end Dec.,
mid-Jan.–mid-Feb.
A la carte: 30–35€.

In this orange and red marine-style restaurant on the quay, Carole Dumont exudes good humor as she serves up appetizing, shrewd dishes based on local produce. At the counter or a table by the blackboard that lists the day's dishes, we enjoy grilled crab, the Indian-style squid, lamb kidneys and crème brûlée, all washed down with a lively wine.

● Café de la Cale SIM

Quai Guerveur, in Sauzon.
Tel. 02 97 31 65 74.
Closed Nov. 1–Easter.
A la carte: 45€.

By the lighthouse, Bruno Loiseau spins like a dervish, dashing from his teak terrace to the dining room decorated with souvenir photos. We feast on stuffed crab served in the shell, steamed Atlantic sea bass, rack of Belle-Ile lamb and spiced poached pears.

BELLEFOSSE see **COLROY-LA-ROCHE**

BELLEVILLE

54940 Meurthe-et-Moselle. Paris 356 – Nancy 18 – Metz 41 – Pont-à-Mousson 13 – Toul 28.
A simple gourmet port-of-call on the Moselle, near the magnificent abbey in Pont-à-Mousson.

 RESTAURANTS

● **Le Bistroquet** ◎ V.COM
97, rte Nationale.
Tel. 03 83 24 90 12. Fax 03 83 24 04 01.
le-bistroquet@wanadoo.fr
www.le-bistroquet.com
Closed Sat. lunch, Sun. dinner, Mon.,
2 weeks end July, 1 week beg. Aug.
Prix fixe: 31€ (weekday lunch),
46€ (lunch), 56€ (dinner). A la carte: 75€.

Guests continue to flock to Marie-France Ponsard's restaurant to sample its French cuisine reinterpreted in a lighter vein. In the 1900-style dining room, a langoustine salad with citrus vinaigrette, strips of John Dory with a foamy beurre blanc and a rare sirloin steak served with a creamy tarragon-seasoned sauce are simple and precise. Obeying the same principles, desserts include a hot soufflé with mirabelle plum liqueur. All these generous dishes are beautifully accompanied by Yvan Pesusic's selection of wines.

BELLEVILLE

69220 Rhône. Paris 417 – Mâcon 24 – Lyon 50 – Bourg-en-Bresse 43.
This welcoming town is the crossroads of the Beaujolais district.

 HOTELS-RESTAURANTS

● **Le Beaujolais** COM
40, rue du Maréchal-Foch.
Tel. 04 74 66 05 31. Fax 04 74 07 90 46.

Closed Sun. dinner, Tue. dinner, Wed.,
1 week Christmas–New Year's,
3 weeks Aug.
Prix fixe: 17€, 25€, 13€ (child).
A la carte: 45€.

In his ochre dining room equipped with rustic furniture, Sébastien Rumeaux serves market-inspired dishes that bow to tradition. Terrine of young rabbit, pikeperch served over lentils and bacon, veal kidney fricassée with whole grain mustard sauce and a caramelized apple charlotte are gently priced.

In Saint-Jean-d'Ardières (69220). 5 km nw via D18 and D69.

■ **Château de Pizay**
Saint-Jean-d'Ardières.
Tel. 04 74 66 51 41. Fax 04 74 69 65 63.
info@chateau-pizay.com
www.chateau-pizay.com
Closed 23 Dec.–6 Jan.
59 rooms: 119–194€. 3 suites: 221€.
Prix fixe: 37€, 59€. A la carte: 65€.

This fine residence with one wing surrounded by vineyards and dating back to the 17th century provides large, practical rooms, a swimming pool, tennis courts and a fitness trail. In the elegant dining rooms, we savor the classics interpreted by Aurélien Merot: poached duck foie gras, whitefish meunière, Charolais beef and traditional millefeuille flavored with Bourbon vanilla. A Beaujolais from the property is just the thing to wash all this down without hiking up the check.

BELLEY

01300 Ain. Paris 506 – Aix-les-Bains 33 – Bourgen-Bresse 76 – Lyon 98.
ot-belley@club-internet.fr.
This is the land of epicure-in-chief Brillat-Savarin, and Lucien Tendret, who gave his name to a Bresse blonde poulltry liver individual terrine and eulogized his gourmet predecessor at the local assembly. The old town has some very beautiful Renaissance courtyards.

● RESTAURANTS

● La Fine Fourchette

Rte de Chambéry, N504.
Tel. 04 79 81 59 33. Fax 04 79 81 55 43.
Closed Sun. dinner, Mon.,
mid-Dec.–mid-Jan., mid-Aug.–end Aug.
Prix fixe: 23,50€, 28,50€, 33€, 39,50€,
54€, 10€ (child).

The contemporary dining room in salmon tones is very welcoming. Guy Delouille prepares a green bean salad with crayfish tails, individual poultry liver terrine with tomato sauce, whitefish with Chardonnay sauce, perch with sorrel, Bresse poultry with cream sauce and a strawberry gratin. A huge terrace with a view of the lake.

● Le Bouchon SIM

21, rue Saint-Martin.
Tel.-Fax 04 79 81 49 24.
Closed Sun. dinner, Mon. dinner.
Prix fixe: 11,50€ (weekday lunch), 23€.
A la carte: 35€.

The name of the place says it all. The cuisine concocted here by Daniel Daujat pays tribute to Lyon, with escargots, perch filet, skirt steak with shallots and a sour cherry frozen soufflé, all delightful. Amiable checks.

BENFELD

67230 Bas-Rhin. Strasbourg 29 –
Colmar 40 – Obernai 14 – Sélestat 19.
grandried.ot.benfeld@wanadoo.fr.
A town on the highway by the Ried river, with a historic past and an antique dealers' village.

 RESTAURANTS

● Le Petit Rempart COM

1, rue du Petit-Rempart.
Tel. 03 88 74 42 26. Fax 03 88 74 18 58.
www.petit-rempart.fr
Closed Mon. dinner, Tue. dinner, Thu. dinner,
2 weeks Feb., 3 weeks Aug.
Prix fixe: 9,30€, 24€, 29€, 7,90€ (child).
A la carte: 45€.

Jean-Marie and Francis Grass run their little family establishment meticulously. In the dining room, with its woodwork and coffered ceiling, Jean-Marie prepares traditional regional dishes that Francis serves with gusto: duck foie gras seasoned with Gewurztraminer, pike-perch with Pinot Gris sauce, beef filet medallion Rossini with duck foie gras and a mint charlotte with chocolate coffee sauce, all very well crafted.

BENODET

29950 Finistère. Paris 565 – Quimper 18 –
Concarneau 20 – Fouesnant 9 – Quimperlé 49.
tourisme@wanadoo.fr.
This is family Finistère by the sea, just a step away from the Bigouden region. The Cornouaille bridge and cruises on the river Odet are next door.

◼/● HOTELS-RESTAURANTS

◼ Ker-Moor

Corniche de la Plage.
Tel. 02 98 57 04 48. Fax 02 98 57 17 96.
kermoor-hotel@wanadoo.fr / www.kermoor.com
Closed 10 days end Dec., 1 week beg. Jan.
86 rooms: 65–130€.
Prix fixe: 30€, 8€ (child). A la carte: 55€.

The sea stretches away behind this thirties hotel complex, mirroring the marine decoration of the rooms and the wonderfully fresh cuisine. Proof is in the warm scallops on a bed of greens, poached turbot with hollandaise sauce, honey-glazed duck breast and a frozen vacherin.

◼ Domaine de Kereven

Rte de Quimper, 1,5 km from Bénodet.
Tel. 02 98 57 02 46. Fax 02 98 66 22 61.
Closed Oct.–mid-Apr.
12 rooms: 48–70€.

Renovated rooms, studio apartments to rent, an attentive welcome, moderate prices and twenty hectares of grounds make Sylvie and Christian Berrou's establishment an excellent base for a tour of the region.

■ Kastel

Corniche de la Plage.
Tel. 02 98 57 05 01. Fax 02 98 57 29 99.
hotel-kastel@wanadoo.fr / www.hotel-kastel.com
Closed 2 weeks Dec.
22 rooms: 66–121€.
Prix fixe: 28€ (weekdays.), 32€, 10€ (child).

This family hotel by the beach has very spacious rooms. In the dining room, the tender crab with fresh tomatoes, the pan-tossed rouget with vegetable risotto and an orange soup with spiced caramel work an effortless charm. Very reasonable prices.

BERCHERES-SUR-VESGRE see HOUDAN

BERG see SARRE-UNION

BERGERAC

24100 Dordogne. Paris 538 – Périgueux 48 – Agen 91 – Bordeaux 94.
tourisme-bergerac@aquinet.tm.fr.
Here in Cyrano country, fine wines and old stone coexist harmoniously. Do not miss the tobacco and inland fleet museums housed in handsome antique residences.

 HOTELS-RESTAURANTS

■ La Flambée

49, av Marceau-Feyry.
Tel. 05 53 57 52 33. Fax 05 53 61 07 57.
la.flambee2@wanadoo.fr / www.laflambee.com
20 rooms: 53–85€.
Prix fixe: 27€, 38€. A la carte: 45€.

Patrice and Isabelle Delage's hostelry is welcoming indeed with its flower-filled grounds, swimming pool, tennis facilities and spacious rooms, some with a terrace. In the kitchen, Laurent Lainte prepares a pan-seared escalope of foie gras, Atlantic sea bass presented with a sprinkling of fleur de sel, grilled sirloin steak with bone marrow and chocolate profiteroles, all served in the refined dining room with its fireplace.

■ Hôtel de Bordeaux

38, pl Gambetta.
Tel. 05 53 57 12 83. Fax 05 53 57 72 14.
www.hotel-bordeaux-bergerac.com
Closed mid-Dec.–7 Jan.
40 rooms: 46–90€.

The Manant family runs this establishment. The regularly refurbished rooms are always a delight.

● L'Imparfait   COM

8, rue des Fontaines.
Tel. 05 53 57 47 92.
Closed mid-Dec.–end Feb.
Prix fixe: 21€ (lunch), 37€, 47€.

Jean Rolland offers a heartfelt welcome in his 12th-century establishment in the middle of the old town. At the stove, the faithful Philippe Séguy delights us with a foamy crayfish soup with foie gras profiteroles, delicious veal trotter stew served with legumes and the pastry plate. Alain Mesclop presents his shrewd selection of wines from neighboring properties.

In Montbazillac (24240). 8 km rte de Mont-de-Marsan.

● La Tour des Vents   COM

At the Moulin de Malfourat.
Tel. 05 53 58 30 10. Fax 05 53 58 89 55.
www.tourdesvents.com
Closed Sun. dinner (exc. summer),
Mon. (exc. summer), Tue. (exc. summer),
Jan.–beg. Feb.
Prix fixe: 23,50€, 33,50€, 39,50€, 49€.
A la carte: 55€.

Marie Rougier, a modern *mère* of Périgord, wages a charm offensive in her contemporary establishment, which contrasts with the 15th-century mill standing next to it and watching over the vineyards. Her cuisine is also a marriage of tradition and modernity. The tasting plate of three duck fois gras, a roasted lobster accompanied by a vanilla-seasoned vegetable purée, a crisp covered pie containing veal sweetbreads and ceps and the strawberry shortbread cookie are all tours de force.

In Saint-Julien-de-Crempse (24140). 12 km ne via N21 and D107.

■ Manoir du Grand Vignoble   ❀⌂

Le Grand Vignoble.
Tel. 05 53 24 23 18. Fax 05 53 24 20 89.

www.manoirdugrandvignoble.com
42 rooms: 59–111€. 2 suites: 149–240€.
Prix fixe: 24€, 46€. A la carte: 45€.

This 17th-century manor stands tall at the heart of a vast estate with tennis court, swimming pool and fitness center. The rooms are refined and the cuisine in the same vein. Thierry Cottereau deftly formulates a vegetable tartare with crab jus and pistachio oil, pan-fried Atlantic sea bass with asparagus tip wheat risotto, spice-glazed duck breast and a pain perdu with milk caramel ice cream, accompanied by a pleasant selection of Bergeracs.

BERGERES-LES-VERTUS see **VERTUS**

BERGHEIM

68750 Haut-Rhin. Paris 450 – Sélestat 8 – Colmar 14 – Strasbourg 50.
Ancient alleyways, high gates and fine fortifications. The world seems to be unaware of this winegrowing village despite its wealth of attractions.

 HOTELS-RESTAURANTS

■ Chez Norbert

9, Grand-Rue.
Tel. 03 89 73 31 15. Fax 03 89 73 60 65.
labacchante@wanadoo.fr
www.cheznorbert.com
Closed 10 days beg. Nov., 3 weeks Mar.,
1 week beg. July, Rest. closed Wed. lunch,
Thu., Fri. lunch.
10 rooms: 60–90€. 2 suites: 115€.
Prix fixe: 22€, 48€, 9€ (child).
A la carte: 35€.

At this rustic winegrowing farm, the functional rooms are furnished in contemporary style. In the restaurant, La Bacchante, chef Adrien Kliem serves duck foie gras, a snail and walnut cassolette, grilled salmon served over sauerkraut, tender roasted oxtail and a Kirsch-seasoned frozen kouglof, and Sabine Schalck recommends the proper wine.

● La Wistub du Sommelier

SIM

51, Grand'Rue.
Tel. 03 89 73 69 99. Fax 03 89 73 36 58.
www.wistub-du-sommelier.com
Closed Tue. dinner, Wed., 2 weeks Jan.,
2 weeks July.
Prix fixe: 16€, 19,90€. A la carte: 35–40€.

Patrick Schneider's *winstub* is an institution on the wine route. Wooden tables, banquettes and ceramic stove set the tone in this eatery that still has its antique stamp. Here, we savor beautifully crafted local dishes. Head cheese in aspic terrine with vinaigrette, goose foie gras, a pike and crayfish quenelle, veal kidney with creamy mustard sauce and a poached Williams pear with semolina flan.

● L'Auberge des Lavandières

N ☎ SIM

48, Grand'Rue.
Tel. 03 89 73 69 96. Fax 03 89 73 37 02.
contact@leslavandieres.fr
Closed Mon., Tue.
Prix fixe: 19€, 27,50€. A la carte: 38€.

Frédéric Ancelot from Bayon, who learned his trade at the Bistroquet in Belleville, has taken an innocuous inn and turned it into a very good, low-priced restaurant. Together with his wife Nathalie, a native of Guebwiller who formerly worked in the dining room at the Fer Rouge, he presents the freshest produce of the moment. Foie gras slow-cooked in the ultra-gentle heat of a steam oven accompanied by a dried fruit chutney, jumbo shrimp with sesame in salad, pike-perch filet served on pissaladière, cod filet with zucchini mousse in a lasagne mille-feuille, tartes flambées (thin crusted local tarts garnished with cream, onions and bacon) served at lunch and dinner and a house frozen kouglof make a marvelous impression. All the village's winegrowers feature on a list that is fraught with temptation.

BERGUES

59380 Nord. Paris 279 – Lille 65 – Calais 52 – Saint-Omer 31 – Dunkerque 9.
bergues@tourisme.norsys.fr

A stone's throw from Dunkerque and the sea, a walled town that still has its Flemish feel.

● RESTAURANTS

● **Le Cornet d'Or** ◎V.COM
26, rue Espagnole.
Tel.-Fax 03 28 68 66 27.
Closed Sun. dinner, Mon.
Prix fixe: 25€, 36€, 52€. A la carte: 67€.

In the heart of the walled town, this elegant 16th-century Spanish abode holds a trim dining room equipped with antique cabinets. The menu drawn up by Jean-Claude Tasserit pays tribute to Northern France, with scallops rolled in bacon, pan-simmered cod with eggs, veal tenderloin medallions and sweetbreads with chanterelles and frozen violet flower parfait with syrup from the same flowers. The service is first class and we are greeted like old friends.

BERNAY

27300 Eure. Paris 155 – Rouen 60 –
Evreux 50 – Louviers 52.
office.tourisme.bernay@wanadoo.fr.
Peaceful Eure, to be explored at a stroll.

 HOTELS-RESTAURANTS

■ **Hostellerie du** ❀ 🏠
Moulin Fouret
3,5 km s via rte de Saint-Quentin-des-Isles (D33).
Tel. 02 32 43 19 95. Fax 02 32 45 55 50.
lemoulinfouret@wanadoo.fr
www.moulin-fouret.com
Closed Sun. dinner and Mon. (exc. summer).
8 rooms: 55€.
Prix fixe: 39€, 55€. A la carte: 75€.

Rest is guaranteed in the peaceful rooms of this 16th-century mill, looking out onto wooded, flowered grounds. Edwige Deduit provides a friendly smile at the desk, while at the stove her husband François whips up Norman dishes with a modern air. Escalope of foie gras completed with the savors of pain d'épice,

pan-seared turbot with salted butter accompanied by an herbed champagne emulsion, squab served in an individual cocotte with chanterelles and a thin apple tart serve the region with honor.

BERRWILLER see **GUEBWILLER**

BERRY-AU-BAC

02190 Aisne. Paris 161 – Reims 17 –
Laon 30 – Soissons 48.
Champagne lies in sight. We come to pay our respects on the fields of the Great War and walk the Chemin des Dames, site of the Battles of the Aisne, but also to feast in a convivial inn.

● RESTAURANTS

● **La Cote 108** V.COM
N44.
Tel. 03 23 79 95 04. Fax 03 23 79 83 50.
www.lacote108.com
Closed Sun. dinner, Mon., Tue., Christmas–mid-Jan., mid-July–end July.
Prix fixe: 23€, 36€, 47€, 58€.
A la carte: 52€.

Christophe Gilot has decided to settle down in this roadside restaurant opposite World War I Hill 108 after leaving his native Ardennes for Toulousy in Toulouse, then the French Embassy in New York. His classical training has left him with a repertoire of traditional recipes that he masters rather well. Although we might enjoy a slightly more imaginative touch, we have to admit that pressed foie gras terrine with beet chutney, cod filet with citrus seasonings, braised pork cheeks and the soft-centered caramel dessert are neatly done and sensibly priced.

BESANÇON

25000 Doubs. Paris 408 – Dijon 95 –
Belfort 94 – Mulhouse 134.
otsi.besancon@caramail.com.
The birthplace of Victor Hugo still has its citadel, 17th-century facades, beautiful location on the Doubs river, antique brown tiles and old-fashioned air. This city of art and history a step away

from Switzerland, and not far from Franches-Montagnes and the Loue valley painted by Courbet, is charming in all its finery.

 HOTELS-RESTAURANTS

■ Charles Quint

3, rue du Chapitre.
Tel. 03 81 82 05 49. Fax 03 81 82 61 45.
hotel-charlesquint@wanadoo.fr
www.hotel-charlesquint.com
Closed 1 week Feb.
9 rooms: 82–135€.

Just above the cathedral, this antique, aristocratic, 18th-century residence with its mini-garden and new swimming pool boasts delightful rooms in contemporary style and gray tones (often small, unfortunately, but in excellent taste).

■ Hôtel Castan

6, square Castan.
Tel. 03 81 65 02 00. Fax 03 81 83 01 02.
art@hotelcastan.fr / www.hotelcastan.fr
Closed Christmas–beg. Jan., 3 weeks Aug.
10 suites: 95–170€.

By the cathedral, this 17th-century town house provides charming, refined rooms with antique furniture and ornate bathrooms. A fine interior courtyard and a delicious welcome.

■ Novotel

22 bis, rue Trey.
Tel. 03 81 50 14 66. Fax 03 81 53 51 57.
h0400@accor.com / www.accor.com
107 rooms: 59–122€.
Prix fixe: 25€, 47€, 55€, 8€ (child).
A la carte: 30€.

The modern rooms here are perfectly equipped and Hugues Bauman's cuisine neatly phrased. Potato and cod casserole with sundried tomatoes and the vanilla crème brûlée are flawless. A heated swimming pool.

● Le Champagney   V.COM

37, rue Battant.
Tel. 03 81 81 05 71. Fax 03 81 82 19 76.

contact@restaurant-le-Champagney.fr
www.restaurant-le-Champagney.fr
Closed Sun.
Prix fixe: 15,80€, 19,80€, 26,50€, 32€.
A la carte: 40€.

Thierry Garni has taken over this fine establishment. On the terrace or in the historic 16th-century dining room, we savor Alexandre Arnaud's dishes. Morels poached in Vin Jaune and served in puff pastry, roasted pike-perch with Savagnin sauce, quail brochette with country bacon and a pecan crème brûlée are not bad.

● Christophe Menozzi   N·COM

11, rue Jean-Petit.
Tel. 03 81 81 28 01.
Closed Sun., Mon., 10 days mid-Aug.
Prix fixe: 16€ (weekday lunch), 20€, 40€.
A la carte: 45€.

Exit the Mungo Park. By the Doubs, Christophe Menozzi (who was Georges Wenger's sommelier at the Noirmont for fifteen years) provides a refined cuisine and sound wines. Benoît Rostchi, Jocelyne Lotz-Choquart's former lieutenant, carries on at the stoves in simpler fashion (although not all that simple) and fine vintages follow. The beef muzzle salad with balsamic vinegar and asparagus, trout filet with Poulsard wine sauce and a poultry filet with almond milk and oyster mushrooms are pleasant. Do not miss the desserts (raspberry ice cream with Sureau liqueur cream sauce and pain d'épice glazed with orange marmalade and Macvin ice cream), which are the house forte.

● Le Chaland   COM

Promenade Micaud, near the pont Brégille.
Tel. 03 81 80 61 61. Fax 03 81 88 67 42.
chaland@chaland.com / www.chaland.com
Closed Sun. dinner.
Prix fixe: 19€ (lunch), 29,50€, 39,50€, 49,50€. A la carte: 51–58€.

Patrick Bertin closed his promenade Micaud barge for four months to carry out renovation work. Now it is good as new again, open for business in its berth by the Brégille bridge. A cheerful waitress welcomes us with a smile, while Patrick prepares fried cod cakes, foie gras and vegetables slow-cooked in a ceramic dish and breaded and fried sardines that will transport us to other climes. The splendid morel mushroom-stuffed chicken simmered in a cream and Vin Jaune sauce, like the Fougerolle sour cherry vacherin, are the stuff that childhood memories are made of, and bring us back to Franche-Comté. Fine set menus.

● Le 1802 `COM`

Pl Granvelle.
Tel. 03 81 82 21 97. Fax 03 81 82 05 61.
Closed Christmas–New Year's.
Prix fixe: 20€. A la carte: 35€.

Founded to mark the bicentenary of Victor Hugo's birth, this contemporary brasserie is fresh as ever. Its feat is to provide a set menu at 20 that offers noble dishes at base prices. Green lentil and Morteau smoked sausage salad, minced poultry with Cajun seasonings and the Macvin crème brûlée make an excellent impression. We can also be contented with a composed salad or a carpaccio with the great house fries. Note the choice of Tissot or Pupillin Jura wines at giveaway prices (from 15,50 to 21).

● Le Poker d'As `COM`

14, square Saint-Amour.
Tel. 03 81 81 42 49. Fax 03 81 81 05 59.
Closed Sun. dinner, Mon., Christmas–New Year's, 3 weeks July, 1 week Aug.
Prix fixe: 17€, 23€, 32€, 44€,
10€ (child). A la carte: 50–55€.

Jeannette Ferreux in the rustic strawberry and yellow dining room and Vincent Ferreux at the stove serve potato cakes with pan-tossed ceps, oven-browned oysters with mild garlic, a duckling breast with honey and spices and a ginger cream dessert with slow-cooked pineapple and lime jelly, a fine repertoire presenting a frank exchange of views between Doubs and Mediterranean flavors.

● La Table des Halles `N` `SIM`

22, rue Gustave Courbet.
Tel. 03 81 50 62 74. Fax 03 81 50 66 42.

Closed Sun., Mon., 2 weeks Feb.,
2 weeks beg. Aug.
Prix fixe: 16€ (lunch), 20€ (dinner).
A la carte: 35€.

Jean-Pierre Billoux has opened a relaxed tavern on two floors of a former Carmelite cloister by the market. We come to celebrate fried eggs with golden toast, escargot spring rolls, trout filet served with crunchy bacon, a beef daube with sauce gribiche (caper and pickle mayonnaise) and a frozen absinthe parfait, in the capable hands of chef Pierre-Loïc Béard and manager Emmanuel Dumont. The wine list catalogues highly spirited elixirs at bargain prices.

● L'Avant-Goût `SIM`

4, rue Richebourg.
Tel.-Fax 03 81 81 48 86.
avant.gout@free.fr
Closed Sat. lunch, Sun., Mon., Feb. vac.,
1 week at Easter, end July–beg. Aug.
Prix fixe: 16€ (lunch), 33€ (dinner).
A la carte: 36€.

After training with Chevrier and Girardet in Switzerland, Thierry Perrod returned home to share his skills with the people of Besançon. Many regulars hurry here at lunchtime to enjoy the region's finest produce enlivened by occasional exotic flavors at a lower price. Scallop tartare with tomatoes, pork tenderloin with hazelnuts, a pork chop with Arabica-seasoned jus and frozen coffee parfait meet with unanimous approval.

● L'Annexe `N` `SIM`

11, rue du Palais-de-Justice.
Tel. 03 81 53 17 12.
Closed Sun., Mon., 1 week beg. Feb.,
2 weeks mid-Aug.
Prix fixe: 12,50€ (lunch), 15€ (lunch).
A la carte: 45€.

David Jamen has taken over this small contemporary restaurant—something of a deluxe diner—with its lively bar, back room and teak mini-patio. Depending on the vagaries of the market, we enjoy shrewd, contemporary dishes, such as gnocchi with tomatoes and shrimp, a veal sweetbread medallion with reduced balsamic jus, sirloin steak with whole grain mustard sauce and pear tarte Tatin served with pain d'épice ice cream. Aunt Claudine handles the service and the jury returns a unanimously favorable verdict on the lunchtime dish of the day.

● L'O à la Bouche
9, rue du Lycée.
Tel. 03 81 82 09 08. Fax 03 81 82 16 38.
Closed Sat. lunch, Sun., Mon. dinner.
Prix fixe: 11,50€ (weekday lunch), 14,50€ (weekday lunch), 18€ (weekday lunch), 21€ (weekday lunch), 25,50€ (dinner), 35€ (dinner), 45€ (dinner). A la carte: 40€.

Former Guy Savoy pupil Eric Aucant prepares a delicate, honest Southern French cuisine. In the contemporary dining room, marinated salmon with pepper compote, pike-perch in a walnut crust with Savignin cream sauce, wild duck with whelks and a flavorful juniper berry sauce, dark chocolate fondant and rum-flambéed bananas with vanilla ice cream and Sichuan peppercorns are moderately priced.

● Le Temps des Copains
12, rue Richebourg.
Tel. 03 81 61 97 90.
Closed Sun.
Prix fixe: 21€, 26€. A la carte: 30€.

Laurent Fonquernie concocts traditional dishes in a rustic burgundy dining room. Mushrooms in puff pastry, pan-tossed scallops and mussels, veal escalope with ginger seasoning and an assortment of different chocolate mousses make up a fine convivial spread.

In Geneuille (25870). 13 km N. via N57 (rte de Vesoul) and D1.

■ Château de la Reine Blanche
Chemin de la Goulotte.
Tel. 03 81 57 64 64.
Rest. closed Sun. dinner, Mon.
8 rooms: 72–149€.
Prix fixe: 25€ (weekday lunch), 35€, 42€, 58€.

This mansion set in a landscaped garden boasts comfortable, travel-themed rooms (Mykonos, Bruges, Florence) and refined cuisine under the guidance of Jean-François Maire, who left Ecole-Valentin to offer good advice here. In the well-groomed dining rooms with their molded ceilings, we savor flawless, refined, classical dishes. Foie gras terrine, a generous poultry with morels, pike-perch with meat jus, duck breast served with Fougerolles sour cherries and a raspberry dacquoise or variations on the chocolate theme are accompanied by a fine, knowledgeably presented selection of wines.

In Montfaucon (25660). 9 km via N54, D464, D146.

● La Cheminée
3, rte de la Vue-des-Alpes.
Tel. 03 81 81 17 48. Fax 03 81 82 86 45.
restaurantlacheminee@wanadoo.fr
Closed Sun. dinner, Wed., Feb. vac.
Prix fixe: 22€, 46€, 14€ (child).
A la carte: 50–60€.

Philippe Gavazzi and Sylvette Bessei run this charming, rustic establishment. The produce is carefully selected, the combinations subtle and the preparations precise, as shown by the creamy lobster soup with risotto topped with parmesan shavings, roasted Atlantic sea bass with dill-seasoned butter, veal sweetbreads pan tossed with pain d'épice, warm mirabelle plums perfumed with Macvin and Tahitian vanilla ice cream.

BESSE-EN-CHANDESSE

63610 Puy-de-Dôme. Paris 467 – Issoire 31 – Le Mont-Dore 25 – Clermont-Ferrand 47. Fax 04 73 79 52 08. superBesse@laposte.fr. Discover the "absolute" Auvergne so dear to Vialatte, with its black lava houses, Pavin lake and Puy de Montchal volcano.

HOTELS-RESTAURANTS

■ Les Mouflons
Avenue du Sancy.
Tel. 04 73 79 56 93. Fax 04 73 79 51 18.
www.hotel-mouflons-besse.com
Closed mid-Nov.–mid-Dec.

Rest. closed end Oct.–mid-Dec.
50 rooms: 60–90€.
Prix fixe: 12,50€, 26€, 10€ (child).
A la carte: 35€.

Revolution has come to this seventies brown and yellow chalet. Bruno Vesval is now at the helm, watching over Albert Boudet's cuisine. The burgundy rooms are equipped with fine wooden furniture. The swimming pool and fitness center help us burn off a few calories after sampling the country terrine, the salmon filet with beurre blanc sauce and lentils, the steak with Bleu d'Auvergne sauce and frozen nougat with the house honey.

■ **Hostellerie du Beffroy**
26, rue de l'Abbé-Blot.
Tel. 04 73 79 50 08. Fax 04 73 79 57 87.
lebeffroy@orange.fr / wwww.lebeffroy.com
Closed Mon. and Tue. (exc. Feb., July–Aug.),
beg. Nov.–end Dec.
11 rooms: 53–61€. 1 suite: 99–110€.
Prix fixe: 25€, 34€, 42€, 60€.

In this 15th-century establishment, Thierry Legros cooks in contemporary style, preparing gazpacho served with thin slices of thyme-seasoned swordfish, foie gras in yogurt, a salmon trout served whole, country pork chops and fresh fruit crumble in an amusing confiture jar, all beautifully crafted. The eleven rooms have been restored in period fashion.

BETHUNE

62400 Pas-de-Calais. Paris 214 – Calais 83
– Lille 39 – Arras 35 – Amiens 93.
The Grand-Place, belfry and cellars, the memory of the executioner immortalized by Dumas and the red brick art deco houses should be more than enough to attract gourmets to this Northern stronghold where a very gifted chef practices his art.

 HOTELS-RESTAURANTS

■ **Le Vieux Beffroi**
48, Grand-Place.
Tel. 03 21 68 15 00. Fax 03 21 56 66 32.

www.levieuxbeffroi.fr
16 rooms: 50–75€.
Prix fixe: 10,70€, 22,90€, 6€ (child).
A la carte: 32€.

In the center of town, this good, classical hotel provides contemporary rooms all in beige or blue (depending on the floor) and honest dishes at the Bruxelles Café. Bone marrow with sel de Guérande, a local fish stew, Flemish carbonade and finally a traditional crème brûlée are easily enjoyable.

In Busnes (62350). 12 km n via rte de Calais.
● **Marc Meurin**
Le Château de Beaulieu
1098, rue de Lillers.
Tel. 03 21 68 88 88. Fax 03 21 68 88 89.
contact@chateaudebeaulieu.fr
www. chateaudebeaulieu.fr
Closed 1 week beg. Jan., 3 weeks Aug.
Rest. closed Sat. lunch, Sun. dinner, Mon.
16 rooms: 140–260€. 4 suites: 320–400€.
Prix fixe: 55€, 85€, 110€ (wine inc.), 145€
(wine inc.). A la carte: 125€.

Deep in Béthune country ("nowhere land", as he likes to remind us), Northern wizard Marc Meurin and his colorful wife Claudine have acquired this château which would not look out of place in Wonderland. The setting stands on the border between classical architecture and contemporary art, with boldly decorated rooms and suites and elegant salons offering sauna, massage and therapy of all kinds. In the kitchen, the crack team put together by genial redhead Marc, including faithful lieutenants Philippe Géniteau, Franck Hochedez and Sébastien Morand, prepares magnificently balanced dishes cooked to perfection. Landais duck foie gras bathed in Port on the grill and served with celery root ravioli, langouste in a crust of chorizo, line-fished Atlantic sea bass served on a seasoned bed of New Zealand spinach and the raw oysters are rare jewels. Tribute to the Flanders produce he loves so much takes the form of the savory "well-brought-up" squab, served with gnocchi in sauce and coriander-seasoned chard, but also the country lamb, its roasted chops accompanied by a mild onion gratin and bathed in thyme flower–seasoned pan juices. The frozen Béthune strawberry parfait with marshmallow syrup provides a delightful conclusion. The first-rate service and selected wines keenly recommended by Christian Caron—vintages that match the high standards of the stunning cuisine—help to make the Château de Beaulieu one of the finest restaurants in France.

In Gosnay (62199). 5 km sw via N41 and D181.

■ Chartreuse du Val Saint-Esprit

1, rue de Fouquières.
Tel. 03 21 62 80 00. Fax 03 21 62 42 50.
levalsaintesprit@lachartreuse.com
www.lachartreuse.com
65 rooms: 120–250€. 1 suite: 380€.
Prix fixe: 32€, 55€, 70€. A la carte: 96€.

This 18th-century château built on the ruins of an antique Carthusian convent offers spacious guest rooms in bright colors, recently renovated with an eye to preserving the spirit of the past, including period furniture. All have a view of the grounds. Genuine banquets organized by Franck Gilabert take place in the luxurious dining room. Guests feast on veal sweetbreads glazed in a sauce flavored with orange zest, line-fished sea bass in pastry, blanquette de veau with chanterelles, a roasted veal cutlet served with heirloom vegetables before the flambéed crêpes, or may just settle for a less expensive bite at the neighboring brasserie, the Vasco.

BETTENDORF see ALTKIRCH

LE BETTEX see
SAINT-GERVAIS-LES-BAINS

14430 Calvados. Paris 217 – Caen 30 – Cabourg 15 – Lisieux 27 – Pont-l'Evêque 32.
One of the prettiest villages in Normandy, with its central square, antique market, old houses and manor.

● RESTAURANTS

● Le Pavé d'Auge

Beuvron-en-Auge.
Tel. 02 31 79 26 71. Fax 02 31 39 04 45.
Closed Mon. and Tue. (exc. July–Aug.), end Nov.–end Dec., 1 week Feb. vac.
Prix fixe: 32,50€, 45€, 48,50€.

It's worth going out of our way to sample Jérôme Bansard's regional cuisine. On the Normandy Landing route, we take time out to pause at this neo-rustic restaurant under the covered market and taste the quahog clams with slices of garlic, John Dory with green and red tomato compote and a grilled veal belly accompanied by spring vegetables in sage-seasoned sauce. The roasted apricots with honey and rosemary ice cream provide an excellent conclusion. A delightful welcome and reasonable check.

27210 Eure. Paris 177 – Honfleur 15 – Le Havre 32 – Deauville 31 – Evreux 77.
office-de-tourisme-beuzeville@wanadoo.fr.
This large, hospitable village with its main square and admirable inns is the gateway to the finest beaches on the Normandy coast.

 HOTELS-RESTAURANTS

■ Le Petit Castel

Pl du Général-de-Gaulle.
Tel. 02 32 57 76 08. Fax 02 32 42 25 70.
auberge-du-cochon-dor@wanadoo.fr
www.le-cochon-dor.fr
Closed mid-Dec.–mid-Jan.
13 rooms: 55–96€.
Half board: 65–116€.

This adjunct to the Cochon d'Or, is a restful halt, with its well-kept, comfortable rooms all in pink and its garden, pleasant indeed when the sun shines.

● Le Cochon d'Or

64, rue des Anciens-d'AFN.
Tel. 02 32 57 70 46. Fax 02 32 42 25 70.

www.le-cochon-dor.fr
Closed beg. Jan.–beg. Feb. Rest. closed Mon.
16 rooms: 60–76€.
Prix fixe: 18€, 25€, 32€ (dinner), 42€
(dinner), 12€ (child). A la carte: 38–48€.

Madame Rouillon has bought this 1900 Norman hostelry providing traditional rooms and cuisine to match. Stéphane Breval whips up chitterling sausage with Camembert sauce, sole meunière, Calvados-seasoned tripe and a tarte Tatin with cider caramel.

LES BEZARDS

45290 Loiret. Paris 139 – Auxerre 79 – Orléans 74 – Joigny 57 – Montargis 23 – Gien 18.
This milestone on the highway immortalized in song by music hall legend Charles Trénet is also a choice stop between the forest of Orléans and the banks of the Loire.

 HOTELS-RESTAURANTS

● **Auberge des Templiers**
N7, Les Bézards.
Tel. 02 38 31 80 01. Fax 02 38 31 84 51.
templiers@relaischateaux.fr
www.lestempliers.com
Closed 3 weeks Feb.
22 rooms: 110–275€. 8 suites: 295–650€.
Prix fixe: 55€, 120€. A la carte: 120€.

Fall is the great time of year in Les Bézards, with its belling stags and magnificent hunting season spreads. However, this particular property by the N7 highway, with its peaceful garden, luxury cottages and rooms refurbished in period style is a delightful place to stay all year round. Philippe Dépée, exemplary host and Relais & Châteaux pioneer, watches over his inn like a protective father. He is aware of the smallest detail in the life of the kitchen and cellar. At the stove, Hervé Daumy teases precise flavors from high-quality produce. The langoustine marinade, pigeon with herb-seasoned foie gras, wild Atlantic sea bass with spinach, cod filet with virgin olive oil and tomato sauce, Montargis praline-glazed pigeon or the sirloin steak with slow-cooked shallots remain firmly on track, faithful to theme of rejuvenated classics. In the game season, the entire menu celebrates the local hare and deer. For dessert, the tarte Tatin is a model of the genre and the gently spiced slow-cooked tomatoes are well worth the effort too. Excellent service and a fine English-style bar prolong our pleasure with cigars and brandies.

BEZIERS

34500 Hérault. Paris 767 – Perpignan 92 – Marseille 234 – Montpellier 70.
mairie.de.beziers@wanadoo.fr.
The Saint-Nazaire cathedral, Saint-Jacques garden, banks of the Orb and nine locks of the Canal du Midi are the outstanding features of this lowland town in the heart of sweet France.

 HOTELS-RESTAURANTS

■ **Imperator**
28, allée Paul-Riquet.
Tel. 04 67 49 02 25. Fax 04 67 28 92 30.
info@hotel-imperator.fr
www.hotel-imperator.fr
45 rooms: 51–85€.

In the famous alleyways of Béziers, Marie-Louise Planes' hotel boasts rooms, each decorated in a different color, and a delightful patio.

■ **Champ de Mars**
17, rue de Metz.
Tel. 04 67 28 35 53. Fax 04 67 28 61 42.
www.hotel-champdeMar.com
10 rooms: 30–48€.

Mr. Schuller has bought this hotel just outside the center with its calm blue and yellow rooms. Renovation in progress.

● **L'Ambassade**
22, bd de Verdun.
Tel. 04 67 76 06 24. Fax 04 67 76 74 05.
lambassade-beziers@wanadoo.fr
Closed Sun., Mon., end May–beg. Jan.
Prix fixe: 28€, 36€, 52€.

In the spacious dining room with its resolutely contemporary décor in aluminum, frosted glass and pale woodwork, Patrick Olry's flavors are firmly ensconced in their region and day. We yield to the lure of chilled egg custard sauce with pork ears, cut into cubes served over dandilion salad, the red tuna in a sesame crust or a stuffed rack of lamb served with variety cut brochettes seasoned with garam masala. Desserts including the tender waffle with Gariguette strawberries and mascarpone conjure up childhood memories. The wines are up to the same standard and it is hard to choose from the 700 on offer, including top of the bill Languedoc and Roussillon vintages.

● **L'Octopus**

12, rue Boïeldieu.
Tel. 04 67 49 90 00. Fax 04 67 28 06 73.
www.restaurant-octopus.com
Closed Sun., Mon., Christmas–New Year's,
1 week beg. Jan., mid-Aug.–beg. Sept.
Prix fixe: 20€ (lunch), 28€ (lunch), 48€,
68€. A la carte 65€.

This refreshingly imaginative modern restaurant is now up to speed. In the kitchen, Fabien Lefebvre, formerly at the Bristol and Juana, reinterprets dishes from the greater South of France in an ultracontemporary style. The results are the crunchy and tender pork "lollipop", the roasted John Dory with simmered purple artichokes and shellfish and the farm-raised pork with roasted squid, served with an individual cocotte of young broad beans and new potatoes. Desserts revised with equal care, such as the "nitro-chlorophyl", are just as successful. The wines are shrewd and the check reasonable.

● **Les Caves de la Madeleine** SIM

2, pl de la Madeleine.
Tel.-Fax 04 67 28 17 08.
Closed Sat. lunch, Sun.
Prix fixe: 12€ (lunch), 14€ (lunch),
17€ (lunch), 20€. A la carte: 45€.

This vaulted, contemporary-style basement with summer terrace serves fresh

dishes at low prices. Foie gras terrine with slow-cooked caramelized onion, pan-seared scallops with baby hearts of endive and beet soup, lamb tenderloin medallions seasoned with thyme flower and served wih a potato cake and the crème brûlée with coconut ice cream and chocolate ganache are well crafted.

● **Le Vieux Siège** SIM

6, pl des Trois-Six.
Tel. 04 67 28 96 12.
Closed Tue. dinner.
Prix fixe: 12,90€ (lunch), 18,90€, 26€
(wine inc.), 34€, 7,90€ (child).
A la carte: 35€.

The Cléments have turned their salmon and burgundy retro bistro into an essential eatery. We enjoy the oven-roasted oysters, foie gras in puff pastry with apples or a veal escalope in cream sauce before the chocolate moelleux for dessert.

In 34490 Lignan-sur-Orb. 7 km nw via D19.

■ **Château de Lignan** ❀ 🏨

Place de l'Eglise.
Tel. 04 67 37 91 47. Fax 04 67 37 99 25.
chateau.lignan@wanadoo.fr
48 rooms: 92–114€. 1 suite: 122–150€.
Prix fixe: 25€, 39€, 62€. A la carte: 58€.

This former bishop's residence converted into a modern hotel is just the thing for travelers seeking rest. The atmosphere is delightful, with wooded grounds, the Orb river nearby, Jacuzzi, outdoor swimming pool and spacious rooms in green and red. In the care of Eric Faverolle, we recharge our batteries with the frog legs and truffles, the marbled duck foie gras terrine, the stuffed salmon trout, the oven-crisped pork trotter and the berry vacherin.

In 34370 Maraussan. 6 km via D14.

● **Parfums de Garrigues**

33, rue de l'Ancienne-Poste.
Tel.-Fax 04 67 90 33 76.
Closed Tue., Wed.
Prix fixe: 23€, 35€, 40€, 55€,
10€ (child). A la carte: 50€.

If Jean-Luc Santuré learned one thing as a pupil of Witzigman in Munich, Trois-gros in Roanne and Maximim in Nice, it was to select the right produce and treat it with respect. Now he is preparing it in his own inspired, gourmet fashion. In a dining room in the colors of Oc, we savor marbled foie gras terrine with figs and honey, the roasted wild Mediterranean sea bass, leg of lamb with chops, accompanied by assorted garden vegetables and then a caramelized mille-feuille with light strawberry mousse. Delicious Languedoc wines into the bargain.

BIARRITZ

64200 Pyrénées-Atlantiques. Paris 776 – Bayonne 9 – Saint-Sébastien 50 – Bordeaux 199 – Pau 124.
biarritz.tourisme@biarritz.tm.fr.
The gourmet, society, seaside capital of the Basque country is still true to its time-honored image. The beach of kings (and king of beaches) is here, home to the Basque Coast surfing community and the fashionable bars where they drink sherry and cider, as in Seville and Donostia. Will a mention of the Bellevue casino's slender silhouette by the vast ocean, excursions leading out to sea and the covered market with its country fair ambiance be enough to sum up a town so often dismissed as a watering place for tourists in search of a round of golf or a tan? Biarritz is not a rustic town (that is Bayonne) or a frontier one (Hendaye), but simply home to a rather European good taste, with produce found only in the region: touron au chocolat, a Basque-style nougat, local cod and squid. The cuisine here has an accent and its chefs are riding high.

■	HOTELS

■ Hôtel du Palais

1, av de l'Impératrice.
Tel. 05 59 41 64 00. Fax 05 59 41 67 99.
reception@hotel-du-palais.com
www.hotel-du-palais.com
121 rooms: 260–520€. 33 suites: 500–3500€.

A gift from Napoleon III to the Empress Eugénie, this opulent palace by the ocean brims with luxury. From the Empire-style furniture equipping the guest rooms to the seawater swimming pool, hushed lounges and refined cuisine served at the Rotonde, Villa Eugénie and Hippocampe (see Restaurants), not to mention the extraordinarily high standard of service, nothing is too much for the guests here, not even the prices, fit for an Empress too! This year, a sizable fitness center brings a contemporary dimension to the hotel.

■ Sofitel Thalassa Miramar

13, rue Louison-Bobet.
Tel. 05 59 41 30 01. Fax 05 59 24 77 20.
h2049@accor-hotels.com / www.thalasssa.com
110 rooms: 267–446€.

A combination of great comfort and the benefits of thalassotherapy make this luxury hotel a choice destination for vacationers mindful of their health and welfare. It offers rooms with a terrace overlooking the sea, indoor and outdoor swimming pools, steam bath and Jacuzzi, not to mention numerous personalized therapy packages and health cuisine at the Pibales. (See Restaurants: Le Relais Miramar.)

■ Château du Clair de Lune

48, av Alan-Seeger, rte d'Arbonne.
Tel. 05 59 41 53 20. Fax 05 59 41 53 29.
hotel-clair-de-lune@wanadoo.fr
www.chateauduclairdelune.com
17 rooms: 70–130€.

Enjoy the high life in this superb 1900 residence bordered by gardens and offering elegantly decorated rooms named for flowers. The old hunting lodge is fitted out in a more contemporary but equally comfortable style.

■ Mercure Thalassa Régina & Golf

52, av de l'Impératrice.
Tel. 05 59 41 33 00. Fax 05 59 41 33 99.
h2050@accor.com / www.mercure.com
58 rooms: 125–240€. 8 suites: 215–380€.
Prix fixe: 38€. A la carte: 60€.

The Miramar thalassotherapy center, a renowned golf course, a fitness center, Jacuzzi and heated swimming pool: there is plenty to do at this Belle Epoque hotel with its refined rooms and refined health cuisine.

■ Radisson SAS
1, carrefour Hélianthe.
Tel. 05 59 01 13 13. Fax 05 59 01 13 14.
reservations.biarritz@radissonsas.com
www.biarritz.radissonsas.com
150 rooms: 150–310€. 9 suites 190-470€.
Prix fixe: 27€ (wine inc.).

Not far from the sea, this hotel's hi-tech architecture draws businessmen and surfers from far and wide. All enjoy the comfortable rooms decorated with bullfight posters and pictures, numerous facilities (fitness center, panoramic rooftop swimming pool) and chic brasserie cuisine. The Onyx restaurant has been fully renovated.

■ L'Alcyon
8, rue Maison-Suisse.
Tel. 05 59 22 64 60. Fax 05 59 22 64 64.
www.hotel-alcyon-biarritz.com
Closed Jan., Feb.
15 rooms: 70–110€.

Renovated in a contemporary style by the designer of the Maison Garnier, this 1900 rocaille corner hotel near the center is deceptive indeed. Charm, joviality and restraint reign on every floor. A cozy lounge.

■ Mercure Plaza Centre
Av Edouard VII.
Tel. 05 59 24 74 00. Fax 05 59 22 22 01.
www.groupe-segeric.com
69 rooms: 125–260€.

Behind the art deco facade of this seafront hotel, the rooms have finally been renovated in thirties style. A very pleasant lounge bar.

■ Altess
19, av Reine-Victoria.
Tel. 05 59 22 04 80. Fax 05 59 24 91 19.

altess@wanadoo.fr / www.altesshotel.com
Closed Nov.
44 rooms: 70–200€.

The very central location, delectable welcome and comfortable modern rooms and duplexes make this a practical stopover.

■ Le Caritz
14, rue Port-Vieux.
Tel. 05 59 24 84 84. Fax 05 59 24 19 41.
lecaritz@aol.com / www.lecaritz-biarritz.com
12 rooms: 72–133€. 2 suites: 110–165€.

A step away from Port-Vieux beach, this modern hotel boasts comfortable rooms with terraces overlooking the sea. The Jacuzzi and fitness center are very pleasant. There remain the prices, rather high given the quality of service.

■ Edouard VII
21, av Carnot.
Tel. 05 59 22 39 80. Fax 05 59 22 39 71.
www.hotel-edouardVII.com
Closed Feb.
18 rooms: 70–120€.

This English-style Biarritz villa and garden have great charm. We like the well-kept rooms in light shades with their Louis XV furniture and refined bathrooms. The location near the market and Côte des Basques beach is also an asset.

■ Tonic Hôtel Biarritz
58, av Edouard-VII.
Tel. 05 59 24 58 58. Fax 05 59 24 86 14.
tonic.biarritz@wanadoo.fr / www.tonichotel.com
55 rooms: 155–295€. 6 suites: 295–395€.

Overlooking the main beach and casino, this hotel provides modern rooms in varied tones, first class balneotherapy and a quality restaurant (see Restaurants: La Maison Blanche).

■ Maison Garnier
29, rue Gambetta.
Tel. 05 59 01 60 70. Fax 05 59 01 60 80.
www.hotel-biarritz.com
Closed 2 weeks Jan., 2 weeks Feb.
7 rooms: 90–130€.

Yves Gelot greets guests warmly in his delightful 19th-century Biarritz residence. We enjoy the minimalist charms of the guest rooms with their art deco furniture and polished décor.

■ Auberge du Relais

44, av de la Marne.
Tel. 05 59 24 85 90. Fax 05 59 22 13 94.
www.auberge-biarritz.com
Closed 3 weeks Dec. (exc. Christmas),
3 weeks Jan. Rest. closed Tue.
12 rooms: 57€. 1 suite: 110€.
Prix fixe: 21€, 31€. A la carte: 45€.

This inn with its trim, rustic rooms and two modern lounges takes us on a delicious trip through time. The dining room pays tribute to tradition. The lobster with arichokes, wild turbot with pattypan squash, a grilled veal kidney and an apple tart with caramel ice cream are flavorsome.

■ Maïtagaria

34, av Carnot.
Tel. 05 59 24 26 65. Fax 05 59 24 27 37.
www.hotel-maitagaria.com
Closed 2 weeks beg. Dec.
11 rooms: 66–69€. 4 suites: 72–90€.

Eric Irubetagoyena runs this very distinctive hotel with its neat rooms. The pleasant garden terrace is the perfect place to relax and the prices are affable.

■ Palacito

1, rue Gambetta.
Tel. 05 59 24 04 89. Fax 05 59 24 33 43.
www.hotel-palacito.com
Closed 1 week Nov.
27 rooms: 36,50–94,50€.

The steps leading directly to the main beach are a powerful asset and the regularly redecorated rooms practical. The Romance tearoom is charming.

■ Le Petit Hôtel

11, rue Gardères.
Tel. 05 59 24 87 00. Fax 05 59 24 32 34.
www.petithotel-biarritz.com

Closed 2 weeks end Nov., 2 weeks Feb.
12 rooms: 56–77€.

This fine, practically located hotel, with its small, colorful, comfortable rooms and warm welcome, is a very pleasant place to stay.

■ Le Président

Pl G.-Clemenceau.
Tel. 05 59 24 66 40. Fax 05 59 24 90 46.
www.lepresident-biarritz.com
64 rooms: 65–210€.

Right in the center of town, this seventies tower with its practical, well-equipped rooms offers very handy accommodation. The welcome we receive has room for improvement.

■ Romance

6, allée des Acacias.
Tel. 05 59 41 25 65. Fax 05 59 41 25 83.
hotel-la-romance@wanadoo.fr
Closed mid-Jan.–beg. Mar.
10 rooms: 50€.

Just outside the town center, this modern hotel boasts peaceful rooms decorated in bright colors and a friendly welcome.

In Anglet (646000). 4 km se via N10.

■ Le Château de Brindos

1, allée du Château.
Tel. 05 59 23 89 80. Fax 05 59 23 89 81.
info@chateaudebrindos.com
www.chateaudebrindos.com
Closed 20 Feb.–10 Mar.
Rest. closed Sun. dinner, Mon.
24 rooms: 215–305€. 5 suites: 275–530€.
Prix fixe: 32€ (lunch, wine inc.), 50€, 90€.
A la carte: 68€.

Former French rugby captain Serge Blanco has breathed new life into this fine 1900 residence set in ten hectares of grounds bordered by a lake. The guest rooms are luxurious and comfortable, and the fitness center and swimming pool relaxing. The cuisine by Antoine Antunès is served in the circular dining room. Tuna carpaccio with sundried tomato petals, Basque-style crab-stuffed tomatoes, the rare cod with kokotxas (a Basque country delicacy using the head of the fish), breaded and pan-fried saddle of milk-fed lamb, veal sweetbreads seasoned with aromatic herbs and a chocolate soufflé play to a subtly modernized gourmand Basque score.

RESTAURANTS

● Villa Eugénie
& La Rotonde
At Hôtel du Palais, 1, av de l'Impératrice.
Tel. 05 59 41 64 00. Fax 05 59 41 67 99.
reception@hotel-du-palais.com
www.hotel-du-palais.com
Prix fixe: 55€, 100€. A la carte: 110€.

For more than fifteen years, Jean-Marie Gautier has been part of the Hôtel du Palais. Adopted by the Basque country, this native of Berry has taken its local culinary traditions to heart. In the small dining room known as the "Villa Eugénie" and in the great Rotonde opening onto the sea, spider crab in a fine cream-enriched soup, the rouget with pan-tossed little squid accompanied by creamy squid ink-flavored rice and duck foie gras, pan-seared and napped with carrot jus form topical, local produce-based meals. For dessert, if only the "instant chocolate" dessert lasted for hours! Very professional service and a regal wine list. (See Hotels.)

● Relais Miramar
At Sofitel Thalassa Miramar,
13, rue Louison-Bobet.
Tel. 05 59 41 30 00. Fax 05 59 24 77 20.
h2049@accor-hotels.com
Prix fixe: 55€, 70€, 65€. A la carte: 80€.

Whether preparing dishes for the health food eatery (the Pibales) or the gourmet restaurant (the Relais), Patrice Demangel lets produce guide his touch. In the hands of this sturdy native of the Vosges, the best of land and sea reveals all its flavors. The other evening, the gentle Patrice prepared a lasagne of jumbo shrimp, cucumber and celery root, served with a foamy fish bouillon and a grilled grouper with a crushed tomato and fine aromatic herb sauce for a very cheerful dining room full of residents here for their health (showing that slimming need not be a punishment). Dessert was an orange moelleux in a silky dark chocolate crust with vanilla-seasoned Suzette sauce. All beautifully crafted work.

● Les Platanes
32, av Beau-Soleil.
Tel. 05 59 23 13 68.
www.campagneetgourmandise.com
Closed Sat. lunch, Mon., Tue. (Sept.–June), lunch July–Aug.
Prix fixe: 35€ (lunch), 63€.

Bruno Locatelli, who worked with Patrick Pignol at the Relais d'Auteuil in Paris for thirteen years, has enthusiastically taken up the torch in this small establishment where Arnaud Daguin was such a success. The décor has been improved and enhanced with attractive pictures and ornaments. In the dining room, the escargot fricassée with a parsley emulsion and chitterling sausage jus, the foie gras served with quince and sea lettuce, the grilled John Dory in a citrus and lemongrass infusion, served with artichokes and mashed potatoes worthy of Robuchon, are an incitement to attend on a regular basis. Pan-tossed milk-fed lamb chops and tenderloin medallions and the tender shoulder, with basil flavored cooking juices, are a testament to genuine talent, as is the soft-boiled egg with Jurançon cream and passion fruit. An address to remember.

● Campagne et Gourmandise
52, av Alan-Seeger.
Tel. 05 59 41 10 11. Fax 05 59 43 96 16.
www.campagneetgourmandise.com
Closed Sun. dinner (exc. July–Aug.), Mon. lunch, Wed., 2 weeks Feb.–beg. Mar.
Prix fixe: 43€, 65€, 20€ (child).
A la carte: 30–60€.

With its fine view of the Pyrénées, Annick and André Gauzère's 18th-century farmhouse serves up the region on a platter. André selects the finest local produce and prepares it with great simplicity.

In the chic, rustic dining room with its stone and beams, we savor the rabbit mosaic, the veal sweetbreads with foie gras, jumbo shrimp medallions with prunes and asparagus, roasted milk-fed lamb with parsley-seasoned breading and the dark chocolate croustillant with pralines and passion fruit sauce.

● L'Opale

17, av Edouard VII.
Tel. 05 59 24 30 30.
Call for opening days, hours.
A la carte: 55€.

This terrace brasserie (formerly the Operne) offers a view of the main beach. Refurbished in contemporary fashion and relaunched by a team from Bordeaux, it serves a topical cuisine that could do with a touch more simplicity. Carpaccio, a goat cheese "bonbon" salad, grilled small squid (with an unnecessary pesto) and the lamb brochette with curry-seasoned yogurt cream are not bad. The desserts (variations on the strawberry theme, the chocolate mint cup) are pleasant, however, the wine is rather expensive.

● Café de la Grande Plage `COM`

1, av Edouard VII.
Tel. 05 59 22 77 77. Fax 05 59 22 77 83.
www.lucienbarriere.com
Prix fixe: 18,50€ (lunch), 27€,
9,50€ (child). A la carte: 37€.

This Biarritz Coupole refurbished contemporary-style in red and green serves toast with eggplant spread, small squid with Serrano ham, lamb shank braised with rosemary and pain perdu bread pudding. Oysters in grand quantity.

● La Maison Blanche `COM`

At Tonic Hôtel Biarritz, 58, av Edouard VII.
Tel. 05 59 24 58 58. Fax 05 59 24 86 14.
www.tonichotel.com
Prix fixe: 39€, 69€, 12€ (child).

Behind the impersonal, modern hotel facade, a lively restaurant serves a creative cuisine. Newcomer Rémy Le Bretton prepares roasted langoustines with

Serrano ham chips, turbot served with mashed potatoes with pine nuts, breaded veal sweetbreads with almonds and osso buco jus and finally, a pretty variation on the theme of the pina colada.

● Sissinou

5, av Foch.
Tel. 05 59 22 51 50. Fax 05 59 22 50 58.
restaurant.sissinou@wanadoo.fr
Closed Sun., Mon.,Nov. 1, Feb. vac.
Prix fixe: 42€. A la carte: 50€.

Michel Cassou-Debat's restaurant, Sissinou, has more going for it than just a contemporary, minimalist setting. This Troisgros, Crillon and Grand Véfour veteran also concocts fresh, lively dishes. The breaded and fried sardines with tomato and cilantro, the rouget filet sprinkled with spicy jalapeno juice, a poultry fricassée with young vegetables and the pan-simmered cherries accompanied by rice pudding have an easy charm.

● Philippe ○`SIM`

30, av du Lac-Marion.
Tel. 05 59 23 13 12.
lafarguephilippe@hotmail.com
Closed lunch, Mon., Tue., 2 weeks Nov.,
2 weeks Mar.
Prix fixe: 50€ (dinner), 65€ (dinner).

Our 2006 discovery is doing well. In his meticulously designed contemporary workshop, Philippe Lafargue looks cheerful indeed, as do his fans, who are delighted to savor the culinary treats prepared by this Ducasse and Chibois veteran formerly at the Palais and Miramar. The monkfish liver with hazelnut and coriander, the St. Jean de Luz-style tuna belly and the wood fire-roasted suckling pig are entertaining new takes on local dishes. The desserts meet the same high standards, including the excellent cherry-, chocolate- and peach-based preparations. Given the quality of the cellar too, you might as well reserve a table for your next meal as you leave.

● Le Clos Basque

12, rue Louis-Barthou.
Tel. 05 59 24 24 96. Fax 05 59 22 34 46.

Closed Sun. dinner, Mon., 2 weeks Oct.,
2 weeks Feb., 1 week at end June.
Prix fixe: 24€. A la carte: 29€.

This eatery with its very pleasant patio is a discreet but friendly establishment. The wonderfully inexpensive set menu compiled by Béatrice Viateau offers a flavorsome fennel and dill soup with a wheat tortilla and monkfish osso buco with white beans and little cuttlefish, then has us agonizing over whether to choose the rouget or the sirloin steak, before ending with a strawberry charlotte.

● Le Chalut ⓃSIM
"Venta Biarriote"
46, av Edouard VII.
Tel. 05 59 22 07 37.
Closed lunch, Sun., Thu.

Half bistro, half restaurant, this pleasant eatery with its ethnic crimson and chocolate décor is worth a visit for the tapas-style dishes—fried cod cakes, monkfish a l'ajillo (with garlic), Basque veal stew (axoa), whiting with chorizo—and sensibly priced wines (Rioja, Irouléguy). The players from the Biarritz Olympique rugby team love it here.

● Bistro Aroma SIM
18, rue de la Bergerie.
Tel. 05 59 22 09 37.
Closed Sun., Mon., 3 weeks June.
A la carte: 38€.

Natacha and Guillaume Teissier serve up Italy at reasonable prices. In the dining room with its waxed wooden tables, we make short work of the eggplant and zucchini carpaccio, jumbo shrimp tempura, veal escalope Milanese and the tiramisu.

● Le Bistro des Halles SIM
1, rue du Centre.
Tel.-Fax 05 59 24 21 22.
Closed Sun., end Nov.–beg. Dec., 2 weeks June.
Prix fixe: 12,80€ (lunch). A la carte: 36€.

We are favorably impressed by this bistro with its sea- and bullfight-themed

décor and old posters advertising the aperitifs of yesteryear. Benoît Mathelié delights food lovers with his finely balanced market-based dishes. The atmosphere has a rough good humor and the cuisine is in good taste. Oven-crisped scallops with black olives, Atlantic sea bass in a salt crust, veal kidneys in parsley and garlic and the fruit sabayon with raspberry sauce are very honest.

● Chez Albert SIM
At the port des Pêcheurs.
Tel. 05 59 24 43 84. Fax 05 59 24 20 13.
www.chezalbert.fr
Closed Wed. (exc. July–Aug.), 2 weeks beg. Dec., beg. Jan.–mid-Feb.
Prix fixe: 38€, 13€ (child).
A la carte: 45–50€.

Biarritz society flocks to this seafood bistro on the harbor to feast on Serge Caumont's cuisine. Lobster gazpacho, salmon and langoustine sushi, Spanish-style sea bream, duck breast and a pear financier are equal to their task. The fine wines from close at hand or further afield are chosen by Bruno Garcia.

● L'Huîtrier et la Plancha SIM
22, rue Harispe.
Tel. 05 59 41 01 41. Fax 05 59 23 48 85.
www.chezbenat.com
Prix fixe: 17€ (lunch). A la carte: 35€.

Like a protective father, Bernard Benat watches over this seafood restaurant with its dining room all in blue and yellow. The plates of Parra charcuterie, the grilled scallops, fish cooked at the table on a hot stone (pierrade), the boneless rib steak with sea salt and the flambéed apple tart go down without a hitch.

● Le Saint-Amour SIM
26, rue Gambetta.
Tel. 05 59 24 19 64.
Prix fixe: 16–18€ (lunch). A la carte: 40€.

Recently renovated, this tiny place by the market serves fine regional produce. The ceps presented in a jar, foie gras in terrine, fresh cod served on a bed of lentils, rack of lamb in an aromatic herb crust and the house crumble have the wholesome flavor of simplicity. A modest check into the bargain.

● La Tantina de Burgos

2, pl Beaurivage.
Tel. 05 59 23 24 47. Fax 05 59 23 71 67.
Closed Sun., Mon., 3 weeks Christmas–New Year's.
Prix fixe: 9€ (child). A la carte: 37€.

David Arruabarrena and Stéphane Tellechea have successfully maintained the streetwise ambiance of this restaurant. We come here for the friendly atmosphere, the grilled baby squid, the Spanish-style whiting, Basque veal stew (axoa) with Espelette peppers and crème brûlée. The wood décor in burgundy shades is decorated with pictures by the painter Aski.

In Anglet (64600). 4 km se via N10.

● Rio Grande Saloon

62, av de Bayonne, N10.
Tel. 05 59 15 12 86. Fax 05 59 31 00 36.
Prix fixe: 18€, 25€, 6,90€ (child).
A la carte: 30€.

Jérôme Woerth moseys on over to the stove of this Western saloon–style eatery and cooks up a mess of guacamole, wings, minced salmon, beef fajitas and barbecued bananas.

In Arcangues (64200). 8 km, past la Négresse on D254 / D3.

● Le Moulin d'Alotz

Chemin Alotz Errota, 3 km via rte d'Arbonne.
Tel. 05 59 43 04 54.
benoitsarthou@hotmail.fr
Closed Tue., Wed., 15 days Nov., Jan., 1 week at end June.
A la carte: 60€.

Sole master aboard his mill, Benoît Sarthou is the happiest of men. In the dining room or on the teak terrace, this spirited chef and owner serves up a delightfully shrewd regional cuisine. The oven-crisped tuna with spring onions, the pork tenderloin in a mild garlic cream sauce and the potato risotto with ceps are a joy. The desserts too, like the slow-cooked fruit served with pistachio cake, know that the way to our heart is through our stomach. The regional wines perfectly complement these honest dishes.

BIDARRAY

64780 Pyrénées-Atlantiques. Paris 803 – Biarritz 36 – Cambo-les-Bains 17 – Saint-Jean-Pied-de-Port 21.
A true Basque village with its pelota court, hills dotted with sheep and Pont d'Enfer (Bridge of Hell) spanning the waters of the Nive.

HOTELS-RESTAURANTS

■ Ostapé

Domaine de Chahatoa.
Tel. 05 59 37 91 91. Fax 05 59 37 91 92.
contact@ostape.com
www.ostape.com
Closed mid-Nov.–mid-Mar. Rest. closed Mon.
22 suites: 220–540€.
Prix fixe: 43€, 58€.

As we put this guide to bed, Alain Ducasse has announced that he is moving away from this little corner of paradise where he has had a certain amount of bad luck. In any case, this extensive Basque residence is worth a visit for its forty-five hectares of hilly land and scattered houses with whitewashed facades and bull's blood shutters. The stud farm, panoramic swimming pool, cozy rooms and friendly, paneled dining room have great character, as do the dishes prepared by Alain Souliac (who opened the neighboring Iparla inn), served according to the menu of the day. Red tuna from Saint-Jean-de-Luz, grilled small squid, sea lamprey cooked in wine with vegetables and herbs, rack of lamb bathed in cooking juices, a tender veal medallion, the pretty apricot Tatin and the pineappple ravioli with white chocolate mousse are among his triumphs.

■ Barberaennea

Pl de l'Eglise.
Tel. 05 59 37 74 86. Fax 05 59 37 77 55.
www.hotel-barberaennea.fr
Closed mid-Nov.–beg. Apr.
9 rooms: 32–59€.
Prix fixe: 16€, 22€, 7,50€ (child).
A la carte: 20€.

Country peppers in an omelet, cod-stuffed piquillos napped in a red pepper coulis, duck rondo (breast, foie gras, Port sauce) and the apple and pear tarte Tatin: the menu here is staunchly loyal to its region. The Basque country is everywhere in this typical inn, from the rustic rooms to the warm welcome.

● Auberge Iparla

Pl du Fronton.
Tel. 05 59 37 77 21. Fax 05 59 37 78 84.
iparla2@wanadoo.fr / www.alainducasse.com
Closed Wed. (off season).
Prix fixe: 22€. A la carte: 40€.

At the foot of the mountains, this hikers' inn taken over by Alain Ducasse is a simple joy. The rustic décor and traditional cuisine go well together. By the huge fireplace, we make short work of the Landes foie gras, the cod-stuffed pimientos, the slow-cooked pork which is then seared on the grill just before serving, the famous blood sausage and a traditional gâteau Basque. The service is lively and the tab minds its manners.

BIDART

64210 Pyrénées-Atlantiques. Paris 782 – Biarritz 7 – Bayonne 16 – Pau 124 – Saint-Jean-de-Luz 9.
bidarttourisme@wanadoo.fr.
A Basque village and its fine inland restaurant perched on high ground overlooking the ocean.

 HOTELS-RESTAURANTS

■ Villa l'Arche

Chemin Camboénéa.
Tel. 05 59 51 65 95. Fax 05 59 51 65 99.
villalarche@wanadoo.fr / www.villalarche.com

Closed mid-Nov.–mid-Feb.
6 rooms: 95–145€. 2 suites: 170–255€.

This charming Basque-style residence has been turned into a fully equipped hotel, with attractive, renovated rooms that almost all enjoy a sea view. The garden has direct access to the beach.

■ Domaine de Bassilour

Rue Burruntz.
Tel. 05 59 41 90 85. Fax 05 59 41 87 62.
www.domainedebassilour.com
13 rooms: 85–120€. 3 suites: 120–140€.

With its half-timbered farmhouse, Second Empire château and engaging rooms with antique furniture, this is the ideal place for a refreshing stay in the country.

■ Hôtel du Fronton

Place Sauveur-Atchorena.
Tel. 05 59 54 72 76.
www.hoteldufronton.com
Closed 20 Nov.–20 Dec. Rest. closed Mon.
8 rooms: 140–180€.

We first met Eric Lataste in Saint-Jean-de-Luz's Bar Basque. Now the owner of the Tantina de la Playa has redesigned this fine village hotel. The contemporary rooms, some with a balcony overlooking the square and sea, boast elegant materials, wood in gray tones, bright colors and regional paintings by local artists. A bar on the first floor and a terrace.

■ Ouessant-Ty

Rue Erretegia.
Tel. 05 59 54 71 89. Fax 05 59 47 58 70.
www.ouessant-ty.com
8 rooms: 65–100€.

This Basque-Breton hostelry is ideal for families with its marine décor and honest *crêperie*. Equipped with rattan furniture, the rooms are spacious and comfortable.

● Les Frères Ibarboure

S via N10, rte d'Ahètze, chemin de Ttlaliénéa, in Guéthary.
Tel. 05 59 47 58 30. Fax 05 59 54 75 65.

contact@freresibarboure.com
www.freresibarboure.com
Closed mid-Nov.–mid-Dec., 2 weeks Jan.
Rest. closed Wed. (off season).
12 rooms: 115–200€.
Prix fixe: 18€ (lunch), 34€ (lunch), 44€,
49€, 65€, 98€ (child). A la carte: 72€.

Inseparable brothers Martin and Philippe Ibarboure have opened this extensive estate in the countryside—with fully equipped, cheerful, pink lounges, luxurious rooms and a swimming pool in the garden—just a step away from the Basque Coast and their parents' establishment (the Briketenia in Guéthary). We come here for the warm welcome, opulent wine list, reasonable prices and the brothers' trademark, traditional cuisine prepared with dedication. Ceps served three ways, squid stuffed with pork trotters, tuna belly with sauce gribiche (caper and pickle mayonnaise), foie gras served hot with rhubarb and roasted peach and the dessert palette (superb frozen cherry and Lzarra parfait) are Basque and flavorsome. This is the kind of hostelry we are always pleased to see.

● La Cucaracha ✺SIM
Rue de l'Uhabia.
Tel.-Fax 05 59 54 92 89.
Closed Tue., Wed., mid-Nov.–mid-Dec.,
2 weeks beg. Jan.
A la carte: 38€.

Enjoying Philippe Hyppolyte's cuisine, we soon forget that his restaurant is on the busy N10 highway. In the friendly, colorful dining room, gratinéed mussels from Spain, fresh cod filet, grilled lamb chops, splendid boneless rib steak and the baba au rhum are paragons of reliability. The Irouléguy wines are splendid and the atmosphere (above all in the evening) fantastic. Make sure you reserve!

● La Tantina de la Playa ✕SIM
Plage du centre. (Town-center beach.)
Tel. 05 59 26 53 56.
Closed mid-Nov.–mid-Dec.
A la carte: 38€.

This beachside restaurant with its large dining room decorated with a fresco, wooden tables and terrace, serves honest preparations based on the best of the day's catch, and more. Fried cod cakes (acras de morue), fish soup, tuna belly, grilled baby squid, pan-tossed locally fished sole (céteau) and the lamb chops are tremendously good. Frozen nougat and gâteau Basque, too. We wash all this down with a pleasant, light Bordeaux red and imagine ourselves on the far side of the world.

● Blue Cargo SIM
Plage d'Ilbarritz.
Tel. 05 59 23 54 87. Fax 05 59 23 55 73.
blucar@wanadoo.fr
Closed Oct.–Apr.
A la carte: 45€.

This is a favorite meeting place for the privileged children of wealthy local and Parisian families. In the two restaurants by the ocean, they enjoy the music as they feast on a vegetable and mozzarella cake, swordfish steak with lime and peppers, grilled rib eye steak and the chocolate mi-cuit, a soft-centered chocolate cake, before beginning another night's festivities with a manzana verde or two.

● La Plancha d'Ilbarritz SIM
Plage d'Ilbaritz.
Tel.-Fax 05 59 23 44 95.
Closed Wed. (winter), mid-Nov.–Christmas.
A la carte: 35–55€.

Packed in summer, this beach bistro offers a warm welcome and faultless regional cuisine, including the Spanish-style cod, grilled sea bass with lemon butter, rib eye steak on the bone and a pineapple gazpacho for dessert.

BILLIERS

56190 Morbihan. Paris 464 –
Nantes 88 – Vannes 28 – La Baule 44 –
La Roche-Bernard 17.
Morbihan, a sentinel standing at the gates of the Atlantic, with the Pointe de Penlan as its ultimate bulwark.

HOTELS-RESTAURANTS

● **Domaine de** ○ ❀
   Rochevilaine
Pointe de Penlan-Sud.
Tel. 02 97 41 61 61. Fax 02 97 41 44 85.
domaine@domainerochevilaine.com
www.domainerochevilaine.com
33 rooms: 126–367€. 3 suites: 235–490€.
Prix fixe: 39€ (weekday lunch), 66€,
98€, 120€. A la carte: 75–90€.

Standing on the ridges of rock by the sea, this hamlet, with its indoor and outdoor swimming pools, consists of a Breton-style manor and fishermen's and salt marsh workers' cottages. The manor is home to a balneotherapy center and the cottages house spacious guest rooms. In the restaurant, Patrice Caillaut pays tribute to the fine local produce. In the hands of this Taillevent veteran, cold lobster in consommé, fisherman-style cod served with ratatouille, sea bass baked in a salt crust served with fennel-seasoned béarnaise sauce, sliced rib eye steak and the raspberries in their juice with sorbet are refreshing.

BIOT

06410 Alpes-Maritimes. Paris 917 – Cannes 19 – Nice 23 – Antibes 6 – Cagnes 11 – Grasse 21.
tourisme.biot@wanadoo.fr.
In this Provençal hinterland near the coast nestles a village of potters, with its inns, museum dedicated to Léger and Rosary reredos in the church.

 HOTELS-RESTAURANTS

■ **Domaine du Jas**
625, rte de la Mer.
Tel. 04 93 65 50 50. Fax 04 93 65 02 01.
www.domainedujas.com
Closed mid-Nov.–beg. Mar.
19 rooms: 100–235€.

Surrounded by extensive grounds with a heated outdoor swimming pool, these modern villas offer well-equipped studios and apartments, which is about all we can say for this hotel, with its barely decent board cuisine, unexceptional facilities and high prices.

● **Les Terraillers** ○ V.COM
11, rte du Chemin-Neuf.
Tel. 04 93 65 01 59. Fax 04 93 65 13 78.
lesterraillers@tiscali.fr / www.lesterraillers.com
Closed Wed., Thu., mid-Oct.–end Nov.
Prix fixe: 59€, 75€, 95€, 115€.

Chantal and Pierre Fulci's 16th-century pottery is a choice eatery. We like the kiln converted into a private dining room and the bright colors of the old-fashioned main dining room. We also appreciate Claude Jacques and Mikael Fulci's topical Provençal dishes, which they prepare together. The lobster ravioli in bisque, Mediterranean sea bass baked in a salt crust with squid "croutsicroutons" (crunchy croutons) and a rabbit trilogy with lemon-infused sauce tack deftly between tradition and modernity. At the end of the meal, the thin apricot tart with almond ice cream lasts but a second. The service is assiduous and the cellar well stocked.

● **Le Jarrier** COM
30, passage de la Bourgade.
Tel. 04 93 65 11 68. Fax 04 93 65 03 61.
www.lejarrier.com
Prix fixe: 19€, 23€, 30€. A la carte: 80€.

The young, dynamic, determined team here continue to run this once-famous residence with great energy. Fabien Ageloux, a dining room veteran of the Trois Marches, Louis XV and Cigalon; Sébastien Broda, formerly at the Palme d'Or and Belle Otéro; and lastly pastry chef Pascal Picasse, who served at the Pyramide and Belles Rives, manage it meticulously. The cozy setting, attractively set tables, welcoming lounge bar and walls decorated with contemporary and neo-impressionist paintings make this a charming spot indeed. The creamy cauliflower soup, roasted jumbo shrimp with curry-infused oil, Mediterranean sea bass with asparagus and morels, veal cutlet with chanterelles and the chocolate mille-feuille are worth the trip. Unfortunately, the prices à la carte tend to soar.

● **Chez Odile**   **SIM**
Chemin des Bachettes.
Tel. 04 93 65 15 63.
Closed lunch (exc. off season), Wed. (off season), Thu. (off season), beg. Dec.–beg. Feb.
Prix fixe: 19€ (lunch), 30€.

Provence holds its salon in the Toscanos' rustic inn. By the open kitchen or on the flowered terrace, we feast on the reliable cuisine concocted by André. Eggplant served with a pepper coulis, escargots in puff pastry with creamed garlic sauce, a boneless rabbit saddle with tapenade stuffing and an osso buco with prunes cooked in red wine are all up to scratch. Odile welcomes us with great warmth.

BIRIATOU see HENDAYE

BIRKENWALD

67440 Bas-Rhin. Paris 460 – Strasbourg 33 – Molsheim 22 – Saverne 11.
A village at the foot of the Vosges, a step away from Dabo rock in the heart of Alsace's "Little Switzerland".

◨   HOTELS-RESTAURANTS

● **Au Chasseur**
7, rue de l'Eglise.
Tel. 03 88 70 61 32. Fax 03 88 70 66 02.
hotel.au-chasseur@wanadoo.fr
www.chasseurbirkenwald.com
Closed Jan. Rest. closed Mon., Tue. lunch, Thu. lunch.
21 rooms: 60–83€. 3 suites: 120€.
Prix fixe: 15€ (lunch), 39€, 52€, 65€, 10€ (child). A la carte: 55€.

Times are still changing at the Gasses' establishment. Refurbished with wood paneling, the dining room in this Relais du Silence hostelry is charming indeed, like the hunting-themed bistro the Jägerstübe, friendlier than the seven-ties facade. The luxurious rooms, swimming pool and fitness center make this hotel a good-natured stopover. The cuisine—always prepared with refinement by Roger, the father—has become light, fresh and a touch Southern in the hands of Yann, the son, formerly at the Ducasse restaurant in Monaco. There is no pretension on the plates here, just dishes that sparkle with freshness and truth. The game terrine, a poultry and aspic terrine, scallop carpaccio, grilled turbot served with creamy chanterelle risotto, veal kidney with hand-rolled egg noodles and mustard sauce and a tender veal cutlet with vegetables served from a cocotte at the table are splendid, exemplary variations on theme of pure, fresh produce. The desserts follow the same rules: a frozen vacherin, local steamed bread with preserved fruit (dampfnüdle) and a hot fruit soufflé are tailored classics.

BITCHE

57230 Moselle. Paris 436 – Strasbourg 74 – Saverne 51 – Sarreguemines 34.
office-tour@ville.bitche.fr.
Huddled between its native Moselle and Alsace, the German-speaking capital of Bitcherland conceals a wealth of wonders among its golf course, citadel, lakes, crystal factories and forests.

◨   HOTELS-RESTAURANTS

■ **Relais des Châteaux Forts**
6, quai E.-Branly.
Tel. 03 87 96 14 14. Fax 03 87 96 07 36.
hotelrelaisdeschateaux@wanadoo.fr
Rest. closed Thu., Fri. (Oct.–Mar.), Jan.
30 rooms: 40–50€.
Prix fixe: 11€ (weekday lunch), 18€, 26€, 8,40€ (child). A la carte: 35–45€.

This good traditional hotel located at the foot of the citadel offers comfortable blue rooms in period style and a simple *pension* cuisine served in an orange-yellow dining room. Lamb shanks with Provençal vegetables and flambéed Grand Marnier crème brûlée make an excellent impression.

YOUNG CHEF OF THE YEAR

● Le Strasbourg 🏠Ⓞ V.COM

24, rue du Colonel-Teyssier.
Tel. 03 87 96 00 44. Fax 03 87 96 11 57.
le.strasbourg@wanadoo.fr
www.le-strasbourg.fr
Closed 2 weeks Feb. Rest. closed Sun.
dinner, Mon., Tue. lunch.
10 rooms: 45–85€.
Prix fixe: 22€, 29€, 40€, 52,50€.
A la carte: 56€.

Young, energetic and well trained (at the Auberge de l'Ill in Illhaeusern, the Vieux Couvent in Rhinau and the neighboring Arnsbourg in Baerenthal), Lutz Janisch forges ahead, innovating tirelessly. We like him just as he is at this inn in the center of town, now a select hostelry whose exotic, travel-themed rooms offer a touch of the modern. A German from Kottbus who moved to Bitcherland for love of the delightful, smiling Cynthia, he not only renovated this local institution, but changed its character completely. The cuisine followed suit, reflecting the training of a highly gifted pupil who turns all he touches into gold. There is no pretension or flashiness here, just a lively, shrewd, appetizing menu that is reasonably priced given the delights it holds. Gravlax-style marinated veal tongue with caper blossoms, a wonderful mix of rustic and sophisticated, the tender shredded wild watercress with a chanterelle emulsion and Serrano ham and fresh frog legs perfumed with roasted garlic provide a lesson in tradition reinterpreted with a topical flavor. Then comes, roasted skin-side down, the rouget served with brandade, pine nuts and black olives. Next? Veal sweetbreads served in hollowed-out bread, plus a creamy mushroom ragout and the tender Argentinian Angus beef filet with fried onions, fine red wine sauce and a purée of gratin dauphinois, a way of showing that the dynamic young chef is also perfectly at home in a classical vein, expressing his creativity without losing sight of the basics. For dessert, the peach soup with raspberry wine served with lovage ice cream and the white chocolate mousse with sour cherry ice cream are marvelously fresh delights. A young, very keen sommelier presents an outrageously broad selection of wines at every price. Visit the Strasbourg now before all the dedicated followers of fashion catch on!

● Auberge de la Tour   COM

3, rue de la Gare.
Tel. 03 87 96 29 25. Fax 03 87 96 02 61.
restaurant.la.tour@wanadoo.fr
Closed Mon., Tue. dinner, vac. Mar.
Prix fixe: 23€, 52€, 9€ (child). A la carte: 50€.

Marc Steffanus has taken over the reins of this turreted, neo-1900 bistro originally opened by his parents. A young veteran of the Strasbourg Bueheriesel, he concocts dishes that blend Provençal and Asian notes, including Black Tiger shrimp sautéed in curry spices, roasted Atlantic sea bass filet with eggplant caviar, lamb chops in an herb crust with flavorful jus and stuffed pineapple carpaccio sprinkled with honey and served with coconut ice cream. A restaurant to watch closely.

BIZE-MINERVOIS

11120 Aude. Paris 815 – Narbonne 21 – Béziers 23 – Saint-Chinian 17.
A small Minervois village between the limestone plateaus and vineyards.

 HOTELS-RESTAURANTS

● La Bastide Cabezac   Ⓞ🏠

18-20, hameau de Cabezac (hamlet of Cabezac).
Tel. 04 68 46 66 10. Fax 04 68 46 66 29.
www.labastidecabezac.com
Closed 1 week at end Nov., 2 weeks Dec., Feb. vac. Rest. closed Mon. lunch, Tue. lunch, Wed. lunch.
9 rooms: 75–130€. 3 suites: 220€.
Prix fixe: 16€ (lunch), 25€, 46€, 69€, 12€ (child). A la carte: 65€.

In the heart of Minervois wine country, this 18th-century post house attracts a good deal of attention. Hervé Dos Santos' cuisine deserves to be enjoyed with a healthy appetite. This veteran of the Appart' in Paris, formerly with Guérard, Drouant and Lapérouse, concocts restorative Southern dishes. In the old-fashioned dining room, the langoustine cut in strips served with crushed tomatoes, turbot filet with a fresh herb risotto and the lamb medallion with red onions taste simple and ring true. The more finely crafted desserts, including the dark chocolate dessert with a mild spice syrup, also have their charm. After this substantial spread, it is time for a nap in one of the rooms styled in ochre.

BLAESHEIM

67113 Bas-Rhin. Paris 491 – Molsheim 15 – Strasbourg 19 – Sélestat 34.
A step away from Strasbourg-Entzheim airport, an urbane village in the heart of the sauerkraut fields.

 HOTELS-RESTAURANTS

■ Le Boeuf
32, rue du Maréchal-Foch.
Tel. 03 88 68 68 99. Fax 03 88 68 60 07.
auboeuf.resa@wanadoo.fr
www.hotel-au-boeuf.com
Closed 2 weeks beg. Jan., 2 weeks end July–mid-Aug. Rest. closed Fri., Sat. lunch.
22 rooms: 56–130€.
Prix fixe: 15€, 25€, 8,50€ (child).
A la carte: 45€.

This village inn is a handy halt on the airport road. Sandra and Eric Walter provide comfortable, contemporary guest rooms and dishes like the dining rooms, in a very Alsatian style. They include presskopf, head cheese and aspic terrines, fish choucroute, three-game and potato baekeofe and a cold quince dessert or the kirsch parfait, all reliably prepared.

● Schadt
8, pl de l'Eglise.
Tel. 03 88 68 86 00. Fax 03 88 68 89 83.

schadt@wanadoo.fr
Closed Sun. dinner, Mon., end July–beg. Aug.
Prix fixe: 30€, 45€, 60€. A la carte: 60€.

We love the rough good humor of this inn opposite the church. In the dining room with its frescos by Tomi Ungerer, Raymond Waydelich and Christian Geiger, we make short work of the roguish dishes concocted by the mercurial Philippe Schadt. Duck foie gras in brioche, pike-perch filet with morel mushrooms, the divine fried catch of the day, the beef Rossini and a seasonal fruit vacherin are washed down with first-rate Alsatian wines.

BLAMONT

54450 Meurthe-et-Moselle. Paris 454 – Sarrebourg 25 – Phalsbourg 35 – Nancy 70 – Saverne 45.
Near the regional park and lakes, this crossroads community between Alsace and Lorraine is well worth a visit for its church and old houses.

 HOTELS-RESTAURANTS

■ Hostellerie du Château
2, rue Florent-Schmitt.
Tel. 03 83 42 09 07
06 71 04 30 28 (for hotel on Sun. and Mon.).
Fax 03 83 42 58 44.
Rest. closed Sun. dinner, Mon.
7 rooms: 43–50€.
Prix fixe: 17€, 24€, 40€.

The Leyendecker brothers, who worked at the Verte Vallée in Munster, have taken over this town center hostelry and meticulously renovated it. It now offers spacious rooms, along with polished cuisine in its spruce dining room. Daniel at the tables and Benoît in the kitchen have a constant eye to their guests' enjoyment, amply ensured by foie gras terrine infused with vanilla flavors, arborio risotto with mushrooms, a braised pike-perch with Toul escargots and saddle of rabbit stuffed with mirabelle plums. A rare jewel.

BLAUZAC see **UZES**

BLENOD-LES-PONT-A-MOUSSON see
PONT-A-MOUSSON

BLERE

37150 Indre-et-Loire. Paris 233 – Tours 27 –
Blois 46 – Montrichard 17.
tourisme@blere-touraine.com.
If you have read *Pour venger Pépère*, the
superb Touraine crime thriller by **ADG**, you will
already be familiar with this pretty town on the
south bank of the Cher.

 HOTELS-RESTAURANTS

● **Le Cheval Blanc**
Pl de l'Eglise.
Tel. 02 47 30 30 14. Fax 02 47 23 52 80.
le.cheval.blanc.blere@wanadoo.fr
www.lechevalblancblere.com
Closed Jan.–mid-Feb. Rest. closed Sun.
dinner, Mon., Fri. lunch.
12 rooms: 58–78€.
Prix fixe: 21€, 42€, 48€, 59€.
A la carte: 60€.

In the heart of town, Michel Blériot's 17th-
century building provides a charming
welcome. Its guest rooms overlook a flower-
filled courtyard, and the heated swimming
pool is a bonus, but the hostelry's special gift is its regional cuisine, flawlessly
expressed by the master of the house. The
pan-tossed langoustines, pike-perch with
beurre blanc sauce, minced veal sweetbreads, pan-simmered butterflied wild
duck filet and the divine Grand Marnier-
flavored puffed crêpes are perfectly in tune
with tradition and our expectations. A fine
cellar, especially well stocked with Vouvray,
Montlouis and Chinon vintages.

BLESLE

43450 Haute-Loire. Paris 491 – Aurillac 95
– Brioude 24 – Issoire 38 – Saint-Flour 37.
This delicious Haute-Loire village has two claims
to celebrity: its fine church of Saint-Pierre and
its fictitious elementary school teacher, star of
a hit French television series.

 HOTELS-RESTAURANTS

■ **La Bougnate**
Place du Vallat.
Tel. 04 71 76 29 30. Fax 04 71 76 29 39.
contact@labougnate.com
www.labougnate.com
Closed mid-Jan.–mid-Mar.
8 rooms: 55–85€.
Prix fixe: 20€, 25€, 35€.

Jean-Philippe Ferraro and his wife have
taken over the 18th-century inn made
famous by popular French TV series
"L'Instit". The trim rooms are very much
fit for purpose, but we mainly enjoy the
casual good humor of the bistro and its
honest dishes. A marbled slow-cooked
pork cheek and lentil terrine, pike filet with
polenta, veal filet with honey and a verbena-infused sorbet score full marks.

BLIENSCHWILLER

67650 Bas-Rhin. Paris 505 – Strasbourg 43
– Sélestat 11 – Dambach 3.
An unobtrusive halt on the wine route, this
authentic village has charm to spare with its
pleasant cellars, great wine (Winzenberg) and
the Vosges mountains nearby.

 HOTELS-RESTAURANTS

■ **Hôtel Winzenberg**
58, rte des Vins.
Tel. 03 88 92 62 77. Fax 03 88 92 45 22.

Winegrowing family the Dresches have
had the bright idea of providing rustic,
typically Alsatian guest rooms in their
home. The breakfasts here are enough
to coax the latest of risers from their bed
and the check is well behaved.

● **Le Pressoir de Bacchus** SIM
50, rte des Vins.
Tel. 03 88 92 43 01.
lepressoirdebacchus@wanadoo.fr
Closed Tue., Wed. lunch, Christmas,
Feb. vac., 2 weeks beg. July.
Prix fixe: 24€, 9€ (child). A la carte: 43€.

Good humor is the rule in this authentic *winstub*. The local wines selected by Gilles Grucker are hard to resist. We first met his wife Sylvie at her parents' Clos des Délices back in Ottrott. Now she delights us with her hunter's salad with wild pigeon filet and raspberry-infused vinegar, her carp ravioli with minced young onions and a light smoky cream sauce and the pheasant filet with a side of creamy polenta flavored with chanterelles and a fine lingonberry sauce. The crème brûlée duo is not bad and the prices remember their manners.

BLOIS

41000 Loir-et-Cher. Paris 184 – Orléans 61 – Tours 65 – Le Mans 111.
info@loiredeschateaux.com.

Once, it was not noted for its epicurean delights, but Blois has now come to terms with its status as a superb beacon of the Loire Valley and provided us with new restaurants, fine bistros, fashionable chefs and culinary artisans. They are all as deserving of a visit as the handsome château, where the Duke of Guise was slaughtered on the King's orders in 1588. Do not miss the art gallery, the church of Saint-Nicolas, the convent of the Jacobins, the cathedral of Saint-Louis or the Evêché gardens.

 HOTELS-RESTAURANTS

■ Holiday Inn Garden Court
26, av Maunoury.
Tel. 02 54 55 44 88. Fax 02 54 74 57 97.
holiblois@wanadoo.fr
www.holiday-inn.com/blois
Rest. closed Sat. lunch, Sun. lunch.
78 rooms: 75–96€.
Prix fixe: 16,50€, 20€, 7,30€ (child).
A la carte: 35€.

Handily located near the corn exchange, this chain hotel holds no surprises: functional rooms, useful facilities and a run-of-the-mill *pension* cuisine.

■ Mercure Blois Centre
28, quai Saint-Jean.
Tel. 02 54 56 66 66. Fax 02 54 56 67 00.
h1621@accor.com
www.mercure.com
96 rooms: 91–118€.
Prix fixe: 14,50€. A la carte: 35€.

On the Loire châteaux route, this hotel offers all modern conveniences. Along with the fitness center, Jacuzzi and heated swimming pool, the rooms equipped with contemporary furniture, cozy lounge bar and traditional local cuisine ensure a pleasant stay.

● Hôtel Médicis
2, allée François-Ier.
Tel. 02 54 43 94 04. Fax 02 54 42 04 05.
le.medicis@wanadoo.fr
Closed Jan.
Rest. closed Sun. dinner (off season).
12 rooms: 87–115€.
Prix fixe: 21€, 68€. A la carte: 35–50€.

The cozy rooms with their attractive period furniture make for a restful stay in this 1900 establishment run by the Garanger family. The renovated dining room is now decked out in red, black and gold. In this Hungarian-style setting, Monsieur Garanger's dishes express all their subtlety and exuberance. A tender duck flavored with cocoa, with young vegetables in bouillon with a drizzle of Arabica-infused vinaigrette, the sirloin steak, the mix of varied beans with sweet peas and pears, beef prepared two ways (brasied and roasted) served with slow-cooked lentils with Roquefort as well as the acidulated raspberry with passion fruit dessert and the chocolate dessert with berry sorbet are focused works of imagination. Grégory Broussard, the owners' new associate, manages the generous wine list.

■ Hôtel Anne de Bretagne
31, av du Dr-Jean-Laigret.
Tel. 02 54 78 05 38. Fax 02 54 74 37 79.
annedebretagne@free.fr
Closed beg. Jan.–beg. Feb.
27 rooms: 45–58€.

A step away from the château, Eric Coullon's establishment has ample charm, particularly the third floor with its delightful garrets. All the classically styled rooms combine good taste and comfort and are decorated in different colors. A pleasant welcome and a steam bath.

● L'Orangerie du Château ○ V.COM

1, av du Dr-Jean-Laigret.
Tel. 02 54 78 05 36. Fax 02 54 78 22 78.
contact@orangerie-du-chateau.fr
www.orangerie-du-chateau.fr
Closed Sun. dinner, Wed.,
mid-Feb.–mid-Mar.
Prix fixe: 33€, 68€. A la carte: 80€.

This restaurant occupying a converted outbuilding of the François I château serves refined dishes in an equally elegant setting. The building, which dates from the 15th century, has lost none of its splendor down the ages. Enchanted by the long, bright dining room that opens onto a terrace, we succumb to the attractions of the cuisine meticulously prepared by Jean-Marc Molveaux and smilingly served by his wife Karine. We savor the fennel carpaccio with rouget and a citrusy vinaigrette and sorbet, an oven-cooked John Dory in shellfish bouillon, as well as a delicate squab breast in a spicy crumble with the thighs oven-browned and crispy, before succumbing to the variations on a raspberry theme for dessert. The wines also know how to work their charm. Watch out, though: the awakening can be rude indeed when the check arrives.

● Rendez-Vous des Pêcheurs ○ COM

27, rue du Foix.
Tel. 02 54 74 67 48. Fax 02 54 74 47 67.
www.rendezvousdespecheurs.com
Closed Sun., Mon. lunch, 3 weeks Aug.
Prix fixe: 28€ (lunch), 49€, 74€.
A la carte: 79€.

Having trained with Bernard Loiseau, Christophe Cosme knows how to get the most out of his fine, selected produce of land and sea. We delightedly sit down to slow-cooked saffron-seasoned carrot flan, oysters and poached quail eggs, whipped sweet potatoes, pike-perch in papillote, cold sliced tête de veau with sauce ravigote, oven-crisped veal sweetbreads with foie gras, pan-seared Charolais sirloin steak served with baker's-style potatoes and the pear dessert, with warm cake, a lightly salted crumble and chocolate sorbet, all in a relaxed atmosphere with attentive, individualized service.

● L'Espérance   COM

189, quai Ulysse-Besnard.
Tel. 02 54 78 09 01. Fax 02 54 56 17 86.
lesperance.habault@wanadoo.fr
Closed Sun. dinner, Mon., 2 weeks Aug.
Prix fixe: 19,50€, 29,50€, 39,50€,
12€ (child). A la carte: 45€.

Eric Habault's restaurant is a gourmet eating place towards the N152 highway. In its brightly colored, contemporary setting, his elaborate, lively dishes live up to their promise. We enjoy a crab and asparagus tip salad, rabbit saddle slow cooked with thyme and served with a citrusy vinegar emulsion and the Breton shortbread cookies with pan-tossed apples or frozen walnut parfait. The Loire wines meet the same standards.

● Au Bouchon Lyonnais   SIM

25, rue des Violettes.
Tel.-Fax 02 54 74 12 87.
www.aubouchonlyonnais.com
Closed Sun. (exc. July and Sept.),
Mon. (exc. July and Sept.), 24 Dec.–16 Jan.
Prix fixe: 19€. A la carte: 35€.

Frédérick Savy serves true Lyonnaise cuisine in his easygoing, *bouchon*-style restaurant. We savor an individual duck foie gras terrine, pike fish quenelles, tête de veau and tongue with sauce ravigote, apple and pear crumble with vanilla ice cream, all washed down with a Coteau Lyonnais as fresh as the morning dew.

● Le Triboulet   SIM

Pl du château.
Tel. 02 54 74 11 23. Fax 02 54 56 16 57.
www.letriboulet.com

Closed New Year's, Mar.
Prix fixe: 15€, 20€, 25€.
A la carte: 50–55€.

Just to the left of the château, Marie-Jo and Joël Saugier have turned this small rustic inn, with its exposed stone and cheery fire in the winter, into a tasteful halt. They regale us simply, with the foie gras terrine and figs, sole meunière, veal sweetbreads with sour cherries, a wine-poached prune tarte Tatin and a mandarin orange sorbet. A fine choice of Touraine wines at unpretentious prices.

BLUFFY (COL DE)

74290 Haute-Savoie. Paris 551 – La Clusaz 24 – Albertville 38 – Megève 51 – Annecy 11. At the foot of a jagged mountain, the pass and its eponymous inn.

 HOTELS-RESTAURANTS

● **Auberge des** SIM
  Dents de Lanfon
Tel. 04 50 02 82 51. Fax 04 50 02 85 19.
Closed Jan., 2 weeks end June.
Rest. closed Mon., Tue. (exc. July–Aug.).
7 rooms: 50–70€.
Prix fixe: 19€, 35€. A la carte: 38€.

Right at the foot of a jagged rock formation called the Dents de Lanfon, Sylvain Bonnet and Sandrine Sarkissian's Savoy chalet piles on the charm. A marbled foie gras terrine, crayfish gratin and a roasted whiting filet with scallop carpaccio and shellfish cream sauce are delightful. The brochette of duck breast, caramelized with mountain honey, is not bad, and the omelet *norvégienne* (baked Alaska) conjures up childhood memories. Afterwards, we enjoy a welcome nap in one of the Savoy-style, wood-trimmed guest rooms.

BOERSCH

67530 Bas-Rhin. Paris 488 – Strasbourg 36 – Molsheim 12 – Obernai 4 – Rosheim 3. A village on the wine route with its theater square, fine Renaissance houses and riot of flowers in season.

● RESTAURANTS

● **Le Châtelain** N COM
41, rue Monseigneur-Barth.
Tel. 03 88 95 83 33. Fax 03 88 95 80 63.
contact@lechatelain.com
Closed Mon., Tue. lunch, Thu. lunch,
3 weeks end Jan.–mid-Feb.
Prix fixe: 22€, 48€, 22–24€ (winstub).

In this 1722 cellar, Désiré Schaetzel, wine-grower and owner of the Clos des Délices hotel in Ottrott, organizes wine tastings and serves polished meals. Next to the dining room, where we savor foie gras carpaccio or pan-tossed jumbo shrimp, a little corner of a *winstub* allows one to snack, at a reasonable price, on blood sausage with apples or tête de veau. The house red is readily drinkable.

BOIS-L'ABBESSE see LIEPVRE

BOIS DE LA CHAIZE see NOIRMOUTIER-EN-L'ILE

LE BOIS-D'OINGT

69620 Rhône. Paris 450 – Lyon 35 – Villefranche-sur-Saône 17. In the land of golden stone and Beaujolais.

● RESTAURANTS

● **Gudefin** N SIM
Place de la Libération.
Tel. 04 74 71 60 61.
Closed dinner (exc. weekends), Mon., Aug.
Prix fixe: 19,50€, 26,50€, 30€.

Yves and Lucette Gudefin run this reliable village inn with its very simple bistro setting, neon, Formica counter, naïve frescos framing a huge fireplace and timeless dishes. Mushroom terrine, warm sausage, frog legs tossed in garlic and parsley, pan-seared boneless rib steak and chicken in cream and mushroom sauce slip down smooth as velvet.

LE BOIS-PLAGE-EN-RE see ILE DE RE

BOLLENBERG see ROUFFACH

BONLIEU

39130 Jura. Paris 444 – Champagnole 23 –
Morez 24 – Lons-le-Saulnier 33.
In the Haut-Doubs district, this village offers
forests, fresh air and cross-country skiing
routes used as backpacking trails in the summer, not to mention the panoramic view from
the Dame Blanche, giving a fuller picture of the
superb scenery.

 | HOTELS-RESTAURANTS

■ **La Poutre**   ⌂
25, Grande-Rue.
Tel. 03 84 25 57 77. Fax 03 84 25 51 61.
Closed Mon. (exc. July–Aug.), Tue. (exc.
July–Aug.), end Oct.–beg. May.
8 rooms: 39–59€.
Prix fixe: 20€, 40€, 65€, 9€ (child).
A la carte: 50–55€.

François and Sandrine Moureaux run
this 1734 farm with its classical rooms
and colorful, paneled dining room. François concocts new takes on traditional
dishes, based on the season and market produce. Escargots in seafood broth,
thin-sliced trout with Morteau smoked
sausage, minced veal kidneys with sorrel cream sauce and the praline crêpes
are well crafted. Excellent wines to be
discovered.

BONNE-FONTAINE see PHALSBOURG

BONNETAGE

25210 Doubs. Paris 468 – Belfort 69 –
Besançon 65.
At a height of 960 meters, not far from Swiss
Franches Montagnes, a village open to nature.

 | HOTELS-RESTAURANTS

● **L'Etang du Moulin**   ⌂
1,5 km via D236.
Tel. 03 81 68 92 78. Fax 03 81 68 94 42.

etang.du.moulin@orange.fr
Closed 10 days at end Dec., Jan., 1 week beg.
Feb. Rest. closed Tue. (Sept.–June),
Wed. (exc. dinner July–Aug.).
19 rooms: 48–65€.
Prix fixe: 22€, 30€, 42€, 85€.

This large chalet in a lush setting provides simple, snug rooms with a view of
the lake. However, we are more interested in what takes place in the kitchen,
supervised by Jacques Barnachon, who
prepares local produce with skill and
dedication. The morels in puff pastry
with Vin Jaune-seasoned cream sauce,
a white truffle risotto, trout poached
in Chardonnay or duck foie gras with
berries and the simmered lentils and
smoked bacon are enchanting. The welcome is delectable, the prices unpretentious and the sweets (such as the
blueberry dessert, flavored with licorice
and served with sorbet) are a regression
to our childhood. Sandrine Boissenin,
the chef's sister, provides expert advice
on the fine Franche-Comté wine list.

BONNEUIL-MATOURS

86210 Vienne. Paris 322 – Bellac 79 –
Le Blanc 51 – Châtellerault 17 –
Montmorillon 42 – Poitiers 25.
An old village in the heart of the Châtellerault
district and its fine Romanesque church.

● | RESTAURANTS

● **Le Pavillon Bleu**
Le Port D749.
Tel. 05 49 85 28 05. Fax 05 49 21 61 94.
c.ribardiere@wanadoo.fr
Closed Sun. dinner, Mon., Wed. dinner (Oct.–
May), 2 weeks Oct., 1 week Feb.
Prix fixe: 17,60€, 31€, 34€.

By the suspension bridge spanning the
Vienne, Claude Ribardière has turned
this old post house into a modern inn.
The red and green dining room and set
menus that change each month have a
Mediterranean feel to them. Claude likes
to combine local and Southern French

flavors in topical dishes, including a foie gras in sangria aspic with sangria fruit chutney or a creamy scallop soup with a sea urchin emulsion and a wasabi-seasoned tea cake, the pepper-glazed monkfish with quinoa couscous and squid rissoles and the veal sweetbreads served with cep cannelloni. Turning to dessert, a cherry Tatin with whipped cream flavored with Guignolet (a cherry liqueur) is a treat from a bygone age. The wines are from every region and the prices keep a cool head. Christelle, though, provides a delightfully warm welcome.

BONNEVILLE

74130 Haute-Savoie. Paris 559 – Annecy 41 – Chamonix 55 – Thonon-les-Bains 45.
A sizable country town in Savoy, between Lake Geneva and the finest ski resorts in the French Alps.

 RESTAURANTS

In 74130 Vougy. 5 km e via N203.

● **Le Capucin Gourmand** `V.COM`
1520, rte de Genève.
Tel. 04 50 34 03 50. Fax 04 50 34 57 57.
www.lecapucingourmand.com
Closed Sat. lunch, Sun., Mon., 1 week Jan.,
3 weeks Aug.
Prix fixe: 34€, 52€, 54€.
A la carte: 50–75€.

Christine and Guy Barbin have plenty going for them: they offer an unfailingly friendly welcome and in their kitchen, regional produce metamorphoses into subtle, gourmet preparations. In the contemporary dining room decorated in bright tones, we savor a salmon trout salad with shrimp, fish from Mr. Rubeaux in Cluzes, a veal sweetbread medallion with wild myrtle and vanilla-seasoned mashed potatoes as well as pain de Gênes (almond cake) with wild blueberries. A more modest package is on offer at the Bistro du Capucin.

BONNIEUX

84480 Vaucluse. Paris 724 –
Aix-en-Provence 44 – Apt 11 –
Carpentras 44 – Cavaillon 26.
ot.bonnieux@axit.fr.
A hill village in the heart of the Luberon district, with a superb view, fine hostelries and peace and quiet off season.

■ ● HOTELS-RESTAURANTS

● **La Bastide**
de Capelongue
Rte de Lourmarin, les Claparèdes.
Tel. 04 90 75 89 78. Fax 04 90 75 93 03.
contact@capelongue.com
www.capelongue.com
Closed mid-Nov.–mid-Mar.
16 rooms: 160–380
At the Capelongue farm, 14 suites
and studios: 320–750€.
Prix fixe: 60€, 121€, 160€.
A la carte: 130€.

Deep in the Provençal *garrigue*, this large traditional farmhouse is the home of Edouard Loubet, a native of Savoy converted to the Luberon cause. The property has splendid guest rooms overlooking the roofs of the picturesque village, a dining room opening on the hills, a romantic terrace and a first-rate welcome and polished service: in short, everything we could wish. The master of the house, a pupil of Chapel and Veyrat (whose niece he married), has returned to the Bastide founded by his mother Claude. Her ambition was to turn it into the best restaurant in the Luberon. Now, its subtle cuisine flatters the finest produce of Provence in fine, fresh, sophisticated, elaborate preparations, which often bring to mind the early Veyrat. We delight in foie gras served two ways, confit and pan-seared, with sundried green tomatoes and caramelized sauce infused with Sylvestre pine sap, a flan-like spinach soufflé served with pan-tossed chanterelles, grilled sea bream with roasted garlic, meat sauce with golden purslane salad, langoustine tails with parsley and a Chartreuse-infused sauce and finally the rack of lamb seasoned with smoked wild thyme and served with a lemon thyme-seasoned home-style gratin, which happily harmonize with sommelier Cédric Brisson's expertly chosen, sunny wines. The dessert menu offers some delightful surprises, such as a peach with a sorrel infusion glazed with currant jelly, aromatic herb ice cream and balsamic-infused mint chips.

■ Auberge de l'Aiguebrun

Domaine de la Tour. D943.
Tel. 04 90 04 47 00. Fax 04 90 04 47 01.
www.aubergedelaiguebrun.fr
Closed Jan.–end Feb. Rest. closed Tue. lunch (lunch and dinner off season), Wed. lunch.
4 rooms: 140–170€. 3 suites: 170–240€.
Prix fixe: 35€ (weekday lunch), 55€.
A la carte: 70€.

Cicadas serenade this refined Provençal inn with its off-white tones and wood furniture, now in the care of Francis Motta. The rooms are attractive and bright and visitors frequently fall in love with the four bungalows by the river. In the kitchen, Francis prepares only fresh, organically farmed produce, which gives unique flavor to his pistou soup with aged parmesan, his Pastis-seasoned cod bouillabaisse, his specialty dish of Marseille-style tripe and variety cuts (pieds paquets), as well as his strawberry gratin with honey from the house hive and lavender ice cream.

■ Le Prieuré

Rue Jean-Baptiste-Aurard.
Tel. 04 90 75 80 78. Fax 04 90 75 96 00.
www.hotelprieure.com
Closed 10 Nov.–end Mar.
11 rooms: 100–180€.
Prix fixe: 18€, 25€, 32€.

Catherine Saint-Guilhem receives us in this fine stone château, once a hospital in the heart of the village. The old-style rooms have been prettily refurbished and the wine bar serves light dishes. A fish tart, rockfish with tapenade, apricot tagine and the princess almond tart are all well crafted.

● Le Fournil

5, pl Carnot.
Tel. 04 90 75 83 62.
Closed Mon., 20 Nov.–mid-Dec., 10 Jan.–23 Feb.
Prix fixe: 20€ (lunch), 27€ (lunch), 38€, 48€.

This troglodytic eatery carved into the rock and looking out on a charming little square with a fountain has been refurbished in contemporary style by Jean-Christophe Lèche and Guy Malbech. Veterans of Chapel and Baumanière, they regale their guests with the spiced fig marmalade, roasted monkfish with mild garlic, slow-cooked lamb with eggplant, toro steak and a chocolate dessert with berry marmalade. The lunchtime set menus are a bargain.

BORDEAUX

33000 Gironde. Paris 581 – Nantes 320 – Bayonne 183 – Pau 191 – Toulouse 248.
otb@bordeaux-tourisme.com.
With its haughty architecture, wrought-iron balconies, windows looking out over the Garonne, great wines at its gates, select clientele and assiduous gourmet appetites, the (gastronomic) city of Bordeaux is not like any other: it amuses itself unobtrusively, appearing only to feast surreptitiously, although restaurants of every kind—gourmet, traditional, chic, pleasant, easygoing and affected—abound here. We are fond of its 18th-century beauty—Stendhal rightly saw it as one of the most enchanting cities in Europe—waterfronts, quais des Chartrons, noble homes, stone and iron bridges, and cabins, too, looking towards the opulent place de la Bourse. Bordeaux takes time to enjoy life and its little pleasures—chocolates, cheeses and rum cakes—and makes a show of disparaging its culinary stars. To put it bluntly, it is hard not to like Bordeaux.

■ HOTELS

■ Burdigala

115, rue Georges-Bonnac.
Tel. 05 56 90 16 16. Fax 05 56 93 15 06.
burdigala@burdigala.com / www.burdigala.com
77 rooms: 180–280€. 6 suites: 390–480€.

With its handsome 18th-century facade, this city center hotel has plenty of character. The renovated rooms are comfortable and equipped with period furniture. In the Jardin de Burdigala, the local cuisine delights guests seated around the central well of light that infuses the circular dining room.

■ Le Bayonne Etche-Ona

4, rue Martignac.
Tel. 05 56 48 00 88. Fax 05 56 48 41 60.
www.bordeaux-hotel.com
Closed Christmas–New Year's.
63 rooms: 75–120€. 1 suite: 250€.

These two 18th-century houses not far from the Grand Théâtre have undergone a salutary restoration. The rooms are now spruce indeed.

■ Mercure Cité Mondiale

Cité Mondiale, 18, parvis des Chartrons.
Tel. 05 56 01 79 79. Fax 05 56 01 79 00.
h2877-dm@accor-hotels.com
www.mercure.com
96 rooms: 87–97€. 1 suite: 200–250€.
A la carte: 30€.

The comfort and practicality of this chain hotel are what we have come to expect, but it also offers the attractions of a perfect location in the Cité Mondiale convention center and quality regional cuisine at both lunch and dinner in its restaurant, Le 20.

■ Mercure Château-Chartrons

81, cours Saint-Louis.
Tel. 05 56 43 15 00. Fax 05 56 69 15 21.
www.hotel-mercure-bordeaux.com
144 rooms: 57–170€. 1 suite: 160€.

Behind the 18th-century facade of a former liquor storehouse in the Chartrons quarter lie functional, spacious rooms below a roof terrace planted with vines. The wine bar serves flawless dishes.

■ Mercure Mériadeck

5, rue Robert-Lateulade.
Tel. 05 56 56 43 43. Fax 05 56 96 50 59.

h1281@accord.com / www.mercure.com
192 rooms: 97–106€. 2 suites: 190€.

Despite its exterior architecture, this seventies chain hotel boasts neat rooms and an offbeat, movie-themed décor.

■ La Maison Bord'eaux

113, rue du Dr-Albert-Barraud.
Tel. 05 56 44 00 45.
contact@lamaisonbordeaux.com
20 rooms: 150–200€.

Wine lovers will find plenty to slake their thirst for knowledge here in the tasting classes organized by Brigitte Lurton, who has made the most of this fine 18th-century town house set in a garden.

■ Grand Hôtel Français

12, rue du Temple.
Tel. 05 56 48 10 35. Fax 05 56 81 76 18.
www.grand-hotel-francais.com
31 rooms: 97–125€. 4 suites: 115–147€.

This 18th-century town house is impressive, with its wrought-iron balconies, imposing stairs and fine period lounges. Contemporary rooms.

■ Hôtel de Sèze & Royal Médoc

23, allée de Tourny / 3-7, rue de Sèze.
Tel. 05 56 52 65 54. Fax 05 56 48 98 00.
http://hotelsezemedoc.free.fr
69 rooms: 45–69€.

Located between the Grand Théâtre and the Quinconces quarter, this establishment consists of two buildings with elegant stone facades. The Hôtel de Sèze is an 18th-century edifice and the Royal Médoc a seventies construction. The rooms vary in size but are all well cared for.

■ 4 Soeurs

6, cours du 30-juillet.
Tel. 05 57 81 19 20. Fax 05 56 01 04 28.
4soeurs@mailcity.com / http://4soeurs.free.fr
34 rooms: 65–90€.

Set in the "golden triangle", this historic hotel where Richard Wagner stayed has small, carpeted, fully equipped rooms.

■ La Maison du Lierre

57, rue Huguerie.
Tel. 05 56 51 92 71. Fax 05 56 79 15 16.
www.maisondulierre.com
Closed 18 Feb.–end Mar.
12 rooms: 73–90€.

This city guesthouse with its breakfasts on the patio, handsome décor and charming welcome is worth a visit. Hélène Deveze has a gift for putting her guests at ease and they all soon feel at home.

In Bouliac (33270). 8 km via rocade 630, exit 23.

■ Hôtel Hauterive

3, pl Camille-Hostein.
Tel. 05 57 97 06 00. Fax 05 56 20 92 58.
reception@saintjames-bouliac.com
www.saintjames-bouliac.com
15 rooms: 155–225€. 3 suites: 260–390€.

This 12th-century winegrower's residence stands in the center of a group of buildings inspired by the old tobacco drying houses, with a décor by Jean Nouvel. Vines stretch to the horizon beneath the windows of the guest rooms with their designer furniture. We enjoy our breakfast by the swimming pool in the garden, and dinner at the Bistroy, Espérance or Saint-James (see Restaurants).

In Créon (33670). 25 km se via D936, D671.

■ Château Camiac

Rte de Branne.
Tel. 05 56 23 20 85. Fax 05 56 23 38 84.
info@chateaucamiac.com
www.chateaucamiac.com
Closed mid-Oct.–mid-Apr. Rest. closed Mon., Oct.–end Apr.
6 rooms: 160–250€. 4 suites: 360€.
Prix fixe: 32€, 50€. A la carte: 60€.

There is plenty to do in this château that stands between Saint-Emilion and Bordeaux. The eight-hectare estate, tennis facilities, heated swimming pool, air conditioned rooms in period style and 1832 dining room set the tone. We come to enjoy Sébastien Richard's well-crafted traditional cuisine. The foie gras terrine with fig chutney, the turbot with salted butter, the duck magret with pain d'épice and a chocolate mille-feuille with chestnut cream are enchanting.

In Martillac (33650). 9 km via rocade A630 s, exit 18, N113.

■ Les Sources de Caudalie

Chemin de Smith-Haut-Lafitte.
Tel. 05 57 83 83 83. Fax 05 57 83 83 84.
sources@sources-caudalie.com
www.sources-caudalie.com
Closed 1 week Jan.
40 rooms: 240–275€. 10 suites: 390–600€.

Caudalie spring water, rich in minerals and trace elements, has many qualities. We appreciate its benefits, applied at the spa standing among the vineyards of Smith-Haut-Laffite. The evocatively named rooms—Bastide des Grands Crus (Great Vintage Farmhouse), Maison du Lièvre (Hare House), etc.—are havens of peace. The swimming pool, fitness center and golf course provide a little exercise before we head off to lunch or dine at the Grand'Vigne in its 18th-century orangery or the Table du Lavoir, whose name alludes to the grape harvesters' washhouse, faithfully reconstructed in a former wine store (see Restaurants).

● | RESTAURANTS

● Le Chapon Fin

5, rue Montesquieu.
Tel. 05 56 79 10 10. Fax 05 56 79 09 10.
contact@chapon-fin.com
Closed Sun., Mon., end July–end Aug.
Prix fixe: 28€ (lunch), 48€, 76€.
A la carte: 100€.

This Bordeaux institution is enjoying a second youth. Brought in by Jean-Michel Cazes, owner of Lynch-Bages, Nicolas Frion serves up an elaborate, invigorating cuisine. In the hands of this former student of Boyer, Bocuse and Marx, fine regional produce is combined in contrasting preparations. The toasted strips of fish with oysters and cilantro mousse, the roasted John Dory served with a cold lentil cake and a veal tenderloin wrapped in eggplant with ground cocoa beans and hot peppers display remarkable imagination and skill. For dessert, the pressed pain d'épice Tatin-style dessert with cinnamon ice cream is enchanting, like the wine list.

● Le Pavillon des Boulevards   Ⓞ V.COM

120, rue Croix-de-Seguey.
Tel. 05 56 81 51 02. Fax 05 56 51 14 58.
pavillon.des.boulevards@wanadoo.fr
Closed Sat. lunch, Sun., Mon. lunch,
beg. Jan., 3 weeks Aug.
Prix fixe: 40€ (lunch), 65€, 100€.
A la carte: 100€.

The Francs' eatery is one of the city's better finds. Nelly's very friendly welcome and her husband Denis' topical cuisine have an easy charm. In the mini-garden and contemporary dining room, we savor Aquitaine caviar with chestnut cream, a steamed Atlantic sea bass with herbs and raisin pulp and braised veal sweetbreads served with apricot compote and puffed potatoes. The desserts, including a tartare of tomato and strawberries accompanied by iced milk and mint tea, display the same creativity.

● Jean Ramet   Ⓞ V.COM

7-8, pl Jean-Jaurès.
Tel. 05 56 44 12 51. Fax 05 56 52 19 80.
jean.ramet@free.fr / www.ramet-jean.com
Closed Sun., Mon., 1 week Jan., 1 week Apr.,
3 weeks Aug.
Prix fixe: 30€ (lunch), 50€, 60€.
A la carte: 85€.

Bordeaux society has adapted easily to the Ramets' restaurant. Raymonde's warm welcome and especially her husband Jean's fine cuisine are still a great success. The former Troisgros disciple prepares polished dishes, with an allusion to current trends here and there. On the table, this translates as oysters presented in puff pastry, roasted jumbo shrimp served with mango ravioli, veal sweetbreads braised with vegetables and, for dessert, a mango macaron. From the best vineyards (but not the most famous), the wines recommended by Isabelle Dupuy are just the thing.

● La Table Calvet   Ⓝ V.COM

81, cours du Médoc.
Tel. 05 56 39 62 80.
Closed Sun., Mon., 10 days Christmas–New Year's, beg. Aug.–end Aug.
Prix fixe: 20€ (lunch), 26€, 32€, 52€.
A la carte: 70€.

On the first floor of this 19th-century, neo-Renaissance house, we take our seats in the bright dining room with its well-trained staff to savor the deliciously fresh set menus. Sweet pea and Pata Negra soup, tender young chicken breast steamed over a bergamot infusion and a frozen raspberry parfait on a dacquoise, with a pot of cocoa cream, all part of the 26 "discovery" menu, are delightful indeed. Of course, Chef Pierrick Célibert, who received excellent training from Guérard, Cagna and Loiseau, and at the Pavillon des Boulevards, knows the score. The wine list is not exclusively Bordeaux oriented and focuses on quality.

● Le Vieux Bordeaux   V.COM

27, rue Buhan.
Tel. 05 56 52 94 36. Fax 05 56 44 25 11.
www.le-vieux-bordeaux.com
Closed Sat. lunch, Sun., Mon.
Prix fixe: 19€ (lunch), 28€, 39€, 50€.
A la carte: 45–65€.

In this contemporary dining room all in gray and red, we stick with a crab and quinoa salad, roasted Atlantic sea bass perfumed with Key limes, lamb shoulder with a rosemary-infused sauce and a mousse-like chocolate cake served with coffee rum sauce, all remarkable. Nicole and Michel Bordage continue to run their business with great energy and the set menus are still bargains.

● Oenetria   Ⓝ COM

10, rue d'Ausone.
Tel. 05 56 79 30 30. Fax 05 56 44 75 02.
oenetria.restaurant@orange.fr
Closed Sat. lunch, Sun., 3 weeks Aug.
Prix fixe: 25€ (lunch), 35€, 60€.
A la carte: 70€.

Exit the Jardin d'Ausone. Samuel Ingelaere, who has renamed the place, recommends both wine (from the encyclopedic list) and cuisine with gusto. The dishes are prepared by Christophe Dupuis, formerly at the Rosalp in Verbier and Chèvre d'Or in Eze. His *"contraste de foie gras"*, variations on the theme of langoustine, wild rabbit in cream sauce and, for dessert, variations on theme of chcocolate, are full of energy. The superb board presents cheeses aged by Daniel Boujon in Thonon and the vaulted cellars are furnished in a delightful contemporary style.

● La Tupina ○COM

6, rue de la Porte-de-la-Monnaie.
Tel. 05 56 91 56 37. Fax 05 56 31 92 11.
latupina@latupina.com / www.latupina.com
Prix fixe: 35€, 55€ (dinner).
A la carte: 55€.

A chic bistro, a Southwestern French inn and a favorite eatery: this restaurant run by Jean-Pierre Xiradakis, an artisan of select produce and flawless traditional cuisine, is all these things. By the hearth, in dining rooms repainted in blue and beige, we make short work of a coddled egg with foie gras, garlic-seasoned cod, spit-roasted Chalosse poultry, braised lamb shoulder and seasonal fruit clafoutis. These grandmotherly recipes are washed down with fine wines from the cellar. The same spirit reigns in the adjoining annex.

● Gravelier ●COM

114, cours de Verdun.
Tel. 05 56 48 17 15. Fax 05 56 51 96 07.
restogramelier@yahoo.fr
Closed Sat., Sun., 1 week Feb., Aug.
Prix fixe: 20€ (lunch), 26€, 34€, 50€.

Anne-Marie Gravelier has inherited a true talent for team management from her father, Pierre Troisgros. Meanwhile, her husband Yves pulls his weight in the kitchen with precise, stylish dishes. In a contemporary setting in eggplant and anise green tones, we settle down to bite-sized fried asparagus and mozzarella, a fish brochette with three sauces, grilled pigeon speared with wild licorice and a chocolate dessert.

● Les Bonheurs du Palais Ⓝ COM

72/74, rue Paul-Louis-Lande.
Tel. 05 56 94 38 63.
Closed lunch, Sun., Aug.
Prix fixe: 38€.

Only open in the evening, this restaurant is one of the best-kept secrets in Bordeaux. Here, André and Tommy Shan present their superb Franco-Chinese cuisine. Fresh salmon with chili- and spice-infused oil, fried sea bream with Yu Xiang aromatic spices and Gong Bao chicken delight their guests, who include aficionado Thierry Marx from Cordeillan Barges, regularly in attendance. A fine house wild rose sorbet rounds off the proceedings. The changing set menu takes us on a tour of eternal China.

● Le Grand Théâtre Ⓝ COM
"Chez Greg"

29, rue Esprit-des-Lois.
Tel. 05 56 31 30 30.
Prix fixe: 9,50€. A la carte: 45€.

We knew Greg (alias Grégoire de Lépinay) when he was the understated star of the Quai de la Monnaie. Now he has struck a decisive blow at Le Grand Théâtre with a sharp, minimalist, chic and very contemporary bistro/brasserie, noisy and cheerful. It boasts superb, often rather obscure wines, quality produce, prompt young waitstaff and affable prices: we would be happy with less. Oysters served hot, a foie gras terrine, a beautiful fireplace-roasted skirt steak served with thick-cut fries made with duck fat, pasta served *al dente* (linguini with crab, penne with duck breast) are all unfussily enjoyable. By the time the dessert trolley arrives (baba au rhum, the house ice creams), we have realized exactly why this place is full all the time.

● La Table de Didier Gélineau Ⓝ COM

34, rue Huguerie.
Tel. 05 56 51 32 83.
Closed Sun., Mon.
Prix fixe: 22€ (lunch), 41€, 52€.
A la carte: 60€.

Didier Gélineau is back in a contemporary setting with a lounge area. The dishes prepared by this native of the Mayenne (who once trained at the Gerbe de Blé) have a vintage eighties feel to them, with their excess of bits of chervil, mousses and broccoli. The spoon of smoked eel compote with pear and ginger flavors, the cod with three peppers or the seared tuna (slightly dry) with slow-cooked onions leave us thoughtful. The desserts (fruit gratin that wasn't fully cooked) are banal and the service is not yet running smoothly.

● **Le Loup**   COM
66, rue du Loup.
Tel. 05 56 48 20 21.
www.restaurant-du-loup.com
Closed Sun., Mon., 1 week Christmas–New Year's, 3 weeks Aug.
Prix fixe: 16€ (lunch, wine inc.), 23€, 32€, 11€ (lunch).

Martine Peiffer greets the guests, Pierre-Eric Faure prepares the traditional cuisine and in the red and pink-tinted dining room, there are no complaints about the oven-crisped pink shrimp with spicy tomato coulis, pork tenderloin with red pepper and onion confiture, nor the roasted lamb saddle with dates and whole grain mustard. The wreath of wine-poached prunes with flavors of tea and citrus is quite digestible.

● **Philippe**   COM
"Chez Dubern"
44, allées Tourny.
Tel. 05 56 81 83 15. Fax 05 56 51 60 38.
www.philippe-chez-dubern.com
Closed Sun., 1 May, 15 Aug.
Prix fixe: 18,50€ (weekday lunch, wine inc.), 15€ (child). A la carte: 55€.

Dominian Hossein has taken over this noble Bordeaux establishment with its fine woodwork. Philippe Téchoire, formerly at the Place du Parlement, handles the service and Philippe Dublé officiates at the stove. The lobster salad, the sea bream carpaccio with truffles, the Atlantic sea bass with cep risotto, boneless rib steak with Bordelaise sauce and chocolate desserts are pleasant dishes.

● **Café du Théâtre**
Pl Pierre-Renaudel (square Jean-Vautier).
Tel. 05 57 95 77 20. Fax 05 57 95 65 91.
Closed Sun., Mon., mid-July–end Aug.
Prix fixe: 12€ (lunch), 18€ (lunch), 29€ (dinner). A la carte: 40–45€.

In this modern black and red setting on the first floor of the Port de la Lune theater, Jean-Marie Amat reminds us of his singular credentials as he briskly serves us fresh, light, spicy dishes: a roasted tuna with satay sauce, squid served in their ink, a tuna steak with slow-cooked onions and peppers and a quietly exotic slow-roasted lamb shoulder with apricots. The desserts (honey- and saffron-flavored creams, a berry-flavored blanc-manger) deserve high praise indeed. A fine repertoire of wines, including some shrewd Bordeaux, and well-mannered prices.

● **Le Bouchon Bordelais**
30, rue du Pont-de-la-Mousque.
Tel. 05 56 44 33 00.
Closed Sat., Sun.
Prix fixe: 11€ (lunch), 26€. A la carte: 35€.

Bordeaux society discreetly flocks to this popular restaurant and cellar, opened by Nicolas Lascombes, veteran of the Tupina dining room. Tractable prices, quality produce and fresh preparations are the sources of his success. We make short work of the sausage and apple brochette before hungrily eyeing our neighbor's country terrine plate, then hesitate over whether to take the Bayonne ham with scrambled eggs and the ratte potatoes with cubes of pan-tossed foie gras. The grilled salmon steak and the free-range chicken fricassée with onions make a fine impression. The ambiance is noisy, full of life and extremely cheerful. The tart Tatin and the profiteroles bring back childhood memories. A huge range of wines at angelic prices.

● **Quai Zaco**   
80, quai des Chartrons.
Tel. 05 57 87 67 72. Fax 05 57 87 34 42.

www.cartesurtables.fr
Closed Sat. lunch, Sun., 2 weeks Aug.
Prix fixe: 13€ (lunch). A la carte: 35€.

This former wine warehouse taken over by Denis and Nelly Franc is the well-behaved adjunct of the Pavillon des Boulevards. In its charming, neo-rustic setting, the energetic Magali Canet serves a tasteful domestic cuisine. We enjoy the spring vegetable and shrimp cannelloni, sea bream with preserved lemons, veal sweetbreads braised with chanterelles and an apricot Tatin.

● **Le Café Bordelais**   Ⓝ🔝SIM

15, allées de Tourny.
Tel. 05 56 81 49 94.
Prix fixe: 15€ (lunch), 24€. A la carte: 45€.

This old café with its woodwork, banquettes, painted glass and bottle racks has plenty of atmosphere. It serves a timeless, uncomplicated cuisine. Gazpacho, shimp cocktail, skirt steak with shallots, marinated pork ribs preceed a pear tart or fresh seasonal fruit salad; all make an excellent impression. Stéphane Fournier deftly supervises his staff.

● **Le Bistro du 20**   ⓃSIM

20, rue des Piliers de Tutelle.
Tel. 05 56 52 49 79.
Closed Sun., Mon., 1 week Feb., 3 weeks Aug.
Prix fixe: 15€ (lunch). A la carte: 35€.

Christophe Faveau and Paul Névière, two food and wine buffs, have left the business world to make a career of their hobby. With its inviting blackboard menus, counter near the door and selected vintages, their two-story bar is an appealing proposition. We come to sample some of the sixteen wines and four champagnes served by the glass. A poultry liver terrine, a plate of Corsican charcuterie, slow-poached foie gras terrine, poached eggs with red wine sauce, veal cutlet with oyster mushrooms, grilled AAAAA chitterling sausage and crème Catalane are enjoyable.

● **Le Cinq**   ⓃSIM

5, allées de Tourny.
Tel. 05 57 87 36 50.

Closed Sun.
Prix fixe: 18,50€ (lunch).

This new, chic bistro boasts a modern décor of bare stone and contemporary furniture. Bruno Portillo has taken on young staff and presents pleasant dishes at affable prices. Tomato Tatin, tuna tartare, cod and vegetable pie slow-cooked in a ceramic dish, a spring garlic-seasoned pork tenderloin served with creamy risotto, parsley- and garlic-seasoned calf's liver and a pineapple carpaccio or a baba au rhum are all good.

● **Le Petit Commerce**   ⓃSIM

22, rue du Parlement-St-Pierre.
Tel. 05 56 79 76 58.
Closed Sun. lunch, 1 week beg. Jan.
Prix fixe: 12€ (lunch). A la carte: 30€.

The local café décor, bar run by Fabien Touraille and wall picture menu set the tone. We savor the extremely fresh seafood: langoustines cut in two and quick grilled, a turbot as thick as your forearm or little rougets (depending on the catch) are very pleasant.

● **Le Bistro du Sommelier**   SIM

163, rue Georges-Bonnac.
Tel. 05 56 96 71 78. Fax 05 56 24 52 36.
www.bistrodusommelier.com
Closed Sat. lunch, Sun.
Prix fixe: 12,50€, 15,50€. A la carte: 50€.

Natives of Médoc like to meet in this contemporary bistro to "slum it" a little at modest prices, feasting on cod and tomato salad, salmon with herb butter, duckling filet with seasonal fruits followed by a rice pudding. Hervé Valverde chooses his wines with remarkable flair.

● **Le Boudoir-Café Cantine**   SIM

7, rue Traversanne.
Tel. 05 56 94 20 45 / 05 58 91 55 16.
Fax 05 56 94 20 45.
Closed Sun. dinner, Mon. dinner, Tue. dinner.
Prix fixe: 9€ (lunch), 14€ (dinner).
A la carte: 25€.

We enjoy the tasteful domestic cuisine in this canteen *cum* boudoir. The Swiss chard

tart, blood sausage with apples, cod lasagne, veal tagine with fruit and a fruit clafoutis attractively prepared by Fabienne
Biehler slip down smoothly, accompanied
by a specially selected little Bordeaux.

● Le Café Gourmand   SIM
3, rue Buffon.
Tel. 05 56 52 10 98. Fax 05 56 52 03 45.
cafe.gourmand@free.fr / www.cafegourmand.fr
Closed Sun., Mon. lunch.
Prix fixe: 19€ (lunch), 28€.

Fried crab cakes with tomato tartare,
roasted grapefruit-seasoned cod, stir-fried
lamb and a lime mille-feuille with mango
coulis offer a change of air at friendly
prices in this Parisian café in the heart
of Bordeaux. Bruno Oliver, Raymond's
grandson, picks up the gauntlet successfully each day.

● Le Café Maritime   SIM
1, quai Armand-Lalande.
Tel. 05 57 10 20 40. Fax 05 57 10 20 41.
contact@cafemaritime.com
www.cafemaritime.com
Closed Sun.
Prix fixe: 18€ (wine inc.). A la carte: 40€.

This large, lively riverside café located in
a former warehouse combines a relaxed
atmosphere and fusion cuisine. Thai-
seasoned mussels served in a cocotte at
the table, fennel-seasoned Atlantic sea
bass with sundried tomatoes, pan-tossed
calf's liver served with slow-cooked red
onions and a coconut and cinnamon rice
pudding mousse are not unpleasant.

● Café du Port   SIM
1-2, quai Deschamps.
Tel. 05 56 77 81 18. Fax 05 56 77 81 39.
www.lecaféduport.com
Closed Sun., Mon.
Prix fixe: 16€ (lunch). A la carte: 40–45€.

The dishes are honest and the service pleasant in this bodega with its direct view of the
port. Jean-Christophe Mass concocts tasteful classical dishes: seafood carpaccio, calf's
liver deglazed with sherry vinegar and a
delicious almond and strawberry dessert.

● L'Estaquade   SIM
Quai de Queyries.
Tel. 05 57 54 02 50. Fax 05 57 54 02 51.
www.lestaquade.com
Closed Christmas–New Year's.
Prix fixe: 16€ (weekday lunch).
A la carte: 50€.

This cabin built on pilings has been redecorated in burgundy shades and offers
supremely fresh, creative dishes. Foie gras
and truffle ravioli with licorice root–flavored mousse, a duo of scallops and frog
legs, veal sweetbreads and morels served
in a cocotte at the table with polenta and
the hibiscus soup and poached pears provide an excellent accompaniment to the
wines selected by Yann Buissière.

● Le Mogador   SIM
19, rue Castéja.
Tel.-Fax 05 56 44 68 06.
Closed lunch, Sun., Aug.
Prix fixe: 16€, 22€. A la carte: 27€.

In this compact Moorish lounge with its Fez
earthenware, low tables and banquettes,
Souad and Lyazidi, natives of Rabat, serve
the Moroccan-style salads, pigeon pastilla,
lamb tagine and couscous royale before the
honey-sweetened pastries and crescent-
shaped Moroccan almond cookies.

● L'O de l'Hâ   SIM
5, rue du Hâ.
Tel. 05 56 81 42 21.
www.o-de-lha.com
Closed Sun., Mon.
Prix fixe: 13€ (lunch). A la carte: 40€.

Nicolas Nadau (who trained with Greg)
and Virginie Duquesne officiate good
naturedly in this relaxed eatery. The
grapefruit and crunchy vegetable salad,
langoustines with peanuts, catfish filet
with mango salad, cod and pumpkin
with orange sauce, veal cutlet with tarragon and fennel and the lemon leaf crème
brûlée are amusing indeed.

● L'Olivier du Clavel   SIM
44, rue Charles-Domercq.
Tel. 05 57 95 09 50. Fax 05 56 92 15 28.

fgclavel@wanadoo.fr
www.olivierduclavel.com
Closed Sat. lunch, Sun., Mon., Aug.
Prix fixe: 28€. A la carte: 55–60€.

Francis Garcia has kept only this part of his former empire. In the refined, bistro setting with its wood, ecru and white décor, David Rousseau's affably priced set menu plays to a Southern score. A rabbit, hazelnut, crayfish and mild garlic salad, scallops in mushroom-infused broth, foie gras escalope with grapes or a vanilla-seasoned red wine granité with pear salad all make an excellent impression.

● La Patte Casset   SIM
12, rue du Maréchal-Joffre.
Tel. 05 56 44 11 58. Fax 05 56 52 32 11.
pattecasset@free.fr
Closed Sat. lunch, Sun., Thu.
A la carte: 45–50€.

This wooden cabin with its terrace continues to appeal to hip locals. In the kitchen, Stéphane Casset prepares refined, fresh dishes: pan-tossed langoustines with chanterelles, monkfish with rosemary, home-style chopped veal sweetbreads and the citrus tapioca are accompanied by wines that his brother Laurent shrewdly selects.

● Le Port de la Lune   SIM
58, quai de Paludate.
Tel. 05 56 49 15 55. Fax 05 56 49 29 12.
www.leportdelalune.com
Call for opening days, hours.
Prix fixe: 22€, 6€ (child). A la carte: 35€.

We are fond of the old-fashioned bistro setting and jazz ambiance of this riverside repair. The lively, fresh cuisine includes variations on the theme of foie gras, a salad with hot goat cheese on toasts, Spanish-style whiting, whole duck breast and Catalan-style crème brûlée. A new dining room opened in 2007.

● Chez Vincent   SIM
15, rue Frères-Bonnie.
Tel. 05 56 44 43 59.
chezvincentnumericable.fr

Closed Sat. dinner, Sun., Mon. dinner.
Prix fixe: 13,50€, 17€, 20€.
A la carte: 45€.

Bruno Bissrier has eagerly taken up the reins at this friendly bistro frequented by the Bar of Bordeaux. Lawyers set aside their court attire to quietly enjoy escargots in puff pastry, pan-tossed squid, foie gras terrine, cod filet poached in Merlot and minced kidneys with parsley and garlic, followed by house chocolates for dessert.

In Bouliac (33270). 8 km via rocade 630, exit 23.

● Le Saint-James
At Hôtel Hauterive 3, pl Camille-Hostein.
Tel. 05 57 97 06 00. Fax 05 56 20 92 58.
reception@saintjames-bouliac.com
www.saintjames-bouliac.com
Closed Sun., Mon., 2 weeks beg. Jan.
Prix fixe: 30€ (lunch), 57€ (wine inc.), 88€, 153€ (wine inc.). A la carte: 120€.

This 17th-century winegrower's house has survived Jean-Paul Amat's departure. Michel Portos' deft tricks have brought a new vitality to the place. In the dining room, the traditional regional recipes are fresher and more modern. Pan-seared hot foie gras served with avocado and pickles, Aquitane caviar with chive-seasoned yogurt, a pork trotter cake wrapped in caul lace delight both ageing gourmets and fashionable youngsters. For dessert, the basil-seasoned strawberries served with lime sorbet provide a refreshing, sweet conclusion. Then the tab comes and our credit card goes into overdrive...

● Le Bistroy
At Hôtel Hauterive, 3 pl Camille-Hostein.
Tel. 05 57 97 06 06 / 05 57 97 06 00.
Fax 05 56 20 92 58.
www.saintjames-bouliac.com.
Closed Sun., Wed., 2 weeks end Jan.,
3 weeks Aug.
Prix fixe: 19€ (weekday lunch),
26€ (weekday lunch), 34€ (dinner).
A la carte: 50€.

In the hands of Jennifer Mendes in the dining room and Laurent Lehocq at the stove, this offbeat bistro with its hyper-realist paintings presents dishes to reflect the vicissitudes of the market. Mushroom cake, langoustines with arugula, John Dory filet with mashed celery root and flavorful chicken sauce, roasted veal served in its jus and the all-chocolate macaron with mandarin orange sorbet are works of art. The wine list pays tribute to the region as a whole.

● L'Espérance   SIM

At Hôtel Hauterive, 10, rue de l'Esplanade.
Tel.-Fax 05 56 20 52 16.
www.saintjames-bouliac.com
Prix fixe: 15€ (lunch), 29€, 47€,
10€ (child).

With its two dining rooms, bar, covered terrace, changing blackboard menu and hors d'oeuvre buffet, this village café opposite the church is just the kind of place where we would to have our own table. Nicholas Dubosq whips up a country terrine, Basque-style tuna, roasted chicken served with thick-cut fries, before the chocolate tart or the Tropézienne, which together form a pleasant spread indeed.

In Le Bouscat (33110). 3 km nw.

● Le Père Ouvrard   COM

39, av de la Libération.
Tel.-Fax 05 56 02 02 04.
Closed Sat. lunch, Sun.,
Christmas—New Year's vac., Aug.
Prix fixe: 15,50€ (lunch). A la carte: 45–55€.

On the edge of Bordeaux, this 18th-century town house ambles on affably. In the winter garden and neo-rustic dining room, we enjoy the market-based cuisine chalked up on the blackboard. The smoked cod with basil vinaigrette, pan-simmered monkfish and onions, veal sweetbread mille-feuille and almond croustillant with warm chocolate sauce are easily up to specifications.

● La Cape   🅿️◎COM

9, allée de la Morelette.
Tel. 05 57 80 24 25. Fax 05 56 32 37 46.
restaurantlacape.over-blog.com
Closed Sat., Sun.,

Christmas—New Year's, Aug.
Prix fixe: 22€, 34€, 50€, 65€.

Marinated red tuna, a roasted slice of avocado with wasabi green apple ice cream, cod cooked slowly at a low temperature served with coriander-seasoned caramelized orange, a quick-grilled Brittany lobster, sage-seasoned caramelized pork and the house chocolate dessert provide some idea of the fine, spirited, creative cuisine prepared by Nicolas Magie. His brother Emilien recommends the wines. On the garden terrace or in the contemporary violet dining room of this curious chalet *cum* lodge, we completely forget the proximity of the shopping mall opposite. The set menus have a certain repartee.

In Martillac (33650). 9 km via rocade A630 s, exit 18, N113.

● Grand'Vigne

At Les Sources de Caudalie, chemin de Smith-Haut-Lafitte.
Tel. 05 57 83 83 83. Fax 05 57 83 83 84.
sources@sources-caudalie.com
www.sources-caudalie.com
Closed Mon., Tue., 1 week Jan.
Prix fixe: 40€, 60€ (wine inc.), 82€.
A la carte: 75€.

In terms of customer welfare, Les Sources de Caudalie's vinotherapy spa has nothing on its restaurant. On the porch looking out over the lake and vines, Franck Salein, who trained with Guérard and Charial, serves up beautifully crafted delights. The herb-seasoned tuna tartare with a sweet pepper coulis, quick-grilled John Dory served with cumin-seasoned orange pulp and thyme-seasoned lamb tenderloin medallions accompanied by spaghetti with zucchini and thyme sauce form fresh, lively meals. The same attention shows when the dessert arrives: strawberry soup served with verbena ice cream. Turning to the wine, the cellar put together by Christophe Santos offers its share of pleasures too.

● La Table du Lavoir

At Les Sources de Caudalie, chemin de Smith-Haut-Lafitte.
Tel. 05 57 83 83 83. Fax 05 57 83 83 84.

www.sources-caudalie.com
Closed 1 week Jan.
Prix fixe: 32€.

The Sources de Caudalie's bistro is also a great success. It is a popular place, with its elegantly rustic setting, view of the vineyards from the terrace, modest check, friendly welcome and, especially, its well-crafted domestic dishes. Proof comes in the form of roasted vegetable salad, grilled Atlantic sea bass filet with tomatoes and mozzarella, a grilled boneless rib steak and a warm soft-centered chocolate cake.

BORMES-LES-MIMOSAS

83230 Var. Paris 877 – Toulon 40 –
Hyères 21 – Le Lavandou 4 – Saint-Tropez 35.
mail@bormeslesmimosas.com.
In the high season, this picturesque old town on the heights above the sea draws crowds of tourists attracted by its Provençal style.

 RESTAURANTS

● **Lou Portaou** SIM
Rue Cubert-des-Poètes.
Tel.-Fax 04 94 64 86 37.
Closed lunch, Tue., mid-Nov.–20 Dec.
Prix fixe: 22€ (lunch), 39€,
12€ (child's dinner). A la carte: 45–50€.

Philippe Cavatore provides a good-humored welcome to his charming bistro. Served according to the availability of fresh produce, pissaladière (an onion-, anchovy- and olive-topped baked flatbread, in this case the chef adding sardines and thyme), a monkfish cassolette and a lamb Chartreuse with eggplant are the pleasant fare served in this old watchman's house decorated with pictures, ornaments and antique furniture.

● **La Tonnelle** SIM
Pl Gambetta.
Tel. 04 94 71 34 84.
www.la-tonnelle-bormes.com
Closed Wed., Nov., Mar.
Prix fixe: 27€, 38€, 48€, 16€ (child).
A la carte: 55€.

Pascale and Gil Renard offer a relaxed welcome in their chic rustic inn. Polished wooden floors, linen tablecloths and napkins, gleaming silverware and a charming sales area set the tone. The cuisine proudly plays on flavors from every Southern clime. The zucchini with fish soup-style brandade, an individual onion tart with sardines, John Dory napped with satay sauce, lamb sautéed in Indian spices and roasted figs with honey and rosemary are fitting fare.

LA BOUEXIERE

35340 Ille-et-Vilaine. Paris 348 –
Nantes 106 – Vitré 22 – Rennes 16.
A small town in the green countryside of the Rennes district.

 HOTELS-RESTAURANTS

● **La Ferme Gourmande** N SIM
27, rue de Vitré.
Tel.-Fax 02 99 04 43 90.
fermegourmande@wanadoo
Closed 1 week Christmas–New Year's.
3 rooms: 38–52€.
Prix fixe: 32€.

At the heart of a two-hectare property, this typically Rennes-style longhouse offers three trim guest rooms in different colors, as well as a neo-rustic restaurant with a fireplace and view of the swimming pool. In the hands of Joël Feuguer, bacon-wrapped scallops served with a chestnut purée, a roasted Atlantic sea bass with shellfish and bergamot seasoning, pork tenderloin in an herb crust served with mushrooms and a strawberry soup are very appealing tricks.

BOULIAC see BORDEAUX
BOULIGNEUX see VILLARS-LES-DOMBES

BOULOGNE-SUR-MER

62200 Pas-de-Calais. Paris 263 – Amiens 128 – Lille 118 – Le Touquet 30 – Calais 38.
boulogne@tourisme.norsys.fr.

This major port, devoted to the herring, with its town heights, ramparts, basilica, sea museum and fine stores, is well worth a trip along the Côte d'Opale.

 HOTELS-RESTAURANTS

■ La Matelote

70, bd Sainte-Beuve.
Tel. 03 21 30 33 33. Fax 03 21 30 87 40.
tony.lestienne@la-matelote.com
www.la-matelote.com
28 rooms: 110–160€. 1 suite: 215€.

Located on the sea front by the harbor, this thirties establishment has found a new lease on life in the hands of Tony Lestienne, leading chef on the Côte d'Opale. The spacious guest rooms redecorated in red and gold have an easy charm.

● La Matelote

80, bd Sainte-Beuve.
Tel. 03 21 30 17 97 / 03 21 30 33 33.
Fax 03 21 83 29 24.
tony.lestienne@la-matelote.com
www.la-matelote.com
Closed Sun. dinner, Thu. lunch,
22 Dec.–mid-Jan.
Prix fixe: 35€, 48,50€, 72€.
A la carte: 80€.

In Tony Lestienne's restaurant, the Côte d'Opale's finest produce is king. The spirited Northerner prepares mischievous but honest regional dishes for the guests in his red and gold dining room. The squid with hot chili pepper-seasoned risotto, a turbot filet with crayfish, squab breast with foie gras and the raspberry and vanilla mousseline millefeuille are a lively guide to the region.

● Le Nausicaa

Bd Sainte-Beuve.
Tel. 03 21 33 24 24. Fax 03 21 30 15 63.
Closed Mon. dinner (off season).
Prix fixe: 20,50€, 8€ (child).
A la carte: 40–45€.

Located in the Centre National de la Mer (National Sea Center), the Matelote's lit-

tle sister is doing well. Jean-Jacques Bernard and Jean-Yves Fournier concoct reliable, solid dishes, such as flamiche (a regional savory pie), crêpes filled with smoked herring and cream, fish choucroute and the whipped chocolate dessert. A panoramic view of the harbor.

● Aux Pêcheurs d'Etaples

31, Grand-Rue.
Tel. 03 21 30 29 29. Fax 03 21 87 01 02.
www.auxpecheursdetaples.com
Closed Sun. dinner.
Prix fixe: 13€, 16€ (wine inc.), 25€,
6€ (child). A la carte: 40€.

Formerly at the Brocante in Wimille, David Sergent learned to prepare sole, cod, rouget, Atlantic sea bass and turbot supplied by the fishermen's cooperative at Etaples-sur-Mer. In the blue and white dining room, we feast on a mackerel charlotte, a slow-simmered fish stew, sole meunière and a brown sugar tart. Conscientious service.

In Pont-de-Briques (62360). 5 km s via N142.

● Hostellerie de la Rivière

17, rue de la Gare.
Tel. 03 21 32 22 81. Fax 03 21 87 45 48.
www.hostelleriedelariviere.com
Closed Sun. dinner, Mon.,
Tue. (exc. rest. dinner), 3 weeks Jan.
8 rooms: 60–75€.
Prix fixe: 30€ (lunch, wine inc.), 36€, 55€,
20€ (child). A la carte: 70€.

This rustic but chic establishment boasts a few comfortable guest rooms and a contemporary restaurant with beige paneling, where we sample Dominique Martin's reliable (if a little overcomplicated) dishes. A pan-tossed rouget with bitter orange sauce served with pear salad, a baked rolled sole filled with mushroom "caviar", boneless roasted pigeon served over rustic potato cakes and a mini-omelet norvégienne (similar to baked Alaska) served with a banana pineapple brochette and sprinkled with amber rum are finely crafted fare.

LE BOURG-DUN

76740 Seine-Maritime. Paris 186 –
Dieppe 20 – Saint-Valéry-en-Caux 15 –
Rouen 56.
On the chalky plateau of Caux, a village and its
inn straight out of Maupassant.

 RESTAURANTS

● **Auberge du Dun**
3, rte de Dieppe.
Tel. 02 35 83 05 84.
Closed Sun. dinner, Mon., Wed. dinner,
2 weeks Jan.
Prix fixe: 27€, 42€, 73€. A la carte: 85€.

Gourmets need no urging to visit Pierre
Chrétien's restaurant opposite the village church. In the Norman-style dining
room, they enjoy his lively, offbeat preparations. A pan-seared duck foie gras with
apples, skate rolled with spring onions,
a veal sweetbread encrusted with walnuts and served with slow-simmered
legumes in Meax mustard sauce and a
green-peppercorn-seasoned banana soufflé accompanied by a passion fruit sorbet
are refreshingly out of the ordinary. A pity
that the wine list is less adventurous.

BOURG-EN-BRESSE

01000 Ain. Paris 425 – Mâcon 37 – Annecy
113 – Lyon 68 – Genève 112.
The capital of the Bresse region, with its fine
museum, recumbent effigies of Brou and tombs
has a number of claims to fame. Among them
is its natural culinary culture, not the least of
its virtues.

 HOTELS-RESTAURANTS

■ **Mercure**
10, av de Bad-Kreuznach.
Tel. 04 74 22 44 88. Fax 04 74 23 43 57.
h1187@accor.com / www.mercure.com
Rest. closed Sat. lunch.
60 rooms: 82–100€.
Prix fixe: 11,50€. A la carte: 45€.

The strong points of this chain hotel
are its recently renovated, contemporary rooms and simple *pension* cuisine.
A cheerful welcome.

■ **Le Prieuré**
49, bd de Brou.
Tel. 04 74 22 44 60. Fax 04 74 22 71 07.
www.hotelduprieure.com
14 rooms: 75–90€.

Charm guaranteed at this hotel overlooking a park opposite Brou church.
The rooms renovated in pink tones and
equipped with period furniture are very
popular with romantic couples.

■ **Hôtel de France**
19, pl Bernard.
Tel. 04 74 23 30 24. Fax 04 74 23 69 90.
www.grand-hoteldefrance.com
44 rooms: 75–92€.

Near the markets, this old-fashioned
hotel is something of an institution. We
enjoy its 1900 lobby, very friendly welcome, large rooms and Georges Blanc
brasserie (see Restaurants: Chez Blanc).

■ **Logis de Brou**
132, bd de Brou.
Tel. 04 74 22 11 55. Fax 04 74 22 37 30.
citotel@logisdebrou.com
www.logisdebrou.com
30 rooms: 52–71€. 2 suites: 129€.

A flowered garden and terrace, delicious
breakfasts and trim rooms are this personalized hostelry's main assets.

● **Auberge Bressane**
166, bd de Brou.
Tel. 04 74 22 22 68. Fax 04 74 23 03 15.
www.aubergebressane.fr
Closed Tue.
Prix fixe: 19€–24€ (lunch), 35€, 46€,
59€, 69€.

Opposite Brou church, this large, traditional inn serves an appropriate regional
cuisine. On the covered terrace or in the
well-appointed dining room, we feast on
a the duck foie gras "gourmandise" served

with a little pot of crayfish in aspic, a pike fish quenelle served with pike-perch soufflé, Bresse chicken with morels and the hot apricot tart, lovingly prepared by the generous Jean-Pierre Vullin.

● Le Français   COM

7, av d'Alsace-Lorraine.
Tel. 04 74 22 55 14. Fax 04 74 22 47 02.
Closed Sat. dinner, Sun.,
1 week Christmas–New Year's, 1 week May,
3 weeks Aug.
Prix fixe: 23€, 50€. A la carte: 60€.

In the heart of town, this Belle Epoque brasserie with its moldings, stucco and banquettes regales us with frog legs in fines herbes, sole meunière, chicken with creamy morel sauce and the lemon tart, all washed down with a carafe of spirited Beaujolais.

● Chez Blanc   COM

At Hôtel de France, 19, pl Bernard.
Tel. 04 74 45 29 11. Fax 04 74 24 73 69.
www.georgesblanc.com
Prix fixe: 17€, 27€, 38€, 45€,
12€ (child).

This brasserie bearing the Georges Blanc seal is a must. In the 1900 bistro décor, gourmets delight in its revised Bresse classics. A blonde Bresse poultry liver terrine served with slow-cooked onions, tuna steak seasoned with spicy oil, Bresse poultry in cream sauce and a pan-seared sirloin steak with fleur de sel and grilled bone marrow are all very well done. The citrus-seasoned blanc-manger slips down delectably.

● La Reyssouze   COM

20, rue Charles-Robin.
Tel. 04 74 23 11 50. Fax 04 74 23 94 32.
Closed Sun. dinner, Mon., 2 weeks beg. Aug.
Prix fixe: 25€, 30€, 40€, 54€.
A la carte: 70€.

Here in the town's other "landmark", Alain Détain improvises on Bresse tradition in his sensibly priced set menus. In the dining room with its fine woodwork and yellow tones, the frog legs sautéed in fines herbs, quick-seared Atlantic sea bass seasoned with aromatics, Bresse poultry with morels in cream sauce and the thin caramelized apple tart with cinnamon ice cream weave deftly between past and present.

In Péronnas (01960). 3 km e via N83.

● La Marelle   COM

1593, av de Lyon.
Tel. 04 74 21 75 21. Fax 04 74 21 06 81.
www.lamarelle.fr
Closed Sun. dinner, Tue., Wed.,
20 Aug.–mid-Sept.
Prix fixe: 22€ (lunch), 39€, 45€, 55€.
A la carte: 65€.

Despite the rather unprepossessing surroundings, all Bresse flocks to Didier Goiffon's eatery. This former disciple of Pierre Gagnaire and Jean-André Charial leads his guests down paths less trodden between highways of tradition and modernity. In the dining room, this translates as blue lobster meat with cilantro and pickled seaweed, pan-simmered turbot and chanterelles served with ajowan-glazed sweet pea pulp and grilled Miéral pigeon. The desserts, including the Vin Jaune–marinated pear and assorted house ice creams, are just as appealing. The modern, colorful setting and large terrace, Sandra's welcome and the shrewd counsel supplied by sommelier Yannick Bernardin do the rest. A restaurant to watch.

BOURG-DES-COMPTES

35890 Ille-et-Vilaine. Paris 360 – Redon 50 – Rennes 25.
A pretty village of longhouses in the heart of the Rennes district, between Vilaine and Semnon.

●	RESTAURANTS

● Auberge du Relais
de la Place

16, pl de l'Eglise.
Tel. 02 99 57 41 12. Fax 02 99 57 41 57.
www.auberge-lefranc.com
Closed Sun. dinner, Mon., Tue. dinner,
1 week at end Jan.
Prix fixe: 16€, 26€, 31€, 42€, 8,50€ (child).

In the heart of the village, the Lefranc's inn is a paean to inland Brittany. Huguette in the dining room and Jean-Claude in the kitchen delight guests with their friendly smiles and reliable market-based preparations. The duck foie gras, monkfish with bacon, chicken grilled over a wood fire and the île flottante have the good taste of simple fare.

BOURGES

18000 Cher. Paris 246 – Châteauroux 66 – Nevers 69 – Orléans 123.
tourisme@www.ville-bourges.fr.
The heart of France lies here, of course, in this calm, good-natured town of 75,000 souls, which has managed to preserve and even enrich its heritage. In the very center, the maze of streets, large quiet gardens, pleasant marshlands and bountiful mansions—their collection of antiques intact—have an immediate charm.

 HOTELS-RESTAURANTS

■ Hôtel de Bourbon
Bd de la République.
Tel. 02 48 70 70 00. Fax 02 48 70 21 22.
h1888@accor-hotels.com
www.hoteldebourbon.fr
53 rooms: 80–145€. 4 suites: 155–175€.

This ancient abbey turned into a modern hotel has lost none of its character. Garden and rooms are well kept, and the service and reception are very friendly. (See Restaurants: L'Abbaye Saint-Ambroix.)

■ Christina
5, rue de la Halle.
Tel. 02 48 70 56 50. Fax 02 48 70 58 13.
infos@le-christina.com / www.le-christina.com
71 rooms: 46–77€.

The sixties architecture here is hardly the stuff that dreams are made of, but the location opposite the corn exchange, air conditioning and rooms refurbished in lively shades make this a practical, comfortable stopover.

■ Hôtel d'Angleterre
1, pl des Quatre-Piliers.
Tel. 02 48 24 68 51. Fax 02 48 65 21 41.
www.bestwestern-angleterre-bourges.com
Closed 1 week Christmas–New Year's.
31 rooms: 79–89€. 2 suites: 108€.

In the heart of the old town near the Palais Jacques-Coeur, this hotel's strong points are its modern rooms in cheerful colors and assiduous service, rather than its distant welcome.

● L'Abbaye Saint-Ambroix
60, av Jean-Jaurès.
Tel. 02 48 70 70 00. Fax 02 48 70 21 22.
www.abbayesaintambroix.fr
Closed Mon., Tue.
Prix fixe: 45€, 80€. A la carte: 81€.

The 17th-century abbey's former chapel houses this gourmet haunt with a menu by François Adamski. This winner of the 2001 Bocuse d'Or award has plenty of ideas on how to enjoyably update a classical repertoire that relies on modernity and creativity. We savor the Breton sardine tart, crunchy fennel with crushed tomatoes, quick-grilled Atlantic sea bass seasoned with fresh oregano, oven-crisped veal sweetbreads, Swiss chard turned in butter and veal jus, the tender vanilla-seasoned pears and the Mandarin Imperiale flambéed crêpes graced with passion fruit. The service is delightfully attentive and the Loire wines numerous and well chosen.

● Le Jardin Gourmand
15 bis, av Ernest-Renan.
Tel. 02 48 21 35 91. Fax 02 48 20 59 75.
www.jardingourmand.com
Closed Sun. dinner, Mon., Tue. lunch,
mid-Dec.–mid-Jan., 3 weeks July.
Prix fixe: 15€, 23€, 30€, 38€, 45€.
A la carte: 45–50€.

The Chauveaus' Jardin is delightful. Along with Colette's welcome, its location by the marshlands and three successive dining rooms work an immediate charm. In the kitchen, Christian turns regional produce into deftly crafted dishes, including pan-seared foie gras with glazed radishes, lobster fricassée, free-range chicken with chanterelles in cream sauce and the Arabica-seasoned Guanaja chocolate fondant, all sensibly priced.

● **Le Bourbonnoux**

44, rue Bourbonnoux.
Tel. 02 48 24 14 76. Fax 02 48 24 77 67.
www.tablegourmandeduberry.com
Closed Fri., Sat. lunch, Sun. dinner, 2 weeks
Sept., 1 week Feb., 1 week Apr.
Prix fixe: 18€, 23€, 30€. A la carte: 37€.

Set among the local stores lining the street, Jean-Michel and Marie-France Huart's restaurant boasts a trim dining room where the woodwork and bright colors blend harmoniously. Jean-Michel deftly gratifies his guests with subtle, lively dishes presented in shrewd set menus. The nut bread with eggplant cream and chives, the sea trout seasoned with wild dill, slow-cooked carrots with preserved lemons, veal with pain d'épice sauce and sesame seeds and the strawberry pastry made with lentil flour served with a strawberry and lemon thyme sauce are splendid.

● **Le Beauvoir** COM

1, av Marx-Dormoy.
Tel. 02 48 65 42 44. Fax 02 48 24 80 84.
didierguyot@club-internet.fr
www.lebeauvoir.com
Closed Sun. dinner, 3 weeks Aug.
Prix fixe: 18€, 27€, 32€. A la carte: 65€.

On the outskirts of town, the Guyots' restaurant offers authentic gourmet amusements. In a modern setting in yellow and burgundy, Didier prepares the original, concise dishes that make up his gently priced set menus. The scallops with rice wine vinegar and soy sauce, pike-perch in Menetou wine, real beuchelle tourangelle (a local veal kidney and sweetbread dish) and a pear and chestnut gratin are vigorous fare.

73370 Savoie. Paris 533 – Annecy 44 –
Aix-les-Bains 10 – Chambéry 13.

office.tourisme@bourgetdulac.com.
"O time, arrest your flight," Lamartine wrote here. The shores of the lake still listen to the silence of the hours and the abbey of Hautecombe reflect the full measure of this haven.

	HOTELS-RESTAURANTS

● **Ombremont &**
   Bateau Ivre

N504.
Tel. 04 79 25 00 23. Fax 04 79 25 25 77.
www.hotel-ombremont.com
Closed Nov. Rest. closed Mon. lunch, Mon.
dinner (exc. July– Aug.), Tue. lunch,
Thu. lunch.
12 rooms: 165–245€. 5 suites: 265–345€.
Prix fixe: 30€, 45€, 55€ (lunch), 65€,
80€, 150€.

Change has come to this establishment run by Jean-Pierre Jacob, who presides over the heights of Courchevel in winter: he is now opening the hotel—with its view of Mount Revard and the lake—year round. The peaceful rooms, friendly service and the breakfast one comes to expect in a Relais & Châteaux monument are enchanting. Furthermore, the cuisine is lively and inspired, prepared by an efficient team and served on the terrace as well as in the contemporary dining room. Roasted langoustines with oven-crisped potatoes, soft-boiled egg with acidulated Saint-Jean truffle sauce, filet of wild Mediterranean sea bass, roasted lake fish with slow-cooked carrots, Limousin rack of lamb with summer vegetables and pepper-infused oil and the veal sweetbread fricassée with crayfish tails are meticulous work indeed. The desserts (chocolate mousse soufflé, coconut sorbet, house ice creams and sorbets infused with essences of hay, praline, orange, raspberry, mint and basil) are equally charming. The wine list, which travels beyond the Savoy region, is giddying.

● **Auberge Lamartine**

Route du Tunnel, in Chat: 3,5 km n via N504.
Tel. 04 79 25 01 03. Fax 04 79 25 20 66.
www.lamartine-marin.com

Closed Sun. dinner, Mon., 23 Dec.–15 Jan.
Prix fixe: 26€ (lunch), 39€, 61€, 80€.
A la carte: 73€.

Lamartine would have enjoyed the superb panorama spread before our eyes on the terrace, which looks out on both lake and mountain. Marie-Christine Marin greets her guests with great warmth and we soon feel at home in the dining room with its impressive fireplace. Meanwhile, Pierre is hard at it in the kitchen, achieving a perfect marriage of forthright flavors and delicate preparations in such dishes as the quail in salad, poultry breast in a potato crust, slow-cooked poultry thigh served with a poached egg, lake salmon trout meunière or the pan-braised veal sweetbread with a summer vegetable risotto and a spicy reduction sauce made from veal trotter. The daydream continues with the cocoa and vanilla cream mille-feuille and chocolate ice cream with flecks of cocoa bean and a coffee sauce. The glass-walled cellar reveals its secrets and we choose from among the finest Savoy wines.

● **La Grange à Sel**
La Croix Verte.
Tel. 04 79 25 02 66. Fax 04 79 25 25 03.
info@lagrangeasel.com
www.lagrangeasel.com
Closed Sun. dinner, Wed., Jan.–mid-Feb.
Prix fixe: 26€ (lunch), 37€, 47€, 75€.

We soon feel at home in the exposed beam and stone setting of this salt barn. Annie and Jean-François Trépier's welcome is exemplary and Gilles Blonay's cuisine a sweet invitation. This veteran of the Bateau Ivre in Courchevel deftly weds regional produce to Southern French flavors. The pan-seared perch in salad with squid and soy sauce–seasoned oyster nectar, the salmon trout cooked in butter, the ris de veau parmentier seasoned with with truffle essence and the lemon and chocolate croquant served with tea ice cream are delightful, as are the service and shrewd set menus.

BOURGOIN-JALLIEU

38300 Isère. Paris 505 – Lyon 43 – Bourg-en-Bresse 84 – Grenoble 67.
The rugby club, writer Frédéric Dard (aka San Antonio) and Guy Savoy, the star Parisian chef, are just some of the delights we owe to this sizable Dauphiné town, which is well worth closer inspection. Apart from its 19th-century drawings and paintings, the museum has a room devoted to weaving and the fabric printing that made the town's name.

HOTELS-RESTAURANTS

■ **Domaine des Séquoias**
54, vie de Boussieu.
Tel. 04 74 93 78 00. Fax 04 74 28 60 90.
www.domaine-sequoias.com
Rest. closed Sun. dinner, Mon., Tue. lunch, Christmas–New Year's, Aug.
18 rooms: 110–130€. 1 suite: 180€.
Prix fixe: 28€, 74€. A la carte: 90€.

In the heart of grounds shaded by 100-year-old trees, with a swimming pool, this 18th-century dwelling provides rooms with a refined décor. Turning to the restaurant, Eric Jambon prepares lively, topical dishes. These fine tricks include a pumpkin soup with aged Beaufort, chestnuts and bacon, a tuna steak cooked in white sesame oil and the riz de veau in cocotte with new potatoes and black olives.

BOURGUEIL

37140 Indre-et-Loire. Paris 283 – Tours 47 – Angers 81 – Saumur 24 – Chinon 17.
otsibourgueil@wanadoo.fr.
"I like wines that smell of feet", laughed the late great actor Jean Carmet, a son of this vinic region.

HOTELS-RESTAURANTS

■ **Thouarsais**
10, pl Hublin.
Tel.-Fax 02 47 97 72 05.
23 rooms: 25–50€.

Right in the heart of the village, the three small houses that make up this hotel are built around a pretty little yard. After a pleasant night in one of the simple, practical guest rooms here, breakfast lives up to its promise. A modest check.

In Saint-Nicolas-de-Bourgueil (37140).

● **Saint Nicolas Gourmand** `SIM`
28, av Saint-Vincent.
Tel. 02 47 97 77 37. Fax 02 47 97 97 48.
www.tourainegourmande.com
Closed Sun. dinner, Mon., Jan.
Prix fixe: 17€, 39,50€, 12€ (child).
A la carte 40–50€.

Didier Marnay's yellow and pink establishment opposite the church is a paean to the region. His wines take place of honor in both dish and glass. We enjoy the duck foie gras terrine served with a glass of sweet Vouvray, the eel simmered in Saint Nicholas de Bourgueil, Touraine pigeon with rosemary and wild thyme and the cherries with cherry Marnier dessert.

BOURRAN see **RODEZ**

BOURRON-MARLOTTE

77780 Seine-et-Marne. Paris 73 – Fontainebleau 9 – Melun 26 – Nemours 11.
A pretty, old-fashioned village surrounded by Fontainebleau forest.

| | RESTAURANTS |

● **Les Prémices** `V.COM`
12 bis, rue Blaise-de-Montesquiou.
Tel. 01 64 78 33 00. Fax 01 64 78 36 00.
www.restaurant-les-premices.com
Closed Sun. dinner, Mon., Tue., Christmas,
1 week Feb., 1 week Aug.
Prix fixe: 55€, 60€, 75€.
A la carte: 80–90€.

Dominique Maes is celebrating ten years in this modern restaurant housed in the outbuildings of the château of Bourron-Marlotte. This excellent classical chef who once worked with Morot-Gaudry in Paris can also perform a more modern repertoire, with refined preparations showcased in topical presentations. The roasted jumbo shrimp wrapped in angelhair pastry (kadaif), accompanied by lobster coconut bisque, a salad with pesto and aged parmesan, a pork fat–enriched rabbit saddle with veal trotter stuffing and the variations on theme of seasonal fruits (such as Corsican mandarin orange) are all very pleasant. Voluble sommelier Laurent Piro enthusiastically chooses the right wine for these spreads.

LE BOUSCAT see **BORDEAUX**

BOUXWILLER

67330 Bas-Rhin. Paris 447 – Saverne 15 – Bitche 34 – Strasbourg 42.
tourisme.bouxwiller@wanadoo.fr.
Once witches celebrated their Sabbath on Batsberg hill. Today, the city hall has acquired a stately air. As a bonus, the village boasts two museums, one of them devoted to Judaism in Alsace.

 HOTELS-RESTAURANTS

■ **La Cour du Tonnelier** ⌂
84, Grand-Rue.
Tel. 03 88 70 72 57. Fax 03 88 70 95 74.
www.courdutonnelier.com
Closed 2 weeks Christmas–New Year's,
3 weeks Aug. Rest. closed Sun. dinner, Mon.
16 rooms: 52–97€.
Prix fixe: 8,50€ (weekday lunch), 24–28€.
A la carte: 45€.

Jérôme Veit has taken over this modern establishment with gusto, equipping it with comfortable rooms, a busy bar and a decent restaurant. Thomas Kapp charms his guests with duck foie gras terrine, the house-prepared escargots, a poached cod filet with chervil sauce, an Argentinian sirloin steak with slow-cooked leeks and the frozen berry soufflé. The swimming pool and garden are bonuses.

In Imbsheim (67330). 3 km sw via D6.

● **S'Batsberger Stulwel** `SIM`

25, rue Principale.
Tel.-Fax 03 88 70 73 85.
Closed Mon., Tue. dinner, 1 week Sept.,
1 week Jan., 3 weeks June.
Prix fixe: 14€, 18€, 35€.

Anny Reixel offers a keen welcome in her country *winstub*. With its profusion of flowers, the plants, paintings and inscriptions, the house has plenty of character, as do the local dishes, presented with zest. Regional flat savory tarts called "tartes flambées", slow-simmered beef and noodles and the stuffed pork trotter are monuments of popular art.

34140 Hérault. Paris 756 – Marseille 194 – Montpellier 30 – Nîmes 80.
Bouzigues, a little typically Mediterranean fishing village, still honors its traditions and displays an old-fashioned charm. Be sure to visit the Etang de Thau museum.

	RESTAURANTS

● **Le Saint-Julien** `SIM`

2, pl du Port.
Tel. 04 67 53 27 70.
Closed Mon., Tue., Nov.–beg. Apr.
Prix fixe: 14€ (lunch), 18€ (lunch), 28€.
A la carte: 32€.

Next door to the Etang de Thau museum, the Graniers' restaurant has no trouble finding customers. Housed in an old basement, it has been tastefully fitted out. The white walls and wrought-iron and stained wood furniture have a simple air. Shellfish star on the menu, preferably seasoned with aromatic herbs or spices and served grilled, echoing the flavors of the Mediterranean. We yield to the urgings of the marinated anchovies, the grilled tuna or the delicious tabletop grilled lamb. The raspberry tart and the chocolate fondant are choice conclusions.

41250 Loir-et-Cher. Paris 184 – Orléans 63 – Blois 19 – Romorantin 30.
At the gates of Chambord forest and the Sologne region, a village of ancient markets that keeps alive the memory of the Three Musketeers.

●	RESTAURANTS

● **Le Relais de Bracieux**

1, av de Chambord.
Tel. 02 54 46 41 22. Fax 02 54 46 03 69.
relaisbracieux.robin@wanadoo.fr
www.relaisdebracieux.com
Closed Tue., Wed., mid-Dec.–end Jan.
Prix fixe: 38€, 60€, 95€, 140€.
A la carte: 112€.

On the Loire châteaux route, very close to Chambord, the Relais de Bracieux is a first-rate place to stay and also offers an opportunity to dine delightfully on Bernard Robin's fine fare. This former student of Barrier is a past master in the art of modernizing great classics. In a predominantly pink, modern décor, we savor the oven-crisped lobster with sundried tomatoes and the black and white sole with cream and caviar before following with the turbot, French-style sweet peas and game served with potatoes or a minced oxtail parmentier. The spell grips us right up to the last mouthful of the Sologne strawberries in puff pastry and the chocolate fondant. The cellar, which focuses on Loire wines, is managed by Patrick Limonta, who is never sparing of good advice to help you make your choice. Attentive hostess Christine offers a delightful welcome. The level of service is high indeed, as is the check, but for such extraordinary dishes...

BRANSAC see BEAUZAC

24310 Dordogne. Paris 478 – Angoulême 59 – Périgueux 27 – Limoges 86 – Thiviers 26.
This exquisite village, the Venice of green

Périgord, boasts a maze of canals, an abbey—where Pierre Bourdeilles, author of *La Vie des Dames Galantes*, was once master—ancient, white dwellings and a circular layout.

 HOTELS-RESTAURANTS

● **Moulin de l'Abbaye**

Av P.-de-Bourdeilles.
Tel. 05 53 05 80 22. Fax 05 53 05 75 27.
moulin@relaischateaux.fr
www.moulin-abbaye.com
Closed end Oct.–beg. May.
13 rooms: 190–230€. 5 suites: 265–295€.
Prix fixe: 55€, 75€, 90€.

On the Dronne river, Régis Bulot's Relais & Châteaux establishment works its charm. In the mill and the priest's and miller's houses, the old-fashioned guest rooms offer all modern conveniences. In the restaurant, Bernard Villain (trained by Toulousy, Passard and Etchebest) serves up a tasteful domestic cuisine. A lobster and veal sweetbread duo, langoustine tail fricassée, a boned squab, stuffed with foie gras and then braised, showcase both tradition and noble produce. For dessert, the strawberry gratin with wine and lime jelly is deliciously refreshing. A fine wine list.

■ **Chabrol**

57, rue Gambetta.
Tel. 05 53 05 70 15. Fax 05 53 05 71 85.
www.lesfrerescharbonnel.com
Closed Sun. dinner (exc. July–Aug. and Bank holidays), Mon. (exc. July–Aug. and Bank holidays), mid-Nov.–mid-Dec., Feb. vac.
17 rooms: 55–75€. 3 suites: 90–110€.
Prix fixe: 28€, 68€. A la carte: 50–60€.

The Charbonnel brothers provide comfortable rooms renovated in an antique style. In the kitchen, Jean-Claude prepares a tasteful, grandmotherly cuisine. A pork trotter and pike-perch salad in vinaigrette, truffle-seasoned pike-perch, foie gras-stuffed pigeon and then strawberry champagne soup go down like velvet on the covered terrace.

● **Au Fil du Temps**

1, chemin du Vert-Galant.
Tel. 05 53 05 24 12. Fax 05 53 05 18 01.
fildutemps@fildutemps.com
www.fildutemps.com
Closed Mon., Tue., Jan.
Prix fixe: 12–23€, 35€. A la carte: 40€.

Régis Bulot is wearing a smile in the Moulin de l'Abbaye's rustic adjunct, as are its regulars and passing tourists. Across from the patinated bar in the Louis XV-style dining room, creamy cep and poached egg soup, grilled Atlantic sea bass, spit-roasted chicken and caramelized apples seasoned with cinnamon are a delight, washed down with charming local wines.

● **Au Fil de L'Eau** SIM

21, quai Bertin.
Tel. 05 53 05 73 65. Fax 05 53 35 04 81.
fildeleau@fildeleau.com
www.fildeleau.com
Closed Sun. (exc. July–Aug.),
Wed. (exc. July–Aug.), mid-Oct.–mid-Apr.
Prix fixe: 24€, 29€.

Frédéric Chassin presides over this seafood subsidiary created by Régis Bulot: a *guinguette*-style establishment with a cheerful atmosphere. Simply, coolly, we enjoy the fried fish with onion, herb, caper and mustard mayonnaise, lentils with goat cheese on toast, the whiting and ratatouille, duck confit with garlic-seasoned potatoes and a plum rice pudding that takes us back to our childhood.

In 24310 Bourdeilles. 10 km sw via D78.

■ **Les Griffons**

Le Bourg.
Tel. 05 53 45 45 35. Fax 05 53 45 45 20.
griffons@griffons.fr / www.griffons.fr
Closed end Oct.–beg. Apr.
Rest. closed lunch (exc. July–Aug.).
10 rooms: 95–130€.
Prix fixe: 28€, 35€, 10€ (child).

This 16th-century hostelry overlooking the Dronne has an easy charm with its rustically furnished antique guest rooms featuring exposed beams. In the dining room and on the terrace, the dishes are soberly classical. We have happy memories of a duck foie gras terrine, rouget served on a bed of risotto with spring fennel sauce and the tarte Tatin.

In 24530 Champagnac-de-Bel-Air. 6 km ne via D78 and D83.

● **Moulin du Roc**
Tel. 05 53 02 86 00. Fax 05 53 54 21 31.
moulinduroc@aol.com / www.moulinduroc.com
Closed beg. Jan.–beg. Mar. Rest. closed Tue., Wed. lunch, Wed. dinner (off season).
10 rooms: 170–205€.
Prix fixe: 35€ (lunch). A la carte: 65€.

This mill on the Dronne river with its flowered garden, swimming pool, tennis court and luxurious, refined rooms is an enchanting setting. In the restaurant, chef and boss Alain Gardillou, who trained with his mother, the great Solange, pays tribute to the region with a truffle-seasoned creamy potato soup, the cod filet in a shellfish broth, a veal sweetbread escalope served with brasied endives and chestnuts and a cinnamon-seasoned apple marguerite in puff pastry. The 800 wines in the cellar have no trouble finding takers.

BRAY-ET-LU

95710 Val-d'Oise. Paris 70 – Gisors 26 – Pontoise 36 – Mantes 24 – Vernon 18.
The castle of Baudemont and its 11th-century remains are worth the trip to this little village between the Norman and French Vexin regions.

 HOTELS-RESTAURANTS

■ **Les Jardins d'Epicure**
16, Grande-Rue.
Tel. 01 34 67 75 87. Fax 01 34 67 90 22.
info@lesjardinsdepicure.com
www.lesjardinsdepicure.com
Closed Jan. Rest. closed Wed. (off season).
6 rooms: 100–225€. 1 suite: 225€.
Prix fixe: 30€, 39€, 75€, 105€.
A la carte: 75–80€.

Rest and relaxation in an imperial setting refurbished with a modern touch. This large house dating from 1850, with its private lounge, Napoleon III–style rooms, grounds with tall trees, heated swimming pool, steam bath and solarium, has everything you could want. Its fine restaurant and terrace provide culinary delights listed in a changing, varied menu that reflects the talented William Boquelet's inspiration.

BRECA see **SAINT-LYPHARD**

BRELIDY

22140 Côtes-d'Armor. Paris 500 – Saint-Brieuc 45 – Guingamp 14.
Between Lannion and Saint-Brieuc, a charming village not far from the Trégor coast.

 HOTELS-RESTAURANTS

■ **Château de Brélidy**
La Noblance.
Tel. 02 96 95 69 38. Fax 02 96 95 18 03.
chateau.brelidy@worldonline.fr
www.chateau-brelidy.com
Closed Jan.–Mar.
13 rooms: 80–123€. 2 suites: 144–164€.
Prix fixe: 28€, 34€, 9€ (child).

In this handsome 18th-century château, we make the most of the fitness center, Jacuzzi and swimming pool before heading back to our old-fashioned rooms with their neo-rustic furniture, then on to the restaurant decorated with large tapestries. In this setting heavy with history, William Langlet concocts refined dishes with a modern touch, including a mackerel charlotte with pears and cardamom-seasoned cream, a salmon tagine made with local beer, chamomile-seasoned minced duck and small round pastries filled with cream, called puits d'amour, for dessert.

LA BRESSE

88250 Vosges. Paris 440 – Colmar 54 – Epinal 57 – Gérardmer 14.
info@labresse.net.

A Vosges mountain resort at a height of 900 to 1350 meters, famous for its cross-country pistes.

■ Les Vallées

31, rue Paul-Claudel.
Tel. 03 29 25 41 39. Fax 03 29 25 64 38.
hotel.lesvallees@remy-loisirs.com
www.labellemontagne.com
Rest. closed 3 weeks Oct.
54 rooms: 56–160€.
Prix fixe: 21€, 42€, 10,50€ (child).
A la carte: 40€.

Large families and parties of friends flock to this huge hotel complex with its covered swimming pool, Jacuzzi, practical rooms and fairly spacious studio apartments. They lunch rapidly at the Slalom at the foot of the slopes and dine in more sophisticated style at the Diamant in the complex itself. The pan-seared duck foie gras, the grilled salmon trout seasoned with thyme and lemon, the roasted duck breast with chanterelles and a violet-flavored berry soup are delightful.

● Clos des Hortensias   SIM

51, rte de Cornimont, 3 km via D486.
Tel. 03 29 25 41 08. Fax 03 29 25 65 34.
Closed Sun. dinner, Mon., 2 weeks Nov.
Prix fixe: 15,50€ (weekday lunch),
21€ (weekday lunch), 25€ (weekday dinner),
29€ (weekday lunch).

The Renards' residence is a pleasant stop. As François prepares his refined, seasonal, market-based dishes, his wife greets guests warmly. Cod with sauce ravigote (a spicy mustard, pickle and caper vinaigrette), sorrel-seasoned pike-perch, stuffed quail and a praline meringue and nougat dessert have the delightful taste of simple fare.

● Auberge du Pêcheur   SIM

76, rte de la Vologne.
Tel. 03 29 25 43 86. Fax 03 29 25 52 59.
www.auberge-du-pecheur.com
Closed Tue., Wed. (off season),
2 weeks beg. Dec., 2 weeks end June.

4 rooms: 47–52€.
Prix fixe: 14€, 21€, 26€, 8€ (child).
A la carte: 35€.

This rustic chalet at the foot of the slopes offers a chic visual and gourmet tour of the region. The charming, wood-trimmed rooms have been renovated this year. Saffron-seasoned Mediterranean sea bass, boudin blanc (white veal sausage) with pike-perch and crayfish with ceps, country ham braised with whiskey and the mirabelle plum croustillant served with bergamot ice cream will bring roses to your cheeks.

● Le Slalom   SIM

Rte du Col-des-Feignes.
Tel. 03 29 25 41 71. Fax 03 29 25 68 50.
Closed Oct.–Nov.
A la carte: 30€.

Summer and winter, this mountain self-service restaurant delights backpackers and cross-country skiers, who all appreciate the generosity and reliability of its dishes. The appetizer buffet, the salmon filet with lentils, escalope with cream sauce and the frozen nougat go down without a hitch, especially at such reasonable prices.

79300 Deux-Sèvres. Paris 364 – Angers 84 – Cholet 45 – Nirot 64 – Poitiers 82.
Famous for its fairs, this ancient hub of the Vendée Gâtine is one of France's meat capitals. The fine church of Notre-Dame with its Renaissance bell tower is well worth a visit.

■ La Boule d'Or

15, pl Emile-Zola.
Tel. 05 49 65 02 18. Fax 05 49 74 11 19.
hotel-labouledor@wanadoo.fr
www.labouledor.fr
Closed Sun. dinner, Mon. lunch,
mid-Feb.–beg. Mar., 3 weeks Aug.
20 rooms: 43–53€.
Prix fixe: 12€ (weekday lunch), 16€, 27€, 34€.

Near the train station, Didier Coutineau's establishment boasting simple, recently renovated rooms is full of regional spirit. The two dining rooms in orange tones with their neo-Louis XIII furniture have also been renovated. In the kitchen, Stephane Lechelard concocts a cuisine with the delightful fragrance of the local countryside: the pan-seared foie gras with berry sauce, the jumbo shrimp brochette seasoned with Pineau de Charentes, minced monkfish with chanterelles and rack of lamb with slow-roasted garlic have an effortless charm. For dessert, the almond craqueline, angelica mousse and fresh fruit tartare are a wonderful surprise.

BREST

29200 Finistère. Paris 596 – Lorient 134 – Quimper 71 – Rennes 245 – Saint-Brieuc 144.
office.de.tourisme.brest@wanadoo.fr.
It does not always rain in Brest. Poet and traveler (and great sailor, of course) Olivier de Kersauzon says that its sky sometimes wells with "tears of emotion". Jacques Prévert's *Barbara* no longer frequents the rue de Siam. The merchant harbor, now a fashionable quay and marina, boasts one of the finest aquariums in the world: Océanopolis. Brest, city of the Arsenal, stronghold of the French Navy, was destroyed in World War II, but still has its old Recouvrance district and imposing fortress. There are charming strolls to be had down the broad streets in the center. If not beautiful, Finistère's great, unjustly obscure capital is at least a pleasant, gastronomical place. An army of young chefs deftly prepare the region's produce. Gifted artisans are shy, but to be found, and there is a smile behind every door.

■ | HOTELS

■ L'Amirauté
41, rue Branda.
Tel. 02 98 80 84 00. Fax 02 98 80 84 84.
amirautebrest@oceaniahotels.com
www.oceaniahotels.com
84 rooms: 99–119€.

Spacious and practical, this establishment close to the city center offers excellent, perfectly kept modern rooms, some of them equipped for disabled guests. It also boasts a restaurant of note (see Restaurants: L'Amirauté).

■ Le Continental
Square de la Tour-d'Auvergne.
Tel. 02 98 80 50 40. Fax 02 98 43 17 47.
continental.brest@oceaniashotels.com
www.oceaniashotel.com
73 rooms: 120–160€. 1 suite: 300€.

This hotel near the town's museums has an art deco flavor. Its postwar setting holds beautifully styled rooms and the welcome and service are very professional.

■ Océania
82, rue de Siam.
Tel. 02 98 80 66 66. Fax 02 98 80 65 50.
oceania-brest@hotel-sofibra.com
www.hotel-sofibra.com
82 rooms: 58–107€. 1 suite: 115€.

This freshly renovated hotel a step away from the convention center and rail station is under new management. The pleasant, spacious rooms overlook the street dear to Jacques Prévert. (See Restaurants: Océania.)

■ Hôtel de la Paix
32, rue d'Algésiras.
Tel. 02 98 80 12 97. Fax 02 98 43 30 95.
www.hoteldelapaix-brest.com
Closed Christmas–New Year's vac.
29 rooms: 63–105€.

A step away from the Océanopolis discovery park, this hotel provides a friendly welcome and appealing breakfast buffet. The rooms are equipped with contemporary furniture to match the meticulous décor. Fitness center and Internet.

■ Relais Mercure
2, rue Y.-Collet.
Tel. 02 98 80 31 80. Fax 02 98 46 52 98.
mercure.voyageur@free.fr
Closed Christmas–New Year's.
40 rooms: 72–108€.

Behind the conventional facade are rooms in different styles (contemporary, art deco) with bright colors and modern conveniences. A friendly welcome.

● RESTAURANTS

● La Fleur de Sel   ◎V.COM

15 bis, rue de Lyon.
Tel. 02 98 44 38 65. Fax 02 98 44 38 53.
lafleurdesel@wanadoo.fr
www.lafleurdesel.com
Closed Sat. lunch, Sun., Mon. lunch,
10 days beg. Jan., 3 weeks Aug.
Prix fixe:.30€, 50€.

The Plassard's restaurant is the rock on which the city's cuisine is built. Caroline still welcomes us with a smile and her husband Yann continues to concoct shrewd regional dishes. This former disciple of Peyrot, Cagna and Vigato prepares gourmet fare that harmoniously marries tradition and modernity. In the bright, contemporary dining room, we revel in the spider crab cream in aspic served with potatoes and a fig and herb vinaigrette, Atlantic sea bass with creamy lettuce sauce, partidge mille-feuille with green cabbage and the walnut ice cream, Breton shortbread and mascarpone mousse. To make our pleasure complete, the check minds its manners.

● Le Nouveau Rossini   V.COM

22, rue du Cdt-Drogou.
Tel.-Fax 02 98 47 90 00.
Closed Sun. dinner, Mon., 1 week Aug.
Prix fixe: 25€ (weekday lunch), 40€, 66€.
A la carte: 65€.

In the heart of a flower-filled garden, Maurice Mevel's 1900 Breton establishment is charming indeed. We like the modern dining room in bright colors, warm atmosphere, affable service and restrained prices, and are equally fond of the concise, authentic cuisine. Rouget and arichokes in vinaigrette, a blanquette of turbot, an herb-marinated Atlantic sea bass cake and a pigeon breast, served with its thigh and wing cooked with spinach, garlic and peppers, like the dark chocolate fondant, are very flavorsome and precise.

● Océania   V.COM

At the Océania, 82, rue de Siam.
Tel. 02 98 80 66 66. Fax 02 98 80 65 50.
www.hotel-sofibra.com
Closed Sat., Sun., mid-July–mid-Aug.
Prix fixe: 20€, 27€, 33€. A la carte: 50€.

Franck Guest concocts neoclassical dishes organized into appealing set menus in this good hotel restaurant. A shiitake and cep risotto, monkfish medallion with Espelette chili peppers, roasted pigeon infused with garlic and rosemary and the thin lemon tarte served with a crumble are delightful, as are the wines at sensible prices.

● L'Amirauté   COM

At L'Amirauté. 41, rue Branda.
Tel. 02 98 80 84 00. Fax 02 98 80 84 84.
www.oceaniahotels.coma
Closed Sat., Sun., 15 July–15 Aug.
Prix fixe: 28€, 40€, 50€.

Brest society's fine, fashionable refectory is hidden away in a modern chain hotel. Yvon Morvan (who served with Bocuse, Duquesnoy and Robuchon) prepares a subtle, fresh, precise cuisine based on quality produce. Creamy soup with raw oysters and watercress, aromatic herb-stuffed squid cannelloni, rosemary-seasoned John Dory strips served with a cauliflower gratin and the Breton shortbread and seasonal fruit mille-feuille make up interesting set menus.

● Maison de l'Océan   COM

2, quai de la Douane, at the port.
Tel. 02 98 80 44 84. Fax 02 98 46 19 83.
www.maisondelocean.com
Closed 24 Dec.
Prix fixe: 15€, 19,50€, 26,50€,
7,50€ (child). A la carte: 55€.

Opposite the harbor, this smart marine brasserie devotedly serves fine seafood and more. A seafood degustation platter, the whelk gratin with a shellfish coulis, grilled line-fished Atlantic sea bass, sirloin steak with shallots and the vacherin put us back on our feet. Watch out for the à la carte prices.

● **Le Ruffé** COM

1 bis, rue Y.-Collet.
Tel. 02 98 46 07 70. Fax 02 98 44 31 46.
www.restaurateurs-pointe-bretagne.com
Closed Sun. dinner, Mon.
Prix fixe: 19€, 28€, 35€, 7,50€ (child).
A la carte: 47€.

Georges Garkouchevsky's gourmet ocean liner remains firmly on course with a cuisine reflecting modern tastes. At the stove, Jean-Michel Faijean prepares market produce-based dishes assembled in refined set menus. In the modern, ship's cabin-style dining room, the lobster "discovery", the foie gras-stuffed hamburger, skate with spices, Lyon-style chitterling sausage and the Calvados apple pyramid dessert impress us favorably.

● **Ma Petite Folie** 🏠SIM

Port du Moulin-Blanc.
Tel. 02 98 42 44 42. Fax 02 98 41 43 68.
mapetitefolie@wanadoo.fr
Closed 1 Jan.
Prix fixe: 15€ (lunch), 21,50€, 27,50€.
A la carte: 35€.

This handsome vessel is on a steady course. The crew—consisting of Caroline and Yan Plassard, with Stéphane Bazile in the galley—is splendidly attentive and the menu first-rate: the rockfish soup, skate wing with caper butter, a tarragon-seasoned poultry fricassée and the berry crumble with violet ice cream promise delicious adventures at an amiable price.

● **L'Adagio** ⓝSIM

8, rue de Siam.
Tel. 02 98 80 64 70.
Closed Sun. lunch.
Prix fixe: 28€.

Teddy Beuzet, who worked with Ducasse in Paris and Raymond Blanc in Oxford, has turned this ochre-tinted brasserie into a busy, gourmet spot. The thin crust pizzas, goat cheese spring rolls, quick-seared rolled tuna and the Caesar salad strike the right note and the crab ravioli and the scallop tagine look healthy indeed. A choice of quality Italian wines.

● **La Brocherie** ⓝSIM

61, rue Louis-Pasteur.
Tel. 02 98 44 07 69.
www.labrocherie.com
Closed Sat. lunch, Sun., Christmas.
Prix fixe: 18€, 25€.

Pleasant, modern, inexpensive and very red, Jean-Jacques Butynska's restaurant is something of a Breton log hut. Country terrine with sauce gribiche (caper and pickle mayonnaise), the lemongrass-seasoned salmon céviche, cod filet with lobster sauce and the pear Belle Helene do us a power of good.

● **Le Crabe Marteau** ⓝSIM

Quai de la Douane.
Tel. 02 98 33 38 57.
Closed Sun., Christmas–New Year's,
Feb. vac.
A la carte: 30€.

Martine and Pierre Cosmao have turned this stone-clad tavern by the harbor with its wooden tables, bar and beams into a convivial eatery. We quietly enjoy the crab served in various forms (in salad, with avocado, oven crisped, in spicy mayonnaise), the abalone, the scallops and the Chouchen cider crêpes.

● **L'Olive** ⓝSIM

6, pl de la Liberté.
Tel. 02 98 46 05 78.
Closed Sat. lunch, Sun.
Prix fixe: 19€, 28€.

This chic, contemporary snack bar just opposite the market plays mischievously on olive green and black and fills its dishes with sunshine. Goat cheese and sundried tomatoes on toast, red tuna in a sesame crust, rouget, tapenade and the slow-cooked apples and hazelnut-flavored crème brûlée incite us to travel.

● **Amour de Pomme de Terre**

23, rue des Halles.
Tel. 02 98 43 48 51. Fax 02 98 43 61 88.
www.amourdepommedeterre.com
Call for opening days, hours.
A la carte: 45–50€.

This relaxed chain of restaurants has scored a clear success in Brittany. Its strong points are its friendly atmosphere, gentle prices and unfussy regional food. A seafood fricassée, a slice of beef rump roast and the crème brûlée pep us up.

BREITENBACH see HOHWALD

LE BREUIL-EN-AUGE

14130 Calvados. Paris 194 – Caen 54 –
Lisieux 9 – Deauville 21.
A corner of the Auge district a step away from the fine resorts of the Normandy coast.

● RESTAURANTS

● **Le Dauphin** ◎|COM|

2, rue de l'Eglise.
Tel. 02 31 65 08 11. Fax 02 31 65 12 08.
dauphin.le@wanadoo.fr
Closed Sun. dinner, Mon.,
mid-Nov.–beg. Dec., Feb. vac.
Prix fixe: 35€, 42€.

In his typically Norman half-timbered inn, Régis Lecomte plays on the region's culinary traditions with the greatest respect for his produce. Sea urchin in its shell with an egg and green asparagus, abalone zarzuela, little neck crabs, langoustines and sole, pike-perch filet with spring vegetables, slow-cooked squab stew, white Vire chitterling sausage and the thin rhubarb tart with milk caramel ice cream change little, but remain reliably good. A delectable welcome and solid gold set menus.

BREVIANDES see TROYES

BRIGNOGAN-PLAGES

29890 Finistère. Paris 585 – Brest 41 –
Landerneau 27 – Morlaix 49.
An obscure little jewel in North Finistère, between Abers and Léon.

 HOTELS-RESTAURANTS

■ **Castel Régis**

Tel. 02 98 83 40 22. Fax 02 98 83 44 71.
castel-regis@wanadoo.fr / www.castelregis.com
Closed end Sept.–beg. May.
22 rooms: 73–145€.
Half board: 77,50–155€.

A collection of houses and a main building form this pleasant hotel "village" with its large garden and swimming pool. The rooms are comfortable and the *pension* meals reliable. The fitness center is a bonus.

BRINON-SUR-SAULDRE

18410 Cher. Paris 191 – Orléans 57 –
Bourges 65.
With its little brick houses and church with a *caquetoir* (gossip gallery, or small porch), this village seems to have slipped straight from the pages of Maurice Genevoix's *Raboliot*.

 HOTELS-RESTAURANTS

■ **La Solognote** ❀🏠

34, Grande-Rue.
Tel. 02 48 58 50 29. Fax 02 48 58 56 00.
lasolognote@wanadoo.fr
www.lasolognote.com
Closed 2 weeks Mar. Rest. closed Tue. (off season), Wed. (off season).
13 rooms: 58–92€.
Prix fixe: 22€, 26€, 45€, 68€.
A la carte: 36–64€.

With its brick facade, small, neat rooms, hexagonal red floor tiles, ceiling beams and antique furniture, this inn has charm to spare. In the dining room with its large fireplace, we enjoy the fresh dishes based on seasonal produce. Escargots in a crêpe pouch, nutmeg-seasoned pike mousse, veal kidneys, lattice-cut potatoes and broccoli and, as a surprise dessert, the "*douceur de la Solognote*" are all very pleasant.

BRIOLLAY

49125 Maine-et-Loire. Paris 288 – Angers 15 – Château-Gontier 41 – La Flèche 40.
This gentle, rustic, idyllic little corner of Anjou exemplifies the Loire Valley Ronsard style.

 HOTELS-RESTAURANTS

● **Château de Noirieux**
26, rte du Moulin.
Tel. 02 41 42 50 05. Fax 02 41 37 91 00.
noirieux@relaischateaux.com
www.chateaudenoirieux.com
Closed Sun and Mon. (Nov.–Apr.), mid-Feb.–mid-Mar., 1 Nov.–29 Nov. Rest. closed Sun. dinner, Mon., Tue. lunch (Nov.–Apr.).
18 rooms: 175–350€. 1 suite: 160€.
Prix fixe: 57€, 105€.

Anja and Gérard Côme have turned this Anjou manor into a charming hostelry indeed. We do not come here for the fresh, refined rooms, handsome grounds and swimming pool alone, but also for Gérard's subtle, light, modern, but refined cuisine, presented in the form of appealing set menus. The Breton oysters, pan-seared smoked duck foie gras, grilled scallops, oven-crisped langoustines, a juicy venison medallion in hunting season and the pigeon breast roasted in a cocotte showcase quality produce. The desserts (dark caramel "barrel", a pineapple carpaccio and a Cointreau and lime soufflé) conjure up scenes from our childhood. The cellar is an ode to Loire wines.

BRION see JOIGNY

BRISSAC

34190 Hérault. Paris 736 – Nice 366 – Nîmes 67 – Montpellier 43.
This distinctive little village on the way from the Hérault gorges is just a stone's throw from

the Grotte des Demoiselles, one of the deepest of underground "cathedrals".

 RESTAURANTS

● **Le Jardin aux Sources** `COM`
30, av du Parc.
Tel.-Fax 04 67 73 31 16.
www.lejardinauxsources.com
Closed Sun. dinner, Mon., Wed. lunch,
3 weeks Nov. 1 vac., 3 weeks Jan.
Prix fixe: 29€, 41€, 68€.

Jérôme Billod-Morel's 1900 stone establishment brings the flavors of the South to its contemporary dining room. A pear and Roquefort "mosaic" with crunchy puff pastry, the fig cake and rouget filets, the hunter's sampler plate with three kinds of game, a country tart and a cold chocolate nougat play on local recipes with a certain sense of adventure. A brand new swimming pool relieves us of a few calories. Isabelle provides an exquisite welcome.

BRIVE-LA-GAILLARDE

19100 Corrèze. Paris 482 – Limoges 91 – Clermont-Ferrand 171 – Sarlat 52.
tourisme.brive@wanadoo.fr.
Administratively part of the Limousin, Brive flirts with Quercy and rubs shoulders with Périgord. It is surrounded by viaducts bisecting the landscape, green hills and farms raising veal calves. Famous for its poultry fairs in winter, Georges Brassens market all year and book fair in the fall, it enjoys an easygoing existence in any season. It has nurtured a literary school that has its luminaries—Claude Michelet, Denis Tillinac, Michel Peyramaure and Claude Signol—but remains convivial and rustic. It has a passion for rugby, articulately promotes its love of food and boasts plenty of good restaurants. The excellent artisans here provide violet mustard, fine buckwheat crêpes and walnut liqueur. Quality canners—princes of foie gras and confit—abound in the area. All Brive needs is a little self confidence to become a culinary capital in the heart of France.

HOTELS-RESTAURANTS

■ Mercure

Rte d'Objat, le Griffolet, 6 km via D901 and
D170.
Tel. 05 55 86 36 36. Fax 05 55 87 04 40.
h0358@accor-hotels.com
www.mercure.com
54 rooms: 72–87€.
Prix fixe: 18€, 26€, 8€ (child).
A la carte: 40€.

Its practical location a stone's throw
from the Bordeaux and Toulouse turnpike, swimming pool, modern rooms
recently renovated and decent *pension*
cuisine are the main attractions of this
chain hotel.

■ La Truffe Noire

22, bd A.-France.
Tel. 05 55 92 45 00. Fax 05 55 92 45 13.
www.la-truffe-noire.com
Closed Christmas.
27 rooms: 95–120€.
Prix fixe: 35€, 50€, 65€. A la carte: 65€.

For more than 110 years, this solid residence has celebrated hospitality on
its every floor. The regularly redecorated, traditional rooms are just the
place for a refreshing nap after a solid
meal enjoyed by the hearth in winter or on the terrace shaded by ancient
trees in summer. The fare includes
duck foie gras with fig compote, a cod
filet enrusted in chorizo served with a
chickpea purée, pan-seared beef steak
and a baba au rhum.

■ Le Collonges

3-5, pl Winston-Churchill.
Tel. 05 55 74 09 58. Fax 05 55 74 11 25.
lecollonges@wanadoo.fr
24 rooms: 48–57€.

This hotel in the center of town has large
rooms refurbished art deco style. Jean-
Pierre Castera's welcome is hospitality
itself.

■ Le Quercy

8 bis, quai Tourny.
Tel. 05 55 74 09 26. Fax 05 55 74 06 24.
www.contact-hotel.com
54 rooms: 50–60€.

This hotel is delightfully located opposite
the market made famous by singer-songwriter Georges Brassens and hosting the
book fair each year. With its sixties rooms
and popular bar, it is a handy halt.

● Les Arums

15, av d'Alsace-Lorraine.
Tel. 05 55 24 26 55. Fax 05 55 17 13 22.
restaurant.lesarums@wanadoo.fr
www.lesarums.fr
Closed Sat. lunch, Sun. dinner, Mon.,
1 week Mar., end Aug.–mid-Sept.
Prix fixe: 27€ (weekday lunch, wine inc.),
37€, 45€, 82€. A la carte: 60€.

In their ultracontemporary setting, Béatrice and Christophe Champagnac receive
the cream of town society. She runs the
dining room brightly, while he busies
himself in the kitchen, preparing fare
with a topical touch. A langoustine and
sundried tomato tian with vinaigrette, a
rouget mille-feuille with artichokes and
peppers and a ten spice–seasoned squab
with chanterelles are modern interpretations of yesterday's recipes. To conclude,
a passion fruit cannelloni adds a tasteful
touch of freshness. All this is served on
the shady terrace in summer.

● La Toupine

27, av Pasteur.
Tel.-Fax 05 55 23 71 58.
Closed Sun., Mon., 2 weeks Feb. vac.,
2 weeks Aug.
Prix fixe: 12€ (lunch), 24€, 28€.
A la carte: 40€.

As a pupil in the grandest of establishments (the Palm Beach in Cannes and
Pralong 2000 in Courchevel), Olivier Maurin learned to exercise care and precision. This son of Clermont-Ferrand now
devotes his skills to preparing a tasteful,
modern-rustic cuisine. In the Toupine's
refined, contemporary setting, we make

short work of a tuna carpaccio with tomato sorbet, a grilled rouget filet with mushroom- and ham-stuffed artichokes simmered in wine, a pork cheek fricassée with violet mustard and frozen strawberry tulips served in a "cloud" of coconut and banana caramel.

● La Crémaillère `COM`

53, av de Paris.
Tel. 05 55 74 32 47. Fax 05 55 74 00 15.
hotel.restaurant-la.cremaillere@wanadoo.fr
Closed 1 week Christmas–New Year's,
1 week beg. July. Rest. closed Sun.
8 rooms: 44–47€.
Prix fixe: 28,50€, 36€, 40€ (wine inc.)
15€ (child). A la carte: 60–70€.

This long famous restaurant's rustic surroundings continue to enchant. Christophe Forget, a veteran of the Périgourdine, rather successfully concocts a minced veal sweetbread with truffles, a whole lobster with beurre blanc sauce, a Limousin farm-raised veal cutlet with salted butter served with pan-tossed wild mushrooms and the hot Grand Marnier soufflé with house chocolate ice cream, served in the dining room or in the shade of the lime trees on the terrace.

● Chez Francis `SIM`

61, av de Paris.
Tel. 05 55 74 41 72. Fax 05 55 17 20 54.
chez.francis@wanadoo.fr
Closed Sun., Mon., 10 days Feb. vac.,
beg. Aug.–mid-Aug.
Prix fixe: 15€ (weekdays), 23€.
A la carte: 55€.

This Parisian family bistro exerts its charm, especially on writers in town for the book fair. Its retro décor, convivial atmosphere and seasonal cuisine are hard to resist. Francis Tessandier and his son Franck concoct artichoke and summer truffle tartines (on toast), roasted cod filet with chorizo-seasoned potatoes, milk-fed veal with an accompaniment of pan-tossed mushrooms and a white chocolate mousse with raspberries: solid fare, like the region's wine.

● Le Kiosque `SIM`

Pl Jean-Paul Lartigue.
Tel. 05 55 23 27 73.
Closed Sun., Tue. dinner.
Prix fixe: 9,50€ (lunch), 11,50€ (lunch, wine inc.), 18€ (dinner), 25€ (dinner).

Lucie Puech welcomes us with a smile, while Amédée Leymarie (who worked at the Arums and Pont de l'Ouysse, and trained in Paris at the Carré des Feuillants) prepares a simple, pleasant, rural cuisine with a modern flavor. Cucumber and feta gazpacho drizzled with an olive purée, a tomato, mozzarella and basil tart, wild seasonal fish served with slow-cooked fennel and the duck parmentier with sweet potatoes look appetizing indeed. The desserts (fruit in puff pastry with a light cream sauce and the chocolate dessert with a passion fruit center) are imaginative and the place settings (Guy Degrenne plates and Spiegelau glasses) polished. In short, with its little set menus, an eatery to watch and encourage.

● L'Amphitryon `SIM`

12, av d'Alsace-Lorraine.
Tel. 05 55 84 87 04.
amphitryongastro@wanadoo.fr
Closed Sun. dinner, Mon., Tue.
Prix fixe: 15€ (lunch), 30€ (dinner).
A la carte: 50€.

Admittedly, the cod-stuffed piquillos and Espelette peppers, the grilled scallop brochette with creamy risotto, roasted sea bream seasoned with garlic petals, tête de veau cassoulet with porcini and the brioche pain perdu with caramel ice cream are rich, but they are well prepared too. We like Olivier Grelier's authentic cuisine, enjoyed in the dining rooms or on the patio. Sensible set menus.

● Le Bistro du Brune `SIM`

13, av de Paris.
Tel. 05 55 24 00 91.
www.le-brune-brive.com
Closed Sat. dinner (exc. summer), Sun., Wed. dinner (exc. summer), 1 week Jan.
Prix fixe: 7,50€, 10€, 17€, 22€.
A la carte: 30€.

Until late at night, Jean-Hugues Célérier's "Parisian" café standing by the statue of Marshal Brune welcomes guests for a full dinner or simply a drink. In the dining room with its old posters, banquettes and attractive lighting, a duck terrine with slow-cooked caramelized onions, a gizzard confit salad with goat cheese, the tête de veau and the crème brûlée are washed down with a pleasantly priced Bergerac.

In Varetz (19240). 10 km via D901 and D152.

● **Château de Castel Novel**
Tel. 05 55 85 00 01. Fax 05 55 85 09 03.
www.castelnovel.com
Hotel closed mid-Dec.–mid-Jan.
35 rooms: 90–270€. 2 suites: 250–340€.
Prix fixe: 29€ (lunch), 38€, 47€, 67€,
15€ (child). A la carte: 70–90€.

Experienced hosts the Parveaux (also owners of the Alpes du Pralong in Courchevel) provide a polished welcome in their 12th-century, red sandstone château, which boasts fine, comfortable, rustic rooms where Henry de Jouvenel and Colette once stayed. In the grounds shaded by ancient trees, sport and relaxation are on the agenda, with a swimming pool, three hole golf course and fitness center. The restaurant presents Patrick Boulouton's regional cuisine. A duck foie gras confit and its fat with pepper on toasted country bread, a grilled John Dory with cumin-seasoned zucchini and a creamy herb mousse, golden brown veal sweetbreads glazed with ceps served with a pot of seasonal vegetables and the light Armagnac and orange soufflé served with cocoa-flavored ice cream are successful and deft. The fine wines on the list make up for the dishes' occasional lack of originality.

LES BRIZARDS see QUARRE-LES-TOMBES

BRUMATH

67170 Bas-Rhin. Paris 470 – Haguenau 11 – Strasbourg 17 – Saverne 30.
The 1870 war took its toll here, but the town still has its ancient houses, signs of a rich past evinced by the Gallic-Roman archeological digs.

HOTELS-RESTAURANTS

■ **L'Ecrevisse**
4, av de Strasbourg.
Tel. 03 88 51 11 08. Fax 03 88 51 89 02.
www.hostellerie-ecrevisse.com
Closed 2 weeks end July–mid-Aug.
Rest. closed Mon. dinner, Tue.
17 rooms: 50–85€. 2 suites: 100€.
Prix fixe: 45€, 75€. A la carte: 65–70€.

This typically Alsatian inn with its swimming pool has been in the Orth family for seven generations. Tradition rhymes with quality here. The delightful welcome, comfortable guest rooms and elaborate cuisine concocted by Michel (possibly a touch too ornate on occasion, but perfectly in line with local tradition) attract our attention here. Foie gras served three ways, crayfish tail cassolette, individual fresh and smoked fish terrines, the game (in hunting season) and the pretty chocolate dessert board are fine, classical fare, generous and carefully prepared. The luxurious dining room has style and the extensive wine list of 120 vintages is well worth perusing.

● **Krebs'tuebbel**   ■SIM
4, av de Strasbourg.
Tel. 03 88 51 11 08. Fax 03 88 51 89 02.
www.hostellerie-ecrevisse.com
Closed Mon. dinner, Tue., 1 week at end July,
2 weeks beg. Aug.
Prix fixe: 9,50€ (lunch), 17,50€, 31€.
A la carte: 33–42€.

Michel Orth's inn (an adjunct to the Ecrevisse) serves traditional Alsatian dishes. Apart from the shrewd regional tapas, these include shrimp soup, poached Fontaine salmon, slow-simmered chicken in creamy white sauce and a frozen apple nougat dessert. A fine selection of wines and beers.

In Mommenheim (67170). 6 km nw via D421.

● **Castel San Angelo**　SIM
53, rte de Brumath.
Tel. 03 88 51 61 78. Fax 03 88 51 59 96.
Closed Sun. lunch, Mon. dinner, Wed. dinner.
Prix fixe: 30€ (Sun. lunch).
A la carte: 40€.

Angelo Bulone and his Sicilian family run this very neo-rustic Castel with great good humor. We dine pleasantly on Provençal-style frog legs, stuffed squid, a Sicilian meat dish and the tiramisu.

In Mommenheim.

● **Chez Clément**　SIM
"à la Gare"
1, rue de la Gare.
Tel. 03 88 51 61 17. Fax 03 88 51 69 61.
restclement67@aol.com
Closed Tue. dinner, Wed. dinner.
Prix fixe: 10€ (weekday lunch), 12€, 15€, 28€, 32€, 8€ (child). A la carte: 45€.

Joséphine and Clément Gilbert's eatery provides a pleasant welcome and efficient service. The check is modest and the cuisine well crafted. We reserve a table to feast on a marbled duck foie gras with fig chutney, a veal filet with morels and the fruit gratin served with vanilla ice cream. Amiable set menus at lunchtime.

BRUYERES

88600 Vosges. Paris 39 – Epinal 25 – Gérardmer 23 – Remiremont 20 – Saint-Dié 25. Not far from the Vologne river, a crossroads leading to the Hautes Vosges.

●	RESTAURANTS

● **L'Escale**　COM
22, rue Abel-Ferry.
Tel. 03 29 50 10 08.
Closed Sun. dinner, Mon., Wed. dinner.
Prix fixe: 12€. A la carte: 35€.

Stéphane Melloni is now presiding over this neo-art nouveau restaurant in pastel tones where he concocts conventional, but well-crafted dishes. Foie gras in pain perdu, pike-perch filet with Meuse truffles, veal kidney flambéed in Cognac and a pear crème brûlée are sensibly priced.

LE BUGUE

24260 Dordogne. Paris 522 – Périgueux 43 – Sarlat 31 – Bergerac 48.
A small town between Dordogne and Vézère, where we take time out to admire the Périgord Noir district's caves and châteaux.

 HOTELS-RESTAURANTS

■ **Oustalou**　❀🏠
At the Royal Vézère, pl du Royal-Vézère.
Tel. 05 53 07 20 01 (hotel)
05 53 07 66 63 (rest.). Fax 05 53 07 66 90.
restaurant.loustalou@wanadoo.fr
Closed 1 Nov.–end Mar.
49 rooms: 50–90€. 4 suites: 115–130€.
Prix fixe: 20€, 27€, 42€, 47€.

The Cantets have taken over this hotel and its traditional restaurant with gusto. We still enjoy the terrace overlooking the Vézère, the rooms in pastel tones with their period furniture and the uncontentiously priced classical dishes, including lobster in salad, a pan-seared foie gras escalope, pike-perch filet, a beef rib eye and strawberry charlotte.

● **Auberge la Vieille Cure**　SIM
7 km, Saint-Chamassy, Le Bourg.
Tel. 05 53 07 24 24. Fax 05 53 54 39 44.
Closed Sun. dinner (off season), Mon. (off season), end Nov.–mid-Mar.
Prix fixe: 25€, 49€. A la carte: 50€.

Françoise and Michel Compostella have turned this priest's house into an easygoing inn. We feast on foie gras with slow-cooked apples, langoustine risotto, strips of duck breast with morels in sauce and the frozen nougat while savoring some fine Bergeracs.

LE BUISSON-DE-CADOUIN

24480 Dordogne. Paris 536 – Bergerac 38 – Sarlat 35 – Périgueux 53.

The Périgord Noir district is a true wonderland with its walled towns, fine squares bordered by arcades and Cadouin cloister, whose vaults are in the purest Gothic style: a marvel not to be missed.

 HOTELS-RESTAURANTS

● **Manoir de Bellerive**

Rte de Siorac.
Tel. 05 53 22 16 16. Fax 05 53 22 09 05.
manoir.bellerive@wanadoo.fr
www.bellerivehotel.com
Closed beg. Jan.–mid-Mar. Rest. closed Mon. lunch, Tue. lunch, Wed. lunch.
4 rooms: 155–240€. 1 suite: 400€.
Prix fixe: 45€, 55€. A la carte: 100€.

There is something for everyone in Marcel Clévenot's Napoleon III manor. The more athletic among us will enjoy sessions in the fitness center, swimming pool, Jacuzzi and steam bath, while late risers may prefer the comfort of the rooms overlooking the landscaped grounds. All, however, will agree that the two restaurant dining rooms are a very good thing indeed. In the kitchen, Jean-Luc L'Hourre—a Breton winner of the Meilleur Ouvrier de France award from Les Abers (we met him in Lannilis)—concocts a refined domestic cuisine that includes a foie gras charlotte with arichokes, slice of turbot, duckling roasted two ways and a lime mousse. The service is truly perfect and the wine list presents many excellent finds.

BULGNEVILLE

88140 Vosges. Paris 338 – Epinal 51 – Nancy 78 – Vittel 8.
A village on the Vosges plain, a step away from the mineral water towns, at the gates of the Champagne district.

● RESTAURANTS

● **La Marmite Beaujolaise**

34, rue de l'Hôtel-de-Villle.
Tel.-Fax 03 29 09 16 58.
Closed Sun. dinner, Mon.

Prix fixe: 15€ (lunch), 22,50€ (weekday lunch), 30€, 41,50€.

Xavier Gutehrlé, a disciple of Marc Veyrat and Jean-Claude Aiguier, shrewdly reinterprets his region's gourmet traditions. In his bucolic eatery with its rustic dining room, we feast on slow-cooked peppers with thick slices of smoked salmon in an herbed yogurt sauce, a marbled beef cheek terrine with slow-cooked caramelized onions, salmon croustillant with meat sauce, veal kidney with shallots and mustard sauce and a mirabelle plum cream in gelatin. A fine wine list.

BURBACH see **SARRE-UNION**

BUSCHWILLER

68220 Haut-Rhin. Paris 482 – Mulhouse 29 – Altkirch 26 – Colmar 64 – Saint-Louis 6.
A corner of Sundgau with flowers, orchards and verdant countryside a stone's throw from Basel and Saint-Louis.

● RESTAURANTS

● **La Couronne**

6, rue du Soleil.
Tel. 03 89 69 12 62.
Closed Mon.
Prix fixe: 8,50€ (lunch). A la carte: 40€.

This large village house converted into a rustic brasserie in green, brown and beige tones is energetically run by Anne-Rose Oser. A young veteran of the Armes de Bâle in Gewenheim, she performs a light repertoire that has its charms. A chanterelle gratin, sirloin steak with morels, frozen kouglof and a house millefeuille dessert strike the right note.

14390 Calvados. Paris 218 –
Caen 31 – Deauville 19 – Lisieux 35 –
Pont-l'Evêque 33.
cabourg.tourisme@wanadoo.fr.
This "Balbec" is a heartland of Proustian nostalgia, from the promenade by the sea to the Grand Hôtel and casino gardens.

 HOTELS-RESTAURANTS

■ Grand Hôtel

Promenade Marcel-Proust.
Tel. 02 31 91 01 79. Fax 02 31 24 03 20.
h1282@accor-hotels.com
www.grandhotel-cabourg.com
Rest. closed Mon. (exc. July–Aug.),
Tue. (exc. July–Aug.).
68 rooms: 180–315€. 2 suites: 400–600€.
Prix fixe: 43€, 50€.

Under the sign of Mercure today, the Proustian heart of the legendary Grand Hôtel beats on. Marcel's bust in the lobby, the cozy rooms, a dining room that has adopted the name given it by Proust (the Aquarium) and the view of the seawall and beach all add to its charm. Pascal Clerc's neo-Norman cuisine is highly apposite. A foie gras terrine with fleur de sel and green tomato marmalade, Atlantic sea bass with Grenaille new potatoes, spicy roasted lamb and the frozen strawberry and pistachio macarons have plenty of appeal.

■ Mercure Hippodrome

Av Michel-d'Ornano.
Tel. 02 31 24 04 04. Fax 02 31 91 03 99.
h1223@accor.com / www.mercure.com
Rest. closed lunch
76 rooms: 90–210€. 1 suite: 200–250€.
Prix fixe: 14€, 17€. A la carte: 29€.

This hotel's two buildings in Norman style next to the racecourse boast modern rooms, a fitness center with a swimming pool and a dining room looking out onto the racetrack. A chitterling sausage cake, sea bream filet with tomato-infused oil, boneless rib steak with oven-roasted potatoes and chive-seasoned cream and tarte Normande provide suitable refreshment.

■ Cabourg

5, av de la République.
Tel. 02 31 24 42 55. Fax 02 31 24 48 93.
hotellecabourg@wanadoo.fr
www.hotel-cabourg.fr
8 rooms: 110–180€. 1 suite: 180–250€.

Right in the heart of town, this Second Empire villa wages a triumphant charm offensive with its spruced-up, renovated rooms.

■ Le Cottage

24, av du Général-Leclerc.
Tel. 02 31 91 65 61. Fax 02 31 28 78 82.
www.hotellecottage.com
Closed 3 weeks Jan.
14 rooms: 50–99€. 1 suite: 110€.

Dany Rival offers a warm welcome in this stylish Belle Epoque establishment. Guests are delighted by the pleasant gardens and charming rooms, two of them equipped with balneotherapy facilities. Breakfast enchants.

● Le Royal

37-39, av de la Mer.
Tel. 02 31 91 81 39. Fax 02 31 91 83 28.
Closed Sun. dinner, Mon. dinner (off season),
Tue. dinner, Jan.
A la carte: 35€.

Françoise and Marc Monoury's warm-hearted welcome, relaxed atmosphere, well-mannered checks and market cuisine attract plenty of customers to this good-natured brasserie. Mussels, seafood choucroute, chitterling sausage and chocolate mousse are splendid.

In Bavent-Ranville (14860).

■ Hostellerie du Moulin du Pré

7 km w via D513 and rte de Gonneville-en-Auge.
Tel. 02 31 78 83 68. Fax 02 31 78 21 05.
Closed Oct., 2 weeks beg. Mar. Rest. closed Sun. dinner, Mon. (exc. Bank holidays), Tue. (exc. Bank holidays).

10 rooms: 40–59€.
Prix fixe: 36,50€, 49€.

Lost in the countryside, the Hamchin-Holtzes' old farm boasts rustic rooms and a tasteful regional restaurant. Hot pâté with oyster mushrooms, sorrel-seasoned turbot, poultry with morels and the hazelnut parfait are very impressive.

In Dives-sur-Mer (14160).

● **Chez le Bougnat** SIM
25, rue Gaston-Manneville.
Tel. 02 31 91 06 13. Fax 02 31 91 09 87.
chezlebougnat@aol.com
www.chezlebougnat.fr
Closed Sun. dinner, Mon. dinner, Tue. dinner.
Prix fixe: 15,90€, 20,90€, 24,90€.
A la carte: 35€.

François Teissonnière has turned this former hardware store into a refined bistro. Minced duck spread, escargots, veal kidneys in cream sauce and chocolate profiteroles provide simple enjoyment.

CABRIERES-D'AVIGNON

84220 Vaucluse. Paris 711 – Avignon 34 – Apt 24 – Cavaillon 13 – Carpentras 26.
Mount Luberon, its hills, pine groves and pastoral villages.

 | RESTAURANTS

● **Le Vieux Bistro** COM
Grand-Rue.
Tel. 04 90 76 82 08. Fax 04 90 76 98 98.
levieuxbistro @wanadoo.fr
www.vieuxbistro .com
Closed Mon.
Prix fixe: 16€ (lunch), 35€, 37€.

At the gates of the Luberon district, the attractive Aude Fouiller and the energetic Vincent Lantelme have taken over this bistro, a jewel at the heart of the village, and are running it with gusto. They have hired Thierry Château, a reliable chef who formerly worked at the Bastide de Gordes and Andéols. The relaxed atmosphere and bright tastes go well together in the colorful dining room and on the terrace. An eggplant mille-feuille with vegetables worked into local ewe's cheese, honey- and spice-glazed duck with figs, thyme-marinated goat cheese and an exotic passion fruit timbale make an excellent impression.

LA CADIERE-D'AZUR

83740 Var. Paris 819 – Aix-en-Provence 64 – Marseille 44 – Toulon 22.
A small town with neighboring vineyards, the sea close by and noble, authentic Provence all around.

 | HOTELS-RESTAURANTS

● **Hostellerie Bérard**
Av Gabriel-Péri.
Tel. 04 94 90 11 43. Fax 04 94 90 01 94.
berard@hotel-berard.com
www.hotel-berard.com
Closed Jan.–mid-Feb.
Rest. closed Sat. lunch, Mon. lunch.
37 rooms: 85–208€. 3 suites: 229–263€.
Prix fixe: 30€, 47€, 64€, 134€ (for 2), 25€ (child). A la carte: 85€.

The Bérards' hostelry is ambitious indeed, offering grounds planted with olive trees and cypresses, houses of character (including an 11th-century convent), tennis court, gym, Jacuzzi, steam bath and heated outdoor swimming pool. The old-fashioned rooms in the colors of Provence do justice to the setting. In the kitchen, René Bérard has an eye to fashion, but never strays too far. His pain d'épice with a foie gras and green apple chutney topping, grilled sea bream served with stir-fried vegetables and herbs and a lamb tagine with prunes and preserved lemons are an incitement to exploration. For dessert, the lavender crème brûlée pays delicious tribute to the region, as does the cellar, focusing on Bandol and its district.

CAEN

14000 Calvados. Paris 233 – Cherbourg 124 – Le Havre 86 – Rennes 184 – Alençon 105.

toudismefo@ville-caen.fr.

Destroyed in 1944, then rebuilt (although a few of its treasures are still intact: the Abbaye aux Hommes, the Abbaye aux Dames and some old homes in the rue Saint-Pierre), this Norman capital is also a crossroads on the way to the Normandy Landing beaches. Do not miss the art gallery in the château itself.

 HOTELS

■ Holiday Inn

4, pl du Maréchal-Foch.
Tel. 02 31 27 57 57. Fax 02 31 27 57 58.
holiday-in-caen@wanadoo.fr
www.holiday-in.com/caen-cityctr
Open daily. Rest. closed Sat. lunch, Sun.
88 rooms: 81–128€.
Prix fixe: 10,50€, 15€, 7,50€ (child).
A la carte: 35€.

By the Parc de la Prairie, this fifties chain hotel offers large, modern rooms that are regularly refurbished. At the Bistro Foch, we quietly enjoy the refined cuisine, which reflects regional tastes.

■ Hôtel Moderne

116, bd du Maréchal-Leclerc.
Tel. 02 31 86 04 23. Fax 02 31 85 37 93.
info@hotel-caen.com
www.bestwestern-moderne-caen.com
9 rooms: 75–150€.

The functional rooms, upper-story breakfast hall overlooking the city's roofs, sauna, swimming pool and fitness center all make an excellent impression when we visit this hotel (which was "modern" when it was built, after the war).

■ Mercure Port de Plaisance

1, rue de Courtonne.
Tel. 02 31 47 24 24. Fax 02 31 47 43 88.
h0869@accor-hotels.com / www.mercure.com
Rest. closed Sat. lunch, Sun. lunch.
110 rooms: 89–109€. 4 suites: 170€.
Prix fixe: 16€, 21€.

This practical hotel is suitably located near the Saint-Pierre basin, château and Abbaye aux Dames. Its renovated rooms

are fully equipped and the Brasserie la Londe (Tel. +33 (0)2 31 47 24 56) will delight aficionados of bistro cuisine.

● **RESTAURANTS**

● Le Pressoir

3, av Henri-Chéron.
Tel. 02 31 73 32 71. Fax 02 31 26 76 64.
info@restaurant-le-pressoir.com
www.restaurant-le-pressoir.com
Closed Sat. lunch, Sun. dinner, Feb. vac.,
3 weeks Aug.
Prix fixe: 29€ (weekday lunch), 46€, 68€.
A la carte: 70€.

The Vautiers' restaurant is still the city's great gourmet attraction. Sandrine welcomes and serves patrons with a ready smile, while Ivan (formerly with Boyer, Le Divellec and Bruneau in the days of the Bourride) shrewdly prepares fine local produce. The fruits of his labor include a pork trotter sausage and a langoustine in crisp pastry, pan-tossed John Dory with shellfish paste, squab baked in a salt and rye flour crust and the fresh fig macaron with raspberry sauce, all very appealing propositions.

● P'tit B.

15, rue du Vaugueux.
Tel. 02 31 93 50 76. Fax 02 31 93 29 63.
leptitb@wanadoo.fr
Prix fixe: 30€. A la carte: 41€.

This stylish bistro serves Norman produce prepared with a modern touch. Crab confit and smoked salmon with tomatoes, two kinds of shrimp seasoned with lime and grilled on the barbecue, lemon- and almond-seasoned cockerel pastilla and an exotic fruit tian glazed with jelly infused with island flavors add color and vitality to local recipes.

● Alcide COM

1, pl de la Courtonne.
Tel. 02 31 44 18 06. Fax 02 31 94 47 45.
Closed Christmas.
Prix fixe: 15,95€, 24,50€, 6,50€ (child).
A la carte: 35–40€.

This fifties bistro institution is still firmly on track. Refurbished in salmon tones with burgundy furniture, the dining room serves a sober cuisine with no frills. The foie gras, cod filet, scallops flambéed in Calvados, pork tenderloin medallions and tarte Normande are first-rate dishes.

● Le Carlotta   COM

16, quai Vendeuvre.
Tel. 02 31 86 68 99. Fax 02 31 38 92 31.
reservation@lecarlotta.fr / www.lecarlotta.fr
Closed Sun.
Prix fixe: 22€, 25€, 38€, 13€ (child).
A la carte: 50€.

In this large, art deco-style brasserie, dishes past and present make up pleasant meals. We feast staunchly on royal-style shrimp, roasted foie gras, Provençal-style cod, lamb shoulder with Middle Eastern spices and a gratin of seasonal fruits.

● Le Costa   COM

32 bis, quai Vendeuvre.
Tel. 02 31 86 28 28. Fax 02 31 86 28 38.
www.lecosta.com.
Closed Sun.
Prix fixe: 18,50€, 22,50€, 36€.
A la carte: 45–55€.

A step away from the Carlotta, this other art deco establishment (with a terrace) is irreproachably reliable. Martine Besnier welcomes us with a smile, while Michel prepares fresh foie gras, monkfish brochette with roasted scallops, sole meunière and a pretty house baba au rhum. A good choice of wines by the glass.

● A Table   COM

43, rue Saint-Sauveur.
Tel.-Fax 02 31 86 57 75.
Closed Sun., Mon., 2 weeks Aug.
Prix fixe: 13,90€, 19€.

Inexpensive, pleasant and dependable, Eric Darcy's little eatery serves local dishes that reflect the market produce of the day. A boudin sausage Tatin, oven-crisped frog legs, cod brandade, chitterling sausage par-

mentier with mustard sauce and the apple fondant with Calvados caramel sauce slip down smooth as velvet.

● Le Bouchon du Vaugueux   SIM

12, rue Graindorge.
Tel. 02 31 44 26 26. Fax 02 31 79 04 15.
Closed Sun., Mon.
Prix fixe: 13–18€ (lunch), 25€ (dinner).

Stéphane Bertin is a shrewd chef and his market-based cuisine (served only in set menu form) is quite a bag of tricks. His thirties-style bistro in sand and coffee shades has recently been repainted. Served by the lady of the house, foie gras with fig chutney, roasted cod with peach sauce, duck breast medallions glazed with blackberry liqueur sauce, mint-seasoned citrus soup with spice-flavored shaved ice genially transgress the mores of tradition. The astute little wines from every region of France are angelically priced.

● Le Bistro Basque   SIM

24, quai Vendeuvre.
Tel.-Fax 02 31 38 21 26.
Closed Sun., Christmas–New Year's.
Prix fixe: 13,20€ (lunch), 17€ (lunch),
20€ (dinner), 8€ (child). A la carte: 30€.

Stéphane Liot offers an easygoing ambiance, amiable prices and generous helpings. The little squids, the pan-tossed shellfish, the Spanish-style cod, a grilled sirloin steak and the chocolate "Basque beret" dessert by Jérémy Laze are washed down with an Irouléguy, as between Hendaye and Biriatou.

● Café Bois Charbon   SIM

30, quai Vendeuvre.
Tel. 02 31 86 36 82. Fax 02 31 86 26 29.
Closed Christmas.
Prix fixe: 10€ (weekday lunch, wine inc.),
13€, 7,50€ (child). A la carte: 40€.

Open every day, Richard Bretteville's *guinguette*-style café puts on something of a theatrical performance with its waitstaff in caps or berets and tables draped with oilcloth. Philippe Jacqueline's cuisine has charm to spare. The charcuterie board, house fish stew, duck breast with pepper and the apple and berry crumble are splendid. A festive atmosphere on weekends.

CAGNES-SUR-MER

06800 Alpes-Maritimes. Paris 919 –
Nice 14 – Antibes 11 – Cannes 21 –
Grasse 25 – Vence 11.
cagnes06@aol.com.
The seaside resort we only visit in passing. The Provençal village soon takes our mind off the beach so near at hand.

 HOTELS-RESTAURANTS

● **Domaine Cocagne**
Colline de la rte de Vence, 2 km n via D36 and secondary road.
Tel. 04 92 13 57 77. Fax 04 92 13 57 89.
hotel@domainecocagne.com
www.domainecocagne.com
Hotel closed Nov.–mid-Dec.
Rest. closed Nov.–beg. Dec.
17 rooms: 177–308€. 7 suites: 268–808€.
Prix fixe: 40€, 60€.

This vast estate with its extensive grounds offers rest and relaxation with its swimming pool, tennis court and contemporary rooms and apartments. In the restaurant, Martin Roberts prepares his (sometimes excessively) crafted seasonal dishes. Spicy crab and salmon tian, served with an Espelette pepper–seasoned avocado mousse, pan-simmered pigeon breast with its thigh braised old-fashioned style, cabbage with ham and the variations on theme of the strawberry are pleasant, even if a little more simplicity would not go amiss.

● **Le Cagnard** ○▯▯
Rue Sous-Barri, in Haut-de-Cagnes.
Tel. 04 93 20 73 21. Fax 04 93 22 06 39.
cagnard@relaischateaux.com
www.le-cagnard.com
Rest. closed Mon. lunch, Tue. lunch,
Thu. lunch.
20 rooms: 135–270€.
Prix fixe: 55€ (lunch, wine inc.), 72€, 95€.

Félix Barel's Relais & Châteaux establishment is the epitome of charm. On the walls of the old town, its 14th-century foundations, antique rooms with a view and Renaissance lounge (with a ceiling that opens to reveal the sky in season) make an excellent impression. The Cagnard is ideal for a romantic weekend, especially with the rather lively Southern score composed by Jean-Yves Johanny and Didier Agnies in the kitchen. An aspargus risotto with chanterelles, chorizo-seasoned Mediterranean sea bass accompanied with simmered artichokes, pigeon browned in a cocotte and served in its pan juices with mixed vegetables and the fresh berries with mascarpone mousse show plenty of character and precision.

● **Fleur de Sel**
85, montée de la Bourgade,
in Haut-de-Cagnes.
Tel.-Fax 04 93 20 33 33.
contact@restaurantfleurdesel.com
www.restaurant-fleurdesel.com
Closed Wed., Thu. lunch, Nov. 1 vac.,
2 weeks beg. Jan., 1 week beg. June.
Prix fixe: 23€, 39€, 52€, 15€ (child).
A la carte: 45€.

Close to the church, Philippe Loose's Provençal inn is cordially modest. The veteran of Guérard, Meneau, Willer and Bardet has opted for simplicity and there are no complaints about his well-crafted repertoire. A parmesan and anchovy biscuit, sea bream and artichoke tian, cod and potato purée and whelks in aïoli and the beef strips with beef stew jus favorably impress. Pascale Loose offers useful advice on the choice of wine.

● **Josy-Jo**
2, rue du Planastel, in Haut-de-Cagnes.
Tel. 04 93 20 68 76. Fax 04 93 22 60 83.
info@restaurant-josyjo.com
www.josyjo.com
Closed Sat. lunch, Sun., mid-Nov.–Christmas,
1 week beg. Feb.
Prix fixe: 26€ (lunch), 40€ (lunch).
A la carte: 60€.

The more things change, the more they stay the same at Josy Bandecchi's eatery. On the edge of the old village, this Provençal lady's inn has a rustic charm and her skill is legendary. Provençal-style stuffed vegetables, breaded and fried zucchini flowers, the fish of the day, grilled lamb saddle and the boneless rib eye for two cooked over hot coals, like the country lemon mousse, are simple, fresh and authentic.

In Cros-de-Cagnes (06800). 2 km se.

● Loulou la Réserve

91, bd de la Plage.
Tel. 04 93 31 00 17.
Closed lunch (exc. July–Aug.), Sat. lunch, Sun., during Cannes festival in May.
Prix fixe: 39€, 45€. A la carte: 70–85€.

Joseph Campo has joined his brother Eric at the stove, which gives us one more reason to visit this establishment with its friendly welcome. Connoisseurs gather in its baroque-contemporary dining room, attracted by the menu, first-rate in both substance and form. Deftly, precisely, the pair prepare an authentic fish soup, grilled sea bream, Simmenthal boneless rib steak and a berry gratin. The dishes and wines are delicious and we have a marvelous time.

CAHORS

46000 Lot. Paris 582 – Agen 88 –
Brive-la-Gaillarde 102 – Montauban 61.
cahors@wanadoo.fr.
They are proud of their bridge (Valentré, much finer than the one in Avignon) and old town, with its worn paving, crooked lanes and wood-framed houses. The inhabitants of Cahors also love their spring festival, which always begins on the brink of summer and attracts photographers from all over the world, who converge here on the banks of the Lot. Wine and photography have long been happily married in Cahors. The local exhibition center—the Espace Clément-Marot—has named its various rooms for great châteaux: Cèdre, Haute-Serre, Bouysses, Mercuès and, of course, Lagrezette, which is something of a social, vinic and artistic powerhouse. From there, it is but a short step to proclaiming Cahors a fashionable town, Quercy chic and its vintages in vogue.

 HOTELS-RESTAURANTS

■ Terminus

5, av Charles-de-Freycinet.
Tel. 05 65 53 32 00. Fax 05 65 53 32 26.
terminus.balandre@wanadoo.fr
www.balandre.com
Closed Nov.–mid-Dec.
21 rooms: 60–130€. 1 suite: 160€.

The 1900 building has a fair degree of charm, as do the lounges and communal areas decorated with art nouveau stained glass. The rooms are meticulously decorated and comfortably equipped (see Restaurants: Le Balandre).

■ La Chartreuse

Faubourg Saint-Georges.
Tel. 05 65 35 17 37. Fax 05 65 22 30 03.
la-chartreuse@wanadoo.fr
www.hotel-la-chartreuse.com
50 rooms: 51–72€.
Prix fixe: 15€ (weekday lunch), 26€, 31€, 38€, 7€ (child). A la carte: 30–50€.

This seventies hostelry by the Lot provides functional rooms with a view over the river. Its bright restaurant serves a sober *pension* cuisine.

■ L'Hôtel de France

252, av J.-Jaurès.
Tel. 05 65 35 16 76. Fax 05 65 22 01 08.
hdf46@hoteldefrance-cahors.fr
www.hoteldefrance-cahors.fr
Closed 2 weeks Christmas–New Year's.
80 rooms: 44–92€.

This large building boasts a location near the rail station and Valentré bridge, and spacious rooms with all modern conveniences.

● Le Balandre

At the Terminus, 5, av Charles-de-Freycinet.
Tel. 05 65 53 32 00. Fax 05 65 53 32 26.
terminus.balandre@wanadoo.fr
www.balandre.com

Closed Sun. (exc. dinner July–Aug.),
Mon. lunch, 2 weeks Nov.
Prix fixe: 38€, 56€, 60€, 76€, 85€.

Gilles Marre, a veteran of Taillevent and the Auberge de l'Ill, serves up beautifully balanced, subtle dishes that are simultaneously roguish and chic. In the art deco dining room, we feast on "Crème Esau" with lentils, chestnuts and truffled whipped cream, the pan-seared scallops with herb-seasoned vegetables and veal tenderloin medallions served with truffled Jerusalem artichokes and leeks in white sauce. For dessert, Victoria pineapple poached in a vanilla-infused sauce and flambéed passion fruit warm our hearts. The fare here is giddyingly fragrant in the truffle season. Madame Marre's welcome is generosity itself and the cellar watched over by Gilles' brother Laurent a goldmine.

● **Le Marché**   N🖼COM

27, pl Capou.
Tel. 05 65 35 27 27.
restaurant.le.marché@cegetel.net
www.restaurantlemarche.com
Closed Sun., Mon.
Prix fixe: 18€ (lunch), 28€.

A contemporary setting in a delightful square next to the cathedral, designer furniture and dishes with a topical flavor that change to match the market: these are the wonderful surprises sprung up on us by Cécile and Hervé Bourg in Cahors. Hervé, former chef at the Foux in Paris, deftly prepares a "Between Quercy and Provence" mille-feuille dish, foie gras with pain d'épices, a potato tourte with ceps, rouget over mixed salad with tapenade and a calf's liver in parsley butter. The apple crumble and the nectarines in verbena syrup are in the same vein.

● **L'O à la Bouche**   N🖼COM

134, rue Ste-Urcisse.
Tel. 05 65 35 65 69.
Closed Sun., Mon. (exc. dinner July–Aug.),
2 weeks beg. Oct., 2 weeks Apr.
Prix fixe: 25€.

Jean-François Dive, a Belgian from Mons who trained at the Villa Lorraine and Ecailler du Palais Royal in Brussels and was senior sous chef at the Château de Mercuès, has made local news with this fine restaurant, where bricks and wood form the décor. Variations on theme of the tomato (in gazpacho, stuffed with fish tartare, in terrine with Rocamadour goat cheese), an iced cauliflower soup with smoked duck breast, a parmesan biscuit with curry-seasoned zucchini caviar, seafood risotto, foie gras ravioli with cep jus, apricot disks roasted and served with almond pastry cream and a frozen pistachio parfait prove that this keen technician who once worked on a luxury catamaran is an elegant, subtle culinary explorer.

● **Le Rendez-Vous**   COM

49, rue Clément-Marot.
Tel. 05 65 22 65 10. Fax 05 65 35 11 05.
Closed Sun., Mon., 1 week beg. Oct.,
1 week Feb.
Prix fixe: 23€. A la carte: 45€.

Ancient and modern, this little restaurant near the cathedral continues modestly on its way in the hands of Stéphane Brugoux, who learned his art in the great restaurants of the Côte d'Azur. Rouget filet with tabouli, a duck confit samosa, roasted pike-perch with red wine sauce, duck breast with honey-lemon sauce and the strawberry dessert follow the dictates of a generous set menu. Véronique Iglésias provides an exuberant welcome.

● **Au Fil des Douceurs**   SIM

90, quai de la Verrerie.
Tel. 05 65 22 13 04. Fax 05 65 35 61 09.
Closed Sun., Mon., 3 weeks Jan.,
1 week at end June–beg. July.
Prix fixe: 13,50€ (lunch), 20,50 –33,50€,
48€. A la carte: 45–65€.

From Philippe Larguille's barge moored at a quay on the Lot, Cahors looks rather like San Gimignano, with its towers rising above the water. On our plates, a foie gras lasagne with honey and Banyuls wine sauce, sirloin steak with a cep cake, Rocamadour cheese served in salad and a frozen coffee parfait are just the thing. The sweet Rotier Gaillac and the Pineraie Cahors flow like elixirs of youth.

In Caillac (46140). 15 km w via rte de Villeneuve-sur-Lot.

● **Le Vinois**   **SIM**

Le Bourg.
Tel.-Fax 05 65 30 53 60.
www.levinois.com
Closed Tue., Wed. (exc. dinner summer), mid-Nov.–mid-Feb.
Prix fixe: 17€ (weekdays, lunch), 29,90€, 45€, 14€ (child). A la carte: 40€.

An urban bistro in the countryside! Jean-Claude and Elisabeth Voisin offer a friendly welcome in their antique establishment refurbished in designer black and white. We come here for the ambiance and the shrewd set menu presenting a lively, modern cuisine. Sardines in tempura, a pork trotter and cep gratin, the Causse lamb trilogy (roasted rack, braised in a charlotte, and milk-fed lamb sweetbreads and tenderloin medallion with preserved lemons) make a splendid impression. Roasted almond-flavored nectarines served with almond ice cream are a worthy delicacy.

In Espère (46090). 10 km nw via D911 (rte de Villeneuve-sur-Lot).

■ **Domaine de Labarthe**

Domaine de Labarthe.
Tel. 05 65 30 92 34. Fax 05 65 20 06 87.
Open daily (by reserv.).
3 rooms: 65–90€. 1 suite: 80–100€.

At the heart of the estate with its dovecote and swimming pool, enamored couples savor the calm and comfort offered by this 18th-century manor. The small rooms are well cared for and the breakfasts exquisite.

In Lamagdelaine (46090). 7 km n via D653.

● **Claude Marco**   **V.COM**

Le Bourg.
Tel. 05 65 35 30 64. Fax 05 65 30 31 40.
info@restaurantmarco.com
www.restaurantmarco.com
Closed 1 week at end Oct., beg. Jan.–beg. Mar. Rest. closed Sun. dinner, Mon. (exc. dinner July–Aug.).
16 rooms: 110–145€.
Prix fixe: 30€, 40€, 46€, 75€.
A la carte: 75€.

After training with the greats of the Spanish Basque country (Berasatégui, Arzak, Zuberoa), Richard has returned to his father Claude and taken his place in the kitchen. Of course, change always goes smoothly in the Marco family. With its handful of rooms, swimming pool and vaulted dining room, this delightful establishment exudes charm. Crème Dubarry (cauliflower in cream) with truffles and foie gras, a foie gras escalope with spices and pears or with artichoke hearts and cep sauce, the tuna belly and lamb with thyme-seasoned meat jus are enchanting. The produce is superb, the accomplished preparation meticulous, the young waitstaff quick and the desserts delicate (saffron-seasoned pineapple carpaccio and almond milk ice cream). The wine list leaves room for the stars of Cahors' vinic firmament.

In Lascabanes (46800). 19 km w rte de Moissac.

■ **Domaine de Saint-Géry**

Domaine de Saint-Géry.
Tel. 05 65 31 82 51. Fax 05 65 22 92 89.
duler@saint-gery.com
www.saint-gery.com
Closed beg. Oct.–mid-May. Rest. closed lunch
4 rooms: 175–343€. 1 suite: 374–486€.
Prix fixe: 85€.

The Dulers' farmhouse inn is a delight… that comes at a price! Pascale's welcome, the many facilities (fitness center, heated swimming pool, etc.), traditional rooms and flavorsome *table d'hôte* are admirable indeed. In the kitchen, Patrick adds a modern touch to his local menu, with roasted foie gras served on a rosemary-seasoned apricot compote, veal in parsley and garlic with eggplant and spanish pork belly and the chocolate marquise with orange chips. But then the check arrives…

In Mercuès (46090). 10 km w rte de
Villeneuve-sur-Lot.

● **Château de Mercuès**

Tel. 05 65 20 00 01. Fax 05 65 20 05 72.
mercues@relaischateaux.com
www.chateaudemercues.com
Rest. closed Mon., Tue. dinner.
24 rooms: 180–280€. 6 suites: 380–400€.
Prix fixe: 65€, 110€.

The view of the Lot river and the majesty of the medieval architecture make an exceptional setting of this ancient residence of Count Bishops turned into a modern Relais & Châteaux establishment by Georges Vigouroux. We are drawn by the château's beauty, the comfort of the period-style rooms—some modernized by designer François Champsaur (the contemporary bar and new dining room are particularly successful)—and Philippe Combet's steadfast, subtle cuisine. In the hands of this young veteran of the Palme d'Or in Cannes and Oasis in La Napoule, Quercy embraces the Mediterranean in a series of sophisticated dishes. Pan-seared duck foie gras served with a peach crumble, cooked and raw vegetables and mushrooms served with escargots, a slice of turbot in truffles with herb ravioli, lamb tenderloin medallion and chops in papillote with bacon and walnut butter and the raspberry mille-feuille with vanilla-seasoned cream are enchanting. The Cahors-centric wine list focuses on the owner's vintages (Haute-Serre and Mercuès).

In Saint-Henri (46000). 7 km n via rte de Brive
and N20.

● **La Garenne**

Tel. 05 65 35 40 67.
Closed Mon., Tue. dinner, Wed., 2 weeks Mar.
Prix fixe: 18€ (weekday lunch), 25€, 45€.

This former stable converted into a tasteful restaurant is the domain of Jacqueline and Michel Carrendier. Jacqueline, a native of Lorraine from Thionville, greets guests with a smile, while Michel, a son of Montauban who has adopted the Cahors region, energetically prepares new wave Quercy dishes. Washed down with local wines at good prices, his lobe of foie gras

with fruit chutney, monkfish medallion with saffron-seasoned oil, pork trotter cake with tarragon-seasoned mustard, thyme-seasoned country lamb and the roasted peaches with pain d'épice ice cream are polished work.

CAHUZAC-SUR-VERE

81140 Tarn. Paris 657 – Albi 30 –
Montauban 60 – Rodez 85 – Toulouse 70 –
Gaillac 10.
The bucolic splendor of a land of plenty.

	HOTELS-RESTAURANTS

● **Château de Salettes**

3 km via D922 in Salettes.
Tel. 05 63 33 60 60. Fax 05 63 33 60 61.
salettes@chateausalettes.com
www.chateaudesalettes.com
Closed beg. Jan.–mid-Jan., 2 weeks Feb.–
Mar. Rest. closed Mon., Tue.
13 rooms: 131–165€. 5 suites: 259–310€.
Prix fixe: 33€, 80€.

Among the vines, this 13th-century château with swimming pool was the property of a younger branch of the Toulouse-Lautrec family. Attractively renovated, it holds large rooms in a refined, contemporary style, some of them equipped with balneotherapy baths. The restaurant is the special preserve of Pascal Auger. A veteran of Chez Serge in La Rochelle whom we met at the Saint-Ambroix in Bourges, he prepares modern dishes rich in flavors and contrasts. In the designer dining room, foie gras strips grilled with honey, cinnamon and caramelized pumpkin, an orange zest-seasoned roasted monkfish served with corn and a spicy avocado purée, duck with sugared almonds and red cabbage marmalade and the chocolate flan served with shortbread made with arugula-seasoned butter show no deficiency of precision or imagination. To be continued.

● **La Falaise**

Rte de Cordes.
Tel. 05 63 33 96 31. Fax 05 63 33 96 31.

www.lafalaiserestaurant.com
Closed Sun. dinner, Mon., Tue. lunch,
2 weeks Jan., 2 weeks Dec.
Prix fixe: 20€, 31€, 43€. A la carte: 50€.

At the end of Grésigne forest, in the rustic dining room of this former wine storehouse with its veranda and terrace, we feast on ceps on toast, fish filet with citrus and ginger sauce, tender wild rabbit medallions and the mango and kiwi tartare with passion fruit. A breath of fresh air!

CAILLAC see **CAHORS**

CALAIS

62100 Pas-de-Calais. Paris 290 – Boulogne 38 – Dunkerque 45 – Ostende 96 – Saint-Omer 41. ot@ot-calais.fr.
"From Calais on, I made myself drunk with English beer," noted Stendhal. Today, the British are more likely to visit this corner of the Manche district in search of liquor, cheaper in France. The ferries continue to sail to and fro from Dover, and lace is still made in the workshops.

 HOTELS-RESTAURANTS

■ Holiday Inn
Bd des Alliés.
Tel. 03 21 34 69 69. Fax 03 21 97 09 15.
holidayinn@holidayinn-calais.com
www.holidayinn.fr/calais-nord
Closed Christmas, New Year's.
Rest. closed Sat. lunch, Sun. lunch.
63 rooms: 125–167€. 8 suites: 145–167€.
Prix fixe: 22€. A la carte: 35€.

This modern chain hotel by the marina boasts spacious rooms, some of them overlooking the sea.

■ Meurice
5, rue Edmond-Roche.
Tel. 03 21 34 57 03. Fax 03 21 34 14 71.
meurice@hotel-meurice.fr
www.hotel-meurice.fr
Rest. closed Sat. lunch.
39 rooms: 79–130€. 2 suites: 159€.
Prix fixe: 18€, 25€, 35–38€, 43€, 50€,
15€ (child). A la carte: 50€.

Right in the heart of town, this institution still attracts visiting celebrities and tourists with its vast lobby, attractive antique rooms and traditional restaurant.

■ Métropol Hôtel
43, quai du Rhin.
Tel. 03 21 97 54 00. Fax 03 21 96 69 70.
metropol@metropolhotel.com
www.metropolhotel.com
Closed mid-Dec.–beg. Jan.
40 rooms: 46–66€.

Behind the red brick facade of this practical hostelry opposite the rail station are trim, functional rooms and a pleasant English-style lounge bar. The welcome is warm and the check affable.

● Aquar'aile   COM
255, rue Jean-Moulin.
Tel. 03 21 34 00 00. Fax 03 21 34 15 00.
f.leroy@aquaraile.com / www.aquaraile.com
Closed Sun. dinner.
Prix fixe: 22€, 28€, 40€, 10€ (child).
A la carte: 55€.

This modern restaurant on the harbor provides an unobstructed view of the English Channel, the North Sea and even the coast of England. The dishes by Jean-Pierre Morichon are the soul of reliability. The lobster in salad, a sole meunière, rosemary- and honey-seasoned roasted lamb and an apple tartelette are washed down with selected wines.

● Le Channel   COM
3, bd de la Résistance.
Tel. 03 21 34 42 30. Fax 03 21 97 42 43.
www.restaurant-lechannel.com
Closed Sun. dinner, Tue., end Dec.–end Jan.,
end July–mid-Aug.
Prix fixe: 19,50€, 28,50€, 36,50€, 49€.
A la carte: 45–70€.

Those who regularly pass through this port tend to call in at the Crespos' culinary stopover. In the kitchen, Jérôme prepares supremely fresh dishes, generally of the marine persuasion. In the dining room refurbished in art deco style, the smoked salmon plate, Mediterranean sea bass with chanterelles, pikeperch mozzarella gratin and the dessert cart have no trouble finding takers.

● Au Côte d'Argent COM

1, digue Gaston-Berthe.
Tel. 03 21 34 68 07. Fax 03 21 96 42 10.
lefebvre@cotedargent.com
www.cotedargent.com
Closed Sun. dinner, Mon., Christmas–New Year's, Feb. vac., end Aug.–beg. Sept.
Prix fixe: 18€, 23€, 32€, 38€.
A la carte: 55€.

We watch the slow ballet of the Channel ferries from this reliable restaurant with its nautical décor. Turbot filet with hollandaise sauce, sole with grapefruit butter and a beef filet with foie gras emulsion are good classic dishes.

● Les Saisons COM

2, pl de Suède.
Tel. 03 21 97 50 00. Fax 03 21 34 76 69.
lessaisons@wanadoo.fr
Closed Sun. dinner, Mon. dinner.
Prix fixe: 12€, 25€, 39€, 11€ (child).
A la carte: 40€.

In his brightly colored, rustic-modern dining room, Thierry Buffet looks to the sun. A jumbo shrimp and scallop duo, a cod wrapped in caul, the guinea hen and lobster waterzoi (a Belgian poultry dish with cream and leeks) and a chicory-infused crème brûlée reconcile Northern France with the Mediterranean.

CALLAS

83830 Var. Paris 875 – Castellane 52 – Grasse 46 – Draguignan 16.
The breathtaking view from this village in a Var canyon makes it well worth a visit.

 HOTELS-RESTAURANTS

● Les Gorges de Pennafort

Rte de Muy: 7 km se via D25 toward Callas.
Tel. 04 94 76 66 51. Fax 04 94 76 67 23.
info@hostellerie-pennafort.com
www.hostellerie-pennafort.com
Closed mid-Jan.–mid-Mar.
Rest. closed Sun. dinner (exc. July–Aug.), Mon. (exc. dinner July–Aug.).
12 rooms: 130–210€. 4 suites: 210–380€.
Prix fixe: 42€ (lunch), 53€, 69€, 130€, 18€ (child).

The days of the Parisian Chiberta are long gone. Now, Philippe Da Silva happily whiles away the hours on the heights of the Var hinterland. In this sunny country house with its swimming pool, guests enjoy the comfort of rooms in Southern shades before sitting down to eat in the restaurant. The cuisine with its very Provençal flavor faithfully reflects the setting. We enjoy a poultry terrine with asparagus, sea bream with cep risotto, veal kidneys served with capers and horseradish and the mandarin orange baba with assorted sorbets. A superb welcome.

CALUIRE-ET-CUIRE see LYON

CALVINET

15340 Cantal. Paris 592 – Aurillac 34 – Figeac 40 – Rodez 57 – Maurs 18.
Cantal with its cheerful meadows and rivers.

 HOTELS-RESTAURANTS

● Beauséjour ◯⌂

Rte de Maurs.
Tel. 04 71 49 91 68. Fax 04 71 49 98 63.
beausejour.puech@wanadoo.fr
www.cantal-restaurant-puech.com
Closed beg. Jan.–end Feb. (by reserv. only).
6 rooms: 60–70€. 3 suites: 100–140€.
Prix fixe: 25€, 37€, 45€, 60€, 15€ (child).

Louis-Bernard Puech's inn is an ode to Southern Auvergne. In the kitchen, he champions his native region, adding a modern touch to timeless produce. A hot cep pâté with garlic-seasoned meat jus, cod filet roasted with smoked bacon, lamb charlotte with slow-cooked eggplant and the old-fashioned little pot de crème served with pan-simmered cherries, washed down with engaging local wines. After these delights, our dreams in one of the modern, demure rooms are sweet indeed.

CAMBRAI

59400 Nord. Paris 179 – Saint-Quentin 40 – Amiens 87 – Arras 37 – Lille 76.
cambrai@tourisme.norsys.fr.
The land of bêtises (the local candy) has a fine ancient heritage. Rubens' *Burial* in the church of Saint-Géry alone would make it worth a visit.

 HOTELS-RESTAURANTS

■ Château de la
Motte-Fénelon
Square du Château, by allée Saint-Roch.
Tel. 03 27 83 61 38. Fax 03 27 83 71 61.
contact@cambrai-chateau-motte-fenelon.com
www.cambrai-chateau-motte-fenelon.com
36 rooms: 57–110€. 4 suites: 240€.
Prix fixe: 25€, 38€. A la carte: 45€.

Hittorff, the Parisian architect of Ledoyen and the church of Saint-Vincent-de-Paul, had this château built in 1850. It boasts rooms of character, period furniture and, under the brick vaults of the renovated cellars, a gourmet restaurant with a penchant for traditional cuisine.

● L'Escargot   `COM`
10, rue du Général-de-Gaulle.
Tel. 03 27 81 24 54. Fax 03 27 83 95 21.
restaurantlescargot@wanadoo.fr
Closed Fri. dinner, Wed., 1 week Dec.,
1 week at end July.
Prix fixe: 26€, 37€, 13,50€ (child).
A la carte: 45€.

Timeless standards are served in the rustic dining room and mezzanine of this restaurant. The escargots en croustade, a local tart made with many layers of thin pastry, also with local Tomme de Cambrai cheese, poached turbot with hollandaise sauce, brasied veal sweetbreads with morels and the house frozen nougat offer an opportunity to revise our classics without undue damage to our pockets.

CAMBREMER

14340 Calvados.
Paris 211 – Caen 38 – Deauville 28 –
Lisieux 15.
The geographic and gourmet heart of the Pays d'Auge.

 HOTELS-RESTAURANTS

■ Château Les Bruyères   ⓝ ❀ 🏠
Rte du Cadran.
Tel. 02 31 32 22 45. Fax 02 31 32 22 58.
contact@chateaulesbruyeres.com
www.chateaulesbruyeres.com
Closed beg. Jan.–end Jan.
Rest. closed lunch, Mon., Tue.
13 rooms: 85–360€.
Prix fixe: 35€, 41€, 65€.

The historic manor that welcomed Proust when he came to Cabourg for his health has acquired vegetable and herb gardens, an apple orchard and a stud farm. There is also a fine restaurant supervised by chef and boss Phillipe Harfaux, who champions the local produce. Oysters served hot with Camembert, foie gras marinated in Pommeau wine, a John Dory simmered in cider and herb-seasoned lamb chops with chard gratin are accompanied by selected ciders.

CAMPIGNY see PONT-AUDEMER

CANCALE

35260 Ille-et-Vilaine.
Paris 394 – Saint-Malo 16 –
Dinan 35 – Fougères 81 –
Avranches 63.
ot.cancale@wanadoo.fr.
Like the *Bisquine* in times gone by, boats are moored in the harbor leading majestically out to the bay and the Chausey Islands. Oyster farmers watch over their beds. Walkers stroll down the quai de la Houle, then set off for the Pointe du Groin that conceals the Ile des Landes and its bird sanctuary. If happiness is not to be found in Cancale, who knows where it could be hiding?

HOTELS-RESTAURANTS

■ Les Rimains

Rue des Rimains.
Tel. 02 99 89 64 76. Fax 02 99 89 88 47.
bricourt@relaischateaux.com
www.maisons-de-bricourt.com
Closed mid-Dec.–mid-Mar.
4 rooms: 165–265€.

It is hard to resist the charms of this thirties cottage and garden beside the Sentier des Douaniers and its two New England-style coastal *gîtes*. After enjoying the four English-style rooms and fabulous breakfasts, guests offer yet another vote of thanks to Olivier Roellinger.

■ Pointe du Grouin

Pointe du Grouin, 4,5 km via D201.
Tel. 02 99 89 60 55. Fax 02 99 89 92 22.
hotel-pointe-du-grouin@wanadoo.fr
www.hotelpointedugrouin.com
Closed mid-Nov.–end Mar.
Rest. closed Tue., Thu. lunch (off season).
16 rooms: 82–100€.
Prix fixe: 21€, 67€. A la carte: 70€.

The Ile des Landes lies just opposite this hotel with its comfortable, old-fashioned rooms and Louis XV-style restaurant with a panoramic view of the surrounding scenery.

■ Le Continental

Quai Thomas.
Tel. 02 99 89 60 16. Fax 02 99 89 69 58.
hotel-conti@wanadoo.fr
www.hotel-cancale.com
Closed mid-Nov.–1 Dec., 10 Jan.–10 Feb.
Rest. closed Wed., Thu.
16 rooms: 88–148€.
Prix fixe: 17€ (weekday lunch), 24€, 37€, 13,50€ (child). A la carte: 34–55€.

Christophe Wasser's hotel looking out on the harbor has rooms in different shades. The restaurant dining room with its woodwork and seascapes, and the veranda with its view of the fishing fleet, provide a pleasant setting as we sit down to William Basle's cuisine. Artichokes in sauce ravigote, duck foie gras terrine served with with fig and pear chutney, sole meunière, a veal kidney with fresh pasta and slow-cooked potatoes before the "all caramel" profiteroles are not bad.

■ Le Querrien

7, quai Duguay-Trouin.
Tel. 02 99 89 64 56. Fax 02 99 89 79 35.
le-querrien@wanadoo.fr / www.le-querrien.com
15 rooms: 59–159€.
Prix fixe: 16€ (weekdays), 26,90€, 9€ (child). A la carte: 37–54€.

Yves Rallon's Breton establishment looks out on the open sea. It has rooms named for boats, colors that reflect the ocean, a veranda on the quay and a marine dining room. Concocted by Stéphane Jourdan, the sardine mille-feuille with herb butter, the lobster, scallop and vegetable dish, fish served choucroute-style, are unalloyed delights. A hot orange soufflé provides a pleasant conclusion.

■ Le Cancalais

12, quai Gambetta.
Tel. 02 99 89 61 93. Fax 02 99 89 89 24.
www.lecancalais.com
Closed beg. Dec.–end Jan.
Rest. closed Sun. dinner, Mon. (exc. vac.).
10 rooms: 45–90€.
Prix fixe: 17€ (weekday lunch), 28€, 38€.
A la carte: 50–65€.

Jean-Claude Pierpaoli, who formerly ran the Mère Poulard, is still the perfect host. He welcomes his guests like old friends, takes good care of his spruce rooms overlooking the port and serves lively, appealing dishes in the traditional dining room. Guéméné andouille in a buckwheat crêpe with cider butter, blue lobster ravioli with mild spices and an oven-roasted wild turbot served with baked truffle-seasoned potatoes and onions are fine tricks indeed.

■ Auberge de la Motte Jean

2 km via D355.
Tel. 02 99 89 41 99. Fax 02 99 89 92 22.
hotel-pointe-du-grouin@wanadoo.fr
www.hotelpointedugrouin.com

12 rooms: 65–78€. 1 suite: 110–130
Half board: 77–154€.

In the heart of the Cancale countryside, this former farmhouse set in a large garden provides calm, comfortable rooms.

■ Hôtel Duguay-Trouin

11, quai Duguay-Trouin.
Tel. 02 23 15 12 07.
www.hotelduguaytrouin.com
7 rooms: 70–105€.

Providing simple, neat, spruce, contemporary-style rooms by the harbor, this recently opened hostelry offers good value for money. Just the thing for a peaceful stay in Cancale.

■ Le Chatellier

Rte de Saint-Malo, 1 km via D355.
Tel. 02 99 89 81 84. Fax 02 99 89 61 69.
hotelchatel@aol.com
www.hotellechatellier.com
Closed mid-Dec.–end Jan.
13 rooms: 45–60€. 2 suites: 73€.

Lost in the Cancale countryside, this family establishment provides a delightful view of the surrounding landscape, renovated old-fashioned rooms, comfortable first floor suites opening onto the garden and delicious breakfasts.

● Maison de Bricourt

1, rue Duguesclin.
Tel. 02 99 89 64 76. Fax 02 99 89 88 47.
info@maisons-de-bricourt.com
www.maisons-de-bricourt.com
Closed Mon. lunch, Tue. lunch, Wed.,
mid-Dec.–mid-Mar.
Prix fixe: 90€ (lunch), 117€,
165€ (lunch).

Still a modest man, he has kept the faith, a sense of proportion, reasonable prices for so much quality and a determination to maintain and even raise his standards. Although the Michelin guide has, ten years after everyone else, finally recognized Olivier Roellinger's rightful place at the peak of his profession, neither the man nor his world have changed. We still visit this Prince of Brittany to taste the ne plus ultra of today's oceanic cuisine; honest, untainted matches between the freshest fish and exotic spices. We savor John Dory served two ways, in cubes seasoned with ginger-infused vinegar and in strips with celtic vinegar, the oysters served warm with an herb-infused jus and rye, the foie gras with cuttlefish, spring fennel and rosemary, the sea bream seasoned with bay, Atlantic sea bass served whole, sherry- and cocoa-seasoned lobster served with apples and raisins, catfish and asparagus with seaweed-flavored gravy, the lamb saddle roasted with "Grande Caravane" spice mix. Olivier Roellinger turns food into a journey. Like the magnificent desserts, the rum molasses "duck" is a masterpiece crafted by an artist of sweet delicacies. We love fresh fruits from faraway islands, with pepper and fleur d'oranger-seasoned yogurt ice cream and the frozen cinnamon parfait with chocolate sorbet and tapioca. An apple dessert plate served with a crumble has us melting. The wines are conscientiously recommended, the service is enthusiastic and the set menus' honesty is unquestionable. After our meal in this fine Saint Malo–style residence with its playful garden, all we want to say is "Don't change a thing, Olivier, we like you just the way you are."

● La Maison de la Marine

23, rue de la Marine.
Tel.-Fax 02 99 89 88 53.
www.maisondelamarine.com
Closed Mon., Tue. (off season), Jan.
5 rooms: 120–150€.
Prix fixe: 22€ (lunch), 30€, 35€, 40€.

Christian Pousset has opened an original hostelry here in the former shipping office building. The piratical baroque dining room decorated with wall paintings has its share of charm. In the kitchen, young Frédéric Laloyaux, a veteran of Robuchon in Monaco and Bruno in Lorgues, concocts a subtle world cuisine. Tuna maki in paella, a langoustine risotto, monkfish tagine with Middle Eastern spices and a duck breast with sweet and sour sauce served with vegetable sushi are an agile balancing act. Warm brioche with caramelized apples and a mango and passion fruit mousseline aptly complete the house repertoire. Excellent rooms.

● **Le Troquet**
19, quai Gambetta.
Tel. 02 99 89 99 42.
Closed Thu. (exc. vac.), Fri. (exc. vac.),
mid-Nov.–beg. Feb.
Prix fixe: 26€, 38€. A la carte: 48–64€.

This eatery has walls, tables and chairs in wood, and old-fashioned orange cloths on which its original oceanic spreads are served. Laurent Hellue inventively prepares shrimp and chorizo brochette served with a parmesan risotto, a roasted cod with smoked bacon and served with polenta and pork cheeks with slow-cooked shallots and potatoes. Based on seasonal produce, the dishes maintain their appeal right up to the dessert: caramelized apples in a crêpe pouch. Guests can also opt for seafood (lobster, langoustes, etc.), a house specialty.

● **Au Vieux Safran**
2, quai Gambetta.
Tel. 02 99 89 92 42.
Closed Tue. (exc. vac.), Wed. (exc. vac.), Jan.
Prix fixe: 12–25€, 32€. A la carte: 45€.

In the lower part of town by the sea, Sylvain and Jérôme Grastien's red and green restaurant pays tribute to the region. In their modern rustic dining room, we savor Guémené chitterling sausage served warm with slow-cooked caramelized onions, steamed Atlantic sea bass with asparagus, sirloin steak with shallots and a far breton, the local flan-like dessert.

● **Le Surcouf** SIM
7, quai Gambetta.
Tel. 02 99 89 61 75. Fax 02 99 89 76 41.
www.lesurcouf.fr
Closed Tue., Wed., Dec.–end Jan.
Prix fixe: 16€, 25€, 32€, 42€.
A la carte: 60–65€.

Jérôme Pierpaoli, whose father runs the neighboring establishment, has made

a gourmet haunt of this affable bistro. Langoustines pan-tossed in truffle oil, lobster stew in a buckwheat crêpe with cream, a thyme flower-seasoned lamb medallion and a Sichuan peppercorn–seasoned pineapple brochette are truly gratifying.

In Saint-Méloir-des-Ondes (35350). 6,5 km via D76 and D155 and secondary road.

■ **Château Richeux**
Point du Jour, route du Mont-Saint-Michel.
Tel. 02 99 89 64 76. Fax 02 99 89 88 47.
www.maisons-de-bricourt.com
Closed 18 Dec.–28 Dec., 7 Jan.–30 Jan.
Rest. closed Sun. dinner (off season), Mon.,
Tue. lunch.
11 rooms: 160–290€. 2 suites: 290–310€.
Prix fixe: 29€, 50€, 56€, 18€ (child).

Olivier Roellinger has turned this twenties villa into one of the most enchanting hotels in France. Its 2,500 plant species, panoramic view of Mont-Saint-Michel Bay, art deco furniture, 19th-century pictures and exquisite rooms all wield their charm. In the kitchen, apt pupil Julien Perrodin practices his superlatively simple art with gratined crab-stuffed vegetables, oven-browned sole with mashed potatoes, a squab cooked over coals and the dessert cart. Relais & Châteaux.

66140 Pyrénées-Orientales. Paris 850 –
Argelès-sur-Mer 20 – Narbonne 65.
This beach close to Perpignan already has something of the Costa Brava about it.

● | RESTAURANTS

● **La Vigatane**
2, rue des Remparts.
Tel. 04 68 73 16 30.
vigatane@wanadoo.fr
Closed Mon., Tue.
Prix fixe: 10€, 14€. A la carte: 25€.

Former rugby player and dynamic innkeeper, Yves Henrich champions the brightest colors of Catalonian cuisine. In his former wine cellar converted into a highly stylish tavern, grilled fish, anchoïade, meats grilled over a wood fire and cargolade (a local dish of escargots cooked over charcoal) make a very favorable impression. We drink Malavella water and Clos de Paulilles *rosé*, allowing the ambiance of the moment to carry us away.

CANNES

06400 Alpes-Maritimes.
Paris 903 – Aix 150 – Marseille 163 – Nice 34 – Toulon 125.
semoftou@palais-festivals-cannes.fr.
This town partnered with Beverly Hills puts on quite a show. The hotels on the Croisette esplanade are monuments we come to admire. A convention and festival center, Cannes is also a port on the Côte d'Azur by the marina, an ancient Provençal settlement in Le Suquet and a small provincial town proud of its pedestrian credentials around the rue d'Antibes and rue Meynadier. Riviera chefs gather at the Forville market. Local gastronomy is a majestic affair from one great name to the next. Culinarily speaking, this relatively small municipality outclasses its rivals. We discover the soul of Cannes as we stroll along a carless street or down a crooked lane overlooking the coast, lined by palm trees whose heads always seem about to be whipped away by the wind.

■	HOTELS

■ Hôtel Intercontinental Carlton Cannes

58, bd de la Croisette.
Tel. 04 93 06 40 06. Fax 04 93 06 40 25.
carlton@ichotelsgroup.com
www.ichotelsgroup.com/cannes
338 rooms: 260–520€.
36 suites: 615–2370€.
Prix fixe: 39€, 49€.

Hitchcock shot parts of *To Catch a Thief* here. You will feel like a star on the private beach of this luxury hotel with its two turrets, immaculate facade, sea view terrace and huge lobby. The Carlton

offers a fashionable brunch. Seven luxury suites on the eighth floor.

■ Majestic Barrière

10, bd de la Croisette.
Tel. 04 92 98 77 00. Fax 04 93 38 97 90.
majestic@lucienbarriere.com
www.majestic-barriere.com
Closed mid-Nov.–end Dec.
305 rooms: 215–925€.
23 suites: 420–5200€.

Opposite the Palais des Festivals and casino, this twenties jewel stands tall as a wave, with its art deco white facade, outdoor swimming pool heated all year, private beach, first-rate service, immensely stylish rooms and suites and select cuisine (see Restaurants: La Villa des Lys and Le Fouquet's).

■ Martinez

73, bd de la Croisette.
Tel. 04 92 98 73 00. Fax 04 93 39 67 82.
martinez@concorde-hotels.com
www.hotel-martinez.com
395 rooms: 260–900€.
27 suites: 800–32000€.

The art deco facade is very elegant in a simple style. Refined suites and rooms, penthouses with balconies overlooking the sea, Givenchy spa bath, heated outdoor swimming pool, private beach and ambitious restaurants (see Restaurants: Relais Martinez and Palme d'Or) complete the hotel's prestige offerings.

■ Le Grand Hôtel

45, bd de la Croisette.
Tel. 04 93 38 15 45. Fax 04 93 68 97 45.
info@grand-hotel-cannes.com
www.grand-hotel-cannes.com
Closed Nov.
76 rooms: 200–460€.
2 suites: 700–2700€.

A refurbished legend set back from the Croisette esplanade, with a large garden to shelter it from the noise of traffic and rooms with a full view of the sea. Ebony veneer, designer furniture, teak balconies and rose and gray or yellow and mauve décors form a sixties backdrop that only needs Peter Sellers or Austin Powers to complete the scene. Add the ebony bar with its iridescent panels, Pré Carré restaurant—something of a lounge-style deluxe coffee shop with white taffeta drapes and a large terrace outside—and you have a retro pearl turned into a dazzling designer setting.

■ Gray d'Albion

38, rue des Serbes.
Tel. 04 92 99 79 79. Fax 04 93 99 26 10.
graydalbion@lucienbarriere.com
www.gray-dalbion.com
Rest. closed Sun., Mon.
191 rooms: 149–445€. 8 suites: 450–1550€.
Prix fixe: 38€ (wine incl.), 19€ (lunch).

The seventies architecture is dated, but the standardized interior comfort remains. The hotel also boasts a private beach and the once-famous Royal Gray restaurant (+33 (0)4 92 99 79 60) still has delights to offer (scallop and mushroom tartare, veal and artichoke tagine) under Alain Roy.

■ Hilton Cannes

50, bd de la Croisette.
Tel. 04 92 99 70 00. Fax 04 92 99 70 11.
sales.cannes@hilton.com
www.hiltoncannes.com
Rest. closed Mon., Tue.
187 rooms: 269–999€. 47 suites: 359–3149€.
Prix fixe: 49€.

This great cubic "thing" adjoining a casino holds luxury suites and rooms, as well as a swimming pool, Jacuzzi, fitness center and theater. The Scala serves Italian cuisine by Philippe Artaud.

■ Sofitel le Méditerranée

1, bd Jean-Hibert.
Tel. 04 92 99 73 00. Fax 04 92 99 73 29.
h0591@accor.com / www.sofitel.com
149 rooms: 150–340€. 6 suites: 530–700€.

The forties look of this modern tower on the edge of the Big Blue is charming indeed. The Provençal-style rooms, bar,

terrace and panoramic swimming pool are bonuses. It also has a gourmet restaurant—La Méditerranée—and a brasserie—Chez Panisse (see Restaurants).

■ Trois Quatorze

5, rue François-Einesy.
Tel. 04 92 99 72 00. Fax 04 92 99 72 12.
www.trois-quatorze.hotel.com
Rest. closed lunch
96 rooms: 120–500€. 15 suites: 450–1500€.
A la carte: 55€.

The Partouche Group has turned this contemporary hotel into a designer stopover not far from the Croisette. Hi-tech comfort, bright colors and the Mahatma restaurant set the tone. Chef Mario d'Orio, whom we knew at the Majestic, concocts a rather successful fusion cuisine (crab sushi, tandoori chicken).

■ Splendid

4, rue Félix-Faure.
Tel. 04 97 06 22 22. Fax 04 93 99 55 02.
accueil@splendid-hotels-cannes
www.splendid-hotel-cannes.fr
44 rooms: 112–244€. 18 suites: 202–264€.

Looking like a pocket luxury hotel, this establishment is actually a family hostelry that takes good care of its guests. The rooms with antique furniture have been meticulously renovated and some of them have a view of the harbor.

■ Cristal

13-15, rond-point Duboys-d'Angers.
Tel. 04 92 59 29 29. Fax 04 93 38 64 66.
reservation@hotel-cristal.com
www.hotel-cristal.com
Closed 20 Nov.–end Dec., 1 week Jan.
43 rooms: 125–295€. 7 suites: 205–690€.
Prix fixe: 10€, 13€, 23,50€.
A la carte: 50–55€.

The resort's best value for money. This compact thirties luxury hotel with its modern rooms, Jacuzzi, solarium, fitness center and two restaurants is a delightful place to stay.

■ Villa Toboso

7, allée des Oliviers.
Tel. 04 92 99 35 00. Fax 04 93 68 09 32.
contact@charmhotel.com
www.charmhotel.com
15 rooms: 45–140€.

On the heights of the Mont-Fleury neighborhood, this hotel looks out over the roofs of the town. The grounds shaded by olive and palm trees, summer swimming pool, steam bath and refined rooms in Provençal style provide a perfect setting for relaxation.

■ Le Cavendish

11, bd Sadi-Carnot.
Tel. 04 97 06 26 00. Fax 04 97 06 26 01.
reservation@cavendish-cannes.com
www.cavendish-cannes.com
Closed 3 weeks Dec., 2 weeks Feb.
26 rooms: 130–245€. 8 suites: 195–275€.

Built in 1897, this Belle Epoque hotel with its twenties lift, bar in bright colors and charming rooms with Provençal furniture works its spell.

■ Hôtel Cézanne

40, Bd d'Alsace.
Tel. 04 93 38 50 70. Fax 04 93 38 20 44.
29 rooms: 120–200€.

In an oasis of greenery, this recently renovated, peaceful establishment with steam bath, fitness center and private garage is just a ten-minute walk from the Palais des Festivals. Its contemporary decoration and many services are strong assets.

■ Fouquet's

2, rond-point Duboys-d'Angers.
Tel. 04 92 59 25 00. Fax 04 92 98 03 39.
info@le-fouquets.com / www.le-fouquets.com
Closed end Nov.–mid-Mar.
10 rooms: 120–260€. 1 suite: 160–300€.

Large rooms with modern furniture and a pleasant corner lounge await visitors to this convivial hotel on a quiet traffic circle.

■ Hôtel de Paris

34, bd d'Alsace.
Tel. 04 93 38 30 89. Fax 04 93 39 04 61.
reservation@hotel-de-paris.com
www.hotel-de-paris.com
Closed 18 Nov.–26 Dec.
50 rooms: 105–245€. 3 suites: 225–315€.

This 19th-century establishment a step away from the expressway is perfectly soundproofed. We enjoy its wooded garden, steam bath, Jacuzzi and swimming pool. The rooms with their Louis XVI furniture and pastel tones offer rest and relaxation.

■ Hôtel de Provence

9, rue Molière.
Tel. 04 93 38 44 35. Fax 04 93 39 63 14.
contact@hotel-de-provence.com
www.hotel-de-provence.com
Closed end Nov.–end Dec.
29 rooms: 56–102€. 1 suite: 132€.

A stone's throw from the Croisette esplanade, the Portiers' hotel is a wonderful find. The flowered garden, rooms in the colors of Provence and family welcome are delightful.

■ California's

8, traverse Alexandre-III.
Tel. 04 93 94 12 21. Fax 04 93 43 55 17.
nadia@californias-hotel.com
www.hotel-californias.com
33 rooms: 86–296€.

Here in the heart of Cannes, we could imagine ourselves on Ocean Drive as we stand before these two villas surrounded by a flower-filled garden with swimming pool. Some of the bright, trim rooms have a terrace.

■ Hôtel Renoir

7, rue Edith-Cavell.
Tel. 04 92 99 62 62. Fax 04 92 99 62 82.
contact@hotel-renoir-cannes.com
www.leshotelsdeprovence.com
Closed end Dec.–beg. Jan.
21 rooms: 85–140€. 5 suites: 170–235€.

Near the beaches by the Croisette esplanade and the Palais des Congrès convention center, this twenties stopover offers Provençal-style rooms with handy kitchenettes.

■ La Villa Tosca

11 rue Hoche.
Tel. 04 93 38 34 40. Fax 04 93 38 73 34.
contact@villa-tosca.com
www.villa-tosca.com
Closed end Dec.–beg. Jan.
20 rooms: 61–149€. 2 suites: 139–169€.

Just three minutes from the Croisette esplanade, this little building with its twenty-two contemporary rooms and delightful lounge is the perfect place to relax. It is equipped with the latest technologies for vacationers and business guests. Sensible prices.

● | RESTAURANTS

● La Villa des Lys   ⓒⓞⓛⓤⓧ

At the Majestic-Barrière,
14, bd de la Croisette.
Tel. 04 92 98 77 41. Fax 04 93 39 97 90.
villadeslys@lucienbarriere.com
www.lucienbarriere.com
Closed Sun., Mon., mid-Nov.–end Dec.
Prix fixe: 65€, 95€, 115€.

The discreet dining room has a half-English, half-Napoleon III feel to it with its gold leaf walls and veranda opening to the sky. The young waitstaff are keen and the cellar well stocked. The cuisine is dazzling in the hands of chef Bruno Oger, staunch Breton and Georges Blanc's former lieutenant in Vonnas. A dynamic man in his forties, his roots and training have left him with a strong sense of professionalism and a fervor second to none. His reinterpretation of the great classics of the Mediterranean, the Côte d'Azur and its hinterland, which assimilate flavors of the Atlantic, hit the right note every time. His latest triumphs are Burrata cheese and spring garden vegetable ravioli, langouste simply marinated in champagne vinegar served with caviar in aspic, a line-fished Mediterranean sea bass served with slow-cooked tomato, basil, onion and zucchini or the medal-

lions of turbot sautéed in marrow with a shallot and wine compote. His fine essays on the theme of meat (24-hour roasted Limousin veal knuckle stuffed with garlic and the Bresse chicken breast with Lardo di Colonnata and braised potatoes) and airy desserts (sautéed fresh fruit, chocolate ice cream) are entirely successful. In short, this star restaurant does its job with rare talent.

● La Palme d'Or   ⓁⓊⓍ

At the Martinez, 73, bd de la Croisette.
Tel. 04 92 98 73 00. Fax 04 93 39 67 82.
lapalmedor@hotel-martinez.com
www.hotel-martinez.com
Closed Sun., Mon., beg. Nov.–mid-Dec.
Prix fixe: 75€, 98€, 145€, 168€.
A la carte: 200€.

The end of an era on the Cannes Croisette: Christian Sinicropi has taken over from the shrewd Christian Willer, now retired. So why not say it? The new tricks he has introduced in what was one of the great restaurants on the Côte d'Azur are not really to our liking. The renovated art deco setting on the second floor of the luxury twenties hotel may be elegant and the service fast and efficient, but the high fashion dishes, cheap poetry and surfeit of sweet and savory make us wince. Wild red poppies with seasonal vegetables dressed in a red cabbage and chocolate emulsion, a tuna carpaccio with red tabouli, couscous vegetables and a verbena emulsion, a farm-raised rabbit with mustard, lemon, and crisp pralines (!) served with a grated potato cake and garlic confit are uninspiring, although the fish (rouget with grilled tomatoes and the zucchini and Mediterranean sea bass presented in a jar) puts on a better show. The desserts (pistachio and cherry crumble) are too rich. We already miss the Willer touch.

● Le Mesclun

16, rue Saint-Antoine.
Tel. 04 93 99 45 19.
mesclun.cannes@wanadoo.fr
www.lemesclun-restaurant.com
Closed lunch, Sun., Feb.
Prix fixe: 39€. A la carte: 85–95€.

And what if Christian Willer's true heir in Cannes were Olivier Bouzerand? This highly precise Burgundian veteran of the Martinez who went into business for himself at the Patio in Saint-Jean-de-Luz has now marked out his territory in this charming Suquet haunt with its paneled walls, pictures and period furniture. The menu presents a modern take on Riviera cuisine. Lobster ravioli with a broth from its shell, soy-marinated red tuna, sea bream filet with a white bean ragout, sole meunière with a Menton lemon butter emulsion and thyme-seasoned roasted rack of lamb, served with olive oil fork-mashed potatoes are finely crafted dishes based on quality produce. The souffléed orange crêpes with orange zest confit and caramelized hazelnut butter are refreshingly classic. Anna Bouzerand provides a charming welcome.

● Brasserie Carlton `COM`

At Hôtel Intercontinental Carlton,
58, bd de la Croisette.
Tel. 04 93 06 40 21. Fax 04 93 06 40 25.
carlton@ichotelsgroupe.com
www.ichotelsgroupe.com
Prix fixe: 39€, 49€. A la carte: 85€.

This unusual brasserie has found itself a niche in the sun with its prettily crafted dishes and relatively mild checks. A local artichoke and scallop risotto, Mediterranean sea bass, veal tenderloin sautéed with hazelnuts, a simply roasted thick rib eye steak, the house chocolate mousse and roasted cinnamon-seasoned figs leave us with fond memories. A fashionable brunch on the weekend.

● Comme Chez Soi `COM`

4, rue Batéguier.
Tel. 04 93 39 62 68. Fax 04 93 38 20 65.
info@commechezsoi.net
Closed Mon.
Prix fixe: 25€, 20€ (child).
A la carte: 80–90€.

Behind the Croisette, Sophie Meissonnie offers a warm welcome in her cozy, charming, bric-a-brac-style setting. A team of delightful waitresses present its market-based dishes. Mediterranean sea bass carpaccio, coriander-seasoned shellfish salad, jumbo shrimp cannelloni with niçoise vegetables and fresh herbs, fried John Dory with a parmesan-seasoned broccoli purée and a roasted Bresse squab with béarnaise sauce are not bad at all.

● Côté Jardin `COM`

12, av Saint-Louis.
Tel.-Fax 04 93 38 60 28.
cotejardin@wanadoo.fr
www.restaurant-cotejardin.com
Closed Sun., Mon., Nov. 1 vac.,
1 week Jan., 1 week Feb.
Prix fixe: 22€, 28€, 36€, 12€ (child).

Far from the madding Croisette, the Treffots have taken over this restaurant with its garden, shady terrace and dining room in ochre tints. Carine recommends wine to suit the dishes prepared by Philippe. The goat cheese ravioli in an herb foam, rouget filet with tapenade, pan-seared hanger steak with panisses (regional chickpea cakes) and rice pudding with apple and pear marmalade make up incisive spreads.

● Félix `COM`

63, bd de la Croisette.
Tel. 04 93 94 00 61. Fax 04 93 94 06 90.
www.cannes-felix.fr
Closed Sun., Mon., 20 Nov.–20 Dec.
Prix fixe: 43€. A la carte: 55€.

The people of Cannes still love this chic brasserie and terrace on the Croisette, so arm yourself with patience if you wish to taste its frog legs sautéed in garlic, parsley and butter, the grilled fish of the day, rack of lamb with a vegetable mille-feuille and the dessert trolley.

● Le Fouquet's `COM`

At the Majestic Barrière,
10, bd de la Croisette.
Tel. 04 92 98 77 05. Fax 04 93 38 97 90.
fouquetscannes@lucienbarriere.com
www.lucienbarriere.com
Closed 2 weeks Christmas–New Year's.
Prix fixe: 28€ (lunch), 30€ (dinner), 40€, 20€ (child). A la carte: 65€.

The Majestic's other eatery is this Fouquet's. The décor by Garcia features red carpet and chairs, yellow walls and blackboards. The menu supervised by Bruno Oger features classics reinterpreted in a contemporary manner: chicken breast with coriander, melon with Parma ham, whole grilled fennel-seasoned Mediterranean sea bass, sole meunière, a beautiful rib eye steak for two and a Madagascar vanilla bean-flavored crème brûlée. All are reliable and well presented.

● Mantel `COM`

22, rue Saint-Antoine.
Tel.-Fax 04 93 39 13 10.
noel.mantel@wanadoo.fr
Closed Wed. (off season), Thu. lunch (off season), 10 days beg. Aug.
Prix fixe: 34€, 58€. A la carte: 65–80€.

Ducasse taught Noël Mantel to love Southern French produce and prepare it at its freshest. The dining room in warm shades (beige, ochre and red) provides a welcoming setting for the finely crafted feasts here. Lobster ravioli with shellfish sauce, cep risotto, pan-seared Breton cod, grilled line-fished Mediterranean sea bass, caramelized veal knuckle that has been slowly simmered and glazed in its own jus favorably impress as does the dessert buffet .

● Palm Square `COM`

At the Splendid, 1, allée de la Liberté.
Tel. 04 93 06 78 27. Fax 04 93 06 78 29.
info@palm-square.fr / www.palm-square.com
Closed 1 week at end Dec.
Prix fixe: 35€ (dinner), 45€ (dinner) 15€ (child).

The menu is endless and the décor half nightclub, half Buddha Bar-style fusion restaurant, but everything served here under the guidance of Claude Sutter, who trained at the Crocodile in Strasbourg and with Guérard and Boyer, is worth trying. Scallop and bacon risotto, shrimp croustillant with young rabbit, a ginger carpaccio with coconut milk and a grilled sea bream with olives are well crafted.

● Le Restaurant Arménien

82, bd de la Croisette.
Tel. 04 93 94 00 58. Fax 04 93 94 56 12.
infos@lerestaurantarmenien.com
www.lerestaurantarmenien.com
Closed Mon., 10 days Dec.
Prix fixe: 42€.

The setting is kitsch, the stained glass amusing, the atmosphere friendly and Lucie Panossian's cuisine a fine tribute to her ancestral Armenia. Sausage pizza, cracked wheat salad, an Armenian phyllo pastry called beurek, meatballs with herbs, grilled sausages and the filo and nut pastries are genuinely gratifying.

● Les Trois Portes `COM`

16, rue des Frères-Pradignac.
Tel. 04 93 38 91 70. Fax 04 93 38 95 52.
roussel3portes@aol.com / www.troisportes.com
Closed Sun.
Prix fixe: 29€, 55€. A la carte: 50€.

The contemporary setting in shades of beige and dishes dripping with sunshine go well together in Patrick Rousset's restaurant. Atanasian Aram meticulously prepares a chilled melon soup with fresh mint, Mediterranean sea bass with bouillabaisse broth, an oven-roasted leg of lamb and a warm bittersweet chocolate cake with vanilla sauce, all of which make a fine impression.

● Aux Bons Enfants

89, rue Meynadier.
No tel.
Closed Sat. dinner (Oct.–Apr.), Sun., beg. Aug.–beg. Sept., 22 Dec.–2 Jan.
Prix fixe: 20€.

Tables cannot be reserved (at least by telephone) in this Cannes *bouchon*-style restaurant which reflects the Nice Meranda model, but the welcome is warm and the single set menu at 20 something of a steal. Grilled sardines, a wonderful artichoke terrine with pancetta and mozzarella, niçoise-style lamb stew, apricot clafoutis and the house-made fruit tarts are reliably prepared by Luc Giorsetti, a former trainee at the Martinez. No checks or credit cards.

● **Le Maschou**   N SIM

15, rue Saint-Antoine.
Tel. 04 93 39 62 21.
Closed lunch, Sun. (off season).
Prix fixe: 41€.

This cozy, slightly rustic restaurant with
its exposed stone and candles on the tables
presents a single, generous option that
begins with a glass of sangria offered on
the house, prosciutto and melon, and a
basket of crudités and dip. The choice
of grilled meats (charcoal grilled rib
eye steak, rack of lamb or grilled young
chicken), served with potatoes roasted
in hot coals and the all-you-can-eat desserts are timelessly classical. Alain Viotti
manages this enterprise with generosity,
warmth and efficiency.

● **Le Suquetan**   N SIM

6, rue Saint-Dizier.
Tel. 04 93 99 20 10.
Closed Sun., Mon., end Dec.–beg. Jan.
Prix fixe: 19€ (lunch). A la carte: 25€.

Fréderic Lafargue, former tennis teacher,
and François Garcin, international career
chef and Taittinger Prize finalist, have
taken over this small restaurant and terrace by the place du Suquet. The changing menu reflects the produce supplied by
the market nearby, with pears and Roquefort, honey-seasoned duck confit and an
apple crumble.

● **Astoux et Brun**   SIM

27, rue Félix-Faure.
Tel. 04 93 39 21 87. Fax 04 93 39 98 54.
astouxetbrunrestaurant@wanadoo.fr
A la carte: 45€.

This brasserie with its terrace continues to
delight night owls. We quietly savor oysters and other shellfish, house-smoked
salmon, fish stew, grilled sirloin steak and
chocolate mousse, all simply gratifying.

● **La Cave**   SIM

9, bd de la République.
Tel. 04 93 99 79 87. Fax 04 93 68 91 19.
restaurantlacave@free.fr
www.restaurant-lacave.com

Closed Sat. lunch, Sun.,
1 week at end Aug.–beg. Sept.
Prix fixe: 22€, 28€. A la carte: 55€.

This modern bistro with its faux leather
banquettes and posters on the walls provides a spirited welcome from Marc Ber-
rut and a selection of authentic dishes.
The plate of Provençal specialties, vegetables with aïoli, oven-roasted Mediterranean sea bass and a tiramisu are very
well crafted.

● **Le Caveau 30**   SIM

45, rue Félix-Faure.
Tel. 04 93 39 06 33. Fax 04 92 98 05 38.
www.lacaveau30.com
Call for days/hours.
Prix fixe: 22€, 32€. A la carte: 40–60€.

Near the Palais des Festivals and marina,
this neo-thirties brasserie serves honest
Provençal cuisine. Fisherman's soup, veal
kidneys and the crème brûlée are good
classics.

● **Le Comptoir des Vins**   SIM

13, bd de la République.
Tel. 04 93 68 13 26.
comptoirdesvins@cegetel.net
Closed Sun., 1 week Feb., 1 week June.
Prix fixe: 16€ (lunch). A la carte: 30–35€.

This cellar, wine bar and restaurant in
green, brown and cream shades is a likable little eatery. Laurent and Live Heu-
kem offer a warm welcome, while Hervé
Decaux prepares coddled eggs with foie
gras, cod filet served over slow-roasted
fennel and a duck parmentier, all accompanied by selected vintages.

● **La Mère Besson**   SIM

13, rue des Frères-Pradignac.
Tel. 04 93 39 59 24. Fax 04 92 18 93 11.
lamerebesson@wanadoo.fr
Closed Sun., Christmas.
Prix fixe: 27€, 32€. A la carte: 45–50€.

Yves and Margaret Martin continue to cher-
ish the memory of Mère Besson. Curious clients flock to this institution refurbished in
yellow and olive green. A sardine escabeche,

fish soup, rockfish filets, Provençal-style leg of lamb with tomatoes and a soft-centered chocolate cake don't fall short.

● Mi-Figue Mi-Raisin · SIM

27, rue du Suquet.
Tel.-Fax 04 93 39 51 25.
philippelevy546@hotmail.com
Closed Wed., 10 days Dec.
Prix fixe: 19€, 29€. A la carte: 50€.

On the heights of Le Suquet, Philippe Lévy pays sincere tribute to the region's produce in this colorful bistro. We make short work of the fried zucchini blossoms, monkfish medallions with chanterelles, a whole duck breast with a thyme-infused sauce or the Malaga-style caramelized rice pudding cake.

● L'Ondine · SIM

On the beach, la Croisette.
Tel. 04 93 94 23 15. Fax 04 93 94 10 71.
www.ondineplage.com
Closed dinner, Wed., mid-Nov.–mid-Dec.
A la carte: 90€.

This beach eatery is sure of its celebrity. To the sound of the waves, we savor Jean-Pierre Silva's dishes, meticulously prepared with fine produce: marinated fish, grilled Mediterranean sea bass, sea bream accompanied by an eggplant tartine with cep coulis, rack of Sisteron lamb and and crêpes Suzette. The check is not for those of a nervous disposition.

● Chez Panisse · SIM

At the Sofitel Méditerranée,
2, bd Jean-Hibert.
Tel. 04 92 99 73 10. Fax 04 92 99 73 29.
Call for days/hours.
Prix fixe: 18€, 21€, 27€. A la carte: 45€.

This hotel bistro's Provençal décor and comfortable banquettes put guests at their ease. The cuisine plays to a regional score and the prices are well mannered. Provençal-style stuffed vegetables, eggplant and mozzarella bruschetta, grilled Mediterranean sea bass with olive oil, the rack of lamb and the dessert buffet leave us in high good humor. Apposite wines.

In Cannes La Bocca (06150). 3 km.

● Le Saint-Barth · SIM

6, rue Barthélemy.
Tel.-Fax 04 93 48 91 10.
sylvette.manet-martin@wanadoo.fr
Closed Mon. dinner (off season), Tue.,
2 weeks Nov.
Prix fixe: 23€, 32€, 11€ (child).
A la carte: 40–45€.

Guaranteed relaxation at this restaurant in the pedestrian zone. The warm welcome puts us at our ease and the old-fashioned décor works its charm. On the food side, the spider crab soup, Mediterranean sea bass with chestnuts, sautéed calf's liver meunière and the thyme-infused pears served with rosemary sorbet are well crafted.

CANNES LA BOCCA see CANNES
CAP D'ANTIBES see ANTIBES
LE CAP D'AGDE see AGDE

CAPBRETON

40130 Landes. Paris 752 – Biarritz 31 – Mont-de-Marsan 88 – Bayonne 24.
tourisme.capbreton@wanadoo.fr.
A beach, its casino, harbor, family ambiance and summer vacation feel.

 HOTELS-RESTAURANTS

■ L'Océan

85, av Georges-Pompidou, in the harbor area.
Tel. 05 58 72 10 22/ 05 58 72 06 50.
Fax 05 58 72 08 43.
www.hotel-capbreton.com
Rest. closed end Nov.–22 Dec.,
beg. Jan.–beg. Feb.
25 rooms: 54–88€.
Prix fixe: 15€, 24€, 32€.
A la carte: 40–50€.

This peaceful hotel by the channel linking the marina and fishing harbor offers rooms (with balconies) in pastel tones. The restaurant, refurbished in marine style, serves well-mannered dishes in local colors: seafood, foie gras or the mixed seafood grill.

● Le Régalty `V.COM`

At port de plaisance, quartier de la Pêcherie.
Tel.-Fax 05 58 72 22 80.
leregalty@cegetel.net
Closed Sun. dinner, Mon.,
mid-Nov.-end Nov., mid-Jan.-end Jan.
Prix fixe: 25€. A la carte: 50-55€.

On the first floor of a contemporary building, Jean Durand and Michel Bondi's establishment is refined and good natured. The Basque-style squid, turbot braised with aromatic vegetables and foie gras with grapes are precise and flawless.

● MB `N.COM`

26, rue du Général-de-Gaulle.
Tel. 05 58 72 12 02.
Closed Mon.
Prix fixe: 14€ (weekday lunch), 45€.
A la carte: 38€.

Nomadic Burgundian Marc Buffet worked in Boston (the Méridien) and Paris (Le Grand Véfour), before becoming chef at the Château de Montcaud in the Gard region. He has turned this little corner restaurant in the town center, refurbished in modern neocolonial style with white laths and ceiling fans, into a tasteful bistro serving a fresh, flavorsome cuisine. As we savor a tomato-mozzarella Tatin, rouget with artichokes, sautéed roasted veal with snow peas and radishes in squash seed oil, we begin to think about moving in. The bittersweet chocolate fondant with a bugne (a Lyon-style fried pastry) and the house ginger ice cream are splendid. The friendly Nathalie offers a gracious welcome.

● Café Bellevue `COM`

Av Georges-Pompidou, quartier de la plage.
Tel. 05 58 72 10 30. Fax 05 58 72 11 12.
Closed mid-Nov.-mid-Feb.
Prix fixe: 16€ (weekday dinner), 25€, 30€.
A la carte: 40-50€.

A step away from the harbor, this marine brasserie with its retro décor overlooks the channel connecting marina to port. At the oyster bar or in the dining room with its porch, we angle for fresh, well-crafted culinary suggestions. Foie gras with cured duck, Atlantic sea bass with Serrano ham and a soft-centered chocolate cake are gratifying.

● Le Pavé du Port `N.SIM`

Quai Mille Sabords, Port de Plaisance.
Tel. 05 58 72 29 28.
Closed Mon. lunch, Tue., Wed. (exc. dinner Apr.-Sept.).
Prix fixe: 17€, 27€. A la carte: 45€.

They worked in London's luxury hotels, then for the King of Jordan, and are now keenly running this modern harbor-side bistro with its large terrace looking out on the marina. Aurélie Macquet vibrantly presides over the dining room and bar, while Nicolas prepares the catch of the day. Tuna carpaccio, grilled calamari, sole meunière, grilled rouget and drum fish served with vegetable croustillant are washed down with Château Beau Puits.

CAP-FERRET

33950 Gironde. Paris 654 – Bordeaux 71 – Arcachon 8 – Lacanau-Océan 60.
This peninsula at World's End with its tiny hamlets clustered around the Arcachon Basin is the best-kept secret in the Gironde.

■	HOTELS-RESTAURANTS

■ La Maison du Bassin

5, rue des Pionniers.
Tel. 05 56 60 60 63. Fax 05 56 03 71 47.
www.lamaisondubassin.com
Closed Jan. Rest. closed lunch (exc. July-Aug.), Tue. (exc. July-Aug. and Bank holidays).
11 rooms: 120-215€.
Prix fixe: 25€, 39€, 12€ (child).
A la carte: 65€.

A stone's throw from the Ferret lighthouse and oyster beds, the Joinaus have turned this old hotel into a charming establishment indeed. It continues to enchant with its delightful nautical rooms of every size (soon to be equipped with air conditioning), bistro cuisine (especially the grandmotherly desserts) and wines.

■ La Frégate

34, av de l'Océan.
Tel. 05 56 60 41 62. Fax 05 56 03 76 18.

Around the pleasant swimming pool, the Hourquebie family has converted different buildings into neat guest rooms and apartments with kitchens. Handy for clans on vacation.

■ Hôtel des Pins

23, rue des Fauvettes.
Tel. 05 56 60 60 11. Fax 05 56 60 67 41.
Closed Jan.–mid-Feb. Rest. closed Mon.,
weekdays (Nov.–Dec., exc. school vac.).
12 rooms: 55–85€. 2 suites: 125–160€.
Prix fixe: 15€ (Sat., Sun., lunch),
24€ (dinner), 32€ (dinner), 9€ (child).
A la carte: 40€.

Art deco reigns supreme in this peaceful hotel, from its comfortable rooms to the bar and porch. In the restaurant, Stéphane Vivier prepares dishes in the colors of Southwest France (foie gras terrine, cuttlefish with black olives, free-range chicken medallions).

■ Hôtel de la Plage

1, rue des Marins, at the oyster farm.
Tel.-Fax 05 56 60 50 15.
Closed Jan.–mid-Feb.
Rest. closed dinner (exc. Sat.), Mon.
(exc. July–Aug.).
10 rooms: 42–45€.
Prix fixe: 18€, 27€. A la carte: 30–40€.

Janine Condou and Michel Soleil have turned this colonial-style residence into one of the peninsula's great secrets. The rooms with their balconies and straw yellow dining room welcome guests in search of something straightforward and different. We dine on unfussy oysters and sausages, squid and a duck breast with peaches.

● Chez Hortense   SIM

Av du Sémaphore, at the Pointe.
Tel. 05 56 60 62 56. Fax 05 56 60 42 84.
Closed weekdays (beg. Sept.–end Mar.).
Prix fixe: 36€, 41€, 16€ (child).
A la carte: 55€.

Bernadette Lescaret welcomes Bordeaux society, which flocks to her chic cabin to "slum it", admire the view of the Pilat dune and savor uncomplicated classics. The mussels stuffed with ham, grilled sole or turbot, duck confit and the chocolate fondant are faultless.

● Chez Yvan, le Mascaret   SIM

17, rue des Goélands.
Tel. 05 56 03 75 74. Fax 05 56 03 75 65.
Closed Wed., Feb.
Prix fixe: 22€. A la carte: 40€.

The Villes have turned this charming cabin into a convivial gourmet spot. The welcome is friendly indeed and Jeoffroy Isasti's home cooking deft enough. Shrimp fricassée, cod cassoulet, steak tartare and a cherry clafoutis make up pleasant domestic spreads.

● Côté Phare   SIM

32, av Nord-du-Phare.
Tel. 05 57 70 80 35.
Closed Mon. (exc. July–Aug.),
Tue. (exc. July–Aug.), Tue., Feb.
Prix fixe: 16€, 28€, 9,50€ (child).
A la carte: 45€.

A step away from the lighthouse, Christophe Lafon cheerfully presides over this convivial bistro. Beneath the high ceiling or on the terrace, we enjoy the seasonal cuisine, which focuses on the produce of greater Southwest France. Shrimp carpaccio, tuna with aromatic herbs and spices, rib eye steak and panna cotta are very much equal to their task.

● L'Escale   SIM

2, av de l'Océan, Bélisaire jetty.
Tel. 05 56 60 68 17. Fax 05 56 03 77 93.
www.restaurant-cap-ferret.com
Closed Jan.
Prix fixe: 16€ (lunch), 23€ (dinner).
A la carte: 40–45€.

When the weather is fine, the Escale's terrace near to the wharf is a great hit. Visitors flock here to enjoy a place in the sun and a few pleasant dishes. Tuna carpaccio, cod with aïoli, rack of lamb with caramelized jus and garlic confit and the crème brûlée slip down smoothly.

● Pinasse Café `SIM`

2 bis, av de l'Océan.
Tel. 05 56 03 77 87. Fax 05 56 60 63 47.
www.pinassecafe.com
Closed mid-Nov.–end Feb.
Prix fixe: 20€ (weekday lunch), 25,50€, 31,50€. A la carte: 50€.

By the port and the Pilat dune, this bistro with its terrace is a monument in itself. Laurent and Alexandra Tournier provide a professional welcome. The décor in wood, red and blue delights, as do the dishes. Emmanuel Goncalvez surfs on waves of fashion with never a wipe out. Fried squid with onion-, herb-, caper- and mustard-seasoned mayonnaise, cod filet with aïoli, grilled ginger-seasoned Atlantic sea bass and crème brûlée make a fine impression.

● Le Rond-Point de l'Herbe `SIM`

2, bd plage de L'Herbe.
Tel. 05 56 60 51 32.
www.lerondpointdelherbe.com
Call for days/hours.
Prix fixe: 13€, 20€, 28€, 47€.

Ophélia Bazeugeaud is the fairy godmother of Cap Ferret. In this former fisherman's cabin, she presents her treats of the day, in the shape of bargain set menus and changing fare. Bernard Perrot, a veteran of the Maison du Fleuve in Camblanes, tends to the stove with great good will. We enjoy the unpretentious gazpacho, the red tuna tartare, the spaghetti with littleneck clams, beef sirloin grilled at the fireplace and served with béarnaise sauce.

CARANTEC

29660 Finistère. Paris 554 – Brest 68 – lannion 54 – Morlaix 15.
carantec.tourisme@wanadoo.fr.
In the Léon district, this small port looking out on the great bay of Morlaix is worth a visit for its views, fine church and neat homes trimmed with flowers.

HOTELS-RESTAURANTS

● L'Hôtel de Carantec

20, rue du Kelenn.
Tel. 02 98 67 00 47. Fax 02 98 67 08 25.
patrick.jeffroy@wanadoo.fr
www.hoteldecarantec.com
Closed 2 weeks Nov., 2 weeks Jan.
12 rooms: 112–220€.
Prix fixe: 32€, 56€, 79€, 108€.

Why stop here in particular? Because of the art deco hotel refurbished in contemporary style with a perfect view of a superb bay, cozy rooms and Patrick Jeffroy's brilliant cuisine, of course! A master of fare wedding land and sea, including combinations of langoustines and roasted foie gras, giant oysters and andouille sausage, red mullet and pig's feet, this son of Morlaix, who has returned to his roots, inspires us with his pan-fried oats with roasted bacon and buttermilk. Nothing that leaves his kitchens goes unnoticed. Advised by the colorful Christine Tommeler, the Arletty of great Breton restaurants, we willingly succumb to the house's latest temptations. Breton lobster with purple artichokes and shellfish butter, cured Iberian ham, rack of lamb in an herb crust or better yet the "salmis", a rich roasted free-range pigeon ragout served with a cocotte of summer vegetables, are dazzlingly truthful dishes. In conclusion, chocolate and coffee cake, bitter chocolate ganache with cassis sorbet or the mille-feuille of crêpes dentelle (a dried paper-thin rolled crêpe) with bergamot cream and berry sorbet are supreme examples of a refined genre: the unsweetened dessert. The wine list is a trove of excellent finds. In short, this establishment is close to our heart.

● Le Cabestan & la Cambuse `SIM`

7, rue du Port.
Tel. 02 98 67 01 87. Fax 02 98 67 90 49.
lecabestancarantec@wanadoo.fr
www.lecabestan.fr
Closed Mon. (exc. July–Aug.), Tue., Nov.
Prix fixe: 18€, 32€. A la carte: 40–45€.

Daniel and Denis Godec have two strings to their bow. On the first floor, the Cambuse pays tribute to the sea in a range of simple preparations. Upstairs, the Cabestan presents more sophisticated dishes. Tasting the tuna carpaccio with lime-seasoned pesto, avocado and jumbo shrimp salad, pollock with oven-browned mushrooms and skate "Moqueca", a Brazilian fish stew, we feel an urge to set sail with the next tide. A fine sea view.

● **La Chaise du Curé**

3, pl de la République.
Tel. 02 98 78 33 27. Fax 02 98 67 08 85.
Closed Wed., Thu. (off season), 2 weeks Nov., mid-Jan.–mid-Feb.
Prix fixe: 15€ (weekday lunch), 19€, 25€, 32€. A la carte: 40–45€.

Florence and Frédéric Lechat offer a warm welcome in this village bistro by the church. The salmon tartare served with lentils, the swordfish with whole grain mustard, the honey and blueberry seasoned duck breast and the mille-feuille with orange cream are frankly gratifying.

CARCASSONNE

11000 Aude. Paris 790 – Perpignan 114 – Toulouse 92 – Albi 110 – Narbonne 61.
carcassonne@fnotsi.net.
The ancient fortified town and Saint-Nazaire basilica are the essential sights in this fabulous medieval fortress.

■/◉ HOTELS-RESTAURANTS

● **Hôtel de la Cité**
  & la Barbacane

Pl de l'Eglise.
Tel. 04 68 71 98 71. Fax 04 68 71 50 15.
reservations@hoteldelacite.com
www.hoteldelacite.com
Closed end Nov.–end Dec., end Jan.–beg. Mar.
61 rooms: 275–500€.
40 suites: 400–1250€.
Prix fixe: 70€, 110€, 170€.

The Orient-Express group has restored the respectability of this Gothic palace. Its charming, stylish rooms, view of the Saint-Nazaire basilica, vast lobby with attractive frescos, swimming pool and oasis-inspired gardens are impressive indeed. In the majestic dining room with its fireplace, stained glass windows and walls emblazoned with arms and escutcheons, we make short work of the restorative dishes prepared by Jérôme Ryon, Taittinger prizewinner. "Castelnaudary" cassoulet with sage, a gratin of Mediterenean sea urchins, ceps and crémant de Limoux and a whole line-caught sole served with chanterelles and cockles are brilliantly crafted in a revised Southwestern French spirit. The desserts (chocolate financier, wild strawberries with vanilla-scented olive oil) are a delightful experience. The service is spirited and the cellar packed with fine surprises (also see Chez Saskia).

● **Domaine d'Auriac**

Rte de Saint-Hilaire, 3 km se via D104.
Tel. 04 68 25 72 22. Fax 04 68 47 35 54.
auriac@relaischateaux.com
www.domaine-d-auriac.com
Closed 1 week beg. Jan.
Rest. closed Sun. dinner, Mon.
24 rooms: 110–380€. 4 suites: 400–450€.
Prix fixe: 60€, 90€. A la carte: 95€.

Set in the heart of a seventy-five-hectare estate boasting an eighteen-hole golf course, tennis court, swimming pool and steam bath, this fine 19th-century establishment renovated by the Rigaudis family with an eye to modern tastes is appealing indeed. Its old-fashioned rooms have an easy charm and appreciative gourmets flock to the renovated dining room in shades of red to enjoy Philippe Ducos' fine ideas. A disciple of Guérard, Coussau and Arrambide, he deftly prepares a generous anchovy platter, golden grilled langoustines in a creamy shellfish fumet, or better yet, the "crépinette" sausages with truffled pig's feet. To conclude, the warm peach with frozen apricot soufflé offers a cool note. There is also an inexpensive bistro near the golf course.

● Le Parc Franck Putelat Ⓝ◯V.COM

80, chemin des Anglais.
Tel. 04 68 71 80 80.
fr.putelat@wanadoo.fr
www.leparcfranckputelat.com
Closed Sat. lunch, Sun. dinner, Mon., Jan.
Prix fixe: 24€ (lunch)–70€. A la carte: 65€.

A smart town house standing in its own grounds, courteous service with good advice on the choice of wine from Stéphane Bayart and, of course, Franck Putelat's shrewd, passionate cuisine have made this establishment the event of the year at the foot of the walled town. We are curious to see the new domain of the man who took the cuisine of the Barbacane at the Hôtel de la Cité to such heights. A native of Franche Comté who trained with Georges Blanc and holder of the Bocuse d'Argent award, Putelat is an energetic exponent of Southern French cuisine. His foie gras with verjus, lobster and piquillos peppers and pigeon poached in licorice-infused milk are appealing propositions.

● Robert Rodriguez ◯COM

39, rue Coste-Reboulh (near the Post Office).
Tel.-Fax 04 68 47 37 80.
rodrigezro@wanadoo.fr
www.rodrigez.robert.com
Closed Sun., Mon., 2 weeks Feb.,
2 weeks Aug.
Prix fixe: 19€ (lunch), 33€, 45€, 61€ (wine inc.). A la carte: 70€.

The Rodriguez family has made a lasting name for itself here. After studying with some great chefs on the coast, Father Robert moved into this tiny restaurant in the lower part of town, where he opened an extra dining room. With the help of his son, the pastry chef, and his daughter, who looks after the dining room, he serves up invigorating produce-based dishes. The line-fished Atlantic sea bass tartare, the roasted whole lobster, the grilled sirloin brochettes and the warm chocolate tart served with chocolate sorbet make up splendid menus, washed down with fine local wines. On the downside, the prices à la carte mount up slowly but surely.

● Comte Roger COM

14, rue Saint-Louis, la Cité.
Tel. 04 68 11 93 40. Fax 04 68 11 93 41.
restaurant@comteroger.com
www.comteroger.com
Closed Sun. (exc. July–Aug.), Mon. (exc. Bank holidays), mid-Feb.–mid-Mar.
Prix fixe: 32€, 42€, 15€ (child).
A la carte: 55€.

The shady terrace inspires an urge to move in here in the historic heart of town. Pierre Mesa prepares wild duck filets breaded with hazelnuts, grilled scallops, cassoulet with Gascon black pork and a sweet almond panna cotta served with citrus soup, all of which pack a punch.

● Chez Saskia COM

Hôtel de la Cité, pl Auguste-Pierre-Pont, la Cité.
Tel. 04 68 71 98 71. Fax 04 68 71 50 15.
jhamburger@hoteldelacite.com
www.hoteldelacite.com
Closed lunch, Tue., Wed., end Nov.–end Dec., end Jan.–beg. Mar.
Prix fixe: 25–45€. A la carte: 55€.

Managed by the Hôtel de la Cité, this contemporary brasserie serves a deftly crafted bistro cuisine. Andalusian gazpacho, monkfish medallions, grilled beef sirloin and a soft-centered chocolate cake make up cheerful meals.

● Auberge de Dame Carcas SIM

3, pl du Château, la Cité.
Tel. 04 68 71 23 23. Fax 04 68 72 46 17.
Closed Wed., 10 days beg. Oct.,
1 week Christmas–New Year's, 2 weeks Feb., 10 days beg. June.
Prix fixe: 16–16€, 24,50€.

In the heart of town, this rustic inn leaves us replete without breaking the bank. The antique setting in red and white has plenty of character, as does the cuisine. Pan-seared foie gras with berries, a duck gizzard salad, a honey-glazed grilled suckling pig and generous crêpes make up solid spreads.

● L'Ecurie

43, bd Barbès.
Tel. 04 68 72 04 04. Fax 04 68 25 31 90.
www.restaurantlecurie.fr
Closed Sun. dinner.
Prix fixe: 15€ (lunch), 22€ (weekdays),
29€, 35€, 65€.

These former 18th-century stables redesigned by Christophe Foulquier serve honest feasts in the colors of the greater South of France. Foie gras terrine, a grilled eggplant and zuchini salad with Serrano ham, a mixed seafood grill (parrillada) and veal chop with a morel cream sauce favorably impress. The pear tart Tatin with licorice ice cream makes a choice conclusion.

In Cavanac (11570). 7 km s via rte de Saint-Hilaire.

■ Château de Cavanac

Tel. 04 68 79 61 04. Fax 04 68 79 79 67.
infos@chateau-de-cavanac.fr
www.chateau-de-cavanac.fr
Closed beg. Jan.–end Feb., 2 weeks Nov.
Rest. closed Mon.
24 rooms: 65–155€. 4 suites: 152–155€.
Prix fixe: 40€.

In the heart of a vast winegrowing property, this 17th-century château offers individualized guest rooms with enchanting names: Belle de Nuit (Beauty of the Night), Couronne Impériale (Imperial Crown), Tour Capucine (Capuchin Tower) and so on. The four-poster beds and period furniture are part of the décor and the view of the vineyards a bonus. The stables have been converted into a restaurant, where we treat ourselves to pan-seared foie gras with figs, a half lobster over a bed of mixed greens, scallops with fleur de sel, a honey roasted suckling pig and profiteroles.

CARLA-BAYLE

09130 Ariège. Paris 799 – Foix 30 –
Pamiers 29.
This citadel fortified in the 14th century still has all its original charm.

● RESTAURANTS

● Auberge Pierre Bayle

Rue Principale.
Tel.-Fax 05 61 60 63 95.
phadeo@wanadoo.fr
Closed Mon., Tue. dinner (exc. summer),Wed. (exc. summer), 3 weeks end Dec.–10 Jan.
Prix fixe: 25€, 30€. A la carte: 50€.

This fine inn's rustic dining room overlooks the entire region. The view is enough to whet our appetite before we sit down to duck breast carpaccio with spices, roasted monkfish with garlic and citrus fruits, a seven-hour lamb with grilled eggplant and a white chocolate croustillant with strawberries.

CARNAC

56340 Morbihan. Paris 490 – Vannes 31 –
Auray 13 – Lorient 36 – Quilberon 18.
ot.carnac@ot-carnac.fr.
"The rocks won't know we're talking about them," sang Guillevic. The poet's voice has been silenced now, but the granite standing stones are still there in all their enigmatic beauty.

◧ HOTELS-RESTAURANTS

■ Novotel

Av de l'Atlantique.
Tel. 02 97 52 53 00. Fax 02 97 52 53 55.
h0406@accors.com / www.thalasso-carnac.com
Closed Jan.
109 rooms: 107–176€. 1 suite: 206–323€.
Prix fixe: 28€. A la carte: 50€.

This thalassotherapy hotel with its sixties facade, slate and practical rooms has a bright, charming, designer health restaurant: Secret de Table. Dominique Mauge, a Breton from Malestroit, prepares its ambitious cuisine. We adore the salmon tartare with chive-seasoned cream sauce and Atlantic sea bass with seaweed.

● La Calypso

Le Pô.
Tel. 02 97 52 06 14. Fax 02 97 52 20 39.

Closed Sun., Mon. (exc. vac.), Dec., Jan.
A la carte: 60€.

Marc Brosolo presides with gusto over this roadside establishment near the oyster beds, cooking the cream of the catch in his hearth. Sardine, mullet, brill, John Dory, turbot, lobster and monkfish brochettes emerge beautifully cooked from the embers to grace our plates. We eat near to the fireplace and strike up a conversation with our neighbors. Atlantic sea bass carpaccio or broiled oysters and flambéed apple cake or the house tea and mint *succés* to conclude and the two dining rooms purr with contentment.

● **La Côte**   `COM`

At Kermario, 2 km n, near the megaliths.
Tel. 02 97 52 02 80.
lacote@tele2.fr
Closed Sat. lunch (off season), Sun. dinner (off season), Mon. (off season), 1 week beg. Oct., 1 week at end Nov., beg. Jan.–end Feb., 4 days mid-Mar.
Prix fixe: 23€ (lunch), 33€, 43€, 53€, 85€. A la carte: 55€.

Laetitia Michaud is the most gracious of hostesses and Pierre, her chef husband who worked with the Ibarboure brothers in Bidart and at Le Pressoir in Saint-Avé, prepares his regional produce with commitment and creativity. His menus are bargains. A smoked salmon ballottine stuffed with crab and leeks, the broiled pollock filet with chorizo butter and a Tatin-style Breton shortbread and fromage blanc dessert with lemon sorbet star in the 33 option. The Atlantic sea bass with sautéed fava beans, cockles and asparagus served over polenta (from the "Discovery" menu at 43) is splendid.

● **La Brigantine**   `N` `SIM`

3, rue Colary.
Tel. 02 97 52 17 72.
Closed Sun., Mon. (exc. Easter, summer), 1 week beg. Oct., Jan.–mid-Feb., 1 week beg. June.
Prix fixe: 19€, 29€, 59€.

Daniel Béveno, an architect with a consuming passion for gastronomy, has turned this town center establishment with its cute nautical setting in wood, white and blue into a pleasant restaurant. We come here to enjoy the honest seafood platter, langoustine ravioli, John Dory with Muscadet risotto and Atlantic sea bass in papillote with Thai rice and come to grips with some of the fine wines on the exhaustive list.

84330 Vaucluse. Paris 680 – Nyons 35 – Avignon 36 – Carpentras 10.
otcaromb@axit.fr.
At the foot of Mont Ventoux, a Provençal village with ancient lanes where the living is easy.

 HOTELS-RESTAURANTS

■ **La Mirande**   ⌂

Pl de l'Eglise.
Tel. 04 90 62 40 31. Fax 04 90 62 34 48.
www.mirandecaromb.com
Rest. closed Sun. dinner, Tue. dinner, Wed., Jan.
10 rooms: 45–48€.
Prix fixe: 12€, 32€. A la carte: 40€.

This practical hotel at the foot of Mont Ventoux boasts pleasant contemporary rooms and Sébastien Royer's enchanting home cooking. The mixed greens with chicken livers, salmon in papillote, grilled veal medallions and the tart Tatin offer an easy pleasure.

● **Le Four à Chaux**   `COM`

2 km via rte de Malaucène.
Tel. 04 90 62 40 10. Fax 04 90 62 32 62.
www.lefourachaux.com
Closed Mon., Tue. (exc. dinner in summer), mid-Nov.–beg. Dec., Jan.
Prix fixe: 24€, 32€, 40€, 12€ (child).
A la carte: 50€.

Corinne Laugier has taken over this former lime kiln, now a distinctive rustic restaurant with its shady terrace. The cuisine has the fragrance of Provence and the taste of simplicity. Local spelt wheat soup and the milk-fed veal with morel mushrooms offer an authentic flavor.

CARPENTRAS

84200 Vaucluse. Paris 682 – Avignon 28 – Dignes-les-Bains 142 – Gap 147 – Marseille 105.

tourist.carpentras@axit.fr.

At the gate of the Ventoux region, the home of berlingot candy and heart of the Comtat Venaissin enclave is well worth a visit for its cathedral of Saint-Siffrein and ancient synagogue.

 HOTELS-RESTAURANTS

■ Le Comtadin

65, bd Albin-Durand.
Tel. 04 90 67 75 00. Fax 04 90 67 75 01.
le.comtadin@wanadoo.fr
www.le-comtadin.com
Closed 20 Dec.–end Jan.
20 rooms: 54–99€.

Near the church of Saint-Siffrein, this 18th-century town house offers rooms in various bright colors. Looking out on either patio or boulevard, they are perfectly soundproofed.

■ Hôtel du Fiacre

153, rue Vigne.
Tel. 04 90 63 03 15. Fax 04 90 60 49 73.
contact@hotel-du-fiacre.com
www.hotel-du-fiacre.com
17 rooms: 56–100€. 1 suite: 130€.

In a former 18th-century convent, the Cazeauxs have fitted out fine rooms opening onto the patio, with Louis-Philippe furniture and Aubusson tapestries.

● Franck Restaurant   COM

30, pl de l'Horloge / Rue des Halles.
Tel.-Fax 04 90 60 75 00.
www.franckrestaurant.com
Closed Tue., Wed., 2 weeks Mar.
Prix fixe: 26,50€. A la carte: 50–55€.

Franck Deligny has refurnished this town center establishment in contemporary style. The dishes, including a salmon tartare, grilled Atlantic sea bass or the lamb with arugula pesto and purée of ratte potatoes, have character. A lollipop degustation with chocolate, vanilla milkshake and toasted marshmallow provides an amusing conclusion.

● Chez Serge   SIM

90, rue Cottier.
Tel. 04 90 63 21 24. Fax 04 90 11 70 68.
restaurant@chez-serge.com
www.chez-serge.com
Closed Sun.
Prix fixe: 17€ (lunch), 30€ (dinner), 37€.
A la carte: 40€.

Here in the shadow of the plane trees, Serge Ghoukassian leaves chef Alain Gallo free to focus on local produce. Foie gras Tatin with Muscat des Beaumes de Venise, seared sea bream with dill, Chinese-style duck and a lemon meringue tart are appealing indeed. A fine choice of Ventoux vintages.

In Le Beaucet (84210). 11 km se via D4, D39.

● Auberge du Beaucet   COM

Rue Coste-Chaude.
Tel. 04 90 66 10 82. Fax 04 90 66 00 72.
www.aubergedubeaucet.fr
Closed Sun., Mon., Jan.
Prix fixe: 39€, 44€.

Pierre Cote has taken over this formerly famous inn. The sober, rustic setting, view of the valley from the terrace and exposed beams all have their charm. We savor the deftly crafted cuisine with its healthy dose of regional character. Seared lamb sweetbreads with tomato and eggplant purée, turbot bourride (a Provençal fish soup with tomatoes, garlic, onions, herbs and aioli) or crisp roasted lamb with roasted garlic and rosemary, served with olive polenta, are very well conceived. To conclude, a fine Arabica cappuccino with its bitter chocolate biscuit, West Indian rum syrup and whipped cream.

In Mazan (84380). 7 km e via D942.

■ Le Château de Mazan
Pl Napoléon.
Tel. 04 90 69 62 61. Fax 04 90 69 76 62.
chateaudemazan@wanadoo.fr
www.chateaudemazan.com
Closed beg. Jan.–beg. Mar.
Rest. closed Mon. (off season), Tue.
22 rooms: 95–270€. 8 suites: 215–400€.
Prix fixe: 35€, 55€, 75€. A la carte: 70€.

This 18th-century residence, once the home of the Marquis de Sade, still has its neat garden, period moldings and elegant furniture. The tastefully refurbished rooms and cuisine served in a restaurant opening onto a magnificent shady terrace play on elegantly classical notes. A mussel salad served with Andalusian gazpacho, grilled toro brochettes, chilled dessert with calisson (a Provençal sweet) and a cocktail made from almond milk are appealing in every way.

In Monteux (84170). W via D942 (rte d'Avignon).

● Le Saule Pleureur   V.COM
145, chemin du Beauregard.
Tel. 04 90 62 01 35. Fax 04 90 62 10 90.
www.le-saule-pleureur.com
Closed Sat. lunch, Sun. dinner, Mon.,
2 weeks beg. Nov., 1 week beg. Jan.,
2 weeks beg. Mar., 1 week Aug.
Prix fixe: 29€ (weekday lunch),
39€ (dinner), 59€, 89€. A la carte: 115€.

Laurent Azoulay now tends to the fortunes of this restaurant, with its garden, refurbished in contemporary style. In the dining room in chocolate and anise shades, he plays to a modern score, serving up foie gras with Carpentras strawberry macarons, John Dory poached in shrimp broth with turmeric, milk-fed lamb baked in clay and hay with lamb-stuffed cannelloni. The desserts by Nicolas Bichon, 2005 vice-champion Pâtissier de France, such as the variations on theme of chocolate with five grands crus and nine textures, are sweet works of art.

CARQUEFOU see NANTES

06510 Alpes-Maritimes. Paris 936 – Nice 21 – Cannes 37 – Grasse 45.
In this village in the Nice hinterland, the call of the mountains already rings in our ears.

●   RESTAURANTS

● La Forge   N·SIM
Av Fernand Barbary, Carros-Village.
Tel. 04 93 29 31 50. Fax 04 93 20 57 28.
Closed lunch (Mon.–Thu. in summer), Tue. (winter), Wed. (winter),
2 weeks end Oct.–beg. Nov.,
2 weeks Christmas–New Year's.
Prix fixe: 15€ (weekday lunch), 25€.
A la carte: 45€.

This former smithy converted into a restaurant has just been taken over by Claude Scureti and his wife, who have brought a delightfully fresh ambiance to the place. Here in the heart of the village, warm brie with truffles, seared tuna with Provençal vinaigrette, seasonal risotto with market flavors, grilled lobster or a rib eye steak grilled over a wood fire provide a pure moment of delight.

13620 Bouches-du-Rhône. Paris 772 – Marseille 34 – Aix-en-Provence 39 – Martigues 20.
ot.carrylerouet@visitprovence.com.
The great comic movie star Fernandel was fond of this "residential suburb" of Marseille, whose harbor, villas and pines have lost none of their charm.

●   RESTAURANTS

● L'Escale   V.COM
Promenade du Port.
Tel.-Fax 04 42 45 00 47.
Closed Sun., Mon., Jan.
Prix fixe: 35€. A la carte: 70–80€.

This residence with its terrace and sea view had its moment of glory. The dining room has been entirely renovated contemporary fashion in green, blue and fuchsia on a travel theme. We savor the delicious classical dishes. Lobster salad, foie gras terrine, grilled rouget, veal tournedos flavored with Bayonne ham and a large assortment of desserts are reliable and untheatrical.

CARSPACH see **ALTKIRCH**

CASSIS

13260 Bouches-du-Rhône. Paris 804 – Marseille 30 – Aix 50 – La Ciotat 9 – Toulon 42.
omtcassis@enprovence.com.
Creeks, harbor and cruises draw the crowds when the sun shines. But when Cassis is empty ...

 HOTELS-RESTAURANTS

■ Royal Cottage
6, av du 11-Novembre.
Tel. 04 42 01 33 34. Fax 04 42 01 06 90.
info@royal-cottage.com
www.royal-cottage.com
Closed Christmas–New Year's.
25 rooms: 88–162€. 4 suites: 154–237€.

This hotel with its swimming pool offers rooms in a modern style, some of them with a view of the harbor. A fitness center and lush garden complete the picture.

■ La Rade
1, av des Dardanelles.
Tel. 04 42 01 02 97. Fax 04 42 01 01 32.
larade@hotel-cassis.com
www.hotel-cassis.com
27 rooms: 90–145€. 1 suite: 240–285€.

This old-fashioned establishment with its swimming pool has been entirely refurbished. Its rooms in beige tones with their patinated Provençal furniture are comfortable. Some have a sea view.

■ Le Jardin d'Emile
Plage Bestouan
via av de l'Amiral-Ganteaume.
Tel. 04 42 01 80 55. Fax 04 42 01 80 70.

provence@lejardindemile.fr
www.lejardindemile.fr
Closed mid-Nov.–mid-Dec.
Rest. closed Mon.
7 rooms: 82–132€.
Prix fixe: 36€. A la carte: 55€.

Lost in its pine grove not far from the harbor, Fabrice and César Morand's residence is a restful place. The Provençal rooms refurbished in a modern style and charming restaurant with terrace and garden are refreshing. We enjoy the anchovy marinaded in lemon, the fisherman's stew, the Rossini-style beef filet medallions and a chilled peach soup with mint.

■ Hôtel Cassitel
Pl G.-Clemenceau.
Tel. 04 42 01 83 44. Fax 04 42 01 96 31.
cassitel@hotel-cassis.com
www.hotel-cassis.com
31 rooms: 60–90€.

Near the harbor and beach, this hotel providing practical Provençal rooms is perfect for night owls.

● La Presqu'île
Rte de Port-Miou, quartier de Port-Miou.
Tel. 04 42 01 03 77. Fax 04 42 01 94 49.
restaurantlapresquile@wanadoo.fr
www.restaurant-la-presquile.com
Closed Sun. dinner, Mon., beg. Jan.–mid-Feb.
Prix fixe: 30€, 46€, 15€ (child).
A la carte: 65–70€.

On the creek road, this coastal villa with terrace has an easy charm. In the contemporary style blue-tinted dining room, we savor sautéed Provençal-style cuttlefish, lobster in salad with citrus vinaigrette, the house bouillabaisse-style soup and simply grilled Mediterranean sea bass with olive oil and lemon. Huguette Bertoleotti's welcome is delightful as always.

● La Goccia d'Olio
19, rue Michel-Arnaud.
Tel. 04 42 01 38 31.
Closed Sun., lunch (July–Aug.), Jan.
A la carte: 60€.

Alfredo, a member of the Faiola clan (his five brothers run the Stresa in Paris), has founded a quality Italian embassy in this side street near the port of Cassis. Tasting the twenty-five-month-aged Jambon de Langhirano, eggplant spiced with garlic and mint, ravioli stuffed with fresh Brousse cheese, linguine with arugula and mozzarella—among the pastas made in house—we have a sudden urge to get away from it all across the Alps. A former bakery with walls of pinkish local stone, the restaurant is charming indeed. A bottle of Montepulciano Lodola Nuova matches the setting beautifully.

● Chez Panisse   SIM
4, pl Mirabeau.
Tel. 04 42 01 93 93. Fax 04 42 01 33 15.
Closed Sun. dinner, Mon., beg. Nov.–24 Dec.
Prix fixe: 24€, 30€. A la carte: 40€.

Jean-Claude Saindrenan is a charming host indeed. How could his restaurant by the harbor be anything other than a success, with its terrace, delightful waitresses and flawless regional cuisine? Soccer legends Michel Platini and Jean Tigana, and Franz-Olivier Giesbert, director of *Le Point* magazine, adore the green peppercorn-marinated salmon tartare, the chadurée (an Atlantic version of bouillabaisse made with Muscadet), the chocolate croquant and the tiramisu.

● Romano   SIM
At the port, 15, quai Barthélemy.
Tel. 04 42 01 08 16. Fax 04 42 90 09 05.
restaurant.romano@wanadoo.fr
www.restaurant-romano.com
Closed Sun. dinner (off season).
Prix fixe: 23,50€, 29,50€, 10,50€ (child).
A la carte: 45€.

By the harbor, this marine bistro with its contemporary décor boasts a rough good humor and reliable Provençal cuisine. Pan-tossed catch of the day, lobster ravioli, sirloin steak and the lavender-scented crème brûlée are straightforwardly enjoyable.

04120 Alpes de Haute-Provence. Paris 793 – Digne 55 – Draguignan 59 – Grasse 64 – Manosque 95.
office@castellane.org.
This crossroads village perched in the heart of the Alpes de Haute-Provence is an excellent starting point for excursions to the Grand Canyon du Verdon and Point Sublime.

   HOTELS-RESTAURANTS

■ Nouvel Hôtel du Commerce   ⌂
Pl de l'Eglise.
Tel. 04 92 83 61 00. Fax 04 92 83 72 82.
accueil@hotel-fradet.com
www.hotel-fradet.com
Closed beg. Oct.–end Feb. Rest. closed Mon. lunch (exc. off season), Tue. (Sept.–June), Wed. lunch.
35 rooms: 57–70€.
Prix fixe: 20€, 29€. A la carte: 50€.

We like the location of the Fradet family's hotel at the foot of the Notre-Dame-du-Roc chapel, the neat rooms and the dining room with porch. Quail and chanterelle risotto, Mediterranean sea bass with asparagus served with leeks in truffle sauce, roasted milk-fed lamb and the soft-centered chocolate cake napped with sour cherry sauce are always very deft.

In 04120 La Garde. 6 km e via N85.

■ Auberge du Teillon   ⌂
Rte Napoléon.
Tel. 04 92 83 60 88. Fax 04 92 83 74 08.
contact@auberge-teillon.com
www.auberge-teillon.com
Closed Sun. dinner (exc. July–Aug.), Mon. (exc. July–Aug.), Tue. lunch (exc. off season), mid-Nov.–mid-Mar.
8 rooms: 49–55€.
Prix fixe: 20€, 30€, 38€, 44€, 10€ (child).

The Lépines' inn on the Route Napoleon provides fine rooms and meticulous cuisine. Patricia at the desk and Yves in the kitchen leave no stone unturned to make sure that their guests enjoy their visit. Smoked leg of lamb, calamari stuffed with brandade, steamed monkfish medallions with fennel and lobster sauce, roasted boneless squab stuffed with seared foie gras and the chocolate and candied orange terrine make a fine impression.

CASTELNAUDARY

11400 Aude. Paris 735 – Carcassonne 42 – Foix 70.
At the heart of the Tarn Lauragais district, the capital of cassoulet is also a center for fine meat in the ''land of plenty''.

 HOTELS-RESTAURANTS

■ Hôtel du Canal
2 ter, av Arnaud-Vidal.
Tel. 04 68 94 05 05. Fax 04 68 94 05 06.
hotelducanal@wanadoo.fr
www.hotelducanal.com
38 rooms: 48–59€.

On the bank of the Canal du Midi, this former lime factory, now a practical hotel, provides neat, contemporary rooms.

● Le Tirou   COM
90, av Monseigneur-de-Langle.
Tel. 04 68 94 15 95. Fax 04 68 94 15 96.
letirou@wanadoo.fr / www.le-tirou.com
Closed dinner (exc. Sat.), Mon.,
20 Dec.–20 Jan.
Prix fixe: 18€, 27€, 32€. A la carte: 40€.

At the Vissentins' place, tradition serves its purpose. The brick and salmon décor is charming and the garden and terrace perfect for relaxation. We enjoy the puff pasty with escargots and hazelnuts, cassoulet with duck confit and a chocolate marquise.

CASTELNAU-LE-LEZ see MONTPELLIER

CASTELNAU-DE-MONTMIRAIL

81140 Tarn. Paris 648 – Toulouse 70 – Cordes-sur-Ciel 24 – Gaillac 12.
This 13th-century walled town in the heart of the ''land of plenty'' still possesses all its Old World charm.

● RESTAURANTS

■ Hôtel des Consuls   ⑩⌂
Place des Consuls.
Tel. 05 63 33 17 44 (hotel),
05 63 40 63 55 (rest.).
Rest. closed Mon., Tue., beg. Nov.–end Feb.
13 rooms: 55–85€.

On the central village square, these old houses hold new or renovated rooms and a pleasant restaurant with exposed stone walls and hexagonal red floor tiles that serves a tasteful, traditional cuisine. The Vin de Noix–seasoned foie gras terrine, lamb sweetbreads with brown sugar and dark beer, the roasted pigeon with rosemary and the molten chocolate cake with a cherry and orange reduction sauce make up choice spreads.

CASTERA-VERDUZAN

32410 Gers. Paris 714 – Auch 26 – Agen 62 – Condom 21.
In the heart of the Gers district, a small spa resort with its theater and Castéra Vieux chapel.

 HOTELS-RESTAURANTS

■ Ténarèze   ⌂
Av de la Ténarèze.
Tel. 05 62 68 10 22. Fax 05 62 68 14 69.
hotel.tenareze@wanadoo.fr
www.hote-tenareze.com
23 rooms: 35–45,50€.

This hotel near the lake offers neat rooms, a warm welcome and a modest check.

● Le Florida   ⬛COM
Rue Principale / Rue du Lac.
Tel. 05 62 68 13 22. Fax 05 62 68 10 44.
Closed Sun. dinner, Mon., Feb. vac.
Prix fixe: 13,50€ (lunch), 23,50€, 34€, 50€.

Cooking comes as naturally to Bernard Ramounéda as song to a nightingale. Loyal to tradition, he pays tribute to local produce, deftly preparing vintage recipes just as his grandmother Angèle (who founded

Le Florida in 1935) did before him. A salad of warm house-made sausages, golden apples and Gascon mustard, the magnificent cep daube of Grandmother Yvonne (his mother-in-law, a fine cook), the roasted guinea fowl with julienned vegetables and garlic cream and Grandmother Angèle's tender lemon tart are delightful delicacies. The welcome is pleasant, the table attractively set, the atmosphere relaxed and the unrefined dishes charming (Oh, the oven-crisped pig's feet!).

CASTILLON-DU-GARD see PONT-DU-GARD

CASTRES

81100 Tarn. Paris 736 – Carcassonne 67 – Toulouse 71 – Albi 43.
Renaissance mansion the Hôtel de Nayrac and the Goya and Jean-Jaurès museums make this Tarn subprefecture a popular tourist destination. The road to the Sidobre plateau lies very close by.

HOTELS-RESTAURANTS

■ Le Renaissance
17, rue Victor-Hugo.
Tel. 05 63 59 30 42. Fax 05 63 72 11 57.
www.hotel-renaissance.fr
20 rooms: 45–90€.

Behind the 17th-century half-timbered facade lie individualized rooms in various styles, and a convivial lounge.

● Le Victoria   COM
24, pl du 8-Mai-1945.
Tel.-Fax 05 63 59 14 68.
Closed Sat. lunch, Sun.
Prix fixe: 12€ (weekday lunch), 17,50€ (weekday lunch), 21,50–29,50€,
10,50€ (child). A la carte: 55€.

David Gasc has taken over this restaurant with its three successive dining rooms in a vaulted basement. There, he serves reliable regional dishes. A trio of foie gras, mixed seafood grill (parrillada), beef filet medallions with morel mushrooms, roasted rack of lamb in

an herb crust and the warm chocolate beignets with caramelized pistachios and praline ice cream make an excellent impression.

● La Table du Sommelier   SIM
6, pl Pélisson.
Tel.-Fax 05 63 82 20 10.
Closed Sun., Mon.
Prix fixe: 12,50€, 15€, 25€, 30€,
10€ (child).

The décor of this wine restaurant is warm and rustic. Philppe Subira provides a heartfelt welcome and presents fine vintages to go with Patrick Brenac's dishes. A goat cheese tartare with thinly sliced figs, puff pastry with chicken and a light mushroom sauce, cod with caramelized onions or the guinea hen encrusted with spices are well crafted.

CATTENOM see THIONVILLE

CAUSSADE

82300 Tarn-et-Garonne.
Paris 620 – Cahors 39 –
Gaillac 50 – Montauban 25.
Quercy on the Tarn-et-Garonne side, not far from Rouergue, seen from a small town in the "land of plenty", also France's straw hat capital.

HOTELS-RESTAURANTS

■ Larroque   ⌂
16, av du 8-Mai.
Tel. 05 63 65 11 77. Fax 05 63 65 12 04.
hotel.larroque@club-internet.fr
www.perso.club-internet.fr/hotel.larroque
Closed Christmas, 1 Jan.
Rest. closed Sat. lunch, Sun. dinner (off season), 21 Dec.–15 Jan.
12 rooms: 42–65€. 6 suites: 53–100€.
Prix fixe: 14,50€, 20€, 28€,
7,50€ (child's lunch). A la carte: 45€.

Some pleasures are simple indeed, among them the rest and relaxation offered in Daniel Larroque's house and garden. We like the regularly redecorated modern rustic rooms and are equally fond of new chef

Frédéric Bédé's cuisine. A foie gras terrine, grilled Mediterranean sea bass with slow-roasted fennel, thinly sliced duck with fresh seasonal fruit and the corn cakes (galettes de millas) with honey served with ice cream make up spirited meals.

In Monteils (82300). 3 km e via D17.

● **Clos Monteils**   ♨ SIM

Gasherbes.
Tel.-Fax 05 63 93 03 51.
Closed Sat. lunch, Sun. dinner, Mon.,
mid-Jan.–mid-Feb.
Prix fixe: 17€ (weekday lunch),
27€ (dinner), 31–35€ (weekday lunch),
39€ (dinner), 49€ (dinner).

Knock on the door of this former presbytery and discover a world of charm. In the dining room and on the terrace, the Bordaries family provides a delightful welcome and excellent fare. Very much in the local spirit, the set menus include herb-stuffed piquillo peppers and hake with a fennel emulsion, seared tuna with citrus zest, duck fricassée with pine nuts, and a frozen pyramid dessert that conjugates the flavors of passion fruit, parsley, and almond syrup.

CAVAILLON

84300 Vaucluse. Paris 707 – Avignon 25 –
Arles 44 – Aix-en-Provence 60.
tourisme@cavaillon.com.
This melon capital is an authentic Provençal town with its Roman arch, ancient lanes, synagogue and historic Hôtel-Dieu, which now houses an archeological museum.

 HOTELS-RESTAURANTS

■ **Mercure**   ⌂

601, av Boscodomini.
Tel. 04 90 71 07 79. Fax 04 90 78 27 94.
h1951@accor.com / www.mercure.com
Rest. closed Sat. lunch (Oct.–Mar.),
Sun. lunch (Oct.–Mar.).
45 rooms: 85–117€.
Prix fixe: 15€, 20€, 22€, 10€ (child).
A la carte: 36€.

Just outside the town center, this chain hotel boasts practical, modern rooms, a swimming pool, a tennis court and tasteful Southern French dishes.

● **Prévot**   V.COM

"La Maison du Melon"
353, av de Verdun.
Tel. 04 90 71 32 43. Fax 04 90 71 97 05.
jean-jacques@restaurant-prevot.com
Closed Sun. (exc. Bank holidays), Mon. (exc.
Bank holidays), 1 week beg. Jan.,
1 week at end Feb.–beg. Mar., 2 weeks Aug.
Prix fixe: 30€ (lunch), 35€, 43€, 67€, 85€.

At Jean-Jacques Prévot's eatery, melon is king. Both the décor of his comfortably appointed dining room and the imaginative dishes on the menu pay tribute to Cavaillon's cherished Cucumis melo. From May to mid-September, a special menu celebrates the "melon festival". The roasted squash and cured ham, crumble-style, with guinea hen sot-l'y-laisse, the red mullet with seasonal roasted fruit served over a galet de la Durance (a local chocolate-covered almond specialty), lobster pistou served in a cocotte with melon, goat cheese tartare (with melon) and the *fusion aphrodisiaque sucrée*, a slice of melon caramelized with rum and ginger served with a vanilla ice cream stick, are a delightful surprise. Although the special tasting menu weighs in at a spectacular 85 , the lunchtime "bistro" option (with an asparagus parmentière tart, spiced lamb tagine and frozen nougat) is a bargain.

In Cheval-Blanc (84460). 5 km e via D 973.

● **Auberge de Cheval Blanc**   COM

481, av de la Canebière.
Tel. 04 32 50 18 55. Fax 04 32 50 18 52.
www.auberge-de-chevalblanc.com
Closed Mon. dinner (exc. July–Aug.),
Tue. (exc. dinner July–Aug.), Wed. lunch,
Nov. 1, Feb. vac.
Prix fixe: 23€ (lunch), 28€, 48€, 68€.

Hervé Perrasse, who worked with Yvan in Paris, has tired of the stress of life in the capital. On the edge of Cavaillon, his inn is a haven of peace with its garden and fountain. The lady of the house, Sabrina, provides a graceful welcome and the little set menus are an inducement to visit on a regular basis. The "Terre de Provence" option offers macaroni with a lamb bolognese sauce, sea bream with sesame, chèvre with perfumed oils and the chocolate and strawberry house dessert, while news of the "Maréchal-Ferrant" (Blacksmith) menu at 23 , wine included, which changes daily, has spread far and wide on the local grapevine.

In Maubec (84660). 9 km e via D2.

● **Maison Gouin** SIM
100, route Nationale.
Tel. 04 90 76 90 18. Fax 04 90 76 85 35.
Closed Sun., Wed.
Prix fixe: 13€ (lunch), 35€ (dinner),
15€ (child).

Since 1928, the Gouins have been welcoming visitors to this butcher's store, which doubles as a delicatessen and grocery. Olivier, fourth of the name, has added a restaurant. In the Provençal-style dining room, we make short work of his sunny home cooking. Provençal stuffed vegetables, sautéed red mullet with vanilla, pears and ginger, a roast-pigeon breast with foie gras, cabbage stuffed with a ragout of variety meats and the tutti-frutti tart are in a very gourmand Provençal style.

CAVALIERE

83980 Var. Paris 886 – Fréjus 55 –
Le Lavandou 9 – Saint-Tropez 31 – Toulon 51.
On a dreamy road by the sea, between the Corniche des Maures and the Col du Canadel.

 HOTELS-RESTAURANTS

■ **Le Club de Cavalière**
Tel. 04 98 04 34 34. Fax 04 94 05 73 16.
www.clubdecavaliere.com
Closed Oct.–1 May.
34 rooms: 530–600€. 3 suites: 780–950€.
Prix fixe: 48 (lunch), 60€, 80€.

This Relais & Châteaux establishment by the sea is a dream in colors of the South of France, with its Provençal rooms refurbished in contemporary style, swimming pool and private beach. In the restaurant, with its roof that opens to the sky and shady terraces, we savor the cuisine concocted by Marc Dach, who prepares delicate, sunny dishes. We have a good time (as long as we remember not to dwell on the prices) with the langoustine tempura with lemon balm, wild Mediterranean sea bass cooked skinside down with littleneck clams and seaweed butter, rack of lamb with thyme baked in a pastry cocotte and finally the raspberry sable and a semi-sweet chocolate mousse with almond-milk ice cream.

CAVANAC see CARCASSONNE

CAZAUBON

32150 Gers. Paris 705 – Auch 75 –
Condom 50 – Barbotan-les-Thermes 3.
Verdant, peaceful, jovial Gers with spa center Barbotan nearby.

 HOTELS-RESTAURANTS

■ **Château Bellevue**
19, rue Joseph-Cappin.
Tel. 05 62 09 51 95. Fax 05 62 09 54 57.
www.chateaubellevue.org
Closed beg. Jan.–12 Feb.
20 rooms: 67–99€. 2 suites: 115€.
Prix fixe: 20€, 30€. A la carte: 60€.

In the heart of extensive grounds shaded by ancient trees, this manor with swimming pool offers neat rooms. In the refined dining room, Charlotte Latreille serves highly subtle classical dishes. The sautéed langoustines, grilled line-caught Atlantic sea bass with fresh herb jus, roasted squab served over a slice of grilled eggplant and the prune and Armagnac parfait achieve a perfect score. The mother, Michèle Consolaro, provides a delectable welcome with a kind word for everyone.

LA CELLE

83170 Var. Paris 811 – Marseille 66 –
Aix-en-Provence 58 – Toulon 52.
A Var village near Brignoles, with its abbey, cloister, Roman vaults and ambulatory.

HOTELS-RESTAURANTS

● Hostellerie de l'Abbaye de La Celle

Pl du Général-de-Gaulle.
Tel. 04 98 05 14 14. Fax 04 98 05 14 15.
contact@abbaye-celle.com
www.abbaye-celle.com
9 rooms: 205–300€. 1 suite: 300–350€.
Prix fixe: 42€, 57€, 76€. A la carte: 70€.

In the middle of a wooded estate with a swimming pool, this 18th-century building next to a Benedictine abbey delights its guests, which included General de Gaulle some years ago. Its guiding spirit Alain Ducasse has brought in a man he trusts to run the kitchen: Benoît Witz. This veteran of the Bastide in Moustiers builds his art on fine produce. On the table, this produces tuna marinated with herbs and garnished with lemon, monkfish tail roasted with fresh young garlic and sautéed vegetables with basil, a whole veal kidney slow roasted with rosemary and creamy potatoes and the strawberry rhubarb sablé.

CELLES-SUR-BELLE

79370 Deux-Sèvres. Paris 398 – Niort 24 – Poitiers 70 – Saint-Jean-d'Angély 50.
A halt in the Pays Mellois, famous for its royal abbey.

HOTELS-RESTAURANTS

■ Hostellerie de l'Abbaye

1, pl des Epoux-Laurant.
Tel. 05 49 32 93 32. Fax 05 49 79 72 65.
www.hotel-restaurant-abbaye.com
Closed 2 weeks Oct. Nov., 3 weeks Feb.
Rest. closed Sun. dinner.
20 rooms: 46–64€.
Prix fixe: 13€ (weekdays), 21€, 29€, 42€, 9€ (child). A la carte: 41–49€.

This hostelry below the abbey provides practical rooms. In the gray and red dining room or on the terrace when the weather is fine, we enjoy its regionalist cuisine: an escalope of foie gras with Port, monkfish pot-au-feu spiced with garlic in an herbed broth, veal tenderloin and sweetbreads browned with salted butter, served with tarragon jus. The slices of pain perdu served with licorice ice cream are a childhood delight and the extensive wine list covers every region.

CENON see BORDEAUX

CERET

66400 Pyrénées-Orientales. Paris 884 – Perpignan 32 – Port-Vendres 38 – Gerone 80.
office.du.tourisme.ceret@wanadoo.fr.
This pioneering capital of Cubism, a second home to Picasso (originally brought here by the sculptor Manolo), is a jewel of the Rousillon, austere in appearance and famous for its museum and healthy air.

HOTELS-RESTAURANTS

■ La Terrasse au Soleil

Rte de Fontfrède.
Tel. 04 68 87 01 94. Fax 04 68 87 39 24.
terrasse-au-soleil.hotel@wanadoo.fr
www.terrasse-au-soleil.com
Closed Jan.–mid-Feb.
35 rooms: 90–239€. 2 suites: 200–339€.
Prix fixe: 31€, 46€, 13€ (child).
A la carte: 57€.

We look fondly on this Catalan country house frequented by Charles Trenet. Surrounded by extensive grounds, it has a swimming pool and fitness center, as well as neat rooms, each in a different color. The dining room with its faïence, Provençal furniture and exposed stone has great character. The large terrace offers a view of the Canigou *massif*. The menu drawn up by Gérard Perreau promises wonderful surprises with crisp pasty with tomato, basil and mozzarella cheese with a cucumber sorbet, monkfish osso bucco with a bouillabaisse jus, lamb and pistachio croustillant and the soft-centered bittersweet chocolate cake with orange sauce and pistachio ice cream.

■ Mas Trilles

At pont de Reynès: 3 km via rte d'Amélie.
Tel. 04 68 87 38 37. Fax 04 68 87 42 62.
mastrilles@free.fr / www.le-mas-trilles.com
Closed beg. Oct.–end Apr.
8 rooms: 98–225€. 2 suites: 150–225€.

This 17th-century Catalan residence boasts five hectares of wooded grounds and modern rustic rooms with a terrace or private garden.

● Les Feuillants   V.COM

1, bd La-Fayette.
Tel. 04 68 87 37 88. Fax 04 68 87 44 68.
contact@les-feuillants.com
Closed mid-Dec.–1 Feb. Rest. closed Sun. (off season), Mon. (off season).
4 rooms: 80–120€. 2 suites: 100–140€.
Prix fixe: 25€, 35€, 50€. A la carte: 50–55€.

This Belle Epoque villa in the town center stands in the shade of the plane trees. David Tanguy watches over the art deco suites and rooms as well as the elaborate cuisine. Cep cappuccio with pan-seared foie gras, roasted sea bream with walnuts, grilled duckling breast infused with smoked tea and an exotic combination of roasted pineapple, flambéed bananas and coconut sorbet make a splendid impression. The fine Roussillon wines are enthusiastically presented by Frédéric Szentes. The Brasserie le Carré offers a more informal option.

CESSON see SAINT-BRIEUC

CESSON-SEVIGNE see RENNES

CHABLIS

89800 Yonne. Paris 183 – Auxerre 21 Avallon 39 – Tonnerre 19.
ot-chablis@chablis.net.
The reputation of this beautiful old medieval village is built on wine. Its name is famous throughout the world, but the entire district deserves a visit.

 HOTELS-RESTAURANTS

● Hostellerie des Clos

18, rue Jules-Rathier.
Tel. 03 86 42 10 63. Fax 03 86 42 17 11.
host.clos@wanadoo.fr
www.hostellerie-des-clos.fr
Closed mid-Dec.–mid-Jan.
26 rooms: 55–86€.
Prix fixe: 38€, 46€, 53€, 16€ (child).
A la carte: 80€.

Built on the foundations of an old hospice, this hostelry offers traditional but well-equipped rooms, four duplex apartments, a fitness center, snug lounges and especially a restaurant. In the kitchen, Michel Vignaud prepares impressive regional dishes. The fricassée of escargots with a parsley coulis and slow-roasted garlic, Chablis-style salmon trout, Charolais beef tournedos with mushrooms and the crème brûlée with pain d'épice, served with a fresh fruit salad, strike the right note.

CHABRITS see MENDE

CHAGNY

71150 Saône-et-Loire. Paris 328 – Beaune 16 – Chalon 19 – Autun 45 – Mâcon 77.
ot.chagnybourgogne@wanadoo.fr.
This unpretentious town offers a gourmet break on the Côte Châlonnaise route running from Rully to Buxy via Mercurey.

 HOTELS-RESTAURANTS

● Lameloise

36, pl d'Armes.
Tel. 03 85 87 65 65. Fax 03 85 87 03 57.
jacques@lameloise.fr
www.lameloise.fr
Closed lunch Mon.–Thu., 12–18 July, 19 Dec.–18 Jan.
16 rooms: 130–285€.
Prix fixe: 75€ (weekday lunch), 90€, 135€.
A la carte: 130€.

Is Jacques Lameloise the best loved of Burgundy's great chefs? This modest man who seems to care little for the limelight has a charmingly mocking manner that contrasts with the seriousness of his rural cuisine, rooted in the land. We like the cozy feel of his village hostelry and the rooms refurbished with a certain sophistication (handsome marble bathrooms) and admire his cuisine, which is riding high. Grilled ratte potatoes with Burgundy escargots, red wine and parsley cream sauce, a blue lobster mille-feuille, mixed greens over a tomato emulsion sauce with herbs, red mullet over slowly-cooked potatoes, with tomato, celeriac, and parmesan cheese and whole roasted turbot with a razor clam and periwinkle sabayon show that the "born classicist" is not resting on his laurels. Then there are squab cooked in a pig's bladder served with fresh pasta and pan-seared foie gras or the famous oxtail compote with black truffle-seasoned mashed potatoes, not to mention the stunning Bresse chicken with leeks and its blonde liver royale. The desserts have always been one of the house's strong points and remain so today, with marinated wild griottine cherries and dark chocolate and sorbet over orange marmalade, the crisp pastry leaves with caramel and chocolate raspberries, the crème brûlée ice cream or the chicory parfait with Djion-style pain d'epice dacquois. The wine list pays special tribute to the three great Côtes—Beaune, Nuits and Chalonnaise—in all their splendor. Precise but stress-free service and a delectable welcome from Nicole Lameloise.

CHAILLY-LES-ENNERY see METZ

CHAILLY-SUR-ARMANÇON see POUILLY-EN-AUXOIS

CHALAIS

16210 Charente. Paris 495 – Angoulême 46 – Bordeaux 85 – Périgueux 68.
This nobiliary village in the heart of Montmorélien, the Angoumois Champagne, was a principality in the 12th century.

● RESTAURANTS

● Relais du Château
15, rue du Château.
Tel. 05 45 98 23 58. Fax 05 45 98 00 53.
relaisduchateautalleyrand@wanadoo.fr
Closed Sun. dinner, Mon., Tue. lunch,
3 weeks Nov.
Prix fixe: 17€ (weekday lunch), 23,50€, 29,50€, 10€ (child). A la carte: 40–44€.

Crossing the château drawbridge, you find yourself in the Middle Ages. The stone dining room with its large fireplace still displays all its ancient glory. The lord of the manor, Jean-Louis Bruneau, has turned it into a convivial eatery and Christophe Vine at the stove concocts well-phrased market-based dishes. Fresh foie gras terrine with chutney, steamed scallops with a champagne sauce, veal tenderloin with lemon and ginger and a raspberry mille-feuille slip down easily. The wine list is rich in fine Bordeaux and Bergerac vintages. Sensible prices.

LA CHALDETTE

48310 Lozère. Paris 580 – Mende 63 – Marvejols 47 – Clermont-Ferrand 161 – Espalion 60.
ot.nasbinals.free.fr.
In the heart of Aubrac on the banks of the Bès, in a bucolic rural setting, this small spa resort famed in the 1850s is enjoying a strong resurgence.

 HOTELS-RESTAURANTS

■ La Chaldette
36, pl d'Armes.
Tel. 04 66 31 37 00.
chaldetterestaurant@yahou.fr
Closed end Nov.–beg. Feb.
16 rooms: 52–120€.
Prix fixe: 13€ (weekday lunch), 29€, 6€ (child). A la carte: 50€.

Out in the fields, this hotel residence stands next to the spa treatment and convalescence center, with its swimming pool, steam bath and various therapies. The practical apartments are fully equipped. In the restaurant, Emile Fangin serves up reliable dishes, such as foie gras terrine with apples and cinnamon, red mullet croustillant with garlic, filet of beef with morel mushrooms and a pear feuillantine with chocolate croustillant.

CHALLANS

85300 Vendée. Paris 437 – Nantes 59 –
La Roche-sur-Yon 42 – Cholet 84.
ot.challans@free.fr.
This decent-sized market town overlooked by
a tall church with a free-standing bell tower is
the capital of quality free-range duck.

 HOTELS-RESTAURANTS

■ Château de la Vérie

Rte de Saint-Gilles-Croix-de-Vie: 2,5 km s
via D69.
Tel. 02 51 35 33 44. Fax 02 51 35 14 84.
verie@wanadoo.fr
www.chateau-de-la-verie.com
Closed Jan.–end Feb.
Rest. closed Sun. dinner, Mon., Tue. lunch.
21 rooms: 56–158€.
Prix fixe: 15€ (lunch), 19€, 22€, 30€,
35€, 11€ (child).

This 16th-century château surrounded by
an estate with swimming pool, rivers and
marshes, has changed hands yet again.
Jansen Vanhouhen now tends to the comfort of guests staying in its antique guest
rooms. In the Louis XVI-style restaurant,
Yves Nergeau serves an intricate cuisine,
exemplified by the foie gras streussel with
rhubarb, red mullet layered with radicchio
caramelized in balsamic vinegar, chicken
parmentier and oxtail with parmesan and
Vendée ham and the banana croustillant
with caramel passion fruit mousse.

■ Antiquité

14, rue Gallieni.
Tel. 02 51 68 02 84. Fax 02 51 35 55 74.
antiquitehotel@aol.com
www.hotelantiquite.com
Closed 1 week Christmas.
16 rooms: 40–79€.

Charmed by the Bellevilles' warm welcome, chiné furniture, refined rooms,
swimming pool and gentle prices, we
quickly forget the modern nature of their
hostelry.

● Chez Charles

8, pl du Champ-de-Foire.
Tel. 02 51 93 36 65. Fax 02 51 49 31 88.
chezcharles85@aol.com
www.restaurantchezcharles.com
Closed Sun. dinner, Mon., Christmas–end Jan.
Prix fixe: 19€ (lunch), 25–35€, 51€,
12€ (child).

On the town's main square, this resourceful bistro with its friendly welcome and
smiling service presents deftly prepared
regional dishes. The foie gras, the assorted
shellfish plate, the stewed cuttlefish and
floating island put us back on our feet. The
check keeps its head down.

CHALLES-LES-EAUX see CHAMBERY
CHALLUY see NEVERS

CHALONS-EN-CHAMPAGNE

51000 Marne. Paris 165 – Reims 48 –
Dijon 257 – Metz 160 – Nancy 163 –
Troyes 84.
off.tourisme.chalons-en-Champagne@
wanadoo.fr.
This town is an unjustly overlooked child of
Champagne. With its rich stained glass, fine
churches, astonishing museums, old hotels,
parks (the attractive Jard with its handsome
trees) and peaceful views, it has an unostentatious charm.

 HOTELS-RESTAURANTS

● Hôtel d'Angleterre

19, pl Monseigneur-Tissier.
Tel. 03 26 68 21 51. Fax 03 26 70 51 67.
hot.angl@wanadoo.fr
www.hotel-dangleterre.fr
Closed Christmas–New Year's vac.,
mid-July–mid-Aug.
Rest.closed Sat. lunch, Sun., Mon. lunch.
19 rooms: 85–140€. 6 suites: 125–150€.
Prix fixe: 58€, 72€, 95€. A la carte: 90€.

In the hands of Jacky Michel, helped by
decorator Dominique Honnet, this post-
war building has revealed unsuspected
charms. The rooms in pastel shades with
marble bathrooms have an immedi-

ate appeal. For visitors to the elegantly rustic dining room, the master and chef concocts subtle, gourmet preparations, such as the trio of foie gras (one slowly cooked, the second made with spices and the third with leeks), roasted wild turbot with baby carrots and caraway seeds and spit-roasted pigeon stuffed with sweetbreads and fois gras. The pain perdu with strawberries and fromage blanc ice cream is irresistible.

■ Le Renard

24, pl de la République.
Tel. 03 26 68 03 78. Fax 03 26 64 50 07.
lerenard51@wanadoo.fr / www.le-renard.com
Closed 10 days Christmas–New Year's.
Rest. closed Sat. lunch, Sun.
32 rooms: 65–87€. 3 suites: 100€.
Prix fixe: 18€, 42€, 11€ (child).
A la carte: 65€.

This classic hotel with its patio garden is a fine place to stay. Its friendly welcome, functional rooms and meticulous cuisine (foie gras poached in Bouzy wine, duck breast with spices) are immediately appreciated.

■ Le Pot d'Etain

18, pl de la République.
Tel. 03 26 68 09 09. Fax 03 26 68 58 18.
hotellepotdetain51@wanadoo.fr
www.citotel.com
30 rooms: 63–84€.

In the town center, this antique hostelry boasts comfortable, perfectly sound-proofed rooms.

● Le Carillon Gourmand

15, pl Monseigneur-Teissier.
Tel. 03 26 64 45 07. Fax 03 26 21 06 09.
Closed Sun. dinner, Mon., Wed. dinner,
1 week Feb. vac., 1 week Apr., 3 weeks Aug.
Prix fixe: 18€, 22€, 29,50€.

This pleasant bistro continues to delight its guests. Philippe Kerman's welcome, the porch open to the street and Gisèle Morançay's home cooking find plenty of takers. Red tuna tartare splashed with veal jus, the roasted sea bream cooked

skin-side down with green anise, magret duck breast with cherries and sautéed red cabbage and the seasonal fruit terrine with citrus jelly pep us up without denting our bank balance.

In L'Epine (51460). 8,5 km e via N3.

● Aux Armes de Champagne

31, av du Luxembourg.
Tel. 03 26 69 30 30. Fax 03 26 69 30 26.
www.aux-armes-de-Champagne.com
Closed 3 weeks Jan. Rest. closed Sun.
dinner (Oct.–Jan.), Mon. (Oct.–Jan.).
35 rooms: 85–265€. 2 suites: 250–305€.
Prix fixe: 24€ (lunch), 42€, 59€, 89€.
A la carte: 110€.

Jean-Paul Pérardel's vintage establishment with its swimming pool and tennis court leads a happy existence. Attentive host Pascal Fouassier warmly welcomes his guests, before showing them to their classic, comfortable rooms. In the restaurant, Philippe Zeiger concocts shrewd, invigorating fare. Crafted by this pupil of Loiseau, Bardet and Willer, the diced crabmeat with avocado and tomato, red mullet with stuffed zucchini blossoms, the rabbit saddle with sundried tomatoes and slow-cooked apples with sage and the rhubarb tart with spiced sangria coulis keep us in high good humor until the hour of reckoning comes around…

CHALON-SUR-SAONE

71100 Saône-et-Loire. Paris 336 – Besançon 129 – Dijon 69 – Lyon 128 – Mâcon 59.
chalon@chalon-sur-saone.net.
Formerly on the medieval fair route, this sprawling crossroads town still has some fine remnants of its rich past. Noble facades and the magnificent banks of the Saône.

■ HOTELS-RESTAURANTS

■ Le Saint Régis

22, bd de la République.
Tel. 03 85 90 95 60. Fax 03 85 90 95 70.
saint-regis@saint-regis-chalon.fr
www.saint-regis-chalon.fr

Rest. closed Sat. lunch, Sun. dinner.
32 rooms: 72–150€. 4 suites: 150–210€.
Prix fixe: 16,50€, 42€, 52€, 12€ (child).
A la carte: 45€.

This early 20th-century hostelry cannot be faulted. The charming welcome, vintage rooms refurbished in different styles, wonderfully snug lounge and restaurant serving tasteful regional cuisine raise our spirits.

■ Le Saint-Georges

32, av Jean-Jaurès.
Tel. 03 85 90 80 50. Fax 03 85 90 80 55.
www.le-saintgeorges.fr
Rest. closed Sat. lunch, Sun. dinner, 1 May,
10 days at end July, 3 weeks Aug.
50 rooms: 73–150€.
Prix fixe: 16€, 45€, 12€ (child).
A la carte: 60€.

Here by the rail station, Claude Choux provides a friendly welcome. The tasteful rooms and simple dishes prepared by her husband Yves meet with universal approval. In the dining room refurbished in contemporary style, young Bresse chicken terrine stuffed with foie gras, grilled Breton sole meunière, pan-seared filet of beef with a marrow and Mercurey wine sauce and the lemongrass poached pears with sabayon are deftly crafted. The Petit Comptoir next door offers a sensible set menu and modest check.

● Da Nunzio `COM`

3, rue de Strasbourg.
Tel. 03 85 48 39 83. Fax 03 85 48 72 58.
da.nunzio@wanadoo.fr
Closed Tue., Wed.
Prix fixe: 14€, 17€, 24€, 27€.
A la carte: 40–45€.

At this restaurant on the Ile Saint-Laurent, we enjoy Iacono Nunzio's subtle transalpine dishes. As we savor the buffalo mozzarella and tomato salad with olive oil, slow-roasted vegetables and chèvre terrine, a plate of prosciutto with balsamic vinegar and the grilled fish (red tuna, swordfish and shrimp), we long for our summer vacation.

● Rôtisserie Saint-Vincent `SIM`

9, rue du Blé.
Tel. 03 85 48 83 52. Fax 03 85 48 01 83.
Closed Sun., Mon., 2 weeks Christmas–New
Year's, 3 weeks Aug.
Prix fixe: 17€ (lunch), 41,50€ (wine inc.).
A la carte: 35€.

In the ancient town center, this antique 12th-century residence offers the perfect setting for a restaurant with an eye firmly on Burgundian heritage. Guillaume Bouchet regales us with a thin potato tart, salmon mille-feuille with garlic, whole veal kidneys roasted with mustard seeds and then dark chocolate spring rolls with preserved fruit.

● Chez Jules `SIM`

11, rue de Strasbourg.
Tel. 03 85 48 08 34. Fax 03 85 48 55 48.
Closed Sat. lunch, Sun., 2 weeks Feb.,
3 weeks Aug.
Prix fixe: 18€ (weekday lunch), 20,50€,
26€, 34€. A la carte: 40€.

This is one of the star eateries on the Ile Saint-Laurent. In its hushed, rustic dining room, Alain Ducroux plays to a charming, modern rustic score. Pan-seared medallions of foie gras with apple, fisherman's blanquette with baby vegetables, a roasted filet of duckling with caramelized peaches and the soft-centered chocolate cake served warm with vanilla ice cream are gratifying.

In Saint-Loup-de-Varennes (71240). 7 km s via
rte de Mâcon.

● Le Saint Loup

13, RN6.
Tel. 03 85 44 21 58.
Closed Sun. dinner, Mon. dinner, Tue. lunch,
1 week Sept., 1 week Christmas–New Year's.
Prix fixe: 15€ (lunch), 18€, 24€, 34€, 12€
(child). A la carte: 42–56€.

By the RN6 highway, this inn combines a pleasant rustic setting with traditional cuisine. In the hands of Yannick Loppin, we enjoy pan-seared foie gras deglazed with crème de Bourgogne, mountain trout filet, Bresse chicken with sautéed morel mushrooms before concluding with the chocolate profiteroles. A deftly crafted repertoire at modest prices, washed down with fine Burgundies.

In Saint-Marcel (71380). 3 km e via D978.

● **Jean Bouthenet** `COM`
19, rue de la Villeneuve.
Tel. 03 85 96 56 16. Fax 03 85 96 75 81.
Closed Sun. dinner, Mon., Tue., 1 week Feb.,
2 weeks Aug.
Prix fixe: 16,50€, 30€, 39€, 46€.
A la carte: 55€.

For the Bouthenets, cooking is a family tradition. Jean and Laurent, father and son, prepare original, gourmet dishes. Meaux mustard with red tuna tartare, oysters and tomato chutney, scallops with celery jus and green apples and a veal kidney Tatin with a potato crust and licorice-infused sauce are fine tricks indeed. The wines by the glass are well chosen.

In Saint-Rémy (71100). 4 km via N6 and N80.

● **Le Moulin de Martorey** ○`V.COM`
Saint-Rémy.
Tel. 03 85 48 12 98. Fax 03 85 48 73 67.
moulindemartorey@wanadoo.fr
www.moulindemartorey.fr
Closed Sun. dinner, Mon., 2 weeks Feb.,
2 weeks Aug.
Prix fixe: 39€, 51€, 65€, 80€.
A la carte: 90€.

This handsomely renovated 19th-century flour mill is home to a first-rate restaurant. Jean-Pierre Gillot, chief miller, presides at the stove, preparing regional dishes that pay homage to tradition. Escargots prepared three ways, filet of sole with fish fumet, roasted lobster and also the ritual Bresse chicken, served in two courses, as well as a chocolate fondant with praline feuilleté, all have the fine flavor of precision. Pierrette Gillot offers a warm welcome, the service is efficient and the cellar well stocked with Burgundy vintages.

CHAMAGNE

88130 Vosges. Paris 378 – Epinal 36 –
Nancy 39 – Lunéville 31.

At the gates of the Vosges, this village was the birthplace of great 17th-century landscape artist Claude Gellée, known as "Le Lorrain".

● | RESTAURANTS

● **Le Chamagnon** `SIM`
236, rue Claude-Gellée.
Tel.-Fax 03 29 38 14 74.
Closed Sun. dinner, Mon., Wed. dinner,
Nov. 1 vac., 1 week Christmas–New Year's,
3 weeks July.
Prix fixe: 19€, 29€, 35€, 43€.
A la carte: 38–48€.

In this village where the great artist Le Lorrain was born, Charles Vincent draws inspiration from market produce to broaden his already supremely flavorsome palette. The resolutely contemporary style of the two dining rooms and highly attentive service go hand in hand with the smoked salmon followed by the jumbo shrimp tempura, the young rabbit confit served in a cocotte and then for dessert, the almond croquant with baked apples, prepared Tatin-style. The wine list makes room for a few foreign libations.

CHAMALIERES see CLERMONT-FERRAND

CHAMBERY

73000 Savoie. Paris 564 – Grenoble 56 –
Annecy 51 – Lyon 102 – Turin 206.
info@chamberytourisme.com.
Chambéry, whose historic role in the Duchy of Savoy is well documented, is now the gateway to the region's ski resorts with its major high-speed train link. Its château and antique residences still remind us of its momentous past.

■/● | HOTELS-RESTAURANTS

● **Château de Candie** 🏠○
In Chambéry-le-Vieux: 5 km n via N201
toward Chambéry le Haut,
rue du Bois-de-Candie.
Tel. 04 79 96 63 00. Fax 04 79 96 63 10.
candie@icor.fr / www.chateaudecandie.com
Closed Nov. 1 vac., Spring vac.

20 rooms: 110–220€.
Prix fixe: 28€ (weekday lunch), 46€, 58€,
69€, 92€. A la carte: 90€.

In the middle of a six-hectare estate, this
14th-century building has a great deal
going for it: the smiling welcome, outdoor
swimming pool, rooms with their antique
furniture and views of the neighboring
mountains and double dining room with
its white and patinated woodwork. Cédric
Campanella looks after the guests, while
his brother Boris (formerly with Troisgros,
the Martinez and Chabran) prepares a
subtle, sunny cuisine deeply rooted in its
region. A soft-boiled egg with ratte potatoes and truffles, Lake Léman crayfish
with chicken quenelles, tender veal with
a parmesan cappuccino, venison with
juniper berries and bay leaves are ambitious dishes. The desserts, including the
fiendishly tempting as well as subtle variation on a passion fruit theme in the form
of an airy warm soufflé, are in the same
vein. The excellent choice of wines is presented by a friendly, competent young
sommelier.

■ **Hôtel des Princes**　　　　🄽⌂
4, rue Boigne.
Tel. 04 79 33 51 18.
hoteldesprinces@wanadoo.fr
45 rooms: 62–75€.

This fine family hotel handily located
in the heart of town is being renovated
little by little. Themed rooms (travel or
Savoy).

■ **Mercure**　　　　　　　　⌂
183, pl de la Gare.
Tel. 04 79 62 10 11. Fax 04 79 62 10 23.
h1541@accor-hotels.com / www.mercure.com
81 rooms: 66–160€.

The modern, spacious rooms in this hotel
by the high-speed rail station are functional and well designed. A pleasant
lounge bar.

● **L'Essentiel**　　　　　　　◎ V.COM
183, pl de la Gare.
Tel. 04 79 96 97 27. Fax 04 79 96 17 78.

www.l-essentiel-restaurant.com
Closed lunch
Prix fixe: 25€, 40€, 58€. A la carte: 95€.

Jean-Michel Bouvier, who has stood culinary guard opposite the high-speed rail
station for fifteen years now, has changed
his approach. The first floor here is still
devoted to select gastronomy, but the second floor is now a "lounge", dedicated
to more casual dishes and finger food,
served nonstop from 7 p.m. to midnight.
We are fond of his attractive, refined but
unpretentious fare. At the start of the winter season, we enjoyed a superb meal of
New Wave Savoy dishes in his restaurant.
Warm frog leg terrine with an escargot tapenade (made from real escargot which are
chopped, their parsley butter more like a
sweet cream of garlic) were superb. Then
there was the amusing appetizer based
on polenta with preserved pork sausage,
along with cod poached with preserved
lemon served with mashed ratte potatoes
and hazelnut oil (a wonderful exercise of
style), a perfectly cooked pigeon, lightly
breaded with a delicate almond crust,
served with sweet potatoes and a coffee
cappuccino sauce and finally mango soup
with caramelized raspberries and coconut milk. In short, this radiantly precise
herald of Savoy presents his region with
impressive enthusiasm. And with his loud
mouth and ample girth, he is irresistibly
persuasive!

● **Le Saint-Réal**　　　　　🄽 V.COM
Pl Pierre-Dumas.
Tel. 04 79 70 09 33.
www.restaurant-saint-real.com
Closed Sun., 10 days Aug.
Prix fixe: 38€, 69€, 92€.

With its walls of bare gray stone or clad in
flowery fabrics, and its first-rate service
supervised by Nicole Girod and her son
Pascal, this former church of the Pénitents Blancs is now a traditional restaurant showcasing the produce of Savoy with
precision and freshness. Creamy pumpkin
soup with spices and parmesan, a shellfish mille-feuille with Mondeuse wine
and roasted Vercors squab with chestnut

flower honey and rosemary are in very good taste.

● La Maniguette

99, rue Juiverie.
Tel. 04 79 62 25 26.
Closed Sun., Mon., Tue. dinner, Christmas–New Year's, 2 weeks July.
Prix fixe: 28€.

Patrick Turpin and Fanny Palluel have turned this rustic Savoy establishment, with its exposed beams and modern lamps, into a gourmet haunt. Inspired by market produce and spices, Patrick, a veteran of the Chabichou in Courchevel and Petrus in Paris, presents a revised set menu. Beef sushi with lentils and Beaufort cheese, creamy polenta with sautéed calf's liver and balsamic vinegar or the tournedos of salmon with crispy fidés (small vermicelli noodles) win our approval. The chocolate and hazelnut pastilla with salted caramel ice cream is absolutely irresistible.

● L'Hypoténuse

141, Carré-Curial.
Tel. 04 79 85 80 15. Fax 04 79 85 80 18.
resto.hypo@wanadoo.fr
Closed Sun., Mon., end July–end Aug.
Prix fixe: 17,50€ (lunch), 22€, 33€, 44€.

Bernadette and Hubert Bonnefoi founded this small, bright, industrious, reliable establishment fifteen years ago. Quartered in a former barracks built in the Napoleonic era, it offers set menus at splendid prices. The "Agrément" (Pleasure) option includes an hors d'oeuvre buffet, fried pike-perch filets with ravioles du Royans (tiny herb- and cheese-filled ravioli), the venison civet (a stew traditionally thickened with blood) and polenta, and finally the soft-centered chocolate cake with an orange salad. The roasted langoustine brochettes with a cauliflower and curry cream sauce is exemplary in its attention to detail.

● Le Z

12, av des Ducs de Savoie.
Tel. 04 79 85 96 87.

www.zorelle.fr
Prix fixe: 15,50€ (lunch), 23,50€.

Alain Zorelle, who owned the Hôtel des Princes, has opened this successful, contemporary, Parisian-style brasserie. The combination of sixties style and hi-tech furniture, orange lighting and designer chairs is explosive. The highly sober cuisine has an easy charm: line-fished Atlantic sea bass napped in Syrah sauce, veal tenderloin and sweetbreads with morel mushrooms and cream, steak tartare with French fries and a Charolaise beef rib steak hit just the right note. A platter of Gillardeau oysters is invigorating.

In Barberaz (73000). 2,3 km se. Access via N201 / E712 exit 19.

■ Altédia Lodge

61, rte de la République.
Tel. 04 79 60 05 00.
info@hotel-altedia.com / www.hotel-altedia.com
36 rooms: 80–97€. 8 suites: 120€.
Prix fixe: 19,50€ (lunch), 32€.

This new hotel with its contemporary décor in gray and red, designer rooms, minimalist bar and spa tub has chic to spare. Unfortunately, there is also the view of the expressway. The modern, colorful restaurant—the Maison Rouge—serves dishes created by Gilles Hérard, who was such a success at the Château de Candie and Kilimandjaro in Courchevel. Grilled Atlantic sea bass, veal paupiette wrapped in bacon with mushroom polenta and the lobster-filled puff pastry shell remind us that he learned his trade with Ducasse, Senderens and Rochedy.

In Barberaz.

● Le Mont Carmel

1, rue de l'Eglise.
Tel. 04 79 85 77 17. Fax 04 79 85 16 65.
www.le-mont-carmel.com
Closed Sun. dinner, Mon., Wed. dinner.
Prix fixe: 25€ (weekday lunch), 37€, 45€, 55€, 75€.

The main asset of this traditional residence with its comfortable dining room equipped with neo-Louis XVI chairs and cheerfully managed by Manuel Tarouco is its panoramic view of Chambéry. Tasting the fresh, refined but spirited classical cuisine by Yves Vincent, who trained with Georges Blanc, we decide we would like to eat here on a regular basis. The delightful foie gras with quince chutney, grilled red mullet with a salad of Puy lentils and smoked bacon, the salmon trout with creamy ratte potatoes and the roasted rack of lamb with a bacon and cardoon gratin never stale. Sensible set menus.

In Challes-les-Eaux (73190). 7 km sw via N6.

■ **Le Château des Comtes**
de Challes
243, montée du Château.
Tel. 04 79 72 72 72. Fax 04 79 72 83 83.
info@chateaudescomtesdechalles.com
www.chateaudescomtesdechalles.com
Closed Nov. 1 vac.
46 rooms: 60–148€. 6 suites: 180€.
Prix fixe: 25€ (weekdays), 38€, 55€.

A hotel since 1860, this 15th-century château is good-naturedly run by the Trèves. Set in four hectares of grounds with swimming pool and terrace, it offers timelessly elegant period guest rooms. In the Salle des Comtes de Challes dining room, with its French-style ceiling, high fireplace and parquet flooring, we sit down to savor the meticulous Pascal Colliat's cuisine. Pan-seared foie gras in a macaron with mango chutney, salmon trout with a purée of potato with crayfish and saddle of hare in a cocoa crust are polished dishes.

In Voglans (734200. 7 km via rte d'Aix-les-Bains.

■ **Le Cervolan**
Rte de l'aéroport (Airport road).
Tel. 04 79 52 03 10.
cerfvolanthotel@wanadoo.fr
www.cervolan.com
Closed Sat. lunch (exc. summer),
Sun. lunch (exc. summer).
41 rooms: 69–187€.
Prix fixe: 32€, 10€ (child).

Renovated in a contemporary designer fashion, this eighties building favorably impresses with its gray and red décor,

mountain views, swimming pool, two hectares of grounds and fusion restaurant (Dropping Zone or DZ). Chef Frédéric Graglia, who learned his art with Jean-Michel Bouvier and trained with Ducasse, improvises easily on a world cuisine theme. Cubes of tuna with sesame and wasabi and the Atlantic sea bass baked in a clay crust are stunning dishes.

CHAMBOLLE-MUSIGNY see
GEVREY-CHAMBERTIN

LE CHAMBON-SUR-LIGNON

43400 Haute-Loire. Paris 579 – Le Puy-en-Velay 46 – Annonay 48 – Lamastre 33.
"Le Chambon, savior village" is the glorious title of this Protestant commune that rescued Jewish children during the war. At a height of nearly 1,000 meters, its fresh air and view of Mount Gerbier-de-Jonc have made it a location of choice for summer camps and pleasant vacation homes.

■◢ HOTELS-RESTAURANTS

■ **Bel Horizon**
Chemin de Molle.
Tel. 04 71 59 74 39. Fax 04 71 59 79 81.
hotel.bel.horizon@free.fr / www.belhorizon.fr
Closed Jan.–end Mar.
Rest. closed Sun. dinner, Mon.
20 rooms: 55–108€.
Prix fixe: 20€, 29€, 40€.

Guillaume Chazot's modern hotel has more than one string to its bow. There are plenty of leisure activities, including a swimming pool, tennis court, fitness center and many delightful local walks. After all this exercise, guests greatly appreciate the renovated rooms and *pension* cuisine with its topical flavor (venison galantine—boneless stuffed venison sliced and served chilled—foie gras parfait and chocolate parfait with Velay verbena).

■ **Clair Matin**
Les Barandons.
Tel. 04 71 59 73 03. Fax 04 71 65 87 66.
clairmatin@hotelclairmatin.com

www.hotelclairmatin.com
Closed Mon. (off season), Tue. lunch (off season), beg. Dec.–end Dec., beg. Jan.–end Jan.
25 rooms: 50–120€.
Prix fixe: 15–23€, 39€, 10€ (child).
A la carte: 45–50€.

Opposite the mountains, this modern chalet set in its own grounds boasts a range of facilities (swimming pool, tennis court, fitness center), regularly redecorated contemporary rooms and a modern restaurant serving regional cuisine with a topical taste (baked trout medallions and the chocolate cake with a soft blueberry center, accompanied by a milkshake).

CHAMESOL

25190 Doubs. Paris 453 – Besançon 91 – Belfort 43 – Morteau 50 – Montbéliard 30.
A delightful vacation resort in the Haut-Doubs region, surrounded by firs at a height of 730 meters.

 RESTAURANTS

● **Mon Plaisir**
22, rue Journal.
Tel. 03 81 92 56 17. Fax 03 81 92 52 67.
Closed Sun. dinner, Mon., Tue.,
1 week at end Dec., end Aug.–mid-Sept.
Prix fixe: 28€, 70€.

The "pleasure" here is the Pillouds', as they offer a spirited welcome in their rustic establishment decorated with appealing ornaments. Patricia charmingly recommends wines and dishes, while Christian (Luc Piguet's pupil at the Charrue d'Or, he has also worked in Switzerland, notably at the Richemond in Geneva) delicately prepares the produce of Franche Comté. Frog leg meat in spring rolls, crawfish tail gratin, foie gras with tomato confit, pot-au-feu of escargot with cream, duck breast with wild cherries and a grand cru chocolate cake with ice cream are delicate work indeed.

CHAMONIX-MONT-BLANC

74400 Haute-Savoie. Paris 613 – Albertville 68 – Annecy 95 – Genève 82.
info@chamonix.com.
The only star here is Mont Blanc, a magical mountain exalted by scientists such as Saussure and held sacred by mountaineers, its opened routes an open book for its guides, who formed their Company in 1823. In a fitting symbol for this Catholic region, its headquarters are next to the church.

■ **HOTELS-RESTAURANTS**

● **Hameau Albert 1er**
38, rte Bouchet.
Tel. 04 50 53 05 09. Fax 04 50 55 95 48.
infos@hameaualbert.fr
www.hameaualbert.fr
Closed beg. Nov.–beg. Dec.
Rest. closed Tue. lunch, Wed., Thu. lunch.
27 rooms: 116–340€.
Prix fixe: 66€ (lunch), 112€, 140€.

Pierre Carrier has successfully modernized his family hotel, turning it into an updated Relais & Châteaux establishment with a modern adjunct, which combines the materials of a former farmhouse with designer furniture, swimming pools and a fitness center. In the kitchens, he works with produce from the immediate area and further afield, in light preparations and harmonious gustatory blends. Lately, he has even begun to stray from his Savoyard frame of reference. Seared langoustines royale in a reduced seafood broth served with spring salad, turbot medallion brochettes with aged balsamic vinegar, peas, fava beans, artichokes and romaine lettuce cooked *en cocotte*, the line-fished Atlantic sea bass with a chanterelle mushroom crust, chicory foam and ratte potato purée boldly improvise on marine flavors, but as we continue our feast, the Carrier of the high mountains makes a comeback with the pan-seared milk-fed veal chop with vegetables cooked *en cocotte* and crispy bacon, along with the sautéed sweetbread hearts with white beans and chanterelles, plus a purée of ratte potatoes with black truffles, enchanting in a proficient rural manner. The warm soufflé with Poire William and cocoa sorbet provide an elegant conclusion and the very Alpine wine list wanders prettily into the neighboring lands of Switzerland and Italy.

■ Le Mont-Blanc et le Matafan

62, allée Majestic.
Tel. 04 50 53 05 64. Fax 04 50 55 89 44.
www.bestmontblanc.com
Closed Oct., Nov.
32 rooms: 115€. 8 suites: 260–537€.
Prix fixe: 40€, 70€. A la carte: 65€.

Set in the heart of the resort, this Belle Epoque luxury hotel has an immediate charm. Garden, swimming pool, renovated vintage rooms, cozy lounges and the convivial bar area put us at our ease. At the Matafan, the fare prepared by new chef Marc Florian lightly blends the region's fine produce with Mediterranean flavors. A fine choice of wines, with Jean-Charles Gauthey to sing their praises.

■ Auberge du Bois Prin ❀⌂

69, chemin de l'Hermine.
Tel. 04 50 53 33 51. Fax 04 50 53 48 75.
infoatboisprin.com / www.boisprin.com
Closed Nov., 2 weeks May.
Rest. closed Mon. lunch, Wed. lunch.
8 rooms: 200–340€. 2 suites: 268–410€.
Prix fixe: 49€. A la carte: 65€.

Denis Carrier's Savoyard chalet offers an easygoing luxury. Its paneled rooms with their balconies, and sauna and Jacuzzi promise rest and well being. The old-style dining room and terrace provide a breathtaking view of Mont Blanc. A monkfish carpaccio with saffron, sea bream with a borage emulsion, duckling mille-feuille with peaches and a berry crisp follow.

■ La Savoyarde ❀⌂

28, rte des Moussoux.
Tel. 04 50 53 00 77. Fax 04 50 55 86 82.
lasavoyarde@wanadoo.fr
www.lasavoyarde.com
Closed 2 weeks Nov., 2 weeks May.
Rest. closed Tue. lunch, Wed. lunch.

14 rooms: 85–160€.
Prix fixe: 20€. A la carte: 40€.

Massimiliano Molino has taken over with gusto in this huge 19th-century chalet situated at the foot of the Brévent cable car. The rooms in light wood look out on Mont Blanc and the *pension* dishes are spirited (marinated smoked salmon, scallops with lime, pork tenderloin with curry and chocolate cake with creamy custard sauce).

■ Beausoleil ❀⌂

Tel. 04 50 54 00 78. Fax 04 50 54 17 34.
www.hotelbeausoleilchamonix.com
Closed 2 weeks May, 20 Sept.–20 Dec.
Rest. closed lunch (exc. July–Aug.).
17 rooms: 45–128€.
Prix fixe: 13,50€, 17€, 28€.
A la carte: 45€.

This attractive chalet has trim mountain-style rooms and a reliable restaurant serving *pension* cuisine, with the added appeal of a modest check.

● L'Atmosphère

123, pl Balmat.
Tel. 04 50 55 97 97. Fax 04 50 53 38 96.
www.restaurant-atmosphere.com
Prix fixe: 21€, 29€, 10€ (child).
A la carte: 42–56€.

A very "mountain" atmosphere reigns here, full of exuberance and brightness in the expert hands of Dominique Balson, formerly sommelier at the Hameau Albert 1er, and chef Mickael Guibert. The cuisine is highly appealing with its eggplant caviar tart, diced tuna with argan oil and vegetable tagliatelle, thyme-seasoned roasted rack of lamb and the puff pastry with strawberries and mascarpone cheese. A wide range of French and foreign wines.

● La Maison Carrier

Rte du Bouchet.
Tel. 04 50 53 00 03. Fax 04 50 55 95 48.
infos@hameaualbert.fr / www.hameaualbert.fr
Closed Mon. (exc. July–Aug.),
mid-Nov.–mid-Dec., 2 weeks beg. June.
Prix fixe: 26€, 39€, 13€ (child).

This authentic imitation farm reconstructed by Pierre Carrier offers a taste of the true Savoy, with its *thuyés* (a fireplace where pork products are smoked), delightfully roguish dishes (a delicious tête de veau with a sauce gribiche), home-style cabbage soup, pastas (macaroni with ceps) and favorite wines (Marin, Mondeuse). He has scored a success in this chic rustic adjunct, where we feast simply on the pork trotter with béarnaise sauce and the pike fish quenelles with crayfish sauce. The dessert buffet is a trove of childhood treats.

In Le Lavancher (74400). 6 km via N506.

■ **Jeu de Paume**
705, rte du Chapeau.
Tel. 04 50 54 03 76. Fax 04 50 54 10 75.
jeudepaumechamonix@wanadoo.fr
www.jeudepaumechamonix.com
Closed mid-Sept.–beg. Dec.,
mid-May–mid-June.
Rest. closed Tue. lunch, Wed. lunch.
22 rooms: 128–224€.
Prix fixe: 38€, 49€, 58€. A la carte: 52€.

At the foot of the Aiguille Verte, this traditional chalet with its predominantly wood décor is a refined setting with its renovated rooms and a view of Mont Blanc. Among the chiné furniture and large bay windows of the restaurant, we make short work of tuna prepared three ways, cream of rutabaga soup with saffron, the John Dory fish with coriander and butter, stuffed quail breast and strawberry aspic with mascarpone cream and lemon basil sorbet.

In Praz (74400). 2,5 km n.

■ **L'Eden**
35, rte des Gaudemays.
Tel. 04 50 53 18 43. Fax 04 50 53 51 50.
relax@hoteleden-chamonix.com
www.hoteleden-chamonix.com
Rest. closed Tue., beg. Nov.–mid-Dec.
12 rooms: 65–158€.
Prix fixe: 27€, 37€. A la carte: 48–55€.

This century-old establishment boasts a view of Mont Blanc, fully equipped modern rooms and a reliable fusion cuisine

in its restaurant with porch (and terrace in season). Pan-seared foie gras served with a fig tart and mango salsa and tataki tuna served with a citrus salad and avocado are a sample of the delights on offer. Fine wines too.

CHAMPAGNAC-DE-BEL-AIR see BRANTOME
CHAMPAGNIER see GRENOBLE
CHAMPCEVINEL see PERIGUEUX
CHAMPEAUX see AVRANCHES

CHAMPIGNE

49330 Maine-et-Loire. Paris 290 – La Flèche 40 – Angers 25 – Château-Gontier 25.
Lush Anjou and a golf course on the Cheffes road nearby.

▪️◯ HOTELS-RESTAURANTS

■ **Château des Briottières**
3 km nw.
Tel. 02 41 42 00 02. Fax 02 41 42 01 55.
briottieres@wanadoo.fr
Closed mid-Feb.–beg. Mar., Christmas–New Year's. Rest. closed lunch
16 rooms: 120–320€.
Prix fixe: 40€.

A fine 18th-century château set in its own grounds, boasting tastefully furnished, spacious rooms, cozy, relaxing lounges and a dining room for residents.

CHAMPILLON-BELLEVUE see EPERNAY

CHAMPTOCEAUX

49270 Maine-et-Loire. Paris 358 – Nantes 33 – Angers 64 – Cholet 50 – Ancenis 11.
An island in the Loire, the Promenade de Champalud trail and all the delights of the valley brought together in a single village.

▪️◯ HOTELS-RESTAURANTS

● **Les Jardins de la Forge**
1, pl Piliers.
Tel. 02 40 83 56 23. Fax 02 40 83 59 80.
jardins.de.la.forge@wanadoo.fr

www.jardins-de-la-forge.com
Closed 2 weeks beg. Oct., 1 week at end
Feb.–beg. Mar., 1 week beg. July.
Rest. closed Sun. dinner, Mon., Tue.
2 rooms: 80–95€. 5 suites: 110–140€.
Prix fixe: 30€ (weekdays), 48€, 58€, 92€,
23€ (child). A la carte: 70–85€.

Just by the 13th-century château, Paul Pauvert's former smithy with swimming pool delights his guests. All enjoy the convivial, contemporary rooms and the master's refined dishes, served in the bright dining room with its porch. Lobster medallions with asparagus tips and a truffle oil vinaigrette, sautéed scallops and eel, roasted squab with a morel mushroom sauce and Anjou pears, poached then caramelized with pain d'épice ice cream, pay tribute to the Loire, as does the cellar.

CHANCEAUX-SUR-CHOISILLE see TOURS
CHANCELADE see PERIGUEUX

CHANTILLY

60500 Oise. Paris 52 – Pontoise 41 – Compiègne 45 – Beauvais 55 – Meaux 51.
An ancient town with its fine château run by the Institut de France, Living Museum of the Horse in the great stables, vast park and forest and surroundings, where we stroll and relax.

 HOTELS-RESTAURANTS

■ Château de
Montvillargenne
Av François-Mathet.
Tel. 03 44 62 37 37. Fax 03 44 57 28 97.
chateau@montvillargenne.com
www.chateaudemontvillargenne.com
120 rooms: 160–300€.
Prix fixe: 36€, 45€, 67€, 18€ (child).

In the heart of a huge wooded estate, this 19th-century château works its charm. The indoor swimming pool, fitness center, large rooms (each one dedicated to a country), bathrooms with whirlpool tubs and old-fashioned dining room with mezzanine are all very impressive. In the kitchen, Sylvain Marcaille assiduously prepares

modern rustic dishes that especially focus on fish and crustaceans.

■ Dolce Chantilly
Rte d'Apremont Vineuil-Saint-Firmin.
Tel. 03 44 58 47 77. Fax 03 44 58 50 11.
Info-chantilly@dolce.com
www.chantilly.dolce.com
Closed 10 days Christmas–New Year's.
200 rooms: 200–250€. 25 suites: 250–400€.
Prix fixe: 57€, 62€.

To keep us fit, an eighteen-hole golf course, fitness center and two heated pools (outdoor and indoor); to keep us fed, three restaurants (the Swing, Etoile and Carmontelle); to keep us rested, handsome renovated rooms: that is the agenda in this modern hotel complex. Alain Montigny's refined cuisine delights the athletically inclined, who will not turn their noses up at roasted langoustines with cauliflower purée, roasted rouget with celery root, braised rabbit sausage with foie gras or express any qualms over a praline-coated milk chocolate dome.

■ Hôtel du Parc
36, av du Maréchal-Joffre.
Tel. 03 44 58 20 00. Fax 03 44 57 31 10.
bwhotelduparc@wanadoo.fr
www.hotel-parc-chantilly.com
57 rooms: 80–180€.

A step away from the racetrack and forest, this practical hotel boasts a peaceful garden, English-style bar and refined modern rooms, some with a terrace.

In Apremont (60300). 6 km from Senlis.

● La Grange aux Loups COM
8, rue du 11-Novembre.
Tel. 03 44 25 33 79. Fax 03 44 24 22 22.
lagrangeauxloups@wanadoo.fr
www.lagrangeauxloups.com
Closed 10 days beg. Sept., 10 days beg. Jan.
Rest. closed Sat. lunch, Sun. dinner, Mon.
4 rooms: 80€.
Prix fixe: 28€, 50€, 60€ (wine inc.)
8€ (child).

Jean-Claude Jalloux greets his guests like old friends. They are delighted by the convivial dining room all year round and terrace in summer. The good-natured chef regales them with solid, meticulously executed fare. Marbled foie gras terrine seasoned with blueberry fortified wine, turbot medallions with a Chardonnay cream sauce, a lamb saddle encrusted in herbs and the chocolate royale with a banana caramel milkshake are all splendid. A fine list of wines from around the world and four traditional rooms for a night's stay.

● La Tour d'Apremont COM

Apremont, golf course.
Tel. 03 44 25 61 11. Fax 03 44 25 11 72.
www.club-albatros.com
Closed dinner
Prix fixe: 25€ (groups). A la carte: 40€.

This clubhouse restaurant is anything but par for the course. In the kitchen, Philippe Suarez concocts an authentic, inventive cuisine. Foie gras and scallop crème brûlée, simmered sea bream served over grated potato cakes, orange roughy with hazelnuts and bay-seasoned potatoes and the roasted cod with Asian spices have their charm, especially since the prices remember their manners.

LA CHAPELLE-D'ABONDANCE

74360 Haute-Savoie. Paris 603 – Evian 36 – Thonon 34 – Morzine 32 – Châtel 6 – Annecy 108.
ot-chapelle@portesdusoleil.com.
The ski slopes and snowfields have not destroyed the soul of this old village with its fine church and splendid location, solidly implanted in the heart of traditional Savoy.

 HOTELS-RESTAURANTS

■ Les Cornettes

Tel. 04 50 73 50 24. Fax 04 50 73 54 16.
www.lescornettes.com
Closed mid-Oct.–mid-Dec.,
mid-Apr.–beg. May.
40 rooms: 60–130€.
Prix fixe: 22€, 60€. A la carte: 55€.

This year, Philippe and Bernard Trincaz have renovated the wood-paneled rooms and studio apartments in this traditional 19th-century chalet. Do not worry, though: the fitness center and heated pool remain untouched and pleasant as ever. The dining room is equally gratifying with its pressed quail terrine, lake whiting filet with morels, truffle-seasoned squab and the prince de Savoie, the house soufflé with a raspberry coulis, paying delightful tribute to their region.

■ Les Gentianettes

Rte de Chevenne.
Tel. 04 50 73 56 46. Fax 04 50 73 56 39.
bienvenue@gentianettes.fr
www.gentianettes.fr
Closed mid-Sept.–mid-Dec., Easter–Ascension.
Rest. closed Mon. (off season), Tue. (off season).
32 rooms: 85–125€.
Prix fixe: 18€, 19€, 25€, 36€, 44€, 46€, 59€. A la carte: 55€.

Claude Trincaz's chalet wages an unstoppable charm offensive. The sauna, steam bath, Jacuzzi, swimming pool and wood-trimmed rooms with balconies overlooking the surrounding mountains have an easy charm. At mealtimes, the master of the house takes over with a regional cuisine that includes charcuterie, crayfish tail gratin, escalope savoyarde (a gratin of turkey, ham, Réblochon cheese and cream) and a frozen Génépi soufflé.

■ Le Vieux Moulin

Rte de Chevenne.
Tel. 04 50 73 52 52. Fax 04 50 73 55 62.
www.hotel-vieuxmoulin.com
Closed mid-Apr.–mid-May, mid-Oct.–mid-Dec.
Rest. closed Wed.
15 rooms: 45–50€.
Prix fixe: 22€, 45€. A la carte: 40€.

In this traditional inn, the well-kept rustic rooms and honest regional cuisine invite us to linger a while.

LA CHAPELLE-EN-SERVAL

60520 Oise. Paris 42 – Compiègne 43 –
Beauvais 65 – Chantilly 10 – Senlis 10.
A Picardy village like a foray into the forest.

 HOTELS-RESTAURANTS

■ Château Hôtel Mont-Royal

2 km e via D118.
Tel. 03 44 54 50 50. Fax 03 44 54 50 21.
www.chateau-mont-royal.com
Rest. closed lunch, Sun. dinner.
100 rooms: 255–575€.
Prix fixe: 40€.

This extended, renovated hunting lodge
set in its own grounds with swimming
pool, fitness center, tennis courts and
luxury rooms is superbly conducive to
rest and relaxation. Its refined cuisine is
prepared under the eye of Bruno Ledru.
Pressed foie gras and duck terrine, chilled
crab and tomato tartare salad, smoked
Atlantic sea bass with fennel and a trio
of macarons with berry sorbet are finely
crafted work. Excellent service.

LA CHAPELLE-JANSON

35133 Ille-et-Vilaine. Paris 312 – Rennes 65
– Laval 40 – Fougères 10.
On the edge of Mayenne's woods and pastures,
a village in the Pays de Fougères.

 RESTAURANTS

● La Petite Auberge

La Templerie, RN12.
Tel.-Fax 02 99 95 27 03.
Closed Sun. dinner, Mon., Tue. dinner, 1 week
Oct., 1 week beg. Jan., end July–mid-Aug.
Prix fixe: 18€ (lunch weekdays), 22€, 24€,
28€, 33€, 9€ (child). A la carte: 45€.

The dining room of this small inn with its
pastel tones and modern furniture works
its charm. Didier Godineau's reliable cuisine wins us over with such convincing
arguments as duck foie gras, roasted
Atlantic sea bass with tomato vinegar,

tarragon-seasoned veal and the frozen
apricot parfait. Laurence Godineau provides a smiling welcome and attentive
service.

CHARLEVILLE-MEZIERES

08000 Ardennes. Paris 241 – Reims 89 –
Sedan 24 – Luxembourg 129 – Liège 168.
Arthur Rimbaud called it "Charlestown". His
native burg still boasts its fine, arcade-lined
square, the twin of Paris' place des Vosges.

 HOTELS-RESTAURANTS

■ Le Paris

24, av G.-Corneau.
Tel. 03 24 33 34 38. Fax 03 24 59 11 21.
hotel.de.paris.08@wanadoo.fr
www.hoteldeparis08.fr
25 rooms: 41,50–49,50€. 2 suites: 74,50€.

Near the place Ducale, this hotel made
up of three turn-of-the-century buildings
offers contemporary rooms renovated this
year, along with a courteous welcome.

● La Clef des Champs   COM

33, rue du Moulin (waridon).
Tel. 03 24 56 17 50. Fax 03 24 59 94 07.
courrier@laclefdeschamps.fr
www.laclefdeschamps.fr
Closed Sun. dinner.
Prix fixe: 23€, 32€, 60€, 12€ (child).

Christophe Melin has turned his little eatery into a first-rate restaurant. We enjoy
the foie gras served two ways (one marinated in Cognac, the other poached and
served with pain d'épice), the red mullet
tartelette with parmesan, a free-range
chicken with herb butter and the chocolate desserts and exotic fruit served with
mascarpone.

● La Côte à l'Os   COM

11, cours A.-Briand.
Tel. 03 24 59 20 16.
lacotealos@aol.com
Closed Sun. dinner (exc. summer).
Prix fixe: 15€, 25€, 32,50€.
A la carte: 45€.

The carefully prepared domestic dishes served on the first floor and Alsatian cuisine presented in the *winstub* on the second strike the right note in this lively brasserie. We enjoy the duck foie gras terrine, roasted pike-perch, veal sweetbreads with morels and a dark chocolate truffle in all their simplicity. Alain Colignon provides a friendly welcome.

● **Amorini**

46, pl Ducale.
Tel. 03 24 37 48 80.
Closed dinner, Sun., Mon., 3 weeks Aug.
A la carte: 25€.

Fernandino De Matteo prepares subtle, light dishes with fresh, sunny flavors. In the dining room with its gourmand shelves and neat tables, the carpaccio, an assortment of antipasti, agnolini with Gorgonzola and the tomato and basil tortellini are touchingly sincere. The frozen chocolate truffle is splendid.

In 08090 Fagnon. 8 km via D139 and D39.

■ **L'Abbaye**
   de Sept-Fontaines

Tel. 03 24 37 38 24. Fax 03 24 37 58 75.
abbaye-7-fontaines@wanadoo.fr
www.abbayeseptfontaines.fr
22 rooms: 84–145€. 1 suite: 197€.
Prix fixe: 29€, 38€, 54€, 15€ (child).
A la carte: 60€.

General de Gaulle had his quarters in this 17th-century abbey when he visited his fiancée Yvonne. Today, he would approve of the warm welcome and the comfort of the large rooms looking out over the countryside. The cuisine lives up to the same high standards. Chef Eric Bronner prepares finely crafted dishes that tack between tradition and modernity. A carrot soup with mussels, scallops with fleur de sel served on a cep velouté and Ardennes-style young rabbit provide a seasonal interpretation of local produce. Crunchy caramelized quince dessert and a frozen vanilla parfait offer a delicious sweet conclusion.

CHAROLLES

71120 Saône-et-Loire. Paris 365 –
Mâcon 54 – Autun 79 – Roanne 61.
O.T.CHAROLLES@wanadoo.fr.
In the heart of the Brionnais district, this Burgundian Tuscany is the capital of Charolais beef and the trademark blue-glazed earthenware.

▣ | HOTELS-RESTAURANTS

■ **La Poste**

Av de la Libération.
Tel. 03 85 24 11 32. Fax 03 85 24 05 74.
www.la-poste-hotel.com
Hotel closed Sun. dinner, Mon.
Rest. closed Sun. dinner, Mon., 2 weeks Feb.,
12 Nov.–beg. Dec.
13 rooms: 55–110€. 2 suites: 120–130€.
Prix fixe: 23€ (weekdays), 35€, 55€,
70€, 11€ (child). A la carte: 60€.

This imposing Burgundian building flanked by an entirely renovated adjunct, the Villa des Kiwis, and a pleasant flowered terrace offers luxurious rooms with handsomely furniture. In the contemporary dining room, the regional cuisine gains in lightness and originality with the poached eggs in red wine sauce with an escargot fricasse, monkfish tail with chorizo and fresh spinach, beef filet medallions Rossini and a baked apple with pralines and ice cream.

LA CHARTRE-SUR-LE-LOIR

72340 Sarthe. Paris 215 – La Flèche 58 –
Le Mans 50 – Saint-Calais 31 – Tours 40.
Anjou Maine, the sweep of the Loir and a landscape colored by fortresses and ruins.

▣ | HOTELS-RESTAURANTS

■ **Hôtel de France**

20, pl de la République.
Tel. 02 43 44 40 16. Fax 02 43 79 62 20.
hoteldefrance@wordonline.fr
Closed Sun. dinner (exc. July–Aug.),
Mon. (exc. July–Aug.), 10 days Christmas–
New Year's, Feb. vac.

24 rooms: 44–68€. 1 suite: 68€.
Prix fixe: 14€ (weekdays), 24€, 38€,
8€ (child). A la carte: 40–54€.

In their 100-year-old post house set in its garden on the bank of the Loir, Francis and Sylvia Pasteau have combined a traditional French atmosphere with modern comfort, classic rooms, terrace, heated pool and WiFi. At the stove, Eric Lematelot reinterprets traditional fare with talent: the duck foie gras with rose confit, pan-tossed langoustines with orange sauce, braised pike-perch served on a bed of endive or the veal sweetbread and wild mushroom cassolette have an easy charm. Try the house "three perfumes" dessert in conclusion.

CHARTRES

28000 Eure-et-Loir. Paris 89 – Orléans 77 – Evreux 78 – Le Mans 115 – Tours 142.
chartres.tourism@wanadoo.fr.
Venerable Chartres, a place of pilgrimage and gourmet delights, has always been fond of solid fare and subtle flavors. Apart from its imposing cathedral, its glory lies in a game pâté—not blackbird, but plover.

 HOTELS-RESTAURANTS

● **Le Grand Monarque** ○🏛
22, pl des Epars.
Tel. 02 37 18 15 15 / 02 37 21 00 72.
Fax 02 37 36 34 18.
info@bw-grand-monarque.com
www.bw-grand-monarque.com
Rest. closed Sun. dinner, Mon.
47 rooms: 115–165€. 5 suites: 195–235€.
Prix fixe: 46€, 56€. A la carte: 65€.

The young Jallerat generation has eagerly renovated this 16th-century post house with its well-cared-for rooms and suites, fine red, pink, beige and blue fabrics, Flamant furniture and Jouy linen. When mealtimes come round, we can choose between the simple dishes on the blackboard of the Madrigal or the modern reinterpretation of domestic cuisine in the great dining room named by Bertrand for

Georges, his father. The Chartres-style foie gras pâté, the crab, potato, and asparagus Chartreuse, the John Dory with truffles tucked under its skin served with spider crab and zucchini ravioli or the superb local Didier Grandvillain signature poultry, served with Touquet ratte potatoes and country bacon by Laurent Clément, make up stately spreads for gourmet gentlefolk. The coda consists of traditional desserts (Grand Marnier soufflé, heirloom Reinette apples with cider butter). The best of the Loire stars on the first-rate wine list. Excellent, lively, prompt service.

● **La Vieille Maison** V.COM
5, rue au Lait.
Tel. 02 37 34 10 67. Fax 02 37 91 12 41.
rest.la.vieille.maison@wanadoo.fr
www.lavieillemaison.newfr.net
Closed Sun. dinner, Mon., Tue. lunch.
Prix fixe: 26€, 32€, 44€. A la carte: 60€.

Near the cathedral, Bruno Letartre's "old house" is deceptive. Its antique décor of exposed stone and beams, patinated furniture and large fireplace provide the setting for a very contemporary cuisine. The fresh duck foie gras, the roasted turbot with vegetable caviar and asparagus with chorizo-seasoned butter, the braised veal sweetbread medallion served with aged vinegar and mushrooms and the thin hot apple tart with milk caramel are reliably prepared.

● **Le Saint-Hilaire** ▪COM
11, rue du Pont-Saint-Hilaire.
Tel.-Fax 02 37 30 97 57.
Closed Sun., Mon., 1 week Oct., Christmas, 1 week at end July–mid-Aug.
Prix fixe: 26€, 33€, 42€, 12€ (child).
A la carte: 50€.

This appealing 16th-century abode at the end of a bridge over the Eure has been taken over with gusto by Sébastien Brémaud, former sommelier of the Grand Monarque, who cheerfully extols the finest wines of the Loire (not the best known). In the kitchen, the young Julie Lucas reliably espouses the cause of regional produce in her seasonal dishes. In the neo-rustic, green and white décor, escalope of foie gras with green lentils, a jar of Le Conie signature escargots and leeks, saddle of Verdigny rabbit served with home-style mashed potatoes and the crunchy chocolate dessert served with a light coffee mousse strike just the right note. The whole is attractive indeed and its keen championing of Eure and Loir produce warms our heart.

● **Le Bistro de la Cathédrale**   SIM

Cloître Notre-Dame.
Tel. 02 37 36 59 60.
Prix fixe: 21€, 22€, 25€.
A la carte: 30–35€.

Under the cathedral, this chic bistro with its terrace, bar and long, narrow, modern dining room at the back provides fine wines and a splendid, roguish cuisine of the day. Lionel Couasnon, whom we met at the Petit Bistro opposite the market, runs the place with alacrity, serving his favorite Bourgueils and Chinons, while Mario Bocchialini, who worked at the Grand Monarque, prepares a smartly turned-out domestic cuisine. We enjoy the pâté in a pastry crust, poached egg with morel cream sauce, tête de veau served cold and thinly sliced, carpaccio-style, poule au pot and the rice pudding with salted-butter caramel.

CHARTRES-DE-BRETAGNE see RENNES

CHASSELAY

69380 Rhône. Paris 444 – Lyon 21 – Villefranche-sur-Saône 16.
Chasselay's pear orchards are famous, as are the Monts d'Or, which lend a sense of rustic adventure to the Lyon region.

●	RESTAURANTS

● **Guy Lassausaie**   ○ V.COM

Rue de Bellecize.
Tel. 04 78 47 62 59. Fax 04 78 47 06 19.
guy.lassausaie@wanadoo.fr
www.guy-lassausaie.com
Closed Tue., Wed., 10 days Feb. vac.,

3 weeks Aug.
Prix fixe: 40€, 52€, 65€, 15€ (child).
A la carte: 80€.

Guy Lassausaie's traditional establishment is pleasant indeed. We enjoy its cozy smoking room and contemporary lounges with their impressive collection of Lyon silk scarves. In the kitchen, the 1993 Meilleur Ouvrier de France award winner prepares beautifully crafted neo-classical dishes. Oven-baked lobster with caper-seasoned eggplant, Mediterranean sea bass filet served with a rye crêpe topped with caviar, a veal roast seasoned with licorice root, accompanied by a veal knuckle with spring carrots, deftly reinterpret tradition. In the same excellent spirit, the desserts include green verbena–flavored ice cream served in a cone with a berry compote. A reliable restaurant.

CHASSENEUIL-DU-POITOU,
AU FUTUROSCOPE see POITIERS

CHATEAU-D'OLONNE see
LES SABLES-D'OLONNE

CHATEAU-THEBAUD see NANTES

CHATEAU-ARNOUX

04160 Alpes de Haute-Provence. Paris 724 – Digne-les-Bains 25 – Forcalquier 30 – Manosque 41 – Sault 69.
ot.district@wanadoo.fr.
Haute-Provence with its clear sky and bright air, dubbed the "land of nonexcess" (the simple life) by novelist Giono.

	HOTELS-RESTAURANTS

● **La Bonne Etape**   ○ 🏨

Chemin du Lac.
Tel. 04 92 64 00 09. Fax 04 92 64 37 36.
bonneetape@relaischateaux.com
www.bonneetape.com
Closed Nov. Rest. closed Mon. (off season), Tue. (off season), Wed. lunch (off season), end Nov.–mid-Dec., beg. Jan.–mid-Feb.
11 rooms: 160–220€. 7 suites: 220–350€.
Prix fixe: 42€, 68€, 100€, 22€ (child).

Novelist Jean Giono's region is epitomized by the Gleize's Relais & Châteaux establishment, an enduring tribute to tradition. Its meals are a celebration of the senses: no frills or pretension, just authentic produce. "That lamb's genuine," comments Pierre the father, as he serves up fine Hautes-Alpes lamb in a daube served cold with vinaigrette or a guarrigue thyme–seasoned jus, accompanied by Jany's local chickpea cakes (panisses): two delicacies! But first, we savor the admirable eggplant purée–stuffed zucchini blossoms, salted cod with garlic sauce and the Mediterranean sea bass served on a local onion tart called the pissaladière. In conclusion, we enjoy a magnificent honey ice cream served with a honeycomb. The list of wines from the Rhône Valley and further afield is magnificent, the service friendly, the rooms exquisite and the swimming pool a joy. A restaurant? No, a dream destination!

● **L'Oustaou de la Foun**   V.COM

Rte N85.
Tel. 04 92 62 65 30. Fax 04 92 62 65 32.
loustaoudela-foun@wanadoo.fr
Closed Sun. dinner, Mon., Nov. 1 vac.
Prix fixe: 20€ (weekday lunch), 30 €, 40€,
60€, 11€ (child). A la carte: 65€.

Gérald Jourdan is the mad dog of Haute Provence gastronomy. Trained by Sammut and Ducasse, he deftly explores his region's cuisine, reconstructs its traditions and innovates boldly here in his bastion off the highway towards Sisteron. His starters are enchanting tapas—including a slice of slow-roasted eggplant, jumbo shrimp, green tabouli and an avocado with curry, orange, crab and coconut milk—followed by Espelette pepper marinated and roasted tuna or every part of the lamb, with the tomato *"à boire et à manger"* (to eat and drink). We savor Jabron valley fresh goat cheeses and ultimately pay tribute to a generous variation on the strawberry, raspberry and lemon. In dealing with Gérald Jourdan, tedium is not an option.

● **Au Goût du Jour**

14, av du Général-de-Gaulle.
Tel. 04 92 64 48 48.
Closed beg. Jan.–10 Feb.
Prix fixe: 24€.

The Gleizes' bistro is simple and delicious. In the capable hands of Pierre and Jany, we eat exquisitely without breaking the bank. The blackboard displays four starters, four dishes and four desserts, changing each day. A Brousse ewe's cheese and vegetable terrine, stuffed rabbit saddle and a frozen honey-flavored nougat with a strawberry coulis are things of joy. We wash them down with a chilled Coteaux de Pierrevert and offer up heartfelt thanks that such sweet restaurants exist.

CHATEAUBERNARD see COGNAC

35220 Ille-et-Vilaine. Paris 328 – Rennes 23 – Angers 113 – Châteaubriant 52 – Fougères 43.
This patch of Rennes countryside is a classic halt on the road from Paris to Brittany.

 HOTELS-RESTAURANTS

■ **Ar Milin'**   ❀ 🏠

30, rue de Paris.
Tel. 02 99 00 30 91. Fax 02 99 00 37 56.
resa.armilin@wanadoo.fr / www.armilin.com
Closed end Dec.–beg. Jan.
Hotel closed Sun. night (winter).
Gourmet rest. closed Sat. lunch, Sun. dinner.
31 rooms: 70–145€. 21 suites: 170–200€.
Prix fixe: 27€.

This former flour mill dating from the 19th century makes a charming stopover in its five hectares of grounds on the bank of the Vilaine. Its rooms are restful and in its dining room and riverside porch, we enjoy dishes prepared with gusto by Pascal Ribault, eagerly devouring summer vegetables cooked and served in a cocotte, a red mullet, fennel, roasted tomato, black olive and spring onion dish, a sirloin steak with new potatoes seasoned with fleur de sel and the thin apricot tart with Amaretto shaved ice.

In Domagné (35113). 5 km via rte de Chancé.

■ Le Ricordeau
1, rue Saint-Pierre.
Tel. 02 99 00 06 06. Fax 02 99 00 00 32.
t.malotaux@cegetel.net
Rest. closed Fri. dinner, Sun. dinner.
12 rooms: 39–44€.
Prix fixe: 9,50€, 33€. A la carte: 35–40€.

Everything here breathes a rustic charm: the pleasant rooms, Françoise Malotaux's attentive welcome and the cuisine concocted by Thierry, who trained with Amat in Bordeaux and Fulgraff in Colmar. The quality of the produce, simply prepared, shines through in the curry-seasoned oyster ravioli, scallops with chitterling sausage, poultry drumstick cooked in cider and a caramel bavaroise, all amiably priced.

In Saint-Didier (35220). 6 km e via D33.

■ Pen' Roc
Tel. 02 99 00 33 02. Fax 02 99 62 30 89.
hotellerie@penroc.fr / www.penroc.fr
Closed vac. Christmas, Feb. vac.
Rest. closed Sun. dinner (Oct.–May).
29 rooms: 85–150€. 2 suites: 145–225€.
Prix fixe: 22,50€ (weekdays), 31€, 45€, 14€ (child).

There is plenty to do at Joseph and Mireille Froc's hostelry. In the swimming pool and fitness center, we exercise to our hearts' content, while the charming rooms, some with a private terrace, are relaxing to a fault. The rustic and contemporary dining rooms serve prettily crafted, mischievous dishes: pan-simmered abalone with a creamy truffle sauce, line-fished Atlantic sea bass served with squid stuffed with mussels, the squab cooked twice and its pan of poultry variety meats with cream sauce and a Grand Marnier soufflé.

44110 Loire-Atlantique. Paris 355 – Angers 70 – Laval 63 – Nantes 60 – Rennes 60.

The medieval château, Romanesque church, 15th-century Maison de l'Ange and 18th-century Hôtel de la Houssaye deserve far more than a cursory glance.

 | RESTAURANTS

● Le Poêlon d'Or
30 bis, rue du 11-Novembre.
Tel.-Fax 02 40 81 43 33.
Closed Sun. dinner, Mon., 1 week Feb., 2 weeks Aug.
Prix fixe: 16,50€, 24,50€, 33€, 39€, 48€.
A la carte: 65€.

In their gracious inn with its polished décor, Catherine and Cédric Ponche serve reliable, classic dishes, such as crab-stuffed scallops, Atlantic sea bass with beurre blanc sauce, chateaubriand seasoned with Sichuan peppercorns and a soft-centered chocolate cake.

58120 Nièvre. Paris 281 – Autun 40 – Clamecy 65 – Nevers 65.
This Morvan village is worth a detour for its hillside location, museum of the Presidency, Niki de Saint-Phalle statue, panoramic view from the wayside calvary and Château promenade.

 | HOTELS-RESTAURANTS

■ Le Vieux Morvan
8, pl Gudin.
Tel. 03 86 85 05 01. Fax 03 86 85 02 78.
hotel.restaurant@auvieuxmorvan.com
Closed mid-Dec.–end Jan. Rest. closed Sun. dinner, Mon. (off season).
24 rooms: 48–65€.
Prix fixe: 16€, 26€, 32€. A la carte: 45€.

This was one of President François Mitterrand's haunts. The regularly redecorated, old-fashioned rooms and view of the Morvan from the dining room are always pleasant. The *pension* cuisine is reliably good. The scallop carpaccio, curry-seasoned rockfish and a steak with chanterelles are enjoyable.

CHÂTEAUDOUBLE

83300 Var. Paris 879 – Castellane 48 –
Draguignan 13 – Fréjus 43 – Toulon 100.
Discover this cliffside medieval village between
the Gorges de Châteaudouble and the Nartuby
river.

 | RESTAURANTS

● **La Tour** SIM
Pl Beausoleil.
Tel.-Fax 04 94 70 93 08 / 04 94 70 90 57.
philippe.obriot@wanadoo.fr
Closed Wed., 1 Dec.–15 Dec.
Prix fixe: 23€, 33€, 40€, 8€ (child).

On your way to the Gorges du Verdon,
make sure you call in at Philippe Obriot's
gîte. The pleasant welcome, rustic dining
rooms and shady terrace have an easy
appeal, as does the apposite Southeastern French cuisine. The cold scrambled
eggs with fresh chevre and mint, rouget
in papillote with dill and star anise, rolled
chicken stuffed with basil, garlic, parmesan and pine nuts or a cinnamon-seasoned
apple tart cater to everyone's tastes.

CHATEAUGIRON

35410 Ille-et-Vilaine. Paris 350 – Rennes 20.
This fine village with its magnificent fortress
more than justifies a foray into the heart of the
Rennes region.

 | RESTAURANTS

● **La Loriette** ⓃSIM
2, bd Julien-et-Pierre-Gourdel.
Tel.-Fax 02 99 37 41 35.
Closed Mon., Christmas, New Year's.
Prix fixe: 11,50€ (lunch), 9,50€ (child),
6€ (child). A la carte: 25€.

In their old-fashioned dining rooms
equipped with bric-a-brac furniture,
Laetitia and Nicolas Piton are cheerful
indeed, sure in the knowledge that their
guests will be delighted by the Périgordine
salad, the ocean cake (scallops, shrimp

and slow-cooked leeks), the mushroom-
seasoned escalope and a crêpe with chestnut cream.

CHATEAU-DU-LOIR

72500 Sarthe. Paris 235 – Langeais 45 – Le
Mans 45 – Tours 40 – Vendôme 60.
The Loir Valley in the heart of Anjou Maine,
with its charming villages and châteaux.

 | HOTELS-RESTAURANTS

■ **Le Grand Hôtel** Ⓝ🏠
Pl de l'Hôtel-de-Ville.
Tel. 02 43 44 00 17. Fax 02 43 44 37 58.
www.grand-hotel-chateau-du-loir.com
Closed Fri. dinner (Nov.–mid–Mar.), Sat.
lunch (Nov.–mid–Mar.), 1 week beg. Nov.,
1 week at end Dec.
18 rooms: 51–61€.
Prix fixe: 20€, 26€, 35€, 12€ (child).
A la carte: 42–52€.

This 19th-century tufa post house boasts
a delightfully antique style, converted stables, wall and ceiling frescoes, stained
glass and a terrace beneath the wisteria.
The modern or English-style rooms are
fully equipped. Guy Aveline has entrusted
the kitchen to Françis Brisset and Jean-
Luc Dane. At lunchtime, we sit down to a
brasserie-style meal in one of the orange
pink, thirties dining rooms. In the evening, dinner is a semigastronomic affair.
Foie gras in brioche, monkfish with saffron-seasoned sauce, tête de veau and the
beef filet medallions with morels followed
by a red wine–poached pear terrine with
orange coulis pay tribute to tradition. The
à la carte dishes and set menus change
every three months. Local vintages are
well represented on the wine list.

CHATEAUMEILLANT

18370 Cher. Paris 302 – Argenton-sur-
Creuse-Châteauroux 54 – La Châtre 19.
ot.chateaumeillant@wanadoo.fr.
A fine traditional village in the vineyards of Berry.
Visit the choir of the church of Saint-Genès.

HOTELS-RESTAURANTS

● **Piet à Terre**
21, rue du Château.
Tel. 02 48 61 41 74. Fax 02 48 61 41 88.
lepietaterre@wanadoo.fr
www.le.piet.a.terre.free.fr
Closed Jan.–end Feb. Rest. closed Mon. lunch
(exc. July–Aug.), Tue. lunch (exc. July–Aug.),
Wed. lunch (exc. July–Aug.).
5 rooms: 50–80€. Prix fixe: 37,50€,
42,50€, 62,50€, 120€. A la carte: 110€.

The Piets' inn by the vineyards is a delightful hostelry. The fine refurbished facade, Sylvie's warm welcome and the quiet of the contemporary rooms have an immediate appeal. Thierry's cuisine follows (or should we say overtakes?). In the dining room and porch, we feast on shrewd, fresh fare. The red tuna cooked like ham, braised John Dory and oysters served hot with citrus seasoned vegetables, a whole pigeon steamed over hay in a cocotte and a white peach poached in wine are a treat for the eyes and the taste buds.

CHATEAUNEUF see CHAUFFAILLES

CHATEAUNEUF-DU-PAPE

84230 Vaucluse. Paris 673 – Avignon 18 –
Carpentras 22 – Orange 10.
tourismechato9-pape@wanadoo.fr.
The wine is famous, the village well worth the detour and the light of the Vaucluse a unique experience.

 HOTELS-RESTAURANTS

■ **Hostellerie Château**
 des Fines Roches
Rte de Sorgues.
Tel. 04 90 83 70 23. Fax 04 90 83 78 42.
www.chateaufinesroches.com
Closed mid-Oct.–mid-Dec. Rest. closed Mon., Tue.
8 rooms: 130–206€.
Prix fixe: 22€, 60€. A la carte: 75–90€.

Behind the stone walls of a castle built in 1870, Christophe Vessaire serves a spirited but subtle cuisine: oven-browned slow-cooked vegetables served with fresh goat cheese and a garlic and red pepper coulis, a rosemary-seasoned monkfish brochette served on a bed of slow-cooked fennel with orange, pigeon marinated in red wine with seasonal vegetables and the two chocolate dessert with light cream. We like the small, cozy lounges, perfect for sharing secrets, and the Provençal rooms with their view of the vineyards.

CHATEAUNEUF-EN-AUXOIS

21320 Côte-d'Or. Paris 278 – Beaune 35 –
Dijon 44 – Avalon 73 – Montbard 67.
A handsome village and castle on the Burgundy heights, visible from the A6 turnpike, ideally situated high on the Monts de l'Auxois, near the ''roof of the Western world'' dear to Burgundian bard Henri Vincenot.

 HOTELS-RESTAURANTS

■ **Hostellerie du Château**
Rue du Centre.
Tel. 03 80 49 22 00. Fax 03 80 49 21 27.
www.hostellerie-chateauneuf.com
Closed Mon. (exc. July–Aug.),
Tue. (exc. July–Aug.), end Nov.–beg. Feb.
17 rooms: 45–70€.
Prix fixe: 23€, 29€, 39€,
15€ (weekday lunch), 15€ (child).

This house with garden is the medieval castle's little neighbor. We while away happy hours in the renovated guest rooms, dining room and porch (which opens onto a terrace in summer). Escargots, foie gras, salmon steaks, Charolais beef filet and a crème brûlée with sour cherries warm the cockles of our hearts.

CHATEAU-D'OLERON see ILE D'OLERON

CHATEL

74390 Haute-Savoie. Paris 605 –
Thonon-les-Bains 39 – Annecy 113 –
Evian 38 – Morzine 38.
touristoffice@chatel.com.
In the heart of the Val d'Abondance, the picturesque chalets of an authentic mountain
village.

 HOTELS-RESTAURANTS

■ Macchi

Tel. 04 50 73 24 12. Fax 04 50 73 27 25.
elisabeth@hotelmacchi.com
www.hotelmacchi.com
Closed mid-Sept.–mid-Dec., end Apr.–mid-June.
30 rooms: 52–152€. 2 suites: 80–152€.
Prix fixe: 22€, 49€, 10€ (child).
A la carte: 50€.

A rather curious building, this chalet of
Austrian design! Its comfortable rooms
are equipped with balconies overlooking the Val d'Abondance. The welcome,
swimming pool, fitness center and simple *pension* cuisine are very satisfactory.

● Ripaille   `SIM`

Résidence le Moulin.
Tel. 04 50 73 32 14. Fax 04 50 73 20 21.
Closed Mon., mid-Dec.–mid-Apr.,
1 July–mid-Sept.
Prix fixe: 15€, 20€, 8€ (child).
A la carte: 30–40€.

At the foot of the slopes, Michel Trincaz sets the tone, serving up very honest
dishes that include the house salad, trout
meunière, beef filet medallions with chanterelles and crêpes with ice cream.

● Le Vieux Four   `SIM`

Tel. 04 50 73 30 56. Fax 04 50 73 38 12.
Closed Mon., mid-Sept.–beg. Dec., May.
Prix fixe: 15€, 25€, 31€,
41€, 9€ (child). A la carte: 45–50€.

The menu of this Savoyard restaurant
housed in the wood décor of an 1852
farmhouse comes straight to the point.
Foie gras escalope served warm with pain

d'épice and sweet-and-sour jus, a scallop
risotto, the duck breast sliced and presented in a fan formation with pain d'épice
sauce and the pears simmered in Dariole
wine with chocolate are tasteful dishes.
South African and Australian wines provide the perfect accompaniment.

CHATELAILLON-PLAGE

17340 Charente-Maritime. Paris 470 –
La Rochelle 16 – Niort 63 – Rochefort 23 –
Surgères 29.
mairiecahtelaillon@office.fr.
A fine Charentes beach not far from La
Rochelle and its softly shaded coast.

 HOTELS-RESTAURANTS

■ Les Trois Iles

At la Falaise.
Tel. 05 46 56 14 14. Fax 05 46 56 23 70.
hrcm3iles@aol.com
Closed Nov., Christmas–New Year's.
79 rooms: 60–117€.
Prix fixe: 22€ (lunch), 45€, 52€.

This vast seaside hotel complex has a swimming pool, tennis court, Jacuzzi, fitness
center, neat, practical rooms and a restaurant serving honest *pension* dishes.

● Le Relais de la Bernache   `COM`

1, rue Félix-Faure.
Tel.-Fax 05 46 56 20 19.
Closed Sun. dinner, Mon., Tue.
Prix fixe: 24€, 36€, 52€, 72€.
A la carte: 55€.

Alain Duprat sets the tone here. The house
foie gras terrine with fig compote, sole filet
with ceps, eel in Bordelaise sauce, beef
filet with morels and the baba dessert with
fresh berries, marmalade and fruit sauce
are well-phrased dishes that bring out the
quality of the produce. An elegant dining
room and pleasant service.

CHATELLERAULT

86100 Vienne. Paris 300 – Châteauroux 100
– Cholet 132 – Poitiers 38 – Tours 70.

The Henri IV bridge, Hôtel Sully and Maison Descartes are three jewels to see in this ancient town.

| | RESTAURANTS |

● La Grillade

In Naintré, 9 km via N10.
Tel. 05 49 90 03 42. Fax 05 49 90 06 75.
contact@lagrillade.com
www.lagrillade.com
Closed Sun. dinner, 2 weeks Aug.
Prix fixe: 16€, 20,50€, 31€, 38,50€,
8€ (child). A la carte: 30–43€.

The Chevrés have no surprises up their sleeves: the grilled meat promised on the sign is very much in evidence, but there is other fare too. In this cottage-style establishment, Jacques, the chef here since 1976, prepares easily enjoyable classics (stuffed escargots, a scallop brochette with beurre blanc sauce, tête de veau with sauce gribiche). The wood-fired rotisserie is much in demand with its rib eye steak grilled in the fireplace. Dessert takes the form of the chef's cold fruit cream in gelatine. The produce comes fresh from the morning market. Annik waits table and recommends a suitable vintage from the list of 120.

CHATENOIS see SELESTAT

CHAUFFAILLES

71170 Saône-et-Loire. Paris 390 – Lyon 81 – Mâcon 64 – Roanne 34 – Charolles 33.
The Brionnais, "Burgundy's Tuscany," is a land of handsome churches and green hills.

| | RESTAURANTS |

In Châteauneuf (71740). 7 km w via D8.

● La Fontaine ○ COM

Au Bourg.
Tel.-Fax 03 85 26 26 87.
Closed Sun. dinner (exc. summer),
Tue. dinner, Wed., 1 week Nov.,
mid-Jan.–beg. Feb.
Prix fixe: 15€ (weekday lunch, wine inc.),

19,50€ (exc. holidays), 25€, 29,50€,
9,60€ (child). A la carte: 45€.

This former weaving mill with its art deco design has been given a new lease on life. Bocuse veteran Yves Jury has turned it into a restaurant serving shrewd dishes. Following Anne Jury's sound advice, we happily savor venison fricassée with asparagus, a monkfish cheek "cushion" with lobster sauce and a pork trotter and cheek dish with oyster mushrooms. In conclusion, licorice crème brûlée with seasonal fruits is very digestible, as is the check.

CHAUMONT-SUR-AIRE

55260 Meuse. Paris 270 – Bar-le-Duc 21 – Saint-Mihiel 25 – Verdun 33.
In a corner of the Meuse on the edge of the Argonne, an unspoiled patch of countryside and its inn.

| ● | RESTAURANTS |

● Auberge du Moulin-Haut COM

Rte de Saint-Mihiel.
Tel. 03 29 70 66 46. Fax 03 29 70 60 75.
auberge@moulinhaut.fr / www.moulinhaut.fr
Closed Sun. dinner, Mon., 1 week Oct.
Prix fixe: 25€, 90€. A la carte: 48–58€.

Marc Imbach prepares dishes rooted in rural tradition, timeless and flavorsome. The proof is in the truffles and foie gras, poached turbot served with a hollandaise sauce, veal kidney fricassée with pan-simmered ceps and a crunchy flambéed mirabelle plum dessert. This 18th-century mill with its low ceilings, exposed beams and large fireplace has charm to spare.

CHAUMONT-SUR-THARONNE

41600 Loir-et-Cher. Paris 168 – Orléans 36 – Blois 53 – Romorantin 32 – Salbris 31.
This authentic Sologne village with its little central square, church, old houses and woods nearby is well worth a visit.

HOTELS-RESTAURANTS

■ La Croix Blanche de Sologne

5, pl de l'Eglise.
Tel. 02 54 88 55 12. Fax 02 54 88 60 40.
www.hotel-sologne.com
Rest. closed Tue. lunch, Wed. lunch,
Thu. lunch, 2 weeks Jan.
15 rooms: 50–105€. 3 suites: 105–145€.
Prix fixe: 30€, 42€, 55€, 12€ (child).
A la carte: 55€.

This inn has had a rich history. It was once home to Gisèle Crouzier, one of the Sologne's most famous *Mères*. Now, Michel-Pierre Goacoulou welcomes his guests with a smile before showing them to their neat, rustic rooms. Françoise Richard watches over the stove, while Christelle Very presents the wine list of 450 bottles. A foie gras tourte, locally-caught lake fish, pike-perch filet with citrus sauce, veal kidneys, Jean-Gabriel Albicocco signature rabbit and the house tart are beautifully crafted. Efficient, pleasant service.

CHAUMOUSEY see EPINAL

CHAUNY

02300 Aisne. Paris 125- Compiègne 40 – Saint-Quentin 30 – Laon 36 – Soissons 33.
On the edge of Compiègne forest, not far from the Oise Valley, a welcoming town in Picardy.

 HOTELS-RESTAURANTS

● La Toque Blanche

24, av Victor-Hugo.
Tel. 03 23 39 98 98. Fax 03 23 52 32 79.
info@toque-blanche.fr / www.toque-blanche.fr
Rest. closed Sat. lunch, Sun. dinner, Mon., Feb. vac., 3 weeks Aug.
6 rooms: 62–88€.
Prix fixe: 33€ (lunch, wine inc.), 44€, 56€, 71€. A la carte: 80€.

Set in well-kept grounds, this twenties villa deserves more than a cursory glance, as Véronique Lequeux's smiling welcome and her husband Vincent's topical cuisine prove. In the art deco setting of the dining room, we spend a happy hour or two with lobster with mango chutney, a roasted filet of turbot with thyme-seasoned vegetable fricassée, the veal "soyeux" with argan oil and a soft-centered chocolate cake with sour cherries.

CHAUVIGNY

86300 Vienne. Paris 335 – Bellac 65 – Châtellerault 32 – Montmorillon 28 – Poitiers 27.
The town heights, the church of Saint-Pierre, the Gouzon keep and the abbey of Saint-Savin nearby offer an idea of the medieval marvels of this delightful corner of Poitou.

 HOTELS-RESTAURANTS

■ Lion d'Or

8, rue du Marché, ville basse.
Tel. 05 49 46 30 28. Fax 05 49 47 74 28.
Closed Christmas–mid-Jan.
26 rooms: 43–58€.
Prix fixe: 18€, 25€, 28€, 38€, 7€ (child).

Down in the lower part of town, this fairly contemporary hotel works its charm. The yellow and green décor is often original (like the ivy trellis ceiling and wrought-iron open work) and is peppered with art deco touches (the chairs). Each rooms is different. Jean-Pierre Thévenet concocts traditional dishes with Provençal leanings. Langoustine ravioli, a rouget with eggplant caviar and duck breast medallions seasoned with pepper slip down smoothly, as does the soft-centered chocolate cake with frozen custard cream. The wine list is extensive.

CHAVOIRES see ANNECY

CHEMILLY-SUR-YONNE see AUXERRE

CHENAS

69840 Rhône. Paris 409 – Mâcon 18 – Lyon 62 – Villefranche-sur-Saône 27.
The name of both a typical Beaujolais village and one of its ten vintages.

RESTAURANTS

● **Les Platanes de Chénas** COM
Les Deschamps.
Tel. 03 85 36 79 80. Fax 03 85 36 78 33.
chgerber@wanadoo.fr
www.platanes-chenas.com
Closed dinner (mid-Nov.–mid-Mar. exc. by
reserv.), Tue. (exc. July–Aug.), Wed. (exc.
July–Aug.), 1 week Christmas–New Year's,
1 week beg. Jan., Feb.
Prix fixe: 24€, 35€, 45€, 58€, 13€ (child).

Exposed beams, polished wooden floors, a
large fireplace and a shady terrace set the
tone in this Beaujolais inn. Setting aside
the memory of his native Alsace, Christian Gerber prepares dependable dishes
here. A French bean salad with salt-cured
foie gras, choice bits of lobster gratin with
bone marrow quenelles, the veal sweetbreads and kidneys with sherry vinegar
and whole grain mustard and a blackcurrant vacherin with the house coulis
are irreproachable.

LE CHENE see APT

CHENEHUTTE-LES-TUFFEAUX see SAUMUR

37150 Indre-et-Loire. Paris 235 – Tours 31
– Amboise 12.
It takes time to tour the château properly and
the village is well worth a visit.

 HOTELS-RESTAURANTS

● **Le Bon Laboureur** ○🏠
6, rue du Dr-Bretonneau.
Tel. 02 47 23 90 02. Fax 02 47 23 82 01.
laboureur@wanadoo.fr
www.bonlaboureur.com
Closed mid-Nov.–mid-Dec.,
beg. Jan.–beg. Feb. Rest. closed Tue. lunch.
20 rooms: 75–145€. 4 suites: 185–225€.
Prix fixe: 29€, 69€. A la carte: 80€.

A stone's throw from the Château des
Dames, this gourmet institution is looking good. Three generations of the Jeudi

family have turned it into a tasteful hostelry with its individual houses, traditional rooms and small yards. In the
kitchen, Antoine prepares subtle, refined,
traditional fare. In the luxurious dining
room opening onto a shady terrace, crayfish cream with basil-seasoned crushed
tomatoes, pan-tossed monkfish seasoned
with coriander seed and lemongrass, veal
sweetbreads liaised with tête de veau and
variations on the chocolate theme strike
a proficient balance between past and
present.

50100 Manche. Paris 355 – Brest 399 –
Le Mans 278 – Rennes 208 – Caen 124.
ot-cherbourgcotentin@wanadoo.fr.
A seawall, a port, a panorama, a stretch of
coast: this is the capital of the Cotentin, point
of departure for an excursion to La Hague and
the Nez de Jobourg. Do not miss the Fort du
Roule and the War and Liberation museum.

 HOTELS-RESTAURANTS

■ **Mercure** 🏠
Ferry terminal, allée du Président-Menut.
Tel. 02 33 44 01 11. Fax 02 33 44 51 00.
h0593@acco.com / www.mercure.com
84 rooms: 82–115€.
Prix fixe: 15€, 24€, 8€ (child).
A la carte: 35€.

By the ferry terminal, this good hotel built
in the seventies provides functional, modern rooms, a snug bar and a reliable nautical restaurant.

● **L'Aigue Marine** 🆕COM
16, quai de Caligny.
Tel. 02 33 23 95 69.
Closed Sat. lunch, Sun., Bank holidays,
Christmas–mid-Jan.
Prix fixe: 17€, 21€, 30€.

The elegant, blonde Nelly Bonhomme in
the dining room and her son Romain Yer-
naux, who learned his trade at the Troquet in Cancale, tend to this harbor eatery
in mauve shades. The tables are smartly

set and the sea's bounty fills our plates, in the form of sardines with tabouli, the coast's oysters served on the half shell, pollock with chitterling sausage and a carrot-seasoned jus and oven-browned sole with salted butter. Pork ribs with barbecue sauce and a thin apple tart served hot are also delightful.

● **Café de Paris** COM

40, quai de Caligny.
Tel. 02 33 43 12 36. Fax 02 33 43 98 49.
cafedeparis.res@wanadoo.fr
www.mangegastronomie.com
Closed Sun. (exc. off season), Mon. lunch (exc. off season), 3 weeks Nov.
Prix fixe: 18€, 21€, 25€, 34,50€.
A la carte: 40€.

This pleasant brasserie with its contemporary décor and tastefully prepared regional cuisine is an address to remember. Citrus-seasoned quick-seared veal sweetbreads, roasted catfish filet, Contentin lamb chops and a Calvados-flambéed apple croustillant make it worth a detour.

● **Le Vauban** COM

22, quai de Caligny.
Tel. 02 33 43 10 11. Fax 02 33 43 15 18.
Closed Sat. lunch, Sun. dinner, Mon., Nov. 1 vac., Feb. vac.
Prix fixe: 22€ (weekdays), 30€, 38€, 58€, 12€ (child).

Daniel Imbert, a native of Berry who has spent time in Alsace and the Marée in Grandcamp, has finally found a berth here on the waterfront, convivially refurbishing the contemporary setting where his wife Murielle welcomes guests so gracefully. The dishes are sparkling, elegant classics. A pressed individual terrine with oxtail and foie gras, olive oil roasted monkfish, fish soup featuring a shellfish broth and the variations on theme of lamb with a sage-infused jus are first-rate. A fruit *verrine* with ginger syrup and also variations on theme of chocolate provide excellent conclusions. The set menus are generous and the wine list highly resourceful.

CHEVAL-BLANC see CAVAILLON

01410 Ain. Paris 507 – Bellegarde-sur-Valserine 17 – Bourg-en-Bresse 80 – Gex 40. In the heart of the Pays de Gex with its mountains and dairies, the tradition of blue-veined cheese is judged a fine art.

 HOTELS-RESTAURANTS

■ **Le Commerce-Blanc** ⌂

Locale known as l'Abbaye.
Tel. 04 50 56 90 67. Fax 04 50 56 92 54.
www.hotelducommerce-blanc.fr
Closed Tue. dinner, Wed. dinner. (exc. school vac.), Oct.–Jan., 1 week Mar.
8 rooms: 42–50€.
Prix fixe: 13€, 35€. A la carte: 35€.

The old-fashioned rooms, polished parquet flooring and a wood oven promise happy hours ahead. At the stove, Catherine Blanc prepares tasteful classics. Hot cooked sausage, trout meunière, free-range chicken and the dessert cart are all splendid.

37500 Indre-et-Loire. Paris 287 – Tours 47 – Poitiers 80 – Châtellerault 51 – Saumur 30. tourisme@chinon.com.
"Chinon, Chinon; small town, great fame, seated on ancient stone; above it, the wood; below, the Vienne." These words are still firmly rooted in reality. With its green, broad-leaved forest, ruined château where the Kings of France once had their court, "Caves Painctes" cellars dear to Rabelais and medieval quarter, it would be hard to find a town more French than this one.

 HOTELS-RESTAURANTS

■ **Hôtel de France** ⌂

47-49, pl du Général-de-Gaulle.
Tel. 02 47 93 33 91 (hotel),
02 47 98 08 08 (rest.). Fax 02 47 98 37 03.
elmachinon@aol.com
www.bestwestern.com/fr/hoteldefrancechinon
30 rooms: 62–100€. 1 suite: 155–180€.
Prix fixe: 20€, 54€. A la carte: 60€.

This tasteful modern hotel with its attractive rooms occupies two 16th-century houses with a view of the town walls. At the Chapeau Rouge restaurant, we enjoy regional dishes that include A mixed fish grill, beef filet Rossini with truffles and a tender pear poached in Chinon.

■ Diderot

4, rue de Buffon / 7, rue Diderot.
Tel. 02 47 93 18 87. Fax 02 47 93 37 10.
hoteldiderot@hoteldiderot.com
www.hoteldiderot.com
Closed 2 weeks Feb.
27 rooms: 41–73€.

An 18th-century residence boasting neat rooms with antique furniture and a breakfast room with a 15th-century fireplace.

● Au Plaisir Gourmand

Quai Charles-VII.
Tel. 02 47 93 20 48. Fax 02 47 93 05 66.
Closed Sun. dinner, Mon., Tue. lunch,
mid-Feb.–mid-Mar.
Prix fixe: 28€, 39€, 49€, 62€, 12€ (child).

Jean-Claude Rigollet, former chef at the Templiers in Les Bézards and the Tortinière in Montbazon, is seconded by his son Jérôme at the stove and Cédric in the dining room. He cultivates a convivial atmosphere and watches over the traditional cuisine of this quality establishment. Touraine escargots, thin slices of monkfish and oxtail braised in Chinon strike just the right note and the soft-centered chocolate cake is splendid. With Loire wines in attendance, we have everything we need in this comfortable restaurant with its precious hangings and finely worked furniture, housed in a 17th-century tufa residence with a flowered courtyard.

● L'Océanic

13, rue Rabelais.
Tel. 02 47 93 44 55. Fax 02 47 93 38 08.
oceanicrestaurant@club-internet.fr
Closed Sun. dinner, Mon.
Prix fixe: 24€, 34€, 65€.

Patrick and Marie-Paule Descoubes' marine restaurant has an easy charm.

Patrick relies greatly on fresh produce and invariably treats it well in return. Proof is in the red tuna served three ways, straight from the islands, skate with Camembert, a monkfish medallion with vanilla-infused butter and the langoustine salad with pan-seared foie gras. Marie-Paule reliably recommends local vintages.

In Marçay (37500). 9 km via D116.

● Château de Marçay

Tel. 02 47 93 03 47. Fax 02 47 93 45 33.
marcay@relaischateaux.fr
www.chateaudemarcay.com
Rest. closed Sun. dinner (off season),
Mon. (off season), Tue. lunch (summer),
mid-Jan.–beg. Mar.
28 rooms: 120–270€. 6 suites: 295€.
Prix fixe: 52€, 68€, 95€.

Also at the Hautes Roches in Vouvray, Philippe Mollard watches over this 15th-century fairytale castle surrounded by trees and vineyards. With its turrets and high tufa facade, it is a tremendously stylish Relais & Châteaux establishment. The neat rooms, antique furniture, dining room in bright colors and heated swimming pool make an excellent impression. In the kitchen, Frédéric Brisset prepares remarkable, sophisticated dishes, such as the bergamot-seasoned roasted langoustines, seared John Dory strips served with a sweet pea shell bouillon, sautéed squab with chanterelle risotto and for dessert, the strawberries served with a rhubarb and anise-seasoned compote. Ideal for a romantic weekend.

65800 Hautes-Pyrénées. Paris 842 –
Lourdes 25 – Pau 55 – Tarbes 10.
A breath of Pyrenean fresh air in the heart of the Tarbes region.

HOTELS-RESTAURANTS

■ Ferme Saint-Ferréol

20, rue des Pyrénées.
Tel. 05 62 36 22 15. Fax 05 62 37 64 96.
contact@ferme-saint-ferreol.com

www.ferme-saint-ferreol.com
Closed 1 week Feb. vac., Nov. 1 vac.,
Sun. dinner (exc. summer). Rest. closed Sat.
lunch (exc. summer), Sun. dinner (exc.
summer), Sat., Sun., (winter exc. by reserv.).
14 rooms: 50–62€. 1 suite: 90€.
Prix fixe: 16€, 19€, 25€, 32€, 39€,
10€ (child). A la carte: 40€.

Deep in the Bigourdane countryside, this
large 18th-century farmhouse flanked
with two square towers has been meticulously renovated by Bernardette Dalat.
Its brightly colored rooms with their
refined décor take us from one country
to another. In the restaurant, regional
cuisine is king, as delightfully evinced
by an oven-crisped pork trotter with
nettle sauce, mountain trout with Tarbais haricots, caramelized suckling pig
with dried fruits and nuts and the dessert assortment.

CHONAS-L'AMBALLAN see VIENNE
CHOREY-LES-BEAUNE see BEAUNE
CIBOURE see SAINT-JEAN-DE-LUZ

CLAIRAC

47320 Lot-et-Garonne. Paris 693 –
Bordeaux 115 – Agen 35 – Tonneins 4.
tourisme@clairac.com.
Located at a natural crossroads between Quercy
and Gascony, Clairac overlooks the Lot, which flows
into the Garonne nearby. The abbey has been turned
into a museum illustrating the lives of the monks,
boatmen, fishermen and winegrowers here.

	RESTAURANTS

● **L'Auberge de Clairac**
12, av du Général-de-Gaulle.
Tel. 05 53 79 22 52. Fax 05 53 94 15 98.
aubergedeclairac@cegetel.net
www.aubergedeclairac.com
Closed Sun. dinner, Wed.,
Christmas–New Year's vac., 2 weeks Mar.
Prix fixe: 20€, 35€, 49€.

They left behind Agen and Los Aucos to
settle in this 19th-century farmhouse,
now an inn. Anne Soisson greets the

guests, while in the kitchen, husband
Jean-Luc prepares his dishes, reliably
based on regional produce. In the hands
of this former oenologist who trained
with Ducasse, a whole foie gras in terrine, a daurade with yarrow-infused
sauce and the Espelette pepper–seasoned duck breast are delicious odes to
nature. For dessert, the apple tourtiere
displays great proficiency.

CLEDEN-CAP-SIZUN

29770 Finistère. Paris 613 – Audierne 10 –
Quimper 47 – Douardenez 28.
This is land's end, between Cap Sizun with its
bird sanctuary, the Pointe du Raz, the Pointe
du Van and the Baie des Trépassés.

●	RESTAURANTS

● **L'Etrave**
Rte de la Pointe-du-Van.
Tel. 02 98 70 66 87.
Closed Tue., Wed., beg. Oct.–beg. Apr.
Prix fixe: 19€, 50€, 8€ (child).
A la carte: 45€.

At the stove in this modern inn with its
bay windows opening wide on land's
end, Breton mother Huguette Le Gall
pays homage to sea produce. Stuffed spider crab, the seaweed-seasoned monkfish in a buckwheat crust and a lobster
presented at the table in its pot are
inducements to settle here. For meat aficionados, the slice of lamb saddle in an
herb crust is a fine cut and the strawberry
croquant dessert slips down unaided.
The ocean view is a bonus. Well-mannered prices.

CLEEBOURG see WISSEMBOURG

CLERMONT-EN-ARGONNE

55120 Meuse. Paris 236 – Bar-le-Duc 47 –
Sainte-Menehould 15 – Verdun 29.
A crossroads village between Champagne and
Lorraine, looking down on the green lands of
Argonne from its heights.

HOTELS-RESTAURANTS

■ **Le Bellevue**
Rue de la Libération.
Tel. 03 29 87 41 02. Fax 03 29 88 46 01.
hotel.bellevue.jpc@wanadoo.fr
Closed Christmas–10 Jan.
Rest. closed Wed.
7 rooms: 48–55€.
Prix fixe: 16€, 26€, 40€, 11€ (child).
A la carte: 40–45€.

Françoise and Jean-Pierre Chodorge offer a warm welcome in their aptly named hostelry. In the blue-tinted art deco dining room and on the terrace with its view of the countryside, escargots in their shells, goat cheese with bacon, grilled pike-perch, veal flavored with Rataifa liqueur and the mirabelle plum cold cream dessert summon us to a rustic feast. The fine modern rooms accommodate affordably.

CLERMONT-FERRAND

63000 Puy-de-Dôme. Paris 424 –
Grenoble 299 – Lyon 171 – Marseille 478 –
St-Etienne 148.
tourisme@clermont-fd.com.
A short walk down the rue Pascal and through the crooked side streets of the center makes it clear that although Clermont lives in the shadow of volcanoes, there is much more to the city than that. Although it served as the setting for Eric Rohmer's movie *Ma nuit chez Maud* (*My Night at Maud's*), it is actually the capital of short features, hosting their international festival once a year. It has a major media library in the modern setting of La Jetée and a center for new music at the Coopérative de Mai. A legendarily understated city, it can also kick up a din at the place de Jaude and display its popular, gourmand side in the place du Marché-Saint-Pierre without losing sight of tradition's guiding light. We are touched by its devotion to the solid fare of yesteryear (which a few souls reinterpret, but not too radically). The promise of a potée or aligot, even a lightened version, brings us hurrying to this corner of France.

HOTELS-RESTAURANTS

■ **Mercure**
82, bd F.-Mitterrand.
Tel. 04 73 34 46 46. Fax 04 73 34 46 36.
h1224@accor.com / www.accorhotels.com
Rest. closed Sat. lunch, Sun. lunch.
122 rooms: 115–200€. 1 suite: 230€.
Prix fixe: 25€, 30€, 34€, 9,50€ (child).

An impressive lobby, smart, practical rooms and a first-rate regional restaurant are the attractions of this central chain hotel standing behind the place de Jaude. A practical bar and interesting seasonal set menus.

■ **Kyriad Prestige**
25, av de la Libération.
Tel. 04 73 93 22 22. Fax 04 73 34 88 66.
accueil@hotel-kyriadprestigeclermont.com
www.hotel-kyriadprestigeclermont.com
Rest. closed Sat., Sun., Bank holidays, 1
week Christmas–New Year's, 2 weeks Aug.
76 rooms: 99–105€. 6 suites: 125–180€.
Prix fixe: 17,50€ (lunch), 19,50€ (lunch),
20,50€, 25€.

This hotel by the Coubertin stadium boasts functional rooms and a restaurant—the Bistro des Congrès—offering flavorsome dishes at modest prices. The grilled Atlantic sea bass with fennel sauce and the rib eye steak with an Auvergnat wine reduction are finely crafted.

■ **Dav'Hôtel Jaude**
10, rue des Minimes.
Tel. 04 73 93 31 49. Fax 04 73 34 38 16.
contact@davhotel.fr / www.davhotel.fr
28 rooms: 40–54€. Half board: 65–79€.

Modern rooms in a dominant blue shade provide practical accommodation at reasonable prices near the central place de Jaude.

■ **Holiday Inn Garden Court**
59, bd F.-Mitterrand.
Tel. 04 73 17 48 48. Fax 04 73 35 58 47.
www.holidayinn-clermont.com
Rest. closed Fri. dinner, Sat., Sun.

94 rooms: 70–162€.
Prix fixe: 14€, 16,50€, 21€, 7€ (child).
A la carte: 35€.

In the heart of the city, this modern hotel has contemporary rooms and a reliable restaurant, the Gergovia (salmon and crab rilettes, Saint-Nectaire cheese tart). A courteous welcome.

■ Des Puys Arverne

16, pl Delille.
Tel. 04 73 91 92 06. Fax 04 73 91 60 25.
contact@hoteldespuys.fr / www.hoteldespuys.fr
47 rooms: 70–112€. 5 suites: 135–145€.

Built in the eighties, this hotel near the center provides colorful, modern rooms.

■ Bordeaux

39, av Franklin-Roosevelt.
Tel. 04 73 37 32 32. Fax 04 73 31 40 56.
www.hoteldebordeaux.com
31 rooms: 42–62€.

Its central location, meticulously kept classic rooms and very gentle prices argue in favor of this small hotel.

In Chamalières (63400).

■ Hôtel Radio

43, av Pierre-et-Marie-Curie.
Tel. 04 73 30 87 83. Fax 04 73 36 42 44.
resa@hotel-radio.fr / www.hotel-radio.fr
Closed 1 week Jan., 1 week Feb.,
1 week May, 2 weeks Oct.
25 rooms: 79–135€.

This thirties hotel still has its art deco style, even in the rooms overlooking the Auvergne Valley. The restaurant is worth a visit (see Restaurants).

In Pérignat-les-Sarlièves (63170). 8 km s via D978.

■ Hostellerie Saint-Martin

Allée de Bonneval, BP 5.
Tel. 04 73 79 81 00. Fax 04 73 79 81 01.
www.hostelleriestmartin.com
Rest. closed Sun. dinner (Nov.–Mar.).
32 rooms: 90–135€. 1 suite: 120–190€.
Prix fixe: 26€, 32€, 44€, 65€.
A la carte: 48€.

In a former 14th-century Cistercian abbey, this hostelry offers appealing rooms combining ancient and modern aspects: a swimming pool, tennis court, Jacuzzi, garden and domestic cuisine in the hands of Jacky Delalande.

● | RESTAURANTS

● Jean-Claude Leclerc

12, rue Saint-Adjutor.
Tel. 04 73 36 46 30. Fax 04 73 31 30 74.
Closed Sat., Sun., Bank holidays,
1 week beg. Jan., 1 week beg. May.
Prix fixe: 35€, 58€, 75€,
25€ (weekday lunch). A la carte: 80–90€.

The former Cavé has been renamed for its chef. This emblematic restaurant in the city center is looking good indeed. Discreet gourmets slip into the light, bright dining room, their mouths watering, to savor Jean-Claude Leclerc's excellent tricks. This native of Touraine who trained at Baumanière, the Centenaire and in Mougins with Vergé prepares a subtle, light cuisine focused on the Auvergne. A delicious cep dish, foie gras–seasoned braised oxtail, a butter-poached yellow pollock with an acidulated jus, the roasted half-pigeon with garden vegetable lasagne and oven-braised cabbage, like the fine chocolate criss-crossed biscuit served with coffee ice cream deserve a round of applause. The fine set menus illustrate Jean-Claude's extensive talents without too much damage to our pocket.

● Emmanuel Hodencq

Pl du Marché-Saint-Pierre.
Tel. 04 73 31 23 23. Fax 04 73 31 36 00.
emmanuelhodencq@wanadoo.fr
www.hodencq.com
Closed Sun., Mon. lunch, 2 weeks Aug.
Prix fixe: 27€ (lunch), 35€, 65€, 98€.
A la carte: 110€.

This contemporary dining room opening onto a flowered terrace directly above the Saint-Pierre market building is an extraordinary place! We succumb to the temptations placed in our way by Emmanuel Hodencq, who trained at the Carlton in Brussels with Alain Passard, then at the Paris Céladon. Everything this shrewd technician serves is the soul of dependability. A pheasant hen consommé served with truffled chestnut cream, a filet of sole served with truffle-seasoned white boudin veal sausage, and a slow roasted rabbit saddle with onions and blood sauce are examples of finesse without fault. The local cheese platter turns our head. The desserts are slightly less remarkable (slow-cooked apricot and a soft-centered chocolate cake), but very good all the same.

● Amphytrion Capucine   N COM
50, rue Fontgièvre.
Tel. 04 73 31 38 39.
Closed Sun., Mon., 3 weeks Aug.
Prix fixe: 20€ (lunch), 25€, 35€, 50€.

Originally from Marseille, Christophe Kovacs (who worked for fifteen years with Prouhèze in Aumont-Aubrac) has opened this fine establishment with its pastel, bucolic boudoir style. Yellow walls, ceilings with bluish beams and tablecloths in yellow and red set the tone in this snug, softly lit haunt. The set menus are well chosen, offering polished, finely crafted fare based on quality produce. Duck foie gras sandwiches, a root vegetable terrine with truffles, cod and pepper tartlettes and the venison with grated tonka beans make an excellent impression. We end delightfully with the "all is chocolate" dessert.

● Pavillon Lamartine   N COM
17, rue Lamartine.
Tel. 04 73 93 52 25. Fax 04 73 93 29 25.
Closed Sun., Mon. dinner,
Christmas–New Year's, 2 weeks Aug.
Prix fixe: 27€, 45€.

Exit Gérard Anglard. The young Julien Bénard and Mathieu Andanson, formerly at the Pavillon Montsouris in Paris, have taken over this large establishment refurbished in a bright, modern style with tables set well apart. Foie gras terrine, the creamy cep soup served an herb-infused whipped cream, grilled cod with rata-

touille cannelloni and a sage-seasoned pork cheek served with mashed potatoes with bacon impress us very favorably. The variations on the theme of chocolate and the thin Tatin-style tart with milk caramel are choice delicacies.

● L'Alambic   COM
6, rue Sainte-Claire.
Tel.-Fax 04 73 36 17 45.
www.restaurant-alambic.com
Closed Sun., Mon. lunch, Wed. lunch, 1 week Feb., 1 week at Easter, mid-July–mid-Aug.
Prix fixe: 24€, 34€, 10€ (child).
A la carte: 36€.

Bruno Pichon commendably champions his region's fare. In the two smart dining rooms in shades of green, we enjoy the solid dishes prepared by Cyril Da Silva. Pounti (a local herb cake with eggs and prunes), a roasted pork trotter sliced thin and served carpaccio-style, salmon trout, aligot (a local potato and fresh young Tomme cheese purée) or the truffade (with the same cheese but oven browned with sliced potatoes) pay tribute to the Auvergne in all its glory. The famous pain perdu and local vintages are on the agenda.

● Le Comptoir des Saveurs   SIM
5, rue Sainte-Claire.
Tel.-Fax 04 73 37 10 31.
Closed Sun., Mon., Feb. vac., Aug.
Prix fixe: 22€ (lunch), 30€, 40€.

Here in Clermont, Philippe Laurent has succeeded in creating what seems rather like a more laid back version of the Atelier de Robuchon. In a contemporary gourmet snack bar setting, twenty-five guests and no more yield to the temptation of the tapas-style dishes. A pupil of Gagnaire and Le Stanc in Nice, Philippe is a maestro of flavorful mouthfuls. Opposite the delicatessen area, we savor a lively, invigorating rabbit, foie gras, and veal sweetbread individual pressed terrine, jumbo shrimp with pasta shells, Atlantic sea bass with slow-cooked fennel, a lamb saddle seasoned with chili peppers and soy sauce and the pan-tossed strawberry and rhubarb dessert, all of which strike just the right note. The service is attentive and the cellar well stocked.

● **Le Pile Poêle**   Ⓝ SIM
9, rue Saint-Dominique.
Tel. 04 73 36 08 88. Fax 04 73 37 69 33.
Closed Sun.
Prix fixe: 11€ (lunch), 17€, 32€.

Odile Nicolas-Driss runs her cheerfully refurbished city center bistro with a smile. We come to taste the dishes of the day chalked up on the blackboard and savor (depending on the "regionalistic" menu) pounti, truffade, a stuffed pork trotter with mustard sauce, the veal sweetbreads with ceps and a slice of calf's liver with parsley and garlic, which do us a power of good. The lunchtime set menu is a splendid bargain.

● **Le Vésuve**   Ⓝ SIM
9, pl des Bughes.
Tel. 04 73 92 36 68.
Closed Sun., Mon., Aug.
A la carte: 22€.

If you know Marseille's king of pizza (Chez Etienne in the Panier district), this pleasant, friendly eatery on the first floor of an innocent-looking building will seem familiar. Etienne Cassaro's daughter Michèle has been supervising the dining room for nearly three decades, enlivening the place with her smile and extolling the open oven–roasted lasagne, sausage and ravioli, shrimp cooked in the-style of Provence, as well as the crisp, aromatic pizzas slid from the oven under the keen eye of her brother Joseph—jewels of the genre in nine versions.

● **Brasserie Danièle Bath**   SIM
Pl du Marché-Saint-Pierre.
Tel. 04 73 31 23 22.
restaurant.bath@wanadoo.fr
Closed Sun., Mon., Bank holidays, Feb. vac.,
2 weeks end Aug.
Prix fixe: 24€. A la carte: 40–60€.

Danièle Bath runs this convivial Saint-Pierre market restaurant with gusto. The setting is friendly, with its bright red shades, patinated woodwork and rough good humored atmosphere, and the dishes are reliable. The pan-seared foie gras with quince eau-de-vie, the cod and potatoes, a veal cutlet with morel mushroom ravioli and the chocolate marquise are simply but surely gratifying.

● **Le Brézou**   SIM
51, rue Saint-Dominique.
Tel. 04 73 93 56 71. Fax 04 73 35 38 30.
Closed Sat., Sun., Aug.
Prix fixe: 15€, 24€.

Marie-Anne Duchet greets her guests with a charming smile before singing the praises of Annie Mazenet's home cooking. Duck foie gras with slow-cooked caramelized onions, pike-perch with beurre blanc sauce, Salers beef with ceps and l'oeuf à la neige are washed down with exquisite wines.

● **Le Caveau**   SIM
9, rue Philippe-Marcombes /
Rue de la Tour-de-la-Monnaie.
Tel. 04 73 14 07 03. Fax 04 73 31 32 44.
Closed Sun., end Oct.–beg. Nov.
A la carte: 40€.

Opposite City Hall, Francis Lalysse's bistro and cellar welcome ravenous carnivores in a relaxed atmosphere. They make short work of the simple, well-crafted dishes: duck rilettes with foie gras, coq au vin, sirloin steak with morels and crème caramel. Cool, exquisite wines.

● **Le Marché de Nathalie**   SIM
4, rue des Petits-Gras.
Tel.-Fax 04 73 19 12 12.
lemarchedenathalie@club-internet.fr
Closed Sun., Wed., 1 week mid-July,
1 week mid-Aug.
Prix fixe: 15€ (lunch), 10€ (child).
A la carte: 40€.

In the heart of the old town, Nathalie Vigier has handed the kitchen over to Jean-René Hoarau and Maria De Jesus, and now tends energetically to the dining room. She still serves an honest market-based cuisine at moderate prices. Escargot cassolette, skate with Saint-Nectaire cheese, flank steak of milk-fed veal and the blueberry or apple crumble are honest dishes.

● **Le Rallye** SIM
2, av de la République.
Tel. 04 73 92 53 78. Fax 04 73 92 49 59.
Closed Sat. lunch, Sun.
A la carte: 25€.

In this corner brasserie, André Tourette, a former butcher, serves fine meats sold by weight. Calf's liver, skirt steak, beef sirloin and rib steak, but also terrine, carpaccio and tartare, flank and leg of lamb, accompanied by good fries or green beans, are gratifying in their simplicity.

In Chamalières (63400).
● **Hôtel Radio** V.COM
43, av Pierre-et-Marie-Curie.
Tel. 04 73 30 87 83. Fax 04 73 36 42 44.
resa@hotel-radio.fr / www.hotel-radio.fr
Closed Sat. lunch, Sun., Mon. lunch, end Oct.–beg. Nov., 3 weeks Jan., end July–beg. Aug.
Prix fixe: 37€ (lunch, wine inc.), 46€, 60€, 90€. A la carte: 85€.

We like this restaurant on the outskirts of the city. The art deco setting, Caroline Mioche's welcome and Frédéric Coursol's deft tricks raise our spirits. Fine produce from the region and further afield provides the basis for shrewd, precise dishes. The lobster and the veal tartare, the poached wild turbot with beurre noisette and the pigeon filet speared with licorice wood tack deftly between tradition and modernity. For dessert, the tube of meringue and wild strawberry tartare is entertaining.

In 63830 Durtol. 3,5 km nw
● **Bernard Andrieux** LUX
Rte de la Baraque.
Tel. 04 73 19 25 00. Fax 04 73 19 25 04.
Closed Sat. lunch, Sun. dinner, Mon., end Dec.–beg. Jan., 1 week May, end June–20 Aug.
Prix fixe: 23€, 45€, 55€, 70€.
A la carte: 70€.

Renamed for its chef and master, the former Auberge des Touristes is enjoying a second youth. Robert Andrieux, who has worked at some great establishments (Thuriès in Cordes, Blanc in Vonnas, Wenger at the Noirmont in Switzerland), has joined his father Bernard, which explains the inn's fresh start. We are pleased to (re)discover such delicately crafted, topical dishes as the peach surprise, Fontaine salmon with a chestnut sauce and a veal sweetbread with coarse ground black pepper served with a morel chutney. To conclude, a slow-simmered cherry croustillant plays on contrasting textures, but with an eye to flavor.

In Orcines (63870). 13 km via rte du Puy-de-Dôme.
● **Le Mont Fraternité** COM
At the summit of the Puy de Dôme.
Tel. 04 73 62 23 00. Fax 04 73 62 10 30.
Closed Mon. (exc. July–Aug.),
beg. Nov.–beg. Apr.
Prix fixe: 30€, 38€, 45€.
A la carte: 45–50€.

Marlène Chaussemy, who studied with the best teachers, sets the tone with her modern cuisine at the peak of the Puy de Dôme. The modern chalet dining room has a view of the volcano range, but our eyes are firmly on our plates: the criss-cross of foie gras and poultry served with a warm almond biscuit, oven-browned pollock filet with beurre noisette and a roasted rack of lamb served in its cooking juice are finely crafted dishes. The restaurant has scheduled a makeover this year.

CHEESEMONGER OF THE YEAR

Fromagerie Nivesse
23, pl Saint-Pierre
Tel. 04 73 31 07 00. Fax 04 73 31 07 10.

Olivier Nivesse is the new cheese star of Clermont: unassailable on Salers, matchless on Saint Nectaire and unbeatable on Cantal. Born in Thiais in the Val de Marne, this 34-year-old started out in the restaurant business. He was head waiter at the Huîtrière in Lille, with Guérard at the Ferme des Grives in Eugénie and with Bernard Andrieux at the Touristes in Durtol. After training with the two great cheesemongers of Southwest France (Xavier in Toulouse and Bachelet in Pau), he decided to go it alone in Clermont, directly opposite the Saint-Pierre market that has its share of good cheesemongers. Provocation? Hardly. This apt pupil, who chose the Auvergne out of a love for the region, is assiduous indeed. His store is not much to look at from the outside and the characterless, modern interior is little better. However, everything on display is of the highest farmhouse quality. The Bethmale d'Ariège, Crayeux de Roncq from Pas de Calais, Pont-l'Evêque from Spruitte in Saint-Philbert-des-Champs are simply a credit to rural France. Add a choice of wines from every region, with special favorites from Languedoc, Loire and Alsace to taste on the premises, and this cheesemonger and wine merchant turns out to be an Ali Baba of new Auvergne gastronomy.

CLIMBACH

67510 Bas-Rhin. Paris 474 – Strasbourg 63 – Bitche 38 – Haguenau 30 – Wissembourg 9.
A crossroads community on the border of the Palatinate, at a meeting of ways that run through the forest village of Wingen and the Col du Pigeonnier to the lost trails of the Northern Vosges.

| ■/● | HOTELS-RESTAURANTS |

■ Le Cheval Blanc
2, rue de Bitche.
Tel. 03 88 94 41 95. Fax 03 88 94 21 96.
Closed Sun. dinner (mid-Nov.–mid-Mar.), Tue. dinner, Wed., mid-Jan.–mid-Feb., 1 week July.
12 rooms: 45–51€.
Prix fixe: 15,50€, 25€, 36€, 8,50€ (child).

The Freys' charming family inn has discreetly changed hands. We are planning a quick visit to find out more. The last we heard was that both the neat rooms with their modern furniture and the Alsace cuisine were looking good.

CLISSON

44190 Loire-Atlantique. Paris 384 – Nantes 29 – Niort 129 – Poitiers 150 – La Roche-sur-Yon 54.
ot@clisson.com.
Views of the château and the banks of the Sèvre Nantaise paint a cloudless portrait of French *dolce vita*.

| ● | RESTAURANTS |

● Bonne Auberge
1, rue Olivier-de-Clisson.
Tel. 02 40 54 01 90. Fax 02 40 54 08 48.
labonneauberge2@wanadoo.fr
Closed Sun. dinner, Mon., Tue. lunch, Christmas, New Year's, 2 weeks end Feb., mid-Aug.–end Aug.
Prix fixe: 18,50€ (weekday lunch), 23€ (weekday lunch), 37€ (dinner), 58€ (dinner), 12€ (child). A la carte: 75€.

Serge and Chantal Poiron's village establishment has three elegant dining rooms refurbished in lively shades. They provide a suitable setting for the distinctive cuisine, based on exceptionally fresh produce. Lobster mille-feuille, Atlantc sea bass filet with asparagus, veal medallion and sweetbreads with chanterelles, frozen Grand Marnier soufflé with vanilla ice cream form a tasteful, classic menu. The weekday set menus are a bargain.

● La Gétignière `COM`
In 44190 Gétigné. 3 km se via N149.
3, rue de la Navette.
Tel. 02 40 36 05 37. Fax 02 40 54 24 76.
Closed Sun. dinner, Mon., Tue. dinner, 2 weeks Christmas–New Year's, 3 weeks Aug.
Prix fixe: 19€, 26€ (wine inc.), 32€, 35€, 11€ (child). A la carte: 55€.

Jacky and Véronique Renard's vintage, Provençal-style inn with its garden terrace serves a market-based cuisine. A thin sardine and tomato tart, sea bream baked in a salt crust, duck breast strips with mushrooms and the soft-centered chocolate cake with vanilla ice cream are flawless, classic dishes. The wine list includes some fine discoveries.

CLOUANGE see AMNEVILLE

28220 Eure-et-Loir. Paris 143 – Orléans 64 – Blois 55 – Chartres 56 – Châteaudun 12.
The gentle banks of the Loir and an ancient village on the pilgrims' road to Santiago de Compostela.

 HOTELS-RESTAURANTS

■ **Le Saint-Jacques**
Pl du Marché-aux-Œufs.
Tel. 02 37 98 40 08. Fax 02 37 98 32 63.
info@lesaintjacques.fr / www.lesaintjacques.fr
Closed 3 weeks end Feb.–mid-Mar.
Rest. closed Sun. dinner, Mon. lunch.
19 rooms: 65–145€. 1 suite: 160€.
Prix fixe: 18€, 33€, 13€ (child).
A la carte: 45–60€.

This former post house run by the Paulets is worth a visit. The partially renovated rooms go well with the carefully crafted dishes. Stéphane prepares his topical fare with a sure, precise touch. Pan-seared scallops, ginger-seasoned mango and papaya salad, pan-tossed langoustines with creamy risotto and a parmesan biscuit, roasted rabbit saddle with honey and rosemary caramelized carrots and rum-flambéed banana with vanilla ice cream and orange sauce are delightfully exotic. The P'tit Bistro serves simpler dishes at gentler prices.

71250 Saône-et-Loire. Paris 384 – Mâcon 26 – Tournus 33.
cluny@wanadoo.fr.
Well worth a detour with its fine old abbey and adjacent national stud farm.

 HOTELS-RESTAURANTS

■ **Hôtel de Bourgogne**
Pl de l'Abbaye.
Tel. 03 85 59 00 58. Fax 03 85 59 03 73.
contact@hotel-cluny.com
www.hotel-cluny.com
Rest. closed Tue., Wed., beg. Dec.–end Jan.
14 rooms: 80–94€. 2 suites: 150€.
Prix fixe: 24€, 41€, 9,50€ (child).
A la carte: 45–60€.

Michel Colin keeps a close eye on this hostelry opposite the Benedictine abbey. The rooms furnished in Empire style, boudoir and dining room with fireplace and high ceiling are full of character. In the restaurant with its pastel tones, we enjoy the escargots in puff pastry, cod with slow-cooked caramelized shallots, duckling with sour cherries and the chocolate feuille à feuille.

74220 Haute-Savoie. Paris 568 – Annecy 33 – Chamonix 63 – Albertville 38.
infos@aclusaz.com.
This exquisite mountain village at a height of a thousand meters offers open air activities in any season. Cordiality and local color are its pleasant characteristics.

 HOTELS-RESTAURANTS

■ **Les Chalets de la Serraz**
3862 Rte du Col-des-Aravis.
Tel. 04 50 02 48 29. Fax 04 50 02 64 12.
contact@laserraz.com / www.laserraz.com
Closed Oct., May. Rest. closed lunch
10 rooms: 100–165€.
Prix fixe: 38€ (dinner). A la carte: 50€.

This hotel village consisting of Alpine chalets and a converted sheepfold offers a swimming pool, spa tub, steam bath, gardens and mountain rooms with a view of the surrounding peaks. In the dining room, the Beaufort terrine with AOC Grisons beef, a lemongrass-seasoned monkfish medallion, sirloin steak with mushroom sauce and the dessert cart are fit for purpose.

COARAZE

06390 Alpes-Maritimes. Paris 953 – Nice 23 – Sospel 32.
"A village in the sun," says a sign lost in a huddle of olive trees, but who could miss the sundials on the ancient walls?

 HOTELS-RESTAURANTS

■ Auberge du Soleil
5, camin de la Beguda.
Tel. 04 93 79 08 11. Fax 04 93 79 37 79.
auberge.du.soleil@wanadoo.fr
www.notreaubergedusoleil.com
Closed Nov.–mid-Feb.
8 rooms: 56–84€.
Prix fixe: 23€. A la carte: 30€.

At Yvonne Jacquet's, the welcome is as sunny as the smart rooms. The blue dining room presents discreet dishes for our approval. When the sun shines, we savor a warm jumbo shrimp salad, the salt cod and potato purée, Provençal-style daube, the macaronade (a Provençal specialty with macaroni), herb-seasoned sausage and tomato and the frozen honey nougat with berry coulis on the terrace looking out on the Paillon river.

COCURES see FLORAC

COGNAC

16100 Charente. Paris 480 – Angoulême 43 – Bordeaux 120 – Niort 82 – Saintes 26.
office@tourisme-Cognac.com.
The venerable storehouses, François I park, twists of the Charente, old alleys and "angel's share" of evaporated brandy fumes that black-ens the houses all paint the picture of a certain French *dolce vita*.

 HOTELS-RESTAURANTS

■ Domaine du Breuil
104, rue Robert-Daugas.
Tel. 05 45 35 32 06. Fax 05 45 35 48 06.
info@domaine-du-breuil.com
www.domaine-du-breuil.com
Closed 20 Dec.–10 Jan.
Rest. closed Sat. lunch, Mon. lunch.
24 rooms: 56–95€.
Prix fixe: 20€ (lunch), 29€, 45€,
14€ (child). A la carte: 45€.

With its extensive wooded grounds, swimming pool, fitness center, cozy lounges and old-fashioned rooms, this 19th-century manor is a quality setting. We savor a duck foie gras terrine, a roasted rockfish served on a saffron-seasoned risotto, and rack of lamb in its jus, served with parmesan gnocchi in a luxurious circular dining room.

■ Les Pigeons Blancs
110, rue J.-Brisson.
Tel. 05 45 82 16 36. Fax 05 45 82 29 29.
www.pigeons-blancs.com
Rest. closed Sun. dinner, Mon. lunch.
6 rooms: 55–105€.
Prix fixe: 22€ (weekdays), 32€.
A la carte: 50–70€.

We are always delighted to stop off at the Tachet family's 17th-century post house, jointly run by Jean-Michel and Catherine, brother and sister. We eagerly sit down to lobster cake with flambéed langoustines, roasted Atlantic sea bass with pancetta, the venison with juniper berries and the traditional thirteen dessert cart served in the comfortable dining room or on the terrace in summer. A fine wine list from the region and further afield.

In Châteaubernard (16100). Via N141. D15, quartier l'Echassier.

■ Château de l'Yeuse
65, rue de Bellevue.
Tel. 05 45 36 82 60. Fax 05 45 35 06 32.

chateauyeuse@wanadoo.fr / www.yeuse.fr
Closed Jan.
Rest. closed Sat. lunch, Sun. dinner.
21 rooms: 95–162€. 3 suites: 211–323€.
Prix fixe: 27€ (lunch), 47€, 67€.
A la carte: 72€.

Overlooking the Charente Valley, this 19th-century manor provides rooms furnished in an antique style, a fitness center with steam bath, swimming pool and Jacuzzi and a dining room with a pleasant terrace where we enjoy a foie gras crème brûlée, the roasted lobster with vanilla oil–seasoned artichokes and a veal cutlet with morels and French-style sweet peas. Before moving on to the "Cognac and Cigar" lounge, we succumb to the entices of a the traditional Cognac or Grand Marnier soufflé served hot.

COGOLIN

83310 Var. Paris 684 – Fréjus 33 – Sainte-Maxime 13 – Saint-Tropez 9 – Toulon 60.
info@cogolin-provence.com.
A stone's throw from the most prized peninsula on the coast, this village famous for its pipes boasts the added attraction of a fine, unspoiled Provençal spirit.

 HOTELS-RESTAURANTS

■ La Maison du Monde

63, rue Carnot.
Tel. 04 94 54 77 54. Fax 04 94 54 77 55.
www.lamaisondumonde.fr
Closed , mid-Nov.–mid-Dec.,
beg. Jan.–beg. Feb., end Feb.–end Mar.
12 rooms: 70–165€.

By a wooded garden, this comfortable residence with its refined rooms, exotic furniture and delightful welcome exerts an easy charm.

● Grain de Sel   SIM

6, rue du 11-novembre.
Tel. 04 94 54 46 86.
phianne2@wanadoo.fr
www.restaurant-cogolin.com
Closed Sun., Mon., Feb. vac.

Prix fixe: 31€.
A la carte: 40–45€.

Nice-style petits farcis (stuffed vegetables), peppers in anchoïade (a local anchovy spread), fish in bouillabaisse jus, Corrèze veal with preserved lemons and sautéed fruits with licorice ice cream are deftly prepared by Philippe Audibert. All are flavorsome, well-phrased and unfussy, served with warmth according to the fiat of the blackboard in this charming bistro.

LA COLLE-SUR-LOUP

06480 Alpes-Maritimes. Paris 924 – Nice 19 – Antibes 15 – Cannes 25 – Grasse 19 – Vence 8.
The Nice hinterland, the road to Vence and Saint-Paul and homes of greater or lesser charm lending a new form to the scenery.

 RESTAURANTS

● Le Blanc Manger   SIM

1260, rte de Cagnes, quartier Grange Rimade.
Tel. 04 93 22 51 20. Fax 04 92 02 00 46.
leblancmanger@wanadoo.fr
Closed Mon. (exc. July–Aug.), Tue.,
2 weeks beg. Dec.
Prix fixe: 35€. A la carte: 25–35€.

Brigitte Guignery proficiently runs her rustic establishment in orange shades, where wrought-iron and rattan set the tone, presenting set menus of well-crafted dishes. The rouget cooked in virgin olive oil, the hot foie and beef cheek duo and the pear mille-feuille are fine examples.

COLLIAS see PONT-DU-GARD

COLLIOURE

66190 Pyrénées-Orientales.
Paris 890 – Perpignan 30 – Céret 35 – Port-Vendres 2.
collioure@littlefrance.com.
A Catalan Saint-Tropez? Possibly in more modest form, but above all a cradle of art set on the edge of the Big Blue, an authentic harbor that

could have been drawn by Derain, dreamt by
Matisse or visualized by the Fauvists.

 HOTELS-RESTAURANTS

■ Relais des Trois Mas et la Balette

Rte Port-Vendres.
Tel. 04 68 82 05 07. Fax 04 68 82 38 08.
Closed end Nov.–end Jan. Rest. closed
Tue. (off season), Wed. (off season).
19 rooms: 95–150€. 4 suites: 330–450€.
Prix fixe: 35€, 56€, 73€.

This orange pink hostelry clinging to the
rock by village and harbor is Collioure's
delight. The sea is like a backdrop. The
rooms—even the smaller ones—are
charming and the suites enchanting with
their balconies. The cuisine prepared
by Carcassonne's José Vinal, who once
trained on the Côte d'Azur at the Martinez and at the Château Saint-Martin, is
highly appealing in a modernized local
manner. On the terrace by the beach or in
the fine panoramic dining room, we savor
a wreath of anchovies with Banyuls vinegar served over slow-cooked onion and
pepper compote, bowls of picolat (veal
and seaoned pork meatballs) with piquillo
peppers and escalivade (a Catalan roasted
summer vegetable dish) or the thin-sliced
cod with tapenade oil. The anise-flavored
hazelnut rousquilles (sugar-coated ring-
shaped cookies, a local specialty) with
almond pistachio ice cream and a licorice lace biscuit are a rare treat.

■ Casa Païral

Impasse des Palmiers.
Tel. 04 68 82 05 81. Fax 04 68 82 52 10.
www.hotel-casa-pairal.com
Closed Nov. 1–Easter.
27 rooms: 80–182€.

A lush green patio lulled by the whisper of a fountain, air conditioned rooms,
a swimming pool and snug lounges are
among the many charms of this central
19th-century establishment expertly run
by Jacqueline Lormand and Alix Guiot.

■ L'Arapède

Rte de Port-Vendres.
Tel. 04 68 98 09 59. Fax 04 68 98 30 90.
hotelarapede@yahoo.fr / www.arapede.com
Closed end Nov.–beg. Feb.
Rest. closed lunch (exc. weekends).
19 rooms: 53–138€. 1 suite: 88–158€.
Prix fixe: 18€, 25€, 34€. A la carte: 50€.

Thiebaut Le Sage's Southern French cuisine is imaginative—possibly a little too
much so. Mussels with squid ink–colored
ravioli drizzled with curry sauce, with typical Catalan stuffing and served on a saffron-seasoned seafood foam, the whole
topped with a mussel brochette, set the
tone. Then there are monkfish served
on pan-simmered feves, rump steak
napped with a reduced sauce seasoned
with Banyuls and an organically farmed
suckling pig served with tender potato
cakes. The crème catalane, served with
a quenelle of Marc-flavored sorbet provides a fine conclusion. Swimming pool,
terrace and rooms with painted wooden
furniture and a sea view ensure our well-
deserved rest and relaxation.

■ Les Templiers

12, quai de l'Amirauté.
Tel. 04 68 98 31 10. Fax 04 68 98 01 24.
www.hotel-templiers.com
Closed Jan. Rest. closed Tue. (off season),
Wed. (off season).
24 rooms: 41–80€.
Prix fixe: 22€, 9,50€ (child).
A la carte: 40–45€.

Picasso, Matisse and Derain were regular
visitors to this establishment in old Collioure. Now Manée Pous has taken up the
reins of the hostelry with its brightly colored rooms. In the white dining room, we
make short work of Daniel André's dishes:
assorted fried fish, bouillabaisse, slow-
roasted lamb with sweet garlic and crème
catalane slip down without a hitch.

● Le Neptune

9, rte de Port-Vendres.
Tel. 04 68 82 02 27. Fax 04 68 82 50 33.
fmourlane@yahoo.fr
Closed Tue., Wed., 10 days Dec., Jan.

Prix fixe: 30€ (lunch), 49,50€, 66€, 79€.
A la carte: 85€.

The fabulous sea view from the terrace opposite the bar and the meticulous interior décor in pastel tones have their charm, but the gourmet clientele comes to taste the fare served up by the colorful Jean-Claude Mourlane, a wandering native of Toulouse who has spent time in England and Germany, and is seconded here by the young Frédéric Baquié, formerly at the Almandin and Coutanceau in La Rochelle. The lightly fried camerone (a large shrimp) paired with internationally inspired condiments, oven-browned monkfish medallions with a light saffron jus and the Aveyron lamb prepared two ways, the chop grilled with zucchini blossoms, the medallions steamed with pesto, are great delicacies. The warm Burlat cherry gratin sautéed with Collioure wine and the Saint Honoré cake with cherries, sorbet and a pistachio mousse will sweep you off your feet. A fine list of wines from Roussillon and elsewhere presented by Stéphane, Jean-Claude's son.

COLLONGES-AU-MONT-D'OR see LYON

COLMAR

68000 Haut-Rhin. Paris 447 – Strasbourg 73 – Bâle 68 – Fribourg 51 – Nancy 142.
info@ot-colmar.fr.
With its fine chefs throughout the surrounding winegrowing district, restaurants in the town itself, pleasant stores and appealing market, Colmar welcomes visitors with a smile. As its reputation dictates, "the most Alsatian of Alsace towns"—proud of the illuminations that shift and change as we stroll, its Unterlinden museum and the canals of its Little Venice—remains faithful to the postcards by "Hansi," Jean-Jacques Waltz, the town's native portraitist. When we visit Colmar, we look upwards and count the picture book signs he painted before we sit down to eat at the Rendez-Vous de Chasse, JY's, the Neuland, Brenner's or the Maison des Têtes.

■ HOTELS

■ Hôtel les Têtes
19, rue des Têtes.
Tel. 03 89 24 43 43. Fax 03 89 24 58 34.
les-tetes@calixo.net / www.maisondestetes.com
Closed Feb.
17 rooms: 91–175€.
3 suites: 209–245€.

This hotel owes its name to the hundreds of sculpted heads decorating its facade. Dating back to 1609, it has an enchanting interior courtyard. The passages that lead to its typically Alsatian rooms were decorated by a local artist. In the dining room, we are charmed by the regional specialties (see Restaurants: La Maison des Têtes).

■ Le Colombier
7, rue Turenne.
Tel. 03 89 23 96 00. Fax 03 89 23 97 27.
www.hotel-le-colombier.fr
Closed Christmas vac.
28 rooms: 70–190€. 3 suites: 150–190€.

The décor here successfully reconciles the Renaissance components of this 15th-century establishment with the contemporary, neo-art nouveau furniture that equips the rooms. The bar is delightfully relaxing and the welcome wonderfully attentive.

■ Grand Hôtel Bristol
7, pl de la Gare.
Tel. 03 89 41 10 10 / 03 89 23 59 59.
Fax 03 89 23 92 26.
www.grand-hotel-bristol.com
92 rooms: 65–145€. 15 suites: 99–145€.
Half board: 85–185€.

The rail station just opposite was built in 1900, like the hotel. Inside, the comfortable rooms are undergoing renovation. The brasserie is popular, the restaurant renowned and the welcome highly professional. (See Restaurants: L'Auberge and Le Rendez-Vous de Chasse.)

■ **Mercure Champ-de-Mars** ⌂

2, av de la Marne.
Tel. 03 89 21 59 59. Fax 03 89 21 59 00.
h1225@accor-hotels.com / www.mercure.com
75 rooms: 107–127€.

A park provides the setting for this seventies chain hotel with all the functional aspects provided by establishments of that period.

■ **Le Maréchal** ⌂

4, pl des Six-Montagnes-Noires.
Tel. 03 89 41 60 32. Fax 03 89 24 59 40.
www.hotel-le-marechal.com
28 rooms: 80–215€. 2 suites: 245€.
Prix fixe: 35€, 55€, 75€, 11€ (child).
A la carte: 70€.

These 16th- and 17th-century Alsatian houses with their view of the Lauch form a delightful hotel complex run by Romantik Hotels. The old-fashioned rooms look out on the canal and the regional cuisine is up to the same high standard in the Echevin restaurant with its smart terrace.

■ **L'Amiral** ⌂

11b, bd du Champ-de-Mars.
Tel. 03 89 23 26 25. Fax 03 89 23 83 64.
www.hotel-amiral-colmar.com
47 rooms: 49–95€. 1 suite: 110€.

This former malting plant opposite a park in the town center provides modern rooms in warm tones, a fitness center and WiFi, as well as a snug bar.

■ **Mercure-Unterlinden** ⌂

15, rue Golbery.
Tel. 03 89 41 71 71. Fax 03 89 23 82 71.
h0978@accor-hotels.com / www.mercure.com
76 rooms: 97–107€. 4 suites: 135€.

The main attraction here is the immediate proximity of the Unterlinden museum and a shopping mall. A professional welcome, smiling service, modern rooms and a wine bar with a hushed ambiance.

■ **Novotel** ⌂

At the airdrome, 49, rte de Strasbourg.
Tel. 03 89 41 49 14. Fax 03 89 41 22 56.

h0416@accor.com / www.novotel.com
66 rooms: 78–107€.
Prix fixe: 15€, 8€ (child).

This chain hotel built in the seventies is still a headquarters for business visitors. The rooms are functional, the swimming pool and garden pleasant places to relax and the cuisine honest.

■ **Saint-Martin** ⌂

38, Grand'Rue.
Tel. 03 89 24 11 51. Fax 03 89 23 47 78.
colmar@hotel-saint-martin.com
www.hotel-saint-martin.com
Closed beg. Jan.–beg. Mar.
40 rooms: 89–129€. 2 suites: 149€.

The Louis XVI facade, turret, Renaissance stairway, meticulously decorated rooms and warm welcome have an immediate appeal. A charming address to remember.

■ **Le Turenne** ⌂

10, rte de Bâle.
Tel. 03 89 21 58 58. Fax 03 89 41 27 64.
turennecol@aol.com / www.turenne.com
82 rooms: 47–68€.

Not far from "Little Venice", this half-timbered hotel with a very Alsatian touch is an agreeable place to stay.

In Horbourg-Wihr (68180). 3 km e

■ **L'Europe** ❀ ⌂

15, rte de Neuf-Brisach.
Tel. 03 89 20 54 00. Fax 03 89 41 27 50.
reservation@hotel-europe-colmar.fr
www.hotel-europe-colmar.com
111 rooms: 125–156€. 10 suites: 168–700€.
Prix fixe: 25€, 64€. A la carte: 45€.

This vast hotel complex with its imposing neo-Alsatian architecture and spacious, comfortable rooms offers a range of facilities (swimming pools, tennis court, meeting rooms). The Jardin d'Hiver serves local dishes and the Eden a more sophisticated cuisine. Duck foie gras with fig chutney, pike-perch medallions with Pinot Noir sauce served on a bed of sauerkraut, organic steak tartare with tomato, white wine, Cognac and butter sauce are splendid.

In Sainte-Croix-en-Plaine (68420). 10 km se via N422 and D1.

■ Le Moulin

Rte d'Herrlisheim.
Tel. 03 89 49 31 20. Fax 03 89 49 23 11.
www.aumoulin.net
Closed beg. Nov.–31 Mar.
Rest. closed lunch, Sun.
17 rooms: 45–70€.
A la carte: 40€.

A stone's throw from the town, this old mill lost in the countryside offers large rooms at bargain prices, some of them renovated this year. Its little museum of rural items and regional restaurant serving residents only are first-rate.

●   RESTAURANTS

● Le Rendez-Vous de Chasse

At Grand Hôtel Bristol, 7, pl de la Gare.
Tel. 03 89 23 15 86. Fax 03 89 23 92 26.
reservation@grand-hotel-bristol.com
www.grand-hotel-bristol.com
Prix fixe: 42€, 69€, 80€. A la carte: 85€.

A native of Westphalia in Germany who trained at the Armes de France, Valet de Coeur and Auberge de l'Ill, Michaela Peters presides over the kitchens of this institution with its luxurious décor, tables set well apart, elite staff and splendid wine list. The boss, Richard Riehm, has an eye to every detail, but even so, little Michaela has successfully imposed her style and marked her territory. Her lightly Alsatian manner is subtle and free of frills and frontiers. We like the foie gras degustation, the sautéed frog legs with chanterelles or the tender veal roast ("Cousin" Michaela's Alsace is a trove of energy and charm). There follow the fish prepared with finesse (a cod filet served with herb-seasoned jumbo shrimp or the monkfish medallions stuffed with truffles and served with spaghettini and arugula) and the game in season (sautéed venison medallions

with a delicate cherry sauce). References to local culture, which we felt were lacking here two years ago, now feature on the changing menu, even among the fine desserts, which include the splendid Alsatian-style plums in Pinot Noir with pain perdu ice cream.

● La Maison des Têtes

At Hôtel les Têtes, 19, rue des Têtes.
Tel. 03 89 24 43 43. Fax 03 89 24 58 34.
les-tetes@calixo.net
www.maisondestetes.com
Closed Sun. dinner, Mon., Tue. lunch,
Feb. vac.
Prix fixe: 65€, 12,50€ (child).
A la carte: 60–65€.

Behind the 105 sculpted heads that grace the facade of this fine Renaissance residence lies a dining room of character where Marc Rohfritsch enthralls his audience with tasteful classical dishes. Riesling-seasoned goose foie gras, frog legs in a parsley cream sauce, sea bream roasted skin-side down with braised fennel and a balsamic vinegar jus, roasted pigeon breast with potatoes slow-roasted in goose fat or a crème brûlée with brown sugar perfumed with Marc de Gewurz are a keen tribute to regional tradition. The remarkable Carmen's service is spirited and there are 150 fine wines to discover. (See Hotels.)

● JY'S

17, rue de la Poissonnerie.
Tel. 03 89 21 53 60. Fax 03 89 21 53 65.
www.jean-yves-schillinger.com
Closed Sun., Mon., mid-Feb.–beg. Mar.
Prix fixe: 29€ (lunch), 49€, 67€.

In the heart of the "Little Venice" district, Jean-Yves Schillinger's restaurant stuns and startles. Behind the facade decorated with a neo-Gothic fresco by Edgar Mahler, the cuisine in the contemporary dining room designed by Olivier Gagnère is apposite indeed. Jean-Yves plays on contrasting textures and flavors with never a slip. Ginger-marinated red tuna tartare, the steamed scallops and shrimp, roasted pigeon breast served with ceps and an aligot wine foam and the cherry gazpacho and caramelized pistachios over an orange sablé cookie conjure up visions of distant climes and set heads spinning.

● L'Arpège COM
24, rue des Marchands.
Tel. 03 89 23 37 89. Fax 03 89 23 39 22.
restaurant.arpege@wanadoo.fr.
Prix fixe: 27€, 32€, 52€, 10€ (child).
A la carte: 50–55€.

Patrice Kayser concocts succulent dishes that reflect both his inspiration and especially the changing produce available at the market. Potato gratin with foie gras, scallops with orange, coriander and olive oil, milk-fed veal chops simmered with garlic and preserved lemons or the Alsatian squab with cumin-infused carrot jus and pain d'épice tiramisu with salted-butter caramel ice cream are proof that this fine technician (who trained here with Alberto Bradi) has not lost his touch.

● Bartholdi COM
2, rue des Boulangers.
Tel. 03 89 41 07 74. Fax 03 89 41 14 65.
restaurant.bartholdi@wanadoo.fr
Closed Sun. dinner, Mon.,
end Jan.–beg. Feb., 2 weeks June–July.
Prix fixe: 18,50€, 21€, 49€.
A la carte: 40–50€.

Roland and Thierry Foit tend with gusto to the dining room in this gourmet brasserie, and Bernard Schwartz's reliable bistro fare is up to the same high standard. Washed down with wines produced by the place's owners—including the rosy cheeked Jacky Cattin—the goose and duck foie gras, duck breast in salad, pike-perch braised in red wine, tête de veau served with vinaigrette and a frozen meringue dessert with whipped cream fail to disappoint.

● Meistermann COM
2a, av de la République.
Tel. 03 89 41 65 64. Fax 03 89 41 37 50.
info@meistermann.com
www.meistermann.com
Closed Sun. dinner, Mon., Feb. vac.

Prix fixe: 17€.
A la carte: 40–45€.

Gino Di Foggia breathes life into this central brasserie with her singsong accent, while Jean Vandredeuille cooks judiciously. Chicken oysters and foie gras over mixed greens, pike-perch filet over choucroute with a smoked bacon cream sauce, the famous choucroute garnished with five meat cuts and the pears caramelized with licorice charm the gourmand clientele here.

● Aux Trois Poissons COM
15, quai de la Poissonnerie.
Tel.-Fax 03 89 41 25 21.
Closed Sun. dinner, Tue. dinner, Wed.,
Nov. 1 vac., 1 week Christmas–New Year's,
2 weeks July.
Prix fixe: 21€, 27€, 45€, 8€ (child).
A la carte: 55€.

After training in England, Gilles Seiler eagerly took up the reins of his father Jean's establishment. On a bank of the Lauch, he focuses on both land and sea produce with equal attention to detail. Pan-seared foie gras served over an autumn salad, catfish filet with crisp vegetables in an herb-seasoned butter, pike-perch served over a bed of sauerkraut with a beurre blanc sauce and the honey and Sichuan peppercorn–seasoned duck make an excellent impression before we move on to the ritual kouglof glacé.

● Auberge du Neuland Ⓝ 🍽 SIM
2, chemin du Neuland.
Tel. 03 89 23 49 37. Fax 03 89 41 56 95.
Closed Tue. dinner, Wed.,
Thu. dinner (Nov.–Easter).
Prix fixe: 8,40€ (lunch), 11,50€ (lunch),
19€. A la carte: 30€.

Lost in the countryside, this modern establishment, unremarkable in appearance, is worth a detour. Muriel Jamm, a lively blonde, elegantly attends to the guests, while her husband Joël concocts lively, well-crafted dishes. This fine technician (who trained at the Chambard in Kaysersberg, then the Schoenenbourg in

Riquewhir) has chosen a studiedly modest style here. Escargots in their parsley and garlic butter, wild boar terrine served with a quince purée, fried carp with an onion, herb, caper and mustard mayonnaise, tête de veau served with a cocotte of sautéed potatoes, puff pastry with blood pudding and apples (fleischkiechke) almost eat themselves. The prices are affable, the desserts blameless (kouglof glacé and a charlotte made with pain d'épice) and the local wines well chosen.

● **Jules**   Ⓝ🍴SIM

5, rue Conseil-Souverain.
Tel. 03 89 24 42 21.
Closed Sun., Mon., 2 weeks Nov.
Prix fixe: 18€ (lunch), 28€, 36€.

In the shadow of the Koifhus, this is a restaurant to try. Julien Spiegel made quite a career for himself (Schillinger, Haeberlin, Bocuse, Dutournier, Savoy and the Elysée) before opening this refined establishment. The harmony of the décor, where rusty steel melts into subtle off-white shades, offers a charming contrast. The innovative cuisine takes the form of shrewd set menus. A foie gras Tatin, sea bream with a ginger seasoned cannelloni, pike-perch cooked skin-side down with cabbage and cumin, yakitori-style duck brochettes and variations on theme of strawberry (cappuccino, marinated in balsamic vinegar and sorbet) are well crafted. The service is smooth and the genuine mastery of produce and deft touch are surprising.

● **Wistub Brenner**   🍴SIM

1, rue Turenne.
Tel. 03 89 41 42 33. Fax 03 89 41 37 99.
Closed Tue., Wed., 1 week Nov., Christmas–
New Year's, 2 weeks Feb., 1 week June.
Prix fixe: 8€ (child). A la carte: 33–47€.

Gilbert Brenner, a former pastry chef by trade with a passion for all good things, presents the ne plus ultra of tradition in a burlesque cloak. His tripe in Riesling sauce are a wonderful thing. Gilbert, who prepares pork shank, pork shoulder, the tourte de la vallée (an Alsatian pastry baked with Munster cheese and ground pork), the choucroute, the hanger steak seasoned with garlic as happily as smoked salmon served with green lentils, refreshes his traditional repertoire (aimed at preserving good local recipes) on an ever-changing blackboard. In a lively *winstub* setting open to the outside world, we delight in the marbled veal and parsley and the herb-seasoned chicken, pâté in a pastry crust with Riesling aspic or a delicately pressed zucchini, tuna and feta terrine, which give an idea of the contribution this traditional *winstub* with its Southern French leanings is making to the rejuvenation of the genre. All the local winegrowers come to savor the delights on offer here.

● **L'Auberge**   🏠SIM

At Grand Hôtel Bristol, 7, pl de la Gare.
Tel. 03 89 23 59 59. Fax 03 89 23 92 26.
reservation@grand-hotel-bristol.fr
www.grand-hotel-bristol.com
A la carte: 40€.

This brasserie opposite the rail station has remained loyal to the region's cuisine. The 1900 setting with its wall frescos, antique woodwork and old stove breathes its charm. The house terrine with prunes, vineyard-keeper's salad, fish filets over a bed of choucroute, tête de veau with vinaigrette sauce and a chilled mousse with kirsch slip down smoothly.

● **Anadolu**   SIM

31, rue Vauban.
Tel. 03 89 23 71 71.
gurbuz.t@wanadoo.fr / www.anadolu.fr
Closed Sun. lunch, Mon., Sept.
Prix fixe: 30€, 24€. A la carte: 35€.

This small Turkish tavern with its terrace on a pedestrian street is efficiently run by Talat Gurbuz. The appealing cuisine includes delicious mezzé (assorted Lebanese appetizers), lamb in many forms, chicken brochettes and a mild kadaïf (honey- and almond-seasoned angel hair pastry with fresh lemon). The short wine list completes our journey to the East with a few Ottoman vintages. The cost of the fare for this change of air (and fare) remains modest.

● Caveau Saint-Pierre   SIM

24, rue de la Herse.
Tel. 03 89 41 99 33. Fax 03 89 23 94 33.
Closed Mon., Jan.
Prix fixe: 17€. A la carte: 35€.

Tourists are fond of the exposed stone
and beam décor and "Little Venice" surroundings, but the cuisine here also has
its charms: foie gras, herb-encrusted cod,
grilled beef tenderloin and the vacherin
dessert slip down effortlessly.

● Chez Hansi   SIM

23, rue des Marchands.
Tel.-Fax 03 89 41 37 84.
Closed Wed., Thu., Jan.
Prix fixe: 18€, 44€. A la carte: 40–50€.

In his typical Old Colmar cellar, Marc
Gautier makes a fine ambassador for his
region. The woodwork, Alsatian furniture,
waitstaff in traditional costume and local
dishes go together perfectly. An onion
tart, goose foie gras, pike-perch in Riesling
sauce, choucroute with smoked sausage,
bacon and pork and a frozen kouglof with
kirsch are models of their genre.

● Au Cygne   SIM

15-17, rue Edouard-Richard.
Tel. 03 89 23 76 26. Fax 03 89 24 39 31.
Closed Sat. lunch, Sun., Mon. dinner,
1 week Christmas–New Year's, 1 week at
Easter, 15 Aug.
Prix fixe: 10€, 16€, 6€ (child).
A la carte: 35–40€.

The tarte flambée (a thin-crusted savory
tart with cream, onions and bacon), fish
simmered in red wine, sirloin steak served
with marrow and pear croustillant here
are neatly crafted, vibrant traditional
dishes. Kathy and Bertrand Roth uphold
the *winstub* spirit.

● Hammerer   SIM

3, pl Hastinger.
Tel.-Fax 03 89 41 52 43.
Closed Sun., Wed. dinner, Bank holidays,
end July–beg. Aug.
Prix fixe: 9,50€ (lunch), 27€ (lunch).
A la carte: 30€.

Francis Staub, the dandy of cookware, is
an admirer of this paneled dining room
where we savor the classic dishes concocted by Jean Warth. The presskopf (a
head cheese and aspic terrine) as well as
a steak with "real" house made French
fries are monuments of their kind. The
set menus are a bargain.

● Au Koïfhus   SIM

2, pl de l'Ancienne-Douane.
Tel. 03 89 23 04 90. Fax 03 89 23 66 00.
Prix fixe: 18€, 19,50€, 23,50€, 7€ (child).
A la carte: 35€.

The salad gourmande (duck breast, gizzards
and foie gras), salmon in puff pastry over
sauerkraut, beef tenderloin with shallots
and with bone marrow and a Strasbourg-
style veal steak with spätzle followed by a
delicious kouglof glacé are good indeed.
Eric Libbra's charming, wood-trimmed
winstub attracts plenty of customers.

● Le Restaurant du Marché   SIM

20, pl de la Cathédrale.
Tel. 03 89 24 93 88.
f.kurtz@libertysurf.fr
www.restaurantdumarché.fr
Closed Sun., Mon., 1 week Nov. 1,
Feb. vac., 2 weeks Aug.
Prix fixe: 14,50€ (weekday lunch).
A la carte: 45€.

Frédéric and Laurence Kurtz provide a
charming welcome and serve a healthy
market-based cuisine that strikes just the
right note. Ginger-seasoned crisp breaded
pork trotters, orange spotted flounder
with endives, veal roast with slow-roasted
potatoes, crisp bacon and ceps and the
frozen bittersweet chocolate truffles are
pleasant indeed.

● Le Temps des Délices   SIM

23, rue d'Alspach.
Tel. 03 89 23 45 57. Fax 03 89 23 82 95.
angelsteraneo@aol.com
Closed Sun., Mon., 1 week beg. Jan.,
1 week beg. Aug.
Prix fixe: 19€ (lunch), 35€ (dinner).
A la carte: 50–55€.

Although Michelangelo Straneo is somewhat neglecting the fine Italian cuisine that used to delight us so much in his wood trimmed chalet, his foie gras terrine with spiced aspic, sautéed cod filet, tender veal medallions and a suave tiramisu are still tasteful classics. The dining room has its charm with its yellow walls, wood banquettes and library.

● **La Ville de Paris**   SIM
4, pl Jeanne-d'Arc.
Tel. 03 89 24 53 15. Fax 03 89 23 65 24.
Closed Mon. dinner, Tue.
Prix fixe: 21€.
A la carte: 40€.

This central *winstub* had its moment of glory under Gibert Brenner. It continues on an even keel with Claudine Bartholomé at the helm. We still enjoy the escargots, foie gras, salmon in a Riesling sauce, tête de veau, liver quenelle and the caramel flan, all reliably prepared by Steve Mergenthaler.

In Sigolsheim (68240). 6,5 km nw via N 83 then D10.

● **Auberge du Pont**   SIM
   de la Fecht
Tel. 03 89 41 48 12. Fax 03 89 24 51 44.
Closed Mon., Tue., Bank holidays.
Prix fixe: 9€ (lunch), 12€ (lunch),
18€, 28€. A la carte: 25–30€.

The Wiss' inn is worth a foray into the forest. Visitors young and old enjoy the garden, terraces and dining rooms. Monique at the tables and Hubert in the kitchen gratify their regular guests with presskopf (a local head cheese and aspic terrine) vineyard-keeper's salad, pork shank stuffed with horseradish, braised pork shank, beef served with sea salt and a frozen vacherin dessert.

COLOMBEY-LES-DEUX-EGLISES

52330 Haute-Marne. Paris 248 –
Chaumont 25 – Bar-sur-Aube 16 –
Châtillon-sur-Seine 63.
This village of 660 souls with its Boisserie museum and General de Gaulle memorial is a rather impressive place of Gaullist pilgrimage.

   HOTELS-RESTAURANTS

● **Hostellerie de la Montagne**
Rue Pisseloup.
Tel. 03 25 01 51 69. Fax 03 25 01 53 20.
www.hostellerielamontagne.com
Closed Mon., Tue., 10 days Sept., 1 week Christmas, 10 days end Jan.–beg. Feb.
8 rooms: 110–160€. 1 suite: 160€.
Prix fixe: 46€, 56€, 90€, 15€ (child).
A la carte: 110€.

Gérard Natali has created a picture postcard inn here. The furniture with its patina of age, the exposed stone and beams and the spacious, old-fashioned rooms breathe rest and relaxation. The dining rooms have been refurbished contemporary style and son Jean-Baptiste, trained in great establishments worldwide (the Connaught in London, Martinez in Cannes, Boulud in New York and Mamounia in Marrakech), serves topical dishes that still bow to tradition: the chilled soft-boiled eggs and lobster in aspic, the grilled John Dory with an acidic green and red tomato jus, the venison filet breaded with almonds and pine nuts or the slow-cooked apricots stuffed with flavors of the Mediterranean. Fine work!

■ **Les Dhuits**
RN619.
Tel. 03 25 01 50 10. Fax 03 25 01 56 22.
hotel.dui.colombeylesdeuxeglises@wanadoo.fr
www.relais-sud-Champagne.com
Closed 10 days at end Dec., 10 days beg. Jan.
40 rooms: 60€.
Prix fixe: 16,50€, 24€, 35€, 10€ (child).
A la carte: 35€.

Near the Boisserie and Memorial, this seventies hotel has well-kept modern rooms and a restaurant serving local cuisine. Round slices of chitterling sausage in puff pastry, salmon filet in champagne sauce and the berry sabayon are very honest.

COLOMIERS see TOULOUSE

COLROY-LA-ROCHE

67420 Bas-Rhin. Paris 407 – Sélestat 31 –
Strasbourg 67 – Molsheim 38 – Lunéville 70.
A step away from the industrious Bruche and
Ban de la Roche valleys, here is a Vosges village surrounded by forest, full of thickets where
the inhabitants gather wild berries and hunt in
the autumn. The last thing you might expect to
find here is a luxury hotel, but …

 HOTELS-RESTAURANTS

■ La Cheneaudière

3, rue du Vieux-Moulin.
Tel. 03 88 97 61 64. Fax 03 88 47 21 73.
www.chenaudiere.com
25 rooms: 90–260€. 7 suites: 255–420€.
Prix fixe: 45€, 49€ (lunch, wine inc.), 110€.

Mireille François is the charming hostess
of this Vosges Relais & Châteaux establishment. We come here for the relaxing
atmosphere, indoor swimming pool, forest walks and cozy, paneled rooms. Chef
Roger Bouhassoun meticulously prepares the house standards, served in a
vast, luxurious dining room with bay
windows looking out on the surrounding greenery. Fresh Scottish salmon
tartare prepared tableside, a pairing of
goose and duck foie gras, lobster fricassée with thick basil pasta, salmon trout
baked in salt, simmered veal sweetbreads with morels and cream in sauce
and the warm soufflé flavored with plum
eau-de-vie from Lorraine are all in very
good taste.

In 67130 Bellefosse. 9 km ne.

● Auberge de la Charbonnière

Col de la Charbonnière, Champ du Feu.
Tel. 03 88 08 31 17. Fax 03 88 08 31 38.
col-charbonniere@aol.com
Closed Mon. dinner, Tue., 2 weeks Nov.,
2 weeks Mar.
Prix fixe: 14€, 18€, 21€.

Christian Brüls and Michel Felden run
this easygoing chalet a step away from
the ski trails. Michel manages the dining
room with gusto, while Christian prepares

his unfussy cuisine. Fondues, raclettes
and chapeaurade (meat in bouillon with
grated vegetables) are served in the evening. At lunchtime, we make short work
of escargots, cervelas sausage with vinaigrette, pork cheeks with Pinot Noir sauce
and large grilled pork ribs served with a
caramelized Chinese sauce.

In 67420 Ranrupt. 2 km sw.

● Ferme-Auberge Promont

37, Hauts-des-Près, col de Steige, toward
Champ-du-Feu, forest road on left off D214.
Tel.-Fax 03 88 97 62 85.
Closed dinner, Fri., 1 Dec.–26 Dec.
Prix fixe: 16€, 18€.

In this friendly, panoramic Vosges farmhouse, Maryse and Corine Schym-
noll champion their region's cuisine at
unbeatable prices. Covered meat pies,
roasted duck or veal and kirsch-flavored
mousse are washed down with a well-
chosen Pinot Noir.

COMBLOUX

74920 Haute-Savoie. Paris 596 – Chamonix-
Mont-Blanc 31 – Annecy 78 – Megève 6.
combloux@wanadoo.fr.
With its fine bell tower and view of Mont Blanc,
this mountain resort has soul.

 HOTELS-RESTAURANTS

■ Aux Ducs de Savoie

253, rte du Bouchet.
Tel. 04 50 58 61 43. Fax 04 50 58 67 43.
info@ducs-de-savoie.com
www.ducs-de-savoie.com
Closed end Apr.–beg. June, beg. Oct.–mid-Dec.
50 rooms: 110–170€.
Prix fixe: 28€, 33€.

We enjoy a delightfully peaceful stay in
this chalet with its view of Mont Blanc
and the Aiguilles de Warrens. The cozy
lounge with its fireplace, mountain-style
rooms, simple regional and seasonal
cuisine and numerous facilities (heated
swimming pool, gym, Jacuzzi, WiFi)
make this a first-rate stopover.

Le Coeur des Prés

152, chemin du Champet.
Tel. 04 50 93 36 55. Fax 04 50 58 69 14.
hotelaucoeurdespres@wanadoo.fr
www.hotelaucoeurdespres.com
Closed end Oct.–mid-Dec., 1 Apr.–1 June.
32 rooms: 80–127€. 1 suite: 160€.
Prix fixe: 28€, 30€, 35€.

Perched on the resort's heights, Monique
and Nicolas Paget's chalet has many
delights to offer. Jacuzzi, sauna, stationary bicycles, heated outdoor pool and
Savoyard-style rooms offer rest and recreation, while the restaurant serves a tasteful regional cuisine.

Le Coin Savoyard

300, rte de la Cry.
Tel. 04 50 58 60 27. Fax 04 50 58 64 44.
coin-savoyard@wanadoo.fr
www.coin-savoyard.com
Closed Mon. (June, Sept.), end Sept.–10 Dec.,
mid-Apr.–end May.
14 rooms: 90–140€. A la carte: 40€.

Well-equipped traditional-style rooms,
stone bathrooms, warm shades and a
great deal of wood lend their appeal to
this mountain hostelry. At the stove, Benjamin Gonnet concocts frog legs, roasted
salmon with braised leeks, duck breast
with blueberry sauce and crème brûlée.

● Au Coeur de Combloux SIM

65, rte de Megève.
Tel.-Fax 04 50 58 67 70.
Closed Mon., Tue. (off season), mid-Nov.–
mid-Dec., 3 weeks mid-June–beg. July.
Prix fixe: 14,90€ (lunch), 24,90€, 34,90€,
7,30€ (child). A la carte: 40€.

A staunchly regional restaurant, honest
dishes (warm foie gras served over mixed
greens, honey-seasoned duck breast,
tarte Tatin) and a delightful welcome are
the attractions of the Pierious' place.

35270 Ille-et-Vilaine. Paris 387 – Rennes 41
– Dinan 25 – Fougères 49 – Saint-Malo 37.
ot@combourg.org.

"Combourg, my keep," sighed Chateaubriand,
who has a square named for him here. The castle is still standing and open to visitors.

 HOTELS-RESTAURANTS

Hôtel du Château

Pl Chateaubriand.
Tel. 02 99 73 00 38. Fax 02 99 73 25 79.
hotelduchateau@wanadoo.fr
www.hotelduchateau.com
Closed mid-Dec.–mid-Jan., Sun. dinner (off
season), Mon. (off season). Rest. closed Sat.
lunch, Mon. lunch, Sun. dinner.
32 rooms: 56–160€. 1 suite: 139–170€.
Prix fixe: 26€, 36€, 55€, 10€ (child).
A la carte: 55–65€.

Below the château, Marie-Thérèse Pelé's
establishment is a pleasant halt where
modern rustic rooms offer comfort and
relaxation. Her son Antoine's cuisine combines different flavors. His sautéed scallops seasoned with garlic and herbs and
served with a sweet potato purée and chitterling sausage chips, roasted turbot with
Puy lentils in a rich wine sauce, grilled beef
filet with chateaubriand sauce and Grand
Marnier soufflé are easily enjoyable.

Hôtel du Lac

2, pl Chateaubriand.
Tel. 02 99 73 05 65. Fax 02 99 73 23 34.
hoteldulac@tiscali.fr
www.hotel-restaurant-du-lac.com
Closed Feb., Fri. (off season), Sun. dinner (off
season). Rest. closed Fri. (exc. dinner in
season), Sun. dinner (off season).
28 rooms: 48–75€.
Prix fixe: 14€ (weekday lunch), 25€,
9€ (child). A la carte: 55€.

At the entrance to the old town, just a step
away from the towers of the castle, Françoise and Bertrand Hamon provide a generous welcome. The place is charming and
the rooms are practical. Oysters served
warm with orange-seasoned butter, lobster gratin in sabayon, rack of lamb with
a pain d'épice crust and a soft-centered
chocolate cake with buttermilk mischievously reinterpret regional classics.

● L'Ecrivain SIM

Pl Saint-Gilduin, across from the church.
Tel. 02 99 73 01 61. Fax 02 23 16 46 31.
Closed Sun. dinner (exc. July–Aug.),
Wed. dinner (exc. July–Aug.), Thu.,
2 weeks Nov., Feb. vac.
Prix fixe: 14,60€, 21€, 35€, 9,50€ (child).

Surrounded by his collection of antique books and inkpots, Gilles Menier is an attentive host. The scallop profiteroles with smoked bacon–infused sauce, warm foie gras tartine with artichokes, catfish with a coriander-seasoned sauce, duckling filet with vineyard peaches and the crispy chocolate and praline dessert have character. The garden is pleasant and the exhibitions of paintings a bonus.

COMBREUX

45530 Loiret. Paris 122 – Orléans 38 –
Châteauneuf-sur-Loire 14 – Gien 51.
This delightful village in the forest of Orleans is just the place for quiet, pleasant walks.

 HOTELS-RESTAURANTS

■ Auberge de Combreux

35, rte du Gâtinais.
Tel. 02 38 46 89 89. Fax 02 38 59 36 19.
aubergec@compuserve.com
www.auberge-de-combreux.fr
Closed mid-Dec.–mid-Jan. Rest. closed Sun.
dinner (Nov.–Mar.), Mon. lunch.
19 rooms: 60–79€.
Prix fixe: 19€ (weekdays), 29€, 36€,
15€ (child).

Lovers will enjoy a weekend stay in this former post house clad in Virginia creeper, with its charming cottages and garden and swimming pool in season. The food is simple and flavorsome (scallop croustillant, sea bream with a red pepper coulis, veal sweetbread cassolette with a cep gratin and a citrus flavored sabayon).

■ Auberge de la Croix Blanche

46, rte du Gâtinais.
Tel. 02 38 59 47 62. Fax 02 38 59 41 35.
7 rooms: 56€.

Prix fixe: 19€ (weekday lunch), 27€, 39€,
10€ (child). A la carte: 55€.

Estelle Boré and Dany Cochard tend convivially to this antique inn with its old-fashioned rooms and restaurant with fireplace. A lentil cappuccino with smoked trout, lobster cassolette with an oyster cream sauce, young wild boar stew with cranberries, flaky pastry with quince filling and and nougat cream with dried fruit make an excellent impression.

COMMERCY

55200 Meuse. Paris 268 – Nancy 53 –
Bar le Duc 40 – Toul 31.
On the left bank of the Meuse, in the capital of the madeleine, Stanislas' château still stands and is now the town hall. The Saint-Charles hospital with its fine pharmacy and the ceramics museum are worth a visit.

 HOTELS-RESTAURANTS

● Côté Jardin COM

40, rue de Saint-Mihiel.
Tel. 03 29 92 09 09. Fax 03 29 92 09 10.
www.hotelcommercy.com
Rest. closed lunch, Fri., Sat.
11 rooms: 45–68€.
Prix fixe: 18€, 40€, 48€, 15€ (child).

We like the simple pleasures on offer at the Bous' hostelry. In the circular dining room, Annie Bou delights her guests with novel takes on traditional dishes. We have happy memories of the scallops with leeks and the green tea– and mandarin orange–seasoned venison. An excellent choice of wines from the Greater East. On the accommodation side, the yellow and blue rooms ensure a pleasant stay.

COMPIEGNE

60200 Oise. Paris 81 – Amiens 82 –
Beauvais 6 – Saint-Quentin 70 – Soissons 39.
otsi@mairie-compiegne.fr.
Memories of the Second Empire are legion here. We visit the château and its carriage and car museum and the grounds running gently down to

the vast forest. A stroll through the old town is like a leisurely journey back into the past.

 HOTELS-RESTAURANTS

■ Hostellerie Royal-Lieu

9, rue de Senlis.
Tel. 03 44 20 10 24. Fax 03 44 86 82 27.
www.host-royallieu.com
Closed 3 weeks Feb., 2 weeks beg. Aug., Sun.
dinner. Rest. closed Sun. dinner, Mon., Tue.
12 rooms: 83€. 3 suites: 105€.
Prix fixe: 30€. A la carte: 65€.

This picture postcard inn on the edge of the forest has a great deal of charm. We like to relax in its garden and snug rooms and enjoy chef Angelo Bonechi's mushroom ragout, monkfish risotto with sweet garlic, Tuscany-style beef and the berry feuillantine.

■ Les Beaux-Arts

33, cours Guynemer.
Tel. 03 44 92 26 26. Fax 03 44 92 26 00.
www.bw-lesbeauxarts.com
50 rooms: 67–76€. 12 suites: 90–185€.

This hotel by the Oise river offers comfortable rooms in different shades and a lounge serving delicious breakfasts.

● Hôtel du Nord   V.COM

1, pl de la Gare.
Tel. 03 44 83 22 30. Fax 03 44 90 11 87.
Rest. closed Sat. lunch, Sun. dinner,
3 weeks Aug.
20 rooms: 49–55€.
Prix fixe: 23€, 35€. A la carte: 65–80€.

The traditionally styled rooms in yellow, blue and red tones and fine home cooking make this a charming stopover. We watch as sautéed langoustines, the turbot with Sauternes sauce and the veal chop with salted butter are prepared in the open kitchen. The dessert trolley looks very appetizing.

● La Part des Anges   V.COM

18, rue de Bouvines.
Tel. 03 44 86 00 00. Fax 03 44 86 09 00.

www.lapartdesanges.com
Closed Sat. lunch, Sun. dinner, Mon.,
1 week Dec., 3 weeks Aug.
Prix fixe: 18€, 28€ (lunch), 36€, 46€,
52€. A la carte: 50€.

Under the fresco illustrating "the angel's share", Jean-Jacques Moissinac's dishes are very enjoyable. Sautéed langoustines with creamed cauliflower, Atlantic sea bass simmered in Lillet and served with an artichoke mousse, seven-hour lamb served with a dried tomato compote or the waffle served warm with chocolate whipped cream have plenty of energy.

● Rive Gauche   V.COM

13, rue Guynemer.
Tel. 03 44 40 29 99. Fax 03 44 40 38 00.
rivegauche@wanadoo.fr
http://perso.wanadoo.fr/rivegauche
Closed Mon., Tue.
Prix fixe: 35€, 48€. A la carte: 70–90€.

Franck Carpentier's restaurant pays tribute to seasonal produce and the dishes reflect the market's cycle. A warm lobster salad with lemon-infused oil, roasted wild turbot with balsamic vinegar, beef tenderloin from the Aubrac with vineyard-keeper's sauce and a vanilla-seasoned pineapple soup with coconut milk served with mango sorbet and a butter brioche cookie keep their promises. The wine list boasts 350 bottles.

● Bistro des Arts   ■SIM

35, cours Guynemer.
Tel. 03 44 20 10 10. Fax 03 44 20 61 01.
Closed Sat. lunch, Sun.
Prix fixe: 18€, 26€. A la carte: 35–39€.

A step away from the banks of the Oise, Yves Méjean, who trained with Michel Guérard and Bruno Cirino, has a style that falls somewhere between domestic cuisine and the bistro spirit. This results in precise, subtle dishes at reasonable prices, including the sundried tomato tart, cod filet with artichokes, tarragon-seasoned veal or the upside down apricot tart, all pleasantly crafted. An amusing neo-Parisian setting.

In Rethondes (60157). 10 km.

● **Alain Blot**

21, rue du Maréchal-Foch.
Tel. 03 44 85 60 24. Fax 03 44 85 92 35.
alainblot@netcourrier.com / www.alainblot.com
Closed Sat. lunch (exc. Bank holidays), Sun.
dinner, Mon., 1 week Feb., 3 weeks Sept.
Prix fixe: 35€ (wine inc.), 52€, 61€, 82€.
A la carte: 90€.

Here on the edge of the forest, Alain Blot likes to sing the praises of his beloved Brittany. This fine classicist who trained at Carantec and in a wealthy private household displays a taste for finely crafted but unfussy dishes, which he prepares with a certain audacity, but also a lightness of touch, providing the dining room staff, sophisticated table settings and fine silverware with an opportunity to express themselves. For visitors to his luxurious dining room with its Louis XVI furniture and porch opening onto the garden, he prepares Breton produce with an eye to tradition. The proof lies in his langoustine tail dish, grilled Atlantic sea bass with red onion jam, the "simple expression of the sea", duck parmentier with morel mushrooms and the all-chocolate plate. The 300 items on the wine list have no trouble finding a match.

CONCARNEAU

29900 Finistère. Paris 548 – Quimper 22 – Brest 93 – Lorient 51 – Vannes 103.
OTSI.concarneau@wanadoo.fr.
This authentic port was once one of the greatest in France. Inspired by the memory of eminent painters and the beauty of the walled town with its fishing museum, we could amble through its streets endlessly.

 HOTELS-RESTAURANTS

■ **Hôtel Kermoor**

Plage des Sables-Blancs.
Tel. 02 98 97 02 96. Fax 02 98 97 84 04.
kermoor@lespiedsdansleau.com
www.hotel-kermor.com
11 rooms: 95–170€.

This 19th-century establishment run by the Violant family delights aficionados of the open sea. On the one side, they enjoy the lounge and studio housed in a genuine boat hull; on the other, they revel in the ocean view from the terraces of the traditional-style rooms.

● **Chez Armande** COM

15 bis, av du Dr-Nicolas.
Tel.-Fax 02 98 97 00 76.
Closed Tue. (exc. July–Aug.), Wed.,
3 weeks Nov.
Prix fixe: 12,50€, 19,80€, 25,80€.
A la carte: 55€.

Claude Maury remains a staunch classicist, as is apparent from his braised sweetbread feuilletés and vermouth-seasoned lobster, turbot in white cream sauce, farm-raised veal tenderloin and the mandarin soufflé, served by the waterfront in a typically Breton setting. Sensible set menus.

● **La Coquille** COM

1, rue de Moros.
Tel. 02 98 97 08 52. Fax 02 98 50 69 13.
sicallac@wanadoo.fr
www.lacoquille-concarneau.com
Closed Sun. dinner, Mon., 2 weeks Nov.
Prix fixe: 29€, 45€, 60€, 14,50€ (child).

He was the chef of the Tour d'Argent for seven years. Now Jean-François Sicallac, a native of Auray, has returned to Brittany to run this modest establishment next to Concarneau harbor. The Coquille has a past. Jean-François has restored it to its former glory and Marie, his wife from the Meuse, adds a smile. We like marinated pollock with blinis and tarama, langoustine lasagne with Basque vegetables and Atlantic sea bass cooked skin-side down with parsley and garlic-seasoned ceps served with extra virgin olive oil–seasoned mashed potatoes. Mirabelle plums with salted-butter caramel and the croustillant with rosemary ice cream will have you melting. All this deserves a keen round of applause. Simple, tasty meals are served on the bistro side.

● Le Buccin SIM

1, rue Duguay-Trouin.
Tel. 02 98 50 54 22. Fax 02 98 50 70 37.
Closed Sat. lunch (off season), Sun. dinner
(off season), Mon. lunch, 2 weeks Nov.
Prix fixe: 19€ (weekday lunch), 25€, 31€,
38€. A la carte: 45–50€.

In the yellow dining room decorated with paintings by local artists, Patrick Couvert serves up a fine, flavorsome cuisine. The stuffed and oven–browned clams, John Dory served with a chestnut jus, the rack of lamb with a pain d'épice crust and slow-roasted garlic and the chocolate marquise with banana confit and a green tea crème anglaise are well crafted. Jocelyne provides a delectable welcome.

CONDEAU see NOGENT-LE-ROTROU

CONDE-NORTHEN

57220 Moselle. Paris 351 – Metz 20 –
Thionville 48 – Pont-à-Mousson 52 –
Sarrelouis 36.
A corner of Moselle countryside holding a church, farms and modern houses that seem to have sprung up by mistake behind a clump of bushes, as well as a tasteful hostelry.

 HOTELS-RESTAURANTS

■ La Grange de Condé

41, rue des Deux-Nieds.
Tel. 03 87 79 30 50. Fax 03 87 79 30 51.
www.lagrangedeconde.com
17 rooms: 95€. 3 suites: 220–240€.
Prix fixe: 14,50€, 20€, 30€, 46€.

Jean-Marie Visilit, formerly seen only in the most elegant of establishments (the Golf in Crans, Belles Rives in Remich and Relais de Margaux), has now opted for simplicity in his family farmhouse, converted into a convivial halt. The special talent of this lord of Lorraine catering is regional dishes based on exceptional produce whose suppliers are thanked in print on the appetizing menu. The fare includes traditional Messina-style suckling pig in aspic, Boulay-style frog legs in gratin, home-style vol-au-vent, beef rib eye steak with a tomato béarnaise sauce and the desserts around a plum theme, with a chilled soufflé to make you melt. The rustic dining rooms have a vintage charm and the guest rooms a sober luxury. The service is smiling, the rear terrace a joy and the wine cellar and cigar box goldmines. Jean-Marie Visilit has raised simplicity to a fine art!

CONDOM

32100 Gers. Paris 729 – Agen 41 –
Auch 46 – Toulouse 121.
A little capital of foie gras and Armagnac-based gastronomy, its ancient houses putting on a picturesque show for visitors.

 HOTELS-RESTAURANTS

■ Les Trois Lys

38, rue L.-Gambetta.
Tel. 05 62 28 33 33. Fax 05 62 28 41 85.
hoteltroislys@wanadoo.fr / www.lestroislys.com
Closed Feb. Rest. closed Sun., Mon. lunch,
Thu. lunch.
8 rooms: 50–150€. 2 suites: 140–170€.
Prix fixe: 22€, 32€. A la carte: 50€.

Relaxation guaranteed in this central town house with its garden, swimming pool and traditional but well-equipped rooms. In the dining room, the home cooking and fusion dishes delight guests.

● La Table des Cordeliers ○ V.COM

1, rue des Cordeliers.
Tel. 05 62 68 43 82. Fax 05 62 28 15 92.
www.latabledescordeliers.fr
Closed Sun. dinner, Mon.
Prix fixe: 20€, 36€, 46€, 55€,
15€ (child). A la carte: 60€.

Having worked as an expert chocolate maker with his in-laws, the Lerouxs, in Quiberon, Eric Sampietro has now returned to the Gers. Unwilling to do things by half, he has taken the famous Taverne des Cordeliers—which owes its celebrity to Jean-Louis Palladin—by storm. Refurbished designer fashion with its 18th-century chapel, sober lounges and contemporary furniture, the restaurant is enjoying a second youth. The cuisine has followed suit with sweet and savory notions inspired by fashion. Formerly with Raymond Blanc at the Manoir des Quatre Saisons near Oxford, Eric is not short on ideas and combines local traditions with more exotic allusions. The foie gras served warm with ground coco beans and balsamic vinegar, red mullet with a sesame crust with ratte potatoes in red wine and the "*souvenir de Catherine*" desserts, in honor of his Breton wife (buckwheat crêpes, salted-butter caramel ice cream, frozen parfait cream with Vanuatu de Tahiti beans), are masterpieces.

CONDRIEU

69420 Rhône. Paris 500 – Lyon 41 – Annonay 34 – Rive-de-Gier 22 – Vienne 13. The name of this village by the Rhône is familiar indeed, since it is shared with a great vintage pressed from the viognier grape, with its fine bouquet of peach and apricot.

 HOTELS-RESTAURANTS

● **Hôtellerie du Beau Rivage**
2, rue du Beau-Rivage.
Tel. 04 74 56 82 82. Fax 04 74 59 59 36.
www.hotel-beaurivage.com
16 rooms: 95–145€. 12 suites: 175–220€.
Prix fixe: 38€ (lunch), 54€, 75€.
A la carte: 80€.

The snug rooms in a recent wing, view of the Rhône, pleasant welcome, dining room opening onto a terrace and topical cuisine all provide a new vitality in this hostelry made famous by Paulette Castaing. We are charmed by Reynald Donet's fine tricks. A disciple of Troisgros and Passédat, he reliably prepares a lobster salpicon with a pike fish quenelle, foie gras terrine, salmon trout meunière, lamb tenderloin with a basil-seasoned flan and the fresh fruit brochette. Turning to the cellar, the best vintages of Condrieu and Côte Rôtie are a natural accompaniment.

● **La Reclusière**
14, rte Nationale.
Tel. 04 74 56 67 27. Fax 04 74 56 80 05.
lareclusiere@free.fr / http://lareclusiere.free.fr
Closed Nov. 1 vac. Rest. closed Tue., Wed.
8 rooms: 46–74€.
Prix fixe: 20€, 35€, 50€, 10€ (child).

Set in its grounds, this comfortable residence with a handful of well-appointed guest rooms provides a contemporary setting. The cuisine by Martin Fleischmann, a veteran of the Buerehiesel and Auberge de l'Ill, follows suit. Skate wing and mussels in salad, sea bream with wine sauce, pigeon breast and grilled tête de veau followed by the chocolate squares with spiced caramel sauce marry precision and creativity. A round of applause for the premier set menus, very well chosen.

CONFOLENT see BEAUZAC
CONLEAU see VANNES

CONNELLES

27430 Eure. Paris 107 – Rouen 38 – Les Andelys 13 – Vernon 35 – Evreux 33.
In a small valley frequented by Arsène Lupin, the great gentleman burglar of French fiction, this vintage Norman setting offers lush landscapes and houses from another era.

 HOTELS-RESTAURANTS

■ **Le Moulin de Connelles**
40, rte d'Amfreville-sous-les-Monts.
Tel. 02 32 59 53 33. Fax 02 32 59 21 83.
moulindeconnelles@moulindeconnelles.com
www.moulindeconnelles.com
Rest. closed Sun. dinner, Mon. (off season), Tue. lunch.
7 rooms: 120–170€. 6 suites: 145–295€.
Prix fixe: 33€, 42€, 56€, 12€ (child).
A la carte: 63€.

This half-timbered Anglo-Norman manor surrounded by a large estate on an island in the Seine is a haven of peace. Half-Romantic, half-Impressionist, it is an enchanting place for lovers. The rooms have an antique charm with their Jouy fabric and bathrooms in old Rouen faïence. We relax in the swimming pool and Jacuzzi before sitting down to eat. Stéphane Cavalier classically prepares asparagus in puff pastry with morel cream sauce, monkfish medallions prepared in the Norman style, beef filet Rossini and the frozen Benedicine liqueur–flavored soufflé.

CONQUES

12320 Aveyron. Paris 611 – Figeac 45 – Aurillac 53 – Rodez 37 – Espalion 51.
conques@conques.com.
Set in a village found in a little lost valley in Rouergue, the church of Sainte-Foy is a marvel with its tympanum and treasures.

 HOTELS-RESTAURANTS

● **Le Moulin de Cambelong**
Cambelong, 3 km s via D901.
Tel. 05 65 72 84 77. Fax 05 65 72 83 91.
www.moulindecambelong.com
Closed end Oct.–end Mar.
10 rooms: 120–180€.
Prix fixe: 45€.

This 18th-century mill is a charming place. It boasts guest rooms decorated with fine wall fabrics, neat dining rooms, Dominique's delicious welcome and an audacious, scholarly cuisine concocted by Hervé Busset, a keen, curious, self-taught chef. The aromatic herbs that grow down the paths by the Dourdou river blend easily with a range of local produce. We adore Galabar blood sausage with tea-seasoned Aubrac onion confit on toast, the melted Tomme cheese from Laguiole, roasted milk-fed Aveyron lamb served with hazelnut couscous and napped with a chickpea sauce, delicious Fario trout filet with a lentil emulsion sauce and the lightly spiced duck medallions, served with wild chestnut flour gnocchi. Pineapple carpaccio with sorbet and the caramel croustillant with berries will whet the most jaded of appetites.

■ **Hostellerie Sainte-Foy**
Rue Principale.
Tel. 05 65 69 84 03. Fax 05 65 72 81 04.
hotelsaintefoy@hotelsaintefoy.fr
www.hotelsaintefoy.fr
Rest. closed Nov. 1–Easter.
12 rooms: 110–187€. 4 suites: 199€.
Prix fixe: 18€ (lunch), 24€ (lunch), 37€, 51€. A la carte: 70€.

A warm welcome, refined rooms in a neo-rustic manner and *pension* dishes await you in this 17th-century residence with its view of the abbey.

LE CONQUET

29217 Finistère. Paris 617 – Brest 24 – Brigognan 56.
ot-conquet@wanadoo.fr.
This Brest beach at World's End lines the point of land leading out to the islands of Ouessant and Molène. The abbey, lighthouses and harbor are all worth a visit.

■ HOTELS-RESTAURANTS

■ **Le Relais du Vieux Port**
1, quai du Drellac'h.
Tel. 02 98 89 15 91.
Closed Jan.
7 rooms: 42–60€.
Prix fixe: 25€, 9,50€ (child). A la carte: 40€.

Behind its austere facade, this stone house on the harbor offers cozy, nautical-style rooms and a restaurant serving a decent *pension* cuisine. The crab parmentier, sautéed scallops, sautéed veal scallops in cream sauce and the apple crumble are honest.

In Locamaria-Plouzané (29280).
● **La Coromandière** SIM
Plage de Trégana.
Tel. 02 98 48 92 53. Fax 02 98 34 06 92.
A la carte: 25-35€.

One of the best *crêperies* in Brittany? That would be Dominique Morvan's place, housed in an old abode with a fine sea view. The typically Breton setting and delicious buckwheat crêpes with either goat cheese, shellfish or Molène sausage, accompanied by a glass of cider, will steal your heart away.

In La Pointe-Saint-Mathieu (29217). 4 km s.

■ Hostellerie de la Pointe Saint-Mathieu

Tel. 02 98 89 00 19. Fax 02 98 89 15 68.
saintmathieu.hotel@wanadoo.fr
www.pointe-saint-mathieu.com
Closed mid-Jan.–end Feb.
Rest. closed Sun. dinner.
19 rooms: 75–145€. 8 suites: 130–160€.
Prix fixe: 35€, 70€, 10€ (child).

The sea stretches to the horizon from Philippe Corre's trim establishment. Guests in need of a little peace and fresh air enjoy the heated indoor pool, sauna, cozy lounges and spacious rooms. In the rustic dining room, the master of the house concocts subtle fare. We enjoy the local Iroise seafood crumble with cashews, cod filet with pickled seaweed and passion fruit sauce, John Dory fish with creamy risotto, veal sweetbreads *en cocotte* with a Port wine reduction and the cart with house desserts.

88140 Vosges. Paris 337 – Epinal 48 – Langres 68 – Nancy 81 – Neufchâteau 28.
contrex.tourisme@wanadoo.fr.
Made fashionable in the 18th century by Stanislas, Duke of Lorraine, who was followed here by all the courts of Europe, this spa resort still has charm to spare. What memories remain of the Shah, Grand Duke Vladimir and the Prince of Greece, who came to drink from the Pavillon spring, source of urological wonders?

HOTELS-RESTAURANTS

■ Cosmos

13, rue de Metz.
Tel. 03 29 07 61 61. Fax 03 29 08 68 67.
contact@cosmos-hotel.com
www.cosmos-hotel.com
Closed 3 weeks beg. Dec.
Rest. closed lunch (Nov.–Mar.).

77 rooms: 90–115€. 6 suites: 115–130€.
Prix fixe: 29€, 12€ (child).
A la carte: 40€.

Few remain unimpressed by this Belle Epoque hotel with its imposing lobby, refined rooms and many facilities (spa center, swimming pool surrounded by extensive grounds and driving range). In the entirely refurbished 1900 dining room, the traditional and health fares make a good impression.

■ La Souveraine

Domaine thermal.
Tel. 03 29 08 09 59. Fax 03 29 08 16 39.
contact@-hotel.com
www.souveraine-hotel.com
Closed mid-Oct.–end Mar.
31 rooms: 55–70€.

Once the residence of Grand Duchess Vladimir, Patrice Paris' hotel still has its stucco, moldings and high ceilings. The rooms are modern and the place boasts a fitness center, steam bath, Jacuzzi and heated swimming pool.

81170 Tarn. Paris 665 – Toulouse 82 – Albi 26 – Rodez 87 –
Villefranche-de-Rouergue 45.
officedutourisme.cordes@wanadoo.fr.
"In Cordes, everything is beautiful, including regret", Camus wrote of this hilltop village suspended in the sky. The fine Renaissance residences here are a visual feast.

HOTELS-RESTAURANTS

● Le Grand Ecuyer

Above the city.
Tel. 05 63 53 79 50. Fax 05 63 53 79 51.
grand.ecuyer@thuries.fr / www.thuries.fr
Closed mid-Oct.–Easter.
Rest. closed lunch, Mon. (exc. July–Aug.).
12 rooms: 95–160€. 1 suite: 250€.
Prix fixe: 59€, 73€.

Raymond VII's former hunting residence is a splendid setting indeed. Yves Thuries, doctor of chocolate and holder of the Meilleur Ouvrier de France award, now shares the stove with his nephew Damien. Together, they create trilogies of local and more exotic flavors. As we sit surrounded by woodwork, antique rugs and suits of armor, a beef pot-au-feu with warm foie gras and Vietnamese-style sautéed langoustines and grilled veal medallions napped with a light sesame jus served with steamed squab and Vietnamese-style sautéed Keffir limes entertain and delight us. The same goes for the desserts: a composed dessert plate with a dark chocolate soup, wild strawberry and lemon gratin and the luscious sautéed pan perdu brioche.

■ Hostellerie du Vieux Cordes

21, rue de Saint-Michel.
Tel. 05 63 53 79 20. Fax 05 63 56 02 47.
vieux.cordes@thuries.fr
www.thuries.fr
Closed beg. Jan.–mid-Feb.
Rest. closed Sun. dinner (Oct.–Apr.),
Mon. (Oct.–Apr.), Tue. lunch (Oct.–Apr.).
18 rooms: 50–90€. 1 suite: 129€.
Prix fixe: 22€, 46€, 10€ (child).
A la carte: 50€.

In his second establishment housed in a former monastery, Yves Thuriès offers traditional rooms, each one unique, a terrace overlooking the valley and a shady patio. The cuisine by Yannick Pouget is affably priced and very much produce oriented. Atlantic sea bass tartare, skate with brown butter, traditionally prepared sautéed veal and the apple tart with a rhubarb compote and cinnamon ice cream are good examples. Sommelier Jérémy ably assists us in choosing among the 300 items on the wine list.

■ Hostellerie du Parc

Les Cabannes.
Tel. 05 63 56 02 59. Fax 05 63 56 18 03.
www.hostellerie-du-parc.com
Closed Sun. dinner (exc. July–Aug.),
Mon. (exc. July–Aug.), mid-Nov.–mid-Dec.
13 rooms: 55–75€.
Prix fixe: 22€, 31€, 38€, 48€, 11€ (child).

Set in grounds with a swimming pool, Claude Izard's 19th-century hostelry is a first-rate establishment. We enjoy the pleasant welcome from the master of the house, trim rooms and forthright, sincere country cooking served with warmth. We savor the solid foie gras and slow-roasted onion-stuffed duck neck, lobster gratin, venison stew and the stuffed duck and even acquire a few jars to take home.

74700 Haute-Savoie. Paris 592 –
Chamonix 32 – Sallanches 4 – Megève 11.
ot.cordon@wanadoo.fr.
An onion bell tower with a view of Mont Blanc, an authentic Savoyard village and its maze of paths, skiing in winter and walks in summer: a postcard portrait of the French Alps.

 HOTELS-RESTAURANTS

● Les Roches Fleuries

Locale known as la Scie.
Tel. 04 50 58 06 71. Fax 04 50 47 82 30.
info@rochesfleuries.com
www.rochesfleuries.com
Closed beg. Apr.–beg. May,
mid-Sept.–mid-Dec. Rest. closed Mon. (exc. vac.), Tue. lunch (exc. vac.).
20 rooms: 125–235€. 5 suites: 220–415€.
Prix fixe: 32€, 47€, 69€. A la carte: 90€.

On the village heights, this luxurious chalet welcomes mountain lovers. As they step out on its flowered balcony, Mont Blanc rises before them. In the kitchen, Vincent David prepares dishes that wander beyond the region's borders with a nod to the South. In the pistou soup, oven-browned blue lobster, pan-fried veal sweetbreads and the roasted peaches, the Alps and the Mediterranean are wed for better, not worse. After all this, how could our dreams in the trim rooms of this favorite hostelry be anything less than sweet? The same spirit reigns at a more modest price in its bistro adjunct, La Boîte à Fromages.

■ Le Chamois d'Or

4 km sw from Sallanches via D113.
Tel. 04 50 58 05 16. Fax 04 50 93 72 96.
hotellechamoisdor@wanadoo.fr
www.hotel-chamoisdor.com
Closed mid-Sept.–20 Dec., mid-Apr.–1 June.
Rest. closed Wed. lunch, Thu. lunch.
26 rooms: 80–170€. 2 suites: 175–270€.
Prix fixe: 24€, 30€, 12€ (child).
A la carte: 42€.

The Petit-Jeans have been running this village chalet where life's pace is measured by the passing of guests for four generations. All enjoy its Savoyard-style paneled rooms, view of Mont Blanc, swimming pool and garden. The fine dishes prepared by Laurent Brèches meet the same high standards. They include jumbo shrimp in salad with a balsamic dressing, seared scallops with Apremont wine, the duck breast cooked with raspberry vinegar and the Bourbon vanilla crème brûlée.

■ Le Cordonnant

Les Darbaillets.
Tel. 04 50 58 34 56. Fax 04 50 47 95 57.
lecordonnant@wanadoo.fr
Closed Oct.–mid-Dec., mid-Apr.–mid-May.
16 rooms: 57–88€.
Prix fixe: 23€ (weekdays), 32€.

The warm atmosphere and meticulous cuisine go together in this village chalet. We like the Alpine décor, painted wood and rooms with balconies.

CORRENS

83510 Var. Paris 827 – Aix-en-Provence 71 – Toulon 63 – Brignoles 16.
This little jewel in the high Var is well worth a visit for its peaceful fields and love of the good things in life.

 HOTELS-RESTAURANTS

■ Auberge du Parc

Pl du Général-de-Gaulle.
Tel. 04 94 59 53 52. Fax 04 94 59 53 54.
contact@aubergeduparc.fr
www.aubergeduparc.fr

Closed Sun. dinner–Thu. lunch (Nov.–Mar.), Tue. (Apr.–Oct.).
5 rooms: 100€. 1 suite: 130€.
Prix fixe: 32€, 45€, 10€ (child).

This old inn run by Philippe Austruy is charming indeed. After relaxing by the pool or in one of the guest rooms decorated with frescos, trompe-l'oeil and 18th-century furniture, we are ready for dinner. Bertrand Lherbette's market-based cuisine is highly enjoyable. The changing menu offers crayfish ravioli with truffles, stuffed lamb saddle, pigeon in puff pastry with foie gras and a peach gazpacho, all with plenty of energy.

COSQUEVILLE

50330 Manche. Paris 358 – Cherbourg 21 – Barfleur 12.
A small port in the Val de Saire, near the Vicq beach and Cap Levi.

 HOTELS-RESTAURANTS

● Au Bouquet de Cosqueville

Hameau Remond.
Tel. 02 33 54 32 81. Fax 02 33 54 63 38.
www.bouquetdecosqueville.com
Closed Tue. (exc. Aug.),
Wed. (exc. July–Aug.), Jan.
7 rooms: 45–50€.
Prix fixe: 19,50€, 28€, 35€, 50€, 55€.

Formerly at the Marine in Carteret, Eric Pouhier has been running this ivy-covered inn for twenty years. He acquires his produce from reliable sources: fish from Cosqueville or the Cherbourg market, farmhouse meats and local vegetables. The oysters and herb cream, tuna tartare served with little mackerels, mussels and plaice presented in a shellfish bouillon and the Lestre guinea hen with a dried fruit brochette and cider vinegar jus make an excellent impression. For dessert, the hot apricot tart and the raspberry dessert with Tagada strawberry candy are childhood treats.

LE COTEAU see ROANNE
LA COTINIERE see ILE D'OLERON

COUDEKERQUE-BRANCHE see DUNKERQUE
COUERON see NANTES

COUILLY-PONT-AUX-DAMES

77860 Seine-et-Marne. Paris 45 –
Coulommiers 21 – Lagny-sur-Marne 12 –
Meaux 9 – Melun 47.
In the heart of gourmet, Brie, a fine spot to
break our journey and savor some simple,
rustic pleasures.

| ● | RESTAURANTS |

● Auberge de la Brie
14, av Boulingre.
Tel. 01 64 63 51 80. Fax 01 60 04 69 82.
www.aubergedelabrie.com
Closed Sun., Mon.,
2 weeks Christmas–New Year's, 3 weeks Aug.
Prix fixe: 58€, 66€.

The Pavards' Brie cottage and flower-filled
garden have an immediate charm. Céline
greets guests with remarkable warmth,
while in the kitchen, her husband Alain
thinks only of their welfare. Proof takes
the form of the set menus presented by
this veteran of Meneau and the Auberge
de Condé, who has a gift for traditional
chic. In the redecorated dining rooms,
pan-seared duck foie gras with rhubarb,
roasted John Dory with chanterelles and a
meat reduction and the slow-roasted rabbit saddle and sundried tomatoes achieve
heights of mastery and mischief. For dessert, the hot Grand Marnier soufflé served
with orange sorbet lends us wings.

COULOMBIERS

86600 Vienne. Paris 350 – Parthenay 45 –
Poitiers 20 – Lusignan 7.
A Poitou village in the land of the fairy
Mélusine.

| | HOTELS-RESTAURANTS |

■ Le Centre Poitou
39 rue Nationale, RN 11.
Tel. 05 49 60 90 15. Fax 05 49 60 53 70.

hotelcentre-poitou@wanadoo.fr
ww.centre-poitou.com
Closed Feb. vac., Nov. 1 vac.
Rest. closed Sun. dinner (exc. July–Aug.),
Mon. (exc. July–Aug.).
13 rooms: 45–120€.
Prix fixe: 8,50€ (lunch), 13,90€ (lunch,
wine inc.), 25€, 36€, 48€, 72€.
A la carte: 62–80€.

Whether you are stopping off on the way
to Santiago de Compostela or touring the
region, this gracious inn offers a delightful welcome and a convivial atmosphere,
with its décor in wood and shades of red,
beams, ancient flagstones, piano lounge,
garden and terrace beneath an arbor.
France Authé-Martin has brought in Luc
Massé, who prepares a cuisine that weds
tradition and flavor in a contemporary
manner: pan-seared scallops with sweet
potato cream and coffee emulsion, ginger-seasoned vermouth-braised turbot
and the lamb Viennoise with citrus flavors, served with heirloom vegetables,
make an excellent impression, before we
move on to the variations on the theme of
chocolate (airy saffron-seasoned sorbet,
warm soft-centered walnut praline cake).
Wines from every region.

COULON

79510 Deux-Sèvres. Paris 420 – La Rochelle
63 – Fontenay-le-Comte 25 – Niort 11.
ot@villecoulon.fr.
A gateway to the Marais Poitevin marshes and
the starting point for your exploration of this
serene natural cathedral.

| | HOTELS-RESTAURANTS |

■ Au Marais
46, quai Louis-Tardy.
Tel. 05 49 35 90 43. Fax 05 49 35 81 98.
information@hotel-aumarais.com
www.hotel-aumarais.com
Closed mid-Dec.–1 Feb.
18 rooms: 70–75€.

These two old boatmen's houses make up
a quiet hotel with bright, neat rooms. The

welcome is warm and the check affable. Steam bath and WiFi in the bargain.

● Central   🏠COM

4, rue d'Autremont.
Tel. 05 49 35 90 20. Fax 05 49 35 81 07.
le-central-coulon@wanadoo.fr
www.hotel-lecentral-coulon.com
Closed Sun. dinner, Mon., 2 weeks beg. Oct., Feb. vac.
Prix fixe: 18€, 22,50€, 26€, 29€, 38€.
A la carte: 44–50€.

Jean-Paul Guenanten, whose mother Anny Monnet was the muse of Marais Poitevin Niort cuisine in this very hostelry, has taken over its kitchen with gusto. He deftly delights his guests with an escargot crumble seasoned with Charentes wine, smoked eel rillettes seasoned with lime, pike-perch served with Vendée coco beans and twice-cooked wild rabbit served with foie gras. The Kamok-flavored crème renversée almost eats itself. Hervine Guenanten provides a charming welcome and the handsome guest rooms have been brightly refurbished.

● Auberge de l'Ecluse   SIM

La Sotterie.
Tel.-Fax 05 49 35 90 42.
www.aubergedelecluse.com
Closed Sun. dinner (off season),
Mon. (off season), Tue. dinner (off season),
mid-Dec.–mid-Jan.
Prix fixe: 17€, 27€, 40€, 8€ (child).
A la carte: 35–40€.

Loyal to the region, Pierre Couillaud showcases local produce in his judicious preparations. In the vintage décor of this appealing inn, Corine Couillaud presents with a smile traditional farci Poitevin, eel poached in red wine, veal kidneys and chocolate profiteroles.

COURCELLES-SUR-VESLE

02220 Aisne. Paris 122 – Reims 37 – Fère-en-Tardenois 19 – Soissons 21.
Peaceful Aisne, watered by the Vesle and peppered with churches, old villages and *châteaux*, such as this one.

 HOTELS-RESTAURANTS

● Château de Courcelles 🏠○❀🏯

8, rue du Château.
Tel. 03 23 74 13 53. Fax 03 23 74 06 41.
reservation@chateau-de-courcelles.fr
www.chateau-de-courcelles.fr
16 rooms: 275–340€. 3 suites: 340–345€.
Prix fixe: 45€, 85€. A la carte: 110€.

Set in twenty hectares of grounds with a heated swimming pool and riding center, this aristocratic Relais & Châteaux establishment neatly reconciles a 17th-century facade, period guest rooms (Louis XV and Empire) and lounges with a modern flavor. Thibault Serin-Moulin's cuisine is just as successful, combining noble produce and fine, topical ideas to make up a modernized traditional menu. In the dining room with its porch and Napoleon III furniture, duck foie gras escalopes wrapped in cabbage leaves, grilled Breton lobster with an artichoke risotto, roasted rack of lamb served with a Swiss chard gratin and a strawberry and basil soufflé are accompanied by fine wines from all over Champagne.

COURCHEVEL

73120 Savoie. Paris 660 – Albertville 52 – Chambéry 99 – Moûtiers 25.
pro@courchevel.com.
Courchevel is not only located in the largest ski area in Europe (the Trois-Vallées region has over 600 kilometers of slopes), it is also the only gourmet resort, with two restaurants whose first-class status has been recognized for a number of years now: Chabichou and the Bateau Ivre. The intelligently designed village continues up to a height of 2,000 meters. Its hotels are built around the foot of the slopes, enabling easy access.

 HOTELS-RESTAURANTS

■ Les Airelles   🏠🏯

Le Jardin Alpin.
Tel. 04 79 00 38 38. Fax 04 79 00 38 39.
info@airelles.fr / www.airelles.fr

52 rooms: 625–1700€.
7 suites: 2900–8000€.

A star of luxury mountain accommodations, this pastiche Austrian-style hotel, designed by Raymonde Fenestraz, offers high Alpine chic, superb rooms, elegant service, a Jacuzzi, swimming pool, fitness center and two worthwhile restaurants (the Coin Savoyard and Table du Jardin). The prices reflect all this.

■ Byblos Courchevel

BP 98. In Le Jardin Alpin.
Tel. 04 79 00 98 00. Fax 04 79 00 98 01.
courchevel@byblos.com / www.byblos.com
Closed beg. Apr.–mid-Dec.
64 rooms: 400–930€.
12 suites: 835–1060€.
Prix fixe: 75€. A la carte: 60–80€.

Courchevel's luxury hotel provides huge, opulent rooms, some with balconies overlooking the forest. The décor offers a fashionable new take on traditional Savoyard chic, successfully combining patinated paneling, antique furniture and fabric. The fireside lounge area, terrace, sauna, swimming pool and fitness center are ideal settings for rest and recreation. At mealtimes, guests can choose between Lebanese cuisine at the Oriental and French food at the Bayadère (pan-seared foie gras escalopes, Reinette apple Tatin with cherries and eau-de-vie, beef Rossini with sautéed artichokes and grilled porcini glazed in Madeira sauce and the mille-feuille of crêpes and roasted pears with pear sorbet).

■ Le Cheval Blanc

Tel. 04 79 00 50 50.
www.chevalblanc.com
Closed mid-Apr.–mid-Dec.
34 rooms: 790–990€.
A la carte: 120€.

Bernard Arnault's ambition was in the ascendant when he sprang this hotel on an unsuspecting Courchevel. With its Givenchy spa, luxury suites, refined rooms in a chic Alpine manner (wood, leather and velvet, designed by Sybille de Margerie) and half-Savoyard, half-Provençal cuisine orchestrated by Wout Brut, the Flemish chef from Eygalières, it is stylish indeed. Named for his favorite wine, the Cheval Blanc is the talk of the town and already a success.

■ Le Kilimandjaro

Rte de l'Altiport.
Tel. 04 79 01 46 46. Fax 04 79 01 46 40.
welcome@hotelkilimandjaro.com
www.hotelkilimandjaro.com
Closed mid-Apr.–mid-Dec.
17 rooms: 690€. 18 suites: 1060–4540€.

Luxurious stone and wood chalets equipped with "modern Savoyard"-style rooms make up this hotel hamlet, with its swimming pool, sauna, steam bath, Jacuzzi, boutiques, hairdressing and massage salon, beauty parlor and restaurant, the Coeur d'Or.

■ Le Mélézin

Rue de Bellecôte.
Tel. 04 79 08 01 33. Fax 04 79 08 08 96.
lemelezin@amanresorts.com
www.amanresorts.com
Closed mid-Apr.–mid-Dec.
26 rooms: 650–980€.
5 suites: 1900–2700€.
A la carte: 90€.

Refined, bright rooms with contemporary furniture, a pure, almost minimalist décor and unfussy fare are the attractions of this discreetly luxurious hotel, where we enjoy the Jacuzzis, steam bath and massage facilities. The slopes are just opposite.

■ Annapurna

Rte de l'Altiport.
Tel. 04 79 08 04 60. Fax 04 79 08 15 31.
info@annapurna-courchevel.com
www.annapurna-courchevel.com
Closed mid-Apr.–mid-Dec.
61 rooms: 480–570, 660–780€.
9 suites: 1240–1430, 3870–4050€.
A la carte: 70€.

At the highest point of the resort, this modern hotel offers bright, paneled rooms with balconies looking out onto the surrounding mountains. With its cocktail bar, children's playroom, spa with beautician and physiotherapist, heated pool, broadband Internet access in the rooms and restaurant with a terrace facing the slopes, it is a supremely comfortable haven after a day on the pistes.

■ **Alpes Hôtel du Pralong**

Rte de l'Altiport.
Tel. 04 79 08 24 82. Fax 04 79 08 36 41.
pralong@relaischateaux.com
www.hotelpralong.com
Closed 9 Apr.–mid-Dec.
57 rooms: 392–928€.
8 suites: 928–1494€.
Prix fixe: 50€ (lunch), 70€.
A la carte: 100€.

This former Relais & Châteaux establishment on the airport road has plenty of spirit. It boasts spacious rooms bathed in light, a pleasant piano bar, a lounge looking out onto the slopes, a heated mosaic swimming pool, a fitness center, steam bath and Jacuzzi, and, as a bonus, a refined restaurant serving good quality fare.

■ **Bellecôte**

Rue de Bellecôte.
Tel. 04 79 08 10 19. Fax 04 79 08 17 16.
message@lebellecote.com
www.lebellecote.com
Closed mid-Apr.–mid-Dec.
52 rooms: 225–330€. 4 suites: 440–510€.

This luxury hotel offers a combination of styles. Furniture, doors and statuettes from Afghanistan, India and Cambodia embellish the mountain-style rooms, some of them with balconies. In the cozy dining room, the cuisine is carefully prepared and the service assiduous.

■ **Carlina**

Rue de Bellecôte.
Tel. 04 79 08 00 30. Fax 04 79 08 04 03.
message@hotelcarlina.com
www.hotelcarlina.com
Closed mid-Apr.–mid-Dec.
58 rooms: 275–390€. 5 suites: 405–520€.
Prix fixe: 50€ (lunch), 70€ (dinner).

In the heart of the resort, this huge chalet provides an impressively sumptuous reception. The large rooms looking out onto the slopes, fitness center, Jacuzzi, steam bath, heated swimming pool and restaurant with its sunny terrace offer a great sense of well being. Chef Thierry Mathiauld's contribution involves rockfish soup, duck breast with Vin de Noix sauce and the local crozet pasta baked with Beaufort.

■ **Le Lana**

BP 95 (73121).
Tel. 04 79 08 01 10. Fax 04 79 08 36 70.
info@lelana.com / www.lelana.com
Closed mid-Apr.–mid-Dec.
57 rooms: 375–780€ (half board).
19 suites: 720–1230€ (half board).
A la carte: 85€.

The Tourniers have turned this impressive chalet with its different styles into a star attraction. The kitsch setting with its dark woodwork and bright colors, fitness center, baroque heated swimming pool, Clarins spa, rooms in shades of yellow, vaulted lounges and raspberry-colored restaurant are amazing.

■ **Hôtel des Neiges**

Tel. 04 79 08 03 77. Fax 04 79 08 18 70.
welcome@hoteldesneiges.com
www.hotel-des-neiges.com
Closed mid-Apr.–mid-Dec.
43 rooms: 170–930€.
5 suites: 550–1600€.
Prix fixe: 52€, 75€.

Between the town center and the slopes, this famous hotel has survived changing hands. A smiling welcome, attentive service, convivial rooms and an individualized *pension* cuisine.

■ **Le Saint-Joseph**

Rue Park-City.
Tel. 04 79 08 16 16. Fax 04 79 08 38 38.
info@lesaintjoseph.com / www.lesaintjoseph.com
Closed mid-Apr.–mid-Dec. Rest. closed lunch
10 rooms: 330–750€. 4 suites: 330–6002€.
A la carte: 80€.

The Tourniers have turned what was the first hotel in the resort into an ornately opulent residence: Alpine rooms and suites straight from the movies and two restaurants, the easygoing Grand Café and the more gastronomical Hussard with its select cuisine.

■ Chabichou

Quartier des Chenus.
Tel. 04 79 08 00 55. Fax 04 79 08 33 58.
chabi@chabichou-courchevel.com
www.chabichou-courchevel.com
Closed Sept.–end Nov., mid-Apr.–end June.
41 rooms: 200–335€. 3 suites: 310–480€.

Two white wood chalets with rooms renovated in bright colors, a fitness center with gym, steam bath and swimming pool, cozy lounges and a quality restaurant make this hotel complex one of the resort's star establishments (see Restaurants).

■ La Sivolière

Quartier des Chesnus.
Tel. 04 79 08 08 33. Fax 04 79 08 15 73.
lasivoliere@sivoliere.fr
www.hotel-la-sivoliere.com
Closed end Apr.–beg. Dec.
26 rooms: 300–720€.
13 suites: 1000–2000€.
Prix fixe: 55€, 15€ (child).
A la carte: 75–80€.

The rooms with their vintage charm have been refurbished in modern style and offer a delightful view of the neighboring fir forest. In the convivial dining room, we sit by the fire to enjoy traditional local dishes.

■ Les Grandes Alpes

Rue de l'Eglise, BP 1.
Tel. 04 79 08 03 35. Fax 04 79 08 12 52.
www.lesgrandesalpes.com
Closed 22 Apr.–beg. Dec.
35 rooms: 300–830€. 10 suites: 690–1150€.
Prix fixe: 35€, 55€.

Above the shopping arcade, the rich stone facade marks a modern hotel with spacious Alpine-style rooms and a range of facilities (steam bath, swimming pool,

Jacuzzi, therapy center). The restaurant keeps pace and even pulls ahead.

■ La Pomme de Pin

Quartier des Chenus.
Tel. 04 79 08 36 88. Fax 04 79 08 38 72.
info@pommedepin.com
www.pommedepin.com
Closed mid-Apr.–mid-Dec.
39 rooms: 275–386€. 1 suite: 554–706€.

Jean-François Trépier runs the Jacob family's hotel, home of the Bateau Ivre (see Restaurants), with a sure touch. The rooms are immaculate, bright and neat.

■ Le Rond-Point des Pistes

Rue de Park-City.
Tel. 04 79 08 04 33. Fax 04 79 01 04 29.
reservations@rppcourchevel.com
www.courchevel.com
Closed beg. May–mid-Dec.
32 rooms: 170–525€. 7 suites: 560–1495€.
Prix fixe: 38€ (lunch), 45€ (dinner),
13€ (child).

This contemporary hotel with its strategic location by the slopes offers rooms renovated in an Alpine style, a cozy lounge, a fully equipped fitness center and a restaurant serving simple *pension* dishes.

■ Courcheneige

Rue de Nogentil.
Tel. 04 79 08 02 59. Fax 04 79 08 11 79.
info@courcheneige.com
www.courcheneige.com
Closed mid-Dec.–mid-Apr.
81 rooms: 132–172€ (half board).
4 suites: 205–318€ (half board).

This impressive chalet on the slopes offers reasonable rates (for Courchevel!). The rustic rooms, fitness center and Jacuzzi have an easy appeal. Internet and WiFi.

■ La Loze

Rue Park-City.
Tel. 04 79 08 28 25. Fax 04 79 08 39 29.
info@la-loze.com / www.la-loze.com
Closed mid-Apr.–mid-Dec.
26 rooms: 280–490€. 1 suite: 550–750€.

Raymonde Fenestraz's second hostelry pays modest tribute to Austria. We enjoy its friendly atmosphere, comfortable rooms—all painted differently and furnished in Tyrolean style—sauna, steam bath and cozy lounge.

● Le Bateau Ivre ⬤Ⓥ.COM

At La Pomme de Pin, quartier des Chenus.
Tel. 04 79 00 11 71. Fax 04 79 08 38 72.
www.pommedepin.com
Closed lunch (exc. weekends),
mid-Apr.–mid-Dec.
Prix fixe: 85€, 170€. A la carte: 150€.

This year, Jean-Pierre Jacob has managed to be in two places at once: Le Bourget du Lac (the Ombremont is his) and the heights of Courchevel, in this hushed, red, panoramic dining room on two levels. A former pupil of Vergé in Mougins and Lacombe in Cologny, he deftly prepares only the finest produce. Foie gras terrine with toasted pain d'épice and tender roasted fruits, roasted langoustines with potato croustillant and shavings of truffle, lobster with beet sauce, berries and vanilla-seasoned sweet potato mousseline, spruce-flavored pigeon with pear sauce and arugula cake are acrobatic exercises. The wines are chosen with flair, the desserts well conceived (caramelized apples, pain perdu with truffles, sorbet, quartered pear placed on a lime parfait and dusted with cocoa) and the prices unmistakably Courchevel.

● La Table du Jardin ⓋⓋ.COM

At Les Airelles, rue des Clarines.
Tel. 04 79 00 38 38. Fax 04 79 00 38 39.
info@airelles.fr / www.airelles.fr
Closed mid-Apr.–mid-Dec.
Prix fixe: 120€ (lunch), 150€ (dinner),
58€ (child).

The Fenestrazes' hotel has a restaurant that reflects the standards of its wealthy clientele. Stéphane Lavigne's reliable mountain cuisine has a contemporary flavor. Foie gras with berry chutney, grilled Atlantic sea bass served with potatoes Anna, roasted veal cutlet with flavorful jus and the traditional omelet norvégi-enne (baked Alaska) are subtle, lively, elegant dishes. Magnificent service (seen at the Pinède in St. Tropez in summer) and an encyclopedic cellar.

● Le Chabichou ⬤Ⓥ.COM

At the Chabichou, quartier des Chenus.
Tel. 04 79 08 00 55. Fax 04 79 08 33 58.
www.chabichou-courchevel.com
Closed mid-Apr.–end June, Sept.–end Nov.
Prix fixe: 38€ (lunch), 90€, 180€.
A la carte: 150€.

Michel Rochedy is the Ardèche's most Savoyard son. This native of Saint-Agrève has turned his Chabichou into *the* restaurant in Courchevel. The gastronomy lesson he gives here involves top-quality produce, short cooking times, shrewd combinations and a total lack of frills. The results are a fabulous lake fish soup (with whitefish, salmon trout, curry-seasoned perch and crayfish tails) served with fried croutons, foie gras terrine perfumed with spices, beet ravoili in a rhubarb chutney with dried fruits and nuts, acidulated potato mikado: quite an agenda. The langoustine risotto is a masterpiece. The big lake trout with porcini-infused oil is superb, as is the Cantal pork, with its rolled sparerib slow-cooked in mountain pork fat, with Mondeuse wine sauce and sage-seasoned young garden carrots. The boneless pork trotter layered with potato and foie gras is not to be missed. The sexagenarian chef stands at the peak of his art and retirement seems a very remote option! The chocolate-themed dessert is delightful; the wine list giddying. The setting is cozy in a convivial *pension* hotel.

● Le Kilimandjaro ⓋⓋ.COM

At the Kilimandjaro, rte de l'Altiport.
Tel. 04 79 01 46 46. Fax 04 79 01 46 40.
www.hotelkilimandjaro.com
Closed mid-Apr.–mid-Dec.
Prix fixe: 20€ (child). A la carte: 120€.

Alexandre Ongaro takes great care of his produce, preparing a flavorsome cuisine that happily strays from the well-trodden path of Savoy's culinary tradition, with a duck foie gras terrine compressed with mango and served with pain d'épice, frog legs in mild garlic sauce and garden herb bouillon, a pan-seared line-fished pollock, baked crab with Jerusalem artichokes and the ultra slow-cooked pigeon breast, its thighs in confit, with sautéed pumpkin, salsify and chesnuts, for instance. We end cheerfully with Fougerolle sour cherries with Sichuan peppercorns in ravioli with pistachio ice cream. A fine wine list.

● Le Chalet de Pierres   COM
In Le Jardin Alpin.
Tel. 04 79 08 18 61. Fax 04 79 08 38 06.
www.chaletdepierres.com
Closed Oct.–end Nov., end Apr.–10 July.
Prix fixe: 55€ (groups). A la carte: 60–85€.

Yvette Saxe is the brilliant guiding light of this Alpine Brasserie Lipp. Celebrities, sports personalities and anonymous aficionados gather here to enjoy the comfortable, sunny terrace, keen service and Loïc Larteau's steadfast regional cuisine. A Beaufort tart, the chalet soup, olive oil–seasoned grilled Mediterranean sea bass, cod, pormonier (a local sausage made with pork and greens such as spinach and chard), rib eye steak topped with bone marrow and the gargantuan cake buffet will sate even the healthiest appetite. The prices are very Courchevel.

● Le Genépi   COM
Rue de Park-City.
Tel. 04 79 08 08 63. Fax 04 79 06 51 43.
le-genepi@wanadoo.fr
Closed dinner (June, Sept.–Nov.), Sat.,
Sun. (Sept.–Nov.), end Apr.–end May,
beg. July–beg. Sept.
Prix fixe: 25€, 37€ (lunch), 47€ (dinner),
65€, 18€ (child). A la carte: 70–75€.

This good-natured cottage has charm to spare with its refined, friendly setting, welcoming hearth and lounge bar. We also enjoy the dishes served up by Thierry Mugnier, a veteran of the Vivarois and Martinez, who ably weds Savoyard and Mediterranean flavors. Pressed sardines and sundried tomatoes in terrine, mussel and chanterelle soup, salmon trout lightly cooked with a Genepi-infused mousse, oxtail parmentier and the blood orange pain perdu are handsome dishes indeed.

● La Mangeoire   COM
Rue de Park City.
Tel. 04 79 08 02 09 / 04 79 01 05 37.
Fax 04 79 08 06 85.
lamangeoire@aol.fr
Closed lunch, mid-Apr.–mid-Dec.
Prix fixe: 50–100€.

In the heart of the resort, this elegantly rustic restaurant keeps tradition alive, serving classic mountain dishes in a Savoyard setting. Fondue and raclette restore our strength.

● La Saulire   COM
Pl du Rocher.
Tel. 04 79 08 07 52. Fax 04 79 08 02 63.
info@lasaulire.com / www.lasaulire.com
Closed end Apr.–beg. Dec.
Prix fixe: 29€ (lunch), 40€ (lunch),
19–24€ (child dinner). A la carte: 90–95€.

With his fine, native good humor, Jacques Trauchessec, a son of Aveyron summoned to the Alps, breathes life into this restaurant with its wood décor, vintage posters, engravings and antique tools. In the dining room, crab and crayfish ravioli in a shellfish bouillon, porcini and chanterelle fricassée with truffle-infused vinaigrette, roasted wild Atlantic sea bass, grilled salmon trout and the lamb medallions served with a ratatouille crumble make a fine impression. The thin apple tart with caramel ice cream is a classic. The house's special charm lies in its splendid cellar boasting more than 1,000 vintages, including a few bottles of Pétrus from different years.

● L'Anerie   SIM
Pl du Forum.
Tel. 04 79 08 29 15. Fax 04 79 08 10 40.
tournier.freres@wanadoo.fr
Closed end Apr.–mid-Dec.
A la carte: 58–66€.

This barn provides simple pleasures. In a relaxed atmosphere, on the terrace or at the bar, we make short work of bistro dishes with a stylish air. Croûte au fromage (Savoie cheeses oven-browned over bread soaked in the local wine), minced tuna, grilled beef and the berry tiramisu slip down smoothly.

● Le Cap Horn   SIM
Altiport.
Tel. 04 79 08 33 10. Fax 04 79 08 39 25.
caphorn1850@wanadoo.fr
Closed Sun. dinner, end Apr.–beg. Dec.
Prix fixe: 60–90€.

A step away from the airport, the Tourniers have turned this barn into an enchanting, chic brasserie with charming service, a sunny terrace and tasteful dishes. Sushi, Beaufort tart, oven-baked lobster, sole meunière, spit-roasted Bresse chicken and the sirloin steak with morels slip down without a hitch. The dessert buffet is copious, as is the check.

● La Fromagerie   SIM
Rue des Tovets.
Tel. 04 79 08 27 47. Fax 04 79 08 20 91.
Closed lunch, beg. May–end Nov.
Prix fixe: 26€, 28€, 60€.
A la carte: 40–50€.

Joëlle Chevallier runs this easygoing restaurant with an expert touch. Its handsome Savoyard dining room serves well-crafted local dishes at sensible prices (especially for this resort). We feast on a local terrine, porcini fricassée, pan-seared perch filets, Creole-style poultry curry, Chartreuse-infused crème brûlée. A recent major makeover with a few antiques.

COUR-CHEVERNY

41700 Loir-et-Cher. Paris 196 –
Orléans 73 – Blois 14 – Châteauroux 87 –
Romorantin-Lanthenay 28.
This village's handsome white château inspired Captain Haddock's Marlinspike Hall in Hergé's Adventures of Tintin. Devoted to hunting, it has an impressive pack of hounds, as well as some fine furniture.

 HOTELS-RESTAURANTS

■ Château du Breuil   ❀ 🏨
Rte de Fougères, Le Breuil.
Tel. 02 54 44 20 20. Fax 02 54 44 30 40.
info@chateau-du-breuil.fr
www.chateau-du-breuil.fr
Closed beg. Jan.–end Feb.
16 rooms: 106–185€. 2 suites: 208–245€.
Prix fixe: 38€.

This 18th-century château is a first-class stopover for visitors to the Sologne. Its thirty hectares of wooded grounds, trim lounges and spacious rooms have an immediate appeal. Now, it is possible to eat here, too, and rather well, with salmon medallions, bream filet, beef steak and a soft-centered chocolate cake.

■ Hôtel des Trois Marchands   🏨
Pl de l'Eglise.
Tel. 02 54 79 96 44. Fax 02 54 79 25 60.
hotel-des-trois-marchands@tiscali.fr
www.hoteldes3marchands.com
Closed Mon., mid-Feb.–mid-Mar.
24 rooms: 42–55€.
Prix fixe: 24€, 35€, 9,50€ (child).

The Bricault family has been providing a charming welcome in this old-fashioned inn for 140 years now. Jean-Jacques, latest of the name, watches over the stone and wood rooms, refurbished antique style. In the kitchen, chef Jean-Claude Berchon astutely prepares his fine classics. Marinated salmon salad with oyster mushrooms, sole meunière, roasted wild duck with porcini and the frozen Grand Marnier soufflé raise our spirits, as does our friend Périco Legasse, long a regular.

COURSEULLES-SUR-MER

14470 Calvados. Paris 252 – Caen 20 –
Arromanches 14 – Bayeux 24.
tourisme.courseulles@wanadoo.fr.
Historic Normandy with its Allied landing

beaches: it was here that General de Gaulle set foot on French soil again on the 14th June 1944. Today, oyster beds have replaced the battlefields.

 HOTELS-RESTAURANTS

■ La Crémaillère 🏠
Bd de la Plage. Avenue de la Combattante.
Tel. 02 31 37 46 73. Fax 02 31 37 19 31.
cremaillere@wanadoo.fr
www.la-cremaillere.com
40 rooms: 45–100€. 11 suites: 60–150€.
Prix fixe: 19€, 28€, 36€, 7€ (child).
A la carte: 45–55€.

This establishment with its annex charms tourists who have come to visit the Normandy Landing beaches. They enjoy the bright, comfortable rooms in burgundy and blue and the fitness center. In the dining room, refurbished in contemporary style with a glass wall providing a panoramic view of the Côte de Nacre, they savor locally farmed foie gras served with chutney and honey-seasoned apricots, grilled langoustines with beurre blanc, the pretty sole meunière and tripe slow simmered with tomato, before the ritual tarte Tatin with crème fraîche. Well-chosen wines by the glass.

■ Hôtel de Paris 🏠
Pl du 6-Juin.
Tel. 02 31 37 45 07. Fax 02 31 37 51 63.
hoteldeparis-normandie@wanadoo.fr
www.hoteldeparis-normandie.fr
Closed mid-Nov.–10 Feb.
27 rooms: 45–50€.
1 suite: 100–116€.
Prix fixe: 15€, 25€, 36€, 7€ (child).
A la carte: 55€.

A step away from the beach where General de Gaulle landed, this quiet hotel boasts neat rooms and a dining room with porch serving a simple *pension* cuisine.

● La Pêcherie COM
Pl du 6-Juin.
Tel. 02 31 37 45 84. Fax 02 31 37 90 40.
pecherie@wanadoo.fr / www.la-pecherie.fr
6 rooms: 45–90€.

Prix fixe: 17€ (weekdays), 19,50€, 23€, 37€, 11€ (child).

The handful of rooms in boat cabin style have been refurbished recently, but the gourmet clientele here is more interested in the dining room, with its oars, portholes and storm lamps. Pascal Derick delights his guests with new takes on traditional dishes. House smoked salmon with chives, braised veal sweetbreads with morel cream sauce, grilled turbot with fleur de sel, monkfish in red wine sauce and the glazed duck breast with sesame are all finely crafted. The thin apple tart with cider caramel is a model in its genre.

COURTENAY

45320 Loiret. Paris 119 – Auxerre 56 – Nemours 44 – Orléans 102 – Sens 26.
A crossroads town linking Gâtinais to Burgundy. The fine inns here owe allegiance to both regions.

 HOTELS-RESTAURANTS

● Auberge La Clé des Champs V.COM
Rte de Joigny, les Quatre-Croix.
Tel. 02 38 97 42 68. Fax 02 38 97 38 10.
info@hotel-lacledeschamps.fr
www.hotel-lacledeschamps.fr
Closed Tue., Wed., 2 weeks end Oct.,
3 weeks Jan.
7 rooms: 71–75,50€.
Prix fixe: 25€, 36€, 45€.
A la carte: 50–55€.

If you need a break from the stress of modern living, head straight for Marc Delion's 17th-century farmhouse. Seen from the terrace and rustic dining room, the countryside stretches off to the horizon. We savor the classic dishes prepared with the chef's special touch: escargot fricassée with mushrooms and garlic cream sauce, monkfish medallion with saffron-seasoned sauce served with a spinach flan, pan-seared sirloin steak with anchovy sauce and the soft chocolate cake with pistachio ice cream are washed down with Burgundy and Loire wines.

In Ervauville (45320). 9 km nw via N60, D32, D34.

● **Le Gamin**
Le Bourg.
Tel. 02 38 87 22 02. Fax 02 38 87 25 40.
Closed Sun. dinner, Mon., Tue.
Prix fixe: 46€, 56€. A la carte: 95€.

This former village grocery store and bar has been converted into an elegant inn with terrace and garden. Surrounded by mirrors, ornaments and brick, Joël Desmurs welcomes his guests with a broad smile, sure of his chef's talent. Yannick Ris deftly concocts subtle classics. The truffle in puff pastry, shelled lobster seasoned with Bourbon vanilla, veal sweetbreads with morels, quince tart with almond cream and apple and candied orange tart served with pain d'épice delight connoisseurs of high tradition.

CREON see BORDEAUX
LE CRESTET see LAMASTRE
CRESTET see VAISON-LA-ROMAINE

CREUTZWALD

57150 Moselle. Saint Avold 15 – Metz 45.
A frontier town with its mining history, Balthus le Lorrain cultural center, forest, lake and many stores.

● | RESTAURANTS

● **La Forge des**
   Grands Aigles
43, rue de la Houve.
Tel. 03 87 93 04 08.
Closed Sun. dinner, Mon.
Prix fixe: 19,50€, 26,50€, 41,50€.

Elvis and Geneviève Valsecchi have bought this place from her parents (his in-laws), keeping the handsome ceramic stove (kachelofen) that gave the place its name. They plan to open a hotel here, but for the moment, we feel at home with the terrace, makeshift décor and open window at the end of the dining room giving the place a Provençal feel. Elvis combines local and seasonal produce, tradition and

fashion, in the thin vegetable and smoked salmon tart, slice of foie gras seasoned with Gewurtz, pike fish poached in Riesling or the foie gras-stuffed pork trotter, before the frozen mirabelle plum parfait.

● **Le Baron Rouge** ⓝ SIM
60, rue de la Gare.
Tel. 03 87 90 13 35.
Prix fixe: 12€ (lunch). A la carte: 25€.

The bar, tables, bistro chairs and enameled plaques set the tone in this pure Parisian café setting. We come here to savor stylish vintages by the glass and feast on the studiedly roguish fare. The lunchtime menu offers beer-poached rabbit in salad, blood sausage with apples and an escalope cordon bleu, before a baked apple. An opportunity not to be missed.

CRILLON-LE-BRAVE

84410 Vaucluse. Paris 694 – Avignon 40 –
Carpentras 15 – Vaison-la-Romaine 26.
This fine, historic village at the foot of Mont Ventoux is enjoying a second youth.

■ ◆ | HOTELS-RESTAURANTS

■ **Hostellerie de**
   Crillon-le-Brave
Pl de l'Eglise.
Tel. 04 90 65 61 61. Fax 04 90 65 62 86.
www.crillonlebrave.com
Closed end Oct.–mid-Mar.
27 rooms: 200–400€.
5 suites: 500–600€.
A la carte: 67€.

Canadians Craig Miller and Peter Chittick have fallen in love with Provence and turned a few 17th-century houses into an elegant Relais & Châteaux establishment. The Italian-style terrace overlooking the Ventoux plain, shady swimming pool, rooms bathed in light, superb suites and La Tour apartment are impressive indeed. Philippe Monti, who trained with Pic, Haeberlin and Meneau, manages the modern bistro devoted to regional dishes and the gourmet restaurant in a converted cellar. Seared Landes foie gras, jumbo shrimp with a tomato, basil and licorice root–seasoned sauce, pan-seared red tuna served with stuffed zucchini and the simple roasted leg of lamb are delightful. The strawberry blanc-manger takes us back to our childhood.

● **Le Vieux Four**   SIM

Rue du Vieux-Four.
Tel. 04 90 12 81 39. Fax 04 90 12 87 43.
Closed lunch, Mon., end Nov.–end Feb.
Prix fixe: 26€.

This former bakery turned Provençal restaurant is packed in the summer. The terrace is very popular with its view of Mont Ventoux, but Catherine Fauque's cuisine has a hand in the place's popularity too. Foie gras terrine with slow-cooked caramelized onions, brandade with onion, herb-, caper- and mustard-seasoned mayonnaise, basil-seasoned roasted salmon and the lamb medallion with a creamy garlic sauce will whet the most jaded appetite. The apple cake with caramel sauce conjures up visions of childhood and the menu is angelic.

CRIQUEBOEUF see HONFLEUR

LE CROISIC

44490 Loire-Atlantique. Paris 464 –
Nantes 88 – La Baule 9 – Vannes 78.
At the end of the Guérand peninsula and the Côte Sauvage, this port with its coastal appendages reminds us of the Brittany of old.

 HOTELS-RESTAURANTS

● **Le Fort de l'Océan**   ◑✿𝄞

Pointe du Croisic.
Tel. 02 40 15 77 77. Fax 02 40 15 77 80.
fortocean@fr.oleane.com / www.fort-ocean.com
Rest. closed Sat. lunch, Sun. lunch,
mid-Nov.–mid-Dec.
6 rooms: 170–250€. 2 suites: 280€.
Prix fixe: 45€, 62€.

The Côte Sauvage stretches out endlessly from the swimming pool, restaurant and sheltered terrace of this 17th-century Vauban-style fort. Attentive host Gérard Louis makes sure his guests are comfortable in the elegant rooms decorated by Catherine Painvin. In the kitchen, Guillaume Brizard plays his part, too. Roasted langoustine tails, simply cooked John Dory, beef sirloin steak and a spiced fresh peach dessert are simple and strike the right note.

■ **Les Vikings**   𝄞

In Port-Lin.
Tel. 02 40 62 90 03. Fax 02 40 23 28 03.
24 rooms: 71–111€.

Gérard Louis has carved out a small empire in Le Croisic (the Océan and Fort de l'Océan are his also). He has a knack of making his guests feel at home in convivial modern settings with spacious rooms. The most popular afford fine views of the Côte Sauvage from their bay windows.

● **Grand Hôtel de l'Océan**   ◑𝄞

Plage de Port-Lin.
Tel. 02 40 62 90 03. Fax 02 40 23 28 03.
12 rooms: 85–200€.
A la carte: 80€.

The restaurant dining room of this hotel, perched on the rocks by the sea, offers a stunning view. Gérard Louis tends to his guests attentively, while Gérald Samson serves up the best sea produce in a series of simple, fresh preparations, such as a seafood platter, lobster bisque, Atlantic sea bass in a salt crust (requiring a ritual performance at a side table), langoustes fresh from the tank, as well as a boneless rib steak and the baba au rhum. After our meal, the bright, practical rooms are just the thing!

■ **Castel Moor**   𝄞

Baie du Castouillet.
Tel. 02 40 23 24 18. Fax 02 40 62 98 90.
castel@castel-moor.com
www.castel-moor.com
Rest. closed Sun. dinner (Oct.–Mar.).
18 rooms: 58–79€.
Prix fixe: 20€ (weekday lunch), 23,50€,
41€, 10,50€ (child). A la carte: 40–50€.

Anne Guillou has just taken over this substantial villa on the Côte Sauvage road. The bright, modern rooms are restful indeed and the blue and straw yellow semicircular dining room and porch have a splendid sea view. All this helps to sharpen her guests' appetites, adding to their enjoyment of the sunny cuisine. Langoustines breaded in orange zest–seasoned breadcrumbs, monkfish medallions with bacon and pine nuts, rack of lamb with baby vegetables and the hot Grand Marnier soufflé are flawless.

● **Le Quai 11**
11, quai de la Petite-Chambre.
Tel. 02 40 23 00 51. Fax 02 40 23 18 32.
quai11@hotmail.fr
www.restaurant-de-bretagne.com
Closed Tue.
Prix fixe: 13,50€, 18€, 27€, 10€ (child).
A la carte: 45€.

Refurbished in contemporary style, this fine restaurant with a porch serves Brittany on a platter. The cuisine does honor to the region in a series of fresh, lively preparations: crab- and whelk-stuffed ravioli, basil-seasoned tuna carpaccio, roasted Atlantic sea bass with beurre blanc, pan-simmered veal with chanterelles and a fruit crumble are all finely crafted.

● **La Bouillabaisse Bretonne** SIM
12, quai de la Petite-Chambre.
Tel. 02 40 23 06 74. Fax 02 40 15 71 43.
Closed Mon., Tue., beg. Jan.–end Mar.
Prix fixe: 20€, 35€. A la carte: 55€.

We are fond of Philippe and Michelle Marcilly's restaurant by the harbor. The sea view, warm welcome and fresh, light cuisine prepared by son Alexandre go well together. Langoustines in salted butter, artichoke- and foie gras-stuffed ravioli, sole meunière, pan-tossed John Dory with preserved lemons and the roasted lamb medallions with bacon are not bad. The rum- and vanilla-flavored brioche with passion fruit and pineapple sorbet forms a delightful coda.

CROS-DE-CAGNES see CAGNES-SUR-MER

80550 Somme. Paris 193 – Amiens 21.
Gray mist over the Baie de Somme, shifting skies and the Marquenterre bird sanctuary nearby form the basis of a delightful weekend stay for Parisians seeking a change of air.

■ HOTELS-RESTAURANTS

■ **Les Tourelles**
2-4, rue Pierre-Guerlain. BP 90036.
Tel. 03 22 27 16 33. Fax 03 22 27 11 45.
lestourelles@nhgroupe.com
www.lestourelles.com
Closed 3 weeks Jan.
33 rooms: 40–62€.
Prix fixe: 21€, 31€, 9€ (child).
A la carte: 45€.

By the Baie de Somme, Gilles and Dominique Ferreira Da Silva are the charming hosts of this Gustavian hotel in marine tones. The gray, blue and beige shades are restful, the rooms quiet and pleasant (six have just been fitted out in the "Priest's House" at the bottom of the garden) and the dormitory for children is a fine idea. We dine on the tasteful regional cuisine: the Marquenterre escargot quiche, line-fished Atlantic sea bass with pickled seaweed, Breton salt marsh lamb (pré-salé) and the strawberry cheesecake delight appetites sharpened by the ocean wind.

CROUTELLE see POITIERS

74350 Haute-Savoie. Paris 540 – Genève 27 – Bonneville 35 – Bellegarde 44 – Annecy 20.
Verdant Savoy, peaceful and discreet, a stone's throw from Switzerland and Lake Geneva.

■ HOTELS-RESTAURANTS

■ **L'Ancolie**
1050, lac des Dronières.
Tel. 04 50 44 28 98. Fax 04 50 44 09 73.
info@lancolie.com / www.lancolie.com
Closed Nov. 1 vac., Feb. vac.

Rest. closed Sun. dinner, Mon.
10 rooms: 79–113€.
Prix fixe: 27,50€ (weekday lunch), 39,50€,
47,50€, 65€, 20€ (child).
A la carte: 60–75€.

Yves Lefebvre's chalet is a haven of peace
offering snug, bright rooms with a view of
the lake. Savoyard tradition reigns in the
dining room. The oak-smoked salmon,
Lake Léman crayfish tail gratin, veal tenderloin medallions simmered with morels
and a pear charlotte in a chocolate shell,
served with pistachio cream, are well
phrased.

● L'Horloge

55, rue Léonce-Brieugne.
Tel. 04 90 77 12 74. Fax 04 90 77 29 90.
horlog@wanadoo.fr
www.horloge.netfirms.com
Closed Mon. dinner (mid-Sept.–mid-Apr.),
Tue. dinner, Wed., beg. Feb.–mid-Mar.
Prix fixe: 16€, 38€.

This 14th-century oil presshouse has
been converted into a colorful, bucolic
restaurant. It offers a good-natured welcome, gentle prices and changing menus
in the colors of Provence.

CUERS

83390 Var. Paris 837 – Toulon 24 –
Brignoles 25 – Marseille 84.
A Var of vineyards and hills with the sea not
far away.

| ● | RESTAURANTS |

● Le Lingousto

Rte de Pierrefeu.
Tel. 04 94 28 69 10. Fax 04 94 48 63 79.
www.lingousto.com
Closed Sun. dinner, Mon., Wed. dinner,
2 weeks Oct., 2 weeks Feb.
Prix fixe: 74€, 88€. A la carte: 70€.

Alain Ryon's Provençal dwelling has a
charming authenticity and consistency.
Its vines, vegetable garden, terrace shaded
by plane trees and cozy dining room in

ochre shades put us in the right frame of
mind to enjoy the reliable, creative cuisine.
The crabmeat, tomato, ginger and lobster
dish, the cold potato cream with parmesan
and Saint Jean truffles, herb-marinated
bream tasting of the sea, grilled Mediter-
rranean sea bass with olive oil–seasoned
mashed potatoes and the pork trotter sausage cake served with pan-seared duck foie
gras keep their promises.

LA CURE see LES ROUSSES

CURZAY-SUR-VONNE

86600 Vienne. Paris 371 – Poitiers 29 –
Lusignan 13 – Niort 53 – Parthenay 36.
Just next to Poitiers and its Futuroscope, discover the gentle banks of the Vonne, a fine gray
stone church and a stained glass museum.

| | HOTELS-RESTAURANTS |

● Château de Curzay

Tel. 05 49 36 17 00. Fax 05 49 53 57 69.
info@chateau-curzay.com
www.chateau-curzay.com
Closed beg. Nov.–mid-Apr.
Rest. closed lunch (exc. Fri., Sat. Sun.).
19 rooms: 165–280€. 3 suites: 320–340€.
Prix fixe: 60€, 75€, 80€ (wine inc.).
A la carte: 100€.

In their 18th-century château converted
into a modern Relais & Châteaux establishment, Brigitte de Gastines and Eric
Cachart provide a host of delights. The
120-hectare estate with its river, heated
swimming pool and private stud farm,
and the guest rooms in pastel colors,
charm walkers, fitness buffs and late risers. All gather in the Cédraie restaurant
to savor Nicolas Isnard's noble produce-
based cuisine. This shrewd technician
prepares inventive, invigorating dishes,
such as foie gras served in two novel ways
(on a stick and compressed), John Dory
presented like a "club sandwich", squab
in a vegetable tagine with preserved lemons and variations on the pineapple theme
(crunchy, frozen, and soft). Smiling, assiduous service.

57850 Moselle. Paris 442 – Strasbourg 45 – Saverne 19 – Sarrebourg 26 – Phalsbourg 20. The high rock perched above the forests with the Saint-Léon chapel at its peak is something of a Vosges Mont Saint-Michel.

 HOTELS-RESTAURANTS

● Auberge Katz   SIM
2, pl du Village.
Tel. 03 87 07 40 04.
www.ot-dabo.fr/katz.htm
Prix fixe: 9,50€. A la carte: 35€.

Patricia Spurny runs both the kitchen and dining room of her little village eatery, which is doing well. We enjoy the chef's salad, the tartes flambées, the salmon rösti and the cordon bleu with Munster cheese, not forgetting the frozen mirabelle plum dessert. A generous welcome and well-behaved prices.

In La Hoube (57850). 6 km n via D45.

■ Hôtel des Vosges   ⌂
Tel. 03 87 08 80 44. Fax 03 87 08 85 96.
www.hotel-restaurant-vosges.com
Closed 10 days Oct., Feb.
Rest. closed Tue. dinner, Wed.
9 rooms: 30–45€.
Prix fixe: 19€, 25€, 7€ (child).
A la carte: 30–35€.

This reliable family hotel has a garden with an unobstructed view of the Saint-Léon rock. The rooms are simple and neat. The dishes concocted by Jean-Luc Schwaller, formerly with Emile Jung, include cured ham, pike-perch in puff pastry, veal with sage-seasoned cream sauce and a thin apple on toast dessert, all impeccable.

● Le Zollstock   SIM
11, rte du Zollstock.
Tel. 03 87 08 80 65. Fax 03 87 08 86 41.
Closed Mon. lunch, Thu. dinner, Christmas–New Year's, end June–beg. July.
Prix fixe: 9,30€ (weekday lunch), 30€.
A la carte: 25–30€.

On a bend in the road, Jean-Louis Fetter's excellent inn is a dependably regionalistic eatery. We staunchly savor meat and cream sauce in puff pastry cups, trout with almonds, veal medallion with chanterelles, leg of venison and ice cream.

67120 Bas-Rhin. Paris 476 – Saverne 28 – Sélestat 41 – Strasbourg 23 – Molsheim 6.
With its ramparts, château and church, this trim village by the Bruche is well worth a detour.

 RESTAURANTS

● Auberge de la Bruche   COM
1, rue Principale.
Tel. 03 88 38 14 90. Fax 03 88 48 81 12.
www.auberge-bruche.com
Closed Sat. lunch, Sun. dinner, Wed.,
12 days at end Dec.–beg. Jan.,
mid-Aug.–end Aug.
Prix fixe: 26€, 64€. A la carte: 52–60€.

Hubert Raugel has turned his fine inn on the bank of the Bruche into a charming little gourmet halt. These days, the service has slipped a tad, but we cannot fault the schniederspätle (local stuffed dumplings) with foie gras, pike-perch with morels in ravioli nor the beef filet medallions served with gnocchi, which all carry the hallmark of true skill. The fleur d'oranger parfait with chocolate sauce is well crafted and the Alsatian wines by the glass very palatable.

67650 Bas-Rhin. Paris 426 – Obernai 19 – Sélestat 9 – Strasbourg 46 – Saverne 61.
otdlv@netcourrier.com.
The main square is splendid indeed with its bear fountain and Renaissance houses. The best view of the village's old roofs is to be had walking from the Saint-Sébastien chapel in the heart of the vines to the foot of the Vosges mountains.

HOTELS-RESTAURANTS

■ Au Raisin d'Or   ⬒
28 bis, rue G.-Clemenceau.
Tel. 03 88 92 48 66. Fax 03 88 92 61 42.
au-raisin-dor@wanadoo.fr
www.au-raisin-dor.com
Closed 20 Dec.–20 Jan., Mon.
Rest. closed Mon., Tue. lunch.
8 rooms: 42–46€.
Prix fixe: 8€, 28€, 8,50€ (child).
A la carte: 40€.

This Alsatian-style guesthouse stands on the wine route. The rooms are rustic and neat, and Michel's welcome does justice to Anne Imbs' cuisine. With the house vintages, we wash down monkfish medallions with ham, frog legs in puff pastry and the pigeon filet with orange-seasoned mustard sauce.

■ Le Vignoble   ⬒
1, rue de l'Eglise.
Tel. 03 88 92 43 75. Fax 03 88 92 62 21.
Closed Jan.
7 rooms: 54–74€.

A step away from the church, this converted barn dating back to 1765 offers trim little rooms. The atmosphere is rustic, Caroline Martin's welcome warm, the breakfast generous and the prices restrained. WiFi.

DANJOUTIN see BELFORT

DANNEMARIE

68210 Haut-Rhin. Paris 448 – Mulhouse 25 – Belfort 24 – Altkirch 10.
A traditional halt on the Sundgau fried carp route.

● RESTAURANTS

● Ritter
5, rue de la Gare.
Tel. 03 89 25 04 30. Fax 03 89 08 02 34.
Closed Mon. dinner, Tue., Thu. dinner, Christmas–New Year's vac., Feb. vac.,

1 week July.
Prix fixe: 9,50€ (lunch), 15€, 22€, 30€, 9,50€ (child). A la carte: 40€.

Richard Enderlin reliably runs this fine 1900 residence with its farm museum décor of tankards and tools. We savor the duck foie gras medallion, duckling with mirabelle plum sauce and the frozen Kirsch mousse. A pleasant choice of wines by the glass.

DAX

40100 Landes. Paris 733 –
Biarritz 60 – Mont-de-Marsan 54 – Pau 88 – Bordeaux 153.
tourisme.dax@wanadoo.fr.
The heart of the Landes, its sentinel and crossroads. The cathedral of Notre Dame, Borda museum, Gallo Roman walls and arenas are essential tourist attractions, not to mention the spas for mud and hot bath treatments, Potinière casino for gambling aficionados and automat museum, a treat for children.

HOTELS-RESTAURANTS

■ Grand Hôtel   🛏️🏨
Mercure Splendid
Cours Verdun.
Tel. 05 58 56 70 70. Fax 05 58 74 76 33.
h2148@accor-hotels.com / www.mercure.com
Closed beg. Jan.–end Feb.
106 rooms: 95–165€. 6 suites: 150–165€.
Prix fixe: 26€, 38€, 10€ (child).
A la carte: 35€.

Near the Adour river, this pure art deco hotel built in the thirties is a first-rate stopover. Its practical location in the town center, spacious beige and yellow rooms, pleasant spa and polished *pension* cuisine make a fine impression. Chef Laurent Mura takes a fresh, seasonal look at local Landes cuisine.

● L'Amphitryon   COM
38, cours Gallieni.
Tel. 05 58 74 58 05.
Closed Sat. lunch, Sun. dinner, Mon., 3 weeks Jan., 2 weeks end Aug.–beg. Sept.

Prix fixe: 20€, 26€, 38€.
A la carte: 40–45€.

The off-white dining room with its royal-blue tablecloths has been redecorated in a warmer style. In the kitchen, Eric Pujos prepares Landes recipes in his usual spirited way, with an eye to the Basque country. Grilled foie gras with local Ente prunes, monkfish escalope simmered with Spanish cured pork fat and served with an octopus fricassée, saffron-seasoned twice-cooked tripe and the Isarra-flavored mille-feuille make us wish we could eat here on a regular basis. Affable prices and well-chosen wines.

● **Une Cuisine en Ville** 🆕◎⟦SIM⟧
11, av G.-Clemenceau.
Tel. 05 58 90 26 89.
Closed Mon., Tue., mid-Aug.–beg. Sept.
Prix fixe: 32€, 52€.

Philippe Lagraula revolutionized the gourmet criteria of his town when he opened this elongated gastronomic arena with its modern chairs, beige and brown tones and open kitchen "lab". A veteran of the Bocuse school, who worked with Bras and Le Bec, and at Market in Paris, Lagraula presents modern, creative, tapas-style set menus. His smoked eel with slices of foie gras and tarama, the red tuna with a mango pepper and a combava oil bonbon, the "baby blanc pizza" with fresh white ewe's cheese and pickled seaweed, sea bass with bulgur risotto, marinated pigeon with spices and sauce chistora are finely crafted works. The desserts (the ice cream cones, with Maldon salted-butter caramel and limoncello yogurt and a hazelnut and strawberry concoction) are rare treats.

In Saint-Paul-les-Dax (40990). 3 km.
● **Moulin de Poustagnacq** ⟦V.COM⟧
Rue René-Loustalot, chemin de Poustagnacq.
Tel. 05 58 91 31 03. Fax 05 58 91 37 97.
Closed Sun. dinner, Mon., Tue. lunch,
Christmas–New Year's vac., Feb. vac.
Prix fixe: 29€, 39€, 69€, 15€ (child).
A la carte: 75€.

The mill has its charm, but then so does Thierry Berthelier's cuisine, a paean to tradition and the season. On the lakeside terrace by the woods or in the old-style dining room, we feast on salty jumbo shrimp grilled with piquillo peppers and served with gazpacho, a cod and potato mille-feuille, tender cooked pigeon breast with a reduction sauce and the crisp waffle and chocolate cappuccino. The welcome is delectable, the service enthusiastic and the cellar well stocked with Bordeaux vintages.

DEAUVILLE

14800 Calvados. Paris 199 – Caen 47 – Le Havre 41 – Evreux 101 – Lisieux 30 – Rouen 90.
infodeauville@deauville.org.
"In Deauville," said Tristan Bernard, "there's the sea too." The sea aside, the town has a gourmet temperament, with reliable restaurants, lively brasseries, affable stores and artisans modernizing Norman tradition. Then there is nostalgia. Nothing has changed since 1966, when Lelouch came here to shoot his movie *A Man and a Woman*. A love story between Jean-Louis Trintignant and Anouk Aimée, it is set in the typically Auge-style station, at the Hôtel Normandy and on the Planches promenade. It made the resort famous the world over. Its Normandy in winter was built of lone figures, soft dawns and shifting light on the beach. Out of season, Deauville is enchantingly peaceful. "Chabadabada again, it all starts over, life moves on." You only have to sit on the terrace at Miocque's or listen to Martine at Marthe's, telling the latest stories...

■	HOTELS

■ **Le Royal Barrière**
Bd E.-Cornuché.
Tel. 02 31 98 66 33. Fax 02 31 98 66 34.
royal@lucienbarriere.com
www.lucienbarriere.com
Closed mid-Nov.–beg. Mar. Rest. closed lunch
230 rooms: 177–509€.
22 suites: 500–3888€.
Prix fixe: 42€, 52€, 25€ (child)
A la carte: 74€.

This great twenties luxury hotel is a palace dedicated to the stars who have a named suite there (including Dustin Hoffman and Liz Taylor). Lavishly redesigned by Garcia, the rooms look out over the sea and Planches promenade. The hotel also boasts an outdoor pool and two restaurants (the traditional Côté Royal and the gastronomic Etrier).

■ Le Normandy XI
38, rue Jean-Mermoz.
Tel. 02 31 98 66 22. Fax 02 31 98 66 23.
www.lucienbarriere.com
257 rooms: 307–533€.
34 suites: 658–831€.
Prix fixe: 53€.

This 1912 Norman chalet where Claude Lelouch shot *A Man and a Woman* transcends fashion. The renovated rooms are in different colors. The restaurant is Belle Epoque, the inner courtyard charmingly Norman in style, the swimming pool indoor, the bar hushed and concierge Gérard Feuillie competent indeed. In the hands of André Plunian, the food is amiably universal.

■ Le Golf
Le Mont Canisy New Golf.
Tel. 02 31 14 24 00 / 02 31 14 24 23.
Fax 02 31 14 24 01.
www.lucienbarriere.com
Closed beg. Nov.–end Dec. Rest. closed lunch
178 rooms: 165–400€.
10 suites: 310–625€.
Prix fixe: 38€, 55€, 20€ (child).

This huge, half-timbered hotel with sea and country views offers rest and recreation at any hour, with massages, pedicure and manicure, golf course, swimming pool, spacious rooms and fine spreads in the two restaurants, the Pommeraie and Club House, where the dishes concocted by Christophe Bezannier are approved by all.

■ Hostellerie de Tourgéville
Chemin de l'Orgueil. 6 km s via D278.
Tel. 02 31 14 48 68. Fax 02 31 14 48 69.
www.hostellerie-de-tourgeville.fr
Rest. closed lunch (exc. Bank holidays),
3 weeks Feb.
6 rooms: 125–175€. 19 suites: 190–330€.
Prix fixe: 39€, 57€.

This neo-Norman manor surrounded by greenery is highly conducive to relaxation. Each with its own décor, the rooms are all named for movie stars. Director Claude Lelouch is the owner. The facilities include a projection room, gym, tennis court, two swimming pools, bicycles and table tennis and billiard tables, enough to keep us occupied for a quiet weekend. In the rustic dining room opening onto a patio, we enjoy tuna carpaccio, vanilla-seasoned John Dory, stuffed rabbit and a soft-centered chocolate biscuit.

■ L'Augeval
15, av Hocquart-de-Turtot.
Tel. 02 31 81 13 18. Fax 02 31 81 00 40.
info@augeval.com / www.augeval.com
32 rooms: 54–218€.

Between the church and the race track, this charming 19th-century manor with a hushed ambiance has a terrace, heated swimming pool, gym and neat rooms. A fine refectory (see Restaurants).

■ Continental
1, rue Désiré-Le-Hoc.
Tel. 02 31 88 21 06. Fax 02 31 98 93 67.
www.hotel-continental-deauville.com
Closed mid-Nov.–mid-Dec.
42 rooms: 54–93€.

Built in 1880, this hotel is ideally located near the station and the Quai de la Marine. It has guest rooms with double glazing and a pleasant breakfast room.

■ Hélios
10, rue Fossorier.
Tel. 02 31 14 46 46. Fax 02 31 88 53 87.
www.hotelheliosdeauville.com
45 rooms: 49–79€. 1 suite: 140–200€.

In the center of the resort, this modern hotel with its small swimming pool has contemporary guest rooms and a pleasant breakfast room. A complete renovation is scheduled for next year.

■ **Mercure Yacht Club**   🏠

2, rue Breney.
Tel. 02 31 87 30 00. Fax 02 31 87 05 80.
h2876@accor.com
www.mercure-hotel.com
Closed beg. Jan.–beg. Feb.
53 rooms: 93–166€.

This modern hotel with its neat, practical rooms offers views of the yachts and park. The breakfasts are very generous.

■ **Le Trophée**   🏠

81, rue du Général-Leclerc.
Tel. 02 31 88 45 86 (hotel); 02 31 88 28 46 (rest.). Fax: 02 31 88 07 94 (hotel) / 02 31 87 52 27 (rest.).
information@letrophee.com
www.letrophee.com
25 rooms: 54–199€. 10 suites: 119–199€.
Prix fixe: 18€ (lunch), 37€, 46€.
A la carte: 65€.

Right in the center, this hotel boasts bright, comfortable rooms (some with a balcony or balneotherapy tub), as well as its Flambée rotisserie, where Fabrice Vingtrois prepares a contemporary cuisine.

■ **Côte Fleurie**   🏠

55, av de la République.
Tel. 02 31 98 47 47. Fax 02 31 98 47 46.
www.hoteldelacotefleurie.com
Closed 3 weeks Jan.
15 rooms: 63–76€.

Near the Touques racetrack, this Deauville hostelry with its brightly decorated rooms and patio is a delightful place to stay.

In Villers-sur-Mer (14640). 7 km. sw.

■ **Domaine de Villers**   🅽♣🏠

Chemin du Belvédère.
Tel. 02 31 81 80 80. Fax 02 31 81 80 70.
www.domainedevillers.com
Closed 10 days end Jan.–beg. Feb. Rest. closed lunch (exc. Fri., Sat. Sun.), Wed.
17 rooms: 120–245€.
Prix fixe: 32–44€.

This fine manor by the sea offers fine grounds and a swimming pool. The contemporary, art deco and Directoire rooms are spacious, the bar welcoming and the restaurant serves a voguish take on Norman cuisine.

● | RESTAURANTS

● **L'Etrier**   ⦿**LUX**

At Le Royal, bd Cornuché.
Tel. 02 31 98 66 33. Fax 02 31 98 66 34.
royal@lucienbarriere.com
www.lucienbarrierre.com
Closed beg. Nov.–beg. Mar.
Prix fixe: 62€ (dinner), 92€ (dinner).

Although he works closely with Ciro's in an advisory role, Eric Provost is still the maestro of the Royal. This pupil of Ghislaine Arabian who worked with Alain Ducasse prepares a meticulous cuisine based on fine produce from Normandy and further afield. We are charmed by duck foie gras cooked in mild spices, served with a small blood sausage, whole lobster with lemon flowers and the slow-braised veal shank seasoned with soy sauce and cider. The desserts, such as orange-flavored caramelized lemon confit tart served with carrot and citrus ice cream are also very impressive. The fine cellar boasts 100 vintages and the waitstaff are young and conscientious.

● **Le Ciro's**   **LUX**

Bd de la Mer, promenade des Planches.
Tel. 02 31 14 31 31. Fax 02 31 88 32 02.
casinodeauville@lucienbarriere.com
www.casinodeauvillelucienbarriere.com
Closed Tue., Wed. (Oct.–Apr.), 3 weeks Jan.
Prix fixe: 39€ (weekdays, lunch),
25€ (child). A la carte: 75€.

This star restaurant on the Planches promenade has adopted a new strategy. Joël Malebranche, who knows all there is to know about the region's cheeses, is still master of the house, but the kitchen is now in the hands of Eric Provost from the Etrier, who has brought a new zest to the menu. Quick-seared tuna perfumed with coriander, anchovies in fleur de sel, thick-cut Atlantic sea bass filet with a flavorful sundried tomato-flavored pasta and the turbot with its button mushrooms and gray shrimp are examples of his cutting edge perfomances. Fine desserts (strawberry vacherin, pineapple carpaccio, fruit minestrone) and meticulous service.

● L'Augeval V.COM

15, av Hocquart-de-Turtot.
Tel. 02 31 81 13 18. Fax 02 31 81 00 40.
info@augeval.com / www.augeval.com
Prix fixe: 20€ (lunch), 42€, 60€,
14€ (child). A la carte: 45–65€.

In this discreet manor next to the church, Thierry Legrix continues to serve enchanting dishes. The "petals" of duck foie gras accompanied by a smoked oil–seasoned mixed green salad, sole meuniere served in all of its simplicity and glazed chestnut mousse with vanilla cream and Curacao-flavored ice cream are washed down with a well-chosen wine by the glass (see Hotels.)

● Le Brummel COM

At the Casino, 2, rue Edmond-Blanc.
Tel. 02 31 14 31 14. Fax 02 31 14 66 71.
casinobarriere@lucienbarriere.com
lucienbarriere.com
Prix fixe: 25€. A la carte: 50€.

The décor of this rococo brasserie is signed Garcia. Philippe Lechanoine's cuisine is charming indeed, with his Italian vegetable tart, tender cod with tomatoes and a lovely surprise in the grilled lamb chops. The fried Bounty candy bar in sorbet, the strawberries in mousse and Tagada candy take us back to our childhood days.

● Le Spinnaker COM

52, rue Mirabeau.
Tel. 02 31 88 24 40. Fax 02 31 88 43 58.
Pascal732@aol.com / www.adeauville.com
Closed Mon. (off season), Tue. (off season),
2 weeks Nov., Jan., 1 week at end June.
Prix fixe: 30€, 40€ (wine inc.), 45€.
A la carte: 60€.

In his contemporary, blue-tinted restaurant, Pascal Angenard is the soul of reliability. His foie gras with four spices, chitterling

sausage fricassée with potatoes, locally fished sole with a reduced jus and the turbot with shallots are finely crafted. In conclusion, we turn to the pastry cart. There are a few good wines by the glass.

● Les Trois Mages COM

1, av de la Terrasse.
Tel. 02 31 88 55 00. Fax 02 31 88 86 13.
les3mages@wanadoo.fr
Closed Tue. (off season), Wed. (off season).
A la carte: 70–80€.

On the Planches promenade, this fashionable restaurant serves a voguish cuisine. Salmon maki with goat cheese and apples, Spanish-style steamed rouget, lamb medallion served Middle Eastern style and a waffle with pralined fruit mousse are effective. An indifferent welcome.

● Yearling COM

38, av Hocquart-de-Turtot.
Tel. 02 31 88 33 37. Fax 02 31 88 33 89.
www.le-yearling.fr
Closed Mon., Tue., 2 weeks Jan.
Prix fixe: 15€, 21€, 34€. A la carte: 65–75€.

Revived by Christophe Joumaa, who used to work in the dining rooms of Ciro's and the Normandy, this English-style bistro is a discreet retreat by the racetrack. Foie gras terrine with slow-cooked apples, grilled langoustines with raspberry vinegar, duck breast with sweet and sour sauce and the sorbets presented on a painter's palette are quietly enjoyable.

● Le Temptation N·SIM

77, rue du Général-Leclerc.
Tel. 02 31 98 25 45. Fax 02 31 98 91 56.
temptation-deauville@wanadoo.fr
Closed weekday dinner (exc. vac.).
Prix fixe: 15€ (weekday lunch),
19€ (weekday lunch). A la carte: 45–50€.

Isabelle Piquenet has changed the name of the Bagdad Café and turned it into a tasteful eatery. Her fisherman husband sails on a trawler and brings the best of his catch here, which explains the freshness of the tuna tartare, basket of shrimp tempura, turbot filet and the Provençal-style pan-fried scallops served with truffle risotto. The oxtail parmentier and the apple tiramisu are also very commendable. Couscous is served on the weekend in memory of the Temptation's former name.

● Le Dosville　　SIM
70, rue Gambetta.
Tel. 02 31 88 30 75. Fax 02 31 88 30 79.
le.dosville@free.fr
Closed Tue. (exc. Bank holidays and vac.),
Wed. (exc. Bank holidays and vac.).
Prix fixe: 19,50€, 14,50€ (weekday lunch),
34,50€, 42,50€. A la carte: 63€.

A veteran of Bocuse, the Tour d'Argent and Rostang, Patrick Mari has opted for a modest approach here. The set menus are simple and the dishes conventional, but the preparations strike the right note and his touch never falters. Pan-fried John Dory seasoned with sesame seeds, scallops with potato cakes and the kirsch- and cream-seasoned morel-stuffed pigeon are among his useful tricks.

● Le Drakkar　　SIM
77, rue Eugène-Colas.
Tel. 02 31 88 71 24. Fax 02 31 88 49 27.
www.restaurant-le-drakkar.com
Closed Christmas.
Prix fixe: 26,60€. A la carte: 45–50€.

Hervé Van Colen, who has several businesses in Trouville, takes great care of this paneled brasserie in the center of town. Fish soup, grilled Atlantic sea bass, sole meunière, escalope with cream sauce and a fruit crumble slip down smoothly.

● Le Garage　　SIM
118 bis, av de la République.
Tel. 02 31 87 25 25. Fax 02 31 87 38 37.
Closed mid-Dec.–beg. Jan., 1 week Feb. vac.,
May 1.
Prix fixe: 18€, 28€, 12,50€ (child).
A la carte: 40–50€.

The Le Roys have turned this modest brasserie into a generous, reliable restaurant. Under the fresco of cars on the wall and among the brass and pictures of actors, we savor simple, reliable home

cooking in a noisy, relaxed atmosphere: mussels in cream, skate with beurre noisette, a lamb shank and the tarte Tatin with fresh cream.

● Chez Julie　　SIM
29-31, rue Mirabeau.
Tel. 02 31 87 22 11.
www.restaurantchezjulie.com
Closed Mon. (exc. July–Aug.), Tue. (exc. July–Aug.), Jan.
Prix fixe: 15€ (weekday lunch), 25€.
A la carte: 38€.

Julie Mabille enthusiastically tends to this stylish restaurant in orange and mauve shades. The Thai salad, rare-cooked salmon with Indonesian-style shrimp and the honey-glazed chicken brochet are deftly crafted by Olivier Delante.

● Chez Miocque　　SIM
81, rue Eugène-Colas.
Tel. 02 31 88 09 52.
Closed Tue., Wed., Jan.
A la carte: 50€.

There has been a revolution here: Jacques Miocque has retired and his disciple Jérôme Peuset is now at the helm. The Fiftiess café setting with its imitation leather banquettes and mirrors is the same as ever and the cuisine has not changed a jot. The mussels in cream, spinach salad, sole meunière, 500-gram rib eye steak and the crème brûlée are still very honest.

DELME

57590 Moselle. Paris 365 – Metz 33 –
Nancy 31 – Château-Salins 12 –
Pont-à-Mousson 29.
communedelme.free.fr.
A village in the Metz countryside where the old synagogue has been turned into a museum.

■ HOTELS-RESTAURANTS

■ A la Douzième Borne　　⌂
6, pl de la République.
Tel. 03 87 01 30 18. Fax 03 87 01 38 39.

XIIborne@wanadoo.fr
www.12eme-borne.com
Rest. closed Sun., Mon. dinner.
16 rooms: 49–70€. Prix fixe: 20€, 33€, 45€.

Bernard, Jean, Michel and René François (the first two in the kitchen, the others in the dining room) are brothers. Behind their establishment's impressive facade, modernity and tradition cohabit cordially. The rooms are practical and the set menus polished. The store sells local produce and the food and wine are reliably presented. Duck foie gras with quince, sole meunière, duckling with orange marmalade and a mirabelle plum dessert are washed down with selected wines.

DENGOLSHEIM see SESSENHEIM

LES-DEUX-ALPES

38860 Isère. Paris 642 – Grenoble 78 – Le Bourg d'Oisans 26 – Vienne 40.
les2alp@les2alpes.com.
A mountain setting at 1,660 meters, with panoramic terraces looking out on the Croix and Cimes and expeditions to the Croisière-Blanche and Ecrins national park.

 HOTELS-RESTAURANTS

● Le Chalet Mounier

2, rue de la Chapelle.
Tel. 04 76 80 56 90. Fax 04 76 79 56 51.
doc@chalet-mounier.com
www.chalet-mounier.com
Closed beg. May–mid-June,
beg. Sept.–mid-Dec. Rest. closed lunch (exc. Sun. and Bank holidays).
47 rooms: 90–145€.
Prix fixe: 35€, 44€, 48€, 55€.

This kitschy rustic chalet with its carved woodwork is impossible to miss. In the hands of Alban Mounier, the ex-Auberge Balme provides neat rooms, a heated swimming pool, a steam bath and a first-rate restaurant. Guests in the dining room with its operetta décor sit down to Eric Sana's local cuisine with its southern French touch. The cold tomato soup

with crayfish tails, the John Dory seasoned with garden herbs served in a cocotte, the farm-raised pigeon, like the strawberry and creamy lemon macarons, warm our hearts, as does the impressive collection of wines.

● Le Diable au Coeur   SIM

Télécabines du Diable.
Tel. 04 76 79 99 50.
www.lediableaucoeur.com
Closed dinner (exc. group reserv.), beg. Sept.–mid-Dec., beg. Apr.–mid-June.
Prix fixe: 11€ (child), 19€.
A la carte: 41€.

At the top of the Diable cable car line, the Mouniers provide a generous welcome in their eatery near the pistes. Anthony Bertaux prepares polished Alpine dishes. Crozets (the local pasta) in Beaufort gratin, pork tenderloin medallion in a Réblochon cheese crust and the wild blueberry crumble make an excellent impression.

DIEBOLSHEIM see RHINAU
DIEFFENBACH-AU-VAL see VILLE

DIEFMATTEN

68780 Haut-Rhin. Paris 536 – Mulhouse 21 – Colmar 49 – Belfort 23 – Thann 14.
This is where gourmet Sundgau begins, in a simple, neat village that seems to have been transported from another age.

 HOTELS-RESTAURANTS

● Le Cheval Blanc   V.COM

17, rue de Hecken.
Tel. 03 89 26 91 08. Fax 03 89 26 92 28.
patrick@auchevalblanc.fr
www.auchevalblanc.fr
Closed Mon. (exc. lunch Bank holidays), Tue. (exc. lunch Bank holidays), 2 weeks mid-Jan., 2 weeks end July.
8 rooms: 54–99€.
Prix fixe: 23€ (weekday lunch), 52€, 34€, 39€. A la carte: 70€.

This former farm in pastel blue has been converted into a modern hostelry. Patrick

Schlienger, son of the family and disciple of Bocuse, Jung and Willer, presides over the stove. His parents tend to the dining room with a smile, while sommelier Daniel Gresser recommends fine wines from Alsace and elsewhere. Savoring the foie gras confit, grilled sole with a saffron-seasoned foam, guinea hen breast in caramelized cream, cherry soup with almond milk ice cream and the strawberry profiteroles with pistachio ice cream, we wish we could eat here on a regular basis. A terrace, pleasant grounds and eight trim rooms for an overnight stay.

DIEMERINGEN see SARRE-UNION

DIEPPE

76200 Seine-Maritime. Paris 195 – Abbeville 68 – Caen 172 – Le Havre 110 – Rouen 65.
66.officetour.dieppe@wanadoo.fr.
With its chalk cliffs, château museum and ferries crossing to England, this seafaring town has a taste of distant horizons.

 HOTELS-RESTAURANTS

■ Aguado
30, bd de Verdun.
Tel. 02 35 84 27 00. Fax 02 35 06 17 61.
chris-bert@tiscali.fr / www.hoteldieppe.com
56 rooms: 39–92€. 4 suites: 102€.

This cozy seafront hotel offers English furniture, impeccable rooms in gentle shades and a relaxing bar.

■ Hôtel de l'Europe
63, bd de Verdun.
Tel. 02 32 90 19 19. Fax 02 32 90 19 00.
www.hoteldieppe.com
Closed Jan.
60 rooms: 85–88€.

Alain Bert runs this hotel, with its wood and concrete facade, equipped with bright rooms in beige and blue tones, furnished in rattan and looking out over the sea. Internet.

■ Hôtel de la Plage
20, bd de Verdun.
Tel. 02 35 84 18 28. Fax 02 35 82 36 82.
plagehotel@wanadoo.fr / www.plagehotel.fr.st
40 rooms: 45–80€.

Gentle prices, neat rooms bathed in light and the sea stretching out to the horizon. WiFi.

● La Mélie
2, Grande-Rue du Pollet.
Tel. 02 35 84 21 19. Fax 02 35 06 24 27.
Closed Sun. dinner, Mon.
Prix fixe: 20€ (weekday lunch), 28€ (weekdays, wine inc.), 35€, 48€.

Do not judge this discreet restaurant in blue and champagne by its cover. The old-fashioned facade conceals a delightful dining room with a changing menu. In the hands of François Hue, who trained with Vigato and Loiseau, the fine produce of the Dieppe tides and the land around the Baie de Somme express themselves to the full. On the table, lobster in season, pan-seared scallops, turbot (poached or grilled to your liking), Houdan poultry and Breton salt marsh lamb (pré-salé) tend towards subtle, fresh, personal preparations. Kazuyo Hue's delightful smile brightens the dining room.

● Bistrot du Pollet
23, rue de la Tête-de-Boeuf.
Tel. 02 35 84 68 57.
Closed Sun., Mon., 2 weeks Apr., 4 days mid-Aug.
Prix fixe: 11€. A la carte: 35€.

Pleasant, inexpensive and located very close to the harbor, this marine bistro is looking healthy indeed. Xavier Hericher's sea catch changes from day to day. A few oysters, tarragon-seasoned catfish served whole and a Calvados soufflé are highly enjoyable.

● La Musardière
61, quai Henri-IV.
Tel.-Fax 02 35 82 94 14.
www.restaurant-lamusadiere.com
Closed Wed. (exc. July–Aug.), 1 week Nov., Jan.

Prix fixe: 12€, 15,50€, 20€, 26€,
8€ (child). A la carte: 30–40€.

Laurent Duriez has turned this restaurant in pink shades with its terrace overlooking the marina into a lively place. Fish soup, scallops with garlic cream sauce, sirloin steak with foie gras and the tarte Normande make a fine impression.

DIEUE-SUR-MEUSE see **VERDUN**

26220 Drôme. Paris 627 –
Valence 67 – Montélimar 28 – Nyons 30 –
Orange 58.
ot.dieulefit@wanadoo.fr.
Between Provençal Drôme and the wonders of Tricastin, a corner of contentment for lovers of peace, quiet and light.

 HOTELS-RESTAURANTS

In Poët-Laval (26160). 5 km w via D 540.
■ **Les Hospitaliers**
Vieux Village.
Tel. 04 75 46 22 32. Fax 04 75 46 49 99.
www.hotel-les-hospitaliers.com
Rest. closed Mon. (off season),
Tue. (off season), mid-Nov.–mid-Mar.
20 rooms: 70–140€. 2 suites: 145–160€.
Prix fixe: 25€, 39€, 53€. A la carte: 61€.

In the heart of a fine Drôme village overlooking the Rhône Valley, this charming hotel occupying old stone houses enchants travelers in search of authenticity. Garden, swimming pool, fitness center, rooms of character and a fine restaurant all go to make our stay a pleasant one. Whether we choose to eat on the panoramic terrace or in the rustic dining room with its blond stone and large beams, we relish the white bean ice cream and goat cheese quenelle, roasted monkfish with langoustine reduction sauce, roasted guinea hen and cardamom-seasoned apricot crumble served with salted-butter caramel.

04000 Alpes de Haute-Provence. Paris 748 –
Aix-en-Provence 109 – Cannes 136 – Gap 89.
info@ot.dignelesbains.fr.
This modest capital of the Provençal highlands is a crossroads on the Alpine route.

 HOTELS-RESTAURANTS

■ **Le Grand Paris**
19, bd Thiers.
Tel. 04 92 31 11 15. Fax 04 92 32 32 82.
www.hotel-grand-paris.com
Closed 1 Dec.–1 Mar.
Rest. closed Mon. lunch (off season), Tue. lunch (off season), Wed. lunch (off season).
16 rooms: 80–165€. 4 suites: 130–170€.
Prix fixe: 31€, 43€, 58€, 65€.
A la carte: 67–77€.

Hotel and restaurant have been renovated in this former 17th-century convent, now a family hostelry. Here, we have everything we need, right down to the fitness center. Jean-Jacques Ricaud provides a solid cuisine based on polished classic recipes. The scallops with white bean mousseline and sherry sauce, monkfish with pesto, lamb tenderloin medallion in the style of chef Casimir Moisson and the warm lime soufflé never stale, especially with Noémie helping us to choose a wine that will flatter the food.

■ **Villa Gaïa**
24, rte de Nice, 2 km s via N85.
Tel. 04 92 31 21 60. Fax 04 92 31 20 12.
hotel.gaia@wanadoo.fr / www.hotelvillagaia.fr
Closed 20 Oct.–mid-Apr., 1 week beg. July.
Rest. closed weekdays lunch
10 rooms: 55–92€. Prix fixe: 26€ (dinner).

This large house set in wooded grounds is a haven of peace and comfort with its lounge, library and individualized rooms. Anne-Françoise Martin concocts eggplant salad, oven-browned cod, herb-seasoned rabbit with polenta and a frozen meringue dessert with fruit, while her husband Georges Eric offers a warm welcome.

DIJON

21000 Côte-d'Or. Paris 311 –
Auxerre 152 – Bâle 255 – Besançon 91 –
Genève 190 – Lyon 194.
infotourisme@ot-dijon.fr.

O happy city! Every inch Burgundian and passionately French. Venturing along the rue de la Liberté and rue Musette, we enjoy a provincial ambiance that has hardly changed in more than a century. On our way, we come across a splendid cast-iron market which takes on a theatrical air when it grows busy, full of incomparable cheesemongers, tasteful bakers, pork butchers ready to defend "their" jambon persillé (a local specialty—parsley and ham terrine) and chocolate makers who just will not throw in the towel. Dijon is a paean to Burgundian produce, and tradition is perpetuated in its Old World stores behind retro facades. They shelter not only impassioned artisans, but also local specialties with a worldwide reputation: mustard, pain d'épice, Cassis and of course l'escargot. In the heat of the moment, we could almost forget that the Côte de Nuits vineyards begin at its gates.

■	HOTELS

■ Sofitel la Cloche   🏬

14, pl Darcy.
Tel. 03 80 30 12 32. Fax 03 80 30 04 15.
h1202@accor-hotels.com
www.hotel-lacloche.com
53 rooms: 150–195€. 15 suites: 245–400€.

Under the Accor flag, this 1900 luxury hotel has kept its ornate facade and old-fashioned ambiance. The suites on the top floor, piano bar and gym make a good impression. The fine restaurant is called the "Jardins de la Cloche". (See Restaurants.)

● Hostellerie du   ◐🏬
Chapeau Rouge

5, rue Michelet.
Tel. 03 80 50 88 88. Fax 03 80 50 88 89.
www.chapeau-rouge.fr
Rest. closed 2 weeks beg. Jan.
30 rooms: 125–260€.
Prix fixe: 38€ (lunch), 100€. A la carte: 76€.

This 1863 hostelry provides modern rooms and a suitable restaurant. In the entirely red dining room, William Frachot, who trained in England, Montreal and New York, serves up a spirited, hybrid cuisine. Pan-fried langoustines in their shells with an aged goat cheese risotto, wild Atlantic sea bass in a seaweed and shellfish salad with a ginger-seasoned veal reduction sauce, veal sweetbreads served with a vegetable and noodle stir fry and the warm coffee biscuit with mandarin orange jelly are washed down with wines from all over the world.

■ Hôtel Mercure   🏬
& le Château Bourgogne

22, bd de la Marne.
Tel. 03 80 72 31 13. Fax 03 80 73 61 45.
www.mercure.com
116 rooms: 85,50–124€.
7 suites: 142,60–155€.
Prix fixe: 29€, 45€. A la carte: 59€.

This chain hotel next to the Palais des Congrès is very practical. The functional rooms, professional welcome and contemporary restaurant supervised by Gonzalo Pineiro (escargots in their shells, pantossed cod and a mint-glazed strawberry soup) strike just the right note.

■ Le Jacquemart   🏠

32, rue Verrerie.
Tel. 03 80 60 09 60. Fax 03 80 60 09 69.
www.hotel-lejacquemart.fr
28 rooms: 49–59€. 3 suites: 79€.

In the heart of the city, this 17th-century building with its antique furniture provides a friendly welcome and renovated town house guest rooms.

■ Philippe Le Bon   🏠

18, rue Sainte-Anne.
Tel. 03 80 30 73 52. Fax 03 80 30 95 51.
www.hotelphilippelebon.com
32 rooms: 78–196€.

The rooms are functional and some of them have a view over the roofs of Dijon. A medieval restaurant: Les Oenophiles (see Restaurants).

■ Wilson ⬆

Pl Wilson, 1, rue de Longvic.
Tel. 03 80 66 82 50. Fax 03 80 36 41 54.
hotelwilson@wanadoo.fr
www.wilson-hotel.com
27 rooms: 73–91€.

This 17th-century post house in Louis-Philippe style boasts a pleasant inner courtyard and rooms refurbished in light shades, all just next to the Derbord restaurant.

■ Hôtel du Palais ⬆

23, rue du Palais.
Tel. 03 80 67 16 26. Fax 03 80 65 12 16.
hoteldupalais-dijon@wanadoo.fr
11 rooms: 38–68€. 2 suites: 48–93€.

In the heart of the old city, this 17th-century establishment offers charming rooms, a pleasant welcome and affable prices.

● RESTAURANTS

● Le Pré aux Clercs ◉LUX

13, pl de la Libération.
Tel. 03 80 38 05 05. Fax 03 80 38 16 16.
billoux@club-internet.fr
www.le-pre-aux-clercs.com
Closed Sun. dinner, Mon., 1 week Feb. vac.,
2 weeks Aug.
Prix fixe: 35€ (weekdays lunch, wine inc.),
48€, 90€.

Gourmet king of Dijon for almost twenty years, Jean-Pierre Billoux now works with his son Alexis in the kitchen, but still defends his title as Burgundy's great classicist, championing dishes that have been forgotten elsewhere. Escargots in red wine sauce, pike-perch with mustard sauce and the chicken with red wine in the style of Alexandre Dumaine (who taught Billoux everything during his retirement in Digoin) are the fare we find in this dining room with its French-style ceiling, fine leather armchairs and sober, timeless décor. Coriander-seasoned squab in aspic, sesame-seasoned poultry with frog legs served with watercress vinaigrette, scallop brochette with stuffed endives and poultry livers, sauce prepared with beer, Bresse hen with pistachio-seasoned sausage and spelt risotto, Burgundy cheeses (Citeaux, Epoisses), strawberry soufflé, crème brûlée and the Paris-Brest (a choux pastry ring with almonds and butter cream) are just some of the irrefutable facts provided by the house *cuisine de vérité*. Sommelier Patrice Gillard has been here for more than thirty years and serves Burgundies of great character (such as Hudelot or Denis Mortet Gevrey-Chambertin) to accompany these delights.

● Stéphane Derbord ◉V.COM

10, pl Wilson.
Tel. 03 80 67 74 64. Fax 03 80 63 87 72.
www.restaurantstephanederbord.fr
Closed Sun., Mon. lunch, Tue. lunch,
1 week Feb., 2 weeks beg. Aug.
Prix fixe: 25€ (weekday lunch), 45€, 55€,
65€, 15€ (child). A la carte: 80€.

Stéphane Derbord plays to a lively score in this modern restaurant, serving up topical Burgundian dishes. Escargots in broth served with a crisped veal trotter flavored with mild garlic, pike-perch in crème brûlée with celery and orange caramel and Charolais sirloin steak with horseradish oil and mustard sauce display a focused creativity. For dessert, poached pain d'épice–seasoned whipped egg whites with almond milk ice cream are a charming allusion to the region. The 780 vintages on the wine list here turn our heads.

● Les Œnophiles 🏠V.COM

At the Philippe-le-Bon, 18, rue Sainte-Anne.
Tel. 03 80 30 73 52. Fax 03 80 30 95 51.
www.hotelphilippelebon.com
Closed Sun., lunch (Aug.).
Prix fixe: 21€ (lunch, weekdays), 29€, 60€.
A la carte: 62–72€.

The wine museum cellar, Gothic courtyard, collection of historical figurines, medieval dining rooms and reproductions of period paintings are impressive, and Stéphane Catane's cuisine is equally studied. Frog legs grilled with oysters in a mild garlic cream sauce and sirloin steak with foie gras and pain d'épice are not bad. The pralined puffed rice cake provides a sweet conclusion.

● La Côte Saint-Jean 🏠🔲COM

13, rue Monge.
Tel. 03 80 50 11 77. Fax 03 80 50 18 75.
Closed Tue., Wed., 2 weeks Jan.,
3 weeks Aug.
Prix fixe: 16€ (lunch), 27,50€, 39€.

Stephen Houchin trained at the Savoy in London before losing his heart to rural France and coming over to the Continent. He has turned this cozy restaurant with its moldings, exposed stone and green facade into a temple devoted to fine Burgundian produce. We enjoy his pain d'épice, foie gras, fresh Gilly cheese, broiled escargot and bacon-stuffed artichoke hearts with Chartreuse sauce, breast of guinea hen in the style of Gaston Gérard and a light cassis mousse with pain d'épice ice cream. The French countryside is sweet indeed when viewed through the eyes of this artisan from Albion!

● La Dame d'Aquitaine 🔲COM

23, pl Bossuet.
Tel. 03 80 30 45 65. Fax 03 80 49 90 41.
dame.aquitaine@wanadoo.fr
Closed Sun., Mon.
Prix fixe: 29€, 33,80€, 42€.
A la carte: 55€.

This vaulted 13th-century crypt has changed hands. Laurent Perriguey now serves a sound, well-crafted cuisine here. Slow-cooked lasagne with foie gras, roasted pike-perch, rabbit saddle served with its kidneys and a flambéed pain d'épice ice cream and meringue dessert express an unfussy regionalism.

● Le Gastronome 🔲COM

19, rue d'Auxonne.
Tel. 03 80 66 12 40.
Closed Sun., Mon., 3 weeks Aug.
Prix fixe: 15,50€ (lunch), 30€, 33€, 40€.

Cyrille Riandet, a native of Beaune who worked at the Bénaton, Jardin des Remparts and Ecusson, has taken over the former Gourmandin with gusto, and given it a significant new name. Lightly reinterpreted tradition is his "thing", expressed in precise preparations of choice fresh produce. The marbled "all beef" terrine with foamy mustard emulsion, a crab and horseradish mille-feuille, fireplace-grilled duck breast and a waffle made to order are works well done.

● Ma Bourgogne 🔲COM

1, bd Paul-Doumer.
Tel. 03 80 65 48 06. Fax 03 80 67 82 65.
Closed Sat., Sun. dinner, Feb. vac.
Prix fixe: 22€ (weekdays), 28€, 33€.

Bernard Minot, a fine local classicist, serves unsurprising but flawless dishes. The minced quail with foie gras, Armagnac-flambéed kidneys and a pain d'épice charlotte are in good taste.

● Le Cézanne 🔲COM

38, rue de l'Amiral-Roussin.
Tel. 03 80 58 91 92. Fax 03 80 49 86 80.
Closed Sun., Mon. lunch, 1 week Christmas–New Year's, 2 weeks Aug.
Prix fixe: 17,50€, 28€, 38€, 13€ (child).

In the heart of Dijon's historic center, the Ardoint brothers (Benoît in the dining room and David in the kitchen) play to a light Provençal score. Rouget in escabeche, pike-perch with mushroom- and ham-stuffed artichokes simmered in wine, honey and lavender, lemon-seasoned strips of duck breast and a creamy apricot dessert with thyme ice cream are enchanting surprises.

● Le Théâtre des Sens 🔲🔲SIM

31, rue Chabot-Charny.
Tel. 03 80 31 39 53.
Closed Sat. lunch, Mon., mid-July–mid-Aug.
Prix fixe: 22€, 32€.

Christophe Chartelet, who studied with a number of fine Beaune chefs (Crotet, Monoir and Morillon) and then in Paris (with Savoy and Le Divellec), has now opened this mischievous bistro with its red walls and modern lighting. The message here is a fresh modern take on traditional cuisine, producing Dombe-style frog legs, pike-perch with black mustard sauce, chanterelle-stuffed suckling pig, tender tête de veau served with royale-style slow-cooked beef cheeks. The tarte Tatin with thick caramel is a delicacy.

● Le Bistrot des Halles   SIM

10, rue Bannelier.
Tel. 03 80 49 94 15. Fax 03 80 38 16 16.
billoux@club-internet.fr
Closed Mon., Thu. dinner, 1 week Christmas–
New Year's.
Prix fixe: 16€ (lunch). A la carte: 35€.

Although this authentic, old-fashioned bistro looks as if it has been standing here by the market forever, it is actually just fourteen years old. An unannounced adjunct of the Pré aux Clercs, it is prized by good food buffs. The lentil salad with chitterling sausage or with cold asparagus cream, spit-roasted pork tongue, beef Bourguignon and fresh white cheese or slice of berry tart on the 16 menu the other day were exquisite. Jean-Pierre Billoux has put together an efficient team and offers some of the best value for money in the city.

● La Fringale   N SIM

Chez l'Polo
53, rue Jeannin.
Tel. 03 80 67 69 37.
Closed Sun., Mon., Aug.
Prix fixe: 11€ (lunch), 16€, 24€.

Jean-Paul Seurat, alias l'Polo, works on fresh fish with gusto. Steamed salmon with a curry sauce, grilled rouget with basil, simply prepared Breton sole meunière, scallops in a seafood broth or speared on brochettes and the turbot with olive oil and sel de Guérande cut no corners where quality is concerned. A cozy décor with blue checked tablecloths for marine enthusiasts.

● Le Chabrot   SIM

36, rue Monge.
Tel. 03 80 30 69 61. Fax 03 80 50 02 35.
lechabrot@wanadoo.fr
Prix fixe: 9,50€ (lunch), 20,50€, 30€.
A la carte: 35€.

We enter through the handsomely converted wine cellar on the street side, where we select our wine by the glass or bottle with 250 temptations to choose from. We then snack in the bistro or dine upstairs on chef M. Daperon's stylish creations: ham and parsley terrine, salmon filet pan seared on one side and finished under the broiler, coq au vin with pain perdu, concluding with a flavorful pain d'épice sorbet, made all the more digestible by a mild-mannered check.

● Les Jardins de la Cloche   SIM

14, pl Darcy.
Tel. 03 80 30 12 32. Fax 03 80 30 04 15.
h1202@accor-hotels.com
www.hotel-lacloche.com
Prix fixe: 26€ (weekday lunch), 31€, 40€
(wine inc.), 12€ (child). A la carte: 65–75€

This hotel restaurant provides a true feast for 31 . Behind its late-19th-century facade, the Jardin has enjoyed a modern makeover. The subtle enchantments of its menu are woven by René Villard and Romain Detot, working together. Poultry liver salad with radishes and crunchy bacon, crisped veal sweetbreads with grapes and endive and a praline dacquoise with whiskey-seasoned mousse look good indeed.

In Marsannay-la-Côte (21160). 8 km s via N74.

● Les Gourmets   V.COM

8, rue du Puits-de-Tet.
Tel. 03 80 52 16 32. Fax 03 80 52 03 01.
www.les-gourmets.com
Closed Sun., Mon., Tue. lunch,
mid-Jan.–10 Feb., 2 weeks Aug.
Prix fixe: 29€, 38€, 59€, 78€,
18€ (child). A la carte: 80–110€.

In his winegrowing village on the Côte de Nuits, Joël Perreaut is a font of wisdom. His opulent green and yellow dining room with its terrace in summer has a vintage eighties air. The dishes are tasteful indeed. The traditional poached eggs in Chardonnay sauce with garlicky escargots, pork ear and trotter and white beans in salad, poultry breast

293

with morels and a veal cutlet served in a cocotte with its flavorful cooking juices and a Carnaroli risotto are delightfully reinterpreted in a fashionable light. The Burgundian wine list is superb, with sommelier Grégory Jacquelin offering shrewd advice. The desserts are tempting (crêpes Suzette flambéed tableside, the light Grand Marnier soufflé and pan-simmered golden apples seasoned with lemongrass and the chestnut waffles). Nicole Perreault provides a marvelous welcome.

In Prenois (21370). 12 km nw via N71 and D104.

● **Auberge de la Charme**   ◎COM

12, rue de la Charme.
Tel. 03 80 35 32 84. Fax 03 80 35 34 48.
davidlacharme@aol.com
Closed Sun. dinner, Mon., Tue. lunch, Feb. vac., 10 days beg. Aug.
Prix fixe: 18€ (weekdays lunch, wine inc.), 41€, 57€, 75€, 10€ (child).

Just a few kilometers from Dijon, this former smithy is home to one of the brightest young hopes of the culinary world. David Zuddas, formerly Jeunet's lieutenant in Arbois, creates subtle, original dishes that are suitably complemented by the extensive wine list. In the dining room with its exposed stone, the celery remoulade with jumbo shrimp, cod with verjus-marinated vegetables and veal sweetbreads served with kumquats and broccoli amuse, startle and enchant. The desserts, including a fruit and date medjoul served with buttermilk and Argan-seasoned ice cream, are from the same mold. A restaurant to watch.

DINAN

22100 Côtes-d'Armor. Paris 401 – Saint-Malo 32 – Rennes 55 – Saint-Brieuc 59 – Vannes 119.
infos@dinantourisme.com.
This adorable old town perched above the Rance is tremendously Breton in appearance, with its ancient houses, Tour de l'Horloge, Duchesse Anne promenade and château.

 HOTELS-RESTAURANTS

■ **D'Avaugour**   🏨

1, pl du Champ.
Tel. 02 96 39 07 49. Fax 02 96 85 43 04.
www.avaugourhotel.com
Closed mid-Nov.–end Dec., 1 Jan.–12 Feb.
21 rooms: 72–170€. 3 suites: 120–260€.

This old stone building backed up against the town walls in the center of Dinan houses a lavish hotel with meticulously appointed renovated rooms overlooking the square or garden. In summer, breakfast is served on the terrace.

■ **Jerzual**   🏨

26, quai Talards.
Tel. 02 96 87 02 02. Fax 02 96 87 02 03.
www.dinan-hotel-jerzual.com
Rest. closed Sat. dinner, Sun. (off season), 3 weeks Nov.
52 rooms: 89–157€. 2 suites: 165–215€.
Prix fixe: 24€, 32€, 15€ (child).
A la carte: 52€.

Here by the harbor, Serge Lucas keeps a firm hand on the helm of this hotel with its Breton cloister silhouette, terrace, swimming pool, Jacuzzi and spacious rooms in yellow and blue. Philippe Colignon's traditional cuisine is very persuasive. Oysters, sole served grilled or meunière style, rack of lamb with creamy garlic sauce and a soft-centered chocolate cake are washed down with selected wines.

■ **Le Challonge**   🏨

29, pl Duguesclin.
Tel. 02 96 87 16 30. Fax 02 96 87 16 31.
lechallonge@wanadoo.fr / www.hotel-dinan.fr
18 rooms: 52–76€.

By the old fairgrounds, this hostelry is charming indeed with its cozy, colorful, renovated rooms. Modern furniture, delicious breakfasts and modest prices.

● **La Mère Pourcel**   🍴V.COM

3, pl des Merciers.
Tel. 02 96 39 03 80. Fax 02 96 39 49 91.
chezlamerepourcel@wanadoo.fr

Closed Sun. dinner, Mon., 3 weeks Jan.
Prix fixe: 19,40€ (lunch, weekdays), 63€.
A la carte: 55€.

This historic, 15th-century, half-timbered, wood-framed merchant's home with its beams and woodwork is under new management. House foie gras terrine, fresh fish of the day, Breton salt marsh lamb and a thin apple tart continue to make an excellent impression.

● **L'Auberge du Pélican**　

3, rue Haute-Voie.
Tel. 02 96 39 47 05. Fax 02 96 87 53 30.
Closed Mon. lunch (exc. July–Aug.), Thu. dinner (exc. July–Aug.), Sat. lunch (exc. off season), mid-Jan.–mid-Feb.
Prix fixe: 16,50€, 54€.

Nestling in the heart of the old town, this tasteful restaurant presents a menu that changes with the seasons. The Briats serve traditional fare and seafood in their contemporary dining room in marine shades or on the terrace, weather permitting.

● **Fleur de Sel**　COM

7, rue Sainte-Claire.
Tel. 02 96 85 15 14. Fax 02 96 85 16 66.
Closed Sun. dinner, Mon., Tue. lunch.
A la carte: 40€.

Laurent Maurin has turned this Parisian bistro into a convivial restaurant. Crab crème brûlée, roasted pike-perch with cured ham, pigeon breast encrusted in pistachio nuts and the strawberry tiramisu leave us with happy memories.

● **Le Cantorbery**　SIM

6, rue Sainte-Claire.
Tel. 02 96 39 02 52.
Closed Wed. (off season), mid-Feb.–end Feb., 10 days beg. July.
Prix fixe: 16€ (lunch), 25€.
A la carte: 40–50€.

On the first floor as well as the second, where the white paintwork sets off the stone and beams of this 17th-century town house, we enjoy the flavorsome dishes prepared on the stove and in the huge stone hearth by Eric Houis: grilled sardines, roasted Saint-Pierre served on a bed of leeks, rack of lamb with fleur de sel and the chocolate moelleux.

DINARD

35800 Ille-et-Vilaine. Paris 421 – Saint-Malo 12 – Dinan 22 – Rennes 75 – Dol-de-Bretagne 29.
dinard.office.de.tourisme@wanadoo.fr.
Its historic villas, perfect setting on the Rance and the Pointe du Moulinet, Ecluse beach and Clair-de-Lune promenade have turned this place from a quiet little town in the 19th century into a perennially fashionable seaside resort.

■ / 　HOTELS-RESTAURANTS

■ **Grand Hôtel Barrière**　

46, av George-V.
Tel. 02 99 88 26 26 / 02 99 88 26 25.
Fax 02 99 88 26 27.
grandhoteldinard@lucienbarriere.com
www.lucienbarriere.com
Closed end Nov.–end Mar. Rest. closed lunch
90 rooms: 145–600€. 8 suites: 520–600€.
Half board: 32€.
Prix fixe: 38€, 50€. A la carte: 60€.

This charming luxury hotel run by the dynamic Arnaud Bamvens is enjoying a second youth. The rooms with their panoramic views of Saint-Malo and the ramparts have been redecorated British-style by Jacques Garcia. The music bar, the lobby with its carved woodwork and the old elevator set the tone. The cuisine served by Daniel Legenand at the Blue B is a delightful surprise. The scallops with licorice root-seasoned Chantilly, spinach with poached eggs in wine sauce with grilled toast strips, the rouget served whole with ratatouille chutney as well as the roasted rack of lamb served with puréed Paimpol coco beans are delicately crafted work. Add the gourmand desserts (the "choco-ramel", citrus-flavored puffed crêpes) and wine list rich in unfamiliar Bordeaux vintages at sensible prices and we would be happy to eat here on a regular basis.

■ Villa Reine Hortense

19, rue Malouine.
Tel. 02 99 46 54 31. Fax 02 99 88 15 88.
reine.hortense@wanadoo.fr
www.villa-reine-hortense.com
Closed beg. Nov.–25 Mar.
7 rooms: 150–235€. 1 suite: 385
Half board: 180–300€.

The Belle Epoque lives on in the magic of this 19th-century mansion. Originally commissioned by the Russian Prince Vlassov as a tribute to Queen Hortense de Beauharnais, the villa still has all its vintage charm and offers private access to the Ecluse beach, individualized rooms with a sea view and luxurious bathrooms where we happily linger.

■ Novotel Thalassa

1, av Château-Hébert.
Tel. 02 99 16 78 10. Fax 02 99 16 78 29.
www.accorhotels.com, www.novotel.com
Rest. closed 3 weeks Dec.
106 rooms: 119–163€.
Prix fixe: 28€. A la carte: 48€.

On the Pointe de Saint-Enogat, this hotel complex devoted to health care has sixty-seven fully equipped studio apartments, bright rooms with a sea view and a state-of-the-art thalassotherapy center, along with a beauty salon, swimming pool, steam bath and Jacuzzi. On the terrace overlooking the Channel, we make short work of gazpacho served with langoustines, Atlantic sea bass filet, duck breast and the St. Malo craqueline, a local specialty.

■ Manoir de la Rance

Jouvente, 7 km se.
Tel. 02 99 88 53 76. Fax 02 99 88 63 03.
Closed beg. Jan.–mid-Mar.
7 rooms: 80–160€. 2 suites: 120–230€.

At the end of a private drive, this fine manor set in its gardens has lost none of its vintage charm. The English-style decoration in pink shades, glass wall and antique furniture are all conducive to a peaceful stay on the banks of the Rance.

■ Hôtel Crystal

15, rue Malouine.
Tel. 02 99 46 66 71. Fax 02 99 88 17 73.
hcrystal@club-internet.fr
www.crystal-hotel.com
24 rooms: 79–132€. 2 suites: 160–180€.

A stone's throw from the Pointe de Malouine with its handsome residences, this modern, seventies hotel with wood-trimmed décor offers large, well-kept rooms. Ask for one with a sea view.

■ Roche Corneille

4, rue G. Clemenceau.
Tel. 02 99 46 14 47. Fax 02 99 46 40 80.
roche.corneille@wanadoo.fr
www.dinard-hotel-roche-corneille.com
Rest. closed lunch, Mon. (off season).
28 rooms: 65–155€.
Prix fixe: 28€, 35€, 45€, 55€,
10€ (child). A la carte: 55–60€.

In this historic, late-19th-century villa, François Garrigue welcomes his guests with the accent of Southwest France. The ochre, gray and beige shades, teak and light beech flooring give the rooms a handsome touch. In the restaurant, Jean-Yves Bor presents dishes with a local flavor: Cancale oysters on the half shell, bay-fished Turbot with beurre blanc, thyme-seasoned rack of lamb and tarte Tatin with whipped cream slip down smoothly.

■ Améthyste

Place du Calvaire.
Tel. 02 99 46 61 81. Fax 02 99 46 96 91.
hotel-amethyste@wanadoo.fr
www.hotel-amethyste.com
Closed end of Nov. 1 vac.–beg. Apr.
19 rooms: 72–85€.

The Oléron family greets guests with a smile before showing them to the contemporary rooms in flawless pastel tones.

■ Balmoral

26, rue du Maréchal-Leclerc.
Tel. 02 99 46 16 97. Fax 02 99 88 20 48.
info@hotels-balmoral.com
hotels-balmoral.com
31 rooms: 48–46€.

This old building in the town center still has its rustic feel after the recent renovation. The orange tones are soothing and we feel at home in the small, handsome rooms after a stroll along the coast.

■ Hôtel de la Plage   ⓝ⌂

3, bd Féart.
Tel. 02 99 46 14 87. Fax 02 99 46 55 52.
hotel-de-la-plage@wanadoo.fr
Closed Sun. dinner.
18 rooms: 55–100€.

This hotel by the Ecluse beach with its marine décor offers pleasant, renovated rooms and breakfast on the terrace when the skies are clear.

■ Hôtel des Tilleuls   ⓝ⌂

36, rue de la Gare.
Tel. 02 99 82 77 00. Fax 02 99 82 77 55.
hotel-des-tilleuls@wanadoo.fr
www.hotel-des-tilleuls.com
Rest. closed Sat. lunch, Fri. dinner (off season), Sat. (off season), 18 Dec.–mid-Jan.
53 rooms: 43–75€.
Prix fixe: 11,50€, 15€, 25€, 9,50€ (child).
A la carte: 35€.

This sixties building has a cheerful ambiance. Stanislas Carfantan offers a delightful welcome. The Liberty-style rooms are in blue and green and the dining room in pink. Didier Hoffman prepares timeless dishes, including Breton-style scallops, fisherman's-style choucroute (fish over sauerkraut), duck breast with pepper sauce and a three-chocolate cake served with custard cream.

● Hôtel de la Vallée   ⓝCOM

6, av George-V.
Tel. 02 99 46 94 00.
www.hoteldelavallee.com
Closed Sun. dinner, Mon. (off season), mid-Nov.–20 Dec., beg. Jan.–beg. Feb.
23 rooms: 50–150€. A la carte: 45€.

Francis Marx, formerly at the Surcouf in Cancale, has taken over this old hotel by the sea. The rooms will have to wait a while for renovation, but the modern décor of the restaurant is charming indeed. The cuisine concocted by this son of Strasbourg who trained at the Valentin-Sorg is reliable and fresh: pork terrine, scallop carpaccio seasoned with citrus, fresh cod served with chitterling sausage and the grilled John Dory have character. A fruit crumble and a cocoa tirmaisu served in *verrine* are pleasant delicacies.

● Didier Méril   COM

1, place du Général-de-Gaulle.
Tel. 02 99 46 95 74. Fax 02 99 16 07 75.
www.restaurant-didier-meril.com
Closed Wed. (exc. summer),
mid-Nov.–beg. Dec.
4 rooms: 50–120€.
Prix fixe: 22€ (weekday lunch), 29€, 45€,
75€, 12€ (child). A la carte: 60–75€.

Didier Méril has moved his flagship to a place by the Prieuré beach. The view from the terrace plunges down to the sea and the panoramic dining room is chic. The contemporary furniture and design are appealing in a cheerful, minimalist manner. Our plates tend to be a little overloaded with enthusiastic, generous portions. Lobster carpaccio, orange-seasoned langoustine salad, raw crab and salmon spring rolls, turbot served with a pretty vegetable purée with roasted pistachios, small sole filets served with an abundance of vegetables and various presentations of lamb set the tone. The desserts (all-chocolate or a compostion on the theme of rhubarb) are appealing. Four rooms and two suites complete the offer here.

● La Salle à Manger   COM

25, bd Féart.
Tel. 02 99 16 07 95.
la.salleamanger@wanadoo.fr
Closed Sun. dinner (exc. summer), Mon. (exc. summer), 2 months winter.
Prix fixe: 18€. A la carte: 40€.

Yannick Lalande's dining room is as fresh and colorful as his cuisine. Depending on the seasonal set menu, we savor oysters served warm in a champagne and beet juice reduction, salted cod with coco beans, duck breast with peanut sauce and foie gras. The "school days memory", an apple Tatin with rum and cider grog, provides a fine conclusion.

● Le Bistrot de Didier

6, rue Yves-Verney.
Tel. 02 99 46 81 90.
didiermeril@wanadoo.fr
Closed Wed., Thu. (off season).
Prix fixe: 12,50€ (lunch).
A la carte: 25–40€.

Didier Méril has turned his antique restaurant into a friendly modern bistro, whose success is due to a relaxed atmosphere, simple dishes and late service. The tartiflette, the house mackerel rillettes, the beef carpaccio and the roasted Atlantic sea bass with thyme are simply gratifying.

In Saint-Briac (35800). 8 km nw D786.

■ Hôtel de la Houle

14, bd de la Houle.
Tel. 02 99 88 32 17. Fax 02 99 88 96 11.
hoteldelahoule@wanadoo.fr
www.hoteldelahoule.com
Closed beg. Nov.–Easter vac.
14 rooms: 50–85€. 2 suites: 110€.

The rooms of this bric à brac hotel with its garden have been renovated in a cheerful riot of color and furniture. Its second building is furnished with patinated items.

In Saint-Lunaire (35800). 5 km via D786.

● Le Décollé   SIM

1, pointe du Décollé.
Tel.-Fax 02 99 46 01 70.
www.escalesgourmande.com
Closed Mon., Tue. (exc. July–Aug.), Wed., Dec.–end Jan.
Prix fixe: 19€ (weekday lunch), 29€, 39€.
A la carte: 55–60€.

With its unobstructed view of the sea and Saint-Lunaire beach, this point at World's End provides an ideal setting to enjoy scallop carpaccio, John Dory with mushroom-and-ham-stuffed artichokes simmered in wine, oxtail parmentier with foie gras and the baba au rhum served with a Bourbon vanilla-seasoned pineapple minestrone and mango sorbet. Eric Lemale looks after his guests well.

86130 Vienne. Paris 322 –
Châtellerault 10 – Poitiers 18.
A Poitou village with all the charm of yesteryear. Do not miss the wall paintings in the chapel at the château.

■ HOTELS-RESTAURANTS

● Le Binjamin   COM

N10.
Tel. 05 49 52 42 37. Fax 05 49 62 59 06.
binjamin1@aol.com
Closed Sat. lunch, Sun. dinner, Mon.
10 rooms: 44–51€.
Prix fixe: 26€ (weekdays), 52€.

Madame Daubis offers a warm welcome in this modern hostelry standing back from the highway. The cuisine is in the colors of Poitou. A circular dining room and neat rooms in painted wood, practical for an overnight stay.

● Le Clos Fleuri   SIM

Rue de l'Eglise.
Tel. 05 49 52 40 27. Fax 05 49 62 37 29.
Closed Sun. dinner, Wed.
Prix fixe: 17€, 24,50€, 29,50€.
A la carte: 35–40€.

Near the church, in a courtyard where a venerable chestnut tree stands, the Berteaus' establishment charms us with its simplicity and traditional dishes. Foie gras, tête de veau, catch of the day, beef and the profiteroles slip down smoothly. Set menus at gentle prices.

DIVES-SUR-MER see CABOURG

DIVONNE-LES-BAINS

01220 Ain. Paris 491 – Gex 10 – Thonon 51 – Bourg 129 – Genève 18.
divonne@divonnelesbains.com.
This peaceful spa resort with its famous casino

is one of the jewels of the Gex district, a stone's throw from Switzerland.

 HOTELS-RESTAURANTS

● **Grand Hôtel**
Domaine de Divonne
Av des Thermes.
Tel. 04 50 40 34 34 / 04 50 40 34 18.
Fax 04 50 40 34 24.
info@domaine-de-divonne.com
www.domaine-de-divonne.com
Closed Wed., Thu., lunch exc. Sun.,
Mon. and Tue. (July, Aug.).
119 rooms: 190–490€,
14 suites: 465–2760€.
Prix fixe: 25€ (lunch), 34€ (dinner).
A la carte: 45€.

The casino, golf course and thirties grand hotel delight the Swiss neighbors who come to call. The rooms in various styles (art deco, contemporary, etc.) are spacious and comfortable. The suites have a view of the Alps. In the kitchens of the huge Léman brasserie dining room, Daniel Gobet prepares well-crafted, domestic regional dishes. The bouquet of asparagus with roasted bacon, the dab, sole and crayfish ballotine with sauce Nantua, roasted sirloin with tender slow-cooked orange-seasoned turnips and the dessert buffet are accompanied by delightful wines from Switzerland, Savoy and Jura.

■ **Château de Divonne**
115, rue des Bains.
Tel. 04 50 20 00 32. Fax 04 50 20 03 73.
divonne@grandesetapes.fr
www.chateau-divonne.com
27 rooms: 145–330€. 7 suites: 440–510€.
Prix fixe: 26€ (lunch), 39€ (lunch), 53€
(lunch), 46€ (dinner), 57€ (dinner), 70€
(dinner), 90€ (dinner). A la carte: 89€.

This 19th-century establishment was built on the ruins of an 11th-century fortified manor. With its extensive wooded grounds, shady terrace, old-fashioned rooms reached by way of a monumental stairway, painted woodwork, mirrors, flowery fabrics, view of Lake Geneva and

swimming pool, it has a wealth of arguments in its favor. Then there is the added inducement of Laurent Belissa's dishes, including duck foie gras terrine with preserved lemons, lake whitefish seasoned with fennel and dill, honey- and lavender-glazed suckling pig or the Burlat cherries, pan simmered in pistachio jus, served with a Breton shortbread and a frozen mascarpone quenelle.

● **Auberge du Vieux Bois**
Rte de Gex.
Tel. 04 50 20 01 43. Fax 04 50 20 17 74.
Closed Sun. dinner, Mon.,
10 days Nov. 1 vac., Feb. vac.,
10 days beg. July.
Prix fixe: 12€, 40€, 10€ (child).
A la carte: 40–45€.

On the edge of the Mont-Mussy woods, we spend a happy hour or two relaxing over Marc Tritten's seasonal produce–based cuisine. On the terrace or in the bucolic dining room, the trout tartare, pike fish quenelle with sauce Nantua, veal medallion with crayfish and the frozen hazelnut vacherin are simply remarkable.

DOL-DE-BRETAGNE

35120 Ille-et-Vilaine. Paris 372 –
Saint-Malo 27 – Rennes 58 – Dinan 26 –
Fougères 53.
office.dol@wanadoo.fr.
Mont-Saint-Michel nearby, the rail station and the curious Mont-Dol attract crowds of tourists to this crossroads town. Do not miss the ancient cathedral of Saint-Samson.

 HOTELS-RESTAURANTS

■ **Le Bretagne**
Pl Chateaubriand.
Tel. 02 99 48 02 03. Fax 02 99 48 25 75.
Closed Oct.
Rest. closed Sun. dinner (off season).
27 rooms: 31–60€.
Prix fixe: 12€, 30€. A la carte: 20–27€.

In the center of the antique episcopal city, the Haellinge's family hotel offers simple, neat rooms in various colors and a rustic dining room decorated with ornaments. A dozen oysters, pollock meunière, the beef cut of the day with wine sauce and the local flan-like dessert give an idea of the reliable *pension* cuisine.

● Grabotais   SIM

4, rue Ceinte.
Tel.-Fax 02 99 48 19 89.
Closed Sun. dinner (off season), Mon.,
2 weeks Jan.
Prix fixe: 16€ (lunch), 18€, 24€, 30€.
A la carte: 35€.

This 15th-century merchant's home enchants us from the outset with its fireplace and exposed beams and stone. In the traditional dining room brightened by a yellow décor, Nicolas Girot serves sound foie gras, seafood brochette, grilled lamb chops and tarte Tatin.

DOLANCOURT see BAR-SUR-AUBE

DOLE

39100 Jura. Paris 364 – Beaune 65 –
Besançon 53 – Dijon 50.
This fine Jura town straddling the Doubs and Canal du Rhône au Rhin is also the setting for *La Grande Patience*, the Franche Comté masterwork by writer Bernard Clavel. Do not forget to visit the Chaux forest nearby, whose trees inspired the title of his *Colonnes du Ciel* (*Columns of the Sky*) opus.

 HOTELS-RESTAURANTS

■ La Chaumière
& la Découverte

346, av Maréchal-Juin.
Tel. 03 84 70 72 40. Fax 03 84 79 25 60.
la-chaumière.info.com
Closed 1 week Christmas–New Year's.
Rest. closed Sun. (exc. July–Aug.).
18 rooms: 65€.
Prix fixe: 31€, 45€, 53€, 75€, 12€ (child).

This cottage is rustic, simple and very comfortable with its pleasant rooms overlooking the swimming pool and garden.

In its restaurant refurbished in contemporary style, Joël Cesari serves splendidly ingenious dishes prioritizing creativity and local produce. Escargots in Gentiane-seasoned cream and the cauliflower carpaccio and whitefish filet display well-honed skills, as does rolled hen and morels poached in Vin Jaune, served with basmati rice. The cellar is well worth inspection with its fine selection of Jura wines knowledgeably presented by Olivier Soppis.

● Brasserie les Templiers

35, Grande-Rue.
Tel. 03 84 82 78 78 / 06 15 93 15 81.
Fax 03 84 82 31 90.
Closed Sun. dinner, Mon.
Prix fixe: 14€, 24€, 6€ (child).
A la carte: 40€.

Under the Gothic vaults of this 13th-century chapel, Yann Jacquemin's bistro dishes bring a smile to our faces. The escargots in puff pastry, pike-perch filet with garlic butter, veal kidneys with Madeira sauce and the tarte Tatin are reliability itself.

● Le Bec Fin

67, rue Pasteur.
Tel. 03 84 82 43 43.
fassenet.romu@orange.fr
www.le-bec-fin.com
Closed Mon., Tue. (exc. dinner July–Aug.),
Wed. (Sept.–June), 11–21 Sept.,
24 Dec.–18 Jan.
Prix fixe: 25–60€. A la carte: 70€.

Romuald Fassenet has caused a stir, taking over this antique establishment with its vaulted dining room and turning it into the rising star here in Dole. This veteran of Vernet in Paris (in the days of Alain Soliveres) and Jeunet in Arbois offers a light, fresh take on Franche Comté cuisine, adding an occasional touch of charm here and there. Crayfish salad with asparagus, a goose liver escalope served with local corn cakes (gaudes) and a mango and sour cherry chutney, pan-simmered frog legs with hazelnuts on Carnaroli risotto and, finally, the house specialty, a breast of free-range poultry with Vin

Jaune, strengthen our conviction that something enchanting is happening in this modest but charming dining room near the Pasteur house. The desserts (pistachio and raspberry macaron, apple-pear crumble and the hazelnut dessert seasoned with Macvin) meet the same high standards. The fine wine list presents Jura vintages and more. Catherine Fassenet welcomes us gracefully indeed and provides shrewd advice.

● La Romanée `COM`

13, rue des Vieilles-Boucheries.
Tel. 03 84 79 19 05. Fax 03 84 79 26 97.
la-romanee.franchini@wanadoo.fr
Closed Sun. dinner (exc. off season), Wed.
(exc. off season), 1 week Aug.
Prix fixe: 12€, 18€, 25€, 30€,
10€ (child). A la carte: 45€.

Still with its antique meat hooks, this former butcher's store built in 1717 is striking indeed, boasting a vaulted dining room refurbished in yellow and green. Valérie and Patrick Franchini's good humor is infectious and the food does them justice. Escargots served in buckwheat crêpes, pike-perch in thin slices with julienned morels, the Bresse poultry and the dessert cart fail to disappoint.

DOLUS-D'OLERON see ILE D'OLERON
DOMAGNE see CHATEAUBOURG

DOMFRONT-EN-CHAMPAGNE

72240 Sarthe. Paris 215 – Alençon 55 –
Laval 78 – Le Mans 22 – Mayenne 57.
A Champagne Mancelle village in the heart of
a grain-growing region.

●	RESTAURANTS

● Midi

D304.
Tel. 02 43 20 52 04. Fax 02 43 20 56 03.
www.restaurantdumidi.com
Closed Mon., 1 Feb.–mid-Mar.
Prix fixe: 12,90€ (weekday lunch), 18,90€,
26€, 35€, 7,80€ (child). A la carte: 35€.

This village inn is refreshing indeed with its orange shades, contemporary furniture, tables set well apart and cuisine with a topical flavor meticulously prepared by Jean-Luc Haudry. Foie gras-stuffed ravioli with morel-infused cream sauce, scallops with slivered endives, basil-seasoned lamb roast and the fresh fruit tartare go down readily.

DOMMARTEMONT see NANCY

DOMMARTIN-LES-REMIREMONT see
REMIREMONT

DOMME

24250 Dordogne. Paris 542 – Cahors 52 –
Sarlatla-Canéda 12 – Fumel 52 –
Périgueux 76.
infos@domme-tourisme.com.
Famous for its old houses, a delightful village
perched on a cliff above the winding Dordogne
river.

	HOTELS-RESTAURANTS

■ L'Esplanade

Tel. 05 53 28 31 41. Fax 05 53 28 49 92.
www.esplanade-perigord.com
Rest. closed Mar.–Apr. (exc. dinner May–
Oct.), Wed. lunch (Mar.–mid-Nov.).
15 rooms: 77–148€. 5 suites: 128–216€.
Prix fixe: 30€ (lunch), 47€, 90€,
18€ (child). A la carte: 87€.

Overlooking the Dordogne, René Gillard's Périgord hostelry is welcoming indeed with its rooms renovated in bright colors, antique furniture and elegant dining room in blue and yellow. The dishes concocted by Pascal Bouland with their regional accents—scrambled eggs with truffles, Quercy lamb cutlet served with its sweetbreads and an Espelette pepper–seasoned carrot purée, and, finally, the orange trilogy with a mini-soufflé, shaved ice and a mousseline—make a fine impression.

DONZENAC

19270 Corrèze. Paris 469 – Brive 11 –
Tulle 27 – Uzerche 26.
infos@domme-tourisme.com.
On the border of Quercy and Périgord, this Corrèze village famous for its slate is a charming
place.

 HOTELS-RESTAURANTS

● Le Périgord   **N·COM**

9, av de Paris.
Tel. 05 55 85 72 34.
Closed Mon. dinner, Wed.,
Feb. vac.
Prix fixe: 20€, 30€.
A la carte: 45€.

Johnny Thouvenin and his wife Carine
have taken over this wayside halt on the
road from Paris to Brive, which is now
fully refurbished. The existing antique
bar has been tastefully restored and
there are now two dining rooms, one in a
chic rustic style, the other more modern.
The generous set menus display a well-
tempered regionalism (duck leg confit,
foie gras terrine with a fig compote center, sirloin steak with porcini-seasoned
potato gratin). A la carte, the Limousin
beef carpaccio with thick shavings of
aged Cantal and walnut oil, scrambled
eggs and truffles, tomato gazpacho, a
fresh fromage blanc and herb quenelle
with olive cake, a foie gras escalope
cooked in the pan with seasonal mushrooms, honey-glazed pork ribs and the
Limousin beef sirloin are unadulterated
delights. Do not miss the walnut crème
brûlée: superb!

DORMANS

51700 Marne. Paris 118 –
Reims 42 – Château-Thierry 24 –
Epernay 25 – Meaux 71.
office.tourisme.dormans@wanadoo.fr.
This village close to the A4 turnpike in Champagne sings an ode to the gently nodding vines
on the bank of the Marne.

● RESTAURANTS

● La Table Sourdet   **COM**

6, rue du Dr-Moret.
Tel. 03 26 58 20 57. Fax 03 26 58 88 82.
Closed Mon., 2 weeks July.
Prix fixe: 36€, 45€, 50€, 62€,
10€ (child). A la carte: 40–55€.

Six generations of the Sourdet family have
been providing for the people of Champagne in this village bordered by bobbing
vines. In the sumptuous dining room, we
enjoy Marc Maréchal's regional fare: pan-
seared foie gras with chanterelles, cham-
pagne-poached turbot, Bouzy-seasoned
monkfish medallions, veal sweetbreads
comptesse Marie and the berry gratin with
champagne sabayon are accompanied by
a fine list of 350 wines. Bistro dishes at La
Petite Table.

DORNACH see **MULHOUSE**

DOSSENHEIM-SUR-ZINSEL

67330 Bas-Rhin. Paris 452 – Saverne 8 –
La Petite-Pierre 16.
A gateway to the Northern Vosges with hid-
den, ruined châteaux, as in Hunebourg nearby.
The Petite-Pierre and its forest are just a step
away.

 RESTAURANTS

● Chez Clauss   **SIM**

154, montée des Tilleuls.
Tel. 03 88 70 00 81. Fax 03 88 70 05 27.
www.restaurant-clauss.com
Closed Sat. lunch, Mon.
Prix fixe: 14,90€ (lunch, weekdays), 20,90€
(weekdays), 30€ (Sun.).

Roby Clauss has been running this affable inn with its woodwork, sandstone and
fine paintings for many a year now. Guests
have long gathered there on weekends
to enjoy the loggers' plate with grilled
sausage, tartes flambées and the flambéed fruit brochette, a traditional repertoire enthusiastically performed by this

expert tennis timekeeper. But now his son, Philippe, has returned from a tour of duty with the greats (Arnsbourg, Crocodile, Palme d'Or) and revolutionized the house style. His set menus are bargains, the wines well chosen and the dishes too sophisticated for the setting: marinated sardines added to tomato gazpacho in a glass, chanterelle risotto with green vegetables and the sea bream with Coppa ham and slow-cooked caramelized fennel. To be continued.

DOUAINS see **VERNON**

DOUARNENEZ

29100 Finistère. Paris 588 – Quimper 24 – Brest 76 – Lorient 91 – Vannes 143.
tourisme.douarnenez@wanadoo.fr.
This authentic port is steeped in Breton charm. Georges Perros, the poet of *Papiers Collés*, spoke nostalgically of the misty drizzle falling on the bay. Do not miss the harbor museum.

 HOTELS-RESTAURANTS

■ **Le Clos Vallombreuse**
7, rue d'Estienne-d'Orves.
Tel. 02 98 92 63 64. Fax 02 98 92 84 98.
clos.vallombreuse@wanadoo.fr
www.closvallombreuse.com
25 rooms: 52–120€.
Prix fixe: 18€, 26€, 35€, 40€, 54€, 10€ (child). A la carte: 60–91€.

Set in a wooded garden by the bay, the Rubin sisters' manor is a haven of peace. As guests enjoy the enchanting rooms and swimming pool, the wonderfully named Denis Lecuisinier, veteran of La Tour d'Argent, meticulously prepares the finest fresh local produce, combining classical sobriety and a sense of innovation in his appealing dishes. The marbled langoustine terrine, grilled turbot seasoned with curry, rack of lamb in a salt crust and a thin apple tart with milk caramel are accompanied by an alluring choice of wines.

■ **Ty-Mad**
Plage Saint-Jean.
Tel. 02 98 74 00 43.
info@hoteltymad.com / www.hoteltymad.com
Closed mid-Nov.–mid-Mar. Rest. closed lunch
16 rooms: 55–154€.
Prix fixe: 25€ (dinner) 9€ (child).
A la carte: 33€.

Among the attractions of this hotel with its terrace and flowered garden overlooking the beach of Saint-Jean are rooms decorated with works of art, Arnaud and Armelle Raillard's friendly welcome, gentle prices and WiFi. In the restaurant with its wood, whitewashed and beige décor, Gérard Tanter's cuisine is an added argument: sardines in salt, langoustines in a savory pastry turnover, sole with Roquefort sauce and the cod in aïoli are not bad.

● **Crêperie Tudal**   SIM
36, rue Jean-Jaurès.
Tel.-Fax 02 98 92 02 74 / 06 62 68 17 80.
Closed Sun., Mon. (off season and vac.),
2 weeks end June.
Prix fixe: 9€, 14€, 19€. A la carte: 12–17€.

With its contemporary setting, this *crêperie* and grocery store has a delightful simplicity. It serves buckwheat crêpes with bacon or marinated sardines as well as sweet wheat crêpes with cider jelly.

In Tréboul (29100). 3 km nw.
■ **Thalasstonic**
Rue des Professeurs-Curie.
Tel. 02 98 74 45 45 / 02 98 74 45 63.
Fax 02 98 74 36 07.
info@hotel-douarnenez.com
www.hotel-douarnenez.com
48 rooms: 45–61€. 2 suites: 104–130€.
Prix fixe: 17€, 23€, 9€ (child).
A la carte: 30–35€.

A step away from the sea, this contemporary hotel provides bright, spacious rooms, direct access to the thalassotherapy center and a modern restaurant, where the health food includes grilled tuna served on a bed of leeks, toasted veal medallions with new potatoes and a cinnamon-seasoned poached pear, all at gentle prices.

DOUE-LA-FONTAINE

49700 Maine-et-Loire. Paris 320 –
Angers 42 – Châtellerault 85 – Cholet 52 –
Saumur 20.
The ruins of the collegiate church of Saint-Denis, the stone arenas hosting performances and the 10th-century Carolingian house are the jewels of this treasure trove in the Pays de l'Aubance.

 HOTELS-RESTAURANTS

■ Hôtel de France
19, pl du Champ-de-Foire.
Tel. 02 41 59 12 27. Fax 02 41 59 76 00.
www.hoteldefrance-doue.com
Closed 22 Dec.–22 Jan.
Rest. closed Sun. dinner, Mon.
17 rooms: 41–62€.
Prix fixe: 16€, 21€, 29€, 38€,
8€ (child). A la carte: 42€.

Refined, comfortable rooms, a dining room in traditional style and dishes to match delight the guests of the day in this central hotel. Prepared by Didier Jarnot, the duck foie gras, pike-perch with beurre blanc, beef filet medallions seasoned with pepper and the Cointreau-flavored crème brûlée strike the right note.

■ La Saulaie
2 km, rte de Montreuil-Bellay.
Tel. 02 41 59 96 10. Fax 02 41 59 96 11.
hoteldelasaulaie@wanadoo.fr
Closed 22 Dec.–7 Jan.
44 rooms: 37–55€.
This new establishment offers bright, spacious, functional rooms, a professional welcome and copious breakfasts.

● Auberge Bienvenue
104, route de Cholet.
Tel. 02 41 59 22 44. Fax 02 41 59 93 49.
auberge.bienvenue@wanadoo.fr
www.aubergebienvenue.com
Closed 22 Dec.–10 Jan.
Rest. closed Sun. dinner, Mon.
10 rooms: 46–70€.
Prix fixe: 22€, 50€, 8,50€ (child).
A la carte: 50€.

We like this inn refurbished in a modern style, with its spacious, comfortably equipped rooms. Michel Roche is an affable host and reliable cook. In his friendly dining room opening onto a flowered terrace, guests savor the citrus-seasoned pan-simmered langoustine tails, monkfish medallion with morel cream sauce, rack of lamb with pine nuts and the Cointreau-flavored frozen parfait.

DOUSSARD

74210 Haute-Savoie. Paris 555 – Annecy 20
– Albertville 27 – Megève 42.
A village at the end of Lake Annecy, just below the Dents de Lanfon.

 RESTAURANTS

● Chez Ma Cousine
Bout du lac. (At the end of the lake.)
Tel. 04 50 32 38 83. Fax 04 50 32 91 66.
info@chezmacousine.fr
www.chezmacousine.fr
Closed Tue. (exc. summer), Wed. (exc. summer), end Oct.–end Jan.
Prix fixe: 17€, 26€, 33€.
A la carte: 33–41€.

The bay windows and terrace look out onto the lake, paintings by local artists are shown on the walls and a serene charm reigns. Famous in Talloires, Sophie Bise runs her unobtrusive inn with an expert touch. The restaurant, which serves grilled meats and more topical dishes prepared by Hervé Getenet, does the place justice. Green tomato gazpacho with crab, lake whitefish meunière, rosemary-seasoned grilled lamb chops and a berry tiramisu give us every reason to enjoy ourselves. A pleasant wine list with a few foreign labels.

DRAGUIGNAN

83300 Var. Paris 896 – Fréjus 31 –
Marseille 126 – Nice 90 – Toulon 82.
Contact@coeurdeprovence.com.
One of the crossroads of Provence, which is the subject of its Museum of Folk Arts and Traditions.

HOTELS-RESTAURANTS

● Lou Galoubet SIM
23, bd Jean-Jaurès.
Tel. 04 94 68 08 50. Fax 04 94 50 33 82.
lougaloubet@orange.fr
Closed Mon. dinner, Tue. dinner, Wed.,
mid-July–mid-Aug.
Prix fixe: 29€, 24€, 10€ (child).
A la carte: 55–60€.

This red and white restaurant with its retro brasserie appeal is looking healthy. Boss Nicole Michel and chef Laurent Lalou have a firm hand on the helm. In the kitchen, all is fresh as the morning dew: only the finest seasonal produce is accepted here. Scallops in salad, turbot, John Dory or grilled Mediterranean sea bass, the sirloin steak with morels and the duck breast dish make an excellent impression.

In Flayosc (83780). 7 km via D557.

■ La Vieille Bastide
306, rte du Peyron.
Tel. 04 98 10 62 62. Fax 04 94 84 61 23.
lavieillebastide@tiscali.fr
www.lavieillebastide.fr
Rest. closed Sun. dinner, Mon.
7 rooms: 55–121€.
Prix fixe: 22,90€ (lunch), 27,90€, 45€,
57€, 21,90€ (child).

It is hard to resist the charms of Isabelle and Alain d'Aubreby's country house. We like the cheerful welcome, garden, shady terrace, swimming pool and colorful rooms, and are equally fond of Marie-Denise and Frédéric Guigoni's Southern French culinary partnership. The escargots in puff pastry with shellfish broth, monkfish with Parma ham, pigeon in a pastry crust with sweet pea purée and a blanc manger in sweet syrup with grated coconut and peach marmalade are very New Wave Provence.

In Flayosc.

● L'Oustaou SIM
5, pl Joseph-Brémond.
Tel. 04 94 70 42 69. Fax 04 94 84 64 92.
Closed Sun. dinner (Oct.–May), Mon.,

Wed. (Oct.–May), Nov. 1 vac., Feb. vac.
Prix fixe: 20€ (weekday lunch), 26€, 34€,
39€, 15€ (child). A la carte: 50–55€.

Mathieu Cassin serves up dishes with a modern flavor in this charmingly refurbished former post house. Served in a dining room furnished with bits and pieces, or on the terrace, the foie gras with pain d'épices, hot Cabecou goat cheese with eggplant, the jumbo shrimp, porcini and gnocchi and the rabbit thigh simmered with onions are finely crafted work. The house mango coconut baba au rhum is to die for.

DUNIERES

43220 Haute-Loire. Paris 549 – Le Puy 52 –
Saint-Agrève 30 – Saint-Etienne 37.
This was the silk capital of the Velay district until 1914. Today, it is the terminus of miniature tourist train "La Galoche".

HOTELS-RESTAURANTS

■ La Tour
7 ter, rte du Fraisse.
Tel. 04 71 66 86 66. Fax 04 71 66 82 32.
www.hotelrestaurantlatour.com
Rest. closed Sun. dinner, Mon., Feb.
11 rooms: 45–59€.
Prix fixe: 20€, 26€, 30€, 47€.
A la carte: 50€.

We can but admire this hostelry, with its rooms tastefully decorated by Laurence Roux and inspired cuisine from Régis Marcon pupil Gilles Roux. The four set menus and highly imaginative à la carte dishes are based on local produce: the escargot brochette seasoned with Grazac, a panfried salmon trout, roasted veal shoulder with porcini flan and a potato fricassée and the frozen verbena parfait.

DUNKERQUE

59140 Nord. Paris 292 – Calais 46 –
Amiens 154 – Lille 73 – Ypres 54.
dunkerque@tourisme.norsys.fr.
Destroyed in 1945, Dunkerque rose magnifi-

cently from its ashes and is now an ultramodern port. The waterfront factories are the sign of its dynamic nature. The town's high good humor finds expression in its annual carnival.

 HOTELS-RESTAURANTS

■ Europ' Hôtel

13, rue Leughenaer.
Tel. 03 28 66 29 07 / 03 28 65 08 05.
Fax 03 28 63 67 87.
europehotel@wanadoo.fr / www.europehotel.fr
68 rooms: 67–74€.

Near the Leughenaer, a remnant of the town's 14th-century fortifications, this seventies building is now a hotel boasting modern, comfortable rooms.

● L'Estouffade   COM

2, quai de la Citadelle.
Tel.-Fax 03 28 63 92 78.
Closed Sun. dinner, Mon.,
end Aug.–end Sept.
Prix fixe: 26€ (exc. Sun. and Bank holidays),
37€, 14€ (child). A la carte: 52€.

Maurice Claeyssen fishes for ideas on the waterfront by his eatery, so freshness abounds in its refurbished white and orange-yellow dining room. The scallop tartare, roasted langoustine tails served with a watercress emulsion, fish filets in bouillabaisse jus and oven-roasted fresh figs with reduced Corsican honey and the muscat sabayon meet with unanimous approval.

● Au Petit Pierre   SIM

4, rue de Dampierre.
Tel. 03 28 66 28 36. Fax 03 28 66 28 49.
www.aupetitpierre.com
Closed Sat. lunch, Sun. dinner.
Prix fixe: 17,50€, 24€, 31,50€.
A la carte: 35€.

This 18th-century establishment's attractions are its setting, atmosphere and inspired regional cuisine. Pierre Neville offers a warm welcome, while chef Arnaud Deschilodre prepares a Bergues cheese gratin, mixed local fish and

vegetable stew, stuffed sole in the style of Ostend, with oysters and shrimp in cream sauce, veal kidneys flambéed in fleur de bière and chicory-flavored crème brûlée, just to show that the low country has a (gourmet) contribution to make too.

In Coudekerque-Branche (59210). 4 km s via D916.

● Soubise   V.COM

49, rte Bergues.
Tel. 03 28 64 66 00. Fax 03 28 25 12 19.
restaurant.soubise@wanadoo.fr
Closed Sat., Sun.
Christmas–New Year's vac., 1 week at Easter, 1 week at end July–mid-Aug.
Prix fixe: 25€, 34€, 40€, 47€, 58€, 10€ (child). A la carte: 49–62€.

With its harmonious champagne tones, Louis XIII furniture and pictures on the walls, this renovated former post house is a veritable charm offensive. The refined, flavorsome dishes deftly concocted by Michel Hazebroucq enchant as they change with the seasons. Duck foie gras, sole with almonds, Flemish squab with potato cakes and the pan-simmered veal kidneys are honest and tasty. Two pastry cooks prepare delicious desserts (fresh almond pastry cream with pears served glazed in gelatin) and the house bread. A fine selection of wines from all over France.

In Malo-les-Bains (59240). 3 km.

● Au Bon Coin   COM

49, av Kléber.
Tel. 03 28 69 12 63. Fax 03 28 69 64 03.
www.au-bon-coin.com
Closed Sun. dinner, Mon.
Prix fixe: 32€, 47€, 53€.

Patrick Philippon is still running this good restaurant, but now with a new team in the kitchen. The three set menus of no great originality feature duck foie gras, sea bream, veal cutlet and the chocolate moelleux. Fortunately, the fine wine cellar offers a little excitement.

In Teteghem (59229). 6 km se via N1 and D204.

■ La Meunerie

At Galghouck, 174, rue des Pierres.
Tel. 03 28 26 14 30. Fax 03 28 26 17 32.
meunerie@wanadoo.fr / www.lameunerie.com
Closed 1 week at end Feb., end July–beg. Aug.
Rest. closed Sun. dinner, Mon. lunch.
9 rooms: 90–122€. 1 suite: 218€.
Prix fixe: 28€, 39€, 53€ (wine inc.), 61€,
84€ (wine inc.).

The Caudrons good naturedly tend to
this former steam mill, still in working
order. Fanny greets her guests and shows
them to their trim rooms, while David
sets to work at the stove. No à la carte
dishes, just set menus matching the mood
of the chef, the season and the market's
wares, all verbally presented. The rolled
stuffed Atlantic sea bass, smoked herring
foam with saffron-seasoned butter, foie
gras served pressed with artichokes and
crushed hazelnuts, the Atlantic sea bass
and potatoes with seafood foam and the
olive-seasoned Liques rabbit saddle make
our mouths water.

DURTOL see CLERMONT-FERRAND
DURY see AMIENS

EBERSMUNSTER

67600 Bas-Rhin. Paris 508 – Strasbourg 40
– Obernai 23 – Saint-Dié-des-Vosges 55 –
Sélestat 9.
This Ried village is famous for its magnificent
abbey church in the Austrian baroque style. The
Ill runs serenely through the village.

● | RESTAURANTS

● Les Deux Clés ⓝCOM

72, rue du Général-Leclerc.
Tel. 03 88 85 71 55.
Closed Mon., Thu.
Prix fixe: 30–33€. A la carte: 40€.

This old-style inn opposite the abbey
church is friendliness incarnate. One
comes here for the family welcome, the
neat dining room with its curved ceiling and the cozy atmsophere. Add to this
a poultry liver terrine, the breaded and
fried eel, Mère Baur's wine-simmered fish,
pike-perch with cream sauce, the roasted
stuffed breast of guinea hen, the "almond
mount" dessert and the frozen Vielle Fine
soufflé. Fine choice of local wines.

● Restaurant de l'Ill ⓝSIM

52, rue du Général-Leclerc.
Tel. 03 88 85 75 40.
Closed Mon., Tue.
Prix fixe: 8,50€ (lunch), 25,50€, 27€.

An amusing kitsch décor with souvenirs
of the 1870 war, antique furniture, Betsch-
dorf pots and art nouveau lamps. There is a
small terrace and a smiling reception from
Josiane. The chef, an ex-antiques dealer,
cooks up in exquisite fashion frog legs
wrapped in greens and a tasty fried carp
with spicy mayonnaise. The day's special
(crunchy vegetables, stuffed chicken) is
generous. In short, this is a lively place
that should be sought out.

LES ECHETS

01700 Ain. Paris 455 – Lyon 19 – Bourg-en-
Bresse 47 – Villefranche-sur-Saône 29.
A stone's throw from Lyon but already with a

foothold in La Dombes, a gastronomic village that is like a gourmet oasis on the country route.

HOTELS-RESTAURANTS

■ **Christophe Marguin**

916, rte de Strasbourg.
Tel. 04 78 91 80 04. Fax 04 78 91 06 83.
www.christophe-marguin.com
Closed Sun. dinner, Mon., 23 Dec.–6 Jan.,
end July–25 Aug.
7 rooms: 60–80€.
Prix fixe: 22€ (lunch), 28€, 43€, 50€.
A la carte: 70€.

Christophe Marguin, known as "Marguin of La Dombes" (the title of his fine book of recipes) gives a relaxed welcome to his Logis de France establishment which has the feel of a friendly, local bar, an old-style restaurant and a rough joint all at once. One enjoys delicious salmon and caviar with fried egg, herb-seasoned sautéed frog legs or ravioli, poultry with morel cream sauce or the Grand Marnier soufflé. A house with heart!

EGUISHEIM

68420 Haut-Rhin. Paris 445 – Rouffach 10
– Mulhouse 39 – Colmar 7.
info@oteguisheim.fr.
Ancient ruins seem to show that this is the "cradle" of vineyards. In addition there is the site at the foot of the Husseren towers, the route through the old houses and the high-quality winemaking.

HOTELS-RESTAURANTS

■ **Hostellerie du Château**

2, rue du Château.
Tel. 03 89 23 72 00. Fax 03 89 41 63 93.
www.hostellerieduchateau.com
10 rooms: 65–114€. 1 suite: 115–155€.

Modern, and in the heart of the village, this hotel has cheerful rooms with bright colors.

■ **Hostellerie du Pape**

10, Grand-Rue.
Tel. 03 89 41 41 21. Fax 03 89 41 41 31.
www.hostellerie-pape.com
Rest. closed Mon., Tue., 3 weeks Jan.,
10 days beg. Feb.
33 rooms: 65–95€.
Prix fixe: 17€, 48€, 10€ (child).

Maurice Huber is the professional manager of this modern hotel with functional rooms situated at the edge of the town, while Jean-Marie Boucheseche gives a heartfelt rendition of traditional dishes. The pan-seared duck foie gras with ceps, pressed pheasant with hazelnuts, pike-perch in thin slices with potatoes and the venison medallions with red cabbage are extremely well prepared. Local wines are on the program.

■ **Auberge Alsacienne**

12, Grand-Rue.
Tel. 03 89 41 50 20. Fax 03 89 23 89 32.
www.auberge-alsacienne.net
Closed 20 Dec.–10 Feb.,
1 week at end June–beg. July.
Rest. closed Sun. dinner, Mon.
17 rooms: 55–64€. 2 suites: 70€.
Prix fixe: 20€, 27,50€, 7,50€ (child).

An inn like they used to be. Sweet rooms and serious cuisine are on offer from Thierry Peter, relieved in the kitchen by Stéphane Laurent. Local dishes have their voice here, but one that has been vigorously reinterpreted. The escargots and mushrooms in a crêpe pouch, pike-perch with leek cream, goose breast with raspberry vinegar and the apple and raisins marinated in Gewurtz, served in streudel, are finely done.

● **Le Caveau d'Eguisheim**   COM

3, pl du Château.
Tel. 03 89 41 08 89. Fax 03 89 23 79 99.
Closed Mon., Tue., 3 weeks Feb.–mid–Mar.,
1 week July.
Prix fixe: 37€, 59€, 20€. A la carte: 65€.

The serious chef of the village is Jean-Christophe Perrin. The man we knew from La Galupe in Urt and Toiny in Saint-Barth has transformed this winemaker's house on two floors into a quality establishment. His fine handling of themes based on pork (a wonderful presskopf), his carp ravioli in white wine bouillon, the tuna on a tarte flambée (a flat savory tart), the "squab in a woodcock's nest" and the beautiful Salers beef in glossy Bordelaise sauce are spirited exercises in style that highlight the produce. The wines labelled Beyer and Wolfberger, both shareholders in the restaurant, follow suit.

● **La Grangelière**   COM

59, rue du Rempart-Sud.
Tel. 03 89 23 00 30. Fax 03 89 23 61 62.
lagrangeliere@wanadoo.fr
www.lagrangeliere.com
Closed Sun. (off season), Thu. (off season),
3 weeks Mar.
Prix fixe: 22€ (wine inc.), 29€, 65€,
10€ (child). A la carte: 60€.

Discreet but very correct, Alain Finkbeiner, who was chef at the Château d'Isenbourg in Rouffach, has not forgotten the great lessons he learned on the Côte d'Azur, principally with Chibois in Cannes. Duck carpaccio with soy sauce vinaigrette, fennel seed–seasoned John Dory, the foie gras mille-feuille served hot, the veal tenderloin medallion as well as the pan-simmered pêche de vigne with house ice cream make a very good showing. Ad hoc wines suggested by Karine.

● **Au Vieux Porche**   COM

16, rue des Trois-Châteaux.
Tel. 03 89 24 01 90. Fax 03 89 23 91 25.
vieux.porche@wanadoo.fr
Closed Tue., Wed., 1 week Nov., end Feb.–
end Mar., 10 days end June–beg. July.
Prix fixe: 23€, 8,50€ (child).
A la carte: 45€.

This 18th-century winemaker's house is run with dynamism by Pascal and Betty Feuermann. Both he, a former sommelier with Chambard, and she, daughter of an owner-grower, cannot be pried from the surrounding vineyards. On the cuisine side, their chef Eddy Fischer produces the goods. The rustic dining room

with stained glass windows, beams and wooden fittings is the scene for classic feasts. A marbled foie gras terrine, pike-perch simmered in Riesling and a frozen kirsch-flavored dessert look very good.

● **Pavillon Gourmand**   SIM

101, rue du Rempart-Sud.
Tel. 03 89 24 36 88. Fax 03 89 23 93 94.
http//perso.orange.fr/pavillon.schubnel/
Closed Tue., Wed., Christmas.
Prix fixe: 16€, 25€, 30€, 60€,
9€ (child).

Pupil of star establishments (Bocuse, Vergé, Haeberlin and Tantris), Pascal Schubnel, former chef of Le Caveau, now succeeded in the kitchen by his son David, serves regional cooking modestly but efficiently. His onion tart, his pike-perch and Riesling soufflé, his choucroute and his Gewurtz sorbet are models of their kind.

ELSENHEIM

67390 Bas-Rhin. Paris 449 – Colmar 18 – Sélestat 14 – Strasbourg 61.
In an otherwise anonymous village consisting of several houses planted in the Ried, just above Ill-haeusern on the route to Marckolsheim, sits one stately home with wrought-iron balconies.

● | RESTAURANTS

● **Le Cottage**   SIM

22, rue Principale.
Tel. 03 88 92 51 59. Fax 03 88 74 98 00.
lecottage@evc.net
Closed Mon., Tue. dinner, Wed. dinner,
2 weeks Feb., 2 weeks Aug.
Prix fixe: 12€ (lunch), 35€. A la carte: 50€.

Gilbert and Dominique Zeyssolff run this village inn with professionalism, offering a smiling welcome, quality produce and traditional dishes, without forgetting the wines of their vinicultural friends. Fish in red wine sauce, scampi cassolette, pike-perch simmered in Riesling, veal kidneys in mustard sauce and frozen cherry parfait are eaten with pleasure.

ENGENTHAL-LE-BAS see WANGENBOURG ENTZHEIM see STRASBOURG

ENSISHEIM

68190 Haut-Rhin. Paris 467 – Mulhouse 15 – Colmar 24 – Guebwiller 14.

This former capital of the Austrian *landgraviat*, decimated by the last world war, is proud of its town hall with arched vaults and its Jesuits' church, and a little less of its sadly famous prison.

 HOTELS-RESTAURANTS

■ La Couronne

47, rue de la 1er-Armée.
Tel. 03 89 81 03 72. Fax 03 89 26 40 05.
la-couronne@wanadoo.fr
9 rooms: 65–99€. 4 suites: 65–165€.
Prix fixe: 30€, 42€, 72€, 10€ (child).
A la carte: 70€.

Jean-Marc Pflimlin is the spirited newcomer to this establishment with a good reputation. Housed in a building dating from medieval times, the rooms mix modern comfort and old-fashioned charm, while the seasonal fare is precisely designed. Jumbo shrimp and escargot ravioli served with small vegetables, spice-glazed Atlantic sea bass with three-rice ratatouille, squab breast with "flavors of the forest", chocolate and acidulated cream soufflé served hot are finely-crafted dishes that manage to blend with one of the 1,000 wines in the cellar.

● Le Thaler

47, rue de la 1er-Armée.
Tel. 03 89 26 43 26. Fax 03 89 26 40 05.
la-couronne@wanadoo.fr
Closed Sun. dinner.
Prix fixe: 12€ (lunch). A la carte: 35€.

This friendly drinking place is the inexpensive annex to La Couronne. Tête de veau with vinaigrette, Munster cheese in puff pastry served in salad and a slice of herb-seasoned kidneys are peasant dishes in the best taste. Good choice of wines by the glass.

EPERNAY

51200 Marne. Paris 142 – Reims 27 – Châlons-en-Champagne 34 – Château-Thierry 48.
tourisme@ot-epernay.fr.

The second Champagne town or the first? For you to decide, as you walk along the avenue that bears the name of the blond wine.

■ Le Clos Raymi

3, rue Joseph-de-Venoge.
Tel. 03 26 51 00 58. Fax 03 26 51 18 98.
closraymi@wanadoo.fr
www.closraymi-hotel.com
7 rooms: 100–150€.

Under the management of Rachel-Raymi Woda, this former establishment of the Chandons has been happily renovated in an art deco style. From the rooms to the sitting room, including the breakfasts, charm abounds.

● Les Berceaux

13, rue des Berceaux.
Tel. 03 26 55 28 84. Fax 03 26 55 10 36.
les.berceaux@wanadoo.fr
www.lesberceaux.com
Rest. closed Mon., Tue., 3 weeks Feb.,
2 weeks Aug.
27 rooms: 77–86€.
Prix fixe: 22€ (weekday lunch), 48€,
64€ (Sat., Sun. lunch). A la carte: 80€.

Patrick Michelon's domain sparkles to the rhythm of his adopted Champagne. This native of Mulhouse, long won over to the cause of the blond wine, directs his little kingdom with a masterly hand. The rooms, renovated in lively colors, are comfortable and the upper class cuisine, which combines tradition with finesse, is very seductive. Crab-stuffed zucchini flower tempura, Breton lobster *verrine* with Vendee beans, whole wild turbot, simply roasted and the crispy suckling pig with mild spices make up a tempting menu.

● Les Cépages `COM`

16, rue de la Fauvette.
Tel. 03 26 55 16 93. Fax 03 26 54 51 30.
www.lescepages-epernay.com
Closed Sun., Wed.
Prix fixe: 18€, 69€.

Fresh, quality produce is the basis of the cuisine of David Mathieu, who devises his menu according to the market. The rigorous execution does not include flights of fancy. Honey-seasoned foie gras nougat, langoustines with chanterelles (in season), rosemary-seasoned veal and a pineapple gazpacho are flawless and offered in gourmet special menus.

● Le Théâtre `COM`

8, pl Mendès-France.
Tel. 03 26 58 88 19. Fax 03 26 58 88 38.
www.epernay-rest-letheatre.com
Closed Sun. dinner, Tue. dinner, Wed., 1 week Christmas, Feb. vac., 2 weeks beg. July.
Prix fixe: 22€, 28€, 44€, 10€ (child).

Lieven Vercouteren, a Belgian who has adopted Champagne, has perfectly mastered the region's cuisine—with the addition of his own little touches—which he offers in his brasserie. People queue up for boneless pork trotter, slow-simmered monkfish in red wine sauce, cod with grape sauce, crispy veal sweetbreads braised with green cabbage and the mirabelle plum Tatin. The Sparnaciens (inhabitants of Epernay) are not wrong!

● La Table Kobus `SIM`

3, rue du Dr-Rousseau.
Tel. 03 26 51 53 53. Fax 03 26 58 42 68.
www.latablekobus.com
Closed Sun. dinner, Mon., Thu. dinner,
2 weeks Christmas–New Year's, 1 week Apr.,
2 weeks Aug.
Prix fixe: 19€, 26€, 35€, 43€.

The quality of the reception and the cuisine are not coincidental to the success of this 1900s-style brasserie. Serge Herscher, who used to work in the restaurant with Boyer, and chef Thierry Sidan, formerly of Le Crillon, ensure the excellent running of a very straightforward establishment.

We can do nothing other than recommend the cold cumin-seasoned carrot soup, the skate wing with spicy pan perdu, the pretty veal cutlet and the chocolate île flottante, washed down with carefully chosen wines (unless one brings one's own wine, without corkage!).

● La Table de Tristan `N` `SIM`

21, rue Gambetta.
Tel. 03 26 51 11 44. Fax 03 26 32 42 39.
www.latabledetristan.fr
Closed Sun., Mon., 2 weeks Feb.
Prix fixe: 16€ (lunch), 27€ (dinner).
A la carte: 50€.

The Dauvissats have taken over, and rechristened, the Bacchus Gourmet, leaving the reins in the hands of chef Martin Arnaud, who offers a high-quality regional cuisine. Foie gras served cold in aspic with seasonal fruit, pike-perch filet with champagne sauce, veal with Ratafia sauce, Troyes chitterling sausage with Chaource cheese and the lychee and raspberry shaved ice dessert with Reims biscuits, or the pretty tart with fresh grapes simmered in champagne are classical little dishes that we liked very much.

In Champillon-Bellevue (51160). 6 km n via N51.

● Royal Champagne

Bellevue.
Tel. 03 26 52 87 11. Fax 03 26 52 89 69.
royalChampagne@relaischateaux.com
www.royalChampagne.com
Closed beg. Dec.–beg. Jan.
Rest. closed Mon., Tue. lunch.
21 rooms: 195–340€. 4 suites: 320–360€.
Prix fixe: 60€, 80€, 100€, 20€ (child).
A la carte: 105€.

This coaching inn turned Relais & Châteaux has kept its former character. From the neat rooms and suites the view of Epernay, the vineyards and the Marne, enchants. On the cooking side, one enjoys the delectable fare of Philippe Augé, who works skillfully. This wise disciple of Alain Ducasse serves up finely prepared market dishes, both classic and contemporary: duck foie gras confit marinated in Bouzy wine, chorizo-seasoned cod, seven-hour lamb shoulder with little stuffed vegetables and the soufflé served hot with Reims biscuits are accompanied by a very fine list of Champagne wines.

In Vinay (51530). 6 km s via D951.

● **Hostellerie la Briqueterie**

4, rte de Sézanne.
Tel. 03 26 59 99 99. Fax 03 26 59 92 10.
info@labriqueterie.fr / www.labriqueterie.fr
Closed 1 week Dec. Rest. closed Sat. lunch.
40 rooms: 170–190€. 2 suites: 280€.
Prix fixe: 80€ (dinner), 65€ (dinner), 30€,
38€. A la carte: 85–90€.

This country inn—which joined Relais & Châteaux last year—with its garden, health center, friendly bar and neat rooms, is the ideal place for a stay centered on relaxation. Gérard Pommier and Alix Philippon watch over things while in the kitchen Gilles Goess skillfully puts regional produce to culinary music. The breadth of the wine list makes one hesitate but one practical option is the house champagne as an accompaniment to the duck foie gras terrine with a light fig marmalade, roasted lobster with fork-mashed ratte potatoes and a Reims vinegar sauce, Fromentières pigeon stuffed with young lettuce shoots, served with sweet pea cream and the vanilla panna cotta.

EPINAL

88000 Vosges. Paris 384 – Belfort 96 –
Colmar 92 – Mulhouse 107 – Nancy 71.
tourisme.epinal@wanadoo.fr
The beautiful images by Pellerin, the museum of ancient and contemporary art, the old town, the basilica and the château grounds make one want to stop off in the capital of Vosges.

 HOTELS-RESTAURANTS

■ **Manoir des Ducs** ❀

5, avenue de Provence.
Tel. 03 29 29 55 55. Fax 03 29 29 55 56.
manoir-hotel@wanadoo.fr
www.manoir-hotel.com
Rest. closed Sun. dinner.
10 rooms: 78–199€. 2 suites: 139€.

Prix fixe: 32€ (weekday lunch), 42€, 58€,
92€, 16€ (child). A la carte: 95€.

Next to the restaurant Les Ducs de Lorraine (see below), this grand hotel houses elegant rooms, a health center, hammam and Jacuzzi.

■ **La Fayette**

Parc économique Le Saut-le-Cerf.
Rue Bazaine.
Tel. 03 29 81 15 15. Fax 03 29 31 07 08.
hotel.lafayette.epinal@wanadoo.fr
www.bestwestern-lafayette-epinal.com
Closed 24 Dec. dinner.
57 rooms: 80–95€. 1 suite: 180€.
Prix fixe: 18,50€, 28,50€, 34,50€,
42,50€, 10€ (child).

This modern hotel run by Gérard Claudel is a boon. Golf course nearby, heated swimming pool, Internet and WiFi await you, in addition to a careful cuisine from Philippe Perrosé. The pike-perch and crayfish ravioli with morels and the pan-fried veal sweetbreads with dried fruits give their money's worth.

■ **Kyriad**

12, av du Général-de-Gaulle.
Tel. 03 29 82 10 74. Fax 03 29 35 35 14.
hotel-kyriad-epinal@wanadoo.fr
www.kyriad.fr
Closed 1 week at end Dec.
48 rooms: 59–64€. 3 suites: 78€.

With its gaily colored rooms, this chain hotel benefits from an ideal location opposite the station.

■ **Hôtel Mercure**

13, pl E.-Stein.
Tel. 03 29 29 12 91. Fax 03 29 29 12 92.
www.mercure.com / www.accor-hotels.com
Open daily. Rest. closed Sat. lunch,
Sun. lunch.
61 rooms: 119–129€. 4 suites: 119–160€.
Prix fixe: 18€, 21€, 24€, 8€ (child).

Jacuzzi, sauna, hammam and swimming pool add to the enjoyment of the stay in this functional hotel. The rooms are immaculate and the cuisine of chef

Sylvio Zanin accomplished when it follows regional traditions.

● **Les Ducs de Lorraine**   Ⓥ.COM

5, rue de Provence.
Tel. 03 29 29 56 00. Fax 03 29 29 56 01.
obriot.ringer@wanadoo.fr
www.ducsdelorraine.fr
Closed Sun. dinner.
Prix fixe: 30€ (weekday lunch),
45€ (weekend dinner). A la carte: 100€.

This grand 19th-century house is a quiet refuge of these illustrious Spinaliennes (inhabitants of Epinal). The cuisine created together by the experienced Claudy Obriot and Stéphane Ringer, tender young shoot who has shot up the career ladder, rework the classics with a light touch. The lobster tartare, Meuse truffle-seasoned turbot filet, rabbit ravioli with wild thyme as well as the emblematic mirabelle plum soufflé are delicate, precise, finely-crafted dishes. The fine wines selected by Bruno Collin make high-class accompaniments to the meal.

● **Le Petit Robinson**   COM

24, rue R.-Poincaré.
Tel. 03 29 34 23 51. Fax 03 29 31 27 17.
www.lepetitrobinson.fr
Closed Sat. lunch, Sun., mid-July–mid-Aug.
Prix fixe: 18,50€, 10€ (child).
A la carte 40–45€.

François Aubertin, the modest man of Epinal, chooses his produce with confidence and cooks it without frills and flounces. One doesn't tire of the salmon quenelles with herb sauce, grilled red mullet with white sauce, duck breasts served with prunes and the light puff pastry with strawberries and fruit coulis. Engaging welcome to a distinctive wooded setting.

● **Le Bagatelle**   SIM

12, rue des Petites-Boucheries.
Tel.-Fax 03 29 35 05 22.
le-bagatelle@wanadoo.fr
www.le-bagatelle.com
Prix fixe: 11,90€, 40€, 15€ (child).
A la carte: 35€.

Pascal Dannenmuller's cuisine goes on a voyage. In a contemporary setting in shades of yellow one enjoys glazed crab bavaroise, red mullet soufflé served with bouillabaisse broth, roasted Atlantic sea bass, rustic but chic grilled pork trotter and the all-chocolate plate, sensibly priced.

● **Le Bistro de Serge**   SIM

18, rue du Général-Leclerc.
Tel. 03 29 38 23 16. Fax 03 29 38 27 17.
le.bistro .de.serge@wanadoo.fr
Closed Sun., Mon., Bank holidays,
2 weeks Christmas–New Year's, 3 weeks Aug.
Prix fixe: 17€ (weekday lunch), 28€.
A la carte: 35€.

Serge Ferraro has created a real bistro where he offers fine wines by the glass in friendly surroundings while talking up the well-made dishes of his chef Denis Cladire. Tuna tartare, quail salad with foie gras, shallot- and cream-stuffed cutlass-fish, sirloin steak flambéed with Cognac and mascarpone mousse with berries slip down without a murmur.

In Chaumousey (88390). 10 km w via D36 and D460.

● **Le Calmosien**   COM

37, rue d'Epinal.
Tel. 03 29 66 80 77. Fax 03 29 66 89 41.
lecalmosien@wanadoo.fr / www.calmosien.com
Closed Sun. dinner, Mon., 2 weeks July.
Prix fixe: 21€, 31€, 51€, 10€ (child).

Jean-Marc Béati offers regionalism touched with a note of Provence in this smart restaurant, renovated in modern style in shades of salmon pink. Quail salad with foie gras, simmered escargots in thick sauce, rouget prepared with tapenade, an herb-seasoned rack of lamb, hot lemon soufflé and the filo pastry with Quetsche and mirabelle plums make one want to become a regular here.

L'EPINE see **CHALONS-EN-CHAMPAGNE**
L'EPINE see **NOIRMOUTIER-EN-L'ILE**

ERMENONVILLE

60950 Oise. Paris 51 – Compiègne 42 –
Beauvais 66 – Meaux 24 – Senlis 14.
ot-ermenonville@wanadoo.fr.
The village has an aristocratic appeal. The memory of Jean-Jacques Rousseau remains, with his sealed tomb located in the justly famous park. Close by are the sea of Sable and the abbey of Chaalis.

 HOTELS-RESTAURANTS

■ **Château d'Ermenonville**
Rue René-Girardin.
Tel. 03 44 54 00 26. Fax 03 44 54 01 00.
ermenonville@leshotelsparticuliers.com
www.chateau-ermenonville.com
50 rooms: 90–270€. 2 suites: 270€.
Prix fixe: 30€, 42€, 52€, 85€.
A la carte: 64€.

This old château, known by the wider public for its appearance in the film *Les Visiteurs*, remains a place of privilege. Firstly because of the comfort of its renovated rooms and then for the classic, well-handled cuisine of Nicolas Mouton. Lobster in an Andalou-style gazpacho, the salmon filet roasted skin-side down, duck breast served in its cooking juices and the raspberry mille-feuille acquit themselves without disgrace.

ERNEE

53500 Mayenne. Paris 300 – Domfront 48 –
Fougères 21 – Laval 30 – Vitré 30.
On two hillsides overlooking the Mayenne, the former capital of Bas-Maine displays its old houses along the length of the gentle river.

 HOTELS-RESTAURANTS

● **Le Grand Cerf**
19, rue Aristide-Briand.
Tel. 02 43 05 13 09. Fax 02 43 05 02 90.
info@legrandcerf.net / www.legrandcerf.net
Closed Sun. dinner, Mon. (exc. hotel by reserv.), mid-Jan.–1 Feb.
7 rooms: 38–48€.

Prix fixe: 15€ (weekday lunch), 23€, 32€,
12€ (child). A la carte: 50€.

In this modern hotel with rooms that are all different, Mayenne is represented in the pictures on the walls, in the restaurant with its exposed stonework decorated with numerous sculptures and in the local dishes reworked by Hugues Cérémie and Pierre Beaugeais. Parsley-seasoned slow-cooked beef with new potatoes and tapenade, the oven-baked grenadier served with crushed tomatoes with basil and cider butter and the guinea hen stuffed with chickpeas and fresh peppermint and served with dark chocolate sauce are enjoyed effortlessly. For dessert, Calvados baba with fresh fromage blanc sorbet hits the right note. Fine wine list from all over France in the good hands of Noëlle Cérémie.

● **La Coutancière**
At La Coutancière,
9 km e, Vautorte (53500).
Tel. 02 43 00 56 27. Fax 02 43 00 66 09.
Closed Tue. dinner, Wed.,
2 weeks July–beg. Aug.
Prix fixe: 14,90€, 23,90€, 29€, 45,70€.

Wooded grounds bordering the forest, a dining room in autumnal shades and an attentive reception: this is an inn where one feels at home, to enjoy the fine preparations of Eric Couteau. Escargot-stuffed brioche, Atlantic sea bass pan simmered with chestnuts and oyster mushrooms and the oven-roasted venison served with potato and a lingonberry Tatin give pleasure, as does the variation on the chocolate theme which makes a nice suprise at the end of the meal.

ERNOLSHEIM-LES-SAVERNE see SAVERNE

ERQUY

22430 Côtes-d'Armor. Paris 452 –
Saint-Brieuc 33 – Lamballe 21 – Dinard 39.
tourisme.erquy@wanadoo.fr.
The "scallop capital" is a Breton pearl overlooking the ocean, all decked out in pink sandstone.

■ Le Beauséjour 🏠

21, rue de la Corniche.
Tel. 02 96 72 30 39. Fax 02 96 72 16 30.
www.beausejour-erquy.com
Closed mid-Nov.–mid-Feb. Rest. closed Sun.
dinner, Mon. (exc. July–Aug.).
15 rooms: 47–64€.
Prix fixe: 18€, 25€, 33€, 9,50€ (child).
A la carte: 35€.

Situated near the port and the beach, this guesthouse, with garden, is a pleasant place to stay. The rooms have all been renovated and one eats the honest fare in view of the sea.

● L'Escurial COM

Bd de la Mer.
Tel. 02 96 72 31 56. Fax 02 96 63 57 92.
lescurial.denisfroc@wanadoo.fr
www.lescurial.com
Closed Sun. dinner, Mon., Jan.
Prix fixe: 21€. A la carte: 60€.

Denis Froc, previously of Roellinger in Cancale and of Rachel Gesbert's in Rennes, displays creativity in his glass establishment opposite the sea. In tune with the markets, he serves up strips of marinated Atlantic sea bass and scallops, tarragon-seasoned rouget filet and a vanilla-seasoned roasted duckling. Variations on the strawberry theme makes a good impression.

● La Cassolette SIM

6, rue de la Saline.
Tel.-Fax 02 96 72 13 08.
delangle-lacassolette@wanadoo.fr
Closed Wed., Thu., Nov.–Feb.
Prix fixe: 15€ (weekday lunch), 24€, 32€, 40€, 14€ (child). A la carte: 56€.

Christine Delangle directs this discreet establishment with enthusiasm and leaves the cooking reins in the hands of her chef Patrick Briend, who serves up a cuisine with local tastes. In the old-style dining room or the oriental terrace, one enjoys langoustine cassolette with orange sauce, Breton beer-simmered pike-perch, sirloin steak with Sichuan peppercorns and the salted-butter caramel charlotte.

In Saint-Aubin (22430). 2,5 km se via D68, rte de la Bouillie.

● Relais Saint-Aubin SIM

Tel. 02 96 72 13 22. Fax 02 96 63 54 31.
gilbert.josset@wanadoo.fr
Closed Mon., Tue. (mid-Nov.–mid-Mar.),
Wed. (mid-Nov.–mid-Mar.), 1 week Oct.,
Feb. vac.
Prix fixe: 17€, 55€.

The food around Gilbert Josset's hearth is worth stopping off for. The garden, terrace, rustic décor and old stones also deserve a look. One enjoys a seafood fricassée with bacon and cider, grilled Atlantic sea bass served with a Breton artichoke compote, rack of lamb encrusted in herbs and prunes simmered in wine and aromatic spices.

67150 Bas-Rhin. Paris 418 – Strasbourg 24 – Colmar 49 – Molsheim 27 – Sélestat 25.
grandried.oterstein@wanadoo.fr.
This is the homeland of Alsace sugar, the road between Ried and Vosges with a cuisine awaiting discovery.

 HOTELS-RESTAURANTS

■ Crystal Hôtel 🏠

41, av de la Gare.
Tel. 03 88 64 81 00. Fax 03 88 98 11 29.
baumert@hotelcrystal.info
www.hotelcrystal.info
Hotel closed 1 week Aug.
Rest. closed Fri. dinner, Sat. lunch, Sun.,
1 week Christmas–New Year's, 3 weeks Aug.
Prix fixe: 30€.

This hotel marries functionality and charm. The renovated rooms are comfortable, the garden welcoming, the bar friendly and there are meeting rooms for seminars. The cuisine is not lacking in daring or character. A pressed shrimp and vegetable terrine, roasted Atlantic sea bass with whole grain mustard sauce, duckling served with kumquat and foie gras and the frozen mandarin orange mousse are among our good memories.

● Jean-Victor Kalt

41, av de la Gare.
Tel. 03 88 98 09 54. Fax 03 88 98 83 01.
jean-victor.kalt@wanadoo.fr
Closed Sun. dinner, Mon., 1 week at end July,
10 days beg. Aug.
Prix fixe: 28€, 45€, 65€. A la carte: 75€.

The surroundings of this business district are hardly enchanting but Jean-Victor Kalt's restaurant deserves the detour. This disciple of Pierre Gagnaire serves up a cuisine balanced between peasant and aristocratic produce, tradition and modernity. In the dining room with its nineties setting, marbled terrine of smoked sausage and two types of foie gras, veal tenderloin medallion with morels and the raspberry and Bourbon vanilla-seasoned tiramisu give great joy, as does the cellar, rich in wines from all over France.

ERVAUVILLE see COURTENAY

ESPALION

12500 Aveyron. Paris 601 – Rodez 31 –
Aurillac 70 – Millau 82.
otespali@infosud.fr.
The location beside the Lot, the château and the beautiful old houses are worth a stop on the road between Aubrac and Conques.

● | RESTAURANTS

● Méjane

8, rue Méjane.
Tel. 05 65 48 22 37. Fax 05 65 48 13 00.
Closed Sun., Mon. (exc. dinner summer),
Wed. (summer), Mar., 4 days June,
Christmas.
Prix fixe: 17€ (lunch), 22,50€, 33€,
12€ (child).

A few hundred meters from the Lot and the old château, the Caralps' establishment is full of charm. Philippe, trained with his parents-in-law at the Voyageurs in Saint-Chély-d'Aubrac, delights his guests with his reworked traditional recipes. In the art deco-inspired dining room one enjoys pork trotter and head cheese sliced thin and served cold in carpaccio style with basil-seasoned vinaigrette, sea bream on a thin mustard-seasoned tomato tart and the duck breast medallions in a pistachio crust. The desserts are equally wonderful, with the astounding frozen coffee crumble with nougat and chickory cream served in a cone. Fantastic reception from Régine.

ESPALY-SAINT-MARCEL see
LE PUY-EN-VELAY

ESPELETTE

64250 Pyrénées-Atlantiques. Paris 790 –
Pau 119– Cambo 6 – Bayonne 22.
The village of the famous Basque pepper, with the dried ones hung on the fronts of the red and green timbered houses that run down to a tributary of the Nive, the high 17th-century church built like a fortress and the cemetery with its stone disks. The château, now the town hall, tells of the town's wealth of history.

■/● | HOTELS-RESTAURANTS

■ Euzkadi

285, Karrika-Nagusia.
Tel. 05 59 93 91 88. Fax 05 59 93 90 19.
hotel.euzkadi@wanadoo.fr
hotel-restaurant-euzkadi.com
Closed 1 Nov.–20 Dec.
Rest. closed Mon. (exc. July–Aug.), Tue.
31 rooms: 52–77€.
Prix fixe: 16,24€, 27,31€. A la carte: 33€.

André Darraidou is the mayor of Espelette and his beautiful inn covered in the peppers proudly affirms his region. No one complains for the rustic rooms are pleasant and the owner's cooking—assisted in the restaurant by his wife—is stamped with Basque authenticity. It is a joy to discover, at a gentle price, local specialities such as the tripoxta (a Basque veal variety meat specialty), the sautéed squid served with its ink in creamy rice, axoa (the Basque veal stew) with Espelette chili peppers and a corn meal–based Basque tart.

ESPERE see CAHORS

ESQUIULE

64400 Pyrénées-Atlantiques. Paris 816 –
Pau 49 – Mauléon-Licharre 19 – Oloron 15.
The last Basque town just before the "border"
of Béarn.

	RESTAURANTS

● **Chez Château**   SIM

Le Bourg, place de l'Eglise.
Tel. 05 59 39 23 03. Fax 05 59 39 81 97.
jb.hourcourigaray@wanadoo.fr
Closed Mon.
Prix fixe: 10€, 19€, 30€ (dinner), 55€,
12€ (child).

Jean-Bernard Hourcourigaray was eleven
times the French Basque pelota champion.
He runs his rustic inn with presence and
has given over the kitchen to Jean-François Leclerc, who serves smoked trout with
fresh liver and green apples, monkfish and
jumbo shrimp gratin, roasted cod, garlic-seasoned rack of lamb and the pan-
fried lamb sweetbreads with ceps, not
to omit the odd soft-centered chocolate
cake seasoned with Espelette chili peppers served with a raspberry and piquillo pepper sorbet.

ETRAT see SAINT-ETIENNE

ETRETAT

76790 Seine-Maritime. Paris 205 –
Le Havre 29 – Fécamp 17 – Rouen 87.
ot.etretat@wanadoo.fr.
Arsène Lupin looked for the treasure of the kings
of France in the Hollow Needle in the sea at
Etretat. His creator, Maurice Leblanc, settled
in the Clos Lupin, a literary museum that one
can now visit.

	HOTELS-RESTAURANTS

■ **Dormy House**

Rte du Havre. BP 2.
Tel. 02 35 27 07 88. Fax 02 35 29 86 19.
dormy.house@wanadoo.fr
www.dormy-house.com

60 rooms: 87–87€. 1 suite: 205–215€.
Prix fixe: 21€ (weekday lunch), 48€,
36,50€, 41€, 18€ (child).

This manor house and outbuildings dating from 1870 and facing the cliff of Amont
overlooks the village. The grounds guarantee quiet and tranquillity, while the
rooms have the charm of yesteryear. In
the art deco–style dining room, or on the
terrace overhanging the coast line, one
enjoys regional products such as the crab
verrine served with a consommé prepared
from its shells, a symphony of fish from
the Albâtre coast, a rib eye steak served
with sucrine lettuce, shallot confit and
béarnaise sauce as well as the melon in
rhubarb soup with berries and spicy garden mint sorbet.

■ **Le Donjon-Domaine**
  Saint-Clair

Chemin Saint-Clair.
Tel. 02 35 27 08 23 / 02 35 10 22 81.
Fax 02 35 29 92 24.
info@hoteletretat.com / www.hoteletretat.com
17 rooms: 90–250€. 4 suites: 220–330€.
Prix fixe: 39€, 49€, 20€ (child).
A la carte: 100€.

This manor house that inspired Maurice
Leblanc has become a place of leisure with
grounds, swimming pool, finely decorated
rooms, English-style sitting rooms and
cooking that reflects the mood of the time.
Wilfrid Chaplain seduces with the foie
gras macaron, the roasted John Dory with a
quinoa risotto, sirloin steak with potatoes
and the pan-simmered cherries served
with berry marmalade.

● **Le Galion**   COM

Bd René-Coty.
Tel. 02 35 29 48 74. Fax 02 35 29 74 48.
www.etretat.net-le-galion
Closed Tue., Wed., mid-Dec.–end Jan.
Prix fixe: 22€, 30€, 38€, 11€ (child).

Jean-Marc Hartmann offers, in his old
house, a fresh cuisine in which seafood
has pride of place. Espelette pepper-seasoned roasted langoustines, fish duo with
nasturtium-infused cream sauce, monk-

fish in a wild rice crust, a veal sweetbread cassolette with mushrooms and the chocolate mousse with salted-butter caramel are very well prepared.

40320 Landes. Paris 736 –
Mont-de-Marsan 26 – Dax 78 – Pau 58.
ville-eugenie-les-bains.fr.
This little Landes village is renowned the world over for its weight loss cures and its great cook.

  HOTELS-RESTAURANTS

● **Les Prés d'Eugénie**
Tel. 05 58 05 06 07. Fax 05 58 51 10 10.
reservation@michelguerard.com
www.michelguerard.com
Closed 2 weeks Dec., beg. Jan.–end Mar.
Rest. closed weekdays lunch (exc. July–Aug.), Mon. dinner.
29 rooms: 270–340€. 15 suites: 390–510€.
Prix fixe: 140€, 160€, 190€.

When one is tired of fashionable cooking with its emulsions, juices, mousses, jellies and pretension, a cure with Guérard will do the trick. This young cook of seventy-three years of age has kept intact the faith of his early career. He still has the enthusiasm of the apprentice *pâtissier* of Vétheuil who became the passionate bistro chef in Asnières at the time of Le Pot au Feu, opening "nightclub" restaurants for Régine, before going into exile in the middle of the Landes of Chalosse. Here he has found the source of eternal youth, the elixir of creativity and the spring of perpetual intelligence. Fashionable stars (Ducasse or Chibois) learned all they know from him. Many curious gourmets come to take lessons in *savoir-vivre* with this king of diet cooking transformed into the prince of "natural" cuisine. This magician is first and foremost a poet, a peasant in aristocrat's clothing who knows how to charm with words as much as with food. What could be more exquisite to the taste and to the eye, as well as to the ear, than the tender oyster mushrooms

and morels with local asparagus, oven-roasted locally-fished cod in the style of Grande Iode and the squab with a simple jus. Everything with Guérard is good and beautiful, not only this old cure establishment of Napoleon III, renovated by lady of the house Christine, who has an idea a minute, with its thermal farm that has the air of a Landais museum, the new dining room with its stone floor and beamed ceiling. Also, and above all, the magical dishes that make even the satiated salivate. The oyster on the half shell served with whipped green coffee cream constitutes an Atlantic masterpiece. The egg with Aquitaine caviar and parsley mousse, diced smoked eel and a cool salad and burnet-infused vegetable bouillon bowls one over. Like the pan-seared rouget under a layer of lace-like buttered bread, served with Venetian-style aïoli. The top dish of the moment? The duckling cooked just rose colored, "Chinese gardener's style", its skin glazed and crisp like Bigorre black pork belly, with its flesh tender and juicy: a miracle of taste and contrast. Try and find fault after that with the best desserts in the world (soft Marquis de Bechamel cake with melting rhubarb ice cream, the Suzy crumble, crêpes with aged Armagnac), without forgetting the list of grand Bordeaux at sympathetic prices and the delicious Tursans, including those of maestro Guérard who is also baron of Bachen. It is true: this enchanter is eternal.

■ **La Maison Rose**
Tel. 05 58 05 06 07. Fax 05 58 51 10 10.
www.michelguerard.com
Closed beg. Dec.–10 Feb.
26 rooms: 77–180€. 4 suites: 135–220€.

The guesthouse of Michel Guérard makes one see life through rose-colored glasses. The warm welcome, the rooms in Liberty of London colors, the cozy sitting room, the swimming pool and the Jacuzzi afford delicious moments of relaxation.

● **La Ferme aux Grives**
Tel. 05 58 05 06 07. Fax 05 58 51 10 10.
reservation@michelguerard.com
www.michelguerard.com

Closed beg. Jan.–beg. Feb.
Rest. closed Tue. dinner (exc. Bank holidays
and day before Bank holidays and from mid-
July to end Aug.), Wed. (exc. Bank holidays
and day before Bank holidays and from mid-
July to end Aug.).
Prix fixe: 43€.

One falls in love with the Guérard establishments and one does the same with this
farm converted into a timeless restaurant.
The rustic-chic setting (fireplace, beams
and traditional red tiles), the wine casks
at the bar and the rural dishes full of character all give pleasure. One enjoys oven-
glazed ham pâté pierced with foie gras and
cabbage, vegetables, monkfish marinière,
Marennes oysters and mussels with herbs
as well as the Castille-style stuffed suckling pig. One's mouth waters just hearing
the description and the "coquin" raspberry tiramisu makes one want to have
a siesta in the sublime suite situated just
above. What a wonderful inn!

EURODISNEY see **MARNE LA VALLEE**

EVIAN-LES-BAINS

74500 Haute-Savoie. Paris 580 –
Thonon-les-Bains 10 – Annecy 84 –
Chamonix-Mont-Blanc 109.
otevian@icor.fr.
Evian-les-Bains is not just the border town
invaded by its neighboring Swiss game lovers, who come from as far as Lausanne. It has
its own rhythm, composed of gentle tender-
ness and gaiety and clarity. The waters of Lake
Léman (Lake Geneva) are an intense blue, taking on the color of the sky. Looking at this flat
stretch of land in front of the snowy mounts
gives a moment of inner peace. Here one does
not talk about peace but about "*molle*". Having
the *molle* of the lake is to understand the spirit
of Evian, which offers the anti-stress tool of a
microclimate. Few things are needed: a walk
along the banks, near the neat gardens, a golf
area, a gentle mountain walk into the gentlest
of hinterlands, a more or less prolonged visit
to the casino taken over by one-armed bandits.
Don't worry: they haven't managed to change
the spirit of the place.

■	HOTELS

■ Hôtel le Royal
Royal Parc Evian,
south shore of Lake Geneva.
Tel. 04 50 26 85 00. Fax 04 50 75 38 40.
reservation@royalparcevian.com
www.royalparcevian.com
Closed 12 Nov.–22 Dec.
130 rooms: 205–890€.
24 suites: 890–1050€.

Overlooking the town and the lake, this
Belle Epoque luxury hotel is an Alpine
star. Grounds, golf course, luxury suites,
panoramic view of the mountains and a
fitness center called "Living Better" set
the tone. (See Restaurants: Café Royal
and Jardin des Lys.)

■ La Verniaz
Av d'Abondance, in Neuvecelle-Eglise.
Tel. 04 50 75 04 90. Fax 04 50 70 78 92.
verniaz@relaischateaux.com
www.relaischateaux.com
Closed mid-Nov.–mid-Feb.
32 rooms: 120–250€. 6 suites: 250–550€.

This traditional Relais & Châteaux is
comprised of a group of chalets. Jean Verdier keeps a careful eye on reception, the
grounds, the swimming pool, the tennis
court and the warm rooms with view of
the lake (see Restaurants).

■ L'Ermitage
Royal Parc Evian,
south shore of Lake Geneva.
Tel. 04 50 26 85 00. Fax 04 50 75 29 37.
hotelermitage@royalparcevian.com
www.royalparcevian.com
91 rooms: 95–290€. 4 suites: 190–330€.

L'Ermitage is the luxury annex of Le
Royal and has the setting of a typical
turn-of-the-century chalet, with wood
everywhere in the décor of the guest
rooms, dining room and sitting room,
with its large fireplace. Relaxation is not
forgotten, thanks to the swimming pool
and fitness center. (See Restaurants: Le
Gourmandin.)

■ **Alizé**

2, av J.-Léger.
Tel. 04 50 75 49 49. Fax 04 50 75 50 40.
alize.hotel@wanadoo.fr
www.alizehotelevian.com
Closed mid-Nov.–1 Feb.
Rest. closed Mon., Tue. (exc. July).
22 rooms: 65–102€.
Prix fixe: 20€, 28€.

Mme Gruber, on the hotel side, ensures the comfort of her guests, while in the Grand Café (tel. 04 50 75 46 73), Franck Delale serves an honest, traditional cuisine. Duck foie gras, the mountain salad, perch or whiting filet, lamb shanks, house tart and the chocolate mousse are charged at a gentle rate.

■ **Le Bourgogne**

Pl Charles-Cottet.
Tel. 04 50 75 01 05. Fax 04 50 75 04 05.
www.hotel-evian-bourgogne.com
Closed Dec. Rest. closed Mon.
30 rooms: 59–95€.
Prix fixe: 15€, 45€, 8€ (child).
A la carte: 35€.

Situated in the center of town, this intimate-style hotel offers large, comfortable rooms. Christophe Riga serves up for our pleasure the house foie gras, perch simmered in white wine, bacon-seasoned salmon trout, duck breast with orange sauce and desserts like pain d'épices and caramel.

■ **Le Littoral**

Quai de Blonay.
Tel. 04 50 75 64 00. Fax 04 50 75 30 04.
www.littoral-evian.com
Closed Nov. 1 vac.
30 rooms: 63–95€.

This modern hotel offers comfortable rooms with view of the lake. Very reasonable prices.

■ **Hôtel de France**

59, rue Nationale.
Tel. 04 50 75 00 36. Fax 04 50 75 32 47.
www.hotel-france-evian.com
Closed mid-Nov.–26 Dec., 1 week Feb.
45 rooms: 42–91€.

The assets of this hotel remain its location, its comfortable rooms and its accessible prices.

● | RESTAURANTS

● **Le Café Royal**   ◎ V.LUX

At Hôtel le Royal,
south shore of Lake Geneva.
Tel. 04 50 26 85 00. Fax 04 50 75 38 40.
restaurantroyal@evianroyalresort.com
www.royalparcevian.com
Closed lunch, mid-Nov.–end Dec.
Prix fixe: 90€, 145€. A la carte: 130€.

On the banks of the Léman (Lake Geneva), under frescoes by Jaulmes, one is speechless at the refinement of this high place of gastronomy with its tables all lined up straight as a die. Michel Lentz, former assistant to Bonin at Le Crillon, is the maestro reigning over the cuisine served to his soon-to-be-delighted customers. His fine, contemporary dishes give voice to extremely fresh produce. The royal garden's black heirloom tomato, Lake Léman salmon trout with a wild herb infusion, the Abondance beef sirloin steak cooked in the "virtual oven" testify to an experienced technical skill. Philippe Deflon's desserts are not to be outdone, with the likes of the soft Caribbean chocolate biscuit, nor are the wines selected by Loic Chavasse-Frette. (See Hotels: Le Royal).

● **La Verniaz**   ◎ V.COM

At La Verniaz, rte d'Abondance,
in Neuvecelle.
Tel. 04 50 75 04 90. Fax 04 50 70 78 92.
verniaz@relaischateaux.com
www.relaischateaux.com/verniaz
Closed mid-Nov.–mid-Feb.
Prix fixe: 38€, 53€, 70€.

A warm and intimate Relais & Châteaux with comfortable, idyllic chalets. Jean Verdier steers the establishment with care and professionalism while Patrick Dutartre in the kitchen serves up a classic cuisine in which regional products have pride of place: foie gras terrine, Lake Léman whitefish cooked skin-side down served with vegetables, signature salmon trout with whipped butter, chicken with the flavors of Brittany, spit-roasted over a wood fire, and the crunchy fruit tart or frozen vacherin are eaten with pleasure. Local wines (from coastal or inland vineyards) share in the feast.

● Le Gourmandin   `V.COM`

At L'Ermitage, in Neuvecelle.
Tel. 04 50 26 85 54. Fax 04 50 75 29 37.
hotel-ermitage@royalparcevian.com
www.royalparcevian.com
Closed weekdays lunch
Prix fixe: 50€, 70€, 22€ (child).

Michel Mottet prepares a refined cuisine for the chalet. His crunchy fruit tart or frozen vacherin, his Atlantic sea bass filet roasted skin-side down with zucchini and peppers, sprinkled with crushed olives, like his French veal tenderloin medallion breaded in peanuts and gently sautéed, make a good impression. The sweet chocolate desserts (grand cru fondant, soft-centered Guanaja, dried fruits poached in Crimée liqueur) are mouth-wateringly delicious. (See Hotels: l'Ermitage.)

● Jardin des Lys   `COM`

At Hôtel le Royal,
south shore of Lake Geneva.
Tel. 04 50 26 85 00. Fax 04 50 75 38 40.
Prix fixe: 60€, 70€.

Health cuisine can be a pleasure, as proved by Michel Lentz with his "lightness", "balance", "recharge" or "purity" menus, eaten in a calm, minimalist setting. Enjoy, without putting on weight, tomato sprinkled with fleur de sel, frozen purslane juice, a turbot with sorrel-infused soy emulsion and the roasted sea bream wrapped in green cabbage—nothing but pleasure. A fine sweet moment is to be had with a roasted mango brochette with Espelette chilis and kiwi sorbet.

● Le Chalet du Golf   `SIM`

Evian Masters Golf Club, rte du Golf.
Tel. 04 50 75 56 34. Fax 04 50 75 65 54.
www.royalparcevian.com

Closed dinner (exc. summer),
beg. Dec.–beg. Feb.
Prix fixe: 29€ (lunch), 10€ (child).
A la carte: 45€.

Gourmet golfers in a hurry between holes discuss their exploits around the rich and varied buffets offered them by chef Thierry Buttay.

● Histoire de Goût   `SIM`

1, av du Général-Dupas.
Tel. 04 50 70 09 98. Fax 04 50 70 10 69.
www.histoiredegout.fr.st
Closed Mon., 2 weeks beg. Jan.,
2 weeks beg. June.
Prix fixe: 15€, 18€, 21€, 23€, 34€,
10€ (child).

Sébastien Douyère offers dishes full of energy in this gourmet cavern. Duck foie gras, salmon tartare with basil, monkfish blanquette with saffron-seasoned sauce and the sirloin steak with ceps are well prepared, like the frozen local raspberry soufflé. Dominique Froissard and Christine Maire form a crack team at the helm of this friendly cellar with numerous bottles to discover.

● Le Liberté   `SIM`

Casino Royal.
Tel. 04 50 26 87 50. Fax 04 50 78 48 40.
Closed Christmas.
Prix fixe: 25€, 38€.

Delicious hot goat cheese salad with grilled vegetables, jumbo shrimp enveloped in coriander-seasoned sushi, perch, beef filet with cep butter and the chocolate profiteroles are some of the joys served in this brasserie where the major asset is the beautiful terrace.

● Le Paris   `SIM`

Quai de Blonay.
Tel. 04 50 75 27 20. Fax 04 50 75 14 19.
Closed Wed., Thu., Dec.–Jan.
Prix fixe: 22€, 27€, 31€.
A la carte: 35–40€.

An honest brasserie cuisine for dinner with friends, or for two, without ceremony.

EVOSGES

01230 Ain. Paris 483 – Belley 35 –
Bourg-en-Bresse 53 – Lyon 78 – Nantua 31.
In the heart of Bugey, a calm corner of the mountain with its picture-postcard inn.

 HOTELS-RESTAURANTS

■ **L'Auberge Campagnarde**   ●❀☐
Rue de l'Auberge.
Tel. 04 74 38 55 55. Fax 04 74 38 55 62.
auberge-campagnarde@wanadoo.fr
www.logis-de-france.fr
Closed 1 week Sept.,
mid-Nov.–end Nov., Jan.
Rest. closed Tue. dinner, Wed.
15 rooms: 43–77€.
Prix fixe: 22€, 27€ (Sat., Sun., lunch),
10€ (child).

This old farm makes a pleasant refuge for lovers of walks in the forest and for anglers. The inn rooms have a rustic style while Jeanne-Marie Merloz's cuisine brings an attractive personal touch to the regional heritage. A slow-simmered escargot stew, black pollock filet cooked meunière style, veal with Bleu de Bresse cheese and the Mondeuse de Bugey tart are effortlessly enjoyable.

EVREUX

27000 Eure. Paris 97 – Rouen 55 –
Caen 134 -Chartres 78 – Alençon 119.
information@Evreux-tourisme.org.
The capital of Eure is worth the detour for its Notre Dame cathedral, ramparts and edifying museum.

 HOTELS-RESTAURANTS

■ **Normandy**   ◍▐▌☐
37, rue Edouard-Feray.
Tel. 02 32 33 14 40.
www.normandyhotel.eu
Closed 10 days mid-Aug. Rest. closed Sun.
20 rooms: 66–93€.
Prix fixe: 23,50€ (weekdays), 34€.

This old timbered hotel, which could be straight out of a Maupassant story, has had a makeover. The rooms have been refreshed, with beautiful bathrooms in soft colors. On the cuisine side, seared foie gras with chestnuts and smoked bacon, cod in mille-feuille with smoked salmon and the pan-tossed calf's liver seasoned with cider vinegar are served with professionalism in a wood-paneled dining room, with beams on the ceiling, parquet flooring and a huge fireplace, that has kept its old charm.

■ **Hôtel de France**
29, rue Saint-Thomas.
Tel. 02 32 39 09 25. Fax 02 32 38 38 56.
www.hoteldefrance-evreux.com
14 rooms: 16–70€.
Prix fixe: 23€, 38€, 16€ (child).
A la carte: 40–45€.

The high-quality, rustic-style rooms with WiFi and Internet and the quietly classic cuisine make Jean-Luc Wantier's establishment a pleasant stopover.

■ **Mercure**
Bd de Normandie.
Tel. 02 32 38 77 77. Fax 02 32 39 04 53.
h1575@accor.com / www.mercure.com
Closed Christmas, 31 Dec., 1 Jan.
60 rooms: 90–99€.
Prix fixe: 16€, 20€, 22€, 9€ (child).

This well-sited Mercure offers rooms with the expected comforts. Langoustines and marinated baby vegetables in salad, pike-perch poached in red wine and served on a bed of asparagus and the apple clafoutis with a milky coulis are honest fare.

● **La Croix d'Or**
3, rue Joséphine.
Tel. 02 32 33 06 07.
Prix fixe: 14,50€ (weekdays), 20€, 30€.

Joséphine de Beauharnais, who stayed here long ago, paid with a golden cross. Today, this good inn sited on the corner of busy streets welcomes 250 covers with a dynamic team. A marbled smoked salmon terrine, pork trotter gratin with cider vinegar, seafood, a slice of grilled turbot and the butcher's choice meat cuts give real pleasure. Professional reception by Francis Fargeau.

● **L'Orient**
25, rue Edouard-Féray.
Tel. 02 32 39 30 02.
Prix fixe: 12,90€, 13,50€, 17,90€,
58€ (for 2).

The owners are Cambodian, the cuisine Vietnamese, Thai and Chinese and the produce from Normandy: in short, contrary to Kipling's adage, East and West meet in the Orient. Rolled meat or imperial style pâté, vermicelli in beef soup (pho) or the spicy shrimp (tom yum koong), glazed duck, ginger-seasoned chicken and grilled Atlantic sea bass presented in a banana leaf give a true taste of authenticity in surroundings very recently redecorated in black and red.

● **Vieille Gabelle** COM
3, rue Vieille-Gabelle.
Tel.-Fax 02 32 39 77 13.
Closed Sat. lunch, Sun. dinner, Mon.,
Christmas–New Year's, 1 week Apr.,
3 weeks Aug.
Prix fixe: 15€, 26€.

Michel Potrimol is the nice manager of this Norman house with timbers and fireplace. The dining room is warm and the cuisine works flawlessly in tune with the market. The scallop fricassée with endives, cider-seasoned turbot, oven-browned sole with shrimp, cod filet with basil cream sauce, veal sweetbreads with sorrel and the Calvados-flavored apple "tulip" and cinnamon ice cream, are eaten with pleasure.

● **La Gazette** SIM
7, rue Saint-Sauveur.
Tel. 02 32 33 43 40. Fax 02 32 31 38 87.
xavier-buzieux@wanadoo.fr
Closed Sat. lunch, Sun., 3 weeks Aug.
Prix fixe: 22€ (weekdays), 31€, 42€, 52€.

Star of his adopted town, the Roannais Xavier Buzieux has turned his old bistro into a modern, light, contemporary res-

taurant with a touch of minimalism, with its gray monotints. The place, enlarged thanks to the purchase of a neighboring shop, is now chic. And this pupil of the Roux brothers in London has not lost his touch, charming his clientele with well-produced menus. The apple-seasoned foie gras terrine, gnocchi with creamy cep sauce, trout brandade napped with a beet coulis, a potato and chitterling sausage cake, rabbit thigh with dates and the frozen pear matchsticks all look good.

In Parville (27180). 4 km w via N13.

● **Côté Jardin** COM
Rte de Lisieux.
Tel. 02 32 39 19 19. Fax 02 32 31 21 85.
Prix fixe: 17€, 27€, 37€.

On the route to Lisieux, Emmanuel Dossemont Lambert gives a warm welcome and creates his menus with market and seasonal produce. Duck foie gras seasoned with Sauternes, marinated sea bream, cod filet with mozzarella, lamb saddle in an herb crust and the vanilla-seasoned pear tartare go down without a murmur.

EYBENS see **GRENOBLE**

13810 Bouches-du-Rhône. Paris 704 –
Avignon 30– Saint-Rémy-de-Provence 12 –
Marseille 81.
Alpilles country with, in this beautiful village with its colors of Provence, the memory of painter Mario Prassinos and his sparkling hillside.

 HOTELS-RESTAURANTS

■ **Mas de la Brune**
Rte de Saint-Rémy.
Tel. 04 90 90 67 67. Fax 04 90 95 99 21.
contact@masdelabrune.com
www.masdelabrune.com
Closed Nov. 1–Easter.
9 rooms: 240–270€. 1 suite: 370€.

This very charming guesthouse set in an old oil mill and its Renaissance *mas* offers cozy, comfortable rooms. The swimming pool and herbalist's garden complete the picture.

■ Le Mas du Pastre ❀⌂

Quartier Saint-Sixte, rte d'Orgon.
Tel. 04 90 95 92 61. Fax 04 90 90 61 75.
contact@masdupastre.com
www.masdupastre.com
Closed mid-Nov.–mid-Dec.
Rest. closed Sun. (exc. off season).
15 rooms: 100–180€. 3 suites: 130–220€.
Prix fixe: 29€, 45€, 68€. A la carte: 55€.

The swimming pool, Jacuzzi, hammam and old-style but very functional rooms make this former sheep farm a charming guesthouse. In the restaurant, one enjoys regional cuisine created by Sébastien Jiraud. Foie gras escalope with ratatouille confiture, red sea bream served on bayaldi (a Provençal vegetable gratin), lavender honey-glazed duck breast and a soft fromage blanc and almond blanc-manger with a duo of tomato and tarragon sorbets are delightful.

● Le Bistro d'Eygalières ○COM

Rue de la République.
Tel. 04 90 90 60 34. Fax 04 90 90 60 37.
sbru@club-internet.com / www.chezbru.com
Closed mid-Jan.–mid-Mar., 1 week Aug.
Rest. closed Sun. dinner (off season), Mon.,
Tue. lunch.
2 rooms: 115–130€. 2 suites: 160€.
A la carte: 70–90€.

In the heart of this picture postcard village, Wout Bru's bistro charms all. The mini-patio, the attractively laid tables, the smiling welcome from Suzy and, of course, the cooking of the master of the place are all staggering. This native of Flanders who trained at hotel school in Bruges, T'Couvent in Ypres, Le Mas des Herbes Blanches in Joucas, then at Le Cabro d'Or and L'Oustau in Baumanière, has made Provence into his country of adoption and inspiration. The sautéed ratte potatoes with Parma ham and truffles, roasted bacon-wrapped monkfish in a rosemary-infused bouillon, roasted rack of lamb with an eggplant and lamb trotter mille-feuille and the pan-tossed berries

with pain d'épice and balsamic pay delicious homage to the land of cicadas.

LES–EYZIES-DE-TAYAC

24620 Dordogne. Paris 517 – Périgueux 47 – Sarlat 21 – Brive 63.
ot.les.eyzies@perigord.tm.fr.
The world capital of prehistory is right here. The Grand-Roc grotto, national museum and circuit of Vézère are not to be missed.

 HOTELS-RESTAURANTS

■ Le Moulin de la Beune 🏚

2, rue du Moulin-Bas.
Tel. 05 53 06 94 33. Fax 05 53 06 98 06.
contact@moulindelabeune.com
www.moulindelabeune.com
Closed Nov. 1–Apr. 1
Rest. closed Sat. lunch, Tue. lunch,
Wed. lunch.
20 rooms: 59–70€.
Prix fixe: 29€, 40€ (wine inc. dinner), 55€,
10€ (child). A la carte: 70€.

Calm is guaranteed in this former mill with rustic, white-walled rooms and traditional red tiles. On the cooking side, the fine work of Georges Soulié wakes up the tastebuds with escargots in a golden pastry crust, a scallop and cep fricassée, veal sweetbreads with morels and the hot Grand Marnier soufflé. The only problem is the check …

■ Hostellerie du Passeur 🏚

Pl de la Mairie.
Tel. 05 53 06 97 13. Fax 05 53 06 91 63.
www.hostellerie-du-passeur.com
Closed 1 Nov.–1 Apr.
Rest. closed Sat. lunch (exc. summer),
Tue. lunch (exc. summer).
20 rooms: 72–115€.
Prix fixe: 17€ (lunch), 23€ (lunch), 27€
(dinner), 37€ (dinner) 11€ (child).

Gérard Brun has renovated (but in an old style) the rooms of this guesthouse. In the kitchen, he is just as efficient and meticulous in his creation of bistro dishes. Nothing to criticize in jumbo shrimp tail salad, pike-perch served with a virgin olive oil viniagrette, veal sweetbread escalope with ceps and hot marbled orange and chocolate soufflé.

■ Hôtel des Roches

15, av de la Forge, rte de Sarlat.
Tel. 05 53 06 96 59. Fax 05 53 06 95 54.
www.roches-les-eyzies.com
Closed Nov. 1–mid-Apr.
41 rooms: 72–90€.

The rooms of this friendly hotel offer every comfort. The establishment has a swimming pool and the walks in the large grounds with its river are very pleasant indeed.

EZE-VILLAGE

06360 Alpes-Maritimes. Paris 943 – Nice 12 – Monaco 8 – Menton 20.
eze@webstore.fr.
A village perched up high like an eagle's nest, an exotic garden, a sheer cliff opposite the great blue ocean—in sum, this is a magical place, an exotic garden like a belvedere overlooking the Mediterranean.

 HOTELS-RESTAURANTS

● Le Château de la   ○❀**LUX** Chèvre d'Or

Rue du Barri.
Tel. 04 92 10 66 66. Fax 04 93 41 06 72.
reservation@chevredor.com
www.chevredor.com
Closed end Oct.–beg. Mar.
29 rooms: 270–805€.
3 suites: 1260–2640€.
Prix fixe: 65€ (lunch), 85€, 120€ (lunch, wine inc.), 168€ (dinner). A la carte: 180€.

The view of Cap Ferrat and Cap d'Ail, the gardens, the terraces and the private swimming pools reached directly from the spacious and neat rooms make this an idyllic Relais & Châteaux. The restaurant is not to be outdone. Philippe Labbé, a Meilleur Ouvrier de France trained by Loiseau, Boyer, Lorain, Vergé and Willer and formerly of the Château de Bagnols,

creates fine dishes that are respectful of tradition and which are often very rich, but pleasurable, as demonstrated by goose and duck foie gras in two services, roasted Mediterranean sea bass with pepper sauce, milk-fed veal cutlet with ceps and sweet melon with a local sugared almond sweet, served with iced sweet almond soup. Extremely fine wine list, knowledgeably explained.

■ Château Eza   ❀

Rue de la Pise.
Tel. 04 93 41 12 24. Fax 04 93 41 16 64.
infos@chateaueza.com
www.chateaueza.com
Closed beg. Nov.–mid-Dec.
6 rooms: 150–1050€. 4 suites: 1050€.
Prix fixe: 37€, 47€, 90€. A la carte: 76€.

This high-up 14th-century house offers an exceptional panorama of the coast from its terraces. The rooms are elegant and the cuisine of Pierre Daret, who has taken over the kitchen, full of canny skill: lobster medallion poached in an aromatic herb-seasoned bouillon with mango and ginger vinaigrette, pan-seared tuna steak glazed in balsamic vinegar and the sautéed veal with a penne, zucchini and olive fricassée, served with a parmesan croustillant, have everything they need to please.

● Le Troubadour   **COM**

Rue du Brec.
Tel. 04 93 41 19 03.
troubadoureze@wanadoo.fr
www.troubadoureze.fr
Closed Sun., Mon., mid-Nov.–20 Dec., end Feb.–beg. Mar., 1 week beg. July.
Prix fixe: 32€, 47€.

Gérard Vuille's establishment and cuisine are still in the best of taste, the passing years not undermining this beautiful building in the center of the village. Rabbit in aspic, stuffed zucchini flowers, turbot cooked in Sancerre, the parsley and garlic–seasoned rack of lamb and the frozen nougat make a good impression. Attentive reception.

F

FAGNON see **CHARLEVILLE-MÉZIÈRES**

FALAISE

14700 Calvados. Paris 221 – Caen 36 –
Argentan 23 – Lisieux 46.
falaise-tourism@mail.cpod.fr.
Deepest Normandy, when it leaves the Orne,
becomes ''little Switzerland'' as it approaches
the plain of Caen. William the Conqueror's castle is worth a glimpse!

 HOTELS-RESTAURANTS

■ La Poste

38, rue G.-Clemenceau.
Tel. 02 31 90 13 14. Fax 02 31 90 01 81.
hotel.delaposte@wanadoo.fr
Closed Fri. dinner (May–Sept. exc. by
reserv.), Sun. dinner, Mon., 3 weeks Jan.
15 rooms: 52–95€. 2 suites: 75€.
Prix fixe: 15,50€ (exc. weekend lunch), 25€,
32€.

In their post-war house, Bernadette
Boutmy and Christine Lefèvre offer neat
rooms in pastel colors. In the dining room
with its sunny colors, the classic meals are
honestly priced. The house duck foie gras
terrine, rolled sole with asparagus, a lamb
medallion with thyme flower and goat
cheese and the dark chocolate fondant are
executed with finesse by Bernadette.

● La Fine Fourchette   V.COM

52, rue G.-Clemenceau.
Tel. 02 31 90 08 59. Fax 02 31 90 00 83.
Closed Tue. dinner (off season), Feb. vac.
Prix fixe: 14,80€, 19€, 29,50€, 50€.
A la carte: 53€.

Gilbert Costil serves up personalized
dishes according to his imagination. Langoustines pan tossed with thyme flower,
lemongrass-seasoned sole with fried
leeks, traditional pan-simmered tête de
veau seasoned with fines herbes and a little caramelized apple soufflé served Tatin
style, with cider jelly and apple sorbet, are
right on target.

● L'Attache   COM

1,5 km nw via rte de Caen.
Tel. 02 31 90 05 38. Fax 02 31 90 57 19.
Closed Tue., Wed., 2 weeks July.
Prix fixe: 19€, 30,50€, 35,50€, 43,50€. A
la carte: 60€.

Alain Hastaing's former coaching inn with
its smart exterior still seduces through
its welcome, its redecorated setting in
salmon, green and white, its gentle prices
and its tasty cuisine. Tête de veau cake,
pan-seared beef filet medallions with
Sichuan pepper, Pacific tuna and the
chocolate craquant, all accompanied by
selected wines, are right on target.

FALICON see **NICE**

LA FAUCILLE (COL DE)

01170 Ain. Paris 481 – Bourg-en-Bresse 108
– Genève 32 – Gex 12 – Nantua 60.
Giving, at almost 900 meters, a splendid view
of the Léman, this is a classic staging post in
the Alps-Jura route, bordering Gex country.

 HOTELS-RESTAURANTS

■ La Mainaz

Rte du col de la Faucille. 1 km s via N5.
Tel. 04 50 41 31 10. Fax 04 50 41 31 77.
mainaz@club-internet.fr / www.la-mainaz.com
Closed end Oct.–beg. Dec. Rest. closed Sun.
dinner, Mon. (exc. school vac.).
22 rooms: 60–90€.
Prix fixe: 26€, 40€, 15€ (child).

This chalet facing the Léman (Lake
Geneva) always offers comfort and carefully prepared menus with classic dishes
(smoked salmon, sole with Vin Jaune
sauce, beef with morels) at gentle prices.
Wonderful welcome.

■ La Petite Chaumière

Rte du col de la Faucille.
Tel. 04 50 41 30 22. Fax 04 50 41 33 22.
www.petitechaumiere.com
Closed mid-Oct.–20 Dec., 3 weeks Apr.
34 rooms: 46–76€. Half board: 49€.

This is the destination of sporty types seeking the authenticity of serious cuisine and a friendly atmosphere. No one is disappointed by this professional establishment.

FAY-SUR-LIGNON
see **LE CHAMBON-SUR-LIGNON**

FAYENCE

83440 Var. Paris 891 – Castellane 55 – Draguignan 30 – Fréjus 35 – Grasse 27.ot. fayence@wanadoo.fr.
This old-fashioned town is an example of pretty Upper Var, offering lovely views of the valley from the belvedere of the church.

 HOTELS-RESTAURANTS

■ Moulin de la Camandoule
Chemin Notre-Dame-des-Cyprès,
via rte de Seillans.
Tel. 04 94 76 00 84. Fax 04 94 76 10 40.
www.camandoule.com
Rest. closed Wed., Thu., 2 weeks beg. Jan.
10 rooms: 105€. 1 suite: 170€.
Prix fixe: 30€ (lunch), 45€. A la carte: 60€.

This 17th-century oil mill surrounded by grounds crossed by a Roman aqueduct is irresistible! Its immaculate, colorful rooms, swimming pool and Provençal dining room extended with a terrace compete for guests' well being. The crispy jumbo shrimp with spicy jus, a pan-fried Mediterranean sea bass with olive paste, served with raw and cooked artichokes, the poultry filet stuffed with escargots and served in a creamy white sauce and the Sichuan pepper–infused crème brûlée with roasted apricots are major assets.

■ Les Oliviers
Quartier de la Ferrage, rte de Grasse.
Tel. 04 94 76 13 12. Fax 04 94 76 08 05.
hotel.oliviers.fayence@free.fr
22 rooms: 73–96€.

Here, in this meeting place for wind-surfing addicts, there is no pretension: simple rooms with Provençal colors, gentle prices and a rooftop swimming pool.

● Castelleras   V.COM
461, chemin de Peymeyan.
Tel. 04 94 76 13 80. Fax 04 94 84 17 50.
contact@restaurant-castelleras.com
Closed Mon., Tue., 2 Jan.–6 Feb.
Prix fixe: 45€, 60€, 12€ (child).
A la carte: 70€.

Perched up on the heights of Fayence, Alain Caro's restaurant opens onto the town and the valley. The view takes your breath away, but not your appetite: pan-seared foie gras escalope seasoned with vanilla and rhubarb, a pan-seared scallop with mushroom- and ham-stuffed artichokes simmered in wine and a rack of lamb served in a pistachio-seasoned crumble with stuffed baby vegetables are skillful interpretations of the Provençal classics. The wines of the Grand Midi flow readily from their source. The soft-centered chocolate cake with a cherry confit center fulfils its duty.

● La Farigoulette   SIM
Pl du Château.
Tel.-Fax 04 94 84 10 49.
lafarigoulette@wanadoo.fr
Closed Sun. (July–Aug.), Tue., Wed. (exc. dinner July–Aug.), end Jan., 1 week Feb., end June.
Prix fixe: 19,50€ (lunch), 36€.
A la carte: 50€.

Hervé Quesnel, in his former stables, serves up classic and ingenious dishes according to the weather and the seasons, as brilliantly demonstrated by creamy squash and chestnut soup, served with pan-seared slices of duck foie gras, the monkfish, jumbo shrimp and chorizo brochette served with artichoke and parsley-seasoned fried bread, piglet cheeks served with an emusion of cooking juice and lentils and the pineapple carpaccio with piña colada sauce and pineapple sorbet.

● La Table d'Yves   SIM

1357, rte de Fréjus.
Tel. 04 94 76 08 44. Fax 04 94 76 19 32.
contact@latabledyves.com
www.latabledyves.com
Closed Wed. (exc. July–Aug.), Thu. (exc.
lunch July–Aug.), Nov. 1 vac., Feb. vac.
Prix fixe: 28€, 39€, 52€,18€ (child).
A la carte: 50–55€.

Yves Merville, whom we knew from Cagnes, has made his nest in this Provençal bistro decorated in yellow, ochre and blue. He is an attentive presence, promoting quality dishes in menus inspired by the market. Pan-seared foie gras with seasonal fruits, truffle salad with poached egg, line-fished Atlantic sea bass with creamy asparagus and the seven-hour lamb shoulder make a good impression. The pistachio and salted-butter cookie is a gastronomic indulgence.

FECAMP

76400 Seine-Maritime. Paris 202 –
Le Havre 44 – Dieppe 66 – Rouen 74.
The town has hardly changed since *La Maison Tellier*. As well as Maupassant's memory, there is the abbey church of the Trinity and the Benedictine house devoted to the precious liqueur.

 HOTELS-RESTAURANTS

■ Le Grand Pavois

15, quai de la Vicomté.
Tel. 02 35 10 01 01. Fax 02 35 29 31 67.
le.grandpavois@wanadoo.fr
www.hotel-grand-pavois.com
32 rooms: 78–150€. 3 suites: 110–248€.

Danielle Paumier has endowed this former jam factory, which opens onto the port, with Internet and WiFi. Rooms in light colors and modern furniture set the tone of a pleasant stopover.

■ Auberge de la Rouge

Rte du Havre.
Tel. 02 35 28 07 59. Fax 02 35 28 70 55.
auberge.rouge@wanadoo.fr
www.auberge-rouge.com

Rest. closed Sat. lunch, Sun. dinner, Mon.
8 rooms: 60€.
Prix fixe: 14,50€ (weekday lunch), 19€,
29€, 35€, 11€ (child). A la carte: 60€.

The sun is in attendance, as much in the garden as in the rooms and the cuisine. Paul-Aymeric Durel in the kitchen serves up Landes duck foie gras escalope with Granny Smith apples, minced rare-cooked Atlantic sea bass with masala seasoning and wasabi cakes, slice of Atlantic sea bass with potato garnish and grated black truffles, wild duck served with foie gras-enriched gravy and, to finish, the pleasant hot Benedictine soufflé. Extremely serious work, which is reproduced in an annex in town: La Plaisance (02 35 29 38 14), 33, quai de la Vicomté.

■ Ferme de la Chapelle

Côte de la Vierge, via rte du Phare.
Tel. 02 35 10 12 12. Fax 02 35 10 12 13.
fermedelachapelle@wanadoo.fr
www.fermedelachapelle.fr
Rest. closed Mon. lunch.
17 rooms: 60–140€.
Prix fixe: 20€, 35€.

On the cliff, near the sailors' chapel, this former farm with rooms and apartments in the Norman style offers a rigorously executed traditional cuisine. Thomas Buchy concocts foie gras terrine with veal sweetbreads and currant sauce, citrus-seaoned catfish soufflé, pepper-seasoned sirloin steak served with spicy slow-cooked vegetables and the Benedictine and chocolate cake, which all slip down without a murmur.

FEGERSHEIM see STRASBOURG

FERE-EN-TARDENOIS

02130 Aisne. Paris 109 – Reims 50 –
Château-Thierry 23 – Laon 56 –
Soissons 27.
tardenois@aol.com.
A green piece of countryside between grassy hillsides and valley. The town, which has an ancient marketplace and a château with medieval ruins, is worth seeing.

HOTELS-RESTAURANTS

● Château de Fère

3 km n via D967, rte de Sisme.
Tel. 03 23 82 21 13. Fax 03 23 82 37 81.
chateau.fere@wanadoo.fr
www.chateaudefere.com
Closed beg. Jan.–10 Feb.
Rest. closed Mon. lunch (Nov.–Mar.).
19 rooms: 150–350€. 7 suites: 230–400€.
Prix fixe: 35€, 49€, 88€. A la carte: 95€.

Near the château of Anne de Montmorency, this Renaissance castle commands respect. Its grounds with heated swimming pool, refined rooms and dining room exude history. On the food side, Dominique Quay, trained with Adolphe Bosser in Audierne, creates a technical, cross-bred cuisine in the best taste. The langoustine, wrapped in angel-hair pasta and then fried, John Dory filet accompanied by shellfish and soybean sprout risotto, two-spice-glazed Barbary duckling and the crème brûlée pastilla with crushed rosemary-seasoned apricots find their match in a wine cellar representing all of France.

FERNEY-VOLTAIRE

01210 Ain. Paris 502 – Thonon 44 –
Bellegarde 37 – Geneva 10 – Gex 11.
otferney@ccpays-de-gex.fr.
Gex country harbors the village of Voltaire, the lord of Ferney, with his château in its grounds and his statue in the pedestrian center as reminders.

RESTAURANTS

● Le Pirate

Rue de Genève.
Tel. 04 50 40 63 52. Fax 04 50 40 64 50.
contact@lepirate.fr / www.lepirate.fr
Closed Sun., Mon., 1 week beg. Jan.,
3 weeks Aug.
Prix fixe: 37€ (lunch, wine inc.), 30€ (lunch),
40€, 59€, 16€ (child). A la carte: 62€.

The setting is modern—if a touch dated—in shades of violet pink. But Pierre-Franck and Valérie Salamon form a crack team who make you see life through rose-colored glasses. Pierre-Franck, who trained with Blanc, Guérard, Willer and Marchesi and is a winner of the Taittinger prize, was brought up in Bresse country and practices a cuisine that is precisely measured in its cooking and perfectly balanced in terms of flavors. We could cite as proof the gourmet dish called "taste everything", the monkfish and salmon duo with hazelnuts and artichokes, the pan-tossed rouget with pesto and Provençal-style pain perdu, the beef Rosigny and the soft chocolate biscuit with pain d'épice glazed in an exotic fruit coulis which all demonstrate a lovely technical prowess. One enjoys the fine selection of 400 wines in the prolific list.

FERRETTE

68480 Haut-Rhin. Paris 529 – Altkirch 19 –
Colmar 79 – Mulhouse 37 – Bâle 27.
infotourisme@jura-alsacien.net.
Enchanting and dreamy, this is the former capital of Sundgau, with the château of the Counts of Ferrette, little streets that cascade down, greenery everywhere and wanton vegetation.

HOTELS-RESTAURANTS

● Au Cheval Blanc

3, rue Léon-Lehmann.
Tel. 03 89 40 41 30. Fax 03 89 40 49 08.
Closed Mon., 1 week at end Dec., June.
Prix fixe: 22€, 23€, 25€.
A la carte: 25–30€.

Local dishes, a rustic, simple atmosphere and sensible prices are the assets of this unpretentious village restaurant. Munster cheese in puff pastry, fried carp filet, fried lamb and the apple streudel are delicious.

● Le Jura

33, rue du Château.
Tel.-Fax 03 89 40 32 09 .
restdujura.dietlin@laposte.net
www.restdujura-dietlin.com
Closed Tue. dinner, Wed. dinner, Christmas,
1 week July.

Prix fixe: 15€, 28€, 7,50€ (child).
A la carte: 35€.

Alsace is on the program with Jean and Mireille Dietlin: well-laid tables, décor of a neat inn with wood fittings, yellow and green colors and a classic but light cuisine. One enjoys the autumn salad, escargots, pike-perch sautéed in oil with white wine, brandy, garlic, shallots and tomatoes, the veal kidneys flambéed in Cognac and the house chocolate charlotte and seasonal fruit tarts.

In Ligsdorf (68480). 4 km s via D432.

■ **Le Moulin Bas**
1, rue de Raedersdorf.
Tel. 03 89 40 31 25. Fax 03 89 40 37 15.
info@le-moulin-bas.fr / www.le-moulin-bas.fr
Rest. closed Tue.
8 rooms: 65–85€.
Prix fixe: 12€, 32€, 60€. A la carte: 50€.

Right on the Swiss border, this 18th-century mill deserves a stop as much for the place as for the cuisine. The refined rooms in a rustic style, the two tennis courts and the terraces, one of them new, are an invitation to true relaxation. The classic cuisine impresses: a fine carpaccio, tuna croustillant with tomato, roasted pigeon with yellow peaches and the strawberry millefeuille are extremely well conceived.

In Lutter (68480). 8 km se via D23.

■ **Auberge Paysanne**
1, rue Wolschwiller.
Tel. 03 89 40 71 67. Fax 03 89 07 33 38.
aubergepaysanne2@wanadoo.fr
www.auberge-hostellerie-paysanne.com
Closed 2 weeks Feb., 2 weeks beg. July, Christmas, Mon. (exc. by reserv.). Rest. closed Mon., Tue. lunch.
16 rooms: 49–69€.
Prix fixe: 9,50€ (weekday lunch), 18€, 23€, 29€, 9,50€ (child). A la carte: 45€.

With the arrival of Carmen Guérinot, this 17th-century village farm is experiencing a second youth. The repainted exterior, smart breakfasts and renovated rooms on a rustic theme are all seductive. The guesthouse cuisine (salmon crêpe, jumbo shrimp with preserved lemons, pork tenderloin medallion in an herb crust, floating island) created by Andréas Andréou has the merit of being reasonably priced.

In Moernach (68480). 5 km w via D473.

■ **Au Raisin**
85, rue des Tilleuls.
Tel. 03 89 40 80 73. Fax 03 89 08 11 33.
contact@auraisin.com / www.auraisin.com
Open daily. Rest. closed Mon.
8 rooms: 36–44€.
Prix fixe: 15€, 36€, 7€ (child).

The Schneiders have for three generations offered both regulars and tourists the comfort of their rooms, their smart dining room and the seriousness of their regional, traditional cuisine, currently created by Robert.

LA FERTE-BERNARD

72400 Sarthe. Paris 165 – Alençon 54 – Chartres 80 – Châteaudun 63 – Le Mans 52. This little capital of the Perche Sarthois region allows a rural stop and detours. Don't miss the church of Notre Dame des Marais.

■◢
●◣ HOTELS-RESTAURANTS

● **La Perdrix**
2, rue de Paris.
Tel. 02 43 93 00 44. Fax 02 43 93 74 95.
http://monsite.wanadoo.fr/laperdrix
Closed Mon. dinner, Tue., Feb.
7 rooms: 46–58€.
Prix fixe: 17€ (weekdays), 26€, 38€.
A la carte: 45€.

Near the motorway, the Thibauts' establishment offers a muted, discreet atmosphere, a refined décor in which orange dominates and freshly redecorated rooms. On the restaurant side, Serge cooks in rhythm with the market. Chanterelles in puff pastry and a poached egg with shallot sauce, turbot served meunière style with an amusing Curaçao-seasoned butter sauce, and the sirloin steak with fresh pasta and foie gras, served with Worcestershire sauce, are well conceived. The sweet dark chocolate dessert with a crunchy nougat and puffed rice cake goes down a treat. Ice cream, bread and croissants are made in-house. Fine wine list, highlighting the Loire.

● Le Dauphin

3, rue d'Huisne.
Tel. 02 43 93 00 39. Fax 02 43 71 26 65.
Closed Sun. dinner, Mon., 1 week Mar.,
2 weeks Aug.
Prix fixe: 15€, 23,80€, 31,50€, 39€,
11,50€ (child).

In this 16th-century house in the heart of the old town, the Guimiers blend ancient and modern: classic dining room in shades of ochre with fireplace and contemporary furniture and crockery. The traditional cuisine is also reinterpreted to today's tastes. Pan-tossed langoustines, artichokes and peppers served with an olive-seasoned sabayon, poached catfish in a milk fumé, gray shrimp coulis and rolled eggplant and a duckling filet with green asparagus and pancetta, napped with a pear reduction, make happy customers. The variation on the theme of the strawberry makes a light ending to the meal. A rich wine list with a hundred or so vintages from every vineyard.

LA FERTE-IMBAULT

41300 Loir-et-Cher. Paris 195 – Bourges 68 – Orléans 70 – Romorantin 19.
In the heart of rural Sologne, an amazing village, famous for its church and (private) château.

 HOTELS-RESTAURANTS

■ La Tête de Lard

13, pl des Tilleuls.
Tel. 02 54 96 22 32. Fax 02 54 96 06 22.
www.aubergealatetedelard.com
Closed Sun. dinner, Mon. (exc. Bank
holidays), Tue. lunch, 2 weeks Jan.–beg. Feb.,
2 weeks Sept.
11 rooms: 48–74€.
Prix fixe: 17€ (weekdays), 24€ (weekdays),
29€, 34€, 42€, 49€. A la carte: 50€.

Jean-Marie Benni's inn remains a friendly stopover with its smiling welcome and its rustic restaurant with finely crafted dishes. Leek and cep terrine, pike-perch with morels, a veal sweetbread escalope served in its cooking juices and the frozen chestnut parfait with pear sauce are extremely well made. A sweet, personalized room in a Sologne-style building.

LA FERTE-SAINT-AUBIN

45240 Loiret. Paris 156 – Orléans 23 – Blois 63 – Romorantin 45 – Salbris 34.
One can visit the château where Jean Renoir filmed *La Règle du jeu* and go off hunting or walking in the thickets of rural Sologne.

 HOTELS-RESTAURANTS

■ Château les Muids

On the N20.
Tel. 02 38 64 65 14. Fax 02 38 76 50 08.
info@chateau-les-muids.com
www.chateau-les-muids.com
21 rooms: 65–145€. 1 suite: 195€.
Prix fixe: 20€ (lunch), 43€, 18€ (child).
A la carte: 65€.

In the middle of beautiful grounds with swimming pool, tennis court and mini-golf, this 18th-century château houses rooms of character. In the kitchen, the rapid turnover of chefs continues. Let us hope that this last one will survive with his cold orange-seasoned tomato soup served with crab tartare, scallop fricassée and lemongrass-seasoned pike-perch, duck medallions with sour cherries and the cinnamon-seasoned roasted pineapple.

● Ferme de la Lande

3 km via rte de Marcilly, D921.
Tel. 02 38 76 64 37. Fax 02 38 64 68 87.
solignote@fermeland.com
www.fermedelalande.com
Closed Sun. dinner, Mon., 3 weeks Jan.
Prix fixe: 35€, 47€, 15€ (child).
A la carte: 72–82€.

This part of an old farmhouse bordering a wood has the charm of the past. Julien

Thomasson's cuisine is traditional but light, highlighting quality produce: Breton lobster ravioli, escargots from a small producer, wild John Dory, roasted milk-fed veal and a chocolate soufflé.

● **Les Brémailles** `COM`

195 RN20 (At the northern approach to la Ferté-Saint-Aubin).

Tel. 02 38 76 56 60. Fax 02 38 64 68 04.

restaurant.les bremailles@wanadoo.fr

Closed Sun. (exc. summer), Mon. dinner (exc. summer), Tue. (exc. summer).

Prix fixe: 21€, 8,50€ (child). A la carte: 50€.

This hunting lodge made of brick and wood next to the RN20 offers high-quality classic dishes: the salmon smoked in-house, pike-perch in a sesame crust with fennel-seasoned beurre blanc, sirloin steak with morels and a pineapple carpaccio with cardamom and a scoop of ice cream, all washed down with selected wines.

FIGEAC

46100 Lot. Paris 572 – Rodez 66 – Aurillac 65 – Villefranche 36.

figeac@wanadoo.fr.

Champollion was born here; a museum found down a narrow alleyway recalls his life and work. The Causse is a paradise for ramblers, who step briskly across the GR (long-distance footpath) that crosses the town. Capital of Upper Quercy, it deserves a stop for its Hôtel de la Monnaie.

 HOTELS-RESTAURANTS

■ **Château du Viguier du Roy & la Dînée du Viguier**

Rue Droite, 4, rue de Boutaric.

Tel. 05 65 50 05 05 / 05 65 50 08 08.

Fax 05 65 50 06 06.

www.chateau-viguier-figeac.com

Hotel closed mid-Oct.–end Apr.

Rest. closed Sat. lunch (off season), Mon. (off season), 3 weeks Feb.

16 rooms: 160–365€. 3 suites: 325–500€.

Prix fixe: 42€, 75€, 20€ (lunch), 28€.

This is a 12th-century house with 16th-century keep, a cloister, a chapel, delightful sitting rooms with beautiful medieval furniture that give onto the rooms renovated with a light décor, the library, the heated swimming pool, the terraced gardens and the spa. In the Dînée du Viguier, Daniel Authié cooks up a pleasant squab wrapped in pastry served with foie gras, a turbot filet, John Dory with chestnuts and a delicious lamb tenderloin filet. Fine cellar with a focus on the best Cahors.

■ **Le Champollion**

3, pl Champollion.

Tel. 05 65 34 04 37. Fax 05 65 34 61 69.

10 rooms: 43–49€.

Right in the center of town, this medieval building houses clean, modern and air-conditioned rooms at competitive prices.

● **Cuisine du Marché** `COM`

15, rue de Clermont.

Tel.-Fax 05 65 50 18 55.

cuisinedumarche@wanadoo.fr

Closed Sun.

Prix fixe: 18€ (lunch), 29€, 40€.

A la carte: 55€.

Joël Centeno and Christophe Bourdon both run this friendly restaurant in old Figeac. They produce fresh, unpretentious dishes: tomato and mozzarella mille-feuille, crisp bundles of haddock, simple pan-tossed Atlantic sea bass, Mont-Royal pigeon and a chocolate macaron with mascarpone cream and vanilla, which one enjoys without paying through the nose.

FLAVIGNY-SUR-MOSELLE see NANCY

FLAYOSC see DRAGUIGNAN

LA FLECHE

72200 Sarthe. Paris 245 –

Angers 50 – Laval 70 – Le Mans 45 – Tours 70.

The military school, the wood decorations in the Notre Dame des Vertus chapel and also the Têtes Rouges zoo are the treasures to be discovered in this gateway to the châteaux of Val.

■ HOTELS

■ Le Relais Cicero

18, bd d'Alger.
Tel. 02 43 94 14 14. Fax 02 43 45 98 96.
hotel.cicero@wanadoo.fr / www.cicero.fr
Closed vac. Christmas, 2 weeks beg. Aug.
21 rooms: 59–110€. 7 suites: 110–120€.

This former 17th-century convent, located in a garden that removes it from the world, is a haven of peace. Henry Chérel skillfully marries contemporary style and authenticity with period furniture and beautiful ornaments.

FLEURIE

69820 Rhône. Paris 413 – Mâcon 22 – Villefranche 28 – Bourg 46 – Lyon 62.
One of the small beacon towns of Beaujolais country whose name is synonymous with solid, honest wine.

 HOTELS-RESTAURANTS

■ Grands Vins

La Lie, D119.
Tel. 04 74 69 81 43. Fax 04 74 69 86 10.
www.hoteldesgrandsvins.com
Closed Dec., Jan.
20 rooms: 66–75€.

This hotel with nice rooms, situated between Chénas and Chiroubles on the edge of vineyards, makes a pleasant stop conducive to enjoying vintage wines. Garden and swimming pool.

● Auberge du Cep

Pl de l'Eglise.
Tel. 04 74 04 10 77. Fax 04 74 04 10 28.
Closed Sun., Mon., Dec., Jan.
Prix fixe: 35€, 55€, 65€, 85€.
A la carte: 75€.

Opposite the church, Chantal Chagny's establishment is still the rigorous and charming ambassador of Beaujolais. We like her consistent preparation of traditional recipes and the highlighting of local produce. The restaurant is refined, the atmosphere rustic and the dishes to match: fines herbes–seasoned roasted frog legs, eel braised in wine, Charolais sirloin steak with Beaujolais sauce and Beaujolais-marinated prunes. On the wine side, the region has, as is to be expected, pride of place. Begin with those of the great neighbor Duboeuf.

FLEVY see METZ

FLORAC

48400 Lozère. Paris 629 – Mende 40 – Alès 67 – Millau 78.
otsi@ville-florac.fr.
In the middle of nowhere, this Lozère town has the ridge of the Cévennes and the Tarn gorges as its beautiful horizon.

 HOTELS-RESTAURANTS

■ Grand Hôtel du Parc

47, av Jean-Monestier.
Tel. 04 66 45 03 05. Fax 04 66 45 11 81.
grand-hotel-du-parc@wanadoo.fr
www.grandhotelduparc.fr
Closed mid-Nov.–mid-Mar.
Rest. closed Sun. dinner (off season),
Mon. lunch, Tue. lunch (off season).
60 rooms: 47–68€.
Prix fixe: 21€, 28€, 38€, 8,50€ (child).
A la carte: 35–40€.

This hotel is a very pleasant place, surrounded by wooded grounds with swimming pool. The old-style rooms are comfortable and the hotel cuisine quite well made: the foie gras terrine with figs, crayfish sautéed in olive oil with white wine, garlic and tomato, the lamb prepared with the flavors of the Cévennes mountains and the wild blueberry tart make it a flawless stopover.

● Adonis & Gorges du Tarn

48, rue du Pêcher.
Tel. 04 66 45 00 63. Fax 04 66 45 10 56.
gorges-du-tarn.adonis@wanadoo.fr
www.hotel-gorgesdutarn.com
Closed beg. Nov.–Easter.

Rest. closed Wed. (exc. July–Aug.).
27 rooms: 45–60€.
Prix fixe: 17€, 22€, 25€, 28€,
15€ (child).

The Tarn gorges begin here, in this family house with comfortable rooms and serious cooking. Mireille Paulet wears a big smile, while in the kitchen her husband Martial applies himself to Cévennes produce that changes with the seasons. On the plate, this transforms into Pélardon goat cheese-stuffed ravioli with mushroom cream, served in a hen bouillon, trout and Swiss chard served as a sandwich between two layers of polenta, roasted lamb flanked by pan-simmered summer vegetables and the crunchy frozen pistachio nougat served with roasted apricots.

● **La Source du Pêcher**   SIM
1, rue Remuret.
Tel. 04 66 45 03 01. Fax 04 66 45 28 82.
Closed Wed., Nov. 1–Easter.
Prix fixe: 24€, 16€, 32€.
A la carte: 55–65€.

Pascal Paulet runs this old, carefully-equipped establishment with great professionalism. Chef Didier Commandre reworks tradition, preparing a foie gras terrine with Aubrac tea aspic, monkfish with saffron-seasoned sauce, quick-seared salmon trout with vineyard-keeper's sauce, minced duck breast with Mont Lozère wild blueberries and a hot oven-browned Pélardon goat cheese with Cévennes honey. Rooms were opened in late 2007.

In Cocurès (48400). 5,5 km ne via N106 and D998.

■ **La Lozerette**   ●□
Tel. 04 66 45 06 04. Fax 04 66 45 12 93.
lalozerette@wanadoo.fr
www.lalozerette.com
Closed Nov. 1–1 Apr.
21 rooms: 52–78€.
Prix fixe: 17€ (weekday lunch), 22€, 35€,
46€, 11€ (child). A la carte: 45€.

Overlooking the Cévennes national park, Pierrette Agulhon's sweet establishment

offers luminous, neat rooms, a meeting room and floral, aromatic gardens. In the fuchsia dining room with exposed beams, a Pélardon and sundried tomato samosa, a thyme-seasoned lamb saddle and a seasonal fish with a lemon thyme sauce are very pretty things cooked by Jorges Borges.

LA FLOTTE see **ILE DE RE**

FOIX

09000 Ariège. Paris 780 – Carcassonne 89 – Saint-Girons 44.
Ariège is both rough and soft country at the same time, to which this welcoming town with its old houses, its pretty location and site and its count's château makes a pleasant showcase.

 HOTELS-RESTAURANTS

■ **Hôtel Lons**
6, pl G.-Duthil.
Tel. 05 61 65 52 44 / 05 34 09 28 00.
Fax 05 61 02 68 18.
www.hotel-lons-foix.com
Hotel closed Christmas–New Year's vac.
Rest. closed Sat. lunch,
Christmas–New Year's vac.–end Jan.
37 rooms: 52–65€. 1 suite: 73€.
Prix fixe: 11,30€ (weekday lunch), 13,50€,
24€, 7,60€ (child). A la carte: 30€.

This hotel in the heart of the old town only gets better over the years: neat, comfortable rooms and well-prepared cuisine from Charles Lons. Slow-roasted duck gizzards in salad, traditional cassoulet with duck confit and a trout meunière leave room for equally well-made sweets such as a Musketeer-themed dessert or the frozen meringue.

● **Le Médiéval**
42, rue des Chapeliers.
Tel. 05 34 09 01 72. Fax 05 34 09 01 73.
Closed Sun., Mon. (exc. dinner by reserv.).
Prix fixe: 22€, 30€, 40€. A la carte: 60€.

This restaurant on two floors attracts the cream of Foix society. Chef-owner Eric

Lemoine skillfully re-enacts tradition and his guests appreciate onion Tatin with pan-seared foie gras and fig sorbet, cod filet with rhubarb compote, veal sweetbread with ceps and the all-chocolate dessert plate (mousse, soft-centered cake and sorbet).

● Phoebus

3, cours Irénée-Cros.
Tel.-Fax 05 61 65 10 42.
www.arriege.com/le-phoebus
Closed Sat. lunch, Mon., 1 week Feb.,
mid-July–mid-Aug.
Prix fixe: 18€ (weekday lunch), 27€, 35€, 49€.

An idyllic location above the Ariège for this establishment that is both modern and classic with décor in the heraldic style of ancestral flags and coats of arms, shades of yellow and above all lots of glass with fantastic views of the château of Gaston Phoebus. In the kitchen, Didier Lamotte serves up well-handled traditional dishes: foie gras in terrine as an appetizer, scallops on melted mozzarella and the pigeon served on a caul lace–wrapped oxtail bundle. You should try the amusing "Cuban ashtray".

● Le Sainte-Marthe COM

Pl Lazema / 21, rue N.-Peyrévidal.
Tel. 05 61 02 87 87. Fax 05 61 05 19 00.
restaurant@le-saintemarthe.fr
www.le-saintemarthe.fr
Closed Tue. dinner, Wed., 2 weeks Jan.
Prix fixe: 22€, 27€, 34€, 38€,
10€ (child). A la carte: 40–45€.

Florence and Geneviève Chabot are the fairy godmothers of this welcoming establishment. Geneviève, in the kitchen, creates foie gras served two ways with figs, foie gras profiteroles, Provençal-style tuna steak, stuffed duck breast with truffle jus, house cassoulet, not to mention the meringue tower and an orange-flavored chocolate ganache truffle. These dishes can be eaten in the restaurant or taken away.

FONDETTES see TOURS

FONTAINEBLEAU

77300 Seine-et-Marne. Paris 65 – Melun 18 – Montargis 52 – Barbizon 11 – Orléans 89. The royal château with its great staircase and grounds attract huge crowds. Don't forget the Napoleonic museum and the large forest nearby.

■ / ● HOTELS-RESTAURANTS

■ L'Aigle Noir

27, pl Napoléon-Bonaparte.
Tel. 01 60 74 60 00. Fax 01 60 74 60 01.
hotel.aigle.noir@wanadoo.fr
www.hotelaiglenoir.fr
Closed 22 Dec.–7 Jan., 3 weeks Aug.
18 rooms: 120–160€. 3 suites: 220–360€.

This large hotel sited in a 15th-century town house makes a good impression. A covered swimming pool, rooms in soft, muted colors with 17th-century furniture, meeting rooms, bar and fitness suite are on the agenda.

■ Hôtel Napoléon

9, rue Grande.
Tel. 01 60 39 50 50. Fax 01 64 22 20 87.
info@naposite.com / www.naposite.com
56 rooms: 120–155€. 1 suite: 210€.
Prix fixe: 32€ (lunch), 40, 55€,
15€ (child).

A hundred meters from the château where Napoleon said his farewell to the imperial guard in 1814, sits this coaching inn converted into a warm family house. André Zahar and his son Frédéric watch over the establishment with a protective eye. In La Table des Maréchaux, opposite the patio, a marbled foie gras terrine, saffron-seasoned risotto with langoustines, honey-seasoned duck breast and a crunchy puff pastry with lightened cream are finely executed by Antony Assis, sensibly priced and served with distinction in a discreet, muted dining room with yellow striped walls and red velvet armchairs.

■ Mercure Royal Fontainebleau 🏛

41, rue Royale.
Tel. 01 64 69 34 34. Fax 01 64 69 34 39.
h1627@accord.com / www.accord.com
Rest. closed 10 days Christmas–New Year's,
3 weeks Aug.
91 rooms: 120–135€. 6 suites: 165–200€.
A la carte: 35€.

This comfortable chain hotel in warm colors, with functional rooms and nestled in grounds, deserves a stopover. The affable Richard Duvauchelle welcomes you and puts the relaxation and health facilities at your disposal. In the equestrian-style restaurant with terrace, a Cognac-seasoned crayfish tulip, scallop brochettes with sesame, lamb curry seasoned with almonds and the "café-plaisir" signature dessert by Jean-Michel Guilloteau are very pleasant.

● Croquembouche   COM

43, rue de France.
Tel. 01 64 22 01 57. Fax 01 60 72 08 73.
info@restaurant-croquembouche.com
www.restaurant-croquembouche.com
Closed Sat., Sun., Christmas–New Year's,
2 weeks Aug.
Prix fixe: 27€ (weekdays), 35€.
A la carte: 55€.

In his intimate little restaurant in shades of gray, Claude Maison d'Arblay, who used to work in Paris at Beauvilliers and Le Toit de Passy before going to cook in Madrid, seduces with an inspirational cuisine prepared as closely as possible to the markets and the seasons. Scallop carpaccio, a guinea hen quenelle served with lentil cream, roasted cod with celery and bacon ravioli, lamb sweetbread fricassée with capers and the Gâtinais pain d'épice tiramisu make one want to become a regular.

● La Petite Alsace   N SIM

26, rue de Ferrare.
Tel. 01 64 23 45 45. Fax 01 64 22 68 86.
lapetitealsacefontainebleau@orange.fr
Prix fixe: 12,50€ (lunch), 15€.
A la carte: 28€.

Multiple versions of "tarte flambée" (a regional flat savory tart), onion tarts, traditionally prepared beef cheeks and the pork shank served over sauerkraut look good in this simple, friendly *winstub* which makes the center of Fontainebleau seem like the rue des Hallebardes in Strasbourg.

PASTRY CHEF OF THE YEAR

Frédéric Cassel

71/73, Rue Grande.
Tel. 01 64 22 29 59. Fax 01 64 22 84 17.

An unassuming champion of chocolate (ah, his "macarré", mixing pralined almonds and crushed macaron cookies or his ganache with finely crushed Tonka beans!), an expert in new takes on classic pastry making (his hazelnut mille-feuille will have you melting on the spot and his Saint-Honoré (puff pastry with chantilly and pastry cream) is to die for, this maestro of sweet (but never sickly) treats, a native of Abbeville who trained with Fauchon and Pierre Hermé, improvises according to the season. A Grand Marnier flavored macaronade, a lighter version of the macaron, chocolat cube—a fresh approach to Sacher cookies with chocolate raspberry chantilly, the Frisson with macaron cookies, lemon mousseline with fruit preserves, or as an encore the peanut and milky ganache Rigoletto with caramel chips are delicacies of the highest order. Yet this master of the genre (who chairs the prestige Relais Desserts association) has not let talent go to his head. In his magnificent, modern, recently enlarged store, we choose, examine and listen to the appropriate explanations. In short, we yield to temptation.

FONTENAY-SUR-LOING see MONTARGIS

FONTETTE see VEZELAY

FONTEVRAUD-L'ABBAYE

49590 Maine-et-Loire. Paris 308 –
Chinon 21 – Loudun 23 – Saumur 15 –
Angers 78.
The buildings of the monastery, which was
a famous prison, are well preserved. In the
Romanesque church the effigies of the Planta-
genets can be admired. The monumental kitchens
date from the second half of the 12th century.

 HOTELS-RESTAURANTS

■ **Prieuré Saint-Lazare**
In the royal abbey, rue Saint-Jean-de-l'Habit.
Tel. 02 41 51 73 16. Fax 02 41 51 75 50.
www.hotelfp-fontevraud.com
Closed Nov.–end Mar.
52 rooms: 60–112€.
Prix fixe: 18€ (weekday lunch),
22€ (weekday lunch), 38€, 49€.

A place unique for its history as well as for
the quality of its cuisine. In the gardens
of the largest royal abbey in Europe, dating from the 12th century, the ancient
priory where lepers were cared for now
houses comfortable rooms with, in the
little cloister, the restaurant in which Eric
Bichon serves a contemporary cuisine.
Duck foie gras marinated in Coteaux-du-
Layon, langoustine brochettes with Serrano ham, turbot filet in an herb crust, the
roasted lamb and its crispy slow-cooked
shoulder are extremely well conceived.
Carine Boucher's advice is very valuable
in choosing among the 400 listed wines,
principally featuring the Loire.

● **La Licorne**
Allée Sainte-Catherine.
Tel. 02 41 51 72 49. Fax 02 41 51 70 40.
www.la-licorne-restaurant.com
Prix fixe: 27€ (weekday lunch), 40€, 55€,
72€.

Fabrice Bretel has taken over this pretty
18th-century building edged with a small
walled garden but is continuing to give his
customers what they are used to. Jean-
Michel Bézille is still setting the trends
with his cuisine, served in the medieval-
style dining room, that offers sincere,
finely-crafted regional dishes. Escargots in
chilled absinthe-seasoned custard sauce,
cut in cubes and served over spinach, pike-
perch served in a saffron-seasoned mussel crust, olive-seasoned roasted duck and
a frozen nougat with slow-cooked fruits
and a Chinon wine coulis are accompanied by vintages selected by the estima-
ble Fabien Montier.

FONTJONCOUSE

11360 Aude. Paris 826 – Narbonne 32 –
Perpignan 66 – Carcassonne 56.
You get to the heart of Corbières country by a
narrow road that zigzags across the mountain.

 HOTELS-RESTAURANTS

● **Auberge du Vieux Puits**
5, rue Saint-Victor.
Tel. 04 68 44 07 37. Fax 04 68 44 08 31.
www.aubergeduvieuxpuits.fr
Closed Sun. dinner, Mon. and Tue. (mid-
Sept.–mid-June), beg. Jan.–beg. Mar.
13 rooms: 105–170€. 1 suite: 215–230€.
Prix fixe: 55€ (weekday lunch), 90€, 110€,
20€ (child). A la carte: 120€.

This inn with a swimming pool has the
charm of the past with its rustic rooms
that are bathed in light. On the cuisine
side, Gilles Goujon, Meilleur Ouvrier de
France, who has worked at Le Moulin in
Mougins and Le Petit Nice in Marseille,
reproduces Mediterranean dishes with
invention and skill. Sardines cooked Mor-
rocan style with garlic and spices in a thin
bread crust, oven-baked red mullet and
brandade, roasted black pig served with
slow-cooked ratte potatoes, mushrooms
and onions and the peaches in raspberry
syrup, served on a salted sugar cookie,
combine, to best effect, authenticity and
gastronomic indulgence.

FONTVIEILLE

13990 Bouches-du-Rhône. Paris 715 –
Avignon 30 – Marseille 90 – Saint-Rémy 18
– Arles 10.

ot.fontvieille@visitprovence.com.
This beautiful village in the Alpilles contains Daudet's mill, where he wrote his *Letters*.

HOTELS-RESTAURANTS

■ Auberge La Regalido
Rue Frédéric-Mistral.
Tel. 04 90 54 60 22. Fax 04 90 54 64 29.
la-regalido@wanadoo.fr
www.laregalido.com
Hotel closed mid-Oct.–beg. Mar.
Rest. closed Sat. lunch, Mon., Tue. lunch,
end Oct.–beg. Mar.
15 rooms: 125–260€. 2 suites: 260€.
Prix fixe: 20€ (lunch), 25€ (lunch).
A la carte: 82€.

This former olive oil mill inspired several beautiful letters from Alphonse Daudet. Today it is a cheerful inn run by the Michels. The rooms, in the colors of Provence, have each been christened with the name of a flower or spice. The vaulted dining room extending into the terrace is the place of gastronomy where one succumbs to a mussel and spinach gratin, roasted whole Mediterranean sea bass with soft-cooked Beaux olive oil–seasoned tomatoes, slow-roasted garlic and lamb and the signature desserts by Thomas, presented on a cart.

● La Table du Meunier
42, cours Hyacinthe-Bellon.
Tel. 04 90 54 61 05. Fax 04 90 54 77 24.
latabledumeunier@wanadoo.fr
Closed Tue., Wed., Nov. 1 vac.,
1 week Christmas–New Year's, Feb. vac.
Prix fixe: 23€, 30€. A la carte: 35€.

Former trainee of Lenôtre, Marie-France Fel composes a daily ode to Provence. The light-filled setting, the reception of her husband Thierry and the home-style cooking all enchant: marbled rabbit terrine with slow-cooked caramelized onions, Mediterranean sea bass with fresh tomatoes, delicious lamb in pesto and lavender-infused crème brûlée. Sunny wines are a marvelous accompaniment to a very fresh cuisine.

F FORBACH

FORBACH

57600 Moselle. Paris 385 – Metz 57 –
Sarreguemines 21 – Sarrebrück 14.
This used to be coal-mining country. Today it shares the green frontier with Sarre.

RESTAURANTS

● Le Schlossberg
13, rue du Parc.
Tel. 03 87 87 88 26. Fax 03 87 87 83 86.
Closed Sun. dinner, Tue. dinner, Wed., 10 days
beg. Jan., 1 week at end July, 10 days beg. Aug.
Prix fixe: 20€ (weekdays), 29€, 36€, 47€.
A la carte: 55€.

This old neo-Gothic manor house run by the Beckendorfs is a cheery stopover with a peaceful view of the Schlossberg park. On the cooking side, Pascal proposes pan-seared foie gras with quetche plums, escargot ravioli with Roquefort cream sauce, olive oil–seasoned grilled Atlantic sea bass, pigeon and veal sweetbreads with truffle-seasoned jus and the frozen bergamot-flavored nougat. In the restaurant, Laurence and Thierry ensure good advice for both food and wine.

In Rosbruck (57600). 6 km sw via N3.

● Auberge Albert-Marie
1, rue Nationale.
Tel. 03 87 04 70 76. Fax 03 87 90 52 55.
Closed Sat. lunch, Sun. dinner, Mon.,
2 weeks beg. Aug.
Prix fixe: 25€ (weekday lunch),
30€ (dinner), 36€ (weekday lunch), 40€
(Sat., Sun.), 10€ (child). A la carte: 65€.

This large Lorraine inn is the kingdom of the Sternjacobs. In the kitchen, Pierre serves up traditional dishes which he reproduces with taste and skill. Pressed lobster, smoked salmon, foie gras, Marseille-style fish soup, pan-seared scallops with ceps, John Dory with Paimpol white beans, venison filet with pepper sauce and pork trotter cakes are reinvigorating classics. His brother Patrick gives advice on wine and readily looks to Alsace to accompany pineapple carpaccio or roasted peaches with vanilla ice cream. Nicole and Dorothée give an attentive welcome and advice.

In Stiring-Wendel (57600). 3 km ne via N3.

● **La Bonne Auberge**

15, rue Nationale.
Tel. 03 87 87 52 78. Fax 03 87 87 18 19.
Closed Sat. lunch, Sun. dinner, Mon. (exc. Bank holidays), 1 week Christmas–New Year's, 2 weeks at Easter, 2 weeks Aug.
Prix fixe: 40€ (weekday lunch), 50€, 85€.
A la carte: 90€.

Isabelle and Lydia Egloff, the sommelier and the cook, form one of those female duos that are the most highly successful in contemporary cooking. In their modern house situated near the national route and a stone's throw from the border with Sarre, they set the pace for a cuisine that is inventive and constantly evolving. Lorraine is their region and the South their direction of preference. Wines and food therefore achieve a skillful balance between the traditions of the great East and the affection for other regions, with an inclination towards the Mediterranean. Truffled goose foie gras served with fresh figs (a house creation dating to 1983), eggplant ravioli with reduced jus and whipped goat cheese, sliced sole seasoned with bergamot, pan-tossed escargots with green coffee oil and quinoa tabouli with grapefruit jelly, a lavender honey-glazed rack of lamb with dried cep ravioli or the breadcrumb-coated and fried veal kidneys served with beer-braised endive are tempting dishes. The desserts, like the violet-flavored "brûlée glacé" with milk chocolate syrup and a chocolate sangria cigar or the formidable Irish coffee–flavored crème soufflé, are the forte of the house. A wonderful place.

04300 Alpes de Haute-Provence.
Paris 754 – Digne 54 – Aix-en-Provence 80 – Manosque 23 – Apt 42.
oti@forcalquier.com.
Here, the sky is lavender blue. This is the country of Giono and *Chant du monde*.

■	HOTELS-RESTAURANTS

■ **Auberge Charembeau**

4 km e via N100, rte de Niozelles.
Tel. 04 92 70 91 70. Fax 04 92 70 91 83.
contact@charembeau.com
www.charembeau.com
Closed mid-Nov.–1 Mar.
22 rooms: 55–89€. 2 suites: 90–125€.

Set in the middle of undulating grounds dotted with sheep, this 18th-century farm with heated swimming pool and tennis court has the advantages of neat rooms, peace and quiet and delicious breakfasts.

● **La Table & Co** SIM

3, rue des Cordeliers.
Tel. 04 92 75 00 75. Fax 04 92 75 01 00.
Closed Mon. dinner (exc. July–Oct.),
Tue. (exc. July–Oct.), Feb., Mar.
A la carte: 33€.

As he did in his Parisian Chavignol—our Parisian Bistro of the Year 2002—Régis Lebars attracts lovers of good food and "natural" wines. Produce is at the height of quality and gastronomic ideas are in full flow. In rhythm with the markets, a saffron-seasoned gazpacho served with arugula sorbet, skate cheeks with mild garlic cream sauce, slow-cooked lamb shank served cold with vegetables in curry vinaigrette or an apricot Tatin with rosemary sorbet delight the customer.

29940 Finistère. Paris 553 – Quimper 16 – Concarneau 8 – Pont-L'Abbé 22.
accueil@foret-fouesnant.tourisme.com.
This pretty town of south Finistère is known for its sweetness. Pierre-Jakez Hélias made it his last home in the countryside.

■	HOTELS-RESTAURANTS

■ **Hôtel du Port**
  & Petit Comptoir

4, corniche de la Cale.
Tel. 02 98 56 97 33. Fax 02 98 56 93 95.

hotelduport29@wanadoo.fr
www.hotelduport.fr
Closed Sun. dinner, Mon. dinner, beg. Dec.–
beg. Mar. Rest. closed Sun. dinner, Mon.,
Tue. lunch (off season).
6 rooms: 40–62€. 3 suites: 62€.
Prix fixe: 13,50€, 18€, 32€.
A la carte: 35€.

The Paugams give a kind welcome to both their bistro and their hotel with its sweet rooms in shades of yellow. Stéphane serves up artichoke and goat cheese in salad, soft-cooked potatoes with cod, a tourte of veal sweetbread and mushrooms and pears in puff pastry with salted-butter caramel sauce, which are in very good taste.

● Auberge Saint-Laurent   `COM`

Rte côtière de Concarneau.
Rte de Beg-Menez.
Tel.-Fax 02 98 56 98 07.
Closed Mon. dinner (off season), Tue. dinner
(off season), Wed., Nov. 1 vac., Feb. vac.
Prix fixe: 20€, 35€, 15€ (weekday lunch)
10€ (child).

In the lively dining room of this rustic establishment, Philippe and Véronique Le Gac offer a seasonal cuisine that goes down very well. Sundried tomatoes in a lobster shell with citrus sushi, pan-tossed langoustines seasoned with truffles, coriander-seasoned yellow pollock with shallots, sage-seasoned Atlantic sea bass filet, glazed duck breast and pecan brownies for dessert are effortlessly enjoyable.

79380 Deux-Sèvres. Paris 400 –
Bressuire 15 – Niort 60 – Nantes 60.
In the middle of Bressuire countryside, bordering the Vendée, this is an historical town that bore witness to the Royalist insurgencies during the French Revolution and which has a château.

 HOTELS-RESTAURANTS

● Auberge du Cheval Blanc   `N` `SIM`

36, rue de Lattre-de-Tassigny.
Tel. 05 49 80 86 35. Fax 05 49 80 66 75.

auberge.du.cheval.blanc@wanadoo.fr
Closed Mon. dinner (exc. hotel season),
end Jan.–mid-Feb.
4 rooms: 33,50–42,50€.
Prix fixe: 12,50€ (weekdays), 18,50€,
22,50€, 33,50€.

This former coaching inn has kept the charm of the past. Joël Barbion offers authenticity, as much in the simple, rustic rooms as in the old-style restaurant with its beautiful Henri IV fireplace. One can choose the second, modern, dining room to enjoy the cuisine of Marie-France Meynard. Jumbo shrimp brochettes flambéed in Cognac, a rouget and scallop duo napped with a saffron sauce, a sliced beef filet with slow-cooked caramelized shallots and a frozen Cognac soufflé are good standard dishes, reworked and altered according to the markets.

76440 Seine-Maritime. Paris 117 –
Amiens 72 – Rouen 45 – Beauvais 52.
officeforegesleseaux@wanadoo.fr.
The forges have been replaced by the casino and the greenery of Bray country is all around.

 HOTELS-RESTAURANTS

■ La Paix   🏠

15, rue de Neufchâtel.
Tel. 02 35 90 51 22. Fax 02 35 09 83 62.
contact@hotellapaix.fr / www.hotellapaix.fr
Closed 10 days at end Dec., 2 weeks beg. Jan.
Rest. closed Sun. dinner (off season),
Mon. lunch.
18 rooms: 56–75€.
Prix fixe: 19,80€, 26€, 35,40€,
10,50€ (child).

Nicolas Brynsteel and Michel Rémy offer a smiling welcome, simple, neat rooms and friendly guesthouse cuisine. Rouen-style duck terrine, veal sweetbread cassolette, poached eel with sorrel sauce, catfish in cider, duck breast canapés and the Benedictine-flavored frozen nougat cannot be criticized.

In Le Fossé (76440). Rte de Gournay, 2 km
via D915.

● **Auberge du Beau Lieu** ◎COM

2, rue du Montadet.
Tel. 02 35 90 50 36. Fax 02 35 90 35 98.
aubeaulieu@aol.com
www.auberge-du-beau-lieu.com
Closed 8 Jan.–8 Feb.
Rest. closed Tue., Wed. lunch (exc. July–
Aug.), Fri. lunch (exc. July–Aug.).
3 rooms: 49–57€.
Prix fixe: 19€ (weekday dinner), 37€, 47€,
57€, 13€ (child).

The Ramelets' inn deserves its name of
"Beautiful Place". Three sweet little rooms,
the chiné furniture and carefully chosen
colors all blend harmoniously. Here, good
food is served. Marie-France in the restaurant and Patrick in the kitchen work hard
to serve regional dishes of rare quality, as
demonstrated by the pan-seared foie gras
with slow-simmered apples in cider, lobster tail with Vin Jaune and aged Comté
cheese risotto, wild duck with red wine,
duck liver with shallot sauce and a soft-
centered chocolate cake that accompanies
a green Chartreuse-flavored ice cream.

FOSSETTE-PLAGE see LE LAVANDOU

FOUDAY

67130 Bas-Rhin. Paris 408 – Strasbourg 62
– Saint-Dié 34 – Saverne 56 – Sélestat 37.
The Bruche valley road leads to Upper Vosges and
meanders through bucolic Ban de la Roche.

 HOTELS-RESTAURANTS

■ **Julien**

12, rue Nationale.
Tel. 03 88 97 30 09. Fax 03 88 97 36 73.
hoteljulien@wanadoo.fr / www.hoteljulien.com
Closed 2 weeks Jan. Rest. closed Tue.
36 rooms: 77–121€. 10 suites: 121€.
Prix fixe: 12€ (lunch), 15€, 18€, 22€,
9€ (child), 28€ (Sun.), 36€ (Sun.).
A la carte: 43–50€.

Modern and charming, with its wooded
surroundings and flowers, this large

building is situated in the middle of a
park in the heart of the Bruche valley. The
comfort of the rooms, the quality of the
facilities (swimming pool, sauna, hammam and fitness center) and the sensible
prices are golden assets. Gérard Goetz's
menus draw on local sources. The pan-
seared foie gras with apples as well as
his variation on theme of the presskopf
(with foie gras, a marvel!), the roasted
scallops with lemon butter, the veal kidney and sweetbread fricassée with morels
and the soft-centered Guanaja chocolate
cake with vanilla ice cream make the hotel
guests very happy. The large wine list is the
domain of Bernard Heng, while reception
and restaurant services are delivered with
the warm personality of Hélène Goetz.

FOUESNANT see LA FORET-FOUESNANT

FOUGERES

35300 Ille-et-Vilaine. Paris 322 – Avranches
45 – Laval 55 – Le Mans 130 – Rennes 50.
The 12th- to 15th-century château, the flamboyant Gothic St.-Sulpice church, the wood-
paneled houses in the Marchix quarter and the
upper town with its belfry are some of the treasures of this pearl of Upper Brittany, which
overlooks the Lançon valley.

● RESTAURANTS

● **Le Haute-Sève** №■COM

37, bd Jean-Jaurès.
Tel. 02 99 94 23 39. Fax 02 99 94 99 75.
Closed Sun. dinner, Mon., 2 weeks beg. Jan.,
Feb. vac., mid-July–mid-Aug.
Prix fixe: 19,50€ (weekday lunch), 22€,
28,50€, 39,70€.

Thierry Robert's timbered house has kept
the character of the past while opening
itself to today's tastes. The good-natured
reception, the dining room decorated
with paintings by local artists and the
cuisine blending tradition and modernity easily find takers. The cod tartlette
with sundried tomatoes and langoustine
caramel, the pollock in papillote with
slow-simmered shallots and the andou-

ille chitterling sausage with new pota- toes, the lamb filet with rosemary honey, like the olive oil–roasted mango and date Tatin allow one to predict a wonderful future for this establishment with heart.

In Landéan (35133). 8 km ne via D177, rte de Caen.

● **Au Cellier**

29, rue Victor-Hugo.
Tel.-Fax 02 99 97 20 50.
Closed Sun. dinner, Mon., Wed. dinner,
2 weeks Jan., 2 weeks July Aug.
Prix fixe: 11,50€ (weekday lunch), 16,30€,
22,30€, 41€, 7,80€ (child).
A la carte: 45€.

Philippe Ripoche has taken over this pretty little house covered in Virginia creeper. Its country-style dining room decorated with a 19th-century painting witnesses a procession of high-quality traditional dishes served by Philippe's wife Maryannick. Salmon tartare, pike-perch with vinegar, shallot and pickle butter, the duck breast with blueberries and the frozen nougatine with a berry coulis all make a good impression.

FOUGEROLLES

70220 Haute-Saône. Paris 376 –
Epinal 49 – Luxeuil 10 – Remiremont 26.
accueil@otsifougerolles.net.
Franche-Comté on the Vosges side, in the mid-dle of Griotte cherry country (visit the ecomu-seum!) and bordering the little-known "thousand ponds" area.

● RESTAURANTS

● **Au Père Rota**

8, Grande-Rue.
Tel. 03 84 49 12 11. Fax 03 84 49 14 51.
Closed Sun. dinner, Mon., Tue. dinner, Jan.
Prix fixe: 24€, 32€, 54€, 13,50€ (child).

Jean-Paul Kuentz, Vosgien through and through and trained at Baumanière and La Mère Poulard, has been handling the Griotte cherry in all its forms for thirty years. Other things too. In a modern set-

ting of pastel tones, he offers a superb duck terrine with local sour cherries served with slow-cooked caramelized onions, a pretty rabbit mosaic terrine with Morteau sausage and Arbois wine aspic, guinea hen breast with morels and Vin Jaune and finally, the signature oven-baked crêpes with sour cherries. A wonderful establish-ment with attentive service and a cellar rich in 250 French wines.

FOURCES

32250 Gers. Paris 725 – Agen 53 –
Auch 59 – Condom 13.
In the heart of Gers, a charming walled town, famous for its old houses, its château and... Michel Cardoze's moustache!

 HOTELS-RESTAURANTS

■ **Château de Fourcès**

Tel. 05 62 29 49 53. Fax 05 62 29 50 59.
contact@chateau-fouces.com
www.chateau-fources.com
Closed beg. Dec.–beg. Mar.
Rest. closed Wed., Thu., beg. Nov.–1 Apr.
12 rooms: 100–155€. 6 suites: 214–230€.
Prix fixe: 29€, 35€, 47€. A la carte: 50€.

This medieval château, surrounded by grounds with a river running through, has pretty rooms in the towers that have recently been redecorated. In the dining room with its exposed stonework, marbled foie gras terrine in fig jelly, duck confit with almonds and pistachios, veal kidneys pan tossed with Armagnac and the apple croustade, a local tart made with many layers of thin pastry, hold their attrac-tive own.

FOURGES

27630 Eure. Paris 74 – Rouen 63 –
Les Andelys 26 – Evreux 47 – Mantes 23 –
Vernon 14.
A wonderful site with the bubbling Epte flow-ing through, the nearby château of Villarceaux and its golf course and the neighboring ruins of La Roche-Guyon.

●	RESTAURANTS

● Moulin de Fourges

38, rue du Moulin.
Tel. 02 32 52 12 12. Fax 02 32 52 92 56.
www.moulin-de-fourges.com
Closed Sun. lunch, Mon., weekdays Nov.–Mar.
Prix fixe: 21€, 31€, 38€, 15€ (child).
A la carte: 48€.

This former mill beside the Epte, covered in Virginia creeper, has bucolic charm. Anthony Dalençon's Normandy cuisine is rich in know-how and finesse. A vegetable terrine and lobster medallion, the Atlantic sea bass, seared skin-side down and finished under the broiler, beef filet medallions with a foie gras sauce and a mille-feuille for dessert seduce effortlessly.

LE FOUSSERET

31430 Haute-Garonne. Paris 730 –
Tarbes 105 – Toulouse 56 – Muret 34.
Between Volvestre and Comminges, a gateway in the heart of nature to the lower Pyrénées.

●	RESTAURANTS

● Les Voyageurs   N COM

1, Grand-Rue.
Tel.-Fax 05 61 98 53 06.
Closed dinner, Sat., beg. Aug.–beg. Sept.,
1 week at end Dec.
Prix fixe: 11€ (weekday lunch), 23€,
29€, 37€.

René Molinard's inn welcomes gourmet travelers to timeless classic dishes, thoroughly accomplished. The foie gras terrine, scallops in puff pastry with slivered endive, green peppercorn-seasoned duck breast and a berry gratin seasoned with fleur d'oranger give, very simply, pleasure. Nice reception from Maryse.

FREHEL

22240 Côtes-d'Armor. Paris 438 –
Saint-Malo 44 – Dinan 43 – Saint-Brieuc 48
– Lamballe 48.

Fréhel, with its wild coastline, headland, two lighthouses, beach and town is like a potted version of Brittany. Don't miss the Latte fort.

●	RESTAURANTS

● Le Victorine   COM

Pl de la Mairie.
Tel. 02 96 41 55 55. Fax 02 87 41 55 55.
Closed Sun. dinner, Mon., Nov. 1 vac.,
Easter vac.
Prix fixe: 20€, 28€.
A la carte: 40€.

Thierry Teffaine works skillfully with the seasons and the market. His loyal customers enjoy his generous special menus of fish soup, house foie gras, scallops in puff pastry with juniper berry cream sauce, rabbit saddle with thyme-infused jus and the kouign-amann ice cream with caramel sauce. A rich wine list acts as counterpoint.

● La Fauconnière   SIM

At cap Fréhel.
Tel. 02 96 41 54 20.
Closed dinner, Wed. (off season),
Oct.–end Mar.
Prix fixe: 13,50€ (weekday lunch), 19€,
25€, 30€. A la carte: 35–40€.

Pascal Havy, in this thirties concrete building with a full view of the sea, has the sole aim of making his customers happy. The gently priced special menus remain boons. Oysters, surf and turf salad, John Dory or pollock, a pork and chitterling sausage duo, the butcher's choice cut and the "rum route" dessert bring nothing but happiness.

FREJUS

83600 Var. Paris 875 – Cannes 39 –
Hyères 90 – Nice 65.
frejus.tourisme@wanadoo.fr.
The cathedral with its cloister and font make this old Roman town, also a huge seaside resort, a place of architectural treasures to be discovered.

HOTELS-RESTAURANTS

■ L'Aréna

145, rue du Général-de-Gaulle.
Tel. 04 94 17 09 40. Fax 04 94 52 01 52.
info@arena-hotel.com / www.arena-hotel.com
Closed 10 days at end Dec., 1 week beg. Jan.
39 rooms: 70–160€. 1 suite: 170–220€.
Prix fixe: 25€ (lunch), 40€, 55€,
15€ (child). A la carte: 60–65€.

Smiling welcome, smart rooms overlooking a pleasant patio and a lively cuisine are the reasons why people want to stay in this charming Provençal resort which lodged Napoleon on his return from the campaign in Egypt. Dominique L'Honoré serves up precisely executed and sunny dishes. Lobster ravioli with shellfish sauce, Mediterranean sea bass with fennel aïoli, lamb in an herb crust served with a vegetable tart and the blanc-manger with peach coulis rework local traditions to today's tastes.

● Port-Royal   V.COM

Pl du Tambourinaire, in Port-Fréjus.
Tel. 04 94 53 09 11. Fax 04 94 53 75 24.
Closed Sun. dinner (exc. summer),
Mon. lunch (summer),
Tue. dinner (off season), Nov. 1–beg. Mar.
Prix fixe: 29€, 35€, 49€. A la carte: 60€.

The exterior is boring but the interior warm, in shades of salmon and claret with neo-Louis XVI furniture. Marcel Chavanon offers delicious, reliable and well-made dishes: truffles, turbot cooked according to season, beef filet Rossini, chocolate fondant served hot and the thin apple tart are serious dishes.

● Les Potiers   ■ SIM

135, rue des Potiers.
Tel. 04 94 51 33 74.
Closed Tue., Wed. lunch, lunch exc. Sun.
(July–Aug.), 1 Dec.–21 Dec.
Prix fixe: 23€, 34€. A la carte: 45–56€.

The Potiers' very small inn has a lot of charm. In old Fréjus, the atmosphere and the cuisine here have a wonderful air of Provence. Richard François and his colleague in the restaurant, Maria Fortunato, offer exquisite fare. Lobster ravioli with tarragon-seasoned tête de veau, wild oven-roasted sea bream, crisp slow-cooked lamb with basil-seasoned seafood carpaccio and a painter's palette of crème brûlée (vanilla, orange, chickory, pistachio and pralined nut) are very well made.

● Au Mérou Ardent   SIM

157, bd de la Libération.
Tel. 04 94 17 30 58. Fax 04 94 17 33 79.
patrickdelpierre@wanadoo.fr
Closed Wed. (exc. July–Aug.), Thu. (exc.
July–Aug.).
Prix fixe: 14,50€, 24€, 36€,
6,50€ (child). A la carte: 40–45€.

Patrick Delpierre puts the sea in everything, from the décor to the food. Smoked salmon tartare with notes of Asian flavors, the seafood macaronade (a Provençal pasta dish), scallop risotto with basil and cream sauce. Or, for meat-lovers, a duck and two-purée parmentier or a sirloin steak with morel sauce. The lemon charlotte with crunchy bits of nougatine is well conceived.

44580 Loire-Atlantique. Paris 423 –
Nantes 42 – La Roche-sur-Yon 65 –
Saint-Nazaire 50.
A rural village betweene Nantes, the Vendéen Breton marshes and the Pornic peninsula.

 RESTAURANTS

● Le Colvert   N COM

14, rte de Pornic.
Tel. 02 40 21 46 79. Fax 02 40 21 95 99.
Closed Sun. dinner, Mon., Wed. dinner,
1 week Jan., mid-Aug.–beg. Sept.
Prix fixe: 16€ (weekday lunch), 25€, 32€,
46€, 11,50€ (child).

After having toured the kitchens of France, Fabrice Praud and his saucepans have landed in this traditional bistro with well-set tables. In tempting special menus, his guests enjoy sautéed escargots and duck gizzards in a thin tart, Atlantic sea bass with shellfish, a wild boar medallion with nuts and dried fruit and rice pudding in puff pastry with caramelized apples, served with crème brûlée–flavored ice cream.

FREUDENECK see WANGENBOURG
FROENINGEN see MULHOUSE
FROHMUHL see LA PETITE-PIERRE
FURDENHEIM see MARLENHEIM
LA FUSTE see MANOSQUE
FUTEAU see SAINTE-MENEHOULD

81600 Tarn. Paris 671 – Toulouse 58 –
Albi 26 – Montauban 50.
A little wine capital with a good-natured feel.

 HOTELS-RESTAURANTS

■ La Verrerie

1, rue de l'Egalité.
Tel. 05 63 57 32 77. Fax 05 63 57 32 27.
contact@la-verrerie.com
www.la-verrerie.com
Rest. closed Sat. lunch (off season),
Sun. dinner (off season).
14 rooms: 53–68€.
Prix fixe: 23€, 30€, 13€ (weekday lunch),
60€, 10€ (child).

This former glassworks converted into a tranquil hotel has an energetic décor, pleasant rooms and modern dining room with colors of the South and a terrace. Gilles Segur's cuisine is also not bad. Basil-seasoned tomato tartare with iced tomato and pan-tossed butterflied shrimp with garlic, cod filet in a fennel shell served with a light coco bean bouillon and the lamb served two ways, roasted with Lautrec garlic, preceed the simmered strawberry crème brûlée and deliver the goods attractively in light, creative style.

● Les Sarments

27, rue Cabrol.
Tel.-Fax 05 63 57 62 61.
www.restaurantlessarments.com
Closed Sun. dinner, Mon., Wed. dinner,
1 week at end Dec., 10 days beg. Jan.,
end Feb.–mid-Mar.
Prix fixe: 28€, 33€, 46€. A la carte: 45€.

Next to the wine house, this medieval wine store converted into a refined restaurant with arches and pretty paintings by Bernard Bisson, is nearly always full. Its fifteen covers are quickly taken by guests delighted to taste crispy sardines and duck confit, a red onion pastilla anchoïade, the caramel-deglazed scallops and prunes in papillote, around a large choice of local wines.

● **La Table du Sommelier** `SIM`
34, pl du Grifoul.
Tel.-Fax 05 63 81 20 10.
Closed Sun. (exc. July–Aug.), Mon.
(exc. July–Aug.).
Prix fixe: 13€ (lunch, wine inc.), 16€, 26€,
7,50€ (child).

In Daniel Pestre's bistro, the menu is king and the wines run the gamut of Chile, Argentina, Australia and Bulgaria. The dishes are what might be called "tradition revisited": the escargot and parsley roll, minced sardines with squid ink risotto, the wild boar simmered in Gaillac and the sour cherry and cream sabayon hit the target. It is good to eat on the teak terrace in summer.

GAILLON-EN-MEDOC see LESPARRE-MEDOC

GAILLON-EN-MEDOC see LESPARRE-MEDOC

GAP

05000 Hautes-Alpes. Paris 687 –
Avignon 169 – Sisteron 53 – Grenoble 108.
office.tourismegap@wanadoo.fr.
The principal town of the Upper Alps is worth a visit for its maze-like old town, its museum and the clean area of Champsaur, the country of Chant du monde.

▓ HOTELS-RESTAURANTS

■ **La Porte Colombe** ⌂
4, pl Euzières.
Tel. 04 92 51 04 13. Fax 04 92 52 42 50.
hotel.portecolombe@wanadoo.fr
Rest. closed weekdays lunch, Sun.
27 rooms: 45–70€. 1 suite: 70€.
Prix fixe: 22€, 28€, 11€ (child).
A la carte: 35€.

In an old gateway of the town, this recent hotel is worth staying in for its comfortable, clean rooms as well as its terrace-solarium with a splendid view of the valley.

● **Le Patalain** `V.COM`
2, pl Ladoucette.
Tel.-Fax 04 92 52 30 83.

sarl-le-patalain@wanadoo.fr
Closed Sun., Mon., 1 week at end Oct.–beg.
Nov., Christmas–mid-Jan., 1 week beg. May.
Prix fixe: 17,50€ (lunch), 34€ (dinner), 38€
(dinner).

Gérard Périnet is the good-natured overseer of this smart establishment. Seated outside on fine days, shaded by trees, or in the neat restaurant with well-spaced tables one can enjoy the warm asparagus, foie gras in terrine, creamy risotto, the fish of the day or the rabbit saddle bathed in mustard, honey and rosemary. In the bistro, the special menu of the day (at 17.50) offers soft ewe's cheese and Coppa ham in terrine, a Provençal-style sea bream and a roasted duckling with spicy jus, just right.

● **Les Olivades** `N` `COM`
Rte de la Garde.
Tel. 04 92 52 66 80. Fax 04 92 52 67 20.
www.restaurant-les-olivades.com
Closed Sun. dinner, Mon.,
Christmas–mid-Jan.
Prix fixe: 18€, 22€, 26€, 30€.

Cédric Manzoni, a native of Gap and mad about Corsica (you will find a Corsican menu with cold meats and cheeses) has worked at Baumanière, Le Bacon in Cap-d'Antibes, La Voile d'Or in St. Jean-Cap-Ferrat and at Levernois in Beaune. Returning home, he has set up on the green heights of the town in this charming house. Special menus in the garden, meals under roughcast stone arches and lively service make one want to become a regular. The Olivades platter of local specialties (stuffed vegetables, pissaladière and mushroom- and ham-stuffed artichokes simmered in wine), the Mediterranean sea bass baked in filo with soft local ewe's cheese and served with seaweed-seasoned basmati rice plus the strawberry tiramisu are well turned-out.

● **Le Pasturier** `COM`
18, rue Pérolière.
Tel. 04 92 53 69 29. Fax 04 92 53 30 91.
pasturier.rest@wanadoo.fr
Closed Sun. dinner (exc. Bank holidays),

Mon. (exc. Bank holidays), Tue. lunch (exc. Bank holidays), 2 weeks beg. Jan., 10 days at end June, 10 days beg. July.
Prix fixe: 25€, 39€, 41€, 11€ (child).
A la carte: 60–65€.

New yellow decoration for the Dorches in the center of town. Djema is all smiles, while her husband Pascal skillfully handles the menus. We love his sun-filled dishes such as the goat cheese mille-feuille with slow-cooked artichokes, peppers and onions, the bouquet of asparagus served with a truffle mousseline and the leg of lamb roasted with herbs, with its cooking juices infused with lavender. The vanilla and Tagada strawberry candy vacherin with fresh and dried fruit makes an attractive end to the meal and wines from the Rhône valley and Provence are sensibly priced.

● **Le Bouchon**   N SIM
4, La Placette.
Tel. 04 92 46 02 43.
Closed Sun.
Prix fixe: 26,90€.

Next to the Bertrand cellars, this bistro offers lively, unpretentious fare as accompaniment to the best bottles at the lowest price. Beef cheeks in terrine, anchoïade, salmon tartare and rack of lamb are eaten with pleasure.

LA GARDE see CASTELLANE

26700 Drôme. Paris 626 – Montélimar 21 – Nyons 40 – Pierrelatte 6.
The Tricastin of wonders is to be found in the south of Drôme. Here there is already a feeling of majestic Provence.

 HOTELS-RESTAURANTS

■ **Logis de l'Escalin**   ✿ ⌂
1 km via D572, quartier Les Marteaux.
Tel. 04 75 04 41 32. Fax 04 75 04 40 05.
info@lescalin.com / www.lescalin.com

Rest. closed Sun. dinner, Mon.
14 rooms: 68–80€. 1 suite: 90–135€.
Prix fixe: 25€, 30€, 35€, 42€.
A la carte: 70€.

Overlooking the Rhône valley, the local house of Serge Fricaud expresses all the character of the region with bright, cheery rooms and a lively southern cuisine. Summer truffles floating on cold lobster soup, spicy tuna medallions, oven-roasted rabbit haunch seasoned with lemongrass and a poached peach served on a thin almond tart are precise and to the point.

48800 Lozère. Paris 615 – Alès 60 – Florac 71 – Mende 58.
A medieval village with its panoramic keep, on the ancient Regordane road that linked the Auvergne to Languedoc, lost in the middle of Lozère and full of rural charm.

 HOTELS-RESTAURANTS

■ **Auberge Regordane**   ⌂
In Prévenchères.
Tel. 04 66 46 82 88. Fax 04 66 46 90 29.
pierre.nogier@free.fr / www.regordane.com
Closed mid-Oct.–mid-Apr.
15 rooms: 54–65€.
Prix fixe: 18€, 26€, 35€, 10€ (child).
A la carte: 45€.

Above the Chassezac gorges, the Nogiers' 16th-century inn remains a dependable institution. We love Pierre's reception, the old-style rooms with lime-washed walls and polished parquet and the vaulted dining room. Philippe's regional cuisine reproduces the region's dishes with finesse. Pike-perch rillettes with roasted hazelnuts, beef filet with a potato and cep gratin or the mixed citrus fruits with a fruit jelly are well conceived.

79270 Deux-Sèvres. Paris 420 – Fontenay-le-Comte 30 – Niort 12 – La Rochelle 62 – Saint-Jean-d'Angély 60.

A peaceful stop in the heart of Niortaise Sèvre and Poitou marshes.

● | RESTAURANTS

● Les Mangeux de Lumas

78, rue des Gravées.
Tel. 05 49 35 93 42. Fax 05 49 35 82 89.
Closed Mon. dinner, Tue., Wed. dinner (exc. summer), 2 weeks end Jan.
Prix fixe: 19€, 48€, 11 .

This large inn right beside the marsh has doubtless lost a little of its personality by increasing in size. It offers, of course, the escargots (lumas) in red wine sauce, the parsley-seasoned eel and white mojette beans with Vendée ham. Beware of the droves of tourists in summer!

GARONS see NIMES
GASSIN see SAINT-TROPEZ
GEISPOLSHEIM see STRASBOURG

GEMENOS

13420 Bouches-du-Rhône. Paris 783 –
Marseille 25 – Toulon 51 –
Aix-en-Provence 39.
contact@gemenos.com.
The pretty park of St. Pons makes an idyllic romantic walk near this lively town on the outskirts of Marseille.

 | HOTELS-RESTAURANTS

■ Relais de la Magdeleine

Rte d'Aix, rond-point de la Fontaine.
Tel. 04 42 32 20 16. Fax 04 42 32 02 26.
contact@relais-magdeleine.com
www.relais-magdeleine.com
Closed mid-Nov.–mid-Mar.
Rest. closed Mon., Wed. lunch.
24 rooms: 115–185€. 1 suite: 220€.
Prix fixe: 30€ (lunch), 42€, 55€.
A la carte: 65€.

This elegant 18th-century building, typically Provençal with its antique furniture, traditional red tiles, printed fabric and its grounds that resonate with the song of the cicadas, has a feel that charms. The comfort and quiet of the rooms harmonizes, without a wrong note, with Philippe Marignane's regional cooking. The swimming pool beneath the sun is an asset. While Philippe's dishes—tomato and basil gazpacho presented with a bouquet of shrimp, the sea bream filet with crunchy fennel and ratatouille jus or rack of lamb in a pistachio crust, with white beans and chanterelles—seduce effortlessly.

GENERARGUES see ANDUZE

GENESTON

44140 Loire-Atlantique. Paris 400 –
Cholet 62 – Nantes 22 – La Roche-sur-Yon 45.
A town that is already in the Vendée, bordering the area of Retz and Grand-Lieu lake, very near the Ognon valley.

● | RESTAURANTS

● Le Pélican

13, place Georges-Gaudet.
Tel.-Fax 02 40 04 77 88.
Closed Sun. dinner, Mon., Wed., Feb. vac., Aug.
Prix fixe: 20€, 30€.

Behind its pretty exterior of painted wood, Pascal Vilaseca delights his guests, comfortably installed in the brightly-colored dining rooms, with well-conceived regional dishes. No one would criticize marbled vegetable and foie gras terrine, a roasted Atlantic sea bass with potatoes and smoked eel, duck in stewed vegetables or the brioche pain perdu with apples, napped in salted-butter caramel sauce. Several wines can be had by the glass, to keep the check to a sensible level.

GENEUILLE see BESANÇON

GENNES

49350 Maine-et-Loire. Paris 306 –
Angers 33 – Cholet 68 – Saumur 20.
The softness of Angevin Val and the beauty of the nearby church of Cunault.

HOTELS-RESTAURANTS

■ Aux Naulets d'Anjou
18, rue de Croix-de-Mission.
Tel. 02 41 51 81 88. Fax 02 41 38 00 78.
www.hotel-lesnauletdanjou.com
Closed Christmas–New Year's, Jan.
Rest. closed lunch, Tue. dinner (mid-Oct.–mid-Apr.).
19 rooms: 49–55€.
Prix fixe: 21–24€, 35€, 9€ (child).

Between Anjou and Saumurois, vineyards and châteaux, the Bouleries' establishment welcomes you with open arms. At your disposal are the immaculate rooms, the pleasant garden, the heated swimming pool and the cheerful cuisine of Pierre. In the colorful dining room, thyme-seasoned foie gras, Atlantic sea bass with fennel, skirt steak with shallots and baked apples with rose-infused syrup are simple and good.

GERARDMER

88400 Vosges. Paris 424 – Colmar 52 – Epinal 41 – Saint-Dié 28 – Thann 51.
info@gerardmer.net.
The "pearl of Vosges" with its lake, its Cuves waterfall and its gentle jewelery box of a mountain is a haven in fresh air. The international fantasy film festival that takes place annually in winter has not made it lose its good rustic character.

HOTELS-RESTAURANTS

■ Grand Hôtel & Le Grand Cerf
Pl du Tilleul, BP 12 (Grand Hôtel) /
17-19 rue Charles-de-Gaulle (le Grand Cerf).
Tel. 03 29 63 06 31. Fax 03 29 63 46 81.
gerardmer-grandhotel@wanadoo.fr
www.grandhotel-gerardmer.com
Rest. closed lunch (exc.Sun. and Bank holidays).
58 rooms: 76–196€. 14 suites: 120–350€.
Prix fixe: 25€, 45€, 55€, 85€, 11€ (child).

Claude and Fabienne Remy watch carefully over this 19th-century monument of a hotel in the middle of wooded grounds. Redecorated rooms, suites with balneotherapy, bar, chic bistro (see Le Coq à l'Ane) and gastronomic restaurant (Le Pavillon Petrus), with Thierry Longo's classic and masterly cuisine, effortlessly please the stars who come for the Fantastica festival. A foie gras terrine seasoned with pine-flavored caramel and served with fruit chutney, crayfish and spring leek cannelloni with sauce Nantua (crayfish sauce), John Dory served with thin-sliced scallops, braised squab medallions or the roasted pineapple with a milk caramel mille-feuille make a good impression.

■ Le Manoir au Lac
59, chemin de la Droite-du-Lac.
Tel. 03 29 27 10 20. Fax 03 29 27 10 27.
www.manoir-au-lac.com
Closed 2 weeks Nov.
10 rooms: 150–190€. 2 suites: 270–330€.
Half board: 190–410€.

Claude Valentin has turned this Vosgien chalet of 1830 frequented by Maupassant to good account, combining the exterior timbers with a warm decoration, antique furnishings and lace fabric. The tearoom in which a piano has pride of place offers a superb view of the lake while the refined rooms are perfect. Add sauna, hammam and heated swimming pool, as well as the proximity of the ski runs and you have all you need to satisfy the most demanding guests.

● Beaurivage
Esplanade du Lac. 2, av de la Ville-de-Vichy.
Tel. 03 29 63 22 28. Fax 03 29 63 29 83.
www.hotel-beaurivage.fr
48 rooms: 67–182€. 4 suites: 160–340€.
Prix fixe: 22,50€ (weekdays), 36€, 48€, 68€, 11€ (child). A la carte: 65–70€.

The luminous and wood-decorated rooms, the modern suites, the spa, the swimming pool, the Jacuzzi and the fitness suite, as well as the fantastic view of the lake: all the ingredients for a happy stay are here. Michel Harasse's hotel, now managed by Elisabeth Ragaezozi, attracts gourmets to its light dining room where Jean-Michel Costa, previously of Schillinger's in Colmar, who we knew in Metz at Le Bouquet Garni, delights with his reworked traditional dishes. The composed foie gras platter (breaded, spiral, in a baked cream and chilled in custard), the grilled turbot and roasted lobster in its shell, layered in fresh tomatoes, lamb filet medallions with rosemary-seasoned cooking jus, served with herb-seasoned gnocchi and a fresh ewe's cheese quenelle and the nougatine dessert fall within the real anchors of the *terroir*. Le Toit du Lac, a new restaurant created in the hotel, remains to be tested.

■ **L'Auberge de Martimprey**   ⌂

26, col de Martimpré, 2 km out of town.
Tel. 03 29 63 06 84. Fax 03 29 63 06 85.
www.auberge-martimprey.com
Rest. closed Sun. dinner (off season),
Mon. (off season), Tue. lunch (off season).
10 rooms: 49–79€. 1 suite: 79€.
Prix fixe: 19€, 8€ (child). A la carte: 40€.

Elisabeth and Yves Ragalozzi offer regional dishes rigorously cooked by Grégory Jacquot in their pretty chalet beside the road. Wild boar terrine, foie gras with a balsamic reduction and slices of toast, pikeperch seared skin-side down and finished under the broiler, wild boar and potato casserole with slow-cooked chestnuts and the wild blueberry tart with almonds, served warm with vanilla ice cream, hit the bull's-eye.

■ **Hôtel de Jamagne**   ⌂

2, bd de la Jamagne.
Tel. 03 29 63 36 86. Fax 03 29 60 05 87.
hotel@lajamagne.com / www.jamagne.com
Closed mid-Nov.–end Nov., 3 weeks Dec.
48 rooms: 50–150€.
Prix fixe: 13€, 40€, 8€ (child).
A la carte: 30–45€.

The Jeanselme family have been going strong, since 1905, in this town chalet. The rooms decorated in yellow and blue, the rustic furnishings, the swimming pool, the fitness center and the regional cuisine all encourage one to stay. On the food side, Julien Jeanselme creates

marbled foie gras terrine served with smoked duck, quick-seared tuna served tataki style, twelve-hour beef cheeks, the mirabelle plum dessert and a crisp, fresh spiced pear dessert, which pleasantly reflect the region's cuisine.

● **L'Assiette du Coq à l'Ane**   ☎SIM

At Grand Hôtel, pl du Tilleul.
Tel. 03 29 63 06 31. Fax 03 29 63 46 81.
www.grandhotel-gerardmer.com
Prix fixe: 17€, 22€, 25€.

The good deal of the resort? The Remys' Grand Hôtel, with its cheerful neo-mountaineers' tavern. The warmth of the wood blends with the cuisine of Dominique Arnold, who concocts traditional fare with a light touch: foie gras with mirabelle plum chutney, pike-perch and salmon wrapped in thin-sliced potatoes, veal with onions, plums, vinegar and white wine and variations on the theme of the wild blueberry.

● **Le Bistro de la Perle**   SIM

32, rue du Général-de-Gaulle.
Tel.-Fax 03 29 60 86 24.
Closed Tue. dinner (off season), Wed. (off season), 2 weeks Oct., 1 week beg. July.
Prix fixe:10,30€ (weekday lunch), 16€, 22,50€. A la carte:30€.

The reception is a little anonymous but the checks are always reasonable and the regional dishes well prepared. An escargot cassoulet with creamy garlic sauce, duck breast with mirabelle plums, pork cheeks simmered in Pinot Noir and wild blueberry clafoutis are very nice.

● **La Chaume**   SIM

23 bis, bd Kelsch.
Tel.-Fax 03 29 63 27 55.
lachaume2@wanadoo.fr
Closed Sun. dinner (exc. vac., Bank holidays),
Mon. (exc. vac., Bank holidays),
2 weeks end Nov., 1 week beg. June.
Prix fixe: 12€, 15€, 5,50€ (child).
A la carte: 25–30€.

In his rustic inn situated a stone's throw from the lake, Jean-François Marchal delights with his duck and lentil mille-feuille with horseradish mousse, crisp potatoes and smoked trout with chive and strawberry-seasoned cheese, rabbit fricassée with noodles and the Lorraine-style frozen madeleine, which are eaten without fuss.

In Les Bas-Rupts (88400). 4 km sw on rte de la Bresse.

● **Les Bas-Rupts**

181, rte de la Bresse.
Tel. 03 29 63 09 25. Fax 03 29 63 00 40.
basrupts@relaischateaux.com
www.bas-rupts.com
23 rooms: 145–190€. 3 suites: 250–480€.
Prix fixe: 32€ (weekday lunch), 45€, 60€, 80€, 15€ (child). A la carte: 110€.

In the heart of the Vosgien forest, this vast mountain chalet makes a high-flying Relais & Châteaux. Its strong points? The exuberant welcome from Sylvie and Philippe Witdouck, expert on choice Burgundies, the large wood-decorated rooms and suites, the heated swimming pool, the Jacuzzi, the hammam and the restaurant. Michel Philippe continues to watch—from afar—over the kitchen, while François Lachaux cooks up a meticulous cuisine that situates itself between land and sea. In the pink wooden dining room, sliced cold tête de veau served carpaccio style with truffle oil and roasted langoustines, a poached pike-perch quenelle served with crab, the "whole pig" platter, the young Bresse chicken in Vin Jaune and morels and the *lait de poule*, an eggnog-like drink served in an eggshell as well as the spiced pear sorbet effortlessly blend with one of the 3,000 wines in a cellar developed by Serge Andert.

In Les Bas-Rupts.

● **Cap Sud**   COM

144, rte de la Bresse.
Tel. 03 29 63 06 83. Fax 03 29 63 20 76.
olivier.colonna@club.fr
Closed Mon.
Prix fixe: 14,90€ (lunch), 25€ (dinner), 35€.

In the heart of the Vosges, this restaurant—now the playing field of Olivier Colonna—decorated like an ocean liner with portholes and a view of the mountains has an unsettling effect. The maritime cuisine plays with charming contrasts. Variations on theme of Vosges trout, the more exotic pan-seared scallops with curry, the sea bream tagine with preserved lemons, osso bucco served with an Italian minced parsley and garlic sauce called gremolata and the variations on a pineapple theme for dessert take one on a voyage with a light touch.

In Liézay (88400). 2 km via rte d'Epinal.

■ **Auberge Produits du Terroir**

9, rte du Saucefaing.
Tel. 03 29 63 09 51. Fax 03 29 60 85 08.
www.liezey.fr
Closed 1–15 Dec.
Rest. closed Mon., Tue. (exc. school vac.).
7 rooms: 52–56€.
Prix fixe: 14,80€, 30€, 6,50€ (child).
A la carte: 30–35€.

Serge Bertrand and Jean-François Marley give a warm welcome to their farm/inn beside the lake. They offer, the former in the restaurant and the latter in the kitchen, culinary creations linked to regional tradition but not lacking in ingenuity. Rustic but very functional rooms in an authentic hotel that can only seduce.

In Xonrupt-Longemer (88400). 6 km w.

■ **Auberge du Lac**

2887, rte de Colmar.
Tel. 03 29 63 37 21. Fax 03 29 60 05 41.
www.aubergedulac-gerardmer.com
Closed mid-Nov.–mid-Dec.
Rest. closed Mon. (off season), Tue. (off season).
16 rooms: 48€. A la carte: 20€.

This large chalet in shades of beige and blue, 200 meters from the lake, offers mountain-style rooms for families, as well as a brasserie cuisine served in a wood-decorated and cozy room. Buckwheat crêpes with cumin-seasoned Munster cheese, Vosges-style salad, fresh trout cooked to order and the pork and charcuterie served on a bed of sauerkraut make a good impression.

GERTWILLER see BARR

GEVREY-CHAMBERTIN

21220 Côte-d'Or. Paris 315 – Beaune 33 –
Dijon 12 – Dôle 61.
gevrey.info@wanadoo.fr.
Celebrated the world over for its great Burgundian vintage, this little Côtes de Nuits village is also a famous gourmet stopping place.

 HOTELS-RESTAURANTS

■ Grands Crus
Rue de Lavaux.
Tel. 03 80 34 34 15. Fax 03 80 51 89 07.
hotel.lesgrandscrus@nerim.net
www.hoteldesgrandscrus.com
Closed Dec.–beg. Mar.
24 rooms: 75–85€.

A stone's throw from the vineyards, this village house is worth the visit for its warm welcome, its nicely appointed rooms, its neat garden and its cozy sitting room with fireplace. Cyclists are welcomed.

● Rôtisserie du Chambertin
Rue du Chambertin.
Tel. 03 80 34 33 20. Fax 03 80 34 12 30.
rotisserieduchambertin-bonbistro@wanadoo.fr
www.rotisserie-bonbistro .com
Closed Sun. dinner, Mon., Tue. lunch,
3 weeks Feb., 2 weeks beg. Aug.
Prix fixe: 32€, 38€, 45€, 70€,
13€ (child). A la carte: 55–65€.

The setting of this 11th-century vaulted cellar has kept its historic charm. Jean-Pierre Nicolas, for his part, concocts quite attractive things that are a combination of past and present. Oven-crisped pork trotters with an herb salad, a pan-seared duck foie gras escalope with slow-cooked apples and sorrel, roasted pike-perch with a wine and vegetable sauce, free-range grain-fed chicken simply roasted and served with a spicy honey sauce and an almond milk panna cotta make a good impression.

● Chez Guy & Family
3, pl de la Mairie.
Tel. 03 80 58 51 51. Fax 03 80 58 50 39.
chez-guy@hotel-bourgogne.com
www.hotel-bourgogne.com
Closed Christmas, New Year's.
Prix fixe: 26€, 29,50€, 34€.

The best price-quality-cheerfulness ratio in Burgundy is still to be found with Guy Rebsamen, who has become the representative of the gastronomy of his region in an inn renovated in a modern style with its light and luminous wood panels. His special menu (starter, main dish and dessert) at 29.50 is unbeatable. His daughters Natacha and Sandrine run the restaurant and advise on wines, while his son, Yves, attends the ovens. Escargots with slow-cooked tomatoes drizzled with a parsley jus, a house-prepared ham and parsley terrine, pollock with slow-cooked leeks, twelve-hour red wine–braised beef cheeks, a tender apple crumble and a roasted pineapple panna cotta served with clafoutis, pineapple sorbet and coconut mousse take one straight back to childhood. The best Côte de Nuits wines form a counterpoint.

In Chambolle-Musigny (21220). 5,6 km to the north.

■ Château André Ziltener
Rue de la Fontaine.
Tel. 03 80 62 41 62. Fax 03 80 62 83 75.
chateau.ziltener@wanadoo.fr
www.chateau-ziltener.com
Closed mid-Dec.–1 Mar.
3 rooms: 200€. 7 suites: 250–350€.

Luxury, calm and sensual pleasure are all on the agenda in this 18th-century establishment with rooms in the style of Louis XV. A little visit to the Museum of Wine is called for because it forms an integral part of the place.

GEX

01170 Ain. Paris 492 – Genève 21 –
Pontarlier 93 – Saint-Claude 43.
ot.paysdegex@wanadoo.fr.
The old capital of the Gex region looks towards Mont Blanc, which can be admired just behind

the church dating from 1860. The old houses—built by the holders of royal titulaires and merchants attracted by the fiscal immunity—testify to its past glory.

 HOTELS-RESTAURANTS

■ Auberge des Chasseurs
In Echenevex, 4 km s via D984 and secondary road.
Tel. 04 50 41 54 07. Fax 04 50 41 90 61.
aubergedeschasseurs@wanadoo.fr
Closed Nov.–beg. Mar.
Rest. closed Sun. dinner, Mon., Tue. lunch.
15 rooms: 85–150€.
Prix fixe: 33€, 41€, 13€ (child).
A la carte: 55€.

Mont Blanc can be seen in all her beauty from the terrace. Heated swimming pool, old-style dining room, small, nicely appointed rooms: this inn is a real joy, offering in addition simple, high-quality food. Nothing to criticize in the dishes offered by Jean Hatte: house-prepared foie gras, fish mousseline, saffron-seasoned monkfish medallion, poultry with morels and crème brûlée.

■ L'Hôtel du Parc
58, passage de la Couronne.
Tel. 04 50 41 50 18. Fax 04 50 42 37 29.
hotel.parc@wanadoo.fr
www.hotelduparc-gex.com
Closed Sun., Jan.
14 rooms: 56–68€.

Sweet, calm little rooms, flowered terrace, soft and muted bar/sitting room, smiling welcome and friendly prices are on offer here. Nothing but joy.

GIENS

83400 Var. Paris 867 – Toulon 29 – Carquerainne 11 – Hyères 10.
This peninsula and its village, at the gateway to Hyères, is the departure point for Porquerolles and the site of the Tour-Fondue. St. John Perse, who loved these lyrical places, rests in the cemetery.

 HOTELS-RESTAURANTS

■ Le Provençal
Pl Saint-Pierre.
Tel. 04 98 04 54 54. Fax 04 98 04 54 50.
le.Provençal@wanadoo.fr
www.Provençalhotel.com
Closed end Oct.–beg. Apr.
41 rooms: 72–165€.
Prix fixe: 26€, 33€, 49€, 13€ (child).

The flower- and tree-filled grounds of this house opposite Porquerolles goes down in terraced levels to the sea. Provençal rooms, swimming pool and beach are invitations to total relaxation. Laurent Batz in the kitchen offers a lively cuisine with fish soup, John Dory with tomato-seasoned béarnaise sauce, the breaded lamb saddle and puffed oven-baked crêpes served Lido style.

● Le Tire-Bouchon
Pl Saint-Pierre.
Tel. 04 94 58 24 61. Fax 04 94 58 15 37.
Closed Tue. (exc. July–Aug.), Wed., mid-Dec.–mid-Jan.
Prix fixe: 25€, 34€. A la carte: 45–50€.

Christian Beaumont has taken over this little village establishment near the church with its terrace looking towards the islands. Escargots in puff pastry, fisherman's stew, a small pigeon breast served with foie gras, veal kidneys with ceps and the Grand Marnier tiramisu are of great quality.

GIGNAC

34150 Hérault. Paris 724 – Montpellier 31 – Béziers 52 – Sète 59.
A tranquil village, with shady plane trees, in the Hérault valley.

 RESTAURANTS

● Liaisons Gourmandes
3, bd de l'Esplanade.
Tel. 04 67 57 50 83. Fax 04 67 57 93 70.
liaisonsgourmandes.capion@wanadoo.fr

Closed Sat. lunch (off season), Sun. dinner,
Mon. (off season), Mar.
Prix fixe: 17€ (lunch), 28€, 45€.
A la carte: 36,50–41€.

This smart house with its colorful exterior is welcoming. One can enjoy, in the restaurant or on the terrace, the cuisine of Jacques Calmet-Capion who is equally effusive with his truffle-seasoned poultry croquettes, sea bream simmered in red wine, grilled toro steak and a pear gratin with orange sabayon.

GIGONDAS

84190 Vaucluse. Paris 665 – Avignon 38 –
Nyons 31 – Orange 19.
ot-gigondas@axit.fr.
This wine-making village just before Ventoux carefully guards its famous Côtes-du-Rhône vintage.

 HOTELS-RESTAURANTS

■ Les Florets

2 km e, rte des Dentelles.
Tel. 04 90 65 85 01. Fax 04 90 65 83 80.
acceuil@hotel-lesflorets.com
www.hotel-lesflorets.com
Closed beg. Jan.–mid-Mar. Rest. closed Mon.
dinner (off season), Tue. (off season), Wed.
14 rooms: 90–125€. 1 suite: 120€.
Prix fixe: 25€, 39€, 52€, 15€ (child).

Thierry and Martine Bernard's hostelry is situated at the foot of the Dentelles of Montmirail mountains. No surprise, then, that the chef Daniel Chiocca draws inspiration from them. In the Provençal dining room or on the shaded terrace, the soft-cooked eggplant and tomatoes served with melon balls drizzled with vinegar caramel, the cod and Drome ravioli duo, quick-seared lamb with chorizo and the delicious frozen lime dessert served with a berry macaron sing the praises of the "païs" with a contemporary feel. This is the stuff with which to feed sweet dreams in the peaceful rooms.

● L'Oustalet   SIM

Pl de la Mairie.
Tel. 04 90 65 85 30. Fax 04 90 12 30 03.
www.restaurant-oustalet.fr
Closed Mon. (off season).
Prix fixe: 25€ (weekday lunch), 32€, 42€,
55€, 15€ (child). A la carte: 55–60€.

In this 19th-century house in the heart of the village, Cyril Glémot concocts flawless dishes: pan-seared duck foie gras with quince marmalade, catfish filet pan tossed in a Gigondas beurre rouge sauce, pork tenderloin and pork belly millefeuille and the Jivara chocolate cannelloni served with roasted cocoa bean caramel slip down effortlessly. Local wines are on the program.

GILLY-LES-CITEAUX see VOUGEOT
GIMBELHOF see LEMBACH

GIMONT

32200 Gers. Paris 730 – Toulouse 55 –
Auch 25.
The little Gers capital of foie gras on the doorstep of Toulouse, Gimont has two of the great French producers in the domain: the Countess of Barry and the Dukes of Gascogne.

 HOTELS-RESTAURANTS

■ Château de Larroque   Ⓝ ✿ 🏠

Rte de Toulouse.
Tel. 05 62 67 77 44. Fax 05 62 67 88 90.
chateaularroque@free.fr
www.chateau-larroque.com
Closed 3 weeks Nov., 1 week beg. Jan.
Rest. closed Sun. dinner (off season), Mon.
(off season), Tue. lunch (off season).
16 rooms: 84–176€. 1 suite: 176–191€.
Prix fixe: 24€, 37€, 55€, 10€ (child).
A la carte: 55€.

This beautiful early 19th-century château with its twisted staircase is run with great passion by the Fagedets. Brother and sister André and Rose-Marie play a duet of great flavors in the kitchen and smiles in the restaurant. One comes here to relax and unwind in the beautiful grounds of ten hectares, to rest in one of the old-style rooms which have recently been redecorated and to taste the generous dishes that do honor to the Gers region. The pan-seared foie gras escalope seasoned with Bigarreaux, parsley-seasoned duck breast and foie gras, line-fished tuna served in the style of Gascony and the rack of lamb with spring garlic shoots are eaten with pleasure. Olivier, André's son, who has trained with Trama and Guérard, looks after the *pâtisseries* with heart: croustade (a local tart made with many layers of thin pastry) served with cinnamon ice cream slips down without a murmur.

GIROUSSENS see LAVAUR

GIVET

08600 Ardennes.
Paris 264 – Charleville-Mézières 56 – Rocroy 40 – Fumay 23.
ot-givet@dial-oleane.com.
This edge of France, bordering Meuse, is a geographical curiosity pointing like a finger towards Belgium. The nuclear power station of Chooz can be visited.

 HOTELS-RESTAURANTS

■ Les Reflets Jaunes

2, rue du Général-de-Gaulle.
Tel. 03 24 42 85 85. Fax 03 24 42 85 86.
reflets.jaunes@wanadoo.fr
www.reflets-jaune.com
Rest. closed Mon.,
10 days Christmas–beg. Jan.
17 rooms: 61–67€. 13 suites: 80–115€.
Half board: 73–139€.

This 17th-century house has become a contemporary hotel offering functional and very relaxing rooms in shades of yellow, blue and green. A very honest cuisine is found in its brasserie L'Hôtel de Ville at 10, pl. Carnot (03 24 42 06 36).

GIVORS

69700 Rhône. Paris 484 – Lyon 25 – Rive-de-Gier 17 – Vienne 13.

office.tourisme.fleuve@wanadoo.fr.
Between Rhône and Isère, near the great river and the greenery of Pilat.

● RESTAURANTS

● Mouton-Benoît COM

35, rte Nationale.
Tel. 04 78 07 96 36. Fax 04 72 49 99 94.
Closed Sat., 2 weeks Aug.
Prix fixe: 23€, 47€, 60€. A la carte: 50–60€.

This 18th-century coaching inn is the domain of Philippe Mouton-Benoît, who gives a dynamic welcome and who cooks with verve: fresh pan-seared foie gras with cabbage, sautéed scallops with truffle-seasoned artichokes, grilled turbot with beurre blanc sauce and a mango and passion fruit crème brûlée.

GOLFE-JUAN

06220 Alpes-Maritimes. Paris 905 – Antibes 5 – Cannes 6 – Grasse 23 – Nice 29.
A beach, golf course, terraces on the sea and the golden coast.

 HOTELS-RESTAURANTS

■ Beau Soleil

Golfe-Juan, 6, impasse Beau-Soleil.
Tel. 04 93 63 63 63. Fax 04 93 63 02 89.
contact@hotel-beau-soleil.com
www.hotel-beau-soleil.com
Closed beg. Nov.–beg. Mar.
30 rooms: 51–127€.

A stone's throw from the N7, towards Antibes, this is a modern hotel with functional rooms a moment from the beach.

● Tétou COM

8, av des Frères-Roustan, Golfe-Juan, on the beach.
Tel. 04 93 63 71 16.
Closed Wed., Nov.–end Feb.
A la carte: 140€.

If you want to eat a quality bouillabaisse right beside the water, this gourmet establishment is the place. Extra-fresh fish, well prepared, savory soup and rouille make a great impression. The service is meticulous, the red and blue setting neat and the prices on a par with the reputation of the place.

GONDRIN

32330 Gers. Paris 755 – Agen 57 – Auch 44 – Condom 16.
A green stopover in Armagnac country.

 HOTELS-RESTAURANTS

■ Le Pardaillan

25, av Jean-Moulin.
Tel. 05 62 29 12 06. Fax 05 62 29 11 79.
le.pardaillan@wanadoo.fr
www.le-pardaillan.com
Closed Jan.
Rest. closed Sun. dinner (exc. July–Aug.).
25 rooms: 42–49€.
Prix fixe: 11,50€ (weekday lunch), 16€, 20€, 31€, 8€ (child). A la carte: 40€.

Next to a leisure activity center and its stretch of water, this modern establishment houses practical, comfortable rooms. The rather classic dining room opens onto a garden and is the setting for a procession of honest, home-cooked dishes: pan-seared foie gras with seasonal fruit, salmon simmered in champagne, the veal cutlet with morels and an apple Tatin.

GORDES

84220 Vaucluse. Paris 715 – Apt 21 – Avignon 38 – Carpentras 26 – Cavaillon 17.
office.gordes@wanadoo.fr.
A gateway, the heart of Luberon society or a secret village in winter: everything depends on one's perspective. Perched up high, this much-praised town (the reception here sometimes exceeds the norm) has retained the charm of timeless Provence.

 HOTELS-RESTAURANTS

■ Les Bories

Rte de l'Abbaye-de-Sénanque.
Tel. 04 90 72 00 51. Fax 04 90 72 01 22.

lesbories@wanadoo.fr
www.hotellesbories.com
Closed beg. Jan.–10 Feb.
Rest. closed Sun. dinner (mid-Nov.–mid-Mar.), Mon. (mid-Nov.–mid-Mar.).
27 rooms: 175–380€. 2 suites: 450–810€.
Prix fixe: 55€, 88€, 68€, 20€ (child).

These modern stone *bories* (traditional Provençal beehive-shaped dwellings) set amid scrubland are one of Gallon's properties. The colorful rooms, the spa, the swimming pool and Pascal Ginoux's cooking all seduce effortlessly. Pressed lobster, tomato and artichokes, foie gras with figs served two ways, Mediterranean sea bass slow-cooked at a low temperature and the thyme-smoked country rack of lamb are dishes full of delicacy. Fine cellar.

■ La Bastide de Gordes

Le Village.
Tel. 04 90 72 12 12. Fax 04 90 72 05 20.
mail@bastide-de-gordes.com
www.bastide-de-gordes.com
Closed beg. Jan.–mid-Feb.
45 rooms: 170–355€. 5 suites: 420–690€.
Prix fixe: 25–32€, 39€ (lunch),
59€ (dinner), 89€ (dinner), 20€ (child).
A la carte: 108€.

This country house dating from the 16th century offers cleverly renovated rooms facing the valley or the village, a fitness suite, hammam, Jacuzzi and swimming pool. In the elegant yellow Provençal dining room, extended by a shaded panoramic terrace, one can enjoy such good regional products, prepared with heart by Olivier Bouzon, as crab, foie gras, rouget, John Dory, beef, lamb and a fig and chocolate dessert, a menu that changes with the seasons and the markets.

■ La Bastide des 5 Lys

Chemin du Moulin, in Les Beaumettes, 5,5 km s via D15 and D103.
Tel. 04 90 72 38 38. Fax 04 90 72 29 90.
info@bastide-des-5-lys.fr
www.bastide-des-5-lys.fr
Closed Oct.–Mar.
12 rooms: 130–261€. 1 suite: 232–261€.
Prix fixe: 34€, 48€, 74€, 18,50€ (child).

The turnaround of chefs continues in this rural country house. Christian Née, now at the helm, offers a southern cuisine full of ideas: foie gras terrine with Beaune de Venise Muscat, John Dory with truffles and celery parmesan ravioli and the Ventoux rack of lamb served with anchovy and piquillo-seasoned fried polenta strips. The Victoria pineapple with vanilla bean served with a baba au vieux rhum makes an attractive ending to the meal. The elegant avenue of cypress trees, the Louis XV-style rooms, the golf course, the swimming pool and the tennis court are all encouragements to unwind.

■ Domaine de l'Enclos

Rte de l'Abbaye-de-Sénanque.
Tel. 04 90 72 71 00. Fax 04 90 72 03 03.
www.avignon-et-provence.com/domaine-enclos
Rest. closed Sun., Mon.
10 rooms: 100–180€. 4 suites: 160–320€.
Prix fixe: 38€.

The Laffites' establishment makes a charming hotel. There is the welcome of Nadia and Serge, the comfortable rooms with terrace or private garden, the moments in the Jacuzzi or the heated swimming pool. In the restaurant, Jérôme Dufaure effortlessly delights with a curry-seasoned crab tartare served with a thin roasted tomato tart and goat cheese ice cream and a lamb tenderloin wrapped in herbs. The mint- and basil-infused strawberry soup served with a chocolate truffle and mango ice cream is well prepared.

■ La Ferme de la Huppe

Rte de Goult, Les Pourquiers, D156.
Tel. 04 90 72 12 25. Fax 04 90 72 01 83.
www.lafermedelahuppe.com
Rest. closed lunch (exc. Sun.), Wed., Thu., mid-Nov.–mid-Mar.
9 rooms: 80–165€.
Prix fixe: 45€, 18€ (child).

While the swimming pool and the rustic rooms of this little 18th-century farm are attractive, it is the cuisine of Gérald Konings that makes people stay. In the

borie-style restaurant, the baked foie gras crème seasoned with sherry vinegar, cod filet with grilled vegetables, rabbit saddle stuffed with sage and served on ratatouille with black olives and the white peach clafoutis makes up a finely crafted menu.

● L'Estellan

Rte de Gordes, quartier La Dragonne.
Tel.-Fax 04 90 72 04 90.
estellan@wanadoo.fr / restaurant-estellan.com
Closed Wed., Thu. (off season).
Prix fixe: 36€. A la carte: 50€.

Charm is definitely on the agenda at Philippe Debord's establishment, as much in the shaded terrace as in the pretty bistro that pays homage to Mistral and Daudet. His lunch menu is a gift. Squash soup with coconut milk and smoked bacon, gently cooked Mediterranean sea bass with black pasta carbonara, rosemary-seasoned lamb shanks served on a local onion tart and the crêpe mille-feuille topped with berries put sun in the plate. Fine local wines.

● Le Mas Tourteron

Rte des Imberts, chemin Saint-Blaise.
Tel. 04 90 72 00 16. Fax 04 90 72 09 81.
elisabeth.bourgeois1@wanadoo.fr
Closed Mon., Tue., weekdays (Nov. 1–mid-Dec.), mid-Dec.–beg. Mar.
Prix fixe: 37€, 59€.

Elizabeth Bourgeois is the mother of local cuisine, to be discovered in her charming *mas*. Her delightful special menus change according to the seasons and the market. We have a good memory of the truffle-seasoned gnocchi, the local fish soup and the soft fromage blanc served with Apt candied fruits. Philippe, her husband, will take you on a passionate voyage of discovery of local wines.

35350 Ille-et-Vilaine. Paris 385 – Saint-Malo 14 – Dinan 25 – Dol-de-Bretagne 13 – Rennes 65.
The rural station of St. Malo makes a beautiful countryside stop.

HOTELS-RESTAURANTS

● Tirel-Guérin

1, Le Limonay.
Tel. 02 99 89 10 46. Fax 02 99 89 12 62.
resa@tirel-guerin.com / www.tirel-guerin.com
Closed mid-Dec.–beg. Feb.
Rest. closed Mon. lunch (exc. Bank holidays).
56 rooms: 65–198€. 2 suites: 190–198€.
Prix fixe: 25€ (weekdays), 29,90€ (Sat.,
Sun.), 35€ (weekdays), 46€, 62€, 78€,
105€. A la carte: 80€.

The family house of the Tirels and the Guérins is more famous than the station just opposite. A legendary reception, cozy rooms, intimate sitting rooms and various facilities (heated swimming pool, Jacuzzi, health center) soon make one feel at home. In the kitchen, Jean-Luc Guérin and Guillaume Tirel create between them finely-crafted dishes that marry Brittany with far away places. Langoustines in filo pastry with garden herbs, poached turbot and cauliflower with grapefruit vinaigrette, the farm-raised squab with Penja vanilla-seasoned pepper and a strawberry and raspberry dessert served with a superb licorice root–seasoned crème, make one happy to wait for the next train.

GOUMOIS

25470 Doubs. Paris 510 – Besançon 94 –
Montbéliard 53 – Morteau 48.
The Swiss border is here, just below the river.
Visit the Franche-Comté with its prow of the
Corniche de Goumois.

HOTELS-RESTAURANTS

■ Taillard

Rte de la Corniche.
Tel. 03 81 44 20 75. Fax 03 81 44 26 15.
hotel.taillard@wanadoo.fr
www.hoteltaillard.com
Rest. closed Mon. lunch, Wed. lunch,
Wed. dinner (off season), Nov.–beg. Mar.
18 rooms: 65–90€. 3 suites: 120–160€.
Prix fixe: 22€ (lunch), 32€, 44€, 55€,
75€, 100€ (wine inc.). A la carte: 80€.

This charming hostelry on the Corniche de Goumois, surrounded by nature, is a rambler's reward. The reception of Jean-François Taillard, the sweet, quiet rooms, particularly those in the annex, and the thirties restaurant guarantee rest and well being. The local dishes concocted by Jean-Michel Lehongre (duck foie gras served two ways, trout meunière, the braised veal sweetbreads and morels served with an old-fashioned potato purée and the frozen absinthe parfait) are instantly restorative. The wine list, rich in more than 400 items from all over the world, deserves lingering over.

■ Le Moulin du Plain

Tel. 03 81 44 41 99. Fax 03 81 44 45 70.
www.moulinduplain.com
Closed Nov.–end Feb.
Prix fixe: 16€ (weekdays), 20€, 34€.

An isolated house on the edges of French-Swiss Doubs in the middle of a wild valley. Pleasant, comfortable rooms and cuisine based around river fish and Franche-Comté classics (trout simmered in Vin Jaune, a mushroom turnover and hot smoked ham). A fishermen's paradise.

GOURDON

46300 Lot. Paris 546 – Cahors 45 –
Sarlat 26 – Bergerac 90 – Brive 66 –
Figeac 64.
gourdon@wanadoo.fr.
In the heart of hospitable Quercy, Gourdon's old rue du Majou, the Cordeliers' church with its baptismal font and the view of the Causse from the esplanade are beacons reminding you to take your time.

HOTELS-RESTAURANTS

■ Domaine du Berthiol

1 km e via D704.
Tel. 05 65 41 33 33. Fax 05 65 41 14 52.
www.hotelperigord.com
Closed Christmas–New Year's, Jan.–end Mar.
Rest. closed Sun. dinner (off season),
Mon. (off season).
27 rooms: 67–84€. 2 suites: 125–142€.

Prix fixe: 24€, 38€ (dinner), 48€ (dinner), 11€ (child). A la carte: 50€.

Lost in Quercy, in the middle of wooded grounds with swimming pool and tennis court, this manor house with sixties appeal offers luxurious rooms, some of which have their own terrace. David Halais' cuisine delivers pleasant herb-seasoned mushroom ravioli with foie gras sauce, Atlantic sea bass cooked in its skin with basil and olive oil sauce, pan-seared sirloin steak, vineyard keeper's–style, and a spicy pineapple brochette. It all blends well with wine from Cahors.

■ Hostellerie de la Bouriane

Pl du Foirail.
Tel. 05 65 41 16 37. Fax 05 65 41 04 92.
hostellerie-la-bouriane@wanadoo.fr
www.hotellabouriane.fr
Closed 10 days Oct., mid-Jan.–mid-Mar.
Rest. closed Sun. dinner (off season), Mon.
20 rooms: 67–104€.
Prix fixe: 23€, 46€, 12€ (child).
A la carte: 55–65€.

This century-old hospitable establishment seduces without trying. Everything is harmonious: charming reception, rustic rooms and Jessica Boegly's careful cooking. Pan-seared fresh duck foie gras with grapes, a halibut gratin, veal sweetbreads and truffles served in croustade, and the Marsala-seasoned crêpe soufflé are attractively done. Rich cellar.

GRAMAT

46500 Lot. Paris 537 – Cahors 56 – Brive 57 – Figeac 35 – Gourdon 38 – Saint-Céré 22.
gramat@wanadoo.fr.
The little capital of Upper Quercy looks attractive, perched up above the Causse, with its large square with up-and-coming residences and the proximity of the large site of Rocamadour.

HOTELS-RESTAURANTS

■ Château de Roumégouse

4,5 km via N140 and secondary road to Brive.
Tel. 05 65 33 63 81. Fax 05 65 33 71 18.
roumegouse@relaischateaux.com
www.chateauderoumegouse.com
Closed beg. Apr.–mid-Sept. Rest. closed lunch (exc.Sun.), Tue. lunch (exc. July–Aug.).
15 rooms: 300–390€.
Prix fixe: 35€ (lunch), 40€ (lunch, wine inc.), 45€ (lunch, wine inc.), 50€ (dinner).

This beautiful medieval-style castle dating from the 19th century is branded with the Relais & Châteaux label. It won the favor of General de Gaulle in the seventies and remains a haven of rest with its rooms full of character, cozy sitting rooms and bar/library. The food served in the Louis XV dining room exudes the flavors of the region, care of Jean-Louis Lainé, whose wife Luce gives a marvelous reception and who has developed a seductive *savoir faire* (she formerly worked in Paris at the Boutique de la Maison de Marie-Claire). Langoustines and asparagus, saffron-seasoned cod filet and rack of lamb in an herb crust are tasty offerings.

■ Le Lion d'Or

8, pl de la République.
Tel. 05 65 38 73 18. Fax 05 65 38 84 50.
liondorhotel@wanadoo.fr
www.liondorhotel.com
Closed Sun. dinner (off season), Mon. (off season), beg. Jan.–end Jan., 10 days beg. Feb.
15 rooms: 40–80€.
Prix fixe: 30€, 40€, 70€ (wine inc.), 10€ (child). A la carte: 73€.

His name is Bond. Peter Bond. Having taken over this famous establishment on the large square, he highlights the produce of Quercy—with a fine accent from other places—served up by chef Jérôme Roseau in unexpected combinations such as the duck foie gras served with Cahors-marinated strips of duck breast and Calvados caramel with fried celery and the deboned wild rabbit saddle with pepper sauce, served with Saint-Jean pears and mushroom- and ham-stuffed artichokes simmered in wine, which make one want to take up residence during the hunting season. The desserts (a pineapple carpaccio with Sichuan pepper and pear ice cream quenelles) are inventive. Modern rooms and recent redecorations. An establishment to watch.

■ Relais des Gourmands

2, av de la Gare.
Tel. 05 65 38 83 92. Fax 05 65 38 70 99.
gcurtet@aol.com
www.relais-des-gourmands.fr
Closed Feb. vac. Rest. closed Sun. dinner
(exc. July–Aug.), Mon. (exc. July–Aug.).
16 rooms: 54–62€.
Prix fixe: 17€ (weekday lunch), 19€ (Sat.,
Sun., lunch), 42€, 8,50€ (child).
A la carte: 35€.

Rooms decorated in pink, yellow and blue, a swimming pool and garden and a lively restaurant where one can enjoy the food of Gérard Curtet await you in this modern building opposite the train station: lamb sweetbread in salad with a sweet-and-sour sauce, sautéed farm-raised lamb simmered with trumpet mushrooms and a frozen walnut soufflé served over custard sauce. Suzy Curtet combines food and wine with skill.

GRAND-BALLON

68760 Haut-Rhin. Paris 497 – Colmar 44 –
Guebwiller 20 – Mulhouse 37.
The most intoxicating of the Alsace mountain towns, reaching more than 1,424 meters, with its belvedere monument symbolizing, in the midst of peaceful Vosges, the end of the wars and European reconciliation.

HOTELS-RESTAURANTS

■ Chalet-Hôtel du Grand Ballon ✿ ⌂

Rte des Crêtes,
at the summit of the Grand Ballon.
Tel. 03 89 48 77 99. Fax 03 89 62 78 08.
www.chalethotel-grandballon.com
25 rooms: 23,65–30,50€.
Prix fixe: 14,50€, 21,50€, 28€,
8€ (child). A la carte: 32€.

Lovers of nature like this place for its peace and quiet, gentle prices and very spruce rooms. Regional fare without any pretension has pride of place: the house-

prepared country terrine, pork cuts and choucroute, and the house tarts are very authentic.

GRAND-BORNAND

74450 Haute-Savoie. Paris 567 – Annecy 33
– Albertville 47 – Bonneville 23.
otsigrambois@wanadoo.fr.
A real old-style village at 934 meters altitude, transformed into an Alpine resort without losing its lovely character.

 HOTELS-RESTAURANTS

■ Les Cimes ⌂

In Les Chinaillon, 5,5 km n via D4.
Tel. 04 50 27 00 38. Fax 04 50 27 08 46.
www.hotel-les-cimes.com
Closed mid-Apr.–mid-June,
end Aug.–beg. Dec.
10 rooms: 75–155€. Half board: 76–152€.

A sauna, hammam, carefully furnished cozy rooms and half-board at the very close-by restaurant are on offer from this mountain chalet renovated in contemporary style.

■ La Croix Saint-Maurice ⌂

Pl de l'Eglise.
Tel. 04 50 02 20 05. Fax 04 50 02 35 37.
www.hotel-lacroixstmaurice.com
Closed Oct.
22 rooms: 47–83€. 3 suites: 82–160€.
Prix fixe: 17,50€, 21€, 26,50€,
8,50€ (child). A la carte: 35€.

A very simple chalet with sweet and cozy rooms, a smiling welcome and inventive dishes at a reasonable price are offered by Jérôme and Pierre Missillier. Réblochon and potatoes, whiting filet, Savoie sausages simmered in white wine and a traditional blueberry and egg dessert called matafan are quiet marvels.

■ Le Vermont ⌂

Rte du Bouchet.
Tel. 04 50 02 36 22. Fax 04 50 02 39 36.
www.hotelvermont.com
Closed mid-Sept.–mid-Dec.,

mid-Apr.–mid-June.
23 rooms: 60–160€. Half board: 90–220€.

This chalet with Savoie-style rustic rooms and a swimming pool and fitness center, a stone's throw from the cable car at La Joyère, fulfils its function admirably.

● **La Ferme de Lormay**   ⛵SIM
Vallée du Bouchet. Locale known as Lormay et Grand-Bornand.
Tel. 04 50 02 24 29. Fax 04 50 02 26 15.
Closed Tue., weekend lunch (off season),
10 Sept.–20 Dec., mid-Apr.–mid-June.
A la carte: 40€.

The regional cuisine served up by Albert Bonamy is a worthy offering. After exploring the valley of Bouchet, it is a delight to eat the pork belly soup, locally fished trout meunière, chicken with crayfish and seasonal tarts, enjoyed alongside restorative Savoie wines.

● **L'Hysope**   SIM
Pont de Suize, rte du Bouchet.
Tel.-Fax 04 50 02 29 87.
Closed Wed. (off season), Thu. (off season),
3 weeks Oct.
Prix fixe: 28€, 39€, 69€, 11€ (child).

Jean-Christophe Prat skillfully marries sweet and savory tastes in this village restaurant decorated with wood paneling. His foie gras escalope served hot with balsamic vinegar and an apricot compote, like the sirloin steak with Mondeuse wine sauce and cocoa-infused sauce, are two good examples. One ends with the chocolate croustillant served over custard sauce with Chartreuse-flavored ice cream and the feeling that life is good. Thanks also to Vanessa Prat, who will dig out the wines that bring out the best in these daring dishes.

GRAND-COMBE-CHATELEU see MORTEAU

34280 Hérault. Paris 752 – Montpellier 28 – Aigues-Mortes 11 – Lunel 16 – Nîmes 45 – Sète 46.

infos@otlagrandemotte.fr.
Obviously, one doesn't come here to this large "coastal village" reminiscent of a suburb in the 1970s for romantic reasons, but for the beach and the sand, with their great holiday air.

■◢●   HOTELS-RESTAURANTS

■ **Hôtel les Corallines**
Quartier Point Zéro.
Tel. 04 67 29 13 13. Fax 04 67 29 14 74.
info@thalasso-grandemotte.com
www.thalasso-grandemotte.com
Closed Christmas–end Feb.
39 rooms: 92–161€. 3 suites: 158–258€.
A la carte: 50€.

Opposite the sea, this hotel complex is worthwhile for its light-filled, contemporary rooms, thalassotherapy center, two swimming pools, panoramic terrace and two honest restaurants with reliable guesthouse cooking.

■ **Mercure**   🏠
140, rue du Port.
Tel. 04 67 56 90 81. Fax 04 67 56 92 29.
h1230@accor.com / www.mercure.com
99 rooms: 105–150€. 18 suites: 175–210€.
Prix fixe: 25€. A la carte: 45€.

This contemporary chain hotel beside the sea, decorated in shades of yellow and beige, has nautical-style rooms that are undergoing complete renovation, very attentive service and the honest guesthouse cooking of Sébastien Arcanger. Other assets? Air conditioning and terrace, private sitting room and secure parking, Internet and WiFi, swimming pool, numerous meeting rooms.

■ **Novotel**
1641, av du Golf.
Tel. 04 67 29 88 88. Fax 04 67 29 17 01.
h2190@accor.com / www.novotel.com
81 rooms: 65–130€.
Prix fixe: 16€, 23€, 8,50€ (child).

At the entrance to the golf course, this contemporary hotel with its grand lobby houses spacious rooms in rainbow colors, a health center, a swimming pool and a classic restaurant where Frédéric Deliancourt dispenses a welcome brasserie cuisine. Salmon lasagne, baked duck and potatoes and a chestnut vanilla ice cream are washed down with superb wines at Mercure prices.

■ Golf Hôtel ❀🏠
1920, av du Golf.
Tel. 04 67 29 72 00. Fax 04 67 56 12 44.
golfhotel.montpellier@hotelbestwestern.fr
www.bestwestern-golfhotel34.com
39 rooms: 81–139€. 6 suites: 140–302€.

Ideally situated opposite the golf course and Ponant Pond, this contemporary chain hotel is worthwhile for its functional rooms with spacious balcony and its garden swimming pool.

■ Azur Bord de Mer 🏠
Esplanade de la Capitainerie, rue du Casino.
Tel. 04 67 56 56 00. Fax 04 67 29 81 26.
hotelazur34@aol.com / www.hotelazur.net
20 rooms: 90–129€. 2 suites: 140–180€.
Half board: 105–210€.

This hotel with the sea for a neighbor offers pleasant a swimming pool and functional rooms, some with a teak terrace.

■ Europe 🏠
Allée des Parcs.
Tel. 04 67 56 62 60. Fax 04 67 56 93 07.
hoteleurope@wanadoo.fr
www.hoteleurope34.com
Closed Dec.–end Jan.
34 rooms: 61–115€.

This family hotel offers swimming pool, rooms with exotic décor and Moroccan-style sitting room, all at reasonable prices.

● Alexandre V.COM
Esplanade Maurice-Justin.
Tel. 04 67 56 63 63. Fax 04 67 29 74 69.
michel@alexandre-restaurant.com
www.alexandre-restaurant.com
Closed Sun. dinner (exc. July–Aug.), Mon.,
Tue. (Nov.–Mar. exc. Bank holidays), Jan.
Prix fixe: 43€, 58€, 73€, 15€ (child).
A la carte: 70€.

This establishment, run with the masterly hands of Michel and Dany Alexandre, has the status of an institution. One comes for the view of the boats and for the pleasures of the palate. The menu, which honors the great expanse of Languedoc-Roussillon, changes five times a year and delivers gems. Pan-seared foie gras with figs, grilled squid and shellfish brochettes, the fresh cod in tapenade with olive oil–seasoned vegetable purée, grain-fed pigeon prepared according to the season and a Grand Marnier crêpe soufflé make a good impression. The rich cellar with its 350 items is one of the assets of the house. Quality cuisine at a bistro special menu price (menu: 28).

● La Cuisine du Marché SIM
89, av du Casino.
Tel. 04 67 29 90 11.
etiennelechef@aol.com
Closed lunch, Mon. (exc. July–Aug.), Tue.
(exc. July–Aug.).
Prix fixe: 26€, 31€, 33€, 11€ (child).

Etienne Collignon delivers a clean, unpretentious cuisine that, above all, creates an appetite. Tarragon-seasoned sardines on toast, bouillabaisse served without bones, sirloin steak with morels and the pear and puff pastry tart seduce without trying. It is all fresh, generous and authentic.

GRAND-VILLAGE-PLAGE see
ILE D'OLERON

GRANGES-LES-BEAUMONT

26600 Drôme. Paris 560 – Valence 16 –
Grenoble 85 – Vienne 70.
Between Romans and Valence, in the heart of
wine-making Drôme, a peaceful village with its
beautiful inn.

| ● | RESTAURANTS |

● Les Cèdres ◎◎LUX
Rue Henry-Machon.
Tel. 04 75 71 50 67. Fax 04 75 71 64 39.

www.restaurantlescedres.fr
Closed Sun. dinner (exc. summer and day
before Bank holidays), Mon., Tue., Dec.–beg.
Jan., 1 week mid-Apr., 20 Aug.–beg. Sept.
Prix fixe: 35€ (weekday lunch), 69€, 95€,
25–30€ (child).

In the middle of Drôme, the inn of the
Bertrand brothers stands out like a jewel.
The dining room, redecorated in contemporary, designer, minimalist mode,
opens onto a smart garden and awak-
ens the senses. Jean-Paul's reception is
seriously professional while the cooking of his brother Jacques is fine, subtle
and simple. With Pic in Valence and Gleize in Château-Arnoux, this modest man
learned the art of selecting the best produce from the locality without forgetting
preparation with a light touch and precise cooking. The red tuna tartare with
pickles and capers, served with slow-
cooked tomato coulis and a vegetable
julienne, lamb carpaccio marinated with
truffles and with olive oil and the herring caviar served over a creamy Mona
Lisa potato cappuccino are powerful,
spirited moments in a festive meal. Add
to this a beautiful Angus beef steak simply pan seared, served sliced and accompanied by shallots which have been
slow-cooked in goose fat. For dessert, the
tender apricot dessert with almonds and
a fresh mint ice cream. These are all presented in delicious homage to the Rhône
valley. As for the cellar, the best Crozes-
Hermitages, St-Pérays and Côtes-du-
Rhône are praised with professionalism
by the sommelier Olivier Sebrer and reasonably priced.

GRANVILLE

50400 Manche. Paris 336 – Saint-Lô 57 –
Saint-Malo 93 – Avranches 26.
office.tourisme@ville-granville.fr.
The number one coastal resort in Cotentin since
the 19th century has found new vigor, with its
thalassotherapy and festival of writers of the
sea. People come here for the fresh air, to
depart for the Chausey islands or to stroll along
the ramparts that adorn the upper town.

HOTELS-RESTAURANTS

■ Le Grand Large
5, rue de la Falaise.
Tel. 02 33 91 19 19. Fax 02 33 91 19 00.
infos@hotel-le-grand-large.com
www.hotel-le-grand-large.com
Closed 2 weeks Dec.
51 rooms: 48–124€.

Perched up on the cliff and within the
precincts of the thalassotherapy center
(sauna, hammam and Jacuzzi), this hotel
gives one a great breath of sea air. The
rooms are decorated in energizing colors of red, yellow or blue, guaranteeing
modern comfort.

■ Hôtel des Bains
19, rue G.-Clemenceau.
Tel. 02 33 50 17 31. Fax 02 33 50 89 22.
hotel-bains@wanadoo.fr
www.hoteldesbains-granville.com
54 rooms: 42–95€. 1 suite: 80–105€.

A lively ensemble is formed by the casino,
where the restaurant is found, the thalassotherapy center for relaxation and this
century-old hotel. The rooms, set out in
contemporary style, offer a balcony with
view of the sea.

● La Citadelle COM
34, rue du Port, BP 624.
Tel. 02 33 50 34 10. Fax 02 33 50 15 36.
citadelle@club-internet.fr
www.restaurant-la-citadelle.com
Closed Tue. (off season), Wed. (off season),
mid-Nov.–mid-Dec.
Prix fixe: 18€, 22€, 27€, 33€, 10€ (child).
A la carte: 40–45€.

Patrick Duret, specializing in fish, follows the tides closely. Everything here
is fresh and tasty: oysters topped with
cream and broiled, an Atlantic sea bass
filet with a grapefruit sauce, local Normandy scallops in fricassée, veal piccata
served with mushrooms and a strawberry puff pastry dessert with a pastry
cream lightened with Italian meringue.
All are at their best.

GRASSE

06130 Alpes-Maritimes. Paris 911 –
Cannes 17 – Nice 41 – Draguignan 57.
tourisme.grasse@wanadoo.fr.
The town of perfume has become one of gastronomy. After a walk in the historic center don't miss the paintings by Rubens in the old Notre Dame cathedral.

 HOTELS-RESTAURANTS

● La Bastide Saint-Antoine

48, av Henri-Dunant.
Tel. 04 93 70 94 94. Fax 04 93 70 94 95.
info@jacques-chibois.com
www.jacques-chibois.com
11 rooms: 200–380€. 5 suites: 460–860€.
Prix fixe: 59€ (lunch), 150€ (dinner).

When we say that Jacques Chibois is the rigorous father of Côte d'Azur cuisine, we have said it all. This man from Limoges who adopted Provence has been trained both in sweet and savory cuisine, formerly with Delaveyne, Guérard, Outhier and Vergé. He has proved that he knows how to do everything in the kitchen. And, seasoned loner that he is, he has spent the last ten years putting the finishing touches to his solitary retreat just outside the perfume capital of Grasse. To this *bastide* he has added an annex with contemporary-style rooms, a terrace and a host of olive trees, as well as an elegant, very "southern" dining room, in short, it is an exemplary Relais & Châteaux establishment. Such is the lair of this businessman who acts in silence, having the good taste to focus on the essentials. Having become the specialist on olive oil, pulses, condiments, mushrooms and other woodland wonders, Jacques Chibois has not forgotten how to roll up his sleeves. Still young at the age of fifty, he reinterprets the cuisine of the uplands, the *garrigues* and the Riviera in his own down-to-earth way that is both carefully crafted and precise. He delivers up an ode with the sweet-scented perfume of pastures and damp earth. There is the purple asparagus with a truffle-infused glaze and foie gras, a creamy mushroom mousse with shavings of black truffle, the amusing "caviar" pasta "Isabelle", fine like a risotto, with scallops, oyster mushrooms, almond milk and Alba truffles, the rouget on a bed of mint-seasoned cucumber with tomato-enriched bergamot jus, lemongrass and blood orange-seasoned sole, and also the wild rabbit saddle cooked rare, served with quince confit and dates. Most of all, don't miss the desserts, moments of sublime pleasure. We would travel to Grasse solely for the poached pear with caramelized licorice root-flavored honey nougatine, the poached cherries and the figs. Great art indeed. Great service and a rich cellar to match.

● Café Arnaud   SIM

10, pl de la Foux.
Tel. 04 93 36 44 88.
Closed Sun.
Prix fixe: 11€, 15€, 18€. A la carte: 35€.

In the vaulted dining room and on the little summer terrace the fresh market cuisine is crisp, straightforward, changes each day and is reasonably priced. Guy Fovez, the manager, and Christophe Duminy, the chef, form an effective team at the helm of this amazing establishment. Tête de veau with sauce gribiche (caper and pickle mayonnaise) in salad, ravioli carbonara, country-style quail fricassée and a delicious chocolate dessert do not fail to please. Alongside we drink the Marquis de Fonséguille Vacqueyras that works its magic wherever it goes.

● Le Moulin des Paroirs   SIM

7, av Jean-XXIII.
Tel. 04 93 40 10 40. Fax 04 93 36 76 00.
moulindesparoirs@wanadoo.fr
Closed Sun., Feb. vac.
Prix fixe: 16€ (lunch), 25€, 41€, 58€.
A la carte: 50–60€.

Valérie Touseau and Stéphane Lepesme make a dynamic duo in this 18th-century former olive oil mill. The locally inspired dishes are examples of well-mastered classicism, as demonstrated by the house foie gras served three ways, the fine salmon rillettes, sautéed scallops with coriander cream sauce, quail with ceps in Bordelaise sauce and, finally, a chocolate fondue.

GRAUFTHAL see LA PETITE-PIERRE

GRAULHET

81300 Tarn. Paris 694 – Albi 39 – Toulouse 63 – Castres 31.
This capital of tanning is reputed for working the hides of Mazamet sheep. It is worth visiting for the old 13th-century bridge, the Panessac district with its rich medieval houses, the Moulin des Seigneurs and the Porte du Gouch.

| ● | RESTAURANTS |

● La Rigaudié
Rte de Saint-Julien-du-Puy.
Tel. 05 63 34 49 54. Fax 05 63 34 78 91.
www.larigaudie-restaurant.com
Closed Sat. lunch, Sun. dinner, Mon.,
1 week beg. May, 2 weeks end Aug.
Prix fixe: 18€ (weekday lunch), 22€, 54€,
10€ (child).

José Poser has given this 19th-century mansion house a new lease on life. Sitting in the shade of the plane trees or in the very genteel dining room, we taste Stéphane's dishes: duck carpaccio with slices of parmesan, Catalan-style squid, the pan-fried sea bream, oven-crisped pork trotter, escargots served by the dozen and the slow-cooked lamb shoulder served with quenelles and a creamy garlic sauce. A house to watch.

GRENADE-SUR-L'ADOUR

40270 Landes. Paris 724 – Mont-de-Marsan 15 – Orthez 50 – Saint-Sever 14.
The square with the *bastide* with the arches and the Adour flowing nearby constitute a charming image of the Landes.

| ◪ | HOTELS-RESTAURANTS |

● Pain, Adour et Fantaisie
14-16, pl des Tilleuls.
Tel. 05 58 45 18 80. Fax 05 58 45 16 57.

pain.adour.fantaisie@wanadoo.fr
Closed mid-Nov.–mid-Dec.
Rest. closed Sun. dinner (off season),
Mon. (off season), Wed. lunch (off season).
11 rooms: 70–164€.
Prix fixe: 38€, 82€. A la carte: 75€.

This half-timbered 17th-century mansion house on the banks of the Adour and just off the square offers cozy rooms and Philippe Garret's imaginative cuisine. In the hands of this former student of Guérard and Savoy, the Jurançon-seasoned duck foie gras terrine served with fig and walnut marmalade, roasted scallops with smoked pumpkin and green asparagus, the seared duck foie gras with peppers, dried fruits and nuts and ceps and the caramelized pear ice cream with slices of panettone, prepared in the style of pain perdu, yield up their heady scents. It is also good value for money.

GRENDELBRUCH

67190 Bas-Rhin. Paris 476 – Strasbourg 42 – Molsheim 18 – Obernai 11 – Urmatt 6.
A mountain village that has retained the Old World charm of the Vosges.

| ● | RESTAURANTS |

● L'Auberge de la Grenouille [SIM]
26, rue de l'Eglise.
Tel.-Fax 03 88 95 52 27.
Closed Mon., Tue., mid-Feb.–end Feb.
Prix fixe: 27€, 35€, 8€ (child).
A la carte: 40–45€.

Goose foie gras in a covered pie, pepper-seasoned smoked herrings served cold, fennel-seasoned Atlantic sea bass, leg of venison and the crème brûlée: young Ludovic Hyolle, who has taken over a house in this mountain village, has returned to a straightforward cuisine that enhances produce and avoids futile sophistication.

● Ferme-Auberge du Pâtre [SIM]
27, rue de la Victoire.
Tel.-Fax 03 88 97 55 71.

gross.andre@wanadoo.fr
www.bienvenue-a-la-ferme.com
Closed weekdays (exc. Fri. lunch July–Aug.),
Christmas–New Year's vac.
Prix fixe: 16€ (lunch), 22,50€ (lunch).

We visit the farm and have lunch at the inn. Céline and André Gross do all the work themselves, particularly with their goats, and produce menus at unbeatable prices: the house tourte served with salad, rabbit terrine, slow-simmered lamb shoulder and the house tart make merry feasting.

GRENOBLE

38000 Isère. Paris 566 – Chambéry 56 – Genève 146 – Lyon 105 – Saint-Etienne 153. office-de-tourisme-de-grenoble@wanadoo.fr. Stendhal's town cannot be understood except in terms of the mountain. Every Friday evening the townsfolk are thinking of only one thing: the peaks. On the Uriage route its Vercors leading to Chambousse, chalets and ski-tows await them, but also a pristine Nature that offers up its fruits. The water from springs and torrents that issues from Grenoble faucets is reputed to be the purest tap water in all of France. Could this be the reason why Grenoble, abandoned at the end of the week, looks poorish in spite of its market selling regional produce on the Place Hoche, the renovated 1850s covered market on the Place Sainte-Claire, a selection of goodly restaurants and a lively local tradition? "We are a cul-de-sac whereas Lyons is a storehouse and a hub", according to Henri Ducret, owner of the Park Hotel and tourist counselor extraordinaire. If all the people of Grenoble were like him, we would hear more about their delicious cardoons, the everlasting gratin dauphinois, the ravioli, Chartreuses and walnuts for which the neighboring communes have stolen the credit.

| ■ | HOTELS |

■ Park Hôtel Concorde
10, pl Paul-Mistral.
Tel. 04 76 85 81 23. Fax 04 76 46 49 88.
resa@park-hotel-grenoble.fr
www.park-hotel-grenoble.fr
Closed 22 Dec.–beg. Jan., Aug.
50 rooms: 130–250€. 1 suite: 515–690€.

Henri Ducret, the indefatigable Rhône-Alp tourism promoter, has made this downtown hotel into a star in its category. Vast space, much storage room, carefully chosen furnishings and warm colors in the rooms and suites: everything here revolves around the twin concepts of comfort and charm. See also the Parc restaurant.

■ Grand Hôtel Mercure Grenoble Président
11, rue du Général-Mangin.
Tel. 04 76 56 26 56. Fax 04 76 56 26 82.
h2947@accor-hotels.com
www.mercure.com
105 rooms: 128–140€. 3 suites: 167€.

Like all the other hotels in the chain, this one, managed by Dominique Combriat, has many advantages such as WiFi, game consoles, conference rooms, a sauna and a Jacuzzi. The bar takes us on a trip to Africa and the rooms are functional and comfortable.

■ Mercure Centre Alpes Hôtel
12, bd du Maréchal-Joffre.
Tel. 04 76 87 88 41. Fax 04 76 47 58 52.
H0652@accor.com / www.mercure.com
Rest. closed Sat., Sun.,
1 week Christmas–New Year's.
88 rooms: 115–125€.
Prix fixe: 15€ (weekday lunch).
A la carte: 25–30€.

This listed building was constructed for the 1968 Olympic Games. It is close to Paul-Mistral Park and the Palais des Sports and offers well-equipped rooms, a wine bar and a fitness center.

■ Novotel Grenoble Centre
Pl Robert-Schuman.
Tel. 04 76 70 84 84. Fax 04 76 70 24 93.
h1624@accor-hotels.com / www.novotel.com
116 rooms: 107€. 2 suites: 160€.

Many businessmen pass through the Europole district and stop in this hotel where comfort and practicality go hand-in-hand. The modern rooms in clear tones and the brightly lit bathrooms are comfortable.

■ Gambetta

59, bd Gambetta.
Tel. 04 76 87 22 25. Fax 04 76 87 40 94.
hotelgambetta@wanadoo.fr
www.hotel-resto-gambetta.com
Closed 1 week Christmas–New Year's,
10 days at end July, 10 days beg. Aug.
Rest. closed Fri. dinner, Sat., Sun.
45 rooms: 49–68€.
Prix fixe: 11,90€, 28,90€, 10€ (child).

Dating from 1924, this hotel has modern
rooms and a contemporary garden-style
restaurant with a renovated aquarium. An
escargot fricassée and the frozen Chartreuse soufflé are good value for money.

■ Hôtel des Alpes

45, av Félix-Viallet.
Tel. 04 76 87 00 71. Fax 04 76 56 95 45.
hotel-des-alpes@wanadoo.fr
www.hotel-des-alpes.fr
67 rooms: 49–68€.

A strong point: the prices. Practical
because it's only a few steps from the train
station, this seventies hotel offers clean
and tidy modern rooms at very reasonable prices.

In Eybens (38320). 5 km se.

■ Château de la Commanderie

17, av d'Echirolles.
Tel. 04 76 25 34 58. Fax 04 76 24 07 31.
resa@commanderie.fr / www.commanderie.fr
Rest. closed Sat. lunch, Sun., Mon.,
2 weeks Christmas–New Year's.
25 rooms: 87–169€.
Prix fixe: 37,50€, 46,50€, 57€, 66€,
15€ (child). A la carte: 78€.

This former commandery of the Knights
Templars has character. The de Beaumont family maintains the well-polished
parquet floors, antique furniture, family
portraits, Aubusson tapestries, 18th-cen-
tury lounges, bedrooms with old-style
furnishings, the billiard room and the
vast dining room and terrace. The luxurious lifestyle also means strolling in the
grounds, lounging by the swimming pool
and carefully crafted meals. Tuna sushi,
lake whiting on a bed of artichokes, a
beef Rossini mille-feuille, variations on
theme of chocolate and Nutella ice cream
are not bad at all.

● RESTAURANTS

● Auberge Napoléon

7, rue Montorge.
Tel. 04 76 87 53 64.
caby@auberge-napoleon.fr
www.auberge-napoleon.fr
Closed lunch, Sun., beg. Aug.–end Aug.
Prix fixe: 45€, 67€, 89€.

Napoleon Bonaparte was a guest here.
Chandeliers, dishes and table linens bring
the yellow Empire-style dining room
to life. Frédéric Caby receives us while
Agnès Chotin cooks up precious dishes:
foie gras and date pastilla, scallops with
squid ink risotto, roasted monkfish with
Noirmoutier potatoes, beef with morels
in red wine sauce and a peanut mousse
with absinthe sorbet and basil ice cream.
A fine cellar.

● L'Escalier V.COM

6, pl de Lavalette.
Tel. 04 76 54 66 16. Fax 04 76 63 01 58.
lescalier@wanadoo.fr
Closed Sat. lunch, Sun., Mon. lunch.
Prix fixe: 32€, 56€, 69€. A la carte: 60€.

Wooden beams, exposed stonework, nicely
set and spaced tables: Alain Girod has preserved the soul of this restaurant near the
museum with its shining silverware and
fresh market produce. Frog legs with ceps,
sea bream prepared in the local style with
butter, capers, and lemon, Atlantic sea
bass stuffed with spinach, mascarpone
and mushrooms, roasted wild duck, in
season, and a baba au Chartreuse Jaune
work their subtle charm in the capable
hands of Boris Roginski.

● La Glycine

168, cours Berriat.
Tel.-Fax 04 76 21 95 33.
Closed Sun., Mon., 2 weeks Aug.
Prix fixe: 30€, 39€.

Philippe Rostang has returned to his homeland after training with Troisgros, Senderens, Delaveyne, Le Cirque in New York and with papa Jo in La Bonne Auberge in Antibes. He has taken over the former Bistro Lyonnais, renamed it and now produces food that is precise, well thought out and prepared with heart. The fennel spring rolls, a pike fish quenelle soufflé and duck and potatoes served with hot foie gras describe the evolution of a chef who has learned in the course of his adventures to add spice, sparkle and a dash of color to his native Dauphiné cuisine. A pistachio fondant with Chartreuse has flair. The wine list continues to improve. The rustic setting has retained its Old World charm with the terrace in the shade of the wisteria, the decorated ceiling, the exposed stonework, old posters, framed labels and copper furnishings.

● A Ma Table   COM

92, cours Jean-Jaurès.
Tel.-Fax 04 76 96 77 04.
Closed Sat. lunch, Sun., Mon., Aug.
A la carte: 55€.

Michel Martin opts for quality produce in this intimate restaurant. Crayfish tartare served with two types of salmon, Lake Léman whiting or red mullet, pan-seared sirloin and the pineapple meringue dessert with creamy rum sauce go down without any difficulty.

● Dialogue Café   COM

11, av d'Alsace-Lorraine.
Tel.-Fax 04 76 46 18 03.
Closed Sun., Mon. dinner, Aug.
Prix fixe: 15€, 18€. A la carte: 35€.

The service in this neo-1900s Parisian brasserie is always efficient, the prices have hardly changed and the cuisine remains consistent. Classic smoked herrings and potatoes in oil, a sweet pepper-themed platter, salmon steak, lightly cooked salmon in thin slices, the tête de veau served in a cocotte and the tarte Normande live up to our expectations.

● Le Petit Paris   COM

2, cours Jean-Jaurès.
Tel. 04 76 46 00 51. Fax 04 76 46 80 67.
restaurant@lepetitparios.fr
www.lepetitparis.fr
Closed Christmas, 1 Jan. dinner, 1 May.
Prix fixe: 15€, 25€, 35€, 45€.
A la carte: 60–70€.

The Estève father and son make a friendly team. The cuisine by young Sylvain becomes increasingly more sophisticated. Michel, the father, lauds the anchovies with tapenade, the tuna carpaccio with foie gras, pan-simmered Mediterranean sea bass with shellfish, slow-cooked rabbit haunch and the lemon-themed dessert. The wine list always includes some good bottles.

● Ciao a Té   SIM

2, rue de la Paix.
Tel. 04 76 42 54 41.
Closed Sun., Mon.
A la carte: 25–35€.

We encounter Italy in the rustic dining room with exposed beams and in the sunny dishes. Cannelloni alla zagaglia (ricotta, spinach, tomato, basil), oven-gratined tortellini, lasagne alla calabrese, ravioli alla nuovo take us on a journey from one end of the boot to the other. The Parma ham, the carpaccio and the tiramisu are very presentable.

● La Panse   SIM

7, rue de la Paix.
Tel. 04 76 54 09 54. Fax 04 76 42 64 54.
Closed Sun., Bank holidays, 1 week beg.
May, mid-July–mid-Aug.
Prix fixe: 14€ (lunch), 17€ (dinner),
20€, 32€, 13€ (child). A la carte: 25–30€.

Dominique Chauveau's bistro is the cheerful meeting place in the antiques district. The cuisine based on fresh market produce is faultless and we delight in a whiskey-seasoned herring pâté, hot oysters with spring vegetables, catfish with sorrel and grilled beef filet with béarnaise sauce. The frozen Chartreuse soufflé is amazing.

● **Le Parc**

10, pl Paul-Mistral.
Tel. 04 76 85 81 23. Fax 04 76 46 49 88.
resa@park-hotel-grenoble.fr
www.park-hotel-grenoble.fr
Closed Sat. lunch, Sun. lunch, Christmas–
New Year's vac., Aug.
Prix fixe: 29€, 32€, 54€.
A la carte: 40–55€.

The fashionable set in Grenoble likes to pack into this chic rustic hotel tavern where David Casillas cooks up irreproachable classic dishes. Foie gras terrine, cod in a vegetable broth, Charolais beef filet in morel sauce and Chartreuse-flavored profiteroles are a delight.

In Champagnier (38800). 9 km s via N85 and D64.

● **L'Etable**

Rue du Bourg.
Tel. 04 76 98 34 82.
letable@wanadoo.fr
Closed Sun., Mon.
Prix fixe: 15€ (lunch), 17€ (lunch), 25€.

Lionel Achard's country inn is attractive. Here we celebrate well-prepared family cuisine in the fixed-price and à la carte menus that change with the seasons. Crayfish in salad, a fish and shellfish stew, strips of duck breast with morels in cream sauce and the roasted nectarines served in pistachio pastry cream all look good.

In Montbonnot-Saint-Martin (38330). 7 km ne via N90.

● **Alain Pic**

"Les Mésanges"
876, rue du Général-de-Gaulle.
Tel. 04 76 90 21 57. Fax 04 76 90 94 48.
info@restaurant-alain-pic.com
www.restaurant-alain-pic.com
Closed Sat. lunch, Sun. dinner (all day summer), Mon., 2 weeks end Aug.
Prix fixe: 25€, 40€, 48€, 15€ (child).
A la carte: 70€.

Alain Pic's very discreet and genteel roadside establishment is all in good taste. The terrace and flower garden offer guests an unbeatable view as they savor the traditional cuisine cooked up by the former maestro of Valence. In the welcoming dining room, the mushroom and foie gras tartelette, turbot with ceps, free-range chicken with baby vegetables and fruits in puff pastry maintain the gold standard. The wines selected by Marie-Hélène Pic form a perfect accompaniment for these choice dishes.

In Saint-Martin-le-Vinoux (38950). 2 km via A48 and N75.

● **Pique-Pierre**

1, rue Conrad-Kilian.
Tel. 04 76 46 12 88. Fax 04 76 46 43 90.
info@pique-pierre.com / www.pique-pierre.com
Closed Sun. dinner, Mon., Aug.
Prix fixe: 25€, 32€, 39€, 59€.
A la carte: 50€.

Jacques Douvier has transformed his genteel residence into a charming restaurant. Wood furnishings, mirrors, lighting fixtures, wood paneling and the terrace set the tone for the décor. The cuisine takes its inspiration from the traditional dishes of the Rhône valley. We enjoy the escargot fricassée with potatoes and cheese, whiting with buttered vegetables, lamb medallions prepared southern style and the tarte Tatin. The regional wines selected by Laure Douvier are an excellent accompaniment for these carefully crafted dishes.

GRIGNAN

26230 Drôme. Paris 632 – Montélimar 24 – Nyons 24 – Pont-Saint-Esprit 34.
The château where Madame de Sévigné's daughter once lived overlooks the beautiful lavender-scented countryside of Provençal Drôme. It is also a country of truffles and delicious food.

■□ HOTELS-RESTAURANTS

■ **Manoir de la Roseraie**

Chemin des Grands-Prés.
Tel. 04 75 46 58 15. Fax 04 75 46 91 55.
roseraie.hotel@wanadoo.fr
www.manoirdelaroseraie.com
Closed Tue. (off season), Wed. (off season),

mid-Oct.–mid-Mar.
18 rooms: 160–250€. 3 suites: 330–380€.
Prix fixe: 30€ (weekdays), 47€, 58€,
20€ (child). A la carte: 75€.

Under the watchful eye of Véronique Martinez this 19th-century manor set in its own grounds at the base of the château has lost none of its charm. The hotel has considerable advantages: Internet, WiFi, air conditioning, a swimming pool, tennis court and rooms renovated in the old or Provençal style. In the circular dining room in sandy and wine-red tones we discover the foie gras pot-au-feu with grated Tricastin truffles, Atlantic sea bass with quick-marinated vegetables and apricots with a lemon-seasoned fresh fromage blanc sorbet, all prepared by chef Frédy Trichet.

■ Le Clair de la Plume
Pl du Mail.
Tel. 04 75 91 81 30. Fax 04 75 91 81 31.
plume2@wanadoo.fr / www.clairplume.com
10 rooms: 90–165€.

At the base of the château that was so dear to the Marquise de Sévigné, we find a delightful hotel in a 17th-century residence with some colorful rooms and an exquisite tearoom. In it we savor the tea chosen from a rich menu, the soft-centered chocolate cake, the orange or lemon flavored galopin (a small thick pancake), tarte Tatin as well as grilled chicken and salad and the tomato with mozzarella carpaccio. It is simple, charming and very good, for one or several nights.

■ La Maison du Moulin
Rte de Montélimar.
Tel. 04 75 46 56 94 & 06 23 26 23 60.
www.maisondumoulin.com
4 rooms: 75–100€. 1 suite: –145–190€.

Bénédicte and Philippe Apples put their hearts into renovating this charming old water mill. We come here for a few days of peace and quiet, not to mention the food. Salade niçoise, a stuffed tomato served with a tian of roasted vegetables, local cheeses and a strawberry croustil-

lant dessert, accompanied by red, white or *rosé* of the Domaine de Montine, all slip down effortlessly. It's as easy as pie and free as the air. A house that makes us feel happy.

GRIMAUD

83310 Var. Paris 865 – Fréjus 32 – Saint-Tropez 11 – Sainte-Maxime 11 – Toulon 65.
bureau.du.tourisme.grimaud@wanadoo.fr.
This charming old-style village with its terraces, church, chapel, ruined castle and little lanes overlooks the gulf of Saint-Tropez. Miracle of miracles: it has retained its charm.

■ HOTELS-RESTAURANTS

■ Athénopolis
Rte de la Garde-Freinet, quartier Mouretti.
Tel. 04 98 12 66 44. Fax 04 98 12 66 40.
hotel@athenopolis.com
www.athenopolis.com
Closed end Oct.–beg. May.
Rest. closed Wed. (exc. July–Aug.).
20 rooms: 82–125€. A la carte: 35€.

This semi-Grecian, semi-Provençal house with its white facade and blue shutters, swimming pool and bright rooms is a pleasant stopover in the heart of the Massif des Maures. Unpretentious food with all the colors of Provence.

■ La Boulangerie
Rte de Collobrière.
Tel. 04 94 43 23 16. Fax 04 94 43 38 27.
www.hotel-laboulangerie.com
Closed 1 Oct– 1 May.
10 rooms: 106–128€. 1 suite: 200–250€.

This *mas* with a view of the surrounding mountains offers us quiet and comfortable rooms, a tennis court, swimming pool, ping pong, a basketball court and good seasonal food.

■ Le Coteau Fleuri
Pl des Pénitents.
Tel. 04 94 43 20 17. Fax 04 94 43 33 42.
coteaufleuri@wanadoo.fr
www.coteaufleuri.fr

Closed end Oct.–20 Dec.
Rest. closed Mon., Tue., Fri. lunch.
14 rooms: 46–115€.
Prix fixe: 45€, 68€, 15€ (child).
A la carte: 65–75€.

Jean-Claude Paillard concocts tasty and simple dishes while Jacques Minard sings the praises of his eloquent wine list. The dining room is rustic, with an open fireplace and a terrace with a view of the Massif des Maures. The rooms are comfortable and the prices are reasonable, making it a pleasant stopover.

● Les Santons

3, rte Nationale.
Tel. 04 94 43 21 02. Fax 04 94 43 24 92.
lessantons@wanadoo.fr
Closed Wed., Thu. lunch.
Prix fixe: 35€ (lunch, wine inc.), 49€, 79€.
A la carte: 110€.

Far from culinary trends and experiments, Claude Girard pays passionate homage to his region. In this Provençal house with its shining copper utensils, his classics continue to charm our palate with their timeless harmonies. The lobster salad with herb vinaigrette sauce, a house fish stew, veal sweetbreads and truffle jus in croustade and a dark chocolate soufflé meet with unanimous approval, as do the sassy wines selected from all winegrowing regions.

● La Bretonnière   COM

Pl des Pénitents.
Tel.-Fax 04 94 43 25 26.
Closed Sun. dinner, Mon.,
mid-Nov.–mid-Mar.
Prix fixe: 18€, 28€, 35€.
A la carte: 50–55€.

Yves Ducobu always treats fine produce with respect and diligence in this carefully tended establishment. A potato waffle with foie gras, creamy shellfish risotto with a lacy parmesan biscuit, mustard-seasoned cod with walnut oil and lemon potato purée, a poultry charlotte with duck liver pan tossed with ceps, followed by a caramelized apple Breton-

style crêpe all make a good impression. The house is charming with its Louis-Philippe furniture against tones of blue and yellow. The terrace is being renovated. A fine wine list.

● Le Mûrier   COM

Quartier La Boal, D14.
Tel. 04 94 43 34 94. Fax 04 94 43 32 65.
dubourglemurier@wanadoo.fr
Closed Sat. lunch (exc. July–Aug.),
Sun. dinner (off season), Mon. (off season),
Nov., 2 weeks Jan.
Prix fixe: 25€ (lunch), 40€, 60€,
15€ (child).

We quickly succumb to the charm of Jean-Philippe Dubourg's pretty *mas* with its veranda opening out on the flower garden. Old terra cotta tiles, wooden chairs, pastel tones: it feels good to be in Provence. However, the stout Jean-Philippe, who is built like a rugby player, is proud of his origins in the Southwest of France though he continues to work the produce of the Var. A native of Marmande, he trained with Daguin, Guérard and Trama, and reworks the Provençal classics with delicacy. The little dish of cold soup with sweet peas and sorrel, stuffed mushroom macaroni with John Dory, asparagus and morels, squab served with foie gras and a thin-sliced eggplant and anisette cream dish are some of his delightful preparations.

● La Cousteline

Plaine de Grimaud, RD 14.
Tel. 04 94 43 29 47.
Closed lunch (July–Aug.), Sat. lunch (winter),
Tue. (winter), Wed. lunch (winter),
end Nov.–end Jan.
Prix fixe: 33€.

Danièle Poulad, the mother, and Virginie, the daughter, come together to manage this charming house in a verdant setting. We come here for simple country dishes that are lively and well prepared. A mushroom omelet, an ewe's cheese mille-feuille served on a bed of greens, the country terrine, duck confit, the mushroom- and ham-stuffed artichokes simmered in wine, a slow-simmered wild boar stew and the roasted young capon with herbs go down without any fuss. At 18 a bottle, the Domaine de la Sanglière comes in three colors.

GRUISSAN

11430 Aude. Paris 796 – Carcassonne 73 – Narbonne 15 – Perpignan 76.
This resort in the Aude is the "in" beach for the people of Narbonne.

 HOTELS-RESTAURANTS

■ Le Phoebus Casino
At the casino, bd de la Sagne.
Tel. 04 68 49 03 05 (hotel) /
04 68 49 39 02 (rest.). Fax 04 68 49 45 04.
hotel-gruissan@g-partouche.fr
www.phoebus-sa.com
50 rooms: 60–90€.
Prix fixe: 20€, 26€, 39€, 7,50€ (child).

Located in the casino complex, this charming modern hotel has decorated its rooms with themes relating to the South of France and nautical practices. The rooms have been renovated and the cuisine is in the hands of Frédéric Lejeune. The menus are still a bargain and the dishes are tasty though simple. Foie gras terrine with Cartagène jus and raisin marmalade, a traditional omelet with ceps, Noilly vermouth-seasoned scallops, monkfish brochette with sauce inspired by old-style fish stew, a slow-cooked lamb shank served with couscous and raisins and a frozen blackcurrant parfait with cocoa-flavored Genoa cake are not bad. The grill formula is popular around the swimming pool.

GUEBERSCHWIHR

68420 Haut-Rhin. Paris 452 – Colmar 11 – Mulhouse 42 – Strasbourg 86.
An adorable winegrowing village with a vast grand-place, a Romanesque bell tower and old houses open up each year for the Fête de l'Amitié (Feast of Friendship), not to mention the famous slopes (Goldert and Steinert) and the highly reputed Muscat in its cellars.

 HOTELS-RESTAURANTS

■ Relais du Vignoble   ⌘ ⌂
& Belle Vue
33, rue des Forgerons.
Tel. 03 89 49 22 22. Fax 03 89 49 27 82.
relaisduvignoble@wanadoo.fr
www.hotelrelaisduvignoble.com
Closed 1 week Dec., Feb.
Rest. closed Wed. lunch, Thu.
30 rooms: 46–89€.
Prix fixe: 16€, 28,50€. A la carte: 40€.

Situated next to the family cellar, the Roths' recent construction is a choice stopover on the wine route. The contemporary rooms, some with a balcony, promise rest and repose. The domain wines are served in the restaurant and on the terrace overlooking the vineyards and accompany the fine country dishes (pâté in pastry served hot, the fish choucroute, a duckling filet with pepper sauce and the frozen vacherin).

● La Taverne Médiévale   SIM
11, rue Haute.
Tel. 03 89 49 20 79. Fax 03 89 49 28 62.
tavernemedievale@wanadoo.fr
Closed Tue., Wed., 1 week beg. Nov., 3 weeks end Feb.–mid-Mar., 1 week at end June.
Prix fixe: 20€, 35€, 8€ (child).
A la carte: 35€.

In their cheerful rose-colored sandstone tavern Jean-Michel and Sylvie Schmidt serve up food that is rooted in the local region. The proof is in the duck foie gras terrine, the house choucroute, beef filet Ganseliesel (a local specialty) and frozen kouglof, all washed down by local wines.

GUEBWILLER

68500 Haut-Rhin. Paris 475 – Mulhouse 23 – Belfort 51 – Colmar 26 – Strasbourg 104.
ot.guebwiller@wanadoo.fr.
An industrious town, a wine town with small production vineyards, a sunny microclimate and four grands crus: enough to make its reputation, along with the Schlumberger dynasty and its hardy winegrowers far from the beaten track.

HOTELS-RESTAURANTS

■ Château de la Prairie

Allée des Marronniers.
Tel. 03 89 74 28 57. Fax 03 89 74 71 88.
info@chateau-prairie.com
www.chateau-prairie.com
15 rooms: 55–179€. 3 suites: 115–179€.

This 19th-century genteel residence in the heart of its two-hectare grounds offers peace and relaxation in functional rooms and nicely appointed lounges. Cécile and Franco Fancello welcome us with a smile.

■ L'Ange

4, rue de la Gare.
Tel. 03 89 76 22 11. Fax 03 89 76 50 08.
hoteldelange@wanadoo.fr
www.hotel-ange.com
Rest. closed Sat. lunch (exc. by reserv.).
36 rooms: 50–65€.
Prix fixe: 29€, 32€. A la carte: 35€.

Franco Fancello is again at the helm of what used to be a maternity hospital. The rooms are functional and Carl Jacquot's cuisine is carefully crafted. The recipes are true to tradition, with allusions to the South of France. Arugula salad with parmesan, escargots prepared in the style of Alsace (stuffed with spiced butter and herbs and cooked in local wine), pike-perch on a bed of sauerkraut, sea bream in a salt crust, the house tiramisu and the frozen Marc de Gewurztraminer mousse all shimmer gently.

● La Taverne du Vigneron   SIM

7, pl Saint-Léger.
Tel. 03 89 76 81 89. Fax 03 89 74 87 42.
Closed Mon., mid-Jan.–end Jan.
Prix fixe: 8,50€, 17,50€, 19,50€.
A la carte: 30€.

This tavern is true to a cheerful tradition. Vineyard-keeper's salad, a head cheese and aspic terrine, trout poached in Riesling, veal escalope with cream sauce, a frozen kouglof and a slice of apple tart go down pleasantly in a relaxing atmosphere.

In Berrwiller (68500). 9 km s.

● A l'Arbre Vert   COM

96, rue Principale.
Tel. 03 89 76 73 19. Fax 03 89 76 73 68.
www.restaurant-koenig.com
Closed Sun. dinner, Mon., 3 weeks July.
Prix fixe: 20€, 28€, 45€.

A sterling reception, a floral atmosphere, a cuisine that is true to tradition but enriched by contemporary influences; in short, everything is pleasing here. Mathieu, the son, is precise when he prepares breaded veal sweetbreads and green asparagus served in salad, oven-roasted scallops with whole vanilla beans, a roasted squab breast in an herb and pine-nut crust and the strawberry tiramisu with rhubarb sorbet. The wine list, in the hands of Robert, the father, offers carefully chosen bottles where Alsace, naturally, has pride of place.

In Hartmannswiller (68500). 7 km se via D5.

■ Meyer-l'Amphitryon

49, rte de Cernay.
Tel. 03 89 76 73 14. Fax 03 89 76 79 57.
www.hotel-meyer-alsace.com
Closed Sun., 2 weeks Feb.
9 rooms: 47–70€.
Prix fixe: 23€, 7€ (child).

This rustic and (ahead of its time) strictly non-smoking establishment has classic and nicely appointed rooms. Jean Mayer, who trained in the Fer Rouge in Colmar and the Abbesses in Remiremont, serves up regional cuisine that changes with the seasons. Salad with crayfish Florentine served in the cooking dish at the table, the fisherman's plate with an anise-seasoned beurre blanc, the hunter's plate and a pain d'épice crème brûlée all make a good impression.

In Soultz (68360). 3 km via D430.

● Metzgerstuwa   SIM

69, rue du Maréchal-de-Lattre-de-Tassigny.
Tel. 03 89 74 89 77. Fax 03 89 76 14 63.
Closed Sat., Sun., Christmas–New Year's, end June–beg. July.
Prix fixe: 7,50€ (lunch), 22€. A la carte: 30€.

A discreet star of Alsace gastronomy, Gilbert Schluraff—our Charcutier of the Year in 2005—still works wonders in his cheerful and pleasant *winstub*. The charcuterie plate, generously carved pork cuts, variations on the pork trotter, the poached salmon, escalope with cream sauce and the frozen kouglof is healthy, simple and nourishing food. It reveals true know-how and the prices are heaven sent.

GUECELARD

72230 Sarthe. Paris 220 – Le Mans 20 – Château-du-Loir 40 – La Flèche 25 – Le Grand-Lucé 40.
The village, the forest, the river and the national road near Le Mans.

● | RESTAURANTS

● La Botte d'Asperges

49, rue Nationale.
Tel.-Fax 02 43 87 29 61.
Closed Sun. dinner (exc. Bank holidays), Mon., Mar., Aug.
Prix fixe: 16€, 26€, 36€, 48€, 8€ (child). A la carte: 44–65€.

Flowers on the side of a national road? Yes, here. Once we go through the door of this old post house, we are surrounded by paintings and frescoes with floral motifs and we eagerly sit down to the traditional dishes cooked up by Karine using the changing market produce. Lobster salad, sole in papillote and a boneless pigeon with veal sweetbreads and foie gras charm us without any difficulty, as does the chocolate soufflé as a light way to end the meal.

LA GUERINIERE see
NOIRMOUTIER-EN-L'ILE

GUETHARY

64210 Pyrénées-Atlantiques. Paris 780 – Biarritz 9 – Bayonne 19 – Saint-Jean-de-Luz 7.
A beautiful seaside village on the Basque coast with colorful houses and an atmosphere that suggests summer vacations.

■ | HOTELS

■ La Villa Catarie   🏨

415, av du Général-de-Gaulle.
Tel. 05 59 47 59 00. Fax 05 59 47 59 02.
info@villa-catarie.com / www.villa-catarie.com
Closed beg. Nov.–mid-Feb.
13 rooms: 145–180€. 3 suites: 135–250€.

The interior of this 17th-century hotel matches its charming facade. It is carefully decorated with a focus on comfort and its location in the heart of the village is an added attraction.

GUEWENHEIM

68116 Haut-Rhin. Paris 459 – Mulhouse 21 – Altkirch 23 – Belfort 26 – Thann 9.
In the extreme south of Alsace, on the D466 linking the Aspach bridge to Masevaux, a choice stopover, a monument to wine.

● | RESTAURANTS

● Restaurant de la Gare   COM

2, rue Soppe.
Tel. 03 89 82 51 29. Fax 03 89 82 84 62.
restaurant.gare@tv-com.net
Closed Tue. lunch, Wed., Feb. vac., 3 weeks July Aug.
Prix fixe: 27€, 30€, 42€, 65€, 8,50€ (child). A la carte: 55€.

Disregard the facade of this train station restaurant: the wine list is a monument! The Seidel family has run this establishment for four generations and everything they offer is worth a visit. The cuisine: tender scallops, the pressed hen and goose foie gras, roasted Atlantic sea bass, truffle-seasoned pork trotter wrapped in a caul lace bundle and a fruit gratin with an island-style marquise are a testament to Michel's talent as he devotes himself passionately to his cuisine.

GUICHE see URT

GUINGAMP

22200 Côtes-d'Armor. Paris 483 –
Saint-Brieuc 32 – Carhaix-Plouguer 48 –
Lannion 31.
We know this town at the meeting of roads on
the Armor coast for its football team but also
for its Basilica of Notre-Dame de Bon-Secours
and its central square with granite houses.

●	RESTAURANTS

● **La Boissière**

1 km, route Yser.
Tel. 02 96 21 06 35. Fax 02 96 21 13 38.
Closed Sat. lunch, Sun. dinner
(exc. July–Aug.), Mon., Christmas,
2 weeks Mar., 2 weeks beg. July.
Prix fixe: 15,35€ (weekday lunch).
A la carte: 42–54€.

This century-old mansion house decorated in tones of beige with wood furnishings is a good-quality stopover. Thomas Monfort selects market produce to concoct seasonal traditional dishes with a touch of fantasy. A buckwheat flour far (a local flan-like savory dish) with Guéméné chitterling sausage, pike-perch quenelles with white wine, shallots and tomatoes and the quail breast and foie gras in spices with slow-cooked apricots go down effortlessly. For dessert, the chestnut crème brûlée with chocolate sauce makes a good impression.

● **Clos de la Fontaine** Ⓝ SIM

9, rue du Général-de-Gaulle.
Tel. 02 96 21 33 63. Fax 02 96 21 29 78.
Closed Sun. dinner, Mon., Feb. vac.,
2 weeks July.
Prix fixe: 14,50€ (weekday lunch), 22€,
42€. A la carte: 50€.

Stéphane Ollivier uses a little of everything in his classic restaurant with its pleasant terrace-patio. He is present both at the reception and in the kitchen and he serves up sunny dishes with a smile, such things as the turmeric-seasoned scallop salad, a roasted Atlantic sea bass with preserved lemons, duck parmentier with foie gras and slow-cooked spice-seasoned fennel served with vanilla ice cream.

GUJAN-MESTRAS

33470 Gironde. Paris 640 – Bordeaux 56 –
Andernos-les-Bains 26 – Arcachon 10.
Oyster country by the Bassin d'Arcachon.

■ / ●	HOTELS-RESTAURANTS

● **La Guérinière** ○ 🏠

18, cours de Verdun.
Tel. 05 56 66 08 78. Fax 05 56 66 13 39.
lagueriniere@wanadoo.fr
www.lagueriniere.com
Rest. closed Sat. lunch,
Sun. dinner (Oct.–May).
23 rooms: 95–160€. 2 suites: 220€.
Prix fixe: 35€ (Sat., Sun.), 45€ (weekdays
lunch, wine inc.), 60€, 110€, 20€ (child).
A la carte: 70€.

The spacious Japanese-style rooms in this contemporary hotel, located a short distance from the main oyster port in the Bassin d'Arcachon, guarantee us peace, but it is mainly the food that attracts passing tourists and regular customers. Thierry Renou, who trained at the Ferme Saint-Siméon in Honfleur and the Beau Rivage in Gien, cooks up regional produce with imagination. In the modern dining room the oysters simmered in Sauternes, the roasted sturgeon with poached eggs in red wine sauce and eggplant caviar, a rack of lamb roasted with herbs and caramel parfaits with bits of crunchy nougatine meet with no resistance.

● **Les Viviers** SIM

Port de Larros.
Tel. 05 56 66 01 04. Fax 05 57 73 08 26.
melimat@wanadoo.fr
Closed Tue. dinner, Wed., Thu. dinner,
1 week at end Nov., 1 week at end Dec.,
3 weeks Jan.
Prix fixe: 19€, 25€. A la carte: 55€.

Sébastien Maréchal is the prudent manager of this terrace diner. Soup with aïoli, sturgeon in salad with smoked Aquitaine caviar, a monkfish brochette with mussels and oysters, chopped duck breast simmered in Lillet and a large crêpe for dessert are lively dishes at reasonable prices. The à la carte prices are a little steep.

GUNDERSHOFFEN

67110 Bas-Rhin. Paris 464 – Strasbourg 48 – Haguenau 16 – Sarreguemines 62.
The gateway to the northern Vosges, the suburb of Niederbronn where passing visitors stop to admire the half-timbered houses and enjoy the gourmet eateries.

■ / ● HOTELS-RESTAURANTS

■ Le Moulin

7, rue du Moulin.
Tel. 03 88 07 33 30. Fax 03 88 72 83 97.
hotel.le.moulin@wanadoo.fr
www.hotellemoulin.com
Rest. closed Sun. dinner, Mon., Thu.,
1 week Feb., 3 weeks Aug.
10 rooms: 84–210€.
Prix fixe: 42€, 53€, 70€, 90€.
A la carte: 92€.

This renovated old grain mill has ten customized rooms in a chic rustic style that have been adapted to today's tastes by the painter Edgar Mahler. Grounds, a watercourse and a large breakfast buffet. Au Cygne is just 300 meters away.

● Au Cygne

35, Grande-Rue.
Tel. 03 88 72 96 43. Fax 03 88 72 86 47.
sarl.lecygne@wanadoo.fr / www.aucygne.fr
Closed Sun. dinner, Mon., Thu.,
mid-Feb.–beg. Mar., 3 weeks Aug.
Prix fixe: 42€, 53€, 70€, 88€.
A la carte: 95€.

Annie and François Paul have taken a village inn and transformed it into a major eatery in a region that is not lacking in such establishments. The half-timbered blue-ish facade, the warm colorful interior, the paintings by Walch and frescoes by Mahler, the beautiful Annie's charming welcome and the subtle cuisine of François—who trained with Mischler in Lembach—skillfully reworks tradition with refinement, modernity and a deliberate touch of the South but without abandoning the rich region of Alsace. The ham served with schniederspätle (local stuffed dumplings), lobster salad with crunchy vegetables seasoned with citrus zest, roasted John Dory with artichokes and sundried tomatoes, ginger-seasoned langouste tails, the rack and tenderloin of lamb with curry-seasoned golden raisin sauce, roasted thick-cut pork tenderloin with pine nuts, olive oil and basil, as well as the chocolate dessert platter and the Quetsches plum beignets with spice ice cream, are wonders of their kind. The wine list is full of delicious temptation, the menus are reasonable and the charming nearby mill is worth visiting.

● Le Soufflet `COM`

13, rue de la Gare.
Tel.-Fax 03 88 72 91 20.
lesoufflet@free.fr
www.lesoufflet.free.fr
Closed Sat. lunch, Mon. dinner, Wed. dinner.
Prix fixe: 26€, 54€. A la carte: 50–55€.

Facing the station and the town hall, Franck and Armande Chateauroux have opted for a dual vocation: serious and finely wrought cuisine in a stylish dining area and country cuisine in the *winstub* (Bahnstubel). Foie gras served three ways, pan-tossed jumbo shrimp, an orange roughy in cream sauce, ostrich filet, variations on the theme of wild woodruff and a frozen lime parfait are very good indeed.

HAGENTHAL-LE-BAS

68220 Haut-Rhin. Paris 480 – Mulhouse 40
– Altkirch 27 – Colmar 74 – Bâle 12.
One of the keys to the Sundgau region and a discreet gateway to Switzerland amidst the greenery of the orchards.

 HOTELS-RESTAURANTS

● Jenny

84, rue de Hegenheim.
Tel. 03 89 68 50 09. Fax 03 89 68 58 64.
reception@hotel-jenny.fr / www.hotel-jenny.fr
Rest. closed Sun., Christmas, end July–beg. Aug.
26 rooms: 60–140€.
Prix fixe: 13,50€, 26€ (lunch), 39€,
50€, 58€, 10€ (child).

Stay at Jenny's. You won't be disappointed by the bright, well-kept and functional rooms or by the extra attractions—a heated swimming pool, terrace, private lounge, two conference rooms, Internet, WiFi —nor by Monique Koehl's winning smile or Emmanuel Lambelin's vegetarian or gastronomic cuisine. He has worked with Westermann and is the ex-chef of the nearby Ancienne Forge. Not a vegetarian? In that case, go for the Landes duck foie gras prepared in house with pepper and fleur de sel, pan-seared Atlantic sea bass with mild spices served in a lovage-seasoned shellfish bouillon, venison medallions in a flavorful red wine sauce with crushed shallots with creamy cep polenta and a mango clafoutis with coconut and ginger ice cream; all are full of vigor.

HAGENTHAL-LE-HAUT

68220 Haut-Rhin. Paris 481 – Mulhouse 36
– Altkirch 27 – Colmar 73 – Bâle 12.
Still in verdant Sundgau and the county gateway to Switzerland.

● RESTAURANTS

● A l'Ancienne Forge   COM

52, rue Principale.
Tel. 03 89 68 56 10. Fax 03 89 68 17 38.
baumannyves/a-lancienne-forge.html
Closed Mon. lunch, Tue., Wed. lunch.
Prix fixe: 28€, 38€, 48€. A la carte: 40€.

The Baumanns made a judicious resolution to lower their prices and to offer every day a fixed-price menu and an à la carte menu with wine served by the glass. They also returned to fundamentals: creamy pumpkin soup, salmon with shrimp sauce, Brazillian beef, in addition to Sylvie Bauman's signature caramel panna cotta, are not to be sniffed at. Yves is attentive in the dining room and we gravitate towards peace in this old forge with its painted beams.

HAGETMAU

40700 Landes. Paris 737 –
Aire-sur-l'Adour 34 – Dax 45 –
Mont-de-Marsan 29 – Orthez 25.
An ideal town from which to visit the Chalosse and the Grandes Landes.

 HOTELS-RESTAURANTS

■ Les Lacs d'Halco

3 km sw via rte de Cazalis.
Tel. 05 58 79 30 79. Fax 05 58 79 36 15.
www.hotel-des-lacs-dhalco.fr
24 rooms: 64–98€.
Prix fixe: 20€ (weekdays), 27€, 50€.

This contemporary house with light and sparsely decorated designer bedrooms offers us the peace of the forest, a view of water and a circular restaurant. The temptation to stay overnight is strong indeed.

■ Le Jambon

245, rue Carnot.
Tel. 05 58 79 32 02. Fax 05 58 79 73 80.
9 rooms: 45–60€.

This peaceful and welcoming house situated in the town has a courtyard garden, a swimming pool, smart functional rooms and a cuisine that reflects the colors of the region.

HAGONDANGE

57300 Moselle. Paris 329 – Metz 19 –
Thionville 15 – Amnéville 7.
This old "iron town" is becoming a genteel and
peaceful provincial town.

 HOTELS-RESTAURANTS

■ Agena

50, rue du 11-Novembre.
Tel. 03 87 70 21 32. Fax 03 87 70 11 48.
reservation@hotel-agena.fr
www.hotel-agena.fr
Closed Sun. dinner.
Rest. closed Sat. lunch, Sun. dinner.
40 rooms: 54–70€.
Prix fixe: 18€ (lunch), 28€, 35€.
A la carte: 50€.

Norbert and Gaëtan Leonhard's peaceful
and relaxing contemporary hotel is located
next to a pond. The reception is warm
and friendly, the rooms are colorful and
Emmanuel Oudert's cuisine in the Restaurant du Lac is creative and based on quality
produce. The foie gras escalope served hot
with honey vinaigrette and the monkfish
and langoustine blanquette with Sauternes
sauce, served with a creamy chanterelle
risotto, are two good examples.

● Méligner   COM

69, rue de la Gare.
Tel. 03 87 71 24 98. Fax 03 87 71 53 21.
Closed Sun. dinner, Wed.
Prix fixe: 23€ (weekdays), 32€, 39€,
10€ (child).

Located across from the station, the San-
drinis' establishment has been renovated
in a tasteful contemporary style. Alexandra extends a warm and friendly welcome and it is a pleasure to savor Frédéric's
carefully prepared dishes. Lobster with
tomatoes, artichokes and spring onions,
mushrooms cooked in goose fat served
with oven-crisped potatoes and a poached
egg, sherry-seasoned sautéed skate and
a tender monkfish medallion wrapped
in bacon and served with a pumpkin
risotto and Noilly vermouth sauce provide an inspired echo of the South. The
slow-roasted pear served with vanilla flan
and salted-butter caramel ice cream is a
nice way to finish off the meal.

HAGUENAU

67500 Bas-Rhin. Paris 480 – Strasbourg 33
– Baden-Baden 42 – Karlsruhe 61.
tourisme.haguenau@wanadoo.fr.
A little Strasbourg with its shopkeepers, talented
pastry chefs, a lively town center and, just on
the edge of town, a view of the large local forest from above.

 HOTELS-RESTAURANTS

■ Les Pins

112, rte de Strasbourg.
Tel. 03 88 93 68 40.
www.hotelrestaurantlespinshagueneau.com
Closed 24 Dec. dinner.
23 rooms: 68€.
Prix fixe: 17,50€ (lunch), 23,50€, 29€,
37€, 50€.

Eric Fuchs is a wine lover (his wine list is a
monument) who takes this curious American-style motel, dating from the sixties,
very seriously. The rooms are carefully
appointed, the rear garden is a pleasure,
the *winstub*-style wood-toned dining
room is welcoming and the cuisine by
Yannick Rosley, formerly of the Coq Hardi
in Verdun, is very good. The house puff
pastry, small herring in an old-style marinade, pike-perch with a meat stuffing, veal
with chanterelles and a frozen Fleur de
Bière-flavored soufflé look good.

■ Europe

15, av du Professeur-René-Leriche.
Tel. 03 88 93 58 11. Fax 03 88 06 05 43.
europe.hotel1@wanadoo.fr
www.europehotel.fr
Rest. closed Sat. lunch.
72 rooms: 48–75€.
Prix fixe: 10€ (weekday lunch), 19€, 35€,
6,50€ (child). A la carte: 40€.

Freddy Naegely and his daughter Sandrine gracefully manage this recent

construction that is a bit from the center. Two swimming pools (indoors and out), a sauna, a veranda dining room overlooking the water and functional rooms all set the tone. In the restaurant, salmon carpaccio, pan-fried rouget with lemon tabouli and Aurélien Rust's signature berry soup make a good impression.

● **Le Jardin** `V.COM`
16, rue de la Redoute.
Tel.-Fax 03 88 93 29 39.
Closed Tue., Wed., Nov. 1 vac., Feb. vac., end July–beg. Aug.
Prix fixe: 17€ (weekday lunch), 18,50€, 29€, 34,50€, 46€.

The Jardin does not have a terrace but it does have a fine dining room with a caisson ceiling, colorful frescoes and nicely appointed tables. It immediately charms us with its painted facade and rich stained glass in the vestibule. The chadurée (an Atlantic version of bouillabaisse, this version seasoned with saffron), shrimp tartare served with guacamole and grilled Atlantic sea bass with a tropically inspired sauce prove that Damien Meyer, who trained with Mischler in Lembach, knows what he is doing when preparing fresh fish with art and originality. He serves up generous portions and then offers choice desserts: a rhubarb crème brûlée, praline-flavored frozen nougat and a strawberry pastilla. The service by his gracious wife lends charm and vibrancy to the house.

● **L'Essentiel** `SIM`
2, pl du Marché-aux-Bestiaux.
Tel. 03 88 73 39 47. Fax 03 88 73 29 48.
rlessentiel@wanadoo.fr
Closed Sat. lunch, Sun., Mon. dinner.
Prix fixe: 12€–13,50€ (lunch), 29–35€ (dinner).

The essential here is the red and brown décor, the atmosphere of a Parisian bistro and especially the seductive cuisine. Pierre Weller (La Source des Sens in Morsbronn) and his brother-in-law Laurent Ritter have succeeded in creating a style with eclectic influences and with the help of

their chef Alexandre Rubler. The produce is of good quality and the preparations nicely inspired: a salad with smoked duck breast and foie gras, grilled tuna with olive oil and peppers, quick-seared veal kidney with mustard sauce and strawberries in their jus served with white chocolate ice cream. An interesting wine list includes some Spanish vintages.

● **Chez Monique** `SIM`
13, rue Meyer.
Tel. 03 88 93 30 90.
www.buerehiesel.com
Closed Sun., Mon., Bank holidays, 2 weeks beg. Sept., 1 week Christmas–New Year's, 1 week at end May.
A la carte: 35€.

Monique Baumann knows how to receive us in her *winstub* next to the theater. We enjoy her good, family cooking that is typical of the region—things like the tourte, the braised pork shank served with Munster cheese sauce, the choucroute and the warm mirabelle plum gratin. Her many regular customers enjoy the friendly atmosphere and the service fit for a king. The prices toe the line.

In Marienthal (67500). 6 km s via D48.
● **Epices et Sens** `V.COM`
1, rue du Rothbach.
Tel. 03 88 93 43 48. Fax 03 88 93 40 35.
contact@epicesetsens.com
www.epicesetsens.com
Closed Sun. dinner, Mon., 3 weeks Sept., 2 weeks Mar.
Prix fixe: 32€, 42€, 48€. A la carte: 60€.

René Fieger, who trained with Mischler in Lembach, Outhier in La Napoule and also in Canada and Shanghai is a traveling chef who offers us a sophisticated Franco-Asian cuisine with its eyes "on the horizon". We are not sure that the baroque setting of this stopover near a hermitage suits the experimental dishes he prepares with gusto: a slice of head cheese and aspic terrine served "New Wave style" with foie gras ice cream and arugula, the jumbo shrimp with soba (Japanese buckwheat noodles), glazed duck served with vegetable spring rolls or the grilled thick-cut Iberian pork tenderloin served with a corn flan. The berry panna cotta is slightly gelatinous, but the melon simmered in Pineau is freshness itself.

In Niederschaeffolsheim (67500). 6 km s via N63.

■ Au Boeuf Rouge

39, rue du Général-de-Gaulle.
Tel. 03 88 73 81 00. Fax 03 88 73 89 71.
www.boeufrouge.com
Closed 2 weeks Feb. Rest. closed Sun. dinner, Mon., Tue. dinner, 3 weeks July.
13 rooms: 64–68€.
Prix fixe: 25,50€ (weekday lunch), 34€, 47€, 57€, 68€, 10€ (child).
A la carte: 65€.

Since 1880, generations of Gollas have succeeded each other at this good inn. François, the latest in the line, is in charge of the kitchen and trained with Loiseau in Saulieu and Savoy in Paris. He is very good at playing with the produce of both land and sea. Foie gras served three ways, langoustines with vermicelli, pan-sizzled truffle-seasoned turbot and potatoes and meat layered in puff pastry look good. The game is well prepared in season and the pineapple refreshed with mint, served with piña colada sorbet, is an extremely cool way to finish off. Anne Golla recommends the great wines in the cellar.

In Oberhoffen-sur-Moder (67240). 7 km ne via D29.

● Au Cerf

2, rue Principale.
Tel. 03 88 63 22 64. Fax 03 88 53 88 94.
Closed Sun. dinner, Mon., Thu. dinner, end Jan.–beg. Feb., 3 weeks Aug.
Prix fixe: 10,80€ (lunch), 22,50€, 29,50€, 43,50€.

The Dorns have created a warm atmosphere in this cozy traditional establishment. The à la carte menu is generosity itself, offering us carefully prepared gastronomic dishes at moderate prices. The business menu offers (for 29,50) shrimp and monkfish with Middle Eastern seasonings in puff pastry or foie gras served two ways, pike-perch with a crayfish coulis or duck breast with ceps and a mirabelle plum vacherin or a berry soup served with crème brûlée. Marie-José smiles as she welcomes us and serves while Francis concocts the generous cuisine. The wine list is a mine of good things. The overall impression is one of simplicity and authenticity and wins our affection.

HAMBACH see **SARREGUEMINES**

HAMEAU-DANNEVILLE see **SAINT-GERMAIN-DES-VAUX**

HANDSCHUHEIM

67117 Bas-Rhin. Paris 460 – Marlenheim 4 – Strasbourg 17 – Saverne 23.
A little commune in Kochersberg, not far from Strasbourg on the N4 and much appreciated by lovers of the tarte flambée.

● RESTAURANTS

● L'Espérance

5, rue Principale.
Tel. 03 88 69 00 52. Fax 03 88 69 10 19.
Closed lunch, Mon., Tue., Jan.
A la carte: 25€.

This temple of the tarte flambée offers us one of the most successful of the genre, with a thin and crunchy crust, creamy base and either onions and smoked bacon or mussels with garlic and parsley butter or perhaps Munster cheese or fresh goat cheese. They are cooked up in the wood-fired oven by the constantly moving Michel Schott. Two rooms, one old style with a patina and the other, more modern, in green pastel shades, with marquetry and Spindler engravings, have the charm of a friend's house. In addition, there are little *winstub*-style dishes like ham cooked over hay, served with exquisite grumbeerekiechle (potato cakes), bibeleskäs (garlic-, onion- and chive-seasoned fresh white cheese), and a presskopf (head cheese and aspic terrine).

HARDELOT-PLAGE

62152 Pas-de-Calais. Paris 257 – Calais 55 – Boulogne-sur-Mer 15 – Le Touquet 24.
A beach on the Opal Coast devoted to golf and our English friends.

 HOTELS-RESTAURANTS

■ Hôtel du Parc
111, av François-Ier.
Tel. 03 21 33 22 11. Fax 03 21 83 29 71.
parc.hotel@najeti.com
www.hotelduparc-hardelot.com
81 rooms: 95–140€. 25 suites: 185–250€.
Prix fixe: 27€, 39€, 11€ (child).
A la carte: 60€.

The park, the sauna, the golf club and the heated outdoor swimming pool guarantee pleasant moments of relaxation, as do the vast comfortable bedrooms. In the restaurant, Eric Poing delights his guests with his marbled langoustine terrine with peppers and eggplant, pan-tossed sole with truffle oil, veal tenderloin medallion served Provençal style and the calisson (a regional sugar-coated almond paste specialty), glazed with Grand Marnier.

HARTMANNSWILLER see GUEBWILLER

HASPARREN

64240 Pyrénées-Atlantiques. Paris 783 – Bayonne 24 – Biarritz 34 – Cambo-les-Bains 9.
A Basque village in the Labourd region on the road to Lower Navarre.

 HOTELS-RESTAURANTS

● Hégia
Chemin de Curutcheta, quartier Celhai.
Tel. 05 59 29 67 86.
info@hegia.com / www.hegia.com
5 rooms half board: 480–700€

Don't be fooled: this typically Basque farmhouse dating from the 18th century is an amazing restaurant. The "family" concept of a restaurant is the hip new place

to go, with designer and New Age minimalist décor. The kitchen is in the center, surrounded by the guests attracted by the owners' good food and the unusual welcome. Véronique and Arnaud Daguin, formerly in the Platanes in Biarritz, don't like monotony. Pan-tossed squid with roasted onions, cod with Mendigorria tomatoes, Duplantier's signature poultry roasted and served boneless on Rosevals potatoes and pork belly, in addition to a frozen Ursuya blueberry and citron-seasoned crème, are enchanting. The dishes change according to the seasons and the moods of the chef. No à la carte here, just one menu that we savor and share as if we were at home.

■ Les Tilleuls
1, pl de Verdun.
Tel. 05 59 29 62 20.
hotel.lestilleuls@wanadoo.fr
Closed Sat. (off season), Sun. dinner (exc. long weekends and summer), mid-Feb.–mid-Mar.
10 rooms: 45–52€.
Prix fixe: 15€ (weekdays), 23€, 28€.

This large Basque house offers cheerful rooms, a friendly welcome and no-nonsense regional cuisine.

HAUTE-GOULAINE see NANTES

HAUTELUCE

73620 Savoie. Paris 606 – Albertville 24 – Annecy 62 – Megève 31.
www.lessaisies.com.
With its pretty onion-domed bell towers, Beaufortain is a mountain fit for a postcard.

 HOTELS-RESTAURANTS

■ La Ferme du Chozal
Tel. 04 79 38 18 18. Fax 04 79 38 87 20.
informations@lafermeduchozal.com
www.lafermeduchozal.com
Closed end Oct.–mid-Dec., end Apr.–end May.
Rest. closed Sun. dinner, Mon.,
Tue. (summer).
10 rooms: 120–195€.
Prix fixe: 25€, 35€, 45€.

Anne-Christine and Frédéric Boulanger have tastefully restored this old farmhouse making it into a little paradise with its cozy atmosphere and bright, half Savoy-, half contemporary-style rooms. The young Cyril Suet, who trained with Chapel and in the Chapeau Rouge in Dijon, cooks up a menu that changes every day. Crayfish and leeks presented in a jar, whiting with a fish reduction, pork spareribs with vegetable chips and a passion fruit ravioli make delightful munching. A fine cellar with Alpine wines from around the border (Savoie, the Southern Tyrol, the Valais).

LES HAUTES-RIVIERES

08800 Ardennes. Paris 263 – Charleville-Mézières 22 – Dinant 68 – Sedan 39.
The Ardennes have always been the "land we never reach" described by André Dhôtel. We realize this as we near the end of the world in this pretty valley in Linchamps.

 HOTELS-RESTAURANTS

■ Auberge en Ardenne

15, rue de l'Hôtel-de-Ville.
Tel. 03 24 53 41 93. Fax 03 24 53 60 10.
auberge.ardenne@wanadoo.fr
www.aubergeenardenne.com
Closed Christmas–New Year's vac.
Rest. closed Sat. lunch, Sun. dinner.
14 rooms: 49–55€.
Prix fixe: 23€, 9€ (child). A la carte: 30–35€.

We immediately feel good in André Willaime's inn. The reception is charming, the rooms comfy and cozy and the setting on the banks of the Semoy is heavenly. In fine weather we can have lunch on the terrace with only the river before us. Nicolat Cosenza applies himself diligently in the kitchen preparing Ardenne ham, trout, wild boar sauté and apple vôte (the local crêpe). The prices are very reasonable.

● Les Saisons COM

5, Grand-Rue.
Tel. 03 24 53 40 94. Fax 03 24 54 57 51.

Closed Sun. dinner, Mon., Wed. dinner,
1 week Feb., mid-Aug.–end Aug.
Prix fixe: 18€, 36,50€.
A la carte: 35–45€.

Seasons come and go and Claude Poirson continues on his merry way. He knows his job (he learned in the Auberge de l'Ill) and delights his guests, in the beautiful rustic dining rooms renovated in a luminous apple green, with cassolette of escargots simmered in champagne, scallop salad, trout meunière, monkfish in Pinot Noir sauce, wild duck with peaches and simmered lamb shank. The pleasure of the linger-in-the-mouth dishes is matched only by the reasonable prices.

LE HAVRE

76600 Seine-Maritime. Paris 198 – Amiens 182 – Caen 86 – Lille 292 – Nantes 374 – Rouen 88.
office.du.tourisme.havre@wanadoo.fr.
It was bombed in 1944, then rebuilt in concrete under the iron rule of Auguste Perret. It has been included in the World Heritage List. The city of Dufy and Braque, of Salacrou and René Coty, is a charming stranger in this modern guise. A stretch of beach at Sainte-Adresse, the sea air around the harbor, the quietly impressive restaurants around the charming and comely covered market: obviously enough to attract customers. It must also be said that there are many good stands of all kinds and even a famous bookshop that has a quality tea/coffee house.

■ HOTELS

■ Pasino

Pl Jules Ferry.
Tel. 02 35 26 00 00. Fax 02 35 25 62 18.
www.partouche.com
Open daily.
Rest. Havre des Sens: closed Sun. dinner, Mon.
40 rooms: 120–250€. 5 suites: 170–350€.

The successful neo-fifties design of the unassuming bedrooms with a view of the harbor: a brand new luxury hotel with casino, lounge bar, spa, brasserie (with rather sinister mauve décor), a gastronomic restaurant (Le Havre des Sens) and a snack bar (the Paz) dedicated to the foods of the world with Patrick Picard at the helm.

■ Novotel

Quai Colbert, 20, cours Lafayette.
Tel. 02 35 19 23 23. Fax 02 35 19 33 25.
h5650@accor.com
134 rooms: 105–120€.
10 suites: 120–250€.
Prix fixe: 28€, 8,50€ (child).

This new designer-style Novotel offers us contemporary lines, bright and simple furniture, views of the port and the new Chamber of Commerce. Mickaël Roy, formerly chef at Ciro's in Deauville and at the Passerelle, prepares a cuisine based on nice sea-inspired ideas (a leek and salmon terrine, steamed cod and fines herbes and the Breton shortbread prepared with Isigny butter and seasoned with peppered mango).

■ Le Mercure

Chaussée G.-Pompidou.
Tel. 02 35 19 50 50. Fax 02 35 19 50 99.
h0341@accor.com / www.mercure.com
Closed lunch Sat., Sun. and Bank holidays.
92 rooms: 99–117€. 4 suites: 115–135€.
Prix fixe: 15€, 18€, 7,50€ (child).

Right on the Bassin du Commerce, a very practical hotel with a conference center, functional rooms and carefully prepared cuisine.

■ Vent d'Ouest

4, rue de Caligny.
Tel. 02 35 42 50 69. Fax 02 35 42 58 00.
contact@ventdouest.fr / www.ventdouest.fr
38 rooms: 88–135€.

This charming hotel makes a pleasant stopover with designer wood furniture in the bedrooms and a warmly welcoming library/lounge. To complete the picture, the excellent breakfasts enable us to start out on the right foot to discover the surroundings or to face a day's work.

■ Art Hôtel

147, rue Louis-Brindeau.
Tel. 02 35 22 69 44. Fax 02 35 42 09 27.
arthotel@free.fr / www.bestwestern.fr/arthotel
31 rooms: 79–105€.

Ideally situated just a short distance from the Bassin du Commerce and surrounded by a few good restaurants, this hotel can also pride itself on very comfortable rooms and a cozy lounge.

■ Le Marly

121, rue de Paris.
Tel. 02 35 41 72 48. Fax 02 35 21 50 45.
contact@hotellemarly.com
www.hotellemarly.com
37 rooms: 71–97€.

This seventies hotel with its well-kept rooms, classic and functional furniture and pastel shades is a practical stopover for a stay in the center.

■ Les Voiles

3, pl G.-Clemenceau.
Tel. 02 35 54 68 90. Fax 02 35 54 68 91.
voilesaccueil@wanadoo.fr
www.lapetiterade.com
16 rooms: 90–149€.
Prix fixe: 22€, 39€, 42€,
16€ (weekday lunch). A la carte: 33–47€.

The Hôtel des Bains has hoisted its sails and changed its crew. Renovated in a marine style with lots of color, it is sure to please. Some of the rooms have balconies overlooking the sea. The Petite Rade serves up good fare in the form of a shrimp brochette, rouget served over a chorizo mousse, poultry breast with lingonberries and a seasonal fruit dacquoise.

● | RESTAURANTS

● La Villa du Havre

66, bd Albert-Ier / 1, rue G.-de Maupassant.
Tel. 02 35 54 78 80. Fax 02 35 54 78 81.
info@lavilladuhavre.com
www.villaduhavre.com
Closed Sun., Mon., 2 weeks Jan.,
mid-July–beg. Aug.

Prix fixe: 29€ (weekday lunch, wine inc.),
39€, 84€, 12€ (child). A la carte: 120€.

Madness of this caliber is usually picked up and locked up. Jean-Luc Tartarin, a native of Caen, was maestro in the Folie du Bois des Fontaines in Forges-les-Eaux after learning his trade with Gill in Rouen and Boyer in Reims. He is now installed in Armand Salacrou's old 1890s villa on the seafront with its high ceilings, stucco work, contemporary décor, amusing paintings, art deco furniture and efficient service. His wife, the lovely Annabelle, runs the show with feeling and dignity. He innovates furiously, presenting the produce of the moment and the season but has a tendency to take his guests for laboratory guinea pigs. He is provocative and allusive and conducts stylish exercises using exceptional produce. As a starter, we like his variation of the classic herrings and potatoes in oil (as an emulsion), creamed cauliflower with squid ink and the beef tartare presented with a sardine. Next comes the marvelous judiciously grilled langoustine served with sauce flavored with their shells and an olive oil caramel. The red mullet gets the same treatment with a Campari-flavored sauce, served with fresh escargots, monkfish slowly cooked at a low temperature with sumac powder and napped with an arugala and pine nut sauce and the Salers rib eye steak with lightened béarnaise and a creamy potato gratin served in a Staub cocotte —gourmets land on their feet. It is obvious that Tartarin has a seed of genius mixed in with a dash of madness. We would like to see him more prudent, more restrained. Seeing him in this genteel residence by the edge of the sea, we conclude that he has the finest restaurant in a range of 200 km around Paris. His desserts (the mille-feuille, soufflé, themes and variations on the season's fruits and chocolate) are worth a nod. With him, Le Havre finally has an establishment with a future that is worthy of its past.

● **Wab**   **N·COM**

33, rue d'Iena.
Tel. 02 35 53 03 91.

Closed Sat. lunch, Sun., Mon. dinner,
3 weeks Aug.
Prix fixe: 17€ (lunch).

Omar Abo-Dib, owner of the *domaine* Saint Clair at Etretat, has transformed this old port warehouse into a fashionable, good-quality restaurant. In a predominantly red setting we savor Olivier Da Silva's cunningly wrought dishes: fried salt cod cakes (acras de morue), pan-tossed mushrooms served with a poached egg, pollock with cabbage and bacon and the nice grilled sirloin served with fried potato wedges. The place has cachet and the desserts have punch (a spéculos cinnamon cookie–flavored milk shake). The wines are well chosen.

● **Le Zgorthiote**   **N·COM**

110, rue Jules-Siegfried.
Tel. 02 35 43 34 97.
Closed Sat. lunch, Sun.
Prix fixe: 13€ (lunch).

For the last fifteen years Ayman Al Choubli has been the gourmet ambassador of the land of the cedar tree across from the Palais de Justice. In this colorful and carefully appointed setting with tables nicely laid with red and white tablecloths we enjoy the various mezze (hummus, tabouli, falafel, spiced sausage called makanek, moutabbal), kibbe, chwarma, chich tabouk (lemon-seasoned chicken on skewers) and baklava.

● **L'Odyssée**   **COM**

41, rue du Général-Faidherbe.
Tel.-Fax 02 35 21 32 42.
Closed Sat. lunch, Sun. dinner, Mon.,
Feb. vac., 3 weeks Aug.
Prix fixe: 22€, 28€, 38€. A la carte: 55–60€.

The nearby fishing port provides Pierre Hebert with most of the fresh produce for his cuisine. The rest is in the technique. Worth savoring: marinated salmon with whipped fresh white cheese, langoustine tempura, roasted turbot, beef sirloin with morels and the Vergoise sugar cookie with apples or the almond cream berry dessert.

● **La Petite Auberge**   COM

32, rue de Sainte-Adresse.
Tel. 02 35 46 27 32. Fax 02 35 48 26 15.
Closed Sun. dinner, Mon., Wed. lunch,
1 week Feb. vac., 3 weeks Aug.
Prix fixe: 20,50€ (weekdays), 28€, 40€.
A la carte: 60€.

True to his reputation as a faithful defender of the culinary heritage of Le Havre, Lionel Douillet receives us in his pastel green contemporary-style restaurant and serves up nice regional dishes such as sole sautéed wih chanterelles, turbot with zucchini spaghetti, veal sweetbreads with wild mushrooms, roasted squab with foie gras sauce followed by a pretty pineapple and vanilla mille-feuille.

● **Le Sorrento**   COM

77, quai de Southampton.
Tel. 02 35 22 55 84. Fax 02 35 41 12 34.
Closed Sat. lunch, Sun.
Prix fixe: 24€, 32€. A la carte: 45€.

Salvatore Vespoli has taken over the establishment that makes people take Le Havre for Sorrento. The arugula salad with shrimp and parmesan, littleneck clam fricassée, Atlantic sea bass baked in a salt crust, veal escalope with lemon sauce and tiramisu awaken the desire to visit Campania.

● **Café des Grands Bassins**   ⓝSIM

23, bd Amiral Mouchez.
Tel. 02 35 55 55 10.
Prix fixe: 14,50€ (lunch).

An amusing makeover: this café we found in the docks area with its red benches, counter and an eternal bistro ambiance. The modest cuisine follows suit. Egg and salmon in aspic, a covered poultry tart, tongue with spicy sauce, sole meunière and the prune charlotte are not to be sniffed at.

● **Le Bistro des Halles**   SIM

7, pl des Halles.
Tel. 02 35 22 50 52. Fax 02 35 22 96 70.
Closed Sun.
Prix fixe: 13,50€ (lunch), 29,90€.
A la carte: 40–50€.

Located on the Place des Halles, this "bistro Lyonnais" is a favorite with the people of Le Havre. Popular for its friendliness, moderate prices and good cuisine, it is never empty. At lunch time and in the evening, it serves bone marrow spread on toast and topped with fleur de sel, grilled cod, beef hanger steak, pain perdu and crème brûlée.

● **L'Entrecôte**   SIM

23, rue Buffon.
Tel. 02 35 25 12 47. Fax 02 35 26 59 84.
restaurant.entrecote@cegetel.net
Closed Sun. (exc. Bank holidays), dinner (exc. weekend), 3 weeks Aug. A la carte: 28€.

Meat lovers are served in L'Entrecôte from 8 a.m. thanks to the proximity of the *abattoirs*. Nobody balks at the tête de veau and tongue with sauce ravigote (a spicy mustard, pickle and caper vinaigrette), the sirloin napped in a wine sauce and served with its bone marrow and the T-bone for three. An apple tart and crème brûlée finish off the meal on a pleasant note.

● **Le Grignot**   SIM

53, rue Racine.
Tel. 02 35 43 62 07. Fax 02 35 21 67 60.
grignot@tiscali.fr / www.legrignot.com
Closed Sun., Bank holidays, 3 weeks Aug.
A la carte: 35–40€.

Ludovic Ferey and Arnaud Samson cultivate the retro style with cheerful bric-a-brac across from Niemeyer's volcano. The ambiance quickly warms up and the non-stop bistro cuisine proves to be authentic. An asparagus terrine, poached skate with caper and cream sauce, calf's liver, great sirloin steak and baba au rhum are perfectly executed classics.

● **Le Petit Bouchon**   SIM

42-44, rue Louis-Philippe.
Tel. 02 35 43 22 43.
restaurant-le-petit-bouchon@wanadoo.fr
Closed Sun., Mon., 2 weeks Christmas–New Year's, 3 weeks Aug.
Prix fixe: 23€, 35€, 7,50€ (child).
A la carte: 45€.

Yann Falsarella gave a new lease on life to this contemporary-looking bistro and we are happy to be tempted by the foie gras crème brûlée, the frog legs with garlic, roasted Atlantic sea bass, T-bone steak and blanc manger napped with berry coulis.

● La Petite Brocante   SIM

75, rue Louis-Brindeau.
Tel. 02 35 21 42 20. Fax 02 35 43 26 48.
Closed Sun., 10 days Christmas–New Year's,
1 week beg. May, 3 weeks Aug.
Prix fixe: 13€ (weekday lunch), 25€.
A la carte: 40–45€.

Across from the covered market, we always have a soft spot for this friendly brasserie with its fifties décor. The bistro classics and the choice of little wines are mouthwatering and do not let us down. As we can see with fish terrine, haddock served with beurre blanc, veal kidneys over tagliatelli and chocolate profiteroles.

● La Strasbourgeoise   SIM

90, rue Voltaire.
Tel. 02 35 41 20 84.
Closed Sun. dinner, Mon., 3 weeks Aug.
Prix fixe: 12€ (lunch, wine inc.), 17€, 25€.
A la carte: 35€.

This dyed-in-the-wool *winstub* is located across from the volcano. The lively and cheerful atmosphere, reasonable prices and dishes by its chef-manager, Jean-Luc Meichel from Strasbourg, attract gourmets from all around. An escargot and Riesling fricassée, haddock with beurre blanc served on a bed of sauerkraut and the apple streudel are impeccable, as are the Dolder and Rolly-Gassmann wines.

● Wilson   SIM

98, rue du Président-Wilson.
Tel.-Fax 02 35 41 18 28.
Closed Sun. dinner, Tue. dinner, Wed.,
1 week Easter vac., 2 weeks Aug.
Prix fixe: 16,50€ (weekdays), 23,50€,
33,50€.

Friendliness is the key word in Florence and Luc Lefèvre's establishment. We savor an imaginative and judiciously prepared cuisine in a blue-and-white marine décor. Oven-browned seafood cassolette, cod with tomato butter and basil, chopped duck breast served in blackcurrant sauce and the caramelized apple in puff pastry with cider butter and vanilla ice cream make a good impression.

HEDE

35630 Ille-et-Vilaine. Paris 370 –
Avranches 70 – Dinan 35 –
Dol-de-Bretagne 30 – Rennes 24.
This part of upper Brittany holds marvels in store in the form of the Château de Montmuran and the Iffs church.

●   RESTAURANTS

● La Vieille Auberge   N COM

Rte de Tinténiac, Le Perrau,
At the base of Virages de Hédé.
Tel. 02 99 45 46 25. Fax 02 99 45 51 35.
www.lavieilleauberge35.fr
Closed Sun. dinner, Mon., 3 weeks Feb.,
2 weeks end Aug.–beg. Sept.
Prix fixe: 17€ (weekday lunch), 26€, 35€,
41€, 15€ (child).

The Leffondrés put their hearts into restoring this old 17th-century mill situated by the side of a pond and overlooking a flower garden. On the terrace in summertime and in the country-style dining room, we savor Jean-Marc's carefully prepared local dishes. Grilled langoustine with chili pepper, roasted turbot served with potato slices, veal sweetbreads with morels and the "old boy" baba are faultless.

HEGENHEIM see SAINT-LOUIS

HEILIGENSTEIN

67140 Bas-Rhin. Paris 437 – Strasbourg 38
– Colmar 36 – Barr 3.
One of the little-known capitals of Alsatian wine next to the Vosges Piedmont, this is where we find the rarity that bears the name of the commune: a Klevener, or the old Traminer made from pink Savagnin.

HOTELS-RESTAURANTS

■ Le Relais du Klevener

51, rue Principale.
Tel. 03 88 08 05 98. Fax 03 88 08 40 83.
relaisduklevener@wanadoo.fr
www.alsacelogis.com
Closed Mon., Wed., Thu. lunch,
22 Dec.–mid-Feb.
29 rooms: 42–53€. A la carte: 38€.

Olivier Meckert's inn makes a good impression. We savor game in season, perch filet with mushrooms, beef with chanterelles and an apple tart with almond cream. Rustic bedrooms for a well-deserved rest.

● Le Raisin d'Or

38, rue Principale.
Tel. 03 88 08 95 23. Fax 03 88 08 26 81.
auraisindor@wanadoo.fr
Closed Tue., Wed., Feb. vac.,
2 weeks beg. July.
Prix fixe: 19€, 24€, 27€, 8€ (child).
A la carte: 35€.

Olivier Heyd, who worked at l'Ami Fritz in Ottrott and at Beau Site in the glorious days of the Schreiber brothers, has taken over this roadside *winstub* where he plans to renovate the rustic dining room. For the moment, he delights his guests with a fairly spiced-up local cuisine, as we find with fleichschnacka (a local specialty, pasta stuffed with duck sausage), head cheese and aspic terrine served with crunchy vegetables, pike-perch poached in Riesling, crayfish cassolette with mushrooms and vegetables, a beef roast with Pinot Noir sauce and mushrooms and a frozen kouglof flavored with Marc. We only wish there were more of this prudent classicism around!

64700 Pyrénées-Atlantiques. Paris 804 –
Biarritz 31 – Saint-Jean-de-Luz 15 –
Saint-Sébastien 20.
tourisme.hendaye@wanadoo.fr.
A seaside resort in the Basque country just north of Spain.

 HOTELS-RESTAURANTS

■ Hôtel Serge Blanco

125, bd de la Mer.
Tel. 05 59 51 35 35 / 08 25 00 00 15.
Fax 05 59 51 36 00.
info@thalassoblanco.com
www.thalassoblanco.com
Closed 3 weeks Dec.
90 rooms: 63,50–101€.
Prix fixe: 28€.

Between the beach and the marina, this hotel complex with thalassotherapy treatments is devoted to relaxation. We appreciate the bright contemporary rooms, the cocktails in the bar and the carefully crafted cuisine. Dominique Ochin's cuisine in the modern dining room offers a subtle reinterpretation of regional classics. Landes foie gras cooked in terrine with dried figs and pear and pineapple chutney, the roasted Atlantic sea bass served with a simple Jerusalem artichoke purée and truffle-seasoned gravy, the roasted grain-fed half-pigeon with rosemary-seasoned brochettes served with lentils and bacon make a good impression.

In Biriatou (64700). 4 km se via D258.

● Bakéa

Le Bourg.
Tel. 05 59 20 76 36. Fax 05 59 20 58 21.
contact@bakea.fr / www.bakea.fr
Rest. closed Mon., Tue.
30 rooms: 53–120€.
Prix fixe: 32€, 43€, 63€, 15€ (child).
A la carte: 60€.

The Duvals' inn, garden and peaceful rooms overlook the valley of the Bidassoa. This is where Eric, who trained at the Ritz, finds his inspiration. A native of Normandy, he has completely adopted the Basque culinary traditions as we can see with fresh basil-marinated anchovy lasagne, pan-simmered tuna belly and lemongrass- seasoned vegetables, veal sweetbreads with green asparagus and a fruit mille-feuille. Corinne's smile in the dining room and her precious advice on wines are also worth the stopover.

HENNEBONT

56700 Morbihan. Paris 492 – Lorient 12 –
Vannes 49 – Concarneau 57 – Quimperlé 27.
The bell tower of the basilica of Notre-Dame-de-
Paradis and the nearby citadel of Port-Louis are
not-to-be-missed monuments in this little Breton
town on the banks of the Blavet river.

 | HOTELS-RESTAURANTS

● **Château de Locguénolé**
Rte de Port-Louis.
Tel. 02 97 76 76 76. Fax 02 97 76 82 35.
www.chateau-de-locguenole.com
Closed beg. Jan.–mid-Feb. Rest. closed lunch
(exc.Sun.), Mon. dinner (winter).
27 rooms: 112–289€. 4 suites: 325–405€.
Prix fixe: 42€, 69€, 94€, 26€ (child).
A la carte: 100€.

We find the life of luxury between Vannes
and Lorient in the heart of a 120-hect-
are domain overlooking the coast. In
this fine 18th-century complex the perfectly equipped (sauna, Turkish bath)
old-style rooms offer sweet moments of
relaxation. Jean-Bernard Pautrat's cuisine is equally impressive. He has now
reached the age of maturity, having been
second in command to Marc Meneau at
Vézelay and mentor to Olivier Roellinger
at Gérard Vié's. The refined dishes based
on the best of local produce include an
individual sardine and slow-cooked
pepper terrine seasoned with wild
thyme and lobster medallions in a shellfish crust, under a lemon leaf foam with
spinach risotto. The cooking is precise
and the preparations limpid, as we can
see from the suckling pig riblets glazed
in spices, served with pan-sizzled Chinese cabbage, apples and raisins, seasoned with curry. The veal tenderloin
medallion served with a lemon crumble,
little pineapple chutney-stuffed artichokes and a licorice root-infused jus
is an exquisite delicacy. The little raspberry vanilla waffle, with a kiwi coulis
and ice cream, savored in the light of the
setting sun, is a moment of sheer magic
in this enchanting setting. In addition,
the fine, well-stocked cellar rich with its
many surprises and the full dress service
constitute the ingredients for a wonderful experience orchestrated by the ever-
discreet Bruno de la Sablière.

L'HERBAUDIERE see
NOIRMOUTIER-EN-L'ILE

HERBIGNAC

44110 Loire-Atlantique. Paris 453 – Nantes
77 – La Baule 22 – Saint-Nazaire 29.
The Brière, canals, lime-washed houses,
thatched roofs, all the poetry of this land where
earth and water mingle.

● | RESTAURANTS

● **La Chaumière des Marais** [COM]
Ker Moureau,
6 km s via D774, rte de Guérande.
Tel.-Fax 02 40 91 32 36.
lachaumieredesmarais@wanadoo.fr
Closed Mon. (exc. July–Aug.), Tue.,
mid-Oct.–mid-Nov., Feb. vac.
Prix fixe: 18€, 28€, 38€, 40€.
A la carte: 52€.

Hervé Michels does justice to the local produce in his thatched house that is typical
of the Brière region. Marinated foie gras,
frog legs and chanterelles in Muscadet-
seasoned sauce, the slivered cabbage simmered with wine, shallots, seaweed and
herbs and the squab with rhubarb are
finely crafted. We like the terrace with
the view of the kitchen garden.

HESINGUE see **SAINT-LOUIS**

HEUDICOURT-SOUS-LES-COTES see
SAINT-MIHIEL

HEUGUEVILLE-SUR-SIENNE

50200 Manche. Paris 342 – Avranches 52 –
Cherbourg 80 – Coutances 7 – Saint-Lô 35.
The church at Orval and Coutances cathedral
are two of the region's treasures. Lost between
the hedgerows and the sea, this little village is
worth a stopover.

	RESTAURANTS

● Le Mascaret

3 rue de Bas.
Tel. 02 33 45 86 09. Fax 02 33 07 90 01.
lemascaret@wanadoo.fr
www.restaurant-lemascaret.fr
Closed Sun. dinner, Mon., Wed. dinner,
end Nov.–beg. Dec., 3 weeks Jan.
Prix fixe: 29€, 39€, 67€, 19€ (lunch).
A la carte: 70€.

Nadia and Philippe Hardy watch over one of the most closely kept secrets of the Cotentin region. They have renovated the village presbytery and turned it into a charming establishment and are preparing to move to an old school with a few bedrooms in Blainville-sur-Mer. For the moment we can discover their colorful setting, enthusiastic Nadia's warm welcome and Philippe's modern Norman dishes with a hint of faraway places. Spider crab, leeks and asparagus presented in a champagne flute with a burnet emulsion, squid with a coffee and red wine reduction, turbot, slow-cooked at a low temperature, served with an herb jus and the seven-hour lamb served with ratte potatoes surprise but stay on track. The desserts, all of smoke and music woven, give Nadia an opportunity for a nice exercise in gueridon service. A magical house.

HINSINGEN

67260 Bas-Rhin. Paris 406 – Saint-Avold 35 – Strasbourg 90.
On the edge of the Moselle region, a village with an ambiguous profile. We see hilly Alsace here, but also the simple landscapes and farms of the Lorraine plateau.

●	RESTAURANTS

● La Grange du Paysan   SIM

8, rue Principale.
Tel. 03 88 00 91 83. Fax 03 88 00 93 23.
Closed Mon., 2 weeks winter, Good Friday,
1 week summer.

Prix fixe: 10 € (weekdays), 20€, 25€,, 28€, 32€, 40€.

Everything here—setting, décor, produce, cuisine—derives from peasant traditions. This old farmhouse offers essentially local produce that has been prepared with much finesse. Head cheese and aspic terrine (presskopf), smoked sausage, chitterling sausage, potato sausage and the white veal or blood sausage are happy to have the authentic smokey taste of bygone days. Jean-Luc Rieger cooks as naturally as a bird sings. The regional flat savory tart is a Rolls Royce of its kind, thin and crispy, with its naturally tart cream, its country bacon with a real smokehouse taste: it has a finesse that is rare and, moreover, it is sliced in the dining room and served on to the plate,, which is quite unusual. We don't regret the stuffed pork belly, the tête de veau, the braised ham, the liver quenelles served on a bed of sauerkraut or the cold aspic-glazed raspberries served over hot white chocolate.

HIRTZBACH see **ALTKIRCH**

HOCHFELDEN

67270 Bas-Rhin. Paris 466 – Strasbourg 23 – Saverne 15.
Beer is center stage in a brasserie that is a monument, the frontier with the Hanau region and Kochersberg, the route toward the North of the Vosges: Hochfelden offers all this.

●	RESTAURANTS

● L'Orchidée d'Asie

42, rue du Général-Lebocq.
Tel. 03 88 89 03 03.
Closed Sat. lunch, Mon.
Prix fixe: 31€ (for 2), 44€ (for 2).
A la carte: 25€.

The Trang family and chef Ding accomplish wonders in this roadside Vietnamese restaurant. We have to face the difficult task of choosing between Chinese, Vietnamese and Thai gastronomy and we enjoy stuffed crab claws, cod with spicy pepper or ginger sauce, glazed duck, beef with black mushrooms and the flambéed apple beignets.

HOERDT

67720 Bas-Rhin. Paris 484 – Strasbourg 17 – Haguenau 16 – Molsheim 44 – Saverne 46. This is the land of asparagus, in the Ried region on the banks of the Rhine with its fertile alluvial soil.

● | RESTAURANTS

● A la Charrue

30, rue de la République.
Tel. 03 88 51 31 11. Fax 03 88 51 32 55.
lacharrue@wanadoo.fr / www.lacharrue.fr
Closed Mon., Christmas–New Year's vac.,
3 weeks July.
Prix fixe: 9€ (lunch), 11€, 27€, 35€.
A la carte: 35–45€.

Asparagus has its temple in Fabienne Haegel's half-timbered Alsatian residence with its vast courtyard. We can enjoy the white vegetable in multiple preparations from April 1st to June 15th, after which the menu changes with the seasons. Excellent goose foie gras, head cheese and aspic terrine, pike-perch simmered in wine, veal medallions with wild mushrooms and frozen kouglof with macerated raisins make a nice impression.

HOHRODBERG

68140 Haut-Rhin. Paris 462 – Colmar 27 – Gérardmer 37 – Munster 8.
A nice setting overlooking the Munster valley, its gentle mountain decked with forests and its thatch roofs.

 | HOTELS-RESTAURANTS

■ Le Panorama

3, rte Linge.
Tel. 03 89 77 36 53. Fax 03 89 77 03 93.
www.hotel-panorama-alsace.com
Closed 2 weeks Nov., 24 Dec.,
beg. Jan.–beg. Feb.

30 rooms: 44–71€.
Prix fixe: 16,50€, 19,80€, 26,50€, 37€.
A la carte: 40–50€.

Gilbert Mahler keeps an attentive eye on this establishment with its magnificent panorama overlooking the Munster valley. The modern rooms, heated swimming pool and carefully appointed dining room encourage us to stay overnight. In the restaurant, Arnaud Marschall serves fresh new Munster cheese in puff pastry, roasted pike-perch on a bed of sauerkraut, grilled sandwiches, grilled rib eye steak and a streudel-style apple dessert. The local wines go down without difficulty and the prices are reasonable.

■ Roess

16, rte du Linge.
Tel. 03 89 77 36 00.
www.hotel-roess.fr
25 rooms: 35–62€.
Prix fixe: 19–31€.

This large 19th-century chalet was renovated and enlarged in the sixties and is worth a visit for its friendly family atmosphere, welcoming interior, sumptuous view of the Upper Vosges and its very nice regional cuisine.

LE HOHWALD

67140 Bas-Rhin. Paris 430 – Sélestat 26 – Molsheim 33 – Strasbourg 53.
ot.lehohwald@wanadoo.fr.
A mountain resort in the heart of the fir forests: people come here in winter to go ski touring and all year round for the fresh air.

 | HOTELS-RESTAURANTS

■ Grand Hôtel

16, rue Principale.
Tel. 03 88 08 36 00. Fax 03 88 08 36 01.
resa-hohwald@monalisahotels.com
www.monalisahotels.com
65 rooms: 65–110€. 7 suites: 90–140€.
Prix fixe: 16€, 54€, 7€ (child).
A la carte: 40€.

Samuel Moreau manages this hotel that has been completely renovated in a contemporary designer style. In addition to its unassuming and carefully appointed rooms, this late-19th-century Grand Hotel offers all the usual spa features: a superb indoor swimming pool, sauna, Turkish baths and Jacuzzi. The modern restaurant in shades of beige, green and red serves a foie gras and potato mille-feuille, salmon trout filet, rack of lamb and a thin apple tart accompanied by French wines which may be served by the glass.

■ Le Clos Ermitage

34, rue du Wittertalhof.
Tel. 03 88 08 31 31. Fax 03 88 08 34 99.
info@clos-ermitage.com
www.clos-ermitage.com
19 rooms: 50–60€.
Prix fixe: 16€, 19€.

This fine 19th-century property is ideal for seminars or sports/health getaways. It has twelve conference rooms (two new ones added this year), a spa, two swimming pools (one of them heated), a sauna and a Jacuzzi. The rooms with their pastel shades are comfortable and the menus are light, particularly if we avoid the "chocolate temptation dessert".

■ Villa Mathis

Col du Kreutzweg, 2 km, in Breitenbach (67220)
Tel. 03 90 57 27 00. Fax 03 90 57 27 13.
www.villa-mathis.com
Rest. closed Mon.
Prix fixe: 12€ (lunch, weekdays), 25€.

Catherine Comau, who worked in the dining rooms for Julien at Fouday and in the Strasbourg Hilton, has transformed this thirties residence and its grounds, once the home of a famous automobile manufacturer and then a children's home, into a high-tech vacation resort. The rooms are bright and cheerful, looking out on the mountains, and we enjoy the cuisine in the spirit of the times. A citrus-marinated salmon carpaccio, rabbit terrine with a vinaigrette-seasoned beet and parsley duo, sirloin steak or hanger

steak with mushrooms, veal kidney with mustard sauce and a frozen vacherin hit the spot.

■ La Forestière

10A, chemin du Eck.
Tel. 03 88 08 31 08. Fax 03 88 08 32 96.
http://laforestiere.fr.monsite.wanadoo.fr
Rest. closed lunch
3 rooms: 65–95€. 2 suites: 85–90€.
Prix fixe: 25€, 35€.

Catherine Marchal has put her heart into this new-look guesthouse that reminds us of a lodge in the Vosges. Exotic wood, slate, ceramic decoration and other fine materials have been used in a minimalist and restful style. In the restaurant, which is mainly reserved for guests, the chestnut soup, leg of wild boar and the chocolate brownies served with pan-simmered apricots hit the right spot.

■ Marchal

12, rue du Wittertalhof.
Tel. 03 88 08 31 04. Fax 03 88 08 34 05.
www.reperes.com/marchal
Closed 2 weeks Nov., 2 weeks Jan.
15 rooms: 45–68€. 2 suites: 75€.
Prix fixe: 17,40€, 23,30€, 26,60€.
A la carte: 35€.

Nelly Tastor has renovated this fine mountain inn. Each room is decorated to suggest a country. In the restaurant, Pierre Kazemi blends local produce with faraway flavors as in the pike-perch filet served with cumin- and orange-seasoned carrots, the veal sauté with pomegranate and walnut sauce served with saffron-seasoned rice and the frozen pineapple mousse.

● La Petite Auberge

6, rue Principale.
Tel. 03 88 08 33 05. Fax 03 88 08 34 62.
www.lapetiteauberge-hohwald.com
Closed 1 week Nov., Jan.,
1 week at end June.
Rest. closed Tue. dinner, Wed.
7 rooms: 61€.
Prix fixe: 14,90€, 26,70€.

A little close to the road but charming, this country inn with duplex rooms with terraces is very welcoming. Assisted by his wife in the dining room, Robert Hubrecht concocts a cuisine that remains true to the Alsatian tradition, with smoked trout mousse, pike-perch filet with cream sauce, pork cuts and charcuterie served on a bed of sauerkraut and a generous dessert plate of good quality.

HOHWARTH see VILLE

HOHWILLER see WISSEMBOURG

HONFLEUR

14600 Calvados. Paris 185 – Caen 64 – Le Havre 24 – Lisieux 34 – Rouen 75.
The miracle remains intact: Eugène Boudin's and Alphonse Allais' hometown has remained "untouched" with its half-timbered houses, slate and brick. The roofs in the old town, the lieutenancy in the old harbor, the church of Saint Catherine with its roof in the form of an upside-down hull of a boat: they are all charming, moving and win us over. But there is also the Côte de Grâce, the Val de Seine extending here as far as the estuary, the tortuous little lanes in the upper city, the adorable inns, the fine restaurants and the charming hotels. Just a short distance from Paris by the highway, Honfleur is better than a postcard from the past: a sort of Norman image of time recovered.

■	HOTELS

■ La Ferme Saint-Siméon

Rue Adolphe-Marais.
Tel. 02 31 81 78 00. Fax 02 31 89 48 48.
accueil@fermesaintsimeon.fr
www.fermesaintsimeon.fr
30 rooms: 220–450€. 4 suites: 550–850€.

In the hands of the Boelens the old inn favored by the Impressionists has become a modern Relais & Châteaux establishment. The spa with swimming pool, sauna and Turkish bath do not detract from the charm of this large half-timbered, slate-roofed cottage. (See also Restaurants.)

■ Le Manoir du Butin

Phare du Butin (Butin lighthouse).
Tel. 02 31 81 63 00. Fax 02 31 89 59 23.
accueil@hotel-lemanoir.fr
www.hotel-lemanoir.fr
Closed 2 weeks Nov., 3 weeks Jan.
10 rooms: 120–350€.

Installed in a superb 18th-century half-timbered manor house, the annex to the Ferme Saint Siméon has cozy old-style rooms, a snug lounge with an open fireplace and a dining room where it is pleasant to savor the nicely reworked local cuisine. (See Restaurants.)

■ L'Ecrin

19, rue Eugène-Boudin.
Tel. 02 31 14 43 45. Fax 02 31 89 24 41.
hotel.ecrin@honfleur.com / www.honfleur.com
28 rooms: 95–170€. 2 suites: 200–250€.

This gay and lively 18th-century house just a short distance from the center of town is full of charm with its antique furniture and rooms in the colors of the sea. The sauna, swimming pool and spa add to the pleasure.

■ La Maison de Lucie

44, rue des Capucins.
Tel. 02 31 14 40 40. Fax 02 31 14 40 41.
info@lamaisondelucie.com
www.lamaisondelucie.com
Closed 20 Nov.–mid-Dec.
4 rooms: 125–210€. 2 suites: 285–315€.

The new owners, who run a seafood bistro in the old harbor, have transformed Lucie Delarue-Mardrus' old residence into a contemporary hotel. In Honfleur's historic center, Haddad Daridon now devotes himself to the comfort of his guests in the snug but functional rooms.

■ Les Maisons de Léa

Pl Sainte-Catherine.
Tel. 02 31 14 49 49. Fax 02 31 89 28 61.
www.lesmaisonsdelea.com
27 rooms: 85–295€. 2 suites: 235–275€.

In the most beautiful part of the town, across from the wooden church, each of these four houses evokes a different theme and has exquisite rooms.

■ Castel Albertine 🏨

19, cours A.-Manuel.
Tel. 02 31 98 85 56. Fax 02 31 98 83 18.
info@honfleurhotels.com
www.honfleurhotels.com
Closed Jan.
25 rooms: 75–150€. 1 suite: 150–170€.

Albert Sorel, a native of Honfleur, was once the owner of this splendid manor house dating from the 19th century. It now lodges travelers to the little Norman port town in nicely restored rooms and a pleasant shady veranda.

■ La Diligence 🏨

53, rue de la République.
Tel. 02 31 14 47 47. Fax 02 31 98 83 87.
hotel.diligence@honfleur.com / www.honfleur.com
38 rooms: 85–240€.

Situated close to the Vieux Bassin, the hotel has an exotic air with its Thai portal, decorative objects and Asian canopies. We fancy ourselves on board a yacht sailing for faraway horizons and find ourselves dreaming of traveling in one of the comfortable rooms.

■ Mercure 🏨

4, rue des Vases.
Tel. 02 31 89 50 50. Fax 02 31 89 58 77.
h0986@accor.com / www.mercure.com
56 rooms: 70–109€.

A central location for this chain hotel with good-quality rooms. Opt, however, for those in the rear, which are quieter.

■ La Tour 🏨

3, quai de la Tour.
Tel. 02 31 89 21 22. Fax 02 31 89 53 51.
www.hotelhonfleur.biz
Closed 28 Nov.–27 Dec.
48 rooms: 57–105€.

The slate facade and roof of this seventies building give it a Norman look. It is situated not far from the harbor and the rooms have been renovated in varied colors.

■ Le Cheval Blanc 🏠

2, quai des Passagers.
Tel. 02 31 81 65 00. Fax 02 31 89 52 80.
lecheval.blanc@wanadoo.fr
www.hotel-honfleur.com
Closed Jan.
31 rooms: 70–200€. 2 suites: 325–425€.

Vincent Dubost has redecorated this 15th-century residence, with its fine Norman architecture, in a contemporary style. The rooms are rustic and colorful and most of them overlook the harbor.

■ Le Dauphin 🏠

10, pl Pierre-Berthelot.
Tel. 02 31 89 15 53. Fax 02 31 89 92 06.
info@hoteldudauphin.com
www.hoteldudauphin.com
34 rooms: 69–113€.

In the heart of the old town, a well located hotel with cozy rooms with rattan furniture, some equipped for balneotherapy. Free WiFi.

In Barneville-la-Bertran (14600). 5 km sw via D62 and D279.

■ Auberge de la Source 🏨

Tel. 02 31 89 25 02. Fax 02 31 89 44 40.
Closed mid-Nov.–mid-Feb.
16 rooms: 61–105€.

A pleasant and restful country inn on the edge of a wood with charming little rooms overlooking the flower garden and apple trees.

In Criqueboeuf (14600). 6 km via the coast road.

■ Le Manoir de la Poterie 🏵🏨

Chemin Paul-Ruel.
Tel. 02 31 88 10 40. Fax 02 31 88 10 90.
info@honfleur-hotel.com
www.honfleur-hotel.com
Closed 20 Nov.–20 Dec.,
Christmas–New Year's.
18 rooms: 116–230€.

This vast neo-Norman residence equipped with Turkish baths, heated swimming pool and a new spa overlooks the sea and countryside, as do its Louis XVI and Directoire rooms. The lounge with an open fireplace is an invitation to relax and the gastronomic restaurant offers delicious feasting. (See Restaurants.)

In Vasouy (14600). 3 km via rte du Littoral.

■ La Chaumière
Rte du Littoral.
Tel. 02 31 81 63 20. Fax 02 31 89 59 23.
www.hotel-chaumiere.fr
Closed 2 weeks Nov., 2 weeks Feb.
8 rooms: 150–230€. 1 suite: 450€.

This 17th-century farmhouse is an ideal Relais & Châteaux getaway for those in search of a little peace. The vast grounds overlook the Seine estuary and the cozy rooms are tastefully furnished. (See Restaurants.)

■ Le Romantica
Chemin du Petit-Paris.
Tel. 02 31 81 14 00. Fax 02 31 81 54 78.
www.romantica-honfleur.com
25 rooms: 60–70€. 10 suites: 120€.
Prix fixe: 25€, 35€, 11€ (child).
A la carte: 35–40€.

Although half-timbered, this welcoming house with a view of the sea is a recent construction. It offers rest and comfort in neo-rustic rooms and simple family cuisine (chitterling sausage with cream and apples, duck breast with Morello cherries). Swimming pool and garden.

● | RESTAURANTS

● La Ferme Saint-Siméon
Rue Adolphe-Marais.
Tel. 02 31 81 78 00. Fax 02 31 89 48 48.
accueil@fermesaintsimeon.fr
www.fermesaintsimeon.fr
Closed Tue., Wed. lunch.
Prix fixe: 75€ (weekday lunch, wine inc.), 90€ (lunch), 125€ (dinner), 20€ (child).
A la carte: 117–137€.

Would Eugène Boudin and his painter friends still recognize their historic residence? It has been modernized in the hands of the Boelens and the cuisine, by

Patrick Ogheard, an Auvergne native who formerly labored under Alain Ducasse in Monaco, has adapted to today's tastes. It now leans more toward the Mediterranean than toward the Norman coast but it has many fine points: langoustines with a vegetable pizzetta, crayfish and frog legs in herb soup, Atlantic sea bass and shellfish with white beans, milk-fed veal with ceps and Breton salt marsh lamb with chard and black truffles. The service is both precise and professional. The wine list has many great Bordeaux at a variety of different prices. The desserts based on theme of raspberries or chocolate make a good impression. And the collection of house Calvados is a monument. We are inclined to forget the prices …

● L'Absinthe
10, quai de la Quarantaine / 1, rue de la Ville.
Tel. 02 31 89 23 23. Fax 02 31 89 53 60.
antoine.ceffrey@wanadoo.fr
www.absinthe.fr
Closed mid-Nov.–mid-Dec.
6 rooms: 105–135€. 1 suite: 225€.
Prix fixe: 31€, 52€, 62€.
A la carte: 90–95€.

Antoine Ceffrey is the attentive father watching over this residence dating from the 15th and 17th centuries. Xavier Bertrand concocts a cuisine that is both very contemporary and nevertheless true to its roots. The 31 menu is a bargain and the à la carte menu is full of temptation. Pan-seared escalope of foie gras, sole meunière in a cep crust, squab (first roasted and then finished in wine sauce and served with a grapefruit sabayon) make a good impression. Some nice rooms in an annex.

● Le Butin de la Mer
Phare du Butin (Butin lighthouse).
Tel. 02 31 81 63 00. Fax 02 31 89 59 23.
accueil@hotel-lemanoir.fr
www.hotel-lemanoir.fr
Closed Mon. lunch, Wed., Thu.,
2 weeks beg. Nov., 3 weeks Jan.
Prix fixe: 35€, 48€. A la carte: 72€.

This elegant 17th-century house in the undeclared annex of the Boelens of the

Ferme Saint-Siméon introduces us to the subtle and fine cuisine of Yannick Bernouin. Warm langoustine salad, sea bream carpaccio, tuna minestrone, roasted duck filet and seasonal plums in puff pastry make a good impression in a finely appointed rustic yet refined setting.

● SaQuaNa

22, pl Hamelin
Tel. 02 31 89 40 80
www.alexandre-bourdas.com
saquana@alexandre-bourdas.com
Closed lunch (exc. Sat., Sun.), Thu.
Prix fixe: 40€, 60€.

Alexandre Bourdas created the sensation of the year when he opened this unassuming restaurant last year. Formerly with Guérard, Marcon and Bras, for whom he ran a restaurant in Toya, Japan, his fusion cuisine is finely tuned and subtle. His large "Green Olive" fixed-price menu is a faithful reflection of this. Lime-seasoned poached lobster with celery and coriander served in a clear coconut and combava oil bouillon, pan-seared scallops with a mild Cévennes onion borscht with a foamy grilled shrimp jus, a pan-sizzled Atlantic sea bass (curiously encrusted in duck cracklings, its jus incorporated with walnut oil), the roasted squab breast and pepper-seasoned peach, espresso crème and bulgur in arugula jus, the rolled pear biscuit with ginger caramel sorbet, a praline and hot hazelnut-infused milk. This succession of off-beat flavors is accompanied by choice wines. The most unusual experience that Normandy has to offer for the moment.

● La Terrasse et l'Assiette   ◎COM

8, pl Sainte-Catherine.
Tel. 02 31 89 31 33. Fax 02 31 89 90 17.
Closed Mon., Tue. (exc. July–Aug.),
10 days beg. Jan.
Prix fixe: 28€, 49€. A la carte: 85€.

The sign tells all, or almost all. Across from the church of Saint Catherine, the Bonnefoys' terrace is an open invitation. The dishes are equally attractive. Gérard, whom we know from Carentan, derives considerable satisfaction from reworking local produce with his own light touch. Between the brick walls and half-timbered walls of the dining room, the oysters in a vinegar-seasoned tomato sauce with spring onions, the cod with Vire chitterling sausage served with lemon-seasoned potatoes in white sauce, the veal sweetbreads with cabbage and bacon accompanied by fresh sweet peas, and the frozen Calvados soufflé served with a crunchy almond cookie make up an à la carte menu that is rich in color and flavor. Anne-Marie Bonnefoy's warm and friendly smile is an added attraction, as is the fine wine list.

● Le Bréard   ⌂■COM

7, rue du Puits.
Tel. 02 31 89 53 40. Fax 02 31 88 60 37.
lebreard@wanadoo.fr
Closed Tue. lunch, Wed. (exc. July–Aug.),
Thu. lunch, 2 weeks beg. Dec.,
3 days at Christmas.
Prix fixe: 25€, 32€, 18€ (weekday lunch).
A la carte: 60€.

Fabrice Sébire, a native of Honfleur who worked in L'Absinthe and with Gérard Bonnefoy before going to the "great Parisians" (Tour d'Argent, Véfour, Lucas Carton), has made a discreet return to the Norman countryside. In an updated and modernized setting with a heated and covered patio, he offers us fine and carefully crafted dishes with a distinctive presentation. Slow-cooked rabbit terrine, tuna served three ways, pan-seared sea bream and the cod seasoned with ras el-hanout are cunningly crafted. A light apple croustillant with manzanilla with mint-infused green tea jelly is a light and exotic way of returning to Normandy.

● Entre Terre et Mer

12-14, pl Hamelin.
Tel. 02 31 89 70 60. Fax 02 31 89 40 55.
info@entreterreetmer-honfleur.com
www.entreterreetmer-honfleur.com
Closed Wed., 20 Jan.–beg. Feb.
Prix fixe: 19€ (lunch), 49€.
A la carte: 60€.

As the name indicates, this restaurant, with its two rustic dining rooms extending to a terrace, serves up local food from land and sea. In the kitchen, Stéphane Lévesque, who did a stint at Le Grand Véfour, with Troisgros and at L'Absinthe, skillfully elaborates pressed foie gras flavored with vanilla in an individual terrine, wild turbot in a pork trotter crust, rabbit medallion with herbs and a crunchy chocolate bonbon.

● Auberge du Vieux Clocher   `COM`

9, rue de l'Homme-de-Bois.
Tel. 02 31 89 12 06. Fax 02 31 89 44 75.
Closed Tue., Wed., 3 weeks Jan.,
1 week at end June.
Prix fixe: 20€, 25€. A la carte: 50€.

Here we find the whole picturesque aspect of the Sainte-Catherine district. The little pastel-colored dining rooms and the fine collection of old plates sets the tone. Monique's smiling welcome and Serge Pérou's cuisine do the rest. Duck foie gras with a fig compote, pan-roasted cod, tender poultry with Calvados-seasoned cream sauce and the Reinette apple gratin with Calvados-flavored milk caramel are a true pleasure.

● Champlain   `COM`

6, pl Hamelin.
Tel. 02 31 89 14 91. Fax 02 31 89 91 84.
Closed Thu., Fri., beg. Jan.–10 Feb.
Prix fixe: 16,50€, 27€. A la carte: 40€.

The newly refurbished facade and the new terrace furniture give us an even greater appreciation for this discreet address. Christophe Bouvachon, formerly with Blanc in Vonnas, Gleize in Château-Arnoux and Bourdin at the Connaught, presents prudent, simple and reasonably priced regional dishes that always please. Pan-tossed langoustine tails and foie gras served in salad, local fish stew, chopped poultry in cream sauce and the spiced apple terrine are deliciously generous.

● La Fleur de Sel   `COM`

17, rue Haute.
Tel.-Fax 02 31 89 01 92.
www.restaurantshonfleur.com
Closed Tue. (exc. Bank holidays), Wed. (exc.

Bank holidays), Jan., 1 week at end June.
Prix fixe: 25€, 35€, 40€, 12€ (child).

This old fisherman's bistro refurbished by Vincent Guyon, formerly of the Ferme Saint-Siméon and the Assiette Gourmande, offers dishes that blend tradition and modernity. Duck foie gras with ginger marmalade, tuna carpaccio with a mango and passion fruit marinade and the cod filet served with green Puy lentils with a hazelnut oil and coconut milk sauce are chic and exotic. The winter fruit crumble with caramel ice cream takes us straight back to childhood.

● Au Vieux Honfleur   `COM`

13, quai Saint-Etienne.
Tel. 02 31 89 15 31. Fax 02 31 89 92 04.
Closed Christmas.
Prix fixe: 29€, 49,50€. A la carte: 58€.

The first floor, terrace and ground floor afford an unbeatable view of the Vieux Bassin. There is a friendly welcome and Jean-Pierre Villey's cuisine is designed to please us. We willingly sit down to mussels in cream sauce, sole meunière, duck in cider sauce and the Calvados-flambéed warm apple tart.

● L'Ancrage   `SIM`

12, rue de Montpensier.
Tel. 02 31 89 00 70. Fax 02 31 89 92 78.
Closed Tue. dinner (exc. July–Aug.),
Wed. (exc. July–Aug.), 2 weeks Mar.
Prix fixe: 15€, 17€, 20€, 32€,
8€ (child). A la carte: 35€.

You don't have far to go from the Bassin to drop your anchor in this friendly family bistro with its well-made regional dishes. Mussels in cream sauce with shallots and garlic, cod with farmer's cream, rib eye steak with slow-cooked caramelized shallots and the citrus terrine with honey jelly are not to be sniffed at. Reasonable prices.

● Ascot   `SIM`

76, quai Sainte-Catherine.
Tel. 02 31 98 87 91. Fax 02 31 89 38 72.
Closed Wed. (off season), Thu. (off season),

beg. Jan.–beg. Feb.
Prix fixe: 22,50€, 28,50€.
A la carte: 45€.

Whether on the terrace overlooking the Vieux Bassin or in the dining room with its retro charm and minimalist décor, we praise Claude Le Roux's nice knack. A scallop carpaccio, grilled Atlantic sea bass with virgin olive oil, the house chicken dish, frozen nougat and the lemon tart are all good quality.

● **Les Boucaniers** `SIM`

35, rue Haute.
Tel. 02 31 88 25 64. Fax 02 31 89 01 92.
Closed Tue., Wed., 3 weeks Jan.
Prix fixe: 17,90€, 23€, 8€ (child).
A la carte: 38€.

Jérôme Vaussy is following in the tracks of his brother-in-law, Vincent Guyon, who is enjoying the fruits of the success of La Fleur de Sel. The Boucaniers also give the lion's share to sea produce and more generally to local produce: Camembert in puff pastry with Calvados caramel, mussels in pastry with celery-infused cream and a grilled Atlantic sea bass. The slow-cooked apples served in a cider mousseline is a nice Norman way to finish off the meal.

● **La Grenouille** `SIM`

16, quai de la Quarantaine.
Tel. 02 31 89 04 24. Fax 02 31 89 53 60.
reservation@absinthe.fr / www.absinthe.fr
Closed mid-Nov.–mid-Dec.
Prix fixe: 16€, 24€. A la carte: 35–45€.

Corinne Ceffrey, whose husband Antoine runs L'Absinthe, is perfectly happy in this Parisian-style bistro. A scallop carpaccio, curry-seasoned salmon crumble with Chinese cabbage, sole meunière with steamed potatoes, the house-prepared tripe and fruit salad are the delights of the day.

● **L'Hippocampe** `SIM`

44-46, quai Sainte-Catherine.
Tel.-Fax 02 31 89 98 36.
Closed Wed. (off season), 3 weeks Dec.,
2 weeks Jan.
Prix fixe: 21,30€, 29,80€. A la carte: 40€.

Philippe Crochard has made this waterfront bistro into a place for gourmets. Fish and langoustine cassolette, pretty oysters, jumbo shrimp brochette, tripe slow simmered in tomato and onions and chocolate profiteroles go down effortlessly.

● **Au P'tit Mareyeur** `SIM`

4, rue Haute.
Tel. 02 31 98 84 23. Fax 02 31 89 99 32.
www.auptitmareyeur.com
Closed Mon., Tue., 1 week at end Nov., Jan.,
1 week at end June.
Prix fixe: 21€, 43€.

In a typically Norman setting of stone, wooden beams and half-timbered walls, Julien Domin offers us a contemporary cuisine based on Norman classics. Comfortably settled on favric-covered chairs, we set about discovering the changing fixed-price and à la carte menus. Escargots and Vire chitterling sausage with oyster mushrooms, steamed skate ballotine served on a bed of pan-tossed sauerkraut with basil-infused cream sauce and plaice in foamy butter with slow-cooked onion and garlic-seasoned peppers make a good impression. Pretty apple and milk caramel tart "graced with fleur de sel".

In Criqueboeuf (14600). 6 km via the coast road.

● **Manoir de la Poterie** `COM`

Chemin Paul-Ruel.
Tel. 02 31 88 10 40. Fax 02 31 88 10 90.
www.manoirdelapoterie.com
Closed lunch, Mon., Thu., Christmas,
1 week beg. Jan.
Prix fixe: 32€, 65€, 46€.

The neo-Louis XVI-style room looks out at the sea from the heart of this modern Norman manor house and Olivier Davoust's dishes are in harmony. Triple-X Norman duck foie gras cooked in sea salt, strips of red mullet with chard ravioli and the hot apple soufflé are very well made.

In Pennedepie (14600). 5 km via rte de Trouville.

● **Le Moulin Saint-Georges** `SIM`

Tel. 02 31 81 48 48.
Closed Tue. dinner, Wed., mid-Feb.–mid-Mar.

Prix fixe: 15€, 24€, 8€ (child).
A la carte: 35€.

The least we can say is that the entrance to this restaurant is original: you first have to go through the roadside bar-tabac, then through the kitchen where you can admire the coal stove where Patrick Lelièvre prepares family-style dishes the way we like them. Duckling terrine, John Dory with sorrel, pepper-seasoned steak and poached meringue in custard sauce please us without ruining us.

In Vasouy (14600). 3 km via rte du Littoral.

● **La Chaumière**
Rte du Littoral.
Tel. 02 31 81 63 20. Fax 02 31 89 59 23.
www.chaumiere-honfleur.com
Closed Tue., Wed. lunch, Thu. lunch,
2 weeks Nov., 2 weeks Feb.
Prix fixe: 40€, 60€.

This charming 17th-century cottage facing the sea with its grounds extending all the way to the estuary is the annex to the Ferme Saint-Siméon, an enchanting place dedicated to a cuisine that is light and precise. In the hands of Mickaël Lelièvre, a native of Alençon who has worked at Pré Catelan and Rochevillaine, criss-crossed strips of Atlantic sea bass and artichokes, hot seared foie gras with apple vinaigrette, roasted lobster in its shell with asparagus, roasted veal with vegetables and the pain perdu with salted-butter caramel ice cream are amazing.

HORBOURG-WIHR see COLMAR

HOSSEGOR

40150 Landes. Paris 756 –
Biarritz 29 – Mont-de-Marsan 91 –
Bordeaux 177 – Dax 38.
hossegor.tourisme@wanadoo.fr.
The Les Landes resort par excellence with its lake, windy beach, blond sand and pine trees, an eternal profile that never changes whatever the period.

■/● HOTELS-RESTAURANTS

■ **Les Hortensias du Lac**
Av du Tour-du-Lac.
Tel. 05 58 43 99 00. Fax 05 58 43 42 81.
www.hortensias-du-lac.com
Closed beg. Nov.–1 Apr.
19 rooms: 155–225€. 5 suites: 225–375€.

We are sure to relax and unwind in this thirties building on the banks of the sea-water lake. Stress disappears quickly when we settle into the contemporary bedrooms and duplexes with balconies and terraces or relax in the lounge with its panoramic view or by the side of the swimming pool.

■ **Lac'otel**
Av du Touring-Club-de-France.
Tel. 05 58 43 93 50. Fax 05 58 43 49 49.
lacotel@wanadoo.fr / www.lacotel.fr
Rest. closed Sun. dinner (off season),
Mon. (off season), mid-Dec.–mid-Jan.
42 rooms: 59–96€. 4 suites: 59–96€.
Prix fixe: 12€ (lunch, wine inc.),
19€ (lunch), 48€ (dinner) 10€ (child).
A la carte: 38–50€.

The hotel takes its name from the sea-water lake next to it where surfers and water-lovers enjoy themselves. Surrounded by pines, we settle into one of the bright, colorful finely appointed rooms for an invigorating stay by the ocean. Unadventurous cuisine in the Marée Bleue restaurant: grilled lobster with crayfish butter, squab (roasted and then finished in wine sauce) and brioche pain perdu with caramelized pears.

■ **Le Pavillon Bleu**
1053, av du Touring-Club-de-France.
Tel. 05 58 41 99 50. Fax 05 58 41 99 59.
pavillon.bleu@wanadoo.fr
www.pavillonbleu.fr
Rest. closed Mon., Christmas–mid-Jan.
21 rooms: 70–135€. 6 suites: 86–151€.
Prix fixe: 21€, 31€. A la carte: 65€.

Teddy and Jenny Bretelle run a modern hotel facing the lake where a charming welcome and the cuisine of the prudent Philippe Béraud, based on local produce, awaits us in the large bright dining area. The brother and sister team look after their guests tactfully and there are no complaints about the langoustines in cream sauce with sweet peas and ricotta, the monkfish in cocotte, the cod with asparagus and lamb presented in a pastoral composition.

■ Hôtel de la Plage

94, place des Landais.
Tel. 05 58 41 76 41. Fax 05 58 41 76 54.
www.hoteldelaplage.net
Closed 3 weeks Nov., 2 weeks beg. Jan.
12 rooms: 57–113€.

This hotel facing the sea merits its name and offers us the comfort of renovated rooms with balconies, completely new showers and a terrace where we can cool off in summer. A small unpretentious restaurant.

● La Tetrade

1187, av du Touring Club de France.
Tel. 05 58 43 51 48.
Prix fixe: 19€, 26€, 98€ (for 2).

The Carlier brothers, Laurent the chef and Olivier the maitre d' – who run the Tetrade in Cap Breton—have rejuvenated and added a chic touch to the Huîtrières du Lac while also giving it a new name and an impressive new look. The unassuming and minimalist décor with shades of yellow, beige and brown, the terrace giving onto the lake and the fresh and simple dishes adapted to today's tastes, though free of frills: that's what we like about it. Fashionable folk from Bordeaux and Toulouse come here to relax and rub elbows with each other at reasonable prices. Crab gazpacho, mariscada (a Spanish shellfish stew), parillada, grilled mixed seafood, wild turbot with creamy rice and mushrooms and Spanish-style grilled sea bream, served from a gueridon trolley, make a good impression.

In Saint-Vincent-de-Tyrosse (40230). 7 km e via D33.

● Le Hittau

1, rue du Nouaou.
Tel. 05 58 77 11 85. Fax 05 58 77 19 61.
duccanya@aol.com

Closed Tue., Wed., 2 weeks Oct., Feb. vac., 1 week at end June.
Prix fixe: 32€, 42€, 45€, 65€, 12€ (child).

The Ducs, whom we know from the Tourasse in Jean-de-Luz, have done a charming job of rehabilitating this magical sheepfold surrounded by a flower garden. Nathalie has a charming welcome for us while Yannick in the kitchen implements the lessons he learned with Caule in Mimizan, Darroze at Langon and in the Cannes Carlton. We delight in the vegetable cannelloni with lobster, mixed salad with rouget and stuffed squid, an individual terrine of leeks in a mosaic of foie gras, the Thai-style cod stew and the pan-cooked pigeon with wine-enriched jus. The chocolate "conversation" is a delight and the Bordeaux are reasonably priced.

LA HOUBE see DABO

78550 Yvelines. Paris 61 – Chartres 45 – Dreux 20 – Mantes-la-Jolie 28 – Versailles 41.
The land of black-headed poultry with white rings around the neck has many charming establishments worth visting.

 HOTELS-RESTAURANTS

● La Poularde de Houdan

24, av de la République.
Tel. 01 30 59 60 50. Fax 01 30 59 79 71.
contact@alapoularde.com
www.alapoularde.com
Closed Sun. dinner, Mon., Tue.,
1 week Nov. 1, 1 week Feb.
Prix fixe: 22€ (weekday lunch), 33€ (weekday lunch), 35€, 47€, 15€ (child).

His father taught him to appreciate food, then he studied with Delaveyne and Guérard. Now Sylvain Vandenameele extols the generous cuisine of bygone days. Before tasting the meat, we can observe the hens he raises as they scatter about in the garden of this genteel residence. Ravioli with lobster and shellfish sauce with hellishly hot sauce, roasted sea bream with a sea-food tuile, breast of local young hen with wild mushrooms, tête de veau with tongue and brain and the champagne peach soup make a good impression. A rich cellar.

In Berchères-sur-Vesgre (28560). 7 km nw via D933.

■ Château de Berchères
18, rue du Château.
Tel. 02 37 82 28 22. Fax 02 37 82 28 23.
chateau-de-bercheres@wanadoo.fr
http://www.chateaudebercheres.com
19 rooms: 130–215€. 3 suites: 255€.

Vast grounds, a magnificent 18th-century château built by a disciple of Ledoux, amusing interior décor on theme of fruit and vegetables and charming rooms: this is what awaits us in Lina Sicard's charming Château. Don't miss the breakfast.

L'HOUMEAU see LA ROCHELLE
HUNINGUE see SAINT-LOUIS
HURIGNY see MACON

68420 Haut-Rhin. Paris 482 – Colmar 9 – Eguisheim 3 – Guebwiller 22.
The highest village in the vineyard (380 meters), the proximity of the Vosges, tours of the ruined château and neighboring Eguisheim: We almost forgot to admire the winegrowers' signs.

 HOTELS-RESTAURANTS

■ Husseren-les-Châteaux
Rue du Schlossberg.
Tel. 03 89 49 22 93. Fax 03 89 49 24 84.
www.hotel-husseren-les-chateaux.com
Closed 10 days Jan.
37 rooms: 113–135€. 1 suite: 230€.
Prix fixe: 21€ (lunch), 28,50€, 39€, 53€.
A la carte: 55€.

Perched on a hill in the midst of trees this contemporary hotel offers us an unbeatable view of the valley of the Rhine. After exercising in the swimming pool, a round of tennis or a sauna in the spa, we deserve a break in one of the Scandinavian-style duplex bedrooms. In the restaurant, Christophe Loche elaborates a classically aristocratic cuisine such as the duck foie gras escalope with berries, Cognac-flambéed jumbo shrimp, beef filet medallions with Port-enriched morel sauce and the crème brûlée trilogy.

83400 Var. Paris 858 – Toulon 20 – Aix-en-Provence 101 – Cannes 122.
ot.hyeres@libertysurf.fr.
Hyères is well worth a visit, and not just for its islands and airport: the Château des Aires, the chapel of Notre-Dame-de-Consolation with its esplanade, the Place Saint-Paul with its belvedere, the view of the Parc Saint-Bernard and the house of the Vicountess of Nouailles designed by Mallet-Stevens are all attractions in this charming stopover.

 HOTELS-RESTAURANTS

■ Mercure
19, av Ambroise-Thomas.
Tel. 04 94 65 03 04. Fax 04 94 35 58 20.
h1055@accor.com / www.mercure.com
84 rooms: 85–185€.
Prix fixe: 12€ (weekday lunch), 14€, 28,50€. A la carte: 36€.

This chain hotel run by Olivier Herphelin has been renovated in an unassuming style. It is situated in the heart of the business district and is easily accessed from the freeway. Comfortable, well-insulated rooms, a terrace, valet car parking service, conference rooms, swimming pool, Internet, WiFi. In the white dining room with marine décor we savor Michel Best's dishes served up by Frédéric Navalon: fish soup, scallop and monkfish duo with cream sauce, duck breast in honey and the soft-centered chocolate cake go down well.

■ Hôtel Bor
3, allée E.-Gérard, in Hyères Les Palmiers.
Tel. 04 94 58 02 73. Fax 04 94 58 06 16.
contact@hotel-bor.com / www.hotel-bor.com
20 rooms: 100–150€. 2 suites: 250€.

This hotel with an enviable location—it is practically on the beach—offers rooms in a contemporary spirit.

■ Hôtel du Soleil

Rue du Rempart.
Tel. 04 94 65 16 26. Fax 04 94 35 46 00.
soleil@hotel-du-soleil.fr / www.hoteldusoleil.fr
22 rooms: 30–92€.

In the upper part of the old city this establishment of character proves to be a pleasant hotel with impeccably kept rooms.

■ Ibis Thalassa

Allée de la Mer, à la Capte.
Tel. 04 94 58 00 94. Fax 04 94 58 09 35.
h1559@accor-hotels.com / www.thalassa.com
Closed 3 weeks Jan.
95 rooms: 60–128€.

Between the harbor and Etang des Pesquiers a chain hotel with thalassotherapy thrown in. The rooms have all modern comforts and the diet cuisine is good quality. A heated sea water swimming pool.

● La Colombe   V.COM

663, route de Toulon.
La Bayorre, 2,5 km via rte de Toulon.
Tel. 04 94 35 35 16. Fax 04 94 35 37 68.
www.restaurantlacolombe.com
Closed Sat. lunch, Sun. dinner, Mon.
Prix fixe: 27€, 35€. A la carte: 65€.

Nadège and Pascal Bonamy run a cheerful neo-Provençal restaurant at the foot of the Massif des Maurettes. The colors are warm, like the cuisine, which looks southward for its flavors. Fresh spider crab with ratatouille, shrimp with pistachio vinaigrette, John Dory with chanterelles, baked crab and lobster, veal sweetbread escalope seasoned with verbena and the chocolate temptation dessert make a good impression.

● Les Jardins de Bacchus   COM

32, av Gambetta.
Tel. 04 94 65 77 63. Fax 04 94 65 71 19.
santionijeanclaude@wanadoo.fr
www.les-jardins-de-bacchus.com
Closed Sat. lunch, Sun. dinner, Mon.

Prix fixe: 33€, 43€, 55€, 11€ (child).
A la carte: 70€.

We may look askance at the slightly kitsch décor presenting Bacchus and his gardens in the frescoes decorating the walls of the atrium-like dining room. However, we have to raise our hats to Jean-Claude Santioni who delights his guests with scallops with leeks, Mediterranean sea bass served over peppers and onions, monkfish medallions with Middle Eastern spices, stuffed pigeon with grated potato cake and pear. The fig crumble with a sorbet made from calissons, the local sugar-coated almond paste specialty, makes a choice way to end the meal.

● Le Bistro de Marius   SIM

1, pl Massillon.
Tel. 04 94 35 88 38.
bistro demarius@free.fr
Closed Mon. (exc. Bank holidays), Tue. (exc. Bank holidays), mid-Nov.–beg. Dec.
Prix fixe: 17€, 26€, 32€.

This old bistro situated on the square in the old city offers quality cuisine concocted from changing products at the local markets. We are easily pleased by the citrus-seasoned rouget in salad, royal sea bream, the duck breast with chestnut honey and the frozen nougat.

● Chez Lucas   SIM

3, rue des Porches.
Tel.-Fax 04 94 35 86 22.
Closed Sun. (exc. July–Aug.),
Mon. (exc. July–Aug.), 2 weeks end Nov.,
10 days at end Dec.–beg. Jan.,
10 days beg. Feb.
A la carte: 35€.

You have to be lucky to find a seat at this little restaurant, especially because reservations are not accepted, but once we succeed, we are happy to savor the pizzas and soccas (chickpea flour cake, a local specialty), the minced chicken on toast and the roasted purple figs.

IGE

71960 Saône-et-Loire. Paris 398 –
Mâcon 14 – Cluny 13 – Tournus 41.
The gently rolling hills of the Mâcon region
with their vineyards with châteaux, abbeys and
old villages nestling among them!

 HOTELS-RESTAURANTS

■ Château d'Igé

Rue du Château.
Tel. 03 85 33 33 99. Fax 03 85 33 41 41.
ige@chateauxhotels.com
www.chateaudige.com
Closed beg. Dec.–end Feb.
Rest. closed lunch (exc. weekends).
8 rooms: 95–150€. 8 suites: 177–210€.
Prix fixe: 35€, 49€, 56€, 13€ (child).
A la carte: 70€.

Dating from 1235, this Mâcon château run
by Françoise Leury-Germond on the wine
route works its charm on us. The rooms
with their old-style furniture and Olivier
Pons' neoclassical cuisine have no difficulty in putting their spell on us. Under the
veranda with its terrace extending into the
garden, we are easily tempted by crab and
herring caviar with with cabbage, bacon
and avocados, the roasted jumbo shrimp
in olive oil, a sirloin steak with mushroom
cannelloni and the Grand Marnier soufflé served hot.

ILE-AUX-MOINES

56780 Morbihan. Paris 474 – Vannes 14 –
Auray 15 – Quiberon 46.
Whether we come from Conleau or Port-Navalo,
we always find something new in this part of the
Morbihan. Rediscover this little paradise!

● RESTAURANTS

● Les Embruns   SIM

Rue du Commerce.
Tel. 02 97 26 30 86. Fax 02 97 26 31 94.
Closed Wed., 2 weeks beg. Oct., Jan. Feb.
Prix fixe: 18€, 25€, 8€ (child).
A la carte: 35€.

This bar/restaurant run by the Le Mauff
family offers good quality classic dishes.
House fish soup, crayfish, tarragon-seasoned monkfish brochette, beef with
béarnaise sauce and house profiteroles
at reasonable prices.

ILE-DE-BREHAT

22870 Côtes-d'Armor. Access from la pointe
de l'Arcouest (02 96 20 00 11),
Saint-Quay-Portrieux, Binic or Erquy.
syndicatinitiative.brehat@wanadoo.fr.
This pearl in the Côtes d'Armor department
just a short distance from Paimpol and the
Pointe de l'Arcouest demands that we make a
little effort: we have to get about on foot.

 HOTELS-RESTAURANTS

■ Hôtel Bellevue

Port-Clos.
Tel. 02 96 20 00 05. Fax 02 96 20 06 06.
Closed 11 Nov.–20 Dec., beg. Jan.–mid-Feb.
17 rooms: 87–127€.
Prix fixe: 24,60€, 36€.

Functional rooms and the fish dishes
served in the panoramic dining room
satisfy us in the form of scallop carpaccio, Atlantic sea bass with pickled seaweed and grilled lobster, accompanied
by reasonably priced wines. A renovation in 2007.

■ La Vieille Auberge

Au Bourg.
Tel. 02 96 20 00 24. Fax 02 96 20 05 12.
www.bretagnehebergement.com
Closed Nov.–Easter.
14 rooms: 71–101€.
Prix fixe: 17€, 20€, 40€, 8€ (child).
A la carte: 33€.

The peace and quiet, functional rooms,
dining room decorated with fishing nets,
flowering courtyard and the reliable seafood cuisine make for a pleasant stay in
this old corsair hideout converted into
a pleasant stopover by Jacqueline and
Nathalie Lamidon.

ILLHAEUSERN

68970 Haut-Rhin. Paris 439 – Sélestat 13 –
Colmar 17 – Strasbourg 60.
The most famous village in Alsace? In terms of
food, definitely. The houses were rebuilt after
the last war, as was the bridge over the Ill. The
tall church dates from 1957 and the stork has
returned to its nest.

 HOTELS-RESTAURANTS

■ Hôtel des Berges

4, rue des Collonges.
Tel. 03 89 71 87 87. Fax 03 89 71 87 88.
hotel-des-berges@wanadoo.fr
www.hoteldesberges.com
Closed Feb., Mon., Tue.
7 rooms: 252–287€. 6 suites: 342–497€.

The hotel annex to the Auberge de l'Ill
charms us discreetly with its garden. On
the banks of the river, and laid out like
a tobacco barn with a charming fisherman's hut, the residence has very finely
appointed rooms and suites with wood
furnishings. Breakfast is a real meal.

■ La Clairière

50, rte d'Illhaeusern.
Tel. 03 89 71 80 80. Fax 03 89 71 86 22.
hotel.la.clairière@wanadoo.fr
www.hotel-la-clairiere.com
Closed Jan., Feb.
25 rooms: 78–202€. 2 suites: 240–260€.

Located next to the Forêt de l'Ill, this con-
temporary-styled Alsatian residence has
a heated swimming pool and a tennis
court. Peace and quiet are guaranteed.

■ Les Hirondelles

In the village.
Tel. 03 89 71 83 76. Fax 03 89 71 86 40.
hotelleshirondelles@wanadoo.fr
www.hotelleshirondelles.com
Closed 1 week at end Dec.,
beg. Feb.–20 Mar.
19 rooms: 62–80€.

Comfort and rustic authenticity are what
give this old village farmhouse its charm.

The open-air swimming pool is an added
attraction in fine weather. WiFi.

● L'Auberge de l'Ill

Rue de Collonges-au-Mont-d'Or.
Tel. 03 89 71 89 00. Fax 03 89 71 82 83.
aubergedelill@auberge-de-l-ill.com
www.auberge-de-l-ill.com
Closed Mon., Tue., 1 Jan.–8 Jan.,
Feb.–beg. Mar.

A fine setting, high-class service, great
cuisine, an extensive wine list, a warm
welcome and an atmosphere to match it:
few establishments have all these assets
together. The Haeberlins do, plus one
more: the natural comeliness of a unique
house anchored in its surroundings, proud
of its roots and bringing together a well-
bonded team (Michel Scheer, the master
of the house, has been here for more than
thirty years!). Ranging from Paul, who is
over eighty years old and who extends a
welcome and is in the kitchen every morning; to Jean-Pierre, who is elegance itself;
to Danièle, who looks after guests in the
dining room and in the garden; to the
mother Marie, who comes round at the end
of the meal to make sure that everything
was just perfect; and of course Marc, the
prodigy, son and chef who orchestrates
more than twenty chefs. We conclude that
this house is the manifestation of a family
commitment. The Haeberlins don't work,
they share a unique experience, as do their
guests who anticipate their stay well in
advance. They know that joy will come
from the encounter with this unique place,
the discovery of a new dish (the creamy
Thai herb and shrimp soup garnished with
a coconut emulsion) or from rediscover-
ing an eternal classic (the famous salmon
soufflé, the royal lobster Prince Wladimir
with a bisque sauce), a wine discovered by
accident among the immense listings or
recommended by Serge Dubs, the exceptional *sommelier* who long ago won the
title of best in the world in his category. A
unique establishment? We were just about
to say that. The other day, watching the
majestic course of the Ill river, there was
something fairy-tale-like about the bridge,
the bank and all the flowers, the play of

light and shade in the garden. There were the little toasts with foie gras, the little flat savory tarte flambée, with thick cream, the cool Muscat de Josmeyer à Wintzenheim. Then in an unassuming mother-of-pearl dining room with bay windows giving onto the exterior, walls lit up by Muhl's canvases, these unique moments were punctuated with splendid dishes: the terrine, served as an *amuse-gueule*, with the house-prepared sardines that are marinated, punctuated with a few grains of caviar and placed on a mound of ratte potato. Sublime in a rustic-yet-refined register, the tripe in a salad with broad beans and goose foie gras and, already a classic in the same mode, the pike-perch filet with a fine red wine sauce and fried eel with herb sauce; mouthwatering Atlantic sea bass and tomato-stuffed cannelloni, pesto and Jabugo ham—exotic and so fresh. The masterpiece disguised as a main dish: a reworking of a Rhône-Alps classic, the poached and truffled Miéral à Montrevel signature Bresse poultry with small stuffed cabbages, and the thighs cooked again with spring vegetables in truffle vinaigrette. Or the venison filet with a dried fruit compote, wild mushrooms and soft fromage blanc knepfles (similar to quenelles). On top of that, the desserts are always a sensation here because of our nostalgia for childhood (home-style frozen vacherin, an oven-baked crêpe with sour cherries served with Tahitian vanilla ice cream, the house ice creams). We wash it all down with a kirsch by Windholtz in Ribeauvillé, telling ourselves that we have not had a unique meal, a sublime experience but rather that we have quite "simply" lived through something completely exceptional.

● **A la Truite**   `SIM`

17, rue du 25-Janvier.
Tel. 03 89 71 83 51. Fax 03 89 71 88 15.
Closed Tue. dinner, Wed.,
3 weeks mid-Feb.–beg. Mar.
Prix fixe: 18€, 26€, 39€. A la carte: 35–45€.

Jean Louis and Christophe Poujol form a twosome to cook up dishes that are reasonably priced and are anchored in the local region, as witnessed by head cheese and aspic terrine (prepared in house), the fish stew made by Marie-Louise, the fried carp filets, the capon simmered in Riesling and the frozen kouglof (also prepared in house), all served in the warm and friendly atmosphere of an inn with a pleasant terrace on the banks of the river bordered with willow trees.

ILLKIRCH-GRAFFENSTADEN see **STRASBOURG**
ILLZACH-MODENHEIM see **MULHOUSE**
IMBSHEIM see **BOUXWILLER**

INGERSHEIM

68040 Haut-Rhin. Paris 443 – Colmar 4 – Turckheim 3.
This suburb of Colmar with its high-quality winegrowers and gourmet artisans is the starting point for hikes through the Vosges.

●	RESTAURANTS

● **Taverne Alsacienne**

99, rue de la République.
Tel. 03 89 27 08 41. Fax 03 89 80 89 75.
tavernealsacien@aol.com
Closed Sun. dinner, Mon., Thu. dinner,
1 week Jan., 1 week at end July,
2 weeks beg. Aug.
Prix fixe: 11€ (lunch), 15€ (lunch), 18€, 53€.

Jean-Philippe Guggenbuhl runs the family tavern with an expert hand. The cuisine is based on local produce: foie gras with mango and passion fruit coulis, braised pike-perch with truffle-seasoned vegetable purée, the beef in Alsatian Pinot Noir sauce and the raspberry croustillant dessert delight us. A nice wine list with the comments of Béatrice Groell.

INGOUVILLE-SUR-MER see **SAINT-VALERY-EN-CAUX**

INGWILLER

67340 Bas-Rhin. Paris 469 – Haguenau 25 – Sarre-Union 39 – Saverne 23 – Strasbourg 45.
tourisme@pays-de-hanau.com.

This town, a crossroads in the Northern Vosges with its famous onion-domed synagogue and old houses, is at the heart of a fine region that seems to have emerged from one of Hansi's dreams.

 HOTELS-RESTAURANTS

■ **Aux Comtes de Hanau**
139, rue du Général-de-Gaulle.
Tel. 03 88 89 42 27. Fax 03 88 89 51 18.
www.aux-comtes-de-hanau.com
Rest. closed Mon. dinner, Wed. dinner,
Feb. vac.
11 rooms: 38,50–71,50€.
Prix fixe: 10€, 50€, 9,50€ (child).
A la carte: 25–35€.

Since 1848 the Futterer family has welcomed guests to this inn situated at a corner on the road to the Northern Vosges. The rooms are clean and tidy. In the kitchen Louis Futterer cooks up traditional dishes that are served in the three dining rooms. The house-prepared head cheese and aspic terrine, the seafood pizza, enormous oven-roasted pork shank, delicately sautéed veal kidneys and a rum-raisin frozen kouglof are not to be sniffed at.

INXENT see MONTREUIL

95290 Val-d'Oise. Paris 41 – Compiègne 66 – Chantilly 24 – Pontoise 13.
A handsome forest town on the banks of the Oise with memories of painters from bygone centuries.

● **RESTAURANTS**

● **Le Gai Rivage** COM
11, rue Conti.
Tel. 01 34 69 01 09.
Closed Sun. dinner, Mon., Tue. dinner,
1 week Christmas–New Year's, 1 week Aug.,
1 week beg. Sept.
Prix fixe: 34€. A la carte: 35–50€.

This inn, with its terrace and large windows on the banks of the Oise river, makes a pleasant break. Marie-Odile Ménier extends a warm and friendly welcome while Eddy Vernier cooks up good-quality classics. We like the scrambled eggs with morels, the John Dory with asparagus, the duck confit with local apple biscuits and the seasonal fruit tarts.

86150 Vienne. Paris 374 – Confolens 30 – Niort 105 – Poitiers 55.
The gentle green stretches of the Poitou region and the peaceful valley of the Vienne.

 HOTELS-RESTAURANTS

■ **Val de Vienne**
In Port de Salles, 7 km.
Tel. 05 49 48 27 27. Fax 05 49 48 47 47.
www.hotel-valdevienne.com
Closed Christmas, New Year's.
20 rooms: 65–78€. 2 suites: 110–130€.
Half board: 81–162€.

Situated in the middle of the countryside and on the banks of the Vienne river, Emmanuelle Prat's hotel offers simple modern comforts. Practical rooms, a terrace, a heated swimming pool, a lounge/bar on the veranda make for a very pleasant stay.

84800 Vaucluse. Paris 696 – Avignon 23 – Apt 34 – Carpentras 17 – Cavaillon 11.
officetourisme.islesur-sorgue@wanadoo.fr.
"I was ten. The Sorgue enshrined me". The little town in the Vaucluse in the interlacing of its canals still remembers René Char although the antique dealers have snatched some of its local glory from the poet of Les Busclats.

 HOTELS-RESTAURANTS

■ **Mas de Cure-Bourse**
Carrefour de Velorgues, 120 chemin serre.
Tel. 04 90 38 16 58. Fax 04 90 38 52 31.
www.masdecurebourse.com
Rest. closed Mon., Tue. lunch (exc. Bank holi-

days), 3 weeks Nov., 2 weeks Jan.
13 rooms: 85–215€.
Prix fixe: 30€. A la carte: 50€.

Orchards surround the rooms deco-rated with Souleiado fabrics and Francky Schlosser's sunny cuisine. This 18th-century *mas* run by Nadine Pomarede is a fervent celebration of Provence, as we can see with the asparagus risotto with slices of parmesan, the Provençal-style cod, the veal scallops with mushroom- and ham-stuffed artichokes simmered in wine and the soft local goat cheese tart with lemon.

● La Prévôté   COM

4 bis, rue Jean-Jacques-Rousseau.
Tel.-Fax 04 90 38 57 29.
contact@la-prevote.fr / http://la-prevote.fr
Closed 3 weeks Nov., 3 weeks Feb.
Rest. closed Tue. (exc. July-Aug.), Wed.
4 rooms: 80–160€. 1 suite: 140–180€.
Prix fixe: 25€, 43€, 55€, 65€.
A la carte: 75€.

In this old convent where the Sorgue flows, Jean-Marie Alloin, disciple of Raymond Blanc in the Manoir des Quatre Saisons and Pierre Carrier in Chamonix, has installed a cozy establishment where he cooks up Provençal cuisine in all its forms. The house has five charming guest rooms. We are won over by the lobster ravioli with a creamy coffee cappuccino, the Provençal-style lamb Tatin and the Saville orange soufflé served with a dark chocolate-filled crêpe.

● Le Jardin du Quai   ⌂SIM

91, av Julien-Guigue.
Tel. 04 90 20 14 98. Fax 04 90 20 31 92.
danielhebet@aol.com / www.lejardinduquai.com
Closed Tue., Wed., Jan.
Prix fixe: 27€ (lunch), 40€ (dinner).

A traveler from Charentes who was discovered in Paris in the Petit Bedon, surfaced again in the Mirande in Avignon, then in the Andéols in the Luberon, Daniel Hébet has finally settled down in a hidden bistro in a garden across from the station in the flea market capital. In a fun décor with

lots of old signs, the slate of the day offers good counsel, the wines of the moment are pleasant and this lively technician has lost none of his style. The other day, for 27 , he was offering a lunchtime fixed-price menu of marinated tomato and mozzarella, monkfish with asparagus and a melon and strawberry gelatin dessert with grilled pistachios. Sheer pleasure!

● L'Oustau de l'Isle   SIM

147, chemin du Bosquet (crossing the route d'Apt).
Tel.-Fax 04 90 20 81 36.
www.restaurant-oustau.com
Closed Tue., Wed. (exc. dinner in summer), 3 weeks Nov., 3 weeks Jan.
Prix fixe: 25,50€, 35,50€.
A la carte: 40–45€.

In his backyard sheltered from the noise of the city, Sylvain Bourlet enjoys preparing dishes that stimulate the palate: green salad with truffle oil, parmesan and smoked duck breast, the boneless trout encrusted in almonds served with a potato cake, the lemon- and ginger-seasoned poultry ballotine served with Asian noodles and finally the macaron and chocolate rose cookies are welcome. A nice cellar. A *gîte* to rent over the restaurant.

● Le Paradis de la Sorgue   SIM

53, rte de Carpentras.
Tel.-Fax 04 90 21 15 78.
contact@leparadisdelasorgue.fr
www.leparadisdelasorgue.fr
Closed Sat. lunch, Sun. dinner, Mon., Christmas–New Year's vac.
Prix fixe: 12,90€ (weekday lunch), 18€, 25€, 8,50€ (child). A la carte: 40€.

Lilian Nondedeu, who has taken over the oven of this Provençal bistro, is a skillful chef. Goat cheese marinated in olive oil and tapenade served with eggplant caviar and a tomato compote, the rouget with parsley-seasoned cream sauce, the lamb served with goat cheese and thyme-seasoned tomatoes and finally the honey-flavored peach mousse are local classics that go down well in the three modern dining rooms decked out in the local colors.

In Velleron (84740). 6 km n via D938.

■ La Grangette

Chemin Cambuisson.
Tel. 04 90 20 00 77. Fax 04 90 20 07 06.
hostellerie-la-grangette@club-internet.fr
www.la-grangette-provence.com
Closed mid-Nov.–mid-Feb.
Rest. closed Tue., Wed.
16 rooms: 89–249€.
Prix fixe: 42€, 48€. A la carte: 60€.

In the middle of its grounds, this old barn transformed into a charming inn is a choice stopover. The brightly colored rooms, the swimming pool and spa and lastly Brigitte Blanc-Brude's Southern cuisine meet with no resistance. The creamy cep risotto, Mediterranean sea bass served with thin slices of zucchini, the lamb shank with orange confiture and the chocolate ispahan offer us delicious moments.

89440 Yonne. Paris 210 – Auxerre 49 – Avallon 17 – Tonnerre 39 – Montbard 33. This pretty village in Burgundy, a short distance from the marvels of Noyers and Montréal, is worth visiting for its rustic solitude and its fine inn.

 HOTELS-RESTAURANTS

● Auberge du Pot d'Etain

24, rue Bouchardat.
Tel. 03 86 33 88 10. Fax 03 86 33 90 93.
potdetain@ipoint.fr / www.potdetain.com
Closed Feb., mid-Oct.–end Oct.
Rest. closed Sun. dinner, Mon.,
Tue. lunch (exc. July–Aug.).
7 rooms: 56–69€. 2 suites: 75€.
Prix fixe: 25€, 33€, 39,90€, 49,90€,
8,50€ (child). A la carte: 60€.

The Pécherys' inn in an old post house works its charm on us. We like Alain and Catherine's welcome, the finely appointed rooms and their son Fabien's carefully crafted cuisine. With the selection of Burgundy wines, we delight in the cannelloni stuffed with herbed goat cheese and smoked trout, the grilled cod filet served

with oven-baked potatoes and beets, Charolais beef, a veal trotter and red wine ragout and finally an Anis de Flavigny-flavored crème brûlée. The service is attentive and the check reasonable.

83380 Var. Paris 884 – Fréjus 11 – Draguignan 40 – Saint-Raphaël 14 – Sainte-Maxime 9. A balcony looking out on the big blue sea from the sinuous coast of the Var region.

 HOTELS-RESTAURANTS

■ Hodeo

Corniche des Issambres.
Tel. 04 94 49 52 52. Fax 04 94 49 63 18.
info@saintelme.com / www.saintelme.com
17 rooms: 150–200€.
13 suites: 400–670€.
Prix fixe: 62€, 100€, 23€ (child).
A la carte: 60–90€.

Exit the Villa Saint-Elme: enter Hodeo, an apparently meaningless name but it would seem to be easier for foreigners to pronounce. Edith Piaf and Charles Trenet both frequented this thirties residence. The charming rooms with a view of the sea, the renovated terrace, the restaurant and its brand new décor help us to forget the neighboring national road. A sea breeze blows through chef Laurent Tanguy's cuisine. Minced tuna in vinaigrette served with tapenade and pepper and tomato sorbet, lobster navarin revisited in the style of Provence, quail stuffed with Agen prunes and flavored with Armagnac as well as the crunchy praline and chocolate dessert with blackberries and the chocolate and grapfruit sphere are promising.

● Chante-Mer

At the Calanque des Issambres, in the village.
Tel. 04 94 96 93 23.
Closed Sun. dinner (Oct.–Easter), Mon., Tue. lunch, mid-Dec.–end Jan.
Prix fixe: 22–35€.

This charming little inn has a dining room with wood furnishings and the colors of Provence on the nicely set tables. A pleasant terrace in summertime.

ISSOUDUN

36100 Indre. Paris 247 – Bourges 37 – Châteauroux – Tours 131.
tourisme@villeissoudun.fr.
The setting for Balzac's novel, *La Rabouilleuse*. Don't miss the local inn for a lesson on the gourmet history of the Berry region.

 HOTELS-RESTAURANTS

● La Cognette

Bd Stalingrad (rest.) / rue des Minimes (hotel).
Tel. 02 54 03 59 59. Fax 02 54 03 13 03.
lacognette@wanadoo.fr / www.la-cognette.com
Closed Jan. Rest. closed Sun. dinner (Oct.–May), Mon. (Oct.–May), Tue. lunch (Oct.–May).
14 rooms: 75–125€. 3 suites: 150–200€.
Prix fixe: 25€. A la carte: 80€.

"La mère Cognette" reigned over the kitchens in this inn that Balzac used in *La Rabouilleuse*. Today, Jean-Jacques Daumy, with his father-in-law watching over him, cooks up old-style dishes that are straightforward and generous, but reworked according to today's tastes. The creamed lentils, an escargot and garlic cream turnover, the home-style carp filet, the oyster-stuffed cannelloni, truffle-seasoned veal sweetbreads, pork ribs with pepper caramel and the massepain d'Issoudun (green lentils with goat cheese) are washed down with the nice little wines of the Loire and the Berry region. It's enough to set us dreaming delicious dreams in the snug little rooms with a terrace and illustrious names like "Napoleon" and "Lamartine".

ISTRES

13800 Bouches-du-Rhône. Paris 789 – Marseille 55 – Arles 46 – Salon-de-Provence 25 – Martigues 14.
otistres@visitprovence.com.
Between the Etang de Berre and the deserted Crau plain, a commune dedicated to aeronautics. The museum of old Istres presents a recreation of an old Provençal kitchen.

● RESTAURANTS

● La Table de Sébastien

7, av Hélène-Boucher.
Tel. 04 42 55 16 01. Fax 04 42 55 95 02.
lesdeuxtoques@aol.com
www.latabledesebastien.fr
Closed Sun., Mon., Christmas–New Year's vac., 2 weeks end Aug.–Sept.
Prix fixe: 28€, 72€, 13€ (child).
A la carte: 80–85€.

Sébastien and Mylène Richard co-manage this fine establishment. The ochre-red rustic dining room with exposed beams and stonework contribute to the pleasure, as does the terrace, which is pleasant in summer. We rejoice with the cep and light cream Tatin with shellfish jus, the John Dory with shellfish and spinach, sautéed veal sweetbreads, potatoes and ceps, pheasant with autumn flavors, not to omit the "never before seen" Espelette pepper macaron, with Roves ewe's cheese and served with a natural wine sorbet, brought by Sébastien, who used to work in Senderens and the Cheval Blanc in Nîmes in the days of Thierry Marx. A large list of French and foreign wines.

ITTENHEIM see STRASBOURG

ITTERSWILLER

67140 Bas-Rhin. Paris 429 – Sélestat 14 – Molsheim 24 – Strasbourg 40.
The location between the vines and Vosges is worthy of a postcard. The grand rue looks toward the slopes that are heavy with grapes and the *winstub* inn has sprouted annexes across the town.

 HOTELS-RESTAURANTS

■ Arnold

98, rte du Vin.
Tel. 03 88 85 50 58. Fax 03 88 85 55 54.
arnold-hotel@wanadoo.fr

www.hotel-arnold.com
Closed 2 days at Christmas.
Rest. closed Sun. dinner (Nov.–May),
Mon. (Nov.–May).
29 rooms: 77–110€. 1 suite: 120–315€.
Prix fixe: 23€, 32€ (Sat., Sun., lunch), 46€,
58€, 11€ (child). A la carte: 55€.

Comfortable rooms with a view of the vineyards. The boutique selling local produce and Simon Bruno's cheerful *winstub* attract an increasingly large public. All appreciate Yves Fritsch's happy knack in the kitchen in the form of the goose foie gras, pike-perch in Riesling, mushroom-stuffed poultry breast and the frozen pain d'épice mille-feuille.

ITXASSOU

64250 Pyrénées-Atlantiques. Paris 792 – Biarritz 24 – Saint-Jean-de-Luz 36 – Cambo 4. The village cherry trees clinging to the hillsides produce wonderful black fruit, the jam of which is the ideal accompaniment for Basque sheep's cheese.

 HOTELS-RESTAURANTS

■ Le Chêne

Near the church.
Tel. 05 59 29 75 01. Fax 05 59 29 27 39.
hotel.chene.txassou@wanadoo.fr
Closed Christmas–New Year's, Jan.–end Mar.
Rest. closed Mon., Tue. (Oct.–June).
16 rooms: 34–38€.
Prix fixe: 16€, 22€, 24€, 40€.
A la carte: 40–48€.

Nothing could be more Basque than Geneviève Salaberry's old inn at the foot of the village church. The décor and the charm of the rooms are perfectly attuned to the spirit of the place. Fabrice Davoust's cuisine seduces us with regional dishes reworked in accordance with today's tastes: duck carpaccio with slices of ewe's cheese, roasted sea bream on a bed of mild peppers, the twice-cooked beef tripe with ceps and the baked apple with caramel sauce and cinnamon ice cream look good.

■ Le Fronton

La Place.
Tel. 05 59 29 75 10. Fax 05 59 29 23 50.
reservation@hotelrestaurantfronton.com
www.hotelrestaurantfronton.com
Closed 1 week Nov., Jan.–mid-Feb.
Rest. closed Wed.
25 rooms: 25–55€.
Prix fixe: 17€, 20€, 26€, 8€ (child).
A la carte: 35€.

This Basque village inn with its very pleasant old-style rooms and no-nonsense cuisine flies the Basque flag high. We continue to like the piperade, the duck filet with cherries and, of course, the gâteau Basque.

IVRY-LA-BATAILLE

27540 Eure. Paris 77 – Anet 7 – Dreux 22 – Evreux 33 – Pacy-sur-Eure 18.
The beautiful Château d'Anet is nearby. This is where the Normandy of hedgerows begins, as does gourmet Normandy, in the Moulin.

 RESTAURANTS

● Le Moulin d'Ivry COM

10, rue Henri-IV.
Tel. 02 32 36 40 51. Fax 02 32 26 05 15.
Closed Mon., Tue., 2 weeks Oct., Feb. vac.
Prix fixe: 29€ (weekdays), 46€.
A la carte: 75€.

Arnaud Vadepied has replaced Gilles Beaudrillier in the kitchen and prepares impeccable classic dishes: langoustines in salad, fresh duck foie gras, turbot with mushrooms, cider-poached pike-perch, kidney napped with Meaux mustard sauce and home-style apple charlotte. The meal takes on a festive atmosphere in this rustic old mill.

JARNAC

16200 Charente. Paris 470 – Barbezieux 31 –
Bordeaux 115 – Cognac 15 – Angoulême 29.
officetourisme-pays-de-jarnac@wanadoo.fr.
In addition to the beautiful warehouses on
the banks of the Charente, this pretty capital
of homemade Cognac is also the birthplace of
François Mitterrand.

 | RESTAURANTS

● **Restaurant du Château**   `COM`
15, pl du Château.
Tel. 05 45 81 07 17. Fax 05 45 35 35 71.
contact@restaurant-du-chateau.com
www.restaurant-du-chateau.com
Closed Sun. dinner, Mon.
Prix fixe: 26€, 38€, 43€, 15€ (child).

Ludovic Merle is the sprightly manager
of this establishment next to the Château Courvoisier. Parsley- and garlic-
seasoned country whelks, the John Dory
with chanterelles and escargots, the
thick slice of sole sautéed in wine sauce
and shallots with spring vegetables, veal
sweetbreads with morels and the frozen
Cognac and nougatine vacherin make a
good impression.

In Bourg-Charente (16200). 6 km w via N141
and secondary road.

● **La Ribaudière**   `V.COM`
Pl du Port.
Tel. 05 45 81 30 54. Fax 05 45 81 28 05.
la.ribaudiere@wanadoo.fr
www.laribaudiere.com
Closed Sun., Mon., Tue. lunch, Feb.
vac., mid-Oct.–1 Nov.
Prix fixe: 35€, 45€, 50€, 70€,
12,50€ (child). A la carte: 75€.

This contemporary restaurant on the
banks of the Charente serves up sharply
distinctive dishes in its elegant dining
room. Thierry Verrat, who trained with
Loiseau, skillfully blends the local produce with Mediterranean flavors. On the
plate this gives us langoustines and sundried tomatoes in puff pastry with saffron-
seasoned citrus sauce, a bay-seasoned

John Dory with baby broad beans and
Iberian ham, lamb saddle medallions
with almonds and the raspberry "transparence" with granulated sugar and
light cream. Charente wines and ageless
Cognac warm the heart.

JARVILLE-LA-MALGRANGE see NANCY

JAUSIERS

04850 Alpes-de-Haute-Provence. Paris 747
– Barcelonnette 9 – Gap 63 – Cannes 152 –
Digne 79.
In the heart of the valley of the Ubaye, the great
outdoors of the Southern Alps under an azure-
blue sky.

 | HOTELS-RESTAURANTS

● **Villa Morélia**
Rue Principale.
Tel. 04 92 84 67 78. Fax 04 92 84 65 47.
www.villa-morelia.com
Closed Apr., mid-Nov.–mid-Dec.
Rest. closed Sun., Mon., Tue. (off season).
7 rooms: 110–185€. 3 suites: 280€.
Prix fixe: 35€ (lunch), 52€ (dinner), 75€,
20€ (child).

Robert Boudard, a Burgundian who fell
in love with the region, welcomes us with
the good faith of the passionate self-taught
man. There are eleven charming rooms
in this old house. Vincent Lucas' dishes
are cunning, vivifying and creative but
lacking in extravagance. This 33-year-old
Niçois, who did a stint in the Fermes de
Marie de Megève, then in the Parisian
Cantine des Gourmets, cooks as naturally
as a bird sings. He changes his menu every
day, taking his inspiration from the changing seasons. The other day, facing the sun
above the Pain de Sucre and the Croix de
l'Alpe that still had some lingering snow, it
was a sheer pleasure to be on the terrace.
Foie gras served hot with a melon coulis
and fennel grains, a tuna steak marinated
in pine nut oil, seasoned with coriander
and served with buckwheat pasta, salmon
confit in spicy oil, with a lettuce salad with
capers and olives, spicy pork tenderloin

medallion served with crunchy asparagus fricassée, Robert Bedot signature pastas and an exquisite rum and pineapple-vanilla milk shake with medlar berries and strawberries in honey, plus the carefully chosen and fairly priced wines. In a word, a house with a heart, and one to discover.

53250 Mayenne. Paris 225 – Alençon 35 –
Bagnoles-de-l'Orne 19 – Le Mans 70.
A green break in the Mancelles Alps.

● | RESTAURANTS

● **La Terrasse**
30, Grande-Rue.
Tel. 02 43 03 41 91. Fax 02 43 04 49 48.
www.terrasse.fr
Closed Tue., Wed. exc. Bank holidays,
2 weeks July, 10 days Nov. 1 vac.,
1 week Feb. vac.
Prix fixe: 19–44€.

This village house has been transformed into a charming and welcoming establishment. Nice cuisine served in a contemporary dining room using the changing local market produce. A choice cellar.

89300 Yonne. Paris 144 – Auxerre 28 –
Montargis 60 – Sens 33 – Troyes 76.
ot.joigny@libertysurf.fr.
The bell tower on the Yonne, the nodding houses huddled together, the Côte Saint-Jacques wine– in short, a picture of a peaceful France not far from the capital.

■/● | HOTELS-RESTAURANTS

● **La Côte Saint-Jacques**
14, faubourg de Paris, BP 197.
Tel. 03 86 62 09 70. Fax 03 86 91 49 70.
lorain@relaischateaux.com
www.cotesaintjacques.com
Closed Jan. Rest. closed Mon. (winter),
Tue. (winter).

32 rooms: 210–260€. 5 suites: 420–540€.
Prix fixe: 35€ (lunch), 112€ (lunch),
155€ (lunch).

Jean-Michel Lorain, with stints at Taillevent, Girardet and Troisgros, was not content to inherit the family business founded by his grandmother and brought to the pinnacle of its career by his father Michel. He has his own tune to play. The building overlooking the Yonne was completely renovated from top to bottom with new contemporary-style rooms. The dining room has been adapted to today's tastes and the cuisine follows suit. His flagship dishes: a dish on the theme of the oyster, a lobe of duck foie gras with celery root and slow-cooked red onions, a slice of turbot poached in a pig's bladder with quinoa, fennel and artichokes and presented with flavorful squash jus, a langoustine gazpacho served hot with creamed zucchini, a roasted pigeon and sweet peas with mild garlic- and fines herbes–seasoned whipped cream and ginger-seasoned veal sweetbread medallions with pearl onions, rhubarb and radishes, the work of a precise artist who has mastered his palette. The desserts (a mille-feuille with rose ice cream, variations on the theme of the hazelnut) are more great moments in a festive meal, the mandatory classics (the blood sausage with light whipped potatoes, Bresse hen steamed over champagne) are true to form and the great Burgundies, from Chablis to Volnay, Chambolle-Musigny to Mercurey, all raise their glasses.

■ **Rive Gauche**
Chemin du Port-aux-Bois.
Tel. 03 86 91 46 66. Fax 03 86 91 46 93.
contact@hotel-le-rive-gauche.fr
www.hotel-le-rive-gauche.fr
Rest. closed Sun. dinner.
42 rooms: 68–107€.
Prix fixe: 18€ (weekday dinner), 24,50€,
28€, 34€, 9,50€ (child). A la carte: 45€.

On the left bank of the Yonne, the annex of the Côte Saint-Jacques is never empty. Guests appreciate Madame Lorain's welcome and the comfort of the modern rooms. In the kitchen, Philippe Mathieu and David Limare elaborate finely crafted local dishes. The escargot cakes with mashed potatoes, scallops with creamed Puy lentils, beef cheeks simmered in red wine presented in a cocotte and the vanilla crème brûlée honor tradition.

JOINVILLE

52300 Haute-Marne. Paris 244 – Bar-le-Duc 54 – Bar-sur-Aube 47 – Chaumont 44 – Saint-Dizier 32.
office-tourisme@wanadoo.fr.
It is worth stopping in this large town in the Haute-Marne for the Château du Grand-Jardin and the Musée de l'Auditoire. The chronicler of Saint Louis was the local lord here in the 13th century.

 HOTELS-RESTAURANTS

■ **Le Soleil d'Or**
9, rue des Capucins.
Tel. 03 25 94 17 90. Fax 03 25 94 15 66.
info@hotelsoleildor.com
www.hotelsoleildor.fr
Closed 1 Feb.–15 Feb., 1 Aug.–8 Aug.
Rest. closed Sun. dinner, Mon., Tue. lunch.
22 rooms: 45–130€.
Prix fixe: 14,50€ (lunch)., 20€ (weekdays), 40€.

Christophe Quackelbeen extends a warm welcome in this 17th-century aristocratic house that offers us the comfort of sparsely furnished rooms and good food in the shadow of the statues from the old Jacobin convent. Foie gras served three ways, oven-roasted cod with chestnut butter, beef Rossini and the little Tagada strawberry candy and basil vacherin, cooked up by Rudy Robbe, make a good impression. Julien Briois provides valuable advice on the wines.

● **La Poste**
Pl de Grève.
Tel. 03 25 94 12 63.
Closed Sun. dinner, Mon. lunch, 2 weeks Jan.
Prix fixe: 12,50€ (lunch), 23€, 32€, 7€ (child).

This serious central establishment has opted for a touch of Zen to welcome guests to its *nouvelle vague* dining room. The cuisine in harmony with the changing seasons meets with no resistance. The menu served at lunch time and in the evening is heaven sent.

JOSSELIN

56120 Morbihan. Paris 428 – Vannes 44 – Dinan 84 – Lorient 74 – Rennes 80.
ot.josselin@wanadoo.fr.
The sturdy fortress that is the Château des Rohan and the basilica of Notre-Dame-du-Roncier are two not-to-be-missed monuments.

 HOTELS-RESTAURANTS

■ **Hôtel du Château**
1, rue du Général-de-Gaulle.
Tel. 02 97 22 20 11. Fax 02 97 22 34 09.
www.hotel-chateau.com
Closed Sun. dinner, Mon., 1 week Nov., 1 week at end Dec., Feb.
36 rooms: 33–72,50€.
Prix fixe: 10,50€ (weekday lunch), 15–23€, 48,50€.

On the banks of the Oust, the Bonieux's pleasant inn stands across from the Château des Rohan, the walls of which can be seen from some of the rooms and from the terrace where good local fare is served up, though we can also enjoy it in the medieval-style dining room.

JOUCAS

84220 Vaucluse. Paris 719 – Avignon 43 – Cavaillon 21 – Carpentras 32 – Apt 14.
A little Provençal village in the heart of Saint-Luberon-des-Prés.

 HOTELS-RESTAURANTS

■ **Le Mas des Herbes Blanches**
Rte de Murs, 2,5 km.
Tel. 04 90 05 79 79. Fax 04 90 05 71 96.
www.herbesblanches.com

Closed beg. Jan.–10 Mar.
19 rooms: 149–495€. 3 suites: 310–495€.
Prix fixe: 49€ (weekday lunch), 69€,
95€ (weekday dinner). A la carte: 95€.

Lost in the *garrigue*, Evelyne Juillard's Provençal *mas* is an excellent Relais & Châteaux establishment. We like the peace and comfort of the rooms with balconies and private gardens and the pleasant moments spent by the side of the swimming pool or on the tennis court. In the restaurant, we are equally equally impressed by Benoît Vidal's skillful sleight of hand. The shredded crab and cucumber seasoned with white balsamic vinegar, the roasted blue lobster served in a bouillon from its shell and seasoned with cocoa, the pigeon breast with strawberry marmalade and the chocolate croustillant with an apricot reduction are a testament to his exuberant creativity and great mastery.

● **Hostellerie le Phébus**   ○✿🏠

Rte de Murs.
Tel. 04 90 05 78 83. Fax 04 90 05 73 61.
phebus@relaischateaux.com /
resphebus@wanadoo.fr / www.lephebus.com
Closed beg. Nov.–end Mar. Rest. closed Tue.
lunch, Wed. lunch, Thu. lunch.
24 rooms: 175–605€.
11 suites: 265–605€.
Prix fixe: 50€ (lunch), 70€, 110€,
20€ (child). A la carte: 110–135€.

Having joined the major league after studying under Hiély, then Vergé, Vié and Robuchon, Xavier Mathieu has become one of the finest defenders of the new Provençal cuisine. His main advantage: the technique he acquired over the years and which he knows how to use to give a new dimension to the local produce of the region. Facing the Luberon, his stone *mas*, once the headquarters of a Knights Templars domain, with luxury rooms and suites, bears the Relais & Châteaux seal of approval. The private swimming pools and soft colors are a hymn to Provence. Nothing has been left to chance either in the décor or in the dishes. Carefully thought out and executed, Xavier's prep-

arations are light as air and weighed down with just the right amount of regional tradition. The langoustine tails and Aquitaine caviar with green apple and ginger sauce served with a parmesan biscuit, leek-seasoned salt cod and potato gratin, a monkish stew, rouget with tomatoes, onions and sweet peppers and a lamb confit are served up zealously by a young and attentive team. The tables and dishes are very nicely presented. The rum flambée dessert and the lavender poached peach with semolina take us straight back to childhood.

JOUY-AUX-ARCHES see METZ

JUAN-LES-PINS

06160 Alpes-Maritimes. Paris 917 –
Aix-en-Provence 162 – Nice 25 – Cannes 9.
accueil@antibes-juanlespins.com.
The beach, the sea and Golfe-Juan on the horizon. Tender is the life, as Scott Fitzergerald might have said when he stayed at Belles Rives. Of course the architectural disorder and the profusion of boutiques of all sorts gives the seafront at Juan the aspect of an open-air market. But there are also some beautiful art deco facades which, if painted in pastel colors, would remind us of Miami and Ocean Drive.

 HOTELS-RESTAURANTS

● **Belles Rives**   🏠○🍴🏠
  & la Passagère

33, bd Edouard-Baudoin.
Tel. 04 93 61 02 79. Fax 04 93 67 43 51.
info@bellesrives.com / www.bellesrives.com
Closed beg. Jan.–beg. Feb.
43 rooms: 140–730€. 5 suites: 450–1360€.
Prix fixe: 75€ (dinner), 95€. A la carte: 120€.

The facade, the art deco furniture in the lobby and clocks showing the time all round the world remind us of the heydays of this residence that Marianne Estène-Chauvin has preserved untouched, exactly as it was in the thirties. Scott and Zelda Fitzgerald lived *Tender is the Night* here. The beach and the pontoon have not changed. The novelty:

Frédéric Buzet's fine cuisine served in the ocean liner–style dining room. Formerly he worked with Véfour whom we know from the Saint-Paul in Saint-Paul-de-Vence. The lobster- and red pepper–stuffed cannelloni, the truffle-seasoned potatoes cooked like a risotto, the gently cooked thick-sliced tuna served with slow-roasted beefsteak tomatoes, the Mediterranean sea bass with local lemons and finally the farm-raised lamb served with chickpea cakes and an eggplant compote deserve our applause and to be awarded a plate this year. Moreover, Radhouane Zaiter's excellent desserts are equally attractive. The chocolate or coffee feuille-à-feuille, made with the local almond cake and glazed in caramel emulsion and the Breton shortcake served with mango and purple figs napped in a reduced ginger infusion are mouthwateringly good.

■ **Hôtel Juana**   ⏥
  La Terasse Club
La Pinède, av G.-Gallice.
Tel. 04 93 61 08 70. Fax 04 93 61 76 60.
reservation@hotel-juana.com
www.hotel-juana.com
Rest. closed lunch
37 rooms: 210–495€. 3 suites: 495–1200€.
A la carte: 90€.

Mariane Estène-Chauvin of Belles Rives bought her art déco neighbor and cousin. The rooms, which have been renovated in a contemporary style, still retain their charm. The Lounge cuisine is simple but not simplistic, thanks to Jean-Laurent Depoile. Lobster with slow-cooked fennel or seasoned with citrus flavors, foie gras served plain or in crème brûlée with figs and the variations on the theme of whatever fruits are in season make a good impression. A much-frequented bar, heated swimming pool, spa, Turkish bath and Jacuzzi.

● **Les Pêcheurs**   ◎Ⓥ.COM
10, bd du Maréchal-Juin, port du Crouton.
Tel. 04 92 93 71 55 / 13 30 (La Plage).
Fax 04 92 93 15 04.
www.lespecheurs-juan.com

Closed lunch (summer), Tue., Wed. (summer), mid-Nov.–20 Dec.
Prix fixe: 40€ (lunch), 77€, 95€.
A la carte: 110€ (La Plage: 60€).

Francis Chauveau is very serious about this chic restaurant with its contemporary décor overlooking the sea. The à la carte menu by the ex-chef at the Amandier in Mougins and Belle Otéro in Cannes gives pride of place to the best local seafood, though not exclusively. In the marine dining room, red lobster with mint tabouli, sage-seasoned John Dory served with zucchini carpaccio and a Limousin rack of lamb presented with a Provençal gratin energetically revisit the traditions of the region. Marc Janodet, whom we know from the Juana, is the man behind the delicious moments that come to us in the form of a wild strawberry mille-feuille with lemongrass-seasoned strawberry sauce and a fromage blanc sorbet. Attentive service, a cellar that is rich with wines from the South of France and a very New Wave Riviera check. Simpler cuisine and service at La Plage.

● **Bijou Plage**   COM
Bd du Littoral.
Tel. 04 93 61 39 07 / 04 93 67 69 72.
Fax 04 93 67 81 78.
bijou.plage@free.fr / www.bijouplage.com
Prix fixe: 21€, 30€, 49€.
A la carte: 55–70€.

One of the finest sand beaches of the Alpes Maritimes, facing the Lérins islands, this Bijou has not usurped its name. Stéphane Sino prepares a very tasty Mediterranean cuisine. The warm jumbo shrimp served in salad, rockfish soup, scorpion fish filet, John Dory with truffle butter and lamb shanks napped in spring onion jus leave just enough space to allow us to fully appreciate Ludovic Touyers' pastries. Exquisite Tatins.

JULIENAS

69840 Rhône. Paris 405 – Mâcon 14 –
Bourg-en-Bresse 50 –
Villefranche-sur-Saône 32 – Lyon 66.

This winegrowing village welcomes us from cellar to cellar without forgetting to feed guests gracefully.

RESTAURANTS

● Le Coq à Juliénas
Pl du Marché.
Tel. 04 74 04 41 98. Fax 04 74 04 41 44.
leon@relaischateaux.com
www.coq-julienas.com
Closed Wed., mid-Dec.–mid-Jan.
Prix fixe: 22€, 10€ (child).
A la carte: 30–50€.

Nicely situated on the Place du Marché, staunchly faithful Lyonnais Jean-Paul Lacombe's bistro is entirely devoted to the virtues of Beaujolais products. A local ham and parsley terrine with whole grain mustard sauce, grilled cod with black olive sauce and hen bouillon, poultry fricassée prepared like a coq au vin and a large vanilla-flavored meringue served with Beaujolais wine syrup over shaved ice are punctuated unequivocally by Juliénas and other local vintages.

JUNGHOLTZ

68500 Haut-Rhin. Paris 475 – Colmar 32 – Mulhouse 23 – Belfort 62 – Guebwiller 6.
Close by the Notre-Dame de Thierenbach place of pilgrimage with its onion-domed church, a village surrounded by the forest. Famous also for its very moving Jewish cemetery.

HOTELS-RESTAURANTS

● Les Violettes
Thierenbach.
Tel. 03 89 76 91 19. Fax 03 89 74 29 12.
lesviolettes2@wanadoo.fr
www.les-violettes.com
Rest. closed Mon., Tue., 2 weeks beg. Jan.
19 rooms: 70–195€. 3 suites: 210–300€.
Prix fixe: 28€ (weekday lunch), 47€, 63€, 12€ (child). A la carte: 67€.

On the edge of the forest, facing the pilgrims church, this chic *table d'hôte* looks good. The red sandstone building, polished up by the wonder boy of home hairdressing, Philippe Bosc, marks his return to his birthplace. Rooms with wood furnishings give it a rustic mountainy feeling, the dining rooms are decorated with good paintings and the terrace is panoramic: all dedicated to the glory of Alsace. Sébastien Sattler's food alternates between simplicity and sophistication: fresh foie gras trio (one marinated in Port, another rolled in smoked duck breast and the last one breaded in crushed hazelnuts), rockfish- and basil-stuffed cannelloni with tapenade and the roasted duckling served with stir-fried vegetables, bulgur risotto and a sweet pepper sauce make us want to travel and remind us that Jean-Yves Schillinger established the house cuisine. For dessert, the soft-centered Cuban chocolate cake with pralines and almond milk ice cream is a wonder. A post-prandial stroll along the neighboring woodland paths is *de rigueur*.

● Biebler COM
Thierenbach.
Tel. 03 89 76 85 75. Fax 03 89 74 91 45.
la-roseraie-biebler@wanadoo.fr
www.biebler.com
Closed Jan. Rest. closed Tue., Wed.
5 rooms: 46–70€. 2 suites: 75€.
Prix fixe: 22€, 25€, 30€, 36€, 10€ (child). A la carte: 45–50€.

Fabrice Biebler, alone at the helm, cooks good quality classic cuisine in this roadside inn: a puff pastry cup filled with meat in creamy white sauce, a rabbit terrine, a pike-perch and salmon duo, beef in sauce made with local wine and the plate of house dessert specialties, all washed down with nice local wines. Three renovated rooms for a well-deserved siesta.

● La Ferme des Moines SIM
Across from the church in Thierenbach.
Tel. 03 89 76 93 01. Fax 03 89 74 37 45.
www.lafermedesmoines.fr
Prix fixe: 12,90€ (weekday lunch), 20€, 8€ (child). A la carte: 35€.

This old farmhouse that once belonged to the Thierenbach monks has now become a large inn with Philippe Bosc watching over it and his wife Francine and Daniel Florenc in the kitchen. The dishes are best enjoyed with family or friends. Duck foie gras, head cheese and aspic terrine, fish simmered in Riesling, tête de veau with vinaigrette and apple streudel with vanilla ice cream are amazing. Watch out for the hustle and bustle on Sundays!

KATZENTHAL

68230 Haut-Rhin. Paris 441 – Munster 18 – Saint-Dié 48 – Colmar 7.
At the foot of Wineck castle, which gives its name to the local grand cru, this welcoming winegrowing village with its white bell tower was entirely rebuilt after the last war.

 HOTELS-RESTAURANTS

■ A l'Agneau

16, Grand-Rue.
Tel. 03 89 80 90 25. Fax 03 89 27 59 58.
www.agneau-katzenthal.com
Closed 1 week Nov., 1 week at end Dec., 2 weeks at end Jan., 1 week July
Rest. closed Wed., Thu.
12 rooms: 45–60€. 1 suite: 80–110€.
Prix fixe: 19€ (lunch), 21€, 45€, 8€ (child).

Patricia and Christophe Munch are very serious about this little modern hotel with its cozy rooms. The welcome is friendly and reassuring, the regional *winstub*-style cuisine combined with wines from René Meyer's nearby vineyard make it a very Alsatian stopover. Riesling-seasoned pâté in pastry crust, sturgeon filet with sauerkraut, a stuffed quail and the kirsch dessert are good standards.

KAYSERSBERG

68240 Haut-Rhin. Paris 436 – Colmar 12 – Sélestat 26 – Guebwiller 35.
ot.kaysersberg@calixo.net.
How beautiful Doctor Schweitzer's city is! With its houses on the banks of the Weiss, its deposed château, time-worn cobblestones, flamboyant sandstone, comely *auberges* and the call of the Vosges flirting with its vines.

 HOTELS-RESTAURANTS

● Le Chambard

9-13, rue du Général-de-Gaulle.
Tel. 03 89 47 10 17. Fax 03 89 47 35 03.
info@lechambard.fr / www.lechambard.fr
Rest. closed Mon., Tue. lunch, Wed. lunch.
20 rooms: 96–114€. 3 suites: 195€.

Prix fixe: 29€ (lunch), 47,50€, 64€, 75€, 15€ (child). A la carte: 75–100€.

The Nasti brothers' house at the entrance to the village with its vast "zebra-colored" rooms, modern-style suites and most of all its choice cuisine make it a "must" on the wine route. In the kitchen, Olivier adds touches of the south to Alsatian culinary tradition. The dishes? Foie gras and country bacon, a vegetable and potato dish presented with style at the tableside, Atlantic sea bass, the lemon-seasoned lobster in its shell or the pike-perch served on a bed of julienned white and red radishes and with a beer vinegar- infused jus: in short, food that is lively, tasteful, sharp and that leaves your palate clean and fresh and ready to taste the cheeses matured by Jacky Quesnot in the Ferme Saint-Nicolas in Colmar, followed by then the amazing desserts, like the Victoria pineapple served with rum grog, the exotic fruits served with matcha tea sorbet and the cherry compote (savory) with a Piedmont pistachio cream … Nice work! (See also La Winstub du Chambard.)

■ A l'Arbre Vert

1, rue Haute-du-Rempart.
Tel. 03 89 47 11 51. Fax 03 89 78 13 40.
hotel-restaurantarbrevert@kaysersberg.com
Closed beg. Jan.–mid-Feb. Rest. closed Mon.
20 rooms: 59–73€.
Prix fixe: 23€, 27€, 10€ (child).

Eliane Wittmer extends a warm welcome while Gaspard Batista produces good solid food in this beautiful regional establishment. House terrine, oven-roasted half quail with foie gras, pike-perch served on a bed of sauerkraut, the honey-, Marc de Gewurztraminer- and lemon-seasoned duck breast and a crème brûlée close fine meals that take their inspiration from the local region. The charming setting, the flowery facade, the reasonable prices, the *winstub*-style dining room and the wood furnishings are all extra attractions that explain the success of the house.

■ Hôtel Constantin

10, rue du Père-Kohlmann.
Tel. 03 89 47 19 90. Fax 03 89 47 37 82.
www.hotel-constantin.com
20 rooms: 50–71€.

Denis and Christine Kohler are the driving force behind this tastefully appointed winegrower's house. The rooms swing between the Alsatian and the modern style. Breakfast is served in the luminous glass-roofed dining room enhanced by a superb earthenware stove. Reasonable prices.

■ Les Remparts

4, rue de la Flieh.
Tel. 03 89 47 12 12. Fax 03 89 47 37 24.
www.lesremparts.com
41 rooms: 66–84€.

On the edge of the old city this modern hotel situated in a residential district offers functional rooms. Ask for a room with a terrace or balcony. A sauna and game room to help us relax. WiFi.

● Au Lion d'Or `COM`

66, rue du Général-de-Gaulle.
Tel. 03 89 47 11 16. Fax 03 89 47 19 02.
auliondor@wanadoo.fr / www.auliondor.fr
Closed Tue. dinner, Wed., mid-Jan.–end Feb.
Prix fixe: 18€, 25€, 36€. A la carte: 38€.

An affordable Alsace: that's what this goodly inn dating from 1521 offers us. The Ancel brothers run this house that has been in their family since 1764. Daniel is at the reception, Jean-Marc serving and Jean-Joseph in the kitchen: duck foie gras, fish choucroute, tripe simmered in Riesling and regional flat savory tarts called "tarte flambée", plain or with cheese. A dining room with a large open fireplace and courtyard garden.

● La Vieille Forge

1, rue des Ecoles.
Tel. 03 89 47 17 51. Fax 03 89 78 13 53.
Closed Wed. (exc. Bank holidays), Thu. (exc. Bank holidays), Feb. vac., 2 weeks July.
Prix fixe: 19€, 20€, 25€, 32€, 9€ (child).

There is no room for frills in this old 15th-century forge transformed into a beige and rose-colored inn with exposed stonework and wood. The charming Marie Gutleben welcomes us while Christophe Grivel cooks up a cuisine that is both generous and finely crafted, anchored in the Alsatian countryside. Salad with soft mountain cheese and smoked ham, mushroom and escargot cassolette, pike-perch filet with crispy crêpes, served with sauerkraut, slow-cooked venison and onion stew with house spätzle and the frozen terrine dessert with pain d'épices delight the guests. The menus are a blessing.

● La Winstub du Chambard   ⬛SIM

9-13, rue du Général-de-Gaulle.
Tel. 03 89 47 10 17. Fax 03 89 47 35 03.
info@lechambard.fr / www.lechambard.fr
Closed Mon., Tue. lunch, Wed. lunch,
beg. Jan.–beg. Feb.
Prix fixe: 24€, 10,50€ (child).
A la carte: 40€.

We also find the Nastis in this *winstub* with yellow and pine décor right next to their gastronomic restaurant. They delight their customers with suckling pig presskopf, foie gras terrine with dried fruits similar to the Alsatian holiday cake called bereweke, pike-perch simmered in wine, the house choucroute and the frozen vacherin, all accompanied by a judicious selection of smart wines in which Alsace has pride of place.

● Flamme & Co   ⓃSIM

4, rue du Général-de-Gaulle.
Tel. 03 89 47 16 16.
Closed lunch, Mon., Tue. (off season).
A la carte: 20€.

They created a sensation in their village by opening this modern "tarte flambée" eatery. From 6:00 pm to midnight, the Chambard Nastis serve twenty-five sorts of "flammeküche" in an old *winstub* that has been modernized. Oven-browned with cheese, but also with fresh herbs, tomatoes and parmesan or with smoked salmon and herbs, these classic garnished pies are deservedly famous.

● Le Château   SIM

38, rue du Général-de-Gaulle.
Tel. 03 89 78 24 33. Fax 03 89 47 37 82.
Closed Wed. dinner, Thu., 1 week at end
Nov., 2 weeks Jan., 1 week at end June.
Prix fixe: 16,50€, 18€, 19€, 26€, 32€,
8€ (child). A la carte: 30–35€.

The Kohlers, who own the Hotel Constantin, are also the driving force behind this rustic establishment with white and wood shades. Faithful gourmets come to savor Jean-Yves Bill's dishes. An onion tart, escargots prepared in the style of Alsace (stuffed with spiced butter and herbs and cooked in local wine), smoked trout with horseradish sauce, the coq au Riesling and the crème caramel are delightful and reasonably priced.

KEMBS-LOECHLE

68680 Haut-Rhin. Paris 493 – Colmar 60 –
Mulhouse 25 – Altkirch 26 – Bâle 16.
On the edge of Alsace's Petite Camargue, an old commune of boatmen that is famous for its dam.

●	RESTAURANTS

● Les Ecluses   SIM

8, rue de Rosenau.
Tel. 03 89 48 37 77. Fax 03 89 48 49 31.
restaurant.les.ecluses@freezbee.fr
Closed Sun. dinner, Mon., Wed. dinner (Oct.–
Apr.), Nov. 1 vac., Feb. vac.
Prix fixe: 14,50€, 39€, 8,50€ (child).
A la carte: 38€.

The dining room is unassuming and contemporary with red-orange cherrywood furnishings. Bertrand Welte delights his clients with crayfish salad seasoned with citrus and coriander, the Bismarck herring served on salad with green apples, mushrooms and sherry- seasoned cream sauce, Alsatian-style fish simmered in wine, venison shoulder with chestnuts and currants and frozen nougat with a berry coulis.

KERBOURG see SAINT-LYPHARD
KERVIGNAC see HENNEBONT

KIENTZHEIM

68240 Haut-Rhin. Paris 433 – Colmar 13 – Munster 28.
At the foot of the Sigolsheim cemetery, this historic village whose château is home to the Saint-Etienne fraternity and a wine museum, deserves a visit and some tasting.

 HOTELS-RESTAURANTS

■ Hôtel de l'Abbaye d'Alspach
2/4, rue Foch.
Tel. 03 89 47 16 00. Fax 03 89 78 29 73.
www.abbayealspach.com
Closed beg. Jan.–mid-Mar.
28 rooms: 68–105€. 5 suites: 140–180€.

The charm of the old blends with modern comfort in these outbuildings of a 13th-century convent converted into a hotel. Rustic furniture, sauna, conference rooms.

■ Hostellerie Schwendi
2, pl Schwendi.
Tel. 03 89 47 30 50. Fax 03 89 49 04 49.
www.hotel-schwendi.com
Rest. closed Wed., Thu. lunch,
Christmas–10 Mar.
25 rooms: 65–98€.
Prix fixe: 22€, 30€, 36€, 46€, 9€ (child).

On a charming cobblestone square in the heart of the winegrowing village, Anita and René Schillé have transformed an 18th-century wine cellar into a charming stopover with a half-timbered facade, exposed stonework and wooden beams. The rooms are rustic and finely appointed and the dishes prepared by their son Fabien are good quality. Pan-seared foie gras with sour cherries, onion tart, trout and vegetable soufflé, breast of guinea hen with mushrooms and beer-macerated berries over shaved ice meet with no resistance.

KIFFIS

68480 Haut-Rhin. Paris 541 – Altkirch 31 – Colmar 90.

On the Swiss frontier the village stands as a sentinel overlooking the gently sloping hillsides of the Jura.

● RESTAURANTS

● Le Cheval Blanc   SIM
21, rue Principale.
Tel. 03 89 40 33 05. Fax 03 89 40 36 66.
agnes.walther@tiscali.fr
Closed Mon., 2 weeks Jan., 2 weeks July.
Prix fixe: 13,50€, 22€, 30€, 45€,
8,50€ (child). A la carte: 35€.

A warm eggplant and goat cheese dish, pheasant terrine with baby vegetables, herb-stuffed trout, a veal steak with Munster sauce and the frozen kouglof make a good impression in this old-style inn. André Walther pampers his guests in this welcoming house with solid oak parquet floor and massive wooden beams. We slip easily into the sheer pleasure of eating.

KILSTETT

67840 Bas-Rhin. Paris 489 – Strasbourg 14 – Haguenau 23 – La Wantzenau 5.
The silt from the Reid and the banks of the Rhine.

 HOTELS-RESTAURANTS

■ Oberlé
11, rte Nationale.
Tel. 03 88 96 21 17.
www.hotel-oberle.fr
Closed 2 weeks Feb., mid-Aug.–beg. Sept.
Rest. closed Thu., Fri. lunch.
31 rooms: 30–51€.
Prix fixe: 10€ (weekdays), 21€, 36€,
10€ (child).

Modern but old style, a large family inn with practical rooms, a warm welcome, *table d'hôte* cuisine and the *plat du jour* attracting lots of people for lunch.

● Le Cheval Noir   COM
1, rue du Sous-Lieutenant-Maussire.
Tel. 03 88 96 22 01.

Closed Mon., Tue., 10 days end July,
10 days beg. Aug.
Prix fixe: 12€ (weekday lunch), 25€, 45€.

A fine 18th-century half-timbered Alsatian house with its carefully appointed dining room decorated with a fresco representing a hunting scene, a welcoming family that has received people for five generations and a regional cuisine that has adapted to the tastes of today.

KINTZHEIM

67600 Bas-Rhin. Paris 432 –
Sélestat 5 – Colmar 22.
At the foot of Haut-Koenigsbourg castle, Monkey Mountain and the Eagle Park, this spirited winegrowing village offers a hearty welcome.

●   RESTAURANTS

● Auberge Saint-Martin   SIM

80, rue de la Liberté.
Tel. 03 88 82 04 78. Fax 03 88 82 26 20.
Closed Wed. (exc. July–Aug.),
1 week at end Nov., 3 weeks Jan.
Prix fixe: 9€ (weekday lunch), 19€, 21€,
8,50€ (child).
A la carte: 35–45€.

People used to stop here in days gone by for the tartes flambées. Patrice Blutzer set up shop in this roadside inn on the wine route and delights his customers with the house-prepared duck foie gras, the Tomme du Ried cheese salad, pike-perch in Pinot Noir sauce, oxtail braised in red wine and a sweet version of the regional tarte flambée, with apples and Grand Marnier. A fine wine list with 100 listings.

 KNUTANGE see THIONVILLE

KOENIGSMACKER

57970 Moselle. Paris 349 – Thionville 9 –
Metz 39 – Luxembourg 41.
Near the valley of the Moselle, a village waiting to be discovered, a church with baroque furniture.

■   HOTELS

■ Moulin de Méwinckel   N❀⌂

Tel. 03 82 55 03 28.
5 rooms: 40–70€.

In what used to be the stable of a peasant mill where the paddle wheel still turns, five quiet and brightly decorated rooms. A warm welcome.

KRAUTERGERSHEIM

67880 Bas-Rhin. Paris 492 –
Strasbourg 25 – Obernai 9 – Molsheim 16.
The name of the commune literally means "Cabbagetown", so we are not surprised that cabbage is the star vegetable in the neighboring fields.

●   RESTAURANTS

● Le Chou'Heim   SIM

2, rue G.-Clemenceau.
Tel.-Fax 03 88 48 18 10.
eric.ivens@hotmail.fr
www.lechouheim.com
Closed Sat. lunch, Mon., Wed. dinner.
Prix fixe: 33€, 7€ (child).

Eric Ivens who took over this picturesque residence welcomes us while Jean-Marie Albrecht, who is in charge of the kitchens, is respectful of regional traditions, as we can see with escargots prepared in the style of Alsace (stuffed with spiced butter and herbs and cooked in local wine), smoked duck breast served on a bed of julienned cabbage, a salmon and pike-perch duo, the Cordon Bleu with morels and a house-prepared chocolate mousse. The prices are reasonable. A new stone cellar has opened.

KRUTH

68820 Haut-Rhin. Paris 453 –
Gérardmer 31 – Mulhouse 40 – Thann 20.
The high valley of the Thur at the southern end of the Alsatian Vosges. Don't miss the Saint-Nicolas waterfall.

HOTELS-RESTAURANTS

■ Auberge de France

20, Grand'Rue.
Tel. 03 89 82 28 02. Fax 03 89 82 24 05.
aubergedefrance@wanadoo.fr
www.aubergedefrance.fr
Closed beg. Jan.–beg. Feb., 2 weeks June.
Rest. closed Wed. dinner, Thu.
16 rooms: 46–53€.
Prix fixe: 11€ (weekday lunch), 17€, 39€,
8,50€ (child).

A pleasant old-style inn, with billiards, a
bowling pitch, tidy rooms, a rustic dining
room and Alsatian dishes with the colors
of the mountains.

KUTZENHAUSEN see
MERKWILLER-PECHELBRONN

LABAROCHE

68910 Haut-Rhin. Colmar 14 –
Gérardmer 51 – Munster 25 – Saint-Dié 52.
One of France's largest townships. Hamlets
tucked into the landscape, thatched roofs, woodland paths can all be found at a height of 750m
right in the heart of the Vosges.

HOTELS-RESTAURANTS

■ Au Tilleul

385, La Place.
Tel. 03 89 49 84 46. Fax 03 89 78 91 88.
au-tilleul@wanadoo.fr / www.hotel-tilleul.fr
Closed Jan.
30 rooms: 37–70€.
Prix fixe: 15€ (weekday lunch).

Martine and Christiane Munier's benevolent gaze watches over this family *pension*
boasting lots of charm in its cozy rooms.
Taste tranquillity as well as Christiane's
cooking, whose treats include her individual chicken liver terrine, pâté in a short
crust with assorted raw vegetables, leg of
venison and her house-made éclair.

■ La Rochette

Rte des Trois-Epis.
Tel. 03 89 49 80 40. Fax 03 89 78 94 82.
www.larochette-hotel.fr
Closed 2 weeks Nov., mid-Feb.–mid-Mar.
Rest. closed Mon. dinner (exc. hotel cli-
ents), Tue.
6 rooms: 52–55€. 1 suite: 58€.
Prix fixe: 16€, 28€, 37€, 43€.
A la carte: 38€.

Pretty rooms in a verdant setting with
breakfasts served on the veranda. The dining room with its large French windows
giving on to the garden lends a final touch
of charm. You won't tire of the individual
escargot and potato casserole (baekeofe),
filet of turbot served over risotto and the
layered casserole of pork tail and potato.

LABARTHE-SUR-LEZE

31860 Haute-Garonne. Paris 698 –
Toulouse 20 –Muret 6.

An escape to the South of the Toulousain countryside.

● | RESTAURANTS

● **La Rose des Vents**
2292, route du Plantaurel.
Tel. 05 61 08 67 01. Fax 05 61 08 85 84.
Closed Sun. dinner, Mon., Tue., Feb. vac.,
2 weeks Aug.–Sept., 1 week Christmas.
Prix fixe: 15€ (lunch), 22–29€, 39€.
A la carte: 60€.

A classical culinary experience in the dining room or on the veranda where Joel Lamotte concocts genuine home cooking such as vanilla-seasoned pan-fried slice of foie gras, filet of sole with ceps, the duo of veal sweetbreads and kidneys with small onions and a chilled creamy chocolate mousse.

LACABAREDE

81240 Tarn. Paris 755 – Béziers 70 – Carcassonne 55 – Castres 37 – Mazamet 20 – Narbonne 60.
A foray into the green heartland of the land of plenty.

◨ | HOTELS-RESTAURANTS

■ **Demeure de Flore**
106, route Nationale.
Tel. 05 63 98 32 32. Fax 05 63 98 47 56.
www.demeuredeflore.com
Closed Mon. (off season), Jan.
10 rooms: 89–100€. 1 suite: 140–190€.
Prix fixe: 26€ (lunch), 34€ (dinner),
19€ (child).

Set in the middle of two hectares of parkland, this house—built in 1890—oozes charm. Francesco Di Bari is responsible for both hotel and kitchen. Elegant rooms in vibrant tones vie with an attentive cuisine. In the old-fashioned, highly-polished dining room, dishes such as potato gnocchi with a jumbo shrimp jus, vanilla-seasoned roasted scallops, squab with hazelnuts and honey and the chocolate and Grand Marnier dessert are equally enchanting.

LACAPELLE-MARIVAL

46120 Lot. Paris 557 – Cahors 63 – Figeac 21 – Rocamadour 31 – Gramat 20.
Set high on the Causse at an altitude of 375 meters, this corner of Quercy countryside feels like the end of the world.

◨ | HOTELS-RESTAURANTS

■ **La Terrasse**
Across from the château.
Tel. 05 65 40 80 07. Fax 05 65 40 99 45.
hotel-restaurant-la-terrasse@wanadoo.fr
www.hotel-restaurant-la-terrasse-lot.fr
Closed Jan., Feb.
Rest. closed Sun. dinner, Mon., Tue. lunch.
13 rooms: 43€.
Prix fixe: 19€, 24€, 35€, 55€.
A la carte: 60€.

Close to the church and 13th-century castle, Lucien Vanel's venerable establishment, currently run by Stéphane Almaric, beckons seductively. In the dining room, which has a view of the ramparts, Almaric—who worked at Toulousy in Toulouse and Albano in Agde—serves up a high-flying cuisine including blue lobster-stuffed ravioli, sole pan fried in butter, garlic and parsley, young pigeon prepared two ways and the mango and coconut spring rolls. After such a feast, choose between a stroll in the garden or a nap in one of La Terrasse's elegant rooms.

LACAUNE

81230 Tarn. Paris 710 – Albi 65 – Béziers 90 – Castres 49 – Millau 70 – Montpellier 130.
Famed for its ham, this casino town makes for a perfect stopover in Tarn country.

◨ | HOTELS-RESTAURANTS

● **Calas**
4, place de la Vierge.
Tel. 05 63 37 03 28. Fax 05 63 37 09 19.

hotelcalas@wanadoo.fr
www.pageloisirs.com/calas
Closed Fri. dinner, Sat. lunch (Oct.–Apr.),
Sun. dinner (Oct.–Apr.), 20 Dec.–10 Jan.
16 rooms: 42–55€.
Prix fixe: 15€, 21,50€, 28€ (Sun. lunch),
34€, 10€ (child). A la carte: 40€.

Four generations of Calases have presided over this family-run establishment and are responsible for its continuing success. Guests flock in increasing numbers to enjoy the delights of the swimming pool, the quirky, individually-styled bedrooms and the frescoed dining room where Claude puts on a great show with dishes like creamy corn soup served with foie gras ice cream, salmon "wallet" with a light white wine sauce, cep-stuffed guinea hen and the creamy bitter orange meringue dessert.

LACAVE

46200 Lot. Paris 533 – Brive 52 – Sarlat 42 – Cahors 58 – Gourdon 26.
The winding rivers of the Dordogne, roads leading to castles, the Quercy and the Périgord just a hop, skip and a jump away, combine to give a perfect, peaceful picture of France.

 HOTELS-RESTAURANTS

● **Château de la Treyne**
3 km w via D23 and D43.
Tel. 05 65 27 60 60. Fax 05 65 27 60 70.
treyne@relaischateaux.com
www.chateaudelatreyne.com
Closed beg. Jan.–end Mar. Rest. closed lunch
12 rooms: 180–380€. 2 suites: 480–580€.
Prix fixe: 42€ (lunch), 82€ (dinner), 25€ (child).

Built in the 14th and 15th centuries, this Quercy-style castle overlooking the Dordogne river was turned into a Relais & Châteaux Hotel de Charme to great effect by Michèle Gombert. Philippe, Michèle's lawyer son, masterfully manages the estate. He is also behind the Château de Bastille, a more modest establishment in nearby Cales. At the Château de la Treyne every-

thing is set to impress. There are formal French gardens, 120 hectares of parkland, sumptuous bedrooms, pink marble bathrooms and vast reception areas. Meals are served in a cozy, richly decorated dining room complete with paneling and coffered ceiling. Chef Stéphane Andrieux, who worked at Pic, Meneau and the Lion d'Or at Romorantin, manages to modernize classic fare with great dexterity. Just try his slice of foie gras pan fried, served with quince jelly, fresh variations on the tomato (confit with fennel, with cabeou goat cheese, in sorbet and in a tart with mixed island spices), monkfish in curry foam, veal sweetbread medallions braised with truffles and, for dessert, a delicate variation on the cherry, all prepared with a real artist's touch. A good wine list with wines of the Southwest taking pride of place.

● **Le Pont de l'Ouysse**
Tel. 05 65 37 87 04. Fax 05 65 32 77 41.
pont.ouysse@wanadoo.fr
www.lepontdelouysse.fr
Closed mid-Nov.–beg. Mar. Rest. closed Mon. (exc. dinner in season), Tue. lunch.
12 rooms: 138–145€. 2 suites: 160–180€.
Prix fixe: 46€, 82€. A la carte: 120€.

Along the banks of the Ouysse sits the pretty maison Chambon. Marinette—here since the establishment was founded in what was the family home—welcomes guests with great aplomb while husband Daniel plays his stove like a musical instrument. He "composes" with local produce but knows when to take flight and sing with nobler, more exotic products. His salad of artichokes in a peppery truffle vinaigrette, duck liver with onions and peppers with port caramel, lobster ravioli with foam reduction, red mullet served two ways, grilled Atlantic sea bass with fennel and thyme served with a pepper and mango purée, as well as the pan-sautéed crayfish in garlic and tomato sauce, are highly satisfying. Everyone adores his meat duos such as Limousin beef tenderloin served with marrow, salt crystals, potato and beef tail cream, delicious braised veal sweetbreads with langoustine tails and the desserts (coconut milk tapioca, coconut sorbet with berries, peach soup with vanilla ice cream and a soft biscuit inspired by chef Lucien Vanel) are lapped up. A good cellar with the best Cahors wines to choose from. The rooms are charmingly in the style of the South of France, the swimming pool beckons and the shaded terrace is a delight.

LAGUIOLE

12210 Aveyron. Paris 579 – Aurillac 78 – Rodez 53 – Espalion 22.
ot-laguiole@wanadoo.fr.

High up on the Aubrac plateau (1000 meters), this town is renowned for its statue of a bronze bull by the sculptor Pompon (which sits on the place du Foirail), its cheese and the famous knife which carries its name. Last but not least, for the great chef who put it on the map.

 HOTELS-RESTAURANTS

● Michel Bras   ⬤⬤❀ 🏠
Rte de l'Aubrac.
Tel. 05 65 51 18 20. Fax 05 65 48 47 02.
info@michel-bras.fr / www.lucienbarriere.com
Closed end Oct.–beg. Apr. Rest. closed Mon.,
Tue. lunch (exc. July–Aug.),
Wed. lunch (exc. July–Aug.).
15 rooms: 178–370€.
Prix fixe: 100€, 160€, 18€ (child).

If you've never been to Laguiole or to the Bras, expect a cultural shock and forget everything you've ever seen elsewhere! Prepare for encounters of another kind with Michel, the young patriarch who turned sixty this year, his son Sébastien, his wife Ginette, their close team of workers and the Argentinian wine steward, Sergio Calderone, who presides over a highly sensible and interesting wine list. Where to begin? The enchantingly austere rooms high up on the Aubrac plateau or the exterior hallway which runs along like a sheep track or the dining room in the shape of a Zen retreat. Then comes the menu. Let's call it a hymn to Bras' inspiration in which pastoral poetry is

underscored by technique. The result is a famous spring vegetable, multi-grain and herb gargouillon with elderberry oil, simply served foie gras, seasonal salads, lassi, saffron potatoes. The catch of the day reads like one of Rousseau's confessions: "Simply braised, farmed langoustines garnished with sorrel-seasoned potatoes, served with an oil treated as if it were cream", or still "perfume in all tonalities for a Béganton turbot poached and simmered in sweet curry butter; in cooking, a touch of pesto with delicately perfumed basil and sweet young garlic". Meat dishes are deliciously and profoundly earthy "To bring us back to an ancient tradition: young spit-braised leg of ewe; a mixture of sweet Lézignan spring onions and orange-braised ham" and of course the rib eye steak from pure Aubrac beef, spit roasted and served with butter mousse, green beans and garlic. This cuisine is thoughtful, subtle and deeply rooted. Desserts are marvels of their kind: warm coconut biscuit with strawberries/raspberries that embody the idea of the "lava cake" created in 1981 and reproduced worldwide, sugar crystallized balsamite leaves and house chocolate ice cream. In short, this "otherworldly" establishment on the windswept, sweetly seductive heights of the Aubrac, absolutely deserves a visit.

■ Grand Hôtel Auguy   ◯🏠
2, allée de l'Amicale.
Tel. 05 65 44 31 11. Fax 05 65 51 50 81.
contact@hotel-auguy.fr / www.hotel-auguy.fr
Closed beg. Nov.–mid-Mar.
Rest. closed Sun. dinner (exc. July–Aug.),
Mon. (exc. dinner July–Aug.),
Tue. lunch (exc. July–Aug.).
22 rooms: 72–98€.
Prix fixe: 30€ (weekday lunch), 55€, 60€,
75€, 15€ (child).

Isabelle Auguy and Jean-Marc Muylaert run their establishment with great care. Bedrooms are simple, refined and always welcoming. Isabelle's cooking is underscored by a good wine list and Jean-Marc's service is frank and sincere. The menus—including the very good "Discover the *ter-*

roir of l'Aubrac" – as well as the à la carte offerings are strong on fresh, local produce cooked with a personal touch. You won't turn your back on the black pudding with pan-seared foie gras and apple cider-seasoned potato purée, green asparagus and frogs legs in an emulsion of smoked bacon and olive oil, veal sweetbreads braised in a ginger-seasoned reduction, new spring carrots with preserved shallots. The spice "cigars" over a caramelized pear with honey ice cream and ginger and a passion fruit dessert have what it takes.

LAMAGDELAINE see **CAHORS**

LAMARQUE

33460 Gironde. Paris 543 – Bordeaux 66.
A port on the Gironde estuary at the end of the Médoc peninsula.

 HOTELS-RESTAURANTS

● **Le Relais du Médoc** `SIM`
70, rue Principale.
Tel. 05 56 58 92 27.
lerelaisdumedoc@club.fr
Closed Sun. dinner, Mon.,
1 week at end Jan., 1 week beg. Feb.
Prix fixe: 12€ (weekday lunch), 19€, 25€,
33€, 5,50€ (child). A la carte: 35–40€.

Joel Tilatti and David Walzack have chosen a classical repertoire linked to the local *terroir*. Witness the Bordeaux-style escargots, Médoc-style salad, line-fished Atlantic sea bass with lemon sauce, duck breast medallions with foie gras and soft-centered chocolate cake with a berry sauce. The dining room has recently been refurbished.

LAMASTRE

07270 Ardèche. Paris 575 – Valence 39 – Privas 56 – Le Puy 73 – Saint-Etienne 92.
This is Ardèche in vacation mode, complete with tall houses, deep gorges and forests, pleasing inns and a little train that huffs and puffs as it chugs up the peaks.

 HOTELS-RESTAURANTS

● **Le Midi "Perrier"**
Pl Seignobos.
Tel. 04 75 06 41 50. Fax 04 75 06 49 75.
Closed Fri. dinner, Sun. dinner, Mon.,
mid-Dec.–mid-Feb.
10 rooms: 62–98€.
Prix fixe: 38€, 78€.

The atmosphere is a little faded but the authentic cuisine of Bernard Perrier is as much a part of yesterday as it is of today. Gorge yourselves on warm salad with duck foie gras and mushrooms, crayfish cake with lobster sauce, Bresse hen poached in a pork bladder and the frozen chestnut soufflé. The solid dishes cry out for a choice Côtes-du-Rhône before retiring to your old-fashioned room for a peaceful night's slumber.

■ **Château d'Urbilhac**
2 km se via rte de Vernoux-en-Vivarais.
Tel. 04 75 06 42 11.
info@chateaudurbilhac.com
www.chateaudurbilhac.com
12 rooms: 115–146€.

This 19th-century neo-Renaissance "castle", set in a vast park of thirty hectares overlooking the Doux valley, offers up lots of peace and quiet. Old-fashioned rooms with some choice pieces of furniture, a swimming pool and tennis court.

In Le Crestet (07270). 8 km e.

■ **L'Escapade**
Le Groubon.
Tel.-Fax 04 75 06 33 90.
josiane.scherle@aliceadsl.fr
www.lamastre.com/escapade
Closed Feb. vac.
9 rooms: 38–40€.
Prix fixe: 12€ (weekday lunch, wine inc.),
15€, 19€, 28€, 8€ (child). A la carte: 30€.

The dynamic Josiane Scherlé has just taken over the reins of this establishment. The hotel and restaurant are being renovated. A hot goat cheese–stuffed tomato, trout and ravioli, squab with grated potato cakes and the honey and lavender crème brûlée are first-class and sensibly priced. Extras include a gym, swimming pool and WiFi.

LAMBALLE

22400 Côtes-d'Armor. Paris 430 – Dinan 40 – Rennes 80 – Saint-Brieuc 20 – Saint-Malo 48.

The town is nestled close to the bay of Saint-Brieuc and boasts a national stud farm, the Mathurin-Méheut museum and a collection of ancient granite, half-timbered houses that add to its cachet.

 HOTELS-RESTAURANTS

■ Le Manoir des Portes

La Poterie.
Tel. 02 96 31 13 62. Fax 02 96 31 20 53.
contact@manoirdesportes.com
www.manoirdesportes.com
Rest. closed Sun., Mon.
12 rooms: 55–86€. 3 suites: 112–141€.
Prix fixe: 23€. A la carte: 35€.

This 16th-century manor house with comfortable, recently renovated bedrooms sits a mere trot from a riding center, in the middle of a leafy garden. The pleasant dining room has exposed beams and a fireplace. Hervé Jamin serves up dishes using produce to its best effect as well as foie gras, catfish filet with veal reduction, grilled chitterling sausage and the kouign-amann.

■ La Tour des Archants

2, rue du Docteur-Lavergne.
Tel. 02 96 31 01 37. Fax 02 96 31 37 59.
latourdesarchants@wanadoo.fr
Rest. closed Sat.
16 rooms: 50–70€.
Prix fixe: 18€, 25€, 32€, 9€ (child).

Claude Mounier's 14th-century timber-framed house nestles in the center of town. On offer: simple, modern bedrooms as well as two dining rooms, one rustic, the other contemporary, in which to taste ageless fare (mussels in cream or a pepper-seasoned steak) and unbeatable desserts (the house crème brûlée, a tart Tatin).

● Le Connétable

9, rue Paul-Langevin.
Tel.-Fax 02 96 31 03 50.
Closed Sun. dinner, Mon., 1 week Oct., 2 weeks Jan., 1 week June.
Prix fixe: 11€, 14€, 19€, 28€, 7,50€ (child). A la carte: 35€.

Hervé Nicholas' local cuisine is both lively and polished. A guinea hen terrine, yellow pollock filet with langoustines, braised side of milk-fed veal, foie gras and the apple hazelnut crumble are most satisfying, especially as prices show restraint. His wife, Marie-Laure, watches over the service.

LAMBERSART see LILLE

LAMOTTE-BEUVRON

41600 Loir-et-Cher. Paris 173 – Salbris 21 – Orléans 37 – Blois 60 – Romorantin 39.

This Sologne village is famous for the Tatin sisters who invented their upside-down apple tart.

 HOTELS-RESTAURANTS

■ Hôtel Tatin

5, av de Vierzon, across from the train station.
Tel. 02 54 88 00 03. Fax 02 54 88 96 73.
hotel-tatin@wanadoo.fr / www.hotel-tatin.fr
Closed Sun. dinner, Mon., Christmas–New Year's vac., Feb. vac., 2 weeks beg. Aug.
13 rooms: 52–77€. 1 suite: 120€.
Prix fixe: 27€, 51€, 9€ (child).

Don't forget it was here that the Tatin sisters invented their famous, eponymous tart. Martial Caillé serves up well-made dishes: quail terrine with foie gras, grilled pike-perch with foie gras, roasted partridge with grilled ham and the original tart Tatin. Moderate prices and a good wine cellar. Modern décor in the rooms.

LAMPAUL PLOUARZEL

29810 Finistère. Paris 584 – Saint-Brieuc 162 – Quimper 80 – Brest 25 – Landerneau 14.
omt.lampaul-plouarzel@wanadoo.fr.

On the road to the Abers, a pleasant halt in the Northern Finistère region.

| ● | RESTAURANTS |

● Auberge du Vieux Puits `COM`
Pl de l'Eglise.
Tel.-Fax 02 98 84 09 13.
Closed Sun. dinner, Mon., 2 weeks Sept., end Mar.–beg. Apr.
Prix fixe: 32€, 42€.

Jean-Pierre Stéphan, the previous incumbent at Benodet, has made his nest in this pleasant inn. He works with market produce to propose a number of sparkling dishes: rosemary-seasoned roasted shrimp, an aromatic broth with shellfish and langoustines, simply prepared seasonal fish, beef cheek braised with grilled smoked bacon and a chicory crème brûlée. Marie-Louise Stéphan has a warm welcome.

LANDERSHEIM

67700 Bas-Rhin. Paris 462 – Saverne 13 – Strasbourg 25.
The rich and fertile countryside between Strasbourg and Saverne is known as the Kochersberg. This village, with its white church and timber-framed houses, is typical of the area.

| ■ | HOTELS |

■ Auberge du Kochersberg
2, rte de Saessolsheim.
Tel. 03 88 69 93 08.
18 rooms: 80–130€ (by reserv. only).

Following several changes of ownership, a local group of investors has just reopened this mythical landmark. Ten rooms have been entirely renovated in a very comfortable style to put this establishment back in the class it deserves. (It once served as the luxurious "canteen" of the Adidas group). Banquets and restaurants are run by Kieffer catering.

LANDSER

68440 Haut-Rhin. Paris 475 – Mulhouse 11 – Bâle 32 – Colmar 54.

This little town in the Sundgau, not far from Mulhouse and its museums, has a great gastronomic future before it.

| ● | RESTAURANTS |

● Hostellerie Paulus `V.COM`
4, pl de la Paix.
Tel. 03 89 81 33 30. Fax 03 89 26 81 85.
Closed Sun. dinner, Mon., 1 week Christmas–New Year's, 2 weeks Aug.
Prix fixe: 25€ (weekdays) 44€, 59€, 69€.

Hervé Paulus now serves his wonderful, small menu (at 25) at lunch and dinner. He doesn't compromise on quality, offering balanced menus which reflect his daily market purchases, seasonal ingredients, traditional Alsatian as well as other influences. The chocolate-colored interior has just been redone and the teakwood terrace on the back is a pleasure on fine days. Pan-seared slice of foie gras, langoustine brochette with crunchy fresh sweet pea carpaccio, John Dory with broad beans and Serrano ham, pike-perch with a stir fry of bok choy and bacon, veal sweetbreads with small French peas and steak with buttered potatoes reveal a neoclassicist of stupendous talent who plays skillfully on a register of tastes while avoiding the chi-chi like the plague. His thyme-seasoned roasted peaches and poached apricots with almond cake are choice. Top Alsatian wines form part of the feast and blond, smiling Stéphanie Paulus' charming welcome warms the heart.

LANGEAIS

37130 Indre-et-Loire. Paris 262 – Saumur 41 – Tours 24 – Angers 96 – Chinon 28.
otsi@neuronnexion.fr.
Louis XI's castle is an impressive pile in this small, Old World town.

| ◨◉ | HOTELS-RESTAURANTS |

● Errard
2, rue Gambetta.
Tel. 02 47 96 82 12. Fax 02 47 96 56 72.

info@errard.com / www.errard.com
Closed Sun. dinner (off season), Mon. (off
season), Tue. (off season), Dec.–end Jan.
8 rooms: 69–79€. 1 suite: 106€.
Prix fixe: 29€, 39€, 51€, 15€ (child).
A la carte: 65€.

This is a family operation run by Yannick
Errard in an ancient coaching inn dating from 1653 and harboring a few old-
fashioned rooms. He is a proponent of
Loire valley cuisine and treats his guests to
duck foie gras with spiced poached pears,
escargots and mushrooms in puff pastry,
eel stewed in wine with onions and Bou-
gueil wine, spice-glazed pork chops and
pineapple, mango, passion fruit, banana
and cardamom spring roll soaked in aged
rum. From a list brimming over with Loire
wines you're bound to find the ideal bottle
to accompany your meal. An excursion to
the nearby château makes for a good post-
prandial digestive.

In Saint-Patrice (37130). 10 km w via rte de
Bourgueil.

■ **Château de Rochecotte**
Tel. 02 47 96 16 16. Fax 02 47 96 90 59.
chateau.rochecotte@wanadoo.fr
www.chateau-de-rochecotte.fr
Closed end Jan.–end Feb., end Nov.–10 Dec.
35 rooms: 134–222€. 3 suites: 291€.
Prix fixe: 39€ (lunch), 51€, 58€ (wine inc.).

On the road of the Loire châteaux lies the
ancient and well looked-after property of
the Prince de Talleyrand. Here, the Pas-
quiers welcome you to cozy, tastefully
decorated rooms. It is a delight to wander in the park towards the chapel, taking in the French-style gardens and the
swimming pool. The restaurant is up
to par. In the 18th-century-style dining
room, Emanuelle delights guests with
langoustines in salad, line-fished Atlantic sea bass escalope with artichokes and
basil, pork chop glazed with spicy sauce
and the chocolate and ginger biscuit,
while Gérard and Isabelle keep a solemn
eye on proceedings.

33210 Gironde. Paris 628 – Bordeaux 49 –
Bergerac 82 – Libourne 55.
office-du-tourisme-langon@wanadoo.fr.
The heart of the Graves and the good-natured
Sauternes region: this is the essence of this particular wine country of which this large town
is the capital.

	HOTELS-RESTAURANTS

● **Claude Darroze** ○⬒
95, cours du Général-Leclerc.
Tel. 05 56 63 00 48. Fax 05 56 63 41 15.
restaurant.darroze@wanadoo.fr
www.darroze.com
Closed mid-Oct.–mid-Nov., 5 Jan.–23 Jan.
15 rooms: 58–110€.
Prix fixe: 40€, 58€, 74€, 15€ (child).
A la carte: 85–104€.

This venerable coaching inn boasts pretty,
comfortable rooms and a terrace under
beautiful plane trees. As for the cuisine,
it remains faithful to a classical tradition dear to Claude Darroze's heart and
is mastered with the help of his second-
in-command, Sébastien Putrabey. Under
the trompe-l'oeil décor of the dining room
and according to season: braised red mullet with slow-cooked tomato and basil,
fresh milk-fed lamb, game (like the wild
rabbit à la royale), and the warm soft chocolate cake. Serge Oppillard's wine list has
a good showing from the Médoc, Pessac-
Léognan region.

● **Chez Cyril** 🅿🟩SIM
62, cours des Fossés.
Tel. 05 56 76 25 66. Fax 05 56 63 25 21.
cyril.baland@wanadoo.fr
Closed Sat. lunch, Sun. dinner, Mon. dinner.
Prix fixe: 12€ (weekday lunch), 22€, 32€
12€ (child).

Low-cost menus and market-based dishes
in a pretty, contemporary-style décor of
ivory and wood. Cyril Balland has managed to make a name for himself, with
simmered escargots with hazelnuts, cod
filet with garlic potato purée, a mush-

room-stuffed breast of guinea hen, soft chocolate cake with cocoa syrup and mandarin orange sorbet and spiced poached oranges, all sampled with pleasure. Plus, a lively welcome from Karine and nice wine list with foreign and French offerings.

LANGUIMBERG

57810 Moselle. Paris 413 – Nancy 60 – Lunéville 43 – Sarrebourg 19 – Saverne 48.
The road through the natural park of Lorraine meanders wantonly and dreamily among the pond lands of Moselle.

 | RESTAURANTS

● **Chez Michèle**
57, rue Principale.
Tel. 03 87 03 92 25. Fax 03 87 03 93 47.
Closed Tue. dinner, Wed., 22 Dec.–10 Jan.
Prix fixe: 17€ (lunch weekdays), 25€, 27€, 48€, 65€, 12€ (child). A la carte: 57–62€.

Michèle and Serge Poiré's inn is a quality stop in this country of ponds and forests. There are generally four hands in this kitchen but Serge is giving son Bruno, trained at Blanc in Vonnas and Westermann in Strasbourg, an increasingly free reign to develop his own talents. Mother Michèle orchestrates in the dining room and guides the gourmet through a wine list full of temptations. The cuisine reflects the tastes of today while drawing inspiration from the heritage of Lorraine, enriched by Mediterranean flavors. The *amuse-gueules* definitely herald what's coming next. Feast on a foie gras brochette with mirabelle plum jam, pike-perch with accompanying squid ink spaghetti, pigeon breast with polenta, browned under the grill with mascarpone cheese, before finishing with a cheese plate by Philippe Olivier and a strawberry rhubarb crème brûlée. This cuisine—both rich in flavor and full of well-balanced and thoughtful surprises—gives great pleasure. Be it in the dining room or on the terrace, the various menus cannot fail to seduce and the service is quite charming.

LANNEMEZAN

65300 Hautes-Pyrénées. Paris 825 – Auch 65 – Tarbes 33.
This industrial center (chemical products, reinforced concrete, a nearby institute on atmospheric research) is the most active in the Pyrenean range. Nearby is the valley of the Gers and the ancient chapel of Notre-Dame de Garaison.

■ | HOTELS-RESTAURANTS

■ **Hôtel des Pyrénées**
33, rue de Diderot, rue G.-Clemenceau.
Tel. 05 62 98 01 53. Fax 05 62 98 11 85.
Rest. closed Sun. dinner.
30 rooms: 39–54€.
Prix fixe: 14€, 22€, 28€, 40€,
7€ (child). A la carte: 35€.

A decent hotel harking back to 1900 with old-fashioned rooms full of wood paneling and a rustic dining room done in shades of pink. Jean-Jacques Nogues serves up an ad hoc *terroir* cuisine with no concession to fashion: foie gras served hot with simmered apples, trout with almonds, grilled duck magret with green peppercorns and a seasonal fruit tart go down well.

LANNION

22300 Côtes-d'Armor. Paris 515 – Saint-Brieuc 63 – Brest 96 – Morlaix 39.
tourisme.lannion@wanadoo.fr.
This town in the Côtes d'Armor has a definitive Breton flavor thanks to its old houses and close proximity to the sea.

● | RESTAURANTS

● **La Ville Blanche**
At the locale known as La Ville-Blanche, via rte de Tréguier, 5 km via D786.
Tel. 02 96 37 04 28. Fax 02 96 46 57 82.
www.la-ville-blanche.com
Closed Sun. dinner (exc. July–Aug.), Mon., Wed. (exc. July– Aug.), 18 Dec.–26 Jan., 1 week at end June–beg. July.
Prix fixe: 44€, 54€, 72€, 112€ (wine inc.), 15€ (child). A la carte: 65–70€.

One of the curiosities of the Ville Blanche is without a doubt the herb garden where Jean-Yves Jaguin grows the aromatic plants which he uses in his cooking. This attraction to quality is demonstrated in all the dishes of this pork-butcher and caterer who is master of the stove since the departure of his brother. If the garden is worth a visit so is the classic dining room where you can taste quintessential dishes with a modern touch. The warm oysters in a hen broth served with foie gras flan, shelled lobster and Paimpol beans in a thyme and lemon emulsion, braised carrots tossed in pumpkin seed oil, licorice-seasoned veal sweetbreads with a terrine of baby vegetables and variations on the peach (verbena peach ice cream, caramelized or peach and raspberry cocktail) or on the apple (mille-feuille or an iced mousse dessert with Calvados) are high flyers as is the selection of wines presented by Sébastien Balard.

● **Le Serpolet** **ⓝSIM**

1, rue Félix-Le-Dantec.
Tel. 02 96 46 50 23.
Closed Sat. lunch, Wed.
Prix fixe: 16,50€, 20€, 24€.
A la carte: 35€.

In this historic town, the green and pink house of Emmanuel Le Coadou does not go unnoticed. Likewise his cooking. Sheltered by stone walls and old beams, tuck into lamb confit in terrine with green lentils, red mullet pan fried with saffron butter, pan-tossed calf's liver with grapes and walnuts and a gratinéed fresh fruit sabayon. Vanessa is in charge of the dining room and cellar.

● **La Gourmandine** **SIM**

23, rue Roger-Barbé.
Tel. 02 96 46 40 55. Fax 02 96 37 11 39.
Closed Sat. lunch, Sun., Mon.
Prix fixe: 12€ (weekday lunch),
25€ (dinner) 7,50€ (child). A la carte: 38€.

In the center of Lannion is a place you'll want to return to for the aubergine and violet décor, the welcome and cooking of Sandrine and Gilles Vomscheid, not

to mention the unbeatable prices. Scallops in puff pastry flambéed with Noilly on a bed of slow-simmered leeks, wood fire-grilled line-fished Atlantic sea bass with herbs, wood fire–grilled pork shank with mustard sauce and browned goat cheese- and pear-filled filo pastry with caramel balsamic slip down nicely.

LAON

02000 Aisne. Paris 141 – Soissons 37 – Reims 62 – Saint-Quentin 48.
tourisme.info.laon@wanadoo.fr.
The upper town crowned with Notre Dame cathedral, its steeple and the Midi rampart. The Ardon gate is worth a detour, though can be admired from afar. Don't miss the Saint-Martin abbey or the Soissons gateway. There is a good museum in the Templar chapel.

● | RESTAURANTS

● **La Petite Auberge**

45, bd Brossolette.
Tel. 03 23 23 02 38. Fax 03 23 23 31 01.
palaon@orange.fr
Closed Sat. lunch, Sun. (exc. Bank holidays), Mon. dinner, 1 week Feb., 1 week at Easter, 2 weeks Aug.
Prix fixe: 19€, 25€, 32€, 41€, 10€ (child). A la carte: 63€.

Willy-Marc Zorn's La Petite Auberge, like his more modest Bistro Saint-Amour, are faithfully regional in inspiration. With veritable know-how, his offerings include langoustine-stuffed ravioli with rosemary-seasoned rhubarb compote, red mullet filet accompanied by squid ink risotto, Liques poultry filet with pasta shells and chanterelles and variations on fruits or chocolate. Excellent service by Nicolas Lovet.

LAPLUME see AGEN

LAPOUTROIE

68650 Haut-Rhin. Paris 457 – Colmar 20 – Sélestat 35 – Saint-Dié 36 – Munster 24.
A welcoming craft village with all the charm of the Vosges, fresh air, thatched roofs, cheese

makers, the scent of distilling and savory scents wafting from the inns.

 HOTELS-RESTAURANTS

■ Les Alisiers

Follow signs from the church, 3 km to the sw via secondary road.
Tel. 03 89 47 52 82. Fax 03 89 47 22 38.
hotel@alisiers.com / www.alisiers.com
Closed beg. Jan.–beg. Feb.,
4 days at Christmas. Rest. closed Mon., Tue.
15 rooms: 50–122€. 1 suite: 180€.
Prix fixe: 15€ (weekdays), 28€, 39€, 45€,
10€ (child).

This old farmhouse dating back to 1819 houses a charming inn. Under the watchful eye of Ella Degouy and with the help of her son Matthias, you can make the most of colorful, contemporary rooms, a hammam and a regional cuisine served in the luminous dining room or on the terrace overlooking the valley. The foie gras served hot, salmon filet with bacon-seasoned cream, Limousin lamb platter and Marcel Manthermann's kirsch-flavored iced mousse dessert put you right on track.

■ Le Faudé

28, rue du Général-Dufieux.
Tel. 03 89 47 50 35. Fax 03 89 47 24 82.
info@faude.com / www.faude.com
Closed 3 weeks Nov., 3 weeks Mar.
Rest. closed Tue., Wed.
30 rooms: 42–92€. 2 suites: 128–164€.
Prix fixe: 19€, 26€, 31€, 52€, 9€ (child).

A kindly welcome awaits you at Thierry and Chantal Baldinger's enlarged and modernized village house. Three dining rooms (one in green tones, the other in orange and the third in mauve) allow traditional gourmets a choice of venue. A garden runs along the river, and cozy rooms, a fitness center with a heated pool, hammam and sauna, make you want to move in. At the stoves, Thierry and his second-in-command José Di Luca are multi-faceted and do not fail to deliver: The foie gras and white wine, caramel and sauerkraut

chutney, pike-perch filet over sauerkraut, trilogy of tuna with tomato reduction, tête de veau with sauce gribiche (caper and pickle mayonnaise). The frozen layered nougat and meringue house dessert is staggering, as is the 500-bottle wine list.

LARRAU

64560 Pyrénées-Atlantiques. Paris 835 – Saint-Jean-Pied-de-Port 47 – Oloron 43 – Pau 77.
This town at the edge of the Iraty woods is a stopover on the way to St-James of Compostella. In the fall, wood pigeon is hunted here.

 HOTELS-RESTAURANTS

■ Etchemaïté

Tel. 05 59 28 61 45. Fax 05 59 28 72 71.
hotel.etchemaite@wanadoo.fr
www.hotel-etchemaite.fr
Closed 1 week beg. Dec., Jan.
Rest. closed Sun. dinner, Mon.
16 rooms: 42–58€.
Prix fixe: 18€ (exc. Sun. and Bank holidays),
24€, 34€, 8€ (child). A la carte: 50€.

Here in Pyrenean territory, a stay at the Etchemaïté brothers' family inn will warm the heart. An all-smiling Martin welcomes you at reception knowing that in the kitchen, Pierre—an old disciple of Constant at the Crillon and Cambdeborde at the Régalade—will ensure a well-cooked regional cuisine: stuffed squid with veal trotter and sweetbread, tuna steak with fennel sauté, squab served two ways and the pain perdu dessert are guarantees of delicious siestas in pleasant bedrooms.

■ Despouey

Tel. 05 59 28 60 82. Fax 05 59 28 64 10.
Closed mid-Nov.–1 Apr.
7 rooms: 34–50€.

Right in the heart of the high Soule, this family *pension* is welcoming. Recently renovated rooms with old-fashioned furnishings guarantee your comfort.

LASCABANES see **CAHORS**

LASTOURS

11600 Aude. Paris 800 – Montpellier 169 –
Narbonne 88 – Carcassonne 15.
This is an ancient village at the foot of its ruined
castle deep in Cathar country.

 RESTAURANTS

● Le Puits du Trésor

21, rue des Quatre-Châteaux.
Tel.-Fax 04 68 77 50 24.
contact@lepuitsdutresor.com
www.lepuitsdutresor.com
Closed 2 weeks beg. Jan., mid-Feb.–end Feb.
Prix fixe: 37€, 53€, 70€. A la carte: 75€.

You can't miss the chimney of this old textile factory situated at the foot of the castle. The latter houses a country brasserie
with a terrace devoid of chi-chi or osten-
tation but also a modern and comfortable
gastronomic restaurant. Here Jean-Marc
Boyer, a disciple of Pacaud at l'Ambroisie, is
as precise and modest as his mentor in his
treatment of noble products cooked with
respect to tradition. Marbled foie gras terrine with artichokes, lobster and pigeon, a
lobster slow-cooked with garlic and chanterelles show a fine-honed artistry. The
lemon preserves with mascarpone cheese
ends the meal on a sunny touch. Team
these up with the new wines of the great
South under Laurent Prunet's guidance.

LATTES see MONTPELLIER

LAUTERBOURG

67630 Bas-Rhin. Paris 519 – Wissembourg
19 – Haguenau 41 – Strasbourg 63.
tourisme.lauterbourg@wanadoo.fr.
This border town with its demolished ramparts
alongside the Rhine river is the town furthest
from the sea in the whole of France.

 HOTELS-RESTAURANTS

● La Poêle d'Or

35, rue du Général-Mittelhauser.
Tel. 03 88 94 84 16. Fax 03 88 54 62 30.
info@poeledor.com / www.poeledor.com
Closed Wed., Thu., 3 weeks Jan.,
end July–beg. Aug.
Prix fixe: 26€ (lunch), 40€, 73,50€.
A la carte: 60€.

This half-timbered house is a village institution where François and Marie-Odile
Gottar match a gourmet tradition with a
faultless welcome. Four hands man the
stove—those of Jean-Marc and his father
François, who has had a stint with some
of the greats (Cerf at Marlenheim, Buerehiesel at Strasbourg). Be it in the Renaissance dining room or on the flowered
terrace, treat yourselves to truffled foie
gras, classic Alsatian choucroute made
with fish instead of charcuterie, veal kidneys with whole grain mustard, pigeon
simply roasted and served in its own cooking dish and a strawberry and raspberry
feuilleté. Jean-Claude Wendling is good at
pairing dishes with local wines.

In Munchhausen (67470). 6 km s via D248.

● A la Rose

35, rue du Rhin.
Tel. 03 88 86 51 86. Fax 03 88 86 15 99.
Closed Mon. (exc. Bank holidays),
Tue. (exc. Bank holidays), 2 weeks beg. Feb.,
2 weeks July.
Prix fixe: 9,50€, 11,50€, 22€.
A la carte: 45€.

Thierry Lehmann devises compact *terroir*
dishes in this traditional inn. The house
prepared goose foie gras, meat stew with
onions, herbs and Riesling wine, a venison filet steak and the crème brûlée are
accompanied by Alsatian wines at reasonable prices. The flowered terrace is
highly popular in good weather.

LAVAL

53000 Mayenne. Paris 279 – Angers 78 –
Le Mans 85 – Rennes 74.
office.tourisme.laval@wanadoo.fr.
Its location on the Mayenne, its old houses, the
castle and its keep, its embankments and the
de la Perrine garden all conspire to make you
want to stop over in Laval.

HOTELS-RESTAURANTS

■ Grand Hôtel de Paris

22, rue de la Paix.
Tel. 02 43 53 76 20. Fax 02 43 56 91 83.
hotelparislaval@wanadoo.fr
Closed 22 Dec.–2 Jan.
50 rooms: 61–160€.

This hotel built in 1950 is situated in the town center. It has recently modernized its rooms in tones of red and yellow. The walls are hung with the paintings of artist friends. Internet. WiFi.

● Le Bistro de Paris   V.COM

67, rue Val-de-Mayenne.
Tel. 02 43 56 98 29. Fax 02 43 56 52 85.
bistro.de.paris@wanadoo.fr
Closed Sat. lunch, Sun. dinner, Mon., Aug.
Prix fixe: 26€ (Sat., Sun., dinner),
31€ (Sat., Sun., dinner), 47€, 12€ (child).
A la carte: 49€.

This neo-art nouveau bistro cuts quite a dash. The décor is charming, the prices are right and Guy Lemercier's cuisine manages both tradition and current trends with dexterity. This modest Meilleur Ouvrier de France is sure of his art as demonstrated by his well-balanced menus. Warm langoustine salad, turbot filet with spices, veal sweetbreads seasoned with Arabica coffee and the chocolate macaron hold up well. The wine list presided over by Jean-François Pavoine is representative of all France's wine regions.

● Le Capucin Gourmand   V.COM

66, rue Vaufleury.
Tel. 02 43 66 02 02.
capucingourmand@free.fr
http://capucingourmand.free.fr
Closed Sun. dinner, Mon., Tue. lunch, 3 weeks Aug.
Prix fixe: 21€ (weekdays), 47€.

The setting is pleasant with beams, paneling, wicker chairs and a patio. The cooking isn't bad either. Scallop sausages, escargot-stuffed profiteroles, squab cooked in almonds and the fruit crumble leave a good impression.

● L'Antiquaire   COM

5, rue des Béliers.
Tel. 02 43 53 66 76.
Closed Sat. lunch, Sun. dinner, Wed.,
Feb. vac., 3 weeks mid-July–beg. Aug.
Prix fixe: 18€, 39€.

In the center of the old town this lively establishment impresses with its art deco dining room done in ochre, salmon pink and black tones. Gilles Hubert fiddles with local fare, not hesitating to give it a push in a more modern direction. Warm beef cheek salad with foie gras, poached pike-perch filet with cider beurre blanc, pan-seared lamb chops with a garlic-seasoned new potato purée and a Reinette apple crumble with almonds are real delicacies.

● La Gerbe de Blé   COM

83, rue Victor-Boissel.
Tel. 02 43 53 14 10. Fax 02 43 49 02 84.
gerbedeble@wanadoo.fr / www.gerbedeble.com
Closed 1 week beg. Jan., 1 week at end July,
3 weeks Aug. Rest. closed Sun., Mon. lunch.
8 rooms: 72–100€.
Prix fixe: 18€ (weekday lunch), 26€, 37€,
12€ (child).

Not far from the Prefecture, Eric Jouanen's establishment boasts eight agreeable little rooms and a good table. Hailing from Nîmes, Jouanen marries local cuisine with that of the great West in some lively concoctions. Beams and a fireplace grace the dining room where you can feast on green bean salad with foie gras, line-fished Atlantic sea bass grilled in an herb crust, Maine beef rib eye steak. The strawberry tempura hits the spot.

● A la Bonne Auberge   COM

170, rue Bretagne.
Tel. 02 43 69 07 81.
labonneauberge@free.fr
Closed Fri. dinner, Sat., Sun. dinner,
10 days Christmas–New Year's.
Prix fixe: 18€ (weekdays), 40€.

On the road between Rennes and Vitré, this Virginia creeper–clad residence catches the eye. A modern dining room is the venue for tasty little meals thanks

433

to sensible menus—inexpensive on week-days. Local chitterling sausage on blinis with Camembert cream, pike-perch with crayfish, rack of lamb in an herb crust and spelt wheat cake slip down nicely.

LE LAVANCHER see
CHAMONIX-MONT-BLANC

LE LAVANDOU

83980 Var. Paris 877 – Fréjus 64 –
Cannes 102 – Toulon 42.
info@lelavandou.com.
"Tonight the sea and the sky made a rendez-vous, to create a dreamlike world in the Lavan-dou," wrote songster Henri Salvador. Indeed, the beach and its pier facing the Hyères islands are redolent of the Côte d'Azur of the sixties revised in the seventies.

 HOTELS-RESTAURANTS

■ Auberge de la Calanque
62, av du Général-de-Gaulle.
Tel. 04 94 71 05 96. Fax 04 94 71 20 12.
www.aubergelacalanque.com
Closed mid-Oct.–mid-Apr.
32 rooms: 155–275€. 2 suites: 275
Half board: 190–310€.

Although Provence takes pride of place, this establishment could pass for a haci-enda. Colors abound inside and out while the blue and white bedrooms look out to sea. The swimming pool in the garden is a little piece of paradise.

■ Le Rabelais
2, rue Rabelais.
Tel. 04 94 71 00 56. Fax 04 94 71 82 55.
hotel.lerabelais@wanadoo.fr
www.le-rabelais.fr
Closed 20 Nov.–20 Dec.
20 rooms: 45–105€.

A comfortable hotel in the Provençal style, facing the marina with bright, colorful rooms. Breakfasts are served on the ter-race and prices are reasonable.

● L'Atlas   SIM
27, quai Gabriel-Péri.
Tel.-Fax 04 94 64 73 10.
atlas.restaurant@wanadoo.fr
Prix fixe: 17€, 25€, 35€, 12€ (child).
A la carte: 40€.

Moroccan soup, filo pastry with egg, grou-per tagine, couscous with assortment of meats and Middle Eastern pastries for des-sert are lovingly and efficiently cooked by Zoubida Rezgaoui. Across from the port.

● L'Auberge Provençale   SIM
11, rue Patron-Ravello.
Tel. 04 94 71 00 44. Fax 04 94 15 02 25.
aubProvençale@yahoo.com
Closed Mon., Tue. lunch, 10 Nov.–20 Dec.
Prix fixe: 28€, 42€.
A la carte: 51€.

Annie Pennavayre loves this fifties bistro in the heart of the old village where Chris-tophe Janvier serves up pleasant dishes with local color. Mediterranean sea bass roasted with thyme flowers, thin tomato slices braised with balsamic and artichoke reduction, foie gras-stuffed beef tender-loin with red wine reduction and the rasp-berry mille-feuille are quite alluring.

● Les Tamaris   SIM
Plage de Saint-Clair.
Tel. 04 94 71 07 22 / 04 94 71 02 70.
Fax 04 94 71 88 64.
Closed Tue. (exc. dinner in season),
beg. Nov.–mid-Feb.
A la carte: 45–65€.

Christian Jacquinet's table is an oasis on the beach. Yellow flowered tablecloths and dishes such as breaded and fried zucchini, grilled sardines, bouillabaisse, lamb chops and chocolate cake. Saint-Baillon *rosé* and ice-cream from Del Monte in Bormes are lapped up without moderation.

In Aiguebelle (83980). 4,5 km w via D559.

● Les Roches
1, av des Trois-Dauphins.
Tel. 04 94 71 05 07. Fax 04 94 71 08 40.
www.hotelprestige-provence.com
Closed mid-Jan.–mid-Feb.

32 rooms: 365–750€. 6 suites: 680–1400€.
Prix fixe: 62€, 95€.

The latest of the "the highly rated of the Côte d'Azur", Mathias Dandine—formed at the Oasis in la Napoule, Chibois in Grasse and Tarridec at the Roches—has just bought the restaurant of the latter establishment and abandoned his restaurant, the Escoundudo at Bormes, for this terrace facing the Golden Isles. While brother Fabien holds sway over the dining room, Mathias is in the kitchen preparing a generous, high-quality, deeply rooted Provençal cuisine with brio. A marvelous bouillabaisse with poached egg and salt cod potato purée, rouget with stuffed squid, duckling roasted with chestnuts and olive jus seduce us. Everything from the wines to the dessert (a layered chocolate and pepper dessert) have perfect pitch. An idyllic experience. Pretty nautical rooms with terra cotta–tiled bathrooms and a more modest poolside restaurant.

In Aiguebelle.

● **Le Sud**

Av des Trois-Dauphins.
Tel. 04 94 05 76 98.
Closed Jan.
Prix fixe: 59€, 20€ (child).

Christophe Pétra is a mischievous ex-pupil of Vergé, Chibois, Outhier and Bocuse and has turned this roadside establishment into a charming bistro with carefully cooked delicacies. In a Provençal-style dining room he distils his know-how via a menu where products from the daily catch and the Varois hinterland are the stars. After the *amuse-bouches* based on the truffle, set your heart on a Mediterranean sea bass with white beans and young spinach, snapper in thin-sliced potatoes served with vegetables, four-hour roasted rabbit with pine nut polenta before ending with a rich "avalanche" of small desserts. A selection of Provençal wines by Gérard Combec accompanies these dishes. A taxi shuttle is available to guests.

In Fossette-Plage (83980). 3 km e via D559 (rte de Saint-Tropez).

■ **83 Hôtel** 🏨

Av du Levant.
Tel. 04 94 71 20 15. Fax 04 94 71 63 42.
hotel83@wanadoo.fr / www.83hotel.com
Closed beg. Oct.–beg. Apr.
30 rooms: 120–350€.
Prix fixe: 36€, 17€ (child).

You'll want to spend time in this hotel with its bright, spacious rooms, two swimming pools (indoor and outdoor), a tennis court and a terrace from which to sample tasty specialities. A local tuna and citrus dish, wild rouget on a bed of fennel in pesto sauce, wood fire–grilled lamb chops with an eggplant and thyme cake and the strawberry mille-feuille hold up well.

LES LAVAULTS see **QUARRE-LES-TOMBES**

81500 Tarn. Paris 700 – Albi 51 – Castres 40 – Toulouse 44.
Visit this medieval city for its ancient houses and the cathedral of Saint Alain.

 HOTELS-RESTAURANTS

In Giroussens (81500). 10 km nw via D87.

● **L'Echauguette** COM

Pl de la Mairie.
Tel. 05 63 41 63 65. Fax 05 63 41 63 13.
www.restaurant-echauguette.com
Closed Sun. dinner (exc. July–Aug.), Mon. (exc. July–Aug.), mid-Sept.–end Sept., Feb.
3 rooms: 26–45€.
Prix fixe: 11€ (weekday lunch), 18€, 25€, 48€, 7€ (child). A la carte: 25–30€.

Built in the 13th and 19th centuries, this good, rustic establishment has three pleasant rooms and well-made classical dishes. Francis Fachetti admirably succeeds in his preparation of duck foie gras, tuna steak served on a bed of sauerkraut, traditional cassolette and veal kidney poached in Gaillac wine. To finish, a coconut mousse and a pineapple carpaccio slip down easily. The terrace and the interior are in a nautical style. Pretty view.

In Saint-Lieux-lès-Lavaur (81500). 7 km nw via D 630.

■ **Château des Cambards**

Les Cambards.
Tel. 05 63 81 10 00.
moulin-de-matti@wanadoo.fr
6 rooms: 75–125€.

This 17th-century manor house makes for a charming and stylish stopover, thanks to its wooded parkland, swimming pool, terrace, piano bar and cozy rooms.

LAVELANET

09300 Ariège. Paris 798 – Foix 28 – Carcassonne 71 – Castelnaudary 53 – Pamiers 42.
lavelanet.tourisme@wanadoo.fr.
The Ariège is also known as the rough country; 500 metres above sea level are green peaks studded with castles to be visited at a leisurely pace.

| ■ | HOTELS-RESTAURANTS |
| ● | |

In Palot (09300). 10 km w via D117.

■ **Relais des Trois Châteaux**

Tel. 05 61 01 33 99. Fax 05 61 01 73 73.
lerelaisdestroischateaux@wanadoo.fr
www.troischateaux.com
Closed mid-Nov.–end Nov., end Jan.–mid-Feb.
Rest. closed Sat. lunch, Sun. dinner, Tue.
7 rooms: 53–65€.
Prix fixe: 25€, 38€, 48€, 7€ (child).

An agreeable stay in the Ariège château country in an old farmhouse complete with overhead beams, fireplace and period furniture. Take advantage of the covered pool and fitness center after sampling some well-turned-out dishes by Gérard Gardinal which include a slice of duck foie gras, medallion of monkfish with blackberry cream, veal sweetbreads in Madeira wine and the dessert cart.

LAVENTIE

62840 Pas-de-Calais. Paris 230 – Lille 29 – Béthune 18 – Arras 46.
Hospitality collides with good cooking in the Nord-Pas-de-Calais.

| ● | RESTAURANTS |

● **Le Cerisier**

3, rue de la Gare.
Tel. 03 21 27 60 59. Fax 03 21 27 60 87.
eric.delerue@wanadoo.fr / www.lecerisier.com
Closed Sat. lunch, Sun. dinner, Mon.,
1 week Feb., Aug.
Prix fixe: 29€, 48€, 66€, 15€ (child).
A la carte: 81–93€.

This typically bourgeois house with its stone and brick facade and contemporary interiors admirably suits the fancy cuisine of Eric Delerue. Like his mentor Marc Meurin, he likes to work with quality produce and invent tasty combinations such as a lobe of foie gras with tart cherry sauce, rouget seasoned with Thai herbs and sesame oil, Tahitian vanilla–seasoned squab and sticks of steamed shortbread. The small chocolate cake with a caramel filling, served hot, and the peanut macaron are tip-top. Julien Lombard advises from a good wine list and Isabelle Delerue's service is briskly efficient.

LAXOU see NANCY
LAY-SAINT-CHRISTOPHE see NANCY

LECTOURE

32700 Gers. Paris 708 – Agen 39 – Auch 35 – Condom 26.
ot.lectoure@wanadoo.fr.
This little hillside town charms mightily thanks to its wonderful situation, cathedral and limestone dwellings.

| ■ | HOTELS-RESTAURANTS |
| ● | |

■ **Hôtel de Bastard**

Rue Lagrange.
Tel. 05 62 68 82 44. Fax 05 62 68 76 81.
www.hotel-de-bastard.com

Closed Christmas–end Jan. Rest. closed Sun. dinner, Mon., Tue. lunch.

28 rooms: 46–70€. 3 suites: 90–122€.

Prix fixe: 16€ (weekday lunch), 29€, 48€, 62€ (wine inc.), 10€ (child).

The old 18th-century town house of the Sire of Bastard St Denis remains a prime hotspot in this city in the Gers. Everyone may take advantage of the convivial welcome, the air-conditioned rooms (some of them with mansard roofs), the bar, the swimming pool, the garden and the regional cuisine of Jean-Luc Arnaud. Formerly at Senderens, Arnaud proposes a spiffy à la carte menu based around a duck foie gras served three ways, snapper in crust with diced seasoned tomatoes, veal sweetbreads medallion with potato and chanterelle gnocchi and an Armagnac-soaked prune soufflé.

LEERS see **LILLE**

LEMBACH

67510 Bas-Rhin. Paris 461 – Wissembourg 15 – Bitche 32 – Strasbourg 55.
info@ot.lembach.com.

A forest town at the tip of Northern Alsace and an exquisite layover on the road to the region's fortified castles. Do not miss the ruins of Fleckenstein.

 HOTELS-RESTAURANTS

■ Hôtel du Cheval Blanc & Rossel'Stub

3, rte de Wissembourg.
Tel. 03 88 94 41 86. Fax 03 88 94 20 74.
info@au-cheval-blanc.fr
www.au-cheval-blanc.fr
Closed 2 weeks end Jan.–10 Feb., 10 days at end Aug., 1 week beg. Sept.
Rest. closed Fri. lunch, Mon., Tue.
Rossel'Stub closed: Wed., Thu.
3 rooms: 107–138€. 3 suites: 199€.
Prix fixe: 26€. A la carte: 35–40€.

An exquisite hotel with bright, cozy rooms in a chic rustic style. On the ground floor is a *winstub* offering great value for money.

There are wooden tables, an open kitchen, prompt service and light versions of traditional home cooking. Sure-fire successes, the boneless roast duck in wine sauce, a salmon terrine with cured herring with horseradish cream, a pike fish quenelle with shellfish sauce, pork trotter wrapped in caul lace and served with mustard sauce and the rhubarb and strawberry soup are models of their kind.

■ Le Relais du Heimbach

15, rte de Wissembourg.
Tel. 03 88 94 43 46. Fax 03 88 94 20 85.
www.hotel-au-heimbach.fr
16 rooms: 55–70€. 2 suites: 107€.

A kindly welcome from Martin Biehler in this half-timbered house opposite the Cheval Blanc. Well-tended, homespun rooms and generous breakfasts make you want to take up residence.

● Le Cheval Blanc ⓒⓒⓄLUX

4, rte de Wissembourg.
Tel. 03 88 94 41 86. Fax 03 88 94 20 74.
info@au-cheval-blanc.fr
www.au-cheval-blanc.fr
Closed Fri., Mon., Tue., 10 days Aug., 2 weeks beg. Sept.
Prix fixe: 34€ (lunch), 56€, 69€, 89€.
A la carte: 130€.

This 18th-century coaching inn is in full renewal. Fernand Mischler, the father, and Franck, his son, are committed to quality. They, more than anyone, know how to work a product in traditional and innovative ways. Take the frogs legs: served as soup, as a tiny canapé, or crispy, ham-style served on a garlic flan with parsley jus, they are enough to make you faint as you lick the plate. The Mischler's plush, grand dining room with its coffered ceiling and elaborate fireplace definitely has a soul; here, everything is at the service of good taste. Loiseau used to say that "the star in the kitchen is the product", a sentence which could easily be appropriated by these outstanding artisans who, were they able to, would wear their modesty emblazoned across their front. With them mussel stew with saffron cream sauce, parsley and shallots and a langoustine tail in its bouillon gives the impression of having just been pulled out of the water that morning in a port in the Finistère. Everything else is just as pleasing. The hot duck foie gras pan tossed with acidic melon, grilled rouget served over polenta, turbot in a pastry crust and its little oyster soup seems to have just jumped out of the sea. The product and nothing but the product: that's what one thinks when tasting the simply roasted lobster with salted butter, a rack of milk-fed lamb from the Aveyron in a crust of herbs, juicy venison with chanterelles and berry jelly and Cyrille Lhoro's cheeses (ah the Gouda, the Abondance, the Fougeru and the Munster!) with amazing breads introduced to us in the dining room with gusto by a master baker wearing a beret (a symbolic innovation). Everything is followed by regal desserts: the soft raspberry dessert with champagne jelly and lemongrass sorbet, a peach variation with a light saffron pastry cream and Muscat wine sorbet or a lemon cream under the guise of *"après-dessert"*. In short it's always "plus" for the Mischlers who are definitely the Haeberlins of the North.

In Gimbelhof (67510). 10 km n via D3 and forest road.

■ Ferme du Gimbelhof ✿ 🏠

Tel. 03 88 94 43 58. Fax 03 88 94 23 30.
info@gimbelhof.com
Closed 20 Nov.–26 Dec., Feb. vac.
Rest. closed Mon., Tue.
8 rooms: 45–55€.
Prix fixe: 11,50€ (lunch), 28€, 6€ (child).

Nothing has changed in these wooded surroundings. Not the view of the Fleckenstein ruins, nor the simplicity of this verdant inn. Simple rooms and *terroir* cooking make this a peaceful stop.

LENCLOITRE

86140 Vienne. Paris 320 – Châtellerault 20 – Mirebeau 11 – Poitiers 32 – Richelieu 25. The Romanesque church with its 15th-century fortified facade is well worth a look in this pretty Poitevin town.

■ HOTELS-RESTAURANTS

■ Château Hôtel de Savigny 🄽 ✿ 🏠

6, rue du Château.
Tel. 05 49 20 41 14. Fax 05 49 86 76 38.
www.chsfrance.com
Closed beg. Jan.–mid-Feb.
Rest. closed weekdays lunch (off season).
10 rooms: 180–290€.
Prix fixe: 38€, 60€, 80€, 30€ (child).
A la carte: 65–98€.

This Renaissance château run by Pascal Faure since 2006 will take you beyond time and far from the madding crowd! Refined comfort abounds. You'll find a smoking parlor, rooms with a view of the parkland, Louis XV furniture, Laura Ashley wall coverings, a terrace and two dining rooms, one of which has a fireplace. Michel Hastain's up-to-date cuisine is perfectly in keeping. Try the duck foie gras confit, dried figs in Morilles wine and China flowers, oven roasted line-fished sea bass garnished with crab, veal sweetbreads served in a small pot with Grelot onions and glazed carrots. Totally seductive, as is the pain d'épice mille-feuille with a side of quince preserves.

● Champ de Foire 🄽 ● COM

18, pl du Champ-de-Foire.
Tel. 05 49 90 74 91. Fax 05 49 93 33 76.
champdefoire@wanadoo.fr
Closed Sun. dinner, Mon., Tue. dinner, 2 weeks Jan., 1 week Feb., 1 week at end June, 2 weeks end Aug.
Prix fixe: 21€, 27€, 41€, 46€.

This appealing restaurant situated alongside the medieval marketplace is definitely worth a stop thanks to its warm welcome and seasonal menus which change weekly. Richard Toix lovingly prepares contemporary dishes such as roasted langoustines with chestnut cream, thinly sliced filet of John Dory, new potatoes and bacon, broiled veal sweetbreads and chanterelle risotto with fresh almonds, which slip down effortlessly. To finish, the oven-crisped sour cherry pastry with sour cherry sorbet is gobbled up. The Langue-doc takes pride of place among the 150 references on the wine menu.

LENS

62300 Pas-de-Calais. Paris 200- Lille 37 –
Arras 19 – Béthune 19.
lensoftour@aol.com.
A mining town which has become a soccer capital. Go Lens!

 HOTELS-RESTAURANTS

■ Espace Bollaert

13c, rte de Béthune.
Tel. 03 21 78 30 30. Fax 03 21 78 24 83.
hotelbollaert@nordnet.fr
www.espace-bollaert.com
Closed Aug. Rest. closed Sun. dinner.
54 rooms: 68–89€.
Prix fixe: 22€.

The one and only address in Lens for soccer fans; Bruno and Isabelle Parrain's Espace Bollaert sits right across from the stadium. The rooms are modern and practically decorated in green and blue tones. The honest *pension* cooking appeals, particularly on match evenings with its set menu. A Tatin of foie gras, halibut with blackcurrant mustard, rump steak and the chocolate fondue slip down nicely in the "blood red and gold" dining room.

● L'Arcadie II   COM

13, rue Decrombecque.
Tel.-Fax 03 21 70 32 22.
arcadie.2@wanadoo.fr / www.arcadie.2.com
Closed Sat. lunch, Mon. dinner,
Tue. dinner (exc. groups).
Prix fixe: 16,50€, 26€ (weekday lunch),
30€, 45€, 15€ (child).

Hervé Wacquiez continues to regale the citizens of Lens with his foie gras with chestnut and cep chutney, frog leg tartare with beets, pike-perch filet with slow-simmered celery root, the pumpkin, broad bean and monkfish stew, stuffed truffled breast of guinea hen with poppy seeds and the pineapple mille-feuille.

In Vendin-le-Vieil (62880). 3,5 km.

■ Lensotel

Centre commercial Lens 2.
Tel. 03 21 79 36 36. Fax 03 21 79 36 00.
lenshotel@wanadoo.fr
www.lenshotel.com
69 rooms: 73–92€. 1 suite: 66€.
Prix fixe: 19€, 25€, 31€, 15€ (child).
A la carte: 45€.

This modern hotel situated in the commercial center of town offers comfortable, Provençal-style rooms, a few of which give onto the garden. In the brick-walled dining room with its fireplace and a veranda facing the swimming pool, you'll like pike-perch with foie gras, medallions of lamb with garlic en chemise and the classic Grand Marnier frozen soufflé lovingly prepared by chef Xavier Manzoni.

LESPARRE-MEDOC

33340 Gironde. Paris 543 – Bordeaux 66 –
Soulac-sur-Mer 30.
Lesparrre and its port are a world away right at the tip of the Médoc peninsula.

 HOTELS-RESTAURANTS

In Gaillon-en-Médoc (33340). 2 km nw via N215.

■ Château Layauga

Tel. 05 56 41 26 83. Fax 05 56 41 19 52.
chateaulayauga@wanadoo.fr
www.chateaulayauga.com
Closed Jan.
7 rooms: 110–130€. Half board: 200€.

Stéphane Noar's enchanting 19th-century residence, complete with elegant rooms filled with Louis XV–style furniture and a garden with a pond, sits in the heart of the Médoc vineyards.

LETTENBACH see ABRESCHVILLER
LEUTAZ see MEGEVE

LEUTENHEIM

67480 Bas-Rhin. Paris 501 – Haguenau 22 –
Karlsruhe 46 – Strasbourg 45 –
Soufflenheim 5.

L'Outre Forêt with its flower-filled village and potters' houses.

 RESTAURANTS

● **Auberge du Vieux Couvent**

Locale known as Koenigsbruck,
2 km nw via D163.
7, rue du Vieux-Moulin.
Tel. 03 88 86 39 86. Fax 03 88 05 28 78.
Closed Mon., Tue.,
1 week Christmas–New Year's,
1 week at end Feb.–beg. Mar.,
1 week at end Aug.–beg. Sept.
Prix fixe: 26€, 36€.

A hop, skip and a jump from some convent ruins stands a 17th-century house with a timber-covered terrace for outside dining and a dining room covered with inscriptions in dialect. This is the home of Catherine and Damien Hirschel, who once worked at the Crillon in Paris. Back on native soil they fell in love with the house. The locals have been right in heaping laurels on the two menus, which are a steal. Delicious beef in salad with an egg vinaigrette, rabbit terrine with aspic and a foie gras or crayfish *verrine*, tuna steak with peppers in filo, duck confit and the Charolais beef sirloin with red wine sauce slip down nicely, not forgetting to praise the exquisite strawberry tiramisu with berry sorbet and pan-tossed apricots in acidulated sauce and the spéculos ice cream. A good-natured atmosphere and prompt service by a trio of adorable waitresses gives this country manor an air of great civility.

LEVERNOIS see BEAUNE

LEZOUX

63190 Puy-de-Dôme. Paris 436 –
Clermont-Ferrand 30 – Issoire 43 – Riom 28
– Thiers 16 – Vichy 41.
The Livradois peaks and the volcanoes of the Puys chain are the jewels of this land of well-sharpened knives.

HOTELS-RESTAURANTS

● **Château de Codignat**

In Bord-l'Etang, 8 km se via D223 and D309.
Tel. 04 73 68 43 03. Fax 04 73 68 93 54.
codignat@relaischateaux.com
www.codignat.com
Closed Nov. 1–mid-Mar.
Rest. closed lunch (exc. weekends).
14 rooms: 370–670€. 5 suites: 670€.
Prix fixe: 54€, 72€, 95€.
A la carte: 95–106€.

Superbly situated in a medieval setting with up-to-date comfort and imbued with French history, this beautiful castle was a Relais & Châteaux establishment before being taken over by le Polito. Dine in the keep on Stéphane Dupuy's wonderful repasts where produce is treated with respect and flavors are highlighted. After the duck foie gras cooked in a saffron-seasoned bouillon with a fine mousse of small young peas and spring vegetables, John Dory roasted in chorizo sausage crust, creamy polenta with osso buco jus, Landes pigeon breast with a wine reduction, end with raspberries and fraises de bois with Breton shortcake, a light pepper mousse and fennel sorbet.

LIEPVRE

68660 Haut-Rhin. Paris 422 – Colmar 34 –
Ribeauvillé 20 – Saint-Dié 30 – Sélestat 15.
ot.valargent@rmcnet.fr.
The forest of Vancelle and Frankenbourg castle mark the limits of the countryside in this industrial town along the road to the Vosges of Lorraine.

● **RESTAURANTS**

In Bois-l'Abbesse (68660). 2 km w.

● **La Vieille Forge**

13, Bois-l'Abbesse.
Tel. 03 89 58 92 54. F ax 03 89 58 43 58.
alavieilleforge@wanadoo.fr
Closed 2 weeks Feb., 2 weeks Aug.
Prix fixe: 20€, 32€. A la carte: 40€.

An old forge, transformed into a congenial stopover, offering regional specialities at bargain prices. In the cozy paneled dining room, you'll enjoy escalope of foie gras with chutney, pike-perch cooked in Sancerre with morels, pan-tossed veal sweetbreads and kidneys and the delicious lemon pastry.

LIEZAY see GERARDMER
LIGNAN-SUR-ORB see BEZIERS

LIGNY-EN-CAMBRESIS

59191 Nord. Paris 194 – Saint-Quentin 34 – Arras 52 – Cambrai 17 – Valenciennes 41.
This beet country was home to Matisse who hailed from nearby Cateau. A good place to discover the verdant North.

 HOTELS-RESTAURANTS

● **Château de Ligny**
2, rue Pierre-Curie.
Tel. 03 27 85 25 84. Fax 03 27 85 79 79.
contact@chateau-de-ligny.fr
www.chateau-de-ligny.fr
Closed Sun. dinner, Mon., Tue., Feb.,
2 weeks beg. Aug.
10 rooms: 120–200€. 16 suites: 220–440€.
Prix fixe: 48€, 82€. A la carte: 90€.

Set amidst ample grounds, this 12th- and 15th-century fortress guarantees relaxation. After sessions in the hammam, Jacuzzi, swimming pool or fitness center, repair to spacious, peaceful rooms for some well-deserved rest. In the dining room, situated in the old guard room, Gérard Fillaire's lovingly prepared fish and Raymond Brochard's meat dishes are highly successful. The rosemary-seasoned rouget, lobster risotto with duck foie gras, oven-broiled veal sweetbreads, lemon-seasoned linguine and the chicory-seasoned soufflé for dessert are all enchanting.

LIGSDORF see FERRETTE

LILLE

59000 Nord. Paris 223 – Bruxelles 119 – Luxembourg 310 – Strasbourg 522.
info@lilletourisme.com.
The capital of the Nord-Pas-de-Calais is a mere hour away from Paris thanks to the TGV which discharges its passengers either at the aptly named Lille-Flanders station or at Lille-Europe whose very name hints at a future vocation. But Lille is no suburban town. This city certainly doesn't lack exoticism thanks to the safeguarding of its specific character by the renovation of its lovely facades or the sprucing up of its Grand-Place (main square). Also apparent is the legendary warmth of Northern people. Thanks to its belfry, its old stock exchange, its alleyways, its renovated houses, its gay Place Ribour and the large, popular and cosmopolitan market of Wazemmes, Lille has an air of a Flemish bazaar. The city overflows with delights which are all its own: sweet, salty, frothy … The rue de Béthune is softly scented with the aroma of mussels, french fries and beer, making choosing a table quite hard as you flit between restaurants. It takes no time to feel right at home in Lille or to be adopted by its citizens who are quick to raise a glass and are great gourmets at heart.

■ HOTELS

■ **L'Hermitage Gantois**
224, rue de Paris.
Tel. 03 20 85 30 30. Fax 03 20 42 31 31.
contact@hermitagegantois.com
www.hotelhermitagegantois.com
67 rooms: 195–390€. 8 suites: 390€.
Prix fixe: 30€, 39€
(Estaminet Gantois, prix fixe: 19€, 23€).

This old almshouse and its chapel date from 1460 but have had a modern and somewhat daring makeover. It boasts lovely, guest-friendly rooms and a lobby under a glass ceiling. Stéphane Blanche's refined cuisine stars a sardine and vegetable tart and veal kidneys with an olive purée. The best bet is the Estaminet Gantois with its local dishes (rabbit with prunes and a local fish stew with aromatic herbs and vegetables called waterzoi) and its low prices. A clever way to discover this above-average spot.

■ Alliance   🏨

Couvent des Minimes
17, quai du Wault.
Tel. 03 20 30 62 62. Fax 03 20 42 94 25.
alliancelille@alliance-hospitality.com
www.alliance-lille.com
Rest. closed Mon. (mid-July–mid-Aug.).
83 rooms: 195–225€. 8 suites: 289–379€.
Prix fixe: 15€ (weekday dinner), 35€, 40€.

Situated between old Lille and the citadel, this 17th-century convent houses a top-of-the-line hotel. Modern rooms overlooking the garden and the cloister converted to a dining room under a huge glass pyramid charm instantly. From the kitchen, cold jumbo shrimp purée, monkfish brochette with escargot sauce, pork loin with a browned mozzarella topping and the fig and berry soup are reassuring.

■ Carlton   🏨

3, rue de Paris.
Tel. 03 20 13 33 13. Fax 03 20 51 48 17.
carlton@carltonlille.com
www.carltonlille.com
54 rooms: 169–226€. 5 suites: 259–1215€.

Facing the old stock exchange, this early-20th-century luxury hotel is highly attractive with its lavish suites, period rooms, marble bathrooms, fitness center and English bar. Excellent service.

■ Grand Hôtel Bellevue   🏨

5, rue J.-Roisin.
Tel. 03 20 57 45 64. Fax 03 20 40 07 93.
www.grandhotelbellevue.com
60 rooms: 125–155€.

This handsome 18th-century town house boasts a semi-circular lobby, adorned with friezes and gilt, and old-fashioned rooms, some of them giving onto the Grand-Place. Its lounges are dedicated to Mozart and Verdi, who stayed here at one time. Internet and WiFi.

■ Mercure Lille Centre Opéra   🏨

2, bd Carnot.
Tel. 03 20 14 71 47. Fax 03 20 14 71 48.
h0802@accor.com / www.accor.com
101 rooms: 80–162€. 1 suite: 263€.

Next to the central post office and the Opera house, this early 20th-century edifice happily combines old-fashioned décor with modern comfort. Beams and bricks adorn the entrance lobby and lounges. Rooms are done in wine-colored tones. Pretty conference room.

■ Novotel-Lille-Centre   🏨

116, rue de l'Hôpital-Militaire.
Tel. 03 28 38 53 53. Fax 03 28 38 53 54.
h0918@accor.com / www.novotel.com
104 rooms: 89–189€.
Prix fixe: 9,50€ (child). A la carte: 26–42€.

Centrally located near the Grand-Place, this highly practical hotel has comfortable rooms, done in blue, pink or orange, junior suites and a restaurant serving dependable, seasonal dishes cooked by Eric Wullai (diced and seasoned vegetables with crab, rouget escabèche). Fitness center, WiFi.

■ Le Brueghel   🏨

5, parvis Saint-Maurice.
Tel. 03 20 06 06 69. Fax 03 20 63 25 27.
www.hotel-brueghel.com
65 rooms: 65–120€.

This hotel, with its typically Flemish facade, is situated opposite the church of Saint-Maurice in a pedestrian area and is not without charm. It has an Old World feel thanks to its wooden elevator and its small rooms decorated in pastel tones. Internet and WiFi connections make this a convenient place to stay.

■ Hôtel de la Treille   🏨

7-9, pl Louise-de-Bettignies.
Tel. 03 20 55 45 46. Fax 03 20 51 51 69.
hoteldelatreille@free.fr
www.hoteldelatreille.com
42 rooms: 70–130€. 2 suites: 90–180€.

The charm of the old with its colonnades, mosaic floors and glass walls in the lounges. The colorful and comfortably modern rooms and their marble bathrooms are wisely priced.

● RESTAURANTS

● A l'Huîtrière

3, rue des Chats-Bossus.
Tel. 03 20 55 43 41. Fax 03 20 55 23 10.
contact@lhuitriere.fr
www.lhuitriere.fr
Closed Sun. dinner, Aug.
Prix fixe: 43€ (weekday lunch), 120€.
A la carte: 120€.

Since 1928, L'Huitrière has seen generations of the Proye family come and go, while quality has remained a constant. Now, in an effortless changeover of roles, son Antoine has left L'écume des Mers—the next door annex—to take over from his father Jean who has retired. Antoine, who represents the fourth generation of his family, is, like his father before him, devoted to the finest products of both surf and turf. He respects homey Northern values and treats his clients to fine table-side service. Chez Proyes there are no compromises: scallops pan-seared with truffle jus or grilled and served with a warm preserved ginger vinaigrette, roasted turbot with marrow-topped toasts, oven-roasted line-fished sea bass with roasted oysters and the sole, pan-fried in butter, garlic and parsley with gray shrimp, cooked by the faithful thirty-year-old incumbent Philippe Lor, marry the same style of calm perfection. Meats are also treated with verve, in the manner of veal kidney in salt crust, finely sliced with shallot sauce and served with a divine endive gratin topped with marrow—a cunning Flemish side dish which could be a meal in itself. Add some stylish desserts: the table-side preparation of crêpes Suzette is quite a ritual, and chicory and juniper eaux-de-vie, the first as an iced dessert mousse, the second in sabayon, refer to a simple local custom. The wine list reads like an anthology and prices are not too lofty. The collection of juniper liqueurs signs off on a great work of art by a Northern institution situated behind France's most beautiful fish store—an art deco residence in all its glory.

● Le Sébastopol

1, pl Sébastopol.
Tel. 03 20 57 05 05. Fax 03 20 40 11 31.
n.germond@restaurant-sebastopol.fr
www.restaurant-sebastopol.fr
Closed Sat. lunch, Sun. dinner, Mon. lunch,
3 weeks Aug.
Prix fixe: 50€ (wine inc.), 65€.
A la carte: 76–80€.

With its lovely center-city facade, its art déco interiors and its cheerful atmosphere, Le Sébastopol remains one of Lille's flagship establishments. Jean-Luc Germond, who was Robert Bardot's second in command in the days of Le Flambard, likes to combine Northern inspiration with Southern charm. Following the seasons, products are carefully selected for their quality and relevancy to current tastes. Crispy rouget with cannelloni, zucchini and parmesan, oven-roasted John Dory served with a side of sundried tomatoes and slow-cooked fennel, truffled breast of pigeon with a crêpe pouch of drumstick meat and eggplant and the beet and spiced berry syrup over shaved ice for dessert underscore the chef's talent. An interesting wine list and a fine welcome by Nicole Germond.

● Bistro Tourangeau

61, bd Louis-XIV.
Tel. 03 20 52 74 64. Fax 03 20 85 06 39.
Closed Sat. dinner, Sun.
Prix fixe: 28,50€.

Behind this red-painted wooden front nestles a dynamic restaurant dedicated to the Loire valley. Hugues Hochart welcomes and watches over his guests while, in the kitchen, brother Hervé gives serious thought to escargots in their shell, monkfish wrapped in bacon, lamb shank braised in local wine and fresh fruit with a Coteaux-de-layon sabayon. Naturally, the Loire valley takes pride of place on the wine list.

● La Coquille

60, rue Saint-Etienne.
Tel.-Fax 03 20 54 29 82.
dadeleval@nordnet.fr

www.lestablesgourmandes.com
Closed Sun.
Prix fixe: 16€ (lunch), 24€,
29,50€ (wine inc.). A la carte: 45€.

This 18th-century establishment boasts choice fare. Dany Deleval's welcome is all smiles and the market-based dishes of husband Olivier are a delight. Under the old beams of the contemporary dining room, pressed poultry with foie gras and vegetables, truffled turbot filet roasted with five spices, veal cutlet with spring mushrooms and the crisp and creamy frozen desserts based on the mint candy, Bêtise de Cambrai, slip down just fine.

● L'Ecume des Mers   COM

10, rue de Pas.
Tel. 03 20 54 95 40. Fax 03 20 54 96 66.
aproye@nordnet.fr / www.ecume-des-mers.com
Closed Sun. dinner.
Prix fixe: 15€ (lunch), 20€ (dinner).
A la carte: 45€.

With one eye on the Huitrière and one on this, the next-door annex, with its chic pub look, the ubiquitous Antoine Proye is everywhere at once. Market-fresh fish and vegetables determine the daily menu. At the stove, Christian Leroy has a light, deft touch with classic fare. Tuck into haddock salad with lentils, skate with brown butter, rouget with dill and lemon, pepper-seasoned beef tenderloin and the quetsche plum crumble.

● Brasserie André   COM

71, rue de Béthune.
Tel. 03 20 54 75 51. Fax 03 20 15 13 99.
Closed New Year's.
A la carte: 55–60€.

This handsome, Flemish-style brasserie has a lot of style. Jean-Claude Heusel runs the establishment with verve while Fabrice Ponceau puts dash into the pan-tossed forest mushrooms, line-fished sea bass with asparagus, herb-roasted rack of lamb and the peach and raspberry dessert, which can be washed down with a franziskaner beer served in a stoneware mug.

● Le Compostelle   COM

4, rue Saint-Etienne.
Tel. 03 28 38 08 30. Fax 03 28 38 08 39.
compostellelille@aol.fr
www.lecompostelle.fr
Prix fixe: 27€, 32€. A la carte: 50€.

Close to the Grand-Place, this former 16th-century coaching inn has recently changed hands. Philippe Vallette assures an enthusiastic welcome while Christophe Nabot puts his skills into a classic cuisine without any hitches. Foie gras with figs, grilled turbot filet, sweetbreads pan fried in butter, garlic and parsley and crème brûlée in three Northern flavors are a pleasure to eat.

● Les Remparts   COM

Logis de la Porte-de-Gand, rue de Gand.
Tel. 03 20 06 74 74. Fax 03 20 06 74 70.
contact@terrassedesremparts.fr
www.terrassedesremparts.fr
Closed lunch
Prix fixe: 31€. A la carte: 40€.

This 17th-century fortified tower is part of the city's history. Alexander Lecocq watches over the establishment with care while Sylvain Fievet cooks up well-balanced, up-to-date dishes. Delight in veal tongue with a garnish of truffles, foie gras, cockscombs and Madeira wine, the duck foie gras, grilled tuna, grilled Mediterranean sea bass, veal hanger steak and the orange and caramel crisp, served with a smile.

● Baan Thaï   COM

22, bd J.-B.-Lebas.
Tel. 03 20 86 06 01. Fax 03 20 86 72 94.
gtbi@wanadoo.fr
www.baanthai-lille.com
Closed Sat. lunch, Mon.,
Christmas–New Year's.
Prix fixe: 23€ (weekday lunch), 41€, 45€,
49€. A la carte: 40€.

This lovely bourgeois town house, pleasantly run by Pramod Palabnak, is a fine showcase for Thai cooking. Solicitous service, an enticing menu and an exotic modern décor combine to make this a likable venue. Peppery beef salad, fried pork-stuffed sea bass, duck with a sushi sauce and the green curry beef are carefully prepared. The pineapple and melon duo with honey caramel is a nice conclusion.

● Banyan `COM`

189, rue de Solférino.
Tel. 03 20 57 20 20. Fax 03 20 57 16 16.
www.lebanyan.com
Closed Sat. lunch, Sun.
Prix fixe: 14€ (lunch), 25€ (lunch),
35€ (dinner), 55€ (dinner) 12€ (child).
A la carte: 45–50€.

This attractive 1880s establishment complete with stucco, mirrors, parquet floors and exotic, bare tables, has style. The attentive staff hails straight from Thailand and Laos. The seafood brochette, grilled sea bass in banana leaf, ground rump steak seasoned with basil, leg of lamb with ka chaï seasoning and the dark chocolate spring rolls take you on a tasty journey.

● Champlain `COM`

13, rue Nicolas-Leblanc.
Tel. 03 20 54 01 38. Fax 03 20 40 07 28.
le.champlain@wanadoo.fr
www.lechamplain.fr
Closed Sat. lunch, Sun. dinner, Mon. dinner, Aug.
Prix fixe: 25€, 30€, 37€, 45€.

Close to the Beaux Arts museum, this 19th-century residence is highly seductive. Denis and Sylvie Gaboriau greet you with gusto and will enchant you with their top-quality, crisp, fairly creative yet well-executed cuisine. Raw oysters on a fennel remoulade, roasted whole sea bass, magret de canard with caramelized spiced pears and vineyard peaches poached with sour cherries go down a treat. Good wine list.

● Clément Marot `COM`

16, rue de Pas.
Tel. 03 20 57 01 10. Fax 03 20 57 39 69.
clmarot@nordnet.fr / www.clement-marot.com
Closed Sun. dinner.
Prix fixe: 34€, 42,50€, 52€.

Not as poetic as its namesake, our own Lille-based Clément Marot concocts classic dishes with a local flavor that fit perfectly with the spirit of this brick house with its English-style interior. The langoustine tail salad, seared foie gras served hot, turbot with hollandaise sauce, poultry with endives and a Northern-style chickory-seasoned crème brûlée are a treat. Bruno Waniez is in charge of a wine cellar of 250 choices.

● Le Barbue d'Anvers `N` `SIM`

1 bis, rue de St-Etienne.
Tel. 03 20 55 11 68.
www.lebarbuedanvers-restaurant-lille.com
Closed Sun., Mon.,
3 weeks end July–mid-Aug.
Prix fixe: 32€. A la carte: 35–45€.

Philippe Galliaerde has turned a 16th-century brick house into a preppy watering hole where Lille's trendy set can go to party. The attentive staff reel off the day's specials as well as the usual offerings such as gray shrimp cake served with a jus and shrimp emulsion, veal tongue with a garnish of truffles, foie gras, cockscombs and Madeira wine with duck carpaccio, a mushroom flamiche (the local covered pie) and rack of lamb seasoned with Guérande salt. The cod stew with aromatic herbs and vegetables comes in generous portions as do the mussels simmered in shallots and white wine served with fries. Desserts include a frozen chicory parfait with waffles and a tiramisu (with juniper!). Maredsous, Hoegaarden or Bécasse beers are natural choices.

● Le Square d'Aramis `N` `SIM`

52, rue Basse.
Tel. 03 20 74 16 17.
Closed Christmas.
Prix fixe: 19,90€. A la carte: 35€.

Valérie and Eric Galliaerde have given this house in old Lille a baroque look with paintings and antiqued walls, turning it into a setting for conviviality and indulgence. Valérie in the kitchen and Eric in the dining room bring life to this charming spot. You can choose from the lightened-up regional fare on the blackboard or go for a menu true to the grand tradition of the Nord. A Maroilles cheese tart, a terrine with slow-cooked onions, a cod filet with sesame and the local meat and aromatic herb stew are all a hymn to the culinary virtues of Flanders. The desserts (fruit crumble, crème brûlée) are perfectly in tune.

● L'Assiette du Marché   ⬡SIM

61, rue de la Monnaie.
Tel. 03 20 06 83 61. Fax 03 20 14 03 75.
www.assiettedumarche.com
Closed Sun., 3 weeks Aug.
Prix fixe: 13€, 16€, 20€. A la carte: 35€.

The Huîtrière's other branch is in the capable hands of Thomas Proye, Jean's younger brother. His task is to attend to the well being of his guests in this 18th-century residence that was once the city treasury. Be it in the adjoining dining rooms, under the courtyard's glass veranda or on the summer terrace, Patrick Patou serves market fare on a silver platter with his coddled eggs with morel cream, roasted tuna with onions and bacon, oxtail in pot-au-feu and the cannelés. Good wine cellar at reasonable prices.

● Aux Moules   🔒SIM

34, rue de Béthune.
Tel. 03 20 57 12 46. Fax 03 20 12 90 92.
www.auxmoules.fr
Closed Christmas–New Year's.
Prix fixe: 18,50€. A la carte: 30€

This brasserie is worth a detour for its 1920 ceramic interiors, its beer on tap and its simply presented Northern dishes. The shrimp croquettes, fish stew with aromatic herbs and vegetables, the mussels with garlic cream sauce, the local meat stew with fries and salad and the giant chocolate éclair are honest fare.

● Le Toucouleur   ⓝSIM

146, rue du Molinel.
Tel. 03 20 48 23 33. Fax 03 20 48 23 36.
www.letoucouleur.com

Closed Sat. lunch, Sun., Aug.
Prix fixe: 13€ (lunch), 18,50€, 24,50€, 30€ (wine inc.).

Médoune Fall hails from Saint-Louis-de-Sénégal and has created an exotic, quality venue. The Antilles go hand-in-hand with Africa to produce spicy dishes. Fried cod cakes, the stuffed crab, the spicy sausage, the chicken yassa, veal colombo, the tieboudiene (rice, fish, vegetables, tomato) are cooked as they should be. Wooden sculptures, plaid chair covers and red tablecloths make for a highly colorful experience.

● Le Bistro de l'Opéra   SIM

58, bd Carnot.
Tel. 03 20 13 08 88. Fax 03 20 13 03 61.
www.bistro opera.com
Closed Sat. lunch, Sun., Mon. dinner,
3 weeks Aug.
Prix fixe: 16€ (weekday lunch), 22€,
11€ (child). A la carte: 45€.

Laurent Cusin worked in the dining room at Scholteshof at Hasselt and at Bocuse and runs this updated bistro with gusto. In the kitchen, Vincent Valenton treats his faithful clientèle to a local-style mille-feuille with white beer, sea bass stew with aromatic herbs and vegetables, a slice of veal sweetbreads with Madeira wine and the crème brûlée flavored with vanilla beans, all of which please the palate. A choice selection of wines is available at the bar or under the glass roof of the red and gray dining room.

● Le Bistro de Pierrot   SIM

6, pl de Béthune.
Tel. 03 20 57 14 09. Fax 03 20 30 93 13.
pierrot@bistro -de-pierrot.fr
Closed Sun., Bank holidays, Mon.,
2 weeks Aug.
A la carte: 37€.

The Ledieus have taken over Pierre Coucke's bistro while he stays on at Capinghem. In the kitchen, Stéphane Delobel carries on with the local covered pie (called flamiche) with morels, the sole meunière, beef tenderloin with gray pepper and the pain perdu. Beaujolais and wines from small producers are served by the glass. Obviously missing is good old Pierrot's chatter.

● Le Bouillon de Louis   SIM
65, bd Louis-XIV.
Tel. 03 20 52 57 40. Fax 03 20 85 06 39.
hhochard@laposte.net
Closed Sat., Sun.
Prix fixe: 8,50€, 9,50€. A la carte: 25€.

In their red and ochre diner graced with a brick wall, the Hochart brothers, who also own the Bistro Tourangeau, offer up lightly smoked salmon with potatoes in oil, slow-cooked oxtail with condiments, rare-cooked tuna in ratatouille, Flemish carbonnade (a regional beef and beer stew) and a dark chocolate and walnut dessert. Good fare and the menus are a steal.

● Les Compagnons   SIM
de la Grappe
26, rue Lepelletier.
Tel. 03 20 21 02 79. Fax 03 28 36 82 77.
les-compagnons-de-la-grappe@wanadoo.fr
Closed Sun.
A la carte: 30€.

This bistro run by two women (Danielle Lechevin out front and Francine Rosier in the kitchen) is attractive with its art déco interior, designer lamps and red and yellow tones and is just waiting to be discovered down a quiet and narrow alleyway. On offer: foie gras with seasonal chutney, cod filet with beurre blanc, oven-browned veal sauté with Maroille cheese and assorted ice creams.

● Lakson   SIM
21, rue du Curé-Saint-Etienne.
Tel. 03 20 31 19 96. Fax 03 20 31 79 01.
contact @lakson.fr / www.lakson.fr
Closed Sun., Mon.
Prix fixe: 17€ (weekday lunch, wine inc.), 19€ (weekday lunch), 23€ (weekday dinner), 38€ (dinner), 15,50€ (child).
A la carte: 40€

This restaurant *cum* caterer opens out onto a flowered courtyard and is devoted

to Scandinavian cuisine. Inside or out on the heated terrace, the smoked venison and mushrooms in puff pastry, a choice of various smoked herrings, a cod filet poached in a spicy broth and the beef tenderloin in a spicy crust with grated potato cakes hit the spot. The pear truffle poached in Glog (Swedish spiced wine) and the Småland cheesecake slip down effortlessly.

● Le Passe-Porc   SIM
155, rue de Solférino.
Tel. 03 20 42 83 93. Fax 03 20 07 62 77.
Closed dinner (exc. Fri.), 3 weeks Aug.
Prix fixe: 10€, 16€, 7€ (child).
A la carte: 32€.

Former horse dealer Christian Descampiaux chooses his meat with skill. Numerous are the city's carnivores who flock to sit and savor his tripe cassolette, Vilette-style hanger steak, spider crab with garlic and the house tart.

In Capinghem (59160). 6 km nw via D933.
● La Marmite de Pierrot   ●SIM
93, rue Poincaré.
Tel. 03 20 92 12 41. Fax 03 20 92 72 51.
pierrot@bistro -de-pierrot.com
Closed Sun. dinner, Tue. dinner, Wed. dinner, Thu. dinner, Mon.
Prix fixe: 22€ (lunch), 30€, 10,50€ (child).

Pierre Coucke, aka "Pierrot of Lille", has left his rue de Béthune address to install himself in the countryside in an old-fashioned inn. Checked tablecloths, wooden counter-tops, back rooms and jolly diners make for lots of charm. People come slumming in search of tripe stew, a cassolette, tête de veau, calf's liver pan-fried in butter, garlic and parsley, stuffed port trotter and veal sweetbread croquettes— all kinds of delicious things which are moistened and smoothed with Sancerre Rouge de Pinard or the Trois Monts beer. "I'll never let Nouvelle Cuisine in here", clamors Pierrot, always game for a laugh, who also animates a culinary program on France 3 Nord-Pas-de-Calais, suggesting mouth-watering desserts in stentorian tones. A brown sugar tart, pain perdu or crêpes Suzette make a sweet finish to a fabulous feast.

In Lambersart (59130). 2 km nw.

● **La Laiterie**

138, av de l'Hippodrome.
Tel. 03 20 92 79 73. Fax 03 20 22 16 19.
lalaiterie@wanadoo.fr / www.lalaiterie.fr
Closed Sun., Mon., 3 weeks Aug.
Prix fixe: 38€, 15€ (child).
A la carte: 75€.

This characterful establishment in Lille's residential suburbs owes a great deal to the personality and dynamism of its owner-chef Benoit Bernard. Modern architecture combined with big bay windows looking onto the garden set the stage for a creative cuisine which refuses to give itself airs. The menu is filled with discoveries from far-flung travels and touched with the spirit of the age: smoked eel mille-feuille, smoked herring eggs in whipped cream, the roasted line-fished Atlantic sea bass with ketchup and tomato sushi, milk-fed veal chops, pan-tossed chanterelles with parsley and a raspberry mille-feuille. The wines are tastefully selected by Francois-Xavier Dassonneville. It's easy to see why this "dairy" is a great success.

In Leers (59115). 20 km ne via rte de Roubaix.

● **La Buissonnière** `SIM`

72, rue Pierre-Catteau.
Tel. 03 20 83 90 26. Fax 03 20 02 40 96.
aubergelabuissonniere@wanadoo.fr
wwww.la-buissoniere.fr
Closed dinner (exc. weekends), Mon.,
Feb. vac., 3 weeks Aug.
Prix fixe: 26€, 35€, 10€ (child).
A la carte: 40€.

Deep in the countryside, this old farm with its stables, beams and bricks is run with great vim and vigor by the Veroone brothers. Luc welcomes guests, while Olivier feeds them on rabbit terrine seasoned with Blonde d'Esquelbecq, North Sea langoustines in cappuccino, fresh cod in tapenade, caramelized stir-fried pork tenderloin medallion and a spiced caramel brioche perdu.

In Wattignies (59139). 7 km s via D759.

● **Le Cheval Blanc** `COM`

110, rue du Général-de-Gaulle.
Tel.-Fax 03 20 97 34 62.
le-cheval-blanc3@wanadoo.fr
Closed Sat. lunch, Sun. dinner, Mon. dinner,
Feb. vac., Aug.
Prix fixe: 26€. A la carte: 55–65€.

Salad with citrus-seasoned langoustines, drum fish with pain perdu, roasted duckling filet and a chocolate and licorice flan are precisely concocted by Jérôme Follet in this stone-built inn with its neat, modern décor.

LIMOGES

87000 Haute-Vienne. Paris 394 – Angoulême 104 – Brive 92 – Châteauroux 125.
ot.limoges.haute-vienne@en-france.com.
Always discreet, Limoges enchants thanks to its cathedral, stained glass, string of churches, the enamel museum in the episcopal palace and its bridges spanning the Vienne. A culinary awakening is also in the making.

■	HOTELS

● **Domaine de Faugeras**

Allée de Faugeras.
Tel. 05 55 34 66 22. Fax 05 55 34 18 05.
infos@domainedefaugeras.fr
www.domainedefaugeras.fr
Rest. closed Sun. dinner, Mon., Tue.
18 rooms: 95–450€.
Prix fixe: 45€ (lunch). A la carte: 80€.

Set in a business park in a large green area, Eric and Pierre Verger have created a lovely modern hotel in an old 18th-century château which once belonged to a family of porcelain manufacturers. Tranquility, luxury and culinary delights are on offer at Philippe Redon's table. Formerly with Jacques Chibois, this chef's progressive and authentic cuisine shows a lot of talent. Roasted basil-seasoned lamb with parmesan served with slow-cooked onions and artichokes, lobster in Vin Jaune sauce, thyme-seasoned roasted rack of lamb with an eggplant tian and the black figs in balsamic jus served with olive oil basil ice cream slip down nicely. The large cellar and the attractive setting add to the pleasure of this lovely Limoges establishment.

■ Royal Limousin 🏨

1, pl de la République.
Tel. 05 55 34 65 30. Fax 05 55 34 55 21.
h5955@accor / www.accor.com
77 rooms: 68–120€.

This modern, comfortable hotel, situated on a pedestrian square right next to the Présidial Palace and the church of Saint-Pierre-du-Queyroix, is a perfect spot from which to visit the town. At night, light meals can be enjoyed in your light wood, pastel-toned room.

■ Etap Hôtel 🏨

14, rue Chinchauvaud.
Tel. 08 92 68 11 18. Fax 05 55 77 90 47.
h5634@accor.com / www.etaphotel.com
120 rooms: 40–46€.

Laurent Gauze and Sophie Barret run this hotel with its well-appointed rooms. The railway station is near by.

■ Jeanne d'Arc 🏨

17, av du Général-de-Gaulle.
Tel. 05 55 77 67 77. Fax 05 55 79 86 75.
www.hoteljeannedarc-limoges.fr
Closed Christmas–New Year's.
50 rooms: 60–91€.

This 19th-century coaching inn near the station and the Champ-de-Juillet gardens is a choice stopover thanks to its tranquil atmosphere and its old-fashioned furnishings.

■ Luk Hôtel 🏨

29, pl Jourdan.
Tel. 05 55 33 44 00. Fax 05 55 34 33 57.
www.lukhotel-limoges.com
Closed Christmas–New Year's, 1 week summer.
57 rooms: 42–49€.

Jacques and Annie Marquet are at the helm of this appealing hotel with its colorful, individually decorated rooms.

This well-kept establishment is a venue of choice in Limoges.

■ Le Richelieu 🏨

40, av Baudin.
Tel. 05 55 34 22 82. Fax 05 55 34 35 36.
info@hotel-richelieu.com
www.hotel-richelieu.com
32 rooms: 63–98€.

Modern architecture at this hotel situated near the public library. Bright, neat and well- soundproofed rooms. Irreproachable welcome and service.

■ Hôtel de la Paix 🏨

25, pl Jourdan.
Tel. 05 55 34 36 00. Fax 05 55 32 37 06.
31 rooms: 38–64€.

A collection of old gramophones fills the ground floor of this 19th-century building. The rooms are filled with a motley assortment of furniture that add to their old-fashioned appeal.

●	RESTAURANTS

● Le 27 🍴COM

27, rue Haute-Vienne.
Tel. 05 55 32 27 27. Fax 05 55 34 37 53.
www.le27.com
Closed Sun., Bank holidays.
Prix fixe: 12€ (lunch), 15€ (lunch),
16€ (lunch), 22€ (dinner). A la carte: 45€.

Lord of the Chapelle Saint-Martin, Gilles Dudognon is more relaxed in this pleasant annex that offers moderately-priced market-based dishes. In the red and white contemporary dining room or on the terrace, crowds come to taste Nicolas Prodhomme and Jérome Gérardin's fried shrimp ravioli, the steamed drum fish with vegetable tian, lamb saddle seasoned with sundried tomatoes and the roasted apricots with vanilla ice cream which make for fresh, sunny meals.

● Amphitryon ◎COM

26, rue de la Boucherie.
Tel. 05 55 33 36 39. Fax 05 55 32 98 50.

amphitryon87000@aol.com
Closed Sun., Mon., 1 week Jan.,
1 week at end Aug.–beg. Sept.
Prix fixe: 19€ (weekday lunch),
24€ (weekday lunch), 36€, 60€,
15€ (child). A la carte: 80€.

The Lequets have enthusiastically taken over this family house in the quartier des Bouchers. The neoclassical décor has been redone in yellow and green tones. Richard provides a lively welcome while Pascal uses the market as inspiration for his up-to-date cuisine. Langoustines served with a sweet pea cappuccino, Atlantic sea bass, seared on one side and finished under the broiler, served with raw and cooked asparagus and the pigeon breast with a half lobster, grilled with artichokes, are all lovely. To end, the strawberry and vanilla dessert and the oven-crisped orange pastry are both light versions of great classic desserts. Stay tuned.

● Chez Alphonse   SIM

5, pl de la Motte.
Tel.-Fax 05 55 34 34 14.
bistrot.alphonse@wanadoo.fr
Closed Sun., Bank holidays.
Prix fixe: 12,50€ (lunch). A la carte: 30€.

This fifties bistro with its formica-topped bar, its checked tablecloths, its old posters and its mustachioed maitre d' is totally seductive. Enjoy scrambled eggs with morels, yellow pollock with broccoli, veal medallions and the Bourbon vanilla ice cream-stuffed choux pastry.

● La Cuisine   SIM

21, rue Montmailler.
Tel.-Fax 05 55 10 28 29.
restaurantlacuisine.com
Closed Sun., Mon., 2 weeks end Jan., Aug.
Prix fixe: 15€ (lunch), 25€, 30€,
11€ (child). A la carte: 45–55€.

Escargots in herb-seasoned bouillon, roasted jumbo shrimp, hummus with country bacon, Marseille-style stuffed squid, marjoram-seasoned roasted lamb saddle and the chocolate pistachio cone: these are some of the daily delights thought up by Guy Quéroix. There's a new menu every day in this contemporary bistro. Great prices at lunchtime; can get expensive at night but no one's complaining.

● Firenza   SIM

1, rue François-Chenieux.
Tel. 05 55 77 53 24. Fax 05 55 77 30 00.
Closed Sat. lunch, Sun., Christmas.
Prix fixe: 7€ (child). A la carte: 30€.

Lionel Germanaud runs this brightly colored trattoria with panache. Poached eggs served with fried and oven-browned risotto, fresh squid with sundried tomatoes, the veal escalope in bocconcini, house tiramisu, Milan-style shortbread with preserved lemons and the meringue with Limoncello sauce are easy to eat. Truffle pizzas and penne pasta in tomato sauce are exquisite.

● Les Petits Ventres   SIM

20, rue de la Boucherie.
Tel. 05 55 34 22 90. Fax 05 55 32 41 04.
emavic-sarl@wanadoo.fr
www.les-petits-ventres.fr
Closed Sun., Mon., 2 weeks Sept., Feb. vac.,
Easter vac.
Prix fixe: 21€, 26,50€, 28€, 32€,
7€ (child). A la carte: 40€.

This 15th-century, half-timbered house is home to a charming, rustic dining room where Pierre Granero treats his guests to leek and salmon mille-feuille, red mullet with poppy seeds, braised veal sweetbreads with blinis and, for dessert, brioche pain perdu served with milk caramel and an exquisite Breton shortbread ice cream.

14100 Calvados. Paris 176 – Caen 63 –
Evreux 73 – Le Havre 56 – Rouen 93.
officelx@clubinternet.fr.
The basilica attracts thousands of pilgrims even though its architectural beauty is far from obvious (according to philosopher François George, it could even be "a proof" of the non-existence of God). But the old town and the Auge riverbanks are attractive.

HOTELS-RESTAURANTS

■ Mercure

2,5 km, rte de Paris.
Tel. 02 31 61 17 17. Fax 02 31 32 33 43.
h1725@accor.com / www.accor.com
69 rooms: 80–95€.
Prix fixe: 15€, 17€, 21€, 22€.
A la carte: 29–35€.

This hotel next to the basilica has modern rooms—some are under the eaves on the top floor. Next to the pool, in the restaurant decorated in tones of red, feast on tasty classics: tuna and tapenade mille-feuille, grilled Atlantic sea bass with anise-seasoned butter over wild rice, rosemary-seasoned lamb shanks and a soft-centered chocolate cake.

● Le France `COM`

5, rue au Char.
Tel.-Fax 02 31 62 03 37.
lefrancerestaurant@wanadoo.fr
Closed Sun. dinner (exc. July–Aug.), Mon.
Prix fixe: 16€, 24€, 9,50€ (child).

Right next to the cathedral, Evelyne Leroux's market fresh, seasonal cooking will easily seduce you. Pressed oxtail and foie gras, veal hanger steak with chive butter and a delicious dark chocolate dessert with coffee crème will make you want to return for every meal in this old-fashioned décor graced with an old press, gramophones and bright copper utensils.

● Aux Acacias `COM`

13, rue de la Résistance.
Tel. 02 31 62 10 95. Fax 02 31 32 59 06.
Closed Sun. dinner, Mon.,
Wed. dinner (exc. summer).
Prix fixe: 16€, 23€, 39€, 8,50€ (child).
A la carte: 55€.

The interior design of this Norman inn is inspired by Laura Ashley's English style. Flowered curtains, pastel wallpaper, dried bouquets and painted wood have a nice effect. In the kitchen, classic chic will enchant you with duck foie gras, roasted Atlantic sea bass simply seasoned with

salt, the sirloin steak with truffle oil and an apple in a crêpe purse with vanilla ice cream.

In Ouilly-du-Houley (14590). 10 km e via D510 and D262.

● La Paquine `COM`

Rte de Moyaux. The church.
Tel.-Fax 02 31 63 63 80.
Closed Sun. dinner, Tue. dinner, Wed.,
1 week Sept., 2 weeks end Nov., 1 week Mar.
Prix fixe: 31€. A la carte: 65€.

In his charming inn in a flower-filled country setting, Emmanuel Champion offers lovingly prepared dishes based on the best of local products: pork trotter and escargot fricassée, Atlantic sea bass filet and potato casserole with a foamy shellfish sauce, oven-crisped veal sweetbreads served with slow-cooked carrots, roasted pineapple with exotic jus and a confiture of sweet pepper. A large choice of cider and Calvados selected by Ginette Champion.

LOBSANN see
MERKWILLER-PECHELBRONN
LOCAMARIA-PLOUZANE see LE CONQUET

LOCHES

37600 Indre-et-Loire. Paris 261 – Blois 68 – Châteauroux 72 – Châtellerault 56 – Tours 42. Reasons to stop here: The royal castle, medieval houses, the annual "*forêt des livres*" book fair organized by author Gonzague Saint-Bris at the end of August.

● **RESTAURANTS**

● Le Vicariat `N` `COM`

4, pl Charles-VII.
Tel. 02 47 59 08 79.
le-vicariat@wanadoo.fr
www.auberge-le-vicariat.com
Closed Sun. dinner, Mon.
Prix fixe: 16,50€ (lunch, exc. Sun.),
20€, 39€.

In full costume, Yves and Caroline Krier invite you to taste their medieval-style cooking in their inn across from the castle and its garden. Quail salad with walnuts, basil-seasoned pike-perch, hunter's-style venison and an anise-seasoned fig gratin are carefully prepared by Philippe Sully, formerly of the Manoir Saint-Thomas at Amboise, and served in an old stone dining room with a glass roof.

LOCQUIREC

29241 Finistère. Paris 535 – Lannion 22 – Morlaix 23 – Guingamp 52.
The beaches of Bruyères and Saint-Michel-en-Grève, the château of Rosanbo, the high point of Beg-en-Fry, the treasury of the church of Saint-Jean-du-Doigt, the chapel of Notre-Dame-de-la-Joie: These are some of the treasures of Locquirec.

 HOTELS-RESTAURANTS

■ Le Grand Hôtel des Bains

15 bis, rue de l'Eglise.
Tel. 02 98 67 41 02. Fax 02 98 67 44 60.
hotel.des.bains@wanadoo.fr
www.grand-hotel-des-bains.com
Rest. closed lunch
36 rooms: 128–303€. 2 suites: 460–533€.
Prix fixe: 34€. A la carte: 65€.

Behind this pretty twenties facade on the Locquirec Point nestle a number of seaside-inspired rooms with a contemporary twist. After a walk in the waterside garden or a few strokes in the covered pool, Michel Nicol's cooking arrives just at the right moment. We love the scallop ravioli and slow-cooked spring leeks, fennel-seasoned Atlantic sea bass with caramelized veal jus, lamb medallion with mint honey and the Grand Marnier soufflé served hot.

● Le Gibus

56, rte de Plestin.
Tel. 02 98 67 41 07. Fax 02 98 79 31 28.
Closed Mon. (exc. July–Aug.), 2 weeks beg. Jan.
Prix fixe: 16€, 20€, 25€, 29,50€.
A la carte: 45€.

In this old-fashioned décor, Patrick Theolade cooks simple dishes inspired by surf and turf. The grilled shrimp, monkfish brochettes, thick rib eye steak and the crème brûlée hit the spot.

● Brasserie de la Plage

Port de Locquirec.
Tel. 02 98 79 30 70.
Closed dinner (exc. summer), 1 week Dec.
Prix fixe: 24€, 13€ (child). A la carte: 35€.

This laid-back annex of the Hotel de la Plage has been revamped. Simple dishes (three fish terrine, sole meunière, duckling filet with slow-cooked caramelized shallots, tarte Tatin) marry well with the very Côté Ouest décor consisting of wooden slats in tones of beige and pale yellow.

LOCTUDY see PONT-L'ABBE

LODS

25930 Doubs. Paris 441 – Besançon 37 – Baumeles-Dames 52 – Pontarlier 23.
itsi.ornans@wanadoo.fr
The peaceful Loue valley was the source of Courbet's dreams at Ornans and attracts Kirsch lovers to Mouthier-Haute-Pierre. The site, with its waterfalls, is superb.

 HOTELS-RESTAURANTS

■ La Truite d'Or

40, rte de Besançon.
Tel. 03 81 60 95 48. Fax 03 81 60 95 73.
la-truite-dor@wanadoo.fr / www.la-truite-dor.fr
Closed Sun. dinner (off season),
Mon. (off season), mid-Dec.–beg. Feb.
11 rooms: 46–54€.
Prix fixe: 16,50€, 21€, 33€, 43€,
9€ (child). A la carte: 45€.

In this old stone-cutter's mill alongside the Loue, Gilles and Sylvie Vigneron propose well-turned classics. Morel cassolette, trout braised in Savignin wine, venison medallions with red wine sauce and the roasted pear or crème brûlée slip down easily. The simple rooms overlooking the river are comfortable.

LOGUIVY-DE-LA-MER see PAIMPOL

LOIX see ILE DE RE

LONGEVILLE-LES-SAINT-AVOLD see
SAINT-AVOLD

LONGUYON

54260 Meurthe-et-Moselle. Paris 315 –
Metz 80 – Nancy 135 – Sedan 71 –
Thionville 58 – Verdun 44.
Belgium is nearby. This is a part of the world
known as the "Pays Haut". This piece of
Meurthe-et-Moselle, which used to be part of
Moselle, escaped being annexed in 1870 and
is still searching for an identity. Verdant paths
have replaced the steel mills.

 HOTELS-RESTAURANTS

● **Le Mas**   ○COM
65, rue Augistrou.
Tel. 03 82 26 50 07. Fax 03 82 39 26 09.
mas.lorraine@wanadoo.fr
www.lorraineetmas.com
Closed beg. Jan.–beg. Feb. Rest. closed Mon.
(exc. Bank holidays), Tue. lunch.
14 rooms: 49–68€.
Prix fixe: 21€, 42€ (Sat., Sun., lunch),
13€ (child). A la carte: 56–61€.

This establishment belongs in the strong
tradition of Lorraine with its family atmosphere, its warmhearted welcome and its
pleasant comfort. The cuisine reflects
generous workmanship by Gérard Tis-
serant, a wine steward turned chef after
meeting Jean-Pierre Billoux. Sit by the
fireplace or on the terrace in summer and
choose from a market-based
menu: langoustines and julienned morels
in puff pastry, roasted Atlantic sea bass
with curry vinaigrette-seasoned vegetable
spaghetti and bacon sauce, a free-range
chicken, oyster fricassée, sautéed duck
foie gras served with a Vitelotte potato
cake, followed by the dessert cart.

In Rouvrois-sur-Othain (55230). 7,5 km via
N18.

● **La Marmite**   COM
7,5 km via N18.
Tel. 03 29 85 90 79. Fax 03 29 85 99 23.

gerardsilvestre55@orange.fr
Closed Sun. dinner, Mon., Tue.,
10 days beg. Jan., 10 days at end Aug.
Prix fixe: 15€, 34€, 53€, 12€ (child).
A la carte: 45–55€.

Gérard and Martine Silvestre spare no
effort at this ancient village café. Gérard's
locally based cuisine offers bourgeois
dishes that combine with the sunny atmosphere to provide moments of real pleasure. Salad with a boneless twelve-hour
pork trotter served warm with vinaigrette,
boneless red mullet filet grilled with pesto,
the Dombes quail, also boneless, served
with wild mushrooms and the frozen bergamot-flavored nougat are eaten in the
classically comfortable dining room.

LONS see PAU

LONS-LE-SAUNIER

39000 Jura. Paris 412 – Bourg-en-Bresse 71
– Chalon-sur-Saône 63 – Besançon 84.
The Franche Comté triumphs in this lovely old
town. The rue du Commerce with its handsome
houses, theater and the pharmacy of the Hotel-
Dieu are the jewels in its crown.

 HOTELS-RESTAURANTS

■ **Hôtel du Parc**   🎁
9, av Jean-Moulin.
Tel. 03 84 86 10 20. Fax 03 84 24 97 28.
Rest. closed Sun. dinner (off season).
16 rooms: 50–54€.
Prix fixe: 15€, 23€, 6€ (child).
A la carte: 30–35€.

The rooms are functional and the cuisine
is inspired by local tradition, as attested
by Morteau sausage salad prepared vineyard-keeper's style with grape leaves,
the perch filet with almonds, pan-tossed
boneless rib steak with Cancoillotte (a
runny white cheese) gratin dauphinois
and green salad. The chocolate and pear
truffle makes a nice finish. The restaurant was redecorated in 2007.

In Courlans (39000). 6 km via N78.

● **Hôberge de Chavannes**

1890, rte de Chalon.
Tel. 03 84 47 05 52. Fax 03 84 43 26 53.
nicolas.pourcheresse@auberge-de-chavannes.com
www.auberge-de-chavannes.com
Closed 2 weeks beg. Jan., 10 days Feb.,
10 days Apr.
Rest. closed Sun. dinner, Mon., Tue. lunch.
11 rooms: 80–140€.
Prix fixe: 28€ (weekday lunch), 55€, 75€,
25€ (child).

The Carpentiers' old inn keeps getting younger. Under the leadership of Nicolas Pourcheresse has emerged a brand new hotel with minimalist rooms, decorated according to geographical themes (Oceanic, Asian, Gypsy, Mediterranean). In the contemporary Zen dining room, this former chef of the Chaumière in Dôle delivers gastronomic and original dishes such as the Luberon asparagus served with milk Chantilly and smoked herring caviar, the catfish braised in Vin Jaune, Bresse poultry cooked whole in a pastry shell and the strawberries and raspberries served with star anise–flavored ice cream.

LORETTE

42420 Loire. Paris 500 – Rive de Gier 5 –
Saint-Etienne 20 – Lyon 43.
This industrial suburb which used to house steel mills manages to offer some pretty green spots in the valley of Giez and the Pilat.

●	RESTAURANTS

● **La Table d'Elsa**

54, rue Eugène-Brosse.
Tel. 04 77 73 72 56. Fax 04 77 73 72 58.
Closed Sun. dinner, Mon.
Prix fixe: 22€ (lunch), 33€, 45€.

Marc Di Bartolomeo, who worked in some of the grand hotels on the Adriatic and at the Richelieu on the Ile de Ré, has transformed this bourgeois residence into a fine dining establishment with its high ceilings and well-spaced tables. Braised foie gras served with rhubarb compote, avocado and crab, a roasted monkfish with a zucchini cake and the squab ragout, served with carrot tagliatelli and fennel, are tempting. The desserts (roasted pineapple with almond cream and chocolate sorbet or the apricot clafoutis with Madagascar vanilla ice cream) are successful.

LORGUES

83510 Var. Paris 845 – Fréjus 39 –
Brignoles 33 – Draguignan 13 – Toulon 74.
lorotsi@aol.com.
This patch of the Haut Var, in truffle and wine country, home to the Université François Rabelais, is worth a detour.

◪	HOTELS-RESTAURANTS

■ **Château de Berne**

Chemin de Berne (rte de Salernes, D10).
Tel. 04 94 60 43 60. Fax 04 94 60 48 89.
auberge@chateauberne.com
www.chateauberne.com
Closed beg. Jan.–Mar. 1, beg. Nov.–end Dec.
13 rooms: 195–410€. 6 suites: 325–790€.
Prix fixe: 49€ (wine inc. dinner),
20€ (child). A la carte: 65€.

Set in the middle of parkland and vines, Christine Monteil's château certainly doesn't lack attractions: the organic kitchen garden, the oenology, cooking and watercolor courses, the exhibitions, concerts, sporting activities by the pool or in the fitness center and siestas in the Provençal-decorated rooms enrich your stay. In the restaurant, Philippe Migo carefully refines truffle-seasoned lobster gazpacho, Mediterranean sea bass with a thyme-infused fish stock, veal medallion browned in the oven with a pain d'épice topping and pan-simmered apricots.

● **Bruno**

3 km via rte des Arcs.
Tel. 04 94 85 93 93. Fax 04 94 85 93 99.
chezbruno@wanadoo.fr
www.restaurantbruno.com
Rest. closed Sun. dinner, Mon. (off season).

3 rooms: 100–200€. 3 suites: 260–306€.
Prix fixe: 58€, 120€, 20€ (child., lunch).

Truffles, nothing but truffles! Clément Bruno has eyes only for truffles. All the monomaniacs of the black nugget gather in his farmhouse surrounded by vineyards with its three pretty Provençal-style rooms. In the hands of Gérard Puigdellivol, Eric Barbe and Yann Sandrini, the foie gras ravioli with Alba white truffle coulis, the scallops with truffled, slow-cooked leeks, veal sweetbreads with chanterelles and truffle sauce, the dark chocolate desserts and an orange and amerena cherry crème brûlée are not lacking in character. That goes, too, for the nectars of winemaker friends.

LORIENT

56100 Morbihan. Paris 503 – Quimper 68 – Vannes 58 – Hennebont 12.
tourismelorient@azimail.com.
Destroyed in 1943, the town presents a new face. The national Marine has a lot to do with its near future. One can visit the submarine base, the art nouveau quarter of Merville and the cours Chazelles, the art deco facades and the rue Madame-de-Sévigné. This modern "Bretonne" needs to be rediscovered.

 ■ HOTELS-RESTAURANTS

■ Mercure 🏨
31, pl Jules-Ferry.
Tel. 02 97 21 35 73. Fax 02 97 64 48 62.
h0873@accor.com / www.mercure.com
58 rooms: 88–98€.

In a commercial district, next to the Palais du Congrès and the old port, this welcoming hotel—recently renovated in warm colors—offers irreproachable comfort and furnishings.

● L'Amphitryon ⓒⒸ Ⓥ.ⒸⓄⓂ
127, rue du Col.-Muller.
Tel. 02 97 83 34 04. Fax 02 97 37 25 02.
contact@amphitryon-abadie.com
www.amphitryon-abadie.com
Closed Sun., Mon., 2 weeks beg. Sept.,

10 days beg. Jan., 20 May–mid-June.
Prix fixe: 58€, 89€, 115€, 15€ (child).
A la carte: 110€.

Jean-Paul Abadie, self-taught wizard of Morbihan cuisine and native of the plateau of Lannemezan in the Pyrénées, knows his Breton repertoire by heart. In the resolutely contemporary interior of his comfortable dining room, magic strikes with the discovery of his "taste everything" menu, an ode to his lightened version of Brittany's gastronomy. Ah! The savory royale and spider crab "transparence" seasoned with licorice root, rouget with blackcurrant and lemon-seasoned artichokes, little medallions of tasty red tuna seasoned with lovage and crisped in the oven. Everything is royal yet seems so simple, such as the classic Atlantic sea bass braised in champagne and the boneless stuffed pan-steamed Pouhinec squab. This joyful experience carries on through dessert—the creamy cherry and pecan frozen dessert and the marvelous citrus fruit cannelloni with spicy rhubarb sorbet. The wine cellar is opulence itself with more than a thousand references. Véronique has a praiseworthy knowledge of wine (she was our Sommelière of the Year 2005) and is an outstanding hostess for whom wine is a feast to be shared with whomever wishes to take flight. She is utterly competent.

● Le Jardin Gourmand ⓄⒸⓄⓂ
46, rue Jules-Simon.
Tel. 02 97 64 17 24. Fax 02 97 64 15 75.
Closed Sun., Mon., 3 weeks Feb.,
15 Aug.–2 Sept.
Prix fixe: 26€ (lunch), 38€, 50€ (dinner),
13€ (child).

This charming house has a garden with a pergola, a soberly elegant dining room and a charming welcome. Fresh, regional products provide the fine, basic ingredients for Natalie Beauvais' cuisine which overflows with tasty ideas. Thanks to the straightforward menus, you will enjoy Quiberon oysters, Guidel cider-braised monkfish and tomatoes with an artichoke and sage-seasoned veal stuffing, before being seduced by the rice pudding with caramelized slow-cooked apples. Service and the choice of wines from a well-balanced list are under the careful guidance of Arnaud Beauvais.

● La Cuisine `SIM`

17, bd du Maréchal-Franchet-d'Espérey.
Tel.-Fax 02 97 84 04 04.
Closed Sun., Mon., 1 week Christmas–New Year's, 2 weeks Aug.
Prix fixe: 11,50€ (weekday lunch), 15,35€ (weekday lunch). A la carte: 30–35€.

In her turmeric-colored bistro, Joëlle Libé attracts diners who enjoy armchair traveling. Her fusion cooking hits the spot with the carrot and tarragon terrine, the catch of the day, chicken marinated in Moroccan spices, lamb tagine and spicy poached pears which slip down easily.

● Le Pécharmant `SIM`

5, rue Carnel.
Tel. 02 97 21 33 86. Fax 02 97 35 11 01.
Closed Sun., Mon., 1 week beg. Jan., 10 days end Apr.–beg. May, 3 weeks July.
Prix fixe: 22€, 39€, 49€, 69€, 11€ (child).

Serge Hacquet, who used to work with Delaveyne at the Camélia in Bougival, has not lost his touch in this good neighborhood bistro. He treats his faithful clientèle to poached eggs with crab quenelles and mushrooms, braised sea bream with seaweed-flavored melted butter, roasted squab with Breton honey and Sichuan pepper and a soft-centered chocolate cake to die for.

● Le Pic `SIM`

2, bd du Maréchal-Franchet-d'Espérey.
Tel. 02 97 21 18 29. Fax 02 97 21 92 64.
Closed Sat. lunch, Sun.
Prix fixe: 18,50€, 28€, 38€. A la carte: 45€.

This jolly brasserie, decorated in red and black, is vivaciously run by Marc and Nathalie Saulou. The former cooks with simplicity, while the latter welcomes you with alacrity. Langoustine tail brochettes with pain d'épice croutons, Atlantic sea bass with oyster vinaigrette, Limousin rump steak with bacon-seasoned potato cakes, the frozen mint parfait and the chocolate croustiillant stand up well. Fine wines by the glass.

LOUBRESSAC

46130 Lot. Paris 534 – Brive 47 – Cahors 74 – Saint-Céré 10 – Gramat 16.
saint-cere@wanadoo.fr.
A fortified village of the Quercy with the castle of Castelnau-Bretenoux dominating the Lot, which meanders majestically through the landscape.

■ ◆ HOTELS-RESTAURANTS

■ Le Relais de Castelnau

Rte de Padirac.
Tel. 05 65 10 80 90. Fax 05 65 38 22 02.
rdc46@wanadoo.fr
www.relaisdecastelnau.com
Closed end Oct.–Easter.
Rest. closed Sun. dinner, Mon.
40 rooms: 55–105€. 1 suite: 120€.
Prix fixe: 18€, 25€, 29€, 45€, 10€ (child). A la carte: 55€.

This modern establishment is in a dream spot overlooking the valleys of the Bave and the Dordogne and right opposite the castle of Castelnau-Bretenoux, but that isn't its only trump card. There are the practical and comfortable rooms and especially the wily cooking of Rémi Pradier. The farm-raised lamb sweetbread and Port cassolette, quick-seared salmon served with slow-cooked leeks, beef tenderloin served with pommes Maxime (thinly sliced and arranged in a rosette before baking) and the chocolate fondant honor the region, following the example of the wines of Cahors.

■ Lou Cantou

Le Bourg.
Tel. 05 65 38 20 58. Fax 05 65 38 25 37.
Closed end Oct.–11 Nov., 2 weeks Feb.
Rest. closed Sun dinner, Mon. (off season).
12 rooms: 47–57€.
Prix fixe: 12€, 25€, 32€, 7€ (child).
A la carte: 34€.

At the heart of the fortified village, Hubert and Marie-Claude Cayrouse's inn offers the comfort of simple, clean rooms, some of them with a view of the Bave valley. In the rustic dining room, we still love the foie gras terrine and the Quercy lamb plate, cooked up by Hubert.

LOUDUN

86200 Vienne. Paris 310 – Angers 80 – Châtellerault 45 – Poitiers 58 – Tours 70.
The old town on the hill, the Tour Carré and the dwellings of the lower town which include that of Théophraste Renaudot deserve a careful visit.

■ HOTELS

■ Renaudot
40, av de Leuze.
Tel. 05 49 98 19 22. Fax 05 49 98 94 22.
29 rooms: 36–57€.

In the center of town, not far from the church of Saint-Pierre, a simple and practical stopover with functional rooms and low prices.

LOUE

72540 Sarthe. Paris 230 – Laval 58 – Rennes 126 – Le Mans 29.
villedeloue@wanadoo.fr.
This is the country of the lovely, red-feathered fowl where long ago François Reichenbach filmed *La France Tranquille*.

■ HOTELS-RESTAURANTS

■ Ricordeau
13, rue de la Libération.
Tel. 02 43 88 40 03. Fax 02 43 88 62 08.
hotel-ricordeau@wanadoo.fr
www.hotel-ricordeau.fr
Rest. closed Sun. dinner, Mon.
10 rooms: 85–125€. 3 suites: 125–150€.
Prix fixe: 26€, 80€. A la carte: 70–75€.

The Hermans continue to take flight in this 19th-century coaching inn set along the banks of the Vègre. Pleasant rooms and comfortable lounges make for a restful stay and a heated pool provides relaxation. The old-style decoration is appealing right down to the dining room with its fireplace and flagstones. Here, or on the terrace overlooking the garden, you'll be able to taste explosive cuisine, for Jean-Yves, who hails from Franche-Comté, has also lingered in Switzerland, Burgundy and the Jura and delivers an elaborate score: lamb sweetbreads and oysters served warm with a ginger-seasoned carrot jus as an appetizer, Atlantic sea bass filet, cuttlefish and morels, breast of local Loué chicken stuffed with chanterelles, veal cutlet, potatoes with escargots and delicious desserts, like the pistachio macaron and apricots poached in lavender syrup served with lavender ice cream. Also try the annex, the simpler Coq Hardi and the Bistro at Le Mans.

LOURDES

65100 Hautes-Pyrénées. Paris 848 – Bayonne 145 – Pau 46 – St-Gaudens 88 – Tarbes 20.
The site of the famous pilgrimage center dedicated to the apparition of the Virgin. There is also a fortified castle and a museum of the Pyrénées.

■ HOTELS-RESTAURANTS

■ Grand Hôtel de la Grotte
66, rue de la Grotte.
Tel. 05 62 94 58 87. Fax 05 62 94 20 50.
booking@hoteldelagrotte.com
www.hotel-grotte.com
Rest. closed beg. Nov.–end Mar.
80 rooms: 64–158€.
Prix fixe: 18–24€ (brasserie). A la carte: 60€.

This large and traditional establishment at the foot of the castle offers stylish rooms, some of which have a view of the Basilica. No miracles in the kitchen, but there is a brasserie formula with buffet dining, a terrace under the chestnut trees and classic cuisine in the modest dining room.

● Le Magret

10, rue des Quatre-Frères-Soulas.
Tel.-Fax 05 62 94 20 55.
contact@lemagret.com / www.lemagret.com
Closed 2 weeks Jan., 1 week at end June–beg.
July. Rest. closed Mon., Tue. (off season).
Prix fixe: 13€ (weekday lunch), 26€, 33€,
9,50€ (child). A la carte: 45€.

In the gaily colored, rustic dining room filled with shiny copper pots, Philippe Pène greets you with a big smile. Tourists and locals alike habitually stop here for a meal consisting of the black pig platter, a pike-perch served with creamy Tarbais haricots, slowly braised squab served with pan-tossed porcini and a chocolate "farandole".

LOURMARIN

84160 Vaucluse. Paris 738 – Apt 19 –
Aix 33 – Cavaillon 34 – Digne 112.
ot-lourmarin@axit.fr.
"We have ceased to talk with him whom we love and this is not silence" wrote Char in *L'Eternité à Lourmarin* about his friend Camus. The latter lies here in the village next to Henri Bosco. One comes here for the peace, the pretty village, the castle, the view over the hills of the Luberon. And the gastronomy!

■ HOTELS-RESTAURANTS

● Auberge La Fenière

Rte de Cadenet via D943.
Tel. 04 90 68 11 79. Fax 04 90 68 18 60.
reine@wanadoo.fr
www.reinesammut.com
Closed Jan. Rest. closed Mon., Tue. lunch.
7 rooms: 160–300€.
Prix fixe: 78€, 115€, 35€ (child).
A la carte: 120€.

Reine Sammut reigns gracefully over the hillcrests of the great Luberon. Her inn is an invitation to discover her adopted region. How not to love the large garden, the terrace and its view, the warm atmosphere of the rooms decorated with themes from the arts and crafts? Reine and Guy Sammut have added a bohemian zest for living thanks to two ravishing caravans which their performer friends love to visit. (Pierre Arditi and Guy Bedos are regulars.) With the support of Guy who is a heartfelt proponent of her cuisine, the aptly-named Reine continues her quest for flavors and savors, lovingly turning out the best of what's currently on the market, combining Tuscany with Provence with a few touches of Catalonia. Curiosity is the driving force of this little woman from Frizon in Lorraine, whether it takes her to the shores of Sicily or Greece. Summer purslane salad with spiny lobsters cooked in olive oil served with ginger confit, truffle oil-seasoned risotto, zucchini flower tempura with summer truffles, simply grilled rougets served with a fine olive oil-infused potato purée and the farm-raised squab braised in cocotte with slow-roasted garlic, served with red Camargue rice and spicy sauce, all to be sampled with the crisp, regional white wines of the region or the magnificent reds made by neighboring alchemist and friend, Tardieu-Laurent. As for the desserts (the Thé de Lu biscuits with sour cherries and pistachio butter crumble with ice cream), they are an open invitation to dream in such an enchanting spot.

■ Le Moulin de Lourmarin

Rue du Temple.
Tel. 04 90 68 06 69. Fax 04 90 68 31 76.
infos@moulindelourmarin.com
www.moulindelourmarin.com
Rest. closed Wed.
20 rooms: 120–190€. 1 suite: 350€.
Prix fixe: 30€, 55€, 70€, 12€ (child).

This Provençal abode has become the annex of Edouard Loubet, currently at Capelongue. Under his guidance, Cedric Carjuzaa's market-based cuisine highlights local flavors through its ever-changing menus. The grilled truffle on toasts, Bourbon vanilla-seasoned jumbo shrimp served with a cardamom-seasoned pear and ginger sauté, the rack of lamb stuffed with fresh goat cheese and the multi-chocolate marquise show mastery and promise true pleasure, which the bill does nothing to dispel. Pretty, well-appointed rooms.

■ Le Mas de Guilles ❀🏠

Rte de Vaugines.
Tel. 04 90 68 30 55. Fax 04 90 68 37 41.
hotel@guilles.com / www.guilles.com
Closed end Oct.–Easter. Rest. closed lunch
29 rooms: 80–150€. 1 suite: 150€.
Prix fixe: 44€, 15€ (child). A la carte: 65€.

Situated in parkland surrounded by olive trees, vines and fruit trees, this 17th-century Provençal farmhouse doesn't lack panache. Its rustic Provençal-style rooms, its swimming pool and Patrick Lherm's sunny cuisine warm the heart.

● L'Antiquaire COM

9, rue du Grand-Pré.
Tel.-Fax 04 90 68 17 29.
Closed Sun. dinner, Mon., Tue. lunch,
2 weeks Nov., 2 weeks Jan.
Prix fixe: 29€. A la carte: 40€.

The white dining room is the setting for the composed cuisine of David Dubouchet. Tuck in with gusto to an oven-baked brandade, thin mushroom tart, beef cheek and potato casserole and lamb confit and the nice assortment of desserts. Sensible prices.

● Maison Ollier COM

Pl de la Fontaine.
Tel. 04 90 68 02 03. Fax 04 90 68 36 47.
Closed Tue. (off season), Wed. lunch,
Wed. dinner (off season), mid-Nov.–mid-Dec.
Prix fixe: 15€ (weekday lunch), 21€, 29€.
A la carte: 40–45€.

In this old hotel which has kept its Provençal style, Michel Théron orchestrates fresh produce in Mediterranean tones. Throw in your lot with pressed foie gras and figs served with chutney, jumbo shrimp tempura, the mixed fish grill with vegetables, beef kefta served with couscous and the strawberry tiramisu served with sorbet.

● Le Bistro de Lourmarin SIM

2, av Ph.-de-Girard.
Tel. 04 90 68 29 74. Fax 04 90 68 37 44.
lebistro delourmarin@wanadoo.fr
Closed Thu., Fri. lunch, Christmas–New

Year's, 3 weeks Jan., 1 week at end Aug.
Prix fixe: 16,50€, 26€. A la carte: 38€.

The terrace has a view of the Lubéron hills and the local castle. Regional inspiration and Lyonnais tradition meet in a love match under the guidance of Jérôme Bulan. Grilled squid and pepper salad, rouget and slow-cooked leek gratin, the cod bouillabaisse and the pistachio-specked sausage with steamed potato salad are smashing. The hot caramelized apples served on vanilla ice cream with chocolate sauce and Grand Marnier are fine finales.

LUCELLE see OBERLARG
LUCEY see TOUL

LUCHE-PRINGE

72800 Sarthe. Paris 240 – Angers 70 –
La Flèche 13 – Le Mans 40.
This old village sits on the right bank of the Loir. It has a church with a Pieta dating from 1500 and a 13th-century Plantagenet chancel.

 HOTELS-RESTAURANTS

● Auberge du Port des Roches 🅝COM

In Port des Roches Est, 2,5 km. via D13 and D214.
Tel. 02 43 45 44 48. Fax 02 43 45 39 61.
Closed 1 week at end Oct.–beg. Nov., Feb.
Rest. closed Sun. dinner, Mon., Tue. lunch.
12 rooms: 46–65€.
Prix fixe: 23€, 35€, 46€, 9€ (child).

In their cozy inn on the road to the châteaux with its garden-terrace set on the banks of the Loir, the Lesiourds aim for conviviality and a country spirit. Rooms are bright and the cream and red dining room with its Louis XV chairs are ideal for enjoying Thierry's of-the-moment cooking. The menus vary according to season. Pommeau-seasoned foie gras served with an apple compote, the monkfish in a lavender infusion, braised veal sweetbreads with pigs ears and then the chocolate financier with creamy caramel sauce slip down with no effort at all. Good regional wines. Renovations planned for this year.

85400 Vendée. Paris 438 –
La Roche-sur-Yon 33 – Cholet 89 –
Fontenay-le-Comte 30 – La Rochelle 43.
This town where Richelieu was crowned bishop in 1608 has a cathedral and ancient dwellings.

●	RESTAURANTS

● **L'Ardoise Gourmande**
52, rue G.-Clemenceau.
Tel. 02 51 56 35 10.
Closed Sun., Mon. dinner, Tue. dinner, vac.
Christmas, 10 days beg. Aug.
Prix fixe: 17€.

Philippe Boucard is in the dining room while his sister Béatrice Lacarin shares the kitchen with her husband Jean-Philippe. This trio's shared experiences with some of the great Parisians (Ritz, Savoy, Rostang, Besson) led them to create this funky, town-based "country" bistro. Engaging décor; simple and tasty cooking. An oven-crisped goat cheese and walnut dish, the salmon terrine with fines herbes, the pollock filet with cabbage, rabbit with whole grain mustard sauce and the pineapple syrup panna cotta are well prepared and appear on a very reasonably priced menu.

LE LUDE

72800 Sarthe. Paris 245 – Angers 65 –
Chinon 65 – La Flèche 21– Le Mans 44 –
Tours 50.
This castle in the Sarthe is one of the marvels of the valley. Don't miss the Sound and Light show.

■●	HOTELS-RESTAURANTS

● **La Renaissance**
2, av de la Libération.
Tel. 02 43 94 63 10. Fax 02 43 94 21 05.

www.renaissancelelude.com
Closed Sun. dinner, Mon., Nov. 1 vac.,
Feb. vac., 1 week beg. Aug.
8 rooms: 46–56€.
Prix fixe: 14€ (weekday lunch), 22€, 30€,
36€, 8,50€ (child). A la carte: 49–53€.

Next to the castle, the Lenoirs' inn is resolutely contemporary: décor and rooms are modern in style and the cooking is inventive. At the stove, Dany breaks with tradition thanks to some crafty combinations. Try the simmered scallops in sauce with a crust of lentils and tulip jus, the lobster consomme with foie gras and a cactus infusion, oven-browned pike-perch with a crust of hazelnuts and ceps and the tender beef and Camembert, which have no trouble slipping down, just like the soft fresh goat cheese and the orange tea sorbet—an explosive ending.

LUNEVILLE

54300 Meurthe-et-Moselle. Paris 341 –
Nancy 36 – Epinal 64 – Metz 95 –
Strasbourg 131.
The "Versailles of Lorraine"—château and gardens—has suffered a large disaster (a fire in 2003 which destroyed much of the château) which the whole region is trying to make everyone forget. Restoration is under way. The old town and the near-by porcelain works of Saint-Clément are also worth a detour.

■●	HOTELS-RESTAURANTS

● **Château d'Adoménil**
Tel. 03 83 74 04 81. Fax 03 83 74 21 78.
adomenil@relaischateaux.com
www.adomenil.com
Closed Jan., Feb. vac. Rest. closed Sun. dinner, Mon., lunch (exc. weekends).
9 rooms: 160–200€. 5 suites: 220–260€.
Prix fixe: 44€ (weekday dinner), 89€,
23€ (child). A la carte: 84–91€.

The 18th-century castle and its various outbuildings stand in a splendid park. The nobility of the surroundings and the luxurious rooms with all modern conveniences as well as the warm, stylish bourgeois dining room, make this a choice address. Under the direction of Michel Million, his son-in-law Cyrille Leclerc signs off on a sophisticated cuisine, which reflects contemporary tastes and new ideas without turning its back on local flavors. Hard to resist the pigeon salad with foie gras pan-seared with coriander-seasoned sugar, pike-perch with shallots slow-cooked in Pinot Noir, the pigeon breast served with a brochette of its organ meats and a mildly spicy jus and desserts such as a cherry clafoutis. Moreover, the lush wine list presented by Bernadette Million and Sophie Leclerc's service add to the pleasures of dining.

■ Hôtel des Pages

5, quai des Petits-Bosquets.
Tel. 03 83 74 11 42. Fax 03 83 73 46 63.
les.pages@wanadoo.fr
37 rooms: 53–70€. 9 suites: 95–120€.
Half board: 119–220€.

Facing the castle, on the opposite bank of the Vezouse, this modern hotel offers pretty, individualized rooms done up in warm tones. Internet and WiFi.

● Le Floréal   COM

1, pl Léopold (2nd floor).
Tel. 03 83 73 39 80. Fax 03 83 73 29 89.
rest.floreal@wanadoo.fr
Closed Sun. dinner, Mon.
Prix fixe: 15€, 24€, 30€, 37€,
8€ (child). A la carte: 40€.

Right next to the Saint-Jacques church, the Brideys run a most reliable house. Stéphane at the stove and Arnaud in the yellow-orange dining room filled with paintings and plants, offer a classic, well turned-out cuisine. Tomme de Pierre-Percée cheese in puff pastry, roasted monkfish with a cep risotto, pan-seared scallops with crayfish tails, pork trotters stuffed with foie gras and the mirabelle plum cream baba are lovingly cooked.

● Marie Leszczynska   SIM

30, rue de Lorraine.
Tel. 03 83 73 11 85. Fax 03 83 73 00 34.
Closed Sun. dinner, Mon., Tue. dinner,
1 week Christmas–New Year's,
1 week Jan., 2 weeks Aug.
Prix fixe: 13,60€, 23€, 28,50€, 37€,
6,90€ (child). A la carte: 38€.

This establishment bearing the name of Louis XV's wife is very close to the castle. The king here is Benoît Joliot who concocts fresh market-based dishes for his clients in a dining room with red tablecloths. Crayfish and smoked salmon in salad, turbot in puff pastry with juniper berry-flavored butter, oven-crisped veal sweetbreads in pastry with morels and the mirabelle plum parfait with caramel sauce are highly regarded. Nice wine list.

64660 Pyrénées-Atlantiques. Paris 832 –
Pau 45 – Lourdes 61 – Tardets 29 –
Oloron 10.
The Béarn with its countryside, its forest, its fresh air and an up-and-coming health resort.

 HOTELS-RESTAURANTS

● Au Bon Coin

Rte des Thermes.
Tel. 05 59 34 40 12. Fax 05 59 34 46 40.
thierrylassala@wanadoo.fr
www.thierry-lassala.com
Closed Jan.
Rest. closed Mon. lunch, Tue. lunch.
18 rooms: 55–86€.
Prix fixe: 22€ (weekday lunch), 38€, 50€,
10€ (child).

Bordering the Parc National de Pyrénées, Thierry Lassala's large establishment is right next to thermal baths. Tranquility and the plush comfort of both rooms and dining room will put you to rest. The flavorful cuisine by this disciple of Guérard and Arrambide underscores a great fidelity to the Basque-Béarnais spirit. The rouget filets and artichokes in a peppery vinaigrette, the Saint-Jean-de-Luz tuna belly, the Galice beef strips and the duo of caramel and chocolate fondants are an open pleasure, enhanced by a remarkable wine list and very considerate service.

LUSIGNAN

86600 Vienne. Paris 362 – Angoulême 97 –
Confolens 75 – Niort 55 – Poitiers 25.
A Romanesque church and recollections of the
lords of Lusignan revive the legend of the fairy
Mélusine.

 HOTELS-RESTAURANTS

■ Le Chapeau Rouge
1, rue Chypre.
Tel. 05 49 43 31 10. Fax 05 49 43 31 20.
Closed Sun. dinner (Oct.–May),
Mon. (exc. dinner June–Sept.), Nov. 1 vac.
8 rooms: 42–53€.
Prix fixe: 17€, 43€.

This 17th-century coaching inn has kept
its Old World panache with its rustic rooms
and a dining room graced with a lovely fireplace with a turning spit. Regional cuisine
of Poitou and a personalized welcome.

LUSSAC-LES-CHATEAUX

86320 Vienne. Paris 355 – Bellac 40 –
Châtellerault 50 – Poitiers 39 – Ruffec 51 –
Montmorillon 12.
Mme de Montespan was born in this feudal town
on the right bank of the Vienne. Don't miss the
prehistoric grottoes or the Mérovingian necrop-
olis at Civaux.

 HOTELS-RESTAURANTS

■ Les Orangeries
12, av du Docteur-Dupont.
Tel. 05 49 84 07 07. Fax 05 49 84 98 82.
orangeries@wanadoo.fr / www.lesorangeries.fr
Closed mid-Dec.–mid-Jan.
7 rooms: 65–110€. 3 suites: 95–165€.
Half board: 105–205€.

The simple paneled, rustic décor of this
18th-century house has lots of character.
Add the garden at the back and the swimming pool, and you have a pleasant base
from which to visit the Poitou.

LUTTER see FERRETTE

LUTZELBOURG

57820 Moselle. Paris 438 – Strasbourg 63 –
Metz 110 – Sarrebourg 19 – Phalsbourg 5.
lutzelbourg@wanadoo.fr.
A corner of the Vosges, between the canal of
the Zorn and some romantic ruins. We're still
in Lorraine but Alsace is nearby.

 HOTELS-RESTAURANTS

■ Hôtel des Vosges
149, rue Ackermann.
Tel. 03 87 25 30 09. Fax 03 87 25 42 22.
info@hotelvosges.com / www.hotelvosges.com
Rest. closed Sun. dinner (exc. groups),
Wed. (exc. groups).
10 rooms: 55€.
Prix fixe: 10€ (lunch), 19€ (dinner), 25,50€
(wine inc.), 28,50€ (wine inc.) 9,50€ (child).

Kindness and simplicity are the hallmarks of this large inn (circa 1900), with
its beige wood décor, right on the edge of
the Marne Rhine canal. The rooms have
old-fashioned furnishings and there are
two dining rooms—one huge and kitsch,
the other more intimate and rustic—and
a traditional if a bit dated cuisine which
seems to please. Pierre Bouvier and Marc
Corriger team up to prepare a marbled
foie gras terrine, fresh trout cleaned and
cooked to order, boneless rib steak with
green peppercorns, duck breast with
honey, blood sausage on a bed of shallots and a Lorraine-style cold dessert
in jelly with caramel sauce, all of which
are easy to enjoy. Charming welcome by
Régine Lorang.

LUXE see MANSLE

LUYNES

37230 Indre-et-Loire. Paris 250 – Tours 12
– Chinon 42 – Langeais 14 – Saumur 57.
otsiluynes@wanadoo.fr.
The somber fortress of the château de Luynes is
not open to the public, but the surrounding countryside is agreeable, and there is a fine modernized, old manor house in which to stay.

HOTELS-RESTAURANTS

■ Domaine de Beauvois

Le Pont-Clouet, 4 km nw via D49.
Tel. 02 47 55 50 11. Fax 02 47 55 59 62.
beauvois@grandesetapes.fr
www.beauvois.com
Rest. closed Mon., Tue.
34 rooms: 180–240€. 2 suites: 270–300€.
Prix fixe: 38€, 47€, 65€.

This 16th- and 17th-century manor-house, surrounded by a large park, is one of the Loire valley stars of the Traversac group. The traditionally furnished rooms, fine furniture, reception areas, fitness center, pond and endless paths make for a long perfect weekend. Add Régis Gilpin's trendy, pleasing cuisine: the bacon tempura with zucchini and basil sauce, cod encrusted in hazelnuts, pike-perch browned in its skin and the farm poultry stuffed with mushrooms and horseradish cream. The wine list is an ode to the Loire.

LYON

69000 Rhône. Paris 450 – Genève 152 – Grenoble 107 – Marseille 315 – Saint-Etienne 61 – Turin 310.
lyoncv@lyon-france.com.
Ancient capital of the Gauls, now a modern-day capital of gastronomy. Lyon couldn't care less about trends. This city of generous appetites eschews nitpicking and remains the queen of good value for money. With few great tables to its name, Lyon makes up for it with fine inns, pleasant eateries, embassies of regional cooking where old-fashioned savoir faire is valued, wine by the carafe slakes the thirst and hearty fare is everywhere. Lyon is at a crossroads. A window on the Rhône, a gateway to Switzerland, this ancient gallo-Roman site with its Italian influences is the silk weavers' city and above all, one huge larder. Culinary craftsmen abound, likewise fine products: Rhône valley fruit, Beaujolais wine, poultry from the Bresse, fish from the lakes of Savoie and the ponds of La Dombes, cheese from the Drome are all to be found in Lyon, on the Quai Saint-Antoine and in the modern covered market of La Part-Dieu. A town tailor-made for the hungry gourmet!

HOTELS

■ La Cour des Loges

2/8, rue du Boeuf (5th arr.).
Tel. 04 72 77 44 44. Fax 04 72 40 93 61.
contact@courdesloges.com
www.courdesloges.com
62 rooms and apartments: 230–590€.

The Sibuets, reigning monarchs of Megève with colonies in Ramatuelle and the Luberon, have turned these Renaissance courtyards, with their colorful rooms, into a contemporary jewel. Health spa with sauna and heated pool. (See Restaurants.)

■ La Villa Florentine

25, montée Saint-Barthélemy (5th arr.).
Tel. 04 72 56 56 56. Fax 04 72 40 90 56.
florentine@relaischateaux.com
www.villaflorentine.com
28 rooms: 310–360€. 9 suites: 515–800€.

Nestled against the Fourvière hill, this former 17th-century convent has been turned into a charming Relais & Châteaux establishment. Renaissance fresco in the entrance hall, elegant rooms and a terrace with a panoramic view set the tone. A fine restaurant (see Terrasses de Lyon).

■ Grand Hôtel Mercure Château Perrache

12, cours de Verdun-Rambaud (2nd arr.).
Tel. 04 72 77 15 00. Fax 04 78 37 06 56.
h1292@accor-hotels.com
www.accor-hotels.com
111 rooms: 98–182€.

To a great extent, this 1906 station hotel has preserved its art nouveau cachet thanks to its Majorelle furniture and wood paneling, wrought iron and stained glass. Spacious and bright rooms; Restaurant Les Belles Saisons.

■ Hilton

70, quai Charles-de-Gaulle (6th arr.).
Tel. 04 78 17 50 50. Fax 04 78 17 52 52.
rm-lyon@hilton.com / www.hilton.com
179 rooms: 139–330€.
9 suites: 300–1200€.

Right in the heart of the Cité international site of the convention center, casino and contemporary art museum, this modern, international inn provides spacious rooms, a fitness center, a cozy bar, a Belgian brasserie and a Thaï restaurant (The Blue Elephant). Located between the Rhône and the Tête d'Or park.

■ Radisson SAS Hôtel Lyon   ▥

129, rue Servient (3rd arr.).
Tel. 04 78 63 55 00. Fax 04 78 63 55 20.
info.lyon@radissonsas.com
www.radissonsas.com
Rest. closed Sat. lunch, Sun., Bank holidays, mid-July–1 Sept.
245 rooms: 110–330€.
Prix fixe: 38€, 48€, 56€ (wine inc.), 20€ (child), 19€ (Bistro de la Tour).

Not far from the station, Lyon's landmark skyscraper le Crayon (the pencil) houses a modern hotel and two restaurants. On the 32nd floor is the Arc-en-ciel with Christian Lherm's refined cuisine (foie gras served hot with cherry vinegar and slow-cooked veal belly with Thai-style basil-infused milk). The Bistro de la Tour is on the ground floor. Fine panoramic view.

■ Sofitel   ▥

20, quai du Dr-Gailleton (2nd arr.).
Tel. 04 72 41 20 20. Fax 04 72 40 05 50.
h0553@acco / www.sofitel.com
138 rooms: 285–315€. 26 suites: 435
2 presidential apartments: 1200€.

Eric Oboeuf is the attentive manager of this modern star of the center-city hotels. Cubist architecture, luxurious furnishings, luxury rooms with mahogany and blond wood furniture create a warm atmosphere. A brasserie ambiance at the Sofishop. More refined dining at the Trois Dômes. (See Restaurants.)

■ La Tour Rose   ▥

22, rue du Boeuf (5th arr.).
Tel. 04 78 37 25 90. Fax 04 78 42 26 02.
contact@tour-rose.com / www.tour-rose.com
9 rooms: 230–355€.

This magnificent Renaissance town house is worth it for its glassed-in courtyard, its stair tower, its terraced gardens and its baroque-modern rooms. (See Restaurants: La Tour Rose.)

■ Boscolo Grand Hôtel   ▥

11, rue Grolée (2nd arr.).
Tel. 04 72 40 45 45. Fax 04 78 37 52 55.
reservation@lyon.boscolo.com
www.boscolohotels.com
113 rooms: 94,95–211€.
27 suites: 158,25–399,80€.

The ex-hotel Concorde has kept its flair: witness the art deco-, Empire- or contemporary-style rooms. Comfort guaranteed near the city center and not far from the Rhône.

■ Carlton   ▥

4, rue Jussieu (2nd arr.).
Tel. 04 78 42 56 51. Fax 04 78 42 10 71.
h2950@accor.com / libertel-hotels.com
79 rooms: 78–157€. 4 suites: 148–166€.

The combination of styles between the fifties rotunda and the opera-style bar is fairly successful in giving this hotel an old-fashioned feel. English-style or art deco rooms.

■ Globe et Cécil   ▥

21, rue Gasparin (2nd arr.).
Tel. 04 78 42 58 95. Fax 04 72 41 99 06.
globe.et.cecil@wanadoo.fr
www.globeetcecilhotel.com
58 rooms: 99–150€.

Nicole Renart greets her guests in her art deco den with a warm welcome and a smile. A beautiful building with quality furniture which turns each room into a personalized space.

■ Grand Hôtel   ▥
Mercure Saxe-Lafayette

29, rue de Bonnel (3rd arr.).
Tel. 04 72 61 90 90. Fax 04 72 61 17 54.
h2057@accor.com / www.mercure.com
Rest. closed 2 weeks Aug.
156 rooms: 107–188€. 1 suite: 381€.
Prix fixe: 21€, 17€ (lunch). A la carte: 37–42€.

Located near the convention center in the business district, this hotel offers all modern conveniences: functional, spacious rooms, fitness center, Jacuzzi, jazz bar, conference rooms. In memory of the old garage that once stood here, the dining room is decorated in chrome, red and black, thirties style. Tasty, home-style cooking: foie gras, scallops in tagine broth, ginger-seasoned veal and a dark chocolate craquelin dessert.

■ Hôtel des Beaux-Arts   ⛫

75, rue du Pdt-Herriot (2nd arr.).
Tel. 04 78 38 09 50. Fax 04 78 42 19 19.
h2949@accor-hotels.com / www.accorhotels.com
75 rooms: 74–157€.

The Place Bellecour is not far from from this 1900-style hotel with a number of rooms decorated by contemporary artists. A happy marriage.

■ Lyon-Métropole   ⛫

85, quai J.-Gillet (4th arr.).
Tel. 04 72 10 44 44. Fax 04 72 10 44 42.
metropole@lyonmetropole-concorde.com
www.lyonmetropole-concorde.com
117 rooms: 150–250€. 1 suite: 395€.
Prix fixe: 20,50€, 25,50€, 12€ (child).

A hotel for sports lovers with its Olympic pool, spa, fitness center, tennis and squash courts and driving range. The rooms are well appointed and the cuisine well done. Mozzarella bruschetta, beef carpaccio with spices and the Charolais beef tartare served in a nautical-style brasserie with its terrace aren't half bad.

■ Le Phénix Hôtel   ⛫

7, quai de Bondy (5th arr.).
Tel. 04 78 28 24 24. Fax 04 78 28 62 86.
reception@hotel-le-phenix.fr
www.hotel-le-phenix.fr
36 rooms: 124–166€.

Charmingly set on the banks of the Saône, the modern rooms (some with fireplaces) and the glassed-in breakfast room make this a pleasing romantic stopover.

■ Sofitel Royal   ⛫

20, pl Bellecour (2nd arr.).
Tel. 04 78 37 57 31. Fax 04 78 37 01 36.
H2952@accor-hotels.com
www.accorhotels.com
74 rooms: 111–170€. 4 suites: 293–450€.

The 19th-century facade sets the tone for the restoration of this building but some liberties were taken in fitting out a few of the rooms in a comfortable, contemporary style. Windows open onto the Place Belle-cour or the Rhône in the distance.

■ Hôtel du Collège   ⛫

5 pl Saint-Paul (5th arr.).
Tel. 04 72 10 05 05. Fax 04 78 27 98 84.
contact@college-hotel.com
www.college-hotel.com
39 rooms: 105–140€.

We still have a soft spot for this amusing little hotel in the Saint-Paul quarter which has fun recreating the atmosphere of an old school with its classroom, its fifties and sixties furniture and its neat, minimalist rooms.

■ Hôtel des Artistes   ⛫

8, rue Gaspard-André /
Pl des Célestins (2nd arr.).
Tel. 04 78 42 04 88. Fax 04 78 42 93 76.
hartiste@club-internet.fr
www.hoteldesartistes.fr
45 rooms: 80–120€.

Actors from the Célestins theater are habitués of this charming hotel near the rue Mercière and the Saint-Antoine market. The rooms are stylish and sunny. The breakfast room has a fresco by Cocteau and modernity has made its entrance with WiFi.

■ Hôtel des Savoies   ⛫

80, rue de la Charité (2nd arr.).
Tel. 04 78 37 66 94. Fax 04 72 40 27 84.
hotel.des.savoies@wanadoo.fr
www.hoteldessavoies.fr
46 rooms: 46–100€.

This hotel is rooted in Savoie and proud of it. The small, renovated rooms, reached by a circular, central, wrought-iron staircase will afford you many agreeable moments. A thoughtful welcome and a handy garage.

■ Hôtel du Théâtre

Place des Célestins, entrance 10,
rue de Savoie (2nd arr.).
Tel. 04 78 42 33 32. Fax 04 72 40 00 61.
contact@hotel-du-theatre.fr
www.hotel-du-theatre.fr
24 rooms: 55–81€.

This is the best value for money in town with its neat rooms, courteous welcome and location in an island of leafy tranquility. As a bonus, there is a view of theater and the Célestins, between Bellecour and the Saint-Jean quarter.

● RESTAURANTS

● Léon de Lyon LUX

1, rue Pleney (1st arr.).
Tel. 04 72 10 11 12. Fax 04 72 10 11 13.
leon@relaischateaux.com
www.leondelyon.com
Closed Sun., Mon., 3 weeks Aug.
Prix fixe: 59€ (lunch), 118€, 150€.

One can never say enough about Jean-Paul Lacombe, that quarter century institution of Lyon's grand culinary tradition. His respect for fine regional products and the delight on the faces of his diners at the end of a brilliant repast in the paneled and absolutely comfortable dining room attest to his masterful craft. As the first French restaurateur to develop a gourmet empire with his bistro branches, he has nevertheless known how to remain a quietly modest artisan. Cantal farm-raised pork served with foie gras and slow-cooked caramelized yellow onions, big roasted langoustines with slow-cooked fennel, pan-seared line-fished Atlantic sea bass served with preserved lemons: small pleasures distilled by the crafty Jean-Paul are numerous in lively and savory dishes such as pigeon with herbs stuffed under the skin then simply roasted, or the milk-fed veal filet simply pan fried. On the dessert side, the wild strawberry tart cooked to order

and the roasted Muscat-flavored apricots seasoned with lemon thyme become delicious exercises in style. Dynamic service mirrors the cooking: faultless. Add a wonderful cellar, rich in wines of the Rhône valley, Burgundy and the Beaujolais, selected by Georges Duboeuf (the father-in-law) himself, and you will understand that Jean-Paul Lacombe makes you wish you could be a lifelong regular in this great gourmet establishment.

● Pierre Orsi V.LUX

3, pl Kléber (6th arr.).
Tel. 04 78 89 57 68. Fax 04 72 44 93 34.
orsi@relaischateaux.com / www.pierreorsi.com
Closed Sun., Mon. (exc. Bank holidays).
Prix fixe: 80€ (dinner), 23€ (child).

Pierre Orsi has long been a major name in Lyonnaise gastronomy. He owes it to his exacting professionalism, his precision, his classical cuisine, the impeccable welcome of the lovely Geneviève and the refined elegance of the dining rooms, rose garden and dome of this Relais Gourmand. Tucked among the various menus are the well-known foie gras ravioli with Port and truffle-enriched jus, the saffron-seasoned John Dory filet, Charolais beef sirloin with a wine sauce and the desserts like the crêpes Suzette with orange butter. In addition, the luxurious Lyonnaise bistro, the Cazenove (04 78 89 82 92), makes a good annex.

● Les Terrasses de Lyon LUX

25-27, montée de Saint-Barthélemy, at the Villa Florentine (5th arr.).
Tel. 04 72 56 56 56. Fax 04 72 40 90 56.
florentine@relaischateaux.com
www.villaflorentine.com
Prix fixe: 45€ (lunch), 60€ (lunch, wine inc.), 98€, 125€. A la carte: 107–134€.

From the heights of Fourvière, the panorama is splendid and the terrace of the Renaissance-inspired villa has an exceptional view of the old town. The setting and décor of this Relais & Châteaux establishment are of an elegance and refinement that perfectly concur with the fine cuisine perfected by David

Tissot, who worked with Régis Marcon, Jacques Maximin and was made Meilleur Ouvrier de France in 2004. Let yourselves be conquered by the roasted jumbo shrimp glazed with shellfish jus served with an asparagus tip tartelette, the sautéed John Dory with grilled vegetables and panisses (fried chickpea cakes) pan-tossed with rougail (a spicy diced tomato, ginger, onion and birds-eye pepper condiment), a veal sweetbread medallion with crunchy risotto and chanterelles with Savagnin sauce as well as the little stuffed seasonal fruits.

● **La Tour Rose**   V.COM
22, rue du Boeuf (5th arr.).
Tel. 04 78 37 25 90. Fax 04 78 42 26 02.
contact@tour-rose.com / www.tour-rose.com
Closed Mon. lunch, Sun.
Prix fixe: 17€, 29€, 40€.

Jacques Champion has taken over the reins of this superb Renaissance house with its glassed-in courtyard and ushered in a new era. The young Denis Davidoff proposes a contemporary cuisine which is well made but still looking for a style. Creamed peppers in a tuna carpaccio, grilled jumbo shrimp with eggplant and risotto cannelloni, simmered veal sweetbreads served in a cocotte and tossed with potatoes and bacon and the rice pudding with a ginger infusion, accompanied by mango marmalade, are off to a good start. To be followed.

● **Christian Têtedoie**   V.COM
54, quai Pierre-Scize (5th arr.).
Tel. 04 78 29 40 10. Fax 04 72 07 05 65.
restaurant@tetedoie.com / www.tetedoie.com
Closed Sat. lunch, Sun., Mon. lunch,
1 week at end Feb., end July–20 Aug.
Prix fixe: 44€, 52€, 65€, 85€. A la carte: 85€.

Set along the Saône, Christian Têtedoie's table continues to attract seekers of fine products. For the guests in this bourgeois dining room with its ochre tones, this former chef at Bocuse, Vergé and Blanc concocts contrasting dishes, between surf and turf, modernity and tradition. On the plate this gives us foie gras

chilled in cold savory egg custard, cubed and served with meat jus, a rouget with a tomato emulsion, lobster, slow-cooked tête de veau and a cold jelly-covered pear and almond paste dessert. Same rigor at a lesser price in its neighborhood annex, the Contretête (04 78 29 41 29).

● **Les Trois Dômes**   V.COM
20, quai du Dr-Gailleton (2nd arr.).
Tel. 04 72 41 20 20 / 04 72 41 20 97.
Fax 04 72 40 05 50.
h0553@accor-hotels.com
www.les-trois-domes.com
Closed Sun., Mon., 1 week Feb.,
end July–end Aug.
Prix fixe: 51€ (lunch), 73€, 88€, 126€, 30€ (child). A la carte: 91–108€.

On the Rhône, the 8th floor of the Sofitel Bellecour offers not only a great view of the city and its three domes but also a very good table. Chef Alain Desvilles unrolls his art with mastery, signing off on dishes accompanied by subtly chosen wines by the glass which add a judicious counterpoint to the food. Happiness comes in the form of the crab and avocado mille-feuille with ginger- and lemon-infused oil, a verbena-seasoned lobster with a zucchini composition, milk-fed Limousin lamb shoulder slow-cooked and served with grilled pesto-seasoned vegetables and a vanilla mille-feuille served with caramel ice cream. All is accompanied by a faultless service.

● **La Mère Brazier**   V.COM
12, rue Royale (1st arr.).
Tel. 04 78 28 15 49. Fax 04 78 28 63 63.
info@lamerebrazier.com
www.lamerebrazier.com
Closed Sat. lunch, Sun. lunch (summer),
Sun. dinner, 1 week Feb. vac., 3 weeks Aug.
Prix fixe: 18€ (lunch), 22€ (dinner), 50€ (dinner). A la carte: 65€.

This year we were disappointed by La Mère Brazier, now taken over by Philippe Bertrand. The quenelle served with a tasteless and heavy potato gratin, the artichoke hearts and duck foie gras without much flavor at all, the pale-tasting shell pasta with truffles didn't turn us on. Nor did the Bresse chicken demi-deuil with white creamy sauce (overcooked) or the chestnut sorbet with chocolate sauce with a Bresse-style cookie, which left us unsatisfied. In short, is this venerable establishment, with its succession of old, wood-paneled dining rooms, under threat?

● La Cour des Loges

28, rue du Boeuf (5th arr.).
Tel. 04 72 77 44 44. Fax 04 72 40 93 61.
contact@courdesloges.com
www.courdesloges.com
Rest. closed Sun., Mon.
Prix fixe: 55€ (Warhol),
75€ (Grande Cour).

Less in the news since Nicolas Le Bec's departure, La Cour des Loges remains a good address with refined dishes orchestrated by Anthony Bonnet. We still love the foie gras, the egg surprise and the chocolate fondant served hot, along with its flavorful lollipops. Love is in the air…

● Auberge de l'Ile

On the Ile Barbe (9th arr.).
Tel. 04 78 83 99 49. Fax 04 78 47 80 46.
info@aubergedelile.com
www.aubergedelile.com
Closed Sun. (exc. Easter and Mothers Day),
Mon., Aug.
Prix fixe: 45€ (weekday lunch), 90€, 120€.

A minor event on the île Barbe set smack on the Saône: Jean-Christophe Ansanay-Alex has become a member of the Relais & Châteaux chain as a Relais Gourmand. This establishment has charm: ivy-covered walls, alfresco service in the evening for drinks in the garden and modern restrooms on the first floor. Add the contemporary surroundings, menus which are "set" but never in a rut. The chef, who trained at Orsi, likes complication. We like the boiled egg crumbled over a chanterelle fricassée, lobster with figs acidulated with passion fruit and the late grape harvest reduction, thin slices of Atlantic sea bass with a cep sabayon and the pigeon pot-au-feu (even if the latter is overwhelmed by the lemon leaf bouillon), not omitting the creamy mush-

room soup served cappuccino style with bacon and foie gras. The young staff is a bit slow, struggles with serving the red wine at the correct temperature, forgets to change cutlery between two desserts (poached peaches and bitter almond ice cream). *In fine*, everyone was reconciled by the licorice ice cream served in a cone.

● Nicolas le Bec

14, rue Grolée (2nd arr.).
Tel. 04 78 42 15 00. Fax 04 72 40 98 97.
restaurant@nicolaslebec.com
www.nicolaslebec.com
Closed Sun., Mon., 1 week Jan.,
3 weeks Aug.
Prix fixe: 48€, 98€ (dinner),
118€ (weekday dinner), 128€ (dinner).

He was once the star of Megève at the Fermes de Marie. He's now the star of trendy Lyon. Nicolas le Bec, who trained at Vigato, is still shaking up Lyon's gourmet scene. His modern interior in caramel and chocolate tones is full of charm, but his true talents of invention are constantly renewed on the plate. As for the latest, gray littleneck clams "too hot to handle" served home style with shellfish and seaweed-scented butter, the zucchini flower with basil and diced green tomatoes, cod poached in a saffron-seasoned rockfish bouillon, a slice of turbot, thick and oven-browned, with a steamed asparagus terrine and fresh verbena-infused jus make for fresh, light, explosive dishes. Add: the milk-fed veal cutlet "matured" in green apples and sucrine lettuce hearts with chickory-seasoned jus, the roasted Bavière beef tenderloin, his flourless mild onion tart, his beef jus heightened with Tio Pepe and smoked cardamom-seasoned milk, equally delicious. The yummy desserts (dark chocolate soup, soft-centered sweet biscuit, Brazilian coffee-flavored ice cream and a Muscat sabayon with almond and angelica) are enchanting. Every year the wine list boasts new nectars.

● L'Alexandrin

83, rue Moncey (3rd arr.).
Tel. 04 72 61 15 69. Fax 04 78 62 75 57.

Closed Sat. lunch (May–Aug.), Sun., Mon.,
10 days Christmas–New Year's.
Prix fixe: 38€ (wine inc., lunch), 60€, 80€.

Laurent Rigal, chef at the l'Alexandrin for the last ten years, has just taken over this fine establishment which has long been a choice Lyonnais venue. In the bright, up-to-date dining room you'll dine on spicy fare as well as dishes from the Rhône valley presented in amusing, themed menus. Laurent selects his products with care before skillfully combining them. Witness the artichoke and caper rilettes mille-feuille with a date and almond milk coulis, the line-fished Atlantic sea bass, eggplant cannelloni, fine ratatouille and potato purée, truffleseasoned veal filet and the winter vegetable ragout served with truffle butter. Same happy marriage for the desserts; for example, lightly simmered and spiced cherries served on a sugar cookie and the pistachio ice cream served with a raspberry tartelette and rose confiture.

● Fleur de Sel ○COM
3, rue des Remparts-d'Ainay (2nd arr.).
Tel. 04 78 37 40 37. Fax 04 78 37 26 37.
Closed Sun., Mon., 1 week Jan.,
3 weeks Aug.
Prix fixe: 19€ (lunch), 29€, 49€.
A la carte: 55€.

It's an about-face for Cyril Nitard who's lowering his prices but not the flag. Trained by Senderens in Paris, Marchesi in Milan and Le Stanc in Monte-Carlo, he continues to give his own spin to Lyonnais market-based cooking in a modern, green and yellow dining room. Always delicious are the open langoustine ravioli, the rarecooked tuna with pan-tossed vegetables, his sweet pea and garlic ravioli, his sirloin steak with eggplant stuffed with slow-simmered veal trotter and finally the fine pineapple and mango ravoili.

● Le Gourmet de Sèze ○COM
129, rue de Sèze (6th arr.).
Tel. 04 78 24 23 42. Fax 04 78 24 66 81.
legourmetdeseze@wanadoo.fr
Closed Sun., Mon., Bank holidays,

1 week Feb., 1 week May, Aug.
Prix fixe: 35€, 43€, 60€, 66€.

Numerous are the gourmets who appreciate the cooking and style of Bernard Mariller. Formerly of Troisgros, Robuchon and the Auberge des Templiers at Les Bézards, he has what it takes to delight. In a contemporary chocolate-and-cream-toned dining room, his clever and precise dishes hit the spot. Slow-cooked pork trotters with mustard, John Dory filet with a new potato and bacon fricassée, an onion-stuffed saddle of rabbit served with rosemary-seasoned jus and the assortment of four desserts are faultless.

● Mathieu Viannay ○COM
47, av Foch (6th arr.).
Tel. 04 78 89 55 19. Fax 04 78 89 08 39.
Closed Sat., Sun., Bank holidays, 1 week
Feb. vac., Aug.
Prix fixe: 34€ (lunch), 49€, 85€.
A la carte: 75€.

For Mathieu Viannay, both setting and cuisine play on a register of sagacious modernity. Surrounded by stone walls, colorful seating and neo-baroque light fixtures, you'll enjoy the abalone and pine nut fricassée with hazelnut oil, the frogs legs, arugula and horseradish risotto, lamb curry with shavings of butter-simmered mango and warm honey madeleines served with fresh fromage blanc ice cream. The good wine list and the lunch menu are equally welcome.

● Le Splendid
3, pl Jules-Ferry (6th arr.).
Tel. 04 37 24 85 85. Fax 04 37 24 85 86.
lesplendid@georgesblanc.com
www.georgesblanc.com
Prix fixe: 23€, 28€, 31€.

The Mères Lyonnaises, those legendary lady chefs of Lyon past whose portraits adorn the walls, seem to watch over this rejuvenated brasserie across from the Brotteaux train station. Georges Blanc artfully upholds their tradition. His thin vegetable cakes, roasted cod, pan-seared Atlantic sea bass, duckling filet with honey as well as the vanilla mille-feuille and the soft-centered chocolate cake look great. Well-priced menus.

● Le Nord 🔲🔲 COM

18, rue Neuve (2nd arr.).
Tel. 04 72 10 69 69. Fax 04 72 10 69 68.
www.bocuse.com
Prix fixe: 8,50€, 21,80€, 28€.
A la carte: 35€.

Paul Bocuse and Jean Fleur's first annex is in fine form. The bordeaux-colored seats of this 1900 brasserie are seldom empty. Amateurs of a decent, regional, bistro-type cuisine flock here to eat the duck foie gras in terrine, the pike fish quenelle, the "bourgeoise"-style tête de veau and the baba au rhum.

● Les Oliviers 🔲COM

20, rue de Sully (6th arr.).
Tel. 04 78 89 07 09. Fax 04 78 89 08 39.
Closed Sat., Sun., Bank holidays, Christmas–New Year's, 1 week May, Aug.
Prix fixe: 16€ (weekday lunch), 31€ (dinner), 46€ (dinner). A la carte: 34–42€.

You can almost hear the cicadas at Mathieu Viannay's original restaurant, now his annex. Stone walls and lots of yellow and green exude the perfume of Provence. Olivier Canal's up-to-date cuisine is just as sunny: Provençal-style rouget in escabèche, cod and aïoli served cold, oven-baked snapper served with thyme-seasoned garlic purée, rosemary-seasoned slow-cooked lamb shank and the chocolate cigar with orange and thyme marmalade all put you in a good mood as does the bill. With a glass of Côtes-du-Rhône in hand, you might just as well be under real-life olive trees.

● Alex COM

44, bd des Brotteaux (corner of rue Vauban).
Tel. 04 78 52 30 11. Fax 04 78 52 34 16.
chez.alex@club-internet.fr
Closed Sun., Mon., Bank holidays, Christmas, Aug.
Prix fixe: 26€, 41€, 18€ (child).
A la carte: 55€.

In his modern beige and mauve setting, Alex Tournadre serves up moderately priced menus. We liked his lobe of foie gras slow cooked in its fat, served with a balsamic and grape aspic, red mullet cake in a walnut crust served with a Jerusalem artichoke mousseline and a hazelnut emulsion, tender glazed Cantal pork ribs served with a split pea purée jus and chestnuts and the crusty honey madeleines with caramel ice cream.

● Le Caro de Lyon COM

25, rue du Bât-d'Argent (1st arr.).
Tel. 04 78 39 58 58. Fax 04 72 07 98 96.
carodelyon_reception@libertysurf.fr
www.carodelyon.com
Closed Sun.
Prix fixe: 27€, 38€.

Lounge bar and book-lined walls, paneling and Murano glass: this is the décor conceived by Jean-Claude Caro for his trendy restaurant. Frédérique Côte lovingly cooks dishes which follow fashion such as green olive soup, the fresh crab, rougail (a spicy diced tomato, ginger, onion and birds-eye pepper condiment) and bread salad, the lobster sausage, diced mushrooms in reduced cream with a lime-seasoned soy emulsion, pan-seared foie gras with figs and tea-infused sauce, sprout salad and a spicy chocolate fondant with peach marmalade and Port-seasoned caramel.

● Le Grenier des Lyres COM

21, rue Creuset (7th arr.).
Tel.-Fax 04 78 72 81 77.
philippe.vincent@numericable.fr
Closed Sat. lunch, Sun., Mon., 2 weeks Aug.
Prix fixe: 20,50€ (weekday lunch), 29,50€ (weekday lunch), 35,50€ (dinner), 49€ (dinner), 69€ (foie gras menu), 17,50€ (child). A la carte: 40€.

Hugo Czechowicz, a pupil of Thierry Gache, then of Têtedoie, is currently at the stove of this cozy restaurant run by Philippe Vincent. This is a funky place, with its Beaubourg-style pipes and its diode lighting with fiber optics in the ceiling. Color and taste meet on the plate with the melon and cider gazpacho, salmon in a sesame crust, the trout in a pastry turnover with fresh goat cheese, duck breast roasted with spices, the green asparagus cake with a beet and fig sauce and the frozen chocolate truffle soufflé mille-feuille for dessert.

● **Jean-Claude Pequet** COM
59, pl Voltaire (3rd arr.).
Tel. 04 78 95 49 70. Fax 04 78 62 85 26.
Closed Sat., Sun., Bank holidays, Aug.
Prix fixe: 32€, 45€. A la carte: 48€.

Pattypan squash in a salad with tartare of tomato, the artichoke and sea bream mille-feuille, the duck medallions with vineyard peaches and the crêpes Suzette, not to mention the chilled chocolate cream dessert, are fine fare *chez* Jean-Claude Pequet. This award-winning chef of fine lineage is no slouch when it comes to quality. The terrace set up under the plane trees on the square and the modern dining room are equally pleasing.

● **Le Passage** COM
8, rue du Plâtre (1st arr.).
Tel. 04 78 28 11 16. Fax 04 72 00 84 34.
restaurant@le-passage.com / www.le-passage.com
Closed Sun., Mon., 3 weeks Aug.
Prix fixe: 35€, 48€, 45€. A la carte: 50€.

He's Lyon's most discreet host. Vincent Carteron welcomes guests as if to his own home at this address hidden in the shadow of a *traboule* (Lyonnais covered passageway between streets). The art deco armchairs and the intimacy of the interior set the tone of the place. Christian Bacque, who trained at La Mère Brazier, convicingly cooks market produce of the moment. A marbled foie gras and fig terrine, cumin-seasoned lobster stew and sea bream in a whelk cream sauce are top notch.

● **Raphaël Béringer** COM
37, rue Auguste-Comte.
Tel.-Fax 04 78 37 49 83.
www.raphaelberinger-restaurant.com
Closed Sun., Mon. lunch, July.
Prix fixe: 34€, 45€.

Raphaël Béringer makes this traditional, *bouchon*-style establishment rhyme with dependability and freshness. In this chic brasserie setting with its modern gray-and-brown décor, Raphaël, John and Sherry skillfully turn out beef-stuffed ravioli with pan-seared foie gras, a smoked salmon tempura, braised pork belly, farm-raised red-label chicken with crayfish tails and creamy polenta before the walnut parfait and coconut and pineapple spring roll.

● **La Voûte** COM
"Chez Léa"
11, pl Antonin-Gourju (2nd arr.).
Tel. 04 78 42 01 33. Fax 04 78 37 36 41.
Closed Sun.
Prix fixe: 27,50€. A la carte: 40–45€.

The century-old dining rooms on the first floor have a lot of style and Philippe Rabanel's cuisine remains faithful to the traditions of Lyon's lady chefs of yore. Regale yourselves with hot sausage poached in Mâcon wine, a fish quenelle with crayfish sauce, the traditional tablier de sapeur (white wine–marinated, breaded and fried wedge of beef tripe), vinegar-glazed chicken and the frozen Chartreuse soufflé that easily enthuse.

● **Yinitial** COM
14, rue du Palais-Grillet (2nd arr.).
Tel. 04 78 42 14 14. Fax 04 72 40 98 07.
palais.grillet@wanadoo.fr
Closed Sun., 3 weeks Aug.
Prix fixe: 20€, 26€. A la carte: 50€.

Joëlle Garious hired Nicolas Alia who wields a wicked, fusion cuisine. Red tuna tartare with marinated zucchini, pork brochette served with crunchy salad, steamed salmon dim sum, stir-fried lamb with tabouli and a traditional soft-centered chocolate cake are well received. The open plan kitchen and tables set between thick stone walls, under venerable 17th-century beams, have a lot of character.

● **L'Etage** ○SIM
4, pl des Terreaux (1st arr.).
Tel.-Fax 04 78 28 19 59.
Closed Sun., Mon., end July–end Aug.
Prix fixe: 22€ (lunch), 33€.

A curious establishment, this restaurant located on the second floor of a house looking out over the Place des Terreaux. For his guests seated in the cozy dining room, Jérôme Soonberg, trained by Gagnaire at Saint-Etienne and in Paris, concocts a skillful and refined cuisine, such as the pan-seared foie gras with wine aspic, scallops with slow-cooked eggplant, lamb sweetbreads with artichokes in escabeche sauce and the warm chocolate fondant accompanied by a frozen banana mousse.

● En Mets Fais   🅿🏠SIM
ce qu'il te Plaît

43, rue Chevreul (7th arr.).
Tel. 04 78 72 46 58. Fax 04 72 71 89 46.
Closed Sat., Sun., 3 weeks Aug.
Prix fixe: 19€ (lunch), 21€ (lunch),
35€ (dinner).

At any hour, you can sample the foie gras terrine with pistachios, pan-tossed cuttlefish salad, veal kidneys in foie gras sauce, the roasted pigeon with its jus and a jasmine-flavored crème brûlée in the small, modern dining room or on the veranda. Katsuli Ishida rewrites his score three times a week. Lyon's fresh market products bond well with Japanese tradition.

● Thomas   🅿🏠SIM

6, rue Laurencin (2nd arr.).
Tel.-Fax 04 72 56 04 76.
info@restaurant-thomas.com
www.restaurant-thomas.com
Closed Sun., Mon., Christmas–New Year's,
2 weeks beg. May, 2 weeks Aug.
Prix fixe: 16€ (weekday lunch),
35€ (weekday dinner). A la carte: 40€.

Thomas Ponson, a pupil of Lacombe, Chabran and Ansanay-Alex, has made a justified hit in his establishment next to the Musée des Tissus. His wood and red-toned, chic bistro underscores a cuisine of market products at the service of a revamped classicism. A blood sausage and apple Tatin served with crique (an Ardèche-style grated potato cake), grilled sea bream with slow-cooked fennel and olives, young Charolais beef with

pommes dauphine and tomato béarnaise sauce and the frozen chestnut vacherin, whipped cream and Valrhona chocolate coulis are all delicious.

THIS YEAR'S
VALUE-FOR-MONEY
AWARD

● Magali & Martin   🅝🏠SIM

11, rue des Augustins (1st arr.).
Tel. 04 72 00 88 01.
Closed Sat., Sun. lunch,
3 weeks Dec.–mid-Jan., 3 weeks Aug.
Prix fixe: 17€ (lunch).
A la carte: 25€.

With their restaurant on two floors, their reasonable prices, their revamped home cooking and their lovely surroundings, Martin and Magali Schmied have created the event of the center city. He is Viennese and has worked with the Obauer brothers in Werfen—Austria's best table—as well as at Ducasse, Ledoyen and Taillevent. She is a returning native of Lyon having worked at Astrance in Paris' 16th arrondissement. Together they have put all their heart into this small, low-key, chic and tidy establishment where market products triumph. The other day, Piedmont-style veal-, tuna-, and caper-stuffed courgettes, veal belly stuffed with fresh coco beans served with the jus from the roast and a café liégeois served with madeleines were simply marvelous. An address worth its weight in gold. But be warned, since it opened, it's been full up. Reservations are a must!

● Le Verre et l'Assiette   🅝🏠SIM

20, Grande-Rue de Vaise (9th arr.).
Tel. 04 78 83 32 25.
Closed Sat., Sun., Tue. dinner, 1 week Feb.,
3 weeks Aug.
Prix fixe: 21€ (lunch, wine inc.).
A la carte: 26–31€.

Maryline and Olivier Delbergues offer the finest of the fine in their little pad much beloved by Vaise regulars. Overhead beams, old stones and black and white photographs easily delight. There are three à la carte menus. Pan-seared foie gras, seasoned with Granny Smith apples and hibiscus, big escargot-stuffed ravioli with frog legs, grilled swordfish, pork tenderloin served with potatoes and pancetta and the soft-centered chocolate cake or the fresh figs poached in citrus juice are not too sweet or heavy.

● Le Comptoir des Marronniers

8, rue des Marronniers (2nd arr.).
Tel. 04 72 77 10 00. Fax 04 72 77 10 01.
leon@relaischateaux.com
www.leondelyon.com
Closed Sun., Mon. lunch, 3 weeks Aug.
Prix fixe: 22,80€, 10€ (child).

In Jean-Paul Lacombe's other bistro, photographs of the region's great chefs grace the walls of an animated dining room. Here, Guillaume Mouchel serves sunny, polished dishes such as eggplant terrine with a tomato emulsion, pike-perch mousseline with lemon butter, pan-seared duck breast with yellow peach coulis and a rhubarb tart, at very reasonable prices.

● L'Est

14, pl Jules-Ferry, gare des Brotteaux (6th arr.).
Tel. 04 37 24 25 26. Fax 04 37 24 25 25.
www.bocuse.com
Prix fixe: 19,50€, 25€ (Sat., Sun., dinner),
9,80€ (child). A la carte: 40€.

In the old Brotteaux train station, Paul Bocuse and Jean Fleury's trendy brasserie marches to the hum of electric trains and agreeable, Southern fare: Andalusian-style gazpacho, rouget filet served niçoise style, spit-roasted Bresse poultry and the baba au rhum.

● Le Gailleton

5, pl du Dr-Gailleton (2nd arr.).
Tel. 04 78 38 70 70. Fax 04 78 38 70 71.
www.leondelyon.com
Closed Sun., Mon. dinner, 10 days Aug.
Prix fixe: 11€, 22,80€, 11€ (child).

The menus are well thought out and lovingly cooked by the young Vincent Khramos, come to rejoin the Lacombe team. Dishes change regularly and delight the regulars who lap up pure Lyonnaise fare at affordable prices. Damien Livrozet manages the service with flair and offers the best of his cellar.

● Maison Villemanzy

25, montée Saint-Sébastien (1st arr.).
Tel. 04 72 98 21 21. Fax 04 72 98 21 22.
leon@relaischateaux.com
www.leondelyon.com
Closed Sun., Mon. lunch, 23 Dec.–9 Jan.
Prix fixe: 22,80€. A la carte: 30€.

Up on the heights of the Croix-Rousse, Jean-Paul Lacombe has transformed the old home of a doctor-colonel of the military hospital into a trendy spot. In the designer dining room or out on the terrace overlooking the city, Olivier Gelles serves up a snappy, fresh cuisine somewhere between the Rhône and the Mediterranean: carpaccio with pesto, cod parmentier, pork roast and the mascarpone crème are tops.

● L'Ouest

1, quai du Commerce (9th arr.).
Tel. 04 37 64 64 64. Fax 04 37 64 64 65.
commercial@brasserie-bocuse.com
www.brasseries-bocuse.com
Prix fixe: 19,50€. A la carte: 50€.

Paul Bocuse and his sidekick Jean Fleury are everywhere, from North to South to East and also West along the Saône. In their immense modern loft with counter, giant screen and open-plan kitchen, accomplished fusion dishes sail by, such as fried cod cakes or cod filet, both with Asian flavors. The spit-roasted Bresse poultry and the frozen berry vacherin are marvels of simplicity.

● Le Petit Léon

3, rue Pléney (1st arr.).
Tel. 04 72 10 11 11. Fax 04 72 10 11 13.
leon@relaischateaux.com
www.leondelyon.com
Closed dinner, 3 weeks Aug.
Prix fixe: 19€.

In this annex situated on the ground floor of Léon de Lyon, Jean-Paul Lacombe proposes good classic dishes on a constantly changing menu. Julien Gauthier cooks homegrown fare; savory baked Lyon-style pork cake with country-style salad, fennel-seasoned pollock, pan-sizzled beef with olives and a brown sugar crème brûlée, served with wines from the region, give a lot of pleasure. A pretty paneled interior hung with old advertising plaques.

● Le Sud   SIM

11, pl Antonin-Poncet (2nd arr.).
Tel. 04 72 77 80 00. Fax 04 72 77 80 01.
www.paulbocuse.com
Prix fixe: 19,50€, 21,80€, 9,80€ (child).
A la carte: 35€.

True to its name, in this other annex of Paul Bocuse and Jean Fleury, the Mediterranean is served up on a platter. In a warm, blue and yellow décor, oven-crisped jumbo shrimp, the fisherman's platter, served bouillabaisse style, and thyme-seasoned roasted lamb chops are dishes redolent of sunshine.

● Brasserie Georges   N SIM

30, cours de Verdun-Perrache (2nd arr.).
Tel. 04 72 56 54 54. Fax 04 78 42 51 65.
brasserie.georges@wanadoo.fr
www.brasseriegeorges.com
Closed 1 May.
Prix fixe: 19,50€, 21,50€, 24,50€,
9€ (child). A la carte: 35–40€.

Classic bistro offerings are regular staples of this immense art deco brasserie with its yellowy orange tones and its restored frescoes. Traditional salade Lyonnaise, with bacon, poached egg and croutons, the house pike fish quenelle, pistachio-seasoned sausage and baba au rhum hold their own. "Good beer and good fare since 1836" remains the house motto.

● Café Comptoir de Lyon   N SIM

4, rue Tupin (2nd arr.).
Tel. 04 78 42 11 98.
Closed Sun.

Prix fixe: 13€ (lunch), 16€ (dinner),
23€ (dinner). A la carte: 40€.

Remy Barrier is at the helm of this old-fashioned bistro with its stucco interior, art deco clock and imposing bar counter. Pleasure comes in the form of the individual poultry liver terrine, the pan-seared fresh scallops, the veal escalope in cream sauce and tender tarte Tatin. Nice Côtes by the jug.

● Jols   N SIM

283, av Jean-Jaurès (7th arr.).
Tel. 04 78 72 10 10. Fax 04 78 72 10 68.
contact@jols.fr / www.jols.fr
Closed Sun.
Prix fixe: 15€ (lunch), 18€ (lunch),
23€ (dinner), 8€ (child). A la carte: 38€.

Méhu and Carpentier, pupils of Bocuse and creators of Assiette et Marée, have turned this art deco market into a seafaring establishment with wind in its sails. Fresh herb-seasoned salmon tartare, grilled tuna steak with Middle Eastern seasonings, fresh cod with thyme flower, as well as the grilled "butcher's choice", fries made from potatoes with their skins and the Sichuan pepper–seasoned chocolate tart: fresh, snappy and well-cooked.

● Benoît   N SIM

5, rue Tupin (2nd arr.).
Tel. 04 78 42 38 12.
Closed Sun.
Prix fixe: 13€, 16€, 24€, 28€.
A la carte: 38€.

Benoît Toussaint has taken over at the helm of this establishment once dedicated to fish and shellfish. Earthier products now play a greater part. Shellfish and squid ink risotto, baked salt cod and potatoes, a whole roasted veal kidney served with two mustards and brioche perdu with apples and maple syrup slip down nicely.

● Le Bistro de Lyon   SIM

64, rue Mercière (2nd arr.).
Tel. 04 78 38 47 47. Fax 04 78 38 47 48.
www.leondelyon.com

Prix fixe: 16,50€ (lunch, wine inc.), 23,40€, 26,50€, 50€, 10€ (child).
A la carte: 45€.

For thirty years, Jean-Paul Lacombe's first bistro has been treating customers to the house pâté in a pastry crust, warm sausage tart, pike fish quenelles, the house pork dish called the "Saint-Cochon", a local sausage called sabodet and gnafron, another specialty of the house, washed down with a Beaujolais from father-in-law Duboeuf.

● **La Brasserie de la Bourse** SIM
45-47, rue de la Bourse (2nd arr.).
Tel. 04 78 92 82 96. Fax 04 78 92 82 75.
www.brasserielabourse.com
Prix fixe: 19€, 25€, 29€, 10€ (child).
A la carte: 45€.

Jacques Lafargue's cuisine revisits his vacations in Thailand while escaping Lyonnais culinary tradition. Sushi and sashimi with sesame seeds, cod with slow-cooked eggplant, the Thai-style duck curry and the soft-centered chocolate cake with fleur de sel make this brasserie next to the Bourse a hangout for lovers of stylish dishes.

● **Chez Maurizio** SIM
1, pl Eugène-Wernert (5th arr.).
Tel.-Fax 04 78 25 83 63.
www.restaurant-chez-maurizio.com
Closed Sun., Mon., Christmas–New Year's vac., 2 weeks beg. May.
Prix fixe: 13€ (weekday lunch), 27€.
A la carte: 35–40€.

This trattoria may change hands but it continues to seduce. Under Karine Sonigo's direction in the dining room and Giovanni de Maio's at the stove, you will enjoy the antipasti plate, langoustine risotto, the stuffed squid with basalmic sauce, the giant Alba truffle ravioli and the house tiramisu, served without ceremony in a rustic décor.

● **Les Lyonnais** SIM
1, rue Tramassac (5th arr.).
Tel. 04 78 37 64 82. Fax 04 78 37 58 35.

www.restaurant-lyonnais.fr
Closed Sun. dinner, Mon.,
1 week Christmas–New Year's, 3 weeks Aug.
Prix fixe: 17,50€, 22€. A la carte: 40€.

Photographs of Lyon's famous citizens are displayed on the walls of this modern Lyonnais *bouchon*. In an informal atmosphere, enjoy the tête de veau with sauce gribiche (caper and pickle mayonnaise), pike fish quenelle soufflé with lobster sauce, the foie gras escalope with sour cherries and the praline tart. The reasonable prices are a plus.

● **Le Musée** SIM
2, rue des Forces (2nd arr.).
Tel. 04 78 37 71 54.
Closed Sun., Mon. dinner, Tue. dinner.
Prix fixe: 18€ (lunch), 20€, 22€ (dinner). A la carte: 30€.

Luc Minaire deftly runs this simple *bouchon*. Imitation leather seats, a brass bar, rendered walls and a "monastic" fresco are part of the décor. The house bread is delicious. As for his wife Sylvie's cooking, it goes down a treat. Try tripe soup, marinated shredded skate, the cardoons with bone marrow and the orange chocolate tart; toast with a Rhône or Beaujolais.

● **Sushido** SIM
169, rue Cuvier (6th arr.).
Tel. 04 78 52 70 35 / 04 78 27 96 06.
Fax 04 78 17 48 83.
contact@sushido.com / www.sushido.com
Closed Sat. lunch, Sun., Mon.
Prix fixe: 14€ (lunch), 18€ (dinner).

Two gourmand trips are possible: serve yourselves from the carousel downstairs or head up to the restaurant under the direction of Tan Loc with chef Doan Doan in the kitchen. The "sushis saké" with salmon, tekkamaki (tuna roll), namban (fried fish), temaki maguro (red tuna) and mint mango ice cream go down a treat.

In Caluire-et-Cuire (69300). 5 km ne.
● **L'Auberge de Fond Rose**
23, quai Clemenceau.
Tel. 04 78 29 34 61 Fax 04 72 00 28 67.

www.aubergedefondrose.com
Closed Sun. dinner, Mon., Feb. vac.
Prix fixe: 38€ (lunch, wine inc.), 51€, 63€,
78€, 18€ (child). A la carte: 80€.

For gourmets, the Auberge de Fond Rose is the perfect spot in which to satisfy their appetites. This twenties establishment, with its beautiful dining room, fireplace and terrace is grand and refined. Voted Meilleur Ouvrier de France in 1996, Gérard Vignat's dishes are models of inspiration. The tataki-style tuna with its aspic, the Lake Léman whiting with caviar, sundried tomato-stuffed lamb saddle and the painter's palette of crèmes glacées and sorbets are artful novelties. Isabelle Rouquette will have no trouble finding your wine of choice from a selection of 500.

In Caluire-et-Cuire.

● **La Terrasse Saint-Clair**   SIM
2, grande-rue de Saint-Clair.
Tel. 04 72 27 37 37. Fax 04 72 27 37 38.
leon@relaischateaux.com
www.leondelyon.com
Closed Mon., 3 weeks Christmas–New Year's,
2 weeks Aug.
Prix fixe: 22,80€.

On the banks of the Rhône, Jean-Paul Lacombe's open-air café with its terrace stretching out onto the Place Bellevue serves up carefully cooked, reasonably priced fare. The warm Burgundy escargot-stuffed ravioli, light cod mousseline, the veal shank and slow-cooked vegetable tian and the meringue and grapefruit sorbet in a crêpe pouch make for a mouth-watering menu.

In Collonges-au-Mont-d'Or (69660). 12 km along the banks of the Saône. D433 and D51.

● **Paul Bocuse**   VLUX
Pont-de-Collonges Nord, 40, rue de la Plage.
Tel. 04 72 42 90 90. Fax 04 72 27 85 87.
paul.bocuse@bocuse.fr / www.bocuse.fr
Closed Christmas.
Prix fixe: 115€, 155€, 195€, 19€ (child).
A la carte: 140€.

This "young", old softie has just turned eighty-one and continues to affect us all

with his happy personality, his polish and his passion. We love this emblematic character who has marked an era, a century, a world and a city—just as he is. We not only love the businessman who has set up brasseries in all four corners of the globe—at Epcot and elsewhere—but also the man of passion. At home in the Pont-de-Collonges establishment, the cuisine is the stuff of memory and flavor. Served by a team of Meilleur Ouvriers de France with maitre d' François Pipala presiding in the dining room and a gaggle of chefs—Jean Fleury, Christian Bouvarel, Christophe Muller and Gilles Reinhardt—who work in pool in the kitchen under his name, the cooking remains devilishly seductive. The always sensational VGE (created for the president of the Republic in 1975) truffle soup, the Maine lobster salad (!) prepared Parisian style, the rouget in oven-crisped thin-sliced potatoes, Mediterranean sea bass in a crust with sauce Choron (a tomato-flavored béarnaise), the pigeon in puff pastry with cabbage sprouts and the Bresse fricassée with creamy morel sauce have hardly aged. Trends are what go out of fashion. Bocuse knows this, doesn't go in for modish emulsions, makes fun of everything which kills taste and puts himself and his entire team at the service of the perrenial product. Simple Miéral signature Bresse poultry spit roasted and served with a macaroni gratin makes the whole world jump for joy. Add the cheeses from Renée Richard, the grand dessert cart where Bernachon's signature President cake resides with the Sirio crème brûlée, as well as the best of Burgundy, Beaujolais and Rhône wines recommended by that master of his art, John Euvrard, and you'll know you've just eaten a meal which is in the image of the master: generous and enduring.

In Rillieux-la-Pape (69140). 7 km via N83 and N84.

● **Larivoire**   V.COM
26, chemin des Iles.
Tel. 04 78 88 50 92. Fax 04 78 88 35 22.
bernard.constantin@larivoire.com
www.larivoire.com
Closed Sun. dinner, Mon. dinner, Tue.,
16 Aug.–30 Aug., 1 week Feb.

Prix fixe: 33€ (weekday dinner), 44€, 64€, 80€, 17€ (child). A la carte: 81–117€.

In his lovely bourgeois establishment, Bernard Constantin lovingly cooks a classical yet contemporary repertoire where quality products have pride of place. For proof try the coddled eggs with langoustines and morels, grilled rouget filets with a big tomato- and parmesan-stuffed macaroni topped with red wine and bone marrow sauce, the Dombes duckling glazed with honey and pepper and the Grand Marnier soufflé served hot. An ample wine list and pleasant service by Chantal Constantin.

In La Tour-de-Salvagny (69890). 11 km via N7.

● **La Rotonde**   ◉LUX

200, av du Casino.
Tel. 04 78 87 00 97. Fax 04 78 87 81 39.
www.restaurant-rotonde.com
Closed Sun., Mon., 10 days at end July, 3 weeks Aug.
Prix fixe: 51€ (weekday lunch), 85€, 115€, 140€. A la carte: 140€.

Up on the flowered heights of Charbonnières, the Casino du Lyon Vert houses one of the region's surefire chefs. Philippe Gauvreau, who trained at Jacques Maximin, turns fine products from all four corners of France into lively, sunny dishes. Breton lobster in salad with a white asparagus carpaccio, John Dory in lemongrass bouillon with coconut, spit-roasted Challans duck served with blood sauce and the dark chocolate cannelloni with crème brûlée-flavored ice cream go happily with the cellar's fine offerings. Glitzy décor, efficient service and a sumptuous cellar.

●	BOUCHONS

Local atmosphere, old-fashioned bistro décor, jolly wines and local fare: they represent the soul of Lyon.

● **Le Vivarais**   ●COM

1, pl du Dr-Gailleton (2nd arr.).
Tel. 04 78 37 85 15. Fax 04 78 37 59 49.
Closed Sat. lunch, Sun., end July–end Aug.
Prix fixe: 21€ (lunch), 26€, 35€.
A la carte: 45€.

Right near the Rhône and the Ainay quarter, Robert Duffaud's chic *bouchon* is always full. This old disciple of Alain Chapel skillfully turns out fare full of character: seafood in puff pastry, pike fish quenelles with mushroom bisque, the lamb plate (medallion, brain, tongue and sweetbreads) and a praline tart.

● **La Tassée**   COM

20, rue de la Charité (2nd arr.).
Tel. 04 72 77 79 00. Fax 04 72 40 05 91.
jpborgeot@latassee.fr / www.latassee.fr
Closed Sun.
Prix fixe: 25€ (lunch), 31€, 38€, 49€, 70€, 10,50€ (child). A la carte: 50€.

A skip and a hop from the Place Bellecour, Jean-Paul Borgeot's bistro with its 1950's bacchanalia-type fresco is worth a detour. By day or late into the night, feast without fuss on the apple and blood sausage in puff pastry with chive-seasoned beurre blanc sauce, thyme-seasoned roasted Atlantic sea bass and stuffed baby squid served with an olive oil-flavored potato purée, veal sweetbread in cocotte and the frozen Arquebuse (a Lyonnais liqueur) parfait with warm chocolate sauce.

● **Le Jura**   SIM

25, rue Tupin (2nd arr.).
Tel. 04 78 42 20 57.
Closed Sat. and Sun. (May–Sept.), Sun. and Mon. (Oct.–Apr.), Aug.
Prix fixe: 19,80€. A la carte: 30€.

With its thirties décor, this authentic *bouchon* is the delight of Lyonnais and tourists alike. Under the attentive eye of Brigitte Josserand, each and every diner can tuck into slow-simmered veal trotter served cold and sliced in salad, a pike-perch filet with beurre blanc sauce, the tablier de sapeur (white wine–marinated, breaded and fried wedge of beef tripe) and the lemon meringue tart. These traditional dishes are washed down with liters of Chénas and Chiroubles wine. Son Benoît now waits on tables.

● Daniel & Denise   ⌂SIM

156, rue de Créqui (3rd arr.).
Tel.-Fax 04 78 60 66 53.
Closed Sat., Sun., Bank holidays,
end Dec.–beg. Jan., Aug.
A la carte: 37–50€.

Hailing from the Vosges, Joseph Viola, formerly the second-in-command of Lacombe at Léon de Lyon and named Meilleur Ouvrier de France in 2004, is one of the foremost guardians of Lyon's soul. In this friendly *bouchon* with its white and red tablecloths, he reworks traditional dishes using quality merchandise to produce mouth-watering fare: crayfish omelet, pike fish quenelle, individual poultry liver terrine served with tomato coulis and floating islands with pralines all slip down all by themselves as do the pots of Beaujolais or Côtes-du-Rhône. No evil surprises from the bill.

● Le Mercière   ⌂SIM

56, rue Mercière (2nd arr.).
Tel. 04 78 37 67 35. Fax 04 72 56 06 48.
www.le-merciere.com
Prix fixe: 12,60€ (weekday lunch),
14,40€ (weekday lunch), 17,45€ (weekday
lunch), 25,50€. A la carte: 38€.

The Lyonnais *bouchon* par excellence. Jean-Louis Manoa knows his stuff and better than anyone how to put atmosphere into his dining room as well as on the plate. The menu changes often but his truffle pasta, fresh parsley-seasoned frog legs fricassée, Bresse poultry with cream and potato crêpes and his Lyonnaise-style cake with apples and pralines are sinful. Beaujolais and Côtes-du-Rhône add to your good humor.

● Au Petit Bouchon   ⌂SIM
"Chez Georges"

8, rue du Garet.
Tel. 04 78 28 30 46.
Closed Sat., Sun., Aug.
Prix fixe: 17€ (lunch), 24€ (lunch).
A la carte: 35€.

The Deschamps *bouchon* in the historic city center draws devotees of hot sausage with lentils, pike fish quenelles with sauce nantua (crayfish, cream and tomato), chitterling sausage with mustard sauce and tarte Tatin. France cooks with subtlety and dexterity while Michel waits on tables with celerity. Good Beaujolais. An old-fashioned bistro setting which stirs the heart.

● Chez Abel   ⌂SIM

25, rue Guynemer (2nd arr.).
Tel. 04 78 37 46 18. Fax 04 78 37 17 31.
Closed Sat., Sun., Bank holidays, Christmas–
New Year's, Aug.
Prix fixe: 17€ (lunch), 24€ (dinner),
31€ (dinner). A la carte: 40 €.

Everything here sings of the 50's, from the parquet floor to the wood paneling and the menus which offer only great classic dishes: salade Lyonnaise (with a poached egg, bacon and croutons), pike fish quenelle, kidneys in Madeira sauce, tête de veau and chocolate mousse.

● Le Café des Fédérations   ⌂SIM

8-9-10, rue du Major-Martin (1st arr.).
Tel. 04 78 28 26 00. Fax 04 72 07 74 52.
yr@lesfedeslyon.com
www.lesfedeslyon.com
Closed Sun., 1 week Christmas–New Year's,
1 week at end July, 3 weeks Aug.
Prix fixe: 19,50€ (lunch), 24€ (dinner).

Still the headquarters of the "federated" who tuck into authentic, generous, highly local dishes reflected by the giant sausages hanging over the counter. Plentiful salade Lyonnaise, caviar de la Croix-Rousse, a local lentil dish, charcuterie and wild boar terrine, pike fish quenelles, tablier de sapeur and the praline tart cooked up this year by Thierry Bisquay.

● Le Garet   ⌂SIM

7, rue du Garet (1st arr.).
Tel. 04 78 28 16 94. Fax 04 72 00 06 84.
legaret@wanadoo.fr
Closed Sat., Sun., Bank holidays,
end July–end Aug.
Prix fixe: 17,50€ (lunch), 22€ (dinner).
A la carte: 35€.

Nothing changes here: neither the worn décor with its wood paneling and old paintings or the crew of regulars eating the dishes cooked by Julien Emmanuelli and served by Emmanuel Ferra. The pork variety meat salad, skate wing, pike fish quenelle, tête de veau with sauce ravigote and the house crème caramel with wine sorbet go down nicely.

● Chabert et Fils   SIM
11, rue des Marronniers (2nd arr.).
Tel. 04 78 37 01 94. Fax 04 78 37 79 18.
degipa@club-internet.fr
www.chabertrestaurant.fr
Closed Christmas, New Year's.
Prix fixe: 17€, 22,90€, 33€.
A la carte: 30€.

A postcard décor where Jean-Pierre Gillin does honor to the reputation of this *bouchon* with his traditional cuisine beloved of all. Gnafron (flan with chitterling sausage, cabbage and garlic cream), the saladier Lyonnais (beef muzzle chilled and sliced thin, coco beans, smoked herring and veal trotter, also chilled and sliced thin), the pike fish quenelle with crayfish coulis, chitterling sausage and the praline tart are washed down with the emblematic Beaujolais.

● Chez Hugon   SIM
12, rue Pizay (1st arr.).
Tel.-Fax 04 78 28 10 94.
Closed Sat., Sun., Aug.
Prix fixe: 23€, 25€, 33€.

Another authentic Lyonnais *bouchon* where chef Arlette Hugon concocts, using quality produce, immutable fare such as the potato and smoked herring salad, rockfish pan fried in butter, garlic and parsley, blanquette de veau, poultry liver terrine and a decent praline tart.

● La Meunière   SIM
11, rue Neuve (1st arr.).
Tel.-Fax 04 78 28 62 91.
www.la-meuniere.fr
Closed Sun., Mon., 1 week Christmas–New Year's, mid-July–mid-Aug.
Prix fixe: 18€ (lunch), 24€, 29€.
A la carte: 30€.

This Lyonnais *bouchon* is always full. The reason for its success is its 1920's atmosphere, its kindly welcome and its standard, regional dishes at low prices. It's very pleasurable to tuck into slow-simmered, then chilled, beef muzzle and veal trotter sliced thin in salad, skate wing, tête de veau with sauce gribiche and red wine–simmered pears and prunes.

LYONS-LA-FORET

27480 Eure. Paris 105 – Rouen 35 –
Les Andelys 20 – Gisors 30 –
Gournay 25.
At the heart of one of the loveliest beech forests in France is a village with fine houses such as the one in which Ravel composed the *Tombeau de Couperin*. Don't miss the Abbey of Mortemer close by.

 | HOTELS-RESTAURANTS

■ La Licorne
27, pl Isaac-Benserade.
Tel. 02 32 49 62 02. Fax 02 32 49 80 09.
licorne-hotel-lyonslaforet@wanadoo.fr
www.licorne-hotel.com
12 rooms: 68–95€. 6 suites: 100–133€.
Half board: 87–100€.

This village inn was aquired by Fabrice Levêque and has pretty, comfortable rooms revamped almost every year. Last year, a restaurant was added.

■ Les Lions de Beauclerc
7, rue de l'Hôtel de Ville.
Tel. 02 32 49 18 90.
Closed Wed.
6 rooms: 59–75€.

Cozy rooms, low prices, charming décor within the walls of a brick house. Ideal for a snug weekend.

● La Halle   SIM
6, pl Isaac-Benserade.
Tel. 02 32 49 49 92. Fax 02 32 49 07 52.
Closed Wed.
Prix fixe: 18,50€, 28€, 9€ (child).

This wood-paneled dining room across from the market has a lot of pizzaz. Here Benoît Paris serves with a smile, seconded by the efficient Perrine Delivet, while in the kitchen Bruno Langlois concocts classic, simple dishes. Feast happily on jumbo shrimp flambéed in Armagnac, salmon steak served with zucchini fricassée, beef tenderloin with new potatoes and the mint-seasoned pineapple.

MACON

71000 Saône-et-Loire. Paris 392 – Bourg-en-Bresse 37 – Chalon-sur-Saône 59 – Lyon 74.
macon.tourisme@wanadoo.fr.

This is the first town to herald the South as you head down to the Midi. With its lively streets, flowered squares, embankments along the Saône and its ancient Saint-Laurent bridge with its twelve arches, Mâcon brings to mind a langorously sleepy Italian city batting its eyes at the prosperous Bresse across the river. Don't miss the Lamartine museum and be aware that the vineyards of the Beaujolais and Pouilly-Fuissé are just beyond the TGV train station.

■ HOTELS-RESTAURANTS

■ Park Inn
26, rue de Coubertin.
Tel. 03 85 21 93 93. Fax 03 85 39 11 45.
www.parkinn.com
64 rooms: 90–155€.
Prix fixe: 18€, 28€.

In grounds along the Saône, this hotel-restaurant with swimming pool and terrace offers beneficial tranquility. The spacious rooms look out onto the Saône. In the Fourchette restaurant, Jérôme Broux concocts escargots, a Charolais beef confit and potato dish and Calvados-flambéed cold apple cake.

■ Hôtel Bellevue
416, quai Lamartine.
Tel. 03 85 21 04 04. Fax 03 85 21 04 02.
www.ila-chateau.com/bellevue
Closed end Nov.–mid-Dec., 2 weeks beg. May.
20 rooms: 85–140€. 4 suites: 155€.

Its downtown style, view of the embankment and strategic situation along the N6 make this the No. 1 address. Pretty, revamped rooms and a well-designed staircase.

■ D'Europe et d'Angleterre
92, quai Jean-Jaurès.
Tel. 03 85 38 27 94.
www.hotel-europeangleterre-macon.com
Closed Sun. (Dec., Jan.).
29 rooms: 45–60€.

Low rates, an adorable welcome and a position along the Saône are the main attractions of this 19th-century hotel which has been modernized but kept its old furniture.

■ Hôtel de Bourgogne

6, rue Victor-Hugo.
Tel. 03 85 21 10 23. Fax 03 85 38 65 92.
www.hoteldebourgogne.com
Open daily. Rest. closed lunch, Sun.,
3 weeks Jan.
50 rooms: 55–95€.
Prix fixe: 18€ (dinner), 29€ (dinner),
8€ (child).

This old 19th-century coaching inn has been rejuvenated thanks to modern rooms in pastel colors. Burgundian cooking in the restaurant La Perdrix.

● Pierre

7, rue Dufour.
Tel. 03 85 38 14 23. Fax 03 85 39 84 04.
contact@restaurant-pierre.com
www.restaurant-pierre.com
Closed Sun. dinner, Mon., Tue. lunch,
10 days beg. Feb., 3 weeks July.
Prix fixe: 27,50€, 33€, 44,50€, 54,50€,
63€, 72€, 12€ (child),
A la carte: 65–75€.

Isabell Gaulin is there to help you choose your dish or your wine. Christian applies himself with precision to regional products: duck foie gras served three ways with a gelatinous pear confit, roasted turbot with creamy clam sauce, black truffle croustade (a local tart made with many layers of thin pastry) and a warm Grand Marnier soufflé served with a thin tuile cookie all win top votes. We love the stone walls and beams, the winter garden and the moderate bill. A happy experience which encourages one to try out the Auberge des Deux Roches (pl. de l'Eglise à Vergisson—03 85 35 86 50) also owned by the Gaulins.

● L'Amandier

74, rue Dufour.
Tel. 03 85 39 82 00. Fax 03 85 38 92 21.

Closed Sat. lunch, Sun. dinner, Mon.,
Feb. vac., 2 weeks Aug.
Prix fixe: 16€, 34€, 45€, 50€.
A la carte: 61€.

In this old establishment with its modern interior, you'll be served a serious cuisine combining regional produce with original garnishes. Florent Segain is a traditionalist. Try his foie gras terrine, the herb-seasoned half lobster, rack of lamb with thyme-seasoned jus, soft-centered chocolate cake and the frozen tea and honey parfait. Reasonable rates and polished service and welcome.

● Le Rocher de Cancale

393, quai Jean-Jaurès.
Tel. 03 85 38 07 50. Fax 03 85 38 70 47.
www.restaurant-aurocherdecancale-macon.com
Closed Sun. dinner, Mon.
Prix fixe: 15€ (lunch, wine inc.), 20€ (wine
inc.), 29€, 33€, 38€, 10€ (child).

In this 200-year-old establishment, Chantal Bock maintains quality through a plethora of offers. Take-away dishes, market menus or menus based on lobster as well as formula menus of two or three dishes easily attract. As does, in the dining room with its view of the Saône, the red tuna and salmon duo served with horseradish sauce, the whiting filet served with star anise–seasoned herb butter, Bresse poultry in pot-au-feu and the lime crêpes soufflé that are faultless. Great menus.

In Saint-Amour-Bellevue (71570). 11 km s
via A6.

■ Auberge du Paradis

Le Plâtre Durand.
Tel. 03 85 37 10 26.
www.aubergeduparadis.fr
Closed Jan.
Rest. closed Sun. dinner, Mon., Tue.
4 rooms: 85–105€. 3 suites: 120–180€.
Prix fixe: 25€, 40€.

After a lovely welcome by Valérie, guests are taken to their table or to one of the seven charming modern rooms filled with antique furniture. In a warm, black and red decorated dining room with comfortable "club" armchairs, the cuisine of Cyril Laugier—formerly with Blanc—takes off. Parsley- and onion-stuffed quail fritters, the ras-el-hanout-seasoned lamb kebab with shallots and lemon served with rutabaga purée or the pear compote with truffle oil and a thyme-seasoned fromage blanc sorbet are carefully cooked and up to date. Valérie Bugnet gives good counsel on wine. A pool has been added.

In Saint-Laurent-sur-Saône (01750). On the left bank.

● **L'Autre Rive**

143, quai Bouchacourt.
Tel. 03 85 39 01 02.
www.lautrerive.fr
Closed Sun. dinner, Mon.
Prix fixe: 21€ (weekdays), 28€, 35€, 40€.

Smack across from Mâcon, the Rivons' restaurant appeals thanks to its well-set tables, its terrace on the Saône, its neo-rustic chairs and the cooking behind the scene. Vincent worked at the Rocher de Cancale, at La Mère Vittet and at Têtedoie. He has a light touch with local products, using traditional recipes to good measure. Parsley- and garlic-seasoned frog legs, pike-perch with fleur de sel served with risotto and the poultry in cream sauce make up well-thought-out menus. Smiling service. We're still in the Bresse.

In Saint-Laurent-sur-Saône.

● **Le Saint-Laurent** SIM

1, quai Bouchacourt.
Tel. 03 85 39 29 19. Fax 03 85 38 29 77.
www.georgesblanc.com
Prix fixe: 27€ (weekday dinner), 30€, 40€, 45€, 12€ (child).

This 1930's-style bistro/brasserie *cum* open-air café along the Saône is piloted from afar by Georges Blanc and does honor to the region. In the kitchen, Stéphane Chevauchet gives serious attention to an individual poultry liver terrine, a ham and parsley terrine, fried pike-perch or Saone river fish, the Vin Jaune-braised veal and a mille-feuille. Faultless welcome and service.

LA MADELEINE-SOUS-MONTREUIL see MONTREUIL

MAGESCQ

40140 Landes. Paris 725 – Biarritz 54 – Mont-de-Marsan 67 – Dax 16.
This pretty town at the crossroads of the beaches and the Basque country is the gastronomic beacon of the Landes.

 HOTELS-RESTAURANTS

● **Le Relais de la Poste**

24, av de Maremne.
Tel. 05 58 47 70 25. Fax 05 58 47 76 17.
poste@relaischateaux.com
www.relaisposte.com
Closed mid-Nov.–mid-Dec.
Rest. closed Mon., Tue. lunch, Thu. lunch.
10 rooms: 225–390€.
Prix fixe: 51€, 71€, 100€.
A la carte: 95–110€.

At the Coussaus', tradition is never boring. Brothers Jean and Jacques, who are as close as can be, rule the kitchen. The former cooks dishes based on the best local products while the latter presides over a swift service and is a natural at carving at the table. Witness the adroit removal of the skin of an Adour salmon steak, with its light béarnaise sauce—the work of a master craftsman. We won't say this out loud in case they raise their prices, but the modestly priced classy offerings on the wine list reflect a generosity which belongs to innkeepers of old. Each season brings its parcels of pleasure. The Gillardeau oysters, in sea water aspic with watercress and Aquitaine caviar, glisten with their perfume of the sea, the pan-seared escalope of foie gras, at the same time juicy and crusty, served with chanterelles, truffles, and a mild Gascon wine-enriched reduction and the famous salmon served with artichokes and ham: This is what awaits you in the renovated dining room, which nevertheless looks quite antiquated. Wood, brick, large windows, space and comfortable fifties-style armchairs set the tone of a coaching inn which—thanks to its "Zen-style" rooms plus spa—has morphed into a modern Relais & Châteaux establishment.

● Le Cabanon

1129, av des Landes.
Tel. 05 58 47 71 51. Fax 05 58 47 75 19.
http://monsite.wanadoo.fr/lecabanon40
Closed Sun. dinner (exc. July–Aug.), Mon.
Prix fixe: 25€, 35€, 48€.
A la carte: 47–54€.

Claude Bories puts his clients at ease and there is a good-humored, party atmosphere in his *cabanon* (cottage). On the kitchen side, Landes of course takes pride of place with the cep cassolette, the glorious foie gras plate, the veal sweetbreads with morels and grilled pine nut-flavored frozen nougat. Everything, including the bill, is bound to please.

MAGNY-COURS see NEVERS

89660 Yonne. Paris 196 – Auxerre 30 – Avallon 32 – Clamecy 21.
This curious town owes its name to a fortress perched above the Yonne and the Nivernais canal. The main square, with its houses all strung together and its red-tiled roofs, looks like a painting by Peynet.

 HOTELS-RESTAURANTS

■ Le Castel

Pl de l'Eglise.
Tel. 03 86 81 43 06. Fax 03 86 81 49 26.
lecastelmailly@aol.com
6 rooms: 69€. 2 suites: 84–99€.
Half-board: 35€.

Guaranteed relaxation in Elisabeth and Dominique Meuterlos' village house with its five prettily fitted out rooms. Bountiful breakfasts.

MAISONSGOUTTE see VILLE
MALATAVERNE see MONTELIMAR

25160 Doubs. Paris 457 – Besançon 74 – Pontarlier 16 – Saint-Claude 73.
ot.malbuisson@worldonline.fr.
Come and discover the lac de Saint-Point—France's third largest natural lake. The town offers cross-country skiing in winter, hiking in summer and rambles all year long. With a bit of imagination, you'll think you were somewhere between Québec's Laurentians and the Swedish Värmland.

 HOTELS-RESTAURANTS

● Jean-Michel Tannières

17, Grande-Rue.
Tel. 03 81 69 30 89. Fax 03 81 69 39 16.
contact@restaurant-tannieres.com
www.restaurant-tannieres.com
Closed Jan. Rest. closed lunch, Mon., Tue.
4 rooms: 60–100€.
Prix fixe: 38€, 45€. A la carte: 65€.

Set beside a stream, the Tannières' village house is an invitation to spend a few delicious moments at the Bistro d'Angèle with its quick and inexpensive set menus or at its gastronomic restaurant where Jean-Michel is faultlessly true to his region with dishes such as creamy morel and green asparagus soup, langoustines pan-tossed in Macvin, chicken with morels and Vin Jaune and a frozen Pontarlier-flavored soufflé. Solid fare which guarantees solid slumber in one of the four attractive rooms of this kindhearted establishment.

■ Le Lac

In the village, Grande-Rue.
Tel. 03 81 69 34 80. Fax 03 81 69 35 44.
hotellelac@wanadoo.fr / www.hotel-le-lac.com
Closed mid-Nov.–mid-Dec.
50 rooms: 39–87€. 4 suites: 125–183€.
Prix fixe: 18€ (weekday lunch), 23€ (Sat., Sun., lunch), 43€, 8€ (child).

The rooms with a view on the lac de Saint-Point are highly agreeable and comfortable. Breakfasts are true to their name and the straightforward cuisine makes this a more than honorable table. Jean-Georges

Maur reinterprets Chauvin family rec-ipes: slice of foie gras, morels in cream, pike mousseline with crayfish coulis are carefully prepared. Frédérique Chauvin's dessert trolley is worth a detour. Nearby is a cheese restaurant in which to feast on fondue, tartiflette, mushrooms and Morteau smoked sausage gratinéed with Comte cheese in salad and pear or Morbier cheese quiche at decent prices.

● **Le Bon Accueil**

Rue de la Source.
Tel. 03 81 69 30 58.
Fax 03 81 69 37 60.
marcfaivre@le-bon-accueil.fr
www.le-bon-accueil.fr
Closed Sun. dinner (exc. July–Aug.), Mon., Tue. lunch, 1 week Nov. 1, mid-Dec.–mid-Jan., 1 week at Easter.
12 rooms: 64–94€.
Prix fixe: 22€ (weekday lunch, wine inc.), 27€, 38€, 49€, 15 € (child).
A la carte: 60€.

Marc Faivre has just finished renovat-ing the cozy rooms of his chalet next to the lake. Cooking-wise, this former pupil of Blanc, Lameloise and Gagnaire sings the praises of his region via clever, top-ical dishes. A Morteau smoked sausage and pan-wilted leek tart, the absinthe-seasoned Alpine lake whitefish, rabbit saddle with Savagnin sauce and a juni-per berry sorbet served with grapefruit macaronade are accompanied by superb local wines and a smile from Catherine Faivre. A gold-plated welcome.

MALICORNE-SUR-SARTHE

72270 Sarthe. Paris 235 – Château-Gontier 50 – La Flèche 15 – Le Mans 30.
A pleasant stopover in one of France's gentle heartlands.

●	RESTAURANTS

● **La Petite Auberge** 🅽 **COM**

5, pl Du-Guesclin.
Tel. 02 43 94 80 52. Fax 02 43 94 31 37.
Closed dinner (exc. Sat. Oct.–Mar.), Mon.,

beg. Jan.–end Feb.
Prix fixe: 17€ (weekday lunch), 22€ (weekdays), 25€ (Sat., Sun.), 29€ ((weekdays), 32€ (Sat., Sun.), 9€ (child).

Dominique Bourneuf presides over four differently toned dining rooms with old-style decorations in which we feast on traditional fare. At the stove, Loïc Lami concocts chicken oysters in salad with a truffle oil vinaigrette as an appetizer followed by oven-browned scallops with smoked salmon, pike-perch with verjus or veal kidneys in Port sauce. Pleasurable to the end, that is, dessert (apple tart served warm with caramel ice cream), especially if seated next to the beautiful 13th-century fireplace or on the waterside terrace.

MALO-LES-BAINS see DUNKERQUE
MALROY see METZ

MANCIET

32370 Gers. Paris 720 – Agen 79 – Auch 72 – Mont-de-Marsan 53 – Nogaro 9.
A small crossroads town in the Gers, not far from the Landes and its pretty stone houses.

●	RESTAURANTS

● **La Bonne Auberge** 🅽 **COM**

Pl du Pesquerot.
Tel. 05 62 08 50 04.
Closed Sun. dinner, Mon., 3 weeks mid-Jan.–beg. Feb.
Prix fixe: 25€, 35€, 50€.

In this establishment on the village square, Simone aka Pepita is welcom-ing, the dining room is pleasantly plush and local products are well treated by Pepito. This is what is on offer at the San-pietros, whose son Eric runs La Table des Cordeliers at Condom. The range is more modest here, yet not that restrained: the marbled foie gras terrine with figs or in crème brûlée, the Gascon beef in a wine velouté and the pork trotter medallions with minced hot liver are good, hearty Gersois fare. Generosity abounds here.

The wine list, menus and desserts (exquisite chilled fruit soup) are all the confirmation you need.

MANDELIEU-LA-NAPOULE

06210 Alpes-Maritimes. Paris 896 – Cannes 9 – Fréjus 30 – Draguignan 54 – Nice 37.
ota@ot-mandelieu.fr.
This residential suburb of Cannes is famous for its golf course, its casino and its chic addresses.

 HOTELS-RESTAURANTS

■ **Sofitel Royal Hôtel Casino**
605, av du Général-de-Gaulle.
Tel. 04 92 97 70 00. Fax 04 93 49 51 50.
h1168@accor.com / www.sofitel.com
213 rooms: 200–429€.
Half board: 233–495€.
Prix fixe: 27€, 38€ (dinner).
A la carte: 25–35€.

This seaside hotel is true to its name. Live like a king in the vast, sunny rooms, lounge around the pool or in the casino. Last but not least is the gastronomic dining room, Le Féréol. Variations on tuna tartare, the Atlantic sea bass with garlic butter and mashed potatoes, the veal cutlet and mozzarella gratin and the dessert buffet sing a Mediterranean song. Brasserie cooking at reasonable prices at the Terrasse du Casino.

■ **Ermitage du Riou**
Av Henri-Clews.
Tel. 04 93 49 95 56. Fax 04 92 97 69 05.
www.ermitage-du-riou.fr
41 rooms: 126–301€. 4 suites: 341–529€.
Prix fixe: 25€, 39€ (wine inc.), 54€, 80€.
A la carte: 70€.

With its unbeatable view over the Mediterranean and the Lérins islands, a golf course and swimming pool near by, this establishment is worth a detour. The rooms are well appointed and spacious and the uneventful cooking offers traditional fare: fish soup, roasted swordfish with papaya and lime and a duck breast with mango and sweet potatoes. The cellar is worth discovering for some good property-bottled wines.

■ **Domaine d'Olival**
778, av de la Mer.
Tel. 04 93 49 31 00. Fax 04 92 97 69 28.
www.sejoursdusud.com
29 rooms: 86–149€. 7 suites: 128–285€.

Twenty rooms and suites as well and always the same enchantment. This superb, regional-style establishment is set in tropical surroundings between two branches of the Siagne river. Charming welcome and high-grade service.

● **L'Oasis**
Rue Jean-Honoré-Carle, La Napoule.
Tel. 04 93 49 95 52. Fax 04 93 49 64 13.
www.oasis-raimbault.com
Closed Sun. dinner (off season), Mon. (off season), mid-Dec.–mid-Jan.
Prix fixe: 54€ (lunch), 64€ (lunch), 72€ (lunch, wine inc.), 82€ (lunch, wine inc.), 120€, 145€. A la carte: 120–140€.

This Relais Gourmand has quite an original role as a place where Mediterranean products meet spicy, Asia-based flavors. In the seductive spaces of the dining rooms, veranda or patio, the Raimbault brothers—Stéphane is at the stove—offer a creative cuisine with highly varied dishes and several menus. The Tahitian vanilla-seasoned marbled duck foie gras terrine served with a pineapple and green peppercorn chutney and a side of green mango salad, the langouste with stir-fried spring vegetables in a Thai-seasoned fricassée, the star anise– and Sichuan pepper–seasoned caramelized veal sweetbreads and the dessert "caravan" make a great showing. Interesting wine list under the expert guidance of Pascal Paulze and very attentive service.

MANDEREN see SIERCK-LES-BAINS

MANIGOD

74230 Haute-Savoie. Paris 561 – Annecy 26 – Chamonix 70 – Thônes 6.

manigod@club-internet.fr.
A balcony on the Aravis, this village's inhabitants are all named Veyrat, or nearly all …

HOTELS-RESTAURANTS

■ Chalet de la Croix-Fry

Rte du Col-de-la-Croix-Fry.
Tel. 04 50 44 90 16. Fax 04 50 44 94 87.
www.hotelchaletcroixfry.com
Closed mid-Sept.–mid-Dec.,
mid-Apr.–mid-June. Rest. closed Mon., Tue.
7 rooms: 145–230€. 3 suites: 350–410€.
Prix fixe: 25€ (weekday lunch), 76€.
A la carte: 75–90€.

The Veyrat family is definitely at home in Savoie, and this authentic log cabin, fitted out with care and all creature comforts, is their den. Marie-Ange Guelpa-Veyrat is the mistress of the house with her daughter Isabelle at reception. The latter married Edouard Loubet—that will-o'-the-wisp from Lourmarin—and the cuisine served up here by his disciple Luc Morel is definitely under the influence. Local products, flowers and mountain plants are well matched. A risotto of locally gathered wild mushrooms and parmesan with a truffle sauce, the duck foie gras terrine and wild blueberry bonbons, the Alpine lake whitefish or Montremont salmon trout served whole with a licorice root emulsion or the simmered rabbit seasoned with wild thyme, served with a nasturtium gratin, are in essence half Veyrat, half Loubet (the latter was the pupil of the former). In short, a feast for all. Good choice of desserts prepared at the table.

MANOM see THIONVILLE

MANOSQUE

04100 Alpes de Haute-Provence. Paris 761 – Digne 59 – Aix 57 – Avignon 92.
ots@ville-manosque.fr.
Is this really the hometown of the *Husard sur le Toit*, with its church of Notre-Dame-de-Romogier and its 18th-century hôtel de ville? The medieval structure remains but there have been inroads of concrete. Do not miss the Giono museum.

HOTELS-RESTAURANTS

■ Pré Saint-Michel

Tel. 04 92 72 14 27. Fax 04 92 72 53 04.
pre.st.michel@wanadoo.fr
www.presaintmichel.com
24 rooms: 55–100€. Half board: 113–150€.

The comfortable, modern rooms of this hotel look out over the town's rooftops. A huge garden, swimming pool and delicious breakfasts will embellish your stay.

● Le Luberon   SIM

21 bis, pl du Terreau.
Tel.-Fax 04 92 72 03 09.
Closed Sun. dinner, Mon., 2 weeks Oct.
Prix fixe: 13,50€ (weekday lunch), 18,50€,
27,50€, 37,50€. A la carte: 48–58€.

Jean-Pierre de Greeter is a no-nonsense cook. His cuisine is straightforward and very fresh—inspired by market products. The flaked cod worked into aïoli in the manner of rilettes, sea bream filet with tapenade and the six-hour lamb shoulder, served with spelt wheat risotto, are extremely palatable. The honey and lavender crème brulée makes for a joyful finish. Give yourselves a treat with the little "*Terroir et Patrimoine*" menu—a nice homage to the region.

In La Fuste (04210). 6,5 km via rte de Valensole.

■ Hostellerie de la Fuste

Rte d'Oraison.
Tel. 04 92 72 05 95. Fax 04 92 72 92 93.
lafuste@aol.com / www.lafuste.com
Closed end Oct.–mid-Mar.
Rest. closed Sun. dinner, Mon.
12 rooms: 95–185€. 2 suites: 200–270€.
Prix fixe: 46€, 56€, 85€, 20€ (child).
A la carte: 95€.

Set in the heart of the Vemensolais plateau, this 17th-century construction is an ideal point of departure for a visit to the region. The rooms are refined and quiet. Equally seductive are a library hung with chandeliers, a wood-burning fireplace and a modern dining room with a view of the garden. The cooking of Daniel Jourdan (truffle-seasoned scrambled eggs, trout in a shellfish broth, oven-roasted rack of lamb and the creamy mascarpone) makes up the rest.

LE MANS

72000 Sarthe. Paris 202 – Angers 97 – Nantes 186 – Rennes 153 – Tours 83.
officedutourisme@ville-lemans.fr.

In the magnificent old center of Le Mans—which was a choice background for Philippe de Broca's film, *Le Bossu*—the cathedral of St-Julien and Queen Berengaria's house would alone justify a trip to the capital of the Sarthe, made easily accessible from Paris thanks to the TGV. The town also boasts an automobile museum as well as its racing circuit where numerous prestigious events take place, including the famous twenty-four hours of Le Mans.

 HOTELS-RESTAURANTS

■ Mercure le Mans Centre
19-21, rue de Chanzy.
Tel. 02 43 40 22 40.
H5641@accor.com
68 rooms: 105–115€. 5 suites: 180–250€.

The hotel event of the city? This recent Mercure installed in the old headquarters of the Mutuelles du Mans, circa 1883. The place has conserved the appearance of a grand bourgeois establishment, thanks to the colonnaded lobby and the grand staircase with stained glass, while equipping itself with modern rooms and suites decorated in a contemporary style with corner workstations and flat screen TVs.

■ Concorde
16, av Général-Leclerc.
Tel. 02 43 24 12 30. Fax 02 43 24 85 74.
www.concordelemans.com
Rest. closed Sat., Sun.
52 rooms: 70–150€. 4 suites: 150€.
Prix fixe: 15€, 21€.

This brick house dates from the beginning of the 20th century. Within its walls nestles a charming hotel with period furniture and warm tones. The constantly

renovated rooms are spacious and soundproof. Patrick Fer is at the stoves of the Amphytrion, serving up a light and well-thought-out cuisine. An assortment of mushrooms in cream, presented in puff pastry, salmon rilettes with horseradish cream and the grenadier filet served with mustard sauce and risotto make for nice rearrangements of classic recipes. Exemplary welcome and service.

■ Hôtel Levasseur
Restaurant La Mendigotte
5, bd Levasseur.
Tel. 02 43 39 61 62.
Rest. closed Sat. lunch, Sun., Mon.
37 rooms: 52–70€.
Prix fixe: 12,50€ (lunch). A la carte: 25€.

This good, city center hotel has been gaily renovated with contemporary, colorful rooms. On the ground floor is an equally colorful brasserie with a zinc-topped bar, a pleasant atmosphere and simple fare.

■ Le Saint-Pierre
25, rue des Chanoines.
Tel. 02 43 87 25 39.
3 rooms: 69€.

This old canon's house situated in front of the cathedral has been tastefully and simply done up by Jean-Claude Ciaramella. Three delectable bedrooms (moderately priced), nice breakfasts and a wide-angle view over the rooftops set the tone. WiFi for all.

● Beaulieu
3, pl des Ifs.
Tel. 02 43 87 78 37. Fax 02 43 87 78 27.
Closed Sat., Sun., Bank holidays, Feb. vac., Aug.
Prix fixe: 28€ (lunch), 38€, 49€, 59€.
A la carte: 85€.

It was a beacon of the old town. Here it has come fully into its own. More space, a corner cocktail bar in the entrance, a few salons, a background in various tones of red, nicely set tables: everything points to a successful move. Olivier Boussard's little defects remain—a tendency to be too showy and to overload dishes with useless small herbal offerings (such as sprigs of chervil all over the place). But this disciple of Henri Seguin at the Pressoir in Paris and Firmin Arrambide at Saint-Jean-Pied-de-Port has returned to his roots and knows his stuff. Fine langoustine and crab in aspic with a saffron emulsion sauce or the langoustine "in all of its forms" (in a tian, in aspic and infusion, with a soft-boiled egg and rolled in Middle Eastern angelhair pastry called kadaïf), variations on the oyster theme (aspic, in sea water, warm, with lime, with ginger, sorbet), foie gras in a croustillant of figs and truffles are rich enough works of art to constitute a meal in themselves. The house signature dish? Poultry from the Patis farm in Coulans-sur-Gée, offered in two servings, the thighs in pot-au-feu, presented in their jus and delightfully tender, served with seasonal mushrooms and a foie gras-topped soft-boiled egg: this is great art! Add some scrumptious desserts (citrus fruit and lemongrass ravioli, an apple and cinnamon croustillant followed by caramel ice cream) and a wine list which includes regional offerings. A terrific establishment.

● Le Fontainebleau   COM

12, pl Saint-Pierre.
Tel. 02 43 14 25 74.
Closed Mon. dinner, Tue., 1 week Feb.,
3 weeks mid-Sept.–beg. Oct.
Prix fixe: 17€, 27€, 39,50€.
A la carte: 30–35€.

Laurent Mauboussin knows how to bring regional products up to date by playing with cooking methods, spices and sweet-and-sour flavors with undeniable talent. The crab tartare with tomato caviar, the Atlantic sea bass filet with a bread crust and lemon crumble, the spicy duckling with honey or the thin apple tart served hot with cinnamon and vanilla have seduced Le Mans' inhabitants who relish these inventive dishes in the newly renovated dining room or, in fine weather, on the terrace.

● La Ciboulette   ●SIM

14, rue Vieille-Porte.
Tel. 02 43 24 65 67. Fax 02 43 87 51 18.
laciboulettelemans@aol.com
Closed Sat. lunch, Sun., Mon. lunch,
1 week Jan., 1 week May, 2 weeks Aug.
Prix fixe: 14,50€, 20,80€, 29,90€.
A la carte: 55€.

Laurent Lachat likes to spoil gourmets and a festival of surprising flavors awaits each visitor. Lachat worked at Patrick Cirotte's Grenadin in Paris and then in Las Vegas before settling in Le Mans next to the cathedral. His cuisine is inventive but never airy-fairy: the foie gras crumble, fresh cod with sundried tomatoes, duck breast with spice caramel and the liquid-centered chocolate cake dessert, all with wines chosen for the occasion.

● Auberge des Sept Plats   SIM

79, Grand-Rue.
Tel. 02 43 24 57 77.
Closed Sun., Mon., Tue. lunch,
1 week Christmas–New Year's.
Prix fixe: 14,90€, 16,90€, 18,90€,
8€ (child).

Right next to the town hall, Jean-Louis Nouchet and Fabrice Goutard's establishment offers a delightful menu. The rustic dining room done in Bordeaux-red tones is cozy. Périgord-style terrine with pigeon and foie gras, the mountain tartine with ham, pork tenderloin medallions with chanterelles and the apple tart with vanilla ice cream and milk caramel leave a good memory.

● Le Nez Rouge   SIM

107, Grand-Rue.
Tel.-Fax 02 43 24 27 26.
Closed Sun., Mon., Feb. vac., 3 weeks Aug.
Prix fixe: 19,90€, 31€. A la carte: 48€.

The décor with its wooden beams in the heart of the old city is amusing and Thierry Blot's cuisine seduces thanks to a few small touches of originality. An apple, foie gras and pan-roasted duck Tatin, scallop brochette with mango cooked in clarified butter, braised veal sweetbreads with crayfish and cep cream and the strawberry meringue dessert with a lavender sauce are enchanting.

● **Le Plongeoir** SIM

55, Grand-Rue.
Tel. 02 43 23 27 37.
www.le-plongeoir.com
Closed Sun., Mon., 2 weeks Oct.,
2 weeks Apr.
Prix fixe: 13€, 25€. A la carte: 35€.

Stéphanie Vavasseur and Nicolas Wielic-zko energetically run this purple-colored establishment with its ethnic ground floor dining room and Zen lounge on the first floor. Nicolas Wieliczko cooks according to the season and what he brings back from his travels. Lebanese-style mezze, snapper filet with pineapple and quinoa salsa, grilled octopus with lime, squid ink spaghetti and chicken with peanut sauce are not bad. The "American Dream" dessert with maple syrup, fig confiture and chestnut cream is an event of its own.

In Arnage (72230). 10 km toward Angers on D147.

● **Auberge des Matfeux** V.COM

289, av Nationale.
Tel. 02 43 21 10 71. Fax 02 43 21 25 23.
matfeux@wanadoo.fr
www.aubergedesmatfeux.fr
Closed Sun. dinner, Mon., Tue. dinner,
10 days beg. Jan., 1 week at end July, Aug.
Prix fixe: 37€, 50€, 71€, 17€ (child).
A la carte: 65€.

Le Mans' gastronomes are well acquainted with this address which has spent the last forty years offering quality cuisine. Xavier Souffront has handed over his place at the stove to Dominique Louveau, who is charged with giving a breath of fresh air to the establishment. A red tuna and foie gras tartare, langoustine ravioli, the mixed seafood plate, Loué red label chicken oysters and a sour cherry and pistachio macaron have renewed the repertoire. Highly professional welcome and service. Good cellar presided over by Fabrice Guihéry.

MANSLE

16230 Charente. Paris 420 – Angoulême 25 – Cognac 55 – Limoges 95 – Poitiers 90 – St-Jean d'Angély 60.
The Charente river runs through this pretty town with its 16th-century stone bridge. Every July, Mansle plays host to a circus festival.

 HOTELS-RESTAURANTS

■ **Beau Rivage** ●□

Pl Gardoire.
Tel. 05 45 20 31 26. Fax 05 45 22 24 24.
Closed Sun. dinner (off season),
3 weeks Nov., 3 weeks Mar.
31 rooms: 49–54€. 1 suite: 75€.
Prix fixe: 13€, 30€, 7,50€ (child).
A la carte: 40–45€.

Alain Louis' establishment sits along the banks of the Charente. Its severe facade hides attractive rooms, a terrace with a panorama of greenery and a pretty garden. In the huge dining room, dine on traditional dishes such as the goat cheese and spinach quiche seasoned with truffles, the roasted Atlantic sea bass with hazelnuts or the duck breast with orange sauce. To finish, the crêpe with meringue-lightened pastry cream is a sweet from childhood.

In Luxé (16230). 6 km w via D739.

● **Auberge du Cheval Blanc** ●COM

La Gare.
Tel. 05 45 22 23 62.
Closed Sun. dinner, Tue. dinner, Mon., 1–10 Sept., Feb.
Prix fixe: 13,50€ (lunch, weekdays), 25€, 35€.

A rustic, flowery restaurant with an exquisite welcome and a refined, well-cooked regional cuisine based on market buys, is what most pleases in this century-old establishment. The menus are veritable gifts.

In Saint-Groux (16230). 3 km nw via D361.

■ Trois Saules

Le Bourg.
Tel. 05 45 20 31 40. Fax 05 45 22 73 81.
les3saules.faure@voilà.fr
Closed Fri. dinner (off season), Sun. dinner,
Mon. lunch end Oct.–end Nov.,
2 weeks Feb.–beg. Mar.
10 rooms: 33–50€.
Prix fixe: 10€ (weekdays), 28€.

The Charente runs parallel to this pleasant inn spread out over two buildings, offering partially renovated rooms which are neat and functional. A genial welcome and a simple, regional cuisine.

MANZAC-SUR-VERN see PERIGUEUX
MARAUSSAN see BEZIERS
MARÇAY see CHINON

MARGAUX

33460 Gironde. Paris 604 – Bordeaux 31 – Lesparre-Médoc 42.
At the beginning of the Médoc peninsula, this classy appellation is deemed to produce more "feminine" wines. The lovely village which bears this name is welcoming.

HOTELS-RESTAURANTS

■ Relais de Margaux

5, route de l'Ile-Vincent.
Tel. 05 57 88 38 30. Fax 05 57 88 31 73.
relais-margaux@relais-margaux.fr
www.relais-margaux.fr
Rest. closed lunch (exc. weekends), Mon.
96 rooms: 150–320€.
14 suites: 350–390€.
Prix fixe: 32€, 45€, 75€.

In the heart of the vineyards, this charming abode with swimming pool and fitness center offers the latest in water spa treatments as well as luxurious rooms. But what most seduces here is Laurent Costes' cuisine. The lobster sushi, the basil-seasoned John Dory, the boneless pigeon with foie gras and the frozen cherry macaron happily blend modernity and tradition.

■ Pavillon de Margaux

3, rue Georges-Mandel.
Tel. 05 57 88 77 54. Fax 05 57 88 77 73.
le-pavillon-margaux@wanadoo.fr
14 rooms: 63–115€.
Prix fixe: 28€, 38€, 45€, 51€,
10€ (child). A la carte: 45€.

This old village school built in the 19th century in Bordeaux stone houses fourteen classic-style rooms and an art deco restaurant. The menu is not very original but well-priced. Salmon tartare with vegetables in a beet vinaigrette, pan-roasted cod with creamy saffron risotto, sirloin steak with a creamy chanterelle sauce and the raspberry dessert served in a glass with pistachio cream are appreciated, as are the low prices.

● Le Savoie

1, place de la Trémoille.
Tel.-Fax 05 57 88 31 76.
Closed Sun. dinner, Mon. dinner,
1 week Christmas–New Year's.
Prix fixe: 18€ (weekday lunch), 26€, 32€,
42€, 15€ (child). A la carte: 50€.

Philippe Vilet has started renovations on a winter garden for all seasons and has composed a new menu with traditional recipes using good, fresh products. Star anise–seasoned ratatouille and escargots in puff pastry, monkfish filet with a Margaux wine sauce, lamb cutlet with foie gras and cep duxelles in a lace caul pouch, liver with potatoes and the chocolate marquise presented in a *verrine* with a biscuit are straightforward and very pleasing dishes.

In Arcins (33460). 6 km nw via D2.

● Le Lion d'Or

11, rte de Pauillac.
Tel. 05 56 58 96 79.
Closed Sun., Mon., July.
Prix fixe: 13,50€. A la carte: 45€.

Along the Grand Cru route of the Médoc, Jean-Paul Barbier's establishment has become the rallying point for local producers who don't hesitate to bring their own bottle—the wine racks form the bulk of the restaurant's décor. Apart from the wines, everyone appreciates the sausage, the tête de veau, the eel simmered in Bordelaise, sirloin steak with shallots cooked over grapevines, the roasted pigeon presented on a foie gras canapé and the traditional cannelé for dessert. A heart-warming address.

MARIENTHAL see **HAGUENAU**

MARLENHEIM

67520 Bas-Rhin. Paris 465 – Strasbourg 20 – Haguenau 35.
Rendezvous on August 15 for the feast of l'Ami Fritz to discover the joyful soul of this first town along the region's wine route. Otherwise all year round the Hussers at the Cerf show gastronomic Alsace at its very best.

 HOTELS-RESTAURANTS

● **Le Cerf**
30, rue du Général-de-Gaulle.
Tel. 03 88 87 73 73. Fax 03 88 87 68 08.
info@lecerf.com / www.lecerf.com
Rest. closed Tue., Wed.
12 rooms: 90–140€. 2 suites: 200€.
Prix fixe: 39€ (lunch), 85€, 98€,
23€ (child). A la carte: 105€.

Under the direction of Michel Husser and his wife, Cathy, the place has recently been given a facelift. The waiters are now dressed in black, like avant-garde chefs' assistants, there is modern lighting and new chairs which have brought a note of clarity and gaiety to the Alsatian-style paneled dining room with its marquetry work by Spindler and its huge canvas by Loux. The house, however, stays obstinately true to tradition. The best proof of the Hussers' attachment to old recipes is the *plaisir* menu at 39 , served at lunchtime, which distills everything one loves and is often forgotten by more trendy establishments. Thus the paté in a pastry crust (named *royale*, with veal sweetbreads and morels), the thick-cut smoked salmon with a horseradish mousse, then puff pastry cups filled with veal sweetbreads and served with poultry quenelles and a creamy mush-

room sauce, the civet of venison, slow simmered with onions and red wine served with the house-made chestnut spätzle noodles. Nothing but good, serious classic dishes which can be accompanied— thanks to the good idea of a competent sommelier—by wines by the glass of winemaker friends and neighbors. Traditional desserts include ice creams according to season or the Alsatian-style baba, as well as daily meat and fish choices which allow for a reasonably priced meal for a high class establishment. But one could go on and on about the foie gras terrine with mango chutney, the eel and escargot brochette with lentils and local pesto (garlic and parsley in addition to basil), the grand duck liver ravioli in a pot-au-feu and the famous and wonderful suckling pig choucroute, with medallions of caramelized meat, fare full of character which manages to lighten up dishes without straying too far from tradition. The house desserts are as good as the rest: baba au Kirsch served with cherry compote and a vanilla-flavored whipped cream and the frozen vacherin with fine meringue cut into matchsticks, all of which are wonderful creations in the spirit of the region.

● **Au Tonneau** SIM
2, pl du Kaufhaus.
Tel.-Fax 03 88 87 75 02.
Closed Fri., Christmas–New Year's.
Prix fixe: 14,70€, 17,30€, 22€, 24€, 34€,
8,50€ (child). A la carte: 36€.

A *winstub* atmosphere, friendly welcome, generous little dishes and local wines contribute to the success of this genial address. The barrel-covered walls give you a hint of what it's all about so order a glass of wine and feast on foie gras, pike-perch over sauerkraut, sirloin steak with morels and chocolate mousse or crème caramel.

■ **Hostellerie Reeb** COM
2, rue du Dr-Schweitzer.
Tel. 03 88 87 52 70. Fax 03 88 87 69 73.
info@hostellerie-reeb.fr
www.hostellerie-reeb.fr
Closed 3 weeks Jan.
Rest. closed Sun. dinner, Mon.

26 rooms: 50€. 2 suites: 87€.
Prix fixe: 19,50€, 24,50€, 31€, 44€,
12€ (child). A la carte: 40€.

Fredy Reeb is a welcoming host in his half-
timbered house at the entrance to the
village. Be it in the rustic or classic-style
dining rooms, his cooking should be tasted
with a good Alsatian wine. The foie gras
with fruit chutney, the Munster cheese
and bacon in puff pastry and pike-perch
in paupillette served with sauerkraut have
character. The neighboring *winstub* offers
local specialities. The rooms are charming and quiet, worthy of this Alsace village and quality address.

In Furdenheim (67117). 5 km e via N4.

● **La Ferme des Trois Frères** SIM

15, rte de Strasbourg.
Tel. 03 88 69 00 86. Fax 03 88 69 14 20.
Closed Sat. lunch, Mon., 2 weeks Oct.,
2 weeks Jan.
A la carte: 25€.

Dominique Schmitt has transferred his
Marmoutier farm to the ex-Feldfof and
made it into a charming mountain refuge.
Dominique, a true lover of Savoie (he used
to work at the Totem in Flaine) is a proponent of cooking with cheese. In his perfect chalet, the fine pasta from the Savoie
and other regions are proposed in cheese
sauce, Provençal style, pan tossed, Italian
style or rolled with meat. Add a few of the
best tartes flambées, the local savory flat
pastries with cream and bacon, including
the whole wheat peasant version, and his
success at week's end is clear.

MARNE-LA-VALLEE

77206 Seine-et-Marne. Paris 27 – Meaux 28
–Melun 41.

■	HOTELS

■ **Disneyland Hôtel**

In Disneyland Park.
Tel. 01 60 45 65 00. Fax 01 60 45 65 33.
www.disneyland.com
496 rooms: 355–483€.

At the entrance to the park, an enchantingly decorated hotel boasting refined
rooms, an indoor pool, fitness center and
elegant restaurants, including the gourmet California Grill.

■ **New York**

In Disneyland Park.
Tel. 01 60 45 73 00. Fax 01 60 45 73
33.dlp.nwy.frontoffice@disney.com
www.disney.com
565 rooms: 214–614€. 27 suites: 1050–2050€.

Red exterior piping, thirties décor and a
lake: suddenly, you are at the Rockefeller
Center. Enjoy the neo–art deco rooms
and the Parkside restaurant, straight out
of an Edward Hopper painting.

■ **Newport Bay Club**

In Disneyland Park.
Tel. 01 60 45 55 00. Fax 01 60 45 55 33.
dlp.npb.front.office@disney.com
www.disney.com
1093 rooms: 196–331€.
13 suites: 395–675€.

It is rather pleasant, this reproduction
vacation resort beside a lake, complete
with lighthouse. We might almost be
in Westport (Connecticut) or Newport
(Rhode Island). The indoor and outdoor
pools, sauna, Jacuzzi and massage parlor are a bonus, as is the Cape Cod restaurant with its refreshing seafood cuisine.

■ **Séquoia Lodge**

In Disneyland Park.
Tel. 01 60 45 51 00. Fax 01 60 45 51 33.
www.disneyland.com
1011 rooms: 164–291€. 10 suites: 410–420€.

The sequoias surrounding the hotel were
brought from America and provide a surprisingly restful effect here. The steam
bath-sauna-Jacuzzi complex and cozy
lounges heighten this feeling. The only
hitch is the simplistic rooms.

■ **Le Cheyenne**

In Disneyland Park.
Tel. 01 60 45 62 00. Fax 01 60 45 62 33.

www.disneylandparis.com
1000 rooms: 125–197€.

The most family friendly hotel in the Disneyland park with its rooms for four decorated in Wild West fashion. Do not miss brunch in the saloon, ideal for the kids.

 | RESTAURANTS

● **California Grill** `V.COM`
Disneyland Hotel.
BP 111.
Métro: Marne-la-Vallé-Chessy (RER A).
Tel. 01 60 45 65 00 / 01 60 45 65 76.
Fax 01 60 45 65 33.
marieangele.duffrey@disney.com
www.disneylandparis.com
Prix fixe: 44€, 46€, 71€, 15€ (child).

Eric Leautey continues to fly the flag of French quality in a land where children are king. This student of Robuchon plays to a tasteful neoclassical score, serving up grilled jumbo shrimp, creamy asparagus soup presented with an Aquitaine caviar-flavored whipped cream, grilled lobster with spring vegetables and dill butter and the lamb shank served with gnocchi and polenta, which all display an effortless charm. The strawberry-flavored butter biscuit served with ewe's milk ice cream provides a delightfully fresh conclusion. A fine establishment with a Victorian flavor, a generous cellar and meticulous service.

MARQUISE

62250 Pas-de-Calais. Paris 274 – Calais 22 – Arras 116 – Boulogne 17 – Saint-Omer 51.
This stopover town points its nose towards cape Gris-Nez, the Channel tunnel and neighboring Albion.

 | RESTAURANTS

● **Le Grand Cerf** ○`COM`
34, av Ferber.
Tel. 03 21 87 55 05. Fax 03 21 33 61 09.
s.pruvot@legrandcerf.com

www.legrandcerf.com
Closed Sun. dinner, Mon., Thu. dinner.
Prix fixe: 27€, 37€, 47€.
A la carte: 46–70€.

From the Côte Saint-Jacques to the Opal Coast may seem like a great step but not so for this fine coaching inn. Stéphane Pruvot, who used to work with Lorain at Joigny, perfectly demonstrates a wisely creative cuisine using the best products of turf and surf. The dining room is modestly elegant and the menu full of tasty offerings such as the fennel seed-marinated scallops, the roasted langoustines with onion compote, a beer-braised ox cheek dish accompanied by orange-seasoned slow-cooked carrots and the chocolate symphony with passion fruit and kiwi coulis. To crown it all, a seductive wine list under the guidance of Bernard Poly comes with charming service.

MARSANNAY-LA-COTE see DIJON

MARSEILLAN

34340 Hérault. Paris 760 – Montpellier 48 – Béziers 31 – Sète 24.
Highlights of this port on the Thau lagoon include the apse of the church of Saint Jean-Baptiste, Noilly-Prat warehouses (you can visit them), the old black stone market hall. The beach is a few steps away.

 | RESTAURANTS

● **Chez Philippe** ●`SIM`
20, rue de Suffren.
Tel.-Fax 04 67 01 70 62.
chezphilippe@club-internet.fr
Closed Mon., Tue. (off season),
mid-Nov.–mid-Feb.
Prix fixe: 26€. A la carte: 30€.

In this 1930's-style bistro, Jeanne Lecointre is all smiles. Her new chef, Antonio Diaz, treats his guests to up-to-date fare. The tuna roll, the Mediterranean sea bass salad, a licorice root-flavored lamb brochette with almond milk and the chocolate and cardamom duo go well with nice wines from the Languedoc-Roussillon region and a moderately priced bill.

MARSEILLE

13000 Bouches-du-Rhône. Paris 772 –
Lyon 314 – Nice 191 – Toulon 64 –
Aix-en-Provence 31.
info@marseille-tourisme.com.

The Pharo corniche, the cove of Maldormé, Kennedy Boulevard, Prado beach, the picturesque Panier quarter, the crowded yacht basin of the Vieux-Port, comings and goings on the Cours D'Estienne-d'Orves: This is Marseille-on-Charm, an engaging city on the French Riviera to be discovered through her 19th-century facades and her Greek and Italian villas. Stroll to the Vallon des Auffes, stopping to peer at the maze of fishermen's huts lining narrow streets named after fish, sit awhile in cafés and gaze out across the little harbor, or visit the monument to the heroes of the Orient and experience that call of the sea. Marseille doesn't just make you long to travel, she takes you on a voyage. Each tourist becomes a wanderer. Here, gastronomy is as natural as its city, the daughter of Provence, the love child of the Mediterranean.

■	HOTELS

■ Sofitel Palm Beach

200, corniche Kennedy (7th arr.).
Tel. 04 91 16 19 00. Fax 04 91 16 19 39.
h3485@accor.com / www.sofitel.com
160 rooms: 249–285€. 10 suites: 455€.

True comfort and a minimalist design. Add to that the Mediterranean and the Château-d'If on the horizon: that's what the revamped Sofitel, managed by the experienced Domenico Basciano, has to offer. Refined rooms, several lounges, a swimming pool and fitness center set the tone. (Restaurant: see La Réserve.)

■ Sofitel Vieux Port

36, bd Charles-Livon (7th arr.).
Tel. 04 91 15 59 00. Fax 04 91 15 59 50.
H0542@accor.com / www.sofitel.com
131 rooms: 250–400€.
3 suites: 695–995€.

Loïc Fauchille is in charge of this grand old hotel on the Vieux-Port. Comfortably appointed rooms, swimming pool, fitness center and a famous restaurant. (See les Trois Forts). Classy welcome and service.

■ Le Petit Nice

Anse de Maldormé, 160, corniche Kennedy (7th arr.).
Tel. 04 91 59 25 92. Fax 04 91 59 28 08.
passedat@relaischateaux.com
www.passedat.com
Closed Jan., Feb.
13 rooms: 190–275€. 3 suites: 610–810€.
Half board: 290–1010€.

Looking over the Mediterranean, this Relais & Châteaux hotel has a sunlit swimming pool, quiet rooms and a high-flying restaurant. (See Restaurants.)

■ New Hotel of Marseille
"Le Pharo"

71, bd Charles Livon (7th arr.).
Tel. 04 91 31 53 15. Fax 04 91 31 20 00.
www.newhotelofmarseille.com
100 rooms: 180–270€.
Prix fixe: 25€, 29€.

A few steps from the Vieux-Port and across from the Sofitel, this new designer hotel has created quite a stir. The entrance in the former Pasteur Institute is awfully chic and the cuisine of the Victor Café terribly contemporary, beguiling but not outrageous. The dining room, with its Warhol and Basquiat reproductions, and the staff, in American-style shirts, are great fun. A creamy Pastis-seasoned mussel soup, the poached egg in red wine sauce, the yellow risotto with garlic sauce and the ratatouille-stuffed squid go down a treat. The caramelized quince in a crêpe bundle and the wine list showcasing the new Provençal wines are wonderful surprises.

■ Grand Hôtel
Mercure Beauvau

4, rue Beauvau (1st arr.).
Tel. 04 91 54 91 00. Fax 04 91 54 15 76.
H1293@accor.com / www.accor.com
65 rooms: 134–235€. 8 suites: 400€.

Reserve a room on the Vieux-Port and you're sure to find yourself in the heart of the city. The bar and breakfast room renew that pleasure. In their day, George Sand, Maupassant and Chopin all stayed here and the décor, although comfortably renovated, has kept that link with the past.

■ Mercure Prado

11, av de Mazargues (8th arr.).
Tel. 04 96 20 37 37. Fax 04 96 20 37 99.
H3004@accor.com / www.mercure.com
98 rooms: 65–115€. 2 suites: 170€.

Designer furnishings lend personality to this chain hotel. This contemporary, mid-town address is managed with talent by Stéphanie Grataloup, who watches over the comfort and well-being of her clients.

■ New Hôtel Bompard

2, rue des Flots-Bleus (7th arr.).
Tel. 04 91 99 22 22. Fax 04 91 31 02 14.
www.new-hotel.com
45 rooms: 75–140€. 4 suites: 135–250€.

City life bustles under the windows of this peaceful hotel. A comfortable edifice with well-appointed rooms which is well worth a visit. Prices are moderate.

■ Novotel Vieux Port

36, bd Charles-Livon (7th arr.).
Tel. 04 96 11 42 11. Fax 04 96 11 42 20.
H0911@accor.com / www.novotel.com
110 rooms: 120–168€.

Opening on to the Vieux-Port, this chain hotel is pleasant because it is practical: WiFi, swimming pool, conference rooms and a restaurant are all at hand.

■ Résidence du Vieux Port

18, quai du Port (2nd arr.).
Tel. 04 91 91 91 22. Fax 04 91 56 60 88.
www.hotelmarseille.com
43 rooms: 91–135€. 7 suites: 162–200€.

This welcoming hotel with its view on the Vieux-Port and Notre Dame de la Garde

has delightful rooms. Breakfast is extra but the price is right.

■ Océania Hôtel

5, la Canebière (1st arr.).
Tel. 04 91 90 61 61. Fax 04 91 90 95 61.
www.oceaniahotels.com
43 rooms: 81–103€. 2 suites: 95–136€.

Strategically situated and easy to get to, the rooms of this modern establishment have been renovated in tones of gray. Professional welcome and service, moderate prices.

■ Hermès

2, rue Bonneterie (2nd arr.).
Tel. 04 96 11 63 63. Fax 04 96 11 63 64.
www.hotelmarseille.com
29 rooms: 47–90€.

The Paulins, who manage the Residence du Vieux-Port and who recently opened the Hotel du Palais (26, rue Breteuil, 04 91 37 78 86), offer moderately priced, contemporary rooms—some with a terrace. A pleasant welcome is guaranteed and the panoramic view from the rooftop solarium is always a delight.

■ New Hôtel Vieux Port

3 bis, rue Reine-Elisabeth (1st arr.).
Tel. 04 91 99 23 23. Fax 04 91 90 76 24.
www.new-hotel.com
42 rooms: 135–250€.

A bit more costly than elsewhere but the idea is so charming that one accepts the price. Each floor of this hotel is decorated in the style of a country or continent: Mexico, India, Morocco, Africa or Asia are the ideal settings for your sweet dreams.

■ Saint-Ferréol

19, rue Pisançon (1st arr.).
Tel. 04 91 33 12 21. Fax 04 91 54 29 97.
www.hotel-stferreol.com
Closed 17 Dec.–27 Dec.
19 rooms: 73–97€.

Van Gogh, Gauguin and Cézanne, among others, inspired the decorators of this ideally situated hotel 200 meters from the Vieux-Port in the tranquility of a lively pedestrian street. The moderate prices and courteous welcome are much appreciated.

●	RESTAURANTS

● Le Petit Nice   CO LUX

At Le Petit Nice, 160, corniche Kennedy (7th arr.).
17, rue des Brabes.
Tel. 04 91 59 25 92. Fax 04 91 59 28 08.
passedat@relaischateaux.com
www.passedat.com
Closed Sun. lunch, Mon. lunch.
Prix fixe: 55€, 180€.

Gérald Passédat, star of the Kennedy Corniche and beloved of food critics, has managed to keep his feet firmly on the ground. This good-natured ruler of the Maldoré cove improves his domain by skillfully renewing his agile palette. The sea is his vocation. It is the field of his passion, the place of his imagination. A few of his stellar dishes? The slice of Mediterranean sea bass cooked in olive oil "the way Lucie Passédat liked it" or the "bouillabaisse" with Middle Eastern spices, his version of the national dish. But you can also come to this establishment perched on the sea, graced by quality service, to taste the daily specials which are a fusion of the senses. Among the most recent creations, the tender sea anemones redolent of the ocean, served with a caviar mousse and light beignets, the lobster with marinated ginger-seasoned shredded crab and lemongrass and the rougets pan tossed with pistachio and star anise. No one is ever bored at the Petit Nice.

● L'Epuisette   ○ V.COM

138, rue du Vallon-des-Auffes (7th arr.).
Tel. 04 91 52 17 82. Fax 04 91 59 18 80.
contact@l-epuisette.com / www.l-epuisette.com
Closed Sun., Mon., beg. Aug.–beg. Sept.
Prix fixe: 45€, 65€, 105€.
A la carte: 97–102€.

The seaside location sets the tone for this paneled, chic, warm, bright and modern establishment. Bernard Bonnet runs the dining room with tact and enthusiasm, while Guillaume Sourrieu serves up the flavors of the Mediterranean with pleasure. What do we like? His way of teasing the sea without pushing too far. His variation on the langoustine (in tartare, one grilled, one on a brochette, with celery in spicy truffle-seasoned mayonnaise and with his ultra-reduced cream). Or the oysters from the Blue Coast in a violet emulsion and with his seafood "floating islands", not to forget the lobster in tagine with slow-cooked baby vegetables, meat jus, and Middle Eastern spices. In short, the freshest from the sea mingling maliciously with flavors from afar.

● Miramar   ○ V.COM

12, quai du Port (2nd arr.).
Tel. 04 91 91 10 40. Fax 04 91 56 64 31.
contact@bouillabaisse.com
www.bouillabaisse.com
Closed Sun., Mon.
A la carte: 75–80€.

Well situated on the Vieux-Port, the Miramar has regained its youth thanks to Christian Buffa, who trained with Bocuse and Vergé. In the elegantly bourgeois dining room, which has kept its fifties flair, or on the sunlit terrace, dine on the traditional local fish stew presented with a grilled red langouste, the pieds et paquets (a local variety meat dish), the sirloin steak with béarnaise sauce and gratin dauphinois and the *"chichi frégi"* dessert, frozen in the center and served over vanilla egg custard cream. Pleasant service and wines extremely well chosen by Guillaume Ambrocio.

● Les Trois Forts   ○ V.COM

At the Sofitel Vieux-Port,
36, bd Charles-Livon (7th arr.).
Tel. 04 91 15 59 56. Fax 04 91 15 59 50.
h0542@accor.com / www.sofitel.com
Prix fixe: 43€ (lunch), 53€, 83€,
35€ (child). A la carte: 70€.

The dining room with it nautical décor sets the tone straight away. Dominique Frérard does honor to the noblest representatives of the marine world. Lobster in salad, pike-perch filet and the sea bream, hide behind their apparent simplicity, a wealth of aromas and authentic tastes. Sirloin steak and a veal cutlet compete for the meat lovers. The deserts, crème brûlée or strawberry charlotte, add a sweet touch. The service is excellent as is the wine list, presented with know-how by Karine Tinon. (See Hotels)

● Une Table au Sud ◎COM

2, quai du Port (2nd arr.), 2nd floor.
Tel. 04 91 90 63 53. Fax 04 91 90 63 86.
unetableausud@wanadoo.fr
www.unetableausud.com
Closed Sun., Mon., Christmas,
1 week beg. Jan., 3 weeks Aug.
Prix fixe: 34€ (lunch), 48€, 66€, 88€.
A la carte: 90€.

Across from the Vieux-Port, Lionel Lévy, a young up and coming chef, is still being talked about. The modern setting of his restaurant and his up-to-date Southern cuisine will delight you with the bouillabaisse milkshake, the daily catch accompanied by a slice of rhubarb and Noirmoutier new potatoes, quail with pear and licorice root and the chocolate and salted-butter caramel mille-feuille. Alas, the bill is not exactly reasonable.

● Calypso N COM

3, rue des Catalans (7th arr.).
Tel. 04 91 52 40 60.
A la carte: 60€.

This establishment had its moment of glory in the late sixties. Light, modern, panoramic, it has become more modest. The picture windows give on to the sea with the same view of the Frioul islands. Today it boasts—on a short menu which is always a good sign—fish soup, parsley- and garlic-seasoned cuttlefish, bouillabaisse, bourride, the "live" grilled langouste, red sea bream in season (and always grilled with fennel) and the garlic- and parsley-seasoned scorpion fish. Mayor Jean-Claude Gaudin is a regular.

● Les Mets du Sud N COM

8, pl de l'Amiral-Muselier (8th arr.).
Tel. 04 91 77 88 25. Fax 04 91 71 82 46.
www.lesmetsdusud.com
Closed Mon., Tue., 1 week Feb.
Prix fixe: 32€, 9€ (child). A la carte: 65€.

Michel and Florence Stefanini have taken over this cozy Provençal house in the Prado district from René Alloin. She in the kitchen, he in the dining room give a congenial no-nonsense twist to the establishment. Thin scallop tart with a citrus-seasoned reduction and roasted fruits and vegetables with cider vinegar, monkfish medallions with chanterelles, squid tempura and jumbo shrimp fricassée with an Amaretto foam are lively, fresh, light dishes. The Piña Colada transparence makes a choice finish.

● Les Arcenaulx COM

25, cours d'Estienne-d'Orves (1st arr.).
Tel. 04 91 59 80 30. Fax 04 91 54 76 33.
www.les-arcenaulx.com
Closed Sun., 2 weeks mid-Aug.
Prix fixe: 24€ (lunch), 32€, 54€,
10€ (child). A la carte: 55€.

Simone and Jeanne Laffitte, famous booksellers and gastronomes of repute, are at the head of this establishment situated in the arsenal of the royal galleys. In the kitchen, Eric Cornilleau prepares lovely Provençal dishes with refinement. Who could tire of the Provençal-style stuffed vegetables, mushroom- and ham-stuffed purple artichokes simmered in wine, the bouillabaisse plate and traditional Marseille pieds et paquets, a local variety meat specialty. The almond cake with praline pastry cream and "literary ice creams" are pleasant endings.

● Le Charles Livon COM

89, bd Charles-Livon (7th arr.).
Tel. 04 91 52 22 41. Fax 04 91 31 41 63.
www.charleslivon.fr
Closed Sat. lunch, Sun., Mon. lunch,
Christmas–New Year's, Aug.
Prix fixe: 25€ (lunch), 34€, 68€,
12€ (child). A la carte: 62€.

The setting in gray and red with its Moroccan wall lamps has charm and Christian Ernst shows faultless talent in the kitchen. Roasted scallop and cep mille-feuille, the jumbo shrimp cannelloni, the line-caught fish with shellfish risotto and a composition of duck in a pepper crust with the thigh stuffed with foie gras are well prepared. The variations on the chocolate theme leave pleasant memories.

● Chez Loury   `COM`

3, rue Fortia (1st arr.).
Tel. 04 91 33 09 73. Fax 04 91 33 73 21.
loury@loury.com / www.loury.com
Closed Sun., 1 week Christmas–New Year's,
1 week Sept.
Prix fixe: 18€, 28€, 29€. A la carte: 55€.

Bernard Loury, the Burgundian of the Vieux-Port who trained with Garin, does not go in for half measures when it comes to the freshness of his products, weather permitting. The sea urchins presented in strips, in scrambled eggs, Spanish style (with tomatoes, peppers, onions and garlic), stuffed vegetables with mussels or smoked bacon as well as the bouillabaisse, are worth a visit. Add the covered terrace on a lively street, the first-rate service, the smiling welcome and the heavenly menus and you are apt to make a reservation.

● Le Comptoir des Savouille   `COM`

44, rue Sainte (1st arr.).
Tel. 04 96 11 03 11. Fax 04 96 11 03 14.
perso.wanadoo.fr/comptoirsavouille
Closed Sat. lunch, Sun.
Prix fixe: 13€ (weekday lunch).
A la carte: 45€.

Philippe Mehouas has turned this convivial spot into a gastronomic destination. People flock here to taste classic dishes brought up to date. The fish soup, spaghetti with squid ink, traditional Marseille pieds et paquets and tiramisu for dessert are not half bad. Cool prices.

● Chez Fonfon   `COM`

140, rue du Vallon-des-Auffes (7th arr.).
Tel. 04 91 52 14 38. Fax 04 91 52 14 16.
chezfonfon@aol.com / www.chez-fonfon.com
Closed Sun., Mon. lunch, 2 weeks beg. Jan.
Prix fixe: 40€, 55€, 12€ (child).
A la carte: 70€.

Nothing has changed *chez* Fonfon since his nephew, Alexandre Pina, took over this institution that backs up against the cove, with the little harbor on the horizon. Fish soup, langoustines in tapenade, rockfish mille-feuille, roasted fish with an olive oil–seasoned celery root purée are proof of some serious cooking which merits attention. Yellow tones and windows facing the boats have warmed up the décor. One almost forgets to mention the bouillabaisse (at 45): a monument of its kind.

● La Réserve   `COM`

At the Sofitel Palm Beach,
200, corniche Kennedy.
Tel. 04 91 16 19 00. Fax 04 91 16 19 39.
h3485@accor.com / www.sofitel.com
Prix fixe: 45€ (lunch, wine inc.).
A la carte: 70€.

Is this Marseille or Santa Monica? Here at the end of the corniche are the futuristic lines of a cubic construction, a refined and contemporary dining room and Belgian-born Thierry Bayot's seafood concoctions that show how easily he has slipped into a Mediterranean mold. Mediterranean sea bass served over rougail (a spicy diced tomato, ginger, onion and birdseye pepper condiment), with a chocolate and lime emulsion, roasted grouper in two textures with rings of sautéed cuttlefish, the grilled tuna steak served with heirloom vegetables seasoned with island spices give an exotic touch to this spot. The great idea: thick fish steaks, simply grilled, such as fennel-seasoned Mediterranean sea bass or sole with lemon butter.

● Chez Maurice Brun   `COM`
"Aux Mets de Provence"

18, quai de Rive-Neuve (7th arr.), 3rd floor.
Tel. 04 91 33 35 38. Fax 04 91 33 05 69.
Closed Sat. lunch, Sun., Mon. lunch,
2 weeks beg. Aug.
Prix fixe: 40€ (lunch, wine inc.),
46€ (wine inc. dinner), 40€ (child).

Naturally this is not the Maurice Brun of yore, but this jazzed-up institution facing the Vieux-Port has kept its charm. Tried and true dishes include grilled sea bream with slow-cooked fennel and veal kidneys with artichokes. A smiling welcome but the service drags a bit.

● Michel `COM`
"Brasserie des Catalans"
6, rue des Catalans (7th arr.).
Tel. 04 91 52 30 63. Fax 04 91 59 23 05.
A la carte: 77€.

The photograph dates from 1967. Here is Jeanne (the mother, in the kitchen), Michel (who founded the establishment in 1946), Tony (their son, in a red pullover) and Paul (as a modest young man wearing a tie), who now presides over the establishment and its offerings of the catch of the day. All Marseille, including mayor Jean-Claude Gaudin as well as happy-go-lucky celebs, flock here for parsley- and garlic-seasoned cuttlefish, the ritual bouillabaisse (58) and the fish (sea bream, Mediterranean sea bass, John Dory, scorpion fish, depending on the day's catch). Let the service carry you along before giving in to a classic yet perfect dessert (mille-feuille with "runny" cream and the pralined dacquoise *castel*). The Pibarnon *rosé* is a pleasure to drink.

● Péron `COM`
56, corniche Kennedy (7th arr.).
Tel. 04 91 52 15 22. Fax 04 91 52 17 29.
www.restaurant-peron.com
Prix fixe: 56€, 68€.

Esthete owners Roger Misraki and Denis Barral have given a contemporary look to this open air café with its brown-toned, teak terrace. The youthful service is very relaxed and the menu—not exactly cheap—reveals the talents of young Oliver Caparros who used to work with the Pourcels. Fish soup, foie gras terrine with fig marmalade and a sardine croustillant make for bracing starters. The main dishes nudge towards outrageous sophistication (the jumbo shrimp married with

veal cheeks, grilled squid with an overwhelming lemon jus). The desserts—by a pastry chef formed at Pic—are the real surprise: divine spiced coffee with green apple jelly and a baba absolutely gorged with vanilla and pineapple.

● Le Café des Epices
4, rue du Lacydon (2nd arr.).
Tel.-Fax 04 91 91 22 69.
cafedesepices@yahoo.fr
Closed Sat. dinner, Sun., Mon.,
Dec., Feb., Aug.
Prix fixe: 15€, 19€, 23€, 35€ (dinner).

This modern *bouchon* behind the town hall, with its six inside tables and as many on its terrace, is nearly always full. In the open plan kitchens, Arnaud Carton de Grammont, who worked with Blanc at Vonnas, Lacombe in Lyon and Banzo in Aix, concocts dishes that give pause. The cold Espelette pepper-seasoned ratatouille with grilled langoustines, John Dory with fresh almonds and sundried tomatoes, the mildly spiced veal brochette and the pan-simmered apricots accompanied by a verbena ice cream are affordable treats. A new annex on the Vieux-Port.

● Au Bord de l'Eau `N` `SIM`
Port de la Madrague Montredon, 15, rue des Arapèdes (8th arr.).
Tel. 04 91 72 68 04.
Closed Mon. lunch (summer), Tue. (exc. dinner summer), Wed (exc. dinner summer), beg. Dec.–beg. Feb.
A la carte: 50€.

A waterside, open-air café with terrace on the Madrague port: Nicolas Ravanas is an easygoing host. On the program: the catch of the day, grilled and offered at 6,50 per three ounces (sole, rouget, sea bream, striped sea bream, Mediterranean sea bass), grilled marinated seafood (salmon, squid in thin strips, tuna, jumbo shrimp, monkfish or the mixed grill), not to mention the seafood brochettes. Pasta, pizza and meat dishes are also on offer but who would come to this heavenly spot overlooking the fishing boats and not go for the wonders of the surf?

● Café des Arts   Ⓝ SIM

122, rue du Vallon-des-Auffes (7th arr.).
Tel. 04 91 31 51 64.
Closed Sat. lunch, Sun. lunch, Wed.,
1 week Christmas–New Year's,
3 weeks Aug.–mid-Sept.
Prix fixe: 15€ (lunch), 28€.
A la carte: 30–40€.

A garden with a patio, two olive trees, terra cotta floor tiles, wooden tables, a humidor and a daily menu with very reasonably priced dishes: this establishment situated not far from the Vallon des Auffes is one of Marseille's best-kept secrets. People come to Georges Jacomino for the wood fire-grilled meats, a Charolais sirloin steak, an Argentinian rib eye, the fried zucchini flowers, slow-cooked beef stew with pasta, mushroom-and ham-stuffed artichokes simmered in wine, as well as the catch of the day, finishing with a crème brûlée, all of which make for simple pleasures.

● La Grotte   Ⓝ SIM

Calanque de Callelongue (8th arr.).
Tel. 04 91 73 17 79.
A la carte: 30–100€.

The three dining rooms with their chandeliers, mirrors, 19th-century canvases, a patio plus a terrace, make for a baroque setting for lunching with friends in an atmosphere of romantic dining. Neighboring fishermen bring back their catch to be cooked simply (Mediterranean sea bass, rouget, one spot sea bream, turbot and sole). Rockfish soup, fried Mediterranean shellfish or squid stuffed with shallots and tomatoes and simmered in white wine are easy to eat. Kids, too, adore various pizzas (anchovy, goat cheese, Provençal). The pewter countertop and the old brass cash register give the impression you've stepped into the past.

● Le Lunch   Ⓝ SIM

Calanque de Sormiou (9th arr.).
Tel. 04 91 25 05 37.

Closed mid-Oct.–mid-Mar.
A la carte: 65€.

A sought-after little paradise at the end of a beach nestled between two rocks. Christophe Négrel has taken over at the stove with a vengeance. This home-grown lad has stopped in many fine establishments (Ducasse, Martinez, Fenière at Lourmarin, Icône at Aix) before coming home to roost. His agenda: reworking the freshest products of the ocean fished by Jean-Claude Bianco, using simple, good ideas based on the season, a spirit of adventure and lightness of fare. The cuttlefish fry, the octopus with hummus, the stuffed scorpion fish braised in the local style, bouillabaisse in two courses and a simply grilled catch of the day are moments of true happiness.

● La Marine   Ⓝ SIM

16, rue Désiré Pellaprat (8th arr.).
Tel. 04 91 25 28 76.
www.restaurant–marseille.net
Closed beg. Jan.–10 Feb.
Prix fixe: 24€. A la carte: 40€.

This fisherman's hut *cum* brasserie, with its terrace overlooking the Goudes port, is an informal address although Fabrice Garaut is a serious manager. This former sailor and skipper has been docking here for a year now. Low prices and a 24 lunch menu are a steal. Fish raised in the neighboring farm along with the catch of the day, oven-browned mussels and almonds, grilled sea bream or Mediterranean sea bass and a pan-fried seafood brochette (jumbo shrimp, scallops, mussels) won't ruin the passing shopper any more than the regular customer happy to get such a bargain.

● Carbone   SIM

22, rue Sainte (1st arr.).
Tel.-Fax 04 91 55 52 73.
Closed dinner (July–Aug.), Sun.
Prix fixe: 10€ (lunch), 15€ (lunch),
18€ (lunch), 30€ (dinner). A la carte: 50€.

The décor is modern and cozy. Yohann Paolaci's cooking follows and Christian

Planel is a tactful host. Not much new to say about the artichoke-stuffed ravioli, duck carpaccio wth soy sauce, duck breast with honey and sesame, strawberry mille-feuille with vanilla-flavored cream and the warm green apple and chocolate spring rolls. This spot is trendy but good.

● **Chez Etienne** SIM

43, rue de Lorette (2nd arr.).
No tel.

Pizza means Etienne aka Cassaro aka le Panier. This is the only place to eat extra-thin pizza with tomato and mozzarella just how you like it. There's no phone and booking is doubtful, but what makes this place is its simplicity. A few nicely cooked pastas and exquisite meats complete the house's range.

● **504** SIM

34, pl aux Huiles (1st arr.).
Tel. 04 91 33 57 74. Fax 04 42 50 60 91.
Closed Mon. lunch, Christmas, 1 May, Aug.
Prix fixe: 30€ (wine inc.) 10€ (child).
A la carte: 55€.

Akim Berkani is an attentive ambassador of this Moroccan outpost. Feast on various stuffed filo pastries, the fish trio, a red spice-seasoned tagine, the royal-style couscous or spit-roasted lamb. Wines from the Maghreb stand up for themselves and the dessert (a chocolate pastilla) is imaginative.

● **L'Escale** SIM

2, bd Alexandre-Delabre (8th arr.)
Les Goudes.
Tel. 04 91 73 16 78. Fax 04 91 73 52 12.
Closed Mon. (off season), Tue. (off season).
A la carte: 60€.

This famous institution of the Goudes, prettily overlooking the Mediterranean, has been taken over by André Agobian, owner of La Grotte. This design buff is about to freshen up the décor (perhaps it will be done the day you decide to check in here). In the kitchen, the bounty of the sea takes pride of place. The fare, which is served in the boat cabin-style dining room or on the terrace overlooking the horizon, may not be exactly haute cuisine but is perfectly straightforward. An octopus salad, oven-browned mussels, the Mediterranean sea bass carpaccio, spaghetti with langouste, local bourride (a fish stew with aïoli) or bouillabaisse, monkfish stew and jumbo shrimp with Bandol wine jus slip down nicely.

● **Honoré** SIM

121, rue Sainte (1st arr.).
Tel. 04 91 33 08 34. Fax 04 91 33 00 36.
www.honore-online.com
Closed Sun., Mon., Aug.
A la carte: 27€.

In her children's clothes boutique, Annick Lestrohan has opened a welcoming Spanish restaurant with slate walls and rattan chairs. The Pata Negra ham, gazpacho, zucchini with coriander-seasoned honey, squid in its ink and the house berry crumble sustain an attractive menu.

● **La Ferme** SIM

23, rue Sainte (1st arr.).
Tel. 04 91 33 21 12. Fax 04 91 33 81 21.
restaurant.la.ferme@wanadoo
Closed Sat. lunch, Sun., 1 week beg. Jan., Aug.
Prix fixe: 30€ (wine inc.), 39€, 44€.

There's something for everyone in this rural farm. Dig in happily to the shellfish cannelloni, zucchini flowers stuffed with rouget mousse and served with mushroom sauce, the big langoustine ravioli with scallops and the mixed fish grill with anchovy sauce. Nothing chichi, just a well-thought-out menu.

MARTEL

46600 Lot. Paris 511 – Brive 34 –
Cahors 78 – Saint-Céré 31.
martel2@wanadoo.fr.
The town with seven towers proudly exhibits its ancient houses. The lovely Place des Consuls is a must-see on market day.

■ **HOTELS-RESTAURANTS**

■ Relais Sainte-Anne

Rue du Pourtanel.
Tel. 05 65 37 40 56. Fax 05 65 37 42 82.
www.relais-sainte-anne.com
Closed mid-Nov.–mid-Mar.
11 rooms: 70–160€. 5 suites: 135–245€.

Pierre Bettler has turned this ancient parochial school into a charming hotel with pastel-colored rooms done up in a contemporary style. The warm welcome, swimming pool and flower-filled garden are an added balm.

● Au Hasard Balthazar   [SIM]

Rue Tournemire.
Tel. 05 65 37 42 01. Fax 05 65 37 42 09.
www.lesbouriettes.com
Closed Mon., Oct.–Easter.
Prix fixe: 15,50€, 24,50€, 8€ (child).
A la carte: 32–38€.

Products are for sale and there are lots of yummy things to taste: everything in this real/faux old-fashioned café is chic and bohemian. Under the watchful eye of Philippe and Patrick Beille, Philippe Aubertin cooks up Quercy. A goat cheese timbale, foie gras with fleur de sel, a duck breast with Cahors-style sauce and the tiramisu with walnut sauce are pleasing. Nice wine list.

MARTRES-TOLOSANE

31220 Haute-Garonne. Paris 765 –
Toulouse 60 – Saint-Gaudens 32 –
Bagnères de Bigorre 97.
A pleasant stop on the road to Comminges.

■ **HOTELS-RESTAURANTS**

■ Castet

44, av; de la Gare.
Tel. 05 61 98 80 20. Fax 05 61 98 61 02.
hotelcastet@wanadoo.fr
Closed Sun. dinner, Mon.
12 rooms: 36–39€.
Prix fixe: 25€, 27€, 45€. A la carte: 55€.

Gilles Sales' country hotel with its swimming pool and rustic rooms doesn't just lay claim to comfort. His table makes it a gastronomic high spot. In the newly renovated dining room, big pan-fried langoustines served in truffle-seasoned bouillon, a lobster with leeks and celery root emulsion sauce, veal roast braised in a cocotte with ceps and a poached pear with grapes, served with house brioche, slip down very nicely.

MARTILLAC see BORDEAUX

MASEVAUX

68290 Haut-Rhin. Paris 441 – Altkirch 30 –
Colmar 57 – Mulhouse 29.
ot.masevaux@wanadoo.fr.
At the gateway of the Territoire of Belfort, this peaceful town is one of the frontiers of the province. The ballon d'Alsace is not far nor is the Asfeld lake and its attractive walks in the nearby woods.

■ **HOTELS-RESTAURANTS**

■ Hostellerie Alsacienne

16, rue du Maréchal-Foch.
Tel.-Fax 03 89 82 45 25.
http://perso.wanadoo.fr/hostellerie.alsacienne
Closed 3 weeks Oct., 1 week Christmas–New Year's.
Rest. closed Mon.
8 rooms: 44–53€.
Prix fixe: 12€ (lunch), 24€, 38€, 43€, 9,15€ (child). A la carte: 44€.

Philippe Battman takes you under his wing in order to help you discover his version of regional recipes. Pan-seared duck foie gras, fish choucroute, almond-crusted trout with shredded rutabaga salad, pork cheeks simmered in amber beer and the slow-cooked figs seasoned with star anise and served hot with pistachio ice cream make for a nice finish. A typically regional décor with carved paneling and well-balanced prices make this a choice address. Pretty rooms redone in 1930's Alsatian style.

MASSAGUEL

81110 Tarn. Paris 670. Castres 15 –
Mamazet 21 – Lautrec 26 –
Castelnaudary 29 – Carcassonne 37.
A stopover in pastel country right in the heart
of the land of plenty.

| | RESTAURANTS |

● **Auberge des Chevaliers**
Pl de la Fontaine.
Tel.-Fax 05 63 50 32 33.
Closed Mon. dinner, Tue., 2 weeks Feb.
Prix fixe: 13€, 20,50€, 24€, 29,50€,
10€ (child).

In his picture-postcard inn with its old
beams and sparkling copper pots, Serge
Lavigne is an honest-to-goodness traditionalist. Pick from a number of tasty
menus, his country-style escargot brochette with smoked bacon, the cod filet
with lentils and coriander seeds, pork
trotter and ceps wrapped in caul lace and
the apple meringue pie.

MASSIGNAC

16310 Charente. Paris 440 – Angoulême 45
– Nontron 56 – Rochechouart 18 –
La Rochefoucauld 23.
Lots of Romanesque churches, the death lantern
at Cellefroin and the château of Rochebrune at
Etagnac are an indication of what you may find
in this lovely Charentais countryside.

| | HOTELS-RESTAURANTS |

■ **Le Domaine des Etangs**
Tel. 05 45 61 85 00. Fax 05 45 61 85 01.
info@domainedesetangs.fr
www.domainedesetangs.fr
Closed beg. Jan.–mid-Mar. Rest. closed Sun.
dinner (exc.July–Aug.), Mon., Tue. (exc.
July–Aug.).
22 rooms: 130–165€.
2 suites: 210–400€.
Prix fixe: 28€ (weekday), 36€, 45€.
A la carte: 50–65€.

This estate is the stuff of legend thanks
to its hamlet of houses and their bedrooms dotted around numerous ponds,
the swimming pool, tennis court, restaurant in the old stables, kitchen garden
and… Limousin cattle-raising operation. A subtle mix of luxury and simplicity, contemporary design, old stones, wood
paneling and glass. Everything has been
thought out down to the last detail by
that master, Marc Aupiais, including what
goes on in the kitchen: a simple seasonal
vegetable soup, a monkfish and vegetable mille-feuille with a beet caramel and
carrot reduction, the Barbachon poultry
breast stuffed with foie gras served with a
tarragon sauce, the hot pastilla with dried
fruit and caramel sauce. Finally, nothing
like a boat trip to top your pleasure.

MAUBEC see CAVAILLON

MAUSSANE-LES-ALPILLES

13520 Bouches-du-Rhône. Paris 714 –
Avignon 29 – Arles 19 – Marseille 82 –
Martigues 44.
contact@maussane.com.
The green heart of the Alpilles, which produces
a world-famous olive oil.

| | HOTELS-RESTAURANTS |

■ **Val Baussenc**
122, av de la Vallée-des-Baux.
Tel. 04 90 54 38 90. Fax 04 90 54 33 36.
www.valbaussenc.com
Closed beg. Nov.–end Feb.
Rest. closed lunch (exc. July–Aug.), Wed.
22 rooms: 69–199€.
Prix fixe: 25€, 30€, 33€, 12€ (child).
A la carte: 50–61 €.

Cool rooms in the summer, heated pool
in the winter: this large, Provençal house
is highly frequentable. Add the warmth
of the staff, the discreet service and the
sun-filled dishes on offer. Sit down with
alacrity to savor an eggplant papeton with
cool tomato coulis, the vanilla-seasoned
jumbo shrimp, a toro rib eye pan roasted
with garlic butter and a verbena-seasoned

fresh fruit minestrone. You won't be disappointed.

■ Castillon des Baux

Quartier du Touret.
Tel. 04 90 54 31 93. Fax 04 90 54 51 31.
www.castillondesbaux.com
Closed Jan.
15 rooms: 80–120€.

The valley of les Baux, the Alpilles and the Camargue are a stone's throw from this Provençal farmhouse where Mireille and Alain Clavel invite their guests to step out of time. The rooms are large and perfectly appointed, with views over the countryside, the cypresses and the olive trees. The swimming pool is an ideal spot from which to bask in the song of the cicadas.

● Ou Ravi Provençau `COM`

34, av de la Vallée-des-Baux.
Tel. 04 90 54 31 11. Fax 04 90 54 41 03.
infos@ouravi.com / www.ouravi.com
Closed Tue., Wed., 11 Nov.–mid-Dec.
Prix fixe: 32€, 10€ (child).
A la carte: 47–55€.

Jean-François Richard has many tasks: he is there to welcome you, at the stove and in the cellar, to better serve his clients. This old-fashioned inn with its flowered garden is his den and his menus have some great offerings. In season, mushroom- and ham-stuffed purple artichokes simmered in wine, rouget filet with tapenade and an Alpilles rack of lamb with sage and roasted whole garlic share pride of place. A tip-top caramel flan for dessert and a bottle chosen in the underground cellar, which opens out onto the vineyards, completes a faultless meal.

● La Place `SIM`

65, av de la Vallée-des-Baux.
Tel. 04 90 54 23 31.
Closed Tue., Jan.
Prix fixe: 30€. A la carte: 40€.

The décor is cozy and up to date in this modern bistro in the heart of an authentic Alpilles village. A quality team led by Jean-André Charial of the Oustau guarantees a

good time. In the dining room Marco Giudicelli serves with a smile dishes lovingly prepared by Violaine Cocault, who used to work at Baumanière and who trained at the Crillon and at Arpège. A parmesan and marinated sardine tart, cod pan roasted with chorizo, the spicy lamb shoulder roast with snow peas and a thin apple tart meet with success.

In Paradou (13520). 2 km w via D17.

■ Du Côté des Olivades

Locale known as de Bourgeac.
Tel. 04 90 54 56 78. Fax 04 90 54 56 79.
www.ducotedesolivades.com
9 rooms: 95–204€. 1 suite: 195–268€.
Prix fixe: 38€, 48€, 52€. A la carte: 70€.

At Les Baux-de-Provence, this house surrounded by olive trees boasts a few modern rooms and a pleasant swimming pool, but it is mainly Nancy Bourguignon's lively cooking that draws the crowds. The pan-tossed ceps, rouget in pesto, the lamb dish and the apple tart for dessert are a delight.

● Bistro de la Petite France `COM`

55, av de la Vallée-des-Baux.
Tel. 04 90 54 41 91. Fax 04 90 54 52 50.
Closed Wed., Thu. (exc. dinner July–Aug.),
mid-Oct.–1 Dec.
Prix fixe: 25€.

After stints with Gagniere, Pinchorri in Florence and Garcia in Bordeaux, Thierry Maffré-Bogé is really at home in Le Paradou. His single daily menu offers up inspired cuisine based on market-fresh products. The house fish soup, an anise-seasoned filet of haddock and the lamb shoulder roast with slow-roasted garlic do not appear by chance any more than the generous dessert plate, composed of four desserts (baba au rhum, a three-chocolate cake, a tarte Tatin and caramel ice cream), which is irresistible. The service is prompt and guests are warmly greeted.

● Bistro du Paradou `SIM`

"Chez Jean-Louis"
57, av de la Vallée-des-Baux.
Tel.-Fax 04 90 54 32 70.

bistro .paradou@wanadoo.fr
Closed Sun., Mon., Nov., mid-Jan.–mid-Feb.
Prix fixe: 42€ (wine inc.) 20€ (child).

Regional cooking has no secrets for Mireille Pons. She knows her Provençal-style eggplant, the pot-au-feu and the leg of Alpilles lamb, her crème caramel and her tarts, with berries from local gardens, by heart. In the dining room or at the reception, considerate and smiling Jean-Louis is sure to leave you feeling pampered by your hosts.

MAZAGRAN see **METZ**

MAZAMET

81200 Tarn. Paris 740 – Albi 65 – Carcassonne 52 – Castres 20 – Toulouse 90.
A friendly flower-filled city in the heart of the Haut-Languedoc regional park at the foot of the Montagne Noire.

 | HOTELS-RESTAURANTS

■ **Mets et Plaisirs**
7, av Albert-Rouvière.
Tel. 05 63 61 59 63.
www.metsetplaisirs.com
Closed 2 weeks beg. Jan., 2 weeks end Aug.
Rest. closed Sun. dinner, Mon.
11 rooms: 42–55€.
Prix fixe: 15€ (weekdays), 23€, 50€.

In the town center across from the post office, this 1900 house, meticulously run by Jean-Pierre and Marie Bancard, has vintage style. The rooms are being renovated, the dining room is cozy and the cuisine is resolutely of Southern tradition. Cep- and ham-stuffed ravioli, a lamb blanquette with basil and the white chocolate soufflé are well done. Well-thought-out set menus.

MAZAN see **CARPENTRAS**

MEGEVE

74120 Haute-Savoie. Paris 602 – Chamonix-Mont-Blanc 36 – Albertville 31 – Annecy 61.

megeve@megeve.com.
Just before the 1920s, Baroness Maurice de Rothschild decided to found in France a prestigious Alpine resort which, summer and winter alike, would compete favorably with rivals on the other side of the Alps. The result was Megève, which has been able to hold on to its village charm. Main square, priory, museum of the Val-d'Arly, antique dealers, high-tech stores: Megève is picture-book Savoie. Add to this the benchmark establishments created by the Sibuets whose Fer à Cheval, Fermes de Marie, Mont-Blanc, and Lodge Park hotels provide a string of charming lodgings, and you understand why this gem of a resort is the summit of Alpine chic. In Megève's chalet setting, gastronomy reaches Olympian heights. Baroness Rothschild's dining room in the capable hands of Alexandre Faix, the restaurants of the Hotels de Montagne (from the Fermes de Marie to the Lodge Park) already add up well. The figurehead? Of course it is Marc Veyrat whose winter residence here has become a seasonal fixture. But you will also find his pupil Emmanuel Renaut at the Flocons de Sel, Rémy Coste, the gifted baker, Nano, who gives the warmest greetings at La Sauvageonne and Le Refuge and Paolo Venezian, the authentic Italian of Il Mirtillo. All this combines to create a culinary crossroads of the first order.

■ | HOTELS

■ **Chalet du Mont d'Arbois**
447, chemin de la Rocaille.
Tel. 04 50 21 25 03. Fax 04 50 21 24 79.
montarbois@relaischateaux.fr
www.chalet-montarbois.com
Closed mid-Oct.–mid-Dec.,
mid-Apr.–mid-June.
30 rooms: 315–990€. 8 suites: 850–3800€.
Half board: 373–1048€.

Baroness de Rothschild has transformed her home into an intimate Relais & Châteaux with a view of the surrounding mountains. Comfort and charm are the hallmarks of the rooms and the expensive suites in the Noémie chalet. Magnificent breakfasts; the spa and massage salon are relaxing.

■ Les Fermes de Marie   ✿🏠

Chem. de Riante-Colline.
Tel. 04 50 93 03 10. Fax 04 50 93 09 84.
contact@fermesdemarie.com
www.fermesdemarie.com
Closed Oct.–mid-Dec., end Apr.–mid-June.
71 rooms: 140–572€. 12 suites: 368–1285€.
Half board: 210–740€.

Jocelyne Sibuet carefully oversees this hotel which has become the benchmark of chalet style. Bedrooms, suites and public rooms have a Savoyard look and exude relaxation. Four packages allow you to taste of all the gastronomic pleasures: *pension chic, gastro, grill* and *fromagerie*. (See Restaurants.)

■ Lodge Park   🏠

100, rue d'Arly.
Tel. 04 50 93 05 03. Fax 04 50 93 09 52.
contact@lodgepark.com / www.lodgepark.com
Closed end Mar.–mid-Dec.
50 rooms: 210–350€.
11 suites: 515–1100€.
Half board: 350€.

This grand old twenties hotel set in grounds in the center of town has been redone in Adirondack style straight from the pages of a magazine with alpine rooms and suites filled with pretty wooden furniture. Fusion food. (See Restaurants.)

■ Fer à Cheval   🏠

36, rte du Crêt-d'Arbois.
Tel. 04 50 21 30 39. Fax 04 50 93 07 60.
www.feracheval-megeve.com
Closed mid-Apr.–mid-June,
mid-Sept.–mid-Dec.
49 rooms: 309–387€. 14 suites: 406–720€.
Half board: 368–505€.

Sibuet family property for generations, this warm and friendly hotel has typically Savoyard rooms. Lounging by the pool in summer is pure bliss. (See Restaurants: Alpage and Fer à Cheval.)

■ Le Mont-Blanc   🏠

Place de l'Eglise.
Tel. 04 50 21 20 02. Fax 04 50 21 45 28.
contact@hotelmontblanc.com / www.c-h-m.com
Closed 1 week at end Apr., May,
1 week beg. June.
29 rooms: 130–250€. 11 suites: 240–306€.

This local institution once haunted by Cocteau and his acolytes continues successfully under the auspices of the Sibuets. The fireside, patio, swimming pool and Jacuzzi all provide pleasant places to relax, as do the sumptuous rooms and suites. Come morning, the breakfasts make you glad you stayed.

■ Grange d'Arly   🏠

10, rue des Allobroges.
Tel. 04 50 58 77 88. Fax 04 50 93 07 13.
contact@grange-darly.com
www.grange-darly.com
Closed 1 Oct.–mid-Dec., 1 Apr.–end June.
22 rooms: 92–156€. 2 suites: 152–205€.
Half board: 122–216€.

Christine and Jean-Marie Allard have created a warm environment at their hotel where faithful clients feel at home. Cuisine and décor are typically Savoyard.

■ Chalet Saint-Georges   🏠

159, rue Monseigneur-Conseil.
Tel. 04 50 93 07 15. Fax 04 50 21 51 18.
www.hotel-chaletstgeorges.com
Closed mid-Mar.–20 June,
mid-Sept.–mid-Dec.
19 rooms: 110–470€. 5 suites: 235–650€.
Half board: 160–570€.

Winter and summer alike guests are delighted by this chalet. The heated pool, fitness center, carefully furnished rooms and two fine restaurants (the Table du Trappeur and the Table du Pêcheur) are pure bliss.

■ Au Coin du Feu   🏠

252, rte de Rochebrune.
Tel. 04 50 21 04 94. Fax 04 50 21 20 15.
contact@coindufeu.com
www.coindufeu.com
Closed mid-Apr.–mid-Dec.
23 rooms: 200–345€. Half board: 246€.

If you are looking for a friendly hotel that won't break the bank, head for the mountain home of Mireille Baud. The warm welcome, practical rooms, the family-style fare of the Saint-Nicholas and the evenings around the fire are seductive.

■ La Chaumine

36, chemin des Bouleaux.
Tel. 04 50 21 37 05. Fax 04 50 21 37 21.
Closed mid-Apr.–beg. July, 1 Sept.–22 Dec.
11 rooms: 71–105€.

Megève's best value for money? No doubt this 19th-century farmhouse where you get an adorable welcome and eleven rooms that look out over the Alpine meadows and the village below.

■ Terass Park Hôtel

377, rte d'Odier.
Tel. 04 50 21 04 76. Fax 04 50 58 78 78.
terrasspark@wanadoo.fr
www.terrasspark.com
Rest. closed lunch, 1 Oct.–mid-Dec.,
mid-Apr.–1 July.
18 rooms: 80–130€.
Prix fixe: 28€, 15€ (child).

Delphine Reverberi carefully manages this friendly chalet which boasts renovated rooms and baths and a sauna. The spacious terrace overlooks the cross-country ski trails and the lounge with fireplace set the tone. The half-board cuisine is copious and Thursday's Savoyard evening full of fun.

■ Au Coeur de Megève

44, rue Charles-Feige.
Tel. 04 50 21 25 30. Fax 04 50 91 91 27.
info@hotel-megeve.com
www.hotel-megeve.com
Rest. closed Tue. (off season), Wed. (off season).
29 rooms: 85–180€. 7 suites: 131–400€.
Prix fixe: 20€ (lunch), 30€, 37€,
8,50€ (child). A la carte: 45€.

In the heart of the village, the flower-filled garden, the pretty rooms, the thoughtful welcome and the cozy lounge set the tone. Thierry Salagros' fine cuisine is a combination of Savoyard products and flavors from afar.

■ Ferme Hôtel Duvillard

3048, rte du Mont-d'Arbois.
Tel. 04 50 21 14 62. Fax 04 50 21 42 82.
ferme.duvillard@wanadoo.fr
Closed Oct.–mid-Dec., 10 Apr.–mid-June.
19 rooms: 121–262€.

Even under new management, the Duvillard's chalet has kept its Alpine style thanks to a sunlit terrace and summer swimming pool.

■ La Prairie et le Chalet des Griottes

407, rue Charles-Feige.
Tel. 04 50 21 48 55. Fax 04 50 21 42 13.
www.hotellaprairie.com
Closed Oct.–end Nov., May.
32 rooms: 79–150€.

The wood paneled interiors add warmth to this tranquil hotel. Les Griottes, across the way, is a seven-room chalet ideal for a stay with family or friends. Terrace.

■ Au Vieux Moulin

188, rue A.-Martin.
Tel. 04 50 21 22 29. Fax 04 50 93 07 91.
www.vieuxmoulin.com
Closed Oct.–mid-Dec., beg. Apr.–end May.
38 rooms: 145–240€. 1 suite: 320–390€.

Family atmosphere at this hotel with comfortable rooms where the swimming pool, beauty-fitness center and lounge provide activities for all. Quality home cooking and reasonable prices.

■ La Crémaillère

288, rte du Crêt-du-Midi.
Tel. 04 50 21 21 49. Fax 04 50 58 78 40.
www.lacremaillere.megeve.com
Closed mid-Apr.–mid-June,
mid-June–mid-Dec.
15 rooms: 85–117€.
Prix fixe: 26€.

Denis and Laurence Devesa have added a family touch to their establishment. The well-conceived rooms can accommodate up to five people. The town center is nearby and the cuisine is classic (trout, blanquette, apple tart, gâteau Basque).

● RESTAURANTS

● **Chalet du Mont d'Arbois**

At the Chalet du Mont d'Arbois,
447, chemin de la Rocaille.
Tel. 04 50 21 25 03. Fax 04 50 21 24 79.
montarbois@relaischateaux.fr
www.chalet-montarbois.com
Closed weekdays lunch (exc. vac.),
Mon. (exc. vac.), mid-Oct.–mid-Dec.,
mid-Apr.–mid-June.
Prix fixe: 60€, 110€, 25€ (child).
A la carte: 110€.

Authenticity and refinement are the happy twin attributes of this spacious Alpine-style dining room. Service is punctilious under the leadership of Philippe Standaert. Wise advice and contagious good humor add to the pleasure of choosing one of Olivier Bardoux's tasty delicacies. Bardoux, who used to work with Laurent in Paris and Haeberlin at the Aubege de l'Ill, cooks lively dishes like the parmesan biscuit with eggplant caviar and sardines, strips of Atlantic sea bass slow-cooked at low temperature and served with osciètre caviar and cauliflower cream, calf's liver in a bed of arugula and fried onion and the traditional soufflé. A continuous joy completed by a cellar boasting of 900 different wines.

● **Flocons de Sel**

75, rue Saint-François.
Tel. 04 50 21 49 99. Fax 04 50 21 68 22.
restaurant@floconsdesel.com
www.floconsdesel.com
Closed Mon. lunch (off season),
Tue. lunch (off season),
Thu. lunch (off season), Nov., June.
Prix fixe: 55€ (lunch), 100€.

Emmanuel Renaut, "Manu" to his friends, is the rising star of Megève. His goal? The creation, on the heights of Rochebrune, of a hotel-restaurant worthy of his talent. Meanwhile, this former right-hand man of Marc Veyrat, Meilleur Ouvrier de France laureate, formerly chef at Claridge's in London, continues to cook up a storm in his charming chalet in the middle of the resort. In a warm, intimate, wood-paneled setting, you will taste cuisine with a crisp and lively personal style, up to date yet rooted in the traditions of this hard-working Northern Frenchman who has taken to the Savoie with gusto. The creamy sea urchin, Jerusalem artichoke cakes with artichokes and cardoons served with a butter-enriched truffle bouillon, crayfish in aspic served over creamed corn, vegetable mille-feuille with chanterelles in vinaigrette and the farm-raised pigeon with wild blueberry sauce undoes, shocks and seduces us. The balloon-like chocolate puff, flambéed with pear liqueur, is magical, an experience not to be missed. Everything this golden-fingered wonder-boy does is admirable.

● **L'Alpage**

At the Fer à Cheval, 36, rte du Crêt-d'Arbois.
Tel. 04 50 21 30 39. Fax 04 50 93 07 60.
www.feracheval-megeve.com
Closed Mon., Tue., lunch (exc. vac.),
beg. Apr.–mid-Dec.
A la carte: 57€.

Marc Sibuet has turned this chic chalet-style annex into a shrine of regional goodies: raclettes, tartiflettes, fondues and Réblochonnades, all delicious, are served in front of the fireplace. A berry tart to conclude and it's time to rest up before heading back to the ski slopes. Another address, Les Molliettes, is open for lunch in the summer; nature lovers, especially, will enjoy the Alpine swimming pool.

● **Lodge Park**

At the Lodge Park, 100, rue d'Arly.
Tel. 04 50 93 05 03. Fax 04 50 93 09 52.
contact@lodgepark.com / www.lodgepark.com
Closed beg. Apr.–mid-Dec.
A la carte: 80€.

Thierry Guinot left the Vosges to come to Savoie where he offers up-to-date cuisine in a warm, modern *rôtisserie* setting. His delicate, structured dishes are a tasty recital. Witness the big crab claw stir fry, the foie gras hamburger with a cinnamon apple, salmon trout with sautéed chanterelles with parsley and garlic sauce and the bison shoulder roast with a sweet potato emulsion. Huge dessert table and a clever wine list.

● **La Taverne du Mont d'Arbois** `COM`

2811, rte Edmond-de-Rothschild.
Tel. 04 50 21 03 53. Fax 04 50 58 93 02.
www.chalet-montarbois.com
Closed 1 Nov.–mid-Dec., 1 May–mid-June.
Prix fixe: 40€ (weekday dinner),
50€ (wine inc. dinner). A la carte: 64–79€.

The tavern, under the guidance of Alexandre Faix of the Mont d'Arbois, goes its merry way with the rigorous Eric Souverain at the stove. Beamed ceilings and wood paneling give a warm feeling to the establishment. Smoked salmon, the tomato mozarella tart, lake whitefish, slow-cooked lamb shank and the famous Paris-Brest (a choux pastry ring with almonds and butter cream) are a delight. Attentive service with a smile.

● **L'Esquinade** `COM`

201, rue de la Poste.
Tel.-Fax 04 50 93 15 32.
www.lesquinade-megeve.com
Closed lunch (summer), beg. Apr.–mid-June, beg. Sept.–mid-Dec.
A la carte: 65€.

A revolving menu with variations on fusion food at this trendy spot with its narrow bar, long counter, minimalist décor with a few Alpine touches, background music and designer restrooms. From 7 pm to 2 am, Gérard Dalzotto enlivens this fine establishment where you can try a foie gras duo, roasted Mediterranean sea bass in a salt crust and the enormous grilled shrimp, prepared with care by the serious Loïc Normand.

● **L'Atelier** `SIM`

2811, rte Edmond de Rothschild.
Tel. 04 50 21 03 53.
montdarbois@relaischateau.fr
Closed lunch, Mon., Tue., mid-Apr.–end June, mid-Sept.–mid-Dec.
Prix fixe: 50€.

This chic rustic "studio" with designer lighting and wood paneled décor is all charm. The service is polished, the combinations clever and the cuisine of Bernard Ferrand full of wit. Scallop carpaccio, the Réblochon bonbon with a truffled Jerusalem artichoke sauce and the roasted monkfish with mandarin and Espelette pepper sauce will leave you with happy memories. Nice wines from the domaine Rothschild and elsewhere (Roussette, Mondeuse).

● **Idéal** `SIM`

3001 route Edmond-de-Rothschild, Idéal 1850.
Tel. 04 50 21 31 26. Fax 04 50 93 02 63.
Closed dinner, mid-Apr.–mid-Dec.
Prix fixe: 17€ (child). A la carte: 50€.

The terrace touches Mont Blanc, the interiors are full of Alpine charm, the chic rustic cuisine is spit-roasted and the clientele is laid back. In short, this is the finest Alpine restaurant in Savoie. Creamy pumpkin soup, a bacon and Beaufort cheese tart, roasted leg of lamb and poultry with morels and polenta are classics we never tire of. Attentive service under the leadership of Vincent, who keeps an eye on everything.

● **Puck**

31, Rue Oberstdorf.
Tel. 04 50 21 06 61. Fax 04 50 21 68 22.
Closed Sun. dinner, Mon.
Prix fixe: 28€ (lunch, wine inc.),
15€ (child). A la carte: 40€.

Just behind the ice rink, this annex of Emmanuel Renaut's Flocons de Sel serves up sunny cuisine all day and well into the night. Slow-cooked eggplant with thyme and orange, lake whitefish with lemon risotto, pork tenderloin medallion with wild mushrooms and a white chocolate mousse served in a glass with apricot come with a wide choice of wines by the glass or by the bottle. Service is relaxed, the welcome warm and the terrace pleasant.

● Face au Mont-Blanc   N SIM

7310, rte du Jaillet.
Tel. 04 50 93 07 15. Fax 04 50 21 51 18.
www.hotel-chaletstgeorges.com
Closed dinner, beg. Apr.–end June,
beg. Sept.–mid-Dec.
Prix fixe: 27€ (lunch), 32€ (lunch),
38€ (lunch), 14€ (child, lunch).

In this mountain-top restaurant Yves Fourmier offers an appetizer buffet, jumbo shrimp brochette, spicy braised lamb shank and a dessert buffet which please the skiers hungry after a morning on the slopes. At the foot of the Jaillet ski-lift, the atmosphere is guaranteed and the prices are moderate.

● L'Alpette   SIM

Massif de Rochebrune.
Tel. 04 50 21 03 69.
www.restaurant-alpette.com
Closed lunch, Sept.–mid-Dec., mid-Apr.–
beg. July.
Prix fixe: 22€, 29€. A la carte: 50–60€.

The perfect place to regroup at noon after a morning on the slopes. Skiers and hikers will rejoice in the morels in brioche, tuna steak with pain d'epices and the lamb shank with acacia honey. Tartiflette and raclette are also on offer. The terrace is lively, the service is relaxed, the setting sumptuous—only the prices are a bit too steep.

● Chalet du Radaz   SIM

4800, rte de la Cote-2000. 8 km se.
Tel. 04 50 58 94 44.
Closed dinner, end Sept.–mid-Dec.,
beg. May–10 July
A la carte: 45€.

This restaurant set in the Alpine meadows has been completely redone since becoming the rendezvous for skiers who, under Brigitte Blanchet's watchful eye, are happy to treat themselves to the hot Réblochon salad, charcuterie and country cheeses, blanquette and pot-au-feu produced by Emmanuel Clus. House tarts and the crème brûlée slip down nicely.

● Le Cintra   SIM

196, pl de l'Eglise.
Tel. 04 50 21 02 60. Fax 04 50 91 90 04.
lecintra@wanadoo.fr
Closed mid-Apr.–mid-June.
Prix fixe: 38,70€, 11€ (child).
A la carte: 55€.

In the heart of town, this famous brasserie is low key, with quick service and good standard fare. Evelyne and Patrick Mourot, with chef Stéphane Burnous, serve game terrine, roasted sea bream with onion sauce, sole meunière, tête de veau, a slice of calf's liver and a Paris-Brest for dessert, always in top form.

● La Cote 2000   SIM

3461, rte de la Cote-2000, 8 km se.
Tel. 04 50 21 31 84. Fax 04 50 93 02 63.
www.chalet-moutarbois.com
Closed mid-Apr.–mid-June,
mid-Oct.–mid-Dec.
Prix fixe: 15€ (child). A la carte: 65€.

Alexandre Faix, master of the domain of the Mont d'Arbois, has turned this spacious chalet into the success story of Megève. On the heights of the Mont d'Arbois, outside on the terrace if it is fair, inside if it is not, you will find Réblochon samosas, salmon trout seasoned with parsley and garlic and pan fried in butter, a Beaufort tourte and a honey-roasted pear. Careful of the hot-tempered service when everyone comes in from the slopes.

● Les Drets   SIM

2803, rte de la Cote-2000, 8 km se.
Tel. 04 50 21 31 78.
Closed end mid-Sept.–mid-Dec.,
end Apr.–mid-June.
Prix fixe: 21,50€ (lunch). A la carte: 25€.

Straightforward and fun, this Alpine inn offers fine homey dishes prepared by Serge Cayuela. A house terrine, endive salad, locally hunted wild rabbit served with polenta and the blueberry tart slip down well.

● Le Matou `SIM`

At the foot of téléphérique de Rochebrune.
Tel. 04 50 58 97 77.
le.matou@tiscali.fr
Closed Oct.–end Nov., mid-Apr.–end May.
Prix fixe: 10€ (child). A la carte: 35€.

Fabien Donoyan is the sweetheart of the skiers at the foot of Rochebrune. In his wood-paneled tavern with a terrace, he serves tasty, fresh, inexpensive dishes that express all the best of Savoie. You'll never tire of Réblochon spring rolls, the house terrine with pistachios, morels in puff pastry and chitterling sausage with mustard sauce. The desserts (notably a raspberry and lychee clafoutis) are a delight.

● Auberge du Bel Alpage `SIM`

489, rte Nationale.
Tel. 04 50 21 26 82.
www.auberge-du-bel-alpage.com
Closed Mon. (off season), Tue. (off season),
Wed. (off season), 3 weeks Dec.,
Easter–end May.
Prix fixe: 28€, 33€.

François Ando has made his mark in this neat roadside inn decorated in wood and linen. Foie gras mille-feuille, the salmon trout filet with truffles and the slow-roasted lamb shank seasoned with spices and orange are carefully prepared. For dessert, the berry sabayon slips down nicely. Great set menus.

● Le Vieux Megève `SIM`

58, pl de la Résistance (across from the central parking lot).
Tel. 04 50 21 16 44. Fax 04 50 93 06 69.
www.py-internet.com/vieux-megeve
Closed mid-Sept.–mid-Dec.,
mid-Apr.–mid-June.
Prix fixe: 22,50€ (lunch), 24,50€ (lunch),
9,50€ (child). A la carte: 50€.

The Delacquis have made their old chalet one of Megève's institutions. The fifties décor has style and the food is in keeping with its tone. Charcuterie, smoked salmon, coq au vin, escalope viennoise and the raspberry cup are all in the best tradition.

In Leutaz (74120). 4 km sw via rte du Bouchet.

● La Sauvageonne `COM`

"Chez Nano"
Hameau de Leutaz.
Tel. 04 50 91 90 81. Fax 04 50 58 75 44.
www.sauvageonne-refuge.com
Closed mid-Sept.–mid-Dec., mid-Apr.–beg. July.
Prix fixe: 30€ (lunch), 10€ (child).
A la carte: 70€.

Jean-Marc Fanara, Nano for short, has turned this old chalet into a unique spot with a thirties bar and smoking room and a beautiful dining room with a beamed ceiling and wood carvings. Clients come to please the eye as well as the palate with authentic dishes that combine Savoyard and Mediterranean tastes. The truffle-seasoned slow-simmered meat stew, the duck confit and cep cannelloni, the roasted cod with licorice root–seasoned slow-cooked fennel bulbs, the Middle Eastern–style slow-cooked lamb shank and the mountain honey soufflé are just right. Anyone who is anyone in Megève or Paris parties here until the wee hours.

In Leutaz.

● Le Refuge `SIM`

Rte de Leutaz.
Tel. 04 50 21 23 04. Fax 04 50 91 99 76.
www.sauvageonne-refuge.com
Closed Sun. dinner (off season),
Mon. (off season), Tue. (off season),
mid-June–mid-July, mid-Oct.–mid-Nov.
Prix fixe: 22€ (lunch), 27€ (lunch).
A la carte: 52€.

Nano of La Sauvageonne sold his annex to his chef Franck Soyer who plays in a serious register. Poached egg with morels and a slice of foie gras, a chestnut Chartreuse, a spit-roasted lamb shank with a Grenaille new potato fricassée and a fruit minestrone look fine. The wines are chosen with flair and the lunchtime set menus a godsend. Pretty chalet setting.

57960 Moselle. Paris 440 –
Sarreguemines 38 – Saverne 40 – Bitche 12
– Strasbourg 62.

In the heart of glass country, an art center in a museum in an old factory draws people from around the world.

 HOTELS-RESTAURANTS

■ **Auberge des Mésanges**

2, rue du Tiseur.
Tel. 03 87 96 92 28. Fax 03 87 96 99 14.
www.aubergedesmesanges.com
Closed 1 week Christmas–New Year's, Feb.
vac. Rest. closed Sun. dinner, Mon.
20 rooms: 33–51€.
Prix fixe: 9,50€ (weekday lunch), 17€,
7€ (child). A la carte: 33€.

In this modern inn in his adopted village, Pascal Walter, born in Sarreguemines, trained by Schneider at Saint-Walfrid, then at the Grand Hôtel de la Reine in Nancy, proves that you can give good value for money and renew your repertoire. In a 1980-90s hotel, he set up an old-fashioned tavern with wood furniture that refers back to the traditional style of Lorraine. From the kitchen you will enjoy the duck foie gras wrapped in smoked ham, oven-baked mixed fish and potatoes and a rabbit and mushroom tourte. This cleverly developed cuisine lightens and modernizes traditional fare while tipping its hat to days gone by. Tidy rooms.

MELLE

79500 Deux-Sèvres. Paris 390 – Niort 32 –
Poitiers 62 – Saint-Jean-d'Angély 47.
In the heart of Poitou, ruled over by Queen Ségolène.

 HOTELS-RESTAURANTS

■ **L'Argentière**

In St-Martin, 2 km. via rte de Niort.
Tel. 05 49 29 13 22. Fax 05 49 29 06 63.
hotel-restaurant.largentiere@wanadoo.fr
Rest. closed Fri. dinner (Nov.–Mar.),
Sun. dinner, Mon. lunch.
18 rooms: 41–43€.
Prix fixe: 14€ (weekdays), 20€, 29€.

Buildings with a Mediterranean look house functional, brightly colored rooms. Regional-style cuisine served in a modern dining room or under the garden arbor.

● **Les Glycines**

5, pl R.-Groussard.
Tel. 05 49 27 01 11. Fax 05 49 27 93 45.
www.hotel-lesglycines.com
Closed 2 weeks Jan.
Rest. closed Sun. dinner (off season), Mon.
7 rooms: 39–54€.
Prix fixe: 16,80€, 24,80€, 39€,
12€ (child).

Cozy rooms, a restaurant in the conservatory and a brasserie all add to the charm of this establishment. Eric Caillon and Christopher Auger offer modern cuisine based on regional products. Foie gras bonbons with potatoes, line-fished Atlantic sea bass with thyme, grilled sirloin steak with Anjou wine sauce and a fig trio with salted-butter caramel ice cream as the sweet finish. Fine wines from the West of France.

MELLES

31440 Haute-Garonne. Paris 790 –
Toulouse 115 – Saint-Gaudens 32 –
Luchon 27.
Hikers paradise, a pretty mountain town between the Garonne and Aran valleys on the GR 10 trail.

 HOTELS-RESTAURANTS

■ **Auberge du Crabère**

Tel. 05 61 79 21 99. Fax 05 61 79 74 71.
patrick.beauchet@wanadoo.fr
Closed Tue. (exc. vac.), Wed. (exc. vac.),
11 Nov.–mid-Dec.
6 rooms: 31–40€. 2 suites: 90–125€.
Prix fixe: 25€. A la carte: 45€.

Patrick Beauchet loves his region. In his inn this modest man devotes himself entirely to his craft. Mountain soup, trout in papillote with wild herbs, lamb with duck liver and an Armagnac-flavored cake for dessert make copious meals in front of the fire in winter or on the terrace overlooking the mountains in summer. Welcome with a smile and cozy rooms a plus.

MELUN

77000 Seine-et-Marne. Paris 47 – Fontainebleau 18 – Orléans 104 – Troyes 108. The fine church of Saint-Aspais, old narrow streets, a provincial air on the outskirts of Paris and fine stalls in the market.

● | RESTAURANTS

● Le Mariette
31, rue Saint-Amboise.
Tel. 01 64 37 06 06. Fax 01 64 37 00 47.
Closed Sat. lunch, Sun., Mon. dinner.
3 weeks Aug.
Prix fixe: 26€ (weekday lunch), 36€, 65€.
A la carte: 75€.

Bertrand Barbier, who was chef for four years at the Bas Bréau in Barbizon, has taken over this town center restaurant with gusto. The bright red and blue décor is a bit loud, but the cuisine of this chef who used to work at Lucas-Carton, the Grand-Véfour and La Marée is precise and faultless. Tuna mille-feuille (tartare style), salmon medallions with sesame and the slow-cooked lamb shoulder roast with eggplant cream are great.

● Le Spagho
10, quai Hippolyte-Rossignol.
Tel. 01 64 41 65 97.
Closed Sun.
A la carte: 35€.

Giovanni Sabatino from Puglia has turned this modern red, pink and black den, with the kitchen in the middle of the dining room and a huge zinc bar, into a showcase for sunny Italy right on the Seine. This jolly fellow from Foggia makes his quayside restaurant seem like the shores of the Mediterranean. Squid with hot pepper sauce, arugula panzerotti, mozzarella and parmesan, nettles served with meat balls, veal roll with sage, along with an easy red Salice Salentino from Italy, slip down easily.

● L'Atelier des Saveurs
6, pl Jacques-Amyot.
Tel. 01 64 52 10 92. Fax 01 64 52 41 73.
Closed dinner, Sun., Mon., 1 week beg. Jan.,
3 weeks Aug.
Prix fixe: 19€.

Eddy Creuze sold the Mariette to create this studio-salon where you can sample the dish of the day at lunch (19 plus 5,50 for dessert). The bright modern white, red and black setting sparkles. The menu changes daily (for example, pollock and shrimp soufflé, served with Espelette pepper-seasoned beurre blanc, followed by a pork tenderloin medallion with spicy caramel and hazelnut risotto). Tea is served in the afternoon—a good excuse to try the apple and berry *verrine* and the thin pineapple tart with brown sugar. Evenings from Tuesday to Friday Eddy becomes a cooking teacher for would-be Cordon Bleus.

● La Bodega
18, quai Hippolyte-Rossignol.
Tel. 01 64 37 10 57.
Closed Sat. lunch, Sun., Mon. dinner,
2 weeks end Aug.
A la carte: 35€.

This little showcase for Iberian cuisine allows you to try lively dishes in a colorful setting decorated with paintings and posters of bullfights. Grilled squid, tomato cake, paella, a mixed meat parrillada, as well as turron and crème catalane, produced by Ana Roth from Asturia, are truly authentic. The Mas Rabell de Torrès is easy to drink with it all.

● Yo!
Centre commercial Carré Sénart,
3 allée du Préambule, 77127 Lieusaint.
Tel. 01 60 60 10 98. Fax 01 60 60 08 70.
www.yosushi.com
Prix fixe: 9,90€ (weekday lunch).
A la carte: 20€.

In the middle of the mall, this Asian restaurant has a conveyor belt from which to grab the angelhair pasta (kadaïf)-wrapped Black Tiger shrimp, the Iso Yo roll (sushi where the rice is on the outside and enrobed in tobiko orange, fish eggs and an inner core of salmon and avocado) and truffon. Prices are unbeatable and water, fizzy or still, is on the house.

In Le Plessis-Picard (77550). 10 km n.

● **La Mare au Diable**
Parc du Plessis-Picard.
Tel. 01 64 10 20 90. Fax 01 64 10 20 91.
mareaudiable@wanadoo.fr
www.lamareaudiable.fr
Closed Sun. dinner, Mon., Tue. dinner.
Prix fixe: 25€, 35€, 42€, 47€.
A la carte: 55–65€.

Not much to do with George Sand's novel of the same name, but it remains the house where she met Baron Dudevant and where Michèle Eberwein has been greeting her guests for the last thirty years with kindness and a smile. Laurent Asset came to the kitchen here ten years ago via the Grand Véfour in Paris and Les Charmettes in Barbizon. His menu varies with the seasons and the market, his dishes are always beautiful and his products top quality. The lobster and pan-seared foie gras duo, slightly smoked sea bream filet, Armagnac-flambéed duckling and the duck breast with blueberry sauce are well done. A very good reason to exit the A6 motorway.

In Pouilly-le-Fort (77240).

● **Le Pouilly**
1, rue de la Fontaine, Vert-Saint-Denis.
Tel.-Fax 01 64 09 56 64.
lepouilly@wanadoo.fr
www.lepouilly.com
Closed Sun. dinner, Mon., Christmas,
mid-Aug.–beg. Sept.
Prix fixe: 28€ (weekdays), 43€, 65€.
A la carte: 90€.

The innovative head of the cuisine of Melun, Anthony Vallette, a young dynamic Normand who trained in Chambéry at the Château de Candie and with Carrade at Jurançon, has turned this fine fortified farm into his culinary laboratory. The

dynamic owner Philippe Malherbe is particularly attentive to the service in the dining room where modern dishes come together. Oysters with mango, fresh foie gras with chervil root accompanied by a scoop of beetroot sorbet, John Dory with Aquitaine caviar in a phyllo crust, farm-raised Quercy lamb roasted with purple garlic, Reims lentils and crosnes and a symphony of chocolate with a pepper "Eskimo" that slips down easily.

MENDE

48000 Lozère. Paris 592 – Alès 103 – Aurillac 154 – Issoire 139.
mende.officedetourism@free.fr.
Set between the hills of the Margeride and the Causses, this little capital of France's most rural department brims with bucolic charm. The Tarn gorges are next door, the cathedral of Notre-Dame-et-Saint-Privat, the place du Griffon with its venerable old houses and the bridge of Notre-Dame whose arches span the Lot are worth discovering.

■ HOTELS-RESTAURANTS

■ **Lion d'Or**   🎁
12-14, bd Britexte.
Tel. 04 66 49 16 46. Fax 04 66 49 23 31.
lion-dor48@wanadoo.fr
Closed beg. Nov.–end Mar.
Rest. closed Sat. lunch (exc. July–Aug.),
Sun. dinner (exc. July–Aug.).
41 rooms: 46–76€.
Prix fixe: 18€, 24€, 29€, 12€ (child).

At the entrance to the village, this comfortable member of an international hotel chain offers pleasant rooms, some overlooking the garden, a swimming pool and tasty regional menus: hot goat cheese in hazelnut crust on salad, roasted trout with cured ham and almonds, sirloin steak with ceps and an apple croustade.

■ **Hôtel-Restaurant de France**
9, bd Lucien-Arnault.
Tel. 04 66 65 00 04. Fax 04 66 49 30 47.
www.hoteldefrance-mende.com
Closed 2 weeks beg. Jan.

Rest. closed Sat. lunch, Mon. lunch.
27 rooms: 50–100€.
Prix fixe: 24€, 27€.

This former coaching inn, with its digni-fied yet eclectic rooms, its wood-paneled dining room and its summer patio, has a table of great repute. Luc Boudon, who trained in the dining room of Guérard at Eugénie-les-Bains, greets the guests with verve, while Christophe Robert offers refined seasonal dishes. A fresh vegetable tartare, parmesan biscuit and langoustine brochette, Atlantic sea bass with a spring vegetable gratin and a light mousseline, the roasted squab served in an individual cocotte with chanterelle fricassée and the berry mille-feuille are light and very well prepared.

● **Le Mazel**

25, rue du Collège.
Tel.-Fax 04 66 65 05 33.
Closed Mon. dinner, Tue., mid-Nov.–mid-Mar.
Prix fixe: 14,50€, 19,50€, 22,50€,
27,50€. A la carte: 35€.

Terroir cuisine is alive and well *chez* Jean-Paul Brun. The truffle omelet, escargots in the style of Burgundy, the catch of the day and the duck breast with oyster mush-rooms are as tender as they can be. The desserts are just as good (a lovely frozen vacherin). The service, orchestrated by the smiling Monique Brun, is careful and the prices are right.

In Chabrits (48000). 5 km nw via D42.

● **La Safranière**

Chabrits.
Tel.-Fax 04 66 49 31 54.
Closed Sun. dinner, Mon., 1 week Sept., Mar.
Prix fixe: 22€, 25€, 37€, 45€.

Sébastien Navecth has turned this old stone farmhouse into a choice restau-rant. In the modern welcoming dining room you can enjoy regional cuisine with a contemporary twist. The house smoked duck breast, chadurée (an Atlantic version of bouillabaisse with vegetables), lamb medallion with grilled kidneys and the cherry and strawberry soup with ginger-seasoned wine, served with a fresh from-age blanc ice cream, are light versions of local classics. Service is attentive and the price is right.

84560 Vaucluse. Paris 717 – Avignon 40 –
Aix-en-Provence 55 – Apt 23 –
Carpentras 36.
This hilltop Luberon village, once home to Nico-las de Stael and made famous by Peter Mayle, remains an unspoiled Provençal picture post-card. Don't miss the corkscrew museum.

■ HOTELS-RESTAURANTS

■ **La Bastide de Marie**

Rte de Bonnieux – Quartier de la Verrerie.
Tel. 04 90 72 30 20. Fax 04 90 72 54 20.
bastidemarie@c-h-m.com / www.c-h-m.com
Closed beg. Nov.–20 Apr.
8 rooms: 415–530€. 6 suites: 635–730€.
Prix fixe: 75€ (wine inc.), 85€ (for residents).

Looking for pure bliss in the Luberon? Try a visit to the Sibuets, the finest coun-try house hotel in the world, with its cozy bedrooms, soft tones, antique furniture, whitewashed walls, beautiful spaces, friendly service and choice table. In charge of the latter is the young Gérald Potron, a Niçois by birth who used to work at the Eden Roc at Cap d'Antibes, and who gracefully handles the products of the South. You are sure to enjoy the single menu which changes daily and the com-plimentary white, red or *rosé* wine from the *domaine* along with complimentary mineral water and coffee. Roasted tuna steak served with rhubarb poached with garden verbena and ratte potatoes, the lamb roast rolled in dried fruits and olive pulp, served with simmered chickpeas and chard, and a white chocolate mousse with red-streaked yellow raspberries and served with thin lace poppyseed cookies make you want to take up residence.

■ **Hostellerie le Roy Soleil**

Le Fort, route des Beaumettes, D 103.
Tel. 04 90 72 25 61. Fax 04 90 72 36 55.

hroysoleil@aol.com / www.roy-soleil.com
Hotel closed mid-Dec.–mid-Mar.
Rest. closed mid-Oct.–mid-Mar.
21 rooms: 85–340€.
Prix fixe: 28€ (lunch), 35€, 55€ (dinner),
70€ (dinner), 80€ (dinner).
A la carte: 78–90€.

The wooded park and flower garden which surround this 18th-century *bastide* make a fit introduction. The quiet, cozy rooms have terraces overlooking the Luberon or private gardens. The restaurant is in the hands of Richard Baima who worked for ten years with Senderens. His dishes are lively and well crafted: Italian-style green asparagus with an anchovy tempura, duck foie gras perfumed with corn and artichoke, red mullet with an anchovy sabayon, farm-raised pigeon with oven-crisped saffron-seasoned fennel with orange sauce are great. For dessert, the Provençal "beans", poached in a lemon-thyme infusion, served with hazelnut ice cream with whiskey sauce, are an unusual treat.

LE MENITRE

49250 Maine-et-Loire. Paris 300 –
Angers 28 – Baugé 23 – Saumur 25.
A levee on the river, an abbey and the sweet air of the Loire valley.

 | RESTAURANTS

● **Auberge de l'Abbaye** COM
Port Saint-Maur.
Tel. 02 41 45 64 67. Fax 02 41 57 69 75.
www.destination-anjou.com/abbaye
Closed Sun. dinner, Mon., Tue.,
10 days at end Dec., mid-Feb.–beg. Mar.,
mid-Aug.–beg. Sept.
Prix fixe: 18,50€, 23€, 33€, 37€, 48€,
54€, 64€, 9,50€ (child). A la carte: 59€.

Yannick and Céline Bodin overwhelm with kindness and generosity in their fine dwelling on the banks of the Loire. The moderately priced *prix fixe* menus will allow you to discover the chef's approach to regional specialties. The pan-seared foie gras with

figs, the Loire pike-perch with beurre blanc sauce, the Haut-Anjou hunted squab with sherry and honey and the pear poached in Vin de Champigny with a sour cherry-perfumed granité go down a treat.

MENTON

06500 Alpes-Maritimes. Paris 962 –
Monaco 13 – Cannes 63 – Nice 30.
ot@villedementon.com.

Set on the sea, the Promenade du Soleil, the local version of the Promenade des Anglais, the Cocteau museum and the old town with the church of Saint-Michel and the chapel of the Pénitents-Noirs, add to the charm of this town well known for its lemon trees and beloved of retirees.

 | HOTELS-RESTAURANTS

■ **Les Ambassadeurs**
3, rue Partouneaux.
Tel. 04 93 28 75 75.
info@ambassadeurs-menton.com
Rest. closed Nov.–beg. Feb.
21 rooms: 240–280€.
Prix fixe: 35€ (wine inc.), 50€, 60€.

Near the Palais de l'Europe, this handsome refurbished hotel with its themed floors (poetry, cinema, painting) is charming. The rooms are colorful, attractive and nicely furnished. The cuisine is creative and fun whether served on the veranda or in the library called "Louvre".

■ **Royal Westminster**
1510, promenade du Soleil / 28 av Félix-Faure.
Tel. 04 93 28 69 69 / 04 93 28 69 70.
Fax 04 92 10 12 30.
www.vacancesbleues.com
Closed beg. Nov.–20 Dec.
92 rooms: 58–147€.
Prix fixe: 20€.

This hotel on the shore of the Mediterranean belongs to the Vacances Bleues chain. The soft pink rooms are comfortable, the fitness center is practical and the Belle Epoque facade gives style to the establishment. Sensible cooking, professional reception and service.

■ Napoléon

29, Porte-de-France.
Tel. 04 93 35 89 50.
info@napoleon-menton.com
Rest. closed Sun. dinner, Mon.,
end Oct.–mid-Dec.
41 rooms: 79–129€.

Near the port and the border, this elegant contemporary hotel pays tribute to the writers and actors who have stayed in Menton. Fine food form the grill served at the waterside restaurant.

● Mirazur

30, av Aristide-Briand.
Tel. 04 92 41 86 86.
Closed Mon., Tue.
Prix fixe: 35€ (weekday lunch), 70€.

Italy is right next door. Alain Kerloc'h, a Breton, in the dining room, Mauro Colagreco, an Argentinian, in the kitchen, both having worked for Passard, have taken over this designer terrace, overlooking the stunning sea, once made famous by Jacques Chibois. Their style is refined, light, colorful and divinely simple with every product handled deftly. Squid with lardo di Colonata, a tomato "martini" with garden flowers, egg with asparagus cream and the grilled veal sweetbreads with Menton lemon-seasoned green cabbage are enchantments.

● Au Pistou

9, quai Gordon-Bennett.
Tel. 04 93 57 45 89.
Closed Sun. dinner (winter), Mon.
Prix fixe: 15€. A la carte: 40€.

Smack on the old port, this terraced bistro has been run by the same family for ages. The moderate prices and the fresh fish, as well as the relaxed atmosphere, are a sure success.

LES–MENUIRES

73440 Savoie. Paris 664 – Chambéry 101 – Albertville 52 – Moûtiers 27.
lesmenuires@lesmenuires.com.
Conceived in the sixties under the guidance of

Nicolas Jay, then of Joseph Fontanet, at an altitude of 1800 meters, this is "an urban development in the mountains". Hence the gigantic concrete buildings? Even though La Croisette with its boutiques, its innumerable suppliers devoted to skiing and snowboarding, its slopes, lifts and functional equipment is a success and more ("it's hideous but it works", quipped one magazine devoted to the Alps), the nineties saw typical Savoie-style buildings appear in the chalet-style Sapinière district halfway between La Croisette and Reberty. The newer houses are more regional in style and frankly more human than the giant Ménuires which look like Sarcelles in the Alps.

■ HOTELS-RESTAURANTS

■ Le Kaya

Village de Reberty.
Tel. 04 79 41 42 00. Fax 04 79 41 42 01.
www.hotel-kaya.com
Closed mid-Apr.–mid-Dec.
48 rooms: 665–1664€ (1 week, half board).
Prix fixe: 45€ (lunch), 53€ (dinner).

This large luxury chalet created a sensation in the center of the resort. Wood paneled rooms and suites, modern slate, stone, larch, glass and linen décor, extensive leisure facilities (swimming pool, hammam, sauna) set the tone of the establishment: up market. Add a young, smiling staff, the cuisine of young David Archinard, formerly of Rostang, who plays the Southern register with quality products, and you are sure to agree that this new place is worth a visit. Fine pumpkin cream flavored with Beaufort, the foie gras and pain d'épices, salmon trout meunière, the young guinea hen breast with sweet peas, the rabbit stew and a tasty exotic fruit vacherin are all delightful.

■ L'Ours Blanc

Reberty 2000. 1,5 km se.
Tel. 04 79 00 61 66. Fax 04 79 00 63 67.
www.hotel-ours-blanc.com
Closed end Apr –beg. Dec.
49 rooms: 115€. 2 suites: 230€.
Prix fixe: 18€ (lunch), 20€, 28€, 12€ (child).

This is where Bernardette Chirac and David Douillet celebrated the resort's fortieth anniversary last year. In other words, this large friendly chalet is an institution. The rooms have been redone in Alpine style, the lounge is cozy, the fitness center welcome and the view of the mountains from the dining room is splendid. You will be served salmon tartiflette, salmon trout with chanterelles cooked with Mondeuse wine and the lamb medallion in a cep-seasoned breading. Pascal Casali, who worked in England at the Lygon Arms in Broadway, knows his craft. His wife, born in Worcestershire, greets guests with a delightful British accent.

■ Le Ménuire

Tel. 04 79 00 60 33. Fax 04 79 00 60 00.
info@le-menuire.fr / www.le-menuire.fr
Closed 23 Apr.–1 Dec.
39 rooms: 70–154€. 2 suites: 148–316€.
Half board: 95–204€.

This modern chalet on the edge of town has been redone in a warm rustic style thanks to the skill of master woodworker Gilbert Meilleur. Several pretty paneled rooms and suites. Warm family welcome from Emmanuel and Roxane Martinez. Restaurant La Pierra.

■ Chalet 2000

Reberty-Village.
Tel. 04 79 00 60 57. Fax 04 79 00 22 25.
chalet2000@wanadoo.fr
www.hotel-chalet2000.fr
Closed end Oct.–mid-Dec., beg. May–end June.
17 rooms: 49–126€.
Prix fixe: 18€, 19,50€, 32€.
A la carte: 40€.

Warm rooms, simple regional cuisine with Savoie specialties and a smiling welcome from Serge Udry set the tone of this good no-frills establishment.

● Au Coin du Feu   SIM

Rond Point de la Croisette.
Tel.-Fax 04 79 09 97 52.
www.restaurantaucoindufeu.com
Closed Mon. lunch (exc. July–Aug.),
Tue. lunch (exc. July–Aug.),
Sept.–mid- Dec., Apr.–mid- June.
Prix fixe: 11€. A la carte: 30€.

The Jays' pretty tavern offers a warm welcome for nicely updated market-based cuisine. Coddled eggs with morels, the salmon trout grilled in the fireplace, whole wheat pasta gratin made with local crozets and the fruit crumble are produced by Emily and served with verve by her sister Servanne.

● Chalet les Sonnailles   SIM

In Vieux Hameau des Bruyères.
Tel.-Fax 04 79 00 74 28.
Closed end Apr.–beg. July,
beg. Sept.–end Nov.
Prix fixe: 11€, 8,50€ (child).

Winter, summer, noon (self-service) and night (à la carte), you will enjoy stuffed escargots, the herb-seasoned rack of lamb, grilled meats and a berry gratin which slip down a treat.

● L'Etoile   SIM

Quartier de la Sapinière.
Tel.-Fax 04 79 00 75 58.
jpierrerey@wanadoo.fr
Closed end Apr.–mid-Dec.
A la carte: 40–45€.

Typical all the way, Juliette and Jean-Pierre Rey's establishment does Savoie proud. An old sheepfold where the waiters in local costume serve up bacon and goat cheese salad, scallops with lemon and coriander seed, roasted rack of lamb served in a Beaufort crust as well as an introduction to the "fabulous" house wild blueberry tart. Wines from around the world.

● La Ferme de Reberty   SIM

Reberty-Village.
Tel. 04 79 00 77 01.
lafermedereberty@tiscali.fr
Closed end Apr.–beg. Dec.
Prix fixe: 18€, 25€, 10€ (child).
A la carte: 45–50€.

Young and fun, this mountain brasserie is full late into the night. Eric Stervinou is at the stove concocting lively fresh market-based dishes. Sophie Challant will welcome you with verve. Saint Marcellin salad, pork tenderloin medallion with Armagnac and the fresh fruit brochettes served with hot fudge sauce slip down nicely.

● **La Marmite de Géant** `SIM`
Quartier des Bruyères.
Tel. 04 79 00 74 75. Fax 04 79 00 71 57.
www.marmitedegeant.com
Closed end May–mid-Dec.
Prix fixe: 17€, 24€.A la carte: 38€.

This address is one of the resort's institutions. You will enjoy good simple Savoie specialties: hot goat cheese salad, the salmon trout with pine nuts and lemon butter, duck breast with figs and a waffle with fresh fruits. With family or friends this address is sure to please, right down to the bill.

MERCUES see **CAHORS**

71640 Saône-et-Loire. Paris 345 – Beaune 28 – Chalon-sur-Saône 13 – Autun 40 – Chagny 12.
The "capital" of the Côte Chalonnaise, tucked at the foot of its castle, is worth visiting for its fine old houses and its fine wine — peppery on the nose, pleasant and fresh on the palate.

 HOTELS-RESTAURANTS

■ **Hostellerie du Val d'Or**
140, Grande-Rue.
Tel. 03 85 45 13 70. Fax 03 85 45 18 45.
contact@le-valdor.com / www.le-valdor.com
Closed mid-Dec.–mid-Jan.
Rest. closed Mon., Tue. lunch.
12 rooms: 75–95€.
Prix fixe: 21–24€ (lunch), 39€, 61€, 12€ (child). A la carte: 59€.

One can get carried away by the team in charge of this former coaching inn. In the kitchen Pascal Charreyras prepares his version of traditional French cuisine.

The poached egg in red wine sauce, Val de Saône perch, veal sweetbreads simmered in beet jus and the frozen Marc de Bourgogne soufflé are very good. The cellar is up to par. The prix fixe menus are generous and the rooms stylish.

73550 Savoie. Paris 653 – Albertville 43 – Annecy 87 – Chambéry 91 – Moûtiers 16.
info@meribel.net.
In the middle of the Trois-Vallées, the largest ski area in the world, lies this beautiful village of modern chalets built in traditional style. The English were the first to come to the resort which has carefully preserved its old village.

 HOTELS-RESTAURANTS

● **Allodis** ○⊞
Le Belvédère, BP 43.
Tel. 04 79 00 56 00. Fax 04 79 00 59 28.
allodis@wanadoo.fr / www.hotel-allodis.com
Closed Sept.–mid-Dec., Apr.–beg. July.
32 rooms: 99–210€. 12 suites: 135–289€.
Prix fixe: 42€, 56€, 66€, 72€.

Allodis is Méribel's star table located in the Forni's well-run, charming hotel at the foot of the slopes. The paneled rooms and suites are decorated with taste and refinement. The terrace has a wide angle view of the mountains, the dining room is plush and the swift service greeted with enthusiasm. In the kitchen, Alain Plouzé from Anjou, who came to Savoie fifteen years ago, prepares local products in a creative register. We love his lunch dishes, deceptively simple and frankly good: chestnut and hazelnut soup with Pata Negra ham and foie gras, the Savoie-style pain perdu with pancetta, Réblochon and aged Beaufort, the salmon trout filet with gnocchi and the braised Rippoze poultry breast with the local pasta (crozets) and pormoniers sausage. The dinner menu is more sophisticated but the regional flavors are still treated with care. Mouthwatering rhubarb shortbread cookie with calisson (a Provençal sugared almond paste specialty) ice cream.

■ Le Grand Coeur

Tel. 04 79 08 60 03. Fax 04 79 08 58 38.
www.legrandcoeur.com
Closed mid-Apr.–mid-Dec.
40 rooms: 172,50–1635€. 5 suites: 1635€.
A la carte: 85€.

Central airconditioning, terrace, private
dining room, valet parking, fitness center, hammam, sauna, Jacuzzi, Internet,
WiFi, conference room, massage salon,
health spa (under renovation). Just what
does this Relais & Châteaux, run by the
prestigious Edouard Rutchi in a beautiful
mountain setting, not have? Attentive welcome and service, small cozy rooms, Marc
Dach's fresh carefully prepared dishes
like the Beaufort fondant, line-fished sole
napped with Vin d'Apremont sauce and
served with asparagus, lamb medallion
sautéed with slow-cooked garlic and a
cocoa lace cookie with grilled almonds,
savored with relish.

■ Le Yéti

Rond-point des Pistes.
Tel. 04 79 00 51 15. Fax 04 79 00 51 73.
welcome@hotel-yeti.com / www.hotel-yeti.com
Closed end Apr.–beg. July,
end Aug.–beg. Dec.
27 rooms: 210–540€. 1 suite: 305–335€.
Prix fixe: 42€. A la carte: 50€.

At the foot of the slopes, Frédéric and
Sophie Saint-Guilhem's hotel is a nice
place to stay. The quiet rooms and the
heated pool, open to all, are much appreciated, as is the sunny cuisine. The mozzarella with tomatoes, the Mediterannean
sea bass served with fennel, the grilled
lamb chops and the berry crumble are
simple and good.

■ Alpen Ruitor

Rue des Bleuets.
Tel. 04 79 00 48 48. Fax 04 79 00 48 31.
info@alpenruitor.com / www.alpenruitor.com
Closed mid-Apr.–beg. Dec.
44 rooms: 220–430€. 1 suite: 500–785€.
Prix fixe: 45€ (dinner).

This neo-Tyrolian house is signed Raymonde Fenestraz of Airelles in Courch-

evel. Rooms with balconies overlooking the
slopes are furnished with care. The dining
room is pleasant as is the inspired regional
cuisine (the crisp Réblochon toasts and
ribboned Savoie cured ham on salad, perch
meunière with smoked butter sauce and a
Genepi-flavored crème brûlée).

■ Alba

Rond-point des Pistes.
Tel. 04 79 08 55 55. Fax 04 79 00 55 63.
www.meribel-hotelalba.com
Closed mid-Apr.–mid-Dec.
19 rooms: 139–179€. 1 suite: 258€.
Prix fixe: 40€, 48€, 58€, 12€ (child).

Gilles and Laurence Chardonnet, who run
the Tour de Pacoret at Grésy-sur-Isère in
the summer, have chosen warm paneling
and red and yellow tones to decorate the
guest rooms. At the end of the day guests
meet by the fireside in the lounge, after
a stop at the sauna and hammam. In the
kitchen, Daniel Vichard lovingly prepares
nice dishes (the poultry wing and marinated foie gras salad, lake whitefish with
a Mondeuse wine sauce, slow-simmered
pork cheek and onion stew with chestnuts). Laurence zigzags between the cellar and the dining room to serve up some
fine bottles.

■ La Croix Jean-Claude

Les Allue. 7 km D915 A.
Tel. 04 79 08 61 05. Fax 04 79 00 32 72.
lacroixjeanclaude@wanadoo.fr
Closed Sept.–mid-Dec., Apr.–end June.
13 rooms: 60–110€.
Prix fixe: 21€, 29€, 35€, 10€ (child).

Mado Gacon offers up a bit of Méribel's art
and history in this 1860s chalet that she
runs with love. The colorful wood-paneled setting is a treat and Aurélie Lerieux's
careful cuisine is tasty without preten-
tion. The garlic-seasoned frisée with hot
cheese, an old-style veal blanquette served
with a vegetable gratin, cheeses aged by
Denis Provent in Chambery and the old-
fashioned desserts like the frozen pine
bud parfait, on the 29 menu, slip down
with no trouble. Simple cozy rooms, nice
lounge.

● Le Blanchot   COM

Rte de l'Altiport.
Tel. 04 79 00 55 78. Fax 04 79 08 58 86.
leblanchot@voila.fr
Closed Sun. dinner, Mon. dinner,
1 Sept.–mid-Dec., end Apr.–end June.
Prix fixe: 35€ (lunch). A la carte: 45–70€.

Golf in summer, snowshoeing and cross-country ski trails in winter, this is the view from this mountain restaurant which has redone its décor with an eye on the great outdoors. Monique Touchant greets guests with a smile while Christophe Perrin, who worked in the Caribbean, offers cuisine with an exotic touch. "Savoie style"-sushi, local sausage (diots) terrine, foie gras ravioli, the coddled egg with ceps and lovely meats, each with their provenance labeled on the menu (Aubrac tenderloin, Aveyron red-label veal cutlet) are crowd pleasers. Madagascar vanilla–flavored crème brûlée is a model of its kind.

MERKWILLER-PECHELBRONN

67250 Bas-Rhin. Paris 505 – Strasbourg 48 – Haguenau 16 – Wissembourg 22.
Once the oil capital of Alsace, now a museum city and more recently a gastronomic crossroads.

●	RESTAURANTS

● Auberge du Baechel-Brunn

3, rte de Soultz.
Tel. 03 88 80 78 61. Fax 03 88 80 75 20.
beachelbrunn@wanadoo.fr
Closed Mon., Tue., 2 weeks end Jan.,
2 weeks end Aug.
Prix fixe: 26€ (lunch), 38€, 50€, 65€.
A la carte: 51–58€.

The old family barn has become a modern inn with a bright, elegant, welcoming dining room that can boast of being one of the gastronomic shrines of Alsace. The know-how of Jean-Paul Limmacher, who trained at the Cheval Blanc, and the imaginative verve of Thomas, his son, a pupil of Bueherhiesel, do wonders with the best local seasonal products. Variations on the theme of foie gras, the pike-perch in thin slices of potato, the Alpilles lamb with *garrigue* herbs and the chocolate and garden mint parfait are good examples of this successful partnership. Your enjoyment will be rounded out by wines from a fine list presented by daughter-in-law Esther and by the highly affable service.

In Kutzenhausen (67250). 1 km n.

● Auberge du Puits VI   ◎SIM

20, rte de Lobsann.
Tel. 03 88 80 76 58. Fax 03 88 80 75 91.
www.auberge-puits-6.com
Closed Mon., Tue., Wed. lunch, Jan.
Prix fixe: 34€, 41€, 48€, 60€,
8€ (child). A la carte: 45€–50€.

He is young and talented, his name is Alexandre Fender and his cooking is a heartwarming delight. Marie and Norbert Koehler have created a gastronomic restaurant in this old café where the miners from the potassium mine used to gather to play *boules*. No effort is spared to offer a friendly welcome and incomparable service. Fine products and seasonal offerings, ranging from the Alsatian *terroir* to the four corners of the world, are some of Alexandre's secret ingredients to which he adds a hint of intuition. The cold fresh fromage blanc and shrimp soup, the curry-seasoned swordfish and the rack of lamb seasoned with masala spices are masterpieces. A lemon filled with fresh garden lemon balm sorbet is a divine suprise. This wake up call to the senses can be enjoyed without fear of spending a fortune.

METZ

57000 Moselle. Paris 332 – Nancy 57 – Reims 190 – Strasbourg 163 – Luxembourg 62.
tourisme@ot.mairie-metz.fr.
"No other town can make itself as well-loved as Metz", wrote Barrès in *Colette Baudoche*. In the last century and a half, the town has not changed its soul so much as its geographic situation. It is no longer a garrison town, vigilantly guarding the Eastern approaches, but an active city, right in the heart of Europe, not far from Luxembourg, the Sarre and Belgium. Metz is a crossroads city, with terrific computer technol-

ogy, a solid cultural base as well as a football team. It is ready for the TGV Est as well as the first provincial annex of the Beaubourg museum and loves sweet savors as much as salty ones. Good little eateries and brasseries are its specialties. There are more good tables here than you would think, both in the center of town and in the outlying, verdant countryside and there is a host of fine produce to choose from.

■	HOTELS

■ Hôtel la Citadelle
5, av Ney.
Tel. 03 87 17 17 17. Fax 03 87 17 17 18.
www.citadelle-metz.com
77 rooms: 175–265€. 2 suites: 335
Half board: 210–335€.

Right in the heart of a protected area, this old purveyor of military supplies, situated right behind the arsenal, has been transformed into a luxury hotel. A pleasing welcome and large, comfortable rooms are much appreciated. Choice table (see Restaurants: the Magasin aux Vivres).

■ Holiday Inn
1, rue Félix-Savart.Technopole 2000,
5 km from Metz.
Tel. 03 87 39 94 50. Fax 03 87 39 94 55.
www.holidayinn-metz.com
86 rooms: 105–115€. 4 suites: 125€.
Prix fixe: 25€, 10€ (child).
A la carte: 30–35€.

Facing the eighteen-hole golf course, this modern hotel with swimming pool is worth it for its peaceful, contemporary-style rooms and its honest *pension* cooking at the Alizés.

■ Hôtel du Théâtre
3, rue du Pont-Saint-Marcel.
Tel. 03 87 31 10 10 / 03 87 30 12 29.
Fax 03 87 30 04 66.
www.port-saint-marcel.com
60 rooms: 78–130€. 6 suites: 130–180€.
Half board: 110–205€.

The banks of the Moselle have been turned into a marina which lends a seaside atmo-

sphere to this spot. This hotel, situated nearby, offers pretty, modern rooms as well as a leisure area complete with swimming pool, sauna and hammam. The restaurant is just as pleasant.

■ Mercure Centre Saint-Thiébault
29, pl Saint-Thiébault.
Tel. 03 87 38 50 50. Fax 03 87 75 48 18.
h1233@accor.com / www.mercure.com
112 rooms: 99–139€. 4 suites: 139€.
Prix fixe: 17€, 20€, 8€ (child).
A la carte: 28–44€.

Pastel yellow tones for this chain hotel right near the city center and the railway station, which cannot fail to please, thanks to a smiling welcome and practical rooms. A respectable cuisine with salmon carpaccio, pike fish quenelle, steak tartare and soft-centered chocolate cake.

■ Novotel Centre
Pl des Paraiges.
Tel. 03 87 37 38 39. Fax 03 87 36 10 00.
h0589@accor.com / www.novotel.com
117 rooms: 89–120€. 3 suites: 130€.
Prix fixe: 19€, 8€ (child). A la carte: 30–33€.

Classic chain comfort at this centrally located hotel situated near the commercial center and the Place Saint-Louis: huge, practical rooms, a swimming pool and conference areas. The gastronome will find his pleasure further afield rather than in the snack-bar-style restaurant.

■ Hôtel de la Cathédrale
25, pl de Chambre.
Tel. 03 87 75 00 02. Fax 03 87 75 40 75.
www.hotelcathedrale-metz.fr
19 rooms: 58–95€. 1 suite: 105€.

This 17th-century establishment has old-fashioned, comfortable rooms, some of which give onto the cathedral, as well as a restaurant, the Baraka (see Restaurants) with good, sensible, Moroccan cuisine.

■ Cécil'Hôtel
14, rue Pasteur.
Tel. 03 87 66 66 13. Fax 03 87 56 96 02.

www.cecilhotel-metz.com
39 rooms: 54–63€.

Good value for money at this hotel situated between the railway station and the city center.

In Fey (57420). 11 km sw, via A31 (Nancy).

■ **Les Tuileries**
Rte de Cuvry.
Tel. 03 87 52 03 03. Fax 03 87 52 84 24.
lestuileries@wanadoo.fr
www.hotel-lestuileries.fr
41 rooms: 65–75€. Half board: 100–147€.

In the hands of the Vadala brothers, an old tile factory has been transformed into a hotel blending classical and modern styles, decorated in warm tones and offering all the comforts of a tip-top establishment. There is a shady garden for fine days and one lingers here over regional and seasonal dishes of the restaurant, affiliated with "Moselle Gourmande" (Gourmet Moselle).

In Rugy (57640). 12 km n via D1.

■ **La Bergerie**
10, rue de la Bergerie.
Tel. 03 87 77 82 27. Fax 03 87 77 87 07.
info@la-bergerie.fr / www.la-bergerie.fr
Closed Christmas–New Year's.
48 rooms: 76–90€.

On the way to Luxembourg and Germany, this ancient sheepfold has been transformed into a rustic hotel with comfortable rooms. A warm welcome, diligent service and faultless cooking.

● | RESTAURANTS

● **Restaurant Maire**
1, rue du Pont-des-Morts.
Tel. 03 87 32 43 12. Fax 03 87 31 16 75.
restaurant.maire@wanadoo.fr
www.restaurant-maire.com
Closed Tue., Wed. lunch.
Prix fixe: 23€ (weekday lunch),
31€ (lunch, wine inc.), 43€, 49€, 61€.
A la carte: 65€.

He's the ace of seafood cooking, having been a pupil at the Mouscardins in Saint-Tropez and then at the Santons in Grimaud, and retains a propensity to cook fish with dexterity. Yves Maire offers the scallops, either wrapped in Meuse truffles and served with Chinese noodles with the addition of a white truffle-flavored fine pumpkin cream, or served roasted on a bed of lamb's lettuce and chestnut with a light emulsion sauce. Likewise, the pike-perch is golden brown, served with a thin eggplant tart, or whole, perfectly cooked, and served with Provençal vegetables seasoned with coriander seeds. There is also the Atlantic sea bass filet on a bed of caramelized julinenned endive with a rose petal sauce or the red mullet roasted on rye tabouli with black olives and a balsamic vinaigrette. High praise for the desserts (classic and tasty frozen mirabelle soufflé, a cold cassis and apple cream in gelatin with a spice crumble, a frozen Carribean chocolate dessert with a pistachio center and the pear poached in curry) all low-key and traditional.

● **Le Magasin aux Vivres**
At Hôtel la Citadelle, 5, av Ney.
Tel. 03 87 17 17 17. Fax 03 87 17 17 18.
contact@citadelle-metz.com
www.citadelle-metz.com
Closed Sun. dinner.
Prix fixe: 35€ (lunch), 55€ (lunch).
A la carte: 110€.

Christophe Dufossé is a talented technician capable of all sorts of tricks of today's cuisine scene, but having been the solitary little regent of Burgundy and Champagne, he is having a hard time adapting to Lorraine. His gastronomic register is certainly skilled though hardly regionally-based and often gratuitous. Christophe—who knows how to do everything—proposes a big degustation menu comprised of ten small dishes which change according to the inspiration of the moment. Technically, this works perfectly, but what gustatory interest is there in mixing lobster with raw mango, pink peppercorns and a vinaigrette made with bourbon vanilla? We would rather that the Dufosse revolution, which sweeps up everything in its stride, focus on the region. In short, we praise Christophe D. for his Lorraine escargots in cannelloni, steamed with champagne in the oven, for his chicken oysters in roasting juices which figured the other day on the "little" lunch menu at 33 . Or even, in a more rebellious vein, the potato rosti, with his grilled rouget and signature Humbert chitterling sausage. You can't fault the sea urchins with spring vegetables and Aquitaine caviar or the little pot of duck foie gras with an amusing crunchy cumin-seasoned "finger", and there is inherent bravura in the langoustine in a truffle crust with shellfish cappuccino and grated green asparagus. An address to follow as it raises local gastronomy to new heights.

● Au Pampre d'Or

31, pl de Chambre.
Tel. 03 87 74 12 46. Fax 03 87 36 96 92.
Closed Sun. dinner, Mon. lunch, Tue. lunch,
10 days beg. Jan., 10 days beg. Aug.
Prix fixe: 26€, 35€ (wine inc.), 45€, 60€.
A la carte: 85€.

The Lamaze's 17th-century hotel is full of contrasts. At reception, Catherine is professional and friendly, the setting uncluttered and welcoming and Jean-Claude's cooking sophisticated and natural. Thanks to the know-how of this highly serious native of the Vosges—a disciple of Gaertner and Schillinger—the little cabbages stuffed with snails, the John Dory with fennel, the hot foie gras and cep ravioli, delicious salmon trout with a truffled vegetable purée, the lamb in a crust and the roasted deboned squab are works of art and acts of valor. Don't miss the desserts which are monuments of their kind: raspberries in a fine purée with pistachio ice cream and the strawberries Romanoff, served with vanilla ice cream, are flawlessly fresh. The service is diligent and the wine list plentiful. A sure-fire address.

● Restaurant des Roches

29, rue des Roches.
Tel. 03 87 74 06 51. Fax 03 87 75 40 04.

Closed Sun. dinner, Mon. dinner.
Prix fixe: 27€, 36€, 46€.

A low-ceilinged dining room with beams and stone walls at this establishment alongside the Moselle, warmed up by the cuisine of Michel Chielle, a newcomer to these stoves. Scallops with garlic and parsley, grilled John Dory with virgin olive oil and tomato sauce, sirloin steak with ceps and the frozen soufflé with Lorraine Mirabel plums don't promise any more than they deliver but are nevertheless quality dishes. Well-planned menus.

● El Theatris

2 pl de la Comédie.
Tel. 03 87 56 02 02.
Closed Sat. lunch (exc. fêtes), Sun.
Prix fixe: 20,50€ (weekdays),
45,50€ (dinner). A la carte: 55€.

In the 18th century, this was a military lodge. Today it has become a trendy eatery full of gray tones, baroque furnishings, contemporary design and weathered wood. Jean-Michel Zang greets you with a smile and the chef—Yvon Nicolas, a Breton from Quimperle who worked at Pont-Aven at the Moulin de Rosmadec, at the Fermes de Marie at Megève and at Lea Linster in Munster—knows his stuff. Products are fresh, the combinations of flavors ingenious and the rusic-chic style pleasant. The veal carpaccio with parmesan, the swordfish with roasted sesame seeds and the poultry breast stuffed with chard are well-honed dishes. Nice desserts, including a brioche pain perdu with vanilla caramel and maple syrup, which gives you a clue.

● L'Ecluse

45, pl de Chambre.
Tel. 03 87 75 42 38. Fax 03 87 37 30 11.
Closed Sat. lunch, Sun. dinner, Mon.,
2 weeks beg. Aug.
Prix fixe: 22€, 35€, 65€. A la carte: 69€.

This mariner's "loft" setting facing the Moselle has charm and Eric Maire lots of talent. As for Emmanuelle Maire, she welcomes and advises with verve. The weekday lunch menu is a grand affair at 22. When we were there, it offered thinly sliced smoked salmon on a sprout salad, oven-browned cod served over a purée of white coco beans, served with gnocchi, pork tenderloin braised with prunes and served with rolled sweet peppers and chorizo-seasoned Tarbais coco beans, plus poached fruit and ice cream. The minced crab with an artichoke crème caramel is a little rich as are the roasted langoustines served on a celery root risotto with champagne hollandaise sauce. A young sommelier comments knowledgeably on the wines.

● Flo   COM

2 bis, rue Léon-Gambetta.
Tel. 03 87 55 94 95. Fax 03 87 38 09 26.
orasia@groupeflo.fr / www.flometz.com
Prix fixe: 14,90€, 19,50€, 29,50€,
25,50€, 13€ (child). A la carte: 45€.

This brasserie hides behind a Jugendstil facade, complete with lovely wooden paneling, stucco ceilings, art deco chandeliers and a shellfish bar. People flock here for the sea whelks, the special of the day, the scallop brochette, the nicely cut red meats served with béarnaise sauce and fries, the good service and the mirabelle-flambéed brioche pain perdu with milk caramel. Good wine list. Reasonable prices.

● Georges   COM

"A la Ville de Lyon"
9, rue des Piques.
Tel. 03 87 36 07 01. Fax 03 87 74 47 17.
george-ville-de-lyon@wanadoo.fr
www.alavilledelyon.com
Closed Sun. dinner, Mon., 1 week Feb.,
1 week Aug.
Prix fixe: 17€ (lunch), 23€,
31€ (wine inc.), 38€ (dinner), 42€, 60€.
A la carte: 60€.

Georges Vikloszki has quietly taken over the former Ville de Lyon. He trained on the Côte d'Azur as a student of Vergé at Mougins and then Chibois at Cannes, and has a light touch with Lorraine dishes. His "Rabelais" menu is exemplary of his style. The rabbit aspic flavored with Vin de Conz, Valleroy escargots with saffron jus and slow-cooked garlic with a mirabelle plum sorbet, the fine pork trotter in the form of truffled sausage with mustard sauce and a frozen mirabelle plum parfait with a passion fruit coulis are a succession of regional delights. We also like his frog legs and mushrooms in creamy sauce and his veal sweetbreads braised with morels. True cuisine, precise flavors and reasonable prices can now be found at the Ville de Lyon.

● Le Chat Noir   COM

30, rue Pasteur.
Tel. 03 87 56 99 19. Fax 03 87 66 67 64.
rest-le-chat@wanadoo.fr
Closed Sun., Mon., vac. Christmas,
2 weeks beg. Aug.
Prix fixe: 26€, 45€. A la carte: 60€.

An African décor, dishes from all corners of the globe and a trendy atmosphere. Anne Rossi has a serious grip on things and Sebastien Leman is a dexterous cook who turns out good tender cep risotto, the large langoustine ravioli, cod prepared in the style of Marseille, veal filet with pantossed mushrooms and an exotic fruit gazpacho. The first menu is a real gift, the wine list full of goodies.

● Di Roma   COM

7, rue Lafayette.
Tel. 03 87 56 16 49. Fax 03 87 57 39 46.
bouxci@free.fr
Closed Sat. lunch, Sun.
Prix fixe: 25€, 10€ (child). A la carte: 35€.

This modern trattoria next to the railway staton is well run by Pierre Berdicaro. In the kitchen Thomas Knispen cooks antipasti, bruschetta, grilled Atlantic sea bass, the daily pasta special, saltimbocca and tiramisu like an Italian mama. The bill isn't too brutal.

● La Gargouille   COM

29, pl de Chambre.
Tel. 03 87 36 65 77. Fax 03 87 74 46 34.
www.lagargouille.com
Closed Mon. lunch, Tue. dinner, Wed.,
Christmas, 2 weeks July.

Prix fixe: 19,50€ (lunch, wine inc.),
31€ (wine inc.), 41€ (wine inc.),
10€ (child).
A la carte: 47€.

The neo-1900 décor at the foot of the cathedral is a bit dated, but Pierre Wetzel's cooking, which modernizes local recipes, isn't half bad. Laquenexy escargots in puff pastry with braised spring vegetables, the old-fashioned braised suckling pig cheeks and the frozen mirabelle plum parfait hold up well.

● La Goulue `COM`
24, pl Saint-Simplice.
Tel. 03 87 75 10 69. Fax 03 87 36 94 05.
Closed Sun., Mon., 1 week Jan.
Prix fixe: 32€, 50€. A la carte: 50€.

Yves François is the town's king of fish and shellfish, the place a monument of its kind with wonderfully fresh products served in the École de Nancy bistro setting. Shrimp in Thai-style salad, fish tartare, John Dory with potatoes and the red tuna with sesame are of great quality. The baba with kirsch slips down easily.

● Le Jardin de Bellevue `COM`
58, rue Claude-Bernard.
In Borny, 3 km via rte de Strasbourg.
Tel. 03 87 37 10 27. Fax 03 87 37 15 45.
www.lejardindebellevue.com
Closed Sat. lunch, Sun. dinner, Mon., Feb.
vac., 3 weeks July.
Prix fixe: 22€ (lunch), 35€, 44€ (wine inc.),
14€ (child). A la carte: 65€.

Philippe and Nathalie Jung have made their nest in a century-old bourgeois dwelling with a flower-filled garden. Dishes are refined: langoustine cappuccino, herb-seasoned turbot filet, beef filet and escargots and the mango and mascarpone soup with sorbet are good. Well-proportioned menus.

● Restaurant du Pont Saint-Marcel `COM`
1, rue du Pont-Saint-Marcel.
Tel. 03 87 30 12 29. Fax 03 87 30 04 66.
www.port-saint-marcel.com

Closed Christmas, New Year's.
Prix fixe: 15€, 28€. A la carte: 45€.

This 17th-century establishment with frescoed walls is the modest ambassador for regional recipes and products. Wearing local costume, the waiters bring you dishes of yore: quiche Lorraine, tourte (covered pie), frog legs, pike-perch with crayfish coulis, beef tongue with spicy sauce and a Lorraine-style clafoutis are accompanied by an anthology of good regional vintages.

● La Popote `SIM`
30, rue Clovis.
Tel. 03 87 55 98 99. Fax 03 87 15 13 34.
lapopote@wanadoo.fr
Closed Sun., Mon. dinner, 10 days Christmas–New Year's, 1 week July–Aug.
Prix fixe: 10,50€ (weekday lunch),
12,50€ (weekday lunch), 5,50€ (child).
A la carte: 29–36€.

Gérard Combe invites you to hearty, home-style cooking in his neat little bistro near the Sainte-Therese church. A generous farm salad, pike-perch with Pinot Noir sauce, tartare, tête de veau, hanger steak with shallots and a Lorraine-style plum tart (chaudée), concocted by Bruno Louis, are all delicious and generous, as are the welcome and the agreeable menus. A cozy setting on theme of "*temps des cerises*".

● L'Etude `SIM`
11, av Robert-Schuman.
Tel. 03 87 36 35 32. Fax 03 87 36 35 39.
l-etude@l-etude.com / www.l-etude.com
Closed Sun.
Prix fixe: 15€ (lunch), 21€, 26,30€,
6,50€ (child).

Philippe Rigault runs this brasserie *cum* library with alacrity. The place has charm and Eric Lalouette's cuisine uses daily market fare to concoct pleasing meus. Whelk fricassée with saffron, cod and potato casserole with sundried tomatoes, lamb shanks tagine with dried fruit, beef tartare prepared tableside and the frozen mirabelle plum soufflé are upstanding works. Nice choice of wines from all over and resonable prices for well-devised menus.

● **4 vins 3**   **ⓃⓂSIM**
83, rue Mazelle.
Tel. 03 87 75 20 20.
Closed Sun., Mon. dinner.
A la carte: 35€.

The Cristofaro brothers have taken this former designer wine bistro and turned it into an Italian-Provençal establishment of quality. Formerly of Maximin at the Negresco in Nice and then at the Bel Air at Echternach, Gérome is a subtle cook; Roberto waits on tables with verve. We like the ratatouille ravioli with basil sauce, stuffed niçoise vegetables, vegetable risotto, cod with masala spices and pesto and the herb-stuffed rabbit with polenta wedges cooked in bacon fat. The wines are well chosen, prices are reasonable and the house pasta (penne with country ham and poultry sauce) delectable.

● **Le Sarment**   **ⓂSIM**
21, rue Mazelle.
Tel.-Fax 03 87 17 45 63.
Closed Mon. dinner, Tue., end July–beg. Aug., 10 days Christmas–New Year's.
Prix fixe: 19€, 22€. A la carte: 40€.

Jean-Luc Mazur, who passed through the Xalupa on the port at Saint-Jean-de-Luz, and his brother-in-law David Fasano, formed at the XIIe Borne at Delme then at the Bistro du Port in Porto-Vecchio, are absolute devotees of the Basque country and the Gers region and currently run the city's Basque-Gascony showcase with great ardor. In a warm and family-like setting, tuck into the foie gras terrine with Floc, roasted pike-perch with saffron potatoes and Madiran butter, rack of lamb in an herb crust and the frozen mirabelle plum souf- flé. The place is rustic, the prices reason- able. Lots of character throughout.

● **Thierry**   **ⓂSIM**
   "Saveurs et Cuisine"
Maison de la Fleur Ly, 5, rue des Piques.
Tel. 03 87 74 01 23. Fax 03 87 77 81 03.
www.restaurant-thierry.fr

Closed Sun., Wed., 2 weeks Feb., 3 weeks Aug.
Prix fixe: 15,50€ (lunch), 21,50€ (lunch), 31,50€ (lunch weekends). A la carte: 45€.

Surfing on the wave of fusion cooking, Thierry Krompholtz presides over a com- fortable and eclectic setting in a 16th- century town house where he uses his "melting pot" to marry flavors from East and West. On the plate, this gives us mar- inated tuna and crab rolls with wasabi, tom ka gai (Thai-style coconut chicken soup), spicy fish tagine, caramelized suck- ling pig cheeks and fruit crumble. Don't miss the puff pastry cup filled with sim- mered veal in white sauce or the frozen mirabelle plum soufflé—they are Lor- raine dishes in origin. Good wines from all over the world.

● **Brasserie ABC**   **ⓃSIM**
2, pl Général-de-Gaulle.
Tel. 03 87 66 67 11.
Prix fixe: 17,50€, 30€.

Opposite the railway station, this insi- tution excels in sensible, classic dishes (tartare, tête de veau, chitterling sausage, crêpe Suzette) and proposes a tempting Rabelaisian menu under the guidance of the discreet Emmanuel Sanchez. This classic chef does wonders with his pike- perch poached in beer and his frog legs flan, which is the star dish on the "Rabe- lais" menu and shows that he knows to branch out from strict brasserie fare.

● **Le Père Potot**   **ⓃSIM**
At Kyriad, 8, rue du Père-Potot.
Tel. 03 87 36 55 56.
Prix fixe: 14,50€ (weekdays), 23€.
A la carte: 30€.

This table is better than it looks. The name may evoke a jolly inn but the setting is mod- ern with high, black, bare tables and the cooking contemporary under the dynamic leadership of Stéphane Rolet. Parsleyed escargots and bacon in an unctuous cham- pagne cream, the Lorraine pork ribs in bone marrow crust and the thin fig tart with five-spice ice cream look great.

● Le Toqué 🅽 SIM

27, rue Taison.
Tel.-Fax 03 87 74 29 53.
Closed Sun., Mon., Christmas, 3 weeks Jan.,
10 days beg. Aug.
Prix fixe: 19,90€, 25,50€ (weekday dinner),
30€ (Sat., Sun., dinner),
6,50€ (child). A la carte: 30–40€.

Régis Toulet has taken over the former
Fleur de Sel and updated it in tones of
orange and beige. A foie gras Tatin with
Port wine coulis, the generous smoked
salmon plate, tender beef with foie gras
in red wine sauce and a maple walnut
tart are promising.

● L'Aloyau SIM

3, rue de la Fontaine.
Tel. 03 87 37 33 72. Fax 03 87 76 24 30.
aloyau@wanadoo.fr
Closed Sun. dinner, Mon., mid-July–mid-Aug.
Prix fixe: 15€ (lunch), 24€, 29€.
A la carte: 35€.

Jacques Heitzmann watches over his
fine cuts of meat and his generous cuisine. His menus are terrific and allow you
to feast on a Riesling tart, tête de veau,
prime cut brochette, sirloin steak and
crème brûlée at a decent price. Charming service.

● L'Antre d'Eux SIM

3, rue des Parmentiers.
Tel.-Fax 03 87 37 31 49.
Closed Tue. dinner, Wed.
Prix fixe: 8€ (weekday lunch).
A la carte: 35€.

Denis Pink and Guy Korzinski have
handed over the walls of their convivial
den to local artists. The décor changes
with each new exhibit, the menu according to season. In the kitchen, Guy cooks
unpretentious fare. Chanterelle and garlic cream croustade, tomato and ham
carpaccio with thick slices of parmesan,
scallops in seafood broth and the basil
tomatoes and slow-cooked lamb shanks
are good value for money. The tiramisu
and chocolate mousse slip down a treat.

● L'Auberge du Mini-Golf SIM

Ile du Saulcy.
Tel.-Fax 03 87 30 74 02.
auberge-minigolf@wanadoo.fr
Closed Mon., Thu. dinner,
2 weeks 1 Nov. vac., Feb. vac.
Prix fixe: 27€, 42€. A la carte: 45€.

On an island in the Moselle, the mini-golf
acts as a backdrop for Henri Thomas' restaurant. His spicy, sweet-and-sour dishes
are a pleasant surprise. Fresh foie gras
with peach compote, salmon escalope
with pepper, honeyed duck breast and
the delicious chestnut cream are not bad
at all. Pretty waterside terrace.

● La Baraka SIM

At Hôtel de la Cathédrale,
25, pl de Chambre.
Tel. 03 87 36 33 92. Fax 03 87 75 40 75.
www.hotelcathedrale-metz.fr
Closed Wed., mid-July–mid-Aug.
Prix fixe: 20€, 23€, 25€. A la carte: 25–30€.

All the balm of North Africa finds its way
onto Taher Hocine's plates. His filo wraps,
couscous and tagines, not to mention the
Middle Eastern pastries and the mint tea,
take you on a pleasant detour into this
warmhearted culture. In the dining room,
Sadila waits on tables with a smile.

● Le Bistro de Metz SIM
"Chez Jean-Marie"

9-11, rue des Huiliers.
Tel. 03 87 75 64 72. Fax 03 87 50 56 35.
Closed Sun., Mon. dinner, 1 week Feb.,
1 week July.
Prix fixe: 19€. A la carte: 34€.

Jean-Marie Westelink has turned this center city bistro into a friendly *bouchon*.
Enjoy poached eggs in red wine sauce,
salade Lyonnaise (eggs, bacon chunks and
croutons), cod with potatoes, tête de veau
and figs roasted in rum. Prices are reasonable; the Beaujolais and Côtes-du-Rhônes
flow nicely. A relaxing atmosphere.

● Le Bistro des Sommeliers SIM

10, rue Pasteur.
Tel. 03 87 63 40 20. Fax 03 87 63 54 46.

lebistro dessommeliers@wanadoo.fr
Closed Sat. lunch, Sun., 1 week Christmas–
New Year's.
Prix fixe: 8,50€ (weekday lunch), 15€.
A la carte: 36–41€.

Ex-sommelier at La Goulue, Christophe Bastien carefully chooses wines that will go with Laurent Hoffman's fare. Duck breast and Jerusalem artichokes, chanterelle and parsley fricassée, curried monkfish carpaccio, strugeon escalope with peppers and fennel cream, oven-roasted rack of lamb with pesto, the knife-cut beef tartare and an apple streudel with cinnamon ice cream get everyone's vote.

● Chez Moi   SIM

22, pl des Charrons.
Tel. 03 87 74 39 79. Fax 03 87 74 53 62.
jose.roir@wanadoo.fr / www.chez-moi.fr
Closed Sun., Mon., Christmas–New Year's,
3 weeks Aug.
Prix fixe: 22€, 26€ (wine inc.).
A la carte: 35–45€.

In the historic neighborhood of the Mazelle, regional fare is second nature to José Roir. His Rabelaisian menu offers a bergamot-infused liqueur for aperitif, the parsley-seasoned rabbit with an original beer-flavored sorbet, duck breast with apples and pine honey and a baked mirbelle plum crêpe with an amusing Nancy macaron ice cream. With that, drink the Châteaux de Vaux Pinot Noir at 22 a bottle. The white designer Zen setting is pleasing without being pretentious.

● Chez l'Oncle Ernest   SIM

2 bis, rue des Tanneurs.
Tel. 03 87 75 49 09. Fax 03 87 76 77 79.
Closed Sun. dinner, Mon. dinner, Tue. dinner,
2 weeks beg. Aug.
Prix fixe: 8,90€ (lunch), 15,80€ (weekday
lunch), 24€, 5€ (child). A la carte: 37€.

Slightly to one side of the Place des Paraigues and at the foot of the historic hill of Sainte-Croix lies this old-fashioned bistro. There is quite a contrast between the décor and the modern building in which it is set, but Ernesto Salinas' recipes are

up-to-date renditions of daily selections. Pan-tossed scallops served with smoked salmon, the pike-perch with a beurre blanc, slow-cooked duck legs with roasted potatoes, not to omit the pretty Tatin with vanilla ice cream, are truly fulfilling.

● L'Instant   SIM

32, rue du Coëtlosquet.
Tel. 03 87 65 58 09.
touvier.f@numericable.fr / www.linstant.fr
Closed Sat. lunch, Sun., Mon. dinner.
A la carte: 35–40€.

Franck and Aline Touvier keep late hours in this easygoing spot where Virginie Koch is into fusion cooking. Some lovely surprises erupt with the marinated salmon with passion fruit and ginger, the salmon spring rolls with crunchy baby vegetables, curry-seasoned sesame chicken crumble and pineapple ravioli served on a bed of fruit. Careful service, measured prices: enough to seduce the town's younger clientèle.

● Jadis   SIM

1-3, rue du Grand-Wad.
Tel. 03 87 74 10 38. Fax 03 87 79 28 77.
schmitzd@wanadoo.fr
Closed Sun., Mon.
A la carte: 40€.

Visually, nothing has changed, though the current team has been completely revamped. Recent newcomer David Schmitz is into fresh and fresh produce. Scallops with balsamic vinegar, a salmon trilogy with a red tuna mille-feuille are not bad even if, now and then, things are a tad insipid. To finish, how about a discreet tiramisu or chocolate fondant? An address which is slowly earning its merit.

● La Toscane   SIM

12, rue Dupont-des-Loges.
Tel. 03 87 75 60 73.
Closed Sun. lunch.
A la carte: 32€.

The thin, crusty pizzas are so famous that there is an obligatory queue every night. People also come for the caprese salad, garlic sole, cream involtini and the tarte Tatin that are practically give-aways. Friendly service.

● La Ville de Casa   SIM

14-16, rue Mazelle.
Tel.-Fax 03 87 75 33 70.
Closed Mon., 1 month in summer.
Prix fixe: 15€ (wine inc.), 20€ (wine inc.),
25€ (wine inc.). A la carte: 30€.

The setting is as white as the town which gives its name to this quality showcase of Moroccan cuisine. The service is charming and no one's complaining about tuna wrapped in filo, pepper and tomato salad, the chicken tagine with pears, lamb brochettes, couscous and Middle Eastern pastries. Low prices.

● La Winstub   SIM

2 bis, rue Dupont-des-Loges.
Tel.-Fax 03 87 37 03 93.
Closed Sun., Mon., Christmas–New Year's,
1 week beg. Jan.
Prix fixe: 12,50€ (lunch, wine inc.),
7,90€ (child). A la carte: 30€.

Philippe de Cuyper, who just opened an Italian restaurant (O Tostino, 33, pl. du Quarteau, 03 87 74 46 43), continues to offer Alsatian fare in this easygoing Alsace-Lorraine-style *winstub*. Mixed salad, pike-perch with bacon, choucroute, escalope cooked in Alsatian wine and a sweet version of the regional tarte flambée, with thick cream, apples and Calvados, slip down nicely. Low prices and nice carafe wines.

In Ban Saint-Martin (57050). 1 km e.

● Parmentel   COM

5, rue du Général-de-Gaulle.
Tel. 03 87 32 67 45.
Closed Sat. lunch, Sun. dinner, Mon.,
1 week Feb., 2 weeks Aug.
Prix fixe: 24€ (weekday lunch). A la carte: 45€.

Behind a pedestrian facade on a busy street, this agreeable spot with its Provençal tones and stuccoed walls will attract the eye of many a crafty gourmet. In his open-plan kitchen, Etienne Parmentel, who worked under Roger Vergé at Mougins, concocts wily, light, fresh dishes. The salmon and tuna carpaccio duo with grapefruit, vineyard-keeper's pike-perch filet with a chanterelle ragout, duck breast with peaches and the berry mille-feuille with a light cream are accompanied by nice wines by the glass.

In Chailly-Les-Ennery (57365). 16,7 km from Metz.

● Auberge de Chailly   SIM

25, rue Principale.
Tel. 03 87 77 83 20. Fax 03 87 77 71 85.
Closed Sat. lunch, Sun dinner, Mon.
Prix fixe: 15€, 21€, 23€, 31€.
A la carte: 38€.

Pascal Behr, who used to work at the Buffet de la Gare in Metz, is friends with all the good chefs of the region who come here to make merry on their days off. His clever first menu offers tasty fare based on regional specialties: oven-browned Munster ravioli with Roquefort or the warm leek and cured ham salad with a duck mousse with Port, a salmon cream with potatoes or the classic but juicy sirloin steak simply seared and served with herb butter, before the fruit tart appears on the list. Don't say no! The baked pork trotters, the baked escargots and potatoes and also the pike-perch wrapped in crispy bacon melt in your mouth.

In Flevy (57365). 17 km n via A4, D1, D52C.

● Le P'tit Bouchon   SIM

43, Grand'rue.
Tel. 03 87 73 90 87. Fax 03 87 73 98 14.
gilles.pierre2@wanadoo.fr
Closed Sat. lunch, dinner (exc. weekends),
1 week Christmas–New Year's,
2 weeks beg. Aug.
Prix fixe: 12,50€. A la carte: 28€.

Gilles Pierre runs this modern-style, pleasant country *bouchon*, nicely revamped in red and white. Quiche lorraine, a Munster cheese tart, the two-fish brochette (rouget and Mediterranean sea bass), the Flemish carbonade (a local baked beef and beer stew) and a cherry tart won't make waves.

In Jouy-aux-Arches (57130). 12 km sw via A31, N57.

● **Le Charlemagne**

92, Grand'rue.
Tel.-Fax 03 87 60 86 44.
greg-lecharlemagne@hotmail.com
Closed Sat. lunch, Sun.
Prix fixe: 10€ (dinner), 19€ (lunch), 30€, 50€, 12€ (child).
A la carte: 35€.

Exit the Gallo Roman. Grégory Jeandeau has taken over this rustic dwelling which he's modernized, placing the wise Roger Monvignier at the stove. This good, classic chef is a dab hand at turning out traditional dishes with a light touch. The duck foie gras terrine with Pacherenc de Vic Bihl, poached eggs in red wine sauce with Burgundy escargots, a house bourride (fish stew with aïoli), duck breast with honey and Provençal-style brioche topped with candied fruits and sugar give a sunny touch to this popular Lorraine haunt.

In Malroy (57640). 8 km n via D1.

● **Aux Trois Capitaines** ⬤SIM

43, rue Principale.
Tel. 03 87 77 77 07. Fax 03 87 77 89 78.
george.geringer@wanadoo.fr
Prix fixe: 13,50€, 18€, 32€ (Sat., Sun., lunch). A la carte: 40€.

In this pretty village house with its deliberately old-fashioned dining room complete with fresco, fireplace and parquet floor, Marcel Moureaux refines up-to-date peasant fare with vim and vigor. On the plate, this means foie gras, delicious eggs and potatoes, a tender pike fish quenelle, frog legs with parsley, roasted cod with olive oil mashed potatoes, a braised lamb shank with thyme and baba au rhum. A large choice of quaffable wines.

In Mazagran (57530). 13 km via D954 (rte de Boulay).

● **Auberge de Mazagran** COM

Village Sainte-Barbe,
locale known as Mazagran.
Tel. 03 87 76 62 47. Fax 03 87 76 79 50.
mele-ciass@orange.fr
Closed Sun. dinner, Tue. dinner, Wed. lunch,

2 weeks beg. Jan., 2 weeks Aug.
Prix fixe: 25€, 49€. A la carte: 60€.

Peppy Cyril Monachon has taken over this pretty, old-fashioned inn without disrupting the style of his predecessor, Dominique Decreton. The house has kept up its look of an old 19th-century farmhouse with its garden and rustic interior. Where dishes are concerned, the pressed terrine of artichoke and goat cheese, cod filet with Bigorre ham, the suckling pig medallion with mirabelles and pineapple slow-cooked with Bourbon vanilla beans marry earthiness with refined quality.

In Plappeville (57050). 7 km nw, rte de Ban Saint-Martin.

● **Le Jardin d'Adam** ⬤COM

50, rue du Général-de-Gaulle.
Tel. 03 87 30 36 68. Fax 03 87 30 79 01.
le-jardin-d-adam@numericable.fr
Closed Tue. dinner, Wed.
Prix fixe: 25€, 35€, 60€.

It's easy to give in to the sin of greed in Anne and François Adam's garden. François' fresh and natural cooking has everything to seduce one. His dishes go straight to the essential: you need not look far to find the authentic taste of the duck foie gras with soft-simmered carrots, the roasted turbot with meat jus, the duckling filet served vineyard-keeper's-style (wrapped in grape leaves) and the dark chocolate sorbet with coffee syrup over shaved ice. There's no time to get bored here when the menus and dishes change daily. Some distinguished vintages, not always well known (such as Pascal Oury's white Moselle), are *de rigeur* in this winemaker's house with its refined décor. Anne is wonderful at reception and in the dining room.

In Saint-Julien-les-Metz (57070). 4,4 km nw

● **Au Poivre & Sel**

130, rue du Général-Diou.
Tel. 03 87 36 80 43.
Closed Sat. lunch, Sun., Mon. dinner.
Prix fixe: 15€ (lunch). A la carte: 30€.

It's easy to like this pleasant riverside inn with its luminous interiors, its oak parquet floors kept shiny with linseed oil and its Zen décor. With the help of irascible Mylène Bourlier in the dining room, Claude Thomas runs this establishment with verve. The cooking, signed by a youthful Paul Bie who trained in Savoie, astonishes one by its freshness and obvious talent. Salmon tartare, the escargot and asparagus croustade, a traditional chicken dish, oven-roasted ham accompanied by puffed potatoes and the crème brûlée in three flavors (pistachio, Bourbon vanilla and bergamot) make for a nice finale.

In Vezon (57420). 16 km sw, via A31 (Nancy).

● **Auberge de Vezon**   SIM

58, rue des Vignerons.
Tel.-Fax 03 87 69 91 98.
bernard.germain2@tiscali.fr
Closed Sun. dinner, Tue. dinner, Wed.,
Easter vac., 3 weeks Sept.
Prix fixe: 11€, 25€, 8€ (child).
A la carte: 35€.

A smiling, laid-back ambiance with a convivial cuisine: this is Bernard Germain's recipe for this simple inn in a winemaking village. House terrine, tarragon-seasoned frog legs and escargot cassolette, tête de veau with two sauces and the frozen mirabelle parfait are pleasurable. Reasonable prices.

In Woippy (57143). 5 km nw via D953.

● **Auberge Belles Fontaines**   SIM

51, rte de Thionville.
Tel.-Fax 03 87 31 99 46.
Closed dinner, Sat.
1 week Christmas–New Year's, 3 weeks Aug.
Prix fixe: 24,50€, 38€.

Danielle Marchesini gives you a charming welcome in this country manor. Chef Ludovic Lirhantz juggles with fresh market produce. Mediterranean sea bass tartare with vanilla-seasoned coconut milk, lobster and langoustine gazpacho, tuna medallions with basalmic crushed tomatoes and goose breast confit with garlic and basil make free with Provençal flavors. Nice thin honey and fig tart wih cinnamon ice cream.

01800 Ain. Paris 460 – Lyon 36 –
Bourg-en-Bresse 37 – Genève 119.
La Dombes, water ponds and the pretty town of Pérouges are just beyond this little crossroads town.

 HOTELS-RESTAURANTS

● **Claude Lutz**   COM

17, rue de Lyon.
Tel. 04 74 61 06 78. Fax 04 74 34 75 23.
Closed Sun. dinner, Mon., 3 weeks Nov.,
1 week July.
16 rooms: 40–58€.
Prix fixe: 28€, 42€, 58€.
A la carte: 45–55€.

There's a rumor that Claude Lutz wants to sell. Nevertheless, this fine professional, who trained with Bocuse, continues to turn out good, classic dishes. The marinated raw salmon, foie gras duo, morels in puff pastry with cream, lobster fricassée with Sauternes and the chicken with creamy morel sauce mean serious application. A few rooms for a stayover.

MIETESHEIM see GUNDERSHOFFEN
MIGNALOUX-BEAUVOIR see POITIERS

12100 Aveyron. Paris 644 – Mende 97 –
Rodez 66 – Albi 108 – Montpellier 115.
This panoramic tannery town in the South of the Aveyron is a close cousin of the Languedoc. The Tarn gorges are close by and the GR wanders through the wonders of the Rouergue region.

 HOTELS-RESTAURANTS

■ **Mercure International**   🏨

1, pl de la Tine.
Tel. 05 65 59 29 00. Fax 05 65 59 29 01.
mercure.millau@wanadoo.fr
www.mercure.com
Rest. closed Sun. dinner, Mon. lunch.
57 rooms: 83–122€. 1 suite: 150€.
Prix fixe: 18€, 19€, 24€, 40€.

Built in the seventies, this hotel has classic, welcoming rooms and an honest table done in Mediterranean colors, the Bouchon de la Fontaine, where Eric Guillemin's offerings (the regional degustation plate, a marinated scallop brochette and the tiramisu with orange sauce) slip down with ease.

■ La Musardière 🏛

34, av de la République.
Tel. 05 65 60 20 63. Fax 05 65 59 78 13.
freewebs.com/lamusardiere
Closed 2 weeks Nov., 2 weeks Jan.
Rest. closed Sat. lunch, Sun. dinner, Mon.
14 rooms: 110–175€.
Prix fixe: 25€. A la carte: 50€.

Bertrand Debiossac presides over this 19th-century dwelling in the center of town. Rooms are comfortable, some have a balcony overlooking the park or a bathroom with a Jacuzzi. There's been a change in the kitchen. Jean-Emmanuel Christ serves up tasty, neoclassical fare. The fresh duck foie gras, a fish trio with beurre blanc sauce and the duck breast with crushed sugared almonds are memorable.

■ Château de Creissels 🏛

2 km, rte de Saint-Affrique.
Tel. 05 65 60 16 59. Fax 05 65 61 24 63.
www.chateau-de-creissels.com
Closed Sun. dinner (off season),
Mon. lunch (off season), Jan.–end Feb.
30 rooms: 47–89€.
Prix fixe: 23€, 32€, 38,50€, 50€,
12€ (child). A la carte: 45€.

David and Florence Lassauvetat currently watch over this medieval castle, enlarged in the seventies. The rooms have a great view over the countryside. The restaurant comes up trumps with the Roquefort in puff pastry, the grilled scallops with ceps, monkfish medallion with morels, rack of lamb, pan-seared foie gras escalope and the wild strawberry gratin. The park makes for an ideal leisure area and the billiard table in the library ensures a few happy moments.

● La Terrasse COM

15, rue Saint-Martin.
Tel. 05 65 60 74 89.
Closed Sun. dinner, Mon., Oct.
Prix fixe: 14,50€ (weekday lunch), 21€,
25€, 32€, 8€ (child). A la carte: 37€.

Michel Coffy takes great care over his sunny dishes in his fine Terrasse with its orange and red interior. The brousse (soft white ewe's cheese) cake with thyme-seasoned pan-tossed langoustines, salmon medallions with slow-roasted garlic, cod filet with saffron sauce and minced duck with Roquefort are what you would expect.

● Auberge de la Borie 🛏SIM
Blanque

3 km via rte de Cahors, via D911.
Tel.-Fax 05 65 60 85 88.
Closed dinner (Jan.–Mar. exc. Sat.),
Feb. vac.
Prix fixe: 12€, 19€, 25€.

There's a limitless view of the town from the dining room of Marie-Hélène Negron's restaurant. The cooking, meanwhile, has its eye fixed on Lyon with the sausage and walnut salad, trout in a crêpe pouch, tête de veau with sauce ravigote and the frozen nougat. A warm welcome and a decent bill.

● Capion SIM

3, rue J.-F.-Alméras.
Tel. 05 65 60 00 91. Fax 05 65 60 42 13.
Closed Tue. dinner, Wed., 1 week beg. Jan.,
3 weeks July.
Prix fixe: 18€, 24€, 34€, 13€ (weekday
lunch). A la carte: 29–34€.

The Avelines have managed to create an ambiance and a cuisine which ensures them a daily stream of regulars. The lunch menus are truly low in price and the setting, like the welcome, is pleasing. The menu offers quail with pan-seared foie gras and raspberry sauce, salmon trout filet with beurre rouge, lamb sweetbreads with parsley and shallots and a pastry cart.

MINERVE

34210 Hérault. Paris 814 – Béziers 46 – Carcassonne 44 – Narbonne 32.
Perched on a spur of land, this historic capital of the Minervois is worth a careful visit.

 HOTELS-RESTAURANTS

■ Le Relais Chantovent

17, Grand-Rue.
Tel. 04 68 91 14 18. Fax 04 68 91 81 99.
Closed mid-Dec.–mid-Mar.
Rest. closed Sun. dinner, Mon.
8 rooms: 40–50€.
Prix fixe: 19,50€, 36€, 8,50€ (child).
A la carte: 40€.

Right in the heart of the village, Maïté and Louis Evenou give you a warm welcome and offer you a cozy room. Their son Patrick is at the stove and proposes some serious fare such as well-crafted scrambled eggs with truffles, spicy shrimp fricassée, lamb pastilla and espresso dacquoise with dark chocolate. Coteaux du Languedoc or Minervois wines are suitable accompaniments.

MIONNAY

01390 Ain. Paris 458 – Lyon 22 – Bourg-en-Bresse 44 – Meximieux 25.
The gateway to the Dombes houses the famous *Croquembouche* inn recreated by Fanny Deschamps.

 HOTELS-RESTAURANTS

● Alain Chapel

N83.
Tel. 04 78 91 82 02. Fax 04 78 91 82 37.
chapel@relaischateaux.com
www.alainchapel.fr
Closed Feb. Rest. closed Mon., Tue., Fri. lunch.
12 rooms: 120–140€.
Prix fixe: 105€, 135€, 150€.
A la carte: 120–150€.

What a team! Creative, ambitious, still as open to the world as during the time of the great Alain (Chapel) who is no longer with us …and of that other Alain (Ducasse) who cut his teeth here. Suzanne Chapel—whose son Romain is following in his father's footsteps—captains the ship. She's a constant, smiling presence with a heartwarming word for everyone. Philippe Jousse, seconded by Pierre Mercier, produces dazzling cuisine. It reflects the seasons, the tastes of the *terroir*, with that dash of modernity which underscores a great table. Officially there is no à la carte menu but you can choose between the well-composed set menus. Open your taste buds with ham in anise-flavored Côtes-du-Rhône aspic served with spring vegetables in tarragon cream sauce. The remarkable balance of flavors only gets better with the rouget filet and tender potatoes, heightened with a tomato chutney. Summer shines on the plates, but autumn is full of taste and vigor with the appearance of a game consommé with Soisson white beans and herb-stuffed pasta. Desserts are the domain of Stéphane Levillain who works with the seasons and, at the first nip in the air, offers a frozen chestnut vacherin, an orange carpaccio with candied peel and little yellow Chartreuse candies. Christophe Equille has the keys to the cellar and is always ready to propose some undiscovered gem. Vincent, Michel and Cédric Perugini assure the service which counts in a great establishment. This is an authentic Relais & Châteaux where, in order to truly profit from the dining, you can choose from twelve adorable rooms and an exquisite breakfast with which to prolong the dream.

MIRAMBEAU

17150 Charente-Maritime. Paris 512 – Cognac 47 – Bordeaux 73 – Royan 45.
An ancient village and its château set between the vineyards of Cognac and Bordeaux.

 **HOTELS-RESTAURANTS**

● Château de Mirambeau

1, av Comte-Duchatel.
Tel. 05 46 04 91 20. Fax 05 46 04 26 72.
reservation@chateauxmirambeau.com
www.chateauxmirambeau.com

Closed end Sept.–end Mar.
16 rooms: 200–235€. 3 suites: 460–675€.
Prix fixe: 40€, 50€, 60€, 80€.
A la carte: 75€–95€.

Luxury and elegance are the hallmarks of this magnificent 19th-century château situated not far from the coast of Charente. The few, choice rooms are sumptuous and spacious. The eight-hectare park, the swimming pools and the fitness center are a haven of leisure and relaxation. At table, Fréderic Milan—who trained with Vergé at Mougins—makes the most of seasonal offerings. The marinated salmon carpaccio with pineapple, rosemary and lemongrass-seasoned crabmeat, the lobster with slow-simmered leeks served with vanilla-perfumed lychees and the buttered beef roast with summer truffle–seasoned potatoes, sprout salad and parmesan cream both stun and seduce. Dessert is full of finesse with the Sacher Agaruani biscuit, cardamom-infused apricot compote and apricot raspberry sorbet. The advice of sommelier Aurélien Vincent, the service and the welcome are as good as you'll get in any grand establishment.

MIREPOIX

09500 Ariège. Paris 755 – Carcassonne 50 – Castelnaudary 35 – Foix 38 – Limoux 34 – Pamiers 24.
A historic pearl in the Ariège.

HOTELS-RESTAURANTS

● **Relais Royal**
8, rue du Maréchal-Clauzel.
Tel. 05 61 60 19 19. Fax 05 61 60 14 15.
relaisroyal@relaischateau.com
www.relaisroyal.com
Closed beg. Jan.–beg. Feb.
Rest. closed lunch (Nov.–Apr., exc. Sun.),
Sat. lunch, Mon.
5 rooms: 150–220€. 3 suites: 220–270€.
Prix fixe: 32€, 85€, 18€ (child).
A la carte: 80€.

Built in the 18th century and renovated in 2004, what was once the mayor's residence has been turned into a charming hotel affiliated with the Relais & Châteaux group. A central courtyard, heated swimming pool, terra cotta-tiled floors, marble fireplaces and elegant rooms seduce from the start. In the grandiose setting of the restaurant, Abraham Robert offers up *terroir* dishes up-dated with flair. We like the duck foie gras terrine with spicy apples, the salmon trout with orange and carrot sauce, the veal simmered in amber beer and the dark chocolate fondant. Lovely welcome.

● **Les Remparts**
6, cours L. Pons-Tande.
Tel. 05 61 68 12 15. Fax 05 61 60 80 22.
sarl.lesremparts@wanadoo.fr
www.hotelremparts.com
Closed Mon. lunch.
Prix fixe: 17€ (weekday lunch), 25€, 36€, 50€. 10€ (child).

Géraldine Portoles likes contrast: the backdrop is medieval with lots of bare stone and wood, while the furniture is modern. There are two dining rooms, one bedecked with beams, the other in a vaulted cellar. She marries savors and spices from here and there in some innovative preparations: salmon tartare with citrus, star anise and parmesan, plaice with almonds and preserved lemons, veal sweetbreads with a bay-infused jus, chocolate cake with a melted salted-butter caramel center and apple raisin spring rolls with mint sauce are irresistible.

MISSILLAC

44780 Loire-Atlantique. Paris 438 – Nantes 63 – Redon 25 – Saint-Nazaire 37 – Vannes 54.
On the edge of the natural park of the Brière lies lovely parkland, a golf course, fairy tale château and a village with its church boasting a very fine altar piece.

HOTELS-RESTAURANTS

● **La Bretesche**
Rte de la Baule.
Tel. 02 51 76 86 96. Fax 02 40 66 99 47.
hotel@bretesche.com / www.bretesche.com

Closed mid-Jan.–mid-Mar.
Rest. closed Sun. dinner (off season),
Mon., Tue. lunch.
24 rooms: 200–446€. 6 suites: 275–556€.
Prix fixe: 40€, 60€, 80€, 20€ (child).
A la carte: 65€–75€.

It's a prestigious spot: a 15th-century château on the edge of the regional park of
the Brière. Furnishings are very high class:
splendid rooms, a swimming pool and
eighteen-hole golf course, tennis court,
woods and pond. Gilles Charpy's cooking
delicately harmonizes with the tranquil
surroundings and the season's offerings.
His dishes are sincere and uncontrived.
The wild thyme-seasoned langoustines
with a spring onions and Aquitaine "perl-
ita" caviar, the pan-simmered line-fished
sea bream with stuffed zucchini and mixed
vegetables cooked in butter, fresh herbs
and parmesan, the pork trotter cake with
Paimpol white beans and the pork tenderloin in an herb and young sprout salad
yield carefully studied flavors. The Guanaja
chocolate cake with crunchy "pearls" and
a verbena- and lemongrass-infused sauce,
served with a pine nut crumble and strawberry sorbet, is delicious.

MITTELBERGHEIM

67140 Bas-Rhin. Paris 500 – Sélestat 17 –
Strasbourg 37 – Sélestat 20.
This exquisite Renaissance village on a knoll has
two clock towers as well as hillsides of vineyards,
including the zippy Zotzenberg which makes a
wonderful Sylvaner. Meander through its streets
and go knocking on cellar doors.

 HOTELS-RESTAURANTS

● **Winstub Gilg**
1, rte du Vin.
Tel. 03 88 08 91 37. Fax 03 88 08 45 17.
info@hotel-gilg.com / www.hotel-gilg.com
Closed beg. Jan.–beg. Feb.
Rest. closed Tue., Wed.
15 rooms: 45–85€.
Prix fixe: 20€, 45€, 70€, 11€ (child).
A la carte: 40€–45€.

This typical dwelling where regional
culinary traditions excel sings an ode to
Alsace. Two generations, Georges Gilg
and his son-in-law Vincent Reuschlé,
are firmly and expertly in charge of this
establishment: a good example of the
transmission of tastes and know-how
of the *terroir*. The well-devised recipes
are always topical. The delicious foie
gras with truffle-infused jus in aspic,
the exquisite monkfish medallions with
curry-perfumed sesame seeds and the
lamb medallion served over a ratatouille
seasoned with wild thyme leaves a delicate taste in the mouth. The meal ends
with a light ring-shaped savarin yeast
cake soaked in Kirsch, served with fresh
fruit, which is zingy and fresh. The wine
list merits a detour and there are some
regional steals for less than 25 a bottle. The price is right and the pleasure is
intense.

● **Am Lindeplatzel**   COM
71, rue Principale.
Tel. 03 88 08 10 69. Fax 03 88 08 45 08.
Closed Mon. lunch, Wed. dinner, Thu.,
10 days at end Nov., 3 weeks Feb.,
10 days at end Aug.
Prix fixe: 29€, 34,50€, 52€, 10€ (child). A
la carte: 54€.

A bit of here and a bit of there is what Patrick Durot looks for from his region and
the rest of the world in order to concoct
well-crafted dishes. It's hard to choose,
once you've had the mixed greens,
between sautéed shrimp with Chinese
noodles or rack of lamb with thyme-
infused jus, the chocolate fondant or a
berry vacherin, but everything is worth
a detour.

MITTELHAUSBERGEN see STRASBOURG

MITTELHAUSEN

67170 Bas-Rhin. Paris 475 – Strasbourg 20
– Saverne 22 – Haguenau 18.
This is the Kochersberg, with its large farms,
its fertile fields and a village with its old houses
and inscriptions painted on their facades.

HOTELS-RESTAURANTS

■ A l'Etoile

12, rue de la Hey.
Tel. 03 88 51 28 44. Fax 03 88 51 24 79.
www.hotel-etoile.net
Hotel closed 2 weeks beg. Jan.
Rest. closed Sun. dinner, Mon.,
2 weeks beg. Jan., mid-July–beg. Aug.
24 rooms: 42–53€.
Prix fixe: 9,50€ (lunch), 17€, 26€, 30€, 35€.

Life is so pleasant here that one would like to stay forever at the Bruckmanns. Chantal's welcome is charming, the prices are very reasonable, the rooms little havens of peace and Jacques' cooking, a delight. Trained at Mischler at Lembach, he interprets Alsatian recipes with brio: rabbit and beer aspic terrine, pike-perch pot-au-feu with cream sauce, lamb tenderloin and the soft-centered chocolate cake are irreproachable. The lovely painting *l'Alsacien* by Luc Hueber presides over this venerable establishment.

MITTERSHEIM

57930 Moselle. Paris 413 – Metz 85 – Nancy 64 – Sarrebourg 22 – Sarre-Union 17 – Saverne 39.
mutche@wanadoo.fr.
This village in the heart of the natural park of Lorraine is an ideal stopping point along the romantic route of the ponds of the Moselle.

 HOTELS-RESTAURANTS

■ L'Escale

Rte de Dieuze.
Tel. 03 87 07 67 01. Fax 03 87 07 54 57.
www.lescalemittersheim.fr
Closed beg. Feb.–mid-Feb.
13 rooms: 45–55€.
Prix fixe: 10€ (lunch, weekdays), 15€, 20€, 25€, 8€ (child). A la carte: 35–40€.

You'll feel right at home in this country inn, where you're greeted like a member of the family. The rooms are charming and practical and Jean-Paul Noé's cooking warmhearted. He delights visitors with a house mirabelle plum terrine, pike-perch filet simmered in Riesling, a deboned and stuffed pigeon and a frozen wild raspberry soufflé. Reasonable prices.

MOELAN-SUR-MER

29350 Finistère. Paris 523 – Quimper 46 – Concarneau 28 – Lorient 24 – Quimperlé 10.
otsi.moelan.sur.mer@wanadoo.fr.
Along the artist's route in Cornouaille lies this pretty oyster country along the Merrien inlet.

 HOTELS-RESTAURANTS

■ Manoir de Kertalg

Rte de Riec-sur-Belon, 3 km w via D24.
Tel. 02 98 39 77 77. Fax 02 98 39 72 07.
kertalg@free.fr / www.manoirdekertalg.com
Closed mid-Nov.–end Apr.
6 rooms: 98–180€. 3 suites: 180–230€.

This century-old manor sits in the center of a wooded park. It has large, modern rooms and regularly organizes maginificent exhibitions.

■ Les Moulins du Duc

2 km nw.
Tel. 02 98 96 52 52. Fax 02 98 96 52 53.
www.hotel-moulins-du-duc.com
Closed beg. Dec.–end Feb.
Rest. closed Sun. dinner (off season),
Mon. (off season), Mon. lunch.
20 rooms: 78–150€. 4 suites: 155–189€.
Prix fixe: 29€ (lunch), 36€, 50€, 66€.
A la carte: 65€.

This hotel, composed of a heated indoor pool, a sauna and several Breton houses turned into rooms and duplexes, mainly attracts gourmets. In his millhouse, Thierry Quilfen serves up invigorating regional dishes such as duck foie gras served with a plum reduction, lobster tail poached in bouillon and then browned in the oven, squab wrapped in cabbage and a kouign-amann.

MOERNACH see FERRETTE

MOISSAC

82200 Tarn-et-Garonne. Paris 645 –
Agen 42 – Cahors 63 – Toulouse 74.
On the banks of the Tarn, the tastiest grapes
in France and the oldest cloister in the world
attract gourmets and travelers from around
the world.

 HOTELS-RESTAURANTS

● **Le Pont Napoléon**

2, allée Montebello.
Tel. 05 63 04 01 55. Fax 05 63 04 34 44.
dussau.lenapoleon@wanadoo.fr
www.le-pont-napoleon.com
Closed Sun., Mon., Jan., Nov. 1 vac.,
Christmas (24 and 25 Dec. dinner).
12 rooms: 29–56€.
Prix fixe: 23€, 50€, 65€.

After a stint with Ducasse and at the château de Mercuès, Michel Dussau has come
home and put down his pots by the riverside in this house full of pretty old-fashioned rooms. In the kitchen, taste and
talent are combined in the summer truffle-seasoned green beans and foie gras, the
pan-seared rouget layered with crunchy
vegetables, the dried chorizo with piquillo peppers, the grilled rack of lamb with
fresh legumes and rosemary-seasoned
ratatouille and the upside-down apricot
tart with a verbena-infused cold cream
and gelatin dessert. Wines selected by
Fabienne Maupas and the moderate prices
will add to your pleasure.

■ **Le Chapon Fin**

3, pl des Recollets.
Tel. 05 63 04 04 22. Fax 05 63 04 58 44.
info@lechaponfin-moissac.com
www.lechaponfin-moissac.com
Rest. closed Mon. (off season),
Tue. (off season).
18 rooms: 45–65€. 4 suites: 70–80€.
Prix fixe: 25€, 35€, 10€ (child).
A la carte: 45–52€.

This hotel is right next to the cloister on
the market square. Recently renovated, it
offers lovely, spacious, welcoming rooms.

The cuisine fits in with the family atmosphere. Duck foie gras terrine with slow-
cooked caramelized onions, monkfish
marinated with sweet peppers, lamb
shanks braised with rosemary, like the
delicious fresh seasonal fruits with mascarpone and balsamic syrup, are irreproachable.

● **L'Auberge du Cloître** COM

Pl Durand-de-Bredon.
Tel. 05 63 04 37 50.
Closed Mon., Wed. dinner (off season),
Christmas–New Year's.
Prix fixe: 12,60€, 21€, 24,60€.
A la carte: 50€.

At the entrance to the cloister, this former
coaching inn houses a choice table. In the
rustic dining room or on the sheltered terrace, Christophe Guillossou deftly handles the fine local products. The scallop
salad with basalmic vinegar and truffles,
the grilled tuna with olive oil and basil,
the duck breast with green peppercorns
and the desserts vary with the mood of
the chef and slip down nicely with wines
of Cahors and Bergerac.

MOLITG-LES-BAINS

66500 Pyrénées-Orientales. Paris 907-
Perpignan 51 – Prades 8 – Quillan 55.
A crag, a rock slide, an emerald lake, the green
slopes of mount Paracolis, a Baroque tower and
its outbuildings and, at the foot of the hill, a
stylish spa.

 HOTELS-RESTAURANTS

● **Château de Riell**

Tel. 04 68 05 04 40. Fax 04 68 05 04 37.
riell@relaischateaux.fr
www.relaischateau.com/riell
Closed 1 Nov.–1 Apr.
Rest. closed lunch (exc. weekends).
16 rooms: 142–270€. 3 suites: 280–388€.
Prix fixe: 43€. A la carte: 75€–80€.

Biche Barthélemy has turned what once
was a ruin into a Relais & Châteaux with
a fine park, tennis court and swimming

pool. After relaxation comes rest in the magnificently appointed rooms of the château or in the family cottages. Lionel Migliori, formerly of Guérard's, offers up from the kitchen a symphony of flavors and dishes with a Catalan accent. In the dining room the ballet of the waiters is perfectly orchestrated. Be sure to try the cool tomato soup with a mustard-seasoned ice cream quenelle, the cod filet steamed and served over assorted greens, presented with a vegetable consommé and shellfish-flavored butter, the grilled rack of lamb with a creamy garlic sauce on a bed of spinach and roasted pine nuts and the rhubarb and strawberry crumble, refreshed with lime juice, which are all simply divine.

■ Grand Hôtel Thermal

Tel. 04 68 05 00 50. Fax 04 68 05 02 91.
Closed end Nov.–end Mar.
54 rooms: 52–113€. 12 suites: 110–130€.
Prix fixe: 24€. A la carte: 40€.

The spa has been modernized by the Barthélemys and this old-fashioned hotel welcomes guests to the tune of Pablo Casals. The fifties-style rooms, reception area and hallways are refreshingly retro. The spacious rooms are more modern. The cuisine for residents is far from awkward with the gazpacho and marinated anchovies, grilled salmon, veal tenderloin medallion simmered with lemongrass and peaches and the chocolate dessert.

MOLLKIRCH

67190 Bas-Rhin. Paris 450 – Strasbourg 41
– Molsheim 12 – Saverne 35 – Mutzig 8.
Brisk Vosges air between the Bruche valley and the Grendelbruch mountains.

 HOTELS-RESTAURANTS

■ Fischhutte

30, rte de Grendelbruch.
Tel. 03 88 97 42 03. Fax 03 88 97 51 85.
fischhutte@wanadoo.fr / www.fischhutte.com
Closed 2 weeks end Feb.–mid-Mar., 1 week at end June–beg. July Rest. closed Mon., Tue.
14 rooms: 54–74€. 2 suites: 90€.

Prix fixe: 13€ (dinner), 16€ (dinner), 32€, 45€ (wine inc.), 12€ (child). A la carte: 44€.

Bernard Schahl greets occasional customers and regulars with a smile. The rooms are cute and the cuisine pleasing. His generous poultry salad, spicy duck foie gras, pike-perch filet with spring cabbage choucroute, leg of venison with mushrooms and fresh fromage blanc tart meet with great success. Jacky Bossuet advises on wines with authority.

MOLSHEIM

67120 Bas-Rhin. Paris 475 – Strasbourg 28
– Sélestat 34.
infos@ot-molsheimmutzig.com.
The cars (Bugatti is from here), the wine (Bruderthal grand cru), the beauty of the monuments (Metzig is a major Jesuit church): all contribute to the soul and charm of this city in the round.

 HOTELS-RESTAURANTS

● Diana

14, rue Sainte-Odile.
Tel. 03 88 38 51 59. Fax 03 88 38 87 11.
info@hotel-diana.com / www.hotel-diana.com
Rest. closed Sun. dinner, New Year's.
55 rooms: 78–93€. 1 suite: 170€.
Prix fixe: 26€, 58€. A la carte: 45€.

Swimming pool, sauna and mini-fitness center all add to the pleasure of a stay at Christine and Michel Baly's contemporary establishment. Set in a one-and-a-half-hectare park, spacious comfortable rooms await the guests. At mealtimes, Michel Knipilaire's menu makes your mouth water. His overtly French cuisine is deftly handled and allows a few escapades abroad. Serrano ham with melon, sea bream tagine with mild peppers, spice-rubbed duck breast with orange-infused fennel are pleasant surprises. Olive oil ice cream served with spiced lace cookies form a delicate conclusion. These dishes are washed down with fine wines from Alsace, Bordeaux or Barsac like château Coutet, owned by the Balys. Exemplary welcome and service.

■ Le Bugatti

Rue de la Commanderie.
Tel. 03 88 49 89 00. Fax 03 88 38 36 00.
info@hotel-le-bugatti.com
www.hotel-le-bugatti.com
Closed 24 Dec.–2 Jan.
45 rooms: 47–53€.

Annex of the Diana, this modern establishment bears the name of the nearby car manufacturer and offers pleasant, moderately priced rooms in a modern setting.

● La Metzig

1, pl de l'Hôtel-de-Ville.
Tel. 03 88 38 26 24. Fax 03 88 49 36 27.
Closed Tue. dinner, Wed.
Prix fixe: 7,50€ (child). A la carte: 41€.

In the gothic cellars of this Renaissance house, you will be glad to try escargots, potato cakes, pike-perch with almonds, ham and cheese-stuffed veal escalope and the frozen Marc-flavored kouglof. Local wines flow from the source.

MOMMENHEIM see BRUMATH

32260 Gers. Paris 730 – Aire-sur-l'Adour 105 – Toulouse 100 – Auch 20 – Mirande 19.
In the heart of the tranquil Gers.

■/● HOTELS-RESTAURANTS

● Le Bouchon Gaston

In the village.
Tel.-Fax 05 62 65 48 81.
www.compagniedesvins.com
Closed beg. Oct.–end Apr.
Rest. closed Mon., Tue., Wed.
3 rooms: 40–48€.
Prix fixe: 25€.

Christian Termotte's wine cellar doubles as a popular eatery where you can wash down foie gras with a Pacherenc or marry foie gras terrine seasoned with Pacherenc, stuffed guinea hen breast cooked in a pig's bladder and the crème brûlée with some of the best bottles of the Southwest.

79320 Deux-Sèvres. Paris 401 – Bressuire 15 – Cholet 50 – Niort 55 – La Roche-sur-Yon 80.
In the Sèvre, not far from the Vendée, this spot is an ode to a verdant countryside.

■/● HOTELS-RESTAURANTS

■ Saint-Pierre

Rte de Niort.
Tel. 05 49 72 88 88. Fax 05 49 72 88 89.
lesaint-pierre@wanadoo.fr
Rest. closed Sun. dinner and Fri. (Oct.–Apr.), Sat. lunch.
30 rooms: 43–52€.
Prix fixe: 20€, 48€.

A modern, bright, wooden structure with exposed beams with practical, well-equipped and inexpensive rooms. A professional welcome and a well-crafted cuisine in the Charentais style, which can be savored in the garden in summer.

MONETIER-LES-BAINS see
SERRE-CHEVALIER
MONIEUX see SAULT
MONSWILLER see SAVERNE

31530 Haute-Garonne. Paris 680 – Auch 62 – Toulouse 20 – Pujaudran 16.
The fringes of the Gers in Toulousain country, like an ode to the true countryside of the greater Midi.

■/● HOTELS-RESTAURANTS

■ Le Ratelier

Chemin du Ratelier.
Tel. 05 61 85 43 36. Fax 05 61 85 76 98.
leratelier@wanadoo.fr / www.leratelier.fr
Rest. closed Tue.
26 rooms: 45–60€.
Prix fixe: 14,80€ (weekdays), 18,80€, 22,50€, 23,50€, 29€, 10€ (child).
A la carte: 35€.

A few kilometers from Toulouse, surrounded by a wooded park, lies this old farmhouse gracefully converted by Béatrice Legeay. Some of the comfortable and practical rooms have just been renovated, but it is Eric Lingner's cooking in particular which draws the crowds. In the dining room, with its stone walls and exposed beams, foie gras cappuccino with chanterelles, Atlantic sea bass filet with tapenade, minced duck breast with orange sauce and the frozen prune and Armagnac parfait provide comfort without breaking the bank.

MONTARGIS

45200 Loiret. Paris 110 – Auxerre 21 – Bourges 118 – Orléans 73.
offtourisme-district.montargis@wanadoo.fr.
The "Venice of the Gâtinais" is also the capital of the praline and boasts more than one charm. Don't hesitate to take a detour from the N7 in order to discover its 127 bridges and canals.

 HOTELS-RESTAURANTS

● **Hôtel de la Gloire**
74, av du Général-de-Gaulle.
Tel. 02 38 85 04 69. Fax 02 38 98 52 32.
www.maitrescuisiniersdefrance.com
Closed Tue., Wed., Feb. vac., 2 weeks Aug.
10 rooms: 57–65€.
Prix fixe: 30€, 52€. A la carte: 75€.

At the entrance to the town, Jean-Claude Martin's house offers a few comfortable rooms, all decorated differently, but it is mainly the table of this French master chef which pleases his visitors. In the contemporary dining room, lobster salad, roasted Atlantic sea bass with mustard sauce presented with thinly sliced tomatoes, sautéed veal sweetbread and kidney accompanied by slow-simmered vegetables and the fruit tart from the dessert cart pay due respect to the finest produce of each season.

■ **Le Coche de Briare**
72, pl de la République.
Tel. 02 38 85 30 75. Fax 02 38 93 44 68.

Closed Feb. vac., 3 weeks Aug.
Rest. closed Sun. dinner, Mon., Thu.
10 rooms: 38–47€.
Prix fixe: 19,50€ (weekday lunch), 27,50€, 38€, 12€ (child).

Bernard Daux starts by choosing his products intelligently before transforming them with simplicity. A slice of foie gras served hot, oven-browned pike-perch with crayfish, venison steak (in season), veal sweetbreads with langoustines and the frozen praline soufflé are finely honed work. There are a few quiet rooms for a pleasant stay.

■ **Ibis et Brasserie de la Poste**
2, pl Victor-Hugo.
Tel. 02 38 98 00 68. Fax 02 38 89 14 37.
h0861@accor.com / www.ibishotel.com
Closed Christmas.
59 rooms: 48–67€.
Prix fixe: 11,80€, 19,90€, 22€, 26,90€, 7,50€ (child). A la carte: 26–34€.

The hotel offers no more than moderate comfort but the brasserie-style restaurant is not bad at all. The honey-roasted goat cheese salad, pike-perch and crayfish tails with beurre blanc, an enormous choucroute and the dessert presented on a painter's palette are irreproachable.

In Fontenay-sur-Loing (45210).
Rte de Ferrière via N7.

■ **Domaine de Vaugouard**
Chemin des Bois.
Tel. 02 38 89 79 00. Fax 02 38 89 79 01.
info@vaugouard.com / www.vaugouard.com
Closed 10 days at end Dec.
48 rooms: 120–205€. 3 suites: 160–240€.
Prix fixe: 25€, 42€ (dinner).

Imagine: in the center of a golf course sits an 18th-century manor house with well-appointed rooms, a riding stable and a fitness center. A dream? No, a pleasing reality as is the cooking of Pierre Legrand. A pressed artichoke and foie gras terrine, tempura-style fried John Dory, rack of lamb and the brioche pain perdu make up choice menus.

MONTAUBAN

82000 Tarn-et-Garonne. Paris 643 –
Toulouse 55 – Agen 74 – Albi 72 –
Cahors 61.
officetourisme@montauban.com.
On its spur undercut by a bend in the Tarn river, the town of Ingres reclines langorously. The historic center, the neoclassical houses of the Place Franklin-Roosevelt, the cathedral of Notre-Dame and the embankment along the Pont-Vieux clamor to be visited at length.

 HOTELS-RESTAURANTS

■ Crowne Plaza & Table des Capucins

6-8, quai de Verdun.
Tel. 05 63 22 00 00. Fax 05 63 22 00 01.
contact@cp-montauban.com
Rest. closed Sat. lunch, Sun.
80 rooms: 200–250€. 4 suites: 350–450€.
Prix fixe: 25€ (weekday lunch), 33€, 52€, 70€.

This 18th-century convent transformed into a grand, modern hotel opposite the Tarn has created quite a stir. The rooms are contemporary and very Zen; the modern bar, the cloister promenade and the chapel dedicated to receptions have class. The cherry on the cake? The fine, vibrant cuisine of Hervé Sauton. This native of Chamalières in Auvergne, who was trained by Loiseau in Saulieu before going to the Castellet in the Var, has the means to do well in this setting. The tarragon-seasoned shredded crab, pan-seared foie gras and New Zealand spinach with lemon oil seasoned-potatoes and a berry caramel, free-range poultry with shiitake fricassée and the spicy caramelized pineapple with lime meringue and aged rum ice cream are well-honed dishes. A young yet already experienced sommelier presides over a fine choice of Southern vintages.

■ Mercure

12, rue Notre-Dame.
Tel. 05 63 63 17 23. Fax 05 63 66 43 66.
h2183@accor.co / www.accorhotels.com
44 rooms: 89–120€.

Prix fixe: 14€, 16,50€, 25€, 7€ (child).
A la carte: 35–40€.

A noble, 18th-century town house is now a chain hotel without any great personality. The rooms are practical and the restaurant will satisfy large or lesser appetites. Foie gras with seasonal fruits, salad in the style of Quercy, the galinail (deboned chicken thigh stuffed with garlic), tête de veau served warm with sauce gribiche and the warm blackcurrant soufflé slip down respectably.

■ Hôtel Orsay & Cuisine d'Alain

Pl de la Gare.
Tel. 05 63 66 06 66. Fax 05 63 66 19 39.
www.hotel-restaurant-orsay.com
Hotel closed Sun., 1 week Christmas–New Year's, 1 week May, 2 weeks beg. Aug.
Rest. closed Sat. lunch, Sun., Mon. lunch.
20 rooms: 47–64€.
Prix fixe: 23€, 34€, 58€, 11€ (child).

Alain Blanc is the town's most serious chef. The years may pass, but his grasp remains firm. Pan-seared foie gras escalope with potatoes and caramelized onions, Mediterranean sea bass with tapenade, pigeon served two ways and the saffron- and Armagnac-seasoned tripe are classy. Well-chosen wines, pretty dessert trolley, pleasant rooms.

● Les Saveurs d'Ingres

11, rue de l'Hôtel de Ville.
Tel. 05 63 91 26 42. Fax 05 63 66 28 92.
Closed Sun., Mon.
Prix fixe: 25€ (lunch weekdays), 39€, 52€, 90€.

The modern décor under its brick vault, not far from the Musée Ingres, has charm. Cyril Paysserand—who worked with Dutournier—has concocted a Southwest cuisine brought up-to-date with well-planned dishes and contemporary flavors. Tender foie gras with a squid, lemon and chorizo fricassée, Atlantic sea bass in a seaweed and mushroom crust served with eggplant caviar and the veal sweetbreads and truffles served in a cocotte with heirloom vegetables have character. A nice, local wine list and a smiling welcome from Valérie.

● Au Chapon Fin

1, pl Saint-Orens.
Tel. 05 63 1 .10.
Closed Sat., Sun. dinner, 3 weeks Aug.
Prix fixe: 16,50€ (weekdays, wine inc.), 25€, 35€.

Alain Albert represents the second generation of this establishment next to the Pont-Vieux and follows tradition with pizzazz and character. The pastel-toned dining room with its modern lighting is luminous. The cooking lightly follows current trends and the menus are priced very moderately. Coddled eggs with cream, curry-seasoned crab and asparagus in puff pastry, the braised squid with rosemary, served with an onion, herb, caper and mustard mayonnaise and the duckling filet with orange sauce, served with oven-browned thinly sliced potatoes in white sauce, look great.

● Au Fil de l'Eau COM

14, quai du Dr-Lafforgue.
Tel. 05 63 66 11 85. Fax 05 63 91 97 56.
aufildeleau82@wanadoo.fr
Closed Sun. (exc. lunch off season), Mon., Wed. dinner (off season).
Prix fixe: 18€ (lunch), 31€, 41€, 55€, 9,50€ (child).

There's been a revolution *chez* Jean-François Pech who has refreshed his décor in tones of mauve with a beautiful, modern fireplace and an elegant lobby. On the cooking end, this good, classic chef entices you with smoked salmon tartare in a crêpe bundle, drum fish with a shellfish coulis, milk-fed veal with basil-infused jus and the criss-crossed white and dark chocolate dessert; all are tried and true. This address between the Tarn and the Pont-Vieux is worth a detour.

In Albias (82350). 10 km n via N20.

● Eskualduna SIM

N20.
Tel. 05 63 31 01 58. Fax 05 63 31 13 40.
www.grill.eskualduna.com

Closed Mon., 1 week Christmas–New Year's, 2 weeks beg. June.
Prix fixe: 13,80€ (weekday lunch), 36€, 8€ (child). A la carte: 35€.

Miguel Cabrero plays it hot in this roadside bodega. House sangria, formica tables and checkered linens as well as the Iberian plate (anchovies, peppers and ham, San Juan escargots), the grilled fresh foie gras with potatoes, the line-fished Atlantic sea bass and the rib eye for two deliver on their promises. The flambéed fruit brochette slips down effortlessly.

83440 Var. Paris 895 – Cannes 33 – Draguignan 42 – Fréjus 29 – Grasse 21.
Discover this village in its theatrical setting which lies on the outskirts of the Haut-Var surrounding the hinterland of Cannes and the great lake of Saint-Cassien.

● RESTAURANTS

● Auberge des Fontaines ○COM d'Aragon

Rte de Grasse, 3 km se, quartier de Narbonne.
Tel.-Fax 04 94 47 71 65.
ericmaio@club-internet.fr
www.fontaines-daragon.com
Closed Mon., Tue., Jan.
Prix fixe: 37€ (lunch), 65€, 90€, 20€ (child).

Eric Maio decides at the market what dishes he'll concoct for his sunny lunches. Formerly at Bruno at Lorgues, he adores truffles and highlights them in his cooking. On the menu, green asparagus tips in salad served with a white truffle oil-infused mascarpone quenelle, roasted pike-perch in cocotte served with a creamy black truffle risotto and pigeon stuffed with chard, roasted pine nuts and apples served with a rosemary jus. For dessert, the crunchy cylindrical dessert with lemon cream, slow-cooked vanilla-seasoned carrots and a verbena sorbet is pleasurable. Carine Maio lovingly watches over everything. The garden and house are extremely pleasant.

MONTBAZON

37250 Indre-et-Loire. Paris 250 – Tours 16
– Châtellerault 58 – Chinon 41 – Loches 33.
office-tourismemontbazon@wanadoo.fr.
This is a major stopover at the crossroads to the
châteaux of the Loire. The valley of the Indre is
a veritable haven of peace.

 HOTELS-RESTAURANTS

● Château d'Artigny

Rue de Monts, 2 km sw via D17.
Tel. 02 47 34 30 30. Fax 02 47 34 30 39.
artigny@grandesetapes.com
www.artigny.fr
65 rooms: 160–410€. 2 suites: 410–570€.
Prix fixe: 35€, 50€, 85€. A la carte: 80€.

This 17th-century-style château, built in
1920 by perfumer François Coty, counts
as one of the major French stopovers of its
kind. It certainly doesn't lack prestige: a
park dominating the valley of the Indre,
with French gardens and a private chapel,
for leisurely walks. Inside there are spectacular staircases, reception rooms, comfortable bedrooms and rooms with elegant
furniture, *objets d'art* and paintings worthy of a grand house. For relaxation, there
are swimming pools, a hammam and various fitness rooms. Francis Maignaut is
in charge of the cooking, which is subtle. His classics—the veal sweetbreads,
foie gras, pike-perch, eel, Touraine black
chicken or Poitou-raised lamb—offer a
palette of tastes and harmonious flavors
cleverly underscored by a bottle of wine
chosen from the well-stocked cellar. The
lacy crêpes for dessert have that oh-so-
simple tastiness. Service and welcome
are those one would expect from a grand
establishment.

■ Domaine de la Tortinière

2 km n via N10 and D287.
Tel. 02 47 34 35 00. Fax 02 47 65 95 70.
domaine.tortiniere@wanadoo.fr
www.tortiniere.com
Closed Sun. dinner (Nov.–Mar.),

20 Dec.–1 Mar.
24 rooms: 120–200€. 6 suites: 320€.
Prix fixe: 30€ (lunch, wine inc.),
37€ (lunch, wine inc.).

Xavier and Anne Olivereau are loving ten-
ants of this pretty, Second Empire dwelling. They greet their guests as friends
before showing them to a quiet, spacious
room overlooking the swimming pool. In
the restaurant, David Chartier reworks
the classics with a light touch. Witness
the minced pollock with a mango tartare, red tuna served with thinly sliced
potatoes and ginger, lamb tenderloin with
preserved lemons and a rosemary-infused
gravy and the apple and pear mille-feuille
with salted-butter caramel.

● La Chancelière
& Le Jeu de Cartes

1, pl des Marronniers.
Tel. 02 47 26 00 67. Fax 02 47 73 14 82.
lachanceliere@lachanceliere.fr
www.lachanceliere.fr
Closed Sun. (exc. Bank holidays),
Mon. (exc. Bank holidays),
mid-Feb.–mid-Mar., mid-Aug.–end Aug.
Prix fixe: 32€, 35€ (Sat., Sun., lunch).

The free and independant spirit which
animates the Chancelière & Le Jeu de
Cartes team is a guarantee of orignal-
ity. Under the imaginative direction of
Jean-Luc Hattet and Jacques de Pous,
the twin houses have now become one
with a new, trendy décor and an innovative cuisine. The ever-changing menus—
specialty and otherwise—can be mixed
and matched for a supplement and are
signed by Michel Gangneux. The egg
and watercress cappuccino, salmon
with Avruga caviar and oyster cream,
cod medallions served with potatoes in
Serrano ham, poultry wings with chanterelles poached in lobster and crayfish
butter and the hot Angelique du Marais
Poitevin liqueur soufflé are part of this
joyous and flavorful repast. The service
is affable and there is an interesting wine
list replete with great Loire wines which
won't break the bank.

MONTBELIARD

25200 Doubs. Paris 477 – Belfort 22 –
Besançon 76 – Mulhouse 60.
The Peugeot museum at Sochaux and the hôtel
Beurner-Rossel are a good enough reasons to
visit the second largest city of the Doubs.

 HOTELS-RESTAURANTS

■ La Balance

40, rue de Belfort.
Tel. 03 81 96 77 41. Fax 03 81 91 47 16.
hotelbalance@orange.fr
Closed Christmas.
44 rooms: 55–100€.

This historic 16th-century house has
renovated its rooms. There's a beautiful
wooden staircase and a belle epoque dining room offering a mid-range regional
cuisine of uneven quality.

● Le Saint-Martin

1, rue du Général-Leclerc.
Tel. 03 81 91 18 37.
Closed Sat., Sun., 1 week at end Feb.,
1 week at end Mar., 3 weeks Aug.
Prix fixe: 29€, 55€.

In the heart of the city, not far from the
château, this little bourgeois house with
its small, intimate dining rooms offers
a well-crafted cuisine based on quality
products. A nice wine list showcasing all
the vineyards of the Franche-Comté.

● Chez Joseph

17, rue de Belfort.
Tel. 03 81 91 20 02. Fax 03 81 91 88 99.
Closed Sun., Mon., Aug.
A la carte: 55€.

A native of Calabria, Joseph Morabito
likes to travel. In a contemporary setting he offers a clever cuisine based on
fresh, seasonal products and is audacious
with fish. John Dory with château Chalon sauce, Atlantic sea bass with anchovy
cream sauce, langoustines with veal
sweetbreads, roasted monkfish served
with a red onion tart and a turmeric-
and ginger-seasoned red tuna keep up
with the trends.

● Chez Cass'graine

4, rue du Général-Leclerc.
Tel. 03 81 91 09 97. Fax 03 81 95 43 03.
Closed Sat., Sun. Bank holidays,
Christmas–New Year's, Aug.
A la carte: 42–52€.

This keen bistro is worth a look-in for its
debonair welcome, sympathetic ambiance and market-based, seasonal cuisine
served in a small, quaintly decorated
dining room. Scallops with blood sausage and balsamic caramel, Atlantic sea
bass roasted with sweet peppers, belly
of farm-raised pork served with slow-
cooked red cabbage and a chocolate terrine served with orange salad make you
wish you were a regular. Good, characterful wines.

In Sochaux (25600). 4 km w.

● Brasserie du Musée Peugeot

Carrefour de l'Europe.
Tel. 03 81 99 42 03. Fax 03 81 99 42 06.
Closed dinner, Christmas, New Year's.
Prix fixe: 14€. A la carte: 30€.

An agreeable setting in the heart of the
Peugeot museum serving trendy little
dishes.

MONTBONNOT-SAINT-MARTIN see
GRENOBLE
MONTBOUCHER-SUR-JABRON see
MONTELIMAR
MONTCHENOT see REIMS

MONT-DE-MARSAN

40000 Landes. Paris 711 –
Agen 121 – Bayonne 106 – Bordeaux 131 –
Pau 85.
tourisme@mont-de-marsan.org.
This gourmet crossroads of the Petites Landes,
North of Chalosse de Tursan, is an easy-going
burg. Visit the Despiau-Wlérick in the 16th-cen-
tury castle keep of Lacataye, the remains of the
fortifications and the Romanesque houses. Satisfy your appetite at the local market.

HOTELS-RESTAURANTS

■ **Le Renaissance**

Rte de Villeneuve.
Tel. 05 58 51 51 51. Fax 05 58 75 29 07.
www.le-renaissance.com
Closed 1 Oct.–1 May (exc. by group reserv.).
Rest. closed Sat. lunch, Sun. dinner.
29 rooms: 52–77€. 1 suite: 96€.
Prix fixe: 20€, 28€, 49€, 10€ (child).

Situated on the road to Villeneuve, at the outskirts of town, this hotel is a simple, relaxing stopover. The pleasant rooms give on to the garden and the swimming pool promises leisure time. There's a new chef in the kitchen, Jean-Marie Bijou, who offers dishes full of promise. A foie gras duo with basalmic vinegar coulis, grilled scallop brochette with lime, veal sweetbread medallions in an herb crust and the dark chocolate in puff pastry are not bad at all.

● **Un Air de Campagne**

3, rue Thérèse-Clavé.
Tel. 05 58 06 05 41.
Closed Sat. lunch, Mon., Tue. dinner,
1 week Dec., 1 week Mar., 3 weeks Aug.
Prix fixe: 25€, 36€, 50€. A la carte: 55€.

François Duchet, a native of Limoges who worked with his compatriot Jacques Chibois at Grasse, with Thierry Marx at Cordeillan-Bages and with Philippe Garret at Grenade-sur-Adour, has opened this small, modern, country-style restaurant in town. People flock to taste an unadorned, seasonal and spontaneous cuisine: gazpacho, poached eggs in wine sauce with tender lentils and bacon, grilled cod, veal roast with country bacon and the breast of guinea hen served with caramelized onions. Pretty desserts (passion fruit crème brulee, crunchy orange pastry with light lemon cream and verbena ice cream) and a still-minimal wine list that nevertheless highlights the Southwest all the way to its frontier with Bordeaux.

In Uchacq-et-Parentis (40090). 7 km via N134.

● **Didier Garbage** COM

N134.
Tel. 05 58 75 33 66. Fax 05 58 75 22 77.
restaudidiergarbage@wanadoo.fr
Closed Sun. dinner, Mon., Tue. dinner,
10 days Jan.
Prix fixe: 12–20€ (bistro), 30€ (lunch, weekdays), 35€, 45€.

Bistro or gastro: Garbage has both. Around the bar there are wooden tables and a congenial ambiance; dishes are listed on a blackboard. The price of the menu corresponds to the "main dish." Veal trotter with mashed potatoes and the rice pudding cost 15. The bourgeois dining room is cozier and offers a series of clever, though not necessarily costly, menus. Tricandille salad, beef cheeks braised in Madiran and the clafoutis pay a nice homage to the region.

MONTEILS see also CAUSSADE

12200 Aveyron. Paris 619 – Rodez 68 – Albi 69 – Villefranche-du-Rouergue 11.
In *bastide* country, a pretty, green village, once the home of Monsignor Marty; it has a resident poet, a pleasant inn and a bucolic environment.

 HOTELS-RESTAURANTS

■ **Le Clos Gourmand**

Tel. 05 65 29 63 15. Fax 05 65 29 64 98.
Closed end Oct.–beg. Apr.
4 rooms: 45€.
Prix fixe:13€, 19,50€,29€,8€(child).
A la carte: 22–32€.

Anne-Marie Lavergne has well understood that good things suffice unto themselves. Her cooking is therefore free of pretentiousness: foie gras in salad, trout filet, Aveyron veal with morels and the layered crêpe cake have captivated a truly gourmet clientèle. The garden of this old lawyer's office gets the sun's first rays. The four rooms are adorable as is the welcome.

MONTELIMAR

26200 Drôme. Paris 605 – Valence 46 – Avignon 85 – Nîmes 111.

montelimar.tourisme@wanadoo.fr.

Montélimar is one big nougat which spreads out for miles. This is a false image as are, of course, the bottlenecks of the N7 which disappeared once the motorway was built. In the center of town, the new *allées Provençales* help to make one forget that the N7 used to split the city down the middle. Signs for nougat abound.

 HOTELS-RESTAURANTS

■ Relais de l'Empereur

Pl Max-Dormoy.
Tel. 04 75 01 29 00. Fax 04 75 01 32 21.
www.relaislempereur.com
Closed mid-Nov.–mid-Dec.
27 rooms: 60–88€. 2 suites: 88–128€.
Half board: 92–150€.

This coaching inn has a mildly nostalgic air. Not just because Napoleon I stayed here but also because it was a stopover for numerous vacationers who used the N7 to get to the Mediterranean between the 1950's and '70's. The Latrys' rooms are pleasant and the family smiling and friendly. The cooking could be improved.

■ Le Sphinx

19, bd Marre-Desmarais.
Tel. 04 75 01 86 64. Fax 04 75 52 34 21.
reception@sphinx-hotel.fr / www.sphinx-hotel.fr
Closed 21 Dec.–13 Jan.
24 rooms: 49–69€.

This center city 17th-century town house is cute and inexpensive. The furnishings and décor have style.

● Les Senteurs de Provence   COM

202, rte de Marseille.
Tel. 04 75 01 43 82. Fax 04 75 01 21 81.
lsdp.restaurant@wanadoo.fr
Closed Sun. dinner, Tue. dinner, Wed.
Prix fixe: 16€, 20€, 26€, 40€.
A la carte: 49€.

Pascal Aimé extends a warm welcoming to this classy inn. Jean-Paul Reynes employs his know-how on market-based products where regional specialities take pride of place. The escargot and spinach spring rolls, sea bream filet served with leeks slow-cooked in cream and the roast beef with foie gras and morels are well composed. The frozen nougat parfait and the sorbet plate bring the feast to a sweet ending. Nice wine list.

In Malataverne (26780). 9 km, via N7 and D844, rte Donzère.

■ Domaine du Colombier

Rte de Donzère.
Tel. 04 75 90 86 86. Fax 04 75 90 79 40.
www.domaine-colombier.com
Closed 1 week Feb., 2 weeks 1 Nov. vac.
Rest. closed Mon. (off season).
22 rooms: 77–174€. 3 suites: 189–204€.
Prix fixe: 24€ (lunch, wine inc.), 32€, 38€, 58€. A la carte: 65€.

This nice inn with its neat rooms, pretty, flower-filled park and pleasant swimming pool also offers a good table. The truffle omelet, halibut with mixed peppers, rosemary lamb shank and the dessert cart have gotten simpler and tastier.

In Montboucher-sur-Jabron (26740). 4 km se via D940.

■ Château du Monard

Golf de la Valdaine.
Tel. 04 75 00 71 30. Fax 04 75 00 71 31.
www.domainedelavaldaine.com
31 rooms: 74–99€. 4 suites: 135–202€.
Prix fixe: 25€ (weekday lunch, wine inc.), 29€, 10€ (child). A la carte: 50€.

This establishment, complete with swimming pool, is on the Valdaine golf course and offers attractive rooms in various styles. The restaurant has been completely renovated in tones of orange and chocolate and Philippe Groult has handed it over to Olivier Lévy. The blood sausage Tatin with apples, rouget with tapenade served with sautéed pumpkin and preserved lemons, roasted thyme-seasoned saddle of lamb served with stuffed vegetables and the roasted pear with honey and lavender ice cream perfectly titillate the palate. Same spirit at the Bistro du Monard, but less expensive.

MONTENACH see SIERCK-LES-BAINS
MONTEUX see CARPENTRAS
MONTFAUCON see BESANÇON
MONTFAVET see AVIGNON

MONTFORT-L'AMAURY

78490 Yvelines. Paris 47 – Houdan 16 – Rambouillet 20 – Versailles 27.
This pretty burg in the Ile-de-France is perched on a rise and boasts a Grand-Place, a lovely church, a cemetery with ancient tombstones, cozy dwellings and castle ruins which were the backdrop for the film, *Le Corbeau*. Ravel once lived here.

	HOTELS

■ **Hôtel Saint-Laurent**
2, pl Lebreton.
Tel. 01 34 57 06 66. Fax 01 34 86 12 27.
www.hotelsaint-laurent.com
Closed 3 weeks Aug.
11 rooms: 95–155€. 1 suite: 170€.

In the heart of the village, Christiane and André Delabarre have transformed this old bourgeois house into a very charming hotel with exquisite rooms with marble bathrooms. Breakfasts to die for.

MONTHIEUX

01390 Ain. Paris 440 – Lyon 30 – Bourg-en-Bresse 39 – Meximieux 25.
The Dombes with its ponds, golf courses and forests.

	HOTELS-RESTAURANTS

■ **Hôtel-Golf le Gouverneur**
Château du Breuil.
Tel. 04 72 26 42 00. Fax 04 72 26 42 20.
www.golfgouverneur.fr
Closed 2 weeks Dec., Feb. vac.
45 rooms: 80–110€. 8 suites: 120–160€.
Prix fixe: 36€. A la carte: 52–58€.

Situated on the largest golfing domain of the Rhône-Alpes region, this plant-filled luxury hotel blends comfort and functionality: well-appointed rooms and a clubhouse for relaxation. In the restaurant, duck foie gras with figs, roasted Atlantic sea bass and the herb-encrusted rack of lamb with a rosemary jus are pretty good. For a fresh finish, try the coriander-seasoned mango carpaccio.

MONTICELLO see L'ILE-ROUSSE

MONTJEAN-SUR-LOIRE

49570 Maine-et-Loire. Paris 325 – Angers 30 – Ancenis 28 – Chpateaubriant 65 – Cholet 45.
A town with a panorama, rich in history, on a promontory dominating the regal river.

	HOTELS-RESTAURANTS

■ **Auberge de la Loire**
2, quai des Mariniers.
Tel.-Fax 02 41 39 80 20.
www.aubergedelaloire.com
Closed 1 week Christmas–New Year's,
2 weeks Sept., 2 weeks
beg. Jan., 1 week at end July–beg. Aug.
Rest. closed Sun. dinner (off season), Wed.
8 rooms: 46–53€.
Prix fixe: 19€, 27,50€, 33,50€,
10,50€ (child). A la carte: 60€.

The Gondrées' inn is set alongside the Loire and is full of charm. We love Dominique's welcome and the cozy rooms, four of which overlook the river. We equally appreciate Jean-Claude's regional cuisine. In the Provençal-toned dining room, duck foie gras in terrine, Loire fish served with beurre blanc, sirloin steak with béarnaise sauce and the Cointreau-flavored orange gratin highlight fine local products.

MONTLUÇON

03100 Allier. Paris 331 – Moulins 80 – Bourges 97 – Clermont-Ferrand 111.
The iron works have gone! The economic capital of the Bourbonnais is an ecologically-friendly

town which showcases its old quarter with pride and invites you on a walking tour around the town, the hill of Sainte-Agathe and the Tronçonais forest.

 HOTELS-RESTAURANTS

■ **Château Saint-Jean**

Parc Saint-Jean.
Tel. 04 70 02 71 71. Fax 04 70 02 71 70.
www.chateaustjean.net
Closed Sun. dinner (Nov.–Mar.),
1 week beg. Jan.
16 rooms: 65–125€. 4 suites: 115–125€.
Prix fixe: 21€ (weekday lunch), 34€, 47€,
60€, 12€ (child). A la carte: 56–70€.

An ideal and welcoming setting for a quiet or romantic stay, this 15th-century château offers tastefully furnished rooms and meals served in the starkly decorated old chapel with its white stone walls and green carpet. Here, Tierry Douault follows the seasons and faultlessly concocts foie gras with fleur de sel as an appetizer, red mullet with zucchini and peppers, coriander seeds and citrus sauce and the roasted duck breast with cep and figs. Good cellar.

● **Le Grenier à Sel**

10, rue Sainte-Anne / pl des Toiles.
Tel. 04 70 05 53 79. Fax 04 70 05 87 91.
info@legrenierasel.com
www.legrenierasel.com
Closed Nov. 1 vac., 2 weeks Feb.
Rest. closed Mon. lunch, Sat. lunch (off season), Sun. dinner (off season).
7 rooms: 95–125€. 2 suites: 95–125€.
Prix fixe: 21,50€, 32€, 51€, 66€,
15€ (child). A la carte: 55€–65€.

Under the benevolent and efficient control of Nicole Morlon, dishes come and go in the blue and white dining room or on the terrace when the sun shines. Discover delicacies lovingly cooked by Jacky. Turnovers with morels in wild mushroom cream, pike fish quenelles and lobster and the Auvergne-style duck are flavorful fireworks while remaining simple and generous. You won't leave a spoonful of Jeremy's

chocolate dessert with ginger ice cream. We loved the Laurent family's red and white Saint-Pourçain wines. This lovely bourgeois house covered in ivy is an exquisite spot, the rooms are welcoming, the restaurant modern and convivial and the hosts attentive to your every desire. You can be assured of a successful stay here.

MONTMERLE-SUR-SAONE

01090 Ain. Paris 422 – Bourg-en-Bresse 45 – Lyon 46 – Mâcon 28.
The banks of the Saône lend charm to this town on the edge of the Dombes.

 HOTELS-RESTAURANTS

● **Emile Job** `COM`

12, rue du Pont.
Tel. 04 74 69 33 92. Fax 04 74 69 49 21.
contact@emilejob.com
www.hotelemilejob.com
Closed Sun. dinner (off season), Mon., Tue. lunch (exc. July–Aug.), 3 weeks 1 Nov. vac.,
2 weeks beg. Mar.
22 rooms: 65–88€.
Prix fixe: 19,90€, 52€ 15€ (child).
A la carte: 58€.

Eric Lépine makes sure that Emile Job is still a little part of this establishment. In his memory, the establishment, formerly Le Rivage, now carries his name, but Eric, who worked at Orsi in Lyon and Guérard at Eugénie, has made his mark within these walls thanks to his well-thought-out traditional cuisine. Duck foie gras terrine, fresh frog legs sautéed in garlic and parsley, Bresse chicken with morels in cream sauce and the delicious chocolate praline dessert have won over the locals. Upstairs, the rooms are simple and well-appointed. A very kind welcome and reasonable prices.

MONTMORILLON

86500 Vienne. Paris 359 – Poitiers 51 –
Bellac 43 – Châtellerault 56 – Limoges 83.
office.de.tourisme@worldonline.fr.
The banks of the Gartempe, ramparts, the church of Notre-Dame, the chapel of Saint-Laurent, the Octagon in the cemetery of la Masison-Dieu—all this gives an image of tranquility.

 HOTELS-RESTAURANTS

● **Lucullus et Hôtel de France** ○📠
4, bd de Strasbourg.
Tel. 05 49 84 09 09. Fax 05 49 84 58 68.
www.le-lucullus.com
Rest. closed Sun. dinner, Mon., Tue.
35 rooms: 42–65€.
Prix fixe: 18,50€, 30,50€, 35,50€,
47,50€, 10,50€ (child).

Whether at the bistro or at the haute cuisine resaurant, the Lucullus, chef Gérard Alloyeau has fun juggling tradition and modernity. He fashions, rummages, associates and mixes sweet and salty, French and foreign flavors. The result is stunning. Veal sweetbread Tatin with country honey to start. Drum fish with artichokes and olives and the veal cutlet with pan-tossed chanterelles are more classic as a follow-up. The simmered nectarines, the pistachio macaron and the soft fromage blanc sorbet are the final touch. The unwavering kindness of Marie-Thérèse, from her welcome to her service at table is adorable. So are the part-traditional, part-modern rooms. The bill is more than reasonable.

MONTNER

66720 Pyrénées-Orientales. Paris 860 –
Perpignan 28 – Prades 37 – Amélie-les-Bains 60.
An exquisite winemaker's village with its baroque church dedicated to Saint James.

 HOTELS-RESTAURANTS

● **L'Auberge du Cellier** COM
1, rue de Sainte-Eugénie.
Tel. 04 68 29 09 78. Fax 04 68 29 10 61.

www.aubergeducellier.com
Closed 2 weeks Nov., 2 weeks Mar.
Rest. closed Mon. (off season), Tue., Wed.
5 rooms: 53€.
Prix fixe: 39€, 65€, 85€, 18€ (child).
A la carte: 55–65€.

In his cooking, Pierre-Louis Marin presents every facet of a product: foie gras with Granny Smith apples and raspberries, tender monkfish with vanilla and Marc de Banyuls served with pumpkin and Cerdagne ham and the deboned squab, tender and rosy, with celery root, artichokes and a flavorful natural jus. This ends up being quite a process but the approach is amusing. For dessert, try the "Schiste de Montner", which marries chocolate, pralined nuts, caramel and a Rivesaltes reduction. Béatrice Marin gives advice on what to choose between Roussillon and Coteaux de Languedoc wines in order to highlight these finely wrought dishes. Eight cozy rooms for a stopover.

MONTPELLIER

34000 Hérault. Paris 758 –
Marseille 171 – Nice 328 – Nîmes 52 –
Toulouse 242.
contact@ot-montpellier.fr.
What a curious capital! The Languedoc-Roussillon isn't enough for Montpellier, which sees itself as a "Eurocity" and looks towards Madrid and Barcelona. Thanks to Bofill, the city is ranked for its contemporary artistic heritage. It also has its old town, its walks, towers, charming hotels and lovely Place de la Comédie lit up at night, to tempt the stroller. It forgets to claim its traditions but the surroundings proclaim its riches. Sète, Bouzigues, the vineyards of the Languedoc or the mountains of the Cévennes are its hinterland. The beaches of Palavas and the Grande-Motte, the Thau basin, the nearby Camargue and the Gard are its outskirts. Montpellier is a crossroads that is so filled with ambition it sometimes forgets to look too closely at itself. Its richness is to be that crossroads. The fame of the Jardin des Sens shows that everything is possible here.

■ | HOTELS

■ Le Jardin des Sens
11, av Saint-Lazare.
Tel. 04 99 58 38 38. Fax 04 99 58 38 39.
www.jardindessens.com
Closed Sun., Mon., Tue.
13 rooms: 160–190€. 2 suites: 290–470€.

The contemporary hotel of the Pourcel brothers welcomes a few privileged guests to modern, bright rooms around the pool and of course, at their table. (See Restaurants.)

■ Holiday Inn-Métropole
3, rue du Clos-René.
Tel. 04 67 12 32 32. Fax 04 67 92 13 02.
www.holiday-in.com
80 rooms: 130–175€. 4 suites: 200–230€.

This 19th-century dwelling—whose facade and staircase are original—boasts contemporary décor in the rooms and in the English bar. The terrace is shaded by palm trees and looks out on to the swimming pool. (See Restaurants: La Closerie.)

■ Sofitel-Antigone
1, rue des Pertuisanes.
Tel. 04 67 99 72 72. Fax 04 67 65 17 50.
h1294@accor.com
www.sofitel-montpellier.com
88 rooms: 95–235€. 1 suite: 425€.

The originality of this chain hotel resides in its swimming pool on the roof with an unbeatable view of the new neighborhoods of Montpellier and Antigone. Irreproachable comfort in well-planned rooms, a fitness center, Jacuzzi, conference rooms and regional cuisine in the circular restaurant.

■ Suite Hôtel
45, av du Pirée.
Tel. 04 67 20 57 57. Fax 04 67 20 58 58.
h6017@accor.com / www.suite-hotel.com
140 suites: 95€.

Keep an eye on this hotel with its red and blue tones and agreeable, quiet suites with their office *cum* sitting room nooks. Irreproachable comfort, a fitness center, swimming pool, seating lounge and terrace.

■ Le Guilhem
18, rue J.-J.-Rousseau.
Tel. 04 67 52 90 90. Fax 04 67 60 67 67.
www.hotel-le-guilhem.com
35 rooms: 87–116€. 10 suites: 143€.

Right in the heart of town, this 16th-century house is worth it for its pretty rooms giving on to a garden. Tranquility and low prices are an extra bonus.

■ Hôtel du Palais
3, rue du Palais-des-Guilhem.
Tel. 04 67 60 47 38. Fax 04 67 60 40 23.
www.hoteldupalais-montpellier.fr
26 rooms: 60–102€.

Not far from the Palais de Justice, this charming hotel boasts welcoming rooms at reasonable prices. Service is attentive.

■ Hôtel du Parc
8, rue Achille-Bègé.
Tel. 04 67 41 16 49. Fax 04 67 54 10 05.
www.hotelduparc-montpellier.com
19 rooms: 49–78€.

This 18th-century house, converted into a hotel, offers classy rooms with plaster walls (orange-yellow, red, off-white, ochre) which are very tasteful. Prices are reasonable.

■ La Maison Blanche
1796, av de la Pompignane.
Tel. 04 99 58 20 70. Fax 04 67 79 53 39.
www.hotel-maison-blanche.com
Rest. closed Sat. lunch, Sun.
32 rooms: 76–102€. 2 suites: 140–150€.

The rooms with their bleached wood and the columned facade remind one of Louisiana and are not without charm. There's a garden with exotic trees and a swimming pool.

● RESTAURANTS

● Le Jardin des Sens   LUX

At Le Jardin des Sens, 11, av Saint-Lazare.
Tel. 04 99 58 38 38. Fax 04 99 58 38 41.
contact@jardindessens.com -
www.jardindessens.com
Closed Sun. dinner, Mon., July–beg. Aug.
Prix fixe: 50€, 120€, 190€.

When one talks about the restaurant of Jacques and Laurent Pourcel, those traveling and visionary twins, is one talking about Paris (the Maison Blanche, Sens and Comptoir), Shanghai (the first Relais & Châteaux in China), Singapore (Raffle's), Bangkok, Marrakech (the Plage Rouge, their recent gourmet "trading post" just at the edge of the desert), London (W'Sens in Saint James), Palavas-les-Flots or Saint-Paul-Trois-Châteaux (the Villa Augusta)? We've probably forgotten a few along the way. Whatever. The arugula gazpacho with parmesan that you were so enthusiastic about during your Chinese holidays at the Sens on the Bund and the desserts of the Villa Augusta can now be tasted in their original form here in Montpellier. The Pourcel brothers have artfully experimented with their gift for ubiquity. Along with their wine expert, Olivier Château, they concoct seasonal dishes, carefully lay out tempting menus and make one dream. Sea urchins stuffed with crab, the pressed vegetable, lobster and cured duck terrine and the ratatouille-stuffed squid and langoustines with minced zucchini are some of their best tricks. The roasted pigeon served with its cooking juices and a curried pasta prepared with its giblets is a success. The tender two-chocolate dessert and banana minestrone with coconut sorbet are happy temptations. All the wines of Languedoc lie in waiting. The youthful service is motivated. The amphitheater-shaped dining room doesn't lack style and the garden is a dream spot for an alfresco lunch.

● Prouhèze Saveurs   🍴 V.COM

728, av de la Pompignane.
Tel. 04 67 79 43 34. Fax 04 67 79 71 94.
prouhezesaveurs@wanadoo.fr
Closed Sat. lunch, Sun., dinner (Mon., Tue., Wed.), 20 July–25 Aug.
Prix fixe: 23€, 31€.

In the Prouhèze family, talent is passed around. Father Guy, the owner of this cozy establishment with its Bordeaux-red tones, has transferred his know-how and passion to his son Pierre-Olivier (who worked at Trama, Sarran and Thuriés). There are four hands at the stoves, producing tasty Southern-based cuisine. The reasonably priced semi-gastro, semi-bistro menus follow the seasons and are based on products from the sea, the Aveyron and the Lozère. You'll sigh with ease while tasting cold tête de veau sliced thin and served carpaccio-style with truffle oil and the foie gras in terrine with cinnamon-seasoned fig confiture, scallops pan-tossed with tomatoes and fennel, simmered lamb sweetbreads and chanterelles and the duckling filet with orange sauce. The tender Cevennes chestnut dessert with candied chestnut ice cream takes you back to childhood. A choice of 240 wines crowns it all.

● La Closerie   V.COM

At the Holiday Inn Métropole,
3, rue du Clos-René.
Tel. 04 67 12 32 32. Fax 04 67 92 13 02.
www.holidayinn-montpellier.fr
Closed Sat., Sun., Bank holidays.
Prix fixe: 23,50€. A la carte: 36€.

The setting of this chain hotel doesn't portend a cuisine of such high quality. Gregory Courtial, a new chef full of ideas, lovingly prepares little mushroom and chicken spring rolls, sole and a sautéed sweet pepper and onion duo, excellent lamb with sundried tomatoes and little "red pearl" Napoleon with light vanilla cream, all tip-top. Regional wines predominate. The bill won't ruin you.

● Le Kinoa   V.COM

6, rue des Soeurs-Noires.
Tel. 04 67 15 34 38. Fax 04 67 15 34 33.
restaurantkinoa@wanadoo.fr
Closed Sun., Mon., 2 weeks beg. Nov.,

2 weeks beg. Jan.
Prix fixe: 16,50€ (lunch, wine inc.), 26€,
35€. A la carte: 50€.

Gilbert Furlan and Jean-Marc Forest,
whom we knew from the Chandelier, continue to cook the type of fresh, fun dishes
which made their fame. Shellfish aïoli with
anise and swordfish tartare, cod served
with a warm lime vinaigrette, roasted
lamb shanks with a light tapenade sauce,
plus an apricot and caramelized apple tart
with light almond cream. A friendly welcome and efficient service.

● Cellier Morel ○COM

27, rue de l'Aiguillerie.
Tel. 04 67 66 46 36. Fax 04 67 66 23 61.
contact@celliermorel.com
www.celliermorel.com
Closed Sun., Mon. lunch, Wed. lunch,
3 weeks Sept.
Prix fixe: 28€ (lunch), 47€, 62€, 90€.
A la carte: 85€.

The Lozère is the star in this medieval
town house in the center city, where Eric
Cellier concocts technically and aestheti-
cally impeccable dishes for his clients. We
can't criticize the pan-seared slice of foie
gras with smoked milk mousse, monkfish
cassolette served with a tartare of tomatoes, duckling filet accompanied by a spicy
chutney and the tender coconut cake with
Carambar candy ice cream which show
masterful creativity. One regret, the bill
is a bit steep.

● La Compagnie des Comptoirs COM

51, rue François-Delmas.
Tel. 04 99 58 39 29. Fax 04 99 58 39 28.
www.lacompagniedescomptoirs.com
Closed May–end Aug.
Prix fixe: 18€. A la carte: 60€.

Some good friends ate badly this year at the
Pourcel brothers. Others were delighted
with this address and were well received in
this faux bistro with its colonial airs. Thierry Nicollo is now in charge of the stove
and concocts Italian-style artichokes and
roasted peppers in oil with arugula and
slices of parmesan, spicy jumbo shrimp,

grouper glazed in pepper sauce, sirloin
steak, the braised beef roast and a cappuccino. There's a young, alert team of
waiters.

● Le Mas des Brousses ○COM

540, rue du Mas-des-Brousses, 5 km via A9
exit 29 and D172.
Tel. 04 67 64 18 91. Fax 04 67 64 18 89.
lemasdesbrousses@free.fr
Closed Sat. lunch, Sun. dinner, Mon.
Prix fixe: 19€ (lunch), 40€, 68€, 75€.
A la carte: 65€.

Set right next to the Odysseum, Jérome
Bartoletti's table draws all of Montpellier. Formerly with the Pourcels and Marc
Veyrat at l'Ecusson and the Grand Arbre,
he offers—in every sense of the term—a
refined and inventive cuisine. Behind the
roasted scallops served on slow-roasted
tomatoes with parmesan sorbet, tuna and
foie gras and the whole pigeon served with
celery compote lies meticulous work, perfectly accomplished. The desserts, which
include vanilla-seasoned pear bonbons,
served with soft fromage blanc ice cream,
say it all: this is a top-class restaurant.

● L'Olivier ○COM

12, rue Aristide-Ollivier.
Tel. 04 67 92 86 28. Fax 04 67 92 10 65.
Closed Sun., Mon., Christmas–New Year's,
Aug.
Prix fixe: 27€ (lunch), 32€, 47€.
A la carte: 70€.

Chez the Bretons, classicism is good.
Yvette's welcome and Michel's cooking
show the greatest respect for tradition.
The roasted langoustine tails with sesame seeds, John Dory strips marinated
with coriander seeds, roasted pigeon with
foie gras, veal with chanterelles, crêpes
Suzette with vanilla ice cream and a thin
peach and raspberry tart go best with the
cellar's Languedoc wines.

● L'Ecrin d'Anaïs

15, rue La Fontaine.
Tel.-Fax 04 67 02 14 50.
Closed Sun., Mon., Bank holidays,
1 week Feb., Aug.

Prix fixe: 12€ (lunch), 23€, 34€, 44€.
A la carte: 40–45€.

Always innovative, Patrick Arnaud concocts astonishing dishes in his kitchen, reinventing the use of spices and long cooking times. Sardine tempura, monkfish osso bucco with Sichuan peppercorns and cumin-seasoned carrots, local flatbread with onions and pork tenderloin with Montonet sauce, the citrus "hamburger" and the rosemary-infused rice pudding are mouthwatering. In order to vary pleasures, the main menu changes every three months. The wines are almost exclusively from the Languedoc-Roussillon.

● **Brasserie du Théâtre**

22, bd Victor-Hugo.
Tel. 04 67 58 88 80. Fax 04 67 58 09 29.
www.brasseriedutheatre.com
Closed Sun.
A la carte: 40–60€.

The trump cards of the house are clear: a welcome at any hour, reassuring fare, quick service and acceptable prices. Before or after a show, this twenties establishment has character. Tuna tartare, squid with parsley and garlic, mixed fish grill done in the local style, grilled rib eye or tartare with fries are on offer to a delighted clientèle. The chocolate profiteroles have their fans.

● **Castel Ronceray** COM

130, rue Castel-Ronceray.
Tel. 04 67 42 46 30. Fax 04 67 27 41 96.
www.lecastelronceray.fr
Closed Sun. lunch (exc. for group reserv.),
Mon., Feb. vac., 3 weeks Aug.
Prix fixe: 26€ (weekday lunch), 39,50€,
52€, 62€, 15€ (child). A la carte: 45€.

The Guiltat establishment is pleasant and gives good value for money. Patrick concocts foie gras escalopes served cold in aspic, Atlantic sea bass with chanterelles and black rice, venison with mustard sauce and the white chocolate and pistachio triangle with a crunchy pralined chocolate mousse, while Nathalie adroitly advises on wine. The garden opens its gates at the first ray of sun and service is nicely attentive.

● **Le Séquoia** COM

Port Marianne, 148, rue de Galata.
Tel. 04 67 65 07 07. Fax 04 67 64 50 23.
Closed Sat. lunch, Sun., Wed.,
1 week Christmas–New Year's.
Prix fixe: 38€. A la carte: 65€.

Formerly of Loiseau and the Jardin des Sens, Yann Rio doesn't lack creativity. He likes everything to be in harmony, from the décor to the dishes. The dining room is a mixture of metal and green and red tones and has a view of the boats. The fare is well thought out, with a touch of fusion: the little pot of hot goat cheese and basil savory crumble, a tasting plate of lobster and scallop mousse, rack of lamb glazed with black sesame served with home-style potatoes and a milk caramel crème brûlée.

● **Tamarillos**

2, pl du Marché-aux-Fleurs.
Tel. 04 67 60 06 00. Fax 04 67 60 06 01.
www.cartesurtables.com
Closed Sun., Mon. lunch.
Prix fixe: 18€ (weekday lunch), 29€, 50€,
90€.

Philippe Chapon now offers four menus for every budget. With his passion for combining fruits and flowers, he is constantly inventing new recipes. Having been a pastry chef for ten years with Guy Savoy, he now brings his talent to the service of the people of Montpellier who delight in the tuna tartare with blackcurrant and orange flavors, green vegetables simmered in coconut milk with zucchini beignets and meats and fish cooked with imagination. Desserts are, of course, his particular domain and here you'll find some exquisite surprises. Finally, as well as good service and decent prices, the *fluides de la Septimanie* aka the wines of Languedoc-Roussillon, are terrific. Our "value for money" award refers, of course, to the first two menus.

● **Les Caves Jean Jaurès**   SIM

3, rue Collot.
Tel. 04 67 60 27 33. Fax 04 67 22 05 65.
Closed Sun. lunch, Mon. lunch, Aug.
Prix fixe: 19€. A la carte: 38€.

Marie-Noëlle Vansicote, along with ardent sommelier Frédéric Turpaud, lauds the wines of the Midi with fervor. They can be tasted in a vaulted cellar accompanied by inexpensive little dishes. Duck salad, sea bream, duck breast with fresh seasonal fruits and the delicious chestnut dessert are worth a detour.

● **Le César**   SIM

17, pl du Nombre-d'Or.
Tel. 04 67 64 87 87. Fax 04 67 22 20 39.
Closed Sun.
Prix fixe: 8,50€ (weekday lunch), 23,80€, 32,50€. A la carte: 35€.

This animated Greco-Roman-style brasserie in the Antigone neighborhood offers down-to-earth, regional fare. Scallop brochette with jumbo shrimp, duck strips served with ceps and a prune and milk craquelin hold their own.

● **Sushi Bar**   SIM

20, rue Bernard-Délicieux.
Tel. 04 99 77 06 06.
www.le-sushi-bar.com
Closed Sun., Mon., 1 week Jan., 2 weeks Aug.
Prix fixe: 13€, 24€. A la carte: 30€.

Flore and Olivier Calme have taken up residence on the rue Délicieux and offer Japanese fare: very Zen. It's a pleasure to taste skillfully cooked wakame salad, tuna tartare, pan-tossed shrimp, chicken yakitori and the green tea crème brûlée.

● **Verdi**   SIM

10, rue Aristide-Ollivier.
Tel.-Fax 04 67 58 68 55.
www.le-verdi.info
Closed Sun., 3 weeks Aug.
Prix fixe: 18€, 22€, 26€. A la carte: 55€.

Mimmo Cortese is the good Italian address of the city. His cooking is a ode to the familiar dishes of the boot. Arugula and artichoke salad, grilled squid, turbot with artichokes and potatoes, Roman-style saltimbocca, veal sweetbread medallions with ceps and a light tiramisu are well-cooked and wildly tasty. Well-priced Italian wines contribute to the ambiance.

● **Les Vignes**   SIM

2, rue Bonnier-d'Alco.
Tel.-Fax 04 67 60 48 42.
www.lesvignesrestaurant.com
Closed Sat. lunch, Sun., Wed. dinner, 1 week at Easter, Aug.
Prix fixe: 24€ (weekday lunch), 39€, 55€, 12€ (child). A la carte: 58€.

David Mogicato has fun and talent when transforming local products. Shredded skate with balsamic vinegar, pesto-seasoned tomatoes and beet juice, royal sea bream with leeks cooked in truffle oil, creamy Bouzigues oyster soup, veal kidney with endives and whole grain mustard sauce and the molten chocolate cake with vanilla ice cream and ginger mango compote are pleasant surprises. The welcome is warm and the service dynamic.

In Castelnau-le-Lez (34170). 3,7 km ne

● **L'Authentique II**   V.COM

560, rte de la Pompignane.
Tel. 04 67 52 92 54. Fax 04 67 52 75 24.
Closed Sun., Mon., 2 weeks Aug.
Prix fixe: 28€, 33€, 38€, 48€, 15€ (child).

After a stint at the Grande-Motte, Arnaud Barbot wisely decided to come home. In his functional and trendy dining room and terrace he wavers between tradition and modernity without losing a beat. Pressed duck foie gras with Muscat, grilled Mediterranean sea bass with green crab sauce, the guinea hen, its thigh wrapped in mountain cured ham and roasted and the pan-simmered pears with salted-butter caramel, served with Grisette de Montpelier ice cream, are convincing. Adorable welcome, smiling service and reasonable prices.

In Lattes (34970). 5 km D21.

● **Domaine de Soriech**

Av de Boirargues.
Tel. 04 67 15 19 15. Fax 04 67 15 58 21.
michel.loustau@domaine-de-soriech.fr
www.domaine-de-soriech.fr
Closed Sun. dinner, Mon., Feb. vac.
Prix fixe: 29,50€ (weekday lunch), 42€,
55€, 74€, 18,50€ (child). A la carte: 65€.

Michel Loustau's neo-California villa has
charm, as does his cooking. He prepares
refined fare that follows the seasons. Duck
carpaccio served with foie gras in terrine, red mullet with almond butter and
foamy oyster bouillon, country rack of
lamb with parsley and garlic, served with
a slow-roasted garlic infusion and the desserts (pineapple cocktail with spices and
a banana mousse with Languedoc fig ice
cream and berry coulis) feel like home-
cooked food with a difference. Prices have
a tendency to soar.

MONTRACOL

01310 Ain. Paris 430 – Bourg 9 – Mâcon 22
– Lyon 60.
This is the peaceful Bresse, with its squat farm-
houses, white-feathered fowl and cozy inns.

●	RESTAURANTS

● **Le Frometon**   SIM

Le village.
Tel. 04 74 24 28 90.
Closed Sat. dinner, Mon., Nov. 1 vac.,
2 weeks July.
Prix fixe: 22,50€, 19,50€.

With their unpretentious family style,
the Vernes are choice hosts. Paul and his
son Jérémie are in the kitchen while Liliane kindly welcomes and serves her clients. The terrifically priced menu offers
a country poultry liver salad, home-style
carp, Bresse chicken in cream sauce and
the house apple tart which would tempt
a saint.

MONTREAL-DU-GERS

32250 Gers. Paris 725 – Agen 57 – Auch 59
– Condom 16 – Mont-de-Marsan 65.
otsi.montrealdugers@wanadoo.fr.
A beautiful Gascon *bastide* which has preserved its character.

●	RESTAURANTS

● **Chez Simone**   SIM

Across from the church.
Tel. 05 62 29 44 40. Fax 05 62 29 49 94.
Closed Mon., Tue.
Prix fixe: 15€ (lunch), 25€.

Bernard Daubin, the son of Simone, who
started the restaurant, pursues tradition
with verve. The portions, like the prices,
are truly generous. Honest fare all the
way with simply presented foie gras,
the house ham, slow-roasted red peppers, guinea hen with garlic and lemon,
Armagnac croustade, veal sweetbreads
with oyster mushrooms and a slow-simmered eel and onion stew. Neighbor
Michel Cardoze de Fourcès is a regular
and loudly hails his belief in this "truthful cuisine".

MONTREUIL

62170 Pas-de-Calais. Paris 232 – Calais 72
– Abbeville 49 – Arras 80 – Lille 116.
This ancient city—its ramparts, its hilly alleyways, white-washed brick houses—were dear to
the Victor Hugo of *Les Misérables* (it is here that
takes place the episode in which Jean Valjean
gives himself up in order to save someone falsely
accused). The town has remained faithful to its
image of the past.

◤�😊	HOTELS-RESTAURANTS

● **Château de Montreuil**

Chaussée des Capucins.
Tel. 03 21 81 53 04. Fax 03 21 81 36 43.
reservation@chateaudemontreuil.com
www.chateaudemontreuil.com
Closed mid-Dec.–beg. Feb.
Rest. closed Mon., Tue. lunch, Thu. lunch.

18 rooms: 175–260€. 3 suites: 260€.
Prix fixe: 38€, 63€, 80€.

This cozy Relais & Châteaux boasts a good table. Christian Germain's classic dishes give sure value. You can order duck foie gras, Norman oysters, monkfish tail, Atlantic sea bass, veal cutlet or locally raised lamb with your eyes closed. From salty to sweet, the various dishes are light and delicate. Products are not tampered with, just tinkered with enough to make them wonderful. Lindsay and her team provide authentic, deft service. With its handful of rooms and apartments, this lovely, English-style house offers hospitality for anyone wanting a short or long stay. A golden welcome.

■ **Hermitage** ⌂

Place Gambetta.
Tel. 03 21 06 74 74. Fax 03 21 06 74 75.
www.hermitage-montreuil.com
100 rooms: 107–135€. 2 suites: 305€.

You couldn't wish for a more historic setting than this hotel situated in the heart of the city on the site of the Hôtel-Dieu. Founded in 1200 by Gauthier de Maintenay, Lord of Montreuil, it was rebuilt by Napoleon III before being turned into what it is today. Rooms are bright, spacious and quiet with great bathrooms. Apart from the restaurant (see Le Jéroboam), the intimate atmosphere of the bar is most agreeable.

● **Le Jéroboam** 🏠COM

At the Hermitage, pl Gambetta.
Tel. 03 21 86 65 80. Fax 03 21 81 36 43.
Closed Sun. (off season), Mon. (off season), Jan., 1 week Sept.
Prix fixe: 16€ (lunch), 25€, 29€, 58€.
A la carte: 55€.

The loft-style setting with bricks and contemporary lighting is reassuring. Céline and Olivier Germain—whose parents run the nearby Château—have turned this annex of the former Hotel-Dieu into a trendy brasserie. Quaff crisp wines and sup on up-to-date fare: delicious cold sweet pea soup, mint and radishes (a delight), langoustines in salad with ginger and the more rustic stuffed pork trotter are full of vigor.

● **Le Clos des Capucins** COM

46, pl du Général-de-Gaulle.
Tel. 03 21 06 08 65. Fax 03 21 81 20 45.
clos-des-capucins@wanadoo.fr
Closed 1 week Nov., Feb. vac.,
1 week at end June.
Rest. closed Sun. dinner, Mon.
6 rooms: 38–76€. 1 suite: 100€.
Prix fixe: 15,60€ (weekday lunch), 19,50€, 30€, 40€, 10€ (child).
A la carte: 33–41€.

Jean-Luc has a friendly welcome for his guests. His time at the Westminster in Le Touquet imparted a serious knowledge of the products of the sea which he cooks with care: grilled langoustines with basil, Breton sardines marinated in Muscadet and green celery, roasted salmon with slow-cooked cabbage, tarragon-seasoned duck legs and the three-chocolate pyramid with pistachio ice cream. There is real value for money here. The rooms are pleasant.

In Inxent (62170). 9 km n via D127.

■ **Auberge d'Inxent** ⌂

318, rue de la Course.
Tel. 03 21 90 71 19. Fax 03 21 86 31 67.
auberge.inxent@wanadoo.fr
Rest. closed Tue., Wed. (exc. July–Aug.), mid-Dec.–mid-Jan.,
1 week at end June–beg. July.
5 rooms: 65–72€.
Prix fixe: 15€, 22€, 26€, 38€.
A la carte: 35€.

The ancient 17th-century presbytery of Jean-Marc Six still affords the same old pleasure. It's easy to relax in one of the six Louis-Philippe style rooms before sitting down to tried and true escargots in puff pastry, river trout, home-style chicken the way our grandmothers prepared it and the frozen juniper berry mousse.

In La Madeleine-sous-Montreuil (62170).

● **Auberge de la Grenouillère**

2, rue de la Grenouillère.
Tel. 03 21 06 07 22. Fax 03 21 86 36 36.
auberge.de.la.grenouillere@wanadoo.frou
contact@lagrenouillere.fr
www.lagrenouillere.fr
Closed mid-Dec.–end Jan.
Rest. closed Tue., Wed.
4 rooms: 75–100€. 1 suite: 120€.
Prix fixe: 30€, 50€, 75€. A la carte: 85€.

A native of Dôle, trained in Alsace at the Cerf and the Crocodile, Roland Gauthier cooks dishes from his Northern region with passion. He has now decided to hand over his stove to his son Alexandre, who has come home after paying his dues at Marcon in Saint-Bonnet-le-Froid, Lasserre in Paris and La Pinède at Saint-Tropez. The latter takes lots of risks with his food combinations, throwing sweet-and-sour flavors around, adding spices everywhere, in short shedding the parental mantle. Although the establishment has kept its style of wooden beams, low ceilings, stone floors and frescoes on a frog theme, Junior's excesses could have resulted in a catastrophe. But quite to the contrary, high praises are drawing delighted clients to this remote corner of the Marais de la Canche to feast on the carrot in all of its forms, langoustines cooked and raw with galagangal, littleneck and razor clams with mango, pomegranate and a salmon caviar emulsion, which go from all-out gimmicky cooking to the frankly sublime. One can imagine that 55-year-old Roland is quite astonished to see his 27-year-old son Alexander grabbing the bit so fiercely in order to turn tradition upside down. However there is nothing better than white truffle-seasoned gnocchi, a monkfish tail presented whole on the plate in its cooking juice, a Licques pigeon prepared to order and the local lamb, tender and juicy, with crispy caramelized skin, served with minced artichokes. Desserts are easily seductive such as the fine raspberry mille-feuille. One can only hope that the *terroir* will help temper the creative ardor of the son. But whatever else one can say, this Grenouillère, with its four rustic rooms, affords one a great deal of pleasure.

49260 Maine-et-Loire. Paris 333 –
Angers 55 – Châtellerault 72 – Chinon 40 –
Cholet 61 – Saumur 15.
The local château is one of the Renaissance gems of the Loire valley.

	HOTELS-RESTAURANTS

● **Hostellerie Saint-Jean**

432, rue Nationale.
Tel. 02 41 52 30 41. Fax 02 41 52 89 02.
Closed Sun. dinner, Mon., 1–6 Mar.,
24 July–6 Aug.
Prix fixe: 14,50€ (lunch), 38€.

This Loire valley hostelry has kept its old-fashioned charm. The large, rustic dining room has style and the wine list, featuring wines from Saumur and Savennières, produces the goods. Regional products (vegetables, pike, poultry) are highlighted by careful preparations. A very nice welcome.

01340 Ain. Paris 397 – Mâcon 24 –
Saint Amour 25 – Tournus 36.
This is the heart of the Bresse with its world-famous white poultry and animated agricultural fairs which are called the "glorieuses".

	HOTELS-RESTAURANTS

■ **Le Pillebois**

Rte de Bourg-en-Bresse: 2 km s via D975.
Tel. 04 74 25 48 44.
lepillebois@wanadoo.fr
http://hotellepillebois.com
Hotel closed Sun. dinner (Oct.–Apr.).
Rest. closed Sat. lunch, Sun. dinner.
32 rooms: 66–100€.
Prix fixe: 17€ (lunch), 27€, 32€, 45€.

Marie-Paule Laventure's pretty clutch of modern, neo-Bresse buildings offer bright, functional rooms and carefully tended cuisine. Olivier Chardigny—formerly of Blanc—turns out very a promising crumble made with cod, crushed potatoes and herbs and a duck breast in sweet-and-sour sauce, served with a celery root purée and quince fricassée.

● Chez Léa

10, rte d'Etrez.
Tel. 04 74 30 80 84. Fax 04 74 30 85 66.
lea.montrevel@free.fr
www.restaurant-lea.com
Closed Sun. dinner, Mon. dinner, Wed.,
end Dec.–mid-Jan., end June–beg. July.
Prix fixe: 25€, 34€, 50€, 62€.
A la carte: 75–90€.

In this charming flower-filled inn right in the heart of the Bresse farmland, Marie-Claude Monnier follows the path blazed by her mother Léa with just enough rejuvenating touches to keep alive those traditional dishes of a region renowned for its gastronomy. Fresh, seasonal products are what makes Louis Monnier's cuisine so attractive and you'll delight in perfectly cooked dishes such as the Bresse chicken liver terrine with lobster sauce, topped with crayfish, the Breton catch of the day (following the tides), the lobster gratin in the style of Eugénie Brazier and the Bresse hen with morels and cream sauce before ending with a delicious dark chocolate marquis with vanilla sauce and candied oranges. A straightforward and masterful cuisine which will enchant even the most exacting gourmets.

● Le Comptoir ⌂🛏SIM

9, Grand-Rue.
Tel. 04 74 25 45 53. Fax 04 74 30 85 66.
lea.montrevel@free.fr
www.restaurant-lea.com
Closed Sun. dinner (exc. July–Aug.),
Tue. dinner (exc. July–Aug.), Wed.,
1 week Christmas–New Year's,
end June–beg. July.
Prix fixe: 19,50€, 27€, 31€.
A la carte: 30€.

In this Lyonnais *bouchon*, Cédric Monnier—the son of Marie-Claude and

Louis—produces terrific recipes just like home. His individual chicken liver terrine with a celery remoulade, his duckling filet roasted with rosemary jus and served with lentils and bacon and the baba au rhum with whipped cream are definitely mouthwatering. The menus are not expensive even with a bottle or glass of the excellent Saint-Vérans, Mâcons or Beaujolais.

MONTRIOND see AVORIAZ

MONTROND-LES-BAINS

42210 Loire. Paris 445 – Saint-Etienne 31 –
Lyon 61 – Montbrison 15 – Roanne 49.
This small spa town of 4000 souls has a casino, the Forez hills as a backdrop and the Bastie d'Urfé (a 17th-century château) as a historic gem. Montrond is also proud of its great table.

 ■ HOTELS-RESTAURANTS

● Hostellerie La Poularde ○⌂🏨

2, rue Saint-Etienne.
Tel. 04 77 54 40 06. Fax 04 77 54 53 14.
la-poularde@wanadoo.fr
www.la-poularde.com
Closed 3 weeks Jan., 2 weeks Aug.,
Sun. dinner (exc. Bank holidays),
Mon. dinner (exc. Bank holidays).
Rest. closed Sun. dinner, Mon., Tue. lunch.
7 rooms: 92–132€. 3 suites: 167–248€.
Prix fixe: 54€ (exc. Sat. dinner and Sun. lunch), 60€ (exc. Sat. dinner and Sun. lunch), 120€, 22€ (child).

Gilles Etéocle, Meilleur Ouvrier de France par excellence, has cultivated a wise old man look, thanks to his long hair and white beard. Nothing has changed for ages in this famous old inn where Etéocle also artfully cultivates classicism and a taste for authentic flavors. In a comfortable, 1980 dining room, top-notch staff serve grilled veal sweetbreads with a crayfish brochette, rolled in grains, on a truffle-scented "bed", pike-perch with green apples and cider-infused cream or the "case" containing a truffled young Bresse hen, cooked whole, with a spring vegetable ragout. There's a whiff of old-style class in all this. But everything here rings true, including the fine-honed desserts (frozen raspberry soufflé, thick chocolate cake and a lemon fondant). The wine list is exceptional and the old-fashioned rooms have been renovated to suit the times.

LE MONT-SAINT-MICHEL

50116 Manche. Paris 329 – Avranches 22 – Saint-Malo 52 – Fougères 47.
A marvel of the Western world with its abbey on its windswept granite rock rising from the sea: one of the most beautiful sites in the world.

 HOTELS-RESTAURANTS

● **La Mère Poulard**
Grande Rue.
Tel. 02 33 89 68 68. Fax 02 33 89 68 69.
www.mere-poulard.fr
60 rooms: 100–190€. Prestige: 280€.
1 suite: 370€.
Prix fixe: 55€, 65€, 75€, 85€.
A la carte: 100€.

Michel Bruneau—who had tried to make his mark in this famous establishment at the foot of the rock—has thrown in the towel. His former second-in-command—Cédric Ménard, who used to be at the P'tit B in Caen—has taken over and is bravely doing his best to whip up the omelets cooked over an open wood fire, the lobster fricassée with mushrooms, tender beef roast served with vegetables in sauce ravigote, roasted Atlantic sea bass with potatoes, spit-roasted poultry with thyme and the chocolate trilogy dessert. The room renovations are yet to be completed.

MONTSOREAU

49730 Maine-et-Loire. Paris 290 – Angers 74 – Châtellerault 68 – Chinon 20 – Poitiers 80 – Saumur 10 – Tours 55.
A sleeping beauty on the banks of the Loire and its château. Visit the nearby collegiate church at Candes-Saint-Martin.

 HOTELS-RESTAURANTS

■ **Le Bussy**
4, rue Jehanne-d'Arc.
Tel. 02 41 38 11 11. Fax 02 41 38 18 10.
hotel.lebussy@wanadoo.fr
www.hotel-lebussy.fr
Closed Dec.–end Jan.
12 rooms: 51–66€.

The rooms of this 18th-century house, with its cellar breakfast nook, overlook the château of the lady of Monsoreau. A pleasant welcome from Dominique Roi.

● **Diane de Méridor**
12, quai Ph.-de-Commines.
Tel. 02 41 51 71 76. Fax 02 41 51 17 17.
dianedemeridor@wanadoo.fr
Closed Tue. (exc. July–Aug.),
Wed. (exc. July–Aug.), 3 weeks Jan.,
2 weeks Nov.
Prix fixe: 13,50€ (weekday lunch), 24€,
30€, 40€, 50€, 65€ (wine inc.),
10€ (child). A la carte: 65€.

Bertrand and Stéphanie Deze's limestone building looks out onto the Loire. The rustic-modern dining room with its terra cotta floor tiles and orange fabric, fireplace and beams, is the setting for a parade of cleverly updated local dishes. Witness the eel sushi on a bed of smoked wasabi, the roasted pike-perch with crayfish coulis and mashed potatoes, the sage and mint-seasoned veal belly served in an individual cocotte and a Granny Smith apple compote served with a dried fruit nougatine.

MORET-SUR-LOING

77250 Seine-et-Marne. Paris 74 – Fontainebleau 10 – Melun 27 – Nemours 17 – Sens 44.
The ancient bridge on the Loing, the site itself, the old city: Everything attracts the eye in this lovely village much-loved by artists which was a fief of the Impressionists. An absolute must-see: The "live" pageant in summer makes the town's history come alive again.

HOTELS-RESTAURANTS

● **Hostellerie**
  du Cheval Noir
47, av J.-Jaurès.
Tel. 01 60 70 80 20. Fax 01 60 70 80 21.
contact@chevalnoir.fr
www.chevalnoir.fr
Closed 2 weeks beg. Jan., 1 week Aug.
Rest. closed Sun. dinner, Mon., Tue. lunch.
8 rooms: 80–125€. 1 suite: 150€.
Prix fixe: 30€, 40€, 48€, 53€, 68€,
16€ (child). A la carte: 65€–95€.

Gilles de Crick's house along the Loing has lots of character and offers a personal, refined and tasty cuisine. The pressed terrine of rabbit confit is flavored with cardamom. The roasted pike-perch is served with a red wine butter sauce and a sweet garlic purée. Beef tenderloin suprises us with garden vegetable mixture, an acidulated cocktail of fresh herbs and a cola emulsion. The pear tarte Tatin with salted-butter caramel makes for a more restrained finish. We applaud the charming welcome, the energetic service and the cozy rooms.

● **Le Relais de Pont-Loup** COM
14, rue du Peintre-Sisley.
Tel. 01 60 70 43 05. Fax 01 60 70 22 54.
relaispontloup@wanadoo.fr
Closed Mon.
Prix fixe: 28€ (weekday lunch), 38€,
25€(child). A la carte: 43€.

Marie-Lucie Robert greets and cooks with aplomb. The décor definitely has style. Pretty plates show off traditional fare: artichoke hearts in sauce, catch of the day, Vendée quail with cherries and a fine caramelized fruit tart. The park along the river is a peaceful backdrop. Well-chosen wines and a smiling welcome.

MORLAIX

29600 Finistère. Paris 538 – Brest 59 –
Saint-Brieuc 87 – Quimper 77.
There are many attractions in this pretty town of the Northern part of Finistère, with its viaduct, old houses, bay and port. The TGV has put it at just four hours from Paris.

 HOTELS-RESTAURANTS

■ **Hôtel de l'Europe** ⌂
1, rue d'Aiguillon.
Tel. 02 98 62 11 99. Fax 02 98 88 83 38.
www.hotel-europe-com.fr
Closed 2 weeks Christmas–New Year's.
57 rooms: 60–150€. 3 suites: 150–250€.
Half board: 90–210€.

This hotel has been here for two centuries, welcoming visitors into its 17th-century, wood-paneled interior. The staircase is also worth a detour. Prices remain steep.

● **Les Bains Douches** ∏SIM
45, allée du Paon-Ben.
Tel.-Fax 02 98 63 83 83.
Closed Sat. lunch, Sun., Mon. dinner,
2 weeks Nov., 2 weeks May.
Prix fixe: 12,80€ (weekday lunch), 15,30€
(weekday lunch), 19€ (weekday dinner)
7€ (child). A la carte: 31€.

Situated in the old public baths of the town, this bistro stands out as much for its décor as for its cooking. Tony Pilon concocts apple and foie gras crumble, John Dory with spring vegetables, duck breast Rossini and the chocolate coconut fondant, sure to please. Nice atmosphere and reasonable prices.

● **Brasserie de l'Europe** SIM
Pl Emile-Souvestre.
Tel. 02 98 88 81 15. Fax 02 98 63 47 24.
contact@brasseriedeleurope.com
www.brasseriedeleurope.com
Closed Sun., 1 week Jan., 1 week May.
Prix fixe: 12€, 15€, 8€ (child).
A la carte: 31€.

He's from the Loire valley, has worked in Paris at the Pressoir and Petit Pré and has returned to the country of his first love. Laurent Chauvin deftly handles surf and turf. He doesn't confine himself to the most expensive products of either and, along with his associate Christophe Guillot—late of the Roux Brothers in London—offers them to delighted guests. There's a wine bar in the basement with wines by the glass and savory tarts.

MORNANT

69440 Rhône. Paris 479 – Lyon 25 – Saint-Etienne 37 – Givors 12 – Vienne 24. South of the hills of the Lyonnais, in what is known as the Pilat, lies this tranquil stopover town.

 HOTELS-RESTAURANTS

■ La Poste

5, pl de la Liberté.
Tel. 04 78 44 00 40. Fax 04 78 44 19 07.
Rest. closed Sun. dinner.
11 rooms: 45–70€.
Prix fixe: 14€ (weekday lunch), 17,50€, 32€, 9,30€ (child). A la carte: 34€.

A keen welcome from Philippe Bajard and some serious cooking from Daniel Vergnon in this orange-toned house with its family atmosphere. Marbled foie gras terrine, sausage with slow-cooked apples, fresh frog legs prepared in the style of Provence, sea trout with creamy tomato and pepper soup, Monts du Lyonnais venison with a Grand Veneur sauce and the chocolate mousse are not bad at all. Nice rooms.

MORSBRONN-LES-BAINS

67360 Bas-Rhin. Paris 499 – Strasbourg 46 – Haguenau 11 – Wissembourg 28.
A picture postcard village set in the outer forest to be visited for its restorative properties and, as of now, a good table.

 HOTELS-RESTAURANTS

● Hôtel de la Marne et La Source des Sens

19, rte de Haguenau.
Tel. 03 88 09 30 53. Fax 03 88 09 35 65.
info@hoteldelamarne.com
www.hoteldelamarne.com
Closed 1 week beg. Nov., end Jan.–mid-Feb., 2 weeks July.
Rest. closed Sun. dinner, Mon.
13 rooms: 50–85€.
Prix fixe: 13,50€ (lunch), 22€, 40€, 60€, 13€ (child). A la carte: 55€–60€.

We had discovered Pierre Weller after his return home from his various experiences: Ducasse in Monaco, Bateau Ivre at Courchevel, Cheval Blanc at Lembach, Buerehiesel before Brazil and Japan as advised by Emile Jung. Now he's turned the interior of this establishment upside down, creating a large, modern dining room where he has preserved the pretty wood paneling but added contemporary seating and a screen which shows you what's going on in the kitchen. This restaurant pulls out all the stops and an inquisitive clientèle is beating down the doors. The tuna sashimi with foie gras beignet is the *amuse-bouche*; cep fricassée with sautéed artichokes in an arugula and green lentil salad and the sea bream with potato gnocchi with sausage and a pepper coulis are edging towards greatness. We also love the thick wedge of calf's liver in a hazelnut and pesto crust served with ratte fingerling potatoes and a lemon thyme jus and finally the thick-cut Iberian pork tenderloin grilled pink and juicy, served with an *al dente* risotto are nearing perfection. One reproach: desserts seem keener to transgress tradition than to provide pure pleasure, *viz à viz* chocolate mille-feuille (without pastry) with berries and a pepper sorbet and an upside-down tart (with phyllo, no short crust, no puff pastry, nor sweet pastry crust) with apricots, cardamom and pistachio. But youth must have its way…

MORTAGNE-AU-PERCHE

61400 Orne. Paris 157 – Alençon 39 – Chartres 80 – Lisieux 88 – Le Mans 73.
office-mortagne@wanadoo.fr.
Hills and stud farms characterize the Perche region. A jolly, smiling and convivial Normandy is at its best in this pretty town renowned for its blood sausage festival.

HOTELS-RESTAURANTS

■ Hôtel du Tribunal

4, pl du Palais.
Tel. 02 33 25 04 77. Fax 02 33 83 60 83.
hotel.du.tribunal@wanadoo.fr
www.perso.wanadoo.fr/hotel.du.tribunal.61
.normandie
Closed Christmas, New Year's.
18 rooms: 50–80€. 3 suites: 90–100€.
Prix fixe: 18€, 40€, 9€ (child).
A la carte: 45–50€.

The rooms of this historic coaching inn have a charming rustic appeal. Jean-François Leboucher offers a heartfelt welcome while Régis Peltier concocts the duck foie gras duo, cod filet with aromatic herbs, pan-roasted beef tenderloin with foie gras and a fine apple tart with cinnamon ice cream. The flower-filled garden is pleasant in good weather.

MORTEAU

25500 Doubs. Paris 469 – Besançon 64 –
Pontarlier 32 – Neuchâtel 39.
o.val.de.morteau@freesbee.fr.
This large town in the Haut-Doubs near the real Swiss mountains is the home of sausages smoked in local farms with high chimneys. Visit the neighboring village of Grand-Combe-Chateleau.

 RESTAURANTS

● Auberge de la Roche

Pont de la Roche.
Tel. 03 81 68 80 05. Fax 03 81 68 87 64.
www.ifrance.com/aubergedelaroche
Closed Sun. dinner, Mon., Tue. dinner,
mid-Jan.–end Jan.
Prix fixe: 26€ (weekdays), 40€, 75€.

Philippe Feuvrier plays on local tradition and follows the seasons. We like the friendly welcome at his attractive, colorful inn. The menu changes but his variations on the Morteau smoked sausage, crayfish and salmon in a crêpe pouch, pike mousseline served with buttered cabbage, venison medallion with lingonber-

ries, roasted goose liver with Vind e Paille caramel and the deboned Bresse poultry with a creamy Vin Jaune-seasoned stuffing are timeless feats that don't pale. The little charlotte with a walnut cookie and blonde caramel slips down nicely.

MORZINE

74110 Haute-Savoie. Paris 593 –
Thonon-les-Bains 33 – Annecy 79 –
Genève 62.
touristoffice@morzine-avoriaz.com.
This pretty resort at 960 meters in altitude and has kept its feeling of an old Savoie town. You reach the Nyon point (2000 meters high) via the Pleney ski lift.

 HOTELS-RESTAURANTS

■ Dahu

293 Le Mas-Metout.
Tel. 04 50 75 92 92. Fax 04 50 75 92 50.
info@dahu.com
www.dahu.com
Closed mid-Sept.–mid-Dec.,
mid-Apr.–mid-June.
39 rooms: 61–189€. Half board: 93–254€.
Prix fixe: 25€, 40€, 15€ (child).
A la carte: 35–40€.

Le Dahu remains one of our favorite spots in this resort. There's an unbeatable view down the valley, two swimming pools and a welcoming alpine setting. The Heu family are charming hosts and the rooms of their chalet are clean and pleasant. On the restaurant's menu, the hot goat cheese salad with honey, a veal navarin with spring vegetables and the brown sugar pain perdu with vanilla ice cream are not bad at all.

■ Le Samoyède

Pl de l'Office du Tourisme.
Tel. 04 50 79 00 79. Fax 04 50 79 07 91.
info@hotel-lesamoyede.com
www.hotel-lesamoyed.com
Closed end Sept.–mid-Dec., mid-Apr.–mid-June.
7 rooms: 35–75€. 18 suites: 115–215€.

The lively hotel of the Baud-Pachon has been a landmark of this resort since the 1950's. The bar fills up at sundown and the restaurant, run by son Alexandre, is an agreeable eatery. (See Restaurants: La Taverne.)

■ Le Chalet Philibert

Le Putey.
Tel. 04 50 79 25 18. Fax 04 50 79 25 81.
info@chalet-philibert.com
www.chalet-philibert.com
Closed 24 Apr.–20 May, 24 Sept.–10 Oct.
14 rooms: 65–140€. 4 suites: 125–240€.
Prix fixe: 35€, 45€, 50€, 15€ (child).

Comfortable, wood-paneled rooms in this Savoie chalet with swimming pool taken over by the Baud family. Errico David is at the stove and enlivens winter evenings in the alpine dining room. Traditional, rustic, warm...

■ La Bergerie

Rte du Téléphérique.
Tel. 04 50 79 13 69. Fax 04 50 75 95 71.
info@hotel-bergerie.com
www.hotel-bergerie.com
Closed mid-Sept.–mid-Dec.,
end Apr.–end June.
25 rooms: 70–230€. 2 suites: 160–260€.

This famed hotel of the resort has known many generations of the Marullaz family and the establishment is still run with utmost dedication. The heated, covered pool can be enjoyed year-round and the rooms are charming. The studios, some of which have a kitchenette, are functional and appealing with their typical wood paneling and green and red checked fabric. The welcome, like everything else here, is charming.

■ La Clef des Champs

Av de Joux-Plane.
Tel. 04 50 79 10 13. Fax 04 50 79 08 18.
hotel@clefdeschamps.com
www.clefdeschamps.com
Closed beg. Sept.–mid-Dec.,
beg. Apr.–end June.
30 rooms: 60–100€. Half board: 123–181€.

Sylvie and Pierre Leblanc have put their hearts into renovating, enlarging and modernizing their house, particularly where the rooms are concerned. Some are duplexes and offer an up-to-date Savoyard look. The lounges with their pale paneling are welcoming and the *pension* cooking is effective. Prices are very reasonable. Jacuzzi and heated pool.

■ Fleur des Neiges

Tel. 04 50 79 01 23. Fax 04 50 75 95 75.
fleurneige@aol.com
Closed Sept.–mid-Dec., mid-Apr.–end June.
37 rooms: 50–66€. Half board: 52€.

Canadian hockey player David Archambault has adopted the region thanks to his wife. They've renovated the family chalet and turned it into a welcoming spot where you'll feel right at home. Prices are reasonable and the regional cuisine looks great. There's a bar with a fireplace, terraces with panoramic views, a hammam, hot tub and heated swimming pool.

■ Les Lans

Tel. 04 50 79 00 90. Fax 04 50 79 15 22.
hotel-les-lans@wanadoo.fr / www.leslans.com
Closed Sept.–mid-Dec., mid-Apr.–end June.
32 rooms: 45–100€.

Bernadette Marullaz runs this chalet on the route to the Avoriaz ski lift. A fierce Savoyarde, she recounts tales of the old village with enthusiasm. At reception, her daughter is a smiling hostess. The common areas are paneled and the *pension* cuisine is familial and reasonably priced.

● La Taverne & L'Atelier   COM

At Le Samoyède, pl de la Crusaz.
Tel. 04 50 79 00 79. Fax 04 50 79 07 91.
info@hotel-lesamoyede.com
www.hotel-lesamoyede.com
Closed lunch (exc. Sun. winter),
Thu. lunch (summer), Fri. lunch (summer),
Sat. lunch (summer), Sun. (summer),
20 Sept.–mid-Dec., mid-Apr.–mid-June.
Prix fixe: 30€, 64€. A la carte: 58€.

Alexandre Baud-Pachon cut his teeth at the Relais Louis XIII in Paris, at the Chat

Botté in Genève and at the Bateau Ivre in Courchevel before rejoining the familial homestead. His preparations are refined, light and fresh. The frog leg ravioli with sweet garlic and a mushroom emulsion, whitefish with slow-cooked vegetables, sirloin steak with breaded celery root cakes and a crispy banana and cocoa mille-feuille with roasted Fressinette strawberries with honey are nicely done.

● **La Chamade** `SIM`

Pl de la Crusaz.
Tel. 04 50 79 13 91. Fax 04 50 79 27 48.
restaurant@lachamade.com
www.lachamade.com
Closed 10 days at end Nov.,
10 days beg. Dec., May.
Prix fixe: 42,50€. A la carte: 60€.

Thierry Thorens presides over two dining rooms—one of them folksy and the other in a rustic mountain style—which nicely sum up the atmosphere of Savoie. Formerly with Bocuse, he offers dishes full of sensible ideas. An escargot fricassée, mushrooms in puff pastry, fish pot-au-feu and the Savoie wine sabayon with fruit and sorbet won't let you down. An easygoing welcome and service. Not quite so for the prices.

● **Le Matafan** `SIM`

Av de Joux-Plane.
Tel. 04 50 79 27 74.
Closed mid-Sept.–mid-Dec.,
mid-Apr.–end June.
Prix fixe: 17€, 32€.

Michel Blanc treats you to sensibly priced Savoie specialties (raclette, "rebloche", matafan, fondue, tagliatelle carbonara, cep omelet) in a relaxed setting.

LA MOTHE-ACHARD

85150 Vendée. Paris 433 –
Les Sables d'Olonne 15 –
La Roche sur Yon 15 – Nantes 83.
A verdant stopover on the road leading to the beaches of the Vendée.

 HOTELS-RESTAURANTS

■ **Domaine de Brandois**

La Forêt.
Tel. 02 51 06 24 24.
www.domainedebrandois.com
29 rooms: 125–170€.
Prix fixe: 30€.

This 18th-century château, with its verdant estate, horses, park, forest, location not far from the Sables d'Olonne and the sea, designer rooms in the château, the priory or the orchard, its contemporary furniture and its open-plan bathrooms, is the brand new hotel created by two former employees of Novotel, Didier Robard and Jean-Pascal Roger. In the dining room, with its modern tables and Philippe Starck-style chairs, you can enjoy an up-to-date cuisine: guacamole served in a glass with tomato and shredded crabmeat, a saffron- scented fish and shellfish tajine, seared tuna steak with sesame seeds and a berry sugar biscuit for dessert.

MOUCHARD

39330 Jura. Paris 395 – Besançon 39 –
Arbois 10 – Dole 36.
This town is best known for its TGV station, a few steps away from the vineyards of Arbois.

 HOTELS-RESTAURANTS

■ **Chalet Bel'Air**

7, pl Bel-Air.
Tel. 03 84 37 80 34. Fax 03 84 73 81 18.
www.besac.com/chaletbelair
Closed Sun. dinner, Tue., Wed., 1 week at end Nov., 1 week beg. Dec., 1 week at end June.
9 rooms: 85–97€. 1 suite: 50–69€.
Prix fixe: 23,50€, 44€, 53€, 74€,
12€ (child).

Monique and Bruno Gatto have turned this chalet into an establishment where you'll feel right at home. The rooms are small, homey and agreeable and the cooking—rustic-style in the rotisserie, more sophisticated in the restaurant—slips down nicely. Bruno is at the top of his form with his duck foie gras escalope with reduced currant juice and a Comté cake, marinated salmon with pine honey, sautéed scallops with a Noilly vermouth sabayon, lamb bacon in a tarragon crust and his Caraque chocolate Saint-Eve. Nice local wines.

MOUDEYRES

43150 Haute-Loire. Paris 572 – Le Puy-en-Velais 26 – Aubenas 64 – Langogne 59.
Right near mount Gerbier-de-Jonc, in the heart of the Velay, sits this adorable village which has managed to maintain its old-fashioned feel and its breezy good manners.

 HOTELS-RESTAURANTS

■ Pré Bossu
Le Bourg.
Tel. 04 71 05 10 70. Fax 04 71 05 10 21.
Closed beg. Nov.–beg. May.
Rest. closed lunch
1 room: 95€. 5 suites: 120–140€.
Prix fixe: 38€, 42€, 58€, 20€ (child).

With its thatched roof and flowers, this cottage surrounded by fields has a great deal of charm. Carlos Grootaert uses his own vegetables or those of his neighbors. His exclusively local products—even the wines come from small vineyards around here—are excellent. The fiddlehead cassolette, the wild Saint-Front lake pike-perch, the lamb shank and the licorice root–flavored ice cream impart an incomparable taste of the *terroir*.

In Saint-Front (43550). 12 km e via D39.
■ L'Herminette
Bigorre-les Maziaux.
Tel. 04 71 59 57 58. Fax 04 71 56 34 91.
www.auberge-pays-auvergne.com
Rest. closed Sun. dinner, Mon.
6 rooms: 50–64€.
Prix fixe: 19€.

Catherine Mathieu and Régis Van Nieuwenhuyze run a tight ship at their admi-

rable inn. Country charcuterie, the hot goat cheese salad, Auvergne-style beef stew, simmered lentils and bacon and a fruit tart go down a treat. The surroundings deserve a stay for one or several nights in one of the six pretty rooms.

MOUGINS

06250 Alpes-Maritimes. Paris 908 – Cannes 8 – Antibes 13 – Grasse 11 – Nice 32.
tourisme@mougins-coteazur.org.
This pretty, gourmet village in the hinterland of Cannes has long been famous for its tourist attractions. This is the place to have a good time in the open air.

 HOTELS-RESTAURANTS

● Le Mas Candille

Bd Clément-Rebuffel.
Tel. 04 92 28 43 43. Fax 04 92 28 43 40.
candille@relaischateaux.com
www.lemascandille.com
Rest. closed Mon. (exc. dinner July–Aug.),
Tue. (exc. dinner July–Aug.), Jan.
39 rooms: 340–615€. 1 suite: 665–845€.
Prix fixe: 70€, 105€, (exc. March festival,
May and the Monaco grand prix).
A la carte: 140€.

Up on the heights of Cannes, this 18th-century Provençal farmhouse, surrounded by four hectares of parkland planted with olive trees and cypresses, makes for a very charming Relais & Châteaus. The luxurious rooms, the superb Shiseido spa and the two swimming pools guarantee wellbeing, as does the restaurant. Serge Gouloumes concocts a clever cuisine inspired by his travels and current trends. The Armagnac-seasoned foie gras Tatin, the langouste bouillabaisse, roasted pigeon with quinoa soufflé served with its thighs in spring rolls and peaches served in a lemon-thyme seasoned broth are very satisfying. Wonderful service.

■ Manoir de l'Etang

Bois de Font-Merle, 66 allée du Manoir.
Tel. 04 92 28 36 00. Fax 04 92 28 36 10.
manoir.etang@wanadoo.fr

www.manoir-de-letang.com
Closed end Oct.–beg. Apr.
16 rooms: 125–250€. 4 suites: 275–360€.
Prix fixe: 29€ (lunch), 39€ (lunch).
A la carte: 64€.

You'd never believe you were just ten minutes from the Croisette in this pretty park with its lotus-flower pond. Nestled here is a 19th-century house offering rooms decorated in all the colors of Provence with a restaurant offering all those of Italy. Zucchini flowers with semi-dried cherry tomatoes, red tuna with a green ratatouille, grilled sirloin with minced parmesan and truffle vinaigrette and the berry tiramisu give joy all around. The bill is a bit of a killjoy but the service is irreproachable.

● **Moulin de Mougins**   LUX
In Notre-Dame-de-Vie, 2,5 km se via D3.
Tel. 04 93 75 78 24. Fax 04 93 90 18 55.
reservation@moulindemougins.com
www.moulindemougins.com
Closed Mon.
7 rooms: 140–130€.
Prix fixe: 58€ (lunch, wine inc.), 98€, 115€, 170€.

Taking on Roger Vergé's establishment was a gamble and Alain Lorca has succeeded in making his mark, while keeping some of the star dishes of this great chef of the Côte d'Azur with whom he never worked and to whom the town paid tribute just this year. In any case, here—virtually intact—is this restaurant dedicated to a cuisine of the sun. Lorca plays on a register that takes flight, is refined, up-to-date and full of zeal, with dishes such as hot foie gras with roasted verbena-seasoned figs and a fresh almond cappuccino, a duck, foie gras and black truffle pâté in a pastry crust served with a generous salad, the Mediterranean sea bass simmered with green tomatoes and fennel and served with fried chickpea cakes (panisses) and turbot cooked with mushroom- and ham-stuffed artichokes simmered in wine. The roasted veal sweetbreads with buttered green beans, almonds and fresh coriander seasoned peaches and the veal kidney wrapped in

a crust and served with a slow-simmered chanterelle daube make for some good, earthy fare. The desserts (the dark chocolate cake with basil-seasoned strawberries and raspberries) are in the same tone. This a great house in top form.

● **La Terrasse**   COM
31, Bd Courteline.
Tel. 04 92 28 36 20. Fax 04 92 28 36 21.
www.la-terrasse-a-mougins.com
Closed Mon., Tue. lunch, beg. Jan.–mid-Feb.
4 rooms: 105–150€.
Prix fixe: 25€ (lunch), 35€ (lunch), 45€.
A la carte: 70€.

Roger Vergé knew how to gather qualified personnel around him who, in their turn, set up shop in the region. This is the case of Jean-Luc Gaufillier who has breathed life into this bijou address with a rotisserie, a terrace, palm trees and a view of Cannes and the Lérins islands. Chef Laurent Martinez cooks up market-based dishes such as chard and pine nut tourte, pumpkin risotto, braised pork cheeks served with a pleasant olive oil–infused potato purée and the plum clafoutis with pistachio ice cream, which give you a good idea of what's on offer. The lunch menus are great deals.

● **L'Amandier de Mougins**   COM
In the village.
Tel. 04 93 90 00 91. Fax 04 92 92 89 95.
lamandierdemougins@wanadoo.fr
www.aurendezvous-mougins.com
Prix fixe: 15€, 19,80€, 25€.
A la carte: 60–70€.

This establishment with its bright rooms and peaceful terrace was Roger Vergé's first address at Mougins and the place still has as much charm as ever. Nowadays, Christophe Ferré runs the kitchen. His dishes are full of sun and products like small niçoise-style ravioli with basil and tomato sauce, Mediterranean sea bass cooked crisp, squab breast served on a canapé and the miniature roasted pears. Various menus help to tamper down the bill. Classic local wines are always agreeable.

MONHOUDOU

72260 Sarthe. Paris 200 – Alençon 32 –
Le Mans 40.
A tranquil corner of the Sarthe.

 HOTELS-RESTAURANTS

■ Château de Monhoudou

2 km s via D117.
Tel. 02 43 97 40 05. Fax 02 43 33 11 58.
monhoudou@aol.com / www.monhoudou.com
6 rooms: 89–155€.
Prix fixe: 39€ (wine inc.) 20€ (child).

This Renaissance château, which has
been the property of the Monhoudou
family for nineteen generations, won't
fail to charm, thanks to its English-style
grounds inhabited by wild animals, its
large, elegant rooms with old-fashioned
furnishings and its drawing room with
fireplace and library. In the restaurant,
Marie-Christine, the lady of the manor,
uses her antique porcelain plates to serve
up traditional dishes. Scallops served
over soft-simmered leeks, then salmon
in a sorrel crust or the duck confit with
peaches, are pleasant fare. The house
seasonal fruit tart brings back memories
of childhood. Dinners are candlelit.

MOULINS

03000 Allier. Paris 299 – Bourges 101 –
Clermont-Ferrand 104 – Nevers 55 –
Roanne 99.
o.t.moulins@wanadoo.fr.
A famous stopping point on the N7, this is the
capital of the Bourbonnais and a crossroads from
which to visit the spa towns and châteaux of the
region as well as the bucolic valley of the Besbre—
dear to René Fallet—which is nearby.

 HOTELS-RESTAURANTS

■ Hôtel de Paris

21, rue de Paris.
Tel. 04 70 44 00 58. Fax 04 70 34 05 39.
www.hoteldeparis-moulins.com
22 rooms: 64–100€. 5 suites: 122€.

The cozy and modern rooms compensate
for the loss of the once highly popular restaurant. You'll appreciate the efficient service and the quality of the welcome.

● Le Clos de Bourgogne ⓥ.COM

83, rue de Bourgogne.
Tel. 04 70 44 03 00. Fax 04 70 44 03 33.
www.closdebourgogne.fr
Closed Sat. lunch, Sun. dinner, Mon., Christ-
mas, 2 weeks Aug.
Prix fixe: 20€ (lunch), 27€, 45€, 57€.
A la carte: 65€.

This manor house surrounded by a verdant park in the heart of town won't fail
to charm. Its hard to be indifferent to its
large stateroom and three bourgeois sitting rooms with their 18th-century and
Empire furniture. In the kitchen, Hervé
Chandioux also knows how to seduce.
Formerly of Flo in Paris, he has worked
with Gilles Goujon at Fontjocouse and
Georges Blanc in Vonnas and cooks up
technically accomplished as well as imp-
ish fare. The cucumber served with goat
cheese sorbet, herb- and lime-seasoned
risotto served with a grilled sea bream
filet, beef tenderloin with a young sprout
salad and a cinnamon-seasoned Breton
shortbread with berry gelatine revisit
the classics with ingenuity. The service
is attentive, the wines of Sancerre and
Reuilly appealing.

● Restaurant des Cours ⓥ.COM

36, cours J.-Jaurès.
Tel. 04 70 44 25 66. Fax 04 70 20 58 45.
patrick.bourhy@wanadoo.fr
www.restaurant-des-cours.com
Closed Tue. dinner, Wed., Feb. vac.,
1 week at end June, 10 days Aug.
Prix fixe: 20€, 50€, 10€ (child).
A la carte: 55€.

Patrick Bourhy has taken the time to create a setting to his taste. The décor is
Empire-style and the color red predom-
inates. Sit down to feast on the Puy lentil risotto served with a poached egg and
marinated salmon, the catch of the day,
grilled and served with a saffron beurre

blanc, beef with truffle sauce and the signature praline and Hervé Courtais roasted cocoa bean dessert. A very kind welcome and efficient service.

LE MOULLEAU see ARCACHON

MOUSTIERS-SAINTE-MARIE

04360 Alpes de Haute-Provence. Paris 775 – Digne-les-Bains 49 – Aix-en-Provence 92 – Draguignan 62 – Manosque 51.
moustiers@wanadoo.fr.
The lovely earthenware, the scent of lavender, the approach to the Gorges of the Verdon: All of this can be found in this lovely village with its tortuous streets and old houses, which stands out like a pearl on the touristic map of the Haute-Provence.

 HOTELS-RESTAURANTS

■ Bastide de Moustiers
Chem. de Quinson. D952 S.
Tel. 04 92 70 47 47. Fax 04 92 70 47 48.
www.bastide-moustiers.com
Closed end Nov.–mid-Dec.,
10 days at end Jan.
12 rooms: 155–315€. 1 suite: 275–330€.
Prix fixe: 44€, 58€, 75€, 15€ (child).

Alain Ducasse's secret weapon is in Haute Provence: it is this charming *bastide* with its twelve delicious rooms, its antique furniture, its cozy dining rooms and its young team devoted to serving an inspired and market-based cuisine. Eric Santalucia from Toulouse uses no tricks in producing the ideas of the master ("Better a turbot without genius than genius without a turbot") in a menu that changes with each meal. Marbled foie gras terrine with figs, John Dory cooked with fennel, Saint-Jurs lamb rubbed with garlic and served with golden-brown chickpea cakes, zucchini and spring onions, goat cheese in all of its forms and ages and the fruit minestrone with a verbena sorbet and a fresh chocolate mint cup make you want to take up residence. A knowledgeable sommelier sings the praises of the best wines between Provence and the Rhône valley (white from the château Rasque, Cornas from Vôge).

● La Treille Muscate
Pl de l'Eglise.
Tel. 04 92 74 64 31.
Closed Wed. (dinner off season),
Wed. (July–Aug.), Thu. (off season),
mid-Nov.–mid-Feb.
Prix fixe: 26€, 35€.

Mireille Servan is Moustiers' good fairy. Her welcome is genuinely accented and she is a warm presence on her terrace across from the church, as are the yellow tones of her table overlooking the river and its shady banks. The stuffed vegetables (potatoes with octopus fricassée, zucchini with goat cheese mousse), asparagus with shavings of chorizo, sea bream with olives and the seared sirloin with slow-simmered shallots cooked by her husband Gaston are artful, well-made and with no pretentions other than to give pleasure.

● Les Santons COM
Pl de l'Eglise.
Tel. 04 92 74 66 48. Fax 04 92 74 63 67.
www.lessantons.com
Closed Mon. (dinner)., Tue. (off season).
Prix fixe: 25€, 34€.

Perched above the torrent, this house has charm with its fireplace and its terrace under a vine-filled arbor. Jean-Marie Marre delights with tomato Tatin with goat cheese and toasted fennel seeds, beef with morels and a chocolate tartlette with peach sorbet. A smiling and discreet welcome.

MOUTHIER-HAUTE-PIERRE

25920 Doubs. Paris 443 – Besançon 39 – Pontarlier 21 – Salins-les-Bains 42.
Peaceful and cool valley of the Loue as Courbet painted it. It continues to produce wonderful cherries.

 HOTELS-RESTAURANTS

■ La Cascade
4, rue des Gorges-de-Noailles.
Tel. 03 81 60 95 30. Fax 03 81 60 94 55.
hotellacascade@wanadoo.fr
Closed beg. Nov.–20 Mar.

17 rooms: 60–67€.
Prix fixe: 20€, 35€, 47€.

René and Madeleine Savonet are always there when you need them, welcoming clients with a smile and showing them to quiet, comfortable rooms or to a table in order to sample René's cooking. Morels in puff pastry, turbot filet, minced chicken in Vin Jaune sauce, quail filet with berry sauce and the seasonal fruit charlotte are unpretentious.

MOUZON

08210 Ardennes. Paris 245 – Charleville-Mézières 40 – Sedan 18 – Verdun 63.
Here the Ardenne flirts with the Meuse, gazing towards the lovely game-filled forests, rich with boar. Do not miss the Domaine de Belval.

| ● | RESTAURANTS |

● Les Echevins
33, rue du Général-de-Gaulle.
Tel. 03 24 26 10 90. Fax 03 24 29 05 95.
Closed Sat. lunch, Sun. dinner, Mon., 1 week at end Dec., 1 week beg. Jan., 3 weeks Aug.
Prix fixe: 25€, 37€, 50€. A la carte: 50€.

Pascal Oudéa's 17th-century, half-timbered house reflects Southern climes. Witness his sunny, well-crafted dishes such as the marbled tuna, eggplant and tomato terrine with a tapenade vinaigrette, grilled scorpion fish with basil and simmered arichokes, duck medallions cooked to a golden brown with rosemary and a berry dessert with rose-flavored biscuits accompanied by a rhubarb mint coulis. The service is terrific and the bill reasonable.

MUHLBACH-SUR-MUNSTER

68380 Haut-Rhin. Paris 461 – Colmar 24 – Gérardmer 38 – Munster 6.
The Munster valley with its bucolic byways, fresh air and its farms-turned-inns where cheese dishes are still lovingly cooked the old way.

| | HOTELS-RESTAURANTS |

■ Perle des Vosges
22, rte du Gaschney.
Tel. 03 89 77 61 34. Fax 03 89 77 74 40.
www.perledesvosges.net
Closed beg. Jan.–beg. Feb.
40 rooms: 40–73€. 5 suites: 106–117€.
Prix fixe: 13€, 65€, 8,50€ (child).

Ernest André Benz, formerly of Chapel, Jung and Ducasse, has come home to roost in this charming Vosgesian chalet perched on a hill. The rooms give onto the woods and the cuisine does honor to the region. In the Louis XII-style dining room, hikers and cross-country skiers are treated to escargot ravioli, pan-tossed rouget with herb-seasoned minced artichoke hearts and a veal cutlet served in an individual cocotte with mushrooms and spinach. The anisette-flambéed strawberries are a flamboyant dessert. One wants to return.

MULHOUSE

68100 Haut-Rhin. Paris 464 – Strasbourg 117 – Bâle 35 – Colmar 43 – Belfort 42.
ot@ville-mulhouse.fr.
Mulhouse is probably sick and tired by now of its has-been and antiquated image of an "Alsatian Manchester". Mulhouse not Alsatian? Come now, there are *winstub*s or *"wistuwa"*, taverns serving fleischnacka, wines by the pitcher and a smart atmosphere. There are also those stars of the gastronomic arts, worthy of the region, be they named Jacques or the Bouton d'Or. But the museums alone would justify a visit here. From fine tables to good hotels (the Parc and her art deco appearance), this great Southern city opens wide its doors to each passing gourmet.

| ■ | HOTELS |

■ Le Parc
26, rue de la Sinne.
Tel. 03 89 66 12 22. Fax 03 89 66 42 44.
contact@hotelduparc-mulhouse.com
www.hotelduparc-mulhouse.com
79 rooms: 95–170€. 7 suites: 250–450€.

This 1930's grand hotel, with its lovely facade, is just across from theater. With its characterful entrance hall, period furniture, well-appointed rooms and white-marbled bathrooms, it ranks high. Charlie's bar is cozy and the Steinbach restaurant fancy. (See Restaurants.)

■ La Bourse

14, rue de la Bourse.
Tel. 03 89 56 18 44. Fax 03 89 56 60 51.
www.bestwestern.com/fr/hoteldelabourse
Closed 24 Dec.–31 Dec. (exc. groups).
46 rooms: 39–115€. 2 suites: 120–212€.
Half board: 54–150€.

After a stroll along the nearby Rhin-Rhône canal, we like to end up here, pampered by a thoughtful team in the oh-so comfortable rooms (some are themed) or in the little bar. Delicious breakfast served in an interior garden.

■ Bristol

18, av de Colmar.
Tel. 03 89 42 12 31. Fax 03 89 42 50 57.
lebristol@clubinternet.fr
www.hotelbristol.com
73 rooms: 55–120€. 10 suites: 75–250€.

Comfortable and practical: this is how to define this hotel strategically situated near the historic center and the town's various points of interest. The rooms offer you the possibility of languishing in a jaccuzi bathtub, while the art deco lounge is a relaxing spot.

■ Mercure-Centre

4, pl du Général-de-Gaulle.
Tel. 03 89 36 29 39. Fax 03 89 36 29 49.
H1264@accor.com / www.mercure.com
96 rooms: 105–125€.

To judge this hotel only by its 1970's-style facade would be a mistake because the rooms are well-conceived, the service and welcome are agreeable and the proximity to the railway station and the modern town, a plus. The Torpedo bar is pleasant.

■ Kyriad Mulhouse Centre

15, rue Lambert.
Tel. 03 89 66 44 77. Fax 03 89 46 30 66.
kyriad@hotel-mulhouse.com
www.hotel-mulhouse.com
60 rooms: 53–90€.

The Place de la Réunion is right next door to this city center hotel. The business rooms are roomy and functional. Fitness center with sauna and hammam.

In Froeningen (68720). 7 km sw via D8.

■ Auberge de Froeningen

2, rte d'Illfurth.
Tel. 03 89 25 48 48. Fax 03 89 25 57 33.
www.alsanet.com/froeningen
Closed Sun. dinner, Mon., Tue., 3 weeks Jan., mid-Aug.–1 Sept.
7 rooms: 55–65€.
Prix fixe: 13€ (lunch), 58€.

This typically Alsatian inn has a few ad hoc rooms, some with a balcony and a view of the village, the garden or the Ill. In the restaurant, Christophe does the region proud with goose foie gras in terrine, poached white halibut served on a bed of chanterelles vinaigrette, the signature Klapperstein beef tongue and the fresh figs poached in Pinot Noir, served with a verbena sorbet.

In Sausheim (68390). 6 km ne via N422A.

■ Mercure-Sausheim

N 422.
Tel. 03 89 61 87 87. Fax 03 89 61 88 40.
h0556@accor.com / www.mercure.com
98 rooms: 107–135€. 2 suites: 305€.

Situated next to the Peugeot factories, this hotel offers all the usual benefits of the chain. Everything is unsurprisingly classical except for the Alsatian décor and the eiderdowns on the beds. The swimming pool and tennis court are very welcome. The restaurant serves a local, down-to-earth cuisine.

● | RESTAURANTS

● Le Steinbach   `V.COM`

At Le Parc, 26, rue de la Sinne.
Tel. 03 89 66 12 22. Fax 03 89 66 42 44.
www.hotelduparc-mulhouse.com
Closed Sat. lunch, Sun., mid-July–end Aug.
Prix fixe: 18€ (weekday lunch), 23€.
A la carte: 60€.

Cindy Lachaux is a newcomer to the stoves of this pretty art deco hotel where she composes a classical yet tuneful score with a slice of duck foie gras, steamed cod, a little nest of veal sweetbreads and Marc de Gewurztraminer sorbet. The menus are a steal and the service irreproachable.

● Il Cortile   `◎COM`

11, rue des Franciscains.
Tel. 03 89 66 39 79. Fax 03 89 36 07 97.
www.ilcortile-mulhouse.fr
Closed Sun., Mon., 2 weeks Jan., 20 Aug.–beg. Sept.
Prix fixe: 23€, 35€, 52€. A la carte: 60–65€.

Stefano D'Onghia knows how to play host at his table and how to plunge us into the heart of gastronomic Italy. Tried and true dishes are craftily interpreted, like the monkfish carpaccio, a cool tartare with balsamic or a rouget mille-feuille with eggplant caponata accompanied by sweet potato and banana ravioli. Then there's the veal saltimbocca, an herb- and rosemary-seasoned pasta and the raspberry tiramisu, fresh and creamy. The décor of the contemporary dining room has been revamped with charm and restraint.

● Le Poincaré Deux & le Bistro   `COM`

6, porte de Bâle.
Tel. 03 89 46 00 24 / 03 89 06 16 65.
Fax 03 89 56 33 15.
Closed Sat., Sun.
Prix fixe: 19€, 35€, 10€ (child).
A la carte: 42–60€.

The second of its kind, Laurence and Renaud Chabrier's new Poincaré is a quality table where traditional cooking takes pride of place. Next door, the bistro is aptly named, offering well-cooked classics: the signature Jean Ducloux poultry liver terrine, scallops with "a thousand" caravan spices, beef with Bordelaise wine sauce served with bone marrow and the timeless Grand Marnier soufflé. It's simple, good and it works. The 1950's red and beige décor is wearing well.

● Restaurant de la Tour de l'Europe   `COM`

3, bd de l'Europe.
Tel. 03 89 45 12 14. Fax 03 89 56 18 28.
restaurant@tour-europe.com
Closed Mon.
Prix fixe: 25€, 28€, 34€. A la carte: 42€.

One comes to the top of the Tour de l'Europe primarily for the unbeatable view over the town. The menus—especially the *terroir* menu—are worth the detour. The sliced escargots flambéed in Cognac, salmon escalope roasted with slices of foie gras, tender beef tenderloin and a soft frozen nougat do not lack skill.

● La Table de Michèle   `COM`

16, rue de Metz.
Tel. 03 89 45 37 82.
michele.brouet@wanadoo.fr
Closed Sat. lunch, Sun., Mon.,
end Dec.–beg. Jan., 2 weeks Aug.
Prix fixe: 17€, 10€ (child).
A la carte: 55€.

Michèle Brouet, whom we encountered at the l'Auberge du Canon at Zillisheim, has turned this corner house into a modern and gourmand chalet. All of Mulhouse rendezvous here to taste the market-based cooking of this self-taught chef who is assisted by an enthusiastic, all-female team. Duck foie gras, grilled Mediterranean sea bass, oven-roasted lamb shank and figs poached in Port with a pain d'épice ice cream deliver what they promised as do wines selected by Michèle's daughter.

● La Tour de Jade   `COM`

3, rue de Metz.
Tel. 03 89 66 10 18. Fax 03 89 66 00 79.
tourdejade@free.fr / www.tourdejade.com
Closed Mon.

Prix fixe: 9,60€ (lunch), 17,40€ (lunch), 20€ (lunch). A la carte: 22–35€.

Sam Nang welcomes you with a smile to this exquisite Asiatic table. Chef Bora Dham scientifically concocts imperial pâté, spring roll, monkfish with spicy sauce, pork ribs and the Jade Tower cup, dedicated to the imperial Hué tower. Alsatian red, white or *rosé* wines or tea are available.

● Le Petit Zinc 🏠SIM

15, rue des Bons-Enfants.
Tel. 03 89 46 36 78.
Closed Sun., 3 weeks Aug.,
Christmas–New Year's.
Prix fixe: 8,50€ (lunch). A la carte: 35€.

The neo-1900 setting is a bit dated but the Weills still welcome the hoards of night-owls with a smile. We love Alain and Myriam's welcome. We also appreciate Claude Gresser's traditional cooking. The creamy split pea soup, trout with Riesling sauce, slow-cooked pork cheek and the frozen kouglof are washed down with some keen little wines. Agreeable service and reasonable prices.

● Au Fourneau des Halles SIM

6, rue des Halles.
Tel.-Fax 03 89 66 57 07.
Closed Sat. lunch, Sun. lunch, Mon. dinner,
Christmas, 2 weeks beg. Aug.
Prix fixe: 7,50€ (weekday lunch), 18€,
6,90€ (child). A la carte: 32€.

A lot of people file through this center city brasserie between 11:30 pm and 1:30 am. People meet up over the vineyard-keeper's salad, pike-perch simmered in sparkling wine, sirloin steak with pepper and the apple tart. A dynamic atmosphere and a generous cuisine.

● Aux Caves du Vieux Couvent SIM

23, rue du Couvent.
Tel. 03 89 46 28 79. Fax 03 89 66 47 87.
philippe-thuet@wanadoo.fr
www.cavesduvieuxcouvent.com
Closed Sun. dinner, Mon., Wed. dinner,
1 week Christmas–New Year's.

Prix fixe: 11€, 16€ (wine inc.), 26€ (wine inc.), 19€, 6€ (child). A la carte: 35€.

Philippe Thuet pays homage to the city and its traditions in his cellars. The walls are decorated with frescoes detailing the history of Mulhouse. Typical dishes include country-style head cheese in aspic terrine, fish choucroute, veal kidneys with Pinot Noir sauce and Beerawecka-flavored ice cream, which are simple and delicious.

● La Bruschetta SIM

1, rue de Mittelbach.
Tel. 03 89 45 22 62. Fax 03 89 56 49 57.
Closed Sun., Mon.
Prix fixe: 12,50€ (lunch), 14€ (lunch).
A la carte: 38–51€.

Lino Rodi runs this modern trattoria with verve, offering Italian cooking based on market availability. One is regaled with the octopus carpaccio, swordfish with honey and balsamic sauce, saltimbocca with risotto and tiramisu. The minimalist décor with its ivory and sky-blue tablecloths is very restful. Wines can be had by the glass and the bill is not hefty.

● Winstub Henriette

9, rue Henriette.
Tel. 03 89 46 27 83.
Closed Sun., Mon., Bank holidays, Christmas.
Prix fixe: 7,62€ (weekday lunch).
A la carte: 34€.

Marie-Christine Musslin is everywhere, from the dining room to the kitchen, from the cellar to the terrace. Her center city *winstub* attracts a cheerful clientèle with good appetites. Munster cheese in puff pastry with crunchy vegetables, salmon filet on a bed of sauerkraut, local potato and meat casserole served with green salad and the apple streudel breathe sincerity.

● Zum Mehlala SIM

7, rue d'Illzach.
Tel. 03 89 59 41 32.
Closed Sun., Mon.
Prix fixe: 9€ (child). A la carte: 25–30€.

One loses track of time in this inn. Marie-Thérèse Reithinger knows how to please her clients who are mad for her tartes flambées (local flat pies, often with cream and bacon), fleischschnaka (meat-filled hand-rolled pasta), bibelekäs (fresh fromage blanc and herbs), not to mention sauerkraut, chicken liver salad and the broiled steak, all good ideas. The rhubarb soup is light after all those rich dishes. Reasonable prices.

● **Zum'Sauwadala**   SIM
13, rue de l'Arsenal.
Tel. 03 89 45 18 19. Fax 03 89 46 16 09.
www.restaurant-sauwadala.com
Closed Sun., Mon. lunch.
Prix fixe: 9,40€ (lunch), 16€ (lunch), 25€.
A la carte: 35€.

An unpronounceable name but filled with humor. Jacques Serpin's place is warm and does honor to regional cooking. The tender onion tart, vineyard-keeper's salad, a three-fish choucroute, baeckeofe (a local meat and potato casserole), Fleur de Bière sorbet and the frozen kouglof are typical and well made. The atmosphere is convivial and the bill just right.

In Dornach (68200). 3 km nw
● **Au Canon d'Or**   SIM
40, rue de Belfort.
Tel. 03 89 43 50 63. Fax 03 89 42 61 76.
Closed Sat. lunch, Sun. dinner, Mon. dinner,
1 week Christmas–New Year's, 3 weeks July.
Prix fixe: 11€ (weekday lunch),
21,50€ (weekdays). A la carte: 55€.

Gilles Reeb leaves nothing to chance, supplying himself from producers he knows and preparing the classic recipes which have gained him his reputation. Along with his wife Marie-Laure, he breathes life into this old 1686 coaching inn with its pleasant boLudeis interior. Feast on the foie gras trilogy (with pain d'épice, with Sichuan pepper, pan-seared), the stuffed poached sole with white sauce, mushrooms, truffles and lobster, the pigeon with chanterelle and trumpet mushrooms and the vanilla crème brûlée. A smiling, sincere welcome.

In Illzach-Modenheim (68110). 5 km ne via D422.
● **La Closerie**
6, rue Henry-de-Crousaz.
Tel. 03 89 61 88 00. Fax 03 89 61 95 49.
restaurant.closerie@wanadoo.fr
www.la-closerie.fr
Closed Sat. lunch, Sun., Mon. dinner, Christmas–New Year's, mid-July–beg. Aug.
Prix fixe: 35€, 40€, 50€, 12€ (child).
A la carte: 57€.

A bourgeois interior but full of fantasy, light and warmth. Hubert Beyrath offers some gourmet moments over serious dishes concocted by Bertrand Sicard. The goose foie gras terrine with slow-cooked pear, fresh pasta gratin with broad beans served with rolled lobster claw, beef filet with bone marrow and red wine sauce served with a potato cake and the delicious lemon mille-feuille show off a mastery of cooking times and skills. The wine list is hefty, the menus well-planned and the service diligent.

In Riedisheim (68400). 2 km.
● **Le Relais de la Poste**   ◎ V.COM
7, rue du Général-de-Gaulle.
Tel. 03 89 44 07 71. Fax 03 89 64 32 79.
contact@restaurant-kieny.co
www.restaurant-kieny.com
Closed Sun. dinner, Mon., Tue. lunch, Feb.
vac., end July–mid-Aug.
Prix fixe: 27€, 37€, 57€, 80€.

The Kienys have been in this house since the middle of the 19th century. Jean-Marc, the latest of that name, offers a cuisine that is not afraid to be innovative. A vegetable tarte with pepper raspberry sorbet, the "local fair"-style waffle with potatoes and marinated minced salmon, the grilled John Dory served with an escargot, parsley and garlic ragout, catfish filet meunière served with butter, stir fried vegetables with fresh ginger, the slice of goose foie gras served hot, as well as the veal medallions in paupiette with peppercorn-seasoned jus, are artfully honed dishes. The chic, paneled tavern, decorated in coaching inn style, is warmly welcoming. The desserts, a "sweet version of Alsatian traditions" or a "revamped Black Forest cake", are tasty and thoughtful. The cellar tempts and Mariella Kieny is a fine hostess.

In Riedisheim.

● **Auberge de la Tonnelle** COM
61, rue du Maréchal-Joffre.
Tel. 03 89 54 25 77. Fax 03 89 64 29 85.
Closed Sun. dinner, Wed.
Prix fixe: 25€ (lunch), 38€, 45€, 78€.
A la carte: 65–70€.

Roland Burger has filled this famous establishment in a suburb of Riedsheim with warmth. You can feel the efforts being made so that customers will leave happy and contented. Business men have their lunch habits and there are lots of faithful clients at the weekend. Each and every one appreciates the variations on theme of foie gras, the catch of the day, a rack of Limousin lamb and a Tasmanian chocolate dessert. A convivial atmosphere and prompt and serious service. The menu prices are acceptable.

In Rixheim (68170). 6 km se via N66.

● **Le Manoir Runser** ◎ V.COM
65, av du Général-de-Gaulle.
Tel. 03 89 31 88 88. Fax 03 89 31 88 89.
info@runser.fr / www.runser.fr
Closed Sun., Mon.
Prix fixe: 20€, 40€, 50€, 70€.
A la carte: 55–68€.

This large, grand manor house set in the middle of parkland not far from Mulhouse is light and airy—a white facade on the outside and yellow tones on the inside—with a refined elegance that perfectly suits Eric Runser's cooking. This is a cuisine which, along with a great deal of precision and sincerity, depends on quality produce to express the best of itself. We praise the subtlety and richness of the flavors developed by the "Sentier des Saveurs" menu or à la carte, the salmon and lobster tartare, curry-seasoned scallops, the squab baked in a crust and the apricot streudel. This is meticulous work, good to look at as well as to eat, improved by a wine list which gives pride of place to Alsatian wines but also has other offerings fom France and elsewhere. Service is very attentive.

In Rixheim.

● **Le Petit Prince** SIM
100, rue de l'Aérodrome.
Tel. 03 89 64 24 85. Fax 03 89 64 05 21.
Closed Sun., Mon., 1 week Christmas–New Year's, end Aug.–beg. Sept.
Prix fixe: 32€, 42€, 52€.

You could stop by Laurent and Stéphanie Haller's every month and not find the same dish twice. Laurent regularly offers a new theme on which he imposes seasonal products. These can be the tartares, fresh hay, apple or chocolate, but there's always a surprise in the flavors. His work on the preparations, aromas, fruits, or vegetables, with recipes from here and elsewhere, is constant and works its charm. The sole served on a stone from the Rhine river, accompanied by a slice of seaweed-seasoned rice cake with oyster, hot wine and vinegar sauce, pan-roasted veal wrapped in a bamboo leaf with smoked tea, served with a shiitake noodle gratin and the fried ball of crème brûlée with wild blueberries refreshed with a yogurt sorbet reveal a huge overflow of ideas. Prices are measured and the welcome friendly.

In Zimmersheim (68440). 5 km s toward Bâle via rte du parc zoologique.

● **Jules** V.COM
65, rue de Mulhouse.
Tel. 03 89 64 37 80. Fax 03 89 64 03 86.
info@restojules.fr / www.restojules.fr
Closed Sat., Sun., 2 weeks Feb.,
2 weeks Aug.
Prix fixe: 19€ (lunch).

The setting is warmly friendly and the dishes are written up in chalk on a blackboard. Juliette, aka "Jules" and Philippe Breitenstein run this village inn with energy and talent. They value fresh produce and follow the seasons. Bistro dishes (variety meat plate, wonderful tripe simmered in Riesling, chitterling sausage) find great favor.

MUNCHHAUSEN see LAUTERBOURG

MUNSTER

68140 Haut-Rhin. Paris 443 – Colmar 19 – Mulhouse 57 – Strasbourg 89 – Saint-Dié 53.
tourisme-munster@wanadoo.fr.
This great Protestant town has risen from the ashes of World War II without sacrificing its austere style. Here is the gateway to nearby trails, the valley, pastureland and forests.

 HOTELS-RESTAURANTS

■ Hôtel Verte Vallée

10, rue Alfred-Hartmann.
Tel. 03 89 77 15 15. Fax 03 89 77 17 40.
verte.vallee@wanadoo.fr
www.vertevallee.com
Closed beg. Jan.–beg. Feb.
100 rooms: 77–115€. 7 suites: 160€.
Prix fixe: 22€, 29€, 36€, 49€.

Set in tranquil parkland on the banks of the Fecht, this hotel near the city center has many assets: huge, light rooms, a fitness center, swimming pool, an aqua-gym course, hammam, Jacuzzi, conference rooms and WiFi. And if you want to get away from it all, two mountain chalets for six people each. The cooking highlights regional products and isn't half bad. On the menu, the duck foie gras with Port, smoked pike-perch served on a bed of choucroute, venison medallions served with a mushroom and foie gras cake and the lightly cooked cherry tartelette served with house ice creams are most pleasurable. Yvon Gauthier, who used to be a sommelier on the Côte d'Azur, presides over 400 different wines.

● L'Alsacienne   SIM

1, rue du Dôme.
Tel. 03 89 77 43 49. Fax 03 89 77 58 52.
Closed Tue. dinner, Wed., 10 days Sept.,
10 days Mar., 10 days June.
Prix fixe: 8,50€ (weekday lunch), 13,50€,
27,50€. A la carte: 30€.

A kindly house where—late into the night—you can enjoy typical Alsatian dishes lovingly cooked by Etienne Claude-Pierre. Inexpensive Munster quiche with salad, pike-perch filet, boneless pork trotter stuffed in the house style and the chocolate cake cut quite a dash.

● La Schlitte   SIM

7, rue de la République.
Tel. 03 89 77 50 35.
bschlitte@hotmail.com
Closed Mon., Tue. dinner, 1 week beg. Jan.,
2 weeks June July.
Prix fixe: 12,90€ (weekday lunch), 16€,
22,50€, 7,50€ (child). A la carte: 30€.

Delmina welcomes you with a smile while Bruno Savary cooks to please his guests. He delights them with Munster tourte, basil-seasoned salmon and braised ham shank with potato salad, a house specialty.

In Wihr-au-Val (68230). 6 km via D417 E.

● La Nouvelle Auberge   COM

9, rte Nationale.
Tel. 03 89 71 07 70. Fax 03 89 71 08 97.
www.nauberge.com
Closed Sun. dinner, Mon., Tue., Nov. 1 vac.,
Christmas, Feb. vac., 1 week beg. July.
Prix fixe: 25€, 29,50€.

Simple fare has its merits. The proof: this old road stop run by Bernard Leray. In the rustic dining room, this former disciple of Bernard Loiseau puts his heart into a pigeon pâté in pastry, pike-perch with red wine sauce, braised kidneys with shallots and a vanilla cream dessert bursting with sincerity. These are well-cooked dishes, genuine and fresh.

MURAT

15300 Cantal. Paris 525 – Aurillac 52 – Brioude 59 – Saint-Flour 24.
ot.murat@auvergne.net.
The site of this town perched 930 meters up in the Cantal mountains and the volcanoes of the Auvergne, is definitely worth a detour.

 RESTAURANTS

● Jarousset   V.COM

Rte de Clermont-Ferrand.
Tel. 04 71 20 10 69. Fax 04 71 20 15 26.

www.restaurant-le-jarousset.com
Closed Mon., Tue., Dec., Jan.
Prix fixe: 14€, 22€, 32€, 45€.
A la carte: 55€.

A simple reading of the menu designed by Jérôme Cazanave says a lot about the skilled ways of this disciple of Bocuse, Bras and Westermann. Seasonal products—which are treated to bring out the most of their flavors—reign supreme. The local farçou and escargots in their shells with herb butter, rouget and seasonal squash in all of its forms, pork trotter in egg custard that is chilled and cut in cubes and served with foie gras and green vegetables and the season's berries presented in a baba pay delicious homage to the surrounding nature. Isabelle's welcome is pleasant as is the service.

MURBACH

68530 Haut-Rhin. Paris 470 – Strasbourg 103 – Colmar 28 – Mulhouse 26 – Guebwiller 5.
Secret paths through the Vosges forest: byways to stroll down, a Romanesque abbey in pink stone and a gourmet address.

 HOTELS-RESTAURANTS

■ **Saint-Barnabé**
53, rue de Murbach.
Tel. 03 89 62 14 14. Fax 03 89 62 14 15.
hostellerie.st.barnabe@wanadoo.fr
www.hostellerie-st-barnabe.com
Rest. closed Sun. dinner.
24 rooms: 56–150€. 3 suites: 183€.
Prix fixe: 13€ (lunch), 21€, 38€, 65€, 12€ (child). A la carte: 41–54€.

Right in the heart of the forest of the Vosges, Eric and Clémence Orban's hotel seduces one with its charm, the warmth of its welcome and the refined talent of the chef who has worked at the château d'Isenbourg at Rouffach. A thin vegetable tartelette with Scottish salmon, seafood platter with foamy butter mousseline and spiny artichokes, farm-raised quail with pan-tossed chanterelles and a gen-

tly spiced dessert with fennel seed-infused creamy caramel and raspberry sauce are scaling the heights. Not so the prices which remain reasonable.

■ **Domaine Langmatt**
Locale known as Domaine Langmatt.
Tel. 03 89 76 21 12. Fax 03 89 74 88 77.
info@domainelangmatt.com
www.domainelangmatt.com
Closed 1 week Apr.
Rest. closed Mon. lunch.
21 rooms: 96–190€.
Prix fixe: 28€, 63€. A la carte: 46–62€.

The *ballon* of the Vosges is the background of this hotel where you come to breathe the air. Aside from the comfortable rooms, the swimming pool, sauna and fitness center will ensure you get into shape here. The table honors the region with mountain-cured ham, trout with almonds, sirloin steak with morels and the incontrovertible dessert made with Langmatt digestive liqueur.

MUR-DE-BARREZ

12600 Aveyron. Paris 575 – Aurillac 39 – Rodez 76 – Saint-Flour 57.
otmurdebarrez@wanadoo.fr.
The North of the Aveyron nudges the Cantal at this spot in this town full of pretty gray stone houses.

 HOTELS-RESTAURANTS

■ **Auberge du Barrez**
Av du Carladez.
Tel. 05 65 66 00 76. Fax 05 65 66 07 98.
auberge.du.barrez@wanadoo.fr
www.aubergedubarrez.com
Closed Jan.
18 rooms: 38–76€.
Prix fixe: 13,50€, 22€, 26€, 37€, 8€ (child).

Christian Gaudel has a warmhearted welcome. The setting of his inn is rather modern but the rooms are most agreeable. At meal times, in the blue-toned dining room, an updated regional cuisine slips down nicely. Upside-down foie gras tart, the crique (an Ardèche-style grated potato cake) served with crayfish, pike-perch with ceps and an herb-seasoned rabbit make one wish for a permanent place at the table. A spot one likes to return to, especially as prices are moderate.

MUR-DE-BRETAGNE

22530 Côtes-d'Armor. Paris 458 – Saint-Brieuc 43 – Guingamp 46 – Pontivy 17.
This is Brittany of the interior on the carefree road that leads from Rennes to Quimper. Check out the lac de Guéledan.

 HOTELS-RESTAURANTS

● **Auberge Grand'Maison**
1, rue Léon-le-Cerf.
Tel. 02 96 28 51 10. Fax 02 96 28 52 30.
auberge-grand-maison@wanadoo.fr
www.auberge-grand-maison.com
Closed 2 weeks Feb., 2 weeks Oct.
Rest. closed Sun. dinner, Mon., Tue. lunch.
10 rooms: 50–98€.
Prix fixe: 26€, 36€, 42€, 57€, 71€, 90€.

The Le Furs' inn by the side of the National is a choice stopping point. Mireille's smiling welcome and the Belle Epoque-style rooms are highly seductive. The same can be said for the cuisine. Over the course of various, well-balanced menus, Christophe treats regional products with skill and inventiveness, as witnessed by the asparagus and Aquitaine caviar milkshake, roasted John Dory with poppy, veal sweetbread cake served with a morel and meat jus ragout and a fine lime cream dessert with banana sorbet.

MUTZIG

67190 Bas-Rhin. Paris 478 – Obernai 12 – Strasbourg 28 – Saverne 31.
A fortified gateway, the proximity of the Vosges and wine but no longer, alas, any beer. Only the name lives on.

 HOTELS-RESTAURANTS

■ **Hostellerie de la Poste**
4, pl de la Fontaine.
Tel. 03 88 38 38 38. Fax 03 88 49 82 05.
hostellerie.pfeiffer@wanadoo.fr
www.hostellerie-la-poste.com
Closed mid-Nov.–end Nov. Rest. closed Mon.
17 rooms: 44–55€.
Prix fixe: 8€ (weekday lunch), 18€, 30€, 9,50€ (child). A la carte: 36€.

This half-timbered Alsatian house with its tasteful rooms breathes authenticity. The local cuisine is one of quality: witness the duck terrine with crunchy spring vegetables, sea trout with crayfish, sirloin steak with Roquefort and the chocolate charlotte with coffee sauce. The local wines make good companions to the food.

■ **L'Ours de Mutzig**
Pl de la Fontaine.
Tel. 03 88 47 85 55. Fax 03 88 47 85 56.
hotel@loursdemutzig.com
www.loursdemutzig.com
47 rooms: 49–84€.
Prix fixe: 15€ (weekday lunch), 18€, 25€, 9€ (child). A la carte: 33€.

The rooms are charming and squeaky clean; the house is decorated around a bear theme. The cooking is faithful to the *terroir*. Escargots prepared in the style of Alsace (stuffed with spiced butter and herbs and cooked in local wine), pike-perch simmered in Riesling and served over noodles, beer-braised pork cheeks with fromage blanc quenelles and the apple streudel with cinnamon ice cream are infinitely edible.

● **Au Nid de Cigogne** SIM
25, rue du 18-Novembre.
Tel.-Fax 03 88 38 11 97.
Closed Sat. lunch, Wed.
A la carte: 36€.

Cédric Zimmermann is alone at the helm of this old tavern that was once the canteen of the workers from the local brewery. He is quality conscious and, seated next to the pretty green stove, you'll enjoy pork cheeks in aspic, grilled scallops and Atlantic sea bass with chanterelles, goose breast served on sauerkraut with pan-seared foie gras and the profiteroles served hot with vanilla ice cream. Saturday and Sunday night, tartes flambées take pride of place.

12270 Aveyron. Paris 627 – Rodez 76 – Albi 50 – Cahors 86 – Gaillac 49.
otsi.najac@wanadoo.fr.
The delights of a village perched in the heart of rural Aveyron, with its château and inns.

 HOTELS-RESTAURANTS

■ L'Oustal del Barry

Pl du Faubourg.
Tel. 05 65 29 74 32. Fax 05 65 29 75 32.
oustal@caramail.com
www.oustaldelbarry.com
Closed 1 Nov.–31 Mar.
Rest. closed Mon., Tue. lunch (off season).
18 rooms: 52–74€.
Prix fixe: 18,50€ (lunch), 23€, 49€.

L'Oustal is a fine hotel in the heart of the medieval walled town of Najac. It offers a sumptuous view and very pleasant, comfortable rooms. Rémy Simon, who trained with the Pourcel brothers, is genuinely hospitable and serves up a cuisine in which traditional Aveyron cooking rubs shoulders with less conventional, more creatively open dishes. Based on fine regional produce, his range of set menus changes regularly. They feature duck foie gras terrine, oven-crisped perch, boneless pigeon seasoned with four spices, pineapple brochette and other highly accomplished, spirited preparations with their fair share of charm.

54000 Meurthe-et-Moselle. Paris 307 – Chaumont 118 – Dijon 217 – Metz 57 – Reims 194 – Strasbourg 151.
tourisme@ot.nancy.fr.
Ducal Nancy is a good natured, gourmet city. It is pleasant indeed to stroll through its covered market, where the stalls of the poultry sellers, cheesemongers, greengrocers and pork butchers suggest a Lyon in miniature. The city aspires to grandeur around the place Stanislas with its golden railings, bourgeois solidity among its art nouveau houses, and virtuous conviviality in the bistros on the edge of Saint-Epvre. The rue des

Maréchaux is nicknamed "rue gourmande", since it is entirely devoted to food. Its young chefs are busily rejuvenating the Lorraine art of fine fare, with a thought for the traditional bergamot, quenelle, smoked meats and frogs' legs. If gourmet King Stanislas I were to return to his city today, he would be delighted.

■	HOTELS

■ Grand Hôtel de la Reine

2, pl Stanislas.
Tel. 03 83 35 03 01. Fax 03 83 32 86 04.
nancy@concorde-hotels.com
www.hoteldelareine.com
42 rooms: 145–225€. 4 suites: 290–360€.

This luxury 18th-century establishment is the hotel of choice for stars visiting the ducal city. It boasts refined rooms equipped with period furniture, elegant lounges, a magnificent staircase and a highly fashionable bar. Ask for a room overlooking the square. (See Restaurants: Le Stanislas.)

■ Park Inn Nancy

11, rue Raymond-Poincaré.
Tel. 03 83 39 75 75. Fax 03 83 32 78 17.
emmanuel.duhoux@rezidorparkinn.com
Rest. closed Sat. (exc. by reserv.), Sun. (exc. by reserv.), Christmas–New Year's vac., 2 weeks Aug.
192 rooms: 89–150€.
Prix fixe: 15,80€ (weekday lunch), 20,80€ (weekday lunch), 22€, 10€ (child).

Opposite the station, this former Mercure hotel has a lot going for it, including smart rooms in pastel tones and an honorable cuisine concocted by Stéphane Fife (hot foie gras over cabbage, steamed cod with vegetables and dill, two types of crème brûlée: caramel and bergamot).

■ Crystal

5, rue de Chanzy.
Tel. 03 83 17 54 00. Fax 03 83 17 54 30.
hotelcrystal.nancy@wanadoo.fr
Closed 22 Dec.–2 Jan.
58 rooms: 90–156€.

Near the station, this practical stopover for city center pedestrians is run by Gérard Gatinois. Its spacious, spruce, neat rooms have been renovated in various shades and contemporary style. Enjoyable breakfast.

■ Mercure Centre Stanislas

5, rue des Carmes.
Tel. 03 83 30 92 60. Fax 03 83 30 92 92.
h1068@accor.com / www.mercure.com
80 rooms: 84–169€.

The attractions of this good chain hotel run by Bernadette Daout are its ideal location between the place Stanislas, shopping streets and station and its small but neat modern rooms in burgundy shades.

■ Hôtel Américain

Pl André-Maginot.
Tel. 03 83 32 28 53. Fax 03 83 32 79 97.
www.americain-hotel.com
20 rooms: 40–100€.

A step away from the station and the stores in the rue Saint-Georges, this modest hotel boasts smart rooms in various colors along with two meeting rooms. Breakfast is served in an attractive vaulted cellar.

■ Hôtel de Guise

18, rue de Guise.
Tel. 03 83 32 24 68. Fax 03 83 35 75 63.
contact@hoteldeguise.com
www.hoteldeguise.com
42 rooms: 48–86€. 6 suites: 73–109€.

Near the Musée Lorrain (Lorraine Museum), this "aristo-rustic" establishment boasts rooms in red and gold tones with parquet floors, contemporary furniture, an 18th-century staircase and friendly prices.

■ Portes d'Or

21, rue Stanislas.
Tel. 03 83 35 42 34. Fax 03 83 32 51 41.
www.hotel-lesportesdor.com
20 rooms: 50–66€.

The proximity of the station, friendly welcome, small contemporary rooms and well-mannered prices all make for an enjoyable experience.

 RESTAURANTS

● Le Capucin Gourmand   ○ V.COM
31, rue Gambetta.
Tel. 03 83 35 26 98. Fax 03 83 35 99 29.
info@lecapucingourmand.fr
www.lecapu.com
Closed Sat. lunch, Sun. dinner, Mon.,
1 week Aug.
Prix fixe: 28€ (lunch), 32€, 75€,
19€ (child). A la carte: 80€.

Restyled by Hervé Fourrière, the Capucin is elegant indeed with its majestic chandelier commanding the beige dining room, Louis XIV-style chairs and tablecloths, woodwork, fine parquet flooring and ornate moldings, all revisited in contemporary fashion. His personal touch is also apparent in the dishes, prepared with a generous, capable hand. We confidently explore the delights of his refined menu: terrine of lobster in aspic, jumbo shrimp with salted butter in pastilla, foie gras nougat, braised turbot and summer vegetables and the pigeon breast wrapped in greens all display a charmingly revised classicism. The seasonal fresh fruit salad, crème vanilla and sorbet provide a graceful conclusion. The dining room staff are wonderfully attentive and Hubert Quaggiotto has time to spare to describe the treasures concealed in his cellar.

● Cap Marine   V.COM
60, rue Stanislas.
Tel. 03 83 37 05 03. Fax 03 83 37 01 32.
cap.marine@wanadoo.fr
www.restaurant-capmarine.com
Closed Sat. lunch, Sun., Wed. lunch, 1 week
Nov., 1 week Feb., 1 week May, 2 weeks Aug.
Prix fixe: 25€, 33€, 50€. A la carte: 65€.

Patrick Antoine stands guard just a step away from the place Stanislas. A self-taught chef, he prepares the day's catch with dexterity, cunningly shaping it to reflect modern ideas. The langoustines with mild peppers, Atlantic sea bass carpaccio with Parma ham, grilled turbot with thyme-marinated squid and John Dory fish presented with rolled pigs foot are lively, invigorating dishes with an eye to freshness. The marvelous raspberry beignets and mint granité provide a light conclusion to the meal.

● Le Grenier à Sel   ○ COM
28, rue Gustave-Simon.
Tel. 03 83 32 31 98. Fax 03 83 35 32 88.
grenierasel@chez.com
www.chez.com/grenierasel
Closed Sun., Mon., 1 week at end July, 2
weeks beg. Aug.
Prix fixe: 30€ (lunch), 37€ (dinner),
55€ (dinner). A la carte: 90€.

Just a step away from the place Carnot, the Fréchins' restaurant has a staunchly modern touch. In the neoclassical, yellow and green dining room revised in simple, contemporary style, Patrick—who notably trained in the Swiss luxury hotel sector—concocts inventive, technical dishes. On the menu, foie gras cubes enrobed in velvety chocolate, red mullet filet broiled on one side and steamed over mushroom broth with asparagus, poached young pigeon with Fougerolles cherries and a Krieck reduction and the strawberry olive compote served with olive ice cream are highly meticulous preparations. On the oenological side, Christophe Lemoine has built up an impressive cellar of more than 300 different wines.

● Le Stanislas   V.COM
At Grand Hôtel de la Reine, 2, pl Stanislas.
Tel. 03 83 35 03 01. Fax 03 83 32 86 04.
www.hoteldelareine.com
Closed Sat. lunch (exc. off season),
Sun. dinner (exc. off season),
Mon. (exc. off season).
Prix fixe: 25€ (lunch, wine inc.), 31€, 43€.
A la carte: 82€.

On the first floor of an 18th-century house at the head of the square, this elegant restaurant renovated in orange and beige tones and period style makes an excellent impression. In its tasteful setting, where the pomp of bygone days is very much in evidence, Olivier Hubert devises a succulent cuisine tinged with modernity, sun-kissed flavors, balance and wit and served to perfection. The langoustines and cauliflower, fresh green peas and caviar, turbot with green asparagus and grapefruit, young duck with rhubarb, turnips with tonka beans and the poached peach with vanilla, saffron and lime flowers are readily enjoyable. The cellar offers one pure-bred vintage after another.

● L'Excelsior Flo 🏠COM

50, rue H.-Poincaré.
Tel. 03 83 35 24 57. Fax 03 83 35 18 48.
www.brasserie-excelsior.com
Prix fixe: 22,50€ (weekday lunch), 29,50€,
14€ (child). A la carte: 45€.

The finest brasserie in France? This art nouveau monument with its high ceilings, stucco, pegs, Majorelle woodwork, Gruber glasswork and yellow velvet benches, of course. The service is spirited and the cuisine strives for excellence. The creamy asparagus tip risotto, foie gras with mirabelle chutney, the salmon spread, the quiche Lorraine, monkfish "osso bucco" and boneless rib steak with tomato béarnaise sauce are thoroughly gratifying.

● Grand Café Foy 🅝●🏠COM

1, pl Stanislas.
Tel. 03 83 32 15 97.
http://grandcafefoy.fr
Prix fixe: 20€, 25€.

This corner brasserie with its 18th-century décor has been fashionably and deliciously revamped by Valéry Claussin. The setting is chic, with its stucco, moldings, mirrors, charming terrace on the square and cozy second floor. The cuisine from the young Julien Clément, formerly with Pétrus in Paris and Veyrat in Annecy, is splendid. The regional allusions (quiche Lorraine with goat cheese, snails and cauliflower in *verrine*, terrine of carrots and pike-perch in aspic, small pork sausage wrapped in caul fat with mirabelle plums, pike-perch with meat jus and crispy bacon), fine meats (beef rib eye steak with fries and béarnaise sauce) and delightful desserts (mirabelle

plum or raspberry tarts, baba Stanislas, bergamot-infused crème brûlée) go well together. As we drink the Domaine Régina Gris de Toul or Frères Lelièvre Pinot Noir, we think to ourselves that the Foy is something of a Nancy Café Costes with added value for money.

● Le Cul-de-Poule 🔲COM

24, pl de l'Arsenal.
Tel.-Fax 03 83 32 11 01.
Closed Sun., Mon., 1 week Jan., 1 week May,
mid-Aug.–end Aug.
A la carte: 40€.

Alain Gobert's good-natured establishment never empties. In this friendly bistro, the Pavillon Anatole veteran delights his guests with his successful, wayward dishes, including rabbit in rosemary aspic, Alpine lake trout with garden herbs, breast of guinea hen stuffed with fennel and the cherry blanc-manger. To add to our pleasure, the check is uncontentious.

● Les Agaves 🔲COM

2, rue des Carmes.
Tel. 03 83 32 14 14. Fax 03 83 37 13 31.
les-agaves.durand-gilles@wanadoo.fr
Closed Sun., Mon. dinner, Wed. dinner,
1 week at end Feb., 2 weeks beg. Aug.
A la carte: 50€.

Gilles Durand plays the Mediterranean card majestically in his neo-Provençal restaurant decorated with black and white fifties photos. His lively dishes are very contemporary, though. Along with the delightful Italian wines recommended by Babette, we enjoy tomato mille-feuille with goat cheese and pancetta, *al dente* garlic risotto with grilled squid, red mullet filet and house ratatouille, veal with onions and peppers with Marsala crème and the whiskey tiramisu.

● Arôm 🔲COM

26, rue Héré.
Tel. 03 83 35 08 24.
arom8@wanadoo.fr
www.restaurant-arom.com
Closed Sat. lunch, Sun. dinner, Wed.,
2 weeks Oct.

Prix fixe: 16€ (weekday lunch), 22€, 28€, 35€, 10€ (child). A la carte: 40€.

Patrick Gros, a designer devoted to gastronomy, has turned this former art gallery into a fine modern eatery. The bamboo flooring, fluted chairs, wrought-iron chandelier and dessert counter under glass set the tone. Presented on a holder with a spiral binding, the set menu improvises lightly on the flavors of the South of France. Small beef ravioli with wild herbs, smoked salmon cannelloni with vegetable caviar, vegetable risotto with thinly sliced cod and the pear poached in a spicy jus are an encouragement to eat here on a regular basis.

● Bistro Héré   COM
24, rue Héré.
Tel. 03 83 30 49 69. Fax 03 83 32 78 93.
bistrohere@aol.combistrohere@aol.com
Closed Sun. dinner.
Prix fixe: 10€ (weekday lunch),
16€ (weekday lunch), 22€, 26€, 34€.
A la carte: 38€.

Paul and Martine Ariztégui have created a gourmet but relaxed establishment. The elongated dining room is stylish, with stucco, mirrors and pastel walls. Martine gives guests an unfailingly friendly welcome and the set menu options are unbeatable. Paul, who worked in Franche-Comté, then at the neighboring Café du Commerce, prepares simple, savory dishes. Zucchini and goat cheese carpaccio, grilled Munster cheese tartine, oven-crisped whiting, pike fish quenelle with basmati rice, beef cheek braised in wine and the iced mirabelle plum parfait are gratifying.

● Les Feuillants   COM
27, rue Gambetta.
Tel.-Fax 03 83 35 81 33.
Closed Sun. dinner, Mon., Tue. lunch,
Christmas–New Year's, Aug.
Prix fixe: 24€, 34€, 48€ (wine inc.), 44€.
A la carte: 48€.

Jean-Marc Guyot has turned his neo-classical establishment in ivory and burgundy tones into a temple of good taste.

Guests come to enjoy the reliable, generous dishes. Grilled jumbo shrimp with pesto, roasted pike-perch with chanterelles and smoked lentils, duck three ways (with Banyuls wine and with figs, with chestnut mousse and with bitter chocolate and pistachio) are full of energy.

● La Mignardise   COM
28, rue Stanislas.
Tel. 03 83 32 20 22. Fax 03 83 32 19 20.
www.lamignardise.com
Closed Sun. dinner, 1 week at end July.
Prix fixe: 16€ (weekday lunch by reserv.),
23€, 32€ (Sun. lunch by reserv.),
53€ (Sat., Sun.), 15,30€ (child).

The elegant, refined setting and Didier Metzelard's solid cuisine still weave their spell. Following the vagaries of market and season, he offers up a successful score: his pan-tossed scallops and frog legs with an onion béchamel sauce, smoked carp pastille and lobster stew with tea infusion, variations on the theme of duck with Madeira truffle sauce and the frozen licorice nougat with salted-butter caramel delight his patrons. Discreet, efficient service and a fine cellar.

● La Toque Blanche   COM
1, rue Monseigneur-Trouillet.
Tel. 03 83 30 17 20. Fax 03 83 32 60 24.
restaurant@latoqueblanche.fr
Closed Sun. dinner, Mon., 1 week Feb.,
1 week at Easter, 3 weeks end July–mid-Aug.
Prix fixe: 24€, 34€, 50€, 65€, 15€ (child).

Bertrand Heckmann, formerly at the Lucas Carton and Les Crayères, changes his menu to reflect the whims of the market. His sober, elegant, comfortable beige restaurant has two dining rooms providing a bright, intimate ambiance, one of them decorated with a Harlequin fresco. Lobster and veal sweetbreads ravioli with coral sauce, fileted breast of pigeon with spiced caramel and a carrot mousseline and the soft chocolate and pistachio cake served hot are evidence of his sound technique and skills. The 200 wines in the cellar have tremendous wit.

BISTRO OF THE YEAR

● **Chez Tanésy**   ◎SIM

23, Grande-Rue.
Tel. 03 83 35 51 94. Fax 03 83 36 67 23.
Closed Sun., Mon., 1 week Nov.,
1 week Feb., mid-Aug.–end Aug.
Prix fixe: 22€ (lunch), 30€, 40€.
A la carte: 50€.

He is to today's gourmet Nancy what Stanislas was to Lorraine in the century of the Enlightenment: a champion of heritage and a free-thinking conservative (although on a more modest scale). Patrick Tanésy has left his Gastrolâtre on the place Jacques Callot for a cozy bistro setting in the heart of the old town. Like an exclusive club, it has space for barely twenty loyal followers to enjoy its ritual dishes that showcase local tradition: a fine pork terrine, frog legs salad with small snails and foie gras vinaigrette, Italian-style piglet in aspic and a twelve-hour roasted beef with veal foot sauce and polenta sticks. We adore his tributes to France's Greater East in general, featured in an ode of a set menu that revisits layered foie gras and potato casserole and poultry in cream sauce with Vin Jaune and morel mushrooms. An unassuming, modest, greathearted native of Aix, son and grandson of artisan chefs, Tanésy adopted Nancy as his home city thirty years ago. He is indeed the most "Lorrain" of generous restaurateurs, a bearded gourmet who has served his city well. His frozen egg-based custard dessert is a marvel and baba poached with saffron is a model of the genre. His entire wine list is a treasure trove of good vintages. A man, a cuisine and a very special restaurant.

● **Les Pissenlits**   ■SIM

27, rue des Ponts.
Tel. 03 83 37 43 97. Fax 03 83 35 72 49.
pissenlits@wanadoo.fr / www.lespisssenlits.fr
Closed Sun., Mon., 2 weeks beg. Aug.
Prix fixe: 18,50€, 24,20€, 9,50€ (child).

Both at lunch and dinner, Jean-Luc Mengin's restaurant is packed. The appeal of his two rustic dining rooms lies in the welcome we receive from Danièle (who offers shrewd advice on the choice of wine), cheerful atmosphere, well-behaved prices and efficiently executed regional dishes. Dandelion and bacon salad, pike-perch simmered in red wine, tête de veau with a pickle and caper sauce and iced meringue dessert are accompanied by one of the 750 wines from the cellar. Les Pissenlits has a bistro adjunct, "Vins et Tartines".

● **Petit Repas Entre Amis**   ●SIM

17, rue des Quatre-Eglises.
Tel.-Fax 03 83 30 05 87.
www.petitrepasentreamis.com
Closed Sun., Mon. dinner, Tue. dinner,
1 week Feb.
Prix fixe: 13€ (weekday lunch),
15€ (weekday lunch), 18€ (weekday lunch).
A la carte: 35€.

This small restaurant near the market serves up entertaining sweet and savory dishes. In its purple surroundings, we enthusiastically savor the langoustines with grilled bacon and grated green apples, sole cooked in vermouth, duck breast in spicy caramel and pineapple and Sichuan pepper Tatin with salted butter, all at friendly prices.

● **Chez Marie-Pierre**   SIM

Pl Henri-Mengin.
Tel. 03 83 35 31 49. Fax 03 83 47 08 36.
sarl-schaller@wanadoo.fr
www.poissonnerieschaller.com
Closed dinner, Sun., Mon., 2 weeks beg. Feb.,
3 weeks Aug.
A la carte: 35€.

In the heart of the market, a gourmet vessel appears among the stands: this is the domain of Marie-Pierre Schaller, sea and river *raconteuse*, who provides only the freshest produce with a smile into the bargain. Leeks with skate, lean roasted pork rump roast with ginger-seasoned jus, sole meunière with "grandmother's" purée as well as Gewurztraminer Marc crème brûlée.

● Le Léz'art SIM
93, Grande-Rue.
Tel. 03 83 37 60 18. Fax 03 83 32 55 91.
patricemarchand@wanadoo.fr
Closed Sun. dinner, Mon.
Prix fixe: 16€ (lunch), 23€.
A la carte: 38€.

Patrice Marchand, the city's star cheese-monger, runs this "literary café" remotely. Its changing menu offers a strong fusion cuisine accompanied by wines of every provenance. In the new-look library setting, visitors enjoy scallop and chorizo mille-feuille with four cheese risotto, monkfish korma with basmati rice, chopped beef tenderloin seasoned with lemongrass and ginger, the mirabelle plum crumble or the pain d'épice.

● Le Muscovado SIM
41, rue des Maréchaux.
Tel. 03 83 30 59 03. Fax 03 83 37 21 21.
www.muscovado.net
service traiteur: www.annemarielaumond.com
Closed Sun., Mon., 1 week Jan.
Prix fixe: 14€, 20€, 26€. A la carte: 35€.

Anne-Marie Laumond, a cook of great character, has turned her tapas bar into one of the city's better ports of call. Its frequently updated menu offers pigs trotter carpaccio with cep vinaigrette, grilled squid with preserved lemons, lamb shank tagine with spiced apricots and a Carambar (caramel toffee candy) crème brûlée, which all slip down effortlessly.

● Les Nouveaux Abattoirs SIM
4, bd d'Austrasie.
Tel. 03 83 35 46 25. Fax 03 83 35 13 64.
Closed Sat. lunch, Sun., Christmas,
New Year's.
Prix fixe: 17€, 22€, 29€, 5,50€ (child).
A la carte: 32–40€.

In the old slaughterhouse district, this paneled bistro taken over by Jean-Marc Lerondeau still holds a very sixties charm. It specializes in meats. Carnivores of every kind meet there to savor the dishes deftly prepared by Jean-Philippe Corbé. Beef muzzle salad, tête de veau, half-pound beef tartare and a fresh fruit tart will whet the most jaded appetite.

● Les Petits Gobelins SIM
18, rue de la Primatiale.
Tel. 03 83 35 49 03. Fax 03 83 37 41 49.
Closed Sun., Mon., vac. Apr., 3 weeks Aug.
Prix fixe: 22€, 35€, 48€, 12€ (child).

This pocket restaurant on a pedestrian street provides a modern setting in an 18th-century house. It is the lair of Patrice Grosse, who polishes refined, market-based dishes with an eye to current trends. Oven-crisped langoustines with turmeric-seasoned carrots, foie gras carpaccio with Serrano ham and mild Spanish chili peppers, marinated monkfish seared on one side and finished under the broiler, chanterelles with braised veal sweetbreads with diced country smoked bacon and the mirabelle plum pastry cream filled beignets with Bourbon vanilla ice cream are full of good intentions.

● Le P'tit Cuny SIM
97-99, Grande-Rue.
Tel. 03 83 32 85 94. Fax 03 83 32 55 91.
marchand-patrice@wanadoo.fr
www.lepetitcuny.com
Closed Mon. lunch.
Prix fixe: 11,50€ (weekday lunch),
15€ (weekday lunch), 24€, 39€.
A la carte: 35–40€.

Opposite the Musée Lorrain, this rustic tavern with its exposed stone, checked tablecloths and tankards decorating the ceiling is watched over by local cheese kings the Marchands. New chef Alexandre Lartillot handles the classical repertoire very capably. Foie gras and mirabelle plum aspic with slow-cooked onions, Riesling-simmered pike-perch on a bed of sauerkraut, rotisserie piglet with potatoes sautéed in goose fat and bergamot crème brûlée are very much in the spirit of the region.

● Le V-Four SIM
10, rue Saint-Michel.
Tel.-Fax 03 83 32 49 48.
Closed Sun. dinner, Mon., 2 weeks beg. Sept.,

end Jan.–beg. Feb.
Prix fixe: 16€ (weekday lunch), 24€, 35€.
A la carte: 60€.

In a pedestrian street in the old city, Bruno Faonio's intimate dining room with its Starck chairs, refined linen and elegant tableware has a solid reputation in Nancy gastronomic circles. Bruno bases his dishes on changing seasonal produce. Guests savor the escargot fricassée with basil emulsion, the lobster, jumbo shrimp and scallops served in an aromatic olive oil broth, veal sweetbreads first poached then marinated in honey with fork-mashed potatoes and red wine reduction and the soft chocolate cake with mint-infused chocolate sauce.

In Dommartemont (54130). 8 km e via St-Max.

● **Ermitage de la Ferme**   🏠◎V.COM
Sainte-Geneviève
2, chemin du Pain de Sucre.
Tel. 03 83 29 99 81. Fax 03 83 20 87 23.
Closed Sun. dinner, Mon., Wed. dinner,
Nov. 1 vac., Christmas–New Year's vac., Feb.
Prix fixe: 34€, 40€, 55€, 75€,
16€ (child). A la carte: 90€.

Vincent Dallé, who long upheld his reputation as a wonder boy at the Mirabelle in the rue Héré in the heart of the city, has joined his family, who run a seminar center with suitable catering in an ex-farmhouse. Just for Vincent, they have equipped a small, stylish, red and black dining room with seven tables, providing around thirty places, no more. There, he offers a personalized service. The prices reflect this approach in what is very much an upscale restaurant. We can only praise the escargots in pastry with parsley and garlic butter, lake trout with asparagus and cured ham, wild Atlantic sea bass coated in egg, breaded and fried with fennel, veal rib eye steak and the fileted breast of young pigeon with ceps, all of which remind us that Vincent, a still youthful veteran of Rostang in Paris, Les Templiers in Bézards, Les Vannes in Liverdun and Adoménil, has plenty of experience and ideas. The coconut mille-feuille with ganache, like the raspberry sorbet in a white chocolate cappuccino, are choice conclusions.

In Dommartemont.

● **Le Bistro de la Ferme**   Ⓝ SIM
Sainte Geneviève
2, chemin du Pain au Sucre.
Tel. 03 83 29 13 49. Fax 03 83 20 87 23.
Closed Sun. dinner, Mon., Wed. dinner,
2 weeks Nov., 1 week Jan., 2 weeks Feb.
Prix fixe: 16€ (weekdays), 26€ (Sat., Sun.).
A la carte: 35€.

Vincent Dallé and his assistant Patricia Mékong serve good, inexpensive food in this cozy, paneled farmhouse tavern, with tin bar and low ceiling. Slow-roasted rabbit in aspic, European walleye and Toul snail stew, pork foot wrapped in caul fat, beer-roasted piglet and the rhubarb frozen nougat form a delightful regional repertoire.

In Flavigny-sur-Moselle (54630). 16 km via A330.

● **Le Prieuré**   ◎V.COM
3, rue du Prieuré. BP 3.
Tel. 03 83 26 70 45. Fax 03 83 26 75 51.
rjoelroy@aol.com
Closed Sun. dinner, Mon., Wed. dinner,
New Year's, 2 weeks Feb.
Prix fixe: 46€, 79€. A la carte: 100€.

Near the "inspired hill" of Sion, the Roys' country establishment lays on delicious spreads. Joël, holder of the Meilleur Ouvrier de France award and former disciple of Jacques Maximin at the Negresco, serves up shrewd dishes of rare aptness. In the old-style dining room, we enjoy the carpaccio with truffle vinaigrette, monkfish quiche and pigeon poached in red wine with foie gras ravioli. For dessert, both the mirabelle plum soufflé and thin apple tart conjure up scenes from our childhood. We wash down these dependable dishes with fine vintages, before retiring to one of the four rooms in the cloister.

In Jarville-la-Malgrange (54140). 2 km e.

● **Les Chanterelles** `SIM`

27, av de la Malgrange.
Tel.-Fax 03 83 51 43 17.
Closed Sun. dinner, Mon., Aug.
Prix fixe: 18€, 25€, 32€, 45€,
8,50€ (child). A la carte: 50€.

Just a step or two away from the History of Iron Museum, Audrey and Fabien Stoquiaux offer a smiling welcome to guests at their cozy restaurant in soft shades. We take pleasure in the authenticity of the dishes, unobjectionable prices and precise regional offerings. Apple duo with honeyed foie gras, roasted cod with grilled bacon, magret de canard, mille-feuille with mirabelle plums and bergamot reduction and apple quarters pan-tossed in butter, cinnamon and red wine syrup are effortlessly enjoyable. They are washed down with attractive wines by the glass.

In Laxou (54520). 4 km.

● **La Gargote** `SIM`

12, rue Edouard-Grosjean.
Tel. 03 83 28 22 10.
lechef@lagargote.com
www.lagargote.com
Closed Sat., Sun. 31 July–20 Aug.
Prix fixe: 18€ (weekday lunch),
25€ (weekday lunch), 28€ (weekday dinner),
34€ (weekday dinner).

Jean-François Rubbo's stone and wood chalet is no dive. The shrewd set menus are accompanied by an unusual cellar, with discoveries recommended by dining room maestro Eddy Pharose. While the two kinds of savory profiteroles filled with fingerling potato and smoked herring and avocado with salmon jus, roasted lake trout and celery root soufflé with a champagne zabaglione sauce, guinea-hen kebab with coriander and vegetables in a turmeric emulsion, raspberry panna cotta with ice cream and crispy caramel accompaniment may be a little complicated, they do reveal a determination to do things properly.

In Lay-Saint-Christophe (54690). 7,7 km n.

● **Auberge de Courcelles** `SIM`

11, rue Baron-de-Courcelles.
Tel.-Fax 03 83 22 73 95.
Closed Sun. dinner, Mon., Wed. dinner,
1 week Christmas–New Year's,
mid-Aug.–end Aug.
Prix fixe: 17€ (weekday lunch), 27€.
A la carte: 38€.

The Pernots energetically run this farmhouse and terrace in the country just outside town, boasting a refined setting in burgundy tones. Christine, who trained with Boyer in Reims, offers shrewd advice on the choice of wines, while Thierry prepares suitable market dishes. Duck foie gras in terrine with a red onion confiture, salmon filet on white cabbage, tête de veau with Toul gray snails, pan-tossed quince with Creole seasoning and the pistachio ice cream make an excellent impression.

In Villers-lès-Nancy (54600). 7 km sw.

● **La Cuisine du Pré** `COM`

36, av de Maron.
Tel. 03 83 28 16 25.
Closed Sun.
Prix fixe: 18,50€ (lunch), 25€ (lunch), 32€
14€ (child).

Jean-Jacques and Chantal Bonnet serve up a choice, inventive cuisine in their highly refined, traditional, yet contemporary restaurant in shades of moleskin beige. Guests enjoy parmesan shortbread with eggplant spread, chanterelles with potatoes in a basil sauce with cubes of foie gras, scallops with Middle Eastern seasonings and slow-cooked vegetables, roasted free-range chicken breast with a purée and chorizo jus and soft chocolate fondant with vanilla custard sauce. Well worth a visit.

NANS-LES-PINS

83860 Var. Paris 801 – Aix-en-Provence 45 – Brignoles 26 – Marseille 43.
nanslespins-tourisme@wanadoo.fr.
Not far from Saint-Maximin Abbey at the foot of the Sainte-Baume mountains, a village dedicated to eternal Provence.

HOTELS-RESTAURANTS

■ Domaine de Châteauneuf

Rte de Marseille, 3 km n via N560 toward Saint-Zacharie/Marseille.
Tel. 04 94 78 90 06. Fax 04 94 78 63 30.
info@domaine-de-chateauneuf.com
www.chateauneuf@relaischateaux.com www.
domaine-de-chateauneuf.com
Closed Jan.–beg. Apr. Rest. closed lunch
26 rooms: 150–490€. 4 suites: 320–590€.
Prix fixe: 47€ (dinner), 43€ (lunch),
55€ (dinner).

There is no shortage of leisure activities for visitors to this 18th-century residence set in its own grounds and standing at the heart of a golf course. Thanks to Alain Batteux, the greens, pool, park, tennis courts, giant chess game and *pétanque* facilities attract plenty of guests. At the end of the day, they enjoy the comfort of the neat rooms, the terrace and the masseuses. They also delight in Pierrick Berthier's domestic cuisine, including langoustine carpaccio, filet of turbot with mild garlic cream, pigeon breast cooked on the bone and a chocolate savarin.

NANTES

44000 Loire-Atlantique. Paris 384 –
Anger 91 – Bordeaux 325 – Quimper 232 –
Rennes 110.
www.nantes-tourisme.com.
Nantes is the belle of the west, grey and insular, with its houses on the Ile Feydeau decorated with grotesque masks, set between Brittany—whose capital it once was—and Vendée, marking the dividing line. Nantes is a succession of islands whose shores have been filled. We think of it as 19th century, revolving around the "semi-pedestrian" rue Crébillon and the magical passage Pommeraye, but it turns out to be magnificently medieval near the cathedral, the old place du Pilori and the château of the Dukes of Brittany. Move on just a few meters and it already has a foothold in the 22nd century. Its latest cultural hotbed? The "Lieu Unique", housed in the former Lu biscuit factory, which has been renamed, but kept the same initials, its tall, symbolic tower rebuilt. André Breton set his

Nadja there: "Nantes, where some gazes burn for themselves in a surfeit of flames, where a spirit of adventure beyond all adventures lives on in certain souls; Nantes, from where friends can still come to me."

■	HOTELS

■ Grand Hôtel Mercure Nantes

4, rue du Couëdic.
Tel. 02 51 82 10 00. Fax 02 51 82 10 10.
www.accorhotels.com. / www.mercure.com
152 rooms: 150–160€.
10 suites: 190–350€.

The 19th-century facade, modern lobby and functional rooms with their neo-art deco furniture set the tone in this modern, practical establishment. The Bistro de l'Echanson provides appealing set menus combining dishes and wines.

■ La Pérouse

3, allée Duquesne,
cours des Cinquante-Otages.
Tel. 02 40 89 75 00. Fax 02 40 89 76 00.
information@hotel-laperouse.fr
www.hotel-laperouse.fr
46 rooms: 69–136€. 2 suites: 102–143€.

A central location and above all ultra-contemporary design by Bernard and Clotilde Barto, with Zen rooms all in black and white: this is what you can expect from this unique hotel boasting a fitness center, steam bath and Jacuzzi.

■ Mercure Ile de Nantes

15, bd A.-Millerand.
Tel. 02 40 95 95 95. Fax 02 40 48 23 83.
H0555@accor.com / www.accor.com
Closed 24–31 Dec.
100 rooms: 93–125€. 2 suites: 175€.
Prix fixe: 19€, 25€.

The spacious, comfortable rooms are in orange and chocolate tones, some of them overlooking the Loire. Among the other attractions are tennis, the outdoor swimming pool and bar, as well as the Nautilus restaurant and its gastronomic journeys.

■ Novotel Cité des Congrès
3, rue de Valmy.
Tel. 02 51 82 00 00. Fax 02 51 82 07 40.
H1571@accor.com / www.novotel.com
103 rooms: 90–125€. 2 suites: 200€.

The Saint-Félix canal runs peacefully below the windows on one side of this contemporary hotel. Standing just by the Palais des Congrès conference center, it is meticulously managed by Anne-Marie Thiault.

■ Hôtel de France
24, rue Crébillon.
Tel. 02 40 73 57 91. Fax 02 40 69 75 75.
hoteldefrance.nantes@oceaniahotels.com
www.oceaniahotels.com
73 rooms: 52–120€. 1 suite: 140€.

Near to theater and the place Graslin, this tranquil 18th-century hotel attracts visiting artists with its registered porch, grand lobby and Louis XVI- and Regency-style rooms, duly soundproofed.

■ Pommeraye
2, rue Boileau.
Tel. 02 40 48 78 79. Fax 02 40 47 63 75.
info@hotel-pommeraye.com
www.hotel-pommeraye.com
50 rooms: 43–84€.

This central hotel has plenty of charm with its designer lobby, clocks giving the time in distant cities and contemporary rooms.

■ L'Amiral
26 bis, rue Scribe.
Tel. 02 40 69 20 21. Fax 02 40 73 98 13.
amiral@hotel-nantes.fr
www.hotel-nantes.fr
46 rooms: 42–68€. 3 suites: 92–130€.

Near the place Graslin, the modern, comfortable rooms in this contemporary hotel have been refurbished with green wood and brass. The corridors are currently being renovated.

■ Jules Verne
3, rue du Couëdic.
Tel. 02 40 35 74 50. Fax 02 40 20 09 35.
hoteljulesverne@wanadoo.fr
www.arcantis-hotel.com
65 rooms: 45–99€.

This central hotel with its neat, refined, practical, modern rooms just a step away from the place Royale has a top floor view over the roofs of Nantes.

In Orvault (44700). 4 km via rte de Rennes.

■ Domaine d'Orvault
Chemin des Marais-du-Cens.
Tel. 02 40 76 84 02. Fax 02 40 76 04 21.
contact@domaine-orvault.com
www.domaine-orvault.com
41 rooms: 84–112€. 2 suites: 144€
Half board: 135–246€.

In the heart of a residential neighborhood, this former Relais & Châteaux establishment is enjoying a second youth. The warm welcome from Sylvain Lejeune, the rooms overlooking the garden, the fitness center and the pool, as well as the restaurant and terrace, all have their appeal.

In Les Sorinières (44840). 12 km s via rte de la Roche-sur-Yon and D178.

■ Abbaye de Villeneuve
Rte de la Roche-sur-Yon.
Tel. 02 40 04 40 25. Fax 02 40 31 28 45.
villeneuve@leshotelsparticuliers.com
www.abbayedevilleneuve.com
20 rooms: 85–125€. 8 suites: 205€.
Prix fixe: 30€, 42€, 65€, 16€ (child).
A la carte: 55€.

Every aspect of this Cistercian abbey with its magnificent 18th-century buildings exudes charm: the English-style rooms, refined lounges, cloister, grounds, swimming pool and ponds. Sébastien Burgaud's cuisine is equally impressive. Served in the stately dining room looking out on the garden, the tuna carpaccio, parsleyed eel, rib eye steak with flakes of sea salt and dark chocolate terrine are faultless.

● **RESTAURANTS**

● L'Atlantide   ©V.COM

Centre des Salorges, 16, quai E.-Reynaud.
Tel. 02 40 73 23 23. Fax 02 40 73 76 46.
jygueho@club-internet.fr
www.restaurant-atlantide.net
Closed Sat. lunch, Sun., 1 week Christmas–
New Year's, Aug.
Prix fixe: 28€ (lunch), 35€ (dinner), 55€,
70€, 95€.

Jean-Yves Guého dominates the gourmet scene in Nantes from this contemporary building, designed by Wilmotte, just opposite the harbor. Guého, who learned his trade at the Auberge de l'Ill before moving to Louisiana and Hong Kong, then finally joining the Méridien Montparnasse in Paris, maintains the house's culinary standards. In a light, refined, minimalist, modern setting, guests savor the "traveling" cuisine, which has a certain style. Crabmeat with avocado served with a slow-cooked tomato and peppered mango emulsion, lobster *verrine* with artichoke, foamy tomato and summer truffle bouillon, red mullet seared on one side and finished under the broiler, pan-steamed arugula with butter, sundried tomato sorbet and spit-roasted turbot as well as crayfish tails and chanterelles with pan drippings are proof of his skillfully assimilated marine inspiration. The spit-roasted young breast of pigeon and local lobster in thick slices with a lobster and poultry jus, like the lightly grilled veal sweetbreads with macaroni crayfish timbale, are an appealing return to dry land. Brilliant desserts follow (spherical hot and cold chocolate nectarine dessert, kouign-amann with caramel-roasted pear and brown sugar ice cream) and the wine list features vintages from all over the world.

● Le Manoir de la Régate   ©V.COM

155, route de Gachet.
Tel. 02 40 18 02 97. Fax 02 40 25 23 36.
info@manoir-regate.com
www.manoir-regate.com
Closed Sun. dinner, Mon.,
1 week Christmas–New Year's.

Prix fixe: 18,50€ (weekdays),
31€ (weekdays), 44€ (wine inc.),
53€ (wine inc.), 67€. A la carte: 55–60€.

This fine 19th-century building on the bank of the Erdre boasts luxurious lounges and a superb summer terrace. After training (notably with Senderens in Paris and Albert Roux in London), the Pascal brothers and Loïc Pérou created this fine restaurant, a showcase for their inspired, high precision cuisine. Guests come to enjoy the calm surroundings, while savoring the crayfish consommé with herbs and shellfish, the monkfish medallions with squid and broiled quahogs, beef tenderloin with wild mushroom duxelles (minced and creamed) with green asparagus and the strawberry pistachio macaron with strawberries in lemongrass-scented syrup and pistachio ice cream. All is impeccably served by Guillaume Rouault and washed down with wines from a well-chosen list.

● L'Abelia   ⓝ○COM

125, bd des Poilus.
Tel. 02 40 35 40 00.
Closed Sun., Mon., 2 weeks Christmas–New Year's, 3 weeks Aug.
Prix fixe: 29€, 35€, 49€.

We knew Vincent Berthomeau as a modest, inspired cook at the Esquinade. Now we find him at his peak in this 1900 establishment set in its own garden, with period, rustic dining rooms refurbished in a modern style. His lively wife provides a charming welcome and the dishes prepared by this hardworking Vendéen (a pleonasm!) are truth itself. Scallops with endive, veal sweetbreads pan fried in butter, garlic and parsley and chanterelles with an aciduated sauce, duck foie gras with frog legs and diced vegetable toss and the wild duck with figs and slow-cooked red cabbage are works of art. The buckwheat blinis with warm apples and quince caramel sorbet will send you into raptures, while the Domaine de Bel Air Marsaules Bourgueil rolls over the tongue like an elixir of youth. This is quite obviously a great establishment of the future.

● Brasserie Félix COM

1, rue Lefèvre-Utile.
Tel. 02 40 34 15 93. Fax 02 40 34 46 23.
contact@felixbrasserie.com
www.brasseriefelix.com
Prix fixe: 15€. A la carte: 40€.

On the first floor of a recent building by the harbor, Christian Thomas-Trophime's pop brasserie is enjoyed by both visitors and residents of Nantes. They all appreciate the vision of this former chef at the Manoir de la Comète in Saint-Sébastien-sur-Loire, who has come up with a bistro-style menu modernizing the genre. In the hands of Gérard Bellanger, the iced melon with orange blossom water and Parma ham, grilled Atlantic sea bass with chanterelles sautéed in herbs and butter, rabbit saddle with olives and the raspberry blanc-manger are excellent tricks indeed.

● Maison Baron-Lefèvre COM

33, rue de Rieux.
Tel. 02 40 89 20 20. Fax 02 40 89 20 22.
barron-lefevre@wanadoo.fr
Closed Sun., Mon., 2 weeks beg. Aug.
Prix fixe: 18€ (weekday lunch), 25€.
A la carte: 40€.

This much talked about establishment with its New York loft look, vegetable greenhouse and delicatessen provides a touch of the exotic. The Loire, Chilean and Italian wines selected by Damien Chauveau go well with Jean-Charles Baron's market-based cuisine, and there are no complaints about the pan-tossed jumbo shrimp, cuttlefish and quahogs, Atlantic sea bass in salt crust, beef tenderloin Rossini and the thin apple tart.

● L'Océanide COM

2, rue Paul-Bellamy.
Tel. 02 40 20 32 28. Fax 02 40 48 08 55.
www.restaurant-oceanide.com
Closed Sun., Mon., mid-July–mid-Aug.
Prix fixe: 18,50€, 26€, 39,50€, 55€,
12€ (child).

David Garrec has both feet planted firmly in the city and puts into practice the most valuable lessons he learned during his time with Boyer, Gagnaire and Soliveres at the Vernet. The set menus are very carefully priced and the dishes are prepared with skill and intelligence. Crab ravioli poached in its jus, shellfish with basil, Atlantic sea bass filet with butter and mousseline of Jerusalem artichokes and the roasted pigeon breast, its legs confit with foie gras and cooking juices heightened with coffee, are memorable delights. The cheeses are from Bordier in Saint-Malo and the fruit-themed desserts live up to the same high standards.

● Au Verre Bouteille COM

9, rue Kervégan.
Tel. 02 40 08 22 08. Fax 02 40 36 70 22.
Closed Sat. lunch, Sun., Mon. lunch,
2 weeks beg. Sept.
Prix fixe: 24€, 35€, 17€ (lunch).

Nantes society gathers in the rustic dining room of this fine establishment on the island of Ile Feydeau. Trained by Alain Ducasse, Abder Abbou puts together shrewd set menus with stirring Southern French notes. Among the dishes are lobster risotto with langoustine jus, monkfish medallion with foie gras, fileted breast of young pigeon with a layering of different colored cabbages and Brittany shortbread with raspberries.

● La Cigale COM

4, pl Graslin.
Tel. 02 51 84 94 94. Fax 02 51 84 94 95.
lacigale@lacigale.com / www.lacigale.com
Prix fixe: 12,90€ (lunch), 23,90€ (lunch),
16,50€ (dinner), 26,30€ (dinner)
7,50€ (child). A la carte: 35€.

Immortalized by Jacques Demy and Anouk Aimée in *Lola*, decorated with ceramics, glass and woodwork, this art nouveau brasserie across from the Opéra charms guests with its simple cuisine. The seafood platter, pan-seared duck foie gras, red mullet grilled in the local style with spicy oil, grilled chitterling sausage and the chocolate tart and salted-butter caramel are very appealing and reasonably priced.

● Le Kadre   **N·COM**

2 bis, rue Fénelon.
Tel. 02 40 89 21 47.
Closed Sat. lunch, Sun. lunch, Mon. dinner.
Prix fixe: 12,50€ (lunch), 20€.
A la carte: 38€.

Olivier Quint and Christian Karembeu have got it just right with this modern, friendly restaurant, amusing, delicious and just a step away from City Hall. It owes its success to their friends Sadok and Hedy Sellami, and especially the charming Marie Chartier who receives guests with a smile. We like the décor of exposed stone alternating with white-washed walls, imitation metal tables, modern pictures and attractive lighting. The fusion cuisine is restrained and straightforwardly pleasant. Salmon and whiting terrine, jumbo shrimp risotto, skate wing with shallot and vanilla cream sauce, Indian-style veal with basmati rice and a Berber-style chicken tagine with preserved lemons all make an excellent impression.

● Le Rive Gauche   **N·COM**

10, Côte Saint-Sébastien.
Tel. 02 40 34 38 52. Fax 02 40 33 21 20.
www.restaurant-lerivegauche.com
Closed Sat. lunch, Sun. dinner, Mon., 1 week Christmas–New Year's, vac. Apr., Aug.
Prix fixe: 21,50€ (weekday lunch), 29,50€, 33€, 40€.

On the bank of the Loire, this large restaurant with its banqueting rooms and enclosed terrace is run by the dynamic Christophe Fouré, a Norman from Flers. Having trained with Lenôtre and Robuchon, he meticulously prepares both land and sea produce. Pressed foie gras terrine with forest mushrooms and wild hare conserves, scallops in a citrus broth, John Dory fish with mild Spanish peppers and langoustine ravioli, beef cheeks, slow roasted to melting, served with potato purée seasoned with local chitterling sausage and the Breton salted butter shortcake and piña colada sorbet are neatly done.

● Auberge du Château   **COM**

5, pl de la Duchesse-Anne.
Tel. 02 40 74 31 85. Fax 02 40 37 97 57.
Closed Sat. lunch, Sun., 2 weeks beg. Aug.
Prix fixe: 15€ (weekday lunch), 22€.
A la carte: 30–35€.

Opposite the château, Vincent Queruel's inn offers a gourmet touch. This veteran of the Pressoir in Paris prepares his reliable market-based cuisine in an intimate setting whose classicism is brightened by orange and green shades. Bouchot mussels with chanterelles, cod filet with mashed potatoes and seven-hour leg of lamb and potatoes with Epoisse and the creamy chocolate dessert with dried fruits are true to their promise.

● La Poissonnerie   **COM**

4, rue Léon-Maître.
Tel. 02 40 47 79 50.
lestroisas@orange.fr
Closed Sat. lunch, Sun., Mon., 23 Dec.–beg. Jan., Aug.
Prix fixe: 13,50€ (lunch).
A la carte: 55–60€.

Yves Scaviner has taken over this marine haunt where the dishes based on the day's catch auctioned in La Turballe. Guests are welcomed with a smile in the two bright dining rooms with their fine wooden flooring. The mixed salad with scallops and citrus fruits and turmeric, lox-style smoked salmon, Atlantic sea bass filet with chanterelles and the lime soufflé served hot carry out their duties.

● Les Temps Changent   **COM**

1, pl Aristide-Briand.
Tel. 02 51 72 18 01. Fax 02 51 88 91 82.
Closed Sat., Sun., 10 days beg. Jan., 3 weeks Aug.
Prix fixe: 17,60€ (lunch), 18,70€ (lunch), 23,50€ (lunch), 25€,36€, 41€,45€.

The colonial décor here is changeless with its oiled rattan chairs and shady terrace. The bistro atmosphere and tables (unadorned at lunchtime; attractively draped in the evening) have their charm, as does the blackboard where Laurent Le

Bouler chalks up his occasionally off-beat fare: the pan-tossed jumbo shrimp, ceps and cuttlefish with poultry cocoa jus, veal hanger steak with soft-cooked apples or fressinette bananas, and morels with milky caramel harmonize with vintages whose praises are sung with conviction by Marina Le Bouler.

● Le Pressoir ⬛SIM

11, allée de Turenne.
Tel. 02 40 35 31 10.
lepressoirnantes@yahoo.fr
Closed Sat. lunch, Sun., Mon. dinner,
1 week Feb., 1 week at Easter, Aug.
A la carte: 40€.

On the first floor of an 18th-century building, this quiet restaurant has an insider appeal and continues to delight those in the know. Johey Verfaille caters to the guests' needs, while Stéphane Gawlowicz serves up a sincere, even shrewd, market-based cuisine. The oven-crisped pork trotter, red tuna steak in an herb crust, pan-fried veal kidneys with mustard and local sparking wine with raspberries gratify without emptying the pocket. Good wines from the surrounding area.

● Christophe Bonnet ⓃSIM

6, rue Mazagran.
Tel. 02 40 69 03 39.
www.christophebonnet.com
Closed Sun., Mon.,
1 week beg. Jan., Aug.–beg. Sept.
Prix fixe: 30€ (lunch), 33€ , 38€, 43€.

Christophe Bonnet, the city's oddball, worked in Lyon and La Plaine-sur-Mer before returning home. In his tiny kitchen, the inspired maestro dreams up dishes that startle, stir, shock and finally charm. Sashimi-style tuna somewhat overwhelmed by the spiced yogurt, langoustine roasted with olive oil, leeks and tarragon, slices of saddle of lamb with coffee infusion and the caramelized pear in an infusion of royal lotus and crème poire Williams, are explosive. The cozy "bits and pieces" décor is colorful and the waitstaff take the trouble to smile. The fact remains that there is an amazing com-

mittment and enthusiasm to be found here, just opposite the church of Notre-Dame du Salut.

● In Gusto ⓃSIM

4 bis, rue du Chapeau-Rouge.
Tel. 02 40 35 35 95.
Closed Sun.
A la carte: 25€.

This modern snack bar dreamt up by keen Italophiles Nicolas Seguier and Christophe Piers, with its paneled décor, beige and red tones, bar and terrace near the busy rue Boileau, is well worth a visit. Dried or fresh pasta, marvelous Parma ham (aged for twenty-four months), biscotti, delicious little dishes (peppers and tuna, fettuccini carbonara, tomato and zucchini frittata, vegetable lasagne, pesto risotto) go well with the selection of Italian vintages (Montepulciano des Abruzzes, Sangiovese de Molise) at friendly prices.

● Nota Bene ⓃSIM

3, rue St Denis.
Tel. 02 40 12 47 22.
Closed Sun.
Prix fixe: 11€ (lunch). A la carte: 30€.

A colorful décor, a mosaic bar, red lighting and a long, cozy dining room… We soon feel suitably apart from our everyday world in this modern trattoria offering a professional welcome. Mushroom risotto, mozzarella and tomatoes, four-cheese penne gratin or salmon tagliatelle have no great culinary pretensions, but sharpen our taste for travel. The pizza Marguerite is just like they make it in Naples and the pan-fried veal escalope is evidently Milanese.

● A Ma Table SIM

11, rue Fouré.
Tel. 02 40 47 01 18.
amatable@aliceadsl.fr
amatable.com
Closed Sat., Sun., 3 weeks Aug.
Prix fixe: 15€, 20€, 24€.

This old-style bistro next to the former LU biscuit factory provides an introduction to Albert Guillem's gourmet creations. Among his simple, well-prepared, market-based dishes are house duck terrine, pollock filet with leek and curry cream, fileted breast of guinea hen with cider and the soft chocolate cake.

● Le Bistro de l'Echanson `SIM`

At Grand Hôtel Mercure, 4, rue du Couëdic.
Tel. 02 51 82 10 00. Fax 02 51 82 10 10.
h1985@accor.com / www.accor.com
Closed Sun.
Prix fixe: 9,50€ (wine inc.).
A la carte: 30€.

This contemporary bistro in red and black plays on combinations of wines and dishes, with a selection of shrewd fare coupled with great vintages sold at cost. Sommelier Marie-Gabrielle Dupont offers sound advice on how to best accompany Sébastien Moreau's cuisine: vegetarian spreads, creamed pumpkin with aged goat cheese garnish, young duck in blood sauce and slow-cooked apple kouign-amann with mascarpone, bathed in Calvados.

● L'Embellie `SIM`

14, rue Armand-Brossard.
Tel.-Fax 02 40 48 20 02.
francoistroquin@yahoo.co.uk
Closed Sun., Mon., 3 weeks Aug.
Prix fixe: 14€, 16€, 23€, 32€ (wine inc.),
12€ (child, beverage inc.).

François Troquin and Nicolas Barbier have taken over this small eatery with great enthusiasm. Troquin worked with Senderens in Paris and at the Eden Rock in Saint-Barth, Barbier at the Atlantide and the Manoir des Lys at Bagnoles-del'Orne. The quiet dining room in burgundy and yellow is set off by a cob wall. The set menus are balanced and vibrant, promising "dynamite fresh" delights such as shrimp and langoustine ravioli with creamy deglazed crustacean sauce, pan-fried Atlantic sea bass seasoned with lemongrass or rack of lamb in a garlic crust. The quince and pain d'épice sizzled to a golden crust make a fine impression.

In Basse-Goulaine (44115). 8 km via N149.

● Mon Rêve `V.COM`

2, levée de la Divatte.
Tel. 02 40 03 55 50. Fax 02 40 06 05 41.
contact@villa-mon-reve.com
www.villa-mon-reve.com
Closed 2 weeks Nov., 2 weeks Feb.
Prix fixe: 22€, 12€ (child).
A la carte: 47–65€.

This charming establishment nestling on the bank of the Loire, sheltered from the winds of passing fashion, is still loyal to the fine produce and traditions of the Nantes region. The coziness of the dining room and delights of the terrace sharpen our enjoyment of the levelheaded dishes on which Gérard Ryngel's reputation has been built. His balanced, judicious, innovative cuisine is focused on tastes, successively offering local crayfish gazpacho, frog legs simmered in local Gros Plant wine, roasted Challand duck with Muscadet caramel and the local flan incorporating Muscat and raspberries. Entrusted to Jean-Michel's son, the wine list has a remarkable selection of purebred Muscadets and Cécile Ryngel's service is very attentive.

In Carquefou (44470). 5 km ne via D178.

● Auberge du Vieux Gachet `N``SIM`

Vieux Gachet.
Tel. 02 40 25 10 92. Fax 02 40 18 03 92.
Closed Sun. dinner, Mon.
Prix fixe: 16€ (weekday lunch), 31€,
15€ (child). A la carte: 65€.

On the bank of the Erdre, Walter Lescot's inn and terrace offer a choice destination for food lovers. In the ochre dining room with its exposed stone, the young chef prepares classical dishes with lively, precise flavors. Lobster with citrus butter and buckwheat blinis, roasted monkfish dusted with olive powder and thin slices of tomato, sautéed veal medallion and foie gras escalope with pan-tossed chanterelles and the Menton lemon gratin are in great demand.

In Château-Thébaud (44690). 15 km s via D.58, rte de Vertou.

● Auberge la Gaillotière SIM

Locale known as La Gaillotière.
Tel. 02 28 21 31 16. Fax 02 28 21 31 17.
Closed Tue. dinner, Wed., Feb.,
2 weeks beg. Aug.
Prix fixe: 17,50€, 22€, 24,50€, 13€
(weekday lunch), 10€ (child).

This imposing winegrower's house and terrace has been in the Debailly family for several generations. Fifty or so Loire wines accompany the forthright dishes based on local farm produce. In the traditional wood-trimmed dining room, we savor duck foie gras terrine with green tomatoes, cod with capers, pollock with chorizo, rabbit roasted in rosemary and the apple and orange marmalade with pain d'épice.

In Coueron (44220). 16,5 km w.

● Le François II

5, place Aristide-Briand.
Tel.-Fax 02 40 38 32 32.
Closed Sun. dinner, Mon., Thu. dinner,
1 week beg. Jan., 1 week at end Feb.,
1 week beg. May, 3 weeks Aug.
Prix fixe: 19,50€, 26€, 29,50€, 35€,
10,50€ (child).

Near the marshes on the banks of the Loire, this rustic dining room with its exposed stone, rugs and sheer curtains pays a stirring tribute to the region. Jérôme Evain offers a brilliant take on tradition with solid, roguish dishes. These include a timbale of crunchy vegetables and melted Camembert, salted cod with Paimpol coco beans and chorizo, beef cheek and tail tourte and a slow-cooked banana with rum and caramel and lime sorbet.

In Haute-Goulaine (44115). 14 km via N149 and D119.

● Manoir de la Boulaie V.COM

33, rue de la Chapelle-Saint-Martin.
Tel. 02 40 06 15 91. Fax 02 40 54 56 83.
www.manoir-de-la-boulaie.fr
Closed Sun. dinner, Mon., Wed., vac.
Christmas, 3 weeks Aug.

Prix fixe: 30€ (lunch), 58€, 85€, 105€,
16€ (child). A la carte: 60–90€.

Laurent Saudeau's success is obvious: lively, cheerful dining rooms in a manor surrounded by a park on the outskirts of the Muscadet winegrowing region, along with a comfortable décor and diligent service supervised by his smiling wife. Laurent, a native of Nantes formerly at the Négresco, the Bonne Auberge in Antibes and the Bories in Gordes, serves up sun-drenched dishes that are often too rich, but such are the hazards of generosity. Foie gras with cep-flavored yogurt and pigeon confit, variations on the scallop or the Paimpol coco bean presented in all of its forms form the basis for repeated exercises in style. The cuisine is appealing and flavorsome, despite its excesses. Red mullet with Gillardeau oysters and cataplana of slow-cooked lamb and chorizo are bites that display bravura. The desserts (coconut milk sushi or mandarin orange dessert) are a delightful experience.

77730 Seine-et-Marne. Paris 75 – Meaux 27 – Melun 87.
The last town you can reach with your Paris region transport card and the first in Champagne. Twenty-five hectares of vines and one special day in the year: St. Vincent's Day, the 22nd of January.

●	RESTAURANTS

● Auberge du Lion d'Or

2, rue du Bac.
Tel. 01 60 23 62 21. Fax 01 60 23 71 96.
Closed Sun. dinner. Rest. closed Sun. dinner,
Wed., Christmas, mid-Aug.–beg. Sept.
9 rooms: 39,50–44,50€.
Prix fixe: 12€, 20€, 26€, 8€ (child).
A la carte: 35€.

In the direction of Champagne on the bank of the Marne, this country inn boasts nine neat and tidy rooms and a market-based restaurant of genuine worth. In the dining room and at the stoves, Luc Masson does an excellent job, favoring guests with an authentic smile, Brie feuilleté, sole meunière, grape-stuffed quail and an apricot tart. In season, game plays a central role.

NANTUA

01130 Ain. Paris 478 – Annecy 67 – Bourg-en-Bresse 51 – Genève 66 – Lyon 91. nantua.tourisme@wanadoo.fr. The Bugey, the Jura mountains, the land of lakes, crawfish and Nantua sauce.

 HOTELS-RESTAURANTS

■ L'Embarcadère

13, av du Lac.
Tel. 04 74 75 22 88. Fax 04 74 75 22 25.
hotelembarcadere@wanadoo.fr
www.hotelembarcadere.com
Closed 20 Dec.–beg. Jan.
49 rooms: 53–71€.
Prix fixe: 24€ (weekdays),
31€ (Sat., Sun.,), 38€, 61€, 14€ (child).

This hotel with its modern, air-conditioned rooms provides an unobstructed view of the lake of Nantua and the surrounding mountains. In the circular dining room, lobster with raspberry vinegar, garlicky turbot with ceps, Bresse hen with morels and local Savignin wine, roasted mango crumble and exotic sorbet favorably impress.

NARBONNE

11100 Aude. Paris 796 – Béziers 28 – Carcassonne 61 – Montpellier 95 – Perpignan 65.
office.tourisme.narbonne@wanadoo.fr.
"Narbonne, mon amie," sang Trénet, a native of these parts. With its Gothic monuments, including the Saint-Paul basilica and Saint-Juste cathedral, this charming capital of Narbonne Gaul, once an archbishopric, is also a mini-metropolis of wine, a port and a seaside outpost between Corbières and Mediterranean.

 HOTELS-RESTAURANTS

■ Château de l'Hospitalet

10 km via D168, rte de Narbonne-Plage.
Tel. 04 68 45 28 50. Fax 04 68 45 28 78.
resa-narbonne@monalisahotels.com
www.monalisahotels.com
Rest. closed Mon., Tue. lunch.
22 rooms: 75–100€. 3 suites: 95–150€.
Prix fixe: 36€, 45€, 80€.
A la carte: 50–60€.

On the way to the beach, at the foot of the mountains, in a village boasting museums, art studios, stores and a swimming pool, this modern, comfortable hotel provides appealing Provençal rooms. On the culinary side, the Grange serves such delights as pressed terrine of slow-cooked peppers and fresh anchovies, red mullet, an oven-crisped milk-fed veal chop and a crunchy Caribbean dessert with a tea and jasmine emulsion. Less gastronomic, but very fair, the Olivet bistro is also an excellent culinary port of call.

■ La Résidence

6, rue du 1-Mai.
Tel. 04 68 32 19 41. Fax 04 68 65 51 82.
hotellaresidence@free.fr
www.hotelresidence.fr
24 rooms: 53–85€. 2 suites: 86–96€.

Actors Jean Marais, Louis de Funès and Michel Serrault and singer Georges Brassens have all signed the impressive guest book here, testifying to the quality of this traditional hotel in the heart of town, near the Archbishop's Palace and the Saint-Juset-Saint-Pasteur Cathedral, in an attractive 19th-century residence. Under the supervision of Monsieur and Madame Lorme, the rooms in contemporary style and the reasonable prices also have their charm.

● La Table Saint-Crescent

68, av du Général-Leclerc, at the palais du Vin.
Tel. 04 68 41 37 37. Fax 04 68 41 01 22.
saint-crescent@wanadoo.fr
www.la-table-saint-crescent.com
Closed Sat. lunch, Sun. dinner, Mon.,

2 weeks beg. Sept., 1 week Mar.
Prix fixe: 20€ (weekday lunch), 36€,
42€ (wine inc.), 58€, 69€ (wine inc.).
A la carte: 75–94€.

Beneath the vaults of a 7th-century oratory, the dining room is decorated in gentle, light tones. The terrace looks out on the vineyards of the Corbières. Claude Giraud's cuisine focuses on aromas, flavors and colors inextricably linked to nature in the Languedoc region, and today his son is turning the wealth of the Mediterranean into a series of remarkably dynamic, precise dishes. A veteran of the Ritz, Chibois, Guérard and Cabro d'Or, Lionel serves up the langoustine carpaccio with chickpea purée, broiled tuna belly with fennel, rabbit and olive confit with broad beans and roasted almonds and a frozen lemon thyme "eskimo". To round it all off, the wine list offers a perfect panorama of the region's vineyards.

● Le Bistro du Chef en Gare   `SIM`

1, av Carnot.
Tel. 04 68 32 14 52. Fax 04 68 32 29 94.
Closed dinner
Prix fixe: 11€ (lunch, wine inc.),
14,50€ (lunch, wine inc.), 17,50€ (lunch,
wine inc.) 6,50€ (enf., lunch, wine inc.).
A la carte: 28€.

This bistro located in the former train station of singer-songwriter Charles Trenet's home town is now run by the Elior group. The 1900-style décor and background music pay tribute to the artist. The cuisine has become rather simple, with country salad, salmon paupiette in the Norman style, rabbit with mustard sauce and floating island with red berries.

● L'Estagnol   `SIM`

5, cours Mirabeau.
Tel. 04 68 65 09 27. Fax 04 68 32 23 38.
Closed Sun., Mon.
Prix fixe: 17€, 21€, 28€, 8€ (child).
A la carte: 33–38€.

The brasserie in Narbonne where artists dine after theater is in fine shape. In the second floor room that looks out on the

canal and cathedral, or on the terrace, guests enjoy the cheerful atmosphere, friendly service and market-based cuisine. The toast with hot goat cheese and eggplant, roasted Mediterranean sea bass with chanterelles, tête de veau with a gribiche sauce, classic pain perdu and the soft financiers are unpretentious.

In Coursan (11100). 7 km n via N113, rte de
Béziers.

● L'Os à Table   🍴`COM`

88, rue J.-Jaurès, rte des Plages.
Tel. 04 68 33 55 72. Fax 04 68 33 35 39.
losatable-coursan@wanadoo.fr
Closed Sun. dinner, Mon., 1 week Sept.,
2 weeks beg. Jan.
Prix fixe: 24€, 33€, 38€, 46€,
10€ (child). A la carte: 45€.

The Aude rolls peacefully through the heart of the village and the living is easy in the lounges of this house on the riverbank in the building that shelters Claude Fridrici's restaurant. Each day, the market provides him with inspiration for his delicate cuisine. The hamburger stuffed with fois gras, quick sauté of poultry and jumbo shrimp served with a Venere black rice risotto and twice-cooked duck in citrus caramel are among the dishes of the moment, prepared and served with care. On a sweeter note, the "hot, cold and chocolate" promises an intense revelation.

NESTIER

65150 Hautes-Pyrénées. Paris 790 –
Auch 75 – Bagnères-de-Luchon 47 –
Lannemezan 15 – Saint-Gaudens 25.
A peaceful hamlet at the foot of the Pyrénées.

  HOTELS-RESTAURANTS

■ Relais du Castéra   🟡N🏠

Place du Calvaire.
Tel. 05 62 39 77 37. Fax 05 62 39 77 29.
www.hotel-castera.com
Closed Sun. dinner, Mon., Jan., 1 week beg. June.
6 rooms: 46–65€.
Prix fixe: 25€, 32€, 45€, 18€ (weekday
lunch), 9€ (child).

Ghislaine and Serge Latour welcome their guests with open arms in this former post house with its snug rooms. In the restaurant, where the old farmhouse table and fireplace set the tone, they offer an introduction to their region in the form of solid, lively dishes, including creamed pumpkin with pan-seared foie gras, gray sea bream with piquillo peppers, black pig ventreche, young pigeon with ceps and Swiss chard and the rice pudding with pear and red wine jam.

NEUF-BRISACH

68600 Haut-Rhin. Paris 464 – Colmar 16 – Sélestat 31 – Mulhouse 39 – Bâle 62.
Built by Vauban, the walls remain intact, but the town is new. The frontier still lies close by.

 HOTELS-RESTAURANTS

In Vogelgrün (68600). 3 km e via N415.

■ L'Européen
Ile du Rhin.
Tel. 03 89 72 51 57. Fax 03 89 72 74 54.
rene.daegele@wanadoo.fr
www.europeen-hotel.com
Closed mid-Jan.–mid-Feb.
40 rooms: 98–124€. 5 suites: 98–220€.
Prix fixe: 20€, 37€, 70€. A la carte: 55€.

On the Rhine, just a step away from the German border, this motel belonging to the Daegelé family has large, bright, modern rooms, a fitness center, swimming pool, fine terrace and choice restaurant. In the traditional dining room, foie gras, the red wine stew with five varieties of fish, the beef filet with a béarnaise sauce and the crème brûlée are right on target.

In Vogelgrün.

■ Le Caballin
Ile du Rhin.
Tel. 03 89 72 56 56. Fax 03 89 72 95 00.
leranch@lecaballin.fr / www.lecaballin.fr
Closed Christmas–New Year's.
20 rooms: 53–73€.
Prix fixe: 18€, 25€, 34€, 10€ (child).
A la carte: 30–45€.

Set in a riding center, Roland Schmidt's hotel has well-equipped rooms in orange and burgundy tones. In the restaurant, the view over the lake is delightful and the regional cuisine is good. We enjoy the frog legs, pike-perch poached in Riesling, duck breast with pink peppercorns and the frozen Kouglof.

NEUFCHATEAU

88300 Vosges. Paris 323 – Belfort 154 – Epinal 75 – Verdun 106.
ot.neufchateau@wanadoo.fr.
This small Vosges town is worth a visit for the fine stairs of the Hôtel de Ville and the opulent Saint-Nicolas church with its sculptures.

 HOTELS-RESTAURANTS

■ L'Eden
1, rue de la Première-Armée-Française.
Tel. 03 29 95 61 30. Fax 03 29 94 03 42.
hotel-eden@wanadoo.fr / www.leden.fr
Rest. closed Sun. dinner, Mon. lunch,
2 weeks beg. Jan.
26 rooms: 43–80€. 1 suite: 80–90€.
Prix fixe: 24€, 26€, 33€, 45€, 10€ (child).

This contemporary hotel and restaurant offers neat, functional rooms with a variety of colors and furnishings. Jean-Christophe Gros, who has taken over the establishment, presents dishes with a modern flavor. Warm langoustine salad with melon balls and a liquory wine, oven-crisped red mullet on a julienne of vegetables with saffron, foie gras in puff pastry with Granny Smith apples and chocolate fondue with fresh fruit, marshmallows and chunks of pain d'épice incite us to return on a regular basis.

● Le Romain `COM`
74, av du Président-Kennedy.
Tel.-Fax 03 29 06 18 80.
Closed Sun. dinner, Mon.,
1 week at end Aug., 1 week beg. Sept.
Prix fixe: 16€, 21€, 27€, 33€.
A la carte: 32€.

This well-kept roadside establishment is a pleasant surprise in this Vosges town. It offers a modern décor in white tones, alert service and well-prepared dishes. Bruno Mangin presents the marbled duck foie gras terrine with quince jelly, tête de veau finished in the pan with a shallot vinaigrette, roasted Mediterranean sea bass in an herb crust and a duck brochette with mirabelle plums followed by frozen nougat with mirabelle plum sauce, all prepared by Jordan Schoindre.

NEUVILLE-DE-POITOU

86170 Vienne. Paris 337 – Châtellerault 35 – Parthenay 40 – Poitiers 15 – Saumur 80 – Thouars 50.
An astute little town in the heart of Haut Poitou winegrowing country.

● | RESTAURANTS

● Saint-Fortunat   Ⓝ SIM
6, rue Bangoura-Moridé.
Tel. 05 49 54 56 74. Fax 05 49 53 18 02.
fabien.dupont@voila.fr
Closed Sun. dinner, Mon., 2 weeks Jan.,
2 weeks Aug.
Prix fixe: 12€ (lunch), 17€, 28€, 33€, 45€.

In this former farm refurbished in modern style by the Duponts, Aurélie in the dining room and Fabien at the stove serve up innovative dishes. "Vaporeux" of oysters, quinoa, poultry livers and smoked herring as an appetizer, then wild turbot, turnips in sauerkraut, chorizo in an artichoke sauce or simmered veal kidney with ras el-hanout dates are straightforwardly enjoyable. The selection of five desserts changes with the season (passion fruit soufflé and sorbet).

NEVERS

58000 Nièvre. Paris 241 – Orléans 167 – Moulins 55 – Bourges 69.
We come to learn the secrets of Nevers negus (not the sword thrust that so intrigued Lagardère) in this glorious, sweet toothed town.

 | HOTELS-RESTAURANTS

■ Mercure Pont de Loire   🏨
Quai Médine.
Tel. 03 86 93 93 86. Fax 03 86 59 43 29.
h3480@accor.com / www.accorhotels.com
Rest. closed Christmas, New Year's.
59 rooms: 82–110€.
Prix fixe: 21€, 30€, 10€ (child).

On the banks of the Loire opposite the Maison de la Culture (Cultural Center), this pleasant establishment offers a friendly welcome, piano bar, pleasant rooms refurbished in blue and yellow and a dining room in salmon shades. Roger Christian's regional cuisine makes reliable use of fine produce: the creamy escargot, garlic and parsley broth with a small goat cheese cake, whiting mille-feuille with forest mushrooms, beef filet with morels in cream sauce and the chocolate Marquise slip down effortlessly.

● Jean-Michel Couron   ◎ COM
21, rue Saint-Etienne.
Tel. 03 86 61 19 28. Fax 03 86 36 02 96.
info@jm-couron.com / www.jm-couron.com
Closed Sun. dinner, Mon., Tue. lunch,
2 weeks beg. Jan., mid-July–beg. Aug.
Prix fixe: 20€ (weekdays), 28€, 48€.

Both in the vaulted chamber of the former cloister of the Church of Saint-Etienne and in the small adjoining rooms, Jean-Michel Couron serves an inventive, accessible cuisine. Having acquired valuable experience during his time with Bras, he delights us with crab tomato aspic surrounded by a lime cream, langoustine-stuffed peppers with dried apricots and yogurt basil "milk-shake" or Charolais beef served with quenelles of young shallots in fresh fromage blanc and honey. For dessert, brown sugar-roasted apricots with beet root sorbet add a sweet coda to these creative gourmet ballads. Marie-Hélène's welcome and the cellar's treasures do the rest.

● **Le Puits de Saint-Pierre**   🍴COM

21, rue Mirangron.
Tel.-Fax 03 86 59 28 88.
natadolny@wanadoo.fr
Closed Sun. dinner, Mon., Tue. lunch,
1 week beg. Jan., 3 weeks Aug.
Prix fixe: 19,50€, 26€ (wine inc.), 28€,
34€ (wine inc.), 45€ (wine inc.).

Provence pays a visit to Nevers in this period building with a well and a dining room in ochre and olive green tones. An affable hostess and attentive chef, Nathalie Nadolny concocts the dishes from today's South of France that feature on the inviting set menus. The mushroom and goat cheese ravioli, Mediterranean sea bass filet in an orange and coriander emulsion, braised pork cheeks in tea sauce and cherry preserves with five-spice crumble are easily matched with one of the 300 wines from all over France.

● **Cour Saint-Etienne**   COM

33, rue Saint-Etienne.
Tel. 03 86 36 74 57. Fax 03 86 61 14 95.
restaurantlacour@wanadoo.fr
Closed Mon., Tue., 1 week beg. Feb.,
3 weeks Aug.
Prix fixe: 20€, 30€, 10€ (child).

The dynamic Jean-Claude Larrivée has taken over this neat restaurant with its terrace and view of the Church of Saint-Etienne, where he prepares a staunchly flavorsome, generous cuisine. There is no à la carte choice, only selected set menus. Langoustines with a tomato basil sauce, turbot with beurre blanc, quail and foie gras tourte or rhubarb honey crumble with red berry sauce are competent enough.

● **Le Morvan**   COM

28, rue du Petit-Mouësse.
Tel. 03 86 61 14 16. Fax 03 86 61 81 00.
Closed Sun. dinner.
Prix fixe: 13€, 17€, 26€, 30€, 45€,
11€ (child), 45€.

Lionel Lorrain has taken over this contemporary restaurant in green and orange tones with its winter garden, frescos and paintings showing scenes of the Morvan region. On the menu, the jumbo shrimp salad with pink grapefruit, bouillabaisse-style fish stew served with croutons and rouille, sage-seasoned magret de canard with Port wine sauce and the mandarin orange sorbet with a financier are very well-prepared.

● **L'Assiette**   🅽SIM

7 bis, rue Ferdinand-Gambon.
Tel.-Fax 03 86 36 24 99.
Closed Sun., dinner (exc. Fri., Sat.).
Prix fixe: 23€, 28€.

Nadège Pélissou, Florent Passard and Eric Nobécourt run this restaurant with its refined, charming décor. The assorted set menus featuring Tatin-style liver tart, turmeric-seasoned crayfish cassolette, pan-seared scallops, magret de canard and the crispy mascarpone and chocolate chip pastry, all meticulously prepared.

In Challuy (58000). 3 km s via N7.

● **La Gabare**   COM

171, rte de Lyon.
Tel. 03 86 37 54 23. Fax 03 86 37 64 49.
restaurant@lagabare.fr
Closed Sun. dinner, 1 week at end July,
2 weeks beg. Aug.
Prix fixe: 18€ (weekdays), 26€, 40€,
10€ (child). A la carte: 40€.

As well as a terrace, this former farm has two rustic dining rooms with exposed beams, sand-colored walls and a large fireplace. There, Dominique Dany offers a new, light take on Nevers classics at accessible prices. The oven-crisped pork trotters with foie gras, skate terrine with herbs, Atlantic sea bass in olive oil emulsion, veal sweetbreads with morels and the cherry jubilee are fine preparations indeed.

In Magny-Cours (58470). 12 km s via N7.

● **La Renaissance**   ◯🏠

2, rue de Paris.
Tel. 03 86 58 10 40. Fax 03 86 21 22 60.
www.hotel-la-renaissance.fr
Rest. closed Sat. lunch, Sun. dinner, Mon.,
Feb., 2 weeks Aug.
6 rooms: 84–92€. 3 suites: 107–153€.
Prix fixe: 35€, 40€, 70€, 85€.

Jean-Claude Dray welcomes guests with a bright smile, confident of the charm displayed by his former coaching inn converted into an elegant domestic establishment with classically furnished rooms in various styles. However, it is mainly his shrewd dishes combined in gourmet set menus that draw the crowds. On the Morvan sandstone terrace or in the elegant dining room with its beige and burgundy toned classicism, guests delight in pan-tossed spicy langoustines served on green apple, the sole meunière, seared rump steak with a Sancerre reduction sauce and the dessert cart.

NICE

06000 Alpes-Maritimes. Paris 930 – Cannes 33 – Marseille 190 – Gênes 199 – Lyon 472. info@nicetourisme.com.

With its stucco and luxury hotels, Nice still holds all the charm of a Belle Epoque metropolis. We muse on its past as an Italian city as we wander down the alleys that lead to the cours Saleya. Each morning, an exuberant, colorful flower market enlivens this esplanade close to the sea. We enjoy hot socca at the loquacious, stentorian Theresa's stall, then inspect the fresh vegetables and the day's catch. In the rue Droite and rue Sainte-Réparate, the stores have a retro charm and the facades of the houses are red, as in neighboring Liguria. The Palais Lascaris in the Genoese style, with its painted ceilings, post-Renaissance stairs and facade with marble balconies set on consoles garnished with grimacing masks, is one of the city's greatest symbols. So is Nice French? In any case, it is exotic and flavorsome. Its select, chic, deceptively casual restaurants and tasteful trattorias still have their local accent.

■ | HOTELS

■ Negresco

37, promenade des Anglais.
Tel. 04 93 16 64 00. Fax 04 93 88 35 68.
direction@hotel-negresco.com
www.hotel-negresco-nice.com
145 rooms: 315–525€. 5 suites: 670–800€.
Half board: 343–577€.

This 1912 vintage hotel-museum features an eclectic collection of art and makes a virtue of immoderation. The glass dome designed by Eiffel, rococo rotunda, carousel-style brasserie (La Rotonde), uniformed staff, luxury rooms and suites where four centuries converge, gym, meeting rooms and Chantecler restaurant make this a legendary haunt indeed. Under the supervision of Jeanne Augier and management of Nicole Spitz, it is as ever a fabled luxury hotel of vivid charm. (See Restaurants.)

■ Beau Rivage

24, rue Saint-François-de-Paule.
Tel. 04 92 47 82 82. Fax 04 92 47 82 83.
info@nicebeaurivage.com
www.nicebeaurivage.com
107 rooms: 180–350€. 11 suites: 310–640€.
A la carte: 50€.

Close by the old town and cours Saleya, this hotel refurbished in contemporary style by Jean-Michel Wilmotte was frequented by Matisse, Nietzsche and Chekhov. Now, it is enjoying a second youth under Antoine Attia. Its large rooms decorated in the colors of Provence and its private beach are persuasive arguments indeed. The designer restaurant has a catering service in line with the changing seasons.

■ Elysée Palace

59, promenade des Anglais.
Tel. 04 93 97 90 90. Fax 04 93 44 50 40.
restauration@elyseepalace.com
www.elyseepalace.com
143 rooms: 200–330€.
22 suites: 330–660€.
Prix fixe: 19€ (lunch), 29€ (lunch),
13€ (child).

This architecturally futuristic establishment displays a reliable charm with its Sosno sculptures, roof pool, terrace overlooking the city and rooms and suites renovated in various tones. Its restaurant is of the same standard, serving dishes with a modern flavor: a lobe of duck foie gras, sea bass pan-tossed with Menton lemons, veal medallion with sweet green peas and pink peppercorn panna cotta.

■ Le Méridien Nice

1, promenade des Anglais.
Tel. 04 97 03 44 44. Fax 04 97 03 44 46.
mail@lemeridien-nice.com
www.lemeridien-nice.com
20 suites: 235–560€.

This contemporary central hotel on the seafront is striking indeed with its renovated rooms furnished in a Mediterranean style. Its swimming pool and eatery on the panoramic roof, gym, beauty salon, hi-tech meeting rooms, neocolonial restaurant and cocktail bar are all significant assets.

■ Palais Maeterlinck

30, bd Maurice-Maeterlinck.
Tel. 04 92 00 72 00. Fax 04 92 04 18 10.
info@palais-maeterlinck.com
www.palais-maeterlinck.com
12 rooms: 345–480€.
28 suites: 620–3000€.
Prix fixe: 45€, 75€, 26€ (child).

On the lower corniche road, Maurice Maeterlinck's former villa overlooks the sea. The neo-baroque decoration, colorful rooms and swimming pool adjoining the garden set the tone. In the Mélisande—the Venetian-style restaurant with its collection of orientalist paintings—the slow-cooked eggplant, Mediterranean sea bass filet with stuffed pasta shells, lamb saddle in pain d'épice with ceps and orange ravioli with Grand Marnier butter sauce make an excellent impression.

■ Le Palais de la Méditerranée

15, promenade des Anglais.
Tel. 04 92 14 77 00. Fax 04 92 14 77 27.
bfontaine@concorde-hotels.com
www.lepalaisdelamediterranee.com
188 rooms: 280–830€.
12 suites: 1100–2500
Half board: 355–901€.

Behind the preserved, majestic art deco facade overlooking the sea are a brand new casino and an extremely elegant modern hotel that boasts rooms furnished in contemporary style, sunny suites overlooking the baie des Anges, a fitness center and the Pingala Bar. The Padouk restaurant serves refined dishes.

■ HI

3, av des Fleurs.
Tel. 04 97 07 26 26. Fax 04 97 07 26 27.
hi@hi-hotel.net / www.hi-hotel.net
38 rooms: 210–395€. 1 suite: 680€.

A step away from the sea, this thirties building is home to a stylish hotel designed by Matali Crasset. Its entertaining features and poetic rooms with their colored furniture delight the chic, urban clientele. The fitness center, steam bath, Jacuzzi, swimming pool, modern bar and organic meals for guests also promise a variety of pleasures.

■ Masséna

58, rue Gioffredo.
Tel. 04 92 47 88 88. Fax 04 92 47 88 89.
info@hotel-massena-nice.com
www.hotel-massena-nice.com
111 rooms: 125–160€.
17 suites: 160–265€.

Although it is in the heart of the city between new Nice and the old town, this cheerful, welcoming hotel has a very Provençal fragrance. Belle Epoque in style, this 100-year-old establishment offers a variety of attractive rooms, each with its own charm.

■ West End

31, promenade des Anglais.
Tel. 04 92 14 44 00. Fax 04 93 88 85 07.
hotel-westend@hotel-westend.com
www.hotel-westend.com
110 rooms: 235–600€. 10 suites: 690€.
Prix fixe: 29€, 42€, 14€ (child).

Behind its Riviera facade, this registered hotel conceals comfortable rooms refurbished in various styles with Belle Epoque furniture and a chic restaurant in theatrical red: the Siècle. A pot of gray snails in garlic cream, langouste tagliatelle, Mediterranean sea bass in a vegetable broth or crêpes Suzette flambéed at the table closely reflect the classical tone of the establishment.

■ Grimaldi

15, rue Grimaldi.
Tel.-Fax 04 93 16 00 24.
zedde@le-grimaldi.com / www.le-grimaldi.com
46 rooms: 80–190€. 2 suites: 165–230€.

In the heart of a shopping district, this modern hotel offers visitors a warm welcome from Johanna and Yann Zedde, a very cozy lobby, bar and lounge area, rooms in Provençal tints and small terraces on the top floor.

■ Windsor

11, rue Dalpozzo.
Tel. 04 93 88 59 35. Fax 04 93 88 94 57.
www.hotelwindsornice.com
57 rooms: 85–165€.
Half board: 118–231€.

Surrounded by a garden, this hotel—freely decorated by contemporary artists—provides amusing rooms in an eclectic style, a pool and a relaxation center. The bar serves light dishes in summer among the palm trees and bougainvillea.

●   RESTAURANTS

● Le Chantecler   LUX

At the Negresco, 37, promenade des Anglais.
Tel. 04 93 16 64 00. Fax 04 93 88 35 68.
www.hotel-negresco-nice.com
Closed Mon., Tue., beg. Jan.–beg. Feb.
Prix fixe: 45€, 90€, 130€.

When we speak of the sea at Nice, how could we fail to mention the Chantecler, especially now the chef is named Bruno Turbot? This aptly named technician scored a success at the Paris Sofitel before opting for a chance to work with more coastal flavors. In an elegant Regency dining room with Venetian paneling and sumptuous Aubusson tapestries, we savor his shrewd dishes. The pressed red mullet with sundried tomatoes, artichoke hearts with arugula jus, grilled filet

of John Dory with creamy risotto and preserved Menton lemons, Mediterranean sea bass stuffed with coriander-seasoned artichokes and peppers and finally the langoustines steamed in the shell with morels and parsley velouté show that Bruno Turbot has become a full-time Niçois. Efficient service supervised by the meticulous Fréderic Mutter.

● Keisuke Matsushima

22 ter, rue de France / pl Croix-de-Marbre.
Tel. 04 93 82 26 06. Fax 04 93 16 81 02.
info@keisukematsushima.com
Closed Sun., Mon.
Prix fixe: 28€ (lunch), 35€ (lunch),
75€ (dinner), 90€ (dinner).
A la carte: 90–100€.

Ensnared by Gallic gastronomy, Keisuke Matsushima has fallen in love with France. After working for the Pourcels in Montpellier, Marcon in Saint-Bonnet-le-Froid and Banzo in Aix, "Kei" opened his restaurant right in the heart of Nice. In its tiny dining room, guests admired and savored glamorized, appetizing dishes based on a spicy Mediterranean approach and featured on a menu that changed weekly. Victim of his own success, unable to push back the walls, he overcame the urge to head up to Paris, and was then lucky enough to find neighboring premises that enabled him to expand. Staunchly modern, with light wood panels (some of them decorated with foliage in a style reminiscent of Japanese interiors), the new dining room showcases his cuisine and well-trained staff. Sébastien Gibert is master of the cellar, guiding guests towards the wine that will best accompany each remarkable dish, including rosemary-seasoned local squid brochette with a Provençal fried chickpea cake (panisse), slow-roasted Mediterranean sea bass with potato gnocchi with basil, braised beef cheek, sucrine lettuce heart with parmesan and the caramelized quince and pain d'épice mille-feuille with fresh fromage blanc sorbet. Great French art refined in the Japanese manner!

● L'Ane Rouge

7, quai des Deux-Emmanuel.
Tel. 04 93 89 49 63. Fax 04 93 26 51 42.
anerouge@free.fr
www.anerougenice.com
Closed Wed., Thu. dinner, Feb.
Prix fixe: 26€ (lunch), 48€ (dinner), 68€
(dinner). A la carte: 75€.

Located on the old harbor opposite the Château, this gourmet institution is enjoying a second youth. Under the guidance of Michel Devillers, the dining room, redesigned in contemporary style, is a meeting place for connoisseurs of niçoise cuisine with a modern flavor. The highly attractive changing fare includes braised John Dory with pissala (niçoise salt-fish paste), roasted lobster over a stuffed pig's food and a spiced wine reduction, Mediterranean sea bass seared on one side and finished under the broiler with artichokes. The pleasure continues at the end of the meal with the pear poached in red wine and the chocolate mousse. On the cellar side, the wines selected by Lionel Compan provide a wealth of choice.

● Jouni

"La Réserve de Nice"
60, bd Franck-Pilatte.
Tel.-Fax 04 97 08 14 80.
contact@jouni.fr / www.jouni.fr
Closed Sun. (exc. off season),
Mon. (exc. off season), 3 weeks Dec. Jan.
Prix fixe: 100€. A la carte: 85€ – 90€.

Jouni and his associate Giuseppe have moved their "Taste Workshop" into a fine art deco building near the harbor. The light reflected in its mirrors echoes the glint of the Mediterranean. A breath of elegance runs through the premises, with its patinated wood, stone, scraped walls and period furniture in pastel and light ochre tones. The captain of the vessel, Jouni Tormanen, is Finnish, but his masters have more Southern leanings: Le Stanc at the Negresco, Ducasse in Paris and Monaco and Ferran Adria at El Bulli. A talented, exemplary student, Jouni skillfully applies lessons learned in the pursuit of a lively, agile, noble Provençal cuisine.

Lobster salad with ceps, Imperial-style Corsican fish, beef tenderloin and soft chocolate tarts display such precision that any hint of chance can be ruled out. Yannick Mehat, wine expert, will find the proper red or white, Spanish or Italian pearl to grace your glass. Jouni's store, "L'Atelier du Goût" (The Taste Workshop) has opened its doors at 8, rue Lascaris. The private smoking room is a haven for those ensnared by the lure of tobacco.

● Don Camillo

5, rue des Ponchettes.
Tel.-Fax 04 93 85 67 95.
doncamillo.creations@cegetel.net
Closed Sun.
Prix fixe: 36€, 48€, 19€ (lunch),
24€ (lunch).

Change has come to the this former fifties haunt, renovated in contemporary style with gray walls and paintings in cheerful colors, previously run by Stéphane Viano and Franck Cerrutti. Marc Laville, who worked in Saint-Barth, has taken over with enthusiasm, running the place in partnership with Christophe Louche, Issautier's erstwhile lieutenant. The tempting set menu has an appealing fusion style. Oven-crisped truffle risotto, bagna cauda–style stuffed squid, oven-crisped crab with broad beans, prepared like a paella, jumbo shrimp, chorizo and chicken wings and the jasmine and hazelnut duckling filet, with crisp duck confit and date-filled samosa, invite us on a sedentary journey. Veal kidney in red wine mustard with a bacon, potato and goat cheese cake and a pan toss of ceps offers a fine, classical excursion. At dessert, we fall for home-style baked apples with Carambar candy and pain d'épice pain perdu with green apple emulsion that conjures up our childhood.

● La Petite Maison

11, rue Saint-François-de-Paule.
Tel. 04 93 92 59 59. Fax 04 93 92 28 51.
Closed Sun.
A la carte: 47–66€.

Just a step away from the Promenade des Anglais and Old Nice, the Petite Maison is—let's make no bones about it—a great restaurant! In this inordinately charming corner eatery, Nicole Ruby serves authentic niçoise and Mediterranean specialties. Under the pictures by local painters, guests enjoy the open, friendly, warm, refined atmosphere. The Petite Maison is a meeting place for a number of connoisseurs and celebrities who come to savor the fried zucchini flowers, purple artichoke salad with local anchovy spread, various dishes based on the truffle (in scrambled eggs, macaroni, risotto), pan-simmered or oven-roasted fresh Mediterranean sea bass "done like we like it", whole farm-raised chicken stuffed with foie gras (for two) and dark chocolate mousse with mint sorbet. This generous, delightful cuisine is based on fine produce and dedication and prepared with a master's touch. Accompanied by chosen vintages, it is served by Cécile, the daughter of the house.

● **L'Univers**   ◎COM

54, bd J.-Jaurès.
Tel. 04 93 62 32 22. Fax 04 93 62 55 69.
plumailunivers@aol.com
www.christian-plumail.com
Closed Sat. lunch, Sun., Mon. lunch.
Prix fixe: 20€, 42€, 70€.
A la carte: 65–71€.

In the heart of the city, Christian Plumail artfully prepares dishes that offer a very personal take on Nice's heritage. His market-based cuisine is primarily concerned with quality of produce and suitability of taste. The décor of this former brasserie is tastefully simple and the food displays all the charm of its perfectly mastered, candid Mediterranean and Provençal flavors. Both the set options and the menu will gratify food lovers with squid cannelloni with a salad of young shell beans and artichokes, pan-fried rock mullet with accompanying pot of purple artichokes and Italian broccoli, veal cutlet pan-fried with young shell beans and a soufflé of local lemons accompanied by a fruit compote seasoned with star anise. No pretension, just appealing sincerity and service to match.

● **Stéphane Viano**   ◐COM

26, av Victor-Hugo.
Tel. 04 93 82 48 63.
Closed Sun.
Prix fixe: 22€ (lunch), 42€, 62€.

We met him before at the Don Camillo in the rue des Ponchettes. Stéphane Viano, who trained at the Nice Hotel School and went on to the Réserve de Beaulieu, the Massoury in Villefranche and the Relais Saint-Jean in Aspremont, has moved into this cheerful establishment in a sunny building. Pastis-flambéed shrimp or wild Mediterranean sea bass along with a pot of simmered vegetables are classic but highly conscientious preparations. The house specialty? The lunchtime blackboard at 22, offering the freshest market produce daily. The other day at noon, a poached egg salad with tagliatelli and carrots, drum fish filet with rice and zucchini and the chocolate zabaglione presented in a stem glass looked particularly appealing. The little Méguières *rosé* at 19,50 slips down effortlessly.

● **L'Allegro**   COM

4, pl Guynemer.
Tel. 04 93 56 62 06. Fax 04 93 56 38 28.
Closed Sat. lunch, Sun., Aug.
Prix fixe: 18,30€ (weekday lunch), 22,90€ (weekday lunch), 27,50€ (weekday lunch), 30,50€ (weekday lunch), 35€ (dinner), 40€ (dinner), 53€ (dinner), 35€ (dinner), 40€ (dinner), 53€ (dinner). A la carte: 50€.

Jean-Pierre Skrlj and Olivier Bloise are the new duo in charge of this restaurant with its trompe-l'oeil décor, frescos showing characters from the Commedia dell'Arte and pleasant terrace. Diners here savor the fresh Mediterranean cuisine, even if they sometimes miss the more trans-alpine manner of the predecessor, Dante Cortese. The Piedmont-style polenta, grilled rockfish, the rack of lamb with herbs and garlic in its jus and the tiramisu are not bad.

● **Aphrodite**   COM

10, bd Dubouchage.
Tel. 04 93 85 63 53. Fax 04 93 80 10 41.

reception@restaurant-aphrodite.com
www.restaurant-aphrodite.com
Closed Sun., Mon., 3 weeks Jan.
Prix fixe: 23€ (weekday lunch), 35€,
19€ (child). A la carte: 65–70€.

David Faure's studied, light preparations gently revamp regional classics.
In the dining room in Southern shades,
where the antique rubs shoulders with
the modern, local-style stuffed anchovies, lobster in garlic, butter and parsley, octopus, lamb rump roast and the
orchard fruit marmalade and vanilla ice
cream show no lack of precision or personality. You can trust Franck Russo to
recommend the right Provençal wine.

● Brasserie Flo   COM

2/4, rue Sacha-Guitry.
Tel. 04 93 13 38 38. Fax 04 93 13 38 39.
nbourdon@groupeflo.fr / www.flonice.com
Prix fixe: 14,90€ (weekday lunch), 22,50€,
29,50€. A la carte: 50–55€.

This Bordeaux brasserie in a thirties theatre has plenty of chic. The cuisine by
Michel Betis takes its share of liberties
with the usual Flo style. The bresaola
(cured beef) carpaccio, whole royal snapper flavored with tastes from the region,
pan-seared foie gras escalope with apple
tart and the brioche pain perdu with milk
caramel are long on character.

● Coco Beach   COM

2, av Jean-Lorrain.
Tel. 04 93 89 39 26. Fax 04 92 04 02 39.
cocobeach@cocobeach.fr
Closed Sun., Mon. (exc. July–Aug.),
mid-Feb.–mid-Mar.
Prix fixe: 39€ (lunch), 45€ (lunch).
A la carte: 58€.

This hut perched on the heights and overlooking the sea offers a taste of paradise.
The Quirino-Cauvin family's warm welcome, the view of Nice and Pierre Quiri-
no's unfailingly fresh seafood cuisine are
pure delights. Mussels "Coco", fish soup,
grilled catch of the day and the Grand
Marnier soufflé or house-made tart slip
down effortlessly.

● Les Viviers   COM

22, rue Alphonse-Karr.
Tel. 04 93 16 00 48. Fax 04 93 16 04 06.
viviers.bretons@wanadoo.fr
www.les-viviers-nice.fr
Closed Sat. lunch, Sun., 1 week at end July,
3 weeks Aug.
Prix fixe: 35€, 55€, 69€, 12€ (child).
A la carte: 55–60€.

Jacques Rolancy, who received the Meilleur Ouvrier de France award in 1996 (the
same year as Philippe Legendre of the V),
has enthusiastically taken over this twin
establishment devoted to the sea: on one
side, the restaurant; on the other, the bistro. In both cases, we enjoy excellent food
under the supervision of this true professional, who worked in Paris at Laurent,
Robuchon and Taillevent, as well as with
Chapel in Mionnay and at the Auberge
des Templiers in Les Bézards. Returning to more modest endeavors, he now
runs the dining room, takes the orders,
replaces chef David Vaqué at the stove
and conscientiously supervises the fare in
both versions of his Viviers. Pan-fried langoustines and Charolais beef ravioli with
emulsioned jus, layered meat and potato
casserole and the pan-tossed leeks and
red mullet with roasted fennel are proof
that Jacques Rolancy, his eye on everything, has a brilliant grasp of both land
and sea produce.

● Terre de Truffes   SIM

11, rue Saint-François-de-Paule.
Tel. 04 93 62 07 68. Fax 04 93 62 44 83.
www.terredetruffes.com
Closed Sun. dinner, Mon.
Prix fixe: 40€ (lunch). A la carte: 80–85€.

The place has changed hands, but the
spirit remains in this old-fashioned,
paneled bistro and delicatessen devoted
to the truffle, the "black diamond". Duck
foie gras with Brumale truffles, poached
egg with Albuféra sauce, beef filet
Rossini, milk-fed shoulder of lamb and
the soft-centered dark chocolate cake do
their jobs very well.

● **La Merenda** ◯ SIM

4, rue Raoul-Bosio (formerly rue de la Terrasse).
No tel.
Closed Sat., Sun., 1 week Feb.
A la carte: 30–40€.

The rue de la Terrasse has become the rue Raoul Bosio and, unnoticed by its regulars, Nice's most famous exclusive restaurant has changed its address. Aside from that, in these unexceptional surroundings—beaded curtain entrance, close-set tables, stools and open kitchen—Dominique and Danièle Le Stanc continue to delight their guests with pepper tart, fried zucchini flowers, pasta with pesto, stuffed sardines and niçoise-style tripe, all displaying a direct integrity and divine delicacy. The wine list is now worth a look and the direct pressing Château des Crostes *rosé* is a marvel.

● **La Maison de Marie** SIM

5, rue Masséna.
Tel. 04 93 82 15 93. Fax 04 93 88 20 93.
lamaisondemarie@wanadoo.fr
www.lamaisondemarie.com
Closed Christmas.
Prix fixe: 19€, 10€ (child). A la carte: 45€.

Elegant and peaceful, Jean-Paul Villa and Jocelyne Lambalot's eatery is located on the edge of the pedestrian zone. In the kitchen, Alain Rous has added flavorsome sweet and savory recipes to the house's famous dishes, such as the beef stew or Marie's assorted grilled fish dish (parillade), duck foie gras terrine with papaya chutney, Mediterranean sea bass with slow-cooked fennel with orange and the magret de canard seasoned with blackcurrants. On the dessert side, a soft chocolate cake is served with refreshing mandarin orange ice cream. Regional French and Italian wines crown this refined feast.

● **La Zucca Magica** SIM

4 bis, quai Papacino.
Tel. 04 93 56 25 27. Fax 04 93 56 59 76.
www.lazuccamagica.com
Closed Sun., Mon.
Prix fixe: 17€, 27€,
Children under 12: free.

Because vegetables play an important part in Italian cuisine, Marco Folicaldi, a Roman at heart, prepares them in many different ways in his pumpkin-themed eatery. Included on set menus at reasonable prices, gazpacho with yogurt, vegetables and aromatic herbs, lemon-seasoned eggplant and arugula cake, stuffed tomatoes with a side of spaghetti with olives, mozzarella and oregano and the peach soup and Amaretto ice cream are wonderfully colorful dishes. The Ligurian wines are shrewdly chosen.

● **Boni** N SIM

21, rue Barla.
Tel. 04 93 56 35 39.
Closed Sun., Mon.
A la carte: 35€.

Paolo Bonizzoni and his brother Stefano have turned a commonplace bistro into a trattoria worthy of the Rialto. Paolo, the designer, chooses produce in Ventimiglia and offers an enthusiastic welcome, while Stefano, formerly with the RAI, presides at the stove. Plexiglas chairs, interior awnings and white walls, one of them decorated with a tabletop complete with plates and cutlery: the scene is set. Fresh grilled squid, an artichoke salad with parmesan, oven-warmed Piedmont cheese, honey and pine nuts or the Tuscan soup with chickpeas and bacon are representative of the starters. Fried rougets with mixed salad and tomatoes, breaded and fried sardines, mixed salad with potatoes and the tagliatelle with artichokes and parmesan are fine achievements. Desserts are very much a part of the occasion: homemade tiramisu, panna cotta and crème brûlée. We should also point out that the Réserve de Boni, a delicatessen and *table d'hôte*, is just opposite at No. 16.

● **Karr** N SIM

10, rue Alphonse Karr.
Tel. 04 93 82 18 31.
Closed Sun.
Prix fixe: 15€ (lunch). A la carte: 40€.

Welcoming, lively and stylish, Albert Benaïm's contemporary café in black and white is looking good. Patrons enjoy the up-to-the-minute dishes conscientiously prepared by Breton Patrick Gouiller: fish tartare with herbs, goat cheese in crunchy pastry crust with honey and almonds, big pan-fried shrimp brochettes with rosemary and the calf's liver cooked English style. Fish (Mediterranean sea bass, snapper, goatfish, John Dory) are presented according to the catch and cooked to order, grilled or pan-fried, accompanied by a saffron risotto. Crêpes Suzette and the thin apple tart slip down effortlessly.

● Le Grand Balcon   SIM
10, rue Saint-François-de-Paule.
Tel. 04 93 62 60 74. Fax 04 93 62 44 58.
legrandbalcon@wanadoo.fr -
www.legrandbalcon.com
Closed Sat. lunch, Sun. lunch.
Prix fixe: 25€ (lunch). A la carte: 55€.

At Carine and Marcel Marot's restaurant, the Mediterranean in its broadest sense unfolds in a series of sun-drenched, precise preparations. Accompanied by an Italian or California wine, salad with parmesan shavings, warm red mullet salad on eggplant spread, Mediterranean sea bass fricasée with purple artichokes, lamb shank cooked Middle Eastern style with orange preserves and the passion fruit macaron with dark chocolate ice cream titillate the taste buds.

● Lou Pistou   SIM
4, rue Raoul-Bosio (old rue de la Terrasse).
Tel. 04 93 62 21 82.
Closed Sat., Sun. Bank holidays,
1 Nov.–13 Nov.
A la carte: 35€.

Michel Vergnaud serves the essence of Nice on your plate with a smile as he presides over this unassuming canteen in yellow next to the law courts. Breaded and fried zucchini flowers, Mediterranean sea bass cannelloni, wild snapper in papilotte, tripe niçoise and the chocolate profiteroles are free of frills.

● Nissa-Socca   SIM
7, rue Sainte-Réparate.
Tel. 04 93 80 18 35.
Closed Sun., Thu. lunch, 11 Nov.–11 Dec.
Prix fixe: 12,50€ (lunch), 15€, 17,50€,
24€. A la carte: 30–35€.

In the heart of the old town, Fabrice Lemere runs this *bouchon*-style restaurant with its black and white photos of Nice in the old days. The dishes are highly classical: plate of niçoise specialties, grilled peppers, Brousse (fresh local goat cheese), stuffed ravioli, veal escalope with tarragon-seasoned vinegar and white wine sauce and the tiramisu slip down easily.

● Oliviera   SIM
8 bis, rue du Collet.
Tel.-Fax 04 93 13 06 45.
nb@oliviera.com / www.oliviera.com
Closed Sun. dinner, Mon. dinner.
A la carte: 45€.

Nadim Beyrouti presides energetically over his pale green dining room, touting the benefits of the Mediterranean's finest oils, which enhance his tasteful Southern dishes. We enjoy the feuilleté in the style of Crete, aubergine with olives, fish tartare, the house rabbit dish and the tiramisu, which leave very little room for complaint.

● La Part des Anges   SIM
17, rue Gubernatis.
Tel. 04 93 62 69 80. Fax 04 93 54 76 04.
part.des.anges@wanadoo.fr
Closed Sun., 2 weeks Dec., 1 week at end Aug.
A la carte: 35€.

This wine bar in off-white tones and wood is supervised with gusto by Olivier Labarde. The menu, which changes with the seasons, combines mischievous beverages and shrewd dishes. The avocado with crayfish tails, smoked quail salad with parmesan, rare tuna steak or pantossed zucchini with crayfish tails, the black Bigorre pork ribs in a caramelized honey sauce, the vanilla panna cotta and the raspberry and fruit mousse are all by Julien Besson this year.

● Sapore [SIM]

19, rue Bonaparte / Pl du Pin.
Tel.-Fax 04 92 04 22 09.
www.caveaumorakopf.fr
Closed lunch, Sun., Mon., Christmas–New
Year's, 3 weeks Aug.
Prix fixe: 28€ (weekday dinner).
A la carte: 20€.

This contemporary bistro run by Anthony
Riou is a delightful surprise. In his modern dining room in gray and burgundy
shades, the former Le Stanc pastry cook at
the Negresco delights his guests with fresh
tapas at unobjectionable prices. Complemented by Spanish wines, the artichoke
bruschetta, swordfish cannelloni, hand-
chopped beef tartare and the warm soft
chocolate cake are well-conceived.

● La Table Alziari [SIM]

4, rue François-Zanin.
Tel. 04 93 80 34 03.
Closed Sun., Mon., 2 weeks beg. Oct.,
2 weeks Dec., 10 days Jan., 1 week beg. June.
A la carte: 35€.

Anne-Marie and André Alziari's enchanting establishment stands on a small hillside
street in old Nice. It boasts a Provençal-
style dining room, paintings on yellow
walls, a few places outside, bottles of Alziari olive oil on the tables, a short menu on
the blackboard, produce from Nice's cours
Saleya market and dishes with delightful
local flavors by Anne-Marie and Michel.
Stuffed sardines, niçoise cod, a regional
specialty of meat rolls called "alouettes
sans tête", and a soft-centered chocolate
cake are washed down with a glass of Châ-
teau-la-Coste.

● Vin sur Vin [SIM]

18 bis, rue Biscarra.
Tel. 04 93 92 93 20. Fax 04 93 92 25 20.
vinsurvin00@aol.com
Closed Sun., Bank holidays, Christmas,
New Year's.
A la carte: 40€.

When he is not working on his cheese
brand Baud et Millet, Franck Caramel
looks after visitors to his *bouchon*-style

restaurant in wine colored tones. He suggests they choose a bottle, shows them
to their table in the dining room and—
according to the dictates of Cédric Calderone's changing menu—serves them
mille-feuille with eggplant and ricotta,
roasted Mediterranean sea bass with virgin olive oil, pan-fried sirloin steak with
fresh fries and the soft chocolate cake,
accompanied by wines from a list of 200
with descriptions by Jacques Marozny.

In Falicon (06950). 9 km sw via D114.

● Parcours ○[SIM]

1, pl Marcel-Eusebi.
Tel. 04 93 84 94 57. Fax 04 93 98 66 90.
jmdparcourslive@rivieramail.com
www.parcourssliverestaurant.com
Closed lunch, Mon., Tue., 2 weeks beg. Jan.,
1 week beg. Sept.
Prix fixe: 37€, 38€ (wine inc.), 52€,
20€ (child).

The place is modern, the interior chocolate, off-white and yellow. You will under-
standably find your mouth watering as
plasma screens show your food being prepared in real time. Annie and Jean-Marc
Delacourt run the Parcours with great
enthusiasm. The menu matches the surroundings: the thin parmesan shortcake,
house-preserved eggplant and simply-
served anchovies, grilled snapper filet,
thick-cut sirloin steak with slow-cooked
potatoes and lettuce hearts served with
jus, the fruit minestrone with slow-cooked
fennel and the lemon cream with mango
and licorice sorbet are enchanting. Jean-
Marc Delacourt, who presided at the Ritz
in Paris, the Terrasses in Divonne and the
Chèvre d'Or in Eze, has found a restaurant
to suit his chef's whites and ideas.

NIEDERBRONN-LES-BAINS

67110 Bas-Rhin. Paris 451 – Saverne 39 –
Strasbourg 54 – Haguenau 22.
office@niederbronn.com.
The "Marienbad of Alsace" offers thermal
baths, pure springs and the delicious air of
the Northern Vosges mountains. Congeniality,
flowers and the fresh waters of the Steinbach
set the scene in this restful halt.

HOTELS-RESTAURANTS

■ Mercure Grand Hôtel &⚘🏨
16, av Foch.
Tel. 03 88 80 84 48. Fax 03 88 80 84 40.
H5548@accor-hotels.com / www.mercure.com
59 rooms: 75–95€. 4 suites: 114–130€.
Half board: 93–131€.

The fifties charm is a thing of the past:
this hotel now conforms to the chain's
codes: a professional reception, modern
rooms and suites and tennis courts.

■ Muller 🏨
16, av de la Libération.
Tel. 03 88 63 38 38. Fax 03 88 63 38 39.
hotel.muller@wanadoo.fr
www.hotelmuller.com
Closed 3 weeks Jan.
Rest. closed Sun. dinner, Mon.
43 rooms: 47–68,50€.
Prix fixe: 9,50€ (weekday lunch), 8€ (child).

This good, classical hotel appeals with
its woodwork, beige tones, warm welcome, swimming pool, fitness center
and spacious rooms. In a dining room
with veranda, we savor the escalope of
goose foie gras with apricot pain perdu,
house-smoked salmon, pike-perch with
sorrel, medallions of venison and frozen
kouglof.

■ Cully 🏨
35, rue de la République.
Tel. 03 88 09 01 42. Fax 03 88 09 05 80.
hotel-cully@wanadoo.fr / www.hotel-cully.fr
Rest. closed Sun. dinner, Mon., Feb. vac.
33 rooms: 46–65€. 2 suites: 65€.
Prix fixe: 11€ (weekday lunch), 20€, 30€,
8€ (child).

Located in a busy street, this hotel
housed in two buildings has an antique
charm. The rooms are simple and neat,
and offer a range of styles and colors. In
the paneled dining room, Daniel Cully
prepares an improvised regional cuisine. House goose foie gras, smoked
ham, fresh poached trout "au bleu", the
vineyard-keeper's guinea hen (wrapped

in grape leaves) and an iced vacherin
(a meringue and nougat dessert) are
shrewdly crafted.

■ Bristol 🗄
4, pl de l'Hôtel-de-Ville.
Tel. 03 88 09 61 44. Fax 03 88 09 01 20.
hotel.lebristol@wanadoo.fr
www.lebristol.com
Closed 2 weeks Nov., mid-Jan.–beg. Feb.
27 rooms: 45–80€. 2 suites: 70–90€.
Prix fixe: 9€ (weekday lunch), 15€ (weekday lunch), 20€ (lunch), 25€ (dinner), 8€
(child).

This year, Claude Foeller has opened
five new rooms in addition to the hotel's
older, efficiently soundproofed accommodation. Equipped with wooden furnishings, they offer an easy charm. In
the bright, beige-tinted dining room, we
savor Claude Foeller's cuisine. The dozen
escargots prepared in the style of Alsace
(stuffed with spiced butter and herbs and
cooked in local wine), vegetable-stuffed
pike-perch, lamb chops with rosemary
and honey and a frozen kouglof with
sauce are very honest.

● La Villa du Parc `V.COM`
Au Casino, 10, pl des Thermes.
Tel. 03 88 80 84 88. Fax 03 88 80 84 86.
www.casinodeniederbronn.com/events
Closed Christmas.
Prix fixe: 20€ (weekday dinner),
25€ (weekday dinner). A la carte: 42€.

The casino's two restaurants provide
different options. The first serves exotic
dishes in neocolonial surroundings,
while the second offers a chance to sample regional recipes in a *bierstub* atmosphere. Clear consommé sprinkled with
coriander, a jumbo shrimp and vegetable stir fry, Mexican-style beef tenderloin with peppers and guacamole and
the Guauaquil chocolate truffle with
milk caramel ice cream offer an entertaining range of exotic flavors.

67280 Bas-Rhin. Paris 479 – Saverne 32 –
Strasbourg 39.
With the Gothic church and its 135-foot spire, the
Grand Ringelsberg crowning the village nearby
and the Nideck ruins that inspired Chamisso, a
rich tapestry lies at the end of the street.

 HOTELS-RESTAURANTS

■ La Pomme d'Or

36, rue Principale.
Tel. 03 88 50 90 21. Fax 03 88 50 95 17.
lapommeniederh@wanadoo.fr
http://monsite.wanadoo.fr-lapommedor
Closed Sat. lunch, Sun. dinner, Mon.,
2 weeks Mar., 10 days July.
19 rooms: 32–47€.
Prix fixe: 10,70€, 20€, 25€.

Pierre Abelhauser's establishment is pleasant indeed. Its flowered facade and sober
but neat, traditionally furnished rooms in
blue and green tones go well with the market-based cuisine at gentle prices.

NIEDERMORSCHWIHR

68230 Haut-Rhin. Paris 444 – Colmar 7 –
Les Trois-Epis 5.
Perched above the vines and clinging to the
Vosges mountains, this winegrowing village is
famous for its houses with oriel windows and
inclined church bell tower, as well as its taverns and star confectioner.

 HOTELS-RESTAURANTS

■ Hôtel de l'Ange

125, rue des Trois-Epis.
Tel. 03 89 27 05 73. Fax 03 89 27 01 44.
hotel-ange@wanadoo.fr / www.hotelange.fr
Closed 10 days Nov., Jan.–Easter.
20 rooms: 50–62€.
Prix fixe: 12€, 20€, 8€ (child).
A la carte: 35–45€.

In the heart of the village, the Boxler and
Wiss families' half-timbered establishment is well worth a visit. Its rooms are

inviting with their fine woodwork and
antique furniture. There is no longer a
hotel restaurant, but there are many *winstubs* nearby.

● Caveau Morakopf

7, rue des Trois-Epis.
Tel. 03 89 27 05 10. Fax 03 89 27 08 63.
caveau.morakopf@wanadoo.fr
Closed Sun., Mon. lunch, 1 week Jan.,
1 week Mar., 1 week Nov.
A la carte: 40€.

This celebrated basement eatery on the
wine route still has its appeal. Anne Gui-
dat's smiling welcome, the cozy décor, the
stained glass decorated with the Moor's
head that gives the place its name, the rear
terrace and the regional dishes prepared
by Chantal Herque are enchanting. As we
savor the tête de porc in aspic, salted pork
tongue, steak with shallots, a real choucroute and the chocolate cake, we soon
forget how tough it was to get a table.

● Le Caveau des Chevaliers de Malte SIM

127, rue des Trois-Epis.
Tel. 03 89 27 09 78.
c.malte@wanandoo.fr
Closed lunch (exc. Sun.), Tue.,
2 weeks beg. Jan., 2 weeks beg. July.
Prix fixe: 5,30€ (child). A la carte: 28€.

We are fond of this simple tavern with its
pleasant atmosphere, rustic décor and
tables and stools made from old barrels,
run by Raymonde Wolff who watches over
both kitchen and dining room. Carafes
of amiable Alsatian wines accompany
escargots, vineyard-keeper's salad, hot
pâté in pastry crust, sautéed ham and
potatoes and a frozen kouglof prepared
with feeling.

● Caveau des Seigneurs SIM

124, rue des Trois-Epis.
Tel. 03 89 27 12 75.
Closed lunch, Thu.
A la carte: 28€.

Simple, enjoyable and easygoing, Liliane
Hassenfrantz's eatery combines simplic-

ity and good humor with a singular lack of fuss. The rustic cellar setting is ageless and the dishes honest rituals: we delight in the onion tart, tourte, pâté in a pastry crust and the ham and potato salad with fresh crunchy vegetables in season, all delightfully fresh.

NIEDERSCHAEFFOLSHEIM see HAGUENAU

NIEDERSTEINBACH

67510 Bas-Rhin. Paris 453 – Bitche 24 – Strasbourg 64.
The castles of Northern Alsace, the course of the Steinbach, the sweet solitude of the fir forests and nothing more.

 HOTELS-RESTAURANTS

■ Le Cheval Blanc
11, rue Principale.
Tel. 03 88 09 55 31. Fax 03 88 09 50 24.
contact@hotel-cheval-blanc.fr
www.hotel-cheval-blanc.fr
Closed 1 week at end Nov.–beg. Dec.,
beg. Feb.–mid-Mar., 20 June–mid-July
Rest. closed Thu.
26 rooms: 49–69€. 1 suite: 100€.
Prix fixe: 25€, 35€, 45€, 53€,
8€ (child).

When you pay a visit to Michel Zinck, you enter an entertaining, refined world with the Vosges forest on the horizon. From the swimming pool to the giant chessboard, billiard table and *pétanque* ground, everything has been tailored for the enjoyment of guests. The cozy, invariably tasteful rooms and dining room are instantly relaxing. In the hands of the chef, who trained with Blanc, Lameloise, Bocuse and Robuchon, the flawless, quality produce is meticulously prepared: frog legs, pike quenelles, roasted quail with old-fashioned stuffing and the dessert cart do not disappoint. Thierry Leichtman tends to the generously stocked cellar.

NIEUIL

16270 Charente. Paris 440 – Angoulême 40 – Confolens 26 – Limoges 65.
A corner of the gentle region of Charentes, from hill to forest and park to castle.

 HOTELS-RESTAURANTS

■ Château de Nieuil
Tel. 05 45 71 36 38. Fax 05 45 71 46 45.
www.chateauxnieuilhotel.com
chateauxnieuilhotel@wanadoo.fr
Closed beg. Nov.–beg. Mar.
11 rooms: 115–210€. 3 suites: 220–350€.
Half board: 136–252€.

Once a hunting lodge belonging to François I, more recently a Relais & Châteaux hostelry, this small Renaissance castle has lost none of its splendor over the centuries. Its elegant rooms, formal garden with heated summer pool, tennis court and gourmet Grange aux Oies restaurant continue to exert their charm.

● La Grange aux Oies
At the château de Nieuil.
Tel. 05 45 71 81 24. Fax 05 45 71 81 25.
www.grange-aux-oies.com
Closed Sun. dinner, Mon., Tue., Nov.
Prix fixe: 45€ (wine inc.). A la carte: 45€.

In this contemporary establishment occupying the former stables of the Château de Nieuil, Pascal Pressac pays tribute to the Charente region. He turns fine local produce into a modern gourmet repertoire, including free-range chicken breast terrine with foie gras, grilled cuttlefish in sauce ravigote (a spicy mustard, pickle and caper vinaigrette), beef filet with roasted tomato and eggplant compote and the thin orange chocolate tart. As for the wine, Patrice Devaine will offer all the advice you need to make your visit here delightful.

NIMES

30000 Gard. Paris 711 – Montpellier 56 – Aix-en-Provence 108 – Avignon 47 – Marseille 124.

info@ot-nimes.fr.

A strange city. Green and peaceful, Nîmes seems to be slumbering in a delicious torpor, waking only for its annual seven days of glory: *Féria* week in September. During the *Féria*, the city becomes a crazy, chic, giddying whirl. The downside is that Nîmes spends all the rest of the year anticipating, preparing, rousing itself… Admittedly, it has programmed a new *Féria* in February, but is the city's heart in it? A French Rome rich in Gallo-Roman buildings, Nîmes is worth more than a visit one week a year. Not least because of its market, which offers all the fine produce of a region bridging Provence and Languedoc. Cévennes and Camargue are just next door, and here, gastronomy has the local accent (if not always the energy). In any case, the pickled olives, salt cod purée, Pélardon goat cheese, lamb and fish, not to mention croquant cookies and Costières de Nîmes wine, have plenty of character.

■	HOTELS

■ Imperator Concorde

Quai de la Fontaine.
Tel. 04 66 21 90 30. Fax 04 66 67 70 25.
hotel.imperator@wanadoo.fr
www.hotel-imperator.com
57 rooms: 130–200€. 3 suites: 180–220€.

In the city center, this turn-of-the-century establishment is particularly busy during the *Férias*. Long-time regulars or curious visitors come to enjoy the charms of its old-fashioned rooms, the tranquility of the inner courtyard and flower garden, the elegant bar formerly frequented by Ernest Hemingway and the restaurant's delicately crafted cuisine. (See Restaurants: L'Enclos de la Fontaine.)

■ Novotel Atria

5, bd de Prague.
Tel. 04 66 76 56 56. Fax 04 66 76 56 59.
H0985@accor-hotels.com
www.accor-hotels.com
112 rooms: 89–113€. 7 suites: 142–150€.

Yves Dautigny has brought character to this chain hotel, brightening the rooms up with lively colors. Attention has naturally been paid to the more functional aspects, too, with fourteen meeting rooms and a conference center. But when business is done, the bullrings are just a step away and the restaurant serves a typically regional cuisine.

■ L'Orangerie

755, rue Tour-de-l'Evêque.
Tel. 04 66 84 50 57. Fax 04 66 29 44 55.
hr-orang@wanadoo.fr / www.orangerie.fr
31 rooms: 75–79€. 1 suite: 105€.

Although the building dates back to the 18th century, the hotel has been modernized and the rooms are tastefully fitted, each in a different shade. There is plenty of room for relaxation in the gardens, swimming pool, gym and sauna and Erik Bachewiig titillates the taste buds with his regional cuisine.

■ Jardins Secrets

3, rue Gaston Maruejols.
Tel. 04 66 84 82 64.
www.jardinssecrets.net
4 rooms: 195–260€.

A delightful secret sanctuary set in an enclosed garden, with richly decorated rooms (four at the moment, thirteen soon), marble bathrooms, choice fabrics, period furniture and fine paintings. Annabelle Valentin watches over her hostelry conscientiously.

■ New Hôtel la Baume

21, rue Nationale.
Tel. 04 66 76 28 42. Fax 04 66 76 28 45.
nimeslabaume@new-hotel.com
www.new-hotel.com
26 rooms: 105–210€. 8 suites: 155–230€.

Near the food market and Maison Carrée, this old Nîmes town house with its magnificent staircase offers a happy blend of tradition and modernity, from its contemporary rooms with original décor in various shades to its old-style lobby.

■ Royal Hôtel

3, bd Alphonse-Daudet.
Tel. 04 66 58 28 27. Fax 04 66 58 28 28.

rhotel@wanadoo.fr
www.royalhotel-nimes.com
23 rooms: 50–100€.

Central, inexpensive and charming: this
is an address to remember in the heart
of Nîmes, run by Anne Carbo. The rooms
are neat, all in white with antique-style
furniture. The lobby, with its old-fashioned stucco and modern pictures, has
an immediate appeal. The Bodeguita
next to the place d'Assas provides pleasant, tapas-based, light meals.

■ **La Maison de Sophie**   ⌂
31, av Carnot.
Tel. 04 66 70 96 10. Fax 04 66 36 00 47.
hotel-lamaisondesophie@wanadoo.fr
www.hotel-lamaisondesophie.com
5 rooms: 120€. 2 suites: 203–290€.

In the city center, this elegant 1900s town
house is enchanting indeed. Its refined
rooms with their art déco furniture and
highly polished bathrooms, swimming
pool and breakfasts draw the crowds.

● | RESTAURANTS

● **L'Enclos de la Fontaine**
At the Imperator. Quai de la Fontaine.
Tel. 04 66 21 90 30. Fax 04 66 67 70 25.
hotel.imperator@wanadoo.fr
www.hotel-imperator.com
Prix fixe: 30€, 50€, 65€, 15€ (child).
A la carte: 70€.

Pascal Chamalet has taken over the
kitchen of this fine old-fashioned hotel.
Guests eat in the gleaming dining room
or on the porch that looks out onto the
garden. We have no complaints about
the foie gras poached in red wine syrup,
pan-fried Mediterranean sea bass served
on a heap of vegetables, beef tenderloin
cooked fisherman's style and a chocolate
pistachio or vanilla soufflé, all quite well
done (although a little dull). Pierre Rein-
hard, the maître d', carefully tends to his
guests, helping them to choose among
the hundred wines from the region.

● **Le Darling**   Ⓝ·COM
40, rue de la Madeleine.
Tel. 04 66 67 04 99.
Closed lunch (exc. Sun.), Wed.
Prix fixe: 36€, 39€. A la carte: 65€.

This new, creative restaurant is on its way
up! Together with his wife and mother-in-
law, Vincent Croizard, originally from New
Caledonia, is running this new, charming
city eatery, where he serves up successful, delicate, spicy light meals: foie gras
and quail glazed with a tangy green apple
sauce, roasted veal sweetbreads with preserved lemons, oysters and turbot served
with endives and peppers, juicy veal in a
licorice root-seasoned crust and the dark
chocolate dessert with frozen mint lollipop. We balk a little at the fresh hay-sea-
soned beef with a grain clafoutis (a little
dry), green olive tiramisu with gelatine
(slightly sticky), but the cuisine as a whole
surprises, teases, captivates and enchants.
Gisèle, Vincent's wife, gives sound advice
on the equally offbeat wine list, while
Mireille takes turns serving. Definitely
one to watch.

● **Le Lisita**   Ⓟ○COM
2 bis, bd des Arènes.
Tel. 04 66 67 29 15. Fax 04 66 67 25 32.
restaurant@lelisita.com / www.lelisita.com
Closed Sun., Mon.
Prix fixe: 31€ (weekday lunch), 48€, 72€,
15€ (child). A la carte: 100€.

The stars of the city center? Olivier
Douet and Stéphane Debaille, who have
turned Lisita—opposite the bullrings—
into a light, bright, cheerful contemporary restaurant. Olivier, who trained at
the Côte d'Or in Saulieu, the Moulin in
Mougins, then at Le Gavroche in London,
and Stéphane, his dining room associate,
have refurbished their corner dining room
with a certain sense of simple modernism,
but avoided any chilliness. The waitstaff
are as youthful as they are considerate.
The cuisine focuses on clear-cut produce
prepared at the peak of its freshness and
veracity, as preached by Saint Bernard of
Saulieu, who brought these two young
people together. Obeying the dictates of

the market, they regale their guests with scallops with buttered Jerusalem artichokes, foie gras served hot (excellently sliced) with escargots and a mild herbed oil and garlic emulsion, a cod and potato dish with apple jelly (unusual, but fortifying), the signature Allaiton lamb from the Aveyron served with lemon thyme-seasoned mutton trotter. The sautéed Fressinette bananas and a mango carpaccio with a praline puff pastry will have you melting. A fine restaurant indeed.

● Le Bouchon et l'Assiette 🏠COM

5 bis, rue de Sauve.
Tel. 04 66 62 02 93. Fax 04 66 62 03 57.
www.bouchon-assiettte.com
Closed Tue., Wed., 2 weeks Jan.,
3 weeks Aug.
Prix fixe: 15€ (lunch), 20€ (lunch),
44€ (dinner), 11€ (child). A la carte: 38€.

Nomadic native of Strasbourg Lionel Geiger has enthusiastically poured himself into the mold of Gard tradition. In a slightly cluttered, bric-a-brac-style setting, we make short work of the reliable suggestions included on his menu, which changes every two months. In the traditional, sun-colored dining rooms, artichoke mousse with vegetable terrine, rouget filet with citrus vinaigrette, Atlantic sea bass tasting of the sea with oysters and artichoke risotto, venison rump steak with a mix of exotic peppers, Algerian polenta and a creamy chestnut soup and the light chocolate marquise and crêpes with mandarin orange preserves, citrus and Grand Marnier show remarkable flavor and delicacy, the fruit of imagination and skill. The set menus are quite simply the best in town.

● Jardins du Sud 🅽COM

21, rue du Grand Couvent.
Tel. 04 66 36 87 48.
Closed Sun.
Prix fixe: 22€ (lunch), 32€, 45€.

Isabelle Dumas and Claudine Araiz, culinary enthusiasts who formerly worked in the banking business, have taken over this central restaurant with a vaulted ceiling that dates from its previous incarnation as a convent (this used to be the Jardins du Couvent), renovating, brightening and enlivening it with great energy and wit. In the kitchen, Pascal Giordano (who spent seventeen years at the Imperator) deftly prepares lamb ravioli with curry and a split pea velouté, lamb in an herb crust with garlic jus, pan-fried cod filet with almonds, rouget with tomatoes and rosemary and breast of farm-raised chicken with mushroom sauce. Fine desserts follow (soft chestnut cake, prune crumble, vanilla crème brûlée) and the wine list does it all justice.

● Jardin d'Hadrien COM

11, rue Enclos-Rey.
Tel. 04 66 21 86 65. Fax 04 66 21 54 42.
Closed Sun. (exc. lunch off season), Mon.
lunch (July–Aug.), Tue. dinner (exc. summer),
Nov. 1 vac., Feb. vac., 10 days at end Aug.
Prix fixe: 18€, 29€, 42€, 11,50€ (child).
A la carte: 40–45€.

Michel Nicol and Alain Vinouze may be the most laid-back pair in Nîmes catering. The Parisian in the dining room and the Breton in the kitchen recount the region's flavors with all the devotion of converts who have adopted a new home through sheer enthusiasm. The antique, rustic setting, with its exposed beams and stone, and the round tables and fireplace have charm and to spare. On the shady patio, savor zucchini flower soufflé with brandade, peppers stuffed with goat cheese and basil, little toasts with olive spread, olive oil–roasted cod filet, lamb pieds paquets (local offal specialty) sautéed in the local style and a frozen crème de menthe parfait.

● Magister COM

5, rue Nationale.
Tel. 04 66 76 11 00. Fax 04 66 67 21 05.
le.magister@wanadoo.fr
Closed Sat. lunch, Sun.
Prix fixe: 20€, 25€, 35€, 46€, 12€ (child).

Martial Hocquart's cuisine changes with the market and season. In his elegant restaurant dining room, fitted with fine woodwork and now enjoying a new youth, local produce is king. The proof is in a house-style salt cod and potato purée, duck foie gras terrine with pear chutney and soft wheat bread made with squid ink, monkfish with a seaweed-flavored veal jus, rack of lamb with tarragon and the lemon and almond pudding. These fresh dishes are accompanied by the finest Southern French vintages, recommended by the vivacious Marie-Claire.

● Bel Ami Café   Ⓝ SIM

8, rue de la Maison-Carrée.
Tel. 04 66 67 48 49.
Closed Sat. lunch, Sun. lunch, 1 week beg. Jan., 4 days after each Féria (Pentecost and Sept.).
Prix fixe: 11,50€ (lunch), 17€ (lunch), 26€, 27€ (dinner).

In this fine old-fashioned bistro, the walls are adorned with pine wainscoting, the tables well set and the feminine welcome charming. It is well worth a visit for its shrewd set menus and bright suggestions. We steadfastly savor the plate of local Gers specialties, foie gras, Provençal tuna, duck confit, herbed lamb chops and lemon tart or chocolate fondant.

● L'Exaequo   ⚓ SIM

11, rue Bigot.
Tel. 04 66 21 71 96. Fax 04 66 21 77 96.
l.exaequo@wanadoo.fr
www.exaequorestaurant.fr
Prix fixe: 15€ (lunch), 26€ (dinner), 37€ (dinner), 75€.

With its white walls and red leather armchairs, this modern bistro run by Jean-Philippe Delaforge and Valentin Lerch is an ongoing event. Valentin, who trained at the Crocodile and the Cerf in Marlenheim, serves up dishes as precise and flawless as the décor. Crispy vegetable and shrimp fry, barracuda filet in a pastry crust served with a tea-infused emulsion, sliced veal sweetbreads braised with olive oil-sautéed vegetables and a cherry mille-feuille are washed down with delightful vintages selected by Jean-Philippe. Appealing set menus and wines to match.

● Aux Plaisirs des Halles   ⚓ SIM

4, rue Littré.
Tel. 04 66 36 01 02. Fax 04 66 36 08 00.
www.auxplaisirsdeshalles.com
Closed Sun., Mon., 1 week Nov. 1, 2 weeks beg. Feb., 1 week beg. May.
Prix fixe: 20€ (lunch), 37€, 44€, 55€.

Sébastien Granier runs a delightful eatery. This veteran of the Spinnaker in Port-Camargue and Pagès in Vialas has turned his Halles bistro into a modern restaurant. On the menu are charming wines from Languedoc and further afield and well-mastered market-based dishes. Hot seared tuna on a bed of warm potatoes, rockfish with black olive oil, grilled veal cutlet with creamy polenta and a lime bavarois with a slice of soft farmers cheese and raspberries will warm the cockles of your heart.

● Wine Bar   Ⓝ SIM
"Chez Michel"

1, pl des Arènes.
Tel. 04 66 76 19 59.
Closed Sun., Mon. lunch.
Prix fixe: 18€, 26€. A la carte: 25–30€.

We knew Michel Hermet as a knowledgeable sommelier in his Wine Bar on the square de la Couronne. A cheery fellow who has lost nothing of his good humor, he has transported his bistro and fine Languedoc wines to the first floor of the Cheval Blanc, just opposite the bullrings. Jean-Michel Nigon, formerly at the Imperator, concocts reliable, carefree dishes. Lentil cream with bacon, parsleyed mussels hot from the broiler, eggplant and tomato terrine, the fish and sauce of the day, grilled black Bigorre pork trotters, slow-cooked local beef stew prepared in the old style, grilled Pyrénées lamb saddle and the Charolais beef steak for two make an excellent impression.

In Garons (30128). 13 km s.

● Alexandre   ◎ LUX

Rte de l'Aéroport.
Tel. 04 66 70 08 99. Fax 04 66 70 01 75.
restaurant.alexandre@wanadoo.fr
www.michelkayser.com

Closed Sun. dinner, Mon., Tue., Feb. vac.,
2 weeks end Aug.–beg. Sept.
Prix fixe: 56€, 69€, 91€, 24€ (child).
A la carte: 106€.

At the gates of Nîmes, Michel Kayser, the loner from Garons, goes from strength to strength. We salute this poet of pots and pans who has successfully turned his large villa and vast dining room looking out on the garden into a genuine, Provençal oasis. This quiet native of Bitche, our 2005 Discovery of the Year, who trained in Moselle at the Auberge Albert Marie, Rosbruck, then in Isère at the Bouvarel hostelry in Saint-Hilaire-du-Rosier, continues to work on his technical, modern style, developing a solidly rooted Provençal cuisine free of meaningless frills. We like his work in the role of an artist reinterpreting local recipes: a magnificent savory version of floating island seasoned with local truffles, cep-stuffed tielle (a local fried bread specialty), Nimes brandade "in the original". In fine form, he takes on Camargue salt marsh-grazed toro and amazes us with his roasted John Dory and squid with squid ink churros. The deft Lionel Delsol ably suggests appropriate libations from a remarkable cellar devoted to Languedoc wines. Turning to the desserts, the generous scoop of chocolate and licorice ice cream and the remarkable frozen Grand Marnier soufflé will have you melting.

NIORT

79000 Deux-Sèvres. Paris 410 – La Rochelle 66 – Nantes 141 – Poitiers 76.
indo@ot-miort-paysniortaispoitevin.fr.
Within easy reach of Paris by TGV, the capital of the Deux-Sèvres district boasts a distinctive old town, the nearby Marais poitevin marshlands and fine dairies that are the pride of Poitou. Echiré and its butter are just round the corner.

 HOTELS-RESTAURANTS

■ Niort Marais Poitevin

27, rue de la Terraudière / 90, avenue de Paris.
Tel. 05 49 24 29 29. Fax 05 49 28 00 90.
www.accorhotels.com

77 rooms: 101–141€. 2 suites: 141–181€.
Prix fixe: 18€, 27€, 10€ (child).

Near the center, this contemporary hotel offers a number of attractions: a swimming pool, huge, peaceful rooms, a dining room with a veranda and Claude Moinet's reliable market-based cuisine (salmon and shellfish with anise butter, pan-fried calf's liver with raspberries and Poire Williams sorbet).

■ Hôtel du Moulin

27, rue Espingole.
Tel. 05 49 09 07 07. Fax 05 49 09 19 40.
34 rooms: 46–52€.

In this recent hotel overlooking the Sèvre river, a step away from the "Moulin" (a cultural center located on the far bank), the neat, comfortable, renovated rooms with contemporary furniture and inoffensive prices win unanimous approval.

● La Belle Etoile   V.COM

115, quai Maurice-Métayer.
Tel. 05 49 73 31 29. Fax 05 49 09 05 59.
info@la-belle-etoile.fr / www.la-belle-etoile.fr
Closed Sun. dinner, Wed. dinner, Mon.,
3 weeks Aug.
Prix fixe: 22€, 29,50€, 42,50€,
79€ (dinner, wine inc.).

An old hand at Niort cuisine, Claude Guignard has been reigning over his Sèvre river waterfront for three decades. A great champion of his region's produce, he still keeps a tight rein on his restaurant, although he has now decided on a successor, offering a prominent role to his son-in-law Jean-Philippe Vouhé, who trained first with him, then at the Nord in Parthenay and finally at the Régalade in Paris. Their working relationship runs smoothly and sweetly, as shown by the fine ideas featured in the balanced set menus that pay tribute to local tradition: parsley- and garlic-seasoned lettuce and purée with escargots, oxtail and a winter vegetable mille-feuille, crisped veal sweetbreads with a splendid Vendée bean purée. To conclude, the chocolate apple Cognac dessert and green Manzana sorbet works wonders and the Thouarsais whites and reds taste like elixirs of youth. Precise, cheerful, assiduous service.

● La Table des Saveurs

9, rue Thiers.
Tel. 05 49 77 44 35. Fax 05 49 16 06 29.
Closed Sun. (exc. Bank holidays).
Prix fixe: 17€, 25€, 35€, 40€.
A la carte: 50–55€.

"Intuition, curiosity, pleasure": this is the credo of Daniel Houinounou, who has refurbished his restaurant a step away from city hall in a light, warm, contemporary style in white and brown shades. This native of Lyon, who trained in Switzerland (in Crans-Montana and Gruyère) plays from a Niort culinary score with a distinctive lightness of touch. Duck foie gras seasoned with five flavors served with a Pineau blanc aspic, langoustine fricasee with leeks, pan-seared scallops with smoked bacon risotto and the grilled beef tenderloin with chorizo and potato crêpe display energy and character. The desserts, including eleven different forms of chocolate, no less, and others on a fruit theme (golden apple tart served with a Guérande salted cream), are divine surprises.

NITRY

89310 Yonne. Paris 195 – Auxerre 36 – Avallon 23 – Vézelay 31.
Close to the A6 freeway, on the edge of the Morvan district, a green springboard for a dive into bucolic Burgundy.

 HOTELS-RESTAURANTS

■ La Beursaudière

5/7, rue Hyacinthe-Gautherin.
Tel. 03 86 33 69 70 (hotel) /
03 86 33 69 69 (rest.). Fax 03 86 33 69 60.
www.beursaudiere.com
Closed 2 weeks Jan.
11 rooms: 70–110€.
Prix fixe: 18,50€, 36€, 46€, 9€ (child).

We surrender to the charms of this Morvan hostelry with its medieval dovecote, rustic-style rooms and terrace, especially since the cuisine also works its charm. In the able hands of Gérald Carpentier, Burgundy and Morvan are celebrated in a succession of sunny dishes: beef carpaccio with colza oil, thick-cut monkfish with saffron-seasoned citrus butter, wood-fire grilled andouillette and a berry hibiscus soup.

NOGARO

32110 Gers. Paris 730 – Agen 90 – Auch 64 – Mont-de-Marsan 44 – Pau 70.
A Gers village famous for its motorcycle and automobile contests on the Paul-Armagnac racing circuit.

 HOTELS-RESTAURANTS

■ Solenca

Av Daniate.
Tel. 05 62 09 09 08. Fax 05 62 09 09 07.
www.solenca.com
48 rooms: 54–59€.
Prix fixe: 11,50€ (lunch), 14,50€, 39€.

Former rugby player Gérard Ducès has opened this hotel, which offers a blend of comfort and modernity. In the Occitan dialect, *solenca* means a celebration after the harvest. The pink-tiled roofs of this recent construction rise from its attractive grounds, with garden, tennis court and swimming pool. The Gers cuisine is in good taste.

NOGENT-LE-ROI

28210 Eure-et-Loir. Paris 77 – Rambouillet 27 – Chartres 27 – Ablis 35 – Maintenon 10.
The 16th-century half-timbered houses, the high Gothic church and the old Coulomb Abbey make it well worth visiting this fine centre region town where the Eure river spreads its many arms.

● RESTAURANTS

● Le Relais des Remparts

2, rue. du Marché-aux-Légumes.
Tel.-Fax 02 37 51 40 47.

Closed Sun. dinner, Mon. (exc. lunch Feb.–
Nov.), Tue. dinner, 2 weeks Feb.,
3 weeks Aug.
Prix fixe: 17€ (weekday lunch), 22€ (weekday dinner), 28,50€, 35€.

In the center, this traditional dining room
with its flowered fabrics is the best bargain
in town. The smiling welcome, prompt
service, reasonable check and Thierry
Wagner's local cuisine are approved by
all. Duck foie gras, swordfish filet with
basil butter, beef filet Rossini and the
"macumba" are flavorsome accomplish-
ments indeed.

● Le Capucin Gourmand　　SIM
1, rue de la Volaille.
Tel. 02 37 51 96 00. Fax 02 37 51 90 31.
www.capucingourmand.fr
Closed Sun. dinner, Mon., Thu. dinner,
2 weeks Mar., 2 weeks end Aug.–beg. Sept.
Prix fixe: 15€ (lunch), 20,50€, 35€,
11,50€ (child).

In his narrow half-timbered 15th-cen-
tury house, in a dining room in shades of
yellow, Alain Pique readily applies inspiration with a modern touch. Crayfish
croustade, Armagnac-infused foie gras
with fig chutney, vanilla-seasoned filet
of sole and pan-tossed brioche with pain
d'épice ice cream are not bad at all.

NOGENT-LE-ROTROU

28400 Eure-et-Loir. Paris 148 – Alençon 65
– Le Mans 75 – Chartres 56.
This small ancient town is a first stop on the jour-
ney to Brittany. Visit the Château Saint-Jean.

 HOTELS-RESTAURANTS

■ Sully　　⌂
51, rue des Viennes.
Tel. 02 37 52 15 14. Fax 02 37 52 15 20.
www.hotel-sully-nogent.com
Closed Christmas–New Year's.
40 rooms: 54–68€.

A neat, modern hotel with practical, simple rooms, offering reasonably priced

accommodations in a quiet neighborhood. Private parking, WiFi.

● La Papotière　　
3, rue Bourg-le-Comte.
Tel. 02 37 52 18 41. Fax 02 37 52 94 71.
Closed Sun. dinner, Mon.
Prix fixe: 12,50€, 28,50€, 39,50€,
6€ (child). A la carte: 55€.

Between the foot of the Château Saint-
Jean and the church of Saint-Laurent,
this welcoming 16th-century inn has
more than one string to its bow. The
carved wooden door, fireplace, exposed
beams and stone add an unmistakable
distinction to its bistro. Marie-Claude
Bisson's market-based cuisine is not bad
either. Crayfish in scrambled eggs, turbot filet with hollandaise sauce, veal
sweetbreads with morel mushrooms and
an authentic tarte Tatin have a delightful
tang of simplicity.

In Condeau (61110). 11 km n via D918 and
D10.

■ Moulin et Château　　❀⌂
de Villeray
Tel. 02 33 73 30 22. Fax 02 33 73 38 28.
www.domainedevilleray.com
32 rooms: 75–250€. 6 suites: 180–390€.
Prix fixe: 26€, 34€, 49€, 69€,
15€ (child). A la carte: 75€.

Muriel and Christian Eelsen have turned
this 16th- to 18th-century château set in
its own grounds and the watermill on the
bank of the Huisne into an enchanting
hotel, offering attractive rooms, comfortable lounges and a range of leisure
activities (heated swimming pool, riding
center, tennis, canoeing). In the modern
dining room that leads out onto a terrace by the river, Ludovic Brunret serves
a noble cuisine that includes fine tart with
ceps and langoustines, grilled John Dory,
pigeon parmentier and the soft chocolate truffle.

NOIRLAC see SAINT-AMAND-MONTROND

NOIRMOUTIER-EN-L'ILE

85330 Vendée. Paris 473 – Nantes 89 –
La Roche-sur-Yon 88.

Linked to the mainland by a concrete bridge that offers an alternative to the Passage du Gois route (which is submerged at high tide), this Vendée island has lost none of its character. With its noble houses, aristocratic hotels, château, fine churches and mills, as well as the Bois de la Chaise wood, the Plage des Dames beach and the Herbaudière harbor, Noirmoutier seems very much like another world.

 HOTELS-RESTAURANTS

■ Le Général d'Elbée

Pl du Château.
Tel. 02 51 39 10 29. Fax 02 51 39 08 23.
elbee@leshotelsparticuliers.com
www.generaldelbee.com
Closed beg. Oct.–end Mar.
4 rooms: 90–178€. 1 suite: 230€.

A famous Vendée general has lent his name to this 18th-century private residence with its garret rooms upstairs and more conventional accommodation on the first floor, looking out onto the garden and swimming pool.

■ Fleur de Sel

Rue des Saulniers (behind the church).
Tel. 02 51 39 09 07. Fax 02 51 39 09 76.
contact@fleurdesel.fr / www.fleurdesel.fr
Closed beg. Nov.–mid-Mar.
Rest. closed Mon. lunch, Tue. lunch.
35 rooms: 79–160€.
Prix fixe: 25,50€, 35€, 46€.

Deep in parkland, the Wattecamps' pampered hostelry offers cabin-style rooms in yew, waxed pine and striped fabrics, as well as free ADSL access. Swimming pool, Jacuzzi and tennis court provide opportunities for leisure before we sit down in the bright dining room, where Eric Pichou plays on themes of sea and market produce. Tuna cannelloni with eggplant, pan-fried rockfish with bok choy, grilled snapper with mixed sautéed peppers and little squid and the minced young Challans duck with exotic fruit chutney are not bad, even if they tend to err on the side of complexity rather than simplicity. A pretty apricot tart Tatin with a Breton-style shortbread crust and basil-infused cream and Carambar (caramel) ice cream.

■ Les Douves

11, rue des Douves.
Tel. 02 51 39 02 72. Fax 02 51 39 73 09.
hotel-les-douves@wanadoo.fr
Closed Jan.
22 rooms: 46–93€.

Although this hotel run by Bernadette Maisonneuve on the place d'Armes opposite the château may not boast any very distinctive attractions, it does have practical, neat, modern rooms, a meeting room and a pleasant swimming pool on the patio.

■ La Maison de Perle

20, rue de Banzeau.
Tel. 02 51 39 12 08 / 02 51 39 08 22.
Fax 02 51 39 86 33.
perleja@voila.fr
www.lamaisondeperle.com
5 rooms: 80€. 1 suite: 160€.

This 1621 stone establishment makes a delightful guesthouse. Perle and Daniel Jamet provide a warm welcome. Tidy rooms with an old-fashioned charm and a fine interior garden.

■ Autre Mer

32, av Joseph-Pineau.
Tel. 02 51 39 11 77. Fax 02 51 39 11 97.
contact@autremerhotel.fr
www.autremerhotel.fr
Closed mid-Nov.–beg. Apr.
25 rooms: 51–79€. 2 suites: 60–82€.

On the Bois de la Chaise road, this sixties building offers modern, neat rooms of immaculate white and sea green against a marine décor. Neighboring restaurant the Bleu Tomate serves shrewdly chosen little dishes.

● **Côté Jardin** `COM`

1 bis, rue du Grand-Four.
Tel. 02 51 39 03 02. Fax 02 51 54 64 58.
Closed Sun. dinner (exc. July–Aug.), Wed.
dinner (exc. July–Aug.), Thu. (exc. July–
Aug.), 11 Nov.–beg. Feb.
Prix fixe: 16€, 24€, 23€, 36€, 8€ (child).
A la carte: 45€.

This bucolic, ivy-clad restaurant by the château serves up an extremely apt, regional cuisine. José Corbrejaud concocts suitable dishes: pan-sizzled escargots and white beans with garlic cream, Atlantic sea bass filet in a green tea infusion, a rack of lamb cooked with dried apricots and the orange and chocolate tart. Guests can choose between the charming terrace on the patio or the traditional dining room in yellow and blue tones.

● **L'Etier** `COM`

Rte de l'Epine.
Tel. 02 51 39 10 28. Fax 02 51 39 23 00.
restaurant.etier@wanadoo.fr
Closed Mon., Tue. (exc. July–Aug.),
10 Dec.–end Jan.
Prix fixe: 16€, 24€, 35€, 50€, 10€ (child).

In this restaurant on the banks of the Arceau canal and on the pleasant terrace and veranda, Patrice Milliasseau works industriously on local fish, meat, vegetables and fruit to compose his appetizing set menus. In the soberly rustic dining room, pan-seared escalope of foie gras with ceps served on a potato cake with Noirmoutier salt, scallops with ceps and truffle jus, thick turbot filet steamed over seaweed then sizzled to a crisp, young Challans duck cooked hunter's style and the Paris-Brest, a choux pastry ring with almonds and butter cream, favorably impress.

● **Le Grand Four** `COM`

1, rue de la Cure.
Tel.-Fax 02 51 39 61 97.
renee.vetele@wanadoo.fr
www.legrandfour.com
Closed Sun. dinner (exc. vac.),
Mon. (exc. vac.), Dec. Jan.
Prix fixe: 18,50€, 23,50€, 30€, 38,50€,
54€, 65€, 85€, 12,50€ (child).

Concealed behind the château, this comfortable, ivy-covered family home three centuries old houses Patrice Vételé's restaurant. The two refined Renaissance-style dining rooms are charming, the set menus balanced and the best of regional produce—spiced up here and there by Southern French flavors—wins unanimous approval. Accompanied by the appropriate wine (recommended by Patrice Rabiller), duck foie gras served with dried apricot brioche, langoustine and lobster medley with parsley cream and the royal-style rabbit served with root vegetable mousseline are all accomplished work indeed. The pan-simmered apples in mille-feuille napped with salted-butter caramel sauce is a delicacy.

● **Le Manoir** `COM`

11 a, rue des Douves.
Tel. 02 51 35 77 73.
laurenthoue@wanadoo.fr
Closed Sat. dinner, Mon.
Prix fixe: 16€, 13€, 26€. A la carte: 45€.

Laurent Houé provides a friendly welcome in this pastel-toned dining room. Scallops in savory buckwheat crêpes, Atlantic sea bass filet seasoned with star anise, pan-seared magret de canard cooked with raisins and grated potatoes, duo of shoulder and rack of lamb with a wild thyme-seasoned jus and served with white bean purée and slow-roasted garlic and the roasted pineapple with banana caramel are not bad at all. There is a view of the medieval château through the three fine bay windows.

● **Le Vélo Noir**

13, rue du Vieil-Hôpital.
Tel.-Fax 02 51 35 85 29.
levelonoir@tele2.fr
Closed Sun. dinner (off season),
Tue. (off season).
Prix fixe: 15€, 18€. A la carte: 40€.

This delightful bistro is the island's best-kept secret: even the Michelin has missed it! We love the cute setting with its pine wainscotting and the slate with the dishes of the day. A veteran of the Fleur de Sel, Willy Herbet deftly prepares fresh, savory, light concoctions organized into bargain set menus: red tuna tartare with onions and coriander, sardine, red pepper and yellow squash mille-feuille, rouget filet with an eggplant spread, grilled lamb chops in a white bean tagine, fruit salad with peaches and anise and the fennel-infused apricots are the magnificent options.

● **Le Petit Bouchot**   SIM

3, rue Saint-Louis.
Tel. 02 51 39 32 56.
lepetitbouchot@yahoo.fr
Closed Mon. (July–Aug.), Tue. (off season),
Wed. (off season), mid-Dec.–end Jan.
Prix fixe: 16€, 24€, 7€ (child).

This unpretentious restaurant wins us over with its garden, trim surroundings, enthusiastic service and sensible set menus. In the classical dining room with its burgundy red tones, we yield to the charms of the oven-crisped langoustine with pan-seared foie gras, oven-roasted turbot filet with orange butter, veal kidney casserole seasoned with paprika and dark chocolate mousse with salted-butter caramel.

In Bois de la Chaize (85330). 2,2 km nw via D948.

■ **Les Prateaux**   ❀🏠

8, allée du Tambourin.
Tel. 02 51 39 12 52. Fax 02 51 39 46 28.
contact@lesprateaux.com
www.lesprateaux.com
Closed mid-Nov.–mid-Feb.
Rest. closed Tue., Wed. lunch.
19 rooms: 88–160€.
Prix fixe: 24€, 36€, 58€. A la carte: 47–62€.

Near to the Plage des Dames beach, Jean-Paul Blouard's hotel, surrounded by a charming garden, is the preferred haunt of preppy Noirmoutiers society, which appreciates the tidy, comfortable rooms and excellent classical restaurant, brightly decorated in blue and white. Deftly prepared by Anthony Pirault, the stuffed littleneck clams, sole meunière, orange-seasoned minced duck and the Grand

Marnier soufflé have an easy charm. The fine wine list favors the Loire.

In Bois de la Chaize.

■ **Saint-Paul**   🏠

15 av Maréchal-Foch. Bois de la Chaize.
Tel. 02 51 39 05 63. Fax 02 51 39 73 98.
christian.buron@wanadoo.fr
www.hotel-saint-paul.net
Closed Sun. dinner, Mon., beg. Nov.–beg. Mar.
37 rooms: 75–145€.
Prix fixe: 29€, 39€, 63,50€. A la carte: 70€.

This cozy establishment offers many attractions: wooded, flowery grounds, charming welcome afforded by Christian Buron, the bar lounge, renovated rooms, swimming pool and meeting rooms. The cuisine at the Anse Rouge deftly mirrors the cycle of the tides and tradition. Jean-Marie Lepolles' creations are served in the luxurious dining room with its exposed beams: roasted langoustines with caviar cream, pan-seared Atlantic sea bass filet served with buckwheat cake topped with artichoke cream, rack of lamb in a salt crust and the creamy praline-flavored dessert served with an ice cream cone.

In Bois de la Chaize.

■ **Les Capucines**   🏠

Bois de la Chaize.
Tel. 02 51 39 06 82. Fax 02 51 39 33 10.
capucineshotel@aol.com
www.logis-de-France.fr
Closed 1 Nov.–mid-Feb.
Rest. closed Wed. and Thu. (off season).
21 rooms: 40–98€.
Prix fixe: 23€, 28€, 37€,
16€ (weekday lunch), 9,50€ (child).

This small hotel complex near the Plage des Dames beach has two buildings, one on each side of the swimming pool; its rooms are comfortable and practical. Pan-tossed langoustine and foie gras salad with tomato chutney, frog legs in vol-au-vent with Muscadet wine sauce, cassolette of veal sweetbreads and kidneys deglazed with Pineau wine and the chocolate dessert plate stay the course.

In La Guérinière (85680). 5,2 km s via D948 and D95.

■ Punta Lara

Rte de la Noure.

Tel. 02 51 39 11 58. Fax 02 51 39 69 12.

puntalara@leshotelsparticuliers.com

www.hotelpuntalara.com

Closed 1 Oct.–beg. May.

59 rooms: 110–160€. 2 suites: 190–255€.

Prix fixe: 22€, 28€, 35€, 12€ (child).

A la carte: 50–55€.

Philippe Savry has taken up the reins of this hotel, open to the sea and sun, both in its white bungalows with their rattan-furnished rooms and balconies offering a view of the waves and in its Atlantide restaurant, bordered with bay windows giving onto the terrace and swimming pool. Under an upturned boat hull, we eagerly enjoy shrewd dishes that ebb and flow with the tides and seasons: aniseed-seasoned jumbo shrimp with rice, whole Atlantic sea bass with vanilla- and ginger-seasoned jus, brandade with celery, spicy beef, Noirmoutier potatoes with rosemary and the royal-style chocolate dessert.

In L'Herbaudière (85330). 4,8 km ne via D5.

● La Marine

On the harbor.

Tel.-Fax 02 51 39 23 09.

Closed Sun. dinner (exc. July–Aug.),

Tue. dinner (exc. July–Aug.),

Wed. (exc. July–Aug.), 3 weeks Oct.

Prix fixe: 17€ (weekday lunch).

A la carte: 56–65€.

On the Herbaudière harbor, the Marine offers a blend of audacity and wit. Its thoroughbred Noirmoutier cuisine retains a very local touch, although its style owes much to a taste for experimentation. Alexandre Couillon, who trained with Guérard, Georges Paineau (Questembert) and Pierre Lecoutre (Nantes), introduces us to bite-sized red tuna medallions in a sweet-and-sour sauce with shallot confit and caramelized tomato with a peppered mint sorbet, John Dory seasoned with Key limes and served with carrot salad with peanuts and coriander and the squab served with rutabaga "sau-

erkraut", its legs stuffed with dates and chorizo. Fine work.

37210 Indre-et-Loire. Paris 231 – Tours 20 – Amboise 11 – Blois 44 – Vendôme 50.

In the Loire châteaux region, a peaceful village and its vineyards, allied to Vouvray.

 HOTELS-RESTAURANTS

■ Château de Noizay

Rte de Chançay.

Tel. 02 47 52 11 01. Fax 02 47 52 04 64.

noizay@relaischateaux.com

www.chateaudenoisay.com

Closed mid-Jan.–mid-Mar.

Rest. closed Tue. lunch, Wed. lunch,

Thu. lunch.

19 rooms: 135–275€.

Prix fixe: 46€, 59€, 72€, 18€ (child).

Dominating the village and its vineyards, this 16th-century château has an immediate charm. The grounds, with their hundred-year-old trees, swimming pool and elegant rooms equipped with period furniture, make this a very stylish Relais & Châteaux establishment. In the luxurious dining rooms, the seasonal regional dishes are accompanied by appealing wines from the Loire and elsewhere.

73590 Savoie. Paris 585 – Albertville 25 – Annecy 54 – Megève 20 – Chamonix 43.

www.notredamedebellecombe.com.

On the edge of the Val d'Arly valley, the gateway to Beaufortin, land of the Savoy "onion" bell tower.

 RESTAURANTS

● Ferme de Victorine

Le Planay Est: 3 km via rte des Saisies.

Tel. 04 79 31 63 46.

www.lafermedevictorine.com

Closed Sun. dinner, Mon. (mid-Apr.–mid-June, Sept.–Nov.), mid-Nov.–mid-Dec.,

2 weeks end June.
Prix fixe: 20€ (weekday lunch), 25€, 40€.

This former Savoy farm has become a gourmet retreat bent on preserving the region's heritage under the supervision of the dynamic James Ansanay-Alex. At the stove, Denis Vinet refines traditional dishes (just a touch), maintaining an old-fashioned inn-style simplicity. A poultry liver terrine, a creamy squash soup presented with truffle-seasoned whipped cream, duck breast served with "blueberry blood", frozen polenta parfait and the slow-roasted apples with salted-butter caramel work wonders. A bar with a view of the stables, a friendly atmosphere and mountain décor make this restaurant a special favorite of ours.

NOTRE-DAME-DU-PE

72300 Sarthe. Paris 260 – Angers 50 – La Flèche 30 – Nantes 138 – Le Mans 60.
A pretty, green vista in the Sarthe countryside. Church and presbytery still have all their antique charm.

 HOTELS-RESTAURANTS

■ La Reboursière ⓝ✿⌂
1 km s.
Tel.-Fax 02 43 92 92 41.
gilles.chappuy@wanadoo.fr
www.lareboursiere.fr.st
4 rooms: 52–65€. Half board: 104–171€.

Gilles Chappuy has preserved the traditional spirit of this old farm, a rustic, 19th-century longhouse typical of the region, with rooms furnished in an antique style and a stone-walled dining room. The traditional cuisine is based on seasonal produce, including crispy leek and fennel croustade, monkfish brochette with smoked bacon, beef tenderloin in a pastry crust and the chocolate fondant. The local wine makes its own way down.

NOUAN-LE-FUZELIER

41600 Loir-et-Cher. Paris 179 – Orléans 55 – Blois 59 – Lamotte-Beuvron 8.
nouan.otsi@wanadoo.fr.
The heart of the Sologne, with ponds, hunting, châteaux and thickets.

● RESTAURANTS

● Le Dahu COM
14, rue H.-Chapron.
Tel. 02 54 88 72 88. Fax 02 54 88 21 28.
ledahu.restaurant@wanadoo.fr
Closed Tue. dinner (off season), Wed., Thu., mid-Nov.–1 Dec., beg. Jan.–1 Feb., mid-Mar.–end Mar., 1 week at end June.
Prix fixe: 31€, 12€ (child).
A la carte: 55€.

Self-taught virtuoso Jean-Luc Germain, a mathematician by training, presides over the rustic dining room and kitchen of this carefully renovated, hundred-year-old sheep barn in the middle of a lush garden, equipped with a terrace in summer. On the menu? A spirited market-based cuisine accompanied by selected wines. In the rustic dining room with its exposed timbers, Marie-Thérèse serves oysters in sea water aspic with red wine, monkfish medallion with eggplant spread served with mustard and raspberry vinegar sauce, wild Beauce rabbit dry roasted with blood sauce, honey-roasted pears with fennel grains and jasmine ice cream.

● Raboliot COM
Av de la Mairie.
Tel. 02 54 94 40 00. Fax 02 54 94 40 04.
phenrynouan@aol.comwww.raboliot.com
Closed Sun. dinner (exc. Bank holidays), Mon. (exc. Bank holidays), Feb.
Prix fixe: 32€, 38€, 23€ (wine inc.), 16€, 10€ (child). A la carte: 52€.

The village café has become a tasteful restaurant. The warm welcome, the naïve décor of the two dining rooms and Philippe Henry's mischievous cuisine fully justify a visit. Introduced to a range of vintages from every French region, Chile,

Argentina and South Africa by Armahn Sahin, we succumb to the temptation of warm Loire baby pigeon in salad, John Dory filet dry roasted with young leeks and veal jus, a duo of veal sweetbreads and kidneys with Sologne chantarelles and the hot biscuit dripping with Caribbean chocolate sauce.

NOYAL-SUR-VILAINE see RENNES

NOYANT-DE-TOURAINE see SAINTE-MAURE-DE-TOURAINE

NUITS-SAINT-GEORGES

21700 Côte-d'Or. Paris 320 – Beaune 22 – Chalon sur Saône 45 – Dijon 22.
An "unsung" capital of the Côtes-de-Nuits, with its great climate, famous winegrowers and fine, noble châteaux and country folk.

 HOTELS-RESTAURANTS

■ La Gentilhommière

13, vallée de la Serrée (direction Meuilley).
Tel. 03 80 61 12 06. Fax 03 80 61 30 33.
contact@lagentilhommiere.fr
www.lagentilhommiere.fr
Closed mid-Dec.–end Jan.
Rest. closed Sat. lunch, Tue., Wed. lunch.
20 rooms: 85–200€. 11 suites: 200–250€.
Prix fixe: 45€, 55,50€, 59,50€.

This 16th-century hunting lodge deserves a visit. The distinctive rooms with their harmonious blend of rustic and modern charm, themed suites, outdoor swimming pool, massage service, lazy hours spent alfresco, strolls by the river and René Pianetti's cuisine, enhanced by great local vintages, draw gourmets from far afield. In the rustic, exposed stone dining room, flavors from the South of France are blended in precise, if somewhat complex, preparations: mozzarella balls with cherry tomatoes, cod filet with parmesan risotto, boneless veal rib steak with rosemary and the hot "Mon Cheri" soft-centered cake are not badly crafted.

26110 Drôme. Paris 656 – Orange 42 – Valence 96 – Sisteron 99.
ot.nyons@wanadoo.fr.
A delightful town, the mini-capital of lavender, Nyons has lent its name to a black olive and been rewarded by official certification of its fine oil, used to flavor appetizing local dishes.

 HOTELS-RESTAURANTS

■ Le Colombet

53, pl de la Libération.
Tel. 04 75 26 03 66. Fax 04 75 26 42 37.
info@hotelcolombet.com
www.hotelcolombet.com
Closed Dec.–end Jan.
25 rooms: 55–109€.
Prix fixe: 11,90€ (weekday lunch), 15,30€ (weekday lunch), 18,40€ (weekday lunch), 19€, 14,70€ (child). A la carte: 33€.

Benoît Thévenet's hotel is a jewel in the center of town. Its neat rooms with their traditional Provençal furniture and varied colors offer a view of surrounding nature. New chef Christophe Toucas deftly prepares poultry liver terrine with olives and pistachios, Provençal aïoli, grilled chops from Alpine-grazed lamb and the almond pear tart with dark chocolate sauce washed down by delightful vintages from the Rhône Valley.

● Le Petit Caveau

9, rue Victor-Hugo.
Tel. 04 75 26 20 21. Fax 04 75 26 07 28.
Closed Sun. dinner, Mon.,
Wed. dinner (off season), mid-Dec.–end Jan.
Prix fixe: 23€ (lunch), 32€, 35€, 50€, 20€ (child).

The charm of this fine establishment in the old town lies in its discreet location and Provençal ambiance. Under the dining room's rustic vaults, all the sunny flavors of Provence shine through in the cuisine prepared by Laurent Lecompte, who trained with Blanc, Lorain and Gauvreau. Regional traditions are seen anew through the prism of a lively imagination:

crab and arugula ravioli, spider crab with artichokes served with a verbena-infused shellfish emulsion, monkfish medallion with San Daniele cured ham and Provençal vegetables, a pigeon tagine with slow-cooked eggplant, peppers and spiced honey jus and the peach trilogy. A talented, pleasurable cuisine, punctuated by a fine selection of mainly regional wines served by the dedicated Laure Poumier.

● **La Charrette Bleue**   ●COM
Rte de Gap, 7 km via D94, quartier la Bonté.
Tel. 04 75 27 72 33. Fax 04 75 27 76 14.
Closed Tue. (exc. July–Aug.), Wed.,
mid-Dec.–end Jan.
Prix fixe: 18€ (lunch), 24€, 31€, 38€.

This old limestone farm with its shady terrace is a charming place to pause for refreshment. In the brightly colored, rustic dining room, Françoise Roussel pays enthusiastic tribute to the regional cuisine prepared by her husband Paul. Light goat cheese flan, cod filet in bouillabaisse, roasted rabbit saddle with sage and the berry terrine with *rosé* wine jelly marry seasons and surrounding nature for better, not for worse.

OBERHASLACH

67280 Bas-Rhin. Paris 426 – Strasbourg 40 – Molsheim 18 – Saverne 31.
The Nideck honored by Chamisso, waterfalls and ruins, the great forest of the Vosges, lively streams and an 18th-century chapel are the charms of this quiet village.

 HOTELS-RESTAURANTS

■ **Saint-Florent**   ⌂
28, rue du Nideck.
Tel. 03 88 50 94 10. Fax 03 88 50 99 61.
hotel.stflorent@wanadoo.fr
www.hostelleriereeb.fr
Closed 28 Dec.–1 Feb.
Rest. closed Sun. dinner, Mon.
24 rooms: 40–56€.
Prix fixe: 16€, 25€, 31€. A la carte: 25–30€.

We heard he was leaving, yet Francis Reeb is still running this fine establishment, offering attractive rooms and very respectable dishes: house terrine, roasted pike-perch on a bed of Puy lentils, magret de canard seasoned with citrus and soft spices and the chocolate dessert.

● **Ruines du Nideck**   SIM
2, rue de Molsheim.
Tel. 03 88 50 90 14. Fax 03 88 50 93 58.
Closed Mon. dinner, Tue. dinner, Wed.,
3 weeks Jan., 2 weeks Aug.
Prix fixe: 18€, 34€, 8€ (child).
A la carte: 33–40€.

We visit Cyril Munch to taste his specialty (flambéed tarts), but he just as skillfully concocts pan-tossed frog legs with Riesling, crayfish in cassolette, veal kidney with mustard sauce, crème brûlée and a soft-centered chocolate cake. The menu changes regularly.

OBERHOFFEN-SUR-MODER see HAGUENAU

OBERLARG

68480 Haut-Rhin. Paris 470 – Mulhouse 49 – Colmar 90.
The Largue river meanders nearby through

scenery peppered with green, wooded hills. The ruins of Lucelle Abbey and the Swiss border are excellent destinations for a walk.

 RESTAURANTS

● A la Source de la Largue
19, rue Principale.
Tel. 03 89 40 85 10. Fax 03 89 08 19 86.
Closed Tue., Wed., Thu.
Prix fixe: 19,80€ (lunch). A la carte: 35€.

With great modesty, Jean-Marie Hirtzlin—who notably trained with Bocuse and Vergé—has returned from Riedisheim and the Tonnelle to the paternal inn and chosen to concentrate on a brilliantly simple regional cuisine. In the rustic dining room, his wife Martine extols his rabbit presskopf, fried carp, tête de veau and a frozen rhubarb parfait.

In Lucelle (68480). 3 km e.

■ Le Petit Kohlberg
Tel. 03 89 40 85 30. Fax 03 89 40 89 40.
petitkohlberg@wanadoo.fr
www.petitkohlberg.com
Rest. closed Mon., Tue.
35 rooms: 42–68€.
Prix fixe: 16€, 62€, 6,90€ (child).
A la carte: 26–50€.

The Meister family's inn continues to enchant us. Nestling in a magnificent park populated by roe deer and does, it offers a spectacular view of the Jura Mountains. The Swiss border is close by and there are fruit trees everywhere. The setting is genuinely delightful and can be enjoyed together with the Munster cheese in a crêpe pouch, garnished fried carp, ham and the frozen kouglof prepared by Jean-Pierre. The warm welcome at this fine establishment does it justice.

67330 Bas-Rhin. Paris 456 – Haguenau 19 – Ingwiller 7 – Pfaffenhoffen 4.
The Pays de Hanau district with its orchards, high houses featuring neat half-timbering and

North Vosges mountain route is almost a secret country.

 HOTELS-RESTAURANTS

■ Ernenwein
11, rue de la Gare.
Tel. 03 88 90 80 08. Fax 03 88 90 86 62.
info@ernenwein.com / www.ernenwein.com
Closed 1 week beg. Mar., 2 weeks end Aug.
Rest. closed Thu.
12 rooms: 40–46€. Prix fixe: 9€ (lunch),
27€, 40€, 6,50€ (child). A la carte: 36€.

Roland Ernenwein brings his energy to this inordinately charming hotel by the rail station. The welcome is warm; the rooms simple and well kept. The cuisine pays tribute to the region and the dishes are generous. Why deny ourselves the pleasure of a duck presskopf with foie gras, pike-perch, de-boned guinea hen stuffed with foie gras? For dessert, the grapefruit gratin is remarkable.

67210 Bas-Rhin. Paris 485 – Sélestat 23 – Strasbourg 30 – Colmar 45.
otobernai@sdv.fr.
Alsace in brief. With its shadow of Sainte-Odile, place du Marché, belfry, town hall with oriel windows and well at Six Seaux, this model community proves that the image of Alsace as pretty and gastronomic is no pipe dream.

 HOTELS-RESTAURANTS

■ La Cour d'Alsace
3, rue de Gail.
Tel. 03 88 95 07 00. Fax 03 88 95 19 21.
info@cour-alsace.com / www.cour-alsace.com
Closed 24 Dec.–25 Jan.
41 rooms: 119–179€. 2 suites: 159–279€.
Prix fixe: 29€, 48€, 13,70€ (child).
A la carte: 75€.

At the foot of the old walls in the heart of town, this former tithe barn, refurbished with an ample helping of charm by the Hagers, delights its guests. They all appreciate its comfortable, handsome, neat rooms and there are no complaints about Olivier Gerber's fine cuisine. Served in the Jardin des Remparts (the gourmet restaurant and terrace) and the Caveau du Gail (the chic tavern), the carefully crafted dishes prepared by this Auberge de l'Ill veteran are enchanting: pressed quail terrine with a prune confit, turbot filet with sea salt flakes, veal filet with chanterelles and the raspberry gratin.

■ Le Parc

169, rte d'Ottrott, w via D426.
Tel. 03 88 95 50 08. Fax 03 88 95 37 29.
info@hotel-du-parc.com
www.hotel-du-parc.com
Closed 10 Dec.–mid- Jan.
Rest. closed Sun. dinner (exc. La Table),
Mon., dinner (exc. La Table).
56 rooms: 100–180€. 6 suites: 245–295€.
Prix fixe: 45€, 55€ (Sat., Sun., lunch), 60€
(Sat., Sun., lunch), 75€, 16€ (child).
A la carte: 80€.

Relaxation guaranteed in Marc Wucher's establishment! Say goodbye to stress in its comfortable, contemporary rooms (some with fireplaces), two swimming pools (summer and winter), fitness center, brand new Jacuzzi and spa with Moroccan-style massage rooms. In the Table restaurant, Jacky Schweighoffer serves up a modern take on local cuisine, including a fresh lobster and crab dish served with sisho sprouts, monkfish medallion with Iberian ham, veal sweetbreads and potato baeckeofe and variations on theme of the apricot. (See Restaurants: Stub du Parc.)

■ Le Colombier

6-8, rue Dietrich.
Tel. 03 88 47 63 33. Fax 03 88 47 63 39.
info@hotel-colombier.com
www.hotel-colombier.com
36 rooms: 83€. 8 suites: 111–130€.

Michel Baly, also owner of the Colombier in Colmar and the Diana and Bugatti in Molsheim, has turned this old hotel into a pleasant port of call where we enjoy a workout in the fitness center.

■ La Diligence Résidence Bel Air

23, pl du Marché.
Tel. 03 88 95 55 69. Fax 03 88 95 42 46.
hotel.la.diligence@wanadoo.fr
www.hotel-diligence.com
25 rooms: 35–81€.

If you are looking for a traditional, practical hotel in the center of town, where each room is individualized and boasts an alcove, the Diligence is just the place. Or, you may prefer the Résidence Bel Air on the Obernai high corniche road, one kilometer from the center, in a relaxing, green setting.

■ Duc d'Alsace

6, rue de la Gare.
Tel. 03 88 95 55 34. Fax 03 88 95 00 92.
ducdalsace@ducalsace.com
www.ducdalsace.com
19 rooms: 53–95€.

Opposite the station, this fine, half-timbered establishment offers small but renovated rooms. The Fourchette des Ducs restaurant is on the first floor.

■ Les Jardins d'Adalric

19, rue du Maréchal-Koenig.
Tel. 03 88 47 64 47. Fax 03 88 49 91 80.
jardins.adalric@wanadoo.fr
www.jardins-adalric.com
44 rooms: 53–95€. 2 suites: 160–205€.

A dependably warm welcome and renovated, comfortable rooms, all in a setting where classical and modern styles meet.

● La Fourchette des Ducs

6, rue de la Gare.
Tel. 03 88 48 33 38. Fax 03 88 95 44 39.
Closed lunch (exc. Sun., Bank holidays), Sun.
dinner, Mon., 10 days end Dec.–beg. Jan.,
1 week at end Jan.–beg. Feb.,
1 week beg. May, 3 weeks July–Aug.
Prix fixe: 75€, 95€, 12€ (child).

Twenty-five places and no more, three wait and five kitchen staff, two set menus, two dining rooms (one of them boudoir-style with a twenties Spindler fireplace), soft colors, no hullabaloo and reservations required with all tables taken. Oh, and did we mention that the restaurant is closed at lunchtime, except on Sunday? In short, we feel we are among a select few here. Serge Schall, who supervises the dining room, and Nicolas Stamm, master of the stoves, formerly at Haguenau, compete in the "enlightened amateurs" category. Having taken a look at what the best are doing elsewhere, they have decided to do better or do something else. In fact, their eatery is like no other... except the one run by their friends at the Arnsbourg, from whom they quietly "borrowed" the idea of successive succulent morsels to "rouse the palate" Parmesan and truffle cone, caramelized tomato and jumbo shrimp beignets with sesame, as well as the "appetizer trilogy" (truffles in scrambled eggs with a hazelnut mousse, crab and green apple tartare with apricot purée and oysters with balsamic vinegar) could be terribly affected, but are actually precise, fresh, easily digested and unpretentious. The rest of the food is in the same vein, including the langoustine duo (in a tart and in aspic) and the cauliflower mousse with caviar, suggesting one of the great Robuchon's famous creations, a sea-scented, tender recipe with an ambitious market garden touch (the cauliflower). The fine ravioli with young sweet peas or pumpkin in a frothy truffle butter and the lobster medallion with chanterelles and a foie gras emulsion are precise and uncomplicated. The meats are in the same style: sophisticated, but not overly so, like the Alsatian squab with a rose supreme, its leg slow roasted on a bed of caramelized pear with an unsweetened chocolate reduction, or juicy medallions of lamb with cabbage or vegetable flan, fresh and Provençal. Then there are the desserts, which hit the mark: chocolate cappuccino, an exotic fruit brunoise and the vanilla cream with pears and Chantilly before the real dessert which is an Ethiopian mocha jelly with a soft ganache and frozen mixed spice cream. This is great art.

● Le Bistro des Saveurs

35, rue de Sélestat.
Tel. 03 88 49 90 41. Fax 03 88 49 90 51.
Closed Mon., Tue., 3 weeks Oct.,
24 Jan.–10 Feb., 25 July–11 Aug.
Prix fixe: 32€ (lunch), 44€, 70€.

Anything is possible, even a delicious meal in the eatery run by Thierry Schwartz, a gifted pupil of the Robuchon school! Previously at the Taverne du Mont d'Arbois in Megève, he has now made his nest in a chic mountain bistro setting with whitewashed walls. Our former qualms are forgotten. The hour of simplicity has arrived, bringing some fine, rustic moments: the "simple" carrots from the Truttenhausen farm, cooked four hours and served with a jus made from poultry bouillon and cumin, fresh young Munster cheese, with shallots, in the "Bibelesskäs" style, skate in romaine salad with capers, slow-roasted milk-fed veal confit cannelloni, without forgetting the amusing Vosges snack (an egg over easy with toast and smoked sausage) featured on the "back from the market" set menu the other day. The cheese plate is an ode to the art of unpasteurized dairy production in the Vosges. The desserts (vanilla éclair, Piedmont-style Tatin and Picon Bière cocktail, a tribute to Yolande Haag) are fine efforts. The young waitstaff is energetic and the wine list has a range of regional libations (not the most famous of vintages). In short, the restaurant now displays a delightful sincerity and enthusiasm.

● La Stub du Parc

169, rte d'Ottrott.
Tel. 03 88 95 50 08. Fax 03 88 95 37 29.
info@hotel-du-parc.com/ www.hotel-du-parc.com
Closed dinner, Sun., Mon., 10 Dec.–mid-Jan.
Prix fixe: 14€ (child). A la carte: 40€.

Marc Wucher has pulled off an ongoing underhanded trick here with this paneled dining room to the right of his celebrated hotel's entrance. Open only at lunchtime, it enchants guests with its woodwork, banquettes, nooks, fine wooden flooring, superb stained glass, engravings, marquetry, Italian lamps and hushed atmosphere beneath a low ceiling. We savor grandmotherly dishes that are often forgotten elsewhere. In fact, the menu is an anthology of traditional Alsatian delights: the smoked herring tartare, oven-crisped tête de veau, Munster cheese grumbeerekiechle (a regional potato cake) with its green salad, spice-seasoned goose foie gras with toast are all splendid. Great cuisine at bistro prices? Yes, you could say that. The Saint-Léonard duckling in cocotte, stuffed and oven-roasted pork trotters and mushroom schniederspättle (the local stuffed dumplings) with veal jus are simply remarkable. They are accompanied by Haute Forêt Noire beer, with a smooth head, and local wines—not the most familiar of vintages—which are quite dazzling. Then there are the tastefully classical desserts: Malabar and Carambar ice creams, a frozen meringue dessert and the strawberry Melba. In short, pure delight distilled with precision and generosity in a rare ambiance.

● La Cour des Tanneurs 🏠SIM
Ruelle du Canal-de-l'Ehn.
Tel. 03 88 95 15 70. Fax 03 88 95 43 84.
Closed Tue., Wed., 20 Dec.–5 Jan.,
2 weeks beg. July.
Prix fixe: 20€ (weekday lunch), 25€, 35€.
A la carte: 45€.

Roland and Martine Vonville are dependable as ever, and give a warm welcome indeed to their "court". Tribute is paid to seasonal and regional produce in the kitchen run by Cour d'Alsace and Parc veteran Roland. Shrimp brochette with curry on a bed of lentils, pike-perch served with seasonal vegetables, veal cutlet with morels and the frozen walnut kouglof are prepared with admirable precision. Each day brings its share of appealing suggestions and the splendid Loew Pinot Gris still features prominently on the excellent wine list.

● Chez Gérard 🏠SIM
46, rue du Général-Gouraud.
Tel. 03 88 95 53 77. Fax 03 88 47 09 37.
gerard.eckert@free.fr / www.chez-gerard.net
Closed Tue. dinner, Wed., Thu. lunch, Jan.,

2 weeks Nov.
Prix fixe: 9,50€ (lunch), 12,50€ (lunch), 16,50€ (lunch), 26€. A la carte: 40€.

Among the town's best value for money is this good-natured *winstub* with its warm welcome and sincere cuisine. Gérard Eckert, who was chef at the Cour d'Alsace and our Bistro of the Year award winner, is said to have an urge to travel to the Far East. For the moment though, this rosy-cheeked, generous innkeeper is still at work, deftly and inexpensively preparing duck foie gras, choucroute done fisherman's style, oven-crisped head cheese and pork totters and a frozen meringue and nougat dessert in the style of Alsace. The unpretentious wines are in the same vein.

● La Halle aux Blés 🏠SIM
Pl du Marché.
Tel. 03 88 95 56 09. Fax 03 88 95 27 70.
www.halleauxbles.com
Prix fixe: 6,50€ (child). A la carte: 35€.

A congenial brasserie that only closes one day of the year is a useful address to know. Francis Kern's reliable, versatile cuisine is sufficiently well prepared, so guests flock to this former medieval covered market, rejuvenated by Daniel Irion, where they make short work of an onion tart, goose foie gras, choucroute with fish, meat cuts, spare-ribs and the Hans dessert cup with Gewurztraminer.

● L'Agneau d'Or SIM
99, rue du Général-Gouraud.
Tel. 03 88 95 28 22. Fax 03 88 95 40 66.
alagneaudor@orange.fr
Closed Mon., Tue.
Prix fixe: 24€, 29€, 31€, 8€ (child).

This *winstub* has been taken over by Laurent Wolf, who has maintained its traditional tavern feel and reliable cuisine. A head cheese and wine aspic terrine with vinaigrette, garlic-seasoned frog legs, grilled salmon filet with bacon, pikeperch on sauerkraut cooked with Riesling, Armagnac-seasoned veal kidney and the stuffed rabbit saddle with Pinot Noir sauce are very honest.

67710 Bas-Rhin. Paris 463 – Molsheim 26 – Strasbourg 66 – Saverne 16.

An airy village in the heart of Alsace's little Switzerland, a step away from the Rocher de Dabo and the Moselle border. The Vosges mountains, hiking trails and pilgrimages.

 HOTELS-RESTAURANTS

■ Hostellerie Belle-Vue

16, rte de Dabo.
Tel. 03 88 87 32 39. Fax 03 88 87 37 77.
hostellerie.belle-vue@wanadoo.fr
www.hostellerie-belle-vue.com
Closed beg. Jan.–beg. Apr. Rest. closed Sun.
(off season), Mon. (off season).
25 rooms: 78€. 3 suites: 108€.
Prix fixe: 25€, 40€, 12€ (child).
A la carte: 60€.

While enjoying your relaxing break, why not pay a visit to Jean-Paul and Cécile Urbaniak? They are attentive in so many little ways and their rooms are as comfortable as you could wish. On the restaurant side, Sébastien Henry, who trained at the Soldat de l'An II in Phalsbourg and with Mathis in Sarrebourg, prepares first-class regional dishes. In the rustic dining room, escargot cassolette, pikeperch with a beurre blanc, saddle of rabbit and a coffee pyramid served with an English tea sauce are faultless.

OBERSTEINBACH

67510 Bas-Rhin. Paris 451 – Bitche 22 – Wissembourg 25 – Strasbourg 66.

A step away from the Palatinate, this one-street village stands at the foot of a line of ruined castles along the border. This is first-rate walking country in the heart of the Vosges nature reserve.

 HOTELS-RESTAURANTS

● Anthon

40, rue Principale.
Tel. 03 88 09 55 01. Fax 03 88 09 50 52.
info@restaurant-anthon.fr
www.restaurant-anthon.fr
Closed Jan. Rest. closed Tue., Wed.
7 rooms: 48–60€. 1 suite: 98€.
Prix fixe: 24€, 45€, 61€.

Barely thirty, but boasting solid experience acquired with great chefs (at the Côte d'Or in Saulieu, the Pinède in Saint-Tropez, the Chabichou in Courchevel and the Buerehiesel in Strasbourg), Georges Flaig has taken up the torch brilliantly in this establishment founded by his great-great-grandfather in 1860. In the heart of the Northern Vosges nature reserve, in the village of Obersteinbach, we are delighted by this former post house converted into a welcoming hostelry. The dishes concocted by the spirited young chef, who focuses on timeless recipes and the region's fine produce, are a model of creativity and precision. Carpaccio of fresh Obersteinbach goat cheese (supplied directly by a neighboring farm) sprinkled with walnuts and grated apples, Schniederspaetle-style ravoli with salmon trout and shallot confit, lamb saddle with ratatouille and cumin-seasoned chickpea curry and the duckling filet with peaches display unfailing integrity of taste. Add a flower sorbet with white chocolate mousse and apricots stuffed with almond cream, served with Amaretto ice cream, along with a wine list based on Alsatian wines (but not exclusively), and you begin to realize that this place is quite a find. Most of the redecorated rooms look out on the romantic ruins. Some even still have their old-fashioned paneled alcoves with fitted beds.

■ Alsace-Village

49, rue Principale.
Tel. 03 88 09 50 59.
www.alsacevillage.com
Closed beg. Jan.–mid-Feb.
Rest. closed Wed., Thu.
12 rooms: 42–52€.
Prix fixe: 25€. A la carte: 30–35€.

A hotel in a natural setting that will smooth away your stress day and night. The renovated, peaceful rooms offer a well-earned rest after a day spent traipsing about the region. However, before you retire, take your time at the dinner table, savoring Christelle Zerafa-Ullmann's suggestions, which are often prepared from organic produce. A taste of the goat cheese with almonds and honey, duck flambéed with Alsatian prune liqueur and the baked apples with caramel sauce and almonds and you will be wishing you could move in.

ODENAS

69460 Rhône. Paris 428 – Lyon 49 – Villefranche 15 – Mâcon 32 – Bourg-en-Bresse 54.
Beaujolais, its gently nodding vines, rounded hills and image of French tranquility.

● RESTAURANTS

● Christian Mabeau `SIM`

Le Bourg.
Tel. 04 74 03 41 79. Fax 04 74 03 49 40.
christian.mabeau@france-beaujolais.com
Closed Sun. dinner, Mon., 1 week beg. Jan., end Aug.–beg. Sept.
Prix fixe: 45,50€, 51€.

We are delighted to take our seats in Christian Mabeau's establishment, which looks out onto the vineyards. Foie gras pan-seared with currants, grilled wild Atlantic sea bass with lemon butter, a medallion of veal sweetbreads with Port, Charolais beef with a Brouilly wine sauce are accompanied by the house's favorite Beaujolais wines. To finish, the coupe vigneronne (blackcurrant sorbet and blackcurrant sauce with Marc de Bourgogne) rounds off the meal prettily.

OIRON

79100 Deux-Sèvres. Paris 325 – Parthenay 40 – Poitiers 55 – Thouars 11 – Loudun 14.
Madame de Montespan's château with its formal gardens, charming covered gallery, guard hall and Cabinet des Muses is a wonderful example of Renaissance art. A fine Gothic church, tombs and reredos.

■ HOTELS-RESTAURANTS

● Relais du Château `N` `COM`

17, pl des Marronniers.
Tel. 05 49 96 54 96. Fax 05 49 96 54 45.
relaisduchateau@aol.com
www.le-relais-du-chateau.com
Closed Sun. (exc. rest. dinner),
Mon. (hotel open), dinner Bank holidays,
1 week beg. Jan., 2 weeks beg. Feb.
12 rooms: 36–41€.
Prix fixe: 16€ (exc. Sun.), 24€, 32€, 7€ (child).

Right on the village square, the Hotots' hotel in light colors boasts modern rooms and a bright restaurant that opens onto a courtyard terrace. In the kitchen, Loïc concentrates on local produce and loves to innovate: lamb sweetbread salad with mild spices, crispy savory tart with foie gras, Atlantic sea bass filet grilled skinside down with bright red butter and beef filet served with fingerling potatoes, oyster mushrooms and foie gras slip down effortlessly. The soup from fruits in season with ginger and lemongrass provides a fresh conclusion. The dynamic Sylvia recommends wines from the West of France.

OISLY

41700 Loir-et-Cher. Paris 208 – Tours 60 – Blois 27 – Châteauroux 79 – Romorantin-Lanthenay 32.
The Sologne of sands, lakes, clearings and vines.

● RESTAURANTS

● Le Saint-Vincent `P` `COM`

Le Bourg.
Tel.-Fax 02 54 79 50 04.
Closed Mon. dinner, Tue., Wed., beg. Dec.–mid-Jan., 1 week beg. Aug.
Prix fixe: 25€ (lunch), 32€, 52€.
A la carte: 45–60€.

Anyone planning to stop over in the heart of the Sologne will be enchanted by this inn, with its décor in light shades. Christophe Picard, formerly at Taillevent, the Bristol and with Barrier in Tours, concocts unexpected, flavorsome dishes with an exotic touch, using carefully selected produce and well-chosen spices that blossom delicately in the mouth. Enjoy the surprising lobster sausage seasoned with red curry, John Dory poached in a ginger court-bouillon and a veal sweetbread fricassée seasoned with Espelette and piquillo peppers. For dessert, the unctuous warm chocolate dessert with a salted-butter caramel sauce and white chocolate ice cream are to die for. A local wine recommended by Catherine Picard will wash down these delights pleasantly. An explosive address where the check holds no fears. The lunchtime set menu is a bargain.

ILE–D'OLERON

17550 Charente-Maritime. Paris 520 – La Rochelle 81 – Marennes 22 – Rochefort 43 – Saintes 62.
France's largest Atlantic island offers pearly beaches, deep blue sea and plenty of hospitality. Oysters are celebrated all year round and mimosa in March in Saint-Trojan.

 HOTELS-RESTAURANTS

In Château-d'Oléron (17310).
● Jardins d'Aliénor   N COM
11, rue du Maréchal Foch.
Tel. 05 46 76 48 30.
www.lesjardinsdalienor.fr
Closed 3 weeks Mar. Rest. closed Mon. (off season exc. vac.), lunch (July–Aug. and off season exc. by reserv.).
4 rooms: 75–95€.
Prix fixe: 23€, 29€, 39€.

Waging a charm offensive in Oléron is this former town hall converted into an enchanting hostelry with four delightful rooms, startling bathrooms (including a double shower in the Pierre d'Argencourt suite!), warm, gray tones and a delicious patio open to the island's blue sky. Laetitia and Marc Le Reun have achieved their dream. Laetitia, a former corporate controller, provides a warm welcome. Marc, formerly with Goumard, the Copenhague and the Maison Blanche in Paris, prepares unfussy dishes. The set menus are shrewdly put together. Tuna mousse, salmon tartare, pan-fried skate with chives and mashed potato and the chocoate mille-feuille with salted-butter caramel are equal to their task. More attention to the seasoning (watch out for too much or too little salt) and everything will be just right.

● Les Goélands   N SIM
Av du Port.
Tel. 05 46 47 78 48.
Closed Wed., Dec.–end Mar.
Prix fixe: 15€, 20€, 28€.

On the harbor opposite the fortress, Pascale and Philippe Bodard offer a warm welcome in their hut, simplicity itself. In the dining room or on the terrace, we enjoy the fresh, genuine, uncomplicated dishes. House foie gras terrine using Pineau wine, grilled Atlantic sea bass with Maureuil wine, boneless rib steak with ceps and the flambéed meringue and strawberry dessert are specialties.

In La Cotinière (17310).
● L'Assiette du Capitaine   N SIM
2, bd du Capitaine-Leclerc.
Tel. 05 46 47 38 78.
lzindel@club-internet.fr
Closed Wed. (off season exc. vac.), mid-Nov.–beg. Feb.
Prix fixe: 32€.

Luc Zindel is crazy about the Caribbean and left his heart in Guadeloupe, which explains this fun bistro with its red and white pine wainscotting, bar offering a collection of punches and rums, seafood baskets and blackboard changing daily to reflect the latest catch. Mackerel rilettes, seafood tagine, fruit brochettes and pain d'épice go down deliciously.

In Dolus-d'Oléron (17550).
■ Le Grand Large   ❀ ⌂
Baie de la Rémigeasse,
2 km w via secondary road.

Tel. 05 46 75 77 77. Fax 05 46 75 49 15.
contact@le-grand-large.fr
www.le-grand-large.fr
Closed Nov. 1–Easter.
24 rooms: 42–162€. 4 suites: 102–209€.
Prix fixe: 29€. A la carte: 40–55€.

Inexpensive but still congenial and located in the finest setting on the island—a magnificent beach—this sixties establishment is still the perfect place to stay on your ideal vacation. Among its attractions are a swimming pool and bar housed in a Le Corbusier-style wing, handsome panoramic rooms, Philippe Villa's distinctive welcome and meticulous dishes supplied by the faithful Joël Lebeaupin, there for nearly three decades. He now prepares a 29 menu that changes daily. On the day of our visit, a rabbit terrine with red onion chutney, cuttlefish stew in the Saintongeais style, little medallions of lamb in a rustic pastry crust and the frozen parfait with praline sauce served with little dark chocolate cakes made a fine impression.

In Grand-Village-Plage (17370).

● **Le Relais des Salines**   **Ⓝ** SIM
Port des Salines.
Tel. 05 46 75 82 42. Fax 05 46 75 16 70.
Closed Sun. dinner (off season),
Mon. (off season), end Nov.–mid-Mar.
Prix fixe: 15€ (lunch), 30€.

This dazzlingly authentic oyster farmer's hut was put together from scratch thirteen years ago by James Robert, who provides a distinctive, heartfelt welcome. His grandfather and father were fishermen and he serves up the best seafood from the quays of La Cotinière. Chalked up on the blackboard or presented by word of mouth, grilled sardines, mouclade (mussels with a shallots and cream sauce), tuna steaks, oysters "from the neighbor", lentils and cod with bacon, grilled cuttlefish, rougets with bone marrow and local sole are all frankly delicious.

In Saint-Pierre-d'Oléron (17310). D 734.

■ **L'Ecailler**   ⌂
At La Cotinière, 65, rue du Port.
Tel. 05 46 47 10 31. Fax 05 46 47 10 23.

ecailler@club-internet.fr
www.ecailler-oleron.com
Closed Dec.– Jan.
8 rooms: 51–89€.
Prix fixe: 19,80€, 25€, 28,80€, 38€,
10,50€ (child). A la carte: 35–40€.

The Hervés from Saint-Pierre d'Oléron's Saint-Pierre have taken over this hotel on the harbor, with its sunny rooms in shades of blue, its terrace where guests can watch the boats come and go, and its dining room with exposed stone walls. Chef Laurent Le Mellay has a refined repertoire: fish soup, fried colin served *en colère* (with its tail in its mouth), fried sole and the cod with a sauce Calabraise (hot pepper-spiced tomato sauce) are down to earth.

● **Le Petit Coivre**   ■SIM
10, av Bel-Air. D. 734.
Tel. 05 46 47 44 23. Fax 05 46 47 33 57.
lepetitcoivre@free.fr
Closed Sun. dinner, Mon., Wed. dinner,
Feb. vac.
Prix fixe: 25€. A la carte: 40€.

Gilles and Sylvie Beaudrillier have enthusiastically taken over this attractive inn, now reinterpreted in a congenial bistro style. There is a busy road outside and a shopping mall has rather unattractively risen opposite, but here, no hint of a shadow blights our delight. The dining room has beams, pine wainscotting, a large fireplace and a rustic décor featuring farm tools. The blackboard offers duck terrine made with Cognac and foie gras, crispy shrimp salad, sardines with a mustard and wine sauce, pollock cooked with apples and cider, creole pineapple soup and a strawberry tiramisu. Gilles, a native of Champagne who learned his trade at the Cheval Blanc in Sept Saulx, has lost none of his skills.

● **Saveurs des Iles**   Ⓝ■SIM
18, rue de la Plage, La Menounière.
Tel. 05 46 75 86 68.
saveursdesiles@wanadoo.fr
Closed Mon., Tue. lunch, beg. Jan.–end Mar.
Prix fixe: 23€, 35€.

Patrick and Cécile Daudu left the Ile de Ré (and the Chasse-Marée where Patrick was chef) for this quiet patch of garden near La Cotinière. Local produce and exotic spices are the thing in this restaurant run with talent. Pan-seared tuna breaded with flax seeds, ginger-seasoned fish tartare, rougets with summer vegetables, vanilla-seasoned drum fish with rice and coconut milk and the frozen Arabica coffee parfait with Cognac cream are washed down pleasantly with a little Coulon Oléron *rosé* at 10 : a steal.

In Saint-Trojan-les-Bains (17310).

■ Les Cleunes ⓃⰢ

25, bd de la Plage.
Tel. 05 46 76 03 08. Fax 05 46 76 08 95.
www.hotel-les-cleunes.com
Closed mid-Nov.–beg. Feb.
40 rooms: 80–230€.
Prix fixe: 28€, 37€, 54€.

With its spacious, well-appointed rooms, swimming pool, warm welcome and meticulous service, this luxurious residence opposite the road and the sea makes an excellent impression. Ginette Quintard looks after the hotel side, while her son Thierry Seguin presides over the dining room with great energy. Chef Franck Thierry's cuisine is classical and polished. Gillardeau oysters wrapped in seaweed, soft-cooked monkfish fricassée and deboned squab in its juices are finely crafted dishes.

■ Le Homard Bleu ⓃⰢ

10, bd Félix-Faure.
Tel. 05 46 76 00 22. Fax 05 46 76 14 95.
Prix fixe: 28,80€, 39,50€.

Lively, skilled chef Jean-Pascal Ratier, formerly at the Le Rouzic in Bordeaux, tends to the kitchen in this light, bright hotel opposite the sapphire sea. His sister Nelly looks after the premises. In the panoramic dining room, we celebrate sensibly, with old-fashioned-style oysters with garlic and breadcrumbs, pressed rouget terrine with ham and Provençal compote, cod filet in an olive crust, rack of lamb in a sage reduction sauce and a frozen chocolate cannelloni that concludes the tempting set menu at 28,80 .

■ L'Albatros ⓄⰤ

11, bd du Docteur-Pineau.
Tel. 05 46 76 00 08.
www.albatros-hotel-oleron.com
Closed beg. Nov.–beg. Feb.
13 rooms: 57–99€.
Prix fixe: 27€, 79€.

The view, location and beachfront amenities explain the success of this hotel. It offers simple rooms overlooking the ocean (some renovated) and especially conscientious dishes prepared by Alain Oblin, a genuine old-fashioned chef, who pays tribute to lobster on a set menu dedicated to the king of crustaceans, along with (depending on the market) fried cod cakes, Provençal-style grilled monkfish, fried sole seasoned with cumin, curry-seasoned drum fish and the butcher's cut of the day served with house fries.

OLIVET see ORLEANS

OLIVET see ORLEANS

OMONVILLE-LA-PETITE

50440 Manche. Paris 380 – Cherbourg 25 – Nez de Jobourg 7 – Barneville-Carteret 45.
Prévert lived in this delicious, flowery village in La Hague. Travelers visit his home and the garden dedicated to him and pay tribute at his grave in the cemetery.

■ | HOTELS

■ La Fossardière Ⓝ⚘Ⱔ

Hameau de la Fosse.
Tel. 02 33 52 19 83. Fax 02 33 52 73 49.
10 rooms: 40–64€.

Gilles Fossard opens his family home to guests who stay for a day or more. Actors shooting *Le Passager de l'été* stayed here for three months. Charm, peace and simplicity are the trusted trinity here.

ONZAIN

41150 Loir-et-Cher. Paris 203 – Tours 45 –
Amboise 22 – Blois 18 – Montrichard 22.
On the bank opposite Chaumont-sur-Loire and its
fine château, this small rural town off the royal
route also produces pleasant wines.

 HOTELS-RESTAURANTS

● **Domaine des Hauts** ○❀ 🏛
 de Loire

3 km nw via D1 and private road.
Tel. 02 54 20 72 57. Fax 02 54 20 77 32.
hauts-loire@relaischateaux.com
www.domainehautsloire.com
Closed Dec.–end Feb.
Rest. closed Mon. (exc. Bank holidays),
Tue. (exc. Bank holidays).
22 rooms: 130–290€. 10 suites: 320–450€.
Prix fixe: 50€, 75€, 90€, 145€, 25€ (child).

The Bonnigals have turned this 19th-
century country seat into a model Relais
& Châteaux establishment. The rooms
are easy on the eye, the grounds relaxing
and the restaurant—run by Rémy Giraud,
who has worked there for two decades
and was a pupil of Frédy Girardet—full
of charm. The crispy eel in salad with a
shallot vinaigrette, duck foie gras with
chanterelles cooked in Vouvray, roasted
pike-perch roasted skin-side down with
parsley cream, John Dory with a langoustine tartare, creamed potatoes with summer truffles, beef tenderloin poached in
Montlouis wine and a young Vendôme
pressed pigeon with jus deserve nothing
but praise. The desserts (old-fashioned
thick chocolate cake with pralines and a
mint soufflé) are up to the same standard.
A fine Loire wine list.

ORBEC

14290 Calvados. Paris 169 – L'Aigle 39 –
Alençon 80 – Bernay 17 – Lisieux 22.
omar.orbec@wanadoo.fr.
At the southern tip of the Pays d'Auge, an old-
fashioned town straight from a Maupassant
tale.

● RESTAURANTS

● **Au Caneton** 🏠 V.COM

32, rue Grande.
Tel. 02 31 32 73 32. Fax 02 31 62 48 91.
Closed Sun. dinner (exc. Bank holidays),
Mon. (exc. Bank holidays),
Tue. (Nov.–Easter), 2 weeks beg. Jan.,
2 weeks beg. Sept.
Prix fixe: 20€, 30€, 46€, 75€.
A la carte: 70–90€.

This 17th-century inn is an ode to Normandy, with its brasses, collection of
plates, half-timbering and fireplace.
Didier Tricot's cuisine is in the same vein:
classical, solid and generous. Oysters prepared three ways, lobster fricassée, turbot
cooked in cider, spit-roasted wild duck
and a Calvados soufflé are dependability itself. Led by Chantal, the service is
unstoppable. If it were not for the prices
à la carte...

ORBEY

68370 Haut-Rhin. Paris 427 – Colmar 20 –
Munster 25 – Gérardmer 41.
A community covering thirty-eight hamlets in
the heart of the Pays du Munster. The scenery is pastoral and countless excursions can be
enjoyed on foot or ski.

 HOTELS-RESTAURANTS

■ **Au Bois le Sire** 🏛

20, rue du Général-de-Gaulle.
Tel. 03 89 71 25 25. Fax 03 89 71 30 75.
boislesire@bois-le-sire.fr
www.bois-le-sire.fr
Closed beg. Jan.–beg. Feb. Rest. closed Sun.
dinner (off season), Mon. (exc. July–Aug.).
34 rooms: 44,50–68€.
1 suite: 153,50–168,50€.
Prix fixe: 9€ (weekday lunch), 15,50€, 48€,
8€ (child).

With its swimming pool, sauna, Jacuzzi
and play area, this modern hotel—half-
traditional, half-motel—with renovated,
comfortable rooms is a good place to stay.

After a hike, all agree that Olivier Ducoudard's cuisine is just the thing. Duck foie gras with potatoes and celery root, escargot brochettes with bacon, Alpine lake trout with potato saffron emulsion and the duck breast with lingonberries are classics that never stale, like the frozen vacherin. Reasonable prices.

■ Wetterer

206, Basses-Huttes.
Tel. 03 89 71 20 28. Fax 03 89 71 36 50.
info@hotel-wetterer.com
www.hotel-wetterer.com
Closed end Jan.–beg. Feb., 2 weeks Mar., beg. Nov.–beg.Dec. Rest. closed Mon. (Dec., Jan.), Tue. (Dec., Jan.), Wed.
15 rooms: 34–51€.
Prix fixe: 14€, 7,50€ (child). A la carte: 35€.

Bertrand Wetterer welcomes passing or regular patrons as if they were friends, so they naturally feel at home in the cozy rooms, sauna and rustic dining room, with its reliable regional cuisine (poultry liver terrine, fresh poached trout *au bleu*, classic choucroute and the frozen vacherin).

■ La Croix d'Or ⬠

13, rue de l'Eglise.
Tel. 03 89 71 20 51. Fax 03 89 71 35 60.
hotel-croixdor@wanadoo.fr
www.hotel-croixdor.com
Closed 10 days Nov., 2 weeks Jan., 2 weeks end June–beg.
July, Mon. Rest. closed Sat. lunch, Mon., Thu. lunch.
16 rooms: 45–49€.
Prix fixe: 11,60€ (weekday lunch), 14,80€, 18,50€, 23€, 32€, 9€ (child), 32€.

Pascal Macé watches over this family guesthouse with care. The neat and tidy rooms, restrained cuisine, terrace and rustic dining room put visitors at their ease. House terrine with crunchy vegetables, local trout with almonds, duck with blueberries and the pain d'épice crème brûlée slip down effortlessly.

ORCINES see CLERMONT-FERRAND

45000 Loiret. Paris 132 – Le Mans 142 – Tours 116 – Blois 61 – Caen 273.
office-de-tourisme.orleans@wanadoo.fr.
Too near or too far from Paris? We tend to forget this city. Yet, the "Belle de Loire" has no lack of charm. Pleasant restaurants—not always as we imagined them—and gourmet artisans who work hard to get things right: a good reason to take another look at Orléans, its cathedral, art gallery and Loire riverbanks.

■	HOTELS

■ Mercure

44, quai Barentin.
Tel. 02 38 62 17 39 / 02 38 62 96 10 30.
Fax 02 38 53 95 34.
h0581@accor-hotels.com
www.mercure.com
111 rooms: 101–145€. 1 suite: 183€.

All the advantages of a chain hotel, with guaranteed comfort and professional service first and foremost. The swimming pool and terrace are deliciously relaxing. The restaurant has its attractions too.

■ Hôtel d'Arc ⌂

37, rue de la République.
Tel. 02 38 53 10 94. Fax 02 38 81 77 47.
hotel.darc@wanadoo.fr / www.hoteldarc.fr
35 rooms: 79–145€.

This charming hotel has recently been completely renovated. Furnished in Louis-Philippe style, the rooms are comfortable and colorful. An ideal location in the city center.

■ Terminus

40, rue de la République.
Tel. 02 38 53 24 64. Fax 02 38 53 24 18.
terminus.orleans@wanadoo.fr
www.terminus-orleans.com
Closed Christmas–beg. Jan.
47 rooms: 65–95€.

Practical and close to the rail station in the heart of the new pedestrian center, Jean-Paul Norée's hotel provides smart rooms in different styles: Zen, Oriental, African and maritime.

■ Hôtel des Cèdres

17, rue du Maréchal-Foch.
Tel. 02 38 62 22 92. Fax 02 38 81 76 46.
contact@hoteldescedres.com
www.hoteldescedres.com
32 rooms: 55–90€.

The conservatory lounge looks out on the cedars in the garden. The renovated rooms are appealing and so are the prices.

In Olivet (45160). 5 km s via av. du Loiret on the banks of the Loiret.

■ Le Rivage

635, rue de la Reine-Blanche.
Tel. 02 38 66 02 93. Fax 02 38 56 31 11.
http://monsite.wanadoo.fr/le.rivage.olivet
Closed Christmas–20 Jan.
Rest. closed Sun. lunch.
17 rooms: 80–110€.
Prix fixe: 28€ (exc. Sun.), 30€, 42€, 60€.

Jean-Pierre Bereaud conscientiously runs this country inn with terrace and garden on the bank of the Loiret. It boasts neat rooms and an excellent restaurant. In its spruced-up dining room, we discover Franck Lemaître's flavorsome domestic cuisine.

●	RESTAURANTS

● Les Antiquaires

2, rue au Lin.
Tel. 02 38 53 52 35. Fax 02 38 62 06 95.
www.restaurantlesantiquaires.com
Closed Sun. dinner, Mon.,
Tue. lunch (July–Aug.), 1 May.
Prix fixe: 38€ (weekdays wine inc.), 46€, 66€, 22€ (child). A la carte: 70–75€.

Philippe Bardau, formerly with Maximin, Outhier and Huyart, continues on his quest for perfect, refined flavor. He works with produce of the highest quality and displays unfailing inventiveness, although the menu changes four or five times a year. Proof comes in the form of an original series of frog legs–themed

tapas in five plates, John Dory dusted in olive powder, cuttlefish pastilla with a light bouillon, a pan-seared beef and foie gras mille-feuille and a pan-tossed raspberry dessert with its "sushi" and "milkshake". Pascale Lemoine offers advice to those fortunate food lovers who have come to savor these delicious creations, helping them to choose the right wine among a selection that favors Loire vintages, but crosses oceans too.

● Eugène

24, rue Sainte-Anne.
Tel. 02 38 53 82 64. Fax 02 38 54 31 89.
www.cartesurtables.fr
Closed Sat. lunch, Sun., Mon. lunch,
1 week May, 3 weeks Aug.,
1 week Christmas–New Year's.
Prix fixe: 22,50€, 31,50€ (lunch, wine inc.),
35€, 38€, 15€ (child). A la carte: 55€.

Alain Gérard works wonders with Southern French produce to prepare his subtle, lively dishes. Duck breast carpaccio with anchoïade, tuna steak and tomatoes with shallot confit, oven-browned veal with seasoned anchovy paste, summer vegetable lasagne and the dried fruit dessert with roasted figs and pink peppercorns and served with cardamom ice cream leave us with a captivating sense of creativity and mastery.

● La Chancellerie

27, pl du Martroi.
Tel. 02 38 53 57 54. Fax 02 38 77 09 92.
lachancellerie.fr
Closed Sun. dinner.
Prix fixe: 16,50€, 26€, 36€, 8,50€ (child).

Bernard, Annie, Laurent and Fabien Lefèvre—all four of them—run this bistro brasserie in the city center. The welcome is flawless and chef Pascal Letarmeck's cuisine is in a skillfully mastered classical vein. The rabbit terrine, profiteroles stuffed with pike-perch, crunchy potatoes with smoked salmon, Jargeau chitterling sausage grilled with herbs and an apricot tart practically eat themselves.

● L'Epicurien COM

54, rue des Turcies.
Tel. 02 38 68 01 10. Fax 02 38 68 19 02.
lepicurien orléans
Closed Sun., Mon., 3 weeks Aug.
Prix fixe: 25€, 30€ (lunch, wine inc.), 40€,
15€ (child).

The Philippot brothers are the double act in this yellow restaurant with exposed beams, bright as a new pin. Guillaume (in the kitchen) prepares the day's market produce and Sébastien (in the dining room and cellar) sings its praises. Foie gras "bonbons", a thin pike-perch tart with beurre rouge in the local style, hazelnuts with chocolate in season and home-style pain d'épice pain perdu are all very appealing. A fine wine list and sensible set menus.

● La Promenade & Le Martroi COM

1, rue Adolphe-Crespin.
Tel. 02 38 42 78 18. Fax 02 38 42 15 01.
lemartroi@wanadoo.fr
Closed mid-Sept.–1 Mar.
Prix fixe: 16€, 22€, 35€, 10€ (child).

Michel Trognon has set things straight in this two-tier restaurant: an art deco second floor and a more bistro-like first floor (Le Martroi, 02 38 42 15 00). The cuisine is respectable and the friendly welcome is back. No complaints about the trout and leek terrine, skate wing with capers, chicken tagine and the tarte Tatin. Very reasonable prices.

● Le Chalut SIM

59, rue Notre-Dame-de-Recouvrance.
Tel. 02 38 54 36 36. Fax 02 38 75 11 46.
www.lechalut.fr
Closed Sun., Mon., 1 week beg. May,
end July–mid-Aug.
Prix fixe: 15€ (weekdays), 19,80€.
A la carte: 40€.

Chalut is (almost) exclusively focused on fish: a décor in woodwork and salmon shades and a very sea-oriented cuisine. Laurent Legivre concocts enjoyable light dishes that reflect the vagaries of the market. Pan-tossed langoustines, liver with alfalfa sprouts, pan-fried skate with a sweet potato purée and green asparagus and the beef tenderloin with pepper sauce are faultless. To conclude, we cannot resist the raspberry mille-feuille and the mascarpone dessert with pistachios and lime sorbet. Fine wines and takeaway dishes.

● La Dariole SIM

25, rue Etienne-Dolet.
Tel.-Fax 02 38 77 26 67.
Closed Mon. lunch, Easter vac., 3 weeks Aug.
Prix fixe: 16,50€, 21€, 8€ (child).
A la carte: 40€.

This enchanting half-timbered 15th-century house with its terrace in season serves up flavorsome, market-based dishes. At the stove, Hervé Pichonnet reliably prepares shellfish ragout on a bed of julienned vegetables with saffron, scallop ravioli with a soy reduction and dry braised green cabbage and pork shank in a pot-au-feu, seasoned with coriander.

In Saint-Jean-de-Braye (45000). 4 km e.

● Les Toqués N COM

71, chemin du Halage.
Tel. 02 38 86 50 20. Fax 02 38 84 30 96.
lestoques@noos.fr
Closed Sun., Mon., 2 weeks Jan.,
2 weeks Aug.
Prix fixe: 18€ (weekday lunch), 29€,
8€ (child).

Exit the Vaudésir. Now the dynamic Frédéric Jenot runs this delightful establishment on the banks of the Loire, with its charming Japanese-style décor in shades of red. The cuisine is well conceived and we can only praise the crispy shrimp in a Thai sauce, Atlantic sea bass in papillote with basil, braised beef cheek and foie gras and the roasted apples with rum-raisin brioche. The set menus are splendid.

ORNANS

25290 Doubs. Paris 429 – Besançon 25 –
Morteau 53 – Pontarlier 35.
The land of Courbet and the valley of the Loue still have all the rustic charm of 19th-century paintings.

HOTELS-RESTAURANTS

■ **Hôtel de France**

51-53, rue Pierre-Vernier.
Tel. 03 81 62 24 44. Fax 03 81 62 12 03.
contacts@hoteldefrance-ornans.com
www.hoteldefrance-ornans.com
Closed Fri. dinner (off season), Sat. lunch (off
season), Sun. dinner (off season),
beg. Nov.–mid-Nov., 3 weeks Christmas–New
Year's–mid-Jan.
27 rooms: 60–80€. 2 suites: 80–140€.
Prix fixe: 19€, 24€, 27€, 34€,
12€ (child). A la carte: 55€.

In this post house, where generations have
come and gone, the Vincent sons have a
firm grip on the helm. Xavier at the stove
and Stéphane in the dining room serve up
discreet, reassuring dishes. Trout filet with
morels and Vin Jaune, veal sweetbreads
with morels and the house chocolate profiteroles are excellent work. The rooms are
handsome with their white tones. Also
note the Vincents' second establishment:
Hôtel de la Vallée, 25, av du Président-Wilson. Tel. 03 81 62 40 43.

● **Le Courbet**

34, rue Pierre Vernier.
Tel. 03 81 62 10 15.
restaurantlecourbet@orange.fr
Closed Sun. dinner, Mon., Tue. lunch (exc.
July–Aug.), mid-Feb.–mid-Mar.
Prix fixe: 17€, 37€.

Exquisite, congenial and inexpensive: this
establishment dedicated to the great local
painter (his birthplace is just a minute
away) is well worth a visit for Bertrand
Lhôte's market-based cuisine focused on
fish. The menu changes monthly (the trout
poached in Vin Jaune is a great achievement, while the foie gras is not bad and
there is game in the fall). A fine view of the
Loue from the two covered terraces.

ORTHEZ

64300 Pyrénées-Atlantiques. Paris 769 –
Pau 47 – Bayonne 74 – Dax 39 –
Mont-de-Marsan 57.

In the heart of the Béarn, this great poultry,
ham and foie gras market enchants us with its
old humpback bridge, church of Saint-Pierre
and Moncade keep.

 HOTELS-RESTAURANTS

■ **Au Temps de la Reine Jeanne**

44, rue du Bourg-Vieux.
Tel. 05 59 67 00 76. Fax 05 59 69 09 63.
www.reine-jeanne.fr
Rest. closed Sun. dinner (off season).
30 rooms: 45–88€. A la carte: 50€.

This inn, where style and comfort are by
no means mutually exclusive, is a pleasant
place to stay in the Pyrénées. The rooms,
all different, offer peace and well-being.
The sauna and Jacuzzi are ideal for relaxation. Served in a paneled dining room
in white and orange-red shades, the cuisine is up to the same high standard.
Laurent Remangon prepares foie gras
terrine, whiting sautéed in white wine
with brandy, garlic, shallots and tomatoes,
pan-seared pork filet with herbs and a hot
prune and rhubarb compote tart.

● **Auberge Saint-Loup**

20, rue du Pont-Vieux.
Tel. 05 59 69 15 40. Fax 05 59 67 13 19.
aubergedesaintloup@hotmail.com
Closed Sun. dinner, Mon.
Prix fixe: 15€ (lunch), 21€, 34€, 45€.

On the medieval pilgrimage route to
Santiago de Compostela (the Way of St.
James) this gracious inn provides congenial sanctuary. In the entirely renovated
dining room in yellow and cream tones,
we eagerly savor the neoclassical dishes
whipped up by Aurélien Cathelin. A scallop, endive and mushroom flan, a sole
mille-feuille made with "la Vache qui rit"
cheese product, beef tenderloin Rossini
and the crème brûlée are delights.

ORVAULT see NANTES

OSSES

64780 Pyrénées-Atlantiques. Paris 804 – Biarritz 33 – Cambo-les-Bains 19 – Bidarray 5.
This small corner of Basse-Navarre provides the ideal base for a tour of the hills of Basque Labourd.

 HOTELS-RESTAURANTS

■ Mendi-Alde

Pl de l'Eglise.
Tel. 05 59 37 71 78. Fax 05 59 37 77 22.
www.hotelmendialde.com
Closed Sun. dinner (off season), Mon. dinner (off season), Tue. (off season), Dec.
24 rooms: 46–90€.
Prix fixe: 14,50€ (lunch), 20,80€, 29€.

Jean-Michel Noullet, who was once Grégoire Sein's lieutenant at the Biarritz Palais, displays a studied modesty in this little village hotel that offers polished comfort. A native of Alsace from Wissembourg who trained with Blanc, Bocuse and Lorain, he enchants us with a succession of simple but refined dishes. Slow-cooked mixed peppers and onions and ventreche (a French-style pancetta), whiting cassolette with sweet green peas, a raspberry dacquoise and apple strudel are very well done.

OSTHEIM

68150 Haut-Rhin. Paris 435 – Colmar 11 – Sélestat 13.
What is still here to remind us of Ostheim's fine prewar Grand-Place but a section of wall with a stork nest?

 HOTELS-RESTAURANTS

■ Au Nid de Cigognes

2, rte de Colmar.
Tel. 03 89 47 91 44. Fax 03 89 47 99 88.
hotelauniddecigognes@wanadoo.fr
Closed 15–Feb.–mid-Mar. Rest. closed Sun. dinner (Jan.), Mon. (Jan.), Thu. dinner (Jan.).
50 rooms: 40–64€.

Prix fixe: 13€ (lunch weekdays), 24€, 37€, 9€ (child). A la carte: 40–50€.

On the Colmar road, we enjoy our stay with Danielle and Martin Utzmann. Aside from the comfortable rooms, we are impressed by the dishes prepared by their daughter, Céline Utzmann-Houx: a delicate panorama of regional produce and recipes. House goose foie gras, crisp layered tart with pike-perch and "flavors of the forest", venison medallion with morels and a frozen meringue and nougat dessert called the *nid de cigognes* (stork's nest) offer a delicious suggestion of the superb surrounding rivers and forests. The fine wine list has been compiled by David Houx. An excellent breakfast.

OSTHOUSE

67150 Bas-Rhin. Paris 501 – Strasbourg 29 – Obernai 18 – Sélestat 23 – Erstein 4.
A simple Ried village and with a fine inn.

 HOTELS-RESTAURANTS

■ A la Ferme

10, rue du Château.
Tel. 03 90 29 92 50. Fax 03 90 29 92 51.
www.hotelalaferme.com
2 rooms: 83–88€. 5 suites: 114–130€.

In the hands of Jean-Philippe and Brigitte Hellmann, this 18th-century farm has become a modern hostelry. For better, not for worse, the rooms wed tradition to design, particularly in the former tobacco-drying area.

● L'Aigle d'Or

14, rue de Gerstheim.
Tel. 03 88 98 06 82. Fax 03 88 98 81 75.
Closed Mon., Tue., 3 weeks Aug.
Prix fixe: 32,50€, 49,50€, 72€.
A la carte: 60€.

The Aigle d'Or is a family business. During his time at the Cerf in Marlenheim, l'Auberge de l'Ill in Illhaeusern and the Tour d'Argent in Paris, the son, Jean-Philippe Hellmann, refined his talent for flavorsome dishes, often of classical inspiration. We enjoy the pan-tossed frog legs on a layer of garlic potato purée, snapper pot-au-feu, pigeon breast and chocolate drops with ripe cherries and admire the woodwork and superb painted lacunar ceiling of the elegant dining room. The wine list offers plenty of choices and the discreet but attentive service does justice to the quality of the dishes. Visitors may prefer to opt for the simplicity of the regional dishes served in the relaxed atmosphere of the *winstub*.

OSTWALD see STRASBOURG

OTTROTT

67530 Bas-Rhin. Paris 489 – Strasbourg 20 – Colmar 45.
A trim village overlooking the vines, a panoramic view of the Vosges mountains, fine hotels and a thriving tourism business: Ottrott is Saint-Paul-de-Vence with added gourmet pleasures and mischievous red wine.

 HOTELS-RESTAURANTS

■ Hostellerie des Châteaux   ❀ 🏨
11, rue des Châteaux.
Tel. 03 88 48 14 14. Fax 03 88 48 14 18.
leschateaux@wanadoo.fr
www.hostellerie-chateaux.fr
Hotel closed Feb. Rest. closed Sun. lunch (off season), Mon. (off season), Feb., 1 week at end July, 1 week beg. Aug.
61 rooms: 100–265€. 66 suites: 245–265€.
Prix fixe: 36€ (weekdays), 55€, 80€, 16€ (child). A la carte: 85€.

There are plenty of reasons to visit Sabine and Ernest Schaetzel: the charming, entirely renovated rooms, the swimming pool and the "spa and beauty" facility with its sauna, Jacuzzi and treatments. Added to these pleasures are the delights on offer in the restaurant, run by the master of the house. Layers of sauerkraut, smoked and marinated salmon, rouget with puréed nettles, veal cutlet with roasted chicory jus and the lemon cream soufflé make a delicious spread.

■ Beau Site   🏨
Pl de l'Eglise.
Tel. 03 88 48 14 30. Fax 03 88 48 14 18.
lebeausiteott@wanadoo.fr
www.hotel-beau-site.fr
Closed Feb. Rest. closed Sun. dinner (off season), Mon. (off season).
18 rooms: 89–162€.
Prix fixe: 19€, 31€, 54€, 10€ (child).
A la carte: 40–45€.

The Schaetzels, who also own the Châteaux, have made this their second establishment. Pascal Heppe's cuisine offers a meticulous take on tradition. The two types of duck foie gras in terrine, salmon with garden savory, oven-crisped tête de veau with baby vegetables and a sweet frozen beer eau-de-vie soufflé with cinnamon are well-conceived. The hotel also boasts attractive rooms and a warm Alsatian décor.

■ A l'Ami Fritz   🍴❀🏨
8, rue des Châteaux.
Tel. 03 88 95 80 81. Fax 03 88 95 84 85.
ami-fritz@wanadoo.fr / www.amifritz.com
Closed 2 weeks Jan. Rest. closed Wed.
19 rooms: 69–90€. 3 suites: 105–140€.
Prix fixe: 23€, 39€, 60€.

The Fritz hostelry offers bright rooms and a quality regional restaurant. In the kitchen, Patrick carefully complies with local culinary tradition, serving up such dishes as an individual pressed rabbit and tarragon terrine with foie gras, pike fish quenelles with crayfish, duck pieces served over sauerkraut ("choucroute" style) and the frozen prune digestif soufflé. Jean-Dominique Gessner recommends wines that provide a flavorsome accompaniment to the dishes. Pleasant service on the terrace in summer and well-chosen set menus.

■ Le Moulin   ❀🏨
32, rte de Klingenthal, 1 km nw via D426.
Tel. 03 88 95 87 33. Fax 03 88 95 98 03.
domaine.le.moulin@wanadoo.fr
www.domaine-le-moulin.com
Closed 3 weeks Jan. Rest. closed Sat. lunch, Sun. dinner, Mon. lunch.
20 rooms: 68–76€. 3 suites: 107–150€.
Prix fixe: 27€, 55€. A la carte: 32–48€.

This former mill presided over by the Schreiber family is a very congenial hostelry. Its yellow and pink tones, cozy rooms, terrace and good-natured welcome all contribute to a refreshing break. At the stove, Olivier concocts regional dishes. The presskopf, trout, choucroute and the house dessert cup are well-prepared and gratifying.

■ Le Clos des Délices

17, rte de Klingenthal, 1 km nw via D426.
Tel. 03 88 95 81 00. Fax 03 88 95 97 71.
contact@leclosdesdelices.com
www.leclosdesdelices.com
Closed Sun. dinner, Bank holidays.
22 rooms: 46–72€. 1 suite: 92–104€.
Prix fixe: 26€, 39€, 49€, 58€,
15,50€ (child). A la carte: 40–45€.

In both winter and summer, Désiré Schaetzel's fine forest hostelry offers a park, swimming pool, sauna, solarium and stylish rooms refurbished in a modern manner. After your walk, the restaurant looks very enticing, with dishes prepared by Ludovic Van Anvers Mael, who plays very tunefully to a regional score. A regional meat and potato casserole called the baeckeoffe with goose foie gras on a Pinot Gris sauce and garnished with a crispy parmesan disk, pie filled with salmon, vegetables and hard boiled eggs, seasoned with green tea and served with a pumpkin potato purée and the dessert of crêpes with orange and milk cream provide a delightful accompaniment to the wines from the family property.

OUCHAMPS

41120 Loir-et-Cher. Paris 200 – Tours 56 – Blois 19 – Montrichard 18 – Romorantin 39.
On the fringe of the beautiful, forested Sologne region, looking down on the Loire Valley, a rustic stop on the route of the royal châteaux.

■ HOTELS-RESTAURANTS

■ Le Relais des Landes

Tel. 02 54 44 40 40. Fax 02 54 44 03 89.
info@relaisdeslandes.com
www.relaisdeslandes.com
Closed mid-Nov.–beg. Mar.
28 rooms: 90–145€.
Prix fixe: 38€, 45€.

Behind the gates of this country seat on the Sologne moors lies a very special setting, with grounds and swimming pool offering an alternative to a tour of local châteaux. The snug rooms are ideal for a well-deserved break. In the kitchen, Xavier Palmieri makes it a point of honor to use only seasonal market produce. Duck foie gras with grape tomato chutney, pike-perch filet in thin slices of potato with mushroom sauce, lamb medallions in thyme-seasoned jus with a zucchini cake and the warm apple and raisin spring roll with caramel ice cream shrewdly blend flavors without losing sight of the proper taste.

ILE D'OUESSANT

29422 Finistère.
Access by boat: from Brest (2 h 15),
from Le Conquet (1 h) or Camaret (1 h 15).
www.ot-ouessant.fr.
"He who sees Sein sees his end; he who sees Ouessant sees his blood" goes the proverb. Discover this superb island, the westernmost point in France.

HOTELS-RESTAURANTS

■ Ti Jan Ar Ch'Afé

Kernigou.
Tel.-Fax 02 98 48 88 15.
Closed 11 Nov.–Christmas.
8 rooms: 68–88€.

Reservations are essential for those happy souls who are ready to enjoy the charming rooms and delicious breakfasts of this house of character run by Odile Thomas.

■ Roc'h-Ar-Mor

In Lampaul.
Tel. 02 98 48 80 19. Fax 02 98 48 87 51.
hotel@rocharmor.com
http://pagesperso-orange.fr/rocharmor

Closed mid-Nov.–mid-Dec.,
beg. Jan.–beg. Feb.
Rest. closed Sun. dinner, Mon.
15 rooms: 55–87€.
Prix fixe: 18€, 28€, 8€ (child).

In Ouessant, all the sea views are extraordinary. You will be impressed by the sweep of Lampaul Bay to be seen from some of the rooms in this hotel that offers board and lodging. Marie-Pierre provides a smiling welcome and Jean-Louis Le Gall prepares monkfish brochette, fish choucroute, grilled chitterling sausage and a kouign-amann like no other.

● **Ti à Dreuz** ▪SIM▪
Bourg de Lampaul (at the base of Le Bourg).
Tel. 02 98 48 83 01.
Closed Sun. dinner (exc. July–Aug.),
Mon. (exc. July–Aug.), end Sept.–end Mar.
Prix fixe: 15–30€.

We come here for the buckwheat crêpes with egg and regional chitterling sausage and the "ouessantine" (potatoes, Emmental cream, and local smoked sausage called "silzig"). Christine and Michel Legall have turned this blue and white establishment into a solid gold *crêperie*. The cider is a must.

● **Ty Korn** ▪SIM▪
Bourg de Lampaul.
Tel.-Fax 02 98 48 87 33.
Closed Sun. dinner, Mon.,
1 week at end Nov.–beg. Dec., 3 weeks Jan.
Prix fixe: 15–20€ (lunch), 28€.
A la carte: 45€.

This is definitely one of the spots to visit on the island. A good time is had by all at the Dunand-Sauthiers' pub restaurant. First, a drink on the first floor in a bar with a boat cabin décor; then up to the second floor to enjoy the well-crafted domestic cuisine. Opposite the marine frescoes, we make short work of pollock tartare, Atlantic sea bass poached in red wine, oven-roasted rack of lamb and the dark chocolate dessert.

OUILLY-DU-HOULEY see LISIEUX

09140 Ariège. Paris 814 – Foix 60 – Saint-Girons 17.
In the heart of the Ariège, this is rough, proud country. A village of character at a height of around 500 meters and an appealing hostelry.

 HOTELS-RESTAURANTS

■ **Hostellerie de la Poste**
Rue Principale.
Tel. 05 61 66 86 33. Fax 05 61 66 77 08.
www.ariege.com/hoteldelaposte
Closed beg. Jan.–Easter, Nov. 1–20 Dec.
Rest. closed Mon. lunch, Tue. lunch.
19 rooms: 29–66€. 6 suites: 53–66€.
Prix fixe: 15€, 21€, 27€. A la carte: 40€.

In this 1900 establishment with its summer terrace and swimming pool, Anne-Marie Andrieu welcomes her guests with a smile before showing them to their charming rooms, some of them renovated. In the kitchen, her husband Philippe prepares delicious board dishes: crisp savory pasty with goat cheese, thyme-seasoned snapper, slow-cooked pork trotter and a lemon mille-feuille.

OUVEILLAN

34310 Hérault. Paris 790 – Montpellier 92 – Béziers 20 – Narbonne 21.
A quiet village on the Minervois vineyard route.

● RESTAURANTS

● **Le Relais de Pigasse**
Domaine de Pigasse, D11 and D5.
Tel. 04 67 89 40 98. Fax 04 67 89 40 18.
www.relaispigasse.com
Closed Sun. dinner, Mon., Tue. lunch, Nov.–end Mar.
Prix fixe: 75€, 110€. A la carte: 80€.

On the canal bank, Robert Eden's former post house delights gourmets. At the stove, Franck Renimel (who trained with Garrigues, Toulousy, Guérard and the

Pourcels) prepares local dishes with a modern flavor. They include venison presented in a flavorful aspic with mashed Vitelotte potatoes, mosaic of Mediterranean sea bass and wild lobster, beef tenderloin served four ways, a strawberry dessert served in a crunchy spun-sugar cage and herbal teas. All these shrewd dishes are marvelously accompanied by Minervois and other regional wines.

PACE see RENNES

OYONNAX

01100 Ain. Paris 490 – Bourg-en-Bresse 63 – Nantua 21 – Bellegarde 32.
The Bugey with its green mountains, lakes and natural love of food.

 | RESTAURANTS

● **La Toque Blanche** COM
11, pl Emile-Zola.
Tel. 04 74 73 42 63. Fax 04 74 73 76 48.
la.toqueblanche@club-internet.fr
www.toques-blanches-lyonnaises.com
Closed Sat. lunch, Sun. dinner, Mon.,
1 week beg. Jan., 3 weeks Aug.
Prix fixe: 19€, 23€, 31€, 43€, 60€,
11€ (child).

Richard Soibinet, who learned his trade with Lacombe, Blanc and Point, works to recapture the "true" taste of produce in this old-fashioned inn refurbished in pastel colors, peach and apricot. Crayfish gratin with frog legs cooked in Vin Jaune, turbot in champagne sauce, young Bresse chicken with morels and Savagnin sauce, pineapple brochette and bananas roasted in coconut milk will revive your appetite.

PAIMPOL

22500 Côtes-d'Armor. Paris 494 – Saint-Brieuc 47 – Guingamp 29 – Lannion 33.
The old town is intact. Its shipowners' homes and seaport still harbor fond memories of "An Iceland Fisherman" and Théodore Botrel. The delightful dock with its landing stages, the half-timbered buildings in the rue de la Vieille-Poissonnerie and des Huit-Patriotes, the Neo-Gothic parish church, the place de Verdun and the monument dedicated to Botrel all form a charming Breton scene.

 | HOTELS-RESTAURANTS

■ **K'loys**
21, quai Morand.
Tel. 02 96 20 40 01. Fax 02 96 20 72 68.
www.k-loys.com
17 rooms: 55–180€.

Guy Conan provides an enthusiastic welcome in this shipowner's house right by the harbor. British décor, woodwork, period and local furniture andf fabrics and a hushed lounge set the tone in this cozy haunt.

● **La Marne** COM
30, rue de la Marne.
Tel. 02 96 20 82 16. Fax 02 96 20 92 07.
hotel.marne22.restaurant@wanadoo.fr
www.hotelrestaurantdelamarne.com
Closed Sun. dinner, Mon., Tue. (off season),
2 weeks beg. Oct., Feb. vac.
9 rooms: 58€.
Prix fixe: 28€, 45€, 48€, 55€, 15€.

Stéphane Kokoszka, holder of the Master Cook of France award, is a fine, discreet chef. This wise man offers a revolutionary cuisine based on delightfully interpreted fresh fish and vegetables from local growers. We enjoy the langoustine "cappuccino", a "virtual" foie gras with creamed potatoes, lobster poached in hen jus, John Dory Rossini, rare veal cutlet with savory. The two chocoate mille-feuille with carrot cream and pepper sorbet are amusing. The wine list brims with splendid finds. A place to watch. Rustic rooms for overnight stays.

● La Vieille Tour   COM

13, rue de l'Eglise.
Tel. 02 96 20 83 18. Fax 02 96 20 90 41.
Closed Sun. dinner (exc. July–Aug.),
Wed. (exc. July–Aug.), 1 week at end June.
Prix fixe: 26€, 37€, 40€, 47€,
12€ (child). A la carte: 50€.

This 16th-century establishment in the heart of the old town has its charm. Andrée and Alain Rosec provide a generous welcome. Alain prepares a charmingly light, market-based cuisine. Flaked crab with a crisp buckwheat cake, skate with two cabbages and a lamb shank served with a hazelnut purée are well-crafted.

● La Cotriade   SIM

16, quai Armand-Dayot.
Tel. 02 96 20 81 08. Fax 02 96 55 02 51.
www.la-cotriade-paimpol.com
Closed Fri. dinner, Sat. lunch, Mon.,
10 days end Oct.–beg. Nov., 1 week Christmas–New Year's, 2 weeks June–July, 10 days end Aug.–mid-Sept.
Prix fixe: 22€, 27€, 35€, 100€.

Marie-Chantal and Henri Butel have dedicated their restaurant to the sea. The terrace is opposite the harbor and the menu focuses on the best of the latest catch. Henri, formerly at the Crillon and the Royal Evian, delicately cooks langoustines, foie gras and cabbage, scallops with Paimpol white beans, strawberry gratin with Génépi and a vanilla sabayon with oven-crisped caramelized pineapple.

In Loguivy-de-la-Mer (22620). 5,2 km n

■ Au Grand Large

Port.
Tel. 02 96 20 90 18. Fax 02 96 20 87 10.
augrandlarge@wanadoo.fr
Closed Sun. dinner, Mon. (off season), 2 weeks end Nov., beg. Jan.–beg. Feb.
6 rooms: 48–60€.
Prix fixe: Menus: 16€, 29€.

An adorable harbor, a practical address, modern rooms, a panoramic dining room and local dishes. The oysters, seafood, monkfish cassolette, salmon filet with bacon and Paimpol white beans are amiable.

In La Pointe de l'Arcouest (22620). 6 km via D789.

■ Le Barbu

Tel. 02 96 55 86 98. Fax 02 96 55 73 87.
hotel.lebarbu@wanadoo.fr / www.lebarbu.fr
19 rooms: 60–110€.
Prix fixe: 17€ (lunch, weekdays), 27€, 38€, 8€ (child).

Opposite the Ile de Bréhat, equipped with a heated swimming pool and sauna, the Barbu has charm and to spare. The rooms are spacious and the cuisine as local as you could wish: oven-crisped scallops, slow-cooked leeks and scallops in cream sauce will make your mouth water.

In 22500 Pont de Lézardrieux.

■ Relais Brenner

Rte de Saint-Julien.
Tel. 02 96 22 29 95. Fax 02 96 22 22 72.
direction-relaisbrenner@wanadoo.fr
www.relais-brenner.fr
Rest. closed Sun. dinner, Mon., Tue. lunch.
13 rooms: 65–105€. 5 suites: 130–150€.
Prix fixe: 35€, 55€, 30€ (child).
A la carte: 40–59€.

Spacious and charming, the English-style rooms in this luxurious inn offer a view of the Trieux estuary. The restaurant provides a subtle take on local produce under the supervision of new chef Jérôme Renault. The house salad, Ajonc honey-glazed John Dory, beef tenderloin and the Guéméné chitterling sausage taste good.

PALOT see LAVELANET

PALUD-DE-NOVES see SAINT-REMY-DE-PROVENCE

PARADOU see MAUSSANE-LES-ALPILLES

PARAY-LE-MONIAL

71600 Saône-et-Loire. Paris 360 – Mâcon 67 – Roanne 55 – Montceau-les-Mines 37.
This place of culinary and religious pilgrimage leads to the Basilica of the Sacred Heart.

 HOTELS-RESTAURANTS

■ Terminus
27, av de la Gare.
Tel. 03 85 81 59 31. Fax 03 85 81 38 31.
terminus.paray@club-internet.fr
www.terminus-paray.fr
Closed Nov. 1 vac., Sun.
Rest. closed lunch, Sun (off season).
16 rooms: 50–60€.
Prix fixe: 16€, 22€.

Opposite the station, this 1900 hotel has lost none of its character, although it is now equipped with modern, practical facilities. Tasteful rooms and fare for residents.

In Poisson (71600). 8 km via D34.
■ Poste et Hôtel la Reconce
Tel. 03 85 81 10 72. Fax 03 85 81 64 34.
Closed Mon. (exc. July–Aug.), Tue. (exc. July–Aug.), 2 weeks Oct., Feb.
7 rooms: 56–85€.
Prix fixe: 30€ (weekdays), 80€ (wine inc.).

A congenial establishment with attractive rooms in an annex, a friendly welcome and local cuisine, celebrating escargots, Charolais beef and Burgundy wines. Grounds and pool.

PARÇAY-MESLAY see TOURS
PARVILLE see EVREUX

PARIS

What if we dreamed of Paris? Come rain or shine, the City of Light is the world's most beautiful, most gourmet capital, offering a wider culinary choice than any other. The whole world (even New York, London and Sydney, each of which has hosted its own gastronomic big bang) envies us our fine, inexpensive bistros and successful grand restaurants. In this guide, we have opted for simplicity. Every two years, we publish a *Pudlo Paris* reviewing 2,300 addresses (not only restaurants, but also shops and rendezvous). Included here are the best restaurants (the ones awarded plates), and those providing good value for money (marked with a pot). We have also added a small selection of hotels. For a broader, more detailed view, see *Pudlo Paris 2007–2008*.

NOTE: Two additional symbols appear in the Paris listings: the euro ●, which identifies restaurants where it is possible to have a meal for less than 30€; and the broken plate, ⊙, which identifies restaurants that have recently proved disappointing.

PARIS 1ST ARR

■ HOTELS

■ Meurice
228, rue de Rivoli.
Métro: Concorde, Tuileries.
Tel. 01 44 58 10 10. Fax 01 44 58 10 15.
concierge@meuricehotel.com
www.reservationsmeuricehotel.com
120 rooms: 610–850€.
40 suites: 1380–10000€.

The Napoleonic décor of this dream location opposite the Tuileries gardens turns our heads with its gilt, mirrors, glass roofs and elegant lounges. It boasts two first class restaurants (one of them Yannick Alleno's star establishment), a wellness center partnered by Caudalie and a gym. Sumptuous rooms and period furniture.

■ Rennaissance Paris Vendôme
4, rue du Mont-Thabor.
Métro: Tuileries.
Tel. 01 40 20 20 00. Fax 01 40 20 20 01.
www.marriott.com
97 rooms: 299–380€. 3 suites: 490–700€.

Very close to the Tuileries gardens, the 19th-century facade conceals modern rooms in warm colors decorated by Pierre-Yves Rochon, as well as a fitness center, steam bath, sauna and swimming pool. A

Chinese bar and Alain Dutournier's Pinxo restaurant.

■ Costes 🏛

239, rue Saint-Honoré.
Métro: Tuileries, Concorde.
Tel. 01 42 44 50 00. Fax 01 42 44 50 01.
79 rooms: 350–1200€.
3 suites: 700–2400€.

The Napoleon III décor designed by Jacques Garcia continues to attract jet setters, great names in showbiz and super-models. Its success can be attributed to its fine lounges, cozy rooms (some of which are not that spacious), swimming pool, relaxed chic eatery and stylish bar.

■ Hôtel de Vendôme 🏛

1, pl Vendôme.
Métro: Tuileries, Opéra, Concorde.
Tel. 01 55 04 55 00. Fax 01 49 27 97 89.
reservations@hoteldevendome.com
www.hoteldevendome.com
29 rooms: 390–940€.
9 suites: 880–1270€.

This 18th-century hotel offers luxurious, charming, sensuous rooms with antique furniture, marble and hi-tech comfort. Assiduous service and a restaurant on the second floor.

■ Castille 🏛

37-33, rue Cambon.
Métro: Madeleine, Concorde.
Tel. 01 44 58 44 58. Fax 01 44 58 44 00.
castille.paris@starhotels.it
www.starhotels.com
107 rooms: 330–380€.
7 suites: 660–760€.

This discreet hotel near Chanel is famous for its Italian restaurant, Il Cortile. Refined rooms in line with contemporary tastes.

■ Novotel les Halles 🏛

8, pl Marguerite-de-Navarre.
Métro: Châtelet.
Tel. 01 42 21 31 31. Fax 01 40 26 05 79.
h0785-re@accor-hotels.com
www.accor-hotels.com
280 rooms: 190–300€. 5 suites: 305–450€.

This fully equipped hotel with a view of the church of Saint Eustache boasts a décor inspired by Japanese interiors.

■ Hôtel Place du Louvre 🏛

21, rue des Prêtres-Saint-Germain-l'Auxerrois.
Métro: Pont-Neuf, Louvre-Rivoli.
Tel. 01 42 33 78 68. Fax 01 42 33 09 95.
hpl@espritfrance.com
www.esprit-de-france.com
20 rooms: 100–188€.

The attractions of this smart luxury hotel are its modern rooms (some of which look out onto the Louvre and Saint-Germain-l'Auxerrois), breakfast in a vaulted 14th-century basement and sensible prices.

●	RESTAURANTS

● Le Meurice ⓒⓞ V.LUX

At the Meurice, 228, rue de Rivoli.
Métro: Concorde, Tuileries.
Tel. 01 44 58 10 55. Fax 01 44 58 10 76.
restauration@meuricehotel.com
www.meuricehotel.com
Closed Sat., Sun., Feb., beg.– end Aug.
Prix fixe: 75€ (lunch), 190€.
A la carte: 205€.

The décor in the dining room is inspired by the Salon de la Paix at Versailles Palace, and Yannick Alleno's cuisine mirrors it perfectly: grandiose, but not pompous. The master of ceremonies takes his duties as a maestro of flavors to heart. With a squad of seventy sous-chefs under his command, this discreet native of the Lozère district wages battle without compromise, producing a spectacular cuisine that leaves nothing to chance, from the choice of raw materials to the methods of preparation and subtlety of cooking and seasoning to the presentation of the dish. This is great art, refined, delicately crafted and never found wanting. The smoked salmon and scallop coulibiac, the heart of celtuce—a delicious but little-known vegetable in the asparagus family—with caviar, the cod glazed with seaweed, the tender wild Adour river salmon served rare with Choron sauce (hollandaise with a touch of tomato purée), the Bresse hen with truffles and foie gras served with a celeriac and horseradish ravioli, the roasted suckling pig with blood sausage and creamed corn or the spit-roasted rack of milk-fed Pyrénées lamb provide a splendid feast. There is a bit of Carême, Escoffier and Vatel [considered to be the fathers of French cuisine] in Alleno. He unearths forgotten tastes, tracks the finest flavors to their lairs and gives pleasure without trying to impress. The mille-feuille "as you like it" (vanilla, coffee or chocolate, made to order, as it should be) is a high point, and the paper-thin ravioli, iced with red fruit, topped with a champagne- and basil-infused whipped cream and gavotte fourrée (a crisp, thin, rolled-up pancake) are more sophisticated but equally irresistible. Turning to the cellar, you can choose from some 700 wines, with Nicolas Rebut to help you select the appropriate nectar. This is clearly one of the very greatest establishments in Paris today.

● L'Espadon   ⊙ VLUX

At the Ritz, 15, pl Vendôme.
Métro: Madeleine, Pyramides.
Tel. 01 43 16 30 80. Fax 01 43 16 33 75.
food-bev@ritzparis.com / www.ritzparis.com
Prix fixe: 75€ (lunch), 180€ (dinner), 260€ (dinner, wine inc.). A la carte: 160–190€.

First, there is the grandiloquent setting dreamt up by César Ritz more than a century ago, with its gilding, stucco, wall hangings and painted ceiling. Then there is the repertoire of a virtuoso chef. Trained at the Ritz, where he has served loyally for more than twenty years (a two-year escapade at Lasserre aside), Michel Roth, holder of the Meilleur Ouvrier de France award and first winner of the Bocuse d'Or prize, is now running the kitchens of this luxury Paris hotel. His cuisine is both traditional and inventive, paying tribute to the culinary conventions that Auguste Escoffier made his trademark. The spider crab with avocado and citrus fruit couldn't be fresher. The asparagus, served with foie gras, Comté and sauce Périgueux (a rich sauce flavored with Madeira and truffles)

have never tasted so good. The Dover sole, braised in shellfish broth and served with zucchini aïoli, is a marvel of refinement and the Pauliac lamb with foie gras, truffles and salsify reveals a myriad of flavors. Every last note of the delightful sweetbreads with baby artichokes and citrus polenta is calculated. Turning to the desserts, close your eyes and savor the iced chocolate dessert with milk bonbons or the Ritz's signature mille-feuille. Some great vintages feature among the thousand wines the cellar has to offer, all harmonizing with these delicately crafted dishes.

● Le Grand Véfour

17, rue de Beaujolais.
Métro: Palais-Royal, Pyramides, Bourse.
Tel. 01 42 96 56 27. Fax 01 42 86 80 71.
grand.vefour@wanadoo.fr
Closed Fri. dinner, Sat., Sun., Aug.
Prix fixe: 78€ (lunch). A la carte: 200€.

Guy Martin has been conducting his orchestra in the kitchens of the Véfour for nearly fifteen years. This native of Savoie (formerly of the Château de Coudrée, then the Château de Divonne overlooking Lake Geneva) is very much at home in this restaurant made fashionable by Raymond Oliver. The historic setting, with its red velvet seats, view of the Palais Royal, and plaques dedicated to eminent figures such as Balzac, Colette, Hugo, Cocteau, Berl, Malraux and Napoléon has the elegance of a Directoire shrine. Turning to the cuisine, Guy Martin reconciles tradition and modernity, exotic flavors and provincial produce. The golden frog legs with a delicate sorrel sauce and the foie gras terrine with mango confit and ras el-hanout (an exotic blend of Moroccan spices) set the tone. Follow with the monkfish encrusted with mild spices and a light smoked cucumber emulsion, roasted Breton lobster with fennel, tomato and shiso (an aromatic Japanese green), filet of lamb with wasabi, baby fava beans and hearts of baby romaine lettuce or oxtail parmentier with truffles and potatoes. The melon fondant with sorbet and wild strawberries forms a dainty conclusion, while the hazelnut and milk chocolate lollypop with salted caramel ice cream offers a moment of delight. The 750 items on the wine list allow some highly appropriate matches, with Patrick Tamisier providing astute advice.

● Le Carré des Feuillants ⓒⓒ LUX
14, rue de Castiglione.
Métro: Tuileries, Concorde.
Tel. 01 42 86 82 82. Fax 01 42 86 07 71
carre.des.feuillants@wanadoo.fr
www.carredesfeuillants.fr
Closed Sat., Sun., Aug.
Prix fixe: 65€ (lunch), 150€.
A la carte: 140€.

The refined Alberto Bali décor of this gourmet establishment is divided into four interconnecting rooms around an inner courtyard. Behind the scenes, Alain Dutournier, native and champion of the Landes region, beguiles his elegant guests with the cuisine of Southwestern France, fine-tuned to reflect his travels and ideas. He has adopted a philosophy handed down by his mother and grandmother, a "bare minimum" approach that, in his case, results in dishes that are virtual masterpieces. The quality of the ingredients cannot be faulted, and imagination, audacity and unusual permutations do the rest. Diners delight in the foie gras and sweetbreads with crayfish jelly, the baby artichokes cooked with black truffles or, better still, Marennes oysters bathed in seawater jelly, Aquitaine caviar, seaweed tartare and creamy foam or thick slices of John Dory fish with potato, tender cabbage lasagne and an aromatic horseradish mousse or the roasted rack of Pyrénées milk-fed lamb, its leg slowly cooked in a clay pot, paired with lightly curried vegetables. All will conjure sighs of satisfaction from your lips. The journey ends on a sweeter note with wild Andalusian strawberries, rose and lychee macarons, mango and passion fruit ravioli or sweet beignets filled with mango and cardamom or pineapple and coconut. Alain Dutournier has constructed a wine cellar rich in surprises, devoting as much care to choosing the nectars that will match his flavors as he does to devising today's and tomorrow's cuisine.

● Goumard ⓒⓒ LUX
9, rue Duphot.
Métro: Madeleine.
Tel. 01 42 60 36 07. Fax 01 42 60 04 54.
goumard.philippe@wanadoo.fr
www.goumard.fr
Prix fixe: 46€, 30€ (child). A la carte: 135€.

Philippe Dubois, our Restaurateur of the Year 2006, is still riding high. First, his elegant establishment is a visual delight. We never tire of the woodwork, chandeliers and inlays by Lalique, or the engraved glass facade. The food is also a constant source of pleasure, thanks to the skills of Olivier Guyon. Having trained at Vernet and Daniel in New York, he is a master in the preparation of fish of every kind, using select produce to concoct brilliantly simple dishes. Charm does its work in the sautéed crayfish with green asparagus and peanuts, the roasted line-caught sea bass with sweet peas, baby artichokes and heirloom radishes and the sautéed wild squid served with a ricotta and savory ravioli, finished with lobster broth. The culinary display concludes with croustillant filled with wild strawberries, citrus mousse, fresh mango and sorbet of red fruits. Add attentive service and wines to match the exceptional nature of the dishes, and you have a recipe for maritime delight in the course(s) of a dinner or lunch to remember.

● Gérard Besson ⓞ LUX
5, rue Coq-Héron.
Métro: Louvre-Rivoli, Palais-Royal.
Tel. 01 42 33 14 74. Fax 01 42 33 85 71.
gerard.besson4@libertysurf.fr
www.gerardbesson.com
Closed Sat. lunch, Sun., Mon. lunch,
3 weeks Aug.
Prix fixe: 105€. A la carte: 130€.

Classical and timeless: Gérard Besson has prospered for nearly thirty years in this unobtrusive street near the former wholesale food market. Tremendously experienced and a holder of the prestigious Meilleur Ouvrier de France award, he has successfully combined tradition with faultless technique in a cuisine that cares nothing for fashion. His restaurant is luxurious with its widely spaced tables and cozy nooks. Guests come to enjoy mushrooms, truffles and game in season. The fresh green asparagus from Pertuis with morel mushrooms and just a touch of cream, the filet of sole with morels served with pasta stuffed with wild mushroom duxelles, the sautéed blue lobster "Georges Garin" with truffle butter and savory fennel flan and the scallops of sweetbreads lightly sautéed in butter served with asparagus tips and a purée of sweet peas and savory are demanding, polished dishes. The unusual caramelized fennel served with Tahitian vanilla bean ice cream served as a dessert, and the mini–baba au rhum with fresh pineapple and almond milk ice cream is memorable. We are left in no doubt: Besson is still Besson.

● **Hôtel de Vendôme**

1, place Vendôme.
Métro: Tuileries, Opéra, Concorde.
Tel. 01 55 04 55 00. Fax 01 49 27 97 89.
reservations@hoteldevendome.com
Prix fixe: 35€, 40€.

On the second floor of this charming hotel with its prestigious address, the dining room offers a change of scenery in the British manner. Chef Frédéric Fallope presents a golden opportunity with the set menu: delicious puff pastry "cigars" of duck confit, chilled crab appetizer, perfectly cooked swordfish steamed in banana leaves, roasted scallops and desserts that could have been better—overly sweet chestnut meringue and ordinary sorbets. The service could be more conscientious.

● **Il Cortile**

At the Castille, 37, rue Cambon.
Métro: Concorde, Madeleine.
Tel. 01 44 58 45 67. Fax 01 44 58 45 69.
ilcortile@castille.com / www.castille.com
Closed Sat., Sun.,
1 week Christmas–New Year's, Aug.
Prix fixe: 38€ (lunch), 48€ (lunch),
95€ (dinner). A la carte: 95€.

This was *the* Alain Ducasse Italian restaurant. Now, after a period of uncertainty, it

is carrying on without him . . . and looks the picture of health! The tables on the patio—in the open air when the weather is fine—the young, assiduous waiters, the vast range of Italian wines at every price and the chef from Modena, Vittorio Beltramelli, who not only knows the score but performs it with an inspiration that mirrors the changing of the seasons: All is a recipe for success. Cream of celery root with littleneck clams or chilled spaghetti with Mediterranean bottarga served as an appetizer, calf's tongue with sweet and sour vegetables, pumpkin risotto with diced crisp prosciutto or mint, scallops with white truffle oil are right on target. The desserts, ranging from the classical (a giant creamy tiramisu) to the modern (a chilled soufflé with ginger and a pina colada sauce) also hit the mark. We drink selected wines by the glass, such as a Conte della Vipera white from Antinori and Ladoucette in Umbria and a Morgante Nero d'Avola from Sicily, delighted to be enjoying this fine restaurant again.

● **Chez Vong**

10, rue de la Grande-Truanderie.
Métro: Les Halles, Etienne-Marcel.
Tel. 01 40 26 09 36 / 01 40 39 99 89.
Fax 01 42 33 38 15.
chez-vong@wanadoo.fr / www.chez-vong.com
Closed Sun.
Prix fixe: 23,50€ (lunch). A la carte: 85€.

After twenty-five years of loyal service, Vong Kai Kuan seems as lively as ever, and his restaurant, certainly one of the best purveyors of Chinese cuisine in Paris, has in no way lowered its standards; quite the contrary. The dishes presented on the menu reflect the culinary traditions of Canton and Vietnam, competing in subtlety and range of flavor. The service is not fast, but remarkably unobtrusive and polite. The produce is carefully selected and nothing is left to chance. You can savor the steamed ravioli, line-caught sea bass salad, live young turbot (steamed to order) Sichuan beef filet, Peking duck or, ordered in advance, the famous Bresse chicken (also Peking style), sorbets, beignets and steamed cakes. Our host has not neglected the wine list, which promises some shrewd pairings. If the evening goes on long enough, he will even come and chat for a while at your table, taking his duties seriously enough to see you to the door, all with a delightful smile.

● Macéo

15, rue des Petits-Champs.
Métro: Palais-Royal, Bourse, Pyramides.
Tel. 01 42 97 53 85. Fax 01 47 03 36 93.
info@maceorestaurant.com
www.maceorestaurant.com
Closed Sat. lunch, Sun., 3 weeks Aug.
Prix fixe: 30€, 36€. A la carte: 60€.

Just a step away from the Palais-Royal, the late Mercure Galant is enjoying a second wind, thanks to Mark Williamson, who has selected 250 wines from areas as far flung as the Rhône Valley, Burgundy, Spain and the United States. His choices perfectly complement the appealing dishes prepared by Thierry Bourdonnais. Who could resist the tuna tartare with asparagus tips, foie gras with apples and figs in sangria caramel, duck prepared in two ways with mixed vegetables, pineapple and mascarpone macarons, especially when they are served with good humor and promptness? The setting (in a listed 18th-century building) plays on contrasting bright shades and contemporary paintings, offering a note of cheer.

● Le Bar Anglais

At the Régina, 2, pl des Pyramides.
Métro: Tuileries, Palais-Royal, Pyramides.
Tel. 01 42 60 90 34. Fax 01 40 15 95 16.
banqueting@regina-hotel.com
www.regina-hotel.com
Prix fixe: 24€. A la carte: 55€.

With its new English lounge look, the Régina's restaurant is cozier than ever. Hervé Riebbels' straightforward dishes are served in a British bar atmosphere. The chilled tomato and coriander soup and the arugula salad with artichokes and goat cheese are cool fare for warm days. The grilled tuna with wok-seared vegetables reflect current trends, the tender

hand-chopped steak tartare slips down easily and the crème caramel *de grand-mère* is unpretentious.

● Café Marly

93, rue de Rivoli, the Louvre.
Métro: Palais-Royal.
Tel. 01 49 26 06 60. Fax 01 49 26 07 06
s.a.marly@wanadoo.fr / www.marly.fr
A la carte: 60€.

With its unobstructed view of the Louvre pyramid, this Costes brasserie has two great arguments in its favor: the Second Empire décor and the elegant cuisine—as long as price is no obstacle. The mache salad with endive and truffles, the sea bass with a balsamic reduction sauce and parmesan, the grilled lamb tenderloin chops with haricots verts and the petits macarons all deserve attention. However, the service falls short of perfection.

● L'Atelier Berger

49, rue Berger.
Métro: Louvre-Rivoli, Châtelet, Les Halles.
Tel. 01 40 28 00 00. Fax 01 40 28 10 65.
atelierberger@wanadoo.fr
www.restaurant-atelierberger.com
Closed Sat. lunch, Sun., Christmas.
Prix fixe: 14€ (lunch), 36€, 58€.
A la carte: 41€.

The French-Norwegian Jean Christiansen has made the most of his dual roots, as well as his experience with Rostang, Cagna and Vié. Here in his atelier he invites us to taste the end result. We are convinced by the tuna tartare, the smoked eel with marjoram sorbet, the lobster, parmesan, and penne gratin, the roasted veal kidneys, the pig's feet with slowly simmered vegetables and rosemary and the caramelized bananas, tapioca with passion fruit, and bitter chocolate ganache.

● Hôtel Costes

239, rue Saint-Honoré.
Métro: Tuileries, Concorde.
Tel. 01 42 44 50 25. Fax 01 42 44 50 01
Cont. service.
A la carte: 60–80€.

The Costes brothers have turned this discreet hotel and restaurant into one of the most "in" places in the capital. The Café Florian ambiance, Venice fashion, with Napoleon III alcoves and patio have a certain chic. Well-heeled aficionados go straight for the lobster salad or haricots verts salad, spicy penne, line-caught sea bass, "tigre qui pleure" ("crying tiger" beef), generous veal rib chop and warm chocolate cake. And remember: The house serves until late.

● **Le Restaurant du Palais-Royal**

43, rue de Valois / 110, galerie de Valois.
Métro: Bourse, Palais-Royal.
Tel. 01 40 20 00 27. Fax 01 40 20 00 82.
palaisrest@aol.com
www.restaurantdupalaisroyal.com
Closed Sun., 20 Dec.–mid Jan.
A la carte: 70€.

Immediately by the gardens of the Palais Royal, the terrace is one of the prettiest in Paris. The décor is elegant while its cheerful hues, while the food served up by Bruno Hees, formerly of the Récamier, is subtle, carefully prepared and made from fine ingredients, its only fault being its high price. In any case, we have no complaints about the sea bass tartare, eggplant caviar with Ibérico ham, grilled sea bass with olive oil or sautéed calf's liver with a spiced crumble.

● **Chez Pauline**

5, rue Villedo.
Métro: Pyramides, Palais-Royal.
Tel. 01 42 96 20 70. Fax 01 49 27 99 89.
chez.pauline@wanadoo.fr
www.chezpauline.com
Closed Sat. lunch, Sun.
Prix fixe: 27€ (lunch), 45€ (lunch),
55€ (dinner). A la carte: 70€.

A step away from the Palais Royal, André Génin's picturesque circa 1880 bistro is hidden behind an appealing paneled facade. The man's choice of friends suggests a true love of gourmet cooking: Lacombe in Lyon, Chabran in Pont-de-l'Isère and Rostang in Paris. He offers a warm welcome in this little treasure chest of stucco, mirrors, red benches and other jewels of bygone times. His cuisine has character to spare, and the skillfully chosen produce is prepared with unfailing care. The terrine of parsleyed ham, lobster sautéed with new potatoes and shallots, sweetbreads baked in puff pastry "father Génin–style" and an enormous helping of Cognac baba with mixed nuts, dried fruit and a touch of whipped cream are exemplary. Ideally, the wine list should be a little more substantial.

● **Pinxo**

At the Plaza Paris Vendôme, 9, rue d'Alger.
Métro: Tuileries.
Tel. 01 40 20 20 00. Fax 01 40 20 72 02.
www.pinxo.fr
Closed Aug.
A la carte: 45€.

Lunches for shopping enthusiasts from the chic Colette boutique or a business clientele: Pinxo's patrons vary, but the service invariably runs smoothly. Obviously, we would expect nothing less of Alain Dutournier, who has made a great success of this adjunct to the Carré des Feuillants—a chic refectory version—in the heart of the Plaza Vendôme hotel. Surrounded by its minimalist décor (Japanese-inspired tendencies all in black and white by Alberto Bali), we relax as we study the mouthwatering menu devised by Fabrice Dubos, formerly of the Café Faubourg. In no particular order, it offers sautéed small squid with garlic chips, rare sesame-glazed tuna, Aquitaine sirloin steak served both raw and seared and smoked pear with a dark chocolate cake and green tea sorbet. The wines are from all over the world. Apart from being well chosen, they are presented in a novel manner, according to price range, another way of looking at the question.

● **A Casa Luna**

4-6, rue de Beaujolais.
Métro: Palais-Royal.
Tel. 01 42 60 05 11. Fax 01 42 96 16 24.
acasaluna@noos.fr / www.acasaluna.com
Prix fixe: 15€ (lunch on weekdays), 20€.
A la carte: 35€.

Fond of Corsica? Well, here it is in Paris, just opposite the Palais Royal. Its charm is not restricted to the backdrop of old stone vaults, tables spread with crimson cloths, and attractive drapes, posters and photos but also lies in the cuisine, with its particularly Corsican accent, and the welcoming smile of Christine Sanna-Lefranc. Christine, who ran L'Alivi in the Marais quarter, has created a gastronomic showcase here for her native island. The savory tart infused with marjoram, the sardines marinated in fennel and olive oil, the cannelloni stuffed with brocciu (a Corsican goat cheese) and the lamb shank served in its own juices with butter beans are remarkable, even though young chef Laurent Benoit does tend to add pointless sprigs of dill and awkward pink berries to all his dishes. The food is accompanied by wines produced in vineyards from Sartène (exquisite red Fiumicicoli) to Patrimonio, along with Orezza water and finally a complimentary myrtle liqueur that lends the world a rosy glow. Don't miss the shortbread with a lime pastry cream; what is actually a fine tarte sablée au citron frais makes a stunning, sweet (but not excessively so) dessert. It will have you melting on the spot!

● L'Argenteuil   🍷 COM

9, rue d'Argenteuil.
Métro: Pyramides, Palais-Royal.
Tel. 01 42 60 56 22.
Closed Sat., Sun.
Prix fixe: 16€ (lunch), 29,50€.

The Viennes have taken over from the Schaeffers at this small, local restaurant with its boudoir chic. In the kitchen, Sylvain produces daring, lively, sometimes unexpected compositions, and Laetitia, his charming wife, welcomes guests with a smile. The crisp duck foie gras with Banyuls caramel and shallot confit, grilled sea bass with eggplant cannelloni, braised sweetbreads and chanterelles or raspberry macaron with pistachio cream have an easy charm, like the short but shrewd wine list with an astute selection of wines by the glass, so you can enjoy yourself without breaking the bank.

● Pharamond   🏠 COM

24, rue de la Grande-Truanderie.
Métro: Etienne-Marcel, Les Halles.
Tel. 01 40 28 45 18. Fax 01 40 28 45 87.
jmc.corver@wanadoo.fr
www.le-pharamond.com
Closed Sun., Aug.
A la carte: 80€.

Sylvain Lebarbier from L'Ami Louis has discreetly taken over this registered establishment dating back to 1832. The dining room has been dusted down, the banquettes reupholstered in purple velvet and the private rooms on the second floor reopened. In the hands of the young Stéphane Auger, the foie gras in terrine, Burgundy-style escargots, the famous slow-braised and tomato-seasoned tripe, the puff pastry cup filled with meat in creamy white sauce or the braised beef cheeks are an essay in modernized domestic cuisine, just like the poule au pot with fresh truffle-infused mashed potatoes and the lovely Auge Valley veal chops (38!), dishes that demonstrate the restaurant's progress. The prices may have risen, but the quality of the produce is unmistakable. Calvados-flambéed baked apples or the baba au rhum provide an excellent conclusion.

● Au Pied de Cochon   🏠 COM

6, rue Coquillière.
Métro: Châtelet-Les Halles.
Tel. 01 40 13 77 00. Fax 01 40 13 77 09.
de.pied-de-cochon@blanc.net
www.piedecochon.com
Cont. service.
Prix fixe: 24€. A la carte: 50€.

This monument of the former Les Halles wholesale market has been successfully exploring the theme of pig's feet for more than fifty years. At any hour of the day or night, its two persistently packed floors welcome tipsy Parisians and tourists. The onion soup makes an excellent start to the proceedings, which continue with sole meunière or the famous "temptation of Saint Antoine" (pig's tail, ears, snout, and feet), baba au rhum and the ritual crêpes flambéed with Grand Marnier.

● **Zimmer**   🍴 COM

1, pl du Châtelet.
Métro: Châtelet.
Tel. 01 42 36 74 03. Fax 01 42 36 74 04.
lezimmer@wanadoo.fr / www.lezimmer.com
Cont. service.
Prix fixe: 19,90€. A la carte: 40€.

Entirely made over by Jacques Garcia, this discreet Châtelet brasserie has also acquired a new chef, Stéphane Graf, responsible for a welcome change in the menu, which was beginning to run out of steam. Now, we are very happy with the cream of carrot and spring pea soup, cod baked in a spice crust with passion fruit, Venetian steak tartare with parmesan, basil and olive oil and sautéed pears with gingerbread and vanilla ice cream.

● **L'Absinthe**   🍴 SIM

24, pl du Marché-Saint-Honoré.
Métro: Pyramides, Tuileries.
Tel. 01 49 26 90 04. Fax 01 49 26 08 64.
www.michelrostang.com
Closed Sat. lunch, Sun.
Prix fixe: 29€, 36€.

Caroline Rostang, who was our 2006 Hostess of the Year, is still running her excellent eatery with boundless energy. The great Michel's daughter has turned this New York loft–style bistro into an elegant but relaxed establishment, carefully constructed around a large glass wall with a combination of rough materials (concrete, wood, aged metal) and antique tables, Thonet chairs and industrial glass. As for the food, the tastes of the South of France add a ray of sunshine to Laurent Montgillard's roguish cooking. We cheerfully savor Roman ravioli with fresh tomato and verbena, the seared tuna with spices served with wheat risotto, a roasted veal steak with slow-roasted shallot confit, remembering to end on chocolate and coffee fondant. The wine list covers all of France and ventures well beyond its borders, to Italy, New Zealand and Chile.

● **Café Ruc**   SIM

159, rue Saint-Honoré.
Métro: Palais-Royal.
Tel. 01 42 60 97 54. Fax 01 42 61 36 33.
A la carte: 55€.

With its red velvet chairs, this Costes café opposite the Comédie Française suggests a diminutive theater itself. The food is improving and the perfectly choreographed service leaves nothing to chance. The baby artichokes, the grilled sesame-crusted tuna steak, the filet of beef with béarnaise sauce and the raspberry macarons deserve a touch of applause.

● **Le Dauphin**   🍴 SIM

167, rue Saint-Honoré.
Métro: Palais-Royal, Pyramides.
Tel. 01 42 60 40 11. Fax 01 42 60 01 18.
Closed Christmas.
Prix fixe: 25€ (lunch Mon.–Sat.), 37€.
A la carte: 55€.

Didier Oudill and Edgar Duhr have been together for a long time. The two companions studied with Guérard at Eugénie, then went into partnership at the Café de Paris in Biarritz, before taking over this bistro institution: Le Dauphin. The menu has the singsong accents of Provence and the Southwest, and the generous dishes overflow with sun-drenched flavors as the succession of the Provençal-style escargot, a salmon in crispy phyllo pastry with asparagus, duck brandade with thick Morteau smoked sausage, a tangy sauce and chanterelles and beggar's purse with honey ice cream and raspberry sorbet unfolds. Sheer joy!

● **L'Ardoise**   🍴 SIM

28, rue du Mont-Thabor.
Métro: Tuileries, Concorde.
Tel. 01 42 96 28 18.
lardoise1@yahoo.fr
Closed Sun. lunch, Mon., beg.–end Aug.
Prix fixe: 31€. A la carte: 45€.

At Pierre Jay's Ardoise, you will find classics of good home cooking, sometimes reinterpreted, but always perfectly prepared. This veteran of La Tour d'Argent has no shortage of confidence or ideas (if not diffidence), as is shown by the dishes he concocts with ease. The yellow and ochre walls have a soothing effect, and when the food arrives, you will scarcely be disappointed by the langoustine ravioli, the foie gras terrine, the grilled scallops with sautéed shiitakes, the veal loin sautéed with morels and cream or the feuillantine of Gariguette strawberries. A fine selection of wines by the glass.

● Willi's Wine Bar

13, rue des Petits-Champs.
Métro: Bourse, Pyramides.
Tel. 01 42 61 05 09. Fax 01 47 03 36 93.
info@williswinebar.com
www.williswinebar.com
Closed Sun., 2 weeks Aug.
Prix fixe: 25€ (lunch), 34€ (dinner), 19,50€ (lunch). A la carte: 40€.

Mark Williamson's wine bar is astonishingly good. Cultivating his passion for the divine nectar, this quiet Englishman has gradually built up an impressive cellar that reflects a weakness for the Rhône Valley but is not limited to France alone. By taking on a chef of François Yon's stature, he has also invested in quality cuisine. The result is convincing, with tuna tartare, the antipasti plate, sea bass filet, roasted cod with green vegetable risotto, pan-seared veal chops with sage and chocolate terrine.

● Le Rubis

10, rue du Marché-Saint-Honoré.
Métro: Tuileries.
Tel. 01 42 61 03 34.
Closed Sat. dinner, Sun., school vac., Christmas–New Year's, 2 weeks Aug.
A la carte: 25€.

Beaujolais, Bordeaux, Loire wines and Côtes du Rhône: These are the pearls in the cellar stocked by Albert Prat, who provides a family welcome in his fifties-era bistro with its original zinc counter lit by neon. In great simplicity, among the barrels and Formica tables, patrons relish the pig snout salad, homemade rillettes, pork knuckle with lentils, calf's head with mayonnaise, capers, herbs and hard-boiled egg and rice gâteau. There is also a very nice selection of charcuterie.

● Aux Bons Crus

7, rue des Petits-Champs.
Métro: Bourse, Palais-Royal.
Tel. 01 42 60 06 45.
Closed Sun., Mon. dinner, 2 weeks Aug.
A la carte: 30–35€.

A new team has taken over this circa 1900 bistro, which still makes an excellent impression with its freight elevator and zinc bar. At the stove, Stéphane Porte adds a Mediterranean touch to the appetizing house fare. The paper-thin beggar's purse filled with goat cheese, tomatoes and tapenade, the swordfish with beurre blanc, the rib eye steak with morels, the lamb brochette with thyme and the pistachio crème brûlée raise the tone.

● Au Chien qui Fume

33, rue du Pont-Neuf.
Métro: Châtelet, Les Halles.
Tel. 01 42 36 07 42. Fax 01 42 36 36 85.
auchienquifume@club-internet.fr
www.au-chien-qui-fume.com
Closed Christmas.
Prix fixe: 23€, 29€, 30€, 36€.
A la carte: 50€.

Founded in 1740, Au Chien qui Fume is an outstanding monument of the old Les Halles quarter. You can bring your canine friends and order the house standards until late: the escargots with wild mushrooms and garlic, medallions of monkfish with a wild mushroom sauce, kidneys braised in Chablis and fresh fruit gratin with Grand Marnier sabayon.

● Chez Clovis

33, rue Berger.
Métro: Châtelet, Les Halles.
Tel.-Fax 01 42 33 97 07.
Closed Sun., 10 days from Christmas–New Year's, 1 week Aug.
Prix fixe: 19,50€, 25,50€. A la carte: 40€.

This thirties bistro with its patinated décor is something of an institution in the Les Halles quarter. Its devotees have made it their dining room and, over the years, tirelessly continued to revel in the trio of terrines, fish of the day, slowly stewed calf's head, strip steak of Salers beef in red wine and shallots and chocolate profiteroles.

● Paul ⛺ SIM

15, pl Dauphine / 52, quai des Orfèvres.
Métro: Châtelet, St-Michel, Pont-Neuf.
Tel. 01 43 54 21 48. Fax 01 56 24 94 09.
restaurantpaul@wanadoo.fr
Closed Mon., mid Aug.–end Aug.
A la carte: 50€.

Chantal and Thierry Dieuleveut, owners of the neighboring Caveau du Palais, have made absolutely no changes to the décor of this timeless bistro or its trademark domestic repertoire, which is reliable and modest. The stewed escargots, skate in caper sauce, smoked haddock with beurre blanc, honey-glazed duck medallions, sautéed calf's liver with a vinegar sauce, warm chocolate cake and baba au rhum with whipped cream and Bing cherries are cheerfully dependable.

● La Poule au Pot ⛺ SIM

9, rue de Vauvilliers.
Métro: Louvre-Rivoli, Les Halles.
Tel. 01 42 36 32 96.
www.lapouleaupot.fr
Closed lunch, Mon. Cont. service.
Prix fixe: 30€. A la carte: 55€.

They serve until late in this traditional-style bistro, boldly boasting a cuisine no longer in vogue. Night owls come here to sup on eggs with foie gras, the house chicken salad, salmon with champagne sauce, duck confit and chocolate profiteroles.

● Aux Tonneaux des Halles ◉⛺ SIM

28, rue Montorgueil.
Métro: Les Halles.
Tel. 01 42 33 36 19.
Closed Sun.
A la carte: 30€.

Patrick Fabre has turned his traditional bistro into a refuge for those with solid appetites, nostalgic for the old Les Halles market. Patrons sit beneath vine branches and savor the pleasures of bygone days. Dried country sausage, Mediterranean scorpion fish sautéed with leeks, calf's head with a thick, tart vinaigrette and steamed potatoes and tarte Tatin all slip down easily. A good ambiance fueled by quality Beaujolais.

● La Tour Montlhéry ⛺ SIM

5, rue des Prouvaires.
Métro: Louvre-Rivoli, Les Halles.
Tel. 01 42 36 21 82. Fax 01 45 08 81 99.
Closed Sat., Sun., mid-July–mid-Aug.
A la carte: 55€.

An institution in the old Les Halles quarter, the Tour Montlhéry has seen many great figures pass through its portals. Still today, many journalists, politicians and other personalities continue to seat themselves around its tables under the gaze of General de Gaulle and Jeff Kessel, sketched by the late, much-lamented artist Moretti, to savor the homemade fois gras, the chef's terrine, braised salmon with mustard sauce, prime rib roast, sautéed calf's liver, mille-feuille and baba au rhum. The cellar is well stocked and the service prompt.

	HOTELS

■ Hôtel Westminster ⌂

13, rue de la Paix.
Métro: Opéra.
Tel. 01 42 61 57 46 / 01 42 61 77 41.
Fax 01 42 60 30 66.
www.warwickhotels.com /
www.hotelwestminster.com
80 rooms: 450–580€. 21 suites: 750–2500€.

Volker Zach tends to this discreetly opulent residence in the Opéra-Vendôme district. It provides perfectly equipped rooms—some offering high luxury (the Louis Cartier suite)—marble bathrooms, a fitness center partnered by Orlane with a view of the roofs of Paris, a Gothic bar where guests can eat, smoke cigars and listen to jazz (Duke's), and a gourmet restaurant (Le Céladon).

■ Park Hyatt Vendôme

3, rue de la Paix.
Métro: Opéra.
Tel. 01 58 71 12 34. Fax 01 58 71 12 35.
vendome@paris.hyatt.com
www.paris.vendome.hyatt.com
143 rooms: 580–670€.
35 suites: 790–4940€.

Models and pop stars congregate in this refined, contemporary establishment designed by Ed Tuttle. Minimalist rooms with a view of the Place Vendôme, an open bar and quality restaurants (Pur' Grill and the Orchidées). A stylish pearl near the fashion houses and great jewelers.

■ Favart

5, rue Marivaux.
Métro: Quatre-Septembre,
Richelieu-Drouot, Les Halles.
Tel. 01 42 97 59 83. Fax 01 40 15 95 58.
favart.hotel@wanadoo.fr
www.hotel–favart.com
37 rooms: 95–145€.

This was the name of the old comic opera house, which can be seen from certain rooms in this charming hotel where the painter Goya stayed. Mostly refurbished in Louis XVI style. The practical location and sensible prices also argue in its favor.

■ Vivienne

40, rue Vivienne.
Métro: Grands-Boulevards, Bourse.
Tel. 01 42 33 13 26. Fax 01 40 41 98 19.
paris@hotel-vivienne.com
45 rooms: 71–110€.

This refined hotel with its renovated rooms in beige tones and enlarged lobby provides tasteful accommodation on the Grands Boulevards. To make our pleasure complete, the prices keep a low profile.

● RESTAURANTS

● Le Céladon

At Hôtel Westminster, 15, rue Daunou.
Métro: Opéra.
Tel. 01 47 03 40 42. Fax 01 42 61 33 78.
infos@leceladon.com / www.leceladon.com
Closed weekends, Aug.
Prix fixe: 55€ (lunch, wine inc.),
71€ (dinner), 110€ (dinner). A la carte: 100€.

In a French Regency style by designer Pierre-Yves Rochon, decorated with Oriental touches, celadon walls and Chinese porcelain, Christophe Moisand gives free reign to his gastronomic inclinations. This conscientious chef, a graduate of Le Coq Saint-Honoré, deploys the full range of his skills. Meticulousness, subtlety and creativity are the watchwords of his expert repertoire. King crab with spring vegetables open the dance, followed by Breton langoustines, squid, farm-raised veal and Poitou rabbit. The desserts stay the course with wild strawberries, a tapioca pudding with ginger ice cream and a lemon sorbet and vodka float. On weekends, Le Céladon changes its décor to become Le Petit Céladon. The atmosphere is intentionally more relaxed, the tablecloths vanish from the tables and families come to eat after a tour of the Louvre or a stroll in the Tuileries. An astute set menu at 55€, including wine and coffee, and a well-devised children's menu help guests keep the cost down.

● Drouant

18, pl Gaillon.
Métro: Opéra, Quatre-Septembre, Pyramides.
Tel. 01 42 65 15 16. Fax 01 49 24 02 15.
www.drouant.com
Closed 3 weeks Aug.
Prix fixe: 42€ (lunch). A la carte: 90€.

Drouant has become "Drouant by Antoine Westermann." The master of the Strasbourg Buerehiesel has turned the venerable establishment that hosts the Goncourt literary awards into a modish, Zen, gourmet brasserie offering a series of meticulously prepared hors d'oeuvre and dishes. The vegetables, fish or classical dishes served on small plates tapas-style, cold asparagus cream soup, foie gras pâté en croûte and Simmental rib eye steak with slow-roasted shallots: All await you here among a thousand other delights that change from season to season in a gaily refurbished setting in shades of yellow, or on the teak terrace. The desserts, rhubarb croquante in vanilla syrup, millefeuille filled with light cream and baba au rhum, are one of the house's strong points, as are the wines. The service is more relaxed than it was, and the cellar is resourceful. In short, Drouant has been rejuvenated. If France's literary giants can adjust to that, why not you?

● **A la Fontaine Gaillon**

1, pl Gaillon / 1, rue de la Michodière.
Métro: Opéra, Quatre-Septembre.
Tel. 01 42 65 87 04. Fax 01 47 42 82 84
www.la-fontaine-gaillon.com
Closed Sat., Sun., 1 week Feb., 3 weeks Aug.
Prix fixe: 38€ (lunch). A la carte: 65€.

Gérard Depardieu and Carole Bouquet have turned this town house built by Jules Hardouin-Mansart into their gourmet showcase. When the sun is out, opposite the fountain that gives the restaurant its name, the terrace enjoys the restful sound of lapping water. Inside, five private dining rooms are available for more personal repasts. Laurent Haudiot is a conscientious chef. His menu reveals a staunch traditionalism and changes with the seasons. The cold-dressed crab in vinaigrette sauce, langoustine ravioli, whole deep-fried whiting, pan-fried John Dory with mashed potatoes, rack of lamb served in its natural juices or milk-fed veal chop are handled with skill. The praline millefeuille and Gariguette strawberries with mint leaves provide a delightful conclusion. The cellar is well stocked, mainly with wines from small growers, but there are also Sicilian vintages among its shrewd selection at friendly prices.

● **Le Pur'Grill** 🏠 ○ V.COM

At the Park Hyatt Vendôme, 5, rue de la Paix.
Métro: Opéra.
Tel. 01 58 71 10 60. Fax 01 58 71 10 61.
www.paris.vendome.hyatt.com
A la carte: 110€

Elegant, expensive, glamorous, fashionable and super (in the model sense)—in short, very much at home in its location between Cartier and Boucheron—this exquisite, charming hotel, simple in grayish beige, has acquired a chef of great character. Jean-François Rouquette, an engaging beanpole from the Aveyron region who formerly trained under Constant at the Crillon before moving to the Bourdonnais and then Les Muses at the Hôtel Scribe, has caused a stir in Rue de la Paix by bringing letters patent to the house cuisine, both in the lobby patio (Les Orchidées) or the gourmet restaurant known as the Pur'Grill. The place now seems less "fusional" and more regional (but with no awkwardness, just a certain mischief). We delight in a lightened lobster bisque, langoustines sliced lengthwise and seasoned with lemongrass—clean, crisp and natural, scallops with a caramelized cep mushroom sauce and a veal filet served with broccoli and zucchini sautéed in butter. The desserts, with their geometric composition (the apple-themed example is exquisite), avoid gimmickry and licorice-flavored macarons will have you melting. In a word, this is an establishment that deserves proper recognition. Superb wines by the glass, including a La Lagune that will leave you speechless.

● **Mori Venice Bar** ○ COM

2, rue du Quatre-Septembre.
Métro: Bourse.
Tel. 01 44 55 51 55. Fax 01 44 55 00 77.
mori@massimomori.fr / www.massimomori.fr
Closed Sat. lunch, Sun., Aug. Cont. service.
A la carte: 40–100€.

Massimo Mori, the dining room maestro from the Armani Caffé, has gone into business for himself opposite the Palais Brongniart, home of the French stock exchange, where he aspires to the role of Arrigo Cipriani at Harry's Bar, Venice. With a wave of his magic wand, this charming restaurateur works his spell, creating the illusion that the heart of Paris is actually the Grand Canal. The wood and leather décor designed by Philippe Starck provides a jewel case for the produce-based cuisine here. Mustard-seasoned beef carpaccio, shellfish soup, the langoustine escabeche done in the style of sardines in saor: the enchantment abounds. Then there is veal tripe in cream sauce, squid ink risotto and the linguini with clam sauce: reliable, subtle and juicy, a cuisine that delights us heart and soul. Everything here breathes refinement and flavor, including the wines by the glass. The desserts provide a delightful interlude (creamy fruit panna cotta) and the service is quick to satisfy our every wish.

● L'Escargot Montorgueil   COM

38, rue Montorgueil.
Métro: Les Halles, Etienne-Marcel.
Tel. 01 42 36 83 51. Fax 01 42 36 35 05.
escargot-montorgueil@wanadoo.fr
www.escargot-montorgueil.com
Closed 2 weeks beg. Jan., 3 weeks Aug.
A la carte: 80€.

L'Escargot d'Or, founded in 1832, has recaptured a second youth with Laurent Couegnas, who has taken over this Second Empire pearl, a listed historical monument, restoring it to a pristine state. Its stucco, moldings and red velvet seats have a nice effect. The Provençal-style sautéed frog legs with chopped garlic and parsley, Breton lobster flambé with whiskey, veal sweetbreads stewed with vinegar and fresh foie gras and crêpes Suzette are up to standard, even though the prices tend to soar.

● Old Jawad   COM

1, rue Monsigny.
Métro: Quatre-Septembre.
Tel. 01 42 96 16 61.
Prix fixe: 12€ (lunch), 18€, 23€.
A la carte: 35€.

Opposite the Théâtre des Bouffes Parisiens, Nazim Hussain enthusiastically presents his authentic Indian fare. The appetizers from the tandoori oven (chicken tikka, shish kebab), chicken biryani, saffron-seasoned basmati rice, eggplant curry, lamb korma, butter chicken and interesting vegetarian dishes strike the right note, as does the concluding kulfi. The setting is charming with its nooks, banquettes and cushions, and the service is delightfully attentive.

● Gallopin   🛍 🍴 COM

40, rue Notre-Dame-des-Victoires.
Métro: Bourse, Grands-Boulevards.
Tel. 01 42 36 45 38. Fax 01 42 36 10 32.
administration@brasseriegallopin.com
www.brasseriegallopin.com
Cont. service.
Prix fixe: 19,50€, 33,50€. A la carte: 40–50€.

This former stockbrokers' refectory has just celebrated its 130th birthday and has lost none of its splendor, with its woodwork, mahogany bar, superb historic glass veranda and original chandeliers. The uniformed waiters are extremely attentive and serve the subtly prepared brasserie dishes gracefully. The beef and vegetables terrine, tuna tartare with French fries and green salad, pork medallion au gratin with almonds and pistachios, spiced fresh fruit soup with red fruit sorbet are of the best. They can be washed down with a selected Bordeaux or a *gallopin* of beer: 20 centiliters instead of the usual 25 in a silver tankard, a house invention.

● Le Versance   🍴 COM

16, rue Feydeau.
Métro: Bourse, Grands-Boulevards.
Tel. 01 45 08 00 08. Fax 01 45 08 47 99.
contact@leversance.fr / www.leversance.fr
Closed Sat. lunch, Sun., Mon., Aug.
Prix fixe: 32€ (lunch, wine inc.),
38€ (lunch, wine inc.). A la carte: 50€.

Exit Le Petit Coin de la Bourse of gastronomic memory. Some of 19th-century stucco remains, but the place has acquired a more contemporary look in the hands of the dynamic Samuel Cavagnis. Atmosphere, staff and menu have all been rejuvenated. In any case, we cannot find fault with the seared foie gras with artichoke crumble, filet of sea bream in aniseed broth with slow-roasted tomatoes and white beans, slow-roasted lamb shank with dried apricots or tear-shaped chocolate and praline pastry with mango sauce.

● Le Grand Colbert   🍴 COM

2, rue Vivienne.
Métro: Bourse.
Tel. 01 42 86 87 88. Fax 01 42 86 82 65.

le.grand.colbert@wanadoo.fr
Cont. service.
Prix fixe: 19€ (lunch), 28€ (lunch),
34€ (dinner). A la carte: 50€.

Opposite the National Library, this 19th-
century brasserie was featured in *Something's Gotta Give*, starring Keanu Reeves,
Jack Nicholson and Diane Keaton, explaining the fondness of American tourists for
this quiet establishment. It has lived up to
their expectations, though, and there will
be few complaints about the baked onion
soup, sole meunière, pan-fried calf's liver
with caramelized pearl onions and profiteroles with warm chocolate sauce.

● **Le Vaudeville**
29, rue Vivienne.
Métro: Bourse.
Tel. 01 40 20 04 62.
www.groupeflo.fr
Prix fixe: 22,90€, 29,90€. A la carte: 45€.

This is the archetypal Parisian brasserie with its background murmur, typical thirties art deco style, beige marble
and timeless menu, not to mention exemplary service, a reception that copes easily with the establishment's continuing
success in the hands of Laurent Carsault
and Paulo Abate and a cuisine that aspires
to more than just standard, tried-and-
trusted dishes. In the company of staff
from the neighboring banks and AFP press
agency, visitors enjoy duck foie gras in terrine, beautiful oysters, perfect grilled sole,
appetizing caper-seasoned skate, tête de
veau, andouillette AAAAA and a millefeuille, all splendid and fresh. The choice
of wines meets the same high standards
without overly inflating the check.

● **Bistro Volney**
8, rue Volney.
Métro: Opéra.
Tel. 01 42 61 06 65.
Closed Sat., Sun., dinner (Mon.–Wed.), Aug.
Prix fixe: 24€, 32€, 40€. A la carte: 35–50€.

Aurélien Laffon and François Roger have
restored vitality and youth to this old-
style bistro reliant on its charm, with its

large bar, wine racks and attractive, blue-tinted lights. Guests come for the atmosphere, simple cuisine and choice of
shrewd vintages from an extravagant list.
The salad with poached egg and mushrooms, the bouquet of shrimp, or well-prepared kidney served with soft French
fries nicely accompany the Domaine
Gauby Côtes du Roussillon.

● **Silk & Spice** SIM
6, rue Mandar.
Métro: Etienne-Marcel, Sentier.
Tel. 01 44 88 21 91. Fax 01 42 21 36 25.
Closed Sat. lunch, Christmas–New Year's.
Prix fixe: 25€ (lunch), 47€ (wine inc.), 65€.
A la carte: 50–60€.

The flavors of Thailand fill this restaurant,
whose elegance is equaled only by the subtlety of its dishes. We savor the breaded
and fried squid, red curry shrimp, tamarind-seasoned fried Atlantic sea bass,
beef stir-fry, sautéed lamb and the coconut milk flan. On the weekend, the exotic
brunch is well worth the visit.

● **Aux Lyonnais** SIM
32, rue Saint-Marc.
Métro: Bourse, Richelieu-Drouot.
Tel. 01 42 96 65 04. Fax 01 42 97 42 95.
auxlyonnais@online.fr
Closed Sat. lunch, Sun., Mon., Christmas–
New Year's, Aug.
Prix fixe: 28€. A la carte: 60€.

Eric Mercier provides the unshakable
"Ducasse" smile in this circa 1900 bistro
where not a single element is missing: mirrors, woodwork, moldings, counter and
lighting. Here we are happily reunited
with the classics of Lyonnaise cuisine,
Alain Ducasse–style, which apt pupil
Sébastien Guénard prepares by the book.
Taste buds are in for a treat with the pike
quenelles with crayfish, calf's liver with
chopped garlic and parsley, quick-sautéed beef Lyonnaise style and the Grand
Marnier soufflé, not to mention the hazelnut cream tart that will knock you off
your feet. The Beaujolais, Burgundies and
Côtes du Rhône selected by Mathieu Buffet make an excellent impression.

● Dalva Ⓝ 🍴 SIM

48, rue d'Argout.
Métro: Sentier.
Tel. 01 42 36 02 11. Fax 01 42 36 02 27
Closed Sat. lunch, Sun., Mon. dinner.
Prix fixe: 14€ (lunch), 18€ (lunch).
A la carte: 35€.

An eye-catching red facade, a clean and simple bistro entrance, a bay window with a terrace in the summer, then, on the second floor, an attractively decorated room with two dining areas and a Murano chandelier; you soon feel at home in François Lelièvre and Agnès Clément's restaurant. Bruno Schaeffer, previously at L'Argenteuil, organizes the menu with skill. Spinach and smoked haddock ravioli in Charroux mustard sauce, cream of shellfish soup with croutons, roast cod and olive oil fork-mashed potatoes, tender rib eye steak with small roasted potatoes are splendid, as is crème brûlée flavored with bergamot. The somewhat spare cellar is young and reasonable.

● Le Mellifère 🍴 SIM

8, rue Monsigny.
Métro: Quatre-Septembre.
Tel. 01 42 61 21 71. Fax 01 42 61 31 71.
a.mellifere@libertysurf.fr
Closed Sat. lunch, Sun., Mon. lunch.
Prix fixe: 30€ (lunch), 34€ (dinner).

Ideal for refueling after a show at the neighboring Théâtre des Bouffes Parisiens, Alain Atibard's friendly bistro provides a delicious market produce–based cuisine that draws much of its inspiration from Southwest France. Having trained with the greats (Dutournier, Senderens, Lorain and Cagna), our playful, modest chef gives a faultless performance with eggs baked in a ramekin with foie gras, cod brandade, Basque blood sausage with old-fashioned mashed potatoes and Basque cake, a jam-filled butter pastry. Note the free set menu for children under ten.

● Chez Pierrot 🍴 SIM

18, rue Etienne-Marcel.
Métro: Etienne-Marcel.
Tel. 01 45 08 00 10. Fax 01 42 77 35 92.

Closed Sun., 1st week Jan., 3 weeks Aug.
A la carte: 40€.

This elegant, relaxed, antique bistro refurbished in contemporary style is now decked out in fine brown and plum shades that offer a certain warmth. We are pleasantly surprised by the roasted and marinated bell peppers with mozzarella, red mullet with beurre blanc sauce, Aubrac rib-eye steak served with genuine French fries, rare-cooked veal kidneys and homemade chocolate profiteroles. The Beaujolais and Rhône Valley wines encourage us to wholeheartedly raise our glass.

● Clémentine 🍴 SIM

5, rue Saint-Marc.
Métro: Bourse, Richelieu-Drouot, Grands-Boulevards.
Tel. 01 40 41 05 65.
reservation@restaurantclementine.com
www.restaurantclementine.com
Closed weekends.
Prix fixe: 27,50€. A la carte: 35€.

Franck Langrenne provides a warm welcome in this 1906 bistro on two floors, where he serves honest, generous dishes. We treat ourselves to sautéed duck hearts with garlic and parsley, sauerkraut with smoked haddock, cassoulet made with Tarbais beans and strawberry vacherin. A fine selection of wines from small vineyards.

● Aux Crus de Bourgogne 🍴 SIM

3, rue Bachaumont.
Métro: Sentier, Les Halles.
Tel. 01 42 33 48 24. Fax 01 40 26 66 41.
Prix fixe: 27€ (dinner). A la carte: 52€.

Not far from rue Montorgueil and the former Les Halles wholesale market, this distinguished bistro with its listed historic facade has stuck to its traditions. The service is formal but relaxed, the menu time-honored and the clientele made up of journalists from Le Figaro newspaper or Le Nouvel Observateur magazine who are attached to their ways. Like them, we easily enjoy the terrine of parsleyed ham, sole meunière, beef tenderloin with morels and baba au rhum.

● Chez Georges

1, rue du Mail.
Métro: Bourse, Sentier, Palais-Royal.
Tel. 01 42 60 07 11
Closed weekends, Bank Holidays, Aug.
A la carte: 52€.

This typical Parisian bistro has managed to preserve its turn-of-the-century décor (as shown by the counter, seats, stucco and mirrors) and proprietor Arnaud Brouillet ensures that great recipes of yesteryear continue to delight. Regulars or tourists in search of authenticity sit down to such classics as smoked herring and potato salad, salmon steak in sorrel sauce, grilled veal kidney Henri IV–style and iced profiteroles with warm chocolate sauce.

● La Grille Montorgueil

50, rue Montorgueil.
Métro: Etienne-Marcel.
Tel. 01 42 33 21 21. Fax 01 42 33 70 21.
Prix fixe: 14€ (lunch). A la carte: 35€.

The counter that French film star Jean Gabin leaned on in the 1937 movie *Gueule d'Amour* (*Lady Killer*) is still intact, proof of its robustness. The same is true of the chalkboard, presenting classics of domestic cuisine. We make short work of the whole duck foie gras, grilled sea bass, hand-chopped steak tartare and poached pear with chocolate sauce.

PARIS 3RD ARR

■ | HOTELS

■ Murano

13, bd du Temple.
Métro: Filles-du-Calvaire.
Tel. 01 42 71 20 00. Fax 01 42 71 21 01.
42 rooms: 400–650€. 9 suites: 750–2500€.

This fine, contemporary, designer hotel with its Starck furniture, colorful rooms and chic bar is very much in vogue. Visit and wonder. (Also see Restaurants.)

■ Pavillon de la Reine

28, pl des Vosges.
Métro: Chemin-Vert.
Tel. 01 40 29 19 19. Fax 01 40 29 19 20.
www.pavillon-de-la-reine.com
30 rooms: 350–430€. 26 suites: 500–800€.

Under the celebrated arcades, this hotel offers a blend of elegance and refinement. The rooms in orange and red shades have a classical chic, with four-poster beds, paintings, red hexagonal floor tiles and half timbering. The lobby has its charm.

■ La Villa Beaumarchais

5, rue des Arquebusiers.
Métro: Chemin-Vert, St-Sébastien-Froissart.
Tel. 01 40 29 14 00. Fax 01 40 29 14 01.
beaumarchais@leshotelsdeparis.com
www.leshotelsdeparis.com
50 rooms: 280–380€. 4 suites: 780–900€.

Neat rooms, a sauna, Jacuzzi, fitness center and delicious breakfasts served in the inner winter garden are the attractions on offer at this hotel near Bastille and the Marais.

■ Hôtel du Petit Moulin

29, rue de Poitou.
Métro: Filles-du-Calvaire.
Tel. 01 42 74 10 10. Fax 01 42 74 10 97.
contact@hoteldupetitmoulin.com
www.hoteldupetitmoulin.com
17 rooms: 180–350€.

Behind the facade of this perfectly restored former bakery is a very haute couture hotel by Christian Lacroix. Its seventeen rooms provide a delightful blend of silky and decorated fabrics and retro-modern furniture. A very charming establishment.

■ Austin's Arts et Métiers Hôtel

6, rue Montgolfier.
Métro:Arts-et-Métiers.
Tel. 01 42 77 17 61. Fax 01 42 77 55 43.
austins.amhotel@wanadoo.fr
www.austinshotel.com
29 rooms: 99–135€.

In a quiet street opposite the Arts et Métiers museum, this hostelry offers rather smart, renovated rooms at good prices, some still with their original beams.

■ Le Vieux Saule 〇

6, rue de Picardie.
Métro: Filles-du-Calvaire, République.
Tel. 01 42 72 01 14. Fax 01 40 27 88 21.
reserv@hotelvieuxsaule.com
www.hotelvieuxsaule.com
30 rooms: 95–170€.

Behind the balconies of this hotel's flowered facade lie rooms in combinations of pink, blue and yellow. Air conditioning for hot summers and a sauna to keep in shape. WiFi in the rooms and free computers in the small lounge.

● RESTAURANTS

● Le Murano V.COM

13, bd du Temple.
Métro: Filles-du-Calvaire.
Tel. 01 42 71 20 00. Fax 01 42 71 21 01
paris@muranoresort.com
www.muranoresort.com
A la carte: 70€.

Jérôme Foucault and chef Julien Chicoisne, formerly of the Sketch in London and Les Fermes de Marie in Megève, run this chic hotel restaurant with brisk efficiency. The style is neo-Starck in shades of white and plum. A private dining room, terrace and valet parking are all available to its well-heeled customers, who appreciate the meticulously prepared dishes showcasing flavors from all over the world. White bean purée, Japanese-style langoustines, gilthead sea bream or grilled Kobe beef with a purée of "forgotten" vegetables (crosnes, Jerusalem artichokes, rutabagas) impress favorably. The Guanaja chocolate sabayon completes the banquet beautifully. There is brunch on Saturdays and Sundays.

● L'Ambassade d'Auvergne V.COM

22, rue du Grenier-Saint-Lazare.
Métro: Rambuteau, Etienne-Marcel.
Tel. 01 42 72 31 22. Fax 01 42 78 85 47.
info@ambassade-auvergne.com
www.ambassade-auvergne.com
Prix fixe: 28€. A la carte: 40€.

Right in the heart of Paris, Françoise Petrucci tends this country inn with its attentive service and rustic setting. The experience is complete: an old-fashioned dining room with exposed beams and communal tables, comfortable chairs and local produce from the Auvergne, played on deftly by new chef Emmerich de Backer. The pressed leek and Salers cheese terrine, the vegetable and walnut oil croustillant, chitterling sausage with an Auvergne-style cheese and potato purée, farm-raised guinea fowl with roasted garlic and a trio of crèmes are superb.

● Le Pamphlet ○ COM

38, rue Debelleyme.
Métro: Filles-du-Calvaire,
St-Sébastien-Froissart.
Tel. 01 42 72 39 24.
Closed Sat. lunch, Sun., Mon. lunch,
1st 2 weeks Jan., 3 weeks Aug.
Prix fixe: 33€, 55€.

A native of Pau trained at the Crillon by Christian Constant, Alain Carrère has not rested on his laurels. The cuisine comes directly from the region and displays great character. The thin potato tart with marinated wild salmon, sea bream with vegetable fritters and pimiento jus, seared mixed grill of meats served with Swiss chard with green peppercorns and roasted breast of Challans duckling win our ready approval. The pistachio crumble and the roasted pear with ice cream and chocolate sauce are childhood delights.

● L'Auberge Nicolas Flamel 🔨 COM

51, rue de Montmorency.
Métro: Etienne-Marcel, Rambuteau.
Tel. 01 42 71 77 78.
nicolas-flamel@tele2.fr
www.auberge-nicolas-flamel.fr
Closed Sat. lunch, Sun., 3 weeks Aug.
Prix fixe: 30€ (lunch, wine inc.), 49€, 59€.
A la carte: 60€.

In a medieval atmosphere (the restaurant is one of the oldest in Paris, dating from

1407), the cuisine is inventive and of good quality. Creamy risotto with sautéed peas and morels or delicious Noirmoutier potatoes mashed with sea snails and periwinkle butter are two of new chef Frédéric Le Guen-Geffroy's successful offerings. To end, the chocolate hazelnut dessert is delightful.

● **Chez Jenny**   🔲 COM
39, bd du Temple
Métro: République
Tel. 01 44 54 39 00. Fax 01 44 54 39 09
chezjenny@blanc.net / www.chez-jenny.com
Cont. service.
Prix fixe: 19€, 23,50€, 28€. A la carte: 45€.

Its red facade, twinkling lights, sumptuous woodwork, collection of Spindler marquetry offer a change of scenery. The Alsatian quiche, haricots verts salad with smoked duck, salmon with sorrel with Alsatian pasta, grilled rib-eye steak with béarnaise sauce and Alsatian apple tart served à la mode with gingerbread are effortlessly accompanied by a Pinot Gris or Riesling.

● **Le Petit Pamphlet**   🆖🍴SIM
15, rue Saint-Gilles
Métro: Chemin-Vert
Tel. 01 42 71 22 21
Closed Sat. lunch, Sun., Mon. lunch,
Christmas, 1st week Jan., 3 weeks Aug.
Prix fixe: 31€. A la carte: 38€.

His Pamphlet in rue Debelleyme was not enough for him. Alain Carrère has opened a good-natured offshoot just a step away from the parent establishment and not far from place des Vosges. The lump crab with tomato and avocado tartare, Piquillo peppers stuffed with brandade of smoked haddock with chorizo chips, parmesan risotto with grilled shrimp or breast of duckling with seasonal fruit are delicious, as is the engaging spiced cherry chaud-froid with vanilla ice cream.

● **Chez Nénesse**   🍴🔲SIM
17, rue de Saintonge
Métro: République, Filles-du-Calvaire
Tel. 01 42 78 46 49. Fax 01 42 78 45 51

Closed Sat., Sun., Bank Holidays, Christmas–
New Year's, Aug.
A la carte: 23€.

The Leplu family runs this charming, friendly, traditional bistro without affectation. Roger, who presides at the stove, is a veteran of Prunier, Le Grand Véfour and Pierre au Palais-Royal. His cuisine is classical, sober, meticulous and unfussy. The smoked herring and potatoes marinated in olive oil, veal chops pan-fried with butter, lemon and parsley and raspberry clafoutis are of excellent character. Appealing wines.

● **Au Bascou**   🍴SIM
38, rue Réaumur.
Métro: Arts-et-Métiers, Réaumur.
Tel.-Fax 01 42 72 69 25.
Closed Sat., Sun.,
1 week Christmas–New Year's, Aug.
Prix fixe: 18€ (lunch). A la carte: 40€.

Bertrand Guéneron, former Senderens lieutenant at the Lucas-Carton, has preserved the Basque atmosphere in this ochre bistro. The menu breathes the sweet scent of the Pyrénées and Atlantic Ocean, captured in the piperade (sautéed sweet bell peppers with onion and garlic), sautéed squid with Espelette chili peppers and a Basque-style chocolate dessert. A fine choice of Irouléguys reflects the general ambience.

● **Café des Musées**   🍴SIM
49, rue de Turenne.
Métro: St-Sébastien-Froissart, Chemin-Vert.
Tel. 01 42 72 96 17. Fax 01 44 59 38 68.
Closed mid-Aug.–beg. Sept.
Prix fixe: 12,50€ (lunch), 19€ (dinner).
A la carte: 35€.

A step away from the Picasso and Carnavalet museums, this corner café has been taken over by François Chenel, who trained at Fouquet's. Its express lunch option is a steal and the menu of the day up on the blackboard suggests dishes full of vitality, truth and freshness. We love the watercress soup, the slow-simmered poultry and morels as well as the loin of black

Bigorre pork. The fine desserts (Lorrain-style chocolate cake) and wines by the carafe are a mine of common sense.

● **L'Ami Louis**   SIM

32, rue du Vertbois
Métro: Arts-et-Métiers
Tel. 01 48 87 77 48
Closed Mon., Tuesday, mid-July–mid-Aug.
A la carte: 135€.

Of course, guests at L'Ami Louis are not short of a dollar or two; the prices are catastrophic, but if you are not afraid to share the dishes, which are huge, the check can prove manageable. Foie gras, escargots from Burgundy, beautiful seasonal asparagus, milk-fed lamb with sautéed garlic potatoes, whole roasted chicken served with a mountain of French fries have style to spare. The extraordinary wines do nothing to lighten the tab.

● **Chez Omar**   SIM

47, rue de Bretagne
Métro: Filles-du-Calvaire, Arts-et-Métiers, République.
Tel. 01 42 72 36 26.
Closed Sun. lunch.
A la carte: 30–45€

Our favorite Franco Algerian refectory and melting pot: in this twenties to fifties bistro with its banquettes, bar and wooden tables, Omar Guerda serves pastilla, royal couscous, as well as swordfish filet and beef, to one and all: natives of North Africa, businesspersons in suits and hip youngsters. All his dishes are meticulously prepared and served with a smile.

● **Robert et Louise**   SIM

64, rue Vieille-du-Temple
Métro: St-Paul, Filles-du-Calvaire, Hôtel-de-Ville.
Tel. 01 42 78 55 89.
Closed Sun., Mon., beg. July–end Aug.
Prix fixe: 12€ (lunch). A la carte: 38€.

Pascale Georget has taken up the torch of her recently deceased father, Robert. With her mother, Louise, she lovingly tends to the fortunes of this inn, always a delight with its rustic atmosphere and food cooked at the fire with feeling: grilled boudin, escargots, roasted prime rib, grilled lamb, homemade chocolate cake and seasonal fruit tarts are remarkable.

■ | HOTELS

■ **Le Jeu de Paume**

54, rue Saint-Louis-en-l'Ile.
Métro: Pont-Marie.
Tel. 01 43 26 14 18. Fax 01 40 46 02 76.
info@jeudepaumehotel.com
www.jeudepaumehotel.com
30 rooms: 145–335€. 3 suites: 350–445€.

Curiously set in a 17th-century tennis court, this hotel boasts comfortable guest rooms, lounges and billiard, sauna and music rooms.

■ **Bourg Tibourg**

19, rue du Bourg-Tibourg.
Métro: Hôtel-de-Ville.
Tel. 01 42 78 47 39. Fax 01 40 29 07 00.
hotel@bourgtibourg.com
www.hotelbourgtibourg.com
30 rooms: 60–250€. 1 suite: 350€.

In the heart of the Marais, this charming hotel provides rooms in warm tones and Eastern or neo-Gothic styles. Attentive service, a warm welcome and moderate prices complete the picture.

■ **Beaubourg**

11, rue Simon-le-Franc.
Métro: Rambuteau, Hôtel-de-Ville.
Tel. 01 42 74 34 24. Fax 01 42 78 68 11.
www.hotelbeaubourg.com
28 rooms: 118–140€.

A step away from the Pompidou Center, this entirely renovated hotel has comfortable, well-appointed rooms, some of them with exposed stone and beams.

■ **Bretonnerie**

22, rue Sainte-Croix-de-la-Bretonnerie.
Métro: Hôtel-de-Ville.

Tel. 01 48 87 77 63. Fax 01 42 77 26 78.
hotel@bretonnerie.com / www.bretonnerie.com
22 rooms: 116–185€. 7 suites: 180–205€.

In this 17th-century town house, the rooms with their different fabrics are in the purest period style, boasting beams, four-poster beds and antique furniture.

■ Les Deux Iles

59, rue Saint-Louis-en-l'Ile.
Métro: Pont-Marie.
Tel. 01 43 26 13 35. Fax 01 43 29 60 25.
hotel.2iles@free.fr / www.2iles.com
17 rooms: 150–170€.

In the heart of the Ile Saint-Louis, this traditional hotel delights American tourists. Cozy rooms renovated in light shades, rattan furniture, a lounge with a fireplace and a flowered patio.

■ Lutèce

65, rue Saint-Louis-en-l'Ile.
Métro: Pont-Marie.
Tel. 01 43 26 23 52. Fax 01 43 29 60 25.
hotel.lutece@free.fr / www.hoteldelutece.com
23 rooms: 185€.

This little hotel on the Ile Saint-Louis has an easy, rustic appeal. The rooms repainted in yellow shades have French ceilings and fine antique furniture.

■ Saint-Merry

78, rue de la Verrerie.
Métro: Châtelet, Hôtel-de-Ville.
Tel. 01 42 78 14 15. Fax 01 40 29 06 82.
hotelstmerry@wanadoo.fr
www.hotelmarais.com
11 rooms: 160€. 1 suite: 335–407€.

Occupying part of the church of Saint-Merri with its flying buttresses, this Gothic hotel is a friendly repair. Its light tones, carved woods, fine objects, beams and garrets are very stylish.

● RESTAURANTS

● L'Ambroisie   LUX

9, pl des Vosges.
Métro: Bastille, St-Paul.
Tel. 01 42 78 51 45.
Closed Sun., Mon., Christmas vac., Feb.,
end July–end Aug.
A la carte: 245–300€.

A true classicist, refusing to skimp on produce or quality, reassuring us in these days of designer food, unwilling to "deconstruct" dishes but able to deftly span the gap between yesterday's and tomorrow's cuisines: This is Bernard Pacaud, the discreet artisan of L'Ambroisie. The lobster gazpacho, with a very Robuchon air about it, herb and escargot cannelloni in a creamy star anise–flavored broth, soft-boiled eggs and asparagus with a watercress and caviar sabayon sauce, roasted foie gras glazed with onion caramel, served with caramelized turnips and turnip greens, Bresse chicken breast with crayfish and creamed morel mushrooms are enchantingly correct, verging on a serene perfection. There is a kind of timelessness in this beautiful setting, an 18th-century residence restyled by François Joseph Graf, with parquet flooring, tapestries and velvet chairs. The wines, described with shrewd precision by Pierre le Mouliac (unbeatable on the Rhône Valley, brilliant on Burgundy), Daniel Pacaud's serene welcome, Pascal Vetoux's distinguished but unstilted dining room management and the meticulously crafted desserts such as delicate chocolate shortbread tart, vanilla ice cream, thin caramelized puff pastry cookies served with fromage blanc, oven-dried lemon and rhubarb crisps: Here we recognize the discretion that once moved us at Alain Chapel's establishment in Mionnay. A craftsman of French cuisine, never faulted, the overly discreet Bernard has more than earned the three plates we readily return to him after too long an interlude.

● **Don Juan II**   COM

In front of 10 bis du quai Henri-IV.
Métro: Quai-de-la-Rapée, Sully-Morland.
Tel. 01 44 54 14 70. Fax 01 44 54 14 75.
contacts@yachtsdeparis.fr
www.yachtsdeparis.fr
Prix fixe: 165€ (dinner), 190€ (opera cruise).

Jean-Pierre Vigato at the stove, Marc Bungener at the desk and Jean-Luc Paris serving the wine steer this white wood yacht with its brass and mahogany trim on a gourmet cruise down the Seine. Carrots with lobster emulsion, the spiced and roasted Atlantic sea bass, Provencal vegetable-stuffed cannelloni, the breast of young duck served with parsley-seasoned ceps, an assortment of cheeses and variations on the theme of chocolate form the charming set menus.

● **Benoît**   ○ COM

20, rue Saint-Martin.
Métro: Châtelet, Hôtel-de-Ville.
Tel. 01 42 72 25 76. Fax 01 42 72 45 68
restaurant.benoit@wanadoo.fr
Closed Christmas, New Year's, beg.–end Aug.
Prix fixe: 38€ (lunch). A la carte: 70–90€.

Alain Ducasse, gentleman globetrotter, and Thierry de la Brosse from L'Ami Louis previously worked together on the aggiornamento of Aux Lyonnais in rue Saint-Marc. Now they have taken over this bistro revered by Americans, just a step away from the Hôtel de Ville. They have retained both the spirit of the place and its postcard-bistro décor, with counter, brass coat pegs and banquettes perfectly intact. To replace the great Michel, they have brought in Frédéric Rouen. The cuisine of David Rathgeber, who was formerly at Aux Lyonnais, has not changed an iota. Langue Lucullus (smoked ox tongue stuffed with foie gras), frog legs with chopped garlic and parsley, herring-style smoked salmon marinated in oil, cod brandade, oven-roasted shoulder of Pauillac lamb and signature tête de veau—a masterpiece of the genre—are simply superb. Good news: Visa cards, once refused, are at last welcome!

● **Coconnas**   COM

2 bis, pl des Vosges.
Métro: Bastille, St-Paul.
Tel. 01 42 78 58 16. Fax 01 42 78 16 28
info@marcannibaldecoconnas.com
www.latourdargent.com
Closed Mon.
Prix fixe: 25€ (lunch), 32€,
15€ (child). A la carte: 45–65€.

There have been changes in this Terrail bistro under the place des Vosges arcades. A young team has arrived, bringing a more vital approach and a return to tradition. At a polished wooden table, we savor deliciously prepared dishes that have a strong sense of identity. Frédéric Salaün, formerly at La Tour d'Argent, orchestrates the service enthusiastically in the dining room, while Aymeric Kräml, a young Breton veteran of Ducasse, Savoy and Crillon, presides over the kitchen with flair. The results? Tasteful, roguish, rustic dishes. The porcini tart, grilled calf's head with beets and coffee tiramisu are marvels included in the set menu at 32€. A la carte, the poule au pot (stewed stuffed chicken with vegetables and cream sauce) served in two stages is very much an institution.

● **Bofinger**   COM

5-7, rue de la Bastille.
Métro: Bastille.
Tel. 01 42 72 87 82. Fax 01 42 72 97 68.
eberne@groupeflo.fr / www.bofingerparis.com
Prix fixe: 29,90€, 13,50€ (child).
A la carte: 40–66€.

This monument of the brasserie world with its Belle Epoque setting featuring a glass roof dated 1880, Panzani inlays and Hansi paintings attracts all kinds of customers, including those who leave the chore of parking to a valet. Dining room manager Jean-Luc Blanlot directs a flawlessly choreographed ballet. The seafood platter, foie gras, sole meunière, choucroute, spit-roasted lamb saddle served in its jus and the individual baba au rhum are professional indeed.

● Le Dôme du Marais COM

53 bis, rue des Francs-Bourgeois
Métro: Rambuteau, Hôtel-de-Ville, St-Paul
Tel. 01 42 74 54 17. Fax 01 42 77 78 17
domedumarais@hotmail.com
Closed Sun., Mon., 1st week Jan., mid-Aug.–beg. Sept.
Prix fixe: 17€ (lunch), 23€ (lunch)
A la carte: 32€, 45€.

We are awed by the sense of history here under the dome of this former Mont de Piété auction gallery, now run by Brittany's Pierre Lecoutre. The appealing covered terrace and blaze of white and gold in the round hall have plenty of style. The realistically priced set menus offer langoustine spring rolls, John Dory with foamy shellfish and coriander oil sauce, roasted loin of Bigorre black pig with Sicilian lemon and warm Chartreuse soufflé.

● Chez Julien COM

1, rue du Pont-Louis-Philippe.
Métro: Pont-Marie, St-Paul, Hôtel-de-Ville.
Tel. 01 42 78 31 64. Fax 01 42 74 39 30.
Closed Sat. lunch, Sun., Mon. lunch, Christmas, 3 weeks Aug.
Prix fixe: 25€ (lunch), 29€. A la carte: 55€.

Outside and in, from the enchanting 1900s bakery facade to the discreet, romantic interior here on the edge of the Marais quarter, on the riverbank opposite the Ile Saint-Louis, this idyllic setting is perfect for lovers who have not yet plucked up the courage to confess their feelings. The candlelit meal is served on a prettily dressed table in surroundings of antique woodwork and warm hues: foie gras terrine with champagne, sautéed scallops with basil, five-spiced beef tenderloin and strawberries Romanoff accompanied by carafes of Bordeaux or Burgundy.

● Mon Vieil Ami SIM

69, rue Saint-Louis-en-l'Ile.
Métro: Pont-Marie.
Tel. 01 40 46 01 35. Fax 01 40 46 01 36.
mon.vieil.ami@wanadoo.fr
www.mon-vieil-ami.com
Closed Mon., Tue., 1st 2 weeks Jan., 1st 2 weeks Aug.
Prix fixe: 39€.

Antoine Westermann founded his first Parisian annex before Drouant in this modern black and white setting. Adrien Boulouque welcomes and serves the guests, while Frédéric Crochet presides at the stove. Simmered vegetables served warm, foie gras pâté wrapped in pastry, stuffed duck breast, rhubarb compote and pistachio biscuits are meticulous, generous and reliable. The restaurant is open on Sunday.

● Napoli Food SIM

6, rue Castex.
Métro: Bastille.
Tel. 01 44 54 06 61. Fax 01 44 54 00 33.
delizieitaliane@wanadoo.fr
Closed Sun., Mon. lunch, 1 week Christmas–New Year's, Easter, 3 weeks Aug.
Prix fixe: 15€ (lunch). A la carte: 35€.

The success of Fabio Grossi's authentic trattoria continues virtually unabated. The stylish dishes prepared by Neapolitan Antonio Pacchiano change to reflect market produce. Cheerful colors have given the dining room a much younger feel. Mixed homemade vegetable antipasti with buffalo mozzarella, sea bass or lobster simmered with Vesuvian tomatoes, exquisite penne all'amatriciana for two served in a skillet and ricotta cake with pears or figs are tasteful and tasty to the last.

● Brasserie de l'Ile Saint-Louis SIM

55, quai de Bourbon.
Métro: Pont-Marie.
Tel. 01 43 54 02 59. Fax 01 46 33 18 47.
Closed Wednesday, Christmas, New Year's, Aug.
Cont. service.
A la carte: 35–47€.

Choucroute and draft beer are on the menu in this Alsatian brasserie more than a hundred years old, along with smoked Baltic herring in rémoulade sauce with warm potato salad, skate in brown butter sauce, parsleyed calf's liver fried in butter, home-made chocolate mousse and ice creams and sorbets from nearby Berthillon. You only pay for the part of the bottle of wine you drink as you while away the time delightfully, watching the Seine flow by.

● Grizzli Café 🔟 SIM

7, rue Saint-Martin.
Métro: Châtelet.
Tel. 01 48 87 77 56. Fax 01 48 87 34 12.
grizzlicafe@wanadoo.fr
Cont. service.
A la carte: 40€.

With all his usual taste, Didier Kerveno has brought an agreeable, modern, unsnobbish touch—with wooden chairs, brown banquettes and dumbwaiters—to this friendly, early-20th-century bistro, where the lime hues of the first floor blend with the browns and beiges of the attractively redecorated second, reached by a spiral staircase. Eric Law Kwang has adopted a tasteful, lively approach in his spiced crab and avocado appetizer, prawn risotto with red curry sauce, duck breast with five spices and caramelized banana in crisp phyllo pastry. A combination of regional produce and fusion, it slips down effortlessly.

● Le Petit Bofinger 🔟 SIM

6, rue de la Bastille.
Métro: Bastille.
Tel. 01 42 72 05 23. Fax 01 42 72 04 94.
Prix fixe: 19,90€, 28,50€.
A la carte: 32–35€.

There is the main Bofinger and then there is this little brother opposite with its bistro décor, Parisian fresco, gentle prices, conscientious service and well-mannered cuisine. Stéphanie Leblanc prepares tuna rilettes, fish choucroute, the pan-tossed veal liver and a rich chocolate cake.

● Vins des Pyrénées 🔟 SIM

25, rue Beautreillis.
Métro: Sully-Morland, Bastille, St-Paul.
Tel. 01 42 72 64 94. Fax 01 42 71 19 62.
Closed Sat. lunch, 2 weeks Aug.
Prix fixe: 12,50€ (lunch, wine).
A la carte: 38€.

Old postcards, wooden wall seats and grandmotherly drapes feature in this former wine cellar, whose dishes now offer excellent value for the price. The intriguing platter of starters, the herbed salmon roll with stewed fennel, roasted beef prime rib and roasted pineapple brochette are all gratifying, as is the wine list.

PARIS 5TH ARR

■	HOTELS

■ Les Grands Hommes 🏠

17, pl du Panthéon.
Métro: Maubert-Mutualité, Luxembourg.
Tel. 01 46 34 19 60. Fax 01 43 26 67 32.
reservation@hoteldesgrandshommes.com
hoteldes grandshommes.com
32 rooms: 225€. 3 suites: 395€.

Refined rooms in an Empire style and a central location are the attractions of this practical hotel on the place du Panthéon.

■ Le Jardin des Plantes 🏠

5, rue Linné.
Métro: Jussieu.
Tel. 01 47 07 06 20. Fax 01 47 07 62 74.
jardin-des-jardins@timhotel.fr
www.timhotel.com
33 rooms: 75–140€.

Right in the heart of Paris, this hotel by the Jardin des Plantes (botanical gardens) is a charming halt. The rooms refurbished in contemporary style (and named for flowers), sauna, concerts staged in the vaulted hall and breakfast on the terrace in summer are all enchanting.

■ Hôtel Le Colbert 🄽🏠

7, rue de l'Hôtel-Colbert.
Métro: Maubert-mutualité, St-Michel.
Tel. 01 56 81 19 00. Fax 01 56 81 19 02.
reception@lecolbert.com / www.steinhotels.com
37 rooms: 335–415€. 2 suites: 500€.

Between Maubert and the Seine, this delightful 17th-century building houses a refined hotel with functional rooms looking out on the towers of Notre Dame. Guests also enjoy the trim garden.

■ Hôtel du Levant

18, rue de la Harpe.
Métro: St-Michel.
Tel. 01 46 34 11 00. Fax 01 46 34 25 87.
hlevant@club-internet.fr
www.hoteldulevant.com
47 rooms: 73–320€.

The charms of this fine family hotel dating from 1875 are its practical rooms with modern furniture, corridors lined with twenties photos and breakfast room in yellow shades, decorated with a fresco.

■ Jardin de Cluny

9, rue du Sommerard.
Métro: Maubert-Mutualité,
St-Michel-Notre-Dame.
Tel. 01 43 54 22 66. Fax 01 40 51 03 36.
reservation@hoteljardindecluny.com
www.hoteljardindecluny.com
40 rooms: 159–219€.

The black wood and glass entrance leads to rooms in warm colors. Over the last two years, a lot of work has been done on this hotel (quilts, wall fabrics, flat screens) to bring it up to the latest standards while maintaining all its warmth.

■ Jardins du Luxembourg

5, impasse Royer-Collard.
Métro: Luxembourg.
Tel. 01 40 46 08 88. Fax 01 40 46 02 28.
jardinslux@wanadoo.fr
www.les-jardins-du-luxembourg.com
26 rooms: 140–150€.

Sigmund Freud stayed in this charming hostelry just a step away from the Luxembourg Gardens. Contemporary rooms with British and Provençal furniture, a sauna and a friendly welcome.

■ Hôtel des Grandes Ecoles

75, rue du Cardinal-Lemoine.
Métro: Cardinal-Lemoine.
Tel. 01 43 26 79 23. Fax 01 43 25 28 15.
www.hotel-grandes-ecoles.fr
51 rooms: 105–130€.

Harmony reigns throughout, from the dining room with its slightly dated ambiance heightened by decorative mats and point de Hongrie flooring, to the floral rooms with their lace bedspreads.

■ Esmeralda

14, rue Saint-Julien-le-Pauvre.
Métro: St-Michel-Notre-Dame.
Tel. 01 43 54 19 20. Fax 01 40 51 00 68.
19 rooms: 35–95€.

This 1640 building is home to one of the oldest hotels in the capital. The rooms have attractive exposed stone walls and a view of Notre Dame. Angelic prices.

■ Maxim Quartier Latin

28, rue Censier.
Métro: Censier-Daubenton.
Tel. 01 43 31 16 15. Fax 01 43 31 93 87.
info@hotelmaxim.fr / www.hotelmaxim.fr
36 rooms: 95–130€.

Near the Jardin des Plantes (botanical gardens), we enjoy the soft, cheerful shades of the small rooms here, their walls covered with Jouy linen. Some garret accommodation.

■ Sélect Rive Gauche

1, pl de la Sorbonne.
Métro: Cluny-La Sorbonne, Luxembourg.
Tel. 01 46 34 14 80. Fax 01 46 34 51 79.
info@selecthotel.fr / www.selecthotel.fr
67 rooms: 159–219€.

A step away from the Sorbonne, this contemporary hotel has a pleasant lounge giving onto a luxuriant patio under a glass roof. The rooms refurbished in pearl gray tones are charming indeed.

● RESTAURANTS

● La Tour d'Argent

15–17, quai de la Tournelle.
Métro: Maubert-Mutualité, Cardinal-Lemoine.
Tel. 01 43 54 23 31 / 01 40 46 71 11.
Fax 01 44 07 12 04.
www.latourdargent.com

Closed Mon., Tue. lunch.
Prix fixe: 70€ (lunch), 200€, 230€.
A la carte: 200€.

From his vantage point, he must be proud to see that, while the world moves on, it is business as usual for the Tour. Claude Terrail has left his son André to run his establishment. Stéphane Haissant, a veteran of Guérard, Loiseau and Senderens, looks after the stoves and the house cuisine is still successful. Of course, no one visits this establishment (which was already in vogue in the sixteenth century) in search of trendy dishes that will be obsolete as soon as the latest fad has peaked, but rather for a master class in a great, ambitious, classical tradition. In fact, the house offered amuse-gueules (with their mustard-seasoned beignets), the appetizers full of vigor, like foie gras and truffles in a sea urchin sauce, the pike fish quenelle, so silky, served with mushroom duxelles, the canard à l'orange with puffed potatoes and a spinach gratin, the whole veal kidneys cooked to rare perfection, accompanied with crayfish in Vin Jaune sauce and a passion fruit guava parfait are at the height of their ambition. We should also mention that they work their magic as part of a lunchtime set menu at 70 . The service in wing collar and tails and the panoramic setting overlooking the Seine still exert all their ineffable charm. Supervised by the expert David Ridgway, the wine list is still one of the most splendid in the world. Finally, the pear "Vie parisienne", with chunks of poached pear in a vanilla and pear liqueur-infused cream presented under a layer of crisp caramel, remains one of the most irresistible confections of all time. Marvelous Tour!

● **La Truffière**   V.COM

4, rue Blainville.
Métro: Place-Monge, Cardinal-Lemoine, Luxembourg.
Tel. 01 46 33 29 82. Fax 01 46 33 64 74.
restaurant.latruffiere@wanadoo.fr
www.latruffiere.com
Closed Sun., Mon., Christmas, Aug.
Prix fixe: 20€ (lunch). A la carte: 90€.

In the intimate, rustic setting of this 17th-century establishment with its two vaulted rooms, fireplace, cigars and aged spirits, we are ready to try one of the 2,400 wines from its stunning cellar. Sommelier Vincent Martin can point you to the right vintages to properly accompany Jean-Christophe Rizet's sophisticated dishes: Crayfish with asparagus and leeks, bread with olive oil, tomato and garlic topped with a fried egg yolk and cream infused with squid ink, tuna and foie gras croustillant served with caramel marinated carrots or pigeon, its roasted breast and legs stuffed with creamy barley, all make a fine impression. To finish, warm berries with fresh mint and coconut milk served with cassis sorbet is pleasantly refreshing. Supervised by Christian Sainsard, the service is faultless.

● **Mavrommatis**   ○ COM

42, rue Daubenton.
Métro: Censier-Daubenton.
Tel. 01 43 31 17 17. Fax 01 43 36 13 08.
info@mavrommatis.fr / www.mavrommatis.fr
Closesd Sun., Mon., 3 weeks Aug.
Prix fixe: 22€ (weekday lunch), 34€.
A la carte: 60€.

Precise, simple flavors, the taste of fresh local produce from sunny Greece. The Mavrommatis brothers invite us on a gourmet pilgrimage in their fine establishment, where you could imagine yourself to be in Limassol or the Cyclades. On a pleasant little square by the Mouffetard market, their restaurant stands opposite a terrace surrounded by imposing olive trees. The interior breathes 19th-century Athens: mainly pale yellow shades, wooden furniture and black-and-white photos. We begin with tzatziki (cucumber yogurt sauce), taramasalata (a creamy mixture of carp roe, olive oil, lemon and breadcrumbs), dolmadès (stuffed grape leaves) or sardines marinated in spicy oil and marinated "giant" beans, then set about a delicious grilled red mullet filet, a splendid roasted lamb with an eggplant and feta casserole or delicately roasted quail wrapped in grape leaves with honey and thyme. Then we have just enough room left for a date parfait or rice pudding with dried fruit and spiced caramelized pears. Excellent wines from the Peloponnese and the islands accompany this sun-kissed meal.

● **L'Equitable**

47 bis, rue Poliveau.
Métro: St-Marcel.
Tel. 01 43 31 69 20. Fax 01 43 37 85 52
Closed Mon. lunch, Tuesday lunch, Aug.
Prix fixe: 22€ (lunch), 30,50€.
A la carte: 41€.

Very close to the Jardin des Plantes botanical garden, this inn—which deserves its name—has a loyal clientele who appreciate its excellent value for money. Yves Mutin, formerly at Le Jules Verne and L'Ambassade d'Auvergne, has a personal, inventive way of preparing regional produce and choreographing his set menus. The crab salad with julienned vegetables and tomato sorbet, seared pike-perch with crispy skin and a celery root and potato parmentier, duck breast encrusted with coriander, raspberries in a warm strawberry jus with fromage blanc sorbet) are pure delights.

● **Tao**

248, rue Saint-Jacques.
Métro: Cluny-La Sorbonne.
Tel. 01 43 26 75 92. Fax 01 43 25 68 69.
Closed Sun., end July to end Aug.
A la carte: 35€.

We feel at ease in the refined, very Zen surroundings of the Truong's long, narrow establishment, simply decorated with photos of Vietnam. Aficionados can choose between different sizes of dish, depending on how hungry they are. We are tempted by the XL version of steamed dumplings, tender pork simmered in coconut milk and herbed jelly for dessert. Subtle, fresh, tasty, authentic and all made on the premises by chef Kim Nguyen.

● **Le Coupe-Chou**

11, rue Lanneau.
Métro: Maubert-Mutualité.

Tel. 01 46 33 68 69. Fax 01 43 25 94 15.
lecc@lecoupechou.com
www.lecoupechou.com
Prix fixe: 22€, 25€, 32€. A la carte: 45€.

In this discreet street in the Montagne Sainte Geneviève quarter, Christian Azzopardi has turned his restaurant, spanning three 14th-, 16th- and 17th-century buildings into a haven of charm. Enjoy the country duck pâté with Cassis-infused onion jam, monkfish with olive oil, tomatoes and garlic, rack of lamb with fresh mint and strawberry gratin with sabayon by candlelight in one of the adjoining rooms connected by a maze of passages and stairs.

● **Les Bouchons du 5e**

12, rue de l'Hôtel-Colbert.
Métro: Maubert-Mutualité, St-Michel.
Tel. 01 43 54 15 34. Fax 01 46 34 68 07.
www.lesbouchonsdu5.fr
Closed Sat. lunch, Sun., Mon. lunch.
Prix fixe: 20€ (lunch, wine inc.), 26€ (lunch, wine inc.), 30€, 65€. A la carte: 55–75€.

The former name of this restaurant, now run by Denis Blin, has begun to fade from memory. The young Savoy and Gagnaire veteran has discreetly become his own master. Like the restaurant's simply modernized historic décor, the cuisine has grown more exuberant, astute and cheerful. Between the exposed stone walls of the vaulted 12th-century cellar or in the 17th-century first floor dining room, we happily savor goose foie gras prepared three ways, turbot and potatoes roasted in salt, spit-roasted pigeon with truffle risotto, and certainly the individual babas with dark rum, roasted pineapple and coconut. If it were not for the prices . . . .

● **Marty**

20, av des Gobelins.
Métro: Les Gobelins.
Tel. 01 43 31 39 51. Fax 01 43 37 63 70.
restaurant.marty@wanadoo.fr
www.marty-restaurant.com
Noon–11 PM. Cont. service.
Prix fixe: 30€ (lunch), 33€ (dinner).
A la carte: 40–55€.

This former coaching inn turned Parisian brasserie, established in 1913 by the grandparents of current proprietor Geneviève Péricouche, has style to spare with its thirties décor and comfortable terrace. Seafood platters are the specialty, but new chef Emilien Cilia takes a novel approach to tradition with the cured salmon with chive cream, codfish filet with fava beans, old-fashioned calf's head and molten chocolate cake with nougat chips.

● **Christophe**   Ⓝ 🍽 SIM

8, rue Descartes.
Métro: Cardinal-Lemoine.
Tel. 01 43 26 72 49.
Closed Mon.
Prix fixe: 16€ (lunch), 19€ (lunch).
A la carte: 38€.

Opposite the Ecole Polytechnique engineering school, this little bistro with its (very) unassuming décor is run by the brilliant Christophe Philippe. The 26-year old former lieutenant of Eric Briffard at the Plaza and Vernet, who joined Pic and finally the Grill de Monaco, is very much at home here. He delights us with Basque pork belly and black pudding in spring rolls, a quartet of basil-seasoned langoustines in crisp pastry, seared and broiled bream, slow-roasted and delicately-seasoned lamb shoulder and the butter-fried and parsley-seasoned veal sweetbreads served with silky Pompadour potatoes. A cinnamon-seasoned caramelized pineapple dessert is a fine conclusion. The prices are unassuming, but remember to reserve!

● **Ribouldingue**   Ⓝ 🍽 SIM

10, rue Saint-Julien-le-Pauvre.
Métro: St-Michel.
Tel. 01 46 33 98 80.
Closed Sun., Mon., Christmas, New Year's,
2 weeks Aug.
A la carte: 35€.

Nadège Varigny in the dining room and Claver Dousseh in the kitchen perform an original, amusing score in this successor to the former Fogon. Catching on quickly,

lovers of tripe, lamb's brain fried in butter, crispy cow's udder salad, calf's head carpaccio with mayonnaise, capers and herbs, roasted veal kidneys with potatoes au gratin and pig's snouts have set up their headquarters in this elongated restaurant with its close-set tables. For dessert, the rice pudding *grand-mère* or Guanaja dark chocolate mousse are attractive propositions indeed.

● **Au Buisson Ardent**   🍴 🛏 SIM

25, rue Jussieu.
Métro: Jussieu.
Tel. 01 43 54 93 02. Fax 01 46 33 34 77.
info@lebuissonardent.fr
www.lebuissonardent.fr
Closed Sat. lunch, Sun., Bank Holidays,
New Year's, Aug.
Prix fixe: 13€ (lunch), 16€ (lunch),
29€ (dinner). A la carte: 38€.

Chef Stéphane Mauduit (who trained with Michel Rostang) and Jean Thomas Lopez (devotee of wines and music and a graduate of a major business school) were eager to take on this establishment, which still has its 1925 frescos. Market produce, inspired home cooking, a friendly welcome, prompt but not rushed service and reasonable prices are a winning combination. We enjoy croustillant with asparagus, mozzarella cheese and citrus and the veal and pork sausage with sage, served with a Swiss chard fondue. Among the desserts, chocolate and pistachio ganache with Amarena cherries provides a delightful conclusion. To this, add selected wines and the superb house bread.

● **Chantairelle**   🍴 SIM

17, rue Laplace.
Métro: Maubert-Mutualité.
Tel. 01 46 33 18 59.
info@chantairelle.com / www.chantairelle.com
Closed Sat. lunch, Sun., 1 week Aug.
Prix fixe: 16€ (lunch), 21€ (lunch), 30€.
A la carte: 40€.

Do not be put off by its modern exterior: Frédéric Bethe's little Livradois cabin has plenty of character. We savor the poached eggs with fourme d'ambert blue cheese, salmon trout with green Puy lentils or old-fashioned stuffed cabbage, without leaving out the blueberry cake, accompanied by wines (Chanturgue, Châteaugay) and mineral waters from the region.

● Les Délices d'Aphrodite   ⌂ SIM

4, rue de Candolle.
Métro: Censier-Daubenton.
Tel. 01 43 31 40 39. Fax 01 43 36 13 08.
infos@mavrommatis.fr / www.mavrommatis.fr
Prix fixe: 18€ (lunch). A la carte: 38€.

In this blue and white tavern, it's easy to imagine yourself in the Greek Isles. The Mavrommatis brothers maintain the illusion with their succulent cuisine. Pikilia micri (an assortment of appetizers, a Greek Cypriot specialty), pan-seared octopus with olive oil and parsley, jumbo shrimp with garlic and chopped tomato, grilled lamb stuffed with shallot confit and flavored with aged vinegar and cinnamon, orange-infused cream and toasted pistachios delight us with their sun-drenched flavors.

● L'Estrapade   ⌂ SIM

15, rue de l'Estrapade.
Métro: Place-Monge.
Tel. 01 43 25 72 58.
Closed Sat., Sun., 1 week at Christmas, Aug.
Prix fixe: 28€. A la carte: 35€.

This intimate bistro still enchants us with its low ceiling, red banquettes, zinc counter and mirrors. Ariane and Frédéric Chalette continue to regale us with farmhouse dishes, often—although not exclusively—from their native Lorraine. We delight in the parsleyed suckling pig terrine, salmon and baby leek timbale, grilled red tuna with pesto jus, free-range pork with sauerkraut and bacon, dark chocolate pot de crème, as well as the fine growers' wines and very gentle prices.

● Les Papilles   ⌂ SIM

30, rue Gay-Lussac.
Métro: Luxembourg, Cluny-La Sorbonne.
Tel. 01 43 25 20 79. Fax 01 43 25 24 35
Closed Sun., 3 weeks Aug.
Prix fixe: 28,50€. A la carte: 38€.

This highly commendable bistro and gourmet shop run by Bertrand Bluy, formerly a pastry chef with Troisgros, Veyrat and Taillevent, is flourishing. It is copious and irreproachable. A young L'Ami Jean veteran accurately interprets the fresh, subtle menu. The plate of assorted cured meats and pâtés, codfish roasted skin-side down, roasted lamb shoulder, citrus salad and chocolate cappuccino make this a delightful spread. It is a good idea to make a reservation.

● La Rôtisserie du Beaujolais   ⌂ SIM

19, quai de la Tournelle.
Métro: Maubert-Mutualité, Pont-Marie.
Tel. 01 43 54 17 47. Fax 01 56 24 43 71.
A la carte: 40€.

Claude Terrail turned this chic bouchon-style restaurant in a prime riverside location into a rendezvous for friends. It is still there, offering quality produce, attentive service and tempting food. The kitchen with its grill and spits is open to the dining room. As the Challans chickens and beefsteaks sizzle, we begin with crayfish marinated in Mâcon white wine, œufs en meurette (poached eggs with wine, bacon and onions), or the leeks vinaigrette, then face a choice. The roast duck and Salers rib-eye steak with a béarnaise sauce are marvelous. A praline mille-feuille concludes the feast beautifully. A major bonus: The place is open on Sunday.

● Balzar   ⌂ SIM

49, rue des Ecoles.
Métro: Cluny-La Sorbonne, Maubert-Mutualité.
Tel. 01 43 54 13 67. Fax 01 44 07 14 91.
www.brasseriebalzar.com
Cont. service.
Prix fixe: 19,90€ (dinner).
A la carte: 40–50€.

Woodwork, mirrors, faux leather seats, clocks and ceramic vases: Today, this brasserie, so typical of the Left Bank of Paris, is in the hands of the Flo group, but it has not changed a jot. Nor has the chef, Christian René, who is sensibly modest enough to remain in the background, behind a timeless cuisine that we enjoy so much each time: pig snout salad, smoked Baltic herring with cream, skate pan-fried in butter, the house cassoulet and baba au rhum. The Sorbonne crowd delights in these dishes. There are no complaints.

● L'Ecureuil,   🛏 SIM
l'Oie et le Canard

3, rue Linné.
Métro: Jussieu.
Tel.-Fax 01 43 31 61 18.
Closed Christmas, New Year's.
Prix fixe: 17€ (lunch), 20€ (lunch),
18€, 21€. A la carte: 40€.

Be warned: This is a den of rugby fans! This luxurious bistro, an ode to Southwest France, capably caters to their heroic appetites after the game (even when it is just on TV). Generous house foie gras marinated in muscat wine, Salers beef tenderloin and flaky puff pastry filled with apples doused with Armagnac. A real treat. Proprietor Jean-Claude Favre's usually jovial welcome may have its moods.

● Moissonnier   🛏 SIM

28, rue des Fossés-Saint-Bernard.
Métro: Jussieu, Cardinal-Lemoine.
Tel.-Fax 01 43 29 87 65.
Closed Sun., Mon., Aug.
Prix fixe: 24€. A la carte: 30–40€.

Opposite the Institut du Monde Arabe, this fifties décor, *bouchon*-style restaurant inspired by Lyonnais and Franche Comté culture in equal measures serves a perennially fashionable traditional menu. Philippe and Valérie Mayet should pay more attention to the Lyonnaise salad bar, fourteen starters of varying quality. The sautéed tripe is too vinegary, but the beef tenderloin with morel mushroom cream sauce is enjoyable and the generous portion of salt pork and the lentils and smoked Montbéliard sausage is respectable. Apart from this, there is a substantial selection of cheeses and desserts like grandmother used to make. The food as a whole is more generous than subtle. The wines are served in carafes—like the 2004 Chiroubles.

● Au Moulin à Vent   🛏 SIM

20, rue des Fossés-Saint-Bernard.
Métro: Jussieu, Cardinal-Lemoine.
Tel. 01 43 54 99 37. Fax 01 40 46 92 23.
alexandra.damas@aumoulinavent.fr
www.au-moulinavent.com
Closed Sat. lunch, Sun., Mon., 1 week
Christmas–New Year's, 3 weeks in Aug.
Prix fixe: 35€ (lunch). A la carte: 60€.

A step away from the Institut du Monde Arabe, we are firmly back in Paris with this typical old-style bistro run by the dynamic Alexandra Damas. The counter is zinc, the ceiling low, the banquettes in faux leather, the furniture wood and the menu prudently classical. We have no complaints about the Lyonnaise salad with chicory, poached egg and bacon, the eggplant and crayfish terrine, frog legs with tomatoes, garlic and herbs, the thick filet of beef tenderloin with peppercorn sauce and baba au rhum. As for the wine, you can trust the proprietor.

● Perraudin   🛏 SIM

157, rue Saint-Jacques.
Métro: Cluny-La Sorbonne.
Tel. 01 46 33 15 75. Fax 01 46 33 52 75.
restaurant-perraudin@wanadoo.fr
www.restaurant-perraudin.com
Prix fixe: 18€ (lunch), 28€.

The dynamic Monsieur Correy has taken over this institution, frequented since time immemorial by Sorbonne university students, without changing its style. Chef Philippe Dubois gently modernizes bistro classics. The pot-au-feu terrine, profiteroles with warm goat cheese, salmon filet with sorrel sauce, sole meunière, bœuf bourguignon and roasted leg of lamb slip down easily. The grandmotherly desserts—apple tart à la mode and homemade profiteroles—are remarkable.

● Chez René   🛏 SIM

14, bd Saint-Germain.
Métro: Maubert-Mutualité.
Tel. 01 43 54 30 23.
Closed Sun., Mon., 10 days Christmas–New Year's, Aug. Open until 10:30 PM.
Prix fixe: 32€ (lunch, wine inc.),
43€ (dinner). A la carte: 42–60€.

Specialties from Lyon and Beaujolais top the bill in this bistro from a bygone era, with its white tables, simple décor and attentive service. Jean-Claude Cinquin, who has a healthy pair of lungs, is the founder's son, while Jean-Yves Monnerie has been officiating in the kitchen for more than a quarter of a century. Assorted charcuterie and pâtés, fish of the day, rib-eye steak or beef bourguignon and the dessert or charlotte of the day are perfectly prepared and will delight enthusiasts.

● **Les Vignes du Panthéon** SIM
4, rue des Fossés-Saint-Jacques.
Métro: Place-Monge, Cardinal-Lemoine.
Tel.-Fax 01 43 54 80 81.
www.lesvignesdupantheon.fr
Closed Sat. lunch, Sun., 2 weeks beg. Aug.
A la carte: 48€.

Under the historic ceiling, near the patinated zinc counter, Lionel Malière gives lovers of good food and drink occasions to remember. The slow-roasted pressed duck and foie gras terrine, pan-seared veal kidneys and iced macaron glacé with pistachios go famously with wines chosen from all the right places.

PARIS 6TH ARR

■ | HOTELS

■ **Lutétia**
45, bd Raspail.
Métro: Sèvres-Babylone.
Tel. 01 49 54 46 46. Fax 01 49 54 46 00.
lutétia-paris@lutétia-paris.com
www.lutétia-paris.com
172 rooms: 230–380€. 58 suites: 530–2500€.

This art deco monument boasts a delightfully ornate facade, Lalique chandeliers, Arman and César sculptures, rooms refurbished in contemporary style, a highly literary bar and a restaurant: the Paris.

■ **Hôtel du Sénat**
10, rue de Vaugirard.
Métro: Luxembourg, Odéon.

Tel. 01 43 54 54 54.
reservations@hotelsenat.com
35 rooms: 180–310€.

A step away from the Palais du Luxembourg, this fine 19th-century building is a convivial hostelry with smart rooms in a contemporary style. A perfect base camp for those exploring the Saint-Germaindes-Près quarter. A friendly welcome.

■ **Bel Ami**
7, rue Saint-Benoît.
Métro: St-Germain-des-Prés.
Tel. 01 42 61 53 53. Fax 01 49 27 09 33.
contact@hotel-bel-ami.com
www.hotel-bel-ami.com
113 rooms: 270–430€. 2 suites: 490–520€.

In the heart of Saint-Germain, this Zen hotel with its minimalist rooms and modern facilities (fitness center, steam bath, meeting rooms and WiFi) surfs on the wave of fashion.

■ **L'Hôtel**
13, rue des Beaux-Arts.
Métro: St-Germain-des-Prés.
Tel. 01 44 41 99 00. Fax 01 43 25 64 81.
reservation@l-hotel.com / www.l-hotel.com
Rest. closed Sun., Mon., Aug., Christmas.
16 rooms: 255–640€. 4 suites: 540–740€.

Oscar Wilde, Mistinguett and Pierre Loti were residents in this baroque institution renovated by Jacques Garcia. Atrium, spiral staircase, swimming pool and steam bath work their charm.

■ **Hôtel d'Aubusson**
33, rue Dauphine.
Métro: Odéon, Pont-Neuf.
Tel. 01 43 29 43 43. Fax 01 43 29 12 62.
www.hoteldaubusson.com
50 rooms: 280–450€.

Set in a 17th-century building, this hotel has fine rooms decorated with Aubusson tapestries and trimmed with mahogany. The jazz evenings held in the bar on weekends bring the place to life.

■ Relais Christine

3, rue Christine.
Métro: Odéon, St-Michel.
Tel. 01 40 51 60 80. Fax 01 40 51 60 81.
contact@relais-christine.com
www.relais-christine.com
51 rooms: 355–725€. 2 suites: 750€.

This 13th-century convent is now a fine hostelry with a paved courtyard, vaulted cellars, Louis XIV furniture and a fitness center with Jacuzzi. The suites have terraces looking out onto the garden.

■ Relais Saint-Germain

9, carrefour de l'Odéon.
Métro: Odéon.
Tel. 01 43 29 12 05 / 01 44 27 07 97.
Fax 01 46 33 45 30.
hotelrsg@wanadoo.fr / www.hotelrsg.com
22 rooms: 210–420€. 1 suite: 420€.

Taken over by the ebullient Yves Camdeborde, this central hotel on the carrefour de l'Odéon is made up of three 17th-century houses with spacious neo-rustic rooms. The street level Comptoir de l'Odéon serves delicious spreads.

■ La Villa

29, rue Jacob.
Métro: St-Germain-des-Prés.
Tel. 01 43 26 60 00. Fax 01 46 34 63 63.
www.villa-saintgermain.com
31 rooms: 260–480€. 4 suites: 440–480€.

The 19th-century facade conceals warm, contemporary rooms with fine bathrooms. Ambiance guaranteed in the basement when jazz concerts are held in the evening.

■ L'Abbaye

10, rue Cassette.
Métro: St-Sulpice.
Tel. 01 45 44 38 11. Fax 01 45 48 07 86.
hotel.abbaye@wanadoo.fr
www.hotel-abbaye.com
37 rooms: 205–380€. 7 suites: 410–472€.

This 17th-century convent has been converted into a charming hostelry with neat, cozy rooms, all different. A favorite haunt of writers out for a good time in the capital, it offers comfortable lounges and a pleasant patio. The WiFi network is a bonus.

■ Angleterre

44, rue Jacob.
Métro: St-Germain-des-Prés.
Tel. 01 42 60 34 72. Fax 01 42 60 16 93.www.hotel-dangleterre.com
27 rooms: 135–260€. 3 suites: 280–310€.

Hemingway was a regular in this hostelry, which used to house the British Embassy. For a long time now, it has been an old-fashioned hotel with paneled ceilings and patinated beams. The rooms looking out onto the flowered patio are delightfully peaceful.

■ Le Clos Médicis

56, rue Monsieur-le-Prince.
Métro: Odéon, Luxembourg.
Tel. 01 43 29 10 80. Fax 01 43 54 26 90.
message@closmedicis.com
www.closmedicis.com
37 rooms: 155–235€. 1 suite: 480€.

A step away from the Luxembourg Gardens, this hotel boasts a refreshing patio and charming rooms in a varied ethnic style.

■ Hôtel Danemark

21, rue Vavin.
Métro:Vavin.
Tel. 01 43 26 93 78. Fax 01 46 34 66 06.
paris@hoteldanemark.com
www.hoteldanemark.com
15 rooms: 118–156€.

This hotel has more of Denmark to it than just the name, starting with the contemporary design of the fixtures and fittings, and the predominantly blue shades of the rooms. Some of the bathrooms have a Jacuzzi.

■ Hôtel Saints-Pères

65, rue des Saints-Pères.
Métro: Sèvres-Babylone,
St-Germain-des-Prés.
Tel. 01 45 44 50 00. Fax 01 45 44 90 83.
hsp@espritfrance.com

www.espritfrance.com
36 rooms: 140–280€. 3 suites: 295€.

A refined décor, antique furniture and harmonious colors set the tone in this town house built in the reign of Louis XIV. We appreciate the quiet of the flowered patio.

■ **Les Marronniers**

21, rue Jacob.
Métro: St-Germain-des-Prés.
Tel. 01 43 25 30 60. Fax 01 40 46 83 56.
www.paris-hotel-marronniers.com
28 rooms: 102–160€.

A charming, rustic halt with its Napoleon III furniture, small, cozy rooms and flowered garden, also to be admired from the porch.

■ **Welcome**

66, rue de Seine.
Métro: St-Germain-des-Prés, Odéon, Mabillon.
Tel. 01 46 34 24 80. Fax 01 40 46 81 59.
welcome-hotel@wanadoo.fr
www.welcomehotel-paris.com
30 rooms: 30–124€.

For a hotel so close to the carrefour de l'Odéon, the prices are unbeatable. A warm welcome and old fashioned rooms, all different.

● | RESTAURANTS

● **Lapérouse**   🏛 LUX

51, quai des Grands-Augustins.
Métro: St-Michel.
Tel. 01 43 26 68 04. Fax 01 43 26 99 39.
restaurantlaperouse@wanadoo.fr
Closed Sat. lunch, Sun., Aug.
Prix fixe: 30€ (lunch, wine inc.),
45€ (lunch, wine inc.), 95€ (dinner),
120€ (dinner). A la carte: 110–140€.

To believe in Lapérouse or not, that is the question. This riverside establishment has been welcoming guests since 1766. The new management team, Dominique Romano and Judith Cohen, seem to have their eye on the future, and chef Alain Hacquard has a sure touch. The roasted langoustines with watercress and sea-urchin sauce, the sea bass, slow roasted skin-side down served with shellfish jus and leeks stewed with bacon as well as the smoked beef tenderloin served with a truffle and Madeira sauce, served with hand-beaten potato and heirloom vegetable purée, are his tours de force. The desserts—lime soufflé, thyme ice cream and creamy warm chocolate pudding with chicory ice cream—are of good character and the cellar still shows flashes of its former glory.

● **Jacques Cagna**   ◎ V.COM

14, rue des Grands-Augustins.
Métro: St-Michel, Odéon.
Tel. 01 43 26 49 39. Fax 01 43 54 54 48
jacquescagna@hotmail.com
www.jacques-cagna.com
Closed Sat. lunch, Sun., Mon. lunch,
Christmas, 3 weeks Aug.
Prix fixe: 42€ (lunch), 95€.
A la carte: 110–130€.

The historic elegance, the dining room with its Flemish paintings, beams and 16th-century woodwork, Anny Logereau's welcome and a wine list rich in fine vintages: All these are the trump cards of Maison Cagna. Not to mention the lunchtime set menu at 42€, which featured omelet Curnonsky (with diced lobster and lobster bisque sauce) the other day: tremendous! In short, Jacques Cagna, who owns L'Espadon and Rôtisserie, is still hale and hearty in his Old Paris establishment. Here, tradition goes hand-in-hand with contemporary tastes. The pan-seared duck foie gras with caramelized fruit, roasted turbot with puréed Granny Smith apples, salt- and rosemary-crusted veal sweetbreads, Vendée pigeon cooked with green Chartreuse (the breast meat roasted, the leg meat ground and baked in phyllo pastry with spices), and Paris-Brest "of my childhood" are fine work indeed.

CHEF OF THE YEAR

● **Hélène Darroze** 🏠 ⓒⓞ V.COM
4, rue d'Assas.
Métro: Sèvres-Babylone.
Tel. 01 42 22 00 11. Fax 01 42 22 25 40.
reservation@helenedarroze.com
www.helenedarroze.com
Closed Sun., Mon.
Prix fixe: 68€ (lunch), 168€.
A la carte: 130–200€.

Yes, the day has come: Little Hélène has come of age. A onetime rookie from the provinces, her naïveté the butt of insidious jokes, a former tosser of salads in Monaco for Cousin Ducasse from Castelsarrasin, having spent years at Supdeco business school, Hélène is now her own mistress, rallying Paris society to her banner. She has published a large, successful book of sentimental recipes entitled *Personne ne me volera ce que j'ai dansé* (*No One Can Take What I Danced from Me*) and continued her ascent, earning the title "little princess of the Landes in Paris." Today, the empty weekday dining rooms that she and her father Francis once faced in Villeneuve-de-Marsan are no more. Now she choreographs the cuisine of her day, era, roots and personality in this elegant contemporary setting in red and gold, with shades of carrot, tomato and eggplant. Cry it from the rooftops: Southwest France has acquired another grand culinary temple to stand alongside Alain Dutournier's Carré des Feuillants. An embassy built on charm? There is something of that, but make no mistake: Hélène Darroze is inspired. Like a great conductor, she brilliantly leads her young, dynamic, keen kitchen and dining room staff. Anything we may taste in her restaurant is undeniably equal to the finest dishes produced by her peers. So Three Plates for her simply poached white asparagus, served with frog legs, the pan-fried milk-fed lamb sweetbreads with tandoori spices, the aerial and sublime citrus and ginger mousse, magnificent wild river salmon grilled on one side, served with fingerling potatoes and a smoked herring and wild sorrel foam, Landais foie gras grilled on a wood fire and the artichoke ravioli served with a light Provençal-style jus with a touch of fermented anchovy paste. Then there are the Basque lamb saddle stuffed with chorizo and roasted with bay leaves, classic desserts such as rice pudding with muscovado sugar, tropical fruit cocktail, lychee jelly, coconut sorbet and Madong chocolate cake with lemon cream and roasted hazelnut sauce. You may have thought you had already tasted this produce unearthed in the freshest of French regions, the heart of the great Southwest, and these tried and trusted recipes elsewhere, but Hélène coaxes entirely new harmonies from them, her music touching us like a great sonata. Add the most seductive of wines presented by competent, articulate sommelier Gilles Mouligneau, a mine of information on the greater South of France and eternal Bordeaux, combined with tempting prix fixe menus and Armagnacs—aged in Hélène's father's cellar and pleading to be uncorked—and a great house is born. We were the first to gauge Hélène's true worth when she came to the capital. Now she looms over the Parisian culinary stage alongside all those she formerly admired. It is time to applaud her.

● **Le Relais Louis XIII** ⓒⓞ 🍴 V.COM
8, rue des Grands-Augustins.
Métro: Odéon.
Tel. 01 43 26 75 96. Fax 01 44 07 07 80.
contact@relaislouis13.com
www.relaislouis13.com
Closed Sun., Mon., Aug.
Prix fixe: 45€ (lunch), 68€ (dinner), 89€.
A la carte: 130–150€.

This former post house's rich, historical décor, Louis XIII furniture, colors (predominantly red and purple) and medieval cellars impress, but it is Manuel Martinez's cuisine that holds our attention. Holder of the Meilleur Ouvrier de France award, trained at Ledoyen, the Bristol and the Crillon and chef at La Tour d'Argent, this maestro of the range proficiently interprets a reliable, flawless classical repertoire but is also at home with lighter dishes. The Breton lobster and foie gras ravioli with a porcini cream sauce, Breton langoustines in puff pastry with green asparagus and truffle juice, line-caught Dover sole with spider crab and herbed potato gnocchi, roasted Challans duck with strong spices and caramelized turnip purée or twice-cooked veal chop in red wine sauce with diced vegetables are his touchstones: academic, but far from dull. Add fine desserts, such as mille-feuille filled with light vanilla cream and seasonal fruit clafoutis with ice cream, and you will realize that this is the perfect place to celebrate a birthday or other happy event in appropriate style. A great cellar of 1,500 wines tended to by the competent Emilie Cousin.

● **La Méditerranée**   ◎ 🍴 V.COM

2, pl de l'Odéon.
Métro: Odéon.
Tel. 01 43 26 02 30. Fax 01 43 26 18 44.
la.mediterranee@wanadoo.fr
www.la-mediterranee.com
Closed Christmas–New Year's.
Prix fixe: 27€, 32€. A la carte: 70–80€.

Things have changed in this fine seafood restaurant opposite the Théâtre de l'Odéon since Geneviève Jabouille turned the kitchen over to Denis Rippa. This veteran of Le Divellec, L'Ambroisie and Taillevent delicately crafts quality produce and adds a very down-to-earth, personal touch to his dishes, with such success that the food in this fifties setting with its Cocteau carpet and drawings by Bérard and Vertès has never been so refined. Red tuna tartare with olive oil, sea bass carpaccio with wholegrain mustard, Mediterranean bouillabaisse, gilthead sea bream glazed with ginger and served with polenta are of excellent quality, although carnivores may prefer the Lozerian lamb chop served with fennel or pan-roasted beef tenderloin served with olive oil French fries. Turn-

ing to the desserts, the shortbread pecan pie served with passion fruit sorbet or, finally, a tangy apple marmalade with Bourbon vanilla crème brûlée make a first-rate impression.

● **Le Paris**   ◎ V.COM

45, bd Raspail.
Métro: Sèvres-Babylone.
Tel. 01 49 54 46 90. Fax 01 49 54 46 00
lutetia-paris@lutetia-paris.com
www.lutetia-paris. com
Closed Sat., Sun., Bank Holidays, Aug.
Prix fixe: 50€ (lunch, wine inc.),
70€, 130€. A la carte: 100–150€.

The décor by Slavik, which echoes one of the dining rooms of ocean liner *Normandie*, is still impressive. The service is elegant and the prix fixe menus tempting. Philippe Renard (who also looks after the house brasserie) has been here for more than a decade, but cannot be accused of resting on his laurels. The proof is in the eating: the morel mushrooms and white asparagus dressed in chervil and hazelnut vinaigrette and the duck foie gras with baby leeks and a mango, lemon and red onion salsa mark a change in the house style. The line-caught sea bass with barberries, snow peas and seaweed and the roasted "blonde d'Aquitaine" veal chop served with chanterelles, apricots and chervil have a charming peasant appeal. The Basque Axuria lamb is a fine cut of meat and, for dessert, the whole roasted Victoria pineapple served with a white rum and tropical fruit granita is a paragon of its genre.

● **La Closerie des Lilas**   🍴 V.COM

171, bd du Montparnasse.
Métro: Port-Royal, Vavin.
Tel. 01 40 51 34 50. Fax 01 43 29 99 94.
closerie@club-internet.fr
www.closeriedeslilas.fr
Prix fixe: 45€ (lunch, wine inc.).
A la carte: 60–90€.

Literary and artistic Parisian society continues to frequent this iconic locale, along with tourists and the curious. To music from a jazz pianist, the elegant crowd soaks up the atmosphere in the three areas that open before it: the bar, the lively brasserie and the restaurant, with its shady terrace sheltered from the street. The mosaic floor, scarlet seats and polished tables form a splendid setting. In the kitchen, Jean-Pierre Cassagne, long at Edgar, prepares his classic dishes with skill. The salmon with Belgian endive and horseradish cream, pike fish quenelles, beef tenderloin in marrow sauce and chocolate quenelles are equal to the house's reputation. Jean-Jacques Caimant, former Robuchon maître d', watches over the dining room.

● Sensing

19, rue Bréa.
Métro: Vavin.
Tel. 01 43 27 08 80. Fax 01 43 27 03 76.
Closed Sun.
A la carte: 65€.

One of the events of fall 2006 was Guy Martin's acquisition of Dominique, once a historic Russian restaurant, now an eatery devoted to the five senses. Designed with elegance, skill and a rather glamorous chic by Jérôme Fayans-Dumas, it has plenty of verve. A former Lasserre lieutenant who worked with Guy Martin at the Véfour, Rémy Van Péthegem has devised a menu full of surprises. The bite-sized "snacks" are amusing. The mackerel and fennel tart, herb-crusted veal and mushroom-stuffed pasta, lemon zest shortbread topped with grapefruit segments and grapefruit sorbet are promising.

● L'Alcazar COM

62, rue Mazarine.
Métro: Odéon.
Tel. 01 53 10 19 99. Fax 01 53 10 23 23.
contact@alcazar.fr / www.alcazar.fr
Prix fixe: 19€ (lunch, wine inc.),
22€ (dinner, wine inc.), 25€ (lunch, wine inc.), 29€ (lunch, wine inc.), 39€ (dinner).
A la carte: 55€.

Attractive, good, inexpensive (if you stick to the reasonable set menus) and relaxed (if you come for Sunday brunch), Sir Terence Conran's Parisian connection, managed by Michel Besmond, is in fine shape.

We love the modern setting with its mezzanine, veranda and open kitchen. At the range, Guillaume Lutard still focuses on freshness: the tuna mille-feuille, pan-tossed langoustines or slow-cooked thyme-seasoned lamb shoulder show precision are polished preparations. The desserts (a raspberry and licorice vacherin) are of a high standard and the selection of wines is full of pleasant surprises.

● Le Restaurant COM

At L'Hôtel, 13, rue des Beaux-Arts.
Métro: St-Germain-des-Prés.
Tel. 01 44 41 99 01. Fax 01 43 25 64 81.
eat@ll-hotel.com / www.l-hotel.com
Closed Sun., Mon.,
1 week Christmas–New Year's, Aug.
Prix fixe: 50€. A la carte: 70€.

This historic hotel is worth a visit for the polished setting with velvet banquettes in this gourmet boudoir by the Ledoux fountain. The young Philippe Bélissent, formerly at Ledoyen, amazes his audience with farm eggs with truffles, scallop carpaccio, Atlantic sea bass with chestnut and red wine sauce and the young Bresse chicken cooked in cocotte, served with its bouillon, its oyster and a fine chard gratin. Pretty variations on the theme of the apple or pineapple (roasted, vanilla-seasoned, in baba with Malaga ice cream).

● Bastide Odéon

7, rue Corneille.
Métro: Odéon.
Tel. 01 43 26 03 65. Fax 01 44 07 28 93.
bastide.odeon@wanadoo.fr
www.bastide-odeon.com
Closed Sun., Mon., 3 weeks Aug.
Prix fixe: 26€, 38€. A la carte: 40–50€.

Cheerful, friendly and flavorsome, Gilles Ajuelos' lair has an appealingly Provençal feel. This Rostang and Maximin veteran adds his own deft touch to familiar classics, teasing fresh notes from them. Since these sound dishes form part of an unpretentious set menu, they rapidly win us to their way of thinking. Macaroni with escargots and chestnut soup, Riviera-style eggplant mille-feuille, roasted turbot with a creamy olive oil potato purée, gilthead sea bream served with crisp cabbage, roasted quail with risotto, a nice two-pound roasted prime rib for two are gratifying. Add to this traditional but striking desserts, such as creamy vanilla millefeuille and first-rate Provençal wines, and you will start to think that this somber eatery with its off-white décor has a lot going for it.

● Fogon   ○ COM

45, quai des Grands-Augustins.
Métro: St-Michel.
Tel. 01 43 54 31 33. Fax 01 43 54 07 00
Closed weekday lunch, Mon., December, 2 weeks Aug. Open until midnight.
Prix fixe: 35€, 40€.

Alberto Herraiz, who formerly prospered near Saint-Julien-le-Pauvre, has now set himself up in a suitable contemporary setting by the Seine with an open kitchen and baroque banquettes straight out of Almodóvar. This grandson of restaurateurs from La Mancha, who came here from Valencia, has become the darling of Parisian diners. Bomba rice, cooked with rabbit, ham, snails, market vegetables, cuttlefish ink, squid, langoustines or shrimp, acquires the aura of a noble dish. The tapas, both savory (garlic soup, mashed cod with potato, fried fresh anchovies) and sweet (rice pudding, crème catalane, turron ice cream with vine-ripened peaches) are equally appealing, while the Rioja, Mancha and Penedes wines will knock you off your feet. Arriba Herraiz!

● Yugaraj   ○ COM

14, rue Dauphine.
Métro: Pont-Neuf, Odéon.
Tel. 01 43 26 44 91. Fax 01 46 33 50 77
Closed Mon., Tuesday lunch, Aug.
Prix fixe: 19€ (weekday lunch),
34€ (dinner).

Kulendran Meyappen, a terribly "British" Sri Lankan gentleman, runs the best Indian establishment in Paris with genuine warmth. The cuisine he serves up is in his image: generous and refined. Entrusted

to the safe hands of chef Joseph Yhangérajha, it leaves little room for improvisation and exerts an easy charm with its authentic dishes and highly elegant wines. The names: salade pattera, fish tikka, chingri bahar and matchli masala, ghost korma and ghost rada, not to mention thene ou chahat nam for dessert, will take on a whole new meaning after this memorable experience. The décor is a little limited, but the gilded wall bases and grayish beige wall coverings are full of character.

● Bouillon Racine   🍴 COM

3, rue Racine.
Métro: Odéon, Cluny-La Sorbonne.
Tel. 01 44 32 15 60. Fax 01 44 32 15 61
bouillon.racine@wanadoo.fr
www.bouillonracine.com
Closed Christmas, Aug. 15th.
Prix fixe: 15,50€ (lunch), 26€.

Bouillon Racine, which has acquired a little brother next door (see Bouillon des Colonies, above), has retained the art nouveau style that forms the basis of its charm. Luc Morand, who looks after both establishments, has entrusted the kitchen to young Alexandre Beltoise, who wields his utensils with great proficiency. We delight in the tarbais bean and smoked bacon soup, scallop carpaccio with truffle oil, pike-perch and spinach baked in phyllo pastry and stuffed suckling pig roasted on a spit served with mashed potatoes. The soft chocolate cake and velvety chestnut mousse flavored with Jack Daniels are not bad.

● Le Procope   🟡 🍴 COM

13, rue de l'Ancienne-Comédie.
Métro: Odéon.
Tel. 01 40 46 79 00. Fax 01 40 46 79 09.
procope@blanc.net / www.procope.com
Prix fixe: 19€, 24€, 30€. A la carte: 55€.

Historic, but nothing to write home about, this eatery once frequented by Voltaire mistakenly imagines itself to be a gastronomic haven. An oil-soaked Sicilian vegetable caponata, a refrigerator-cold duck foie gras with toasted panettone and dried-out salmon steak in beurre blanc sauce are hardly the stuff that dreams are made of. However, the pepper-crusted beef tenderloin and brown sugar crème brûlée are edible.

● Vagenende 🗂 COM

142, bd Saint-Germain.
Métro: Odéon.
Tel. 01 43 26 68 18. Fax 01 40 51 73 38.
www.vagenende.fr
Closed 3 weeks Aug.
Prix fixe: 19€ (lunch), 23€.
A la carte: 55€.

The setting has the edge on the food. The authentic 1900s décor, all woodwork and mirrors, really does make the visit worthwhile. Still, there are very few grounds for complaint with the onion soup au gratin, chicken liver pâté with Armagnac, roasted pike-perch on shredded endive, a thick veal chop in its own juice served with macaroni casserole and a traditional grandmother-style rice pudding. Decent prix fixe menus.

● Armani Caffè ◯ SIM

149, bd Saint-Germain.
Métro: St-Germain-des-Prés.
Tel. 01 45 48 62 15. Fax 01 45 48 53 17.
mori@emporioarmanicaffe.fr
www.emporioarmani.it
Closed Sun. Cont. service.
A la carte: 75–80€.

He manages to divide his time between the Bourse district, where he has his Mori Venice Bar, and this highly fashionable eatery. Mantoua's Massimo Mori copes with success, chatting with the beautiful people as they battle for a table in this packed setting in shades of mouse gray. Everything chef Ivan Schenatti has to offer bears the stamp of quality: light antipasti, Zibello cured ham, steamed then pan-roasted sea bass with mixed grilled vegetables, red tuna seared on a cast-iron grill, boned lamb chop roasted in caul with artichokes, small veal and Swiss chard ravioli with walnuts. Every pasta dish is worth tasting and the risottos are sublime. Then there are the delicious desserts: red fruit and pomegranate

panna cotta, strawberry or Sorrento lemon ice cream, made to order.

● Boo Ⓝ SIM

6, rue du Sabot.
Tel. 01 42 22 21 56.
Closed Sun., Mon., 2 weeks Aug.
A la carte: 36€.

This Old Paris haunt with its exposed beams and ancient stone has been refurbished in a modern style with gray furniture, pink banquettes and light wood flooring. Hélène Avril provides a charming welcome, while chef Stéphane Porte cooks up light, fresh fare. The smoked salmon charlotte with herbs, foie gras and langoustine terrine, curried monkfish medallion, chicken breast with morels, the slow-cooked lamb shank with eggplant caviar are all expertly prepared. The desserts are in the same vein, including a frozen pistachio or pineapple macaron. A fashionable address with a delightfully snug ambiance.

● Barroco SIM

23, rue Mazarine.
Métro: Odéon.
Tel. 01 43 26 40 24. Fax 01 42 36 05 87.
a.d.a1@wanadoo.fr
www.restaurant-latino.com
Closed lunch.
A la carte: 50€.

This fashionable establishment designed by Maurice Savinel and Roland Le Bévillon is a pleasant surprise. The elegance of the setting contrasts with the cuisine, which sets our taste buds dancing to the rhythm of a bossa nova. Tapas brésiliennes, shrimp with olive oil and parsley, chicken with coconut, churrasco (mixed meat grill) and "cocoloco" (sorbet, macaron, liqueur) are washed down with Chilean and Argentinian wines.

● Da Rosa SIM

62, rue de Seine.
Métro: Odéon.
Tel. 01 40 51 00 09. Fax 01 40 51 04 59.
da-rosa@wanadoo.fr
Closed 25 Dec., 15 Aug.

Prix fixe: 21€ (wine inc. weekdays).
A la carte: 25–45€.

José da Rosa has turned this gourmet grocery store into a laid-back restaurant. The terrace is popular when the sun shines and the Garcia décor has plenty of vitality. The produce is splendid. A variety of risottos, Iberian ham, filets of white tuna and desserts from Pierre Hermé all slip down effortlessly.

● Le Comptoir du Relais   ○ SIM

9, carrefour de l'Odéon.
Métro: Odéon.
Tel. 01 44 27 07 97. Fax 01 46 33 45 30.
hotelrsg@wanadoo.fr
www.hotel-paris-relais-saint-germain.com
Prix fixe: 42€ (dinner weekdays).

An unusual restaurant? Absolutely. Yves Camdeborde's bistro, our last year's "event," can scarcely be compared with any other eatery. What you will find there by night is a chic bistro (seating 22 diners) with an impressive prix fixe menu, and at noon, a gourmet café with dazzling dishes and no reservations. At either time, you will need to wait your turn patiently to taste the "pressed" foie gras and porcini terrine served with artichoke purée, the heavenly cod brandade, a superb boned and breaded pig's foot with its wonderful potato purée, chilled wild strawberry and watermelon soup served with ewe's-milk ice cream and nougatine chunks. Fine wines from selected growers are an added bonus.

● Le 21   Ⓝ ○ SIM

21, rue Mazarine.
Métro: Odéon.
Tel. 01 46 33 76 90.
Closed Sun., Mon., Aug.
A la carte: 55€.

Paul Minchelli springs from his ashes like the phoenix. One virtue cannot be denied him: He certainly knows his fish. Under his guidance, handkerchief-sized restaurant La Cafetière has become a "club" for a select few. Here, this highly talented "non chef," who achieved great success at the

Duc serves up a simple seafood cuisine of exceptional quality: marinated mackerel with capers, red mullet poached in olive oil, grilled sardines with sweet potatoes, steamed sea bass with zucchini and chopped fresh tomatoes all have an easy charm. Add a very good baba au rhum. An obstacle to be ignored, if not forgotten, is the slow service, which favors friends of the clan only.

● Ze Kitchen Galerie   ⚐ ○ SIM

4, rue des Grands-Augustins.
Métro: St-Michel.
Tel. 01 44 32 00 32. Fax 01 44 32 00 33.
zekitchen.galerie@wanadoo.fr
www.zekitchengalerie.fr
Closed Sat. lunch, Sun., Christmas,
New Year's, May 1st, July 14th.
Prix fixe: 23€ (lunch, wine inc.),
34€ (lunch, wine inc.). A la carte: 60–70€.

This gourmet loft with its designer furniture, Cuzzini glass lamps, art by Daniel Humair and Starck metal tables and cutlery easily complements the cuisine prepared by William Ledeuil, a Guy Savoy veteran who formerly ran the neighboring Les Bouquinistes. His dishes are modern, inventive and flavorsome to boot. We begin with beet gazpacho with candied ginger, cucumber and shrimp with fresh Thai herbs, green asparagus and Burratta mozzarella fritters, cream of white asparagus with lemongrass and arugula and marinated tuna with coleslaw, green mango and asparagus. Next we turn to shrimp with softshell crab and grilled frog legs, and grilled chicken and veal sweetbreads with carrot-mustard-ginger jus and milk-fed lamb (slow-cooked, then grilled) with lemongrass-kumquat jus and begin to realize that something fine and flavorsome has come to the rue des Grands-Augustins. Nice strawberry, pistachio and lemongrass cappuccino, wasabi emulsion with chocolate cream and caramelized coconut, roasted banana with coconut ice cream and wines from France and further afield that are well worth a glance . . . an assiduous tasting.

● Caméléon   ⬛ ⓝ SIM

6, rue de Chevreuse.
Métro: Vavin, Raspail.
Tel. 01 43 27 43 27.
Closed Sun.
Prix fixe: 30€. A la carte: 50€.

Jean-Paul Arabian has succeeded brilliantly in refurbishing this Montparnasse bistro in contemporary style. With Dany Angelot, a young veteran of Ledoyen, he serves quality cuisine based on exceptional produce. A bar where friends can meet, a flat screen TV for the latest news, service at any hour and a few tables opposite an open kitchen form the setting here, bright as a button. We savor leeks in vinaigrette served warm, Southern-style onions, anchovy and olive bread, exceptional foie gras poached in red wine and the skate and capers. Thick-cut veal liver served with a creamy olive polenta is a supreme example of its genre. Add mischievous wines, a lunchtime set menu and desserts to match the general tone (an apple tart made with salted butter, mirabelle plums with Breton shortbread) and you realize that this is a remarkable, convivial restaurant deserving of our recognition.

● Evi Evane   ⓝ ⬛ SIM

10, rue Guisarde.
Métro: Mabillon.
Tel. 01 43 54 97 86
Closed Sun., 3 weeks Aug. Open until 11 PM.
Prix fixe: 14,90€ (lunch), 19,90€.
A la carte: 30–35€.

In the heart of Saint-Sulpice, this tavern with its exposed stone walls plays on the same delights. Maria Nikolaou's smile brightens the dining room, while sister Dina prepares her delicate dishes. The turnovers with two cheeses served on a bed of greens, mezze composed of very fresh white taramasalata, stuffed grape leaves, eggplant salad and tzatziki. The grilled beef meatballs with aromatic herbs, the lamb chops with sesame seeds and grilled sea bream are of excellent quality. The strawberry jelly, yogurt with honey, sesame halva and lavender ice cream make a splendid impression.

The friendly prices mean that this exploration of all things Hellenic does little harm to our pocket.

● La Ferrandaise   ⬛ ⓝ SIM

8, rue de Vaugirard.
Métro: Odéon, Luxembourg,
Cluny-La Sorbonne.
Tel. 01 43 26 36 36. Fax 01 43 26 90 91.
laferrandaise@wanadoo.fr
www.laferrandaise.com
Closed Sun., Christmas, May 1st, Aug.
Open until 10:30 PM (Fri., Sat. 11:30 PM).
Prix fixe: 30€. A la carte: 35€.

Gilles Lamiot (who owns La Taverne de Nesle), has brought in a young team trained by his celebrated neighbor Manuel Martinez at Le Relais Louis XIII. A dynamic young waiter and chef Nicolas Duquénoy lend a touch of youth to this rather medieval haunt, with its beams from wall to ceiling and exposed stone. The egg and mushrooms baked in a ramekin, layered terrine of beef shin and foie gras, shellfish cream soup, Breton cod and mashed potatoes with andouille, roasted veal with mashed old-fashioned vegetables, farm-raised pork chop in a mustard and gherkin sauce are lively, flavorsome and full of oomph. The charming, thirst-quenching wines do not hike up the tab. The desserts—rum-flavored pineapple gratin, almond cream with dried fruit and nuts—hit the right note.

● Wadja   ⬛ 🛏 SIM

10, rue de la Grande-Chaumière.
Métro: Vavin.
Tel.-Fax 01 46 33 02 02.
Closed Sun., week Aug. 15th.
Prix fixe: 11€ (lunch), 14€ (dinner).
A la carte: 40–50€.

Thierry Coué, who was a chef with Senderens in the days of the Archestrate, has brought his talents to Denise Leguay's kitchen team in this old-style bistro. Without undue harm to our pocket, we delight in the charming, proficiently crafted dishes here. The fresh marinated sardine tart, lamb brain beignets, the cod filet with zucchini, tuna belly with Tarbais white beans and peppers and the head cheese served with lentils in vinaigrette cannot be faulted. The chocolate charlotte with coffee sauce is a choice delicacy.

● L'Epi Dupin

11, rue Dupin.
Métro: Sèvres-Babylone.
Tel. 01 42 22 64 56. Fax 01 42 22 30 42.
lepidupin@wanadoo.fr
Closed Sat., Sun., Mon. lunch, Aug.
Prix fixe: 22€ (lunch), 31€.

François Pasteau fails to disappoint us. In composing his set menus, this François Clerc veteran who honed his skills with the greats decided that modesty was the thing. He has an eye for quality and creates modern domestic dishes replete with ideas and taste. The caramelized endive and goat cheese Tatin, langoustines with chutney, pineapple and ginger, the cod filet with smoked sausage and spinach and a tender cumin-seasoned pork belly are enchanting. The soft centered chocolate and pistachio dessert is a tempting proposition.

● Les Racines

22, rue Monsieur-le-Prince (at rue Racine).
Métro: Odéon, Luxembourg.
Tel. 01 43 26 03 86. Fax 01 46 34 58 33.
Closed Sun.
A la carte: 35€.

This corner café converted into a traditional-style bistro by Jean-François Debert of Maître Paul is a delightful spot with enduring appeal. We like its easygoing ambiance, checked tablecloths, prewar café atmosphere and perfectly maintained taste for home cooking. Among the dishes featured on the blackboard, the slow-roasted rabbit terrine, tuna steak with fork-mashed potatoes, authentic calf's head in gribiche sauce and veal hanger steak in blue cheese sauce hit the mark.

● Aux Saveurs de Claude

12, rue Stanislas.
Métro: Notre-Dame-des-Champs, Vavin.
Tel. 01 45 44 41 74. Fax 01 45 44 41 95.
claudelamin@hotmail.com
www.ausaveurdeclaude.fr
Closed Sun., Mon., 1 week at Easter,
2 weeks Aug.
Prix fixe: 30€. A la carte: 40–50€.

Having trained with Guy Savoy at Cap Vernet and Bistrot de l'Etoile, Claude Lamin has found himself a good, contemporary-style family bistro, with fine produce, precise cooking, clear-cut ideas and not too much fuss. The set menu is striking and the crayfish and leeks in puff pastry (made to order), asparagus, quail eggs and arugula salad, pan-fried scorpion fish with shredded cucumber and blackened spice-crusted tuna steak served with cauliflower fricassée are honest work. A strawberry-balsamic vinegar clafoutis, served with olive oil ice cream provide a superb conclusion.

● Roger la Grenouille

26, rue des Grands-Augustins.
Métro: Odéon.
Tel. 01 56 24 24 34.
Closed Sun.
Prix fixe: 24€ (lunch), 32€ (lunch).
A la carte: 65€.

The Layracs, father and son, already manage Allard just a step away. Demonstrating their love of Saint-Germain institutions, they have recently taken over this charming old bistro with its many memories. The ghost of good old Roger, who as a child was a ward of the State and used to feed the local poor with his nourishing leftovers, lingers in the two dining rooms: the first, simpler and more relaxed in front by the street; the other, hung with red velvet and more suitable for dining tête-à-tête. Here, the Layracs serve uncomplicated classics: Provençal-style frog legs with garlic and parsley, beautiful seasonal asparagus, slow-roasted lamb shoulder, grilled ribeye steak with béarnaise sauce, tarte Tatin and profiteroles. The check makes no concessions, but there are some fine wines (such as the Château Patache d'Aux) that are quite reasonably priced.

● Allard

1, rue de l'Eperon.
Métro: St-Michel, Odéon.

Tel. 01 43 26 48 23. Fax 01 46 33 04 02
Closed Sun., 3 weeks Aug. .
Prix fixe: 24€ (lunch), 32€. A la carte: 65€.

Things have improved at the Layracs':
They have taken over the neighboring Roger la Grenouille, along with this
establishment. No blunders, no strokes
of genius, just good, classic fare from chef
Didier Remay, who remembers the distant days of Fernande Allard. Escargots in
parsley butter, homemade duck foie gras,
Challans duck with olives and a veal chop
sautéed with wild mushrooms are honest dishes. For dessert, baba au rhum and
Paris-Brest continue to appeal. The cellar
still has its points of interest.

● **Aux Charpentiers**   🛊 SIM
10, rue Mabillon.
Métro: Mabillon, St-Germain-des-Prés, Odéon.
Tel. 01 43 26 30 05. Fax 01 46 33 07 98.
auxcharpentiers@wanadoo.fr
Prix fixe: 19€ (lunch, wine inc.),
26€ (dinner). A la carte: 40–50€.

Genial host Pierre Bardèche has turned
his bistro, open seven days a week, into
an oasis of conviviality. No frills, no glit-
ter, just good, plain, simple fare. The
homemade duck foie gras, eggplant caviar with fresh goat cheese, sole meunière,
veal blanquette and cherry clafoutis are
enchantingly straightforward.

● **Joséphine**   🛊 SIM
117, rue du Cherche-Midi.
Métro: Duroc, Falguière.
Tel. 01 45 48 52 40. Fax 01 42 84 06 83
Closed Sat., Sun.
A la carte: 50–75€.

This bistro (which once had its moment
of glory) still boasts the same 1880s' *bouchon*-style brasserie décor with a patina
of age. Not content to simply manage his
legacy, Jean-Christophe Dumonet has
changed the approach that his father
Jean once made fashionable. Fresh duck
foie gras, crisp jumbo shrimp cakes with
bisque vinaigrette, marinated salmon
with potato purée, pigeon mille-feuille
with slow-roasted legs are not bad. A clas-

sic homemade mille-feuille for two is light
and airy, and the selection of great Bordeaux wines will turn your head.

● **Brasserie Lipp**   🛊 SIM
151, bd Saint-Germain.
Métro: St-Germain-des-Prés.
Tel. 01 45 48 53 91. Fax 01 45 44 33 20.
lipp@magic.fr / www.brasserie-lipp.fr
Closed Christmas. Cont. service.
A la carte: 55–60€.

Of course, this is no longer the great
Cazès' brasserie, but dinner can still be
an enjoyable experience opposite the Far-
gue ceramics, on faux leather seats, rubbing shoulders with personalities such as
actors Anouck Aimée, Pierre Arditi and
Philippe Noiret, writer Jean Dutourd or the
Count of Paris (all seated in the same small
area—though not at the same table—on
the evening we were there, a Sunday).
The enduring house classics live up to
our expectations. We never tire of the
cold sliced sausage in creamy vinaigrette
sauce, Bismarck herring, sole meunière,
stuffed pig's feet, baba au rhum and iced
coffee parfait.

● **Le Parc aux Cerfs**   🛊 SIM
50, rue Vavin.
Métro: Vavin.
Tel. 01 43 54 87 83. Fax 01 43 26 42 86.
Closed Aug.
Prix fixe: 23,50€ (lunch), 29€ (lunch),
30€ (dinner), 35€ (dinner). A la carte:38€.

The lighthearted Paul Hayat runs this genuine thirties bistro, whose warm, cozy
nature is still intact. Chef Eddy Grillon's
cuisine plays lucidly on the flavors of
the South of France. We have no complaints about the cabbage and shrimp
salad, Serrano ham with green lentils and
poached egg, sea bass roasted in olive oil
or tuna with capers and arugula. The wal-
nut-crusted veal is not bad and the cool
mango and raspberry dessert provides a
very digestible finale.

● **Le Petit Lutétia**   🛊 SIM
107, rue de Sèvres.
Métro: Vaneau.

Tel. 01 45 48 33 53. Fax 01 45 48 74 59.
Closed Christmas.
Prix fixe: 30€. A la carte: 40–50€.

This pleasant 1900s *bouillon*-style brasserie still has all the charm of its era, with frescos, moldings, mirrors and brass fittings. Raymond Poignant's cuisine is in much the same vein. The broiled stuffed mussels, homemade foie gras, roasted sea bream, steak tartare and duck confit are unpretentious. Rice pudding with orange zest and raisins is a neatly done, grandmotherly dessert.

● Le Petit Saint-Benoît

4, rue Saint-Benoît.
Métro: St-Germain-des-Prés.
Tel. 01 42 60 27 92.
Closed Sun., Aug.
A la carte: 25€.

Despite the constant succession of chefs, this traditional, vintage 1901 bistro is still a model of the genre. After Alain Doviller, it is now Michel Voisin's turn to present his take on its rustic, generous domestic cuisine, in the form of boiled leeks in vinaigrette, fish baked in parchment paper, grilled hanger steak and dark chocolate fondant. To cap it all, the prices remain manageable.

● Polidor

41, rue Monsieur-le-Prince.
Métro: Odéon.
Tel. 01 43 26 95 34. Fax 01 43 26 22 79.
mailletpolidor.com@wanadoo.fr
Prix fixe: 12€ (lunch), 20€.
A la carte: 25–30€.

No revolution at Polidor, which has been serving domestic classics near the Luxembourg gardens since 1845 (veal blanquette, beef bourguignon, tarte Tatin). Writer and critic Paul Léautaud was fond of this place, which still has its old-fashioned flavor. Cream of lentil soup with foie gras, guinea-fowl stewed with cabbage and chocolate mousse are among the essential dishes of this Lyon *bouchon*–style restaurant prized by students.

■ | HOTELS

■ Duc de Saint-Simon

14, rue Saint-Simon.
Métro: Rue-du-Bac.
Tel. 01 44 39 20 20. Fax 01 45 48 68 25.
www.hotelducdesaintsimon.com
29 rooms: 220–280€. 5 suites: 350–375€.

In the heart of Saint-Germain, this hotel offers guaranteed peace and quiet in its old-fashioned rooms and cozy lounges. The welcome is warm and the French breakfast delicious.

■ Montalembert

3, rue Montalembert.
Métro: Rue-du-Bac, St-Germain-des-Prés.
Tel. 01 45 49 68 68. Fax 01 45 49 69 49.
www.montalembert.com
56 rooms: 350–450€. 8 suites: 580–1250€.

Just off the rue du Bac, this recent hotel boasts distinctive designer rooms, a popular restaurant *cum* bar *cum* tearoom (whose walls are lined with detective novels) and a quiet terrace.

■ Pont Royal

7, rue Montalembert.
Métro: Rue-du-Bac.
Tel. 01 42 84 70 00. Fax 01 42 84 71 00.
www.hotel-pont-royal.com
64 rooms: 380–430€. 11 suites: 580–980€.

After remaining closed for a long time, this grand hotel now boasts a very Elysées lobby, which reflects the elegance of the mahogany-trimmed rooms. The welcome is flawless, the service professional and the proximity of the Atelier de Joël Robuchon salutary.

■ Bourgogne et Montana

3, rue de Bourgogne.
Métro: Assemblée-Nationale, Invalides.
Tel. 01 45 51 20 22. Fax 01 45 56 11 98.
www.bourgogne-montana.com
26 rooms: 155–265€. 6 suites: 305–320€.

The golden yellow rooms of this 18th-century hotel provide an unobstructed view of the Palais-Bourbon, where France's National Assembly sits.

■ Lenox Saint-Germain

9, rue de l'Université.
Métro: St-Germain-des-Prés, Rue-du-Bac.
Tel. 01 42 96 10 95. Fax 01 42 61 52 83.
www.lenoxsaintgermain.com
29 rooms: 120–145€. 5 suites: 190–275€.

This hotel with its art deco ambiance is frequented by artists, fashion photographers and European politicians. All enjoy the rooms (garret or not), swimming pool, bar, breakfast room decorated with an Egyptian fresco and room service until late.

■ Quai Voltaire

19, quai Voltaire.
Métro: Rue-du-Bac, Louvre-Rivoli, Palais-Royal.
Tel. 01 42 61 50 91. Fax 01 42 61 62 26.
info@quaivoltaire.fr / www.quaivoltaire.fr
33 rooms: 107–159€.

Baudelaire, Oscar Wilde and Richard Wagner stayed in this abbey converted into a hotel in the 19th century. A retro air surrounds the rooms decorated in antique style with slightly kitsch bathrooms and no television. An unobstructed view of the Seine and the Palais du Louvre.

■ Hôtel d'Orsay

93, rue de Lille.
Métro: Assemblée-Nationale, Solférino.
Tel. 01 47 05 85 54. Fax 01 45 55 51 16.
hotel.orsay@espritfrance.com
www.esprit-de-France.com
41 rooms: 133–185€. 1 suite: 330€.

Between the Seine, the Orsay Museum and the National Assembly, this hotel's two 18th-century houses provide tastefully fitted, pretty, modern rooms. The lounge opens onto a patio planted with trees. Moderate prices and a delightful welcome.

■ Saint-Germain

88, rue du Bac.
Métro: Rue-du-Bac.
Tel. 01 49 54 70 00. Fax 01 45 48 26 89.
info@hotel-saint-germain.fr
www.hotel-saint-germain.fr
29 rooms: 150–210€.

The Empire, Louis-Philippe and designer rooms are all charming. The selected pictures and furniture, library and patio add their individual touch to the ambiance of this tasteful hotel.

■ Varenne

44, rue de Bourgogne.
Métro: Varenne.
Tel. 01 45 51 45 55. Fax 01 45 51 86 63.
info@hoteldevarenne.com
www.hoteldevarenne.com
24 rooms: 120–150€.

This charming little hotel with its rustic, but air conditioned rooms (equipped with flat screen TV) is a slice of the countryside in Paris. In summer, breakfast is served in the little courtyard, whose walls are a riot of Virginia creeper.

■ Walt

37, av de la Motte-Picquet.
Métro: Ecole-Militaire.
Tel. 01 45 51 55 83. Fax 01 47 05 77 59.
lewalt@inwoodhotel.com
www.lewaltparis.com
25 rooms: 250–320€.

The Italian wood flooring, wooden furniture, congruent colors and light, pleasantly lit bathrooms and reproductions of great paintings at the heads of the beds enhance the harmony of the contemporary décor. A quality restaurant and a small terrace.

● RESTAURANTS

● Le Divellec

107, rue de l'Université.
Métro: Invalides.
Tel. 01 45 51 91 96. Fax 01 45 51 31 75.
ledivellec@noos.fr
Closed Sat., Sun., Christmas–New Year's,
1 week at the end July, 3 weeks in Aug.
Prix fixe: 55€ (lunch), 70€ (lunch).
A la carte: 160€.

Jacques Le Divellec's marine restaurant is still on course for freshness. The politicians and celebrities aboard are happy as clams in its elegant nautical setting, with assurance to spare in the galley. Over decades, the place has built up a solid reputation for fish and shellfish at the peak of their form, reliable preparation and precise cooking. Proof comes in the form of the cassoulet of langoustines with truffles, the clam, cuttlefish and sea snail salad with a shellfish broth, the turbot carpaccio with lemon confit, not to mention the thinly sliced raw tuna with seared foie gras. The ocean is there on our plates, vital and magnificent. For dessert, the warm raspberry soufflé with strawberries and the warm chocolate cake, with its melted chocolate center infused with verbena and served with sesame ice cream, are adept takes on current classics. The service comes with a smile and the list of great wines is thorough.

● Le Jules Verne   ⬤⬤ LUX

Eiffel Tower, south pillar, Champ-de-Mars.
Métro: Bir-Hakeim,
Champ-de-Mars–Tour-Eiffel.
Tel. 01 45 55 61 44. Fax 01 47 05 29 41.
Prix fixe: 57€ (lunch on weekdays),
128€ (dinner). A la carte: 130–170€.

As we write these lines, the Eiffel Tower's black restaurant is about to change hands and style. An invitation to tender was announced to inject new life into the place and Alain Ducasse and Sodexho came up with the winning bid. It is too early to tell what will become of the great establishment designed by Slavik and Loup. Ducasse should bring in his special favorite decorator Patrick Jouin to refresh the décor, and the food, so far brilliantly prepared by Alain Reix, should become a modern take on Ducassian cuisine. To find out more, see the next edition of *Pudlo Paris.*

● Le Télégraphe   Ⓝ 🍴 V.COM

41, rue de Lille.
Métro: Rue du Bac, St-Germain-des-Prés.
Tel. 01 42 92 03 04. Fax 01 42 92 02 77.

Closed Fri. dinner, Sat. lunch, 2 weeks Aug.
Prix fixe: 50€. A la carte: 70€.

Expensive, kosher and good. In the heart of the former residence of the Dames des Postes (Post Office ladies), this art nouveau monument serves a creative cuisine prepared by a young Ducasse veteran. Ceps in cream and walnut oil, balsamic-seasoned sundried tomato Tatin, foie gras served three ways, a seared tuna with ginger pear compote and lamb filet served with eggplant caviar are shrewd concoctions. The rich décor with its fine ceramics has a retro charm that reflects contemporary tastes.

● L'Arpège

84, rue de Varenne.
Métro: Varenne.
Tel. 01 45 51 47 33. Fax 01 44 18 98 39.
arpege.passard@wanadoo.fr
www.alain-passard.com
Closed Sat., Sun.
Prix fixe: 130€ (lunch), 340€ (dinner).
A la carte: 250€.

Oblivious to fashion and its diktats, Alain Passard remains true to form, loyal to the produce-based cuisine that is close to his heart. It has been a long time since critics questioned the lack of red meat on his menu. This grandmaster of the vegetable has won them all over with his skills. Creativity, originality, sensitivity and rigor are the everyday watchwords of this Breton trained by Kéréver, Boyer, then Senderens, as he prepares dishes of breathtaking freshness and vivacity. The lemon-infused sweet onion gratin, the thousand-and-one-flavors of the vegetable from the morning's harvest, the Chausey island lobster served thinly sliced and perfumed with Côtes-du-Jura wine and the Breton monkfish with Orléans mustard are odes to nature's gifts from the Mayenne, Finistère, Côtes d'Armor and Ile-et-Vilaine regions. Then, for the launch of the 1998 vintage Perrier Jouët Belle Epoque: raw scallops in a saffron velouté of zucchini blossoms, beechwood-smoked potato with white Côtes-du-Jura wine. The names are simple, the pleasures vast. If any doubts remain, sugar-coated young pigeon with honey wine and the sweetbreads with licorice root provide dazzling proof. Finally, what can we say about the desserts, except that they too attain summits of refinement? The caramelized tomato stuffed "with twelve flavors" refreshed with an orange sauce or the classic mille-feuille offer moments of delight in this trove of elegance and serenity opposite the Rodin museum.

● Chez les Anges   🏠 ○ V.COM

54, bd de La Tour-Maubourg.
Métro: Invalides, La Tour-Maubourg.
Tel. 01 47 05 89 86. Fax 01 47 05 45 56
Closed Sat., Sun., 3 weeks Aug.
Prix fixe: 28€. A la carte: 65€.

First, it was Armand Monassier's Les Anges. Then it became Jean Minchelli's seafood eatery. Now Jacques Lacipière from Au Bon Accueil has restored the original name, and brought an identity and style to the place. The setting in white tones is chic and modern, although slightly neutral, but the restaurant as a whole has refinement in plenty, with its long counter, attractively set tables and banquettes. In the kitchen, there is no cheating over the quality of produce or its preparation at the peak of freshness. Cream of pumpkin soup with smoked bacon, sea urchin with an emulsion of sea water and hazelnut oil, winter vegetables in a spicy marinade and pigeon terrine with dried fruits all featured on the menu the other day, and were served in small ramekins, tapas style. Then there is gray sea bream with tarbais beans and milk-fed veal roast with salsify and a spicy jus. Passion fruit cream or chestnut ice cream with dark chocolate mousse and coffee-hazelnut financier provide a delightful conclusion. The wines by the glass (from Languedoc or the Rhône Valley) have plenty of nose, and character is much in evidence, with the focus on quality.

● Les Ombres   🔃 V.COM

Musée du Quai Branly, 27, quai Branly.
Métro: Pont-de-l'Alma (RER C).
Tel. 01 47 53 68 00.
Prix fixe: 32€ (lunch). A la carte: 80€.

The all-glass architecture by Nouvel, the view of Paris are the appeals of this museum restaurant entrusted to the Elior group has a lot going for it. Arno Busquet, former assistant at Chez Laurent, strives to get it right in reduced circumstances. Dodine de lapin Rex du Poitou en anchoïade (a rabbit and anchovy paste dish), shellfish risotto, seared tuna belly with sesame, duck seasoned with rosemary and regional shortbread cookies with cherry and pistachio, served with whipped creamy mousse and almond milk sorbet, are tempting. The place is new and the service is still finding its feet. An event to watch.

● Beato   V.COM

8, rue Malar.
Métro: La Tour-Maubourg, Pont-de-l'Alma.
Tel. 01 47 05 94 27. Fax 01 45 55 64 41.
beato.resto@wanadoo.fr
Closed Sat. lunch, Sun., mid-July–mid-Aug.
Prix fixe: 23€, 27€. A la carte: 51€.

Giordani Ivano likes to pamper his guests, summoning them to a ceremony that revolves around classics of domestic Italian cuisine. The Capri-style bruschetta, a mixed seafood grill with a market salad, thin slice of cold veal served with an arugula and parmesan salad and the Amaretto tiramisu are full of delicacy and subtly refreshing.

● Maison de l'Amérique Latine   V.COM

217, bd Saint-Germain
Métro: Rue-du-Bac, Solférino
Tel. 01 49 54 75 00. Fax 01 40 49 03 94
commercial@mal217.org / www.mal217.org
Closed Sat., Sun., Bank Holidays, Christmas–New Year's, 10 days July, 3 weeks Aug.
Prix fixe: 40€ (lunch), 55€ (dinner).

The facade of this 18th-century residence conceals one of the finest terraces in Paris. In summer, among the trees and shrubs, the butterflies of the Left Bank admire Pascal Jouan's skills as he dreams up set menus that delicately balance tradition and modernity. The scrambled eggs with truffles and crisp toast, the thyme-seasoned pan-seared cod with spring onion mashed potatoes, the veal chop with sweet garlic and mascarpone polenta and the hot mango soufflé and lime sorbet make up light, fresh meals.

● Café de l'Esplanade

52, rue Fabert.
Métro: La Tour-Maubourg.
Tel. 01 47 05 38 80. Fax 01 47 05 23 75.
Open daily 8 AM–2 AM. Cont. service.
A la carte: 65€.

The Costes brothers have brought their full salvo of winning formulas to bear in their Invalides restaurant. Napoleon III décor by Garcia, beautiful waitresses, a long terrace and stylish, well-prepared dishes: Thai chicken and basil spring rolls, scallops with lemon butter, quick-seared steak seasoned with herbs and raspberry macarons. The check will leave you shell-shocked.

● Le Café de l'Alma COM

5, av Rapp.
Métro: Alma-Marceau, Pont-de-l'Alma.
Tel. 01 45 51 56 74. Fax 01 45 51 10 08
cafedelalma@wanadoo.fr
Cont. service.
A la carte: 50–75€.

This being Alma, people of breeding come to enjoy the large terrace and the contemporary but elegant setting of this chic café. They like its deliberately restrained colors (red, green and lavender), discreet nooks and gentrified popular cuisine. The jumbo shrimp tempura with endive, the salmon medallions with roasted sesame, the farm-raised chicken with dried fruits and nuts served with mashed potatoes and the vanilla crème brûlée gratify Paris society, which explains the size of the check.

● Thiou COM

49, quai d'Orsay.
Métro: Invalides.
Tel. 01 45 51 58 58. Fax 01 40 62 97 30.
Closed Sat. lunch, Sun., 2 Aug.
A la carte: 70–80€.

A chic clientele, pleasant ambiance, uncompromising check and fashionable cuisine: Thiou has made his mark on the ancient Quai d'Orsay. Salmon ceviche, the langoustine mini–spring rolls, soft shell crabs over greens, oven-roasted Atlantic seabass and the "crying tiger" are effective. The exotic fruits with a chocolate dipping sauce are entertaining rather than tasty and the service is a touch impersonal. But what do the happy few care?

● Le Chamarré COM

13, bd de la Tour-Maubourg
Métro: La Tour-Maubourg, Invalides
Tel. 01 47 05 50 18. Fax 01 47 05 91 21
Closed Sat. lunch, Sun., Mon.
Prix fixe: 28€ (weekday lunch),
40€ (weekday lunch), 60€, 80€.
A la carte: 80€.

In the quiet Invalides quarter, this French Mauritian restaurant will excite the most torpid of taste buds. In partnership with Chantal Dias, Antoine Heerah and Jérôme Bodereau concoct an ambitious fusion cuisine. Pupils of Alain Passard, they learned to select produce, prepare it appropriately (but creatively) and cook it to just the right degree under his supervision. As a result, the dishes we savor in this contemporary, simple dining room, with its red vases, origami-style lamps, chocolate-colored leather chairs and golden-brown banquettes are rare and possibly even unique. The slow-roasted Atlantic octopus in Mauritius-style vindaloo curry sauce, crispy shrimp with carrot broth, seared tuna with two types of sesame and red mullet and squid seared in olive oil dart deliciously between sea and sun. The Sarthois suckling pig with a spiced chutney and the roasted pigeon wrapped in crisp phyllo dough with licorice play consummately on a sweet and savory theme. For dessert, roasted Victoria pineapple with vanilla and a baba au rhum leave the palate deliciously sated.

● Le Soleil

153, rue de Grenelle.
Métro: La Tour-Maubourg.
Tel. 01 45 51 54 12.

Closed Sun.
Prix fixe: 32-36€ ("Merenda").
A la carte: 65€.

Louis-Jacques Vanucci has taken over the former Gildo and brought a new soul to the place with Southern French décor, chairs straight from a Provençal garden and sconce-style lighting. The cuisine takes us on a voyage along the Mediterranean coast from Capri to Andalusia, via Cap d'Antibes. In fact, we are reminded of Nice's Cours Saleya district as we savor the squid with white beans, the Menton lemon-seasoned peppers, the Sicilian tomato pizzeta, the fresh bean soup, the salt cod and potato flan served with whelks and the fresh pasta with parmesan. To conclude, with the Coreleone-style sweet cannelloni, Piedmont hazelnut ricotta mousse or the Corsican clementines, our thoughts turn to the pleasures of an afternoon nap. With a Villaret lieutenant in the kitchen and service with a feminine touch and a ready smile, the charming Vanucci has made a success of his move to the capital.

● **Auguste** ◯ COM
54, rue de Bourgogne.
Métro: Varenne, Assemblée-Nationale.
Tel. 01 45 51 61 09. Fax 01 45 51 27 34.
Closed Sat., Sun., 3 weeks Aug.
Prix fixe: 35€ (lunch). A la carte: 45–60€.

Without warning, Gaël Orieux, erstwhile assistant to Yannick Alleno, has become the new celebrity artisan of the culinary seventh arrondissement. In an elegant, modern setting, this unassuming lad (his handsome head full of ideas) regales informed aficionados with fine dishes reflecting the vagaries of the market. We love his oysters and whelks in puff pastry with sea-infused jelly, silky ratte potatoes with glazed chicken oysters, the delicately seasoned and roasted farm-raised pigeon served with Jerusalem artichokes or the veal sweetbreads simmered in Vin Jaune and served with salsify. His lunchtime set menu is impressive.

● **Bruno Deligne** ◯ COM
"Les Olivades"
41, av de Ségur.
Métro: Ségur, St-François-Xavier, Ecole-Militaire.
Tel. 01 47 83 70 09. Fax 01 42 73 04 75
www.deligne-lesolivades.fr
Closed Sat. lunch, Sun.,
Mon. lunch, 1 week Christmas–New Year's,
Aug.
Prix fixe: 12€ (lunch on weekdays),
60€ (tasting menu). A la carte: 70€.

Bruno Deligne's extended resume (Fauchon, Copenhague, Maximin, Girardet, Pic, Ritz, Taillevent) would make him the ideal candidate to run a grand establishment. But no, here he is, perfectly at ease in his restaurant of Southern French inspiration with its warm, simple décor. His sun-drenched cuisine is in the same vein: sincere, authentic and pleasant. The roasted black tiger shrimp with finely minced papaya, pepper and sweet onions, the seared grilled sea bass with gnocchi seasoned with truffle vinaigrette, the rack of lamb and asparagus fricassée seasoned with thyme and lemon and the Grand Marnier soufflé with candied citrus zest warm our hearts.

● **Gaya Rive Gauche** ◯ COM
par Pierre Gagnaire
44, rue du Bac.
Métro: Rue-du-Bac.
Tel.-Fax 01 45 44 73 73.
Closed Sat. lunch, Sun., Aug.
A la carte: 80€.

On two floors, Christian Ghion has dreamed up a bright, bluish, chic, contemporary, seaside cabin décor. On the food front, the chef from the rue Balzac excels himself. The produce is at its peak, the inventive preparations quite unambiguous, the cooking impeccable and the presentation polished. Results include pressed crab cake with salted turnips and a cauliflower mayonnaise sauce, a croque-monsieur sandwich with gray shrimp, Dover sole served grilled, simply pan seared or pan fried in butter and seasoned with parsley and lemon and braised red mullet with Jerusalem artichokes and Spanish chorizo. Equally refined are the desserts, including iced chocolate dessert seasoned with olive oil and served with a thick orange sauce. The service is exemplary and the menu a pure joy. Paris Left Bank society is eager for more of the same.

● Les Ormes ○ COM
22, rue Surcouf.
Métro: La Tour-Maubourg, Invalides.
Tel. 01 45 51 46 93. Fax 01 45 50 30 11.
Closed Sun., Mon., 1 week Jan.,
3 weeks Aug.
Prix fixe: 32€ (lunch), 38€ (lunch), 44€
(dinner), 79€ (dinner). A la carte: 70€.

Stéphane Molé, a Robuchon disciple, produces works of art in his stylish establishment. He is everywhere at once, honing masterpieces worthy of a great chef. We begin dramatically with his mackerel tart with fennel or his pan-seared foie gras over soft caramelized rhubarb and turnips. To follow, who could resist the symphony of flavors offered by brill with sorrel sauce and marinated vegetables or braised beef tenderloin with soft cooked potatoes and foie gras sauce? Strawberries marinated with mint on a Breton shortbread with olive oil offers a soft landing. Attentive service and a beautiful wine list.

● Tan Dinh ○ COM
60, rue de Verneuil.
Métro: Rue-du-Bac, Solférino.
Tel. 01 45 44 04 84. Fax 01 45 44 36 93.
Closed Sun., Bank Holidays, Aug.
A la carte: 54€.

Here, we discover all the wealth and refinement of that great, insufficiently known art that is Vietnamese cuisine. In a simple, freshly renovated Oriental décor in cream and red, the Vifian brothers bring us high fashion. Using fresh, quality produce, they concoct asparagus velouté with crab ravioli, mango and coconut salad, jumbo shrimp beignets, sautéed lamb with Thai ginger and soursop sorbet. Since good things never come singly, these deliciously subtle dishes are set off by an excellent cellar, where Bordeaux, Burgundies and first-rate Australian, Italian and American wines lie side by side. The welcome and service are on a par with the rest.

● Tante Marguerite ○ COM
5, rue de Bourgogne.
Métro: Assemblée-Nationale.
Tel. 01 45 51 79 42. Fax 01 47 53 79 56
tante.maguerite@bernard-loiseau.com
www.bernard-loiseau.com
Closed Sat., Sun., Aug.
Prix fixe: 34€, 65€. A la carte: 60€.

Nostalgic gourmets need not worry: The spirit of Bernard Loiseau continues to permeate this rustic, bourgeois adjunct with its solid, classical dishes. The menu still features a snail and herb ragout, roasted brill with red wine sauce, roasted veal sweetbreads with shallot mashed potatoes and molten Guanaja chocolate cake and coffee ice cream. As ever, the team and service are remarkable in every way and the Burgundies introduced by Gabriel Guibert provide a very apt accompaniment for the cuisine.

● Vin sur Vin ○ COM
20, rue de Monttessuy.
Métro: Pont-de-l'Alma.
Tel. 01 47 05 14 20.
Closed Sat. lunch, Sun., Mon. lunch (exc.
Apr.–Sept.), Christmas–New Year's vac., Aug.
A la carte: 80€.

Knowledgeable connoisseur Patrice Vidal has more than 600 wines on his list, and Pascal Toulza, who once worked at the Arpège, provides ambitious dishes to match. His inspired preparations offer the best of land and sea. The velvety oxtail soup, the foie gras pot-au-feu, the pantossed rougets, spit-roasted farm-raised pigeon, the Salers beef filet and an orange flower-flavored mille feuille for dessert are all shrewdly matched with the right libation. The setting suggests the dining room of a bourgeois home, the tables are meticulously set and the cellar never fails to provide the perfect vintage to add zest to your meal. A rare establishment.

● Le Violon d'Ingres ○ COM

135, rue Saint-Dominique.
Métro: Ecole-Militaire, Pont-de-l'Alma.
Tel. 01 45 55 15 05. Fax 01 45 55 48 42.
violondingres@wanadoo.fr
www.leviolondingres.com
Closed Sun., Mon.
Prix fixe: A la carte: 45€.

Christian Constant has founded a relaxed, gourmet empire a stone's throw from the Eiffel Tower. His Café Constant and Fables de la Fontaine are oversubscribed. Now, his Violon d'Ingres has become a cheerful, lively, amusing gourmet brasserie, with rotisserie dishes and other modish creations. The prices have been halved and the public has poured in, keen to witness this phenomenon of triumphant modesty. With Constant, there is no trickery. Juggling with fresh market produce, he still concocts a changing, appropriate, personal menu. A superb foie gras in terrine, the Atlantic sea bass fried in a crispy almond crust, a pork trotter Tatin served with ratte potatoes, the spit-roasted poultry or a nice grilled prime rib with parsley-seasoned jus offer a chance to indulge without breaking the bank. The desserts focus on seasonal fruits and the cellar has added some affordable wines. In short, a new career is beginning (again) for this native of Montauban, in Ingres country.

● Le Clos des Gourmets 🕮 COM

16, av Rapp.
Métro: Ecole-Militaire, Pont-de-l'Alma.
Tel. 01 45 51 75 61. Fax 01 47 05 74 20.
www.closdesgourmets.com
Closed Sun., Mon.
Prix fixe: 25€ (lunch), 29€ (lunch), 33€ (dinner).

This restaurant with its Louis XVI-style furniture and sunny yellow colors is looking healthy indeed. Arnaud Pitrois, who trained with Savoy and Constant, serves meticulous dishes at egalitarian prices. Sardines fried tempura-style and served with a pepper-seasoned ketchup, shellfish and Atlantic sea bass in cocotte with a star anise infusion, the roasted chicken with chanterelles seasoned with dill seed

and savory dill-seasoned whipped cream cannot be faulted. Add polished service and you will be glad you paid a visit to this pocket temple of gastronomy.

● Le Maupertu 🕮 COM

94, bd de la Tour-Maubourg.
Métro: La Tour-Maubourg, Ecole-Militaire.
Tel. 01 45 51 37 96. Fax 01 53 59 94 83.
info@restaurant-maupertu-paris.com
www.restaurant-maupertu-paris.com
Closed Sun., 1 week Feb., 3 weeks Aug.
Prix fixe: 22€ (lunch), 29€ (dinner).
A la carte: 45€.

Sophie and Alain Deguest are still here, ready to welcome us in their bright establishment with its sought-after terrace. In the kitchen, Mikael Loiseau concocts sterling dishes of the South of France. The brochette of jumbo shrimp enrobed in smoked bacon with mixed greens, sea bass filet with vegetable purée and anise-seasoned cream and breast of farm-raised chicken with cream sauce and a Fourme d'Ambert cheese crust, served with mashed potatoes with Port sauce, will bring roses to your cheeks, as will the kiwi carpaccio, served with red fruit sauce and Bulgarian yogurt ice cream.

● Nabuchodonosor 🕮 COM

6, av Bosquet.
Métro: La Tour-Maubourg, Ecole-Militaire, Pont-de-l'Alma.
Tel. 01 45 56 97 26. Fax 01 45 56 98 44.
www.nabuchodonosor.net
Closed Sat. lunch, Sun., 3 weeks Aug.
Prix fixe: 21€ (lunch), 31€ (dinner).
A la carte: 50–60€.

With the restaurant's blond woodwork, Sienna hues and Venetian blinds, Chef Thierry Garnier, formerly with Guy Savoy, summons you to royal repasts of slow-cooked shrimp and sea snail stew, seared scallops with balsamic vinegar, beef pot-au-feu seasoned with Sichuan pepper. A brioche pain perdu dusted with browned almonds and apricot jam and a caramel and white chocolate cream mille-feuille provide an excellent conclusion.

● La Taverna   🛗COM

22, rue du Champ-de-Mars.
Métro: Ecole-Militaire.
Tel. 01 45 51 64 59. Fax 01 53 59 92 60.
Closed Aug.
Prix fixe: 18€ (lunch), 22€ (lunch), 33€.

With his thin Taleggio tart, arugula and
Parma ham or his eggplant mille-feuille
with smoked cheese, Gustavo Andreoli
exerts an easy charm. His risottos are
legendary and the the lemon- and oreg-
ano-seasoned rouget, flambéed parmesan-seasoned tagliatelle or fusilli with
broad beans and squid are not bad either.
The pineapple and Montepulciano tiramisu bring a smile to our lips.

● Le Basilic   🛗COM

2, rue Casimir-Périer.
Métro: Solférino, Varenne, Invalides.
Tel. 01 44 18 94 64. Fax 01 44 18 33 97.
www.lebasilic.fr
Closed Sat. lunch.
A la carte: 35€.

The new proprietors, Fabrice Naacke and
Boris Dumeau, have left the décor intact,
changing only the lighting. Marc Gram-
fort, a refugee from the Taillevent school,
is still at home on the range. His bone marrow seasoned with Guérlande salt and
the garlic- and hot pepper–seasoned sea
bream are done to a turn and a simmered
regional veal dish with Basque peppers
is cooked to perfection. A marbled mille-
feuille rounds off the meal beautifully.
Organic and natural wines and a covered terrace.

● Thoumieux   🛗COM

79, rue Saint-Dominique.
Métro: La Tour-Maubourg.
Tel. 01 47 05 49 75. Fax 01 47 05 36 96.
bthoumieux@aol.com /
thoumieux@thoumieux.com
www.thoumieux.com
Prix fixe: 20€ (lunch on weekdays), 35€.
A la carte: 50€.

Paris society has been flocking to the Bas-
salert family's Corrèze brasserie since 1923.
Free from the dictates of fashion, guests
gather under its antique beams every day
with friends or family to enjoy its reliable,
solid bistro cuisine. Duck foie gras terrine,
Dover sole filet pan-fried in butter and seasoned with parsley and lemon, grilled sardines, cassoulet, a half-pound steak and
brown sugar crème brûlée are first-rate.

● L'Atelier de Joël   🏠 SIM
Robuchon

5-7, rue Montalembert.
Métro: Rue-du-Bac.
Tel. 01 42 22 56 56. Fax 01 42 22 97 91.
Prix fixe: 98€ (tasting menu).
A la carte: 70–100€.

Black granite, red lacquer and Indian rosewood, a direct view of the kitchen from the
bar and valet parking: Joël Robuchon's
snack bar strays on the side of chic. Need-
less to say, we are in the presence of *grande
cuisine*, inspired by Joël the First and
implemented by his four assistants, Eric
Lecerf, Philippe Braun, Eric Bouchenoire
and Antoine Hernandez, who alternately
tend to the Table de Joël Robuchon in the
sixteenth arrondissement. A virtuoso display! Sautéed squid with artichokes open
the proceedings, followed by a mackerel
tart, deep-fried whiting, tuna belly, eggs
with caviar, milk-fed lamb from the Pyrénées, all executed with tremendous proficiency. If you still have a little room left,
the warm Chartreuse soufflé with pistachio ice cream (a house classic) will fill it
neatly. An impressive cellar of French, Italian, Spanish, Californian and Australian
wines, a produce-oriented tasting menu
and a choice of small or standard portions
à la carte ingeniously complete the range
of this great restaurant's options.

● Aïda   🅝 ◯ SIM

1, rue Pierre-Leroux.
Métro: Vaneau, Duroc.
Tel.-Fax 01 43 06 14 18.
Closed Sat. lunch, Sun. lunch, Mon., 1 week
Feb., 2 weeks Aug.
Prix fixe: 38€ (lunch), 45€ (lunch),
68€ (dinner), 90€ (dinner).

His name is Koji Aida. This young, subtle,
discreet native of Tokyo has studied oenol-

ogy in Burgundy and prepares a remarkably elegant "knife cuisine" in his tiny cubbyhole in the seventh arrondissement. His sushi and sashimi are splendid (and the mackerel superb). The grilled main dishes, cooked teppanyaki style, are the height of perfection. The spinach salad with mushrooms, the radish broth with foie gras, the miso soup and the tender Limousin beef filet (the meat comes from Hugo Desnoyer in the fourteenth arrondissement, who supplies Pierre Gagnaire and L'Ambroisie) are devilishly tempting. Looking around, we see a few tables, a bar where we can admire the master sculptor, a small Japanese-style dining room with tatamis and an area to stretch out our legs. In short, an exquisite, exotic establishment whose little lunchtime set menus are tickets to Tokyo or Kyoto at angelic prices.

● Au Bon Accueil ○ SIM

14, rue de Monttessuy.
Métro: Alma-Marceau.
Tel. 01 47 05 46 11. Fax 01 45 56 15 80.
Closed Sat., Sun.
Prix fixe: 27€ (lunch), 31€ (dinner).
A la carte: 60€.

In the shadow of the Eiffel Tower, Jacques Lapicière's restaurant is true to its name: the "good welcome." Customers are always cordially received, to say the least, even when the proprietor is absent (he divides his time between this establishment and Chez les Anges in avenue de la Tour-Maubourg). The service is prompt and friendly, the décor has been refurbished in the best possible taste (mahogany and beige walls, tablecloths of freshly ironed gray linen) and the menu offers an inspired, market-based gourmet cuisine. The produce is fresh, the quality faultless and the dishes seasonal. We are beguiled by the creamy frog leg risotto, the oven-crisped sea bass filet, green asparagus seasoned with truffle oil, Bresse chicken breast in a white cream sauce and with crayfish tails served with the roasted drumstick and oven-crisp polenta, as well as the raspberry mille-feuille with vanilla cream. Fine wines chosen from every region with flair.

● L'Affriolé 🔔 SIM

17, rue Malar.
Métro: Invalides, Pont-de-l'Alma.
Tel. 01 44 18 31 33. Fax 01 44 18 91 12.
Closed Sun., Mon., bank holidays
(if long weekends), Christmas–New Year's,
3 weeks in Aug.
Prix fixe: 19€ (lunch), 23€ (lunch),
29€ (lunch), 33€.

In a quiet little street, a simple décor and an alluring menu. The silky creamed Tarbais white beans with foie gras, pork trotter in crisp pastry, monkfish tail with smoked pork belly or the quail and foie gras pâté, finally the Guanaja chocolate soufflé with cocoa sorbet or the fried cakes with softened citrus jelly are marvelous. Thierry Verola, a disciple of Senderens and Duquesnoy, is a master of his trade. In the dining room, Maria Verola tends to the customers in three languages. We like the quality of this unobtrusive, creative restaurant.

● L'Ami Jean 🔔 SIM

27, rue Malar.
Métro: La Tour-Maubourg.
Tel. 01 47 05 86 89. Fax 01 45 50 34 79
ami_jean@hotmail.fr
Closed Sun., Mon.,
1 week Christmas–New Year's, Aug.
Prix fixe: 30€.

Photos of Basque country *pelota* games on the walls, green and red colors, rustic furniture and packed tables: Stéphane Jego nails his flag to the mast. Formerly at La Régalade, Jego is full of verve and undeniably talented. His quick-seared squid with Spanish beans is irresistible. Fish plays an important role. Grilled sea bream with lemon and olive oil and l'axoa (a dish of ground veal, onions and espelette chilis), brebis cheese and black cherry confiture have a special (and deserved) place in the cuisine and heart of our amiable Stéphane, who has a gift for transmuting very simple domestic recipes, as shown by the delicious rice pudding he offers as a dessert. A good choice of wines from Southwest France, especially from the Basque country, on both sides of the Pyrénées.

● Café Constant   🍴SIM

139, rue Saint-Dominique.
Métro: Ecole-Militaire, Pont-de-l'Alma.
Tel. 01 47 53 73 34. Fax 01 45 55 00 91.
Closed Sun., Mon.
A la carte: 30€.

Two buildings away from his Violon d'Ingres, Christian Constant has opened this simpler fifties bistro offering a successful new take on domestic standards. So successful, in fact, that customers have to wait in line (no reservations, unfortunately), giving them time to examine the dishes on the blackboard, which change with the season. Try the "terrine de kako" (Basque pork filet) with lentils, a fennel-seasoned cod, the house Toulouse sausage or Aquitaine beef with potatoes and the strawberries done Melba-style to conclude and you need have no worries about the tab.

● Les Fables de la Fontaine   🍴SIM

131, rue Saint-Dominique.
Métro: Ecole-Militaire, Pont-de-l'Alma.
Tel. 01 44 18 37 55.
Closed Sun., Mon.
A la carte: 40€.

These fables are enchanting tales of the sea told by Christian Constant. He has decided to offer up a taste of sea spray in this former oyster bar, with a terrace next to the charming fountain of Mars. We savor fish from the day's catch, as well as gourmet preparations presented as suggestions of the day. These include cold vegetable soup with boneless chicken filets, braised galinette (a fish of the mullet family), olive and parmesan polenta and an excellent Basque cake.

● Le Gorille Blanc   Ⓝ🍴SIM

11 bis, rue Chomel.
Métro: Sèvres-Babylone.
Tel.-Fax 01 45 49 04 54.
Closed Sat., Sun., Christmas, New Year's,
3 weeks Aug.
Prix fixe: 19€ (lunch). A la carte: 35–40€.

We love this local bistro located near the Bon Marché department store, with its counter, wooden tables, ceramic floor and compact summer terrace. Bernard Arény, formerly at L'Ambassade d'Auvergne, has turned his energy to running the place and renamed it the "White Gorilla," confirming his fondness for animal metaphors (he previously owned Le Grizzli in the fourth). A native of the Pyrénées, he has lost none of his Ariège accent or enthusiasm. To officiate in the kitchen, he has brought in the talented Jérôme Catillat, who trained with Dutournier and at Le Crillon. He concocts cunning, fresh, flavorsome dishes. The lentil salad with pig's feet and foie gras, chestnut soup with a frothy porcini emulsion, small squid with squid ink risotto and partridge wrapped in cabbage (served in the hunting season), work wonders, while the simple rabbit fricassée with onions and Corinth raisins is a domestic delight. The desserts—thin dark chocolate tart and hazelnut crème brûlée—slip down readily. Sensibly priced, thirst-quenching wines, such as Chermette "Cœur de Vendanges" Beaujolais, scarcely boost the check. A treasure trove not to be missed.

● Le P'tit Troquet   🍴SIM

28, rue de l'Exposition.
Métro: Ecole-Militaire.
Tel.-Fax 01 47 05 80 39.
Closed Sat. lunch, Sun., Mon. lunch, Aug.
Prix fixe: 30€ (dinner), 19,50€ (lunch), 27€ (lunch). A la carte: 42€.

Everything is a collector's item in Patrick Vessière's twenties bistro in beige and green hues: marble tables, coffee pots and enameled advertisements on the walls. The proprietor and chef takes a fresh approach to regional cuisine with caramelized endive, apple chutney and tangy goat cheese tart, wild drum fish seasoned with soy sauce and black olive–braised rabbit with fork-mashed potatoes. The strawberry, meringue and lemon ice cream "igloo" provides a suitable conclusion for the feast. The portions are generous, and no smoking is allowed in the restaurant.

● Au Babylone

13, rue de Babylone.
Métro: Sèvres-Babylone.
Tel. 01 45 48 72 13.
Closed dinner on weekdays, Sun., Aug.
Prix fixe: 19,50€ (lunch, wine inc.).
A la carte: 25€.

Liliane Garavana has repainted her old bistro, which has a very Parisian charm with its exposed stone and checked tablecloths. The very simple dishes come at truly moderate prices. Duck foie gras terrine, pike fish quenelle and Dover sole pan-fried in butter and seasoned with parsley and lemon, leg of lamb and farm-raised chicken, daily seasonal fruit tart and chocolate cake: good, old-fashioned French home cooking. In fact, those are Liliane's children waiting the tables.

● La Fontaine de Mars

129, rue Saint-Dominique.
Métro: Ecole-Militaire, Pont-de-l'Alma.
Tel. 01 47 05 46 44. Fax 01 47 05 11 13.
cafedelalma@wanadoo.fr
Closed Christmas–New Year's.
Prix fixe: 23€ (lunch). A la carte: 50€.

The art deco setting, cloth-covered tables, patinated walls and terrace are stylish. The cuisine seems to have improved a little (boudin noir sausage with apples and porcini pâté). Then there are cod with aïoli, cassoulet with duck confit and chicken with morel mushrooms washed down with a lively Cahors. Jacques and Christiane Boudon, who run the neighboring Café de l'Alma and Auvergne Gourmande, seem to have taken our advice.

● Au Pied de Fouet

45, rue de Babylone.
Métro: St-François-Xavier.
Tel. 01 47 05 12 27.
Closed Thursday dinner, 1 week Aug.
A la carte: 20–25€.

Today, this former coachmen's haunt enjoys a solid reputation among the capital's gourmet bistros. Perusing a menu that changes each day, you are sure to find something to suit your tastes among, for example, a lentil salad, slow-cooked duck gizzards in salad, sautéed poultry livers, homemade duck confit, crème caramel and soft chocolate cake, all for a truly minimal price.

● La Poule au Pot

121, rue de l'Université.
Métro: Invalides.
Tel. 01 47 05 16 36. Fax 01 47 05 74 56.
Closed Sat. lunch, Sun.,
10 days Christmas–New Year's, 3 weeks Aug.
Prix fixe: 18,50€, 24,50€.
A la carte: 47€.

This bistro with its typical thirties décor instantly works its charm. The setting, the food, the welcome—everything appeals. The tasty, timeless dishes that Jacques Dumond concocts have a tang of authenticity. Crawfish tail salad, salmon tartare, poule au pot farcie d'Henri IV (classic poached stuffed hen) and Armagnac-soaked prunes with accompanying tea cakes will bring color to your cheeks and a smile to your face.

■	HOTELS

■ Four Seasons George V

31, av George-V.
Métro: George-V.
Tel. 01 49 52 70 00. Fax 01 49 52 70 10.
www.fourseasons.com
186 rooms: 680–880€.
59 suites: 1250–9500€.

This grand French hotel refurbished American-style is the height of luxury. The supremely attentive service, marble trimmed lobby, 16th-century-style suites and rooms, Le Cinq restaurant, bar, gallery, swimming pool and spa are all part of the comprehensive experience. The guests here want for nothing (see Restaurants).

■ Crillon

10, pl de la Concorde.
Métro: Concorde.
Tel. 01 44 71 15 00. Fax 01 44 71 15 02.

crillon@crillon.com / www.crillon.com
108 rooms: 695–890€.
49 suites: 1160–8200€.

A jewel on the place de la Concorde. The rooms with their Louis XV furniture, bar decorated by Arman, Guerlain beauty parlor and dishes from Jean-François Piège (who supervises the Obélisque and Ambassadeurs) are charming indeed. (See Restaurants.)

■ Fouquet's Barrière

46, av George V.
Métro: George-V.
Tel. 01 40 70 05 05. Fax 01 40 70 57 00.
www.fouquets-barriere.com
107 rooms and suites: 690–15000€.

The great event in the Golden Square is this French-owned luxury hotel, the only one in Paris! The golden décor is by Garcia and 40% of the accommodation consists of suites up to 535 square meters in size. The large patio, furniture in beige and plum shades, and lobby that Hollywood itself might envy with its collection of fifties and sixties movie photos all contribute to a sense of absolute luxury (see Restaurants: Diane). The hotel also has a spa and bar, and offers more casual catering.

■ Plaza Athénée

25, av Montaigne.
Métro: Alma-Marceau.
Tel. 01 53 67 66 65 / 01 53 67 66 67.
Fax 01 53 67 66 66.
reservation@plaza-athenee-paris.com
plaza-athenee-paris.com
143 rooms: 565–770€.
45 suites: 940–14000€.

Constellations of stars flock to this 18th-century luxury hotel where the last episode of "Sex & the City" was shot. The bar, the chic Relais and Alain Ducasse's restaurant, the rooms and suites renovated in art deco or classical style, the gallery tearoom and the flowered patio make this a great hotel of its time (see Restaurants).

■ Royal Monceau

37, av Hoche.
Métro: Charles-de-Gaulle-Etoile.
Tel. 01 42 99 88 00. Fax 01 42 99 89 94.
www.royalmonceau.com
66 rooms: 550–850€.
10 suites: 1050–6800€.

Omar Sharif, Massimo Gargia and Champs-Elysées society frequent this rococo luxury hotel redesigned by Jacques Garcia. The Belle Epoque facade conceals a fitness center, squash court, swimming pool, bar with music and two exquisite restaurants (the Jardin, Il Carpaccio). Excellent service (see Restaurants).

■ Lancaster

7, rue de Berri.
Métro: Champs-Elysées-Clemenceau, George-V.
Tel. 01 40 76 40 76. Fax 01 40 76 40 00.
www.hotel-lancaster.fr
47 rooms: 410–590€.
11 suites: 790–1650€.

This little luxury hotel opened in 1889 has a British chic. Christian Liaigre's décor, the rooms with their Louis XVI furniture and the first-rate restaurant supervised by Michel Troisgros go together well.

■ Sofitel le Faubourg

15, rue Boissy-d'Anglas.
Métro: Concorde.
Tel. 01 44 94 14 14 / 01 44 94 14 24 (rest.).
Fax 01 44 94 14 28.
H1295@accor-hotels.com / www.sofitel.com
135 rooms: 365–495€.
38 suites: 575–2000€.

With its décor by Pierre-Yves Rochon, this chain hotel offers a combination of elegance and charm. The modern rooms in beige tones, hushed bar, gym and restaurant (Café Faubourg) are all packed when the FIAC International Contemporary Art Fair and fashion shows are on.

■ Vernet

25, rue Vernet.
Métro: George-V.
Tel. 01 44 31 98 00. Fax 01 44 31 85 69.

www.hotelvernet.com
42 rooms: 390–550€. 9 suites: 1000€.

This little turn-of-the-century luxury hotel refurbished to reflect modern tastes has a discreet appeal. Its rooms renovated in blue and yellow shades, swimming pool, Indian bar with a Punjab theme and restaurant with its dome designed by Eiffel are just some the Vernet's charms.

■ Château Frontenac

54, rue Pierre-Charon.
Métro: Franklin-D.-Roosevelt, George-V.
Tel. 01 53 23 13 13. Fax 01 53 23 13 01.
hotel@hfrontenac.com
www.grouefrontenac.com
90 rooms: 265€. 14 suites: 265–385€.

Just off the Champs-Elysées, this classic hostelry is strategically sited. Renovated in sky blue, its Louis XV-style rooms are cozy indeed.

■ Concorde Saint-Lazare

108, rue Saint-Lazare.
Métro: St-Lazare.
Tel. 01 40 08 44 44. Fax 01 42 93 01 20.
stlazare@concordestlazare-paris.com
www.concordestlazare-paris.com
268 rooms: 450–1500€.

Opposite Saint-Lazare rail station, this institution's great attraction is its 1850 lobby designed by Eiffel. The rooms with their traditional English furniture and the restaurant (Café Terminus) are worth a detour.

■ Napoléon

38/40, av de Friedland.
Métro: Charles-de-Gaulle-Etoile.
Tel. 01 56 68 43 21 / 01 56 68 44 68 (rest.).Fax 01 47 66 82 33.
napoleon@hotelnapoleonparis.com
www.hotelnapoleonparis.com
65 rooms: 195–480€. 18 suites: 385–680€.

Orson Welles, Errol Flynn and Josephine Baker were regulars in this traditional hotel that has belonged to the same family since 1928. We like its distinctive Empire-style rooms.

■ Le San Régis

12, rue Jean-Goujon.
Métro: Alma-Marceau, Champs-Elysées-Clemenceau, Franklin-D.-Roosevelt.
Tel. 01 44 95 16 16. Fax 01 45 61 05 48.
message@hotel-sanregis.fr
www.hotel–sanregis.fr
41 rooms: 330–595€.
11 suites: 655–1050€.

Behind the 18th-century facade lies a cozy luxury hotel. The select bar, refined rooms, snug restaurant and perfect service set the tone in this grand establishment.

■ Hôtel Daniel

8, rue Frédéric-Bastiat.
Métro: Franklin-Roosevelt.
Tel. 01 42 56 17 00. Fax 01 42 56 17 01.
danielparis@relaischateaux.com
Rest. closed Sat., Sun., Bank holidays.
19 rooms: 320–440€. 7 suites: 490–690€.
Prix fixe: 40–50€.

A step away from the Champs-Elysées, this snug hotel is a prime example of the Relais & Châteaux spirit in Paris, luxurious and cozy with a feminine refinement. Exquisite dishes prepared by Denis Fétisson and served at the bar.

■ Hôtel de Sers

41, av Pierre 1 de Serbie.
Tel. 01 53 23 75 75. Fax 01 53 23 75 76.
www.hoteldesers.com
46 rooms: 450–600€.
8 suites: 900–2100€.

Opened two years ago, this charming establishment a step away from the Champs-Elysées is a 19th-century town house restyled to reflect 21st-century architectural principles by Thomas Vidalenc, an exponent of the art still in his twenties. The large, peaceful rooms have a staunchly contemporary design. The breakfast service is flawless. The bar and terrace are very popular at the end of the afternoon.

■ Pershing Hall

49, rue Pierre-Charon.
Métro: George-V.

Tel. 01 58 36 58 00. Fax 01 58 36 58 01.
info@pershinghall.com
www.pershinghall.com
18 rooms: 420–520€. 8 suites: 1000€.

Andrée Putman created the décor of this modern hotel occupying General Pershing's former residence. Its bar and vertical garden designed by Patrick Blanc draw crowds of fashionistas.

■ Rochester

92, rue La Boétie.
Métro: St-Philippe-du-Roule.
Tel. 01 56 69 69 00. Fax 01 56 69 69 01.
hotel@hrochester.com
www.hrochester.com
90 rooms: 265€. 10 suites: 335€.

The Champs-Elysées nearby is one of this modern hotel's great attractions. Service with a smile, fully equipped rooms and a fitness center.

■ Franklin-Roosevelt

18, rue Clément-Marot.
Métro: Franklin-D.-Roosevelt.
Tel. 01 53 57 49 50. Fax 01 53 57 49 59.
hotel@hroosevelt.com / www.hroosevelt.com
48 rooms: 265–450€. 1 suite: 550€.

A small Victorian hostelry with snug rooms, a refined lounge, an elegant bar and a winter garden.

■ Vignon

23, rue Vignon.
Métro: Madeleine, St-Lazare, Auber (RER).
Tel. 01 47 42 93 00. Fax 01 47 42 04 60.
reservation@hotelvignon.com
www.levignon.com
28 rooms: 160–325€.

Near the great department stores, this practical hotel provides contemporary guest rooms and a pleasant breakfast room.

■ Monna Lisa

97, rue La Boétie.
Métro: Franklin-D.-Roosevelt.
Tel. 01 56 43 38 38. Fax 01 45 62 39 90.
contact@hotelmonnalisa.com
www.hotelmonnalisa.com
20 rooms: 170–265€. 2 suites: 380€.

This modern Milanese-style designer hotel offers renovated rooms in a neo-art deco setting, as well as a worthwhile transalpine restaurant (Caffé Ristretto).

■ New Orient

16, rue de Constantinople.
Métro: Europe, Villiers, Rome.
Tel. 01 45 22 21 64. Fax 01 42 93 83 23.
new.orient.hotel@wanadoo.fr
www.hotel-paris-orient.com
30 rooms: 82–140€.

This very discreet little hotel offers accommodation in a chic neighborhood at modest prices. Fitted out in a former town house, its rooms have been redecorated in bright tones this year.

● RESTAURANTS

● Les Ambassadeurs   V.LUX

At the Crillon, 10, pl de la Concorde.
Métro: Concorde.
Tel. 01 44 71 16 16. Fax 01 44 71 16 03.
ambassadeurs@crillon.com
www.crillon.com
Closed Sun., Mon. lunch, Aug.
Prix fixe: 70€ (lunch on weekdays).
A la carte: 200€.

The contemporary style of the cutlery, plates and glasses contrasts with the historic surroundings. The scene is set by the dining room manager, Mathieu Foureau, and his young, dynamic and extremely professional team. The most eagerly awaited artist remains in the wings though. The Crillon has found the chef it deserves in the person of Jean-François Piège. Assisted by his loyal lieutenants Yann Meinsel and Christophe Saintagne, who are ready to step forward and play the lead at any moment, he works on the imagination. The appetizers are already a play on words, flirting with a TV dinner concept but diametrically opposed to the kind of experience that might suggest: common, quick and trite. Indeed, they are magnificent and eminently creative: the Lucien Tende–style gâteau, circa 2006, the croustillante with a slice of ham, the cromesquis of fresh peas and the lemonade (!) of tabouli convey their message intelligently. When the curtain rises, the first act, a niçoise salad, Parisian-style and spider crab served with an herbed reduction glows with freshness and truth. The second is an exercise in subtlety though. The line-caught sea bass minestrone and the golden caviar nage with langoustines turn out to be the exclusive stars of the play, their produce prepared in such a way as to underline all their natural qualities and distil their essences. Making their appearance in the third act, deboned pigeon and foie gras in olive oil reduction and the casse-croûte of blue lobster, red chanterelles and lemon confit bring an infinitely delicate twist to the plot. The intermission—in the company of some of France's finest cheeses matured to perfection—only sharpens the suspense, but finally the epilogue, a new take on cherry and verbena clafoutis or a kind of strawberry basil vacherin by pastry chef Jérôme Chaucesse, breathes its irresistible scents. The wine list is endless and David Biraud provides invaluable advice. A standing ovation for so much talent.

● **Le Bristol** ⓒⓞ 𝗩.𝗟𝗨𝗫
At the Bristol,
112, rue du Faubourg-Saint-Honoré.
Métro: Miromesnil.
Tel. 01 53 43 43 00. Fax 01 53 43 43 01.
rcourant@lebristolparis.com
www.lebristolparis.com
Prix fixe: 80€ (lunch), 175€.
A la carte: 200€.

Eric Fréchon continues to amaze us. He has a thousand and one tricks up his sleeve. When unrestricted imagination is brought to bear in the kitchen, the secret of great dishes lies in superior produce and perfect execution. Both are very much in evidence here. The bouillon with cubes of duck foie gras is combined with langoustines cooked "al dente" with ginger, coriander and leeks, sole with a slightly creamed fishbone reduction with Jura

wine, stuffed with chanterelles. The Sargasses eel, cooked in butter and seasoned with parsley, joins exquisitely with mashed smoked fingerling potatoes with parsley jus, seasoned with garlic. The Bresse hen for two, enveloped in a pig's bladder and slow poached in Jura wine, is served with green asparagus, morel mushrooms and a reduction sauce. The dessert prix fixe is a delight. While we especially love the apricots and Caribbean vanilla–flavored risotto with nougat cream; we also have a weakness for the frozen parfait infused with fresh mint, served with whole raspberries and milk chocolate. The welcome here is exemplary and the service, under the eye of Raphaël Courant, first-rate. Sommelier Jérôme Moreau is discreet and provides excellent advice. The check is, of course, open ended: this is one of the most prominent luxury hotels in Paris and the restaurant is absolutely first class.

● **Le Cinq** ⓒⓞ 𝗩.𝗟𝗨𝗫
At the Four Seasons George V,
31, av George-V.
Métro: George-V.
Tel. 01 49 52 71 54. Fax 01 49 52 71 81.
par.lecinq@fourseasons.com
www.fourseasons.com
Prix fixe: 75€ (lunch), 120€,
210€ (dinner). A la carte: 180–200€.

One day they will raise a statue to the glory of Philippe Legendre. He will certainly find the very idea unwelcome, but he deserves such a mark of respect, simply because he turns dinner in his restaurant into a trip to paradise. Although you are overwhelmed by choices when you read the prix fixe, very fortunately, Eric Beaumard and his dining room team are there to point you in the right direction. The large green asparagus with parmesan and truffles with a slow-cooked black olive polenta whet the appetite with a spectrum of scents that excite the palate. The anthology continues with cod seasoned with roasted peppercorns, underlining the aromas of the truffle tart served simultaneously. Roasted pigeon with peppermint and Sauternes takes on a traditional air next to that brilliant creation, farm-raised veal sweetbreads, pan-fried with orzo pasta "paella"-style. The desserts are in the same vein: innovative and high in color and light, such as a crisp layered pastry with simply roasted fresh pineapple frosted with lime and coconut, or soft Guanaja chocolate streussel cake with cocoa sorbet. The cellar is one of the capital's finest.

● **Alain Ducasse**   CO VLUX

At the Plaza Athénée, 25, av Montaigne.
Métro: Alma-Marceau, Franklin-D.-Roosevelt.
Tel. 01 53 67 65 00. Fax 01 53 67 65 12.
adpa@alain-ducasse.com
www.alain-ducasse.com
Closed Sat., Sun., Mon. lunch, Tue. lunch,
Wed. lunch, 1 week at the end December,
mid-July–end July, 3 weeks Aug.
Prix fixe: 200€, 300€. A la carte: 250€.

Obviously, the Master, Alain Ducasse, is not always present, but the kitchen team led by Christophe Moret and his lieutenant Josselin Herland is one of the most brilliant anywhere. Its members put all their heart into their work and their preparations are remarkable, both in the precision of their execution and for their originality. The products are selected with extreme care, when they are not supplied exclusively to the Plaza. The fresh pasta with cream, truffles and giblets is a magnificent starter. Seasons are observed to the letter here. The line-caught sea bass is accompanied by green asparagus and fresh peas in the spring, but comes with citrus fruits, leeks and spring onions in the fall. The smoked tea-glazed pigeon reveals entirely new flavors that bring out the full taste of turnips in sweet-and-sour sauce. Dessert is always a high point, but for those who are happiest straying from the beaten path, there can only be one choice—soft fresh ewe's cheese, peppered caramel and strawberry-tree honey. Supervised by Denis Courtiade, the service attains summits of excellence, and the cellar, governed by Laurent Roucayrol, is extraordinary. The check is, of course, just as striking, but the most contemporary works of art are priceless and "Monsieur Ducasse" is and remains an artist

with an eye to everything, from the décor designed by his associate Patrick Jouin, to minor details with a major impact, such as the cutlery and plates and the style of the glasses.

● **Taillevent**   CO VLUX

15, rue Lamennais.
Métro: George-V.
Tel. 01 44 95 15 01. Fax 01 42 25 95 18.
mail@taillevent.com / www.taillevent.com
Closed Sat., Sun., end July–end Aug.
Prix fixe: 70€ (lunch), 140€, 190€.
A la carte: 200€.

Alongside the "modernists" and their sometimes controversial concoctions, the "classicists" have their place, but must obviously still bring their cuisine into line with today's tastes. This is exactly what Jean-Claude Vrinat had always asked of the chefs at "his" Taillevent, a timeless (but not changeless) restaurant. Alain Solivérès, a creative craftsman who trained with Maximin, Ducasse and Cirino, has planned a prix fixe that seems traditional on first sight. Only when it is explained by the master of the house do you realize that nothing could be further from the truth. This is confirmed when Sault spelt wheat risotto with browned frog legs or John Dory fish with olives arrive. The sun-filled cuisine reaches its zenith with lamb saddle in a reduction sauce seasoned with regional wild herbs. The desserts, such as the feuille à feuille, a layered dessert of three chocolates, or baba au rhum with liquor-soaked raisins seem a million years old but still topical. The wine list is endless and the setting—a Second Empire town house with contemporary art providing interior decoration—exceptional, as is the service. The check rapidly adds up, but this comes as no shock, since the restaurant is at the peak of its achievements.

● **Lasserre**   CO 🛈 VLUX

17, av Franklin-D.-Roosevelt.
Métro: Franklin-D.-Roosevelt,
Champs-Elysées–Clemenceau.
Tel. 01 43 59 53 43 / 01 43 59 67 45.
Fax 01 45 63 72 23.

lasserre@lasserre.fr
www.restaurant-lasserre.com
Closed lunch (except Thursday, Fri.), Sun., Aug.
Prix fixe: 75€ (lunch), 185€ (tasting menu).
A la carte: 180–200€.

Monsieur Lasserre is no longer with us, but his great establishment opposite the Palais de la Découverte science museum marches on, more splendid than ever. Jean-Louis Nomicos, a close associate of Alain Ducasse for years, presents a prix fixe that skillfully reconciles tradition and modernity. Priority is given to produce, and everything here is a question of balance, as evinced by truffle and foie gras macaroni. The Breton lobster in classic simmered stew seasoned with honey, chestnuts and rosemary is always a must, but turbot in a crust of black truffle, artichokes and green pea purée is today's true event. The pigeon served with seasonal fruits and vegetables, the milk-fed veal chops with lemon and ginger cream sauce, the duck à l'orange are feats of bravura. The chocolate soufflé is splendid. The service is fully what you would expect from such a noble establishment and the check reflects that magnificence. The sommelier's name is Antoine Petrus, which already gives food for thought. When the weather is fine, the roof of the elegant dining room opens to the sky. The effect is magical and never stales.

● **Apicius**

20, rue d'Artois.
Métro: St-Philippe-du-Roule,
Franklin-D.-Roosevelt, George-V.
Tel. 01 43 80 19 66. Fax 01 44 40 09 57.
apicius@relaischateaux.com
Closed Sat., Sun., Aug.
Prix fixe: 140€. A la carte: 150–180€.

Jean-Pierre Vigato dazzles Paris society in this town house set in its own grounds. The classical facade, terrace overlooking the garden and elegant dining rooms in contemporary style have an easy charm. The master delights his preppy clientele with half-traditional, half-imaginative dishes. He plays ingeniously on the changing seasons, offers a very personal take on

the hunting season when autumn comes and prepares seafood with invariable constancy. His dishes include hand-cut and lightly grilled langoustines, a spicy turbot for two, tête de veau with sauce ravigote (exemplary in a chic, roguish style) and the roasted parsley-seasoned Pyrénées leg of lamb. Turning to the desserts, the dark chocolate soufflé served with an unsweetened whipped cream wins our vote. The service is a joy. Even if the Hervé Millet discoveries we select from the wine list hike up the check to a slightly higher sum than is reasonable, we have few regrets.

● **Laurent**

41, av Gabriel.
Métro: Champs-Elysées–Clemenceau.
Tel. 01 42 25 00 39. Fax 01 45 62 45 21
info@le-laurent.com / www.le-laurent.com
Closed Sat. lunch, Sun.,
Bank Holidays.
Prix fixe: 75€, 150€. A la carte: 180€.

With Edmond Ehrlich gone, many had their doubts about Laurent's future. They had not reckoned with the determination of its team of great professionals and the arrival of a conscientious chef. In the dining room, the good-humored Philippe Bourguignon welcomes regulars and first-time visitors with equal courtesy. In the kitchen, Alain Pégouret, who has worked with Joël Robuchon and Christian Constant, is at the summit of his art, as shown by pan seared duck foie gras that opens the proceedings. Beneath a classical exterior, red mullet filet seasoned with saffron, bone marrow and caramelized shallot sauce is an exceptionally modern dish. The Corrèze veal flank steak, simply braised and presented with Swiss chard and a reduction sauce, is congenial and tasty, while hot soufflé perfumed with Anis de Pontarlier is a highly successful confection. Patrick Lair always provides good advice when the time comes to choose a wine. The price of all this splendor is reasonable, and there is a terrace for when the sun shines.

Maxim's   🎜 V.LUX

3, rue Royale.
Métro: Concorde.
Tel. 01 42 65 27 94. Fax 01 42 65 30 26.
maxims@wanadoo.fr
www.maxims-de-paris.com
Closed Sat., Sun., Mon. .
A la carte: 250€.

This prestige establishment has become a shrine visited by nostalgics from all over the world keen on its fifties surroundings and old-fashioned service. A la carte, the langoustine salad, Dover sole braised with vermouth, beef filet with morel mushroom sauce and, finally, the Grand Marnier soufflé delight customers in search of a culinary museum. The wine list has riches to spare. Before stepping inside, make sure you do, too.

Ledoyen   ⃝⃝⃝ 🎜 V.LUX

Carré des Champs-Elysées, 1, av Dutuit.
Métro: Champs-Elysées–Clemenceau.
Tel. 01 53 05 10 01. Fax 01 47 42 55 01
pavillon.ledoyen@ledoyen.com
Closed Sat., Sun., Mon. lunch, Aug.
Prix fixe: 85€ (lunch on weekdays), 198€ (lunch on weekdays), 284€ (wine inc. on weekdays). A la carte: 200€.

The Napoleon III style has been lovingly maintained, and guests here lunch or dine in one of the most elegant settings in the capital. Christian Le Squer's cuisine is in tune with these surroundings as he consummately champions the colors of "his" Brittany, enchanting his enthralled audience with oven-crisped langoustines served in a citrus olive oil emulsion sauce. Straying a little further from the beaten path, the *concentré* of assorted Belon and *spéciales* oysters makes a succulent marine starter. Sobriety does not rule out a touch of mischief, and the astute oven-crisped slices of filet of sole acquire a somewhat Jurassic flavor, prepared as they are with Jura wine. The ingenious sautéed spiced suckling pig with gnocchi and semi-dried tomatoes seems native to the land of Brittany and is toothsome to a fault. For dessert, thin crisp dark chocolate sheets with iced pistachio milk will have you swooning. The service is in the delicious style practiced in bourgeois homes. The check climbs rather higher than Brittany's unspectacular Arrée Mountains, but without giving undue offence.

Pierre Gagnaire   ⃝⃝⃝ LUX

6, rue Balzac.
Métro: George-V.
Tel. 01 58 36 12 50. Fax 01 58 36 12 51
p.gagnaire@wanadoo.fr
www.pierre-gagnaire.com
Closed Sat., Sun. lunch, Wednesday lunch,
2 weeks beg. Aug.
Prix fixe: 90€ (lunch), 235€ (lunch).
A la carte: 300€.

Yes, Pierre Gagnaire is controversial, which is no bad thing. This genius of flavors has always been a mine of ideas, constantly revising the thousand and one dishes he invents and his ways of presenting them. The aim here is innovation as well as originality. Thrill to the exhilarating millefeuille with arugula whipped cream seasoned with spring onion jus, the speck ham and peppered mint with cherry juice, the golden Bresse liver gâteau with glazed crayfish nage seasoned with Pouilly-Fuissé accompanied by Perthius asparagus tips, new onions and Menton lemon paste. Gasp at the daring langoustines with a green mango tartare and crunchy sheet of nougatine and mustard currant syrup that are pan-fried with "Terre de Sienne" spices, served with a broth foam and a slice of black radish-chilled consommé dusted with carob powder. The performance is not over yet. We applaud as the curtain rises on rack of Lozere lamb, roasted and poached with oregano, served with crisped fresh herbs and Swiss chard enrobed with pan juices, cloves of garlic, shallots and eggplant and chili-seasoned Madagascar jumbo shrimp cooked with prune eau-de-vie, grilled medallions of lamb with rich lamb sauce, zucchini flowers and cold reduction sauce as a condiment. Barely a moment to recover and Pierre Gagnaire's grand finale is with us: nine desserts inspired by French *pâtisserie*, made with seasonal fruit, lightly sugared confections and chocolates. The service is perfection itself, including the choice of wines, which can be left unreservedly to Raphaël Huet. However, such prodigies come at a price.

● Les Elysées du Vernet ⓒ LUX

At the Vernet, 25, rue Vernet.
Métro: George-V, Charles-de-Gaulle–Etoile.
Tel. 01 44 31 98 98. Fax 01 44 31 85 69.
reservations@hotelvernet.com
www.hotelvernet.com
Closed Sat., Sun., Mon. noon,
end July–end Aug.
Prix fixe: 59€ (lunch), 94€ (dinner),
130€ (dinner). A la carte: 135€.

The Vernet's restaurant is one of the most splendid in the Champs-Elysées area. The décor is extraordinary, with its glass roof designed by Gustave Eiffel. Eric Briffard, long Joël Robuchon's second-in-command in the Jamin days, cultivates discretion, but still displays incomparable skill and, more than just ideas, wit, when planning the prix fixe. He expertly selects the finest produce and develops its promise to the full. The crunchy honey spice cake, pear, and smoked eel lend a mischievous air to the Landes duck foie gras which has been steamed and seasoned with a touch of ginger, and those who enjoy exoticism within reason will then choose blue lobster, salt-cooked and perfumed with aromatics served with fennel, artichokes, and coriander lemon gnocchi for its precise cooking and perfectly sustained flavors. In comparison, young pigeon with five-spice glaze, tamarind reduction, turnips, dates and lemon confit seems more traditional. The splendid conclusion takes the form of Saint Domingues "grand cru" chocolate, raspberry soufflé tart, and green tea sorbet. Go for the set prix fixes at lunch or dinner.

● Diane LUX

At the Fouquet's Barrière, 46, av George V.
Tel. 01 40 69 60 60. Fax 01 40 70 57 00.
www.fouquets-barriere.com
Open daily.
Prix fixe: 165€. A la carte: 150€.

A modern lounge setting designed by Garcia, a circular ceiling, chairs in a gentle

mauve shade, alert service and a menu urging us to spend, spend, spend: there are no half measures here in most recent of Paris' great luxury hotels. Jean-Yves Leuranguer, chef at Fouquet's and holder of the Meilleur Ouvrier de France award, has delegated responsibility for this eatery to his lieutenant Olivier Scola, formerly with Thierry Marx at Cordeillan-Bages and the Plaza-Athénée in the days of Eric Briffard. The produce is first-rate and the preparations are meticulous. Salmon marinated in Marco Polo spices, the Nice-style chickpea cake (socca) with chard and squid ink, sole with ceps and pear chutney, Wagyu beef with red onions served with tarragon-seasoned gnocchi and the slow-cooked black-tailed pork with cabbage and apricots and the chef's caviar provide a polished demonstration of a chic rustic manner. They are followed by mouthwatering desserts from pastry chef Jean-Luc Labat, including the warm fig mille-feuille and the "childhood memory" desserts in five flavors. The fine wines by the glass are inhospitably priced.

● La Maison Blanche LUX

15, av Montaigne.
Métro: Alma-Marceau.
Tel. 01 47 23 55 99. Fax 01 47 20 09 56.
info@maison-blanche.fr
www.maison-blanche.fr
Closed Sat. lunch, Sun. lunch.
Prix fixe: 40€ (lunch),
65€ (lunch, wine inc.). A la carte: 120€.

Reliable staff in both dining room and kitchen, the determination of the Pourcel twins to achieve new heights of quality, a décor in shades of white and a view of the Eiffel Tower over the roofs of Paris are all to be found here. Now there is scarcely any reason not to award a Plate to Thierry Vaissière for his subtle, delicate, slightly Mediterranean fare with its new take on classics. The zucchini and porcini lasagne with truffled reduction broth, a coconut risotto with grilled jumbo shrimp, a baked sea bass with a white bean and olive crust and the minced beef with potato and ham terrine are the picture of health. The desserts are in the same vein—coconut mille-feuille and mojito sorbet, regional shortbread from Brittany and chocolate tart with tea-flavored sauce. The wine list focuses on Languedoc and the Mediterranean. The prices are no one's idea of a joke, but you will still have to fight for a table, especially in the evening.

● **L'Astor**   LUX

At the Astor, 11, rue d'Astorg
Métro: St-Augustin, Madeleine
Tel. 01 53 05 05 20. Fax 01 53 05 05 30
hotelastor@aol.com
www.hotel-astorsainthonore.fr
Closed Sat., Sun., Aug.
Prix fixe: 33€, 47€ (lunch), 49€ (dinner).
A la carte: 80€.

Fine, well-executed fare, where tradition has the edge, despite a few fairly successful modish escapades presented by Jean-Luc Lefrançois. The sea bream tartare, red mullet with a Thai spice stuffing and thin crunchy pastry with chorizo sausage, veal filet with a gingerbread crust, casserole of spring carrot and radishes and then, on the dessert front, variations on the lemon theme: lemon tart, thin sesame tuiles and assorted lemon sorbets are meticulously prepared. The service is perfect. Although the prices come as a blow, the surroundings are relaxing and the welcome warm.

● **Le Jardin**

At the Royal Monceau, 37, av. Hoche.
Métro: Charles-de-Gaulle–Etoile.
Tel. 01 42 99 98 70. Fax 01 42 99 89 94.
restauration@royalmonceau.com
www.royalmonceau.com
Closed Sat., Sun., Mon. lunch, 3 weeks in Aug.
Prix fixe: 59€ (lunch), 95€ (dinner),
125€ (dinner). A la carte: 130€.

Christophe Pelé formerly worked with Cirino, Del Burgo and Gagnaire. These masters taught him to add that light personal touch that is the hallmark of a great dish. It can often be imperceptible: you have to taste the cherry chutney accompanied with a golden duck foie gras to be sure it is really there. Wild fennel and an artichoke mousseline served with John Dory has an additional note that thrills the palate. A cocotte presenting carrots with roasted veal sweetbreads and licorice root-infused jus becomes a unique creation. The desserts are in the same vein, including the spice- and burnet-flavored ice creams and caramelized tofu. Stéphane Lochon points us South to the wines that will best complement the dishes. The welcome and service are first rate and the luxurious, under-glass garden setting in shades of brown revamped by Garcia has its charm.

● **Il Carpaccio**   ◎ V.COM

At the Royal Monceau, 37, av Hoche.
Métro: Charles-de-Gaulle–Etoile.
Tel. 01 42 99 98 90. Fax 01 42 99 89 94.
restauration@royalmonceau.com
www.royalmonceau.com
Closed Aug. Cont. service.
A la carte: 100€.

Orazio Ganci, formerly at Sadler's in Milan after training with Marchesi in Erbusco, has brilliantly succeeded his compatriot Angelo Agliano in this fine transalpine restaurant cheerfully restyled by Garcia. The handpicked staff deftly serves a salad of raw artichokes, parmesan and arugula, a fritto misto of langoustines, shrimp and calamari, saffron risotto with chanterelles and handmade Sardinian-style pasta with sardines and bottarga. We also enjoy the more sophisticated medallions of monkfish with eggplant, cuttlefish and zucchini. The vanilla ice cream with Seville orange is a model of conclusive freshness. The fine wine list covers the whole of Italy and notably includes Tuscan reds chosen by Bruno Malara. The sublime service and the check—(almost) reasonable for such a grand experience—are the trademarks of Paris' finest Italian restaurant.

● **Senderens**

9, pl de la Madeleine.
Métro: Madeleine.
Tel. 01 42 65 22 90. Fax 01 42 65 06 23
restaurant@senderens.fr / www.senderens.fr
Closed Sat. (July–Aug.), Sun. (July–Aug.),
May 1st.
Prix fixe: 105€ (wine inc.), 115€ (wine inc.). A la carte: 90–120€.

"Senderens *nouveau*" is here! Sixty years old but in great shape, with an assistant brought in from L'Ambroisie, a rejuvenated team and modern décor with neat tables in a industrial material and shades of gray. We are fond of the great Alain, even though we are not absolutely certain he can still offer all the magic of the wizard we once knew, the magic of rue de l'Exposition or rue de Varenne in the days of L'Archestrate. The vegetable-stuffed open ravioli, lightly smoked Scottish salmon with ribbon-cut cucumbers, red mullet cooked with seaweed and fennel confit served with olive oil cubes and the veal and langoustine tartare are not bad, even if they are not works of genius. Add to that the ever-persuasive wine-dish pairings, a less alarming tab when compared to the ferocious prices at Lucas Carton and desserts that are obviously the house's strong point (the fine dacquoise seasoned with Sichuan peppercorns and served with lemon marmalade and ginger ice cream) will have you swooning.

● **Chiberta** ◯ V.COM

3, rue Arsène-Houssaye.
Métro: Charles-de-Gaulle–Etoile.
Tel. 01 53 53 42 00. Fax 01 45 62 85 08.
chiberta@guysavoy.comcom
www.lechiberta.com
Closed Sat. lunch, Sun., 1 week Christmas–New Year's, 3 weeks Aug.
Prix fixe: 60€, 100€. A la carte: 80–90€.

One of the most attractive establishments in the capital. With its décor by Jean-Michel Wilmotte, this new Guy Savoy address has quickly reached cruising speed. Gilles Chesneau's cuisine is worthy of the master's and Jean-Paul Montellier's dining room management is exemplary. We delight in the spicy crisp jumbo shrimp served with a spicy avocado salad and corn crisps, whole turbot pan fried in butter and seasoned with parsley and lemon served with artichokes, grilled pigeon and eggplant seasoned with sage. The desserts are in the same vein, the creamy pistachio and rhubarb gelatin served with vanilla ice cream, a must. The wine list is worth

a close look, with some excellent bottles at affordable prices.

● **Relais-Plaza** ◯ V.COM

At the Plaza Athénée, 21, av Montaigne.
Métro: Alma-Marceau.
Tel. 01 53 67 64 00. Fax 01 53 67 66 66
reservation@plaza-athenee-paris.com
www.plaza-athenee-paris.com
Prix fixe: 45€. A la carte: 80€.

A chic eatery, stylish food and a historic setting. The Plaza Athénée's forties brasserie, with its dining room inspired by the ocean liner *Normandie*, and its manager, the elegant Werner Kuchler, featured this year (both the restaurant and Werner himself) in the credits of the Danièle Thompson movie *Fauteuils d'Orchestre* (*Orchestra Seats*). Alain Ducasse, who loves the place, has entrusted the kitchen to the reliable Philippe Marc, who presents classic, flawless, well-made dishes: crab with red curry sauce, tomato and goat cheese tart, vegetable risotto, breaded and fried veal cutlet—the best in Paris—iced vacherin and baba au rhum, all washed down with a thoroughbred Fessy Brouilly. Service fit for a great establishment and a smart clientele.

● **Rue Balzac** V.COM

3-5 rue Balzac (at 8, rue Lord-Byron).
Métro: George-V, Charles-de-Gaulle–Etoile.
Tel. 01 53 89 90 91. Fax 01 53 89 90 94
ruebalzac@wanadoo.fr / www.ruebalzac.fr
Closed Sat. lunch, Sun. lunch, 3 weeks Aug.
A la carte: 75€.

This cult corner establishment cultivates the legend of Johnny Hallyday, France's perennial rock star. Hallyday, born Jean-Philippe Smet, and his pal Claude Bouillon own the place. Like one of the father of French rock's stadium shows, the cuisine is planned down to the last note. Oven-crisped langoustines, house-style boiled and coddled eggs, fine pasta seasoned with green olives and baba au rhum with lightly whipped cream and rum-raisin ice cream are all highly persuasive. The ambiance is pleasant, Vavro's décor stimulating, and while you wait for a table you can relax at the bar, now situated near the door.

● La Luna 🅟 ◯ V.COM

69, rue du Rocher.
Métro: Villiers.
Tel. 01 42 93 77 61. Fax 01 40 08 02 44.
Closed Sun., Christmas, 3 weeks in Aug.
A la carte: 85–100€.

The gracious Catherine Delaunay, who runs her dining room with charm and virtuosity, has refurbished it in gray and burgundy with a certain discreet elegance. The place has chic to spare with its banquettes and nooks. The beautiful hostess sets the quietly convivial tone and now the cuisine reflects the ambience perfectly. The sea bream, tuna and salmon tartare, langoustine cakes served with fresh young leeks, the Noirmoutier sole simply served meunière style, the bream in banana leaf, lobster in cassolette with spring vegetables and the enormous Zanzibar baba with vanilla-infused cream, sprinkled with artisanal rum (a masterpiece of the genre, easily enough for two or three,) all have an easy appeal. The prices take no prisoners, but do reflect the quality.

● La Cour Jardin Ⓝ ◯ V.COM

At the Plaza Athénée, 25, av Montaigne.
Métro: Alma-Marceau.
Tel. 01 53 67 66 02.
Closed mid-Sept.–mid-May.
A la carte: 90€.

The secret Parisian treasure of the Ducasse Group? The patio at the Plaza, with its ivy covered walls, young, enthusiastic dining room staff and Cédric Bechade's marvelously lyrical cuisine. Paella-style risotto, slow-cooked monkfish in its sauce, sardines in tomato sauce and marinated assorted raw vegetables are delightful "in the style of . . ." dishes. Then poached egg in aspic with pepper sauté and onion jus and turbot with salsa verde are a nod to the Basque country, suggesting that the chef, who trained at the Biarritz Palais, has left his heart somewhere between Bayonne and Hendaye. The red mullet with gnocchi in cheese sauce and the admirable desserts (chocolate raspberries or cherries refreshed with almond milk granita and pain perdu) are refined confections indeed. We help all this along with a thoroughbred Fessy Brouilly or Grisard Mondeuse, thinking that life in avenue Montaigne may not be so dull after all.

● Les Saveurs de Flora ◯ V.COM

36, av George-V.
Métro: George-V.
Tel. 01 40 70 10 49. Fax 01 47 20 52 87.
www.lessaveursdeflora.com
Closed Sat. lunch, Sun.,
1 week Feb., 3 weeks Aug.
Prix fixe: 28€ (lunch), 38€, 65€.
A la carte: 80€.

Flora Mikula prepares well-bred, contemporary dishes in these elegant surroundings. Having worked with Alain Passard for a number of years, she shares this philosophy and passion for authenticity with him. The flavors of the lobster spring roll with coriander are underlined by puréed mango and avocado sorbet, the sole stuffed with gray shrimp is accentuated by orange and coriander and served on angelhair pasta, the veal chop seasoned with garlic and rosemary grows more tender and expressive still when accompanied by the spelt risotto seasoned with parmesan. The desserts are small miracles, like the strawberry spring rolls soaked in a mint strawberry sauce.

● Chez Catherine ◯ V.COM

3, rue Berryer.
Métro: St-Philippe-du-Roule, George-V.
Tel. 01 40 76 01 40. Fax 01 40 76 03 96
Closed Sat., Sun., Bank Holidays, New Year's, 1 week beg. May, 3 weeks Aug.
Prix fixe: 40€ (lunch), 45€ (lunch), 50€ (dinner), 65€ (dinner).
A la carte: 75€.

Catherine Guerraz remains true to form. She seems to delight in coming up with new dishes that surprise the most loyal of her regulars with their explosive flavors. Her langoustine and tarragon ravioli with shellfish broth are prepared just so, her minced catfish with a savory/sweet sauce, citrus vinaigrette and mango spaghetti takes your breath away and the smoothness of veal sweetbreads and duck foie gras with asparagus and morel mushrooms leaves you rooted to the spot. The desserts, too, are audacious to a fault, as shown by soft chocolate bonbon and praline ice cream with chocolate mint sauce. The check is on the heavy side, but not exaggeratedly so, thanks to the set prix fixe option and the wines by the glass selected by Frédéric and the young Cyril Denonfoux.

● **Clovis** ◎ V.COM

At the Sofitel Paris-Arc de Triomphe, 14, rue Beaujon.
Métro: Charles-de-Gaulle–Etoile.
Tel. 01 53 89 50 53. Fax 01 53 89 50 51
h1296@accor-hotels.com
Closed Sat., Sun., Bank Holidays, Christmas–New Year's, Aug.
Prix fixe: 39€ (lunch), 85€ (dinner).
A la carte: 80–90€.

How boring this place would be if François Rodolphe were not here to give it color and taste. Mango and sweet citrus marinade prettily grace the fried langoustines, pistou (the traditional Provençal garlic and vegetable soup) brightens steamed sole with herbs and a vegetable tagine, with dates and lemon confit with rosemary, charmingly "orientalizes" lamb from Paulliac. The house baba au rhum and mango and pineapple marinated with lime and coconut milk provide a marvelous conclusion. Olivier Pellier's recommendations are welcome when choosing the wine. The lunchtime set prix fixe is a bonus.

● **Le Copenhague** ◎ V.COM

142, av des Champs-Elysées.
Métro: Charles-de-Gaulle–Etoile, George-V.
Tel. 01 44 13 86 26. Fax 01 44 13 89 44.
floradanica@wanadoo.fr
www.restaurantfloradanica.com
Closed Sat., Sun., Bank Holidays, 3 weeks Aug.
Prix fixe: 51€ (lunch), 70€ (lunch), 110€ (dinner). A la carte: 100€.

As we know, consuls are not always nationals of the countries they represent, and the Ambassador of the Kingdom of Denmark should confer this honor on Georges Landriot, who has turned this eatery into an academy of authentic Danish cuisine. His Danish-style foie gras poached in beer would bring a smile to the lips of the little mermaid, and Andersen would have loved lightly salted cod with a clam foam and glazed cucumbers. Her Majesty Marguerite II herself would appreciate the refined execution of the reindeer medallions with a red wine sauce and Danish-style croustillant filled with speck. Then the crown princes, the future Frederik X and his brother Joachim, would readily share in aquavit-soaked baba, caramelized pineapple and vanilla whipped cream. The check is princely too, but we have no regrets, especially when the weather is good enough for us to dine on the landscaped terrace.

● **Garnier** ◎ V.COM

111, rue Saint-Lazare.
Métro: St-Lazare.
Tel. 01 43 87 50 40. Fax 01 40 08 06 93.
Closed end July–end Aug.
Prix fixe: 30€. A la carte: 55–90€.

Seafood tops the bill in this fine restaurant, whose great attraction is the wood and mirror décor designed by Dominique Honnet. The impeccably fresh shellfish buffet is also an incentive, as are the whole lobster salad with balsamic vinegar and light spiced tomato sauce, cod filet with basil minestrone and Dover sole pan fried in butter and seasoned with parsley and lemon accompanied simply by small potatoes, all prepared with precision and creativity by Ludovic Schwartz. The desserts, such as puff pastry with egg-based chocolate sauce, are in excellent taste.

● **W** ◎ V.COM

At the Warwick, 5, rue de Berri.
Métro: George-V.
Tel. 01 45 61 82 08. Fax 01 45 63 75 81.
www.warwickhotels.com
Closed Sat., Sun., Bank Holidays, Aug.
Prix fixe: 49€. A la carte: 75–85€.

This luxury hotel has a restaurant with a fully justified reputation. Orchestrated by Christophe Moisand (who also officiates at Le Céladon), the prix fixe set to music by disciple Frédéric Lesourd is full of attractions. It is original without straying into excess and meticulously executed. The red tuna seasoned with parmesan sauce and picholine olives, red mullet with stuffed vegetables served with grilled eggplant or pan-fried lamb with basil crust and garlic herb-seasoned reduction sauce make an excellent impression. The desserts are in the same vein, especially frozen crunchy Guanaja chocolate with an accompaniment of sautéed rhubarb. Excellent service and a peaceful ambiance, perfect for a business meal.

● Brasserie Lorraine   V.COM

2-4, pl. des Ternes.
Métro: Ternes.
Tel. 01 56 21 22 00. Fax 01 56 21 22 09.
lorraine@blanc.net
Open daily, cont. serv.
A la carte: 60€.

Open again after being completely restored, this traditional brasserie, now run by the Blanc group, welcomes Parisian society and local customers. All appreciate the neo-fifties décor, original mosaics and crystal chandeliers. The shellfish buffet is impressive, but guests can also enjoy traditional fare, such as foie gras and Montbazilliac aspic, sole meunière served with steamed potatoes and the grilled lamb cutlets with green beans, while the Paris-Brest meets with unanimous approval. The large terrace is an attraction when the sun shines.

● Le Fouquet's   🎀 V.COM

99, av des Champs-Elysées.
Métro: George-V.
Tel. 01 47 23 50 00. Fax 01 47 23 60 02.
evigoureux@lucienbarriere.com
www.lucienbarriere.com
Open daily .
Prix fixe: 78€. A la carte: 75€.

Eating here is no longer the gamble it once was, thanks to Jean-Yves Leuranguer, winner of the Meilleur Ouvrier de France award. Avoiding facile solutions, this seasoned pro—a veteran of the Martinez—serves up classic dishes that are not necessarily devoid of a modern touch. There can be no objections to lobster ravioli, marbled foie gras terrine with spiced wine, crayfish tail in scented aspic and roasted veal chops to share. The light mille-feuille goes down well, too. The prices are still very steep, but the service has improved considerably.

● Annapurna   V.COM

32, rue de Berri.
Métro: Franklin-D.-Roosevelt, George-V.
Tel. 01 45 63 91 56. Fax 01 40 20 03 80.
Closed Sat. lunch and Sun. (exc. mid-July–mid-Sept.).
Prix fixe: 24€ (lunch), 27€. A la carte: 50€.

Northern India has its embassy here. The traditional chicken tikka, shrimp biryani, Annapurna lamb curry and the famous kulfi (frozen pistachio dessert) cannot be faulted. The service is wonderfully friendly and the check—with tea or a lassi rather than wine—is reasonable.

● Diep   V.COM

55, rue Pierre-Charron / 22 rue Ponthieu.
Métro: Franklin-D.-Roosevelt.
Tel. 01 45 63 52 76 / 01 42 56 23 96.
www.diep.fr
Prix fixe: 84€ (for 2). A la carte: 60€.

Two restaurants, two chefs and the same menu (more or less). In any case, definitely the same family (the Dieps) and spirit. Spring rolls, garlic- and pepper-seasoned shrimp, lemongrass-seasoned Atlantic sea bass, lacquered chicken in two services as well as the pepper-seasoned house sirloin steak delight well-heeled guests who are ready to pay the price for quality cuisine and thoughtful service.

● Café Faubourg   ○ COM

At the Faubourg Sofitel,
15, rue Boissy-d'Anglas.
Métro: Concorde.

Tel. 01 44 94 14 14. Fax 01 44 94 14 28.
h1295@accor-hotels.com / www.sofitel.com
Closed Sat. lunch, Sun. lunch, 3 weeks Aug.
A la carte: 70€.

It is good for a hotel of this class to have a restaurant giving such a good image of contemporary French cuisine. Jérôme Videau has put together a prix fixe that changes with the seasons and often has the flavor of the South of France. The crab mille-feuille, red mullet served with a vegetable medley with garlic and pesto sauce and beef strip loin with olive-seasoned mashed potatoes are fine concoctions. Then for dessert we enjoy a classic layered pastry from Gascony served with Armagnac-flavored ice cream, reminding us that the chef worked with Alain Dutournier. A very warm welcome and highly conscientious service.

● La Table du Lancaster   ○COM
At the Lancaster, 7, rue de Berri.
Métro: George-V.
Tel. 01 40 76 40 76. Fax 01 40 76 40 00.
restaurant@hotel-lancaster.fr
www.hotel-lancaster.fr
Closed Sat. lunch, Sun. lunch,
Bank Holidays, Aug.
Prix fixe: 60€ (lunch), 120€.
A la carte: 110€.

Michel Troisgros has made this hotel restaurant into his Paris laboratory. The Master of Roanne has turned his hand to "slow food" with a 300% success rate. He creates and directs, leaving the execution to Fabrice Salvador. The goat cheese cannelloni with olive oil, cod broth with koshi-hikari rice and the glazed suckling pig with green mango salad offer proof of Troisgros' innovative spirit and Salvador's skills. We end on a high note with the light cappuccino truffle, then burn our fingers on the check. The chic bijou décor has a great deal of charm. So much originality and quality are priceless. The service is perfect.

● Hôtel de Sers   ⓃCOM
41, av Pierre-1-de-Serbie.
Métro: George-V, Tel. 01 53 23 75 75.
www.hoteldesers.com
A la carte: 60€.

Contemporary but quite at home in its 19th-century setting, this elegant, modern, discreet designer hotel in the heart of the Paris Golden Triangle also has a good eatery, which doubles as a bar and lounge, and serves voguish light dishes and delicacies. Tuna tartare, scallop carpaccio, veal T-bone steak and tender slow-cooked lamb shank are very successful. Chef Rémy Delbart (who trained with Alain Dutournier) and Eric Briffard must be talented indeed to work effectively in such a small space. Visitors can also snack on a club sandwich or enjoy a cocktail, depending on the hour and their fancy.

● L'Avenue   COM
41, av Montaigne
Métro: Alma-Marceau, Franklin-D.-Roosevelt
Tel. 01 40 70 14 91. Fax 01 40 70 91 97.
A la carte: 70€.

This contemporary brasserie is expensive and snobbish, but still popular with a clientele that frequents the avenue's luxury stores or RTL and Europe 1 broadcasting. The crab mille-feuille, the cod "hakkasan" (silver cod with champagne and roasted honey) and the mandarina crispy duck (a variation on Peking duck) set the tone. A plus mark for the six (really) small macarons to share. The service is excellent.

● 1728   COM
8, rue d'Anjou.
Métro: Concorde, Madeleine.
Tel. 01 40 17 04 77. Fax 01 42 65 53 87.
restaurant1728@wanadoo.fr
www.restaurant-1728.com
Closed Sat. lunch, Sun.,
1 week Christmas–New Year's, Aug.
A la carte: 70€.

This 18th-century town house has been converted into a charming restaurant by Yang Lining, a world class cithara player. The woodwork, period furniture, tapestries and antique paintings set the tone of the décor and the cuisine charms. Yannick Quéré makes a rather good job of the "Thai desire" (strips of sea bream, kippers and squid), "West coast/East coast"(grilled scallop medallions in a froth of curry sauce), the "Chinese crystal" (chicken in banana leaves) and the creamy cocoa truffle in praline-encrusted puff pastry with hot pistachio sauce.

● Senso   COM

16, rue de La Tremoille.
Métro: Alma-Marceau, Franklin-D.-Roosevelt.
Tel. 01 56 52 14 14. Fax 01 56 52 14 13.
senso@hotel-tremoille.com
www.hotel-tremoille.com
Closed Sat. lunch, Sun.
Prix fixe: 32€ (lunch, wine inc.),
39€ (lunch, wine inc.). A la carte: 70€.

This restaurant is a mystery. Depending on what you choose, you get a masterpiece or a mockery. Frédéric Duca is still searching for his individual style and sometimes gets lost. "Limp" grilled jumbo shrimp, but a John Dory fish served with superbly cooked green gnocchi; saddle of rabbit with chard that is not bad at all, but which comes with a sticky parmesan polenta. The licorice soufflé is a great achievement. Everything is in contrast here, even the prices.

● Stella Maris   COM

4, rue Arsène-Houssaye.
Métro: Charles-de-Gaulle–Etoile.
Tel. 01 42 89 16 22. Fax 01 42 89 16 01
stella.maris.paris@wanadoo.fr
www.tateruyoshino.com /www.
stellemarisparis.com
Closed Sat. lunch, Sun., 1 week mid-Aug.
Prix fixe: 43€ (lunch), 53€ (lunch), 85€,
130€. A la carte: 110€.

Tateru Yoshino could have made his fortune in the Land of the Rising Sun, but instead chose to set up in the land of his masters: Troigros, Senderens and Robuchon. Regular customers shower praise on his very French cuisine, mischievously revised in the Japanese manner. They appreciate its originality and lightness. The langoustine ravioli with fish and shellfish couscous and the rabbit tourte with green pea purée are irresistibly charming. For dessert, Traou Mad (a

Breton shortcake biscuit) with rhubarb compote, accompanied by a strawberry sauce and fromage-blanc ice cream, combines Celtic charm with more exotic Japanese notes. Michiko Yoshino's welcome is simply delicious, and although the food cannot be described as cheap, there are no regrets, for this establishment has a pleasantly outlandish feel to it.

● Tante Louise   COM

41, rue Boissy-d'Anglas.
Métro: Madeleine, Concorde.
Tel. 01 42 65 06 85. Fax 01 42 65 28 19.
tantelouise@bernard-loiseau.com
www.bernard-loiseau.com
Closed Sat., Sun., bank holidays, Aug.
Prix fixe: 34€ (lunch), 40€ (dinner).
A la carte: 65€.

Bernard Loiseau's first Parisian establishment with its fine, restyled thirties décor deserves unqualified praise. Pan-seared escalope of foie gras, perfectly cooked Atlantic sea bass served with green asparagus and olive oil sauce with condiments or the rosemary-seasoned roasted lamb saddle are very much in the spirit of the house. The soft-centered Guanaja chocolate cake and the variations on the theme of amerena cherries will bowl you over. The à la carte tab is not cheap, but you can get off more lightly with a set menu, especially if you choose wine by the glass.

● L'Angle du Faubourg

195, rue du Faubourg-Saint-Honoré.
Métro: Charles-de-Gaulle–Etoile,
George-V, Ternes.
Tel. 01 40 74 20 20. Fax 01 40 74 20 21.
angledufaubourg@cavestaillevent.com
www.taillevent.com
Closed Sat., Sun., Aug.
Prix fixe: 35€, 70€ (dinner).
A la carte: 80€.

This second establishment established by Jean-Claude Vrinat (of Taillevent) is a success. Its contemporary setting is a little noisy—especially at lunchtime—but full of light, and it offers vigorous dishes by Laurent Poitevin, who learned his trade with Michel Del Burgo. A sober technician with skills beyond his years, he enables seasonal produce to express itself to the full. Who could resist the onion ravioli with bluefin tuna conserve and creamy artichoke sauce, slow-cooked cod with romaine lettuce cream and avruga caviar and pan-fried foie gras seasoned with Banyuls wine? Then the soft wild strawberry macaron will sweep you off your feet. Marianne Delhomme, the charming sommelier, will help you choose the right wine for each dish. Finally, Fernando Rocha is the kind of dining room manager we should see more often.

● **Dominique Bouchet**

11, rue Treilhard.
Métro: Miromesnil, Villiers.
Tel. 01 45 61 09 46. Fax 01 42 89 11 14.
www.dominique-bouchet.com
Closed Sat., Sun., Bank Holidays,
1 week Feb., Aug.
A la carte: 70€.

This restaurant is small in size, but stands tall in terms of quality. Dominique Bouchet, who was an assiduous pupil of Joël Robuchon before leaving the nest to manage the kitchen of Les Ambassadeurs, has imagination to spare. The produce is fresh and carefully selected, the execution extraordinarily precise and each preparation is a miniature masterpiece. The petit crab charlotte with basil-seasoned tomatoes is exquisitely simple, pasta with lobster and mushroom purée and reduction sauce is worth the visit in itself and grilled brioche-breaded pig's feet cakes napped with truffle reduction sauce can safely be called a great dish. The eclair "Sao-Tomé" (chocolate ganache with black cherry and cocoa ice cream) is a giddying treat. The service is discreetly tasteful, and shrewd sommelier Michaël Cives presents wines by the glass, enabling us to keep the damage down to a manageable sum.

● **Citrus Etoile**

6, rue Arsène-Houssaye.
Métro: Charles-de-Gaulle–Etoile.
Tel. 01 42 89 15 51. Fax 01 42 89 28 67
info@citrusetoile.fr / www.citrusetoile.fr

Closed Sat. lunch, Sun., Bank Holidays,
2 weeks Aug.
A la carte: 60€.

Gilles Epié has made his Paris comeback just a step away from the Arc de Triomphe. Although the dining room is run by his sparkling Californian wife, Elizabeth, he often leaves the kitchen to liven things up a little, moving from table to table and explaining how he works. He has a fertile imagination and produces dishes that are hard to resist. The scallops served on the half shell, prime oysters with white Landais asparagus and grilled tuna with foie gras are works of precision. The coconut ice cream beignets are simply beguiling. Jean-François Marteil oversees the cellar and provides intelligent advice. The prices are in no way excessive, and if you really want to get a table here, a word of advice: Reserve.

● **Marius et Janette**

4, av George-V.
Métro: George-V, Alma-Marceau.
Tel. 01 47 23 41 88. Fax 01 47 23 07 19
Prix fixe: 46€ (lunch, wine inc.), 48€.

Bernard Pinaud is a master of seafood. He does not just cook it to perfection, he seems to change its very nature to serve it with all its freshness and authentic flavor intact. The crunchy fried langoustines, the splendid tuna carpaccio and the fried whiting with tartar sauce, as well as the simple grilled line-caught sea bass all offer confirmation of his skills. The vanilla mille-feuille is a paradigm of sweetness (but not excessively so). The welcome on board this luxury yacht of a bistro is excellent and the service impeccable and urbane. The prices are high, but justifiably so. The wine list is short but has some interesting items.

● **Market**

15, av Matignon.
Métro: Champs-Elysées–Clemenceau,
Franklin-D.-Roosevelt.
Tel. 01 56 43 40 90. Fax 01 43 59 10 87.
prmarketsa@aol.com / www.jean-georges.com
Prix fixe: 34€ (lunch). A la carte: 100€.

New York superstar Jean-George Vongerichten's Paris restaurant is entertaining. The beautiful people that flock there do not look out of place against the Christian Liaigre décor. The dining room staff led by Eric Précigoux and Sylvain Bonnafé is first rate and their comments on the menu will make your mouth water. The "black plateî (brochettes, crispy fried crab, tuna roll, lobster with daikon radish, spicy quail) is a must, but in the kitchen, Wim Van Gorp has more than one string to his bow. His paprikaspiced cod served with potato ravioli and the pepper-seasoned grilled rib-eye served with marinated cucumbers and asparagus are enchanting dishes. For dessert, coconut panna cotta, marinated passion fruit and lychee and green apple sorbet slip down refreshingly. Brunch on the weekend.

● Le Stresa   COM

7, rue Chambiges.
Métro: Alma-Marceau.
Tel. 01 47 23 51 62.
Closed Sat., Sun., vac. Christmas, Aug.
A la carte: 100€.

You can't get anything for 100 right now, except at the Faiola brothers' 1950s-style restaurant. With Tony in the dining room and Marco at the stove, you are transported to the southernmost part of Italy. The clientele is a melting pot of gourmets. Feast on the stuffed zucchini blossoms, pâte feuilletée pizzas, spaghetti carbonara, a white truffle risotto (in season, will melt in your mouth), olive oil- and lemon-seasoned sole, beef filet César or the nougat cake. The best of the wines from across the Alps are on the menu. And the Antinori Peppoli is great by itself.

● Au Fin Bec

7, rue Roy.
Métro: St-Augustin, Miromesnil.
Tel.-Fax 01 45 22 22 46.
Closed Sat., Sun., 1 week Christmas–New Year's, 3 weeks Aug.
Prix fixe: 34€ (wine inc.). A la carte: 55€.

In this twenties Parisian bistro, Daniel Niveau continues to delight a clientele of regulars who are warmly welcomed by Marie-Claude Mousty. We simply savor the seasonal salad with crayfish tails and foie gras medallions, mixed sauté of sole, sea bass, scallops and jumbo shrimp, veal cutlet with oyster mushrooms and, finally, tarte Tatin.

● Mollard

115, rue Saint-Lazare.
Métro: St-Lazare.
Tel. 01 43 87 50 22. Fax 01 43 87 84 17.
espace.clients@mollard.fr / www.mollard.fr
Prix fixe: 39,50€ (wine inc.), 51€.
A la carte: 52–75€.

Edouard Niermans' art nouveau décor and the listed Sarreguemines ceramics and frescos are certainly impressive, but we have also come to enjoy Joël Prodhomme's first-rate French cuisine. The scallop carpaccio with coriander vinaigrette, classic Mediterranean rockfish bouillabaisse, veal kidneys flambéed with Cognac and the house dessert omelet flambéed with Grand Marnier are exquisitely timeless.

● Kinugawa   ○ COM

4, rue Saint-Philippe-du-Roule.
Métro: St-Philippe-du-Roule, Champs-Elysées–Clemenceau, Franklin-D.-Roosevelt.
Tel. 01 45 63 08 07. Fax 01 42 60 57 36
Closed Sat. lunch, Sun., Christmas–New Year's.
Prix fixe: 32€ (lunch), 75€. A la carte: 75€.

This is one of the fashionable Japanese restaurants between the Champs-Elysées and Opéra. The décor is Zen, the dining room team a little less so and the customers not at all when they get the tab. At lunchtime, patrons vie to order their bento boxes as fast as possible. Things are quieter in the evening, when customers enjoy the sushi bar (on the first floor), the sashimi and the makis or sakamushis (fish filet or shellfish braised in sake), unless they are set on meat, in which case they can choose between the thinly sliced beef and vegetables cooked in broth and seared beef with teriyaki sauce.

● A L'Abordage   N ⛵ SIM

2, pl Henri-Bergson.
Métro: St-Augustin.
Tel. 01 45 22 15 49.
Closed dinner (exc. Wed.), Sat., Sun.,
end July–end Aug.
A la carte: 35–40€.

It looks like just another corner café and terrace behind Saint Augustine's church. But it's a rendezvous for gourmets (often famous chefs, who come to play cards after work) and the blackboard displaying the day's dishes. Bernard Fontenille serves up impeccable chow made with fresh produce prepared at its best in a tasteful, "club" atmosphere. A good country-style pork terrine, fresh salmon tartare, superb boneless rib-eye steak, Paris-Brest, crème brûlée or (splendid) baba au rhum washed down with Foillard Morgon. But hush! Let's keep this private haunt our secret.

● L'Arôme   N ⛵ SIM

3, rue Saint-Philippe-du-Roule.
Métro: St-Philippe-du-Roule, Champs-
Elysées-Clemenceau.
Tel. 01 42 25 55 98.
Closed Sun.
Prix fixe: 28€ (lunch), 33€ (lunch).
A la carte: 45€.

Formerly in the dining room at Hélène Darroze's and the Bristol, Eric Martins enjoyed critical acclaim and more at L'Ami Marcel. Now he has opened a first-class, cozy, entertaining, voguish bistro. Presiding over the stoves is Bordeaux's Pascal Bataillé, a veteran chef who previously worked at Lloyd's Bar and L'Estaminet Gaya. His cuisine is spirited and his fall fare (pumpkin soup, Iberian ham, the oxtail and cheek rillettes, duck with risotto, Armagnac-soaked prune beignets with licorice ice cream) was looking good at the opening. Let's hope it lasts.

● Bocconi   🏠 ⛵ SIM

10, bis, rue d'Artois.
Métro: St-Philippe-du-Roule.
Tel. 01 53 76 44 44. Fax 01 45 61 10 08.
Closed Sat. lunch, Sun.
A la carte : 40-60€.

We are fond of Ciro Polge's trattoria with its casual ambiance and contemporary décor, and enjoy the fine ideas presented by this native of Bergame, a Petrini veteran, who grasps the subtleties of a cuisine that others frequently turn into a travesty. Grilled vegetables with ricotta, fried squid, jumbo shrimp and vegetables, osso bucco and tiramisu vie honorably with the flawless pasta (linguine with clam sauce, penne arrabiata). The wines by the glass are superb and white truffles are sold at saintly prices in season.

● Chez André   🏠 SIM

12, rue Marbeuf
Métro: Franklin-D.-Roosevelt
Tel. 01 47 20 59 57. Fax 01 47 20 18 82
restaurant@chez-andre.com
www.rest-gj.com
Open daily. Cont. service.
Prix fixe: 32€, 9,50€ (child).
A la carte 50€.

In this bistro, whose faux thirties style delights Americans, René Ambanelli serves Burgundian snails served in the shell with garlic and herb butter, frog legs sautéed with garlic and half a roasted chicken with tarragon reduction sauce, which all work their casual charm, as do the dark chocolate quenelles with orange zest.

● Les Gourmets des Ternes   🏠 SIM

87, bd de Courcelles.
Métro: Ternes, Courcelles.
Tel. 01 42 27 43 04.
Closed Sat., Sun.,
10 days Christmas–New Year's, Aug.
A la carte: 55€.

Jean-Francois Marie is keeping this fine Parisian bistro in the family. Supervised by the meticulous Dat Hunguyen, the cuisine is well made, traditional and quintessentially French. Artichoke hearts in vinaigrette, white asparagus with goose foie gras, Dover sole pan fried in butter and seasoned with parsley and lemon, grilled beefsteak served with marrow and baba au rhum will entice you back here.

● Royal Madeleine 🍴 SIM

11, rue du Chevalier-Saint-Georges.
Métro: Madeleine, Concorde.
Tel. 01 42 60 14 36.
royal.madeleine@wanadoo.fr
www.royalmadeleine.com
Closed 1 week Jan., Aug.
A la carte: 60€.

An inconspicuous little street, an equally unobtrusive 1900s-style bistro with a classic, seasonal prix fixe: This is the package presented by Laurent Couegnas, who also owns L'Escargot Montorgueil. Foie gras, sole cooked to your taste, simmered sweetbread cassoulet with mild vinegar sauce and warm profiterole of the day with hot chocolate sauce are prepared by Valérie Paget to the delight of Carole Colin's guests. Uncompromising prices.

● Savy 🍴 SIM

23, rue Bayard.
Métro: Franklin-D.-Roosevelt.
Tel. 01 47 23 46 98. Fax 01 47 23 32 05.
Closed Sat., Sun., Bank Holidays, Aug.
Prix fixe: 23,50€ (lunch), 28,50€ (dinner).
A la carte: 40€.

Located just opposite RTL broadcasting, this old-fashioned bistro has always been used as a stylish refectory by the journalists and advertising people who work nearby. Lionel Dégoulange regales his guests with green Puy lentils with vinaigrette, grilled rib-eye steak with marrow and seasonal fruit tarts. The Saint-Nectaire cheese is superb. Prompt service, and the prices are not excessive.

PARIS 9TH ARR

■ HOTELS

■ Ambassador 🏨

16, bd Haussmann.
Métro: Chaussée-d'Antin-La Fayette,
Richelieu-Drouot.
Tel. 01 44 83 40 40. Fax 01 42 46 19 84.
www.hotelambassador-paris.com
294 rooms: 360–450€.
5 suites: 980€.

This Haussmann-era hotel has a vintage chic. Painted wood panels, crystal chandeliers, pink marble columns and Aubusson tapestries decorate the lobby. The rooms have been renovated neo-art deco style in red, blue and mauve. Bidders from the Drouot auction rooms are regulars here. A spirited restaurant.

■ Le Pavillon de Paris

7, rue de Parme.
Métro: Place-de-Clichy.
Tel. 01 55 31 60 00. Fax 01 55 31 60 01.
www.pavillonparis.com
30 rooms: 140–203€.

Between the Europe and Nouvelle Athènes districts, this quiet hotel offers minimalist, contemporary rooms. The hushed ambiance is an incitement to relaxation.

■ Mercure Opéra Lafayette 🏨

49, rue La Fayette.
Métro: Le Peletier, Cadet.
Tel. 01 42 85 05 44. Fax 01 49 95 06 60.
h2802@accor.com / www.accorhotels.com
96 rooms: 99–199€. 5 suites: 180–280€.

This luxurious establishment with its toile de Jouy fabrics is strategically situated between the Grands Boulevards, the Bourse and the Opéra. A bar and small lounge for meetings, and breakfast in the winter garden.

■ Libertel Opéra Franklin 🏨

19, rue Buffault.
Métro: Le Peletier, Cadet.
Tel. 01 42 80 27 27. Fax 01 48 78 13 04.
info@operafranklin.com
www.operafranklin.com
67 rooms: 139–208€.

Wrought-iron, brass and a wall fresco showing a garden in full perspective set the tone in this classic hostelry. Refurbished in red, green and white, the rooms are equipped with Empire or modern furniture.

■ Lorette Opéra

36, rue Notre-Dame-de-Lorette.
Métro: St-Georges.

Tel. 01 42 85 18 81. Fax 01 42 81 32 19.
www.astotel.com/hotel.laurette@astotel.com
84 rooms: 129–300€.

In the heart of the Nouvelle Athènes district, this contemporary hotel with its 19th-century facade has a trim elegance. The standard rooms are neat and unfussy. The passages, lobby and bar with their designer lighting and refined furniture are chic indeed and breakfast is served in a fine, vaulted cellar.

■ Les Trois Poussins

15, rue Clauzel.
Métro: St-Georges.
Tel. 01 53 32 81 81. Fax 01 53 32 81 82.
h3p@les3poussins.com / www.les3poussins.com
29 rooms: 139–222€.

The rooms in this discreet hotel have been refurbished in a convivial style and equipped with modern furniture. Those on the top floor have a view over Paris.

■ Hôtel Amour

8, rue Navarin.
Métro: Notre-Dame-de-Lorette.
Tel. 01 48 78 31 80.
20 rooms: 90–120€.
A la carte: 35€.

Entertaining, pleasant and signed Costes. The brothers' latest coup in the heart of Nouvelle Athènes, this offbeat tribute to the Pigalle hotels of yesteryear is a great success. We like the spruce rooms, amusing décor and photos of contemporary artists in the passages. The restaurant dining room is well planned with its "scrap" style furniture and patio, giving guests the impression they are eating in the country opposite an ivy clad wall. Bistro cuisine.

● RESTAURANTS

● Les Muses

At the Scribe, 1, rue Scribe.
Métro: Opéra, Madeleine.
Tel. 01 44 71 24 26. Fax 01 44 71 24 64.
h0663-re@accord.com / www.accorhotels.com
Closed Sat., Sun., Bank Holidays,

1 week Christmas–New Year's, Aug.
Prix fixe: 45€ (lunch), 75€, 95€.
A la carte: 70–85€.

This chic hotel restaurant, windowless, is in the basement, but the tables are widely spaced and very well set, the service is impeccable and the sommelier a master of his art. Then the food prepared by Franck Charpentier from W, is subtle, precise and polished. His dishes are attractive, good, technically accomplished and shrewd, and exert an effortless charm. We like the Tudy Island oysters with greens and lemon seawater foam, his parmentier fumé (smoked country-style bacon with mashed potatoes and truffles) as well as pan-seared scallops with crisp beef and foie gras–filled pastry served with celery root ravioli. The meats (Vendée pigeon served with a small covered dish of simmered vegetables or pork belly with Colonnata lard, served with truffle and foie gras ravioli) are frankly inspiring. The desserts (spiced pumpkin waffle and a coffee cream infusion) are equally refined.

● Café de la Paix

2, rue Scribe.
Métro: Opéra.
Tel. 01 40 07 36 36. Fax 01 40 07 36 13.
legrand@ichotelsgroup.com
www.paris.intercontinental.com
Prix fixe: 45€ (lunch), 85€ (dinner on weekdays). A la carte: 65€.

Young winner of the Meilleur Ouvrier de France award Laurent Delarbre has added gourmet color to this monument of the Paris brasserie world renovated a few seasons ago. The stucco, moldings and Garnier frescoes have remained. The cuisine, initially a little bland, has found its feet. Crispy pork trotters, traditional-style borsch, fresh duck foie gras, lamb chops served with its jus, veal belly with risotto and a light and gauzy mille-feuille dessert now offer evidence of dazzling skill. A fine choice of wines with world vintages available by the glass.

● **Charlot Roi des Coquillages** V.COM

12, pl de Clichy.
Métro: Place-de-Clichy.
Tel. 01 53 20 48 00. Fax 01 53 20 48 09.
de.charlot@blanc.net / www.charlot-paris.com
Prix fixe: 19,50€ (lunch), 25€ (lunch, wine inc.). A la carte: 75€.

We would like a new décor, a more exciting wine list and more attentive service. Yet with oysters, bouillabaisse and Grand Marnier soufflé served opposite the bay window looking out on place Clichy we still enjoy eating in this seafood restaurant. This year, we have no complaints about the terrine of red mullet, monkfish carpaccio seasoned with ginger and lime, sea bream in salt crust or the filet of Dover sole meunière reliably prepared by chef Elvis Carcel.

● **Le Pétrelle**   ○ COM

34, rue Pétrelle.
Métro: Anvers, Poissonnière.
Tel. 01 42 82 11 02. Fax 01 40 23 05 69.
Closed lunch, Sun., Mon., Christmas–New Year's, mid-July–mid-Aug. Open until 10 PM.
Prix fixe: 27€ (dinner). A la carte: 60€.

This restaurant only opens in the evening, serves a cuisine dear to its heart and has dreamt up a décor all its own: a romantic library style with fine bouquets, shelves of books and choice linen. Jean-Luc André, an almost wholly self-taught native of the Ardèche who has opened Les Vivres, a bistro and grocery store open from noon to 7 p.m., just next door, is a charming loner. The menu is intelligent, the dishes are market produce-based, lively, fresh and light, and the cuisine is cheerfully kitchen garden, all added attractions. Dishes include the white asparagus and morel mushroom fricassée, marinated baby artichokes served with chervil root chips, scallops and truffles in season, line-caught sea bass roasted with sea salt and crispy herbs and leg of lamb with fava beans, seasoned with thyme and lemon. The desserts (slowly cooked rhubarb with wild strawberries and dark chocolate cake) are delightful.

● **16 Haussmann**   🏠🍴 COM

At L'Ambassador, 16, bd Haussmann.
Métro: Richelieu-Drouot, Chaussée-d'Antin–La Fayette.
Tel. 01 48 00 06 38. Fax 01 44 83 40 57.
16 haussmann@concorde-hotels.com
www.hotelambassador-paris.com
Closed Sat. lunch, Sun.,
3 weeks Aug. Open until 10:30 PM.
Prix fixe: 28€, 32€.

Michel Hache, who used to work with Senderens, has never disappointed us with his set menu, considerably kept down to 32€. The place is worth seeing with its modern décor, cheerful coloring in shades of blue, fine woodwork and Starckian chairs. His cuisine, consistent, subtle and fresh, wins converts to its cause with its crab and crayfish with celeri rémoulade, a mushroom salad with purslane, the roasted sea bass with asparagus and the sole cooked in salted butter. The fraîcheur (a dessert of fresh strawberry, lychees and chocolate) fully deserves its name.

● **Romain**   🏠○ COM

40, rue Saint-Georges.
Métro: St-Georges, Nôtre-Dame-de-Lorette.
Tel. 01 48 24 58 94. Fax 01 42 47 09 75.
Closed Sun., Mon., 3 weeks Aug.
Prix fixe: 24€ (lunch), 26€ (lunch), 32€.
A la carte: 60€.

The Châteaubriant's Burcklis have brought their Lorjou and Carzou paintings and innate warmth from rue de Chabrol to this modern den in the Nouvelle Athènes quarter. Guy has lost none of his skill in the kitchen, as we discover when we taste his exceptional Milanese-style risotto made with saffron. Annick still brightens the dining room with her smile and natural charm. She is assisted there by her son Romain, who is in charge of the wines and has modernized the choice of house vintages from both sides of the Alps. The move has been successful: We have never eaten so well at their table. Eggplant lasagne and roasted sardines topped with mozzarella cheese, thin pizza made with a puff pastry crust, a duo of fried shrimp and calamari with tartar sauce, green and white angel hair pasta with a country tomato sauce with foie gras and the ham and squid ink risotto charm us with their generosity. The tiramisu, like the raspberry panna cotta with raspberry coulis, are wonderful concoctions and the 32€ menu is a fabulous bargain.

● La Table d'Anvers 🅿 🏠 COM

2, pl d'Anvers.
Métro: Anvers.
Tel. 01 48 78 35 21. Fax 01 45 26 66 67.
phiphi.colin@wanadoo.fr
www.latabledanvers.fr
Closed Sat. lunch, Sun., 1 week Christmas–New Year's, 2 weeks beg. Aug.
Prix fixe: 15€ (lunch, wine inc.),
23€ (lunch), 29€, 35€ (dinner, wine inc.).

Philippe Collin has the gift of ubiquity. This Girardet veteran who ran the refined Clos Juillet in Troyes manages to be present in both his Why Not in the seventeenth arrondissement and this, the former abode of the Conticinis, now in a modern bistro style. Philippe and his young team work their charm with roguish dishes offering both taste and accent. There is a veal and tuna tartare, pig's foot carpaccio served with a thick vinaigrette with shallots and herbs, the house rabbit terrine, a formidable calf's head with tongue served with mayonnaise, capers, herbs and hard-boiled egg, the classic andouillette de Troyes with champagne sauce, served with the house purée "Léa" (named after the chef's daughter). The wines by the glass (Chablis or Languedoc) are well chosen. The young maîtresse d' is charming and the desserts (soft chocolate cake with Carambar candy ice cream or Sarlat sour cherries and vanilla ice cream) take us back to our childhood.

● Carte Blanche 🏠 COM

6, rue Lamartine.
Métro: Cadet.
Tel. 01 48 78 12 20. Fax 01 48 78 12 21.
Closed Sat. lunch, Sun., Christmas, end July–mid-Aug.
Prix fixe: 25€, 28€, 35€, 38€.

Jean-Francois Renard, former chef at Beauvilliers, has joined forces with Claude Dupont, maître d' with Gagnaire. In a renovated rustic setting of stone walls and wooden tables, they offer a courteous welcome. The place settings and the appearance of the dishes are modish, but not excessively so. Suprising tins filled with tuna, salmon or sardines are as delicious as the presentation is innovative. Foie gras and veal trotter on toast, piquillo peppers stuffed with Basque sausage and Southern-style flatbread with onions and tuna and the sea bass cooked in a Portugese tagine are a success. All these dishes are included in a well-balanced set menu. The desserts are up to the same standard: a praline, chocolate and sour cherry croustillant or the caramel ginger moelleux served with tea cakes.

● Café Guitry 🍴 COM

At Théâtre Edouard VII, 10, pl Edouard-VII.
Métro: Madeleine, Opéra, Auber (RER).
Tel. 01 40 07 00 77. Fax 01 47 42 77 68
www.theatreedouard7.com
Closed Sun., Mon. dinner, 3 weeks Aug.
Prix fixe: 26€ (lunch), 32€. A la carte: 45€.

We like this theater restaurant and not only because of its Napoleon III surroundings, red walls, collection of black-and-white photos of actors and vintage advertising. Its cuisine, refined by chef Philippe Le Guen with intelligent advice from Andrée Zanat-Murat, author of cookbooks and wife of the manager, Bernard Murat, wields a ready charm. The shrimp salad with mango, coriander and lime, the tuna steak baked in a pepper crust served with ratatouille, the roasted cod filet with zucchini and a veal tagine with dried apricots and almonds and served with fine semolina are well done dishes. The rhubarb compote served with whipped mascarpone and strawberries slips down smoothly.

● A la Cloche d'Or 🍴 COM

3, rue Mansart.
Métro: Blanche.
Tel. 01 48 74 48 88. Fax 01 40 16 40 99.
Closed Sat. lunch, Sun., Aug.
Prix fixe: 17€ (lunch), 25€ (lunch), 29€ (lunch), 27€ (dinner). A la carte: 45€.

This restaurant with its rustic fifties charm does not serve as late as before, but still until one in the morning. The service is lively, the welcome friendly, the prices reasonable and the dishes reliably traditional. The foie gras in pastry, baked Camembert, salmon cooked skin-side down with roasted pine nuts, as well as the prime rib, duck confit, rack of lamb and hand-chopped beef tartare are hard to fault, and both the profiteroles and the authentic tarte Tatin slip down effortlessly.

● Au Petit Riche   🏠 COM

25, rue Le Peletier.
Métro: Richelieu-Drouot, Le Peletier.
Tel. 01 47 70 68 68. Fax 01 48 24 10 79.
aupetitriche@wanadoo.fr
www.aupetitriche.com
Closed Sun.
Prix fixe: 22,50€ (lunch), 25,50€, 29,50€,
11€ (child). A la carte: 55€.

Stucco ceilings, engraved glass, faux leather banquettes and lacquered walls: This circa 1880 institution still offers all the charm of Old Paris. The cuisine is in the same vein, playing on tradition and matching timeless dishes to Loire Valley wines. The pork belly confit served with lentils, the eggs baked in ramekins with foie gras, the pike-perch with beurre blanc, English-style poached haddock, a traditional roasted veal chop and calf's head served with a thick vinaigrette with shallots and herbs are all enjoyable. The vanilla mille-feuille is exquisite and the Paris-Brest delicious.

● Casa Olympe   ○ SIM

48, rue Saint-Georges.
Métro: St-Georges.
Tel. 01 42 85 26 01. Fax 01 45 26 49 33.
Closed Sat., Sun., 1 week Christmas–New Year's, 1 week May, 3 weeks Aug.
Open until 11 PM.
Prix fixe: 38€.

Dominique Versini, a.k.a. Olympe, is still as appealing as in the days when she was playing the Paris society luminary in Montparnasse. The intimate décor with its close-set tables, Provençal fabric, stucco-style walls and Murano chandeliers is an exercise in charm. The dishes are precise in tone, well handled, appetizing and sometimes roguish. We delight in the crisp layered pastry filled with blood sausage and served with mixed greens, the sardines marinated in sea salt served with beet rémoulade, tuna with bacon and onions, langoustine ravioli, lamb shoulder for two and beef tenderloin with peppercorn sauce. The desserts (pots of chocolate with red fruit sauce, Paris-Brest, coffee crème brûlée) are in the same vein. A clientele of dedicated aficionados (film director Claude Berri, Francis Ford Coppola when he is in Paris and TV presenter Emmanuel Chain, among others) help to make the place feel like a friendly club.

● Spring   Ⓝ ○ SIM

25, rue Le Peletier.
Métro: Poissonnière, Notre-Dame de Lorette.
Tel. 01 45 96 05 72.
Closed lunch (exc. Fri., Sat.), Sun.
Menu : 36€.

This is the secret restaurant that everyone is talking about under their breath. A few tables providing just sixteen places make up this compact quality establishment behind a sliding glass door. The dedicated chef puts on a one-man show for an audience that has often reserved two weeks in advance. This is Daniel Rose's pocket theater. An enthusiastic, self-taught native of Chicago who trained with some great French names, he cooks simply, using superb produce that changes each day. A single set menu is the rule for all. The pumpkin soup with pigeon jus, apple juice-marinated salmon with pesto, a fine quail salad as well as the rack of lamb roasted with seasonal vegetables preceeding the red wine–poached pears served with a brownie offer an idea of what awaits you here. The comfort is not all it could be (with the slightly awkward "back to the wall" seating), but the quality is there, the setting is original and the Côte du Frontonnais can be quaffed freely without hiking up the check. An experience to be shared.

● Le Jardinier   🏠🍴COM

5, rue Richer.
Métro: Grands-Boulevards.
Tel.-Fax 01 48 24 79 79.
le.jardinier@wanadoo.fr
www.lejardinier.lesrestos.com
Closed Sat. lunch, Sun., Mon. dinner,
1 week July, 2 weeks Aug.
Prix fixe: 30€. A la carte: 40€.

Stéphane Fumaz, a Veyrat and Pré Catelan veteran, has settled here on the kitsch first floor of a retro hotel with nineteenth-century stucco. The set menus teem with ideas: antipasti-style vegetable raviolis, the escargot fricassée with wild mushrooms, pikeperch in a pastry crust along with Tarbais white beans in jus, spicy quetsches plums in pastry or the fine sour cherry vacherin are simply superb. The feminine service is charming, the choice of wine shrewd and the prices unassuming indeed. Success had better not be too long in coming or this talented chef may move on to new pastures.

● L'Art des Choix   🍴😊SIM

36, rue Condorcet.
Métro: Anvers, Cadet.
Tel. 01 48 78 30 61. Fax 01 48 78 16 29
www.e-quartier.com
Closed Sat. lunch, Sun., Mon. dinner,
1 week Christmas–New Year's, 3 weeks Aug.
Prix fixe: 16€, 21€, 23€, 29€.

Patrice Gras, Alain Dutournier disciple, whose local bistro has been refurbished in a cheerful, contemporary style, offers a convincing, light cuisine that adapts to the market produce of the day. The amiability of the prices matches the meticulousness of the preparations. You will not be disappointed by the warm asparagus with soft-boiled eggs and toast strips for dipping, the avocado cassolette with warm goat cheese, pan-seared turbot with Bayonne ham, the beef tenderloin roasted in red wine or the apple-pear gelatin dessert with salted-butter caramel ice cream.

● La Boule Rouge   🍴SIM

1, rue de la Boule-Rouge.
Métro: Grands-Boulevards, Cadet.
Tel. 01 47 70 43 90 / 01 48 00 07 69.

Fax 01 42 46 99 57.
Closed Sun., Aug.
Prix fixe: 25€, 35€. A la carte: 40–45€.

Like singer Enrico Macias, who is more or less at home here, we are happy to spend time with Raymond Haddad. His affable establishment is warm and flavorsome. The setting is pleasant with its desert-themed fresco and the cuisine refuses to be outdone. Gilthead sea bream, cod, a beautiful Dover sole, fried red mullet or gray mullet served grilled or with "the works" are impeccable. Then there are the Moroccan tapas, minina (chicken and egg soufflé), crisp phyllo pastry stuffed with tuna, merguez (spicy lamb or beef sausage), and the couscous bkaïla (with spinach and beans) at lunchtime on Saturday (go for the ambiance), all delightful in this inexpensive kosher restaurant. The service is affable, the Listel *rosé* slides down effortlessly and, for dessert, watermelon, melon, Algerian pastries made with semolina dough or the pastries made with honey are delicious. Sheer enjoyment!

● Fuji-Yaki   🍴😊SIM

20, rue Henri-Monnier.
Métro: Pigalle, St-Georges.
Tel.-Fax 01 42 81 54 25.
Closed Sun. lunch, mid-Aug.–beg. Sept.
Prix fixe: 7,50€, 9€, 12€, 20€.

The simple snack bar setting is rather dull, but the delightfully warm welcome, polished dishes, gentle prices and purity are gratifying. Without fuss, we savor the miso soup, fried dumplings, langoustine tempura, seafood salad flavored with vinegar, spicy tuna maki, salmon and yellowtail tuna sashimi, meat brochettes yakitori and black or white sesame ice cream, which are just splendid. All this is also available to take away.

● Georgette   🍴SIM

29, rue Saint-Georges.
Métro: Nôtre-Dame-de-Lorette.
Tel. 01 42 80 39 13.
Closed Sat., Sun., 1 week May,
1 week at Ascension, Aug.
A la carte: 40€.

Georgette is Marie-Odile Chauvelot, proud mother of her amiable Nouvelle Athènes bistro. We love the amusing setting with its beams and Formica tables and casual atmosphere. We also enjoy the fare, which is delicious and simple. Depending on what the market has to offer, Florys Barbier (who trained at the neighboring Olympe) produces all kinds of delicacies: a poached egg served with mushrooms, grilled fennel and olive oil, dill-marinated salmon and oven-crisped veal served with sautéed potatoes. The desserts (shortbread cookie with cream and salted-butter caramel ice cream conjure up childhood memories.

● La Petite Sirène de Copenhague   🛏 SIM

47, rue Notre-Dame-de-Lorette.
Métro: St-Georges, Nôtre-Dame-de-Lorette.
Tel. 01 45 26 66 66.
Closed Sat. lunch, Sun., Mon., Christmas, New Year's, 3 weeks Aug.
Prix fixe: 28€ (lunch), 32€. A la carte: 55€.

This simple, pleasant, chic, delicious Danish embassy is run by Peter Thulstrup. This expert technician (who trained at Le Crillon, the Kong Hans in Copenhagen and La Tour d'Argent) is a jack of all trades. He moves from kitchen to dining room, promoting the splendid lunchtime option with gusto, along with his aquavits and Cérès beer. He also provides knowledgeable explanations as he presents Danish-style herring, imperial smoked salmon, braised cod filet with red cabbage and a wonderful duck with caramelized potatoes for our approval. The remarkable desserts (warm cherries with cardamom cream) and relaxed atmosphere are an incitement to eat here on a regular basis.

● Le Pré Cadet   🛏 SIM

10, rue Saulnier.
Métro: Cadet.
Tel. 01 48 24 99 64. Fax 01 47 70 55 96.
flomicadet@wanadoo.fr
Closed Sat. lunch, Sun., New Year's, 1 May, 8 May, 3 weeks Aug.
Prix fixe: 30€. A la carte: 40€.

Discreet, rustic and welcoming, with its plaster walls and friendly atmosphere, Michel Le Boulch's "little club" is one of the secret haunts of the ninth arrondissement (Mayor Jacques Bravo is a regular). We enjoy the lively cuisine, prepared with what the market has to offer by the modest José Marquès. It never disappoints. The menu is splendid and the dishes change. Crisp pastry with a basil bouquet, escargots prepared with parsley and garlic butter, cod filet roasted and served with olive oil–seasoned mashed potatoes, sole meunière, poached calf's head terrine, boneless rib-eye steak and the floating island are all first rate.

● Sizin   🏠🛏🌐 SIM

47, rue Saint-Georges.
Métro: St-Georges.
Tel. 01 44 63 02 28.
ekilic@free.fr / www.sizin-restaurant.com
Closed Sun., last 3 weeks Aug.
Prix fixe: 13,90€ (lunch). A la carte: 30€.

Which is the best Turkish restaurant in Paris? This little corner establishment, presided over with sincere warmth by the young Erdal Kilic. The décor has been gently restyled in shades of white, with souvenirs of Anatolia and photos of Istanbul on the walls. The unfailingly charming cuisine consists of light, spicy, eloquent, faultless dishes. The extra fresh mezze, or Turkish tapas (vegetable fritters, pan fried shrimp with paprika, flaky pastry stuffed with cheese, light taramasalata, hummus, stuffed eggplant), exquisite wood-grilled meats (marinated lamb and beef skewers) and ali nazik adana (chopped meat brochette with yogurt and eggplant) are all remarkable. Desserts (baklava and others) follow, the Yakut Kavaklidere slips down easily and the prices are amiable to a fault.

● Velly   🛏 SIM

52, rue Lamartine.
Métro: Nôtre-Dame-de-Lorette.
Tel.-Fax 01 48 78 60 05
Closed Sat., Sun., Bank Holidays, 3 weeks Aug.
Prix fixe: 23€ (lunch), 31€.

This small restaurant run by Alain Brigant is in good shape. The setting, with its low ceiling, art deco lighting and second floor with a few tables, has character. So does the cuisine, as witnessed by the baked goat cheese, avocado and grapefruit "crumble", pan-fried razor clams with spicy sausage, pan-fried curried monkfish served with a broccoli coulis, pollock filet with cabbage, the suckling pig served with fork-mashed potatoes and finally a veal hanger steak with peppercorn sauce that we savor with pleasure. The desserts (baba au rhum and a chocolate palet) are excellent. The service provided by Thierry Lerosey is dynamic.

● **Chartier**   ⊛ 🍴 SIM
7, rue du Faubourg-Montmartre.
Métro: Grands-Boulevards.
Tel. 01 47 70 86 29. Fax 01 48 24 14 68.
bouillon.chartier@wanadoo.fr
www.bouillon-chartier.com
A la carte: 22€.

For more than a century, this *bouillon*-style restaurant (vintage 1896) has been offering salvation for the thrifty in search of uncomplicated sustenance. Neither the décor—revolving door, faux leather banquettes, mirrors and brass work—nor the ballet of black-and-white clad waiters has changed since our student days. Hearts of palm vinaigrette, beef muzzle salad, oven-baked sea bream, flambéed sea bass served with fennel, pot-au-feu, calf's head and the house pastries are all terribly good natured.

● **A la Grange Batelière**   🍴 SIM
16, rue de la Grange-Batelière.
Métro: Richelieu-Drouot.
Tel.-Fax 01 47 70 85 15.
lagrangebateliere@wanadoo.fr
Closed dinner (exc. 1st and 3rd Wed. each month), Sat., Sun., 1 week Christmas–New Year's, beg. Aug.–end Aug.
Prix fixe: 30€ (lunch), 25€ (lunch).
A la carte: 70€.

Actress Mimie Mathy and her cook husband Benoist Gérard have taken over this post–Second Empire bistro successfully. It has kept its counter and pigeonholes but acquired wooden tables and a little space. Dishes of the day are chalked up on the blackboard and showbiz friends come and enjoy the seafood mille-feuille, the crayfish and asparagus in puff pastry, pan-seared scallops served with a mild brandade, as well as the Mediterranean grilled red mullet tartine and the thick sautéed veal chop. The desserts (vanilla, coffee and chocolate creams in little pots) and a croquant of sour red fruits are charming; the prices, sadly, much less so.

● **Le Roi du Pot-au-Feu**   ⊛ 🍴 SIM
34, rue Vignon.
Métro: Madeleine, Havre-Caumartin.
Tel. 01 47 42 37 10.
Closed Sun., Bank Holidays.
A la carte: 30€.

Nothing changes in this authentic bistro with its talkative proprietors, retro décor with neon lighting, brass, mirrors, counter and companionable welcome, serving a pot-au-feu with a bowl of bouillon and tender meat. The house terrine, the hachis parmentier (a ground meat and potato dish similar to shepherd's pie) and the chocolate mousse are equally commendable.

■   HOTELS

■ **Holiday Inn Opéra**   🏚
38, rue de l'Echiquier.
Métro: Bonne-Nouvelle.
Tel. 01 42 46 92 75. Fax 01 42 47 03 97.
tabledupavillon@parisopera.com
www.holiday-inn.com/paris-opera
92 rooms: 150–259€. 5 suites: 259–299€.

The decent-sized rooms are tastefully appointed, underlining the house art nouveau décor. The pleasant restaurant is decorated with woodwork, frescos and a glass ceiling (See Restaurants: La Table du Pavillon).

■ Terminus Nord

12, bd de Denain.
Métro: Gare-du-Nord.
Tel. 01 42 80 20 00. Fax 01 42 80 63 89.
h2761@accor-hotels.com
www.libertel-hotels.com
236 rooms: 99–235€. 8 suites: 260–275€.

The art nouveau stained glass contrasts with the English style of this 1865 hotel. Standing opposite the Gare du Nord rail station, it enjoys a synergy with the brasserie of the same name, run by the Flo group.

■ Albert 1er

162, rue La Fayette.
Métro: Gare-du-Nord.
Tel. 01 40 36 82 40. Fax 01 40 35 72 52.
paris@albert1erhotel.com
www.albert1erhotel.com
55 rooms: 97–137€.

Between the Gare du Nord and Gare de l'Est rail stations, this classic, practical hotel offers good value for money. Modern, efficiently soundproofed rooms.

■ Paris Est

4, rue du 8-May-1945.
Métro: Gare-de-l'Est.
Tel. 01 44 89 27 00. Fax 01 44 89 27 49.
hotelpariest.bestwestern@autogrill.net
www.bestwestern.fr
45 rooms: 99–185€.

This hotel is set majestically in the main courtyard of the Gare de l'Est rail station. Refurbished in modern style with red and yellow drapes, the rooms all look out onto a rear courtyard, ensuring a peaceful stay.

● RESTAURANTS

● La Table du Pavillon

At the Holiday Inn Opéra, 38, rue de l'Echiquie
Métro: Bonne-Nouvelle.
Tel. 01 42 46 98 84. Fax 01 42 47 03 97.
thierry.viot@hi-parisopera.com
www.table-du-pavillon.com
Prix fixe: 16€ (lunch), 21€ (lunch),
37€ (wine inc.). A la carte: 45€.

Originally a hunting lodge belonging to King Henri IV in 1593, then a brasserie in the twenties, this historic abode now houses a traditional restaurant, whose art deco style has remained intact, with mahogany woodwork, mosaics, mirrors and stained glass paneling. The place has style, and the menu lives up to its promise with a combination of tradition and modernity. The foie gras with rhubarb, shellfish ravioli, sea bass cooked with coarse sea salt, herb-marinated lamb, beefsteak in Chivas sauce and chocolate macaron with Bourbon vanilla ice cream are all pleasant surprises, accompanied by an astute selection of wines at gentle prices.

● Chez Michel

10, rue de Belzunce.
Métro: Gare-du-Nord, Poissonnière.
Tel. 01 44 53 06 20. Fax 01 44 53 61 31
Closed Sat., Sun., Mon. lunch.
Prix fixe: 30€.

Thierry Breton, formerly at the Ritz and Crillon, brings together lovers of Brittany and other food enthusiasts over dishes based on regional produce and the ocean. The 1939 vintage dining room is decorated with a few paintings of the Breton coast between Morlaix and Carnac. Slow-cooked tuna with coriander and Breton-style tabouli, thick tuna steak with eggplant caviar, Breton pot-au-feu with buckwheat dumplings and roasted milk-fed veal with young turnips make a fine feast, which ends with the inevitable kouign-amann (Breton flaky butter and sugar pastry) or an outstanding Paris-Brest (choux pastry ring filled with praline cream). The wine list offers a wide range of vintages at reasonable prices. You can also try some excellent ciders from the Cornouaille district as well as Breton beers. We strongly recommend you reserve.

● Brasserie Flo

7, cour des Petites-Ecuries.
Métro: Château-d'Eau, Strasbourg-St-Denis.
Tel. 01 47 70 13 59. Fax 01 42 47 00 80.

www.brasserieflo.com
Prix fixe: 19,90€ (lunch), 22,90€ (lunch).
A la carte: 45€.

Carved woodwork, stained glass, frescos paying tribute to Alsace and the brewer's art and comfortable leather banquettes are all here. The menu is tastefully classical and the preparation has improved. The duck foie gras, spéciales oysters from Gillardeau, French onion soup, salmon grilled on one side, Colmar-style sauerkraut, leg of lamb roasted with thyme and the authentic baba au rhum and chocolate profiteroles will do you a world of good.

● **La Grille**   🔟 COM

80, rue du Faubourg-Poissonnière.
Métro: Poissonnière.
Tel. 01 47 70 89 73
Closed Sat., Sun., 3 weeks Aug.
A la carte: 45€.

Once you have crossed the threshold, you feel you have been plunged into the past, surrounded as you are by the antique ornaments, hat stands and lace that make up the décor here. Geneviève Cullerre offers her guests a smiling welcome, while Yves, her husband, sets to work in the kitchen, concocting brilliant dishes. The homemade duck terrine with hazelnuts, the mackerel stewed in white wine, the celebrated turbot served with beurre blanc, pan-grilled tenderloin chateaubriand and the custard flan and profiteroles à la royale have not dated at all.

● **Hôtel du Nord**   🔟 COM

102, quai de Jemmapes.
Métro: Jacques-Bonsergent.
Tel. 01 40 40 78 78. Fax 01 40 40 99 20.
Prix fixe: 13,50€ (lunch on weekdays).
A la carte: 40€.

Atmosphere is the key in this Hôtel du Nord, refurbished in an art deco brasserie style by Julien Labrousse. The place has become a fashionable haunt for young middle-class bohemians, attracted as much by the relaxed ambiance as by the fine dishes cooked up by Pascal Chenaut, formerly with Janou in rue Verlomme. We make short work of the antipasti (including buffalo mozzarella), monkfish and grilled shrimp brochette, duck breast with a potato and Salers cheese galette, as well as the gingerbread tiramisu. There is a bonus: the terrace, which soon fills up whenever the sun shows its face.

● **Julien**   🔟 COM

16, rue du Faubourg-Saint-Denis.
Métro: Strasbourg-St-Denis.
Tel. 01 47 70 12 06. Fax 01 42 47 00 65.
p.henriques@groupeflo.fr
Prix fixe: 22,90€, 29,90€. A la carte: 50€.

There is the facade, all in wood, then the dining room with its superb art nouveau décor and Majorelle bar, Trézel muses, glass roofs and floral patterns. Then come the culinary delights. The menu pays tribute to the fine tradition of brasserie dishes, regaling us with salmon rillettes, chicken liver terrine, stewed cod with vegetables, sea bass beurre blanc, grilled leg of lamb, ribeye steak with béarnaise sauce and warm chocolate profiteroles. Turning to the cellar, Bordeaux wines predominate, with a few excellent bottles that are reasonably priced. Neither do we have any complaints about the professional, attentive service.

● **Terminus Nord**   🔟 COM

23, rue de Dunkerque.
Métro: Gare-du-Nord.
Tel. 01 42 85 05 15. Fax 01 40 16 13 98.
terminusnord@groupeflo.com
Open daily. Cont. service.
Prix fixe: 19,90€ (after 10:30 PM), 22,90€, 29,90€. A la carte: 35–60€.

While you wait for your train to leave, or after getting off one, you can take refuge in this delightful, authentic Parisian brasserie opposite the Gare du Nord. The interior is richly decorated, fluently blending art deco and art nouveau (mosaic tiling, frescos, high ceilings). The menu tends toward a tasteful classicism and its execution has improved significantly. The smoked herring and potato salad, seafood platters, bouillabaisse, choucroute, pan-roasted farm-raised veal with morel mushroom sauce and fresh tagliatelle and chocolate profiteroles are enough to satisfy any appetite. A courteous welcome, attentive service and a wide choice of wines by the glass.

● La Cantine de Quentin

52, rue Bichat.
Métro : Goncourt, République.
Tel. 01 42 02 40 32
Closed Mon., dinner.
Prix fixe: 14€ (lunch), 16€ (brunch).
A la carte : 30€.

This gourmet grocery store near the Canal Saint-Martin is a deserved success in the hands of Quentin Hoffmann in the dining room and Johann Baron in the kitchen. These two very young veterans of the Savoy school have opted for an easygoing bistro setting and offer first-rate produce, shrewd wines and takeaway condiments. They delight middle class bohemians from the tenth arrondissement (and further afield) with their exquisite preparations: country terrine, scrambled eggs with truffles, the parmesan risotto cooked Milanese style, the cassoulet with duck confit and a divine vanilla crème brûlée. As we toast all this with Lalande Borie at a knockdown price, we congratulate ourselves on a wonderful (almost accidental) find.

● Aux Zingots

12, rue de la Fidélité.
Métro: Gare-de-l'Est, Strasbourg-St-Denis.
Tel. 01 47 70 19 34.
Closed Sun., Mon. lunch.
A la carte: 40€.

Eighteen-eighties brasserie-style, with moldings, stucco and ornate staircase plus fifties-style lighting and banquettes, Aux Zingots has recovered its soul. At the helm, Gilles Bénard, from Chez Ramulaud in the eleventh arrondissement, and Denys Clément, former photographer with the sports daily *L'Equipe*, have restored the restaurant and entrusted the kitchen to Véronique Melloul, previously at the Cafe de l'Homme. We savor the langoustine tartare with pig's feet, beet and foie gras carpaccio with coarse sea salt, marinated grilled beef tenderloin with freshly made fries and béarnaise sauce, codfish in a creamy sauce with braised lettuce and caramelized onions. The desserts range from the traditional to the tastes of today, with brioche pain perdu with creamy caramel or authentic baba soaked with mandarin liquor. Among the 150 items on the wine list, you are bound to find the right bottle to go with your particular spread.

● Chez Casimir

6, rue du Belzunce.
Métro: Gare-du-Nord.
Tel. 01 48 78 28 80. Fax 01 44 53 61 31.
Closed Sat., Sun., Aug.
A la carte: 35€.

This nearby offshoot of Chez Michel is closely supervised by maestro Thierry Breton. We are pleased to find ourselves back here, enjoying the convivial atmosphere and chatting over a drink and generous dishes concocted by Cédric Lefevre. The country terrine, eggplant and goat cheese mille-feuille, cod brandade served with mixed greens, Burgundy-style stewed beef cheeks and pear Belle-Hélène are gratifying and a bargain at the price.

● Le Sporting

3, rue des Récollets.
Métro: Gare-de-l'Est.
Tel. 01 46 07 02 00. Fax 01 46 07 02 64.
www.lesporting.com
Closed Christmas–New Year's.
Prix fixe: 14€ (lunch on weekdays).
A la carte: 40€.

Strolling by the Canal Saint Martin, you come upon this thirties bistro, still with its wooden bar, unvarnished parquet flooring and lacquered walls. Its modish, gourmet clientele comes to savor a fresh market-based cuisine. The dishes are chalked up on the blackboard: homemade foie gras, sea bass filet with fresh green beans, beef tartare with sautéed small new potatoes, crème brûlée and, in season, a succulent strawberry tart. The wines from selected small growers are enjoyable.

● Le Martel   🔒SIM
3, rue Martel.
Métro: Château-d'Eau.
Tel. 01 47 70 67 56. Fax 01 47 70 51 13.
Closed Sat. lunch, Sun., Aug.
A la carte: 40€.

The fashionistas in their dark glasses have discovered a fondness for this old-fashioned bistro with its updated black and white décor. Comfortably seated on their club chairs or banquettes, they enjoy fare that falls midway between Paris and Algeria, made up of Tunisian-style salad, sesame tuna steak, a pepper-seasoned sirloin steak, chicken tagine with figs, real tarte Tatin and Middle Eastern pastries.

● Le Phénix   ●🔒SIM
4, rue du Faubourg-Poissonnière.
Métro: Bonne-Nouvelle.
Tel. 01 47 70 35 40.
lephenixcafe@wanadoo.fr
www.lephenixparis.com
Closed Sat. lunch, Sun., Bank Holidays,
1 week Christmas–New Year's, Aug.
Prix fixe: 12€ (lunch). A la carte: 30€.

This circa-1880 bistro is enjoying a second youth under the aegis of Fabien Gadeau. This young proprietor and sommelier has brought a new sparkle to its bar, stucco and oilcloths, with solid, boarding house cuisine to match. The Lyonnaise sausage, salmon carpaccio, duck confit and chocolate mousse gratify without breaking the bank.

PARIS 11TH ARR

■ | HOTELS

■ Holiday Inn République   🏨
10, pl de la République.
Métro: République.
Tel. 01 43 55 44 34. Fax 01 43 14 43 62.
www.paris-republique.holiday-inn.com
310 rooms: 150–300€. 8 suites: 288–598€.

This hotel with its renovated rooms has been modernized and its guests are now sheltered from the noise of the place de la République. The restaurant is the "10 de la République".

■ Le Général   ⌂
5-7, rue Rampon.
Métro: Oberkampf, République.
Tel. 01 47 00 41 57. Fax 01 47 00 21 56.
info@legeneralhotel.com
www.legeneralhotel.com
47 rooms: 135–225€. 2 suites: 235–265€.

Far from the madding crowd, but very close to the place de la République, this hotel with its refined, designer setting and fitness center suits business customers and passing tourists.

■ Hôtel Croix de Malte   ℕ⌂
5, rue de Malte.
Métro : République, Oberkampf.
Tel. 01 48 05 09 36. Fax 01 43 57 02 54.
www.hotelcroixdemalte-paris.com
29 rooms: 75–95€.

With its breakfasts in the winter garden, highly colorful décor, palms painted on the walls, and rooms in bright colors, this moderately priced hotel is quite a find. Near to the place de la République and a stone's throw from the Marais.

■ Nord et Est   ⌂
49, rue de Malte.
Métro: République.
Tel. 01 47 00 71 70. Fax 01 43 57 51 16.
info@hotel-nord-est.com
www.hotel-nord-est.com
20 rooms: 75–85€.

The yellow and blue décor has a Southern French feel to it and the rooms have been renovated. With its warm welcome and reasonable prices, this hotel is a pleasant port of call.

● | RESTAURANTS

● Le Sérail   ℕCOM
9, rue Saint-Sabin.
Métro: Bastille, Bréguet-Sabin.
Tel. 01 47 00 25 47. Fax 01 43 14 98 32.
le-serail@wanadoo.fr / www.leserail.com

Closed lunch, Mon., 10 days Aug.
Prix fixe: 30€ (weekday dinner), 35€ (Sat., Sun. dinner).A la carte: 35€.

Red and ochre shades, draped fabrics and soft lighting form the highly appropriate setting of Igal Maor's Moroccan restaurant. Eggplant or tomato salad, stuffed filo pastry or chicken pastilla, the chicken tagine with preserved lemons, six different kinds of couscous to choose from and orange cinnamon salad make up celebratory set menus punctuated by Moroccan wines and house bread.

● Blue Elephant COM
43, rue de la Roquette.
Métro: Bastille,Voltaire.
Tel. 01 47 00 42 00. Fax 01 47 00 45 44.
paris@blueelephant.com
www.blueelephant.com
Closed Sat. lunch.
Prix fixe: 44€. A la carte: 40–60€.

A piece of Thai jungle has apparently been transported to this vast restaurant dining room, down to the waterfall cascading in its center. The menu is a voyage in itself. A guaranteed change of scenery with yam hua plee (the banana flower salad with shrimp, roasted and grated coconut and tamarind sauce), the steamed chu-chi (fresh Thai-style salmon curry with coconut milk) the coco cabane (beef with green curry, accompanied by steamed noodles) and the roum mitt (water chestnuts and jack fruit in a flavored coconut milk).

● Mansouria ○ COM
11, rue Faidherbe.
Métro: Faidherbe-Chaligny.
Tel. 01 43 71 00 16. Fax 01 40 24 21 97.
Closed Sun., Mon. lunch, Tuesday lunch, 1 week mid-Aug.
Prix fixe: 30€, 46€. A la carte: 45€.

A native of Oujda, former ethnologist Fatema Hal has always been keen to share her taste for "Cooking Connections", and that is exactly what she does at her restaurant, in her books and more recently with her own grocery brand. Newcomers or regulars, she welcomes her customers like old friends in the four dining rooms decorated in Moorish style. Whether we are there to taste her cuisine for the first time or enjoy its familiar pleasures for the umpteenth, we never fail to wonder at its tremendous refinement and sweetness. Among the essential dishes here, we should mention the flaky phyllo pastry stuffed with roasted pigeon, the mourouzia (a slowly simmered lamb stew flavored with twenty-seven different spices), chicken tagine with walnut-stuffed figs, puff pastry filled with custard and the sliced oranges with orange blossoms.

● Le Repaire de Cartouche COM
8, bd des Filles-du-Calvaire.
Métro: St-Sébastien–Froissart, Filles-du-Calvaire.
Tel. 01 47 00 25 86. Fax 01 43 38 85 91.
Closed Sun., Mon., 1 week Feb., 1 week May, Aug.
Prix fixe: 16€ (lunch on weekdays), 25€ (lunch on weekdays). A la carte: 40€.

This timeless inn with its rustic surroundings and old-fashioned charm owes its name to the famous, hotheaded bandit Cartouche, who is said to have frequented the place. Is that why the restaurant has two entrances? In any case, Rodolphe Paquin, the current master of the house, reserves a warm welcome and a tempting menu for his guests. This staunch Norman concocts generous dishes, including the cold purée of peas with country ham, steamed hake filet with tomatoes, lemon confit and olive oil, the veal sautéed until golden with fava beans, roasted pigeon with baby vegetables and soft chocolate cake with cream. The menu changes to reflect the produce on offer at the market, and the cellar is well stocked.

● Le Villaret ○ SIM
13, rue Ternaux.
Métro: Parmentier.
Tel. 01 43 57 89 76.
Closed Sat. lunch, Sun., Christmas–New Year's, Aug.
Prix fixe: 22€ (lunch), 27€ (lunch), 52€ (dinner). A la carte: 52€.

This ageless bistro has stood up well to the tests of time and fashion without losing its soul or allowing its style to grow stale. The rustic stone and wood are a foil to the precision of dishes appealingly orchestrated by Olivier Gaslain, who has an eye to both tradition and innovation. We are both reassured and pleasantly surprised by the cold cream of tarbais bean soup, langoustine tails with dried tomatoes and crushed avocado, Breton John Dory fish baked in the oven with wild asparagus and caramelized garlic, sweetbreads encrusted with pain d'épice with baby artichokes and tender potatoes or pineapple and mango ice cream sundae with coconut cream and aged rum ice cream. The cellar has plenty of ideas and, in the dining room, Joël Homel is gratifyingly attentive and friendly to a fault.

● Le Chateaubriand

129, av Parmentier.
Métro: Goncourt.
Tel.-Fax 01 43 57 45 95.
Closed Sat. lunch, Sun., Mon.
Prix fixe: 13€ (lunch), 30€ (dinner), 36€ (dinner). A la carte: 40€.

Inaki Aizpitarte, together with his pal Frédéric Peneau, formerly at Café Burq, have changed the lights, kept the banquettes, slapped on a cheerful coat of yellow paint and above all brought a new spirit to the place. So here it is, the new wave of gourmet bistro—very 21st century, with an eye to its roots. The lunchtime option at 13€ for two courses hits the spot. Over the bar pass glasses of Gramenon, Foillard and Dard et Ribo, a tribute to nature and the grape. The food is lively and fortifying, taking shrewd new approaches to traditional ideas. The julienned cucumber with shredded smoked fish, the orange-infused veal stew and the chocolate mousse were resourceful indeed. In the evening, prices soar and the food becomes showier, with mackerel ceviche with tabasco, seared tuna with asparagus and chorizo, sautéed veal medallions with Pompadour potatoes and pork belly with celery root and licorice. Watch your step: The set menu is at 36€ not including drinks, and the enticing bottles on the wine list can clean you out.

● Chez Ramulaud

269, rue du Faubourg-Saint-Antoine.
Métro: Faidherbe-Chaligny, Nation.
Tel. 01 43 72 23 29. Fax 01 43 72 57 03.
Closed 1 week Dec., 1 week Apr.
Prix fixe: 16€ (lunch), 29€ (dinner).
A la carte: 40€.

Market-based dishes, a vintage bistro setting, a personalized welcome and floods of bottles (the cellar numbers nearly 350 vintages) are the arguments in favor of this restaurant, run by the mischievous Gilles Bénard, who has a gift for putting people at their ease. Here we sometimes meet movie director Cédric Klapisch or actor Jean-Pierre Darroussin, who, like us, delight in the fricassée of baby artichokes and langoustines, filet of pageot (a type of sea bream) with hibiscus jus, eggplant compote, oxtail crumble, calf's feet with foie gras and sautéed cherries with black pepper and lemon mousse.

● Astier

44, rue Jean-Pierre-Timbaud.
Métro: Parmentier, Goncourt.
Tel. 01 43 57 16 35.
www.restaurant-astier.com
Prix fixe: 18,50€ (lunch), 23,50€ (lunch), 28€ (dinner).

This sound local bistro, which offers value for money, a relaxed atmosphere, selected wines and refined dishes of the day, has changed hands, but remains true to its calling. Frédéric Hubig, who owns the Café Moderne behind the Paris stock exchange, has taken it over but has refrained from tampering with all those things that have made it a success: smoked herring with potatoes and olive oil, wonderful terrines, roasted monkfish with basmati rice, traditional veal blanquette and crème caramel like grandmother makes are all simple delights.

● **Le Bistrot Paul Bert**   🦀 SIM

18, rue Paul-Bert.
Métro: Faidherbe-Chaligny, Charonne.
Tel. 01 43 72 24 01. Fax 01 43 72 24 66.
Closed Sun., Mon., Aug.
Prix fixe: 16€ (lunch), 30€ (dinner).

Bertrand Auboyneau, who gave up law and the stock exchange because of his love of good food and fine wines, has made a success of his career change. He has turned this bistro into a warm, welcoming place, bringing in Thierry Laurent, who has a talent for fine, generous, flavorsome dishes, playing with produce and the seasons to express his art to the full. Enjoy the superb rib-eye steak on the bone with homemade French fries, the pan-seared veal sweetbreads or delicate apple tart with rhubarb ice cream. The wines are selected with genuine flair (a striking Dard et Ribo Saint-Joseph) and the set menus are a gift. This is a haven for astute food lovers.

● **L'Ecailler du Bistrot**   🦀 SIM

22, rue Paul-Bert.
Métro: Faidherbe-Chaligny.
Tel. 01 43 72 76 77. Fax 01 43 72 24 66
Closed Sun., Mon., Aug.
Prix fixe: 16€ (lunch), 45€ (dinner).
A la carte: 49€.

Cadoret, a familiar name in the world of oyster farming, is the family name of Gwenaëlle, who runs this establishment, and her brother, who supplies her at the source in Riec-sur-Belon. The marennes, pleine mer and spéciales claires oysters provide a wide range of the best produce available. The catch comes from Guilvinec, and we find ourselves caught up in a veritable festival of marine flavors when the tuna tartare, duo of fresh crab with avocado, fresh shellfish platter and brill (a delicate fish similar to turbot) arrive. To finish, the delicious thinly sliced apples with salted-butter caramel really hits the mark. The Loire wines follow naturally and the marine décor with its gleaming woodwork forms a suitable background for this oceanic repast.

● **Le Marsangy**   🦀 ⊖ SIM

73, av Parmentier.
Métro: Parmentier, St-Ambroise.
Tel.-Fax 01 47 00 94 25.
Closed Sat. lunch, Sun., 2 weeks Christmas–New Year's, 2 weeks Easter, 2 weeks Aug.
Prix fixe: 22€.

Francis Bonfillou, who formerly officiated at the Concorde Lafayette under Joël Robuchon, has turned this restaurant into a gourmet haunt. His produce is rigorously selected and deftly prepared. In the dining room, with its old-fashioned pink hues, slates and mirrors, we enjoy the duck confit terrine with foie gras, sea bass filet with white beans in cream, lamb filet with eggplant caviar and chocolate fondant with basil. The cellar, boasting at least a hundred items, pays tribute to Burgundy. The service is prompt and attentive, and the prices behave themselves.

● **Le Temps au Temps**   🦀 SIM

13, rue Paul-Bert.
Métro: Faidherbe-Chaligny.
Tel.-Fax 01 43 79 63 40.
Closed Sun., Mon., 10 days Christmas–New Year's, Aug.
Prix fixe: 12€ (lunch), 14€ (lunch), 16€ (lunch), 28€ (dinner). A la carte: 36€.

Its facade brightened by red shutters, a visit to this pocket bistro definitely ought not to be rushed. Take your time savoring the dishes prepared by Lyon's Sylvain Sendra. The crisp calf's head with foie gras vinaigrette, Mediterranean red tuna with green asparagus and fresh peas, risotto with pig's feet and morel mushrooms and white chocolate ice cream "cappuccino" with a coffee emulsion all point to a perfect mastery of his art. Add fine bottles or biodynamically produced wines and you have the ideal recipe for a very special meal in a unique setting.

● **Au Vieux Chêne**   🦀 SIM

7, rue du Dahomey.
Métro: Faidherbe-Chaligny.
Tel. 01 43 71 67 69.
Closed Sat. lunch, Sun., Christmas–New Year's, 1 week at Easter, end July–mid-Aug.

Prix fixe: 13€ (lunch), 29€ (dinner).
A la carte: 45€.

This old bistro with its patinated counter and whitewashed walls fills lovers of spirited, mischievous cuisine with delight. Concocted by Stéphane Chevassus, the Sot l'y Laisse veteran trained by Rostang, Cagna and Savoy, the oxtail medallion with potatoes and andouille sausage, monkfish with lentils and a shellfish cream sauce, quail filet and thigh with green asparagus and dried tomatoes and the strawberries and rhubarb with almond cream are washed down with highly impressive, shrewd little wines.

● **Chardenoux**   🍴 SIM
1, rue Jules-Vallès.
Métro: Charonne, Faidherbe-Chaligny.
Tel. 01 43 71 49 52. Fax 01 43 71 80 89.
A la carte: 55€.

The Belle Epoque–style of this hundred-year-old bistro is still intact, with mirrors, ceiling painted with clouds and sky and rococo Fallières bar. After his time at Chez Francis, Philippe Roche took over and has breathed new life into this place. Recently promoted to the kitchen, Lydie Dupraz offers her take on a classic menu, including foie gras terrine with gingerbread, duck terrine with figs, codfish with aïoli, lamb stew with baby vegetables, raspberry mille-feuille and jasmine crème brûlée. The cellar is well stocked and you will have no trouble finding the right wine to quench your thirst among its treasures.

● **Le Clown Bar**   🍴 SIM
114, rue Amelot.
Métro: Filles-du-Calvaire.
Tel. 01 43 55 87 35. Fax 01 43 55 38 20.
www.clown-bar.fr
Closed Sun. lunch, 2 weeks Aug.
Prix fixe: 13,50€ (lunch), 25€ (dinner).
A la carte: 35€.

A step away from the Cirque d'Hiver, Joël Vitte's (registered historic) bistro is appealing indeed with its clownish décor, a menu touting timeless classics and attentive service. We happily set off around the

ring to savor œufs meurette (eggs poached in red wine, with bacon and onions), green salad with crispy phyllo-wrapped Saint-Marcellin cheese, cod brandade, spice-encrusted pork medallions and Valrhona Guanaja melted-chocolate cake. Loire, Alsace and Rhône Valley wines accompany this gentle spread.

● **La Galoche d'Aurillac**   🍴 SIM
41, rue de Lappe.
Métro: Bastille.
Tel. 01 47 00 77 15.
www.lagalochedaurillac.com
Closed Mon.
Prix fixe: 25€, 35€ (wine inc.).

The Bonnets' Auvergnat inn contrasts with the fashionable bars of rue de Lappe. It is a genuine pleasure to sit down here under the hanging clogs, hams, traditional musical instruments and farming implements, and taste authentic produce, such as the Auvergnat salad, veal breast stuffed with bacon and vegetables, goose confit with Guérande salt, truffade (layered, fried potato pancake with bacon and Cantal cheese), aligot (mashed potatoes with tomme cheese and garlic) and pounti (pork loaf that typically includes Swiss chard or spinach and prunes), not to mention the delightful conclusion with prunes stewed in wine. A reinvigorating rustic break.

● **Chez Paul**   🍴 SIM
13, rue de Charonne (at rue de Lappe).
Métro: Bastille, Ledru-Rollin.
Tel. 01 47 00 34 57. Fax 01 48 07 02 00.
chezpaul@noos.fr
A la carte: 31€.

The patina in this twenties bistro is genuine. With its old-fashioned charm, the setting is a popular one, and the sensibly priced classics cannot be faulted. The bone marrow with toast, stuffed hard-boiled eggs, salmon filet with sorrel, steak tartare with sautéed potatoes and chocolate charlotte are simple but excellent. A special mention for the service, which is charming and attentive despite the crowds of tourists that fill the place.

■ | HOTELS

■ Sofitel Paris Bercy

1, av des Terroirs-de-France.
Métro: Cour-St-Emilion.
Tel. 01 44 67 34 00. Fax 01 44 67 34 01.
H2192@accor-hotels.com / www.sofitel.com
376 rooms: 370–415€. 20 suites: 565–2700€.

The top floors of this large modern hotel standing guard over the new village of Bercy enjoy an unobstructed view across the Seine. Fitness center, sauna, Jacuzzi and bright, neat rooms. The Café Ké restaurant serves topical dishes.

■ Novotel Bercy

85, rue de Bercy.
Métro: Bercy.
Tel. 01 43 42 30 00. Fax 01 43 45 30 60.
H0935@accor.com / www.accor-hotels.com
150 rooms: 145–175€. 1 suite: 230–250€.

This chain hotel offers guaranteed comfort and professionalism near to Bercy park. A fine view over the Seine.

■ Claret

44, bd de Bercy.
Métro: Bercy.
Tel. 01 46 28 41 31. Fax 01 49 28 09 29.
resa@hotel-claret.com / www.hotel–claret.com
52 rooms: 120–140€.

The fifty-two rooms here take us on a journey round the vineyards of Bordeaux. With its attentive welcome and faultless restaurant and pizzeria, this former post house is a pleasant pied à terre.

■ Paris-Bastille

67, rue de Lyon.
Métro: Bastille, Gare-de-Lyon.
Tel. 01 40 01 07 17. Fax 01 40 01 07 27.
www.hotelparisbastille.com
31 rooms: 155–235€. 6 suites: 235€.

A hotel ideally located in the heart of Paris near the Bastille Opera and a step away from the Gare de Lyon rail station, with modern, comfortable rooms in shades of red.

■ Pavillon Bastille

65, rue de Lyon.
Métro: Bastille, Gare-de-Lyon.
Tel. 01 43 43 65 65. Fax 01 43 43 96 52.
hotel-pavillon@akamail.com
www.france-paris.com
24 rooms: 130–130€.

A small haven of peace with its flowered courtyard, 17th-century fountain and Provençal ambiance, this charming hotel lets guests make the most of their stay in the capital.

● | RESTAURANTS

● Le Train Bleu   V.COM

Gare de Lyon, pl Louis-Armand.
Métro: Gare-de-Lyon.
Tel. 01 43 43 09 06. Fax 01 43 43 97 96.
reservation.trainbleu@ssp.fr
www.le-train-bleu.com
Prix fixe: 45€ (wine inc.), 48€,
15€ (child). A la carte: 70€.

Established in 1901, this restaurant with its sumptuous, rococo décor is still the finest rail station buffet in France. Visitors can admire frescos paying homage to the Paris-Lyon-Mediterranean railroad, as well as the gilding, stucco, moldings, woodwork and crystal chandeliers. Turning to the food, tradition is properly maintained once more with the homemade duck foie gras, sea bream in the style of the South of France, roasted leg of lamb with potato gratin and baba au rhum soaked with amber Saint James rum. A delicious way of passing the time while waiting for a train.

● Les Grandes Marches   V.COM

6, pl de la Bastille.
Métro: Bastille.
Tel. 01 43 42 90 32. Fax 01 43 44 80 02.
Prix fixe: 22,90€, 29,90€, 13,50€ (child).

This establishment is located at the foot of the Bastille Opera. Its refined, modern setting and topical cuisine go hand-in-hand. Chef Tony Rodrigue's dishes have a very contemporary flavor. The avocado and crayfish tartare with hearts of palm in vinaigrette sauce, curried shrimp in crisp phyllo pastry, sesame-crusted tuna steak and the thick-cut calf's liver with salted-butter potato purée are not bad. For dessert, the raspberry mille-feuille filled with light vanilla cream brings you back to earth.

● L'Oulette   V.COM

15, pl Lachambeaudie.
Métro: Cour-St-Emilion, Bercy.
Tel. 01 40 02 02 12. Fax 01 40 02 04 77.
info@l-oulette.com / www.l-oulette.com
Closed Sat., Sun., Bank Holidays.
Prix fixe: 32€ (lunch), 48€ (wine inc.), 70€, 82€ (wine inc.). A la carte: 70€.

With its contemporary décor, terrace sheltered by thujas and a mouthwatering menu with Southwestern French accents, this restaurant belonging to Marcel Baudis, native of Quercy and pupil of Alain Dutournier, encourages us to indulge ourselves, and that is exactly what we do with the baby artichokes with coriander, fresh mint and cured pork loin, the spice-crusted roasted codfish, the sautéed veal sweetbreads with foie gras flan and a Guanaja chocolate mousse served on a bed of pear granita. The interesting wine list focuses on the Southwest, Bordeaux and Languedoc-Roussillon.

● Le Quincy   ◎ COM

28, av Ledru-Rollin.
Métro: Gare-de-Lyon.
Tel.-Fax 01 46 28 46 76.
Closed Sat., Sun., Mon., Christmas–New Year's, mid-Aug.–mid-Sept.
A la carte: 50–70€.

Michel Bosshard, a.k.a. Bobosse, has turned his old-fashioned inn into a compact gourmet theater. He offers a warm welcome and vigorously touts his traditional cuisine. The atmosphere soon grows companionable. With a keen appetite, we dine on the homemade foie gras, farm-style terrine with cabbage and gar-

lic, codfish brandade, a copious stuffed cabbage, oxtail stew and rabbit stew with white wine and shallots, exemplary in their genre. The chocolate mousse has a silky texture; the vanilla ice cream is homemade. Credit cards are still off limits, but the house continues to present devotees with a plum flambé.

● Entre les Vignes   🏠🍴🎋SIM

27 ter, bd Diderot.
Métro: Gare-de-Lyon.
Tel. 01 43 43 62 84.
Closed Sat., Sun.,
Christmas–New Year's, 3 weeks Aug.
Prix fixe: 19€, 23€. A la carte: 35€.

Didier Petak energetically runs this 1908 vintage bistro opposite the Gare de Lyon, which combines a fine atmosphere, quality produce and inoffensive prices. Gendrier Cheverny in a carafe ('Don't have the Fleurie, it's so-so,' advises the master of the house with a laugh), simmered country sausage, warm potato salad, caper-seasoned skate, the hanger steak served with real frites and a frankly exquisite vanilla crème brûlée make a residence here seem an attractive option.

● Au Trou Gascon   ◎ COM

40, rue Taine.
Métro: Daumesnil.
Tel. 01 43 44 34 26. Fax 01 43 07 80 55.
carre.des.feuillants@wanadoo.fr
www.autrougascon.fr
Closed Sat., Sun., Bank Holidays,
1 week Christmas–New Year's, Aug.
Prix fixe: 36€ (lunch), 50€ (dinner).
A la carte: 80€.

Alain Dutournier's first abode is still on the right track. The bistro setting made over by designer Alberto Bali takes a minimalist approach in gray tones. In the dining room, Claude Tessier and Nicole Dutournier's supervision is unfailingly attentive, while the kitchen carries on the traditions of Southwest France (but not exclusively) under the aegis of apt pupil Jean-Charles Paquet. The pan-seared Landais duck foie gras steak with artichoke and asparagus salad, quick-grilled squid with tomato, eggplant and olive stew, hake steak with eggplant and wild mushrooms forge ahead. The cassoulet made with haricots maïs—a regional bean—is still the best in Paris. Finally, the warm and crispy tourtière and the pistachio-filled dacquoise are paradigms of confection. A great Bordeaux cellar and Armagnacs to die for.

● L'Alchimiste

181, rue de Charenton
Métro: Montgallet, Reuilly-Diderot
Tel. 01 43 47 10 38
Closed Sun., Mon., 3 weeks Aug.
Open until 10:30 PM.
Prix fixe: 14€ (lunch), 18€ (lunch), 20€ (dinner), 25€ (dinner).

Jean-Michel Garby runs this tasteful bistro enthusiastically. It is an affable establishment with its beige tones and stenciled frieze, and the set menu with its various options is well thought out. Chef Marc Ranger plays an elegant, neoclassical score that hits the mark with its fine produce. The pan-seared foie gras with gingerbread, sweet onions and cinnamon apples, the gratin of Royans ravioli with saffron, the codfish "baked at the oven door" with bell pepper cream and duck confit baked in phyllo pastry do their jobs beautifully. A dark chocolate fondant with coffee-pecan sauce slips down effortlessly.

● La Gazzetta

29, rue de Cotte.
Métro: Ledru-Rollin.
Tel. 01 43 47 47 05. Fax 01 43 47 47 17.
team@lagazzetta.fr / www.lagazzetta.fr
Closed Sun. dinner, Mon., Christmas,
New Year's, Aug.
Prix fixe: 14€ (lunch), 26€ (dinner).
A la carte: 37€.

Peter Nilsson, who spread the reputation of Les 3 Salons far beyond the walls of Uzès, has come to add a touch of magic to this 1930s bistro near the Aligre market. Octopus and fennel pizzetta, the mackerel and carrots simmered in white wine, tender tuna belly or a lovely hummus-style chickpea purée have an easy charm, confirmed by the pumpkin and nut risotto, the pollock with roasted almonds, lasagne and the poultry livers with sour cherries. We end with chocolate and caramel mousse with mint tea-infused jus or a ricotta, hazelnut, grilled almond and preserved citrus quenelle, confirming that with such truly creative dishes prepared with quality produce, this fine art deco establishment offers some of the best value for money to be had today. As Napoleon's mother said, 'Let us hope it lasts'…

● Les Zygomates

7, rue de Capri.
Métro: Daumesnil, Michel-Bizot.
Tel. 01 40 19 93 04. Fax 01 44 73 46 63
info@leszygomates.fr / www.leszygomates.fr
Closed Sun., Mon., Aug.
Prix fixe: 14,50€ (lunch) 24€, 30€.

Pleasant, inexpensive and shrewd, Patrick Fray's establishment has become part of life in the twelfth arrondissement. In his hands, this 1900s butcher's store has become a modish, gourmet haunt. There are no unpleasant surprises in store with the raw duck foie gras and pine nut salad, roasted codfish with tapenade and the Moroccan-style pigeon pie. The wines are skillfully selected and not unreasonably priced, and the service is fast and friendly. Like the exquisite beggar's purse of apples and almonds in salted caramel sauce, the other desserts are right on target.

● A La Biche au Bois

45, av Ledru-Rollin.
Métro: Gare-de-Lyon, Quai-de-la-Rapée, Bastille.
Tel. 01 43 43 34 38.
Closed Sat., Sun., 1 week Christmas– New Year's, July 25th–Aug. 25th.
Prix fixe: 23,20€. A la carte: 38€.

We are fond of this firmly rooted rural inn near the Gare de Lyon, with more than just one foot in provincial France. Eric Broutin takes his cuisine seriously and to heart, the prices are sensible and Céline and Bertrand Marchesseau's welcome is civility itself. The homemade duck foie gras, country terrine, salmon with wild mushrooms, game in season (from September to March) and whole grilled veal kidney do you a world of good. The Opéra Biche (homemade chocolate Opéra cake with custard sauce) and seasonal fruit tart are polished desserts.

● La Connivence   ⬛SIM

1, rue de Cotte.
Métro: Ledru-Rollin.
Tel. 01 46 28 46 17. Fax 01 46 28 49 01.
Closed Sun., Mon., 2 weeks Aug.
Prix fixe: 14€ (lunch), 17€ (lunch),
17€ (dinner), 25€ (dinner).

Pascal Kosmala, from Bar le Duc in the Meuse district, formerly at the Gastrolâtre in Nancy, the Maison Kammerzell in Strasbourg and Schillinger in Colmar, has settled in this corner of the East of Paris. His cuisine is classical, subtle, flavorful and sensibly priced, and patrons have no trouble finding something to their taste in the prix fixe menus. The brioche stuffed with Burgundy snails in garlic cream, pike-perch stewed with fava beans and bacon, grilled beef hanger steak with chopped olives served in a tart crust, as well as the dessert of three chocolates and the dame blanche (vanilla ice cream with hot fudge sauce) are generous, carefully crafted preparations.

● L'Ebauchoir   ⬛SIM

43-45, rue de Cîteaux.
Métro: Faidherbe-Chaligny.
Tel. 01 43 42 49 31.
www.lebauchoir.com
Closed Sun., Mon. lunch.
Prix fixe: 13,50€ (lunch, wine inc.),
23€ (lunch). A la carte: 38€.

This mustard-yellow and red bistro with its fifties flavor is as cheerful as it is gastronomic. Its lunches are quick and inexpensive; its dinners more elaborate. Thomas Dufour, who has "done" Baumanière, Arpège and Laurent, has a gift for producing flavorsome, fresh dishes at affordable prices. The smoked herring and potato salad, tuna tartare with mashed avocado, whiting with pesto sauce, a surprising grilled tuna steak with white chocolate and black olives, thyme-roasted chicken, and iced vacherin with mango sorbet are right on target. Thierry Bruneau handles the prompt service.

● Jean-Pierre Frelet   ⬛SIM

25, rue Montgallet.
Métro: Montgallet.
Tel. 01 43 43 76 65.
Closed Sat. lunch, Sun., Aug.
Prix fixe: 18,50€ (lunch), 26,50€ (dinner).

His past training with Delaveyne in Bougival and Michel Oliver at the Bistrot de Paris has left Jean-Pierre Frelet with a good sense of produce and a feel for the right taste. In his old-fashioned bistro he provides a well-managed cuisine based on extensive experience. As the market produce changes, his inspiration goes to work again and you will scarcely be disappointed by the stuffed roasted suckling pig, escargots sautéed in anchovy butter, saffron risotto, fresh cod parmentier with young vegetables or calf's liver with carrots and onions. The dark chocolate fondant with Espelette chili pepper is explosive.

● O'Rebelle   ⬛SIM

24, rue Traversière.
Métro: Gare-de-Lyon.
Tel. 01 43 40 88 98. Fax 01 43 40 88 99.
www.o-rebelle.fr
Closed Sat. lunch, Sun., Bank Holidays, Aug.
Prix fixe: 30€, 38€.

Mr. Trappe is more globetrotter than rebel. His establishment has a ready charm, with its modern setting in bright colors, exotic wood tables and pictures by Australian artists. The escargot galette served with polenta, the codfish mille-feuille with Sarawak black pepper, the lamb prepared two ways served with eggplant tagine and mascarpone and the banana and Espelette chili pepper sabayon provide original combinations of flavors. The wine list spans the world.

● **Le Square Trousseau**   🛏 SIM

1, rue Antoine-Vollon.
Métro: Ledru-Rollin.
Tel. 01 43 43 06 00. Fax 01 43 43 00 66.
Closed Sun., Mon.
Prix fixe: 20€, 25€.

Things have improved in this fine 1900s bistro boasting stucco, mirrors and carved wooden bar, which has simply been the victim of its own success. Philippe Damas, a veteran of Le Crillon, deploys his culinary skills to cope with the influx of customers, close-set tables and noisy atmosphere. This year, we have no complaints about the tuna and cucumber tartare, nor the ravioli with basil, tomato and beaufort cheese. The seven-hour roasted lamb shanks hit the right note and the prune "bonbons" roasted with Armagnac are still excellent.

■ | HOTELS

■ **Mercure Place d'Italie**   🏨

25, bd Auguste-Blanqui.
Métro: Place-d'Italie, Corvisart.
Tel. 01 45 80 82 23. Fax 01 45 81 45 84.
h1191@accor.com / www.mercure.com
50 rooms: 110–160€. 5 suites: 140–170€.

Part of a chain offering substantial advantages, this hotel is well served by the blue collar charm of the Butte aux Cailles district.

■ **Villa Lutèce Port Royal**   🏠

52, rue Jenner.
Métro: Campo-Formio.
Tel. 01 53 61 90 90. Fax 01 53 61 90 91.
lutece@hotelsdeparis.com
www.leshotelsdeparis.com
36 rooms: 150–300€. 3 suites: 250–450€.

This hostelry devoted to literature and writers provides simple, elegant rooms all in black and white.

■ **Grand Hôtel des Gobelins**   🏠

57, bd Saint-Marcel.
Métro: Les Gobelins, St-Marcel.
Tel. 01 43 31 79 89. Fax 01 45 35 43 56.
resa@hotel-des-gobelins.com
www.hotel-des-gobelins.com
45 rooms: 85–189€.

On the edge of the Latin Quarter, a charming, recently built hotel providing spruce rooms, a refined welcome and reasonable prices. A handsome lobby and facade, as well as an extensive, typically Parisian porch.

■ **La Manufacture**   🏠

8, rue Philippe-de-Champagne.
Métro: Place-d'Italie.
Tel. 01 45 35 45 25. Fax 01 45 35 45 40.
lamanufacture.paris@wanadoo.fr
www.hotel-la-manufacture.com
57 rooms: 109–230€.

The ancient and modern are reconciled in this Haussmann-era residence converted into a charming hotel. The oak flooring, designer furniture, contemporary pictures and Jouy linen blend tastefully. Delightful little rooms, including number seventy-four with its view of the Eiffel Tower.

■ **Holiday Inn Bibliothèque**   🏠
   de France

21, rue de Tolbiac.
Métro: Bibliothèque-François-Mitterrand.
Tel. 01 45 84 61 61. Fax 01 45 84 43 88.
holidayinnbibliotheque.com
69 rooms: 133–148€.

A very practical, peaceful pied à terre with parking and rooms for one to three. Close to the François Mitterrand national library.

● | RESTAURANTS

● **Café Bibliothèque**   SIM

MK2 Bibliothèque, 128-162, av de France.
Métro: Bibliothèque-François-Mitterrand,
Quai-de-la-Gare.
Tel. 01 56 61 44 00. Fax 01 56 61 44 12.
sandrine.gay@mk2.com / www.mk2.com
Closed Christmas, New Year's. Open until
Prix fixe: 15,90€ (lunch), 20,90€.
A la carte: 30–40€.

Before or after a movie, you can eat in the designer setting of this MK2 multiplex café. Tomato and mozzarella millefeuille drizzled with olive oil, a tuna steak with four spices and crispy pan-fried vegetables, chicken breast with morels and the berry crumble with vanilla ice cream provide a gourmet screenplay with nonstop action thanks to the fast service.

● Le Bambou

70, rue Baudricourt.
Métro: Tolbiac.
Tel. 01 45 70 91 75
Closed Mon.
A la carte: 20€.

Madeleine Nguyen painstakingly presides over this small Viet embassy, where freshness is the demanding master. Large and small bowls of phô (sliced rare beef soup with meat balls and noodles) like those found in Saigon, papaya salad, omelet-style crêpes stuffed with shrimp, bò bun (spring rolls, grilled beef and julienned vegetables over rice noodles), steamed dumplings and fresh mango are simply delightful.

● Virgule

9, rue Véronèse.
Tel. 01 43 37 01 14.
Closed Wednesday, 3 weeks Aug.

French Cambodian Heng Dao smilingly serves us his "local gastronomy." Schooled at Lenôtre and Jules Verne, his dependability never flags. We are, as ever, crazy about his subtle touches of spice and perfectly cooked dishes. Sautéed small scallops served with oyster sauce and celeri rémoulade, monkfish in a wine sauce, whole duck breast with Bing cherries, along with suckling pig with sweet spices and the Baked Alaska make up cheerful meals at moderate prices.

● L'Anacréon

53, bd Saint-Marcel.
Métro: Les Gobelins.
Tel. 01 43 31 71 18. Fax 01 43 31 94 94.
www.restaurant-anacreon.com

Closed Sat. lunch, Sun., Mon.,
1 week Christmas–New Year's,
1 week May, 3 weeks Aug.
Prix fixe: 20€ (lunch), 32€.

Christophe Accary has rejuvenated its classics of bistro cuisine with a touch of modernity and a great deal of lightness. The vine-ripened tomato gazpacho with cucumber foam, the pan-seared scorpion fish with saffron potatoes and argan oil, the sweetbreads braised in Jura wine and the Plougastel strawberry melba are enhanced here and there with highly appealing hints of exotic flavor. The check is civilized.

● L'Appennino

61, rue de l'Amiral-Mouchez.
Métro: Cité-Universitaire.
Tel.-Fax 01 45 89 08 15.
lappennino@wanadoo.fr
Closed Sat., Sun., Bank Holidays,
1 week Christmas–New Year's, 2 weeks Aug.
A la carte: 35–40€.

Vittorino Marzani fervently orchestrates the flavors of Emilia-Romagna in his trattoria. The dishes are generous and the vitello tonnato, tuna with lemon, homemade pasta with Parma ham, like the sabayon, take us on a highly enjoyable journey. The Italian wines presented by Marie-Christine Marzani underline the authentic fare with their sunny notes.

● L'Avant-Goût

26, rue Bobillot.
Métro: Place-d'Italie.
Tel. 01 53 80 24 00. Fax 01 53 80 00 77.
Closed Sat., Sun., Mon., 1 week beg. Jan.,
1 week in May, 2 weeks beg. Aug.
Prix fixe: 31€.

Christophe Beaufront, who trained under Guérard and Savoy, has forgotten none of his illustrious mentors' creative precision. His set menus change along with the seasons and according to his inclinations, and we relish his sharp, fresh dishes. We fondly remember the pairing of fresh goat cheese with tapenade, creamy pea soup with fresh mint, sesame-crusted codfish, spiced pork pot-au-feu and melon soup with anise and a tarragon ice.

● L'Ourcine

92, rue Broca.
Métro: Les Gobelins, Glacière.
Tel. 01 47 07 13 65. Fax 01 47 07 18 48.
Closed Sun., Mon., 1 week at the end July–mid-Aug.
Prix fixe: 16€ (lunch), 28€.

After seconding Yves Camdeborde at the Régalade, Sylvain Danière now supervises his own restaurant. This old-style bistro looks good. It offers impressive value for money and displays plenty of creativity in the content of the set menu, changed every day. The farm-raised parsleyed pork terrine, roasted pollock with olive oil and roasted and stuffed free-range Gers chicken with sautéed Chinese cabbage are among its successful dishes. When it is time for dessert, do not miss miniature chocolate pralines with Valrhona Guanaja chocolate ganache, a true delicacy. Both the welcome and Vassanthy Danière's service are delightful.

● Auberge Etchegorry

41, rue de Croulebarbe.
Métro: Corvisart, Les Gobelins.
Tel. 01 44 08 83 51. Fax 01 44 08 83 69.
Closed Sun., Mon.
Prix fixe: 26€, 32,50€, 37,60€.
A la carte: 38–80€.

Henri Laborde has brought the Basque country to stay in what was formerly a cabaret frequented by Victor Hugo and the entertainer Béranger. The facade remains, but the dining room is now very much of our century and the cuisine is engagingly generous. The seared foie gras medallions with grapes, small squid in its own ink, duck breast with potatoes sautéed in goose fat and traditional Basque cake have the sweet smell of the Pyrenean Southwest.

■ HOTELS

■ Méridien-Montparnasse

19, rue du Cdt-René-Mouchotte.
Métro: Montparnasse-Bienvenüe.
Tel. 01 44 36 44 36. Fax 01 44 36 49 00.
www.lemeridien-montparnasse.com
953 rooms: 320–520€.
27 suites: 650–960€.

Opposite the rail station, a caravanserai of nearly a thousand renovated rooms with two restaurants (the Montparnasse 25 and Justine), a modular meeting room and a fitness center.

■ Sofitel Forum Rive Gauche

17, bd Saint-Jacques.
Métro: St-Jacques.
Tel. 01 40 78 79 80. Fax 01 45 88 43 93.
h1297@accor-hotels.com / www.sofitel.com
732 rooms: 175–225€. 16 suites: 395–480€.

Nearly 800 rooms in this contemporary hotel where light wood and shimmering tones dominate. Many spacious meeting rooms and a cyber area, fitness center and hairdressing salon.

■ Lenox Montparnasse

15, rue Delambre.
Métro:Vavin, Edgar-Quinet, Montparnasse-Bienvenüe.
Tel. 01 43 35 34 50. Fax 01 43 20 46 64.
hotel@lenoxmontparnasse.com
www.hotellenox.com
52 rooms: 135–170€. 6 suites: 160–260€.

The bustle of the boulevard Montparnasse is soon forgotten in this hotel with its refined rooms and cozy lounges. The open yard when the weather is fine and the bar at the end of the day are welcoming spots regularly visited by the fashion world.

■ Delambre

35, rue Delambre.
Métro:Vavin.
Tel. 01 43 20 66 31. Fax 01 45 38 91 76.

delambre@club.fr / www.hoteldelambre.com
30 rooms: 85–115€.

The facade has been renovated this year and the rooms are now air conditioned in this fine stopover near to the boulevard Montparnasse. Founder of surrealism André Breton was a resident here. Good value for money.

●   RESTAURANTS

● Montparnasse 25 LUX

At the Méridien-Montparnasse,
19, rue du Cdt-René-Mouchotte.
Métro: Montparnasse-Bienvenüe, Gaîté
Tel. 01 44 36 44 25. Fax 01 44 36 49 03.
meridien.montparnasse@lemeridien.com
www.m25.fr
Closed Sat., Sun., Bank Holidays,
mid-July–end Aug.
Prix fixe: 49€ (lunch), 108€ (dinner).
A la carte: 105–145€.

You may or may not like the neo-thirties, slightly colonial, exotic "James Bond" style of this great hotel restaurant hidden away upstairs. In any case, you will soon feel at home. The great virtues here are the superb service run by Mauro Croese (previously with Guy Savoy), the excellent wines, with advice on the long wine list provided by Emmanuel Petit, and of course the fine cuisine, which is solid and traditional, but forging ahead in the hands of Christian Moine, one of Paris' least known great chefs. This veteran of Le Meurice and Le Ritz showcases the finest produce with a rare precision and unfailing aptness of tone. His latest creations are crabmeat served in the crab's claw with a foamy, sweet mustard dressing, a terrine of foie gras, veal sweetbreads and tongue, sea bass pan fried on one side with carrot jus, grilled Angus beef with marrow pain perdu and Colman's mustard, served with a ratte potato purée, or "Monsieur Miéral's" Bresse pigeon roasted like a woodcock and served with creamed fresh peas. The desserts—puff pastry fingers with summer fruit, whipped light cream and red fruit jus—are droll and success-

ful. The cheese board is always admirable. Although the à la carte prices are less than friendly, the lunchtime prix fixe is a fabulous bargain. Remember that.

● Le Duc V.COM

243, bd Raspail.
Métro: Raspail.
Tel. 01 43 20 96 30. Fax 01 43 20 46 73.
Closed Sat. lunch, Sun., Mon., 3 weeks Aug.
Prix fixe: 46€ (lunch). A la carte: 120€.

This celebrated restaurant has built its reputation on fresh fish. It has been following its star for more than three decades now, and the yacht décor designed by Slavik long ago still wields a dated charm. The service is well timed and customers pour in, filling the place at noon despite prices verging on the piratical. In fact, the best deal is the splendid lunchtime set menu, offering salmon with two peppers or other fish tartare, oysters or fried smelt, scallops simply cooked in their shells or provençal-style monkfish, not to mention the chocolate cake and baba au rhum, washed down pleasantly with a good Muscadet.

● Pavillon Montsouris   V.COM

20, rue Gazan.
Métro: Cité-Universitaire.
Tel. 01 43 13 29 00. Fax 01 43 13 29 02.
www.pavillon-montsouris.fr
Prix fixe: 49€.

Located in one of the most beautiful parks in Paris, this pretty, Universal Exhibition–style pavillion has a strong appeal. Looking out at the trees, bathed in the generous light that pours through the glass roof, we give in to the temptation of Stéphane Lemarchand's meticulous cuisine under the attentive eye of proprietor Yvan Courault. The shredded crabmeat with tarragon, shrimp, scorpion fish and clam risotto or the roasted pork served with potato purée with truffle oil charm us effortlessly.

● Le Dôme   COM

108, bd du Montparnasse.
Métro: Vavin.
Tel. 01 43 35 25 81. Fax 01 42 79 01 19
A la carte: 72–100€.

Things have improved in this circa-1920 brasserie, with its refurbished seventies décor designed by Slavik. Chef Franck Graux has taken the kitchen firmly in hand and the service is of a very high standard. There are tuna carpaccio, sea bream tartare and marinated raw salmon, authentic Marseille bouillabaise, grilled tiny red mullet and large Dover sole fried in butter from the île d'Yeu served with mashed potatoes worthy of Robuchon. All offer undiluted pleasure. We conclude with a splendid rum and vanilla mille-feuille. The wine list is rich in divine surprises.

● Millésime 62   Ⓝ ⛟ COM

13-15, pl de Catalogne.
Métro: Gaîté, Montparnasse-Bienvenüe.
Tel. 01 43 35 34 35. Fax 01 43 20 26 21
www.millesimes62.com
Closed Sat. lunch, Sun., Bank Holidays,
2 weeks Aug.
Prix fixe: 24€ (lunch), 26€.

Elegant and charming, flavorsome and vinic, this "lounge" is perfect for both business and private meals. Close to the Montparnasse rail station on a square planned by Boffil, it has an easy charm. The cuisine is a wonderful surprise, with its lively, fresh dishes escorted by a stream of selected vintages, served by the glass or in bottles of every size. Under the supervision of Pascal Noizet, a veteran of the Flo group, the spring roll of duck confit with meat and balsamic vinegar jus, whole foie gras terrine, goat cheese and fresh sardine filet on grilled bread, grilled codfish with wok-fried vegetables and tender roasted duck breast with basmati rice are first-rate. The desserts—baba au rhum, lemon tart—are up to the same high standards.

● Auberge de Venise   Ⓝ 🍴 COM

10, rue Delambre.
Métro: Vavin, Edgar-Quinet.
Tel. 01 43 35 43 09. Fax 01 43 20 51 88.
Prix fixe: 15€ (lunch), 19€.
A la carte: 35–45€.

No pizza in this transalpine inn, just good meat dishes and fragrant pasta, including the penne with spicy tomato sauce or the fresh ravioli with basil, washed down with fine Italian vintages. Antipasti, carpaccio, calmari casserole and Venice-style calf's liver spring some delightful surprises on us.

● La Coupole   🍴 COM

102, bd du Montparnasse.
Métro: Vavin.
Tel. 01 43 20 14 20. Fax 01 43 35 46 14.
jtosi@groupeflo.fr / www.flobrasseries.com
Prix fixe: 15€ (lunch), 22,90€, 29,90€.
A la carte: 40–55€.

The newly non-smoking Coupole is doing very well. The seafood platter, salmon rillettes, grilled codfish, generous choucroute, superb grilled rib-eye steak served with thick-cut French fries, the ever-present Indian-style lamb curry and warm soft chocolate cake and roasted pineapple are splendid, served (despite the sea of tables) with promptness and a smile. The twenties setting with its fresco-embellished column capitals continues to hold a strong appeal.

● Ban Som Tam   Ⓝ ⛟ SIM

5, rue Raymond-Losserand.
Métro: Gaîté, Montparnasse-Bienvenüe.
Tel. 01 43 22 65 72. Fax 01 43 22 26 40
www.restoaparis.com, www.e-quartier.com
Closed Sun., Aug. Open until 11 PM.
Prix fixe: 15€ (weekday lunch), 25€, 35€ (wine inc.), 45€. A la carte: 30–40€.

An excellent match here between a French oenologist and a Thai cook. The partnership is highly successful, especially since Franck Poré has built up a carefully composed wine list to flatter the dishes presented by his wife Phannee. We marvel at this festival of flame and flavor: beignets stuffed with red bell pepper, lemongrass soup, raw diced spicey shrimp, fish steamed in banana leaves with thai curry sauce, refreshing chilled desserts and sticky rice cake with banana. The prices are moderate, the décor refined Thai and the atmosphere relaxing.

● L'Amuse-Bouche

186, rue du Château.
Métro: Mouton-Duvernet, Pernety.
Tel. 01 43 35 31 61. Fax 01 45 38 96 60
Closed Sun., Mon., Aug.
Prix fixe: 24,50€, 30,50€.
A la carte: 40€.

Gilles Lambert delights his crowd of faithful guests with fresh, market-based dishes. We fondly remember the langoustine ravioli with tarragon, fresh crab in rémoulade sauce, tuna steak with cracked black pepper and the calf's liver with a gingerbread crust. The local wines and the aptly crafted desserts, such as apple crumble with salted-butter caramel ice cream, certainly hit the mark.

● La Cerisaie

70, bd Edgar-Quinet.
Métro: Edgar-Quinet,
Montparnasse-Bienvenüe.
Tel.-Fax 01 43 20 98 98
Closed Sat., Sun., Christmas–New Year's, Aug.
A la carte: 38€.

The Lalannes manage beautifully in their mini-bistro with its twenty places, serving up generous dishes inspired by Southwestern France, at friendly prices. At the stove, Cyril from the Ariège, who learned his trade in Paris at Le Bascou and Le Louis XIII and in Toulouse with Garrigues and Vanel, skillfully concocts subtle, charming fare. The sardines in phyllo pastry with cumin, grilled tuna steak with piperade, grilled Landais goose breast and spiced roasted peaches and Armagnac-soaked baba will make you melt. Non-smoking.

● Les Fils de la Ferme

5, rue Mouton-Duvernet.
Métro: Mouton-Duvernet.
Tel.-Fax 01 45 39 39 61.
www.lesfilsdelaferme.com
Closed Sun. dinner, Mon., 3 weeks Aug.
Prix fixe: 17€ (lunch), 26€.

The codfish crumble with orange peel and creamy young garlic broth reflect the fine ideas of Stéphane Dutter, who worked with Georges Blanc and Christian Moris-

set at Le Juana and has settled here with his brother Jean-Christophe, who handles the service. The skate fried in red bell pepper butter, tender slow-roasted leg of suckling pig, rhubarb floating island and red fruit macerated in balsamic vinegar are also magnificent.

● Natacha

17 bis, rue Campagne-Première.
Métro: Raspail.
Tel. 01 43 20 79 27. Fax 01 43 22 00 90.
restaurantnatacha@wanadoo.fr
Closed Sun., Sat. lunch, Mon.,
3 weeks Aug.
Prix fixe: 19€ (lunch), 26€ (lunch),
A la carte: 36–44€.

Alain Cirelli, a veteran of L'Ambroisie, has breathed new life into this legendary Montparnasse eatery. We have happy memories of the steamed baby leeks with poached egg and truffle oil, warm calf's head terrine, John Dory roasted on one side served with asparagus and New Zealand spinach, shepherd's pie, country cherry clafoutis and chocolate fondant with cracked pistachios. A timeless bistro setting, revamped in saffron yellow, white and red.

● Parnasse 138

138, bd du Montparnasse.
Métro: Vavin, Port-Royal.
Tel. 01 43 20 47 87. Fax 01 43 22 44 85
Prix fixe: 11,50€ (lunch on weekdays),
13,50€, 17,50€. A la carte: 25–30€.

With an eye for fresh produce, Caroula and Nelson Da Rosa present a choice of at least ten starters, entrees and desserts on each prix fixe menu, with a few additional daily specials: duck terrine with green peppercorns, homemade duck foie gras, sautéed oyster mushrooms and grilled fresh sardines. Grilled duck breast with honey, authentic pot-au-feu with marrow-bone, veal kidneys, rack of lamb with thyme blossoms: With this kind of Prévert-style inventory, the only problem is choosing. The desserts are generous: sorbet in a crispy pastry cup, apple mille-feuille, vanilla crème brûlée. The cellar is small but well chosen, and the prices are sensible.

● Les Petites Sorcières   🎞 SIM

12, rue Liancourt.
Métro: Denfert-Rochereau.
Tel.-Fax 01 43 21 95 68.
lespetitessorcières@wanadoo.fr
Closed Sat. lunch, Sun., Mon. lunch,
mid-July–mid-Aug.
A la carte: 38€.

The "Little Witches" the restaurant is named after take the form of puppets that watch over Christian Teule's cauldron. A disciple of Joël Robuchon, Christian concocts subtle, precise, seasonal dishes. With a wave of his magic wand, he produces a zucchini and mozzarella clafoutis, tomato stuffed with eggplant caviar, sautéed jumbo shrimp and chorizo, roasted duck steak with olives. With iced raspberry and watermelon gazpacho, we end on a cool note. The tab is very civilized.

● La Régalade   🎞 SIM

49, av Jean-Moulin.
Métro: Alésia, Porte-d'Orléans.
Tel. 01 45 45 68 58.
Closed Sat., Sun., Mon. lunch,
1 week at end July–end Aug.
Prix fixe: 32€.

Yes, this is where it all began: the fashion for bistros serving deftly prepared dishes at low prices. Bruno Doucet, veteran of L'Apicius, knows his trade. We enjoy the convivial, noisy, but amiable atmosphere, and we love his prix fixe, with all the delicious, subtle fare it has to offer. For example? The foie gras flan in a creamy chanterelle mushroom broth, Breton cod filet roasted with olive oil, pigeon breast roasted on the bone offer undiluted pleasure, as do the rice pudding with vanilla and salted-butter caramel and the wines, chosen with tremendous flair. It is vital to reserve.

● Le Severo   🎞 SIM

8, rue des Plantes.
Métro: Alésia, Mouton-Duvernet.
Tel. 01 45 40 40 91.

Closed Sat., Sun., 1 week Christmas–New Year's, 1 week at Easter, Aug.
A la carte: 40€.

William Bernet, a conscientious butcher who worked at the Nivernaises and has now turned restaurateur, has made this ordinary looking corner bistro into a gourmet headquarters. His secret? Excellent meat, good food, a very impressive wine list up on the wall next to the blackboard and a cordial welcome. Johnny Béguin, the modest chef, assiduously prepares boned pig's feet, farmhouse blood pudding, steak tartare or grilled rib-eye steak with (real) French fries and chocolate mousse, all of them delightful. Fish is served in neighboring adjunct Le Bis du Severo.

● L'Assiette   🍴 SIM

181, rue du Château.
Métro: Mouton-Duvernet, Pernety.
Tel. 01 43 22 64 86
www.chezlulu.fr
Closed lunch (exc. Sat., Sun.).
Prix fixe: 50€ (dinner, wine inc.).
A la carte: 50–100€.

Lulu livens up the atmosphere with her earthy humor in this former delicatessen turned bistro. The dishes are generous here, as are the prices, more sensible than in the past. We never tire of her mackerel rillettes, homemade pork pâté, skate in lemon butter, blood pudding parmentier and Poitou-style salt-cured duck stew with vegetables. And her chocolate fondant is just as good.

● Les Caves Solignac   🍴 SIM

9, rue Decrès.
Métro: Plaisance, Pernety.
Tel.-Fax 01 45 45 58 59.
Closed Sat., Sun., 1 week Christmas–New Year's, 3 weeks Aug.
Prix fixe: 18€ (lunch), 28€ (dinner).
A la carte: 38€.

Pascal and Philippe Moisant have taken over the reins of this thirties décor wine bar and offer a tremendously fresh, market-based cuisine. Asparagus and polenta, croustillant of mackerel with rhubarb, slow-cooked beef cheeks in red wine and roasted apricots with vanilla ice cream suitably accompany the seventy growers' vintages. A few good Calvados apple brandies and a moderate tab pleasantly conclude the proceedings.

PARIS 15TH ARR

■	HOTELS

■ Hilton Paris

18, av de Suffren.
Métro: Bir-Hakeim.
Tel. 01 44 38 56 00. Fax 01 44 38 56 10.
rm.paris@hilton.com / www.hilton.com
442 rooms: 220–500€.
19 suites: 260–740€.

A prestige hotel a step away from the Eiffel Tower and opposite the Trocadéro. Comfortable, fully equipped rooms and elegant service. The Pacific Eiffel's Californian cuisine offers a taste of America.

■ Sofitel Paris Porte de Sèvres

8-12, rue Louis-Armand.
Métro: Balard.
Tel. 01 40 60 30 20. Fax 01 40 60 30 00.
h0572@accor.com / www.sofitel.com
608 rooms: 207–280€.
12 suites: 470–550€.

Near the Porte de Versailles exhibition center and close to the heliport, a large, very practical hotel complex. Swimming pool and gym run by Club Med. A brasserie and the gourmet Relais de Sèvres.

■ Mercure Tour Eiffel

64, bd de Grenelle.
Métro: Dupleix.
Tel. 01 45 78 90 90. Fax 01 45 78 95 55.
www.mercuretoureiffel.com
77 rooms: 200–300€. 1 suite: 330€.

Seen through the windows of this good, modern hotel, the Eiffel Tower looms majestically. A gym where guests can keep in shape and (on a more practical side) meeting rooms.

■ Le Marquis

15, rue Dupleix.
Métro: Dupleix, La Motte-Picquet-Grenelle.
Tel. 01 43 06 31 50. Fax 01 40 56 06 78.
lemarquis@inwoodhotel.com
www.inwoodhotel.com
36 rooms: 250–320€.

Rest and recreation are guaranteed here in the refined rooms designed by Paul Sastre, lounge, fireside corner and library.

■ Alizé Grenelle

87, av Emile-Zola.
Métro: Charles-Michels.
Tel. 01 45 78 08 22. Fax 01 40 59 03 06.
info@alizeparis.com / www.alizeparis.com
50 rooms: 88–133€.

In this quiet hotel a step away from the Porte de Versailles exhibition center, guests returning from the trade fairs find all they need to work in their rooms. A fine welcome, moderate prices and WiFi.

■ Nouvel Hôtel Eiffel

5, rue des Volontaires.
Métro: Volontaires.
Tel. 01 47 34 77 89. Fax 01 40 56 36 55.
www.nouvelhotel-paris15.com
36 rooms: 55–108€.

An unpretentious hotel offering a warm welcome. Practical rooms and good value for money considering the location.

■ Pasteur Namiki

33, rue du Dr-Roux.
Métro: Volontaires, Pasteur.
Tel. 01 53 58 12 30. Fax 01 53 58 12 31.
http://monsite.wanadoo.fr/hotelpasteur
Closed Aug.
15 rooms: 65–125€. 2 suites: 140–145€.

A charming little hotel whose most pleasant rooms overlook a flowered courtyard. A friendly welcome and moderate prices.

● | RESTAURANTS

● **Chen**   ○ V.COM

"Le Soleil d'Est"

15, rue du Théâtre.
Métro: Charles-Michels, Bir-Hakeim.
Tel. 01 45 79 34 34. Fax 01 45 79 07 53.
Closed Sun., May 1st, Aug.
Prix fixe: 40€ (weekend lunch), 75€,
15€ (child). A la carte: 80–100€.

Patriarch Fung Chin Chen is now in paradise and the family is assiduously carrying on his work. The faithful Jean Le Gloanec, who has been running the dining room for so long, is assisted by Véronique Chen today. In the half-Chinese, half-contemporary décor of the second floor and in the first floor dining room with its historic woodwork, they recommend sautéed frog legs with herbs, fresh ginger and Sichuan pepper, small turbot with exotic spices—a magical delicacy—or mountain-style oxtail served with pan juices and slow-roasted caramelized eggplant, a dash of Chinese vinaigrette. The hot and cold green apple dessert should not be missed. Tea can be chosen to the exclusion of any other beverage and we have no complaints when the check arrives, since quality has its price.

● **Le Ciel de Paris**   V.COM

Tour Montparnasse (56th floor)
33, av du Maine.
Métro: Montparnasse-Bienvenüe.
Tel. 01 40 64 77 64 / 01 40 64 77 67.
Fax 01 43 21 48 37.
ciel-de-paris.rv@elior.com
www.cieldeparis.com
Prix fixe: 33€ (lunch), 56€ (dinner).
A la carte: 75–90€.

We climb to the 56th floor in record time (with the help of the elevator) and find Paris spread at our feet. The service is assiduous and Jean-François Oyon's cuisine offers an inspired take on seasonal produce. Lobster salad, sea bream with zucchini and eggplant chutney and the pan-seared veal kidneys and sweetbreads with horseradish and capers are among his successes. The wine list is worthy and the meal less expensive than an hour over the capital in a helicopter.

● **Le Grand Venise**   V.COM

171, rue de la Convention.
Métro: Convention, Boucicaut.
Tel. 01 45 32 49 71. Fax 01 45 32 07 49.
Closed Sun., Mon., 1 week Christmas–New Year's, Aug.
A la carte: 100€.

Anne is at the helm and Jean-Louis at the stove, while Marina watches over the cellar. The Piprels work as a family and since there is no point in changing a successful menu, the fare still includes antipasti with eggplant "chinchinettes", a rich seafood lasagne, fried shrimp cooked with precision and the formidable Venice-style calf's liver. The tiramisu and the caramel ice cream are delectable conclusions. The check is high, especially if you yield to temptation and order one of the great vintages on the verbose wine list.

● **Thierry Burlot**

8, rue Nicolas-Charlet.
Métro: Pasteur.
Tel. 01 42 19 08 59.
Closed Sat. lunch, Sun.
Prix fixe: 26€, 32€, 59€.

Thierry Burlot has put together a more dynamic and efficient team that maintains the same high standards when the master's away. The dishes are light, the cooking keeps all the flavor intact and the compositions are unexpected and always tasteful: Jumbo shrimp with coriander and wild lime, Dover sole braised with bacon served with lemon confit, roasted lamb shoulder with carrots and orange flower–scented semolina. The desserts, such as the caramel and fleur de sel ice cream, are acrobatic. Aurélie Frazier handles the service amiably, playing the role of sommelier on occasion.

● **Le Gastroquet**

10, rue Desnouettes.
Métro: Convention, Porte-de-Versailles.
Tel. 01 48 28 60 91. Fax 01 45 33 23 70.

Closed Sat. lunch (July–Aug.), Sun.,
Christmas, New Year's,
3 weeks Aug.
Prix fixe: 19,50€ (lunch), 29€.
A la carte: 55€.

Dany and Madeleine Bulot are adorable
people. Whether you are a regular customer or a first timer, they take you in hand
and pamper you as if you were their grand-
child. Madeleine welcomes the guests,
while Dany works in the kitchen, pop-
ping out into the dining room from time
to time to make sure everything is going
well. A genuine, traditional chef, he serves
up food in a fine classical vein, tempered
to suit current tastes. Leeks in Sauternes
aspic, ham and foie gras, de-boned pig's
foot with lentils, lamb shoulder with oriental spices and calf's liver with lemon confit are polished dishes indeed. The apple
crème brûlée with Calvados is mouthwatering. The wine list has plenty of appeal.
Given the quality, the prices are not in the
least excessive.

● **L'Antre Amis** 🏠 COM
9, rue Bouchut.
Métro: Sèvres-Lecourbe, Ségur.
Tel.-Fax 01 45 67 15 65.
contact@lantreamis.fr
www.lantreamis.fr
Closed Sat., Sun., Bank holidays,
1 week Christmas–New Year's.
Prix fixe: 27€, 33€. A la carte: 40€.

This bistro dining room has been redone
in contemporary chic. Stéphane Pion welcomes with a smile, helps you with the
wine and takes pride in Baptist Anguer-
in's well-executed dishes. The menu has
it all and we particularly like the croustillant of marinated shrimp, the tabouli with
curried mussels, sea bass with vegetables
and the roast veal chop with country ham.
We end on these notes: a croquant of dark
chocolate with raspberry mousse and a
Montélimar nougat soufflé. The wines are
well chosen but don't break the bank.

● **La Gauloise** 🍴 COM
59, av de La Motte-Picquet.
Métro: La Motte-Picquet-Grenelle.

Tel. 01 47 34 11 64 / 01 47 34 49 78.
Fax 01 40 61 09 70.
Prix fixe: 22€, 24€. A la carte: 55€.

This neighborhood institution by the
Ecole Militaire has beautiful stucco ceilings from the 1880s and, on nice days, a
terrace. There's no genius in the kitchen,
but there are dishes that can be counted
on, including salmon carpaccio, goat
cheese tartare, the langoustine risotto
and the île flottante for dessert. It's old-
fashioned service, and the house Brouilly
almost drinks itself.

● **Le Bélisaire** ◎ SIM
2, rue Marmontel
Métro: Convention, Vaugirard
Tel.-Fax 01 48 28 62 24
m.garrel@wanadoo.fr
Closed Sat. lunch, Sun., 1 week Christmas–
New Year's, 1 week at Easter, 3 weeks Aug.
Prix fixe: 20€ (lunch), 30€ (dinner),
40€, 15€ (child).

Matthieu Garrel continues to astonish us.
This staunchly traditional Breton produces
a highly colorful cuisine with a very seasonal taste. A glance at the blackboard, presented and commented on by Evelyne, and
we settle down to feast on marinated wild
mushrooms with beefsteak tomato coulis,
scorpion fish in pastry crust with basil and
tagine-roasted baby vegetables, beef cheeks
braised in red wine and foie gras confit.
Proust would have loved the warm madeleines made with salted butter. The wine
list is shrewd and continually updated, and
the set menus are great bargains.

● **Le Casier à Vin** 🏠🍴 SIM
51-53, rue Olivier-de-Serres.
Métro: Convention.
Tel.-Fax 01 45 33 36 80.
Closed Sat. lunch, Sun., 2 weeks beg. Aug.
A la carte: 32–35€.

This wine cellar, grocery store and restaurant is a rising star. There are those
who call in simply to buy a bottle of wine
recommended by Henri and Ingrid, others who come to purchase cured meats,
pâtés and cheeses to enjoy at home, and

then there are the epicures who sit down to savor Iza Guyot's cuisine. Her cooking is lively, cheerful, high in color and never stales, especially since the dishes on the blackboard change almost daily. Why bother telling you that the tartine of ricotta with thin slices of bresaola was perfect, and that the tuna wrapped in pancetta with arugula and virgin oil was magnificent and that the citrus terrine with orange caramel was to die for?

● **L'Ami Marcel**

33, rue Georges-Pitard.
Métro: Plaisance, Convention.
Tel.-Fax 01 48 56 62 06.
lamimarcel@lamimarcel.com
www.lamimarcel.com
Closed Sun., Mon., 3 weeks in Aug.
Prix fixe: 19€ (lunch), 25€ (lunch),
30€ (dinner). A la carte: 30€.

Eric Martins, formerly with Ledoyen and Hélène Darroze, has turned this local café-style bistro into a tasteful restaurant. His new establishment in the eighth arrondissement (L'Arôme) must take up most of his time, but he has put together a young team here, including chef Daniel Saria. The rest follows naturally, starting with the market-based cuisine. Asparagus and marinated salmon flan, the Atlantic sea bass with Basque peppers and onions, roasted veal served with a celeriac gratin and the prune beignets with licorice ice cream look healthy indeed. The set menu option is splendid.

● **Arti**

173, rue Lecourbe
Métro: Vaugirard
Tel. 01 48 28 66 68. Fax 01 45 54 50 15
arunparis@hotmail.com
A la carte: 35€

Arun Sachdeva introduces us to the cuisine of Northern India. The tandoori shrimp, chicken tikka, shrimp masala and lamb bhuna ghost are local dishes high in flavor and fresh on the palate. The setting is restful with its woodwork, statuettes and jewelry collection. The prices remain honest, especially if you accompany your meal from start to dessert—kulfi (a creamy pistachio and almond ice cream flavored with rose)—with tea or a lassi.

● **Le Beurre Noisette**

68, rue Vasco-de-Gama.
Métro: Lourmel, Porte-de-Versailles.
Tel. 01 48 56 82 49.
Closed Sun., Mon., 3 weeks Aug.
Prix fixe: 18€ (lunch), 22€ (lunch),
32€ (dinner).

The simplicity of the décor reflects the nature of the proprietor, Thierry Blanqui, who is quietly continuing his career in this arrondissement after a few years spent with Christian Le Squer at Ledoyen. Featured in set menus at friendly prices, the foie gras cooked in red wine and spices, the fresh fish of the day, the slow-roasted lamb shoulder with lemon confit and cumin and the house baba au rhum are right on target. When the weather is fine, the terrace provides a further attraction.

● **Le Pétel**

4, rue Pétel.
Métro: Vaugirard.
Tel.-Fax 01 45 32 58 76.
www.restaurant.lepetel.oneline.fr
Closed Sun., Mon., 1 week at the end July,
2 weeks beg. Aug.
Prix fixe: 18€ (lunch), 29,90€.
A la carte: 36€.

Michel Marie is still running this restaurant. It is splendidly reliable. We have moving memories of the asparagus ravioli, lamb shanks with risotto and iced nougat with gingerbread, but the emotion would probably have been just as strong if we had opted for crayfish mango salad, veal kidneys with whole-grain mustard sauce or apple gratin with cider butter. A trusted eatery that never lets us down and is easy on the pocket, too.

● **Le Restaurant du Marché**

59, rue de Dantzig
Métro: Porte-de-Versailles, Porte-de-Vanves.
Tel. 01 48 28 31 55. Fax 01 48 28 18 31.
Closed Sat. lunch, Sun., Mon. lunch,
3 weeks Aug.

Prix fixe: 15€ (weekday lunch, wine inc.), 23€, 29€. A la carte: 30–35€.

This place had its moment of glory in the seventies and eighties, in the days of the Massias, ambassadors of Landes cuisine in Paris. The wooden tables have been stripped of their white cloths and the prices lowered (significantly). Francis Lévêque (who trained with Lorain and Vigato) has taken over this legendary bistro, changed its style, introducing a fresh, eloquent, market-based cuisine chalked up on the blackboard. When we visited, pig's foot tartine, salt- and herb-marinated salmon presented en bocal, scallops with celery root purée, spiced and roasted monkfish with simmered vegetables en cocotte and pain perdu with caramel ice cream were godsends—nothing more, nothing less.

● Stéphane Martin   🏠 SIM

67, rue des Entrepreneurs.
Métro: Charles-Michels, Commerce.
Tel. 01 45 79 03 31. Fax 01 45 79 44 69.
restau.stephanemartin@free.fr
Closed Sun., Mon., Christmas–New Year's,
1 week at Easter, 3 weeks Aug.
Prix fixe: 32€. A la carte: 35–40€.

This street corner restaurant is popular with the local inhabitants. Even the firefighters from the station opposite come to eat here. Marie-Lucile's welcome is affable, and in the kitchen, Stéphane Martin (who worked with Alain Dutournier) is an inventive chef. He adds his personal touch, bringing a new flavor to each traditional dish. White asparagus fricassée with parmesan and country bacon, tuna steak with crisp fennel and sorrel, panseared foie gras with lamb's lettuce salad and papaya give a good idea of his unusual cuisine. Strawberry tiramisu with strawberry biscuits and flavored with rose is light and airy.

● Le Troquet   ● SIM

21, rue François-Bonvin.
Métro: Sèvres-Lecourbe, Cambronne,
Volontaires.
Tel. 01 45 66 89 00. Fax 01 45 66 89 83.

Closed Sun., Mon., 1 week Christmas–New Year's, 1 week May, 3 weeks Aug.
Prix fixe: 24€ (lunch), 28€ (lunch),
30€ (lunch), 38€.

Christian Etchebest is a very good chef. Cumin-seasoned eggplant spread, mussels and sea snails in vinaigrette, the salt and pepper red tuna with beef bone marrow and suckling pig shoulder accompanied by beans in pistou are superb, as is the vanilla soufflé with black cherry jam. The service, supervised by Patricia Etchebest, is prompt, but you have to vacate your table punctually, because the customers who have reserved it for the second sitting have begun to arrive. The meal does not come cheap, but in the end, there is very little to grumble about.

● Le Café du Commerce   🏠 SIM

51, rue du Commerce.
Métro: Emile-Zola,
La Motte Picquet–Grenelle.
Tel. 01 45 75 03 27. Fax 01 45 75 27 40.
commercial@lecafeducommerce.com
www.lecafeducommerce.com
Closed Christmas.
Prix fixe: 14€ (lunch on weekdays), 26€.
A la carte: 30–40€.

This son of a Limousin butcher, who turned this huge twenties café with its floors and galleries into a temple to red meat, has put it back on its feet. The pig's ear salad, tuna steak and vegetables with horseradish vinaigrette and baba au rhum are good, but it is his boneless rib steak, back steak and rib-eye that make it all worthwhile. The service is not always attentive.

● Je Thé . . . Me   🏠 SIM

4, rue d'Alleray.
Métro: Vaugirard.
Tel. 01 48 42 48 30. Fax 01 48 42 70 66.
www.restaurantjethemeparis.com
Closed Sun., Mon.,
2 weeks Christmas–New Year's, Aug.
Prix fixe: 33€.

Jacky Larsonneur continues to assuage our appetite with his single prix fixe menu, which we enjoy in this very beautiful late-19th-century setting. The crayfish fricassée with aromatic herbs, spiced tuna tartare, veal kidneys with coarse mustard are perfectly prepared and adapted to current tastes. The house baba au rhum concludes the festival of flavor. This is the kind of restaurant we love.

PARIS 16TH ARR

■ | HOTELS

■ Raphaël
17, av Kléber.
Métro: Kléber.
Tel. 01 53 64 32 00 / 01 53 64 32 11.
Fax 01 53 64 32 01.
management@raphael-hotel.com
www.raphael-hotel.com
54 rooms: 465–730€.
36 suites: 950–3450€.

This luxury hotel dating from 1925 has been elegantly renovated. We are fond of the panoramic terrace with its view over Paris, paneled English bar and refined rooms.

■ Costes K.
81, av Kléber.
Métro: Boissière, Trocadéro.
Tel. 01 44 05 75 75. Fax 01 44 05 74 74.
resak@hotelcostesk.com
83 rooms: 300–550€.

This handsome, minimalist, contemporary setting, whose pure lines were designed by Ricardo Bofill for the Costes brothers, is impressive indeed with its Japanese-inspired patio and charming rooms.

■ Saint-James Paris
43, av Bugeaud.
Métro: Porte-Dauphine.
Tel. 01 44 05 81 81. Fax 01 44 05 81 82.
contact@saint-james-paris.com
www.saint-james-paris.com
38 rooms: 360–510€. 10 suites: 610–770€.

Near the avenue Foch, this 1892 town house with its grounds, fountain, library bar, Jacuzzi, gym and gracious rooms offers a discreet luxury.

■ Sofitel Le Parc
55-57, av Raymond-Poincaré.
Métro: Trocadéro, Victor-Hugo.
Tel. 01 44 05 66 66. Fax 01 44 05 66 39.
h2797-re@accor.com / sofitel.com
95 rooms: 400–620€. 21 suites: 580–620€.

Elegance abounds on every floor of this hotel, with its art nouveau facade, English-style rooms, pleasant patio terrace and Relais du Parc restaurant.

■ Sofitel Baltimore
88 bis, av Kléber.
Métro: Boissière.
Tel. 01 44 34 54 54. Fax 01 44 34 54 44.
welcome@hotelbaltimore.com
reservation@hotelbaltimore.com
102 rooms: 195–650€. 1 suite: 630–1015€.

The renovation has been a success in this classic, antique hotel refurbished in contemporary style. Fitness center, modern rooms and a refined restaurant (the Table du Baltimore).

■ Sezz
6, rue Frémiet.
Tel. 01 56 75 26 26. Fax 01 56 75 26 16.
mailhotelsezz.com / www.hotelsezz.com
13 rooms: 270–450€. 14 suites: 430–700€.

This former Best Western hotel in the heart of Passy is enjoying a second youth. In the hands of architect Christophe Pillet, it has become a boutique hotel, boasting pure lines and elegant rooms. Its champagne bar is already very popular.

■ Le Square
3, rue de Boulainvilliers.
Métro: Passy.
Tel. 01 44 14 91 90. Fax 01 44 14 91 99.
reservation@hotelsquare.com
www.hotelsquare.com
16 rooms: 260–335€. 6 suites: 420–520€.
Prix fixe: 25€ (lunch). A la carte: 40€.

Here, Patrick Derderian has created a minimalist temple in gray marble with modern furniture and hi tech facilities. A stylish brasserie (Zebra Square) on the first floor.

■ **Trocadero Dokhan's**

117, rue Lauriston.
Métro:Trocadéro,Victor-Hugo, Boissière.
Tel. 01 53 65 66 99. Fax 01 53 65 66 88.
reservation@dokhans.com
www.sofitel.com
41 rooms: 400–550€.
4 suites: 850–1200€.

Unobtrusive and peaceful, this Palladian-style hotel works its charm. Frédéric Méniche has created a rich, elegant décor with marble, green fabrics, gray stripes and velvet. A Vuitton trunk-style elevator.

■ **Hôtel Duret**

30, rue Duret.
Métro: Argentine.
Tel. 01 45 00 42 60. Fax 01 45 00 55 89.
reservation@hotelduret.com
www.hotelduret.com
25 rooms: 150–230€. 2 suites: 250–450€.

We enjoy the understated charm of this discreetly renovated hotel. The rooms are enchanting with their modern furniture and dark purple, bracing green and blue tones.

■ **Les Jardins du Trocadéro**

35, rue Benjamin-Franklin,
place du Trocadéro.
Métro:Trocadéro.
Tel. 01 53 70 17 70. Fax 01 53 70 17 80.
jardintroc@aol.com / www.jardintroc.com
20 rooms: 99–499€. 5 suites: 199–599€.

An ideal location, refined rooms and suites, facilities worthy of a luxury hotel (massage, Jacuzzi, treatments and hairdressing in the rooms) and a 50% discount for readers of this guide are all to be found in this Napoleon III-style hotel.

■ **Le Hameau de Passy**

48, rue de Passy.
Métro: Passy.
Tel. 01 42 88 47 55. Fax 01 42 31 83 72.
www.paris-hotel-hameaudepassy.com
32 rooms: 120–175€.

Nestling in a luxuriant side street in the chic Passy district, this smart hotel provides comfort and silence in its flowered garden.

■ **Résidence Bassano**

15, rue de Bassano.
Métro: George-V, Alma-Marceau.
Tel. 01 47 23 78 23. Fax 01 47 20 41 22.
info@hotel-bassano.com
www.hotel-bassano.com
28 rooms: 150–280€. 3 suites: 500€.

A short step from the Arc de Triomphe, Provence has moved into this guesthouse with its red hexagonal floor tiles, wrought-iron furniture and colored fabrics. Charming!

● | RESTAURANTS

● **Le Pré Catelan** ⬡⬡ LUX

Rte de Suresnes, Bois de Boulogne.
Métro: Porte-Maillot, Porte-Dauphine.
Tel. 01 44 14 41 14. Fax 01 45 24 43 25.
www.lenotre.fr
Closed Sun., Mon., 3 weeks Feb.
Prix fixe: 75€ (lunch), 140€ (dinner), 180€ (dinner). A la carte: 180–205€.

In a Belle Epoque style, with pastel shades and Caran d'Ache frescos, this Napoleon III lodge in the Bois de Boulogne is a natural, chic destination for businesspeople and lovers. Formerly with Boyer, Bardot and Robuchon, Frédéric Anton prepares a refined, highly meticulous cuisine. Hardly has roasted Breton lobster begun to whet your appetite with its garlic snow peas, capers, mushrooms and crispy lobster claw, than you find yourself swept out to sea by variations on the theme of the sardine and steamed seaweed-wrapped turbot served with shellfish and white wine stew. The lamb—grilled chops sautéed with fresh green peas, morel mushrooms and lamb sausage—melts deliciously in the mouth. The desserts, light yet intense (caramelized apple with chocolate cream, green apple sorbet, baked apple and apple tartlet), live up to our expectations, as does the cellar, which offers no fewer than 950 French and world vintages under the informed supervision of David Rivière. The service is, of course, perfect.

● La Grande Cascade ○ 🏠 LUX

Allée de Longchamp, bois de Boulogne.
Métro: Porte-Maillot.
Tel. 01 45 27 33 51. Fax 01 42 88 99 06.
grandecascade@wanadoo.fr
www.lagrandecascade.fr
Closed Feb.
Prix fixe: 70€, 165€. A la carte: 175€.

Changes have been made in this Belle Epoque pavilion built for the 1900 Universal Exhibition. Formerly with Senderens, Chef Frédéric Robert has brought new order to the stoves of this fine residence. In the blaze of red of the dining room with its large bay windows, chanterelle-stuffed zucchini blossoms cooked in olive oil and seasoned with lemon and ginger, line-fished Atlantic sea bass with smoked eggplant caviar and spicy green curry sauce, slow-cooked veal sweetbreads with olives, capers and fried croutons, Medieval-style herb soup and a meringue with preserved lemon marmalade and basil ice cream reliably impress, as do the hundreds of vintages enthusiastically recommended by Pierre Ouardes.

● Hiramatsu ◎ LUX

52, rue de Longchamp.
Métro: Trocadéro.
Tel. 01 56 81 08 80. Fax 01 56 80 08 81.
www.hiramatsu.co.jp
Closed Sat., Sun., Aug.
Prix fixe: 48€ (lunch), 95€ (dinner), 130€ (dinner). A la carte: 140–160€.

Given that Hiroyuki Hiramatsu is now running the former Faugeron, some might expect the cuisine in this very comfortable beige setting, with its modern, rather cold look, to be Japanese. They would be wrong. There is nothing Japanese about the precise, light lobster medallion with truffles and green asparagus, the half-smoked salmon with orange and artichoke jus, the pigeon breast with foie gras flavored with cocoa and strong coffee, the tropical fruit salad with pineapple granita, except the meticulousness and subtlety of their preparation. In their simple, delicate way, they pay tribute to France, with their retinue of 800 Gallic and foreign wines.

● Pavillon Noura V.COM

21, av Marceau.
Métro: Alma-Marceau, Iéna, George-V.
Tel. 01 47 20 33 33. Fax 01 47 20 60 31.
noura@noura.com / www.noura.com
Prix fixe: 30€ (lunch), 45€ (lunch), 50€ (dinner), 65€ (dinner). A la carte: 70€.

At Jean-Paul Bou Antoun's elegant, refined pavilion the Beirut diaspora returns to its culinary roots as Hanna Namnour concocts an authentic, generous cuisine—rekakat (phyllo pastry with feta, onion and parsley), salmon, sole, mixed grill, chicken kebabs, baklava—served by Jean Khoury and accompanied by surprising French and Lebanese wines.

● L'Astrance ◎◎ V.COM

4, rue Beethoven.
Métro: Passy.
Tel. 01 40 50 84 40.
Closed Sat., Sun., Mon., 1 week November, Christmas–New Year's, 1 week Feb., Aug.
Prix fixe: 70€ (lunch), 120€ (lunch), 250€ (dinner, wine inc.).
A la carte: 150€.

The minimalist décor with its gray walls, yellow banquettes and mezzanine, the twenty-six place settings and no more at the well-spaced tables and the need to reserve three weeks in advance set the tone in this diminutive grand restaurant with its insider trading ambience. Christophe Rohat manages the highly urbane service in conjunction with a sommelier who knows his stuff, while Pascal Barbot, expert disciple of Alain Passard, creates light, spirited, impudent, ingenious and sometimes explosive dishes, always personal and perfectly refined. With its savory mushroom and buckwheat crêpe with foie gras and preserved lemon, pollock with a Thai-style lemongrass-seasoned emulsion, the watercress-seasoned scallop and walnut quenelles, Touraine poultry with licorice seasoning served with glazed eggplant, white turnips floating in a light truffle-seasoned hen bouillon or the potato soufflé and vanilla-seasoned fromage blanc (the most impertinent of the "predesserts"), this is one of the most cutting edge cuisines in Paris today. The "surprise" lunchtime option (wine + dishes) at 110' is tempting. Three dishes or two? The debate continues.

● **Passiflore** ◎ V.COM

33, rue de Longchamp.
Métro: Trocadéro.
Tel. 01 47 04 96 81. Fax 01 47 04 32 27.
passiflore@club-internet.fr
www.restaurantpassiflore.com
Closed Sat. lunch, Sun., 3 weeks Aug.
Prix fixe: 35€ (lunch), 38€ (dinner),
58€ (dinner). A la carte: 100€.

Roland Durand, the former maestro of Le Relais de Sèvres, is well versed in subtle Franco-Asian harmonies based on wild herbs and rare condiments. Although the surroundings offer quintessentially traditional bourgeois comfort, this Auvergnat gourmet's approach, with its colorful, lively and shrewd dishes, is in complete contrast to the setting. The cream of wild mushrooms with langoustine tails, lobster ravioli in a mulligatawny broth and pigeon roasted with five spices stir our curiosity. Up to and including the dessert—astonishing green, chili-flavored sorbets—the dishes reveal flavors fit for a true citizen of the world.

● **Le Pergolèse** ◎ V.COM

40, rue Pergolèse.
Métro: Porte-Maillot, Argentine.
Tel. 01 45 00 21 40. Fax 01 45 00 81 31
le.pergolese@wanadoo.fr
www.lepergolese.com
Closed Sat., Sun., Aug.
Prix fixe: 38€ (dinner), 48€ (lunch, wine inc.). A la carte: 100€.

Stéphane Gaborieau, who long presided over the stoves at the Villa Florentine in Lyon, has taken over this elegant estab-

lishment. The frog legs and wild garlic in crispy phyllo pastry, Dover sole filet with a bunch of fresh greens and tiny chanterelles or the Bresse chicken cooked two ways, with mushrooms. To conclude, hot raspberry soufflé and berry and basil dessert soup favorably impress. The assiduous service and selected wines meet the same high standards.

● **Le Relais d'Auteuil** ◎ V.COM

31, bd Murat.
Métro: Michel-Ange—Molitor,
Michel-Ange—Auteuil.
Tel. 01 46 51 09 54. Fax 01 40 71 05 03.
relaisdauteuil@wanadoo.fr
Closed Sat. lunch, Sun., Mon. lunch,
Christmas—New Year's, Aug.
Prix fixe: 50€ (lunch). A la carte: 125–150€.

For now, they have refurbished the lighting and banquettes in this very comfortable establishment with its hushed atmosphere and cheerful décor of contemporary paintings and white, green and brown shades. The fish here smells of sea spray and the game has the scent of the countryside. Fortunately, the defiant Laurent Pignol is still running things, both as manager and in the kitchen. Try the langoustines flavored with lemongrass and marjoram, sea bass filet in a pepper crust, suckling pig with chili pepper and ginger, lime soufflé in a shell with a black pepper and vodka coulis charmingly served by Laurence, his wife and muse, and judge for yourselves. The cellar is dazzling with its 2,500 bottles from France and elsewhere, enthusiastically presented by Nicolas Lepinay.

● **La Table du Baltimore** ◎ V.COM

At the Baltimore Sofitel Demeure,
1, rue Léo-Delibes.
Métro: Boissière.
Tel. 01 44 34 54 54. Fax 01 44 34 54 44.
h2789@accor-hotels.com / www.sofitel.com
Closed Sat., Sun., Bank Holidays, Aug.
Prix fixe: 48€ (lunch), 50€, 95€ (wine inc.).
A la carte: 80–90€.

In this modern restaurant with its pale woodwork, chef Jean-Philippe Pérol subtly but surely leads his patrons down roads less traveled. Accompanied by wines selected and presented by Jean-Luc Jamrozik, thin lobster medallions with pressed carrot and cumin terrine, langoustines cooked in lemon balm butter, sautéed lamb saddle and fresh raspberries, served with thin almond nougatine slivers and mousseline cream, are fine tricks indeed.

● **Tang**   ◯ V.COM

125, rue de la Tour.
Métro: Rue-de-la-Pompe.
Tel. 01 45 04 35 35. Fax 01 45 04 58 19.
Closed Sun., Mon., 1 week Christmas–New Year's, 3 weeks Aug.
Prix fixe: 39€ (lunch), 75€ (lunch), 98€ (dinner). A la carte: 90€.

For more than fifteen years, Chinese Charly Tang's restaurant has remained one of the jealously guarded secrets of Paris society. When captains of business and their elegant partners are racked by Oriental culinary cravings, they head for this refined, classical setting in salmon shades, with its wooden banquettes and shining black lacquer. There, David Laxu's delicate, balanced, airy dishes await them. Summer roll with crab, grilled sea bass with a Thai sauce and black rice, farm-raised chicken with banana, croustillant with pineapple blend the flavors of China, Vietnam and Thailand in fine concoctions with a modern feel to them. The service is impeccable and the vintages live up to the expectations of a smart clientele of connoisseurs.

● **Maison Prunier**   🍴 V.COM

16, av Victor-Hugo.
Métro: Charles-de-Gaulle–Etoile, Victor-Hugo.
Tel. 01 44 17 35 85. Fax 01 44 17 90 10.
prunier@maison-prunier.fr
Closed Sun., Aug.
Prix fixe: 59€ (lunch). A la carte: 80–150€.

A thirties décor featuring a fine bar, well-set tables and very refined dishes prepared by Eric Coisel … things have gotten better again for Prunier. We feared the worst and thought this great fish restaurant might turn into a mere "caviar bar." Admittedly, the new boss, Pierre Bergé, associated with Caviar House, promotes Aquitaine caviar in all its forms here, but the king crab ravioli with parmesan slivers, the fresh cod filet roasted with spices and the "genuine" cod brandade are impressive dishes indeed. The two set menus, with their "Balik" smoked salmon or "signature dishes" are bargains. The Clos Saint Jean Pinot Noir goes down well, as does the Pennautier Cabardès Chardonnay. Then there are exquisite desserts (a splendid baba au rhum), not to mention the striking raw herring with onions and apples, just like the fare at the Zurich Kronenhalle.

● **La Table de Babette**   🅝 V.COM

32, rue de Longchamp.
Métro: Trocadéro, Boissière, Iéna.
Tel. 01 45 53 00 07. Fax 01 45 53 00 15
tabledebabette@wanadoo.fr
Closed Sat. lunch, Sun., 2 weeks beg. Aug.
Prix fixe: 22€ (lunch on weekdays), 39€.
A la carte: 55€.

Babette de Rozières, black pearl of French West Indian cuisine, has taken over the former Robuchon-era Jamin without changing its décor at all. The vaguely British pink and green candy box look makes a slightly affected showcase for the colorful, spicy cuisine. The Caribbean boudin, stuffed crab with Antilles chili pepper, cassolette of assorted seafoods, curried shark steak, diced pork fried golden brown, barbecued chicken, coconut tart and banana flambéed with aged rum, meticulously presented here as high points of the genre, have a delectable flavor of Fort-de-France and Pointe-à-Pitre.

● **Yushi 16**   🅝 V.COM

70, rue de Longchamp, corner rue Lauriston.
Métro: Trocadéro.
Tel. 01 47 04 53 20. Fax 01 47 27 81 06.
Closed Mon.
Prix fixe: 18€ (weekday lunch), 35€.
A la carte: 60€.

This pocket temple of fusion-style Sino-Japanese cuisine displays a preference for wok preparations. Isabelle Lwin provides a smiling welcome, while chef Jean-Paul Luu prepares watercress salad with shiitakes, tuna carpaccio, sole in a caramel sauce, salt- and pepper-sautéed squid, duck glazed in apricot sauce, fried chicken strips, a house fruit salad and sugar-glazed tempura, all very well done.

● **Les Arts**   V.COM

9 bis, av d'Iéna.
Métro: Iéna.
Tel. 01 40 69 27 53. Fax 01 40 69 27 08.
maison.des.arts@sodexho-prestige.fr
www.sodexho-prestige.fr
Closed Sat., Sun., Bank Holidays, Christmas–New Year's, Aug.
Prix fixe: 38€. A la carte: 75–80€.

In this handsome, impeccably comfortable town house, with tables set well apart, cozy rooms and garden open in the season, we savor the reliable cuisine of the resident Ritz veteran. Thierry Chevalier produces fresh, polished dishes, including roasted langoustine tails with shredded leeks in truffle vinaigrette, Dover sole fried in butter with morel mushrooms, diced lamb with coriander and chocolate pudding. Afterward we head on to the neighboring Guimet museum, where the arts are less expensive.

● **Port-Alma**   V.COM

10, av de New-York.
Métro: Alma-Marceau.
Tel. 01 47 23 75 11. Fax 01 47 20 42 92.
Closed Sun., Mon., Christmas–New Year's, Aug.
Prix fixe: 25€ (lunch), 29€ (lunch), 35€ (dinner), 39€ (dinner), 12€ (child).
A la carte: 60–70€.

Sonia and Céline Canal have a firm hand on the helm in this pleasant marine establishment in oceanic hues, with bay windows, fine decorative beams and a view of the Eiffel Tower. Brice Goutret (the son-in-law) concocts crab gazpacho, filet of John Dory, flank steak and Grand Marnier soufflé. All these delights are served in the dining room by the charming Céline, who is also a shrewd sommelier, recommend-

ing the Viré white that will complement the dishes perfectly. Fine produce treated with respect, refined preparations and devoted work.

● **Tsé Yang**   V.COM

25, av Pierre-Ier-de-Serbie.
Métro: Iéna, Alma-Marceau.
Tel. 01 47 20 70 22 / 01 47 20 68 02.
Fax 01 49 52 03 68.
www.tseyang.fr
Prix fixe: 25€ (lunch), 42€, 45€.
A la carte: 55–65€.

When you need to escape the city, head for the Tsé Yang, an authentic imitation Beijing tearoom. Pampered by the delightfully attentive waitstaff, we settle down to enjoy the delicious steamed dishes, a real Peking duck and the almond milk jelly, all prepared by a chef who knows his stuff. Now if it were not for the prices…

● **La Table de Joël Robuchon** ⓒⓒ COM

16, av Bugeaud.
Métro: Victor-Hugo.
Tel. 01 56 28 16 16. Fax 01 56 28 16 78.
latabledejoelrobuchon@wanadoo.fr
Prix fixe: 55€ (lunch, wine inc.), 150€.
A la carte: 150€.

In this hushed, non-smoking gourmet club where the dishes are served in gold surroundings on bare tables of precious wood, Joël the First, king of cooks, delegates authority, ideas and talent to his dedicated lieutenants. Antoine Hernandez in the dining room, and range-top virtuosi Philippe Braun and Eric Lecerf, are dedicated soldiers of fortune. The kitchen is run by Frédéric Simonin, who, like pastry chef François Benot, previously worked with Ghislaine Arabian. Everything served here is characterized by an insistence on supreme quality and a love of fine produce. Spider crab and delicate broccoli cream in seawater jelly, red-leg crayfish stewed in white wine with vegetables, whole fried whiting in herbed butter, John Dory fish with southern aromatics and virgin olive oil, sautéed veal chop, "secrets of the woods" (iced wild strawberries with red poppy candy, yogurt-ginger cream), all are part of the latest Robuchon collection. This highly refined restaurant is a work of gastronomic haute couture, designed by a chef who, not content with defining his era, has also proved to be a precursor of fashion.

● Bon

25, rue de la Pompe.
Métro: La Muette.
Tel. 01 40 72 70 00. Fax 01 40 72 68 30
Closed Sat. lunch, Sun. dinner, Aug.
Prix fixe: 25€ (lunch), 30€ (lunch).
A la carte: 55–60€.

Many managers have thrown in the towel at this Starck-designed restaurant with its baroque décor, stubbornly run by Philippe Amzalack today. Fresh crabmeat with broccoli vinaigrette, spice-rubbed codfish with tomato, beef tenderloin with an anchovy and olive jus, thin-crust mango tart, dishes to be enjoyed with French, Chilean, Spanish or California wines.

● Al Mounia

16, rue de Magdebourg.
Métro:Trocadéro.
Tel. 01 47 27 57 28. Fax 01 45 06 18 80.
almounia@wanadoo.fr / www.al-mounia.com
Closed Sun.
Prix fixe: 18,29€ (lunch). A la carte: 40–45€.

We have a weakness for Ali Chérif's oasis here. The refined lounges, enameled ceramic inlays, red rugs, carved cedar, copper platters, Eastern ambiance and polished cuisine—including such classics as the egg kefta, fish tagine, and the spicy simmered chicken and milk pastilla—are all delightful. A house special of spit roasted meats (mechoui) on Friday or Saturday night.

● Le Murat

1, bd Murat.
Métro: Porte-d'Auteuil.
Tel. 01 46 51 33 17. Fax 01 46 51 88 54.
A la carte: 50–68€.

A trendy Costes eatery (associated with Raphaël de Montrémy here) boasting an imperial red décor by Garcia, this estab-lishment offers simple, tasteful dishes. Gazpacho and avocado, grilled tuna steak with coriander, golden-roasted chicken breast and raspberry macaron have a deli-ciously fresh flavor.

● Conti

72, rue Lauriston.
Métro: Boissière.
Tel. 01 47 27 74 67. Fax 01 47 27 37 66.
Closed Sat., Sun., Bank Holidays,
1 week from Christmas–New Year's,
3 weeks Aug.
Prix Fixe: 32€ (lunch). A la carte: 70€.

The waiters in their tuxedos display a certain elegance, as does the fifties Venetian setting in red tones with its bar at the entrance, stucco ceiling and Murano chandeliers. Michel Ranvier trained with Troisgros and used to travel on the Orient Express between the banks of the Seine and the Laguna. His cuisine is reliably enchanting. The proof is in the remarkable options—calf's head carpaccio with tomato pesto, tagliatelle with scallops, panettone pain perdu—that embellish the lunchtime set menu. All the pasta, as well as the traditional dishes, from the bollito misto, Modena-style, to the carnaroli risotto à la Milanaise and the calamari with radicchio, justify a visit here.

● Chez Géraud

31, rue Vital.
Métro: La Muette.
Tel. 01 45 20 33 00. Fax 01 45 20 46 60.
Closed Sat., Sun., Bank Holidays, Aug.
Prix fixe: 30€. A la carte: 65€.

Now, Géraud Rongier has become a discreet, composed, almost serene restaurateur in a quiet Passy street. He has not given up his Homeric tours of the vineyards of Burgundy and the Rhône Valley, though. The proof is in his divine selection of wines, which delight his guests without leaving them penniless, which blend easily with his rational, authentic, healthy cuisine based on first-rate produce. Scrambled eggs with truffles, the catch of the day (a very nice sautéed fresh cod with vegetables), splendid chicken with truffles, magnificent calf's head, painstakingly prepared by the faithful Gérard Vacher, are fine works indeed. Turning to the desserts, we enjoy the ritual Paris-Brest, a ring of choux pastry filled with a perfect praline buttercream. This is one of the best bistros in Paris, brightened by ceramics inspired by Steinlen.

● Le Relais du Parc   🅿 ○ COM

At the Sofitel le Parc,
55/57, av Raymond-Poincaré.
Métro: Trocadéro, Victor-Hugo.
Tel. 01 44 05 66 10. Fax 01 44 05 66 39.
lerelaisduparc@accor-hotels.com
www.sofitel.com
Closed Sat. lunch (winter), Sun. (winter), Mon. (winter), 1 week at Christmas, 2 weeks Aug.
Prix fixe: 45€ (lunch). A la carte: 75€.

Now you can taste Robuchon and Ducasse all in one at the Sofitel le Parc restaurant, which has received a modern makeover. The dining room team is energetically and cheerfully managed by Gonzague, known to us for twenty years at least, who formerly worked at Le Nikko in the service of Joël the First. In the kitchen, following instructions handed down by the two great traveling, multiple-menu chefs, the young Romain Corbière (formerly at the Louis XV) labors with precision and maturity, preparing the dishes that have made his masters famous. If you have not tasted pork pie in the manner of Lucien Tendret, elbow pasta with truffles and ham, cream of pumpkin soup or fried whiting à la Colbert, then do so at once. The same goes for roasted red mullet with Swiss chard (an inspiring preparation worthy of Michel Guérard, who created a similar dish), the pigeon with cabbage and foie gras, crispy pork belly with Dutch-oven-roasted Pompadour potatoes—this is the perfect opportunity to indulge yourself (almost) inexpensively! Small pots of vanilla and chocolate crème and orange gratin with wild tangerine marmalade alone are worth the visit.

● Oum El Banine   ○ COM

16 bis, rue Dufrenoy.
Métro: Porte-Dauphine, Rue-de-la-Pompe.
Tel. 01 45 04 91 22. Fax 01 45 03 46 26.
Closed Sun.
Prix fixe: 29,90€ (lunch). A la carte: 50–55€.

The carved wooden door opens to reveal the elegant, contemporary setting of a Moroccan restaurant: Ahmed Termidi's establishment where the faithful chef Fouad Elgamari busies himself at the stove, concocting delightful, terribly subtle and light dishes of Morocco—one proud of its traditions. Eggplant caviar, a succulent tagine, fish, lamb (with caramelized tomatoes and almonds) or farm-raised chickens and an airy phyllo pastry with almond milk, which concludes the meal sweetly and beautifully. When we leave Oum El Banine (dedicated to the founder of the Al Qarawiyyin university in Fez), we catch ourselves murmuring "hamdulillah"!

● Le Chalet des Iles   🍴 COM

Lac inférieur, Bois de Boulogne,
porte de la Muette.
Métro: La Muette.
Tel. 01 42 88 04 69. Fax 01 42 88 84 09.
contact@lechaletdesiles.net
www.lechaletdesiles.net
Prix fixe: 14€ (lunch), 23€ (lunch),
30€ (lunch). A la carte: 40–50€.

Raphaël de Montrémy, the shrewd, socialite proprietor of Le Petit Poucet and the River Café, has successfully lured Paris society onto this island in the Bois de Boulogne and into his Second Empire lodge, with its charming yellow and red décor. Stéphane Trouillard's cuisine is appealing indeed with its soft-boiled egg with fresh green pea cream, the jumbo shrimp curry, Caribbean-style, served with basmati rice, the milk-fed rack of lamb with potatoes au gratin and the cheesecake, all very well done.

● La Gare   🍴 COM

19, chaussée de la Muette.
Métro: La Muette.
Tel. 01 42 15 15 31. Fax 01 42 15 15 23.
www.restaurantlagare.com
Closed Christmas.
Prix fixe: 18€ (lunch), 30€, 35€,
12€ (child). A la carte: 55€.

An unusual setting! This restaurant inside the former Passy-La Muette rail station (which was running until 1980) is superb. The dining room still has a station concourse feel to it, with an impressively high ceiling, and the terrace is a garden. On the kitchen side, Yann Morel, formerly with Robuchon, Briffard and Yoshino, has to cater for a crowd of 300. The melon and Italian speck with balsamic vinegar coulis, the pollock with black rice and snow peas, slow-roasted lamb shank served with bulgur wheat, dried fruit and fresh pineapple, the light orange blossom cream and coriander financier cake are not of any great interest, to be honest. But do people come here to eat?

● L'Auberge du Mouton Blanc 🍴 COM
40, rue d'Auteuil.
Métro: Michel-Ange–Auteuil.
Tel. 01 42 88 02 21. Fax 01 45 24 21 07.
www.aubergedumoutonblanc.com
Prix fixe: 19,40€ (lunch),
30€ (wine inc.). A la carte: 35€.

In this gracious art nouveau abode run by Gérard Joulie and Patrick Senhadji, Antonio Goncalvès elegantly concocts a traditional crayfish gratin with spinach, sea bream filet with tender carrots, grilled duck breast with honey and roasted pears and chocolate fondant. You may be interested to know that 17th-century literary giants Molière and La Fontaine used to dine in this very inn.

● Cristal Room Baccarat 🍴 SIM
11, pl des Etats-Unis.
Métro: Boissière, Iéna.
Tel. 01 40 22 11 10. Fax 01 40 22 11 99.
cristalroom@baccarat.fr / www.baccarat.fr
Closed Sun. Open until 10 PM.
A la carte: 100–150€.

Anne de Noailles held her salon in this town house acquired by the Maison Baccarat, so it comes as no surprise that Paris socialites flock to its restaurant, redesigned by Starck in a modern romantic style. Do they come to be seen among the chandeliers, shades, bricks, panel-

ing and gilding, or to head upstairs and taste dishes prepared by Thierry Burlot, also proprietor of a restaurant in his own name in the fifteenth arrondissement? Once the extended names have been simplified, Landais foie gras, Mediterranean red tuna, roasted lobster with vanilla, strawberries or mille-feuille turn deftly from classical to contemporary. The price of style, elegance and flavor? Close-set tables, lost waiters and absurd checks, all drowned in fine wines.

● Settebello 🔃 SIM
9, rue Duban.
Métro: La Muette, Passy.
Tel. 01 42 88 10 15. Fax 01 45 25 74 71.
Closed Sat. lunch, Sun.,
1 week Christmas–New Year's, Aug.
Prix fixe: 18€ (lunch), 22€ (lunch, wine inc.), 24€ (lunch, wine inc.).
A la carte: 50€.

Marco Mazzolini enthusiastically presides over this modern trattoria in cheerful Italian green and red, where the freshest of transalpine classics are served. The traditional but expertly prepared dishes are Piedmont-style veal served cold in tuna sauce, sautéed squid, linguini with clams, fried veal and vegetables and Roman-style saltimbocca. The tiramisu is a moment of pure delight.

● Le Petit Pergolèse SIM
38, rue Pergolèse.
Métro: Porte-Maillot, Argentine.
Tel. 01 45 00 23 66. Fax 01 45 00 44 03.
le.petit.pergolese@wanadoo.fr
Closed Sat., Sun.,
1 week from Christmas–New Year's, Aug.
A la carte: 60€.

Albert Corre is still on duty at what once was the adjunct of Le Pergolèse. His contemporary bistro, decorated with sculptures, paintings and drawings by Warhol, Klein, Arman and Calder, is a stylish haunt for art lovers. Cuisine is not bad either. Thin-crust tomato and mozzarella tart, steamed fresh cod with baby spinach, roasted sea bass in truffle vinaigrette, sautéed veal kidneys and sweetbreads, raspberry mille-feuille and chocolate fondant are first-rate. The prices, though, have not improved.

● **Le Tournesol**   🔃 🏠 SIM
2, av Lamballe.
Métro: Passy.
Tel. 01 45 25 95 94.
A la carte: 35€.

Preserved in its own juice, this authentic bistro, dating from the start of the last century, located just a step away from France's national Maison de la Radio broadcasting center, has been snapped up by young Miri Chérif. The Café Marly veteran has cleaned up the décor, brought in an expert team and come up with a delicious menu. The salad with pan-tossed ceps with mixed garden greens and slices of foie gras, veal liver with berry sauce and the stuffed cabbage with mustard sauce are sincere, flavorsome, uncomplicated dishes and the splendid rhubarb crumble and red Menetou slip down effortlessly.

● **Le Petit Rétro**   🏠 SIM
5, rue Mesnil
Métro: Victor-Hugo
Tel. 01 44 05 06 05. Fax 01 47 55 00 48
www.petitretro.fr
Closed Sat. lunch, Sun., Bank Holidays, Christmas, New Year's, 2 weeks Aug.
Prix fixe: 19,50€ (lunch), 24,50€ (lunch), 27€ (dinner), 33€ (dinner). A la carte: 45€.

Gilbert Godfroi's bistro wields an easy charm with its 1900s décor, ceramics, moldings, painted ceilings and mirrors, and its beige, orange and green tones. The polished, old-fashioned cuisine includes escargots and oyster mushrooms baked under a crust, Scottish salmon ravioli with stewed leeks and chive cream, traditional veal blanquette with pearl onions. The service is quite out of touch, though.

● **Le Stella**   🏠 SIM
133, av Victor-Hugo.
Métro: Rue-de-la-Pompe, Victor-Hugo.
Tel. 01 56 90 56 00. Fax 01 56 90 56 01.
A la carte: 60€.

This highly bourgeois, sixteenth arrondissement Lipp has a very forties chic. The place has been beautifully renovated, the service is first-rate and the kitchen puts a lot of care into its daily menu. Salad of fresh green beans with parmesan, thin-crust tomato tart, grilled tuna steak with pesto, grilled fresh cod filet with olive oil, calf's head, iced vacherin with caramel sauce and assorted red fruit plate à la mode are not bad.

■   HOTELS

■ **Concorde La Fayette**   🏨
3, pl du Général-Koenig.
Métro: Porte-Maillot.
Tel. 01 40 68 50 68. Fax 01 40 68 50 43.
www.concorde-lafayette.com
1000 rooms: 450–520€.
400 suites: 680–1500€.

Popular with groups, this thirty-three floor tower provides many services. Meeting rooms and a fitness center near the Palais des Congrès and its boutiques.

■ **Méridien Etoile**   🏨
81, bd Gouvion-Saint-Cyr.
Métro: Porte-Maillot.
Tel. 01 40 68 34 34. Fax 01 40 68 31 31.
www.lemeridien.com
1005 rooms: 450–480€.
20 suites: 680–110€.

A thousand rooms and a modern, sober décor in beige tones and off-white, set off by black granite. The Orénoc restaurant is devoted to flavors of the world.

■ **Hôtel Mercedes**   🔃🏨
128, av de Wagram.
Métro: Wagram, Ternes.
Tel. 01 42 27 77 82. Fax 01 40 53 09 89.
www.paris-hotel-mercedes.com
37 rooms: 180–210€. 1 suite: 340€.

Miguel Cancio Martin, voguish decorator of the Buddha Bar, has just restyled this small, very thirties art deco hotel. The red dining room with its Gruber stained glass and the charming, Japanese-inspired rooms in chocolate shades set the tone. For lovers, the mini-suite on the eighth floor is a haven of peace.

■ Balmoral

6, rue du Général-de-Lanrezac.
Métro: Charles-de-Gaulle-Etoile.
Tel. 01 43 80 30 50. Fax 01 43 80 51 56.
holet@hotelbalmoral.fr / hotel–balmoral.com
57 rooms: 135–165€.

The rooms and bathrooms here are regularly renovated for the guests' greater comfort. More generally speaking, this hotel near the Arc de Triomphe is run with care and professionalism.

■ Regent's Garden

6, rue P. Demours.
Métro: Ternes, Charles-de-Gaulle-Etoile.
Tel. 01 45 74 07 30. Fax 01 40 55 01 42.
hotel.regents.garden@wanadoo.fr
www.paris–hotels.com
39 rooms: 149–279€.

A chic, relaxed ambiance in this town house near the place de l'Etoile, which was once the property of Napoleon III's doctor. The garden and spacious rooms have a great deal of charm.

■ Hôtel Splendid Etoile

1, av Carnot.
Métro: Charles-de-Gaulle-Etoile.
Tel. 01 45 72 72 00. Fax 01 45 72 72 01.
hotel@hsplendid.com
www.hsplendid.com
57 rooms: 225–275€. 3 suites: 370–385€.

Philippe Thomas brings a family atmosphere to this place. He and his staff provide a perfect welcome. The rooms are in handsome shades of blue that go wonderfully with the Louis XV furniture.

● RESTAURANTS

● Guy Savoy

18, rue Troyon.
Métro: Charles-de-Gaulle-Etoile.
Tel. 01 43 80 36 22. Fax 01 46 22 43 09.
reserv@guysavoy.com / www.guysavoy.com
Closed Sat. lunch, Sun., Mon.,
1 week from Christmas–New Year's, Aug.
Prix fixe: 230€, 285€. A la carte: 200€.

At Guy Savoy's, the contemporary décor designed by Wilmotte, the Bram Van Velde and Daniel Humair paintings and the African statuettes seem to have stepped from the pages of a glossy magazine. However, the service (unusually affable for such a superior establishment), the wines presented by Eric Mancio, the head sommelier, and above all the brilliant, appealing cuisine will soon have you feeling at home. Behind the apparent simplicity lies a love—a passion—for shrewdly prepared produce. This results in short preparations with precise flavors: sharp, absolutely flawless and always surprisingly authentic. The truffled artichoke soup with mushroom and truffle-seasoned brioche, oysters over an iced seafood broth, foie gras with salt, grilled sea bass seasoned with mild spices and turbot in egg salad and in soup express the qualities of the vegetable, shellfish or fish, refusing to allow themselves to be sidetracked. The subtle, precise desserts play from the same score, the fabulous crème "minute", served with green apple jus, a masterpiece we found perfectly copied in the restaurant of three-star Londoner Gordon Ramsay. Guy Savoy is clearly one of the subtle maestros of our day.

● Michel Rostang

20, rue Rennequin (at rue Gustave-Flaubert).
Métro: Ternes.
Tel. 01 47 63 40 77. Fax 01 47 63 82 75.
rostang@relaischateaux.fr
www.michelrostang.com
Closed Sat. noon, Sun., Mon. noon,
3 weeks Aug.
Prix fixe: 70€ (lunch on weekdays), 95€ (wine inc. with lunch on weekdays), 175€.
A la carte: 170€.

There are some classic restaurants that we are always pleased to visit again and Michel Rostang's is one of them. The noble, paneled setting with its art deco allusions and impressive collection of Robj porcelain, the exuberant Marie-Claude's kind welcome and the extremely friendly service put us at our ease. Then the maestro's cuisine takes over with a display of skillfully modernized dishes in the grand tradition. Atlantic blue lobster with tomato chutney and rice vinegar, sea bass with crunchy skin and creamy macaroni gratin and the duck with blood sauce served in two courses play dazzlingly on contrasting flavors and textures. When the time comes for dessert, the crunchy "cigar" with La Havane tobacco and Cognac mousse add a touch of originality that bodes well, although even we traditionalists are starting to think this rich style has had its day. In any case, the selection of wines and Alain Ronzatti's advice cannot be faulted, leaving us in need of a good postprandial nap later on.

● **La Maison de Charly**   ◎|V.COM

97, bd Gouvion-Saint-Cyr.
Métro: Porte-Maillot.
Tel. 01 45 74 34 62. Fax 01 45 74 35 36.
www.lamaisondecharly.com
Closed Mon., Aug.
Prix fixe: 33€. A la carte: 40–50€.

The soft lighting, cozy décor and cuisine (just like in Marrakech!) are flawless. Melvin Drigues' set menu provides an opportunity to sample a mosaic of starters: harira, méchouia, zaalouk or kefta d'agneau. The classic dishes are interpreted in a simple, precise manner: couscous and tagines, pastilla, grilled whole Mediterranean sea bass, tangia, or the ten-hour roasted lamb. We end with a milk pastilla and, of course, mint tea, as in Morocco.

● **Sormani**   ◎|V.COM

4, rue du Général-Lanrezac.
Métro: Charles-de-Gaulle–Etoile.
Tel. 01 43 80 13 91. Fax 01 40 55 07 37.
Closed Sat., Sun., 3 weeks Aug.
Prix fixe: 44€ (lunch). A la carte: 60–90€.

Jean-Pascal Fayet is crazy about wine. He's also an actor and a herald of Italian cuisine. He's made this l'Etoile neighborhood establishment a place of elegance and quality. He hasn't done as much with the dishes except for those with winter or summer truffles (ah! his black truffle tortellini fritto misto!). Vitello tonnato and vegetable caponata, an impressive fritto misto, the tarragon-seasoned lobster and a house-made tiramisu topped with coffee ice cream will make you melt. Treat yourself one night and try one of his Sassicaias.

● **Augusta**   V.COM

98, rue de Tocqueville.
Métro: Malesherbes, Villiers.
Tel.-Fax 01 47 63 39 97.
Closed Sat., Sun., 1 week from Christmas–New Year's, Aug.
A la carte: 90€.

Didier Berton celebrates the ocean in this eatery. His cook, Guillaume Capelle, bases his elaborate preparations from here and farther afield on supremely fresh fish and shellfish. The quick-sautéed langoustine tails with poppy seeds, smoked wild salmon seasoned with dill and lemon confit, seaweed-steamed cod filet with fois gras mousse, roasted turbot with green and white asparagus all feature on the lively, meticulous menu, and only the prices make waves. When the time comes for dessert, strawberry shortbread cookies offer a refreshing conclusion.

● **Meating**   V.COM

122, av de Villiers.
Métro: Pereire.
Tel. 01 43 80 10 10.
chezmichelpereire@wanadoo.fr
Closed Sat. noon, Sun., Mon.
A la carte: 65–75€.

For what the format is worth, it has acquired a following. After the starters of the day at 5€, you can move on to a premium Angus steak or 500g of prime Irish Hereford beef, unless you prefer the only fish dish, red tuna steak grilled on a wood fire. The Tanzanian chocolate soup with warm tea cakes, superb. The check is not so sweet.

● Il Ristorante

22, rue Fourcroy.
Métro: Ternes.
Tel.-Fax 01 47 63 34 00.
ilristorante@wanadoo.fr
Closed Sat. lunch, Sun., 2 weeks Aug.
Prix fixe: 27€ (lunch). A la carte: 60€.

This elegant corner trattoria serves meticulously prepared transalpine classics. Formerly at Cecconi's, Rocco Anfuso does Italy honor with his reliable preparations, including the artichoke and parmesan salad, fried langoustines with little squids, eggplant medallions with mozzarella and a seasonal fruit gratin. To wash down these sun-drenched dishes, the wine list has some lively suggestions.

● La Braisière ○ COM

54, rue Cardinet.
Métro: Malesherbes.
Tel. 01 47 63 40 37. Fax 01 47 63 04 76.
labraisiere@free.fr
Closed Sat. noon, Sun., Aug.
Prix fixe: 33€ (lunch). A la carte: 60€.

The décor is refined, the atmosphere hushed, the cellar well stocked and the menu inventive: These are the attractions of this "little firm" (as Prince of Gastronomy Curnonsky used to say) run by Jacques Faussat, who made a name for himself as Alain Dutournier's lieutenant. Today, he shares his ideas with us here, and approval is forthcoming: We just have to taste the foie gras terrine with apricot, pan-seared tuna steak with a galangal glaze and roasted lamb shoulder with thyme, baby artichoke hearts, peppers and green asparagus. The chayote fruit tart with raspberries, served with a rhubarb and star anise sorbet, is succulent. Francine Praly has a gift for unearthing the right bottle from the wide range of small growers' wines of which her list fondly boasts.

● Epicure 108 ○ COM

108, rue Cardinet.
Métro: Malesherbes.
Tel. 01 47 63 50 91
Closed Sat. noon, Sun.,

Mon. dinner, 2 weeks Aug.
Prix fixe: 29€, 43,50€. A la carte: 40€.

When a native of Japan falls in love with France and expresses this passion in the kitchen, the results are never dull. After a career that took him to Emile Jung's and the Haeberlin brothers' establishments, Tetsu Goya has a passion for Alsace, but not exclusively. A mosaic of warmed assorted vegetables with tomato coulis, pan-fried squid with jumbo shrimp and lentils, veal sweetbread torte and eels sautéed with garlic and parsley are ingenious indeed, as are his interpretations of rabbit terrine seasoned with Sylvaner wine and duck with sauerkraut. For dessert, fruit cup with carrot syrup is pleasantly surprising, like the moderate tab and Kumiko Goya's smile.

● Paolo Petrini ○ COM

6, rue du Débarcadère.
Métro: Argentine, Porte-Maillot.
Tel. 01 45 74 25 95. Fax 01 45 74 12 95.
resinfo@paolo-petrini.fr / www.paolo-petrini.fr
Closed Sat. lunch, Sun., 3 weeks Aug.
Prix fixe: 27€, 29€, 34€. A la carte: 60€.

Talented, self-taught maestro Paolo Petrini has trained many good chefs now working all over Paris. He is never short of imagination, even when he prepares simple, market-based dishes. We like the beef carpaccio, which he naturally serves with arugula with shaved parmesan, the Roman-style artichokes, the red mullet filets with tapenade and fennel and the penne with green asparagus and jumbo shrimp. His recipe for profiteroles is unique. The wines from every region of Italy go wonderfully with the food, but to avoid any chance of a mishap, we can follow Jean-Pierre Mullatier's recommendations.

● Taïra ○ COM

10, rue des Acacias.
Métro: Argentine.
Tel.-Fax 01 47 66 74 14.
Closed Sat. lunch, Sun., mid-Aug.–end Aug.
Prix fixe: 35€, 65€ (dinner). A la carte: 55€

Taïra Kurihara, former chef at Prunier, has also worked at Jamin, Le Véfour, Besson and Cagna. He knows exactly how to prepare and serve seafood without any surplus frills. The skills he has acquired here and there are complemented by his delicacy of touch and natural precision. We succumb to the charms of the red tuna tataki, fresh buffalo milk cheese with pan-fried langoustines, squid and basil fricassée, steamed scopion fish and jumbo shrimp with a herb reduction sauce and vegetables and the fresh fruits served with sisho sorbet and one long succession of treats. If only the surroundings were more cheerful, Paris society (which is partial to seafood) would be in the front row here.

● **Caïus**   🅿 🍴 COM

6, rue d'Armaillé.
Métro: Argentine, Charles-de-Gaulle—Etoile.
Tel. 01 42 27 19 20. Fax 01 40 55 00 93
Closed Sat. noon, Sun., Bank Holidays.
Prix fixe: 23€ (lunch), 38€.

A step away from place de l'Etoile, Jean-Marc Notelet's restaurant has finally been refurbished in a cozy, modern, very well-lit, chocolate-colored décor of pale woodwork, mirrors and thick, dark brown velvet. We feel quite at home as we enjoy the set menu of the day put together by this young chef, who trained with Boyer and Meneau and practiced his art at Le Troyon. Littleneck clam cappuccino with whipped celery root and a light savory reduction sauce, the remarkable pain perdu paired with smoked herring caviar, crisp layered pastry with swordfish seasoned with turmeric and ginger and the veal cheeks with ginseng and citron confit pass the time pleasantly. The desserts, such as roasted rhubarb with whipped mascarpone cheese, are up to the same standard.

● **Bath's**   🆕 🍴 COM

25, rue Bayen.
Métro: Ternes.
Tel. 01 45 74 74 74.
Closed Sat. lunch, Sun., Aug.
Prix fixe: 25€. A la carte 55€.

Exit the Béatilles. Jean-Yves Bath, formerly in Sarpoil in the Auvergne, then above the modern market in Clermont, and finally in the rue de la Trémoille, has moved his eponymous establishment here. He now works in the dining room with his son Stéphane and gives free rein to his chef François Le Quillec. Cep risotto, thinly sliced pork trotters served carpaccio style, Iberian ham, sautéed squid and paella and the Basque-style fried baby squid add a Spanish note to this relaxed, modern, paneled setting. The crème Catalane and the Royal Gala Tatin are very much in keeping with the spirit of this modern gourmet haunt. Served at lunch and dinner time, the set menu at 25€ deserves a Pot for good value.

● **Baptiste**   🍴 COM

51, rue Jouffroy-d'Abbans.
Métro: Malesherbes, Wagram.
Tel. 01 42 27 20 18. Fax 01 43 80 68 09.
Closed Sun., Mon., Bank Holidays, Aug.
Prix fixe: 24€ (lunch), 30€ (lunch), 32€ (dinner).

This bistro of character with its cozy thirties surroundings has plenty of convincing arguments on its side: a creative menu, moderate prices and an extremely friendly welcome. Its success is thanks to Denis Croset, master of the range, and Jean-Baptiste Gay, who looks after the service and cellar. We love the coriander-marinated salmon mille-feuille, pan-seared Atlantic cod and mashed fingerling potatoes, lamb shoulder with eggplant caviar and a sesame reduction and the crunchy sugar cookies with strawberries and lemon curd.

● **Chez Georges**   🆕 🍴 COM

273, bd Pereire.
Métro: Porte-Maillot.
Tel. 01 45 74 31 00. Fax 01 45 74 02 56.
Closed 3 weeks Aug.

After some ups and downs, Chez Georges ("Restaurateur since 1926") has just been taken over by the Menut family, who also own the Grande Cascade and the neighboring Ballon des Ternes (among other places). Georges and Bertrand Menut have brought in the most gifted staff from their establishments to get this historic brasserie moving again, so it is now looking thoroughly rejuvenated. Pâté in a pastry crust, the house sea bream tatare, roasted Atlantic sea bass with artichokes and arugula, the Angus beef with a gratin Dauphinois and a crème caramel have a healthy air and all come in XXL size. An interesting cellar and considered prices.

● La Table des Oliviers   SIM

38, rue Laugier.
Métro: Ternes, Pereire.
Tel. 01 47 63 85 51. Fax 01 47 63 85 81.
ww.tabledesoliviers.fr
Closed Sat. noon, Sun., 3 weeks Aug.
Prix fixe: 20€ (lunch), 28€. A la carte: 51€.

The name hints at the content of the dishes prepared by Thierry Olivier. For example? Sea bass carpaccio with Mediterranean spices, langoustine risotto with reduction sauce, Marseille-style bouillabaisse, veal sweetbreads with wild mushrooms and strawberry carpaccio with balsamic vinegar and an almond milk sorbet. We are already on vacation and can almost hear the song of the cicadas.

● Caves Petrissans   🍴 SIM

30 bis, av Niel.
Métro: Ternes, Pereire,
Charles-de-Gaulle–Etoile.
Tel. 01 42 27 52 03. Fax 01 40 54 87 56
cavespetrissans@noos.fr
Closed Sat., Sun., Bank Holidays, Aug.
Prix fixe: 34€. A la carte: 40€.

Since 1895 (Tristan Bernard located his play Le Petit Café here), this establishment has had a long, colorful history, and Marie-Christine and Jean-Marie Allemoz are still writing the latest chapter day after day. Although it is reputed for its excellent cellar, the restaurant is not simply a wine bar. Duck foie gras, smoked salmon with potatoes in oil and skirt steak with shallots, like the chocolate cake with crème anglaise, are beautifully executed. Savoring these dishes, we appreciate the contents of our glass all the more.

● Hier et Aujourd'hui

145, rue de Saussure.
Métro: Villiers.
Tel. 01 42 27 35 55.
Closed Sat., Sun., 2 weeks Aug.
Prix fixe: 17€ (lunch), 26€.

The restaurant is amusing, modern, tasty, pleasant and inexpensive. In fact, it has everything going for it, despite the background noise. Running it is a keen young duo: Karin Ouet, a petite blonde who provides a smiling welcome and prompt service, and Franck Dervin, a chef full of energy, putting on a one-man show in his kitchen behind glass. The loft-style premises have their charm, with bricks, slate and gray walls. Franck paid his dues with Guy Savoy and Alain Dutournier and knows plenty about buying quality produce at the right price. Asparagus salad with mozzarella, tomatoes and pesto, spiced country terrine, the cod served with tomato-seasoned potatoes, a layered lamb and potato dish with eggplant. The desserts are splendid (Paris-Brest filled with praline cream, fluffy baba au rhum using St. James rum). We wash it all down with some delicious wines, often priced under 20€. A fine establishment indeed!

● Ripaille   SIM

69, rue des Dames.
Métro: Rome.
Tel. 01 45 22 03 03. Fax 01 45 22 04 26
Closed Sat. noon, Sun. noon.
Prix fixe: 11€ (lunch, wine inc.),
15€ (lunch), 23€, 29€. A la carte: 30–35€.

Philippe Favré, previously Gérard Faucher's sommelier, invites you to join him in the company of chef Antoine Butez, Van Laer's ex-lieutenant at Le Maxence. The setting is simple with exposed stone walls and unfussy wooden tables. Pumpkin soup with bleu d'Auvergne cheese, pan-seared scallops with broccoli purée, slow-cooked pork cheeks with fennel, cumin and polenta are tasteful dishes with that gratifying extra touch. Soft chocolate cake with pepper ice cream and a frozen whiskey parfait with chestnut shortbread and

Bailey's meet with unanimous approval. The atmosphere is friendly and the convivial service will keep Ripaille's already loyal customers coming back.

● La Villa Monceau

16, rue des Acacias.
Métro: Argentine.
Tel. 01 44 09 85 59.
Closed Sat., Sun., 2 weeks Aug.
Prix fixe: 19€ (lunch), 26€ (lunch).

Richard Lefrançois (who was at the Caves Angevines in the sixteenth arrondissement), his dining room associate Francis and chef Yvan Sternat (who worked for the Loiseau group at Tante Marguerite) have turned this little place not far from Porte Maillot into a convivial village bistro. With the blackboard menu, bar area and well-prepared market-based dishes, the ambiance is informal and quality is never far behind. The parsleyed ham in terrine, rabbit rillettes, the hot Lyonnais-style sausage with lentils, ground beef and mashed potatoes served home style and braised ham are washed down with a straightforward Beaujolais. The fine red meats and grandmotherly desserts (the chocolate tartlette, the pear and apple clafoutis and rice pudding with salted-butter caramel) are very much in keeping with the rest.

● L'Abadache

89, rue Lemercier.
Métro: Brochant.
Tel.-Fax 01 42 26 37 33.
Closed Sat. (exc. group reserv.), Sun. (exc. group reserv.), Aug.
Prix fixe: 15€ (lunch), 19€ (lunch), 26€ (dinner), 10€ (child). A la carte: 36€.

With its open kitchen, woodwork, green plants and ceramic floor, Yann Piton and Emma Hauser's bistro is a haven of relaxation and conviviality. Yann comes to us from the world of theater, and his present role suits him perfectly. We delight in the brochette of langoustines with a salad of crunchy vegetables, whole roasted sea bream, grilled vegetable mille-feuille with pesto, hand-cut beef tartare with basil and

a cherry financier with cocoa sorbet. A fine selection of wines by the glass.

● Chez Bubune

16, rue Jouffroy-d'Abbans.
Métro: Wagram.
Tel. 01 42 67 60 10.
Closed dinner, Sat., Sun., 3 weeks May.
A la carte: 40€.

Formerly at Fauchon and the Crillon, Denise Hodeau has made her native Sologne the focus of this Parisian restaurant, from décor to dishes. In a rustically styled dining room with lilac-colored tablecloths and shining brasses on the walls, we make short work of lightly spiced oyster mushrooms in salad with thin slices of parmesan, duo of jumbo shrimp and scallops with a sherry butter and mushroom risotto, pheasant with reinette apples and a slightly acidulated cream sauce and the indispensable chocolate pot noir de Bubune with a crisp lace cookie.

● Le Café d'Angel

16, rue Brey.
Métro: Charles-de-Gaulle–Etoile,
Tel.-Fax 01 47 54 03 33.
Closed Sat., Sun., Bank Holidays, Christmas–New Year's, 3 weeks Aug.
Prix fixe: 19€ (lunch), 22€ (lunch).
A la carte: 40€.

This bistro just a step away from place de l'Etoile is a great find with its low prices. the shrewd dishes concocted by Jean-Marc Gorsy, Alain Reix's former lieutenant at the Jules Verne. The pan-seared squid with fresh herbs, scorpionfish filet with slow-simmered vegetables, Norman-style rib-eye steak with roasted potatoes and a caramelized garlic and basil jus, chocolate sundae with salted caramel sauce as we sit shoulder to shoulder on the faux-leather banquettes of this deliciously retro establishment.

● L'Entredgeu

83, rue Laugier.
Métro: Porte-de-Champerret.
Tel. 01 40 54 97 24. Fax 01 40 54 96 62.

Closed Sun., Mon., 3 weeks Aug.
Prix fixe: 22€ (lunch), 30€.

We immediately feel at home in Philippe and Pénélope Tredgeu's restaurant. What do we especially like? The simplicity of the unfussy cuisine, the friendly prices and the attentive service. With all these attractions, it is not easy to find a table, but when you do, you are rewarded with the stuffed squid, the Basque-style poached eggs with lamb roast, chorizo and parmesan, a roasted cod with stuffed artichokes, milk-fed lamb and a rice pudding with a rhubarb and strawberry compote. A growing success that looks set to continue.

● Goupil   SIM

4, rue Claude-Debussy.
Métro: Porte-de-Champerret.
Tel. 01 45 74 83 25.
Closed Sat., Sun., 3 weeks Aug.
A la carte: 40€.

Eric Mayot, formerly of Maxim's, has turned this likable bistro near Porte de Champerret into an excellent eatery indeed. Guillaume Monjuré, who trained with Vigato, prepares a very lively market-based cuisine. We delight in his beet carpaccio, lamb's lettuce and crumbled boiled eggs, the Basque-style squid, quick-seared tuna with celery root rémoulade, pan-seared rib-eye for two with sautéed potatoes, juicy pork chop, grilled veal kidneys with béarnaise sauce, baba au rhum and chocolate mille-feuille. Fine, thirst-quenching wines, including an amiable Corbières.

● Leclou   SIM

132, rue Cardinet.
Métro: Malesherbes, Villiers.
Tel. 01 42 27 36 78. Fax 01 42 27 89 96.
le.clou@wanadoo.fr / www.restaurant-leclou.fr
Closed Sat., Sun., 1 week from Christmas–New Year's, 1 week May, 3 weeks Aug.
Prix fixe: 21€ (lunch), 30€ (dinner).
A la carte: 40€.

Unaffected by ephemeral trends and culinary experiments, Christian Leclou is as delighted as ever to concoct duck foie gras terrine, cod with olive oil–enriched mashed potatoes, cooked lamb shoulder slow roasted for five hours and nougat glacé. With Isabelle Lamare's smile as an added bonus, how could you forgo the pleasure of eating here?

● La Rucola   SIM

198, bd Malesherbes.
Métro: Wagram, Malesherbes.
Tel. 01 44 40 04 50. Fax 01 47 63 13 20.
rucola@wanadoo.fr
Closed Sat. lunch, Sun., 3 weeks Aug.
Prix fixe: 15€ (lunch). A la carte: 40€.

The alliance of two great culinary traditions—French and Italian—makes this unique restaurant a favorite for gourmets of every kind. They come here to enjoy wild asparagus, arugula and shaved parmesan salad, Venetian-style scallops, Dover sole with pesto, veal saltimbocca, Parma ham and Scarmoza and a homemade sabayon. Our thanks go to Michel Lukin and Sergio Païs, the men behind this fine concept.

● Aristide   SIM

121, rue de Rome.
Métro: Rome.
Tel. 01 47 63 17 83. Fax 01 47 54 97 55
restaurantaristide@free.fr
Closed Sat. noon, Sun., 2 weeks Aug.
Prix fixe: 22€. A la carte: 45€.

This bistro from the turn of the last century has many regular local customers. We cheerfully take our place on a faux-leather banquette to enjoy the dishes concocted by Jean-Philippe Siegrist, inventively listed on the mirrors covering the dining room walls. The salad of crayfish tails, sea bream with aromatic herbs, the duck confit and sautéed potatoes and house mille-feuille are all splendid.

● Le Bistrot d'à Côté Flaubert   SIM

10, rue Gustave-Flaubert.
Métro: Ternes, Courcelles, Pereire.
Tel. 01 42 67 05 81. Fax 01 47 63 82 75.
bistrotrostang@wanadoo.fr
www.michelrostang.com
Closed Sat. lunch, Sun., Mon., 1 May,

2 weeks Aug.
Prix fixe: 29€ (lunch). A la carte: 60€.

Michel Rostang's first offshoot is already twenty years old. In this former pork butcher's store that still displays all the spirit of a vintage bistro, apt pupil Cédric Tessier dynamically concocts a duck and foie gras terrine in pastry with a sweet and sour sauce, Grenoble lake perch filets served with sorrel-seasoned ratte potatoes or half of a trussed and roasted Bresse chicken for two with diablo sauce and mashed potatoes (in two courses). The little home-style chocolate pots de crème conjure up childhood memories. Fine, thirst quenching wines.

PARIS 18TH ARR

■	HOTELS

■ Kube

1-5, passage Ruelle.
Métro: La Chapelle.
Tel. 01 42 05 20 00.
paris@kubehotel.com
41 rooms: 250–300€.

A luxury hotel in a district where you would not expect to find one, offering contemporary rooms with designer furniture and a chic ambiance. The Ice Kube bar is a temple to vodka. In its glacial atmosphere, visitors will need the house anoraks!

■ Terrass' Hôtel

12, rue Joseph-de-Maistre.
Métro:Abbesses, Blanche, Place-de-Clichy.
Tel. 01 46 06 72 85. Fax 01 42 52 29 11.
reservation@terrass-hotel.com
terrass-hotel.com
85 rooms: 248–295€. 15 suites: 340–355€.

This establishment is under new management. Its top floor rooms overlooking Montmartre cemetery are very popular. The terrace is a pleasant place to brunch.

■ Mercure Montmartre

3, rue Caulaincourt.
Métro: Place-de-Clichy.

Tel. 01 44 69 70 70. Fax 01 44 69 70 71.
h0373@accor.com / www.accor.com
305 rooms: 138–198€.

This modern, functional complex is ideal for visitors exploring Montmartre. The rooms are practical. WiFi on every floor.

■ Crimée

188, rue Crimée.
Métro: Crimée.
Tel. 01 40 36 75 29.
hotelcrimee@wanadoo.fr
31 rooms: 55–77€.

Modern and spirited, this inexpensive hostelry near the Canal de l'Ourcq provides functional rooms.

■ Roma Sacré Coeur

101, rue Caulaincourt.
Métro: Lamarck-Caulaincourt.
Tel. 01 42 62 02 02. Fax 01 42 54 34 92.
hotel.roma@wanadoo.fr / www.hotelroma.fr
57 rooms: 60–195€.

A few flights of steps from the Sacré-Coeur, this hotel has an antique residential style. The rooms are renovated and there is a garden. The welcome is faultless.

●	RESTAURANTS

● A. Beauvilliers

52, rue Lamarck.
Métro: Lamarck-Caulaincourt.
Tel. 01 42 55 05 42. Fax 01 42 55 05 87.
www.abeauvilliers.com
Closed Sun. lunch, Christmas.
Prix fixe: 25€ (lunch), 35€ (lunch),
45€ (dinner), 63€. A la carte: 65€.

Yohann Paran, trained by Alain Passard and the Contcini brothers and formerly at Le Restaurant de la Garde in the fifteenth arrondissement, has purified the handsome décor imagined by Edouard Carlier. We let the enthusiastic young dining room staff guide us through the wonderfully fresh menu, a blend of tradition and innovation. The crunchy crab appetizer with cumin, celery and black radish in remoulade sauce with smoked egg vinaigrette, the grilled scallops in Indian vaduvan spices served with risotto-style rice, the sautéed farm-raised veal chop with stewed winter vegetables and a brioche pain perdu with apples and spices served with baked-apple ice cream all live up to their promises.

● Le Diapason   Ⓝ V.COM

At the Terrass', 12/14, rue Joseph-de-Maistre.
Métro: Abbesses, Blanche, Place-de-Clichy.
Tel. 01 44 92 34 00. Fax 01 44 92 34 30
seminaire@terrass-hotel.com
www.terrass-hotel.com
Closed Sat. lunch, Sun. dinner, Aug.
Prix fixe: 28€ (lunch). A la carte: 55€.

There have been changes at this opulent hotel opposite Montmartre cemetery. The house restaurant has been modernized and now boasts a refined, modern décor, all in sand, gray and black. The new chef, Julien Roucheteau (who studied under Philippe Legendre, then Michel Troisgros at the Lancaster), has taken over the kitchen with gusto. Crispy Oriental-style kebab, vegetables from Joël Thiébaut's market in a warm tapenade and olive oil dip, fish cooked in a Staub Dutch oven with crunchy fresh peas, glazed pork chop and well-made desserts (rhubarb and mango tartlet, berries and lemon verbena sorbet) make an excellent impression. All these earn full points and mean a quality restaurant in this neighborhood spot at the foot of the butte de Montmartre once again.

● Taka   🔶 SIM

1, rue Véron.
Métro: Abbesses.
Tel. 01 42 23 74 16.
Closed lunch, Sun., Mon., New Year's, mid-July–mid-Aug.
Prix fixe: 20€. A la carte: 30–40€.

Japanese from the walls to the dishes, Okamoto Taka's restaurant is as charming as ever. Red tables, screens and kite lanterns set the scene. On the menu are squid with sea urchin cream and fermented soybeans, shrimp and vegetable tempura, smoked eel maki, a Japanese-style fondue

with thinly sliced beef, chicken and vegetables cooked tableside in hot duck stock flavored with seaweed, as well as sushi, sashimi and red beans with green tea ice cream. Mouthwatering!

● Le Moulin de la Galette   🍴 COM

83, rue Lepic.
Métro: Abbesses, Blanche.
Tel. 01 46 06 84 77. Fax 01 46 06 84 78.
Closed Sun., Mon.
Prix fixe: 25€ (lunch, wine inc.).
A la carte: 55–60€.

New in Montmartre! Antoine Heerah from the Chamarré in the seventh has taken over this legendary haunt filled with memories, once frequented by singer Dalida in the days of Graziano. The décor has been refurbished contemporary style: red, black and dark blue walls, banquettes, stucco and fine parquet flooring have restored the Moulin's youth. Antoine and his young team serve a light market-based cuisine prepared with quality produce. Cep and trumpet mushrooms tossed in minced parsley, wild duck terrine with foie gras and the crispy pork are faultless. We also enjoy the cod and potato purée with chips (despite the useless tomato coulis), the traditionally prepared roasted red pheasant with its crispy skin and lovely potato purée. The desserts are in the same tasteful vein, including the baba au rhum with vanilla-infused cream. A fine cellar and a garden terrace when the weather is fine.

● La Mascotte   ⓢ SIM

270, rue du Faubourg-Saint-Honoré.
Métro: Ternes.
Tel. 01 42 27 75 26. Fax 01 42 27 75 22.
Closed Sat. dinner, Sun.,
Christmas, New Year's, 10 days Aug.
A la carte: 40–60€.

New owners the Turlans have changed the décor, putting on a show of comfortable modernity that rejuvenates this newly chic Aveyron café a tad, but chef Yves Moreau is still at the range. Regulars do not seem disconcerted by céleri rémoulade (banal), seasonal fish, Aubrac beef filet with classic blue cheese sauce (overcooked) served with fried potatoes seasoned with green peppercorns and the house recipe of chocolate fondant and vanilla custard sauce. The dining room staff, who forget the half bottles and charge a supplement for a strawberry tart (sodden) topped with a scoop of ice cream is clearly intent on getting customers to spend as much as possible.

● A la Pomponnette   🏠 SIM

42, rue Lepic.
Métro: Blanche, Abbesses.
Tel. 01 46 06 08 36. Fax 01 42 52 95 44.
alapomponnette@hotmail.com
Closed Sun., Mon. lunch, Aug.
Prix fixe: 18€ (lunch), 32€.
A la carte: 45€.

This Montmartre institution has barely changed since it was founded by Arthur Delcroix in 1909. Three generations later, Arthur's descendants are still very much in evidence, led by the founder's granddaughter, Claude Moureau. In a changeless décor of marble, banquettes, pillars and pictures, including some by Poulbot, who was a friend of the house, we enjoy spirited dishes including the rabbit terrine in tarragon jelly, house-style hot marrow bones on toast, grenadier filet baked in parchment with diced vegetables, Armagnac-flambéed veal kidneys and sweetbreads and a crispy mille-feuille.

● Au Poulbot Gourmet   🏠 SIM

39, rue Lamarck.
Métro: Lamarck-Caulaincourt.
Tel. 01 46 06 86 00. Fax 01 46 06 63 14
Closed Sun., 3 weeks Aug.
Prix fixe: 18€ (lunch), 36€ (wine inc.).
A la carte: 50–55€.

This authentic bistro with its 19th-century stucco has been handed over to Renaud Laudigeois. The place remains reliable, even if the prices have risen slightly, and there can be no complaints about the skate salad in pesto dressing, asparagus in mousseline sauce, monkfish with honey and lime, nor the veal tenderloin with Banyuls wine and raisins. The raspberry macaron and tarte Bourdaloue (pear and marzipan) deserve a special mention.

■ HOTELS

■ Holiday Inn Paris La Villette   🏨

216, av Jean-Jaurès.
Métro: Porte-de-Pantin.
Tel. 01 44 84 18 18. Fax 01 44 84 18 20.
hilavillette@alliance-hospitality.com
www.holidayinn-parisvillette.com
178 rooms: 205€. 6 suites: 265€.

A step away from the La Villette park, this large, modern hotel offers spacious, bright, functional rooms. A practical restaurant: the Brasserie de l'Auditorium (see Restaurants).

● RESTAURANTS

● Au Bœuf Couronné   🏠 COM

188, av Jean-Jaurès.
Métro: Porte-de-Pantin.
Tel. 01 42 39 44 44. Fax 01 42 39 17 30.
au.bœuf.couronne@laposte.net
www.rest-gj.com
Pris fixe: 32€ (wine inc.).
A la carte: 45–60€.

Bone marrow on toast to whet your appetite? Then the prime rib of beef "Villette" for two or the grilled steak with béarnaise sauce for just one? Pan-seared hanger steak or rib-eye steak with red wine and shallots, a strip steak or a thick cut of grilled beef? If there were just a single restaurant keeping our memories of the former La Villette meat market alive, it would be Au Bœuf Couronné in the hands of Gérard Joulie. He is still to be found in this rather elegant art deco setting with its air conditioning, private dining room, veranda and burgundy red and chestnut brown shades. Now all that remains is to refresh ourselves with crêpes with orange liqueur, and, under the spell of a great vintage, sing a verse or two of writer, poet and musician Boris Vian's *Les Joyeux Bouchers*: *"C'est le tango, des bouchers d'la Villette"* (It's the tango of La Villette's butchers).

● **La Cave Gourmande** ◎ SIM

Restaurant de Mark Singer

10, rue du Général-Brunet.

Métro: Botzaris.

Tel.-Fax 01 40 40 03 30.

lacavegourmande@wanadoo.fr

Closed Sat., Sun. (ex. groups with res.),
1 week Feb., 3 weeks in Aug.

Open until 10:30 PM.

Prix fixe: 31€ (lunch), 36€. A la carte: 55€.

American in Paris Mark Singer, chef and master of this Cave Gourmande, learned the rudiments of his trade with the greatest names—Robuchon, Vergé, Manière—before moving to this little street near to the Buttes-Chaumont park. Creative and subtle, inspired by the changing nature of market produce, the rolled haddock filets and the oysters with tomato ice, the sage-seasoned cod crumble, wild duck *"deux temps trois movements"*, saffron-seasoned potatoes and chard and the banana cream make a fine impression. The wines are skillfully chosen.

■   HOTELS

■ **Palma** ⌂

77, av. Gambetta.

Métro: Gambetta.

Tel. 01 46 36 13 65. Fax 01 46 36 03 27.

hotel.palma@wanadoo.fr

www.hotelpalma.com

32 rooms: 59–105€.

A stone's throw from Père Lachaise cemetery, a comfortable local hotel with renovated rooms and air conditioning. A warm welcome and very amiable prices.

●   RESTAURANTS

● **Les Allobroges** 🅿 🍴 COM

71, rue des Grands-Champs.

Métro: Maraîchers.

Tel. 01 43 73 40 00. Fax 01 40 09 23 22.

Closed Sun., Mon., Bank Holidays,
1st week November, 1 week at Easter,

end July–end Aug.

Prix fixe: 20€, 29€, 33€.

Olivier Pateyron and his cheerful wife Annette celebrate the Allobroges, a tribe of ancient Gaul, in this East Paris village. The middle class bohemians who pack its two dining rooms in pastel tones (décor designed by Pierre-Yves Rochon, antique engravings from Granville) are right to stray from their more usual haunts. With style and refinement, the set menu presents recipes that reflect current tastes and the changing seasons: terrine of duck foie gras, smoked haddock brandade with basil, roasted duck with Banyuls wine, rum ganache-filled "cigar" pastry. The French wines are a little expensive, but the precise preparations, reliable produce and attention to degree of cooking rarely give cause for criticism.

● **La Boulangerie** ⓝ 🍴 🍷 SIM

15, rue des Panoyaux.

Métro: Ménilmontant.

Tel. 01 43 58 45 45. Fax 01 43 58 45 46.

Closed Sat. lunch, Sun., Christmas–New Year's.

Prix fixe: 16€ (lunch), 28€.

Stucco, ceramics, counter and dishes chalked up on the blackboard: this true, old-fashioned bistro brings color to its fashionable corner of Ménilmontant. Hassan and Nordine Nidhsain, formerly at the Bombis in the twelfth arrondissement, have taken over enthusiastically here, playing on quality produce, carefully selected wines and changing dishes that form mouthwatering set menus. The vegetable and goat cheese terrine, Moroccan-style meat pastries, tuna tartare with fines herbes, the marinated Lozère lamb brochette served with ratatouille, Sarthe farm-raised pork chops with their little Irish potatoes and a rum-soaked pineapple carpaccio served with a creamy coconut sorbet all hit the mark. The wine list is alluring, but includes few or no bottles at less than 20'. However, the 'pay for what you drink' Château Le Queyroux Côtes de Blaye is not bad.

● Le Baratin   🍴 SIM

3, rue Jouye-Rouve.
Métro: Belleville, Pyrénées.
Tel. 01 43 49 39 70.
Closed Sat. lunch, Sun., 1 week Feb., 1 week
May, 3 weeks Aug.
Prix fixe: 14€ (lunch). A la carte: 35€.

From Argentina and France, respectively, Raquel Carena and Philippe Pinoteau bring us lasting pleasure. No, we are not just saying that, we are still as crazy as ever about this wine bar on the slopes of Belleville, where Carena—with smoldering gaze and sure hand—cooks monkfish and galangal broth, sautéed brill with green asparagus, Breton potatoes with ginger and spring vegetables, as well as a remarkable hazelnut pudding. The wines on the blackboard scarcely begin to reflect the 200 items that Philippe Pinoteau tends to in his cellar. Make sure you reserve a table: Le Baratin has been fashionable for a long time now.

● Le Zéphyr   ☺ 🏠 SIM

1, rue du Jourdain.
Métro: Jourdain.
Tel. 01 46 36 65 81. Fax 01 40 33 10 89.
luenee@wanadoo.fr / www.lezephyrcafe.com
Prix fixe: 13,50€ (lunch on weekdays),
28€ (dinner on weekdays).
A la carte: 40–50€.

We always enjoy the art deco look in burgundy shades here, with moleskin banquettes, mirrors and large windows opening onto a shady terrace. However, on the kitchen front, ambition often rhymes with inattention and affectation. At the risk of upsetting chef and proprietor Ludovic Enée, we feel obliged to suggest he take a more rigorous approach toward the flavors, seasoning, marinades and cooking times of the asparagus carpaccio with roquefort (insipid), roasted sea bass stuffed with vegetables (limp), slow-roasted lamb shank with thyme (overcooked) and the crunchy—actually not that crunchy—strawberry dessert with crushed Montélimar nougat. The price to be paid? The check is fairly high for the area, except at noon, when the set menu combines quality with economy.

The downside? The welcome and service (several readers have informed us of serious problems in this area).

PAU

64000 Pyrénées-Atlantiques. Paris 779 –
Bayonne 113 – Bordeaux 200 – Toulouse 198.
smt@ville-pau.fr.
Good King Henri's château, the view of the mountains from the aptly named boulevard des Pyrénées and the art gallery are some of the attractions of this peaceful town facing due south, towards neighboring Spain.

	HOTELS-RESTAURANTS

■ Parc Beaumont   🏨

1, av Edouard-VII.
Tel. 05 59 11 84 00. Fax 05 59 11 85 00.
reza@hotel-parc-beaumont.com
www.hotel-parc-beaumont.com
70 rooms: 185–250€. 10 suites: 490–950€.
Prix fixe: 28€, 35€, 55€, 80€,
15€ (child). A la carte: 85€.

On the edge of a fine park, this contemporary hotel with its modern rooms and designer furniture is an ongoing event. Charm abounds. In the Jeu de Paume restaurant, the stylish cuisine reflects the general ambiance under the hand of Christophe Canati. A reliable technician, formerly at the Hostellerie de Plaisance in Saint-Emilion, he prepares clear, precise, sharp market dishes, including pan-seared foie gras with chanterelles, turbot roasted with shellfish, slow-roasted spicy lamb shoulder and strawberries in sweet broth seasoned with Jurançon wine. Excellent service and a cellar to match.

■ Continental   🏨

2, rue du Maréchal Foch.
Tel. 05 59 27 69 31. Fax 05 59 27 99 84.
hotel@bestwestern-continental.com
www.bestwestern-continental.com
Rest. closed Sat., Sun., (exc. groups),
1 week Christmas–New Year's.
71 rooms: 59–115€. 4 suites: 150€.
Prix fixe: 20€, 25€.

Antique charm and modern comfort, a contemporary dining room and straightforward board cuisine, all at moderate prices, are the attractions of this 1912 vintage institution. The sensible classical cuisine (duck foie gras with fig confiture and sole filet with ceps) is very much in tune with the setting.

■ Hôtel de Gramont 🏨
3, pl Gramont.
Tel. 05 59 27 84 04. Fax 05 59 27 62 23.
hotelgramont@wanadoo.fr
www.hotelgramont.com
Closed 22 Dec.–6 Jan.
33 rooms: 50–98€. 1 suite: 120€.

This prestige hotel is well-situated in a 17th-century post house. Nicole and Alain Pauchard have renovated the rooms in contemporary style. We also enjoy the highly convivial bar and lounge.

■ Hôtel de Roncevaux 🏨
25, rue L.-Barthou.
Tel. 05 59 27 08 44. Fax 05 59 27 08 01.
contact@hotel-roncevaux.com
www.hotel-roncevaux.com
39 rooms: 52–94€.

A solicitous reception in this former town house, whose rooms have been meticulously renovated in different colors.

■ Kyriad-Centre 🏨
80, rue E.-Garet.
Tel. 05 59 82 58 00. Fax 05 59 27 30 20.
kyriad.pau-centre@wanadoo.fr
www.hotel-pau-centre.com
62 rooms: 85–90€. 8 suites: 110€.

This chain hotel has been refurbished in warm red and yellow shades. The décor and contemporary furniture are very refreshing.

■ Mercure Palais des Sports 🏨
106, av de l'Europe.
Tel. 05 59 84 29 70. Fax 05 59 84 56 11.
h0952@accor.com / www.mercure.com
92 rooms: 75–129€.
Prix fixe: 14,50€ (wine inc.), 34€ (wine inc.), 14€ (child).

This functional, well-appointed Mercure hotel is a pleasant place to stay and boasts a swimming pool in the bargain. In the kitchen, Patrick Morgado prepares good classical dishes such as Rébénacq trout with steamed fingerling potatoes and a cherry Gâteau Basque.

● Au Fin Gourmet V.COM
24, av G.-Lacoste.
Tel. 05 59 27 47 71. Fax 05 59 82 96 77.
au.fin.gourmet@wanadoo.fr
Closed Sun. dinner, Mon., Wed. lunch,
Feb. vac., end July–mid-Aug.
Prix fixe: 18€ (weekday lunch),
26€ (weekday lunch), 35€, 58€.

Opposite the station, at the foot of the funicular, this Belle Epoque lodge boasts an elegant restaurant. The Ithurriague family provides a friendly welcome and concocts the tasteful market-based dishes on its sensible, well-crafted set menus. Foie gras in poultry broth, whiting filet with diced mangos and spicy rack of milk-fed lamb are dependability itself.

● Chez Pierre V.COM
16, rue Barthou.
Tel. 05 59 27 76 86. Fax 05 59 27 08 14.
restaurant.pierre@wanadoo.fr
www.restaurant-chez-pierre.com
Closed Sat. lunch, Sun., Mon. lunch,
1 week beg. Jan., 2 weeks beg. Aug.
Prix fixe: 34€. A la carte: 65€.

This eatery with its British club-style surroundings tends to rely on its former glory. In any case, Raymond Casau, who trained at the Tour d'Argent and Maxim's, is still at the helm, good-naturedly entering his fourth decade. The set menu is well-formulated and the classical dishes never grow stale. They include oyster mushroom salad with fresh liver, sole braised in Juançon wine with morels, béarnaise "cassoulet" with corn beans and a chocolate cake with coffee-flavored crème anglaise. The cellar still has its attractions.

● Le Majestic   COM

9, pl Royale.
Tel. 05 59 27 56 83. Fax 05 59 82 87 44.
Closed Sun. dinner, Mon.
Prix fixe: 18€ (weekday lunch), 22€, 26€,
36€. A la carte: 55€.

There is a new take on a garden ambiance in this dining room with its wood and gray and beige tones. Jean-Marie Larrère continues to delight us with distinctive dishes. Oven-crisped pork trotter in salad, a thick slice of turbot with jumbo shrimp and Espelette peppers, braised boneless oxtail with pan-seared duck foie gras and a warm oven-crisped pear in a crêpe pouch with vanilla ice cream are all trouble free.

● Le Viking   COM

33, bd Tourasse.
Tel. 05 59 84 02 91. Fax 05 59 80 21 05.
restaurant.le.viking@wanadoo.fr
www.le.viking.com
Closed Sat. lunch, Sun. dinner, Mon.,
2 weeks beg. Aug.
Prix fixe: 20€, 32€, 43€, 56€.

The rustic, wine-colored setting is satisfying, as are Pascale's welcome and Philippe Maré's dishes, forming balanced set menus. Cold foie gras lasagne with cep fricassée, pan-fried cod set on a langoustine basket with mushroom sauce and oven-crisped duckling with foie gras caramelized with Jurançon wine make an excellent impression.

● Le Berry   SIM

4, rue Gachet.
Tel. 05 59 27 42 95.
Closed Christmas.
A la carte: 32€.

A genuine brasserie and everything that might suggest: a lively atmosphere, reasonable prices and domestic cuisine. This is what we find at François Tillos' fifties "Parisian bistro" establishment. The cheese soup, sole meunière, chateaubriand with béarnaise sauce and crème brûlée are frankly a delightful experience. Prompt service.

● La Table d'Hôte   SIM

1, rue du Hédas.
Tel.-Fax 05 59 27 56 06.
la-table-dhote@wanadoo.fr
Closed Sun., Mon. (exc. dinner July–Aug.),
New Year's, 1 week beg. Jan.
Prix fixe: 23€, 29€, 8€ (child).

With its good-natured ambiance and exposed stone and beams, this rustic restaurant encourages us to roll up our sleeves and set to. Fabrice Juzanx concocts local dishes unstaled by custom. Foie gras served two ways (in terrine and pan seared), pan-tossed fresh cod with lime and piccolo peppers, black Gascon pork brochettes with sage-seasoned ewe's cheese and the pan-tossed exotic fruit with verbena sorbet offer a powerful incentive to make a habit of this old town eatery.

In Jurançon (64110). 2 km sw.

● Chez Ruffet   ◯SIM

3, av Charles-Touzet.
Tel. 05 59 06 25 13. Fax 05 59 06 52 18.
chez.ruffet@wanadoo.fr
www.restaurant-chezruffet.com
Closed Sun. dinner, Mon.
Prix fixe: 25€ (lunch, wine inc.), 62€, 110€
(wine inc.). A la carte: 110€.

We find ourselves reconciled with Stéphane Carrade's cuisine. In his 18th-century restaurant, this veteran of Bardet in Tours and the Scholteshof in Hasselt is again preparing the fine produce of Southwest France with feeling and respect, having set aside his sometimes audacious culinary experiments. On the menu, this means pan-sizzled duck foie gras with lemon tree leaves and grapevine shoots, a thick slice of sole glazed with chicken jus and the lamb pierced with Spanish pork fat and bathed in miso and ginger. For dessert, the frozen peach drops dessert provides a light, sweet conclusion. The cellar holds large numbers of Southern French vintages, while the check holds large numbers, period. Spirited service.

In Jurançon.

● Le Chat Botté   `COM`

34, av Rauski, rte de Gan.
Tel. 05 59 06 60 50.
contact@domaine-lechatbotte.com
www.domaine-lechatbotte.com
Closed Wed., 2 weeks beg. Sept.,
2 weeks beg. Jan.
Prix fixe: 15€ (weekday lunch), 21€, 38€,
70€.

Arnaud Humbert has breathed new life
into this pleasant inn, renamed for the
restaurant he ran in Metz. In this friendly,
rustic setting devoted to the tales of Perrault, the remarkable set menus offer foie
gras poached in Madeira with cinnamon,
crayfish with licorice-flavored vinaigrette,
a tied beef tenderloin poached in truffle
jus and chocolate meringue cream cake,
all very well crafted.

PAUILLAC

33250 Gironde. Paris 560 – Bordeaux 53 –
Blaye 16 – Lesparre-Médoc 23.
tourismeetvindepauillac@wanadoo.fr.
A small Médoc town, its harbor, famous châteaux, prestige wines, seas of vineyards and
soothing strolls.

 HOTELS-RESTAURANTS

● Château
Cordeillan-Bages

Rte des Châteaux.
Tel. 05 56 59 24 24. Fax 05 56 59 01 89.
cordeillan@relaischateaux.com
www.cordeillanbages.com
Closed Nov. 1–mid-Feb.
Rest. closed Sat. lunch, Mon., Tue.
26 rooms: 145–260€. 2 suites: 300–460€.
Prix fixe: 60€ (lunch), 110€ (dinner)
16€ (child). A la carte: 115€.

He is the Zen artist of Cordeillan, the gourmet star of Médoc. Thierry Marx is a remarkable chef with a muscular, action-hero
physique. However, this unusual individual,
who lives in Japan for three months each
year, eats no meat and delights in pitting
himself against his chic young colleagues
(in Le Havre each year, with Ferran Adria
from El Bulli or Michel Bras from Laguiole),
is also a reserved, retiring fellow. A leader
and loner, he wins our admiration with precise, flawless, technical dishes served in the
new, refined setting of Jean-Michel Cazes'
epicurean retreat. Come and taste the simple pan-seared hot foie gras, served on cold
peach preserves with a line of reduced Port
sauce, the pressed individual smoked eel
terrine, as well as the amusing rollmop herring and potatoes with olive oil in aspic
and a soy risotto with oyster and truffle jus
which flirt with gimmickry, although not
outrageously. Other fine stylistic exercises—
the grapevine-smoked blonde Aquitaine
beef filet with slow-roasted potatoes and
the veal sweetbreads spaghetti with ceps
and truffles—are fortunately more down
to earth. Marx, an associate of Chapel and
Maximin among others, has remarkable
technical skills and his fine tricks are never
marred by imprecision. We note the dazzling desserts in a light style—the deconstructed lemon tart, for instance—and bow
to the eminently Bordeaux-centric wine
list, with all vintages available at very reasonable prices and bottles worthy of interest at less than 30'. In short, this "planet
Marx" deserves a further visit. The appealing rooms, cordial service and quiet atmosphere make it a very distinctive Relais &
Châteaux establishment.

● Café Lavinal

Pl Desquet, Bages.
Tel. 05 57 75 00 09.
Closed Sun. dinner, Christmas–beg. Feb.
A la carte: 40€.

This new look bistro with red banquettes,
neo-fifties lighting, café corner and zinc
counter is Jean-Michel Cazes' mas-
terstroke. Thierry Marx has delegated
authority to Hugo Naon, his disciple of
Argentinian extraction, who concocts the
designer dishes here. The roasted sardines,
sausage-stuffed ravioli, squids with mild
spices, tuna steak grilled rare with sesame
vinaigrette, duck medallions with an eggplant mille-feuille and the fried chorizo
with thick-cut house fries are splendid.
The desserts (oven-crisped banana and

chocolate semifreddo and a tarte Tatin with milk caramel ice cream) have an elegant, classical flavor. As we raise a glass of Torrontes La Higueras, we realize that here, on the delightful square of this picture postcard village, we have found Bordeaux's bargain of the moment.

PEILLON

06440 Alpes-Maritimes. Paris 952 – Monaco 28 – Contes 13 – Menton 37 – Nice 21.
This adorable village perched in the Nice hinterland is worth a detour for its setting, period residences, church and frescoes in the Chapelle des Pénitents-Blancs.

 HOTELS-RESTAURANTS

● Auberge de la Madone
2, place Auguste-Arnulf.
Tel. 04 93 79 91 17. Fax 04 93 79 99 36.
madone@chateauxhotels.com
www.chateauxhotels.com
Closed beg. Nov.–23 Dec.,
beg. Jan.–beg. Feb. Rest. closed Wed.
14 rooms: 95–200€. 3 suites: 230–380€.
Prix fixe: 32€ (lunch, wine inc.), 62€.
A la carte: 75–85€.

There can be no doubt: we are in Provence here. The bright, welcoming décor of the rooms is in local colors and accents, as is the dining room, presided over by Marie-José Clavel, co-owner of the hostelry with Christian Millo, and inspired sommelier, with an encyclopedic knowledge of the region's wines. In the kitchen, Christian and his son Thomas masterfully execute dishes steeped in local tradition and reinterpreted with talent. The light herb tourte with a grilled slice of foie gras, Mediterranean sea bass filet poached in almond infusion with wild fennel cappuccino, twice-roasted lamb with thyme flower are exalted by the choice of quality produce. For dessert, a tourte with Swiss chard and tomato confit with niçoise-style ice cream is a success.

PENMARC'H see SAINT-GUENOLE
PENNEDEPIE see HONFLEUR

PENVENAN

22710 Côtes-d'Armor. Paris 520 – Guingamp 35 – Saint-Brieuc 72 – Lannion 15.
An authentic port of call in the Trégor district.

 HOTELS-RESTAURANTS

● Le Crustacé
2, rue de la Poste.
Tel. 02 96 92 67 46.
Closed Sun. dinner (exc. July–Aug.), Mon. (July–Aug.), Tue. dinner (exc. July–Aug.), 2 weeks beg. Nov., 3 weeks Jan.
Prix fixe: 15,50€, 25,50€, 35€, 9€ (child).

Opposite the town church, this little family restaurant charms us with its dining room in rustic guise. In the kitchen, William Buron prepares reliable dishes, such as a scallop and jumbo shrimp brochette with citrus butter, fish choucroute with saffron, beef filet with wine sauce and a warm individual apple tart. Marie-Reine offers a pleasant welcome.

PENVINS see SARZEAU

PERIGNAT-LES-SARLIEVES see CLERMONT-FERRAND

PERIGUEUX

24000 Dordogne. Paris 486 – Agen 139 – Bordeaux 123 – Limoges 94 – Poitiers 197.
tourisme.perigueux@perigord.tm.fr.
This town, which hosts a gourmet book festival every two years, finds it hard to live up to its role as the capital of Périgord (even modestly). Périgueux, a very easygoing place, displays great warmth and a certain discretion. Do not miss the banks of the Isle, the cathedral and the old quarter of Puy-Saint-Front.

 HOTELS-RESTAURANTS

■ Bristol
37, rue Antoine-Gadaud.
Tel. 05 53 08 75 90. Fax 05 53 07 00 49.
hotel@bristolfrance.com
www.bristolfrance.com

Closed Christmas–New Year's vac.
29 rooms: 56–73€.

With its smart rooms in blue, yellow and red, period furniture and central location, the Durupts' hotel is a friendly place to stay.

● **Le Clos Saint-Front**   COM
5-7, rue de la Vertu.
Tel. 05 53 46 78 58. Fax 05 53 46 78 20.
Closed Sat. lunch, Sun. dinner, Mon.
Prix fixe: 25€, 36€, 60€ (wine inc.)
12€ (child).

The dining room has been refurbished in modern style and this adds an original touch to Patrick Feuga's rustic establishment (stone, fireplace). The foie gras terrine with apple compote, Atlantic sea bass with artichokes and chorizo, duck confit with Breton fingerling potatoes and an oven-crisped salted-butter caramel dessert will not leave you cold. The fine wine list is enthusiastically presented by Stéphanie Marchives.

● **Le Rocher de l'Arsault**   COM
15, rue de l'Arsault.
Tel. 05 53 53 54 06. Fax 05 53 08 32 32.
rocher.arsault@wanadoo.fr
Closed Sun. dinner, July.
Prix fixe: 20€, 27€, 31€, 32€, 48€, 79€,
10€ (child).

The kitchen is very much a feminine preserve in this eatery near the Rocher de l'Arsault. Marie Leymarie and her daughter Valérie transform the region's produce into simple, delicate, exquisite dishes that will make your mouth water. The braised veal sweetbread salad with balsamic vinegar, sole with cep cream sauce, Périgord-style meat and vegetable tourte and a walnut cake napped with crème anglaise are splendid.

● **Le Fou du Roi**   COM
2, rue Montaigne.
Tel. 05 53 09 43 77.
Closed Sat. lunch, Sun., Mon. (exc. dinner by reserv.).
Prix fixe: 15€ (lunch), 19€ (lunch), 22€,

27€, 35€, 45€, 48€, 10€ (child).
A la carte: 50–55€.

Virginie Noël hosts this modern rustic establishment in red and yellow. Olivier Magdelaine performs a tasteful, classical repertoire. A slice of pan-fried liver on a bed of potatoes, scallops served three ways, simply prepared fisherman's catch and the house profiteroles put on an excellent show.

● **L'Essentiel**   ⓝSIM
8, rue de la Clarté.
Tel.-Fax 05 53 35 15 15.
Closed Sun., Mon. (exc. dinner July–Aug.),
Nov. 1 vac., Christmas, 4 days beg. Jan.,
1 week at Easter.
Prix fixe: 20€ (weekday lunch), 29€, 59€.

At the foot of the cathedral, the Vidals have taken over the exquisite Guichaoua and are running it with great energy. Full of vigor, the escargot stew with chanterelles, foie gras and poached egg, caramelized tuna steak cooked in olive oil with a spicy saté, turbot roasted in olive oil and pork spare ribs with slow-cooked potatoes go down deliciously in the cheerful dining room or on the pleasant courtyard terrace.

In Champcevinel (24750). 5 km n via av. G. Pompidou.

● **La Table Du Pouyaud**   V.COM
Rte de Paris.
Tel. 05 53 09 53 32. Fax 05 53 09 50 48.
latablepouyaud@yahoo.fr
www.pouyaud&com
Closed Sun. dinner, Mon. dinner, Tue.
Prix fixe: 24€, 12€, 44€. A la carte: 70€.

Hubert Tarbouriech has turned this panoramic hill overlooking Périgueux into a gourmet epicenter. The à la carte prices in the summer are a little excessive, but the set menus are honest and there are no complaints about the cod slices pan-seared then finished under the broiler with soy or the nests of thinly sliced roasted pigeon in a cocotte with oven-crisped blood sausage. A poached pear and caramel gratin served with wild rose ice cream provides a fitting conclusion, savored in a vast modern dining room with widely spaced tables. A giddying wine list.

In Chancelade (24650). 5,5 km nw via D710 and D1.

■ **Château des Reynats & l'Oison**

15, av des Reynats.
Tel. 05 53 03 53 59. Fax 05 53 03 44 84.
www.chateau-hotel-perigord.com
Closed beg. Jan.–mid-Feb.
Rest. closed Sat. lunch, Sun. lunch, Mon. lunch.
32 rooms: 77–180€. 5 suites: 220€.
Prix fixe: 32€ (lunch), 38€ (dinner), 48€.

Set in grounds equipped with a swimming pool and tennis court, this château comes with a peace and relaxation warranty. Its large rooms offer all of today's luxuries. In the classical dining room, Gilles Gourvat, who came here from the Altiport in Méribel, prepares elaborate dishes, including fried langoustines with guacamole, lobster and baby squid with seafood stuffing, veal roast with ceps, duck liver lasagne and cinnamon and raspberry shortbreads.

In Manzac-sur-Vern (24110). N21 then D43.

■ **Le Lion d'Or**

Pl de l'Eglise.
Tel. 05 53 54 28 09. Fax 05 53 54 25 50.
www.lion-dor-manzac.com
Closed 2 weeks end Nov., 3 weeks Feb.
Rest. closed Sun. dinner (exc. July–Aug.), Mon.
8 rooms: 46–53€.
Prix fixe: 15€ (wine inc.), 18€, 25€, 32€.

This former coaching inn in a Périgord Blanc village is equipped with small, neat, modern rooms, as well as a swimming pool. Nelly and Jean-Paul Beauvais, who provide a friendly welcome, present sensible menus featuring dishes with voguish flavors. Cep fricasée with foie gras, individual pressed rabbit terrine with dried fruit, grilled scallops with an orange vanilla sauce, duck breast and vegetables in a pastry-lined mold and roasted bananas make a good impression.

LA PERNELLE see SAINT-VAAST-LA-HOUGUE

PERNES-LES-FONTAINES

84210 Vaucluse. Paris 688 – Avignon 23 – Carpentras 6 – Cavaillon 20.
A pretty town below Mont Ventoux, with its old quarter and springs.

◨ | HOTELS-RESTAURANTS

■ **Mas la Bonoty**

Chemin de la Bonoty.
Tel. 04 90 61 61 09. Fax 04 90 61 35 14.
infors@bonoty.com / www.bonoty.com
Closed 3 weeks Nov., 1 week beg. Dec., beg. Jan.–beg. Feb. Rest. closed Mon. (exc. lunch in season), Tue. (exc. lunch in season).
8 rooms: 70–95€.
Prix fixe: 22€ (weekday lunch), 37€ (dinner), 50€ (dinner), 63€, 16€ (child).
A la carte: 65€.

For an overnight stop or a short stay, this inn set up in a 17th-century farmhouse converted by Richard Ryan is just the thing. The rooms are delightful and the garden and swimming pool deliciously relaxing. The restaurant meets the same high standards. Laurent Tasse deftly concocts rouget and Aquitaine caviar salad, goat cheese lasagne, lobster served in broth and a chocolate bowl with pear nectar.

● **Au Fil du Temps** SIM

Pl Giraud.
Tel.-Fax 04 90 66 48 61.
fildutemps@wanadoo.fr
Closed Sat. lunch (exc. off season), Tue. (exc. July–Aug.), Wed. (exc. off season), 2 weeks Christmas–New Year's.
Prix fixe: 30€, 50€, 70€.

The long dining room in the colors of Provence has its appeal. Frédéric Robert, formerly with Pic in Valence and the Martinez in Cannes, prepares well-crafted set menus reflecting current and regional trends. The potato and truffle soup, basil-seasoned snapper, saddle of rabbit with olives and the warm apple tart with caramel sauce are very appropriate.

PERONNAS see **BOURG-EN-BRESSE**

PEROUGES

01800 Ain. Paris 462 – Lyon 36 – Bourg-en-Bresse 39 – Villefranche-sur-Saône 58.
info@perouges.org.
This masterpiece of a medieval village, sentinel of the Dombes region, has provided a location for many a historical motion picture, starting with the first version of *The Three Musketeers*.

| | HOTELS-RESTAURANTS |

■ Ostellerie du Vieux Pérouges   🏛️🏨
Pl du Tilleul.
Tel. 04 74 61 00 88. Fax 04 74 34 77 90.
thibaut@ostellerie.com
www.ostellerie.com
Closed Feb. vac.
26 rooms: 78–260€. 2 suites: 230€.
Prix fixe: 40€, 46€, 61€, 17€ (child).

This medieval tavern has lost none of its charm. The rooms are fully equipped miniature museums with their period Bresse furniture. Christophe Thibaut's cuisine is also in a regional vein. A local mixed mushroom dish with cream, poultry liver cakes with mushrooms, crayfish prepared in the local style, oven-roasted Bresse chicken and a regional house-made crêpe dessert topped with cream and the waitress in regional costume maintain the tone.

PERPIGNAN

66000 Pyrénées-Orientales. Paris 855 – Béziers 93 – Montpellier 157 – Toulouse 204.
office-contact@smi-telecom.fr.
On the sun-drenched terrace of the Grand Café de la Bourse on the place de la Loge, the South is with us full frame. Catalan is spoken in the old quarters and the tradespersons have a smile to match their accent. Their products have the color, flavor and rich scents of the Roussillon region and the Mediterranean close by. Tradition lives on, revitalized and underlined from restaurant to stall. Everywhere, tribute is paid to the Collioure anchovy, touron (an almond paste candy), cargolade (a Catalan picnic dish of grilled snails, meat and vegetables), boudin (blood sausage) and aniseed bread.

| ■ | HOTELS |

■ Villa Duflot   🏛️
Rd-pt Albert-Donnezan.
Tel. 04 68 56 67 67. Fax 04 68 56 54 05.
contact@villa-duflot.com
www.villa-duflot.com
18 rooms: 120–140€. 7 suites: 160–200€.
Half board: 155–210€.

It is quite a surprise to come across this art deco villa in the middle of a shopping complex. It is refreshingly different, with its rooms furnished in the appropriate style, swimming pool, grounds and flowery patio (see Restaurants).

■ Mas des Arcades   🏛️
840, av d'Espagne.
Tel. 04 68 85 11 11. Fax 04 68 85 21 41.
contact@hotel-mas-des-arcades.fr
www.hotel-mas-des-arcades.fr
Rest. closed Sat. lunch (off season).
101 rooms: 75€. 3 suites: 150€.
Prix fixe: 20€, 28€, 45€, 12€ (child).
A la carte: 40–55€.

Renovated in contemporary style, the rooms in this traditional Provençal country house are charming indeed. The swimming pool, tennis courts and garden are a bonus. In the Relais Jacques Ier restaurant, Yannick Tual concocts inventive, subtle dishes: shrimp tempura lightly seasoned with curry, Mediterranean sea bass roasted in its skin and served with minted butter and the degustation of roasted local lamb with seasonal herbs are fine examples.

■ Park Hôtel   🏛️
18, bd J.-Bourrat.
Tel. 04 68 35 14 14. Fax 04 68 35 48 18.
contact@parkhotel-fr.com
www.parkhotel-fr.com
67 rooms: 65–105€. 2 suites: 180–280€.

The Marguerittes have established their distinctive style here and their delectable welcome makes their hotel an essential port of call, as do the rooms in the Catalan style (some of them refurbished Zen fashion), the contemporary bar and the cuisine at the Chapon Fin (see Restaurants).

■ Mercure Centre
5, cours Palmarole.
Tel. 04 68 35 67 66. Fax 04 68 35 58 13.
h1160@accor-hotels.com / www.mercure.com
59 rooms: 72–88€. 5 suites: 115–125€.

Modern, practical and central, this classic chain hotel provides functional rooms, a fitness center, meeting rooms and WiFi. A pleasant, quiet bar.

● | RESTAURANTS

● Chapon Fin `Ⓞ` `V.COM`
At Park Hôtel. 18, bd J.-Bourrat.
Tel. 04 68 35 14 14. Fax 04 68 35 48 18.
contact@parkhotel-fr.com
www.parkhotel-fr.com
Closed Sun., 2 weeks beg. Jan.,
2 weeks end Aug.
Prix fixe: 25€ (weekday lunch), 49€, 69€,
100€, 15€ (child). A la carte: 105€.

Perpignan's rail station was made famous by Dali, but the city also boasts an emblematic hotel, a haven for travelers in the know. The service supervised by Robert and Monique Margueritte is thoughtful and Alexandre Klimenko in the kitchen demonstrates his reliable taste for produce from the Catalan coast in a series of dazzling creations: the majestic lobster prepared royal style with foie gras and in a hen consommé, shellfish "cloud" with crispy match-sticks, quickly simmered shellfish, seaweed salad with lime and roasted hazelnuts, grilled Mediterranean sea bass with Maldon salt, a suprising roasted rack of lamb with glazed mango and four-spice-seasoned eggplant dish. All this incites us to experiment in the company of a traditional crème Catalane and its deconstruction served with a small glass of Rivesaltes.

● Mas Vermeil `V.COM`
1700, chemin de la Roseraie.
Tel. 04 68 66 95 96. Fax 04 68 66 89 13.
restaurant@masvermeil.com
www.masvermeil.com
Prix fixe: 49€, 65€ (wine inc.), 15,50€
(child).

Gérard Roger has taken over this Provençal country house, which promotes a Catalan cuisine reinterpreted to reflect modern trends, based on fresh produce and prepared by Dominique Molé. In a Mediterranean décor with no dearth of style, we eagerly sit down to curried mango gazpacho and tomato tartare, grilled cod filet with eggplant tapenade, rare roasted Pyrénées veal filet with a sweet pea mousseline and a slice of hot foie gras and the soft-centered chocolate fondant with ice cream.

● Villa Duflot `V.COM`
Rd-pt Albert-Donnezan.
Tel. 04 68 56 67 67. Fax 04 68 56 54 05.
contact@villa-duflot.com
www.villa-duflot.com
Prix fixe: 31€ (dinner, wine inc.), 10€ (child).

We have already mentioned the accommodational attributes of this startling art deco hostelry in the middle of a shopping precinct. Its restaurant, jointly run by Michel Védrines and Alain Ferrer, is set against a Southern French background that is worth seeing in itself. Quality produce and refined preparations result in polished dishes. Proof takes the form of foie gras in escabeche sauce, assorted grilled fish with the deglazed sauce served on the side and a crabmeat mille-feuille.

● Les Antiquaires `COM`
Pl Desprès.
Tel. 04 68 34 06 58. Fax 04 68 35 04 47.
Closed Sun. dinner, Mon., 1 week Jan.,
1 week at end June, 2 weeks beg. July.
Prix fixe: 23€, 32€, 42€.

With its white walls, exposed beams and flea market furniture, the dining room of this establishment in the old town is still a haven where we savor a cuisine that never stales. In the kitchen, Guillaume Aubailly has taken over from his father Michel and is carrying on in the same vein. Balsamic vinegar-seasoned anchovies and puff pastry, a slice of foie gras pan seared with Banyuls, turbot with morels, a deboned and stuffed pork trotter and the Grand Marnier soufflé are timeless classics.

● Clos des Lys   COM
Chemin de la Fauceille.
Tel. 04 68 56 79 00. Fax 04 68 54 60 60.
contact@closdeslys.com / www.closdeslys.com
Closed Sun. dinner, Mon., Wed. dinner (exc. summer), Feb.
Prix fixe: 17€, 20€ (lunch wine inc.), 27€, 31€.

In the heart of a lovely Mediterranean garden, this contemporary establishment offers quality cuisine. Jean-Claude Vila and his son-in-law Franck Séguret energetically reinterpret traditional dishes. The results are light and surprising. Oven-crisped langoustines with angelhair pasta served with red pepper and ginger chutney, fried Mediterranean sea bass with mild onions and garlic, twice-cooked duck tagine and the grilled duck breast and duck leg confit with spices and its rich jus, couscous and dates sweep us off on a journey colored by a delightful sense of exotic flavors. To conclude, the oven-crisped coconut and passion fruit dessert is in the same style.

● Café Vienne   SIM
3, pl Arago.
Tel. 04 68 34 80 00. Fax 04 68 80 69 73.
cafevienne@wanadoo.fr
Prix fixe: 23,50€, 8,50€ (child).
A la carte: 40€.

With its banquettes, wooden tables, mirrors and black and white photos, this neo-art deco bistro has an easy charm. Camille Otero has turned the stove over to Roger Olivier, who prepares a classical, dependable cuisine. Foie gras terrine with a Banyuls wine aspic, grilled squid, beef tartare and a pear gratin are served until midnight.

● La Casa Portuguesa   SIM
Av du Palais-des-Expositions.
Tel.-Fax 04 68 52 79 31.
Closed Mon. dinner, Tue., Aug.
Prix fixe: 13,50€ (weekday lunch), 18€, 25€, 12€ (child). A la carte: 30€.

Low prices and a pleasant atmosphere set the tone in this *casa* drenched with Portuguese sunshine. Silvia and Graciano Gonçalves present their country's finest recipes in its brightly colored dining rooms. Octopus in salad, Portuguese-style cod, boneless rib steak with cheese and a house flan: all good produce subtly prepared.

● Casa Sansa   SIM
4, rue Fabrique-Couverte.
Tel. 04 68 34 21 84. Fax 04 68 34 89 44.
Closed Christmas.
Prix fixe: 12€ (lunch), 19€, 29€, 11€ (child). A la carte: 45€.

Right in the city center, Louis Bonnet's restaurant plays consummately on tradition. In this bistro's vinic décor, we feast on Catalane-style escargots, fish parillada (mixed grill), suckling pig and a jelly-glazed soufflé with Spanish almond paste.

● Le France   SIM
Pl de la Loge.
Tel. 04 68 51 61 71 / 04 68 73 43 57.
Fax 04 68 51 61 75.
Closed Christmas.
Prix fixe: 23,50€, 8,50€ (child).
A la carte: 43€.

The facade of this brasserie occupying the ground floor of the old Bourse is eye-catching, with its Renaissance designs and gargoyles. The contemporary interior is not bad either. Camille Otero gives chef Ludovic Ranval a free rein and there are no complaints about the grilled calamari with garlic in tomato sauce, Basque-style cooked cod with slow-cooked onions and the duck breast with seasonal fruit. The pineapple carpaccio with sorbet slips down effortlessly.

● Laurens'o `SIM`
5, place des Poilus.
Tel.-Fax 04 68 34 66 66.
contact@laurenso.com
www.laurenso.com
Closed Sun., Mon., 2 weeks Sept.,
2 weeks May.
Prix fixe: 15€. A la carte: 35–40€.

Cédric Laurens and Olivier Husson tend to the stove in this establishment devoted to all things Italian. Full of vigor and with an appetizing whiff of the Mediterranean, the dishes are prepared to be eaten in the restaurant or to go. A sundried tomato mille-feuille, scallop cannelloni and a veal escalope Milanese slip down smoothly.

● Le Sud `SIM`
Corner of rue Bausil and rue Rabelais.
Tel. 04 68 34 55 71. Fax 04 68 51 05 53.
Closed lunch (exc. Sun.), Wed.,
beg. Jan.–beg. Apr.
A la carte: 40€.

Marie Lopez has taken over this Argentina- and Morocco-influenced establishment with its whitewashed walls and patio. Sébastien Ausseil watches over the smart Southern cuisine. Scallop carpaccio or spring rolls, pumpkin cream with shavings of parmesan, pan fried monkfish wih ceps, lamb shank confit with orange and cinnamon, vanilla-seasoned brioche pain perdu and pears in syrup and the tiramisu are not bad.

● Les Trois Soeurs `SIM`
2, rue Fontfroide.
Tel. 04 68 51 22 33. Fax 04 68 51 63 36.
www.les3soeurs.com
Closed lunch (Oct.–May), Sun., Mon. lunch.
Prix fixe: 25€, 50€.

The atmosphere is friendly here in Isabelle Sarrobert's establishment. The place is a tapas bar with music, a lounge in the evening. Stéphane Riether's quick-fire tapas, featuring salmon tartare, magret de canard and a dark chocolate fondant, have plenty of repartee.

In Pézilla-la-Rivière (66370). 7 km w.
● L'Aramon Gourmand `COM`
127, av du Canigou.
Tel. 04 68 92 43 59. Fax 04 68 92 39 88.
laramon.restaurant@wanadoo.fr
http://restaurant.aramon.free.fr
Closed Tue. dinner, Wed., 2 weeks Sept.,
2 weeks Jan.
Prix fixe: 26€, 31€, 36€.

This large inn made fashionable by the Galaberts has changed hands. Nathalie Coste in the dining room and her husband Philippe in the kitchen now preside over its fortunes, serving reliably sunny dishes. Grilled red peppers, cod risotto with green asparagus, duck fricassée with olive-flavored potatoes and poached pears for dessert go down effortlessly.

PERROS-GUIREC

22700 Côtes-d'Armor. Paris 527 – Saint-Brieuc 76 – Lannion 11 – Tréguier 19.
The Ploumanach rocks, the marina, Trestraou beach and the Sentier des Douaniers are the landmarks of this great seaside town.

▪ HOTELS-RESTAURANTS

■ L'Agapa
12, rue des Bons-Enfants.
Tel. 02 96 49 01 10.
hotel@lagapa.com / www.lagapa.com
50 rooms: 120–230€. 1 suite: 490–590€.
Prix fixe: 26€ (lunch), 34€ (lunch), 55€,
72€, 105€.

This charming, elegant UFO is an ongoing event on its pink granite coast. A contemporary building all in glass, steel and granite, it has a fitness center that makes it ideal for an invigorating break. Then there is the friendly service and the highly precise cuisine prepared by Franck Marchesi, who trained with Rostang (seared scallops in salted butter, cod filet fried and steamed in the pan and the chocolate panna cotta). In short, quite enough to earn our praise.

■ Le Grand Hôtel

45, bd Joseph-Le-Bihan.

Tel. 02 96 49 84 84. Fax 02 96 49 84 84.

www.grand-hotel-trestraou.com

Closed 29 Oct.–26 Feb. Rest. closed Sat. dinner, Sun. lunch (exc. 12 July–24 Aug.).

45 rooms: 59–102€. 4 suites: 110–170€.

Prix fixe: 25€, 9€ (child).

A la carte: 30–35€.

In a practical location by the beach and thalassotherapy center, this establishment has chic to spare, with its great hall and impressive dining room. The rooms are furnished in period style.

■ Manoir du Sphinx

67, chemin de la Messe.

Tel. 02 96 23 25 42. Fax 02 96 91 26 13.

lemanoirdusphinx@wanadoo.fr

www.lemanoirdusphinx.com

Closed 2 weeks end Nov.–beg. Dec., end Jan.–1 Mar. Rest. closed Fri. lunch (exc. Bank holidays), Sun. dinner (Oct.–Feb.), Mon. (exc. Bank holidays).

20 rooms: 108–127€.

Prix fixe: 30€, 40€, 50€, 12,50€ (child).

A la carte: 65€.

By the sea, this 1900 villa in art deco (and, in places, contemporary) style exerts an immediate charm. Our day is brightened by the rooms in the English manner, view of the islands, garden running down to the water and irreproachably fresh cuisine, including lasagne with langoustines, thick slice of monkfish pierced with rosemary, beef tenderloin with a wine infusion and a small salted-butter caramel cake.

■ Les Feux des Iles

53, bd Clemenceau.

Tel. 02 96 23 22 94. Fax 02 96 91 07 30.

feuxdesiles2@wanadoo.fr

www.feux-des-iles.com

Closed 2 weeks beg. Oct., 1 week Christmas–New Year's. Rest. closed lunch (exc. Sun.), Fri. (exc. July–Aug.), Sun. dinner (exc. July–Aug.).

18 rooms: 54–120€.

Prix fixe: 24€, 37€, 64€, 15€ (child).

The *feux* are the island lighthouses that feature in the view from the dining room

of this stone hostelry, recently extended with a new wing. The Le Roux family—parents and son—provide fine rustic or modern rooms, some of them opening onto the garden, and traditional meals centered on seafood. We savor the scallop and langoustine gratin, Atlantic sea bass fricassée with cider and acidulated apples, beef filet with red wine sauce and bone marrow and the caramelized apple dessert, delicacies indeed.

■ Au Bon Accueil

11, rue Landerval.

Tel. 02 96 23 25 77.

au-bon-accueil@wanadoo.fr

Closed 2 weeks end Dec.–beg. Jan.

Rest. closed Sun. dinner (exc. July–Aug.), Fri. (exc. July–Aug.).

21 rooms: 52–65€.

Prix fixe: 16€ (lunch, weekdays), 20€, 41€.

This classical hotel located in a quiet street is scheduled for renovation. Opposite the harbor, its restaurant with contemporary dining room offers very welcome seafood dishes.

■ Hermitage

20, rue des Frères-Le-Montréer.

Tel. 02 96 23 21 22. Fax 02 96 91 16 56.

hermitage.hotel@wanadoo.fr

www.hotelhermitage-22.com

Closed beg. Oct.–end Mar.

23 rooms: 41–57€.

Prix fixe: 21€, 10€ (child).

Nestling in its garden right in the city center, this old building turns out to be a welcoming oasis. Everything here is refreshing and pleasant, from Madame Cariou's welcome to the neat little rooms. A traditional set menu at a bargain price.

■ Le Levant

91, rue Ernest-Renan.

Tel. 02 96 23 20 15. Fax 02 96 23 36 31.

le-levant@wanadoo.fr

Rest. closed Fri. (off season), Sat. lunch (off season), Sun. dinner (off season), mid-Dec.–beg. Jan.

19 rooms: 55–61€.

Prix fixe: 19€, 27€, 12€ (child).

All the rooms in this old harbor residence have a sea view. Renovated and equipped with balconies, they offer all the comfort you could wish. The panoramic dining room welcomes enthusiasts ready to gorge themselves on seafood. Roasted langoustines, scallops in salad, Atlantic sea bass in cider and rouget in pepper sauce are meticulously prepared by Sébastien Delpine.

● **La Clarté**

At La Clarté, 5 km, 24, rue Gabriel-Vicaire.
Tel. 03 96 49 05 96. Fax 02 96 91 41 36.
laclarte22@aol.com
Closed Sun. dinner, Mon., Wed. dinner,
2 weeks beg. Oct., end Dec.–mid-Feb.
Prix fixe: 24€ (weekday lunch), 38€, 50€,
70€, 10€ (child). A la carte: 65€.

This former workingmen's eatery occupying a typical pink granite house has been fully renovated. It now sports a refined, luxurious décor in burgundy and brown tones, whose opulence is reflected in the substantial checks. At the stove, Daniel Jaguin, formerly at the Villa Blanche near Lannion, prepares fine Trégor produce with dexterity and intelligence. Pan-fried langoustines with artichokes and Piquillo peppers in verbena broth, monkfish in cider, cauliflower and Paimpol white beans, veal sweetbreads in their jus served with snap peas, carrots and mashed potatoes and the strawberry, tomato and passion fruit tartare served with raspberry sorbet are delicious hymns to the surrounding nature.

● **Le Suroît** SIM

81, rue Ernest-Renan.
Tel. 02 96 23 23 83. Fax 02 96 91 18 32.
Closed Sun. dinner, Mon.
Prix fixe: 26€, 40€.

Henri Guégou watches attentively over this harbor eatery. Giselle presents inspired, topical dishes that pay tribute to the sea (but not exclusively). Langoustine and foie gras salad, fish couscous, lamb cooked three ways with rosemary and a frozen nougatine dessert will whet the most jaded of appetites. Attentive ser-

vice in the friendly, wood-trimmed dining room or on the covered terrace.

PETITE-HETTANGE see THIONVILLE

LA PETITE-PIERRE

67290 Bas-Rhin. Paris 433 – Haguenau 40 – Saverne 22 – Strasbourg 60.
tourisme.pays-lapetitepierre@wanadoo.fr.
"I showed you La Petite-Pierre, its woodland dowry, the sky born in the branches, the pollen twice living under the blaze of flowers," wrote René Char. The great national forest is still one of the finest in France, while the village on its sandstone pedestal has become a well-known health resort. The renovated château houses the headquarters of the North Vosges Natural Park. Hiking is the queen of leisure activities here.

■ HOTELS-RESTAURANTS

■ **La Clairière**

63, rte d'Ingwiller.
Tel. 03 88 71 75 00. Fax 03 88 70 41 05.
info@laclairière.com / www.laclairiere.com
50 rooms: 120–182€.
Prix fixe: 32€, 49€, 10€ (child).
A la carte: 60€.

On the edge of the forest, this contemporary hotel managed by Lisbeth and Karen Strohmenger offers cozy, comfortable rooms, grounds with a swimming pool and obstacle course, meeting rooms and a fine spa, very Zen in appearance. In the restaurant, Stéphane Schramm (who trained at the Cerf in Marlenheim) serves a gratifying, elaborate, accomplished cuisine, including a tuna carpaccio marinated in avocado oil, roasted pork ribs and cornbread and a soy milk crème-style dessert.

■ **Les Trois Roses**

19, rue Principale.
Tel. 03 88 89 89 00. Fax 03 88 70 41 28.
www.aux-trois-roses.com
Closed 1 week Jan.
Rest. closed Sun. dinner, Mon.
40 rooms: 46–102€.
Prix fixe: 17€, 45€, 7,50€ (child).

This welcoming 18th-century establishment is overseen with meticulous care by Philippe Geyer. Everything is designed to make the guest comfortable: snug rooms—some with a balcony and a view of the château—cordial lounges, an indoor swimming pool and panoramic dining rooms overlooking the old village and valley, as well as an elaborate, classical cuisine. Foie gras, the "rich" hors-d'oeuvre, almond-crusted trout, wild boar stew with blood sauce, thick-cut boneless rib steak in red wine sauce with bone marrow and the frozen vacherin are a pleasure.

■ Les Vosges

30, rue Principale.
Tel. 03 88 70 45 05. Fax 03 88 70 41 13.
hotel-des-vosges@wanadoo.fr
www.hotel-des-vosges.com
Closed end Feb.–beg. Mar.,
1 week at end July. Rest. closed Tue.
28 rooms: 55–79,50€. 2 suites: 120–170€.
Prix fixe: 23,50€, 54€, 10€ (child).

This mountain inn is run with unquestionable reliability by the Wehrung family. Jean welcomes guests and looks after the cellar, while Eric, the son, has taken over in the office and kitchen. The paneled rooms are in the Vosges style and the dining room has a view of the château, old village and valley. The poached poultry terrine, trout "au bleu", cock in Riesling sauce and the frozen vacherin are classics that never stale. Rich in great Alsatian vintages from the finest years, the house wine list is giddying indeed.

■ Auberge d'Imsthal

On l'étang d'Imsthal, 3,5 km via D178.
Tel. 03 88 01 49 00. Fax 03 88 70 40 26.
reservation@petite-pierre.com
www.petite-pierre.com
Closed end Nov.–beg. Dec.
23 rooms: 49–108€. 1 suite: 154€.
Prix fixe: 10,50€, 25€ (Sat., Sun., lunch),
26€, 7€ (child). A la carte: 38€.

Nature and relaxation. By a lake in the middle of the forest, this half-timbered hostelry equipped with a fitness center, steam bath and Jacuzzi is a pleasant place

to stay. The dishes pay tribute to regional produce, game and fish, with preparations that are often a lost art elsewhere (and very reasonable prices into the bargain). A "Best Value for Money" award this year for the veal in creamy sauce served in puff pastry shells, freshwater fish stew, beef filet in the style of Vieux Strasbourg, a well-presented tête de veau and the real choucroute with its pork cuts and charcuterie. The raspberries served hot with vanilla ice cream deliciously conclude this delightful experience, which we owe to the mayor of the village, Hans Michaely.

■ Le Lion d'Or

15, rue Principale.
Tel. 03 88 01 47 57. Fax 03 88 01 47 50.
contact@liondor.com / www.liondor.com
Closed 10 days beg. July.
42 rooms: 53–98€.
Prix fixe: 19€ (weekday lunch), 29€, 35€,
43€ (wine inc.), 12€ (child).
A la carte: 45–50€.

This family guesthouse with its vast, panoramic dining room, cozier winstub area (Loewestuewel), contemporary rooms and care lavished in the name of arbrothérapie is now run by the son, Philippe, chair of the Young Restaurateurs of France. New Wave dishes go side- by-side with preparations based on local produce: grilled scallops with endives and quinoa, hot oysters with parsnips, foie gras maison, Savoie lake trout ravioli with mushrooms. You might try the mixed salad and pan-fried veal cutlets served with Alsatian potato gratin and his kirsch parfait.

In Frohmuhl (67290). On l'étang du Donnenbach, 4 km via forest road.

● Auberge du Donnenbach

Tel. 03 88 01 57 69. Fax 03 88 01 52 94.
auberge.du.donnenbach@wanadoo.fr
Closed Mon., Tue., Christmas–mid-Jan.
Prix fixe: 7,50€ (weekday lunch),
9€ (weekday lunch), 28€, 7,50€ (child).
A la carte: 35€.

By the lake, Cédric and Myriam Brumm's modern forest inn has the charm of faraway places. Tasting a Beaufort terrine, salmon trout with saffron, poultry breast glazed with honey and the warm quince confit served with vanilla ice cream, we imagine ourselves out there somewhere between Finland and Canada. An extraordinarily refreshing change of air!

In Graufthal (67320). 11 km s via D178 and D122.

■ Au Vieux Moulin

7, rue du Vieux-Moulin.
Tel. 03 88 70 17 28. Fax 03 88 70 11 25.
kavi.moulin@wanadoo.fr
Closed Feb. vac., 1 week at end June–beg.
July. Rest. closed Tue. dinner.
14 rooms: 39–70€. 1 suite: 110€.
Prix fixe: 10€ (weekday lunch), 27€ (weekday lunch), 28€, 32€, 8€ (child).
A la carte: 29–41€.

Wood and bright colors—red, yellow and orange—decorate this attractive hotel standing by a lake in the forest. The friendly Kassel family offers a very Alsace-oriented cuisine concocted by new chef Nicolas Loutre. The smoked wild boar ham, trout meunière, beef tenderloin and the foie gras with Pinot Noir sauce are a delight.

In Graufthal.

● Le Cheval Blanc

19, rue Principale.
Tel. 03 88 70 17 11. Fax 03 88 70 12 37.
www.auchevalblanc.net
Closed Mon. dinner, Tue., Wed. dinner,
2 weeks Sept., 3 weeks Jan.
Prix fixe: 9,50€ (lunch), 24,50€, 27€, 32€.

The Stutzmann's inn enchants its guests, who all appreciate Brigitte's warm welcome, as well as Gilles' very fresh, reliable cuisine, mirroring the vagaries of the market. In the smart dining room or on the terrace, we relish the duck foie gras terrine with spiced aspic, monkfish stew in a shellfish bouillon, a cassolette of veal kidneys and the frozen rhubarb parfait. Sensible set menus.

7350 Indre-et-Loire. Paris 288 – Poitiers 74 – Le Blanc 39 – Châtellerault 36 – Tours 62.

This little-known village off the royal châteaux route in Indre-et-Loire is mainly worth a visit for its fine inn.

●	RESTAURANTS

● La Promenade

11, rue du Savoureux.
Tel. 02 47 94 93 52. Fax 02 47 91 06 03.
Closed Sun. dinner, Mon., Tue.,
2 weeks beg. Oct., Jan.
Prix fixe: 36€, 45€, 78€. A la carte: 78€.

The Dallais family includes the mother, the father, the son and the holy produce of Touraine. Two corner houses connected in modern style, spacious dining rooms, an eighties-style décor and colorful pictures on the wall: no luxury, but good-natured warmth. Jacky, who trained in Paris with Jacques Manière and shares his rough good humor, returned to the home where his father worked as a blacksmith and his mother ran the village bistro. His son, Fabrice, who has taken over there, is a Savoy and Gagnaire veteran, which explains his "New Wave Touraine" fashion of putting together topical, seasonal dishes. Carrot and broad bean bouillon with bacon and savory, a Spanish-style marinated sardine dish with preserved lemons and wild mushrooms, lobster with tomatoes served with buttered and truffled cabbage, the sanguette (a local black pudding) with meat aspic, delicious peas, egg ravioli with truffles and the Geline de Touaine chicken, alternately blowing hot and cold, are just some of the fine Dallais tricks here. The shrewd desserts (slow-cooked apple lasagne topped with sugar, tea sorbet, Granny Smith spaghetti with a quince broth and the dark chocolate cake with coffee and licorice flavors) make stylish conclusions. The best Loire wines accompany this impulsive, sincere cuisine.

PEZILLA-LA-RIVIERE see PERPIGNAN

67350 Bas-Rhin. Paris 458 – Haguenau 15 – Saverne 26 – Strasbourg 36.

Gateway to the Pays de Hanau, this Northern Alsace community is worth a visit for its little museum of painted and popular imagery.

HOTELS-RESTAURANTS

● **L'Agneau** `COM`

3, rue de Saverne.
Tel. 03 88 07 72 38. Fax 03 88 72 20 24.
gisele.ernwein@wanadoo.fr
www.hotel-restaurant-delagneau.com
Closed 2 weeks Sept., 1 week Mar., 1 week June. Rest. closed Sun. dinner (off season), Mon. (off season), Tue. dinner (off season).
12 rooms: 50–68€.
Prix fixe: 13€, 25€, 55€, 65€.

What better name for a former 18th-century sheepcote than "l'Agneau" (the Lamb)? The three Ernweins—mother Gisèle welcomes the guests—have refurbished the place fifties style in shades of ecru and red. The pleasant rooms are tastefully decorated. At the stove, Anne (who trained with Loiseau in Saulieu and Blanc in Vonnas) tinkers with tradition, offering exuberant, sometimes slightly bombastic reinterpretations. Her mischievous dishes—foie gras served with dried fruit chutney, scallop brochettes with Serrano ham "chips", pink garlic-seasoned lamb with basil, a raspberry macaron or the frozen vacherin—are childhood treats. To help you choose among the 250 wines from every region of France, ask for Viviane. Flambéed tarts in the evening on weekends and a charming, flowered facade in season.

● **A l'Etoile d'Or** `SIM`

14, rue de la Gare.
Tel. 03 88 07 70 64.
Closed Mon. dinner, Tue. dinner, Wed.
Prix fixe: 7,65€ (lunch), 11,22€ (lunch), 32,50€ Sun. lunch, 8€ (child).
A la carte: 35–40€.

Behind the fine, painted facade of this friendly establishment, we find a warm welcome and Marie-Reine Steiner's generous cuisine. We feast on good, simple dishes, such as warmed goat cheese salad, seafood stew, boneless rib eye with horseradish and the chocolate fondue with fresh fruits in season. Couscous on the first Tuesday of the month.

PFULGRIESHEIM see **STRASBOURG**

PHALSBOURG

5737 Moselle. Paris 434 – Strasbourg 57 – Saverne 11 – Metz 109.
tourisme.phalqbourg@libertysurf.fr.
Here you will find the gateway to France where G. Bruno's two heirs began their tour of the country, the (Lorraine) gateway to Alsace, the district where Chatrian was born, the museum devoted to the famous duo, two restaurants that owe their names to the pair and lush countryside bordered by the Vosges forest.

HOTELS-RESTAURANTS

■ **Erckmann-Chatrian**

14, pl d'Armes.
Tel. 03 87 24 31 33. Fax 03 87 24 27 81.
hotel.rest.e.chatrian@wanadoo.fr -
http://www.erckmann-chatrian.com
Rest. closed Mon., Tue. lunch.
14 rooms: 61–79€. 2 suites: 85€.
Prix fixe: 13,50€ (weekdays), 17,60€ (weekdays), 20,60€, 31,40€, 33€, 45€, 6,50€ (child).

In restaurant and hotel, Roland and Netty Richert are hard at it on every front in a display of unfailing talent and conviviality. In both rooms and dining rooms, the decoration is warm and colorful. The quality of the dishes is reliable. Given the elegance and luxury of the paneled setting, the little weekday set menus are pure acts of philanthropy! The other day, duck terrine with crisp vegetables in season, grilled duckling, crème brûlée were on offer for 17.60': delicious and easy on the pocket. However, Basque-style tuna, the venison roast with notes of pain d'épices and served with vegetable gnocchi and the juicy lamb shank in a pastry crust show that Roland, a classicist by training, is quite capable of taking modern trends on board. With tempting desserts into the bargain (rum-infused savarin with hibiscus sorbet and little fruit soup served in a glass), we decide that this courteous establishment with its silver ice buckets and lively wine list deserves a further visit.

● **Le Soldat de l'An II**   CO V.COM

1, rte de Saverne.
Tel. 03 87 24 16 16. Fax 03 87 24 18 18.
info@soldatan2.com / www.soldatan2.com
Closed Sun. dinner, Mon., Tue. lunch,
3 weeks Nov., 3 weeks Jan., 2 weeks Mar.
7 rooms: 120–150€.
Prix fixe: 39,50€ (lunch, wine inc.), 68,50€,
74€, 88€, 23€ (child). A la carte: 100€.

The great innovation in this 18th-century barn topped by varnished tiles and updated in a chic restaurant style by Georges Schmitt is the addition of seven rooms (including one mini suite) with fine furniture, superb sheer drapes and tasteful fittings, providing ample accommodation for a delightful stay. The eatery itself has been enlarged, with a long dining room in black and white tones (very contemporary baroque). In the kitchen, the great Georges continues to pull out all the stops, wedding the finest flavors of Alsace and Lorraine to Southern French produce for better, not worse. On the plates, this results in unusual creations: foie gras with white chocolate and black olives, Marenne oysters with kaffir lime, sautéed John Dory with lemon, jam and asparagus and the rabbit medallions in a parmesan crust. In season, game is king, exemplified by the venison roast with chayottes and piña colada. At the end of the meal, the fresh pineapple and little soft banana cup with soft dark rum ice cream add a vaguely chic touch to the spread. Aside from these fine notions, we delight in the capital cellar and the impeccable welcome provided by Brigitte, who darts around the dining room with endless exuberance.

In 57370 Bonne-Fontaine. 4 km via N4.

■ **Notre-Dame-**   ✿ 🏠
 de-Bonne-Fontaine
212, rte de Bonne-Fontaine,
Danne et Quatre-Vents.

Tel. 03 87 24 34 33. Fax 03 87 24 24 64.
ndbonnefontaine@aol.com
www.notredamebonnefontaine.com
Closed 2 weeks Jan., 1 week Feb.
34 rooms: 49–85€.
Prix fixe: 16€, 19,50€, 31€, 43€ (wine inc.), 10€ (child).

In their seventies hotel, the Knopfs stand Mosellian guard at the gates to Alsace. The daughter, Isabelle Santiago, trained in Germany, England and California, is a dedicated champion of Lorraine's culinary heritage. Her sister Patricia officiates in the dining room, as does her husband Fabrice, who offers oenological advice. Guests can stay over in the modest, modern rooms with recently refurbished bathrooms and views of the forest and enjoy the delights of the local produce. A nice and creamy quiche Lorraine, meat in cream sauce served in a puff pastry shell, trout meunière, duck breast with mirabelles and the omelet Norvégienne (a flambéed meringue, cake and ice cream dessert) are extremely affable.

PHILIPPSBOURG

57230 Moselle. Paris 451 – Strasbourg 60 – Haguenau 29 – Wissembourg 46.
Here begins the Pays de Bitche. A church with an onion bell tower and rustic Vosges homes in red sandstone with half-timbering: a Lorraine-Alsace connection.

● | RESTAURANTS

● **Le Tilleul**   ○ COM
117, rte de Niederbronn.
Tel. 03 87 06 50 10. Fax 03 87 06 58 89.
o.tilleul.issler@wanadoo.fr
Closed Mon., Jan.
Prix fixe: 16€, 26,60€, 33€,
7,70€ (child). A la carte: 50€.

Didier Issler's rustic inn is enjoying a second youth. Leaving the setting unchanged, this veteran of the Cheval Blanc in Lembach has turned the eatery into a tasteful restaurant serving polished neoclassical dishes. Warm langoustine salad with citrus-flavored vinaigrette and ham, Atlantic sea bass in a lemongrass foam with slow-cooked fennel and the calf's liver in Pinot Noir sauce with chopped bone marrow play to a delicate, bewitching score. The theme continues when dessert time comes around, with a fromage blanc mousse, berry soup, a chocolate fondant and verbena ice cream. The set menus are splendid, the wines well-chosen, the prices reasonable and the service friendly.

PIERREFITTE-EN-AUGE

14130 Calvados. Paris 193 – Caen 46 – Deauville 20 – Lisieux 15.
Postcard Norman scenery abounds around this pretty village on the edge of the Vallée de la Touques. Don't miss the Saint-Hymer priory nearby.

 | RESTAURANTS

● Auberge des Deux Tonneaux
Le Bourg.
Tel. 02 31 64 09 31. Fax 02 31 64 69 69.
www.aubergedesdeuxtonneaux.com
Closed Sun. dinner, Mon., mid-Nov.–mid-Mar.
Prix fixe: 25€, 20€, 10€ (child).
A la carte: 40–45€.

Behind the British pseudonyms Lord Brett and Major Wells lurk two Parisian gourmets, one of them a famous photographer, who have breathed new youth into this 17th-century cottage. In the kitchen, Joël Victor carries on the tradition of Norman cuisine. Country terrine, grilled fish of the day, top sirloin steak, rice pudding and a thin apple tart are washed down with local cider.

PIERREFONDS

60350 Oise. Paris 90 – Compiègne 15 – Soissons 32 – Villers-Cotterêts 18.
ot.pierrefonds@wanadoo.fr.
Restored by Viollet-le-Duc, the admirable Gothic château alone is worth the trip to this pretty, old-fashioned village on the edge of Compiègne Forest. Enjoy a stroll down the valley in autumn.

| HOTELS-RESTAURANTS

● Aux Blés d'Or
8, rue Jules Michelet.
Tel. 03 44 42 85 91.
Rest. closed Sun. dinner, Tue. dinner, Wed., Christmas.
6 rooms: 43–61€.
Prix fixe: 23€ (weekday lunch), 36€.

This mill's wheels have long since ceased to turn, but it continues to offer a warm welcome, simple rooms and a rustic but polished cuisine in pleasant surroundings. Attractive beams and a traditional welcome.

In Saint-Jean-aux-Bois (60350). 6 km via D85.

■ Auberge à la Bonne Idée
3, rue des Meuniers.
Tel. 03 44 42 84 09. Fax 03 44 42 80 45.
www.a-la-bonne-idee.fr
Closed beg. Jan.–beg. Feb.
18 rooms: 65–105€. 3 suites: 150€.
Prix fixe: 29,50€ (weekday lunch), 45€, 69€, 15€ (child).

Taken over by Yves Giustinianin, this famous, rather rustic inn on the edge of Compiègne Forest has chosen a resolutely Provençal style for its charming rooms. In the kitchen, Gérald Ludec knows his classics and reinterprets them in his own way. Langoustine tails wrapped in kadaïf angelhair pasta, fennel-infused Atlantic sea bass in an aromatic herb salt crust, squab thighs and a house crêpe dessert titillate the taste buds.

PINEY see TROYES

PLAINE-DE-WALSCH

57870 Moselle. Paris 412 – Sarrebourg 10 – Strasbourg 76 – Abreschviller 9.
In Erckmann & Chatrian country, a world of enchanted forests and secret crystal glassworks…

● RESTAURANTS

● **L'Etable Gourmande**   SIM
3, rte du Stossberg.
Tel. 03 87 25 66 34. Fax 03 87 25 63 35.
Closed Mon., Tue., 2 weeks beg. Jan.,
2 weeks beg. Aug.
Prix fixe: 10,50€ (lunch, weekdays), 26,50€,
45€, 7,50€ (child). A la carte: 55€.

Nathalie and Pierre-Eric Mutschler have turned a former stable into an elegant establishment featuring an extended lounge and a dining room with glasswork. The place has its charm and the welcome is solid gold. The son, who worked at the Soldat de l'An II, has brought new life to the place. Although we miss its former simplicity, the frog leg and escargot cassolette with fresh cream and parsley and the golden brown langoustines served with ceps and chestnuts are not bad. Thick-cut Iberian pork tenderloin, Troyes chitterling sausages and the boneless rib steak with bone marrow make a fine impression. In conclusion, the house ice creams in blueberry or raspberry or the coconut lollipop with chocolate sauce plunge us back into our childhood.

LA PLAINE-SUR-MER

44770 Loire-Atlantique. Paris 446 –
Nantes 58 – Saint-Nazaire 28 – Pornic 9.
A "World's End" and the La Gravette harbor. For the inhabitants of St. Nazaire, we are "on the other side of the water".

 HOTELS-RESTAURANTS

● **Anne de Bretagne**   ○🏨
Port de la Gravette.
Tel. 02 40 21 54 72. Fax 02 40 21 02 33.
www.annedebretagne.com
Closed beg. Jan.–mid-Feb. Rest. closed Sun. dinner (mid-Oct.–mid-Apr.), Mon. (summer), Tue. lunch (summer).
20 rooms: 124–260€.
Prix fixe: 20€, 28€ (lunch, weekdays), 52€, 110€.

Michèle and Philippe Vételé's hostelry has all the charms of a genuine seaside establishment, with luxurious renovated rooms, lounge and bar, an ocean view from the fine dining room and a heated swimming pool. In the kitchen, Philippe creatively interprets the best of local produce. Variations on Breton oysters (in sorbet, chilled in aspic, warm poached with shallots and hot with curry cumin sauce), line-fished Atlantic sea bass with sardines and oysters in tartare, whelks and pickled seaweed and Retz country pigeon seared and finished under the broiler with a roasted cocoa jus pastilla are delicious examples, as are pan-tossed strawberries with cool mint and bergamot tea and the mara des bois sorbet. The wine list, drawn up by Michèle with Rodrigue Pavaldo, is up to the same high standard and includes some exceptional vintages.

PLANCOET

22130 Côtes-d'Armor. Paris 418 –
Saint-Malo 27 – Dinan 17 – Dinard 22 –
Saint-Brieuc 45.
siplancoet@libertysurf.fr.
This village has a famous name, shared with an excellent Breton mineral water drawn from a spring that rises nearby.

 HOTELS-RESTAURANTS

● **Crouzil et l'Ecrin**   ○🏨
20, Les Quais.
Tel. 02 96 84 10 24. Fax 02 96 84 01 93.
jean-pierre.crouzil@wanadoo.fr
www.crouzil.com
Rest. closed Sun. dinner,
Mon. (exc. July–Aug.), Tue.
7 rooms: 75–160€.
Prix fixe: 35€, 60€, 80€, 120€.
A la carte: 80–95€.

Now assisted by his son Maxime, Jean-Pierre Crouzi) celebrates the great traditions of Brittany. Both the rooms and dining room here have all the charms of yesteryear, but still provide comforts more appropriate to our century. Much the same is true in the kitchen, where father and son harmoniously wed the region's star produce to more distant flavors. The hot and cold oysters with carrot sabayon, the wood fire-roasted Breton lobster, basted in Lambic beer, pan-fried deboned pigeon with arabica jus accompanied by cabbage and the green tea and mint macaron with lychee sorbet underline the success of this venture, which owes a great deal to the flawless quality of the produce they use. Delightful wines from the list fill in the picture wonderfully.

PLANGUENOUAL

22400 Côtes-d'Armor. Paris 440 – Dinan 38 – Saint-Brieuc 19 – Lamballe 8.
A fine escape back to nature on the moors of Brittany.

 HOTELS-RESTAURANTS

■ Domaine du Val
Tel. 02 96 32 75 40. Fax 02 96 32 71 50.
château-du-val@wanadoo.fr
www.chateau-du-val.com
53 rooms: 75–230€.
Prix fixe: 29€, 36€, 46€, 15€ (child).

In the heart of its wooded grounds, Hervé Joseph's imposing Breton château inspires respect. Its rooms and studios ally comfort with charm, while its swimming pool, gym and squash court provide an opportunity to work up an appetite before heading for the restaurant to enjoy the sterling board and lodging cuisine. Pan-seared foie gras with caramelized apples, scallops in their shells served with garden vegetables, roasted squab and a chocolate fondant slip down smoothly.

PLAPPEVILLE see METZ

PLELO

22170 Côtes-d'Armor. Paris 470 – Lannion 54 – Saint-Brieuc 22 – Guingamp 72 – Rennes 118.

 HOTELS-RESTAURANTS

■ Au Char à Bancs
Moulin de la ville, Geffroy: 1 km n via D84.
Tel. 02 96 74 13 63. Fax 02 96 74 13 03.
charabancs@wanadoo.fr
www.aucharabanc.com
Closed Jan. Rest. closed Sat. dinner (exc. July–Aug.), Sun. lunch (exc. July–Aug.), Tue. (off season).
5 rooms: 65–90€. A la carte: 25€.

This former 17th-century mill has charm to spare. The Lamour family's welcome, the porches looking out onto the valley, the bric-à-brac shop on the first floor, the old-fashioned rooms with their themed décor (seamstress, musicians, birds, etc.) and the *table d'hôte* paying tribute to the region's produce are a delight.

PLENEUF-VAL-ANDRE

22370 Côtes-d'Armor. Paris 447 – Saint-Brieuc 28 – Lamballe 16 – Erquy 9.
Pléneuf and its fine family resort, with its thirties casino, seawall and panoramic headland, make a fine port of call on the bay of Saint-Brieuc.

■ HOTELS-RESTAURANTS

■ George
131, rue G.-Clemenceau.
Tel. 02 96 72 23 70. Fax 02 96 72 23 72.
hotel-georges@casino-val-andré.com
www.casino-val-andre.com
Closed end Nov.–mid-Feb.
24 rooms: 59–99€. 1 suite: 99
Half board: 59–119€.

This hotel refurbished in contemporary style offers guaranteed rest and relaxation in its rooms equipped with hand-chosen pieces of furniture.

■ Grand Hôtel
80, rue de l'Amiral-Charner.
Tel. 02 96 72 20 56. Fax 02 96 63 00 24.
accueil@grand-hotel-val-andre.fr
www.grand-hotel-val-andre.fr
Closed Jan. Rest. closed Sun. dinner (exc.

July–Aug.), Mon. (exc. July–Aug.), Tue. lunch.
39 rooms: 66,50–99€.
Prix fixe: 27€, 37€, 47€, 76€, 15€ (child).
A la carte: 39–61€.

Directly on the beach, this late-19th-century luxury hotel in ocean colors offers fine rooms and a gastronomic restaurant. A whelk fricassée with pepper mousseline, sole rolled and stuffed with mushrooms, duck wings marinated in Grand Marnier and the regional desserts make an excellent impression.

● Au Biniou

121, rue G.-Clemenceau.
Tel. 02 96 72 24 35.
Closed Tue. dinner (exc. July–Aug.),
Wed. (exc. July–Aug.), Feb.
Prix fixe: 15,50€ (weekday lunch), 24,50€,
30,50€, 12€ (child). A la carte: 50€.

The ocean supplies Pascal Hervé with the raw materials for his fine dishes. Claudine waits attentively on her guests, who can always be certain of a treat to come. Scallops served on a sweet pea velouté with cauliflower purée seasoned with bacon and leeks, grilled Atlantic sea bass with pan-simmered garden vegetables and slow-roasted tomatoes in a beetroot reduction, squab served in a cocotte with an orange and ginger jus and the Calvados and apple tiramisu with pain d'épice are polished work.

PLERIN-SOUS-LA-TOUR see SAINT-BRIEUC
LE PLESSIS-PICARD see MELUN
PLOBSHEIM see STRASBOURG

PLOGOFF

29770 Finistère. Paris 316 – Quimper 47 –
Audierne 10 – Douarnenez 30 – Pont-l'Abbé 42.
In Pointe du Raz country, a hospitable "World's End".

 HOTELS-RESTAURANTS

■ Hôtel de la Baie des Trépassés

Baie des Trépassés.
Tel. 02 98 70 61 34. Fax 02 98 70 35 20.

hoteldelabaie@aol.com
www.baiedestrepasses.com
Closed mid-Nov.–mid-Feb. Rest. closed Mon.
(exc. school vac., Bank holidays).
27 rooms: 32–63€.
Prix fixe: 15,50€, 20€, 53,40€,
9€ (child). A la carte: 35€.

The hotel is being re-stuccoed—but don't be put off: the rooms are very comfortable and the kitchen honest.

■ Ker-Moor

Rte de la Pointe-du-Raz, plage du Loch.
Tel. 02 98 70 62 06. Fax 02 98 70 32 69.
kermoor.h.rest@wanadoo.fr
www.hotel-kermoor.com
16 rooms: 80–85€.
Prix fixe: 25€, 30€, 40€, 8€ (child).

The renovated rooms in this ideally located hotel offer a beautiful sea view. The restaurant pays tribute to local produce: a plate of assorted langoustines from the Bigoudian ports, steamed fish of the day served with seasoned butter, pan-fried lamb saddle with truffle juice and kouign-amann on a crêpe with caramelized apples. Who could ask for more?

PLOMEUR see PONT-L'ABBE

PLOMODIERN

29550 Finistère. Paris 562 – Quimper 28 –
Brest 61 – Châteaulin 14 – Crozon 25.
siplomodiern@wanadoo.fr.
The Pays Glazik comes before Le Porzay. In this "World's End", land and levees such as the Menez Hom seem to share their secrets with the sea.

 HOTELS-RESTAURANTS

■ Pors-Morvan

Rte de Lescuz.
Tel. 02 98 81 53 23. Fax 02 98 81 28 61.
christian.nicolas19@wanadoo.fr
Closed Oct.–end Apr. (exc. vac.).
12 rooms: 40–50€. A la carte: 15–20€.

This former farm near beach, lakes and parks has its charm. Everything here is authentic and the rooms have lost none of their character despite renovation. The *crêperie* offers some delightful specialties (buckwheat crêpes with seafood filling and wheat crêpes with Menez Hom goat cheese).

YOUNG CHEF OF THE YEAR

● **Auberge des Glaziks**
7, rue de la Plage.
Tel. 02 98 81 52 32. Fax 02 98 81 57 18.
www.auberge-des-glaziks.com
Closed Mon., Tue., Nov., Mar.
Prix fixe: 40€, 50€, 60€, 100€.

When the sun is out and the wind is high, it is time to visit Olivier Bellin. This local lad, who paid his dues with the Taupinière in Pont-Aven, Coussau in Magescq, Thorel in La Roche-Bernard and Robuchon in Paris, is now master of all he surveys. He has learned his classics, established his style, defined his domain and smartened up the family inn. Now, in a light beige and blue, elegant, refined dining room with widely spaced tables, azure chairs and art deco consoles, guests savor a delicate cuisine that reflects local flavors. Individual tarts with tripe and cuttlefish, rabbit liver fricasee with Celtic vinaigrette (as served by cousins Jeffroy in Carantec and Roellinger in Cancale), lobster brioche divinely combined with beets, hot foie gras and oysters and the pan-sizzled local Far Guwern sausage and vegetables in pot-au-feu are just some of the splendid things that await you here. Then there are pearly catfish with a veil of citrus, carrot and grapefruit confit, head cheese with pear and cep cake and the veal sweetbreads with buckwheat essence and old-fashioned fries, followed by the little "end of meal treats", as they say at the Arnsbourg in Lorraine, where Olivier paid an appreciative visit. Carrot and ginger soda with frozen biscuit is very digestible. The apricot soup with spicy juice with a fresh and crispy almond quenelle and variatioins on rye (in cream, ice cream, macaron and marshmallow) are effortlessly convincing. On the Burgundy side, the wine list is resourceful. The set menus are models of balance. As for the young waitstaff, they make an effort to keep up, for Bellin is nothing if not fast. All Porzay is closely watching the progress of its gifted son, the dazzling newcomer in New Wave Brittany.

PLOUBALAY

22650 Côtes-d'Armor. Paris 410 – Dinan 19 – Dol-de-Bretagne 34 – Lamballe 35 – Saint-Brieuc 55 – Saint-Malo 14.
This inland village is famous for its château, which offers a splendid panoramic view from its terrace.

| ● | RESTAURANTS |

● **Restaurant de la Gare**
4, rue des Ormelets.
Tel. 02 96 27 25 16. Fax 02 93 82 63 22.
Closed Mon. dinner (exc. July–Aug.), Tue. dinner (exc. July–Aug.), Wed., 2 weeks Oct., 2 weeks Jan., 1 week at end June–beg. July.
Prix fixe: 22€, 35€, 48€, 15€ (child).
A la carte: 60€.

In his rustic restaurant opening onto a small garden, Thomas Mureau serves up a spirited cuisine in the modern manner. In his fare, the produce of Brittany's land and sea coexist harmoniously, as evinced by pan-seared foie gras dusted with pain d'épice crumbs, served with pears and spicy figs, the stuffed and grilled John Dory with creamy bouillon and mushrooms and the juicy venison medallions with autumn vegetables and a reduction and the fresh oven-crisped citrus dessert seasoned with verbena.

PLOUFRAGAN see SAINT-BRIEUC

PLOUHARNEL see QUIBERON

PLOUZEVEDE

29440 Finistère. Paris 560 – Brest 50 –
Saint-Pol-de-Léon 14 – Morlaix 22.
The coast close by and the fields of Léon, rich
in fine vegetables.

 HOTELS-RESTAURANTS

● **Les Voyageurs** `COM`

1, rue de Saint-Pol.
Tel. 02 98 69 96 84. Fax 02 98 69 97 89.
voyageurs.berven@wanadoo.fr
Closed Mar. Rest. closed Mon., Tue.
8 rooms: 53€.
Prix fixe: 16,50€ (weekday lunch), 29,50€,
33,50€, 48€. A la carte: 42€.

This old post house has been refurbished
in modern style by Philippe Bardon and
Louis Clavier. The welcome is delightful
and the cuisine appealing. Oven-crisped
chitterling sausage with apples, roasted
pollock, veal sweetbreads with langoustines and morels finished in Vin Jaune
and the thin apple tart with salted-butter caramel make a good impression. A
few charming rooms.

PLUGUFFAN see QUIMPER
POET-LAVAL see DIEULEFIT
LA POINTE DE L'ARCOUEST see PAIMPOL
LA POINTE-SAINT-MATHIEU see LE
CONQUET
POISSON see PARAY-LE-MONIAL

POITIERS

86000 Vienne. Paris 338 – Limoges 121 –
Niort 75 – Tours 103.
accueil-tourisme@interpc.fr.
The Futuroscope has revolutionized tourism in
this ancient city. Even the TGV high-speed train
stops here. Make sure you visit the old quarter, with its maze of silent alleys and string of
fine churches: Saint-Hilaire-le-Grand, Saint-
Pierre, Sainte-Radegonde and especially Notre-
Dame de la Grande, which boasts an impressive,
ornate facade. In a former abbey, the Saint-
Croix museum holds archeological and artistic wonders.

 HOTELS-RESTAURANTS

■ **L'Europe**

39, rue Carnot.
Tel. 05 49 88 12 00. Fax 05 49 88 97 30.
www.hotel-europe-poitiers.com
88 rooms: 51–85€.

On the edge of the pedestrian district,
this hotel surprises us with its architecture and mixture of styles, from contemporary to Louis-Philippe.

■ **Le Grand Hôtel**

28, rue Carnot.
Tel. 05 49 60 90 60. Fax 05 49 62 81 89.
www.grandhotelpoitiers.fr
41 rooms: 65,50–83€. 6 suites: 110€.

Located right in the city center, this art
deco hotel offers strikingly original and
comfortable rooms and bars.

■ **Continental**

2, bd de Solferino.
Tel. 05 49 37 93 93. Fax 05 49 53 01 16.
www.continental-poitiers.com
39 rooms: 46–55€.

Each floor of this fine rail station hotel
refurbished in contemporary style has its
own colors: green and yellow, yellow and
blue or pink. Guests are welcomed conscientiously and the prices are reasonable.

■ **Le France**

215, rte de Paris.
Tel. 05 49 01 74 74. Fax 05 49 01 74 73.
royalpoitou@wanadoo.fr / www.hotel-poitiers.fr
Closed beg. Nov.–mid-Mar.
56 rooms: 80–139€. 2 suites: 139€.
Prix fixe: 17€.

For those who want to visit the Futuroscope without staying too far out of the
city, this establishment is ideal for a short
visit. The rooms are comfortable and the
renovated dining room immensely cheerful. Chef Loïc Bordon serves up foie gras
terrine, a slice of monkfish with a mousseline sauce and lamb with thyme flower,
all very well prepared.

● **Maxime** ◎ V.COM

4, rue Saint-Nicolas.
Tel.-Fax 05 49 41 09 55.
www.maitrescuisiniersdefrance.com
Closed Sun., 1 week beg. Jan., mid-July–mid-Aug.
Prix fixe: 15€, 20€, 31€, 36€, 50€.

A combination of reliability and high standards: this is what we like about Christian Rougier's place. The décor in red and pink tones is a little eighties, but the cuisine has its sights set firmly on 2010, with the oysters prepared with different textures, poultry lollipops with butternut mousseline, scallops with bacon and truffles and the rabbit prepared in a lightened royal style with truffles, which brings us back to terra firma. For dessert, the cube of pear enrobed in mango and strawberries is amusing. Jacqueline Rougier offers a warm welcome, while useful advice on the eclectic wine list is provided by a young sommelier who is very familiar with his subject. A fine establishment.

● **Vingélique** N COM

37, rue Carnot.
Tel. 05 49 55 07 03.
Closed Sat. lunch, Sun., 1 week Christmas,
1 week at Easter, 4 weekdays Aug.
Prix fixe: 10,50€ (lunch), 32€.

Nicolas Barrillot, who worked in Paris at the Vivarois, Vernet and Pressoir, has crossed the street (he owns the Absynthe just opposite) to take over what was the gourmet restaurant of Poitiers. He has turned the Trois Piliers into a chic, modern, epicurean brasserie. The little lunchtime set menu is right on target with its generous dishes (a fine cod with an herb-seasoned purée). However, it is the rouget with polenta, tête de veau and sweetbreads with foie gras cream and the beef cheek in caul lace, braised with gray escargots, all on the gastronomic set menu, that demonstrate his skills. A quince and soft nougat "turban" has flavors that take us back to our childhood.

● **Le Poitevin** COM

76, rue Carnot.
Tel. 05 49 88 35 04. Fax 05 49 52 88 05.
lepoitevin@cegetel.net

Closed Sun. dinner, Christmas–New Year's,
2 weeks July.
Prix fixe: 11€ (lunch), 22€, 27€, 30€,
35€, 11€ (child). A la carte: 55€.

Jean-Pierre Palard is the local boy the inhabitants are rooting for. We sit down in one of his five adjoining dining rooms to enjoy the gently priced local dishes featured on the bargain set menus. Hot oyster ravioli, mouclade (mussels with shallots and cream) with escargot sauce, pollock filet served with slow-cooked leeks, lamb chops with white beans and the vineyard peach crumble slips down smooth as velvet.

● **Bistro de l'Absynthe** N ● SIM

36, rue Carnot.
Tel. 05 49 37 28 44.
Closed Sat. lunch, Sun., 1 week Dec.,
1 week Apr., Aug.
Prix fixe: 22€.

Inexpensive, pleasant and flavorsome, Nicolas and Camita Barrillot's bistro has an amusing neo-1900 look and a corridor-style dining room. The set menu is unbeatable, offering a cep tarte Tatin, escargots, creamy pumpkin soup with foie gras bites on toothpicks, pike-perch with red wine sauce and a slow-cooked wild hare in blood sauce with chestnuts at bargain prices. The pears poached in Guignolet liqueur and the frozen absinthe parfait round off the meal sweetly.

● **Nardo's Bouchon** N SIM

27, pl Charles-de-Gaulle.
Tel. 05 49 52 80 03.
Closed Sun., Mon.
A la carte: 35€.

With its vaulted premises facing the market, straw-bottomed wooden chairs and ceramic tables, this grand, bouchon-style establishment has a Provençal air to it. Marie-Annick, who worked in the dining room at the Hostellerie de Levernois in Beaune, and Thierry Nardo, formerly with Bardet in Tours, have turned it into the most cheerful bargain eatery in the Halles district. She has settled into the kitchen and labors industriously there, while he looks after the wine in the dining room. Among the changing dishes chalked up on the blackboard are pork trotters on toast, "gourmet nibbles", oxtail in creamy mushroom soup, grilled steak and the chicken with chestnuts, which work wonders. The quince tart and the frozen vacherin form an appealing conclusion.

● **Bistro Notre-Dame**   SIM

55, pl Charles-de-Gaulle.
Tel. 05 49 88 35 62.
Closed Sun.
Prix fixe: 9,50€ (lunch), 11,50€ (lunch), 20€, 7€ (child). A la carte: 24€.

Right opposite the market, Jean-Paul Brun's establishment is hospitable to a fault. Guests come for the genuine Parisian-style bistro setting, the graffiti scribbled by stars on the wall (French soccer czar Michel Hidalgo and singer Gilbert Bécaud among them) and the timeless dishes chalked up on the blackboard. Farci poitevin (a regional sorrel and bacon-stuffed cabbage dish), foie gras, calf's liver in parsley and garlic, duck and potato layered casserole and the profiteroles are gratifying.

● **Le Bistro de la Villette**   SIM

21, rue Carnot.
Tel. 05 49 60 49 49. Fax 05 49 50 63 41.
hesteban@club-internet.fr
Closed Sun., 1 week Christmas–New Year's, 1 week beg. Mar., 22 July–beg. Aug.
Prix fixe: 13€, 23€, 9€ (child).
A la carte: 35€.

This neo-Parisian bistro in the center excels in domestic dishes and fine meats. The pan-tossed escargots with grape leaves, foie gras served two ways, a monkfish brochette with dried bacon, rump steak in a salt crust and the veal piccatta with Roquefort are pleasant.

At the Futuroscope, in Chasseneuil-du-Poitou (86360). 12 km n via N10.

■ **Novotel Futuroscope**   ⌂

Téléport 4.
Tel. 05 49 49 91 91. Fax 05 49 49 91 90.
info@novotel-futuroscope.biz
www.novotel.com
128 rooms: 79–177€.
Prix fixe: 12,50€, 16€, 21,50€, 8€ (child).
A la carte: 35–45€.

This chain hotel on the Futuroscope site provides rooms that achieve the expected level of comfort, a swimming pool, meeting rooms and reliable cuisine. Duck foie gras, monkfish in creamy sauce with baby vegetables, grilled beef tenderloin and a brown sugar crème brûlée are good, classical dishes. The glass and steel building fits in with its surroundings.

At the Futuroscope.

■ **Plaza Futuroscope**   ⌂

Téléport 1.
Tel. 05 49 49 07 07. Fax 05 49 49 55 49;
(Rest.) 05 49 49 07 62. Fax 05 49 49 02 76.
www.clarion-futuroscope.com
283 rooms: 98–154€. 4 suites: 290€.
Prix fixe: 20€ (lunch), 23€ (dinner), 34€, 13€ (child).

The vast, bright rooms, swimming pool and gym are practical. The dining room has plenty of character and the dishes are uncontentious: lobster ravioli, duo of monkfish and local Guéméné chitterling sausage, beef filet with Saumur sauce and a thin apple tart with salted-butter caramel, all well chosen.

At the Futuroscope.

■ **Alteora**   ⌂

Téléport 1.
Tel. 05 49 49 09 10. Fax 05 49 49 09 11.
www.hotel-alteora.com
Closed 1 week beg. Jan.
295 rooms: 60–120€.
Prix fixe: 18,50€, 21,50€, 7,50€ (child).

This ultra-contemporary building next to the Futuroscope boasts modern rooms, a gym, a swimming pool and a restaurant serving honest, traditional cuisine (05 49 00 38 58).

At the Futuroscope.

■ **Holiday Inn Express**   ⌂

Av Jean-Monnet, Téléport 3.
Tel. 05 49 49 10 49. Fax 05 49 49 10 48.

info@holidayinn-futuroscope.biz
www.hotels-futuroscope.biz
194 rooms: 75–99€. Half board: 92–132€.

An impersonal welcome, but well-equipped rooms for a stay at the Futuroscope with no unpleasant surprises.

At the Futuroscope.

■ **Mercure Futuroscope**   ⌂
Aquatis
Av Jean-Monnet,Téléport 3.
Tel. 05 49 49 55 00. Fax 05 49 49 55 01.
h2773@accor.com / www.mercure.com
140 rooms: 62–82€.
Prix fixe: 12€ (lunch), 21,50€,
7,50€ (child).

This hotel is right for those in search of modern comfort, direct access to the Futuroscope and simple catering. A friendly welcome.

In Croutelle (86240). 6 km via N10.

● **La Chênaie**   COM
La Berlanderie.
Tel. 05 49 57 11 52. Fax 05 49 57 11 51.
www.la-chenaie.com
Closed Sun. dinner, Mon., 1 week Feb.,
2 weeks July.
Prix fixe: 20€, 26€, 38€, 14€ (child).
A la carte: 50€.

André and Valérie Chenu's flowery farm is just the thing for a gourmet break. Valérie welcomes us and André regales us with appealing dishes he prepares in his own way. We enjoy foie gras pot-au-feu with baby vegetables, a spicy slice of cod, veal kidneys in a sweet-and-sour sauce and an exotic fruit gratin. Denis Guilbault presents a fine wine list.

In Mignaloux-Beauvoir (86550). 10 km sw via N147, rte de Poitiers.

■ **Manoir de Beauvoir**   ❀⌂
635, rte de Beauvoir.
Tel. 05 49 55 47 47. Fax 05 49 55 31 95.
resa-poitiers@monalisahotels.com
www.manoirdebeauvoir.com
45 rooms: 99–129€. 2 suites: 143€.
Prix fixe: 16€, 35€, 39€, 13€ (child).
A la carte: 50€.

In the heart of extensive grounds with a swimming pool and an eighteen-hole golf course, this fine 19th-century building offers comfortable rooms and studio apartments and an honest restaurant.

POLIGNY

39800 Jura. Paris 397 – Besançon 58 – Dole 37 – Lons-le-Saunier 30 – Pontarlier 64.
tourisme.poligny@wanadoo.fr.
The fruiterers' Jura, with its wheels of Comté cheese, white wine and plateaus where erosion has formed blind valleys.

 | HOTELS-RESTAURANTS

■ **Hostellerie des**   ⌂
Monts de Vaux
At the Monts-de-Vaux, Barretaine.
Tel. 03 84 37 12 50. Fax 03 84 37 09 07.
mtsvaux@hoqtellerie.com
www.hostellerie.com
Closed Nov.–end Dec.
Rest. closed Tue. (exc. July–Aug.), Wed.
lunch (exc. July–Aug.).
8 rooms: 115–190€.
2 suites: 220€.
Prix fixe: 29€, 70€. A la carte: 70€.

Opposite the Jura, set in grounds where guests can swim and play tennis, Jean-Marie Carrion's hostelry displays an immediate charm. Its appealing rooms and classical restaurant have an easy attraction. In the kitchen, the son, Xavier, pays tribute to the region with Comté cheese soufflé, a fines herbes–seasoned sole filet, Bresse chicken cooked in Vin Jaune with morels and a wine-simmered pear with pain d'épice ice cream.

POMMIERS

69480 Rhône. Paris 439 – Lyon 37 – Villefranche-sur-Saône 6.
A rural community typical of the Beaujolais region, with its golden stone and 11th-to-15th-century church, surrounded by fine vineyards that run down to the Saône river.

HOTELS-RESTAURANTS

● **Les Terrasses** **N·SIM**
de Pommiers
Buisante.
Tel. 04 74 65 05 27.
Closed Mon. (off season), Tue., 2 weeks Oct.–
Nov.
Prix fixe: 26€, 34€, 39€.

There is a giddying view of the vineyards
and Villefranche here. Although we have
nominally come for the peace and quiet
and the panorama on show in the dining
room (which opens onto a terrace), Julien
Valençot's cuisine still plays a part. This
young chef, who studied under Henriroux in Vienne, Delacourt in Divonne and
at the Chèvre d'Or, improvises smoothly
on Southern flavors. Sardine-, mushroom-
and ham-stuffed artichokes simmered
in wine, mushroom and foie gras ravioli,
bacon-wrapped monkfish in a shellfish
bouillon and a fennel-seasoned pork shank
all offer a delightful change in this setting
dedicated to all things Beaujolais.

PONT-DE-BRIQUES see BOULOGNE-SUR-MER
PONT-DE-L'ISERE see VALENCE
PONT-SAINTE-MARIE see TROYES

PONT-A-MOUSSON

54700 Meurthe-et-Moselle. Paris 327 –
Metz 31 – Nancy 29 – Toul 48 – Verdun 66.
Pont-à-Mousson has two claims to fame: the
fine Prémontrés abbey and the place Duroc,
one of France's few triangular "squares".

HOTELS-RESTAURANTS

■ **Bagatelle**
47, rue L.-Gambetta.
Tel. 03 83 81 03 64. Fax 03 83 81 12 63.
www.bagatelle-hotel.com
Closed Sun. dinner (off season), Christmas–
New Year's.
18 rooms: 48–60€.

When you visit the Prémontrés abbey,
stop over in this small, extremely charming hotel. You will enjoy the comfort and
refinement of the rooms and the peace and
relaxation to be found in the garden.

● **Pierre Bonaventure** SIM
18, pl Duroc.
Tel. 03 83 81 23 54. Fax 03 83 82 09 59.
bonaventurejulien@tiscali.fr
Closed 10 days Christmas–New Year's.
Prix fixe: 13€, 16€, 8,50€ (child).
A la carte: 35€.

The décor alone justifies a visit, with the
bread oven and butcher's block. Meat is
very much the thing here. You are certain to enjoy the bone marrow, pork tail,
a one-pound hanger steak and the mirabelle cream glazed with jelly.

● **Lilaver** SIM
131, rue du Bois-le-Prêtre.
Tel.-Fax 03 83 81 00 47.
Closed Sat. lunch, Sun. dinner, Mon.,
2 weeks Aug.
Prix fixe: 15€ (weekday lunch), 24€,
7€ (child). A la carte: 40€.

Muriel wears a delightful smile as she welcomes guests to the three bluish, modern
dining rooms of the Velfert's restaurant. In
the kitchen, Stéphane concocts a gourmet
cuisine to match the season. Fresh tomato
gazpacho, duck foie gras terrine with
mirabelle chutney, salmon brochettes
with slow-cooked ginger and garlic, a veal
kidney fricassée with chanterelles and the
coconut and apple mille-feuille with saffron sauce are well-prepared.

In Blénod-lès-Pont-à-Mousson (54700). 2 km
via N57.

● **Auberge des Thomas** SIM
100, av V.-Claude.
Tel.-Fax 03 83 81 07 72.
Closed Sun. dinner, Wed., 1 week Jan.,
1 week Apr., 2 weeks Aug.
Prix fixe: 25€, 32€. A la carte: 50€.

In the Thomas' former inn, Jean-Christophe Di Nigro favorably impresses. A
rouget Tatin bathed in beet jus, langoustine and spinach cannelloni, duck breast
medallions with peach sauce and the rich

chocolate cake with a pistachio filling make up balanced set menus.

PONTARLIER

25300 Doubs. Paris 462 – Besançon 60 – Dôle 88 – Lausanne 67.
The former capital of absinthe is an amiable gateway to Switzerland. Do not miss the portal of the old Chapelle des Annonciades.

● RESTAURANTS

● L'Alchimie
1, av de l'Armée-de-l'Est.
Tel. 03 81 46 65 89.
Closed Sun. dinner, Wed., 10 days beg. Jan., 10 days Apr., mid-July–beg. Aug.
Prix fixe: 20€ (weekday lunch), 35€, 49€.

Pierre-Yvan Boos, sorcerer of savor, turns Franche-Comté produce into an array of tastes, reinterpreting a sparkling succession of classics. The duck foie gras and morteau smoked sausage in papillote, crayfish and Vin Jaune fricassée, poached lake whitefish with chili peppers and asparagus, magret de canard glazed with spices and the rich white chocolate cake with mirabelle plum jam ice cream are all promising. A colorful dining room in cheerful shades.

● Côté Pont
2, rue de la République.
Tel. 03 81 46 59 53.
Closed Sun., Mon., dinner Tue.–Thu. (off season), 3 weeks Jan.
Prix fixe: 15€ (weekdays), 20€.

A single set menu of unpretentious dishes reflecting the market. A very warm welcome and an original décor featuring objects turned to a different purpose than their original one. The owner, Arlette Laude, also provides lodgings in Morteau. A pleasant terrace on the riverbank.

PONTAUBERT see AVALLON

PONT-AUDEMER

27500 Eure. Paris 161 – Le Havre 41 – Rouen 51 – Caen 74 – Evreux 68 – Lisieux 36.
tourisme@ville.pont.audemer.fr.
This fine old town with its half-timbered houses, Gothic church and Risle river is truly picturesque in the Norman style. The great Gaston Lenôtre started out here.

■/● HOTELS-RESTAURANTS

● Erawan   COM
4, rue de la Seule.
Tel. 02 32 41 12 03.
Closed Wed., Aug.
Prix fixe: 19,80€, 11€ (child).
A la carte: 37–42€.

It is relatively rare to find good Asian cuisine in such a typically French small town. Here, though, Jean-Claude Huor concocts excellent Thai dishes: breaded and fried shrimp, pork ribs with garlic and green peppercorns, duck with black mushrooms and the exotic fruit cup make it well worth visiting.

In Campigny (27500). 6 km ne via N175 and D29.

■ Le Petit Coq aux Champs   ❀⌂
La Pommeraie-Sud.
Tel. 02 32 41 04 19. Fax 02 32 56 06 25.
le.petit.coq.aux.champs@wanadoo.fr
www.lepetitcoqauxchamps.fr
Closed 3 weeks Jan., 1 week Nov.
Rest. closed Sun. dinner (off season), Mon. (off season).
12 rooms: 135–155€. 1 suite: 164€.
Prix fixe: 38€, 43€ (wine inc.), 64€, 68€.
A la carte: 65€.

This charming Norman hostelry offers attractive grounds, a swimming pool, terrace, renovated rooms and a cozy interior, along with a pleasant, market produce-based restaurant. Jean-Marie Huard reliably prepares pressed vegetable terrine with rouget, cod with a sorrel mousseline, calf's liver brochette and an apple and orange tart.

29930 Finistère. Paris 534 – Quimper 34 – Concarneau 16 – Quimperlé 18.
ot.pont-aven@wanadoo.fr.

Willows, gorse, the blue of the sky and the slate of the houses, the white facades sharp against the green of the trees, the enchantment of the Bois d'Amour and the high chapel of Trémalon, which inspired the *Yellow Christ*, not to mention the confusion of rocks near the harbor...

 HOTELS-RESTAURANTS

■ Les Ajoncs d'Or

1, pl de l'Hôtel-de-Ville.
Tel. 02 98 06 02 06. Fax 02 98 06 18 91.
ajoncsdor@aol.com
www.ajoncsdor-pontaven.com
Closed Sun. dinner (exc. hotel by reserv.),
Mon. (exc. hotel by reserv.), Jan.
20 rooms: 48–52€.
Prix fixe: 23€, 43€, 9€ (child).
A la carte: 43–48€.

This hotel dates from the end of the 19th century and Gauguin stayed here. It has lost none of its charming simplicity. The restaurant is also in excellent taste. The cuisine naturally mirrors the vagaries of the market: langoustine gratin, the "whole pig" plate and the caramelized pears with ice cream are spot on.

● Le Moulin de Rosmadec

Tel. 02 98 06 00 22. Fax 02 98 06 18 00.
moulinderosmadec@wanadoo.fr
Closed Sun. dinner (off season),
Mon. lunch (off season), Wed. (exc. off season), 2 weeks Oct., 3 weeks Feb.
4 rooms: 90€. 1 suite: 110€.
Prix fixe: 30€, 49€, 72€, 15€ (child).
A la carte: 70–80€.

Frédéric and Franck Sébilleau's 15th-century mill is one of Pont-Aven's gourmet attractions. Its authenticity and the charms of its antique furniture, restored décor and garden offer a delightful introduction to the pleasures in store on a menu mainly devoted to sea produce, the two chefs' specialty. The langoustines, filet of line-fished Atlantic sea bass and the rouget delight connoisseurs, while meat-eaters feast on the veal sweetbread medallions and a boneless stuffed pigeon. All join forces again when dessert comes, though, paying tribute to the lemon soufflé.

● La Taupinière

Croissant Saint-André, rte de Concarneau.
Tel. 02 98 06 03 12. Fax 02 98 06 16 46.
lataupiniere@wanadoo.fr
www.la-taupiniere.com
Closed Mon., Tue., 20 Sept.–mid-Oct.
Prix fixe: 53€, 73€, 80€. A la carte: 95€.

Brittany has a charming embassy indeed on the outskirts of Pont-Aven: Guy Guilloux's blue eatery with its thatched roof. Surrounded by his brigade of professionals, this great but modest chef, master of his repertoire, has learned to remain in the background, leaving produce to stand alone in the limelight. However, he is still quite happy to step forward and offer a little advice, choose a fish or chop a few vegetables with a sure hand. In fact, Guy Guilloux knows his art perfectly. His repertoire includes a pan-seared slice of foie gras, langoustine tail with sesame, line-fished Atlantic sea bass with rhubarb and carrot jus and the classic duck filet with blood sauce. All these delicacies meander uninhibitedly between tradition and sensible modernity. The desserts are of the same stamp, including a strawberry and rhubarb vacherin and a house apricot and raspberry pastry cream confection. The check is honest for a restaurant that has been at the peak of its art for a long time now. The attentive, spirited service is led by the exuberant Madame Guilloux.

12290 Aveyron. Paris 654 – Rodez 25 – Albi 88 – Millau 47 – Saint-Affrique 56.
tourisme-levezou@wanadoo.fr.
The heart of the Aveyron. On the GR hiking trail, the path between Millau and Conques, via the cheerful Lévézou.

 HOTELS-RESTAURANTS

■ **Les Voyageurs**

10, av de Rodez.
Tel. 05 65 46 82 08. Fax 05 65 46 89 99.
hotel-des-voyageurs@wanadoo.fr
www.hotel-d-voyageurs.com
Hotel closed Sun. dinner (exc. summer),
Mon. (exc. summer), beg. Nov.–beg. Mar.
Rest. closed Sun. lunch (exc. summer), Mon.
(exc. summer), Feb.
27 rooms: 39–55€.
Prix fixe: 11€ (lunch), 14,50€, 25,50€,
33€, 9€ (child).

A highly convivial stopover where modernity and tradition coexist harmoniously. In the kitchen, Thomas Rivero displays his mastery of oven-crisped roquefort pastry, monkfish in cream sauce, tête de veau with sauce ravigote and the pork trotter. For dessert, the house frozen nougat with raspberry sauce melts in your mouth. Attractive, fully equipped rooms.

PONT-DE-VAUX

01190 Ain. Paris 382 – Mâcon 23 –
Bourg-en-Bresse 39 – Lons-le-Saunier 69.
pont.de.vaux.tourisme@wanadoo.fr.
Crossroads of the Bresse region, the merits of this old-fashioned small market town are its hospitality and legendary appetite.

 HOTELS-RESTAURANTS

■ **Le Raisin** ⌂

2, pl Michel-Poizat.
Tel. 03 85 30 30 97. Fax 03 85 30 67 89.
contact@leraisin.com / www.leraisin.com
Closed Sun. dinner (exc. July–Aug.), Mon.,
Tue. lunch, beg. Jan.–beg. Feb.
18 rooms: 52–62€.
Prix fixe: 22€, 34€, 48€ (wine inc.), 59€,
12,50€ (child).

The charm and friendliness of the Bresse region are everywhere apparent in this fine inn. Its rustic rooms offer every comfort. Gilles Chazot's cuisine is a vibrant tribute to the district and its produce.

We unstintingly savor a three-flavor terrine, roasted pike-perch with mild garlic, Bresse chicken with a morel cream sauce and the fresh fruit gratin served with Bourbon vanilla ice cream and sabayon.

PONT-DU-GARD

30210 Gard. Paris 694 – Arles 38 –
Nîmes 26 – Avignon 27.
The Roman aqueduct here is one of the most magnetic tourist attractions in the Greater South, but the entire district and its lovely villages are worth a detour.

 HOTELS-RESTAURANTS

■ **La Bégude Saint-Pierre** ✿ 🏨

La Bégude, D981.
Tel. 04 66 63 63 63. Fax 04 66 22 73 73.
begudesaintpierre@wanadoo.fr
www.hotel-saintpierre.fr
Closed 11 Nov.–1 Apr.
20 rooms: 65–130€. 3 suites: 150–200€.
Prix fixe: 19€, 35€, 42€, 55€,
15€ (child).

Bruno Griffoul, who completely renovated his 17th-century hostelry after the 2002 floods, provides a warm welcome. The place, which has kept its old post house feel, has a huge courtyard, a swimming pool and well-equipped rooms. The Provençal cuisine is sensibly priced and concocted with commendable care by the young Pascal Relandre, formerly at the Vieux Castillon. The warm individual Fournès honey cakes, Nîmes-style brandade on crushed tomatoes, roasted pollock and the lamb sauté served with stewed root vegetables have an easy charm. Lively service under the supervision of Benjamin Lin, who was formerly with Banzo in Aix. Sensible set menus.

In Castillon-du-Gard (30210). 4 km ne via D19 and D228.

● **Le Vieux Castillon** ◎ ✿ 🏨

10, rue Turion-Sabatier.
Tel. 04 66 37 61 61. Fax 04 66 37 28 17.
vieux.castillon@wanadoo.fr
www.vieuxcastillon.com

Closed beg. Jan.–mid-Feb.
Rest. closed Mon. lunch, Tue. lunch.
29 rooms: 184–305€. 3 suites: 330€.
Prix fixe: 49€ (weekday lunch), 73€, 86€,
107€. A la carte: 77–105€.

Visitors are still reluctant to leave this imitation Provençal village, reconstructed nearly thirty years ago by the Traversacs and affiliated with the Relais & Châteaux group, especially since the cuisine does justice to the hotel's charm. Bernard Roth, who was the discreet Gilles Dauteuil's lieutenant for ten years, with excursions to the Pyramide in Vienne and the Negresco in Nice, has smoothly taken over from the master. There is a certain continuity in his rejuvenated regional (or, if you prefer, light classical) style, which fits in beautifully with the manorial genre of the house. The veal sweetbread terrine with seasonal vegetables and gray forest mushrooms, egg cocotte with foie gras and a tasty herb bouillon, monkfish tail simmered with bay leaves and the lamb medallions simmered with rosemary are flawless work. Appealing rooms, a swimming pool and unfailingly attentive service.

In Castillon-du-Gard.

■ Le Colombier

24, av du Pont-du-Gard.
Tel. 04 66 37 05 28. Fax 04 66 37 35 75.
hotelrestau.colombier@free.fr
18 rooms: 40–50€.
Prix fixe: 18€, 21€, 25€, 8€ (child).

We are fond of this antique establishment with its foliage-laden facade. The bedrooms are snug and peaceful and overlook the garden. The restaurant provides honest domestic cuisine (eggplant terrine with tomato confit, croustillant of salt cod with pesto, pieds et paquets). A terrace when the sun shines.

In Castillon-du-Gard.

● L'Amphytrion   COM

Pl du 8-Mai-1945.
Tel. 04 66 37 05 04.
Closed Tue. (exc. summer),
Wed. (exc. summer), 1 week at end Nov.,
1 week beg. Dec.

Prix fixe: 28€ (weekday lunch), 40€, 60€,
15€ (child).

Stéphane Goudet has brought a fresh touch to this delightful Provençal establishment with its solid vaults, run by Mario Monterroso. An increasing influx of gourmets comes to enjoy his lively, spirited dishes. A tartine with diced ceps, turbot filet in a vegetable stew, a slow-roasted Ségala veal cutlet with chestnuts and a duckling filet with lightly spiced caramel served over a splash of reduced walnut jus are attractive indeed.

In Collias (30210). 7 km w via D 981, D112 and D3.

■ Le Castellas

Grand-Rue.
Tel. 04 66 22 88 88. Fax 04 66 22 84 28.
infos@lecastellas.fr / www.lecastellas.fr
Closed beg. Jan.–mid-Feb. Rest. closed Wed.
(Nov.–Mar. exc. Bank holidays).
15 rooms: 80–130€. 2 suites: 190–230€.
Prix fixe: 30€ (exc. Sun. and Bank holidays),
40€ (exc. Sun. and Bank holidays), 55€,
75€, 100€, 18€ (child).

Chantal Aparis has turned an old stone house in the heart of the village into an enchanting sanctuary equipped with charming rooms. The cuisine prepared by Jérôme Nutile, formerly at the Chabichou in Courchevel and Blanc in Vonnas, offers a succession of daring ideas with a topical flavor. Sometimes, they do not quite work (oyster meringue whipped in the glass!) or are too much of a gimmick (foie gras served three ways, in which one is dusted with Sarawak pepper), but when he combines local produce with new takes on traditional recipes (rouget with eggplant, lamb chops and roast with sautéed vegetables and roasted garlic jus), we are fully convinced. The poached cherries over shortbread with vin d'orange (a fortified wine digestif infused with Seville bitter oranges) with a vanilla ginger ice cream plunges us back into childhood. Alert service and fine Gard wines chosen by the attentive Jean-Luc Sauron, who knows his trade well.

LE PONTET see AVIGNON

PONT-L'ABBE

29120 Finistère. Paris 575 – Quimper 19 –
Bénodet 12 – Douarnenez 33.
otsi.pontlabbe@altica.com.
The capital of the Bigouden region shows off
its treasures to great effect. On the riverbank,
the monument to local ladies sculpted by François Bazin in 1931 offers a pleasing symme-
try to the Lambour church with its captivating
ruins. Do not miss the Chapelle des Carmes, or
the château and its Bigouden museum. On the
edge of town, Kérazan manor and the Kervazé-
gan ecomuseum preserve a history in danger
of oblivion, with the aid of an open passenger
wagon, a cider press and pictures.

 | HOTELS-RESTAURANTS

■ **Le Bretagne**   ⌂
24, pl de la République.
Tel. 02 98 87 17 22. Fax 02 98 82 39 31.
Closed Sun. dinner (off season),
mid-Jan.–mid-Feb. Rest. closed Sun. lunch
(off season), Mon. (exc. dinner in season).
18 rooms: 47,50–67€.
Prix fixe: 12€, 26€, 30€, 48€,
10€ (child). A la carte: 55€.

Ideal for a stay in the region, this small
hotel is well-run and has a very pleasant
manner. The rooms are classical and Bertrand Cossec's cuisine is highly polished.
Oven-crisped lobster with reduced stock
made with its shell, served with julienned
vegetables, langoustine tails roasted and
served with mixed salad and parmesan shavings and the gratin with apples
poached in Lambic beer are well done.

In Loctudy (29750). 6 km via D2.

● **La Mer à Boire**   SIM
At the port de Plaisance.
Tel. 02 98 87 99 65. Fax 02 98 87 48 19.
lameraboire@wanadoo.fr
Closed Wed., mid-Nov.–mid-Mar.
A la carte: 22€.

The view of the harbor from the dining room
is a bonus. Gérard and Delphine Joncour
serve sweet and savory crêpes with seafood
stuffings. Pleasant and inexpensive.

In Plomeur (29120). 5 km w via D785.

● **Le Jardin de la Tulipe**   COM
8, rue Louis-Méhu.
Tel. 02 98 82 04 13. Fax 02 98 82 03 18.
Closed Mon. dinner, 1 week Oct.,
2 weeks beg. Jan.
Prix fixe: 14,50€, 21€, 29€, 40€,
8€ (child). A la carte: 50€.

Whether on the contemporary brasserie or
garden side, Anita Despierres takes good
care of you. Langoustines in salad, roasted
Atlantic sea bass with ceps and a chocolate mille-feuille with fleur de sel and Earl
Grey ice cream are rather shrewd.

PONT-L'EVEQUE

14130 Calvados. Paris 188 – Caen 48 –
Le Havre 40 – Rouen 79 – Trouville 11.
This Norman town in the heart of the Pays d'Auge
has an international reputation. Cider, Calvados
and cheese are obviously the star attractions, but
do not miss the Route des Manoirs.

 | RESTAURANTS

● **Auberge de l'Aigle d'Or**   COM
68, rue Vaucelles.
Tel. 02 31 65 05 25. Fax 02 31 65 12 03.
thierryduhamel@wanadoo.fr
www.laigledor.com
Closed Sun. dinner (off season), Wed.,
Feb. vac., 1 week at end June.
Prix fixe: 26€, 35€, 46€. A la carte: 70€.

This former post house has remained very
authentic, as has the cuisine prepared by
Thierry Duhamel, who successfully interprets classical genres in his own individual style. Raw oysters with a sweet lemon
vinaigrette, monkfish medallions seasoned with ginger, poultry breast stuffed
with morels and poached in Calvados,
brioche pain perdu with raspberry sauce
and an apple liqueur ice cream are sensible dishes.

● **Auberge de la Touques**   COM
Pl de l'Eglise.
Tel. 02 31 64 01 69. Fax 02 31 64 89 40.
Closed Mon., Tue. (off season), Jan.

Prix fixe: 21,50€, 32€, 10€ (child).
A la carte: 50–55€.

Jacky Libralato has taken over this family inn. The precise, modest house style has remained quite unchanged. Escargot feuilleté with Normande sauce, a thick slice of turbot with Pommeau sauce, Auge valley veal served in cutlets and caramelized apple mousse are very much in the local spirit.

PONTLEVOY

41400 Loir-et-Cher. Paris 211 – Tours 52 –
Amboise 25 – Blois 27 – Montrichard 8.
In this little village in the Loir-et-Cher overlooked by its proud conventual building, we take a gourmet break.

 HOTELS-RESTAURANTS

■ Hôtel de l'Ecole   ⌂
12, rte de Montrichard.
Tel. 02 54 32 50 30. Fax 02 54 32 33 58.
Closed Sun. dinner, Mon., 3 weeks mid-Nov.–
beg. Dec., 10 days at end Feb., 3 weeks Mar.
11 rooms: 57€.
Prix fixe: 21,50€, 52€, 13,50€ (child).
A la carte: 50€.

This lodging house with rustic rooms is full of charm. The dining room has been refurbished in antique style and guests enjoy fine regional cuisine there. We have no complaints about the foie gras terrine served with pork trotters and quenelles served in a dish on the side, pike served with crayfish tails, Vourvey eels cooked in wine and the veal sweetbreads and kidneys in a Port sauce. The flowered terrace is delightful.

PONT DE LEZARDRIEUX see PAIMPOL

PONTMAIN

53220 Mayenne. Paris 325 – Domfront 40 –
Fougères 20 – Laval 50 – Mayenne 45.
A small Mayenne village on the border of Brittany and its basilica, a place of pilgrimage.

 HOTELS-RESTAURANTS

■ Auberge de l'Espérance   ⓝ⌂
9, rue de la Grange.
Tel. 02 43 05 08 10.
pontmain@ladapt.org
Closed Christmas vac.
11 rooms: 33–36€.
Prix fixe: 10€ (weekdays), 12,50 (Sun.
lunch), 15, 50€. A la carte: 22€.

A sheltered workshop that provides neat, functional rooms with particular care paid to the needs of the disabled. Modest, market-based cuisine.

PONT-LES-MOULINS see
BEAUME-LES-DAMES

PONT-REAN

35170 Ille-et-Vilaine. Paris 360 –
Châteaubriant 55 – Fougères 66 – Nozay 58
– Rennes 15 – Vitré 55.
A village of character to the south of Rennes with an 18th-century bridge spanning the Vilaine.

 HOTELS-RESTAURANTS

● Auberge de Réan   ⓝ COM
86, rte de Redon.
Tel. 02 99 42 24 80. Fax 02 99 42 28 66.
auberge.de.rean@wanadoo.fr
Closed Sun. dinner, Mon. (rest.), Feb. vac.
9 rooms: 36–56€.
Prix fixe: 17€ (weekdays), 45€.

Opposite the Vilaine bridge, an old inn boasting neat rooms and a bright dining room. Terrace and cuisine in the colors of Brittany.

PORNIC

44210 Loire-Atlantique. Paris 431 –
Nantes 50 – La Roche-sur-Yon 84 –
Saint-Nazaire 104.
This port was once famed for its pottery, but is now devoted to yachting and recreation.

HOTELS-RESTAURANTS

■ Alliance

Plage de la Source.
Tel. 02 40 82 21 21. Fax 02 40 82 80 89.
info.resa@thalassopornic.com
www.thalassopornic.com
Closed end Nov.–beg. Dec.
112 rooms: 110–160€.
8 suites: 240–300€.
Prix fixe: 32€.

This perfectly equipped hotel complex has practical rooms, a thalassotherapy center, swimming pool, fitness center and three restaurants with panoramic views, offering traditional cuisine or health food.

■ Auberge La Fontaine aux Bretons

Chemin de Noelles.
Tel. 02 51 74 08 08 / 02 51 74 07 07.
Fax 02 51 74 15 15.
infos@auberge-la-fontaine.com
www.auberge-la-fontaine.com
Closed Jan. Rest. closed Sun. dinner (Oct.–Mar.), Mon. (Oct.–Mar.).
23 suites: 88€.
Prix fixe: 26€, 14€ (child).

Neat, comfortable rooms, an attentive welcome and regional cuisine: such are the attractions of this hotel in cheerful blue, red and green shades. We enjoy the red tuna medallions and pan-seared swordfish steak, straight from the ocean.

● Le Beau Rivage `COM`

21, rue de la plage de la Birochère.
Tel. 02 40 82 03 08. Fax 02 51 74 04 24.
info@restaurant-beaurivage.com
www.restaurant-beaurivage.com
Closed Mon., Tue. (exc. summer), mid-Dec.–end Jan.
Prix fixe: 26€ (weekdays), 34€, 46€, 60€ (wine inc.), 15€ (child).

Gérard Corchia's cuisine uses the finest regional produce and shows no lack of creativity. Here by the beach, we enjoy the surprising Loire eels in parsley and garlic, Croisic line-fished Atlantic sea bass grilled skin-side down and seasoned with virgin olive oil, roasted Challans squab with Puy lentils and truffle jus and the Breton-style crêpe with creamy pistachio filling and orange cardamom sauce.

PORNICHET see LA BAULE

ILE DE PORQUEROLLES

83400 Var. Paris 873 – Hyères 20 km (of which 4,8 km is by boat) – Toulon 35.
An island? A paradise just a step away from Giens, where we embark at the tip of the peninsula. Lovers of peace and quiet are drawn by the unspoiled beaches, vineyards, neocolonial homes and gentle weather ensured all year round by a benevolent microclimate.

HOTELS-RESTAURANTS

● Mas du Langoustier

Tel. 04 94 58 30 09. Fax 04 94 58 36 02.
langoustier@wanadoo.fr
www.langoustier.com
Closed beg. Oct.–beg. Apr.
45 rooms: 175–225€. 1 suite: 265–310€.
Prix fixe: 55€, 69€, 85€.

Luxury, peace and sensual pleasure abound in this enchanted manor watched over by Salvatore Troia. The hotel stands in the heart of gardens that conceal a swimming pool, tennis courts and a heliport, along with a private beach nestling at the foot of the Petit-Langoustier fort. The sunny rooms provide luxurious comfort, while the billiard room is ideally suited to quiet conversations. Joël Guillet's cuisine does justice to this bewitching setting. Warm octopus salad with merguez and hummus, pan-seared tuna steak and peppers with leek ravioli and the slice of duck breast with dried orange, juniper berries, chives and forest mushrooms promise rare delights. The highly creative desserts, including the raspberry gratin with eucalyptus honey and a dribbling of apricot sauce, served with pine nut ice cream, form a fine conclusion. Amandine Gargallo's wine list has just the right vintages to accompany all this, as it deserves.

■ L'Auberge des Glycines

22, pl d'Armes.
Tel. 04 94 58 30 36. Fax 04 94 58 35 22.
www.aubergedesglycines.com
11 rooms: 69–269€.
Prix fixe: 21,90€, 9,90€ (child).
A la carte: 42€.

Located right in the center, this Proven-çal-style inn all in blue and yellow serves up an appropriate cuisine: octopus fric-assée, seafood stew and the duck breast with apples and honey are all gratifying. The patio at the back is just the place for a refreshing nap.

■ Villa Sainte-Anne

24, pl d'Armes.
Tel. 04 94 04 63 00. Fax 04 94 58 32 26.
courrier@sainteanne.com
www.sainteanne.com
Closed beg. Nov.–Christmas, 1–15 Feb.
25 rooms: 90–135€.
Prix fixe: 23€, 31€, 10€ (child).
A la carte: 35–40€.

This central hotel run by Sébastien Boud-eau offers comfortable rooms and a bistro-style dining room leading onto a terrace. Emmanuelle Lefaure, who works at the stove, concocts an honest traditional cui-sine: fish soup, an oven-crisped fish crum-ble, Provençal stuffed vegetables and an oven-crisped chocolate dessert.

● L'Arche de Noé ⛺COM

12, pl d'Armes.
Tel. 04 94 58 33 71. Fax 04 94 58 30 60.
www. arche-de-noe.com
Closed Tue. (exc. July–Aug.), Oct.–end Mar.
Prix fixe: 16,50€ (weekday lunch), 25€, 34,50€, 42€, 12€ (child).
A la carte: 55–85€.

The attractions of this inn refurbished art deco style, ideally located in the cen-ter of the village, are its warm welcome and fresh cuisine. Mushroom- and ham-stuffed artichokes simmered in wine, octopus and basil salad, the regional bour-ride (a fish stew with aïoli) and a slow-cooked fennel mille-feuille are washed down with simple local wines.

● Les Jardins de l'Escale SIM

2, rue de la Ferme.
Tel. 04 94 58 30 18. Fax 04 94 58 39 32.
Prix fixe: 12€ (lunch), 30€ (dinner), 15€ (child). A la carte: 45–50€.

This chic café-restaurant offers vogu-ish collations and drinks in between. Sea bream carpaccio with soy, pan-seared tuna steak with herbs, lamb shank confit sea-soned with cumin and served with thyme polenta and a fig and almond tart leave pleasant memories. Food in the garden.

● Lou Cigalou SIM

8, pl d'Armes.
Tel.-Fax 04 94 58 39 84.
Closed end Oct.–Apr.
Prix fixe: 13,50€, 30,50€, 8,50€ (child).

Maxime Scotto welcomes his guests on the main square and terrace with Mediter-ranean cuisine at modest prices. Salmon spread with an abundance of herbs, rouget with local olive spread, beef filet Rossini and pears poached in wine and spices are not bad.

● La Plage d'Argent SIM

Chemin des Langoustiers.
Tel. 04 94 58 32 48. Fax 04 94 58 35 71.
www.plagedargent.com
Closed end Sept.–beg. Apr.
A la carte: 48€.

Stéphane Le Ber runs this beach res-taurant with good humor. Jean-Fran-çois Graindorge regales patrons with the Pinède plate (breaded and fried fresh herbs, olive loaf, diced zucchini with anchovies, cherry tomatoes), the fish of the day, herb-seasoned lamb chops with vegetable couscous and a chocolate fon-dant and brownie with house ice cream. The terrace with its sea view offers a taste of paradise.

PORT-ARGELES see ARGELES-SUR-MER
PORT-DU-CROUESTY see ARZON
PORT-JOINVILLE see ILE D'YEU
PORT-NAVALO see ARZON

PORT-CAMARGUE

30240 Gard. Paris 759 – Montpellier 38 –
Aigues-Mortes 10 – Nîmes 48.
The name says it all: a modern marina built
in the Seventies on the Camargue coast near
Grau-du-Roi, Aigues-Mortes and its gulf.

 HOTELS-RESTAURANTS

● Le Spinaker

Pointe de la presqu'île, Le Grau-du-Roi.
Tel. 04 66 53 36 37. Fax 04 66 53 17 47.
spinaker@wanadoo.fr / www.spinaker.com
Closed mid-Nov.–mid-Feb. Rest. closed Mon.
(off season), Tue. (off season), Wed. (off season).
16 rooms: 109–234€. 5 suites: 234€.
Prix fixe: 55€, 62€, 81€, 15€ (child).
A la carte: 80–100€.

Jean-Pierre Cazals is still at the helm opposite the harbor, even if there are rumors
that he is thinking about retirement. The
rooms are pleasant with their contemporary décor. The terrace, garden and swimming pool incite us to relax until it is time to
make our way to the restaurant and discover
the delights of the host's cuisine, which celebrates seafood and regional produce in
fitting fashion. Beef carpaccio with oil and
julienned truffles, the real sole meunière
with that day's local catch and the braised
Hereford beef rib eye deserve only praise.
To conclude, the trilogy of desserts promises a deliciously sweet encounter.

■ Mercure

Rte des Marines, Le Grau-du-Roi.
Tel. 04 66 73 60 60. Fax 04 66 73 60 50.
h1947@accor.com / www.thalassa.com
Closed 3 weeks Dec.
89 rooms: 105€.
Prix fixe: 26€. A la carte: 41€.

By the thalassotherapy center, this chain
hotel boasts well-equipped rooms, a swimming pool and a fitness center. The restaurant serves regional cuisine: monkfish and
sea bream duo in a salt crust.

ILE DE PORT-CROS

83400 Var.
Porquerolles' little sister: greater solitude and
the ever-present, magical sea off the coast of
Le Lavandou and Hyères beach.

 HOTELS-RESTAURANTS

■ Le Manoir

Tel. 04 94 05 90 52. Fax 04 94 05 90 89.
lemanoir.portcros@wanadoo.fr
Closed beg. Oct.–mid-Apr.
18 rooms: 140–200€. 4 suites: 195–200€.
Prix fixe: 43€, 54€, 20€ (child).

On its miraculously conserved island, this
manor is elegant indeed. Built in 1830 by
the Duke of Vicence, it boasts a white
facade decorated with turrets and columns, and its rooms are paved with hexagonal floor tiles. The swimming pool, garden
and convivial bar add to our pleasure and
Sylvain Chaduteau's talented cuisine does
the setting justice. A thin sundried tomato
tart topped with melted brousse (the local
ewe's cheese), steamed John Dory with
basil, beef tenderloin seasoned with pine
sap and the generous all-chocolate dessert
plate enchant effortlessly.

● Hostellerie Provençale ▣SIM

Tel. 04 94 05 90 43. Fax 04 94 05 92 90.
info@hostellerie-Provençale.com
www.hostellerie-Provençale.com
Closed Nov. 1–Easter.
Rest. closed mid-Oct.–Easter.
5 rooms: 99–110€. A la carte: 45€.

With its terrace on the harbor, Régine
and Philippe Anger's establishment
offers an excellent opportunity to dine
simply. The tapas, fish stew, the butcher's choice beef cut with assorted vegetables and the strawberry soup will whet
the most jaded appetite.

PORT-EN-BESSIN

14520 Calvados. Paris 269 – Caen 38 –
Saint-Lô 45 – Bayeux 9 – Cherbourg 93.
Very close to the Normandy beaches where the

Allies landed, this harbor famous for its scallop fishing conjures up a sensation of open sea.

 HOTELS-RESTAURANTS

■ **La Chenevière**

In Escure, route de Commes.
Tel. 02 31 51 25 25. Fax 02 31 51 25 20.
cheneviere@lacheneviere.fr
www.lacheneviere.fr
Closed Jan. Rest. closed weekdays lunch
29 rooms: 151–362€. 3 suites: 362–462€.
Prix fixe: 35€, 65€, 90€.

Set in grounds with a swimming pool, this delightful 19th-century house makes for a charming stay indeed. The peaceful, comfortable rooms (seven of them have just been opened) are an incitement to relaxation. In the contemporary dining room, a succession of refined domestic dishes appears before us, including foie gras terrine with apple jelly, sole cooked in mild spices, a rack of lamb with Espelette peppers and the rich chocolate cake.

● **L'Ecailler**

2, rue de Bayeux.
Tel. 02 31 22 92 16.
lecailler@msn.com
Closed Sun. dinner, Mon. (exc. July–Aug.), beg. Jan.–mid-Feb.
Prix fixe: 24€ (lunch). A la carte: 40–70€.

This pretty marine bistro opposite the harbor works its charm with changing dishes based on the best of the local catch. The décor is simple, but the cuisine delights. A thin sardine and sundried tomato tart, Atlantic sea bass filet with elderberry flower oil and a Spanish caramel mousse with coconut shavings are splendid. Do not miss the scallop festival in the season.

LES PORTES-EN-RE see ILE DE RE
PORTIVY see QUIBERON

PORT-LESNEY

39600 Jura. Paris 399 – Besançon 37 – Arbois 13 – Dole 40 – Lons-le-Saunier 50.

tourisme@valdamour.com.
The peaceful, winding Loue river here inspired Courbet. This modest village was famous in the days when its mayor was minister Edgar Faure. His smiling bust is now displayed in front of the Mairie.

 HOTELS-RESTAURANTS

● **Château de Germigney**

Rue Edgar-Faure.
Tel. 03 84 73 85 85. Fax 03 84 73 88 88.
www.chateaudegermigney.com
Closed Mon. lunch, Tue. lunch, beg. Jan.–beg. Feb.
17 rooms:125–285€. 2 suites: 295–360€.
Prix fixe: 39€ (lunch), 59€ (dinner), 95€ (dinner), 15€ (child, bev. inc.).
A la carte: 90€.

This vast residence set in its own grounds, with romantic rooms, refined décor by Swiss esthete Roland Schön, a first-rate, urbane garden and a "natural" swimming pool, is a delightful place to stay. The other attraction is the reliable cuisine prepared by Strasbourg's Pierre Basso-Moro, who embraces the seasons and local tradition. Pan-seared foie gras with beef and black pepper aspic, pike-perch cooked in wine, Doubs pike with leeks and the truffle and Comté cheese risotto are enchanting. These delicacies are followed by excellent desserts (a pistachio chocolate mille-feuille and a fig tart) and a wine list featuring vintages from near and far to turn your head.

● **Le Pontarlier** ●SIM

Pl du 8-Mai.
Tel. 03 84 37 83 27. Fax 03 84 73 88 88.
www.chateaudegermigney.com
Closed Fri., Sat. and Sun. (off season), beg. Jan.–beg. Feb.
Prix fixe: 22€, 6€ (child). A la carte: 30€.

This genuine old-style bistro, which has been refurbished *bouchon* and *guinguette* style by Roland Schön, has the character of a village café but offers first-rate cuisine. Arnaud Coulet, former chef de partie at Germigney, presents fried local fish, Indian-style nan with vegetables, soft fromage blanc and cucumber, cod poached in Savagnin wine and a delicious mille-feuille with whipped cream and Grand Marnier. With a drop of white Arbois and a shot of absinthe, we let time slip by, like the waters of the Loue flowing past just a stone's throw away.

PORT-LOUIS see LORIENT

PORT-SUR-SAONE

70170 Haute-Saône. Paris 349 – Besançon 62 – Epinal 76 – Vesoul 13.
This green corner of Franche-Comté on the Haute Saône side should be explored at a leisurely pace.

| ● | RESTAURANTS |

In Vauchoux (70170). 3 km s via D6.
● **Château de Vauchoux**
Rte de la Vallée-de-la-Saône.
Tel. 03 84 91 53 55. Fax 03 84 91 65 38.
Closed Mon., Tue., 1 week at end Feb.
Prix fixe: 60€, 75€, 100€.

Louis XV used to meet the daughter of the Duke of Lorraine in this hunting lodge, now converted into an admirable restaurant. Today, it is the scene of different pleasures: a neoclassical Louis XV- and Starck-style décor and traditional fare based on deftly prepared, noble produce. In Jean-Michel Turin's hands, the foie gras terrine, scrambled eggs with truffles, braised pike-perch and rabbit saddle in cocotte have changed little, but remain pleasant table companions, and the same approach is apparent when the meal ends with the chocolate "*magie*". The wines are knowledgeably recommended by Caroline Turin, while Franceline handles the service.

PORT-VENDRES

66660 Pyrénées-Orientales. Paris 881 – Perpignan 32.
Towards the coast of Spain, this corner of France suggests that Catalonia knows no frontiers.

| ● | RESTAURANTS |

● **Ferme Auberge des Clos**
de Paulilles
Baie Paulilles.
Tel. 04 68 98 07 58.
daure@wanadoo.fr
Closed weekdays lunch (exc. Sun.), Sun. dinner (exc. July–Aug.), end Sept.–mid-May.
Prix fixe: 39€ (wine inc.).

A while back, the Daurés opened the gates of their Château de Jau to culinary invaders. Now they have done it again with the Paulilles, which welcomes guests to a gorgeous setting with a vista of vines. The lounge has plenty of charm with its watergreen walls. A step away from the sea, the shady terrace is a genuine delight. An all-inclusive menu offers a taste of the property's different libations with foie gras with sea salt flakes, gazpacho, farm-raised chicken with prunes, ewe's cheese and a chocolate and coffee macaron. The six wines by the glass prove to be its natural companions.

POUILLON

40350 Landes. Paris 742 – Dax 16 – Mont-de-Marsan 69 – Orthez 28 – Peyrehorade 15.
A genuine village in the heart of the great Landes region.

| ● | RESTAURANTS |

● **L'Auberge du Pas**
de Vent
281, av du Pas-de-Vent.
Tel. 05 58 98 34 65.
www.auberge-dupasdevent.com
Closed Sun. dinner, Tue. dinner, Wed.,
1 Nov. vac., 4 days at Christmas, Feb. vac.
Prix fixe: 12€ (weekdays), 19,50€, 24,50€, 33,50€.

Sophie and Frédéric Dubern's gourmet theater is an old-fashioned inn with its beams, game of skittles and shady garden, where delightful suppers are served

in the summertime. The Duberns, natives
of Bordeaux who have fallen in love with
the region (and skittles!), have preserved
this antique hostelry's style and set the
tone with their light, refreshing welcome.
They present generous set menus introducing a heartfelt, seasonal cuisine, promoting Landes produce with a nod to the
Basque country. What should we single out
for praise? The "*cassole*" of slow-cooked
Espelette peppers and onions, the pepper mille-feuille with potato and herb tartare, the flaked cod on garlic toast, the
Chalosse poultry cooked country style,
the whole duck foie gras, millassou (the
local specialty dessert cooked old style
with rum and roasted apples) or the nougat lace with chocolate mousseline and
fresh raspberries? An inn, you say? A house
of delights…

21320 Côte-d'Or. Paris 271 – Dijon 44 –
Avallon 66 – Saulieu 31.
ot.pouilly.en.auxois@wanadoo.fr.
A green and mountainous Burgundy, the region of
châteaux rather than wine. Worth exploring.

 HOTELS-RESTAURANTS

In Chailly-sur-Armançon (21320). 6,5 km w via
rte de Saulieu.

■ **Château de Chailly** ❀ 🏨
Tel. 03 80 90 30 30. Fax 03 80 90 30 00.
reservation@chailly.com / www.chailly.com
Closed mid-Dec.–mid-Jan., 22 Feb.–5 Mar.
Rest. closed Mon. dinner.
37 rooms: 215–340€. 8 suites: 410–610€.
Prix fixe: 60€, 80€, 100€, 16€ (child).
A la carte: 75€.

Next door to the Morvan region, this
Renaissance château boasts grounds
with a swimming pool, golf course, Jacuzzi
and steam bath. The rooms are extremely
refined and the dishes prepared by Jean-
Marc Diop are delicious tributes paid to
the region's produce.

POUILLY-LE-FORT see MELUN

66230 Pyrénées-Orientales. Paris 905 –
Céret 32 – Perpignan 64.
The upper and lower village have their own
individual charms in this Catalan mountain
community (740 meters).

 HOTELS-RESTAURANTS

● **Le Bellavista et Bellevue** ○🏠
Pl Foiral.
Tel. 04 68 39 72 48. Fax 04 68 39 78 04.
lebellevue@fr.st / www.lebellevue.fr.st
Closed Dec.–end Jan., 2 weeks Feb.
Rest. closed Tue., Wed.
17 rooms: 39–50€.
Prix fixe: 19,50€, 33€.
A la carte: 45–55€.

Denis Visellach plies his art at the helm
of this family establishment, to which he
has brought a fresh touch. This veteran of
the Petit Nice in Marseille and the Oustau de Baumanière is a mine of talent and
creativity, which he places at the service
of the region's finest produce. The result
is memorable. Mediterranean sea bass
terrine wrapped in Serrano ham served
with seasonal greens, sea bream filet in
a chorizo crust with a saffron-seasoned
jus with potato gratin and the slow-
cooked lobster stew with Banyuls sauce,
the chef's specialty, offer pleasant proof
of his skills. The desserts, the strawberry
in all of its forms, in an upside-down tart
with its sauce and a house caramel dessert, delight us in much the same way.
The rooms in the small hotel that makes
up the rest of the hostelry are undergoing
discreet renovation.

PRAZ see CHAMONIX-MONT-BLANC
PRENOIS see DIJON

01160 Ain. Paris 456 – Lyon 57 – Bourg 29
– Nantua 39.
Like gentle Bresse, the Dombes lake region was
also a *Pays des mères*.

RESTAURANTS

● La Mère Bourgeois [COM]

Grande-rue de la Cotière.
Tel. 04 74 35 61 81. Fax 04 74 35 43 49.
merebougeois@laposte.net
Closed Wed., Thu., Aug.
Prix fixe: 16€ (weekday lunch), 25€, 35€,
39€, 10€ (child).

Corinne Aube has taken over this Bresse institution, brought in Amandine Chevalier to tend to the kitchen and lowered the prices. The sense of ambition here has also dropped a notch, but the message is amiable. Two salmon spreads, frog legs in parsley, garlic and butter, pike-perch strips, chitterling sausage gratin in white wine and the lemon meringue pie have the flavor of good, simple fare and are by no means ruinous.

07000 Ardèche. Paris 603 – Valence 40 –
Montélimar 35 – Aubenas 31.
Make sure you visit this little "capital" of the Ardèche perched above the Ouvèze.

 HOTELS-RESTAURANTS

■ La Chaumette

Av Vanel.
Tel. 04 75 64 30 66. Fax 04 75 64 88 25.
hotelchaumette@wanadoo.fr
www.hotelchaumette.fr
Closed Nov. 1 vac., 2 weeks beg. Jan.
Rest. closed Sat. lunch, Sun. lunch (exc. off season), Sun. (off season).
36 rooms: 50–98€.
Prix fixe: 28€, 45€, 15€ (child).
A la carte: 48€.

Monique Teyssier energetically runs this providential hostelry with its swimming pool and fitness center, ideal for those who prefer the outskirts to the middle of town. The rooms are comfortable in a contemporary style and the same spirit reigns in the dining room, where Jérémy Clavier presents a cuisine with more than its share

of subtlety. Venison medallions flavored with chocolate, turbot and ceps in a turnover, minced wild duck dusted with nuts and variations on the apple dessert with Manzana sorbet are smart dishes.

32600 Gers. Paris 710 – Toulouse 29 –
L'Isle-Jourdain 8 – Auch 51.
The start of the Gers, in the heart of hilly Savès, where the view stretches out over the vast Garonne plain. Head on to L'Isle-Jourdain to see the monumental place de l'Hôtel-de-Ville and the Saint-Martin collegiate church.

 RESTAURANTS

● Le Puits Saint-Jacques

Pl de la Mairie.
Tel. 05 62 07 41 11. Fax 05 62 07 44 09.
lepuitsstjacques@free.fr
Closed Sun. dinner, Mon., Tue. (exc. Nov. dinner specials), Feb. vac., 2 weeks end Aug.
Prix fixe: 22€ (weekday lunch), 35€, 50€,
105€ (wine inc.), 15€ (child).
A la carte: 90€.

He is the musician artist of eastern Gers, a first-rate soloist who prepares dishes with a modern flavor, displaying a lively sense of sweet-and-sour and unusual combinations. A native of Moissac who put down roots here, not far from Toulouse, seven years ago, Bernard Bach is a modest soul who has found his haven. Nomadic by nature (he has "done" Chibois in Cannes, Trama in Puymirol, the Augeval in Deauville and the Belvédère in Porto-Vecchio), he is at home in this pink brick inn with its fine wrought-iron sign, now a modern restaurant. On the map, Gascony goes hand-in-hand with Catalonia (the native region of Bach's father, a dedicated gardener in Cazes-Mondenard). The cod in foamy milk served over a ratte potato purée with jumbo langoustines, roasted in their shell with parsley and garlic, is a fine marine exercise. The pan-seared slices of foie gras with pain d'épice with beet and acidulated ginger chutney suggest a sharp sense of sweet and savory, as does grilled rouget served with a citrusy caramelized onion and fennel tart. We also enjoy roasted squab with young broad bean stew, local wild herb jus and chorizo accompanied by a fried chickpea cake. The Maury cherry dessert with pistachio ice cream and cinnamon spéculos ice cream carries us back to our infancy.

PUJOLS see VILLENEUVE-SUR-LOT
PULIGNY-MONTRACHET see BEAUNE
PUPILLIN see ARBOIS

PUSIGNAN

69330 Rhône. Paris 476 – Lyon 26 – Meyzieu 5 – Montluel 14.
A step away from Meyzieu and Saint-Exupéry Airport, a gourmet haven.

 | RESTAURANTS

● La Closerie `V.COM`
4, pl de la Gaieté.
Tel. 04 78 04 40 50. Fax 04 78 04 44 05.
lacloserie2@wanadoo.fr
www.lacloserie2.com
Closed Sun. dinner, Mon., Tue. dinner, 6 Aug.–19 Aug.
Prix fixe: 19,50€ (weekdays lunch, wine inc.), 34€, 44€, 55€, 78€ (lobster menu), 13€ (child), 16€ (child).

Jacques Chillioux runs this restaurant with great energy. Gilles Troump, who officiated with Bocuse and Troisgros, remains discreet, but has lost none of his sense of good fare. In this old post house redecorated in Provençal tones, he excels as an exponent of Lyonnaise cuisine with an added touch of sunshine. An opener of escargots in basil cream, pasta stuffed with Italian-style truffled eggplant in salad and olive-oil roasted cod filet served on a bed of pressed ratte potatoes are fine examples of his genre. The frozen soft apricot nougat is a treat.

LE PUY-EN-VELAY

43000 Haute-Loire. Paris 545 – Clermont-Ferrand 130 – Mende 89 – Saint-Etienne 76.

info@otLepuyenvelay.fr.
The splendid surroundings and masterpieces of religious art in this former bishopric, such as the Cathedral of Notre-Dame-du-Puy, famous for its cloister and treasure, or the old town and its alleyways from a bygone age, leave us feeling we have come up in the region. Remember to try the Pagès Verveine produced in this very town!

 | HOTELS-RESTAURANTS

■ Le Régina 🏨
34, bd du Maréchal-Fayolle.
Tel. 04 71 09 14 71. Fax 04 71 09 18 57.
contact@hotelrestregina.com
www.hotelrestregina.com
25 rooms: 66–85€. 3 suites: 89–104€.
Prix fixe: 16,50€, 26,50€, 11€ (child).

This hotel has successfully modernized its vast rooms behind a fine 19th-century facade. On the catering side, the dining room has been refurbished in modern style, but remains just as comfortable as before. At the stove, Stéphane Valentin bows to the season and his own inspiration. Foie gras terrine poached in Côtes-d'Auvergne, pan-fried veal sweetbreads served over a grilled beef tenderloin and a Toblerone-style pyramid of frozen nougat form what promise to be delightful memories.

■ Le Parc 🏠
4, av C.-Charbonnier.
Tel. 04 71 02 40 40. Fax 04 71 02 18 72.
francoisgagnaire@wanadoo.fr
www.hotel-du-parc-le-puy.com
Closed 2 weeks beg. Jan.
21 rooms: 57–75€. 2 suites: 75€.

Apart from François Gagnaire's restaurant, this building houses a well-kept hotel with functional, contemporary rooms. The welcome is friendly and the check reasonable.

● François Gagnaire ◎ V.COM
At Le Parc, 4, av C.-Charbonnier.
Tel. 04 71 02 75 55. Fax 04 71 02 18 72.
francoisgagnaire@wanadoo.fr
www.francois-gagnaire-restaurant.com

Closed Sun., Tue. lunch, Wed., 2 weeks beg.
Nov., 1 week at end June, 10 days beg. July.
Prix fixe: 40€, 55€, 122€,
19,50€ (child). A la carte: 70€.

François Gagnaire has plenty of references: Chapel in Mionnay, Chavent in Lyon, Lassausaie in Chasselay and, of course, his namesake in Paris. However, this chef and restaurateur has successfully plotted a course between produce-based cuisine and original combinations. Variations on AOC Fin Gras de Mézenc beef all on the theme of tartare, butter-braised pollock filet served with simply presented chard with black olive jus and the grilled duck filet accompanied by mushroom- and ham-stuffed artichokes simmered in wine and Grenaille potatoes are tasteful essays in style. At the end of the meal, strawberry soup made with red wine and the rosemary-infused cream dessert bring the feast to a light end.

● Tournayre   ◎ V.COM

12, rue Chênebouterie.
Tel. 04 71 09 58 94. Fax 04 71 02 68 38.
www.restaurant-tournayre.com
Closed Sun. dinner, Mon., Wed. dinner,
1 week beg. Sept., 2 Jan.–1 Feb.
Prix fixe: 21€, 42€, 54€, 70€.
A la carte: 70€.

Few would think twice about accepting an invitation to Eric and Ludivine Tournayre's restaurant. In their 16th-century chapel, they delight their guests with sensibly priced set menus and sharp, traditional dishes. The foie gras, John Dory with asparagus, beef tenderloin Rossini and rack of lamb with lentils and mushrooms have the fine flavor of simplicity, as does the frozen verbena mousse. Turning to the cellar, the 200 vintages selected have no trouble finding takers.

● Le Bateau Ivre   COM

5, rue Portail-d'Avignon.
Tel.-Fax 04 71 09 67 20.
www.lebateauivre.com
Closed Mon. dinner, Tue. dinner, Wed. lunch.
Prix fixe: 10€ (lunch), 12€ (lunch),
15€ (lunch), 20€ (dinner), 30€ (dinner),
8€ (child).

The dynamic Sylvie and Philippe Lasherme have taken over this restaurant decorated in antique style, offering an attentive welcome, playing on regional produce and lowering the prices. We can unstintingly praise the tartare of Vouzac trout, pike-perch filet, duck breast medallions and a soft chocolate verbena-infused cake, which are in the colors of the Velay region.

● Olympe   COM

8, rue du Collège.
Tel.-Fax 04 71 05 90 59.
Closed Sat. lunch (exc. July–Aug.), Sun. dinner, Mon., 10 days end Feb.–end Mar.
Prix fixe: 16€ (lunch), 19€ (lunch weekdays), 24€, 31€, 55€, 13€ (child).

Pierre Fauritte, who studied with Chapel and at the Juana, has turned this restaurant into one of the better bargains in town. His wife Christine welcomes guests with a smile and the cuisine showcases regional produce. In the bright dining room, we feast on a pheasant galantine with foie gras, Vouzac trout with lentils, duck and potato with the meat's jus, a frozen Velay green verbena parfait and a wild blueberry and meringue dessert. Appealing set menus.

● Lapierre   SIM

6, rue Capucins.
Tel. 04 71 09 08 44.
Closed Sun. (exc. July–Aug.), Dec.–end Feb.
Prix fixe: 24€, 32€. A la carte: 37€.

Estelle and Vincent Thivillier continue to deserve their restaurant's success. Served in its very convivial, contemporary setting, Estelle's cuisine pays vibrant tribute to local produce and recipes. Who could resist the poultry liver moussse with verbena, mixed vegetable salad with country-smoked trout, calf's liver with Velay pine honey and lime juice and a dark cocoa cream dessert with orange sauce?

● **Entrez les Artistes** SIM

29, rue Pannessac.
Tel. 04 71 09 71 78.
Closed Sun., Mon., Tue. dinner,
mid-Sept.–end Sept., 1 week Christmas–New
Year's, Feb. vac.
Prix fixe: 13,50€, 19€, 11€ (child).
A la carte: 30€.

Come artists, come all! You will not be
disappointed by the cuisine in Pascale
Suc's bistro: lentil and smoked tripe
salad, breaded and pan-fried pork trotter with sauce ravigote and profiteroles
with melted chocolate sauce.

● **Le Poivrier** SIM

69, rue Pannessac.
Tel. 04 71 02 41 30. Fax 04 71 02 59 25.
robert.redon@wanadoo.fr
Closed Sun. lunch, Sun. dinner (exc. July–
Aug.), Mon. dinner, 2 weeks Nov.1 vac., Feb.
vac., 1 week at end June.
Prix fixe: 15€ (weekday lunch), 20€, 25€,
29,90€, 12€ (child). A la carte: 40€.

This terra-cotta bistro surrounded by old
houses continues to fill its niche. Robert
Redon's cuisine is generous, but the check
is sufficiently restrained. We quietly enjoy
oven-browned Fourme d'Ambert cheese
cassolette, rack of lamb in a hazelnut crust
and a frozen green verbena mousseline.

In Espaly-Saint-Marcel (43000). 3 km via
N102.

■ **L'Ermitage** ⌂

73, av de l'Ermitage.
Tel. 04 71 07 05 05 (rest. 04 71 04 08 99).
Fax 04 71 07 05 00.
hotel.ermitage@free.fr
www.hotelermitage.com
Hotel closed Jan., Feb. Rest. closed Sun.
dinner (off season), Mon., mid-Jan.–mid-Feb.
20 rooms: 50–75€.
Prix fixe: 16€ (lunch), 20€, 27€, 45€,
10€ (child).

A stone's throw from Le Puy, this hotel
offers a beautiful panoramic view of the
town, renovated rooms at reasonable
prices and a very friendly welcome. The
meals are slightly more expensive, but

pike-perch filet, crayfish bisque and the
roasted pigeon with seasonal mushrooms
are excellent fare.

PUYMIROL

47270 Lot-et-Garonne. Paris 649 – Agen 17
– Moissac 34 – Villeneuve-sur-Lot 30.
This pretty walled town in the Lot-et-Garonne
region, lost in Agen country, boasts old houses
and a grand restaurant.

■◆● HOTELS-RESTAURANTS

● **Michel Trama**

52, rue Royale.
Tel. 05 53 95 31 46. Fax 05 53 95 33 80.
trama@aubergade.com
www.aubergade.com
Closed 3 weeks Nov., 1 week at end Jan.,
1 week beg. Feb.
Rest. closed Sun. dinner (off season), Mon.
(exc. dinner in season), Tue. lunch.
9 rooms: 250–450€. 1 suite: 580€.
Prix fixe: 76€ (weekdays), 160€, 215€,
20€ (child).

Michel and Maryse Trama reign over the
culinary world of the Lot-et-Garonne
region from their ancient 13th- and 17th-
century buildings, partly refurbished
by Jacques Garcia. The establishment's
tone can best be described as Middle
Ages with a contemporary flavor. At our
leisure, we feast on innovations by the
great Michel, never short on ideas when
it comes to juggling with the finest produce of Greater Southwest France. His new
classics? Herb-wrapped truffled potatoes
in papillote, foie gras on a stick rolled in
roasted hazelnuts, local line-caught fish
in broth infused with preserved lemon,
lobster lasagne with truffle-seasoned fish
broth, a foie gras-stuffed hamburger with
ceps and duck jus and a spicy roasted
squab with slow-cooked carrots, all polished work indeed. The house dessert with
a peppered tobbaco leaf has a touch of the
gimmick about it, but after all, as long as
there is a demand…

PYLA-SUR-MER

33115 Gironde. Paris 651 – Bordeaux 66 –
Arcachon 8 – Biscarrosse 34.
pyla002@ibm.net.
This seaside resort is Arcachon's chic watering place.

 HOTELS-RESTAURANTS

■ **Maminotte**   ❀⌂
Allée des Acacias.
Tel. 05 57 72 05 05. Fax 05 57 72 06 06.
hotel-maminotte@wanadoo.fr
12 rooms: 50–95€.

Near the beach, this classic hotel with its
swimming pool stands in a peaceful setting. The huge rooms are bathed in light,
particularly the ones with a balcony looking out over the pines.

■ **Côte du Sud**   ⌂
4, av du Figuier.
Tel. 05 56 83 25 00. Fax 05 56 83 24 13.
reservation@cote-du-sud.com
www.cote-du-sud.com
Closed beg. Dec.–beg. Feb.
7 rooms: 59–110€. 1 suite: 84–130€.
Prix fixe: 22€, 28€, 12€ (child).

The rooms intrigue with their exotic décor,
the beach is close by, the setting is top
notch and the restaurant plays to an ethnic score. The langoustine-stuffed spring
rolls, lobster fricassée seasoned with
vanilla and Sauterenes, veal sweetbread
fricassée with ceps and Chinese noodles
and frozen Armagnac-soaked prune soufflé are not bad.

● **Gérard Tissier**   COM
Bd de l'Océan.
Tel. 05 56 54 07 94. Fax 05 56 83 20 98.
restgt@club-internet.fr
Closed Mon. (exc. July–Aug.),
Tue. (exc. July–Aug.), 11 Nov.–1 Feb.
Prix fixe: 16€, 26€, 30€, 55€,
12€ (child).

The "boss" of Pyla is still Gérard Tissier, who hides himself away in his white
establishment with wood-paneled ceiling
and Caribbean-style fan. An electronics
engineer who fell in love with the restaurant business in Archachon, he welcomes
guests with his cheerful wife Evelyne and
shares his current enthusiasms with them.
A carpaccio served with wasabi sorbet, a
monkfish filet with foie gras, Atlantic sea
bass filet with ceps and a vermouth mousseline cream, spicy pigeon and the avocado with raspberries are not bad at all.

● **La Cabane**   SIM
65, bd de l'Océan.
Tel. 05 56 54 50 67. Fax 05 56 66 27 86.
Closed Mon. (off season), Tue. (off season),
Wed. (off season).
A la carte: 40–55€.

With its huge rotisserie fireplace, counter, well-used tables and good natured
atmosphere, Pierre Pion's "cabin" is successful as ever. We easily enjoy eggs in
cocotte with ceps, a flambéed mix of
jumbo shrimp and scallops with fresh
pasta, grilled beef tenderloin with ceps,
pan-seared foie gras and the flambéed
Grand Marnier soufflé.

QUARRE-LES-TOMBES

89630 Yonne. Paris 232 – Auxerre 72 –
Avallon 19 – Château-Chinon 49.
Right in the heart of Morvan, the far north that
is still on the doorstep of Paris and the last
local region to have been inhabited by wolves.
Visit Saint-Léger and the house of Vauban.

HOTELS-RESTAURANTS

■ Le Morvan

6, rue des Ecoles.
Tel. 03 86 32 29 29. Fax 03 86 32 29 28.
etiennelemorvan@wanadoo.fr
www.le-morvan.fr
Closed beg. Jan.–beg. Mar.
Rest. closed Mon., Tue.
8 rooms: 51–71€.
Prix fixe: 20€, 25€, 33,50€, 47,50€,
10,50€ (child).

Etienne Robbé loves Burgundy, of which
his food is a fine reflection. On the hotel
side, the rooms are extremely comfortable. The escargot cake served on a chanterelle fricassée with white bean cream
and smoked bacon, softly steamed monkfish filet with a peppery slow-cooked fennel and light champagne sauce, a veal
medallion simmered in cocotte with
mushroom fricassée and potatoes and
the Tahitian vanilla crème brûlée and
the house sorbet with strawberries from
Morvan will satisfy every appetite. On
the hotel side, the rooms are extremely
comfortable.

In Les Brizards (89630). 8 km se via D55 and
D355.

■ Auberge des Brizards

At les Brizards.
Tel. 03 86 32 20 12. Fax 03 86 32 27 40.
lesbrizards@free.fr
www.aubergedesbrizards.com
Closed Jan.–mid-Feb.
Rest. closed Mon., Tue. (off season).
20 rooms: 39–90€. 4 suites: 115–150€.
Prix fixe: 23€ (wine inc., weekdays),
28€, 46€, 9€ (child).
A la carte: 50€.

In the very heart of Morvan, with its park,
lakes and gardens, the Auberge des Brizards is an establishment full of simplicity
and authenticity. In the kitchen, Jérôme
Besancenot produces talented creations:
the poultry pâté in a pastry crust with
foie gras in aspic, roasted pike-perch with
potato gnocchi and mushroom jus, rabbit saddle stuffed with herbs and cuttlefish pasta with jus, not to overlook the
Reinette apple shortbread and vanilla ice
cream. Rustic, carefully prepared rooms,
plus a caravan.

In 89630 Les Lavaults. 5 km se via D10.

● Auberge de l'Atre

Les Lavaults.
Tel. 03 86 32 20 79. Fax 03 86 32 28 25.
contact@auberge-de-latre.fr
www.auberge-de-latre.com
Closed 1 Feb.–Mar. 1, 20 June–beg. July
Rest. closed Tue. (exc. summer), Wed. (exc.
summer).
7 rooms: 45–105€.
Prix fixe: 27,50€ (weekdays), 42,50€, 52€,
11,50€ (child). A la carte: 50–70€.

Francis and Odile Salamolard also run
the Hôtel du Nord in Quarré-les-Tombes
but that does not mean they neglect this,
their first establishment. The authentic
setting is that of an old Morvan farmhouse with rustic beams and French
ceilings that subtly modernize the terrace of the dining room. The menu offers
a good deal of regional products and recipes, accompanied of course by regional
wines from the cellar. The smoked red
trout salad, a fan of pike-perch served
Burgundy style with beurre blanc and
seasonal mushrooms, a Charolais beef
medallion and the Burgundian Marc
soufflé easily seduce. In autumn, game
is given pride of place.

QUEDILLAC

35290 Ille-et-Vilaine. Paris 390 – Dinan 28
– Lamballe 46 – Loudéac 56 – Ploëmel 45 –
Rennes 40.
Bordering the N12, a crossroads of Brittany
between Rennes and St. Brieuc.

HOTELS-RESTAURANTS

● Relais de la Rance

6, rue de Rennes.
Tel. 02 99 06 20 20. Fax 02 99 06 24 01.
relaisdelarance@21s.fr
Closed Fri. dinner, Sun. dinner,
24 Dec.–20 Jan.
13 rooms: 48–65€.
Prix fixe: 19,50€, 24€, 37€, 45€,
65€ (wine inc.), 15€ (child).

The stone house of the Chevriers and the Guittons (Thérèse and André are brother and sister, André and Chantal their respective spouses) offers well-kept rooms and two dining rooms, one in Louis XVI style, the other more contemporary. The slice of foie gras, grilled wild sea bass, tasting plate of Erquy scallops and the apples in puff pastry are offered for the delectation of delighted clients.

LES QUELLES see **SCHIRMECK**

LES QUELLES see SCHIRMECK

QUESTEMBERT

56230 Morbihan. Paris 447 – Vannes 28 –
La Roche-Bernard 22 – Rennes 99 –
Redon 34.
A secret Morbihan town, with its pillared marketplace, its town hall made of freestone, its greenery-covered *auberge* and its distinctive cooking.

 HOTELS-RESTAURANTS

● Le Bretagne
et sa Résidence

13, rue Saint-Michel.
Tel. 02 97 26 11 12. Fax 02 97 26 12 37.
lebretagne@wanadoo.fr
www.paineaulebretagne.com
Closed 3 weeks Jan., 2 weeks Mar.
Rest. closed Mon., Tue. lunch.
6 rooms: 70–90€. 3 suites: 120€.
Prix fixe: 28€, 34€, 50€, 79€, 115€,
15€ (child). A la carte: 145€.

Alain Orillac came from Charente-Maritime (the Jardins du Lac in Trizay) to take over the establishment of the Paineaus. In what was formerly a grand restaurant in inland Brittany, simplicity is now the order of the day with a market-based cuisine that offers fare that varies with the seasons and the tides. Oven-crisped scallops with seaweed, quick-seared John Dory with tea-infused bouillon, veal sweetbreads in cocotte and the Breton shortbread with chocolate are well conceived. Frédéric, the brother of the new owner-cook, gives an enthusiastic service. Rooms and suites are in the process of being renovated.

QUIBERON

56170 Morbihan. Paris 504 – Vannes 46 –
Auray 28 – Concarneau 98 – Lorient 47.
quiberon@quiberon.com.
The peninsula, the wild coast, health food cures, exquisite savory caramels: this is Brittany all rolled into one.

 HOTELS-RESTAURANTS

■ Sofitel Diététique

Pointe de Goulvars.
Tel. 02 97 50 20 00. Fax 02 97 30 47 63.
h0562@accor.com / www.accorthalassa.com
Closed 3 weeks Jan.
78 rooms: 327–504€. 2 suites: 598€.

People come here to get (back) into shape. The rooms, which have undergone extensive renovation, have a view of the sea. Naturally, there is a swimming pool and the food is gastronomic and light. Patrick Jarno's cooking is a real, simple pleasure and one can enjoy, without guilt, the fish tartare with tapenade, line-fished sea bass with thinly sliced potatoes, the sirloin with sage butter and the souffléed lemon tart. Mineral water is *de rigueur*.

■ Sofitel Thalassa

Pointe de Goulvars.
Tel. 02 97 50 20 00. Fax 02 97 50 46 32.
h0557@accor-hotels.com / www.thalassa.com
Closed 3 weeks Jan.
133 rooms: 140–419€. 16 suites: 272–591€.
Prix fixe: 50€, 20€ (child).

To unwind from a stressful routine, nothing better than a stay in this hotel complex beside the ocean. The rooms have been redecorated with a contemporary décor and are extremely light. On the food side, the exacting Patrick Barbin offers low-calorie cuisine and total freshness, in wooded, chic and marine surroundings. Langoustine papillote with tartar sauce, monkfish medallion with caramelized carrots and spiced orange jus and the chocolate cigar are finely crafted work. The service is attentive.

■ Europa

At Port-Haliguen, 2 km via D200.
Tel. 02 97 50 25 00. Fax 02 97 50 39 30.
www.europa-quiberon.com
Closed beg. Nov.–end Mar.
51 rooms: 55–142,50€.
2 suites: 163,50–245€.
Prix fixe: 24€, 38€, 45€, 65€,
13€ (child). A la carte: 40–55€.

Rooms with a view of the sea, the fitness suite and balneotherapy ensure an enjoyable stay. In the La Marine restaurant, chef Laurent René offers an impressive cuisine. Lobster and vegetable terrine, the Atlantic sea bass with fleur de sel served with star anise–seasoned sauerkraut-style julienned fennel and the coriander seed-infused dark chocolate "bolero" with vanilla ice cream left us with good memories. The nearby beach, the garden and the swimming pool complete the array of comforts.

■ L'Albatros

19, rue de Port-Maria.
Tel. 02 97 50 15 05. Fax 02 97 50 27 61.
Closed mid-Nov.–mid-Dec.
Rest. closed 24 Dec. (dinner),
31 Dec. (dinner).
35 rooms: 60–86€.
Prix fixe: 13,50€, 16,90€, 22,10€,
7,20€ (child's lunch). A la carte: 30€.

Functional rooms (some with balcony) and an honest local cuisine are offered by this modern hotel a stone's throw from the landing stage for the islands.

■ La Petite Sirène

15, bd René-Cassin.
Tel. 02 97 50 17 34 (hotel) /
02 97 30 55 74 (rest.). Fax 02 97 50 03 73.
info@hotel-lapetitesirene.fr
www.hotel-lapetitesirene.fr
Closed beg. Nov.–end Mar.
33 rooms: 60–130€.

The Jarnos give a warm welcome to this family establishment beside the sea. Light rooms and spruce bathrooms. The restaurant has been closed.

● Le Jules Verne COM

1, bd d'Hoëdic, at Port-Maria.
Tel.-Fax 02 97 30 55 55.
Closed Tue. (off season), Wed. (off season), Jan.
Prix fixe: 27€. A la carte: 45€.

Karine and Patrick Grimaudo have taken over this up-and-coming seafood restaurant. A scallop carpaccio, thin sardine tart with crushed tomatoes, sole meunière and the rouget served on a bed of chanterelles, created by Fabrice Leydet, don't make waves.

● Le Relax COM

27, bd Castero.
Tel.-Fax 02 97 50 12 84.
restaurant-lerelax@wanadoo.fr
Closed Mon., Tue. (Oct.–Apr.), Christmas,
beg. Jan.–mid-Feb.
Prix fixe: 19€, 26€, 34€, 9€ (child).

Relaxation in view of the sea and treats for the palate are simultaneously on offer at Jean-Pierre Le Pen's establishment. Scallop brochettes with slow-simmered leeks and beurre blanc sauce, assorted grilled fish, the monkfish with bacon in a pepper coulis and a pineapple soufflé, savored in a white, yellow and wood setting, set high standards.

● La Chaumine SIM

36, pl du Manémeur.
Tel.-Fax 02 97 50 17 67.
Closed Sun. dinner, Mon.,
mid-Nov.–mid-Mar.
Prix fixe: 14,50€ (lunch), 25€, 30€, 35€,
46€.

This seaside inn makes an agreeable stopping place. Séverine Prado welcomes guests with a large smile while serving an aperitif at the bar to her contented regulars. Her brother Cyril Graff presides in the kitchen. Stuffed littleneck clams with lime butter, skate wing with balsamic vinaigrette, poached turbot with salted butter and the berries in almond cream wake one up. Not to spoil the effect, the prices are gentle.

● **La Criée** `SIM`

11, quai de l'Océan.
Tel. 02 97 30 53 09. Fax 02 97 50 42 35.
www.maisonlucas.net
Closed Sun. dinner, Mon., 2 weeks Dec., Jan.
Prix fixe: 18€, 6€ (child). A la carte: 40€.

Michel Lucas, the excellent purveyor and smoker of fish, has entrusted Jean-Pierre Le Guehennec with the task of tending the kitchen in his seafood restaurant. The fish and shellfish are the stars of the menu, the Nordic platter, the hot oysters, the roasted pollock and chitterling sausage and the peach with orange butter dessert slip down effortlessly. The Breton far, a local flan-type dessert, is legendary.

● **Au Safran** `SIM`

20, rue de Verdun.
Tel.-Fax 02 97 50 18 64.
nicolas.moranne@freesbee.fr
www.autourdequiberon.com/ausafran.html
Closed Sun. dinner (exc. July–Aug.), Mon. (exc. July–Aug.), 1 week Oct., 1 week Mar.
Prix fixe: 15,50€, 22,50€, 28€.
A la carte: 40€.

Thierry Bavay and Nicolas Moranne energetically run this lively restaurant located in a shopping center. Thierry serves up the escargot salad with duck confit, the seafood choucroute and a flambéed tarte Tatin with absinthe-flavored ice cream which has devoted fans. Nicolas advises on wines and gives a prompt and smiling service.

In Saint-Pierre-Quiberon (56510). 4,4 km n.

■ **Le Petit Hôtel**
  du Grand Large

Portivy, 11, quai Saint-Ivy.
Tel. 02 97 30 91 61.
www.lepetithoteldugrandlarge.fr
Closed end Sept.–beg. Feb. Rest. closed Tue.
6 rooms: 60–100€. Prix fixe: 24€, 26€.

We have a particular fondness for this portside hotel renovated in the red and gray colors of the west coast style, with its sailing-themed dining room and its charming rooms with seagrass flooring that open out onto the water and the boats. The welcome given by Hervé Bourdon and Catherine Decker is wonderful, the menu tempting and the cuisine, provided by a young veteran of Patrick Jarno at the Sofitel Diététique, tasty. Chitterling sausage with potatoes, the rouget with peppers and a saffron-seasoned sabayon, sea bream with pork cheeks and Grenaille new potatoes are extraordinary. The "mysterious" strawberry dolmen takes one back to childhood.

QUILLAN

11500 Aude. Paris 808 – Foix 64 – Carcassonne 52 – Limoux 28.
tourisme-quillan@wanadoo.fr.
This little town at the foot of the Pyrénées is surrounded by mountains and nestles on the left bank of the Aude. Pretty town houses, the ruins of a 13th-century castle and the old bridge put it on the map.

 HOTELS-RESTAURANTS

■ **Cartier**

31, bd Charles-de-Gaulle.
Tel. 04 68 20 05 14. Fax 04 68 20 22 57.
contact@hotelcartier.com
www.hotelcartier.com
Closed mid-Dec.–mid-Mar. Rest. closed Sat. lunch (Mar.–Apr. and Oct.–Dec.).
28 rooms: 35–62€.
Prix fixe: 18€, 24€, 28€, 8,50€ (child).
A la carte: 30€.

Michel Cartier looks after this beautiful building dating from 1900, with its small but renovated rooms. André Toustou's traditional cooking leaves you with nothing but good memories: foie gras in salad, fish stew in the spirit of bouillabaisse, roasted rabbit with slow-roasted garlic and a crème Catalane slip down easily.

QUIMPER

29000 Finistère. Paris 564 – Brest 71 – Lorient 68 – Rennes 217 – Saint-Brieuc 128. office.tourisme.quimper@wanadoo.fr.
"Kemper" in Breton means "confluence": This is the meeting place of the Steir and the Odet, at the bottom of a verdant valley overlooked by Mount Frugy. Cruise boats reach the sea in two hours. The town, with its beautiful half-timbered houses, is to be explored on foot. The quays with their footbridges and the picturesque streets give it a timeless feel, even if the town plays up its Celtic aspect, hosting Cornish festivals that inject new life into the spirit of the region. One has only to sniff the air, glance at the carefully decorated shop windows, count the number of antique dealers, look round the museums and make for the modern shopping center to have a drink in front of St. Corentin cathedral to realize that Quimper deserves a detailed exploration.

 HOTELS-RESTAURANTS

■ Hôtel Oceania

Rte de Bénodet. 17 rue du Poher.
Tel. 02 98 90 46 26. Fax 02 98 53 01 96.
oceania.quimper@oceaniahotels.com
www.oceaniahotels.com
87 rooms: 100–130€. 5 suites: 125–165€.
Prix fixe: 9,30€, 25€, 9€ (child).

A large chain hotel that has now proven its quality. Here you will find comfort (well-equipped rooms), relaxation (a heated outdoor swimming pool) and honest, traditional cuisine (fish soup and the pollock tart with tomato sauce).

■ Escale Oceania

6, rue Théodore-Le-Hars.
Tel. 02 98 53 37 37. Fax 02 98 90 31 51.
escaleoceania.quimper@oceaniahotels.com
www.oceaniahotels.com
Rest. closed lunch, Sat., Sun.

62 rooms: 45–85€. 1 suite: 65–99€.
Prix fixe: 17€ (weekday dinner) 9€ (child).

Claire Le Du is the genial manager of this hotel near the Odet that has benefitted from renovated bedrooms and dining room. On the food side, one readily enjoys the fish soup, scallop cassolette and tarte Tatin.

■ Le Gradlon

30, rue de Brest.
Tel. 02 98 95 04 39. Fax 02 98 95 61 25.
contact@hotel-gradlon.com
www.hotel-gradlon.com
Closed mid-Dec.–mid-Jan.
22 rooms: 69–155€.

This hotel near the cathedral offers quiet and comfort. The rooms have been redecorated in a traditional style, while the rose-filled courtyard is an invitation to reverie.

■ Mercure

21 bis, av de la Gare.
Tel. 02 98 90 31 71. Fax 02 98 53 09 81.
h1421@accor-hotels.com
61 rooms: 60–150€.

This chain hotel has the assets of a location opposite the station, maritime decoration and functionality. The small but redecorated rooms are well kept.

● Les Acacias   V.COM

88, bd Creac'h-Gwen.
Tel. 02 98 52 15 20. Fax 02 98 10 11 48.
acacias-qper@wanadoo.fr
www.les-acaciasquimper.monsite.orange.fr
Closed Sat., Sun. dinner, 15 Aug.–beg. Sept.
Prix fixe: 18€ (weekday lunch), 28€, 38€, 48€, 12€ (child). A la carte: 53€.

Philippe Hattet runs this warm restaurant with talent. Located near the thriving part of the city, the modern building surprises. The luxurious décor is an invitation to taste the serious cooking of a skillful practioner who offers a powerful and elaborate cuisine. Crab and amandine potato mille-feuille with shellfish jus, langoustine tails simmered in lightly spiced sauce, squab breast served with Paimpol white coco beans and the Plougastel strawberry and spiced-wine gratin are well conceived. A comprehensive wine selection.

● L'Ambroisie `COM`

49, rue Elie-Fréron.
Tel.-Fax 02 98 95 00 02.
gilbert.guyon@wanadoo.fr
www.ambroisie-quimper.com
Closed Mon. (exc. July–Aug.).
Prix fixe: 22€, 35€, 47€, 68€,
15€ (child).

Gilbert Guyon chooses his produce meticulously from the best regional producers and marries them skillfully, with excellent results. His simple and obvious dishes never disappoint. The sautéed langoustines served on an anise-flavored jus with strips of crêpes, John Dory with spicy jus served with mushroom- and ham-stuffed artichokes simmered in wine and the veal sweetbreads braised in a vinegar-infused sauce served with Paimpol carrots and pearl onions ring true, as do the pears roasted with spiced caramel, served with chocolate mousse in puff pastry. The cellar is well stocked.

● La Fleur de Sel `SIM`

1, quai Neuf.
Tel.-Fax 02 98 55 04 71.
Closed Sat. lunch, Sun., Bank holidays,
Christmas–New Year's vac.
Prix fixe: 21€ (weekdays), 25€, 36€,
8€ (child).

The Le Galls' restaurant is a charming and gastronomic bistro beside the Odet and next to the museum of tiling that has a "back from abroad" décor with its African touches and vivid colors. Pascale gives a cheerful welcome while Alain, trained by Lorain at Joigny and at the Château St. Martin in Vence, works skillfully with his market produce. Fleur de sel-marinated salmon, the potato and chitterling sausage Tatin, saffron-seasoned monkfish medallion, fish choucroute, the duck breast with cider sauce and the frozen parfait, seasoned with licorice root, look good.

● Café de l'Epée `SIM`

14, rue du Parc.
Tel. 02 98 95 28 97. Fax 02 98 64 37 73.
www.quimper-lepee.com
Prix fixe: 18€ (lunch), 21€, 31€,
9€ (child).

This brasserie dating from 1900 was the refuge of the Surrealists and Max Jacob. With its stucco, moldings and benches, the room is welcoming and one settles in happily to enjoy the well-prepared food. A salmon tartare flavored with hydromel (a fermented honey drink), roasted cod and Guéméné chitterling sausage, pollock with pickled seaweed and the lamb medallions with creamy cider sauce are conventionally well done.

● Le Rive Gauche `N``SIM`

9, rue Ste-Catherine.
Tel. 02 98 90 06 15.
Closed Sun., Mon. dinner, 1 week mid-Sept.,
1 week beg. Jan.
Prix fixe: 12€ (lunch), 15€, 19,50€,
25,50€.

Patrick and Sylvie Sutour have taken over this modern town center restaurant located not far from the banks of the Odet. The menus are well chosen, offering scallop profiteroles, tartare of salmon or sole meunière before the cider sabayon served with Lambic beer-simmered apples and a fresh fruit brochette served with peach and currant sorbet.

● La 7e Vague `N``SIM`

72, rue Jean-Jaurès.
Tel. 02 98 53 33 10.
laseptiemevague29@free.fr
Closed Sat., Sun.
Prix fixe: 18€ (lunch), 30€.

Thierry and Isabelle Doudard run this pretty restaurant with discretion. It is reminiscent of a galley pub with its bar near the entrance for drinks with pals and its menus written up on slates for suppers with friends. Thierry, who has worked at the Amphytrion in Lorient, handles seafood produce with skill. Salmon salad, the home-style whiting filet, pan-simmered

Atlantic sea bass and mussels and the tarte Tatin use simplicity to good effect.

● **Bleu Marine**   `SIM`

31 bis, rue de Brest.
Tel. 02 98 64 35 90.
Closed Sat. lunch, Sun. lunch, Mon.
Prix fixe: 22€, 26€.

Corinne Le Gall is the energetic manager of this restaurant that invites escape, as much by its décor as its cuisine filled with foreign flavors. Julien Peron concocts dishes that also take one on a journey. The escargots in buttered Chinese cabbage, fish tagine with preserved lemons, bourride (a local fish stew with aïoli) and a banana mille-feuille with chocolate sauce ring true.

● **Le Stade**   `SIM`

12, av Georges-Pompidou.
Tel. 02 98 90 22 43. Fax 02 98 90 39 99.
restaurantlestade.quimper@orange.fr
Closed Sun., Mon. dinner, 3 weeks Sept.
Prix fixe: 24€, 44€, 52€, 65€,
10€ (child).

Joël Treguer has transformed this former workers' canteen into a serious restaurant. His menu evolves according to the seasons and is also innovative. In the traditional dining room, one can enjoy the Cognac-seasoned seafood croustade, grilled scallop and bacon brochettes, a "pan of Breton riches", Magloire langoustes and the grilled rack of lamb with slow-roasted garlic. The wine cellar, closely supervised by Marie-Noëlle Treguer, is well provided with both minor and great wines.

In Pluguffan (29700). 5 km sw via bd Poulguinan.

● **La Roseraie de Bel Air**   Ⓞ `V.COM`

Impasse de la Boissière.
Tel. 02 98 53 50 80. Fax 02 98 53 43 65.
roseraie-de-bel-air@wanadoo.fr
Closed Sat. lunch, Sun. dinner, Mon.,
mid-Sept.–mid-Oct., 1 week May.
Prix fixe: 25€ (lunch), 45€, 58€, 78€.
A la carte: 75€.

The Cornec and Henaff families look after this restaurant and ensure that their customers are happy. In the dining room, Maryvonne, the mother, guides their choices while daughter Frédérique gives judicious advice on wines from a well-stocked cellar. On the cooking side, Louis, the father, and his son-in-law Lionel create lively dishes in tandem. Jumbo langoustines with sweet peas and "chorizon-ions", rock mullet with a spicy diced new carrot rougaille as a condiment and the lamb with stuffed piquillo peppers marry Breton flavors with those of the Grand Sud. The same goes for desserts such as a strawberry harlequin and coconut-strawberry milk. A wonderful restaurant.

In Ty Sanquer. 7 km n via D770.

● **Auberge Ti Coz**   `COM`

Tel. 02 98 94 50 02. Fax 02 98 94 56 37.
www.auberge-tycoz.com
Closed Sun. dinner, Mon., Tue. dinner,
3 weeks Sept.
Prix fixe: 19€ (lunch), 24,50€ (dinner).

Off a country side road, this inn with a neo-rustic dining room is a delight. There are smart little wines, reasonably priced menus and above all the clever handiwork of Jean-Christophe Despinasse. Formerly of Dutournier in Paris, he serves up langoustine tempura with a truffle infusion, sea bream filet in a spice crust, veal filet with chorizo-seasoned jus and chocolate profiteroles.

29300 Finistère. Paris 519 – Quimper 48 –
Concarneau 31 – Pont-Aven 18 – Rennes 171.
ot.quimperle@wanadoo.fr.
The lower part of the town, the church of St. Croix, the old markets dating from 1880, the old houses of the rue Brémond-d'Ars, the archers' house and the museum of Breton traditions all make this a worthy stopping place.

▣   HOTELS-RESTAURANTS

■ **Le Vintage**   ⌂

20, rue Brémond-d'Ars.
Tel. 02 98 35 09 10. Fax 02 98 35 09 29.
hotelvintage@wanadoo.fr / www.hotelvintage.com
10 rooms: 58–110€.

Hiding behind the 19th-century facade of this charming hotel, linked to the Bistro de la Tour, are very comfortable rooms decorated on a wine theme.

■ Novalis

Rte de Concarneau.
Tel. 02 98 39 24 00. Fax 02 98 39 12 10.
novalis.quimperle@wanadoo.fr
www.inter-hotel.com
Rest. closed Sat., Sun.
38 rooms: 53–63€.
Prix fixe: 8€, 15,50€, 23€, 8€ (child).
A la carte: 30€.

On the road to Concarneau, Eric Chalein's cuisine (the stuffed Glénan soft shell clams, seafood broth with langoustines, pollock served with a meat jus and the duck breast in cider vinegar–seasoned sauce) is well devised.

● La Cigale Egarée   N·COM

ZI de la Villeneuve-Braouic.
Tel. 02 98 39 15 53.
www.lacigaleegaree.com
Closed Sun., Mon., 2 weeks Nov.1 vac.
Prix fixe: 32€, 45€, 62€.

Damien Victor Pujebet, who hails from the Southwest, has made his nest in a charming old house with a pink facade, done out in contemporary style, on the edge of an industrial zone. This adventurous and well-travelled young chef marries tastes with great skill. Cod in puff pastry with a "shoot" of lemon verbena, the "friovlity" of langoustines "in three movements", the caramelized lamb pastilla with pine nuts and nettle-infused jus, grilled sirloin steak and the oysters on shaved ice with a red wine sauce tasting of the sea are knockout dishes.

● Le Bistro de la Tour   COM

2, rue Dom-Morice.
Tel. 02 98 39 29 58. Fax 02 98 39 21 77.
Bistrodelatour@wanadoo.fr
www.hotelvintage.com
Closed Sat. lunch, Sun. dinner (exc. July–Aug.), Mon.
Prix fixe: 21€, 30€, 42€, 56€ (wine inc.),
13€ (child).

We very much like this chic bistro in the art nouveau style of the school of Nancy. Bernadette and Jérôme Carriou run the restaurant with distinction and the chef, Arnaud Stanquic, serves up a Breton cuisine that travels well. Creamy cep and scallop soup with Burgundian truffles, foie gras terrine with an Aubance aspic, pan-fried fish with Madagascar vanilla-infused butter and the Breton-style cassoulet with Baye chitterling sausage harmonize with the superb wines chosen with love by Jérôme.

QUINCIE-EN-BEAUJOLAIS

69430 Rhône. Paris 428 – Mâcon 33 –
Bourg-en-Bresse 55 – Lyon 57 – Beaujeu 6.
The heart of Beaujolais, which opens its cellars and shows off its idyllic countryside homes.

 HOTELS-RESTAURANTS

■ Mont Brouilly

At the Pont-des-Samsons, 2 km e via D37.
Tel. 04 74 04 33 73. Fax 04 74 04 30 10.
contact@hotelbrouilly.com
www.hotelbrouilly.com
Closed 1 week Christmas–New Year's, Feb.,
Sun. dinner (off season), Mon. (off season).
Rest. closed Sun. dinner (off season), Mon.,
Tue. lunch.
27 rooms: 59–66€. 2 suites: 77–92€.
Prix fixe: 17,50€ (weekday lunch), 21€,
25€, 32€, 13€ (child). A la carte: 40€.

The modern hotel among the vineyards suits those interested in wine tourism. The establishment is functional, well situated and enjoys a swimming pool that is very pleasant at the end of the day. The rooms are sound proofed. Good local cuisine created by Yves Bouchacourt. Pike-perch with Noilly vermouth-seasoned cream sauce and a tarte Tatin with caramel sauce and vanilla ice cream are extremely well prepared.

QUINGEY

25440 Doubs. Paris 397 – Dôle 36 – Gray 54 – Besançon 23.
The rustic banks of the Loue, painted by Courbet, set the tone of this pretty village.

 HOTELS-RESTAURANTS

■ La Truite de la Loue   ⌂
2, rte de Lyon.
Tel. 03 81 63 60 14. Fax 03 81 63 84 77.
latruitedelaloue@wanadoo.fr
Closed Tue. dinner (off season), Wed. (off
season), beg. Jan.–beg. Feb., Feb. vac.
10 rooms: 37–57€.
Prix fixe: 17,50€, 19€, 23€, 43€,
8€ (child).

This good auberge beside the river offers renovated rooms and honest, simple cooking: one never tires of the morels in pastry, the trout in Vin Jaune sauce and the sirloin steak with morels. Reasonable prices.

QUINTIN

22800 Côtes-d'Armor. Paris 464 – Saint-Brieuc 18 – Loudéac 31 – Lamballe 34.
otsi.pays-de-quintin@wanadoo.fr.
This ancient pearl of Arcoat, in the Brittany interior, offers medieval facades, a castle, a basilica and stone houses.

 HOTELS-RESTAURANTS

■ Hôtel du Commerce   ⌂
2, rue Rochonen.
Tel. 02 96 74 94 67. Fax 02 96 74 00 94.
hotelducommerce@cegetel.net
www.hotleducommerce.fr.cc
Closed Fri. dinner (exc. hotel by reserv.),
Sun. dinner (exc. hotel by reserv.), Mon. (exc.
hotel by reserv.), 1 week Christmas–New
Year's, 2 weeks Easter, 1 week at end Aug.
11 rooms: 45–83€.
Prix fixe: 14€ (weekday lunch), 24€, 42€,
10€ (child).

With its Virginia creeper–covered exterior, this distinctive 18th-century house eas-ily stands out. In addition, one appreciates the welcome, the comfortable rooms and the reworked regional cuisine served in the rustic but luxurious dining room. Christophe Gourdin serves up langoustines and shrimp in salad, a filet of John Dory with herring caviar and crispy duck breast served with thyme-seasoned caramelized apples — all extremely alluring.

RAMATUELLE

83350 Var. Paris 876 –
Saint-Tropez 10 – Sainte-Maxime 16 –
Le Lavandou 37.
ramatuelle@franceplus.com.
The memories of Gérard Philipe, who rests in
the village cemetery, and of Anne, who wrote
Les Rendez-Vous de la Colline here, fill this
pretty site perched on a hill.

 HOTELS-RESTAURANTS

■ Le Baou & la Terrasse

Av Gustave-Etienne.
Tel. 04 98 12 94 20. Fax 04 98 12 94 21.
hostellerie.lebaou@wanadoo.fr
www.alpazurhotels.com
Closed end Sept.–mid-May.
Rest. closed lunch
39 rooms: 190–350€.
2 suites: 320–390€.
Prix fixe: 55€ (dinner), 72€ (dinner).

Not far from the beaches, near the road
and at the foot of old Ramatuelle, this is a
renovated modern building in the Provençal style run by René Guth. Duplex, suites,
floral decoration in the neo-art deco restaurant La Terrasse all create a positive
effect. Daniel Speller crafts sure-fire successes of the pressed duck and foie gras
terrine, roasted whole turbot, veal with
parmesan and the soft-centered chocolate cake served warm with vanilla ice
cream, all delivered with a smile by Anne-
Marie Souzy. Swimming pool, terrace, car
park, garden, air conditioning, Internet
and WiFi are pluses.

RANRUPT see COLROY-LA-ROCHE
RATHSAMHAUSEN see SELESTAT

LE RAYOL-CANADEL-SUR-MER

83820 Var. Paris 887 –
Bormes-les-Mimosas 9 – Cavalaire 11 –
Le Lavandou 13.
A little place tucked away at the end of a
flower-filled road on the Var coast with its
beautiful wooded park.

 HOTELS-RESTAURANTS

■ Le Bailli de Suffren

Av des Américains.
Tel. 04 98 04 47 00. Fax 04 98 04 47 99.
info@lebaillidesuffren.com
www.lebaillidesuffren.com
Closed mid-Oct.–mid-Apr.
53 suites: 160–392€.
Prix fixe: 27€, 32€, 45€.

Situated directly in front of the Levant,
a sixties hotel renovated in contemporary style with Provençal hexagonal floor
tiles, beige monochrome paintings, Toile
de Jouy fabric, swimming pool and the
beach on its doorstep: the place is like
a piece of paradise. In terms of cooking,
the young David Arnichard, formerly of
Rostang, plays majestically with the cuisine of the South using quality produce.
A creamy watercress risotto with basil-
seasoned John Dory, rouget filets with
crispy skin and the caramelized suckling pig riblets served with cep polenta
play a beautiful rustic melody while the
desserts (notably a berry macaron glazed
with vanilla) do not lag behind. Oh! Spend
several idyllic days at the Rayol, near one
of the most beautiful gardens of the Mediterranean…

● A Maurin des Maures   SIM

Av du Touring-Club.
Tel. 04 94 05 60 11. Fax 04 94 05 67 70.
www.maurin-des-maures.com
Closed Christmas, New Year's.
Prix fixe: 13,50€ (weekday lunch), 22,50€,
28€. A la carte: 50€.

Marie-Ange Schehl has taken over this former roadside café with gusto and made
it into a pleasant restaurant. Grilled eggplant mille-feuille, monkfish with tomato
Tatin or the slow-roasted lamb shank are
not bad. Obviously one is nostalgic for
the time when Dédé Delmonte would
serve up bouillabaisse while recounting
local lore… The chocolate cake is created by his brother René Delmonte, who
has been given the Meilleur Ouvrier de
France award.

ILE DE RE

17630 Charente-Maritime. Paris 490 –
La Rochelle 17 – Fontenay-le-Comte 66 –
Luçon 54.

An island? Of course, even if since 1988 it is not separated from the continent, with its three-kilometer toll bridge which seems to swing above the sea. Ré, in figures, has 8,500 hectares, 16,500 permanent residents, 135,000 summer residents, 50,000 campers and 14,000 holiday homes, but also ten villages from Rivedoux to Loix, La Flotte to Portes and eighty kilometers of cycling paths, for a total island length of thirty kilometers. The bungalows—lovingly whitened with chalk—the orange-colored roof tiles, the port of La Flotte and its pretty old marketplace, the old town houses of St-Martin-de-Ré (was formerly an important military site, its famous prison converted into a citadel in 1681, fortified by Vauban), the old arsenal, the Clerjotte hotel and the Ernest-Cognacq museum tell of its past glory. The ancient abbey of Châteliers, the lakeside area of Fier d'Ars and the nature reserve of Lilleau-des-Niges, the Baleines lighthouse, fifty-five meters high, the house on the St.-Clément marsh and the little wood of Trousse-Chemise form part of its legend. There are also, of course, shadows of literary and political life and the society figures who frequent the island in summer, turning it into the twenty-first arrondissement of Paris.

 HOTELS-RESTAURANTS

In Ars-en-Ré (17590).

● **Le Bistro de Bernard** `COM`

1, quai de la Criée.
Tel. 05 46 29 40 26. Fax 05 46 29 28 99.
bistro debernard@wanadoo.fr
Closed Mon., Tue. (Oct.–Mar.),
beg. Dec.–mid-Feb.
Prix fixe: 24€, 32€. A la carte: 50–60€.

Bernard and Catherine Frigère have made their quayside restaurant into a friendly staging post. The crab in salad, orange-flavored fennel cappuccino and the turbot, simply cooked with beurre blanc, are all successes. Lovely desserts such as a hot puff pastry with fruits in season are always delicately flavored. Attentive service and reasonable prices.

In Ars-en-Ré.

● **La Cabane du Fier**

Le Martray.
Tel.-Fax 05 46 29 64 84.
Closed Tue. dinner (off season), Wed. (off season), beg. Apr.–mid-Nov.
A la carte: 38€.

This oyster fishers' cabin makes a worthy address. Christophe Frigière serves marinated sardines, grilled Atlantic sea bass, smoked salmon choucroute and beef rib eye for two in a relaxed atmosphere.

In Le Bois-Plage-en-Ré (17580).

■ **Les Bois Flottais**

Chemin des Mouettes.
Tel. 05 46 09 27 00. Fax 05 46 09 28 00.
contact@lesboisflottais.com
www.lesboisflottais.com
Closed Jan.–end Feb.
8 rooms: 70–144€.

All wood and charm, the modern guesthouse of Aurélie and Johan Lagord easily seduces. We like its airy rooms in pastel colors and its delicious breakfasts. The heated swimming pool is also much appreciated.

In Le Bois-Plage-en-Ré.

■ **L'Océan**

172, rue de Saint-Martin.
Tel. 05 46 09 23 07. Fax 05 46 09 05 40.
info@re-hotel-ocean.com
www.re-hotel-ocean.com
Hotel closed beg. Jan.–beg. Feb. Rest. closed Wed., 2 weeks beg. Dec., beg. Jan.–beg. Feb.
30 rooms: 72–160€.
Prix fixe: 18€ (weekday lunch), 23€, 26,50€ (dinner), 32€, 10€ (child).

Martine and Noël Bourdet have created a lasting decorative event. Their establishment done out in shades of ochre and sand, with garden and balcony, is fully equipped: hammam, Jacuzzi, heated swimming pool, Internet, sitting rooms, private car park. The wood-paneled rooms have the "bleu de Ré" style. In the dining room decorated with paneling and navy blues, Yoann Leraut plays a simple, unaffected culinary tune. The pan-tossed squid (casserons) with Espelette peppers, the thyme-seasoned cod filet served with an olive oil vegetable purée, the rack of lamb with rosemary jus and the Jonchée Charentaise (a local soft cheese), served with confiture, are accompanied by wines as easy to drink in as air.

In Le Bois-Plage-en-Ré.

■ Les Gollandières

Av des Gollandières.
Tel. 05 46 09 23 99. Fax 05 46 09 09 84.
hotel-les-gollandieres@wanadoo.fr
Closed mid-Nov.–mid-Mar.
35 rooms: 97–118€. 1 suite: 120–180€.
Prix fixe: 26€, 31€, 36€, 10€ (child).
A la carte: 45€.

This charming seventies establishment has a slightly retro feel. The rooms are simple and comfortable and one unwinds in the large swimming pool and in the garden. In the kitchen, Joël Coulon works with the regional produce. The shellfish and oysters in salad, seared tuna steak, rabbit saddle with potatoes and the strawberry fountain with rose ice cream win all the votes.

In La Flotte (17630).

● Le Richelieu

44, av de la Plage.
Tel. 05 46 09 60 70. Fax 05 46 09 50 59.
info@hotel-le-richelieu.com
www.hotel-le-richelieu.com
Closed Jan.–Feb. vac.
34 rooms: 125–460€. 6 suites: 370–560€.
Prix fixe: 55€, 65€, 25€ (child).

Away from the activity of the port but beside the beach, this Relais & Châteaux hotel is the ideal place for an exploratory stay on the island. The Gendres give a kind welcome, the service is perfect, the rooms spacious and quiet, the swimming pool very pleasant and the built-in thalassotherapy center ensures rapid recuperation. Richard Prouteau, a Charentais who has returned home after exile in Luxembourg (where he worked at the excellent Speltz), has given a breath of youth to the kitchen. Crispy citrus-marinated langoustines, the blue lobster topped with chutney

and tomatoes in vinaigrette, sole browned in salted butter, served with reduced fish jus and a minced squid and lemon condiment and the basil-stuffed lamb saddle create a good effect. The addition of dark chocolate and caramel dessert with caramelized dried fruit and Ile de Ré fleur de sel ice cream finishes off the meal in gentle style.

In Les Portes-en-Ré (17880).

● Auberge de la Rivière   COM

La Rivière.
Tel. 05 46 29 54 55. Fax 05 46 29 40 32.
Closed Wed. (off season).
Prix fixe: 15€ (lunch), 24€, 35€, 40€,
9€ (child).

Alberto Fonte plies his craft away from the world, but not far from the little wood of Trousse-Chemise, beloved by those who know it. He skillfully seduces with lobster gratin, roasted sea bream with spring vegetables, turbot in thin slices of local potato, grilled beef rib eye with fleur de sel and the fine vanilla and caramel tart.

In Les Portes-en-Ré.

● Le Chasse-Marée

Place de la Liberté.
Tel. 05 46 29 52 03. Fax 05 46 28 00 11.
restaurant.le.chasse-maree@wanadoo.fr
Closed Sun. dinner (exc. summer), Mon.,
Jan.–end Mar.
Prix fixe: 26€, 32€, 12€ (child).
A la carte: 52€.

Sandrine Salgues and Marc Roussel give an easy welcome to this neat bistro with white wood and beige, offering a local cuisine peppered with skillful exoticism. Tuna maki with chopped pickled vegetables, a fine sardine tart with olives and caramelized onions, beef strips grilled and seasoned with wasabi and the strawberry and coconut spring rolls with chocolate sauce take one on a pleasant culinary voyage.

In Saint-Clément-des-Baleines (17590).

■ Le Chat Botté

23, pl de l'Eglise.
Tel. 05 46 29 21 93. Fax 05 46 29 29 97.

hotelchatbotte@wanadoo.fr
www.hotelchatbotte.com
Closed beg. Jan.–10 Feb., end Nov.–mid-Dec.
20 rooms: 66–152€. 3 suites: 190–245€.

The place has charm and relaxation is assured *chez* Géraldine Massé and Chantal Massé-Chantreau. We like the Zen rooms, the pretty furniture, the tea garden, the generous breakfasts, the balneotherapy and being looked after in the Chinese manner.

In Saint-Clément-des-Baleines.

● Le Chat Botté `V.COM`
20, rue de la Mairie.
Tel. 05 46 29 42 09. Fax 05 46 29 29 77.
restaurant-lechatbotte@wanadoo.fr
www.restaurant-lechatbotte.com
Closed Mon. (off season), beg. Dec.–end Jan.
Prix fixe: 22€ (weekdays), 31€, 41€, 70€,
12€ (child).

A stone's throw away from the hotel of the same name, Daniel Massé is continuing the family tradition in this charming inn. Good cooking, gentle atmosphere, well-decorated tables and a civilized garden set the tone. Oysters served hot with a Pineau wine sabayon, cod with truffle-seasoned mashed potatoes and veal kidneys with mustard sauce as well as the cold berry cream dessert are prepared with craftmanship. A wonderful welcome from Marie-Odile Massé who chooses the wines with love.

In Saint-Martin-de-Ré (17410).

■ Hôtel de Toiras
1, quai Job-Foran.
Tel. 05 46 35 40 32. Fax 05 46 35 64 59.
contact@hotel-de-toiras.com
www.hotel-de-toiras.com
Rest. closed Tue., Wed.
17 rooms: 160–310€. 7 suites: 310–560€.
Prix fixe: 60€.

A very recent Relais & Châteaux on the island, this stately 17th-century home, with its recreated tower on the port, is a jewel of its kind. Old-style parquet, bathrooms with pretty traditonal floor tiles, beautiful materials, well-chosen furni-ture, fantastic welcome and attentive staff: Olivia Mathé has given much of herself to the establishment. The refined rooms are romantic and the breakfasts a choice moment. The sitting rooms allow one to take tea in an idyllic world. Thomas Urbanek looks after a small household restaurant, where the star dishes are Cognac-flambéed langoustine tails in salad, Atlantic sea bass with local potatoes and a pretty berry mousse.

In Saint-Martin-de-Ré.

■ La Baronnie
21, rue du Baron-de-Chantal.
Tel.-Fax 05 46 09 21 29.
info@domainedelabaronnie.com
www.domainedelabaronnie.com
3 rooms: 150–210€. 3 suites: 170–310€.

In her 18th-century home, as well as in its spruce annex, Florence Pallardy welcomes guests delighted to take advantage of the park, the garden, the patio and comfortable, non-smoking rooms.

In Saint-Martin-de-Ré.

■ Le Clos Saint-Martin
8, cours Pasteur.
Tel. 05 46 01 10 62. Fax 05 46 01 99 89.
hotelclos.saintmartin@wanadoo.fr
www.le-clos-saint-martin.com
Closed Oct.–end Mar.
28 rooms: 98–245€.

Two minutes away from the activity of the town center, this large house with blue shutters offers spacious, quiet rooms, Jacuzzi and swimming pool around which breakfast is eaten.

In Saint-Martin-de-Ré.

■ La Jetée
23, quai Georges-Clemenceau.
Tel. 05 46 09 36 36. Fax 05 46 09 36 06.
info@hotel-lajetee.com
www.hotel-lajetee.com
24 rooms: 95–160€.

Right on the port, this well laid-out modern establishment around a huge patio offers large rooms with contemporary comforts. The nicest have beautiful views.

In Saint-Martin-de-Ré.

■ **La Maison Douce**

25, rue Mérindot.
Tel. 05 46 09 20 20. Fax 05 46 09 09 90.
www.lamaisondouce.com
Closed beg. Jan.–mid-Feb., mid-Nov.–end Dec.
9 rooms: 105–155€. 2 suites: 185–235€.

Alain Brunel offers a warm welcome to his 19th-century home with its highly decorated rooms, generous breakfasts and enclosed garden. Loan of slickers and boots for fishing, and don't forget tea when one returns.

In Saint-Martin-de-Ré.

● **La Baleine Bleue** COM

Ilot du Port.
Tel. 05 46 09 03 30. Fax 05 46 09 30 86.
info@baleinebleue.com / www.baleinebleue.com
Closed Mon. (exc. July–Aug.), Tue. (Oct.–Mar.), 10 days Dec.
Prix fixe: 24€ (lunch), 28€ (lunch), 32€ (lunch), 45€, 14€ (child). A la carte: 65€.

Philippe Bodart is the gastronomic sentinel of the port. His bistro with terrace and veranda is maritime chic while the atmosphere is relaxed, the wood decoration warm, the service prompt and the cooking of Christophe Rouillé fresh and well-judged. The fish tartare plate, the crab gourmandise, Peruis scallops with violet potatoes and chestnuts and the grilled veal cutlet with a house purée and mushrooms slip down effortlessly. A pretty mirabelle plum mille-feuille with crushed peanuts and nougatine ice cream. Wines are included.

In Saint-Martin-de-Ré.

● **Le Serghi**

15, quai Clemenceau
Tel. 05 46 09 03 92. Fax 05 46 09 20 58.
Closed Sun. dinner (off season), Mon. (off season), 2 weeks end Nov.–beg. Dec.
Prix fixe: 20€ (lunch), 24€.

The décor of an old bistro, with zinc counter, bare wooden tables, red velvet banquettes and beamed ceiling, redecorated in yellow and with oodles of charm, like the nice, generous menus. One enjoys the sardine rilettes, the slow-cooked squid stew and a trilogy of crème brûlées that have only one objective: to give pleasure at low cost. Alexandre Brunner and his young team give a friendly welcome.

In Sainte-Marie-de-Ré (17740).

■ **Atalante**

Port Notre-Dame.
Tel. 05 46 30 22 44. Fax 05 46 30 13 49.
iledere@thalasso.com / www.relaisthalasso.com
Closed 2 weeks Jan.
115 rooms: 111–240€. 1 suite: 233–362€.
Prix fixe: 52€, 62€, 32€.

Well-equipped, with its swimming pool, direct access to the thalassotherapy center and modern, light rooms, this hotel facing the sea has many assets. On the food side, Arnaud Thierry cooks unaffected dishes of lobster salad, pan-tossed rouget filets, lamb sweetbreads and the apple tart, which go down easily.

REALMONT

81120 Tarn. Paris 707 – Toulouse 79 – Albi 20 – Castres 25 – Lacaune 57.
This staging post town in the heart of passionate Tarn still has a gastronomic reputation.

HOTELS-RESTAURANTS

■ **Mont Royal** ⌂

Rue de l'Hôtel-de-Ville.
Tel. 05 63 55 52 80. Fax 05 63 55 69 91.
emmtroyal@aol.com / www.le-mont-royal.com
Closed Sat. lunch (off season), Sun. dinner, Mon., 2 weeks end Feb.–beg. Mar.
7 rooms: 45–65€.
Prix fixe: 20€, 27€, 40€, 50€, 10€ (child). A la carte: 40€.

In the center of town, a modern hotel with rustic rooms and carefully prepared food. Foie gras escalope served hot with sherry-seasoned caramelized shallots and the spicy duck confit Tatin are not bad. The exquisite Sacher torte is the indulgence of owner Elisabeth Maurer.

● Les Secrets Gourmands

72, av du Général-de-Gaulle.
Tel. 05 63 79 07 67. Fax 05 63 79 07 69.
les-secrets-gourmands@wanadoo.fr
Closed Sun. dinner, Tue., 3 weeks Jan.,
1 week at end Aug.
Prix fixe: 19€, 26€, 35€, 50€,
12€ (child).

The location beside the N112 is hardly enticing, but the cuisine of Franck Augé, trained at Rostang's, Juana's and Taffarello's, is worth the detour. One enjoys, without ruining one's pocket, delicious foie gras breaded in a crushed hazelnut crust, grilled rouget filet with Paimpol coco beans and the roasted veal kidney with Lacaune ham served with red wine–simmered shallots. The chocolate tart served hot with a cocoa coulis and a spoonful of ice cream melts in the mouth.

REDON

35600 Ille-et-Vilaine. Paris 412 – Nantes 80 – Rennes 64 – Saint-Nazaire 54 – Vannes 60. The church of St. Sauveur, the 16th-century houses in the high street and the 17th-century salt lofts are worth a glimpse in this Breton town that was enriched by its ship owners. Inland waterways museum.

●	RESTAURANTS

● Moulin de Via

3 km, rte de la Gacilly.
Tel. 02 99 71 05 16. Fax 02 99 71 08 36.
Closed Sun. dinner, Mon., Tue. dinner.
Prix fixe: 15€, 30€, 45€.

In the middle of green countryside, this old water mill is picture postcard pretty. Claudine and Jean-Paul Cheneau, she an affable host, he a passionate cook, offer an enthusiastic welcome and a clever cuisine. In the country dining room with its old beams, the beef muzzle, simmered, chilled, then sliced thin in salad with langoustines and shellfish jus, the scallops in a vanilla-infused butter emulsion, the pepper-seasoned beef and amandine potatoes and the soft-centered chocolate

cake with Carambar candy ice cream soften the heart.

● La Boque

3, rue des Etats.
Tel.-Fax 02 99 71 12 95.
la-bogue@wanadoo.fr
Closed Sun. dinner, Mon.
Prix fixe: 21€, 35€, 45€, 55€.
A la carte: 50€.

This 16th- and 17th-century house, located opposite the marketplace, immediately charms with its rustic interior that has been completely redecorated this year. Under the beams, Ludovic Honnet offers a fine regional cuisine: pan-seared scallops and creamy parsnip soup with hazelnut oil, cod sliced thin with garden root vegetables, pepper-seasoned beef filet medallions with cardamom-spiced figs and a candied orange sorbet. Wines direct from the producers.

REIMS

51100 Marne. Paris 144 – Bruxelles 233 – Châlons-en-Champagne 48 – Lille 206.
visitreims@netvia.com.
We talk a lot about champagne but never or almost never about Champagne. Yet the town charms, set around its cathedral, and its gastronomic character comes naturally to it. Not just the pale yellow wine created in the *"crayères"* of the Butte St. Nicaise. With a little curiosity, here one can find an agreeably piquant mustard (which deserves its name as much as that of the more famous variety from Dijon), an elite charcuterie including Reims ham, little-known but exceptional *pâtisseries*, old-style biscuits, chocolates that tease with well-dominated alcohol. Knock on doors, wander from the place du Forum to the Boulingrin market and be amazed: the town is fertile and devilishly gastronomic—even if it still seems unaware of it.

■	HOTELS

■ Les Crayères

64, bd Henry-Vasnier.
Tel. 03 26 82 80 80. Fax 03 26 82 65 52.
crayeres@relaischateaux.com

www.gerardboyer.com
Closed Christmas–mid-Jan.
16 rooms: 280–485€. 3 suites: 370–485€.

The ancient Pommery château has renovated its rooms into chic bourgeois apartments. Beautiful gardens, refined decorations and elite restaurant (see Restaurants).

■ Grand Hôtel des Templiers ❀ ⬜

22, rue des Templiers.
Tel. 03 26 88 55 08. Fax 03 26 47 80 60.
hotel.templiers@wanadoo.fr
16 rooms: 180–270€. 2 suites: 340€.

A 19th-century town house, a stone's throw from the center, offering rooms that have been redecorated with warmth. Covered swimming pool, sauna and hammam.

■ Holiday Inn Garden Court ⬜

46, rue Buirette.
Tel. 03 26 78 99 99. Fax 03 26 78 99 90.
higcreims@alliance-hospitality.com
www.holiday-inn.com/reims-cityctr
Rest. closed Sat. lunch, Sun.
82 rooms: 90–210€.
Prix fixe: 14€, 19€.

Five minutes' walk from the cathedral and famous cellars, this chain establishment hides modern, renovated rooms and a panoramic roof restaurant behind its 1900s facade. Very decent cuisine and professional welcome and service.

■ Mercure-Cathédrale ⬜

31, bd Paul-Doumer.
Tel. 03 26 84 49 49. Fax 03 26 84 49 84.
h1248@accor-hotels.com / www.mercure.com
Rest. closed Sat. lunch, Sun. lunch.
120 rooms: 74–135€. 6 suites: 151–165€.

Easily accessible from the A4 (exit 24), this hotel offers huge, functional rooms, a champagne bar and a restaurant, Les Ombrages, where a classic cuisine, imaginatively reworked, is served. A pastry-covered duck tart and cod with tapenade are not bad.

■ Grand Hôtel de l'Europe ⬜

29, rue Buirette.
Tel. 03 26 47 39 39. Fax 03 26 40 14 37.
www.hotel-europe-reims.com
54 rooms: 68–101€.

A central location as well as redecorated and soundproofed rooms make this a practical stopover. The Hôtel du Nord near the station (75, place Drouet-d'Erlon, 03 26 47 39 03), which is part of the same group, offers simpler, but equally comfortable rooms.

■ Porte Mars ⬜

2, pl de la République.
Tel. 03 26 40 28 35. Fax 03 26 88 92 12.
www.hotelporteMar.com
24 rooms: 72–115€.

In the very center of town, this establishment offers panelled, neat rooms. Generous breakfasts.

In Tinqueux (51430). 6 km via A4.

■ L'Assiette Champenoise ⬜

40, av Paul-Vaillant-Couturier.
Tel. 03 26 84 64 64. Fax 03 26 04 15 69.
www.assiettechampenoise.com
33 rooms: 140–190€. 22 suites: 160–250€.

A stone's throw from the center and in the middle of large grounds, the house of the Lallements is welcoming, its restaurant well reputed and the modern but old-style rooms extremely comfortable (See Restaurants.)

● RESTAURANTS

● Les Crayères ⬥⬥ V.LUX

At the Château des Crayères,
64, bd Henry-Vasnier.
Tel. 03 26 82 80 80. Fax 03 26 82 65 52.
crayeres@relaischateaux.com
www.lescrayeres.com
Closed Christmas–New Year's.
Prix fixe: 65€ (lunch), 180€, 280€,
295€ (wine inc.).

Young, brilliant, intellectual Didier Elena is a chef unlike any other who has reasserted his credentials at this large house made fashionable by the Boyers and taken over by the Gardiniers. This clever Monagasque, an ex-medical student who trained with Alain Ducasse for whom he ran Essex House in New York, offers a small menu, with lively choices and clean, complex, precise and pure dishes, served on rectangular plates with powerful accompaniments. Examples of this style that is taking Reims and region by storm? The duck foie gras with white mushrooms and black truffles, a flat savory tarte flambée with veal sweetbreads, coriander, onions and smoked bacon, a rouget filet with duck foie gras and slow-cooked peppers and the Atlantic sea bass in almonds with sour cherries, lettuce cream and beurre noisette. One adds this to the fireplace-grilled lamb saddle, served with artichokes in a peppery vinaigrette, the grilled beef served with baked potato puffs, sweet onion tempura, bone marrow and a sauce Choron: what a pleasure to see a contemporary young maestro modify classic and old dishes in the light of the present day. The desserts (a mara des bois strawberries dessert, a cherry liqueur soufflé and a frozen pistachio clafoutis) are of the same ilk. The wine list is fantastic and the setting of the rooms, panelled or with glass walls, equally so.

● Le Foch ◎ V.COM

37, bd Foch.
Tel. 03 26 47 48 22. Fax 03 26 88 78 22.
njackylouaze@aol.com / www.lefoch.com
Closed Sat. lunch, Sun. dinner, Mon.,
Feb. vac., 1 week at end July, 3 weeks Aug.
Prix fixe: 33€ (weekday lunch), 43€, 59€,
75€, 15€ (child). A la carte: 100€.

The Sarthois Jacky Louazé has quickly made his mark in Champagne. In this elegant establishment he does not hesitate to throw over tradition in his preparation of contemporary seafood dishes. The ras el-hanout-seasoned langoustine brochette, the scallop carpaccio with raw oysters, the Atlantic sea bass cooked in clay, the lobster presented in its shell and the poached peach served with verveine sorbet and lavender cream enchant. The service is smiling. The only snag is the price.

● Le Millénaire ◎ V.COM

4-6, rue Bertin.
Tel. 03 26 08 26 62. Fax 03 26 84 24 13.
contact@lemillenaire.com
www.lemillenaire.com
Closed Sat. lunch, Sun.
Prix fixe: 27€ (exc. Sat. dinner), 42€, 68€.
A la carte: 95€.

This beautiful town center house oozes charm. Its two rooms, one modern and the other classic, delight its devotees. The same harmony is assured in Laurent Laplaige's cooking with its sure combinations and lively preparation. The fine rouget, parmesan and tomato tart, the John Dory cooked in olive oil and served with artichokes in a peppery vinaigrette and the veal piccata with an herb-seasoned risotto testify to a great respect for the beautiful produce from the sea and the earth. On the sweet side, the chocolate and raspberry croquant, served with strawberry sauce and nougat ice cream, delights. The waiters are efficient and the menus balanced. The only false note: increased à la carte prices.

● Le Chardonnay

184, av d'Epernay.
Tel. 03 26 06 08 60. Fax 03 26 05 81 56.
restaurant.lechardonnay@wanadoo.fr
Closed Sat. lunch, Sun. dinner, Mon.
Prix fixe: 26€, 35€, 66€, 10€ (child).
A la carte: 65€.

Brother and sister Dave and Audrey Palardelle have taken over this establishment, which had its moment of glory during the time of the Boyers. In the kitchen, Vincent Fraipon carries on the tradition, not without his own ideas. The simple house-prepared foie gras, scallops with local wine sauce and an old-fashioned blanquette de veau are classics reworked with dexterity. The rich chocolate cake served hot with white chocolate ice cream is an easy pleaser. The service is efficient, wine list intelligently created and the bill stays within the realm of the reasonable.

● Le Petit Comptoir   ○ COM

17, rue de Mars.
Tel. 03 26 40 58 58. Fax 03 26 47 26 19.
au.petit.comptoir@wanadoo.fr
www.au-petit-comptoir.com
Closed Sun., Mon., 2 weeks Christmas–New
Year's, 3 weeks Aug.
Prix fixe: 15€ (lunch), 29€, 37€.
A la carte: 45–55€.

Fabrice Maillot, who has left his Jardin des Arts in Marrakesh, now has both feet in his all-wood designer bistro with its white armchairs. One eats here from the special menu of two or three courses. The price? The lunch menu is 15 with main course and dessert plus a glass of wine and coffee. On the day we went, boeuf bourguignon and rich puff pastry cakes filled with almond- and rum-flavored cream were on offer. A coriander-seasoned razor clam fricassée, grilled jumbo shrimp and vegetable stir-fry, the hen stuffed with veal sausage and simmered in bouillon and the "famous" soft-centered chocolate cake with egg custard sauce and vanilla ice cream are of great quality. Low prices, attentive service and debonair atmosphere take care of the rest.

● Brasserie Flo   COM

96, pl Drouet-d'Erlon.
Tel. 03 26 91 40 50. Fax 03 26 91 40 54.
idarocha@groupeflo.fr / www.floreims.com
Prix fixe: 22,50€, 29,50€, 13€ (child).
A la carte: 45€.

We love the neo-art deco setting of this former army officers' bolt hole that now has a chic, relaxed feel. The food is in tune: duck foie gras, seafood platter, monkfish simmered in cocotte, veal rump steak and crêpes flambéed in Grand Marnier are examples of reworked classics. Excellent service and reasonable prices.

● La Vigneraie   COM

14, rue de Thillois.
Tel. 03 26 88 67 27. Fax 03 26 40 26 67.
lavigneraie@wanadoo.fr / www.vigneraie.com
Closed Sun. dinner, Mon., Wed. lunch,
Feb. vac., 1 week at end July, 3 weeks Aug.
Prix fixe: 16€ (weekday lunch), 23€ (week-

day lunch), 30€, 41€, 51€, 62€,
10€ (child). A la carte: 61–66€.

The setting is warm, the tables elegantly set and the smile of Marie-Agnès Badier an invitation to enjoy a good time. The same goes for her husband Hervé's cooking. The food is prettily decorated and the classic dishes meticulously executed. Shellfish spring rolls with guacamole, a fennel-seasoned foie gras escalope served hot, a half pigeon served Wellington style in a pastry crust and the berry tiramisu are well conceived. Good menus for every budget.

■ ● Bistro Henri IV   Ⓝ SIM

29, rue Henri IV.
Tel. 03 26 47 56 22.
Closed dinner, Sun., Mon.
Prix fixe: 14€. A la carte: 30€.

Carole Leperre and Gérard Debant have taken over this relaxed bistro very near the Boulingrin markets. Former antique dealers who have now cheerfully changed direction, he serves generous helpings of Delas Viogner at the bar, she cooks with great joy. Escargots, head cheese pâté, terrine, tripe and tête de veau, plus seasonal dishes, are found on the chalkboard menu. All go down well.

● Le Boulingrin   🔒 SIM

48, rue de Mars.
Tel. 03 26 40 96 22. Fax 03 26 40 03 92.
boulingrin@wanadoo.fr / www.boulingrin.fr
Closed Sun., Christmas, New Year's.
Prix fixe: 17,50€, 24€.
A la carte: 35–40€.

We have a real love for Bernard Victor-Pujebe's art deco brasserie with its wine frescoes, its benches and its atmosphere. On the cuisine side, carpaccio, marinated goat cheese, salmon with béarnaise sauce and veal kidneys with mushrooms are the embodiment of serious cooking.

● Les Charmes   SIM

11, rue Brûlart.
Tel. 03 26 85 37 63. Fax 03 26 36 21 00.
www.restaurantlescharmes.fr
Closed Sat. lunch, Sun., Mon., 3 days beg.

Jan., Easter vac., end July–mid-Aug.
Prix fixe: 14,50€ (lunch), 24€, 29,50€, 33€.

Sylvie gives a polished welcome, with Jacques' cooking to match. In short, you need have no worries with the Goyeuxs. The duck foie gras plate which includes a slice of an autumn fruit terrine, lightly smoked salmon filet with truffle-seasoned tagliatelli and the field rabbit sausage with apples look great, before the ritual house profiteroles with pistachio ice cream and hot fudge sauce.

● **Chez Paul** SIM

9-13, rue Gambetta.
Tel. 03 26 47 22 00. Fax 03 26 47 22 43.
Closed Sun., Mon. dinner, Tue. dinner.
Prix fixe: 13€ (lunch, wine inc.),
16€ (lunch, wine inc.). A la carte: 40€.

Paul Monteil runs this modern bistro, all done up in black and rose, with energy, offering an unstudied chic cuisine for today's taste. Pork trotter terrine, a Tatin-style tomato and basil tart, veal kidneys and the simple chocolate soup with vanilla ice cream make unaffected eating.

In Montchenot (51500). 11 km via N51.

● **Le Grand Cerf** ○ V.COM

50, rte Nationale.
Tel. 03 26 97 60 07. Fax 03 26 97 64 24.
www.le-grand-cerf.fr
Closed Sun. dinner, Tue. dinner, Wed.,
2 weeks Feb. vac., 3 weeks Aug.
Prix fixe: 34€ (weekdays), 58€, 72€, 88€,
15€ (child). A la carte: 110€.

On the way to the Mont de Reims, Dominique Giraudeau's refined restaurant always makes a good impression. Luxurious surroundings, meticulous service and cooking to match: everything works wonderfully. One does well with a well-stocked cellar, particularly for champagnes, and cooking that never strikes a false note. Breton lobster with sweet-and-sour vinaigrette, roasted rockfish with verjus sauce, veal sweetbreads with chanterelles and a berry puff pastry dessert are reminders of how good the classic can be.

In Tinqueux (51430). 6 km via A4.

● **L'Assiette Champenoise** ○ LUX

40, av Paul-Vaillant-Couturier.
Tel. 03 26 84 64 64. Fax 03 26 04 15 69.
www.assiettechampenoise.com
Closed Tue., Wed., Christmas, Feb. vac.
Prix fixe: 140€, 120€. A la carte: 130€.

Apart from the charm of an elegant dining room opening onto the grounds, the food of this former disciple of Alain Chapel and Michel Guérard plays with fashion, not without success. Variations on the theme of the artichoke served with fresh sweet peas, sole with crosnes (an heirloom root vegetable), slow-cooked chanterelles and salsify and a local farm-raised pigeon tourte with ventreche and spring spinach are pretty things that sometimes pull in opposite directions. Then come the cheeses of Philippe Olivier and the themed desserts (a thin Tagada strawberry candy tart and fruits presented in a variety of textures and flavors). The cellar created by Frédéric Bouché sings the praises of champagne, among other wines.

REIPERTSWILLER

67340 Bas-Rhin. Strasbourg 56 – Bitche 21
– Saverne 35 – Haguenau 34.
A town surrounded by forest in the heart of north Vosges, this is a stop for walkers, sportspeople and hunters.

◨ HOTELS-RESTAURANTS

■ **La Couronne**

13, rue de Wimmenau.
Tel. 03 88 89 96 21. Fax 03 88 89 98 22.
sb.kuhm@wanadoo.fr
www.hotel-la-couronne.com
Closed 2 weeks Nov., mid-Feb.–beg. Mar.
Rest. closed Mon., Tue.
16 rooms: 47–60€.
Prix fixe: 18€ (weekday lunch),
28€ (weekday lunch), 37€, 49€.

This modern house on the edge of the forest offers a rural, comfortable setting. The rooms are spic and span, the welcome from Sylvie warm and Bernard Kuhm's cooking gives priority to produce in season without neglecting the regional aspect. House head cheese and wine aspic terrine, foie gras served two ways, pike-perch with morels and celery root purée and veal kidneys served with mustard are accompanied by well-chosen regional wines.

REMIREMONT

88200 Vosges. Paris 412 – Epinal 27 – Belfort 71 – Colmar 80 – Mulhouse 82 – Vesoul 67.
tourisme.remiremont@wanadoo.fr.
Canonnesses gave this old town its focal interest. Don't miss the crypt of the St-Pierre abbey.

● | RESTAURANTS

● Clos Heurtebise `COM`

13, chemin des Capucins.
Tel. 03 29 62 08 04. Fax 03 29 62 38 80.
Closed Sun. dinner, Mon., 2 weeks beg. Jan.
Prix fixe: 18€ (weekdays), 27,50€, 33€, 42€, 60€, 10€ (child). A la carte: 58€.

Ludovic Léné has managed to impose his style in this neo-Provençal enclave. A purple onion and escargot tart, pan-seared foie gras with balsamic vinegar, seared and baked rouget served with mild garlic-seasoned potatoes, simply cooked cod with a foamy coffee-seasoned cream sauce, rabbit saddle in a spicy crust and the kidney bonbons with slow-cooked carrots and a sauce incorporating local blueberries give a Southern treatment to Vosges cuisine.

● La Quarterelle `COM`

3, rue de la Carterelle.
Tel. 03 29 23 98 69.
Closed Tue. dinner, Wed.
Prix fixe: 17€, 19€, 22€, 25€.
A la carte: 33€.

Florence Odille and Christian Pethe both run this exotic establishment, with its Asian feel and ochre shades. From a childhood spent in the Far East, Christian has retained a taste for sweet-and-sour and for spices. Haddock pastilla with apples, figs

and saffron jus, pan-fried cod with vanilla sauce, tête de veau tagine with ginger, pork ribs glazed with maple syrup sauce and a crisp soy-seasoned pastry, chestnut paste and vanilla-seasoned sweet potato dessert give a notion of this lightly handled fusion cooking.

In Dommartin-lès-Remiremont (88200). 5 km se via D23.

● Karélien `COM`

36, rue du Cuchot.
Tel. 03 29 62 44 05. Fax 03 29 62 22 47.
Closed Sun. dinner, Mon., 2 weeks Jan., mid-July–mid-Aug.
Prix fixe: 17€ (weekday lunch), 25€, 32€, 45€.

Fabrice and Laurence Devriese have cheerfully taken over this friendly establishment that is being renovated at a gentle pace. The cream and brown tones are restful, the food pleasantly regional while incoporating elements from elsewhere and the prices remain reasonable. Eel and smoked trout terrine in aspic with horseradish, grilled salmon with slow-cooked leeks, chitterling sausage and potato layered casserole and pork trotters with sausage and mustard sauce on toast set a casual chic note that we much enjoyed. Breton shortbread with pineapple marmalade and yogurt sorbet with Grand Marnier sauce make a delicate end to the meal.

In Saint-Etienne-lès-Remiremont (88200). 2 km ne via D417.

● Le Chalet Blanc `COM`

34, rue des Pêcheurs.
Tel. 03 29 26 11 80. Fax 03 29 26 11 81.
www.lechaletblanc.com
Closed Sun. dinner, 2 weeks Aug.
Rest. closed Sat. lunch, Mon.
5 rooms: 52–66€. 2 suites: 66–75€.
Prix fixe: 20€ (weekday lunch), 29€ (Sat., Sun. lunch), 51€, 65€, 13€ (child).

Nelly and Joël Lejeune have made their chalet at the foot of the Vosges mountains an ideal place to stay. The setting is calm, the walking plentiful and, when one gets back, Joël's cooking comforting. Pan-tossed langoustines in salad with poppy seeds, fresh duck foie gras in apple and grape gelatin and the veal sweetbreads with wild mushrooms are skillfully executed. The rooms are simple and the prices uninflated, if one keeps to the special menus.

RENNES

35000 Ille-et-Vilaine. Paris 349 – Angers 128 – Brest 245 – Caen 182 – Le Mans 154 – Nantes 109.
infos@tourisme-rennes.com.

Is the statement that Rennes is Breton a truism? On the contrary, the town, which houses the old parliament of the duchy of Brittany, governs from a distance a region whose language it no longer speaks, or only at university level. Its Breton character is nonetheless present everywhere: in the facade of its stone and wood houses, in the beams, the half timbers, the winding alleyways of the old town, where one can gaze into the windows of its gastronomic shops or in the arches of its ancient marketplace. The sea is of course elsewhere but not so far and on its mind, Rennes being the place that offers the best of the St-Malo fishing catches in its attractive restaurants. Kouign-amann and lace crêpes also want to have their delicious say.

■   HOTELS

■ Mercure-Colombier

1, rue du Capitaine-Maignan.
Tel. 02 99 29 73 73. Fax 02 99 29 54 00.
h1249@accor.com / www.accor.com
140 rooms: 107–119€. 2 suites: 200€.
A la carte: 25–30€.

Near the station and decorated on the theme of the forest of Brocéliande, functional rooms and a restaurant (the Excalibur) that is worth a stop.

■ Novotel

Av du Canada.
Tel. 02 99 86 14 14. Fax 02 99 86 14 15.
h0430@accor-hotels.com / www.novotel.com
Open daily. Rest. closed weekends (winter).
100 rooms: 96,50€.

At the edge of the Bréquigny park, this hotel offers an outside swimming pool, a restaurant—Côté Jardin—in which an honest local cuisine is served as well as practical, well-sound-proofed rooms.

● Le Coq-Gadby

156, rue d'Antrain.
Tel. 02 99 38 05 55. Fax 02 99 38 53 40.
lecoq-gadby@wanadoo.fr / www.lecoq-gadby.com
Rest. closed Sun., Mon., 2 weeks Aug.
12 rooms: 118–165€. 2 suites: 265–305€.
Prix fixe: 33€ (weekday lunch), 48€, 20€ (child).

This member of Châteaux et Hôtels de France that was a former meeting place for Dreyfus supporters houses extremely comfortable Louis XV and Louis XVI rooms. The garden, the spa, the beauty salon and the health center complete this establishment under the direction of the dynamic Véronique. In the Coquerie restaurant, Marc Tizon, who used to be the talk of the town at Palais, has come back to the region after a detour at Baumanière's in Baux-de-Provence and now offers skillful regional cooking. We liked shredded crab with sundried tomatoes, Atlantic sea bass with lemon chutney, veal sweetbreads in cocotte and a fine vanilla macaron served with chocolate sorbet. An address that is now worth the detour, for its charm as well as its gastronomy.

■ Hôtel Nemours

5, rue de Nemours.
Tel. 02 99 78 26 26. Fax 02 99 78 25 40.
resa@hotelnemours.com
www.hotelnemours.com
29 rooms: 53–130€.

This is the successful renovation that everyone is talking about. Charming rooms in a contemporary style in the heart of the town, flat screen TVs, restrained furnishings and a personalized welcome give the tone of an establishment that is in vogue.

■ Anne de Bretagne

12, rue Tronjolly.
Tel. 02 99 31 49 49. Fax 02 99 30 53 48.

www.hotel-rennes.com
Closed Christmas–New Year's.
42 rooms: 83–98€.

Don't be fooled by the bland exterior—the place is warm. First the welcome, then the bar and finally the rooms decorated in contemporary style.

■ Mercure Pré Botté

Rue Paul-Louis-Courier.
Tel. 02 99 78 82 20. Fax 02 99 78 82 21.
h1056@accor-hotels.com / www.mercure.com
Closed Christmas–New Year's.
104 rooms: 105–139€. 2 suites: 150€.

The former printing plant of the daily newspaper Ouest-France is now a hotel with modern decorations and imprinted with the history of the site. In a quiet street in the town center, it offers, at a reasonable price, practical, if not very large, rooms.

■ Mercure Place de Bretagne

6, rue LanJuneais.
Tel. 02 99 79 12 36. Fax 02 99 79 65 76.
h2027@accor.com / www.accor.com
48 rooms: 66–132€.

Next to the station in the business area and near the Beaux-Arts museum, this is a quality establishment. The rooms are modern and practical.

In Cesson-Sévigné (35510). 6 km via D177.

■ Germinal

9, cours de la Vilaine.
Tel. 02 99 83 11 01. Fax 02 99 83 45 16.
le-germinal@wanadoo.fr / www.legerminal.com
Closed Christmas–New Year's vac.
Rest. closed Sun.
9 rooms: 65–95€.
Prix fixe: 19€ (lunch), 23€ (lunch, wine inc.), 27€, 33€, 45€. A la carte: 50–66€.

The old village mill, converted into a hotel by the Goualin family, has distinction. The balconies of the rooms look out over the Vilaine and the stone bridge. Mikaël Fenot's cooking revisits tradition with its roasted langoustines with pepper and glazed vegetables, Atlantic sea bass with zucchini risotto, veal sweet-

breads braised in Vin Jaune and a fruit cocktail with lemon-infused oil. A pleasant stop-off.

● RESTAURANTS

● L'Escu de Runfao

11, rue du Chapitre.
Tel. 02 99 79 13 10. Fax 02 99 79 43 80.
escuderunfao@wanadoo.fr
www.escu-de-runfao.com
Closed Sat. lunch, Sun. dinner (all day in Aug.), Feb. vac., 3 weeks Aug.
Prix fixe: 28€ (weekdays), 41€, 54€, 87€.
A la carte: 80€.

In the heart of old Rennes, this 17th-century house has aged without wrinkles. The welcome given by Nathalie Duhoux is as charming as ever it was and the culinary skills of her husband Alain as powerfully seductive. In the latter's hands, produce from both sea and land take on Southern flavors. On the plate, this becomes langoustine and asparagus risotto, roasted turbot with summer truffles, lemongrass- and ginger-seasoned veal sweetbreads and roasted peaches in syrup with almond milk ice cream. The wines selected by François Lemercier reassure, as does the service.

● La Fontaine aux Perles

96, rue de la Poterie.
Tel. 02 99 53 90 90. Fax 02 99 53 47 77.
restaurant@lafontaineauxperles.com
www.lafontaineauxperles.com
Closed Sun. dinner (all day Aug.), Mon.
Prix fixe: 20€ (weekday lunch), 25€ (weekday lunch), 32€, 40€, 60€, 75€.
A la carte: 80€.

Several minutes from the center, Rachel Gesbert's manor house is surrounded by greenery. On the terrace, which gives onto the garden, or the dining room with its refined décor, the menu offers tempting choices. One is quickly won over by veal sweetbread and foie gras mimosas with langoustines, John Dory with spices and shredded mango, a catfish cake served with cold slices of chitterling sausage, beef tenderloin served in a crêpe and seasoned with local cider and the three-chocolate plate. Before that, one will have tasted the delicious cheeses made with unpasteurized milk matured by Yves Bordier and found, to accompany this gentle feast, the perfect wine thanks to the advice of Guillaume Nedelec and Julien Ezanic. The service is lively and the check worth the culinary performance.

● **L'Ouvrée** N 🛈 V.COM

18, place des Lices.
Tel.-Fax 02 99 30 16 38.
restaurantlouvree@wanadoo.fr
www.louvree.com
Closed Sat. lunch, Sun. dinner, Mon.,
Easter vac., beg. Aug.–mid-Aug.
Prix fixe: 14,50€, 21,50€, 32€.

Get your eyes and taste buds ready: this house dating from 1659 has a dining room exquisitely decorated in champagne and cherry, where the cooking of Gérard Jéhannin enchants. The owner Joël Langlais advises on which of the 150 wines on the list goes best with shellfish cassolettes with langoustine sauce, roasted salmon with tandoori spices, thyme-seasoned roasted lamb shoulder and, for dessert, the Breton shortbread with strawberries and a lychee sorbet.

● **Auberge Saint-Sauveur** 🛈 V.COM

6, rue Saint-Sauveur.
Tel. 02 99 79 32 56. Fax 02 99 78 27 93.
Closed Sat. lunch, Sun. lunch, Mon. lunch,
2 weeks Apr., 3 weeks Aug.
Prix fixe: 12€, 15€, 18,50€, 27,50€.
A la carte: 30–40€.

Chantal Lamagnère receives a demanding clientele in this neatly decorated former canon's house. She goes out of her way to win you over with the excellence of Jean-François Guinard's cooking. Sardines baked with potatoes, scallops with a vermouth cream sauce, pollock with wilted sorrel, turbot filet with saffron sauce and the acacia honey-seasoned magret de canard are extremely well regarded. Beautiful Tatin and selected wines.

● **Au Four à Ban** 📷 COM

4, rue Saint-Mélaine.
Tel. 02 99 38 72 85. Fax 02 99 63 19 44.
fouraban@wanadoo.fr / www.lefouraban.com
Closed Sat. lunch, Sun., Mon. dinner,
1 week at end July, 2 weeks beg. Aug.
Prix fixe: 19€ (lunch), 25€, 38€, 50€.

Beside the 18th-century oven, Anne and Jacques Faby run a promising market restaurant. The dining room has been entirely renovated on a contemporary theme and offers fresh dishes inspired by the seasons. Formerly of Château de Divonne under Guy Martin and of Juana under Alain Ducasse, Jacques knows the ropes and there is nothing but good to say about lobster and veal sweetbreads in salad, line-fished Atlantic sea bass with red onion jus, roasted pigeon with bite-sized dates and a salted-butter caramel mousse accompanied by fine bottles of wine. Reasonably priced special menus.

● **L'Appart' de Loïc** N COM

67 ter, bd de la Tour-d'Auvergne.
Tel. 02 99 67 03 04.
Closed Sat. lunch, Sun., Mon. dinner,
1 week Christmas–New Year's, Feb. vac.,
3 weeks Aug.
Prix fixe: 18€ (weekday lunch), 28€.

In his contemporary, light-filled loft, Loïc Pasco produces a clever and spirited cuisine. The crab in filo pastry with cauliflower and vinaigrette, Erquy scallops with lentils in a mussel emulsion, country pork ribs with carrots and chestnuts and the chocolate tart swing successfully between tradition and modernity.

● **Le Galopin** N COM

21, avenue Janvier.
Tel. 02 99 31 55 96. Fax 02 99 31 08 95.
legalopin@club-internet.fr / www.legalopin.com
Closed Sat. lunch, Sun., 1 May.
Prix fixe: 17€, 22€, 30€, 45€.
A la carte: 55€.

This luxury brasserie near the station attracts the Rennes smart set with its prompt service and traditional dishes. Olivier Le Denmat, who has taken over his parents' business, has managed to modernize the place while placing his confidence in the same chef, the reliable Sébastien Guihard. In a chic décor of wood and brass, one settles down to Cancale oysters, sole meunière, veal escalope Viennoise, veal kidneys in a Madeira sauce, hot kouign-amann or the exquisite crème brûlée. Rich choice of Loire wines.

● Le Pichet ⓃCOM
17, bd Laval.
Tel. 02 99 75 24 09. Fax 02 99 75 81 50.
le.pichet@laposte.net / www.lepichet.fr
Closed Sun., Wed. dinner, Thu. dinner,
3 weeks Aug.
Prix fixe: 17,50€ (weekday lunch), 24€,
33€, 43€, 10,50€ (child). A la carte: 45€.

The terrace for summer dining right at the edge of the garden and the large chimney for cooler weather set the tone of Anthony Fouchet's establishment. Crab and potatoes, wild Atlantic sea bass with caramelized spinach, oven-roasted rouget with crispy vegetables are examples of an extremely well-mastered seafood cuisine. A mara des bois strawberry tart with verbena panna cotta makes a choice end to the meal.

● Le Puits des Saveurs ⓃCOM
262, rue Chateaugiron.
Tel. 02 99 53 18 14. Fax 02 99 53 16 45.
Closed Sat. dinner, Sun., 1 week at end July,
3 weeks Aug.
Prix fixe: 31€, 34€, 42€, 52€,
13,50€ (child). A la carte: 53–60€.

Throw yourself uninhibitedly into this bistro-lounge in shades of yellow, decorated with exotic woods, glass and zinc. Pascal Jouzel, who was a Relais & Châteaux chef for seventeen years, issues invitations to inventive feasts. Plunge your spoon into pumpkin and scallop mille-feuille soup, pike-perch medallions with Anjou rouge and lightly spiced squab with veal sweetbreads. For dessert, the chocolate plate and pear pudding are mouthwatering.

● Le Piano Blanc COM
315, rte de Sainte-Foix.
Tel. 02 99 31 20 21. Fax 02 99 31 87 58.
le.piano.blanc@wanadoo.fr
www.lepianoblanc.fr
Closed Sat. lunch, Sun.
Prix fixe: 14€ (weekday lunch), 24€, 35€,
12€ (child). A la carte: 55€.

Jérôme Leroy has made this lively restaurant, near the training ground of Rennes football club, into a gastronomic and friendly haunt. The teak terrace, the refined setting and the glassed-in cellar that one can see into from the dining room all create a wonderful effect. Added to this is the cuisine of Jean-Baptiste Adam, originating from Lorraine and with all the Breton qualities, who successfully produces lively dishes that manage to be both rustic and sophisticated. The crab tartare, scallops with pork trotters, monkfish medallion with caramelized pears and a raspberry tiramisu all look very pleasing.

● Le Petit Sabayon Ⓝ🍴SIM
16, rue des Trente.
Tel. 02 99 35 02 04.
lepetitsabayon@free.fr
Closed Sat. lunch, Sun. dinner, Mon.,
2 weeks Feb., 2 weeks beg. Sept.
Prix fixe: 15€ (lunch, weekdays), 23€, 30€.

If you have managed to discover this exclusive yet warm place, think of reserving a table because places are limited. The Tetrels serve well-conceived dishes such as a cep and Cantal tart, sea bream with shellfish jus and a guinea hen breast with walnuts. At the dessert stage, the gastronomy of yesteryear is revisited with a quince and cardamom tarte Tatin with salted-butter caramel. The menus vary with the seasons but the pleasure remains constant.

● Les Quatre B Ⓝ🍴SIM
4, pl de Bretagne.
Tel.-Fax 02 99 30 42 01.
quatreb@wanadoo.fr
www.restaurantquatreb.com
Closed Sat. lunch, Sun., Mon. lunch.
Prix fixe: 13€ (lunch, wine inc.), 18€,
23,50€, 28€. A la carte: 36–45€.

Bernard Anfray has given over his establishment to his daughter Angéline who has redecorated the place in subtle shades of red, white and gray. At lunchtime it is more of a bistro and at night more refined. In both cases one should try out the cooking of Samuel, who plays skillfully with fashionable ingredients. The red tuna tartare, foie gras with fig chutney, Atlantic sea bass simply prepared with pan-sizzled leeks, veal sweetbreads with morels and a caramel dessert with Salidoux salted-butter caramel ice cream are not to be missed. Generous wine list and gentle prices make one want to be a regular here.

● L'Arsouille ● SIM

17, rue Paul-Bert.
Tel. 02 99 38 11 10.
Closed Sun., Mon.
A la carte: 38€.

At Christophe Gauchet's establishment there are no airs and graces and one is among friends. The atmosphere of this fifties-style faux-café is festive and the cooking prepared as it would be at home. One can enjoy duck terrine with hazelnuts, escargots in parsleyed butter and Bleu d'Auvergne cheese, salted cod with green beans from Madame Cordonnier's garden, beef cheeks with trumpet mushrooms, yellow Chatreuse crème brûlée and pear poached in spiced red wine served with fluffy brioche is also not bad. Good "natural" wines.

● Bistro Marc Angelle ● SIM

38, av du Mail.
Tel. 02 99 54 30 12.
marcangelle@aol.com
Closed Sun., Mon. dinner, Bank holidays.
Prix fixe: 21€ (lunch), 33€ (dinner).

Marc Angelle's traditional bistro gets right down to what matters: completely fresh cooking, reasonably priced. Chitterling sausage tartelette with apples, turbot with seasonal baby vegetables, veal cutlet with Cantal cheese and a berry gratin served with raspberry sorbet make up the gastronomic special menus. The lack of comfort fades into insignificance.

● Léon le Cochon ● SIM

1, rue du Maréchal-Joffre.
Tel. 02 99 79 37 54. Fax 02 99 79 07 35.
Closed Sun. (exc. off season).
Prix fixe: 12,50€. A la carte: 30€.

The décor has been reworked in the style of a country inn and Johnny Pottigan is now alone in the kitchen while Yann Paigier, formerly of l'Arpège with Alain Passard, is still at the helm. The dishes are simple and good: classic oeuf en cocotte, grilled red tuna, sausage with apples and the pain perdu with thyme honey and a seasonal berry jelly. Good selection of wines.

● La Chope ● SIM

3, rue de la Chalotais.
Tel. 02 99 79 34 54. Fax 02 99 79 42 20.
brasserie.lachope@laposte.net
Closed Sun.
Prix fixe: 11€, 14€, 7€ (child).
A la carte: 35–45€.

Olivier Le Garo has taken over this thirties brasserie—in which the jurors of the high school Goncourt prize used to meet—without changing its spirit. Many touring artists and writers a little the worse for drink would meet here after shows, conferences and signings to make short work of the house foie gras, scallop and potato casserole, pork shank choucroute, peppered sirloin steak and the profiteroles

● Bistro du Luguen ● SIM

39, rue de Paris.
Tel. 02 99 36 82 65. Fax 02 99 34 11 09.
luguen@wanadoo.fr
www.bistro-du-luguen.com
Closed Sun., Mon., Aug.
A la carte: 40€.

In this pleasant dining room with its bare stone walls, Christophe Lelièvre gives a heartfelt welcome while one gets down to serious home cooking without ruining one's pocket: the duck terrine with mushrooms, eel medallions with potatoes and a rich chocolate cake are very tempting.

● A la Bonne Franquette N SIM

116, allée Saint-Hélier.
Tel.-Fax 02 23 42 19 75.
Closed dinner, Sat., Sun., 2 weeks Aug.
Prix fixe: 14€ (lunch), 18€. A la carte: 32€.

This was a railway workers' bistro near the freight station. Alain Grizard has made it into a sweet little center of gastronomy and delights his customers with menus that change daily: pumpkin and mussel soup, Lyonnais-style beef tongue salad, Bigoudin chitterling sausage with Réblochon potato purée, pan-seared red tuna, country-style pork ribs with potatoes and an iced mango soup with passion fruit. You go to collect your bottle of wine in the cellar. The food is fresh, well conceived and almost given away.

● Hao Yaki N SIM

37, rue Vasselot.
Tel. 02 99 79 05 91.
Closed Sun. lunch, Christmas.
Prix fixe: 9€, 18€, 14,50€, 19,50€.
A la carte: 25–30€.

Japanese through and through, this Zen bistro is worth the detour for its fresh cooking, its sincere welcome and its low prices. Miso soup, sushi, maki, chicken yakitori and pearl tapioca washed down with Kirin or Asahi beer.

● Paris-New York N SIM

276, rue de Fougères.
Tel.-Fax 02 23 21 15 71.
Closed Sat. lunch, Sun., 10 days beg. May, 2 weeks Aug.
Prix fixe: 15€ (weekdays), 22€, 29,50€, 10€ (child). A la carte: 40€.

Karine Brunet gives an enthusiastic welcome to this adventurous restaurant while Frédéric Barbier creates quality fusion dishes with great skill. An escargot fricassée in open ravioli with a smoked-garlic emulsion, pan-seared foie gras with beet and apple chutney and a veal and Marsala "rizotte" with Guinée pepper make a good impression. The parmesan shortbread and a roasted-banana shortbread with pepper coconut sorbet are truly gastronomic.

● La Réserve N SIM

36, rue de la Visitation.
Tel. 02 99 84 02 02.
Closed Sun., Mon.
Prix fixe: 15€ (lunch), 25€, 29,50€.

Sébastien Blot, formerly of the restaurant at the Fontaine aux Perles, has opened this young, lively, good-natured, wooden and airy bistro that feels like a craftsman's workshop. Here you will find the dishes written up on slate boards and clever menus. Foie gras served in a jar with fig chutney, shellfish in broth, roasted fennel-seasoned sea bream with bacon risotto, pork tenderloin wrapped in bacon and bathed in spicy sauce and the salted-butter caramel dessert slip down as easily as a letter into the mailbox.

● Le Tire-Bouchon N SIM

2, rue du Chapitre.
Tel. 02 99 79 43 43.
Closed Sat., Sun., Bank holidays, Feb. vac., 3 weeks Aug.
A la carte: 30€.

In the town's historic center, this thirties brasserie in a listed building continues to attract lovers of bistro classics such as mackerel spread, scallops in their shell with celery root purée, seven-hour lamb and rice pudding.

● L'Atelier des Gourmets SIM

12, rue Nantaise.
Tel.-Fax 02 99 67 53 84.
Closed Sun., Mon., 3 weeks Aug.
Prix fixe: 12€ (weekday lunch, wine inc.), 15€ (weekday lunch), 18€ (weekday lunch), 24€ (dinner), 25€ (dinner), 31€ (dinner).
A la carte: 30€.

Chef André Loyer and head waiter Pascal Régeard both run this good restaurant with its wine-colored and golden décor. Here one enjoys, without fuss, a tempting foie gras terrine, Atlantic sea bass with salsify, slow-cooked lamb in cocotte and coconut and passion fruit truffles. Reasonable prices.

● **Le Café Breton** SIM

14, rue Nantaise.
Tel. 02 99 30 74 95.
Closed Sat. dinner, Sun., Mon. dinner,
2 weeks Aug.
A la carte: 30€.

Karinne Thomas has taken over this "Parisian postcard" bistro where one enjoys the latest trend in Breton dishes. The young Frédéric Niel offers skillfully prepared oven-crisped chitterling sausage with thyme-seasoned potatoes, roasted Atlantic sea bass with fleur de sel and simmered vegetables, a lamb fricassée with sundried tomatoes served over coriander-seasoned tabouli and peach gazpacho with lime. Several good wines by the glass.

● **Le Comptoir des Halles** SIM

17, rue Jules-Simon.
Tel. 02 99 78 20 07. Fax 02 99 79 19 15.
www.lecomptoirdeshalles.com
Closed Sun.
Prix fixe: 30€. A la carte: 38€.

Christophe Boisselier and Yann Peiger ply their skillful culinary trade opposite the marketplace, under the lead of chef Christian Solary. Mackerel terrine with sundried tomatoes, grilled tuna steak, pasta with lobster with parmesan shavings and the oven-baked sausage with potatoes make a good impression. The chocolate volcano with lavender ice cream is a gastronomic delight.

● **La Saint-Georges** SIM

31, rue Saint-Georges.
Tel. 02 99 38 87 04.
www.creperie-saintgeorges.com
Closed Sun., Mon.
Prix fixe: 7,50€. A la carte: 20€.

Pascale and Olivier Kozyk have made this modern *crêperie* into an enjoyable, fresh place. Their famous savory buckwheat crêpes made in commemoration of George are amusing. The Clemenceau (with Camembert) and the Segal (with slow-cooked leeks) are delicious.

In Cesson-Sévigné (35510). 6 km via D177.

● **Le Sarment de Vigne** ◼SIM

54, route des Fougères.
Tel.-Fax 02 99 62 00 13.
contact@lesarmentdevigne.com
www.lesarmentdevigne.com
Closed Sat. lunch, Sun. dinner, Mon.,
3 weeks Aug.
Prix fixe: 18€ (weekday lunch), 25€, 41€,
42€, 12,50€ (child). A la carte: 40€.

Don't stop to look at the exterior but come inside Yannick Olivier's restaurant. You will be delighted by the warm welcome and the finely prepared cuisine. Menus created according to the markets with tiny, exquisite and ultra-fresh details making all the difference: shelled crab, eggplant spread served on a warm tortilla, duck foie gras, Atlantic sea bass risotto, chorizo with tender rice, whiskey-flambéed lobster, a veal cutlet with grapes served in its own cooking dish and the grilled Breton-style chitterling sausage. As the cherry on top, the soft dark chocolate cake served warm with a sour cherry jus has us melting. A hundred wines from every region, a lovely terrace and astonishing quality-to-price ratio. This is guaranteed happiness.

In Chartres-de-Bretagne (35131). 7 km s.

● **La Braise** 🅝 COM

2, avenue de la Chaussairie.
Tel. 02 99 41 21 29. Fax 02 99 41 33 80.
Closed Sat. lunch, Sun. dinner, Mon. dinner,
Feb. vac., 2 weeks Aug.
Prix fixe: 15€, 20€, 40€, 60€.
A la carte: 50€.

Eric Adam's long, low house is comprised of three dining rooms: country-style with a chimney, maritime and burgundy. The owner-chef serves sun-filled home cooking along the lines of Serrano ham and magret de canard in salad, the catch of the day, roasted squab with mushrooms and an almond milk crème brûlée.

In Pacé (35740). 10 km w via N12.

● **La Griotte** 🅝 V.COM

Pont-de-Pacé, 42, rue du Docteur-Léon.
Tel. 02 99 60 15 15. Fax 02 99 60 26 84.

restolagriotte@wanadoo.fr
www.restaurantlagriotte.com
Closed Sun. dinner, Tue. dinner, Wed.,
10 days beg. Mar., 3 weeks Aug.
Prix fixe: 19€ (weekdays), 26€, 35€,
13€ (child). A la carte: 45€.

In the middle of its gardens, this quiet establishment continues to attract the Rennes smart set. In his modern restaurant, Michel Morand offers half-bourgeois, half-peasant cooking that is accompanied by an impressive wine list. A pork trotter and tongue in parsley and garlic, scallops in squid ink with chorizo, duck breast with honey-seasoned apples and its leg in salad and the pain d'épices and coffee millefeuille carry off all the votes.

In Noyal-sur-Vilaine (35530). 12 km via N157.

● **Auberge du Pont d'Acigné** Ⓞ|V.COM|
Le Pont.
Tel. 02 99 62 52 55. Fax 02 99 62 21 70.
Closed Sat. lunch, Sun. dinner, Mon.,
1 week beg. Jan., 3 weeks Aug.
Prix fixe: 24€ (weekday lunch), 32€, 35€
(weekday lunch), 49€. A la carte: 75€.

On the banks of the Vilaine, the Guillemot's mill has been completely redecorated year after year. The place is full of charm, from the welcome given by Marie-Pierre to the food created by her husband Sylvain. This student of Jacques Thorel and Alain Passard places quality produce to the fore and offers clean, fine dishes. His best recipes are oven-crisped sardines and pickled seaweed, pan-tossed ceps with a poultry liver infusion, rouget with Paimpol white beans, veal sweetbreads with rosemary, a local dessert specialty with a licorice jus and the waffle with fresh figs served with orange flower water ice cream. Good wine and sensible menus.

In Le Rheu (35260). 8 km via rte de Lorient, D224.

● **La Muse Bouche** 🔒SIM
Les Landes d'Apigné.
Tel. 02 99 14 60 14. Fax 02 99 14 60 03.
la.musebouche@laposte.fr
www.restaurant-la-muse-bouche.com

Closed Sun., 2 weeks beg. Aug.
Prix fixe: 10,50€ (lunch weekdays), 12,50€
(lunch weekdays), 16€ (lunch), 18€,
24,50€, 32€, 39€.

Several kilometers from the center, this house surrounded by garden with prettily dressed tables serves a reworked Breton domestic cuisine. Soizic Maréchal ensures a good time with sincere smiles and well-crafted dishes. Light crab and haddock spreads, roasted pollock with buckwheat couscous and vegetables, veal kidneys with mustard and a dark chocolate pastilla with dried fruits are offered at a gentle price, as at the Relais Fleuri, the auberge opposite that has modern and comfortable rooms (31–52).

In Saint-Grégoire (35760). 3 km n via D82.

● **Le Saison** Ⓞ|V.COM|
Impasse du Vieux-Bourg.
Tel. 02 99 68 79 35. Fax 02 99 68 92 71.
contact@le-saison.com
www.le-saison.com
Closed Sun. dinner, Mon., 3 weeks Aug.
Prix fixe: 23€ (weekday lunch), 34€, 46€,
62€. A la carte: 73€.

An adopted Rennais with a Breton heart, the Basque David Etcheverry welcomes you to his *longère*—the traditional French long house made of local materials—surrounded by greenery and with a redecorated, contemporary "Zen" interior. Both regionally inspired and modern, his cooking uses the best produce and doesn't hesitate to innovate with masterly confidence. One is surprised and seduced by foie gras with cherries, line-fished Atlantic sea bass with butter-braised New Zealand spinach, veal sweetbreads with roasted hazelnuts, soft-cooked artichokes and white chocolate and the buckwheat and cinnamon parfait with basil and sundried tomato confiture. The welcome, like the service, is brimming with both kindness and energy. Elsa Malette gives enthusiastic advice on wine.

RETHONDES see COMPIEGNE

REUILLY-SAUVIGNY

02850 Aisne. Paris 111 – Reims 49 –
Château-Thierry 16 – Epernay 34.
On the way to Champagne, the course of the
Marne valley and vineyards form a cat's back on
the hillside, opposite a village that is like those of
years ago. In autumn, the colors are poetic.

 HOTELS-RESTAURANTS

● Auberge Le Relais

2, rue de Paris.
Tel. 03 23 70 35 36. Fax 03 23 70 27 76.
auberge.relais.de.reuilly@wanadoo.fr
www.relaisreuilly.com
Closed Feb., 2 weeks Aug.
Rest. closed Tue., Wed.
7 rooms: 74–92€.
Prix fixe: 44€, 55€, 78€. A la carte: 80–110€.

Here one is right beside champagne vineyards, so close to Paris and yet already
in another world. Lyne and Martial Ber-
thuit do not in any way ignore the traditions of their beautiful wine-making
region but also know how to adapt them
to the best of modernity. This is true of the
decoration of the rooms and even more
so for Martial's cooking, where creativity is matched by the excellent quality of
produce. The creamy carrot soup with
langoustines, turbot in beurre blanc on
risotto with beurre blanc-seasoned yellow vegetables, spice-seasoned breast of
young duck and a warm waffle with raspberries and rose-flavored ice cream are
produced with a masterly hand. The à la
carte check is on a par with the chef's talent but the special menus have a very good
price-quality ratio.

REVEL

31250 Haute-Garonne. Paris 725 –
Carcassonne 45 – Castelnaudary 20 –
Castres 30 – Gaillac 60 – Toulouse 55.
This little capital of Lauragais, interesting for
its paved streets and its large market with its
huge structure, is known for wood crafting,
marquetry and antique reproductions.

 HOTELS-RESTAURANTS

■ Le Midi

34, bd Gambetta.
Tel. 05 61 83 50 50. Fax 05 61 83 34 74.
www.hotelrestaurantdumidi.com
Closed Sun. dinner (off season), Mon. lunch
(off season), 1 week Mar. (exc. hotel clients),
11 Nov.–beg. Dec. (exc. hotel clients).
17 rooms: 38–61€.
Prix fixe: 22,50€, 30€, 45€ (wine inc.),
10€ (child). A la carte: 50€.

This 19th-century coaching inn looking
out onto a busy avenue has pastel-colored
rooms; for peace and quiet, choose those
at the back. In the light-filled dining room,
the traditional food created by Bernard
Aymes holds its own, with examples such
as the slice of black pork ham with artichoke salad, rouget in a tapenade crust,
classic cassolette and an oven-crisped
fresh fruit dessert.

● Auberge des Mazies

3 km, rte de Castres.
Tel. 05 61 27 69 70. Fax 05 62 18 06 37.
bienvenue@mazies.com / www.mazies.com
Closed 3 weeks end Oct.–mid-Nov.,
Christmas–mid-Jan.
7 rooms: 52–57€.
Prix fixe: 13€ (lunch, weekdays), 16€, 48€.

One feels at ease in this auberge, a typical
old barn in the middle of fields, with white
walls, paneling and simple rooms. The
Garniers issue a warm invitation to stay
in a countryside atmosphere and to grills
prepared at the large open fire.

● Sucre et Sel

14, rue de Vaure.
Tel.-Fax 05 62 18 90 31.
regis.evenisse@wanadoo.fr
Closed Sun., Mon., Thu. dinner (exc. July–
Aug.), Feb. vac., 3 weeks Aug.
Prix fixe: 9€, 11€, 13€, 6€ (child).

In the region of Toulouse, the Breton *crêperie* of Régis and Bénédicte Evenisse
stands out. In the yellow restaurant, an
abundance of savory buckwheat crêpes

(smoked salmon with leeks, ground beef, ham, cheese, egg…) and the salted-butter caramel crêpes have no trouble finding takers.

In Saint-Ferréol (31250). 3 km se via D629.

■ **Hôtellerie du Lac**

Av Paul Riquet.
Tel. 05 62 18 70 80.
contact@hotellerie-du-lac.com
www.hotellerie-du-lac.com
Rest. closed Sun. dinner (exc. summer),
20 Dec.–mid-Jan. Closed 22 Dec.–15 Jan.
Prix fixe: 36€, 10€ (child).

St.Ferréol, an old walled town built in 1245 perched on its promontory, with a collegial church, a castle, a windmill, sloping houses, a half-timbered marketplace, a commandery and a belfry are worth the stop, which this 19th-century coaching inn in the middle of fields allows. A bucolic restaurant with its fireplace, local cuisine and simple rooms. Swimming pool and garden.

REVILLE

50760 Manche. Paris 351 – Carentan 44 – Cherbourg 30 – Valognes 22.
This sweet little Cotentin village is known for the legend of a famous monk and also for the character of Henry Viard, celebrated gastronomic chronicler, who has his eternal rest in the cemetery.

■ **HOTELS-RESTAURANTS**

■ **La Gervaiserie**

La Gervaiserie.
Tel. 02 33 54 54 64.
la.gervaiserie@wanadoo.fr
www.lagervaiserie.com
10 rooms: 85–110€.

Overlooking the beach, a comfortable stop-off with its modern rooms that are all provided with a terrace or balcony.

■ **Le Moyne de Saire**

Tel. 02 33 54 46 06. Fax 02 33 54 14 99.
au.moyne.de.saire@wanadoo.fr
www.au-moyne-de-saire.com

Closed end Oct.–10 Nov., Feb.
Rest. closed Wed. (off season).
12 rooms: 46–58€.
Prix fixe: 15,50€, 19,50€, 29€, 40€.

Stéphane Marguery cooks with great natural talent and Agnès gives a smiling welcome. Both run this good establishment, with its clean rooms and pure food, with great discretion. Hot oysters served on a bed of stuffing and bacon, cod filet with grilled Vire chitterling sausage, sea bream cooked skin-side down with zucchini and creamed fennel and pork chops with Contentin cream and fresh mushrooms pay distinctive homage to regional produce.

LE RHEU see RENNES

RHINAU

67860 Bas-Rhin. Paris 458 – Obernai 26 – Strasbourg 33.
Overlooking Germany and its dashing Europark, this village on the banks of the Rhine seems to be waiting for an eternal ferryboat. Its stylish auberge creates the link between two borders.

■ **HOTELS-RESTAURANTS**

■ **Aux Bords du Rhin**

10, rue du Rhin.
Tel. 03 88 74 60 36.
Fax 03 88 74 85 98/03 88 74 65 77.
Rest. closed Mon., Tue.
21 rooms: 34–41€.
Prix fixe: 24€, 30€, 8€ (child).
A la carte: 35–45€.

The ferry that crosses the Rhine leaves from just outside the house of the Bernas. The rooms are sweet, Gabrielle gives a kind welcome and Patrice cooks, with a sure hand, goose foie gras, frog legs with garlic and parsley, pike-perch served cooked in wine with noodles, sirloin steak with béarnaise sauce and a frozen meringue dessert with whipped cream. This is well-prepared classic cooking.

● **Au Vieux Couvent**

6, rue des Chanoines.
Tel. 03 88 74 61 15. Fax 03 88 74 89 19.
Closed Mon. dinner, Tue., Wed., 2 weeks
Feb., 3 weeks July.
Prix fixe: 35€, 82€. A la carte: 80–90€.

A stone's throw from the Rhine, the
Albrecht family continues the legend. A
family working together in harmony is a
joy they share with their guests. Jean the
poet—formerly an electrician, even if he
doesn't like to be reminded of it—enchants
with his roaming and unexpected cuisine,
playfully created with his son Alexis and
then passing through the hands of the
Pourcel brothers; this is an Alsatian synthesis of modernism and tradition. He
goes on "herb outings" to discover the
wild plants of the region that find expression in the dishes he develops. The star-
tlingly self-taught chef with the brilliance
of an old pro offers swordfish carpaccio
with balsamic vinegar and herbs, blue lobster with diced root vegetables and saffron
sauce, a slice of Rhin river eel caught by
Martin Thalgott served with a locally produced stuffed ravioli, veal sweetbreads pan
tossed and served with parsley and sorrel
risotto. Everything delights. But the best
is kept for the end, when the magicians of
the ovens reveal their festival of desserts,
a cascade of marvels: a flavorful violet or
strawberry tiramisu, lemon and Campari
panna cotta, a chocolate cookie served hot
and arbutus-berry lollipop... time seems
to stand still. The wine list offers a superb
choice of 500 reputable vintages.

In Diebolsheim (67230). 5,8 km D468 and
D203.

● **A la Couronne** SIM

4, rue Jean-de-Beaumont.
Tel. 03 88 74 81 07. Fax 03 88 74 63 89.
Closed Tue. dinner, Wed., 2 weeks Christmas–
New Year's, 2 weeks beg. Aug.
Prix fixe: 9€ (weekday lunch), 12€, 15€,
18€, 8€ (child). A la carte: 35–42€.

Annabel and Karl Renaut have made
their modern house into a restaurant frequented by families on Sundays. One does
not grow weary of crayfish ravioli with

orange and ginger butter, house duck terrine with poultry livers, pike-perch with
chanterelles and chive butter, tête de veau
with sauce gribiche and a soft dark chocolate cake with mandarin orange sorbet.
Smiling welcome and service; reasonable prices.

68150 Haut-Rhin. Paris 427 – Colmar 15 –
Mulhouse 59 – Sélestat 15.
info@ribeauvilleriquewihr.com.
The first Sunday in September, during the
"Pfifferdaj", the whole vineyard gets together
for a joyful, medieval feast. But Ribeauvillé also
has a gastronomic celebration every day, with
its proud craftsmen, its great vintages, its elite
distillers and its distinguished restaurants.

HOTELS-RESTAURANTS

■ **Le Clos Saint-Vincent**

Rte de Bergheim.
Tel. 03 89 73 67 65. Fax 03 89 73 32 20.
reception.leclos@wanadoo.fr
www.leclossaintvincent.com
Closed mid-Dec.–mid-Mar.
Rest. closed lunch, Tue.
19 rooms: 95–200€. 2 suites: 185–230€.
Prix fixe: 45€.

Surrounded by vineyards on the plain of
Alsace, this sixties house breathes tranquility. The Chapotin family cheerfully
offers rustic chic with its huge, carefully
decorated rooms, the garden and the terrace. Arnaud Chapotin's regional cooking
blends Munster cheese in puff pastry with
Gerwurtz Marc, venison medallions with
red cabbage and a classic tarte Tatin with
vanilla ice cream for dessert.

■ **Les Seigneurs de Ribeaupierre**

11, rue du Château.
Tel. 03 89 73 70 31. Fax 03 89 73 71 21.
Closed Christmas–1 Mar.
6 rooms: 120–150€. 4 suites: 150–170€.

Under the direction of Marie-Madeleine
and Marie-Cécile Barth, this house near
the church has been transformed into a

charming establishment with carefully prepared rooms. Tasty breakfasts.

● Au Valet de Coeur & Hostel de la Pépinière

40, rte de Sainte-Marie-aux-Mines.
Tel. 03 89 73 64 14. Fax 03 89 73 88 78.
reception@valetdecoeur.fr
www.valetdecoeur.fr
Rest. closed Sun. dinner,
Mon. (exc. Bank holidays), Tue. lunch.
17 rooms: 43,50–82€.
Prix fixe: 33,50€ (weekdays), 45€, 62€,
83€. A la carte: 75€.

Trained at the Taillevent and Fer Rouge schools, Jean-Pierre Egert knows how to give guests a wonderful welcome to his large house at the edge of the forest. They are delighted by the covered swimming pool and the calm of the old-style rooms, also appreciating the pretty creations of chef Christophe Cavelier. In the luminous dining room, pigeon in aspic terrine with pistachio oil, monkfish "osso bucco" and lemon-seasoned new potatoes, duck "hamburger" with pan-seared foie gras and the chocolate and raspberry desserts are both precise and creative.

■ Le Ménestrel

27, av du Général-de-Gaulle.
Tel. 03 89 73 80 52. Fax 03 89 73 32 39.
menestrel2@wanadoo.fr / www.menestrel.com
29 rooms: 73–99€.

For those following the wine trail, Jacqueline John's establishment is very practical: the modern rooms are rather well laid out while the sauna, the hammam and the Jacuzzi allow one to recuperate in style; the breakfasts are also superb.

■ La Tour

1, rue de la Mairie.
Tel. 03 89 73 72 73. Fax 03 89 73 38 74.
info@hotel-la-tour.com / www.hotel-la-tour.com
Closed Jan., Feb.
31 rooms: 63–94€.

Françoise Alt-Kientzler, sister of a famous wine-maker, has transformed this former viticultural enterprise in the middle

of a town into a guesthouse. The rooms are cozy and quiet, particularly those overlooking the courtyard. The sauna, the hammam and the spa allow pleasant relaxation.

● Le Relais des Ménétriers   COM

10, av du Général-de-Gaulle.
Tel. 03 89 73 64 52. Fax 03 89 73 69 94.
Closed Sun. dinner, Mon., Thu. dinner,
1 week at end July.
Prix fixe: 11€ (lunch), 22€, 24€, 35€.
A la carte: 40€.

Regional tradition and modern cuisine blend harmoniously in the dishes prepared by Patrick Serreau. Comfortably seated, a good bottle on the table—chosen from the 660 referenced wines—one enjoys, without breaking the bank, potato quenelles served with a medallion of foie gras, a stew of pike-perch with ravioli seasoned with Riesling and a filet mignon with Munster. The strawberry gratin with orange flower water concludes a meal that has been impeccably served.

● Le Zahnacker   SIM

8, av du Général-de-Gaulle.
Tel. 03 89 73 60 77. Fax 03 89 73 66 61.
joseph.leiser@wanadoo.fr
Closed Thu., Jan., Feb.
Prix fixe: 22€. A la carte: 40€.

Seasonal, fresh produce takes pride of place at Joseph Leiser's restaurant. A fine practitioner of his art, this chef formerly with Gaertner contrives to make the mouth water without increased prices. The regional wines easily marry with scallops over salad with an orange vinaigrette, seafood choucroute, veal kidneys with chanterelles and rich chocolate cake napped with an orange sauce. Agreeable atmosphere of a neighborhood winstub and local wines from the owner's cellar.

● Wistub Zum Pfifferhus   SIM

14, Grand-Rue.
Tel. 03 89 73 62 28.
Closed Wed., Thu. (exc. June–Oct.), Jan.–mid-Mar., 2 weeks July.
Prix fixe: 24€. A la carte: 38€.

Non-smoking for a very long time, this historic tavern enables one to get a better appreciation of Roland Langer's cooking, served in a fun, neo-medieval setting. One is guided by Jacques Thomann towards charcuterie salad with grilled gizzards and smoked goose breast, head cheese and wine aspic terrine, pike-perch served over sauerkraut, veal in cream sauce over puff pastry shells with house-made spätzle and almond milk ice cream washed down with Alisier is extremely tasty. The cellar is always full of amazing wines to discover.

● **Auberge à l'Etoile**   SIM

46, Grand-Rue.
Tel. 03 89 73 36 46. Fax 03 89 73 67 28.
henry38@wanadoo.fr
Closed Mon. dinner, Tue., 2 weeks Nov., Jan.
Prix fixe: 16,50€, 26,50€.
A la carte: 45€.

Jean-Marie Henry has made this old 18th-century building into an up-and-coming inn. He offers very carefully prepared home cooking based on local produce. Duck foie gras, veal sweetbreads in terrine, pike-perch with noodles, veal kidneys with old-style mustard sauce and the Alsatian frozen vanilla raspberry vacherin cheerfully hit the spot.

● **Le Cheval Noir**   SIM

2, av du Général-de-Gaulle.
Tel. 03 89 73 37 83. Fax 03 89 73 38 73.
frick.p@wanadoo.fr
Closed Mon., Mar.
Prix fixe: 19,70€, 21€, 8€ (child).
A la carte: 30€.

This restaurant annexed to the Zahnacker is imbibed with a good-natured simplicity. One comes for local flat savory tarts in various flavors, the vineyard-keeper's salad, trout with almonds, pike-perch on sauerkraut, pork cheeks in a stew flavored with Pinot Noir and fresh fromage blanc with blueberries. The prices don't hurt and the atmosphere is equally pleasant.

● **S'Rappschwirer Stebala**   SIM

6, pl de l'Ancien-Hôpital.
Tel. 03 89 73 64 64. Fax 03 89 73 67 28.
Closed Tue. dinner, Wed., 2 weeks Nov.,
2 weeks Jan., 2 weeks Feb.
Prix fixe: 15,50€, 18€, 23,50€.
A la carte: 35€.

Jean-Marie Henry is also on the other side of the high street in this restaurant that bears the name, in Alsatian, of his town. The cooking is simple and cheery. Onion tart, pike-perch with noodles, a veal escalope with chanterelles and crème brûlée go down without a murmur. The paneled décor is charming and the local flat savory tarts to be recommended.

29340 Finistère. Paris 530 – Quimper 39 –
Concarneau 21 – Quimperlé 13.
ot.riec.sur.belon@wanadoo.fr.
In oyster country, charming river banks in a joyous, proud place with a light that inspired painters.

● | RESTAURANTS

● **Chez Jacky**   COM

At the port de Belon.
Tel. 02 98 06 90 32. Fax 02 98 06 49 72.
chez.jacky@wanadoo.fr / www.chez.jacky.com
Closed Sun. dinner (off season), Mon. (exc. Bank holidays), beg. Oct.–end Mar.
Prix fixe: 17€, 32€, 36€, 76€,
8€ (child). A la carte: 32–52€.

At the Noblets, shellfish, fish and seafood have pole position. Belon oysters, mussels steamed in shallots and wine, turbot with beurre blanc sauce and a local dessert similar to a flan called the far Breton are beautiful. Prices are reasonable, the welcome friendly and the setting of this oyster catcher's cabin, with its bay windows opening onto the view of the open sea, heavenly.

RIEDISHEIM see **MULHOUSE**
RILLIEUX-LA-PAPE see **LYON**

RINGENDORF

67350 Bas-Rhin. Paris 463 – Strasbourg 32 – Pfaffenhoffen 6 – Kirrwiller 2.
The country of Hanau, the Alsace of orchards and beautiful half-timbered houses, is to be found right here.

● RESTAURANTS

● **La Ferme de Suzel**
15, rue des Vergers.
Tel. 03 88 03 30 80.
Closed lunch (exc. weekends), Mon., Tue.
2 weeks beg. Sept., 2 weeks Feb. vac.
Prix fixe: 45€. A la carte: 40€.

Prettily decorated as a typical farmhouse, the house of the Suzels, alias Odette Jung, is an enchanting place. Under the welcoming gaze of a good hostess who has her eye on everything, one hesitates before a menu that changes frequently but which is always tempting. A pork trotter terrine with balsamic vinaigrette, Red Label salmon in an Ile de Ré black potato crust, duck leg confit with two cabbages, sour cherries pan tossed with sugar and the frozen vacherin testify to the real know-how of the wonderful Suzel. The check is small in comparison to the generosity of the food.

RION-DES-LANDES

40370 Landes. Dax 25 – Mont de Marsan 25.
A crossroads between Grandes Landes and Chalosse not to be missed for its media star.

● RESTAURANTS

INNKEEPER OF THE YEAR

● **Chez Maïté**
500, av Charles Despiau.
Tel. 05 58 57 18 05. Fax 05 58 57 04 86.
www.chezmaite.com
Closed Fri. dinner (Oct.–Mar.),
Sun. dinner, Mon.
Prix fixe: 20€, 26€, 39€, 45€.

Yes, yes, this is really her, the star of the small screen, the high priestess of the Musketeers' cuisine. Her restaurant is staple, as simple as they come, with its décor that plays with all the cliches of self-confident bad taste: neon lights, bay windows and front door with a PVC opening, machine-made floor tiles, wooden chairs and tables that can be seen in a thousand other places, with green and red tablecloths. And yet the public is in seventh heaven. The establishment is a recent one. Maïté, the Piaf of the kitchen, was the gate keeper at Rion des Landes train track, making the meals for rugby matches in the area before becoming the star of French TV channel France 3. Like Colette, she believes that "you belong to your village before you belong to your country" and she has never abandoned the people she came from. In 2000 she opened this establishment for the enjoyment of all, where she receives her local, and worldwide, fans. The public is certainly older than average. In other words, they are wiser, coming here to take lessons in French *savoir vivre* and to taste good, true and simple fare: the plate with local specialties with foie gras, soup, foie gras rillettes, a goat cheese salad with gizzards ("Forget the salad, you haven't come here to lose weight", says Maïté, although she herself has lost eighteen kilograms), confit with green beans (*al dente* and exquisitely seasoned with garlic), half of a potato with cream, grilled magret and the wood pigeon classically prepared with sauce made from its carcass. In short, here you will find neither pretension nor frills. Added to this are the desserts (created by Carte d'Or, although the house custard with its vanilla ice cream is exquisite), the wines friendly, good, not expensive (for example "Maïté's favorite", an exquisite Côtes de Castillon Château la Roche Mézières generously priced at 14,50). This cooking—honest and homey, tasty and vigorous—has a single aim: to give enjoyment and a moment of pleasure to everyone without fear of breaking the bank. Maïté has arrived. This Latin star is the Abbé Pierre of the kitchen.

RIQUEWIHR

68340 Haut-Rhin. Paris 437 – Ribeauvillé 5 – Sélestat 19 – Colmar 13.
info@ribeauville-riquewihr.com.
The "pearl of the vineyards" has emerged intact, or almost, from the Middle Ages. Its Dolder door has celebrated its 700-year anniversary and its winemakers are proud of their famous hillside vineyards. It has now found a new tourist and gastronomic vocation.

 HOTELS-RESTAURANTS

■ La Couronne

5, rue de la Couronne.
Tel. 03 89 49 03 03. Fax 03 89 49 01 01.
www.hoteldelacouronne.com
36 rooms: 60–68€. 4 suites: 110
Half board: 70–130€.

The rooms of this establishment, made up of typical 16th-century houses, enjoy modern comforts. In the middle of the old town, it is nonetheless quiet. The welcome is delightful and, in the annex, families happily stay in well-equipped apartments.

■ Hôtel du Schoenenbourg

Rue du Schoenenbourg.
Tel. 03 89 49 01 11. Fax 03 89 47 95 88.
www.hotel-schoenenbourg.fr
54 rooms: 50–122€.

The rooms of this modern hotel at the foot of vineyards are light and well equipped for a stay of several days. For the comfort of their guests, Jacques and Mayo Kiener have made available a good-sized swimming pool, gym, solarium and sauna.

■ A l'Oriel

3, rue des Ecuries-Seigneuriales.
Tel. 03 89 49 03 13. Fax 03 89 47 92 87.
info@hotel-oriel.com / www.hotel-oriel.com
21 rooms: 67–97€. 1 suite: 155€.

The house is several centuries old but the rooms, with their rustic décor, include every comfort. Located right in the heart of the town, this hotel makes a good stop-off on the wine route.

■ Le Riquewihr

3, rte de Ribeauvillé.
Tel. 03 89 86 03 00. Fax 03 89 47 99 76.
www.hotel-riquewihr.fr
Closed Jan.–mid-Feb.
44 rooms: 60–90€. 6 suites: 90–115€.

This family hotel offers large comfortable rooms but also a fitness suite, heated swimming pool and Internet.

■ Le Sarment d'Or

4, rue du Cerf.
Tel. 03 89 86 02 86. Fax 03 89 47 99 23.
www.riquewihr-sarment-dor.com
Rest. closed Sun. dinner (exc. Dec.), Mon., Tue. lunch, mid-Jan.–beg. Feb.
10 rooms: 60–80€.
Prix fixe: 20€, 25€, 37€, 48€, 9,50€ (child). A la carte: 50€.

Built in the city fortifications, this charming hotel in a regional setting provides modern, comfortable rooms. Marianne Merckling and her daughter Isabelle give a smiling welcome while the cooking of father Gilbert does the rest, with tuna tartare with herring caviar, whole roasted Atlantic sea bass with olive oil and basil, lamb chops with slow-roasted garlic and cherries in eau-de-vie.

● La Table du Gourmet

5, rue de la 1er-Armée.
Tel. 03 89 49 09 09. Fax 03 89 49 04 56.
latable@jlbrendel.com / www.jlbrendel.com
Closed Tue., Thu. lunch, Wed. lunch, mid-Jan.–mid-Feb.
Prix fixe: 36€, 90€. A la carte: 100€.

After having converted several charming suites in his 16th-century winemaker's house, as well as adopting a new concept, the D'Brendel Stub, Jean-Luc Bernard, known as JLB, has given himself over to energetically working in the kitchens of his restaurant aimed at gourmets. His cooking is both stamped with orginality and anchored in the region. Our man goes exploring in the fields himself for herbs, flowers, berries and roots to go into his dishes. Regulars to the place vote in numbers for corn bread-coated and fried frog legs with pink garlic purée, fire-roasted Breton lobster with old-style preserved tomatoes, veal sweetbreads, thinly sliced cold artichoke with chanterelle cream and a big white fish roasted with almonds and raspberry candies for gourmets who also have great appetites. The smile of his sister Fabienne, who watches over the house, contributes to the prevailing good humor of the place, which seems to continue indefinitely, long after the last mouthful has been swallowed.

● **Auberge du**   ◎ V.COM
   Schoenenbourg

2, rue de la Piscine.
Tel. 03 89 47 92 28. Fax 03 89 47 89 84.
auberge-schoenenbourg@wanadoo.fr
www.auberge-schoenenbourg.com
Closed lunch, beg. Jan.–beg. Feb.
Prix fixe: 35€, 45€, 63€, 78€.
A la carte: 75€.

The architecture of the building, like the interior decoration, is contemporary. The garden of aromatic herbs gives the opportunity for a scented walk and the terrace offers a superb view over the vineyard that stretches into the horizon as well as of the walls surrounding the town. The cooking, also in the spirit of the times, is the work of François Kliener, who trained with Bise in Talloires and at the Auberge de l'Ill. Natural produce has pride of place in a menu that changes according to the rhythm of the seasons. Summer features iced melon soup and crisp ham. The salmon trout with fresh parsley and coriander jus is a real explosion of tastes. Suckling pig tenderloin with old-style mustard sauce is a piece of genius. The raspberry and rhubarb feuilleté with nougatine ice cream makes a light, fruity end to the meal. The service is very attentive, the charm of sommelier Anne Humbrecht equalled by her professionalism

and the prices of the special menus are agreeably reasonable.

● **D'Brendel Stub**   ⓝ SIM

48, rue du Général-de-Gaulle.
Tel. 03 89 86 54 54.
Closed Wed., 3 weeks Jan.
A la carte: 45€.

Jean-Luc Brendel has created a stir with his modern inn in an ancient house. The contemporary setting with its black tones, a visible rotisserie, and a menu with its synthesis of tradition and modern tastes are all offered by the craftsman of La Table du Gourmet. The bottles of local wine (at rather unpleasant prices) accompany clever dishes. A Bargkass-garnished flat savory tart, breaded head cheese and wine aspic terrine, ham, chicken with chanterelles, a caramelized ham shank with sauerkraut, Alsatian brioche and woodfire–smoked cream sauce all make a good impression.

● **Au Tire-Bouchon**   SIM

29, rue du Général-de-Gaulle.
Tel. 03 89 47 91 61. Fax 03 89 47 99 39.
www.riquewihr-zimmer.com
Closed Christmas.
Prix fixe: 16,50€, 17,50€, 19€, 40€,
9€ (child). A la carte: 40€.

The Zimmers have created a winstub out of this winemaker's house. Régine receives the guests while Thierry Marjorie serves the regional cause in the kitchen. Escargot streudel, rouget and veal trotter in an individual pot, foie gras with potatoes, baeckofe-style, beef with flakes of salt and a chestnut biscuit are well conceived. Local wines are offered, at affordable prices.

32400 Gers. Paris 775 – Aire-sur-l'Adour 17
– Auch 71 – Mont-de-Marsan 49 – Pau 59
– Tarbes 5.
A village of golden stones and the parades of Adour, where Gers and Landes meet, which paints a perfect portrait of French tranquility.

● RESTAURANTS

● Le Pigeonneau   N 🖼 COM
36, av de l'Adour.
Tel. 05 62 69 85 64.
Closed Sun. dinner, Mon., Tue., 1 week Nov.,
1 week Jan., 10 days at end June.
Prix fixe: 26€.

He is the odd one out in Gers cooking. James Hooton, born in Malaysia and brought up in Singapore, before becoming a rubber salesman in London, learned cooking in Paris with Roland Durand at the Relais de Sèvres. He has run this well-kept restaurant for ten years, with its spaced tables and tempting menu. People come here for the light reworking of age-old classics. Warm goat cheese salad with balsamic vinaigrette, strips of duck breast in a salad with Asian seasonings, grilled salmon with curry and small vegetables and the pan-seared magret de canard with local cherries take one on a pleasant journey. The roasted squab with Banyuls jus is an agreeable justification of the name of the restaurant. The unique menu is inviting and the desserts (a covered apple pie served with frozen nougat) a gastronomic treat.

LA RIVIERE-THIBOUVILLE

27550 Eure. Paris 138 – Rouen 49 – Bernay 15 – Evreux 35 – Pont-Audemer 34.
Along a branch of the Risle, a hamlet in a bucolic landscape straight out of a picture book.

◢ ● HOTELS-RESTAURANTS

■ So Café   N 🏵 🏠

1, chaussée du Roy. La Rivière-Thibouville.
Tel. 02 32 45 00 08. Fax 02 32 46 89 68.
info@domainedusoleildor.com
www.domainedusoleildor.com
Rest. closed Sun.
12 rooms: 54–90€. 2 suites: 180–230€.
Prix fixe: 12€, 19€, 24€, 30€,
8€ (child).

This open-air establishment is a great success. People come to listen to jazz and to enjoy, if they want, an exciting world cuisine or French classics. In the café, a salad or a ritual tartine, a salmon and eggplant mille-feuille, simmered veal shank and the roasted fig tart give pleasure, as does the after-dinner walk in the orchard or along the river. The rooms are big, laid back and calm.

● Le Manoir du Soleil d'or   COM
23, Côte de Paris.
Tel.-Fax 02 32 44 90 31.
Closed Sun. dinner, Mon., 2 weeks July.
Prix fixe: 23€, 36€, 50€.
A la carte: 45–55€.

The Lebels have created a pleasant restaurant in this pretty Anglo-Norman manor house. Sandra provides the welcome while Dimitri is in the kitchen. The changing menu highlights seasonal produce. Foie gras terrine with figs, Atlantic sea bass and rouget with lime butter, veal sweetbreads and kidneys with a light vegetable gratin and four small desserts (chocolate, fruit, ice cream and crème brûlée) are extremely well conceived. On sunny days, meals are served on the terrace overlooking the valley of the Risle.

RIXHEIM see MULHOUSE

ROAIX see VAISON-LA-ROMAINE

ROANNE

42300 Loire. Paris 398 – Clermont-Ferrand 106 – Lyon 88 – Saint-Etienne 87.
contact@leroannais.com.
When the Briare canal was dug in 1605, Roanne became a principal navigation point for the water coaches making for Paris and Nantes. The town became wealthy and its bargemen's district saw a proliferation of inns and warehouses. The textile industry, Vichy material and plain and purl stitch gave fame to the town. But it remained principally a crossroads, just beside the Loire, between the Rhône and Beaujolais, not far from Auvergne. If the textile boom is over, after the crisis of the 1960s, the town's reputation for good hotels is as strong as ever.

HOTELS-RESTAURANTS

● Maison Troisgros

1, pl Jean-Troisgros.
Tel. 04 77 71 66 97. Fax 04 77 70 39 77.
info@troisgros.com / www.troisgros.com
Closed 10 days beg. Jan., 10 days Feb., 2
weeks beg. Aug., Tue., Wed. Rest. closed
Mon. lunch (Oct.–Feb.), Tue., Wed.
12 rooms: 175–350€. 1 suite: 510
3 apartments: 410-480€.
Prix fixe: 180€, 140€, 40€ (child).

He is a modern heir: he doesn't refuse his heritage but adapts it to his own liking. He has completely transformed the mother house, giving wings to its cuisine, making it both travel and dream, with a nod to both Italy and Japan. Although Michel Troisgros is the son of Pierre, he has forgotten to put on his menu—in a special framed box as used by friends Haeberlin of Illhaeusern and Lorain of Joigny—the signature dishes of the house. He doesn't question salmon with sorrel or beef filet with bone marrow, but he gives them a different kind of attention. His new classics? They are lacy-cut John Dory with fresh ceps and capers, tomato aspic with little ravioli stuffed with summer flavors, a savory Atlantic sea bass bouillon served over Koshi-Kari rice, langoustines served royal-style with beurre rouge, squab, black truffle-stuffed foie gras cooked Kiev-style and the rump steak with ginger and pepper. So many fine, delicate and astonishing things that are like precious little glimpses or lovers' memories. Michel Troisgros, who was a restaurant owner in Moscow (Koumir) and then continued his adventures at the Hyatt in Tokyo, has not finished surprising us. Marie-Pierre gives a stylish welcome and the wines chosen by Jean-Jacques and Christian (Banchet & Vermorel) are fit for kings. The contemporary rooms are world class. In short, this is a legendary establishment at the height of its form.

● Le Central

20, cours de la République.
Tel. 04 77 67 72 72. Fax 04 77 72 57 67.
Closed Sun., Mon.,
Christmas–New Year's vac., 3 weeks Aug.
Prix fixe: 19€ (lunch), 24€ (lunch),
27€ (dinner).

To eat "cheap" Troisgros, go to this happening bistro adjacent to the mother house which is the beautiful annex of Michel and Marie-Pierre T. In the kitchens, the assiduous student Frédéric Garrivier busies himself offering tasty and approachable food. The cold tomato soup with spring vegetables, runny egg ravioli with spinach, pantossed frog legs with garlic and ginger, small variety meat brochettes with marrow jus and the chocolate praline pannini with coffee ice cream effortlessly afford a delicious moment.

In Le Coteau (42120). Right bank of the Loire.

● Auberge Costelloise

2, av de la Libération. Right bank of the Loire.
Tel. 04 77 68 12 71. Fax 04 77 72 26 78.
auberge-costelloise@wanadoo.fr
Closed Sun., Mon., 1 week at end Dec.–beg.
Jan., 1 week beg. May, mid-Aug.–beg. Sept.
Prix fixe: 25€ (weekdays), 35€, 40€, 49€,
66€. A la carte: 65€.

In this establishment on the banks of the Loire, Christophe Souchon has the masterful art of presenting classic dishes with a hint of modernity. The art deco-style restaurant makes a beautiful setting for pan-seared foie gras with a beet coulis, blue lobster with citrus fruits and basil, veal sweetbreads in a Port reduction and an oven-crisped chocolate dessert with sour cherry marmalade. Excellent Rhône wines advised by passionate enthusiast Raphaël Cornet.

In Villerest (42300). 6 km via D53.

● Château de Champlong

100, chemin de la Chapelle.
Tel. 04 77 69 69 69. Fax 04 77 69 71 08.
www.chateau-de-champlong.com
Closed Sun. dinner, Mon., Tue., mid-Nov.–end
Nov., beg. Feb.–beg. Mar.
Prix fixe: 25€ (weekday lunch), 32€, 44€
(wine inc. dinner), 15€ (child).
A la carte: 55–60€.

This 14th-century house with its biblical murals is impressive. Olivier Boizet, who did his apprenticeship with Troigros and Blanc, has settled here with his wife Véronique, and creates his dishes with the precision of an orchestra conductor. The crunchy escargots in wild garlic greens, roasted turbot with velours sauce with fingerling potatoes and foie gras and rare-cooked veal kidneys with violette mustard are bravura pieces. One can take rest in one of the twenty-three rooms with contemporary décor in the Champlong estate.

ROCAMADOUR

46500 Lot. Paris 535 – Cahors 64 – Brive-la-Gaillarde 55 – Figeac 46.
rocamadour@wanadoo.fr.
The site of this very touristy village on the side of a rock is legendary. One comes here for an overnight stop, via the pedestrian route of a marked path or the painless, automated way.

 HOTELS-RESTAURANTS

■ Les Vieilles Tours
Rte de Payrac, 4 km via D673.
Tel. 05 65 33 68 01. Fax 05 65 33 68 59.
les.vieillestours@wanadoo.fr
www.vieillestours-rocamadour.com
Closed beg. Nov.–end Mar.
Rest. closed lunch (exc. by group reserv.).
16 rooms: 72–96€. 1 suite: 115€.
Prix fixe: 39€, 32€, 29€, 10€ (child).
A la carte: 70–75€.

Located in a large park with swimming pool, this warm country manor house blends the old-fashioned charm of its furniture with a modern taste in decoration (swathes of organza and boutis). Cozy comfort and good cooking that follows the seasons.

■ Hôtel du Château
Rte du Château.
Tel. 05 65 33 62 22. Fax 05 65 33 69 00.
hotelchateaurocamadour@wanadoo.fr
www.hotelchateaurocamadour.com
Closed beg. Nov.–end Mar.
Rest. closed Mon. lunch.

60 rooms: 60–95€.
Prix fixe: 14,50€ (lunch), 19,50€ (dinner), 27€ (dinner), 44€, 9,50€ (child).
A la carte: 40–50€.

Contemporary rooms and a modern dining room in shades of salmon pink give a pleasant, new feel to this serene place. In the kitchen, Gilles Labourel plays the regional card and we have good memories of the symphony of foie gras, rouget with cep jus, magret de canard roasted on the bone and an oven-crisped warm pear dessert with dark chocolate. A charming welcome from Michelle and Stéphane Marnac.

■ Domaine de la Rhue
6 km via rte de Brive, D673 and N140.
Tel. 05 65 33 71 50. Fax 05 65 33 72 48.
domainedelarhue@wanadoo.fr
www.domainedelarhue.com
Closed Oct.–beg. Apr.
14 rooms: 70–130€.

A ramblers' path enables one to get to the center of the village from this hotel converted from the 19th-century stables of a former château. Eric and Christine Jooris give the smiling welcome of hosts proud to offer comfortable, meticulously decorated rooms and excellent breakfasts.

■ Beau Site et Jehan de Valon
Cité médiévale.
Tel. 05 65 33 63 08. Fax 05 65 33 65 23.
www.bestwestern-beausite.com
Closed mid-Nov.–10 Feb.
33 rooms: 41–102€. 5 suites: 97–140€.
Prix fixe: 24€, 52€, 10€ (child).
A la carte: 47€.

For two centuries, the Menots have been welcoming passing visitors to the heart of the old city with Martial, the present holder of the name, now at the helm. The rooms have kept their old character and the regional cooking, created by Franck Laubadère, is festive and light of touch. Foie gras terrine served with a mango chutney, the pike-perch with Cahors sauce, a Quercy country leg of lamb carved tableside and a tarte Tatin napped with milk caramel sauce all go down well.

■ **Le Troubadour**

2,5 km via rte de Brive.
Tel. 05 65 33 70 27. Fax 05 65 33 71 99.
www.rocamadour.com
Closed mid-Nov.–mid-Feb.
10 rooms: 55–85€.
Prix fixe: 25€, 35€.

This old, restored farmhouse makes
a pretty stop-off, with its large garden,
swimming pool, sweet little rooms and
reliable cooking. Foie gras mille-feuille,
monkfish filet, lamb shanks with fresh
garden thyme and the oven-crisped apple
pineapple dessert are much enjoyed.

LA ROCHE-L'ABEILLE see
SAINT-YRIEIX-LA-PERCHE

LA ROCHE-BERNARD

56130 Morbihan. Paris 447 – Nantes 71 –
Vannes 41 – Redon 27 – Saint-Nazaire 37.
Perched above the Vilaine, the Morbihan bridge,
the little port and the charming town are three
reasons for making the detour. The large inn
also justifies the trip.

 | HOTELS-RESTAURANTS

● **L'Auberge Bretonne**

2, pl Du-Guesclin.
Tel. 02 99 90 60 28. Fax 02 99 90 85 00.
resa.thorel@wanadoo.fr
www.auberge-bretonne.com
Rest. closed Mon. lunch, Tue. lunch, Thu.,
12 Nov.–26 Dec., 2 Jan.–20 Jan.
10 rooms: 155–230€. 1 suite: 230–280€.
Prix fixe: 35€ (weekday lunch),
105€ (tasting menu), 137€ (tasting menu).
A la carte: 100–120€.

L'Auberge Bretonne: the apparently simple title says everything about its desire to
safeguard regional identity, in terms both
of its immediate locality and its whole cultural heritage. The place has been renovated bit by bit over the years, without
losing its character as a simple establishment. Breton, it has even become almost
Breton-speaking, with its collection of
pictures of characters in local hairstyles
and hats that give it the charm of a folk
museum. The beautiful floor tiles, the
plants, the light well, the corner bar and
the ten rooms: one might be in the simple home of Bécassine, the cartoon character of a naive Breton housewife. Yet
there is no one more wily than this skillful cook, a Breton from Morbihan proud
of his land, who goes to the market at
Vannes or the port of la Turballe to root
out the best produce of the region. He also
cooks with an irrefutable modern know-
how and accompanies his food with the
best wines in the world. Example dishes
are roasted langoustine with asparagus
and coffee sauce, a poached slice of wild
turbot with hollandaise sauce and spit-
roasted guinea hen with foie gras and
truffle macaroni—this is brilliant cooking that belongs to its tradition but which
superb handling transforms into unique
dishes. The unmissable house dessert prepared by Solange and the vanilla mille-
feuille show that sweet dishes are treated
with the same care as the savory ones.
The welcome given by Solange Thorel is
delightful, the service impeccable, the
wine list, explained with a smile by Virginie Grange, wide-ranging and the price
remains reasonable for such great quality.
With their antique furniture and engravings by Laboureur, the rooms of this bourgeois home in guise of Breton guesthouse
are enchanting. Delicious breakfasts
labelled Relais & Châteaux.

■ **Auberge des Deux Magots**

1, pl Bouffay.
Tel. 02 99 90 60 75. Fax 02 99 90 87 87.
aubergelesdeuxmagots.roche-bernard@
wanadoo.fr
auberge-les2magots.com
Closed Sun. dinner (off season), Mon. (off
season), 1 week Oct., end Dec.–mid-Jan.,
1 week at end June.
15 rooms: 45–75€.
Prix fixe: 14€, 24€, 30€, 43€, 55€,
10€ (child). A la carte: 40–45€.

Maryvonne and Joël Morice have made
this town house into a pleasant guesthouse in the center of town. They offer a
seasonal menu that concentrates on sea-

food. The scallops with spring vegetables and citrus butter, warm langoustines in salad, cider-braised Atlantic sea bass or turbot and the steamed whiting with crayfish sauce are honest fare. A house frozen nougat and a maple syrup crème brûlée are real gastronomic treats and the rooms make a calm and cozy base for exploring the region.

■ Le Colibri   △
Rue du Four.
Tel. 02 99 90 66 01. Fax 02 99 90 75 94.
colibri56130@aol.com
Closed Feb. vac.
11 rooms: 42–52€.

Béatrice Loyer's rooms are neat, tastefully decorated and ideal as an inexpensive way of spending a few days in the town.

ROCHECORBON see TOURS

ROCHEFORT

17300 Charente-Maritime. Paris 475 – Limoges 221 – Niort 62 – La Rochelle 38 – Royan 40.
Immortalised by Jacques Demy and his girls, the city of the Corderie Royale offers its Arsenal quarter, the house of Pierre Loti, the art museum and the mercury trades museum.

■/●   HOTELS-RESTAURANTS

■ La Corderie Royale
Rue Jean-Baptiste-Audebert.
Tel. 05 46 99 35 35. Fax 05 46 99 78 72.
corderie.royale@wanadoo.fr
www.corderieroyale-hotel.com
Rest. closed Sun. dinner,
Mon. (Nov.–Easter), Feb.
44 rooms: 58–156€.
Prix fixe: 30€ (weekday lunch), 36€,
120€ (wine inc.).

In the walls of the old royal artillery, this is a historic establishment with its spacious rooms, carefully chosen furniture and views over the port. The swimming pool, the garden, the veranda restaurant where a carefully prepared cuisine

is served (creamy crab soup, sole Viennoise and a beautifully interpreted rabbit saddle) are all pluses.

■ Roca Fortis   N △
14, rue de la République.
Tel. 05 46 99 26 32.
hotel-rocafortis@wanadoo.fr
16 rooms: 39–57€.

These two local houses built around a courtyard terrace where one can sit outside are worth a visit for their reasonable prices, their carefully selected furnishings and cheerful colors. They offer a blend of calm and charm, right in the heart of things.

● Le Tournebroche
56, av Ch.-de-Gaulle.
Tel. 05 46 87 14 32.
letournebroche@free.fr
Closed Sun. dinner, Mon., Tue.,
1 week at end Dec., 10 days beg. Jan.
Prix fixe: 27€, 39€.

A former officers' residence at the time of Colbert, next to the art and history museum, this has become a gastronomic establishment that respects local produce. The large fireplace is well suited to the roasts of the day.

LA ROCHEFOUCAULD

16110 Charente. Paris 445 – Angoulême 24 – Confolens 45 – Limoges 85 – Nontron 40.
This "pearl of the Angoumois" is proud of its splendid château with machicolated keep, its hospital with apothecary's dispensary, its house of Hérault de Gourville and the cloister of its Carmes abbey.

■/●   HOTELS-RESTAURANTS

■ L'Auberivières   N △
Rte de Mansle.
Tel. 05 45 63 10 10. Fax 05 45 63 02 60.
www.hotel-auberivieres.com
Closed Sat., Sun., 1 week Christmas–New Year's, 2 weeks beg. Aug.
10 rooms: 37–40€.

Prix fixe: 12,50€ (weekdays), 28€, 8,50€ (child).

At the foot of the château, the Dumas' house offers small rooms that are tidy and simple, plus two restaurant rooms. All the cooking is homemade, created with love by Thierry: smoked bacon salad and trout with almonds. The special menus are good value.

■ La Vieille Auberge de la Carpe d'Or

1, rue Vitrac.
Tel. 05 45 62 02 72. Fax 05 45 63 01 88.
25 rooms: 37–49€.
Prix fixe: 19€, 35€.

This 16th-century coaching inn with its turret has kept the character of the period. Added to the old-fashioned charm are immaculate rooms. The rustic dining room offers a cuisine with Charentaise touches.

ROCHEGUDE

26790 Drôme. Paris 645 – Avignon 47 –
Bollène 8 – Carpentras 16.
Here is the Tricastin of truffles, wine, lamb and olive trees: a Provence that begins in Drôme and which is dedicated to gastronomy.

■ HOTELS-RESTAURANTS

■ Château de Rochegude

Tel. 04 75 97 21 10. Fax 04 75 04 89 87.
rochegude@relaischateaux.com
www.chateauderochegude.com
Closed Nov.
23 rooms: 136–355€. 2 suites: 384–555€.
Prix fixe: 16€ (lunch, wine inc.), 22€ (lunch, wine inc.), 31€ (lunch, wine inc.), 35€, 55€, 70€, 85€, 110€, 20€ (child).
A la carte: 85€.

Above the vineyards and the fields of olive trees, this château enjoys huge grounds with swimming pool and tennis court. Its very luxurious rooms mix stylish furnishings and Provençal pieces. We appreciated the thoroughly regional cooking of Thierry Frébout, with a truffle-stuffed open ravioli, oven-browned monkfish medallion with basil, foie gras– and fig-stuffed pigeon in a pastry crust and mixed fruits with sorbet.

LA ROCHELLE

17000 Charente-Maritime. Paris 475 –
Angoulême 145 – Bordeaux 186 –
Nantes 135 – Niort 66.
tourisme.la.rochelle@wanadoo.fr.
La Rochelle, open city? Formerly known for its trade and commerce, now for its tourism and music. "People just pass through La Rochelle" lament the hotel owners, who see the holiday-makers leave for the island (of Ré). Yes, but they come back, seduced by the light of this port town built out of white stone, amused by the contrast between Middle Age timbers and 18th-century ship-owners' houses, astonished by the series of streets with archways. Openly devoted to the sea, the town expresses the best of this inexhaustible theme. Lobsters and eels share the limelight on the menu boards of bistros in the port. Nothing overwhelming, but freshness and generosity are always in evidence. The Coutanceaus are on top with their three restaurants where classic dishes are certain of their position. Cognac, pineau or fleur de sel purchases are made at the market or in the surrounding shops where bargains abound—if, that is, you decide not to cross the estuary to explore the St. Nicolas area, a former haunt of sailors where rough bars blend with the secondhand stores.

■ HOTELS

■ Résidence de France

43, rue du Minage.
Tel. 05 46 28 06 00. Fax 05 46 28 06 03.
www.hotel-larochelle.com
5 rooms: 90–155€. 11 suites: 145–300€.
Prix fixe: 19€, 25€.

Elegance and comfort combine in this hotel in the heart of the old city. Awaiting you are light rooms, pretty, old-style furnishings and a pleasant patio restaurant where the food of Jean-Marc Gaborit offers, at moderate prices, traditional gastronomy (Armagnac-flavored foie gras, rouget with slow-cooked caramelized onions).

■ Les Brises

Rue Philippe-Vincent, chemin Digue-Richelieu.
Tel. 05 46 43 89 37. Fax 05 46 43 27 97.
hotellesbrises@aol.com / www.hotellesbrises.com
46 rooms: 62–119€. 2 suites: 185€.

Facing the Minimes port and the sea, this sixties house offers rooms in an ocean liner style. Wonderful welcome.

■ Champlain France-Angleterre

30, rue Rambaud.
Tel. 05 46 41 23 99. Fax 05 46 41 15 19.
www.hotelchamplain.com
36 rooms: 80–120€. 4 suites: 120–145€.

A charming stay near the old port and pedestrian area is offered by this town house with delightful, tree-filled garden. The rooms with their fine 18th-century furniture are like varied little museums.

■ Hôtel de la Monnaie

3, rue de la Monnaie.
Tel. 05 46 50 65 65. Fax 05 46 50 63 19.
www.hotel-monnaie.com
31 rooms: 80–112€. 4 suites: 178–210€.

Prettily situated at the foot of the Lantern tower and the entrance to the old port, the 17th-century house is pleasant, just like the restful and well-thought-out rooms.

■ Yachtman

23, quai Valin.
Tel. 05 46 41 20 68. Fax 05 46 41 81 24.
www.logis-de-france.fr
40 rooms: 84–108€.

This classic address in the town invites you to a dream voyage without leaving the quays of the old port: maritime decoration in shades of blue, wood, spacious room-cabins, marble bathrooms, swimming pool and patio. (See Restaurants: Grill le Midship.)

■ François 1er

13-15, rue Bazoges.
Tel. 05 46 41 28 46. Fax 05 46 41 35 01.
www.hotelfrancois1.fr
Closed Jan.
36 rooms: 60–106€. 1 suite: 200€.

We fell in love with this royal establishment where the rooms were redecorated last winter. The family welcome is warm and the proximity to the beaches and the port ideal.

■ Relais Mercure Océanide

Quai Louis-Prunier.
Tel. 05 46 50 61 50. Fax 05 46 41 24 31.
h0569@accor-hotels.com / www.mercure.com
123 rooms: 105–150€.
Prix fixe: 20€, 8,50€ (child).

The paneled rooms in a maritime setting are fun, opposite the pleasure port, near the aquarium and the Neptunéa museum. A classic cuisine allows one to dine on the premises without worrying; the Sunday brunch is popular.

■ Saint-Nicolas

13, rue Sardinerie.
Tel. 05 46 41 71 55. Fax 05 46 41 70 46.
www.comforthotel-larochelle.com
79 rooms: 66–95€.

In the middle of the old town, this modern hotel has redecorated its rooms in sky blue and white. A fun, tropical conservatory for breakfasts. Attended parking, a warm welcome and moderate prices.

●	RESTAURANTS

● Richard Coutanceau

Plage de la Concurrence.
Tel. 05 46 41 48 19. Fax 05 46 41 99 45.
coutanceau@relaischateaux.com
www.coutanceaularochelle.com
Closed Sun.
Prix fixe: 45€, 85€, 23€ (child).

Dynamic natives of La Rochelle, the Coutanceaus continue to dominate the gastronomic landscape of their town. Son Christopher has joined his father Richard, having trained with the greats (El Bulli, Ducasse…) and together they create a contemporary cuisine that concentrates on taste and authenticity and highlights the great ocean. Roasted langoustines in a creamy fennel sauce, top-grade oysters with sundried tomatoes, lemongrass and ginger jus, black cuttlefish ravioli served on Catalan vegetables glazed in a basil emulsion, turbot filet colored with crunchy asparagus, gnocchi with young parsley shoots and sauce, line-fished Atlantic sea bass on its crispy skin with artichokes and the Serrano ham with a littleneck clam purée are dynamic. The meat (tender braised pigeon glazed with a sesame sauce and the fennel-seasoned Castille milk-fed lamb with cumin and avocado cannelloni) is equally successful. The desserts excite without being too heavy (almond cream-stuffed apricots with salted-butter caramel ice cream, cherries roasted in balsamic vinegar and a sour cherry and pistachio parfait). Maryse Coutanceau looks after the modern, light and contemporary restaurant with verve and the prices remain reasonable for this level of quality.

● Grill Le Midship ℗⬛COM

At the Yachtman. 23, quai Valin.
Tel. 05 46 41 20 68. Fax 05 46 41 81 24.
leyachtman@wanadoo.fr / www.logis-de-france.fr
Closed Sun., 2 weeks end Dec.
Prix fixe: 30€, 24€, 18€ (weekday lunch), 14€ (child).

Parisian star of the sea, Jacques Le Divellec supervises "his" La Rochelle restaurant from a distance. The good pupil Nicolas Meunier cooks fish in his own style and no one complains, in this maritime grill with mahogany paneling and sweet touches. No. 3 Joguet oysters, a nicely presented fish stew, pan-tossed cod with white beans and chorizo, roasted Atlantic sea bass with citrus caramel and boneless rib steak, with fleur de sel and house fries as a way of coming back down to earth, are confident and attractive. Guayaquil chocolate volcano makes a pleasant ending. A cooking pot award for value this year.

● Le Comptoir des Voyages ⬛COM

22, rue Saint-Jean-du-Pérot.
Tel. 05 46 50 62 60. Fax 05 46 41 90 80.
www.coutanceau.com
Prix fixe: 27,50€, 12€ (child).

All the flavors of the world unite in the saucepans of Fabrice Guérinaud for this colorful culinary vogage. The skillful orchestrator Grégory Coutanceau follows every move with a watchful eye. Oven-browned jumbo shrimp, pineapple and bamboo shoots with mild spices, mackerel in a ginger, lime and red onion marinade and pork kidney medallions in a caramel sauce with Vietnamese noodles are great fun. One finishes with soft-centered chocolate cake with passion fruit center and a balsamic reduction. A good atmosphere, wines from the four corners of the earth and moderate prices: it will all make you leave with sharpened tastebuds!

● Les Flots COM

1, rue de la Chaîne.
Tel. 05 46 41 32 51. Fax 05 46 41 90 80.
contact@les-flots.com / www.coutanceau.com
Prix fixe: 24€ (lunch), 39€, 35€, 79€.
A la carte: 60–70€.

Grégory Coutanceau, who watches over the destinies of four restaurants in the town, is theoretically present in the kitchen here. This former chef of Pré Catelan, a worthy son to his father Richard, took some time to return to the local fold, after almost settling down in Paris, where for a time he took over two fashionable restaurants. Here he is back again in a more modest, contemporary cozy setting, next door to the tour de la Chaîne. Langoustines with Espelette peppers with a pressed tomato mozzarella accompaniment, Atlantic sea bass tossed in a wok with vegetables and pickled Ile de Ré seaweed and Simmental beef tenderloin with wine sauce with Ile de Ré potatoes are very fresh and well made. The desserts (an attractive variation on theme of the cherry) are not lacking in well-measured creativity. Question: does the place still deserve one plate?

● Bistro de Rémi Massé ⬛SIM

59, rue Saint-Jean-du-Pérot.
Tel. 05 46 43 56 08. Fax 05 46 43 56 09.
www.bistro-remi-masse.com
Closed Sat. lunch, Sun. lunch, Mon.,
1 week Christmas–New Year's, 2 weeks Feb.

Prix fixe: 13€ (lunch), 24€, 28€.
A la carte: 40€.

He comes from Portes-en-Ré, where he was chef at the Auberge de la Rivière. He is affable, funny, passionate and presides over the kitchen with a masterly hand. Rémi Massé keeps the kind of bistro people like. You sit down eagerly at white pine or brown wenge tables to listen to him defending authentic tastes and seasonal flavors, while also rolling his sleeves up for the pleasure of his guests. Straight from the market, the produce is fresh and simple: the three-fish plate (tuna tartare, grilled cuttlefish and dill-seasoned salmon), assorted grilled local fish, pigeon served boneless and stuffed with foie gras and the exquisite waffle prepared in the old style hit the bull's eye. This is easy, delicious and fun.

● **Les Orchidées**   ■SIM
24, rue Thiers.
Tel. 05 46 41 07 63. Fax 05 46 50 05 16.
www.restaurant-les-orchidees.com
Prix fixe: 19€ (lunch), 24€.

A stone's throw from the town's market, Stéphane Hottlet, trained at Rostang's in Paris, has made this rather ordinary (but flower-filled) place into a sharp and contemporary establishment. In the restaurant, Véronique welcomes and advises customers' choices on an up-to-date menu. Oysters with slow-cooked caramelized shallots, lobster cake with sesame and saffron-seasoned reduction, beef sirloin and foie gras with roasted hazelnuts and a hot strawberry soufflé charm without effort.

● **L'Entracte**   ℕSIM
35, rue Saint-Jean-de-Pérot.
Tel. 05 46 52 26 69. Fax 05 46 41 90 80.
www.coutanceau.com
Prix fixe: 27,50€.

Grégory Coutanceau has changed the formula of his fourth La Rochelle restaurant (after Les Flots, Le Comptoir des Voyages and Le Comptoir du Sud). After Food & Bar, here is "his" French bistro with its wooden interior and relaxed—or, to sum it up, unpretentious—atmosphere. One can enjoy a ham and parsley terrine, tuna carpaccio, langoustine brochettes with beurre blanc, pork ribs with caramelized potatoes and a pain perdu with vanilla ice cream. The cuisine is clean and flawless. The wine list contains wines from around the world.

● **Bar André**   SIM
5, rue Saint-Jean-de-Pérot.
Tel. 05 46 41 28 24. Fax 05 46 41 64 22.
www.bar-andre.com
Closed Christmas, 1 week Jan.
Prix fixe: 19,30€ (lunch), 35€ (wine inc.).
A la carte: 40–45€.

So famous that one forgets him, André has become the leading figure of maritime produce in La Rochelle, opposite the port. Here are ten restaurants all on a maritime theme, each one different, with service that is often run off its feet and dishes that are sometimes rather carelessly prepared, but nonetheless very authentic. The oysters, a mouclade (mussels with shallots and cream), fish soup, grilled or oven-browned sole with lemon, pan-seared tuna steak with foie gras and a roasted pineapple and mango dessert, *chez* André can be the last word in simple happiness.

● **Le Bout en Train**   SIM
7, rue des Bonnes-Femmes.
Tel. 05 46 41 73 74. Fax 05 46 45 90 76.
Closed Sun., Mon., 1 week Christmas–New Year's, 1 week Aug.–beg. Sept.
Prix fixe: 24€. A la carte: 38€.

A stone's throw away from the market, Gildas and Isabelle run this wood-paneled, colorful bistro with good humor. An area for children with their drawings on the wall sets the tone for this spontaneous place. The chef, Harold Delavalle, plies his craft skillfully. Bone marrow tartines with sea salt flakes, shredded crab in guacamole, tuna grilled with first pressing olive oil, garlic and tomato sauce, olive-stuffed lamb saddle and a rich chocolate cake are confidently realized. Good wine that you can choose yourself in the cellar.

● **A Côté de chez Fred**   SIM

30-34, rue Saint-Nicolas.
Tel. 05 46 41 65 76.
chezfred@rivages.net / www.chezfred.net
Closed Sun. (off season), 10 days Dec.
Prix fixe: 13€, 20€, 25€, 35€.
A la carte: 40€.

Gilles Barres, who was a fisherman, has made this relaxed bistro into a friendly meeting place. Here you can enjoy seafood while contemplating the work of local artists. Pan-simmered cuttlefish in parsley and garlic, Japanese-style fish tartare, skate with lemon butter and rouget with olives slip down easily. Pretty tarte Tatin and merry wines by the glass.

● **Le Dit Vin**   SIM

12, rue Saint-Jean-du-Pérot.
Tel. 05 46 27 50 23.
Closed Sun. (off season), Mon. (off season).
Prix fixe: 15€. A la carte: 35€.

Stéphane Puppi opens his gastronomic wine bistro until late. When he goes into the kitchen, he creates a cuisine that is in rhythm with the markets. The basil-seasoned beef carpaccio, oven-crisped blood sausage with balsamic vinegar and sea bream glazed with shellfish sauce are faultless. The atmosphere is friendly, the tiramisu mellow and the wines sold at reasonable prices.

● **Le Mistral**   SIM

10, pl des Coureauleurs, Le Gabut.
Tel. 05 46 41 24 42. Fax 05 46 41 76 14.
restaurant.lemistral@wanadoo.fr
Closed Nov. 1 vac., Feb. vac.
Prix fixe: 11€ (lunch), 15,30€, 23€, 27€,
7,50€ (child). A la carte: 30€.

A new wind is blowing through the second floor of this wooden house with its superb view over the old port. Oysters, jumbo shrimp salad, sole meunière and a boneless rib steak with green pepper sauce are fantastic. The profiteroles melt in the mouth.

● **La Moulinière**   SIM

24, rue Saint-Sauveur.
Tel. 05 46 41 18 16. Fax 05 46 34 57 94.
www.lamouliniere.fr
Prix fixe: 14,80€, 17,90€, 28€,
7,50€ (child). A la carte: 30–35€.

Patrick Collignon offers a simple cuisine, small checks and Basque dishes of quality in this inn that might be in Hasparren or Bidarray. Mussel gazpacho, fisherman's stew, magret de canard glazed with honey and giant profiteroles in a relaxed atmosphere.

In Aytré (17440). 5 km s via rte de Rochefort.

● **La Maison des Mouettes**   V.COM

1, rue des Claires.
Tel. 05 46 44 29 12. Fax 05 46 34 66 01.
www.lamaisondesmouettes.fr
Prix fixe: 36€, 56€, 59€, 75€,
18€ (child). A la carte: 70€.

This villa overlooking the Bay of Aytré combines pleasure of both eye and palate. Johan Leclerre, who has worked with Ducasse, Troisgros, Gagnaire and Lorain, cooks at an amazing speed. Poached lobster medallion with crushed Vendée coco beans and bacon, grilled scallops glazed in spices with zucchini spaghetti and turbot in its cocotte with stuffed squid and creamy tandoori sauce take one on a culinary journey. On the second floor, in a gleaming contempary décor, Stéphanie Leclerre gives every customer a smiling welcome. The first floor, with its casual bistro style, is more relaxed.

LA ROCHE-SUR-FORON

74800 Haute-Savoie. Paris 552 – Annecy 34 – Thonon-les-Bains 42 – Bonneville 8.
info@larochesurforon.com.
A crossroads to the ski routes and an old Savoie town that is worth the detour.

●	RESTAURANTS

● **Marie-Jean**   ○ V.COM

2131, rte de Bonneville.
Tel. 04 50 03 33 30. Fax 04 50 25 99 98.

contact@restaurant-lemariejean.com
www.restaurant-lemariejean.com
Closed Sun. dinner, Mon., Tue. lunch.
Prix fixe: 25€ (weekday lunch), 35€, 46€,
55€. A la carte: 65–80€.

Patrick and Marie-Hélène Mathis took over
this well-known house in the valley three
years ago. They brought with them a fashionable touch, which succeeded in imposing itself thanks to the know-how of Patrick
and the perfectionist welcome of Marie-
Hélène and of Philippe Diana. The freshness of a vegetable garden is found in the
lobster dish accompanied by a field salad
with oil and honey, tandoori-style scallops
with morels cooked with a buttered jus. The
filet of young duck with white balsamic vinegar with vegetables in season seduce with
the precision of their creation and their
taste. One concludes with an apricot frozen
dessert and the calisson with a kiwi crème
de Cassis sauce, ready to cheerfully attack
the route to the ski stations.

LA ROCHE-SUR-YON

85000 Vendée. Paris 421 – Cholet 67 –
Nantes 67 – La Rochelle 76.
info@o-t.roche.sur.yon.fr.
This was "Napoléon-Vendée", a creation of the
First Empire with a checkerboad layout that
centers around the Place d'Armes. Visit the
Maison des Métiers.

  HOTELS-RESTAURANTS

■ Mercure
117, bd Aristide-Briand.
Tel. 02 51 46 28 00. Fax 02 51 46 28 98.
h1552@accor-hotels.com
www.accorhotels.com
67 rooms: 86–106€.
Prix fixe: 14,90€, 18€, 24,90€.

Near the station, this establishment with
swimming pool and terrace makes a pleasant stop-off for those who want to experience the entertainments of Puy-du-Fou.
The coast is twenty-five minutes away.
Functional rooms and classic cuisine of
a chain hotel.

■ Napoléon
50, bd Aristide-Briand.
Tel. 02 51 05 33 56. Fax 02 51 62 01 69.
hotel-nap@wanadoo.fr / www.inter-hotel.com
Closed Christmas–New Year's vac.
29 rooms: 56–82€.

This classic hotel has the assets of its location in the center of town, its Empire-fur-
nished rooms and its unshocking rates.

● Chez Armand   N COM
86, rue du Président-de-Gaulle.
Tel. 02 51 07 08 09. Fax 02 51 37 66 90.
Closed Sat. lunch, Sun., Mon. dinner,
3 weeks Aug.
A la carte: 36€.

The affable M. Privat has energetically
taken over the former Pavillon Gourmand, putting Elise Bernier in the kitchen.
She demonstrates an attractive know-
how with salad with chilled fish coated
with cold sauce and aspic and chitterling sausage terrine. Cod and potato gratin, salmon tartiflette and the old-style
blanquette de veau taste like you've gone
to grandmother's house. The first bite of
the apple raisin crumble is greeted with a
moment of appreciative silence.

● Auberge de la Borderie   COM
Le Petit Bois Massuyeau, Rte des Sables-
d'Olonne.
Tel. 02 51 08 95 95. Fax 02 51 62 25 78.
restaurantlaborderir@wanadoo.fr
Closed Sun. dinner, Mon., Wed. dinner,
10 days Feb., 3 weeks Aug.
Prix fixe: 23€, 29€, 36€, 10€ (child).
A la carte: 35–45€.

Thierry Boucher gives an intelligent
reworking of old recipes and serves a
meticulously executed contemporary cuisine. Scallops and shrimp in puff pastry
with cabbage, a savory sardine crumble,
pollock medallions with tomato, a layered
baked casserole of potato and duck confit and a peach minestrone are welcome
dishes. The service is efficent and the special menus good value.

RODEZ

12000 Aveyron. Paris 632 – Albi 81 –
Aurillac 88 – Clermont-Ferrand 216.
officetourismerodez@wanadoo.fr.
The heart of Aveyron, and its capital, is a staging
post between the Pays des Bastides and Aubrac,
towards Conques and Le Lévézou. This is the land
of rambling walks and solid, sure gastronomy.
Don't forget to visit the Notre-Dame cathedral and
to wander around the old parts of the town.

 HOTELS-RESTAURANTS

■ **Hostellerie de Fontanges** ❀ 🏠
In Onet-le-Château (12850), Rte de Fontanges.
Tel. 05 65 77 76 00. Fax 05 65 42 82 29.
fontanges.hotel@wanadoo.fr
www.hostellerie-fontanges.com
Rest. closed Sat. lunch, Sun. dinner.
44 rooms: 53–79€. 4 suites: 105–153€.
Prix fixe: 19,50€ (lunch), 24€, 30€, 40€.

This 16th-century château has a good-
humored chic. Martine and Bernard Char-
rié offer a warm welcome, the rooms are
colorful and the grounds and the swimming pool conducive to relaxation. The
regional cooking, in the modern style of
Olivier Nolorgues, is not lacking in ideas.
Foie gras terrine, strips of pike-perch
served with stuffed mushrooms, pan-simmered veal rump roast with an olive jus
and a molten chocolate cake with a white
chocolate quenelle are married with red
Marcillac or white wine from Estaing.

■ **Biney** 🏠
7, bd. Gambetta.
Tel. 05 65 68 01 24. Fax 05 65 75 22 98.
hotel.biney@wanadoo.fr /www.hotel-biney.com
26 rooms: 70–155€. 2 suites: 155€.

The charming venue of the town? This
member of Châteaux et Hôtels de France
has Provençal-style rooms decorated with
pretty materials and beautiful wood. Exquisite breakfasts, hammam and Jacuzzi.

● **Goûts et Couleurs** ◎COM
38, rue de Bonald.
Tel.-Fax 05 65 42 75 10.

jean-luc.fau@wanadoo.fr
goutsetcouleurs.com
Closed Sun. (exc. June, July, Aug., Dec.),
Mon. dinner (exc. June, July, Aug., Dec.),
Wed. dinner (exc. June, July, Aug., Dec.),
1 week beg. Sept., Jan., 10 days beg. May.
Prix fixe: 32€, 75€. A la carte: 58€.

Going down a pedestrian street in old
Rodez, one certainly doesn't expect to go
on a journey to another planet; yet this is
what awaits you if you open the door of artist Jean-Luc Fau. These are his tastes and
colors that he invites you to share through
an inventive cooking that takes you far off
the beaten track. Jumbo shrimp carpaccio
with elderberry flower oil, Pierre Soulages'
pan-tossed squid, fennel-seasoned Atlantic
sea bass with peppers and bitter almond,
lobster stew, veal kidneys and pork belly
with a Muscat caramel sauce go down very
well. One remains under the spell with the
desserts, pots of chocolate flavored with
herbs and flowers or sweet tapas. The chef's
pictures brighten the walls. Final surprise:
the check is within reason.

● **Le Saint-Amans** 🍴COM
12, rue de la Madeleine.
Tel. 05 65 68 03 18.
Closed Sun. dinner, Mon., Mar.
Prix fixe: 17€ (lunch), 27€, 10€ (child).

The surroundings surprise with their large
lacquered mirrors, leather chairs and fil-
tered light that transports you to the Land
of the Rising Sun. But the price of the journey is very reasonable and the cooking of
Jacky Amat traditional and inspired. In
the restaurant, Jeanine's service is nothing but smiles. Lamb sweetbreads with
smoked cream sauce, the three-fish toss
steamed over seaweed, grain-fed pigeon
roasted with Banyuls and cocoa and the
soft dark chocolate fondant with pistachio
sauce and candied oranges are astounding. The local wines are welcome.

● **Le Kiosque** SIM
Av Victor-Hugo.
Tel. 05 65 68 56 21. Fax 05 65 68 47 88.
Prix fixe: 13€ (lunch), 18€, 26€, 40€,
13€ (child). A la carte: 45€.

In the middle of a public garden, this gastronomic restaurant seduces with its thirties décor and the quality of its range of seafood. The cep ravioli cassolette, fish parrillada (mixed grill) and the magret de canard stuffed with mushrooms are worth the wait on the veranda. Exquisite thin apple tart with cinnamon ice cream.

In Bourran (12000). 1,5 km via D994 Cahors.

● **Les Jardins d'Acropolis**
Rue d'Athènes.
Tel. 05 65 68 40 07. Fax 05 65 68 40 67.
dpanis@wanadoo.fr
Closed Sun., Mon. dinner, 2 weeks Aug.
Prix fixe: 16€, 22€, 28€, 35€.

In a part of Rodez built over the past ten years, Dominique Panis is working to recreate the Aveyron region with his own light touch. The special menus are good value, following the market and the seasons and taking inspiration from the great regional neighbors. A former trainee of Bras, Gagnaire and Marcon, Panis gives a discreet performance in a way that is both serious and modest. Foie gras–stuffed hamburger, pork trotter cake, lamb belly stuffed with kidneys and a marshmallow and summer fruit brochette are testament to great ideas that reflect the mood of the times and that put the area back on the culinary map.

ROMANECHE-THORINS

71570 Saône-et-Loire.
Villefranche-sur-Saône 25 – Mâcon 25.
This is one of the great crossroads of Beaujolais country: don't miss the Hameau du Vin, under the label of Duboeuf, in the former station turned museum.

HOTELS-RESTAURANTS

■ **Les Maritonnes**
Rte de Fleurie.
Tel. 03 85 35 51 70. Fax 03 85 35 58 14.
reservation@maritonnes.com
www.maritonnes.com
Closed mid-Feb.–beg. Mar., 2 weeks Oct.
25 rooms: 80–140€.

Prix fixe: 28€, 35€, 50€, 20€ (child).
A la carte: 55€.

Hans and Willemina Meijboom welcome guests to their Virginia creeper–covered home with a kindness typical of their native Holland. The grounds with swimming pool, tennis court and golf practice area as well as the modern rooms delight both sporty types and those who want to sleep late. Both gather at the gastronomic restaurant of Thierry Pasquier or for lunch at his more modestly priced bistro. The frog legs fricassée, pike-perch filet with asparagus and the milk-fed lamb with broad beans are all successful.

ROMANSWILLER see WASSELONNE

ROMORANTIN-LANTHENAY

41200 Loir-et-Cher. Paris 204 – Blois 42 – Orléans 67 – Tours 93 – Vierzon 34.
romorantinlanthenay@fnotsi.net.
The banks of the Sauldre, the site of the old windmill, the automobile museum, the beautiful museum of Sologne just above the water in an ancient setting, the old district and the church of Lanthenay explain the charm of Romo, entry point for Sologne, the eternal city.

HOTELS-RESTAURANTS

● **Le Lion d'Or**
69, rue Georges-Clemenceau.
Tel. 02 54 94 15 15. Fax 02 54 88 24 87.
info@hotel-liondor.fr / www.hotel-liondor.fr
Closed 10 days at end Nov., mid-Feb.–end Mar. Rest. closed Tue. lunch.
13 rooms: 165–390€. 3 suites: 250–480€.
Prix fixe: 95€, 150€. A la carte: 120–175€.

In the middle of the capital of Sologne, the house of the Clément-Barrats has kept the chic of an old-style coaching inn. Marie-Christine continues to lean towards scribblings of yesteryear and the memories of Colette, George Sand and Le Grand Meaulnes, while Didier Clément, her chef husband, reinvents the cuisine of the Loire valley in his own serious, discreet and precise way. We are still crazy about the parsley- and garlic-seasoned wild duck and foie gras terrine and a rabbit saddle with bacon with tangy onion shallot cream sauce, figs, pears and oven-crisped pasta. The pheasant or venison still have pride of place here in the hunting season, which is indeed the most important time of the year in the region. But the sea (grilled scallops with elderberry flower vinegar, red tuna Mikado over shallot cream and tarragon-seasoned turbot with foamy potato milk) is also superbly handled, as are the desserts (a pretty caramelized brioche with angelica sorbet). Loire wines make choice accompaniments and the rooms, redecorated by the Trojan Dominique Honnet, have both ancient and modern comforts in extremely good taste.

● **Auberge Le Lanthenay** `COM`
9 rue Notre-Dame-du-Lieu.
Tel. 02 54 76 09 19. Fax 02 54 76 72 91.
le.lanthenay@wanadoo.fr
10 rooms: 46–52€.
Prix fixe: 23€ (weekdays), 33€, 55€.
A la carte: 55–65€.

Philippe Valin, formerly of Dodin-Bouffant during the time of Jacques Manière, is a skillful practitioner of classicism and gives place of honor to game during the hunting season, as testified by his royal-style wild rabbit, poultry liver and crayfish cake with leeks, Lorraine country lake trout with leeks, foie gras-stuffed pigeon and the strawberry sabayon with Vourvay that makes a wonderful ending to the meal. Small, rustic rooms.

ROQUEBRUNE-CAP-MARTIN

06190 Alpes-Maritimes. Paris 958 – Monaco 9 – Menton 3 – Monte-Carlo 8 – Nice 27.
roquebrune-cap-martin@officedutourisme.com.
A window onto the Méditerranean, bordering the rock of Monaco.

 HOTELS-RESTAURANTS

■ **Vistaero**
Rte de la Grande-Corniche.
Tel. 04 92 10 40 00. Fax 04 93 35 18 94.

info@vistapalace.com / www.vistapalace.com
Rest. closed lunch
70 rooms: 189–350€. 15 suites: 298–690€.
Prix fixe: 60€, 52€, 47€.

This is an exceptional place. The setting, which overlooks Monaco and the sea, is superb, the rooms offer luxury and top-of-the-line comfort with the fitness and rejuvenation center, the heated swimming pool, the hammam and the Mediterranean garden adding voluptuous moments. The lobster salad, langoustine tartare, sea bream, veal sweetbreads, apple tart and a chocolate soufflé signal no snobbery but in no way detract from the enchanted stay that one has in this establishment. Obviously, all of this costs money.

■ **Victoria**
7, promenade de Cap-Martin.
Tel. 04 93 35 65 90. Fax 04 93 28 27 02.
www.hotelmenton.com/hotel-victoria
32 rooms: 75–105€.

An uninterrupted view of the ocean blue, intelligently laid-out rooms, a smiling welcome and reasonable prices are the assets of this establishment, where the terrace is conducive to a spontaneous bit of reading or lazing.

■ **Le Roquebrune** `SIM`
100, av Jean-Jaurès.
Tel. 04 93 35 00 16. Fax 04 93 28 98 36.
leroquebrune@wanadoo.fr
www.leroquebrune.com
4 rooms: 100–135€. 1 suite: 155–195€.

A stone's throw from the center of Monaco and of Menton, the charming guest rooms of Marine and Patricia Marinovitch offer a simple, warm refuge, supplemented by wonderful breakfasts.

ROQUEBRUNE-SUR-ARGENS see FREJUS

LA ROQUE-GAGEAC

24250 Dordogne. Paris 535 – Périgueux 71 – Brive 71 – Sarlat 9.
Along the Dordogne of châteaux, the most

beautiful river in the world, this is a village of yellow stone with golden reflections.

 HOTELS-RESTAURANTS

■ La Belle Etoile

Bourg.
Tel. 05 53 29 51 44.
Hotel.belle-etoile@wanadoo.fr
Closed beg. Nov.–beg. Apr.
Rest. closed Mon., Wed. lunch.
15 rooms: 50–75€.
Prix fixe: 24€, 29€, 38€.

Régis Ongaro, born into the family business, trained with Palais in Biarritz, Martinez in Cannes and Bardet in Tours, has created the beautiful riverside place. The summer terrace gives onto the landing stage while the special menus are inviting and angelically priced. A poached terrine of foie gras, coddled egg with morels, cod crumble, a layered veal shank and potato casserole all have energy. Add to this young duck breast with slow-cooked cabbage and a chocolate pastilla and it seems that happiness is right here, in this place filled with the fragrance of summer jasmine right beside the river Espérance. Pretty rooms that are undergoing renovation.

ROSBRUCK see FORBACH

ROSCOFF

29680 Finistère. Paris 564 – Brest 65 – Saint-Polde-Léon 5 – Morlaix 27 – Quimper 100.
The first thalassotherapy center in Brittany and even France, ferries to and from Plymouth, the île de Batz just opposite, good coastal air, the port and the town, gastronomy and the invitation to stroll around: there are all sorts of good reasons for coming to Roscoff and for staying.

 HOTELS-RESTAURANTS

● Le Brittany et le Yachtman

Bd Sainte-Barbe, BP 47.
Tel. 02 98 69 70 78. Fax 02 98 61 13 29.

hotel.brittany@wanadoo.fr
www.hotel-brittany.com
Closed mid-Nov.–end Mar.
Rest. closed lunch, Mon.
23 rooms: 115–255€. 2 suites: 260–315€.
Prix fixe: 39€, 59€, 69€, 19€ (child).

Arriving at the Chapalains, one is immediately seduced by the setting of their beautiful manor house facing the port and the île de Batz. The cozy rooms in muted shades, the heated swimming pool, the hammam, the gardens: all promise a charming stay. The restaurant serves the tasty cooking of Loïc Le Bail, a young Breton who trained with Jeffroy, Gagnaire, Senderens and Savoy, who adapts the culinary traditions of his region in the light of a very contemporary creativity. Fresh lobster with sweet peas, line-fished Atlantic sea bass with a ginger carrot sorbet, lemongrass-seasoned spinach, suckling pig roasted with savory and served with a large grilled sausage and a seasonal fruit dessert with a cinnamon infusion and passion fruit with a milk sorbet are accompanied by one of the great Bordeaux vintages from the cellar. This is close to real happiness. Relais & Châteaux.

● Le Temps de Vivre

Pl de l'Eglise (pl Lacaze-Duthiers).
Tel. 02 98 61 27 28 / hotel: 02 98 19 33 19.
Fax 02 98 61 19 46 / hotel: 02 98 19 33 00.
contact@letempsdevivre.net
www.letempsdevivre.net
Hotel closed 2 weeks Nov., 2 weeks Mar.
Rest. closed Sun. dinner (exc. July–Aug.), Mon., Tue. lunch, 3 weeks Nov., 3 weeks Mar.
13 rooms: 97–220€. 2 suites: 180–266€.
Prix fixe: 39€ (weekdays), 52€, 62€, 98€, 14€ (child).

Jean-Yves Crenn is—we might as well admit it—one of the favorites of this guide. On the first floor of a Hotel Ibis, one that has several "Zen" and exquisitely decorated rooms, he has established his unexpected domain. Line gives a charming welcome, the staff are attentive, the service watchful, the île de Batz (offering the best small apples in the world) just opposite. On the plate? All the happiness that one can imagine in Brittany, produced by an unparalled technician. This former deli man from Cléder is indeed one of the foremost chefs of his region. If you don't believe it, come and taste warm oysters with lettuce sauce, foie gras in apple jelly and peppered oil, cabbage stuffed with crab and Roscoff pink onions, gently-simmered pollock filet with Ile de Batz potatoes, Atlantic sea bass with kouign-patatez, meats, Paul Renault's house poultry (duck or pigeon) and desserts (strawberry soup with lemon jelly and coconut cream and Breton shortcake with apples and caramel mousse) of an unequalled freshness and clarity. How good it is to be with the Crenns.

■ Armen Le Triton

Rue du Docteur-Bagot.
Tel. 02 98 61 24 44. Fax 02 98 69 77 97.
resa@hotel-letriton.com
www.hotel-letriton.com
Closed Jan.–end Feb.
44 rooms: 40–63€.

Very near the thalassotherapy center, this Breton house promotes calm and repose with its functional rooms and a tennis court.

■ Aux Tamaris

49, rue Edouard-Corbière.
Tel. 02 98 61 22 99. Fax 02 98 69 74 36.
www.hotel-aux-tamaris.com
Closed mid-Nov.–mid-Feb.
26 rooms: 47–75€.

Entirely facing the sea, this good family hotel is experiencing a second youth beneath its stone exterior. Soft shades and a smiling welcome set the tone.

■ Hôtel du Centre

5, rue Gambetta.
Tel. 02 98 61 24 25. Fax 02 98 61 15 43.
contact@chezjanie.com / www.chezjanie.com
Closed mid-Nov.–mid-Feb.
Rest. closed Tue. (off season).
16 rooms: 59–98€.
Prix fixe: 13€, 15,80€. A la carte: 25–30€.

The rooms with their warm colors have been redecorated by Jean-Marie Chap-

alain, who has taken over this house on the port. At Janie's, the bar-restaurant allows one to enjoy, on the terrace on fine days, salmon spread, mussels, the catch of the day, local desserts and a local prune flan.

■ Talabardon

Pl de l'Eglise.
Tel. 02 98 61 24 95. Fax 02 98 61 10 54.
hotel.talabardon@wanadoo.fr
www.talabardon.fr
Closed Nov.–Mar. Rest. closed Sun. dinner, Thu. (exc. dinner July-Aug.).
37 rooms: 58–134,50€.
Prix fixe: 25€, 32€, 45€.

Claude and Elisabeth Talabardon's hotel on the Place de l'Eglise, owned by the family since 1890, has character. The rooms have an old-fashioned comfort while the restaurant room offers a view of the sea, seagulls and boats. Pascal Costiou puts on a regional performance with pan-tossed scallops and artichokes, catfish stuffed with endives, beef tenderloin with pepper and a soft-centered chocolate cake with raspberry sauce.

■ Thalasstonic

Rue Victor-Hugo.
Tel. 02 98 29 20 20. Fax 02 98 29 20 19.
imr@thalasso.com / www.thalasso.com
Closed 3 weeks Dec.
74 rooms: 68–132€.
Prix fixe: 23€. A la carte: 30–35€.

The thalassotherapy center is next to this modern hotel where the rooms are both comfortable and quiet. There are two swimming pools (covered and open-air) and one can enjoy the cooking of Bruno Tartrat in either healthy or gastronomic versions, as one chooses. In the latter category, we appreciated pan-fried breast of pheasant with figs in cocoa sauce, steamed cod filet seasoned with white wine and chives and the grilled chitterling sausage with slow-cooked shallots.

● L'Ecume des Jours

Quai d'Auxerre.
Tel. 02 98 61 22 83. Fax 02 98 61 13 01.

www.ecume-roscoff.com.fr
Closed Tue., Wed., Dec., Jan.
Prix fixe: 22€, 28€, 38€, 48€.

Regulars to this hotel are in a hurry to return to the renovated terrace with a view over the sea or to the interior of this beautiful 16th-century house. Michel Quéré responds to these expectations with a well-thought-out menu. Oven-crisped bacon and crab, oven-roasted pollock with a buckwheat crêpe and artichoke purée, magret de canard with charlotte mille-feuille and mushrooms and the famous coffee-flavored menez-bré put a smile on one's face, which the check doesn't wipe off.

● Les Alizés   COM

37, rue de l'Amiral-Courbet, quai d'Auxerre.
Tel. 02 98 69 75 90. Fax 02 98 61 13 22.
Closed Sun. dinner (off season), Mon. (off season), 20 Dec.–mid-Jan.
Prix fixe: 11,90€ (wine inc.), 18€, 30€, 18€, 8€ (child). A la carte: 38€.

This contemporary brasserie with its bay window overlooking the port is the domain of Isabelle and François Abjean. A successful team in the kitchen produces results: a pair of salmon spreads, scallop carpaccio with ginger and a monkfish navarin with raspberry. Charming welcome and prompt service.

● Le Surcouf   SIM

Rue de l'Amiral-Réveillère.
Tel. 02 98 69 71 89 / 02 98 61 16 61.
Fax 02 98 61 10 19.
surcouf@jalima.fr /www.jalima.fr
Closed Tue., Wed.
Prix fixe: 9,80€ (weekday lunch), 14,80€, 25€, 7€ (child).

The brasserie of Pierre and Myriam Botton-Amiot looks good and here one can cheerfully enjoy very lively local dishes. Scallop and langoustine salad with artichokes, pan-tossed pink onions and Atlantic sea bass, oven-roasted lobster, country lamb and the beef tartare are good. The kouign-amann is a monument.

ROSENAU

68128 Haut-Rhin. Paris 493 – Colmar 59 – Mulhouse 24 – Altkirch 25 – Bâle 15.
Between Sundgau and little Camargue, a village of Alsace that flirts with the Rhine and the Huningue canal.

■ ● | RESTAURANTS

● Au Lion d'Or   N-COM

5, rue de Village-Neuf.
Tel. 03 89 68 21 97. Fax 03 89 70 68 05.
Closed Mon., Tue., Feb., 2 weeks Aug.
Prix fixe: 13€ (weekday lunch), 23€, 28€, 41€.

Théo Baumlin offers, on the covered terrace on fine days or otherwise in the attractive restaurant, well-composed menus that change with his moods and the seasons. Foie gras terrine with aspic, arborio risotto with vegetables, chanterelles and parmesan, rabbit leg over noodles, frozen kirsch and a Fougerolle sour cherry kougelhopf make one want to take up residence here. Wonderful welcome.

ROSHEIM

67560 Bas-Rhin. Paris 482 – Strasbourg 31 – Molsheim 7 – Obernai 6.
accueil@rosheim.com.
The long street filled with old monuments, its yellow sandstone church, its pagan house, the oldest in the province, but also Rosenwiller, an almost mountainous neighbor with its countryside vineyards and the Jewish cemetery hidden by the forest, all make it worth the detour.

 | HOTELS-RESTAURANTS

● Hostellerie du Rosenmeer   ◯ 🏠

45, av de la Gare.
Tel. 03 88 50 43 29. Fax 03 88 49 20 57.
info@le-rosenmeer.com
www.le-rosenmeer.com
Closed Feb. vac., 2 weeks end July–beg. Aug.
Rest. closed Sun. dinner, Mon., Wed.
Winstub closed lunch, Mon.
20 rooms: 40–98€.

Prix fixe: 74€ (wine inc.), 110€ (wine inc.).
A la carte: 60€.

Hubert Maetz was for ten years in succession the second in command to Westermann in Buerehiesel. He is also the efficient, but discreet, partner of our colleague Simone Morgenthaler on the TV channel France 3 who illustrates her "sweet and savory" programs in dialect with recipes from people of the region prepared by this serene maestro. At home, the gentle Hubert runs his winstub (known as "D'Rosemer"), looks after the special menus for the regulars (onion soup and pike-perch with käsenäpfle, a local fromage blanc dumpling) and watches over his very comfortable hotel. It is true that, if the whole effect is more functional than charming, his establishment is comfortable, the service smiling and exact, the cellar abundant, without forgetting the good wines produced by papa Maetz. But one comes first and foremost to discover, in a light restaurant with its huge shuttered bay windows opening onto the outside, the ideas of the moment: truffle-seasoned quick-seared minced scallops presented with a layer of raw scallops on top, pan-seared scallops with walnuts and an herb salad, Atlantic sea bass cooked on pine bark with mugwort jus and the duck foie gras carpaccio with Vin Jaune and a foie bonbon. The roasted capon with its firm and delicious meat, deboned and served with the stuffed and rolled drumstick and his delicious buewespaetzle fall in the same vein, with a wink to the region. Add to this superb desserts: orange and saffron salad with mousse and sorbet of the same flavors and roasted and caramelized Victoria pineapple with coconut Chantilly and a meltingly delicious milk sorbet, and you will say to yourself that here is a truly fine place.

■ La Petite Auberge

41, rue du Général-de-Gaulle.
Tel. 03 88 50 40 60. Fax 03 88 48 00 90.
christophe-vasconi@wanadoo.fr
Closed vac. Mar., end June–beg. July.
Rest. closed Wed., Thu.

5 studios: 45-86€. Prix fixe: 20€,
9,50€ (child). A la carte: 45€.

Neat rooms in a paneled hotel and a classic cuisine in a pleasant inn: this is the domain of the modest Richard Vasconi. Scallop salad with lobster butter, spicy roasted sea bream, beef tenderloin with escargots and the frozen kouglof are dishes of which one never tires.

● Auberge du Cerf   COM

120, rue du Général-de-Gaulle.
Tel.-Fax 03 88 50 40 14.
Closed Sun. dinner, Mon., 2 weeks Jan.
Prix fixe: 12€ (lunch), 15€, 20€.
A la carte: 35–45€.

Pierre Eber keeps a wise and watchful eye on this 16th-century house that pays homage to Alsace in all its forms. Escargots in puff pastry with Munster cheese, pike-perch in fish broth, choucroute and a frozen vacherin all slip down without a second thought. The cheerfulness of the establishment is contagious and the checks not too inflated.

ROSTRENEN

22110 Côtes-d'Armor. Paris 488 – Quimper 70 – Saint-Brieuc 60 – Carhaix-Plouguer 21.
Inland Côtes d'Armor also has its charm.

● RESTAURANTS

● L'Eventail des Saveurs

3, place du Bourg-Coz.
Tel. 02 96 29 10 71. Fax 02 96 29 34 75.
www.leventail-des-saveurs.fr
Closed Sun. dinner, Mon., Wed. dinner,
Feb. vac., 2 weeks end June–beg. July.
Prix fixe: 14,50€ (weekday lunch), 25€,
35€, 45€, 7€ (child). A la carte: 55€.

In his brightly colored restaurant, Laurent Pacquer serves a regional cuisine adapted to today's tastes in its preparation style and use of ideas from other lands. A rye spring roll with Guéméné chitterling sausage and orange-seasoned slow-cooked cabbage, pollock filet with creamed garlic and a Jerusalem artichoke purée, a half pigeon cooked with licorice and chocolate and dried fruits "sausage" are well conceived. There is also a play area for children.

ROUBION see VALBERG

ROUEN

76000 Seine-Maritime. Paris 131 – Amiens 121 – Caen 123 – Le Havre 88 – Lille 230 – Tours 275.
ot-rouen@mcom.fr.

Has Rouen changed since the time of Flaubert's retreats at Croisset? Yes—Paris is now an hour and a bit away by the "turbo" that runs out of Paris-Saint-Lazare station. It is with some emotion that one explores the old alleyways around the cathedral immortalised by Monet, Vieux-Marché square where Joan of Arc was burnt, its lovely marketplace, Gros-Horloge street, its up-and-coming shops, but also the extraordinary Aître St. Maclou, a medieval cemetery that accepted plague victims; everything seems to have come right out of the Middle Ages. All this almost makes one forget to explore the many good restaurants with their wood-paneled décor that seem to have come straight out of Gustave Flaubert's *Un Coeur Simple*.

■	HOTELS

■ Mercure Centre
7, rue Croix-de-Fer.
Tel. 02 35 52 69 52. Fax 02 35 89 41 46.
h1301@accor-hotels.com
www.mercure.com
125 rooms: 125–150€. 4 suites: 250€.

This hotel is a surprise in the old town. Surrounded by medieval sites, it is worth the detour for its modern architecture and its art deco foyer but also for its pleasant rooms.

■ Mercure Champ de Mars
12, av Aristide-Briand.
Tel. 02 35 52 42 32. Fax 02 35 08 15 06.
h1273@accor-hotels.com / www.mercure.com
139 rooms: 105–250€. 2 suites: 210–250€.

The dining room opens onto the Champ de Mars and serves a cuisine of quality. The rooms are intelligently set out to maximize comfort and the Seine runs past a stone's throw away.

■ Le Dandy
93, rue Cauchoise.
Tel. 02 35 07 32 00. Fax 02 35 15 48 82.
contact@hotels-rouen.net
www.hotels-rouen.net
Closed Christmas–New Year's.
18 rooms: 68–105€.

Right in the middle of the pedestrian streets, a little hotel with quiet rooms that are all different, in shades of pink and beige, a pleasant welcome and reasonable prices.

■ Hôtel de Dieppe
Pl Bernard-Tissot.
Tel. 02 35 71 96 00. Fax 02 35 89 65 21.
hotel.dieppe@wanadoo.fr / www.bestwestern.fr
Rest closed Sat. lunch.
41 rooms: 60–102,50€.
Prix fixe: 19€, 27€, 36€.

Opposite the station, this building dating from 1880 has gradually renovated its rooms and now enjoys modern facilities. The restaurant, Les Quatre Saisons, offers the ritual Rouennaise duckling.

■ Hôtel du Vieux Marché
15, rue de la Pie.
Tel. 02 35 71 00 88. Fax 02 35 70 75 94.
www.hotelduvieuxmarche.com
46 rooms: 92–143€. 1 suite: 253€.

Elegantly renovated, several meters from the Vieux-Marché, this good hotel offers well-equipped and quiet rooms. For dinner, Les Nymphéas is next door.

■ Hôtel des Carmes
33, pl des Carmes.
Tel. 02 35 71 92 31. Fax 02 35 71 76 96.
www.hoteldescarmes.com
12 rooms: 47–63€.

Ceilings painted in trompe-l'oeil, functional and quiet rooms, low prices and a gorgeous welcome from Hervé and Marie Dorin: these are the assets of this discreet, central hotel.

■ Hôtel de la Cathédrale

12, rue Saint-Romain.
Tel. 02 35 71 57 95. Fax 02 35 70 15 54.
www.hotel-de-la-cathedrale.fr
26 rooms: 49–89€.

Opposite the cathedral, this house with 17th-century wooden frames hides a delightful patio and well-equipped blue and pink rooms. The breakfast room is typical of Normandy.

■ Le Vieux Carré

34, rue Ganterie.
Tel. 02 35 71 67 70. Fax 02 35 71 19 17.
vieux-carre@mcom.fr / www.vieux-carre.fr
Rest. closed dinner, Sun. (exc. tea salon).
13 rooms: 55–60€.
Prix fixe: 13€ (lunch, wine inc.).

Built around a patio, this wood-framed house in the center of town has comfortable rooms and an impressive restaurant-tearoom.

In Saint-Martin-du-Vivier (76160). 8 km.

■ La Bertelière

1641, av du Mesnil-Gremichon.
Tel. 02 35 60 44 00. Fax 02 35 61 56 63.
reception@la-berteliere.fr
www.la-berteliere.fr
42 rooms: 93–98€. 2 suites: 190€.
Prix fixe: 21€ (weekday lunch), 29€, 39€, 49€, 17€ (child). A la carte: 50–60€.

If you want to sleep in rural surroundings five minutes from the center, this country house is very practical. The rooms are decorated in warm shades of orange, red and yellow, the terrace is a haven and the restaurant well-kept.

● RESTAURANTS

● Gill

9, quai de la Bourse.
Tel. 02 35 71 16 14. Fax 02 35 71 96 91.
gill@relaischateaux.com / www.gill.fr
Closed Sun., Mon., Christmas–New Year's, end July–23 Aug.
Prix fixe: 35€, 62€, 87€.

Gilles Tournadre is as one imagines a native of Normandy: silent and insular. He refuses lengthy explanations but expresses himself through pure products, skillful preparation, short cooking times and clever sauces. In his renovated surroundings of the quai de la Bourse, opposite the Seine, the star of Rouen proudly flies the regional flag. Rare cooked salmon in a spicy crust, hazelnut-breaded John Dory with spinach, onions and ginger, clear langoustine broth and pan-seared turbot with capers and preserved lemons take on, in his hands, an exotic air. With a view to the south or even to Asian islands, this Norman astonishes rather than reassures with great local dishes reworked and lightened: the pigeon in the style of Rouen, simmered in blood sauce, with a vinegar-heightened sauce to die for. Something that is normally too rich, fatty and heavy becomes, in Gilles' hand, a cunning dish with a contemporary air. The desserts are in the same vein, for example terrine of slow-cooked apples with caramel cream ice cream. The wines (such as the Sancerres of father-in-law Lucien Crochet) are the best of their kind: fruity, lively and natural. To come to a vital point, everything that is offered here is priced with a rare modesty, which is a reflection of the house itself, with its shades of gray, and of Sylvie's welcome, which is warm but without pretension. Here is tranquil perfection.

● L'Ecaille

26, rampe Cauchoise.
Tel. 02 35 70 95 52. Fax 02 35 70 83 49.
www.lecaille.fr
Closed Sat. lunch, Sun. dinner, Mon.,
1 week May, 1 week beg. Aug.
Prix fixe: 31€, 45€, 75€, 90€.
A la carte: 110€.

A daring bet that has paid off: Marc Tellier has banished meat from the menu of his contemporary restaurant. He also selects, with the greatest care, the fish and other sea produce that go into dishes that are touching in their simplicity, like their names. Softly spiced rouget tagine, grilled langoustines, oven-roasted turbot and John Dory with ginger are unusually to the point. The same approach goes for the desserts: the apple soufflé and the mille-feuille take you straight back to childhood. On the wine side, the great vintages exalted by Nicole are a marvelous accompaniment to these feasts.

● Les Nymphéas

9, rue de la Pie.
Tel. 02 35 89 26 69. Fax 02 35 70 98 81.
lesnympheas.rouen@wanadoo.fr
www.les-nympheas.fr
Closed Sun., Mon., 3 weeks Aug.
Prix fixe: 29,50€, 38€, 48€.
A la carte: 76€.

At the end of a small paved courtyard, this half-timbered house is a beautiful blend of rusticity and modern restraint. The half-shaded, half-sunny terrace is a blessing in summer. Patrice Kukurudz produces dishes of character in a menu built around the flagship products of the region. One enjoys the delectable pan-seared foie gras escalope with its jus heightened with cider vinegar, langoustine ravioli with slow-cooked new cabbage, slow-cooked lobster stew with Sauternes, sliced veal tenderloin, veal sweetbread and morel fricassée and the hot apple soufflé with Calvados. The service is as warm as it is attentive and the menus balanced.

● Les P'tits Parapluies

46, rue du Bourg-l'Abbé.
Tel. 02 35 88 55 26. Fax 02 35 70 24 31.
lespetitsparapluies@hotmail.fr
www.lesptits-parapluies.com
Closed Sat. lunch, Sun. dinner, Mon.,
1 week beg. Jan., 3 weeks Aug.
Prix fixe: 25€, 34€, 44€, 55€.

This 16th-century building, a former umbrella factory, is skillfully run by Marc Andrieu. The dining room in shades of yellow, with ancient beams, is full of charm. One savors pan-tossed langoustine salad with shellfish vinaigrette, grilled Atlantic sea bass with dill jus, pan-tossed veal sweetbreads and chitterling sausage with cider-seasoned ratte potato purée. One must not forget to taste the fine farm cheeses before allowing oneself to be tempted by a pineapple crumble with an island sorbet, so as to finish on a more exotic note. The menus are reasonable and the service irreproachable.

● La Couronne

31, pl du Vieux-Marché.
Tel. 02 35 71 40 90. Fax 02 35 71 05 78.
contact@lacouronne.com
www.lacouronne.com
Prix fixe: 23€ (lunch), 29€, 39€ (wine inc.),
45€, 16€ (child).

This inn in Vieux-Marché square has been part of the history of the town since 1345. Its typical decoration, with wood panels and frescoes dedicated to Joan of Arc, is full of character. In the kitchen, tradition rules and Vincent Taillefer is right in the mold. Pan-seared foie gras escalope, turbot with hollandaise sauce, pan-fried boneless Norman rib steak with shallots and an apple soufflé are faithful to tradition.

● Le Beffroy

15, rue Beffroy.
Tel. 02 35 71 55 27. Fax 02 35 89 66 12.
Closed Sun. dinner, Tue.
Prix fixe: 15,25€ (weekdays), 30,50€, 45€.
A la carte: 56€.

This building, typical of Normandy with its wooden framework, dates from the 16th century. The interior is cozy, with polished beams and regional pictures. The cuisine of Odile Engel constitutes a hymn of praise to tradition and this native of Obernai prepares, with total mastery, local classics such as lobster salad, langoustine with diced assorted vegetables, Rouen-style duck, beef tenderloin with ceps and one of the best chocolate tarts there is. Marcel Engel, for his part, knows his cellar like the back of his hand, with a very particular affection for white wines of Alsace. One can find no fault with the establishment, especially as its prices have barely increased.

● Au Bois Chenu COM

23, pl de la Pucelle-d'Orléans.
Tel. 02 35 71 19 54. Fax 02 35 89 49 83.
Closed Sun. dinner (exc. July–Aug.),
Tue. dinner, Wed.
Prix fixe: 19€, 16,50€, 27€, 34€, 11€ (child).

Eugénie Barrel runs this stylish and modern establishment, in shades of straw yellow, white and blue, a stone's throw from the Vieux Marché. Oysters in seafood broth and langoustines seasoned with fines herbes, tagliatelli and foie gras gratin, scallops with thinly sliced endives and the thin apple tart served hot go down a treat.

● Le Réverbère COM

5, pl de la République.
Tel. 02 35 07 03 14. Fax 02 35 89 77 93.
Closed Sun., 1 week Apr., end July–19 Aug.
Prix fixe: 35€, 45€, 48€, 120€.
A la carte: 52–60€.

José Rato welcomes customers to a clever cuisine in his restaurant, redecorated in black and white, housed in a fifties building very near the riverbank. Scrambled eggs with oysters, preserved herrings as found at Josephine's in the rue Cherche-Midi in Paris, Atlantic sea bass with a ginger infusion and the duck with Thai herbs make a good impression. The vanilla mille-feuille is remarkably light.

● Les Maraîchers SIM

37, pl du Vieux-Marché.
Tel. 02 35 71 57 73. Fax 02 35 70 53 12.
www.les-maraichers.fr
Closed Christmas.
Prix fixe: 15€, 19,90€. A la carte: 35–45€.

This Paris-style bistro, with its enameled panels, mirrors, old posters, family photos, oak floor planks and bar decorated with jugs welcomes people for pleasant suppers. Smoked salmon, tartare, local boneless rib steak and chocolate cake are eaten enthusiastically.

● Le 37 SIM

37, rue Saint-Etienne-des-Tonneliers.
Tel. 02 35 70 56 65.

Closed Sun., Mon., 1 week beg. Jan.,
1 week Apr., 3 weeks Aug.
Prix fixe: 17,50€. A la carte: 39–45€.

Gilles Tournadre's second restaurant is in the spirit of the times. The surroundings are in shades of plum and the cuisine a French-style version of global cuisine. Sylvain Nouin concocts up-to-date dishes (dill-marinated salmon with a potato mango tartare seasoned with basil, roasted tuna with sweet-and-sour hearts of palm, duck leg with lemon and honey and the chocolate pear tiramisu) that easily tease and then please. The menu changes every month and the check remains low.

● Le 16-9ᵉ SIM

130, rue Socrate.
Tel.-Fax 02 35 70 63 33.
Closed Sun.
Prix fixe: 15€ (lunch), 23€, 29€,
8€ (child). A la carte: 40€.

This restaurant in a fashionable square of old Rouen, with its black and white decoration and red lighting, resembles a sixties Italian cinema, although François Poret's cuisine is very contemporary. Foie gras and pain d'épice mille-feuille, Atlantic sea bass roasted in a shellfish and olive oil emulsion, and the pistachio and raspberry tart are amazing. There is a tearoom in the afternoon.

ROUFFACH

68250 Haut-Rhin. Paris 458 – Colmar 15 – Mulhouse 28 – Bâle 60.
General Lefebvre's old native stomping grounds hides several treasures, including a dramatic square containing beautiful houses with oriels and redans and a large church that played host to the birth of the legendary women's revolt. Vineyards all around.

 HOTELS-RESTAURANTS

■ Château d'Isenbourg

Tel. 03 89 78 58 50. Fax 03 89 78 53 70.
isenbourg@grandesetapes.fr
www.isenbourg.com

40 rooms: 57–410€. 1 suite: 530€.
Prix fixe: 45€, 62€. A la carte: 75€.

Overlooking vineyards, this 18th-century château offers many pleasures. Large, comfortable rooms with stylish furnishings, two swimming pools (one covered), a fitness suite, hammam and Jacuzzi contribute to the joy of being there. The cuisine is not to be outdone. Didier Lefeuvre serves his adopted region skillfully with jumbo shrimp fried in angelhair pasta, scallops in an endive tarte Tatin, farm-raised poultry breast simmered in Riesling and a chocolate soufflé. Large cellar in which Alsace plays the main role and excellent service.

■ La Ville de Lyon

1, rue Poincaré.
Tel. 03 89 49 65 51. Fax 03 89 49 76 67.
www.villes-et-vignobles.com
Closed 10 days Christmas–New Year's.
50 rooms: 48–82€. 7 suites: 110€.

This inn makes an ideal base for visiting the region. The rooms furnished in Louis XV, Louis XVI or contemporary styles, the outdoor heated swimming pool, the hammam, the Jacuzzi and the health center immediately make one want to return. (See Restaurants: Philippe Bohrer.)

● Philippe Bohrer   ◎V.COM

1, rue Poincaré.
Tel. 03 89 49 62 49. Fax 03 89 49 76 67.
villedelyon@villes-et-vignoble.com
www.villes-et-vignoble.com
Closed Sun., Mon. lunch, Wed. lunch,
3 weeks Mar., 1 week at end July,
1 week beg. Aug.
Prix fixe: 27€, 38€, 61€, 80€.

Philippe Bohrer has had a dream career: Loiseau, Lameloise, Gaertner, Bocuse, l'Elysée.... Which allows one to forecast the best future for this native of Upper Rhine who has decided to come back to settle in his home of Rouffach. Three dining rooms with a warm décor of welcoming pale wood where one can eat dishes that swing between regional tradition and innovation. One makes quick work of beet ravioli with their caramel, Atlan-

tic sea bass filet with aromatic herbs and black morels, breast of guinea hen with slow-cooked shallots and a hoseradish-seasoned pigeon, poached then oven browned. We finish on a note both sweet and rather acidic with variations on the theme of rhubarb and strawberries served with ice cream. The welcome is wonderful, the service very attentive and the wines selected with discernment.

● Winstub de la Poterne   SIM

7, rue de la Poterne.
Tel. 03 89 78 53 29. Fax 03 89 78 50 28.
www.flaneurvert.com
Closed Sun. dinner, Mon., Wed. dinner, Feb. vac.
Prix fixe: 8,25€ (weekday lunch), 22€, 28€,
7,50€ (child). A la carte: 30–35€.

Jacques Wipff has made this lively tavern into the gastronomic center of his town. Oxtail and foie gras terrine in wine aspic, pike-perch simmered in Riesling with buttered noodles, a liver quenelle and the apple streudel meet with universal acclaim. Friendly service, serious wine list and reasonable prices.

In Bollenberg (68250). 6 km via N83, exit for D15.

● Au Vieux Pressoir   COM
& Hôtel du Bollenberg

Domaine du Bollenberg.
Tel. 03 89 49 60 04 (rest.)
03 89 49 62 47 (hotel). Fax 03 89 49 76 16.
info@bollenberg.com www.bollenberg.com
Hotel closed Christmas.
Rest. closed Sun. dinner (off season).
45 rooms: 45–61€. 1 suite: 105€.
Prix fixe: 25€ (weekday lunch), 26€ (wine inc.), 33€ (Sat., Sun., lunch) 10€ (child).
A la carte: 45–50€.

In the Meyer family, love of hospitality and the culinary arts have been passed down from generation to generation. In the guesthouse, Michel Runner prepares classics such as foie gras, pike-perch cooked in wine, pork trotter medallions accompanied with local Saint Appoline wine and a frozen kouglof with Marc de Gewurtz, created by Blaise Meyer. There is a choice of thirty or so *eaux-de-vie*. One can sleep in one of the comfortable rooms of the hotel where Marie-Madeleine Holt-zheyer gives a warm welcome. Hammam, sauna, fitness suite.

ROUFFIAC-TOLOSAN see **TOULOUSE**
ROULLET-SAINT-ESTEPHE see **ANGOULEME**

LES ROUSSES

39220 Jura. Paris 462 – Genève 42 – Gex 30 – Nyon 22 – Saint-Claude 31.
ot.les.rousses@wanadoo.fr.
This beautiful ski station in French Jura is king of cross-country skiing and rambling. Its greatest specialty, other than Vacherin and morbier? The good air.

 | HOTELS-RESTAURANTS

■ Le France

323, rue Pasteur.
Tel. 03 84 60 01 45. Fax 03 84 60 04 63.
hoteldefrance-lesrousses@wanadoo.fr
Closed 11 Nov.–mid-Dec., 1 week at end Apr., 10 days beg. May.
28 rooms: 63–112€.
Prix fixe: 19,50€, 49€, 10€ (child).
A la carte: 60–65€.

This good mountain hotel offers cozy rooms that are all different, even if with rather outdated decoration, as well as a serious regional cuisine, reworked and amended by Philippe Romanato. He makes a success of foie gras and pain d'épice mille-feuille, simmered monk-fish medallions breaded in a crust of dried fruits and a local suckling pig flavored with lemon and honey. Monique Petit gives an easy welcome while Christophe Barbier looks after the dining room attentively and enjoys helping people discover the wines of Jura.

■ Le Lodge

309, rue Pasteur.
Tel. 03 84 60 50 64.
lelodge@wanadoo.fr
11 rooms: 60–125€.

With a very mountain décor, this new, stylish chalet offers warm and friendly wood-paneled rooms.

In La Cure (39220). 2,5 km se via N5, rte de Genève.

● Arbez Hôtel Franco-Suisse   COM

Rte de Genève.
Tel. 03 84 60 02 20. Fax 03 84 60 08 59.
hotelarbez@netgdi.fr /www.hotelarbez.fr.st
Hotel closed Nov. Rest. closed Sun. dinner (off season), Mon. (off season), Tue. (off season), Nov., 2 weeks beg. Apr.
10 rooms: 59–69€.
Prix fixe: 26€, 33€, 8€ (child).
A la carte: 50–55€.

This mountain inn on the Swiss border has simple but carefully set-out rooms and a very well-prepared cuisine. Bérénice Salino concocts morels in a pastry crust, pike-perch simmered in Savagnin, morel-stuffed chicken breast and a sour cherry crème brûlée that all make a good impression. Wonderful welcome.

ROUSSILLON

84220 Vaucluse. Paris 727 – Apt 11 – Avignon 51 – Bonnieux 10 – Carpentras 37.
ot.p.i.roussillon@wanadoo.fr.
The ochre quarries that surround this beautiful Provençal village make it a choice attraction. Here you are in the nature reserve of Luberon.

■ | HOTELS

■ Mas de Garrigon

In Clavaillan, 3 km via C7 and D2.
Tel. 04 90 05 63 22. Fax 04 90 05 70 01.
mas.de.garrigon@wanadoo.fr
www.masdegarrigon-provence.com
Closed mid-Nov.–end Dec.
8 rooms: 125–135€. 1 suite: 185€.

In the middle of a wooded park, this *mas* with a view of the Luberon has discreet charm. Its cozy rooms, library corner, swimming pool, breakfasts and sun-filled cuisine enable several delighted initiates to share in the pleasures of this house with heart.

■ Les Sables d'Ocre

Quartier Les Sablières, rte d'Apt.
Tel. 04 90 05 55 55. Fax 04 90 05 55 50.
sabledocre@free.fr / www.roussillon-hotel.com
Closed end Oct.–end Mar.
22 rooms: 55–120€.

Right in the heart of the ochre Provençal countryside, this gaily-colored *mas*
houses rooms with modern comforts,
equipped with balconies or individual
terraces. The flower-filled garden, the
swimming pool and the delicious breakfasts offer other pleasures.

■ Résidence des Remparts

Pl Pignotte.
Tel.-Fax 04 90 05 61 15.
http://perso.orange.fr/teatimeinprovence
1 room: 76–133€. 1 suite: 69–160€.

A panoramic terrace, rooms decorated
in the Provençal style with fireplaces,
Jugendstil furniture, the cozy tearoom
and delicious breakfasts delight Lilly
Weiser's guests.

ROUVROIS-SUR-OTHAIN see LONGUYON

ROYAN

17200 Charente-Maritime. Paris 504 – Bordeaux 121 – Périgueux 183.
info@royan-tourisme.com.
Rebuilt after the war, this Charente resort is dedicated to holidays, families and sea bathing.

 HOTELS-RESTAURANTS

■ Novotel

Bd Carnot / Conche du Chay.
Tel. 05 46 39 46 39. Fax 05 46 39 46 46.
H1173@accor.com
83 rooms: 115–175€.
Prix fixe: 23€.

This huge modern establishment overlooks the sea and the beach, offering spacious rooms with balconies, a neighboring
thalassotherapy center and a light, maritime gastronomy.

● La Jabotière

4, esplanade de Pontaillac.
Tel. 05 46 39 91 29. Fax 05 46 38 39 93.
Closed Sun. dinner, Mon., Wed. dinner,
Christmas, Jan.
Prix fixe: 19€ (at "La P'tite Jab"), 26€,
34€, 45€, 58€.

Next to the casino and right opposite the
beach, Claudette Auger's smart restaurant is well kept. The tables are attractive
and spaced out. Chef Patrick Bachelard,
who worked in Nantes with Shigeo Tori-
gai, cooks up a fine seafood cuisine.
Shredded sliced skate with slow-cooked
onions, Atlantic sea bass roasted on its
skin with an artichoke sauce, drum fish
with wine-simmered asparagus and
shallots and locally fished skate with
meat jus are all successful. A friendly
bistro next door under the name of La
P'tite Jab.

● Le Relais de la Mairie

1, rue du Chay.
Tel. 05 46 39 03 15.
Closed Sun. dinner, Mon., Thu. dinner,
mid-Nov.–mid-Dec., 2 weeks Mar.
Prix fixe: 15,50€, 25€, 32,50€.

For two decades, Alain and Danielle
Gédoux have run this cozy little house
bordering the avenue Pontaillac. A long,
narrow décor with shades of red and rose
create an intimate atmosphere. Alain,
who worked with Besson and Jamin in
Paris, cuts no corners with the quality of
his produce. Quail and foie gras terrine,
rabbit and hazelnut spread, whiting with
mushroom- and ham-stuffed artichokes
simmered in wine and a fish stew with
smoked bacon are quality itself. Reasonable prices.

ROYE

80700 Somme. Paris 113 –
Amiens 46 – Compiègne 42 –
Arras 75.
The beautiful art deco square with its town
hall has the Picard charm of the towns of the
North.

RESTAURANTS

● La Flamiche

18-20, pl de l'Hôtel-de-Ville.
Tel. 03 22 87 00 56. Fax 03 22 78 46 77.
restaurantlaflamiche@wanadoo.fr
www.flamiche.com
Closed Sun. dinner, Mon., Tue. lunch,
1 week beg. Jan., 3 weeks Aug.
Prix fixe: 32€, 45€, 61€ (wine inc.), 65€,
134€, 178€ (wine inc.). A la carte: 85€.

Less than an hour from Paris, the establishment of the Borck-Klopps promotes Picardy with skill and creativity. Gérard gives a heartfelt welcome and makes a clever choice of vintages while Marie-Christine, sometimes relieved by her assistant Eric Gachingnard, demonstrates that she is indeed the first lady of this region's cuisine. Market vegetables with local escargots, fish from the North Sea, eel and mushrooms in savory bites, leek flamiche (a local covered pie), rouget with lemon, basil and caper-stuffed tomatoes, John Dory in sorrel jus with slow-cooked onions, pork with crispy caramelized skin, oven-crisped pork shank with paprika and a Genièvre de Houlle liqueur soufflé are choice offerings. The service is attentive and the cellar rich in surprises.

LE ROZIER

48150 Lozère. Paris 634 –
Mende 64 – Florac 57 – Millau 23.
A pretty starting point when visiting the Tarn gorges. Don't miss the chaos of Montpellier-le-Vieux.

HOTELS-RESTAURANTS

■ Grand Hôtel de la Muse
et du Rozier

La Muse, 4 km via D907, right bank of the Tarn.
Tel. 05 65 62 60 01. Fax 05 65 62 63 88.
info@hotel-delamuse.fr
www.hotel-delamuse.fr
Closed 15 Nov.–end Mar. Rest. closed Mon. lunch, Tue. lunch, Wed. lunch.

25 rooms: 85–120€. 10 suites: 125–145€.
Prix fixe: 30€, 45€, 65€ (dinner), 75€ (dinner), 12€ (child).

The location is magnificent and the views of nature, seen from the terrace or through the glass wall, superb. The modern, renovated rooms, the swimming pool, the private beach on the river are all bonuses. The restaurant is no second best and is under the direction of Samuel Breux, trained at Guérard's, who has knowledge of produce and a creative spirit. Light whipped potatoes and morels with foie gras-topped toast for dipping, pan-fried lotte with cinnamon, braised cabbage and slow-cooked peppers and the thin rhubarb tart with strawberries all make one want to take up residence.

RUGY see METZ

SABLE-SUR-SARTHE

72300 Sarthe. Paris 250 – Angers 65 – La
Flèche 26 – Laval 45 – Le Mans 60.
Sablé and its château do not eclipse the nearby
abbey of Solesmes with its 15th- and 16th-cen-
tury sculptures and Masses that perpetuate the
Gregorian chant.

 HOTELS-RESTAURANTS

■ Le Grand Hôtel

16, pl Dom Guéranger.
Tel. 02 43 95 45 10. Fax 02 43 95 22 26.
solesmes@grandhotel.com
www.grandhotel.com
Closed 1 week at end Dec.–beg. Jan.
Rest. closed Sat. lunch (Nov.–Mar.),
Sun. dinner (Nov.–Mar.).
30 rooms: 85–130€.
Prix fixe: 25€ (weekdays), 40€, 64€.
A la carte: 60€.

Facing the Benedictine abbey, this modern resting place (formerly a coaching inn)
with sauna, Jacuzzi, solarium and fitness
suite, is devoted to relaxation. Marie-Louise and Raymond Jaquet have made this
old residence for Benedictine monks into
a pleasant hotel. On the cuisine side, langoustines in a seafood court bouillon with
sage, pan-seared slice of duck foie gras
with quince, eel poached in Anjou wine,
roasted lamb chops in a sesame crust and
the Grand Marnier soufflé served hot give
a meticulous performance.

● Le Martin Pêcheur

5 km via D159 and secondary road to Golf
Sud-Ouest.
Tel. 02 43 95 97 55. Fax 02 43 92 37 12.
mare.marechal@wanadoo.fr
Closed Sun. dinner, Mon. lunch (off season),
Mon. dinner.
Prix fixe: 16€, 21€, 32€, 35€.

There is an uninterrupted view of the
twenty-seven-hole golf course from the
terrace of this modern building, situated
between forest and river. The restaurant
is decorated on a golf theme in shades of
green where René Maréchal prepares tra-

ditional dishes in a changing menu that
follows the seasons. Quail salad with balsamic vinegar, jumbo shrimp brochette
with beurre blanc, beef tenderloin with
a Port sauce and the chocolate fondant
dessert slip down effortlessly. Wonderful wine list, including several Chilean
and Italian wines.

LES SABLES-D'OLONNE

85100 Vendée. Paris 457 – Nantes 104 –
Niort 113 – La Roche-sur-Yon 38 –
Cholet 107.
info@otlessabledolonne.fr.
This beautiful lady dating from 1900 has taken
several hard knocks, particularly those struck
by developers hungry for concrete in the sixties. There remains only the beach of fine sand,
the homes that have kept their charm of yesteryear—next to the less appealing ones—the
good air, the sunny microclimate but also the
fishing area of La Chaume and the beautiful
promenade along the sea known as the Remblai, effortlessly seducing the traveler in search
of quiet exoticism.

 HOTELS-RESTAURANTS

■ Atlantic Hôtel

5, promenade Godet.
Tel. 02 51 95 37 71. Fax 02 51 95 37 30.
info@atlantichotel.fr /atlantichotel.fr
Rest. closed lunch (off season), Fri., Sun.,
Christmas–New Year's.
30 rooms: 76–131€.
Prix fixe: 22€, 45€, 9€ (child).

This charming hotel, with its pastel rooms
that open onto the ocean, has a covered
swimming pool that makes it a year-round
vacation place. It is also a stopover appreciated by seafarers who leave from Les
Sables to conquer the ocean. The cuisine
of Romuald Chevalier is not lacking in
spirit, as demonstrated by the pan-seared
scallops with oyster mushrooms, grilled
Atlantic sea bass, oven-crisped whiting,
grilled lamb chops and a thin apple tart.
The prices are moderate.

■ Mercure-Thalassa

At lake Tanchet.
Tel. 02 51 21 77 77. Fax 02 51 21 77 80.
h1078@accor.com / www.thalassa.com
Closed Jan.
100 rooms: 94–150€.
Prix fixe: 18€, 26€, 12€ (child).

This recent hotel, attached to the thalasso-therapy center, marries comfort and well-being. The huge rooms look out onto the sea and the pine grove and the cuisine, a choice of healthy or gastronomic, is well conceived. Squid in thin slices cooked with artichokes simmered in wine and olive oil, lamb tagine with Middle Eastern flavors and preserved lemons and the pear charlotte with a light orange sauce, prepared by Stéphane Lhérisson, are not bad.

■ Les Roches Noires

12, promenade Georges-Clemenceau.
Tel. 02 51 32 01 71. Fax 02 51 21 61 00.
info@bw-lesrochesnoires.com
www.bw.lesrochesnoires.com
37 rooms: 56–120€.

Jean-Etienne Blanchard, who is also at the helm of Roches Noires and the Atlantic Hôtel, follows here the same recipe of a simple, warm establishment where it is good to relax and unwind, in season as well as during the rest of the year. Superb breakfasts.

■ Les Embruns

33, rue du Lt-Anger.
Tel. 02 51 95 25 99. Fax 02 51 95 84 48.
lesembruns.hotel@wanadoo.fr
www.hotel-lesembruns.com
Closed Nov. Jan.
21 rooms: 42–55€.

Warm welcome, friendly atmosphere, immaculate décor: Eric and Florence Demaria are the hosts of this hotel in the La Chaume district. The fishing port is five minutes away on foot and the beach just a little further. The rooms each enjoy a different setting, the largest accommodating up to four people. The rates are reasonable.

■ Maison Richet

25, rue de la Patrie.
Tel. 02 51 32 04 12.
www.maison-richet.fr
Closed Dec., Jan.
17 rooms: 40–82€.

In the center of town, a stone's throw from the church of Notre-Dame-de-Bon-Port, are these two houses, one dating from 1905, the other from 1960, harmoniously redecorated with immaculate, fresh rooms in cheerful colors and shades of gray or beige. Charming welcome and pretty interior courtyard that is a haven of cool in summer.

■ Hôtel de la Tour

46, rue du Docteur-Canteteau, la Chaume.
Tel. 02 51 95 38 48.
www.hotel-lessablesdolonne.com
9 rooms: 45–75€.

A tiny, charming hotel with its West Coast décor, omnipresent wood, simple but delightful rooms and generous breakfasts in a room "just like home".

● Villa Dilecta

15, bd Kennedy.
Tel. 02 51 23 85 68. Fax 02 51 23 89 53.
Closed Sun. dinner (off season), Mon.,
Tue. (off season).
Prix fixe: 28€ (weekday lunch), 49€, 58€,
63€, 80€, 87€, 109€. A la carte: 68€.

All the art of Jean-Pascal Vallée goes into his "child's" menu, offering langoustine brochette (with hot dogs) with creamy sauce, Atlantic sea bass seared skin-side down and finished under the broiler and house sorbets and ice creams. Perfectionism and thoroughness run through the gastronomic spirit of this beautiful twenties establishment, renovated by a pupil of Legendre, who formerly worked with Taillevent at the George V. Try squid stuffed with crabmeat, mussels seasoned with wild thyme and the turbot with watermelon and coconut milk: the authentic sea is nothing but joy. The coffee cream dessert with coffee liqueur and a fruit baked Alaska are also wonderful. A magician is hiding near the Remblai promenade, assisted by the attentive eye of Véronique who watches over her restaurant with love...

● Le Beau Rivage `V.COM`

1, bd de Lattre-de-Tassigny.
Tel. 02 51 32 03 01. Fax 02 51 32 46 48.
b.rivage@wanadoo.fr
www.le-beau-rivage.com
Closed Sun. dinner, Mon., 2 weeks beg. Oct., 3 weeks Jan.
Prix fixe: 41€ (weekday lunch), 67€, 70€, 90€, 22€ (child). A la carte: 94€.

First of all there is the wide open view of the sea and the Remblai. Secondly, the meticulous service under the leadership of the rigorous Didier Gaultier. And then there is the painstaking and well-enacted cuisine of Joseph Drapeau. Formerly of Barrier's, he has been in the resort for more than thirty years and, for less than a decade, at ease in his calm establishment. He handles local produce with skill and great care. Turbot filet in herb sauce, Atlantic sea bass filet with seasonal mushrooms and the Burgaud's-style Challans duck with blueberries (rare breast, slow-roasted drumstick) are the dishes one joyfully discovers. Added to this is a berry cappuccino with a mascarpone sorbet, the good wines from the region (lively but delicate Sauvignons from the Vendean vineyards) and elsewhere (good collection of semi-grand Medocs).

● Le Clipper `N`·`COM`

19 bis, quai Guiné.
Tel. 02 51 32 03 61. Fax 02 51 95 21 28.
www.leclipper.com
Closed Tue., Wed. (exc. summer), 2 weeks beg. Dec., Feb. vac.
Prix fixe: 16€ (lunch), 23€, 28€, 37€.

Serious and well-kept, with its neo-Louis XV blue armchairs, its parquet floor and its open terrace, this clipper is the "heavyweight" of the port. Smoked salmon millefeuille, a roasted pike-perch served with beurre blanc, cod Tatin with garlic sauce and grilled wild eel slices are tastefully done. Very friendly welcome from Alain Chadi.

● Loulou Côte Sauvage `COM`

19, route Bleue.
Tel. 02 51 21 32 32. Fax 02 51 23 97 86.
louloucotesauvage@aol.com
Closed Sun. dinner, Mon., Wed. dinner, Feb. vac., 3 weeks Nov.
Prix fixe: 23€, 30€, 38€, 40€, 14€ (child).

One comes here for the view of the sea and the rocks but the food is also worth experiencing, as is the welcome of Béatrice and Jean-Marie Guerry. At the stoves, he comes out with pan-seared foie gras with pain d'épice, grilled Atlantic sea bass with shellfish sauce, sole served with stuffed vegetables and red tuna medallions which are professionalism incarnate.

● La Mytillade `COM`

1, bd de Lattre-de-Tassigny, at Le Beau Rivage.
Tel. 02 51 95 47 47. Fax 02 51 32 46 48.
b.rivage@wanadoo.fr / www.le-beau-rivage.com
Closed Sun. dinner, Mon., 2 weeks beg. Oct., 3 weeks Jan.
Prix fixe: 22€ (weekdays), 36€.

The restaurant is on the first floor of the Beau Rivage and Joseph Drapeau takes care of his minor dishes here as he does the great ones upstairs: game terrine, buckwheat crêpe with seafood, tête de veau, brandade, coq au vin, streudel and tiramisu, all enjoyable recreations of classics. The cellar is seductive and the service extremely attentive.

● Fleurs de Thym `N`·`SIM`

2, quai Guiné.
Tel. 02 51 32 00 51.
Closed Mon. dinner, Tue., Wed.
Prix fixe: 13€, 23€, 30€.

Beautiful, new, friendly and right on the port, this very "decorated" bistro, with its ideas borrowed from Provence, à la Pagnol, wins you over with its charm. One enjoys, in the small dining rooms in pastel shades and served on wooden tables, a fresh, unpretentious cuisine based on the cooking of the south. Grilled sardines, beef carpaccio, cod in a spicy crust, grilled sea bream and the tiramisu could not offend anyone. The pizzas are effortlessly good.

● La Pilotine

7-8, promenade G.-Clemenceau.
Tel. 02 51 22 25 25. Fax 02 51 96 96 10.
Closed Sun. dinner (exc. July–Aug.), Mon.,
Tue. (exc. July–Aug.).
Prix fixe: 15€, 22€, 28€, 30€, 35€, 45€.

We knew him from Scribe in Paris and rediscovered him at Fleur des Mers. Here is Philippe Pleuen, trained by Faugeron, established on a corner of the quay, facing the sea and right on the Remblai. The yellow and soft green décor is seductive. Hot lobster and oysters with a creamy Pineau Charentes sauce, roasted salmon with slow-cooked onions and peppers with a separate dish of asparagus and the langoustine and shrimp brochette with a light vegetable flan are the embodiment of respectable cooking.

In Château-d'Olonne (85180). 7 km se via route de la corniche.

● Cayola V.COM

76, promenade de Cayola.
Tel. 02 51 22 01 01. Fax 02 51 22 08 28.
www.le-cayola.com
Closed Sun. dinner (exc. Bank holidays),
Mon. (exc. Bank holidays), 1 Jan.–30 Jan.
Prix fixe: 35€, 50€, 60€, 85€,
12€ (child). A la carte: 80€.

The most beautiful view of the coast is to be had from this glass and wood restaurant facing all the grandeur of the sea. Raphaël Rolland, whom we knew from Goyen's at Audierne, prepares Vendean dishes here with a very Breton sense of care. Oven-crisped crab with beets and asparagus, fresh lobster in its pot, morels and Grenaille de Noirmoutier potatoes and the wild turbot with zucchini flower, grapefruit and tarragon mousse make one want to be a very regular diner here. Apricot and peach in a warm carpaccio with spéculos and ice cream are freshness itself. A shame that the young serving team haven't got what it takes.

● Le Robinson COM

51, rue du Puits-d'Enfer.
Tel. 02 51 23 92 65.
mannariniclo@orange.fr
Closed Sun. dinner (off season), Wed. (off season), Tue. dinner (off season), Nov. 1 vac., Christmas–New Year's, Feb. vac.
Prix fixe: 13€ (weekday lunch),
18€ (dinner), 30€, 9€ (child).

Low prices and solid classical dishes set the tone of a change of regime at Olivier Thomas's. The seafood platter, ham from the Vendee, grilled salmon, Atlantic sea bass pan seared with olive oil, a slice of leg of lamb and the strawberry dessert make sterling suppers. Old-fashioned rustic décor and a wonderful welcome from Claudine who comfortably advises on Vendean wines to accompany her husband's good dishes.

SABLES-D'OR-LES-PINS

22240 Côtes-d'Armor. Paris 458 –
Lamballe 27 – Saint-Brieuc 39 – Saint-Malo 45 – Dinan 46.
This family coastal resort, between fine golden sands and pine woods, had its moment of glory in the 1950s but is undergoing what might be called a happily modest renaissance.

 HOTELS-RESTAURANTS

■ Manoir Saint-Michel ❀🏠

Rue La Carquois.
Tel. 02 96 41 48 87. Fax 02 96 41 41 55.
manoir-st-michel@fournel.de / www.fournel.de
Closed beg. Nov.–Easter.
20 rooms: 47–110€. 2 suites: 110€.

On the way to the Cap Fréhel, don't hesitate to stop off in this 16th-century house surrounded by huge grounds with a private lake. Its delightfully romantic rooms and its breakfasts offer relaxation and well-being.

● La Voile d'Or
   La Lagune

Allée des Acacias.
Tel. 02 96 41 42 49. Fax 02 96 41 55 45.

la-voile-dor@wanadoo.fr
www.la-voile-dor.com
Closed 2 weeks Nov., Jan.
Rest. closed Mon., Tue. lunch, Wed. lunch.
19 rooms: 90–137€. 3 suites: 178–220€.
Prix fixe: 46€, 56€, 71€, 99€,
25€ (child). A la carte: 86€.

Difficult not to succumb to the charm of this sixties hotel with its pretty rooms renovated in contemporary style and earth tones. Marlène and Michel Hellio ran this good family business with diligence and have now gently turned the page, cheerfully transmitting their know-how to their children, Audrey in the restaurant and Maximin in the kitchen. This passionate cuisine, in which produce of land and sea find the best of their form in elaborate, precise dishes, is an invitation to a voyage: pan-seared duck foie gras enhanced with coriander on a bed of bulgur and pear marmalade, roasted John Dory with pressed potatoes and green vegetable jus and the suprising roasted lobster tail with vadouvan (Indian spice mix) salted butter in hen consommé. Each dish presents a new shore of discovery: veal sweetbreads on Breton spinach, onion gratin with a glossy jus. The cellar gathers solid values while the oven-crisped dessert with Araguani chocolate with its angelica mousse napped with a matcha-infused cream is a great adventure in itself.

■ Hôtel de Diane

Allée des Acacias.
Tel. 02 96 41 42 07. Fax 02 96 41 42 67.
hoteldiane@wanadoo.fr / www.hoteldiane.fr
Closed end Oct.–beg. Apr.
27 rooms: 59–95€.
Prix fixe: 19€, 25€, 30€, 45€,
9€ (child).

This quiet hotel, not far from the beach, has undergone major work. The regionally inspired cuisine remains a serious proposition. Cozy garden and sitting rooms.

SACHE

37190 Indre-et-Loire. Paris 262 – Tours 20 – Montbazon 7.

Balzac gave literary respectability to this pretty town where he wrote *Le Lys dans la vallée*. This devourer of both food and words came to write in the château of Margonne, a kind of museum in the fields, which one can visit.

● RESTAURANTS

● Auberge du XIIᵉ siècle   ○COM

1, rue du Château.
Tel. 02 47 26 88 77. Fax 02 47 26 88 21.
Closed Sun. dinner, Mon. lunch, Tue. lunch,
1 week Nov., 2 weeks Jan., 1 week June,
1 week Aug.
Prix fixe: 30€, 48€, 67€, 15€ (child).

The duo formed by Thierry Jimenez and Xavier Aubrun after their meeting at the Barrière de Clichy always gets it right in this restaurant which, as its name states, goes back to the Middle Ages. The region is beautiful, the Loire wines are inviting and the menu well chosen while the cooking of the two chefs orchestrates it all with modern creativity and taste. Hot foie gras with asparagus and hazelnut oil, poached turbot with oysters and fried leeks, the ham and suckling pig chop served with young vegetables and the cold orange dessert in caramelized brioche with oven-crisped almonds deserve praise while the special menus offer a worthwhile quality-price ratio.

SAINT-AGREVE

07320 Ardèche. Paris 580 – Aubenas 73 – Lamastre 21 – Le Puy 52.
ot-stagr@inforoute-ardeche.fr.
This is the north Ardèche of rocks and forests: the promise of great air and escapist hikes around Mont Chiniac.

HOTELS-RESTAURANTS

● Domaine de Rilhac

2 km se via D120, D21 and secondary road.
Tel. 04 75 30 20 20. Fax 04 75 30 20 00.
hotel_rilhac@yahoo.fr
www.domaine-de-rilhac.com
Closed 20 Dec.–15 Mar.

Rest. closed Tue. dinner, Wed., Thu. lunch.
7 rooms: 84–114€.
Prix fixe: 23€ (weekdays), 38€, 54€, 70€,
15€ (child). A la carte: 70€.

The view of the surrounding mountains from this beautiful establishment is breathtaking. The welcome is smiling and the very comfortable rooms immediately tempting while the cuisine of Ludovic Sinz has nothing to be ashamed of. This former student of Chibois, Ducasse, Loiseau and Robuchon develops his clever dishes that swing happily between tradition and modernity, as evidenced by a trout tartare with lentils and walnut oil, the warm beef carpaccio with red wine, a blanquette of lamb à l'ancienne and the frozen nougat with preserved sugared chestnuts.

SAINT-AMAND-MONTROND

18200 Cher. Paris 285 – Bourges 44 – Châteauroux 66 – Nevers 70.
This small town in the valley of Germigny, separated from the Cher by a hillock that gives it its name, is worth a visit for its old houses, its Saint-Vic museum and the nearby abbey of Noirlac.

 HOTELS-RESTAURANTS

■ Mercure L'Amandois ⌂

7, rue Henri-Barbusse.
Tel. 02 48 63 72 00. Fax 02 48 96 77 11.
h1890@accor.com /www.accor.com
Rest. closed Christmas, New Year's.
43 rooms: 62–73€.
Prix fixe: 11€, 17€, 22€, 8,70€ (child).
A la carte: 37€.

The rooms of this town center establishment are functional and the cuisine of L'Amandois classic and carefully prepared. As demonstrated by goat cheese roasted with pears in red wine with lambs lettuce, pike-perch with beurre blanc, Atlantic sea bass with tomato jus, lamb roast with thyme vinaigrette and an oven-crisped chocolate dessert with custard cream and pain d'épice.

■ Le Noirlac ⌂

215, rte de Bourges (2 km n).
Tel. 02 48 82 22 00. Fax 02 48 82 22 01.
info@lenoirlac.fr /www.lenoirlac.fr
Closed Sat., Sun., (Nov. 1–Easter),
1 week Christmas–New Year's.
43 rooms: 60–69€.
Prix fixe: 17,50€, 22,90€, 26,90€,
9,50€ (child).

Several kilometers from the center, this hotel offers swimming pool, tennis court and pleasantly set-out rooms. In the kitchen, a new chef, Ludovic Bridier, concocts with care escargots in croustade, sea bream, Mediterranean sea bass, beef medallion and the whiskey-flambéed pistachio cream dessert.

■ La Poste ⌂

9, rue du Dr-Vallet.
Tel. 02 48 96 27 14. Fax 02 48 96 97 74.
www.logis-de-france.fr
Closed Christmas–New Year's vac., 1 week
Nov., Mon. Rest. closed Sun. dinner, Mon.
lunch, Wed. (off season).
18 rooms: 50–84€.
Prix fixe: 14€, 26€, 10€ (child).
A la carte: 70€.

This 17th-century coaching inn has been energetically taken over by Franck Laville, a student of Guy Savoy who has come back to the family home without forgetting all the valuable lessons he has learned. One enjoys pork shank terrine with trotter and foie gras, poached pike-perch on a bed of spinach with oyster sauce, beef tenderloin with pepper and a potato cake and the fine warm apple puff pastry tart with ice cream. The cellar is dedicated to the Loire and to Berry. The rooms are simple but not without character and the welcome is friendly. The special menus are reasonably priced—the carte, less so.

● Le Saint-Jean ▮COM

1, rue de l'Hôtel-Dieu.
Tel. 02 48 96 39 82. Fax 02 48 60 52 70.
lesaintjean@wanadoo.fr
www.restaurantlesaintjean.com
Closed Sun. dinner, Mon., Tue., mid-Sept.–
beg. Oct., Feb. vac.

Prix fixe: 20€, 30€, 10€ (child).
A la carte: 30–40€.

Philippe Perrichon is an adventurer in the culinary arts. The musings of this curious fellow give birth to astonishing dishes with hitherto unknown flavors that he perfects over time. In the restaurant, Valérie looks after everything with an eye for detail and explains the menu of the moment. Foie gras and pain d'épice mille-feuille, langoustine profiteroles, a guinea hen breast with cherries and a slightly chocolate sauce and the dessert terrine with flavors of pain d'épice and country honey prove that modern cooking is also designed for small budgets. The accompanying regional wines are not to be turned down.

● **Le Mont Rond** `SIM`
86, rue de Juranville.
Tel. 02 48 96 42 72. Fax 02 48 96 33 80.
feve.regis@wanadoo.fr
www.tablegourmandeduberry.com
Closed Mon., Tue. dinner, Wed. dinner (exc. July–Aug.), Feb. vac., Nov. 1 vac.
Prix fixe: 18€, 26€, 33€, 10€ (child).
A la carte: 35€.

Régis Fève was the studious pupil of Gérard Faucher and Jacques Lameloise before opening this town center house. One feels immediately good in this restaurant in pastel shades that extends into a winter garden. Carp soufflé served with a red wine vinaigrette, trout with moutarde violette sauce, pheasant and mushroom tourte and a traditional savarin are carefully executed. Efficient service and gentle prices.

In Noirlac (18200). 4 km via N144 and D35.

● **Auberge de l'Abbaye** `SIM`
de Noirlac
Tel. 02 48 96 22 58. Fax 02 48 96 86 63.
aubergeabbayenoirlac@free.fr
www.aubergeabbayenoirlac.free.fr
Closed Tue. dinner, Wed. (exc. July–Aug.), mid-Nov.–20 Feb.
Prix fixe: 20€, 25€, 32€, 10€ (child).
A la carte: 48€.

In this former Cistercian chapel, Pascal Verdier doesn't play grand symphonies but prettily harmonizes reworked traditional dishes. Cep ravioli with foie gras, a langoustine Tatin seasoned with garlic and basil and sauced with a broth made from the shells, monkfish medallion with a shellfish bisque, farm-fattened pigeon with truffle jus and chanterelle tabouli, the chocolate spring roll and flambéed pineapple with an aged rum sauce are all well handled. The Cher wines are rightly promoted by Colette Verdier, who watches over the restaurant with a smile.

SAINT-AMOUR-BELLEVUE see MACON
SAINT-ANDRE DES-EAUX see LA BAULE

SAINT-ARCONS-D'ALLIER

43300 Haute-Loire. Paris 518 – Le Puy 34 – Brioude 37 – Saint-Flour 59.
A restored village, perched on its basalt spur with a Romanesque church, garden and 16th-century château.

 HOTELS-RESTAURANTS

■ **Les Deux Abbesses**
Le Château.
Tel. 04 71 74 03 08. Fax 04 71 74 05 30.
abbesses@relaischateaux.com
www.lesdeuxabbesses.com
Closed mid-Nov.–mid-Mar. Rest. closed lunch
12 rooms: 420–620€.
Prix fixe: 50€.

Including the domain of the kitchen, Laurence Perceval Hermet is the heart and soul of this elegantly rustic Relais & Châteaux, situated in the green valley of Haut-Allier. She has created a stylish and personalized apartment from each basalt village house set in their paved alleyways, with renovated bathrooms and in organic and idyllic harmony with nature. In the whitewashed restaurant with its beige tones, gray stone floor, 12th-century chandeliers and contemporary paintings. Pierre Hermet serves a menu that changes daily, where the plate of small seasonal vegetables with orange sesame vinaigrette, scallop brochette, poule au pot heightened with lemongrass seasoning and an old-style house charlotte dessert are the epitome of seductiveness and beauty.

SAINT-ARMEL

35230 Ille-et-Vilaine. Paris 365 – Rennes 17 – Châteaugiron 9.
An escape into the countryside of Rennes. Don't forget to explore the fortified castle of Châteaugiron.

 RESTAURANTS

● **Auberge Saint-Armel** Ⓝ SIM

3, rte de Châteaugiron.
Tel.-Fax 02 99 04 73 88.
Closed Sat. lunch, Sun., Mon. dinner, Aug.
Prix fixe: 11€ (weekday lunch), 14,50€, 22€, 29€, 10€ (child).

This quiet inn not far from Rennes has two friendly dining rooms, one of which has the feel of a grocery store. Emmanuel Hunault serves a regional cuisine adapted to modern tastes, with examples such as farm sausage with duck liver, pollock and chitterling sausage, pan-fried veal shank with mustard and pain d'épice and the marquise au chocolat.

SAINT-ARMEL see also SARZEAU
SAINT-AUBIN see ERQUY
SAINT-AVE see VANNES

SAINT-AVOLD

57500 Moselle. Paris 371 – Metz 44 – Sarrebruck 31 – Sarreguemines 29.
otsi.sta@wanadoo.fr.
A crossroads town in active Moselle towards the Sarre, en route to the A4.

 HOTELS-RESTAURANTS

■ **L'Europe** 🏨

7, rue Altmayer.
Tel. 03 87 92 00 33. Fax 03 87 92 01 23.
sodextel@wanadoo.fr / www.hotel-de-europe.com
Rest. closed Sat. lunch, Sun. dinner, Mon.
34 rooms: 60–76€.
Prix fixe: 28€ (lunch), 40€, 50€, 60€.

If the rooms of this modern hotel are neat and tidy, the cooking of Eugène Zirn is classically ornate. One remains faithful to squab terrine with duck foie gras accompanied by an asparagus salad, pike-perch with slow-simmered leeks and a beurre blanc and a sage-roasted suckling pig chop with mashed potatoes. A fresh pineapple carpaccio in an orange-seasoned marinade served with piña colada sorbet make a wonderful ending to the meal. Very fine wine list.

In Longeville-les-Saint-Avold (57740). 5 km nw, via D72.

● **Le Moulin d'Ambach** COM

Rte de Porcelette.
Tel. 03 87 92 18 40. Fax 03 87 29 08 68.
Closed Sun. dinner, Mon., Wed. dinner, 1 week at end Oct.–beg. Nov., Feb. vac., 2 weeks July.
Prix fixe: 27€, 43€, 55€, 20€ (child).
A la carte: 65€.

One is among family on the weekend in this house in the fields where Walter Backes delights his guests with his cross-bred cooking that has a touch of the South. The tone is set with langoustine "bonbons" and the cod in a potato crust, but this native of Lorraine, who worked at Vergé's in Mougins, acquits himself very well with a local gratinéed creamy pasta and venison dish, venison medallions on a bed of mushrooms and the mirabelle plum soufflé.

ST-BERTRAND-DE-COMMINGES

31510. Paris 782 – Toulouse 115 – Tarbes 72 – Saint-Gaudens 20.
The former capital of Comminges is worth a stopover for its cathedral, Saint-Just basilica and time-worn houses.

 RESTAURANTS

In Valcabrère (31510).

● **Le Lugdunum** Ⓝ COM

Les Espouges.
Tel. 05 61 94 52 05. Fax 05 61 94 52 06.

www.lugdunum-restaurant.com
Closed Sun. dinner, 2 weeks Jan.,
1 week Dec.
Prix fixe: 42€, 57€. A la carte: 80€.

Renzo Pedrazzini's curious hotel offers a taste of ancient Roman recipes. In an appropriate setting, one readily joins in this historic and gastronomic game with lentils with coriander-seasoned sausages, sea urchin-stuffed rouget, grain-fed pigeon and the seasonal dessert trilogy. The only snag is the emperor-like à la carte prices !

SAINT-BONNET-LE-FROID

43290 Haute-Loire. Paris 560 – Le Puy-en-Velay 58 – Valence 68 – Saint-Etienne 52.
A simple Velay village directly en route to the Cévennes and the Ardèche, with rough stone buildings, pretty shops, sweet signs and a warm welcome.

 HOTELS-RESTAURANTS

● **Régis et Jacques Marcon** ⓒⓞ❀🏠
   "Le Clos des Cimes"
Le Bourg.
Tel. 04 71 59 93 72. Fax 04 71 59 93 40.
contact@regismarcon.fr
www.regismarcon.fr
Closed Mon. (Apr., May, Nov., Dec.), Tue., Wed., 23 Dec.–31 Mar.
10 rooms: 160–175€. 2 suites: 220–240€.
Prix fixe: 100€, 120€, 150€, 25€ (child).

People used to come to Velay country to visit Mount Gerbier-de-Jonc. Now they come to visit Mount Marcon. Purely self-taught, trained at home in St-Bonnet-le-Froid with mom in her café-inn, Régis left for Sussex to learn English and then returned to settle here, first offering budget-priced menus and then reaching for the stars. He has become the king of Upper Loire, spreading an entire group of good students and exquisite restaurants around him. The artist of mid-Auvergne, the conqueror of the Bocuse d'Or and the winner of the Taittinger prize has remained stubbornly faithful to his village. Even better,

he has moved house without changing locality, settling on the heights in a place called Larsiallas, taking his team with him to a sort of Zen retreat, with a central stone tower, reproducing what was his mother's house, designing a panoramic restaurant opening onto the landscape and its natural beauty. Régis, master in his own house, works with his son Jacques, who worked principally with Philippe Rochat and in Switzerland at Crissier's, and continues to combine the inspiration of old recipes with contemporary products. The chilled dish of mushrooms and warm lobster in sweet-and-sour sauce with honey and almonds, the scallops with truffles, the stuffed cabbage with cep, chanterelle and trumpet mushrooms, the grilled mushroom sabayon, the sole and chanterelles, the Saugues lamb with a cep praline, cheeses from the Auvergne (Sainte-Necatire, garlic-seasoned Gaperon) garnished with confitures and the mini-desserts, hot and cold, all amazing, including a banana brochette with morel caramel and a puff pastry praline biscuit with chocolate mousse and sorbet, delight customers. One wants to celebrate this modern place, in tune with the mood of the times, all season long and to rediscover this great figure who has had the wisdom to remain himself while exploring to the very end of his dreams.

■ **Le Fort du Pré** 🏠🍴❀🏠
At l'Auberge des Cimes.
Tel. 04 71 59 91 83. Fax 04 71 59 91 84.
info@le-fort-du-pre.fr /www.le-fort-du-pre.fr
Closed Sun. dinner (exc. July–Aug.), Mon. (exc. July–Aug.), 20 Dec.–1 Mar.
30 rooms: 66–71€. 4 suites: 90–115€.
Prix fixe: 19€ (weekday lunch), 26€, 32€, 42€, 65€, 12€ (child).

This huge farm, transformed into a modern hotel, has the feel of a contemporary château bordering the town and the forest. It is effortless to stay here, enjoying the immaculate rooms, the reception of Cécile and the cuisine of Thierry Guyot. The latter does not rest on his laurels but is continually evolving ideas based on a light version of classicism and a rooted modernity. Veal sweetbread "bonbons" with cep-seasoned butter, Atlantic sea bass in an herb crust with cep risotto, a five-hour roasted veal shank with polenta and trumpet mushroom cakes and the almond pastry cream toasts, for dipping, with crushed cocoa beans and little pots of chocolate all make a good impression.

● André Chatelard COM

Place aux Champignons.
Tel. 04 71 59 96 09. Fax 04 71 59 98 75.
restaurant-chatelard@wanadoo.fr
restaurant-chatelard.com
Closed Sun. dinner, Mon., Tue. (exc. July–Aug.), 20 Jan.–20 Mar.
Prix fixe: 19€, 26€, 37€, 45€, 60€, 72€, 10€ (child). A la carte: 45–50€.

André Chatelard is "the other" good chef of the village. He moves away somewhat from the region's escargots and trout, to prepare scallop brochettes with grilled sausage and grilled Mediterranean sea bass with a silky champagne and chestnut sauce. In the hunting season, his stuffed rabbit saddle with oyster mushroom tagliatelli is a marvel and the unforgettable dessert cart recalls his pâtissière origins. Delightful welcome from Viviane; cared-for surroundings.

SAINT-BRANCHS

37320 Indre-et-Loire. Paris 257 –
Tours 20 – Chatellerault 67 – Bourges 154 –
Orléans 135.
The rural heart of Touraine.

●	RESTAURANTS

● Le Diable des Plaisirs SIM

2, av des Marronniers.
Tel. 02 47 26 33 44.
Closed Sun. dinner, Wed.
Prix fixe: 16€ (lunch), 20€, 32€, 12€ (child).

Jérôme Fourré, who was chef at the Tortinière in Montbazon and the Château de Rochecotte in Saint-Patrice, has taken over, with his wife Céline, this huge estab-lishment that was the village school. On bare wooden tables one eats a cuisine of local colors reworked to today's tastes. The salmon tartare with oyster sauce and cucumber emulsion, a slice of cod with mashed white beans and a pineapple panna cotta with Java pepper on the 20 special menu go down very well.

SAINT-BRIAC see DINARD

SAINT-BRIEUC

22000 Côtes-d'Armor. Paris 451 –
Brest 144 – Quimper 128 – Saint-Malo 72 –
Rennes 100.
tourisme@cybercom.fr.
The capital of Côtes-d'Armor has a cheerful gastronomy. The sea here provides the best of its fruits, notably the Saint-Jacques of the neighboring bay and of Erquy port. One can visit the history museum and St.-Etienne cathedral and spend time at the fishing port that has given the town its living.

	HOTELS-RESTAURANTS

■ Hôtel de Clisson

36, rue du Gouët.
Tel. 02 96 62 19 29. Fax 02 96 61 06 95.
contact@hoteldeclisson.com
www.hoteldeclisson.com
25 rooms: 55–120€.

Georges and Michelle Fichot give a pleas-ant reception to their house in the old town with its shades of blue and gold. The rooms and bathrooms are peaceful while the large garden is a haven of peace in summer.

■ Quai des Etoiles

51, rue de la Gare.
Tel. 02 96 78 69 96. Fax 02 96 78 69 90.
quaidesetoiles@libertysurf.fr
Closed 20 Dec.–5 Jan.
40 rooms: 46–57€.

In a practical location, a stone's throw from the station, this is a hotel with clas-sic décor and functional rooms in gray and blue.

■ Ker Izel

20, rue du Gouët.
Tel. 02 96 33 46 29. Fax 02 96 61 86 12.
bienvenue@hotel-kerizel.com
www.hotel-kerizel.com
22 rooms: 36–57€.

The Nicolas' have taken over this characterful Breton house. The simple rooms decorated in white and wood have every comfort. There is a family atmosphere, a pleasant swimming pool and delicious breakfasts.

● Aux Pesked V.COM

59, rue du Légué.
Tel. 02 96 33 34 65. Fax 02 96 33 65 38.
lepesked@wanadoo.fr / www.auxpesked.com
Closed Sat. lunch, Sun. dinner, Mon., 2 weeks beg. Jan., 1 week May, 2 weeks beg. Sept.
Prix fixe: 19€ (lunch, wine inc.),
23€ (lunch, wine inc.), 33€ (wine inc.).
A la carte: 65€.

Why has this pretty house beside the sea been so successful? The chic loft surroundings, the discreet welcome of Sophie, but also the cuisine of Mathieu Aumont who has slowly replaced the chef Jean-Marie Baudic. Langoustines roasted with honey and chestnuts, citrus-seasoned slice of Atlantic sea bass with Paimpol beans, roasted milk-fed veal cutlet with parmesan, new potatoes and chanterelles and pan-tossed strawberries on Breton-style shortbread testify to a certain know-how.

● Amadeus COM

22, rue du Gouët.
Tel. 02 96 33 92 44. Fax 02 96 61 42 05.
lamadeus@wanadoo.fr
Closed Sat. lunch, Sun., Mon. lunch,
mid-Feb.–Mar. 1, 1 Aug.–mid-Aug.
Prix fixe: 25€ (lunch, wine inc.),
33€ (weekday dinner), 38€ (weekday dinner), 47€ (weekday dinner).
A la carte: 50–55€.

Christophe Landier makes it a point of honor to choose produce of unrivalled quality. He puts it to culinary music, giving Breton specialities tunes of the South.

Langoustine and mushroom ravioli with shellfish consommé, roasted spicy monkfish with trumpet mushroom-stuffed potatoes, lamb chops with potato cakes and a chocolate biscuit with a melting center are precisely executed.

● Youpala Bistro

5, rue Palasne-de-Champeaux.
Tel. 02 96 94 50 74.
info@youpala-bistro .com
www.youpala-bistro .com
Closed Mon., Tue., 2 weeks Jan.,
end June–beg. July.
Prix fixe: 17€ (lunch), 28€ (lunch),
45€ (dinner).

Jean-Marie Baudic, whom one knows from Pesked, has opened his fashionable bistro in the center of town with fanfare. The décor is cheerful and colorful, while also being simple. Pan-seared mackerel, a John Dory with sweet peas and chorizo and turbot with a "spoon" of carrots demonstrate a playful, seafood-based cuisine. Baudic, who seems as free as the air, cooks as naturally as he breathes and this pleasure is to be embraced. The dessert (pan-tossed cherries with basil and cherry sorbet, maple syrup ice cream) makes one want to become a regular diner here. Go at lunchtime, when the set menus are unbeatable.

In Cesson (22000). 3 km e via N12.

● La Croix Blanche ◎ COM

61, rue de Genève.
Tel. 02 96 33 16 97. Fax 02 96 62 03 50.
www.restaurant-lacroixblanche.fr
Closed Sun. dinner, Mon., Feb. vac.,
3 weeks Aug.
Prix fixe: 21€, 26€, 34€, 40€,
83€ (lobster menu). A la carte: 60€.

The restaurant of the Mahés continues to win universal acclaim. No lover of gastronomy can resist the smiling welcome to the four different atmospheres of the restaurant and above all to Michel's market-based cooking, lively preparations that reflect the times and the expectations of the greatest number. The duck foie gras served hot with apples, raisins and Pommeau caramel, the John Dory filet with orange peel and veal sweetbreads pain perdu with green asparagus bear witness to creative mastery. For dessert, brioche with sour cherry preserves and chocolate mousse take one right back to childhood. For so much attention to detail, the check is more than reasonable.

In Cesson.

● **Manoir Le Quatre Saisons** COM
61, chemin des Courses.
Tel. 02 96 33 20 38. Fax 02 96 33 77 38.
manoirlequatresaisons@hotmail.com
www.manoirquatresaisons.fr
Closed Sun. dinner, Mon., 2 weeks Oct., 2 weeks beg. Mar.
Prix fixe: 16€, 20€ (weekday lunch), 27€, 32€, 42€, 50€, 62€.

Patrick Faucon has given himself the mission of reinterpreting regional cooking in his own clever way. One enjoys his langoustine tail tartare with sundried tomatoes and fried Chinese noodles, fish stew with chanterelles, oven-roasted Guéméné chitterling sausage with home-style mashed potatoes and the pineapple and rice pudding macaron served with passion fruit sorbet. The welcome, like the service, is professional while the special menus are very good value. Finally, the setting of this pretty stone house with its garden make this a pleasant stop.

In Plérin-sous-la-Tour (22190). 3 km ne via Port-Légué and D24.

■ **Les Bleuets**
At St-Laurent-de-la-Mer,
52, rue des Bleuets.
Tel.-Fax 02 96 73 03 41.
www.lesbleuets.com02.com
Closed Sun. dinner, Tue. dinner, Wed., Feb. vac., mid-Sept.–end Sept.
4 rooms: 48–60€.
Prix fixe: 19€, 27€, 35€, 9€ (child).
A la carte: 50€.

Facing the sea and tranquillity, this classic hotel offers sweet little rooms with a floral décor. On the cooking side, Eric Gicquel pays homage to the region with the duck foie gras terrine with fig confi-

ture, the pan-seared scallops with shallots, mushroom-stuffed poultry thigh wrapped in bacon and the apple crêpe flambéed with Calvados.

In Plérin-sous-la-Tour.

● **La Vieille Tour** ○COM
75, rue de la Tour.
Tel. 02 96 33 10 30. Fax 02 96 33 38 76.
ugho777@aol.com / www.la-vieille-tour.com
Closed Sat. lunch, Sun. dinner, Mon., Feb. vac., 1 week at end Aug., 1 week beg. Sept.
Prix fixe: 24€, 35€, 70€, 15€ (child).

The restaurant was completely renovated in 2007, doubtless in response to the competition in St. Brieuc. Nicolas Adam, a little away from things beneath the Tour de Cesson, still has a (small) lead. His proven skill and his preparations, each tastier than the last, are seductive. Scallops presented naturally in their shell with chive-seasoned oil, John Dory with Jerusalem artichokes with farm buttermilk mousse, cooked to the nano-second, the lobster in seaweed with star anise–infused sauce and foie gras-stuffed squab with a potato blini topped with slow-cooked caramelized shallots are cooked to perfection. The raspberry and chocolate chip soufflé with frozen nougat and the deconstructed strawberry dessert with basil and balsamic make two delicious endings to the meal. The service is still just as attentive and efficient, with Solange watching over things.

SAINT-BRIS-LE-VINEUX see AUXERRE

SAINT-CALAIS

72120 Sarthe. Paris 190 – La Ferté-Bernard 35 – Le Mans 48 – Tours 67 – Vendôme 30.
On the banks of the Anille, a pretty town with its washhouses, its gardens and its beautiful Notre-Dame church with a Renaissance exterior.

 HOTELS-RESTAURANTS

■ **Château de la Barre**
3 km n, rte de la Ferté-Saint-Bernard.
Tel.-Fax 02 43 35 00 17.

www.chateaudelabarre.com
Closed mid-Jan.–mid-Feb.
5 rooms: 150–220€. 1 suite: 220€.
Prix fixe: 60€ (wine inc.).

This château surrounded by a large estate has belonged to the family since the 15th century. The Count and Countess Guy and Marnie de Vanssay offer refined rooms with antique furniture and an aristocratic cuisine served in a room in which a superb dresser has pride of place. On the menu, little fish and pie filled with salmon, vegetables and hard-boiled eggs as an appetizer, then the duck breast and the veal tenderloin medallion with morels followed by regional pastries.

● A Saint-Antoine

Pl Saint-Antoine.
Tel.-Fax 02 43 35 01 56.
asaintantoine@wanadoo.fr
Closed Sun. dinner, Wed., end Feb.–beg. Mar.
Prix fixe: 13€, 17€, 23€, 32€,
7,50€ (child).

The former village café has been converted into a dining room in a bistro style. Fabien Tiscar prepares house-made terrine of foie gras with a Port reduction, fish choucroute or a baked minced duck confit and sweet potato casserole served with mushrooms in a crêpe pouch. For dessert, the seasonal dessert with almond tulip and champagne ice cream. Low-priced specials at lunch on weekdays.

SAINT-CAST-LE-GUILDO

22380 Côtes-d'Armor. Paris 428 –
Saint-Brieuc 52 – Dinan 30 – Dinard 22 –
Saint-Malo 30.
A family beach resort as they used to be.

● RESTAURANTS

● Ker Flore

Pl de l'Eglise.
Tel. 02 96 81 03 79.
ker.flore@wanadoo.fr
Closed Mon., Tue. dinner, Wed. dinner, Jan.,
mid-June–10 July.

Prix fixe: 18€, 24€, 10€ (child).
A la carte: 35€.

This charming country inn in the middle of the town offers an extremely well-prepared local cuisine. Scallops in salad, cod with beurre blanc, crispy honey-roasted pork and pain perdu are served with a smile in a very cheerful restaurant.

SAINT-CERE

46400 Lot. Paris 537 – Brive-la-Gaillarde
54 – Aurillac 63 – Cahors 78.
saint-cere@wanadoo.fr.
In the heart of Quercy, on the chalk plateau, this charming town is worth the detour for its old houses, its towers of St.-Laurent—the medieval château—and the tapestries of Lurçat, where one can also visit the workshop-museum.

HOTELS-RESTAURANTS

■ Les Trois Soleils de Montal

Rte de Gramat, at Saint-Jean-Lespinasse.
Tel. 05 65 10 16 16. Fax 05 65 38 30 66.
lestroissoleils@wanadoo.fr
www.lestroissoleils.fr.st
Closed Mon. lunch, 3 weeks Dec.,
2 weeks end Feb.
26 rooms: 75–103€. 4 suites: 120–285€.
Prix fixe: 28€ (lunch), 38€, 68€,
15€ (child). A la carte: 75€.

This large, modern complex near the château of Montal houses neat rooms and an elegant dining room. The 19th-century paintings and Lurçat tapestries brighten the walls. The cooking of Frédéric Bizat, which used to have its highs and lows, now faithfully follows recipes of the region which he reworks in his light, elaborate way. A roasted half-lobe of foie gras with mild spices, the truffle-seasoned pork trotter served with hot bread, the oven-roasted grain-fed squab and a braised veal shank with ceps make a good impression. At the end of the meal, don't miss the attractive upside-down lemon tart. Grounds, tennis court, swimming pool.

● **Villa Ric**
Rte de Leyme.
Tel. 05 65 38 04 08.
hotel.jpric@libertysurf.fr / www.jpric.com
Rest. closed lunch, mid-Nov.–mid-Apr.
5 rooms: 75–105€.
Prix fixe: 33–35€.

This pleasant villa in pastel colors nestled up against a hillside exerts a powerful charm with its several snug rooms, its cozy welcome, its very attractive dining room, its panoramic view over the countryside and its local dishes revamped to contemporary tastes. Foie gras served hot in a potato crust, veal sweetbreads pan-tossed with asparagus and the light pear-flavored pastry cream slip down effortlessly. Heated swimming pool.

SAINT-CHELY-D'APCHER

48200 Lozère. Paris 544 – Aurillac 107 – Saint-Flour 35 – Mende 45 – Le Puy-en-Velay 85 – Rodez 114.
A crossroads-town at an altitude of 1000 meters that looks towards Aubrac and Margeride.

 HOTELS-RESTAURANTS

■ **Les Portes d'Apcher**
1,5 km n on the N9.
Tel. 04 66 31 00 46. Fax 04 66 31 28 85.
Closed Jan.
Rest. closed Fri. dinner (off season).
16 rooms: 47€.
Prix fixe: 16€, 22€, 46€, 7,40€ (child).
A la carte: 15–20€.

Michel Caule brilliantly runs this unpretentious establishment. The welcome is friendly, the rooms simple, unflashy and neat and the regional cooking very well prepared. Reasonable prices.

In Albaret-Sainte-Marie (48200). 9 km via N9, échangeur A75 on N9.

■ **Le Château d'Orfeuillette**
La Garde.
Tel. 04 66 42 65 65. Fax 04 66 42 65 66.
orfeuillette48@aol.com
www.chateauorfeuillette.com
Rest. closed Sat. lunch (off season), Sun. dinner, Mon. (exc. dinner in season).
23 rooms: 60–120€. 5 suites: 140–190€.
Prix fixe: 29€ (lunch), 32€, 42€.

In the middle of a twelve-hectare estate with swimming pool, this château seduces with its large rooms and sauna. At mealtimes, the cooking of Philippe Gardereau takes over, with a cep flan, truffle-stuffed trout, Aubrac beef skirt steak with Bordelaise wine sauce and blueberry crêpes.

SAINT-CHELY-D'AUBRAC

12470 Aveyron. Paris 595 – Rodez 51 – Espalion 20 – Mende 74 – Saint-Flour 72.
Here we are in an Aubrac of plateaux, where Rouergue meets the Auvergne, in the heart of the country.

■ HOTELS-RESTAURANTS

■ **Hôtel des Voyageurs**
Rte d'Espalion.
Tel. 05 65 44 27 05. Fax 05 65 44 21 67.
www.hotel-conserverie-aubrac.com
Closed Wed. (exc. July–Aug.),
mid-Oct.–10 Apr., 1 week at end June.
7 rooms: 43–48€.
Prix fixe: 15,50€, 20€, 22,50€.
A la carte: 25–30€.

The Amilhats know how to receive guests. Brigitte gives a stylish welcome while in the kitchen Patrick creates a cuisine that has the taste of the region. The pan-seared escargots with creamy garlic sauce, ceps and oyster mushrooms, the trout in papillote, the stuffed cabbage and the cold pineapple dessert flambéed with rum just before serving are very well done. The prices remain reasonable and the pastel-colored rooms are restful.

SAINT-CIRQ-LAPOPIE

46330 Lot. Paris 589 – Cahors 25 – Figeac 45 – Villefranche-de-Rouergue 38.
saintcirq.lapopie@wanadoo.fr.
This splendid village perched above the valley of the Lot is worth the journey for its location

and its lovely houses, including the one where poet André Breton lived.

 HOTELS-RESTAURANTS

■ Auberge du Sombral
Le Sombral.
Tel. 05 65 31 26 08. Fax 05 65 30 26 37.
Closed Tue. dinner (Apr.–June), Wed.,
12 Nov.–end Mar.
8 rooms: 50–75€.

Monique and Gilles Hardeveld give a kind welcome to this rustic stopover in the heart of the village.

● Le Gourmet Quercynois   SIM
Rue de la Peyrolerie.
Tel. 05 65 31 21 20. Fax 05 65 31 36 78.
www.restaurant-legourmetquercynois.com
Closed mid-Nov.–mid-Dec., Jan.
Prix fixe: 18,90€, 22,80€, 34€.

Eric Vivien offers a local cuisine and sells regional produce in his pretty 17th-century house. One is eager to taste the solid choices: cep omelet, pan-seared foie gras with berry sauce, pike-perch with mustard sauce, Cahors coq au vin and the Cahors poached pear seasoned with cinnamon. But be careful of the over-hot room in summer.

SAINT-CLEMENT-DES-BALEINES
see ILE DE RE
SAINT-COLOMBIER see SARZEAU
SAINT-COULOMB see SAINT-MALO

SAINT-CYPRIEN

66750 Pyrénées-Orientales. Paris 876 – Perpignan 15 – Céret 32 – Port-Vendres 20.
An artificial port on the coast near Perpignan. But charm is on the menu…

 HOTELS-RESTAURANTS

● L'Ile de la Lagune
Bd de l'Allemande.
Tel. 04 68 21 01 02. Fax 04 68 21 06 28.
hotelilelagune@wanadoo.fr
www.hotel-ile-lagune.com
Closed 2 weeks Feb.
Rest. closed Mon. and Tue. (mid-Sept.–mid-Apr.)
7 rooms: 120–142€. 15 suites: 131–180€.
Prix fixe: 46€, 56€, 98€. A la carte: 90€.

A pleasant hotel right on the water: the delightful welcome, the comfort of the modern pastel-colored rooms, the swimming pool, the tennis court and the beach all embellish one's stay here. On the food side, the Alsatian Jean-Paul Hartmann, who has been in Catalan territory for seventeen years, surfs Mediterranean flavors with precision and imagination. The potato blini with anchovies and tapenade, the simply grilled John Dory, the veal cutlet with tomatoes, onions and garlic and the vanilla soufflé served warm and napped with a chocolate sauce are accompanied by fine wines advised by Stéphane Riard and by the smile of Catherine Hartmann.

■ Mas d'Huston
Saint-Cyprien-Plage.
Tel. 04 68 37 63 63. Fax 04 68 37 64 64.
contact@golf-st-cyprien.com
www.golf-st-cyprien.com
Closed mid-Nov.–mid-Dec. Rest. closed lunch
50 rooms: 100–160€.
Prix fixe: 32€ (wine inc.). A la carte: 65€.

This hotel on the golf course, a stone's throw from the sea, guarantees relaxation. The rooms equipped with balcony or terrace enjoy every modern comfort, particularly those that have just been renovated. On the eating side, the Parasols offer extremely fresh buffet meals and, for dinner, the Mas to enjoy the Mediterranean cooking of Michel Guillaumou. The slow-cooked tomatoes with pesto, the roasted John Dory, the sirloin steak with morels and an apricot cappuccino enchant.

SAINT-DENIS-D'ORQUES

72350 Sarthe. Paris 240 – Alençon 85 –
Laval 40 – Le Mans 43 – Mayenne 48 –
Sablé-sur-Sarthe 25.

A pretty village in Loué country for nature walking.

●	RESTAURANTS

● Auberge de la Grande Charnie   **N·COM**

Av de la Libération.
Tel. 02 43 88 43 12. Fax 02 43 88 61 05.
laumonic@wanadoo.fr
Closed Tue. dinner, Wed.
Prix fixe: 13€ (lunch), 16€ (lunch), 18,50€ (lunch, wine inc.), 20€, 26€, 35€.

The inn of the Truillets has the charm of establishments of the past: bare stone walls, champagne shades, stretched wall fabrics, beams and fireplace. Laurent prepares a seasonal cooking of local dishes that go down well, such as the creamy pumpkin soup with chanterelles and truffle oil, the scallop and langoustine duo with sesame flavors, napped with a Cognac-enriched sauce and the wild boar medallions with beet jus and pepper-seasoned cream sauce. The crème de Cassis poached fig with crunchy pain d'épice melts in the mouth.

SAINT-DIDIER see CHATEAUBOURG
SAINT-DIDIER see CARPENTRAS

SAINT-DIE-DES-VOSGES

88100 Vosges. Paris 395 – Comar 53 – Epinal 53 – Mulhouse 110 – Strasbourg 98.
tourisme@ville-saintdie.fr.
This former garrison town was completely destroyed when the Germans retreated in 1945 but was recreated with post-war architecture. Attractively full of trees, it is the site of an important geography festival and the native town of Jules Ferry and swings between the past (Nôtre-Dame de Galilée cathedral and gothic cloister) and the future (Tour de la Liberté, 1989).

●	RESTAURANTS

■ Ibis   **N·**

5, quai Jeanne-d'Arc.
Tel. 03 29 42 24 22.

h1102@accor.com
58 rooms: 51–67€.
Prix fixe: 17€.

A modern, predictable stopover to sleep in comfort on the banks of the Meurthe. The rooms are small and standardized but well equipped. Bistro-style cooking and a bar dedicated to beer. Smiling welcome.

● Le Petit Chantilly   **N·V.COM**

11, rue du 11-Novembre.
Tel. 03 29 56 15 43.
Closed Sat. lunch, Sun. dinner, Wed.,
2 weeks end Feb., 3 weeks Aug., 14–28 Feb.
Prix fixe: 14€ (lunch), 17,50€, 24€, 27€.

On the banks of the Meurthe, very near the Espace François-Mitterrand, this contemporary, "pure" and luxurious restaurant resonates a discreet, gleaming atmosphere. The Lidermanns offer classic dishes, using seasonal produce and specialities of the Vosges region, such as the poupeton (a local minced meat pie), done in the traditional style, or the cep omelet.

● Le Grand Café   **N·COM**

61, rue Thiers.
Tel. 03 29 56 15 66.
Closed Sun.
Prix fixe: 15€, 30€.

Pascal Renard has taken over his parents' establishment, transforming it into a large, Paris-style café. The menu offers a generous cuisine where a place is given to small, carefully-prepared dishes: veal blanquette, boeuf bourguignon or the tête de veau with a simple vinaigrette. Sea bream with saffron sauce, the pigeon roasted with ceps and a chocolate tart make a good impression.

● Les Voyageurs   **N·V.COM**

22, rue d'Hellieule
Tel. 03 29 56 21 56.
Closed Sun. dinner, Mon., 24 July–7 Aug.,
25–31 Dec.
Prix fixe: 19€, 28,50€.

For over twenty years, the affable Monsieur Durand has assured the continuity of quality in this prestigious restaurant. The luminous dining rooms overlook the Tour de la Liberté. In the kitchen, Fabien Rohrer, trained in-house, has fun with the market and the seasons. Escargots, duck foie gras, the steamed catch of the day with lemon beurre blanc, the veal kidney fricassée and lamb sweetbreads with oyster mushrooms served with a grated potato cake are dishes that do not disappoint.

● **La Table de Manaïs**
64, rue d'Alsace.
Tel. 03 29 56 11 71.
Closed Sun., mid-Aug.–beg. Sept.
10 rooms:44–64€.
Prix fixe: 13,50€, 22,50€, 27,50€.

Gray exterior and garish yellow sign, but the interior is reassuring. There is the smile of Sylvie and the serious, carefully worked menu of Michel Thomas. Wild boar terrine with pistachios, the summer cep and chanterelle fricassée, the country-style pike and the chanterelle-stuffed breast of guinea hen are extremely well made. The desserts, including a peach cassolette served over crumble, are a heavenly surprise. The dishes are generous and the wine list full of pleasant and unexpected choices. Small rooms for a night's stopover.

● **Bistrocéan** N SIM
2, place Saint-Martin.
Tel. 03 29 56 14 55.
Closed dinner, Sun., Mon., 2 weeks Aug.
A la carte: 25–55€.

Eric Lhomel, fishmonger by trade, has converted a former café into a place dedicated to the sea. The concept is simple: one can buy fish, oysters, lobster, langoustines, jumbo shrimp and pink shrimp to take home or eat on the spot. The setting is reminiscent of the inside of a boat; it is prettily done and the adjacent fishmonger's confers a saltwater feel to it all. The service is efficient, the portions solid and the paella is worth the detour.

● **La Veneto** N SIM
Restaurant Pizzeria,Traiteur
La pêcherie, 11, rte Ecoles.
Tel. 03 29 56 33 31.
A la carte: 28€.

A pizza house with bubbling gaiety, a cheerful welcome, a fine rotisserie with attractive spit-roasted meats, excellent rib eyes and aromatic pastas. The menu is gigantic, consisting of more than forty-five pages. The quality-to-price ratio is what you would expect.

SAINT-DYE-SUR-LOIRE

41500 Loir-et-Cher. Paris 174 – Orléans 51 – Beaugency 20 – Blois 17 – Romorantin 43. The banks of the Loire, the proximity to the great Sologne and the park of Chambord make this crossroads town a charming staging post.

■ ■ HOTELS-RESTAURANTS

■ **Le Manoir de Bel-Air** ❀ 🏠
1, rte d'Orléans.
Tel. 02 54 81 60 10. Fax 02 54 81 65 34.
manoirbelair@free.fr / www.manoirbelair.com
Closed mid-Jan.–mid-Feb.
38 rooms: 40–89€. 4 suites: 115–200€.
Prix fixe: 34€, 38€, 44€, 52€, 8€ (child).

Bordering the Loire, this huge manor house has well-kept and tranquil rooms decorated in blue and champagne yellow. The welcome is friendly and the cuisine is today undertaken by Stéphane Abel. A generous salad with truffle vinaigrette and foie gras, the salmon steak with hazelnut cream, quail prepared in the local style and a fresh fruit mille-feuille all effortlessly please.

SAINT-EMILION

33330 Gironde. Paris 587 – Bordeaux 41 – Bergerac 58 – Langon 50 – Libourne 8.
stemilion.tourisme@wanadoo.fr.
There are, of course, the glorious vineyards, but above all there is the old town with its Roman-tiled roofs, its glorious ruins, its Gothic church, its high tower, its winding alleyways and its houses

that have defied time. Here is an island of beauty that neither tourism nor fashion have spoiled.

HOTELS-RESTAURANTS

● **Hostellerie de Plaisance**
Pl du Clocher.
Tel. 05 57 55 07 55. Fax 05 57 74 41 11.
hostellerie.plaisance@wanadoo.fr
www.hostellerie-plaisance.com
Closed 2 Dec.–14 Mar.
Rest. closed Sat. lunch (off season), Sun., Mon.
18 rooms: 140–360€. 3 suites: 390–590€.
Half board: 175–430€.
Prix fixe: 30€ (lunch), 46€, 135€,
20€ (child). A la carte: 90–100€.

Large, tough, as serious as a pope or a grind, Philippe Etchebest has made this Relais & Châteaux overlooking the medieval town into a gastronomic restaurant of great class. The Perses, who own the Pavie and Monbousquet châteaux, were not satisfied with just putting him in the kitchen—they have given him the keys to the establishment. This ultra-efficient workman wins us over every time with his rustic-refined cuisine that is delicate, serious, precise and dynamic. The sausage tart, Atlantic sea bass with Pavie wine sauce, slow-simmered veal served in a cocotte and the soy mille-feuille with Manjari chocolate sauce are dishes of great technical precision. The wines proposed by the very competent Benoît Gelin readily go beyond Bordeaux. The rooms have an old-fashioned comfort, with a luxury that is never oppressive, affording splendid views onto the hillside and the orange-colored roof tiles. In sum, if you are looking for an ideal place in which to have a gastronomic weekend in the heart of the Libournais and its wines, look no further…

■ **Château Grand Barrail**
Rte de Libourne. D243.
Tel. 05 57 55 37 00. Fax 05 57 55 37 49.
welcome@grand-barrail.com
www.grand-barrail.com
Closed end Nov.–end Dec.
Rest. closed Sun. dinner, Mon., Tue. lunch.

33 rooms: 180–250€. 9 suites: 435–510€.
Prix fixe: 40€, 51€, 62€. A la carte: 80€.

In the middle of the vineyards, the house of Friedrich Gross has not always been welcoming. It seems that things are better now. The quiet rooms, the heated swimming pool, the hammam, the Jacuzzi and the health center easily find takers. The restaurant of Christophe Rohmer is just as good. The fresh goat cheese and focaccia, the sea bream served with crayfish and spinach ravioli, the spicy strips of duck and the raspberry and beet root parfait sing the melody of the times without a false note.

■ **Château Franc-Mayne**
243, route de Libourne / 14, la Gomerie.
Tel. 05 57 24 62 61. Fax 05 57 24 68 25.
contacts@chateau-francmayne.com
www.chateaufrancmayne.com
5 rooms: 180–220€.

Bordered by vineyards, this Bordeaux château houses extremely comfortable rooms. Grounds, wine museum and exquisite breakfasts.

■ **Logis des Remparts**
Rue Guadet.
Tel. 05 57 24 70 43. Fax 05 57 74 47 44.
logis-des-remparts@wanadoo.fr
www.saint-emilion.com
Closed mid-Dec.–mid-Jan.
16 rooms: 70–150€. 1 suite: 150–180€.

A terrace, a garden, a swimming pool and vineyards as far as the eye can see at this 17th-century house in the town center that offers pretty, tastefully decorated rooms.

● **Les Epicuriens**
27, rue Guadet.
Tel. 05 57 24 70 49. Fax 05 57 74 47 96.
jean.desmellier@wanadoo.fr
Closed Thu., 10 days end Nov.–beg. Dec.
Prix fixe: 14€ (lunch), 26€, 34€.
A la carte: 48€.

The Jeans are affable hosts who have taken this town center house in hand. Scrambled eggs with Aquitaine caviar, turbot with langoustines napped with a Port reduction, the Espelette pepper–, ham-, and foie gras–stuffed guinea hen and the fresh white farmer's cheese flavored with Bourbon vanilla and served with a berry compote are well crafted.

● L'Envers du Décor   🏠SIM

11, rue du Clocher.
Tel. 05 57 74 48 31. Fax 05 57 24 68 90.
enversdudécor@nerim.fr
Prix fixe: 15€ (lunch), 25€.

François de Ligneris, the boss and owner of Château Soutard, has made this restaurant into the gastronomic headquarters of his village. As a result, all the winemakers of the Libournais like to meet in this stylish bistro. Emilien Mahaux chooses wines with a "just right" nose and the upper-class dishes (duck foie gras, roasted filet of drum fish, grilled top sirloin with shallots and the caramel charlotte) slip down effortlessly. The welcome is friendly and the service attentive.

● Lard et Bouchon   SIM

22, rue Guadet.
Tel. 05 57 24 28 53. Fax 05 57 24 25 18.
lardetbouchon@merim.fr
Closed Sun., Christmas.
Prix fixe: 25€, 30€ (lunch, wine inc.).
A la carte: 44€.

Emmanuel Emonot, who was sommelier at Loiseau's, has made this vaulted 14th-century cellar with low tables, benches, traditional bar and high sideboards a key venue in the heart of St. Emilion. A new chef, Dominique Froustet, offers simple dishes (charcuterie platter, monkfish medallions with raspberry sauce, lamb cutlets roasted with garlic and a crème Catalane), washed down with the best local vintages, sympathetically priced.

SAINT-ETIENNE

42000 Loire. Paris 520 – Clermont-Ferrand 147 – Lyon 61 – Valence 122.
information@tourisme-stetienne.com.
This was the town of the Verts (the Saint-Etienne football team), arms manufacturing and

also Pierre Gagnaire. Now it has rediscovered its natural gastronomy. Cheerful by nature, the old quarter has charm and good craftsmen abound. Its modern art museum and annual book festival give it another appeal.

■/ HOTELS-RESTAURANTS

■ Mercure Parc de l'Europe   🏨

Rue de Wuppertal.
Tel. 04 77 42 81 81. Fax 04 77 42 81 89.
h1252@accor.com / www.mercure.com
Rest. closed Fri., Sat., Sun.,
10 days Christmas–New Year's.
120 rooms: 102–112€.
Prix fixe: 21€, 33€.

The light-colored rooms are functional and most of them overlook the park. The regional cooking of La Ribandière is attractive. Mixed greens presented in a tulip formation with pan-tossed jumbo shrimp, royal sea bream, pork tenderloin medallions prepared tagine-style and the dessert cart are accompanied by selected wines.

■ Albatros

67, rue Saint-Simon.
Tel. 04 77 41 41 00. Fax 04 77 38 28 16.
hotel.albatros.42@wanadoo.fr
www.hotel-albatros.fr
Closed 22 Dec.–beg. Jan., 3 weeks Aug.
Rest. closed Sat., Sun., (winter).
44 rooms: 78–105€. 3 suites: 145–160€.
Prix fixe: 17€, 20€, 24€, 27€,
12€ (child). A la carte: 40€.

The rooms of this modern hotel with Cajun furnishings have personality. The cuisine is simple and good: foie gras terrine with fig compote, veal escalope with morels and the thin apple tart. A pleasant stopover with swimming pool and view over the town; the municipal golf course is a stone's throw away.

● Nouvelle

30, rue Saint-Jean.
Tel. 04 77 32 32 60. Fax 04 77 41 77 00.
Closed Sun. dinner, Mon., 2 weeks Aug.
Prix fixe: 35€, 40€, 50€, 62€, 75€.

Thirty-six years old (the last ten spent in Saint-Etienne) and an almost new establishment: this is the "new-style" Stéphane Laurier. The designer décor of his town center restaurant was created by his ingenious wife Agnès. The tables are spacious, the staff smiling and the wine list full of good things. Stéphane, trained with Troisgros, Henriroux and Lacombe, has fun reconstructing a contemporary cuisine. His appetizers are immediately captivating and the so-called "calendar" menu is well conceived, with lasagne prepared with local ceps, cured ham and a cep emulsion, a sea bream in red wine sauce, slices of endives with (useless) brined citrus and a lemon crème brûlée that immediately melts in your mouth. One forgives the big shrimp, "blugeoned" by an exotic coconut milk and lemongrass sauce and one takes one's hat off to the business lunch menu at 22 , roasted duck with figs with a Sichuan pepper sauce and smoked potato cakes. Good old Laurier!

● André Barcet   V.COM
19 bis, cours Victor-Hugo.
Tel. 04 77 32 43 63. Fax 04 77 32 23 93.
restaurantandrebarcet@wanadoo.fr
www.restaurantbarcet.com
Closed Sun. dinner, Wed., 3 weeks July.
Prix fixe: 22€, 35€, 45€, 65€.
A la carte: 70€.

André Barcet does not seek to astound but to give pleasure. The cooking of this 1986 Meilleur Ouvrier de France winner is thorough with dishes that are well thought out and meticulously and extremely imaginatively prepared: shrimp salad with artichokes and green beans, the baked macaroni and crab served with sea bream and rouget on a bed of ratatouille, variations on the theme of the pigeon (in its cooking juice, served with a lentil cake and with rice pilaf). A milk chocolate mousse and the fruit clafoutis delight the regulars. Attentive service and unshocking prices.

● Le Chantecler   COM
5, cours Fauriel.
Tel. 04 77 25 48 55. Fax 04 77 37 62 75.
lechantecler42@hotmail.fr
Closed Sat. lunch, Sun. dinner,
2 weeks beg. Aug.
Prix fixe: 24€, 31€, 38€, 7€ (child).
A la carte: 45€.

Anthony Riz always has a kind word for each of his customers and, in the kitchen, René Leroux prepares market fresh dishes every day. Mushroom and poultry liver cake, grilled Atlantic sea bass with sel de Guérande, breaded and butter-fried veal sweetbreads, an almond tart and the cheese cart quietly delight.

● Le Régency   COM
17, bd Jules-Janin.
Tel. 04 77 74 27 06. Fax 04 77 74 98 24.
alexis.bessette@laposte.net
Closed Sat., Sun., Aug.
Prix fixe: 28€, 37€, 45€. A la carte: 45–50€.

The cuisine of Alexis Bessette tends to simplicity. It is a difficult thing to bring off but he does it all down the line, developing menus that allow one to treat oneself without breaking the bank. A basil-seasoned scallop carpaccio, grilled Atlantic sea bass with spring vegetables, the ham-and parmesan-stuffed veal and Paris-Brest (choux pastry ring with almonds and butter cream) are splendid. Contemporary décor and alert service.

● Corne d'Aurochs   SIM
18, rue Michel-Servet.
Tel. 04 77 32 27 27.
aurochs42@wanadoo.fr / www.aurochs.fr /
www.cornedaurochs.fr
Closed Sat. lunch, Sun., Mon. lunch,
1 week beg. May, 1 week at end July, Aug.
Prix fixe: 13€, 22€, 28€, 36€.
A la carte: 35€.

In his old-style bistro, Bruno Billamboz has been delighting his guests for more than twenty years with peasant cooking inspired by Lyonnaise housewives. The pot-au-feu terrine with oxtail, the scallops with saffron, the Gargantua plate and the

Saint-Genis praline tart are washed down with local wines, including several pleasant half-liter bottles.

● Les Deux Cageots   SIM

3, pl Grenette.
Tel. 04 77 32 89 85. Fax 04 77 33 04 16.
Closed Sat. lunch, Sun., Mon.
Prix fixe: 18€ (lunch), 25€, 33€.
A la carte: 40–45€.

The bistro of Jacques and Paule Dargnat is always full. Their secret? An alert and attentive welcome, chiné furnishings that are full of character, a terrific atmosphere and traditional dishes that satisfy the appetite. A tuna tartare, Atlantic sea bass filet, duck breast with peaches and the verbena cream dessert in strawberry gelatine give an idea of the feast prepared by Xavier Thély, all for a moderate price.

● La Mandragore   SIM

15, rue des Martyrs-de-Vingré.
Tel.-Fax 04 77 38 50 70.
Closed Sun. dinner, Mon., Christmas, Feb. vac., 2 weeks end Aug.
Prix fixe: 15€ (weekday lunch), 30€, 32€ (dinner).

An establishment with a good price-quality ratio right in the center of town? That is what Nicolas Treuil offers. For 15 at lunch, this native of Yssingeaux, trained with Troisgros and at the Cerf in Marlenheim, recently offered scrambled eggs with chanterelles, pollock in the Norman style and an almond and salted-butter tart. In the simple setting of bare stone walls, he works to the rhythm of a changing menu. The ideas of the moment give pleasure, in the shape of the ham and fresh fromage blanc cannelloni served with a slice of foie gras, the cod carpaccio with salt cod in cold custard cream with a parmesan biscuit and the veal in a sweet pepper and olive crust. Catherine Treuil gives a smiling welcome and the desserts (roasted apricots in crumble with a halva mousseline and pistachio ice cream) have character.

● Nado   N SIM

38, rue des Martyrs-de-Vingré.
Tel. 04 77 37 49 95.
Closed Sun.
Prix fixe: 20€ (lunch), 45€.

Thierry Lakermance, who was assistant to Stéphane Laurier at Nouvelle, after having worked in the Pyramid in Vienna and for Gravelier in Bordeaux, has created a designer and gastronomic "event" in the heart of the pedestrian old quarter. This native of the Landes, of Madagascan origin, plays adroitly with flavors from around the world: young quail seasoned with sage, the foie gras and pickles, lobster with Italian-style vinaigrette, roasted Atlantic sea bass with mushroom- and ham-stuffed artichokes simmered in wine, chorizo-seasoned rabbit saddle and a lemon and ginger cheese cake are gentle invitations to this stationary journey.

● Le Bistro de Paris   SIM

7, pl Jean-Jaurès.
Tel. 04 77 32 21 50. Fax 04 77 33 68 64.
www.bistro-de-paris.com
Closed Sat. lunch, Sun., 1 week Sept., 2 weeks Dec., 1 week May.
Prix fixe: 22,50€. A la carte: 40€.

With his Parisian atmosphere and brasserie décor, Noël Graci remains the king of the kitchen in his town center bistro. The avocado tartare, whole royal sea bream, the beef roast with ceps and a berry crumble are pleasant and fresh.

● L'Escargot d'Or   SIM

5, cours Victor-Hugo.
Tel. 04 77 41 24 04. Fax 04 77 37 27 79.
www.escargotdor.com
Closed Sun. dinner, Mon., 1 week Feb., 1 week May, 3 weeks Aug.
Prix fixe: 14€ (weekday lunch), 21€, 27€, 33€. A la carte: 44€.

Opposite the marketplace, this century-old house welcomes regulars and passing customers with the same good humor. One takes a glass at the bar before going up to the second floor for classic, carefully prepared meals as demonstrated by the escargots in puff pastry, a trilogy of fish, beef filet Rossini and the profiteroles. For a check that is not as high as the summit of Mount Pilat, regional wines such as a Côte-du-Forez do the trick.

● Le Petit Boulogne SIM

5, rue Adrien-Duvand.
Tel. 04 77 74 51 49.
Closed Sat., Sun., dinner (exc. off season), Aug.
Prix fixe: 11€ (lunch), 17€.
A la carte: 20–25€.

In this outlying area, Eric Neussaint offers a simple, good and low-priced buffet of dishes that make up a meal: the simply grilled jumbo shrimp, the veal cutlet cooked to a perfect medium and a tart that the Tatin sisters would not have disowned. Six regional wines served in pitchers satisfy the regular customer.

In Etrat (42580). Route de Saint-Héand. 5 km via D11.

● Yves Pouchain COM

Rte de Saint-Héand.
Tel. 04 77 93 46 31. Fax 04 77 93 90 71.
Closed Sun. dinner, Mon., Wed. dinner,
2 weeks Jan., 2 weeks Aug.
Prix fixe: 20€, 28€, 40€, 52€,
12€ (child). A la carte: 60€.

Yves Pouchain is not lacking in taste. The proof is his 14th-century farm with its collection of antiques and knick-knacks. This former Accor chef serves a personal cuisine that reworks grandmothers' recipes to today's tastes, and so we have the individual pressed goat cheese, tomato and pine nut terrine, the sesame puff pastry with frog legs and escargots in a caraway seed cream sauce, the rabbit haunch seasoned with thyme flower with its oven-crisped shoulder, served with garlic purée, and the frozen verbena parfait. The welcome is warm, the service thorough and the menus reasonable.

In Saint-Victor-sur-Loire (42230). 10 km via D201 and D25 (toward Firminy).

● Auberge de la Grange d'Ant' COM

At the locale known as Bécizieux.
Tel.-Fax 04 77 90 45 36.

Closed Mon., Tue., Wed., 8 Jan.–25 Jan.
Prix fixe: 18€, 46€, 12€ (child).
A la carte: 67€.

A former barn, now restored and equipped, perched up in the hills of Forez, gives a somewhat rustic air to Denis Cros' restaurant. His cooking, with its lilting accent, puts one in a good humor. One enjoys the pleasure of the creamy asparagus soup with morels and scallops, the roasted Atlantic sea bass with artichoke and cardamom, the veal sweetbreads braised with sage and the roasted cocoa bean biscuit with raspberries and licorice ice cream. The service is extremely attentive, the welcome delightful and the wines faithful to the region of St. Etienne.

In Saint-Victor-sur-Loire.

● La Presqu'Ile

Rte du Port.
Tel. 04 77 53 70 08.
Closed 3 weeks Jan.
Prix fixe: 12€, 18€, 24€, 48€,
12€ (child).

Denis Cros' second restaurant is tucked away in the middle of a medieval village. This stone house has terraces and a lovely view over the gorges of the Loire and the peninsula of Châtelet: the place has charm. Not to mention the contents of Roland Charrier's finely elaborated dishes: frog legs in papillote with oyster mushrooms served with a creamy sweet pea soup, the monkfish with chanterelles and asparagus and the poultry in a rosemary potato crust followed by the strawberry and rhubarb tiramisu served with chestnut and honey ice cream; are all delicately crafted. Costs a small fortune.

SAINT-ETIENNE-DE-BAIGORRY

64430 Pyrénées-Atlantiques.
Paris 819 – Biarritz 51 –
Cambo-les-Bains 31 – Pau 112.
Interior Pays Basque, next to the Nive, where Aldudes ham and Irouléguy wine are produced.

HOTELS-RESTAURANTS

■ **Arcé**

Rte du col d'Ispéguy.
Tel. 05 59 37 40 14. Fax 05 59 37 40 27.
reservations@hotel-arce.com
www.hotel-arce.com
Closed mid-Nov.–mid-Mar.
Rest. closed Mon. lunch, Wed. lunch.
21 rooms: 115–135€. 3 suites: 200–215€.
Prix fixe: 25€, 39€, 12€ (child).

Pascal Arcé, who represents the fifth generation in this place, has, with his wife Christine, perfected this hotel overlooking the Nive with the mountains as decorative backdrop. The rooms, renovated in the old style, are brightened with Basque paintings by a local artist. In the dining room, redecorated in shades of red and white, classic but seductive dishes parade through: an appetizing tête de veau, trout carpaccio, grilled Atlantic sea bass with anchovy butter, lamb sweetbreads with ceps in parsley and the caramelized apples in puff pastry. The whole thing is extremely charming.

SAINT-ETIENNE-DE-TULMONT see
MONTAUBAN

SAINT-ETIENNE-EN-DEVOLUY

05250 Hautes-Alpes. Paris 691 – Marseille 206 – Digne 113 – Sisteron 74 – Gap 42.
www.ledevoluy.com.
A resort in the high Alps that enjoys the sun.

 RESTAURANTS

● **Chez Patras**

Les Cypières.
Tel. 04 92 58 82 22.
Closed Mon. (exc. vac.), beg. Sept.–mid-Dec., May, June.
Prix fixe: 18€ (lunch), 22€.

Valérie and René Patras are the dynamic managers of this former barn, converted into a restaurant by René's parents in 1966, where the wonderful produce of the region

is served. The charcuterie plate, covered cheese and bacon pie, tartichèvre (a variation on the tartiflette using goat cheese), trout filet with lemon cream sauce, grilled beef simply seasoned with thyme, but most of all the ewe's cheese and morel mushroom ravioli and the ewe's cheese raclette, are eaten with gusto.

SAINT-ETIENNE-LES-REMIREMONT see
REMIREMONT

SAINT-FELIX-DU-LAURAGAIS

31540 Haute-Garonne. Paris 739 – Toulouse 44 – Carcassonne 58 – Gaillac 65.
Perched on a promontory with its collegiate church and its château, its windmill that no longer turns, its sloping alleyways, its timbered marketplace, its commandery and its belfry, this ancient walled town dating from 1245 has barely lost its wild character. From the circling path near the château one can see the nearby Black Mountain and the whole countryside in all its glory. With its rolling green fields and cypress trees, it readily calls to mind Tuscany in the middle of Haute-Garonne.

 HOTELS-RESTAURANTS

● **Auberge du Poids Public**

Rue Saint-Roch / Rte de Toulouse.
Tel. 05 62 18 85 00. Fax 05 62 18 85 05.
poidspublic@wanadoo.fr
www.auberge-du-poidspublic.com
Closed Sun. dinner (exc. July–Aug.), Jan., 1 week Nov.
11 rooms: 60–98€. 1 suite: 138€.
Prix fixe: 28€, 38€, 48€, 68€.
A la carte: 70€.

In Claude Tafarello's restaurant, the product is king. This former pupil of Roger Vergé and Jacques Maximin draws his ideas from local farmers and producers. On the plate, this means clean and gastronomic dishes such as simmered vegetables served with assorted sorbets, the lobster tail with asparagus, braised veal shank with its cooking jus and millas (caramelized corn cakes), served with orange salad. The really friendly welcome, the comfortable rooms and the gentle checks do the rest.

SAINT-FERREOL see REVEL

SAINT-FLORENT-LE-VIEIL

49410 Maine-et-Loire. Paris 334 – Angers 41 – Ancenis 16 – Cholet 39.
office-de-tourisme-st-florent-49@wanadoo.fr.
In this beautiful village on the banks of the Loire, the facades of the old houses, grouped all together, are reflected in the waters of the royal river.

 HOTELS-RESTAURANTS

■ Hostellerie de la Gabelle

Quai de la Loire.
Tel. 02 41 72 50 19. Fax 02 41 72 54 38.
www.lagabelle.com
Closed Christmas–New Year's vac., 1 week at end Aug. Rest. closed Sun. dinner, Mon. lunch.
14 rooms: 40–44€.
Prix fixe: 15€, 10€ (child). A la carte: 36€.

Don't change anything: that is the motto of this house on the banks of the Loire, which offers clean little rooms without pretension. Franck Redureau cooks local produce with know-how. His very honest foie gras, ceps and lobster with foie gras, eel, veal sweetbreads and frozen nougatine slip down effortlessly.

SAINT-FLOUR

15100 Cantal. Paris 516 – Aurillac 72 – Issoire 66 – Le Puy 114.
This hilltop town has kept its ancient outline with the cathedral as figurehead. Visit the museum of Haute-Auvergne.

 HOTELS-RESTAURANTS

■ L'Europe

12, cours Spy-des-Ternes.
Tel. 04 71 60 03 64. Fax 04 71 60 03 45.
hoteleurope.st-flour@wanadoo.fr
www.saint-flour-europe.com
44 rooms: 42–67€.

Prix fixe: 17€, 22€, 25€, 11€ (child).
A la carte: 34–39€.

One can see the valley from the terraces of the contemporary rooms (in shades of yellow, orange and green) in this hotel on the heights of the town. In the restaurant, one enjoys a cuisine of local color, with blond lentils, pounti (a local herb cake with eggs and prunes, served with prune sauce), the pike-perch with cream sauce, truffade (local potato and cheese purée) with sausage and coupetade (a local dessert), all priced reasonably.

■ Grand Hôtel de l'Etape

18, av de la République.
Tel. 04 71 60 13 03. Fax 04 71 60 48 05.
info@hotel-etape.com / www.hotel-etape.com
Rest. closed Sun. dinner,
Mon. (exc. July–Aug.).
23 rooms: 56–77€.
Prix fixe: 13,90€ (weekday lunch),
20,50€, 27€, 46€, 8,90€ (child).
A la carte: 41€.

Situated in the town , the hotel of Jean-Paul and Dominique Roux offers rooms with modern comfort and a classic cuisine that has, for three generations, promoted local produce: warm Cantal tart, pork trotter braised with lentils and the ice cream and sorbet plate.

In Saint-Georges (15100). 5 km e via N9.

■ Château de Varillettes

Tel. 04 71 60 45 05. Fax 04 71 60 34 27.
varillettes@leshotelsparticuliers.com
www.leshotelsparticuliers.com
Closed mid-Oct.–beg. Apr.
12 rooms: 110€. 1 suite: 205€.
Prix fixe: 28€, 35€, 45€.

The bishops of St. Flour would spend their summers in this 15th-century château. Philippe Savry, whom we know from Noirmoutier and many fine establishments, has made it into a charming hotel where the rooms overlook the grounds with its swimming pool and medicinal and aromatic plants. In the kitchen, Pascal Baduel skillfully prepares standard classics.

SAINT-GALMIER

42330 Loire. Paris 501 – Saint-Etienne 26 –
Lyon 58 – Roanne 59.
A place for fine water (the Badoit factory is
right here), cheeses (Montbrison is very close),
greenery and fresh air.

● | RESTAURANTS

● **Le Bougainvillier**
Pré-Château.
Tel. 04 77 54 03 31. Fax 04 77 94 95 93.
bougain@wanadoo.fr
www.le-bougainvillier.com
Closed Sun. dinner, Mon., Wed. dinner, Feb.
vac., 1 week at end July, 3 weeks Aug.
Prix fixe: 28€ (weekday dinner), 45€, 58€.
A la carte: 70€.

As an attentive host, Gérard Charbonnier
likes to develop generous and surprising
recipes. If they sometimes seem rather
complicated, they are no less delicious
for that. In the refined dining rooms of
this upper-class restaurant, the foie gras
in aspic mille-feuille, turbot served with
jumbo shrimp and vegetables in basil-
infused oil, the marinated and grilled rack
of lamb served with a cep polenta cream
and the praline croustillant with chocolate mousse commit no fault.

SAINT-GAUDENS

31800 Haute-Garonne. Paris 788 –
Bagnères-de-Luchon 46 – Tarbes 65 –
Toulouse 94.
tourisme@stgaudens.com.
On the doorstep of Comminges, the land of
white veal, with the Pyrénées as decoration
and structure.

● | RESTAURANTS

In Valentine (31800). 4 km. Rte d'Encausse-
les-Thermes, D39.
● **La Connivence**
Chemin Ample.
Tel.-Fax 05 61 95 29 31.
Closed Sat. lunch, Sun. dinner (exc. July–

Aug.), Mon., 1 week Feb.,
2 weeks beg. Sept.–beg. Oct.
Prix fixe: 24€, 35€, 12€ (child).
A la carte: 45€.

The country inn of Raphaël and Cédric
Gourdier is not lacking in assets. The green
terrace, the musical evenings and the traditional dishes (saffron-seasoned crab in
a crêpe pouch, sautéed seafood, veal cutlet with morels, the soft-centered chocolate cake) that are very well turned out
guarantee a pleasant time in the rustic
restaurant.

In Villeneuve-la-Rivière (31800). 5 km via N117.
■ **Hostellerie des Cèdres**
Le Village.
Tel. 05 61 89 36 00. Fax 05 61 88 31 04.
information@hotel-descedres.com
www.hotel-descedres.com
Rest. closed Sun. dinner, Mon. lunch,
Tue. lunch (off season).
24 rooms: 52–82€. 2 suites: 140€.
Prix fixe: 22€, 32€, 42€. A la carte: 55€.

This 17th-century château enjoys pleasant
grounds with swimming pool and huge
rooms that guarantee comfort and tranquillity. In the restaurant, the young Mickaël Huillet distills a quiet standard cuisine
with foie gras with toasted nut bread, sea
bream filet with vegetables, braised veal
with tomato Tatin and a white peach gazpacho accompanied by sorbet. The welcome is warm, the service diligent and the
check almost reasonable.

SAINT-GEORGES see SAINT-FLOUR

SAINT-GEORGES-SUR-LOIRE

49170 Maine-et-Loire. Paris 310 – Ancenis
34 – Châteaubriant 65 – Cholet 49 – Angers 20.
The châteaux of the Loire have their Angers
neighbors. Don't miss the one in Serrant!

● | RESTAURANTS

● **Le Relais d'Anjou**
Rte Nationale.
Tel. 02 41 39 13 38. Fax 02 41 39 13 69.

relais-anjou@wanadoo.fr
Closed Sun. dinner, Mon., Tue. dinner,
2 weeks beg. Jan., 1 week beg. July.
Prix fixe: 22€ (weekday lunch), 27€,
34–38€, 45–49€.

Joys are legion at the village restaurant of Patrick Claude. Here there is a very smiling welcome, a charming setting with its bowers outside and bare beams inside and seasonal cooking that plays with current fashions without trickery. The marjoram-seasoned crayfish Tatin, monkfish medallion with creole spices, veal sweetbreads in cocotte with Layon infusions and the roasted pear with caramel ring true.

● **Tête Noire**

27, rte Nationale.
Tel. 02 41 39 13 12.
Closed Sat., Sun. dinner, 2 weeks Feb.,
3 weeks Aug.
Prix fixe: 12€ (weekday lunch), 20€, 70€.

A rustic setting, sympathetic service and a weekday menu at an angelic price all await you in this countryside restaurant. The wall painting on a hunting theme is a sign that game is well handled in season.

SAINT-GERMAIN-DES-VAUX

50440 Manche. Paris 381 – Cherbourg 29 –
Barneville-Carteret 48 – Saint-Lô 105.
Almost at the end of the world, at the very end of the Cotentin peninsula and just beside the Nez-de-Jobourg, is one of the prettiest ports of the Channel.

●	RESTAURANTS

In Hameau-Danneville (50440). 2 km e via D45.
● **Le Moulin à Vent**   SIM

Tel. 02 33 52 75 20. Fax 02 33 52 22 57.
contact@le-moulin-a-vent.fr
www.le-moulin-a-vent.fr
Closed Wed. (winter), Feb.
Prix fixe: 26€ (lunch), 33€. A la carte: 50€.

This adorable little inn has been taken over by the Fernandes who came from Paris. The all-wood surroundings with

its bar for aperitifs and its garden on the sea have a seductive appeal. Audrey gives a charming welcome while Antoine, who worked at the Cantine du Faubourg and with the Costes, plays with regional and seasonal products. Fish tartare, garlic-seasoned roasted turbot, chickory-seasoned squab, grilled lobster with tarragon butter and the rhubarb mille-feuille cause no upset.

SAINT-GERMAIN LAPRADE see
LE PUY-EN-VELAY

SAINT-GERVAIS-EN-VALLIERE

71350 Saône-et-Loire. Paris 325 –
Chalon-sur-Saône 24 – Beaune 18 –
Chagny 18.
The Burgundy of country lovers, off the beaten wine track and yet very close to it.

	HOTELS-RESTAURANTS

■ **Moulin d'Hauterive**

Tel. 03 85 91 55 56. Fax 03 85 91 89 65.
hauterive1@aol.com
www.moulinhauterive.com
Closed Dec.–beg. Feb.
Rest. closed Sun. dinner, Mon.
10 rooms: 70–132€. 10 suites: 145–170€.
Prix fixe: 25€ (lunch), 35€, 49€, 62€.
A la carte: 75€.

On the Dheune, the Moille's 12th-century mill extends an invitation to relax. Both on reception and in the restaurant, Michel quickly puts his guests at ease as he shows them around: here are rustic, very well-prepared rooms and a heated swimming pool and tennis court with a gym, hammam and Jacuzzi a bit further on. Christiane takes over in the kitchen. Her down-home dishes enchant: tartare of two fish, the cod filet with roasted langoustines and vegetables, the veal sweetbread medallion with veal kidney and the chocolate "tears" with sour cherries. In terms of wine, Burgundy, with its vineyards just next door, has pride of place.

SAINT-GERVAIS-LES-BAINS

74170 Savoie. Paris 597 – Chamonix 25 – Megève 12 – Annecy 84 – Bonneville 42.
In the region of Mont Blanc, a thermal resort that is also a mountain resort at between 820 and 2,000 meters.

 HOTELS-RESTAURANTS

■ Val d'Este

Pl de l'Eglise.
Tel. 04 50 93 65 91. Fax 04 50 47 76 29.
hotelvaldeste@voila.fr
Closed mid-Nov.–mid-Dec.
14 rooms: 45–68€.

In the heart of the village and overlooking the valley, a tranquil, solid stopover with rooms that are not always very big, but clean; gentle prices and quite a friendly welcome.

● Le Sérac   SIM

Pl de l'Eglise.
Tel. 04 50 93 80 50. Fax 04 50 93 86 31.
www.hotel-valdeste.com
Closed Wed. (off season), Thu. lunch (off season), 3 weeks Nov.–beg. Dec., 1 week at end Apr.
Prix fixe: 22€, 35€, 58€.

Raphaël Le Mancq, a native of Marseille, who worked with Bras, Veyrat, and Rostang, but also at La Bastide in Saint-Tropez and Lingousto in Cuers, has made this small restaurant looking towards the valley into a good, safe stopping-off point. Marbled foie gras terrine with morels and Vin Jaune, the line-caught sea bass with salt and fried vegetables, the beef filet medallions with Port sauce served with a potato cake and duck foie gras sandwich and the chocolate dessert plate play a seductive little tune that is effortlessly pleasing.

In Le Bettex (74170). 8 km sw via D43.

■ Arbois-Bettex   ❀⌂

Tel. 04 50 93 12 22. Fax 04 50 93 14 42.
arboisbettex@wanadoo.fr
www.hotel-arboisbettex.com

Closed mid-Apr.–end June, beg. Sept.–20 Dec.
33 rooms: 95–180€.
Prix fixe: 27€, 32€, 50€.

Facing Mont Blanc, this old-style chalet has rooms of character and a regional restaurant of real quality.

SAINT-GIRONS

09200 Ariège. Paris 797 – Foix 44 – Auch 111 – Saint-Gaudens 43 – Toulouse 102.
otcouserans@wanadoo.fr.
Ariège is rough territory: here is one of its outposts that is both proud and modest.

 HOTELS-RESTAURANTS

■ Eychenne   ⌂

8, av P.-Laffont.
Tel. 05 61 04 04 50. Fax 05 61 96 07 20.
eychen@club-internet.fr
www.ariege.com/hotel-eychenne
Closed Sun. dinner (off season), Mon. (off season), beg. Dec.–1 Feb.
41 rooms: 65–195€.
Prix fixe: 27€, 55€, 11€ (child).

Michel Bourdau has made this former coaching inn into a hotel of quality. The rooms have the charm of yesteryear but all the comforts of today. The smart dining room easily charms and the cooking of young Zeroual Haddou is a serious rendition of real cooking: duck foie gras terrine, the monkfish tail, deboned pigeon with pesto and the Grand Marnier soufflé, washed down with good-priced wines. Swimming pool, terrace, garden.

■ L'Horizon 117   ⓝ⌂

D117, route de Toulouse.
Tel. 05 61 66 26 80. Fax 05 61 66 26 08.
horizon.117@orange.fr /www.horizon117.com
Closed Sat. lunch, Sun. dinner,
2 weeks beg. Nov.
20 rooms: 49–56€.
Prix fixe: 17,30–23,50€, 31,50€, 7,80€ (child).

At the edge of St. Girons and close to the historic city of St. Lizier, this eighties hotel built by Francis Puech's father offers happy days. Its swimming pool, well-priced rooms and guesthouse cooking with character (escargot ravioli served in a mild garlic bouillon, grilled sea bream with crushed tomatoes, duck strips with raisins, and the rum-flambéed millas, a local corn cake) deserve a visit.

■ La Clairière & Château de Beauregard ⌂

Av de la Résistance.
Tel. 05 61 66 66 66. Fax 05 34 14 30 30.
contact@domainedebeauregard.com -
www.domainedebeauregard.com
Closed 2 weeks Nov.
Rest. closed Fri. dinner, Mon.
26 rooms: 50–80€.
Prix fixe: 27€, 33€;
La Clairière: 20€ (weekdays), 28€, 65€.

Two hotels and their two restaurants in a large wooded park under one management of Angie and Paul Fontvieille. The rooms and apartments enjoy every modern comfort in a tastefully decorated setting. In La Clairière, Paul's cuisine is contemporary without excess while in the Auberge d'Antan, the Gascon dishes are gargantuan; one enjoys potée (an Auvergnat stew with cabbage, ham and potatoes), garbure (a similar stew prepared in the Southwest tradition) and meats grilled over a wood fire accompanied by garden vegetables. As friendly as they come, not too expensive and perfect for discovering the Ariège Pyrénées.

SAINT-GREGOIRE see RENNES
SAINT-GROUX see MANSLE

SAINT-GUENOLE

29760 Finistère. Paris 590 –
Pont-l'Abbé 14 – Le Guilvinec 8 –
Quimper 34.
otpenmarch@wanadoo.fr.
This land's end, on the Penmarch point, is one of the three large Bigouden ports devoted to coastal fishing, particularly of langoustines. Don't forget to visit Eckmühl lighthouse.

■▮ HOTELS-RESTAURANTS

■ La Mer ⌂

184, rue F.-Péron.
Tel. 02 98 58 62 22. Fax 02 98 58 53 86.
Closed 2 weeks end Nov.–beg. Dec.,
3 weeks Jan.
Rest. closed Sun. dinner (exc. July–Aug.),
Mon. (exc. July–Aug.), Tue. (exc. July–Aug.).
10 rooms: 47–60€.
Prix fixe: 19,80€, 32,50€, 43,50€.

Loïc Sannier has made his local establishment into a sought-after address. The rooms have a sweet, friendly feel and the cooking is an ode to Brittany. We again fell in love with the roasted langoustines with cream sauce, poached slice of turbot, pigeon with brown sauce and slowly cooked caramelized shallots and the Locturdy strawberry dessert. The prices are relatively high but justified by the quality of the food.

In 29760 Penmarc'h. 6 km via route du Guilvinec.

● Le Doris ⌂SIM

Quai Lamartine, port Kérity.
Tel. 02 98 58 60 92. Fax 02 98 58 58 16.
Closed mid-Nov.–beg. Apr.
Prix fixe: 15€, 19,80€, 27,40€, 36€, 67€.
A la carte: 30–50€.

Jean-Pierre Gloanec finds his fish and crustacea at the foot of his house, or almost. One comes to Le Doris on the Lamartine quai in Kérity port to enjoy the seafood plate that one eagerly follows up with a John Dory or duck breast Marco Polo, with spices from the east. The tarte Tatin with apple sorbet brings a sweet note. As well as the flawless welcome and service, there are three pretty guest rooms.

SAINT-HYPPOLITE

68590 Haut-Rhin. Paris 434 – Colmar 20 –
Ribeauvillé 7 – Saint-Dié 42 – Sélestat 10.
Across from the Haut-Koenigsbourg and its massive silhouette, this village, crowded in season, is well placed on the wine route.

HOTELS-RESTAURANTS

■ **Hostellerie Munsch**
   & Aux Ducs de Lorraine
16, rte du Vin.
Tel. 03 89 73 00 09. Fax 03 89 73 05 46.
www.hotel-munsch.com
Closed 2 weeks Nov., 10 days at end Jan.,
beg. Feb.–beg. Mar.
Rest. closed Tue. dinner, Wed.
36 rooms: 50–120€. 4 suites: 120–175€.
Prix fixe: 22€, 55€.

The hotel, with its flowery balconies and
sculptured wood exterior, has large rooms
that are prettily decorated and which give
a bird's eye view of the vineyard and the
Haut-Koenigsbourg. Christophe Meyer,
who has worked at Lameloise's and Loiseau's, defends his region passionately
but also goes beyond it. As demonstrated
by the duck foie gras escalope with seasonal fruits, the monkfish medallion with
saffron, the veal medallion croustillant
with herbs and a generous chocolate dessert plate that gives unabating pleasure.
Wines of Alsace have pride of place, skillfully promoted by enthusiastic sommelier
Mike Eschbach.

■ **Le Parc**
6, rue du Parc.
Tel. 03 89 73 00 06. Fax 03 89 73 04 30.
hotel-le-parc@wanadoo.fr / www.le-parc.com
Closed beg. Jan.–beg. Feb., 10 days end
June–beg. July.
Rest. closed Mon. lunch, Tue. lunch.
30 rooms: 72–140€. 1 suite: 155€.
Prix fixe: 20€, 31€, 50€, 10€ (child).

Here is an Alsace of heart and friendship,
in both the welcome and at the table, in the
winstub or in the restaurant where Joseph
Kientzel successfully revisits regional
classics. Rabbit sausage with pumpkin and
foie gras, a cream and black radish palate
cleanser, goose foie gras three ways (house
special with Gewurtz, another spicy, and
the third oven-crisped "crumble" style),
locally fished salmon trout, open ravioli with coq au vin and pistachios and
the aniseed crème brûlée served with an

exotic fruit crumble are carefully worked
and accompanied by an impressive wine
list. Spacious, calm rooms, swimming
pool and sauna—an ideal stopover on
the wine route.

SAINT-JEAN-SAVERNE see SAVERNE
SAINT-JEAN-AUX-BOIS see PIERREFONDS

SAINT-JEAN-CAP-FERRAT

06230 Alpes-Maritimes. Paris 939 – Nice 9
– Menton 32.
An idyllic peninsula surrounded by perfect blue
sea, a pleasure port that leads its peaceful life:
this Côte d'Azur, which deserves the name, has
not changed since the 1950s. Luxury, calm and
also simplicity reign between Passable Point
and the Bay of Fourmis.

 HOTELS-RESTAURANTS

■ **Grand-Hôtel**
   du Cap-Ferrat
71, bd du Général-de-Gaulle.
Tel. 04 93 76 50 50. Fax 04 93 76 04 52.
marketing@grand-hotel-cap-ferrat.com
www.grand-hotel-cap-ferrat.com
Closed beg. Jan.–beg. Mar.
44 rooms: 205–1075€.
9 suites: 775–2525€.
Prix fixe: 32€, 42€, 55€.

This monument of 1908 has undergone
drastic renovation with its eighties rooms
and its very chic lobby. Work is underway
to enlarge the grounds, from which one can
go down to the beach by a funicular railway.
On the cooking side, Didier Anes, from the
Coupole in Monaco, has been charged with
renovating the house style. It is a sure bet
that he will amaze us again with the caramelized seasonal vegetables with fleur de
sel, his John Dory cooked whole and served
with white coco beans and the hot caramel
soufflé with pear liqueur.

■ **La Voile d'Or**
7, av Jean-Mermoz.
Tel. 04 93 01 13 13. Fax 04 93 76 11 17.
reservation@lavoiledor.fr / www.lavoiledor.fr
Closed beg. Oct.–beg. Apr.

41 rooms: 304–735€. 4 suites: 521–839€.
Prix fixe: 48€ (weekday lunch, wine inc.),
68€ (lunch), 80€, 23€ (child).

This is still one of the most charming
hotels on the Côte. The Florentine elegance of the rooms, their views over the
port and the Mediterranean, the garden
flanking the sea, the two swimming pools,
the affable welcome of Isabelle Lorenzi,
who runs her father's house with good
humor and the cooking of Georges Pélissier, an old hand whom we know from
Byblos in St. Tropez and who has made
himself at home here: all this puts one
at ease. One delights in the langoustines
steamed over smoked tea, the grilled John
Dory strips served with kaffir lime-seasoned shellfish broth, the sole braised with
ceps and foie gras, the vineyard peach cassolette and the figs with rice pudding and
a salted-butter caramel sauce that takes
one straight back to childhood.

■ Le Royal-Riviera

3, av Jean-Monnet.
Tel. 04 93 76 31 00. Fax 04 93 01 23 07.
resa@royal-riviera.com / www.royal-riviera.com
Closed beg. Dec.–mid-Jan.
88 rooms: 330–710€.
7 suites: 1550–2360€.
Prix fixe: 36€ (lunch), 49€.

Bordering Beaulieu, opposite Villa Kerylos, this renovated neo-Hellenic contemporary luxury hotel in shades of brown
offers a charming home away from home
for the relaxation of "weekenders". People
come here for intimate suppers, meals
among friends or for big celebrations in
the beautiful courtyard near the swimming pool. In the kitchen, Bruno Le Bolch
puts on a simple but well-maintained performance: the fresh goat cheese with basil
pulp, morel ravioli with pan-tossed langoustines, the oven-browned Mediterranean sea bass with gnocchi and the sea
bream grillade with thyme (beware of
overcooking!). The service is dynamic,
the wines well-thought-out and the prices
reasonable. On the other hand, the desserts need greater effort.

■ Brise Marine

58, av Jean-Mermoz.
Tel. 04 93 76 04 36. Fax 04 93 76 11 49.
info@hotel-brisemarine.com
www.hotel-brisemarine.com
Closed Nov.–beg. Feb.
17 rooms: 140–156€.

We are communicating under cover the
address of this little late 19th-century
"Italian" villa with carefully-prepared
rooms and generous breakfasts. Superb
view of the open sea.

■ Clair Logis

12, av Centrale.
Tel. 04 93 76 51 81. Fax 04 93 76 51 82.
hotelclairlogis@orange.fr
www.hotel-clair-logis.fr
Closed beg. Jan.–beg. Feb., 1 Nov.–20 Dec.
10 rooms: 95–155€. 6 suites: 185–200€.

In the middle of a huge park, several
houses in different styles make up this
group of hotels with rooms that are sometimes narrow but always comfortable.

● Le Provençal

2, av Denis-Semeria.
Tel. 04 93 76 03 97. Fax 04 93 76 05 39.
Closed beg. Nov.–end Feb.
Prix fixe: 35€ (lunch), 79€, 120€, 160€.
A la carte: 109€.

Quality produce, respect for cooking techniques, intact flavors and a touch of innovation: this is the recipe that has been key
to the success of the cuisine orchestrated
by Dominique Calcerano. One is surprised
by the half-lobster in a shell of purple artichokes, the roasted John Dory with fig
leaves, the vanilla-seasoned pan-roasted
turbot and the roasted rack of lamb. The
chef's secret weapon: an assortment of
five desserts devised by Monsieur René,
whose secrets cannot be revealed… What
is certain is that one makes quick work of
them! All this is not exactly given away, but
at least the view of the sea is free.

● Capitaine Cook

11, av Jean-Mermoz.
Tel.-Fax 04 93 76 02 66.

Closed Wed., Thu. lunch, mid-Nov.–end Dec.
Prix fixe: 25€, 30€.

The rustic bistro of wise Lionel Pelletier is a stroke of luck for Cap Ferrat and the oh-so-pretty village of St. Jean. The two menus of this native of Burgundy who emigrated to the coast twenty years ago are delights. His octopus salad and his sea bream filet with tomato and tapenade are eaten with pleasure. The bouillabaisse (38) is cooked to order; his simple fish bisque prepared in the local style (the modest version of the genre with pike-perch, monkfish or rouget) isn't bad at all. The crème caramel and the tarte Tatin slip down without a murmur.

● Le Sloop   SIM

At the pleasure port.
Tel.-Fax 04 93 01 48 63.
www.restaurantsloop.com
Closed Tue. lunch (off season),
Wed. lunch (off season), mid-Nov.–end Dec.
Prix fixe: 28€. A la carte: 62€.

The terrace opens onto the pleasure port and the sea is certainly on the menu of Alain Therlicocq, who nonetheless does not forget that the land of Provence also gives fine produce. Chard-stuffed squid, whole Mediterranean sea bass prepared in the style of Nice, lamb with basil and parmesan and the country raspberry gratin with mascarpone ice cream are extremely well made. The special menu is excellent value.

SAINT-JEAN-D'ARDIERES see BELLEVILLE
SAINT-JEAN-DE-BRAYE see ORLEANS

SAINT-JEAN-DE-LUZ

64500 Pyrénées-Atlantiques. Paris 790 –
Biarritz 18 – Bayonne 24 –
Saint-Sébastien 34.
Don't ask the man in the street in St. Jean if he is Basque—he will laugh in your face. He is Basque, just as the air here is fresh, the grass on the neighboring hills green and the sea that meanders across the bay blue. The young people frequent the *trinquets* where pelota is played. The nocturnal fêtes have as their highlight the

toro de fuego which runs around the large central square. Under the bandstand, the choir performs old local songs. The town lives its folklore and sells it, with pride and talent. It has never been so Basque as it is today. Every shop window in the busy rue Gambetta boasts one or several local items, promotes tourons, kanougas, mouchous, macarons, Basque gâteaux stuffed with custard or black cherry jam and the striped cloth in the local colors. The gastronomy of the Basque country? It has never been as rich as in St. Jean, its beautiful shop window.

■ | HOTELS

■ Le Grand Hôtel

43, bd Thiers.
Tel. 05 59 26 35 36. Fax 05 59 51 99 84.
direction@luzgrandhotel.fr
www.luzgrandhotel.fr
Closed mid-Oct.–beg. Mar.
48 rooms: 200–600€. 4 suites: 680
Half board: 228–655€.

This twenties luxury hotel has rediscovered its youth with its gleaming rooms overlooking the sea. The inside swimming pool, the beach just below and the fitness center makes one want to laze around here. (See Restaurants: Le Rosewood.)

■ Parc Victoria

5, rue Cépé.
Tel. 05 59 26 78 78. Fax 05 59 26 78 08.
parcvictoria@relaischateaux.com
www.parcvictoria.com
Closed mid-Nov.–mid-Mar.
Rest. closed Tue. (off season).
10 rooms: 160–195€. 7 suites: 260–655€.
Prix fixe: 65€, 69€, 80€.

A stone's throw from the beaches, in a huge park, this Victorian-style town house offers rooms decorated in an art deco style and full of pretty knickknacks. Garden and swimming pool complete the picture. In the kitchen, Eric Jorge creates finely-crafted and gastronomic dishes such as the squid lasagne, the lobster pot-au-feu with young broad beans, the braised veal sweetbreads and the flambéed pineapple with Carambar candy ice cream.

■ Chantaco

Opposite the golf course, route d'Ascain.
Tel. 05 59 26 14 76. Fax 05 59 26 35 97.
resa@hotel-chantaco.com
www.hotel-chantaco.com
Closed Nov.–beg. Mar.
20 rooms: 190–200€. 4 suites: 280€.

On the gulf of Ascain and facing the mountains of the Basque country, this thirties house offers light and well-prepared rooms. The garden and swimming pool are an invitation to idleness.

■ Hélianthal

Pl Maurice-Ravel.
Tel. 05 59 51 51 00. Fax 05 59 51 51 01.
helianthal@helianthal.fr / www.helianthal.fr
Rest. closed end Nov.–23 Dec.
94 rooms: 94–226€. 6 suites: 152–269€.
Prix fixe: 39,50€.

Next to the pedestrian area and directly linked to the thalassotherapy institute, this chic establishment offers rooms with thirties furnishings. The Atlantique restaurant is housed in a building designed by Mallet-Stevens, which has an exceptional view of the sea. Scott Serrato's "well being" cuisine lets you look after your figure while enjoying sumptious light dishes.

■ Zazpihotel

21, bd Thiers.
Tel. 05 59 26 07 77. Fax 05 55 26 27 77.
www.zazpihotel.com
5 rooms: 150–450€.

The latest word in Basque country design is what Carmena and Michel Hiribarren have created with their modern mini-hotel in the heart of St-Jean-de-Luz, with its handsome colors, its futuristic lobby furnished with green and white armchairs, its terrace/swimming pool/solarium, its patio and its quietly decorated rooms, all in the old Mendeberri ("new century" in Basque) house dating from 1900.

■ La Devinière

5, rue Loquin.
Tel. 05 59 26 05 51. Fax 05 59 51 26 38.
la.deviniere.64@wanadoo.fr
www.hotel-la-deviniere.com
11 rooms: 120–160€.

In the center, a stone's throw from the port, this 18th-century house offers rooms with antique furniture and rare objects and books. The breakfasts afford some delicious moments, particularly for tea lovers.

■ La Réserve

Rond-point Sainte-Barbe.
Tel. 05 59 51 32 00. Fax 05 59 51 32 01.
lareserve@wanadoo.fr / www.hotel-lareserve.fr
Rest. closed Sun. dinner (off season),
Mon. (off season).
60 rooms: 55–289€.
Prix fixe: 25€, 32€, 37€.

Situated in a park of three hectares beside the sea, with a golf practice area, a swimming pool and tennis court, this hotel offers huge, luminous rooms. The restaurant, which overlooks the garden, offers a traditional cuisine (red tuna tartare, a grilled turbot with a tomato vinaigrette and the roasted rack of lamb with wild thyme). Efficient service.

■ Grand Hôtel de la Poste

83, rue Léon-Gambetta.
Tel. 05 59 26 04 53. Fax 05 59 26 42 14.
contact@grandhoteldelaposte.com
www.grandhoteldelaposte.com
34 rooms: 55–110€.

This 18th-century establishment had its hour of glory when Lafayette passed through en route to America. The cozily-decorated renovated rooms make it a friendly place two minutes away from the beaches.

■ La Marisa

16, rue Sopite.
Tel. 05 59 26 95 46. Fax 05 59 51 17 06.
info@la-marisa.com / www.la-marisa.com
Closed Jan.
15 rooms: 65–145€.

This large Basque house is hidden between the beach and the shopping streets. Decorated with antique furniture, the rooms are comfortable and quiet.

■ Ohartzia

28, rue Garat.
Tel. 05 59 26 00 06. Fax 05 59 26 74 75.
hotel.ohartzia@wanadoo.fr
www.hotel-ohartzia.com
17 rooms: 55–85€.

This typical house in the heart of the town and a stone's throw from the large beach offers functional rooms; one appreciates the tranquility of the garden and the shaded terrace.

■ Hôtel de la Plage

33, rue Garat, chemin Jacques-Thibaud.
Tel. 05 59 51 03 44. Fax 05 59 51 03 48.
reservation@hoteldelaplage.com
www.hoteldelaplage.com
Closed mid-Nov.–beg. Christmas vac., Christmas–beg. Feb. vac.,
end Feb. vac.–beg. Apr.
22 rooms: 70–122€.

This hotel, with its finest rooms overlooking the sea, benefits from an exceptional location. The beach is on its doorstep and the center of town right beside it. Friendly welcome, reasonable rates.

■ Les Almadies

58, rue Gambetta.
Tel. 05 59 85 34 48. Fax 05 59 26 12 42.
hotel.lesalmadies@wanadoo.fr
www.hotel-les-almadies.com
Closed 3 weeks Nov.
7 rooms: 75–125€.

The exotic name of the hotel derives from the fact that Jean-Jacques and Patricia Hargous used to live in Senegal. Very pleasant, classic rooms with a small terrace.

■ Maria Christina

13, rue Paul-Gélos.
Tel. 05 59 26 81 70. Fax 05 59 26 36 04.
mariachristina@wanadoo.fr
www.hotelmariachristina.com
Closed mid-Nov.–mid-Mar.
11 rooms: 46–94€.

In this Basque villa of the previous century, the rooms have a lot of charm, as does the patio with its lemon trees and bougainvillea. Marie Lascombes and Christophe Pfefferle give a friendly welcome.

● RESTAURANTS

● Le Rosewood   V.COM

At Le Grand Hôtel, 43, bd Thiers.
Tel. 05 59 26 35 36. Fax 05 59 51 99 84.
direction@luzgrandhotel.fr
www.luzgrandhotel.fr
Closed mid-Nov.–beg. Mar.
Prix fixe: 29€, 38€ (lunch).

Nicolas Masse has given new energy to this fine restaurant in the round with a view of the sea. The flavors of crab, whiting with piquillo pepper gnocchi, spit-roasted duck breast with an eggplant purée samosa and the thin cherry and blackcurrant tart with Irouléguy wine and raspberry ice are truly fine, while the regional wines suggested by Stéphane Chaput have much to say. At lunchtime on fine days there is a more simple restaurant service in the rotisserie overlooking the ocean.

● Le Kaïku   COM

17, rue de la République.
Tel. 05 59 26 13 20. Fax 05 59 51 07 47.
Closed Tue. (exc. July–Aug.), Wed. (exc. July–Aug.), mid-Nov.–30 Nov., mid-Jan.–30 Jan.
Prix fixe: 35€, 18€ (child).

Serge Latchère, a real professional in his field of managing a restaurant who cheerfully runs this huge, historic stone house dating from the 16th century, has entrusted the kitchen to Gérard Lasbarreres. Formerly of the Ritz and of Taillevent, he gives a light, fine, regional performance that doesn't get into a rut. It is a real pleasure to rediscover tuna studded with Spanish pork fat and seasoned with four spices, rouget on a bed of peppers and olives, wild duck with bitter orange sauce and the baba au rhum. Reasonable prices.

● La Txalupa   COM

Pl Louis-XIV.
Tel. 05 59 51 85 52 / 05 59 51 23 34.
Fax 05 59 51 85 52.
Prix fixe: 24€. A la carte: 50–55€.

There is no imagination in the menu of this port restaurant but the produce is extremely fresh. Our favorites are mountain-cured ham, sea bream, beef rib eye steak and a house gâteau Basque, all accompanied by Spanish wines. A small, convivial menu with fine platters of crustacea.

● **Olatua**

30, bd Thiers.
Tel. 05 59 51 05 22. Fax 05 59 51 32 99.
www.olatua.com
Prix fixe: 14€ (lunch), 18€ (lunch), 27€,
29,90€.

Olivier Lataste and Ramuntxo Berria met in New York. On their return they opened this restaurant with an electric atmosphere where the local cuisine delights the chic and fashionable clientele with foie gras parfait, braised line-fished whiting, duck wings and the chocolate soufflé. The service is dynamic and the check not excessive.

● **Chez Pablo** SIM

5, rue Mademoiselle-Etcheto.
Tel.-Fax 05 59 26 37 81.
Closed Tue. dinner, Wed.
Prix fixe: 18€, 23€, 32€, 7,50€ (child).

This is one of the oldest restaurants of the town, dating from 1935. Discreet, it remains warm and friendly. "Pablo's dish" at 20 is very good value and one effortlessly enjoys crispy fried cod, piquillo peppers, squids in their ink, whiting and jumbo shrimp with rice, all washed down with a wine of Navarre or Rioja.

● **Petit Grill Basque** SIM

2, rue Saint-Jacques.
Tel.-Fax 05 59 26 80 76.
Closed Wed., Thu. lunch (off season),
1 week Oct., 20 Dec.–20 Jan., 1 week May.
Prix fixe: 20€, 28€.

The décor of a Basque inn with its regional cuisine are the good hallmarks of Frédéric de Grégorio's establishment. It is not hard to enjoy oneself with squid in their ink, monkfish in cream sauce, crispy fried

poultry and gâteau Basque. It is all priced at a friendly rate and served diligently.

● **La Taverne Basque** SIM

5, rue de la République.
Tel. 05 59 26 01 26.
www.latavernebasque.fr
Closed Mon. lunch (July–Aug.),
Tue. lunch (July–Aug.).
A la carte: 50€.

The Durands have taken over this gastronomic inn with its friendly setting and more complex culinary register; the ambition of the place has been realized. There are some attractive regional items on the program such as little squid presented in a deglazed sauce with Basque peppers and shellfish risotto, Banca trout brochettes with figs (in season) and almonds, Basque pork filet with mushrooms in mascarpone sabayon, pears poached in Irouléguy Marc and the financier. Watch this space.

● **Zoko Moko** SIM

6, rue Mazarin.
Tel. 05 59 08 01 23. Fax 05 59 51 01 77.
zokomoko@hotmail.com
Closed lunch (summer), Sat. lunch (exc. Bank holidays), Sun. dinner (exc. Bank holidays), 13 Nov.–4 Dec.
Prix fixe: 17€ (weekday lunch), 23€ (weekday lunch), 39€ (dinner), 46€ (dinner)
12€ (child). A la carte: 48€.

The contemporary setting of this relaxed and cheerful restaurant on the square near the port is chic. Charles Olascuaga does the receiving while the cooking is in the hands of Stéphane Poulain and Thomas Deguarie who joyfully give themselves to a Basque cuisine reworked to today's tastes. Melon and ginger gazpacho, grilled wild jumbo shrimp, oven-browned whiting, roasted pigeon with the drumsticks and wings braised with rosemary and the chocolate Mutxiko are fun invitations to new gastronomic journeys.

In Ciboure (64500). 1 km s.

● **Chez Dominique**

15, quai Maurice-Ravel.
Tel.-Fax 05 59 47 29 16.

Closed Sun. dinner, Mon., Tue., mid-Feb.–
mid-Mar.
Prix fixe: 26€ (lunch). A la carte: 65€.

Only the bounty of the sea informs the
creations of Georges Piron. Formerly of
the Ritz and the Bristol, he selects the best
before treating it with the greatest respect.
There is no question but the result is there
on the plate, served in an attractive marine
décor. Tarragon-seasoned langoustine
ravioli, tuna medallions glazed with balsamic vinegar and soy, John Dory filet with
ginger and chives and oven-crisped cannelloni with mascarpone cream offer a
refreshing note that bodes well. The wines
celebrate the region and the welcome, like
the service, is flawless.

In Ciboure.

● **Pantxua**   COM
At the port de Socoa.
Tel.-Fax 05 59 47 13 73.
Closed Mon. (off season), Tue. (off season),
1 Dec.–mid-Dec., Jan.
Prix fixe: 12€ (child). A la carte: 52–58€.

One comes here for the view from the
terrace of the bay of St-Jean-de-Luz. The
place, with its lovely paintings on Basque
themes, and the cooking continue to offer
a taste of the region, as demonstrated by
crunchy fried cod balls, grilled whiting,
monkfish and jumbo shrimp brochettes
with beurre blanc, beef filet Rossini and
a pineapple carpaccio.

In Ciboure.

● **Arrantzaleak**   SIM
Av Jean-Poulou, towpath.
Tel. 05 59 47 10 75. Fax 05 59 47 04 26.
Closed Mon., Tue. (off season), mid-Dec.–
mid-Feb.
Prix fixe: 30€ (lunch). A la carte: 38€.

This maritime hut on the banks of the canal
has its charm. "MAM" is not always present
but nonetheless takes care of the establishment conscientiously. Garlic-stuffed mussels, wild sea bream, grilled bass, roasted
duck breast, the blanc manger with cherry
confiture and the house baba au rhum are
the good work of clever Ramuntxo Courdé.

The establishment is without pretension,
the service friendly and the check small.

In Ciboure.

● **Chez Mattin**   SIM
63, rue Evariste-Baignol.
Tel. 05 59 47 19 52. Fax 05 59 47 05 57.
Closed Sun. dinner, Mon., mid-Jan.–mid-Mar.
A la carte: 37€.

Nothing more straightforward than this
restaurant on the heights where one is
among Basques, native or adopted, enjoying the family cuisine of Michel Niquet and
Jean-Martin Toyos. The Brana Irouléguy
is the best traveling companion for cod
and octopus salad, Basque-style stuffed
crabs, cod filet, the famous ttoro (a local
fish stew), house confits and an ewe's milk
crème brûlée.

SAINT-JEAN-PIED-DE-PORT

64220 Pyrénées-Atlantiques. Paris 823 –
Biarritz 55 – Bayonne 53 – Pau 100.
With its fortifications designed by Vauban, this
"port" in the mountains on the pilgrimage route
of Santiago de Compostella proves a beautiful,
verdant stopover. Visit Domaine Brana with its
vineyard of replanted irouléguy and its high-
quality pear and plum eaux-de-vie.

 HOTELS-RESTAURANTS

● **L'Auberge des Pyrénées**
19, pl Charles-de-Gaulle.
Tel. 05 59 37 01 01. Fax 05 59 37 18 97.
hotel.Pyrénées@wanadoo.fr
www.hotel-les-Pyrénées.com
Closed mid-Nov.–mid-Dec., beg. Jan.–end
Jan. Rest. closed Mon. (off season), Tue. (off
season).
20 rooms: 92–155€.
Prix fixe: 40€, 70€, 85€. A la carte 60–90€.

Tradition reinterpreted with lightness
and finesse: this is the style of mother
and daughter Anne-Marie and Sandrine
Arrambides who give a very friendly welcome to their guests. The rooms are charming and the flowered balconies overlook
the town walls. As for Firmin, the father,

and Philippe, the son, they have reworked with a sure touch the regional spirit of the establishment. Simply poached duck foie gras, cod-stuffed peppers, grilled rouget and squid with ink sauce and langoustine ravioli with Aquitane caviar are fresh, lively, clever and finely crafted dishes. The roasted rack of milk-fed lamb with garlic confit and the grilled "butcher's choice" cut with béarnaise sauce are classics that enchant. Cousins of the neighboring Cousseaus, the Arrambides extol the return to origins without shouting about it. In the dessert department, a soft-centered chocolate cake and warm madeleines, runny apricot preserves and vanilla ice cream go down well. The friendly service is to match. The wine list is a hymn of praise to the great Southwest without exaggerating its prices, while lazing beside the swimming pool is a fine idea after a choice feast in this Relais & Châteaux that has managed to keep its family atmosphere.

● **Etche Ona** SIM

15, pl Floquet.
Tel. 05 59 37 01 14. Fax 05 59 37 35 69.
Closed 2 weeks end Nov., 2 weeks beg. Mar.,
Wed. dinner, Thu.
5 rooms: 50–57€.
Prix fixe: 29€, 37€, 10€ (child).
A la carte: 40€.

Generations pass but quality remains the hallmark of this establishment. Michel Ibargaray, formerly with Dutournier, Biscaye and Etchébest of Paris conjures up in his kitchen escabeche-marinated tuna belly, mackerel in mustard sauce, roasted lamb shoulder with piquillo peppers and the thin chocolate and almond tart. Washed down with a Jurançon from Lacoste or a Brana Irouléguy, this inn delights. There are a few simple, well-kept rooms.

In Aincille (64220). 7 km via D18.

■ **Pecoïtz**

Tel. 05 59 37 11 88. Fax 05 59 37 35 42.
Closed Jan.–mid-Mar.
Rest. closed Fri. (off season).
14 rooms: 40–45€.
Prix fixe: 15€ (weekdays), 23, 34€, 8€ (child).

Though the prices are low, the quality is high. When it comes to culinary enjoyment, Pecoïtz father and son are in cahoots. We like their piquillo peppers stuffed with cod, eels with garlic and parsley, beef filet medallions, and the traditional gâteau Basque tops it all off wonderfully. For a quiet night, you can stay to sleep in one of the old-style rooms in the inn.

44720 Loire-Atlantique. Paris 440 –
Nantes 64 – Redon 41 – Saint-Nazaire 17 –
Vannes 63.
In the heart of the nature reserve of Brière, a land of earth and water, is this landmark town with its chalk houses covered with thatch. Visit the museums of customs and of brides.

 HOTELS-RESTAURANTS

● **La Mare aux Oiseaux**

162, île de Fedrun.
Tel. 02 40 88 53 01. Fax 02 40 91 67 44.
courriel@mareauxoiseaux.fr
www.mareauxoiseaux.fr
Closed 2 weeks Jan., 2 weeks Mar.
Rest. closed Mon. lunch.
10 rooms: 120–140€. 2 suites: 150€.
Prix fixe: 36€, 50€, 60€, 80€.
A la carte: 75€.

Eric Guérin's thatched cottage is in the middle of an enchanted island. One stays, surrounded by greenery, in a décor inspired by the local flora and fauna, notably the birds that nest all around. The rooms, some built on stilts, have reed roofs and are at the bottom of the garden. The restaurant is a proliferation of ideas and dishes that tell a story. Eric, an Alsatian from Saverne and formerly of the Tour d'Argent, who has returned out of passionate loyalty to his region, is never in want of inspiration. One succumbs to ravioli stuffed with melon and blood sausage, goat cheese ravioli in a vegetable broth, steamed pike-perch served with a beurre nantais, pigeon stuffed with crabmeat, veal sweetbreads with lobster and the berry profiteroles with Tagada strawberry candy flavored ice cream. Magical!

● La Hutte Briéronne   SIM

181, île de Fedrun.
Tel. 02 40 88 43 05. Fax 02 40 91 64 26.
Closed Mon. dinner, Tue. dinner, Wed.
Prix fixe: 18€, 38€, 8€ (child).
A la carte: 34€.

In this cabin-inn, Guillaume Guérin plays the card of local produce. Simple, tasty dishes: house foie gras with sel de Guérande, pike-perch, thinly sliced poultry with Muscadet wine and a frozen nougat with raspberry sauce make a good impression.

SAINT-JULIA

31540 Haute-Garonne. Paris 713 – Toulouse 40 – Carcassonne 60 – Castres 40 – Revel 12.
This ancient fortified town in the heart of Lauragais bears witness to a fine architectural heritage.

●	RESTAURANTS

● Auberge des Remparts   SIM

Rue du Vinaigre.
Tel. 05 61 83 04 79.
Closed Sun. dinner, Mon., Tue. dinner.
Prix fixe: 11,50€ (weekday lunch), 25€, 30€, 8€ (child).

Very near the town walls, the inn of the Laffonts has no trouble finding customers. People like its shady terrace, its suite of two restaurants in pastel shades and the attractively turned-out classics, such as slice of duck foie gras in terrine, pike-perch in a citrus emulsion, guinea hen with cabbage seasoned with juniper berries and the puffed orange crêpe.

SAINT-JULIEN-CHAPTEUIL

43260 Haute-Loire. Paris 562 – Le Puy 20 – Saint-Agrève 32 – Yssingeaux 17.
ot.stjulien-chapteuil@wanadoo.fr.
In the country of Jules Romains (don't miss his

local museum), a beautiful mountainous village, with its church and its fine location.

●	RESTAURANTS

● Vidal   V.COM

18, place du Marché.
Tel. 04 71 08 70 50. Fax 04 71 08 40 14.
www.restaurant-vidal.com
Closed Sun. dinner, Mon. dinner, Tue. (exc. July–Aug.), mid-Jan.–end Feb.
Prix fixe: 22€, 32€, 42€, 52€, 56€, 70€, 12€ (child).

Chantal and Jean-Pierre Vidal have made their establishment into a regional restaurant that holds its own. Armed with the lessons learned with the Troisgros, Jean-Pierre gives a lively touch to a cuisine that honors the seasons: mixed lobster and langoustines, a pike-perch and salmon duo and the twelve-hour roasted milk-fed lamb, with a red praline "discovery plate" for dessert. The intermittent special menus are fine invitations to pleasure.

SAINT-JULIEN-DE-CREMPSE see BERGERAC

SAINT-JULIEN-EN-GENEVOIS

74160 Haute-Savoie. Paris 528 – Annecy 36 – Thonon 47 – Genève 11 – Nantua 55.
This border town is the last stage in the Gex region before Geneva and Switzerland.

●	RESTAURANTS

● La Ferme de l'Hospital   ○ V.COM

In Bossey.
Tel. 04 50 43 61 43. Fax 04 50 95 31 53.
jjnogier@wanadoo.fr
www.ferme-hospital.com
Closed Sun., Mon., mid-Feb.–beg. Mar., Aug.
Prix fixe: 37€, 45€, 52€, 70€.
A la carte: 75€.

This old 17th-century farm was previously the property of Geneva Hospital. The Genevans today flock here to celebrate, just on the other side of the border, the cuisine of Jean-Jacques Noguier. The products are superb, the preparation harmonious and the presentation refined. Cold Lehman crayfish cream with Thai spices and ginger coconut sauce, pan-seared tuna steak with piquillo peppers and slow-cooked vegetables, herbs in a soy vinaigrette, rabbit with tomatoes, foie gras, pine nuts and Pimpiolet jus are a successful marriage of regional and exotic. Then comes the chocolate—intense and dark in little tarts—with pan-tossed sour cherries, vanilla syrup and a sour cherry sorbet. The wines are precious, as is the advice of Franck Mazadi who guides us in their choice.

SAINT-JULIEN-LES-METZ see METZ

SAINT-JULIEN-VOCANCE

07690 Ardèche. Paris 553 – Saint-Etienne 56 – Valence 68 – Saint-Bonnet-le-Froid 12. On the high plateaux of the Ardèche, here is the appeal of the open air.

● RESTAURANTS

● **Jean-François Julliat** COM

Locale known as Le Marthouret.
Tel. 04 75 34 71 61. Fax 04 75 34 79 19.
contact@restaurant-julliat.com
www.restaurnt-julliat.com
Closed Tue. dinner, Wed., 1 week beg. Jan., Feb. vac.
Prix fixe: 24€, 28€, 37€, 45€, 75€, 12€ (child).

Jean-François Julliat, a faithful native of Ardèche, has made this old coaching inn on the route to Puy into a friendly restaurant. Solange gives a warm welcome, offering generous and flavorsome menus using regional produce. Devesset escargots with local crêpes in a spice shell with salsify in a poultry jus, roasted rabbit filet seasoned with juniper berries and mushroom spring rolls with quince preserves and licorice jus and the "sweet picnic" dessert are reminders that Régis Marcon and St. Bonnet are not very far away.

SAINT-JUST-SAINT-RAMBERT

42170. Paris 542 – Roanne 74 – Montbrison 18 – Lyon 81 – Saint-Etienne 17.
A town on the banks of the Loire given over to the pleasures of water.

● RESTAURANTS

● **Le Neuvième Art** N V.COM

Pl du 19-Mars-1962.
Tel. 04 77 55 87 15. Fax 04 77 55 80 77.
Closed Sun., Mon., 1 week Christmas, 2 weeks Feb. vac., 3 weeks Aug.
Prix fixe: 52€, 70€, 90€.

This former station has been converted into a gastronomic hotel of great quality by Christophe Roure. This wonder boy of the kitchen, trained at Gagnaire's, Marcon's and Etéocle, uses all available material in a modern, serious environment. He produces dishes each more carefully prepared than the last in subtle, complex presentations free of heaviness or pointless pretension. Pan-seared foie gras with slow-cooked quetche plums, a Lyonnais bugne (fried sugar-coated pastry) and crunchy vanilla-flavored popcorn, large langoustine brochettes wrapped in kadaïf (Middle Eastern angelhair pastry), with a beet risotto and dried beef tartine, variations on the pork theme (milk-fed, served on hay, in its own cocotte) make fine, subtle but explosive food. The desserts ("barman's platter" following an apricot theme and "suggestions from a forest walk" with wild blueberry ice cream and pear and walnut financier) are invitations to a gastronomic dance.

SAINT-LARY-SOULAN

65170 Hautes-Pyrénées. Paris 828 – Auch 105 – Bagnères-de-Luchon 45 – Saint-Gaudens 65 – Tarbes 75 – Arreau 11.
A balcony onto the Pyrénées and a sports resort dedicated to "la glisse", in the upper valley of Aure. Visit the Bear House and the National Park Museum.

■◉ HOTELS-RESTAURANTS

■ La Pergola

25, rue Vincent-Mir.
Tel. 05 62 39 40 46. Fax 05 62 40 06 55.
www.hotellapergola.fr
Closed Nov. Rest. closed Mon. lunch (Dec.–
May), Tue. lunch (Dec.–May).
23 rooms: 59–107€.
Prix fixe: 29€, 39€, 49€, 15€ (child).
A la carte: 55€.

In the ski resort where everyone who's anyone in Bordeaux gathers, the chalet of Jean-Marie Mir cannot be ignored. We appreciate the rustic setting, the cozy sitting rooms and the cheerful, comfortable guest rooms, as well as the cuisine of Thierry Lafenêtre. In the two authentic dining rooms of La Pergola, foie gras terrine with Jurançon wine bouillon, roasted monkfish wrapped in salt-cured Spanish pork fat with piquillo peppers, braised loin of Bigorre black pig served with vegetables in an individual cocotte and a Pastis charlotte with a seasonal fruit compote warm the heart.

● La Grange   N COM

13, route d'Autun.
Tel. 05 62 40 07 14.
www.hotel-angleterre-arreau.com
Closed Tue. lunch, Wed. (exc. dinner in season), beg. Nov.–mid-Dec., end Apr.–mid-May.
Prix fixe: 18–34€.

This former barn has become a cozy, gastronomic hotel. The wooded décor is warm and the cuisine is colored with flavors of the Pyrénées. Good wines from both sides of the border. Wonderful welcome and gentle prices.

● Le Pic'Assiette   N SIM

In Guchan, 3 km, Quartier Pradet.
Tel. 05 62 39 96 24. Fax 05 62 39 95 63.
www.picassiette.net
Closed Mon. (off season).
Prix fixe: 12,50€, 16€, 18€, 23€, 32€, 7€ (child). A la carte: 40€.

At the gates of the national park and the Spanish border, the establishment of Cathy and Jean-Paul Terrigeol offers an unbeatable view onto the surrounding mountains. In the rustic restaurant, the cuisine is both restorative and affordable with duck foie gras two ways with Jurançon wine sauce, grilled Atlantic sea bass with fennel, duck breast with sel de Guérande and gâteau Basque.

SAINT-LAURENT-BLANGY see ARRAS
SAINT-LAURENT-SUR-SAONE see MACON
SAINT-LEGER-FOUGERET see CHATEAU-CHINON

SAINT-LEONARD-DE-NOBLAT

87400 Haute-Vienne. Paris 407 –
Limoges 20 – Guéret 62 – Aubusson 68.
This large town of Limousin is worth the detour for its beautiful church with a Romanesque belfry.

■◉ HOTELS-RESTAURANTS

■ Grand Saint-Léonard

23, av du Champ-de-Mars.
Tel. 05 55 56 18 18. Fax 05 55 56 98 32.
grandsaintleonard@wanadoo.fr
Closed mid-Dec.–mid-Jan. Rest. closed Mon.
lunch (off season), Tue. lunch (off season).
14 rooms: 55–60€.
Prix fixe: 25€, 42€, 59€.

Jean-Marc Vallet's restaurant is the meeting place for the important people of the locality. In a friendly atmosphere they enjoy well-prepared dishes such as scallop ravioli, the sole with ceps, beef filet, oxtail and the Calvados crème soufflé. The welcome is affable, the service attentive and the check moderate. The rooms are not always very large but are thoughtfully equipped.

SAINT-LIEUX-LES-LAVAUR see LAVAUR

SAINT-LOUIS

68300 Haut-Rhin. Paris 549 – Ferrette 24 –
Mulhouse 31 – Colmar 66.
This is both the doorway to Switzerland to the winding Sundgau, a border town in neutral col-

ors that plays host to a book festival. Gastronomy is on the scene.

HOTELS-RESTAURANTS

■ La Cour du Roy

1, rue de Lectoure.
Tel. 03 89 70 33 33.
www.hotelfp-saintlouis.com
Rest. closed Sat. lunch, Sun. dinner, Mon., end Dec.
30 rooms: 54–200€.
Prix fixe: 28–52€.

This former beer warehouse in a Renaissance style, dated 1906, has been converted into a contemporary hotel with very well-prepared rooms. Luxurious restaurant, timbered bar decorated on the theme of medieval beasts: a great overall effect!

■ L'Europe

2, rue de Huningue.
Tel. 03 89 69 73 55. Fax 03 89 67 92 06.
www.hotel-deleurope.com
27 rooms: 55–102€. 1 suite: 90€.

Behind the brick exterior of this 19th-century house with a neo-gothic tower are hidden comfortable, old-style rooms and a much-appreciated French and American billiard room.

■ Berlioz

rue Henner.
Tel. 03 89 69 74 44. Fax 03 89 70 19 17.
info@hotelberlioz.com / www.hotelberlioz.com
Closed 10 days Christmas–New Year's.
21 rooms: 55–70€.

One has the choice between "Louis XVI" or "boat" rooms in this thirties hotel near the station. The welcome of Patrick Valin and the breakfasts make it a pleasant stopover.

In Hégenheim (68220). 7 km sw via D469.

● Auberge du Boeuf Rouge SIM

9, rue de Hésingue.
Tel. 03 89 69 40 00. Fax 03 89 67 78 69.
boeuf.rouge@libertysurf.fr
Closed Sat. lunch, Sun. (exc. groups).

Prix fixe: 11€ (lunch), 22€ (lunch), 10€ (child). A la carte: 38€.

Alsace is totally present in the establishment of Martin Dirrig. The setting is rural, the place warm and the cuisine of Didier Risacher follows suit. Griled marbled duck and goose foie gras, the local flat garnished pies, pork cuts and charcuterie over sauerkraut and slow-cooked quetche plums with little pain perdu croutons and cinnamon ice cream meet with universal acclaim. Rapid service and low prices.

In Hésingue (68220). 4 km w via D419.

● Au Boeuf Noir

2, rue de Folgenburg.
Tel. 03 89 69 76 40. Fax 03 89 67 77 29.
j.giuggiola@tiscali.fr
Closed Sat. lunch, Sun. dinner, Mon., 2 weeks Mar., 2 weeks Aug.
Prix fixe: 28€ (lunch), 36€ (lunch, wine inc.), 45€, 69€. A la carte: 68€.

Jean-Pierre Giuggiola is an artist of multiple facets. He paints, and exhibits his colorful works on the light walls of his restaurant, but it is in the kitchen that he really shows what he's capable of, giving free rein to his imagination to create new combinations of successful flavors. One makes very short work of lobster and truffle salad, oven-browned pike-perch filet with seasonal vegetables, deboned pigeon cut into slices and the berry mille-feuille wih vanilla ice cream. Josiane "Giugiu" is a charming mistress of the house who gives good advice when it comes to selecting wines. The check is not excessive, encouraging one to go back to taste the things one couldn't try the first time.

In Huningue (68330). 2 km e via D469.

■ Tivoli

15, rue de Bâle.
Tel. 03 89 69 73 05. Fax 03 89 67 82 44.
info@tivoli.fr / www.tivoli.fr
Rest. closed Sat., Sun., Christmas–New Year's vac., 1 week at end July, 2 weeks beg. Aug.
41 rooms: 62–150€.
Prix fixe: 13€ (lunch), 24€, 45€.
A la carte: 50€.

Philippe Schneider, student of Jung and of the Hæberlins, excels in reinterpreting traditional dishes with finesse and a light touch. We like his venison terrine with foie gras, salmon trout roasted skin-side down, black tiger shrimp, venison medallion and the classically prepared torche au marron (a chestnut and meringue dessert). Eric Gollentz, a connoisseur of wines from the region and elsewhere, always gives good advice while the service is high quality and the checks remain reasonable. In the brasserie, the fast dishes of the day are executed with care and are very good value. The rooms, decorated in contemporary style, are functional.

In Village-Neuf (68128). 3 km ne via N66 and D21.

● **Le Cheval Blanc**   **N SIM**
6, rue de Rosenau.
Tel. 03 89 69 79 15. Fax 03 89 69 86 63.
www.lechevalblanc.fr
Closed Christmas–beg. Jan.,
3 weeks in summer.
12 rooms: 45–48€.
Prix fixe: 17€, 21€, 39€ (wine inc.), 48€.

Massimo Cataldi, who worked at the Rendez-Vous de Chasse in Colmar, is trying to do a good job in his roadside restaurant. He works seriously with regional products and treats game with solemnity, offering wild boar in various forms: ham, head cheese, sausage, chops, civet, venison saddle or medallions, pheasant, pigeon, wild duck, young partridge and breasts of game hen. Everything is reasonably priced. In the bar corner, where the dish of the day is served (as in the rather kitsch restaurant), the special menus are also dispensed with seriousness. There is nothing to change in the goose foie gras, pike-perch on a bed of slow-cooked leeks and horseradish, nor the desserts (crème brûlée and an apple and walnut oven-crisped dessert).

In Village-Neuf.

● **La Nouvelle Brasserie Runser**   **SIM**
2, rue de Saint-Louis.
Tel. 03 89 67 11 15. Fax 03 89 69 45 08.

Closed Christmas.
Prix fixe: 12€ (lunch), 21€, 29€, 32€.
A la carte: 45€.

Eric Runser has successfully kept this very contemporary brasserie going. One comes here, right on the border, to talk but also to enjoy a slice of foie gras with Port wine jelly, jumbo shrimp brochettes, sole meunière, beef sirloin steak and a frozen kouglof, created by good disciple Denis Beck. Professional service and moderate prices.

SAINT-LOUP-DE-VARENNES see CHALON-SUR-SAONE

SAINT-LUNAIRE see DINARD

SAINT-LYPHARD

44410 Loire-Atlantique. Paris 450 – Saint-Nazaire 22 – Nantes 75 – La Baule 17.
otsi-stlyphard@wanadoo.fr.
A regional natural park since 1970, covering 40,000 hectares and eighteen administrative areas, Brière is the second largest swamp area of France and perhaps the most beautiful. The wealth of thatched roofs, flights of peewits, herons, warblers, mallards, snipe and teals and the sightings of stoat, mink, otters and stone martens make one want to indulge in a little secret fishing behind the reeds.

●	RESTAURANTS

■ **Les Chaumières du Lac**
Rue du Vignonnet.
Tel. 02 40 91 32 32. Fax 02 40 91 30 33.
jclogodin@leschaumieresdulac.com
www.leschaumieresdulac.com
Closed end Dec.–mid-Feb., Tue.
Rest. closed Tue., Wed. lunch.
20 rooms: 64–94€.
Prix fixe: 19,90€, 28,80€, 9€ (child).

The hotel concept of having five little thatched cottages in the very heart of Brière is an original and friendly one. The rooms are large and comfortable while the cooking in the Typhas' inn allows one to eat pleasantly with pan-tossed frog legs and chicken oysters with ceps, rouget and escargots in garlic and parsley, eel in Reims mustard sauce, partridge cooked two ways with chestnut purée, Breton rouelle with salted butter and the Suzette-style peppered mango dessert. The special menus are good value.

● Le Nézil `COM`

Rte de Saint-Nazaire – Le Nézil.
Tel. 02 40 91 41 41. Fax 02 40 91 45 39.
aubergelenezil@wanadoo.fr -
www.paysblanc.com/auberge-nezil/
Closed Sun. dinner, Mon., Wed. (off season),
1 week beg. Oct., mid-Nov.–mid-Dec.
Prix fixe: 28,50€, 38€, 44€,
9,50€ (child). A la carte: 58€.

Hervé Hascoët favors regional dishes into which he incorporates a contemporary touch. One enjoys the pleasurable pan-tossed langoustines with green asparagus, frog legs with local salted butter, lamb tenderloin in an herb crust and puffed crêpes with passion fruit. Armelle's welcome to this typical thatched house with its flower-filled garden is a plus.

In Bréca (44410). 6 km s via D47.

● Auberge de Bréca `COM`

Tel. 02 40 91 41 42. Fax 02 40 91 37 41.
aubergedebreca@wanadoo.fr
www.auberge-breca.com
Closed Sun. (exc. July–Aug.),
Wed. dinner (Nov.–Mar.), Thu. (exc. July–
Aug.), 2 weeks Jan.
Prix fixe: 19,50€, 27€, 35€, 40€,
12€ (child). A la carte: 44–50€.

Françoise and Christian Deniaud give a smiling welcome to their renovated Brière house, offering a cuisine that reflects the region. Mushroom plate with wild boar, pan-simmered pike-perch with cabbage, two types of frog legs, warm chocolate soup and seasonal fruits with marshmallows make a good impression in the rural décor with well-laid tables and a fireplace facing the large port.

In Kerbourg (44410). 6 km via D51.

● Auberge de Kerbourg `COM`

Rte de Guérande.
Tel. 02 40 61 95 15. Fax 02 40 61 98 64.

Closed Sun. dinner, Mon., Tue. lunch,
mid-Dec.–mid-Feb.
Prix fixe: 50€, 55€, 65€, 70€,
15€ (child).

Far from the media and their brouhaha, in the tranquil shelter of an enchanting thatched house dating from 1753, Bernard Jeanson untiringly continues to defend his region with a balanced cuisine in which fine produce of sea and land speak eloquently but not too loudly, as demonstrated by the dishes served in the rather rustic restaurant with its bare stone walls. Stuffed and rolled tuna and duck foie gras with sardine and anchovy cream sauce, monkfish liver with Aquitane caviar, Loire-fished shad in season, veal sweetbread medallions with salted butter and a licorice-flavored carrot jus, the all-citrus tiramisu and pan-simmered cherries with tea-flavored ice cream delight, as does the check, which remains low. Exquisite welcome from Sarah Jeanson.

79400 Deux-Sèvres. Paris 385 – Angoulême 105 – Niort 25 – Parthenay 28 – Poitiers 50. Large agricultural market town famous for its infantry school. Don't miss the ancient cathedral rebuilt in the 17th-century in the Renaissance style.

 HOTELS-RESTAURANTS

■ Le Logis Saint-Martin

Chemin Pissot.
Tel. 05 49 05 58 68. Fax 05 49 76 19 93.
www.logis-saint-martin.com
Closed 1 week Nov., Jan. Rest. closed Sat.
lunch, Mon. (hotel also closed), Tue. lunch.
11 rooms: 120–165€. 1 suite: 165€.
Prix fixe: 28€ (lunch), 48€ (dinner),
75€ (dinner).

The Dalai Lama stayed in this 17th-century manor house in an estate bordering the Sèvre. Since then, Bernard Heintz has restored the restaurant in an oriental style with shades of yellow, ochre and violet. The hotel, hung with blue fabrics, has kept its classical feel. In the kitchen, Emmanuel Parent gives free rein to creativity with oyster ravioli in a sea water aspic and topped with Avruga caviar, line-fished Atlantic sea bass in a hazelnut and juniper berry infusion with simmered ceps, veal sweetbreads simmered in Vin Jaune with heirloom vegetables and suprising desserts, including variations on the beet theme.

SAINT-MALO

35400 Ille-et-Vilaine. Paris 418 – Avranches 67 – Dinan 32 – Rennes 72 – Saint-Brieuc 72. office.de.tourisme.saint-malo@wanadoo.fr. The original city walls, the island of Grand-Bé and the national fort, the Solidor tower, the memories of Surcouf, Jacques Cartier and Chateaubriand, the location just beside the ocean and the boats that float across the horizon: this is the Breton port of St.-Malo, magic intact.

■	HOTELS

■ Grand Hôtel des Thermes

100, bd Hébert, quartier Paramé.
Tel. 02 99 40 75 75 / 02 99 40 75 40.
Fax 02 99 40 76 00.
www.thalassotherapie.com
Closed 2 weeks Jan.
173 rooms: 76–319€. 3 suites: 470–634€.
Prix fixe: 27,50€, 42€, 54€.

This 19th-century luxury hotel facing the sea, enlarged and with an added modern wing, offers rooms with bay windows that look toward the open water. Guests benefit from all the facilities that allow one to rest and recuperate: swimming pool with aquatonic area, hammam and Jacuzzi. Thermal baths are directly accesible for thalassotherapy cures and the beach of fine sand is on the doorstep. The cuisine of Patrice Dugué is health food in La Verrière, gastronomic in Cap Horn (see restaurant). Make sure you don't go overboard on the chocolates of Pascal Pochon.

■ Le Valmarin

7, rue Jean-XXIII.
Tel. 02 99 81 94 76. Fax 02 99 81 30 03.

levalmarin@wanadoo.fr / www.levalmarin.com
12 rooms: 95–135€.
Half board: 105–155€.

Among the beach, the golf course, the riding center, the tennis courts and the covered swimming pool, this 18th-century St. Malo house is worth the visit for its charming welcome, its light and functional rooms, its delicious breakfasts and its honest prices.

■ La Porte Saint-Pierre

2, place du Guet.
Tel. 02 99 40 91 27. Fax 02 99 56 06 94.
www.hotel-portestpierre.com
Closed mid-Nov.–31 Jan. Rest. closed Sun. dinner (exc. July–Aug.), Tue. (exc. July–Aug.), Thu. lunch (exc. July–Aug.).
24 rooms: 62€.
Prix fixe: 28€, 38€, 48€, 8€ (child).
A la carte: 55€.

This little hotel, with its marine décor, houses wood-paneled, practical rooms, some of which overlook the sea. In the restaurant, the owner-chef Anaïck Gaudiche serves a reliable regional cuisine such as fish soup, home-style abalone, chitterling sausage and thin apple tart.

■ La Villefromoy

7, bd Hébert.
Tel. 02 99 40 92 20. Fax 02 99 56 79 49.
villefromoy.hotel@wanadoo.fr.
www.villefromoy.fr
21 rooms: 85–250€.

A coastal house dating from 1900 right beside Rochebonne beach and the sea wall, entirely renovated and exuding charm: this is on offer from Eric and Brigitte Bourdigal-Busnel, along with their friendly welcome. The large sitting room is cozy, the bathrooms modern and the whole effect one of a quietness that is not without warmth. Private closed parking.

■ Le Central

6, Grand-Rue BP 87.
Tel. 02 99 40 87 70. Fax 02 99 40 47 57.
www.hotel-central-st-malo.com
48 rooms: 59–130€. 2 suites: 130–165€.

Prix fixe: 18€, 30€, 12€ (child).
A la carte: 41€.

The name of this hotel is very apt. The rooms are comfortable and the cuisine in La Pêcherie not bad at all. In a nautical, early 20th-century atmosphere, one enjoys the comforting dishes of langoustine salad with citrus-smoked duck breast, pan-tossed John Dory with potatoes and Chouchen (a local-honey based liqueur), lamb medallions with garlic cream and the pear and salted-butter caramel puff pastry dessert with sorbet.

■ La Korrigane

39, rue Le-Pomellec.
Tel. 02 99 81 65 85. Fax 02 99 82 23 89.
contact@lakorrigane.com
www.lakorrigane.com
12 rooms: 90–150€.

Madame Le Carvennec is the hostess of this 19th-century town house. The garden is welcoming and the sitting room/ library restful. The rooms, which bear the names of famous fashion designers, have been carefully decorated.

■ Le Manoir du Cunningham

9, pl Monseigneur-Duchesne.
Tel. 02 99 21 33 33. Fax 02 99 21 33 34.
www.st-malo-hotel-cunningham.com
Closed 15 Nov.–15 Mar.
10 rooms: 90–170€. 3 suites: 200–220€.

Opposite Cunningham's Bar, a friendly place in surroundings that deserve a visit, this 17th-century manor house offers beige, pink or green rooms with furniture in exotic woods. Added attractions are the view of the pleasure port, the island of Cézembre, the bay and the old town.

■ La Rance

15, quai Sébastopol.
Tel. 02 99 81 78 63. Fax 02 99 81 44 80.
hotel-la-rance@wanadoo.fr
www.larancehotel.com
11 rooms: 55–82€.

In this hotel where the marine atmosphere created by Patrick Ray is that of a guest-

house, the rooms are simple and comfortable. Some overlook the Solidor tower and the sea.

■ L'Ascott

35, rue du Chapitre.
Tel. 02 99 81 89 93. Fax 02 99 81 77 40.
www.ascotthotel.com
Closed Jan.
10 rooms: 90–145€. 1 suite: 145€.

The affable host, Patrick Guillon, gives a very smiling welcome to his century-old house with contemporary rooms and designer furniture.

■ Hôtel Beaufort

25, chaussée du Sillon.
Tel. 02 99 40 99 99. Fax 02 99 40 99 62.
www.hotel-beaufort.com
20 rooms: 75–205€. 2 suites: 145–205€.

Ideally situated above the Grande Plage, a stone's throw from the city walls and the thalassotherapy center, the establishment of Sylvie and Mark Peterson offers luminous rooms that open onto the sea. The nicest have a bay window or a balcony.

DISCOVERY OF THE YEAR

● Le Saint-Placide

6, pl du Poncel.
Tel. 02 99 81 70 73. Fax 02 99 81 89 49.
imobihan@wanadoo.fr
www.lesaintplacide.com
Closed Tue., Wed. (exc. dinner July–Aug.),
10 days Feb., 2 weeks end June July,
10 days Nov.
Prix fixe: 18€ (weekday lunch), 24€
(weekday lunch), 42€, 67€, 12€ (child).
A la carte: 70€.

Luc and Isabelle Mobihan don't do anything with the common herd. She seems to have a resemblance to Véronique Abadie at L'Amphitryon in Lorient: the same instinctive charm, serene energy, attention paid to (good) wines from everywhere and the same deliberately unstructured look, care of Marithé and François Girbaud. This comes as no surprise: both of them worked there. What is more, Isabelle is from Lorient (while Luc is from Finistère). He also went to make his fortune at the Auberge des Templiers in Bézards. Then they both earned a reputation at the château de Sully in Port-en-Bessin. Finally, they invested in a former tram station in the St. Servan area, the well-heeled part of St. Malo, gave it a modern overhaul, creating a place in their own style. With the assistance of word of mouth advertising, the establishment is continually full. The products of the day's tide, diver-gathered scallops in a superbly done sesame crust, foie gras married with local smoked chitterling sausage with fig compote, lobster in a shellfish bouillon, perfumed with a sprinkling of coriander and the juicy lamb married with Paimpol coco beans all await you. With clever menus and well-regarded vintages (Vin de Voile from Plageoles, Coteaux du Giennois from Henri Bourgeois, Roc de Cambes des Mitajvile) there is enough to make it the best new discovery. The Mobihans have not got big heads, however. Their *amuse-gueules* are amazing (cep cappuccino, king crab, celery emulsion), their bread, cheeses from Bordier and the marvelous desserts, including the "*route du rhum*" with banana mousse cannelloni, pineapple sorbet and a miniature baba are worth getting hysterical about. In short, everything here merits praise for its combination of cheerfulness and seriousness to best effect, in an unexpected establishment that resembles only itself.

● **Le Cap Horn**

At Grand'Hôtel des Thermes, 100, bd Hébert, Grande Plage du Sillon.
Tel. 02 99 40 75 40. Fax 02 99 40 76 00.
www.thalassosaintmalo.com
Closed 2 weeks Jan.
Prix fixe: 27,50€, 42€, 54€. A la carte: 65€.

The serious and efficient Pascal Dugué, chef of the Grand Hôtel des Thermes, cheerfully delivers his "rush" services in high season. When 400 health cure client guests are hungry, one has to rise to the challenge. Healthy and light at La Verrière, more gastronomic and creative at Le Cap Horn, he seduces, before the grand sight of the high tides on the Sillon, with crab with with an avocado emulsion, a dish of diced langoustines and Pata Negra ham, minced, cooked Atlantic sea bass on the plate with a light sea urchin-flavored butter and John Dory on a bed of seasoned eggplant purée with fennel bouillon. The kouign-amann and the apple mille-feuille with its local buttermilk ice cream and the spéculos cookies in a frozen praline parfait are very attractive items created by expert pâtissier Pascal Pochon. Fine wine list at mild prices.

● **A l'Abordage**

5, place de la Poissonnerie.
Tel.-Fax 02 99 40 87 53.
catherine.nicolas14@wanadoo.fr
www.alabordagesaintmalo.com
Closed Sat. lunch (off season), Sun. (off season), Mon., 3 weeks Jan., 1 week June, 2 weeks end Nov.
Prix fixe: 57€ (tasting menu).
A la carte: 60€.

Laurent Nicolas, who has worked at Guy Savoy's and in Britain (at Tante Claire and Le Gavroche), and his wife Cathy, British sommelier vice-champion, have created a divine, upmarket surprise within their own walls. Chic brown and blue décor, with pretty armchairs, the fine cuisine of the young Gurvan Pencole and amazing choice of wines set the tone of a distinctive place. Shelled langoustines and blood sausage, strips of marinated tuna with pumpkin, wasabi and bitter orange sauce, pan-tossed rouget with artichokes and peppers, veal filet with glazed white turnips and local dessert served with star anise–seasoned coffee while saying to yourself that something delicious is coming this way. This is a place to watch.

● **Le Chalut**

8, rue de la Corne-de-Cerf.
Tel.-Fax 02 99 56 71 58.

lechalutstmalo@aol.com
Closed Mon., Tue. (exc. dinner July–Aug.).
Prix fixe: 24€ (lunch), 37€, 50€, 68€.
A la carte: 55–65€.

Jean-Philippe Foucat's is a good establishment. Formerly of the Ritz and Ledoyen, he plays his own hand in a charming marine setting. "All that comes from the sea", could be his motto (apart from an impeccable spiced foie gras terrine with fig compote). Scallops in salad with truffle oil, cod with creamed pumpkin sauce and Jerusalem artichokes and the turbot with oyster mushrooms, crushed tomatoes and crabmeat are finely-crafted dishes. The Jardin Secret de Sauvion Muscadet makes inspired drinking up here and the desserts (apple pie with caramel ice cream and soft chocolate cake with licorice ice cream) are to be devoured on the spot.

● **Delaunay**   ◎COM
6, rue Sainte-Barbe.
Tel. 02 99 40 92 46.
bdelaunay@wanadoo.fr
www.restaurant-delaunay.com
Closed lunch, Sun., Mon. (off season),
mid-Nov.–mid-Dec., Jan.–end Feb.
Prix fixe: 28€. A la carte: 45–65€.

The restaurant of Didier Delaunay is one of the St. Malo bonnes addresses. Based on extremely fresh produce, his cuisine gives pride of place to fish and other seafood without forsaking meat from the inland. A scallop and oyster carpaccio with hazelnut oil, sesame tuna steak with zucchini and lemon chutney and the leg of lamb served over vegetable couscous are delectable in every way. The chocolate soft-centered biscuit with Bounty candy ice cream is a highly recommended ending to the meal. Brigitte Delaunay gives a most agreeable welcome and advises the appropriate wine with a smile. The special menu represents, at 28 , a stunning price-quality ratio.

● **La Duchesse Anne**   ◎COM
5, pl Guy-la-Chambre.
Tel. 02 99 40 85 33. Fax 02 99 40 00 28.
Closed Sun. dinner, Mon. lunch, Wed. (off

season), Dec., Jan.
Prix fixe: 70€. A la carte: 55€.

This establishment continues to be a choice restaurant. In his old-style setting, Serge Thirouard keeps on turning out high-flying classics. Wine-simmered mackerel filets served cold, seafood gratin, poached turbot with hollandaise sauce, grilled lobster and grilled chateaubriand-cut beef and profiteroles are monuments treated with respect. The gorgeous welcome, the diligent service and the prices that have finally been lowered all enchant.

● **Le Bénétin**   COM
Les Rochers Sculptés, in Rothéneuf.
Tel.-Fax 02 99 56 97 64.
restaurantlebenetin@wanadoo.fr
www.restaurant-lebenetin.com
Closed Sun. dinner, Mon.
Prix fixe: 13€, 17€, 30€, 10€ (child).
A la carte: 40€.

There is a new team in this beautiful chic, loft-style panoramic restaurant, full of wood and light. Patrick Traup, who came from the Cunningham, directs the restaurant while the young Jean-Charles Briquet, who worked at La Mère Pourcel in Dinan, with Tirel-Guérin at La Gouesnière and at Le Flocon de Sel in Megève, has taken over the kitchen with spirit. An oyster and scallop tartare, shellfish stew, veal filet with Jerusalem artichokes and the pineapple carpaccio are promising.

● **La Grassinais**
12, allée de Grassinais, rte de Rennes.
Tel. 02 99 81 33 00. Fax 02 99 81 60 90.
manoirdelagrassinais@wanadoo.fr
saint-malo-hebergement.com
Closed 21 Dec.–31 Jan., Sat. lunch,
Sun. dinner, Mon. (off season).
29 rooms: 59–79€.
Prix fixe: 24€, 36€, 56€, 12€ (child).

As soon as you cross the threshold of this former farm you forget the industrial area that surrounds it. Martine Bouvier, an admirable hostess, doesn't rest until she has won you over. The cuisine of her hus-

923

band Christophe seduces effortlessly. The sea and the land are equally represented. We still like the crab remoulade served with rich zucchini custard cream, sole with artichokes and orange and the seven-hour lamb served with a green cabbage couscous. We appreciate the grand desserts of Caroline and Anne-Sophie. The cellar hides several wonders and the checks remain affordable. A good stopover that has light, functional rooms.

● Le Bistro de Jean   ●SIM

6, rue de la Corne-de-Cerf.
Tel.-Fax 02 99 40 98 68.
Closed Sat. lunch, Sun., Wed. lunch, Christmas–New Year's vac., Feb. vac.
Prix fixe: 14€ (lunch), 19€ (lunch).
A la carte: 33–40€.

This chic wood-decorated bistro is one of our favorites, enthusiastically taken over by Hervé-Jean and Catherine Le Bourhis, who came from La Kammerzell in Alsace. The careful décor, relaxed atmosphere, wine by the glass, the changing menu on the slate and the sober prices: it is all seductive. Sardines with goat cheese (exquisite idea), rouget tart, boneless rib steak with (or without) Gorgonzola sauce and a coffee tiramisu effortlessly delight. The pot of Coteau du Lyonnais from Duboeuf goes down without a murmur.

● Le Bulot   N·SIM

13, quai Sébastopol.
Tel. 02 99 81 07 11.
Closed Sat. (off season), Sun. (off season).
Prix fixe: 13€ (lunch). A la carte: 28€.

Fabienne and Jean-René Boursin and their chef Fico Gautier have made this bistro on the St.-Servan port into a buzzing place. These cheerful souls, who met at the Soupe au Chou in Vitré, set the tone for a joyous, uncomplicated atmosphere. Bar/restaurant, tea tasting, terrace at the foot of the Solidor tower: the place is fun, the décor modern and the chalkboard menu friendly. A salmon tartare (slightly overwhelmed by its potatoes and dill), the house terrine, grill of the day, cod and potato purée cooked in the wok and a soft-

centered chocolate cake make nice suppers among friends.

● Côté Sens   N·SIM

16, rue de la Herse.
Tel. 02 99 20 08 12.
Closed lunch, Mon. (off season),
2 weeks end Nov., 2 weeks end Feb.
A la carte: 35–50€.

Pascal Poisson, who formerly worked at the neighboring Bistro de Jean, has installed himself in this colorful little spot, with its half-height decorative woodwork and its naïve paintings done by a painter friend, where he performs his one-man show in his mini-kitchen open onto the restaurant. British yachtsmen have made it one of their eating places of choice. Quick-seared cuttlefish with pine nuts, crispy jumbo shrimp with mixed herbs, John Dory with seaweed-flavored butter, grilled cod filet with pancetta and a fresh fig pastilla give nothing short of pure pleasure. Well-chosen organic wines form a precise accompaniment to it all.

● L'Epicerie   N·SIM

18, rue de la Herse.
Tel. 02 23 18 34 55.
Closed Sun., Mon., 2 weeks Jan.
A la carte: 35–45€.

The setting is a simple, lively bistro, two large menu slates fixed to the wall, an open kitchen and good-humored service: here is one of the good discoveries of central St. Malo. The chef is a woman who knows her craft. Extremely fresh hors-d'oeuvres, fish just in from the tide, wonderful red meat and wines chosen with "nose" set the tone for a friendly place.

● L'Ancrage   SIM

7, rue Jacques-Cartier.
Tel. 02 99 40 15 97. Fax 02 23 18 03 61.
Closed Tue. (off season), Wed. (off season),
beg. Jan.–beg. Feb.
Prix fixe: 15€ (weekday lunch), 20€, 27€, 34€.

Without a doubt, the excellent price-quality ratio of the special menus explains vacationers' interest in this restaurant near the city walls, but we mustn't forget that the land and sea cuisine of Christophe Bigot is of excellent quality, as demonstrated by the seafood platter, salmon filet smoked with fennel, veal escalope in the style of Normandy, apple puff pastry dessert and sour cherry crêpes. Friendly atmosphere and service, on both the first and second floors.

● La Corderie   SIM

9, chemin de la Corderie,
quartier "Saint-Servan".
Tel. 02 99 81 62 38. Fax 02 99 81 25 14.
lacorderie.restaurant@wanadoo.fr
www.lacorderie.com
Closed Sun. dinner (exc. fêtes), Mon.,
11 Nov.–mid-Feb.
Prix fixe: 17€, 9€ (child). A la carte: 42€.

Denis Gerbert does not seek to amaze the crowds. Although he learned several clever tricks from his brother-in-law, Franck Cerutti, who is in the kitchens of Alain Ducasse at the Louis XV in Monaco, simplicity is always his ground rule: saffron-seasoned fish soup, Atlantic sea bass cooked Provençal-style and a soft-centered carrot and spice cake seduce. Anne Gerbert keeps a watchful eye over the restaurant that opens onto the sea.

● Domaine des Mauriers   SIM

Les Mauriers.
Tel. 02 99 19 85 44. Fax 02 99 19 85 45.
contact@lesmauriers.com
www.lesmauriers.com
Closed Mon., Feb.
Prix fixe: 15€ (weekday lunch), 26€, 31€,
41€. A la carte: 58€.

Daniel Le Héran remains the interpreter of a successful modern cuisine: a turbot cake with Guéméné chitterling sausage, thin scallop tart with smoked morel sauce, lemongrass-seasoned tagine of monkfish medallions, beef filet medallions with bone marrow and spicy red wine sauce and a pain d'épice and white chocolate dessert. The prices remain super low. A wonderful stopping place.

● Gilles   SIM

2, rue Pie-qui-Boit.
Tel.-Fax 02 99 40 97 25.
Closed Wed., Thu. (mid-Oct.–Easter),
20 Nov.–mid-Dec., Feb. vac.
Prix fixe: 19,50€, 20,70€, 24€.

In the rue Pie-qui-boit ("the drinking magpie"), the rare bird Philippe Poignand, a self-taught man, brilliantly creates such dishes as langoustines in puff pastry with vegetables, John Dory with hot oysters and pan-crisped bacon, slow-simmered fish stew with seaweed, cider- and Camembert-seasoned rabbit leg. A crunchy almond wafer and the cider, apple and caramel dessert are not bad. Eliane Poignand explains each dish with great kindness, without revealing all their secrets—the mystery remains on the plate.

In Saint-Coulomb (35350). 11 km ne

● Terre et Mer

La Secouette.
Tel. 02 99 82 12 46. Fax 02 99 82 12 46.
Closed Mon., Tue. lunch, Feb. vac.
Prix fixe: 19€, 25€, 30€, 9,50€ (child).

Marcel Cadieu welcomes his guests with open arms to his rustic restaurant with bare stone walls and beams. Serious classics emerge from his kitchen: pan-tossed scallops with endives, roasted Atlantic sea bass with chanterelles, beef rump roast with shallots and the roasted pear with honey and spices.

SAINT-MARCEL see CHALON-SUR-SAONE

SAINT-MARCEL-DU-PERIGORD

24510 Dordogne. Paris 552 – Bergerac 19 –
Saint-Alvère 10 – Lalinde 8.
At the gentle heart of France, bordering rural Périgord, black and purple.

●   RESTAURANTS

● Auberge Lou Peyrol   SIM

Tel. 05 53 24 09 71.
fiona.wawrin@wanadoo.fr / www.loupeyrol.com

Closed Mon. (exc. off season), Tue. (off season), Wed. (off season),
mid-Jan.–mid-Feb.
Prix fixe: 28€, 33€, 40€, 9€ (child).
A la carte: 45€.

Philippe Wavrin and his wife Fiona give a warm welcome to this tiny village inn and its stone restaurant with its shady terrace overlooking the church. Duck foie gras with apples and beetroot vinaigrette, John Dory pan-tossed with squid ink risotto, the pork trio (loin, blood sausage and oven-crisped meat) with lentils and a warm Armagnac and orange soufflé served with vanilla ice cream make one want to be a regular diner here.

SAINT-MARTIN-DE-BELLEVILLE

73440 Savoie. Paris 653 – Albertville 42 – Chambéry 91 – Moûtiers 15.
lesmenuires@lesmenuires.com.
At 1450 meters altitude, a terrace open onto the pistes of Trois-Vallées.

 HOTELS-RESTAURANTS

■ Le Saint-Martin

Les Grangeraies.
Tel. 04 79 00 88 00. Fax 04 79 00 88 39.
hotelsaintmartin@wanadoo.fr
www.hotel-stmartin.com
Closed mid-Apr.–beg. Dec.
27 rooms: 98–195€.
Prix fixe: 30€, 50€, 80€, 12€ (child).

Right above the village, at the crossroads of the pistes, the welcome here is warm, the rooms wood paneled and the whole effect cozy. The hammam, sauna and mini-club contribute to the well-being of one's stay, as does the New Wave Savoie cuisine served in the Grenier. The whole pig menu (Pormoniers sausage, blood sausage with apples and Savoyard pork with polenta frites) make a good impression. Not to be missed is the caramelized millefeuille from a recent *stagaire* at Fauchon working the pastries in the kitchen. A jewel awaiting discovery.

■ Les Chalets du Gypse

ZAC Places.
Tel. 04 79 09 45 00. Fax 04 79 06 71 89.
Closed beg. Oct.–mid-Dec.,
end Apr.–end June.
Apartments: 1120–2531€ per week.

A new-style chic Savoie residence overlooking the village, with large rooms for families and covered swimming pool.

● La Bouitte

Hameau de Saint-Marcel.
Tel. 04 79 08 96 77. Fax 04 79 08 96 03.
info@la-bouitte.com / www.la-bouitte.com
Closed Sept.–10 Dec., May–beg. June.
Rest. closed Mon.
5 rooms: 242€. 2 suites: 242–366€.
Prix fixe: 47€, 78€, 110€, 150€,
18€ (child). A la carte: 116€.

Here is a father and son, a house growing at an organic pace, a chalet with terrace, sweet little rooms, sauna and choice restaurant. The establishment is the quiet star of the Belleville valley, built up from a little mountain inn that made fondue and raclette, run by René Meilleur. He is a scuba diver at the holiday village of Ménuires, a cabinetmaker by training who created his establishment with the same passion with which he became a chef. René, who has received the revelation of creative cooking, mixes products from here and there without ever forgetting the local land and Savoie. La Bouitte is growing in reputation. René is relieved by his son Maxime, who trained in pâtisserie but also handles savory dishes. There are now special menus named "son's inspiration" and "father's inspiration" that complement each other. The mother, Marie-Louise, who has seen her little world grow bit by bit, watches over everything with feeling. The wooden restaurant has been enlarged with a veranda, but this is no large-scale operation but rather one that has kept its head: there are forty-five covers, no more. Ceps in large thin ravioli with watercress and meat jus, local salmon-trout with whipped butter, finely-minced broccoli cream, black truffles shaved onto potato soup, served with a lace biscuit, the palate-cleansing tomato and Sichuan pepper soda, an immaculately pan-seared half lobe of foie gras with coconut bouillon and the partridge in cocotte with chives and chopped chanterelles: dishes evocative of rural Savoie await you in the guise of a walk through "a thousand and one flavors". The adventure continues with the course of regional cheeses (Bleu de Termignon, Tomme or Beaufort), followed by Maxime's sumptuous desserts (walnut mille-feuille, pralined mousseline and salted-butter caramel ice cream). A sommelier on top of his subject adds to it all with divine wines, proving that Savoie viniculture can be great when it wants to be. It is clear: there is in the hamlet of St. Marcel an excellent and charming establishment that is ready to move up to star status.

■ Alp'Hotel

Rue Notre-Dame.
Tel. 04 79 08 92 82. Fax 04 79 08 94 61.
alphotel@wanadoo.fr /www.alphotel.fr
Closed end Apr.–mid-Dec.
30 rooms: 70–110€. 1 suite: 115–165€.
Prix fixe: 20€, 35€, 50€, 10€ (child).
A la carte: 25–30€.

The renovated rooms of this large chalet in the middle of the resort offer a good level of comfort. The half-boarders enjoy a simple, family cuisine. For one-off guests there is a menu of local specialities: Alpine herb salad, lake whitefish, tartiflette (oven-baked potatoes in Réblochon) and farçons (Savoyard potatoes). Nice welcome and moderate prices. Health center.

■ Edelweiss

Tel. 04 79 08 96 67. Fax 04 79 08 90 40.
www.hotel-edelweiss73.com
Closed end Apr.–beg. July, end Aug.–mid-Dec.
16 rooms: 95–135€. Half board: 140–205€.

This rustic and simple family hotel offers clean rooms as well as a nice guesthouse cuisine.

● Le Lachenal

Tel. 04 79 08 96 29.
lelachenal@orange.com

Closed end Apr.–beg. July,
end Aug.–mid-Dec.
3 rooms: 66–66€.
Prix fixe: 18€, 14€ (child, weekday dinner).

This inn, with its three cozy little rooms, has character. Martine and Laura Vasseur took over this year.

● L'Etoile des Neiges

Chef-lieu.
Tel. 04 79 08 92 80. Fax 04 79 08 90 40.
www.hotel-edelweiss73.com
Closed end Apr.–mid-Dec.
Prix fixe: 24€ (lunch), 29€, 50€.

With its central fireplace and its typical Savoyard wood decoration, this gastronomic chalet reached by ski and on foot makes a friendly little stopover. An omelette with chanterelles, Savoyard salad, lamb chops with crozets (the regional pasta), the raclette and tartiflette are served side by side with a traditional Savoyard gratin. Flawless classic desserts.

● Le Montagnard

Les Places.
Tel. 04 79 01 08 40.
www.le-montagnard.com
Closed lunch (July–Aug.),
beg. May–end June, beg. Sept.–10 Dec.
A la carte: 35€.

This former stable has become a distinguished restaurant under the management of Eric Suchet. This lively cheese producer offers all the specialities of his region in surroundings full of charm and good humor: soup with diots (the local sausage), lake whitefish with slow-cooked vegetables, trout with local pasta and dishes made from local Réblochon cheese or a local dish called paillasse bellevilloise (grated potatoes with goat cheese, mushrooms and green salad) sit together with the *plats du jour*, which vary according to the market. Pretty desserts (sweet rissoles, sweet pear tarts, farcon and lemon tart), fresh wines and ever-present smiles.

SAINT-MARTIN-DE-LA-BRASQUE

84760 Vaucluse. Paris 760 – Aix-en-Provence 34 – Apt 40 – Avignon 79.
A stone's throw from the beautiful château of Ansouis, on the foothills of Luberon, a very tranquil little Provençal village.

●	RESTAURANTS

● La Fontaine
Pl de la Fontaine.
Tel. 04 90 07 72 16.
Closed Sun. dinner (Nov.–Apr.), Mon. (Nov.–Apr.), Tue., Nov. 1, mid-Dec.–mid-Jan.
Prix fixe: 32€. A la carte: 36–40€.

We like the Provence of the Girands. Martine's warm welcome, the ochre surroundings and the happy blend of flavors in Michel's clever dishes: stuffed zucchini flower with artichoke heart mousseline, hot foie gras and fig toast, swordfish, steaks, rabbit and the jumbo shrimp sautéed with onions and peppers. This is all enjoyable stuff, as is a blanc-manger with raspberry sauce and fresh raspberries. The local wines keep things in the South and the check won't make you jump.

SAINT-MARTIN-DE-RE see ILE DE RE
SAINT-MARTIN-DU-TOUCH see TOULOUSE

SAINT-MARTIN-DU-VAR

06670 Alpes-Maritimes. Paris 943 – Antibes 34 – Nice 28 – Cannes 44 – Vence 22.
The route from Nice to Grenoble borders the river and slips between the hollows of the mountain.

●	RESTAURANTS

● Jean-François Issautier
Rte de Digne, D6202.
Tel. 04 93 08 10 65. Fax 04 93 29 19 73.
jf.issautier@wanadoo.fr
Closed Sun. dinner, Mon., Tue., 10 days at end Oct., beg. Jan.–beg. Feb.
Prix fixe: 42€, 55€ (wine inc. dinner), 70€, 110€.

The building, in the twenties hacienda style, calls to mind the Belle Epoque. An old sage of the sea, Jean-François Issautier, lives in the rear. He changes his menu according to the market and the season, using the best vegetables as well as the best Mediterranean fish, still astounding customers with his stuffed zucchini flower presented in a wild mushroom broth, oven-crisped pork trotter, wild Atlantic sea bass in season and the slice of rare-cooked lamb served over puréed potatoes with an herb jus. The deserts play with fruits in season, and the wine list gives pride of place to New Wave Provence. In short, here is a charming dinosaur in very good health.

ST-MARTIN-DU-VIVIER see ROUEN
SAINT-MARTIN-LE-VINOUX see GRENOBLE
SAINT-MAXIMIN see UZES

SAINT-MEDARD-CATUS

46150 Lot. Paris 575 – Cahors 20 – Gourdon 30 – Villeneuve-sur-Lot 59.
Very near the large town of Cahors, this beautiful Quercy village is worth the visit for its tranquillity and its gastronomic skill.

●	RESTAURANTS

● Le Gindreau ◎ V.COM
Le Bourg.
Tel. 05 65 36 22 27. Fax 05 65 36 24 54.
perso.wanadoo.fr/le.gindreau
Closed Mon., Tue., mid-Oct.–beg. Nov., 3 weeks Feb.
Prix fixe: 38€, 50€, 80€, 14€ (child).

In the authentic dining room that was the former school, all the flavors of Quercy converge in the dishes so brilliantly prepared by the duet of Alexis Pelissou and Thierry Thomas. Their joint symphony is a hymn of glory to local produce: foie gras with spices, egg and truffle bundles with truffle-seasoned jus, claw and medallions of Breton lobster, marinated new vegetables and double-cut farm-raised lamb chops pan-tossed with truffles and parsley. Add to this agreeable desserts such as the truffle-marasquin soufflé, the natural smiles of the place, the friendliness of a very attentive service and the Cahors of a cellar jealously guarded by Robert Gassilloud, who has the look of a medieval taskmaster, and you have the ingredients that make St. Médard into a great pleasure trove.

SAINT-MIHIEL

55300 Meuse. Paris 287 – Bar-le-Duc 35 – Nancy 73 – Toul 49 – Verdun 36.
The nature reserve of Lorraine, the hillside routes, the reviving vineyards and the lake of Madine, a huge expanse of water on which sailing sports are practiced: this is what one will discover in the town of sculptor Ligier Richier. Don't miss the sepulcher in the church of St. Etienne.

 HOTELS-RESTAURANTS

In Heudicourt-sous-les-Côtes (55210). 15 km ne via D901, D133.

■ Hôtel-Restaurant du Lac de Madine
22, rue Charles-de-Gaulle.
Tel. 03 29 89 34 80. Fax 03 29 89 39 20.
www.hotel-lac-madine.com
Closed mid-Dec.–end Dec., beg. Jan.–mid-Feb. Rest. closed Mon. lunch.
44 rooms: 53–90€.
Prix fixe: 22,50€, 32€, 56€.

The years go by and this friendly hotel keeps its freshness with its redecorated rooms that have been refurnished in contemporary style. The natural surroundings and the lake lend themselves to some wonderful walks and Franck Herbin's cuisine is expressive. A palette of duck foie gras served three ways, turbot escalopes with thinly sliced potatoes in a beurre blanc sauce, classically prepared veal kidney fricassée and the frozen mirabelle plum soufflé are well-prepared classics.

SAINT-MONT

32400 Gers. Aire sur Adour 18 – Pau 65 – Auch 80.
The land of Gers wine and of jolly Gascony.

 HOTELS-RESTAURANTS

■ Auberge de Saint-Mont
Rue Ste-Barbe.
Tel. 05 62 69 62 59.
auberge.saint-mont@wanadoo.fr
Rest. closed Sun. dinner, Mon. dinner, Tue. dinner, 2 weeks Jan.
16 rooms: 31–48€.
Prix fixe: 10€ (lunch), 16,50€, 23,50€, 29,50€.

Aymeric Saint-Lannes, 26, whose parents run the Ferme aux Cerfs at Houga, learned to cook all by himself the day he took over his adorable village inn, which is a shop for regional products, a hotel and a bistro. The simple sign, the outside eaten away by ivy, the restaurant with its bread oven, deer's head and wooden clock and tables, set the tone of the place. Classic Gascon Garbure, Basque fish stew (ttoro), slow-cooked escargots in duck fat, grilled boneless rib steak with its juice heightened with Armagnac and the covered pie with vanilla ice cream for dessert meet with universal acclaim.

SAINT-NICOLAS-DE-BOURGUEIL see BOURGUEIL

SAINT-PALAIS-SUR-MER

17420 Charente-Maritime. Paris 788 – Bayonne 52 – Biarritz 63 – Dax 60 – Pau 74 – Saint-Jean-Pied-de-Port 32.
www.saint-palais-sur-mer.com.
A resort next to Royan, more upmarket, with its pretty private houses amid the pine trees.

 HOTELS-RESTAURANTS

■ Ma Maison de Mer
21, av du Platin.
Tel. 05 46 23 64 86.
reservations@mamaisondemer.com
www.mamaisondemer.com
6 rooms: 60–170€.

Adorable twenties house has kept its seaside charm while gaining a distinguished British touch thanks to its new owners. Pretty maritime furniture with gray monochrome paintings in the New England style.

● **Les Agapes**

8, rue Marcel-Vallet.
Tel. 05 46 23 10 23.
Closed Sun. dinner, Mon., Tue. (Nov.–Apr.), Nov. 1 vac., Jan.
Prix fixe: 24€, 34€, 46€.

Opposite the market as well as the leisure park and its lake, this former private house has become a high-quality establishment under the management of Patrick Morin, who has worked at the Ritz and at Glénan in Paris. Langoustine and herb salad, smoked salmon terrine with asparagus, catfish filet with a morel risotto and sweet peas and the red tuna brochette (be careful of overcooking) are the work of a careful craftsman. One finishes with a lemon dessert with raspberry jus and pistachio meringue cream cake, without forgetting to do homage to the local Charente chardonnay. Attractive special menus.

SAINT-PATRICE see LANGEAIS

06570 Alpes-Maritimes. Paris 926 – Nice 21 – Antibes 18 – Cannes 28 – Grasse 22.
The pétanque players are still here while the village chatterers gather in the village café. The town itself, beneath high city walls and with its little streets with smooth, slippery pavestones and its thousand shops, has kept its magic intact. Don't miss the Maeght foundation, an open-roofed temple to contemporary art.

 HOTELS-RESTAURANTS

■ **Le Mas de Pierre**

Rte des Serres.
Tel. 04 93 59 00 10.
masdepierre@relaischateaux.com
40 rooms: 173–390€.
8 apartments: 390–770€.
Prix fixe: 42€ (lunch), 65€.

The best-kept secret in St. Paul: this *mas*, newly-elected to the ranks of Relais & Châteaux, at the outskirts of the village with a view of the rocky massif, the Baous and, in the distance, the clustered houses of La Colle-sur-Loup. Beautiful, large rooms in villas spread about a garden make you feel as if you are visiting (wealthy) friends. The whole thing lacks polish but not country charm. At the helm in the kitchen is the young Toulousian Nicolas Navarro, who was trained at nineteen and then went to work at the Villa Belrose in St. Tropez. Creamed potato soup, pistou soup, lobster, John Dory medallions infused with basil (very Thai) and thinly sliced beef and foie gras with sautéed vegetables are dishes of character.

■ **Le Mas d'Artigny**

Rte de La Colle-sur-Loup.
Tel. 04 93 32 84 54. Fax 04 93 32 95 36.
mas@grandesetapes.fr / www.mas-artigny.com
65 rooms: 150–450€. 25 suites: 670–1400€.
Prix fixe: 50€, 30€, 25€, 70€, 16€ (child).

This seventies *mas* on the Côte d'Azur is a special place. Its vast rooms, some of which enjoy a private swimming pool, marry comfort and function. Its health center, sauna and spa compete for your well being, as does the cuisine. Francis Scordel serves a Southern cuisine with full flavors. Grilled langoustine brochettes, green asparagus cut into fans, a lobster and sweet pea fricassée, grilled duck breast and the caramelized puff pastry cookies with light Bourbon vanilla cream testify to a flawless culinary professionalism.

● **Le Saint-Paul**

86, rue Grande.
Tel. 04 93 32 65 25. Fax 04 93 32 52 94.
stpaul@relaischateaux.com
www.lesaintpaul.com
Closed Christmas–New Year's, beg. Jan.–beg. Feb.
15 rooms: 190–410€. 3 suites: 580€.
Prix fixe: 48€ (lunch), 68€, 80€, 92€.

In the heart of medieval St. Paul, this Relais & Châteaux, composed of three charming little houses dating from the 16th century, with a shady terrace and vaulted dining room, makes a romantic getaway. Its large stone walls, frescoes and colored furnishings, as well as its rooms decorated in Provençal style and its murmuring fountain make this establishment a little haven of peace. The new element? Chef Ludovic Puzenat, a Burgundian from Digoin who trained with Billoux and Meneau and who offers a Mediterranean cuisine that doesn't get boring. Marinated eggplant and cod in paupiette, roasted red monkfish with basil- and garlic-stuffed zucchini, slow-cooked asparagus and a slice of foie gras with aged balsamic jus, stuffed zucchini and a roasted Averyon lamb medallion with fresh thyme jus are works of art.

■ La Colombe d'Or

Pl Charles-de-Gaulle.
Tel. 04 93 32 80 02. Fax 04 93 32 77 78.
contact@la-colombe-dor.com
www.la-colombe-dor.com
Closed Oct.–23 Dec.
15 rooms: 275€. 11 suites: 340€.
A la carte: 80€.

Picasso, Braque, Prévert, Montand, Signoret and César were regular guests at this hotel located at the edge of the town. The rooms have recently been redone and the paintings on the walls as well as the mosaic in the swimming pool instantly charm—unlike the food, which is as dull as ever.

■ Hostellerie des Messugues

Domaine des Gardettes, impasse des Messugues.
Tel. 04 93 32 53 32. Fax 04 93 32 94 15.
info@messugues.com /www.messugues.com
Closed Nov.–end Mar.
15 rooms: 85–130€.

This *mas*, hidden away in a pine grove, feels like home. The rooms are functional, even charming, with their furnishings of character, while the swimming pool is an invitation to unwind.

■ Le Hameau

528, route de La Colle-sur-Loup.
Tel. 04 93 32 80 24. Fax 04 93 32 55 75.

lehameau@wanadoo.fr /www.le-hameau.com
Closed mid-Nov.–mid-Feb.
14 rooms: 105–220€. 3 suites: 190–220€.

This fashionable "village" has been rebuilt around an existing building, in this case a former farm. In each little house are very comfortable rooms. The swimming pool, the terrace and the garden allow pleasant moments of relaxation. The prices have become steep.

SAINT-PAUL-LES-DAX see **DAX**

SAINT-PAUL-TROIS-CHATEAUX

26130 Drôme. Paris 634 – Montélimar 28 – Nyons 39 – Orange 33.
st.paul3chxot@wanadoo.fr.
The Tricastin of wonders with its lavender-blue colored sky, its plateau of Clansayes, its former capital and its Romanesque St. Paul cathedral.

 HOTELS-RESTAURANTS

● Villa Augusta

14, rue du Serre-Blanc.
Tel. 04 75 97 29 29. Fax 04 75 97 29 27.
tableaugusta@villaaugusta-hotel.com
Rest. closed Sun. lunch.
24 rooms: 95–230€. 1 suite: 350–400€.
Prix fixe: 26€, 42€, 52€, 85€, 15€ (child).

In the heart of the gastronomic town of St. Paul, this villa joyfully blends old and new. The pretty, colorful rooms make one want to stay here. The Pourcel brothers have delegated the cooking to one of their good students, Christophe Fluck, who uses regional products with dexterity, producing divine dishes that delight guests at both lunch and dinner. There are the "chic nibbles" lunches and stylish dinners in a huge dining room with glass wall where he performs a great culinary concert uniting all the flavors of Provence: zucchini flowers with langoustines presented with a celery carpaccio, rouget with asparagus and ham "chips", turbot with vegetables and a truffle bouillon, wild thyme-seasoned lamb saddle with variations on the sweet pea theme and the crunchy chocolate dessert with pear sorbet and coffee sabayon. It is lively, fine, full of energy, precisely cooked and with a clean marriage of flavors. Seductive use of colors of the great South.

■ L'Esplan

15, pl de l'Esplan.
Tel. 04 75 96 64 64. Fax 04 75 04 92 36.
saintpaul@esplan-provence.com
www.esplan-provence.com
Closed 10 days at end Dec.,
2 weeks beg. Jan.
Rest. closed lunch, Sun. dinner (off season).
36 rooms: 63–110€.
Prix fixe: 23,50€, 35€, 49€, 12€ (child).

Henriette and Claude Paulin are hosts who are continually updating this 16th-century town house. The relaxation center and solarium enable one to unwind while the rooms are welcoming and quiet. In the kitchen, Cédric Denaux offers a cuisine of discovery, although beware: there are still some excesses. Excellent veal sweetbreads in their own cocotte with diced celery. Rodolphe Legal guides wine lovers to local varieties such as Sainte-Cécile-les-Vignes, Gigondas and gives details of local vineyards if one wants to explore the region.

● La Vieille France
"Jardin des Saveurs"

1,2 km, rte de la Garde-Adhémar
Chemin des Goudessarts.
Tel.-Fax 04 75 96 70 47.
vieillefrance.jardindessaveurs@wanadoo.fr
Closed lunch (summer), Mon., Tue. lunch, 3 weeks Nov.–beg. Dec., Christmas, Easter vac.
Prix fixe: 25€ (weekdays), 45€, 110€ (winter truffle menu).

At the Fouillets' there are six tables, no more, and all the happiness in the world. Jean, originally from Régnié-en-Beaujolais, who used to work at Pont des Samsons in Quincé, cooks as naturally as he breathes, offering a limited but seductive menu. Dalia, who was chosen as the "Best Sommelier in France" in 1982, selects the best Côtes-du-Rhône or Tricas-

tin to accompany brandade, individual pressed terrine of foie gras and artichokes, grilled sea bass and the Celas Farm lamb, a seven-hour roasted leg and rare-cooked loin served with spring vegetables. For dessert, pan-tossed cherries served over pain perdu and the rhubarb shortcake with strawberries make one want to return to childhood.

● La Chapelle

5, impasse Ludovic-de-Bimard.
Tel.-Fax 04 75 96 60 88.
Closed Sun. dinner (off season), Mon., Tue. lunch (summer), 20 Sept.–10 Oct., 10 days June.
Prix fixe: 24€ (lunch), 32€, 46€.

Only a few ruins of the original chapel remain in the establishment of the Rollands, with Ginette on reception and Eric in the kitchen. His cooking is full of freshness, as again demonstrated this year by pan-seared foie gras and asparagus pain perdu, fork-mashed sea bream and potato purée and the sundried tomato-stuffed rabbit with fresh goat cheese, which show the extent of his know-how, as does the Tonka bean crème brûlée.

SAINT-PERE-SOUS-VEZELAY see VEZELAY
SAINT-PIERRE-QUIBERON see QUIBERON
SAINT-PIERRE-D'OLERON see ILE D'OLERON

SAINT-POL-DE-LEON

29250 Finistère. Paris 556 – Brest 62 – Morlaix 19 – Roscoff 6.
The former religious center of Léon has kept its beautiful old gray stone edifices, like the old cathedral. Don't miss the belfry on the Kresker chapel or the panoramic view of the region from the tower.

 HOTELS-RESTAURANTS

■ Hôtel de France

29, rue des Minimes.
Tel. 02 98 29 14 14. Fax 02 98 29 10 57.
www.hoteldefrancebretagne.com
22 rooms: 42–90€.

This hotel is in an ideal village setting for those who also want to be close to the center of town and the port. The rooms are light and functional and the garden is a mini-oasis of green.

● La Pomme d'Api `COM`

49, rue Verderel.
Tel. 02 98 69 04 36. Fax 02 98 29 06 53.
yannick.lebeaudour@free.fr
Closed Sun. dinner (exc. July–Aug.),
Mon. (exc. July–Aug.).
Prix fixe: 23€ (weekday lunch), 35€, 45€,
65€ (dinner), 12€ (child).

This 16th-century stone house with exposed beams holds its own. Yannick Le Beaudour is a marvelous cook and his Senegalese wife Khady looks after reception with a smile. One enjoys camus artichokes braised in morel bouillon, Atlantic sea bass cooked skin-side down served on a steaming hot disk of new potatoes, cured country bacon and green asparagus, sautéed veal cutlet with rosemary-seasoned fruits and vegetables and pan-tossed strawberries and salted butter with buckwheat crumble and vanilla ice cream. A wonderful place to stay.

SAINT-POURCAIN-SUR-SIOULE

03500 Allier. Paris 330 – Moulins 32 –
Montluçon 64 – Riom 61 – Vichy 29.
This happy wine-growing Bourbon village has a pretty museum dedicated to vineyards and wine.

 HOTELS-RESTAURANTS

■ Le Chêne Vert 🏨

Bd Ledru-Rollin.
Tel. 04 70 47 77 00. Fax 04 70 47 77 39.
hotel.chenevert@wanadoo.fr
www.hotel-chenevert.com
Hotel closed Closed Sun. dinner (exc. mid-June–mid-Sept.), 2 weeks Jan.
Rest. closed Sun. dinner, Mon., 3 weeks Jan.
29 rooms: 44,50–57€.
Prix fixe: 18€, 26€, 38€, 8€ (child).
A la carte: 33–39€.

This Bourbon establishment offers both classic and contemporary rooms, both of which are well prepared. If one is very or just slightly hungry, one will do justice to Jean-Guy Siret's restaurant, where one can enjoy foie gras crème brûlée, Basque-style tuna steak, young duck breast with grapefruit juice and the "octave" (chestnut cream, blackcurrant mousse and a macaron).

SAINT-QUAY-PORTRIEUX

22410 Côtes-d'Armor. Paris 470 – Saint-Brieuc 23 – Guingamp 28 – Paimpol 26.
saintquayportrieux@wanadoo.fr.
This seaside resort near Erquy has an annual celebration of the St. Jacques scallop, queen of St. Brieuc bay. It gives a year round welcome to health enthusiasts in search of good air as well as lovers of the casino.

■ HOTELS

■ Ker Moor 🏵🏨

13, rue du Président-Le-Sénécal.
Tel. 02 96 70 52 22. Fax 02 96 70 50 49.
ker.moor@wanadoo.fr / www.ker-moor.com
Closed 1 Jan.–end Feb., mid-Nov.–mid-Dec.
28 rooms: 99–155€.

The sea stretching into the horizon, huge, comfortable rooms and delicious breakfasts await you in this fun, Moorish-inspired villa overlooking the bay of Saint-Brieuc.

SAINT-QUIRIN

57560 Moselle. Paris 392 – Strasbourg 91 –
Lunéville 56 – Sarrebourg 19.
The "three roses" of this old woodcutter's town in a clearing are its beautiful churches. Pretty location and cared-for houses.

 HOTELS-RESTAURANTS

■ Hostellerie du Prieuré 🍴🛏

163, rue du Général-de-Gaulle.
Tel. 03 87 08 66 52. Fax 03 87 08 66 49.

tbllorraine@aol.com /www.saint-quirin.com
Closed Nov. 1 vac., Feb. vac., 1 week summer.
Rest. closed Sat. lunch, Tue. dinner, Wed.
8 rooms: 43–58€.
Prix fixe: 17€ (lunch), 26€, 35€, 55€.

If you are traveling through the Moselle
Vosges and want moderate prices and
simplicity without foregoing an inventive, spicy cuisine, stop at the Souliers'
and restore yourself with Didier's food, a
perfect blend of today's tastes and dishes
of the past, taking advice on wine from
the smiling Valérie. The produce, the
cooking, the blends—everything passes
through the sieve of a rigorous perfectionism. One gives oneself over effortlessly to
grilled slice of foie gras with pan-tossed
forest mushrooms, roasted fennel seed-
seasoned sea bass, roasted squab with
blood sauce and a whiskey coffee mousse
with crunchy sugar pearls. By the time the
gentle check arrives, one feels full of grat-
itude. And for a good rate, one of the eight
modern rooms equipped with local furniture will fit the bill.

SAINT-RAPHAEL

83700 Var. Paris 870 – Aix-en-Provence 121
– Toulon 93 – Cannes 42 – Fréjus 4.
saintraphaël.information@wanadoo.fr.
On the southern wing of the bay of Fréjus, a beach
that has become immensely popular, victim of
its real estate success. Several old villas, the
promenade René-Coty and avenue du Touring-
Club are reminders of its rich past.

HOTELS-RESTAURANTS

■ Continental

100, promenade René-Coty.
Tel. 04 94 83 87 87. Fax 04 94 19 20 24.
info@hotels-continental.com
www.hotelcontinental.fr
Closed Nov.–end Feb.
44 rooms: 77–180€. 2 suites: 150–220€.

This hotel is so well located that one gets to
the beach in a few steps. Large, contemporary rooms with Mediterranean-style blue
and white walls and modern comforts.

■ Excelsior

193, bd F.-Martin.
Tel. 04 94 95 02 42. Fax 04 94 95 33 82.
info@excelsior-hotel.com
www.excelsior-hotel.com
36 rooms: 60–175€.
Prix fixe: 26€ (weekdays), 45€.

Jean-François Tagliani is the happy owner
of this building dating from 1900 that overlooks the sea. The redecorated rooms face
the swimming pool or the port. Solid cooking with accents of the Mediterranean
and Provence.

● L'Arbousier   V.COM

6, av Valescure.
Tel. 04 94 95 25 00. Fax 04 94 83 81 04.
www.arbousier.net
Closed Mon., Tue., mid-Dec.–beg. Jan.
Prix fixe: 28€ (weekday lunch), 36€, 46€,
58€. A la carte: 85€.

This is one of the solid values of the old
city. The welcome is friendly and the cooking inspired. Philippe Troncy handles the
beautiful produce of the South with both
art and science. A crunchy sesame and foie
gras mille-feuille, roasted monkfish with
sundried tomatoes, squab cooked in its
own cocotte with fig chutney and a quick
vacherin served with three seasonal fresh
fruit sorbets go down well. Fine wine list in
which Provence is the main focus.

In Valescure (83700). 5 km nw.

● La Tosca   COM

Rte des golfs,
across from the académie golf Maeva.
Tel.-Fax 04 94 44 63 44.
Closed lunch, Sun., Mon.,
1 week Christmas–New Year's.
Prix fixe: 39€, 18€ (child).

To enjoy Italian cooking, you must come
to Maria-Célestine and Germano Agabio's,
opposite the golf course: a swordfish carpaccio, sardine filets with smoked tuna
and octopus, air-cured meat with olive
oil, artichoke hearts with flakes of parmesan and the smooth tiramisu are amazing. Fine wines from the Boot.

Rest. closed Tue., Wed.
27 rooms: 155–380€. 5 suites: 300–600€.
Prix fixe: 42€ (dinner).

SAINT-REMY-DE-PROVENCE

13210 Bouches-du-Rhône. Paris 705 –
Nîmes 43 – Marseille 90 – Avignon 20 –
Arles 26.

This old Provençal town, famous for its Roman monuments and the time that Vincent van Gogh spent here, has become a sort of society cross-roads to the Alpilles, almost another Saint-Tropez, without the port. Fashionable shops, chic hotels and noisy cafés abound while the fashion-able people are a highly visible presence.

 HOTELS-RESTAURANTS

● **Hostellerie du Vallon**
  de Valrugues

Chemin Canto-Cigalo.
Tel. 04 90 92 04 40. Fax 04 90 92 44 01.
resa@valrugues.wanadoo.com
www.hotelprestige-provence.com
Closed fin–Jan.–end Feb.
Rest. closed Sun. dinner, Mon.
40 rooms: 190–280€.
12 suites: 390–1290€.
Prix fixe: 55€, 71€, 92€, 20€ (child).

A little away from the town in a residential area, this large, postcard villa makes a good impression with its garden, Provençal-type rooms and facilities (golf, swimming pool, tennis court and sauna). In the restaurant, Laurent Chouviat, who has worked with Bardet and Senderens, skillfully handles classic and contemporary dishes. One enjoys duck foie gras terrine with black olives and lemon zest, an aromatic herb-seasoned roasted rouget, slow-cooked eggplant purée and squab in the style of Mère Chouviat (with cooking juices and aromatic spices, the leg stuffed like a spring roll and served with creamy polenta and slow-cooked onions with herbs) is full of freshness.

■ **Les Ateliers de l'Image** 🏨

36, bd. Victor-Hugo.
Tel. 04 90 92 51 50. Fax 04 90 92 43 52.
info@hotelphoto.com / www.hotelphoto.com
Closed 10 Dec.–beg. Mar.

On the ring road, the town cinema has become a luxurious hotel under the aegis of Alain and Francine Godard, with its indoor swimming pool and light-filled rooms (some with terrace and view of the Alpilles) equipped with the latest technologies. The cooking has an attractive Southern accent: basket of spring vegetables accompanied with three sorbets, the Mediterranean duo in bouillabaisse, Alpilles rack of lamb with black olive jus and the souffléed lemon gratin on thyme shortbread with mango sauce are carefully crafted.

● **La Maison Jaune**

15, rue Carnot.
Tel. 04 90 92 56 14. Fax 04 90 92 56 32.
lamaisonjaune@wanadoo.fr
www.franceweb.org/lamaisonjaune.fr
Closed Sun. dinner (winter), Mon., Tue. lunch (summer), beg. Jan.–beg. Mar.
Prix fixe: 34€, 52€, 62€, 15€ (child).

In the heights of the town, the terrace of this 16th-century building gives a wonderful view onto the roofs of Saint-Rémy-de-Provence. François Perrault delivers a clever cuisine that well and truly does homage to recipes of the Mediterranean. Lentils graced with vinaigrette and topped with parsley and slices of duck breast, grilled sardine filets with pancetta and red peppers, roasted pigeon served with almonds and grilled ceps, a banana and brown sugar dessert with mangos and sorbet and the roasted pineapples seasoned with ginger and served with nougatine and a passion fruit sorbet are very seductive dishes.

● **Alain Assaud** COM

13, bd Marceau.
Tel. 04 90 92 37 11.
www.fra.cityvox.fr
Closed Sat. lunch (exc. Bank holidays), Wed. (exc. Bank holidays), Thu. lunch (exc. Bank holidays), mid-Nov.–mid-Mar.
Prix fixe: 26€, 41€, 12€ (child).

Alain Assaud rises to the occasion and a meal with him is always a success. After years spent with Troisgros, Guérard, Vergé and at L'Oustau, he has kept his art and know-how: select premium products, treat them with respect so that they preserve their flavors and add a personal touch at the last moment as a kind of signature to each dish. Basil and tomato cakes, fresh cod with aïoli, duck with figs and verbena-seasoned pears effortlessly seduce.

In Palud-de-Noves (13550). 11 km via D30 and D29.

● **La Maison**
Domaine de Bournissac, rte de Noves, montée d'Eyragues.
Tel. 04 90 90 25 25. Fax 04 90 90 25 26.
bournissac@wandoo.fr
www.lamaison-a-bournissac.com
Closed Mon. and Tue. (off season), Jan.–mid-Feb.
9 rooms: 110–230€. 4 suites: 195–255€.
Prix fixe: 43€, 68€, 110€, 15€ (child).
A la carte: 85€.

You need a good road map to reach this gastronomic *mas* hidden away between Verquières and Eyragues. Nestled on a hillside, in the middle of vineyards and olive trees, the establishment, with its panoramic swimming pool and charming rooms, offers a splendid view of greater Luberon and the Ventoux. Christian Peyre, who trained with Hiély in Avignon and then worked at L'Escale in Carry-le-Rouet and at Lorain's in Joigny, produces a creative but "down-to-earth" cuisine. Variations on the theme of asparagus (in foam, breaded with parmesan, raw, in gazpacho), verbena-seasoned pears, Asian-style lobster with soba and soy sauce, pigeon with cherries (its legs slow cooked) and the olive oil and raspberry macarons harmonize with a wine list full of offerings from the Rhône or the nearby hillsides of Baux.

In Verquières (13670). 11 km via D30 and D29.

● **Croque Chou** [SIM]
Pl de l'Eglise.
Tel. 04 90 95 18 55. Fax 04 32 61 15 05.
www.le-croque-chou.fr

Closed Sun. dinner (off season), Mon., Tue. lunch (summer), 1 week beg. Oct., 1 week beg. Jan., end Feb.–beg. Mar.
Prix fixe: 26€ (weekday lunch), 45€, 60€, 90€. A la carte: 56–66€.

Daniel Folz has taken over this 17th-century sheepfold, entrusting the kitchen to his son Sébastien. Here one enjoys a Provençal cuisine that is delicate, fresh and in the spirit of the times. We have a lobster quenelle with cold avocado soup, variations on the egg in its shell with seasonal products, catch of the day cooked with fennel, a mushroom mousseline and a shellfish broth and finally the slow-cooked pork shank wrapped in crisp cured country bacon. Attractive desserts themed around fruit.

29290 Finistère. Paris 601 – Brest 15 – Le Conquet 5.
Just beside Conquet, in the heart of Abers, an old town with its pretty square and 16th-century timbered house.

 HOTELS-RESTAURANTS

■ **Les Voyageurs**
16, rue Saint-Yves.
Tel. 02 98 84 21 14. Fax 02 98 84 37 84.
lesvoyageurs2@wanadoo.fr
www.hotelvoyageurstrenan.fr
Closed Sun. dinner (off season).
30 rooms: 45–65€. 55 suites: 120€.
Prix fixe: 22€, 42€, 9€ (child).
A la carte: 40–44€.

This charming establishment offers functional, light rooms. Michel Le Confec gives a serious handling of foie gras terrine, grilled sea bream on tomato sauce with coriander, beef filet medallion with figs and mushrooms in puff pastry and a frozen nougat with crème anglaise.

SAINT-SATURNIN-LES-APT see APT

SAINT-SAVIN

86310 Vienne. Paris 345 – Montmorillon 20 – Poitiers 45 – Châtellerault 49 – Bellac 60. The medieval bridge on the Gartempe, the abbey church with its 15th-century spire, paintings, crypt and nave are worth the journey to this pretty fishing center.

 HOTELS-RESTAURANTS

■ Hôtel de France
Pl de la République.
Tel. 05 49 48 19 03. Fax 05 49 48 97 07.
hotel-saint-savin@wanadoo.fr
Closed Sun. dinner (exc. July–Aug.),
Mon. lunch (exc. July–Aug.).
15 rooms: 39–53€.
Prix fixe: 17–24€.

This attractively renovated hotel offers gleaming, fresh rooms—not luxurious but often huge and properly equipped. The restaurant room sets a cheerful tone with its pretty parquet and shades of yellow. Carefully-prepared regional cuisine: pike in papilotte and a slow-cooked pork cheek dish are well regarded.

● Christophe Cadieu
15, rue de l'Abbaye.
Tel.-Fax 05 49 48 17 69.
www.cadieu.com
Closed Sun. dinner, Mon., Wed. dinner, Jan.–mid-Jan., mid-Sept.–end Sept.
Prix fixe: 19€ (weekday lunch), 36€, 45€, 51€.

This century-old house near the abbey, with its rustic setting and warm colors, stones and beams, is up and coming. The cuisine of the rigorous Christophe Cadieu is an invitation to taste dishes that closely follow the market and seasons, with the menu changing about every two months. Pan-tossed langoustines with seasonal fresh fruit, lobster cooked in a contemporary style, oven-roasted lamb tenderloin, bacon-wrapped pigeon with artichokes and slivered slow-cooked peppers testify to a fine purchase of produce as well as good treatment. Thick dark chocolate cake served over caramelized almonds is a fine gastronomic treat. Béatrice gives a wonderful welcome and there are attractive wines from every region at modest prices.

SAINT-SEVER

40500 Landes. Paris 726 – Mont-de-Marsan 18 – Aire sur l'Adour 31 – Dax 50.
A rural crossroads at the heart of the "grandes Landes".

 HOTELS-RESTAURANTS

■ Relais du Pavillon Costedoat
Rte de Grenade.
Tel. 05 58 76 20 22. Fax 05 58 76 25 81.
relaispavillon@wanadoo.fr
Closed Sun. dinner, Mon.
Prix fixe: 22€, 12€ (child). A la carte: 38€.

Eric Costedoat and Isabelle Laforge propose poultry terrine with foie gras and ceps, civet of eel slow braised with onions, sliced foie gras and the wonderful apple croustade. The welcome is wonderful.

SAINT-SULPICE-SUR-LEZE

31410 Haute-Garonne. Paris 710 – Auterive 15 – Foix 55 – Saint-Gaudens 65 – Toulouse 35.
South of Toulouse and at the foot of the hills of Volvestre, an old walled town with its arches.

● RESTAURANTS

● La Commanderie
11, pl de l'Hôtel-de-Ville.
Tel. 05 61 97 33 61. Fax 05 61 97 32 60.
www.lacommanderie.venez.fr
Closed Tue., Wed., 2 weeks Feb., 2 weeks Sept.
Prix fixe: 21€ (weekday lunch), 35€.
A la carte: 50€.

In the central square of the town, Jean-Pierre Crouzet's restaurant, a converted former headquarters of 13th-century Knights Templar, is a delight. In its dining room with fireplace one makes short work of hearty dishes such as pressed individual terrine with peppered sausage and saffron potatoes, pan-fried slice of cod with raisins and almond milk, lamb shank braised in white wine and the warm dark chocolate cake. Lively special menus and smiles to go with it.

SAINT-SULPICE-LE-VERDON

85260 Vendée. Paris 430 – Nantes 45 – Montaigu 14 – Cholet 51 – La Roche sur Yon 31. A beautiful stopover in the heart of Vendean country.

■	HOTELS

● Le Logis de la Chabotterie

La Chabotterie.
Tel. 02 51 09 59 31.
restaurant.thierrydrapeau@wanadoo.fr
Closed Sun. dinner, Mon., Tue. lunch,
4 days at end Dec., 1 week beg. July,
2 weeks Aug.–beg. Sept.
A la carte: 60€.

In the middle of a house-museum, near the spot where the War of Vendée ended, is a victorious chef: Thierry Drapeau, who, encouraged by general advice, has made it his home. Formerly the valiant hero of the Château de la Vérie near Challans, here he handles local produce cleanly, intelligently and with a light touch. His specialities are escargots rolled in spinach "lasagne" with local goat cheese in between strips of puff pastry, Atlantic sea bass in a carrot and rye bread crust, sautéed pigeon breast with cauliflower mousseline and baba with aged rum. The fine wine list developed by his accomplice Pascal Chaudoy is wide-ranging. Reasonable prices for so much happiness!

SAINT-SYLVAIN-D'ANJOU see ANGERS

SAINT-SYMPHORIEN

72240 Sarthe. Paris 230 – Laval 66 – Le Mans 30.
The château of Sourches that sheltered des Cars and the numerous 18th-century buildings give character to this old city.

■	HOTELS-RESTAURANTS

● Relais de la Charnie

4, pl Louis-des-Cars.
Tel. 02 43 20 72 06. Fax 02 43 20 70 59.
relais.charnie@wanadoo.fr
Closed Sun. dinner, Mon., Feb. vac.,
2 weeks Aug.
6 rooms: 45–58€.
Prix fixe: 14,90€ (weekday lunch), 18,50€,
24,90€, 29,90€, 10€ (child).

This old coaching inn with its feel of "old France" offers irreproachable rooms and a dining room with large fireplace. In the kitchen, Stéphane, former journeyman and excellent *saucier*, cooks up classics in his own style. Coddled eggs with langoustines and morels, a fisherman's pot-au-feu from Loguivy-de-la-Mer and the beef filet Rossini slip down effortlessly. The chestnut cream terrine with chocolate sauce is scrumptious.

SAINT-SYMPHORIEN-LE-CHATEAU see ABLIS

SAINT-THEGONNEC

29410 Finistère. Paris 550 – Brest 49 – Châteaulin 53 – Morlaix 13 – Quimper 70.
The mountains of Arrée are very close; one comes to this adorable town of inland Brittany to visit the church enclosure.

■	HOTELS-RESTAURANTS

■ Auberge Saint-Thégonnec

6, pl de la Mairie.
Tel. 02 98 79 61 18. Fax 02 98 62 71 10.
contact@aubergesaintthegonnec.com
www.aubergesaintthegonnec.com
Closed 20 Dec.–1 Feb., Sun. dinner.
Rest. closed Sat. lunch, Sun. dinner,
Mon. lunch.
19 rooms: 80–120€.
Prix fixe: 25€, 45€, 15€ (child).

A stone house in the village with cozy rooms. The atmosphere is captivating and the cooking of Emmanuel Nivet a pleasure. Alain Le Coz takes over in the restaurant and on his recommendation you enjoy scallops, Atlantic sea bass filet with slow-cooked fennel, steamed and stuffed John Dory, saffron veal sweetbreads and a pear and pain d'épice mille-feuille.

SAINT-TROJAN-LES-BAINS see
ILE D'OLERON

SAINT-TROPEZ

83990 Var. Paris 874 – Fréjus 35 – Cannes 73 – Toulon 71 – Aix-en-Provence 120.
tourisme@nova.fr.
The most famous port in the world combines every fault and every virtue. As well as the monstrous traffic jams in summer and the parading on the yachts moored in the quay, there is also the calm happiness out of season and the Provençal squares of an old village, an ideal, picture-postcard silhouette outlined against the wide blue sea, a citadel that gives an unbeatable view of a gulf of light and a wonderful market. Add to this hotels that captivate with their charm, quality restaurants, illustrious cafés, delightful terraces, reviving vineyards on the most exquisite hinterland, chefs that play with Provençal flavors with great spirit and craftsmen who practice their art serenely—without forgetting, a divine surprise, rates that are undoubtedly among the lowest on the Côte. It is time to rediscover Saint-Trop'.

| ■ | HOTELS |

■ Château de la Messardière
Rte de Tahiti.
Tel. 04 94 56 76 00. Fax 04 94 56 76 01.
hotel@messardiere.com / www.messardiere.com
Closed mid-Oct.–mid-Mar.
75 rooms: 300–500€.
41 suites: 550–1500€.
Prix fixe: 64€, 95€.

This mad château, with its ten hectares of pines, offers both villas and chic rooms in the colors of the South. The swimming pool overlooks the gulf. In the kitchen, Christophe Cuissard offers a carefully prepared cuisine without arrogance. Duck foie gras, grouper, John Dory, fresh monkfish, Sisteron lamb and Charolais beef are cooked retaining the maximum of freshness. For dessert, Gariguette strawberries with yellow peaches from Provence undergo the same treatment.

■ Le Byblos Saint-Tropez
Av Paul-Signac.
Tel. 04 94 56 68 00. Fax 04 94 56 68 01.
saint-tropez@byblos.com www.byblos.com
Closed beg. Oct.–end Apr.
53 rooms: 290–740€.
44 suites: 700–4200€.

High up in the town, this hotel with eighties rustico-Provençal rooms, magnificent swimming pool and very popular health center is reserved for the privileged few whom one can encounter in the sunny restaurant of Le Bayader, the fusion restaurant Le Spoon (see Restaurants) or at the piano bar (late night, a discothèque) Les Caves du Roy.

■ La Bastide de Saint-Tropez
Rte des Carles. BP 54.
Tel. 04 94 55 82 55. Fax 04 94 97 21 71.
bst@wanadoo.fr
www.bastide-saint-tropez.com
Closed beg. Jan.–10 Feb.
Rest. closed Mon., Tue.
10 rooms: 220–460€. 6 suites: 300–580€.
Prix fixe: 60€.

Hidden in its pine grove away from the center, not far from the road to the beaches, this charming Provençal cottage is one of the gastronomic oases of the village. One comes for the sweet little rooms with bathrooms decorated in Salerne tiles and the swimming pool in the center of the garden. On the cooking side, Franck Broc, previously of the Château de la Messardiere, cooks up sun-filled dishes. Ewe's cheese mixed with fresh herbs and sundried tomatoes in an open ravioli, big roasted spicy shrimp with two kinds of peppers, mushroom- and ham-stuffed artichokes simmered in wine and a dill- and Sichuan

peppercorn–seasoned sea bream make
one want to take up residence.

■ La Pinède

Plage de la Bouillabaisse.
Tel. 04 94 55 91 00. Fax 04 94 97 73 64.
reservation@residencepinede.com
www.residencepinede.com
Closed beg. Oct.–Easter.
35 rooms: 380–920€.
4 suites: 655–1730€.

This dream establishment with its (pri-
vate) beach, heated swimming pool, huge
terrace and rooms that make it a Relais
& Châteaux of distinction belongs to the
Delion family who own La Réserve at
Beaulieu. The welcome and the service
are flawless while the cooking of Arnaud
Donckele is brilliant (see Restaurants).

■ Villa Marie

Rte des Plages, chemin du Val-de-Rian.
Tel. 04 94 97 40 22. Fax 04 94 97 37 55.
contact@villamarie.fr / www.c-h-m.com
Closed mid-Oct.–mid-Apr.
42 rooms: 196–628€. A la carte: 82–145€.

As distinct from their hotels in Megève,
Lyon or Les Ménerbes, Jocelyne and Jean-
Louis Sibuet have made this villa overlooking the bay their pied-à-terre on the Côte
d'Azur. The three hectares of pine grove
provide peace and privacy while one can
enjoy the swimming pool or the spa, the
refined rooms furnished in baroque style
and in pastel shades, as well as the cuisine
of Jean-François Guidon. Cucumber soup
with mint, grilled John Dory, spit-roasted
poultry and the raspberry mille-feuille
make a good impression.

■ La Ponche

3, rue des Remparts.
Tel. 04 94 97 02 53. Fax 04 94 97 78 61.
hotel@laponche.com / www.laponche.com
10 rooms: 215–425€. 5 suites: 295–540€.

Slightly to the side of the old port, this
quiet hotel with luxurious rooms is visited every summer by a chic, avant-garde
clientele. (See Restaurants.)

■ Le Yaca

1, bd d'Aumale.
Tel. 04 94 55 81 00. Fax 04 94 97 58 50.
hotel-le-yaca@wanadoo.fr
www.hotel-le-yaca.fr
Closed mid-Oct.–Easter.
28 rooms: 270–350€. 4 suites: 580–695€.

Right in the center, these three houses
offer rooms that are of differing sizes but
which, with their Provençal furnishings,
are all charming. The patio, the swimming pool and the transalpine cuisine
also contribute to the pleasure of the stay.
(See Restaurants.)

■ Domaine de l'Astragale

Chemin de la Gassine.
Tel. 04 94 97 48 98. Fax 04 94 97 16 01.
message@lastragale.com
www.lastragale.com
Closed mid-Sept.–end May.
34 rooms: 295–415€.
16 suites: 950–1300€.
Prix fixe: 39€ (lunch), 48€.
A la carte: 40–55€.

The managerial duo formed by Julie Nouveau and Thierry Mathiault, one in the
hotel and the other in the kitchen, works
perfectly. This modern hotel offers beautiful rooms with a Provençal feel, pleasant extras such as the swimming pool, the
grounds, the tennis court and the private
beach. Situated outside the building, the
restaurant highlights the colorful cooking of the South.

■ La Ferme d'Augustin

In Ramatuelle (83350), plage de Tahiti.
Tel. 04 94 55 97 00. Fax 04 94 97 59 76.
info@fermeaugustin.com
www.fermeaugustin.com
Closed mid-Oct.–end Mar.
24 rooms: 175–250€.
22 suites: 250–560€.

Several meters from the beach, this former farm delights a smart clientele who
enjoy the Provençal rooms, the balneotherapy facilities and the heated swimming pool.

■ La Tartane

Rte des Salins.
Tel. 04 94 97 21 23. Fax 04 94 97 09 16.
reservation@latartane.com
www.hotel-latartane.com
Closed mid-Oct.–mid-Apr.
20 rooms: 300–650€. 7 suites: 445–900€.
Prix fixe: 18–22€. A la carte: 70–90€.

This is an attractive Provençal faux village with rooms and bungalow suites in a pine grove and a large swimming pool. The whole effect is organic and quiet, with touches of exotic and Provençal décor. Tasty fusion cooking with the oven-crisped shrimp, gingered sea bream wrapped in a banana leaf, curried chicken breasts, minced beef strips with sesame and the chocolate spring rolls.

■ La Maison Blanche

Pl des Lices.
Tel. 04 94 97 52 66. Fax 04 94 97 89 23.
hotellamaisonblanche@wanadoo.fr
www.hotellamaisonblanche.com
Closed Feb.
5 rooms: 240–390€. 4 suites: 550–780€.

On the famous Lices square, this village house with contemporary rooms, garden and champagne bar is one of the popular places in town.

■ La Mistralée

1, av du Général-Leclerc.
Tel. 04 98 12 91 12. Fax 04 94 43 48 43.
contact@hotel-mistralee.com
www.hotel-mistralee.com
Open daily. Rest. closed weekdays off season.
8 rooms: 190–460€. 2 suites: 390–790€.

This 19th-century house in the middle of large grounds, the property of hairstylist Alexandre, offers themed rooms (Tarzan, Chinese, Chanel, Victor Hugo). Heated swimming pool and hammam. Middle Eastern-inspired cuisine.

■ La Bastide des Salins

Rte des Salins.
Tel. 04 94 97 24 57. Fax 04 94 54 89 03.
info@labastidedessalins.com
www.labastidedessalins.com
Closed beg. Nov.–beg. Mar.
13 rooms: 190–310€. 1 suite: 330–480€.

This 17th-century cottage with terrace and swimming pool offers cozy, quietly decorated rooms.

■ Playa

57, rue Allard.
Tel. 04 98 12 94 44. Fax 04 98 12 94 45.
playahotel@aol.com
www.playahotelsttropez.com
11 rooms: 90–175€. 5 suites: 168–235€.

There are reasonably-priced places, even in St. Tropez. This is one, with simple, well-equipped rooms and breakfasts on the patio. Open all year.

In Gassin (83580).

■ Villa Belrose

Bd des Crêtes, dir. Saint-Tropez, N98.
Tel. 04 94 55 97 97. Fax 04 94 55 97 98.
info@villabelrose.com /www.villabelrose.com
Closed end Oct.–beg. Apr.
33 rooms: 140–730€.
3 suites: 700–2200€.

Overlooking the gulf of St. Tropez, this contemporary villa is a haven of peace not far from the Lices square. The rooms with their marble bathrooms are the epitome of elegance and the huge swimming pool, fitness center and beauty salon are wonderful. The cuisine is in keeping with the atmosphere of a top-quality Relais & Châteaux (see Restaurants).

● | RESTAURANTS

● La Pinède

Plage de la Bouillabaisse.
Tel. 04 94 55 91 00. Fax 04 94 97 73 64.
reservation@residencepinede.com -
www.residencepinede.com
Closed beg. Oct.–beg. May.
Prix fixe: 75€ (dinner), 135€ (dinner), 160€ (dinner), 30€ (child).

The cuisine of this top-notch Relais & Châteaux makes the grade. At lunchtime, one eats just beside the water while in the evening one dons a jacket to enjoy the refined dishes of Arnaud Donckele. This native of Normandy who trained with Lasserre, Ducasse, Guérard and at the Plaza handles the beautiful produce of the Mediterranean with finesse and technical skill: bouillon of local rockfish, simply prepared rouget, king crabmeat, crisp romaine salad, a thin tart with tender spring vegetables, heightened with niçoise condiments and anchovy tempura, langoustines roasted with lavender honey, John Dory, shrimp, clams and the razor clams with Thai basil sauce and grated kaffir lime make one want to set sail for distant lands. Suckling pig cooked porchetta style with summer savory, ceps, almonds and chutney and a Bresse chicken breast poached in pig's bladder in an artichoke and basil bouillon, with a truffle-seasoned parmesan macaroni gratin put one's feet back on dry land. The desserts: a wild strawberry mille-feuille with chiboust (a lightened pastry cream seasoned with roses from Grasse) and the vacherin-themed dessert with roasted almonds and apricots and ice creams are of the same high level. Large wine list, distinguised service and prices to match.

● Leï Mouscardins ○Ⓥ.COM
Tour du Portalet (at the port).
Tel. 04 94 97 29 00. Fax 04 94 97 76 39.
info@leimouscardins.com
www.leimouscardins.com
Closed Mon. (off season), beg. Nov.–beg. Apr.
Prix fixe: 59€, 69€, 79€, 89€,
30€ (child).

Laurent Tarridec, whom we already know from his previous experience at Esclimont then at Chabichou de Courchevel and Les Roches du Lavandou, is a small king whose crown has been challenged. If he isn't the unanimous favorite in his town, he remains the star of the port. The lively Provençal dining room with its stripped woodwork, antique furniture, light-colored materials and bay windows looking out onto the expanse of sea is very chic. The food follows suit. Both land and sea products are used in a distinctive Mediterranean cuisine that nods to the native

region of this hard-headed Breton. A platter of escargots with pork trotter and herb jus, pot of cod and potato brandade with croutons, cabbage stuffed with truffles and foie gras and rouget in bouillon with pan-steamed spelt wheat with argan oil are among his special turns. The desserts (the pot of roses, chocolate and raspberries in lime jelly and the cherries with pistachio ice cream, Colette-style) are successes. The service is equally good, the wines have quality and the checks are Tropezian, like the eclectic and gastronomically educated clientele.

● Les Moulins de Ramatuelle ○COM
In Ramatuelle (83350), rte des Plages.
Tel. 04 94 97 17 22. Fax 04 94 97 85 60.
info@christophe-leroy.com
www.christophe-leroy.com
Closed lunch, mid-Nov.–mid-Dec., Jan.
Prix fixe: 39€, 70€. A la carte: 130€.

Christophe Leroy, whom one finds in Avoriaz, Marrakesh and his bistro in St. Tropez, deals in the cool and the fashionable. The clientele is demanding and, at Ramatuelle as elsewhere, many of them come to experience the minimalist décor as well as the ideas of a constantly evolving chef. These guests, who have already been won over, choose lobster salad with ginger and lime sauce, the crunchy vegetable marinade with roasted jumbo shrimp, Mediterranean sea bass with chives, turbot in a salt crust, veal scallops with chanterelles, beef rib eye steak and a vanilla panna cotta, knowing they won't be disappointed. Aimé Stoesser provides a personalized service and valuable help in the choice of wine. Beware of the check, which is geared towards the aforementioned clientele, people not in the habit of having to watch what they spend.

● Spoon Byblos COM
Av Foch.
Tel. 04 94 56 68 20. Fax 04 94 56 68 01.
spoon-byblos@byblos.com / www.byblos.com
Closed Tue. (exc. summer), Wed. (exc. summer), Oct. May.
A la carte: 95€.

St. Tropez, capital of show biz, has, like London, Tokyo and Paris, its Spoon. The spirit of Alain Ducasse blows powerfully over Byblos where his concept has been implemented by Christophe Fiorino. All the classics of "fusion food" figure on the menu: grilled tuna, lamb tagine and a cheesecake served with Malabar candy-flavored ice cream, accompanied by worldwide wines, advised by Clément Gavet.

● Auberge de l'Oumède ⬛ COM

Chemin de l'Oumède.
Tel. 04 94 44 11 11. Fax 04 94 79 93 63.
contact@aubergedeloumede.com
www.aubergedeloumede.com
Closed lunch (1 July–31 Aug.), Wed. (off season), mid-Oct.–Easter.
3 rooms: 189–368€. A la carte: 60–75€.

The three rooms are paradise on earth with their view of the vineyards and the sea below and their private swimming pool. The charm of the hotel is reflected in the welcome given by Carole Frésia and the passionate cooking of Jean-Pierre Frésia. Grilled meats, bouillabaisse cooked to order, line-fished Mediterranean sea bass and fisherman's langouste grilled over a grapevine fire, oxtail and potato layered casserole with pan-seared foie gras and a hot chocolate tartare are very fine. A large list of wines from Provence and Bordeaux. The prices are not too Tropezian.

● Le Girelier ⬛ COM

Quai Jean-Jaurès.
Tel. 04 94 97 03 87. Fax 04 94 97 43 86.
Closed lunch (July–Aug.), Mon. (off season), Nov.–mid-Mar.
Prix fixe: 38€ (lunch), 17€ (child). A la carte: 60–75€.

Yves Rouet runs, with unparalled professionalism, this quiet establishment on the port that has been in his family since 1956. The décor of the restaurant, overlooking the boats, is not garish or hyped. What does the good Yves, formerly of Julius in Genevilliers and Delaveyne in Bougival, offer? The freshest of the day's catch, handled with skill. One enjoys, according to

the day's special menus, rockfish soup, sautéed squid, fried local fish, octopus in salad, grilled sardines and small strips of monkfish presented like frog legs, all with flawless good taste.

● Palm ⬛ COM

26, rue des Charrons.
Tel. 04 94 54 80 38. Fax 04 94 54 82 89.
Closed lunch
Prix fixe: 38€ (dinner), 20€ (child).

There has been a change of team in this cool Zen restaurant where the kitchens are now under the direction of Julien Ferrière. He offers fare that is a little complicated but which gives pleasure, such as the house parmentier dish, Breton lobster with a hazelnut potato mousseline and the roast beef with truffle mashed potatoes. He also serves wild Atlantic sea bass with a citrus reduction sauce, a jar of vegetables with savory-seasoned butter and, to finish, a fresh mint panna cotta, a few wild strawberries with a creamy mascarpone dessert and Tagada strawberry candy-flavored ice cream. The prices, for St. Tropez, seem almost reasonable.

● Le Patio ⬛ COM

At the Yaca, 1, bd d'Aumale.
Tel. 04 94 55 81 00. Fax 04 94 97 58 50.
hotel-le-yaca@wanadoo.fr
Closed Mon. (Easter–May), Nov.–Easter.
A la carte: 70€.

This is the place to come if you want a transalpine cuisine served in pleasant surroundings, with a patio beside the swimming pool or the interior room with its contemporary décor. Carmelo Carnevale cooks squid and shrimp, Cognac-flambéed tagliatelli, linguini with clams and a tiramisu. The service is as nice as it could be and the prices remain within the limits of the reasonable.

● La Ponche ⬛ COM

3, rue des Remparts.
Tel. 04 94 97 02 53. Fax 04 94 97 78 61.
hotel@laponche.com / www.laponche.com
Closed 1 Nov.–mid-Feb.
Prix fixe: 24€, 38€. A la carte: 55–60€.

In the establishment of Simone Duckstein, Christian Geay relies on market and seasonal produce to cook unpretentious dishes. Fish soup, local rouget, beef sirloin with foie gras and an apple puff pastry dessert with cinnamon ice cream seduce effortlessly. The special menus allow one to get away with a very reasonable check.

● Club 55 SIM

43, bd Patch.
Tel. 04 94 55 55 55. Fax 04 94 79 85 00.
Closed dinner, Nov., Feb.–end Mar.
Prix fixe: 75€ (lunch), 85€ (lunch),
95€ (lunch). A la carte: 60–75€.

Patrice de Colmont energetically runs this beautiful white space created by his parents in 1955. Wooden armchairs, benches, a bar, the beach and the deep blue sea are what make up the décor. From Collaro to Carlos, Johnny to Eddy, everyone has come here and returns again and again for an early or late lunch of fried fish, saffron-seasoned fish brochette, tuna steak, escalope Milanais and the tarte Tropézienne while drinking a local rosé (the best local Provençal vintages of the moment). A friendly, understanding service.

● L'Auberge des Maures SIM

4, rue du Dr-Boutin.
Tel. 04 94 97 01 50. Fax 04 94 97 67 24.
Closed lunch, beg. Dec.–end Feb.
Prix fixe: 25€ (child). A la carte: 55€.

One is always taken by surprise by the kindness of the welcome to this town house where Franck Roux cooks up Provence. Little Provençal stuffed vegetables, mushroom- and ham-stuffed artichokes simmered in wine, sea bream filet with local aromatic herb sauce, a Provençal daube, a local tripe specialty called pieds-paquets and the house tiramisu are eaten with pleasure. The whites, reds and rosés of Provence speak for themselves. Pleasant service and a check without nasty surprises.

● Banh Hoï SIM

12, rue du Petit-Saint-Jean.
Tel. 04 94 97 36 29. Fax 04 98 12 91 34.
banh-hoi@wanadoo.fr
Closed lunch, beg. Jan.–Mar.,
mid-Oct.–beg. Apr.
A la carte: 55€.

This small Asian restaurant tucked away in a narrow street is a real find. The welcome is very friendly, the service attentive and the cuisine, Thai or Vietnamese, sincere. One enjoys shrimp soup with lemongrass, monkfish with ginger, beef sirloin steak with satay sauce and fried bananas.

● Le Bistro SIM

3, place des Lices.
Tel. 04 94 97 11 33. Fax 04 94 97 59 70.
info@bistro -saint-tropez.com
www.bistro -saint -tropez.com
Closed Wed. (winter).
Prix fixe: 14€ (lunch), 35€ (dinner),
60€ (dinner).

Frédéric Blanc, from Millésime beach, has taken over this legendary bistro (formerly Des Lices). The setting, with its brown monotints, is contemporary. The market cuisine is this year prepared by Franck Plana. We again liked the smoked salmon in a croque-monsieur or the Provençal chicken club sandwich, offered for lunch, and the "Tokyo-style" sea bream with eggplant chutney.

● Chez Fuchs SIM

7, rue des Commerçants.
Tel. 04 94 97 01 25. Fax 04 94 97 81 82.
fuchssttropez@wanadoo.fr
Closed Sun., Mon., vac. Jan.–mid-Feb.
A la carte: 50€.

Olivier Fuchs, in his olive green restaurant (located in a family house) that has been famous since the early fifties, carries on with the fundamental elements that ensure youthfulness and freshness. In high season, you must reserve a table to enjoy mushroom- and ham-stuffed artichokes simmered in wine, local cuttlefish stew, milk-fed veal cutlet with Sichuan peppercorns and the tarte Tropézienne.

● L'Escale SIM

On the harbor.
Tel. 04 94 97 00 63. Fax 04 94 97 77 50.
chezjoseph@wanadoo.fr
www.joseph-sainttropez.com
Closed 5 Nov.–10 Dec.
Prix fixe: 37€ (lunch). A la carte: 80–90€.

Joseph Geenen, who already owns two restaurants near the town hall, looks after this legendary restaurant beside the sea. Its has a new décor in shades of gray and up-to-date dishes. Pan-tossed squid, langouste (27 for 100 grams), duck breast and soft chocolate cake slip down effortlessly.

● Gandhi SIM

3, quai de l'Epi.
Tel. 04 94 97 71 71 / 04 94 97 83 03.
Fax 04 94 56 19 39.
siva@gandhisai.com / www.gandhisai.com
Closed Mon. lunch (exc. off season),
Wed. (off season), mid-Dec.–end Dec.
Prix fixe: 23€, 8,50€ (child).
A la carte: 34–48€.

It's easy to have a good dinner without breaking the bank in St. Tropez. You have only to go to this Indian restaurant, where everything is good: samosas, rockfish tikka, lamb vindaloo or on a brochette cooked in the tandoori oven, almond and cardamom ice cream and the kulfi, of a distinctive smoothness. In addition there is the smile of Sivanandan Ponudrai and to drink, sweet, savory, or rose-flavored lassi prepared by the new chef Kumar.

● Kaï Largo SIM

Nioulargo-Plage / Bd Patch.
Tel. 04 98 12 63 12. Fax 04 98 12 61 70.
Kaled@nioulargo.fr / www.nioulargo.fr
Closed Tue. (winter), Wed. (winter),
8 Jan.–Feb. vac.
Prix fixe: 65€ (dinner). A la carte: 55€.

A high-quality Asian cuisine, served with a smile by an Indo-Chinese and Mauritian team in the restaurant and kitchen on the sunny beach: this can be found only on Boulevard Patch. Dim sum, sweet-and-sour shrimp, basil-seasoned tuna, lemongrass-seasoned chicken, caramelized pork, chocolate spring roll and iced mango soup are truly delicate.

● Lei Salins SIM

Plage des Salins.
Tel. 04 94 97 04 40. Fax 04 94 97 49 26.
info@lei-salins.com / www.lei-salins.com
Closed lunch (July–Aug.), Nov.–Easter.
A la carte: 45–65€.

M. Massat, the new owner of this small, covered restaurant overhanging Salins beach, has slightly increased the prices but serves stuffed mussels, sea bream, lamb shank, tarte Tropézienne and a chocolate fondant that slip down as effortlessly as a letter into a mailbox.

● Le Petit Charron SIM

6, rue des Charrons.
Tel. 04 94 97 73 78. Fax 04 94 56 55 78.
c-benoit@wanadoo.fr
Closed Sun., mid-Nov.–mid-Dec.,
mid-Jan.–mid-Feb., 2 weeks beg. Aug.
A la carte: 50–55€.

This inn in the town, decorated with flags of La Niourlague, looks good. The Benoits give a kind welcome; Anne-Violène asks you, with a smile, to wait, as there are few spaces available to taste Christian's cuisine. Oven-crisped rouget with artichoke caviar, slow-cooked lamb shoulder, guinea hen roasted with garlic cream served with Italian-style gnocchi and a lavender-flavored crème brûlée are eaten with great pleasure.

● La Plage des Jumeaux SIM

Rte de l'Epi.
Tel. 04 94 55 21 80. Fax 04 94 79 87 41.
Closed dinner (exc. July–Aug.).
A la carte: 50–55€.

Jean-Claude Moreu in the restaurant and Jean-Yves Allaire in the kitchen have watched over this well-kept beach for more than two decades. The blue and white striped terrace makes one dream of long holidays. The salade niçoise, parmesan carpaccio, grilled sardines, pasta with pesto, pan-seared tuna with first pressing olive oil, garlic and tomato sauce, the catch of the day (sea bream, Mediterranean sea bass, John Dory) and a lemon-flavored farm-raised chicken are culinary professionalism itself.

● **La Table du Marché**

38, rue Georges-Clemenceau.
Tel. 04 94 97 85 20. Fax 04 94 97 85 60.
info@christophe-leroy.com
www.christophe-leroy.com
Prix fixe: 18€, 26€. A la carte: 60€.

Christophe Leroy has made this town bistro into a place with heart. We love the simplicity of the place and the good-natured prices of the special menus. A fresh tomato and basil tart, chicken spring rolls, sole meunière with lemons and capers, spit-roasted chicken with mashed potatoes, beef rib eye steak with morel sauce and the local dessert go down without a murmur. Food and wine can be taken away.

In Gassin (83580).

● **Villa Belrose**

Bd des Crêtes, direction Saint-Tropez RN 98.
Tel. 04 94 55 97 97. Fax 04 94 55 97 98.
info@villabelrose.com / www.villabelrose.com
Closed lunch (July–Aug.), end Oct.–Easter.
Prix fixe: 55€ (lunch), 85€, 110€,
170€ (wine inc.).

This white villa with its huge panoramic terrace overlooks the bay. In the kitchen, Thierry Thiercelin, student of Loiseau and Maximin, makes a perfect marriage of traditional dishes and original flavors. Cold slow-cooked vegetables, Moroccan-style rouget stuffed with spinach, leek and cheese and served with polenta, octopus served with squid ink sauce and whole roasted Racan pigeon with grapes, semolina, vegetables and a grappa jus are wonders. The trolley of Robert Bedot's cheeses and the variations on the theme of chocolate give a beautiful ending to the culinary celebration. Large choice of wines, high-class service and resulting prices.

SAINT-VAAST-LA-HOUGUE

50550 Manche. Paris 344 – Cherbourg 32 – Carentan 41 – Saint-Lô 69 – Valognes 19.

office-de-tourisme@saint-vaast-reville.com.
Beautiful oysters, the great wind of Cotentin, stone houses and the bouquets of hortensias are what one comes here to experience, as well as the picturesque port.

	HOTELS-RESTAURANTS

■ **France et Fuchsias**

20, rue du Maréchal-Foch.
Tel. 02 33 54 42 26. Fax 02 33 43 46 79.
france-fuchsias@wanadoo.fr
www.france-fuchsias.com
Closed Mon. (exc. July–Aug.), Tue., Jan.–Feb.
37 rooms: 43–120€.
Prix fixe: 19€ (lunch), 26€, 38€.
A la carte: 35–40€.

The establishment of Isabelle and Jean-Pierre Brix is a traditional house in the heart of the village with charming rooms set among a little clearing in the trees. In the kitchen, Pierre Marion, trained at Chabichou in Courchevel and at Marine de Carteret, is not lacking in ideas. Langoustines roasted on a thin brochette with minced smoked duck, turbot with asparagus, lamb kadaïf with a vegetable brochette, an apple and Camembert charlotte with cider jelly and pan-tossed strawberries with fresh fromage blanc ice cream wake you up, bowl you over and seduce. The "local" menu, with its pressed chitterling sausage and potato, makes one want to be a regular diner. The wine list is full of examples from every vineyard and the Calvados from the neighboring Capelle in Sotteville is the companion to a celebratory meal.

■ **La Granitière**

74, rue du Maréchal-Foch.
Tel. 02 33 54 58 99.
contact@hotel-la-granitière.com
www.hotel-la-granitière.com
10 rooms: 53–81€.

This fifties residence has rooms that are dated but charming. Amusing stained glass window in the stairway and a home-away-from-home atmosphere.

● **Le Chassée-Marée**

8, place du Général-de-Gaulle.
Tel. 02 33 23 14 08.
Closed Mon., Tue. (off season), 3 weeks Jan.
Prix fixe: 15€ (weekday lunch), 19€, 26€.

Well, okay, the boss has his rather particular personality. But the marine restaurant of this port side bistro has charm, and its little menus, which change according to the catch, are privileged offerings of freshness and salt water that represent very good value for money.

In La Pernelle (50630). 6 km se.

● **Le Panoramique**   SIM

1, pl de l'Eglise.
Tel. 02 33 54 13 79. Fax 02 33 54 09 97.
info@le-panoramique.fr
www.le-panoramique.fr
Closed Thu. (exc. July–Aug.).
Prix fixe: 13,90€, 21€, 31€.
A la carte: 35€.

A brasserie, a restaurant and the view of the sea stretching into the distance with a panorama over the countryside of Val-de-Saire. The cuisine of Arnaud Feron, the son of the house, and of Christophe Bourdet certainly makes the grade. Stuffed and rolled pork flavored with cider vinegar, pan-simmered salmon with Guérande fleur de sel, ham cooked on the bone and a Norman-style Calvados-flambéed thin apple tart exude the region.

SAINT-VALERY-EN-CAUX

76460 Seine-Maritime. Paris 189 –
Le Havre 79 – Bolbec 44 – Dieppe 35 –
Rouen 59.
otsi.st.valery.en.caux@wanadoo.fr.
This port in Caux country has lost nothing of its old charm reminiscent of Maupassant. The sloping cliff is the class walk of the area.

■ HOTELS-RESTAURANTS

■ **Hotel du Casino**

Rue G.-Clemenceau.
Tel. 02 35 57 88 00. Fax 02 35 57 88 88.
contact@hotel-casino-saintvalery.com
www.hotel-casino-saintvalery.com
Rest. closed Sun.
76 rooms: 71–125€.
Prix fixe: 21€, 27€, 38€, 9€ (child).

This building, in modern architectural style, on the port, offers functional rooms decorated in shades of green and violet. You don't need to win the lottery to eat the hodge-podge of dishes in this restaurant: chicken oysters, cumin-seasoned sardines in aspic, skate wing with fresh thyme, quail roasted with rosemary and a frozen apricot cream dessert.

■ **La Maison des Galets**

On the waterfront.
Tel. 02 35 97 11 22. Fax 02 35 97 05 83.
la maison des galets@club-internet.fr
www.lamaisondesgalets.fr
14 rooms: 40–100€.
Prix fixe: 18€, 30€, 9€ (child).
A la carte: 45–50€.

This classic hotel on the beach, now the home of Danielle Magne and Yara Barrio, has had a facelift. The decoration has kept its former style, with a restaurant with wood, in colors of vanilla and cinnamon, a large fireplace, a big bar at the old counter and checkerboard tiles. The kitchen flies the regional colors of Caux.

● **Le Port**   COM

Quai d'Amont.
Tel. 02 35 97 08 93. Fax 02 35 97 28 32.
Closed Sun. dinner, Mon., Thu. dinner (exc. summer).
Prix fixe: 21€, 38€.

Olivier Warin runs this establishment on the port with a firm hand, offering an unpretentious cuisine that takes account of the fluctuations in the tides. Warm oysters with tarragon, grilled turbot with hollandaise sauce, tête de veau with sauce gribiche and pears in puff pastry with caramel sauce make a good impression. The décor, in shades of almond green and burgundy, is restful.

In Ingouville-sur-Mer (76460). 4,6 km sw via D925.

● Les Hêtres

24, rue des Fleurs. Le Bourg.
Tel. 02 35 57 09 30. Fax 02 35 57 09 31.
leshetres@wanadoo.fr / www.leshetres.com
Closed beg. Jan.–mid-Feb.
Rest. closed Mon., Tue. (exc. dinner in season), Wed. lunch (off season).
5 rooms: 90–160€.
Prix fixe: 40€, 85€. A la carte: 115€.

In the middle of a huge garden, Eric Liberge's manor house has plenty of character. Chiné furniture and objects give a warm feel to the five rooms of the house. The cuisine follows suit and Bertrand Warin develops lively, precise dishes from Normandy such as crab stuffed with apples and celery root, turbot roasted with a gray shrimp brandade, pigeon roasted with summer savory and the chocolate dessert with salted-butter caramel. With these punchy dishes, wines from all over the world hit the bull's-eye.

SAINT-VALERY-SUR-SOMME

80230 Somme. Paris 201 – Amiens 71 – Abbeville 18 – Le Tréport 25.
With the bay of Somme and its gray tones and Le Crotoy, here is the land of maritime poetry in Picardy that is directly en route to Marquenterre park. Don't miss the sailor's chapel or the eco-museum and wander along the seawall promenade.

 HOTELS-RESTAURANTS

■ Relais Guillaume de Normandy

Quai Romerel.
Tel. 03 22 60 82 36. Fax 03 22 60 81 82.
relaisguillaumedenormandy.akeonet.com
Closed mid-Dec.–mid-Jan. Rest. closed Tue.
14 rooms: 55–72€.
Prix fixe: 18€, 29€, 40€, 10€ (child).

There is a wonderful view over the Bay of Somme from the dining room of this brick manor house. The cuisine of Thierry Dupré gives an intelligent treatment to products of the region, as well as elsewhere. Oven-crisped langoustines and pork trotters with morel cream sauce, roasted Atlantic sea bass with julienned fennel, the house specialty of lamb medallions cooked Estran's way and the pineapple tapioca and a coconut milk emulsion with caramel are a personal performance of high quality. The special menus are well conceived and the rooms allow one to stop over en route to Marquenterre.

■ Picardia

41, quai Romerel.
Tel. 03 22 60 32 30.
contact@picardia.fr / www.picardia.fr
18 rooms: 75–96€.

Between the old town and the sea, this house of regional appeal has been given a contemporary makeover. Rooms with mezzanine and the communal areas are cozy.

■ Du Port et des Bains

1, quai Blavet.
Tel. 03 22 60 80 09.
hotel.hpb@wanadoo.fr
17 rooms: 65–80€.

This hotel facing the port has a full view of the Bay of Somme. Colorful rooms, rattan furniture, local paintings, cuisine with a local color and reasonable prices set the tone for a well-regarded hotel.

SAINT-VERAN-EN-QUEYRAS

05350 Hautes-Alpes. Paris 730 – Briançon 49 – Guillestre 30.
The beauty of Queyras and the highest village in Europe at 2,042 meters altitude. Visit the Soum museum.

HOTELS-RESTAURANTS

■ L'Astragale

Tel. 04 92 45 87 00. Fax 04 92 45 87 10.
astragale@queyras.com
www.astragale.queyras.com
Closed beg. Apr.–mid-June, beg.
Sept.–mid-Dec. Rest. closed lunch
Prix fixe: 23€ (dinner).

It is a joy to take up residence in this house that has mountain peaks as a backdrop. The "mountain"-style rooms are nice and the cuisine highlights local and organic products. Swimming pool, sauna and a traditional Queyras welcome are all pluses.

■ **Châteaurenard**

Tel. 04 92 45 85 43. Fax 04 92 45 84 20.
info@hotel-chateaurenard.com
www.hotel-chateaurenard.com
Closed mid-Nov.–20 Dec.
20 rooms: 65–140€.
Prix fixe: 22€, 32€.

One comes to this chalet in the high mountain pasture for the view and one stays for the comfort of the quietly decorated contemporary rooms and for the sun on the terrace. One also takes the opportunity to try the cuisine of Yves Dubas who gives a fine reworking to local dishes. A chestnut cream cappuccino with ceps and licorice mousse, slow-cooked chamois stew with blackcurrants and caramelized pain perdu have energy. The prices are reasonable and the place friendly.

■ **Beauregard**

Tel. 04 92 45 86 86. Fax 04 92 45 86 87.
info@hotelbeauregard.fr
www.hotelbeauregard.fr
Closed 10 Apr.–10 June, 20 Sept.–20 Dec.
Rest. closed Mon.
15 rooms: 63–78€. 6 suites: 110–129€.
Prix fixe: 21€, 26€, 28€, 9€ (child).

The Strobels are welcoming hosts and one can visit them throughout the year. The ski pistes are just in front while the swimming pool and the tennis court can be used in summer. The mountain-style rooms are well equipped and the cuisine is full of character. After a day of walking or sport, game in feuilleté, coriander-seasoned rouget, Durance rack of lamb flambéed with Meleze liqueur and an herb-seasoned crème brûlée slip down pleasurably.

SAINT-VICTOR-SUR-LOIRE see SAINT-ETIENNE

SAINT-VINCENT-DE-TYROSSE see HOSSEGOR
SAINT-YBARD see UZERCHE

SAINT-YRIEIX-LA-PERCHE

87500 Haute-Vienne. Paris 433 –
Limoges 41 – Brive-la-Gaillarde 63 –
Périgueux 62.
otsistyrieix@free.fr.
Green and tranquil Haute-Vienne. Don't forget to visit the collegial church of Moûtiers.

 HOTELS-RESTAURANTS

In La Roche-l'Abeille (87800). 12 km, ne via D704.

■ **Moulin de la Gorce**

Tel. 05 55 00 70 66. Fax 05 55 00 76 57.
moulindelagorce@relaischateaux.fr
www.moulindelagorce.com
Closed Mon. lunch, Tue. lunch,
end Nov.–beg. Mar.
9 rooms: 75–165€. 1 suite: 245€.
Prix fixe: 44€ (weekdays), 63€, 80€,
25€ (child).

This windmill lost in the heart of the countryside, transformed into a bucolic Relais & Châteaux, is experiencing renewed serenity. The rooms are pretty, large and tranquil; Pierre Bertranet has a rather forthright and traditional way of speaking. Foie gras-stuffed pork trotter, pike-perch with langoustines cooked in a clay crust, wild rabbit (during the hunting season), rolled crêpes with vanilla and orange peel-flavored butter and puff pastries filled with cream and Gariguette strawberries are beautiful offerings. A wonderful cellar full of great vintages from all regions of France.

SAINTE-ANNE-D'AURAY

56400 Morbihan. Paris 475 – Vannes 17 –
Auray 17 – Hennebont 34.
A place of pilgrimage celebrating the appearance of the saint in 1623 to the peasant Yves Nicolazic. The neo-Renaissance basilica and its cloister receive numerous groups, particularly on the 25th and 26th of July.

HOTELS-RESTAURANTS

■ L'Auberge

56, rte de Vannes.
Tel. 02 97 57 61 55. Fax 02 97 57 69 10.
auberge-jl-larvoir@wanadoo.fr
www.auberge-larvoir.com
Closed Mon. (Nov. 1–Easter), Jan.
12 rooms: 80–100€. 2 suites: 120–200€.
Prix fixe: 20€, 34€, 44€, 60€,
10€ (child). A la carte: 61€.

Tradition is good. The proof is to be found with the Larvoirs, in this fine inn where Pope John Paul II stayed. The welcome given by Françoise is always wonderful and the quiet, carefully worked cuisine of Jean-Luc is respectful of dishes of yesteryear, although not exclusively. Variations on the theme of the scallop, duck foie gras with Sureau aspic, John Dory with thinly sliced chorizo, Swiss chard and apple juice, catfish filet with quahog clam ragout, wild rabbit braised with carrots and herb-seasoned pain perdu and a Guanaja chocolate dessert with hazelnuts are really delicate. There are twelve sweet little redecorated rooms that are light, quiet, modern and fairly spacious, allowing one to take up comfortable residence.

SAINTE-ANNE-LA-PALUD

29550 Finistère. Paris 586 –
Châteaulin 20 – Quimper 24 – Crozon 27 –
Brest 67.
A point just across the Channel from Cornwall with its chapel and its indulgences that unites Brittany in pilgrimage, banners flying in the wind, every year at the end of August.

 HOTELS-RESTAURANTS

● Hôtel de la Plage

On the beach.
Tel. 02 98 92 50 12. Fax 02 98 92 56 54.
laplage@relaischateaux.com
www.relaischateaux.com
Closed mid-Nov.–beg. Apr.
Rest. closed Tue. lunch, Wed. lunch,
Fri. lunch (off season).

26 rooms: 166–208€. 4 suites: 255–292€.
Prix fixe: 47€, 84€. A la carte: 100–120€.

Family-based and wonderful, this Relais & Châteaux on the point gives directly onto the beach. It is a house that honors its region, being welcoming and gastronomic. The rooms, some with bay windows, are delightful, the swimming pool inviting and the cuisine of newly arrived Mickael Renard looks beautiful. Add to this Anne and Jean Millau Le Coz, as attentive hosts as one could wish for, watching over the relaxed atmosphere of the place and its fabulous collection of paintings from Mathurin Méheut. Atlantic sea bass with Aquitaine caviar, oysters in cucumber aspic, roasted langoustines with foie gras, grilled blue lobster with beurre blanc sauce and a whole turbot with slow-cooked potatoes are precise and fine. In addition, a seven-hour roasted veal shank and the macaron shells with fresh fromage blanc mousseline and strawberries. Fine cellar and friendly service.

SAINTE-CROIX-EN-PLAINE see COLMAR
SAINTE-MARIE-DE-RE see ILE DE RE

SAINTE-MARINE

29120 Finistère. Paris 571 – Concarneau 26 – Quimper 23 – Pont-l'Abbé 7 – Bénodet 5.
A tiny Breton port, with its harbor, the Cornwall bridge that links it to Bénodet, the start of the journey into Bigouden.

 HOTELS-RESTAURANTS

■ Villa Tri Men

16, rue du Phare.
Tel. 02 98 51 94 94. Fax 02 98 51 95 50.
contact@trimen.fr / www.trimen.fr
Closed mid-Dec.–mid-Jan.
Rest. closed lunch, Sun. dinner (exc. July–Aug.), Mon. dinner (exc. July–Aug.).
20 rooms: 102–235€.
Prix fixe: 33€.

This villa in the pines, overlooking the port of St. Marine, exerts charm with its thirties facades and its quiet, tranquil décor with white monotints. The cuisine of Frédéric Claquin matches; this native of Quimper, trained at La Mer in Saint-Guénolé and at L'Amphitryon in Lorient, practices a refined simplicity: tian of skate wing, crab and cold risotto, simply seasoned langoustines, spicy tuna wrapped in salt-cured Spanish pork fat, John Dory with lemongrass and orange butter. The desserts (Breton shortbread with raspberry or the crispy raspberry and Pougastel srawberry dessert) blend in with the tone.

■ L'Hôtel Sainte-Marine

19, rue du Bac.
Tel. 02 98 56 34 79. Fax 02 98 51 94 09.
contact@hotelsaintemarine.com -
www.hotelsaintemarine.com
Closed beg. Nov.–mid-Dec.
11 rooms: 75–90€.
Prix fixe: 17,50€ (lunch), 27€, 29€, 38€, 48€, 10€ (child). A la carte: 45€.

The eleven rooms are charming with their marine décor and windows opening onto the sea with its boats returning from fishing expeditions. The simple and fresh cuisine served in a smart, marine brasserie setting offers tuna carpaccio, John Dory roasted with aromatic herbs, lamb confit with eggplant caviar and the berry soup served with a lemon crisp, among other attractive items.

SAINTE-MAURE see **TROYES**

SAINTE-MAURE-DE-TOURAINE

37800 Indre-et-Loire. Paris 274 – Tours 39 – Châtellerault 37 – Chinon 31 – Loches 32.
This crossroads town is famous for its exquisite wood-ash-matured goat cheese.

● RESTAURANTS

In Noyant-de-Touraine (37800). 2,5 km w via route de Chinon.

● La Ciboulette COM

78, route de Chinon (across from exit 25 on the A10).
Tel. 02 47 65 84 64. Fax 02 47 65 89 29.
laciboulette@wanadoo.fr / www.laciboulette.fr

Closed Sun. dinner (off season), Mon. dinner (off season), Tue. dinner (exc. weekends, Bank holidays, vac.).
Prix fixe: 15,95€, 18,95€, 24,85€, 28,65€, 8€ (child).

Pascal Daguet, who was chef at the Galant Verre in the rue de Verneuil, Paris, has established himself in a strategic, if less poetic, place in Touraine: near junction 25 of the A10. He and his wife Annick ensure that their guests have a pleasant time and the motivated waitstaff serves a simple, fresh cuisine. Crayfish terrine served warm with a fish reduction–flavored butter, rouget with slow-cooked leeks, veal sweetbreads with Muscat sauce and a pear and chocolate dessert are astounding. Wines from the Loire don't send the check rocketing.

SAINTE-MAXIME

83120 Var. Paris 877 – Fréjus 21 – Cannes 59 – Draguignan 34 – Toulon 74.
office@sainte-maxime.com.
Unfortunately tough to get to, this seaside resort reminiscent of the Côte d'Azur of the past with its pleasure port and its Tourelles château offers a superb view of the gulf of St. Tropez.

 HOTELS-RESTAURANTS

■ Le Beauvallon

Boulevard des collines, N98.
Beauvallon-Grimaud.
Tel. 04 94 55 78 88. Fax 04 94 55 78 78.
reservation@lebeauvallon.com.
www.lebeauvallon.com
Closed 15 Oct.–20 Apr.
Rest. closed lunch (off season).
58 rooms: 205–555€.
12 suites: 770–2400€.
Prix fixe: 65€ (dinner), 80€ (dinner), 20€ (child).

On the other side of the Bay of St. Tropez, this 1913 monument has appeal. The building has been renovated in contemporary style, but not without warmth. There is a swimming pool, beach, private jetty, grounds and neighboring golf course. In the Colonnades restaurant, Jean-Michel Belin produces fashionable dishes. Lobster brochettes with big scallops served on green papaya, tempura-style fried tuna, Angus rib steak from the grill and a caramel and lychee dessert with coconut cream make one want to take up residence. Wonderful beach cuisine, with overtones of fusion food, at Beauvallon Beach.

■ Amarante Golf Plaza   🌺🏠

Rte du Débarquement, domaine du Golf.
Tel. 04 94 56 66 66. Fax 04 94 56 66 00.
reservation@golf-plaza.fr
www.jjwhotels.com
Closed mid-Jan.–mid-Mar.
112 rooms: 127–380€.
Prix fixe: 21€ (lunch), 37€ (dinner),
12€ (child). A la carte: 75€.

Golf course, swimming pools, fitness and health center, hammam and tennis court; the rather chic, sporty clientele of this hotel complex also appreciate its large rooms decorated in Italian country style. The cuisine of Michel Rethore is simple in St. Andrews, more sophisticated in the Relais de Provence. In both cases, it honors the region.

■ Montfleuri   🏠

3, av Montfleuri.
Tel. 04 94 55 75 10. Fax 04 94 49 25 07.
hotelmontfleuri@wanadoo.fr
www.montfleuri.com
Closed mid-Nov.–end Dec.,
beg. Jan.–mid-Mar.
Rest. closed lunch
30 rooms: 45–185€. 1 suite: 150–245€.
Prix fixe: 20,50€, 26,50€, 12,50€ (child).

Ochre-colored rooms in which one feels immediately at home, a garden, a swimming pool and charming hosts are why we like this establishment where one can stay at a price reasonable for the Côte. Quentin Vandevyver is an exemplary master of the house and Martine a cook who conjures up simple, good dishes: goat cheese millefeuille with Provençal vegetables, basil-seasoned salmon, veal shoulder steak with rosemary and a chocolate fondant with crunchy praline dessert are wonderful.

● L'Amiral   COM

Galerie marchande at the port.
Tel.-Fax 04 94 43 99 36.
Closed 15 Jan.–Mar. 1, Tue. dinner, Wed.
Prix fixe: 14€ (lunch), 28€, 49€.
A la carte: 65€.

David Fauveaux, who worked at the Fermes de Marie in Megève and L'Hostellerie du Nord in Auvers-sur-Oise, highlights sea produce in his cooking. Crab stuffed in Moroccan style with spinach, leeks and cheese, lobster lasagne, John Dory with mashed potatoes and a saffron rice pudding served with a pear poached in spiced wine are well conceived. The welcome is friendly and the lunchtime prices very gentle.

● La Gruppi   Ⓝ SIM

82, av Charles de Gaulle.
Tel. 04 94 96 03 61.
Closed Tue. dinner, Wed. (off season),
2 weeks mid-Dec.
Prix fixe: 23–32€.

Right in the center and a stone's throw from the boats, the location is strategic. The cuisine varies according to the day's catch, there is a beautiful covered terrace and very cheerful dining room on the second floor.

● La Marine   Ⓝ SIM

6, rue Ferdinand-Bessy.
Tel. 04 94 96 53 93.
Closed 2 weeks Nov., beg. Jan.–beg. Feb.
Prix fixe: 25€, 48€, 7,50€ (child).

In the heart of the old village, a bistro that has the accents of Provence and Italy combined. A solid cuisine, in rhythm with the market.

SAINTE-MENEHOULD

51800 Marne. Paris 222 – Bar-le-Duc 50 – Châlons 49 – Reims 79 – Verdun 48.
This is the gastronomic capital of Argonne. It gave birth to Dom Pérignon—who was born and died on the same dates as Louis XIV (1639–1715), as testified by the plaque in the street dedicated to him—and to the famous rec-

ipe for tender pork trotter. Don't forget its beautiful central square.

 HOTELS-RESTAURANTS

■ Le Cheval Rouge
1, rue Chanzy.
Tel. 03 26 60 81 04. Fax 03 26 60 93 11.
rouge.cheval@wanadoo.fr
www.lechevalrouge.com
Rest. closed Sun. dinner, Mon.,
18 Dec.–8 Jan.
Prix fixe: 18€, 28€, 50€, 11,50€ (child).

The "serious" establishment of this crossroads-town is run by François and Catherine Fourreau who watch over the careful décor of exposed stonework. The rooms are simple and neat, the menus generous. Chef Jean-Robert Lafois, relieved by his son Matthieu, carefully prepares slow-cooked pork trotter with its bones, a pork trotter cake with truffle jus, perch with sorrel, frozen blackcurrant cream dessert and frozen caramelized vanilla soufflé. Of solid value.

● A Mon Idée
45-47, av de Vitry.
Tel. 03 26 60 83 25.
Closed Sun. dinner, Mon. dinner.
Prix fixe: 12,50€ (lunch), 16,50€, 22,50€, 29,50€.

Neither the outside nor the inside of this café-guesthouse are much to look at, but Cédric and Sandrine Costes—he worked at the Petit Comptoir and Le Coq Hardi in Verdun and she at Les Armes de Champagne in L'Epine—are real pros. A vegetable and shellfish cappuccino presented with a poached egg, tête de veau served cold in thin slices and a fish soufflé are lovely surprises.

In Futeau (55120). 13 km e via N3, D2.
■ L'Orée du Bois
At the edge of the woods.
Tel. 03 29 88 28 41. Fax 03 29 88 24 52.
aloreedubois@free.fr / www.aloreedubois.fr
Closed Tue. (exc. dinner Easter–Sept.), 20 Nov.–end Dec., beg. Jan.–end Jan.

12 rooms: 80–150€. 2 suites: 150€.
Prix fixe: 43€, 65€, 13€ (child).
A la carte: 60–73€.

Paul Aguesse has retained what he learned at the Barrier de Tours. He concentrates on produce and is always trying for more naturelness and lightness in his preparation. In this inn at the edge of the forest, one enjoys crayfish salad with Argonne trumpet mushrooms, scallops and endive charlotte with cardamom jus, squab with beets and jus and a crunchy pear dessert with almond milk ice cream. The rooms are comfortable and sauna, Jacuzzi and hammam enable one to keep fit.

SAINTE-SAVINE see TROYES

73620 Savoie. Paris 600 – Albertville 31 – Beaufort 18 – Megève 23.
Beaufort country is also one of pretty villages with old chalets and domed bells.

 HOTELS-RESTAURANTS

■ Le Calgary
73, rue des Périots.
Tel. 04 79 38 98 38. Fax 04 79 38 98 00.
contact@hotelcalgary.com
www.hotelcalgary.com
Closed end Apr.–mid-June, mid-Sept.–mid-Dec. Rest. closed lunch (exc. weekends).
39 rooms: 62–135€.
Prix fixe: 23€, 35€, 45€.

Franck Picard, Olympic champion in Calgary, watches over his Tyrolean hotel-chalet (with swimming pool, sauna and hammam) with great care. The contemporary rooms in different colors are very pleasant and in the kitchen Didier Vidal takes care of the clever, semi-regional dishes that have been given a contemporary reworking: various smoked fish blinis with eel-seasoned cream, pike-perch with a cep crust, stuffed cod filet with black turnip crème, pigeon breast roasted with onion jus and the Caribbean-style coconut dessert make a good impression.

SALLANCHES

74700 Haute-Savoie. Paris 588 – Chamonix-Mont-Blanc 28 – Annecy 70 – Bonneville 30 – Megève 14.
ot.sallanches@wanadoo.fr.
At the foot of Megève, this crossroads town is famous for its station, its motorway exit and its friendly market.

● RESTAURANTS

■ **Le Cerf Amoureux**
Rte de Nant-Ruy, 3 km s.
Tel. 04 50 47 49 24. Fax 04 50 47 49 25.
contact@lecerfamoureux.com
www.lecerfamoureux.com
Closed 2 weeks beg. Oct., 10 days Apr.
Rest. closed Sun., Mon. (exc. vac.).
11 rooms: 110–350€.
Prix fixe: 34€.

This very new chalet has mountain charm, offering a beautiful view of Mont Blanc and the Aravis, guesthouse cuisine for the residents and a very attentive welcome. Rooms with balconies.

● **Bernard Villemot** `COM`
57, rue du Dr-Berthollet.
Tel. 04 50 93 74 82. Fax 04 50 58 00 82.
Closed Sun. dinner, Mon., 3 weeks Jan., 20 Aug.–mid-Sept.
Prix fixe: 28€, 35€, 45€, 20€ (child).
A la carte: 55–60€.

Before climbing up to Megève or Chamonix, you have to stop at Bernard Villemot's. His regional restaurant deserves some attention for pressed oxtail and foie gras, pike with beurre blanc sauce and crayfish, chopped veal kidney with cep compote and a frozen Chartreux monastery produced Genepi soufflé. Fine food on the horizon.

SALON-DE-PROVENCE

13300 Bouches-du-Rhône. Paris 723 – Marseille 54 – Aix-en-Provence 37 – Arles 45 – Avignon 49.
ot.salon@visitprovence.com.
The town of Michel de Notre Dame known as

"Nostradamus" has become a favored crossroads between the Luberon and the Alpilles.

 HOTELS-RESTAURANTS

● **L'Abbaye Sainte-Croix**
Rte du Val-de-Cuech,
5 km ne via D17 then D16.
Tel. 04 90 56 24 55. Fax 04 90 56 31 12.
saintecroix@relaischateaux.com
www.hotels-provence.com
Closed Nov. 1–Easter.
21 rooms: 160–335€. 4 suites: 422–453€.
Prix fixe: 45€, 70€.

This former abbey dating from the 12th century, built in the middle of scrubland, overlooks Salon-de-Provence and offers an unbeatable view of the foothills of the Alpilles. The rooms converted from the former monks' cells, offering both modern comfort and rustic style, make this Relais a place of retreat and charm. The meals created by Pascal Morel, served in the Provençal restaurant or on the shady terrace, have nothing of the ascetic about them. One begins with lobster salad with an old-fashioned vinaigrette. Then comes the sea bream, the red tuna, sirloin steak and tête de veau—perfectly executed classics that rely on quality produce. One finishes off with a dessert of soft fruit cake and pineapple carpaccio.

■ **Le Mas du Soleil**
38, chemin Saint-Côme.
Tel. 04 90 56 06 53. Fax 04 90 56 21 52.
mas.du.soleil@wanadoo.fr
www.lemasdusoleil.com
Rest. closed Sun. dinner, Mon.
10 rooms: 115–280€. 1 suite: 280€.
Prix fixe: 38€, 62€, 68€, 87€.

Located in a residential quarter, this Provençal villa with light, charming rooms is above all worth the visit for its restaurant. The talented master chef Francis Robin creates good-looking classics such as lobster salad with a fines herbes–seasoned bouquet of green beans, grilled rouget filets with mixed salad and red pepper sauce, roasted leg of lamb with seasonal vegetables and baked Alaska flambéed with Grand Marnier.

55 rooms: 54–100€. 2 suites: 154–166€.
Prix fixe: 18€, 28€, 31€, 35€,
10€ (child). A la carte: 45€.

Damien Durey and his mother Laure are
in charge of an inventive cuisine that is
surprising in this traditional wine-growing town. And so, wok-tossed lobster and
scallops with sweet wine and Thai spices,
rouget tandoori with quinoa cooked three
ways, strips of duck breast with apple vinegar sauce and puréed sweet potatoes and
a crunchy roasted mango dessert with
mango sauce make exotic, charming suppers. The welcome given by Floriane, the
daughter of the house, is perfect while
son-in-law Eric, a good connoisseur of
the wines of the region, is in charge of an
efficient service. The cozy new tearoom
has an unbeatable view over the vineyards in winter. In the same house, the
Panoramic (tel. 02 48 54 22 44) owned
by André Ravenal, offers warm rooms in
shades of raspberry and gray with redecorated bathrooms.

● La Tour
31, Nouvelle Place.
Tel. 02 48 54 00 81. Fax 02 48 78 01 54.
info@la-tour-sancerre.fr
www.la-tour-sancerre.fr
Closed Sun. (mid-Nov.–Mar.),
Mon. (mid-Nov.–Mar.).
Prix fixe: 22€ (weekdays), 25€, 50€.
A la carte: 60€.

This establishment, which owes its name
to the 14th-century tower that tops it,
enjoys two restaurants: an elegant and
rustic one on the first floor and another,
more modern and with a view of the vineyards, on the second. Baptiste Fournier
throws himself into original and seductive compositions: foie gras terrine with
rhubarb served with a mixed salad, tuna
steak with ginger, Sainte-Anned'Auray
squab with smoked fingerling potatoes,
Grand Marnier soufflé with dark chocolate
and an Earl Grey and fine matcha tea tiramisu. The father of the young chef, Daniel Fournier, formerly of Guy Savoy's, looks
after the service. The wine list gives priority to Sancerres; to find your way among

---

SAMOENS

74340 Haute-Savoie. Paris 585 – Chamonix-
Mont-Blanc 63 – Annecy 72 – Genève 54.
samoens@wanadoo.fr.
This is the region of waterfalls, Sixt-Fer-Cheval
and the magnificent air of Savoie. The famous
glacial circle is here.

 HOTELS-RESTAURANTS

■ Neige et Roc
Tel. 04 50 34 40 72. Fax 04 50 34 14 48.
resa@neigeetroc.com / www.neigeetroc.com
Closed mid-Apr.–beg. June, 20 Sept.–20 Dec.
47 rooms: 80–120€. 3 suites: 120–200€.
Prix fixe: 22€ (lunch), 28€, 50€.
A la carte: 60€.

In the center of the village, the chalet of
the Deffaugts offers varied pleasures. In
summer, swimming pool and tennis are
in order while in winter skiing and bubbling hot tubs take over. The mountain-
style rooms are a delight year round, as is
Olivier's modern cusine. Crayfish in aspic
with lime zest, freshwater fish stew with
saffron butter, duck spring roll with soy
sauce and mountain honey and a strawberry and orange dessert flambéed with
Grand Marnier cannot be criticized.

SAN-MARTINO-DI-LOTA see BASTIA

SANCERRE

18300 Cher. Paris 205 – Bourges 46 –
La Charité-sur-Loire 25 – Vierzon 68.
ot.sancerre@wanadoo.fr.
Nestled on its hillock, this beautiful wine-growing village with its castle and its welcoming wine
cellars is also worth visiting for its location,
Chavignol cheese and likable vintages.

 HOTELS-RESTAURANTS

■ Les Augustins & Le Panoramic
Remparts des Augustins.
Tel. 02 48 54 01 44. Fax 02 48 54 13 60.
restaurant-lesaugustins@wanadoo.fr
Rest. closed Mon. lunch (off season).

the 300 varieties, follow the wise advice of Pascal Lassudrie.

● La Pomme d'Or   ⚓SIM

Pl de la Mairie.
Tel. 02 48 54 13 30. Fax 02 48 54 19 22.
Closed Sun. dinner (beg. Nov.–end Feb.),
Tue. dinner (Mar.–end Oct.), Wed. (Mar.–end
Oct.), 1 week Nov. 1, 1 week beg. Jan.
Prix fixe: 18€ (weekdays), 26€, 36,80€,
45€, 18€ (child).

If the pretty landscape that surrounds the dining room is a trompe-l'oeil, the cuisine of Didier Turpin is the real thing. On the menu, which changes according to the markets, are pan-tossed escargots with mild garlic cream, pike-perch with Sancerre sauce, slow-cooked wild boar (in season) and onion stew with blood sauce and the profiteroles with house ice creams that are, without a shadow of a doubt, exquisite and kindly priced. Opposite the church, the Epicerie de la Pomme d'Or has dishes to take away as well as local wines, cheeses, fruits and vegetables from the region's producers.

SARE

64310 Pyrénées-Atlantiques. Paris 799 – Biarritz 26 – Cambo-les-Bains 19 – Saint-Jean-de-Luz 14.
This is the village of Ramuntcho. It was here that Pierre Loti dreamed up the adventures of his Basque smuggler playing games of daring with the nearby border. A superb site perched up in the mountains, beautiful church, pediment and pleasant inn: a little Basque postcard.

HOTELS-RESTAURANTS

■ Arraya   🏠

Place du Village.
Tel. 05 59 54 20 46. Fax 05 59 54 27 04.
hotel@arraya.com / www.arraya.com
Closed beg. Nov.–end Apr.
Rest. closed Sun. dinner (off season),
Mon. (off season), Tue. lunch (off season).
20 rooms: 84–120€.
Prix fixe: 21€, 31€, 10€ (child).
A la carte: 45€.

Arraya, a very regional name for this hotel in the Basque heart of Sare, equipped with a terrace, a garden, the Internet and half-antique, half-modern rooms. No need to be a Saratar to enjoy the comfort, simplicity, moderate prices, quality welcome and service of Jean-Baptiste and Sébastien Fagoaga and of the two Laurences, wives of the two brothers, as well as the cuisine of René Dubès and Marc Tesseire who serve a polished stuffed Spanish crab ravioli served in a shellfish broth, a mix of jumbo shrimp and lamb cutlet with chanterelles and the frozen chocolate nougatine dessert presented with an orange mini-gratin, all very finely done and washed down with a wine from Bordeaux, Burgundy, the Loire or Spain.

SARLAT-LA-CANEDA

24200 Dordogne. Paris 530 – Brive-la-Gaillarde 51 – Bergerac 73 – Cahors 62 – Périgueux 67.
sarlat@perigord.tm.fr.
Given an overhaul under the Malraux law, the capital of black Perigord shows off its old Renaissance town to the traveler taking a magnificent walk through the past. In summer, the pedestrian and nocturnal circuit is a joy.

HOTELS-RESTAURANTS

■ La Madeleine   🏠

1, pl Petite-Rigaudie.
Tel. 05 53 59 10 41. Fax 05 53 31 03 62.
hotel.madeleine@wanadoo.fr
www.hoteldelamadeleine-sarlat.com
Closed beg. Jan.–mid-Feb.
Rest. closed Mon. lunch (exc. July–Aug.),
Tue. lunch (exc. July–Aug.),
mid-Nov.–mid-Mar.
39 rooms: 59–102€.
Prix fixe: 26€, 46€, 11€ (child).

In this town house, Philippe Melot offers an attractive and very regional cuisine. We like, as ever, duck foie gras with brioche toast, roasted monkfish medallion with orange, slow-cooked Cahors goose stew with blood sauce and apples and a frozen soufflé with a glass of Grand Marnier. The check causes no upset while the rooms are simple but offer every comfort.

■ Le Saint-Albert et le Montaigne ⌂

Pl Pasteur.
Tel. 05 53 31 55 55. Fax 05 53 59 19 99.
hotel.stalbert@wanadoo.fr
www.sarlathotel.com
Closed Sun., Mon. (winter), 2 weeks Feb.
25 rooms: 45–58€. 1 suite: 76–82€.
Prix fixe: 11€, 20€, 30€, 8€ (child).

Le Saint-Albert and Le Montaigne are each on one side of the square. The former is a friendly establishment and the latter, a more luxurious building, offers comfortable and modern rooms. In the dining room with its feel of a contemporary bistro, the region is highlighted through attractive wines of Aquitaine and foie gras terrine with onion compote, grilled trout, duck breast with honey sauce and walnuts and a fresh fruit chaud-froid on brochette for dessert. Friendly service and gentle prices.

● Le Présidial 🄽COM

6, rue Landry.
Tel. 05 53 28 92 47.
Closed Sun., Mon. lunch, mid-Nov. Mar.
Prix fixe: 26–40€.

This beautiful 17th-century house with its garden hides a cozy interior, a beautiful terrace and local dishes. Foie gras, confit and duck breast are treated with admirable care.

● La Rapière COM

Pl du Peyrou.
Tel. 05 53 59 03 13. Fax 05 53 30 27 84.
www.larapiere-sarlat.com
Closed Sun. (exc. vac. and Bank holidays),
Mon. lunch (exc. vac. and Bank holidays),
3 weeks Dec., mid-Feb.–mid-Mar.
Prix fixe: 18,50€, 22,40€, 27,30€, 36€. A la carte: 45–55€.

The grandiose cathedral is nearby and one can hear its bells chiming from the restaurant of Gérard Gatinel who receives the blessing of his clients for his unpretentious regional cooking: a pork trotter gratin with garden vinaigrette, trout filet in court bouillon served with beurre blanc sauce, veal sweetbreads with morels and a frozen walnut parfait are well handled.

● Le Relais de la Poste 🄽SIM

Impasse de la Vieille-Poste.
Tel. 05 53 59 63 13.
Closed Tue., Wed. (off season),
3 weeks mid-Nov.–beg. Dec.
Prix fixe: 18–34€.

This rustic establishment in the upper town gives a relaxed welcome and a generous regional cooking. Beneath the beams, foie gras mille-feuille, pike-perch with buttered cabbage and glazed ceps slip down effortlessly.

● Le Grand Bleu SIM

43, av de la Gare.
Tel.-Fax 05 53 31 08 48.
Closed Sat. lunch, Mon.
Prix fixe: 22€. A la carte: 35€.

Those who want to enjoy the pleasure of a cuisine that departs from traditional tracks go to Franck Ruaz's. Langoustine ravioli, monkfish and foie gras mille-feuille, roasted sea bream with Bergerac honey, spiced pears and the trilogy of herb- and flower-flavored ice creams make a good impression. The friendliness of the welcome and the low prices are additional assets.

SARPOIL

63490 Puy-de-Dôme. Paris 460 – Clermont-Ferrand 38 – Issoire 10 – Thiers 60.
This green heart of the Auvergne and of Puys country has kept its charm.

● | RESTAURANTS

● La Bergerie V.COM

Tel. 04 73 71 02 54. Fax 04 73 71 01 99.
cyril.zen@wanadoo.fr
Closed Sun. dinner (exc. July–Aug.), Mon.
(exc. July–Aug.), 3 Jan.
Prix fixe: 15€, 60€. A la carte: 55€.

Audrey and Cyril Zens have just taken over this once-famous (under Jean-Yves Bath, who left for Clermont then Paris) formerly gastronomic "*bergerie*", and are attempting to restore its culinary identity. In addition to a charming welcome, they offer fashionable dishes: crab and lobster aspic, turbot with meat jus, herb-stuffed roasted rack of lamb, rhubarb compote with berries and basil-flavored ice cream and the small blueberry tart with light pistachio cream that are rather promising.

SARREBOURG

57400 Moselle. Paris 439 – Strasbourg 73 – Metz 95 – Lunéville 55.
tourismesarrebourg@wanadoo.fr.
The country of Erckmann-Chatrian, crystal and red brick tiles is also one of canals and forest. Don't forget to visit the Cordeliers' chapel, decorated with a stained glass window by Chagall.

 HOTELS-RESTAURANTS

■ Les Cèdres   ❀ 🏠

Chemin d'Imling (recreation area).
Tel. 03 87 03 55 55. Fax 03 87 03 66 33.
info@hotel-lescedres.fr / www.hotel-lescedres.fr
Closed Christmas–New Year's.
Rest. closed Sat. lunch, Sun. dinner.
42 rooms: 50,70–61,70€.
2 suites: 70,70–89,60€.
Prix fixe: 13,40€ (lunch). A la carte: 50€.

In the middle of a huge forest and numerous lakes, this modern hotel delights lovers of walks and fishing. Guests also appreciate the calm rooms and Benoît Schwartz's sun-filled cuisine. Mediterranean-themed fisherman's salad, monkfish and tapenade mille-feuille, veal filet served on a potato cake and a soft walnut cake with coconut and berries bring balm to the heart.

● Mathis   ◎ COM

7, rue Gambetta.
Tel. 03 87 03 21 67. Fax 03 87 23 00 64.
Closed Mon., Tue. dinner, 10 days beg. Jan., end July–beg. Aug.

Prix fixe: 29,50€, 49,50€ (wine inc. dinner), 75€. A la carte: 80€.

The word is that he's thinking of retirement but he is still as fit as a fiddle, garnering the best produce from the Strasbourg markets and cooking them with passion. Ernest Mathis confidently offers his own version of fusion cooking. In his hands, the wonderful ingredients of France travel with the aid of spices, condiments and dried fruits from other lands. In the quiet, unpretentious dining room, try the orange-flavored langoustine tempura, roasted Atlantic sea bass served with pepperoni-seasoned basmati rice, milk-fed pork tenderloin with large grain mustard and peanut sauce, a cherry and Kirsch dessert and the spice crumble. With these pleasing dishes, the wines of Alsace chosen by Christophe Klein hit the nail on the head. The welcome given by lady of the house Lily is as wonderful as ever.

● L'Ami Fritz   🅿🛏 SIM

76, Grand-Rue.
Tel. 03 87 03 10 40. Fax 03 87 03 31 47.
contact@amifritz.fr / www.amifritz.com
Closed Wed., Thu. dinner, 2 weeks beg. Oct., 2 weeks Feb.
Prix fixe: 18,50€, 25,50–31,50€, 9,50€ (child). A la carte: 35€.

Tino Carapito is the ideal host: smiling, welcoming, giving skillful advice on food or wine, describing dishes and waiting tables with great ease. Formerly of the Petite-Pierre in Vosges, he has created a sober, restyled winstub in the center of town that is a gastronomic establishment always full to the rafters. You sometimes need to be patient to taste sliced tête de veau served cold with herb vinaigrette, steamed halibut on a bed of fennel, potato cakes with Munster stuffing, roasted duck breast with honey and spices and an apple streussel with cinnamon ice cream created by Adrien Meyer, formerly with Mathis. To these finely crafted and inexpensive dishes are added the classic veal in cream sauce over puff pastry shells, tripe with Riesling sauce and tête de veau that afford nothing but pleasure.

● Auberge Le Baeckeoffe

24, rue de la Division-Leclerc.
Tel. 03 87 03 10 26. Fax 03 87 23 72 84.
Closed Sun. dinner, Mon., 2 weeks Aug.
4 rooms: 28–52€.
Prix fixe: 18€, 28€, 36€. A la carte: 40€.

The Zimmermanns have tradition in them, through and through. Josiane gives a kind welcome to her clients while Marc delights them with a beautifully-prepared Alsatian cuisine. The house duck foie gras, pike-perch with chanterelles, veal kidney with whole-grain mustard sauce and hot raspberries with vanilla ice cream are well made and charged at a gentle rate. Several guest rooms to relax in.

● L'Auberge de Maître Pierre SIM

24, rue Saint-Martin.
Tel. 03 87 03 10 16. Fax 03 87 07 11 03.
auberge@maitrepierre.com
Closed Mon., Tue., 2 weeks beg. Sept.,
3 weeks Christmas–New Year's.
Prix fixe: 18,30€, 29€. A la carte: 38€.

Cooked in a wood oven, Daniel Pierre's tartes flambées (the local savory flat pies) are famous but his other specialities (smoked salmon, pike-perch with beurre blanc, beef sirloin steak cooked old Strasbourg style and a frozen nougat with raspberry sauce) are also not bad. Relaxed welcome, generous portions.

● A la Table des Tropiques ⓃSIM

9, rue du maréchal-Foch.
Tel. 03 87 07 89 29.
Closed Mon.
A la carte: 22€.

Gaston-Paul Effa, writer, philosopher and man of taste(s), has made this exotic restaurant with its simple setting the ambassador of cooking from the Antilles and the west coast of Africa. Shrimp with African seasonings, tiep bou dien (Atlantic sea bass cooked in red rice) and chicken with grains from Mali have energy and character.

SARREGUEMINES

57200 Moselle. Paris 396 – Strasbourg 105 – Metz 69 – Sarrebruck 18.
otsgs@wanadoo.fr.
The land of tiles and of the Smart car, the banks of the Sarre, the relationship with the biggest German province makes this crossroads town into a mini-capital of gastronomy.

 HOTELS-RESTAURANTS

● Auberge Saint Walfrid ○⌂

58, rue de Grosbliederstroff.
Tel. 03 87 98 43 75. Fax 03 87 95 76 75.
stwalfrid@free.fr / www.stwalfrid.free.fr
Closed Feb. vac.
Rest. closed Sat. lunch, Sun., Mon. lunch.
11 rooms: 95–158€.
Prix fixe: 25€ (weekdays), 48€, 70€,
12€ (child). A la carte: 75–95€.

Stéphan Schneider, who trained in fine schools (Crocodile, Schillinger, Palme d'Or), has made this former 18th-century farm into a charming hotel with a garden, carefully prepared rooms, luxurious restaurant and choice service. Martin Dahlem, maître d'hôtel and sommelier, takes solemn charge of a huge cellar in which great Burgundies and fine Alsatian wines are reasonably priced. On the cuisine side, the marriage between Provence and Lorraine creates dishes of remarkable finesse. Stéphan concocts, with great passion, a light version of classicism. A few notions of his talent? A poached egg with mushroom foam and chanterelles, grilled turbot served on a bed of vegetables with its cooking juice lightly creamed, without forgetting escargot ravioli with parsley jus in an oxtail bouillon and Hingingen goat cheese marinated in olive oil, which sums up, in its blending of East and South, the spirit of the house. For dessert, slow-cooked apricots with meringue cream cake or pistachio ice cream with almond cream. One should praise the special menu at 20 which offers nibbles, country cured ham, caramelized veal loin with Lorraine-style vegetables before the frozen nougat. This is an establishment that has managed to keep its cultural heritage and defend it with passion.

● Le Vieux Moulin

135, rue de France.
Tel. 03 87 98 22 59. Fax 03 87 28 12 63.
Closed Thu., mid-Jan.–beg. Feb., 1 week Aug.
Prix fixe: 20€, 31€, 51€, 70€.
A la carte: 85€.

Does one still call Thierry Breininger's restaurant "Le Vieux Moulin"? The name of the owner-chef now figures in large letters, like a boastful advertisement, on the outside, just next to the river. After working with the greats (Arnsbourg, Savoy, Crillon, Buerehiesel), will-o'-the-wisp Thierry is master in his own home, instituting his own ways, narrating a cuisine of his times—reminiscent of Lorraine in its intensity and of the Mediterranean in the taste of oils and condiments of the South, fresh in terms of its constant evolution according to the markets. Thinly sliced liver with artichokes and kumquats, scallops in celery bouillon, frog legs with cheese-stuffed ravioli, catfish poached with ginger and served in a lemongrass bouillon and the young Domaine de Hoche pigeon pastilla with cinnamon jus compose a joyful symphony. Alsatian-style frog legs dumplings (fleischnaka), a pan toss of frog legs with escargots, plus the creamed sweet peas with mint, Lorraine-style split pea soup (even if the langoustine toasts were replaced by Antan smoked bacon) – are fun nods to the great eastern region. Strong on the sweet side (his magnificent crunchy and creamy vanilla cream with crisp apples and green apple jus is attributed to Guy Savoy, its creator), Thierry can do it all. There are the same products and the same spirit at the Breiningers' very new grocery/delicatessen (tel. 03 87 95 59 30).

● Winetour

Intersection rue de la Paix, rue du Moulin.
Tel.-Fax 03 87 09 46 06.
Closed Sun., Mon.
Prix fixe: 13€, 25€. A la carte: 40–45€.

Just as the décor blends contemporary and old, the menu offered by Philippe Meyer offers classic dishes like beef Rossini, brioche pain perdu and more recent recipes like a red tuna carpaccio and a grilled scorpion fish; both are equally good. The special menu at 25 is ideal and the prices have noticeably lowered. On the reception side, Mylène Lefrançois is perfect and Daniel Olivieri, previously at the Casino des Sommeliers, knows his cellar like the back of his hand and offers good advice.

● La Bonne Source SIM

24, av de la Gare.
Tel.-Fax 03 87 98 03 79.
guy.adam57@wanadoo.fr
Closed Sat. lunch, Sun. dinner, Mon.,
mid-July–mid-Aug.
Prix fixe: 12€ (weekday lunch), 14€, 22€,
25€. A la carte: 30–35€.

Everything in this winstub is authentic: the plates of Sarreguemines china, the odors of perfumed wood, the kindness of the welcome from Guy Adam and the dishes of François Chatellier. The house country terrine, raw vegetables, pike-perch with potatoes (baeckeofestyle), rippele (grilled pork chops), frozen kouglof and sour cherries flambéed in Kirsch delight at low cost. The pitcher wines are outstanding.

In Hambach (57910). 8 km toward A4.

■ Hostellerie Saint-Hubert

Le domaine de la Verte Forêt,
rue de la Forêt.
Tel. 03 87 98 39 55. Fax 03 87 98 39 57.
www.hostellerie-st-hubert.com
Closed 1 week at end Dec.
51 rooms: 59–62€. 2 suites: 88€.
Prix fixe: 23€, 58€, 8€ (child).
A la carte: 44€.

Michel Roth, from the Paris Ritz, runs his sister-in-law's establishment from a distance. We are on the edge of the forest in a modern, neo-Tyrolean style building with spacious, light rooms. The solid cuisine effortlessly pleases, with foie gras with forest flavors, roasted pike-perch in an herb crust, guinea hen stuffed with foie gras and served with morel sauce and the frozen mirabelle plum parfait with bergamot and caramel ice cream. People come here for seminars (the Swatch factory is nearby) or for the stay in nature.

In Woelfling-les-Sarreguemines (57200). 11 km via N62.

● Pascal Dimofski ⊙COM

2, quartier de la Gare.
Tel. 03 87 02 38 21. Fax 03 87 02 21 36.
pascal.dimofski@gmail.com
Closed Mon., Tue., mid-Feb.–beg. Mar.,
mid-Aug.–beg. Sept.
Prix fixe: 25€ (lunch), 26€, 36€, 46€,
68€, 15€ (child). A la carte: 70–90€.

This former inn at the edge of the wood offers a décor of attractive quietness and a promising welcome, but the best is in the food. Pascal Dimofski is indeed one of those gifted chefs who possess an instinctive intelligence about produce. His cuisine plays cleverly with regional fare, going beyond its borders. His grilled potatoes stuffed with escargots, Atlantic sea bass with tomato marmalade, milk-fed veal cutlet browned with parmesan and a coffee and dark chocolate mousseline dusted with crushed grilled almonds are really dynamic. All of this doesn't come free but there is a large variety of special menus that allow one to leave not too much out of pocket. Attractive wines, particularly from the Rhône valley.

SARRE-UNION

67260 Bas-Rhin. Paris 409 – Strasbourg 84 – Metz 82 – Sarreguemines 23.
The capital of the "hump" of Alsace is unfortunately poor in terms of restaurants, but the surrounding areas contain nice surprises.

● | RESTAURANTS

In Altwiller (67260). 6 km nw via Harskirschen.

● L'Ecluse 16 🔒SIM

Locale known as Bonne-Fontaine.
Tel. 03 88 00 90 42. Fax 03 88 00 91 94.
Closed Mon. lunch, Tue., 2 weeks beg. Mar.,
2 weeks beg. Sept.
Prix fixe: 17€ (weekday lunch), 28€, 42€.

Again this year, we have fallen in love with Jean-Yves Leroux's pretty brick inn, bordering the haulage route. This typical 1900s house offers a tasteful modern interior where one has the pleasant experience of eating well. Lime-seasoned trout with chanterelles, grilled swordfish steak with spicy bibelekäs (fresh fromage blanc with herbs), braised veal sweetbreads with meat jus and frozen pistachio cannelloni, it is a gastronomic sin. The touch of chef Jean-Yves Roux, added to these classic dishes, hits the bull's-eye every time.

In Berg (67320). 12 km se via N61 and D15.

● Bellevue ⓃSIM

Tel. 03 88 00 62 26.
Closed Tue. dinner, Wed.,
10 days Christmas–New Year's.
Prix fixe: 8,50€ (lunch), 21,50€, 25€, 32€.

Sonia Gilger, who works in the kitchen with her sister, while her daughter Carmen gives a smiling reception, cultivates her huge kitchen garden. This blonde and cheerful fairy godmother has made this panoramic establishment in the heart of the hump of Alsace into her little gastronomic domain. There is the café corner, the tables for the dish of the day (salad with sausage and Gruyère, roasted pork tenderloin with pan-tossed potatoes and zucchini) and the winstub room with its collection of engravings, plates and souvenirs. Salad with sausage and Gruyère, and a pork tenderloin with pan-tossed potatoes and zucchini gratin, Head cheese and wine aspic terrine, pâté in pastry crust, escargots, Alsace-style meat dumplings (fleischschnackas), old-style ravioli and tête de veau are like grandma made them.

In Burbach (67260). 10 km se, N 61.

● Le Windhof Ⓥ.COM

3, Windhof.
Tel. 03 88 01 72 35. Fax 03 88 01 72 71.
bernard.kehne@wanadoo.fr
www.windhof.fr
Closed Sun. dinner, Mon., Tue. dinner,
2 weeks Jan., 3 weeks Aug.
Prix fixe: 19€, 27,50€, 42€, 46€, 53€,
61€. A la carte: 50–65€.

On the plateau of Lorraine, this large, exposed farm is deceptive. The wooden interior is luxurious and charming with its vast, double dining room and its well-spaced and well-placed tables. The Kehné family run the establishment with professionalism but it is the son, Laurent, back from his classes with the greats (Crocodile, Auberge de l'Ill, Cerf at Marlenheim, Cygne at Gundershofen), who has bowled the house style over, balancing it with his sense of finesse and lightness: swordfish carpaccio with fennel (served as an amuse-gueule), flat savory mini-tart, surf and turf, niçoise-style tomato and pepper tart with pan-tossed sardines, scallop carpaccio with pan-tossed little squids, pan-cooked sturgeon with truffle oil-seasoned risotto, classic pan-tossed veal kidney with mustard sauce and the strawberry mille-feuille with basil sauce. The wine list is full of wonderful discoveries, nicely charged.

In Siewiller (67320). 12 km se via N61.

● Restaurant de la Gare   SIM
9, rte Nationale.
Tel. 03 88 00 99 46. Fax 03 88 01 20 28.
Closed Mon., Tue. dinner, Sept., 2 weeks Jan.
Prix fixe: 23€, 25€, 8,80€ (child).
A la carte: 32€.

The Benedick's café-restaurant is a joy. Céline on reception is all smiles and in the kitchen, Frédéric, trained by Albrecht in Rhinau, creates delicious tartes flambées at the weekend and serious dishes during the week. Duck breast and foie gras salad, fish stew with horseradish sauce, sirloin steak with ceps and the chocolate profiteroles are eaten in a relaxed atmosphere.

SARS-POTERIES

59216 Nord. Paris 257 – Avesnes-sur-Helpe 12 – Charleroi 46 – Lille 107.
sars-poteries@wanadoo.fr.
This piece of Avesnes huddles up to rural Thiérache, the northern Normandy that produces good cider and wholesome Maroilles cheese.

 HOTELS-RESTAURANTS

● Auberge Fleurie   V.COM
67, rue du Général-de-Gaulle.
Tel. 03 27 61 62 48. Fax 03 27 61 56 66.
fauberge@wanadoo.fr
www.auberge-fleurie.net
Closed Sun. and Mon. night (hotel),
2 weeks Jan., 2 weeks end Aug.
8 rooms: 65–90€.
Prix fixe: 26€, 39€, 55€, 62€.

This flower-filled inn with eight little rooms has a cozy atmosphere while the cooking offers high-quality classics. Foie gras carpaccio with spices and truffles, a poached filet of turbot with a light beurre blanc sauce made with champagne and the milk-fed Pyrénées lamb cannot be criticized and are effortlessly enjoyed. Figs roasted in cinnamon-seasoned red wine with a little pot of cream is reminiscent of the South. Irreproachable service, high prices.

SARZEAU

56370 Morbihan. Paris 479 – Vannes 23 – Nantes 112 – Arzon 10.
office.de.tourisme.sarzeau@wanadoo.fr.
The noble château of Suscinio, the abbey of St. Gildas, the oyster farming area of Tour du Parc, the small ports called Brillac, Logeo, Kerners and Cranhfol: the gentle Brittany of the Rhuys peninsula.

 RESTAURANTS

● Le Petit Port   SIM
Quai des Voileries, port du Logeo.
Tel. 02 97 26 89 87. Fax 02 97 63 97 23.
lepetitport@aol.com
Closed Tue. (off season), Wed. (off season),
beg. Nov.–mid-Mar.
A la carte: 27€.

This Breton straw hut or *paillote* on a pretty little port is one of the joys of the Rhuys peninsula. Dominique Samuel offers fresh fish treated simply and at a low price: fisherman's cold spreads for toast, oysters from neighbor Yvonnick Chalm, grilled tuna steak with tomato, scallop brochettes and Breton far (a flan like dessert) all to be eaten in the open air, under the covered terrace or in the extension of the hut.

In Penvins (56370). 7 km se via D198.

■ **Le Mur du Roy** 🏠

Tel. 02 97 67 34 08. Fax 02 97 67 36 23.
contact@lemurduroy.com
www.lemurduroy.com
Closed mid-Dec.–mid-Jan.
Rest. closed Mon. lunch, Tue. lunch.
10 rooms: 52–86€.
Prix fixe: 32€, 48€. A la carte: 53–58€.

Agnès and Nicolas Boyère have made this Mur du Roy into a welcoming house. The rooms are unpretentious and the good quality beds allow a good night's rest. Agnès gives a smiling reception while Nicolas cooks as naturally as he breathes. Here a contemporary element is added with mushroom bouillon with Burgundy escargots, langoustine and vegetable tempura with an aromatic foam and also béarnaise sauce, cod filet with Swiss chard and shallots and served with an anchovy soup and the pineapple and saffron cream dessert. It's full of surprises and not without charm.

In Penvins.

● **Le Vent d'Ouest** COM

47, rte de la Grée.
Tel.-Fax 02 97 67 42 15.
leventdouest@orange.fr
Closed Tue. (exc. July–Aug.), Wed. (exc. July–Aug.).
Prix fixe: 32€, 44€, 14€ (child).
A la carte: 55–60€.

William Grivet, who has done a tour of duty in Parisian brasseries, notably with the Blanc brothers and the Costes, has energetically taken over this Breton establishment on the side of the road. In the elegant dining room with its stone walls and materials and carpets in shades of blue, one enjoys Burgundy escargots in papillote with baby vegetables and Noilly Prat, roasted haddock with Guéméné chitterling sausage and beurre rouge, duck breast

and potato cake with truffle oil and the crunchy caramelized apple dessert served with apple sorbet.

In Saint-Colombier (56370). 4 km ne via D780.

● **Le Tournepierre** COM

Tel. 02 97 26 42 19. Fax 02 97 43 91 70.
Closed Sun. dinner, Mon., Tue., Nov.
Prix fixe: 19€ (weekday lunch), 29€, 39€, 43€, 55€, 9,95€ (child).

Alain Jouan puts Brittany on the map in this pretty stone house. We fell in love with the scallops with sweet potato purée served with crispy farm bacon, a slice of monkfish in white bean and smoked bacon stew with country sausage, marjoram-seasoned veal scallops glazed with Port-enriched pan juices. The roasted bananas and pineapple served with local pastry flan and Carambar candy sauce and the salted-butter caramel ice cream take one right back to childhood. Very attentive service and really nice special menus.

SAUBUSSE

40180 Landes. Paris 736 – Mont-de-Marsan 72 – Bayonne 43 – Biarritz 50 – Dax 19.
This Landes thermal resort looks towards Adour and the Basque neighbors.

● RESTAURANTS

● **Villa Stings** Ⓝ○ COM

9, rue du Port.
Tel. 05 58 57 70 18.
Closed Sat. lunch, Sun. dinner, Mon., Feb., 1 week June.
Prix fixe: 32–75€.

This large 19th-century stone house right beside the river charms without effort. The dining room is refined, the tables well set out, the cellar well stocked—but it is the food served up by the excellent Francis Gabarrus that immediately seduces and makes one want to return. We like the spontaneous, regional Landes dishes that have been reworked without being betrayed. Sweet pea gazpacho served with toasts with a rabbit spread, smoked eel served warm with spring garlic, Atlantic sea bass with asparagus and young broad beans, a ginger-seasoned slice of foie gras and grilled tuna belly with Sichuan pepper make one want to be a regular here. The reception of Marie, who watches over her guests with a kindly eye, is exquisite, and the desserts (waffles with wild blueberry and lime confiture) take one back to childhood memories.

SAUGUES

43170 Haute-Loire. Paris 532 – Le Puy-en-Velay 43 – Brioude 51 – Saint-Flour 55.
The land of Robert Sabatier, little Olivier and of the book *Noisettes sauvages*…

 HOTELS-RESTAURANTS

■ La Terrasse   🏠
Cours Dr-Gervais.
Tel. 04 71 77 83 10. Fax 04 71 77 63 79.
laterrasse.saugues@wanadoo.fr
Closed Sun. dinner (off season), Mon. (off season), beg. Dec.–end Jan.
8 rooms: 55–65€.
Prix fixe: 25€, 37€, 50€, 10€ (child).

A house in the middle of the village with renovated rooms in a contemporary, quiet décor that allow an enjoyable stay. In the restaurant, Benoît delights his universe by modernizing his regional cuisine. Smoked trout presented in a dome, minced Vourzac trout in a shallot crust, veal with peppers, onions, chestnuts and ceps, a hazelnut, almond and pistachio meringue cake served with a chocolate and orange cream and the frozen rose-flavored parfait make agreeable food. In the dining room, Denis Fargier watches over everything with a seeing eye. Robert Sabatier is a happy regular.

SAULGES

53340 Mayenne. Paris 250 – Château-Gontier 38 – La Flèche 50 – Laval 34 – Le Mans 56 – Mayenne 40.
A rural town of Mayenne dedicated to nature.

 HOTELS-RESTAURANTS

■ L'Ermitage
3, pl St-Pierre.
Tel. 02 43 64 66 00. Fax 02 43 64 66 20.
info@hotel-emitage.fr / www.hotel-emitage.fr
Closed 1 week at end Dec.
Rest. closed Fri. dinner (Oct.–Mar.),
Sun. dinner (Oct.–Mar.).
35 rooms: 59–97€. 1 suite: 90–119€.
Prix fixe: 23€, 37€, 54€, 11€ (child).

This ancient building with its contemporary décor offers two charming perspectives: the countryside that one sees from some of the rooms and the Merovingian church opposite the glass-walled restaurant. Garden, aromatic pathway and heated swimming pool add to the pleasure. Christian Possémé has since January entrusted the cuisine to a new chef who provides traditional meals. Three hundred wines from France and elsewhere.

SAULIEU

21210 Côte-d'Or. Paris 247 – Dijon 76 – Autun 40 – Avallon 38 – Beaune 64.
saulieu.tourisme@wanadoo.fr.
The bronze bull of Pompon, the St. Andoche basilica, the natural regional park of Morvan, the old town with its russet-colored roof tiles: there are all sorts of good reasons to stop here. In addition, gastronomy reigns, with a king named Bernard Loiseau, spiritual son of Dumaine, who has made the Côte-d'Or into a great French establishment.

 HOTELS-RESTAURANTS

● Le Relais Bernard Loiseau   ⚪⚪🏠
2, rue d'Argentine.
Tel. 03 80 90 53 53. Fax 03 80 64 08 92.
loiseau@relaischateaux.com
www.bernard-loiseau.com
Closed beg. Jan.–beg. Feb.
Rest. closed Tue., Wed. lunch.
23 rooms: 150–330€. 9 suites: 260–470€.
Prix fixe: 98€, 120€, 145€, 155€, 180€, 24€ (child). A la carte: 190€.

The classics of Bernard Loiseau (frog legs with garlic purée and parsley jus, pikeperch with slow-cooked caramelized shallots and red wine sauce and the farm-raised poultry breast with pan-seared foie gras and truffle-seasoned purée) still have an important place on the menu. But the restaurant is continuing to evolve at great speed; Dominique Loiseau has taken over the reins of this beautiful house for the man who departed too soon and has found in Patrick Bertron a sure and solid rock. This discreet, hardworking native of Rennes is given spirited support in the kitchen by a team of young, gifted "pros". Together they have overcome all the difficulties and today the place remains one of the most prestigious there is. The hotel has cachet, the rooms and suites have a rustic luxury and the spa fulfills the desire for a completely relaxing weekend. The service is extremely attentive, the breakfasts magnificent and in the restaurant a feeling of celebration continually reigns. The menu changes regularly, giving priority to seasonal products. They are carefully treated, as naturally as possible and all their juices preserved. The balance of flavors is faultless, the cooking precise and the dishes full of color. It is confirmed by the most recent creations of the house: crayfish with mushrooms in a little dish with crayfish jus and foamy sweet clover milk, the turbot with Guéméné chitterling sausage in a Beaune wine and parsley oil–seasoned crust, the spit-roasted veal kidney with a Madeira-enriched jus, slow-cooked shallots and pain d'épice–flavored mustard, pigeon breasts with flavors of sage and licorice and herb gnocchi, the legs stuffed with variety meats, are effortlessly seductive. There is still the superb regional cheese cart allowing one to pause before the arrival of the desserts—all of which are attractive. But one must decide and one will never regret having been tempted by roasted Morvan hazelnut nougatine and the pomme d'amour slow-cooked in cider vinegar and served over a basil-infused crème brûlée with an apple basil sorbet. However, the Burgundian masterpiece of the moment is the violet granité surrounded by a blackcurrant sorbet with local almond cake and popsicle. A fresh, sharp, and easily-digested marvel, as Bernard the First liked them—he who made people want to make the trip from Paris to Saulieu just for him! In the restaurant, the faithful are still there to give, under the management of Eric Rousseau (who has a smile as ever-ready as did the great Bernard) and Pascal Abernot, a smiling, efficient and friendly service. And to make the party really perfect, Eric Goettelmann has several ideas in mind and a cellar that allows one, without breaking the bank, to enjoy oneself. This is still a great place…

■ La Tour d'Auxois

Square Alexandre-Dumaine.
Tel. 03 80 64 36 19. Fax 03 80 64 93 10.
www.tourdauxois.com
Closed Feb.
27 rooms: 97–117€. 8 suites: 137€.
Prix fixe: 21€, 26€, 35€, 57€.

A charming hotel opposite the Côte d'Or, overlooking the gastronomic avenue. The rooms are decorated in Provençal shades and there is a garden, terrace and outdoor swimming pool. The bistro is in the cellar and the restaurant is under the careful management of Nancy native Philippe Brun who has "done" Ducasse, the Pré Catelan, the Miramar in Biarritz, Iparlé and Ostapé with Ducasse in the Basque country. Foie gras seasoned with bergamot, frog legs and hazelnut-stuffed gougères and a grapevine-smoked Charolais sirloin steak make a good impression.

● La Borne Impériale   COM

16, rue d'Argentine.
Tel. 03 80 64 19 76. Fax 03 80 64 30 63.
www.borne-impériale.com
Closed Mon. dinner (exc. July–Aug.),
Tue. (exc. July–Aug.), 10 Jan.–10 Feb.
Prix fixe: 18€ (lunch, wine inc.), 22,80€,
28,50€, 13,50€ (child).

The "great house" next door attracts gourmets from all over the world and other chefs have to sweat blood to maintain the reputation of Saulieu, a Mecca of French gastronomy. Jean Berteau, formerly of the Moulin of Mougins and L'Oasis of La

Napoule, seduces with a staunch classical menu: coddled eggs with escargots, roasted pike-perch, braised ham on the bone with creamy morel sauce and a chocolate dessert. Marie-Christine Berteau is a wonderful hostess, the special menus are really good and the seven rooms allow you not to have to take to the road after enjoying the owners' Burgundies.

SAULT

84390 Vaucluse. Paris 722 – Digne 93 – Aix-en-Provence 81 – Avignon 68 – Carpentras 42. ot-sault@axit.fr.
On the heights of Ventoux, a hotel in the most secret Provence. We are in lavender country here, where wheat is also cultivated and nougat, with the good taste of grilled almonds or honey, is made.

▮◣/◯ HOTELS-RESTAURANTS

▪ Hostellerie du Val de Sault ❀⌂
Rte Saint-Trinit.
Tel. 04 90 64 01 41. Fax 04 90 64 12 74.
valdesault@aol.com / www.valdesault.com
Closed beg. Nov.–end Mar.
Rest. closed lunch, Mon., Tue.
11 rooms: 114–127€. 5 suites: 129–185€.
Prix fixe: 39€, 42€, 87€, 14€ (child).

Opposite Ventoux, Yves Gattechaut's hotel makes a choice stopover. The reception given by Ildiko de Hanny, the flower-filled grounds, swimming pool, Jacuzzi and the carefully prepared rooms offer many pleasures. The cuisine of the master of the place sings the praises of the region with scrambled eggs with truffles, ginger- and lemongrass-seasoned scallops, lamb with blackcurrants and lavender and the raspberry or tarragon sorbet.

▪ Le Louvre ⌂
Pl du Marché.
Tel. 04 90 64 08 88. Fax 04 90 64 14 01.
antoine.scibona@wanadoo.fr
www.louvre-provence.com
Closed Jan.
16 rooms: 45–60€. 1 suite: 60€.
Prix fixe: 14€, 19€, 28€, 10€ (child).

Antoine Scibona has restored this hotel, dating from 1920, situated on the Place du Marché. The rooms are simple, painted in cheerful shades of red and yellow, some with a view of the lavender fields and Ventoux. The cuisine prepared from local produce is created by Philippe Anzallo who offers fresh foie gras, Landaise-style salad, roasted sea bream, a lamb charlotte and an iced nougatine with dried fruits. The prices are gentle and the place makes an ideal point of departure for climbing Ventoux.

● Le Soleil 📷SIM
Quartier de la Promenade.
Tel.-Fax 04 90 64 15 93.
ladelloise@wanadoo.fr
Closed Wed. dinner, Thu. lunch, Feb.–end Mar.
Prix fixe: 20€. A la carte: 30€.

Sophie Bailly is in the kitchen of her simple inn. The welcoming terrace gives a restful view of Ventoux and is accompanied by a glass of one of those fine wines that are enjoyed with dishes that are full of the colors of the South. Goat cheese, sundried tomatoes and black olives in an individual pressed terrine, leg of lamb with thyme and mixed peppers, house spelt wheat pasta with cured ham and garlic and the flambéed apple cinnamon feuilleté with chocolate served with whipped cream and raspberry sauce are wonders. So as not to spoil anything, the prices are low.

In Monieux (84390). 5,5 km.

● Les Lavandes 📷COM
Pl Léon-Doux.
Tel. 04 90 64 05 08. Fax 04 90 64 13 99.
Closed Mon., Jan.–mid-Feb.
Prix fixe: 24,50€, 30€, 40€, 11€ (child).
A la carte: 35–40€.

The fine-tasting Côtes-du-Ventoux and Côtes-du-Rhône are still better served here in the shadow of the century-old trees in the large Léon-Doux square and to the sound of its pretty fountain. Alain welcomes you like an old friend and entrusts the appetites of his enchanted customers to Emmanuel Lopez. His apple-marinated salmon, Mediterranean sea bass in puff pastry, rack of lamb caramelized with honey and lavender and his little chocolate cakes give much pleasure. Beautiful dishes and a good atmosphere at a reasonable price.

SAULXURES

67420 Bas-Rhin. Paris 408 – Strasbourg 62 – Saint-Dié 32.

The road climbs towards the peaks, drifts off towards Hautes-Vosges, leaving the Bruche valley on its right and nodding towards the fir trees. You come to the village and its dome bell, the inn tucked away in a corner.

 HOTELS-RESTAURANTS

■ La Belle Vue

36, rue Principale.
Tel. 03 88 97 60 23. Fax 03 88 47 23 71.
labellevue@wanadoo.fr / www.la-belle-vue.com
Closed 1 week at end Mar.,
10 days end July–beg. Aug., 2 weeks Nov.
Rest. closed Tue., Wed.
4 rooms: 84€. 2 suites: 122–163€.
Prix fixe: 19,50€, 23€ (weekdays), 30€, 33€, 36€, 72€.

We like the enthusiasm of Valérie Boulanger, who is at the helm of this happy house. The very smiling reception, the cozy rooms, the wood décor and the generous breakfasts all give pleasure. The cuisine of Marc Koeniguer follows trends with spicy duck tartare with arugula salad, vanilla-seasoned sea bream, slow-cooked venison with blood sauce served with cabbage and the caramelglazed macaron, even if it isn't always easy to forget that imaginative creator, Denis Boulanger, who departed too soon. On the cellar side, a Zotzenberg Grand Cru Tokay labelled Albert Seltz and a Pinot Noir labelled Trimbach make astounding companions to the meal.

SAUMUR

49400 Maine-et-Loire. Paris 322 – Angers 67 – Le Mans 123 – Poitiers 93 – Tours 66.
infos@ot-saumur.fr.

The town of Cadre Noir and sparkling wines has the Loire running past its slate-roofed houses and its château. Every year, a gastronomic festival unites literature and love of wine.

 HOTELS-RESTAURANTS

■ Château de Verrières

53, rue d'Alsace
Tel. 02 41 38 05 15.
contact@château-verrieres.com
Rest. closed lunch (exc. by reserv. for residents).
9 rooms: 120–280€.
Prix fixe: 39€.

This 19th-century house in the middle of an estate of two hectares offers spacious, refined rooms. There is a cozy sitting room and carefully prepared renovation for the residents.

■ Anne d'Anjou

32, square Mayaud
Tel. 02 41 67 30 30
contact@hotel-anneanjou.com
45 rooms: 76–175€.

This 19th-century town house between the Loire and the château provides a choice reception and stylish rooms with modern comforts.

■ Adagio

94, av Général-de-Gaulle
Tel. 02 41 67 45 30.
contact@hoteladagio.com
38 rooms: 61–145€.

On Offard island, this modern hotel with its pastel-colored contemporary rooms looks good.

● Gambetta   **N COM**

12, rue Gambetta
Tel. 02 41 67 66 66
Closed Sat. lunch, Sun. dinner (summer),

Mon., 3 weeks Nov., 2 weeks beg. Mar.
Prix fixe: 16€ (lunch), 24€, 48€.

Between the Combier distillery and the Cavalerie school, this quiet, old-fashioned establishment offers a fine and inexpensive Loire cuisine that gives pride of place to fish of the Loire and local products. Wonderful list of local wines.

● **Auberge Saint-Pierre**
6, pl St-Pierre
Tel. 02 41 51 26 25
Closed Sun., Mon.
Prix fixe: 14€ (lunch), 25€.

Simple and warm, opposite the St. Pierre church, this bistro set in a 15th-century ropemaker's house offers a well-handled and generous market cuisine. Beautiful fireplace.

In Chênehutte-les-Tuffeaux (49350). 8 km, D751.

■ **Le Prieuré**
Tel. 02 41 67 90 14. Fax 02 41 67 92 24.
prieure@grandesetapes.fr / www.prieure.com
33 rooms: 125–280€. 3 suites: 295–330€.
Prix fixe: 23€ (lunch weekdays), 29€ (lunch weekdays), 32€, 49€, 57€, 74€, 99€ (wine inc. dinner). A la carte: 55–75€.

The soul of the place, cleverly equipped with modern comforts, has been retained. This former priory is a quality hotel with an unbeatable view of the Loire while the food, prepared by Jean-Noël Lumineau, has the colors of the region. Eggplant charlotte with strips of marinated salmon, roasted pike-perch with endives and sea urchin, veal filet with pearl onions and ginger and, finally, the rich chocolate cake with raspberry sauce give pleasure. The magnificent Loire wines such as the Coteaux du Layon, Saumurs and other Chinons are excellent accompaniments.

SAUSHEIM see MULHOUSE

27370 Eure. Paris 125 – Rouen 24 – Evreux 40 – Louviers 19.

Gentle, green and peaceful Eure, to be discovered at random on a country walk.

 HOTELS-RESTAURANTS

● **Manoir des Saules**
2, pl Saint-Martin.
Tel. 02 35 87 25 65. Fax 02 35 87 49 39.
manoir.des.saules@wanadoo.fr
www.manoirdessaules.com
Closed Sun. dinner (Oct.–May), Mon., Tue.,
2 weeks Feb., 3 weeks Nov.
6 rooms: 185–195€. 3 suites: 210–245€.
Prix fixe: 58€ (weekdays), 78€, 118€, 25€ (child). A la carte: 80€.

Couples like to spend a romantic weekend in this timbered manor house with charming old-style rooms and pleasant, flower-filled garden. The cuisine of Jean-Paul Monnaie also offers the opportunity to savor prettily turned-out seasonal dishes such as foie gras terrine, John Dory with baby vegetables, Bresse hen and the apple tart mille-feuille.

SAUTEYRARGUES

34270 Hérault. Paris 761 – Montpellier 30 – Marseille 165 – Nice 330 – Nîmes 43.
The art of glassmaking was a specialty of the hinterland of Montpellier under the Ancien Régime. The ovens had gone out but they regained strength and energy ten years ago. What a pleasure to walk along the glassmakers' street!

● RESTAURANTS

● **Lennys**
266, av Louis-Cancel.
Tel. 04 67 55 37 97. Fax 04 67 54 71 82.
restaurant.lennys@wanadoo.fr
Closed Sat. lunch, Sun. dinner, Mon.,
2 weeks Sept.
Prix fixe: 18€ (lunch, weekdays), 39€, 82€.

The young Ludovic Dziewulski, formerly of Reine Sammut's at La Fenière, freely practices the cuisine of Languedoc-Roussillon. Beef consommé with celery root and foie gras powder ravioli, rouget tempura with seasoned mayonnaise and the roasted lamb with a squash crumble are clever dishes that make one want to take up residence. Kaffir lime crème brûlée that reveals an unexpected Zan mousse makes a wonderful ending to the meal.

● **Le Brice**   SIM

Les Rives. Sauteyrargues.
Tel.-Fax 04 67 55 30 73.
Closed Sun. dinner (exc. July–Aug.), Mon.
Prix fixe: 11€ (lunch, wine inc.), 15€, 20€, 22€. A la carte: 35€.

Friendly and good-natured, Fabrice Lerose's modern restaurant decorated in yellow and blue deserves a visit for its charming welcome and the reasonably priced, seasonal menus. Foie gras terrine, trout tossed in olive oil, wood-fire roasted Aveyron leg of lamb and a rich chocolate cake with crème anglaise are pure pleasure. An opportunity to discover the attractive wines of St. Loup.

SAUVETERRE

30150 Gard. Paris 674 – Avignon 15 – Alès 77 – Nîmes 49 – Orange 16 – Pont-Saint-Esprit 36. Gard country, a stone's throw from the Rhône and its beautiful vineyards.

■ | HOTELS

■ **Château de Varenne**

Pl Saint-Jean.
Tel. 04 66 82 59 45. Fax 04 66 82 84 83.
www.chateaudevarenne.com
Closed Jan.
11 rooms: 98–168€. 2 suites: 180–290€.

In grounds of three hectares, the tower of this 18th-century château has a fantastic view over the Alpilles and the Luberon. The rooms and the swimming pool guarantee relaxation and well-being.

SAUVETERRE-DE-COMMINGES

31510 Haute-Garonne. Paris 799 – Bagnères-de-Luchon 35 – Tarbes 69 – Toulouse 105.

St. Bertrand, its stately religious edifices, old houses, Luchon and the Hospice of France route: discover the beautiful Pyrenean region of Comminges.

 | HOTELS-RESTAURANTS

■ **L'Hostellerie des 7 Molles**

Gesset, 3 km s via D9.
Tel. 05 61 88 30 87. Fax 05 61 88 36 42.
contact@hotel7molles.com
www.hotel7molles.com
Closed mid-Feb.–mid-Mar., Tue. (Oct.–May), Wed. (Oct.–May). Rest. closed Tue. (exc. dinner May–Oct.), Wed. (exc. dinner May–Oct.).
16 rooms: 79–142€. 2 suites: 142–187€.
Prix fixe: 29,50€, 39€, 47€.
A la carte: 50–60€.

The energy of the neighboring mountain is also transmitted through the generosity of Gilles Ferran. The sixties building has a certain charm and offers great facilities such as the tennis court and swimming pool but also attractively set-out rooms. His colleague in the kitchen, Christian Deschamps, creates his compositions with seasonal produce. Hot duck foie gras with blueberries, sea bream with slow-roasted garlic and piquillo peppers, roasted pigeon with slow-cooked onions and a Gascon-style apple feuilleté flambéed with Armagnac are terrific.

SAUVETERRE-DE-ROUERGUE

12800 Aveyron. Paris 650 – Rodez 35 – Albi 54 – Villefranche-du-Rouergue 44.
One of the proud walled towns of Rouergue, with its beautiful arcaded square edged with "covers" (called "*chistas*" here) with 14th- and 15th-century ogival arches.

 | HOTELS-RESTAURANTS

● **Le Sénéchal**

Le Bourg.
Tel. 05 65 71 29 00. Fax 05 65 71 29 09.
le.senechal@wanadoo.fr
www.hotelsenechal.com
Closed Jan., Feb.–mid-Mar.

Rest. closed Mon., Tue. lunch, Thu. lunch.
8 rooms: 100–105€. 3 suites: 135–165€.
Prix fixe: 25€, 51€, 70€, 82€, 120€.

In the middle of one of the most beautiful regions of France, Chantal and Michel Truchon welcome gourmet lovers of authenticity to their beautiful 12th-century house. The comfort of the rooms is, on the other hand, very much of our times and is in the luxury category; the hotel also offers a very pleasant heated swimming pool. In the kitchen, Michel Truchon orchestrates with a master's touch the superb market produce that he chooses from the surrounding area. He isn't afraid to put enduring classics on the menu but brings to them a note of innovation that owes everything to his talent. With him, the lobster salad, foie gras served two ways (hot and cold), line-fished Atlantic sea bass, tête de veau, local meats and poultry and a rich soft-centered chocolate cake also take on an air of discovery. In addition, the wines advised by Christophe Salgues never lack personality and the special menus at a considered price allow one to leave with change in one's pocket.

SAUVIGNY-LES-BOIS

58160 Nièvre. Paris 249 – Autun 99 – Decize 26 – Nevers 10.
The softness of the Nivernais in the land of Amognes. Don't miss the 11th-century Romanesque church.

	RESTAURANTS

● Auberge de Sauvigny   ■SIM
27, rue de l'Etang.
Tel. 03 86 37 17 83.
aubergedesauvigny@wanadoo.fr
Closed Mon. dinner, Tue. dinner,
1 week July–Aug.
Prix fixe: 9,60€ (weekday lunch),
15€ (weekdays), 17€, 25€, 8,50€ (child).
A la carte: 23–28€.

Enter a fairy tale world at Cyril Font's: his traditional recipes, reworked in the light of the 21st century, startle and surprise, taking on flavors that are usually foreign to them.

He is having fun and we like that. Several of his special turns: Burgundy-style sliced ham with avocado and tomato parfait, Loire pike-perch filet with beurre blanc and champagne sauce, tuna steak served with julienned vegetables and beef cheek medallions simmered in red wine. For dessert, try the "Route des délices de Bourgogne" (the plate takes the form of a curvy road!), Cassis-poached pear, velvety berry and ginger cream and the pain d'épice with cider butter caramel. Astonishing, isn't it? And delicious! Like the reception given by Nathalie Boulay. What's more, the check is a gift.

SAVERNE

67700 Bas-Rhin. Paris 447 – Strasbourg 39 – Haguenau 37 – Molsheim 28.
info@otsaverne.fr.
It was from the *col* of Saverne that Louis XIV made his famous comment: "What a beautiful garden!" Also in Saverne are the *Tres Tabernae* ("three taverns") of the Romans that affirmed and began Alsace's ancestral vocation of hospitality extended with good humor and modesty.

	HOTELS-RESTAURANTS

■ Hôtel de l'Europe   🏠
7, rue de la Gare.
Tel. 03 88 71 12 07. Fax 03 88 71 11 43.
info@hotel-europe-fr.com
www.hotel-europe-fr.com
Closed 2 weeks Christmas–New Year's.
27 rooms: 60,50–89,50€. 1 suite: 83–123€.

Each room honors a country of the European Union, conferring an original atmosphere on this hotel. Located near the station, its convenience is also an asset.

■ Chez Jean   🏠
"Rosestiebel"
3, rue de la Gare.
Tel. 03 88 91 10 19. Fax 03 88 91 27 45.
chez.jean@wanadoo.fr / www.chez-jean.com
Hotel closed 2 weeks end Dec.–mid-Jan.
Rest. closed Sun. dinner, Mon.,
2 weeks mid-Dec.–beg. Jan.
25 rooms: 61–83€.
Prix fixe: 27€, 47€.

It was a convent and has become a very good town center hotel. There is the kindness of the Harters, the rooms decorated in Alsatian style, warm and practical, Jean-Pierre's reliable cuisine, the S'Rosestiebel *winstub* as well as Chez Jean, which delights connoisseurs with poultry in aspic, soufflé with lobster sauce, the famous tête de veau, classic and the frozen Grand Marnier soufflé. The terrace is welcoming in summer and the wines of Alsace that are on offer don't make the check rocket.

■ Le Clos de la Garenne

88, route du Haut-Barr.
Tel. 03 88 71 20 41. Fax 03 88 02 08 86.
clos.garenne@wanadoo.fr
www.closgarenne.com
Rest. closed Sat. lunch, Tue. dinner,
Wed. dinner, Feb. vac.
14 rooms: 32–86€.
Prix fixe: 16€ (weekday lunch), 36€ (wine inc.), 45€, 55€, 12€ (child). A la carte: 75€.

In the middle of a pretty wooded park, this very recent family house has been tastefully decorated by Virgine and Sébastien Schmitt. The modern, Savoie-style rooms, as pretty as a picture, are an invitation to spend some wonderful moments, particularly at breakfast time. In the restaurant, Sébastien, past master in the art of making tartes flambées, ventures towards a more modern cuisine. Here one enjoys slow-cooked pears with pan-seared foie gras, big langoustines with pumpkin cream, marbled rabbit terrine with beet purée, game in season and the chocolate and mirabelle plum dessert. The wines offered by Manu Minck are outstanding.

■ Villa Katz

42, rue du Général-Leclerc.
Tel. 03 88 71 02 02. Fax 03 88 71 80 30.
tavernekatz@wanadoo.fr
www.tavernekatz.com
6 rooms: 54–100€. 4 suites: 75–100€.
Prix fixe: 16€ (lunch), 24€, 38€, 42€,
55€, 12€ (child).

Suzy Schmitt, who also has the Taverne Katz, watches lovingly over her Jugend-stil "folly", loved in the past by a descendant of emperor William II, the baron of Holland. The rooms are sweet and comfortable and the good traditional dishes of Franck Pellegrino are worth the detour. A slice of foie gras, fish stew, farm-raised duck and a woodruff-seasoned beignet with compote are irresistible.

● Zuem Staeffele

1, rue R.-Poincaré.
Tel.-Fax 03 88 91 63 94.
michel.jaeckel@wanadoo.fr
www.strasnet.com/staessele.htl
Closed Sun. dinner, Wed., Thu. dinner, Christmas–New Year's, 10 days at end July,
2 weeks beg. Aug.
Prix fixe: 21,50€ (weekday lunch), 29,50€ (weekday lunch), 37€, 52€.
A la carte: 55€.

Opposite the Rohan château, the Jaeckels' house is one of the lasting kind. Michel is modest and industrious and is not content just to deliver local recipes: he is continually reinventing them, using market produce, and is never short of ideas. Langoustine ravioli served over sweet-and-sour sauce and a melon and pan-seared foie gras salad set the tone. There is a pan-tossed monkfish and smoked bacon, duck breast with rhubarb and a curry-seasoned lamb medallion with beans, peaches and almonds. An apricot dacquoise with almond milk ice cream and a simmered peach with green tea sauce make gentle endings to the meal. The wines are a passionate celebration of Alsace, without overlooking other regions. Fabienne, who welcomes her guests as if they were old friends, has a communicative smile and there is a general atmosphere of good humor that isn't undermined by the discreet check.

● Château du Haut-Barr

Tel. 03 88 91 17 61. Fax 03 88 91 86 26.
hautbarr@free.fr
www.notrealsace.com/chateau-du-haut-barr
Closed Mon., Thu. dinner, 1 Nov.,
3 weeks Feb.
Prix fixe: 19€, 28,50€, 30,50€,
7€ (child). A la carte: 38€.

Bernard Baudendiestel is the king of the fortified castle from where one can admire the town and the plain of Alsace. His cuisine is like he is—provocative—but the regional products are treated in a personal way and with heart, as demonstrated by his superb goose foie gras, salmon tagliatelli with trout roe, veal kidneys with whole grain mustard and Armagnac-flavored plum ice cream. The fisherman's catch and tartes flambées in the evening in the brasserie section are another reason for making the stop. Pretty summer terrace.

● **Taverne Katz**

80, Grand-Rue.
Tel. 03 88 71 16 56. Fax 03 88 71 85 85.
tavernekatz@wanadoo.fr
www.tavernekatz.com
Closed Christmas.
Prix fixe: 16€ (lunch), 24€, 38€.

This tavern shines out like a Renaissance pearl, with its wood decoration, beamed ceiling, engravings by Hansi and Untereiner, kelsch tableclothes and dishes that pay reverence to the history of Alsace. The menu even enacts a kind of festival: an escargot, white cabbage, goose gizzards and slow-cooked chestnut salad, horseradish-seasoned pork trotter, grumbeerekiechle (potato cakes), nudelstrudel (rolled stuffed noodles) or the marvelous poultry timbale. It all moves and delights with a childlike feel of playfulness. The establishment is run by Suzy Schmitt, with her son Pierre in the restaurant. The desserts, simple and good (a mirabelle plum chaud-froid or streudel), the wines chosen with "nose", the well-pulled Saverne beer: in short, one sees that the place has kept a spirited role as a retro institution. Pleasant summer terrace.

● **Le Carpaccio** SIM

22, Grand-Rue.
Tel. 03 88 02 07 74. Fax 03 88 91 26 43.
Closed Sun. lunch, Thu.
Prix fixe: 16€ (lunch), 40€ (lunch),
8€ (child). A la carte: 35€.

Mimmo de Calabre has made his crimson and oriel establishment into a nice little advertisement for transalpine cuisine. Carpaccio, pizzas, cheese tortelloni, spaghetti carbonara, saltimbocca and frozen chocolate truffle are simply astounding, served in an amusing Neo-Pompeiian décor. Several fine Pouilles or Abruzzes wines do not increase the check (too much). Slow service.

In Ernolsheim-les-Saverne (67330). 6 km route de Bouxwiller.

● **Le Daubenschlag** SIM

87, rue Principale.
Tel. 03 88 70 30 16.
Closed Sat. lunch, Mon., Tue.
A la carte: 28€.

Pierre Sansig, installed in a former barn, delights his guests with his sweet and savory tartes flambées. They also come for the cured ham plate with raw vegetables, fish brochette and the meats (beef sirloin or veal filet). The wines served in pitchers are good value and the prices not brutal.

In Monswiller (67700). 3 km n via D425.

● **Kasbür**

8, rue de Dettwiller.
Tel. 03 88 02 14 20. Fax 03 88 02 14 21.
www.restaurant-kasbur.fr
Closed Sun. dinner, Mon., 2 weeks Jan,
2 weeks Aug.
Prix fixe: 19€ (lunch), 38€, 46€, 55€.

A "kasbür" is a farmer-cheesemaker, an ancestor of the Kieffer family whose profession is depicted in the fresco decorating the outside of this thirties building with updated décor. Yves Kieffer in the kitchen pays homage to the grand cuisine learned in Paris at the Tour d'Argent and at Vézelay with Meneau. He makes the most of the good regional produce by serving it in original, carefully prepared dishes, in rock bottom-priced formula menus. We enjoy the view of the forest and fields of Haut-Barr while tasting escargots served in parsley soup, Atlantic sea bass filet, pike-perch streudel, rack of lamb and the suckling pig. When it is time for dessert, we hesitate between a strawberry and rhubarb dessert with fresh cheese ice cream, cherry confit on old-fashioned shortbread and the caramel ice cream. The considerate welcome and attentive service of Béatrice persuade us that this was the right choice.

In Saint-Jean-Saverne (67700). 4 km n via D115.

■ **Kleiber**
37, Grand-Rue.
Tel. 03 88 91 11 82. Fax 03 88 71 09 64.
info@kleiber-fr.com /www.kleiber-fr.com
Closed 23 Dec.–mid-Jan.
Rest. closed Sat. lunch, Sun. dinner.
16 rooms: 46–70€.
Prix fixe: 10€ (lunch), 20€, 45€, 10€ (child).

Because of its location next to the regional nature park of Vosges, this family hotel is the headquarters of hikers as well as ATB lovers. In the village, it offers well-equipped rooms in the style of Louis-Philippe and a good, unpretentious cuisine under the management of Stéphane Lorentz, who watches father Georges out of the corner of his eye. Beef stew served pressed into the form of a cake, organic salmon on a bed of vegetables with mushroom risotto, apple and pear regional desserts and the tartes flambées at the end of the week are also right on the mark.

SCEAUX-SUR-HUISNE

72160 Sarthe. Paris 175 – Châteaudun 74 – La Ferté-Bernard 11 – Mamers 40 – Le Mans 37.
The Roches château, the 12th- and 16th-century St. Germain church and its beautiful sculptures are worth a detour into the countryside.

| ● | RESTAURANTS |

● **Le Panier Fleuri**   Ⓝ SIM
1, av de Bretagne.
Tel. 02 43 93 40 08. Fax 02 43 93 43 86.
Closed Sun. dinner, Tue. dinner, Wed.,
10 days Jan., 2 weeks Aug.–beg. Sept.
Prix fixe: 14€ (weekdays), 19€, 29,50€,
9€ (child). A la carte: 45–52€.

A country atmosphere in this 19th-century house. The Vanniers have decorated the long restaurant in yellow chiné antique furnishings and serve clever dishes that follow the seasons. Laurent, digging into the drinks cabinet, serves up duck foie gras, pike-perch roasted skinside down with champagne, veal kidneys with whiskey sauce, venison steak with white rum sauce and grapes and a Grand Marnier soufflé that slip down effortlessly. Of course, the "quiet" dishes are not excluded. Attractive wine list, including several foreigners. Wonderful reception by Hélène Vannier.

SCHARRACHBERGHEIM

67310 Bas-Rhin. Paris 470 – Strasbourg 25 – Marlenheim 5 – Molsheim 8 – Saverne 22.
The start of the wine trail: don't miss villages like Traenheim and Le Dompeter or the baptistry of Dalenheim.

| | HOTELS-RESTAURANTS |

● **Lauth et fils**   SIM
63, rue Principale.
Tel. 03 88 50 66 05. Fax 03 88 50 60 76.
www.brasserie-restaurant-lauth.com
Closed 2 weeks Christmas–New Year's,
2 weeks beg. Aug.
Rest. closed lunch, Mon., Tue.
8 rooms: 35–46€. A la carte: 35€.

This country brasserie, as huge as a concert hall, offers regional specialities astutely reworked by the master of the house, Daniel Lauth. Smoked herring in cream, artisanal head cheese terrine and wine aspic, grilled pork shank basted with beer eau-de-vie and frozen soufflé seasoned with Marc de Gewurztraminer exude authenticity. The beer is brewed on site and the wines are from neighboring producers. It is all good, and not expensive. The nine rooms are simple and tranquil. In addition, in the evening there are exquisite tartes flambées made in a wood-burning oven.

SCHILTIGHEIM see STRASBOURG

SCHIRMECK

67130 Bas-Rhin. Paris 410 – Strasbourg 53 – Sélestat 59 – Saint-Dié 39.
cc.hautebruche@wanadoo.fr.
This crossroads town of the Bruche valley opens out onto a secret, thicketed and wooded Vosges. Here are a string of very rural hamlets with smart inns that make clean little stopovers.

 HOTELS-RESTAURANTS

In Natzwiller (67130). 6 km sw via N420 and D130.

■ **Auberge Metzger**
55, rue Principale.
Tel. 03 88 97 02 42. Fax 03 88 97 93 59.
auberge.metzger@wanadoo.fr
www.hotel-aubergemetzger.com
Closed Sun. dinner, Mon., 3 weeks Jan.,
2 weeks end June–10 July.
16 rooms: 54–75€.
Prix fixe: 13€ (weekday lunch), 19€,
24€ (lunch), 37€ (dinner), 55€ (dinner).

The Metzgers give a passionate account of Alsace, and the cuisine of Yves, who honors local produce, follows suit. Here one enjoys house charcuterie, a half-dozen escargots prepared Alsatian style (stuffed with spiced butter and herbs and cooked in local wine), stuffed pike-perch simmered in Riesling, suckling pig loin in a spicy sauce with morels and crêpes flavored with Kirsch. It is billed at a fair price and it all makes one want to spend several nights in the cozy rooms of this Vosges inn with flower-filled balconies. A very charming reception from Corinne and prompt service.

In Les Quelles (67130). 7 km sw via D420, D261, and forest road.

■ **Neuhauser**
La Broque, Schirmeck.
Tel. 03 88 97 06 81. Fax 03 88 97 14 29.
hotelneuhauser@wanadoo.fr
www.hotel-neuhauser.com
Closed 2 weeks Nov., Feb. vac.
10 rooms: 62–79€. 2 suites: 119–152€.
Prix fixe: 20€, 25€, 34€, 45€,
10€ (child). A la carte: 36–45€.

In this family hotel in open countryside, nestled at the top of a hill in the Bruche valley, one can choose between one of the pretty modern rooms or an apartment in one of the three wooden chalets. Pierre and Michel Neuhauser look after their guests with good local produce: duck foie gras with prunes, salmon trout, stuffed rabbit and wild forest berry dessert. Exquisite *eaux-de-vie* that are distilled in-house.

COL DE LA SCHLUCHT

88400 Vosges. Paris 439 – Colmar 37 – Epinal 56 – Gerardmer 16 – Saint-Dié 36.
The border *col* between the Vosges of Lorraine and of Alsace. One follows the ridge road for the pleasure and the vertigo.

 HOTELS-RESTAURANTS

■ **Chalet-Hôtel le Collet**
Restaurant de Montagne
Tel. 03 29 60 09 57. Fax 03 29 60 08 77.
hotcollet@aol.com
www.chalethotel-lecollet.com
Closed beg. Nov.–beg. Dec.
Rest. closed Wed., Thu. lunch.
19 rooms: 62–72€. 6 suites: 92€.
Prix fixe: 16€ (lunch), 24€, 27€,
8€ (child). A la carte: 40€.

After a day's skiing or walking one is welcomed with a comforting smile to the Lapôtres' establishment. The charming hotel has been recently renovated in mountain style and the rooms are very comfortable. In the kitchen, Olivier busies himself preparing attractive, invigorating dishes of quality. Cold sunny side-up egg served on a vegetable salad, salmon steak grilled with almonds, a grilled beef sirloin steak and, for the most gourmet, the chocolate fondue with seasonal fruit is finger-licking good.

SCHNELLENBUHL see SELESTAT
SCIEZ-BONNATRAIT see
THONON-LES-BAINS

SEDAN

08200 Ardennes. Paris 257 – Charleville-
Mézières 24 – Metz 146 – Reims 105.
ot.sedan@wanadoo.fr.
The football team is in great shape and so is the
town, just next to Belgian Ardenne and its forests and with its fortified castle, a sign of its
past as a stronghold town.

	RESTAURANTS

● **Au Bon Vieux Temps** V.COM

1, pl de la Halle / 1, rue de Mulhouse.
Tel. 03 24 29 03 70. Fax 03 24 29 20 27.
restaurant.au.bon.vieux.temps@wanadoo.fr
www.restaurant-aubonvieuxtemps.com
Closed Sun. dinner, Mon., Wed. dinner,
Christmas–New Year's, mid-Feb.–beg. Mar.,
1 week Aug.
Prix fixe: 15,50€, 21,50€, 25€, 36€,
8€ (child). A la carte: 35–50€.

It's like the good old days: the dining room
is pretty with its naïve-style murals, crafted
ceiling and impeccably laid tables. Alain
Leterme is at the helm in the kitchen and
produces a cuisine of the past, reinterpreted
for today's tastes: tuna terrine, pike-perch
with chanterelles, turbot filet grilled over
a wood fire and the poached veal sweetbreads with chanterelles. Just next door, Le
Marmiton opens only at lunchtime. In the
dining room with its rather famous stained
glass windows, the attractive special menus
of the day revolve around smoked herring
with potatoes in oil, Ardenne ham medallion and duck leg confit.

In Bazeilles (08140). 3 km e via N58.

■ **Château de Bazeilles** ❀ 🏚

Chemin Remilly.
Tel. 03 24 27 09 68. Fax 03 24 27 64 20.
contact@chateau-bazeilles.com
www.chateau-bazeilles.com
Rest. closed Sat. lunch, 1 week at end Dec.
20 rooms: 74–92€.
Prix fixe: 25€, 33€, 15€ (child).
A la carte: 45–50€.

These listed 17th-century buildings harbor
a hotel with contemporary interior. Swimming pool, welcoming rooms, grounds and
orangery surround the restaurant where the
kitchen has been taken over by Frantz Hue-
mer. Pressed veal sweetbreads and foie gras,
turbot with tarragon mousseline, lamb saddle roasted with spices and honey and the
chocolate croquettes with poached pear are
appreciated by gourmets of the region.

In Bazeilles.

● **Auberge du Port** COM

Rte de Rémilly.
Tel. 03 24 27 13 89. Fax 03 24 29 35 58.
auberge-du-port@wanadoo.fr
auberge-du-port.fr
Closed Fri. (exc. dinner Apr.–Oct.), Sat. lunch,
Sun. dinner, Christmas–New Year's vac.,
3 weeks Aug.
Prix fixe: 17,50€ (weekday dinner), 23,50€,
32€, 36€, 45€, 9€ (child). A la carte: 60€.

The special menu selections of Jean-Paul
Vetter are a gift. They allow one to discover, without breaking the bank, the cuisine of this native of Vosges. Vetter, who
worked in Denmark before setting up in
this inn on the banks of the Meuse, honors the Ardennes with a cured ham plate, a
generous plate of wild boar, pigeon breast
salad with pears, Atlantic sea bass with
grilled almonds, venison medallion with
pepper and spices and a chocolate fondant
with crème anglaise.

SEEBACH see **WISSEMBOURG**

SEES

61500 Orne. Paris 186 – Alençon 22 –
Argentan 24 – Domfront 66 –
Mortagne-au-Perche 33.
office-tourisme-sees@wanadoo.fr.
This ancient Roman fortification, which became
a cathedral town, is worth the trip for its old
buildings with their air of nobility and its 12th-
century cathedral.

	HOTELS-RESTAURANTS

● **Le Dauphin** COM

31, pl des Anciennes-Halles.
Tel. 02 33 80 80 70. Fax 02 33 80 80 79.

dauphinsees@wanadoo.fr
Closed Sun. dinner (off season), Mon. (off
season), 1 week Nov., 2 weeks Jan.
6 rooms: 58–85€. 1 suite: 110€.
Prix fixe: 21€, 28€, 41€, 56€.
A la carte: 60€.

How beautiful Normandy is when handled by Roger Bellier, at his place opposite the marketplace. Chitterling sausage with langoustines, roasted salmon, blood sausage, monkfish, pike-perch, Camembert and cider butter stew, pigeon prepared two ways, veal sweetbreads with ceps and the country tart seduce effortlessly. The setting is pleasant, the service smiling and the prices reasonable. Old-style rooms in pastel shades.

SEGOS see AIRE-SUR-L'ADOUR
SEGURET see VAISON-LA-ROMAINE

SEIGNOSSE

40510 Landes. Paris 747 – Dax 32 –
Biarritz 36 – Soustons 11.
www.tourisme-seignosse.com.
The forested part of Landes, a step away from
the sea.

| ■ | HOTELS |

■ La Villa de l'Etang Blanc
Rte de l'Etang-Blanc.
Tel. 05 58 72 80 15.
www.hotel-restaurant-charme-hossegor.com
Closed beg. Jan.–end Mar. Rest. closed Sun.
dinner, Mon.
10 rooms: 50–120€.
Prix fixe: 25€ (weekdays). A la carte: 40€.

This little hotel next to a remote lake, reached through golf course and forest, seems like the back of beyond. Patrick and Janine Nadal have made it into a little island of charm with colorful small rooms, glass-filled dining room and garden. Chef Olivier Valleau, student of Maximin and Amat, whom we know from the Maison du Fleuve at Camblanes, offers an inspirational cuisine based on the seasons and markets. Goat cheese and avocado

mousse, spaghetti with jumbo shrimp and garlic, Atlantic sea bass with tapenade, braised veal shank and the cherry feuilleté make divine surprises.

SELESTAT

67600 Bas-Rhin. Paris 440 – Colmar 22 –
Strasbourg 51 – Mulhouse 63.
accueil@selesta-tourisme.com.
At the crossroads of the rapid Colmar-Strasbourg route, Sélestat is famous for its humanist library, devotional bells and beautiful Renaissance houses as well as for the wine routes of Vosges and the Rhine.

| ■◢ | HOTELS-RESTAURANTS |

● Abbaye de la Pommeraie
8, bd du Maréchal-Foch.
Tel. 03 88 92 07 84. Fax 03 88 92 08 71.
pommeraie@relaischateaux.com
www.relaischateau.com/pommeraie.
www.pommeraie.fr
Rest. closed Sun. dinner, Mon. lunch.
12 rooms: 141–246€. 2 suites: 291–316€.
Prix fixe: 51€, 90,50€. A la carte: 90€.

Christiane and Pascal Funaro run a good-natured Relais & Châteaux. The relaxed atmosphere, smiling service, rooms of sure taste and the pleasant garden are all a joy while the cuisine of Daniel Stein is not to be outdone. In the restaurant, Le Prieuré, beautiful woodwork and perfectly straight tables match the noble, clean food. Crab mille-feuille with slow-cooked vegetables, lobster with market vegetables, venison filet with apricot chutney and eggplant semolina and an Isaphan-themed ice cream sandwich with mascarpone, basil and raspberry make delicious feasts. Sensible checks and attractive Alsace wines complete the picture (see also the winstub S'Apfelstuebel).

■ Auberge des Alliés
39, rue des Chevaliers.
Tel. 03 88 92 09 34 / 03 88 92 28 00.
Fax 03 88 92 12 88.
auberge.allies@wanadoo.fr
www.auberge-des-allies.com

Hotel closed 24 Dec.–2 Jan.
Rest. closed Sun. dinner, Mon., Christmas–
beg. Jan., end June–mid-July.
18 rooms: 48–65€.
Prix fixe: 21€, 26€, 8€ (child).

This old town center inn offers rooms with every comfort in a tasteful Alsatian atmosphere. The reception is courteous and the cuisine of Roland Roesch simple and good. Escargots, goose foie gras, roasted pike-perch with Alsatian red wine sauce and prunes, served in an old-style winstub setting, are generous and not excessively charged.

■ Vaillant

Pl de la République.
Tel. 03 88 92 09 46. Fax 03 88 82 95 01.
hotel-vaillant@wanadoo.fr
www.hotel-vaillant.com
47 rooms: 65–95€.
Prix fixe: 15€, 24€, 29€, 34€,
7,50€ (child).

Claire Faller has gradually redone this modern building, with its tastefully laid out rooms. In the restaurant, creamed chestnuts with morels, paupiette of pike-perch with green vegetables, beef sirloin steak with slow-cooked shallots and a Pinot Gris sauce and an iced Kirsch parfait are eaten with pleasure. This year, a brasserie has been created in the bar.

● S'Apfelstuebel   SIM

At the Abbaye de la Pommeraie, 8, bd du Maréchal-Foch.
Tel. 03 88 92 07 84. Fax 03 88 92 08 71.
pommeraie@relaischateaux.com
www.relaischateaux.com/pommeraie
Prix fixe: 26€ (weekday lunch), 35€ (lunch, wine inc.), 51€ (wine inc.).

This library-style "*stub*", decorated on a theme of apples, is as pretty as a picture. Audrey Meyer chooses the wine to accompany in fine manner the dishes concocted by Daniel Stein: slow-cooked vegetable terrine with smoked salmon, ginger-seasoned emperor fish served on a bed of fresh spinach, veal medallion with eggplant, tomato and basil mille-feuille and

a strawberry Melba with Tagada strawberry bonbons.

● Au Bon Pichet   SIM

10, pl du Marché-aux-Choux.
Tel.-Fax 03 88 82 96 65.
Closed Sun. dinner, Mon. dinner,
2 weeks end Aug.–Sept.
Prix fixe: 15,80€ (lunch), 25€ (dinner).
A la carte: 35–55€.

The old hospital of the town, situated on the edge of the Ill, houses a traditional restaurant equipped with a recently renovated rotisserie room. Without making the check rocket, one can enjoy house terrine, red tuna tartare, a solid boneless rib steak, magnificent veal kidney roasted in its fat and the seasonal fruit tart cooked with heart by the ruddy-faced Roland Barthel, a former butcher who knows his meat like a true expert.

● La Vieille Tour   SIM

8, rue de la Jauge.
Tel. 03 88 92 15 02. Fax 03 88 92 19 42.
vieille.tour@wanadoo.fr / www.vieille-tour.com
Closed Mon.
Prix fixe: 11€ (weekday lunch), 19€, 33€,
44€, 55€.

Samy and Nicolas Rhulmann are giving an uncomplicated new life to this typical house flanked by an old tower. They have redone the restaurant, conserving the traditional style and cooking side by side, interpreting regional dishes with charm. House half-duck, half-goose foie gras terrine with Black Sureau sirop, pike-perch poached in red wine with frog legs, lamb medallions in pastilla with diced mushrooms simmered in cream and the roasted Victoria pineapple with caramel sauce and a house financier with honey ice cream make a good impression. Diligent service and prices that are not excessive.

In Rathsamhausen (67600). 5 km e via D21 and D209.

■ Les Prés d'Ondine

5, route de Baldenheim.
Tel. 03 88 58 04 60. Fax 03 88 58 04 61.
message@presdondine.com

www.presdondine.com
Closed mid-Jan.–mid-Feb.
Rest. closed Sun. dinner, Wed.
8 rooms: 65–105€. 4 suites: 105–135€.
Prix fixe: 32€ (wine inc.).

A stay in this pretty inn beside the Ill is stamped "relaxation". Stéphane Dalibert has decked it out with all the attractions: sweet, cozy rooms, sitting room/library, fitness center, hammam, Jacuzzi. You need to take the time to taste the good food concocted by the master of the house. Alsatian-style salad, trout or pike-perch filet, traditional choucroute and the kouglof pain perdu are extremely well conceived.

In Schnellenbuhl (67600). 8 km via D159 and D424.

■ Auberge de l'Illwald

Locale known as de Schnellenbuhl.
Tel. 03 88 85 35 40. Fax 03 88 85 39 18.
contact@illwald.fr / www.illwald.fr
Closed 24 Dec.–10 Jan.,
1 week at end June–mid-July.
Rest. closed Tue., Wed.
9 rooms: 65–110€.
Prix fixe: 10€ (weekday lunch), 30€ (Sat., Sun.), 8,50€ (child). A la carte: 36€.

Brigitte and Christian Schwartz have very quickly taken the measure of their smart hotel with its Alsatian charm. Eight additional rooms have been created in the two local houses made of pink sandstone. As for the winstub, it has become a landmark in the region. In the packed restaurant with its fresco by Edgar Mahler, one makes quick work of head cheese and wine aspic terrine, pike-perch simmered in red wine, rabbit leg with star anise seasoning and licorice-flavored strawberries. The slate menu board changes every day but the classics of Alsace are faithful to their post.

SELLES-SAINT-DENIS

41300 Loir-et-Cher. Paris 195 – Bourges 71 – Orléans 71 – Romorantin-Lanthenay 16 – Vierzon 26.
A rustic crossroads bordering the Sologne, in the country of Jacques Coeur.

HOTELS-RESTAURANTS

● Auberge du Cheval Blanc   V.COM

Pl du Mail.
Tel. 02 54 96 36 36. Fax 02 54 96 13 96.
auberge@chevalblanc-sologne.com
www.chevalblanc-sologne.com
Closed Sun. dinner (off season),
Tue. dinner, Wed., 1 week Christmas–New Year's, 3 weeks Feb., 1 week Aug.
7 rooms: 49,50–77€. 1 suite: 120€.
Prix fixe: 25,50€, 44€, 52€.

This pretty timbered house in the heart of the village is eye-catching. Through the door one glimpses the patio onto which are beautifully set-out rooms. Chrystèle Poyau has a kind word for her clients while Ludovic, an excellent pâtissier who trained at the Templiers in Bézards then at Chez Robin in Bracieux, skillfully cooks up pan-seared foie gras with simmered green lentils, frog legs, roasted wild duck and an orange and Grand Marnier soufflé. Lunch on the terrace on fine days and attractive vintage wines.

SEMBLANÇAY

37360 Indre-et-Loire. Paris 250 – Blois 76 – Le Mans 70 -Tours 16.
The softness of the Loire valley countryside a stone's throw from Tours and the Val.

HOTELS-RESTAURANTS

■ La Mère Hamard

Pl de l'Eglise.
Tel. 02 47 56 62 04. Fax 02 47 56 53 61.
www.lamerehamard.com
Closed Sun. dinner, Mon., Tue. lunch, mid-Feb.–mid-Mar.
11 rooms: 63–90€.
Prix fixe: 19€ (weekday lunch), 26€, 28€, 31€, 10€ (child).

One can hear the chimes of the church bells from the charming redecorated rooms of this smart establishment, the inn of the Pégués, with Monique on reception and Patrick in the kitchen. Without confining themselves to recipes of the region, they work with local producers and farmers. Individual cassolette pots with scrambled eggs and morels, foie gras, lobster and Paimpol white beans in a cocotte and a nougatine mille-feuille with apples served Tatin-style are invitations to take up residence. The "love at first sight" wines from the Loire are gifts.

SENLIS

60300 Oise. Paris 53 – Compiègne 33 – Meaux 40 – Chantilly 10.
off.tourisme-senlis@wanadoo.fr.
A delightful medieval town celebrated by Daniel Boulanger (*Fouette Cocher*) and immortalized by du Parvis.

● | RESTAURANTS

● Le Bourgeois Gentillhomme [COM]
3, pl de la Halle.
Tel. 03 44 53 13 22. Fax 03 44 53 15 11.
bourgeois-gentillhomme.com
Closed Sat. lunch, Sun., Mon.,
end July–end Aug.
Prix fixe: 25€ (weekday lunch), 38,80€, 70€, 14€ (child).

In Philippe Bourgeois' restaurant, taste and sensuality blend happily. In the refined pink and white dining room or the 12th-century vaulted cellar, one enjoys elaborately crafted and tested dishes. A soft boiled egg served with morel purée, Atlantic sea bass filet roasted skin-side down and served with buttered leeks, breast of guinea hen served with creamed morels and a quince and honey sabayon enchant.

SENS

89100 Yonne. Paris 117 –
Montargis 51 – Fontainebleau 55 –
Auxerre 60.
otsi.sens@wanadoo.fr.
The town's treasure of the St. Etienne cathedral and the museum in the synod palace make it worth the stopover.

 | HOTELS-RESTAURANTS

■ Paris et Poste
97, rue de la République.
Tel. 03 86 65 17 43. Fax 03 86 64 48 45.
www.hotel-paris-poste.com
Rest. closed Sun. dinner, Mon.,
2 weeks beg. Jan., 2 weeks Aug.
30 rooms: 70–150€. 6 suites: 125–150€.
Prix fixe: 23€, 36€, 65€, 13€ (child).

This coaching inn now has its third generation of Godards: Odile on reception and Philippe in the kitchen. The food on offer in the Postillon, a chic brasserie, and in Senon, the elegant restaurant, deserve attention. Seasonally based, it renews itself with ease: mixed salad with ceps and marinated scallops, duck wings, slow-cooked pork cheeks served with simmered trotter and ear and a chocolate marquise make a good impression. The cellar of the large Burgundies is tempting, the check reasonable, the rooms cozy and the breakfasts fantastic.

● La Madeleine
1, rue d'Alsace-Lorraine.
Tel. 03 86 65 09 31. Fax 03 86 95 37 41.
lamadeleine3@wanadoo.fr
www.restaurant-lamadeleine.fr
Closed Sun., Mon., Tue. lunch, Christmas–
New Year's vac., 3 weeks Aug.
Prix fixe: 45€ (weekday lunch), 55€, 68€, 75€, 98€. A la carte: 110€.

Patrick Gauthier loves his work. The names of his dishes are enough to get the imagination and taste buds working: grill-seared duck foie gras "exalted" by saffron-seasoned sautéed apples, Atlantic sea bass filets braised in Chablis with a touch of cream, spit- or oven-roasted squab, "whichever way you like it", Garriguette strawberries with rhubarb compote and almond milk ice cream. Add to that the smiles and advice of Béatrice Gauthier and you will be, as we were, seduced by this house and its cared-for setting.

● Le Crieur de Vin

1, rue d'Alsace-Lorraine.
Tel. 03 86 65 92 80. Fax 03 86 95 37 41.
www.restaurant-lamadeleine.fr
Closed Sun., Mon., Tue. lunch,
2 weeks Christmas–New Year's,
2 weeks June, 2 weeks Aug.
Prix fixe: 22,50€ (lunch), 32–38€, 48€.

A good time is to be had in the annex of La Madeleine. In the atmosphere of a relaxed bistro, one enjoys food washed down with small local wines: the house asparagus dish, sole filet in puff pastry, veal kidneys with rosehips and the chocolate mousseline.

SERRE-CHEVALIER

05220 Hautes-Alpes. Paris 678 – Briançon 7 – Gap 95 – Grenoble 110 – Col du Lautaret 21.
A beautiful resort where one can ski under the sun of the southern Alps.

● RESTAURANTS

● L'Antidote

In Le Monêtier-les-Bains, Serre-Chevallier 1500, at the hotel Alliey.
Tel. 04 92 44 09 74.
Closed Sun., Mon., beg. Sept.–beg. Dec., end Apr.–beg. June.
Prix fixe: 45€, 56€, 62€, 68€.

Being Marc Veyrat's second-in-command for eight and a half years, in Annecy and Megeve, leaves its mark. Stéphane Froidevaux is continually stirring juices, picking mountain herbs and imagining "country soup with the flavors of a forest walk" – glazed with mushrooms—monkfish brochettes with almonds, rack of lamb cooked in larch tree bark and a black truffle cooked in a little bread crust with spelt wheat ice cream and the truffle-seasoned country soup. Poet and countryman, this native of Montbéliard originating from Briançonnais has very quickly become the darling of Serre-Chevalier. His gentle follies, channeled by the proactive Léa, who also worked with Veyrat in the restaurant, give joy to the curious gourmet.

SERVIERS-ET-LABAUME see UZES

SESSENHEIM

67770 Bas-Rhin. Paris 504 – Strasbourg 32 – Haguenau 17 – Wissembourg 44.
The memory of Goethe's love for Frédérique Brion, the daughter of a local pastor, lights up the history of the village. People come here from the other side of the Rhine in a romantic pilgrimage.

● RESTAURANTS

● Au boeuf

1, rue de l'Eglise.
Tel. 03 88 86 97 14. Fax 03 88 86 04 62.
contact@auberge-au-boeuf.com
www.auberge-au-boeuf.com
Closed Mon., Tue.
Prix fixe: 28€ (lunch, weekdays), 43€, 56€, 12€ (child).

This is a picture postcard inn, right out of a drawing by Hansi, and the atmosphere is very friendly. The cuisine of Yannick Germain dusts off classics of the region. Stewed scallop and jumbo shrimp with lobster jus, Kochersberg escargots in mushroom shells, Atlantic sea bass in puff pastry with tomatoes and fennel, Doriath farm duck cooked three times in fine sour cherry sauce and strawberry and lavender dessert with Bourbon vanilla ice cream are top-quality. There is also the visit to the Goethe museum which is part of the house. The cellar is rich in local wines. Adorable reception from Christiane and Claudine.

In Dengolsheim (67770).

● A l'Agneau   COM

11, route de Strasbourg.
Tel. 03 88 86 95 55. Fax 03 88 86 04 43.
Closed Mon., Tue., 2 weeks Feb.
Prix fixe: 26€ (lunch). A la carte: 40–50€.

The Wendlings have based their establishment on friendship. Gérard, in the kitchen, delights his customers with his asparagus and morel mushroom in puff pastry, John Dory filet roasted with sour cherries and the veal escalope with Madeira- and truffle-seasoned foie gras sauce. For dessert, one has a party with the brown sugar-caramelized cherry blinis with acacia milk. Carine gives an extremely kind welcome although the prices are unfortunately less attractive. Lovely summer terrace.

SETE

34200 Hérault. Paris 789 – Montpellier 33 – Lodève 63 – Béziers 56.
tourisme@villesete.fr.
The view of Mont St. Clair and the chapel of Notre-Dame-de-Salette, the old port, the maritime cemetery and the one in which Georges Brassens is at eternal rest: these are the reasons to stop in this southern point of France.

 HOTELS-RESTAURANTS

■ Grand Hôtel et Quai 17
17, quai Maréchal-de-Lattre-de-Tassigny.
Tel. 04 67 74 71 77. Fax 04 67 74 29 27.
www.legrandhotelsete.com
Hotel closed 1 week beg. Jan.
Rest. closed Sat. lunch, Sun.,
2 weeks beg. Jan.
42 rooms: 70–120€. 1 suite: 190–220€.
Prix fixe: 19€ (lunch), 25€, 45€,
12€ (child).

This century-old building is well situated on the banks of the royal canal. It has large rooms that were designed to make one's stay as pleasant as possible. The architecture, with its metal and glass framework, is interesting, and one can enjoy the cool patio when the sun is at its height. The newly-arrived Jean-Pascal Amet offers a finely-made cep tartine with chestnut broth, turbot roasted in an oyster and artichoke emulsion, half pigeon with pan-seared foie gras and the banana and chocolate sauce mille-feuille. The reception and the service are affable and the prices remain moderate. Watch this space.

● L'Amerik Club
Promenade Maréchal Leclerc.
Môle Saint-Louis.
Tel. 04 67 53 02 37. Fax 04 67 51 48 98.
Closed Oct.–Apr.

Prix fixe: 22€ (weekday lunch),
37€ (dinner). A la carte: 45€.

The Pourcel brothers—them again!—have taken over this grill, ice-cream parlor and cocktail bar at the foot of the Vauban fort. At the helm in the kitchen is one of their best students, Antoine Perray, who has also worked at Ducasse's, who performs "happening" feats with a cuisine that is half Languedocan, half Italian. Local fish soup, octopus carpaccio, octopus pie, a pizza-like tart with artichokes, skate wing over semolina, gnocchi made with chicken oysters and diced foie gras with cep jus and a fresh fruit milk shake for dessert make first-class suppers. Attractive wines from the great South.

● La Palangrotte
1, rampe Paul-Valéry, quai de la Marine.
Tel. 04 67 74 80 35. Fax 04 67 74 97 20.
Closed Sun. dinner, Mon. (exc. July–Aug.).
Prix fixe: 14€, 22€, 29€, 32€, 10€ (child).

Alain Gemignani fishes his ideas from the port. Fresh fish and shellfish of the day are quickly prepared in the kitchen: octopus salad with potatoes and aïoli, monkfish with aïoli and vegetables, grilled Mediterranean sea bass with sweet-and-sour orange sauce and pork loin medallions with creamy chanterelle sauce for carnivores. On the dessert side, the excellent Paris-Brest, a choux pastry ring with almonds and butter cream, makes the grade. Fine wines from Languedoc-Roussillon.

SEVENANS see BELFORT

SEVRIER

74320 Haute-Savoie. Paris 541 – Annecy 6 – Albertville 40 – Megève 55.
sevrier@wanadoo.fr.
Facing Annecy, right on the lake.

 HOTELS-RESTAURANTS

■ L'Auberge du Chuguet
823, rte d'Albertville.
Tel. 04 50 19 07 35 (rest.)

04 50 19 03 69 (hotel). Fax 04 50 52 49 42.
achuguet@aol.com / www.hotel-de-chuguet.com
Rest. closed Sat. lunch, Sun. dinner, Mon.
25 rooms: 54–76€. 4 suites: 93–98€.
Prix fixe: 19€ (weekday lunch), 25€, 30€,
38€ (dinner).

You can't, as is well known, judge a book
by its cover. Go through the door of this
large modern chalet and you will discover
a quiet interior. The rooms in shades of
pastel are pleasantly set out and in summer breakfast is taken on the terrace.
The dishes created by Bruno Tenailleau
at L'Arpège are "chic": the shiitake and
slow-cooked shallot bruschetta, Mediterranean sea bass filet in a grain crust
with seaweed-seasoned mustard sauce,
soft-cooked veal cutlet with truffles and
licorice and pineapple ravioli with ginger yogurt cream and coconut foam. The
special menus are well conceived and the
reception friendly.

SEWEN

68290 Haut-Rhin. Paris 452 – Epinal 79 –
Mulhouse 39 – Belfort 32 – Colmar 66.
This area of south Vosges is where the Upper
Rhine joins the Territory of Belfort. In the hol-
low of valleys, this is the green massif.

HOTELS-RESTAURANTS

■ **Les Vosges**
38, Grand-Rue.
Tel. 03 89 82 00 43. Fax 03 89 82 08 33.
info@hoteldesvosges.com
www.hoteldesvosges.com
Closed Sun. dinner, Wed., mid-Dec.–end Dec.,
1 week Jan.
16 rooms: 51–60€.
Prix fixe: 16€ (weekday lunch), 21€, 25€,
33€, 9€ (child).

The advantage with Jean-Michel Kieffer is
that one knows exactly what one is going
to find: a warm welcome, cozy rooms, a
pleasant environment with the river running through the garden and the terrace
to idle on. And then there is the cuisine of
a chef trained in the school of Bocuse and

Crocodile: simmered cabbage with foie
gras, pan-tossed langoustines and wild
mushrooms, chanterelle-stuffed quail and
a frozen kouglof are extremely well made
and reasonably priced.

SIERCK-LES-BAINS

57480 Moselle. Paris 355 – Metz 45 – Luxembourg 38 – Thionville 17 – Trier 51.
Near Luxembourg, not far from the Sarre and
the valley of the Moselle, this rustic area shows
off its old farms and medieval ruins.

HOTELS-RESTAURANTS

In Manderen (57480). 4 km e via N153 and
D64.

■ **Relais du Château**
Mensberg
15, rue du Château.
Tel. 03 82 83 73 16.
www.relais-mensberg.com
Closed end Dec.–end Jan.
Rest. closed Mon. lunch, Tue.
13 rooms: 41–48€.
Prix fixe: 13€ (weekday lunch), 18€, 26€,
34€, 50€, 8,50€ (child).

This old farm at the foot of Malbrouck
château offers the comfort of its neat little
rooms, a friendly reception and a likable
local cuisine in a clean rustic setting.

In Montenach (57480). 3,5 km se via D956.

● **Auberge de la Klauss**
1, route Kirschnaumen.
Tel. 03 82 83 72 38. Fax 03 82 83 73 00.
la-klauss@wanadoo.fr
www.auberge-de-la-klauss.com
Closed Mon., Christmas–New Year's vac.
Prix fixe: 15€, 20€, 29€, 34€, 50€,
16€ (child).

Fréderic Keff has taken charge of the
house established by his father Charles
in this old family farm of 1869. The latter
looks after the manufacturing lab—notably of the foie gras offered for sale to take
away—as well as the selection of wines.
Here, in the atmosphere of a farm/inn, one
tastes dishes reworked to today's tastes:

house pâté and charcuterie, terrines, ham, wild boar ham, fresh-caught trout with almonds, wild boar or venison medallions according to that day's local hunt and the classic frozen mirabelle plum soufflé. The cellar is wonderful, the prices not exaggerated and the house preserves available for sale in the neighboring shop.

SIERENTZ

68510 Haut-Rhin. Paris 483 – Mulhouse 16 – Altkirch 19 – Bâle 17 – Colmar 52.
Bordering Sundgau, this southern area of Alsace is near Switzerland and the Rhine and is a crossroads town of likable proportions.

 HOTELS-RESTAURANTS

● **Auberge Saint-Laurent**
1, rue de la Fontaine.
Tel. 03 89 81 52 81. Fax 03 89 81 67 08.
www.auberge-saintlaurent.fr
Closed 2 weeks Mar., 2 weeks Aug.
Rest. closed Mon., Tue.
10 rooms: 80–100€.
Prix fixe: 39€, 48€, 50€, 70€,
18€ (child). A la carte: 90€.

The whole Arbeit family works for the well-being of their guests in this former coaching inn. The charming receptionist, Anne, who is also the sommelier, is helped by her daughter Marie, while father Marco takes up his position in the kitchen. This technician, who is both joyful and rigorous in his methods, cooks up lively, fresh, light and even inventive dishes that emerge out of local tradition: duck foie gras with cabbage confiture, pike-perch roasted skinside down with slow-cooked and fried leeks, frog legs tossed in parsley, garlic and butter, served with parmesan risotto, pigeon with a smoked bacon cabbage fricassée and a frozen sour cherry soufflé. It all feeds the wonderful dreams that one has in the rustic-modern rooms decorated on countryside themes. Very fine cellar and cared-for surroundings.

SIEWILLER see SARRE-UNION

SIGNY-L'ABBAYE

08460 Ardennes. Paris 218 – Charleville-Mézières 29 – Hirson 40 – Sedan 51.
The road to upper Ardenne goes through this likable village between small valleys and forests.

 HOTELS-RESTAURANTS

■ **Auberge de l'Abbaye**
2, pl Aristide-Briand.
Tel. 03 24 52 81 27. Fax 03 24 53 71 72.
Hotel closed mid-Jan.–beg. Mar.
Rest. closed Tue. dinner, Wed. lunch
9 rooms: 37–56€.
Prix fixe: 14€ (weekdays), 18€, 26€, 36€,
8,50€ (child). A la carte: 30–35€.

Nine simple rooms make this old 17th-century coaching inn a cheerful place to stay. The cooking is reliable: a little flan with nettles in cream, grilled halibut filet, meats direct from the organic farm of the restaurant's owners (rump steak or sautéed lamb) and a meringue-topped rhubarb clafoutis are well made and kindly charged.

■ **Le Gibergeon**
7, rue de l'Eglise.
Tel.-Fax 03 24 52 80 90.
Closed Sun. (off season), 1 week Feb.,
1 week Aug.
6 rooms: 30–45€. 2 suites: 45€.
Prix fixe: 11,50€, 19€, 29€, 7€ (child).
A la carte: 32€.

Daniel Durmois changes his menu according to the market: frog legs sautéed in parsley, garlic and butter, escargot-stuffed tomatoes, grilled lamb chops seasoned with herbes de Provence and the crème brûlée effortlessly seduce. The reception from Patricia, the cozy rooms and the sensible prices all do the same.

SIGOLSHEIM see COLMAR

SIRAN

34210 Hérault. Paris 805 –
Carcassonne 35 – Lézignan-Corbières 19 –
Narbonne 36 – Perpignan 95.

Between Corbières and Minervois, the rural magic of a beautiful village. Visit the chapel of Centeilles.

 HOTELS-RESTAURANTS

■ Le Château de Siran

Av du Château.
Tel. 04 68 91 55 98. Fax 04 68 91 48 34.
contact@chateau-de-siran.com
www.chateau-de-siran.com
Closed mid-Jan.–mid-Feb.
Rest. closed Mon.
11 rooms: 65–130€. 1 suite: 170–250€.
Prix fixe: 17,50€ (weekday lunch), 28€, 7,50€ (child). A la carte: 40€.

There have been changes in this 15th-century building adjoining the village fortifications, with its vaulted reception rooms, charming bedrooms and terrace overlooking the vineyards. It was the Villa d'Eléis and is now the Château de Siran. Martine and Alain Maire have taken over the establishment, leaving the reins of the kitchen in the hands of Grégory, formerly of Veyrat's and Ducasse's. Honey-marinated salmon carpaccio with a small glass of Muscat de Saint Jean, monkfish and scallop blanquette with spinach, roasted foie gras-stuffed duck breast with tapenade cream and a pear and chocolate sabayon, accompanied by Minervois and regional wines advised by Alain, have panache.

SISTERON

04200 Alpes de Haute-Provence. Paris 710 – Digne-les-Bains 39 – Barcelonnette 101 – Gap 52.
office.de.tourisme-sisteron@wanadoo.fr.
This gastronomic capital of Provençal high country marries lamb and nougat, while its citadel, keep and rock of Baume are reflected in the blue waters of the Durance.

 HOTELS-RESTAURANTS

■ Grand Hôtel du Cours

Pl de l'église.
Tel. 04 92 61 04 51.
hotelducours@wanadoo.fr
Hotel closed beg. Nov.–beg. Mar.
Rest. closed beg. Dec.–end Feb.
48 rooms: 56–80€.
Prix fixe: 22€, 28€.

The Michels have run this traditional hotel for a hundred years. Françoise, third of that name, has bought the restaurant part, keeping good chef Jérôme Jullien, who practices Provençal cookery as if it were second nature. In the huge restaurant with its glass bay windows and French doors, one enjoys a solid cuisine created from quality products and offered in generous menus. A salad of pieds-paquets (a local variety meat dish) with sauce gribiche, pollock with anchovy cream, rabbit with olives and polenta, Lou Pastre lamb with olives and pepper and the dessert buffet make a good impression. The Château la Gardette des coteaux de Pierrevert barely increases the check.

● Les Becs Fins   COM

16, rue Saunerie.
Tel. 04 92 61 12 04. Fax 04 92 61 28 33.
becsfins@aol.com / www.becsfins.free.fr
Closed Sun. dinner (exc. July–Aug.),
Mon. (exc. July–Aug.), end Nov.–mid-Dec.,
10 days June.
Prix fixe: 24€, 34€, 43€, 55€.
A la carte: 45–55€.

Jean-Raphaël Videau renews, without excess, the regional repertoire of this restaurant (with terrace) in the pedestrian town center. Lamb terrine with thyme flower and mint, sea bream with white wine sauce, duck breast with apples in a caramel and raspberry sauce and pain d'épice and cinnamon ice cream are extremely honest, as are the wines. Sensible set menus and a more costly à la carte. Fine local chocolates and candies.

SOCHAUX see MONTBELIARD

SOREZE

81540 Tarn. Paris 744 – Toulouse 59 –
Carcassonne 44 – Castelnaudary 27 –
Castres 27.
otsi-soreze@wanadoo.fr.
A beautiful village bordering Lauragais and
its unusual abbey, founded by Pepin the Brief
in 754.

 HOTELS-RESTAURANTS

■ **Hôtellerie de l'Abbaye**
18, rue Lacordaire.
Tel. 05 63 74 44 80. Fax 05 63 74 44 89.
contact@hotelfp-soreze.com
www.hotelfp-soreze.com
Rest. closed Tue.
52 rooms: 90–110€. 8 suites: 145€.
Prix fixe: 20€ (lunch), 26€, 34€,
10€ (child). A la carte: 43€.

You get historical frissons in this 17th-cen-
tury monument where the Benedictines
established this abbey school, which still
houses a school with an excellent reputation. One sleeps in the Pavillon des Hôtes or
in the rather more chic Logis des Pères, in
one of the former monks' cells and forgets
one's cares by sitting down in the old refec-
tories over which the imaginative Stéphane
Cornu reigns. There is a parade of dishes:
pressed foie gras terrine, poached lobster
ravioli, leg of lamb and potato casserole
and his variation on the piña colada. A walk
in the six hectares of grounds is conducive
to both digestion and meditation.

● **Le Tournesol**
26, rue du Maquis.
Tel.-Fax 05 63 74 11 10.
letournesol@hotmail.fr
Closed Mon. dinner, Tue., Jan.
Prix fixe: 24€, 45€, 16€ (child).

The fine and inventive traditional cuisine
served in this splendid 17th-century rustic setting is a pleasant discovery. Three
dining rooms and a smoking room with
two monumental fireplaces form a beautiful backdrop for exhibitions of paintings,
sculptures and ceramics by artists of the
region and also for high-quality feasts.
Brousse (local young ewe's cheese) lasagne, duck breast with pears and a coffee-
flavored gratin are well conceived.

SORGES

24420 Dordogne. Paris 467 – Périgueux 21
– Brantôme 24 – Limoges 76 – Thiviers 15.
This crossroads town between black and white
Perigord is a fine place to gain an understanding
of truffles. The local museum is a must-see.

 HOTELS-RESTAURANTS

■ **Auberge de la Truffe**
N21.
Tel. 05 53 05 02 05. Fax 05 53 05 39 27.
contact@auberge-de-la-truffe.com
www.auberge-de-la-truffe.com
Rest. closed Sun. dinner, mid-Nov.–end Mar.
19 rooms: 51–61€. 4 suites: 90–100€.
Prix fixe: 18€, 23–32€, 42–47€, 100€
(truffle menu), 11€ (child). A la carte: 60€.

Jacqueline Leymarie gives a dynamic welcome to her beautiful modern inn while
Pierre Corre, for his part, seeks to share
his passion for truffles by organizing culinary courses starring the black diamond.
He initiates people to the mysteries of this
curious local tuber by having them taste
dishes that bring out its best. Scrambled
eggs with truffles, sole with ceps, duck
breast stuffed with truffles and hot foie
gras and a hot Grand Marnier soufflé are
washed down with fine wines suggested
by Jean-Marc Caillau, while Sophie Bastide
watches over the room with good humor.
The rooms in warm colors of red, yellow
and orange, the garden and swimming
pool, all make one want to stay over.

LES SORINIERES see **NANTES**

SOSPEL

06380 Alpes-Maritimes. Paris 972 – Menton
18 – Nice 41 – Vintimille 28.
An old village perched up en route to the col de
Tende gives a foretaste of Piémont.

HOTELS-RESTAURANTS

■ Hôtel des Etrangers
& Bel Aqua

Bd de Verdun.
Tel. 04 93 04 00 09. Fax 04 93 04 12 31.
sospel@sospel.net / www.sospel.net
Closed Nov.–beg. Mar.
Rest. closed Tue., Wed. lunch.
30 rooms: 65–115€.
Prix fixe: 20,50€, 32€, 10€ (child).

Every room of the hotel is unique, carefully decorated in Provençal taste. Swimming pool, Jacuzzi, fitness room and hammam are at hand for relaxation, without forgetting the solarium rocked by the rhythm of the river. This establishment, which has been in the same family for many years, is a haven of peace, bathed in the sun and in good living. The Bel Aqua restaurant is in the hands of son Gilles Domerego, a student of Maximin and Robuchon. With great discretion and finesse, he prepares a tomato and basil compote, fish and meats of excellent quality and a puffed raspberry gratin that bowl one over with their authentic tone. Bottles of beautiful local wine are of course on offer, as well as wines from more distant vineyards.

SOUFFLENHEIM

67620 Bas-Rhin. Paris 494 – Strasbourg 48 – Haguenau 14 – Baden-Baden 29.
Bordering the large forest of Haguenau, this is the capital of colored pottery.

● RESTAURANTS

● Au Boeuf
48, Grand-Rue.
Tel. 03 88 86 72 79.
Closed Christmas, New Year's.
Prix fixe: 11€ (weekday lunch), 19€, 25€.

This is a welcoming 17th-century inn converted into a modern, comfortable hotel with terrace and smart dining room. One comes for the gentle atmosphere, well-pulled beers, local vintages and traditional local food.

In Auenheim (67480). 4 km e via N63.

● Au Tisonnier
8, rte de Soufflenheim.
Tel. 03 88 86 32 25. Fax 03 88 53 05 83.
Closed Wed., Thu., mid-Jan.–beg. Feb.
Prix fixe: 8€ (weekday lunch).
A la carte: 40€.

Julien Schmitt-Andt learned his craft at Buerehiesel then worked in the great establishments of Paris and the Basque coast before returning to the kitchens of this family winstub with a modern feel. Head cheese and wine aspic terrine, scallop risotto, cod filet in a pastry crust with mussel sauce, boneless rib steak with coarse-ground black pepper and a quince parfait keep their promises. The service is professionnal and the prices friendly.

SOUILLAC

46200 Lot. Paris 516 – Brive-la-Gaillarde 39 – Sarlat 29 – Cahors 67.
souillac@wanadoo.fr.
This crossroads town on the N20 is the real departure point for the rural routes of Lot.

 HOTELS-RESTAURANTS

■ Les Granges Vieilles
Rte de Sarlat.
Tel. 05 65 37 80 92. Fax 05 65 37 08 18.
www.lesgrangesvieilles.com
Closed mid-Nov.–mid-Mar. Rest. closed lunch
11 rooms: 65–91€.
Prix fixe: 23€, 28€, 35€, 40€,
8€ (child).

The Cayre family watch over the destiny of this neo-Gothic manor house, provided with large functional rooms and a heated swimming pool. They prepares nice little dishes such as crayfish tails in salad, sturgeon filet, grilled lamb saddle and walnut cake with ice cream, which has the taste of authenticity.

■ Grand Hôtel

1, allée Verninac.
Tel. 05 65 32 78 30.
www.grandhotel-souillac.com
Closed beg. Nov.–Mar.
40 rooms: 40–80€.
Prix fixe: 19–27€.

This huge old and central establishment with eclectic charm offers cared-for rooms as well as a local cuisine served on the veranda or in the garden beneath the plane trees.

■ Le Quercy

1, rue Recège.
Tel. 05 67 37 83 56.
25 rooms: 30–65€.

Away from the center with its swimming pool, garden and pleasant rooms, this hotel offers the best price-quality ratio in town.

● Le Redouillé

28, av de Toulouse.
Tel. 05 65 37 87 25.
Closed Sun. dinner (off season), Mon., Jan., 2 weeks beg. Mar.
Prix fixe: 17€ (weekday lunch), 36€, 58€.

Sonia and Stéphane Delombre run this serious restaurant with a smile; it is somewhat out of town but is worth a small detour. The neo-Provençal décor and the terrace are charming, as is the cuisine of young Hossein Chojdal. Brioche with foie gras, simmered pike-perch with Chinese cabbage, simmered veal sweetbreads and duck confit pastilla make a good impression. Finally, keep room for the frozen walnut or local plum soufflé.

SOULTZ see GUEBWILLER

SOULTZMATT

68750 Haut-Rhin. Paris 471 – Colmar 21 – Mulhouse 34 – Guebwiller 11.
With wine, water, forest and roads climbing up to the roads of Hautes-Vosges, Soultzmatt has it all.

HOTELS-RESTAURANTS

■ Vallée Noble

Id Finkwaeldélé.
Tel. 03 89 47 65 65. Fax 03 89 47 65 04.
www.valleenoble.com
Rest. closed Sat. lunch (off season), Sun. dinner (off season).
50 rooms: 59–170€.
Prix fixe: 16€ (vegetarian), 26€ (*terroir* menu), 32€, 40€, 10€ (child).

The Betters run this beautiful establishment with courtesy and efficiency. The rooms are comfortable and the grounds and swimming pool add to the stay. The classic menu is attractively priced.

SOUSCEYRAC

46190 Lot. Paris 544 – Aurillac 47 – Cahors 94 – Figeac 41 – Mauriac 72.
ot-sousc@club-internet.fr.
The Quercy of wonders! Between Causse and the chestnut grove, this is a region of hilly timberland, dark thicket and secret pathways.

 HOTELS-RESTAURANTS

■ Au Déjeuner de Sousceyrac

Pl des Condamines.
Tel. 05 65 33 00 56. Fax 05 65 33 04 37.
Closed Sun. dinner (off season), Mon. (off season), Jan.
10 rooms: 40–60€.
Prix fixe: 15€, 25€, 35€, 45€, 10€ (child).

Beware, you need to book, because this guesthouse is very popular, a modern hotel with delightful rooms that also has finely turned-out food from chef and owner Patrick Lagnès, accompanied by a Cahors wine wisely imposed by the master of the house and cheerfully explained by Eliane Philippe. Pan-seared foie gras and shellfish, cod filet with chestnut cream, farm-raised veal loin with ceps and a pear and almond cream tart marry, through the seasons, flavors of the region and inventive touches.

● Auberge de la Grange aux Oies

2, rue du Gâtinais.
Tel. 02 54 88 40 08.
Rest. closed Mon. dinner, Tue., Wed., 2 weeks
end Dec.–beg. Jan., 1 week June.
Prix fixe: 23€ (weekday lunch), 39€, 51€.

This cute Sologne inn pays homage to its
village with its service in local costume,
carefully chosen knickknacks and antique
furniture. The cuisine follows suit, promoting the Sologne region: game in season and local lake fish. Fine list of Loire
and Berry wines.

STEIGE see VILLE

STENAY

55700 Meuse. Paris 243 – Charleville-
Mézières 57 – Sedan 35 – Verdun 46.
The European museum of beer here attracts
a small group of devotees in a brasserie renovated in a style pleasing to the eye.

◨ HOTELS-RESTAURANTS

■ Le Commerce

16, rue Aristide-Briand.
Tel. 03 29 80 30 62. Fax 03 29 80 61 77.
Gilpin.patrice@wanadoo.fr
Closed beg. Jan.–mid-Jan. Rest. closed Fri.
dinner (off season), Sat. lunch (off season),
Sun. dinner (off season).
16 rooms: 40–65€.
Prix fixe: 11,90€ (weekday lunch), 13,50€
(weekday lunch), 16€, 25,90€,
8,50€ (child). A la carte: 38–48€.

Nothing has changed at Patrice Gilpin's
and so much the better. We love the atmosphere of this house with lovely rooms.
The beer flows freely, accompanying
dishes of character: a quail terrine made
with local beer, scallop and shellfish stew
with white beer, John Dory with Leffe beer,
duck breast with mirabelle plums and
white beer and a white beer sabayon on a
bed of raspberries. The Beer Museum is a
stone's throw away.

STIRING-WENDEL see FORBACH

STRASBOURG

67000 Bas-Rhin. Paris 490 – Bâle 147 –
Karlsruhe 81 – Luxembourg 219.
otsr@strasbourg.com.
The European beauty who has refurbished her
parliament, rebuilt her hotels, cosseted her university site (may Goethe watch over his statue)
and stood her ground on the banks of the Rhine
while continually looking after her green spaces,
pedestrian streets, the flowing Ill and beautiful houses. French and German, playing with its
dual culture and playing the cosmopolitan with
charm, offering up its old districts to be visited, from the cathedral to Petite France but
also the very "Prussian" Place de la République, Strasbourg is obviously nothing like other
French towns. This exotic charm is reflected in
its varied restaurants, its *winstubs* and its star
eating places. Several pages in a guide is not
enough to exhaust its secrets.

■ HOTELS

■ Régent Petite-France

5, rue des Moulins.
Tel. 03 88 76 43 43. Fax 03 88 76 43 76.
rpf@regent-hotels.com / www.regent-hotel.com
Rest. closed Mon.
56 rooms: 235–305€. 16 suites: 465–485€.
Prix fixe: 32€, 37€. A la carte: 60€.

Behind its 300-year-old facade, this hotel
situated in former ice houses at the heart
of Petite France houses extremely well-
equipped rooms and suites in a contemporary décor. The view onto the rushing
flow of the Ill is superb and calm guaranteed in this pedestrian zone. Champagne
bar and Le Pont Tournant restaurant (see
Restaurants). Excellent service and valet
parking.

■ Régent Contades

8, av de la Liberté.
Tel. 03 88 15 05 05. Fax 03 88 15 05 15.
rc@regent-hotels.com / www.regent-hotels.com
45 rooms: 175–225€. 2 suites: 295–420€.
Half board: 293–261€.

Near the Ill, in the old imperial quarter, this 19th-century building is a hotel of charm. The spacious rooms are intelligently set out, the Belle Epoque breakfast room superb and it is a pleasure to drink in the Regency bar. Sauna and Jacuzzi for relaxation.

■ Hilton International

Av Herrenschmidt.
Tel. 03 88 37 10 10. Fax 03 88 36 83 27.
contact@hilton-strasbourg.com
www.hilton-strasbourg.com/
238 rooms: 150–325€.
5 suites: 330–1100€.
Prix fixe: 27–32€ (le jardin Tivoli),
28–34€ (la Table du Chef).

This modern caravanserai offers spacious rooms that have been carefully equipped. Two bars, the Churchill and the Bugatti, and two restaurants, the Jardin du Tivoli and the Table du Chef, make it one of the most popular places in town.

■ Holiday Inn

20, pl de Bordeaux.
Tel. 03 88 37 80 00. Fax 03 88 37 07 04.
histrasbourg@alliance-hospitality.com
www.holidayinn-strasbourg.com
Rest. closed Sat. lunch, Sun. lunch.
170 rooms: 100–250€. 1 suite: 560–660€.
Prix fixe: 22€ (weekday lunch)
26€ (weekday lunch) 9€ (child).

A stone's throw from the Parliament and the Palais de la Musique, this great modern "thing" offers huge, well-equipped rooms. Guests have free access to the health club (swimming pool, sauna, hammam) and the business center. Laid-back and jazzy atmosphere in the lounge bar. In the La Louisiane restaurant there is a choice between local dishes and food with a more Mediterranean accent (red sea bream on a bed of oven-crisped Provençal vegetables, lamb chops with a southern-style vegetable flan and tiramisu).

■ Sofitel

Pl Saint-Pierre-le-Jeune.
Tel. 03 88 15 49 10. Fax 03 88 15 49 99.
h0568@accor-hotels.com

100 rooms: 195–225€.
24 suites: 305–350€.

In the middle of the town, this "historic" Sofitel—it was the first link in the chain—offers cozy rooms, some with a view of the St. Pierre-le-Jeune church. Le Thomann is a desirable meeting place and the house restaurant is supervised by Antoine Westermann (see Restaurants: Inside).

■ Beaucour

5, rue des Bouchers.
Tel. 03 88 76 72 00. Fax 03 88 76 72 60.
info@hotel-beaucour.com
www.hotel-beaucour.com
42 rooms: 66–135€. 7 suites: 163–281€.

This hotel composed of five small old houses gives a home-away-from-home welcome. The wonderful service, the carefully prepared rooms, the delicious breakfasts and the reasonable prices instantly touch the hearts of Guy-Pierre Baumann's guests.

■ L'Europe

38, rue du Fossé-des-Tanneurs.
Tel. 03 88 32 17 88. Fax 03 88 75 65 45.
info@hotel-europe.com / www.hotel-europe.com
Closed 1 week at end Dec.
51 rooms: 62–135€. 9 suites: 140–185€.

It is best to book to secure a room in this hotel next to the cathedral in the pedestrian area. It combines calm and comfort. Attended parking in the basement.

■ Hôtel de France

20, rue du Jeu-des-Enfants.
Tel. 03 88 32 37 12. Fax 03 88 22 48 08.
www.hotel-de-france.com
66 rooms: 95€. 10 suites: 130€.

Good value rooms in the center of town is the secret of this hotel's success, in addition to the charming reception and the attention given to comfort.

■ Grand-Hôtel Concorde

12, pl de la Gare.
Tel. 03 88 52 84 84. Fax 03 88 52 84 00.
le.grand.hotel@wanadoo.fr

www.le-grand-hotel.com
83 rooms: 98€. 2 suites: 149€.

An elegant glass lift serves the rooms of this sixties hotel which has old-fashioned charm but every modern comfort. Varied breakfasts.

■ Maison Rouge

4, rue des Francs-Bourgeois.
Tel. 03 88 32 08 60. Fax 03 88 22 43 73.
info@maison-rouge.com
www.maison-rouge.com
140 rooms: 83–175€. 2 suites: 275–320€.

Every detail of this hotel has been chosen to create an original, harmonious whole: the red facade, the coordinated furniture and paintings and the high-tech facilities are in confident good taste. Both reception and service are perfect.

■ Mercure-Centre

25, rue Thomann.
Tel. 03 90 22 70 70. Fax 03 90 22 70 71.
h1106@accor-hotels.com / www.mercure.com
98 rooms: 99–145€.

In the very center of town, this practical chain hotel combines comfort, professionalism and reasonable prices. Parking.

■ Monopole-Métropole

16, rue Kuhn.
Tel. 03 88 14 39 14. Fax 03 88 32 82 55.
infos@bw-monopole.com
www.bestwestern-monopole.com
90 rooms: 85–134€. 5 suites: 150€.

This hotel near the station is hidden away in a quiet street. More than 100 years old, it offers rooms with old-style or contemporary décor, some decorated by local artists. The sitting rooms house works of the cultural heritage of Alsace. Wonderful reception.

■ Novotel-Centre Halles

4, quai Kléber.
Tel. 03 88 21 50 50. Fax 03 88 21 50 51.
h0439@accor.com / www.novotel.com
98 rooms: 109–159€.
Prix fixe: 22,50€, 31€ (wine inc.), 8€ (child).

This Novotel could serve as a model for its professional welcome, its efficient rooms in white and beige and its Côté Jardin restaurant which serves a well-made traditional cuisine (salads, grilled meats and daily specials).

■ Le Dragon

2, rue de l'Ecarlate.
Tel. 03 88 35 79 80. Fax 03 88 25 78 95.
hotel@dragon.fr / www.dragon.fr
30 rooms: 69–116€. 2 suites: 149€.

In this 17th-century building near the banks of the Ill, Jean Zimmer watches over his designer rooms in shades of gray. Fine view over the roofs of the Jean Sturm school and the top of St. Thomas church. Pretty paved courtyard. The lobby and sitting room hold various exhibitions.

■ Cardinal de Rohan

17-19, rue du Maroquin.
Tel. 03 88 32 85 11. Fax 03 88 75 65 37.
info@hotel-rohan.com / www.hotel-rohan.com
36 rooms: 70–135€.

This charming hotel at the center of the town in the pedestrian zone is the epitome of elegance. Furnished with antiques, the comfortable rooms each have their own personality.

■ Cathédrale

12, pl de la Cathédrale.
Tel. 03 88 22 12 12 / 08 00 00 00 84.
Fax 03 88 23 28 00.
reserv@hotel-cathedrale.fr
www.hotel-cathedrale.fr
47 rooms: 75–160€.

Opposite the cathedral and the Kammerzell house, this building from the Renaissance period is a charming hotel run by Alain Cézard. The reception is pleasant, the rooms attractively set out and in the building next-door five luxuriously equipped apartments allow one to stay the week.

■ Diana-Dauphine

30, rue de la Première-Armée.
Tel. 03 88 36 26 61. Fax 03 88 35 50 07.

www.hotel-diana-dauphine.com
Closed Christmas–New Year's.
45 rooms: 70–135€.

This hotel of discreet charm is well situated. The historical town is a few minutes walk or tram ride away. Cozy rooms and an elegant sitting room have been redecorated in contemporary style. Private parking.

■ Gutenberg

31, rue des Serruriers.
Tel. 03 88 32 17 15. Fax 03 88 75 76 67.
hotel.gutenberg@wanadoo.fr
www.hotel-gutenberg.com
42 rooms: 65–98€.

This house in the center of the old district is worth seeing for its walls dating from 1745 and its elegant flowered facade with crafted balcony. The rooms, some of which look onto the cathedral and the statue of Gutenberg, are furnished in the old style. Sensible prices.

■ Hannong

15, rue du 22-Novembre.
Tel. 03 88 32 16 22. Fax 03 88 22 63 87.
info@hotel-hannong.com
www.hotel-hannong.com
Closed 1 week Jan.
72 rooms: 76–182€.

In the very heart of the town center, on the site of the Hannong pottery works, this charming establishment marries tradition and modernity. It is decorated like a town house, from the lobby, with its elegant wooden staircase, to its contemporary rooms, with original parquet floors and wall fabrics. The sweetest have a sloping ceiling.

■ Hôtel des Princes

33, rue Geiler.
Tel. 03 88 61 55 19. Fax 03 88 41 10 92.
hoteldesprinces@aol.com
www.hotel-princes.com
Closed 10 days beg. Jan., 3 weeks Aug.
43 rooms: 98–125€.

The European Parliament and the Orangerie park are very close to this hotel which, in the heart of the business area, offers large, quiet rooms.

■ Villa d'Est

12, rue Jacques-Kablé.
Tel. 03 88 15 06 06. Fax 03 88 15 06 16.
res.villa@cieldenuit.com
www.hotel-villa-est.com
48 rooms: 105–125€.

This hotel with direct access from the motorway is nonetheless situated in a quiet area. The Palais des Congrès and European Parliament are close by. Some rooms are classic, others more contemporary but all offer modern comforts. Fitness center with hammam, sauna, balneotherapy and exercise bikes.

■ Relais Mercure Saint-Jean

3, rue du Maire-Kuss.
Tel. 03 88 32 80 80. Fax 03 88 23 05 39.
h1813@accor-hotels.com / www.mercure.com
52 rooms: 59–119€.

This hotel is close to the most popular tourist spots of the town. The rooms equipped in functional style and well sound proofed are equipped with high-speed soundproofed WiFi.

■ Villa Novarina

11, rue Westercamp.
Tel. 03 90 41 18 28. Fax 03 90 41 49 91.
www.villanovarina.com
5 rooms: 75–150€.

Christine and Jacques Claus have opened this charming guesthouse not far from the Orangerie park. Swimming pool, garden, relaxation, Internet and delicious breakfasts figure on the agenda.

■ Couvent du Franciscain

18, rue du Faubourg-de-Pierre.
Tel. 03 88 32 93 93. Fax 03 88 75 68 46.
info@hotel-franciscain.com
www.hotel-franciscain.com
Closed Christmas–New Year's.
43 rooms: 39–70€.

In the 14th century, the town of Strasbourg gave the Franciscans the management of this hotel-hospice where poor travelers could find bed and board. Since 1525, private individuals have been owners of the place. Clean rooms and breakfasts eaten under the gaze of gourmet Franciscans in the fresco by André Wenger. Sensible prices and private parking.

■ L'Elégant

Rue du Général-Conrad.
Tel. 03 88 60 02 85. Fax 03 88 61 50 81.
bateaulelegant@free.fr
www.bateau-lelegant.com
Closed Sun., Mon.
39 rooms: 45–60€.
Prix fixe: 12€ (weekday lunch), 27€, 35€, 6€ (child). A la carte: 40€.

This thirties boat with its upper and lower deck cabins is another way of spending a good night in the town. It is moored in the ramparts dock which it sometimes leaves to make river crossings. It serves a good market cuisine (escargot lasagne, monkfish in seafood broth and pain d'épice crème brûlée).

■ Hôtel Suisse

2-4, rue de la Râpe.
Tel. 03 88 35 22 11. Fax 03 88 25 74 23.
info@hotel-suisse.com / www.hotel-suisse.com
25 rooms: 45–99€.

Next to the cathedral and the banks of the Ill, this old hotel offers wood-trimmed rooms equipped with Internet connection. Beautiful terrace and delicious breakfasts.

■ Les Trois Roses

7, rue de Zurich.
Tel. 03 88 36 56 95. Fax 03 88 35 06 14.
www.hotel3roses-strasbourg.com
32 rooms: 47–86€.

An Austrian atmosphere in the rooms, warm wood and soft duvets make a cozy ensemble. The breakfast buffet is copious, the sauna relaxing and the river banks nearby.

In Entzheim (67960). 12 km via A35 (exit 8), D400 and D392.

■ Père Benoît

"Steinkeller"
34, rte de Strasbourg.
Tel. 03 88 68 98 00. Fax 03 88 68 64 56.
hotel.perebenoit@wanadoo.fr
Closed Christmas–New Year's, 3 weeks Aug.
Rest. closed Sat. lunch, Sun., Mon. lunch.
60 rooms: 54–72€.
Prix fixe: 19€, 24€, 6,50€ (child).

Three kilometers from the airport, this 17th-century farm makes a friendly stopover. Welcomed by Denis Massé, one sits down to revive energies with duck foie gras, pork cheeks with mustard, pear gratin with almond milk ice cream and wood fire-flambéed tarts, all washed down with beers or local wines. The prices are sensible and the rooms comfortable.

In Ostwald (67540). 7 km via A35 (exit 7) and route de Schirmeck.

■ Château de l'Ile

4, quai Heydt.
Tel. 03 88 66 85 00. Fax 03 88 66 85 49.
ile@grandesetapes.fr / www.chateau-ile.com
60 rooms: 190€. 2 suites: 715€.
Prix fixe: 30€ (lunch), 35€ (lunch, wine inc.), 49€, 67€, 16€ (child).
A la carte: 35–40€.

This neo-Gothic house hidden away in the middle of wooded grounds bordering the Ill makes a beautiful stopover. The rooms are decorated in an antique style and are well equipped. Spa, sauna, hammam, Jacuzzi, swimming pool and terrace allow moments of relaxation. Yannick Mattern, the new chef, brings finesse to a carefully crafted rustic cuisine in the winstub and more sophisticated fare in the refined restaurant (wild boar terrine with foie gras and chestnuts, roasted pikeperch and variations on the fig).

In Plobsheim (67115). 12 km s via route d'Offenburg.

■ Le Kempferhof

351, rte du Moulin.
Tel. 03 88 98 72 72 / 03 88 98 71 82.
Fax 03 88 98 74 76.

info@golf-kempferhof.com
www.golfkempferhof.com
Closed 22 Dec.–9 Jan.
Rest. closed Sun. dinner.
29 rooms: 150–200€. 4 suites: 200–230€.
Prix fixe: 15€, 32€, 38€, 42€.
A la carte: 45€.

Legendary cinematic scenes serve as décor in the designer, contemporary rooms of this very beautiful 19th-century manor house surrounded by an eighteen-hole golf course. The cuisine of Sébastien Hahn, the new chef, also deserves to be filmed. Crab mille-feuille, roasted monkfish served on a bed of slow-cooked leeks, poultry breast with Vin Jaune sauce and a fresh fromage blanc tiramisu are supervised by boss Guillaume Robuchon, who worked at Au Crocodile.

● | RESTAURANTS

● Au Crocodile

10, rue de l'Outre.
Tel. 03 88 32 13 02. Fax 03 88 75 72 01.
info@au-crocodile.com / www.au-crocodile.com
Closed Sun., Mon., Christmas–New Year's,
1 week beg. Jan., beg. July–beg. Aug.
Prix fixe: 56€ (lunch), 85€ (dinner),
113€ (dinner), 127€ (dinner).
A la carte: 120–130€.

Every year, Emile and Monique Jung dedicate themselves to a historic and gourmet celebration. In 2006, it was Mozart, on the occasion of the 250th anniversary of his birth, with a menu that paid him homage. Oxtail soup with bone marrow flan, duck liver schnitzel with raspberry vinaigrette, horseradish and sherry sauce, swordfish in anchovy spread with olive oil and preserved lemons, grilled young toro steak with artichokes and beans with a smoked butter emulsion interpret, in concrete manner, *The Magic Flute* or *Don Juan*. For dessert, a cloud of whipped mascarpone on a disk of white cake soaked in mocha and rum and a summer fruit dessert with spice sorbet and a lemon cumin elixir are reminders that the composer of *Cosi Fan Tutte* was a great lover of sweet things. An exercise in style? Yes, of course, proving that Emile Jung can do everything, mastering every trick with expertise and awareness. As, for example, in that starter inspired by Heston Blumenthal, the young genius of Bray-on-Thames: a nitrogen-frozen flake of mint that cleans the palate in the blink of an eye. But one can also come here to taste the dishes drawn from the region, which make splendid creations. There is, for example, the sublime cold sweet pea soup with a poached egg, grilled duck liver seasoned with rhubarb and served with a citrus ginger jus, pike-perch and carp in Pinot Noir sauce and carrot purée with julienned leeks and a slab of pork trotters with suckling pig chops and Tarbais beans, served in the style of Luxembourg. Add to this a choice of desserts, which have made a huge leap over the past few years, such as a crispy coffee-flavored confection with a Tahitian vanilla cream and coffee ice cream. The wines, suggested by the expert Gilbert Mestrallet, are the perfect accompaniment. The service, orchestrated by the baton of the indispensable Monique Jung, is really one of the best in France. This is a great establishment.

● Le Buerehiesel

4, parc de l'Orangerie.
Tel. 03 88 45 56 65. Fax 03 88 61 32 00.
westermann@buerehiesel.fr
www.buerehiesel.com
Closed Sun., Mon., 1–20 Jan., 3 weeks Aug.
Prix fixe: 35€ (lunch), 65€, 108€.
A la carte: 90€.

Antoine Westermann has abandoned Strasbourg for Paris (where he runs Drouant and Mon Vieil Ami), leaving his restaurant and the kitchens under the direction of his son Eric, charging him with giving back soul and meaning to the great establishment in the Orangerie park. At the time of publication, it is is too early to predict the future. Eric has changed the style of the house, lowering the prices, selling off the silver, getting rid of some of the grandeur as well as some of the staff. The new Buerehiesel is here. One still has the vinicultural advice of the wise Jean-Marc

Zimmermann, the charm of the place—an old Molsheim farm—with its modern, loft-style room and a cuisine that, through lightened versions of classics, highlights quality produce. There is no reason not to savor veal sweetbreads with parsley and garlic served with chanterelles, pâté wrapped in veal and farm-raised pork with white poultry livers, schniederspaetle (local stuffed dumplings) with frog legs and chervil, a whole Quiberon whiting cooked in butter, garlic and parsley, served with sautéed baby vegetables and the roasted Pyrénées lamb chops and roast with simmered artichokes and peppers and Tarbais beans. And then the desserts, which have always been a strong suit of the establishment: crispy coffee and salted-butter caramel dessert served with coffee ice cream, caramelized beer brioche with roasted pear ice cream. It is too soon to judge or evaluate the establishment. Let us give one plate to begin—and wait to see what gives.

● **Maison Kammerzell** 🏠 V.COM

16, pl de la Cathédrale.
Tel. 03 88 32 42 14. Fax 03 88 23 03 92.
info@maison-kammerzell.com
www.maison-kammerzell.com
Hotel closed Feb. vac. Rest. closed Christmas.
9 rooms: 69–117€.
Prix fixe: 29,50€, 37€, 45€, 8€ (child).
A la carte: 42–52€.

La Maison Kammerzell dates from 1427 (although the present flamboyant architecture is from 1589) and is one of the most beautiful buildings in Strasbourg. Each of its rooms has its history and it is thanks to Guy-Pierre Baumann that it has become a gourmet hotel. He has entrusted the kitchens to faithful Hubert Lépine. Duck foie gras with Gewurztraminer aspic, borsch with tiny diced beets, roasted monkfish filet with summer savory-seasoned young fava beans, wild boar belly stuffed with foie gras and truffles, slow-cooked potatoes and pumpkin purée and a honey milk chocolate mousse with a brownie and chocolate ice cream renew the house repertoire—choucroute remaining the signature of the place. The cellar is full of good intentions, essentially local ones. The almost-secret nine rooms of the Baumann hotel, which are reached by a 16th-century spiral staircase, give a privileged view of the cathedral bells.

● **Maison des Tanneurs** 🏠 V.COM

42, rue du Bain-aux-Plantes.
Tel. 03 88 32 79 70. Fax 03 88 22 17 26.
maison.des.tanneurs@wanadoo.fr
www.maison-des-tanneurs.com
Closed Sun., Mon., 3 weeks Jan.
Prix fixe: 24€ (lunch), 28€ (lunch).
A la carte: 55€.

François Leenhardt attentively looks after this beautiful 16th-century building. The chefs René Breitel and Roland Laemmer always follow tradition with escargots, onion tart, trout with almonds, guinea hen with a green peppercorn stuffing, classic choucroute, roasted ham and a quince tart. One isn't bowled over, true, but there are also no unpleasant surprises.

● **L'Estaminet Schloegel** 🅿○ V.COM

19, rue de la Krutenau.
Tel.-Fax 03 88 36 21 98.
Closed Sat. lunch, Sun., Mon. lunch, Christmas–New Year's, 3 weeks Aug.
Prix fixe: 25€ (lunch). A la carte: 60€.

Himber & Humbert are the new duo heading this former faux café that has become a truly good restaurant. Philippe Himber, formerly at the Western Grill, is the boss. Zealous Stéphane Humbert until recently worked at Pralong 2000 in Courchevel. Their partnership gives rise to professionalism incarnate in a fresh, intimate little restaurant. This is a fine, precise cuisine without embellishments but closer to the truth of the produce. For example, crab salad with fines herbes and grated celery root in mayonnaise with an audacious mango sauce, roasted pike-perch filet with bone marrow on toast and pan-tossed slices of polenta, slow-cooked wild duck stew with hot foie gras, served with baby vegetables in a ginger bouillon and red wine–braised beef cheek and potato casserole with fried parsley. No pretension or pointless frills in the dishes. In short, everything one loves, served with diligence by smiling and motivated waitresses. Add to this wines from Alsace sought out with "nose" (like the pinot noir of Maurice Schoech) and fine, fresh desserts (quince and pear Tatin-style tart with caramel ice cream and a vanilla-seasoned fresh fromage blanc mousse and warm blueberry compote, served with a cookie). Enough to talk, just opposite the Pont au Chat, of "another" event in the Krutenau.

● Le Penjab

12, rue des Tonneliers.
Tel. 03 88 32 36 37. Fax 03 88 32 18 55.
lepenjab@wanadoo.fr
Closed Sun., Mon. lunch, Thu. lunch.
Prix fixe: 21€, 42€, 47€, 9,30€.
A la carte: 55€.

Eric Jenny charges the Paris-Bombay gastronomic ticket at a heavenly price. Quality produce, freshness and proper handling are the ingredients that make up a celebratory meal. Eric, whose mother Harco runs the famous Vietnamese restaurant the Tour de Jade in the avenue des Vosges, offers in a cared-for setting, with its Indian wood decorations, chicken or shrimp samosas, eggplant or onion beignets, shrimp korma with coconut milk, savory cheese nan, mashli masala (spicy fish curry), lamb tandoori and the Kashmir-style chicken with spicy yogurt and saffron rice. Clean flavors and exquisite mild or spicy sauces: everything unfolds with ceremonial grace in these elegant and refined surroundings. The desserts (pistachio ice cream, gulab jamun and a cinnamon beignet) give a smiling end to the meal.

● La Cambuse ○ COM

1, rue des Dentelles.
Tel. 03 88 22 10 22. Fax 03 88 23 24 99.
cambuse@wanadoo.fr
Closed Sun., Mon., 3 Aug., Christmas.
A la carte: 52€.

Everything in Babeth Lefebvre's restaurant evokes the sea. The décor created by her husband Philippe transports us as if by magic into the inside of a boat cabin—and off we go, cruising down the Ill, the sole captain on board, ready to take on everything to sail around the world's oceans. Babeth proudly flies the colors of a cuisine that resembles her: generous, bold and inventive. Nothing of regional cuisine, then. Our destination is the open sea and flavors of elsewhere, far from the little France where she has nonetheless set up home. Pleasure is guaranteed with shrimp with mango and green papaya, matjes mille-feuille with wasabi and apples, never meat, but extremely fresh fish like the pineapple turbot and sea bream with basil-infused olive oil. On the dessert side, one can choose to follow the trip towards the islands with the chocolate tart with coconut cream or to return and anchor nearer to French shores, reminded of its vineyards and orchards with Cognac-flavored peach gratin. The wine list is replete with fine Chilean and American wines rubbing shoulders with the best Alsatian vintages. Philippe has just the right words to persuade and reel in the indecisive. Last surprise—and not the least—is that the check turns out to be reasonable for such an offering.

● Le Pont aux Chats

42, rue de la Krutenau.
Tel.-Fax 03 88 24 08 77.
Closed Sat. lunch, Wed., 2 weeks Feb.,
2 weeks Aug.
Prix fixe: 19€ (weekday lunch).
A la carte: 50€.

Valère and Véronique Diochet, who have been at this former Krutenau winstub for two years, very quickly managed to win over the whole of Strasbourg with a formula that combines tradition and modernity in both its décor and its food. The old windows and contemporary décor in the entirely renovated restaurant are a mirror-like reflection of the local produce that is subjected to unusual but clever interpretations of our friend Valère. His apprenticeship with Westermann, to whom he was second in command, doubtless plays its part, giving him knowledge of all the local producers and farmers from whom he gets high quality products. All that remains is the skillful treatment that produces salad with marinated sardines and artichokes, Label Rouge salmon pan tossed with fresh almonds, a slice of plaice and little pan-fried squids with preserved lemons, oven-crisped lamb shoulder with rosemary jus and poached white and yellow peaches served with blackcurrant jus and lemony thyme-seasoned shaved ice. On fine days, all this is appreciated much more on the terrace installed on the small internal courtyard and it is a year-round pleasure to eat here, punctuated by a glass of wine chosen à la carte on the advice of Véronique. The service leaves nothing to chance and the prices, despite so many good results, continue to be gentle.

● **La Casserole** 🏠COM
24, rue des Juifs.
Tel. 03 88 36 49 68. Fax 03 88 24 25 12.
Closed Sat. lunch, Sun., Mon., Aug.
Prix fixe: 15€ (lunch, weekdays), 27€, 50€.

Eric Girardin was a sommelier at Le Bateau Ivre in Courchevel and at Mischler's in Lembach. Today he is at the helm in the kitchen and no one would criticize him in his new function. Bubbling over with ideas, he changes the menu in its sweet, colorful little frame every few weeks. It is an opportunity for the regulars or passing customers to regularly experience the latest creations of this amateur chef who is mad about good wine and good cuisine. Foie gras with fruit chutney, sea bream with pepper oil, roasted pork tenderloin with slow-cooked cumin-seasoned carrots and a freshly sliced pear carpaccio with vanilla and chocolate truffle ice cream make a very good impression. In the restaurant, the sweet Marylin provides a pleasant, energetic service that adds pleasure to the food. Attractive special menus.

● **Le Festin de Lucullus** 🏠COM
18, rue Sainte-Hélène.
Tel.-Fax 03 88 22 40 78.
caroline.thiercelin@tiscalli.fr
Closed Sun., Mon., end Feb.–beg. Mar.,
3 weeks Aug.

Prix fixe: 14€ (lunch), 27€ (dinner).
A la carte: 40–45€.

The red of the completely renovated restaurant echoes the cuisine of Eric Thiercelin: colorful, energetic and fashionable. The influence of the South is definitely present. Crab seasoned with garden herbs, olive oil and lemon, the grilled tuna steak with summer vegetables, kouglof with slow-cooked wild duck pan-seared foie gras—one doesn't tire of either the scents or the flavors. This good, inexpensive special menu ends wonderfully with the raspberry crème brûlée shortbread with flecks of vanilla.

● **Le Panier du Marché** 🏠COM
15, rue Sainte-Barbe.
Tel. 03 88 32 04 07. Fax 03 88 23 64 52.
lepanierdumarche@hotmail.fr
Closed Sun.
Prix fixe: 19,50€ (lunch), 27€.

Fresh and well-handled is how one could describe the cuisine of Christophe Couvent. Here, only special menus are offered, but always at a tiny price. Pan-seared duck foie gras with spicy chocolate, grilled tuna steak, rack of lamb with artichokes and a small coconut tart with caramelized banana will win over lovers of southern-inspired cooking.

● **Le Thomasien** 🏠COM
12, rue des Dentelles.
Tel. 03 88 32 76 67.
Closed Sat. lunch, Sun., Mon. lunch (exc.
Christmas market days).
Prix fixe: 23€, 29€. A la carte: 35–40€.

Henri Velty doesn't posture. There is nothing more sincere than the food of his stone house in Petite France situated not far from the church of St. Thomas. We have good memories of the duck foie gras prepared two ways, served with fig chutney, seafood brochette (tuna, cod, large shrimp) and the grilled rack of lamb with tandoori spices polished by this native of Bugnéville in Vosges. The wild blueberry and sparkling wine sabayon accompanied by a pink grapefruit sorbet makes a fresh ending to the meal. Efficient service and really nice prices.

● **La Tour de Jade** 🛎COM

57, av des Vosges.
Tel. 03 88 35 14 37.
Closed Sat. lunch, Sun., Mon. lunch,
3 weeks Aug.
Prix fixe: 15€ (lunch), 28€, 35€.
A la carte: 35€.

Harco Jenny is an old-fashioned Vietnamese mother who scolds you if you don't finish her generous portions. But as everything she serves is delicious, no one complains. On the first floor of a smart building dating from 1900, in a room laid out like a private dining room, one enjoys fine, fresh food: pho (like it's served in Hanoi), ban cuon (steamed ravioli), fish of the day cooked with coconut milk, caramelized pork and the ginger ice cream slip down as effortlessly as can be. The great chefs of Alsace have understood the situation and come here to celebrate after their kitchens close.

● **La Cruche d'Or** ℕCOM

6, rue des Tonneliers.
Tel. 03 88 32 11 23.
Rest. closed Sun.,
2 weeks end Feb.–beg. Mar.
14 rooms: 55–60€.
Prix fixe: 24€, 28€. A la carte: 40€.

In the middle of a gastronomic street, Carine and Serge Jung have taken over, with spirit, an old tavern. The wooden, polished surroundings are shiny bright, the service obliging, the restaurant cheerful and there are also hotel accommodations. Serge, who worked at Buerehiesel, looks after both regional specialities and dishes that reflect the times. Slow-cooked onion tart, fine pâté in pastry crust, foie gras with Port aspic and slow-cooked apricots, pike-perch served on noodles, veal escalope Viennoise, fleischschnacka (Alsatian-style meat dumplings) and jumbo shrimp and chanterelle penne make one want to take up residence. Traditional desserts and selected wines.

● **Inside** ℕCOM

At Sofitel, 4, pl Saint-Pierre-le-Jeune.
Tel. 03 88 15 49 05. Fax 03 88 15 49 99.
h0568fb@accor-hotels.com /www.sofitel.com
Prix fixe: 29€ (weekday lunch).
A la carte: 55€.

Antoine Westermann, who supervises the kitchens of the Sofitel gourmet brasserie, has redone the décor in a contemporary style and offers a modern cuisine. A thin tart with marinated tuna, pâté in a pastry crust with foie gras, grilled mackerel filet with chop suey-style vegetables and the roasted pike-perch with potato purée with ceps and onion jus are well conceived. The venison parmentier with Pinot Noir sauce and foie gras makes a fine, modernized version of traditional cooking and, on the dessert side, Breton shortbread with spiced figs and yogurt sorbet takes one straight back to childhood.

● **Le Pont Tournant** ℕCOM

At the Régent Petite France,
5, rue des Moulins.
Tel. 03 88 76 43 00.
www.hotelsregent.com
Closed Sun., Mon., lunch weekdays (winter, exc. groups).
Prix fixe: 30€, 35€.

In the most beautiful hotel in town, this designer restaurant (with its minimalist makeover) and its bare black tables, red and carmine walls and armchairs and gray-beige banquettes is chic. The menu does good business by offering, under the lead of young Cédric Kallenbach, creamed Jerusalem artichokes seasoned with truffles, pan-crisped tête de veau with mustard, grouper seasoned with garam masala and the rack of lamb in a salt crust. The desserts (chocolate and coffee cream) slip down effortlessly.

● **L'Alsace à Table** COM

8, rue des Francs-Bourgeois.
Tel. 03 88 32 50 62. Fax 03 88 22 44 11.
info@alsace-a-table.fr /www.alsace-a-table.fr
Closed 24 Dec. dinner, 1 Jan. dinner
Prix fixe: 22€, 27€, 12€ (child).
A la carte: 50€.

Here is a misleading name for a restaurant! With such a title, one expects to find onion tart and toasted goose choucroute. In fact, Guy-Pierre Baumann has made it into a seafood restaurant. In a 1980 art nouveau setting, one enjoys a well-prepared seafood cuisine. The seafood platter, fish served with sauerkraut, monkfish medallions with seasoned eggplant purée, monkfish soufflé with squid ink tagliatelli and the orange sorbet topped with sangria, created by Patrice Loisse, is eaten simply and without fuss.

● **L'Atable 77** COM

77, Grand'Rue.
Tel. 03 88 32 23 37. Fax 03 88 32 50 24.
latable77@free.fr / www.latable77.com
Closed Sun., Mon., 2 weeks Dec.,
2 weeks July.
Prix fixe: 24€ (lunch), 30€ (lunch), 50€.
A la carte: 60€.

In purified surroundings of gray and orange, Stéphane Kaiser, who was the student of Emile Jung before proving himself at Ledoyen in Paris, has chosen to return to his roots by settling in the Alsatian capital. With him, nothing is left to chance—from the refined presentation to the carefully executed preparation and including the choice of natural produce stuffed with flavors. One is seduced by a fashionable, light cuisine that does not always satisfy one's hunger. But frozen sweet pea cream with whole grain mustard sauce, breaded and fried fish with typical minestrone vegetables in aspic, pan-tossed cod with thinly sliced radishes, tandoori-spiced suckling pig, oven-crisped pain d'épice dessert and an orange cream dessert with anise ice cream are well conceived. The wine list, explained by Guillaume Buecher, is not limited to just this region. The service, like Delphine's attentive welcome, is friendly while the special menus, particularly those for lunch, make one want to become a regular here.

● **Brasserie Kirn** COM

6-8, rue de l'Outre.
Tel. 03 88 52 03 03. Fax 03 88 52 01 00.

www.brasseriekirn.fr
Closed Sun. dinner, Christmas, 1 May.
Prix fixe: 17,50€ (lunch), 19,90€ (lunch),
23,50€ (lunch), 29,50€ (weekday dinner)
9,50€ (child). A la carte: 55€.

Jean-Paul Kirn's neo–Belle Epoque brasserie is the meeting place for those who love grilled monkfish medallions with peanut sauce, bone marrow with Guérande salt, milk-fed veal hanger steak, half-pound boneless rib steak, a sweet take on the regional casserole with apples, pears and grapes and the seasonal seafood buffet. Nice service and prices.

● **Fleur de Sel** COM

22, quai des Bateliers.
Tel. 03 88 36 01 54.
Closed Sun., Mon. lunch, 1 week beg. Jan.,
1 week at end Mar., 3 weeks Aug.
Prix fixe: 12€ (weekday lunch), 15€ (weekday lunch), 16€ (weekday lunch).
A la carte: 45€.

Françoise and Jean-Paul Schaller, who used to run Julien, a neo-art nouveau gourmet and upmarket boudoir, have recreated it in greater simplicity. The decoration of off-white stucco produces a contemporary look. And, on the kitchen side, Steve Meschberger cooks a fashionable bistro-type cuisine. Slow-cooked vegetables in a flat puff pastry, smoked ham, steamed in papilotte, oven-crisped swordfish with basil and tempura-style vegetables, browned cheese-topped lamb medallions with Espelette peppers served with a carrot mousseline and polenta and the rich chocolate cake served with orange sorbet hold their own.

● **Le Mandarin** COM

7, rue du Vieux-Marché-aux-Poissons.
Tel. 03 88 75 52 08. Fax 03 88 65 16 23.
www.restaurantlemandarin.com
Closed Sun. dinner, Mon.
Prix fixe: 44€, 52€, 70€. A la carte: 45€.

This modest Chinese restaurant uses quality produce and produces carefully prepared dishes. Herbert Sin gives a cheerful welcome and steamed dim sum, ginger-seasoned sole, Canton-style beef sirloin steak cooked at the table, half a Peking duck for two and a coconut dessert are invitations to an amazing journey.

● **La Mauresse**   COM

7, rue du Vieux-Marché-aux-Poissons.
Tel. 03 88 75 55 27. Fax 03 90 29 43 85.
www.mangerenalsace.com
Closed Sun. dinner, Mon.
Prix fixe: 8,50€ (weekday lunch), 29€, 54€.
A la carte: 50€.

Jacky Mercier has made discretion and consistency his bywords. Lovers of seafood know that his fish and crustacea are completely fresh. Fish soup, salmon tartare with fresh mint, whole Atlantic sea bass flambéed in Pastis, fish served with sauerkraut and a champagne sauce and the Catalane-style crème brûlée are delicious and the wine selection isn't bad.

● **Le Pont des Vosges**   COM

15, quai Koch.
Tel. 03 88 36 47 75. Fax 03 88 25 16 85.
pontdesvosges@noos.fr
Closed Sun.
A la carte: 50€.

The chic atmosphere, the fifties armchairs and the setting of a lively brasserie on the first floor of a building in the imperial quarter; this Lipp of Strasbourg is run by Annie Leclerc—but it is a gourmet Lipp. Annie, who has piercing blue eyes and who notices everything, is not satisfied with having the most popular establishment in town. She also feeds her guests with refinement and the cuisine of the young Jean-Philippe Schubnel gets everyone on board, with thinly sliced ceps served carpaccio style, monkfish and salmon in individual aspic terrine, smoked herring terrine, veal kidney with mustard sauce (also prepared English style) and the frozen nougat with honey sauce, which give simple pleasure.

● **Le R**   COM

53-55, Grand-Rue.
Tel. 03 88 22 09 25.
Closed lunch, Sun., Mon.
Prix fixe: 15€, 30€, 45€.

This is the "happening" restaurant of Strasbourg, which has taken over. No sign on the outside street—it has all happened by word of mouth. Richard Meier, formerly of La Rivière, has opened a Starckian place on two floors where a serious team works behind a clear screen to produce "intuitive cuisine". On offer, the tapas menu, vegetable spring rolls with spicy foam, scallop sashimi and grilled rouget. The orange flower water-seasoned mousse with a lacy vanilla cookie will surprise you.

● **Villa Casella**   COM

5, rue du Paon.
Tel. 03 88 32 50 50 / 03 88 66 37 96.
Fax 03 88 22 36 47.
info@villacasella.com / www.villacasella.com
Closed Sat. lunch, Sun., 2 weeks Christmas–New Year's, 1 week at Easter,
3 weeks Aug.
Prix fixe: 22€ (lunch, wine inc.), 40€, 50€.
A la carte: 55€.

Antonio Casella has made this good-natured trattoria into the star Italian restaurant of the town center. There are sometimes too many covers and a service that finds it hard to keep up, but the overall effect is effortlessly seductive. A mixed vegetable antipasto, pear and Gorgonzola risotto, monkfish medallion with artichokes, grilled beef tagliata with a balsamic reduction and parmesan and a pistachio panna cotta are well conceived. The transalpine wine list is a fund of good things.

● **Le Village d'Asie**   COM

1, av du Général-de-Gaulle.
Tel. 03 88 61 05 79. Fax 03 88 61 06 19.
Closed Mon., 2 weeks Aug.
Prix fixe: 21€, 26€, 30€. A la carte: 45€.

As its name indicates, this restaurant takes us to the Far East in a little gustatory journey starting in the heart of the Esplanade area. Hong Kong, Peking, Shanghai and Canton are among the destinations to which Alain Li invites us with steamed shrimp, chicken and meat spring rolls, steamed turbot, fish and shellfish stew,

Peking-style glazed duck, honey-seasoned pork roast and flambéed crêpes with mango compote. Friendliness is freely available, as is discretion. In terms of prices, one comes back down to earth very gently.

● Gavroche 🅿️⊙SIM

4, rue Klein.
Tel.-Fax 03 88 36 82 89.
restaurant.gavroche@free.fr
www.restaurant-gavroche.com
Closed Sat., Sun., Christmas–New Year's,
1 week at end Aug.
Prix fixe: 33€. A la carte: 60€.

He was the shy and retiring one, the student of the greats who remained in the shadows. Having learned the craft at Le Buerehiesel, Le Cerf and La Cheneaudière, Benoît Fuchs is now firmly asserting himself. His inn, formerly of unnattractive rough-cast stone, has been redecorated in soft shades, with yellow walls in the tadelakt style and the atmosphere of a private club. There are several tables and twenty or so covers that are taken by storm, as if gourmets have spread the word. Tradition is helped out by creativity and ideas from elsewhere renew the tried and true recipes. Nathalie Fuchs, lively and smiling, explains the menu with spirit, also giving advice on wine. In short, this laboratory of future cooking is devilishly seductive. The other evening, big scallops served in a foamy bouillon, quail brochettes glazed with foie gras sauce, grilled tuna steak medallions with whole grain barley risotto, the wonderful "lamb lollipops" with a side of yogurt seasoned with Indian spices and red bean mousseline were the work of an artist. Work that the desserts live up to: vanilla and passion fruit panna cotta and a shortbread tartlette with pineapple and a mascarpone and lime mousse. It seems that this enthusiastic restaurant is worth the applause (if one overlooks the courtyard toilets). This little Gavroche is undoubtedly a great one.

● L'Atelier du Goût 🅽🍴SIM

17, rue des Tonneliers.
Tel. 03 88 21 01 01.

Closed Sat., Sun., Christmas–New Year's,
1 week Feb., 2 weeks Aug.
Prix fixe: 20,50€ (lunch). A la carte: 35€.

Esther and François Morabito, who ran Le Panier du Marché, have created an event with this refined snack bar in a green and orange design. The black radish and squid tempura, the cep paté in the style of Vosges and the pan-tossed gnocchi and arugula make nifty and fashionable offerings. One feels at ease in this bar/*table d'hôte* to enjoy grilled scallops with a polenta cake, creamy risotto with a summer savory-seasoned suckling pig fricassée and the rare-cooked calf's liver with a carrot mikado and fresh grapes. The desserts are a divine surprise (mango cheesecake, pear and quince sorbet and the local dessert called the quechtartle, with ice cream or fresh fromage blanc and cinnamon). The wines are a fund of good things and the natural beer St. Pierre is drunk with great gusto.

● L'Assiette du Vin 🍴SIM

5, rue de la Chaîne.
Tel. 03 88 32 00 92. Fax 03 88 23 54 71.
Closed Sat. lunch, Sun., Mon. lunch,
3 weeks Aug.
Prix fixe: 15€ (lunch) 23€, 27€, 50€.

Philippe Roth, a former student of the Lyon chefs Orsi, Lacombe and Chavent, doesn't like monotony. He creates his modern and spirited cuisine with products gleaned from the market. His menu board sets out food that is well thought out and precisely executed. Eggplant and goat cheese mille-feuille, grilled squid with marinated summer vegetables, grilled beef and peanut cookies with pan-simmered peaches are all attractive. One washes down this feast with a vintage selected from 650 choices—the name of this restaurant is no accident.

● Lohkäs 🅽🍴SIM

25, rue du Bain-aux-Plantes.
Tel.-Fax 03 88 32 05 26.
Closed Thu., Fri. lunch, 3 weeks Jan.,
2 weeks July.
Prix fixe: 22€, 27€. A la carte: 38€.

This beautiful 1676 inn has kept its distinctive character and its semi-basement setting, with traditional stove upstairs and old-fashioned organ. Hot Munster salad, onion tart, pike-perch simmered in sparkling wine, goose liver simmered with apples and veal kidneys with mustard sauce are, without pretending to be great cuisine, carefully prepared and welcome dishes.

● Alambar ⓃSIM

15, rue du Vieux-Marché-aux-Vins.
Tel. 03 88 75 16 00.
Closed Sat. lunch, Sun.
A la carte: 25–35€.

Albert Schmitt, the head of P'tit Max, Place de l'Homme de Fer, has created a fresh, Italian-style garden setting and a dynamic restaurant team in this cool brasserie. Caramelized fennel salad with an orange foam, salmon steak with beurre blanc, preserved lemons and risotto, seafood linguini, foie gras tagliatelli and pancetta easily hold their own. Pasta (lasagne, penne and fusili) and focaccia and sunny wines all give pleasure.

● Le Bouquet Garni ⓃSIM

41, rte de l'Hôpital.
Tel. 03 88 34 66 86.
www.lebouquetgarni.fr
Closed Sat. lunch, Sun., Mon. dinner,
1 week Christmas–New Year's, 1 week Feb.,
3 weeks Aug.
Prix fixe: 9€ (lunch), 20€. A la carte: 35€.

Gaëtan Serge, formerly of Le Munstertuewel, took over a rather anonymous Neudorf house and has transformed both interior and exterior. The cuisine of Frédéric Olivier, formerly of Le Buerehiesel, is not lacking in character. Goose foie gras terrine with a dried fruit compote, sea bream with fennel sauce, poultry breast with celery cream and a frozen kouglof with local Marc de Gewurz are all attractive offerings on the 20 special menu.

● Canas y Tapas ⓃSIM

12, quai St-Nicolas.
Tel. 03 88 35 05 60.
A la carte: 20-30€.

Jean-Luc Desombre has, with a motivated team, created an Iberian experience on a bank of the Ill. Bar, tiles, tapas and cogollos like those of the Basque country, ham and Catalan-style tomato-rubbed bread with ham make one want to dance the flamenco. The produce is of high quality; the "a Feria" octopus plate and the Andalousian squid strike a marine note that goes down very well. Add to this the rosé Gran Feudo Chivite de Navarre and one has the impression that the cost of the ticket from Alsace to Spain is not expensive.

● Chan Chira ⓃSIM

2, rue des Moulins.
Tel. 03 88 32 68 34.
Closed Sat. lunch, Sun. lunch, Mon. lunch,
3 weeks in winter
A la carte: 45€.

Replacing a charming tearoom, this establishment in Petite France houses a high-quality Thai restaurant on two floors. The house has a quiet atmosphere, with red lamps, beams, exotic furniture and incense. Shrimp spring rolls, papaya salad, beef "lap" and lemon-sautéed chicken are flawlessly professional.

● Le Cornichon Masqué ⓃSIM

17, pl du Marché Gayot.
Tel. 03 88 25 11 34.
Closed Sun., Mon., 1 week at end Dec.,
3 weeks Jan.
A la carte: 35€.

Gilles Moercker knows how to welcome people to this charming building situated on one of the prettiest little squares of the town. The bar as you go in, the daily slateboard menu, the wide-awake waitress, the sensible prices, the dessert selection and the fruity wines: it all seduces. Stuffed goose neck, herring with cream, tuna carpaccio, tongue salad with lentils and cod filet with mashed potatoes go down well with everyone.

● **Gölbasi**　　🅝 SIM

35, Grand-Rue.
Tel. 03 88 75 68 54.
Closed Mon., 4 days Christmas–New Year's.
Prix fixe: 8€ (dish of the day).
A la carte: 25€.

Deniz and Hasan Cihangir, originally from Gölbasi in southeastern Turkey, have opened a modest embassy to their country in the heart of the Grand-Rue. One comes to this relaxed atmosphere to taste the house grilled meats, the doner kebab, with its spit-caramelized meat, the chopped meat kofte and Tavuk Sis (chicken brochettes). The Yakut Kavaklidere is a pleasure to drink.

● **Pierre, Bois, Feu**　　🅝 SIM

6, rue du Bain-aux-Roses.
Tel. 03 88 36 25 59.
Closed Sat. lunch, Sun. lunch, Tue., Wed. lunch.
A la carte: 40€.

Renaud Schneider, who has already roamed around the world a fair bit (in Frankfurt at Bistro 77, at Edel's in Sélestat, in Porto-Vecchio at the Tropicana), has chosen the means of a friendly, smart bistro next to the river and the cathedral, in a wooded, rustic setting, to make his fortune. One enjoys, according to the changing menu, breaded and fried vegetables, coddled egg with foie gras, blood sausage with onions and the boneless rib steak. Everything looks good.

● **Le Pub 38**　　🅝 SIM

38, rue Wimpheling.
Tel. 03 88 60 58 80.
lepub38@free.fr
Closed Sat., Sun., 2 weeks beg. Aug.
Prix fixe: 13,50€ (lunch).
A la carte: 40–55€.

Exit the Villa Médicis. This faux pub has rediscovered its first identity under the management of Hubert Dormann, a tall, attractive man (if a little stiff) who has gathered a serious team around him. The house has been renovated with a contemporary look and offers the fine cuisine of a young former chef of the Villa Casella. Marinated raw tuna, eggplant mille-feuille, San Daniele ham fougasse and spaghetti with clam sauce do not fail to seduce.

● **L'Ami Schutz**　　SIM

1, rue des Ponts-Couverts.
Tel. 03 88 32 76 98. Fax 03 88 32 38 40.
info@ami-schutz.com / www.ami-schutz.com
Closed Christmas–New Year's vac., 1 May.
Prix fixe: 11,85€ (lunch), 20€ (lunch), 22,80€, 24,30€ (lunch), 32,80€, 38,30€.
A la carte: 55€.

Cathy Maisch runs, with brilliance, this bierstub that typifies Petite France. The two wooden rooms, one noisy and the other private, have charm. The summer terrace overlooking the Ill is a joy. On the cuisine side, one enjoys escargots and garlic butter in puff pastry, salmon trout with almonds, pork shank seasoned with beer eau-de-vie and the frozen local Marc-flavored kouglof with wild rose sauce.

● **L'Ancienne Douane**　　SIM

6, rue de la Douane.
Tel. 03 88 15 78 78. Fax 03 88 22 45 64.
anciennedouane.rv@elior.com
www.anciennedouane.fr
Closed Christmas.
Prix fixe: 18€, 19,50€.
A la carte: 30–40€.

Touristy but practical, open every day and bordering the Ill, this large, rather factory-like but friendly brasserie, with its waiters in traditional costume, serves typical dishes at low prices. Head cheese and wine aspic terrine, salmon brochette, a generous choucroute with seven types of pork cut and charcuterie, tête de veau with sauce ravigote and pan-simmered quince with cinnamon ice cream fulfil their function perfectly.

● **Le Beijing**　　SIM

8, quai des Pêcheurs.
Tel.-Fax 03 88 35 39 57.
Closed Sat. lunch, Sun. lunch.
Prix fixe: 15€. A la carte: 30–35€.

Contrary to the impression given by the name, Chan Oi Wang originates from Shanghai and his cooking covers the immensity of China. Nothing to criticize in the steamed ravioli, stuffed crab, oven-crisped duck and the flambéed banana beignet, charged at reasonable prices.

● La Bourse `SIM`

1, pl de Lattre-de-Tassigny.
Tel. 03 88 36 40 53. Fax 03 88 36 35 46.
nathalie@restaurant-de-la-bourse.fr
www.restaurant-de-la-bourse.fr
Closed Christmas, New Year's.
Prix fixe: 8,50€ (weekday lunch), 20€.
A la carte: 35€.

This huge brasserie with its high ceiling does not pretend to do anything other than to feed agreeably and quickly easily-satisfied crowds with cold beef salad with horseradish, salmon grilled skin-side down with basil, lewerknepfle (local liver dumplings), tartes flambées and streusel accompanied by local wine. Friendly atmosphere and reasonable prices.

● Au Coq Blanc `SIM`

9, rue Mélanie.
Tel. 03 88 41 87 77. Fax 03 88 31 61 82.
au.coq.blanc@wanadoo.fr
www.au-coq-blanc.fr
Closed Sun. dinner, 2 weeks Jan.,
mid-Aug.–12 Sept.
Prix fixe: 25€, 31,50€. A la carte: 40€.

This good establishment in Robertsau is warm and the cooking of François Baur, working under the management of owner Lucien Ennesser, equally so. The clientele orders and the ovens get fired. Roasted quail and foie gras in salad, slow-simmered beef stew served with crispy vegetables, four fishes stew poached in wine with noodles, veal kidney with mustard sauce and a frozen meringue with whipped cream respect tradition. Beautiful summer terrace.

● La Grappa `SIM`

5, rue du Vieux-Marché-aux-Vins.
Tel. 03 88 75 98 60.
landosina@wanadoo.fr

Closed Sun., Mon.
Prix fixe: 18€, 25€. A la carte: 55€.

Franck Riegel has made this local Italian restaurant, in the very center of the town, opposite the tram line, an agreeable stopping-off place. The place is friendly and the cooking follows suit. We like the carpaccio, the oven-crisped parmesan dish, penne seasoned with peppers, Roman-style saltimbocca and the tiramisu. The service is pleasing and the restaurant fills quickly, despite the menu prices, which tend to soar.

● La Patrie `SIM`

1, rue des Balayeurs.
Tel. 03 88 35 16 92. Fax 03 88 36 81 92.
Closed Sun., Mon., Christmas–New Year's,
1 week Feb., 3 weeks Aug.
Prix fixe: 21–28€, 32€. A la carte: 33€.

The country referred to is Portugal. Pedro Botijo and his chef Jorge de Almeida offer fried cod cakes, shrimp beignets, fisherman's cod, Portuguese mixed meat platter with seafood and the Molotoff pudding sprinkled with red or white wine. Everything breathes the country between Setubal and Faro. Friendly atmosphere and tight prices.

● Le Rocher du Sapin `SIM`

6, rue du Noyer.
Tel. 03 88 32 39 65. Fax 03 88 75 60 99.
Closed Sun.
Prix fixe: 15,50€, 18€, 22€, 8€ (child).
A la carte: 30€.

This good old "comfort food" brasserie has kept the look and menu of former times. One first goes shopping in the nearby shops and then comes to put down one's bags and taste the terrine of wild boar head cheese and wine aspic with vinaigrette, salmon poached in sparkling wine, pike-perch poached in red wine, cheese-stuffed and breaded escalope and a Black Forest cake. The service is assiduous and the check not inflated.

● Salambo-Amilkar   SIM

2, rue de la Croix.
Tel. 03 88 35 40 50.
Closed Sun., mid-July–mid-Aug.
Prix fixe: 19€, 20€. A la carte: 30€.

In this exotic, softened setting, one has the impression of having been transported to Megara, as in Salambo, and the gardens of Amilkar. Chadia Ganame looks after the egg or tuna in filo pastry, the fine couscous and tagines. The pâtisseries are as sweet as the country and the mint tea, with pine nuts, is served as it should be. It does not cost much to go on the journey here.

● Secrets de Table   SIM

39, rue du 22-Novembre.
Tel. 03 88 21 09 10. Fax 03 88 21 08 18.
secretsdeable@wanadoo.fr
Closed dinner, Sun.
Prix fixe: 8,70€, 9,90€. A la carte: 15€.

Jean Westermann, brother of Eric at Buerehiesel, runs this chic and tasty fast food restaurant which cuts a dash with its modern, designer canteen setting. One munches Caésar salad, tuna cocktail, salmon marinated in sea salt, ham on toast, chicken and pineapple salad with Middle Eastern spices, without hesitation.

● Trattoria Da Giovanni   SIM

1, pl Saint-Thomas.
Tel. 03 88 22 20 99.
Closed Sun., Mon., end July–end Aug.
A la carte: 40€.

This pocket-sized trattoria offers the whole of Italy on a plate. Giovanni Lava watches carefully over the antipasti misti, eggplant gratin, grappa-seasoned salad, saltimbocca and tiramisu. Booking is essential.

● La Vieille Tour   SIM

1, rue Adolphe-Seyboth.
Tel. 03 88 32 54 30.
lercher@hotmail.com
Closed Sun., Mon., 1 week Jan.,
2 weeks July.
Prix fixe: 35€. A la carte: 65€.

Trained by Antoine Westermann, Véronique and Emmanuel Lercher have made this corner house bordering Petite France into a friendly eatery. In a sunny setting of orange walls and blue curtains, one makes short work of house country pâté, mild peppers stuffed with crab, pork trotter cake with ceps, the pistachio crème brûlée and the quetsche plums sautéed with cinnamon. It is well done, even if the à la carte prices give themselves airs.

● La Vignette   SIM

29, rue Mélanie.
Tel. 03 88 31 38 10. Fax 03 88 45 48 66.
lavignetterobertsau@cegetel.net
Closed Sat., Sun., 2 weeks Christmas–New Year's, 3 weeks Aug.
Prix fixe: 8,50€ (lunch). A la carte: 45€.

The fashionable set of Strasbourg congregate in this rural tavern in the heart of Robertsau, where beautiful hostess Danie Douanic and hard-working chef Serge Knapp practice the high art of conviviality and of pleasing the customers. The summer terrace is popular and one enjoys, without holding back, slow-cooked beef terrine with trumpet mushrooms and foie gras, head cheese and wine aspic terrine, grouper roasted with thyme and bay, niçoise-style tripe and the dried fruit dessert with apples and quince. It's lively, relaxed and not too dear.

● Zuem Ysehuet   SIM

21, quai Mullenheim.
Tel. 03 88 35 68 62. Fax 03 88 36 50 67.
www.zuem-ysehuet.com
Closed Sat. lunch, Sun., Oct.–end Apr.
Prix fixe: 18€ (lunch), 26€. A la carte: 45€.

The place, right on the bank of the Ill, skillfully defies fashion. Guido Scheidhauer looks after reception, Sacha Bender after the kitchen and the service on the covered patio at the back is prompt. One eats, without regret, duck foie gras terrine with pears and pistachios, grilled sea bream with fennel and slow-cooked tomatoes, quail stew with shallot confit and the frozen kouglof with Kirsch.

In Fegersheim (67640). 13 km s via N83.

● **La Table Gourmande**   V.COM

43, rue de Lyon.
Tel. 03 88 68 53 54. Fax 03 88 64 94 95.
Closed Sun. dinner, Mon. dinner, 1 week Jan.,
2 weeks July.
Prix fixe: 21€ (lunch), 26€ (dinner),
49€ (dinner). A la carte: 60€.

The Grassers are still energetically looking after this discreet good restaurant.
Trained in Austria, from where Anita
comes, Philippe serves up light, fresh
dishes. The seafood carpaccio, roasted
Atlantic sea bass filet, breast of farm-
raised young duck with a slice of foie gras
and the "all chocolate" dessert are of beautiful quality. The cellar is rich in the finest production of the region. The menus
are well conceived.

In Fegersheim.

● **Auberge du Bruchrhein**   SIM

24, rte de Lyon.
Tel.-Fax 03 88 64 17 77.
Closed Sun. dinner, Mon.
Prix fixe: 17€ (weekday lunch), 23€, 28€.
A la carte: 38€.

This fine village inn allows you to have a
gourmet meal without breaking the bank.
A pressed beef cheek terrine in aspic, seafood choucroute, Atlantic sea bass simmered in dark beer, veal kidney served
with red shallots and local noodles and the
mirabelle plums flambéed with Schnapps
and served with vanilla ice cream are
eaten effortlessly. Gilles Salomon cooks
with care, while Mandy looks after her
customers tenderly.

In Illkirch-Graffenstaden (67400). 5 km via
route de Colmar.

● **A l'Agneau**   COM

185, rte de Lyon.
Tel. 03 88 66 06 58. Fax 03 88 67 05 84.
Closed Sun. dinner, Mon., Tue.,
1 week beg. Feb., Aug.
Prix fixe: 32€, 15€ (child).
A la carte: 55€.

The Kerns work as a family. Guillaume
takes over from his mother Martine in

the kitchen while his father Claude gives a
lively welcome. There is no need to change
a successful menu. Transparent ravioli
stuffed with smoked duck foie gras, pike-
perch in a thin layer of potatoes, slow-
cooked venison stew with blood sauce
infused with cocoa served with a layered
mashed potato casserole and the extra-
dark chocolate fondant with white chocolate mousse hit the target.

In Ittenheim (67370). 12,5 km sw via A35
then N4.

● **Au Boeuf**   SIM

17, rte de Paris.
Tel. 03 88 69 01 42.
info@au-boeuf.com / www.au-boeuf.com
Closed Mon., Tue., 2 weeks June.
Prix fixe: 21,50€. A la carte: 35€.

This roadside inn, pioneer of the tarte
flambée, always scores a bull's-eye. The
setting is friendly, the restaurant rustic
and the welcome charming. Jean-Jacques
and Christian Colin look after the house
food, not only the famous flat tarts, but the
head cheese in wine aspic terrine, salmon
filet and the frozen kouglof. Family atmosphere and gentle checks.

In Mittelhausbergen (67200). 6 km nw via D41.

● **Au Tilleul**   SIM

5, rte de Strasbourg.
Tel. 03 88 56 18 31. Fax 03 88 56 07 23.
autilleul@wanadoo.fr / www.autilleul.fr
Rest. closed Tue. dinner, Wed., Feb. vac.,
2 weeks beg. Aug.
12 rooms: 52–60€.
Prix fixe: 16€ (lunch), 21€, 36€ (dinner),
7€ (child). A la carte: 55–60€.

Lorentzes have run this smart inn since
1888. The rooms are neat and tidy but it is
the cuisine of Jacques, the current Lorentz,
assisted by Eric Moebs, that makes one
want to stay. Pan-seared foie gras with
balsamic vinegar, crayfish and frog legs
in a puff pastry shell with sauce and a venison medallion with vineyard peaches are
full of inspiration. The Black Forest leaves
a good memory and the cellar is full of discoveries from here and elsewhere.

In Pfulgriesheim (67370). 10 km via D31.
● **Bürestuebel** ✿SIM
8, rue de Lampertheim.
Tel. 03 88 20 01 92. Fax 03 88 20 48 97.
restaurant.burestubel@wanadoo.fr
www.burestubel.com
Closed Sun. (Nov.–Jan.), Mon. (Nov.–Jan.),
Tue., Feb. vac., mid-Aug.–end Aug.
Prix fixe: 17€, 26€. A la carte: 35€.

The wise Pierre Meyer swears by Alsace and the richness of its local cuisine. He has retained the lesson learned at Mischler's in Lembach and he zealously sets out his region's tastes, returning to simplicity but in the most superlative way. He looks after the tartes flambées, breaded pork trotters, local liver dumplings and the beer-roasted pork shank. The bread is made in house, like the ice creams, and choosing between the "Gretel cup" (sweet and sour cherry sorbet with eau-de-vie) and Bürestuebel (vanilla ice cream, cinnamon-seasoned fruits simmered in red wine) involves a hard decision. Nothing is left to chance in this former farm with its painted wooden fittings, its flowered courtyard and its timbered facade repainted in yellow. Despite the high number of covers, the service is exemplary and the check moderate.

In Pfulgriesheim.
● **L'Aigle** SIM
22, rue Principale.
Tel. 03 88 20 17 80. Fax 03 88 20 76 76.
Closed Sun., Mon., 2 weeks Christmas–New Year's, 3 weeks July
A la carte: 28€.

In their pleasant roadside inn, Marthe and Lydia Roth look after their customers with the tartes flambées baked in the wood-fired oven, wild rabbit in aspic terrine, grilled sirloin with potatoes and the frozen meringue and Chantilly dessert, all washed down with regional wines. Delightful welcome and very gentle checks.

In Plobsheim (67115). 12 km s via route d'Offenburg.
● **Au Boeuf** ✿SIM
25, rue du Général-Leclerc.
Tel. 03 88 98 58 25. Fax 03 88 98 73 02.

Closed Sat. lunch, Mon., 1 week Jan.,
3 weeks Aug.
Prix fixe: 19€ (lunch), 26€, 32€.
A la carte: 30€.

It would be a mistake to stay outside admiring the beautiful timbered exterior. You have to come in and sit down in the red, wooden décor of the warm dining room. With the educated advice of Marie-Paule Sutter, you hesitate to choose among stuffed pike-perch simmered in red wine, pork cheeks, tête de veau and a seasonal fruit crumble. The portions are generous and the prices moderate and Vincent Sutter, who formerly worked at the Auberge de l'Ill and at La Poste in La Wantzenau, is a skillful craftsman.

In 67300 Schiltigheim. 3 km via D468.
● **Serge & Co** ◎COM
14, rue des Pompiers.
Tel. 03 88 18 96 19. Fax 03 88 83 41 99.
serge.burckel@wanadoo.fr
www.serge-and-co.com
Closed Sat. lunch, Sun. dinner, Mon.,
2 weeks July.
Prix fixe: 48€, 58€, 88€.

After having labored in all four corners of the globe, from St. Louis, Missouri to Hong Kong, via Los Angeles and Orlando, Serge Burckel has finally hung up his hat in an inner suburb of Strasbourg. He has made his mark with distinctive fusion cooking that skillfully reinterprets regional classics in a sure-fire winning formula. His good humor spreads through the restaurant as well as the dishes. With his bandana glued to his head, this wonder boy who is always on duty gives the impression that he is just playing around—yet his creations are hard to forget. With him, the frog legs wink at the escargots and the sweet pea purée is classically prepared and served with a warm smoked bacon aspic. He also makes a fun "soft spring roll" with crabmeat served with a shellfish cream. Regional produce is honored with John Dory with morels and asparagus (also with creamed asparagus), hand-rolled noodles with venison, veal kidney ravioli and the head and tongue served cold, carpaccio style, a carnivorous feast. The desserts are playful, with names that raise a smile but an end result that requires respect. Chocolate cigar and pineapple fritters amuse. On the financial side, the clever special menus put his creations within reach of all budgets.

● La Table Chaude COM

43, rte du Général-de-Gaulle.
Tel. 03 88 81 22 24. Fax 03 88 81 47 95.
www.latablechaude.com
Closed Sat. lunch, Sun., Mon. dinner,
3 weeks Aug.
Prix fixe: 20€, 17€, 32€. A la carte: 48€.

Emilio de Matteis, who opened the pizzeria Riva Destra (12, quai Saint-Nicolas. Strasbourg. Tel. 03 88 35 05 60), has left the kitchens of this *tavola calda* to Dominique Roth. The classics are still on the menu, such as parmesan and basil carpaccio, fritto misto, saltimbocca with basil cream and the tiramisu. Warm welcome but checks a little too high.

● La Taverne de Saint-Malo SIM

12, rue Contades.
Tel. 03 88 18 98 00.
Closed Sat. lunch, Sun. dinner, Mon.
Prix fixe: 14€ (lunch), 18€ (lunch), 20,50€ (lunch), 27€ (lunch). A la carte: 45€.

Brigitte and Kaine Palleau—she from Alsace, he from St. Malo—have made this Breton tavern into a high-quality establishment. One forgets the external appearance of a concrete bunker to concentrate on the warm kitsch setting with its knickknacks on a maritime theme. Marinated smoked herring, seafood tapas, lemon-seasoned sardines with steamed potatoes, fish stew served St. Malo–style, roasted fresh pineapple with caramel and rum raisin ice cream slip down effortlessly.

● WINSTUBS

These wine cafés are the guardians of regional tradition. Warm atmosphere, cozy, wooded décor and simple little dishes, manager (or manageress) of character, wines in jugs and friendly company. To experience a *winstub* is to get a glimpse of the soul of Alsace.

● Chez Yvonne
"S'Burjerstuewel"
10, rue du Sanglier.
Tel. 03 88 32 84 15. Fax 03 88 23 00 18.
info@chez-yvonne.net / www.chez-yvonne.net
Closed Christmas, New Year's.
A la carte: 35–40€.

Jean-Louis de Valmigère has energetically taken over this celebrated *winstub* where Helmut Kohl, Jacques Chirac and Gerhard Schröder, among others, used to junket. The wood setting with its benches and small corners is cute. In the kitchens, Dominique Radmacher offers both regional recipes and produce and contemporary food on the menu slate: goat cheese terrine with peppers, sauerkraut and pork tart, Munster cheese in puff pastry, roasted pike-perch seasoned with orange peel, pork shank braised in beer and Gewurz-flavored ice are very attractive. The wine list elegantly exceeds the orbit of a *winstub*.

● Le Clou

3, rue du Chaudron.
Tel. 03 88 32 11 67. Fax 03 88 21 06 43.
Closed Sun., Wed. lunch, Christmas,
New Year's.
A la carte: 38€.

Marie Sengel is a prominent figure in Strasbourg. With her husband, she delights her world—politicians and theatrical people—in a very charming wood setting, with onion tart, head cheese and wine aspic terrine, pike-perch served over sauerkraut, ham braised in Pinot Noir and the frozen meringue with whipped cream. The wines in jugs contribute to the convivial atmosphere and the prices won't make you climb the wall. All the same, beware of overcooking at the end of the week, particularly when the masters of the house are not there (overcooked shriveled sausage and calf's liver).

● Kobus

7, rue des Tonneliers.
Tel. 03 88 32 59 71.
erkohn@wanadoo.fr
Closed Sun., Mon., 1 week Nov.,

3 weeks mid-Jan.–beg. Feb.
Prix fixe: 14,90€. A la carte: 25–35€.

Eric Kuhn has just moved and has changed the name of his establishment, which he runs in the tradition of L'Ami Fritz. But he still gives a very authentic, simple welcome to the specialities of this town-center establishment. Foie gras terrine, duck leg confit, choucroute and strawberry soup with Pinot Noir served with cinnamon ice cream have the good taste of tradition.

● **Fink'stuebel** ⬛SIM

26, rue Finkwiller.
Tel. 03 88 25 07 57. Fax 03 88 36 48 82.
finkstuebel@noos.fr / http://finkstuebel.free.fr
Closed Sun. (exc. marché de Christmas),
Mon., 1 week beg.
Jan., 1 week Feb., 3 weeks Aug.
A la carte: 40€.

Sophie and Thierry Schwaller have successfully taken over the reins of this *winstub* with respect for the traditions of Alsace. First, in terms of food, with kouglof with pork cheeks and foie gras, crispy pike-perch with sauerkraut, beef served with sea salt and horseradish cream and the frozen kouglof with Kirsch, and then in terms of hospitality, with a friendly atmosphere in which beer and local wines flow freely.

● **Muensterstuewel** ⬛SIM

8, pl du Marché-aux-Cochons-de-Lait.
Tel. 03 88 32 17 63. Fax 03 88 21 96 02.
munsterstuewel@wanadoo.fr
www.strasnet.com/munsterstub.htm
Closed Sun. (exc. Christmas market days),
Mon., 1 week beg. Jan., 2 weeks beg. July.
Prix fixe: 30€ (lunch, wine inc.), 45€ (wine
inc. dinner). A la carte: 40€.

This *winstub* with an unpronouncable name (meaning "wine shop of the cathedral") is run with a masterly hand by Patrick Klipfel, who is constantly innovating, offering entertainment and good little dishes. This semi-finalist for the best sommelier of France, a trainee with Bocuse and Girardet, is backed up by Jean-Louis Ohl in the kitchen. The fish comes

from Quiberon and the meat is of perfect quality. Shrimp tails on caramelized sauerkraut, pork trotter with potatoes in casserole accompanied by a quick-seared goose liver, stuffed and slow-cooked oxtail and the pistachio parfait with quetsche plum sorbet are astonishing.

● **Au Pont-Corbeau** ⬛SIM

21, quai Saint-Nicolas.
Tel. 03 88 35 60 68. Fax 03 88 25 72 45.
corbeau@reperes.com
www.pontcorbeau.com
Closed Sat. (exc. Christmas market days),
Sun. dinner, 1 week Feb., end July–end Aug.
Prix fixe: 11€ (weekday lunch).
A la carte: 35€.

Adorable and one hundred per cent Alsatian, Christophe Andt is a flag carrier for local traditions. His warm *winstub* is decorated in an old style with frescoes by Edgar Mahler and woodwork by Raymon Emile Waydelich. On the plate, an onion tart, grilled ham, chilled pot au feu salad with sautéed potatoes, tête de veau and the dark chocolate and sour cherry terrine seasoned with Kirsch are delicious and very gently priced. Attractive wines in pitchers.

● **Au Coin des Pucelles** ⬛SIM

12, rue des Pucelles.
Tel.-Fax 03 88 35 35 14.
Closed Sun., Sun. dinner, Bank holidays,
mid-July–mid-Aug.
A la carte: 36€.

The house is historic, the banquettes have style and the cuisine of Roland Rohfritsch skillfully signs up with tradition. Head cheese and wine aspic terrine, duck foie gras, choucroute, ham and the frozen vacherin are very honest. Friendly welcome and prices that do not shock.

● **Zum Strissel** ⬛SIM

5, pl de la Grande-Boucherie.
Tel. 03 88 32 14 73. Fax 03 88 32 70 24.
zuem.strissel@orange.fr
Closed Christmas, New Year's.
Prix fixe: 13,70€, 22€, 8€ (child).
A la carte: 32€.

Jean-Louis de Valmigère has taken over this historic house with its colored windows, wine-press room, scupltured casks, wooden benches and old paintings. He has polished up the place and left the old team, who are quietly good and solid, undisturbed. Head cheese and wine aspic terrine with vinaigrette, pike-perch on a bed of sauerkraut, pork shank braised in beer and the apple tart are all nice.

● Au Cruchon

11, rue des Pucelles.
Tel. 03 88 35 78 82.
Closed Sat. lunch (exc. fêtes), Sun. (exc. fêtes), Mon. lunch, 2 weeks Aug.
Prix fixe: 9€ (lunch). A la carte: 35€.

This was an establishment famous for the musical atmosphere led by Fernand Wohl, whose accordion now features as a wall decoration. The young Gilles Spannagel has taken over the house with discretion, dreaming up finely crafted dishes (pumpkin soup with "the spirit" of foie gras and pike-perch on a bed of sauerkraut with Avruga sauce), which does not mean that the presskopf (transformed into a carrot terrine), boudin noir (with parsnip purée) are not on the menu. The evening menu (frog leg tartlet) and the desserts (a quetsche plum gratin with cinnamon ice cream) are worthy of praise.

● Zehnerglock

4, rue du Vieil-Hôpital.
Tel. 03 88 23 17 42.
Closed Mon.
Prix fixe: 22,50€ (lunch). A la carte: 35€.

We knew the Zehnerglock for its rustic atmosphere and its fresco of the historic "ten o'clock bell." Yves and Karine Lutz, plus Rachel Schmitt, Yves' sister, are in charge of the establishment which has kept its antiquated character. Yves, formerly of Zimmer-Sengel and Valentin-Sorg, carefully creates goose foie gras with Gewurtz aspic and dried fruit compote, escargots and little puff pastry shells with meat and white sauce. A place to watch.

● Au Bon Vivant

7, rue du Maroquin.
Tel. 03 88 32 77 81. Fax 03 88 32 95 12.
Closed Thu. (exc. lunch season), Fri.
Prix fixe: 15,90€, 18,90€, 30€,
7,50€ (child). A la carte: 36€.

Cédric Moulot and Michel Reuche of the neighboring Tire-Bouchon have just taken over this old tavern. It is too soon to assess the change, but onion tart, pâté in a pastry crust, spit-roasted chicken, goose breast with sour cherries and a chocolate cream dessert seasoned with Kirsch leave fine memories.

● D'Choucrouterie

20, rue Saint-Louis.
Tel. 03 88 36 52 87 / 03 88 36 07 28.
Fax 03 88 24 16 49.
info@choucrouterie.com
www.choucrouterie.com
Closed Sat. lunch, Sun., 2 weeks Aug.
Prix fixe: 9€ (weekday lunch).
A la carte: 30–35€.

Man of theatre and singer Roger Siffer leaves Théo, conductor of the restaurant, to manage this affable establishment with discernment. Until late into the night, one can eat smoked trout and salmon salad, pike-perch breaded with pain d'épice, local liver dumplings, choucroute served seven different ways and the tarte Tatin, which make a good impression, washed down with edel in pitchers and Météor beer.

● La Petite Mairie

8, rue Brûlée.
Tel.-Fax 03 88 32 83 06.
Closed Sat., Sun.,
Christmas–New Year's vac.
A la carte: 38€.

A stone's throw from the town hall, Maryse Wenger's tavern is always full. The house duck and goose foie gras combination, head cheese and wine aspic terrine, Mediterranean sea bass filet, ham breaded with pain d'épice and the house-made three-chocolate mousse are fantastic, just like the reception.

● **Sel & Poivre** SIM

18, rue du Neufeld.
Tel.-Fax 03 88 34 51 40.
selpoivre@club-internet.fr
Closed Sat. lunch, Sun., 2 weeks Christmas–
New Year's, 1 week Aug.
Prix fixe: 8,50€ (lunch), 9,50€ (lunch),
12,50€ (dinner), 18,50€ (dinner).
A la carte: 38€.

Laurent Man has energetically taken over
this small, cozy restaurant. Thierry Kno-
bloch creates with profesionnal seriousness the "salt and pepper" hors-d'oeuvre,
pike-perch and salmon served over a bed
of sauerkraut, a two-pound beef steak and
the berry charlotte. Small summer terrace
and local wines in a pitcher.

● **S'Thomas Stuebel** SIM

5, rue du Bouclier.
Tel. 03 88 22 34 82.
Closed Sun., Mon., Christmas–New Year's,
3 weeks Aug.
A la carte: 29€.

Next to St. Thomas, Thierry Deylot guards
another secret. Onion tart, head cheese and
wine aspic terrine, pike-perch poached in
Riesling, veal kidneys with local noodles
and the quetsche plum sorbet are nicely
washed down with selected wines.

● **S'Wacke-Hiesel** SIM

Pl de la Foire-Exposition.
Tel. 03 88 36 64 75. Fax 03 90 41 68 09.
swacke-hiesel.fr
Closed Sat. lunch, Sun., Christmas–New
Year's, 2 weeks beg. Aug.
A la carte: 35€.

A stone's throw from Wacken, this faux-
wooden hut is passionately run by two
sisters, Anne and Michèle Leppert. One
comes here to enjoy presskopf, onion tart,
oven crisped pike-perch and hanger steak
with shallots taken directly from traditional cuisine. The prices are reasonable
and the crème brûlée flambée fun.

● **La Taverne du Sommelier** SIM

3, ruelle de la Bruche.
Tel. 03 88 24 14 10.

www.chefstudio.fr
Closed Sat. (exc. Bank holidays), Sun. (exc.
Bank holidays), 2 weeks Aug.
A la carte: 38€.

Martin Schreiber, wine expert, shares his
encyclopedic knowledge with his customers, who are often passionate wine lovers
themselves. His cellar develops along with
his discoveries. Game terrine, braised
monkfish cheeks, duck breast roasted with
quince and spicy pears simmered in red
wine accompany the finds of the day.

● **Le Tire-Bouchon** SIM

5, rue des Tailleurs-de-Pierre.
Tel. 03 88 22 16 32. Fax 03 88 22 60 88.
contact@letirebouchon.fr
www.letirebouchon.fr
Prix fixe: 23€, 32€, 8€ (child).
A la carte: 32€.

With its typical exterior, this *winstub* is
an institution. Cédric Moulot in the restaurant and Michel Reuche in the kitchen
have given it its former dynamism. Pan-
seared foie gras with simmered apples,
whole pike-perch served on sauerkraut
with a Riesling sauce, hand-cut steak tartare prepared at the table, roasted ham
with Munster sauce and an apple streudel with vanilla ice cream are fantastic.
Nice welcome, diligent service and moderate prices.

● **Zum Wynhaenel** SIM

24, rue Sleidan.
Tel.-Fax 03 88 61 84 22.
Closed Sun., 1 week beg. Mar., mid-July–
mid-Aug.
Prix fixe: 12€ (weekday lunch) 10€ (child).
A la carte: 34€.

Raymond Mainberger is the protective
father watching over his rustic tavern
tucked away in an art nouveau building.
One eats escargots, grilled ham, veal kidney with mustard sauce and chocolate
cake without any difficulty. Nice wines
in pitchers, summer terrace.

BAKER OF THE YEAR

Au Pain de mon Grand-Père

58, rue de la Krutenau.
Tel. 03 88 36 59 66.

Patrick Dinel, a native of Nancy, intellectual and keen convert to the cause of authentic baking, is very much at home with his dough. Assisted by his son Bruno, he tends to the leaven in his kneading trough and plies his trade in full view of the customers in his rustic store with its wood-burning oven. What he produces has a delightfully old-fashioned flavor. Charentes-Poitou butter, Breton shortbread, whole grain breads, ciabatta, olive fougasse, spelt wheat Coronne, Pogne de Romans, rye Chaperon, soy flour Bûcheron, the delightfully rustic round loaf of stone-ground wheat flour and the Kamut newly revive the baker's spirit of Alsace. Aficionados of local produce need not worry, though: he also purveys a superb kouglof, streussel, Chinois, pretzel and onion tart all well worth the detour. A word of advice: at peak times, you can expect to join a long line of customers!

STUTZHEIM-OFFENHEIM

67370 Bas-Rhin. Paris 478 – Strasbourg 13 – Saverne 23.
A village of Kochersberg, like a signpost to the countryside, reputed for its taverns that serve tartes flambées.

●	RESTAURANTS

● Le Marronnier

18, rte de Saverne.
Tel. 03 88 69 84 30. Fax 03 88 69 87 82.
Closed lunch (exc. Sun.).
A la carte: 25€.

A former farm transformed into a charming inn with interminable dining rooms. An entire family, the Friedrichs, serve satisfied customers in the very busy restaurant. Exquisite tartes flambées, plain or with cheese, are what one finds at sensible prices every evening. Pretty multicolored wood fittings and wide culinary range (presskopf, tartiflette, caramelized pork ribs or ham shank).

● Le Tigre

Rue Principale.
Tel. 03 88 69 88 44.
Closed Sat. lunch, Mon. dinner, Wed., 1 week Feb. vac., 3 weeks July–mid-Aug.
Prix fixe: 22,50€ (Sun.), 25€ (lunch). A la carte: 28€.

From the road, one can see this establishment with its modern facade and interior, its parasol-covered terrace and its active waitresses. Emmanuel Wolfromm is the talented but modest practitioner of all the culinary arts: a potato and Munster gratin, breaded and fried squid, trout with white summer truffles, spicy pork trotters and tartes flambées in the evening have the best society of the region coming in droves.

TALLOIRES

74290 Haute-Savoie. Paris 552 – Annecy 13 – Albertville 34 – Megève 50.
talloirestourism@wanadoo.fr.
This admirable village is worth a visit for its location, its beauty as a timeless sentinel and its old-world houses with the characteristic charm of Savoie.

 HOTELS-RESTAURANTS

● Auberge du Père Bise

Rte du Port.
Tel. 04 50 60 72 01. Fax 04 50 60 73 05.
reception@perebise.com / www.perebise.com
Closed beg. Dec.–beg. Feb.
Rest. closed Tue. (off season), Wed. lunch (and dinner off season), Fri. lunch.
16 rooms: 250–400€. 7 suites: 400–650€.
Prix fixe: 80€, 125€, 170€.
A la carte: 120–160€.

Sophie and Charlyne Bise celebrate the marriage of tradition and luxury, classicism and modernity. Each of the extremely comfortable rooms has its own color scheme. In the kitchen Sophie Bise works in tandem with Gilles Furtin, reworking classic dishes with very contemporary flavors. The lake fish, Brittany lobster with herb cannelloni, veal scallops with zucchini and chanterelles and the daisy flower soufflé are best enjoyed at your leisure in the beautiful dining room or on the terrace overlooking the lake. Vincent Maduli is in charge of the cellar which, naturally, because of its age, offers more than 1000 listings that illustrate the history and geography of French wines. It can therefore be difficult to choose one, but what dilemma could be more delicious?

■ L'Abbaye

Chemin des Moines.
Tel. 04 50 60 77 33. Fax 04 50 60 78 81.
abbaye@abbaye-talloires.com
www.abbaye-talloires.com
Closed mid-Nov.–mid-Feb. Rest. closed Mon. (off season), Tue. (off season).
33 rooms: 130–290€. 4 suites: 300–550€.
Prix fixe: 29€ (weekday lunch), 40€, 60€, 75€, 20€ (child). A la carte: 85€.

This 17th-century Benedictine abbey in the setting of the lake is an open invitation to rest and repose. The flowery cloister leads to what were once monks' cells, now rooms where comfort goes hand-in-hand with modernity. Each room has its own color scheme to match our different moods. In the kitchen, Frédéric Fouquet juggles with roasted langoustines with sweet peas, bacon and lettuce jus, roasted Atlantic sea bass filet with summer savory-seasoned crushed tomatoes and garlicky pesto, young duck breast rolled in peach caviar with dried fruit risotto, frozen grapefruit macarons and a cone full of minced strawberries. The serving staff is attentive and Dominique Meinder is an excellent guide to help you choose your wine.

■ Le Cottage

Le Port.
Tel. 04 50 60 71 10. Fax 04 50 60 77 51.
cottagebise@wanadoo.fr / www.cottagebise.com
Closed 10 Oct.–end Apr.
35 rooms: 100–230€.
Prix fixe: 39€, 53€.

Facing the pier, Christine and Jean-Claude Bise's three little thirties houses offer timely accommodation. We liked the cozy rooms overlooking the lake, the garden and swimming pool, the refined dining room, the shady terrace and Stéphane Lavigne's classic cuisine. Accompanied by carefully chosen wines, quail salad with hazelnut oil, lake trout seasoned with orange peel, roasted rack of lamb with slow-cooked eggplant and thinly sliced strawberries served with berry jelly are best savored overlooking the lake.

TAMNIES

24620 Dordogne. Paris 508 – Brive-la-Gaillarde 51 – Périgueux 59 – Sarlat 16.
Bucolic black Perigord with its gently sloping hills, its caves and the nearby valley of the Dordogne.

HOTELS-RESTAURANTS

■ Laborderie

Tel. 05 53 29 68 59. Fax 05 53 29 65 31.
hotel.laborderie@wanadoo.fr
www.hotel-laborderie.com
Closed Nov. 1–Easter. Rest. closed Mon.
lunch (exc. July–Aug.), Wed. lunch.
45 rooms: 28–92€.
Prix fixe: 19€. A la carte: 40€.

With its pinnacle, three annexes and large grounds overlooking the valley, this typical construction in the high town square never fails to exercise its charm. Gérard Laborderie, always outgoing and friendly, has created a niche of tranquility with rooms that are both rustic and contemporary, peaceful and cozy. Formerly a barn made entirely of wood and stone, the restaurant is bright and airy. Patrick Baiguera does a lively interpretation of classic dishes that delight us: veal kidneys in puff pastry with financier sauce, roasted trout with fleur de sel, minced tongue and a frozen walnut soufflé. The keynote is generosity, even in the prices.

TANINGES

74440 Haute-Savoie. Paris 570- Chamonix 51 – Thonon-les-Bains 47 – Annecy 65.
This old Savoyard village perched at a height of 640 meters with its old humpback bridge over the Foron has the largest church in the region (fifty-eight meters long).

●   RESTAURANTS

● La Crémaillère   COM

rte du lac Flérier.
Tel. 04 50 34 21 98. Fax 04 50 34 34 88.
Closed Sun. dinner (exc. Bank holidays),
Mon. dinner (exc. Bank holidays), Wed. (exc. Bank holidays), beg. Jan.–beg. Feb., 2 weeks end June–beg. July.
Prix fixe: 25€, 32€, 43€, 12€ (child).

Jean-Pierre Bonjean is at the helm in this goodly lakeside inn that serves delicious regional dishes based on local market products. The large bay windows of the dining room and the vast panoramic terrace are ideal settings in which to enjoy lobster sauce with lime sauce, cured country ham, simmered pork cheeks with polenta and chocolate truffle with orange sauce. It's a good idea to reserve a table as the seating is limited.

TANTONVILLE

54116 Meurthe-et-Moselle. Paris 325 –
Nancy 28 – Epinal 49 – Lunéville 34 –
Toul 37 – Vittel 44.
This old brewery town was the home of the Tourtel family, in close proximity to the Haroué and Thorey-Liautey châteaux and at the foot of the "inspired" hill so dear to Barrès.

●   RESTAURANTS

● La Commanderie   COM

1, rue Pasteur.
Tel.-Fax 03 83 52 49 83.
www.restaurant-la-commanderie.com
Closed Sun. dinner, Mon., Tue. dinner, 1 week beg. Jan., 2 weeks end Aug.–beg. Sept.
Prix fixe: 13,50€ (weekdays), 24€ (weekdays), 29,50€, 35€, 45€, 9,50€ (child), 45€.

Samuel and Céline Lanne work their charm in this renovated old house with its beautiful terrace, its fountain and private parking lot. Enjoy fresh, finely prepared delicacies in the light-filled and elegant restaurant where tones of ochre and sand blend subtly with the cane chairs. Escargots in cassolette with minced chanterelles, shellfish and seafood stew in a spicy bouillon, tête de veau with sauce gribiche, mirabelle plum cold dessert and a bergamot-infused crème brûlée makes us want to stay the night.

TARARE

69170 Rhône. Paris 463 – Roanne 42 –
Lyon 46.
In the land of gold-colored stones, a gourmet sentinel on the Beaujolais route.

● RESTAURANTS

● Jean Brouilly
3 ter, rue de Paris.
Tel. 04 74 63 24 56. Fax 04 74 05 05 48.
restaurant.jean-brouilly@wanadoo.fr
www.tarare.com/brouilly
Closed Sun., Mon., 3 weeks Feb.,
3 weeks Aug.
Prix fixe: 35€, 55€, 70€. A la carte: 69€.

The star of the lower Beaujolais region, the uncrowned king of this gentle land is filled with vines. For a quarter of a century in his smart country residence by the side of the national road, Jean Brouilly, a classic maestro, has honed the regional cuisine with precision and a light touch. A sunnyside-up egg with celery root cream sauce, rabbit simmered with parsley and garlic, lake trout with sage-infused oil, Highland beef sirloin steak with red wine sauce and a soft biscuit with pistachios and blueberries are old reliables that always please us, best savored with the finest vintages of his neighbor Pierre Marie Chermette in the Domaine de Vissoux (Griottes, Coeur de Vendanges, Moulin à Vent) as we contemplate the joys of life in this land of gold-colored stones.

TARASCON-SUR-ARIEGE

09400 Ariège. Paris 775 – Ax-les-Thermes 28 – Foix 17 – Lavelanet 32.
An escapade in the "rugged" country of the Pyrénées.

HOTELS-RESTAURANTS

● Auberge de la Grotte
In Bedeilhac, 3 km, pl du Village.
Tel.-Fax 05 61 02 84 68.
aubergecharaux@aol.com
Closed Wed. (exc. July–Aug.),
10 days end Oct.–beg. Nov.
Prix fixe: 22€ (weekday lunch), 26€, 38€, 50€, 8€ (child).

Xavier Charaux's restaurant on the village square is a choice stopover. At meal times the ochre-toned dining room hosts a parade of well-prepared regional dishes such as open ravioli with escargots and fresh goat cheese, cod filet cooked koshkera style, duck breast in papilotte, a slice of foie gras and the Izarra gâteau Basque with goat's milk ice cream.

TARBES

65000 Hautes-Pyrénées. Paris 795 – Pau 43 – Bordeaux 218 – Lourdes 18 – Toulouse 156.
We visit the cathedral, the Massey garden, the museum devoted to the Hussars, the banks of the Adour river and the lively market with the same enthusiasm as we discover the heart of the provinces.

HOTELS-RESTAURANTS

■ Le Rex Hôtel
8, cours Gambetta.
Tel. 05 62 54 44 44.
Rest. closed Sun. dinner.
80 rooms: 100–165€. 6 suites: 200–300€.
Prix fixe: 18€, 35€.

Colorful and spanking new, this designer-style contemporary establishment is a commitment to modern luxury, transparency and high-tech furniture. The cuisine is creative and carefully prepared to the specifications of the young Ludovic Trémège. Gourmet buffet on Sundays.

■ Henri IV
7, av B.-Barère.
Tel. 05 62 34 01 68. Fax 05 62 93 71 32.
hotel.henri4@wanadoo.fr / www.henri4.fr
23 rooms: 62–98€.

This 19th-century hotel near the cathedral and the birthplace of Marshal Foch is where Serge Phalippou receives guests in warm and luminous rooms that are decked out with a variety of colors and furniture.

● L'Ambroisie ◎ V.COM

48, rue de l'Abbé-Torné.
Tel. 05 62 93 09 34. Fax 05 62 93 09 24.
www.perso.wanadoo.fr/lambroisie
Closed Sun., Mon.
Prix fixe: 34€, 50€, 70€. A la carte: 76€.

This 19th-century ex-presbytery is called upon to serve "divine food", or ambrosia. This is the mission of Daniel Labarrère and he succeeds rather well at it, with the help of good-quality products from the large Tarbes market. Here we can savor all of Gascony with pan-seared slice of foie gras in an almond crust, turbot with Tarbais white beans, roasted meats, grilled young duck breast and a crunchy citrus dessert. Jean Rodrigues, an excellent guide, is in charge of the cellar and service. In addition, the prices are reasonable and the check won't give you a heart attack.

● L'Aragon N V.COM

2 ter, rte de Lourdes, Jullian (4 km on 921a).
Tel. 05 62 32 07 07. Fax 05 62 32 92 50.
www.hotel-aragon.com
Rest. closed Sat. lunch, Sun. dinner.
12 rooms: 45–65€.
Prix fixe: 19€ (wine inc.), 32€, 45€, 55€, 7,50€ (child). A la carte: 60€.

The people of Tarbes don't hesitate to travel the few kilometers that separate them from Bernard Cazaux's hostelry. In the bistro, with its modern dining room, as in the gastro part with its more classic setting, a spell is cast by goose foie gras terrine with a local fougasse, grilled Atlantic sea bass filet with vegetable fricassée with ventrèche, morels stuffed with veal sweetbreads and the all-apple plate. So many hearty preparations invite us to indulge in delicious siestas in theme-based (wine, golf) and tastefully decorated rooms.

● Le Petit Gourmand ● SIM

62, av B.-Barère.
Tel.-Fax 05 62 34 26 86.
Closed Sat. lunch, Sun. dinner, Mon., 1 week beg. Jan., 2 weeks Aug.
Prix fixe: 18€. A la carte: 40€.

Old posters on the walls, a friendly atmosphere and welcoming smiles all inform us that we are going to enjoy ourselves here and the dishes marked on the slate by Guy Espagnacq live up to our expectations. Marie puts her heart into scallops in their shell with salted butter, tuna belly with slow-cooked onions and green peppers, foie gras-stuffed guinea hen breast with mushrooms served with deglazed pan jus as well as the crème caramel with a hint of citrus and a large pistachio tea cake. A very pleasant establishment with moderate prices.

● Le Fil à la Patte N SIM

30, rue Georges-Lassalle.
Tel. 05 62 93 29 23.
Closed Sat. lunch, Sun., Mon., 7–27 Aug.
Prix fixe: 18€, 25€.

This friendly and rustic eatery located not far from the cathedral charms us with its local dishes based on market products. The prices are reasonable. Tuna carpaccio, sole with basil butter, Gascon-style beef daube and duck breast with cherries make a good impression.

● Le Grillon N SIM

37, av du Régiment-de-Bigorre.
Tel. 05 62 93 88 31.
Closed Mon., Tue.
Prix fixe: 17€, 26€. A la carte: 35€.

This slightly old-fashioned restaurant is nevertheless well worth a visit. Just a few steps away from the central Place de Verdun, Roger Odou pays homage to the wonderful produce of the region with rolled sea bream filet with black olive tapenade, dill-seasoned Atlantic sea bass, veal tenderloin medallion and dark chocolate quenelle with orange jelly.

TARDETS-SORHOLUS

64470 Pyrénées-Atlantiques. Paris 817 – Pau 62 – St-Jean-Pied-de-Port 49 – Oloron-Ste-Marie 28.
The little region of Soule watches over the most secret part of the Basque country.

  HOTELS-RESTAURANTS

■ Uhaltia Le Pont-d'Abense
In Alos-Sibas-Abense (64470) via D247,
quartier d'Abense.
Tel. 05 59 28 54 60. Fax 05 59 28 75 91.
uhaltia@wanadoo.fr
Closed beg. Dec.–end Jan. Rest. closed Sun.
dinner, Mon., Wed. dinner.
10 rooms: 28–55€.
Prix fixe: 25€. A la carte: 40€.

Basque country means Basque cuisine: simplicity, quality products and generosity. And Basque cuisine means Isabelle Iraola. She reigns over this traditional establishment, in a green setting, that offers, in addition to its terrace, private lounge and old-style bedrooms, a subtly modulated regional cuisine that always strikes the right note. In the impeccably laid out dining room with wood and warm tapestries, we make short work of the monkfish and salmon duo served cold with shrimp, Basque-style pan-simmered monkfish and green peppers, the tasting plate of the local lamb and a chocolate mousse dome, all accompanied by a local wine or a Bordeaux.

● Les Pyrénées   SIM
Pl du Marché.
Tel. 05 59 28 50 63. Fax 05 59 28 72 85.
Closed 1 week at end Sept., 1 week beg. Jan.
Prix fixe: 15€, 20€. A la carte: 30€.

Throughout the year, Henri Abadie continues his passionate celebration of his region. In his cream-colored contemporary restaurant, a French or Spanish wine goes well with Basque salad with tomato sauce, a liver puff pastry Tatin with apples, trout with ham, lamb medallions and the gâteau Basque, the essence of serious eating.

TAUTAVEL

66720 Pyrénées-Orientales. Paris 866 – Carcassonne 96 – Narbonne 74 – Perpignan 31.
It is worth visiting the little museum of Prehistory in this Catalan village that became famous in 1971 for the discovery of the oldest human skull ever found in Europe.

● RESTAURANTS

● Le Petit-Gris   SIM
Rte d'Estagel.
Tel. 04 68 29 42 42. Fax 04 68 29 40 49.
Closed Mon. (off season), 3 weeks Jan.
Prix fixe: 20€, 25€, 30€, 7€ (child).
A la carte: 40€.

At a short remove from the village, Nathalie and Eric Quilliet offer us the Corbières landscape as far as the eye can see but also on our plate. In the sunny dining room with large bay windows looking out on the vines and the Pyrénées, wood fire-grilled escargots, monkfish with oyster mushroom sauce, a regional fish stew with nine fish, rabbit with aïoli and the crème Catalane prepared by Stéphane Carretero are models of their kind. A friendly atmosphere and no unpleasant surprises in the check.

TAVEL

30126 Gard. Paris 677 – Alès 68 – Nîmes 43 – Orange 22 – Avignon 15.
To the south of the Rhône valley, a gateway to some of the fine *rosé* wines of the Midi in an important wine-growing town.

  HOTELS-RESTAURANTS

■ Le Pont du Roy
Rte de Nîmes. 3 km se via D4 and D976.
Tel. 04 66 50 22 03. Fax 04 66 50 10 14.
contact@hotelpontduroy.fr
www.hotelpontduroy.fr
Closed end Sept.–Easter. Rest. closed lunch
14 rooms: 61–78€.
Prix fixe: 27€, 50€, 11€ (child).

To the south of the Rhône valley, this contemporary Provençal-style *mas* in the midst of the vineyards has a charming effect. Serge and Steve Schorgeré—father and son—redecorated the house with its wood-trimmed and brightly colored rooms, garden and swimming pool. In the dining room, Steve's cuisine, reserved for residents at the hotel and accompanied by local wines, is evocative of Provence and the Mediterranean. Eggplant purée with tomato sauce, sea bream with fleur de sel and olive oil, marinated and grilled leg of lamb and the chocolate fondant all constitute delicious menus.

● La Petite Bouf'   SIM
Rue Frédéric-Mistral.
Tel. 04 66 50 29 53.
lapetitebouf@wanadoo.fr
www.lapetitebouf.fr
Closed Sun., Tue. dinner, Wed. dinner.
Prix fixe: 12€ (weekday lunch).
A la carte: 35€.

Gilles Thomas' table is a must in this wine-growing village. It is difficult to resist the welcome, the atmosphere and the menu so full of character. The old-style Provençal dining room is the backdrop for a spectacle of finely prepared specialities: small Saint-Marcellin cheese tarts served over salad, trout breaded in walnuts and browned in clarified butter, a slice of leg of lamb with garlic cream sauce and the walnut dessert with Vin de Noix go down well with a chilled Tavel rosé.

TENCE

43190 Haute-Loire. Paris 570 – Le-Puy-en-Velay 46 – Lamastre 39 – Saint-Etienne 54.
office.de.tourisme.tence@freesbee.fr.
The heart of the Velay region, the slopes leading to Mont Gerbier-de-Jonc, the high forests and the clear air.

■ / ● HOTELS-RESTAURANTS

■ Hostellerie Placide
1, rte d'Annonay.
Tel. 04 71 59 82 76. Fax 04 71 65 44 46.
placide@hostellerie-placide.fr
www.hostellerie-placide.fr
Closed Sun. dinner, Mon. (exc. July–Aug.),
Tue. (exc. July–Aug.), beg. Jan.–end Mar.
12 rooms: 70–100€.

Prix fixe: 15€ (weekday lunch), 28€, 45€, 55€, 16€ (child). A la carte: 55€.

The Placides have renovated the old 1902 stage coach stop dating from their grandmother's day: conference room, garden, vast rustic and warmly toned bedrooms. Véronique extends a warm and friendly welcome while Pierre-Marie prepares local market produce in season in skillfully wrought regional dishes. In the wood-toned dining room giving onto the garden, we concentrate on Grazac escargots with licorice-infused jus, crayfish tails with Serrano ham, slice of pike-perch simmered in red wine and grilled beef sirloin steak with morel jus and Cantal cheese potato gratin. Nice desserts and a sizable cellar.

TENDE

06430 Alpes-Maritimes. Paris 888 – Cuneo 50 – Menton 56 – Nice 78 – Sospel 38.
Italy is just round the corner. The perfume of Provence sweeps over the heights.

● RESTAURANTS

● Auberge Tendasque   SIM
65, av 16-Septembre 1947.
Tel. 04 93 04 62 26. Fax 04 93 04 68 34.
Closed dinner (exc. Fri., Sat. and Sun.).
Prix fixe: 12€, 14€, 21€. A la carte: 30€.

Close to the Italian frontier the Porqueres' stately inn offers a rustic setting with a charming painted ceiling and a shady terrace. The menus are a delight. Burgundy-style escargots, wild boar terrine, trout mousse, sirloin steak with ceps and a house tart slip down effortlessly.

TETEGHEM see **DUNKERQUE**

THANN

68800 Haut-Rhin. Paris 472 – Mulhouse 22 – Colmar 44 – Guebwiller 25.
office-de-tourisme.thann@wanadoo.fr.
The collegiate church of Saint-Thiébaut, the horizontal donjon known as "the witch's eye"

and the glorious Rangen wine-growing region are sufficient to ensure the reputation of Thann. The valley of Saint-Amarin deploys its verdant ribbon.

 HOTELS-RESTAURANTS

■ La Cigogne

35-37, rue du Général-de-Gaulle.
Tel. 03 89 37 47 33. Fax 03 89 37 40 18.
mangelhotels@yahoo.fr
www.hotellacigogne.com
Closed Feb. Rest. closed Sun. dinner, Mon.
27 rooms: 48–76€.
Prix fixe: 13,50€, 26€, 32€ (dinner),
11€ (child). A la carte: 55€.

The Mangels' modern hotel is known for its efficient service, its comfortable rose-toned rooms and its honest family cooking. In the lemon and blue pastel dining room Claude's dishes—Andalouse-style langoustine tart, pike-perch on sauerkraut, venison medallion with lingonberries and a frozen vacherin—go down well with local wines.

■ Moschenross

42, rue du Général-de-Gaulle.
Tel. 03 89 37 00 86. Fax 03 89 37 52 81.
info@le-moschenross.com
www.le-moschenross.com
Closed 2 weeks beg. July
Rest. closed Sun. dinner, Mon. lunch.
23 rooms: 31–46€.
Prix fixe: 11€ (weekday lunch), 16€, 22€,
46€, 7,30€ (child).

This large red house dating from 1880 in the center of the town has bright and lively colored rooms. The Geyer-Pontals extend a hearty welcome and Isabelle's finely prepared dishes reflect the seasons. The pork trotter served over sauerkraut, escargots, pike-perch served over slow-cooked leeks, veal hanger steak with morels and the chocolate desserts are very well made.

■ Le Parc

23, rue Kléber.
Tel. 03 89 37 37 47. Fax 03 89 37 56 23.
reception@alsacehotel.com
www.alsacehotel.com
Rest. closed 3 weeks Jan.
21 rooms: 65–180€.
Prix fixe: 37€, 17€ (child).
A la carte: 49€.

In their country house set in wooded grounds, the Martins offer period-style furniture in opulent rooms, elegant lounges, a fitness center—sauna, Turkish bath and Jacuzzi—and a swimming pool. In the richly colored dining room, extending onto the terrace in summer, Sonia Kassis presents classic cuisine adapted to today's taste. Foie gras terrine with fruit chutney, grilled pike-perch with pepper sauce, duck breast with honey and figs and a chestnut crème brûlée are all well prepared. Paulo Soarès suggests appropriate wines to match these dishes.

THANNENKIRCH

68590 Haut-Rhin. Paris 436 – Colmar 21 – Bergheim 7 – Sélestat 15.
This pretty forest village on a rise across from the Haut-Koenigsbourg and not far from the wine route, symbolizes bucolic Alsace.

 HOTELS-RESTAURANTS

■ La Meunière

30, rue Sainte-Anne.
Tel. 03 89 73 10 47. Fax 03 89 73 12 31.
info@aubergelameuniere.com
www.aubergelameuniere.com
Closed 20 Dec.–20 Mar.
23 rooms: 63–105€.
Prix fixe: 13€, 17€, 22€, 34€, 36€,
7€ (child).

This picture postcard Alsatian inn overlooking the valley is a haven of peace. The rooms are mountain style, half-rustic, half-modern, and the bay windows of the dining rooms look out on the surrounding countryside. The fitness center, the panoramic terrace and the garden are all enchanting. In the kitchen, Jean-Luc Dumoulin serves up robust and cheerful food using local market produce. In the rustic dining room the crunchy Munster cheese bonbon with lentil salad, perch filet on a bed of cumin-seasoned sauerkraut, veal hanger steak with lemon and ginger, the Reinette apple dessert and crème brûlée left us with delicious memories.

■ Le Touring

Rte du Haut-Koenigsbourg.
Tel. 03 89 73 10 01. Fax 03 89 73 11 79.
touringhotel@free.fr / www.touringhotel.com
Closed beg. Jan.–end Mar.
Rest. closed lunch (exc. weekends).
45 rooms: 50–94€.
Prix fixe: 16€ (weekdays), 21€, 41€.
A la carte: 37–42€.

In the heart of the village and in sight of the pine crests, Antoine Stoeckel's hearty hotel has kept up with the times, with its rooms with wood furniture and its serious cuisine with Jean-Louis Biechler at the helm. In the old-style light wood dining room, foie gras ravioli with vegetable bouillon, rosemary-seasoned and grilled Atlantic sea bass and a strawberry frozen meringue go down without any difficulty.

● S'Waldstebel SIM

24, rue Sainte-Anne.
Tel.-Fax 03 89 73 11 84.
Closed Mon., mid-Jan.–end Feb.
Prix fixe: 12,50€ (lunch), 16,50€, 20€.
A la carte: 30–35€.

With its pine benches and panoramic terrace, this mountain tavern exudes the charm of the Vosges. Eric Bechdolff cooks up timeless dishes and finely wrought concoctions that go well with the rustic wooden dining room when escorted by local wines. House duck foie gras, pike-perch served on sauerkraut with beurre blanc, pork cuts and charcuterie served on sauerkraut and a Kirsch-flavored mousse have no difficulty convincing us, particularly since the Marcaire menu is devilishly generous.

THEOULE-SUR-MER

06590 Alpes-Maritimes. Paris 903 –
Cannes 11 – Draguignan 59 – Nice 42 –
Saint-Raphaël 30.

ot@theoule-sur-mer.org.
A discreet balcony overlooking the Blue Beyond.

 HOTELS-RESTAURANTS

■ Miramar Beach Hotel

47, av de Miramar.
Tel. 04 93 75 05 05. Fax 04 93 75 44 83.
reservation@mbhotel.com
www.mbhriviera.com
56 rooms: 135–315€. 6 suites: 235–350€.
Prix fixe: 24€ (weekdays), 31€ (weekdays),
41€ (wine inc. weekdays), 85€ (dinner)
16€ (child). A la carte: 75€.

Nestling in a creek of red rocks, Peter Van Santen's hotel offers an unbeatable view, charming and brightly colored rooms, as well as a swimming pool and a fitness center: so many invitations to meditation and rest. At the Etoile des Mers, a panoramic restaurant decorated with a wall panel that evokes the nearby Massif de l'Esterel, Jilali Berrakama produces dishes with the flavors of the bright and cheerful South while Ali Hedayat, the sommelier, recommends choice wines to go with the dishes. Cep risotto with parsley served with a simmered rabbit leg, John Dory and sea urchin with aïoli and Italian broccoli and Mediterranean sea bass and chorizo in a quinoa paella with saffron-seasoned shellfish jus are enthusiastic statements in freshness and precision.

THESEE

41140 Loir-et-Cher. Paris 220 – Tours 53 –
Blois 38 – Châteauroux 74 – Vierzon 63.
The beginning of the Sologne region, the banks of the Cher, the easy-on-the-palate wines harvested from sandy soil: that's what we find in the modest vicinity of the Loire Valley.

 HOTELS-RESTAURANTS

■ Hostellerie du Moulin de la Renne

15, impasse des Varennes / 11, rte de Vierzon.
Tel. 02 54 71 41 56. Fax 02 54 71 75 09.

moulindelarenne@yahoo.fr
www.moulindelarenne.com
Closed 1 week Nov., 10 Jan.–10 Feb.
Rest. closed Mon. lunch, Tue. lunch.
13 rooms: 52–93€.
Prix fixe: 17€, 23€, 30€, 40€, 9€ (child).

This old riverside mill hosts a family hostelry enhanced with a shady garden, rooms with Old World charm and good quality cooking at reasonable prices. In the rustic dining room with harmonious tones of yellow and green, or on the summer terrace, the hot goat cheese, oven-browned trout, coq au vin and crème brûlée are serious local classics that go down well with the cheerful wines of the Loire and the Berry regions.

THIERS

63300 Puy-de-Dôme. Paris 392 – Clermont-Ferrand 42 – Lyon 133 – Saint-Etienne 108 – Vichy 37.
A medieval city with its back to a rocky outcrop offers a mosaic of different neighborhoods linked to the different trades of bygone days. Don't miss a visit to the Cutlery Museum.

● | RESTAURANTS

● Le Coutelier SIM
4, pl du Palais.
Tel.-Fax 04 73 80 79 59.
www.le-coutelier.com
Closed Mon. and Tue. (off season), Oct.
Prix fixe: 15€, 16€, 26€, 6€ (child).
A la carte: 40€.

We come to eat but also to visit this old cutlery workshop that doubles as a museum. Jésus Moreno displays old objects and a collection of knives while serving up local recipes. Truffade (local potato and cheese purée) and Auvergne ham, pikeperch seasoned with verjus, sausage with red cabbage and the house apple dessert are particularly successful.

THIONVILLE

57100 Moselle. Paris 340 – Metz 29 – Luxembourg 29 – Trèves 76.
tourisme@thionville.net.
By the banks of the Moselle river, this crossroads city leading to the Grand Duchy of Luxembourg was once the iron capital. The countryside is now verdant between the Guentrange butte, where vines once grew, and the nearby forests.

 | HOTELS-RESTAURANTS

● L'Horizon
50, rte du Crève-Coeur.
Tel. 03 82 88 53 65. Fax 03 82 34 55 84.
hotel@lhorizon.fr
horizon@romantikhotels.com
www.lhorizon.fr
Closed mid-Dec.–mid-Jan. Rest. closed Sat. lunch, Mon. lunch, Fri. lunch.
12 rooms: 98–150€.
Prix fixe: 40€, 47€, 54€.
A la carte: 55–70€.

The residence is classical with its beautiful facade covered with Virginia creeper and the furniture has the charm of bygone days. Bedrooms and lounges receive guests with elegance. The grounds are peaceful and the picturesque panorama of the surrounding countryside justifies the name of the establishment; the name is a heartfelt statement. Jean-Pascal Speck is over the ovens and produces classic dishes with precision and a personal touch. Langoustines tossed with sundried tomatoes, Riesling-roasted cod filet, oven-roasted veal tenderloin medallions with preserved lemons and a mirabelle plum bavaroise seasoned with eau-de-vie hit the right note. We only have to choose the right wine to match the quality of the food. Anne-Marie Speck and her willing smile are there to help you.

● Aux Poulbots Gourmets COM
9, pl aux Fleurs.
Tel. 03 82 88 10 91. Fax 03 82 88 42 76.
philippe.ardizzoia@orange.fr
www.aupoulbotsgourmet.fr

Closed Sat. lunch, Sun. dinner, Mon.,
2 weeks Jan., 1 week at Easter,
end July–mid-Aug.
Prix fixe: 36€, 45€, 55€, 60€, 10€ (child).

In the classic dining room with white and brown tones and on the shady terrace, Philippe Ardizzoia, formerly of the Crillon and the Tour d'Argent, serves up nicely presented market produce in tempting menus. Without the enlightened comments and advice of Pascal Gobeaut it would be easy to get lost in the wine list with 400 vintages from France, New Zealand and Luxembourg. Marbled duck foie gras terrine with ceps, truffle soup, lobster and langoustine risotto, lamb tenderloin medallions with house potatoes and thyme sauce and a hot soufflé with Grand Marnier are unanimous winners.

● **Les Sommeliers**   🅟🅖SIM

23, pl de la République.
Tel. 03 82 53 32 20. Fax 03 82 53 47 85.
restsommelier@wanadoo.fr
Closed Sat. lunch, Sun., Bank holidays,
1 week Christmas–New Year's.
Prix fixe: 15€, 8,50€. A la carte: 35–40€.

Cheeky little wines, a smart and sassy atmosphere and carefully crafted dishes: the formula bears the stamp of Brigitte Gallois, a charming sommelier who has made this establishment with its yellow and green tones, glass roof and brasserie-style décor into a first-class eatery. Laurent Kraemer's attractive dishes charm us: pan-tossed frog legs with garlic and parsley, gratined Camembert with peppered caramel, saffron-seasoned monkfish medallion, tête de veau with two sauces, grilled Argentinian beef medallions with béarnaise sauce, a rich chocolate cake and crème brûlée-flavored ice cream.

● **Au Petit chez Soi**   🅝SIM

23, rue de Luxembourg.
Tel. 03 82 53 62 96.
Closed Sun., Mon., Bank holidays,
10 days Christmas–New Year's, 10 days at Easter, 3 weeks summer.
Prix fixe: 32€, 45€.

Philippe Tessier, who worked with Guillou in Schouweiler, opened this rustic inn in town with its Basque-style pimientos hanging from the walls and its generous and finely crafted cuisine. Foie gras terrine, escargot fricassée with basil and spring garlic, rouget in bouillabaisse broth, beef cheeks simmered in red wine with home-style mashed potatoes and a traditionally prepared tête de veau with sauce gribiche all hit the right spot. The desserts are in the same register (tarte Tatin served with a scoop of caramel ice cream). A winning welcome, charming service and a well-targeted wine list with a good choice of vintages by the glass.

In Knutange (57240). 10 km sw via D13, D952.

● **Remotel**   🏠

75, rue de la République.
Tel. 03 82 85 19 23. Fax 03 82 84 22 01.
remotel@wanadoo.fr / www.remotel.fr
Rest. closed Mon.
27 rooms: 57–87€.
Prix fixe: 11€ (weekdays), 16€, 23€ (wine inc.), 30€, 8€ (child, bev. inc.).

The Remmer family offers a hearty welcome in this downtown hotel/restaurant. The modernly furnished rooms are pleasant and Daniel's robust regional cuisine will never lose its charm. Creamed carrot soup with a topping of goat cheese, sole meunière, pan-tossed slice of veal sweetbread with asparagus tips and the crunchy caramel basket with trilogy of ice creams are honest work.

In Manom (57100). 6 km ne.

● **Les Etangs**   V.COM

Rte de Garche.
Tel. 03 82 53 26 92. Fax 03 82 53 30 12.
www.restaurantlesetangs.com
Closed Sun. dinner, Mon.
Prix fixe: 28€, 34€, 38€, 14€ (child).
A la carte: 52–57€.

Jacqueline and Franck Legile manage, Philippe Fiorini cooks and Olivier Schanne is in charge of the wine service: the young dynamism of this country house with its bay window is always pleasing. The well-balanced menus served in the wine-red contemporary dining room offer chic dishes that change with the tastes of the day. Salmon and monkfish with nori seaweed, stir-fried langoustine spring rolls, lemongrass-seasoned monkfish and jumbo shrimp brochettes with risotto, plus a rack of lamb with chanterelles and young garlic and vegetable ravioli in a pesto emulsion make a good impression even if they tend to make too much of them.

In Petite-Hettange (57480). 12,6 km via N153.

● **Restaurant Olmi**　　🏠⚪COM

11, rte Nationale.
Tel. 03 82 50 10 65. Fax 03 82 83 61 01.
Closed Mon. dinner, Tue. dinner, Wed.,
2 weeks Feb., 2 weeks beg. July.
Prix fixe: 30€ (weekdays), 41€, 60€.
A la carte: 65€.

A UFO in Moselle, that's Jean-Marc Olmi. This modest man who worked with Nachon in the Concorde before the Tuileries at Fey and the Forêt d'Amnéville, is in the process of changing his profile. He took a truckstop eatery (the Relais des Trois Frontières) and made it into a reputable restaurant. He changed the name, put his own name outside and declared his ambitions. He paid careful attention to the presentation, enriched his wine list and extended his range. Sole with vermouth sauce and chives, escargot callelleti in a garden herb bouillon, roasted lobster in sauce with creamy risotto, Dombes poultry cooked in Vin Jaune with morels and the pan-seared beef sirloin steak with wine-enriched pan juices are all excellent quality. In addition, varied and imaginative desserts based on traditional recipes, such as the coffee mille-feuille and caramelized almonds, fresh raspberry dessert with light cream and a crunchy waffle and the composition on the theme of the lemon ("passionnement citron") with an individual tart, crème brûlée and sorbet all tell us that something great and good is happening in Petite Hettange. Corinne's smiling welcome is a constant feature. The formerly country-style décor has developed a finer accent (entrance, lounge, bathrooms, round tables all had a facelift last year) and the local region has been

included in the feast with the produce of the best growers in the region, a welcome innovation.

In Yutz (57970). 3 km via N153.

● **Les Alérions**　　🏠🍴COM

102, rue Nationale.
Tel. 03 82 56 26 63. Fax 03 82 56 26 65.
www.lesalerions.com
Closed Sun. dinner, Mon., Tue. dinner, mid-Aug.–end Aug.
Prix fixe: 16€ (weekday lunch), 21,50€,
29,50€, 38€ (wine inc.), 48€, 10€ (child).
A la carte: 42–48€.

The facade next to the national road is austere, but we would be wrong not to stop here because, on the inside, Frédéric Scheid's cuisine blends the flavors of the Lorraine region with those of the Southwest in carefully crafted and precise dishes that are designed to win our hearts. In the carefully laid out dining room—wood sculptures, tile stove, high ceilings—a procession of oven-crisped oxtails with foie gras and red wine, smoked salmon and mirabelle plum in a crêpe pouch with fresh white cheese, pan-seared scallops with a crispy smoked bacon and cep cappuccino, a half pigeon stuffed with morels and glazed in Port sauce, lastly the frozen mirabelle plum soufflé constitute finely wrought work. Everything is good in Les Alérions—the three beakless and talon-less eagles on the Lorraine coat of arms!

THOIRY

01710 Ain. Paris 527 – Bellegarde-sur-Valserine 27 – Bourg-en-Bresse 100 –
Gex 14.
The heart of the Gex country, between the Crêt de la Neige and the Léman region.

 ◼️ HOTELS-RESTAURANTS

◼️ **Holiday Inn**　　

1, av Mont-Blanc, 1,5 km ne.
Tel. 04 50 99 19 99.
www.holidayinn.com
Rest. closed Sat. lunch, Sun. lunch.

95 rooms: 80–140€.
Prix fixe: 20€, 29€.

Practical and functional, a stopover hotel just down the road from the Geneva-Cointrin airport and the Swiss border. Carefully crafted market cuisine, buffets, well-equipped rooms and service with a smile.

● Les Cépages

465, rue Briand-Stresemann.
Tel. 04 50 20 83 85. Fax 04 50 41 24 58.
contact@lescepages.com / www.lescepages.com
Closed Sun. dinner, Mon., Tue.
Prix fixe: 29€ (lunch, weekdays), 46€, 90€.
A la carte: 80–100€.

In summer, the terrace overlooking the neighboring peaks is a sheer pleasure, but the subtly lit half-classical, half-modern dining room with its straw yellow and orange colors also offers moments of rare pleasure. Jean-Pierre Delesderrier, the little gourmet king of the Gex country, skillfully elaborates a fresh market cuisine that is refined, rooted and elegant, a true technician. On the changing menu, lobster simply seasoned with salted butter, resting in a sweet pea- and mint-seasoned seafood broth, foie gras ravioli poached in a truffle-seasoned poultry broth, roasted sea bream presented on a cold zucchini cream, stuffed Ain hen breast in a creamy Jura wine sauce and a frozen verbena parfait are finely wrought dishes. Isabelle Barros is there to help suggest pertinent wines and the menus are well balanced.

THONON-LES-BAINS

74200 Haute-Savoie. Paris 570 – Annecy 75 – Chamonix 100 – Genève 34.
thonon@thononlesbains.com.
A port on Lake Léman, a medieval chateau, an AOC wine, a fine table and a great cheese: surely this is enough for a joyful stopover?

 HOTELS-RESTAURANTS

■ Arc-en-Ciel   🏠

18, pl de Crête.
Tel. 04 50 71 90 63. Fax 04 50 26 27 47.

info@hotel-arcenciel.com
www.hotelarcencielthonon.com
Closed Christmas–New Year's vac.
Rest. closed Sun. dinner (Dec.–mid-May), Mon. (Dec.–mid-May).
40 rooms: 59–79€.
Prix fixe: 13€ (weekdays), 19€, 25€, 28€, 30€, 9€ (child). A la carte: 35–40€.

This modern hotel run by Bernard and Denis Favre is located not far from the center and is worth visiting for its garden and swimming pool, its functional and comfortable rooms with a balcony or terrace, its fitness center with sauna and gymnasium and its restaurant Les Marroniers, which serves reliable cuisine: lambs lettuce salad with Réblochon melted in puff pastry, a roasted rack of lamb seasoned with wild thyme and the chestnut dessert cup, from chef Jean-François Morand.

■ Savoie et Léman   🏠

40, bd Carnot.
Tel. 04 50 71 13 80. Fax 04 50 71 16 14.
hotel@ecole-hoteliere-thonon.com
www.hotel-savoieleman.eu
Closed Sat., Sun., Nov. 1 vac., Christmas–New Year's vac., Feb. vac., Easter, July–Aug.
34 rooms: 110€.
Prix fixe: 15€, 23€, 10€ (child).

Following a radical renovation, this annex to the hotel school offers a view of Lake Léman, has brand new rooms and a generous and reliable cuisine that reflects the changing seasons.

● Le Prieuré

68, Grand-Rue.
Tel. 04 50 71 31 89. Fax 04 50 71 31 09.
plumex-prieuré@wanadoo.fr
Closed Sun. dinner, Mon., Tue., 2 weeks Nov., 2 weeks beg. Apr.
Prix fixe: 34€ (lunch), 38€, 58€, 72€.

Charlie Plumex celebrates gastronomy in the chapel of the old Thonon priory. In the vaulted restaurant with wooden décor and red and gray colors, this veteran of the Royal-Evian who trained in England offers a new interpretation of regional classics in a lighter and more refined register. We enjoyed lobster salad, duck foie gras, big langoustines with oven-crisped Réblochon-seasoned potatoes, salmon trout with salted butter, beef sirloin steak and a variation on the tête de veau with a touch of madness that gives it its charm. Desserts are in the same register with the thin apple tart and an eau-de-vie-and raspberry-infused soufflé. The wine list has been reduced in quantity but not in quality.

In Anthy-sur-Léman (74200). 6 km via D33.

■ L'Auberge d'Anthy

2, rue des Ecoles.
Tel. 04 50 70 35 00. Fax 04 50 70 40 90.
info@auberge-anthy.com
www.auberge-anthy.com
Closed 10 days Oct.
Rest. closed Sun. dinner, Mon.
16 rooms: 46–62€.
Prix fixe: 13,50€, 23€,: 29€,
37,50€ (wine inc.).

Claude and Catherine Dubouloz run this charming inn. The lake is not far away and you're sure to find peace in the gently colored rooms, as in the lounge and on the terrace kept cool by the nearby fountain. Natural cuisine with good products: any more would be superfluous. Asparagus with a foamy cream sauce, lake trout filet (steamed or meunière style), boneless rib steak and the soft chocolate cake are very well made. The cellar provides an excellent accompaniment with wines from Savoie and the valley of the Rhône.

In Sciez-Bonnatrait (74140). 9 km via N5, rte de Genève.

● Château de Coudrée

Tel. 04 50 72 62 33. Fax 04 50 72 57 28.
chcoudree@coudree.com / www.coudree.com
Hotel closed Nov.
Rest. closed Tue. and Wed. (exc. July–Aug.).
17 rooms: 138–346€.
Prix fixe: 39€ (lunch), 90€. A la carte: 85€.

Catherine Réale Laden's edifice is not lacking in character. Imagine a Middle Ages castle in a 17th-century Italian Renaissance setting with luxurious rooms with 19th-century furniture. Only the cuisine

of Marco Bassi, newly arrived from the Verbier Rosalp, could possibly upstage it. With langoustines in a crunchy crust and served with mango salad, smoked salmon trout with leeks and lime jus, a loin of suckling pig with an acidulated apple compote and a calisson pastry with fresh fromage blanc ice cream. You can trust Max Hardouin to recommend a wine to go with your meal.

THOUARCE

49380 Maine-et-Loire. Paris 320 – Angers 30 – Cholet 45 – Saumur 40.
A wise stopover on your way through the wines of Anjou. Visit the nearby Château de Brissac-Quincé!

| ● | RESTAURANTS |

● Le Relais de Bonnezeaux

1 km, route d'Angers.
Tel. 02 41 54 08 33. Fax 02 41 54 00 63.
relais.bonnezeaux@wanadoo.fr
www.cuisineriesgourmandes.com
Closed Sun. dinner, Mon., Tue. dinner,
end Dec.–mid-Jan.
Prix fixe: 18,50€ (weekdays), 24,50€,
40,50€, 54€ (wine inc.), 11,50€ (child).
A la carte: 40€.

Located in an old train station, this rural stopover offers a pleasant view of the vineyards. In the kitchen, Robert Touchet remains true to tradition and strikes the right note: Vendée escargots with quail eggs in red wine sauce, pike with beurre blanc, roasted squab with reduced wine sauce and a frozen honey and Triple Sec nougat.

THOUARS

79100 Deux-Sèvres. Paris 335 – Angers 70 – Bressuire 30 – Châtellerault 74 – Cholet 55.
An abundance of flowers, the château of the dukes of Trémoille on its rocky outcrop, the beautiful church of Saint-Médard with its rich Romanesque portal. The Old World charm of its houses completes the picture of this medieval city.

HOTELS-RESTAURANTS

■ Hôtellerie Saint-Jean
25, rte de Parthenay.
Tel. 05 49 96 12 60. Fax 05 49 96 34 02.
hotellerie-st-jean@wanadoo.fr
www.hotellerie-st-jean.fr
Closed Sun. dinner, dinner Bank holidays,
Mon. (exc. off season), Feb. vac.
18 rooms: 40–42€.
Prix fixe: 16€, 25€, 32€, 9€ (child).
A la carte: 45–53€.

This building dating from 1970 offers a fine view of the old city. Bright yellow and orange colors in the irreproachable rooms and dining room. Eric Bernier and Xavier Bichon serve up market cuisine that makes a good impression: a thin scallop tart, fennel-seed seasoned Atlantic sea bass with a citrus herb sauce, spicy caramelized veal sweetbreads and a soft-centered chocolate cake served with orange sorbet are very well prepared.

■ Hôtel du Relais
3 km. n, rte de Saumur.
Tel. 05 49 66 29 45. Fax 05 49 66 29 33.
15 rooms: 35–54€.

Its location in the heart of the industrial zone is not ideal but this large villa offers brightly colored rooms and a veranda breakfast room.

THURY-HARCOURT

14220 Calvados. Paris 254 – Caen 28 – Falaise 28 – Vire 41.
otsi.thury@libertysurf.fr.
The crossroads of "Swiss Normandy", gourmet pleasures and country walks.

HOTELS-RESTAURANTS

● Le Relais de la Poste   COM
Rte de Caen.
Tel. 02 31 79 72 12. Fax 02 31 39 53 55.
www.hotel-relaisdelaposte.com
Closed 2 weeks Nov., Mar.
Rest. closed Fri. (off season), Sat. lunch (off

season), Sun. dinner (off season).
9 rooms: 60–140€. 1 suite: 140€.
Prix fixe: 15€ (lunch, wine inc.), 26€, 35€, 40€.

We like this old post house with its ivied walls, its vast enclosed courtyard, old-style rooms and elegant dining room under the wooden framework of the roof. Jean-Marc Harau does not surpass the establishment's former glory under Jean Mauge but serves up genuinely good traditional fare. Vitelotte potato mousse with a lime macaron, citrus-seasoned scallops, sole filet steamed over seaweed, marinated Swiss pigeon, pistachio macaron with a carrot verbena sorbet and a frozen Calvados soufflé make a good impression. A fine wine list presents us with difficult choices.

TIERCE

49125 Maine-et-Loire. Paris 280 – Angers 23 – Château-Gontier 35 – La Flèche 35.
Escape to the peace and tranquillity of the Anjou region.

● RESTAURANTS

● La Table d'Anjou   COM
16, rue d'Anjou.
Tel. 02 41 42 14 42. Fax 02 41 42 64 80.
www.destination-anjou.com/tabledanjou
Closed Sun. dinner, Mon., Tue. dinner (off season), 2 weeks beg. Jan., mid-July–mid-Aug.
Prix fixe: 18€ (weekday lunch), 24€, 33€, 49€, 15€ (child). A la carte: 51–58€.

A winning combination for Catherine and Patrick Linay in the center of the village: bright rooms and a flowery terrace at the rear, a warm welcome, genuinely good local fare that reflects the changing seasons. At the ovens, Eric Boulland concocts duck foie gras served three ways, pike-perch with roasted langoustines and beurre blanc sauce, rabbit saddle with bacon venison sauce and pan-simmered quince and apples served with salted-butter caramel as sweet as childhood memories. A fine cellar reflecting the colors of the Anjou wines.

TIGNES

73320 Savoie. Paris 696 – Albertville 85 –
Chambéry 134 – Val-d'Isère 13.
information@tignes.net.
An alpine location at more than 1,600 meters,
the dam, the lake and the panorama of the
Grande Motte are year-long attractions for
mountain lovers and skiers alike.

 HOTELS-RESTAURANTS

■ Les Campanules

Quartier le Rosset.
Tel. 04 79 06 34 36. Fax 04 79 06 35 78.
campanules@wanadoo.fr
www.campanules.com
Closed May–beg. July, Sept.–beg. Oct.
30 rooms: 100–230€. 12 suites: 160–290€.
Prix fixe: 35€, 48€. A la carte: 65€.

There is no shortage of reasons for visiting Thierry Raymond's mountain chalet: the cozy setting, large and comfortable rooms, heated swimming pool, fitness center, Turkish bath, Jacuzzi and carefully crafted regional cuisine of Stéphane Grignon. In the dining room with its fresco evoking the history of the village that was sunk in 1952, a rolled scallop and smoked salmon carpaccio, roasted salmon trout filet, breaded rack of lamb with crunchy bacon and pan-tossed seasonal fruit served in a jelly jar are a delight.

■ Village Montana

Les Almes.
Tel. 04 79 40 01 44. Fax 04 79 40 04 03.
contact@vmontana.com / www.vmontana.com
Closed Sept.–beg. Nov., May–end June.
79 rooms: 54–150€. 31 suites: 115–250€.
Prix fixe: 20€, 25€, 40€. A la carte: 55€.

This hotel complex consisting of several chalets that are typical of the region offers a panoramic view of the resort and the surrounding mountains. The rooms and suites facing the slopes are refined and the facilities (swimming pool, Turkish bath, Jacuzzi, fitness center) make a good impression. In the Chaumière restaurant, the slow-roasted vegetable risotto, rouget

filets with fennel, grilled sirloin steak and a mandarin orange individual tart introduce a sunny note.

● Le Chalet Bouvier

In Val-Claret, 2 km. sw., at hotel L'Ecrin.
Tel. 04 79 06 99 90. Fax 04 79 07 80 39.
www.chaletbouvier-tignes.com
Closed lunch, Sept.–end Nov., May–end June.
Prix fixe: 25€. A la carte: 40€.

When not at the Essentiel in Chambéry, Jean-Michel Bouvier is high up in this mountain chalet. We appreciate the warm and authentic aspect of the wood in the dining room. The quietly subdued atmosphere is perfect for savoring a pumpkin, young Tomme cheese and bacon "milkshake", grilled salmon trout filet, pork civet with bacon and a comforting chocolate soufflé served hot.

TINQUEUX see REIMS

TONNERRE

89700 Yonne. Paris 199 – Auxerre 38 –
Montbard 45 – Troyes 60 – Avallon 52.
The city of the knight of Eon has retained some fine medieval treasures, like the fosse Dionne and the interior of the old hospital with the painting of the entombment of Christ. The Château de Tanlay and Epineuil vineyards are just down the road.

 HOTELS-RESTAURANTS

■ L'Auberge de Bourgogne

2 km e via rte de Dijon.
Tel. 03 86 54 41 41. Fax 03 86 54 48 28.
auberge.bourgogne@wanadoo.fr
www.aubergedebourgogne.com
Rest. closed Sun. dinner, Mon.,
mid-Dec.–10 Jan.
39 rooms: 50–56€.
Prix fixe: 10€ (weekday lunch), 16€, 29€.

This vast modern residence overlooking the vineyards is useful for visiting the region. Functional rooms, moderate prices and regional cuisine go well together.

● **Le Saint-Père**   ⓝ SIM

2, av Georges-Pompidou.
Tel. 03 86 55 12 84.
Closed Sun. dinner, Tue. dinner (off season),
Wed., Christmas–20 Jan.
Prix fixe: 11€ (lunch), 15€, 40€.

This rustic little house with its collection of coffee mills is always welcoming. We go there for unpretentious regional cuisine. Escargots in Chablis, pike-perch with thinly sliced chorizo, beef flambéed in Marc de Bourgogone and finished in the oven with Epoisses cheese and the seven-hour lamb shanks all look good.

TOUL

54200 Meurthe-et-Moselle. Paris 285 –
Nancy 24 – Bar-le-Duc 61 – Metz 75 –
Verdun 79.
office.tourisme.toul@wanadoo.fr.
The local vineyards, which have made considerable progress, present some pretty slopes. The cathedral of Saint-Etienne and the church of Saint-Gengoult are both jewels.

● | RESTAURANTS

● **Le Dauphin**   ◎ V.COM

Rte de Villey-Saint-Etienne.
Tel. 03 83 43 13 46. Fax 03 83 43 81 31.
christophe.vohmann@wanadoo.fr
Closed Sun. dinner, Mon., Wed. dinner,
1 week at end July, Aug.
Prix fixe: 29€ (lunch exc. fêtes), 59€,
10€ (child). A la carte: 65€.

The industrial zone established on an old American base has one excellent restaurant. Christophe Vohmann has transformed the old officers' mess into a house of taste with pale blond 19th-century wood interiors and nicely laid-out tables. Here this former student of Mère Brazier cooks up a rich cuisine that is adapted to today's tastes. Foie gras and potato mille-feuille with truffle jus, John Dory flavored with sea urchins, breaded and fried foie gras-stuffed pigeon strike a balance between tradition and modernity, as does the round of crunchy shortbread with mirabelle chutney at the end of the meal. The wines selected and recommended by Véronique Vohmann are a perfect match for these fine preparations.

● **Aux Bouchons Lyonnais**   ⓝ SIM

10, rue de la République.
Tel. 03 83 43 00 41.
Closed Sun. dinner.
Prix fixe: 14€ (weekday lunch), 35€.

Céline and Bertrand Dufourcq have addded a sprightly touch to the old Commerce. The dining room is laid out like a 1900s brasserie with red benches, frescoes of Bellevue tiles, one representing Mercury, the other Gambrinus. Bertrand, who has just returned from a stint with Ducasse, offers in addition to chitterling or pistachio sausage from Colette Sibilia in Lyon, daily specials, truffle-seasoned scallops with creamed celery root, turbot served with a champagne sauce, appealing risottos, generous pork cuts and charcuterie over sauerkraut. The baba au rhum and crème brûlée with red Lyonnais-style pralines make a good impression.

In Lucey (54200). 9 km nw via D904, D908.

● **Auberge du Pressoir**   SIM

7, rue Pachenottes.
Tel. 03 83 63 81 91. Fax 03 83 63 81 38.
www.aubergedupressoir.com
Closed Sun. dinner, Mon., Wed. dinner,
Christmas–New Year's vac.,
mid-Aug.–beg. Sept.
Prix fixe: 12,80€, 16,80€, 23,90€, 29€.

The winepress stands before this old village train station. The bright eating area with its bay windows overlooking the vineyards and cherry-plum trees, its peasant objects and sunny terrace offers a nicely crafted and modern version of the local cuisine. Reynald Steschenko succeeds very well with local escargots simmered in red wine, pike-perch filet in a pine nut crust and duck breast with cherries. The chocolate dessert is not bad and the wine list includes all wine-growing areas.

TOULBROCHE see **BADEN**

TOULON

83000 Var. Paris 839 – Aix-en-Provence 85 – Marseille 65.
toulon.tourisme@wanadoo.fr.
The famous harbor, the Mont-Faron corniche, the navy museum and the port attract lovers of the sea to this arsenal city.

 HOTELS-RESTAURANTS

■ Holiday Inn Garden Court
1, av Rageot-de-la-Touche.
Tel. 04 94 92 00 21. Fax 04 94 62 08 15.
higctoulon@alliance-hospitality.com
80 rooms: 103–103€.
Prix fixe: 16€, 20€, 11€ (child).

This modern chain hotel near the station makes a favorable impression with its off-white rooms with classic furniture, its swimming pool and contemporary restaurant in shades of green. The dishes prepared by chef David Dos Santos—salmon tartare with beet vinaigrette, little Provençal-style stuffed vegetables and Provence-inspired sautéed jumbo shrimp—are perfectly good.

■ New Hôtel Tour Blanche
Bd de l'Amiral-Vence.
Tel. 04 94 24 41 57. Fax 04 94 22 42 25.
toulontourblanche@new-hotel.com
www.new-hotel.com
Rest. closed Sat., Sun.
75 rooms: 78–108€.
Prix fixe: 19€, 23€, 8€ (child).
A la carte: 50€.

A splendid view of the city and harbor, rooms with seventies furniture in lively tones, a swimming pool and quality cuisine: all make for a pleasant stopover. However, it is due to close for renovations. Check first!

■ La Corniche
17, littoral Frédéric-Mistral,
presqu'île du Mourillon.
Tel. 04 94 41 35 12, Fax 04 94 41 24 58.
Rest.: 04 94 41 10 04. Fax 04 94 00 91 57.
info@cornichehotel.com

laurent.richard6@wanadoo.fr
www.bestwestern-hotelcorniche.com
Rest. closed Sun. dinner, Mon., Bank holidays.
21 rooms: 85–125€. 4 suites: 105–190€.
Prix fixe: 27,90€, 36€, 45€, 53€, 10€ (child).

Overlooking the bay and close to the Saint-Louis fort and the Mourillon beaches, this sixties construction is a peaceful hotel with white and bright rooms renovated in the old style and overlooking the sea or scented garden. The contemporary restaurant in shades of green and white is the backdrop for the lively gourmet dishes prepared by Nathalie and Laurent Richard. Scallop carpaccio, grilled fish of the day and mixed fresh fruits leave lasting memories.

● Les Pins Penchés
3182, av de la Résistance, at Cap Brun.
Tel. 04 94 27 98 98. Fax 04 94 27 98 27.
infos@restaurant-pins-penches.com
www.restaurant-pins-penches.com
Closed Sun. dinner, Mon., Tue. lunch.
Prix fixe: 48€, 58€.

A sublime setting of pine trees bent by the wind on the sea. The large garden, the aristocratic residence, the terrace, the genteel lounges and the serious and carefully wrought cuisine: everything Stéphane Lelièvre does is charming. Of course the master of the house is often occupied with the group meals that are organized in the large tent in the grounds. But the establishment, with shades of the Pré Catelan, is very resourceful. When it comes to eating, we are tempted by asparagus with a whipped sauce, creamy eggplant soup with black olive mousseline, wild Mediterranean sea bass with mashed potatoes and a mild and bitter orange fondant served with verbena sorbet. A fine cellar that pays homage to Provence.

● Blanc le Bistro
290, av Jean-Jaurès.
Tel. 04 94 10 20 40.
Closed Sun., Mon.
Prix fixe: 18€ (wine inc.), 29€.
A la carte: 30–40€.

A former cinema converted into a contemporary brasserie with red and brown armchairs, amusing lighting and a lively à la carte menu: this is the domain of Thierry Blanc. This former assistant to Ducasse, who designed and organized the Abbaye de la Celle, the Ostapé and the Lyonnais, has brought in the young Laurent Lemal, ex-assistant to Benoît Witz at the Celle, who concocts a symphony that is light and seductive. Chickpea cream with goat cheese-topped puff pastry, a pressed foie gras and quince terrine, sea bream in bouillabaisse, poultry breast seasoned with herbs and traditional pork sausage wrapped in caul lace with braised white cabbage succeed in gentrifying peasant dishes. And the desserts (a raspberry cheese cake and the house tiramisu) take us straight back to childhood.

● **Le Pointilliste**   Ⓝ COM

43, rue Picot.
Tel. 04 94 71 06 01.
Closed Sat. lunch, Sun. dinner,
3 weeks July–Aug.
Prix fixe: 15€ (lunch), 28€, 41€, 55€.

Christophe Janvier, a young veteran of the Jardin du Sommelier, who has worked with Chibois and Llorca in Mougins, knows his scales. The modern décor, with neon lighting and tables laid out with shades of brown and off-white, is a little neutral, but the menus are seductive. Foie gras on toast with caramelized shallots served on a bed of slow-cooked new potatoes, langoustine ravioli with pan-simmered leeks, roasted Atlantic sea bass and chanterelles with mushroom- and ham-stuffed artichokes simmered in wine and thin sirloin steak strips roasted in Sichuan peppercorns make a good impression. The desserts (coconut dacquoise with Bourbon vanilla-seasoned roasted pineapple and piña colada sorbet) leave us with a lingering flavor that tells us to "come back often". A house worth watching.

● **L'Arbre Rouge**   COM

25, rue de la Comédie.
Tel. 04 94 92 28 58.
bmussillon@neuf.fr

Closed Sun., 3 weeks Aug.
Prix fixe: 21€, 29€ (weekday dinner)
9,50€ (child). A la carte: 35–40€.

Just a few steps from the Place d'Armes, this cozy and discreet little establishment with warm tones is the domain of Benjamin Mussillon. Sandrine Viresleau takes her cooking very seriously. The mouth-watering fixed-price and à la carte menus offer us, accompanied by a selection of wines from Provence, pesto-stuffed sardines, duck breast carpaccio with truffle jus, slice of turbot with little shrimp in white wine sauce, curry-seasoned pork tenderloin and a berry tiramisu with Cointreau.

● **Le Gros Ventre**   COM

279, littoral Frédéric-Mistral,
presqu'île du Mourillon.
Tel. 04 94 42 15 42. Fax 04 94 31 40 32.
Closed lunch (July–Aug.), Tue.,
Wed. (exc. July–Aug.).
Prix fixe: 27€, 34€, 48€, 12€ (child).
A la carte: 60–75€.

Facing the Saint-Louis fort, on the ground floor of a modern building on the Corniche, Alain and Clémentine Audibert propose a choice stopover. The straw- and salmon-colored dining room and the terrace in the shade of the ventilated tent make a good impression. A scallop and foie gras salad, fish in a salt crust, beef sirloin steak with truffles and a chocolate truffle dessert are all welcome.

● **Le Jardin du Sommelier**   COM

20, allée de l'Amiral-Courbet.
Tel. 04 94 62 03 27. Fax 04 94 09 01 49.
scalisi@le-jardin-du-sommelier.com
www.le-jardin-du-sommelier.com
Closed Sat. lunch, Sun.
Prix fixe: 31€, 34€, 39€, 49€.

Christian Scalisi smiles but he is serious about this Provençal establishment with its tones of green and orange. The cellar justifies the name and in the kitchen Mikaël Chassigneux presents some pleasant surprises in the changing menus. Foie gras in matchstick strips with pain d'épice, scrambled eggs with crayfish and sea urchins, John Dory filet, pan-tossed lamb with bamboo shoots and mushrooms and the pineapple dessert with guava foam and blue lagoon cocktail sauce are lively and interesting.

● **Lido**   COM
Av Frédéric-Mistral.
Tel. 04 94 03 38 18. Fax 04 94 42 07 65.
lelido@wanadoo.fr / www.lelidodetoulon.com
Prix fixe: 24€, 35€, 12€ (child).
A la carte: 47€.

Feet on the sand and eyes on the horizon, fresh and unpretentious cuisine that makes the right impression: Jean-Claude Grandmanche's restaurant definitely deserves a visit. Michael Bernard effortlessly cooks up dishes that have all the colors of the Var region. Oven-crisped hot goat cheese on toast served over mixed salad, crayfish risotto, swordfish tartare and a rack of lamb with aromatic herbs from the Guarrigue receive unanimous approval.

● **Caffè di Pasta**   Ⓝ🍴SIM
Le Mourillon, 16, rue Castillon.
Tel. 04 94 31 44 15.
Closed Sun., Mon., mid-July–mid-Aug.
A la carte: 36€.

We have seen him shine in the Méribel Antarès and in the Porto Vecchio Belvédère. Now we find Christian Farenasso settling for discretion in the heart of the Mourillon. His colorful and modern Italian bistro is charming and cheerful. The farandole of pasta, like the other fine Italian-style preparations, exudes sincerity and good humor. Eggplant bruschetta with parmesan, fresh local ewe's cheese-stuffed cannelloni, creamy mushroom risotto, penne pasta with pancetta and Gorgonzola cheese, gnocchi in Genovese-style pistou soup, squid in parsley and garlic and the rum tiramisu suggest that this born technician has lost none of his flair.

● **Caffè Florian**   ⓃSIM
121, quai Sinse.
Tel. 04 94 31 52 59.
Closed Sun., Mon. dinner, Tue. dinner.
Prix fixe: 25€. A la carte: 20–30€.

This terrace by the port, with its name evoking La Serenissima, is the little kingdom of the young and dynamic Jennifer Poiret. Food is served outdoors or inside on the red benches, a friendly cuisine that reflects Provence and travel. Octopus daube, carpaccio with parmesan, lamb in spiced cream sauce and tagliatelli with tomato, pepper and basil sauce go down without any difficulty.

● **L'Eau à la Bouche**   SIM
54, rue Muiron.
Tel. 04 94 46 33 09.
Closed Sun., 2 weeks beg. Oct.
A la carte: 40€.

Blue and white, this charming little eatery has a terrace that opens onto a little square in the Mourillon district. The tides and dish of the day are marked on the slate. Fig and parmesan in a crêpe pouch, a two-salmon mille-feuille with vinegar cream sauce, tuna steak with shellfish sauce and pear and cashew crêpes leave a good impression. The sea is everywhere—in the paintings, the knickknacks, the fresh food—and we can see it dancing in the distance.

● **Monte Cassino**   SIM
133, rue Orves / Rue Castillon.
Tel.-Fax 04 94 36 21 26.
Closed Sun., Tue. dinner.
Prix fixe: 10,50€ (lunch), 12,50€ (lunch), 15€ (lunch), 26€ (dinner).

Michel Jaubert is the dynamic man behind this modest and refreshing Mediterranean eatery. In the modern dining area, star anise–seasoned cuttlefish, artichoke lasagne, fish in papillote, lamb shank tagine and the chocolate dessert invite us on a journey that varies in the course of the affordable menus.

● **Au Sourd**   SIM
10, rue Molière.
Tel. 04 94 92 28 52. Fax 04 94 91 59 92.
Closed Sun., Mon.
Prix fixe: 28€. A la carte: 60€.

An artillery man under Napoleon III returned deaf from the war and created this friendly restaurant in the old part of the city. Gourmets listen fondly to the call of the sea as transmitted by Jean-Pierre and Yvan Martellotto. In the dining room or on the sunny terrace, mussel brochettes, langouste salad, fried langoustes, spiny lobsters, rouget, John Dory filet with lavender honey and a fresh fig tart are washed down with the wines of Provence.

TOULOUSE

31000 Haute-Garonne. Paris 699 – Barcelone 321 – Bordeaux 247 – Cahors 113 – Auch 78.

Rose colored, like the bricks that turn red in the setting sun, making it look like the Florence in the Southwest of France, on the banks of the Garonne where a dome reminds us of the quays of the Arno. Toulouse retains its independent spirit, looking more toward Spain than Paris. From the 11th to the 13th century, it was the city of the Capitouls, the twelve consuls who administered the city and made it prosperous. It had a parliament in 1420 and was the headquarters of the Albigensian heresy. It remains the epicenter of the gourmet Midi, with Quercy, Périgord, Gascony and the Languedoc claiming the roots. It cultivates the spirit of companionship, the cult of good wine, confit and rugby. We like it for its colors, its warmth, its good humor and its accent. Of course we would like to see it endowed with more good eating establishments of all kinds, but with its team spirit, its sense of a shared local heritage, its proud and talented artisans, it offers us many pleasures.

 RESTAURANTS

■ Crowne Plaza
7, pl du Capitole.
Tel. 05 61 61 19 19. Fax 05 61 23 79 96.
hicptoulouse@alliance-hospitality.com
www.crowneplaza.com/toulouse
Rest. closed end July–beg. Sept.
176 rooms: 150–325€. 5 suites: 400–1000€.
Prix fixe: 20€ (weekday lunch), 25€, 8€ (child).

Right on the prestigious Place du Capitole, this grand American-style hotel provides spacious and modern rooms in shades of blue, yellow and red, reception rooms, modular lounges and a large amphitheater for seminars. Carefully crafted cuisine in the restaurant opening out to the Florentine patio.

■ Sofitel-Centre
84, allée J.-Jaurès.
Tel. 05 61 10 23 10. Fax 05 61 10 23 20.
H1091@accor-hotels.com
www.accor-hotels.com
119 rooms: 260–280€. 16 suites: 299–322€.
Prix fixe: 14€ (lunch). A la carte: 55€.

This chain hotel in a modern glass and rose brick building provides luminous and modern rooms, well-equipped conference rooms and a fashionable bistro, the SW Café. The chef Franck Lopez cooks up fusion cuisine in a white and unassuming setting. Shrimp tempura and steamed grouper with semolina accompanied by wines from all over the world.

■ Grand Hôtel de l'Opéra
1, pl du Capitole.
Tel. 05 61 21 82 66. Fax 05 61 23 41 04.
contact@grand-hotel-opera.com
www.grand-hotel-opera.com
50 rooms: 175–310€. 16 suites: 370–460€.

In the heart of Toulouse, on the Place du Capitole, this 17th-century convent has been transformed into a modern hotel: elegantly decorated rooms and suites, a fitness center, a pleasant bar/lounge and two restaurants (the Jardins de l'Opéra and the Grand Café de l'Opéra, see Restaurants).

■ Holiday Inn Toulouse Centre
13, pl Wilson.
Tel. 05 61 10 70 70, Fax 05 61 21 96 70.
Rest.: 05 61 21 08 27, Fax 05 61 21 06 70.
hicapoul@guichard.fr / www.hotel-capoul.com
124 rooms: 95–170€. 6 suites: 170–210€.
Prix fixe: 23,90€.

This modern stopover on the Place Wilson is very popular with businessmen who appreciate its professionalism, the glass-roofed reception area, the contemporary-style rooms renovated in green and yellow tones and the Capoul brasserie with its terrace and flamboyant red décor. Brandade-stuffed piquillo peppers and the cassoulet with duck confit are not bad.

■ Mercure-Wilson

7, rue Labéda.
Tel. 05 34 45 40 60. Fax 05 34 45 40 61.
h1260@accor-hotels.com / www.mercure.com
91 rooms: 133–143€. 4 suites: 163–173€.

This very pleasant establishment offers all the comfort of the chain, including WiFi and a central location. Typical of Toulouse, the residence has spacious rooms with contemporary décor. The terrace offers us pleasant times in the sun.

■ Hôtel des Beaux-Arts

1, pl du Pont-Neuf.
Tel. 05 34 45 42 42. Fax 05 34 45 42 43.
www.hoteldesbeauxarts.com
18 rooms: 98–168€. 1 suite: 210€.

On the bank of the Garonne, Francis Fauvel's 18th-century house has charming English-style rooms, some of them giving onto the river. Exquisite buffet breakfasts.

■ Hôtel Garonne

22, descente de la Halle-aux-Poissons.
Tel. 05 34 31 94 80. Fax 05 34 31 94 81.
contact@hotelgaronne.com
www.hotelgaronne.com
11 rooms: 155–180€. 3 suites: 235–259€.

We have a little weakness for the intimate residence of Pierre Courtois de Viçose, who transformed the old Hôtel des Couteliers into a nice stopover with modern Asian décor. Just across from it, the restaurant Le 19 turns over the tables at full speed. (See Restaurants.)

■ Mermoz

50, rue Matabiau.
Tel. 05 61 63 04 04. Fax 05 61 63 15 64.
reservation@hotel.mermoz.com
www.hotel-mermoz.com
52 rooms: 75–115€.

The décor of this modern hotel is based unpretentiously on the history of Mermoz and the Aéropostale. The rooms with balconies and art deco furniture work their subtle charm on us, as does the welcoming inner courtyard, the flowery conservatory, the shady terrace and the Vol de Nuit bar.

■ Athénée

13 bis, rue Matabiau.
Tel. 05 61 63 10 63. Fax 05 61 63 87 80.
www.athenee-hotel.com
Closed end Dec.–beg. Jan.
35 rooms: 64–147€.

Just 500 meters from the basilica of Saint-Sernin, this modern designer-style hotel has bright rooms, functional and classic furniture, a conference room and a lounge with brick and stone walls.

■ Les Capitouls Jean-Jaurès

29, allée J.-Jaurès.
Tel. 05 34 41 31 21. Fax 05 61 63 15 17.
reservation@hotel-capitouls.com
www.bestwestern-capitouls.com
51 rooms: 110–176€. 1 suite: 245€.

Located in an old town house next to a metro station, this establishment has a hall with character—a vaulted ceiling with rose-colored bricks—a conference room and small but comfortable richly toned bedrooms with classic furniture.

■ Hôtel de Brienne

20, bd du Maréchal-Leclerc.
Tel. 05 61 23 60 60. Fax 05 61 23 18 94.
hoteldebrienne@wanadoo.fr
www.hoteldebrienne.com
68 rooms: 67–91€. 3 suites: 105–135€.

Hélène Pieropan's modern hotel, named after the nearby canal, has enduring charm. The facade of rose-colored bricks and glass, the verdant marble hallway opening onto the patio, the carefully appointed modern bedrooms in a delicate blue and two conference rooms offer tranquillity at the heart of the city, everything to win us over.

■ Hôtel Saint Claire

29, place Nicolas Bachelier.
Tel. 05 34 40 58 88. Fax 05 61 57 85 89.
contact@stclairehotel.com
www.stclairehotel.com
16 rooms: 48–108€.

In the heart of a historic neighborhood, between the Garonne and the Canal du Midi, this completely renovated hotel offers a simple and unassuming atmosphere. Particular attention has been paid to the choice of furniture and materials (natural rush carpeting, white furniture, mirrors) and to the layout of the bedrooms in accordance with feng shui principles while still offering WiFi.

■ Ours Blanc Wilson

2, rue Victor-Hugo.
Tel. 05 61 21 62 40. Fax 05 61 23 62 34.
wilson@hotel-oursblanc.com
www.hotel-oursblanc.com
37 rooms: 51–73€.

Close to the Victor-Hugo market, this twenties building has tidy and functional rooms in shades of blue and white, with modern furniture, some of them overlooking the rooftops of the city and the Place Wilson. We reach the rooms in a little elevator dating from the same period.

● | RESTAURANTS

● Les Jardins de l'Opéra

At Grand Hôtel de l'Opéra, 1, pl du Capitole.
Tel. 05 61 23 07 76. Fax 05 61 23 63 00.
www.lesjardinsdelopera.com
Closed Sun., Mon., 1 week Jan., 3 weeks Aug.
Prix fixe: 42€, 70€, 90€, 16€ (child).
A la carte: 97€.

Toulouse's leading restaurant, run by the Toulousys, Les Jardins de l'Opéra underwent an *aggiornamento* under the command of the young Stéphane Tournié, who, along with Yves Thuriès de Cordes, took over this luxury residence hidden behind the Place du Capitole. We must confess that we are a little baffled by the formula which consists in having us taste small portions of several dishes, transforming the gourmet of an evening into a laboratory guinea pig. It has to be said that Stéphane, who has worked in Taillevent in Paris, is talented and knows his job, presenting ideas that are often seductive. Plate number 3 thus has us discovering foie gras rolled in mango and served with its aspic, sautéed coriander and ginger-seasoned vegetables topped with crayfish and the mackerel hamburger with carrot and cabbage slaw: explosive! Plate number 5 introduces us to a soy sauce- and ginger-marinated beef tenderloin with beets, veal scallops with Chinese cabbage and a brown morel sauce and the stuffed rabbit in papillote with mustard and vinegar sauce: fine produce, nicely cooked, but a little tiring for the palate, which is refreshed by the desserts plate (known as plate number 7, which is hardly very poetic), with pineapple spring rolls with crunchy chopstick-style cookies with fennel sorbet, creamy Guanaja chocolate and caramel macaron with vanilla tapioca and caramelized apples with sesame and coriander served aside a little crème brûlée. The wines are steeply priced (the local Côtes du Frontonnais come in at 30 and 45). In a word, it is worth the experience, particularly with such chic service, and the setting still retains the airs and graces of a palace for the nouveau riche of Toulouse.

● Michel Sarran   ○○ V.COM

21, bd Armand-Duportal.
Tel. 05 61 12 32 32. Fax 05 61 12 32 33.
www.michel-sarran.com
Closed Sat., Sun. Wed. lunch, Christmas–New Year's, Aug.
Prix fixe: 45€, 85€, 110€.

Michel Sarran, the quiet man from the Gers region, quickly won over the people of Toulouse. This skilled technician has the happy knack of knowing how to blend the perfumes of the South. We know him from the Mas du Langoustier on Porquerolles island, a man who loves sunny seafood dishes. The bare design of his dining area with its pretty red and green tones charms the eye and his dishes are no less charming. Warm foie gras soup with Belon oysters, blue lobster presented on spiced pineapple, line-fished turbot with grilled chestnuts and Aquitane caviar, light tomato and sea fennel soup with grilled sardines and bulgar and the cucumber and grapefruit are awesome dishes, as are the roasted hazelnut-encrusted veal scallops with potatoes and Bigorre black pig tenderloin served in a cocotte with thyme-seasoned cooking jus and potatoes with wine sauce and country bacon. We conclude that whatever emerges from Michel Sarran's kitchen is necessarily classy and stylish. Pretty cherry tomatoes infused with berry juices, lime and basil Italian ice or shortbread cookies with a strawberry milkshake for dessert leaves us reeling.

● **Le Mas de Dardagna**

1, chemin de Dardagna.
Tel. 05 61 14 09 80.
www.masdedardagna.com
Closed Sat., Sun., Aug.
Prix fixe: 18€ (lunch), 45€, 55€.

The country in the city? This is what the Joffre brothers offer us in the heart of the Rangueil district. Fabrice, the older of the two, worked with Daguin in Auch, in the Vernet in Paris, and with Cirino before opening his own restaurant in Beirut for five years. Sylvain, the younger, "did" Bras at Laguiole. In other words, these two rebels know their way around a kitchen for the greater pleasure and delectation of the smart people who come to their adorable 18th-century "Toulousaine" with its rose-colored stones in checkerboard pattern. The terra cotta tiles on the floor, the wooden chairs and the garden all suggest a "Sunday in the country". The lunch menu offers—and that's the right word with this standard of quality—beef carpaccio with a seasonal greens bouquet, hot asparagus with garlic sauce, cabbage root salad with mackerel and black olives, pollock with summer savory–seasoned sweet peas, Bigorre pork tenderloin and a lamb tagine, finishing off with thyme-infused strawberries in wine and a rhubarb tart, all exquisite delights. For 55 ,

the morels in cream, pan-seared Mediterranean sea bass with thyme, matchsticks of foie gras in terrine with puffed rice, lamb with kasha and a strawberry and rhubarb marmalade with light fresh cheese cream shows us what the Joffre brothers are made of. Obviously a house with a "rosy" future.

● **Le 19** COM

19, descente de la Halle-aux-Poissons.
Tel. 05 34 31 94 84 / 05 34 31 94 80.
Fax 05 34 31 94 85.
www.hotelsdecharmetoulouse.com
Closed Sat. lunch, Sun., Mon. lunch,
2 weeks Christmas–New Year's.
Prix fixe: 35€. A la carte: 55€.

The two vaulted brick rooms with their 16th-century ribbed vaults obviously have lots of character. The young Jean Oliva uses local market produce in the spirit of the times—fresh, spicy and sassy, of course, but not overly so. It is easy to yield to the pleasures of his amazing asparagus duo (green and white) in creamy soup with oyster brochettes, John Dory meunière with sweet pea cream and braised lettuce and the lamb saddle with black Bigorre pork served with their famous white truffle cream gnocchi (a seductive dish), wonderful indeed, and for dessert, the Guanaja chocolate mille-feuille with sauce and a very light fresh farm milk ice cream is an excellent follow-up. An establishment to watch. (See Hotels: Hôtel Garonne.)

● **7, Place Saint-Sernin** COM

7, pl Saint-Sernin.
Tel. 05 62 30 05 30. Fax 05 62 30 04 06.
restaurant.sept.place.saint.sernin@wanadoo.fr
Closed Sat., Sun., Christmas–New Year's.
Prix fixe: 18€ (weekday lunch),
24€ (weekday lunch), 34€ (weekday dinner),
11€ (child). A la carte: 55€.

Benoît Cantalloube's restaurant looks good at the foot of the Romanesque basilica. This student of Guérard at Eugénie, Boulud in New York and Savoy in Paris uses fresh locally sourced produce that varies with the seasons, in a flamboyant décor of red and yellow tones as a backdrop to contemporary paintings. He enchants us with his Landes duck foie gras, a glazed purple Roussilon artichoke fricassée, Bouchot langoustines and mussels, a rack of Pyrénées lamb with herbs, variety meat brochettes and an assortment of crèmes Catalanes, richly seductive. Brice Mialet is an excellent guide to local and less local wines.

● **Valentin Restaurant**   Ⓝ🍽️ⒸⓄⓂ

21, rue Perchepinte
Tel. 05 61 53 11 15.
Closed Sun., Mon.
Prix fixe: 17,50€ (weekday lunch), 32€.

Valentin Neraudeau, 22, worked with Daguin in Auch, where he was elected best apprentice in France in 2001, but also with Bach in Pujaudran and in the château de Larroque at Gimont, before opening this charming stopover in the heart of the Saint-Etienne district. Neither the little upstairs room, reminding us of an antique store, nor the brick cellar is lacking in charm. Sea bream tartare with vanilla-infused oil, pike-perch roasted skin-side down with leek and country bacon tourte and veal sweetbreads with chanterelles make a good impression. For dessert, pistachio gâteau Basque and the sour cherries with vanilla ice cream are irresistible.

● **Le Vélane**   Ⓝ ⒸⓄⓂ

3, pl Montoulieu.
Tel. 05 61 53 60 56. Fax 05 61 53 66 69.
levelane@levelane.com / www.levelane.com
Closed Sat. lunch, Sun., 1 week Aug.
Prix fixe: 17€ (weekday lunch), 25€ (weekday lunch), 37€. A la carte: 70€.

This fashionable lounge managed from afar by Dominique Toulousy is nevertheless a gourmet's delight. We lounge in the shade of the wattle fence on the terrace in summertime or in the baroque Venetian décor of the dining room with its background music as we sample the pleasures of oyster tartare and scallops with coriander, grilled turbot filet with ceps, beef sirloin steak with truffle and macaroni and the dark chocolate cake with a passion fruit center.

● **Brasserie des Beaux-Arts**   ⒸⓄⓂ

1, quai de la Daurade.
Tel. 05 61 21 12 12. Fax 05 61 21 14 80.
sgiroussens@groupeflo.fr
www.brasserielesbeauxarts.com
Prix fixe: 14,90€ (lunch, wine inc.), 22,50€, 29,50€, 12,50€ (child).
A la carte: 50–60€.

On the banks of the Garonne, downtown, the Flo group has made this neo-art deco brasserie into its provincial flagship. In the dining room with noble wood fixtures and mirrors, the amazing foie gras terrine with Jurançon-seasoned aspic, roasted scallops with chanterelles and shiitakes, a T-bone veal steak with cep fricassée and the chocolate dessert all strike the right note. Valet car parking service in the evenings.

● **Grand Café de l'Opéra**   ⒸⓄⓂ

At Grand Hôtel de l'Opéra, 1, pl du Capitole.
Tel. 05 61 21 37 03. Fax 05 61 23 41 04.
www.brasserieopera.com
Closed Sun., Christmas.
Prix fixe: 15,90€ (weekday lunch), 25,90€, 10,90€ (child). A la carte: 40€.

This is the eatery that all Toulouse comes to after an evening at theater, where passing stars can be seen. Jean-Pierre Glaize is in charge of the chic dining room and veranda which, in fine weather, becomes an open-air terrace. We like the carefully selected décor—wood, leather armchairs—and the quality cooking. Although the chefs change (currently Bruno Galou), the same standards of freshness and striking flavors are maintained. Oak-smoked herring salad, skate wing with caper butter, house blood sausage and apples with mashed poatatoes and pain perdu with spéculos ice cream make a very good impression. (See Hotels.)

● **Le Bouchon Lyonnais**   ⒸⓄⓂ
"Laurent Orsi"

13, rue de l'Industrie.
Tel. 05 61 62 97 43. Fax 05 61 63 00 71.
orsi-le-bouchon-lyonnais@wanadoo.fr
www.le-bouchon-lyonnais.com
Closed Sat. lunch (exc. Bank holidays),

Sun (exc. Bank holidays).
Prix fixe: 19,90€, 27€, 33€, 15€ (child).

Lyons has its embassy on Toulouse soil in the form of this thirties-style brasserie with rosewood tones run by Laurent Orsi. The traditional Lyonnais preparations are ardently defended, the menus devote more than their share to Lyonnais produce and seafood. Accompanied by an informative wine list that omits no regions, hot sausage, sardine and tomato mille-feuille, pike fish quenelles with trilogy of fish in first pressing olive oil, garlic and tomato sauce, Toulouse-style cassolette, fleurie chitterling sausage and a frozen Grand Marnier soufflé are delightful. A summer terrace.

● La Pâte Folle `COM`

19, rue de Castellane.
Tel. 05 61 62 34 70.
Closed Sat. lunch, Sun. lunch, 2 weeks beg. Aug.
A la carte: 32–37€.

Patrick Carthery, the happy owner of Copains d'Abord (38, rue du Pont-Guilhemery, 05 62 47 39 99), has made this immaculately decorated and modern establishment his second eatery. In the kitchen, Christophe Llido elaborates simple and sunny preparations. Tomato and mozzarella brochets, whole sea bream, pasta with scallops and traditional lasagne go down without any difficulty.

● Au Pois Gourmand `COM`

3, rue Emile-Heybrard.
Tel. 05 34 36 42 00. Fax 05 34 36 42 08.
www.pois-gourmand.fr
Rest. closed Sat. lunch, Sun., Mon. lunch.
4 rooms: 85–125€.
Prix fixe: 23€ (weekday lunch), 37€, 51€, 59€ (wine inc.), 64€.

Martine and Jean-Claude Plazzotta are hiding out in this neocolonial residence with its straw-colored rooms with white wood furniture. In the cozy dining room with its yellow-orange and cream shades we savor southern cooking that is both frank and generous. Marinated scallops with Aquitaine caviar, grilled Atlantic

sea bass with star anise–seasoned cream sauce and creamed eggplant, veal sweetbreads braised in Banyuls wine and the Victoria pineapple brochet make a good impression.

● Restaurant Emile `COM`

13, pl Saint-Georges.
Tel. 05 61 21 05 56. Fax 05 61 21 42 26.
emile@restaurant-emile.com
www.restaurant-emile.com
Closed Sun., Mon. (exc. dinner summer),
1 week at end Dec., 1 week beg. Jan.
Prix fixe: 18€ (weekday lunch), 30€ (weekday lunch), 35€, 39€, 50€,
10€ (child). A la carte: 50–55€.

Luc Thibault manages with fervor and enthusiasm the three floors and terrace of this lively house. Christophe Fasan's cuisine offers us good quality preparations from both land and sea. Scallops with foie gras, shiitakes and Jerusalem artichokes, local mixed fish grill, cassoulet with duck confit and oven-crisped pigeon with cabbage and foie gras are generous and flavorsome.

● Michel, Marcel, Pierre et les Autres

35, rue de Rémusat.
Tel.-Fax 05 61 22 47 05.
www.michelmarcelpierre.com
Closed Sun., Mon., 1 week Aug.
A la carte: 35–40€.

Along with two friends who are crazy about rugby, cigars, jazz and bullfighting, Michel Sarran created the kind of bistro we no longer find in today's world. On two floors, with a zinc counter on the ground floor, a more cozy art deco-style dining room on the first floor, the walls shades of pastel pink and salmon decorated with old posters and sportsmen's shirts (Robert Pirès' shirt is next to that of Thomas Castaignède), the place has charm. The generous fixed-price menu changes every day. The à la carte menu changes from month to month. We are delighted by the cauliflower in an herb vinaigrette, salmon filet with parsley- and garlic-seasoned zucchini, crème brûlée with rosemary and honey, Maman Pierette's preserved foie gras, the Spanish-style charcuterie from Mr. Garcia at the Victor-Hugo market and an oven-crisped whiting with onion confiture, which go down a treat. Accompanied by the new wines of the Grand Midi, like the superb *"mille vignes"* Fitou from Guérin at La Palme. A house with a warm heart.

● Le Bateau   N·SIM

Promenade Henri Martin, port de la Daurade.
Tel. 05 61 12 29 34.
Closed Sun. (off season), Mon. (off season).
Prix fixe: 15€, 20€ (lunch).
A la carte: 40€.

We knew Bibi Heuillet as a judicious maitre d' at the Grand Café de l'Opéra. We now find this cheerful chap is the enthusiastic captain of this boat moored at the quai de la Daurade, across from the Saint Jacques hospital. All Toulouse sneaks down to greet the bonny Bibi and offer themselves up to the pleasures of lentil and bacon salad, shredded Serrano ham, salt cod and potato dish, grilled squid, veal chops with slow-roasted garlic. The frozen nougat makes a delightful dessert.

● Café Italien   N·SIM

9 bis, pl des Carmes.
Tel. 05 61 25 08 63.
A la carte: 24€.

A *tavola calda* run by a Roman opposite the Carmes market. The wood and zinc counter, the wood or marble tables and the relaxed atmosphere work their charm on us. No pretentiousness in the dishes, just quality produce simply prepared. The pasta and bean soup, spaghetti puttanesca, linguini with pesto Genovese and the simple mozzarella and anchovy crostini have an authentic flavor. The tiramisu and the panna cotta will delight sugar lovers. The little Tuscan Sangiovese goes down easily.

● La Cantine du Curé   N·SIM

2, rue des Couteliers.
Tel.-Fax 05 61 25 83 42.
www.lacantineducure.com

Closed Sun., Mon., 1 week at end Aug.
Prix fixe: 28,50€, 40,50€ (wine inc.).
A la carte: 45€.

King Henri IV used it as a trysting place; it is now a first-class restaurant. Surrounded by bricks and wooden beams, Christophe Aurel serves up delicious foie gras poached in spiced wine on toast, a monkfish cassoulet with Bordelaise wine, a honey-braised pork shank and a chocolate and preserved orange dessert.

● La Corde   N·SIM

4, rue Jules-Chalande.
Tel. 05 61 29 09 43. Fax 05 61 29 09 43.
www.lacorde.com
Closed Sat. lunch, Sun., Mon. lunch.
Prix fixe: 12–18€ (lunch), 24€, 30€,
55€ (dinner), 65€ (dinner), 90€ (dinner).
A la carte: 70€.

One of the oldest eateries in the city installed in a 15th-century building has got people talking. In just three short years Mo Bachir has managed to seduce all of Toulouse with a lively and traditional cuisine. In the two dining rooms, one contemporary, the other baroque, we don't hesitate to savor the truffled foie gras on toast with fleur de sel, steamed pike fish in a basil crust, cassoulet with duck confit and a caramel floating island.

● Le Gallery   N·SIM

8, rue Maury.
Tel. 05 61 99 30 81.
Closed Mon. dinner, Tue. dinner, Sat. lunch,
Sun. dinner.
Prix fixe: 13€ (lunch). A la carte: 35€.

Stéphane Réau, who has worked in London and Geneva, has set up in an artistic setting with "Pop Art" colors, white walls and bare wood tables. The lunchtime slate, offering creamy broccoli soup, gnocchi with pesto, chicken seasoned with four spices and cheese cake, takes us on a journey through the seasons. In the evening, Gorgonzola and coppa risotto and pollock with a green herb sauce is breathtaking. Brunch on Sundays.

● Le Genty Magre Ⓝ SIM

3, rue Genty-Magre.
Tel. 05 61 21 38 60.
Closed Sun., Mon., Tue. dinner, 1 week beg.
Jan., mid-July–end Aug.
Prix fixe: 18€ (lunch), 20€,
30€ (wine inc.).

He worked in New York (with Boulud) and
Tokyo (The Four Seasons) after studying under Toulousy and with Coussau.
In the heart of Toulouse, Romain Brard
recounts his region while taking inspiration from his travels. Kyoto-style marinated black pig, jumbo shrimp wrapped
in angelhair pastry, foie gras with dried
fruits and nuts and a spicy quick-seared
tuna steak with slow-cooked peppers and
onions and chorizo put Toulouse, Singapore and Hong Kong on the same wave-
length.

● La Madeleine de Proust Ⓝ SIM

11, rue Riquet.
Tel. 05 61 63 80 88. Fax 05 61 63 82 46.
www.madeleinedeproust.com
Closed Sun., Mon., 2 weeks Christmas–New
Year's, 2 weeks beg. Aug.
Prix fixe: 17,50€, 22,50€, 27,50€,
8€ (child). A la carte: 45€.

In Philippe Merle's dining room dating
from another era, old toys and grandmother's recipes go hand-in-hand. The
are no objections to the creamy chestnut
and wild nettle soup, cod filet with grilled
vegetables, duck medallions with lingonberries and pain d'épice served with verbena ice cream.

● Le Mauzac Ⓝ SIM

18, bd Lascrosses.
Tel. 05 61 13 94 05.
Closed Sat., Sun., 3 weeks Aug.
A la carte: 25€.

We know Christine and Jean-Michel Del-
houme from the Quartier Latin in Paris,
where they attracted lovers of simple
wines and robust fare to their zinc counter. They adopted the same formula when
they emigrated to Toulouse. Rimbert's
Saint Chinian, Dozon's Chinon or Raquil-
ley Mercurey form gourmet accompaniments for smoked herring with potatoes
in oil, head cheese terrine with herbed
vinaigrette, cod prepared in the style of
Provence, tête de veau with sauce ravigote, rib eye steak for two served with
real fries and a baba au rhum that melts
in the mouth. Although the plain café
décor is hardly eye catching, the joyful
atmosphere of gourmet fellowship very
quickly convinces us to make a habit of
coming here.

● Rôtisserie des Carmes Ⓝ SIM

38, rue des Polinaires.
Tel. 05 61 53 34 88.
Closed Sat., Sun., 25 Dec.–1 Jan.,
4 weeks end July–end Aug.
Prix fixe: 21€ (lunch), 25€.

Alain Chabrier is the charming self-taught
man of the Carmes district. He trained
as a lawyer, sold institutional furniture
and studied under Daguin, Mazère and
Garrigues. The décor looks good with its
yellow tones and modern paintings with
notes of red and crimson. The menus are
a bargain and the produce comes from the
neighboring market. Asparagus in vinaigrette with poached egg, big langoustines
roasted Barcelona-style, pan-seared country veal filet served with fresh tomato-
and basil-seasoned gnocchi make us want
to stay overnight. There is also chicken
served with spicy pepper and tomato
sauce and strawberries in orange flower-
infused cane sugar syrup. In a word, delicious things that know how to be simple
without losing their flavor.

● Le Saint-Germain Ⓝ SIM

31 bis, allée de Brienne.
Tel. 05 61 13 99 06.
germain-lespadon@wanadoo.fr
Closed Sun., Mon., 1 week beg. Jan.,
2 weeks Aug.
Prix fixe: 25€, 30€, 10€ (child).
A la carte: 40€.

Antoine Delavaux's seafood bistro is worth
visiting for its reasonable prices and its
honest-to-goodness dishes like platter of
oysters, whelks and shrimp, jumbo shrimp

and blood sausage fricassée, monkfish blanquette with white wine sauce and the chocolate fondant.

● L'Angelo SIM
4, rue Labéda.
Tel.-Fax 05 61 21 37 24.
Closed Sun., Mon., Aug.
A la carte: 30–35€.

Opposite the Victor-Hugo market, Attilio Carniel flies the Italian colors with well-made classic preparations. We delight in the seafood salad, polenta with parmesan, eggplant parmesan, squid in tomato basil sauce, Vienna-style calf's liver, tiramisu and panna cotta.

● La Bascule SIM
14, av Maurice-Hauriou.
Tel. 05 61 52 09 51. Fax 05 61 55 06 32.
restaulabascule@aol.com
Prix fixe: 15€ (weekday lunch), 22,80€,
10€ (child).

Bright and cheerful guests, smiling waiters, enchanting dishes: everything seems to be just right in this friendly establishment run by Bernard Esquirol. In the classic bright yellow dining room, we savor fresh scallop and asparagus salad, fish of the day in a salt crust, rosemary-seasoned five-hour lamb shoulder roast and a mascarpone and raspberry crumble.

● Le Bon Vivre SIM
15 bis, pl Wilson.
Tel. 05 61 23 07 17. Fax 05 62 30 36 01.
c.meliet@lebonvivre.com
www.lebonvivre.fr
Closed Christmas.
Prix fixe: 22€, 35€. A la carte: 36€.

Day and night this neighborhood eatery comes to life in the capable hands of Cathy Meliet. We enjoy the plain and simple local fare served up in dishes like Gers lentils with beef muzzle salad, Bigorre pork ears, whiting with aïoli, tête de veau with sauce gribiche, Tarbais cassoulet with two confits and a house pain perdu dessert. Simplicity and quality go hand-in-hand.

● Le Colombier SIM
14, rue Bayard.
Tel. 05 61 62 40 05. Fax 05 61 99 10 11.
www.restaurant-lecolombier.com
Closed Sat. lunch, Sun.,
1 week Christmas–New Year's, Aug.
Prix fixe: 19,95€, 32€, 36€,
15,90€ (lunch). A la carte: 60€.

One of the best cassoulets in Toulouse? Always with Gérard Zasso in his charming brick and wood dining room. Oven-crisped goose confit melts in your mouth, extremely fresh sweet corn and other regional specialties: this is what you'll find here, accompanied by choice wines, sautéed foie gras and Armagnac, duck breast stuffed with foie gras in a salt crust and a raspberry gratin. A good house.

● L'Empereur de Huê SIM
17, rue des Couteliers.
Tel. 05 61 53 55 72.
Closed lunch, Tue.
A la carte: 45€.

Marie-Odile in the dining room and Sarah Truong-Qui in the kitchen celebrate the tastes of Vietnam in fine, delicately prepared dishes. Banana flower salad with roasted duck, shrimp soup, sardines seasoned with ginger, garlic and hot pepper and a mild monkfish curry with a touch of lemongrass make a good impression. Don't miss the Saigon dessert (pan-tossed Frecinette bananas with spices and caramel and a farmer's milk ice cream): a delight!

● Au Gré du Vin
10, rue Pléau.
Tel. 05 61 25 03 51.
contact@augreduvin.com
www.augreduvin.com
Closed Sat., Sun. lunch, Mon.
Prix fixe: 14€ (lunch), 18€ (lunch),
26€ (dinner), 35€ (dinner).

Downtown, opposite the Dupuy museum, Sami El Sawi has taken over this intimate eatery. The setting is old-fashioned with exposed stone walls and rose-colored bricks and brass objects hanging from the ceiling, all giving it a certain charm. The menus are enchanting with mild pepper bavarois with vanilla sauce, grilled deboned quail with cep sauce, tuna steak glazed with mustard sauce, a mushroom-stuffed breast of guinea hen and the apricot panna cotta.

● **J'Go**   SIM

16, pl Victor-Hugo.
Tel. 05 61 23 02 03. Fax 05 62 30 36 01.
toulouse@lejgo.com / www.lejgo.com
Closed Christmas, New Year's.
Prix fixe: 13€, 15€, 18€, 24€.
A la carte: 35€.

Opposite the Victor-Hugo market the atmosphere in the evenings is heady, rhythmic and noisy, the cooking is visible. The bar is taken by storm while the two first floor rooms are quieter, but just a tad. People come here to savor, in addition to the eponymous Quercy lamb (rack, saddle, shoulder roast, filet, and, of course, leg), Bigorre pork, Gascon farm-raised chicken, foie gras terrine and scrambled eggs with mild spring garlic. It's friendly, flavorful and inexpensive and the Château de Plaisance goes down easily.

● **Le Pyrénéen**   SIM

14, allée Franklin-Roosevelt.
Tel. 05 61 23 38 88. Fax 05 61 62 89 82.
lacassagne-p@wanadoo.fr
www.lepyreneen.com
Prix fixe: 35€. A la carte: 45€.

This cheerful brasserie with its frescoes dating from 1880 has much charm. It is pleasing to the eye, the taste buds also. Philippe Lacassagne and François-Louis Lapeyre present a cuisine that is unadventurous but carefully crafted. Gillardeau oysters, anise-flambéed Atlantic sea bass, tête de veau with sauce ravigote and crêpes go down a treat.

In Colomiers (31770). 10 km via D112 and D63.
● **L'Amphitryon**   ○○ V.COM

Chemin de Gramont.
Tel. 05 61 15 55 55. Fax 05 61 15 42 30.
contac@lamphitryon.com
www.lamphitryon.com

Prix fixe: 24€ (lunch weekdays), 32€ (lunch), 54€, 98€. A la carte: 95–105€.

Green fields and Aerospace Aérospatiale: Yannick Delpech's cuisine is like his environment, rooted yet modern. A lively thirty year-old, he learned the ropes as a young pastry chef with Michel Belin in Albi and Didier Oudill in Biarritz and has now moved on to concocting authentic and lively dishes that are well balanced. Roasted langoustines, thin shavings of cucumber with Marenne oysters in chutney, fresh knife-trimmed sardines, smoked herring with whiting cream, rouget seared on its skin and finished under the broiler and tomato and poached egg bonbons and the whipped escabeche with piquillos are nothing short of *haute cuisine*. In terms of meat, he opts for a regional flavor with the delightful Laurage young duck in a black pepper crust, young Mont Royal pigeon with the legs made into sausage and stuffed in caul lace packets served with a fresh pear, mango and mint dish. To finish off, the classic dark chocolate soft-centered cake and the cocoa crème brûlée with a passion fruit milkshake is metronomic in its precision. The cellar has pleasant surprises in store and the charming service by the gracious Sandrine Batard is quite simply marvelous.

In Colomiers.
● **Le Canard sur le Toit**   Ⓝ V.COM

58, rue de la Salvetat.
Tel. 05 61 30 37 83. Fax 05 61 15 19 80.
canardsurletoit@wanadoo.fr
www.canardsurletoit.com
Closed Sun. dinner.
Prix fixe: 22€, 26€, 32€, 42€.
A la carte: 45€.

Situated at a short distance from the airport, this 18th-century residence serves pleasant meals, has seven lounges, a terrace and a winter garden. An opportunity to peacefully enjoy such classics as round of duck confit with caramelized onions, turbot filet with saffron, cassolette and a slow-roasted pear served with Muscat sorbet.

In Rouffiac-Tolosan (31180). 12 km ne via N88.

● **O Saveurs**   🅿⊙**COM**

8, pl des Ormeaux.

Tel. 05 34 27 10 11. Fax 05 62 79 33 84.

www.o.saveurs.free.fr

Closed Sat. lunch, Sun. dinner, Mon.,

10 days at end Feb., 10 days beg. May,

mid-Aug.–beg. Sept.

Prix fixe: 22€ (weekday lunch), 34€, 75€,

15€ (child). A la carte: 78€.

Situated just outside the rose-colored city, this little house provides a peaceful stopover in the square of a picturesque village. Daniel Gonzalez, the chef, and David Biasibetti, the pastry chef, serve up a cuisine that is fresh and limpid with today's tastes in well-balanced gourmet menus. On the pleasant terrace or in the two contemporary-style dining rooms with their bright sunny tones, after chosing the wine to harmonize with your feast with the helpful advice of sommelier Jérémy Fombuse, foie gras and pork trotter-stuffed ceps with a side of stew, Atlantic sea bass filet served in cocotte, Saint-Jean truffle-seasoned Canaroli risotto, roasted rack of lamb in a dried fruit crust with trumpet mushroom cream sauce are precise and delicious pleasures. Crunchy Manjari chocolate spring rolls with spicy minted fruit sauce and the Cantonese rice with fruits and chocolate sorbet are light ways to finish off.

In Saint-Martin-du-Touch (31300). 8 km via N124.

● **Le Cantou**   **COM**

98, rue Vélasquez.

Tel. 05 61 49 20 21. Fax 05 61 31 01 17.

le.cantou@wanadoo.fr / www.cantou.fr

Closed Sat., Sun., 10 days at end Dec.,

1 week beg. Jan., mid-Aug.–end Aug.

Prix fixe: 30€ (lunch), 37€, 39,50€, 56€.

This stylishly renovated old farmhouse has its terrace organized around the bucolic charm of its well. Philippe Puel is the high priest of authentic cuisine in a lighter register. On the menu? Pan-seared duck foie gras with fresh figs and fig caramel, grilled Atlantic sea bass with Swiss chard-stuffed piquillo peppers, Rouergue pigeon breast served with the wing and leg

meat stuffed in a crêpe pouch. Not to forget the dessert, a lemon mousseline and its candied zest, orange sauce and a scoop of thyme sorbet. A fine selection—1800 listings!—of wines chosen by the wine waiter Bertrand Ferrer.

In Tournefeuille (31170). 10 km W. via D632.

● **L'Art de Vivre**   Ⓝ**COM**

279, chemin Ramelet-Moundi.

Tel. 05 61 07 52 52. Fax 05 61 06 41 94.

pierre.lartdevivre@wanadoo.fr

www.lartdevivre.fr

Closed Sun. dinner, Mon. dinner, Tue. dinner,

2 weeks Christmas–New Year's,

2 weeks beg. Feb., 3 weeks Aug.

Prix fixe: 23€ (weekday lunch), 34€, 43€,

54€, 13€ (child). A la carte: 75€.

On the banks of the Ossau, the Belgian Pierre Sepulchre has succeeded in charming the people of Toulouse in search of fresh air at his table overlooking the grounds. Everbody enjoys this chef's precise and robust preparations. Pan-seared duck foie gras served with Puy lentil soup, roasted Atlantic sea bass filet with creamy cep sauce, veal kidneys with balsamic vinaigrette and Meaux whole grain mustard and a slow-cooked pineapple glazed cookie bring sweet smiles to the lips of one and all.

In L'Union (31240). 7 km ne via N88.

● **La Bonne Auberge**   Ⓝ**COM**

2 bis, rue de l'Autan-Blanc, N88.

Tel. 05 61 09 32 26. Fax 05 61 09 97 53.

Closed Sun., Mon., 2 weeks Christmas–New

Year's, 2 weeks end Aug.

Prix fixe: 19€ (lunch), 24€, 35€, 45€.

A la carte: 50€.

This tasteful inn enjoys peaceful surroundings. Eric Puel has given it a gentle facelift and rejuvenated the cuisine. In the capable hands of this dynamic chef, jumbo shrimp with chorizo, seafood pot-au-feu, veal cutlet with an Aubrac potato and cheese dish and the chocolate fondant with a pistachio center swing merrily between tradition and modernity.

LE TOUQUET-PARIS-PLAGE

62520 Pas-de-Calais. Paris 243 – Calais 67 – Abbeville 59 – Boulogne-sur-Mer 30.
contact@letouquet.com.

This temple of land yachting, enduro racing and golf galore has long been known to our British neighbors. The town is called "Paris-Plage" because it was discovered by Mr. de Villemessant, a journalist with *Le Figaro* and lover of the place who had the good idea of taking the city-dwellers outdoors in the pre-war years. A pine forest was created here in 1835 then, in the Roaring Twenties, a complex of neo-Gothic and mock Tudor residences was built with maritime themes, today constituting some extremely pleasant architectural promenades.

 HOTELS-RESTAURANTS

■ Le Westminster 🏨🏠

5, av Verger.
Tel. 03 21 05 48 48. Fax 03 21 05 45 45.
reception@westminster.fr / www.westminster.fr
115 rooms: 90–185€. 2 suites: 500–700€.
Half board: 117€.

This thirties palace made of rose-colored bricks retains all its retro cachet with its art deco hallway and old-style elevators. The rooms, with period furniture, are tastefully luxurious and not extravagant. The cocktail bar with its dark wood décor, the swimming pool with its Philippe Starck coffee shop and the Pavillon restaurant are all worth a visit. (See Restaurants.)

■ Le Manoir ⚘🏠

Av du Golf.
Tel. 03 21 06 28 28. Fax 03 21 06 28 29.
manoirhotel@opengolfclub.com
www.opengolfclub.com
Closed beg. Jan.–beg. Feb.
41 rooms: 128–208€. 1 suite: 294–318€.
Prix fixe: 33€. A la carte: 55€.

The golf course is a pretext for staying here but the peace makes us want to enjoy it without playing. This very British neo-Gothic manor is conducive to restful activities with its spacious bedrooms, flowery garden, swimming pool, tennis court and cozy lounges. The traditional cuisine makes a good impression with a foie gras terrine served with cured ham-wrapped duck breast and pistachios in puff pastry, rouget filets seasoned with vanilla and lemon tagliatelli, a rack of lamb braised with Cognac served with simmered artichokes and peppers, the fresh fig Tatin and an exotic fruit gratin with mascarpone.

■ Novotel Thalassa Le Touquet 🏠

Waterfront.
Tel. 03 21 09 85 00. Fax 03 21 09 85 10.
h0449@accord-hotels.com
www.accordhotels.com
Closed 2 weeks Jan.
146 rooms: 101–166€. 3 suites: 216–282€.
Prix fixe: 30€, 13€ (child). A la carte: 45€.

Facing the sea and having direct access to the neighboring thalassotherapy center, this modern chain hotel with bright rooms has been renovated in a contemporary style with light wood furnishings, three conference rooms, a fitness center, an indoor sea-water swimming pool and a panoramic restaurant with bay windows overlooking the coast. The scallops presented in a wreath, sea bream with thyme-infused jus, boneless lamb saddle and the daily house pastries constitute a prudent family cuisine that is mainly dedicated to sea products.

■ Le Bristol 🏠

17, rue Jean-Monnet.
Tel. 03 21 05 49 95. Fax 03 21 05 90 93.
reservations@hotelbristol.fr
www.hotelbristol.fr
52 rooms: 70–160€.

The best value for money in the resort: this thirties hotel was renovated in 1950 and again in 1970. Its refined décor and carefully chosen furniture, comfortable old-style rooms and pleasant Ascot bar all guarantee us a good time.

● Le Pavillon V.COM

At Le Westminster, 5, av Verger.
Tel. 03 21 05 48 48. Fax 03 21 05 45 45.

reception@westminster.fr
www.opengolfclub.com
Closed lunch, Tue. (exc. summer),
beg. Jan.–beg. Feb.
Prix fixe: 50€, 75€, 120€ (lunch, wine
inc.). A la carte: 75€.

William Elliott prudently sticks to the classics in this elegant English-style dining room with its white tones. Duck foie gras, quick-seared tuna steak, rouget with fennel and artichokes, a milk-fed veal cutlet with summer truffles, chocolate and crème de menthe mille-feuille and vanilla rice pudding with a poached egg and caramel ice cream make a good impression. A resourceful cellar.

● **Flavio**   ◉ V.COM
"Le Club de la Forêt"
1 and 2, av du Verger.
Tel. 03 21 05 10 22. Fax 03 21 05 91 55.
flavio@flavio.fr / www.flavio.fr
Closed Mon. (exc. July–Aug.), Jan.
Prix fixe: 20€, 60€, 78€, 120€.
A la carte: 82€.

Flavio Cucco from Monaco created this house in 1949. Guy Delmotte, his son-in-law, has been over the ovens since July 13, 1968. True to style, this fellow traveler of Faugeron at the Berkeley presents a chic and elegant classic cuisine. Langoustines served royal style in a summer truffle-infused soup, roasted turbot with smoked garlic and Marant lamb seasoned with salt-preserved wild lemons border on tranquil perfection. The little 20 menu (mussels served in cocotte, coq au vin, the daily pastry dessert with a glass of wine included) is the bargain of the century.

● **Le Café des Arts**   COM
80, rue de Paris.
Tel. 03 21 05 21 55. Fax 03 21 84 64 20.
www.cafedesarts.fr
Closed Tue. (off season), Wed. (off season),
1 week at end Dec., 2 weeks Jan.
Prix fixe: 20€, 30€, 10€ (child).
A la carte: 47–57€.

For more than twenty years, Jérôme Panni has prowled the nearby markets in search of produce for the menu in his intimate dining room and delights his guests with fresh and inspired dishes. Annie Rousseau recommends the cheeky little number that goes down a treat with the langoustines in their shell, foie gras ravioli with mushroom capuccino, roasted Atlantic sea bass with asparagus, grilled scallops and roasted potatoes with chanterelles, Charolais beef steak with Touquet ratte potato cakes and poultry stew with white sauce, aromatic herbs and vegetables. Rice pudding with violet ice cream and a frozen pistachio parfait with roasted pears are choice desserts.

● **Le Village Suisse**   COM
52, av Saint-Jean.
Tel. 03 21 05 69 93. Fax 03 21 05 66 97.
Closed Sun. dinner (off season), Mon., Tue.
lunch (off season).
Prix fixe: 26€ (weekdays), 37€, 50€,
10€ (child). A la carte: 64€.

Aymeric Cappelle supervises this pleasant regional eatery in a real faux Swiss chalet. Duck foie gras, pan-tossed langoustines with basil, local stew, poultry stuffed with chanterelles and house profiteroles melt in the mouth. The charming Frédérique Lamarque recommends the wines.

● **Les Sports**
22, rue Saint-Jean.
Tel. 03 21 05 05 22. Fax 03 21 05 80 01.
Prix fixe: 16€, 18,90€, 8,80€ (child).
A la carte: 30€.

Les Sports resists fashions and hearsay. We do not come to the rue Saint-Jean for a lesson in applied gastronomy. Created in 1913, overhauled in the eighties and taken over by Laurent Bruloy in 1999, this local institution is renowned for its atmosphere, its benches and its eternal dishes (Saint-Vaast oysters, sole meunière, Welsh rarebit, mussels with shallots and white wine and steak tartare). The mustached and mischievous Gilbert Faucambergue provides a hearty welcome.

● **Ricochet**   Ⓝ SIM
49, rue de Paris.
Tel. 03 21 06 41 36.

www.ricochet-letouquet.com
Closed Wed., 3 weeks Jan.
Prix fixe: 13€ (lunch), 28€ (dinner).

The much-traveled Christelle and Jean-Marc Carelle, (Saint-Barth and Atlanta) have successfully created a designer-style café that makes a good impression with its red bricks, white tables, barstools and bar. It is bright, cheerful and fashionable. People come here to delight in the welcome and fresh produce that graces the changing slate. Thai-style beef salad, ricotta and white truffle ravioli in court bouillon, seafood pasta and an apple and strawberry crumble are tailor-made and the menus are heaven-sent.

● Restaurant du Marché   SIM

33, rue Jean-Monnet.
Tel.-Fax 03 21 05 96 44.
Prix fixe: 18,90€, 25,90€, 8€ (child).
A la carte: 35€.

Alexandre Briche has taken over this debonair eatery just behind the market with lots of flair and a young team. The old-style bistro décor with red faux leather benches and zinc counter looks pleasant and proud. The cuisine is simple but authentic, based on the nearby market. Poultry liver terrine with onion compote, skate with capers and the whitefish poached in cider are unassuming and moderately priced.

● Cosi Più   SIM

74, rue de Metz.
Tel. 03 21 05 32 32.
A la carte: 35€.

Pascal Verrechia's winning smile lights up this debonair trattoria. Tomato and fresh mozzarella crostini, scallop tagliatelli, salmon lasagne with Florentine sauce, saltimbocca and tiramisu make a good impression. The products are for sale in the shop opposite.

TOURNEFEUILLE see TOULOUSE

71700 Saône-et-Loire. Paris 361 – Chalon-sur-Saône 28 – Mâcon 35.
ot.tournus@wanadoo.fr.
The church of Saint-Philibert, the old houses, the Roman tiles, the gentle landscapes provide a portrait of a city of yesteryear, the city of Geuze and the restaurant that bears his name, where good eating comes naturally.

 HOTELS-RESTAURANTS

■ Hôtel de Greuze

5, pl de l'Abbaye.
Tel. 03 85 51 77 77. Fax 03 85 51 77 23.
contact@hotel-de-greuse-bourgogne.com
www.hotel-de-greuse-bourgogne.com
16 rooms: 115–220€. 3 suites: 420–520€.

Situated at the foot of the Saint-Philibert bell tower, this typical Bresse house next to the region's gourmet institution has rooms in various styles—Louis XVI, Directoire, Empire—and a conference room.

■ Le Rempart

2-4, av Léon-Gambetta.
Tel. 03 85 51 10 56. Fax 03 85 51 77 22.
lerempart@wanadoo.fr / www.lerempart.com
Closed Christmas.
Rest. closed Tue. (off season).
34 rooms: 75–115€. 7 suites: 145–200€.
Prix fixe: 30€, 50€, 75€, 15€ (child).

Located on the ramparts of the city, this 15th-century guardhouse run by the Marion family has spacious rooms with contemporary décor, a bar, a lounge, a terrace-patio and a bright and airy dining room, enhanced by vestiges of a Romanesque cloister. The new chef, Fabien Blanc, reinterprets tradition with escargots in their shells with garlic and parsley presented on a Swiss chard leaf, steamed Atlantic sea bass with spring salsify and verbena broth, Bresse chicken fricasee with crayfish and fresh pineapple pan tossed with rosemary butter caramel sauce. The Bistro is a more modest establishment.

● Aux Terrasses

18, av du 23-Janvier.
Tel. 03 85 51 01 74. Fax 03 85 51 09 99.
aux.terrasses@wanadoo.fr
Closed Sun. dinner, Mon., Tue. lunch, Jan.,
1 week Nov., 1 week June.
18 rooms: 60–75€.
Prix fixe: 23€ (weekday lunch), 27€, 35€,
56€, 11€ (child). A la carte: 60€.

Located on the roadside at the gate of
Tournus, this old post house continues to work its charm. We like its provincial atmosphere and its comfortable
rooms with their wine-red and gray color
schemes and we equally appreciate its
local cuisine with hints of the South. In the
hands of Jean-Michel Carette, wild duck in
puff pastry, grilled salmon trout, parmesan shortbread with fennel purée, roasted
pigeon breast served with its leg meat in
pastilla and a soft chocolate cake served
with passion fruit sorbet ring true.

■ Le Terminus

21, av des Gambetta.
Tel. 03 85 51 05 54.
leterminustournus@wanadoo.fr
Closed Wed.
13 rooms: 43–59€.
Prix fixe: 18€ (weekdays), 24€, 41€.

Friendly and welcoming, this traditional-
style hotel across from the train station
looks good with its cheerful rooms and colorful bar. Added to that, we have the wonderful lobby and menus with a local flavor.
Olivier Perrot concocts an adorable menu
at 18 that pays homage to the Charolais
cattle. We may also delight in foie gras and
Morteau sausage in papillote, frog legs
and morels, Miéral Bresse chicken and a
fig tart with basil ice cream. An establishment that is heaven-sent.

● Restaurant Greuze

1, rue Albert-Thibaudet.
Tel. 03 85 51 13 52. Fax 03 85 51 75 42.
greuze@wanadoo.fr
www.restaurant-greuze.com
Closed mid-Nov.–mid-Dec.
Prix fixe: 50€ (lunch), 92€, 100€,
15€ (child). A la carte: 90–120€.

This address has a very good international
reputation. Jean Ducloux, who was intran-
sigent with regard to the purest aspects of
French culinary tradition, made it into a
timeless point of reference. Laurent Couturier took over the ovens, not without
some risks, and did not hesitate to adapt
the classics but never deformed them.
Who could reproach him for trying to
make history rather than endlessly repeat-
ing it? White mushroom risotto with truffle foam, roasted lobster in its shell with
thyme-infused jus, Bresse chicken cooked
two ways (with morels and sautéed in garlic) and the four-chocolate dessert win
unanimous approval. The cellar, in the
capable hands of Gregory Corsin, is worthy of a great house and a great region. For
Burgundy, nothing but the best.

83440 Var. Paris 884 – Nice 58 – Cannes 36
– Grasse 26 – Draguignan 31 – Fréjus 35.
The heart of Fayence country: another world,
just thirteen kilometers from the A8, one hour
from Monaco and Saint-Tropez.

 HOTELS-RESTAURANTS

■ Four Seasons Resort
Provence at Terre Blanche

Domaine de Terres Blanches, D56 toward
Bagnols-en-Forêt.
Tel. 04 94 39 90 00. Fax 04 94 39 90 01.
www.fourseasons.com/fr/provence
Closed Jan.
111 suites: 250–800€.

The great stone gate and the security at
the entrance remind us of dream hotels
on faraway islands. In the main building, surrounded by villas with suites, this
impression is compounded by the architecture consisting of stone, wood and
glass. From the terraces we might expect
to see the beach and the ocean stretching
away to infinity: an ocean of greenery with
the medieval villages of Fayence, Tourrettes, Callian and Montauroux emerg-
ing from it like fantastical islands and in

the background the Provençal massifs of the center of the Var region. Everything is impressive here: suites with private terraces, a spacious bar, four restaurants, including the Faventia, tennis, golf, an infinity pool and magnificent 3000-square meter spa, all basking in a Provençal and contemporary atmosphere.

● Le Faventia

At Four Seasons Resort Provence at Terre Blanche, Domaine de Terres Blanches, D56, Bagnols-en-Forêt.
Tel. 04 94 39 90 00. Fax 04 94 39 90 01.
www.fourseasons.com/fr/provence
Closed lunch, Sun., Mon.,
beg. Jan.–beg. Feb.
Prix fixe: 58€, 75€, 98€. A la carte: 100€.

Philippe Jourdain, Meilleur Ouvrier de France, formerly of Tour d'Argent and Moulin in Mougins, has taken over the kitchen in this magnificent resort where he has made an impression with cooking that respects tastes and seasons. He uses only the best local produce: creamy basil risotto, langoustines pan-tossed with lemongrass, rouget with purple artichokes (raw and cooked in arugula leaves) and the roasted green asparagus and chanterelle-stuffed pigeon. His pastry chef, Nicolas Denis, lately of the George V, orchestrates the desserts menu with a magical touch with a milk chocolate and passion fruit dessert, brown sugar-caramelized Victoria pineapple and a souffléed almond meringue with Sichuan peppercorn ice cream, mouthwateringly good. Guillaume Barbotin's and Fréderic Woelffle's wine list pays a special homage to Provence and also to foreign wines. Under the management of Brice Delclos, formerly of the Palme d'Or in Cannes, the dining room staff is young, affable and conscientious. It is a true pleasure to sit in this restful establishment, with soft lighting on the stone walls of the terrace, and authentic Provence stretching as far as the eye can see.

The old village perched above the Vallée du Loup, is like an ode to timeless Provence.

 HOTELS-RESTAURANTS

■ La Demeure de Jeanne

907, rte de Vence.
Tel. 04 93 59 37 24. Fax 04 93 24 39 95.
yolande6@libertysurf.fr
www.demeuredejeanne.com
Rest. closed lunch, mid-Oct.–mid-Mar.
1 room: 100€. 3 suites: 150
Half board: 200–250€.

Yolande Cohen's guesthouse continues to seduce us with its rooms with balconies, its discreet luxury, its porcelain and enamel from Longwy, its terrace and its shady garden and swimming pool. At dinner time the single *menu-carte*, with aperitif and wine included, is reserved for residents, making them the only ones to enjoy the mistress of the house's happy knack of preparing sweet pea cream with pan-seared foie gras, a line-fished Atlantic sea bass filet with a rockfish sauce, a veal cutlet with artichoke sauce and farm cheeses from Châteaudouble.

● Les Bacchannales

21, Grand-Rue.
Tel. 04 93 24 19 19.
Closed Mon., Wed.,
3 weeks mid-Jan.–beg. Feb.
Prix fixe: 32€, 38€, 48€. A la carte: 41€.

Christophe Dufau has made the Bacchanales into a modern and colorful bistro that offers all the colors of Provence in its changing à la carte menu: salad topped with vegetables and diced cod in cold savory custard, creamed artichoke soup served with ham on toast, the grilled catch of the day prepared with peppers, veal roast in cocotte with lemon and the Carpentras strawberry confiture with pistachio ice cream, all accompanied by pleasant *vins du pays*.

06140 Alpes-Maritimes. Paris 936 – Nice 28 – Grasse 18 – Vence 6.

37000 Indre-et-Loire. Paris 237 – Angers 109 – Chartres 141 – Le Mans 83 – Orléans 116.

info@ligeris.com.

Tours used to be known as the town where the best French was spoken without a trace of either a patois or a local accent. It now prides itself on having what consitutes the richness of a fine provincial city. Starting with products that are the glory of French charcuterie: meat spreads based on goose and pork, chitterling sausages, wild boar or pork headcheese, terrines and braised hams; all French, of course. People come here in search of that which constitutes the sweet singularity of the "garden of France". Not only the straightforward wine, the honest-to-goodness vegetables, the fresh fruit, but also the well-aged meat from cattle that have grazed on good grass, the barley sugar evocative of childhood, stuffed prunes, chocolate that flirts with bitterness, well-presented pastries, old-style bread and innocent confectionery. What city could be more French?

■	HOTELS

■ Jean Bardet
57, rue Groison.
Tel. 02 47 41 41 11. Fax 02 47 51 68 72.
sophie@jeanbardet.com / www.jeanbardet.fr
16 rooms: 140–270€. 5 suites: 330–400€.

Managed by the good-humored Jean and Sophie Bardet this Second Empire château—now transformed into a Relais & Châteaux establishment—and its recent extension in the Tours style in the heart of vast and flowering grounds have no difficulty in charming us. A kitchen garden, swimming pool, intimate lounges, bedrooms with period furniture, delicious breakfasts and elegant table set the tone. (See Restaurants.)

■ Univers
5, bd Heurteloup.
Tel. 02 47 05 37 12. Fax 02 47 61 51 80.
contact@hotel-univers.fr / www.hotel-univers.fr
Rest. closed lunch
85 rooms: 193€. 8 suites: 193–398€.
Prix fixe: 32€, 55€, 75€.

Situated right in the center of town, this palace dating from 1846 is dizzying with its monumental stairs, refined reception rooms, vast bedrooms and suites with 1900s furniture, six lounges, quiet bar and the gallery of portraits of celebrities who have frequented the establishment. In the La Touraine restaurant, Pascal Schenet elaborates lively and precise dishes: panseared foie gras with pears, John Dory steamed over lemongrass, duck breast with raspberries and a fruit charlotte.

■ Quality Hotel Harmonie
13, rue F.-Joliot-Curie.
Tel. 02 47 66 01 48. Fax 02 47 61 66 38.
harmonie.hotel@wanadoo.fr
www.choicehotelseurope.com
Closed 22 Dec.–7 Jan.
54 rooms: 96€. 6 suites: 127€.

Designed for comfort and decorated with bright and noble shades and materials, this hotel is also near the station. Studio apartments with kitchenettes are the delight of families visiting the city.

■ Holiday Inn
15, rue Edouard-Vaillant.
Tel. 02 47 31 12 12. Fax 02 47 38 53 35.
hitours@alliance-hospitality.com
www.holiday-inn.com/tours-cityctr
103 rooms: 115–140€. 2 suites: 155–211€.
Prix fixe: 9€, 15€, 18€, 10€ (child).
A la carte: 30€.

Situated near the station, this hotel offers the advantage of chain hotels with functional and comfortable layout and traditional cuisine.

■ Châteaux de la Loire
12, rue L.-Gambetta.
Tel. 02 47 05 10 05. Fax 02 47 20 20 14.
contact@hoteldeschateaux.fr
www.hoteldeschateaux.fr
Closed mid-Dec.–end Feb.
30 rooms: 50–73€.

Restful and refined bedrooms, both spacious and comfortable with their semimodern semi-classic furniture, a friendly reception, pleasant breakfast room and moderate prices: these are the main advantages of this downtown hotel with its luminous lobby that is run by the cheerful Patrice Dutertre.

■ Holiday Inn Express

247, rue Giraudeau.
Tel. 02 47 77 45 00. Fax 02 47 77 45 01.
www.expressholidayinn.fr
Rest. open for groups only.
45 rooms: 70€. 3 suites: 90€.

The rooms in this modern hotel have been renovated in yellow tones and with contemporary furniture. Discreet and well laid out, with three perfectly equipped seminar rooms and in the modern dining room with green and yellow tones, good reliable family cuisine.

In Rochecorbon (37210). 6 km e via N152.

■ Les Hautes Roches

86, quai de Loire.
Tel. 02 47 52 88 88. Fax 02 47 52 81 30.
www.leshautesroches.com
Closed end Jan.–end Mar.
15 rooms: 135–265€.

A charming Relais & Châteaux establishment has been created in this ancient dwelling overlooking the Loire. Here you can spend delicious moments around the heated open-air swimming pool, in the unassuming rooms and the refined dining room extending to the panoramic terrace. (See Restaurants.)

● RESTAURANTS

● Jean Bardet

57, rue Groison.
Tel. 02 47 41 41 11. Fax 02 47 51 68 72.
sophie@jeanbardet.com / www.jeanbardet.com
Closed 1 Apr.–31 Oct.
Prix fixe: 60€, 125€, 165€, 25€ (child).
A la carte: 130–150€.

For seventeen years he has been to Tours what Bocuse is to Lyons: an institution. Nicely installed in the Château de Belmont with the Relais & Châteaux seal of approval, Jean, the prince of vegetables, discusses cuisine like nobody else, with the flair of an entertainer. We love his aphorisms and his passionate outbursts. We have to admit that he is backed up by the enthusiastic Sophie and her communica-

tive good humor. Always ready, like a Jack-in-the-box, to show us his kitchen garden, his Vouvray wines and other delights from the region, he is the best ambassador of good eating and drinking in Touraine, as demonstrated by these dishes full of heart and spirit that pay homage to the best products of the Valley of the Loire: a lobe of duck foie gras poached in Port, fresh lobster in a citrus vinaigrette with pan-tossed mango and turbot fished off the Breton coast served in a saffron-, coriander seed- and preserved lemon-infused fish broth. For Jean Bardet, "cuisine reflects a way of life, a season, a humor. We must serve products only in season and return to an earlier cuisine". He proves it once again with the amazing breast of young farm-raised Chevillas guinea hen with layered veal sweetbreads, potato and foie gras topped with purslane jus, an artistic reinterpretation of a regional classic. It melts and mingles with the taste buds all through to the desserts. The pan-simmered fruit presented in a crumble goes down effortlessly, accompanied by the finest of Touraine wines and the comments of the expert Gabriel Leconstet.

● Charles Barrier

101, av de la Tranchée.
Tel. 02 47 54 20 39. Fax 02 47 41 80 95.
charlesbarrier@yahoo.fr
Closed Sat. lunch, Sun. (exc. Bank holidays).
Prix fixe: 25€ (weekdays), 49€, 59€, 85€, 15€ (child). A la carte: 91€.

For ten years now, Hervé Lussault, a thirty-five-year-old Laotian, who trained in Artigny and then in Paris with Senderens, has been at the helm of Charles Barrier's illustrious residence. The refined classicism of the décor has been lightened in a more contemporary style where ochre and blue dominate. There is also the veranda and the flowery garden and, of course, the cuisine, a symphony of nuances, oscillating between tradition and modernity. Big crispy langoustines with Madras curry seasoning and slow-cooked vegetables, frog legs browned with mild spring garlic served with oyster mushroom risotto, mullet served with an artichoke fricassée and a breast of black Geline poultry with a pink ginger- and verbena-infused bouillon are extremely well made. A frozen anise parfait with slow-cooked carrots with orange makes a refreshing finish. The wines come from all over the country with 500 rigorously selected listings.

● **La Roche Le Roy**

55, rte de Saint-Avertin.
Tel. 02 47 27 22 00. Fax 02 47 28 08 39.
laroche.leroy@wanadoo.fr
www.rocheleroy.com
Closed Sun., Mon., Feb. vac., Aug.
Prix fixe: 35€ (weekday lunch), 50€, 70€, 14€ (child).

Tradition is Alain Couturier's day-to-day guide. His little manor house is at a slight remove from the center city, and in it, this former student of Charles Barrier and the Roux brothers turns out rigorously elaborate tête de veau terrine served warm, roasted pike-perch filet with slow-cooked leeks, breast of squab with foie gras, braised veal sweetbreads with pommes Anna and a baba dessert. Stéphane Benoît, the maitre d' and knowledgeable sommelier, makes sure everyone is happy. Marylin Courturier, a native of Newcastle-upon-Tyne, has retained her British accent and offers a graceful welcome.

● **La Deuvalière** COM

18, rue de la Monnaie /
15, rue du Petit-Soleil.
Tel.-Fax 02 47 64 01 57.
ladeuvaliere@wanadoo.fr
Closed Sat. lunch, Sun., Mon.
Prix fixe: 22€, 31€.

Because he is curious, Emmanuel Deuval borrows from foreign cuisine in his presentations. Among the excellent menus, we therefore find jumbo shrimp tandoori with almond yogurt sauce, fresh and smoked halibut lasagne with fava beans and cherry tomatoes in a dill emulsion, guinea hen with crayfish risotto and a warm soft chocolate cake with fresh raspberries. Pleasantly original with attentive service.

● **La Chope** COM

25 bis, av Grammont.
Tel. 02 47 20 15 15. Fax 02 47 05 70 51.
www.lachope.info
Closed 2 weeks beg. Aug.
Prix fixe: 18,90€, 23,40€, 8,50€ (child).
A la carte: 41€.

Samuel Gicqueau's brasserie, situated on one of the large boulevards, is always packed. Both tourists and workers flock to this bright and gay Belle Epoque setting to savor good family cuisine. Jumbo shrimp with ginger and sesame, pan-simmered cod with an eggplant purée and sundried cherry tomatoes and duck medallions and foie gras with figs and fried zucchini flowers with Port sauce all look very good.

● **L'Odéon** COM

10, pl du Général-Leclerc.
Tel. 02 47 20 12 65. Fax 02 47 20 47 58.
l.odeon@orange.fr
www.restaurant-odeon.fr
Closed Sun., 3 weeks Aug.
Prix fixe: 22,50€, 32,50€, 47€ (dinner)
12€ (child). A la carte: 50€.

Michel Giraud has energetically taken over this neo-art deco brasserie near the station. Yves Fradier presents a lighter version of classic cuisine. Poached eggs with red wine sauce, duck foie gras terrine, sea bream in a salt crust, pan-tossed oysters with endive and honey cakes are not bad at all. The house dark chocolate profiteroles take us straight back to chilhood.

● **Les Tuffeaux** COM

19, rue Lavoisier.
Tel. 02 47 47 19 89.
Closed Sun., Wed. lunch.
Prix fixe: 25€, 28€, 30€, 36€, 8€ (child).

Across from the museum of history of Touraine, Gildas Marsollier has been preparing Touraine recipes and Mediterranean produce for the last twenty years. In a rustic yet refined setting with tufa walls and wooden beams, a sort of cross between a cathedral and a typical Loire interior, we delight in creamy frog meat soup, the legs served on the side with parsley and garlic, Atlantic sea bass filet with oyster jus and curried eggplant, pan-tossed venison medallions and chestnuts and red beet "parasols" with mandarin orange sauce are all finely wrought preparations.

● **Les Linottes Gourmandes** 🅝🍴SIM

22, rue Georges-Courteline.
Tel. 02 47 38 34 82.
Closed Sun., Mon., 1 week Feb.,
end July–mid-Aug.
Prix fixe: 16€ (lunch), 24€.

Hervé Chardonneau, a native of Montargis who has worked with Bardet, Reine Sammut, Thorel and Guého in Nantes, created quite a little stir by opening this rustic and simple bistro with his co-disciple from the hotel school of Blois, Thomas Legendre. A few tables, wooden beamed ceilings, a little bench and a fixed-price and à la carte menu set the tone. A pork cheek terrine, veal sweetbreads with shiitakes sautéed in butter, a roasted slice of monkfish with foamy butter and a shellfish bouillon and the Atlantic sea bass filet with mutton trotter salad hit the right spot, as do the little vanilla pots de crème with cannelés (little fluted cakes).

● **Le Martin Bleu** 🅝🍴SIM

4/6, pl des Aumônes.
Tel. 02 47 05 06 99.
Closed Sun., Mon., end July–beg. Aug.
Prix fixe: 12,90€ (lunch), 17,50€, 23€.
A la carte: 35€.

Florent Martin, the chef, and Bernard Ghnassia, the man in the dining room, bring life and alacrity to this house near the station. The rough-cast rose-colored walls make a modest setting. The illustrations by Jean-Jack Martin, Florent's father, to whom we owe the fine Chroniques du Martin Pêcheur, spice up the interior, which is also decorated with fishing nets. Here we find freshwater cuisine dedicated to the river god in the form of prudent menus and classic but light preparations. Pike-perch and salmon terrine with asparagus, pike filet with beurre blanc, eel in parsley and garlic with char-

lotte potatoes, three fish from the Loire with crayfish butter, chitterling sausage with a shallot compote all pay pious homage to the region. The tart Tatin with caramel ice cream and red wine–soaked pears is a true delight.

● **L'Atelier Gourmand** 🍴SIM

37, rue Etienne-Marcel.
Tel. 02 47 38 59 87. Fax 02 47 50 14 23.
mail@lateliergourmand.fr
www.lateliergourmand.fr
Closed Sat. lunch, Sun., Mon. lunch,
mid-Dec.–mid-Jan.
Prix fixe: 20€. A la carte: 35€.

Under the vigilant eye of the Bironneau brothers, David and Fabrice, this 15th-century house with its warm tones, wooden beams and stone, located in historic Tours, merrily continues the French tradition of our grandmothers. Now assisted by Marc Gauthier, Fabrice turns out nicely executed dishes that David serves in the dining room or on the newly renovated terrace, while also recommending an ad hoc wine from the Loire region. Duck foie gras with sel de Guérande, slow-cooked tuna and root vegetable stew with anchovy butter, tête de veau with sauce ravigote and the fruit compote with rosemary and salted butter are moderately priced and carefully crafted dishes that combine the tones of Touraine region and the deeper South.

● **Le Bistro de la Tranchée** 🍴SIM

101, av de la Tranchée.
Tel. 02 47 41 09 08. Fax 02 47 41 80 95.
charlesbarrier@yahoo.fr
Closed Sun., Mon., 3 weeks Aug.
Prix fixe: 11,90€ (lunch), 19,60€ (weekday dinner), 8,50€ (child). A la carte: 30 –35€.

Hervé Lussault, the worthy and energetic heir to Barrier, runs this bistro in masterly fashion. Salmon mille-feuille with dill-seasoned whipped cream, Atlantic sea bass filet with fresh herb salad and farm-raised pork tenderloin glazed with soy sauce and served with a carrot mousseline and almond milk make up an aristocratic cuisine. Seasonal fruit clafoutis is not far behind. It is exquisite, refined, inexpen-

sive and bears the stamp of Sébastien Bou-
let, the goodly second in command.

● **La Cuisine de Georges**   Ⓝ𝗦𝗜𝗠
20, rue Georges-Courteline.
Tel. 02 47 36 92 04.
Closed Mon.
A la carte: 22€.

Jacquelin Pujole, formerly of Périgueux,
has transformed this grocery/bistro, with
its old-style atmosphere, into a pleasant place to be. Daily specials (sausage
poached in red wine and a nice vegetable purée), salad (local Sainte-Maure goat
cheese on toast over mixed greens) and
toasts (with foie gras) go well with some
choice wines, condiments and spices.
The service is non-stop from 8:30 am to
8:00 pm. Tea is served with clafoutis and
chocolate cake and groups of friends are
welcome, as are single individuals, at the
host's vast table.

● **Hardouin**   Ⓝ𝗦𝗜𝗠
70, rue Bernard-Palissy.
Tel. 02 47 75 16 62.
Closed Sat., Sun., Easter vac., 3 weeks Aug.
Prix fixe: 12€ (lunch). A la carte: 28€.

We can now have a quick snack of local
pork spreads, the rillons (crunchy) and
rilettes (creamy), chitterling sausage and
Hardouin dried sausages. Julien Garnier
and his family have taken over the Hardouin brothers' Vouvray production factory
and "gone gastronomic", opening a nice
establishment in town. On high chairs or
at relaxing tables, we can savor the seasonal house charcuterie served on a cutting board, salmon rillettes (in season),
baked salt cod and potato purée and quail
stuffed with sausage and braised in Cham-
palou or Turonien wines, without spending a fortune.

● **Le Zinc**   Ⓝ𝗦𝗜𝗠
27, pl du Grand-Marché.
Tel. 02 47 20 29 00.
Closed Sun. lunch, Wed., Christmas–New
Year's, 1 week Aug.
Prix fixe: 18,50€, 23,50€. A la carte: 32€.

Martine and Jean-François Roussaud have
made this bistro, with its wooden beams,
stones and zinc tables, one of the jewels of
the town center. Now at the ovens, she formerly worked the dining room at the Ferme
Saint-Simon in Paris. He, the schoolmaster,
has abandoned the classroom for the love
of fine fare. Basil-seasoned cheese ravioli,
pork trotter salad, tête de veau with sauce
gribiche and the Roulière boneless rib steak
served with homemade French fries is honest fare. Don't miss the Camembert terrine,
much appreciated by the regulars. The desserts (vanilla chestnut pot de crème and a
frozen Carambar candy parfait) and Pierre
Caslot's Bourgueil la Chevalerie complete
the panoply of this warm and friendly
house. A magnificent reception.

● **L'Affiné**   𝗦𝗜𝗠
66, rue Colbert.
Tel. 02 47 61 32 34.
arnaud.gerbier@numericable.fr
www.laffine.com
Closed Sun., Mon., 2 weeks Jan.,
2 weeks beg. Aug.
Prix fixe: 14€ (weekday lunch).
A la carte: 25€.

Arnaud and Audrey Gerbier, natives
of Romorantin and Paris, created this
"cheese bar" that proposes a selection of
carefully chosen well-matured cheeses.
Two relaxing dining rooms, old walls with
wooden beams and the best of wines—
this is what we find in addition to the fine
cheese dishes. A grand platter brimming
with local specialties, Savoie-style tartine, haricot salad with spice-seasoned
local Sainte Maure goat cheese, the copious raclette, goat cheese gratin, Saint Marcellin cheese and the chocolate fondue are
a delight to one and all.

● **Le Boeuf sur la Place**   𝗦𝗜𝗠
35, pl du Grand-Marché.
Tel. 02 47 38 83 84. Fax 02 47 20 66 96.
Closed Sun., Aug.
A la carte: 36€.

The carnivores have their house with
wooden beams and red velvet benches.
With Jean-Marie Arnaud and a good selec-

tion of regional and other wines, they feast on foie gras, sirloin steak, beef filet Rossini, chocolate mousse and brioche pain perdu with caramelized apples, served up in generous portions.

● **Le Charolais** SIM
"Chez Jean-Michel"
123, rue Colbert.
Tel.-Fax 02 47 20 80 20.
Closed Sat., Sun., 10 days Christmas–New Year's, 1 week May, 3 weeks Aug.
Prix fixe: 12€ (lunch). A la carte: 45€.

Jean-Michel Montagu, ex-sommelier at Senderens, Faugeron and Savoy, has made this friendly bistro his favorite establishment. He has added to it Les Pierres Fondues at number 122 in the same street (tel. 02 47 05 14 54). We give ourselves up to poached eggs served with red wine sauce, escargot sausage, seven-hour roasted leg of lamb, oven-crisped pigeon dish and brioche pain perdu, washed down with one of the "lip-smacking" Loire wines from the wine list that is full of surprises.

● **Le Douro** SIM
16, rue de la Grosse-Tour.
Tel. 02 47 38 50 90.
Closed Sat. lunch, Sun., Mon. dinner,
1 week Christmas–New Year's.
1 week at Easter, Aug.
A la carte: 32€.

Portugal turns up in this lively setting with azulejos and carefully laid-out tables. We are won over by the Lusitanian wines and the straightforward cuisine of Tonio Do Vale. Breaded and fried cod, grilled sea bream, suckling pig served with clams and the house rice pudding are washed down with the vinho verde or vinho tinto of the Douro region.

● **L'Hédoniste** SIM
16, rue Lavoisier.
Tel.-Fax 02 47 05 20 40.
Closed Sun., Mon., 2 weeks Feb.,
2 weeks Mar.
Prix fixe: 18€, 24€, 30€, 45€.
A la carte: 42€.

The father and son team Fabien and François Lagelle give us a good humored reception in this wine restaurant. In a setting that is a combination of new and old—stone, fireplace and red-laquered ceiling, with shades of pearl and burgundy—poached eggs with red wine sauce, pike-perch cooked with first pressing olive oil and tomato sauce, pigeon pastilla and the vanilla and strawberry marmalade crème brûlée, concocted by Emmanuel Cesary, are accompanied by a wine list of more than 400 wines from all regions.

● **Le Petit Patrimoine** SIM
58, rue Colbert.
Tel. 02 47 66 05 81.
Closed Sun., Mon., 1 week Christmas–New Year's.
Prix fixe: 8,50€ (lunch), 13,50€ (lunch),
14,80€ (dinner), 31€ (dinner).
A la carte: 29€.

In the street frequented by lovers of good food, Franck Garand runs this friendly and inexpensive regional bistro where he offers us a cuisine that is generous and unpretentious. In the very long room with old stone and photographs from yester-year, the local tourte containg fava and french beans, Loire mullet in an herb crust with layered potatoes and veal simmered in red wine and a frozen nougat by chef Mathias Houpau, escorted by cheerful wines from the Loire Valley, present a moderately priced Touraine.

● **La Trattoria des Halles** SIM
31, pl Gaston-Paillhou.
Tel. 02 47 64 26 64. Fax 02 47 20 14 65.
la-trattoria-tours@wanadoo.fr
Closed Sun., Mon., Aug.
A la carte: 38€.

Olivier Romain and his Russian wife Tatiana run this very French trattoria across from the covered market. Good wines, 80% of them foreign, make an excellent escort for oven-crisped cod and potato purée, monkfish osso bucco, the lemon-seasoned veal piccata with minced artichoke and parmesan served with spinach tortellini and the panna cotta with strawberry sauce and lemon brioche. It's amusing, rather tasty and the prices are fair.

● **Zafferano**   SIM

7-9, rue de la Grosse-Tour.
Tel. 02 47 38 90 77. Fax 02 47 39 26 69.
www.zafferano.com
Closed Sun., Mon., 2 weeks Feb.,
3 weeks Aug.
Prix fixe: 18€, 30€. A la carte: 37€.

Edouardo Pillitteri celebrates all of Italy in this rustic trattoria with its fine summer terrace in the old city. A different region is presented each month, giving us an opportunity to do a tour of the Boot in the form of fish carpaccio, rockfish filet with polenta and basil sauce and sage-seasoned veal wrapped in Parma ham, before the ritual tiramisu or panna cotta.

In Chanceaux-sur-Choisille (37390). 15 km via N10, D76.

● **Le Relais du Moulin**   COM
   de la Planche

Langennerie.
Tel. 02 47 55 11 96. Fax 02 47 55 24 34.
www.moulindelaplanche.com
Closed Sun. dinner, Mon., Tue., 2 weeks Jan.
Prix fixe: 25€ (weekday lunch), 33€, 42€,
55€, 13€ (child).

Claude-Pierre Chauveau has transformed this 15th-century mill and outbuildings into a peaceful stopover with a view of the headrace and the pond, by the side of which we lunch or dine in fine weather. The six little rooms are charming. The ovens have changed hands, but no one complains about vegetable, mushroom and poached foie gras served in an individual cocotte, a monkfish and shellfish ragout with white beans, suckling pig that is at once both crunchy and melting and the white chocolate ice cream with hot fudge sauce. A friendly welcome and homey service, warm atmosphere and menus at reasonable prices.

In Fondettes (37230). 8 km w via N152.

● **Auberge de Port-Vallières**   SIM

Rte de Langeais, RN 152.
Tel. 02 47 42 24 04. Fax 02 47 49 98 83.

www.touraine-gourmande.com
Closed Sun. dinner, Mon.,
Tue. dinner (off season), 2 weeks Feb.,
2 weeks end Aug.–beg. Sept.
Prix fixe: 17€ (lunch), 24€, 35€, 42€.
A la carte: 55€.

Bruno Leroux is the driving force behind this country inn that reminds us of a cheerful guinguette, on the banks of the Loire. In the orange-toned dining room a generous lobster salad with foie gras, roasted pork loin with tomato sauce and fennel, veal sweetbreads braised in Banyuls wine with mushrooms and the pear and licorice liégois with peanut cream sauce make a good impression. The local *vins du pays* provide a light-hearted accompaniment under the attentive eye of Marie-Hélène Leroux.

In Parçay-Meslay (37210). ZI Milletière: 9 km.

● **L'Arche de Meslay**   ⌂🍴COM

14, rue des Ailes.
Tel. 02 47 29 00 07. Fax 02 47 29 04 04.
www.latourainegourmande.com
Closed Sun. (exc. Bank holidays), Mon. (exc.
Bank holidays), 3 weeks Aug.
Prix fixe: 13,50€, 23€, 26€, 36€, 42€,
10€ (child), 42€.

Quite close to Tours, Ludovic and Isabelle Launay run this ark on the side of the national road leading to Paris. It is worth a stop, in spite of the uninspiring industrial surroundings. Surrounded by lawns and flowers, it brings the countryside to the city and offers judiciously priced mouthwatering menus. In the contemporary-style dining room with shades of eggshell, Pompeii-style décor with columns, the Loire pike-perch with Chinon wine sauce and espelette peppers, a local interpretation of bouillabaisse, Racan country pigeon with pain d'épice, honey and lavender and the pineapple tempura with Salidou salted-butter caramel with caramel ice cream deserve praise.

In Rochecorbon (37210). 6 km e via N152.

● **Les Hautes Roches**   V.COM

At Les Hautes Roches, 86, quai de Loire.
Tel. 02 47 52 88 88. Fax 02 47 52 81 30.

www.leshautesroches.com
Closed Sun. dinner, Mon., end Jan.–end Mar.
Prix fixe: 48€, 65€, 90€.

A solitary retreat devoted to good living overlooking the Loire, this 18th-century dwelling built on tufa rocks amazes and shocks us. Breton Didier Edon's cuisine is a perfect match for the classicly refined elegance of the dining room with shades of red and beige marble. This skillful craftsman makes finely wrought dishes that are sometimes too complex for some palates. However, accompanied by a fine list of 250 wines and the helpful advice of sommelier Eric Lopez, the fresh lobster, marbled rabbit terrine, rouget barbet meunière, beef steak with coarse-grained black pepper with young turnips and anchovies offer a wide palette of nicely matched flavors. A feast of taste that we bring to a quiet close with a fig tarte Tatin and the crispy chocolate dessert. (See Hotels.)

LA TOUR-DE-SALVAGNY see **LYON**

TOURTOUR

83690 Var. Paris 832 – Aups 10 – Draguignan 21 – Salernes 11.
This fine village perched in the pine forests of the Upper Var region has retained its Old World nature with its tightly huddled dwellings, its 16th-century oil mill and its view of the *garrigue* and surrounding hills.

 HOTELS-RESTAURANTS

■ La Bastide de Tourtour
Rte de Flayosc.
Tel. 04 98 10 54 20. Fax 04 94 70 54 90.
bastide@verdon.net
www.bastidedetourtour.com
Rest. closed lunch (exc. weekends July–Aug.).
25 rooms: 90–280€.
Prix fixe: 27€, 43€, 49€, 68€. A la carte: 85€.

Dominating the hill, amid the oaks and pines, this house seems to have always watched over the valley. The custom-ized rooms are not lacking in charm and the *bastide* offers the full range of facilities: conference room, library, flowering garden with arbor, swimming pool, tennis and a sports room. Stéphane Martinot's cuisine conjugates all the flavors of Provence. Duck foie gras terrine with pain d'épice and slow-cooked onions in a syrupy raspberry jus, pollock cut in strips and cooked Provençal-style with oilve oil-seasoned mashed potatoes and citrus fruit in a honey and cinnamon infusion served with lemon sorbet go down easily. Joël Feuillerat runs a fine regional cellar and offers pertinent advice.

● Les Chênes Verts
Rte de Villecroze.
Tel. 04 94 70 55 06. Fax 04 94 70 59 35.
Closed Tue., Wed., beg. June–mid-July.
3 rooms: 100€.
Prix fixe: 52€, 135€. A la carte: 105€.

For three decades now this Provençal house has charmed its guests with its rustic yet chic bedrooms and authentic cuisine. Far from fads and fashions, Paul Bajada, a true chef, follows his solitary path, continuing to work the fine regional produce with respect and application. A sure guarantee of success with scrambled eggs with truffles, lightly salted cod with aïoli, stewed lamb medallions with truffles and honey and lavender ice cream, timeless dishes accompanied by one of the 450 cru from his impressive cellar.

TOURTOUR

67310 Bas-Rhin. Paris 470 – Strasbourg 25 – Molsheim 8 – Saverne 22.
The northern part of the wine route. The local glory is an Altenberg *grand cru* that gives splendid Rieslings and Muscats.

● RESTAURANTS

● Zum Loejelgücker
17, rue Principale.
Tel. 03 88 50 38 19. Fax 03 88 76 02 46.
loejelgucker@traenheim.net
www.Loejelgücker-auberge-traenheim.com

Closed Mon. dinner, Tue., Feb. vac.
Prix fixe: 10,40€ (lunch), 16,50€, 26€, 40€.

The heart of Alsace rings out here in Claude Fuchs' magnificent half-timbered house decked out with wood and frescoes illustrating work in the vineyards. The menu and wine list, with nearly 200 listings, proves without any difficulty that here we concentrate on good eating and drinking. The green- and mint tea-marinated tuna carpaccio with grilled eggplant, the roasted cod filet with fresh sweet peas, the fried veal kidneys napped with a mustard-seasoned herb sauce and the white chocolate and sour cherry jelly verrine swing delicately between regional tradition and modernity. A charming inn that we also appreciate for its moderate prices.

TREBEURDEN

22560 Côtes-d'Armor. Paris 524 – Saint-Brieuc 72 – Lannion 9 – Perros-Guirec 14.
tourisme.trebeurden@wanadoo.fr.
The rose-colored granite coast, the houses nestling among the flowers, the fine harbor, even modernized, with its beach and its little marina: everything here invites us to stop and relax.

 HOTELS-RESTAURANTS

● **Le Manoir Lan-Kerellec**
11, allée Centrale-lan-Kerellec.
Tel. 02 96 15 47 47. Fax 02 96 23 66 88.
lankerellec@relaischateaux.fr
www.lankerellec.com
Closed mid-Nov.–mid-Mar.
Rest. closed lunch (Mon.–Thu.).
19 rooms: 100–340€. 4 suites: 320–422€.
Prix fixe: 38€ (lunch), 47€, 58€, 68€.
A la carte: 85€.

Facing the islands, this noble 19th-century Breton manor, classified Relais & Châteaux and isolated at the end of the rose-colored granite coast, is evocative of old tales and legends. The rooms overlooking the ocean, the dining room with its wood-work suggesting the hull of a boat and the warm welcome of Luce and Gilles Daubé

encourage travelers to hang up their hats. The cuisine by poet Marc Briand is a veritable definition of Brittany: spider crab, foie gras and green apples with avocado, pan-simmered Breton lobster with slow-cooked vegetables and a lemon-seasoned polenta topped with a lobster shell reduction sauce, Plougastel strawberries sprinkled with black olive honey and a lime- and basil-infused shaved ice dessert are subtle moments that are improved by the fine wines and comments of Jean-François Ghibaudo.

■ **Ti al-Lannec**
14, allée de Mézo-Guen.
Tel. 02 96 15 01 01. Fax 02 96 23 62 14.
resa@tiallannec.com / www.tiallannec.com
Closed mid-Nov.–beg. Mar.
26 rooms: 85–270€. 9 suites: 325–355€.
Prix fixe: 24€ (lunch), 26€ (lunch), 37€, 76€, 16,50€ (child). A la carte: 80€.

Perched on the rose-colored granite coast, this Ti al-Lannec ("house on the heath") presents little features that make us think of paradise. Its shady grounds running down to the sea, its charming and comfortable rooms and its balneotherapy center are all enchanting. In the kitchen, Dominique Lanos' regional classics continue in the same vein or even break new ground, as witnessed by duck foie gras, Atlantic sea bass filet with roasted eggplant spread, traditionally braised veal sweetbreads and little local-style crêpes.

■ **Ker an Nod**
2, rue de Pors-Termen.
Tel. 02 96 23 50 21. Fax 02 96 23 63 30.
info@kerannod.com / www.kerannod.com
Closed 11 Nov.–end Mar. Rest. closed lunch
21 rooms: 45–65€.
Prix fixe: 23€, 29€, 39€, 12€ (child).
A la carte: 40€.

Facing the windswept islands and the beach, this honest-to-goodness hotel with its granite facade offers an unrestricted view of the sea. Its modern, differently colored rooms and cooking (duck foie gras, Atlantic sea bass filet with roasted eggplant spread, traditionally braised veal

sweetbreads and little local-style crêpes)
encourage us to kick back and relax.

■ Le Quellen

18, corniche du Goas-Treiz.
Tel. 02 96 15 43 18. Fax 02 96 23 64 43.
www.lequellen.com
Closed Sun. dinner (off season), Mon., Tue.
(off season), 3 weeks Nov., 3 weeks Mar.
6 rooms: 41–56€.
Prix fixe: 25€, 35€, 55€, 9€ (child).
A la carte: 55€.

Since 2003, the Goarin brothers have
spared no effort in refurbishing their
charming house. The result? A tidy hotel
with nicely laid out rooms, all in different
styles and two dining rooms, one classic,
the other modern. Olivier serves up serious family dishes like stuffed razor clams,
steamed turbot filet, duck breast with
chanterelles and a frozen citrus nougat.

● Le Goéland SIM

14, rue de Trozoul.
Tel. 02 96 23 53 78. Fax 02 96 15 44 16.
lecastrec1@wanadoo.fr
www.bouchon-breton.com
Closed Mon., Tue. (exc. July–Aug.),
Wed. (exc. July–Aug.).
Prix fixe: 20€, 25€, 30€.

Nothing beats traveling about for a while
before really settling down. This is what
Louis Le Roy did at Porte de France in Lannion, in the Manoir de Coatguelen and in
the Repaire de Kerroch in Paimpol. He is
now perfectly at ease in this bistro and com-
municates his good humor, particularly in
his cuisine. The menus are not excessively
expensive and offer spicy crab cakes, pan-
simmered abalone with Paimpol white
beans, veal tripe cooked in cider and strawberry cookies, finely designed and executed
with talent. The service is impeccable and
the advice on wines is good.

TREBOUL see DOUARNENEZ

22730 Côtes-d'Armor. Paris 526 – Saint-
Brieuc 75 – Perros-Guirec 9 – Lannion 10.
Les Rochers, the aquarium, the island of
Renote: the Breton hideaway of PPDA.

■/● HOTELS-RESTAURANTS

■ Mer et Plage

Plage du Coz-Pors.
Tel. 02 96 15 60 00. Fax 02 96 15 31 11.
www.hoteldelamer.ifrance.com
Closed mid-Nov.–beg. Apr.
14 rooms: 40–35€. 1 suite: 65–85€.

On the beach, facing the sea, this cozy hotel
run by Yvon Le Gaouyat offers a pleasant seaside setting, modern and brightly lit rooms
with good soundproofing, white walls and
blueish textiles, a conference room and the
good quality Transat brasserie.

● Auberge de la Vieille Eglise COM

Le bourg, pl de l'Eglise.
Tel. 02 96 23 88 31. Fax 02 96 15 33 75.
Closed Sun. dinner, Mon., Tue. dinner, Mar.
A la carte: 48€.

Facing the rose-colored granite church,
this flowery inn with its rustic atmosphere
serves up unpretentious regional fare
that makes the right impression. In the
dining room, decked out with stone and
wooden beams, we savor house foie gras
with onion confiture, catfish filet cooked
in cider and apples, monkfish sautéed with
white wine, shallots and tomatoes, a lamb
chop in mustard and a cornucopia of fresh
fruits diligently prepared by Bruno Le Fes-
sant. Catherine provides passionate comments on the wines.

22220 Côtes-d'Armor. Paris 508 –
Saint-Brieuc 61 – Guinguamp 28 –
Lannion 18 – Paimpol 15.
Renan's homeland, cathedral of Saint-Tugdual
and the old houses, the pearl of the Rose Gran-
ite Coast.

HOTELS-RESTAURANTS

■ **Kastell Dinec'h**

2 km sw via rte de Lannion, via N786 toward
Perros-Guirec.
Tel. 02 96 92 49 39. Fax 02 96 92 34 03.
kastell@club-internet.fr
www.kastell-dinech.net
Closed end Dec.–beg. Apr.
Rest. closed Tue. dinner (off season),
Wed. (off season).
15 rooms: 78–135€.
Prix fixe: 32€, 40€, 53€.

The Pauwels tastefully refurbished this
Breton farmhouse and its flowery grounds
complete with menhir. Its well-laid-out
rooms, with three more on the way, overlook the swimming pool and gardens. The
restaurant, which is reserved for guests at
the hotel, invites us to savor good quality family cooking in the mouthwatering
prix-fixe/à la carte menu.

■ **Aigue Marine** 🏠

Port de Plaisance, 5, rue Marcellin-Berthelot.
Tel. 02 96 92 97 00. Fax 02 96 92 44 48.
aiguemarine@aiguemarine.fr
www.aiguemarine.fr
Closed beg. Jan.–end Feb.
Rest. closed lunch exc. Sun. (June–Sept.),
Sat. lunch (Nov.–Mar.), Sun. dinner, Mon.
48 rooms: 78–98€.
Prix fixe: 28€, 32€, 42€, 10€ (child).

Right on the harbor, Jacques and Chantal Chaumet's modern hotel offers peace
and relaxation in its pastel-shaded rooms
overlooking the sea and garden, its fitness room and indoor swimming pool.
In the restaurant with its sunny tones, the
prix-fixe/à la carte menus offers locally
gathered scallops with green asparagus,
beet juice and mixed aromatic herb salad,
oven-browned pollock in a chorizo and
Paimpol white bean crust, duck with a citrus-flavored breading and a marriage of
crème brûlée and chocolate. Skillful cooking by the young chef Yoann Péron.

29910 Finistère. Paris 544 – Quimper 28 –
Concarneau 7 – Pont-Aven 9 – Quimperlé 28.
tregunc@club-internet.fr.

The painters' route in Cornouaille leads through
this authentic Breton village with its menhirs at
the edge of the forest.

 HOTELS-RESTAURANTS

■ **Auberge des Grandes**
 Roches

Rue des Grandes-Roches.
Tel. 02 98 97 62 97. Fax 02 98 50 29 19.
hrlesgrandesroches@club-internet.fr
www.hotel-lesgrandesroches.com
Closed 20 Dec.–end Jan.
Rest. closed Tue., Wed.
17 rooms: 75–130€. 5 suites: 130€.
Prix fixe: 45€, 12€ (child). A la carte: 62€.

This complex of renovated old farmhouses
constitutes charming accommodations.
The rooms are peaceful and nicely decorated, the swimming pool is heated and
the dolmens and menhirs are impressive.
In the kitchen, Nicolas Raday, the owner
and a former student of Mère Brazier,
knows his classics and gives free rein to
his imagination. Jumbo shrimp tempura
tossed together with fries, turbot poached
in a milky vinaigrette with pan-wilted mint,
beef with aged wine sauce and a nectarine
terrine with a lemon biscuit are accurate
and precise. Everything is washed down
with the wine recommended by Maud, the
sommelier and Nicholas' wife.

■ **Le Menhir**

17, rue de Concarneau.
Tel. 02 98 97 62 35. Fax 02 98 50 26 68.
Closed Nov. 1 vac., 3 weeks Feb.
Rest. closed Sun. dinner.
28 rooms: 26–47€.
Prix fixe: 10€ (lunch), 20€, 27€, 33€,
8€ (child). A la carte: 40€.

Both restful and vibrant with energy, like
Brittany itself, this hotel/restaurant is a
choice stopover. The rooms are skillfully
laid out and the cuisine has the good taste

of family recipes. Formerly with Lucas-Carton, Patrice Blomet uses all his know-how to concoct dishes like the scallop tartare, Atlantic sea bass filet with whole grain mustard sauce, the whole pig platter with its gravy and the strawberry mille-feuille. Accompanied by a nice little bottle, we have a highly successful marriage.

● Le Clos du Minaouët

Tel. 02 98 50 29 30. Fax 02 98 50 21 90.
Closed Sun. dinner (off season), Mon. (summer), Tue. (off season), 3 weeks Jan., Feb. vac.
Prix fixe: 20€, 25€, 35€, 45€, 15€ (child).

Jean-Luc Golliot keeps a benevolent eye on things in this gourmet *clos* with its modern bay-windowed dining room in champagne tones. We delight in the sea produce presented in the changing yet balanced menus. Grilled scallops with sautéed onions and peppers in a mille-feuille, steamed lobster with minced vegetables and shellfish cream sauce, steamed John Dory with Kerdruc shellfish and turbot seasoned with dill make a good impression. Karine Even's pertinent comments guide us through a fine selection of wines from all over.

TRELLY

50660 Manche. Paris 324 – Saint-Lô 37 – Avranches 46 – Coutances 11.
The inland Cotentin where *bocage* means cottages nestling amidst the hedgerows. Don't forget to visit the nearby cathedral at Coutances with its fine bell tower that set Proust dreaming.

 HOTELS-RESTAURANTS

■ La Verte Campagne

Le hameau Chevalier.
Tel. 02 33 47 65 33. Fax 02 33 47 38 03.
lavertecampagne@wanadoo.fr
Closed 2 weeks Dec.
Rest. closed Mon. dinner, Wed.
5 rooms: 50–78€.
Prix fixe: 23,50€, 32€, 40€,
13,50€ (child). A la carte: 33–51€.

Something British about this very charming old 17th-century farmhouse with its cozy little rooms, decidedly French cuisine and the whiff of a sea breeze. We appreciate crab and flambéed jumbo shrimp salad, roasted filet of turbot with ham over vegetables, pork tenderloin medallion with mushroom confit and an apple and pear crumble.

LE TREMBLAY-SUR-MAULDRE

78490 Yvelines. Paris 43 – Houdan 24 – Mantesla-Jolie 32 – Versailles 24 – Rambouillet 18.
With its church, château and houses covered with ivy, this village is a lovely postcard for the Ile-de-France region.

 HOTELS-RESTAURANTS

■ Domaine du Tremblay

Pl de l'Eglise.
Tel. 01 34 94 25 70. Fax 01 34 87 86 27.
accueil@domainedutremblay.com
www.domainedutremblay.com
7 rooms: 145–240€.

In the middle of its forty-hectare grounds with a golf course, this 17th-century brick mansion provides old-style carefully renovated bedrooms, a fitness center with a Turkish bath and a brasserie reserved for golfers.

● Laurent Trochain

3, rue du Général-de-Gaulle.
Tel. 01 34 87 80 96. Fax 01 34 87 91 52.
trochain.laurent@wanadoo.fr
www.restaurant-trochain.fr
Closed Mon., Tue., 2 weeks beg. Jan.,
2 weeks Aug.
Prix fixe: 45€, 60€, 75€ (wine inc.).

Laurent Trochain has come a very long way. This northern lad, who trained in the Hasselt Scholteshof, in the Château at Fère-en-Tardenois, at the Abbaye de Tonnerre, along with Christophe Cussac, then with Pierre Gagnaire, took over the former Gentilhommière on the church square and transformed it into a restaurant that measures up to his creative standards. In its nicely laid-out rustic-yet-refined atmosphere we delight in pan-seared duck foie gras with pepper and celery root and an apple reduction sauce, gazpacho with creamy zucchini and fried bread, salmon trout pan-simmered with mango and carrots served with puréed broccoli, chorizo with new potatoes and the pork tenderloin medallions with Indian spices and served with local pasta and bacon. The thin raspberry tart with nuts and crème brûlée and the chocolate gelatine dessert with berry sorbet is the finest and sweetest *haute cuisine*. A wonderful welcome and lovely wines from all regions.

TREMOLAT

24510 Dordogne. Paris 536 – Périgueux 53 – Bergerac 34 – Brive-la-Gaillarde 86.
Quiet flows the Dordogne between gently shaded verdant carpets that seem to have emerged from a British tailor's shop. We observe the *cingle* or loop indicating where the river meanders, the village itself, typical of the Périgord Noir, where Claude Chabrol shot *Le Boucher* (*The Butcher*). The church and the schoolhouse have not changed.

  HOTELS-RESTAURANTS

● **Le Vieux Logis**   ○✿ 🏚
Le Bourg.
Tel. 05 53 22 80 06. Fax 05 53 22 84 89.
vieuxlogis@relaischateaux.com
www.vieux-logis.com
25 rooms: 163–313€. 9 suites: 315–335€.
Prix fixe: 32€ (lunch), 46,50€, 79€, 15,50€ (child). A la carte: 70–100€.

Bernard Giraudel's magnificent residence is the kind of Relais & Châteaux that we dream of. Nestling in the heart of one of France's most beautiful regions, this large and charming 17th-century farmhouse has always remained in the same family. Bernard renovated it with good taste while remaining true to tradition. The rustic furniture is evocative of bygone days but the swimming pool, the conference rooms and the welcoming bar have all the

modern conveniences that we cannot live without. At breakfast or dinner, we take our seats in the vast wood-toned dining room or on the shady terrace and prepare for a true gourmet pleasure. The cuisine of Vincent Arnould, who trained with Passédat and Chiboit, is well worth the visit in its own right. Duck foie gras, small sturgeon presented in little bundles, country lamb with a light stuffing and local wild strawberries served with basil sorbet are so many felicitous orchestrations of local produce and flavors. With vintages from all French regions, the cellar is more than able to provide worthy accompaniments for these delectable feasts of the Périgord.

● **Le Bistro d'en Face**   ♨SIM
Le Bourg.
Tel. 05 53 22 80 69. Fax 05 53 22 84 89.
www.vieux-logis.com
Prix fixe: 11,90€ (lunch), 21€, 28€.
A la carte: 30€.

Across from the schoolhouse where Claude Chabrol shot *Le Boucher* (*The Butcher*), Bernard Giraudel has opened a cheerful and friendly *table d'hôte* bistro and terrace along with a grocery store, an opportunity to savor Pierre-Jean Duribreux's robust dishes in a friendly atmosphere. Formerly in the Bas Bréau in Barbizon and the Vieux Logis, he brews up magical concoctions with pig's head with dates, trout filet with almonds, chicken seasoned with verjus, pan-seared duck breast with morel cream sauce and chocolate mousse. Reservations only.

TREMONT-SUR-SAULX see BAR-LE-DUC

LE TREPORT

76470 Seine-Maritime. Paris 181 – Rouen 95 – Abbeville 44 – Dieppe 31.
officetourismeletreport@wanadoo.fr.
The "pearl of the Alabaster Coast" proudly displays its sand and stone beach framed by the white chalk cliffs speckled with black flint. Admire the panorama from the terraces and the Calvaire des Marins.

HOTELS-RESTAURANTS

■ Hôtel de Calais

1, rue de Paris.
Tel. 02 27 28 09 09. Fax 02 27 28 09 00.
info@hoteldecalais.com
www.hoteldecalais.com
34 rooms: 45–70€.

A panoramic view of the port and coastline: point number one in favor of this brick hotel perched overlooking the port. Mr. Levillain kindly welcomes us to the well-laid-out Louis-Philippe-style bedrooms. Victor Hugo passed through this old post house that is now equipped for WiFi.

● Le Saint-Louis   `COM`

43, quai François-Ier.
Tel. 02 35 86 20 70. Fax 02 35 50 67 10.
Closed mid-Nov.–mid-Dec.
Prix fixe: 17,50€, 24€, 36€ (Sat., Sun.),
50€ (Sat., Sun.), 60€. A la carte: 48€.

Henri Deparis reigns over this eatery, with its large bay windows, situated directly on the quais. This coastal-style brasserie in shades of salmon—retro lighting, copper lamps and old posters—produces a cuisine that is full of freshness: a scallop and parmesan gratin, sole filet pan tossed with shellfish, grilled turbot medallion with béarnaise sauce and the little baba with its Saint-James rum ice cream bear the hallmark of chef Cédric Delahaye.

TRIGANCE

83840 Var. Paris 824 – Digne 74 –
Draguignan 41 – Grasse 72.
Situated at the entrance to the Gorges of Verdon, the village is a sort of ode to untamed Provence, Upper Provence where the air is easy to breathe under the bluest sky in the world.

HOTELS-RESTAURANTS

■ Château de Trigance

Tel. 04 94 76 91 18. Fax 04 94 85 68 99.
chateautrigance@wanadoo.fr
www.chateau-de-trigance.fr

Closed beg. Nov.–end Mar.
10 rooms: 120–170€. 2 suites: 190€.
Prix fixe: 27€, 37€, 47€. A la carte: 67€.

Perched on a rocky outcrop, this 15th-century fortified castle is now a hotel of character: massive walls, watchtowers, battlements and parapets, flags flying from pointed towers, armor and coats-of-arms, everything to take you on a trip back through time, including rooms with four-poster beds and an old medieval dining room with a vaulted ceiling. There's nothing except the cuisine of Philippe Jouffroy to bring us back to the taste of the day: a foie gras surprise, rosehip marmalade on walnut toast with a little basket of salad, roasted jumbo shrimp with vanilla-seasoned breaded and fried zucchini, rice and parmesan crisps and slow-cooked pigeon breast and legs with a baby leek tart. At dessert, fruit with sorbet and local Trigance honey has definite charm.

LA TRINITE-SUR-MER

56470 Morbihan. Paris 490 – Vannes 31 –
Auray 13 – Lorient 40 – Quiberon 22.
tourisme@ot-trinite-sur-mer.fr.
The stones of Carnac are just a stone's throw away. Here in the Gulf of Morbihan, you share the scenery with the passing sailing boats.

HOTELS-RESTAURANTS

■ Le Lodge Kérisper

4, rue du Latz.
Tel. 02 97 52 88 56.
contact@lodgekerisper.com
www.lodgekerisper.com
Closed 2 weeks Jan.
16 rooms: 110–230€.

Travelers and lovers of Africa, Claudie and Philippe Favre dreamed of having their own lodge, like the one they knew from Namibia. They built it in Brittany, just a hundred meters from the port of La Trinité, on the remains of an old 18th-century farmhouse. They called in two cunning architects who extended the existing structure with a splendid thirty-six-square-meter veranda where breakfast is served in fine weather. They also found old wood, mixed with new pine, imagined delicious little nooks, an old-style bar with a zinc counter, modern lighting fixtures (from the king of such things, Ingo Maurer), and used antique furniture. The bedrooms are romantic, bright and unassuming in white and beige tones, with bistro seats or school desks, waxed wooden tables and snug sofas. The lounge/bar is a living room such as we would dream of having at home.

■ Le Petit Hôtel des Hortensias

Pl de la Mairie.
Tel. 02 97 30 10 30. Fax 02 97 30 14 54.
leshortensias@aol.com / www.leshortensias.info
Closed Tue. (exc. dinner in summer), Wed.
lunch, Thu. lunch (in winter), beg. Dec.–beg.
Christmas vac., end Christmas vac.–end Jan.
6 rooms: 99–159€. A la carte: 45€.

A strange structure, this turn-of-the-century seaside villa in the Scandinavian style. Overlooking the port, Nathalie Gauthier and Pierre Le Glohaec have a warm smile and offer their guests cozy English-style rooms and cuisine that is half-ocean, half-Mediterranean. In their marine bistro, l'Arrosoir, whether in the comfort of the woody setting or on the panoramic terrace, we delight in stuffed quahogs, cod with thyme-seasoned butter, honey-roasted rack of lamb and buckwheat flour porridge with raisins and salted-butter caramel.

● L'Azimut & ses Chambres Marines COM

1-3, rue du Men-Dû.
Tel. 02 97 55 71 88 /
02 97 30 17 00 (hotel). Fax 02 97 55 80 15.
www.charme-gastronomie.com
Rest. closed Mon. (July–Aug.), Tue. dinner
(exc. July–Aug.), Wed. (exc. July–Aug.).
6 rooms: 60–110€.
Prix fixe: 20€ (lunch exc. Sun.), 25€
(lunch), 30€, 35€, 45€, 60€, 12€ (child).

Just next to the harbor, the genuine welcome, terrace and nautical-style painted wood dining room attract us. With the

healthy complexion of Nantes, Rudy Deniaud, who trained with Delphin, brews up a daring cuisine (sometimes too daring) using fresh local products. We liked goat cheese ravioli (even though it had raisins), and although we raise an eyebrow at the house "Chinese hat" crab dish, the gently cooked tuna and the fish grilled in the fireplace (superb Atlantic sea bass with beurre blanc) please us. The desserts—strawberry cookie, caramel ice cream and a pear far (a local flan-like dessert)—deserve nothing but praise.

LES TROIS-EPIS

68410 Haut-Rhin. Paris 439 – Colmar 11 – Munster 17 – Gérardmer 50.
The scene of a miracle: it was here that Thierry Schoeré, a resident of Orbey, saw three ears of corn appear in the hand of the Virgin in 1491. Since then, Les Trois-Epis has never ceased to welcome pilgrims who have climbed the 658 meters in search of the benefits of good air.

 | HOTELS-RESTAURANTS

■ Hôtel des Trois Epis

10, rue Thierry-Schoeré.
Tel. 03 89 49 81 61. Fax 03 89 78 90 48.
hotel3epis.1@wanadoo.fr
40 rooms: 80–85€. 2 suites: 145–160€.
Prix fixe: 29,90€, 39,90€, 45€.
A la carte: 50€.

In the middle of its flowery garden, this sixties vacation resort still continues to work its charm. As witnessed by the welcome provided by Helmut Hautzinger and the carefully laid-out rooms with a view of the Vosges. In the rustic dining room, the regional cooking based on organic produce exudes gentle perfumes. Goose foie gras, cod filet cooked skin-side down, slow-cooked pork cheek medallions and a cold yellow nectarine soup leave no room for criticism.

■ Turckheim Croix d'Or

3, rue Thierry-Schoeré.
Tel. 03 89 49 83 55. Fax 03 89 49 87 14.
hostelleriecroixdor@wanadoo.fr

www.hostelleriecroixdor.com
Rest. closed Mon., Jan.
12 rooms: 42–52€.
Prix fixe: 13,10€ (exc. Sun.), 24€, 29€,
7€ (child). A la carte: 36€.

We appreciate the panoramic view of the Vosges from the terrace or the dining room with its large bay windows. The smiling Fabrice Kolb, who trained at Lucas-Carton, Arpège and Taillevent, delights us with simple yet classic dishes that he executes to perfection. Pan-tossed mixed mushrooms, pan-simmered salmon with creamy bacon sauce, veal steak with chanterelles and the berry soup are a pleasure.

TROUVILLE-SUR-MER

14360 Calvados. Paris 199 – Caen 47 –
Le Havre 40 – Lisieux 29 – Pont-l'Evêque 11.
o.t.trouville@wanadoo.fr.
The simple and rustic equivalent to Deauville? Yes, Trouville is partly that, plus the boardwalk, the beach, the pontoon, as seen in the film *A Man and A Woman*, plus the memory of Marguerite Duras who wrote *L'Eté 80* in Les Roches Noires.

 HOTELS-RESTAURANTS

■ Hostellerie du Vallon
12, rue Sylvestre-Lasserre.
Tel. 02 31 98 35 00. Fax 02 31 98 35 10.
hduvallon@wanadoo.fr / www.bestwestern.fr
61 rooms: 98–150€. 1 suite: 250–350€.

In the upper part of the city, this neo-Norman structure has a very well-equipped fitness center, swimming pool, bar, billiard room, conference room, large bedrooms with balconies and hearty breakfasts.

■ Le Flaubert
Rue Gustave-Flaubert.
Tel. 02 31 88 37 23. Fax 02 31 88 21 56.
hotel@flaubert.fr / www.flaubert.fr
Closed mid-Nov.–mid-Feb.
31 rooms: 80–155€. 2 suites: 200€.

Isabelle Caupeil runs this thirties hotel, with its retro décor and charming atmosphere, ideally located at the end of the Trouville boardwalk. Looking like an English manor, it delights us with its position facing the sea and its old-style customized rooms.

■ Mercure
Pl Foch.
Tel. 02 31 87 38 38. Fax 02 31 87 35 41.
h1048@accor-hotels.com
Closed lunch (Nov.–Mar.).
80 rooms: 69–149€.
Prix fixe: 16€, 20€, 10€ (child).

In the center of town, facing the casino, this chain hotel turned toward the interior courtyard has renovated rooms with wine-red tones and modern furniture, three conference rooms and a contemporary restaurant. Grilled sole with garlic, butter and lemon, duck breast with sour cherries and brown sugar crème brûlée make up authentic traditional cuisine.

■ Le Saint-James
16, rue de la Plage.
Tel. 02 31 88 05 23. Fax 02 31 87 98 45.
Closed Jan.
12 rooms: 70–110€.

This family house has a practical location just a few steps from the beach, a quiet lounge with fireplace, a nice bar with a late 18th-century dowry chest and renovated bedrooms that are comfy and cozy.

■ Le Central
5 and 7 rue des Bains (hotel).
158, bd Fernand-Moureaux (restaurant),
Tel. 02 31 88 80 84. Fax 02 31 88 42 22.
central-hotel@wanadoo.fr
http://lecentral.cartesurtable.com
Closed Christmas.
19 rooms: 81–114€. 2 suites: 81–114€.
Prix fixe: 18,50€, 28€, 8,40€ (child).
A la carte: 40–55€.

Less ostentatious than Les Vapeurs across from it, this art deco brasserie bearing the stamp of Van Colen with its counter, heated terrace in winter and lively waiters, fulfills its function. The seafood platter, a fish duo cooked in the local style, sirloin steak with béarnaise or bordelaise sauce and a tarte Tatin with fresh cream are sure bets. The hotel has a reception room on the first floor and, distributed over two buildings, pleasantly renovated well-soundproofed rooms with contemporary furniture.

● Les Vapeurs 🏠 SIM

160, bd Fernand-Moureaux.
Tel. 02 31 88 15 24. Fax 02 31 88 20 58.
jmeslin@lesvapeur.fr / www.lesvapeurs.fr
Closed Christmas.
A la carte: 40€.

Founded in 1927, this brasserie and its annex Les Voiles is run by the enthusiastic Gilbert and Ghislaine Meslin and continues to please us. There is the art deco atmosphere, the zinc counter, the lively service, the simple yet reliable à la carte menu and the much-sought-after terrace. The fish soup, fried whiting, an Auge valley veal escalope and the local Norman-style tart go down without any difficulty. The dining room is always full with passing celebrities dropping in. It is becoming necessary to reserve a place on weekends.

● L'Annexe SIM

4, rue des Bains.
Tel. 02 31 88 10 27.
Prix fixe: 15 (lunch), 25€. A la carte: 45€.

Joël Métony, a native of Pointe-à-Pitre, who trained with his father-in-law Régis Lecomte in the Dauphin du Breuil in the Auge, passed through the Touques and left the Alysés to take charge of the ovens in this contemporary bistro. This modern setting with wooden tables, red and gray walls and pretty lighting fixtures is the undeclared annex of Hervé Van Colen in the Central, but Joël has a free hand when it comes to compiling market menus that brighten up the slate. Langoustine carpaccio, oven-crisped tuna with summer vegetables, a sea bream meunière, vegetable tagliatelli and a steamed young turbot prepared with first pressing olive oil, garlic and tomato sauce, served with julienned sugar snap peas, are freshness incarnate.

● Le Cap Horn SIM

20, rue des Bains.
Tel. 02 31 98 45 06.
Closed Tue.
Prix fixe: 13€, 25€. A la carte: 30€.

Daniel and Martine Letartre left a Parisian suburb for this traditional establishment that effortlessly produces its carefully prepared daily fare. We come for the fried smelt, the mussels cooked in white wine and shallots, poached skate with Norman butter, monkfish slow simmered in white sauce, pike-perch in beurre blanc and the "Cap Horn" stew with cod, Atlantic sea bass, pollock and mussels. In short, all sorts of good things that work wonders wherever we find them.

● La Petite Auberge SIM

7, rue Carnot.
Tel. 02 31 88 11 07. Fax 02 31 88 96 39.
Closed weekdays lunch, Tue. (exc. July–Aug.),
1 week June.
Prix fixe: 28€, 36€.

Just a few steps away from the boardwalk, this inn opts for a regional Norman style at every level. Straw-yellow tones, brightly shining copper and old plates deck the walls of the quietly subdued rustic dining room. Michel Gandoin does justice to the region in the course of his nicely crafted traditional recipes. Breaded filet of sole, a thin minced scallop and mushroom tart, Atlantic sea bass cooked in papillote and a fine apple tart glazed with almonds work their considerable charm.

● Les Quatre Chats SIM

8, rue d'Orléans.
Tel. 02 31 88 94 94.
www.les4chats.com
Closed Mon. lunch, Tue., Wed., Thu. lunch,
mid-Nov.–mid-Dec.
A la carte: 55€.

Serge and Muriel Salmon attract the Paris smart set to their fifties bar with its mini–dining room at the back and mezzanine. They are passionate about cuisine and wine and create a sensation every day in this unusual combination where retro barstools, métro benches, offbeat tables and an open kitchen set a sassy tone. The dishes on the slate are carefully crafted. Langoustine flan with saffron cream, arugula with parmesan, San Daniele cured ham, tuna with sesame, skirt steak with shallots and the ginger-seasoned veal chop swing between a carefully calculated exotic and a light aristocratic cuisine. The desserts (the grapefruit soup and a raspberry tiramisu) go down without any difficulty.

● **Tivoli Bistro** `SIM`
27, rue Charles-Mozin.
Tel.-Fax 02 31 98 43 44.
Closed Wed., Thu., mid-Nov.–10 Dec.,
2 weeks June.
Prix fixe: 18€, 26€. A la carte: 40€.

A relaxed atmosphere in a soft blue and yellow pastel setting, reasonable prices and good country cooking: this is what awaits you at Christiane Dantec's, where our tastebuds provide a warm welcome, when accompanied by a little local wine, for marinated mackerel, foie gras ravioli, skate with beurre noisette, coq au vin, green peppercorn-seasoned steak and chocolate fondant presented by the ever-faithful Gérard Verger.

TROYES

10000 Aube. Paris 171 – Dijon 183 – Nancy 186 – Auxerre 86 – Châlons 83.
troyes@club-internet.fr.
More of a miracle than a city. Preserved from the onslaught of time, the old Troyes has remained intact in spite of the wars, with its string of beautiful churches, flamboyant Gothic edifices, treasures and museums. The wood panel houses make up a precious collection that we discover with our heads raised as we stroll through the easy-to-visit center: it has the shape, indeed, of a champagne cork. Of course, if we come to Troyes, it is often in search of a bargain in the factory shops, but don't forget to pay a visit to the Museum of Modern Art with its collection that includes works by Derain, Delaunay, Dufy and Balthus. And make a quick visit to the nearby cathedral with its admirable stained glass windows, the basilica of Saint-Urbain with its

Virgin with the Grapes and the church of Sainte-Madelaine and its amazing rood screen. Miracle: we are never jostled during these visits and we sometimes have the feeling that we are still making discoveries.

■	HOTELS

■ **Le Champ des Oiseaux** ❀ 🏠
20, rue Linard-Gonthier.
Tel. 03 25 80 58 50. Fax 03 25 80 98 34.
message@champdesoiseaux.com
www.champdesoiseaux.com
12 rooms: 110–220€.

In a cobblestoned lane of the old city, Monique Boisseau had the good taste to restore three corbeled 15th- and 16th-century houses and to build two more. Together they never fail to charm with their wood-beamed rooms and different styles, tiles from Salernes and delicious breakfasts served in the interior courtyard and garden.

■ **Hôtel de la Poste** 🏠
35, rue Emile-Zola.
Tel. 03 25 73 05 05. Fax 03 25 73 80 76.
reservation@hotel-de-la-poste.com
www.hotel-de-la-poste.com
Rest. closed Sat. lunch, Sun. dinner, Mon.
26 rooms: 97–132€. 6 suites: 157€.
Prix fixe: 19€, 29€, 10€ (child).

In the heart of the center, this welcoming hotel has bright and cheerful rooms and apartments, a cozy lounge, two conference rooms, a very comfortable and quietly subdued bar where works by local painters hang and Les Gourmets, a quality restaurant with a seaside atmosphere. Patrick Jolain delights his guests here with finely prepared seaside dishes.

■ **Mercure Troyes Centre** 🏠
11, rue des Bas-Trévois.
Tel. 03 25 46 28 28. Fax 03 25 46 28 27.
h3168@accor-hotels.com / www.mercure.com
63 rooms: 94–111€. 7 suites: 108–150€.

A modern hotel has taken over from the old hosiery factory. The hallway presents a 19th-century loom and the whole atmosphere is nice and snug thanks to the many beautiful materials. The rooms are comfortable and a decent size.

■ Relais Saint-Jean

51, rue Paillot-de-Montabert.
Tel. 03 25 73 89 90. Fax 03 25 73 88 60.
infos@relais-st-jean.com
www.relais-st-jean.com
27 rooms: 85–135€. 3 suites: 135
Half board: 120–205€.

Established in the rue des Orfèvres in the heart of the hosiery capital, this pleasant half-timbered house has contemporary rooms with white walls that open onto the garden or the medieval district, a conference room and a lounge/bar with a billiard table and a subdued atmosphere where musical evenings are organized.

■ La Maison de Rhodes

18, rue Linard-Gonthier.
Tel. 03 25 43 11 11. Fax 03 25 43 10 43.
message@maisonderhodes.com
www.maisonderhodes.com
Open daily. Rest closed lunch
11 rooms: 135–192€. 3 suites: 215–245€.
A la carte: 28–68€.

In the historic center of Troyes, the addition to the Champ des Oiseaux nourishes many dreams. Its U-shaped wood-paneled structure dating from the 12th to the 16th century, its interior courtyard and its delicious rooms with curious bathrooms fill its guests with joy. The same enthusiasm can be found in the restaurant reserved for residents where the Franco-Brazilian chef elaborates delicious dishes.

■ Royal Hôtel

22, bd Carnot.
Tel. 03 25 73 19 99. Fax 03 25 73 47 85.
reservation@royal-hotel-troyes.com
www.royal-hotel-troyes.com
Closed 10 days at end Dec.,
2 weeks beg. Jan.
Rest. closed Sat. lunch, Sun., Mon. lunch.
40 rooms: 64–89€.
Prix fixe: 24,50€, 29,50€, 12€ (child).

Close to the station, this hotel has perfectly soundproofed rooms and a bright and luminous dining room decorated in a contemporary style. Good-quality country house cuisine is served there: a warm cocotte filled with layers of mashed potatoes and foie gras and turbot filet with asparagus risotto make a good impression.

In Bréviandes (10450). 5 km s via N71.

■ Le Pan de Bois

35, av du Général-Leclerc.
Tel. 03 25 75 02 31. Fax 03 25 49 67 84.
vadrot.jose@wanadoo.fr
www.hoteldupandebois.fr
Closed Sun. dinner (off season)
Rest. closed Sun., Mon. lunch, Christmas–
New Year's, 1 week beg. Aug.
41 rooms: 40–70€.
Prix fixe: 17–22€, 12€ (child).
A la carte: 34€.

The Vadrots rule over this complex consisting of two wood-paneled structures. José manages the bright and modern renovated bedrooms while Sylvie and Charles watch over the restaurant. Green and yellow grilled vegetables, a country terrine, salmon in a crêpe pouch, sirloin steak and profiteroles go down well with a regional wine. In summer, service extends pleasantly onto the terrace.

In Piney (10220). 19 km ne via D960.

■ Holiday Inn Forêt d'Orient

Rte de Géraudot-Rouilley-Sacey.
Tel. 03 25 43 80 80. Fax 03 25 41 57 58.
www.holidayinntroyes.com
Rest. closed lunch, Jan.–Mar., Nov.–Dec.
58 rooms: 80–112€. 25 suites: 135€.
Prix fixe: 26,50€ (lunch), 10€ (child).
A la carte: 33€.

Located on a golf course at the edge of large woods, this contemporary chain hotel has a swimming pool, a fitness center and a lounge with a fireplace. Its carefully laid-out, spacious and functional bedrooms guarantee rest and repose. In the dining room with its salmon-colored walls, concocted by Rémi Damien, fresh goat cheese and hazelnut oil in a crêpe pouch, squid sautéed with white wine, shallots and tomatoes, boneless rib steak with pepper sauce and a frozen white mint and chocolate chip parfait are authenticity itself.

●   RESTAURANTS

● Le Bourgogne   ○COM

40, rue du Général-de-Gaulle.
Tel. 03 25 73 02 67. Fax 03 25 71 06 40.
Closed Sun. dinner (exc. last Sun. of the month), Mon., Thu. dinner, 25 July–28 Aug.
Prix fixe: 32€ (weekdays), 45€.
A la carte: 55€.

This must-visit city center eatery continues to win over lovers of great traditional French cuisine. In the dining rooms of this establishment, Aimé Dubois serves up top-flight classics like pan-tossed scallops and fresh truffles, catfish filet with lobster sauce, thyme-seasoned rack of lamb and dark chocolate cake with a pistachio cream for dessert. The palatable prices and the lively service are a plus.

● Le Valentino   ○COM

35, rue de Paillot-de-Montabert.
Tel. 03 25 73 14 14. Fax 03 25 41 36 75.
levalentino@free.fr
Closed Sat. lunch, Sun. dinner, Mon., 2 weeks beg. Jan., 2 weeks Aug.
Prix fixe: 22€ (lunch), 28€, 46€.
A la carte: 60€.

As we wander along a pedestrian walkway in the old city we discover a 16th-century half-timbered house with an enchanting little flowery courtyard. The Andrés run a lively business here. In the cheerful dining room with contemporary works of art, we appreciate Gilles' light and finely crafted cuisine that changes with the seasons and the market. Pork trotter spring rolls served with truffle oil-seasoned salad, roasted rouget with creamed eggplant and mixed artichokes and peppers with Ratafia-seasoned sauce, pan-seared scallops with chopped pistou-seasoned vegetables and roasted fresh figs accompanied by a frozen spice parfait with passion fruit sauce meet with unanimous approval, as do the wines, as recommended by Claudine.

● Le Céladon   ▲COM

31, rue de la Cité.
Tel.-Fax 03 25 80 58 23.
Closed Sat. lunch, Sun. dinner, Mon., 1 week at end Jan.–beg. Feb., 3 weeks Aug.
Prix fixe: 18€ (weekday lunch), 22€, 26€, 11€ (child).

Xavier Delavenne came back to his home country after studying in the Gorges de Pennafort at Callas and in the Château de l'Yeuse at Cognac. Under the beautiful old timber beams, but in a modern décor, he concocts his carefully crafted recipes. Tatin-style duck foie gras tart with duck and blackcurrant gravy, oven-browned plaice in an artichoke and coriander bouillon with lemon and argan oil, sautéed veal sweetbreads with coarse sea salt-seasoned potatoes and Crécy-style gravy are all amazing. The vineyard peach soaked in a verbena infusion goes down all on its own. Cheerful wines from Champagne and Burgundy. We like the youthful spirit and charming menus in this house.

● Le Bistroquet   SIM

Pl Langevin.
Tel. 03 25 73 65 65. Fax 03 25 73 55 91.
Closed Sun. (exc. off season).
Prix fixe: 19,90€, 31,90€, 8€ (child).
A la carte: 38€.

Established in an old cinema, this spacious 1900s-style brasserie is always full. People flock here for its reasonable prices, friendly atmosphere and classic and down-to-earth cuisine consisting of market dishes and regional specialties. On the wine-red banquettes under the old-style lighting fixtures and washed down by a regional wine, chilled and sliced beef muzzle in salad, grilled Atlantic sea bass, AAAAA grade chitterling sausage and the meringue brioche with raspberries make us want to become regulars.

● Le Bon Vivent   SIM

23, rue de Turenne.
Tel.-Fax 03 25 73 23 66.
Closed Tue., Wed.

Prix fixe: 7,80€ (weekday lunch), 11,50€ (weekday lunch), 22€, 7€ (child).
A la carte: 30–40€.

Vincent Chevalarias delights his customers in a little house in the old city transformed into a friendly bistro. Coddled eggs, surf and turf, AAAAA chitterling sausages with an Othe country cider reduction and the brioche pain perdu with caramelized apples go down without any difficulty.

● Aux Crieurs de Vin

4-6, pl J.-Jaurès.
Tel. 03 25 40 01 01.
aux.crieurs.de.vin@wanadoo.fr
www.auxcrieursdevin.com
Closed Sun., Mon., 1 week beg. Jan.,
mid-Aug.–end Aug.
Prix fixe: 10,90€ (lunch). A la carte: 23€.

Jean-Michel Wilmes' and Nicolas Vauthier's cellar/bar is still the friendly wine bistro in the heart of Troyes. The brick walls, wine crates and wooden and zinc tables create the atmosphere. For our pleasure, the slate offers house terrine, sage-seasoned rouget, coq au vin and artisan-produced farm yogurt with chestnut tree honey accompanied by selected wines with a "nose" that is hard to beat.

● L'Illustré SIM

8, rue Champeaux.
Tel. 03 25 40 00 88. Fax 03 25 40 00 29.
Closed Christmas, New Year's, 1 May.
Prix fixe: 13,20€, 24€, 35€, 7,20€ (child).

Sandrine Boutiton is in charge of the three floors of this lively resaurant/bar in the heart of the pedestrian zone. People come here for its relaxed atmosphere, old-fashioned surroundings and modern décor, the lights, the stone fireplace, the wood panels and the red tones. The cuisine in the spirit of the times is not bad either. Potato gratin with foie gras and a morel cream sauce, cod steamed in cabbage leaves and a spice-seasoned duo of beef and foie gras are not bad.

● Les Matines SIM

53, rue Simart.
Tel. 03 25 76 03 82. Fax 03 25 81 06 98.
Closed Sun. dinner, Mon., 2 weeks Jan.,
2 weeks Aug.
Prix fixe: 16,50€, 32,50€, 9€ (child).

A couple of steps away from the cathedral, this salmon-toned establishment run by Coralie Nos and Samuel Rodier charms us with its traditional cuisine served up with a song. Duck foie gras with fig compote, Mediterranean sea bass with lobster bisque, beef tenderloin with morels and a white chocolate and sour cherry dessert meet with no resistance.

● La Taverne de l'Ours SIM

2, rue Champeaux.
Tel. 03 25 73 22 18. Fax 03 25 73 31 86.
www.taverne-ours.com
Prix fixe: 19€, 28€ (wine inc.), 32€.

This 16th-century wood paneled house with its winter garden and vaulted cellar works its charm on us. The cuisine wins us over gently: suckling pig, leg of lamb, crisp vegetables with herb mayonnaise, Troyes chitterling sausage with melted Chaource cheese and the house chocolate profiteroles.

In Pont-Sainte-Marie (10150). 3 km ne via N77.

● Hostellerie de Pont Sainte-Marie

34, rue Pasteur.
Tel. 03 25 83 28 61. Fax 03 25 81 67 85.
Closed Sun. dinner, Tue. dinner, Wed.,
10 days beg. Jan., 3 weeks Aug.
Prix fixe: 43€, 45€ (weekdays lunch,
wine inc.), 50€, 69€, 119€ (tasting menu,
wine inc.). A la carte: 80€.

Situated just across from the Gothic cathedral, this former monument to gourmandize has found a new lease of life. Now in the hands of Christian Chavanon, it presents a selection of inspired gourmet dishes. Eucalyptus-smoked salmon served with an oiled and grilled brioche with mossy whiskey served over shaved ice, mullet in a pan-tossed marinade, an Aquitaine caviar and vegetable mille-feuille, the pork-based preparations and a peach Tatin served with carrot cinnamon ice cream are very nice indeed. Sandra Chavanon recommends wines with charm and rigor.

In Pont-Sainte-Marie.

● **Le Bistro DuPont**   🛏SIM
5, pl Charles-de-Gaulle.
Tel. 03 25 80 90 99. Fax 03 25 40 82 65.
Closed Sun. dinner, Mon., Thu. dinner.
Prix fixe: 17€ (weekday dinner), 23€, 28€.

Yves Brouillet performs multiple roles, at the ovens, where he excels, to managing this fine establishment with an already good reputation. We like the sixties bistro atmosphere and the robust cuisine. Boneless breaded and fried pork trotter served with green salad, pike-perch or cod filet, splendid beef sirloin steak and a pretty apple tart are tailor-made to perfection. The wines are appropriate and the prices are very reasonable.

In Sainte-Maure (10150). 7 km n via D78.

● **Auberge Sainte-Maure**   V.COM
99, rte de Mery.
Tel. 03 25 76 90 41. Fax 03 25 80 01 55.
auberge.saintemaure@wanadoo.fr
Closed Sun. dinner, Mon.
Prix fixe: 26€, 40€, 50€.

An absolutely charming half-timbered house with a terrace overlooking the river. Gérard Martin provides a winning welcome and the dining room, with its old wooden beam roofwork, exudes country charm. People flock to the summer terrace to savor Martine's latest ideas. Variations on the duck foie gras theme, roasted langoustines with carrot sauce, Quercy farm-raised saddle of lamb with a quinoa tabouli and a garlic and sage sauce and pan-simmered fresh figs with rose sorbet prove to be quite delicious and in keeping with today's tastes. A fine list of wines from all over France.

TULLE

19000 Corrèze. Paris 479 – Brive-la-Gaillarde 29 – Aurillac 83 – Clermont-Ferrand 140.

It was here, in this prefecture of the Limousin department that flirts with the Auvergne, that Denis Tillinac, a "local" at the time, wrote *Spleen en Corrèze.*

 HOTELS-RESTAURANTS

● **Le Central**   V.COM
32, rue J.-Jaurès / 12, rue de la Barrière.
Tel. 05 55 26 24 46. Fax 05 55 26 53 16.
Closed Sat., Sun. dinner, 2 weeks beg. Aug.
Prix fixe: 25€. A la carte: 67€.

This rustic establishment is not lacking in character, both on the ground floor—more of a brasserie with a *plat du jour* that is very popular at lunch time—and on the first floor, with its more gastronomic approach. In the flamboyant and rustic dining room—decked out in wood, copper, paintings and fine furniture from yesteryear—Raymond Poumier elaborates serious country cooking based on fine and exceptionally fresh local produce. Pan-seared foie gras on greens, turbot filet, veal sweetbread fricasee with ceps and chanterelles, Limousin beef steak and cream-filled puff pastries go down very well indeed.

● **La Toque Blanche**   🛏COM
Pl Martial-Brigouleix.
Tel. 05 55 26 75 41. Fax 05 55 26 93 95.
www.hotel-latoqueblanche.com
Closed 1 week at end Jan., 1 week beg. Feb., 2 weeks beg. July Rest. closed Sun. dinner, Mon.
8 rooms: 42€.
Prix fixe: 23€. A la carte: 40€.

We like to return to this central inn with its pleasant rooms where rusticity blends with refinement. Bruno Estival extends a hearty welcome and in the kitchen his subversion of regional classics can only be described as inspired. In a setting of yellow and green pastel we need no encouragement to savor the chilled tête de veau, thinly sliced and served carpaccio-style with moutarde violette, before passing on to turbot or rouget in season, sirloin steak with pan-seared foie gras, veal sweetbreads with slow-cooked apricots.

For dessert, the baba au rhum brings back memories of times past. A reputation that remains intact, a home catering service, all at reasonable prices. An address that deserves our unreserved praise.

LA TURBALLE

44420 Loire-Atlantique. Paris 459 – Nantes 84 – La Baule 13 – Guérande 7.
The great harbor of the Guérande peninsula. Come and enjoy the return of the fishing boats.

 RESTAURANTS

● **Terminus**   SIM
18, quai Saint-Paul.
Tel. 02 40 23 30 29.
terminus44420@aol.com
http://laturbale.free.fr/restaurant-terminus.htm
Closed Sun. dinner, Tue. dinner, Wed.
Prix fixe: 16€, 21€, 27€, 45€.
A la carte: 37–47€.

We take a table near the veranda of this fish restaurant facing the harbor and renovated in shades of cream where Marie-Corine and Xavier Chevallier extend a charming welcome. In the course of light preparations based on supremely fresh produce, Xavier is inspired by the ocean. House-smoked salmon, lemongrass-seasoned turbot and cod with curry sauce reveal a true talent. The Breton flan-like far and the seasonal fruit Pavlova are a gourmet's delight.

LA TURBIE

06320 Alpes-Maritimes. Paris 947– Monaco 8 – Menton 16 – Nice 16.
A village nestling at the top of the mountain that the Romans celebrated and Napoleon occupied: many plaques testify to this.

 HOTELS-RESTAURANTS

● **Hostellerie Jérôme**
20, rue Comte-de-Cessole.
Tel. 04 92 41 51 51. Fax 04 92 41 51 50.

hostellerie.jerome@wanadoo.fr
www.hostelleriejerome.com
Closed Dec.–mid-Feb.
Rest. closed Mon. dinner (exc. July–Aug.),
Tue. dinner (exc. July–Aug.).
6 rooms: 120–150€.
Prix fixe: 60€, 110€.

The unrecognized genius of the Mediterranean coast? Bruno Cirino, of course, who put his fine mind at the service of others (La Bonne Auberge at Antibes, Vergé at Mougins, Maximin in the Negresco, Ducasse in Juana), before settling in this charming stopover that has become the much-sought-after refuge of demanding gourmets. We like the simple but refined décor, the bright rooms, the polished wood furniture, the dining room with its painted vaults, the terrace and the arbor. The cuisine focuses on the essentials, hits precisely the right note and steers clear of superfluous fuss. The finest produce from Nice and San Remo are used to create choice interpretations with such dishes as duck foie gras with roasted black figs, chopped spinach salad with aged vinegar, blue lobster, truffle and summer cep risotto, Mediterranean sea bass with wild dill shoots, zucchini flowers slow-cooked in olive oil and milk-fed veal sweetbreads encrusted with chanterelles and topped with truffle jus and Comté cheese. Don't pass on the desserts. The dark chocolate turnover with Piemont hazelnut ice cream, the light Carros cream and a strawberry mille-feuille with vanilla ice cream are knockouts. Make no mistake about it: Cirino is one of the "greats".

● **Le Café de la Fontaine**
4, av du Général de Gaulle.
Tel. 04 93 28 52 79.
Closed Mon. dinner (exc. summer).
A la carte: 35€.

The dishes follow closely on each other as they make their appearance on the slate that Bruno Cirino writes up twice a day. There is no room for boredom in his old-style contemporary bistro that Bruno makes a little more beautiful with each passing year. The cuisine is deliberately cheerful and sunny and brightens up the plate. A salt cod and potato dish with mild peppers, cod in an herb crust, rabbit cooked niçoise-style with tomatoes, garlic, anchovies and olives and the dark chocolate or roasted coffee tart are mouthwatering. The décor is simple, and we can also savor the carefully wrought dishes on the terrace.

TURCKHEIM

68230 Haut-Rhin. Paris 441 – Colmar 7 – Munster 12 – Gérardmer 45.
The night watchman in his greatcoat calling out the hours, the memory of Turenne before the battle, the fortified gates, the *Coteau du Brand*, renowned for its Riesling, its busy winemakers and its gourmet stopovers: a town that is an honor to beautiful Alsace!

 HOTELS-RESTAURANTS

■ Berceau du Vigneron

10, pl Turenne.
Tel. 03 89 27 23 55. Fax 03 89 30 01 33.
www.berceau-du-vigneron.com
40 rooms: 43–85€.

Built on the ramparts of the old city, this half-timbered house with its typical Alsatian rooms that are comfortable and equipped—carpet, hair dryer and television—has an agreeable *winstub*, the Caveau du Vigneron. A buffet lunch in the inner courtyard in summertime costs 8.

● L'Homme Sauvage   COM

19, Grand-Rue.
Tel. 03 89 27 56 15. Fax 03 89 80 82 03.
homme.sauvage.sarl@wandoo.fr
Closed Sun. dinner (exc. off season), Wed. (exc. off season), 1 week Oct., 2 weeks Feb., 1 week at end Aug.
Prix fixe: 13–25€ (weekday lunch), 34€, 9,50€ (child). A la carte: 46€.

There is a satisfying irony in the name of this 1609 inn (The Wild Man), given that John Oed of Strasbourg—who trained in the Cerf de Marlenheim, in the Chambard

and in the Fer Rouge—serves up very civilized cuisine. In the pretty dining room with wooden beams that is both rustic and contemporary or in the cobblestone courtyard in summer, foie gras brochettes with jumbo shrimp and mirabelle plum chutney, sea bream with tapenade served with tapenade-seasoned mashed potatoes, jumbo shrimp, stuffed rabbit saddle with chanterelle risotto and a fresh seasonal fruit mille-feuille with mascarpone cream make up seductive dishes that swing between tradition and modernity.

● Caveau du Vigneron   SIM

5, Grand-Rue.
Tel. 03 89 27 06 85.
Closed lunch, Mon.
A la carte: 40€.

Malou and Coco Helschger have brought youth and vibrancy to this 16th-century cellar with its smart and sassy atmosphere. Masterpieces, old wood paneling and a winepress are the hallmarks of this carefully chosen décor. The traditional cuisine wins us over with the onion tart, escargots, boneless frog legs with parsley sauce, potatoes and braised ham shank, berry soup and the frozen kouglof. Local wines wash it all down artfully.

● Auberge du Brand   SIM

8, Grand-Rue.
Tel. 03 89 27 06 10.
www.aubergedubrand.com
Closed Wed.
9 rooms: 56–110€.
Prix fixe: 23€, 31€, 45€, 9€ (child).
A la carte: 55€.

This goodly inn with its wooden beams and rustic atmosphere has comfortable old-style rooms that are spacious and tastefully furnished. Christian Zimmerlin, who has been through the Ducasse school, serves up very satisfying traditional dishes. Duck foie gras seasoned with eau-de-vie and quince, fish with Riesling cream sauce, beef with Munster sauce and Gewurtz-seasoned roast peaches bring a smile to the lips.

Auberge du Veilleur ● SIM

12, pl Turenne.
Tel. 03 89 27 32 22. Fax 03 89 27 55 56.
auberge.veilleur@wanadoo.fr
Closed Sat. lunch, Tue.
Prix fixe: 19,90€, 29,50€, 7,50€ (child).
A la carte: 38€.

Sabrina Chelly and Nicole Dos Santos have taken over and renovated the *winstub* that Christiane Kretz made fashionable without breaking with the spirit of the place. We are welcomed with a smile to the dining room decked out in the colors of Alsace. Jean-Marc Parlato's regional cuisine is authentic: grilled bone marrow with sel de Guérande, pot-au-feu salad with crisp vegetables, fish choucroute, steak tartare and the frozen kouglof go down a treat.

Le Caveau du Chemin ● SIM
de Ronde

1, rue des Vignerons.
Tel.-Fax 03 89 27 38 27.
lecheminderonde@wanadoo.fr
www.lecheminderonde
Closed Mon. dinner, Jan.–beg. Feb.
A la carte: 36€.

On the ramparts of the old city, this rustic tavern, now in the hands of Franck Heinrich, serves up traditional fare with enthusiasm. The house salad, sirloin steak with béarnaise sauce, beef tartare and pain perdu are authentic.

TURQUANT

49730 Maine-et-Loire. Paris 303 – Tours 60 – Angers 76 – Chinon 21 – Saumur 10.
In the heart of the Anjou vineyards, a pretty village with tufa houses.

■	HOTELS

■ Demeure de la Vignole

Impasse Marguerite-d'Anjou.
Tel. 02 41 53 67 00. Fax 02 41 53 67 09.
demeure@demeure-vignole.com
www.demeure-vignole.com
Closed mid-Nov.–mid-Mar.
7 rooms: 74–95€. 1 suite: 115€.

An original stopover in Anjou. A terraced garden, pretty non-smoking guest rooms and a troglodyte suite in this charming tufa residence built against the side of a hill and run by Monique Bartholeyns. A charming change of scenery with elegance and good taste guaranteed. Breakfast on the terrace amidst the flowers and pools, overlooking the Loire valley.

TURQUESTEIN-BLANCRUPT

57560 Moselle. Paris 395 – Strasbourg 96 – Baccarat 45 – Sarrebourg 24.
The heart of the Vosges forest, on the Lorraine side, and the home of the tales of Erckmann-Chatrian.

	HOTELS-RESTAURANTS

■ Le Kiboki

Le Four. Rte du Donon, D993.
Tel. 03 87 08 60 65. Fax 03 87 08 65 26.
Closed mid-Feb.–20 Mar., Tue.
Rest. closed Wed. lunch.
14 rooms: 110–130€. 2 suites: 68€.
Prix fixe: 22€ (lunch), 24€, 28€,
35€ (dinner), 9€ (child).

This picture-book inn in the woods enjoys peaceful surroundings. Robert Schmitt welcomes with an open smile his long-standing guests who have been won over by the peaceful comfort of the rooms—four-poster solid oak beds—the swimming pool and sauna. Alice's cuisine presents an insightful new take on tradition. Wild boar terrine with pistachios and black trumpet mushrooms, house duck foie gras, river-fished trout breaded and fried with almonds, house duck confit served on a bed of sauerkraut and flambéed mirabelle plums on Bourbon vanilla-flavored ice cream are so many joint homages to Alsace and Lorraine.

TUSSON

16140 Charente. Paris 420 – Angoulême 40 – Cognac 50 – Poitiers 84 – Mansle 15.
Renaissance houses, the vestiges of the Abbaye

des Dames and the museum of rural life make us want to extend our stay in this beautiful city in Charente.

● | RESTAURANTS

● **Le Compostelle** Ⓝ COM

Le Bourg.

Tel.-Fax 05 45 31 15 90.

le-compostelle@wanadoo.fr

Closed Sun. dinner, Mon., Thu., 2 weeks end Sept.–beg. Oct., 3 weeks Jan.

Prix fixe: 14€ (weekday lunch), 22€, 25€, 29€, 38€, 12€ (child). A la carte: 48–58€.

As its name indicates, this typically Charentais restaurant is on the pilgrimage route to Saint James of Compostella. It offers rusticity—wooden beamed ceilings and white tablecloths—and honest-to-goodness simplicity all the way to the kitchen where Laurent Malescot concocts his own version of country dishes. Seafood ravioli with exotic fruit chutney to start, then the Cognac-roasted lobster or the pigeon pastilla with spicy caramel are invigorating. For dessert, a mocha cream in salted-butter puff pastry and the iced cappuccino with Cognac. A fine wine list with vintages from all over France.

TY SANQUER see QUIMPER

UBERACH

67350 Bas-Rhin. Paris 459 – Haguenau 18 – Saverne 32 – Strasbourg 38 – Pfaffenhoffen 2.

An industrious town in the Hanau region at the entrance to the great forest of Haguenau.

● | RESTAURANTS

● **Restaurant de la Forêt** Ⓝ ▪ COM

94, Grand-Rue.

Tel. 03 88 07 73 17. Fax 03 88 72 50 33.

Closed Mon. dinner, Tue. dinner, Wed., 4 days beg. Jan., 3 weeks July–Aug.

Prix fixe: 8€ (lunch), 14,25€ (weekdays), 34€.

This former beer depot has become a fine restaurant in the hands of Caroline and Bernard Ohl. Bernard, who has already worked in the Anthon in Obersteinbach and in the Cygne in Gundershoffen, manages to blend the rustic and refined in masterly fashion. We could come simply for the *plat du jour*, the leek quiche and the braised smoked ham with cream sauce served with a potato gratin, but there are also other things to please us here: the variety meats (kidneys with shallots in Port, oven-crisped tête de veau) or the seafood (scallops and Mediterranean sea bass with olive oil, shrimp salad) or even the classic Alsatian dishes as always (frog legs, a marbled foie gras terrine), not to mention the pretty desserts (frozen praline parfait and cherry soup with vanilla ice cream) or the nicely laid tables and excellent glasses.

UCHACQ-ET-PARENTIS see MONT-DE-MARSAN

UNGERSHEIM

68190 Haut-Rhin. Strasbourg 97 – Mulhouse 18 – Ensisheim 5 – Guezbwiller 8.

All of Alsace summed up in a series of splendidly reconstituted houses: don't miss the ecomuseum!

■ Les Loges de l'Ecomusée

Chemin du Grosswald.
Tel. 03 89 74 44 95 / 03 89 74 44 49.
Fax 03 89 74 44 68.
28 rooms: 38–45€. Prix fixe: 15€, 29€.

By the entrance to the ecomuseum, a very smart modern hotel in the regional style enables us to visit everything without undue hustle and bustle. Pleasant and functional rooms that are also practical for families in the mezzanine. Regional cuisine in a large ground-floor dining room with a counter where draught beer is served.

L'UNION see **TOULOUSE**

URCUIT

64990 Pyrénées-Atlantiques. Paris 762 – Biarritz 21 – Bayonne 14 – Dax 45.
The Adour flows peacefully through this Basque country that is so close to Les Landes.

● Au Goût des Mets SIM

4 km nw via D261.
Tel.-Fax 05 59 42 95 64.
Closed Wed., 1 week Feb. vac.,
1 week beg. July.
Prix fixe: 12€ (weekday lunch), 25€,
8€ (child). A la carte: 35–48€.

Catherine and Christian Capdepuy extend an energetic welcome and serve up country cooking the way we like it. Depending on the market, Christian concocts duck stuffed with ceps, rolled, sliced and served cold, Adour eels with parsley and garlic, roasted doves with fresh ceps and the baked apples with raisins and vanilla bean-infused Agen prunes. The terrace is a blessing in summertime.

URIAGE-LES-BAINS

38410 Isère. Paris 577 – Grenoble 11 – Vizille 11.

A thermal spa from the past where one-armed bandits have replaced baccarat. People still come here for rheumatism and for their respiratory health. We also come for the fresh mountain air and the delicious food.

● Les Terrasses du Grand Hôtel

Place Déesse-Hygie.
Tel. 04 76 89 10 80. Fax 04 76 89 04 62.
grandhotel.fr@wanadoo.fr
www.grand-hotel-uriage.com
Hotel closed 26 Dec.–22 Jan.
Rest. closed Sun., Mon., end Dec.–end Jan.,
2 weeks end Aug.
39 rooms: 115–195€. 3 suites: 235–255€.
Prix fixe: 80€, 100€, 125€, 25€ (child).

Bonnard, Sacha Guitry and Coco Chanel frequented this fine spa hotel in days gone by. Today people come here to be pampered in the fitness center and for the semi-open-air swimming pool but especially for Christophe Aribert's lively and creative cuisine. The manager of the establishment, Stéphane Cano, makes sure the service is exceptional and we enjoy our time here knowing we are sure to love the food. Spiny lobsters roasted with cardamom and served with French beans, chickweed and purslane, pan-seared foie gras with cabbage root and turnip caramel, roasted Léman lake trout, potatoes in cream, leeks and fennel, poached Vercours trout in walnut milk, poached pigeon roasted with celery root, parsley, white Cevenne onions and served with gravy flavored with the liver and the Trièves guinea hen slow-roasted with carrot juice and roasted walnuts, are masterly. The black cherries with morels and fresh milk curds, a four-spice biscuit with mint and passion fruit jelly and the frozen mocha meet the same high standards. A large cellar, dominated by the Rhône and Alp regions.

■ Les Mésanges

94, rte des Mésanges.
Tel. 04 76 89 70 69. Fax 04 76 89 56 97.
www.hotel-les-mesanges.com

Closed end Oct.–beg. Feb.
Rest. closed Sun. dinner (Feb.–May),
Mon. (exc. dinner May–Oct.), Tue.
33 rooms: 55–75€.
Prix fixe: 23€, 28€, 35€, 52€,
10€ (child). A la carte: 50€.

The Prince family puts its heart into this family business with its warmly furnished rooms and pleasant swimming pool. In the restaurant, Eric and Yves serve up great French classics like duck foie gras terrine, Atlantic sea bass with a creamed leek infusion, the pan-roasted rack of lamb with morels and a slice of a frozen Chartreuse cream terrine. The swimming pool enables us to digest our meal peacefully.

URMATT

67280 Bas-Rhin. Paris 421 – Molsheim 17 – Saverne 36 – Wasselonne 22.
A sentinel between the valley of the Bruche and the forest, on the pathway through the rocks and a true village of the Vosges.

 HOTELS-RESTAURANTS

■ Le Clos du Hahnenberg
Chez Jacques

65, rue du Général-de-Gaulle.
Tel. 03 88 97 41 35. Fax 03 88 47 36 51.
clos.hahnenberg@wanadoo.fr
www.closhahnenberg.com
Hotel closed Fri. dinner, Feb. vac.
Rest. closed Fri. dinner, Christmas, New Year's, Feb. vac.
33 rooms: 49,50–61€.
Prix fixe: 13€ (weekday lunch), 19€, 26€
7,50€ (child). A la carte: 37€.

With its renovated bedrooms, games and sports facilities (boules, tennis and swimming pool), this inn is a pleasant stopover. Bruno Baur, whom we know from the Louis XIII in Strasbourg, presents a very pleasant cuisine: goat cheese salad, monkfish slice with Colombo spices, pikeperch with Riesling sauce, a Milan-style piccata and a local steamed bread dessert with mixed spice ice cream make a good impression.

■ La Poste

74, rue du Général-de-Gaulle.
Tel. 03 88 97 40 55. Fax 03 88 47 38 32.
www.multimania/hotelrestlaposte
Closed Sun. dinner, Mon., 1 week Christmas–New Year's, Feb. vac., 2 weeks July.
14 rooms: 40–57€.
Prix fixe: 17,50€, 48€, 8,50€ (child).

Doris Gruber and her brother Jacques run this welcoming inn in the center of town. The rooms are pleasant and the garden is ideal for daydreaming. Installed in the fine dining room, we continue our journey as we enjoy the classic but very well-executed cuisine: quail terrine with foie gras, turbot with beurre blanc sauce and scallops, beef filet medallions with béarnaise sauce and flambéed raspberries served over vanilla ice cream.

URRUGNE

64122 Pyrénées-Atlantiques. Paris 795 – Biarritz 23 – Bayonne 29 – Hendaye 8 – Saint-Jean-de-Luz 3.
The frontier is not far away and there are still the Pyrénées over which this old fortified town looks lovingly. A fine renovated 16th-century church.

 HOTELS-RESTAURANTS

■ Château d'Urtubie

Tel. 05 59 54 31 15. Fax 05 59 54 62 51.
www.chateaudurtubie.fr
Closed 1 Nov.–30 Mar.
10 rooms: 70–150€.

Both a hotel and a museum, this medieval fortified castle provides comfortable rooms, each named after its style of furniture and decoration. The antique furniture adds to the character of this place where Laurent de Coral is attentive to detail. The breakfast is amazing.

URT

64240 Pyrénées-Atlantiques. Paris 758 – Bayonne 16 – Biarritz 24 – Cambo-les-Bains 28 – Pau 98.

The peaceful banks of the Adour and an old sailors' village.

 | RESTAURANTS

● La Galupe

Port de l'Adour.
Tel. 05 59 56 21 84. Fax 05 59 56 28 66.
auberge.galupe@wanadoo.fr
www.lagalupe.com
Closed Sun. dinner, Tue.,
Wed. (Nov.–Easter, Aug.), Feb. vac.
Prix fixe: 30€ (lunch), 77€.

Christian Parra's old establishment still has as many fans as ever. Stéphane Rouville, newly arrived from Alençon, has kept the spirit of this half-timbered rustic house with its wooden beams, tiles and open fireplace. The region still occupies the place of honor in the cuisine with traditional dishes. Grilled royal langoustines, an Adour-fished eel poached in Bordelaise wine, Basque country milk-fed lamb with quinoa and a strawberry vacherin with lemon thyme ice cream are best washed down with delicious regional wines.

19200 Corrèze. Paris 446 – Tulle 59 – Aurillac 100 – Clermont-Ferrand 84.
ot-ussel@wanadoo.fr.
In this northeastern part of the Corrèze, so dear to Chirac, we already have one foot in the Auvergne. The narrow lanes afford glimpses of beautiful turreted houses, including the Hôtel de Ventadour.

 | HOTELS-RESTAURANTS

■ Grand Hôtel de la Gare

Av Pierre-Sémard.
Tel. 05 55 72 25 98. Fax 05 55 96 25 63.
Closed Sun. dinner, Christmas.–beg. Jan.
Rest. closed Sun. dinner, Fri., Christmas.–beg. Jan.
16 rooms: 46–52€.
Prix fixe: 18€ (weekdays), 20€, 32€.

The rooms in this train station hotel are rustic and pleasant. The local cuisine is always generously served: duck breast salad with chestnuts, salmon with mushroom mousse, veal chops with ceps and a raspberry gratin. We feel welcome.

19140 Corrèze. Paris 450 – Brive 38 – Limoges 56 – Tulle 30.
ot.uzerche@wanadoo.fr.
Overlooking the Vézère river, this little town in the Corrèze is an ode to the gentle pace of French provincial life. Don't miss the old 15th- and 16th-century houses, the 14th-century Porte Bécharie and the 12th-century church of Saint-Pierre.

 | HOTELS-RESTAURANTS

■ Hôtel Teyssier

Rue du Pont-Turgot.
Tel. 05 55 73 10 05. Fax 05 55 98 43 31.
www.hotel-teyssier.com
Closed 3 weeks end Dec., Feb. vac.
Rest. closed Tue. (off season), Wed.
14 rooms: 52–75€.
Prix fixe: 19€, 24€, 35€, 10€ (child).

Laurent Benhayoun has put the kitchen in the hands of Benoît Alexandre and gourmets rejoice at his decision. A cascade of shellfish and chorizo, with an olive oil, lemon, vanilla infusion, rouget spread on slices of zucchini, slow-roasted lamb shoulder with Provençal-style tomatoes and big fries, baba au rhum and the orange soup with mint impress us as choice gastronomy. The river is nearby to facilitate digestion.

In Saint-Ybard (19140). 6 km nw via D920 and D54.

● Auberge Saint-Roch

Le Bourg.
Tel. 05 55 73 09 71. Fax 05 55 98 41 63.
www.auberge-saint-roch.fr
Closed Sun. dinner and Mon. (summer), dinner (off season), Christmas–end Jan., mid-June–beg. July.
Prix fixe: 13€ (lunch), 18€, 25€, 38€, 8€ (child). A la carte: 40€.

Right in the middle of the village, Jean-François Moulinier's bar/café, with its shady terrace, is also an inn. Regulars and passing gourmets savor the much-appreciated cuisine based on market produce, including duck foie gras, trout with chanterelles, beef filet with wild blueberries and a frozen walnut parfait.

UZES

30700 Gard. Paris 685 – Montpellier 86 – Arles 50 – Avignon 38 – Nîmes 25.
otuzes@wanadoo.fr.

The oldest duchy in France, with its noble houses, beautiful roofs with rounded tiles that can be seen from the Bermonde tower, the church of Saint-Etienne and the Place aux Herbes which comes to life on market days. It has retained its aristocratic bearing under its relaxed appearance. Enjoy it now before it becomes another Gordes or Saint-Rémy.

 HOTELS-RESTAURANTS

■ Hôtel d'Entraigues

8, rue de la Calade.
Tel. 04 66 22 32 68. Fax 04 66 22 57 01.
www.leshotelsparticuliers.com
36 rooms: 60–170€.
Prix fixe: 15€, 18€, 21€. A la carte: 45€.

Mika Léger and Benjamin Savry co-manage this 15th- to 18th-century structure with its heterogeneous rooms and bright and cheerful bathrooms. In the vaulted dining room and on the terrace Laurent Didier serves up well-made regional dishes such as the eggplant cake with fresh goat cheese and basil, grilled Mediterranean sea bass with herbes de Provence, a pork tenderloin medallion served with tapenade and a frozen chocolate soufflé.

■ Hostellerie Provençale

1, rue de la Grande-Bourgade.
Tel. 04 66 21 11 06. Fax 04 66 75 01 03.
www.hostellerieProvençale.com
Rest. closed Sun. dinner, Mon.,
Tue. lunch, Sun.
9 rooms: 75–135€.
Prix fixe: 25€, 29€.

This old establishment located near the Place aux Herbes provides welcoming rooms. Stone, terra cotta tiles, antique furniture and beautiful textiles constitute a joyful symphony. The cuisine is simple and regional as ever.

■ Mercure

Rte de Nîmes.
Tel. 04 66 03 32 22. Fax 04 66 03 32 10.
www.mercure-uzes-gard.com
Rest. closed Nov., Jan.
65 rooms: 65–95€.
Prix fixe: 15€, 25€, 7€ (child).

A restful chain hotel. We find the comfort we expect and a welcome swimming pool when we return from trekking in the region. Tennis and ping-pong complete the sporting facilities. The welcome is warm and pleasant and the prices are still reasonable. Simple and straightforward cuisine that changes with the seasons.

● Le Bec à Vin

6, rue Entre-les-Tours.
Tel. 04 66 22 41 20.
Closed Mon., Tue. lunch (off season).
Prix fixe: 26€.

Dominique Bécasse, who used to run the Terroirs store on the Place aux Herbes, created this charming restaurant with its interior gardens to replace the old Fontaines. We go there for the simple pleasure of a nicely mixed cuisine based on local produce. Hot Pelardon cheese in a sesame crust, vitello tonnato, a squid and tomato fricassée, lamb tagine with apricots and the osso bucco make a nice loop around the Mediterranean. A nice wine list with wines from all *terroirs*.

● Au Fil de l'Eau

10, pl Dampmartin.
Tel.-Fax 04 66 22 70 08.
Prix fixe: 25€, 29€, 37€.

Paola and Olivier Pierpaoli, who have opened a boutique/restaurant dedicated to Italy right on the Place aux Herbes (the Coin des Pâtes), welcome us to their fine establishment dedicated to the sea and fusion food. Under the arches, in the garden or in the vaulted dining room we enjoy rouget terrine, fried seafood with spicy pickled mayonnaise, simply grilled squid and tuna served on ratatouille with soy sauce vinaigrette.

● **La Taverne** SIM

9, rue Xavier-Sigalon.
Tel. 04 66 22 47 08. Fax 04 66 22 45 90.
Prix fixe: 23€, 24€, 26€. A la carte: 45€.

The cuisine is unpretentious and good and the décor is welcoming with the garden and patio. There is therefore no reason to turn our noses up at this tavern where we can enjoy the local salt cod and potato dish, monkfish medallions with beurre blanc, beef filet with morels and the licorice parfait, all which make a very good impression.

● **Les Trois Salons** SIM

18, rue du Dr-Blanchard.
Tel. 04 66 22 57 34.
Closed Mon., Tue., end Jan.–end Feb.
Prix fixe: 21€ (lunch), 39€ (dinner).
A la carte: 60€.

Pierre Teste's smile makes us want to stay in this beautiful antique dealer's residence to discover the cooking of the new chef, Toby. The beef marinated with mushrooms served with Pelardon cheese, grilled bonito fish with Jerusalem artichokes, prunes and tarragon, suckling pig flanked with quince compote and served with sage-infused potatoes and a chocolate flan with saffron-seasoned pear are not unworthy of the talented fantasies of his famous Swedish predecessor, Peter.

In Arpaillargues-et-Aureillac (30700). 4,5 km via D982.

■ **Château d'Arpaillargues**

Rue du Château.
Tel. 04 66 22 14 48. Fax 04 66 22 56 10.
www.chateaudarpaillargues.com
Closed beg. Oct.–beg. Apr.
26 rooms: 80–120€. 3 suites: 80–260€.
Prix fixe: 26€, 48€, 16€ (child).

Charm and family atmosphere, luxury and relaxation, wood and stone, tradition and rusticity blend harmoniously in this 18th-century residence where Marie d'Agoult, Franz Liszt and François Nourissier liked to stay. The advantages include the grounds, terrace, swimming pool and spacious rooms. Emmanuel de La Rosa now does the cooking while Rémi Courtil chooses the wines to go with the smoked salmon with lime cream, swordfish filet on a bed of crisp vegetables, roast beef in a pastry crust and coriander-seasoned ganache with caramelized pain d'épice.

In Blauzac (30700). 7 km w via D979.

■ **La Maison**

Pl de l'Eglise.
Tel.-Fax 04 66 81 25 15.
www.chambres-provence.com
Closed mid-Nov.–mid-Mar.
3 rooms: 105–130€. 2 suites: 160–180€.

Christian Vaurie and Pierre Berringer have transformed this old 18th-century residence into a very charming guesthouse. The swimming pool, garden and vast bedrooms with all modern comforts contribute to the well-being of the guests, as do the exquisite breakfasts.

In Saint-Maximin (30700). 7 km.

■ **Château de Saint-Maximin**

Rue du Château.
Tel. 04 66 03 44 16. Fax 04 66 03 42 98.
www.chateaustmaximin.com
Closed beg. Jan.–end Feb. Rest. closed lunch, Mon., Tue.
4 rooms: 160–250€. 2 suites: 280–350€.
Prix fixe: 52€.

It is difficult to resist the charm of this château with its sumptuous rooms, masterpieces hanging on the walls, hundred-year-old olive trees, many facilities (heated swimming pool, Turkish bath, Jacuzzi, fitness center) and its very pertinent cuisine based on fresh market produce.

In Serviers-et-Labaume (30700). 6 km via D981.

● **L'Olivier** COM

Traverse des Trois-Ponts.
Tel. 04 66 22 56 01. Fax 04 66 22 54 49.

www.l-olivier.fr
Closed Mon., Jan.–end Feb., 1 week Nov.
Prix fixe: 22€ (weekday lunch), 38€, 55€.
A la carte: 50€.

In their bucolic little village, Odino and
Numa, father and son, are very good at
enchanting us with a cuisine that is redolent of the South. We delight in Italian-style vegetables, shelled and grilled
shrimp on brochettes with fennel and
black olives, lemon- and thyme flower-
marinated rabbit and a frozen bitter
almond praline mousse.

VAAS

72500 Sarthe. Paris 238 – Angers 78 –
Château-du-Loir 9 – Château-la-Vallière 14 –
Le Mans 40.
The verdant and gentle pace of life in the peace-
ful Sarthe.

| | HOTELS-RESTAURANTS |

● **Le Vedaquais**
Pl de la Liberté.
Tel. 02 43 46 01 41. Fax 02 43 46 37 60.
vedaquais@aol.com / www.vedaquais-72.com
Closed 1 week Nov. 1 vac.,
1 week Christmas–New Year's, Feb. vac.
Rest. closed Fri. dinner, Sun. dinner, Mon.
12 rooms: 48–60€. 2 suites: 60€.
Prix fixe: 10,50€ (weekday lunch),
16,50€ (weekdays), 20€ (weekdays),
25€ (weekdays), 7,50€ (child).
A la carte: 46–52€.

A new lease on life for the old town hall/
schoolhouse. Daniel Beauvais and Sylvie Langevin have transformed it into a
bright and cheerful space with a billiard
room and colorful bedrooms. Schoolhouse décor in the dining room complete
with blackboard and slate, where we savor
with more relish than in a school cafe-
teria a cuisine that reflects the taste of
the day: foie gras with pain d'épice, slow-
cooked catfish with Jasnières wine sauce,
morel-stuffed chicken breast and hazelnut crème brûlée. A fine wine list and reasonable menus.

VAILLY-SUR-SAULDRE

18260 Cher. Paris 185 – Sancerre 25 –
Aubigny-sur-Nère 18 – Bourges 56.
A pretty village in the Berry region not far from
the Sologne where we seem to detect the shadow
of Raboliot.

| ● | RESTAURANTS |

● **Le Lièvre Gourmand**
14, Grande-Rue.
Tel. 02 48 73 80 23. Fax 02 48 73 86 13.

contact@lelievregourmand.com
www.lelievregourmand.com
Closed Sun. dinner, Mon., Tue.,
Jan.–beg. Feb.
Prix fixe: 39€, 49€, 59€.

The Australian William Page occupies these old village houses that are typical of the Berry region and creates a cuisine that reflects this: Sologne at heart and exotic by nature. In the dining room with its chic-rustic elegance we delight in lobster salad in two services (the claws in a cup and the tail in tempura), tuna steak served with a tomato curry, pressed terrine of veal sweetbreads and cep aspic and a coconut bavarois with peanut ice cream with satay sauce. The cellar is shared fairly between French and Australian wines. Here again, William knows the ropes and is able to guide you faultlessly toward the most appropriate choice.

VAISON-LA-ROMAINE

84110 Vaucluse. Paris 667 – Avignon 50 – Carpentras 27 – Montélimar 65.
ot-vaison@axit.fr.
Ruins that tell a story and give the city its name, the banks of the Ouvèze, the Upper City, the chapel of Saint-Quénin: is that enough to sing the praises of a city that is chock-a-block with people in summer?

 HOTELS-RESTAURANTS

■ Hostellerie le Beffroi

Rue de l'Evêché – Cité Médiévale – BP 85.
Tel. 04 90 36 04 71. Fax 04 90 36 24 78.
lebeffroi.@wanadoo.fr / www.le-beffroi.com
Hotel closed 4 days at Christmas, end Jan.–end Mar. Rest. closed weekdays lunch, end Oct.–end Mar.
22 rooms: 85–160€.
Prix fixe: 28€, 35€, 45€, 13€ (child).

At the foot of the château, this charming hostelry distributed over two town houses from the 16th and 18th centuries has old-style rooms where we find comfort and authenticity among the wood-trimmed interiors, stone and period furniture. To relax, we can enjoy the garden terrace and the swimming pool. In the newly decorated dining room, Frédéric Peyrol presents a variety of pleasures inspired by Provence. Creamy mussel soup with tomatoes and basil, an escargot tartlette, duck breast with honey and lavender and a local pastry with a Marc de Provence-seasoned apple filling make a good impression. In summer, the salad bar moves to the terrace, offering a light and refreshing alternative in the shade of the belfry.

● Le Moulin à Huile ○ COM

1, quai Maréchal-Foch.
Tel. 04 90 36 20 67. Fax 04 90 36 20 20.
info@moulin-huile.com / www.moulin-huile.com
Rest. closed Sun., Mon.
3 rooms: 130€. 2 suites: 150€.
Prix fixe: 28€ (weekday lunch),
40€ (weekday lunch), 60€, 75€.

Robert and Sabine Bardot have very nicely refurbished this old oil mill on the banks of the Ouvèze. Formerly chef in the Flambard in Lille, he opted for a golden exile in Provence. He is a complete artist, painter, poet and chef who cultivates a passion for spices. Foie gras and Kerala spice rolls, rare-cooked salmon steak cooked in duck fat, rare-cooked rack of lamb with vegetables, bananas roasted in their skin with coconut ice cream, plus a salted-butter caramel testify to his mastery. We prolong the pleasure by lazing on the terrace on the banks of the river and spending a night in one of the cozy rooms. A rare house.

In Crestet (84110). 5 km via D938 and D76.

■ Mas de Magali ❀ 🏠

Quartier Chante-Coucou.
Tel. 04 90 36 39 91. Fax 04 90 28 73 40.
masmagali@wanadoo.fr
www.masdemagali.com/form.html
Hotel closed mid-Oct.–beg. Apr.
Rest. closed lunch, Wed., mid-Oct.–beg. Apr.
20 rooms: 68–75€.
Prix fixe: 27€.

This pretty *mas* with shades of Provence, a swimming pool, garden, welcoming rooms with a terrace and country-style dining room is home to the Bodewes. These Dutch people, who fell in love with the land of cicadas, welcome us with a smile. Magali is in charge of service and Hilbrand chooses the wines while Bastian concocts generous and finely crafted dishes with a local accent. The menu changes every day, presenting a choice of two starters and two main dishes.

In Roaix (84110). 5 km via D975.

● **Le Grand Pré**
Rte de Vaison.
Tel. 04 90 46 18 12. Fax 04 90 46 17 84.
info@legrandpre.com / www.legrandpre.com
Closed Sat. lunch, Sun. dinner, Tue., Nov.–end Feb.
Prix fixe: 32€, 52€, 62€, 72€.
A la carte: 82€.

Raoul Reichrath, who worked just under Bruneau in Brussels, has transformed this old farmhouse into a bright and cheerful gourmet establishment. In the sparingly decorated dining room, brought to life with the work of a Mexican painter, and on the terrace leading to the garden where vegetables and aromatic plants grow, he casts a spell on asparagus cake with foie gras, turbot cooked in spiced oil, oven-roasted squab, variety meat sausage with coffee-flavored gravy and a peach panna cotta with wild blueberry sauce. Flora, the sommelier, offers the wines of the Rhône valley with flair.

In Séguret (84110). 10 km via D977 and D88.

■ **Domaine de Cabasse**
Rte de Sablet.
Tel. 04 90 46 91 12. Fax 04 90 46 94 01.
www.domaine-de-cabasse.fr
Closed Nov.–end Mar. Rest. closed weekday lunch (off season, exc. Wed. and weekends).
13 rooms: 88–107€.
Prix fixe: 29€, 10€ (child).

Carefully decorated rooms, a lively regional cuisine and local wines make this Provençal residence at the foot of the Dentelles de Montmirail a choice stopping point. Tomatoes with mozzarella, paprika-seasoned Atlantic sea bass, tapenade-stuffed poultry and an apricot tart are some of the ideas taken from a menu

that changes every day. The swimming pool is a pleasure.

In Séguret.

■ **La Table du Comtat**
Tel. 04 90 46 91 49. Fax 04 90 46 94 27.
table.comtat@wanadoo.fr
www.table-comtat.com
Closed 19 Nov.–8 Dec., Feb.
Rest. closed Sun. dinner (off season), Tue. dinner (off season), Wed. (off season).
8 rooms: 80–110€.
Prix fixe: 20€ (weekday lunch), 34€, 48€, 13€ (child).

An unforgettable view of the Ventoux and the Dentelles de Montmirail from the bay window. The dishes prepared by Franck Gomez, formerly of the Lutétia, take us from pleasure to pleasure with scallops with smoked country bacon, sole meunière with hazelnuts, farm-raised poultry breast and pan-tossed foie gras with morels. The old-style rooms are cozy and the swimming pool refreshing.

In Séguret.

● **Le Mesclun**
Rue des Poternes.
Tel. 04 90 46 93 43. Fax 04 90 46 93 48.
mesclunseguret@aol.com / www.lemesclun.com
Closed Mon., Tue. (off season), Jan.
Prix fixe: 19€ (lunch), 25€ (lunch), 32€, 38€, 14€ (child).

Situated in the heart of a charming village, this rustic little eatery never ceases to astonish us. In every dish he prepares, Christophe Bonzi, formerly of the Hostellerie de Crillon-le-Brave, adds a little sunshine and something exotic, perhaps reminiscent of Tunis, where he worked for two years. White bean hummus with olive oil, crunchy toasts with slow-cooked lamb spread, lemon-seasoned blanquette de veau and Madagascar vanilla crème brûlée are nicely made. The abundant wine list and Lucie's smile do nothing to take away from this.

VALBERG

06470 Alpes-Maritimes. Paris 815 – Barcelonnette 75 – Castellane 68 – Nice 85 – Saint-Martin-Vésubie 58.
vsa@alpes-azur.com.
Nestling in a preserved environment at 1670 meters, at the gateway to the Mercantour and one hour from the coast, this ski resort has developed harmoniously and retained its character.

 HOTELS-RESTAURANTS

■ Le Chalet Suisse
4, av de Valberg.
Tel. 04 93 03 62 62. Fax 04 93 03 62 64.
info@chalet-suisse.com
www.chalet-suisse.com
Closed Oct.–end Nov., Apr.–end May.
23 rooms: 66–185€.

In this mountain chalet just next to the ski and sled runs, the clean and tidy little rooms are authentic and unpretentious. We appreciate the sauna and Turkish bath both before and after our efforts on the slopes.

■ Blanche-Neige
10, av de Valberg.
Tel. 04 93 02 50 04. Fax 04 93 02 61 90.
www.hotelblancheneige.fr
Hotel closed Nov. Rest. closed lunch, Mon., Tue., Nov., beg. July–end Aug.
17 rooms: 66–112€. Prix fixe: 22€.

This pretty chalet with its colorful walls and furniture offers a blend of the mountain and Provençal styles. We appreciate the family-style but professional cuisine. Half-board in season only (reserve).

In Roubion (06420). 14 km via D30 and D28.
■ La Fripounière
At the col de la Couillole.
Tel. 04 93 02 46 12.
www.lafripouniere.com
14 rooms: 15€.
Picnic: 6€. Half board: 38€. A la carte: 28€.

Next to the Parc du Mercantour, this chalet with its orange-toned wood and textile decorations is a cozy stopover. The Carons

have renovated the rooms, terrace and restaurant dining area, and Anne-Claude and Patrick, a sportsman, an epicurean and ex-manager of a luxury establishment, do their shopping locally and cultivate their own vegetable garden. The croque-monsieur featuring local herbs, Challans quail caramelized with pine honey, local goat cheeses and a wild blueberry tart have cheerful and regional flavors. A fine list of whiskeys.

VALBONNE

06560 Alpes-Maritimes. Paris 912 – Cannes 12 – Antibes 15 – Grasse 13 – Mougins 8.
A true Provençal village, much appreciated by the British, with the checkerboard layout of Roman cities. We visit the Place aux Arcades, the Romanesque church, the old fountain and the artisans' mill.

 HOTELS-RESTAURANTS

■ Les Armoiries
Pl des Arcades.
Tel. 04 93 12 90 90. Fax 04 93 12 90 91.
www.hotellesarmoiries.com
16 rooms: 89–159€.

Right in the middle of the pedestrian zone, this superb 17th-century structure asserts its individuality with its cheerful welcome, cute little rooms and generous breakfasts.

■ Bastide de Valbonne
1288, rte de Cannes.
Tel. 04 93 12 33 40. Fax 04 93 12 33 41.
www.bastide-valbonne.com
29 rooms: 95–115€.

The Ferro family, who run this distinctive *bastide*, has opted for modernism and color. The pleasant rooms are peaceful and simple. We are awakened by the song of the cicada. The garden, terrace and swimming pool complete the relaxed atmosphere.

● Lou Cigalon   ○COM

4-6, bd Carnot.
Tel. 04 93 12 27 07. Fax 04 93 12 09 96.
www.alainparodi.com
Closed Sun., Mon.
Prix fixe: 26€ (lunch), 42€, 69€, 105€.

Alain Parodi's house, like its owner, is warm and welcoming. The large wooden beams, bare stone and antique furniture in the two dining rooms give us a good feeling, which only improves as soon as we taste the sun-kissed cuisine. We take pleasure in shredded crabmeat with mango, coriander and coconut sauce, roasted Atlantic sea bass with chanterelles, rouget with bouillabaisse sauce, whole pigeon with vegetables in an individual pot served with cold diced foie gras and the baba au rhum with seven-year aged rum and Bourbon vanilla-seasoned whipped cream. All are mouthwateringly good and the choice of wines of Provence recommended by Romuald Germain is nothing short of staggering.

● Auberge Fleurie   ✿🛏COM

1016, rte de Cannes.
Tel. 04 93 12 02 80. Fax 04 93 12 22 27.
fleurie.aberge@wanadoo.fr
Closed Mon., Tue., 3 weeks Dec.,
2 weeks Easter.
Prix fixe: 25€, 32€. A la carte: 53–58€.

Jean-Pierre Battaglia is well established in this Provençal-style inn that deserves its name. The cuisine is classic but has a nice twist to it and varies in the amazing menus. Crayfish ravioli with lobster cream, Mediterranean sea bass pan-simmered and served with spinach on toast, sirloin steak with pepper and pear in puff pastry: prudence itself. The terrace is a delight as soon as the sun makes an appearance.

● Daniel Desavie   COM

1360, rte d'Antibes.
Tel. 04 93 12 29 68. Fax 04 93 12 18 85.
Closed Sun., Mon., 2 weeks Nov.,
2 weeks Mar., 2 weeks beg. July.
Prix fixe: 27€, 32€, 37€ (dinner),
47€ (dinner). A la carte: 80€.

Daniel Desavie, who was second to Roger Vergé at Mougins, has settled here for a more modest role, delighting us with exquisitely wrought and inspired dishes. The oxtail consommé with truffle quenelles, shelled lobster in seafood broth and with beurre blanc, center-cut sirloin steak with onions slow cooked in red wine and soft dark chocolate cake with vanilla ice cream make a good impression.

VALCABRERE see
SAINT-BERTRAND-DE-COMMINGES

LE VAL D'AJOL

88340 Vosges. Paris 383 – Epinal 45 – Lux-euil-les-Bains 18 –
Plombières-les-Bains 10 – Remiremont 18.
otsi-valdajol@wanadoo.fr.
This commune, in the depths of a Vosges valley with some sixty hamlets nestling in a verdant setting just next to Franche-Comté, has an abundance of *charcuteries* in its central town that make the wood-smoked local chitterling sausage and minced pork turnovers.

■◪／ HOTELS-RESTAURANTS

■ La Résidence   ✿🛏

5, rue des Mousses.
Tel. 03 29 30 68 52. Fax 03 29 66 53 00.
contact@la-residence.com
www.la-residence.com
Closed end Nov.–end Dec., 2 weeks Mar.
Rest. closed Sun. dinner.
49 rooms: 45,50–90€.
Prix fixe: 23,50€, 24,50€, 28€, 43€,
8€ (child). A la carte: 45–55€.

This fine aristocratic residence situated in large grounds has no lack of attractions: a beautiful veranda restaurant with its open fireplace, comfortable bedrooms installed in the outbuildings, heated swimming pool, the eternal good humor of Maryvonne Bongeot and the little dishes prepared by her son Cédric are quite pleasing. We delight in Val d'Ajol smoked chitterling sausage, a pike-perch tart with bacon vinaigrette, a pan-seared sirloin steak with bone marrow and an amusing strawberry rhubarb milkshake.

VAL-D'ISERE

73150 Savoie. Paris 697 – Albertville 87 – Briançon 137 – Chambéry 135.
info@valdisere.com.
This friendly and relaxing sixties ski resort has recovered its soul after multiple old-style renovations in this Tarentaise setting. Formerly made famous by the Goitschel sisters and Jean-Claude Killy, it had the good sense not to take itself for a star. As a result, we live here in harmony with the countryside almost all year long.

 HOTELS-RESTAURANTS

● **Les Barmes de l'Ours**
Chemin des Carats.
Tel. 04 79 41 37 00. Fax 04 79 41 37 01.
www.hotel-les-barmes.com
Closed beg. May–beg. Dec.
49 rooms: 350–790€.
26 suites: 600–1000€.
Prix fixe: 50€ (lunch, weekdays), 95€, 120€.

Raphaël Tahmazian took over the management of this contemporary hotel with its comfy and opulent semi-mountain, semi-Swedish décor and multiple activities (fitness center, Turkish bath, Jacuzzi, swimming pool, health and beauty care and massage). Chef Alain Lamaison, who left Corsica and the Calvi Signoria for Savoie, is still at the helm of the Pas de l'Ours rotisserie, the Coin Savoyard and the more refined Table de l'Ours, where he continues to serve the region with respect and imagination in the form of thin Léman crayfish ravioli in a creamy soup, artichokes with local sausage (diots), John Dory with bacon-flavored cabbage, veal filet with gravy flavored with wild blueberries, veal sweetbreads with truffles in a cocotte and a hot red praline soufflé, all a gourmand's delight.

■ **Le Christiana** ⌂
BP 48. 50 meters from the bus station.
Tel. 04 79 06 08 25. Fax 04 79 41 11 10.
www.hotel-christiania.com

Closed end Apr.–beg. Dec.
55 rooms: 268–506€.
14 suites: 490–1224€.
Prix fixe: 60€. A la carte: 110€.

The main institution of the resort, managed with flair by Philippe Bertoli, is this chic hotel with its cozy bar, cheerful lounge, perfectly equipped fitness center, heated swimming pool and tidy rooms. In the restaurant, the spirit of the times has modified Philippe Meyzin's menu: composed plate of parsleyed foie gras and pain d'épice, John Dory with ground truffles and pumpkin Mikado and beef filet medallions with a Beaufort and heirloom vegetable gratin.

■ **Aigle des Neiges**
Tel. 04 79 06 18 88. Fax 04 79 06 18 87.
Closed beg. May–beg. Dec.
106 rooms: 206€. 17 suites: 410–850€.
A la carte: 60€.

The former Latitudes hotel, renovated in a very contemporary style, makes quite an impression with its high-tech chic yet unassuming rooms. Those who like fashionable décor will love it. Fashion followers will frequent one of the three gourmand areas supervised by the bubbly Luc Reversade, called Pier (modern mountain style), Paul (baroque gastro) and Jack (tapas bar). Worth discovering.

■ **Le Blizzard** ⌂
BP 64.
Tel. 04 79 06 02 07. Fax 04 79 06 04 94.
www.hotelblizzard.com
Closed beg. May–beg. Dec.
57 rooms: 354–458€. 17 suites: 410–850€.
Prix fixe: 32€ (lunch), 48€.

Elegance at the foot of the ski runs: this large mountain chalet has accomplished its mission. The cozy aspect of the lounges and the style of some of the suites please us without any difficulty. In the kitchen, the young chef Patrice Durand juggles with duality. Certain dishes are daring and audacious, in tune with the times. Others are entirely true to their classic nature. We retain good memories of the creamy artichoke soup with foie gras, as well as veal sweetbreads in an individual cocotte with Swiss chard and truffles. Handsome desserts from the trolley.

■ Le Grand Paradis

At the ski slopes.
Tel. 04 79 06 11 73. Fax 04 79 41 11 13.
grandparadis@wanadoo.fr
www.hotelgrandparadis.com
Closed May–beg.Dec.
36 rooms: 190–275€. 4 suites: 550–892€.
Prix fixe: 42,70€ (dinner), 15€ (lunch).

At the foot of the ski runs, this hotel is 100% mountain-style: warm and friendly as we might expect. Wood, natural tones, a lively welcome and Pascal Noyon's regional yet inventive cuisine are the main advantages of the house.

■ La Savoyarde

Rue Christmas-Machet.
Tel. 04 79 06 01 55. Fax 04 79 41 11 29.
Hotel closed beg. May–mid-July, beg. Aug.–beg. Dec. Rest. closed beg. May–beg. Dec.
38 rooms: 159–222,50€.
11 suites: 235–286€.
Prix fixe: 35€ (lunch), 40€.

Jean-François and Dominique Marie have created a quality hotel with nice bedrooms, a relaxing spa and a laid-back atmosphere. In the kitchen, Damien Landais, formerly of the Allodis at Méribel, is generous, sometimes to a fault, but also inspired. A Beaufort and potato terrine, variations on the crayfish theme and suckling pig chops seasoned with hay are a success.

■ Tsanteleina

BP 201.
Tel. 04 79 06 12 13. Fax 04 79 41 14 16.
info@tsanteleina.com / www.tsanteleina.com
Closed beg. May–beg. July,
end Aug.–beg. Dec.
60 rooms: 224–396€. 11 suites: 336–516€.
Prix fixe: 30€ (lunch), 49€, 95€.

Refined and central, modern and unassuming, this very comfortable hotel in a reworked mountain style provides a charming welcome. Jérôme Labrousse is very expansive in the kitchen. The creamy pumpkin soup with foie gras is a classic.

■ Kandahar

Av Olympique.
Tel. 04 79 06 02 39 / 04 79 06 48 49.
Fax 04 79 41 15 54.
www.hotel-kandahar.com
Closed 2 May–30 Nov.
34 rooms: 80–270€. 7 suites: 105–340€.
Half board: 133–455€.

The name might be suggestive of the Middle East for some, while others may dream of winning the famous ski trophy. Both will sleep the sleep of the just in the cozy mountain-style rooms and all can meet up at the Taverne d'Alsace for a good meal. (See Restaurants.)

■ Le Samovar

La Daille.
Tel. 04 79 06 13 51. Fax 04 79 41 11 08.
samovar@wanadoo.fr / www.lesamovar.com
Closed end Apr.–beg. Dec.
12 rooms: 110–250€. 6 suites: 90–250€.
Prix fixe: 15€ (lunch), 30€, 35€,
10€ (child).

Savoyard and warmly welcoming, this large chalet at the foot of the Funival and the La Daille ski runs is stamped with Savoyard chic. A charming welcome and country cooking in the tavern-style dining room.

■ Les Sorbiers

BP 72. le Vieux Village.
Tel. 04 79 06 23 77. Fax 04 79 41 11 14.
hotelsorbiers@wanadoo.fr
www.hotelsorbiers-valdisere.com
Closed beg. May–mid-July, end Aug.–end Nov.
29 rooms: 142–298€.

This chalet-hotel at the foot of the slopes continues its transformation without losing any of its charm. The omnipresent wood gives the bedrooms and bar a warm and cheerful aspect.

■ La Becca ✿⌂

Le Laisinant, rte de l'Iseran, se.
Tel. 04 79 06 09 48. Fax 04 79 41 12 03.
info@labecca-val.com / www.labecca-val.com
Closed 1 Sept.–end Nov., end Apr.–1 July.
11 rooms: 64€ (summer), 122–159€.
Half board: 153–221€.

This family chalet is the essence of simplicity and good taste. Frescoes and painted furniture give the neat and tidy rooms a mountainy atmosphere. In the kitchen, Emmanuel Voisin carefully crafts a smoked marbled foie gras terrine served with thick quince jelly and pan-seared salmon trout with a pine oil emulsion and spelt wheat risotto. A charming welcome from Dominique and Béatrice Tempesta.

● La Fruitière SIM

La Daille.
Tel. 04 79 06 07 17. Fax 04 79 06 22 81.
lafoliedouce@wanadoo.fr
Closed 1 May–30 Nov.
A la carte: 35–45€.

A real mountain bistro. This cunningly refurbished old dairy right on the slopes is the temple of Luc Reversade, a man from Charentes whose love of the Alps delights one and all with lively and fresh preparations: leeks in a sauce ravigote, simmered lentils and pork cuts, roasted chicken and rack of lamb play on the simplicity of a good child. The desserts, a cream and pralined butter mille-feuille and the tiramisu, are superb. Nice wines chosen for their nose.

● L'Arolay SIM

Fornet.
Tel. 04 79 06 11 68. Fax 04 79 41 91 64.
arolay@wanadoo.fr / www.arolay.com
Closed Sun. dinner, Mon., Sept.–end Nov.,
May–end June.
Prix fixe: 12€, 25€, 16€. A la carte: 38–48€.

Classic is in and good humor is imperative in this charming chalet. François Marion provides a warm welcome while Frank Boehrer makes regional dishes without any difficulty. Soup of the day, the mountain platter, braserade, meats cooked at the table with sauces for dipping and a chocolate fondue meet with no resistance.

● Casa Scara SIM

Pl de l'Eglise.
Tel.-Fax 04 79 06 26 21.
Closed May–end July, Sept.–end Dec.
Prix fixe: 22€. A la carte: 55€.

Across from the church Gérard Scaraffiotti extends a hearty welcome while Alain Pfeffer, the flying Alsatian who, having arrived via Naples and Salerno, now brews up tasty Italian-style dishes. The fritto misto, risotto with truffled cream, minced calf's liver with a vinegar- and herb-seasoned white sauce, saltimbocca à la romana and the tiramisu are a delight. The wines have also crossed the Alps, with elegance!

● L'Etable d'Alain SIM

Ferme de l'Adroit.
Tel. 04 79 06 13 02. Fax 04 79 41 93 91.
Closed beg. Sept.–end Nov.,
beg. May–end June.
A la carte: 35–55€.

The farmhouse décor with stone, wood and the view from the bay windows of a herd of cattle, is charming. Hélène Mattis' welcome and the cuisine with perennial (fondue, raclette, tartiflette) or ephemeral (foie gras and chutney and rack of lamb roasted over hay) specialities is pure pleasure. The local Savoie filled puff pastry and Savoie cake with its milk caramel ice cream are incomparable delights.

● La Folie Douce SIM

La Daille.
Tel. 04 79 06 21 08.
lafoliedouce@wanadoo.fr
Closed May–mid-Dec.
A la carte: 25–35€.

Luc Reversade has created the best self-service restaurant in France. The dishes in jars, the unusual drinks and reworked tradition are presented in a modern way and in various sections. Gourmand skiers come to feed merrily on local buckwheat pasta served with Beaufort cheese sauce, macaroni and cheese, spicy chicken, a wild blueberry tart and rice pudding.

● La Grande Ourse   SIM

Front-de-Neige.
Tel. 04 79 06 00 19. Fax 04 79 41 91 14.
www.grande-ourse.com
Closed mid-May–end Nov.
Prix fixe: 20€ (lunch), 45€ (dinner), 12€ (child, lunch). A la carte: 69€.

This listed old chalet with its fresco by Fautrier charms us. The lunchtime fare is simple and in the evening we we yield to the ideas of Philippe Debize. Foie gras, lobster ravioli, pan-simmered monkfish, a slice of calf's liver and soft-centered chocolate cake are not bad.

● Le Pré d'Aval   SIM

Immeuble le Solaise, av Olympique.
Tel. 04 79 41 14 05. Fax 04 79 41 17 87.
pesenti25@aol.com
Closed June.
Prix fixe: 16€ (weekday lunch), 20€ (weekday lunch), 9€ (child).
A la carte: 45€.

Inexpensive, friendly and central, Alain and Véronique Pesenti's tavern serves a Beaufort and artichoke terrine, rump roast flambéed with Cognac and a chocolate truffle, washed down with Savoie wines or the Côtes du Luberon of Paul Dubrule, a friend of the house.

● La Taverne d'Alsace   SIM

At Hôtel Kandahar, av Olympique.
Tel. 04 79 06 48 49. Fax 04 79 41 15 54.
www.hotel-kandahar.com
Closed lunch, beg. May–beg. Dec.
A la carte: 50€.

Michel Wehrung keeps an attentive eye on the cuisine in this Savoie *winstub* where Pierre-Julien Berthet provides a lively welcome. The woody décor is the same as in Ribeauvillé. Sausage in salad, a flat savory tart, fresh fromage blanc with herbs, baeckeofe (a sliced potato and meat casserole) and choucroute are best with a Riesling or a Pinot Noir.

VALENCE

26000 Drôme. Paris 562 – Avignon 126 – Grenoble 96 – Saint-Etienne 21 – Lyon 102.
info@tourismevalence.com.

Between Provence and the Lyons region, only two and a quarter hours from Paris by TGV, the capital of the Drôme is both a junction and a crossroads. We tend to take it for a town to pass through quickly. Then, the streets in the old city, the Protestant temple of Saint-Ruf, the Place Saint-Jean and the cast-iron covered market, the Maison des Têtes with its playful sculptures, the square so dear to Peynet and his lovers, across from the Rhône and the Ardèche mountains, all work their charm on us. A gourmand capital, it is an excellent town. Don't forget that the Hermitage vintages, Saint-Joseph, Crozes and Cornas are just next door.

 HOTELS-RESTAURANTS

SOMMELIER OF THE YEAR

● Pic

285, av Victor-Hugo.
Tel. 04 75 44 15 32. Fax 04 75 40 96 03.
pic@relaischateaux.com /www.pic-valence.com
Closed 3 weeks Jan. Rest. closed Sun. dinner, Mon., Tue. lunch (exc. off season).
12 rooms: 200–285€. 3 suites: 305–395€.
Prix fixe: 79€ (weekday lunch), 125€, 175€, 26€ (child).

The famous house on the side of the N7 never ceases to change. The latest version: gray, contemporary and triumphant with designer-style minimalist bedrooms. The name of the house is written in giant letters on the unassuming facade. Anne-Sophie Pic and her husband David Sinapian, the cunning manager who orchestrated its entry into orbit, are magnificent representatives of the current generation. We are the first in almost five years to place Anne-Sophie in the Olympus of great French restaurants, thus enabling her to share the glory of her father Jacques and grandfather André. Clear and subtle, her approach is technical. She settles, as Churchill might have said, for the best. Thus, Loctudy langoustines, grilled, placed on a savory purée of sweet peas heightened with cebette onions, perfumed with metholated licorice, the rack of milk-fed Aveyron lamb (a juicy marvel) seasoned with ginger and tomato with artichoke and Agria potatoes as well as the tender Drome pigeon that achieves a formidable marriage with melon are stunning demonstrations. All this daring woman's know-how is summed up in these top-of-the-range products, cooked at peak freshness, condiments added judiciously and conjugated without extravagance. The bluefin tuna makes a pretty marbled pattern with the foie gras and the Rex rabbit performs a harmonious dance with sage and saffron. There is also the fennel-seasoned rouget with anchovies marinated in escabeche, turbot in a rhubarb crust and a soft-boiled egg with escargots from the Eyrieux valley. Great art unleashed! With the help of an enthusiastic team, Anne-Sophie Pic strikes a balance with the *terroir* while retaining a certain flair. Philippe Rigollot, the young pastry chef and winner of the World Pastry Cup, amazes us with superb presentations, including a stunning composition on the themes of pepper, raspberry, kirsch and chocolate. The formidable sommelier, Denis Bertrand, whom we celebrate this year, juggles with the best Côtes du Rhônes creating high-quality marriages of wine and food. His playground: the river and the adjoining slopes with an evident preference for the northern part: from Condrieu (ah, Cuilleron and Vernay!) to Hermitage (the Graillot is a wonder), from Cornas (not forgetting the King Colombo) to Saint-Péray (from maestro Vôge), from Saint-Joseph (Dard & Ribo, Grippa and Combier) to Côte Rôtie (Gaillard and Clusel Roch), not to mention great names like Chave, Guigual, Jaboulet and Chapoutier, all fervently hailed and defended with passion. A great house, a great cellar, a great chef and a great sommelier. QED.

■ Novotel

217, av de Provence.
Tel. 04 75 82 09 09. Fax 04 75 43 56 29.
info@novotelvalence.com
www.novotelvalence.com
107 rooms: 88–105€.
Prix fixe: 22€, 8€ (child).

Its proximity to the highway makes this chain hotel with its functional rooms and straightforward *table d'hôte* cuisine a practical stopover.

■ Hôtel de l'Europe

15, av Félix-Faure.
Tel. 04 75 82 62 65. Fax 04 75 82 62 66.
hoteleurope.valence@wanadoo.fr
Closed Christmas.
25 rooms: 42–65€.

This fine art deco establishment has charming and quite comfortable rooms. Its modest prices and warm welcome make it a choice stop in the center of town.

■ Hôtel de France

16, bd du Général-de-Gaulle.
Tel. 04 75 43 00 87. Fax 04 75 55 90 51.
info@hotel-valence.com
www.hotel-valence.com
34 rooms: 50–80€.

This centrally located modern hotel has recently been refurbished. In tastefully decorated and colorfully toned rooms and cozy lounges we can relax and work with a WiFi connection.

■ Interhôtel de Paris

30, av Pierre-Sémard.
Tel. 04 75 44 02 83. Fax 04 75 41 49 61.
www.hoteldeparis-valence.com
Closed 27 Dec.–2 Jan.
29 rooms: 40–58€.

This contemporary hotel with its modern furniture and rooms that blend wood and orange tones is also notable for its warm welcome and central location.

■ Yan's Hôtel

Quartier Maninet, rte de Montéléger.
Tel. 04 75 55 52 52. Fax 04 75 42 27 37.

info@yanshotel.com / www.yanshotel.com
Rest. closed Sat. lunch, Sun. dinner (May–
Sept.), weekends (mid-Sept.–end May), mid-
Dec.–beg. Jan.
36 rooms: 72–99€. 1 suite: 116–125€.
Prix fixe: 22€, 26€, 32€, 10€ (child).

This eighties building near the hospital and
the D262 offers the comfort of rooms with
bright wood furniture and balconies overlooking the swimming pool and garden. We
can savor a cuisine with today's tastes in
the dining room and on the terrace.

● **Flaveurs**
32, Grand-Rue.
Tel. 04 75 56 08 40. Fax 04 75 43 41 76.
Closed Sun., Mon.
Prix fixe: 25€ (lunch), 35€, 45€, 51€.

Baptiste Poinsot, who worked with Chabran
and in Europe in Avignon, created a sensation in the heart of the old city with this
chic restaurant with wooden beams, colorful paintings, subtle lighting and nicely
laid-out and spaced tables. The creative
and precise cuisine continues in the same
vein, proposing in the balanced menus
slow-cooked foie gras with fig chutney,
cod filet with an acidulated bouillon and
a squab in a citrus crust, its breast pan-
simmered, its jus heightened with Manjari
chocolate. All are distinctive and cheeky.
The desserts (on theme of chocolate salted-
butter caramel or mixed fruits, vineyard
peach and bergeron apricot) make a good
impression. A house to watch.

● **La Ciboulette**
6, rue du Commerce.
Tel. 04 75 55 67 74.
Closed Closed lunch exc. Sun., Mon., Thu.,
1 week Jan.
Prix fixe: 32€ (weekdays), 47€, 70€.

Walter Bellon, who worked with Pic and
Gagnaire, gives free rein to his imagination in this engaging "little eatery".
The foie gras duo (a pan-seared slice and
another served cold in the form of a lollipop), the cubes of escargots suspended in
chilled egg custard sauce and their daring parsley "caviar", as well as variations

on theme of oysters, defy definition. The
salmon trout stuffed with crayfish, the
Charolais sirloin with pot-au-feu bouillon
served in a beer glass and the pigeon with
dates in a lime reduction are also intriguing. The desserts (an Ardèche chestnut
delicacy, Carambar candy and chocolate
in puff pastry) are more seductive. An
unusual wine list where the valley of the
Rhône gets the smallest share.

● **L'Epicerie**
18, pl Saint-Jean.
Tel. 04 75 42 74 46. Fax 04 75 42 10 87.
pierre.fr@free.fr / http//pierre.seve.free.fr
Closed Sat. lunch, Sun., 10 days Christmas–
New Year's, 1 week beg. May,
3 weeks Aug.
Prix fixe: 18€, 24€, 44€, 64€.
A la carte: 40–45€.

Pierre Seve has extended his domain. In
addition to his fine dining room under the
vaulted ceiling across from the cast-iron
covered market, he has created a brasserie
section with a brick counter, yellow and
red armchairs and a non-smoking dining
room in a contemporary style with transparent tables. His cuisine is as rooted and
as generous as ever, and the menus are an
open invitation. Salad with bacon and ravioli, goat cheese nougat with chestnut tree
honey, seven-hour braised Drôme lamb
shanks and boneless Drôme quail with
grapes are fine moments in the regional
menu at 24 .

● **7 par Anne-Sophie Pic**
285 bis, av Victor-Hugo.
Tel. 04 75 44 53 86. Fax 04 75 40 96 03.
pic@relaischateaux.com / www.pic-valence.com
Prix fixe: 17€ (lunch), 30€.

The ex-Auberge du Pin has been converted
into a designer brasserie in homage to
the mythical holiday route. Anne-Sophie
Pic and David Sinapian preside over this
lively, noisy and dynamic feast. Stéphane
Roussillon, the good disciple, cooks from
a simple base, adding spices and condiments here and there that make all the
difference. Scottish salmon marinated
with fennel, grilled squid, local ceps, car-

paccio, a goat cheese verrine, tuna belly, a chitterling sausage gratin, pan-seared veal escalope with coconut and a chocolate currant tart make a good impression. A nice choice of wines, including a striking red Vivarais.

● La Cachette

20, rue Nôtre-Dame de Soyons.
Tel. 04 75 55 24 13.
Closed Sun., Mon., 10 days beg. Jan.,
2 weeks end Apr.–May.
Prix fixe: 18€ (lunch), 25€, 35€.

Masachi Ijichi, originally from southern Japan, has made this out-of-the-way little eatery, with its internal courtyard and cramped seating, into a must. Formerly with Pic and the Pourcels, he skillfully manipulates the full range of modern cuisine. His menus are heaven sent and we take unbridled delight in the shellfish broth with pumpkin gnocchi, marbled vegetable terrine with quail thighs and gizzards, foie gras terrine breaded with pain d'épice, rouget with salt cod and potato cake and shrimp spring roll and the pan-seared veal filet and sweetbreads with mushroom duxelles. The overall effect is light as a feather and the desserts (pear poached in Earl Grey with a cone filled with praline mousse and Bourbon vanilla ice cream) are equally enchanting.

● Bistro des Clercs

48, Grand-Rue.
Tel. 04 75 55 55 15. Fax 04 75 43 64 85.
Closed Sun. lunch.
Prix fixe: 27€, 18€, 11,90€ (child).

Michel Chabranin's old-style bistro across from the Maison des Têtes in the heart of old Valence makes a good impression. The marble counter, the copper coat pegs, the fifties lighting fixtures all plunge us into the atmosphere of bygone bistros. There is a no-nonsense menu. Guillaume Duban, who used to work with Pic, is a master of this cuisine. Pâté in pastry crust, sole meunière, beef hanger steak, pork trotters and crème brûlée are nicely done. Regional wines dominate the list and the enthusiastic Laetitia's welcome sets the tone.

● Café Bancel

7, bd Bancel.
Tel. 04 75 78 35 98.
fred.maillesaud@cegetel.net
Closed Sun.
Prix fixe: 24€, 14€ (lunch). A la carte: 38€.

The fashionable dishes, designer décor and lounge music atmosphere are attractive. The ceramic bar, rose lighting, translucent shelving and high tables set the tone. Fried ravioli in salad, a monkfish tagine and the all-chocolate macaron are not bad.

● Le Resto de Caro SIM

5, pl Saint-Jean.
Tel. 04 75 42 47 33. Fax 04 75 02 19 47.
Closed Sat. lunch, Sun., Mon. dinner.
Prix fixe: 12€ (lunch), 6€ (child).
A la carte: 25–30€.

Pierre Vernière has taken over the ovens in this bouchon Lyonnais across from the Baltard-style covered market. He skillfully proposes gizzards in salad, tête de veau and a thick chocolate cake that can be savored without fuss. Caroline Vartanian serves with a smile and the check is reasonable.

In Pont-de-l'Isère (26600). 9 km n via N7.

● Michel Chabran

29, av du 45e-Parallèle.
Tel. 04 75 84 60 09. Fax 04 75 84 59 65.
chabran@michelchabran.fr
www.michelchabran.fr
Rest. closed Sun. dinner.
12 rooms: 80–135€.
Prix fixe: 36€, 51€, 89€, 155€,
25€ (child). A la carte: 125€.

In his large family house of Rhône shingle Michel Chabran offers a finely-wrought cuisine. Assisted by his faithful lieutenants, Jean-Claude Segard and Sandrine Genaud, he concocts rooted dishes that are an ode to local produce and the joy of life. We willingly give ourselves up to lobster salad married with pork muzzle, Vendée sole filet with langoustines, pan tossed and heightened with a creamy oyster beurre blanc, the savory veal sweetbread fricassée with rouget-perfumed jus, served with ratte potatoes with parsley, garlic and crushed pistachios. In addition, the service by Rose-Marie remains kindness itself and the cellar is a veritable declaration of love of the Rhône valley, from Hermitage to Côte-Rôtie, not to mention Châteauneuf and Saint Joseph.

VALENCE-SUR-BAÏSE

32310 Gers. Paris 734 – Agen 50 – Auch 36 – Condom 9.
A Cistercian abbey in the countryside, the vineyards all around and the producers of Armagnac presiding over the landscape.

 HOTELS-RESTAURANTS

■ La Ferme de Flaran

Rte de Condom.
Tel. 05 62 28 58 22. Fax 05 62 28 56 89.
www.fermedeflaran.com
Closed 10 days end Oct.–beg. Nov.,
10 days at end Dec., Sun. dinner (exc. mid-July–mid-Aug.), Mon. dinner (exc. mid-July–mid-Aug.). Rest. closed Sun. dinner, Mon., Tue. lunch (Oct.–May).
15 rooms: 49–75€.
Prix fixe: 20€, 24€, 28€, 38€.

Nathalie and Pascal Bourlois, natives of the Val de Loire who have traveled to Réunion, Guyana and the French West Indies, energetically took over an old hotel-farmhouse that was an outbuilding of the Flaran abbey. Just a few steps from this Cistercian marvel, their generous menus are an excuse for gourmand pilgrimages. We come to feast without going bankrupt on foie gras terrine with Armagnac and prunes, Atlantic sea bass filet with creamy basil sauce, duck leg confit with Tarbais white beans and a thin apple tart with Armagnac. A few tidy and simple little rooms, a swimming pool and a garden to extend the stay.

VALENCIENNES

59300 Nord. Paris 208 – Lille 54 – Arras 68 – Bruxelles 105.
valenciennes.tourisme@wanadoo.fr.

The Athens of the north has 19th-century charm with its finely wrought facades, its Beaux-Arts museum, its Jesuit library, the nearby Belgian dams and the gentle banks of the Canal de l'Escaut.

 HOTELS-RESTAURANTS

■ Grand Hôtel

8, pl de la Gare.
Tel. 03 27 46 32 01. Fax 03 27 29 65 57.
www.grand-hotel-de-valenciennes.fr
85 rooms: 72–88,50€. 10 suites: 105€.
Prix fixe: 6,50€ (child).
A la carte: 55–65€.

The Zielinger family takes this hotel across from the station very seriously. The art deco facade and interior with many period features and the comfy and cozy rooms make it a "special" place. Two cuisines, one brasserie and the other more gastronomic, present Alsatian and nouvelle cuisine.

■ Auberge du Bon Fermier

64, rue FaMar.
Tel. 03 27 46 68 25. Fax 03 27 33 75 01.
beinethierry@hotmail.com
www.bonfermier.com
Closed 24 Dec.–25 Dec.
16 rooms: 81–126€.
Prix fixe: 26€, 39,50€, 48€, 16€ (child).

Stone and brick at this old 17th-century post house with a cobblestone courtyard and antique furniture. The rooms have been renovated and the restaurant shines with all its new lighting fixtures. Thierry Beine spoils his guests with fine dishes with a regional flavor (lobster gratin, poached in white wine with mussels, shrimp, mushrooms and cream sauce and a North country hen served with lobster). Fish selections according to the day's catch.

■ Le Chat Botté

25, rue Tholozé.
Tel. 03 27 14 58 59. Fax 03 27 14 58 60.
www.hotel-lechatbotte.com
33 rooms: 65–74€.

Jacques Verbaere and Brigitte Zielinger took their inspiration freely from Perrault's Puss in Boots and Gustave Doré's lithographs to decorate this fine hotel facing the station. The modern rooms are not lacking in charm and the cat accompanies you faithfully throughout your stay.

● **Brasserie Arthur** SIM

46 bis, rue Famars.
Tel. 03 27 46 14 15. Fax 03 27 41 62 96.
Closed Sun. dinner, Mon., Christmas.
Prix fixe: 25€, 30€, 9€ (child).
A la carte: 29€.

Jean-Philippe Le Touze has managed to recreate a Parisian atmosphere in this thirties brasserie. The newly arrived Frédéric Dumoux presents rigorously executed classics in the genre: bone marrow, rouget filet, hanger steak with shallots, pain perdu and profiteroles, all good.

VALENTINE see SAINT-GAUDENS

VALESCURE see SAINT-RAPHAËL

VALRAS-PLAGE

34350 Hérault. Paris 773 – Montpellier 77 – Béziers 17 – Agde 25.
On the right bank of the Orb, this seaside resort reputed for its magnificent eight-kilometer-long beach of fine sand retains a little of the cachet of a traditional family resort with its pre-war holiday homes.

 HOTELS-RESTAURANTS

■ **Mira Mar**

Bd du Front-de-Mer.
Tel. 04 67 32 00 31. Fax 04 67 32 51 21.
info@hotel-miramar.org
www.hotel-miramar.org
Closed 30 Oct.–1 Apr.
Rest. closed Sun., Mon. (off season).
27 rooms: 77–89€.
Prix fixe: 19,50€, 25€, 33€, 8€ (child).

Facing the sea, which we can admire from most of the rooms, this beach hotel has every comfort due to its modern infra-

structure. Seafood and Mediterranean cuisine in the restaurant. Cool drinks and ices in the bar/ice cream bar.

● **Le Delphinium** COM

Av des Elysées.
Tel.-Fax 04 67 32 73 10.
ledelphinium@wanadoo.fr
Closed Sat. lunch, Sun. dinner, Mon., Nov. 1 vac.
Prix fixe: 19€, 25€, 30€, 38€, 45€, 12€ (child). A la carte: 60€.

A few steps away from the Casino, the Louros' restaurant cuts a fine figure with its art nouveau look with wrought-iron and bay windows overlooking the sea. Louis, who studied under Guérard and Troisgros, cooks up delicate preparations with all the colors of the Midi: Mediterranean sea bass carpaccio with tomato and basil, rouget with a Luque olive-seasoned ratatouille and a citrus-seasoned roasted duckling. For dessert, the apple and pear Tatin with coriander seed-infused caramel hits the right spot. Delphine, the lady of the house, praises the Languedoc wines deservedly and without excess.

VAL-THORENS

73440 Savoie. Paris 669 – Albertville 59 – Chambéry 107 – Moûtiers 32.
valthorens@valthorens.com.
The highest ski resort in Europe? This is it, at an altitude of 2300 meters. Following its initial success in the 1970s, it has now found a new lease on life in the Savoyard fashion.

 HOTELS-RESTAURANTS

■ **Fitz-Roy**

Place de l'Eglise.
Tel. 04 79 00 04 78. Fax 04 79 00 06 11.
welcome@hotelfitzroy.com
www.hotelfitzroy.com
Closed May–Nov.
32 rooms: 189–480€. 7 suites: 450–1200
Prix fixe: 80€, 110€.

Run by the Luxury Mountain group, this charming and comfortable establishment has undergone a wonderful transformation. The furniture has been changed in the dining room and bedrooms. The décor has continued to evolve in a refined register and the chefs have also changed. Thierry Van Laher is over the kitchens and emphasizes the modern tone of the menu. Lobster spring rolls, foie gras-stuffed turbot, sirloin steak Rossini briefly smoked over a licorice-root fire, the hazelnut and pear Williams crumble, seasoned with thyme and served with pear sorbet, are good. A nice wine list.

■ Le Val Thorens   🏠

Tel. 04 79 00 04 33. Fax 04 79 00 09 40.
contact@levalthorens.com
www.levalthorens.com
Closed beg. May–beg. Dec.
80 rooms: 88-149€.? pens.: 723-1 093€.
Prix fixe: 28€ (dinner), 10€ (child).

This hotel with the ski runs just outside the door is mainly a very comfortable family establishment. The rooms are spacious and cozy. Three restaurants, Savoyard, traditional and gastronomic, offer gourmets a fine selection.

■ Le Bel Horizon   ❀🏠

Rue du Soleil.
Tel. 04 79 00 04 77. Fax 04 79 00 06 08.
info@belhorizon.com / www.belhorizon.com
Closed beg. May–end Nov.
31 rooms: 65-152€. Half board: 152€.

The south-facing balconies mean that there is an abundance of light. The lounge with its open fireplace, the billiard room, the solarium and fitness center are also welcome.

■ Le Sherpa   ❀🏠

Rue de Gebroulaz.
Tel. 04 79 00 00 70. Fax 04 79 00 08 03.
courrier@lesherpa.com / www.lesherpa.com
Closed beg. May–end Nov.
52 rooms: 100-210€. 4 suites: 170-300€.
Prix fixe: 20€, 16€, 30€. A la carte: 44€.

The bedrooms and duplexes in this vast chalet have been renovated in the Savoyard style. It also has a new body care

section complete with Turkish bath and Jacuzzi. In the restaurant, the regional produce takes on a southern flavor. Lake whiting seasoned with thyme flower, star anise–seasoned pollock in papillote, pork loin medallion with Beaufort and paprika and a ravishing blackberry and blueberry gratin with Genepi.

■ Novotel Val Thorens   🏠

Place de la Lombarde.
Tel. 04 79 00 04 04. Fax 04 79 00 05 93.
h0457@accor.com
www.novotelvalthorens.com
Closed 1 May–30 Nov.
104 rooms: 161-206€.
Prix fixe: 14€ (lunch), 17€ (lunch),
23€ (lunch), 30€, 15€ (child).

Situated a few steps away from the ski runs, this chain hotel modernizes the mountain style with functional rooms and wood elements adapted to today's tastes. For families it offers spaces reserved for children with an activity leader, game rooms, films and a special restaurant. It also caters to adults with a fitness center (swimming pool, sauna, Turkish bath, Jacuzzi and fitness training) and theme evenings. The restaurant serves regional fare without any surprises.

■ Trois Vallées   ❀🏠

Grande-Rue.
Tel. 04 79 00 01 86. Fax 04 79 00 04 08.
reservation@hotel3vallees.com
www.hotel3vallees.com
Closed mid-May–mid-Nov. Rest. closed lunch
24 rooms: 105-129€. 5 suites: 129€.
Prix fixe: 24€, 26€, 15€ (child).
A la carte: 36-54€.

A comfortable stopover in this mountain-style hotel with a lounge bar, cozy bedrooms (all bathrooms have been refurbished) and varied cuisine. Hot foie gras in a sesame brioche with mango chutney and glazed duck breast with ginger-seasoned wilted Chinese cabbage are a pleasure. The menus change every day.

● **L'Oxalys**

Tel. 04 79 00 20 51 / 04 79 00 12 00.
Fax 04 79 00 24 39.
oxalys@montagnettes.com
www.montagnettes.com
Closed May–end Nov.
Prix fixe: 36€ (lunch), 48€, 70€, 15€
(child). A la carte: 70–95€.

The resort's flagship establishment: the vast and charming dining room created by Agnès Girard at the foot of the Montagnettes du Soleil residence. Jean Sulpice, who trained with the greats (Veyrat, Jeffroy, the Arnsbourg and ElBulli), is at the helm presenting a daringly revitalized Savoie cuisine. Atlantic sea bass seared skin-side down and finished under the broiler served with passion fruit, the pigeon in a foie gras crust with licorice-seasoned gravy and exotic fruits on a jasmine tea-infused creamy pudding with marbled fresh cheese and passion fruit sorbet surprise us in just the right way. Magalie Sulpice keeps a benevolent eye on the dining room and cellar with its nice wines adding to the charm of the establishment.

● **Le Vieux Chalet**

Rue du Soleil.
Tel.-Fax 04 79 00 07 93.
www.levieuxchalet.com
Closed lunch (exc. Sat. winter and July–Aug.), Sept.–beg. Nov., beg. May–end June.
Prix fixe: 16€ (lunch July–Aug.).
A la carte: 40–60€.

Magalie and Vincent Hudry, cousins of Edouard Loubet, who is a local here and famous at Bonnieux, have taken over this beautiful and very "decorated" chalet with its old-style wood décor. It opens only in the evening but we like to snuggle in here cosily for foie gras served chilled in aspic with a morel crust, lake whiting served in crayfish bisque and the tête de veau with sauce gribiche served up by the young Alexandre Gautreau who trained at Beau Rivage in Sables d'Olonne and who spent four years in the Grand Hotel at Tadoussace in Quebec.

● **Le Chalet de la Marine**

Piste des Dalles.
Tel. 04 79 00 03 12. Fax 04 79 00 04 08.
info@chaletmarine.com
www.chaletmarine.com
Closed dinner, mid-May–mid-Nov.
Prix fixe: 23€ (lunch), 34€ (lunch),
12€ (child). A la carte: 45€.

A new name and new team for this high-up establishment. The Gorinis from the Trois Vallées hotel have taken over this mountain pasture chalet and given it a new life. In the kitchen, David Boyer tries his hand at a simple cuisine which he executes with precision. No objections to pot-roasted beef cheeks in pot-au-feu or the spicy lamb shanks. The dessert buffet will delight young and old alike.

● **La Chaumière**

Immeuble La Vanoise.
Tel. 04 79 00 01 13. Fax 04 79 00 20 56.
ea12@orange.fr
Closed beg. May–beg. Dec.
Prix fixe: 28€ (dinner) 10€ (child).
A la carte: 30–40€.

Marie Albouy's tavern in the heart of the resort welcomes its guests in a lovely long dining room. Garlic-stuffed escargots, foie gras and pain d'épice mille-feuille, a monkfish fricasée with young vegetables, pierrade (three types of meat cooked on a stone at the table) and the "*bolet savoyard*" (vanilla-coffee, hot chocolate with rum), are served with a smile and go down a treat.

LE VALTIN

88230 Vosges. Paris 437 – Epinal 54 – Gérardmer 18 – Colmar 46.
This pretty village in the Vosges, just a short distance from the Col de la Schlucht, is good for getting back to nature.

 HOTELS-RESTAURANTS

● **Le Val Joli**

12 bis, le Village.
Tel. 03 29 60 91 37. Fax 03 29 60 81 73.
contact@levaljoli.com / www.levaljoli.com

Closed mid-Nov.–beg. Dec.
Rest. closed Sun. dinner (exc. vac.), Mon.
(exc. vac.), Mon. lunch (exc. Bank holidays).
7 rooms: 77–82€. 3 suites: 122–155€.
Prix fixe: 17€ (weekdays), 22€ (weekdays),
29€, 35€, 10€ (child). A la carte: 40–70€.

The Laruelles are model innkeepers. There is Papa Jacques, busy as mayor and organizer, brother Jean-Paul in the dining room giving a warm introduction to the village and the son Philippe, a giant of a man who plays the role of the prolific heir. Although he learned the trade with Ducasse in Monaco, Willer in Cannes and Bruno in Lorgues, he remains obstinately true to the region. Of course he has introduced a touch of lightness and freshness here and there that bring sunshine to the local *terroir*, but the Vosges specialities remain. The rooms have been enlarged and redecorated and wood-trimmed suites have been added. The menus have remained reasonable. Smacking our lips, we savor the cold pressed grated potatoes and pan-seared foie gras, lightly smoked trout with a potato papillote and sorrel cream sauce, salmon trout steamed over hay with horseradish cream, sautéed potatoes in Riesling sauce, warm pink trout pâté marinated in white Alsatian wine and the exquisite frangipane-filled cake with a pine bud syrup sorbet.

67730 Bas-Rhin. Paris 420 – Colmar 31 – Saint Dié – Ribeauvillé 17 – Sélestat 12.
The Vosges, the forest and the call of the great outdoors.

 HOTELS-RESTAURANTS

■ Hôtel Elisabeth

5, rue du Général-de-Gaulle.
Tel. 03 88 57 90 61. Fax 03 88 57 91 51.
info@hotel-elisabeth.fr / www.hotel-elisabeth.fr
Closed 8 Jan.–15 Jan., 26 Feb.–12 Mar.,
26 June–3 July
Rest. closed Sat. lunch, Sun. dinner, Mon.
10 rooms: 49€.
Prix fixe: 10€ (weekday lunch), 25€, 32€
(wine inc.), 38€, 12,50€ (child).
A la carte: 45€–50€.

Before wielding kitchen utensils, Gérard Dehaye juggled with figures in an accounting firm. His stays with Bras at Laguiole and Didier Oudill in Paris have enabled him to now present an honorable à la carte menu that is not lacking in flair. The pan-tossed chanterelles with jumbo shrimp in an acidulated reduction, roasted scallops with a creamy saffron-seasoned herb risotto, the thick-cut veal chops accompanied by roasted hazelnut bulgur and Arabica-heightened pan juices and a Gariguette strawberry dessert, a pistachio cream dessert and a house saffron-flavored ice cream are a gourmet's delight. Afterwards we allow ourselves a little nap in one of the hotel's rooms with red and wood tones.

● Auberge Frankenbourg ○🏠

13, rue du Général-de-Gaulle.
Tel. 03 88 57 93 90. Fax 03 88 57 91 31.
info@frankenbourg.com
www.frankenbourg.com
Closed mid-Feb.–10 Mar., end June–10 July.
Rest. closed Tue. dinner, Wed.
11 rooms: 49€.
Prix fixe: 26€, 43€, 56€, 72€ (wine inc.),
14€ (child). A la carte: 55–65€.

This friendly hotel with a considerable reputation is undergoing a gentle renovation. The rooms have been redecorated and the furniture in the restaurant has changed. In the kitchen, Sébastien Buecher has taken over from his father Aimé in the last few years. After training with the best chefs in Alsace—Mischler in Lembach, Jung at the Crocodile, Albrecht in Rhinau and Brendel in Riquewihr—he is reasserting his desire to bring creativity to the fore. Pan-tossed langoustine served on a pork trotter and headcheese cake, served with warm basil aspic, Atlantic sea bass with Swiss chard ravioli and ricotta poached in a broth made with the fish bones, served with polenta frites and the pigeon breast with vegetables in aspic with the thighs wrapped in crunchy angelhair pastry blend local and more exotic flavors with daring and precision. The house chocolate mint dessert is a sweet and extremely tempting way to finish off a meal. Fabien Steip uses his talent to recommend wines that put the finishing touch to this cocktail of gourmet pleasures.

VANDOEUVRE see **NANCY**

VANNES

56000 Morbihan. Paris 460 – Rennes 113 – Saint-Nazaire 77 – Quimper 119.
tourisme@pays-de-vannes.com.
The old city, so typically Breton, with its half-timbered houses, its ramparts and Promenade de la Garenne, is worth a relaxing visit in the heart of the "little sea" of Morbihan. Don't miss the giant aquarium!

 HOTELS-RESTAURANTS

■ Mercure

Le Parc du Golf, 19, rue Daniel.
Tel. 02 97 40 44 52. Fax 02 97 63 03 20.
www.accor-hotels.com
Rest. closed Sat. (off season), Sun.
71 rooms: 86–126€. 6 suites: 116–158€.
Prix fixe: 19€.

This chain hotel stands out by virtue of its location on the gulf and its classy welcome. The rooms are practical and cheerful, the cuisine is pleasant and and in keeping with today's tastes. Don't miss the large aquarium nearby.

■ Villa Kerasy

20, av Favrel-et-Lincy.
Tel. 02 97 68 36 83. Fax 02 97 68 36 84.
info@villakerasy.com / www.villakerasy.com
Closed mid-Nov.–10 Dec., 3 weeks Jan.
11 rooms: 92–165€. 1 suite: 288–330€.

A few steps from the station, this genteel twenties residence works its charm on us with rooms furnished with Compagnie des Indes furniture, the tearoom and the English garden.

● Régis Restaurant   ○COM

Pl de la Gare.
Tel. 02 97 42 61 41. Fax 02 97 54 99 01.

Closed Sun., Mon., 2 weeks end Nov.,
2 weeks Feb. vac., 1 week at end June.
Prix fixe: 29€, 54€, 76€, 16€ (child).

The Mahés establishment across from the station is an old reliable. For more than fifteen years their chic and unassuming medieval tavern has made a good impression. Régis, who trained with Maximin at the Negresco and in the Cantine des Gourmets in Paris, attracts us with his artful preparations. In the course of masterly menus the flavors of seafood from the Morbihan bay and the Rhuys peninsula blend with more exotic perfumes, particularly those of Provence and the Mediterranean. The proof is in the eating, as we find when we taste the Middle Eastern-style rouget, monkfish tagine with lobster and olives and roasted tomatoes served with reduced soup and the delicious seafood dishes (sardines in kefta or marinated, whiting meunière, monkfish, scallops). The desserts are equally well equipped to please us, for example the warm chocolate tart with thick chocolate and salted-butter caramel ice cream.

● La Table des Gourmets   COM

6, rue A.-le-Pontois.
Tel. 02 97 47 52 44. Fax 02 97 47 15 87.
guillaumeetlaura@wanadoo.fr
Closed Sun. dinner (exc. July–Aug.),
Mon. (exc. dinner July–Aug.), Tue. lunch,
1 week at end Jan., 1 week beg. Feb.,
2 weeks June.
Prix fixe: 17€ (weekday lunch), 26€, 38€,
45€, 58€.

Modernism is the order of the day in this restaurant at the foot of the ramparts and just a few steps from the port, in the simply decorated dining room with refined tones of beige and red, as well as in the dishes, where Guillaume Hugué deploys his *savoir faire* turning out local produce with a contemporary flavor. Consider the oysters browned in the oven with curry seasonings, monkfish in an acidulated spring seafood broth, a head cheese and pork trotter potato dish with chitterling sausage gravy and the pan-fried pain d'épice with honey and salted-butter caramel.

● La Table Alsacienne   SIM

21-23, rue Ferdinand-le-Dressay.
Tel.-Fax 02 97 01 34 53.
Closed Sun., Mon., 1 week Christmas,
3 weeks Aug.
Prix fixe: 21€, 7€ (child). A la carte: 30–35€.

The house facing the marina doesn't look like much but when we get to the first floor we find an authentic *winstub* where yellow is the dominant color, with polychrome wood and old signs and engravings. Yves Weiss from Mulhouse concocts the recipes of his homeland with a passion. Foie gras served Strasbourg-style, flammeküeche, pork cheeks, shellfish, potato baeckeofe, a pork and Munster cheese dish and a frozen kouglof, washed down with Alsatian wines, naturally, as we dream of long-legged storks nesting on chimney tops.

● Rive Gauche   SIM

Le Port.
Tel.-Fax 02 97 47 02 40.
Closed Sun., Mon., 2 weeks Oct.,
1 week June, 2 weeks Aug.
Prix fixe: 14€ (lunch), 22€.
A la carte: 40€.

This bistro facing the port makes a very pleasant break. A very well-stocked cellar enables us to choose from great and small wines, with the helpful advice of the masters of the house, Nathalie and Stéphane Berrigaud. We gather round the welcoming counter or sit elbow-to-elbow at the tables to savor Cyril Jorda's cuisine. A veal sweetbread and chanterelle fricassée, pan-seared Atlantic sea bass filet with niçois-style confit and pesto sauce, young duck breasts roasted with mild spices and a frozen caramel soufflé are joined by offerings of the day from the market, all prepared with constant attention.

● Roscanvec   SIM

17, rue des Halles.
Tel. 02 97 47 15 96. Fax 02 97 47 86 39.
roscanvec@yahoo.fr
Closed Sun. (off season), Mon. (off season),
2 weeks beg. Jan.
Prix fixe: 17€, 24€, 34€, 49€.

Gagnaire, Ducasse, the Pourcels (he opened the Sens & Bund for them in Shanghai): thus goes the brilliant track record of Thierry Seychelles who was also chef for a season in the Signoria in Calvi before quietly taking control of this historic restaurant in the old city. There is an amazing contrast between this traditional half-timbered house and his contemporary cuisine with hints of faraway places. The menu has a scent of Asia and the Mediterranean in simply prepared rouget, a Thai curry with potatoes, sea bream, fresh goat cheese, herb and harissa ravioli with shellfish coconut sauce and Poitou-Charentes lamb with apricots, pimientos, almonds, capers and preserved lemons in a marinated condiment. For dessert, pineapple beignets with a chocolate and spice dipping sauce and the fresh fromage blanc and basil ice cream are delightful. Obviously a house to watch.

In Arradon (56610). 7 km via D101.

■ Logis de Parc er Greo

9, rue Mané-Guen.
Tel. 02 97 44 73 03. Fax 02 97 44 80 48.
contact@parcergreo.com
www.parcergreo.com
Closed mid-Nov.–mid-Mar.
14 rooms: 72–125€. 1 suite: 149–199€.

Customized bedrooms, a lounge decked out with watercolors and model ships and a heated covered swimming pool: this is what awaits you in this modern and peaceful hotel located near the gulf.

In Arradon.

■ Les Vénètes

Pointe d'Arradon.
Tel. 02 97 44 85 85. Fax 02 97 44 78 60.
info@lesvenetes.com / www.lesvenetes.com
Closed 2 weeks beg. Jan.
Rest. closed Sun. dinner, Mon. (off season).
8 rooms: 90–130€. 2 suites: 150–200€.
Prix fixe: 35€, 55€, 75€.

Affording an exceptional view of the Gulf of Morbihan, Anita and Christian Tournaire's home offers a charming stay in rooms that have been redecorated in blue and white. In the kitchen, Philippe Estermann steers a steady course toward quality with dishes that are sharp and fresh. Roasted langoustines with chorizo, vegetables in the style of Nice with cherry tomatoes, a slice of monkfish with risotto and wedges of Reggiano parmesan and basil-infused olive oil, center-cut Limousin sirloin from Mr. Ledru, mashed potatoes with foie gras and the pan-simmered peaches with a dark chocolate gratin are all quite simply amazing.

In Conleau (56000). 4,5 km sw

■ **Le Roof**

10, allée des Frères-Cadoret.
Presqu'île de Conleau.
Tel. 02 97 63 47 47. Fax 02 97 63 48 10.
leroof@club-internet.fr
40 rooms: 79–151€.
Prix fixe: 29€, 40€, 12€ (child).
A la carte: 60€.

The view from the bedroom terraces is worthy of a postcard. We sit back and unwind as we contemplate the cove with the boats at anchor. The rooms are renovated regularly and decorated tastefully with marine themes. The restaurant opens onto the Gulf of Morbihan and makes a nice setting in which to savor sea produce like pan-seared scallops, Atlantic sea bass filet in a salt crust, a sole and veal sweetbread fricassée and a light apple tart.

In Saint-Avé (56890). 6 km n via D767.

● **Le Pressoir**

7, rue de l'Hôpital.
Tel. 02 97 60 87 63. Fax 02 97 44 59 15.
le.pressoir.st-ave@wanadoo.fr
www.le-pressoir-st-ave.com
Closed Sun. lunch, Mon., Tue., 3 weeks Oct.,
2 weeks beg. Mar., 1 week beg. July.
Prix fixe: 32€ (weekday lunch), 52€, 69€,
90€, 130€ (wine inc.), 18€ (child).
A la carte: 90€.

On their way to Pontivy, many people take the time to stop off at the flagship restaurant of the Vannes region. Bernard Rambaud unerringly reconciles all genres. In his skillful hands the beautiful produce of land and sea receive full expression in lively preparations that are sometimes classic and sometimes modern. In the neo-rustic dining room decked out with colorful paintings the Breton lobster with tête de veau prepared in the spirit of Saint-Emilion, Atlantic sea bass filet on a bed of basil- and garlic-seasoned summer vegetables with small shellfish and the veal sweetbreads and pork trotters with reduced jus and pan-tossed chanterelles add a lighter touch to grandmother's traditional recipes. When it comes to the desserts, the chocolate cake with almond and pistachio cream is a delight. The wines selected by Yann Le Corsse make a fitting match and the reception, the service and even the check are equally pleasant. A truly great establishment.

VARENGEVILLE-SUR-MER

76119 Seine-Maritime. Paris 200 –
Fécamp 56 – Rouen 66 – Dieppe 10 –
Fontaine-le-Dun 19.
The marine cemetery where Braque, Albert Roussel and Georges de Porto-Riche are buried is worth a trip to this part of the Caux region. Don't forget to visit the Manoir d'Ango and the Parc des Moustiers with its pretty flower beds.

 HOTELS-RESTAURANTS

■ **La Terrasse**

Rte de Vasterival. 3 km nw via D75.
Tel. 02 35 85 12 54. Fax 02 35 85 11 70.
francois.delafontaine@wanadoo.fr
www.hotel-restaurant-la-terrasse.com
Closed mid-Oct.–mid-Mar.
22 rooms: 48–58€.
Prix fixe: 22€, 28€, 35€, 9€ (child).
A la carte: 34€.

On the side of the cliff and facing the sea, this 1900s inn offers rooms that are simple and peaceful, a shady garden and good dishes that take their inspiration from the ocean, such as saffron-seasoned mussel cassolette, the traditional stew called marmite Dieppoise and an apple and almond tart worthy of our grandmothers.

VARETZ see BRIVE-LA-GAILLARDE
VASOUY see HONFLEUR

VAUCHOUX see PORT-SUR-SAONE
VELLERON see L'ISLE-SUR-LA-SORGUE

VENCE

06140 Alpes-Maritimes. Paris 928 – Antibes 20 – Grasse 26 – Cannes 30 – Nice 24.

The Place du Peyra, the narrow streets, the Chapelle du Rosaire by Matisse, the Château de Villeneuve and the Emile-Hugues foundation, like the Galerie Beaubourg in the Château Notre-Dame-des-Fleurs: so many landmarks to visit in this old town with its back to the Baous, or hills.

 HOTELS-RESTAURANTS

■ Château du Domaine Saint-Martin

Av des Templiers, BP 102.
Tel. 04 93 58 02 02. Fax 04 93 24 08 91.
reservations@chateau-st-martin.com
www.chateau-st-martin.com
Closed mid-Nov.–mid-Mar.
34 rooms: 340–600€.
6 suites: 840–1200€.
Prix fixe: 46€ (lunch), 75€, 105€, 62€.
A la carte: 90–200€.

This old Knights Templar château situated on its own grounds in the heights of the Col de Vence offers us absolute luxury and a most magnificent 180-degree view of the coast. The hotel is impressive with classy service, very stylish suites, a swimming pool, tennis court and a host of olive trees. The dining room extending onto the breathtaking terrace is equally magnificent. In the kitchens, the discreet Philippe Guérin, formerly with Chapel and Bardet, tends to make rich preparations. Roasted smoked country bacon and langoustines with pan juices deglazed with balsamic vinegar, asparagus and morel ravioli, strips of sole seasoned with Colombo spices and the John Dory filet with preserved lemons sometimes veer toward excessive sweetness, but overall, he steers a steady course. The desserts (vanilla raspberry marbled dessert and chocolate crème) provide a magnificent moment, the service is classy and the cellar is sumptuous.

■ Diana

Av des Poilus.
Tel. 04 93 58 28 56. Fax 04 93 24 64 06.
www.hotel-diana-vence.com
Closed Nov.
27 rooms: 100–120€. 1 suite: 130€.

The rooms in this hotel are charming, whether they overlook the garden or the street. The seventies facade is interesting and the exhibitions of paintings and sculptures introduce a creative element. It is nicely kept and only a few steps from the old city.

■ Auberge des Seigneurs

Pl Frêne.
Tel. 04 93 58 04 24. Fax 04 93 24 08 01.
Closed 1 Nov.–1 Mar. Rest. closed Sun., Mon.
7 rooms: 60–95€.
Prix fixe: 31€, 45€.

Situated in one of the wings of the Château de Villeneuve, this inn is steeped in history. It has received King François I, Marc Chagall, Pierre Renoir and Modigliani and it has kept its Old World charm. The rooms are pretty, with a view of the Baous, and the cuisine (a local vegetable gratin in an earthenware dish, fish of the day, a wood fire–roasted rack of lamb and a biscuit cookie served with apricot parfait) make a good impression.

■ Villa Roseraie

51, av Henry-Giraud.
Tel. 04 93 58 02 20. Fax 04 93 58 99 31.
accueil@villaroseraie.com
www.villaroseraie.com
14 rooms: 85–140€.

The century-old magnolia trees perfume the garden of this 1900s villa close to the old city. We like its little rooms decorated with Souleiado textiles and dried flowers, its swimming pool and the reasonable prices.

● La Table d'Ami

689, chemin de la Gaude.
Tel. 04 93 58 90 75. Fax 04 93 58 22 86.
jacques.maximin@wanadoo.fr
www.maximin.fr

Closed Mon., Tue., Nov.–end Dec.
Prix fixe: 50€ (wine inc.), 100€.

Jacques Maximin is still at the helm but he did not hesitate to change the name of the establishment (as a nod to his faithful customers or an indication of forthcoming changes?). The affordable menus have had a definitive impact but the master of the house, who formerly reigned over the kitchens of the Negresco after a stint with Roger Vergé and Jo Rostang, concentrates more than ever on a cuisine based on local products. Of course it is inventive but most of all it aims to restitute all the grandeur of the authentic flavors. Fresh tomato, mussel and mozzarella soup, Andalou gazpacho with cool fresh diced red tuna, Laurageais farm-raised chicken sautéed in the style of Nice and local white peaches with a cherry compote do not abandon the southern flavors that this native of the north of France has adapted better than anyone else. The atmosphere is charming and enhanced by the works of contemporary art by great names from the *école de Nice*. The wine list is rich with charming local wines.

● Auberge des Templiers `COM`

39, av Joffre.
Tel. 04 93 58 06 05. Fax 04 93 58 92 68.
lestempliers3@wanadoo.fr
www.restaurant-vence.com
Closed Mon. lunch, Tue. lunch,
Wed. (off season).
Prix fixe: 39€, 49€, 59€. A la carte: 69€.

At the foot of the Col de Vence and at the edge of the village, southern tradition has found a home in this inn renovated in the Provençal style with its veranda, arbor, patio, old stones and wrought-iron. Stéphane Demichelis, who trained in Cannes with Chibois and Willer, delights his guests with pan-tossed fresh morels and asparagus served with shavings of parmesan and a warm vinaigrette, champagne-braised slice of turbot with puréed seafood and shellfish jus, pan-sizzled veal sweetbreads with bone marrow and truffle ravioli, warm pineapples with meringue and island-style ginger-seasoned caramel sauce and coconut ice cream.

● Le Vieux Couvent `COM`

37, av A.-Toreille.
Tel.-Fax 04 93 58 78 58.
levieuxcouventvence@tiscali.fr
www.restaurant-levieuxcouvent.com
Closed Wed., Thu. lunch, mid-Jan.–mid-Mar.
Prix fixe: 27€, 34€, 46€.

The Gascon Jean-Jacques Bissières fell in love with this old 17th-century chapel and opened his restaurant here, presenting classics from the Provençal range inspired by his periods with Vergé and Ducasse. So, no surprises, but we can look forward to enjoying ourselves among the pillars and the ribbed vaulting. We begin with the pressed rabbit confit served on greens with crusty socca, a Provençal fried chickpea cake. Then comes the spicy cod filet with fennel slow-cooked in olive oil and the breast of a free-range chicken roasted with spring vegetables. The fruit sorbet tulip dessert goes down a treat.

● La Farigoule `SIM`

15, rue Henri-Isnard.
Tel. 04 93 58 01 27. Fax 04 93 58 69 09.
bruotp@wanadoo.fr
Closed Sun. dinner, Tue. lunch, Wed. lunch,
New Year's, Feb. vac.
Prix fixe: 22€, 29,50€, 39,50€, 55€,
15€ (child).

A relaxing atmosphere, Provençal cuisine and rock-bottom menu prices are all good reasons to visit Patrick Bruot's establishment. Formerly with Chibois, Ducasse and Maximin, he favors simplicity and market produce in preparations that are fresh and finely wrought. Pistou soup with escabeche-marinated rouget, stuffed Mediterranean sea bass braised in a bouillabaisse-style jus, sautéed veal chop served with a squash and parmesan gratin and napped with chanterelle jus and the caramelized waffles with slow-cooked apples or pears served with a mascarpone ice cream are a pleasure whether in the dining room or on the terrace.

VENDIN-LE-VIEIL see LENS

VENDOME

41100 Loir-et-Cher. Paris 169 – Blois 34 –
Le Mans 78 – Orléans 91 – Tours 56.
Ot-Vendome@wanadoo.fr.
The old Abbey of the Trinity, the abbey church
and the château are the treasures of this old
Val de Loire citadel.

HOTELS-RESTAURANTS

■ Le Saint-Georges

14, rue Poterie.
Tel. 02 54 77 08 18. Fax 02 54 77 09 19.
contact@hotel-saint-georges-vendome.com
www.hotel-saint-georges-vendome.com
Rest. closed Sun. dinner.
24 rooms: 65€. 3 suites: 100€.
Prix fixe: 27€, 39€.

Fabien Gimel, formerly at the Moulin de
Mougins and the Atlanta Ritz-Carlton,
brilliantly assumes the twin roles of hote-
lier and chef. The rooms and studio apartments are decorated to illustrate the idea
of returning home after a long journey. A
relaxed atmosphere reigns in the corridors, bar and restaurant. The cuisine is
also inspired with the flavors of faraway
places blending with local produce.

VENTRON

88310 Vosges. Paris 437 – Epinal 53 –
Mulhouse 51 – Gérardmer 27.
otventron@wanadoo.fr.
In this pretty Vosges location the Leduc sisters,
both ex-skiing champions, along with their nine
brothers and sisters, have established a ski complex near a hermitage and textile museum presenting the richness of the region.

HOTELS-RESTAURANTS

■ Les Buttes

At l'Ermitage du Frère Joseph.
Tel. 03 29 24 18 09. Fax 03 29 24 21 96.
info@frerejo.com / www.frerejo.com
Closed mid-Nov.–mid-Dec.
Rest. closed lunch (exc.Sun.).
26 rooms: 75–179€.

1 suite: 123–205€.
Prix fixe: 16€, 22€, 28€, 10€ (child).

This charming chalet with a view has
cozy rooms, a Turkish bath and a heated
swimming pool. The hot foie gras and
apple mille-feuille, local fish soup with
dill-seasoned Mediterranean sea bass,
the duck breast and honey crumble and
a rhubarb and strawberry cold soup are
irreproachable.

■ Ermitage du Frère Joseph

Tel. 03 29 24 18 29. Fax 03 29 24 16 57.
info@frerejo.com / www.frerejo.com
Closed Sun. dinner–Wed. (Nov.–mid-Dec.).
54 rooms: 49–95€.
Prix fixe: 16,20€, 19,80€, 22,90€.
A la carte: 30–40€.

The Leduc sisters' inn has an unrestricted
view of the Vosges, sporting facilities
(swimming pool, Turkish bath and sauna)
shared with Les Buttes and authentic *table
d'hôte* cuisine.

VERDUN

55100 Meuse. Paris 263 – Bar-le-Duc 54 –
Metz 79 – Nancy 95.
verduntourisme@wanadoo.fr.
This martyred city has become the city of peace.
We visit the upper part with its old hotels,
cathedral and Episcopal palace, underground
citadel and the nearby Douaumont ossuary.

HOTELS-RESTAURANTS

● Le Coq Hardi

8, av de la Victoire.
Tel. 03 29 86 36 36. Fax 03 29 86 09 21.
coq.hardi@wanadoo.fr / www.coq-hardi.com
Rest. closed Fri., Sun. dinner.
32 rooms: 95–135€. 3 suites: 130–250€.
Prix fixe: 44€ (weekdays), 64€, 95€,
18,50€ (child),
Bistro: 20€ (weekdays), 36€.

The Coq Hardi hotel is nearly 200 years
old. It has witnessed some impressive
history, including the tragic period of
this city on the Meuse. Its half-timber-

ing and tower testify to its history but its rooms and décor are not too haughty to make some sacrifices to modernity. It is the best establishment in the city—a sort of institution—managed by Patrick Leloup, honorary president of the Jeunes Restaurateurs de France. He has put the kitchens in the hands of Frédéric Engel, a young chef who has already worked with Loiseau, Ducasse, Senderens, Jung and Westermann. The wiser for his experiences in his personal Tour de France of these great establishments, he very successfully uses the produce and flavors of the East and the South of France to blend tradition with today's tastes. Landes foie gras, a grilled John Dory filet, the black pig and the already-famous house flambéed mirabelle plums with caramel are excellent. We appreciate the old-style service and the pertinent advice of Michael Prévost who reigns over an extremely rich cellar. More modest fare at the Bistro .

In 55320 Dieue-sur-Meuse. 13 km via N35 and D34.

■ Hostellerie du Château des Monthairons

Le Petit Monthairons.
Tel. 03 29 87 78 55. Fax 03 29 87 73 49.
acceuil@chateaudesmonthairons.fr
www.chateaudesmonthairons.com
Closed 1 Jan.–10 Feb.
Rest. closed Mon., Tue. lunch.
23 rooms: 70–180€. 6 suites: 190–280€.
Prix fixe: 49€, 60€, 80€, 13€ (child).
A la carte 55–70€.

This 19th-century château is a veritable fairy tale with its neo-Renaissance facade nestling in its fourteen-hectare grounds. The beach on the river bank and the vast rooms with Old World charm are a delight, as is the welcome extended by Jean-Marie Thouvenin. In the kitchen his son Benoît carefully elaborates regional classics. Chopped young wild boar in sauce, roasted pike-perch, the stuffed young pigeon breast accompanied by a soufflé and a frozen almond parfait hit the right spot.

71350 Saône-et-Loire. Paris 332 – Dôle 49 – Beaune 24 – Chalon-sur-Saône 24 – Dijon 65.
This Burgundy commune that flirts with the Franche-Compté is proud of its canal and its old houses.

 HOTELS-RESTAURANTS

■ Hostellerie Bourguignonne

2, av Président-Borgeot.
Tel. 03 85 91 51 45. Fax 03 85 91 53 81.
hostelleriebourguignonne@hotmail.fr
www.hostelleriebourguignonne.com
Closed 2 weeks end Feb.–mid-Mar.
Rest. closed Sun. dinner (off season), Tue.,
Wed. lunch.
9 rooms: 88–98€.
Prix fixe: 22€ (weekday lunch), 37,80€.

This old inn, which used to be very well known and famous among gourmets, has managed to retain its Old World charm. Beautiful rustic rooms and nicely presented specialities: eggs in red wine sauce, ham and parsley terrine, local pôchouse Verdunoise (fish seasoned with garlic and poached in white wine), Charolaise beef steak and a pear and blackcurrant dessert always make a good impression. An attentive welcome.

27130 Eure. Paris 117 – Chartres 57 – Dreux 38 – Alençon 77.
The large square, the old houses, the promenade on the ramparts, the church of Notre Dame: is this enough to describe the wealth of this beautiful Norman city that watches over the N12?

 HOTELS-RESTAURANTS

● Le Clos

98, rue de la Ferté-Vidame.
Tel. 02 32 32 21 81. Fax 02 32 32 21 36.
leclos@relaischateaux.com
www.hostellerieduclos.fr
Closed Sun. dinner (Nov.–Mar.), Mon., Tue.
lunch, 10 Dec.–26 Jan.

4 rooms: 160–195€. 6 suites: 215–255€.
Prix fixe: 32€ (exc. Sat. dinner and Bank holidays), 52€, 78€, 16€ (child).
A la carte: 60–70€.

The luxurious comfort of this Relais & Châteaux establishment in a fine Norman manor is a delight to Parisians and all lovers of Normandy. Alain and Nadine Simon offer a warm and stylish welcome in their red brick house with its authentic furniture and very cozy and British charm. After a stint in the fitness center or the tennis court, we like to relax in the peaceful quietness of the bedrooms with their old wood beams and waxed wood floors. Thomas Baudet carefully prepares festive fare with truffles in salad, sundried tomatoes with lacy parmesan wafers, turbot and foie gras served hot with a reduced pan gravy and celery root fries, veal sweetbreads simmered in cider and accompanied by slow-cooked leeks and potato puffs and the frozen Calvados soufflé that takes us straight back to childhood. A fine cellar.

■ Le Saumon

89, pl de la Madeleine.
Tel. 02 32 32 02 36. Fax 02 32 37 55 80.
www.hoteldusaumon.fr
Hotel closed mid-Dec.–beg. Jan.
Rest. closed mid-Dec.–beg. Jan., 2 weeks Feb.
29 rooms: 44–64€.
Prix fixe: 11€ (weekdays), 15€, 19€, 26,50€, 49€. A la carte: 30€.

Central and attractive, this old post house continues a long tradition of hospitality. The rooms swing between good classical taste and state-of-the-art modernism in an intimate setting. In the kitchen, Alain Simon opts for simplicity with marinated salmon and scallops, duck thighs and a local tarte Normande with cinnamon ice cream.

VERNON

27200 Eure. Paris 75 – Rouen 63 – Evreux 32 – Mantes-la-Jolie 23.
tourisme.vernon@wanadoo.fr.
This pretty Norman town is the closest to Paris.

The old bridge and a mill on the Seine, the church of Notre Dame and the château de Bizy make interesting visits.

HOTELS-RESTAURANTS

■ Hôtel d'Evreux

11, pl d'Evreux.
Tel. 02 32 21 16 12. Fax 02 32 21 32 73.
contact@hoteldevreux.fr / www.hoteldevreux.fr
Rest. closed Sun. (exc. holidays).
12 rooms: 51–60€.
Prix fixe: 22€, 28€. A la carte: 45–50€.

This 17th-century half-timbered structure, formerly the town house of the counts of Evreux and a post house, has the trace and charm of history still intact. The rustic furniture in the bedrooms, the wood beams and the open fireplace in the dining room all confirm this. In the kitchen, tradition is *de rigueur* though not without a contemporary touch: the Cognac-seasoned venison terrine with hazelnuts, tomato confiture with Sichuan peppercorns, lobster and scallops in puff pastry with slow-cooked leeks, duck breast with chanterelles and a wild strawberry gratin with passion fruit convince us of this.

● Les Fleurs   COM

71, rue Carnot.
Tel. 02 32 51 16 80. Fax 02 32 21 30 51.
lesfleurs@tele2.fr
Closed Sun. dinner (exc. July–Aug.), Mon., 1 week beg. Jan.
Prix fixe: 24€, 35€, 47€, 12€ (child).
A la carte: 50€.

The Lefebvres left their Barbizon establishment to set up in this old building in the heart of Vernon. Frédérique serves in the definitely contemporary dining room while Bernard elaborates a cuisine that is both generous and tasteful. Escargot in puff pastry, bacon-wrapped cod filet, a layered oxtail and potato dish and the veal sweetbreads are some of his successes. The raspberry soufflé is a knockout.

● Côté Marine [SIM]

4, pl de la Chantereine.
Tel. 02 32 51 01 95. Fax 02 32 51 68 91.
Prix fixe: 17€, 27€, 37€, 12€ (child).
A la carte: 42€.

Jean-Claude Lambert, who owns Côté Jardin in Parville, enjoys great success in this pleasing annex with its seaside themes and dining room overlooking the Seine. No objections to the poached turbot with shellfish simmered in white wine with garlic and shallots, the spring garlic-braised lamb shank, roasted pineapple and a coconut mousse with rosemary syrup. Gérard Hue provides good advice on the best wine to choose.

In Douains (27120). 8 km via D181 and D75.

■ Château de Brécourt

Tel. 02 32 52 40 50. Fax 02 32 52 69 65.
brecourt@leshotelsparticuliers.com
www.chateaudebrecourt.com
29 rooms: 90–270€.
Prix fixe: 28€ (lunch, weekdays), 42€, 70€, 16€ (child).

Philippe Savry has always had a penchant for charming residences whether in his native Cantal or adopted Vendée and this is one of the jewels of his collection: a 17th-century château with moats and a vast grounds in the middle of the Norman countryside. The bedrooms with their antique furniture, the wooden beams and old tile flooring, the open fireplaces, the bar in the old guardroom and the main courtyard all win us over with their charm. The enchantment continues at the table thanks to Sébastien Guil who makes nice things with noble products like Landes duck foie gras, the sole meunière, roasted squab and the Mara des Bois strawberry dessert.

VERQUIERES see
SAINT-REMY-DE-PROVENCE

VERSAILLES

78000 Yvelines. Paris 21 – Palaiseau 17 –Rambouillet 32 – Saint-Germain-en-Laye 12.

● | RESTAURANTS

● Les Trois Marches [LUX]

R1, bd de la Reine.
Métro: Versailles-Chantiers (RER C).
Tel. 01 39 50 13 21. Fax 01 30 21 01
25.gerard.vie@westin.com
www.trianonpalace.fr
Closed Sun., Mon., Aug.
Prix fixe: 58€ (weekdays lunch), 99€, 180€. A la carte: 170€.

Gérard Vié's 18th-century orangery, with its sumptuous décor, luxurious lobby, deadpan doormen, Marie-Antoinette bar, liveried waiters and venerable grounds wooded with centuries-old trees, remains a temple of French cuisine. The great Gérard, a native of Couïza in the Aude region, still has a childlike freshness tempered by his mastery of domestic haute cuisine, acquired during his time with the wise André Guillot at the Vieux Marly. He deftly juggles flavors, blending truffle and foie gras in a ravioli with flavorful celery root, or wild escargots and frog legs with creamy Swiss chard purée. The John Dory presented in a green tea bouillon with quinoa, the pigeon with shellfish and the tender beef Rossini are all succulent. Nicolas Duroussau's musk-flavored dark chocolate macaron or the Roquefort cream parfait will sweep you away. Enchanting.

● La Brasserie du Théâtre

15, rue des Réservoirs.
Métro: Versailles-Rive-Gauche (RER C).
Tel. 01 39 50 03 21. Fax 01 30 21 92 69.
Closed 20 July–20 Aug.
Prix fixe: 20€ (lunch, wine inc.).
A la carte: 30–45€.

The red banquettes and mirrors and the photographs on the walls signed by actors Sim, Francis Perrin and Pierre Arditi illustrate the theatrical propensities of this historic thirties brasserie recently taken over by Bertrand Gayot for the Flo Group. On the culinary side, the classic dishes—smoked herring and potatoes, roasted cod with spinach, andouillette AAAAA and rice cake—remain unchanged. The waitstaff is in uniform and the winter garden, veranda and cigars a bonus.

VERTUS

51130 Marne. Paris 139 –
Reims 48 – Châlons-en-Champagne 31 –
Epernay 21.
The southern part of the Champagne vineyards near the Mont-Aimé, which dominates the local countryside. The Chardonnay and Pinot Noir vines coexist merrily.

 HOTELS-RESTAURANTS

In Bergères-lès-Vertus (51130). 3,5 km via D9.
■ Hostellerie de la Reine Blanche
18, av Louis-Lenoir.
Tel. 03 26 52 20 76. Fax 03 26 52 16 59.
www.hotel-reine-blanche.com
Closed Christmas–New Year's vac.,
beg. Feb.–end Feb.
27 rooms: 75–79€. 3 suites: 129€.
Half board: 109–187€.

This vast residence in the heart of the city reminds us of a modern chalet with its unassuming glass and wood and brightly colored comfortable rooms. The breakfasts are particularly good.

In Bergères-lès-Vertus.
■ Le Mont-Aimé
4, rue Vertus.
Tel. 03 26 52 21 31. Fax 03 26 52 21 39.
www.hostellerie-mont-aime.com
Closed Sun. dinner, Feb. vac.
46 rooms: 60–125€.
Prix fixe: 35€, 45€, 60€, 70€,
12€ (child). A la carte: 84–94€.

The renovation of this old village café transformed it into a welcoming establishment with cozy rooms, some of them giving directly onto the garden, and a restaurant with traditional cuisine. In spite of being tempted to leave, Jean Sciancalepore has not lost his smile or his easy knack in the kitchen. Judge for yourself by tasting the lobster salad with balsamic vin-

aigrette, grilled turbot with champagne sauce and the pear Mont-Blanc with Baileys. The Champagne wines encourage us to raise our glasses.

VERVINS

02140 Aisne. Paris 176 – Reims 88 –
Charleville-Mézières 68 – Laon 36.
The smallest sub-prefecture in France, also the capital of the Thiérache in northern Normandy, is worth visiting for its fine series of fortified churches, its ramparts and old houses.

 HOTELS-RESTAURANTS

■ La Tour du Roy
45, rue du Général-Leclerc.
Tel. 03 23 98 00 11. Fax 03 23 98 00 72.
latourduroy@wanadoo.fr
www.latourduroy.com
Rest. closed Mon. lunch, Tue. lunch.
9 rooms: 100–185€. 2 suites: 230€.
Prix fixe: 35€, 50€, 65€, 90€ (wine inc.)
20€ (child).

The tower room is the *chef d'oeuvre* of this renovated manor with its three towers overlooking the ramparts of the city. Proud of the glorious history of her establishment (Anne de Bretagne, Henri IV, Charles de Gaulle and François Mitterrand have stayed here), Annie Desvignes juggles skillfully with the local produce. Wonderful preparations spring from her hands: minestrone-style clear langoustine consommé with vegetables and noodles, sea bream filet with mushroom- and ham-stuffed artichokes simmered in wine, beef filet with puréed mint sauce and desserts with caramelized pears, perfectly accompanied by the bottles that Sylvain Lamblin pulls out of his hat.

VESOUL

70000 Haute-Saône. Paris 358. Belfort 70 –
Besançon 45 – Langres 75.
otvesoul@club-internet.fr.
Jacques Brel sang "*T'as voulu voir Vesoul*".
The church of Saint-Georges, the Ursuline con-

vent, the abundance of flowers in season and the Château de Filain are an excellent cure for sarcasm.

■ Hôtel du Lion

4, pl de la République.
Tel. 03 84 76 54 44.
hoteldulion@wanadoo.fr / www.hoteldulion.fr
18 rooms: 45–50€.

In the heart of the city and close to the shopping areas, a practical stopover with unassuming and contemporary rooms. Breakfast on the terrace in summer.

● Caveau du Grand Puits

Rue Mailly.
Tel.-Fax 03 84 76 66 12.
Closed Sat. lunch, Sun., Wed. dinner,
Christmas–beg. Jan., May, mid-Aug.–beg. Sept.
Prix fixe: 17€ (weekdays), 36€.

This vaulted cellar in the heart of the old city charms us with its stone walls, mezzanine, Franche-Comté cuisine and the dishes based on market produce that are served on the patio in fine weather.

76980 Seine-Maritime. Paris 187 –
Dieppe 27 – Rouen 57 –
Saint-Valéry-en-Caux 8.
mairie-veules-les-roses@wanadoo.fr.
The beach at the end of the chalk cliffs of the Caux country is a windy haven.

● Les Galets

Tel. 02 35 97 61 33. Fax 02 35 57 06 23.
plaisance-les-galets@wanadoo.fr
Closed Tue., Wed., mid-Jan.–mid-Feb.
Prix fixe: 36€, 50€, 72€. A la carte: 66€.

After an invigorating walk on the stone beach, we find refuge in this brick house that is typical of the Caux country. We delight in pan-seared duck foie gras esca-

lope, John Dory filet seasoned with thyme and lemongrass with meat jus and hemp oil gravy, lobster served in a jar with slow-cooked pork cheek and asparagus tips and the veal sweetbreads slowly caramelized with honey and ginger. We spoil ourselves with the berry dessert, pear and spéculos sorbet and mint-seasoned chocolate mousse in a chocolate shell. This is an opportunity to observe that Gilbert Plaisance, a veteran who looks like a local Jean Gabin, and a fellow traveler with Manière in Paris, has not lost his knack. He still knows how to receive his guests, who are delighted to spend some time in his establishment and to share a bottle in his company.

24220 Dordogne. Paris 542 – Périgueux 66 – Brive-la-Gaillarde 63.
Near the Château Beynac and the luminous village of La Roque-Gageac, on the golden route to the Dordogne, a Périgord village that takes the time to breathe.

● Le Relais des Cinq Châteaux

Bourg.
Tel. 05 53 30 30 72. Fax 05 53 30 30 08.
www.bestofperigord.com
Closed Sun. dinner, Mon. (off season),
mid-Feb.–mid-Mar.
14 rooms: 50–130€.
Prix fixe: 22€, 28€, 52€, 11€ (child).

Jacky Vasseur is a modest chef on the châteaux route whom we visit greedily just after our visit to La Roque-Gageac and Beynac-et-Cazenac. This expert technician produces a delicately fine traditional cuisine and has made his house, in the leafy shade of the roadside with its veranda dining room, into a choice stopover. Creamy asparagus soup, wild mushroom-stuffed veal shoulder and a caramelized rhubarb tart with sauce make his 22 menu look like philanthropy.

VEZAC see also AURILLAC

VEZELAY

89450 Yonne. Paris 222 – Auxerre 53 –
Clamecy 23 – Avallon 16.
vezelay.otse@ipoint.fr.

The elevated position of this hill overlooking the
Morvan, the basilica of Mary Magdalene, the
cemetery where Jules Roy, Georges Bataille,
Maurice Clavel and Max-Pol Fouchet rest, the
old medieval village: an inspiring location.

 HOTELS-RESTAURANTS

■ Poste et Lion d'Or

Pl du Champ-de-Foire.
Tel. 03 86 33 21 23. Fax 03 86 32 30 92.
www.laposte-liondor.com
Closed beg. Jan.–end Feb.
37 rooms: 70–90€. 1 suite: 127–160€.

Comfortable rooms overlooking the countryside and a friendly welcome make this
old post house a favorite stopover on the
Promenade des Fossés.

■ Résidence du Pontot

Pl du Pontot.
Tel. 03 86 33 24 40. Fax 03 86 33 30 05.
Closed end Oct.–end Apr.
8 rooms: 105–140€.

In the heart of the town and near the basilica, this old house is not lacking in charm
with its period furniture, enclosed garden
and subdued atmosphere. Parking available for guests.

In Fontette (89450). 5 km e via D957.

■ Crispol

Rte d'Avallon.
Tel. 03 86 33 26 25. Fax 03 86 33 33 10.
www.crispol.com
Closed mid-Jan.–mid-Feb.
Rest. closed Mon. lunch.
10 rooms: 75€. 2 suites: 110–120€.
Prix fixe: 21€, 50€. A la carte: 39–44€.

In their stone house at the foot of the Vézelay hill, Christian and Marie-Paule Schori
extend a warm welcome to passing visitors. We can admire the paintings by the
lady of the house on the walls of the contemporary-style bedrooms. Christian's
talents can be measured in the dishes with
crayfish in a seafood broth, local trout
with shallots, roasted quail and peaches
and the crème brûlée.

In Pierre-Perthuis (89450). 5 km. se via D958.

■ Les Deux Ponts

Tel. 03 86 32 31 31. Fax 03 86 32 35 80.
lesdeuxponts@mail.com
www.lesdeuxponts.com
Hotel closed Feb. vac. Rest. closed Tue. (Feb.
vac. and Easter, June–Sept.), Wed. (Feb. vac.
and Easter).
7 rooms: 50–57€.
Prix fixe: 22€, 29€.

Philippe and Mariane Bariteau took over
this modernized old inn on the side of a
country road near the two bridges over
the Cure. The simply decorated and bright
bedrooms and the carefully prepared food
are an open invitation. Oven-crisped
escargots and sautéed mushrooms, Charolais beef with red wine reduction and shallot butter and the strawberry mille-feuille
are classics that rarely fail to please.

In Saint-Père-sous-Vézelay (89450). 3 km se
via D957.

● L'Espérance

Tel. 03 86 33 39 10. Fax 03 86 33 26 15.
esperance@relaischateaux.com
www.marc-meneau-esperance.com
Closed mid-Jan.–mid-Mar.
Rest. closed Mon. lunch, Tue., Wed. lunch.
30 rooms: 150–450€.
Prix fixe: 90 (lunch), 160€, 220€,
40€ (child).

As we finish this guide there are still
doubts concerning this establishment we
love so much. We have always defended
this passionate self-taught man, an
anarchist and destroyer of trends and
fads who trained in the Strasbourg hotel
school and is a disciple of André Guillot in
the Vieux Marly. This Burgundian loner
announced his bankruptcy with three
months to find a rescuer. But with Marc
Meneau, a divinely-inspired maverick
who has taken up quarters under Vézelay
hill, the worst is never sure. The last time

we ate here, one bucolic day early last fall, whether on the terrace or in the ever-so-slightly "British" dining rooms of his Espérance, we found him in better form than ever. Françoise Meneau, née Plaisir, rigorously orchestrated the service. The wines from the region (Pommard Péze-rolles from Hubert de Montille, Charmes Chambertin from Armand Rousseau) or elsewhere (Champigny Clos Rougeard from Foucauld) are a fine accompaniment for a meal fit for a king. There were the eggs Florentine (with spinach and parmesan in thin pastry) making modern homage to Escoffier, the cep tourte (so light), with the mushrooms raw, marinated and grilled, langoustines with radishes and turnips, cooked in a cocotte, and then the fabulous signature Miéral Poulet de Bresse, stuffed with herbs and served with potatoes. So many odes to great classicism, only younger, lighter, in a word: modernized. The cheese? A unique platter holding two Cantals, one aged eighteen months, the other eight months, made from Salers milk and selected by the master *affineur* Bernard Antony de Vieux-Ferrette. The desserts? Poetry. The strawberry Marie Antoinette, conceived in a cloud of milk for Sofia Coppola, the praline-stuffed meringues, lemon tea cakes and coffee roasted with rose petals. The cuisine? A dream come true in a village in the Morvan part of Burgundy just a short distance from the beautiful village where Saint Bernard once preached the Second Crusade. Marc Meneau, a passionate chef and something of a fighting monk ("a lynx", according to his friend and neighbor Jules Roy), is its indomitable sentinel. Of all our French chefs, he remains the most irrepressible artisan, always vigilant, always ready to spring into action. Let's wish him every chance of returning to full form.

In Saint-Père-sous-Vézelay.

● **L'Entre Vigne** `SIM`

Across from L'Espérance.
Tel. 03 86 33 33 33. Fax 03 86 33 26 15.
Closed Sun. dinner, Mon., Tue. lunch,
beg. Jan.–mid-Feb.

Prix fixe: 25€, 30€, 35€ (Sun.),
15€ (child).

We find Marc Meneau's bistro in this annex where simplicity and quality go hand in hand. We like the warm wood and wrought-iron décor, the generous gourmet dishes and the big Sunday buffet. On the à la carte menu we opt for poached eggs in red wine sauce, sole with young vegetables in herb-seasoned butter, mushroom-stuffed poultry breast seasoned with thyme flower and a thin caramelized apple tart, simply delicious.

VEZON see **METZ**

65500 Hautes-Pyrénées. Paris 774 – Pau 48
– Aire-sur-l'Adour 54 – Auch 60 –
Mirande 38 – Tarbes 20.
A delightful stopover in the Pyrénées on our way to the Gaves rivers.

■ / HOTELS-RESTAURANTS

■ **Le Réverbère** Ⓝ☖

29, rue d'Alsace.
Tel. 05 62 96 78 16. Fax 05 62 96 79 85.
le.reverbere@wanadoo.fr / www.lereverbere.fr
Closed 1 week Christmas–New Year's.
Rest. closed Sat. lunch, Sun. dinner.
10 rooms: 44–46€.
Prix fixe: 11–13€, 22–27€, 33€,
8€ (child). A la carte: 60€.

This charming hotel in the heart of the town has elegantly decorated rooms with bright tones and a goodly table. Xavier Fpadiliero and Cédric Rannou form a twosome to present lobster in salad with balsamic vinaigrette, mixed duck breast and jumbo shrimp dish and an individual cup with dark chocolate and sour cherries.

VIC-FEZENSAC

32190 Gers. Paris 745 – Toulouse 110 –
Mont-de-Marsan 75 – Agen 71 – Auch 32.
A stopover in Armagnac country.

HOTELS-RESTAURANTS

● Hôtel du Midi   ⓝSIM

4, rue de la Treille.
Tel. 05 62 06 35 17. Fax 05 62 58 09 76.
Prix fixe: 12€ (weekday lunch), 14€, 18€,
24€. A la carte: 35€.

When Mr. Navarro and Mrs. Voiseux
arrived they gave the old Treille a new lease
on life, at least with the beige and Bordeaux-colored décor. As for the food, the
pan-seared foie gras, a salmon filet with
sorrel and the pineapple with whipped
cream slip down effortlessly.

VICHY

03200 Allier. Paris 358 – Clermont-Ferrand
55 – Roanne 68 – Moulins 56.
tourisme@villevichy.fr.
A green city, a spa city, rich in sometimes painful history. A literary city (Valéry Larbaud was
born here and a prize still bears his name), it
has kept up with the times without losing its
soul. Parc des Sources, rococo residences, a
convention center and a casino all get along
nicely together. It is becoming increasingly easy
to find good food here.

 HOTELS-RESTAURANTS

■ Sofitel Thalassa Vichy   ⌂
    Les Célestins

111, bd des Etats-Unis.
Tel. 04 70 30 82 00. Fax 04 70 30 82 01.
h3241@accor.com / www.accor.com
Closed Feb.
120 rooms: 160–260€. 11 suites: 350–900€.
Prix fixe: 42€, 47€, 140€, 16€ (child).
A la carte: 70€.

A chain hotel like any other? Not really, if we
are to judge by the passage linking it to the
Célestins fitness center or the panoramic
swimming pool on the seventh floor. The
rooms are unassuming and modern and a
guarantee of rest. In the completely renovated N3 restaurant, the ginger- and pineapple-infused langoustine foam, grilled
John Dory with asparagus, slow-cooked

lamb stew with white sauce seasoned with
fresh coriander and a chocolate mille-
feuille with cocoa ice cream form part of
a tastefully fusion register. The Bistro des
Célestins offers less expensive fare.

■ Aletti Palace Hôtel   ⌂⌂

3, pl Joseph-Aletti, La Véranda.
Tel. 04 70 30 20 20 / 04 70 30 21 21.
Fax 04 70 98 13 82.
www.aletti.fr
129 rooms: 98–146€. 8 suites: 176–236€.
Prix fixe: 21€ (weekdays), 35€, 48€.

Situated opposite the Grand Casino, this
1900s hotel has been modernized but still
retains some of its Old World splendor. A
vast dining room with a veranda offers
us classic food in the form of citrus-seasoned lobster salad, pan-fried Mediterranean sea bass, roasted duck with turnip
purée and a light milk chocolate mousse
served in a chocolate tuile with a saffron-
seasoned pear.

■ Novotel Thermalia   ⌂

1, av Thermale.
Tel. 04 70 30 52 52. Fax 04 70 31 08 67.
h0460@accor-hotels.com
www.accor-hotels.com
128 rooms: 97–119€.
Prix fixe: 13€, 17€, 24€, 8,50 € (child).

The neighboring thermal baths set the
tone. The rooms are functional, the cuisine adapted to dieting with light and
simple recipes. A conservatory restaurant with a summer terrace.

■ Pavillon d'Enghien   ⌂

32, rue Callou.
Tel. 04 70 98 33 30. Fax 04 70 31 67 82.
hotel.pavi@wanadoo.fr
www.pavillondenghien.com
Closed 21 Dec.–beg. Feb. Rest. closed Fri.
dinner (off season), Sun. dinner, Mon.
22 rooms: 60–88€.
Prix fixe: 23€, 33€, 8€ (child).
A la carte: 40€.

This pavilion near the Callou thermal
baths has tastefully furnished customized
bedrooms. The menu offers good family

food such as scallop carpaccio, sirloin steak and the generous dessert cart.

● Jacques Décoret   ⓒⓄⓋⒸⓄⓂ

7, av de Gramont (near rue de Paris).
As of June '08: corner 15 rue de la Paix /10, rue Prunel.
Tel.-Fax 04 70 97 65 06.
jacques.décoret@wanadoo.fr
www.jacquesdécoret.com
Closed Tue., Wed., 1 week Oct., Feb. vac., 3 weeks Aug.
Prix fixe: 40€ (lunch), 105€, 140€ (wine inc.). A la carte: 90€.

No review or discussion between fine gourmets fails to mention Jacques Décoret as a leader of fashionable cuisine. The man who was our Young Chef in 2004 still has the wind in his sails and a persistent rumor has it that his departure is imminent, so don't hesitate to taste the cuisine of this ever-young veteran of Troisgros in Roanne, Marcon in Saint-Bonnet-le-Froid and Passard in Paris, with his 1996 Meilleur Ouvrier of France award. Subtle and poetic dishes full of interesting surprises take shape in his capable hands. The best of land and sea can thus make interesting bedfellows: pressed Normandy crab and squid served on a creamy white tuna velouté, the sole *"filet de Bretagne"* cooked with its bones "to play on the bitter and sour flavors of the endive and pink grapefruit", the corn flour cake, crunchy but soft in the center, served with red cabbage compote and a rabbit saddle. For dessert, the "Grand Suisse", served in its original pot and perfumed with the flavors of the Ivory Coast, invite us on a journey through time and space.

● L'Alambic   ⒸⓄⓂ

8, rue Nicolas-Larbaud.
Tel. 04 70 59 12 71. Fax 04 70 97 98 88.
Closed Sun. dinner, 1 week Christmas–New Year's, 2 weeks Feb., 3 weeks Aug.
Prix fixe: 26€, 45€.

Norman Jean-Jacques Barbot's restaurant in the shopping district is no bigger than a pocket handkerchief but it has charmed both natives of Vichy and passing visitors for the last fifteen years. The technique is simple but it has proved its worth: a friendly atmosphere, attentive service and cuisine using fresh market produce that changes with the seasons and the moods of the chef. We thus find veal sweetbread ravioli and crayfish with cream and herb sauce, the monkfish and wild salmon medallions wrapped in smoked bacon, the veal osso bucco with mushrooms. For the final touch, the frozen soufflé with marinated passion fruit and raspberries is not to be missed.

● L'Envolée   ⒸⓄⓂ

44, av Eugène-Gilbert.
Tel.-Fax 04 70 32 85 15.
Closed Tue., Wed., Feb. vac., mid-July–beg. Aug.
Prix fixe: 18,50€ (weekday lunch), 24€, 30€, 31€, 38€.

We like Marie-France's warm and friendly welcome in this colorful establishment decorated with paintings and Bruno Remont's entirely personal interpretation of classics that shakes tradition a little. Seated behind the glass facade we delight in langoustine ravioli in a celery root infusion, tuna medallion with red wine vinegar-seasoned butter, boneless lamb saddle wrapped in caul lace and poached in a thyme infusion and the frozen rolled cake with orange zest.

● La Table d'Antoine   ⒸⓄⓂ

8, rue Burnol.
Tel.-Fax 04 70 98 99 71.
www.latabledantoine.com
Closed Sun. dinner, Mon., Thu. dinner (off season), Feb., 1 week at end June.
Prix fixe: 38,50€, 47€. A la carte: 55€.

A longstanding reference in Vichy gastronomy, Antoine Souillat's establishment is now something of an institution. The modest know-how of this student of Loiseau and Meneau makes a good impression in a neo-Baltard setting of glass and cast iron. On the terrace giving onto a pedestrian street, we delight in the cold zucchini soup with local Gaperon cheese with a goat cheese and beet quenelle, Atlantic sea bass filet with licorice-infused cream sauce and squid ink pasta, veal scallop with chicory cream sauce and pan-tossed beets and the grapefruit mille-feuille with caramel sauce.

● **Brasserie du Casino** 🍴SIM

4, rue du Casino.
Tel. 04 70 98 23 06. Fax 04 70 98 53 17.
www.allier-hotels-restaurants.com
Closed Tue., Wed., 20 Oct.–mid-Nov.,
1 week at end Feb., 1 week beg. June.
Prix fixe: 15€ (weekday lunch), 25€.
A la carte: 42€.

This brasserie has soul. The thirties décor with faux leather benches and, on the walls, the photos of artists who stirred and inflamed the nearby opera house give this a very charming retro aspect. In the kitchen, Jean-Bernard Dechassat orchestrates classic preparations, producing an irreproachable interpretation of some great old classics. We enjoyed the house foie gras with morels cooked in wine, slow-cooked rouget fricassée with fennel, calf's liver served with a light vegetable purée and to finish, mixed coffee and white chocolate ice creams with coffee liqueur and an espresso nougatine.

● **L'Hippocampe** SIM

3, bd de Russie.
Tel.-Fax 04 70 97 68 37.
Closed Sun. dinner, Mon., Tue. lunch, 3 weeks Oct.–beg. Nov., 3 weeks June.
Prix fixe: 16€ (weekday lunch), 25€, 30€, 50€. A la carte: 40–50€.

Rémy Bourgeois, a Burgundian who worked with Flavio in Le Touquet, serves up a cuisine that is mainly lively and colorful sea fare. In the rustic dining room we savor the langoustine and scallop consommé, wild Atlantic sea bass pan-served with slow-cooked fennel, local Salers beef filet medallions with Saint Pourcin sauce served with a potato gratin. The hot orange and Grand Marnier soufflé is a classic we return to with pleasure.

LE VIEIL see NOIRMOUTIER-EN-L'ILE

38200 Isère. Paris 490 – Lyon 32 – Valence 74 – Saint-Etienne 49.
o-t-vienne@wanadoo.fr.
The cathedral of Saint-Maurice, the temple of Augustus and Livia and the Roman theater attract lovers of fine architecture and archaeology.

 HOTELS-RESTAURANTS

● **La Pyramide** ○🏨

14, bd Fernand-Point.
Tel. 04 74 53 01 96. Fax 04 74 85 69 73.
www.lapyramide.com
Closed 3 weeks Feb., 1 week Aug.
Rest. closed Sun., Mon.
20 rooms: 200–230€. 4 suites: 380€.
Prix fixe: 56€ (lunch), 98€, 105€, 155€, 25€ (child). A la carte: 130€.

Spacious and elegant rooms, a pleasant garden, attentive and diligent service. Patrick Henriroux has made Fernand Point's old home into a remarkable Relais & Châteaux establishment. Originally from Franche-Comté, he studied with Blanc in Vonnas after spending some time at the Ferme des Mougins and now devotes himself wholeheartedly to maintaining the reputation of an establishment with a long history. His cuisine is inventive and the cooking is perfectly mastered: the compilation of foie gras, peaches and Port aspic, whole John Dory served with oven-crisped potatoes and warm chorizo vinaigrette, the tender grilled Salers beef sirloin from Maurice Trolliet, the house chocolate dessert, following the theme of the local "Jazz à Vienne" festival, wins unanimous approval.

● **Le Bec Fin** COM

7, pl Saint-Maurice.
Tel. 04 74 85 76 72. Fax 04 74 85 15 30.
www.vienneonline.com
Closed Sun. dinner, Mon., Wed. dinner, Christmas–New Year's.
Prix fixe: 19,50€, 28,50€, 56€, 10€ (child).

Roger Jolivet is affable and pleasant, like his cuisine: frank and generous, between *terroir* and tradition. We enjoy simple pleasures with scallops in salad, salmon filet with chive sauce, Lyon-style gras-double, beef filet medallions breaded with herbs and served with a vineyard-keeper's sauce and a frozen Grand Marnier soufflé, a model of its kind.

● Le Molière `COM`

9, rue Molière.
Tel.-Fax 04 74 53 08 41.
Closed Sun., Mon., 1 week May, 2 weeks Aug.
Prix fixe: 16€, 20€ (wine inc.), 21€, 29€.
A la carte: 36€.

Isabelle and David Sudant extend a friendly welcome while Cédric Garin puts his stamp on the cuisine in a series of nicely reworked classics. Formerly second in command at the Saint-Martin in Vence, he delights us with little squid and scallops baked into fougasse-style bread, rare tuna steak, mushroom- and ham-stuffed artichokes simmered in wine, boneless quail with artichoke purée, the rich chocolate cake with raspberry confiture and the madeleine cake ice cream.

● Les Saveurs du Marché `SIM`

34, cours de Verdun.
Tel.-Fax 04 74 31 65 65.
Closed Sat., Sun. Bank holidays,
23 July–20 Aug.
Prix fixe: 12€ (lunch), 16€, 28€, 35€.
A la carte: 42–49€.

Just a stone's throw from the Roman amphitheater, this pleasant bistro-style establishment, with a bar and wood furnishings, is designed to please. Sébastien and Valérie Desestret learned the trade in the nearby Pyramide and their menus, particularly the lunchtime menu, are bargains. Escargot ravioli with parsley and red wine reduction, pan-tossed sea bream served with lacy parmesan wafers, vegetable pistou with wild thyme jus, rabbit stuffed with prunes served with new potatoes and a fresh thyme jus and the honey roasted figs with pain d'épice pain perdu, served with cinnamon sorbet, enhance the market produce.

In Chonas-l'Amballan (38121). 9 km s via N7.

● Domaine de Clairefontaine ○❀🏠

Chemin des Fontanettes.
Tel. 04 74 58 81 52. Fax 04 74 58 80 93.
www.domaine-de-clairefontaine.fr
Closed mid-Dec.–mid-Jan.
Rest. closed Mon., Tue.
26 rooms: 52–120€. 2 suites: 80–160€.
Prix fixe: 45€ (lunch weekdays), 60€, 80€,
66€, 98€.

The Girardons' domain in the heart of its three-hectare grounds is an invitation to rest and tranquillity. In the main house, which once belonged to the bishops of Lyons, and the annex with its charming rooms, terrace and tennis court, we quickly forget life's little upsets. Philippe takes up the torch in the kitchen. This 1997 Meilleur Ouvrier de France award winner diligently reworks the classics of French haute cuisine. Lobster and raw tomato mille-feuille with an avocado mousseline (in July and August), boneless frog legs with parsley and oyster mushroom-seasoned garlic cream, farm-raised pigeon in a pastry crust with duck foie gras, the traditionally roasted milk-fed veal filet, stewed vegetables and the peach, apricot and almond crumble are models of their kind. The dark Caraïbes chocolate Stradivarius is also exemplary. Laurence at the reception welcomes us with a smile and Dominique Vialat offers invaluable advice on the Côtes du Rhône wines.

In Chonas-l'Amballan.

■ Hostellerie Le Marais ❀🏠
Saint-Jean

616, chemin du Marais.
Tel. 04 74 58 83 28. Fax 04 74 58 80 93.
contact@domaine-de-clairefontaine.fr
www.domaine-de-clairefontaine.fr
Closed Mon., Tue., mid-Dec.–mid-Jan.
10 rooms: 82–90€. Half board: 110€.

Just a short distance from the A7 highway, this old farmhouse is now a friendly inn with Provençal-style rooms in good taste. The terrace and garden further please the delighted guests.

VIENNE-LE-CHATEAU

51800 Marne. Paris 236 –
Châlons-en-Champagne 52 –
Sainte-Menehould 9 – Verdun 49.
A town in an enclave in the Argonne forest.
Visit the local eco-museum.

 HOTELS-RESTAURANTS

■ Le Tulipier
Rue St-Jacques.
Tel. 03 26 60 69 90. Fax 03 26 60 69 91.
tulipier.le@wanadoo.fr
38 rooms: 53–76€.
Prix fixe: 22€, 35€, 55€.

This vast modern complex, skillfully managed by Richard Dogna, offers rooms that are both functional and comfortable, an indoor swimming pool and a quiet location in the middle of the forest. In addition, the cuisine is carefully crafted and based on quality produce: foie gras with onion confiture, poached eggs with Maroilles cheese, pike-perch with julienned vegetables, beef sirloin steak with morels in cream sauce, whole kidney with whiskey sauce, molded pudding cakes with champagne marc and a house cookie dessert with custard cream sauce.

In Apremont-sur-Aire (08250). 16 km via Binarville.

● L'Argonne
Rue Dessous la Roche.
Tel. 03 24 30 53 88.
5 rooms: 29€.
Prix fixe: 11,60€, 14€, 19€, 24€,

An unpretentious facade next to a modest café masks a village inn that is well worth visiting. Thierry Leblan took over the family business and renovated the culinary style without changing the décor. An Argonne-style fricassée (smoked bacon chunks, croutons, potatoes, Gruyere cheese and eggs), salmon and perch brochettes and the beef, duck breast and wild boar trilogy constitute a pleasant surprise.

VIERZON

18100 Cher. Paris 207 – Bourges 39 –
Châteauroux 58 – Orléans 84.
office-tourisme@ville-vierzon.fr.
Of course its industrial history (forge and porcelain) is not necessarily enchanting, but the old pedestrian center is worth having a look at and the Berry Champagne circuit leaves us dreaming of country escapades.

 HOTELS-RESTAURANTS

■ Le Continental
104 bis, av Edouard-Vaillant.
Tel. 02 48 75 35 22. Fax 02 48 71 10 39.
robertbc87@wanadoo.fr
Closed Christmas, New Year's,
1 week Feb. vac.
37 rooms: 50–67€.

We like the courteous welcome, the renovated and comfortable rooms and the simple but good food reserved for the guests at this hotel a little way from the center.

● La Maison de Célestin
20, av Pierre-Sémard.
Tel. 02 48 83 01 63. Fax 02 48 71 63 41.
lamaisondecelestin@wanadoo.fr
www.lamaisondecelestin.com
Closed Sat. lunch, Sun. dinner, Mon.,
2 weeks Jan., 3 weeks Aug.
Prix fixe: 22€, 30€, 40€,
50€, 60€, 14€ (child).
A la carte: 50–60€.

Annie and Pascal Chaupitre "did" the Côte d'Or at Saulieu and the Petit Comptoir in Epernay before settling in this city of forges. They chose a fine country-style house across from the station with a terrace and veranda giving onto a charming garden. Pascal in the kitchen displays a real talent that justifies a visit—if justification is required. His pressed tuna with slow-cooked vegetables, the salt cod and potato stuffed vegetable plate, the farm-raised wasabi-seasoned rabbit, potatoes and fresh goat cheese and the little lemon pastry dessert are a promise of good times to come. The wine list has a wealth of nice listings, Annie's welcome is warm and the prices remain reasonable. So many good reasons to visit and return to Vierzon.

VIEUX-FERRETTE see FERRETTE
VILLAGE-NEUF see SAINT-LOUIS

VILLAINES-LA-JUHEL

53700 Mayenne. Paris 220 – Alençon 30 –
Bagnoles-de-l'Orne 30 – Le Mans 59 –
Mayenne 27.
At the edge of the Perche region, an old town surrounded by peacefully rolling countryside.

 HOTELS-RESTAURANTS

■ Hôtel Oasis
1 km, rte de Javron.
Tel. 02 43 03 28 67. Fax 02 43 03 35 30.
hoteloasis@hotmail.com / www.oasis.fr
13 rooms: 41–69€. Half board: 61–109€.

An oasis in the countryside, an old farmhouse like Steve Chedor's, a blend of rustic touches (wood and stone décor, wooden beams and terra cotta tiles in the bedrooms, a little garden with a pond) and a variety of equipment (fitness center, Turkish bath, Jacuzzi, mini-golf course).

VILLARD-DE-LANS

38250 Isère. Paris 584 – Voiron 44 –
Grenoble 34 – Lyon 123 – Valence 67.
www.ot-villard-de-lans.fr.
This little ski touring resort still remembers the struggle of the Vercors *maquis* and boasts the beauty of its countryside with the spectacular gorges of the Bourne.

 HOTELS-RESTAURANTS

■ Le Christiana
Av du Professeur-Nobécourt.
Tel. 04 76 95 12 51.
info@hotel-le-christiana.fr
Closed mid-Sept.–mid-Dec.,
beg. Apr.–mid-May.

Rest. closed lunch (exc. July–Aug.).
23 rooms: 70–190€.
Prix fixe: 25€, 50€.

This large wooden chalet with balconies looking out at the mountain is warm and welcoming: nice wood-paneled bedrooms and a friendly reception area. The Tétras restaurant is open in the evening and serves specialities to warm us up after our efforts.

■ A la Ferme du Bois Barbu
Bois-Barbu, 3 km via rte du Col-de-Liorin.
Tel. 04 76 95 13 09. Fax 04 76 94 10 65.
Closed 1 week Oct., mid-Nov.–beg. Dec.,
1 week Apr., 1 week June, Sun. dinner, Wed.
8 rooms: 47–55€.
Prix fixe: 17€, 23€, 35€.

This old farmhouse near the slopes has been transformed into a hospitable and rustic chalet hotel that is cozy and serves good food. Snug little rooms, generous dishes.

● Le Trente Pas
16, rue des Francs-Tireurs.
Tel. 04 76 94 06 75.
Closed Mon., Tue., Nov., Apr.
Prix fixe: 15€ (weekday lunch), 25€, 50€.

Located near the town church, this good country restaurant serves up cheese specialities and dishes based on market produce. Good menus and nice prices.

VILLARS-LES-DOMBES

01330 Ain. Paris 434 – Lyon 36 – Villefranche-sur-Saône 27 – Bourg-en-Bresse 30.
ot.villarslesdombes@caramail.com.
The heart of the Dombes region, ponds, large woods, a bird sanctuary that is magnificent in the fall.

 HOTELS-RESTAURANTS

■ Le Ribotel et la Villardière
Rte de Lyon.
Tel. 04 74 98 08 03 / 04 74 98 11 91 (rest.).
ribotel@wanadoo.fr / www.ribotel.fr
Closed Christmas–New Year's, Jan.

47 rooms: 45–85€.
Prix fixe: 14€ (lunch), 24€, 40€, 9€ (child).

Located a short distance from the bird sanctuary, this goodly establishment provides very simple bed and board. Under the wooden beams of the bright dining room we savor smoked duck breast, frog legs in parsley and garlic, poultry thigh with morels and apple and caramel served hot in puff pastry.

In Bouligneux (01330). 4 km nw via D2.

● **Le Thou** COM

Le Village.
Tel. 04 74 98 15 25 / 04 74 98 15 24.
Fax 04 74 98 13 57.
Closed Sun. dinner, Mon., 3 weeks Oct., Feb. vac.
Prix fixe: 29€, 37€, 44€, 54€.
A la carte: 55€.

Stéphane Köenig's restaurant takes its name from the sluice gates used in the ponds of the Dombes region. Nathalie works diligently to provide attentive service in this charming little flowery inn with a patio and garden. Stéphane concocts a marbled foie gras terrine, carp filet served with thinly sliced potatoes and free-range chicken with morel cream sauce that do justice to the region, not to mention the charming XXL dish known as the "*fin de la faim*" (the end of hunger), a veritable selection of gourmet delights.

VILLE

67220 Bas-Rhin. Paris 418 – Sélestat 16 – Strasbourg 58 – Saint-Dié 39.
tourisme@cccanton-de-ville.fr.
This pastoral and forested region where wild berries drop into our hands and where we only have to raise our arms to pick the fruit from the trees, has an abundance of home distilleries.

HOTELS-RESTAURANTS

■ **La Bonne Franquette**

6, pl du Marché.
Tel. 03 88 57 14 25. Fax 03 88 57 08 15.
bonne-franquette@wanadoo.fr

www.hotel-bonne-franquette.com
Closed Nov. 1 vac., Feb. vac., 1 week at end June–beg. July. Rest. closed Sun. dinner, Mon.
10 rooms: 33,50–53,50€.
Prix fixe: 19,50€, 27,60€, 38,50€, 10€ (child).

A flowery facade, carefully kept rooms and rustic furniture make this attractive, centrally located inn a choice stopover. Véronique's welcome and Pascal Schreiber's cuisine are equally pleasing. Everything here is "informal". A locally smoked trout carpaccio, pike-perch filet with Riesling cream sauce, thinly sliced duck breast with mountain honey and a frozen kirsch mousse go down easily.

LA VILLE-AUX-CLERCS

41160 Loir-et-Cher. Paris 158 – Orléans 71 – Châteaudun 27 – Vendôme 18.
This part of the Loir, between the woods and the river, is a bucolic haven.

HOTELS-RESTAURANTS

■ **Manoir de la Forêt**

Tel. 02 54 80 62 83. Fax 02 54 80 66 03.
www.manoirdelaforet.fr
Closed 1 week Jan.
Rest. closed Sun. dinner (Sept.–Apr.), Mon. (Sept.–Apr.).
16 rooms: 51–80€. 2 suites: 90–120€.
Prix fixe: 27€, 35,50€, 50€, 17€ (child).

Surrounded by woods in the heart of its own grounds, this beautiful 18th-century country residence offers us a verdant setting in which to relax and unwind: rooms with old-style furniture, a subdued atmosphere in the lounges and restaurant where Arnaud Villedieu takes his inspiration from a classic repertoire without undue flourishes. The delicious and generous crab, langoustine and foie gras dish, the beef cheeks, the rump steak with Chinon wine sauce and a rich chocolate cake with candied oranges pass the test.

VILLECOMTAL-SUR-ARROS

32730 Gers. Paris 758 – Pau 72 – Aire-sur-l'Adour 68 – Auch 50 – Tarbes 25.
In the south of the Gers region, between Bigorre and the Landes, a peaceful town gazing at the Pyrénées.

●	RESTAURANTS

● Le Rive Droite

1, chemin de Saint-Jacques.
Tel. 05 62 64 83 08. Fax 05 62 64 84 02.
rivedroite2@wanadoo.fr / www.marciac.fr
Closed Mon., Tue., Wed., Nov. 1 vac.
Prix fixe: 34€.

This elegant 18th-century Chartreuse house where George Sand once stayed is now the property of Myriam and Philippe Piton. A creative and imaginative establishment where pork trotter in paupillette, cod with chanterelles, black pork belly, half of a squab in a cabbage leaf and a walnut crème brûlée adorn an amazing fixed-price/à la carte menu.

VILLEFRANCHE-DE-CONFLENT

66500 Pyrénées-Orientales. Paris 904 – Perpignan 49 – Montpellier 206 – Prades 6 – Narbonne 114.
Thanks to the military architect Vauban, who fortified the city with admirable ramparts and bastions protecting the narrow valley of the Têt, Villefranche is one of the "most beautiful villages in France".

●	RESTAURANTS

● L'Auberge Saint Paul

7, pl de l'Eglise.
Tel. 04 68 96 30 95. Fax 04 68 05 60 30.
auberge-st-paul@wanadoo.fr
http://perso.wanadoo.fr/auberge.stpaul
Closed Sun. dinner, Mon., Tue., 2 weeks Nov., 3 weeks Jan., 1 week at end June.
Prix fixe: 19,50€ (lunch, wine inc.), 33€ (wine inc.), 47€, 85€.
A la carte: 70€.

The Gomez imagination has transformed this old 13th-century chapel into a simply decorated and unassuming restaurant. In the beige and white dining room with modern stained glass and on the shady terrace, we appreciate the peace and tranquillity along with Patricia's cuisine, in which regional produce is used to serve dishes that are frank and generous: langoustines in a mixed grain salad with sesame oil, rouget filet slow-cooked with tomatoes and olives, sage-stuffed rabbit, breaded pork trotter and the nectarine and licorice soup served with orange sorbet. The prices are reasonable, particularly in the set menus.

VILLEFRANCHE-DE-ROUERGUE

12200 Aveyron. Paris 608 – Rodez 58 – Albi 68 – Cahors 61.
infos@villefranche.com.
This rich old *bastide* has many treasures to reveal, with its old bridges, baroque Chapelle des Pénitents, square with the arches and the old cathedral.

	HOTELS-RESTAURANTS

■ Le Relais du Farrou   ⌂

Rte de Figeac.
Tel. 05 65 45 18 11. Fax 05 65 45 32 59.
le.relais.de.farrou@wanadoo.fr
www.lerelaisdefarrou.com
Closed Nov. 1 vac., Christmas,
1 week beg. Jan., Feb. vac.
Rest. closed Sat. lunch (off season),
Sun. dinner (off season), Mon. (off season).
24 rooms: 45,50–84€. 1 suite: 93–110€.
Prix fixe: 22€, 33,50€, 42€, 14€ (child).
A la carte: 55–60€.

On the edge of the town this post house dating from 1792 has kept its Old World charm. The rooms are peaceful thanks to the garden and the river that runs quietly through it. They are spacious and also lead to the indoor swimming pool and Turkish bath. In the dishes, regional flavors dominate with house foie gras, stuffed pigeon breast, tuna steak served with dill-seasoned vegetables baked in a ceramic dish, fresh shrimp and citrus salad and the rich chocolate cake served with a milky tea-infusioned mousse are all equally delicious.

VILLEFRANCHE-DE-LAURAGAIS

31290 Haute-Garonne. Paris 740 – Carcassonne 60 – Toulouse 32.
An old *bastide* in the heart of the Haute Garonne with shades of Tuscany.

　HOTELS-RESTAURANTS

■ Hostellerie du Chef Jean
In Montgaillard-Lauragais,
3 km toward Toulouse.
Tel. 05 34 66 71 34. Fax 05 34 66 71 33.
hostellerie-chef-jean@wanadoo.fr
www.hostellerie-chef-jean.com
Closed beg. Jan.–mid-Feb.
14 rooms: 58–75€.
Prix fixe: 20€, 25€, 35€, 45€,
8,50€ (child). A la carte: 45€.

At the entrance to Toulouse, located opposite a perfectly equipped fitness center, the rooms in this old residence are classical and carefully kept. In the all-brick restaurant dining room, pan-seared scallops with vegetables, anis-ette-flambéed roasted Mediterranean sea bass and the beef filet Rossini are tasteful classics.

VILLEFRANCHE-SUR-MER

06230 Alpes-Maritimes. Paris 936
– Nice 6 – Beaulieu-sur-Mer 4 –
Saint-Jean-Cap-Ferrat 4.
The most beautiful harbor in the world, the citadel, the chapel and memories of Cocteau.

　HOTELS-RESTAURANTS

■ Welcome
3, quai de l'Amiral-Courbet.
Tel. 04 93 76 27 62. Fax 04 93 76 27 66.
www.welcomehotel.com
35 rooms: 68–194€. 1 suite: 305–345€.

Jean Cocteau has a room here, an homage to the man who was a cherished resident and painted the frescoes in the Chapelle Saint-Pierre situated just across from it. The reception is impeccable, the wine bar frequentable and the view of the harbor unbeatable.

■ Versailles
7, bd Princesse-Grace-de-Monaco.
Tel. 04 93 76 52 52. Fax 04 93 01 97 48.
www.hotelversailles.com
Closed end Oct.–beg. Feb.
Rest. closed Mon. (off season).
43 rooms: 85–140€. 3 suites: 155–220€.
Prix fixe: 35€, 40€, 17€ (child).

This seventies hotel with its gray and white rooms enjoys an exceptional location. Overlooking the harbor, the contemporary restaurant and terrace offer an unforgettable panorama. In the kitchen, Yves Duchateau orchestrates classic preparations such as escargots sautéed in mild spring garlic and oven-browned in their serving dish, cod with aïoli, veal kidneys simmered in Port and served with mustard sauce and crêpes Suzette with Grand Marnier.

● La Fille du Pêcheur　COM
13, quai Courbet.
Tel. 04 93 01 90 09. Fax 04 93 01 90 29.
www.lafilledupecheur.com
Closed 2 weeks Jan.
Prix fixe: 12€ (child). A la carte: 42–52€.

Papa Roux provides the raw material for this family restaurant that concentrates mainly on sea produce. Krystel, the fisherman's daughter, provides a friendly welcome and serves Provençal-style pan-seared scallops, Cognac-flambéed jumbo shrimp and an apple tart that meet with no criticism.

● Mère Germaine　COM
9, quai Courbet.
Tel. 04 93 01 71 39. Fax 04 93 01 96 44.
contact@meregermaine.com
www.meregermaine.com
Closed mid-Nov.–end Dec.
Prix fixe: 37€. A la carte: 65€.

Overlooking the fishing port, with its terrace on the sea front, Rémy Blouin's establishment is something of an institution. Fresh produce and delicately wrought preparations are the hallmarks of tuna marinated in lime and coconut milk, grilled Mediterranean sea bass with fennel, the house stuffed sole and an oven-browned fruit sabayon. In short, an establishment with the kind of rustic charm that never goes out of fashion.

● L'Oursin Bleu `COM`

11, quai Courbet.
Tel. 04 93 01 90 12. Fax 04 93 01 80 45.
oursinbleu@club-internet.fr
Closed Tue. (off season), 10 Jan.–beg. Feb.
Prix fixe: 34€, 32€. A la carte: 70€.

With Indonesian-style décor, this restaurant on the waterfront and in the heart of the effervescent port incites us to travel while we stay put. For our delectation, Jérôme Deloncle offers crab in an exotic mille-feuille, small squid served in various styles, a slice of monkfish and the house "exotica" dessert that provides a pleasant escape.

● Michel's `SIM`

Pl Amélie-Pontonnais.
Tel. 04 93 76 73 24. Fax 04 93 76 73 42.
compact@michel-f.net / www.michel-f.net
Closed Tue., Christmas.
A la carte: 42€.

Between the port and the old city, the Garnerys have used their family spirit to support a winning formula that is summed up in a few words: friendliness, fresh produce and reasonable prices. In the dining room or on the terrace we delight in salmon and scallop tartare, John Dory filet with tarragon-seasoned hollandaise sauce, milk-fed veal tenderloin with mustard sauce and a chocolate and grapefruit fondant.

69400 Rhône. Paris 433 – Lyon 35 – Bourg-en-Bresse 54 – Mâcon 45.
ot.villefranche-beaujolais@wanadoo.fr.
The "undeclared" capital of the Beaujolais region. The Saône marks the frontier with the Dombes region.

 HOTELS-RESTAURANTS

■ Hôtel de Plaisance

96, av de la Libération.
Tel. 04 74 65 33 52. Fax 04 74 62 02 89.
www.hotel-plaisance.com
Closed Christmas–New Year's.
68 rooms: 58–93€.
Prix fixe: 24€, 32€. A la carte: 40–45€.

This seventies structure has been carefully renovated with imagination, making it a comfortable hotel with modern and welcoming rooms. Salmon carpaccio, crunchy fennel salad, tuna in a sesame crust, duck breast with an orange sweet-and-sour sauce and a banana and apple duo flambéed with rum have pleasant surprises in store for us.

■ La Ferme du Poulet

180, rue Mangin.
Tel. 04 74 62 19 07. Fax 04 74 09 01 89.
la.ferme.du.poulet@wanadoo.fr
Closed Sun. dinner, Mon., Christmas–beg. Jan.
9 rooms: 105–105€.
Prix fixe: 28€ (weekday lunch), 36€, 48€, 60€, 15€ (child). A la carte: 69€.

The enclosure around this 17th-century farmhouse cuts it off from the neighboring industrial zone. We can thus fully enjoy the contemporary rooms and the restaurant with the wooden beams where Jacques Rongeat serves up carefully prepared dishes: escargots with garlic butter and scallops with zucchini butter.

● Le Juliénas `SIM`

236, rue d'Anse.
Tel. 04 74 09 16 55.
Closed Sat. lunch, Sun., 1 week beg. Jan., mid-July–mid-Aug.

Prix fixe: 13€ (lunch), 16,50€ (lunch),
23,50€, 35€, 8€ (child). A la carte: 38€.

A simple presentation, a friendly welcome
and generous servings: these are the ingredients that constitute the success of Pascal
Quillas' bistro. No objections to the beef
and Beaujolais wine aspic, oven-crisped
cod with star anise–infused sauce, minced
veal kidneys with Port and the frozen cinnamon soufflé.

VILLEMOYENNE

10260 Aube. Paris 186 – Troyes 20 –
Bar-sur-Aube 47- Châtillon-sur-Seine 51.
A little village (fewer than 500 inhabitants),
not a "*ville moyenne*" (average-sized town), in
the Aube countryside.

●	RESTAURANTS

● **La Parentèle**
32, rue Marcellin-Lévêque.
Tel. 03 25 43 68 68. Fax 03 25 43 68 69.
Closed Sun. dinner, Mon., Tue., 2 weeks
Feb. vac., 1 week at end July–mid-Aug.
Prix fixe: 26€, 46€, 66€, 15€ (child).
A la carte: 65€.

The Caironis' old village grocery store has
had a second lease on life since the children, Christophe and Bruno, have taken
over. At every meal the chic and rustic
yet vaguely Japanese dining room and
the terrace garden welcome lovers of the
sun-soaked Champagne cuisine. In the
kitchen David Goubeault and Gaël Koziar
join forces to brew up a cold charteuse of
shrimp in a basil-seasoned shellfish vinaigrette, simply prepared John Dory and a
duck filet with herbs and mushroom- and
ham-stuffed artichokes simmered in wine.
The desserts, in the same style, meet with
an enthusiastic welcome, like the individual praline tart with vanilla ice cream.
Combined with these sweet delights, the
wines selected by Christophe Caironi and
David Chavier hit the right spot.

VILLEMUR-SUR-TARN

31340 Haute-Garonne. Paris 645 – Albi 65 –
Castres 72 – Montauban 25 – Toulouse 40.
Between Toulouse and Montauban, a *bastide*
on the Tarn.

	HOTELS-RESTAURANTS

■ **Auberge du Flambadou**
5 km s via D14.
Tel. 05 61 09 40 72. Fax 05 61 09 29 66.
www.aubergeduflambadou.com
Rest. closed Sun. dinner, Mon. lunch.
5 rooms: 75–130€.
Prix fixe: 15€ (lunch), 18€, 44€.

A nice inn with a large open fireplace
where fish and meat are grilled. Snugly
rustic rooms, a charming welcome.

● **La Ferme de Bernardou**
66, av du Général-Leclerc, route de Toulouse.
Tel. 05 61 09 02 38. Fax 05 61 35 94 87.
Closed Sun. dinner, Mon., Tue. dinner.
Prix fixe: 18,50€ (weekday lunch), 29€,
42€, 13€ (child). A la carte: 45€.

Philippe Iragne has turned his goodly inn
into a genuine gourmet stopover. We like
to go there to enjoy nicely reworked traditional cuisine, as in the tossed mix of
crunchy vegetables, melon and cucumber
pulp, roasted turbot with mushroom ravioli, pan-seared duck breast with peaches
and a strawberry and raspberry cappucino
with rice pudding.

VILLENEUVE-LA-RIVIERE see
SAINT-GAUDENS

VILLENEUVE-LES-AVIGNON

30400 Gard. Paris 682 – Avignon 5 –
Nîmes 46 – Orange 22.
villeneuve.les.avignon.tourisme@wanadoo.fr.
While the popes lived at Avignon, the bishops
were in residence at Villeneuve. The old city
has retained much wealth from this period: the
tower of Phillip the Fair, Fort Saint-André and
the Chartreuse of Val-de-Bénédiction.

HOTELS-RESTAURANTS

■ **Le Prieuré**
7, pl du Chapitre.
Tel. 04 90 15 90 15. Fax 04 90 25 45 39.
leprieure@relaischateaux.com
www.leprieure.fr
Closed end oct–mid-Mar.
Rest. closed Tue. (exc. July–Aug.).
23 rooms: 220€. 10 suites: 420€.
Prix fixe: 45€ (lunch), 65€, 95€, 20€ (child).

This traditional Relais & Châteaux establishment has just changed hands. Jean-André Charial de Baumanière, the new manager, has made the décor more contemporary and put the cuisine in the hands of the young Franck Fage, who formerly worked with Ducasse and in the Cabro d'Or. He serves up a rejuvenated Provençal cuisine that is in tune with the Provence of today. Fine langoustine ravioli, sea bream cooked in Maussane oil with pan-simmered fennel, the rack of lamb roasted in its juice with a vegetable and pepper sauté and the all-chocolate plate are welcome treats. Climbing roses, vast grounds, wooden beams and exposed stone take on a different meaning in this new atmosphere.

■ **La Magnaneraie**
37, rue du Camp-de-Bataille.
Tel. 04 90 25 11 11. Fax 04 90 25 46 37.
magnaneraie.hotel@najeti.com
Closed mid-Feb.–mid-Mar.
Rest. closed Sat. lunch, Sun. dinner, Wed.
29 rooms: 135–235€. 10 suites: 265€.
Prix fixe: 33€, 80€.

This beautiful 15th-century residence complete with garden offers elegant and carefully laid out rooms. A dining room with columns and a shady terrace where the cuisine has all the colors of Provence.

■ **L'Atelier**
5, rue de la Foire.
Tel. 04 90 25 01 84. Fax 04 90 25 80 06.
hotel-latelier@libertysurf.fr
23 rooms: 49–85€.

This 16th-century house has been transformed into a charming hotel with cozy rooms, antique furniture and objects, paintings and sculptures. A pleasant shady patio.

VILLENEUVE-SUR-LOT

47300 Lot-et-Garonne. Paris 598 – Agen 29 – Bergerac 61 – Cahors 74.
The banks of the Lot, the old houses and the home of Paul Guth and the *Agen* prunes.

 HOTELS-RESTAURANTS

In Pujols (47300). 4 km via D118 and C207.
■ **Les Chênes**
Bel Air.
Tel. 05 53 49 04 55. Fax 05 53 49 22 74.
www.hoteldeschenes.com
Closed end Dec.–beg. Jan.
21 rooms: 60–75€.

Across from the medieval village and the valley of the Lot, this building that is both modern and regional has carefully decorated peaceful rooms.

In Pujols.
● **La Toque Blanche**
Tel. 05 53 49 00 30. Fax 05 53 70 49 79.
latoque.blanche@wanadoo.fr
www.la-toque-blanche.com
Closed Sun. dinner, Mon., Tue. lunch,
19 June–beg. July.
Prix fixe: 25€, 38€, 54€, 78€, 14€ (child).

This residence on the flank of a hill offers an incomparable view of the valley of the Lot. The dishes present a festival of fine local and authentic produce. Bernard Lebrun reinterprets the classics of the Southwest with talent and lends them just the right measure of new savors. The foie gras and duck confit duo with truffles, lobster and vegetable stew and squab roasted with spices are mouthwateringly good. The prune dessert with cinnamon ice cream is a dessert that no one can afford to ignore but the many menus have other fine discoveries in store. The cellar where Christophe Basin reigns is remarkably rich.

In Pujols.

● **Lou Calel**
Au Bourg.
Tel.-Fax 05 53 70 46 14.
Closed Tue. lunch, Wed. lunch, Thu. lunch,
2 weeks Oct., 2 weeks Jan., 1 week June.
Prix fixe: 18€ (lunch, wine inc.), 22€, 30€,
38€, 12€ (child).

The ambassador in Pujols of the generous cuisine of the Southwest is Bernard Lebrun who welcomes us with the same warmth as in the Toque Blanche, his first home. The wines, like the menu, are local and as delightful as ever. A lobe of foie gras slow-cooked in garlic, cod filet with slow-cooked fennel, beef cheek daube simmered with Buzet wine and the house baba au rhum are cooked with loving care and just rich enough.

VILLENEUVE-SUR-YONNE

89500 Yonne. Paris 133 – Auxerre 46 –
Joigny 19 – Montargis 45 – Nemours 57 –
Sens 14.
Rich in history (it sheltered Misia Sert and Bernard Clavel), this city stretches along the banks of the Yonne.

HOTELS-RESTAURANTS

■ **La Lucarne aux Chouettes** 🏠
Quai Bretoche.
Tel. 03 86 87 18 26. Fax 03 86 87 22 63.
www.lesliecaron-auberge.com
Closed Sun. dinner (exc. July–Aug.),
Mon., Jan.
4 rooms: 99€. 3 suites: 145–165€.
Prix fixe: 21€ (lunch).

Her performances in *Gigi* and *An American in Paris* showed only a part of Leslie Caron's talents. This great lady is also a hostess who is renowned for her courtesy and consideration. Her paintings decorate the rooms alongside older canvases. Her inn, where grain was once stored, is known for its fine cuisine and rustic décor. Warm quail salad with yakitori, sea bream with slow-cooked tomatoes and basil, oven-crisped rabbit with morels and the strawberries in puff pastry are exquisite delights for which we are indebted to the Japanese chef Daïsuke Inagaki.

VILLEREST see ROANNE

VILLERS-LE-LAC

25130 Doubs. Paris 474 –
Besançon 69 – La Chaux-de-Fond 16 –
Morteau 6.
The Saut du Doubs is opposite, the Lake of Chaillexon is our neighbor and the Swiss communes of Locle and La Chaux-de-Fonds are just down the road.

HOTELS-RESTAURANTS

● **Le France** ◐🏠
8, pl Cupillard.
Tel. 03 81 68 00 06. Fax 03 81 68 09 22.
www.hotel-restaurant-lefrance.com
Closed beg. Jan.–beg. Feb.
Rest. closed Sun. dinner, Mon.
12 rooms: 55–100€.
Prix fixe: 20€ (lunch), 27€, 54€, 68€,
12€ (child). A la carte: 75€.

Four generations of the same family have run this traditional establishment. This history did not prevent them from creating another little lounge next to the lobby and renovating the rooms in a contemporary style. For the guests in the beautifully wood-paneled dining room, Hugues Droz, who trained with Jean-Pierre Billoux in Dijon, pays homage to his region. As witnessed by a pheasant terrine with wild mushrooms, perch filets in fish broth, poultry thighs with morels and Vin Jaune and the frozen nougat in a pine honey cage. A fine cellar with the Jura very much present.

VILLERS-LES-NANCY see NANCY
VILLERS-SUR-MER see DEAUVILLE
VINAY see EPERNAY
VINCELOTTES see AUXERRE
VINEZAC see AUBENAS

VIRE

14500 Calvados. Paris 295 –
Saint-Lô 40 – Caen 62 – Bayeux 61.
office.tourisme.vire@wanadoo.fr.
Although the capital of the andouille sausage
was destroyed in 1944, it is still an authentic stopover crossroads. The clocktower on a
fortified 13th-century gate and the church of
Notre Dame still survive to remind us of the
city of bygone days.

● RESTAURANTS

● **Manoir de la Pommeraie** `V.COM`
2,5 km via D524, rte de Flers.
Tel. 02 31 68 07 71. Fax 02 31 67 54 21.
Closed 2 weeks July, 2 weeks Jan.,
Sun. dinner, Mon.
Prix fixe: 22€ (weekday lunch), 33€,
48,50€. A la carte: 50–55€.

On the road to Flers, this 18th-century
manor offers a rustic setting with its two
dining rooms looking out on century-
old trees. Georges Lesage carefully prepares a refined cuisine while Maryse is
in charge of the service and offers sound
advice on suitable wines. An escargot gratin, salmon steak with balsamic vinegar,
roasted squab seasoned with pepper and
vanilla and a strawberry gratin with rhubarb marmalade get full marks.

● **Au Vrai Normand** `SIM`
14, rue Armand-Gasté.
Tel.-Fax 02 31 67 90 99.
www.vrai-normand.com
Closed Tue. dinner, Wed., Feb. vac.
Prix fixe: 13,50€ (lunch), 19€, 24€, 30€.
A la carte: 35€.

Michaël Wahl serves up good, simple and
fresh food in his rustic establishment.
Hot chitterling sausage with slow-cooked
leeks, rouget à la Provençale, a pork tenderloin braised with bacon and a rum-flamb-
béed banana are scrupulously respectful
of the market and seasons.

VITRAC

24200 Dordogne. Paris 523 – Cahors 53 –
Brivela-Gaillarde 65 – Sarlat 8.
A pretty village in Black Périgord on the road
to the Montfort "loop" and chateau.

 HOTELS-RESTAURANTS

■ **Domaine de Rochebois**
Rte de Montfort, 3 km e via D703.
Tel. 05 53 31 52 52. Fax 05 53 29 36 88.
info@rochebois.com / www.rochebois.com
Closed Nov.–end Apr.
32 rooms: 145–225€. 8 suites: 295–420€.
Prix fixe: 35€, 15€ (child). A la carte: 40€.

Immense grounds, a swimming pool, a
tennis court, a golf course, a terraced garden and carefully decorated rooms: the
reasons for coming to this 19th-century
manor are legion. And then comes the
cuisine: Eric Marsanne studiously prepares duck foie gras, oven-roasted turbot,
roasted rack of lamb seasoned with rosemary and a chocolate mille-feuille.

■ **La Treille**
Le Port.
Tel. 05 53 28 33 19. Fax 05 53 30 38 54.
www.latreille-perigord.com
Closed mid-Nov.–mid-Dec., 2 weeks Feb.–
beg. Mar. Rest. closed Mon. (exc. dinner in
season), Tue. (exc. dinner in season).
7 rooms: 40–52€. 1 suite: 65–70€.
Prix fixe: 16,50€ (weekday lunch), 22€,
30€, 36€, 41€, 10,50€ (child).

With its facade covered with Virginia
creeper, this charming village house has
been the property of the Latreille family since 1866. It is now in the hands of
Philippe, who concocts a regional cuisine
that is lively and inventive. In the dining
room and veranda or on the terrace in the
shade of the arbor, we delight in foie gras
Tatin with citrus jus, a tartare of tomatoes with spices and shredded skate, veal
sweetbreads with morels and a soft-centered dark chocolate cake with beer-flavored ice cream before having a rest in
one of the upstairs bedrooms.

VITRE

35500 Ille-et-Vilaine. Paris 308 –
Châteaubriant 51 – Fougères 32 – Laval 40 –
Rennes 39.
The massive château, the ramparts, the church
of Notre Dame, the Tertres Noirs, the old city
and the houses in the rue Baudrairie. Any intelligent approach to Brittany begins in Vitré.

● | RESTAURANTS

● Taverne de l'Ecu   COM

12, rue Baudrairie.
Tel. 02 99 75 11 09. Fax 02 99 75 82 97.
Closed Sun. dinner (exc. July–Aug.),
Tue. dinner, Wed., 10 days Sept.
Prix fixe: 20€ (lunch), 25€, 44€, 12€ (child).

Charm is guaranteed in this half-timbered
16th-century house. Facing the two beautiful period fireplaces, we savor a cuisine of the period that is both robust and
precise. Tuna tartare with coriander and
coriander seeds with a walnut oil-seasoned vegetable julienne, scallops with
an endive and honey Tatin, grilled duck
breast with roasted figs and an apple pastilla with pastry cream defend both the
colors of the Southwest and Brittany.

● Le Petit Pressoir   N SIM

20, rue de Paris.
Tel.-Fax 02 99 74 79 79.
Closed Sun. dinner, Mon., Wed. dinner,
2 weeks Aug.
Prix fixe: 10,50€ (weekday lunch), 16€,
21€, 29€. A la carte: 35€.

At their welcoming establishment Christelle and Thierry Lebrun serve up good
household cuisine. The foie gras with figs,
the pollock with chanterelles, sirloin steak
with lingonberries and the dessert plate
go down without any difficulty.

VITRY-LE-FRANÇOIS

51300 Marne. Paris 181. Bar-le-Duc 54 –
Châlons-en-Champagne 33 – Verdun 96.
Created by François I, this old stronghold on
the Marne was entirely rebuilt at the end of the
last war. It is in the center of an opulent agricultural *terroir*.

 | HOTELS-RESTAURANTS

■ La Poste

Pl Royer-Collard.
Tel. 03 26 74 02 65. Fax 03 26 74 54 71.
www.hoteldelaposte.com
Closed beg. Dec.–beg. Jan., 3 weeks Aug.
Rest. closed Sun.
28 rooms: 49–95€.
Prix fixe: 24€, 38€, 75€.

This hotel near the cathedral is worth
visiting for its bright rooms with gentle orange tones, some having a Jacuzzi,
for its charming reception and the well-
prepared cuisine. Scallops in salad, the
fennel-seasoned Atlantic sea bass in papil-
lotte, a veal chop with mushrooms and
young vegetables and an exotic tart with
Creole sauce are a pleasure to eat in the
elegant neoclassical dining room. The
wine list is extensive with some nice surprises in store.

■ La Cloche

34, rue Aristide-Briand.
Tel. 03 26 74 03 84. Fax 03 26 74 15 52.
www.hotel-de-la-cloche.fr
Closed New Year's. Rest. closed Sat. (Oct.–May).
22 rooms: 45–100€.
Prix fixe: 26€, 35€, 40€, 60€,
11€ (child).

A veritable institution in the heart of the
city, Jacques Sautet's hotel charms us with
its carefully decorated rooms and its traditional cuisine served in the elegant Louis
XVI dining room. The lobster and ginger
mille-feuille, a sole and cep lasagne, beef
cheeks braised in beer with foie gras and the
Grand Marnier soufflé are finely wrought.

● Le Gourmet des Halles   SIM

11, rue des Soeurs.
Tel. 03 26 74 48 88. Fax 03 26 72 54 28.
Closed Tue. dinner, Christmas.
Prix fixe: 11€, 14€, 16€, 22€.
A la carte: 30€.

Just a short distance from the covered market we find a friendly establishment run by the vigorous Laurent Lecompte. Three dining rooms, one brightened up with a beautiful fresco and a pavement terrace enable us to enjoy house foie gras with Gewurztraminer and champagne Ratafia, pike-perch simmered in Crémant de Bourgogne, beef filet medallions with chanterelles and the "retro" (ice cream, choux pastry and nougatine).

VITTEL

88800 Vosges. Paris 342 – Epinal 43 –
Nancy 71 – Langres 73.
vittel-tourisme@wanadoo.fr.
The water city is less famous than the water itself. It is worth visiting for the spa installations in a domain that Nestlé restored beautifully. The Club Med facilities do not lag behind. A superb park.

 HOTELS-RESTAURANTS

■ L'Orée du Bois

3 km w via rue de la Vauviard.
Tel. 03 29 08 88 88. Fax 03 29 08 01 61.
info@loreedubois.fr / www.loreeduboisvittel.fr
39 rooms: 59–63€.
Prix fixe: 17€, 32€, 8,50€ (child).
A la carte: 42€.

We start by relaxing in the fitness center or the heated swimming pool, Turkish bath or Jacuzzi in order to be able to fully appreciate the chef's dishes. The house foie gras trilogy, pork roast with fleur de sel, and the butcher's cut of the day with morel sauce are very pleasant, not to mention the surprise ending to the meal, the platter of local Lorraine products. The rooms are comfortable.

■ Hôtel d'Angleterre

162, rue Charmey.
Tel. 03 29 08 08 42. Fax 03 29 08 07 48.
www.abc-gesthotel.com
Closed mid-Dec.–end Jan.
53 rooms: 69–115,50€.
2 suites: 126–180€.
Prix fixe: 19€, 25€, 34€, 8,60€ (child).
A la carte: 29€.

This early-20th-century hotel between the station and the spa has retained some of its charm from bygone days. The rooms are spacious and comfortable. The dining room has retained its fine chevron parquet floor. The cuisine proceeds peacefully with Lorraine mirabelle plum terrine, perch with slow-cooked vegetables, the Cognac flambéed partridge and the wild blueberry charlotte.

■ Le Châlet de Vitellius

70, av Georges-Clemenceau.
Tel. 03 29 08 07 21. Fax 03 29 08 91 55.
vitellius@wanadoo.fr
Rest. closed Sun. dinner (off season),
Mon. (off season).
10 rooms: 45–60€.
Prix fixe: 28€, 38€, 16€ (lunch)
8€ (child). A la carte: 45–55€.

Roger Marquaire welcomes us to this charming chalet right in the center. The rooms are elegant and all different and the cuisine has today's tastes. Foie gras nougat with pain d'épice, wild rabbit stew with blood sauce served with fresh pasta and the roasted figs with violet-flavored sauce constitute a frank and straightforward feast.

VIVONNE

86370 Vienne. Paris 355 –
Angoulême 95 – Niort 65 – Poitiers 22 –
Saint-Jean-d'Angély 92.
At the confluence of three rivers, an old town dominated by the ruins of its chateau.

 HOTELS-RESTAURANTS

■ Le Saint-Georges

Grande-Rue.
Tel. 05 49 89 01 89. Fax 05 49 89 00 22.
www.hotel-st-georges.com
Rest. closed Fri. lunch, 1 Dec.–end Jan.
32 rooms: 40–64€.
Prix fixe: 16€, 32€.

An old post house refurbished in accordance with today's tastes offers functional rooms and carefully designed menus with the colors of the *terroir* of Charente. A lounge with an open fire and wonderful welcome.

VONNAS

01540 Ain. Paris 409 – Mâcon 19 – Bourg-en-Bresse 25 – Lyon 72.
otvonnas@club-internet.fr.
In the Bresse, the region where the fine fowl cackle freely outdoors, the flowery village of Georges Blanc.

  HOTELS-RESTAURANTS

● **Georges Blanc**
Pl du Marché.
Tel. 04 74 50 90 90. Fax 04 74 50 08 80.
blanc@relaischateaux.com
www.georgesblanc.com
Closed Jan. Rest. closed Mon., Tue., Wed. lunch.
50 rooms: 160–290€. 8 suites: 550–655€.
Prix fixe: 105€, 160€, 180€, 220€, 26€ (child). A la carte: 120–150€.

Georges Blanc was mocked for a long time: the little Blanc boy, mamma's little favorite (and grandmamma's: according to Curnonsky, Mère Blanc was "the best cook in the world"), the man who couldn't cook, the first in the Thonon hotel school to never wear a tocque, the successful businessman...until people realized that this sixty-year-old in top shape (he is sixty-four but looks ten years younger) and at the summit of his art was not only the survivor of a generation that wanted to conquer the world but also the stars. Loiseau, the leader, is dead, although his establishment lives on. Michelin played yo-yo with Lameloise, Lorain and Meneau. Billoux has become more discreet. In short, of the "Burgundy Six", Blanc stands out as the last conqueror. His domain extends from wine (Mâcon Azenay) to shops on the Vonnas square transformed into a theater set, as well as hotels that can be simple (Les Saules) or very charming (the

Relais & Châteaux establishment bearing his name), with a brand new sumptuous spa, fitness, health and beauty center and a vast indoor swimming pool. Plus, numerous bistro-brasseries: the Ancienne Auberge in Vonnas, Saint-Laurent near Mâcon, Chez Blanc in Bourg and the Splendid in Lyons. We almost forgot to mention the "grand restaurant" that bears his name. His sons, Frédéric and Alexandre, one cautious, the other more inspired, have joined him. Georges, who never loses sight of his target, does not pass on the torch. President of the inter-professional committee of Bresse fowl, he continues to be the incarnation of a product and its region. His menu known as "*Bresse en fête*" recounts the saga of the divine chicken in the course of cunningly crafted preparations. Layers of foie gras and hen with giblets in aspic, chicken oysters and flat ocean oysters with white coco beans in an herb-seasoned seafood emulsion, stuffed poultry wings around a bone marrow cake with truffle jus, a Bresse blonde liver cake with lobster sauce and a crayfish tail broth and the rolled chicken thigh with "*velours*" Syrah wine sauce, root vegetables and mushrooms are, quite simply, great art. In the era of triumphant emulsions, this multi-faceted chef who steers straight ahead, continues to defend what he believes in, cultivating his garden and roots. The panouille (a divine caramel vacherin with milk caramel sauce) is worthy, finally, of applause, as are the great Burgundies, the splendid Mâcons and the delightful Beaujolais drawn from an immense cellar where the faithful Marcel Périnet rules along with a team of young sommeliers. This is certainly a great house and a great chef who deserved to be immortalized by his region while still alive.

■ **Résidence des Saules**
Pl du Marché.
Tel. 04 74 50 90 90. Fax 04 74 50 08 80.
blanc@relaischateaux.com
www.georgesblanc.com
Closed Jan.
6 rooms: 140–170€. 4 suites: 310–678€.

Georges Blanc's annex next to the Ancienne Auberge on the village square and across from the establishment bearing his name offers spacious rooms at reasonable prices behind a facade of flowery balconies and just above a boutique that sells regional produce.

● L'Ancienne Auberge

Pl du Marché.
Tel. 04 74 50 90 50. Fax 04 74 50 08 80.
ancienneauberge@wanadoo.fr
www.georgesblanc.com
Closed Jan.
Prix fixe: 20€, 27€, 30€, 45€.
A la carte: 40–60€.

Georges Blanc continues to perpetuate tradition in this establishment steeped in family history. The period posters and photos, the checkered tablecloths, the counter and the old lemonade bottles evoke a time when the lemonade factory was still in operation before it became his grandmother's inn. It is to her that Georges dedicates his cuisine that is true to the pure Bresse tradition. Lamb and aromatic herb pâté served hot, the silky pike fish quenelle with lobster sauce and a Bresse chicken served with basmati rice and cream sauce form a delicious ensemble. The home-style orange cake with four-flower sorbet is a must in this annex to the mother house.

VOUGEOT

21640 Côte-d'Or. Paris 326 – Beaune 27 – Dijon 17.
One of the most famous wines in the world, the château, the village, the vineyards.

◼/● HOTELS-RESTAURANTS

In Gilly-lès-Cîteaux (21640). 2 km e via D251.

◼ Château de Gilly

Tel. 03 80 62 89 98. Fax 03 80 62 82 34.
gilly@grandesetapes.fr / www.château-gilly.com
Rest. closed weekdays lunch
37 rooms: 156–300€. 11 suites: 405–715€.
Prix fixe: Le Clos Prieur: 42€, 65€;
Côté Terroirs: 20€, 25€.

This magnificent 14th-century Cistercian construction is changing hands again but retains the same quality we praised in years gone by. The omnipresent stone, the vaults and Gothic arches, the tapestries and the antique furniture create a timeless atmosphere. The rooms are not lacking in comfort and modernity has made an appearance: a heated swimming pool, beauty care center and WiFi connection. In the kitchen Jean-Alain Poitevin breathes new life into the hotel's two restaurants. The wiser for his experience with Lameloise and in Crayères (in Boyer's time), he elaborates a gastronomic cuisine in the Clos Prieur and a more family-oriented menu in Côté Terroirs. Among his fine performances, we recall creamy pumpkin soup with country bacon and chestnuts, turbot poached in court-bouillon with Mersault sauce, polenta prepared with beurre d'Echiré, leg of young milk-fed goat served in puffed brioche, a truffle-seasoned charlotte and the soft coconut and mango cake with coconut sorbet.

VOUGY see **BONNEVILLE**

VOUILLE

86190 Vienne. Paris 342 – Châtellerault 45 – Parthenay 35 – Poitiers 19 – Thouars 53.
In the heart of verdant Poitou.

◼/● HOTELS-RESTAURANTS

● Le Cheval Blanc

3, rue Barre.
Tel. 05 49 51 81 46. Fax 05 49 51 96 51.
lechevalblanc.clovis@wanadoo.fr
14 rooms: 46–57€.
Prix fixe: 17€, 45€.

A contemporary dining room in the heart of an old structure with its bay window opening onto the water: the Blondin family receives us with charm and adapts local traditions to produce meals with a regional flavor.

VOUTENAY-SUR-CURE

89270 Yonne. Paris 207 – Auxerre 37 –
Avallon 15 – Vézelay 16.
Situated at the intersection of two roads, this
village looks toward the eternal hill of Vézelay
and stretches languorously along the valley of
the Cure. Beautiful cliffs.

 HOTELS-RESTAURANTS

■ Le Voutenay

Rte Nationale 6.
Tel. 03 86 33 51 92. Fax 03 86 33 51 91.
auberge.voutenay@wanadoo.fr
www.monsite.wanadoo.fr/auberge.voutenay
Closed Sun. dinner, Mon., Tue., 1 week at end
Nov., 3 weeks Jan., 1 week at end June.
5 rooms: 40–65€. 1 suite: 65€.
Prix fixe: 25€, 35€, 45€, 55€,
12€ (child).

Right on the N6, a woody park with a
nearby river acts as the setting for this
18th-century residence with bucolic
charm. Behind the ivy-covered facade,
we find a terrace, a lounge, Jacuzzi, retro
and colorful rooms and, in the ochre and
red dining room, not far from the central
fireplace with its sculpted wood mantel-
piece, fine dishes prepared by Laurent
Poirier. Presented in the menus and served
by Valérie, cold local beer-poached foie
gras, perch filet poached in an Irancy wine
infusion, pigeon breast and thigh in samosas and a tart flambéed with Calvados are
the essence of good sense.

VOUVRAY see **TOURS**

WANGENBOURG

67710 Bas-Rhin. Paris 469 – Strasbourg 42
– Saverne 20 – Molsheim 40.
At the heart of Alsace's Little Switzerland,
a village made for convalescence, relaxation
and quiet strolls in the pure air. In the ruins of
its medieval forest château, you can feel time
standing still.

 HOTELS-RESTAURANTS

■ Parc Hôtel

39, rue du Général-de-Gaulle.
Tel. 03 88 87 31 72. Fax 03 88 87 38 00.
parchotel@wanadoo.fr
www.parchotel-alsace.com
Closed beg. Nov.–end Mar.
31 rooms: 51–84€. 3 suites: 93–109€.
Prix fixe: 16€, 19€, 24€, 33€, 10€ (child).

Set in its grounds overlooking the valley,
the Gihrs' establishment is just the place
to enjoy a little fresh air. Elisabeth's welcome and the tennis court, indoor swimming pool and sauna induce an immediate
sense of well-being. On the food side, son
Olivier prepares dishes of true character,
such as the foie gras and sauerkraut terrine, oven-crisped langoustine with vegetable tartare, Riesling-poached chicken
with buttered pasta and the pear served
two ways, in warm wine and in a spice-
infused aspic.

In Engenthal-le-Bas (67710). Junction D218
and D224.

■ Hôtel des Vosges

5, rue de Winsbourg.
Locale known as Steigenbach.
Tel.-Fax 03 88 87 30 35.
Closed Wed.
8 rooms: 43€.
Prix fixe: 14,50€, 27€.

This inn standing on a crossroads in a
forest clearing is an address to remember. The rustic rooms are full of character, as is the dining room, a hunters'
haven. The theme continues with Cunib-
ert Klerlein's dishes, which include some
very sound traditional cuisine. Game ter-

rine, pike fish quenelles, veal cutlets with mushrooms and a caramel flan slip down smoothly.

In 67710 Freudeneck. 3 km e via D224.

■ Freudeneck

3, rte de Wangenbourg.
Tel. 03 88 87 32 91. Fax 03 88 87 36 78.
hotel-freudeneck@wanadoo.fr
www.hotelfreudeneck.com
9 rooms: 53,50–56,50€.
Prix fixe: 8,50€ (weekday lunch), 15€
(weekday lunch), 18€ (weekday lunch),
20€ (dinner), 7,50€ (child).

This forest inn offers bright, comfortable rooms and a tasteful traditional restaurant. Jean-Claude Wagner stoutly prepares escargots prepared in the style of Alsace (stuffed with spiced butter and herbs and cooked in local wine), mixed pepper-seasoned cod filet, venison steak and a simple fruit sabayon.

LA WANTZENAU

67610 Bas-Rhin. Paris 476 – Strasbourg 12 – Brumath 17.
This town was famous for its "chick". Now, only the bird's name remains. Another tradition has survived, though: the Strasbourg Sunday meal, when local families like to linger at the table.

 HOTELS-RESTAURANTS

● Le Relais de la Poste

21, rue du Général-de-Gaulle.
Tel. 03 88 59 24 80. Fax 03 88 59 24 89.
info@relais-poste.com / www.relais-poste.com
Closed 3 weeks Jan.
Rest. closed Sat. lunch, Sun. dinner, Mon.
12 rooms: 80–130€. 2 suites: 130€.
Prix fixe: 37€ (weekdays lunch, wine inc.),
45€, 68€, 150€, 23€ (child).
A la carte: 92€.

This old post house converted into a "Romantik Hotel" has been completely renovated, but still has the woodwork, frescoes and coffered ceilings that form its Old World charm. The functional rooms are refined but welcoming. Jérôme Daull has turned the restaurant into a gourmet haunt acclaimed for its reliable cuisine. We pay proper tribute to the delicate fresh foie gras served with Muscat aspic on country bread, grilled cod filet with tomatoes served in tartare and also sundried, the home-style roasted young chicken with vegetables and a dark chocolate puff pastry dessert with mandarin orange sorbet. The lush, green terrace is a joy in summer. Highly attentive service.

■ Hôtel du Moulin

3, impasse du Moulin.
Tel. 03 88 59 22 22. Fax 03 88 59 22 00.
moulin-wantzenau@wanadoo.fr
www.moulin-wantzenau.com
Closed Christmas–New Year's.
19 rooms: 67–88€. 1 suite: 101€.
Half board: 71€.

On the Strasbourg road, this former mill is an excellent place to stay. Béatrice Wolf and Andrée Dametti provide a cheerful welcome and the rooms furnished with selected fabrics have plenty of character. (See Restaurants: Au Moulin de Wantzenau.)

● Zimmer V.COM

23, rue des Héros.
Tel. 03 88 96 62 08. Fax 03 88 96 37 40.
zimmer-nadeau@club-internet.fr
www.zimmer-nadeau.fr
Closed Sun. dinner, Mon., Nov. 1 vac.,
Feb. vac.
Prix fixe: 19,70€, 30€, 37€, 59€ (wine
inc.), 15€ (child). A la carte: 64€.

Dominique Nadeau, who trained at the Robuchon school, has refurbished this traditional establishment in white. At the stove, he applies his talents to preparing a solid cuisine that still leaves room for innovation. A layered scallop and potato dish with ceps, sole meunière with Mont Saint-Michel mussels, oven-crisped veal sweetbreads with morels in a sherry sauce and the mirabelle plum crème brûlée served next to a hot soufflé with a quenelle of ice cream are attractive propositions. An excellent cellar.

● Les Jardins Secrets   N 🏠 COM

At Hôtel La Roseraie. 32, rue de la Gare.
Tel. 03 88 96 63 44. Fax 03 88 96 64 95.
www.hotelroseraie.fr
Rest. closed lunch (exc. Sun., Mon., Tue.).
15 rooms: 48–56€.
Prix fixe: 28€, 34€.

The décor is Zen, the welcome serene, the cuisine deft and the set menus well-chosen: here is the restaurant you should try in this gourmet village. Foie gras with Berawecke chutney, black mullet filet with white beans and guinea hen with pumpkin purée make a fine impression. The appealing, classical desserts are finely crafted (crème brûlée with vanilla ice cream and coffee and whiskey served over shaved ice, "Irish coffee" style). You will rise from the table a happier person.

● Les Semailles   🏠 COM

10, rue du Petit-Magmod.
Tel. 03 88 96 38 38. Fax 03 88 68 09 06.
info@semailles.fr / www.semailles.fr
Closed Sun. dinner, Wed., Thu., 3 weeks Feb., 3 weeks Aug.
Prix fixe: 26 (lunch, weekdays), 39€.

Jean-Michel Loessel is a chef with a promising future. The Rosenmeer at Rosheim, the Julien in Strasbourg and the Cheval Blanc in Lembach already feature among his trophies. His crisp foie gras mille-feuille, scallops and shrimp with citrus flavorings, thyme-seasoned roasted lamb, the house strawberry dessert and a light mascarpone mousse are the expression of a skilled, inventive culinary approach. In the dining room, Laurence looks after each of her guests with talent and charm. She will also unearth the right wine to flatter the dish you choose. The prices keep a cool head.

● Au Moulin de Wantzenau   COM

2, impasse du Moulin.
Tel. 03 88 96 20 01. Fax 03 88 68 07 97.
philippe.clauss@wanadoo.fr
www.moulin-wantzenau.com
Closed Sun. dinner, bank holiday evenings, 1 week beg. Jan., 1 May, 3 weeks July.
Prix fixe: 25€ (weekdays), 28€, 34€, 48€, 60€, 14€ (child), 60€. A la carte: 65€.

The comfortable dining room and shady terrace here are delightfully cozy. Philippe Clauss, the prudent heir who trained at the Beau Site in Ottrott and Gavroche in London, presents dishes that are a touch more imaginative than in the past. Crab, avocado and grapefruit tartare, orange-seasoned Atlantic sea bass served with chanterelles and artichokes, venison cannelloni with ceps and foie gras and an exotic fruit cappuccino incite us to come again. The huge cellar was put together by Clauss the elder.

● Le Grillon   🏠 SIM

18, rte de Strasbourg.
Tel. 03 88 96 27 84. Fax 03 88 96 65 40.
Closed Sat. dinner, Sun., Wed. dinner, mid-Dec.–beg. Jan., 1 week at end July, 1 week beg. Aug.
Prix fixe: 20€, 25€. A la carte: 35–40€.

Yves Matter, Jérôme Daull's disciple at the Poste, wins us over with moderate prices and a pleasant ambiance. The terrace is crowded in summer. Guests feast on smoked salmon with house potato chips, pike-perch poached in wine and the duck breast with pan-tossed chanterelles. If you find it impossible to choose between the frozen chocolate truffle and a house berry gratin with vanilla ice cream, remember you can afford both at these prices. The service deserves extra credit. Exquisite flambéed tarts in the evening.

● Il Forchettone   SIM

25a, quai des Bateliers.
Tel. 03 88 96 37 30. Fax 03 90 29 25 18.
restaurantilforchettone@wanadoo.fr
Closed Mon., Tue. lunch, Aug.
Prix fixe: 25€, 36,50€.
A la carte: 45–50€.

The spacious terrace in front of this modern establishment in the heart of a residential neighborhood by the canal is instantly overflowing whenever the sun shines. The service is a ballet of proficiency and the menu focuses on the regions of Italy. Pizza as in Naples, fritto misto as in Campania, mushroom tortelloni as in Emilia-

Romagna, fish tagliolini as in the Veneto and orechiette as in Puglia (the native country of the owners, Tina and Franco Albanese): all this and more awaits you here, prepared with no frills but a great deal of precision. A fine Italian wine list and a tiramisu ice cream to melt the most hardened soul.

● Le Pont de l'Ill `SIM`

2, rue du Général-Leclerc.
Tel. 03 88 96 29 44. Fax 03 88 96 21 18.
aupontdelill@wanadoo.fr
www.aupontdelill.com
Closed Sat. lunch, Aug.
Prix fixe: 22€, 25€, 28€, 30€,
10€ (child). A la carte: 45€.

Pierre Daull, brother of Jérôme at the Poste, manages this neo-1900 brasserie nonchalantly but efficiently. Chef Fabrice Bienvenot tends to the seafood platters and prepares duck foie gras, a fisherman's stew, pike-perch in red wine sauce, goose breast seasoned with pepper and a soft-centered chocolate cake at prices that fail to torpedo our budget.

WASSELONNE

67310 Bas-Rhin. Paris 461 – Haguenau 39 – Saverne 14 – Strasbourg 25.
A welcoming crossroads town, boasting the antique ruins of a castle bombarded by Turenne, timber-framed houses, the wine route just a step away and Alsace's Little Switzerland next door.

 HOTELS-RESTAURANTS

■ Hostellerie de l'Etoile

Pl du Maréchal-Leclerc.
Tel. 03 88 87 03 02. Fax 03 88 87 16 06.
luxetoile@aol.com / www.hostellerie-etoile.com
Rest. closed Sun. dinner, Christmas, New Year's.
33 rooms: 38–48€.
Prix fixe: 11€ (weekdays), 17€, 27€.

On the main square, this traditional hotel offers modern rooms and simple, blameless dishes served in a porch dining room. The oyster mushrooms in puff pastry, pike-perch and salmon filets, lamb

medallion in a pastry crust and rich chocolate cake are unpretentious.

● Au Saumon

69, rue du Général-de-Gaulle.
Tel. 03 88 87 01 83. Fax 03 88 87 46 69.
thierry.welty@neuf.fr
Closed Feb. vac., 2 weeks beg. July.
Rest. closed Sun. dinner, Tue. dinner, Wed.
6 rooms: 40€.
Prix fixe: 11,50€ (lunch, weekdays),
17,50€, 45€, 9€ (child). A la carte: 50€.

Thierry Welty has taken over the family establishment and renovated the place, but refrained from making any radical changes. The bucolic rooms, warm welcome, pleasant dining room and faultless service reflect the quality of the food. The cuisine is regional and first-rate: pan-tossed liver with mushroom ravioli, pike-perch served on a bed of sauerkraut, braised veal sweetbreads served with potato purée and a cinnamon parfait with prunes soaked in Armagnac are appetizing classics that never stale. In the summer, the terrace on the edge of the main square is delightful.

● Dolce Vita `SIM`

17, pl du Marché.
Tel. 03 88 87 27 17. Fax 03 88 87 02 06.
Closed Sun. lunch, Tue. dinner, Wed. dinner.
Prix fixe: 24€, 32€, 8,50€ (child).
A la carte: 40–45€.

Hervé Giagnorio-Schall has turned this very cheerful trattoria into a restaurant worthy of interest. The décor, featuring photos of stars and trompe-l'oeil, is highly imaginative. We cheerfully sit down to our soft melting pizzas, succulent pasta and also the rouget alla Calabraisi, the saltimbocca alla Romana and the panna cotta. The cellar is run by "Bill" Siebenschuh, ex-sommelier at the Kochersberg in Landersheim, who even plays the pizzaiolo, teasing dough into discs (dare we say "whenever kneaded'?).

● La Petite Suisse `SIM`

69, rte de Cosswiller.
Tel. 03 88 87 05 38.

Closed Tue. dinner, Wed., 2 weeks beg. July.
Prix fixe: 15€, 30€, 6,50€ (child).
A la carte: 33€.

This "Little Switzerland", with its mountain refuge air, is run by Hervé Feldis, who trained at the Etoile and then with his stepfather at the Salmon. Sandrine, née Welty, is charmingly attentive as we feast on the simple, plain, local cuisine. The escargots, headcheese and aspic terrine, salmon with sorrel sauce, pork shank with sauerkraut and the profiteroles are delightful. A terrace when the weather is fine.

In Romanswiller (67310). 3,5 km e via D224.

● **Les Douceurs Marines**

2, rte de Wangenbourg.
Tel.-Fax 03 88 87 13 97.
Closed Mon.–Thu. (dinner), Wed. lunch,
Nov. 1 vac., 1 week in summer.
Prix fixe: 11€ (lunch, weekdays), 15€,
17,50€, 23€, 30€, 40€ 7,50€ (child).
A la carte: 36€.

On the border of Little Switzerland, this blue and white house offers a change of air. The shady terrace is a joy when the sun shines. Emmanuelle greets us with all the charm of a hostess welcoming us to her home. Cooking comes as naturally to Claude, who trained at the Métropole Palace in Monaco and the Sporting in Roquebrune-Cap Martin, as song to a thrush. Certain specialties recur throughout the year: bouillabaisse, a simpler local fish soup and fish poached in red wine. The prices are angelically restrained and the set menu at 23 , which, the other day, included the surf and turf salad, then the delicate fish couscous and finally a berry Melba, is quite simply a steal. Add the fish soup, bursting with flavor, Atlantic sea bass in an orange infusion and a frozen marbled coconut and exotic fruit dessert and you will soon come to the conclusion that this affable establishment is a treasure trove, well-worth another visit.

WATTIGNIES see LILLE

68250 Haut-Rhin. Paris 460 – Colmar 21 –
Mulhouse 29 – Thann 26.
In this pretty, unspoiled, rustic village to the south of the wine route, modesty reigns unchallenged, from the shrewd wines to room at the inn.

 HOTELS-RESTAURANTS

● **Au Cheval Blanc**   ○❀🏚

20, rue de Rouffach.
Tel. 03 89 47 01 16. Fax 03 89 47 64 40.
www.auberge-chevalblc.com
Closed 10 days end June–beg. July,
15 Jan.–8 Feb.
Rest. closed Sun. dinner, Mon., Tue. lunch.
10 rooms: 85–100€. 2 suites: 120€.
Prix fixe: 36€, 65€, 76€, 87€,
13€ (child). A la carte: 72€.

The Koehler family have been winegrowers from father to son since 1785. Today, in this luxurious, typically Alsatian establishment, Gilbert Koehler regales guests with his presentation of goose foie gras served three ways, jumbo shrimp served two ways (simply roasted and in a spicy bouillon), the local-style venison medallion served with house spätzle and the berry mille-feuille. Vintages from the family property naturally head the wine list, which focuses on the region's production, but still has room for other libations. The hotel rooms have been fully renovated in bright, warm colors.

68920 Haut-Rhin. Paris 453 – Colmar 8 –
Eguisheim 4 – Ribeauvillé 17.
Travelers pass through this slightly suburban winegrowing village to bypass the city of Colmar to the west. It is the starting point for hikers heading for southern Alsace, where mountain meets vine.

 HOTELS-RESTAURANTS

● **La Palette**   ○❀🏚

9, rue Herzog.
Tel. 03 89 80 79 14. Fax 03 89 79 77 00.

lapalette@lapalette.fr / www.lapalette.fr
Hotel closed 3 weeks Jan.
Rest. closed Sun. dinner, Mon., Tue. lunch,
10 days Jan.
15 rooms: 64–74€. 1 suite: 110€.
Prix fixe: 14€ (lunch), 22€, 25€, 35€,
59€, 10€ (child). A la carte: 52€.

Henri Gagneux, a native of Bonneville in Savoy, who trained with Jacob in Courchevel and at the Bourget-du-Lac, paints from a palette of endless shades, reflected in both the colors of his rooms and the dishes that make up the delicious, demanding menu here. The rooms have been modernized, but the jigsaw-cut wooden ceiling remains intact, gracing a dining room whose walls are now brightened by works from contemporary artists. Assisted by a young reception and waitstaff, Henri puts his skills into practice in the kitchen, teasing the finest produce to perfection. The whole grain cake with lobster, the monkfish medallion with sun-dried tomatoes and a lentil risotto with olives, the duck breast in a cocotte of sweet-and-sour radishes, the rich chocolate or hazelnut cake and the amaretto parfait with hot wine-poached cherries are simply splendid.

WEYERSHEIM

67720 Bas-Rhin. Paris 474 – Brumath 8 – Hoerdt 3 – Strasbourg 15.
Surrounded by bucolic scenery to the north of Strasbourg, a step away from the asparagus fields, the Zorn nods its melancholy way through the countryside.

● | RESTAURANTS

● **Auberge du Pont de la Zorn** SIM
2, rue de la République.
Tel.-Fax 03 88 51 36 87.
Closed Sat. lunch, Wed., Thu., 3 weeks Sept., 2 weeks Feb.
Prix fixe: 32,50€ (Sat., Sun., lunch).
A la carte: 34–42€.

On the bank of the Zorn, Myriam and Hervé Debeer have made a good-natured,

resolutely Alsatian tavern of this country inn. The ambiance is friendly in the dining room and in the garden when summer comes. We happily set to work on the local flat garnished pies cooked in a wood oven, foie gras nougat, rabbit presskopf, pike-perch in a horseradish crust, caramelized pork ribs and the regional flat apple tart.

WIHR-AU-VAL see MUNSTER

WILLGOTTHEIM

67370 Bas-Rhin. Paris 462 – Saverne 16 – Strasbourg 22 – Wasselonne 13.
In the heart of Kochersberg and its lush countryside, an old-style village with timber-framed homes.

● | RESTAURANTS

● **L'Oie Gourmande**
51, rue Principale.
Tel. 03 88 69 90 65.
Closed Sat. lunch, Wed., 2 weeks end Aug.
A la carte: 28€.

Pleasant, inexpensive and fun with its blue facade and picturesque dining rooms adorned with antique furniture and Alsatian engravings, the Schmitt establishment is something of a convivial museum. Sandrine offers a lively welcome and Olivier provides reliable cooking. Sometimes he overdoes it a little, but such are the perils of generosity. The exquisite local flat garnished savory pies, house head-cheese and aspic terrine, pork cheeks with Melfor vinegar and the frozen Kouglof are gratifying.

WIMEREUX

62930 Pas-de-Calais. Paris 269 – Calais 34 – Arras 120 – Boulogne-sur-Mer 6.
tourisme.wimereux@wanadoo.fr.
With its pastel-colored art deco houses, sandy beach, family clientele and unabashed appetite, this resort is a mainstay of charm on the Côte d'Opale.

■/● HOTELS-RESTAURANTS

● **Atlantic Hôtel & la Liégeoise**

Digue de la Mer.
Tel. 03 21 32 41 01. Fax 03 21 87 46 17.
alain.delpierre@wanadoo.fr
www.atlantic-delpierre.com
Closed 1 week at end Jan.–end Feb.
Rest. closed Sun. dinner, Mon. lunch.
18 rooms: 76–123€.
Prix fixe: 34€, 45€, 61€. A la carte: 70€.

Alain Delpierre has been at home here for more than ten years. With its art deco facade rising above the seawall, this hostelry definitely has its charms. Our host's chosen cuisine marries innovation to tradition. Seafood plays the starring role, with the local catch served with a lobser medallion in sauce, turbot with coconut milk and rougail (a spicy diced tomato, ginger, onion and birdseye pepper condiment) and ginger-seasoned Atlantic sea bass, while the rack of lamb encrusted in parsley with spring vegetables caters to more carnivorous appetites. However, meat and fish lovers are naturally reunited over the Tatin style caramel mille-feuille. The cellar is resourceful. The food is served in a panoramic dining room with Louis XVI furniture. The rooms are in pastel or deeper tones. Choose one with a sea view if you can.

● **L'Epicure**

1, rue de la Gare.
Tel. 03 21 83 21 83.
Closed Sun., Wed. lunch, 10 days Christmas–New Year's, 10 days at end Aug.
Prix fixe: 24€ (lunch), 29€ (lunch), 37€.

A chef good as gold? Philippe Carrée labors alone in this modest, street level dining room setting. Trained in the luxury hotels of Geneva, the Côtes d'Armor Breton, with his love of fine produce and incisive flavors, prepares a frank, market-based cuisine. Among his successes are vegetable ravioli with herring eggs, the cod with garden vegetables and veal kidneys with a side of golden brown polenta. Great Bor-

deaux wines are on offer at rock bottom prices and the desserts (the rosemary infused cream, honey seasoned pears and a caramel passion fruit dessert) are quick witted. This little eatery is a special favorite of ours.

● **La Vie est Belle**

44, rue Carnot.
Tel. 03 21 83 19 31.
Closed Sun. dinner, Mon.
Prix fixe: 18,50€ (lunch), 28€ (dinner).

We knew Jean-François Laurent when he was full of ambition at the Brocante in Wimille. Now he is showing a little more modesty in this pretty restaurant. The light shades, pine paneling, attractive lamps and teak tables have plenty of oomph. We enjoy timbale with crab and haddock topped with creamed asparagus, the lamb stew and the poached Atlantic sea bass with sea urchin sauce. Guests can also drop by to taste rice pudding with chestnut honey and a ground almond crumble in the afternoon. Jot this address down in your book of treats.

WINTZENHEIM

68920 Haut-Rhin. Paris 445 – Colmar 6 – Turckheim 5.
A crossroads town in the suburbs of Colmar, on the wine and Vosges mountain routes.

● RESTAURANTS

● **Le Bon Coin** SIM

4, rue de Logelbach.
Tel. 03 89 27 48 04. Fax 03 89 27 51 14.
au-bon-coin2@wanadoo.fr
Closed Tue. dinner, Wed., 3 weeks Feb.,
3 weeks mid-Aug.–beg. Sept.
Prix fixe: 12,50€, 21€, 36€,
6,50€ (child). A la carte: 30€.

The flowered half-timbered facade invites visitors to step inside and taste the dishes prepared by Rémy Haeffelin, who enthusiastically concocts Alsatian classics. We enjoy hot pâté with spring sprouts in salad, the pike-perch poached in Riesling with noodles, the local Wickerschwihr choucroute and the frozen kouglof.

WISSEMBOURG

67160 Bas-Rhin. Paris 483 – Haguenau 33 – Strasbourg 66 – Karlsruhe 41.
tourisme.wissembourg@wanadoo.fr.
The banks of the Lauter, the houses on the quai Anselman and memories of L'Ami Fritz: this is the most regionalist of Alsace towns. It was here that an adaptation of the Erckmann-Chatrian novel was shot in the thirties. The décor has remained intact, like a Hansi drawing.

 HOTELS-RESTAURANTS

■ Au Moulin de la Walk

2, chemin de la Walk.
Tel. 03 88 94 06 44. Fax 03 88 54 38 03.
info@moulin-walk.com / www.moulin-walk.com
Closed 3 weeks Jan.
Rest. closed Sun. dinner, Mon., Fri. lunch,
3 weeks Jan., mid-June–beg. July.
25 rooms: 50–65€.
Prix fixe: 32€, 38€, 50€, 10€ (child).
A la carte: 42–50€.

Peace and greenery in this former mill, and relaxation in its comfortable rooms, five of them attic conversions. We appreciate the Schmidts' thoughtfulness and Eric's polished recipes: his foie gras or game terrine, the roasted lamb tenderloin and the frozen mirabelle plum soufflé.

■ Hostellerie au Cygne

3, rue du Sel.
Tel. 03 88 94 00 16. Fax 03 88 54 38 28.
www.hostellerie-cygne.com
Closed 2 weeks Nov., 2 weeks Feb.–beg.
Mar., 2 weeks beg. July, Wed.
Rest. closed Sun. dinner, Wed., Thu. lunch.
16 rooms: 50–75€.
Prix fixe: 20€ (lunch), 30€, 45€, 60€,
13€ (child).

In the dining room and kitchen respectively, Cathie and Georges Eberhardt go out of their way to make sure the customers and friends who frequent this smartened up old post house enjoy their visit. The

facade is charming and the paneled rooms refined. The cuisine consists of a succession of reliable, updated traditional recipes: a salted pork cheek and aspic terrine with baby vegetables in sauce, salmon trout potau-feu with horseradish-seasoned heirloom vegetables and sel de Guérande, beef filet medallions with Pinot Noir sauce and slow-cooked mushrooms and the chocolate and salted-butter caramel truffle. On the accommodation side, the rooms are snug in a cozy, romantic way.

■ Hôtel d'Alsace

16, rue Vauban.
Tel. 03 88 94 98 43. Fax 03 88 94 19 60.
hotel.d.alsace@wanadoo.fr
www.hotel-alsace.fr
Rest. closed Fri., Sat., Sun.
41 rooms: 41–54€.
Prix fixe: 13€.

The small rooms in this modern hotel slightly outside the center of town, some of them attic accommodations, are all well-equipped. The prices are reasonable and the breakfast generous. Simple catering during the week.

● Le Carrousel Bleu

17, rue Nationale.
Tel. 03 88 54 33 10.
Closed Mon., Wed., 2 weeks beg. Aug.
Prix fixe: 26€, 36€, 46€.

This recent little main street restaurant is not much to look at; the modern setting is a tad neutral in gray tones with brown seats. At the helm, Annabelle and Michael Heid offer flawless, reliable set menus that lure us away to the South. The "cecina" cannelloni (cured beef) with peppers and melon, a tartare of tomatoes and shrimp seasoned with vanilla, pike-perch with chanterelles, a goat cheese–stuffed pork cutlet, raspberry tiramisu and the rosemary-seasoned pan-simmered apricots with lavender ice cream offer a pleasant conclusion.

● **L'Ange**   COM

2, rue de la République.
Tel.-Fax 03 88 94 12 11.
info@restaurant-ange.com
www.restaurant-ange.com
Closed Mon., Tue., Christmas vac.,
2 weeks June.
Prix fixe: 28,50€, 38€. A la carte: 43€.

In his 16th-century post house, Pierre Ludwig seems to have set aside any former excess of ambition. This former lieutenant of Antoine Westermann prepares a multifaceted regional cuisine that sometimes looks to the shores of the Mediterranean for inspiration. In summer, guests are served on a charming courtyard terrace. Although he has done little to renovate his two adjoining dining rooms, pleasant but simple, we are still happy to gorge ourselves on rabbit terrine with foie gras, trout with onion confiture, pork cheeks with crunchy vegetables and pan-seared liver with balsamic vinegar and apples, which do little damage to our pocket. To conclude, the individual wild blueberry tart served with fresh fromage blanc ice cream makes an excellent impression.

In Cleebourg (67160). 3 km via D77.

■ **Le Tilleul**   ⌂

94, rue Principale.
Tel. 03 88 94 52 15. Fax 03 88 94 52 63.
Closed Mon., Tue., Christmas–New Year's vac., 2 weeks beg. Mar.
8 rooms: 40–45€.
Prix fixe: 19€, 29€, 8,50€ (child).

This hotel-restaurant deep in the heart of a winegrowing village is a pleasant place to stay. Martine and Gérard Franck provide attractive, peaceful rooms and respectable dishes. The house foie gras, sole meunière, scallops with endives, veal steak with morels and the frozen meringue dessert are unpretentious.

In Hohwiller (67250). 10 km s via D263.

● **La Grange Fleurie**   SIM

38, rue Principale.
Tel. 03 88 80 55 71.
Closed Sat., Sun.

Prix fixe: 19,50€, 26€, 7,50€ (child).
A la carte: 30–40€.

A delightful inn where we stop to try the cuisine prepared by André Goaziou, who makes deft use of his market produce. We enjoy a fine gourmet salad with foie gras, a mixed fish dish, beef filet medallion Rossini and the rich chocolate cake.

In Seebach (67160). 5 km e via D245.

● **La Vieille Grange**   N SIM

77, rue des Eglises.
Tel. 03 88 53 18 40. Fax 03 88 53 18 39.
Closed lunch, Mon.–Thu.
A la carte: 25€.

Local flat garnished savory pies, mixed local salad, chilled beef muzzle with vinaigrette and sautéed potatoes, smoked beef tongue served on a bed of sauerkraut, potato cakes and bibelaskäs (local fromage blanc specialty) favorably impress in Joanna and Jean-Marc Bayer's establishment. They have turned this old village barn into a tasteful inn.

WOELFLING-LES-SARREGUEMINES see
SARREGUEMINES
WOIPPY see METZ
XONRUPT-LONGEMER see GERARDMER

ILE D'YEU

85350 Vendée.
tourisme@ile-yeu.fr.
This scrap of granite in the Atlantic, with its fishermen's cottages in blue and white, could be a fragment of Brittany mislaid in the Vendée region. However, the flower-covered homes of Saint-Sauveur (oleander, azaleas and rhododendrons) have more of a Grecian flavor and the bucolic byways remind us of Ireland. Port-Joinville, the island's good-natured capital and busy port, has yet to rebrand itself as a Vendée St. Tropez.

 HOTELS-RESTAURANTS

In Port-Joinville (85350).

■ L'Escale
14, rue de la Croix-du-Port.
Tel. 02 51 58 50 28. Fax 02 51 59 33 55.
yeu.escale@voila.fr / www.yeu-escale.fr
Closed mid-Nov.–mid-Dec.
29 rooms: 50–70€.

A short way from the bustle of the port, this typical abode with its traditional blue shutters offers modern yet convivial accommodation. The decoration of the rooms is charming indeed in a staunchly marine style. Major renovation this year.

■ Atlantic Hôtel
3, quai Carnot au Port-Joinville.
Tel. 02 51 58 38 80. Fax 02 51 58 35 92.
atlantic-hotel-yeu@club-internet.fr
www.hotel-yeu.com
Closed beg. Jan.–end Jan.
18 rooms: 41–80€.

This hotel is run by Bernard Hennequin, who owns the fishmonger's below. Each renovated room is a niche promising repose. In the morning, we wake to see the ocean and fishermen's gardens.

● Le Père Raballand L'Etape Maritime   COM
6, pl de Norvège.
Tel. 02 51 26 02 77. Fax 02 51 26 02 78.
lepereraballand@wanadoo.fr
www.lepereraballand.com

Closed Mon., 1 Dec.–1 Mar.
Prix fixe: 19,80€, 28,60€.
A la carte: 40–50€.

Bearded, smiling Jean-Yves Raballand still mans the desk in the establishment bearing his name, even though he has now handed over the kitchen to son-in-law Stéphane Sarrazin, who trained under his watchful eye. We come here for the atmosphere and view of the harbor, as well as the famous tuna tartare, which is a paragon of its kind, with onions and Tabasco, squid stew with a creamy white sauce, cod served couscous-style and the pork shank, oven roasted the old-fashioned way.

● Le Port Baron   SIM
9, rue Georgette.
Tel.-Fax 02 51 26 01 61.
Closed Mon., 2 weeks Oct., mid-Jan.–mid-Mar.
Prix fixe: 21€, 32€.

Patrick Leray prepares an unostentatious cuisine in this vanilla-colored eatery. We can also sit out on the patio to enjoy the crab ravioli with slow-cooked vegetables, tuna medallions Rossini, half of a Challans duck roasted with honey and an apple cinnamon streussel. A fine choice of Loire wines.

● Les Bafouettes   SIM
8, rue Gabriel-Guisthau.
Tel. 02 51 59 38 38. Fax 02 51 58 78 13.
lesbafouettes@aol.com
Closed Sun. dinner, Mon., 1 week at end Oct.,
1 week beg. Nov., Jan.
Prix fixe: 18€ (lunch), 27,50€, 37€, 48€,
13€ (child). A la carte: 56€.

Stéphane Gilot was Belgian before he set out on the road. Now he is married to Mireille, a lady of pure island stock, and serves inventive culinary creations based on the local catch in his cute restaurant just behind the harbor. The crab ravioli, lobster with fenugreek-seasoned onion compote, filet of sole stuffed with Swiss chard and the John Dory with beet greens in a pepper mille-feuille are surprising. A terrace on the patio and attentive service.

● **Le Bistro du Père Raballand** [SIM]
13, quai de la Mairie.
Tel. 02 51 58 74 04. Fax 02 51 26 02 78.
lepereraballand@wanadoo.fr
www.lepereraballand.com
Closed Mon., 30 Nov.–1 Mar.
Prix fixe: 15€, 19,80€, 28,60€.
A la carte: 39–48€.

Père Raballand's second establishment focuses on a simple approach to local cuisine under the supervision of son-in-law Stéphane Sarrazin. Fresh tuna tartare, traditional squid stew with cream sauce, young Challans duck roasted in spiced honey and a crème brûlée are generously served in an amusing marine setting with pine tables.

YSSINGEAUX

43200 Haute-Loire. Paris 569 – Le Puy 28 – Saint-Etienne 51 – Ambert 74.
Famous for its National Pastry Chef School, this Velay town boasts the attractions of a striking 14th-century Hôtel de Ville and hospital museum. The surrounding highlands are ideal for those hankering after a little pure mountain air.

 HOTELS-RESTAURANTS

■ **Le Bourbon**
5, pl de la Victoire.
Tel. 04 71 59 06 54. Fax 04 71 59 00 70.
le.bourbon.hotel@wanadoo.fr
www.le-bourbon.com
Closed Sun. dinner, Mon.,
1 week Christmas–New Year's.
11 rooms: 65–75€.
Prix fixe: 20€, 26€, 30€, 42€, 11€ (child).

This sixties establishment has been given a refreshing makeover. The rooms are cheerful, the welcome attentive and the dishes prepared by André Perrier are based on the finest produce of the moment. The pressed duck foie gras and fig terrine, the Lignon trout filet, a veal cutlet with artichokes and bacon and the frozen pine honey parfait are splendid.

YUTZ see THIONVILLE

76190 Seine-Maritime. Paris 171 –
Le Havre 57 – Rouen 37 – Fécamp 34.
The Pays de Caux and its outlying districts (do not miss Allouville's thousand-year-old oak), seen from a town that was widely rebuilt in the fifties (fine stained glass in the church of Saint-Pierre).

HOTELS-RESTAURANTS

■ **Le Manoir aux Vaches**
8, rue Félix-Faure.
Tel. 02 35 95 65 65.
hotel-du-havre@tiscali.fr
9 rooms: 86–106€.

This new hotel with its nine snug rooms pays tribute to Normandy's beautiful milkmaids.

■ **Auberge du Val au Cesne**
Rte de Duclair: 4 km sw via D5.
Tel. 02 35 56 63 06. Fax 02 35 56 92 78.
valaucesne@hotmail.fr / www.valaucesne.fr
Closed 2 weeks Nov.–beg. Nov., mid-Jan.–beg. Feb., 10 days Aug.–beg. Sept. Rest. closed Mon., Tue.
5 rooms: 90–90€.
Prix fixe: 28€, 50€ (wine inc.) 13€ (child).
A la carte: 57€.

This 17th-century Norman farm is energetically run by Jérôme Carel. The rooms are cheerful, the dining room rustic with its solid beams and the rejuvenated regional cuisine highly polished. Oven-roasted scallops in their shell, sole with a langoustine mousse stuffing, the house poultry escalope dish and a frozen meringue dessert with whipped cream slip down smoothly.

■ **Hôtel du Havre**
Pl des Belges. 2, rue Guy-de-Maupassant.
Tel. 02 35 95 16 77. Fax 02 35 95 21 18.
hotel-du-havre@tiscali.fr
www.hotel-du-havre.fr
Rest. closed Fri. dinner, Sat. dinner, Sun. dinner (beg. Dec.–Easter) (open for groups).
25 rooms: 50–80€.

Prix fixe: 21€, 24€, 8€ (child).
A la carte: 40€.

With a smile, Patricia Maître welcomes us to this hotel offering comfortable rooms at sensible prices. At the Closerie, she concocts dishes that maintain the delicious tang of tradition. Escargot and frog legs profiteroles with garlic cream, cod filet served Norman style, "real" Saint-Romain blood sausage with a buttered apple compote, as well as the unmissable local tarte cauchoise, do us a world of good.

YVOIRE

74140 Haute-Savoie. Paris 566 – Thonon 16 – Genève 26 – Bonneville 41.
One of the most beautiful villages in Savoie, with its medieval skyline, old houses, Cinq Sens (Five Senses) garden and harbor on Lake Geneva.

 HOTELS-RESTAURANTS

■ Le Pré de la Cure
Pl de la Mairie.
Tel. 04 50 72 83 58. Fax 04 50 72 91 15.
lepredelacure@wanadoo.fr
www.pre-delacure.com
Closed mid-Nov.–beg. Mar.
25 rooms: 70–80€.
Prix fixe: 20€ (weekdays), 25€ (weekdays), 32€ (Sun.), 10€ (child). A la carte: 55€.

With its gardens, terraces and indoor heated swimming pool, this lakeside inn is a delightful place to stay. We like the bright, pleasant rooms and cuisine orchestrated by Olivier and Michel Magnin, father and son, who prepare regional produce with subtlety and character. The Léman crayfish fricasée with carrots and leeks, perch with lemon butter, oven-roasted pigeon with a mushroom fricassée and the rich dark chocolate cake with vanilla ice cream have plenty of spirit. A fine wine list with a few vintages from neighboring Switzerland.

■ Les Flots Bleus
At the port.
Tel. 04 50 72 80 08. Fax 04 50 72 84 28.

contact@flotsbleus-yvoire.com
www.flotsbleus-yvoire.com
Closed Nov.–mid-Apr.
14 rooms: 120–160€.
Prix fixe: 22€ (weekdays), 42€, 72€, 11€ (child).

This modern establishment on the harbor offers functional rooms with a view, not to mention refined cuisine with a modern flavor. The crayfish and citrus fruits, Dombe-style frog legs, cured ham platter, the rabbit terrine and an osso bucco done in the local style can be savored alfresco on the shady terrace.

■ Le Vieux Logis
Chemin des Remparts.
Tel. 04 50 72 80 24. Fax 04 50 72 90 76.
contact@levieuxlogis.com
www.levieuxlogis.com
Closed 1 Dec.–mid-Feb.
Rest. closed Sun. dinner, Mon.
11 rooms: 70–88€.
Prix fixe: 19,90€ (weekday lunch), 48,50€, 10€ (child).

Serge Jacquier-Durand, his wife Liliane and his daughter-in-law Nicole welcome you to this 14th-century abode, a charming hostelry indeed. The rooms with balconies are furnished in contemporary style. In the dining room with its period décor—predominantly wood and stone—we discover the cuisine prepared by the proficient son, Paul. We feast on his wild Garenne rabbit terrine, Léman perch meunière, the Saint Yrieix pork roast and a vanilla crème brûlée.

■ Hôtel du Port
Rue du Port.
Tel. 04 50 72 80 17. Fax 04 50 72 90 71.
hotelduport.yvoire@wanadoo.fr
www.hotelrestaurantduport-yvoire.com
Closed Oct.–beg. Mar.
Rest. closed Wed. (off season).
7 rooms: 110–210€. 2 suites: 165–210€.
Prix fixe: 30€, 46€.

This lakeside hotel has opted for a marine décor. The restaurant, which has something of the brasserie about it, offers up traditional cuisine. The pan-seared foie gras on spiced pain perdu, salmon trout meunière, side of porcelet roasted with sorrel and the local baba dessert with ice cream are accompanied by selected wines.

YVOY-LE-MARRON

41600 Loir-et-Cher. Paris 163 – Orléans 35 – Blois 45 – Lamotte-Beuvron 15 – La Ferté-Saint-Aubin 13.
The Sologne of Raboliot, its pink brick houses, timber frames and great forest rich in game.

 HOTELS-RESTAURANTS

■ Auberge du Cheval Blanc
1, pl du Cheval-Blanc.
Tel. 02 54 94 00 00.
auberge.cheval.blanc@wanadoo.fr
Rest. closed Mon., Tue. lunch.
15 rooms: 60–85€.
Prix fixe: 20€ (weekday lunch), 30€, 35€.

This pleasant indigenous inn dear to hunters has been meticulously renovated. The rooms are spruce, snug and well-equipped, and the cuisine, served in a rustic dining room with red hexagonal floor tiles and half timbering, focuses closely on game in the season.

68340 Haut-Rhin. Paris 430 – Colmar 14 – Saint-Dié 45.
Its silhouette is easy to make out on the wine route: a village stretching along the crest of a hillside, just a step away from its big brothers, Hunawihr, Riquewihr and company.

 HOTELS-RESTAURANTS

■ Au Riesling
5, rte des Vins.
Tel. 03 89 47 85 85. Fax 03 89 47 92 08.
auriesling@wanadoo.fr
www.au-riesling.com
Closed end Dec.–1 Mar.
Rest. closed Sun. dinner, Mon., Tue. lunch.
36 rooms: 61–75€.
Prix fixe: 17€, 24€, 29€, 8€ (child).

Surrounded by vineyards, this quiet hotel offers rooms with all modern comforts, some of them just refurbished, and an affable, classical restaurant. Beef carpaccio, pan-seared scallops, pork tenderloin medallions and cherries in Kirsch can hardly be faulted. We naturally drink wines produced by the Rentz family, our hosts.

■ Caveau du Schlossberg
59a, rue de la Fontaine.
Tel. 03 89 47 93 85 / 03 89 49 00 89.
Fax 03 89 47 82 40.
hotel-le-schlossberg@wanadoo.fr
www.eschlossberg.com
Open daily. Winter: by reserv.
7 rooms: 56–115€. 4 suites: 135–198€.
Prix fixe: 29€, 17€ (child).

Charles Maierboerck has turned this welcoming hostelry into a fine stopover on the wine route. Its renovated rooms and suites provide a panoramic view of the surrounding villages and vineyards. The cuisine, which is gratifying but not overdone, includes foie gras, pike-perch in filo pastry, a rabbit haunch in Riesling sauce and Marc de Gewurtz sorbet.

● Maximilien

19a, rte d'Ostheim.
Tel. 03 89 47 99 69. Fax 03 89 47 99 85.
www.le-maximilien.com
Closed Sun. dinner, Mon., Fri. lunch,
Feb. vac.
Prix fixe: 31€ (lunch), 43€, 63€, 79€.
A la carte: 77€.

This neo-Alsatian establishment, standing on the hillside among the vines, belongs to Jean-Michel Eblin, who set up in business near to his parents' property after a conspicuous stay at the Valet de Coeur. His resume also includes Taillevent and the Auberge de l'Ill, a testament to his tried-and-true technique and skills. He knows how to prepare precisely cooked, refined dishes with finely calculated flavors, and offers proof in the form of the shrimp tail tartlette seasoned with basil-infused oil, pan-tossed pike-perch filet with a mixed herb sauce, roasted Mediterranean sea bass filet, pigeon breast, roasted lobster with an orange reduction sauce and the venison medallion with red beet sauce. The elegant dining room looking out onto the vineyards, with the village in the background, is the perfect setting for our feast.

● Auberge du Froehn SIM

5, rte d'Ostheim.
Tel. 03 89 47 81 57. Fax 03 89 47 80 28.
Closed Tue., Wed., 2 weeks end Nov.,
end Feb.–mid-Mar., end June–beg. July.
Prix fixe: 11€ (weekday lunch), 19€, 23€,
26€, 35€, 10€ (child), 35€.
A la carte: 34–39€.

Dedicated to the great local vintage, Jean-Marc and Brigitte Hatterman's cellar offers wine from close at hand and further afield, especially the libations produced by their friends and neighbors, the Beckers. Duck foie gras with fruit compote, pan-seared scallops with herb sauce, herb-encrusted lamb with rosemary sauce and a raspberry sorbet with eau-de-vie are a delightful experience.

ZIMMERSHEIM see MULHOUSE

57330 Moselle. Paris 342 – Luxembourg 19 – Metz 49 – Thionville 16.
Luxembourg is close by. Here, we are still in the green hills of Moselle. The somewhat idealized country setting dispels all thoughts of the neighboring Cattenom nuclear power station.

■ HOTELS-RESTAURANTS

● La Lorraine

80, rue Principale.
Tel. 03 82 83 40 46. Fax 03 82 83 48 26.
info@la-lorraine.fr / www.la-lorraine.fr
Closed 2 weeks Aug.,
2 weeks Christmas–New Year's.
Rest. closed Mon., Tue.
2 rooms: 150€. 1 suite: 190€.
Prix fixe: 38€, 59€, 20€ (child).
A la carte: 85€.

Passing through Lorraine on the road to Luxembourg, we break our journey at this welcoming village hostelry. Apart from its lodging, which takes the form of two spacious, comfortable rooms (one blue, the other green) and a suite, it provides board in a gourmet restaurant run by Marcel Keff, who prepares an updated, topical version of local culinary classics. We are more than a little proud to have discovered this excellent chef before others, still flushed with their own daring, got around to pinning a star on him. We can but applaud his art as we make short work of Cleuri escargots in quiche served with an herb-enriched mixed salad, the cod filet tossed in salted butter served on mashed potatoes enriched with the local cheese and topped with mustard-flavored poultry gravy, juicy Kanfen roasted suckling pig complete with crunchy skin and served with a potato tart, a warm egg with dark chocolate sauce and a rum sabayon. The neighboring Grand Duchy inspires the wine list. The conservatory and terrace on the garden side provide a congenial extension to the dining room. Breakfast matches the quality of the other meals: diabolically delicious!

INDEX

INDEX

S

INDEX

INDEX